Illustrated Dictionary of Gardening

Illustrated Dictionary of Gardening

Derived from The Royal Horticultural Society
Shorter Dictionary of Gardening

MICHAEL POLLOCK

AND

MARK GRIFFITHS

LONDON • NEW YORK • MUNICH
MELBOURNE • DELHI

Produced for Dorling Kindersley by

cobaltid

The Stables, Wood Farm, Deopham Road, Attleborough, Norfolk NR17 1AJ
www.cobaltid.co.uk

ART EDITORS Paul Reid, Rebecca Johns, Darren Bland, Annika Skoog

For Dorling Kindersley
SENIOR EDITOR Louise Abbott
MANAGING EDITOR Anna Kruger
MANAGING ART EDITOR Lee Grifffiths
DTP DESIGNER Louise Waller
PRODUCTION CONTROLLER Mandy Innes
PICTURE RESEARCH Richard Dabb
US SENIOR EDITOR Jill Hamilton
US EDITORS Christine Heilman, Jenny Siklós
US EDITORIAL ASSISTANTS Nicole Turney, Elizabeth Eaton

First American Edition

Published in the United States in 2005 by DK Publishing, Inc.
375 Hudson Street, New York NY 10014

05 06 07 08 09 10 9 8 7 6 5 4 3 2 1

Text copyright © 2005 The Royal Horticultural Society
Illustration and Design © 2005 Dorling Kindersley

DK books are available at special discounts for bulk purchases for sales promotions, premiums,
fundraising, or educational use. For details, contact: DK Publishing Special Markets,
375 Hudson Street, New York NY 10014 or SpecialSales@dk.com.

A Cataloging-in-Publication record for this book is available from the Library of Congress.

ISBN 0-7566-1480-5

Color reproduction by Colourscan, Singapore.
Printed and bound in Germany by Mohndruck.

Discover more at
www.dk.com

Contents

Foreword

The Royal Horticultural Society is dedicated to encouraging excellence in horticulture and informing anyone who is interested in gardening. These goals are well served by this new book, which is derived from *The RHS Shorter Dictionary of Gardening*, published in 1998 as an abridgment of the acclaimed four-volume reference work *The New RHS Dictionary of Gardening*. It gathers in one volume all core horticultural information, together with entries for over 1,900 genera of ornamental and culinary plants.

The compilation of *The RHS Shorter Dictionary of Gardening* was a major task, and the RHS would like to pay tribute to the dedicated work of Michael Pollock, who not only compiled the horticultural and general entries but has now also undertaken the meticulous revision and updating of the text for this illustrated edition, and of Mark Griffiths, who is responsible for all the plant entries in the original edition.

The introduction of carefully chosen color illustrations throughout the book should help this definitive single-volume dictionary achieve its aim of enabling a wider audience to have an informed understanding of plants and horticultural processes. It is written with the interests of vocational and amateur gardeners in mind, as well as the interests of horticultural students and all others concerned with the development and promotion of horticulture as a profession and a fulfilling leisure activity.

The RHS is proud of its association with this comprehensive guide to horticulture. I warmly commend it to all gardeners who wish to expand their knowledge of this fascinating subject.

Sir Richard Carew Pole
President
The Royal Horticultural Society
October 2005

Illustrated Dictionary of Gardening

A – Z

About this book

The horticultural entries of this book cover the principles and practice of horticulture, gardening techniques, crops, relevant science and terminology, pests, diseases, and disorders. All of these are newly reviewed, revised, and supplemented for this edition where necessary. Although the entries refer mainly to current horticultural practice in Great Britain, consideration has been given throughout to other situations, and a few little-used or obsolete terms are included when considered potentially useful.

Limited mention is made of chemical control measures for pests, diseases, and weeds. This emphasizes the need for environmental responsibility and utmost care in selection and application. Always refer to the product manufacturers' recommendations for acceptable, effective, and safe use of garden chemicals.

Plant genera and species were originally selected on grounds of widespread cultivation. Each entry gives a brief description with guidance on garden merit and preferred growing conditions. Recent changes to plant nomenclature have been applied in this edition, and there are some additional ornamental and culinary plant references.

Several of the largest genera have been presented in tables for ease of reference. The botanical plant name appears in bold in the left-hand column, with any synonyms and common names beneath. General information appears in an introductory paragraph that covers advice on cultivation and hardiness.

Noteworthy cultivars are frequently named in the plant and crop entries, but specific, up-to-date guidance should be obtained by consulting current catalogs of nurserymen and seedsmen.

Included on pages 839–864 are tables, illustrations, and lists that will help with the diagnosis of many plant pests and diseases, botanical descriptions, and common names of plants. These sections form useful supplements to parts of the main text.

Plant nomenclature

Botanical names adopted in this book have been adjudicated by members of the RHS Advisory Panel on Nomenclature and Taxonomy. For the most part, names follow those in the *RHS Plant Finder 2004–2005*.

Abbreviations used in this book

cf. : compare
cv : cultivar
cvs : cultivars
f. : forma
q.v. : which see
sp. : species
spp. : species (plural)

subsp./ssp. : subspecies
subspp. : subspecies (plural)
syn. : synonym
var. : variety
× : hybrid
+ : graft hybrid (see *chimera*)

Conversions of weights and measurements

To convert	into	multiply by
millimeters	inches	0.039
centimeters	inches	0.394
meters	feet	3.281
meters	yards	1.094
square meters	square yards	1.196
grams	ounces	0.0352
kilograms	ounces	35.274
kilograms	pounds	2.205
liters	gallons (US)	0.264
liters	gallons (Imperial)	0.222
liters	pints (US)	2.113
liters	pints (Imperial)	1.76

Acknowledgments

For contributions and advice: Chris Prior, Andrew Halstead, Guy Barter, James Armitage, and Janet Cubey (all at Wisley) and Vana Haggerty (for the composite illustration of bud stages on page 854).

Also, for general guidance and advice, Louise Abbott at DK.

abaxial of the surface or part of a lateral plant organ turned or facing away from the axis and toward the plant's base, such as the underside of a leaf; cf. *adaxial*.

Abelia (for Clarke Abel [1780–1826], who discovered *A. chinensis*). Caprifoliaceae. East Asia; Mexico. 15 species, evergreen or deciduous shrubs with small funnel-shaped flowers through summer and early fall. In some species the calyx is showy. Many genus members are not reliably hardy below 0°F (–18°C), but can be grown against south-facing house walls and in sheltered, walled gardens. Plant in a sunny position, protected from harsh winds. Prune early-flowering species immediately after flowering, midsummer- and fall-flowering species in early spring. Propagate from semiripe or ripe-wood cuttings in summer.

A. *chinensis* China; spreading, deciduous shrub to 5 ft (1.5 m) with pairs of fragrant white flowers surrounded by rose-tinted calyces from summer to fall; *A.* 'Edward Goucher' semievergreen hybrid between *A.* × *grandiflora* and *A. schumannii*, with glossy dark green foliage bronze on emergence, and lilac-pink flowers with golden throats; *A. floribunda* Mexico; somewhat tender evergreen with massed, tubular, cherry red flowers in midsummer; *A.* × *grandiflora* semievergreen hybrid between *A. chinensis* and *A. uniflora* with vigorous, arching branches, dark green foliage emerging bronze-pink and turning deep purple-bronze in fall; flowers mildly scented white, pink-tinged and surrounded by attractive, persistent, pink- or red-purple-tinted calyces; 'Francis Mason': leaves emerging in copper tones turning dark green with gold margins, flowers pale with red-bronze sepals; 'Goldsport' and 'Gold

Strike': more solidly gold-variegated; *A. schumannii* Central China; slender-branched, arching semievergreen to 5 ft (1.5 m) tall with rose-pink flowers produced in great abundance throughout the summer; hardier than most other species; *A. triflora* Himalayas; robust, deciduous shrub with an upright habit and sweetly fragrant shell-pink flowers surrounded by feathery red sepals.

Abeliophyllum (the foliage of this genus was thought to resemble that of *Abelia*). Oleaceae. Korea. 1 species, *A. distichum*, the KOREAN or WHITE FORSYTHIA, a deciduous shrub to 6½ ft (2 m), with arching branches and rather dull, ovate leaves. The flowers appear in late winter and early spring on bare, maroon twigs. They resemble a forsythia's in general shape, but are sparkling white and sweetly scented (flushed pink in the cultivar 'Roseum'). Hardy to 0°F (–18°C) if planted against a south-facing wall and given some support on wires or trellis. Cut back flowered shoots in midspring. Propagate by simple or air layering in fall or spring, or by half-ripe cuttings in a propagating case in summer.

Abelmoschus (from Arabic, *abu-l-misk*, "father of musk," alluding to the aromatic seeds of *A. moschatus*). Malvaceae. Old World Tropics and Subtropics. 5 species, annual and perennial, downy herbs with large, palmately lobed leaves, broadly funnel- or dish-shaped flowers close in shape to those of *Hibiscus* (a genus in which *Abelmoschus* is sometimes included) and podlike fruit. *A. moschatus* is a vibrant half-hardy bedding plant for sunny, sheltered situations. Sow seed under glass in early spring. Plant out after the last frost.

A. *moschatus* MUSK MALLOW, SILK FLOWE0R; bushy annual to 24 in (60 cm); flowers 3–4 in (8–10 cm) long in shades of red and cerise, often stained white at the throat; color selections include 'Mischief' (compact and bushy with bright red, white-eyed flowers), 'Pacific Light Pink' (to 16 in/ 40 cm), bushy, flowers large, dark pink at rim fading to pale pink at center), and 'Pacific Orange Scarlet' (flowers vivid scarlet, white-eyed).

Abies (from Latin, *abire*, to rise up, referring to the great height of some species). Pinaceae. North Temperate regions. Central America. FIR; SILVER FIR. Some 50 species, evergreen, coniferous trees with resinous bark and tiered branches in a whorled or candelabra-like arrangement. The needles are linear and flattened, often keeled and with two pale stripes of stomata beneath, and arranged radially, spirally or pectinately on the branchlets. The male cones hang from leaf axils; the female cones (described in the table below) are ovoid to cylindric and appear in spring, standing more or less upright. These trees are mostly from cool, wet mountainous regions.

Avoid soil that dries out rapidly, and exposure to drying winds (*A. cephalonica* and *A. pinsapo* will tolerate drier and more alkaline soil than others). All species grow best in slightly acidic soil. Most resent air pollution, although *A. homolepis* and *A. veitchii* will survive in cities.

Plant young trees in fall or spring on a well-drained site; select those that are 24–40 in (60–100 cm) tall with a single, straight leader (except for dwarf and low-growing cultivars). Keep the bole clear of weeds and mulch around it. Prune away surplus leaders, and the lowermost branch tiers as they die or attempt to resprout. *Abies* is attacked by adelgids, bagworms and caterpillars of the hemlock lopper. It usually fends off fungi, *Armillaria* included.

Abies concolor
This maturing tree shows the conical crown habit typical of many *Abies* species.

ABIES

Name	Distribution	Habit	Leaves	Cones
A. alba A. pectinata SILVER FIR; EUROPEAN SILVER FIR; CHRISTMAS TREE	C & S Europe	large tree (to 200 ft/60 m); crown regular; bark gray; branches whorled	4¾–1¼ in (12–3 cm) long in 2 horizontal ranks, dark glossy green above, silvery-glaucous beneath	to 7 × 1½ in (18 × 3.5 cm), cylindric, bronze-green at first with exserted, reflexed bracts

Comments: Vulnerable to late spring frosts. Includes 'Pendula', medium-sized with weeping branches, and 'Pyramidalis', medium-sized and densely conical.

Name	Distribution	Habit	Leaves	Cones
A. amabilis PACIFIC FIR; RED SILVER FIR; CASCADE FIR	W N America	large tree (to 120 ft/35 m); crown conic; bark silvery; branches tiered; buds very resinous	to 1½ in (3.5 cm) long, crowded on upper side of branches, pectinate beneath, dark glossy green above, silver-white beneath, orange-scented if crushed	to 6½ × 2¾ in (17 × 7 cm), conic-ovoid, purple at first with concealed bracts

Comments: Will not tolerate dry and chalky soil. Includes 'Spreading Star' ('Procumbens'), low-growing (to 3¼ ft/1 m tall), branches wide-spreading, horizontal.

Name	Distribution	Habit	Leaves	Cones
A. balsamea BALSAM FIR; BALM OF GILEAD	N America	medium-sized tree (to 80 ft) (to 25 m); crown conic; bark gray; branches ascending	to 1 in (2.5 cm) long, 2-ranked, glossy dark green above with glaucous patch at tip, 2 gray-white bands beneath, strongly balsam-scented	to 3 × 1 in (8 × 2.5 cm), oblong-cylindric, purple at first, gummy

Comments: Ill-suited to dry chalky soil and arid atmospheres. Often seen in the more tolerant, dwarf, flat-topped Hudsonia Group, of which the dwarf, cushionlike 'Nana' is a good selection for a moist, part-shaded position on the rock garden.

Name	Distribution	Habit	Leaves	Cones
A. bracteata A. venusta BRISTLE CONE FIR; SANTA LUCIA FIR	California	large tree (to 130 ft) (to 40 m); crown dense to open, brown; buds very long and slender **Comments:** Tolerates heat and drought.	to 2½ in (6 cm), 2-ranked, glossy dark green, spine-tipped	to 3 × ¼ in (8 × 0.5 cm), round to ovoid, golden-green, bracts remarkably long, exserted, spine-tipped

Name	Distribution	Habit	Leaves	Cones
A. cephalonica GREEK FIR; GRECIAN FIR	Greece	to 130 ft (40 m); crown conic; branches low, spreading; dark gray	to 1¼ in (3 cm), dark, glossy green, pale beneath, sharp-pointed, arranged around branchlets	to 7 × 1 in (18 × 2.5 cm), cylindric, tapering, brown with bracts exserted

Comments: Disease-resistant and chalk-tolerant; plant where frosts will not damage early new growth. Includes 'Meyer's Dwarf' ('Nana') a broad, low-growing dwarf with short needles.

Name	Distribution	Habit	Leaves	Cones
A. concolor WHITE FIR; COLORADO FIR	W US	large, slow-growing tree to 160 ft (50 m); crown conic-columnar; bark pale gray; branches whorled, spreading	to 2½ in (6 cm), thick, scattered or in 2 ranks, blue-green	to 4¾ × 1½ in (12 × 4 cm), cylindric, tapering, pale-green to purple with a strong bloom

Comments: One of the finest large conifers—slower-growing in warm climates, favoring cool, airy humid conditions. 'Argentea' ('Candicans') has very bright silver-gray or "blue" foliage; 'Compacta' (to 6½ × 6½ ft) (to 2 × 2 m) has an irregular, dense crown and gray-blue needles.

Name	Distribution	Habit	Leaves	Cones
A. concolor Lowiana Group A. lowiana LOW'S FIR; PACIFIC WHITE FIR; SIERRA WHITE FIR	SW US	to 230 ft (70 m); crown narrowly conic; trunk thick; branches short	to 2½ in (6 cm), 2-ranked, gray-green	to 3½ × 1¼ in (9 × 3 cm), green at first

A. alba

A. balsamea

A. concolor

A. homolepis

ABIES

Name	Distribution	Habit	Leaves	Cones
A. delavayi DELAVAYI'S FIR	China, Burma, India	to 80 ft (25 m); crown candelabriform; branches ascending	to 1½ in (4 cm), densely arranged around branchlets, dark green above, silvery beneath, revolute	to 4¾ × 1½ in (12 × 4 cm), cylindric, dark blue to violet ripening black
A. grandis GIANT FIR; LOWLAND FIR; GRAND FIR;	W N America	fast-growing to 250 ft (75 m); crown conic to columnar; bark blistered, brown to ridged and gray-brown; branches arching to ascending	to 1¾ in (4.5 cm), pectinately arranged, grooved and bright green above, with 2 glaucous bands beneath, very aromatic if crushed	to 4 × 1½ in (10 × 3.5 cm), cylindric, tapering, bright green at first

Comments: Somewhat more lime-tolerant than other species, very tall and fast-growing, favors abundant rainfall and humidity. Lower branches may be pruned out to allow underplanting. 'Aurea' has golden-yellow young growth.

Name	Distribution	Habit	Leaves	Cones
A. homolepis *A. brachyphylla* NIKKO FIR	Japan	to 130 ft (40 m); crown broadly conic; bark yellow to pink-gray, flaky	to 1¼ in (3 cm), densely pectinately arranged, dark green above, with 2 white bands beneath, tip blunt or cleft	to 4½ × 1¼ in (11 × 3 cm), cylindric, smooth, gummy, purple at first

Comments: Pollution-tolerant. Includes 'Prostrata' (low, spreading); 'Scottiae' (dwarf); 'Shelter Island' (semiprostrate, growth irregular, golden at first); 'Tomomi' (growth slender, sparse).

Name	Distribution	Habit	Leaves	Cones
A. koreana KOREAN FIR	S Korea	to 50 ft (15 m); crown broadly conic, compact, bark rough	to ¾ in (2 cm), crowded, arranged around branchlets, glossy dark green above, bright white beneath	to 3 × 1 in (8 × 2.5 cm), cylindric, apex tapering, purple

Comments: Slow-growing and suitable for smaller gardens, where plants no taller than 3¼ ft (1 m) will produce cones. Includes 'Flava' ('Aurea') (very small and slow-growing, leaves yellow-green); 'Piccolo' (dwarf, leaves very short, pointing forward and upward); 'Silberlocke' (leaves turned upward showing silver-white undersides).

Name	Distribution	Habit	Leaves	Cones
A. lasiocarpa SUBALPINE FIR; ALPINE FIR	W N America	to 80 ft (25 m), narrowly conical to columnar, slow-growing; bark thin, smooth silver	⅝–1½ in (1.5–4 cm), densely 2-ranked or in a loose, brushlike arrangement, pale gray-green, apex blunt or notched	to 5 × 1¼ in (13 × 3 cm), cylindric-conic, dark purple at first

Comments: Somewhat lime-tolerant; requires fertile, damp soil. Often sold as an alpine. In drier conditions, very slow-growing and likely to lose its regular, narrow outline.

Name	Distribution	Habit	Leaves	Cones
A. lasiocarpa var. **arizonica** *A. arizonica* CORKBARK FIR; CORK FIR	SW United States	bark thick, creamy-white, corky	silver-gray	

Comments: Attractive small tree with distinctive bark; makes a good bonsai. Includes 'Compacta', a slow-growing, compact, conical shrub with bright blue-gray leaves.

Name	Distribution	Habit	Leaves	Cones
A. magnifica CALIFORNIA RED FIR; RED FIR; SILVER TIP FIR	Oregon, California	to 200 ft (60 m), crown narrow-conic; bark smooth, gray to red-brown, fissured; branches rather short, horizontal	to 1½ in (4 cm), gray-green to blue-green throughout, densely pectinate, curving upward	to 10 × 3½ in (25 × 9 cm), broadly cylindric, purple at first

Comments: Very stately, performing best in cool, airy and humid conditions. Used as a Christmas tree in California. Includes the Glauca Group (leaves very strong blue-green); 'Glauca Prostrata' is dwarf, branches spreading.

A. lasiocarpa **var.** *arizonica*   *A. magnifica*   *A. nordmanniana*   *A. pinsapo*

ABIES

Name	Distribution	Habit	Leaves	Cones
A. nordmanniana NORDMANN FIR; CAUCASIAN FIR; CHRISTMAS TREE	NE Turkey	to 180 ft (55 m); crown conic to columnar; branches whorled, downswept	to 1¼ in (3 cm), glossy, dark green above, silvery beneath, densely arranged—forward-pointing and overlapping above on branchlets, pectinate beneath	to 7 × 1¾ in (18 × 4.5 cm), red tinged green, scales long, reflexed

Comments: Resilient, disease-resistant species making a dense cone. Includes 'Golden Spreader' (dwarf, slow-growing, spreading, foliage light yellow) and 'Pendula' (semiprostrate, branchlets pendulous).

Name	Distribution	Habit	Leaves	Cones
A. pinsapo SPANISH FIR; HEDGEHOG FIR	S Spain	to 120 ft (35 m); crown broadly conic; branches crowded, whorled; bark smooth then rough, rusty brown	to ¾ in (1.8 cm), often shorter, rigid and densely arranged around branchlets, dark green above, silvery beneath	to 6 × 1⅓ in (16 × 3.4 cm), green bloomed purple at first

Comments: Drought-and heat-resistant, chalk-tolerant and remaining dwarf for years. Includes 'Aurea' (slow-growing, weak, leaves golden); 'Glauca' (large, leaves blue-gray); var. **marocana** (*A. marocana*) the MOROCCAN FIR, leaves 2-ranked.

Name	Distribution	Habit	Leaves	Cones
A. procera *A. nobilis* NOBLE FIR; CHRISTMAS TREE	W United States	to 230 ft (70 m); crown conic; bark smooth and silver-gray at first then blistered and brown, ultimately fissured	to 1½ in (3.5 cm), arranged along sides and upper surface of branchlets, blue-green	to 9 × 2¾ in (23 × 7 cm), oblong-cylindric, purple with long-exserted, reflexed bracts

Comments: Sometimes used as a Christmas tree; includes 'Glauca' (leaves blue-gray) and 'Prostrata' (dwarf, flat-topped bush, leaves blue-gray).

Name	Distribution	Habit	Leaves	Cones
A. spectabilis HIMALAYAN FIR **Comments:** New growth badly affected by spring frosts.	Himalayas	to 100 ft (30 m); crown conic, broad; branches red brown at first, spreading then ascending; bark rough, scaly; buds large, round	to 2 in (5 cm), tough 4-ranked, dark green above, silvery beneath, tip cleft	to 6 × 2 in (15 × 5 cm), cylindric to oblong-ovoid, blue-gray to violet

Name	Distribution	Habit	Leaves	Cones
A. veitchii **Comments:** Pollution-tolerant.	Japan	to 120 ft (35 m); crown narrowly conic; branches short, spreading; bark gray, smooth above, fluted below	to 1¼ in (3 cm), ranked along upper surface of branchlets, forward-pointing, glossy dark green above, silver beneath, apex truncate, cleft	to 2¾ × 1 in (7 × 2.5 cm), cylindric, purple-blue, bract tips exserted

abiotic disorder a description of poor growth or malfunction in plants which is not caused by a living organism. Abiotic disorder is commonly related to environmental factors or nutritional deficiency.

abortive of reproductive organs; undeveloped or not perfectly developed, and therefore barren: of seeds; failing to develop normally.

Abronia (from Greek, *habros*, "graceful"). Nyctaginaceae. Western North America, Mexico. SAND VERBENA. 35 species, annual or perennial, trailing herbs, often viscid, with rounded, fleshy leaves. Small tubular flowers are carried in stalked, terminal heads and are often highly fragrant, becoming more so at night. Grow in full sun in rather dry, light soil. In virtually frost-free climates they may become perennial, making leafy mats ideal for binding sand or for greening arid banks, retaining walls and rock gardens. In colder areas they are good basket plants for greenhouses and conservatories. For outdoor use as tender bedding plants, *Abronia* should be grown from seed each year or repropagated by cuttings taken from stock plants overwintered under glass. In frost-free regions, sow seed *in situ* in fall; elsewhere under glass at 59°F (15°C) in spring. Prior to sowing, soak the seed for 24 hours and remove the papery husk. Strike softwood cuttings in sand in spring.

A. latifolia YELLOW SAND VERBENA; British Columbia south to California; thick-leaved, clammy trailer with bright yellow flowers; *A. umbellata* PINK SAND VERBENA, BEACH SAND VERBENA; differs from *A. latifolia* in its narrower leaves, red-tinted stems and rose-pink flowers; *A. villosa* resembles a hairy, sticky *A. umbellata*, with flowers of a deeper pink or rosy-purple; is able to tolerate prolonged drought.

abscission, abscissing (abscising) of leaves, branches and fruits; a separating or falling away, caused by disintegration of a layer of plant tissues at the base of the organ (e.g., as the result of environmental conditions or pollination leading to hormonal action), with a subsequent development of scar tissue or periderm at the point of abscission.

Abutilon (from the Arabic name for mallow). Malvaceae. Tropics and subtropics. PARLOUR MAPLE, FLOWERING MAPLE. Some 150 species, annual and perennial herbs, or shrubs and trees with ovate and finely toothed to palmately lobed leaves, and nodding, solitary, bell- or bowl-shaped flowers with 5 showy, obovate petals and a distinct staminal column. The most frequently grown species are evergreen shrubs, slender-branched and more or less glabrous in *A.* × *hybridum*, *A. megapotamicum*, *A.* × *milleri* and *A. pictum*; robust and hairy in *A.*

Types of abutilon
There are two distinct types of abutilon—spindly, half-hardy shrubs, including *A. megapotamicum* (left) and the more robust mallowlike species, such as *A. vitifolium* var. *alba* (right).

Acacia (From Greek *akakia*, a plant name used by Dioscorides). Leguminosae. Subtropical and tropical regions. MIMOSA; WATTLE. Some 1,200 species shrubs, trees, and lianes (those below evergreen trees). The leaves are bipinnate, but are sometimes only present in juvenile stage and later replaced by phyllodes. The flowers are small and numerous, usually yellow and packed in small, powderpuff-like arrangements. These in turn are crowded in globose or spiciform heads, themselves arranged in racemes or panicles.

Several species will tolerate frost: *A. dealbata*, *A. longifolia*, *A. baileyana* to 14°F (–10°C), *A. saligna* to 23°F (–5°C). *A. decurrens*, *A. melanoxylon*, *A. retinodes*, and *A. podalyriifolia* have all been successfully cultivated outside in favored regions of the UK, with the protection of a south- or southwest-facing wall. In cool temperate climates, the smaller *Acacia* species make beautiful specimens for the cool greenhouse or conservatory, often flowering in winter or early spring. *A. dealbata*, *A. melanoxylon*, *A. longifolia*, *A. pendula*, *A. retinodes* and *A. verticillata* are also amenable to tub cultivation under glass. Outdoors, grow in well-drained, neutral to slightly acidic soil in full sun. In zones at the limits of hardiness, plant near the base of a sheltered south- or southwest-facing wall.

Under glass, grow in direct sun in a free-draining, sandy, loam-based medium with leaf mold or compost. When using fertilizers, it should be remembered that a number of Acacia species show sensitivity to high levels of phosphorus. Try to maintain a minimum winter temperature of 41°F (5°C) and ventilate the plants freely when conditions allow. Water moderately when in full growth, sparingly in winter. Move pot-grown specimens outdoors for the summer.

Propagate *Acacia* from seed or semiripe cuttings. Douse seeds with scalding water and allow them to soak in the cooled liquid for 12–48 hours before sowing; viable seeds should swell. and thus be identifiable. Germination at 68–77°F (20–25°C) takes 7–20 days. Strike semiripe heeled cuttings in a sandy propagating mix under mist or cover with gentle bottom heat, at 60–65°F (15–18°C).

ochsenii, *A. vitifolium* and their hybrid, *A. × suntense*. All have attractive flowers, complemented in some cultivars within the first group by variegated leaves.

A. × hybridum (syn. *A. globosum*) CHINESE LANTERN, FLOWERING or PARLOR MAPLE; a varied group of garden hybrids, erect and spreading shrubs to 6½ ft (2 m); their leaves ovate or palmately lobed, serrate, often variegated; flowers pendulous, to 2¾ in (7 cm), white, pink, red, yellow, apricot, and orange, sometimes conspicuously veined and almost always slightly inflated in appearance. *A. megapotamicum* BRAZILIAN TRAILING ABUTILON; Brazil; slender-stemmed trailer or semiclimber to 10 ft (3 m); leaves dark green, cordate-lanceolate; flowers pendulous with pale yellow petals encased in a blood red calyx and with a redblack column; *A.* 'Variegatum'; leaves gold-mottled; *A. pictum* (syn. *A. striatum*) Brazil; shrub or small tree to 12 ft (4 m) with maplelike leaves; flowers solitary, drooping, to 1½ in (4 cm) with conspicuously veined, orange-yellow petals; 'Aureomaculatum': leaves goldspattered; flowers dark-veined, coralred; 'Thompsonii': orange-flowered with an intricate mosaic of emerald, lime and yellow leaf variegation; *A. × milleri* (*A. megapotamicum* × *A. pictum*) slender stemmed, rather loosely upright plants with flowers intermediate between parents; 'Variegatum': leaves marked with a gold, cream and jade green patchwork; calyx rosy; petals rich yellow; staminal column dark carmine.

Tender abutilons like those mentioned above are often grown as dot plants for summer bedding, or as halfhardy specimens for patio pots and baskets in cool temperate zones. They are also grown permanently in the cool greenhouse, conservatory or the home. *A. megapotamicum*, however, is hardy to 14°F (–10°C) and, if mulched, will usually regenerate from the base after hard frosts. It is well worth attempting outdoors as a wall shrub in sheltered situations (min. 0°F/–18°C).

The second group of popular abutilons comprises those robust, downy shrubs and small trees native to Chile and sometimes included in the genus *Corynabutilon*. These thrive on sheltered, sunny walls above 0°F (–18°C). *A. vitifolium* to 25 ft (8 m), usually less; leaves large, palmately 3–5–7-lobed, coated in gray-white felt; flowers 2–3 in (5–8 cm) wide white or purple-blue; white-flowered plants include var. *album* and 'Tennant's White'; 'Veronica Tennant': large, lavender blooms amid hoary foliage; *A. ochsenii* differs from *A. vitifolium* in its 3-lobed leaves, usually less downy, leaves always with 3 lobes and in its smaller, pale lavender to violet flowers, often spotted at the base within; the hybrid between these species, *A. × suntense* includes the whiteflowered 'Gorer's White' and 'White Charm', the dark purple 'Jermyns' and the violet 'Violetta'. Increase by softwood, greenwood or semiripe cuttings stripped of most of their leaves and inserted in a closed case, under glass.

13

ACACIA

Name	Distribution	Height & Spread	Foliage	Flowers
A. baileyana COOTAMUNDRA WATTLE; BAILEY WATTLE; GOLDEN MIMOSA	SE Australia	15–30 × 8–25 ft (5–10 × 2.5–8 m)	to 2 in (5 cm), finely bipinnate glaucous gray- to blue-green	golden-yellow, strongly fragrant balls arranged in racemes in winter and spring

Comments: An exceptional small tree or multi-stemmed shrub with a compact habit and neat, feathery foliage (purple-tinted in 'Purpurea'); thrives on sunny walls in colder areas.

Name	Distribution	Height & Spread	Foliage	Flowers
A. cultriformis KNIFE ACACIA; KNIFE-LEAF WATTLE	New South Wales	to 12 × 12 ft (4 × 4 m)	to 1½ × ⅝ in (3.5 × 1.5 cm), undivided, ovate to deltoid, thinly fleshy, silvery gray	clusters of golden yellow balls in spring

Comments: Multi-stemmed with arching branches; good for screening and dry banks (min. 20°F (–7°C), elsewhere for very sunny and sheltered sites.

Name	Distribution	Height & Spread	Foliage	Flowers
A. dealbata A. decurrens var. dealbata MIMOSA; SILVER WATTLE	SE Australia; Tasmania	to 100 × 80 ft (30 × 25 m)	to 4¾ in (12 cm), finely bipinnate, silver-gray to sea green	pale gold, intensely fragrant balls in large, branching sprays in late winter and spring

Comments: Very popular shrub or small to medium-sized tree; fast-growing with a narrowly erect, then tiered habit and spreading, feathery foliage. Requires a sheltered, warm position but will regenerate from root suckers if cut down by frost. Flowers are commonly sold as florist's mimosa.

Name	Distribution	Height & Spread	Foliage	Flowers
A. decurrens EARLY BLACK WATTLE; GREEN WATTLE	New South Wales	to 40 × 30 ft (12 × 10 m)	to 2¾ in (7 cm), finely bipinnate, dark green	yellow balls clustered in racemes in late winter and early spring

Comments: Resembles a deep green *A. dealbata*; roots and suckers sometimes invasive. **A. mearnsii** (BLACK WATTLE) differs in its branchlets which are not grooved and ribbed.

Name	Distribution	Height & Spread	Foliage	Flowers
A. 'Exeter Hybrid' A. 'Veitchiana'	garden origin	to 20 × 12 ft (6 × 4 m)	undivided, long and narrow on arching branches	rich yellow, fragrant, in spikes in spring

Comments: (*A. longifolia* × *A. riceana*). A free-flowering container or border shrub for the large cool, conservatory.

Name	Distribution	Height & Spread	Foliage	Flowers
A. farnesiana PERFUME ACACIA; MIMOSA BUSH; SCENTED WATTLE; SWEET ACACIA	Tropical America	to 22 × 15 ft (7 × 5 m)	leaves bipinnate, feathery with segments to ½ in (1 cm) long	orange-yellow, fragrant balls throughout the year

Comments: A deciduous, thorny shrub or tree, possibly synonymous with *A. smallii*, a tree with which it is often confused and which is held to be hardier.

Name	Distribution	Height & Spread	Foliage	Flowers
A. longifolia SALLOW WATTLE; SYDNEY GOLDEN WATTLE	Australia, Tasmania	to 22 × 20 ft (7 × 6 m)	to 6 in (15 cm), undivided, oblong-lanceolate, dark green	pale to golden yellow spikes along branches in late winter and early spring

Comments: Fast-growing but short-lived large shrub or tree with a broad open head. Good for screening and soil binding; in coastal regions it sometimes becomes semiprostrate. Drought- and lime-tolerant. Similar and sometimes treated as a variety of this species, **A. sophorae** (COASTAL WATTLE) is hardier and differs in its shrubby habit, and shorter, broader phyllodes.

A. baileyana   *A. cultriformis*   *A. dealbata*   *A. decurrens*

ACACIA

Name	Distribution	Height & Spread	Foliage	Flowers
A. melanoxylon BLACKWOOD; BLACK ACACIA	Tasmania, Australia	to 100 × 30 ft (30 × 10 m)	to 5½ × 1 in (14 × 2.5 cm), undivided, oblanceolate, dark green	pale yellow balls in branching racemes in spring

Comments: Similar to *A. longifolia*, but with pinnate juvenile foliage. Fast-growing, erect tree; responds well to pruning.

A. mucronata VARIABLE SALLOW WATTLE	Australia	**Comments:** Similar to *A. longifolia*, but with narrower phyllodes and looser inflorescences.		

A. paradoxa *A. arreata* HEDGE WATTLE; KANGAROO THORN	New South Wales	to 15 × 12 ft (5 × 4 m)	½–1¼ × ½ in (1–3 × 1 cm), oblong-lanceolate, dark green, on densely and viciously spiny branches	yellow, in solitary balls in late winter and spring

Comments: Flowers when young, making a fine, if thorny container shrub for terraces and conservatories. In warmer areas, a formidable hedge. Includes the weeping to straggling 'Pendula', and var. **angustifolia** with narrow phyllodes.

A. pendula WEEPING MYALL; WEEPING ACACIA;	E Australia	to 20 × 12 ft (6 × 4 m)	to 4 × ½ in (10 × 1 cm), undivided, lanceolate, blue-green	lemon-yellow in short, cylindrical panicles

Comments: A very beautiful small tree with weeping habit, silvery foliage and flowers produced throughout the year.

A. podalyriifolia QUEENSLAND SILVER WATTLE; MOUNT MORGAN WATTLE; PEARL ACACIA	NE Australia	to 20 × 12 ft (6 × 4 m)	to 2 × ¾ in (5 × 2 cm), undivided, rounded to ovate-elliptic, silvery gray, white-tomentose	bright yellow, balls in branched racemes produced from early winter to early spring

Comments: Handsome large shrub or small tree with silvery foliage; can be trained and pruned. Good for large containers on terraces and in cool conservatories.

A. pravissima OVEN'S WATTLE	SE Australia	10–25 × 6½–20 ft (3–8 × 2–6 m)	to ¾ × ⅝ in (2 × 1.5 cm), undivided, deltoid to cuneate, glaucous gray-green with a single spine below the broad apex on the underside	bright yellow, produced in small clusters in early spring

Comments: Small tree or shrub with arching, wandlike branches and unusually shaped phyllodes. Good for conservatories and sheltered walls and terraces.

A. pulchella WESTERN PRICKLY MOSES	W Australia	to 10 × 6½ ft (3 × 2 m)	finely bipinnate with each segment to ¼ in (0.5 cm) long	bright yellow balls clustered 2–3 together

Comments: Small to medium-sized shrub with prickly branches.

A. farnesiana

A. longifolia

A. pravissima

A. retinodes

ACACIA

Name	Distribution	Height & Spread	Foliage	Flowers
A. retinodes A. *floribunda* of gardens SILVER WATTLE; SWAMP WATTLE; WIRILD	S Australia, Tasmania	to 20 × 12 ft (6 × 4 m)	to 7 × ⅝ in (18 × 1.5 cm), undivided, linear, bright mid-green to gray-green	small, highly fragrant pale yellow balls freely produced in large panicles, principally in summer
	Comments: A fairly hardy and lime-tolerant tree with an airy crown of weeping, narrow foliage. An excellent fast-growing, open screen. Flowers last well when cut.			
A. riceana RICE'S WATTLE	S Tasmania	6½–30 × 5–20 ft (2–10 × 1.5–6 m)	to 2¼ × ¼ in (5.5 × 0.5 cm), undivided, narrow, dark green and sharply pointed	pale yellow balls in dense racemes in spring
Comments: A large shrub with slender, arching branches. Distinguished from A. *verticillata* by the phyllodes, which are clustered, not whorled.				
A. saligna A. *cyanophylla*; A. *cyanophyllodes* BLUE-LEAVED WATTLE; GOLDEN WREATH WATTLE	W Australia	to 20 × 15 ft (6 × 5 m) **Comments:** Multi-stemmed and spreading.	6–12 × ½–1¼ in (15–30 × 1–3 cm), undivided, linear-oblong to lanceolate, blue-green	deep yellow balls in clusters in spring
A. ulicifolia A. *juniperina* JUNIPER WATTLE	SE Australia	to 10 × 6½ ft (3 × 2 m)	to ¾ in (2 cm), undivided, needlelike, olive to dark green	solitary, creamy-yellow balls in spring
Comments: 'Brownii' is compact and bushy, to 24 in (60 cm) tall with large, rich yellow flower heads.				
A. verticillata PRICKLY MOSES	SE Australia, Tasmania	to 20 × 12 ft (6 × 4 m)	to ¾ × ¹⁄₁₆ in (2 × 0.2 cm), undivided, needlelike, whorled, dark olive green	pale yellow in short spikes in spring and early summer
Comments: Bushy shrub with dense, prickly growth. A good hedge if pruned, resisting intruders and saline winds. Unpruned, it becomes multi- stemmed and open with snaking branches and mats of gorselike foliage.				

Acaena (from the Greek *akaina*, thorn, a reference to the spiny flower- and fruiting heads). Rosaceae. Southern Hemisphere (those below from New Zealand). NEW ZEALAND BURR; BIDI-BIDI; SHEEP'S BURRS. Some 100 species, small, evergreen, perennial herbs and subshrubs, carpet-forming with pinnate leaves and spring flowers packed in burlike balls to ⅝ in (1.5 cm) diameter. Hardy to –15°F (5°C) or lower if protected with a dry mulch. Plant in light shade or full sun in sharply draining neutral to slightly alkaline soil. Increase by division, or by seed sown in a frame in fall or spring.

A. 'Blue Haze' vigorous spreader to 12 × 39 in (30 × 100 cm) with long, rooting stems, leaves to 4 in (10 cm) long, leaflets widely spaced, ¼–½ in (0.5–1 cm) long, bluntly toothed to lobed, smooth, gray-green to steel blue or pewter; A. *buchananii* to 1½ in (4 cm), making close carpets of pea green to pale gray-green leaves; leaflets fewer and broader than in A. 'Blue Haze', downy beneath; A. *caesiiglauca* taller than the last species to 2 in (5 cm) with larger leaflets of a pale, glaucous blue and rather downy; A. *microphylla* leaves

½–1¼ in (1–3 cm)-long; leaflets of a pale olive to gray-green with a strong, red-brown tint, pronounced and persistent in the cultivar 'Kupferteppich'.

Acalypha (from the Greek for nettle, *akalephe*: Linnaeus thought that the leaves of this genus resembled those of the stinging nettle). Euphorbiaceae. Tropics. Over 400 species, shrubs, trees and annual herbs. Provide a minimum temperature of 50°F (10°C), with filtered sunlight to medium shade, and high humidity. When in growth, water plentifully and liquid-feed semiweekly. In winter, keep barely moist. Propagate from semiripe cuttings in late summer or from soft cuttings in early spring in a closed case with bottom heat.

A. *godseffiana* New Guinea; to 5½ ft (1.6 m); leaves narrowly ovate, bright green, usually deeply cut and fringed and edged, blotched or spattered with ivory, yellow and lime; flowers dull; A. *hispida* CHENILLE PLANT, RED HOT CAT'S TAIL; New Guinea, Malaysia; to 12 ft (4 m), resembles a spectacular, woody love-lies-bleeding (*Amaranthus caudatus*) with 20-in- (50-cm-) long, dark crimson to bright red tassels, and

broad, sap green leaves; A. *wilkesiana* COPPERLEAF, JACOB'S COAT, MATCH-ME-IF-YOU-CAN; South Pacific; to 15 ft (4.5 m); leaves saw-toothed, elliptic to ovate, 8 in (20 cm) long, usually described as copper splashed with pink and red; includes forms with leaves bronze-maroon edged white to pink, or red with bronze and crimson markings, or red-bronze and very large, to broad and coppery black with twisted, crenate, green and red margins or green stippled and blotched orange and red.

Acanthocereus (from Greek *akantha*, thorn and *Cereus*, a related genus—a reference to the fierce spines). Cactaceae. Central and South America. 6 species, large cacti, shrubby, clambering or treelike in habit with ribbed spiny stems and white, funnel-shaped, nocturnal flowers. Provide a minimum temperature of 50°F (10°C), with filtered sunlight to medium shade and high humidity. Plant in a loam-based, medium-fertility mix high in sand and grit and with a pH of 6–7.5. Shade in hot weather and maintain low humidity. Keep dry from midfall until early spring, except for a light misting on warm days in late winter. Propagate by detaching rooted lengths of stems.

A. colombianus (syn. *A. guatemalensis*, *A. pitajaya*) Colombia; differs from *A. tetragonus* in its erect habit and flowers with a perianth tube to 9 in (23 cm) long; *A. tetragonus* (syn. *A. acutangulus*, *A. pentagonus*) S US, W Indies, C America; gaunt shrub to 10 ft (3 m) tall with arching stems; flowers to 10 in (25 cm) long with a perianth tube to 6 in (15 cm).

Acantholimon (from Greek *akantha*, thorn, and *limon*, an allusion to the related genus *Limonium*). Plumbaginaceae. PRICKLY THRIFT. Mediterranean to Central Asia. 120 species, small, evergreen, tufted, perennial herbs and subshrubs with hummocks of needlelike leaves and short spikelets of flowers produced in summer. Suited to rock gardens and alpine troughs, the following species are cushion-forming, dwarf shrublets. Plant in a warm, dry position in full sun in light and sharply draining, gritty soil. Where rain and cold threaten, these plants succeed better in pans or tufa blocks in the alpine house or frame. Propagate by earthing up the bases of older plants: divide these once roots have formed.

A. glumaceum Central Asia; rose flowers with white, downy calyces; *A. ulicinum* Eastern Mediterranean to Asia Minor; pink flowers with white to purple calyces; *A. venustum* Asia Minor; pink flowers with purple-veined, yellow calyces.

Acanthus (from Greek *akanthe*, thorn). Acanthaceae. Old World. BEAR'S BREECHES. 30 species, perennial herbs and shrubs with lanceolate to oblanceolate, toothed to pinnately lobed leaves, and tall spikes of tubular, hooded flowers carried in summer amid heavily veined bracts. All are hardy but prefer a warm, sunny position in fast-draining soil. Increase by seed or division in early fall, or take winter cuttings of the long, narrow roots.

A. dioscoridis Turkey, Iraq, Iran; leaves gray-green, laciniate to lobed; spikes 12–40 in (30–100 cm) with incised dull green bracts and purple-pink flowers; *A. hungaricus* (syn. *A. balcanicus*, *A. longifolius*) Balkans to Greece; leaves dark, glossy green, deeply pinnately cut, the lobes coarsely toothed but not spiny; spikes to 3¼ ft (1 m) with

spiny purple-red bracts and pale pink flowers; *A. mollis* South Europe, Northwest Africa; leaves glossy dark green, broadly pinnately cut, the lobes wide, toothed and softly spiny; spikes to 5 ft (1.5 m) with toothed, mauve-tinted bracts and white flowers; Latifolius Group includes 'Oak Leaf' with large, very broadly and shallowly lobed, scalloped leaves; *A. spinosus* Mediterranean; leaves dark green, often with sparse silver hairs and obscurely silvered veins, 1–3 × pinnately cut, the lobes deep, narrow, rigid with sharply spiny margins; spikes to 3¼ ft (1 m) tall with spiny, green-mauve bracts and white flowers; Spinosissimus Group: hybrids between this and the previous species with larger, softer, but deeply cut and sharply spiny leaves—most plants sold as *A. spinosus* belong here.

acaricide a chemical used to kill parasitic mites such as red spider mites.

acaulescent of a plant whose stem is absent or, more usually, appears to be absent, being subterranean or so short as to be inconspicuous.

Acca Myrtaceae. South America. 2 species, evergreen shrubs or small trees. *A. sellowiana* (syn. *Feijoa sellowiana*), the PINEAPPLE GUAVA, ranges from Southern Brazil to Northern Argentina. It grows to 20 ft (6 m) tall with peeling gray-brown bark and broadly oblong to elliptic, blunt, leathery leaves, dull green above, silvery beneath. Borne singly or in sparse clusters in summer, the flowers are some 1½ in (4 cm) across and fleshy, with showy crimson stamens. The red-tinted, egg-shaped fruit is edible, as are the flowers. Hardy to 5°F (−15°C) given full sun, protection from harsh winds and a well-drained situation. Propagate by seed or semiripe cuttings in a closed case with bottom heat.

accent plant a plant featured in garden design to focus attention on contrasting color, texture or form, which may be natural, as with weeping willow (*Salix babylonica*), or achieved by trimming, as with yew (*Taxus baccata*).

accessory fruit a fruit or aggregate fruit in which the conspicuous and, usually, fleshy parts are distinct from

the pistil, as in the enlarged torus of the strawberry.

acclimation biological and/or physiological modification in plants as they adapt to environmental change.

acclimatization the gradual introduction of a plant to a different climate or environment; most commonly used for the transfer of tender plants from a greenhouse to a frame or the open garden, a process often termed "hardening off." Also refers to a late stage in the process of micropropagation, sometimes known as weaning.

accrescent growing together or becoming larger or longer with age, or after fertilization, as in the lanternlike calyx of *Physalis*.

accumbent (of cotyledons) lying face to face, the edges of one side lying against the radicle in the seed.

Acer (the Classical Latin name). Aceraceae. North and Central America, Europe, North Africa, Asia. MAPLE. Some 150 species, deciduous or evergreen trees and shrubs (those here deciduous), hardy and grown for their foliage, which often colors beautifully in fall, for their bark, which is sometimes attractively marked, and, less frequently, for their flowers and fruits. The leaves are most typically broad and palmately cut or lobed, but may also be ovate or elliptic to lanceolate, with three or no lobes. Small, usually yellow-green or red-brown flowers appear in arching to pendulous racemes or panicles in spring. The fruits hang on slender stalks and consist of a pair of winged nuts (samaras), fused at their ovules, with the wings spreading outward.

The following maples (see table on following pages) are hardy. Most require full sun or light shade, fertile, well-drained soil, preferably neutral to slightly acidic, and ample moisture. The Japanese maples prefer dappled sun or shade, shelter, and moist, fertile soil rich in organic matter. They grow well in containers and small spaces. Propagate by seed sown when ripe, by softwood or semiripe cuttings, or by grafting.

ACER

Name	Distribution	Habit	Bark	Leaves
A. buergerianum *A. trifidum* of gardens THREE-TOOTHED MAPLE; TRIDENT MAPLE	E.China; Korea; Japan	small, bushy tree with a low, spreading habit **Comments:** An attractive, small maple, useful for large containers, patios and bonsai.		to 3 × 4 in (8 × 10 cm), acutely and palmately 3–5-lobed, dark green above, paler beneath with an entire or finely toothed margin, turning fiery red to orange-yellow in fall
A. campestre FIELD MAPLE; HEDGE MAPLE	Europe; W Asia	variable shrub or small tree to 40 ft (12 m) tall with a rounded, bushy crown or an open habit with twiggy, picturesquely gnarled branches	somewhat corky, gray-brown	to 3 × 4 in (8 × 10 cm) bluntly and palmately 3–5-lobed, dull, dark green above, paler and somewhat hairy beneath, with an entire to toothed or lobed margin, turning clear yellow to amber in fall; petioles contain milky sap
Comments: Used in hedging, and a familiar feature of hedgerows. Includes 'Albovariegatum' leaves blotched white; 'Elsrijk' tree with a dense, broadly conical crown and small, dark green leaves, good for street planting; 'Nanum' ('Compactum') densely compact and shrubby			with small, dark green leaves; 'Postelense' small, shrubby, mop-headed tree or shrub, leaves yellow at first, then yellow-green with red-tinted petioles; 'Pulverulentum' leaves blotched and finely flecked white; 'Schwerinii' leaves blood-red at first, turning purple.	
A. capillipes	Japan	large shrub or small tree to 43 ft (13 m) tall with a deep, broad crown of long, spreading, stemlike branches	young shoots bright red, branches ultimately olive green with silvery white stripes	to 4½ in (11 cm) long, ovate and acutely 3-lobed with a tapering tip and serrate margins, emerging coral red, becoming jade green with a red-tinted petiole, turning orange-red in fall
A. cappadocicum *A. laetum* CAPPADOCIAN MAPLE; CAUCASIAN MAPLE;	Caucasus; W Asia; Himalaya	medium-sized to large tree to 70 ft (20 m) tall, often multi-stemmed		to 4¾ × 5½ in (12 × 14 cm), broadly and palmately 5–7-lobed, entire, deep glossy green turning yellow in fall petioles containing milky sap
Comments: Cultivars include 'Aureum' leaves red-tinted at first then gold to yellow-green; 'Rubrum' leaves blood-red at first turning dark green; and 'Tricolor' leaves pink at first then pale green marked cream. ssp. *lobelii* (*A. lobelii*) grows to 60 ft (18 m) tall with ascending branches			in a compact, columnar to conical crown and large, dark green leaves with wavy margins. ssp. *sinicum* has red-brown, punctate shoots and conspicuously punctate leaves.	
A. carpinifolium HORNBEAM MAPLE	Japan	small to medium-sized tree to 30 ft (10 m) tall		to 4½ × 1½ in (11 × 4 cm), obovate with an acute tip, serrate margins and prominent, pinnate veins, fresh pale to mid-green turning yellow to brown in fall
Comments: Leaves strikingly similar to those of *Carpinus betulus* (COMMON HORNBEAM).				
A. caudatifolium *A. morrisonense* FORMOSAN MAPLE; MOUNT MORRISON MAPLE	China; Taiwan	fast-growing, large shrub or tree to 25 ft (8 m) tall, erect then spreading **Comments:** Needs moist, fertile soil.	green striped white	to 4 × 2¾ in (10 × 7 cm), ovate-oblong with three lobes, the midlobe longer and tapering, margins serrate, emerging red, expanding fresh mid-green with red petiole, turning red in fall
A. caudatum subsp. **ukurunduense** *A. ukurunduense*	Japan; Korea	small tree **Comments:** Dislikes chalk.		to 5½ in (14 cm) wide, cordate in outline with 5–7 narrowly ovate, toothed lobes, veins impressed above, hairy beneath, coloring well in fall

A. buergerianum   A. campestre

A. carpinifolium

ACER

Name	Distribution	Habit	Bark	Leaves
A. circinatum VINE MAPLE	W North America	to 40 ft (12 m) tall, habit variable—in shade, a low-branching shrub with slender, sprawling and snaking stems and intricate twigs; in full sun, a single-trunked, small tree		to 4¾ in (12 cm) wide, almost circular in outline with 5–11 lobes and serrate margins, emerging pink-tinted, hardening bright green and turning amber, flame and bright red in fall

Comments: Tolerates dry shade and is an excellent choice for underplanting in woodland gardens where the arching to clambering branches make airy bowers lit with brilliant fall color. The flowers (small, wine red) and fruit (small, deep crimson propellers) are also decorative. 'Monroe' is small and shrubby, the leaves with five distinct lobes with deeply dissected margins.

Name	Distribution	Habit	Bark	Leaves
A. cissifolium	China; Japan	small, spreading tree to 40 ft (12 m) tall		composed of 3 distinct leaflets to 3 in (8 cm) long, ovate and coarsely toothed, dark green turning red and yellow in fall

Comments: Needs light shade and moist, neutral to slightly acidic soil. ssp. **henryi** (*A. henryi*) has gray bark striped with blue-white, and larger, more or less untoothed leaflets, these turn brilliant crimson in fall. Drooping catkins of pale gold flowers appear with the red-tinted new leaves.

Name	Distribution	Habit	Bark	Leaves
A. crataegifolium HAWTHORN MAPLE	Japan	small tree or large shrub to 30 ft (10 m) tall with long, arching branches	purple-red to gray-green with silver-white stripes	variable, to 3 in (8 cm) long, ovate with 3–5, shallow lobes and serrate margins, fresh green to blue-green

Comments: Foliage remarkably like that of the common hawthorn. 'Veitchii' has leaves splashed with lime and white, flushed pink at the base.

Name	Distribution	Habit	Bark	Leaves
A. davidii DAVID'S MAPLE; SNAKEBARK MAPLE	China	shrub or small to medium-sized tree to 50 ft (15 m) tall, often multi-stemmed or low-branching with long, spreading branches	smooth, olive green striped silvery white	to 6 in (15 cm) long, ovate to oblong with a tapering tip, unlobed or shallowly 3-lobed with serrate margins, dark glossy green, turning bright yellow to orange and purple-red in fall

Comments: Ornamental, red-tinted fruits hang in clusters along the branches in fall. Includes the cultivars 'Ernest Wilson' compact with ascending to arching branches and pale green leaves with pink petioles turning amber in fall; 'George Forrest' vigorous and open-crowned with long, spreading branches and large, deep green leaves with red petioles; and 'Madeleine Spitta' columnar with erect branches, leaves turning orange in late fall. One of the finest "snakebarks" is HERS MAPLE, ssp. **grosseri** (*A. grosseri*; *A. hersii*), to 29 ft (9 m) tall with very decorative, white-marbled, gray-green bark and lobed or unlobed, ovate-cordate leaves to 2¾ in (7 cm) long; these turn a deep, glowing red in fall.

Name	Distribution	Habit	Bark	Leaves
A. giraldii	China	medium-sized to large tree to 60 ft (18 m) tall with a spreading crown	young branches flushed red to pink and variably striped white covered with gray-white bloom	to 4½ × 60 in (11 × 15 cm), with 3 broad and shallow lobes, entire to coarsely serrate, dark green above, pale blue-green beneath, petiole pink-tinted

Name	Distribution	Habit	Bark	Leaves
A. griseum PAPERBACK MAPLE	China	small to medium-sized tree to 40 ft (12 m) tall with open, conical to columnar crown of spreading then ascending branches	twigs slender, dark brown and hairy; larger branches and trunk covered in smooth, glossy, red-brown bark that splits and peels	composed of 3 distinct leaflets to 2 in (5 cm) long, ovate-oblong and coarsely toothed, dark green above and glaucous, blue-green beneath, turning purple-red in fall

Comments: Handsome in summer, glowing in fall; contrasts well with hoar-frost and snow in winter.

A. circinatum

A. crataegifolium 'Veitchii'

A. davidii

ACER

Name	Distribution	Habit	Bark	Leaves
A. heldreichii GREEK MAPLE; RED MAPLE	SE Europe	medium-sized tree to 52 ft (16 m) tall		to 5 in (13 cm) wide, lobes 3–5, oblong-lanceolate and deeply toothed, the three terminal lobes cut almost to base, glossy deep green above, paler and somewhat glaucous beneath

Comments: From the Caucasus and SW Asia, RED BUD MAPLE, ssp. **trautvetteri** (*A. trautvetteri*) has red-brown branches with showy red buds in spring; the leaves are large and turn clear yellow in fall; the fruits have conspicuous, red-tinted wings. From the Balkans, ssp. **visianii** has larger leaves and fruit.

Name	Distribution	Habit	Bark	Leaves
A. japonicum FULL MOON MAPLE; JAPANESE MAPLE	Japan	large shrub or small tree to 30 ft (10 m) with a broad canopy		to 5½ in (14 cm) wide, almost circular in outline with 7–11, ovate to lanceolate, deep lobes, the margins toothed to incised, bright green gradually flushing wine red toward summer's end and coloring deep crimson in fall

Comments: Appearing with the new leaves, the flowers are red with yellow stamens and hang in clusters. Includes the cultivars 'Aconitifolium' ('Laciniatum', 'Filicifolium') with deeply and finely cut leaves and good fall color, 'Green Cascade', with deeply divided, emerald leaves on arching branches, and 'Vitifolium' with broadly fan-shaped leaves composed of 10–12 lobes and coloring brilliantly in fall.

The shade-loving cultivar 'Aureum' (slow-growing with pale yellow leaves turning chartreuse green in summer) belongs to the species *A. shirasawanum*, another Japanese native differing from *A. japonicum* in its glaucous shoots. All favor a well-drained position sheltered from strong winds.

Name	Distribution	Habit	Bark	Leaves
A. macrophyllum BIG LEAF MAPLE; OREGON MAPLE	W N America	large, broad-crowned tree to 100 ft (30 m) tall		to 11 in (28 cm) wide, palmately 3–5-lobed, the lobes irregularly toothed to cut, deep, lustrous green turning orange in fall

Comments: Handsome large tree with drooping clusters of small yellow flowers in spring and tawny-bristly fruits. Armillaria-resistant.

Name	Distribution	Habit	Bark	Leaves
A. maximow-iczianum *A. nikoense* NIKKO MAPLE **Comments:**	Japan; C China	round-headed small tree to 50 ft (15 m) tall		composed of 3 leaflets to 4¾ × 2½ in (12 × 6 cm), ovate to oblong and entire to toothed, dull green above, gray-green and hairy beneath, turning brilliant flame in fall
A. mono *A. pictum*	China; Korea	medium-sized tree to 50 ft (15 m) tall		to 6 in (15 cm) wide, palmately 5–7-lobed, the lobes ovate-deltoid, entire and apiculate, bright green and smooth, turning yellow in fall

Comments: var. **tricuspis** has smaller, glossy, 3-lobed leaves.

Name	Distribution	Habit	Bark	Leaves
A. monspessulanum MONTPELLIER MAPLE	SE Europe to W Asia	small, rounded tree to 40 ft (12 m) tall with a twiggy, dense crown, sometimes a shrub		to 3 in (8 cm) wide, with 3 deltoid-ovate lobes, margins variably toothed, smooth, dark green above, paler and hairless beneath, turning yellow-brown in fall

Comments: Differs from *A. campestre* in its hairless leaves and the petioles which lack milky sap; ssp. **turcomanicum**, however, has leaves with tawny-hairy undersides and blunt lobes. Forms from rather arid regions are small and shrubby with very neat foliage—var. **microphyllum**, for example, is of a suitable scale for dry rock gardens.

A. heldreichii

A. japonicum 'Aconitifolium'

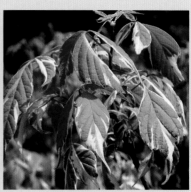

A. negundo 'Variegatum'

ACER

Name	Distribution	Habit	Bark	Leaves
A. negundo ASH-LEAVED ELDER; BOX ELDER; MANITOBA MAPLE	N & C America	fast-growing, broad-crowned tree to 70 ft (20 m) tall, often suckering	ultimately gray; slender young shoots are pithy, smooth, green and somewhat glaucous	to 8 in (20 cm) long, pinnately divided into 3–7, oblong leaflets with toothed to cut margins, bright, pale green above and pale beneath

Comments: Includes the cultivars 'Auratum' with golden leaves, 'Flamingo' with leaves edged and splashed pink to white, 'Elegans' with yellow-edged leaves, and 'Variegatum' with broadly white-margined leaves. var. *violaceum* has frosted, plum-colored new shoots and tassels of pink-tinted flowers. Large trees are sometimes problematic especially in warmer regions—seeding and suckering freely, breaking easily and playing host to box elder bugs.

Name	Distribution	Habit	Bark	Leaves
A. oblongum EVERGREEN MAPLE	Himalaya; China	semievergreen or evergreen shrub or tree to 30 ft (10 m) tall with spreading to upswept branches	peeling, gray	to 4¾ in (12 cm) long, oblong-obovate, usually entire, sometimes 3-lobed, tough-textured, glossy dark green above, glaucous beneath

Comments: New growth emerges bronze-pink. In var. *concolor*, the leaves are pale green throughout.

Name	Distribution	Habit	Bark	Leaves
A. opalus ITALIAN MAPLE	S Europe	medium-sized, rounded tree to 50 ft (15 m) tall		to 4 in (10 cm) wide, with 5, broad and shallow lobes, glossy dark green above and downy to glabrous beneath

Comments: var. *obtusatum* has larger leaves with 5–7, blunt and irregularly toothed lobes and gray-hairy undersides.

Name	Distribution	Habit	Bark	Leaves
A. palmatum JAPANESE MAPLE	Korea; Japan	medium-sized to large shrub or small tree to 25 ft (8 m) tall with a broad tiered crown	gray	to 4 in (10 cm) wide, rounded in outline, palmately and deeply 5–7-lobed, the lobes oblong to lanceolate, finely tapering and toothed to dissected, smooth thin-textured, pale, green, turning gold to bronze

Comments: Small trees and shrubs of great elegance and ideally suited to smaller gardens, especially where a Japanese effect is desired; they also make good tub and bonsai subjects. Perform best in moist and fertile, neutral to acidic soil. Many cultivars developed ranging widely in habit, leaf shape and color. They fall roughly into these categories: **Atropurpureum Group** with red-purple leaves turning scarlet in fall; **Dissectum Group**, round-fiery red or deep headed shrubs with arching branches and leaves scarlet in fall composed of 5–7–9, slender and finely dissected leaflets; **Elegans Group** (Heptalobum group, Septemlobum Group) with 7-lobed leaves, the lobes broader and less finely cut than in Dissectum Group; **Linearilobum Group** with 5–7, very deep slender and toothed lobes. Among the finest cultivars are 'Bloodgood' leaves dark purple-red, turning blood red in fall, fruit red. 'Butterfly' leaves small, deeply cut, emerging pink, turning gray-green with cream margins. 'Osakazuki' (Elegans Group) leaves green turning brilliant, fiery red in fall; 'Sango-kaku' ('Senkaki') young branches and twigs coral pink to sealing wax red, in winter especially, leaves mid-green turning amber in fall.

Name	Distribution	Habit	Bark	Leaves
A. paxii	C China	slow-growing, small, evergreen or semievergreen tree to 30 ft (10 m) tall with a dense, compact crown	initially purple to gray-brown	to 2¾ × 1½ in (7 × 4 cm), obovate, usually 3-lobed, tough, lustrous light green above, pale and glaucous beneath

A. palmatum 'Bloodgood'

A. platanoides 'Crimson King'

A. pseudoplatanus 'Brilliantissimum'

ACER

Name	Distribution	Habit	Bark	Leaves
A. pensylvanicum *A. striatum* GOOSEFOOT; MOOSEWOOD; SNAKEBARK MAPLE; STRIPED MAPLE	N America	small tree or shrub to 40 ft (12 m)₄ in tall, often low-branching or multi-stemmed with long, spreading branches	young branches green to brown striped green and silver-white	to 7 in (18 cm) long, obovate, base subcordate, apex broadly 3-lobed, mid-green turning golden yellow in fall

Comments: Favors neutral to slightly acidic soil and grows well in semiwooded locations. In the cultivar 'Erythrocladum' the young branches become bright coral red in winter. A. 'Silver Vein' (*A. laxiflorum* × *A. pensylvanicum* 'Erythrocladum') is vigorous with arching branches streaked green and white, and large, deep green leaves on long, red petioles turning bright yellow in fall.

A. platanoides NORWAY MAPLE	N Europe to Caucasus, naturalized N America	broad-crowned, large tree to 100 ft (30 m) tall	dark gray	to 7 in (18 cm) wide, broad with 5, ovate-deltoid lobes, the tips tapering with sparse but sharp, broadly angular teeth, thin-textured and smooth, mid- to dark green, rather glossy above, turning clear yellow to amber in fall

Comments: Racemes of bright yellow flowers appear before the leaves. Includes the cultivars 'Crimson King' (leaves dark purple-red to bronze-maroon), 'Crimson Sentry' (habit narrowly columnar, leaves deep purple-red). 'Drummondii' (leaves green deeply edged creamy white), 'Emerald Queen' (vigorous with lustrous, dark green leaves), 'Globosum' (small tree with a mop of short branches), 'Laciniatum' (EAGLE CLAW MAPLE, leaf lobes 5 with slender, talonlike tips), 'Palmitifidum' ('Lorbergii') (leaves with 5 lobes, their tips slender and pointing upward) and 'Schwedleri' (young growth bright red, turning purple-green, then fiery orange in fall).

A. pseudoplatanus PLANETREE MAPLE; SYCAMORE	Europe to W Asia, British Isles	small, untidy and suckering, or large, single-stemmed and broad-crowned tree to 130 ft (40 m)	dirty gray to gray-brown and flaking	to 6 in (16 cm) wide, cordate in outline with 5, ovate and crenate-serrate lobes, dull dark to mid-green above, gray-green beneath, turning yellow in fall

Comments: Fast-growing tree, widely naturalized, often to the point of nuisance. Includes Atropurpureum' (leaves purple beneath), 'Brilliantissimum' (small, slow-growing tree, leaves emerge pink, turn yellow-green, then mid-green), 'Leopoldii' (leaves yellow-pink turning green, splashed pink and creamy yellow), 'Prinz Handjery' (small and slow-growing, differs from 'Brilliantissimum' in its larger leaves tinted purple beneath), 'Purpureum' (leaves tinted purple beneath), and 'Simon Louis-Frères' (leaves pink at first, then green splashed white).

A. rubrum RED MAPLE; SCARLET MAPLE; SWAMP MAPLE	N America	large tree to 130 ft (40 m) tall	gray	to 4 in (10 cm) long, broadly cordate in outline, with 5–7, deltoid lobes, toothed and tapering, smooth dark green above, glaucous beneath, turning brilliant scarlet to yellow in fall

Comments: Best fall color achieved in neutral to acidic soil. Cultivars include 'Columnare' (habit broadly columnar, fiery red in fall), 'October Glory' (fall color deep crimson, long-lasting), 'Red Sunset' (habit dense, erect, leaves bright red in fall),'Scanlon' (crown broadly ovate to conical, good fall color), 'Schlesingeri' (leaves to 4¾ in (12 cm) long with a truncate base and 3, large lobes, turning scarlet early in fall).

A. rufinerve	Japan	medium-sized tree to 40 ft (12 m) tall	green striped white; young branches glaucous blue-white	to 4¾ in (12 cm) long, rounded at base, with 3, spreading, biserrate lobes in apical half, dark green above, paler and red-veined beneath, turning vivid red, gold and amber in fall

Comments: 'Hatsuyuki' ('Albolimbatum') has leaves splashed white at margins and turning red and purple in fall.

A. rubrum 'Schlesingeri'

A. saccharum 'Temple's Upright'

A. tataricum ssp. *ginnala*

ACER

Name	Distribution	Habit	Bark	Leaves
A. saccharinum *A. dasycarpum; A. eriocarpum* SILVER MAPLE;SOFT MAPLE	N America	fast-growing broadly and loosely columnar tree to 130 ft (40 m) tall	gray	to 5½ in (14 cm) long, with 5 deeply cut lobes with tapering tips and toothed to cut margins, light green above, silvery beneath, turning yellow in fall

Comments: Includes f. *laciniatum* with very deep, slender lobes, the margins finely cut, and 'Laciniatum Wieri' with weeping branchlets and finely dissected leaves.

Name	Distribution	Habit	Bark	Leaves
A. saccharum ROCK MAPLE; SUGAR MAPLE	N America	broad-crowned tree to 130 ft (40 m) tall	furrowed, gray	to 5½ in (14 cm) wide, cordate in outline with 3–5, toothed and tapering lobes, thin-textured, smooth, dull green above, gray-green beneath, turning gold, fiery red and scarlet in fall

Comments: Similar to *A. platanoides*. Sap source of maple syrup. Cultivars include 'Newton Sentry' (habit narrowly columnar with short, ascending branches and no distinct leader, leaves turning fiery red in fall), and 'Temple's Upright' (habit narrowly conical to broadly columnar with ascending branches and a distinct leader). ssp. *nigrum* (*A. nigrum*) is the black maple, to 130 ft (40 m) tall with deeply fissured, black bark and usually 3-lobed leaves to 5½ in (14 cm) long, deep, dull green above and gray-green and pilose beneath, turning yellow in fall.

Name	Distribution	Habit	Bark	Leaves
A. tataricum TATARIAN MAPLE	SE Europe to SW Asia	large, spreading shrub or small tree to 30 ft (10 m) tall	green obscurely striped white on young branches	to 4 in (10 cm) long, ovate and finely tapering, biserrate, bright to dull green above, paler and hairy beneath turning yellow in fall; leaves on young shoots may be 3-lobed

Comments: From NE Asia, ssp. *ginnala* (*A. ginnala*) is the AMUR MAPLE, a spreading, large shrub or small tree with 3-lobed, toothed leaves to 3 in (8 cm) long turning bright red in fall. Small, fragrant, yellow flowers are produced in clusters in spring and are followed by red fruit. This subspecies includes the cultivars 'Durand Dwarf' (dwarf with dense, red twiglets and small leaves), 'Flame' (to 22 ft (7 m) tall with fiery fall color), and 'Pulverulentum' (leaves splashed and speckled white).

Name	Distribution	Habit	Bark	Leaves
A. triflorum THREE-FLOWERED MAPLE	Manchuria; Korea	small, spreading tree to 40 ft (12 m) tall	peeling, gray-brown	to 3 in (8 cm) long, composed of 3, ovate to oblanceolate leaflets, dark green above, glaucous beneath, turning fiery red in fall

Comments: Differs from *A. maximowiczianum* in its peeling bark. A choice, slow-growing small tree with brilliant fall color.

Name	Distribution	Habit	Bark	Leaves
A. truncatum PURPLEBLOW MAPLE; SHANTUNG MAPLE	China; Korea	small, broad-crowned tree to 25 ft (8 m) tall		to 4 in (10 cm), base truncate, lobes 5, deltoid, deeply cut, bright green and smooth above, paler and hairy beneath

Comments: Attractive yellow-green flowers appear with the leaves. The cultivar 'Akikaze Nishiki' has leaves variably spotted, splashed and stained white.

Name	Distribution	Habit	Bark	Leaves
A. velutinum *A. insigne*	Caucasus; Iran	large tree		to 6 in (15 cm) wide, base subcordate, broadly and palmately 5-lobed, toothed, bright green above, paler and softly downy beneath

Comments: var. *vanvolxemii*: leaves to 12 in (30 cm) wide, blue-green beneath with hairs on the veins only.

achene a dry, small, indehiscent fruit with a tight, thin pericarp, strictly consisting of one free carpel as in Ranunculaceae, but sometimes applied to Compositae with more than one seed.

achenocarp any dry indehiscent fruit.

Achillea (for the Classical hero Achilles, said to have discovered the medicinal properties of these plants). Compositae. North temperate regions. YARROW; MILFOIL. 85 species, perennial herbs, often aromatic, with entire or finely divided and ferny foliage, and small, buttonlike flower heads in loose clusters or crowded, flat-topped corymbs.

All are summer-flowering, fully hardy and prefer a sunny, well-drained position. The larger species and cultivars thrive in the herbaceous or mixed border; the flower heads are attractive additions to dried flower arrangements. Smaller species are best used in the rock or dry garden, or planted on dry banks and walls. Propagate by division in early spring or fall; take softwood cuttings in late spring.

A. clavennae E Alps, W Balkans; to 4¾ × 8 in (12 × 20 cm); carpeting with silky-silvery, pinnately lobed leaves to 3 in (8 cm) long; flower heads to ½ in (1 cm) diam., bright white with golden centers in loose clusters; *A. clypeolata* Balkans, Romania; to 16 × 12 in (40 × 30 cm); semievergreen herbaceous perennial with finely divided, silvery leaves; flower heads to ⅜ in (0.8 cm) diam., bright yellow, crowded in flat-topped heads; crossed with *A. filipendulina* to produce *A.* 'Coronation Gold', vigorous, to 3¼ ft (1 m) tall with deep golden flower heads that dry well; and with *A.* 'Taygetea' to produce 'Moonshine', with silver leaves and bright yellow flower heads; *A. filipendulina* Caucasus, Iran, Central Asia; semievergreen, herbaceous perennial to 40 × 24 in (100 × 60 cm); leaves green, hairy, deeply and finely pinnately lobed; flower heads to ¼ in (0.5 cm) diam., deep gold, crowded in broad, flat-topped to domed umbels on long stalks drying well; includes 'Altgold' with dark, burnished gold flower heads, 'Gold Plate' with large, deep gold flower heads on long, stout stalks; crossed with *A. ptarmica* to produce the creamy yellow-flowered 'Schwefelblüte'; *A.* × *kellereri* (*A. clypeolata* × *A. ageratifolia*; semievergreen perennial to 6 × 8 in (15 × 20 cm) with feathery, gray-green leaves and loose clusters of daisylike flower heads, white to cream with pale gold centers; *A.* × *lewisii* (*A. clavennae* × *A. clypeolata*; compact semievergreen perennial to 4 × 8 in (10 × 20 cm), with feathery, gray-green leaves; the cultivar 'King Edward' has tight corymbs of tiny, buff-yellow flower heads; *A. millefolium* YARROW erect perennial to 40 × 15 in (100 × 40 cm) with feathery dark green leaves and flat-topped corymbs to 6 in (15 cm) diam., crowded with small, white to pink flower heads; includes 'Burgundy' with wine red flower heads, 'Fanal', with snow-white flower heads in a dense, rosettelike corymb, 'Forncett Beauty' with deep lavender flower heads, 'Fire King' with bright pink flower heads, the magenta 'Kelwayi', and the snowy 'White Beauty'; *A. ptarmica* SNEEZEWORT; erect herbaceous perennial to 40 × 30 in (100 × 75 cm), leaves dark green, lanceolate and toothed but not divided; flower heads to ¼ in (0.5 cm) diam., white in frothy corymbs; includes 'Boule de Neige' with large, snow white, 'double' flower heads; *A.* Summer Pastels, a seed race of herbaceous perennials with soft, gray-green foliage and domed corymbs in shades of pink, rose, buff, salmon, dull orange, purple and gray-lavender; *A.* 'Taygetea', an erect perennial to 24 × 20 in (60 × 50 cm) with feathery, gray-green leaves and flat corymbs of lemon yellow flower heads.

Achimenes (from Greek *chemaino*, to suffer from cold). Gesneriaceae.

CUPID'S PLANT. Central and South America. 35 species, tender, bushy perennials with softly hairy, bushy growth arising annually from underground rhizomes clad with fleshy scales. They are grown for their showy, tubular to funnel-shaped flowers. They may be induced to flower at any time of year. Plant the dormant rhizomes in a fibrous potting mix. Grow in humid conditions, minimum temperature 65°F (18°C), and protect from bright sunlight. Water sparingly at first, increasingly as the new growth emerges. Pinch out the young shoots to encourage bushiness and support if necessary. When in full growth, *Achimenes* benefits from a weak, semiweekly fertilizer and frequent misting (the latter especially if grown in the home). As the flowers fade and the foliage deteriorates, water should be gradually withheld and humidity reduced. Once the top growth has died off, the rhizomes may be stored completely dry and in their pots at a minimum temperature of 45°F (7°C). Separate and clean the maggotlike rhizomes prior to replanting. These are fragile and their inevitable breakup is the principal method of propagation.

A. antirrhina W. Mexico; to 12 in (30 cm); flowers 1¾ in (4.5 cm) long, yellow marked maroon on the exterior with a red-stained throat to bright red-orange with a yellow throat; *A. erecta* (syn. *A. coccinea, A. pulchella*) West Indies, Mexico, Panama; flowers bright scarlet with yellow throats; *A. grandiflora* Mexico, Honduras; 18 in (45 cm); leaves 1¾ in (4.5 cm) long, mauve to maroon with a pink, purple-spotted throat; *A. longiflora* Mexico, Honduras; to 24 in (60 cm); flowers to 2½ in (6 cm), violet, maroon, mauve, magenta or white with various markings. *Cultivars:* 'Ambroise Verschaffelt' (flowers large, white, heavily veined and blotched deep purple); 'Brilliant' (flowers scarlet): 'Glacier' (flowers snow white, tinted icy blue); 'Little Beauty' (flowers deep pink with a yellow eye); 'Paul Arnold' (flowers dark purple, throat white tinged yellow with red dots); 'Peach Blossom' (habit trailing, flowers peach); 'Pearly Queen' (flowers cream tinged pink and lilac); 'Ruby' (flowers small, ruby red); 'Show Off' (flowers profuse, lilac-pink).

achlamydeous of flowers; lacking a perianth.

acicular of leaves; needle-shaped, and usually rounded rather than flat in cross-section.

acidic in gardening, mainly applicable to soil, potting mixtures, and their ingredients, and water having a pH scale value less than 7.0; cf. *alkaline*. See *soils; pH*.

acinaceous of fruit; full of kernels.

acinaciform of leaves; shaped like a scimitar.

Aciphylla (from Greek *akis*, point, and *phyllon*, leaf, referring to the sharply pointed leaves). Umbelliferae. New Zealand; Australia. 40 species, evergreen perennials grown for their rosettes of tough, sword-shaped or compound leaves and spectacular, terminal inflorescences—usually a white or cream, pyramidal panicle composed of many compound umbels packed on candelabra-like branches. All of the species described here are from New Zealand. Male plants are usually held to flower more reliably and impressively than females. They thrive in sharply draining, gritty soil in full sun. In winter they require temperatures no lower than 14°F (−10°C); protect from wet conditions (e.g., a mulch of dry bracken or deep gravel around the crown). Propagate by seed sown under glass in late summer or early spring.

A. aurea dense rosettes of sharply pointed, sword-shaped or pinnate leaves to 3¼ ft (1 m) diam.; flower spikes over 3¼ ft (1 m); *A. colensoi* WILD SPANIARD, SPEARGRASS; swirling rosette of leaves to 20 in (50 cm)-long, coarse, glaucous and rigidly swordlike or pinnate with the lobes sharply tipped and ribbed in sealing wax red; flowers cream in yard-high towers; *A. scott-thomsonii* GIANT SPANIARD; differs from the last species in its more frequently divided leaves to 5 ft (1.5 m) long, emerging bronze and hardening pale gray green with the midribs faintly tinted red; flower spikes to 10 ft (3 m); *A. squarrosa* SPEARGRASS, BAYONET PLANT; rosette to 3¼ ft (1 m) across of rigid olive green leaves, swordlike or

2–3-pinnate, each segment ending in a spine; flower spikes ivory, to 3¼ ft (1 m).

Aconitum (the Classical Latin name, from Greek, *akoniton*). Ranunculaceae. Northern Hemisphere (temperate regions). ACONITE, MONKSHOOD. Some 100 species, biennial or perennial herbs, often tuberous, with erect to scrambling stems, palmately lobed or cut leaves and racemes or panicles of flowers in summer. The flowers consist of five petal-like sepals, the upper three large and forming a domed helmet and extending behind as a spur. All parts of these plants are highly toxic. The following are fully hardy and suitable for herbaceous and mixed borders, woodland gardens, and (the smaller species) for the rock garden. Taller plants may require staking. Grow *A. hemsleyanum* among shrubs or train on pea-sticks. Plant all in moist but well-drained, fertile soil in full sun or part shade. Propagate by division in fall.

A. anthora Galicia; compact, tuberous perennial, erect to 24 in (60 cm); leaves dark green, finely cut into numerous narrow segments; flowers yellow or purple-blue; *A.* × *cammarum* (syn. *A. bicolor*) large group of popular garden hybrids involving *A. variegatum* and *A. napellus*; to 3¼ ft (1 m); leaves to 4 in (10 cm) across and finely divided; flowers some 1½ in (4 cm) long, with high, beaked helmets in open, narrowly pyramidal panicles; cultivars include 'Bicolor' with white and indigo flowers, the tall, slender, violet-blue 'Bressingham Spire', the dull salmon-pink 'Carneum', 'Grandiflorum Album' with large, white flowers, the deep blue 'Newry Blue', and the violet-blue 'Spark's Variety'; *A. carmichaelii* (Asia, North America; erect, tuberous perennial to 5 ft (1.5 m); leaves 3–5-parted, lobed, toothed; flowers deep purple to blue or white, in a dense, erect and narrow panicle; cultivars include the late summer- to fall-flowering, azure blue 'Arendsii'; *A. hemsleyanum* (syn. *A. volubile* of gardens) Asia; stems slender, twining and scrambling with much-lobed leaves and racemes of mauve or lilac to green and blue flowers; *A. lycoctonum* WOLFSBANE, BADGER'S-BANE; Europe, N Africa; tuberous perennial to 5 ft (1.5 m), leaves dark green, 5–7-parted, lobed and toothed; flowers purple to lilac, white or yellow with domed to narrowly cylindric helmets, carried on slender-branched, narrow panicles; subsp. *vulparia*: syn. *A. vulparia*, flowers pale creamy yellow; *A. napellus* MONKSHOOD, HELMET FLOWER, FRIAR'S-CAP, BEAR'S-FOOT; Europe, Asia and N America; erect, tuberous perennial to 5 ft (1.5 m); leaves 5–7-parted, lobed and toothed; flowers blue, violet or lilac with domed, hooded helmets in tall, spirelike panicles in late summer; 'Album': flowers white.

Acorus (Latin name, from the Greek *akoron*, applied in ancient times to both *Acorus calamus*, the sweet flag, and to the superficially similar *Iris pseudacorus*, yellow flag). Araceae (Acoraceae). Northern Hemisphere. 2 species, hardy rhizomatous perennial herbs with sword-shaped leaves and inconspicuous flowers in club-shaped spadices. Both are fully hardy and suited to the bog garden or pond margin. Variegated forms of *A. gramineus* have long been used as bonsai and, more recently, as house plants. Plant in moist or saturated, rich soil, or pot in the same. The roots and rhizomes may be covered by water. Grow in full or dappled sun. Increase by division.

A. calamus SWEET FLAG, SWEET CALAMUS, MYRTLE FLAG, FLAGROOT; Northern Hemisphere, deciduous or semievergreen; leaves to 60 in (150 cm) resembling those of a flag iris, fresh apple green, flushed purple-bronze in 'Purpureus', striped cream and yellow in 'Variegatus'; *A. gramineus* E Asia; evergreen, to 20 in (50 cm) tall; leaves grassy or sedgelike, glossy dark green, tapering finely, in a distinct forward-leaning fan; 'Albovariegatus': dwarf, leaves striped white; 'Oborozuki': leaves vibrant yellow; 'Ogon': leaves variegated chartreuse and cream; var. *pusillus*: very dwarf—seldom exceeds 3 in (8 cm); 'Variegatus': leaves striped cream and yellow.

acropetalous of organs such as leaves or flowers produced, developing or opening in succession from base to apex; cf. *basipetalous*.

Actaea (from Greek *aktea*, the elder tree, a reference to the fruit and leaf shape). Ranunculaceae. Northern

Actaea rubra
The clusters of decorative fruits for which actaeas are chiefly grown rise up from low clumps of divided, elderlike foliage.

Temperate regions (those below from North America). BANEBERRY. 8 species, hardy herbaceous perennials grown for their berries and attractive, foliage. Long-stalked, ternately compound leaves arise in early spring from a thick buried rhizome; their segments are lanceolate-ovate and usually coarsely toothed. A wandlike stem to 32 in (80 cm) tall follows in spring and terminates in a spike of small white or cream flowers. The fruit is beadlike and toxic—pearly white with a blue-black "pupil" in *A. pachypoda*, the WHITE BANEBERRY or DOLL'S-EYES; bright scarlet in *A. rubra*, the RED BANEBERRY or SNAKEBERRY. Plant in the wild or woodland garden in humus-rich, moist soil in part-shade. Increase by division in spring, or from fresh seed (pulp removed) sown in a cold frame.

A. racemosa BLACK COHOSH, BLACK SNAKEROOT; N America; 32–60 in (80–150 cm); raceme to 36 in (90 cm), erect, slender, branched flowers, fragrant; *A. simplex* E Russia, Mongolia, Japan; 24–48 in (60–120 cm); raceme to 12 in (30 cm), erect to bowed; includes Atropurpurea Group, with forms having very dark, purple-bronze leaves—for example, 'Brunette'.

Actinidia (from Greek *aktis*, a ray, alluding to the radiating styles). Actinidiaceae. East Asia. 40 species, largely dioecious, deciduous, woody climbers grown for their fruit, foliage, and small, bowl-shaped, cream flowers. Most Actinidia are familiar as ornamentals in cool temperate gardens. Strongly twining climbers, they are used as wall plants or allowed to scramble through old trees and over arbors, where they provide a bold covering of handsome leaves measuring up to 6 in (15 cm) long, broadly ovate, tapering and deep, smooth green in *A. arguta*, the TARA VINE or YANG-TAO; to 8 in (20 cm) long, broadly elliptic, blunt, tough and hairy in *A. deliciosa* (syn. *A. chinensis*), the CHINESE GOOSEBERRY or KIWI FRUIT; to 6 in (15 cm) long, ovate, tapering finely, emerging chocolate and lime green splashed cream and pink in *A. kolomikta*; and to 4¾ in (12 cm) long, ovate-oblong, tapering, emerging bronze, becoming deep green flecked or mottled silver or cream in *A. polygama*, the SILVER VINE.

In sheltered positions, and especially where rapid growth and wood ripening can be guaranteed by long, hot summers, all of the above will withstand winter lows of 1°F (−17°C). They grow well in part shade, but will require ample sunlight for fruit ripening. Plant in deep and well drained, loamy soil, rich in organic matter (slightly alkaline for *A. kolomikta*; slightly acidic for *A. deliciosa*). Prune in winter to clean out tangled, dead, or exhausted stems. Propagate by semiripe cuttings taken in a case with bottom heat at 70–77°F (20–25°C); also by layering in winter.

Cultivars of *A. arguta* and *A. deliciosa* grown for fruit production are usually selected for sex (i.e., female) and grafted onto seedling rootstocks. A small, male scion may then be grafted on to the established female scion as a built-in pollinator. See *kiwi fruit*.

actinomorphic of regular flowers possessing radial symmetry, capable of division in two or more planes into similar halves.

activator a nitrogenous substance such as sulfate of ammonia, poultry manure, or a commercial product, applied to plant waste in a compost pile to aid decay. Of particular value where nonleafy material is composted during periods of low temperature. Also known as an accelerator

active ingredient (abbrev. **a.i.**) the biologically active component of a pesticide which is toxic to the pest, pathogen or weed it is intended to control.

aculeate prickly, bearing sharp prickles.

aculeiform prickle-shaped.

acuminate of leaves and perianth segments with the tip or, less commonly, the base tapering gradually to a point, usually with somewhat concave sides.

acutangular of stems; sharply angular.

acute of the tips or bases of leaves or perianth segments where two almost straight or slightly convex sides converge to terminate in a sharp point, the point shorter and usually broader than in an acuminate leaf tip.

acyclic plant parts arranged spirally, not in pairs or whorls.

Ada (named after the queen of Caria in Asia Minor). Orchidaceae. South America. 15 species, epiphytic orchids. Native to the Colombian Andes, *A. aurantiaca* is cool-growing (winter minimum 50°F/10°C) and produces arching, 12-in (30-cm) sprays of 1-in-(2.5-cm-) long flowers in late winter and early spring. These are narrow-petaled and appear half-closed, ranging in color from scarlet to dark or bright orange to cinnabar red. Pot in a bark-based orchid mix. Water and feed frequently when in growth; reduce water supplies once the new pseudobulbs are fully formed, only increasing quantities again on the emergence of the flower spikes. Shade from direct sunlight and provide a humid, cool, and airy atmosphere in summer. Increase by division.

adaxial of the surface or part of a lateral plant organ turned or facing toward the axis and apex; sometimes used interchangeably with ventral; cf. *abaxial*.

adelgids (Hemiptera: Adelgidae). Conifer woolly aphids. Sap-feeding insects of conifers, about ¹⁄₁₆–¹⁄₁₆ in (1–2 mm) long, similar to aphids but with shorter antennae, and without the hornlike structure at the base of the abdomen. Many species occur across the Northern Hemisphere.

The SPRUCE GALL ADELGID (*Adelges abietis*) is widespread in Britain, northern Europe, and North America and causes small pineapple-like galls on shoots of *Picea* species during the summer. Infested branches become stunted and the dried-up galls are unsightly. Winged adults emerge from the galls, and fly to infest other spruce trees, depositing a cluster of 20–50 yellow eggs on the needles. After egg-laying, females die in such a position that their wings provide protection for the eggs. Hatched nymphs crawl to the bases of buds to overwinter, and in spring pass through three molts to become stem mothers, producing copious amounts of flocculent white "wool" among which 50 or more greenish eggs are deposited. Nymphs emerge after bud-burst and crawl between developing needles, where their feeding induces pineapple-like galls.

Adelges viridis gives rise to similar galls on *Picea* species but emergent winged forms overwinter on *Larix* species and reinfest spruce in the following spring. *Adelges abietis* causes serious dieback and even death of the silver fir (*Abies alba*), and *Adelges piceae* (the BALSAM WOOLLY APHID of North America), which has a more conspicuous covering of white woolly wax, attacks *Abies alba*, *A. grandis*, and *A. procera*. The stunted shoots of affected trees have swellings often referred to as gouty galls. Tufts of white woolly wax are also associated with the LARCH ADELGID (*Adelges laricis*), and to a lesser extent with *Adelges cooleyi* on Douglas fir (*Pseudotsuga menziesii*) and the SCOTS PINE ADELGID *Pineus pini*. The bark of Weymouth pine (*Pinus strobus*) is most likely to be infested by *Pineus strobi*. It is not feasible to control adelgids on large specimen trees, where damage is rarely serious. Infestations on young conifers—especially Norway spruce (*Picea abies*),

Fluffy white substance secreted on needles

Adelgids

which is extensively grown for Christmas trees in the UK—may be prevented by spraying the conifers with suitable contact insecticides from February to early March.

Adenium (from the Arabic name for this plant, *oddaejn* [Aden]). Apocynaceae. Throughout Africa in arid places. DESERT ROSE; IMPALA LILY; MOCK AZALEA; KUDU LILY; SABI STAR. 1 species, *A. obesum*; a tender succulent, it produces a swollen caudex dividing into a few crabbed branches between 3¼ ft (1 m) and 10 ft (3 m) tall. The leaves are oblanceolate to obovate and are sometimes present only during a short growing season. The flowers are funnel-shaped with five spreading lobes, as much as 2 × 2½ in (5 × 6 cm), and are typically rosy pink or crimson with a white "eye" and throat. Provide a minimum temperature of 59°F (15°C) (these plants in fact thrive in fierce, dry heat). Pot in a gritty and sandy medium. Water freely during periods of high temperatures, scarcely at all otherwise. Grow in full sun; keep free of drafts and damp. Increase by stem cuttings or seed.

Adenophora (from the Greek *aden*, gland, and *phoros*, "bearing"—the style has a glandular base). Campanulaceae. Eastern Europe to Japan. LADYBELLS; GLAND BELLFLOWER. 40 species, hardy herbaceous perennials. They differ from the closely related *Campanula* in their thick, fleshy roots and the swollen disk at the base of the stamens. Rosettes of ovate to lanceolate leaves give rise to arching sprays of pendulous, bell-shaped flowers in summer. Hardy to 5°F (−15°C), they thrive in full sun or part shade. Grow in well-drained, fertile, and preferably slightly alkaline soil. Propagate by fresh seed sown when ripe or from basal cuttings in spring.

A. bulleyana W. China; to 3¼ ft (1 m); flowers pale blue; *A. liliifolia* Eurasia; to 20 in (50 cm) tall, hung with fragrant, white or pale blue flowers; *A. potaninii* W. China; to 36 in (90 cm) arching sprays of lavender flowers; *A. triphylla* to 36 in (90 cm); flowers pale blue or violet.

adherent plant parts usually free or separate (e.g., petals) but clinging or

held closely together. Such parts are sometimes loosely described as united or, inaccurately, as fused, which is strictly synonymous with coherent. Some authors use this word to describe the fusion of dissimilar parts.

Adiantum (from Greek *adiantos*, unwetted or unwettable: the fronds repel water). Adiantaceae. Cosmopolitan. MAIDENHAIR FERN. 200 species, evergreen and deciduous ferns with short, creeping rhizomes and clumps of fronds. These are usually 1–5-pinnately compound with slender, dark stipes, delicate branches and finely textured, wedge- to fan-shaped pinnules. *A. pedatum* and *A. venustum* are among the most desirable hardy ferns for the cool rock garden or shady border. Plant in moist soil rich in leaf mold. Mulch the crowns with garden compost and dry bracken in winter. The remaining species are tender foliage plants for the home, greenhouse, or conservatory. With the exception of the warm-growing *A. peruvianum* and *A. raddianum*, they need a cool, airy atmosphere and a minimum temperature of 50°F (10°C). Plant in an acidic to neutral, well-drained mix high in coir, composted bark, and leaf mold; water throughout the year, but more sparingly in winter, Remove faded fronds. Propagate by division when repotting, ideally in spring just before growth begins.

A. capillus-veneris MAIDENHAIR FERN, SOUTHERN MAIDENHAIR, VENUS'-HAIR FERN; cosmopolitan; fronds to 28 in (70 cm), arching, triangular, 2–3-pinnate, pinnules ½–¾ in (1–2 cm), cuneate to flabellate, emerging pale bronze turning bright lime green; stipe dark brown to black; *A. pedatum* NORTHERN MAIDENHAIR FERN; N America, E Asia; fronds to 20 in (50 cm) tall, slender, black stipes crowned with five pedately arranged pinnae, pinnules emerging bronze-pink turning lime green, to ¾ in (2 cm), obliquely triangular; more crowded and blue-green in var. *subpumilum* (var. *aleuticum*), ALEUTIAN MAIDENHAIR; *A. peruvianum* SILVER DOLLAR MAIDENHAIR; S America; fronds to 3¼ ft (1 m) tall, arching, triangular, 1–3-pinnate; pinnules to 2¾ in (7 cm), diamond-shaped to semicircular, emerging soft silver-rose, turning

pearly gray-green; *A. raddianum* (syn. *A. cuneatum*, *A. decorum*) DELTA MAIDENHAIR FERN; S America; fronds to 24 in (60 cm), narrowly triangular, 3-pinnate, pinnules ½ in (1 cm), cuneate to rhombic, lobed, pale green on very dark stipes; includes 'Fritz Luthii' with pale green fronds, and the much-divided and tasseled 'Grandiceps'; *A. tenerum* BRITTLE MAIDENHAIR FERN; warm Americas; fronds to 40 in (100 cm), arching, broadly triangular, 3–5-pinnate, pinnules rhombic to fan-shaped, sometimes toothed or cleft, stipes black and glossy; includes 'Farleyense' FARLEY MAIDENHAIR, BARBADOS MAIDENHAIR, GLORY FERN, with large, fan-shaped, cut and crisped pinnules; *A. venustum* EVERGREEN MAIDENHAIR; Asia; fronds to 32 in (80 cm), usually smaller, arching, broadly triangular, 3–4-pinnate, pinnules to ½ in (1 cm), ovate-cuneate, tip rounded, finely toothed, coppery at first, becoming fresh pale green and paler beneath, stipes dark, glossy.

adjuvant a substance added to a pesticide formulation or mixture to improve its action, by enhancing spreading, adherence, or penetration, or by reducing phytotoxicity. Adjuvants include so-called spreaders, wetters, and stickers besides surfactants and some antitranspirants. Many are based on refined mineral oil or vegetable oil, and, although not pesticides, are subject to pesticide regulations.

Adlumia (for John Adlum [1759–1836], US soldier and grape breeder). Fumariaceae. Eastern N America, Korea. 1 species, *A. fungosa* (syn. *Fumaria fungosa*), ALLEGHENY VINE, CLIMBING FUMITORY, MOUNTAIN FRINGE. An herbaceous, biennial vine grown for its finely cut, pale green, ferny foliage and drooping panicles of small, spurred flowers. Produced in spring and summer, these are close to those of *Dicentra* in shape and a delicate shade of pink. Hardy to 1°F (−17°C). Sow seed in early spring in light shade in cool, moist soil. Allegheny vine makes a low, bushy plant in its first year; thereafter it quickly climbs to 12 ft (4 m). Provide initial support with brushwood or pea sticks, then allow the stems to scramble through the surrounding vegetation. Self-sows freely.

adnate a plant feature attached by its whole length or surface to the face of an organ.

Adonis (in Greek mythology, the beautiful youth beloved of Aphrodite and killed by a wild boar: this flower was supposed to spring from his spilt blood). Ranunculaceae. Europe, Asia. 20 species, hardy annual or perennial herbs grown for their flowers produced in spring and summer. The stems arise from short, thick rhizomes and bear finely cut foliage beneath a large, solitary, bowl-shaped flower composed of oblong to obovate petals around a boss of anthers. Plant in moist but well-drained soil in sun or light shade with the crowns at a depth of ³⁄₄–1¹⁄₄ in (2–3 cm). Propagate by fresh seed sown in pans in the cold frame in summer.

A. amurensis E Asia; perennial to 6 in (15 cm); flowers to 1¹⁄₂ in (4 cm) diam., with 20–30, yellow petals, sometimes white, rose, or red-striped; includes the fringed, creamy 'Benten', 'Fukurokuju' with very large, double, golden flowers, and the double, yellow to green 'Pleniflora'; in 'Ramosa', flowers are double and bronze-red to brown; *A. annua* PHEASANT'S EYE; Europe to Asia; annual to 16 in (40 cm); flowers to 1¹⁄₄ in (3 cm) diam., with scarlet to crimson petals, their black bases forming an "eye"; *A. aestivalis* is similar and includes forms with yellow flowers; *A. brevistyla* China, Tibet; perennial to 8 in (20 cm) tall; flowers to 1¹⁄₄ in (3 cm) diam., with some 8 white petals tinted blue to lavender on the exterior; *A. vernalis* Europe; perennial to 8 in (20 cm); flowers to 3 in (8 cm) diam., with 12–20 yellow petals, white in 'Alba'.

adpressed, appressed used of an organ that lies flat and close to the stem or leaf to which it is attached.

Adromischus (from Greek, *hadros*, thick, and *mischos*, stem). Crassulaceae. South Africa. 26 species, low-growing, frost-tender, succulent herbs and sub-

shrubs grown for their attractive and often curiously shaped leaves. Plant in an open medium rich in grit and sand. When in growth, allow them to become just dry between waterings and feed with a fertilizer high in potassium and phosphorus but low in nitrogen. In the cooler months, maintain a minimum temperature of 45°F (7°C), with low humidity and full sunlight; water only to prevent excessive shriveling of the leaves. Propagate by leaf and stem cuttings (fallen leaves will often root and grow spontaneously).

A. cooperi (syn. *A. festivus*) PLOVER'S EGG PLANT; clump-former with thickly fleshy, 1¹⁄₂–2³⁄₄-in- (4–7-cm) long leaves shaped like slightly compressed eggs, gray-green speckled red-brown; *A. cristatus* leaves broadening to a squared tip and flattening toward a thin and strongly wavy apical margin; *A. maculatus* leaves broadly oblanceolate to obovate to 4 in (10 cm), rather thinner than in the above two species and gray-green to olive or dull brown with purple-brown blotches, the tip thin, horny-textured and usually wavy.

adsorption the attachment of an ion or molecule to the surface of a soil particle. See *base exchange*.

adult of leaves; the mature foliage of plants that bear leaves of distinctly different shape when young, such as eucalyptus, ivy and gorse; cf. *juvenile*.

adventitious, adventive growth which occurs at an unusual location on a plant—for example, roots arising from a stem or leaf axil. Also used of nonnative plants introduced accidentally or deliberately.

Aechmea (from the Greek, *aichme*, lance head, referring to the hard acute apices of the sepals) Bromeliaceae. C and S America. 170 species, tender, epiphytic, evergreen perennial herbs. Tough, strap-shaped leaves are carried in a stemless rosette, their overlapping and expanded bases forming a cup or funnel in which water collects. From this reservoir, the inflorescence

emerges—a terminal spike or panicle clothed with showy bracts. Although small and often concealed, the flowers are usually brightly colored.

Provide a minimum winter temperature of 50°F (10°C), and bright, filtered light. Plant in a very free-draining, bark-based mix, which should be allowed to become almost dry between waterings. Alternatively, wrap the sparse and wiry roots in a pouch of well-rotted garden compost and sphagnum moss and attach the plant to driftwood, a bromeliad "tree" or a bark slab; water by plunging and misting. Apply weak liquid fertilizer semiweekly in spring and summer. Propagate by detaching roots and offsets.

A. chantinii AMAZON ZEBRA PLANT; leaves spiny-toothed, olive green brightly banded silver-gray beneath in an erect funnel; inflorescence 32 in (80 cm) tall, loosely branched and clothed with brilliant scarlet bracts, lowermost bent downward; flowers waxy and orange-yellow; *A. distichantha* robust, to 3¹⁄₄ ft (1 m) with spreading, mid-green, saw-toothed leaves; inflorescence stout-stemmed, roughly pyramidal; branches short, covered in 2-ranked, overlapping, rose pink to lobster red bracts; *A. fasciata* URN PLANT; funnel spreading with broadly strap-shaped leaves in sea green overlaid and banded with frosty scales; inflorescence 24 in (60 cm) tall, pyramidal and composed of many overlapping bracts, like a candy or flamingo pink torch, picked out with small flowers, shifting with age from pale blue to indigo then dark rose; *A.* Foster's Favorite Group LACQUERED WINE CUP; vigorously offsetting, to 24 × 32 in (60 × 80 cm) with open funnels of glossy garnet leaves and pendulous spikes of small red and blue flowers followed by red berries; *A. fulgens* CORAL BERRY; an open but deep rosette of mid-green, 14-in- (35-cm-) long, oblong to ligulate leaves, glossy above, with gray scales beneath; inflorescence 6–8 in (15–20 cm) tall, branches slender, red clothed with thin, pink bracts; flowers small blue and violet turning deep pink and followed by bright red fruit; *A. nudicaulis* rosette loose; leaves 12–32 in (30–80 cm)-long; black-toothed, strap-shaped and arching from a dark, urnlike base, olive above gray-banded beneath; inflores-

Adonis annua

cence unbranched, to 10 in (25 cm) tall and cylinder-shaped with yellow flowers borne above brilliant red bracts; *A. racinae* CHRISTMAS JEWELS; differs from *A.* 'Foster's Favorite' in its paler, red-bronze leaves, red and yellow flowers and vivid ruby red fruit; *A. recurvata* swollen-based, compact rosette of spiny-toothed, arching, narrowly triangular leaves, mid-green, sometimes flushing red toward their bases at flowering; inflorescence beaconlike, scarcely clearing the leaves and packed with bright red bracts and small, purple, pink or red and white flowers.

Aegopodium (from Greek *aix*, a goat, and *pous*, a foot) Apiaceae. Europe, W Asia. 5 species, fully hardy, low-growing perennial. *A. podagraria*, GROUND ELDER, HERB GERARD, is an invasive weed of gardens, spreading mainly by deep-rooted rhizomes. Up to 36 in (90 cm) in height, with aromatic rootstock. Leaves 1-2-ternate, segments dentate, ovate, acuminate. Small white flowers borne in umbels in early summer. Ground elder (q.v.) colonizes rapidly and can choke all but the most vigorous plants. *A. podagraria* 'Variegata' is a less invasive selection with cream-splashed leaves. It has merit as a ground cover plant on sites where few other species flourish and where its progress can be controlled.

Aeonium (a plant name used by Dioscorides). Crassulaceae. Canaries, Madeira, North and East Africa (all those below from Atlantic Islands). 30 species, mostly perennial, tender shrubs and subshrubs with strap- to wedge-shaped, succulent leaves in wheel-like rosettes and small, yellow flowers packed in cymose, terminal inflorescences. Provide full sunlight and a gritty, loam-based medium that dries out between waterings. If quite dry, these plants may survive short, light frosts and will certainly tolerate a minimum of 41°F (5°C). Propagate by stem tip or leaf cuttings.

A. arboreum stoutly branched, tree-like perennial to 6½ ft (2 m) tall, each branch terminating in a loose rosette of leaves to 6 in (15 cm) long, obovate to oblanceolate, glossy, ciliate and mid-green, dark purple in 'Atropurpureum'; purple-black fading at the base to jade

green in 'Schwarzkopf'; variegated white and cream in 'Variegatum'; *A. canariense* VELVET ROSE; CANARY ISLAND AEONIUM; stemless with a short, unbranched stem; leaf rosette densely crowded, somewhat cupped/to flat leaves oblanceolate to 8 in (20 cm) long, mid-green, dewy with tiny, slightly sticky hairs; *A. haworthii* PINWHEEL; bushy, to 3¼ ft (1 m) tall with loose rosettes of obovate, acute, 2-in- (5-cm-) long leaves, usually glaucous with red margins; *A. tabuliforme* leaf rosettes to 16 in (40 cm) across, stemless, composed of many, overlapping, petal-like leaves, thinly succulent, obovate, acute, apple-green and ciliate.

Aerangis (from the Greek *aer*, air, and *angos*, vessel). Orchidaceae. Africa, Madagascar, Mascarene Islands, Sri Lanka. 50 species, epiphytic and lithophytic orchids with strap-shaped or elliptic leaves in a loose fan or in two ranks along elongated stems. White or ivory, mothlike flowers with long spurs are carried in arching racemes. Provide a minimum winter temperature of 50°F (10°C) and semishaded, humid, and airy conditions. Pot in a very open, bark-based orchid mix, or attach the plant to a pad of sphagnum moss and garden compost and tie it to a suspended raft, cork block, or fiber slab. Syringe daily during warm weather.

A. citrata Madagascar; short-stemmed with broad, 4 in (10 cm)-long leaves and pendulous 10-in- (25-cm-) long racemes packed with rounded ¾-in- (2-cm-) diam. flowers, deep cream to very pale primrose and faintly lemon-scented; *A. ellisii* Madagascar; large plant with distinct stems to 3¼ ft (1 m) long; flowers pure white, nocturnally fragrant in two ranks along a horizontal raceme some 16 in (40 cm) long, each flower with a spur 6 in (15 cm) long pointing straight downward; *A. fastuosa* Madagascar; dwarf, very short-stemmed, broad-leaved, with ¾-2½-in- (2-6-cm-) long racemes of sparkling white 2-in- (5-cm-) wide flowers; *A. kotschyana* Tropical Africa; medium-sized, short-stemmed plant with arching 16-in- (40-cm-) long sprays of 2-in- (5-cm-) wide, white flowers subtly tinted salmon pink with spiraling spurs to 8 in (20 cm) long; *A. luteoalba* Ethiopia to Angola; dwarf, with a few,

strap-shaped leaves to 4 in (10 cm) long—usually shorter—and arching racemes of disproportionately large flowers; var. *rhodosticta*: flowers with a red column).

aeration (1) the exchange of oxygen and carbon dioxide between the atmosphere and soil, which is dependent upon adequate soil pore spaces; cultivation, organic matter content, drainage, plant roots, and earthworm activity are all important influences. (2) the techniques used to relieve compaction, particularly on lawns. See *slitting*; *spiking* (q.v.).

aerator a specially designed hand-operated or mechanical device used to aerate soil or lawns by *slitting* or *spiking* (q.v.).

aerial roots roots borne wholly above ground, either adventitiously, as in *Hedera*, or from the rooting axis, as in many epiphytes.

Aerides (from Greek *aer*, air, due to their apparent ability to thrive on air alone). Orchidaceae. Tropical and subtropical E Asia. 40 species, tender epiphytic orchids grown for their pendulous racemes of fragrant, spurred flowers. They are tall with a single erect stem clothed with 2-ranked, strap-shaped leaves and giving rise to long, aerial roots. Most often grown is *A. odorata*, its flowers to 1¼ in (3 cm) wide and ranging in color from pure white to mauve, but typically sparkling white or cream, faintly and minutely spotted rose-purple on the lip and tipped magenta to purple on the tepals and spur. Provide a minimum temperature of 50°F (10°C). Plant in a coarse, bark-based mix in orchid pots or baskets; suspend in a brightly lit, well ventilated position with high humidity. Mist daily from late spring to fall and water twice weekly by plunging. Reduce water in winter. Propagate by detaching rooted offsets or by cutting long and old stems into rooted sections when repotting.

aerobic of conditions in which oxygen is available; or of organisms, especially bacteria, requiring oxygen for activity or life. Common in descriptions of managing a compost pile where regular turning encourages aerobic conditions and yields a superior product more rapidly than by anaerobic means; cf. *anaerobic*. See *compost pile*.

Aeschynanthus (from Greek *aischyne*, shame, and *anthos*, flower, referring to the red flowers). Gesneriaceae. Indomalaysia. 100 species, tender, evergreen herbs and subshrubs, usually trailing or clambering with thinly leathery leaves and showy tubular flowers, the upper lip 2-lobed, and the lower lip 3-lobed. Fine plants for baskets and hanging pots in the home, greenhouses and conservatories; minimum temperature 64°F (18°C). Provide bright indirect light and medium to high humidity. Plant in a free-draining, fertile mix high in leaf mold and composted bark. Keep moist throughout the year except during cool, dull weather when the plants should be kept rather dry. Root semiripe cuttings in spring and summer in a closed case with bottom heat.

A. marmoratus (syn. *A. zebrinus*) shrubby trailer with stems to 3¼ ft (1 m), leaves pale green with purple marbling, and stained purple beneath; flowers 1¼ in (3 cm) long, olive green flecked maroon); *A. pulcher* (ROYAL RED BUGLER; trailer with slender, cascading stems to 3¼ ft (1 m) long; flowers deep scarlet with a yellow throat, 2½ in (6 cm) long, calyx smooth, yellow-green flushed red above; *A. radicans* LIPSTICK PLANT; trailer with cascading stems to 3¼ ft (1 m) long, flowers deep scarlet, blotched yellow in throat, 2¾ in (7 cm) long emerging from green to maroon calyx cups; *A. lobbianus* differs in its strongly purple-tinted stems, gray-green leaves and deep maroon calyx cups; the flowers are streaked maroon within; *A. speciosus* (syn. *A. splendens*) robust shrubby scrambler to 5 ft (1.5 m) tall; flowers to 2¾ in (7 cm), fiery orange-red above, orange-yellow below, calyx green; *A.* × *splendidus* (*A. parasiticus* × *A. speciosus*; differs from *A. speciosus* in its flowers marked with dark maroon.

Aesculus (Classical Latin name for an oak with edible acorns, applied to this genus by Linnaeus). Hippocastanaceae. N America; Europe; Asia. BUCKEYE; HORSE CHESTNUT. 15 species, hardy deciduous trees and shrubs with large, palmately compound leaves and showy flowers in slender or broad, terminal panicles and racemes in late spring and summer. The seeds are large and woody with a paler hilum and enclosed in a more or less spherical case with a thick, spiny, bumpy or smooth skin. Plant in full sun or light shade in fertile, well-drained soil. Propagate by seed sown in fall, or by grafting in late winter; also by budding in late summer. Physiological scorching of the foliage sometimes occurs in hot, dry summers—this can be alleviated by pruning to reduce total leaf area, and by irrigation. Some US species lose their leaves early in the season (i.e. mid- to late summer).

A. californica CALIFORNIA BUCKEYE; California; small tree or spreading shrub to 40 ft (12 m) tall, often multi-stemmed, with gray bark; glossy dark green leaflets, narrowly oblong, serrate; flowers in erect plumes, white to cream or pink-tinted with rose-mauve filaments, fragrant; *A.* × *carnea* (*A. hippocastanum* × *A. pavia*; RED HORSE CHESTNUT; broad-crowned tree to 80 ft (25 m) tall; leaflets dark green and more or less smooth, toothed, oblong to obovate, often rather puckered and misshapen; flowers in loosely pyramidal panicles, rose to coral red or scarlet blotched orange-yellow; includes 'Briottii', with pale blood red flowers in large panicles; *A. chinensis* CHINESE HORSE CHESTNUT; China; slow-growing, spreading tree to 100 ft (30 m) tall; leaflets large, glossy dark green, toothed, oblong to obovate; flowers in erect spires, white; *A. flava* (syn. *A. octandra*) YELLOW BUCKEYE, SWEET BUCKEYE; North America; broad-crowned tree to 100 ft (30 m) tall; leaflets glossy dark green turning scarlet in fall, obovate; flowers yellow; *A. glabra* OHIO BUCKEYE; C and E US; broad-crowned tree or large shrub to 100 ft (30 m) tall; leaflets dark green and more or less smooth obovate to elliptic; flowers yellow-green with orange anthers; *A. hippocastanum*

spiny green casing splits

seed ("conker")

Aesculus hippocastanum

HORSE CHESTNUT; Balkans; broad-crowned tree to 100 ft (30 m) tall; leaflets mid- to dark green, coarse, with impressed veins, obovate; flowers in large, pyramidal panicles, white blotched rose or yellow, speckled red and fringed, spring; 'Baumannii': a vigorous selection with double, sterile flowers; *A. indica* INDIAN HORSE CHESTNUT; Himalaya; broad-crowned tree to 100 ft (30 m) tall; leaflets large, emerging bronze-pink, hardening smooth, dark green with paler undersides, broadly oblanceolate; flowers similar to *A. hippocastanum* but fewer on a longer, narrower panicle; includes 'Sydney Pearce' a vigorous selection with larger leaves, their petioles persistently red-tinted, and showy, pink-tinted flowers produced in great abundance; *A.* × *neglecta* *A. flava* × *A. sylvatica*; SUNRISE HORSE CHESTNUT; SE US; spreading tree to 70 ft (20 m) tall; leaflets emerging pink, hardening pale green, obovate; flowers yellow suffused red, early summer; 'Erythroblastos' has coral red new growth, amber fall color, and peach to pink flowers; *A. parviflora* SE US; freely suckering, spreading shrub or low-crowned and multi-stemmed tree to 15 ft (5 m) tall; leaflets large, emerging bronze, hardening dark green, smooth obovate; flowers in long, narrowly conical panicles, white with showy, pink-tinted stamens; *A. pavia* RED BUCKEYE; N America; broad-crowned tree or large shrub to 15 ft (5 m) tall; leaflets dark green and glossy, obovate, toothed; flowers carmine to red marked yellow, dark red in 'Atrosanguinea'; *A. turbinata* JAPANESE HORSE CHESTNUT; Japan; broad-crowned tree to 100 ft (30 m) tall; leaflets large, dark green with paler undersides obovate, toothed; flowers creamy white spotted red.

aestivation the arrangement of floral parts within the bud before flowering.

Aethionema (from the Greek, *aitho*, I scorch, and *nema*, thread or filament). Cruciferae. Europe, Mediterranean, W

Asia. STONE CRESS. 40 species, short-lived, semievergreen or evergreen perennial shrublets usually with small and narrow, slightly fleshy leaves and dense, terminal racemes of 4-petalled flowers produced in spring and summer. Most are suited to the rock garden, although *A. grandiflorum* (the largest of the genus) will grace the foreground of herbaceous borders. Plant in light, free-draining and somewhat alkaline soil in full sun. Hardy to 5°F (−15°C). Take softwood cuttings in spring, or sow seed in fall (with many, self-seeding is common).

A. armenum Armenia; tufted shrublet 8 in (20 cm); leaves glaucous; flowers small, pale pink; 'Warley Rose': very compact, leaves blue-gray, flowers rose pink; 'Warley Ruber': flowers deep rosy red; *A. grandiflorum* (syn. *A. pulchellum*) Iran, Iraq; PERSIAN STONE CRESS; loose subshrub to 18 in (45 cm); leaves glaucous; flowers pale rose; *A. iberideum* E Mediterranean to the Caucasus; compact subshrub to 6 in (15 cm); leaves gray-green; flowers fragrant, white; *A. schistosum* Turkey; erect to 4 in (10 cm); stems densely branched; leaves leaden gray; flowers fragrant, rose-pink.

aetiology see *etiology*.

afoliate leafless.

after-ripening a period of air-dry conditioning essential for the germination of some seeds.

agamospermy the development of seed without fertilization. A plant producing seed in this way is called an apomict (q.v.).

Agapanthus (from Greek, *agape*, love, and *anthos*, flower). Liliaceae (Alliaceae). South Africa. AFRICAN BLUE LILY; BLUE AFRICAN LILY; LILY OF THE NILE. 10 species, evergreen or deciduous, perennial herbs with short, thick stems, fleshy roots and strap-shaped leaves. Bell- to trumpet-shaped, the flowers consist of six tepals that meet in a tube below and are outspread at their tips. They are slender-stalked and carried in summer in scapose, rounded umbels. Handsome free-flowering perennials suitable for herbaceous bor-

ders and containers, they are hardy to −10°F (−23°C). Grow in full or dappled sun; keep moist in spring and summer, drier in winter, when the crowns benefit from a dry mulch. Propagate by division in spring, but disturb as seldom as possible.

A. africanus AFRICAN LILY; BLUE AFRICAN LILY; LILY OF THE NILE; to 24 in (60 cm), flowers tubular, to 2 in (5 cm) long, deep violet blue; includes the small, white 'Albus Nanus', and the dark blue 'Sapphire'; *A. campanulatus* to 39 in (100 cm), flowers campanulate, to 1½ in (3.5 cm) long, blue to white; includes the white var. *albidus* (Albus), the lavender-blue, large 'Isis', 'Profusion', free-flowering with pale blue flowers with darker stripes, and 'Variegatus' with cream-striped leaves; *A. inapertus* to 71 in (180 cm), flowers tubular, to 2 in (5 cm) long, bright blue to violet; includes the pale cream 'Albus'; *A. praecox* to 39 in (100 cm) tall, flowers tubular to funnel-shaped, to 2¾ in (7 cm) long, bright to pale blue or white; subsp. *orientalis*: syn. *A. orientalis*, *A. umbellatus*, smaller and clump-forming with stout scapes and pale blue to indigo flowers to 2 in (5 cm) long; includes the white-flowered 'Albus', dwarf 'Nanus', and 'Variegatus' with white-striped leaves. *Cultivars* 'Alice Gloucester' (flowers white); 'Blue Moon' (flowers pale blue), the Headbourne Hybrids (to 3¼ ft (1 m) tall, free-flowering and hardy with flowers in shades of blue), 'Lilliput' (to 18 in (45 cm), small and fine with dark blue flowers), 'Loch Hope' (to 48 in (120 cm) tall, flowers large, dark blue, crowded in broad umbels), 'Peter Pan' (to 12 in (30 cm), dwarf and free-flowering with mid-blue flowers), and 'Rancho White' (12–20 in (30–50 cm) tall, flowers white.

Agapetes (from Greek, *agapetos*, lovely or lovable, referring to the flowers). Ericaceae. East Asia, Pacific, Northern Australia. 95 species, evergreen, semi-scandent shrubs, many of them epiphytes with slender, arching branches and waxy, tubular to urn-shaped flowers, often beautifully marked and hanging from the axils of leathery leaves. Grow in lightly shaded and buoyant, humid conditions, with a minimum

temperature of 41°F (5°C). Plant in small containers in an acidic mix rich in coarse bark and leaf mold. Water and syringe plentifully throughout the growing season, rather less as the days shorten and the flowers develop and open.

A. macrantha NE India; gaunt, arching shrub to 6½ ft (2 m); leaves to 4¾ in (12 cm), laurel-like; flowers 2 in (5 cm), pale candy pink, with dark red chevron markings; *A. rugosa* (syn. *Pentapterygium rugosum*) Khasi Hills; to 3¼ ft (1 m) with rugose leaves to 4 in (10 cm) long; flowers white with purple marbling or red banding; *A. serpens* Nepal, Bhutan and North Assam; to 3¼ ft (1 m); leaves small, crowded; flowers ¾ in (2 cm) long, bright scarlet or fiery red, ivory in 'Nepal Cream', with dark crimson or blood red chevrons; this species has been crossed with *A. rugosa* to produce *A.* 'Ludgvan Cross', intermediate between the parents in habit and leaf form, with white-marked, carmine flowers.

Agastache (from Greek, *aga*, very much, and *stachys*, spike, referring to the abundance of flower spikes). Labiatae. N America; E Asia. GIANT HYSSOP; MEXICAN HYSSOP. 20 species, aromatic perennial herbs with clumped stems, toothed leaves and tubular, 2-lipped flowers whorled in spikes in summer. Hardy to 10°F (−12°C). Plant in full sun in a warm, sheltered situation in free-draining soil. Otherwise, grow in the cool greenhouse or conservatory. Increase by cuttings in late summer.

A. barberi (Arizona to Mexico; to 24 in (60 cm); leaves zestily aromatic, gray-green, toothed, to 2 in (5 cm); flowers rose to purple, but usually glowing coppery orange with an undertone of pink); *A. mexicana* (syn. *Brittonastrum mexicanum, Cedronella mexicana*) Mexico; to 24 in (60 cm), leaves toothed, ovate to lanceolate to 2½ in (6 cm); flowers rose to crimson).

Agave (from Greek, *agauos*, admirable, referring to the handsome appearance of the plants in flower). Agavaceae. Americas (those below from SW US to Mexico). ALOE CENTURY PLANT. Some 300 species, evergreen perennial herbs with rosettes of succulent leaves and erect spikes or candelabra-like panicles of tubular, cream to yellow-green flowers. Robust succulents grown for their handsome foliage and stately habit. The smaller species usually reach flowering size within a decade; larger species may require longer. Leaf rosettes tend to die after flowering. All require full sun and fast-draining, gritty soil. Most need a minimum temperature of 45°F (7°C), although *A. americana* will tolerate lower temperatures and even light and short-lived frosts if dry. Propagate by basal offsets or by plantlets, which sometimes form on spent inflorescences.

A. americana CENTURY PLANT; giant rosette of erect to spreading leaves each to 6½ ft (2 m) long, rigid, lanceolate, gray-green with hooked teeth and terminating in a sharp, dark spine; inflorescence candelabra-like, yellow-green and 12–30 ft (4–10 m) tall; cultivars with white- and yellow-striped leaves are available; *A. attenuata* clump of 3¼-ft- (1-m-) long, ovate to oblong leaves, gray-green with smooth margins; after some years, a short, stout trunk develops; flowers yellow-green, in arching racemes to 10 ft (3 m); *A. filifera* compact with rosettes to 24 in (60 cm) wide; leaves narrow, rigid, dark green, marked with chalky white lines and edged with white fibers; 'Compacta': leaves crowded, to 4 in (10 cm); *A. parryi* low, compact and rounded rosette of broadly obovate leaves to 16 in (40 cm) long, glaucous blue-gray, with short, dark teeth and tipped with a brown spine; *A. victoriae-reginae* ROYAL AGAVE; rosettes slow-growing to 24 in (60 cm) across, dense and domed; leaves tongue-shaped, dark green with smooth white margins and chalky superficial lines.

ageotropic applied to plant parts that are negatively geotropic, i.e., growing upward against the influence of gravity, as in the knee roots of the swamp cypress (*Taxodium distichum*). Also known as apogeotropic.

Ageratum (from Greek, *a*-, without, and *geras*, age; the florets retain their color for a long time). Compositae. Tropical America. 43 species, annual and perennial herbs with buttonlike flower heads. *A. houstonianum* is widely grown as a half-hardy annual suitable for bedding and containers. It is a bushy annual, standing 3–24 in (8–60 cm) tall with rounded, hairy leaves and a broad cap of tightly packed, powderpuff-like flower heads in various shades of blue, lilac and lavender. Cultivars include the taller 'Blue Horizon' and 'Blue Bouquet', the low, hummock-forming 'Blue Blazer', and 'Blue Danube', the pink 'Bengali' and 'Pinkie', and 'White Cushion'. Sow seed under glass in late winter; plant out in late spring, or sow seed *in situ* in late spring. Grow in fertile, moist but free-draining soil in sun. Pinch out faded flower heads regularly.

agglomerate crowded together in a head, as in the flowers of *Scabiosa* species.

aggregate (1) sand, grit, or gravel used as an ingredient of rooting or growing media, or as the basal rooting layer in ring culture of tomatoes; (2) sand, gravel, or ballast used with cement to make concrete; (3) used of soil particles, called crumbs or peds.

aggregate flowers flowers gathered together, usually in a tight rounded bunch or head as in the family Dipsacaceae without being capitulate (as in Compositae).

aggregate fruits a collection of separate carpels produced by a single flower and borne on a common receptacle, as in the fleshy "fruit" of *Rubus*.

Aglaonema (from Greek, *aglaos*, bright, and *nema*, thread, referring to the bright stamens). Araceae. Tropical Asia. 21 species, tender perennial herbs, evergreen, with erect to creeping stems, variegated, oblong to lanceolate leaves and inconspicuous flowers arranged in a club-shaped spadix and enclosed in a green or white, cowl-like spathe. Resilient and popular house plants. Grow in filtered sun or light shade, with a minimum temperature of 50°F (10°C). Propagate by stem cuttings, offsets or division.

A. commutatum to 3¼ ft (1 m); leaves 5–12 in (13–30 cm) long, emerald green banded or spotted yellow-white; includes 'Malay Beauty' with leaves to 12 in (30 cm) long, dark green spattered gray-green and zoned white, 'Treubii' with narrow leaves mottled gray-green or silver, and the heavily white-variegated 'White Rajah'; *A. nitidum* (to 3¼ ft (1 m); leaves to 18 in (45 cm), unmarked or barred and blotched cream; the cultivar 'Curtisii' has leaves marked silver along the main veins; hybridized with *A. pictum* 'Tricolor' to produce 'Silver King' with large leaves heavily streaked silverwhite, and 'Silver Queen' with narrower leaves marbled silvery white; *A. pictum* 12–20 in (30–50 cm) tall, with narrowly elliptic leaves to 6 in (16 cm) long, lustrous jade green blotched silver; includes 'Tricolor' with deep green leaves spattered silver and yellow-green.

AGM The Award of Garden Merit; conferred by the Royal Horticultural Society on any cultivated plant judged to be of outstanding all-around excellence for garden decoration or use in the open or under protection. The AGM was reconstituted in 1992 to replace a similar award dating from 1921, which until the change was the highest accolade in a three-tier system including the respectively lower-ranked, and now defunct, awards FCC (First Class Certificate) and HC (Highly Commended). The AGM is conferred following recommendation by experienced specialists, mostly after field trials. Criteria include: relatively easy cultivation; absence of susceptibility to pests, diseases or disorders; stability of characteristics; and retail availability. Each award is accompanied by a hardiness rating relative to cultivation in the British Isles in the scale H1–H4, with H4 the hardiest. See *hardiness*. AGM plants are identified on labels, in lists and in publications by the letters AGM and/or a "kitemark" consisting of a two-handled cup trophy. The RHS maintains and makes available up-to-date lists of AGM plants. Awards are periodically reviewed and may be rescinded.

Agonis (from Greek, *agonos*, "without angles," referring to the softly drooping and flowing branches of some species). Myrtaceae. Western Australia. 11 species, evergreen shrubs and small trees with fibrous bark, entire leaves and small, clustered flowers with five, rounded petals. Graceful trees for basically frost-free gardens or large, cool greenhouses and conservatories. Even if cut down by mild frosts, they will usually resprout. They tolerate all but wet and heavy soils and thrive in brilliantly sunny, rather dry conditions. Propagate as for *Eucalyptus*.

A. flexuosa WILLOW MYRTLE, PEPPERMINT TREE; to 30 ft (10 m); boughs snaking and arching, branchlets pendulous; leaves to 6 in (15 cm) long, peppermint-scented, linear silky at first; flowers white, ½ in (1 cm)-wide; *A. juniperina* JUNIPER MYRTLE; more erect and shrubby than *A. flexuosa* with very slender, sharply pointed leaves.

Agrostemma (from Greek *agros*, field, and *stemma*, garland). Caryophyllaceae. Mediterranean (naturalized Europe, N America). CORN COCKLE. 4 species, slender annual herbs, erect and hairy with narrow leaves and broadly funnel-shaped, 5-petaled flowers in summer. Fully hardy. Plant in a sunny position in free-draining, rather poor soil. Deadhead regularly. Sow seed *in situ* in spring or late summer, or allow a few plants to set seed and naturalize. *A. githago* to 32 in (80 cm); flowers white, rose or magenta; 'Milas': plum pink; 'Milas Rosea': pale lilac-pink.

Agrostis (from Greek *agrostis*, a kind of grass) Poaceae. Widespread in N Hemisphere. Some 120 species of hardy annual or perennial grasses to 5 ft (1.5 m), stoloniferous or tufted. Grow in well-drained soil in full sun. Propagate by seed or division. *A. tenuis*, BROWNTOP BENT, *A. castellana*, HIGHLAND BENT, and *A. stolonifera* are commonly used in turf grass mixtures. See *lawns*. *A. canina* VELVET BENT GRASS, Europe, is cultivated as a tufted, erect, slender-stemmed border or wildflower meadow perennial. *A. c.* 'Silver Needles' is a noted cultivar having fine leaf blades with silver-margins.

Aichryson (Classical Greek name for a related plant). Crassulaceae. Atlantic Islands, Morocco, Portugal. 15 species, annual or short-lived perennial herbs or subshrubs with thinly fleshy leaves and small, star-shaped yellow flowers in panicles. Plant Aichryson in a

sharply draining, sandy medium, in full sun, with a minimum temperature of 45°F (7°C). Increase by stem cuttings. *A. × domesticum* (*A. tortuosum* × *A. punctatum*) YOUTH-AND-OLD-AGE. Canary Islands; subshrub to 12 in (30 cm), leaves obovate to spathulate, to ½ in (1 cm) long; gray-green; 'Variegatum': leaves white-edged and solid creamy white on the same plant.

Ailanthus (Latinized form of the native name *ailanto*, meaning "reaching for the sky," hence the popular name "tree of heaven"). Simaroubaceae. E Asia to Australia. 5 species, deciduous shrubs and trees with pinnate leaves and small flowers in terminal panicles and followed in late summer by bunches of red-tinted, oblong samaras. A durable, very fast-growing and sometimes invasive tree. Plant on all but the driest or most saturated soils (min. –20°F/–29°C); provide some protection from harsh winds. Increase by rooted suckers and by seed sown in spring. Self-sown seedlings are common and may be a problem. *A. altissima* TREE OF HEAVEN; China; to 100 ft (30 m); canopy broad, much-branched; leaves to 3¼ ft (1 m) long with red-tinted stalks and 15–30 mid-green, lanceolate to ovate leaflets.

air-filled porosity (**AFP**) the percentage by volume of potting mix that is occupied by air when the medium has been saturated and allowed to drain; a measure of aeration.

airplane house a type of greenhouse for commercial cropping, superseded by modern design. Of wood construction, often on a low brick wall, 14–15 ft (4.3–4.6 m) wide, with gutters 6–6½ ft (1.8–2 m) above ground level and a ridge height of about 12¾ ft (4 m).

Ajuga (from Greek *a-*, not, and *zygon*, yoke: meaning obscure but perhaps to do with the calyx, which is not bilabiate). Labiatae. Europe; Asia. BUGLE WEED. 40 species, annual or perennial herbs with low rosettes of obovate leaves, sometimes spreading by stolons, and giving rise in spring and summer to erect stems of tubular, 2-lipped flowers in whorls among leafy bracts. Excellent low groundcover plants, fully

hardy and thriving in sun, shade and a wide range of soils. Propagate by division or detaching rooted stolons.

A. genevensis BLUE BUGLE, UPRIGHT BUGLE WEED; to 16 in (40 cm) tall, usually far shorter, not stoloniferous, with leaves to 4¾ in (12 cm) long; flowers bright blue, to ⅗ in (1.5 cm) long, amid violet to blue-tinted leafy bracts; 'Alba': flowers white; 'Rosea': flowers rosy pink; 'Tottenham': flowers lilac-pink; 'Variegata': leaves mottled creamy white; *A. pyramidalis* PYRAMID BUGLE WEED; creeping, stoloniferous dark green to 4 in (10 cm) long, flowers blue amid leafy, purple-tinted bracts in a pyramidal spike to 6 in (15 cm) tall; 'Metallica Crispa': leaves iridescent, bronze-maroon with crinkled margins; *A. reptans* stoloniferous and carpeting leaves to 3 in (8 cm) long; flowers azure amid purple-blue-tinted bracts in spikes to 12 in (30 cm) tall; 'Atropurpurea'; leaves deep bronze-purple-tinted; 'Braunherz': lustrous dark, purple-black leaves, flowers deep blue; 'Burgundy Glow': leaves silvery variegated green cream, rose and deep red; 'Catlin's Giant': large, luxuriant purple-brown leaves, flowers blue on tall spikes; 'Jungle Beauty': leaves dark green to purple-tinted, wavy-margined; flowers indigo in spikes to 14 in (35 cm); 'Multicolor': leaves dark green overlaid with red-bronze and splashed pink and cream; 'Rosea'; flowers pink.

Akebia (Latinized form of *akebi*, the Japanese name for these plants). Lardizabalaceae. China, Korea, Japan. 2 species, vigorous, woody perennial climbers with slender, twining stems, digitately compound leaves and unisexual flowers in short, drooping racemes. Plant in moisture-retentive and well-drained soil. Grow in full sun or partial shade. Although hardy to –4°F (–20°C), they are sometimes cut down by hard frost, and late spring freezes will kill new growth. The flowers, also produced in spring, are usually unaffected. Increase by stratified seed or by stem cuttings under mist.

A. quinata semievergreen or deciduous; leaves with five, oblong leaflets; flowers strongly vanilla-scented, deep plum purple to dark chocolate or maroon; *A. trifoliata* (syn. *A. lobata*) differs from the last species in being

33

largely deciduous and possessing three leaflets per leaf their margins sometimes shallowly lobed rather than entire; flowers smaller, deep vinous purple, unscented; *A.* × *pentaphylla* leaflets 4–5 (rarely 6 or 7) per leaf; flowers faintly scented.

alate winged; usually used of stems, petioles and fruits where the main body is furnished with marginal membranous bands.

Albizia (for Filippo degli Albizzi, naturalist who returned to Florence in 1749 from an expedition to Constantinople with many new seeds). Leguminosae. Tropics and subtropics. 150 species, deciduous to semievergreen trees, shrubs and lianes with feathery bipinnate leaves and mimosa-like flower heads consisting of bundles of showy stamens in powderpuff-like balls or cylindrical spikes. *A. julibrissin* will grow outdoors (min. temp. –10°F/ –23°C) provided the summers are long, hot, and humid enough to ripen the new growth, or to spur a frosted stump into rapid resprouting. *A. lophantha* may survive outdoors against sheltered walls to 0°F (–18°C), but is otherwise for summer bedding or the cool conservatory. Both flower from midspring to late summer and prefer full sun and fertile, moist soil. Propagate by seed presoaked in tepid water for about twelve hours, or by semiripe cuttings; also by root cuttings in spring.

A. julibrissin SILK TREE; Asia; domed or flat-crowned tree to 20 ft (6 m); flower heads ivory to rosy pink, spherical, to 1½ in (4 cm) wide; *A. lophantha* (syn. *Paraserianthes lophantha*) Australia; tree to 12 ft (4 m); flower spikes to 2½ in (6 cm), cylindrical, lime green to gold.

Alcea (from Greek, *alkaia*, a kind of mallow). Malvaceae. Europe; Asia. HOLLYHOCK. 60 species, hardy hairy biennial or short-lived perennial herbs with broad, rounded to palmately lobed leaves and tall spikes of dish-shaped flowers with five, obovate to cuneate petals. *A. rosea* (syn. *Althaea rosea*) is a summer-flowering biennial, sometimes grown as an annual. An old favorite of cottage gardens, the hollyhock has been much-developed, resulting in cultivars that range in height

from 3¼ to 10 ft (1–3 m), in flower form from the single to semidoubles, full doubles, and peony forms, some with ruffled or lacy petals. Colors run from white to darkest maroon-black through yellow, buff, pale rose, deep pink, and deep red. Full sun is best, together with shelter from strong winds. Sow seed *in situ* in well-drained soil in late summer or spring.

Alchemilla (from the Arabic name for this plant, *alkemelych*). Rosaceae. Cosmopolitan (chiefly Europe and Asia). LADY'S MANTLE. 300 species, hardy evergreen or semideciduous perennial herbs with clumps of slender-stalked, rounded leaves variously toothed, lobed or palmately cut. Produced in spring and summer, the flowers are very small, starry, green-yellow and carried in much-branched panicles. *A. mollis* tolerates sun or shade on all but the wettest or driest soils. It can be grown as a type of "lawn," the foliage sheared regularly. *A. alpina* grows well in full sun on rock gardens and dry banks. Propagate by seed or by division in spring or fall.

A. alpina ALPINE LADY'S MANTLE; low mounds of small leaves with five to seven, toothed, lanceolate-obovate leaflets, dark green and smooth above, silvery-hairy beneath; in gardens, the name *A. alpina* is often misapplied to *A. conjuncta*, a larger plant with flowering stems to 12 in (30 cm) tall and leaves composed of 7–9 lanceolate to elliptic, toothed leaflets, these are smooth and mid-green above and silky-hairy beneath; *A. mollis* LADY'S MANTLE; clump-forming perennial to 16 × 24 in (40 × 60 cm) with circular, toothed and shallowly lobed leaves to 6 in (15 cm) across; these are lime to sea-green and covered in soft, water-repellent down; the plant known as *A. mollis* 'Mr. Poland's Variety', with more deeply lobed leaves that are hairless above, is properly *A. venosa*.

algae primitive unicellular or multicellular photosynthetic plants living in water or moist environments; often a nuisance in ponds or irrigation systems or on damp surfaces.

algal spot a usually red-colored spotting of foliage encountered in warm,

wet regions, caused by algae, especially *Cephaleuros* species. In wet tropical climates or under protected cultivation with overhead watering, the surfaces of many plants are frequently colonized by superficial algae, which are usually harmless except that they can reduce the amount of light available to the plant for photosynthesis. *Cephaleuros*, however, the usual cause of algal spot, is parasitic and grows within the tissues of its host plant, as well as on the surface in the form of raised orange or red hairy patches on foliage and shoots. It is sometimes confusingly referred to as "red rust." The diseases caused by *Cephaleuros* species can be unsightly on ornamentals such as *Anthurium*, *Camellia*, and *Magnolia* and damaging to some crop plants including avocado, citrus, guava, and tea. Generally, they are only a problem if other factors have weakened plants and predisposed them to infection. In serious cases, control can be achieved by treatment with copper-containing preparations. Removal of infected leaves and twigs is advisable to reduce the overall level of inoculum.

algicide a chemical used to control algal diseases and weeds.

alginates seaweed derivatives; used as soil conditioners to enhance crumb stability, and water and nutrient retention.

Alisma (Classical Greek name for this plant). Alismataceae. North temperate regions; Australia. 9 species, aquatic, perennial herbs making a clump of long-stalked leaves that remain partly submerged or stand clear of the water. In summer, many small, 3-petaled flowers are held above the plant on the slender, whorled branches of pyramidal panicles. WATER PLANTAIN, *A. plantago-aquatica*, is found in still or sluggish water and swamps throughout the Northern Hemisphere and Africa. The leaves are elliptic to ovate or lanceolate, ribbed, mid-green, up to 12 in (30 cm) long. The panicles stand 8–24 in (20–60 cm) high and swarm with white flowers on remotely whorled branches. Hardy to –30°F (–34°C), used in ponds, lakes, ditches, and streamsides planted in a loamy mix in submerged baskets, or directly into the banks and bed. Propagate by division, seed, or plantlets, which form on the panicles.

alkaline in gardening, mainly applicable to soil and water having a pH scale value greater than 7.0; cf. *acidic*. See *soils*; *pH*.

alkaloids nitrogenous compounds produced by plants, often as an end-product of nitrogen metabolism. Many have medicinal and/or toxic properties, including morphine, cocaine, nicotine, quinine, colchicine, strychnine.

Allamanda (for F. Allamand [1735–1795], Swiss physician and botanist who collected in Surinam and sent seed of this plant to Linnaeus). Apocynaceae. S America. 12 species, evergreen, usually scandent shrubs with leathery, oblong to lanceolate leaves and showy funnel-shaped flowers. Maintain a humid, airy atmosphere; water and feed freely when in growth; keep barely moist in winter with a minimum temperature of 55°F (13°C). Shade only from the strongest summer sun. Tie in to supports if necessary. Prune after flowering—this varies, but most plants in greenhouse cultivation flower from the late spring through to late winter. Propagate by soft or semi-ripe stem tip cuttings. *A. blanchetii* (syn. *A. purpurea*, *A. violacea*) PURPLE ALLAMANDA; erect or weakly climbing shrub with downy leaves and rich rosy-purple flowers to $3\frac{1}{2} \times 2\frac{1}{2}$ in (9 × 6 cm); *A. cathartica* COMMON ALLAMANDA, GOLDEN TRUMPET; vigorous climber to 50 ft (16 m) with glossy leaves and golden yellow flowers to 4 × $4\frac{3}{4}$ in (10 × 12 cm) with white markings in the throat; 'Grandiflora': flowers very large and freely produced; 'Hendersonii': flowers waxy, orange-yellow, tinged bronze on tube with white spots in throat; 'Nobilis': very large and robust with outsize pure gold flowers; *A. schottii* (syn. *A. neriifolia*) BUSH ALLAMANDA; resembles a more or less self-supporting *A. cathartica*, 5 ft (1.5 m); flowers, to 1 × $2\frac{1}{4}$ in (2.5 × 5.5 cm), golden yellow strongly streaked or stained orange-red to chestnut brown within.

allée a walk or ride cut through dense woodland, or created by the close planting of shrubs and trees; a feature of formal French gardens since the 16th century.

allelopathy the usually harmful direct or indirect chemical effects of one plant on another. An example is the growth-inhibiting effect on other plants of toxic root exudate and leaf drip from the black walnut (*Juglans nigra*). Chemical diffusions from seeds or storage organs have been shown to be effective against microorganisms. However, allelopathic effect is difficult to confirm under natural conditions, and is of limited practical significance in gardens.

Allium (Latin, *allium*, the classical name for garlic, from the Celtic, *all*, meaning "hot"). Liliaceae (Alliaceae). Northern Hemisphere. ONION. Some 700 species, bulbous perennial and biennial herbs with a characteristic "onion" odor. Solitary or clustered bulbs produce leaves ranging in shape from grassy to narrowly tubular, to lanceolate, to elliptic or ovate. The flowers may be star-shaped or campanulate, consist of six tepals, and are carried in scapose umbels usually in spring and summer.

The ornamental species (see table overleaf) are grown for their flowers and foliage, but *Allium* also includes several important culinary herbs and vegetables—*A. cepa* (ONION, SHALLOTS), *A. fistulosum* (WELSH ONION, JAPANESE BUNCHING ONION, JAPANESE LEEK), *A. porrum* (LEEK), *A. sativum* (GARLIC),

Allium cernuum
The dried seed heads of many *Allium* species persist through fall and even into winter, providing long-term decorative interest.

A. schoenoprasum (CHIVES), *A. scorodoprasum* (GIANT GARLIC, SPANISH GARLIC), *A. tuberosum* (CHINESE CHIVES, GARLIC CHIVES, ORIENTAL GARLIC).

The hardy, perennial ornamentals include tall species for the herbaceous and flower border, some of them excellent for cutting and drying, and many smaller species ideal for rock gardens, dry gardens, raised beds, pavement terraces, and pot culture. Species from the western United States (e.g., *A. campanulatum*, *A. unifolium*) tend to be brightly colored in shades of magenta, pink, and red. They are particularly suitable for hot, dry positions in well-drained soil. The taller, Central Asian species (e.g., *A. cristophii*, *A. giganteum*) usually produce large, spherical inflorescences atop long, leafless scapes as the basal foliage withers. They are outstanding when planted among low-growing shrubs such as *Artemisia*, *Cistus*, *Lavandula*, *Salvia*, and *Santolina*, which share their liking for arid, stony soil in full sun. To the front, plant the TURKESTAN ALLIUM, *A. karataviense*, earlier-flowering with attractive, gray leaves and globes of purple to buff flowers. Smaller West Asian species (e.g., *A. carinatum* subsp. *pulchellum*, *A. flavum*) need a position at the front of the border. The smaller clump-formers are suitable for well-drained rock gardens in full sun, among them *A. mairei* and *A. oreophilum*. Himalayan natives, such as *A. beesianum*, require damper, richer soil. Where the ground is especially heavy and winters are wet and cold, some Californian species and dry-growing Asiatics, such as the spectacular *A. schubertii*, are best grown in pans of gritty soil in full sun in a well-ventilated cool greenhouse, alpine house, or bulb frame, and kept dry during the winter months; otherwise, grow them in raised beds.

Plant bulbs in fall or early spring at approximately one-and-a-half times their depth. Clear the foliage once it has withered. If decorative, dead flower heads may be left until they break up. Propagate by offsets, removed when the plants are dormant, or by seed sown in spring at about 55°F (13°C). Divide spring-flowering clump-formers in summer, summer-flowering clump-formers in spring. Pests and diseases of *Allium* crops may also affect ornamentals.

ALLIUM

Name	Distribution	Flowering time	Height	Leaves	Flowers
A. acuminatum	W N America	spring	4–12 in (10–30 cm)	2–4, linear, shorter than scape	deep rose pink to purple-pink or white, 10–30 per 1½–2½ in (4–6 cm) diam. umbel
A. aflatunense **Comments:** Includes 'Purple Sensation' with intense violet umbels on 3¼ ft (1 m) tall scapes.	C Asia	summer	32–60 in (80–150 cm)	6–8, ¾–4 in (2–10 cm) across, ± glaucous, far shorter than scape	pale mauve to violet, small, in dense, 4 in (10 cm) diam. spherical umbels
A. akaka	Turkey, Caucasus, Iran	spring	2–6 in (5–15 cm)	1–3, to 8 × 2½ in (20 × 6 cm), oblong-elliptic, gray-green, low-lying	white to pale lilac pink with red-tinted center, very crowded in spherical 1¼–4 in (3-10 cm diam.), ± stalkless umbels
A. atropur-pureum	S Europe	late spring–summer	1½–39 in (4–100 cm)	3–7, linear, 6–14 in (15–35 cm) diam. umbel	dark purple to near-black in crowded heads, 1¼–2¾ in (3–7 cm) across
A. beesianum **Comments:** Includes the white-flowered f. **album**.	W China	late summer	6–8 in (15–20 cm)	2–4, linear, 6–8 in (15–20 cm), gray-green	bright to deep blue, 6–12, bell-shaped, nodding
A. caeruleum A. azureum BLUE ALLIUM	Siberia, Turkestan	summer	8–32 in (20–80 cm)	2–4, to 2¾ in (7 cm), linear, 3-angled	cornflower blue, 30–50, small, packed in a 1¼–1½ in (3-4 cm) diam. umbel on a slender scape
A. campanula-tum	W US	summer	4–12 in (10–30 cm)	2–3, to 12 in (30 cm), linear	pale pink to white, bell-shaped, 15–40 in a 1–2¾-in- (2.5–7-cm-) diam., hemispherical umbel
A. carinatum ssp. pulchellum A. pulchellum	C & S Europe; Russia; Turkey	summer	12–24 in (30–60 cm)	2–4, to 8 in (20 cm), narrowly linear	purple, cup-shaped, to 30, nodding in a ¾–2 in (2–5 cm) diam. umbel

Comments: The typical *A. carinatum* (KEELED GARLIC) differs in bearing bulbils in its umbels.

Name	Distribution	Flowering time	Height	Leaves	Flowers
A. cernuum LADY'S LEEK; NODDING ONION; WILD ONION	Canada to Mexico	summer	12–28 in (30–70 cm)	4–6, to 8 × ¼ in (20 × 0.7 cm), flat	deep pink to magenta, more rarely white or maroon, cup-shaped, nodding, 10–30 per lax, 1¼–2 in (3–5 cm) diam. umbel
A. cristophii A. albopilosum STARS OF PERSIA	Iran, Turkey, C Asia	summer	6–20 in (15–50 cm)	2–7, 6–16 × ½–1½ in (15–40 × 1–4 cm), glaucous, downy, drooping	purple-violet, starlike, with metallic sheen, long- and slender-stalked, very many in a loose, spherical to hemispherical umbel to 8 in (20 cm) diam.

Comments: Inflorescences very attractive when dried. Includes 'Gladiator' (to 4 ft (1.2 m) with large, lilac-mauve flowers), 'Globus' (*A. cristophii* × *A. giganteum*: to 14 in (35 cm), flowers blue in large heads), 'Lucy Ball' (to 4 ft (1.2 m), flowers dark lilac in compact head), 'Rien Poortvliet' (to 4 ft (1.2 m), flowers lilac).

A. acuminatum   *A. caeruleum*   *A. cernuum*   *A. cristophii*

ALLIUM

Name	Distribution	Flowering time	Height	Leaves	Flowers
A. cyaneum	China	summer	4–18 in (10–45 cm)	1–3, 6 in (15 cm), threadlike, semicylindric	violet-blue to purple veined darker blue, bell-shaped, pendent, 5–18 in a small dense umbel
A. cyathophorum var. farreri A. farreri	China	summer	8–16 in (20–40 cm)	3–6, 7–10 × ¹⁄₁₆–¼ in (18–24 × 0.1–0.5 cm)	maroon to dark mauve, bell-shaped, nodding, 6–30 in a loose umbel
A. flavum SMALL YELLOW ONION	C Europe to W Asia	summer	3–12 in (8–30 cm)	to 8 in (20 cm), narrowly cylindric, glaucous	lemon-yellow, scented, bell-shaped, nodding, slender-stalked, 9–60 in hemispherical ⅝–1¼ in (1.5–3 cm) diam. umbel

Comments: Includes 'Blue Leaf' ('Glaucum') with strongly glaucous, blue-green leaves, and var. *minus*, a smaller plant with contrasting purple stamens.

Name	Distribution	Flowering time	Height	Leaves	Flowers
A. giganteum GIANT ALLIUM	C Asia	summer	32–80 in (80–200 cm)	12–39 × 2–4 in (30–100 × 5–10 cm), gray-green, basal	lilac, mauve or white, star-shaped, very many in a dense, 4–6 in (10–15 cm) diam. umbel
A. insubricum	N Italy	spring–summer	6–12 in (16–30 cm)	4¾–8 × ¹⁄₁₆–¼ in (12–20 × 0.2–0.5 cm), 3–4, flat, glaucous	purple-pink, bell-shaped, rather large and nodding, 3–5 per umbel

Comments: The very similar A. narcissiflorum differs in its fibrous bulb sheath.

Name	Distribution	Flowering time	Height	Leaves	Flowers
A. karataviense ALLIUM	C Asia Turkestan	late spring	4–10 in (10–25 cm)	2–3, 6–8 in (15–20 cm), broad, oblong-elliptic to elliptic, glaucous, gray-blue tinted purple, low-lying	white to pale purple-pink, star-shaped, very numerous in a crowded spherical umbel to 8 in (20 cm) diam.; scape purple-tinted
A. macranthum	W China, Sikkim	summer	8–12 in (20–30 cm)	6–16 × ¼ in (15–40 × 0.5 cm), linear	deep purple, large, bell-shaped, long-stalked, to 20, nodding in a loose umbel
A. mairei	SW China	late summer to early fall	4–16 in (10–40 cm)	to 10 × ½ in (25 × 1 cm), threadlike	white to pink, often spotted red, 2–20, bell-shaped, held erect in a narrow umbel on a wiry stalk
A. moly GOLDEN GARLIC; LILY LEEK	S & SW Europe	summer	4¾–14 in (12–35 cm)	1–3, 8–12 in (20–30 cm), lanceolate, glaucous	golden yellow, star-shaped, fairly large, 10–40 in a 1½–2¾ in (4–7 cm) diam. umbel

Comments: Includes 'Jeannine', with bright yellow flowers in large umbels, 2 scapes produced per bulb.

Name	Distribution	Flowering time	Height	Leaves	Flowers
A. narcissiflorum A. pedemontanum	N Italy, Portugal	summer	6–14 in (15–35 cm)	3–5, 3½–7 × ¹⁄₁₆–¼ in (9–18 × 0.2–0.6 cm), flat, gray green	pure, bright pink to rosy purple, fairly large, bell-shaped, 5–8, nodding

Comments: See A. insubricum.

A. flavum

A. giganteum

A. karataviense

ALLIUM

Name	Distribution	Flowering time	Height	Leaves	Flowers
A. neapolitanum A. cowanii DAFFODIL GARLIC; NAPLES GARLIC	Mediterranean, S Europe, Asia Minor, N Africa	spring	8–20 in (20–50 cm)	2, 3–14 in (8–35 cm), linear-lanceolate	sparkling white, cup- or star-shaped, slender-stalked, small, to 40 per 2–4½ in (5–11 cm) diam., open, hemispherical umbel

Comments: Includes 'Grandiflorum' with large, loose umbels of larger flowers, each with a dark eye.

A. oreophilum A. ostrowskianum	Turkestan, Caucasus, C Asia	spring–summer	2–8 in (5–20 cm)	2, narrow	deep pink to rosy purple, broadly cup-shaped, proportionately large (to ⅝ in (2 cm) across) 10 or more in a loose, spherical umbel

Comments: Includes 'Zwanenberg' with deep carmine flowers.

A. schoenoprasum CHIVES	Europe; Asia; N America; widely naturalized	spring–summer	4–24 in (10–60 cm)	strong onion-scented, 1–5, to 14 in (35 cm), cylindric, hollow	white, pink-mauve or purple, small bell-shaped, crowded in ⅝–2 in (1.5–5 cm) diam. spherical umbels
A. schubertii	E Mediterranean to C Asia	early summer	12–24 in (30–60 cm)	8–18 in (20–45 cm), broadly linear to strap-shaped, wavy, glaucous	white tinted purple or wholly violet, small, narrowly star-shaped in spherical umbels to 2 in (5 cm) diam., but some on far longer, purple-tinted, radiating stalks

Comments: Remarkable for its purple flower heads with very unequal, spokelike flower-stalks.

A. scorodoprasum SAND LEEK; GIANT GARLIC; SPANISH GARLIC	E Europe; Caucasus; Turkey; N Iran	spring–summer	10–36 in (25–90 cm)	to 12 in (30 cm), 2–5, linear	lilac to purple, small in hemispherical umbels, many replaced by purple bulbils

Comments: Culinary herb.

A. senescens GERMAN GARLIC	Europe; N Asia	late spring–summer	2¾–24 in (7–60 cm)	1½–12 in (4–30 cm), 4–9, flat, narrowly strap-shaped	lilac, small, cup-shaped in a ¾–2 in (2–5 cm) diam., hemispherical umbel

Comments: Includes var. **glaucum** with glaucous gray-green leaves growing in a low, swirling configuration.

A. sikkimense A. kansuense	Himalaya; China; Tibet	summer	4–16 in (10–40 cm)	2–5, linear, flat, to 12 in (30 cm)	deep blue or purple, bell-shaped, to 15 in a small nodding umbel
A. sphaerocephalum DRUMSTICK ALLIUM; ROUND-HEADED GARLIC; ROUND-HEADED LEEK	Europe; N Africa; W Asia	summer	to 36 in (90 cm)	2–6, 2¾–14 in (7–35 cm), linear, cylindrical, hollow	purple-pink to maroon, small, bell-shaped, packed in a ¾–1¼ in (2–3 cm) diam., spherical umbel atop a wiry scape

Comments: Flowers sometimes replaced by bulbils; white in sspp. **arvense** and **trachypus**.

A. unifolium	W US	early summer	to 24 in (60 cm)	solitary, gray-green, linear, flat	deep rosy pink, broadly star-shaped, 5–20 in a 2-in (5-cm) diam., hemispherical umbel

A. moly

A. neapolitanum

A. oreophilum

A. schoenoprasum 'Forescate'

Possible problems: onion flies, stem eel worm and onion thrips; bacterial soft rots, onion white rot, rust, smudge and smut.

allogamy see *cross-fertilization*.

allopolyploid a polyploid plant with sets of dissimilar chromosomes from parents of different species, and which is fertile as a result of a doubling of the parental chromosome numbers—for example, rutabaga (*Brassica napus* Napobrassica Group) (4 ×) derived from crossing turnip (*Brassica rapa* Rapifera Group) (2 ×) and rape (*Brassica napus*) (2 ×); cf. *autopolyploid*.

allotment (US, community garden) a piece of land let out by a public authority for cultivation by an individual or family. In the UK, usually a plot measuring 95 × 30 ft (29 × 9.25 m) contained within a group of units.

almond (*Prunus dulcis*) a deciduous tree native of Asia Minor and parts of North Africa, closely allied to the peach. The almond is grown for its nuts or, in cool areas, the attractive pink blossoms in spring. There are two distinct types: the sweet almond, whose nuts are prized for eating raw or cooked, and the bitter almond, which has a poisonous kernel and is used for flavoring and in medicines. In ideal situations, some cultivars may reach a height of 30 ft (10 m). Its chilling requirement is 300–500 hours below 45°F (7°C); early flowering predisposes the blossom and fruitlets to frost damage. Almond is insect-pollinated, and although most cultivars are self-fertile, cropping is improved where a pollinator is grown nearby. Propagation is usually by budding onto seedling almond or peach rootstock; cropping begins within three or four years. Almond is best trained and pruned as a bush peach, removing a proportion of the older wood in spring in favor of the production of fruit bearing one-year-old shoots.

Possible problems: birds; peach leaf curl.

Alnus (Classical Latin name). Betulaceae. Northern Hemisphere, south to Peru and Himalaya. ALDER. 35 species, hardy deciduous or semievergreen trees and large shrubs. The crown is typically ovoid to conical, the bark dark and sooty in appearance and the winter buds gummy. The leaves are ovate to orbicular and tough. The male flowers are small and carried in drooping catkins in winter and (more usually) early spring. Female flowers are borne in shorter, broader catkins that become small, woody "cones." Alders tolerate cold, wind, and a wide range of soil types. All are able to thrive in wet, even waterlogged conditions, *A. glutinosa* especially, but *A. cordata* will also grow in rather dry, poor soil and is proving to be an excellent street tree. Sow seed in fall, or propagate by budding in early fall and cuttings in winter.

A. cordata ITALIAN ALDER; Italy, Corsica; to 100 ft (30 m), crown ovoid to conic; shoots sticky, red-brown; leaves to 4 in (10 cm) long, broadly ovate to rounded, base cordate, margins finely toothed, leathery, deep, glossy green and smooth above, paler beneath, often persisting late into fall; 'Purpurea': new growth bronze-purple; *A. glutinosa* COMMON ALDER, BLACK ALDER; Europe to C Asia, N Africa; to 70 ft (20 m), crown narrowly pyramidal; shoots smooth, sticky; leaves to 4 in (10 cm) long, obovate to rounded, base tapered, margins wavy to toothed, dark green and smooth; includes 'Aurea': new growth yellow aging yellow-green; 'Imperialis': leaves deeply cut; *A. incana* GRAY ALDER; Europe; to 100 ft (30 m), crown conical; shoots gray-downy; leaves to 4 in (10 cm) long, ovate to oval, base rounded to cuneate, toothed, dull green above with corrugated veins, paler beneath with gray down; 'Aurea': shoots yellow becoming orange-red in winter, catkins are yellow-red; 'Ramulis Coccineis': winter shoots and buds red, catkins orange.

Alocasia (from Greek *a-*, without, and *Colocasia*, a genus from which this was split). Araceae. Southeast Asia. ELEPHANT'S EAR PLANT. 70 species, large, tender perennial herbs with tuberous or stoutly rhizomatous roots and long-stalked heart- to arrow-shaped leaves. The flowers are borne in dull, *Arum*-like inflorescences. Grow in a fertile medium rich in humus; water and feed frequently in spring and summer, providing high humidity and protection from full sunlight. Keep barely moist in winter (minimum temperature 50°F/10°C). Propagate by offsets, division of rhizomes or stem cuttings.

A. cuprea (leaves to 12 in (30 cm), oblong to ovate, base cordate, green with a purple or coppery iridescent sheen between black-green zones around the sunken veins above, red-violet beneath; *A. macrorrhiza* GIANT TARO; leaves to 50 in (125 cm), ovate to cordate to sagittate, glossy green above with paler veins; widely grown for its edible rhizomes and shoots; ornamental cultivars include 'Variegata' with leaves blotched cream and dark green, and 'Violacea' with leaves tinged violet; *A. plumbea* similar to *A. macrorrhiza* but with smaller leaves with wavy margins, dark green tinted purple to purple-red or violet-black with dark veins; *A. sanderiana* KRIS PLANT; leaves to 16 in (40 cm), sagittate with wavy margins, metallic violet-black or very dark green with silver-white margins and white veins; *A. veitchii* leaves to 36 in (90 cm), narrowly triangular to sagittate, dark green above, veined and edged gray, red-purple beneath; petiole with dark bands.

Aloe (from the Greek name, related to Hebrew *allal*, bitter). Liliaceae (Aloeaceae). Africa, Madagascar, Cape Verde Islands. Some 325 species, evergreen perennial herbs, shrubs or trees with succulent leaves. The flowers are tubular and consist of six tepals; they are borne at various times of year in long-stalked, narrowly conical racemes or candelabra-like panicles. The larger species are fine plants for dry landscapes in frost-free gardens, or (where frosts are common) cool greenhouses and conservatories. The climbing *A. ciliaris* may be used on pergolas and arbors. Several smaller species, e.g., *A. aristata* and *A. variegata*, are popular, resilient house plants; *A. bakeri* might equally join their ranks. All prefer full sun, a minimum temperature of 45°F (7°C), a dry, airy atmosphere and loamy soil high in grit and sand. Water liberally from late spring to early fall, allowing the soil to dry out between waterings. At other times keep these plants more or less dry, watering only to prevent

ALOE

Name	Distribution	Habit	Leaves	Flowers
A. arborescens CANDELABRA ALOE; OCTOPUS PLANT; TORCH PLANT; TREE ALOE	S Africa; Zimbabwe; Mozambique; Malawi	erect shrub or tree to 20 ft (6 m) tall with a stout trunk and a spreading canopy of candelabriform branches	in terminal rosettes, to 24 in (60 cm) long, gray-green and finely tapering with spiny margins	to 1½ in (4 cm) long, scarlet tipped green-white on an unbranched spike to 3¼ ft (1 m) tall in late winter and summer

Comments: Large shrub for virtually frost-free gardens or conservatories. Withstands drought, salt spray and very mild frosts. Includes 'Spineless' with gray-blue, spineless leaves, and 'Variegata' with leaves striped cream.

A. aristata TORCH PLANT; LACE ALOE	S Africa	stemless forming clusters of dense rosettes.	to 4 × ⅝ in (10 × 1.5 cm), lanceolate, tapering to a slender bristle, strongly incurved, green (red-brown in full sun in poor soil) with scattered white spots in bands and soft, white spiny teeth	to 1½ in (4 cm) long, flame to bright red in a branched inflorescence to 20 in (50 cm) tall in winter and early summer

Comments: Popular dwarf species suitable for shallow containers in the home or glasshouse; used for edging and ground cover in dry, virtually frost-free regions.

A. bainesii	S Africa; Swaziland; Mozambique	tree to 7 in (18 m) tall with a thick, forked trunk and forking candelabriform branches ending in leaf rosettes	24–36 in (60–90 cm) long, sword-shaped, green with scattered, brown-tipped, white marginal teeth	to 1½ in (4 cm) long, rose-tipped green on a branched inflorescence to 24 in (60 cm) tall, in winter

Comments: Stately, slow-growing tree for hot, dry climates.

A. bakeri	Madagascar	plant to 10 in (25 cm) tall with fairly slender, sprawling stems in a freely suckering clump	2¾–6 in (7–15 cm) long, linear-lanceolate and finely tapering with a curving tip and spiny margins, chocolate to green-brown banded brick red or dull pink with scattered green-white spots, or (in inferior forms or if grown in shade), olive tinted red-brown with scattered green-white streaks and spots	to 1¼ in (3 cm) long, apricot to scarlet grading through orange toward yellow-green mouth, on an unbranched spike to 12 in (30 cm) tall in winter

Comments: A fine, miniature aloe ideal for pot culture in the home where foliage and flowers provide interest throughout the year. Requires warm temperatures and is said to favor light shade although leaf color is better in sun. Endangered in the wild, but its generously offsetting habit should guarantee its spread in cultivation.

A. brevifolia	S Africa (Cape Province)	stemless, forming low groups of compact rosettes	to 2½ × ¾ in (6 × 2 cm), triangular-lanceolate, glaucous, gray-green with sparse, soft prickles beneath and toothed margins	to 1¼ in (3 cm) long, pale scarlet with a green mouth on unbranched spikes to 16 in (40 cm) tall in summer

A. ciliaris CLIMBING ALOE	S Africa (Cape Province)	slender, scrambling, leafy stems climbing to a height of 15 ft (5 m)	to 6 × ⅝ in (15 × 1.5 cm), linear-lanceolate, fresh green with white teeth	to 1¼ in (3 cm) long, scarlet to yellow-green at mouth on unbranched spikes to 12 in (30 cm) tall throughout the year

Comments: An unusual climber, tolerant of rather more shade and moisture than other aloes. Train on trellis or pillars in the glasshouse or in frost-free gardens.

A. arborescens 'Variegata'

A. aristata

A. ciliaris

A. distans

ALOE

Name	Distribution	Habit	Leaves	Flowers
A. distans JEWELLED ALOE	S Africa (Cape Province)	stems to 10 ft (3 m) long, decumbent, branching and rooting with clumps of foliage	to 6 × 2¾ in (15 × 7 cm), lanceolate, glaucous, with pale, raised spots, and yellow-white marginal teeth	to 1¼ in (3 cm) long, dull scarlet or lemon yellow marked orange, on a branched inflorescence to 24 in (60 cm) long in summer
A. ferox CAPE ALOE	S Africa (Cape Province)	stem erect, stout, unbranched, to 10 ft (3 m) tall with a large terminal leaf rosette	to 39 × 6 in (100 × 15 cm), lanceolate-ensiform, thickly fleshy, blue-green sometimes tinted red-brown with sharp, red-brown spines on sinuately toothed margins and sometimes covering surface	to 1½ in (3.5 cm) long, scarlet to orange on a branched inflorescence to 24 in (60 cm) tall winter and spring

Comments: Provides a strong, vertical accent for xeriscapes and large succulent collections under glass.

Name	Distribution	Habit	Leaves	Flowers
A. humilis CROCODILE ALOE; HEDGEHOG ALOE; SPIDER ALOE	S Africa (Cape Province)	stemless, forming offsetting clumps of rosettes	to 4 × ⅝ in (10 × 1.8 cm), ovate-lanceolate, tapering, glaucous, tuberculate with white marginal teeth and incurved tips	to 1½ in (4 cm), scarlet to orange on an unbranched spike to 14 in (35 cm) tall in spring

Comments: var. **echinata** (*A. echinata*) is smaller with soft prickles rather than tubercles on the leaf surfaces; 'Globosa' has blue-tinged leaves in a tight, spherical rosette.

Name	Distribution	Habit	Leaves	Flowers
A. marlothii	S Africa; Botswana; Swaziland	stem unbranched, 6½–12 ft (2–4 m) tall	to 60 × 10 in (150 × 25 cm), lanceolate, gray-green with red-brown spines and marginal teeth	to 1½ in (3.5 cm) long, orange to yellow-orange, tipped red-brown to mauve in a candelabra-like inflorescence to 32 in (80 cm) tall in winter

Comments: Slow-growing—small plants are often used in containers and dish gardens.

Name	Distribution	Habit	Leaves	Flowers
A. plicatilis FAN ALOE	S Africa (Cape Province)	much-branched shrub or small tree to 15 ft (5 m) tall	to 12 × 1½ in (30 × 4 cm), in two flattened ranks making fans at the branch tips, strap-shaped and blunt, smooth blue-green	to 2 in (5 cm) long, scarlet tipped green on unbranched spikes to 20 in (50 cm) tall

Comments: Valued for its handsome habit: young plants have a cleanly symmetrical, icy-blue appearance.

Name	Distribution	Habit	Leaves	Flowers
A. saponaria *A. latifolia; A. macracantha; A. picta* SOAP ALOE	S Africa; Zimbabwe; Botswana	stemless, forming suckering clumps of broad rosettes	to 12 × 3–4¾ in (30 × 8–12 cm), broadly lanceolate, pale to deep green with dull white, broken bands and brown marginal teeth	to 1½ in (4 cm) long, yellow to salmon pink, orange or scarlet on a forking inflorescence 20–39 in (50–100 cm) tall

Comments: Fast-spreading and soon-congested, the rosettes may need frequent division.

Name	Distribution	Habit	Leaves	Flowers
A. striata *A. albocincta; A. hanburyana* CORAL ALOE	S Africa (Cape Province)	stem stout, to 3¼ ft (1 m) long, decumbent, unbranched	to 20 × 8 in (50 × 20 cm), ovate-lanceolate, tapering finely, untoothed, unspotted, blue-green with white striations (becoming red-tinted in strong sunlight) and pink to red margins	to 1 in (2.5 cm) long, peach-red to coral-red, on a branching inflorescence to 3¼ ft (1 m) tall in winter and spring

Comments: 'Picta' (*A. striata × A. saponaria*) has dark green leaves striped with cream and banded yellow-green.

A. ferox

A. saponaria

A. striata

A. variegata

ALOE

Name	Distribution	Habit	Leaves	Flowers
A. variegata A. ausana PARTRIDGE BREAST ALOE; TIGER ALOE	S Africa; Namibia	very short-stemmed, each plant composed of leaves tightly packed in an obscure spiral with their expanded bases overlapping	2–6 × ⅜–2 in (5–15 × 1.5–5 cm), triangular in outline and 3-angled with margins folded upward from a sharp keel beneath, thickly fleshy with a hard, smooth surface, dark green with white blotches arranged in bands, tip sharp, keel and margins horny, white	to 1½ in (4 cm) long, flesh pink to dull scarlet on unbranched spikes to 12 in (30 cm) tall in winter
Comments: A very popular dwarf aloe widely grown as a houseplant.				
A. vera A. barbadensis; A. perfoliata BARBADOS ALOE; CURACAO ALOE; MEDICINAL ALOE	Cape Verde Islands; Canary Islands; Mediterranean Region; (introduced to Caribbean and S America)	stem short or absent, the plant a large, sprawling and suckering rosette	to 39 × ⅝ in (100 × 1.5 cm), linear-lanceolate, tapering finely, outspread to incurved, fleshy and sappy, olive to dark gray-green, margins slightly pink-tinged with pale teeth	to 1¼ in (3 cm), yellow on an unbranched spike to 36 in (90 cm) tall produced throughout the year
		Comments: Long used in traditional medicine for its healing and cleansing properties—uses now adopted by the pharmaceutical and cosmetics industries.		

shriveling of the leaves. Propagate by seed, stem cuttings or offsets. See table overleaf.

Aloinopsis (from *Aloe* and Greek *opsis*, resemblance, on account of these plants' supposed similarity to *Aloe*). Aizoaceae. South Africa. 15 species, frost-tender, tuberous perennial herbs making dense, low clumps of succulent, wedge-shaped leaves. The stalkless flowers are daisylike and yellow to pink. Grow in full sun in a dry, well-ventilated environment with a minimum temperature of 45°F (7°C). The growing medium should be high in sand and grit. Water sparingly from midspring to late summer; at other times, merely mist on warm, sunny days. Propagate by seed or division. *A. schooneesii* leaves small, blue-green, broadly spathulate with thick, rounded tips; flowers to ⅝ in (1.5 cm) wide, yellow tinted red.

Alonsoa (for Alonzo Zanoni, Spanish Secretary for Santa Fe de Bogota about 1798). Scrophulariaceae. Tropical Americas. 12 species, small shrubs or perennial herbs with *Nemesia*-like flowers produced in summer and fall. For use as a half-hardy annual in summer bedding, sow seed in early spring and under glass at 65°F (18°C). Alternatively, sow seed *in situ* in late spring. For winter flowering under glass, sow in late summer. Alonsoa can also be propagated also by softwood tip cuttings of nonflowering shoots in late summer. Under glass or in warm climates, treat

as a perennial, pruning hard and repotting after flowering. *A. warscewiczii* (syn. *A. grandiflora*) Peru; MASK FLOWER; a bushy herb or shrub to 24 in (60 cm) tall; flowers ¾ in (2 cm)-wide, scarlet.

Alopecurus (from Greek *alopekouros*, fox-tail). Gramineae. FOXTAIL GRASS. N Temperate regions, S America. 25 species, annual or perennial grasses, usually low to spreading with loosely clumped, short culms and narrow, flat leaf blades. The flower spikes are narrow, hairy and tightly packed, resembling a fox-tail. The following species is fully hardy and will grow in most soils in sun or part shade. Its variegated form makes bright ground-cover, especially if the flower spikes are removed by shearing over. *A. pratensis* COMMON FOXTAIL, FOXTAIL GRASS, LAMB'S TAIL GRASS, MEADOW FOXTAIL; Europe, Asia, N Africa; clump-forming perennial to 3¼ ft (1 m) tall in flower, usually far shorter; 'Variegatus': syn. 'Aureovariegatus', leaves bright green boldly edged and striped gold.

Alophia (from Greek *a-*, without, and *lophos*, crest). Iridaceae. Americas. 4 species, perennial cormous herbs with narrow, plicate leaves and terminal racemes of *Iris*-like flowers in summer. Cultivate as for *Homeria*. *A. drummondii* (syn. *A. caerulea*) US, Mexico; to 16 in (40 cm); flowers to 2½ in (6 cm) wide in shades of violet and indigo fading at the center to white spotted brown.

Aloysia (for Maria Louisa [d. 1819],

princess of Parma and wife of King Carlos IV of Spain). Verbenaceae. Americas. 37 species, glandular shrubs with opposite or whorled leaves and terminal spikes or racemes of small flowers. From Argentina and Chile, *A. triphylla* (syn. *Lippia citriodora*) is LEMON VERBENA. It grows to 10 ft (3 m) tall, but usually makes a lower bush resembling a miniature tree with gnarled and fibrous bark. Lanceolate, to 4 in (10 cm) long and finely tapered, the leaves have an intense lemon perfume. Small, white flowers are produced in spikes and panicles in summer. Given good drainage with a warm position on a south-facing wall, and protection from harsh winds, it will tolerate temperatures to 14°F (–10°C), regenerating from the stem base if given a deep, dry mulch. Grow in full sun. Prune out dead wood and any frosted top growth in late spring, cutting hard back into living wood. Root basal or nodal softwood cuttings in early summer in a closed case with gentle bottom heat.

alpine (1) plant indigenous to sites at high altitude, growing between the tree line and permanent snow line; (2) any plant suitable for a rock garden.

alpine house a greenhouse used for the cultivation of alpines and other perennial plants in containers or beds. Alpine houses are usually unheated, and always freely ventilated.

alpine meadow a garden feature

simulating high-alpine meadow, in which alpine plants are grown among fine grasses. The term is often used to describe a piece of grassland where a variety of plants, especially small bulbs, are naturalized, in a form of wild gardening sometimes called meadow gardening. The grass is not mown until high summer so that the development of bulbous species is not repressed.

Alpinia (for Prospero Alpino [1553–1616], Italian botanist). Zingiberaceae. Asia; Australasia. Some species, tender perennial herbs with stout, aromatic rhizomes and clumped, reedy stems with lanceolate leaves. Waxy and shell-like with a showy lip, the flowers are carried in terminal racemes, sometimes amid highly colored bracts in summer. Provide a minimum temperature of 50°F (10°C) and a humid, airy atmosphere in bright, filtered light. Water and feed freely in spring and summer, sparingly at other times. Increase by division.

A. *purpurata* RED GINGER; South Pacific; to 10 ft (3 m) tall with erect, 8–20 in (20–50 cm)-long, torchlike spikes of overlapping, purple-red bracts; flowers small, white; 'Eileen McDonald': bracts candy pink; 'Pink Princess': bracts rose; 'Tahitian Ginger': bracts deep scarlet; A. *vittata* VARIEGATED GINGER; Solomon Islands; to 5 ft (1.5 m) tall; leaves white- to cream-striped; 'Oceanica': smaller with narrow leaves flashed and striped pure white; A. *zerumbet* PINK PORCELAIN LILY, SHELL GINGER; South East Asia; to 10 ft (3 m); flowers fragrant, waxy to 1½ in (4 cm) long with pink-tinted, white petals and a ruffled golden lip veined wine red, inflorescence pendulous, lacking showy bracts; 'Variegata': leaves striped and zoned yellow and lime; A. *mutica*, the SMALL SHELL GINGER, or ORCHID GINGER, resembles a smaller A. *zerumbet* with more or less erect inflorescences.

Alstroemeria (for Baron Claus von Alstroemer [1736–1794], Swedish naturalist and pupil of Linnaeus). Liliaceae (Alstroemeriaceae). S America. PERUVIAN LILY; LILY OF THE INCAS. 50 species, hardy, fleshy-rooted perennial herbs with erect stems, scattered with ovate to lanceolate leaves and crowned

with an umbel of slender-stalked, funnel-shaped flowers with six obovate tepals. Beautiful summer-flowering perennials hardy to 5°F (–15°C), especially if grown in sheltered borders and thickly mulched in winter. Grow in fertile, free-draining and moisture-retentive soil in sun or part-shade. Propagate by seed sown when ripe, or by division in late summer. Plants may also be grown under glass for winter flowering. They are excellent cut flowers, and many hybrids in the Princess range are grown commercially.

A. *aurea* (syn. A. *aurantiaca*) to 3¼ ft (1 m); flowers 2½–4 in (6–10 cm) across and bright orange to apricot or deep gold, the inner tepals spotted maroon to red; A. Ligtu Hybrids (to 3¼ ft (1 m); flowers ranging in color from carmine to soft pink, salmon, orange or yellow, often with yellow zones and spotted or feathered maroon to red; A. *pelegrina* (syn. A. *gayana*) to 24 in (60 cm); flowers to 4 in (10 cm) across, off-white flushed mauve or pink with a darker center, and inner tepals stained yellow at the base and flecked brown to maroon; A. *psittacina* (syn. A. *pulchella*) to 20 in (50 cm); flowers to 3 in (8 cm) across, green tipped scarlet, overlaid with deep wine red, spotted and streaked dark maroon.

Alternanthera (from Latin *alternus*, alternate, and *anthera*, anther: alternate anthers are sterile in most species). Amaranthaceae. C and S America. JOSEPH'S COAT; CHAFFFLOWER; JOYWEED; BROAD PATH; COPPERLEAF. 200 species, annual or perennial herbs, often with brightly colored leaves and with spikes of small flowers. They are used as perennial foliage plants under glass, as half-hardy annuals outdoors in mild climates, and, in the tropics and subtropics, as permanent edging and groundcover. Grow in full or part sun in moisture-retentive but well-drained soil. Take nodal cuttings in late summer to produce stock plants; overwinter at 55°F (13°C) and water sparingly. Root cuttings in

spring in a humid, closed case with bottom heat at 77°F (25°). Plant out in early summer.

A. *bettzickiana* CALICO PLANT; annual or short-lived perennial to 3¼ ft (1 m) tall; leaves olive green to yellow mottled or stained red to purple; includes dwarf, yellow-leaved 'Aurea Nana', and bright red 'Brilliantissima'; A. *ficoidea* (annual or short-lived perennial widespread in S America and erect to 20 in (50 cm), or creeping and mat-forming; leaves green blotched red and purple or yellow, green, red and orange; 'Versicolor': leaves in copper, blood red and yellow; var. *amoena*: PARROT LEAF, SHOO-FLY, JOYWEED, mat-forming with lanceolate to elliptic leaves variously mottled and veined bronze, red, orange, yellow and purple.

alternate leaves

Anchusa undulata

alternate of leaves, branches, pedicels arranged in two ranks along the stem (see left), rachis, with the insertions of the two ranks not parallel but alternating; cf. *paired*, *opposite*.

alternate host either of two plant species upon which a pest or disease organism spends part of its life cycle, for example the lettuce/poplar aphid (*Pemphigus bursarius*) and wheat/barberry rust (*Puccinia graminis*).

alternation of generations the occurrence of strongly differentiated, alternating sexual and asexual phases within the life cycle of organisms (i.e., the succession of gametophytes and sporophytes), as found in Pteridophytes such as ferns.

Althaea (from Greek *althaia*, a cure) Malvaceae. W Europe to C Asia. 12 species of fully hardy annuals and perennials. Leaves shallowly to deeply lobed. Flowers borne in racemes or panicles, small, pink to blue-purple, midsummer to fall. Distinguished from closely related *Alcea rosea* (q.v.) HOLLYHOCK by smaller, usually stalked flowers.

A. *armeniaca*, to 4 ft (1.2 m), flowers deep rose-pink and A. *cannabina*, to

6 ft (1.8 m), flowers lilac to deep pink are both woody based. *A. officinalis* MARSH MALLOW, to 6½ ft (2 m), flowers pale lilac-pink, gray stellate leaves, culinary and medicinal uses of roots. All three species are strongly erect perennials, suitable for a mixed herbaceous or damp woodland garden. Best grown in fertile, moist soil in full sun. Propagate by seed. Generally less showy than *Alcea*.

Alyogyne (from Greek *aluo*, to be at a loss, and *gyne*, woman, the stigma is virtually obscured by many whorled staminal filaments). Malvaceae. Australia. 4 species, tender evergreen shrubs grown for their *Hibiscus*-like flowers produced throughout the year. Grow in full sun in well-drained loamy soil; avoid waterlogged conditions and keep almost dry in winter (minimum temperature 41°F/5°C). Increase by seed and semiripe cuttings. *A. huegelii* LILAC HIBISCUS; hairy, upright shrub to 8 ft (2.5 m) tall with palmately lobed leaves; flowers shimmering lilac to intense opal blue, to 6 in (15 cm) across, sometimes spotted purple-red at center.

Alyssum (from Greek *a*, against, and *lyssa*, madness: the herb was used against madness and rabies). Cruciferae. Europe to W Asia. 168 species, annual and perennial herbs and subshrubs with small, 4-petaled flowers in headlike racemes in summer. Excellent plants for the rock garden, dry walls and banks, they are fully hardy and prefer full sunlight and free-draining soil. Trim after flowering. Propagate by cuttings in spring or seed in fall.

A. montanum Europe; evergreen, tufted perennial to 8 in (20 cm); leaves small, gray-hairy, flowers fragrant, bright yellow, to ¼ in (0.6 cm) across, in round-headed racemes; *A. wulfenianum* Asia Minor; white-downy, prostrate perennial to 8 in (20 cm) with small, gray leaves; flowers pale yellow to ½ in (1 cm) across in loose corymbs. *A. maritimum* (SWEET ALYSSUM) is now treated as *Lobularia maritima*, and *A. saxatile* as *Aurinia saxatilis*.

Amaranthus (from Greek, *a-*, without, and *maraino*, to wither: the dried flowers of some species are "everlasting"). Amaranthaceae. Cos-

mopolitan. 60 species, annual herbs grown for their foliage and catkinlike racemes. Treat as half-hardy bedding or as potted plants. Sow under glass in early spring at 68°F (20°C) and plant out after the last frost. In warm regions, sow *in situ* in spring.

A. caudatus LOVE-LIES-BLEEDING, TASSEL FLOWER, VELVET FLOWER; 16–40 in (40–100 cm); leaves green, stalks red-tinted; inflorescences tassel-like, strongly pendulous, to 12 in (30 cm) long, crimson to blood red— green in 'Viridis'; *A. hypochondriacus* PRINCE'S FEATHER; 16–60 in (40–150 cm), leaves green; inflorescence dense, composed of dark crimson spikes, erect and grouped together in a broadly pyramidal panicle; 'Erythrostachys': stems and leaves stained purple, spikes deepest blood red; *A. tricolor* TAMPALA, CHINESE SPINACH; to 3¼ ft (1 m); leaves elliptic to ovate leaves to 8 in (20 cm) long; flower spikes small, red-tinted; a species with edible leaves, it also includes the ornamentals 'Joseph's Coat', with leaves flushed scarlet, gold, chocolate and green, and 'Molten Fire' with bronze to maroon leaves flushed scarlet.

× **Amarcrinum** Amaryllidaceae. Garden origin. Intergeneric hybrids between *Amaryllis* and *Crinum*. × *A. memoria-corsii* combines the habit of *Crinum moorei* with the flowers of *Amaryllis belladonna*, bearing large heads of long-lived, fragrant and shell pink flowers in late summer and early fall. The foliage persists year-round unless subjected to severe frost. Grow as for *Amaryllis*.

× **Amarygia** Amaryllidaceae. Garden origin. Intergeneric hybrids between *Amaryllis* and *Brunsvigia*. × *A. parkeri* (*Amaryllis belladonna* × *Brunsvigia josephinae*) is the NAKED LADY LILY, intermediate between the parents, with fragrant flowers ranging from white to deep, clear rose, to carmine. × *A. bidwillii* (*Amaryllis belladonna* × *Brunsvigia orientalis*) differs in its shorter flowers with broader tepals. Grow as for *Amaryllis*.

Amaryllis (the name of a beautiful shepherdess, a character much celebrated in pastoral poetry). Amaryllidaceae. South Africa. 1 species, *A. belladonna* (BELLADONNA LILY, JERSEY

LILY), a bulbous perennial herb with 2-ranked, strap-shaped leaves produced after the flowers. Carried in fall atop stout maroon scapes, the funnel-shaped blooms are 4 in (10 cm) long, sweetly fragrant and glowing candy pink (white, white-eyed, rose and carmine cultivars are also available). Plant in deep, fast-draining loamy soil in a sheltered position in full sun. Keep moist, never wet, from winter until early summer; dry and baked prior to flowering. These bulbs are generally hardy to –10°F (–23°C), performing best beneath a wall and left undisturbed for many years. Apply a winter mulch of dry bracken or straw in cold areas. Propagate by offsets removed during dormancy. The popular tender "amaryllis" is *Hippeastrum*.

Amberboa (from the Turkish name for *A. moschata*). Compositae. Mediterranean to Asia. 6 species, annual and biennial herbs grown for their large, colorful, cornflower-like flower heads. An old favorite in cottage gardens, sweet sultan has a long flowering period and is suitable for cutting. Picked just as they open, the flowers dry well in borax. Sow seed *in situ* in full sun in fall or spring. Protect fall-sown plants where winter temperatures fall below 14°F (–10°C). *A. moschata* (syn. *Centaurea moschata*) SWEET SULTAN; SW Asia; summer-flowering annual to 28 in (70 cm) tall; flower heads, fragrant, long-stalked, to 2¾ in (7 cm) with a rich yellow disk crowned with outspread, finely cut florets in white, cream, yellow, gold-bronze, purple, carmine and pink.

Amelanchier (from amelanchier or amelancier, the Provencal name for *A. ovalis*). Rosaceae. North America; Europe; Asia. JUNEBERRY; SHADBUSH; SNOWY MESPILUS; SERVICEBERRY; SUGAR-PLUM. 25 species, fully hardy deciduous shrubs or small trees with oval leaves. In spring, erect racemes of flowers composed of five white, obovate to lanceolate petals appear; these contrast beautifully with the soft copper of the new growth. The fruits are small pomes, frosty blue-black to plum purple and offset by the fiery reds and oranges of the fall foliage. Hardy to –22°F (–30°C). Grow in full sun or part shade in neutral to acidic soil (*A. alnifolia*, *A. asiatica*, and *A. ovalis* tolerate some lime). Propagate by layering, or by division of suckering species from fall to early spring. Sow seed when ripe. *Amelanchier* hybridizes easily.

A. alnifolia ALDER-LEAVED SERVICE-BERRY; N America; suckering shrub or small tree to 12 ft (4 m) tall flowers fragrant, in erect racemes; 'Alta Glow' columnar with brilliant fall color; 'Regent' fiery fall tints; *A. arborea* (shrub or tree to 70 ft (20 m) tall; leaves red or yellow in fall; flowers fragrant, in drooping racemes; *A. asiatica* graceful shrub or small tree to 40 ft (12 m); leaves turning red-orange in fall; flowers in downy racemes; *A. canadensis* sucker-ing shrub to 25 ft (8 m) tall; leaves, turn-ing orange-red in fall; flowers in erect, downy racemes to 2½ in (6 cm) long; *A. laevis* ALLEGHENY SERVICEBERRY; erect shrub or small tree to 43 ft (13 m) tall; leaves with fiery tints in fall; flowers in nodding racemes to 4¾ in (12 cm) long; *A. lamarckii* graceful, wide-branching shrub or tree to 30 ft (10 m) tall; leaves turning brilliant orange-red in fall; flow-ers in loose racemes to 3 in (8 cm) long; 'Rubescens': flowers soft pale pink.

ament see *catkin*.

American garden a term used in 19th-century European horticulture for a collection of trees, shrubs, and herbs native to N America. The term also came to be used of moist acidic borders.

ammonia a pungent nitrogen-containing gas (NH_3) produced as organic matter decomposes. It can be toxic to plants, but with special soil-injection equipment may be used on a farm scale as a fertilizer. Various ammonium salts are commonly used as fertilizers in gardening—for example, ammonium nitrate, ammonium phos-phate, ammonium sulfate.

ammonification the production of ammonia by soil organisms from organic nitrogen compounds. It is an intermediate step in the mineralization of nitrogen. See *nitrification*.

ammonium nitrate an inorganic fertilizer used as a top-dressing, contain-ing 35% nitrogen, half as nitrate and half as ammonium. It is soil-acidifying, especially applied continually; where for-mulated with lime this effect is avoided.

ammonium phosphate an inor-ganic source of nitrogen and phos-phate used in concentrated compound fertilizer and liquid feed. The forms most usually available are mono-ammonium phosphate (MAP) ($NH_4H_2PO_4$): 12% N, 61% P, and di-ammonium phosphate (DAP) (($NH_4)_2HPO_4$): 21% N, 53% P. Both are water soluble. The pH of MAP is around 3.5 and of DAP around 8.0.

ammonium sulfamate a nonse-lective inorganic contact herbicide, useful against annual, soft perennial, and woody weeds. It is effective in destroying tree stumps when applied as crystals to cut surfaces. An interval of 8–12 weeks is necessary before replant-ing treated ground.

ammonium sulfate an inorganic fertilizer, commonly known as sulfate of ammonia, containing 21% nitrogen. It is quick-acting as a top-dressing, and is also used as an activator for compost piles and as an ingredient of lawn sand. Its use gives rise to soil acidity, and application to chalky soil may result in loss of nitrogen as ammonia.

Amomyrtus (Greek meaning "not *Myrtus*") Myrtaceae. Southern S America. 2 species, evergreen shrubs or trees with flaking bark, leathery leaves, flowers of five, rounded petals with a boss of showy stamens, and small, black, edible berries. *A. luma* favors vir-tually frost-free conditions, growing well in areas of high humidity in full sun or light shade in rich, moist soil. For propagation, see *Myrtus*. *A. luma* (syn. *Myrtus luma*) LUMA; PALO MADRONO; Chile to 70 ft (20 m) tall but more often a bushy shrub to 12 ft (4 m); leaves ovate to lanceolate, 1¼ in (3 cm) emerging coppery red before turning deep glossy green; flowers creamy white, ½ in (1 cm) across, produced in spring and summer.

Amorpha (from Greek *amorphos*, shapeless). Leguminosae. N America. 15 species, aromatic shrubs with glan-dular, pinnate leaves and pealike flow-ers in terminal racemes in summer. Tolerant of poor soil, drought, and lows of −13°F (−25°C), quickly regen-erating if cut down by frost. Plant in sun. Propagate by seed presoaked in hot water for two hours; germination may take three to eight weeks. Increase also by layering, rooted suckers and semiripe cuttings. *A. canescens* LEAD PLANT; gray-downy shrub to 3¼ ft (1 m); flowers violet-blue; *A. fruticosa* BASTARD INDIGO; to 12 ft (4 m) tall with smooth or weakly hairy, glandular growth; flowers may be deep purple, indigo, pale blue or white.

Ampelopsis brevipedunculata
Both the leaves and fruit clusters are similar to those of *Vitis*, hence the name *Ampelopsis*, meaning "resembling a grape."

Ampelopsis (from the Greek, *ampelos*, a grape, and *opsis*, resembling). Vitaceae. North America, Asia. 25 deciduous shrubs and woody vines. Those described here are fast-growing woody climbers, attaching themselves by ten-drils which lack holdfasts (thus differing from *Parthenocissus*). The leaves are palmately lobed or divided or more elaborately compound. Small green-white flowers give rise to grapelike fruits by late summer. The following will toler-ate winter temperatures as low as −13°F (−25°C), especially if given a long, hot summer to ripen their wood. New growth is usually damaged by late frost. Plant in a sheltered position in deep, moderately fertile loamy soil in sun or shade. Provide support. Propagate by leaf bud cuttings in midsummer; treat with rooting hormone and root in a closed case with bottom heat. Green-wood or semiripe cuttings taken in summer may also take root.

A. aconitifolia N China, Mongolia; 30 ft (10 m); leaves to 4¾ in (12 cm) across, with 3–5, lanceolate to rhombic, deeply lobed and coarsely toothed segments in a palmate arrangement, more or less smooth and a fresh green becoming red-orange in fall; fruits small, sloe blue at first, turning orange-red in fine falls; *A. glandulosa* var. brevipedunculata BLUEBERRY IVY; China, Japan, Korea leaves palmately 3- or, rarely, 5- lobed, 2–6 in (5–15 cm) long, basically ovate-cordate in outline, toothed, turning from bright mid-green to red-bronze in fall; fruits turquoise to amethyst; 'Elegans': stems pink-tinted, leaves splashed lime, white or cream; *A. megalophylla* China; to 40 ft (12 m); leaves to 32 in (80 cm), with ovate to oblong leaflets arranged pinnately toward the tip and bipinnately toward the petiole; fruit dark purple ripening black; *A. chaffanjonii* differs in leaves, claret-tinted, not glaucous, beneath, brilliant fall color and fruit red ripening black.

amphicarpic producing two different types of fruit; sometimes used of plants bearing two crops per season.

amphicarpogenous producing buried fruit, as in the peanut (*Arachis hypogaea*).

amphigeal producing two types of flower, one from the rootstock or stem base, the other from the upper stems.

amplexicaul of a leaf base or dilated petiole or stipule enlarged and embracing or clasping the stem.

Amsonia (for Dr. Charles Amson, 18th-century physician and scientific explorer in North America). Apocynaceae. South Europe; Asia; North America. species, perennial herbs and subshrubs with milky sap. Hardy to −4°F (−20°C) or lower if mulched. Plant in full sun or light shade. Propagate by division in spring. *A. tabernaemontana* WILLOW BLUE STAR; SE US; perennial herb to 3¼ ft (1 m); flowers starry, 5-lobed pale to slate blue in terminal panicles in summer.

Anacyclus (from Greek *an*, without, *kuklos*, ring, a reference to the flower

heads). Compositae. Mediterranean. 9 species, annual or perennial herbs with finely cut foliage and daisylike flower heads produced in summer. Hardy to 0°F (−18°C). Grow in full sun in gritty soil with excellent drainage. Remove spent flower heads. Increase by seed sown *in situ* in spring, by cuttings, and by rooted stem sections. *A. pyrethrum* var. *depressus* (syn. *A. depressus*) Spain, Algeria, Morocco; prostrate, short-lived perennial to 2 × 8 in (5 × 20 cm); leaves very fine, with silver down; flower heads to 2 in (5 cm) across, ray florets white above, red-stained beneath, disk florets golden.

anaerobic used of conditions in which oxygen is absent, or of organisms that function in the absence of oxygen; cf. *aerobic*. See *compost pile*.

Anagallis (from *anagallis*, Greek word for this plant, from *anagelao*, to laugh; these herbs were said to dispel sadness). Primulaceae. PIMPERNEL. Cosmopolitan 20 species, hardy annual or perennial herbs with creeping to erect stems and ovate to elliptic leaves. Solitary, dish- to cup-shaped flowers with five broad lobes are produced on slender stalks from the leaf axils in spring and summer. Sometimes thought weedy and invasive, *A. arvensis* is often unwelcome in gardens, but is a bright and delicate groundcover for sunny positions on all but the wettest soil. *A. monellii* favors a warm, rather sandy site and is suitable for rock gardens and the

edges of borders. *A. tenella* should be allowed to colonize in the bog garden and at the margins of streams and ponds in the rockery. Propagate by seed sown *in situ* in spring or under glass in late summer; perennial species also by cuttings in spring.

A. arvensis SCARLET or COMMON PIMPERNEL, POOR MAN'S WEATHER GLASS, SHEPHERD'S CLOCK; Europe; dwarf creeping annual; flowers ¼–¾ in (0.5–1.8 cm) across, typically bright scarlet, also white, pink, yellow and sky blue; *A. monellii* BLUE PIMPERNEL; Mediterranean; erect perennial or biennial to 20 in (50 cm); flowers ½–⅝ in (1–1.5 cm) across, rich blue above, tinted wine red beneath and at the center or wholly blue or wine red; 'Phillippii': flowers large, royal blue; *A. tenella* BOG PIMPERNEL; W Europe; creeping dwarf perennial; flowers ¼–½ in (0.5–1 cm) across, sweetly scented and pale rose or white—deep pink in the cultivar 'Studland'.

Ananas (from *nana*, the Tupi Indian word for the fruit of *A. comosus*). Bromeliaceae. S America. PINEAPPLE. 8 species, tender, perennial evergreen herbs. Dense, conelike spikes of small flowers arise from the center of rosettes of tough, rigid, swordlike leaves with spiny margins. The spikes terminate in a tuft of short, leafy bracts (coma), and swell as they develop, fusing to form an ovoid, fleshy syncarp (the pineapple fruit). Grow in full sunlight with a minimum temperature of 55°F (13°C), and

PROPAGATING ANANAS (PINEAPPLE)

slip or "sucker" shoot

From cuttings
Shoots developing from leaf axils can be detached, dipped in fungicide, dried for a few days, and then rooted in a sandy medium at 70°F (21°C).

From crown shoots
Use a sharp knife to scoop out the tuft or "crown shoot" from a ripe pineapple with about ½ in (1 cm) of the fruit attached. Dip in fungicide and allow to dry for several days. Pot the shoot in a standard cutting medium and provide a minimum temperature of 70°F (21°C). Roots should form in a few weeks.

in high humidity. Water, syringe, and fertilize liberally when in growth, especially in hot weather and during fruit development, but allow the soil to dry slightly between waterings. Keep virtually dry and do not mist in cool dull weather. Propagate by detaching rooted suckers, or by rooting the coma in a moist, sandy mix with bottom heat. Plants usually fruit at about three years of age.

A. bracteatus WILD or RED PINEAPPLE; to 3¼ ft (1 m); leaves olive; inflorescences 4–6 in (10–15 cm)-long, composed of lilac to red flowers and closely clothed in red-tinted bracts; var. *tricolor*, leaves striped cream and yellow and edged with bright red to pink teeth; fruit red-pink, topped with variegated coma; *A. comosus* PINEAPPLE; seedless, edible cultigen taller than the last species with gray-green leaves; inflorescences 6–12 in (15–30 cm)-long; flowers violet-red, with yellow-tinted bracts; syncarp large, orange-yellow when ripe, sweetly fragrant; with 'Porteanus': leaves with a central yellow stripe; var. *variegatus*: leaves striped creamy yellow and sometimes red-pink.

Anaphalis (ancient Greek name for a similar plant). Compositae. Temperate regions. PEARLY EVERLASTING. 100 species, white-hairy perennial herbs with clumps of spreading then erect stems terminating in clusters or flat-topped corymbs of flower heads. These consist of small, yellow florets tightly encased by several series of papery, silver bracts. The following are hardy and flower between midsummer and early fall. They are valued for their silvery effects and long-lasting flower heads. The inflorescences dry well if cut just prior to opening. *A. margaritacea* and *A. triplinervis* are suitable for the herbaceous or mixed border. *A. nepalensis* requires a sunny position in well-drained, gritty soil; var. *monocephala*, smaller still, is suited to rock gardens and alpine sink gardens. Increase by division in early spring.

A. margaritacea N America, Asia and N Europe grows to 32 in (80 cm); leaves gray-green above, silvery beneath; flower heads clothed in pearly white bracts, ½ in (1 cm) wide, in a corymb to 6 in (15 cm) across; var. *yedoensis*: syn. *A. yedoensis*, leaves narrow,

leaves and flower heads somewhat tawny below; *A nepalensis* (syn. *A. triplinervis* var. *intermedia*) Himalaya, Western China; to 12 in (30 cm) tall; leaves gray-green with white-woolly undersides; flower heads ½–⅝ in (1–1.5 cm) wide, silvery, 1–4 per stem; var. *monocephala*: syn. *A. nubigena*, low and tufted with white flower heads, borne one per stem; *A. triplinervis* (temperate Asia; to 36 in (90 cm) tall; leaves gray-hairy; flower heads silver-white ½ in (1 cm) wide, crowded in domed clusters.

anastomosing describing veins that form a network, united at their points of contact.

Anchusa (from Greek, *ankousa*, alkanet, a skin paint—some species were used to make rouge). Boraginaceae. Europe; Africa; Asia. ALKANET; BUGLOSS. 35 species, hardy, coarsely hairy annual, biennial and perennial herbs grown for their flowers. Produced in spring and summer, these are funnel-shaped with five, broad and spreading lobes and are carried in terminal or axillary cymes. Grow *A. azurea* in deep, fertile soil, well-drained but moisture-retentive, and in full sun. Deadhead promptly to maintain a neat habit and promote a second flush of blooms. Increase by division or root cuttings in late winter. *A. caespitosa* requires a very sunny, well-drained position in gritty soil, ideally on the rock garden or in an alpine sink. It is very intolerant of cold, wet conditions. Propagate by offsets in summer. Treated as an annual, *A. capensis* is a fine summer bedding plant, sown *in situ* in spring. As a biennial, it should be overwintered in a frost-free greenhouse.

A. azurea (syn. *A. italica*) Europe, North Africa and Western Asia; spreading, clump-forming perennial to 20 in (0.5 m) tall; flowers ½ in (1 cm) across, deep blue to violet, in showy, terminal clusters; 'Dropmore': to 3¼ ft (1 m) tall, flowers gentian blue; 'Little John': to 16 in (40 cm): flowers small, bright blue; 'Loddon Royalist': to 3¼ ft (1 m) tall, flowers bright blue flowers;

'Opal': to 3¼ ft (1 m) tall, flowers sky blue; *A. capensis* S Africa; CAPE FORGET-ME-NOT; erect, hairy biennial to 24 in (60 cm) flowers in terminal panicles, ½ in (1 cm) wide and bright blue with a white throat; 'Blue Angel': flowers ultramarine; 'Blue Bird': flowers vivid indigo; 'Pink Bird': flowers pink; *A. leptophylla* subsp. *incana* (syn. *A. angustissima*, *A. caespitosa*) Crete; dwarf, tufted perennial to 3 in (8 cm), making mounds of clumped, narrow and bristly leaves; flowers borne 1–3 together on short stalks among the leaf bases, ⅝ in (1.5 cm) wide, dark blue with a white throat.

ancipitous describes stems and fruit with two sharp edges.

androdioecious having male and hermaphrodite flowers on separate plants of the same species, for example marsh marigold (*Caltha palustris*).

androecium the male component of a flower, the stamen or stamens as a whole (see below).

6 stamens make up androecium

Gloriosa superba

androgynous hermaphrodite or, sometimes, monoecious.

Andromeda (for the daughter of Cepheus and Cassiope). Ericaceae. Arctic, temperate Northern Hemisphere. 2 species, dwarf evergreen shrubs, compact or spreading, with short, linear to lanceolate, revolute leaves and small, urn-shaped and 5-lobed flowers nodding in clusters at the branch tips in spring and summer. Fully hardy, *A. polifolia* needs dappled or full sun and moist but porous, acidic soil. Propagate by removal of rooted, creeping branches and suckers, and by simple layering. *A. polifolia* BOG ROSE-MARY, MARSH ANDROMEDA; N Europe, Alps, Carpathians and Russia; to 4¾ in (12 cm) forming dense mounds of spreading to erect stems; leaves to ¾ in (2 cm), dark green above with gray-white undersides; flowers white to pale pink, ¼ in (0.5 cm) long in clusters to 1¼ in (3 cm) across; 'Compacta': compact, leaves gray-green, flowers pink;

'Grandiflora': leaves blue-green, flowers large, white tinted pale pink; 'Minima': dwarf, leaves needlelike, gray-green, flowers pale pink; 'Nana': vigorous, dwarf, flowers small, pink, profuse; 'Nana: Alba': small, compact, leaves silvery beneath, flowers small, white, profuse; 'Red Winter': tall, leaves red-bronze-tinted in fall/winter.

andromonoecious having male and hermaphrodite flowers on the same plant—for example, horse chestnut (*Aesculus hippocastanum*).

Androsace (from Greek *aner*, man, and *sakos*, buckler, from the resemblance of the anther to an ancient buckler). Primulaceae. Northern temperate regions. ROCK JASMINE. 100 species, hardy annual, biennial, or perennial herbs, those here summer-flowering, alpine perennials making dwarf rosettes or cushions of hairy foliage. The flowers are usually white or pink, with a short tube and five broad, outspread lobes; they may be solitary and short-stalked or stemless, or carried in long-stalked umbels. Grow in full sun, with an airy, cool atmosphere and in sharply draining soil. *A. chamaejasme*, *A. imbricata*, and *A. pyrenaica* grow best in a slightly acidic medium; the remaining species are calcicole. High-altitude alpines such as *A. cylindrica*, *A. hirtella*, *A. imbricata* and *A. pyrenaica* grow best in the alpine house or in raised beds that can be covered in cold, wet weather. Lower-altitude species are more tolerant and may be grown in the open in troughs or on the scree and rock gardens; these include *A. carnea*, *A. chamaejasme*, *A. lanuginosa*, *A. primuloides*, and *A. sempervivoides*. Propagate by rooted runners and rosettes of stoloniferous and freely offsetting species, the rest by basal shoot cuttings taken in early summer.

A. carnea W Europe; loosely tufted; leaves to ¾ in (2 cm), linear; scape to 2½ in (6 cm) tall; flowers one to many, white or pink; *A. chamaejasme* Northern Hemisphere; loosely tufted and shortly stoloniferous; leaves oblong to lanceolate; scape to 2¾ in (7 cm); flowers 3–7, white or pink; *A. cylindrica* Pyrenees; densely tufted and cushion-forming; leaves to ½ in (1 cm) long, oblong to lanceolate, persisting after death to form column-shaped shoots; scape to ¾ in (2 cm); flowers solitary, pink with yellow throat; *A. hirtella* Pyrenees; densely tufted and white-hairy; leaves, linear; flowers solitary, very short-stalked, white; *A. imbricata* syn. *A. vandellii*) Alps, Pyrenees; densely tufted, forming rounded cushions; leaves linear to lanceolate, white-hairy; flowers solitary, short-stalked, white with a yellow throat; *A. lanuginosa* Himalaya; prostrate, white-hairy perennial; leaves, lanceolate to obovate; scape to 1½ in (4 cm), flowers many, pink; *A. primuloides* Himalaya; stoloniferous; leaves lanceolate to linear, white-hairy; scape to 2¾ in (7 cm); flowers pink; *A. pyrenaica* Pyrenees; dense, cushion-forming perennial; leaves, linear to oblong, overlapping in columnar shoots; flowers solitary, very short-stalked, white with a yellow eye; *A. sarmentosa* Himalaya; stolons long; leaves lanceolate to ovate, silvery-hairy, scape to 4 in (10 cm); flowers many, deep pink to brilliant carmine; *A. sempervivoides* Kashmir, Tibet; leaves to ¼ in (0.5 cm), ovate to spathulate, densely overlapping in stoloniferous rosettes; scapes to 4 in (10 cm); flowers pink; *A. villosa* Europe, Asia; densely tufted with cushion-forming, domed rosettes; leaves oblong to lanceolate, white-hairy; scapes to 2 in (5 cm); flowers two to three, white with yellow-green centers that turn red; var. *jacquemontii*: flowers purple-pink.

Anemone (From Greek *anemos*, wind, a name used by Theophrastus and reflected in the common name "windflower"). Ranunculaceae. North and South temperate regions. WINDFLOWER. 120 species, hardy perennial herbs with rhizomatous, fleshy, fibrous or woody roots. The leaves are lobed, dissected or compound, rarely entire. Those on the stem are often arranged in a whorl below the inflorescence. Solitary or in cymes, the flowers are dish- to bowl-shaped and composed of numerous, oblong to oblanceolate segments.

The fall-flowering species with a fibrous root-stock such as *A. hupehensis* occur predominantly in damp open woodland. This group, which includes *A. × hybrida*, is well suited to the fall border and woodland garden. They are valued for the long succession of flowers that last well when cut. Plant in dappled shade or part-day sun, in moist, fertile, loamy soil with ample organic matter. *A. hupehensis* will tolerate slightly drier and sunnier conditions, where it will bloom earlier, although flowers will be smaller and of lower quality. Propagate by fresh seed sown ripe, by division or by root cuttings.

Tuberous and rhizomatous species include the spring-flowering *A. blanda*, *A. nemorosa*, and *A. apennina*. They require moist but well-drained, humus-rich soil in the rock or woodland garden, but tolerate dry conditions during their summer dormancy. Also included in this category are taller species with a fibrous or slender-rhizomatous rootstock (e.g., *A. narcissiflora*, *A. sylvestris*). These prefer grittier, more freely draining soil. Light requirements vary from full sun (*A. narcissiflora*) to light shade (*A. sylvestris*). *A. nemorosa* is sufficiently robust for naturalizing in thin sod, where the first mowing occurs after foliage dieback. Smaller species, notably *A. blanda* and its cultivars, are well suited to pot cultivation for the alpine display house. Propagate by fresh seed, rhizomatous species also by division.

Tuberous-rooted plants such as *A. coronaria*, *A. × fulgens*, and *A. pavonina* flower from spring to early summer and are well suited to areas with dry hot summers, where they will grow in light, sandy soil: shade in the hottest part of the day is appreciated. Plants of this type require dry dormancy after flowering. De Caen, Mona Lisa and St. Brigid anemones are a commercial cut-flower crop in milder areas of Europe. Plant in fertile but light-textured soil in sunny borders. In cold areas, mulch for winter protection or lift after flowering and overwinter dry tubers, plunged in sand under frost-free conditions. Under glass, give a winter minimum of 50°F (10°C) and pot tubers in a sandy loam-based mix of medium fertility for flowering 3–4 months later. *A. coronaria* may be flowered under glass almost all year with successive plantings; tubers of this and *A. × fulgens* deteriorate quickly and should be replaced every 2–3 years.

Susceptible to anemone and cucumber mosaic viruses; downy mildew, and anemone smut, which produces swellings on leaf stalks and leaves, bursting to release black spores. Seedlings also susceptible to flea beetle.

ANEMONE

Name	Distribution	Flowering time	Habit	Leaves	Flowers
A. apennina APENNINE ANEMONE	S Europe	early spring	to 6 in (15 cm), rhizomatous, spreading perennial	leaves divided into 3, toothed or lobed segments	solitary, to 1¼ in (3 cm) diam., blue or pink- or white-flushed, with 8–23 oblong tepals

Comments: Includes 'Petrovac' (flowers rich blue, many-tepaled), and 'Purpurea' (flowers soft purple-rose).

Name	Distribution	Flowering time	Habit	Leaves	Flowers
A. biflora	Iran to Kashmir	spring	to 8 in (20 cm), tuberous perennial	leaves divided into 3, lobed segments	2–3 together, nodding, ¾–2 in (2–5 cm) diam., crimson, orange or yellow with 5, narrowly elliptic tepals

Comments: Requires a warm, dry summer rest.

Name	Distribution	Flowering time	Habit	Leaves	Flowers
A. blanda	SE Europe to Cyprus and Turkey	early spring	to 7 in (18 cm), tuberous perennial	leaves divided into 3, lobed segments	solitary, to 1½ in (4 cm) diam., blue, mauve, white or pink with 9–15 narrowly oblong tepals

Comments: Includes 'Ingramii' (('Atrocaerulea') flowers deep blue), 'Blue Shades' (leaves very finely divided, flowers pale to deep blue), 'Bridesmaid' (flowers large, pure white), 'Bright Star' (flowers bright pink), 'Radar' (flowers magenta with a white center), 'Violet Star' (flowers large, amethyst, exterior white), 'White Splendour' (flowers large, white, exterior pink).

Name	Distribution	Flowering time	Habit	Leaves	Flowers
A. coronaria POPPY-FLOWERED ANEMONE	S Europe, Mediterranean	spring	8–24 in (20–60 cm), tuberous perennial	leaves divided into 3, lobed or toothed or cut segments	solitary, to 3 in (8 cm) diam., scarlet, blue, pink, white or bicolored with 5–8, oval tepals

Comments: Many cultivars, dividing roughly into two groups: **De Caen** with single, large, poppy-shaped flowers in white, bright pink, red or purple with showy black anthers, and **St. Brigid** with semidouble to double, large flowers in bright pastels, reds, mauves and bicolors.

Name	Distribution	Flowering time	Habit	Leaves	Flowers
A. × fulgens SCARLET WIND FLOWER	C Mediterranean	spring to early summer	to 10 in (25 cm), tuberous perennial	leaves more or less divided into 3, lobed and toothed segments	solitary, to 2½ in (6 cm) diam., brilliant scarlet with 15 oblong-obovate tepals, center black

Name	Distribution	Flowering time	Habit	Leaves	Flowers
A. hupehensis *A. japonica* of gardens JAPANESE ANEMONE	China, Japan	late summer to fall	to 28 in (70 cm), fibrous-rooted, branching, erect perennial	leaves palmately 3-lobed to 3-parted with sharply toothed margins and thin hairs beneath	several together on long, uneven stalks in sparse umbels, to 2 in (5 cm) diam., white to pink or palest rosy mauve with 5–6 rounded tepals and golden anthers

Comments: This species is often confused with *A. × hybrida*; both have been called *A. japonica*. *A. hupehensis* differs from *A. × hybrida* in its fertile pollen and shorter stature. It includes 'Bressingham Glow' (to 36 in (90 cm), compact, flowers semidouble, petals fluted, deep pink) and 'Prinz Heinrich' (stems slender, flowers deep rosy purple with numerous, flattened tepals). The true *Anemone japonica* is now treated as *A. hupehensis* var. *japonica*. Its flowers have up to 20, pink to rose-mauve tepals.

Name	Distribution	Flowering time	Habit	Leaves	Flowers
A. × hybrida *A. japonica* of gardens CHINESE ANEMONE	garden origin	late summer to fall	to 60 in (150 cm), fibrous-rooted, erect, branching perennial	very similar to *A. hupehensis* but with larger, very slightly hairy leaves	as for *A. hupehensis* but to 3 in (8 cm) diam. with 6–11(–15) tepals

Comments: Differs from *A. hupehensis* in its flowers, usually lacking fertile pollen and taller stature. Many cultivars ranging in height from 28–60 in (70–150 cm), in habit from the bushy and compact to the tall and elegant with very long flower stalks, in flower form from single to double and in color from white to pale pink to deep rosy mauve. They include 'September Charm' with silvery pink flowers.

A. coronaria 'Lord Lieutenant' *A.* × *fulgens*   *A. narcissiflora*   *A. pavonina*

ANEMONE

Name	Distribution	Flowering time	Habit	Leaves	Flowers
A. × lipsiensis A. × seemannii	N and C Europe	early spring	to 6 in (15 cm), rhizomatous, spreading perennial	leaves 3-parted in a ruff below flowers, deeply cut and sharply toothed	solitary, to ¾ in (2 cm) diam., very pale yellow with bright gold and green stamens, tepals 5, ovate-elliptic
Comments: The offspring of *A. ranunculoides* × *A. nemorosa*, a naturally occurring hybrid.					
A. narcissiflora	Europe, Asia, N America	summer	to 24 in (60 cm), rhizomatous perennial	leaves 3–5 parted with narrow, deeply divided and coarsely toothed segments	up to 8 per umbel, to 1½ in (4 cm), white faintly tinted pink or blue beneath, with 5–6, obovate, spreading tepals
A. nemorosa WOOD ANEMONE; WINDFLOWER	N and C Europe	early spring	to 12 in (30 cm), rhizomatous, carpeting perennial	leaves 3-parted with deeply cut, slender segments, some forming a ruff below flower	solitary, to 1¼ in (3 cm) cross, white, occasionally tinted pink or purple with 6–8 (5–12) oblong tepals and golden anthers
Comments: Many cultivars including 'Allenii' (flowers lilac or lavender), 'Flore Pleno' ('Plena') (flowers white, double), 'Robinsoniana' (flowers pearly gray to palest lilac), 'Vestal' (flowers white, center with a buttonlike rose of petaloid segments), 'Vindobonensis' (flowers cream), 'Virescens' (flowers replaced by a pyramid of small, green, leafy bracts), 'Wilk's Giant' (flowers large, single, pure white).					
A. pavonina	Mediterranean	early spring	to 12 in (30 cm), tuberous perennial	leaves 3-parted with much-toothed and divided segments	solitary, to 4 in (10 cm) diam., scarlet, violet, purple, pink, white or yellow with a central boss of black stamens ringed with white, petals 7–9, broadly obovate
Comments: Includes the deep salmon-colored 'Barr Salmon', and the **St.... Bavo Group** with flowers in coral, rose, lavender and violet.					
A. ranunculoides	N and C Europe	early spring	to 6 in (15 cm), rhizomatous, spreading perennial	leaves 3-parted with segments much divided and toothed and held in a ruff below flowers	solitary, to ¾ in (2 cm) diam., deep yellow, tepals 5–6, elliptic
Comments: Includes 'Pleniflora' ('Flore Pleno'), with semidouble flowers, 'Grandiflora' with larger flowers, and 'Superba' with olive-bronze leaves and bright yellow flowers					
A. rivularis	N India, SW China	late spring, early summer	to 36 in (90 cm), swollen-rooted erect, branching perennial	leaves 3, with 3-parted, lobed and toothed segments	2–5 per umbel on slender stalks, ⅝–1¼ in (1.5–3 cm) wide, white stained lavender beneath, with 5–8, oval tepals
A. sylvestris SNOWDROP WINDFLOWER	N India, SW China	late spring, early summer	to 36 in (90 cm), swollen-rooted, erect, branching perennial	leaves palmately 3–5-parted, segments much toothed and divided	solitary, nodding, fragrant, 1–3 in (2.5–8 cm) diam., white, tepals 5+, elliptic
Comments: Includes 'Grandiflora' (flowers large, nodding and held well above plant, 'Elisa Fellmann' (('Plena') flowers semidouble), and 'Macrantha' (very vigorous, flowers large, nodding, strongly fragrant).					

anemone-centered applied to composite flowers, especially chrysanthemums and dahlias, where the disk florets are enlarged to form a central cushion, sometimes of a contrasting color to the ray florets. Also used to describe peonies and camellias with petaloid stamens.

Anemonella (Latin diminutive form of the name *Anemone*, which this plant resembles). Ranunculaceae. 1 species, *A. thalictroides* (RUE ANEMONE), a hardy perennial herb native to eastern North America. Finely divided, ferny foliage arises in spring from tuberous roots. In spring and early summer, 2–5, ¾–1¼ in (2–3 cm)-wide flowers are carried on slender stalks atop a 4–8-in- (10–20-cm-) tall stem and subtended by a compound, leafy ruff. They consist of 5–10 cupped, petal-like sepals, white to pale pink. In the cultivar 'Florepleno', the flowers are double and white, in 'Rosea' pale pink, and in 'Roseaplena' ('Schoaff's Double Pink') double and

rosy pink. Plant in moist, humus-rich sandy soil, in dappled sun or light shade. Mulch in winter. Propagate from fresh seed in summer, or by division of well-established plants.

Anemonopsis (*Anemone*, a related genus, and Greek, *opsis*, resemblance). Ranunculaceae. 1 species, *A. macrophylla* (FALSE ANEMONE), a rhizomatous, hardy perennial herb native to Japan. In summer, the ferny foliage is surpassed by slender stalks to 32 in (80 cm) tall and bearing delicately branched panicles. The nodding flowers are lavender, ¾–1½ in (2–4 cm) wide, and consist of 7–10 cupped, petal-like sepals and ten, far smaller petals. Plant in damp, cool and humus-rich soil in light shade or dappled sunlight. Propagate by division in spring.

Anemopaegma (from Greek *anemos*, wind, and *paigma*, sport, referring to the way in which the wind plays with the stems). Bignoniaceae. C and S America. YELLOW TRUMPET VINE. 40 species, evergreen, woody climbers grown for their showy, tubular to funnel-shaped flowers. The leaves consist of 1–2 pairs of smooth, leathery leaflets to 6 in (15 cm) long and often terminate in a coiling tendril. Plant in a fertile, loamy medium in large pots or tubs in the greenhouse or conservatory (minimum temperature 50°F/ 10°C), in full sun or part shade. Propagate by softwood cuttings.

A. chamberlaynii Brazil; leaf tendrils usually 3-branched; flowers 2 in (5 cm) long, rich golden yellow; *A. chrysoleucum* Mexico to N Brazil; differs from the first species in its unbranched leaf tendrils and larger (2½–4 in (6–10 cm), fragrant flowers borne 1–3 (not 2–8) per axil; these are yellow and usually stained white with orange or purple-brown markings in the throat.

anemophily wind-pollination.

Anethum graveolens
The leaves of this umbelliferous herb, dill, are used for flavoring. It makes a pretty addition to an informal planting.

Anethum (from Greek *anethon*, dill). Umbelliferae. Old World. 2 species, annual and biennial herbs scented of anise with very finely divided leaves and small, yellow flowers in compound umbels. *A. graveolens* is the herb DILL

(q.v.), native to southwest Asia, now widely naturalized in Europe and N America. It grows to 24 in (60 cm) tall, with leaves to 12 in (30 cm) composed of many, threadlike segments.

anfractuose, anfractuous describes plant parts that are closely or tightly sinuous, or spirally twisted.

Angelica (from the ancient name, *Herba angelica*, "angelic plant"—the many herbal properties of this plant were said to have been revealed by an angel). Umbelliferae. Northern Hemisphere. 50 species, biennial, monocarpic or perennial herbs, usually tall and robust with ternately 2–3-pinnate leaves and small, green-white flowers in large, compound umbels. *A. archangelica* is ARCHANGEL, GARDEN ANGELICA, or WILD PARSNIP, a monocarpic herb to 6½ ft (2 m) tall, native to Europe and Asia. The 24-in- (60-cm-) long leaves are smooth and dark green with toothed, oblong segments. The umbels are 4¾–10 in (12–25 cm) wide, massed with white or yellow-green flowers and carried on stout stalks.

Young stems of angelica are crystallized and used for confectionary decoration; they are also eaten fresh, cooked as for asparagus, or boiled with rhubarb to alleviate its tartness. Fresh or dried, the leaves are used in herbal tisanes. The flowers are a valuable nectar source for bees. A stately addition not only to the herb garden, but also to green/white borders and bedding schemes. *Angelica* will usually die after setting seed, but may perform as a perennial if the flower heads are removed soon after fading in summer. Sow seed *in situ* when ripe.

angiosperms plants with their seeds enclosed in an ovary, i.e., flowering plants as opposed to gymnosperms, which are nonflowering plants with naked seeds.

Angraecum (Latinized form of the Malay name *anggrek* or *angurek*, used for epiphytic orchids with aerial roots). Orchidaceae. Tropical and South Africa; Indian Ocean Islands. 150 species, tender, epiphytic orchids usually with leathery leaves arranged in two ranks along erect stems and with

abundant aerial roots. Waxy, starlike and long-spurred, in shades of white, cream, and green, the flowers are produced in axillary clusters and sprays. Grow in light shade in a humid environment, minimum temperature 65°F (18°C). Plant in clay pots or baskets filled with a very open, bark-based medium. Water, fertilize and syringe frequently during warm weather; less often in winter. Increase by offsets and stem cuttings.

A. distichum W Africa; stems to 8 in (20 cm) long concealed by the overlapping bases of two-ranked, short, folded leaves; flowers small, solitary, white; *A. eburneum* Africa, islands in the Indian Ocean; to 3¼ ft (1 m) tall with strap-shaped leaves and arching sprays of 2½ in (6 cm)-wide flowers, green with upturned, shell-like white lips, heavily fragrant at night; *A. sesquipedale* COMET ORCHID; Madagascar; leaves thick, strap-shaped; flowers starry, ivory, thickly waxy in texture, to 7 in (18 cm) across, spicily scented at night with a spur some 12 in (30 cm) long.

angular, angulate of plant parts with laterally projecting angles, as in longitudinally ridged and angled stems.

Anguloa (for Don Francisco de Angulo [*fl.*1790], Spanish naturalist). Orchidaceae. South America. CRADLE ORCHID; TULIP ORCHID. 10 species, terrestrial or epiphytic orchids with large pseudobulbs and long, ribbed leaves. Borne in spring and summer, the flowers are large and solitary, arising on thick stalks alongside the new growth. They consist of broad and waxy, strongly cupped tepals which cradle a small, tonguelike lip. Most are strongly scented of chocolate and wintergreen. Grow in humid, well-ventilated and lightly shaded conditions, minimum winter temperature 48°F (9°C). Pot annually in late winter in an open mix with sphagnum moss and perlite. Water and feed liberally while the new growth develops. Once the new pseudobulbs are complete (usually early fall), allow the plants to dry out thoroughly between waterings and keep in cool, bright conditions; increase water and temperatures when the new growth appears. Increase by backbulbs and division.

A. brevilabris flowers to 4 in (10 cm) deep, tepals olive, interior densely spotted dark blood red, lip short, pale barred blood red with small lateral lobes; *A. clowesii* flowers to 4 in 10 cm) deep, tepals lemon to canary yellow; *A. hohenlohii* (syn. *A. ruckeri* of gardens) flowers to 4¾ in (12 cm) deep, tepals olive, interior densely spotted and stained dark blood red, lip red, larger than in *A. brevilabris*, with distinct, outspread lateral lobes; *A.* × *ruckeri* (*A. clowesii* × *A. hohenlohii*) flowers to 4 in (10 cm) deep, tepals dull yellow to olive, interior yellow spotted blood red; *A. uniflora* flowers to 4 in (10 cm) deep, tepals white faintly flushed rose; *A. virginalis* flowers to 3 in (8 cm) deep, tepals white, interior dotted and lined faintly with pale rose, lip with a kinked base, spotted red.

Anigozanthos (from Greek *anisos*, unequal and *anthos*, flower, referring to the unequal perianth lobes). Haemodoraceae. Australia. CAT'S PAW; KANGAROO PAW. 11 species, evergreen or semideciduous perennial herbs with grassy or irislike leaves in basal fans or clumps and long-stalked spikes or panicles, usually in spring and summer. The flowers are tubular, split on the curving lower side and with five short and acute lobes peeled back on the arching upper side. They are covered in dense and usually colorful felty hairs. Grow in full sunlight in a freely draining, acidic mix. Provide a rather dry, airy atmosphere and a minimum temperature of 41°F (5°C). Water freely during warm weather, sparingly in winter. Propagate by division in spring.

A. flavidus TALL KANGAROO PAW; flowers 1¼–2 in (3–5 cm) long and typically lime green densely covered with sulfur yellow felt with orange anthers, arranged on the ascending branches of erect panicles that stand 3–6 ft (1–2 m) tall; red, pink, buff and orange forms also occur; *A. manglesii* flowers arranged in two rows at the tip of a 12–40-in (30–100-cm) spike, 2¾–4¾ in (7–12 cm) long, yellow-green to emerald with bright red hairs toward the base; *A. rufus* RED KANGAROO PAW; differs from *A. flavidus* in flowers, arranged on outspread branches, basically olive, thickly covered in blood red felt with green anthers.

anion exchange capacity the ability of a soil to adsorb negatively charged ions known as anions. A measure of the retention and availability of such nutrients as phosphate, sulfate, and molybdate.

Anisodontea (from Greek, *anisos*, unequal, and *odous*, tooth, referring to the unequal projections on the mericarps). Malvaceae. South Africa. 19 species, evergreen shrubs or shrubby perennial herbs with lobed leaves. Solitary, cymose, or racemose, the flowers have five spreading, broadly obovate petals and are produced in spring and summer. Grow in full sun or light shade. Needs a minimum winter temperature of 41°F (5°C) with good ventilation, and water plentifully when in growth. Propagate by greenwood or semiripe cuttings in summer.

A. capensis woody-based, bushy perennial to 3¼ ft (1 m) tall; flowers ⅝–1¼ in (1.5–3 cm) wide, pale to deep magenta with darker veins and a basal blotch; *A.* × *hypomadarum* (hybrid of unknown parentage) slender-branched shrub to 10 ft (3 m) tall; flowers ¾–1¼ in (2–3 cm) wide and white or pale pink with deep purple veins merging in a basal blotch.

annual a plant that completes its life cycle of germination, flowering, and seeding within one growing season. Represented, as examples, in the flower garden by cornflower (*Centaurea cyanus*) and in the vegetable garden by lettuce (*Lactuca sativa*).

annual rings

Cross-section, trunk of Pinus muricata

annual rings clearly defined rings of secondary xylem evident in transversely cut woody stems (see above) and roots of plants growing in temperate zones. The rings are due to a seasonal rhythm in the growth of cambium, which is greatest in the spring and gradually falls off toward dormancy. The cycle is repeated each year, so that annual rings provide a means of calculating the age of trees, especially. Also known as growth rings.

annual shoots shoots that live for one year only, produced by herbaceous perennial plants, most bulbs, and some shrubs.

annular, annulate ring-shaped; used of organs or parts in a circular arrangement or forming rings.

annulus (1) the corona or rim of the corolla in Asclepiadaceae; (2) in ferns, an elastic ring of cells that partially invests and bursts the sporangium at dehiscence.

Anoda (from Greek *a-*, without, and Latin *nodus*, joint: the pedicels lack a node). Malvaceae. Tropical and subtropical Americas. 10 species, annual and perennial herbs and subshrubs with hastate, unlobed or lobed leaves and flowers with five, obovate petals carried one to two per axil in erect racemes in summer. Grow under glass (minimum temperature 45°F/7°C) in sun in a well-drained, gritty medium. Water moderately in winter. Alternatively, treat as a half-hardy annual grown in a sunny, sheltered situation. Propagate from seed sown *in situ* in late spring or, earlier, under glass. *A. cristata* erect to sprawling annual or short-lived perennial herb to 5 ft (1.5 m) tall; flowers ⅝–2 in (1.5–5 cm) wide, white, lavender or purple-blue; 'Opal Cup': flowers silvery lilac with an iridescent sheen and mauve veins: 'Snowdrop': flowers pure white.

Anomatheca (from Latin *anomalus*, abnormal, and *theca*, a case, referring to the warty capsule). Iridaceae. Central and South Africa. 6 species, cormous perennial herbs grown for their flowers. Cultivation as for *Babiana. A. laxa Lapeirousia laxa, L.cruenta*; S Africa, Mozambique; leaves sword-shaped, exceeded in summer by a loose, erect to horizontal raceme some 12 in

(30 cm) tall; flowers 1 in (2.5 cm) wide with a straight perianth tube and two groups of three segments, typically red with purple-red markings at the base of the lower three segments; warty seed capsules split to reveal red-brown seeds.

Anopterus (from Greek *ano*, upward, and *pteron*, wing, referring to the winged seeds). Grossulariaceae. Australia; Tasmania. 2 species, evergreen trees and shrubs with leathery leaves and racemes of bell-shaped, 6-parted flowers. Grow in sheltered, humid locations to 10°F (–12°C), or in a cool greenhouse and conservatory. Plant in a neutral to acidic, sandy mix in bright, filtered light or part shade. Propagate by semiripe cuttings in summer. *A. glandulosus* TASMANIAN LAUREL; shrub or small tree to 30 ft (10 m) tall; leaves 2½–7 in (6–18 cm)-long, lanceolate to elliptic leathery, toothed; flowers ¾ in (2 cm) wide, waxy white to pale rose, in 4 in (10 cm)-long racemes in late spring.

Anredera (name derivation unknown). Basellaceae. South America (naturalized Southern Europe). 10 species, woody to herbaceous climbers arising from tuberous roots, with thinly fleshy leaves and small flowers in axillary spikes and racemes. Grow in full sun and with a minimum winter temperature of 41°F (5°C) and sturdy support for the heavy climbing growth. Cut back the previous year's growth to just above ground in spring. Propagate by division of tubers in spring, and by tubercles which may form in the leaf axils. *A. cordifolia* (syn. *Boussingaultia cordifolia*, *B.gracilis* var. *pseudobaselloides*) MADEIRA VINE; MIGNONETTE VINE; vigorous, herbaceous vine; leaves to 20 ft (6 m) fleshy, bright green and smooth, heart-shaped; flowers fragrant white flowers in drooping spikes in late summer; plants named *A. baselloides* are often *A. cordifolia*. True *A. baselloides* differs in its simple, not 3-lobed style.

antemarginal used of veins, sori, and other leaf features lying within, or extending just short of, the margin.

Antennaria (from Latin *antenna*: the pappus hairs of male flowers resemble insect antennae). Compositae. Northern Temperate Regions; Asia; South America. CATS' EARS; EVERLASTING; PUSSY TOES; LADIES' TOBACCO. 45 species, small, often woolly perennial herbs with leaves in basal rosettes and discoid, solitary or clustered flower heads on erect stems in summer. Frost-hardy but intolerant of wet and cold combined. Plant in full sun. Propagate by division in spring. *A. dioica* Europe, N America, N Asia; creeping, evergreen; leaves, spathulate, ¼–1½ in (0.5–4 cm)-long covered in silvery hairs; flower heads to ¼ in (0.5 cm) across in a terminal cluster resembling tiny everlastings, usually white with a silvery pink tint, although deep rose in the compact cultivar 'Nyewoods Variety', rose-pink in 'Rosea' and deep blood red in 'Rubra'.

anterior of the surface or part of an organ turned away from or farthest from the axis and projecting forward or toward the base or (in the case of a flower) any subtending bract; close to abaxial but broader in definition, meaning not only "beneath" but also lower (of two, as in the lower lip of a bilabiate flower) or farthest, as in the tip of an organ, cf. *posterior*.

Anthemis (the Greek name for this herb, from *anthemon*, flower). Compositae. Mediterranean to Western Asia. DOG FENNEL 100 species, hairy, aromatic perennial herbs and subshrubs with finely cut leaves and long-stalked, daisylike flower heads. Evergreen, hardy and summer-flowering. Plant in full sun. Propagate by division in fall or spring, and by basal cuttings in spring or late summer.

A. punctata subsp. *cupaniana* S Europe and N Africa; woody-based perennial making a dense and springy carpet of silvery leaves; flower heads 2½ in (6 cm)-wide, white with yellow centers; *A. tinctoria* GOLDEN MARGUERITE, OX EYE CHAMOMILE; Europe, W Asia; erect, clump-forming, sparsely hairy to woolly perennial to 24 in (60 cm) tall; leaves ferny, mid-green; flower heads to 1¼ in (3 cm)-wide, white to golden or pale cream with golden centers. For *A. nobilis*, see *Chamaemelum nobile*.

anther the pollen-bearing portion of the stamen, either sessile or attached to a filament.

anther cap in orchids, the caplike case enclosing the pollinia.

anther sac a sac-shaped unit containing pollen bearing sacs disposed in two lobes; the tissues separating the members of each pair usually break down prior to anthesis, giving rise to a biloculate (two-celled) anther.

Anthericum (from the Greek *antherikos*, the flowering stem of the asphodel). Liliaceae (Anthericaceae). Southern Europe; Turkey; Africa (those below from Southern Europe). 50 species, fleshy-rooted, rhizomatous perennial herbs with clumps of grassy or straplike leaves and slender, erect, simple to branching spikes of six-parted, starry white flowers. Plant in sun. Where temperatures fall far below 14°F (–10°C), or winter conditions are wet, apply a dry mulch. Propagate by seed, or by division in spring. *A. liliago* ST. BERNARD'S LILY; to 36 in (90 cm) tall with usually unbranched racemes of ¾ in (2 cm)-wide flowers in early summer; *A. ramosum* slightly shorter than the first species with much-branched stems of flowers in summer; leaves gray-green.

anthesis the expansion or opening of a flower; the period in which the anthers and stigmas become functional, allowing fertilization to take place.

anthocorid bugs (Hemiptera: Anthocoridae). Small, usually predacious insects, about ¹⁄₁₆–⅛ in (2–4 mm) long, mostly black or brown and resembling small capsid bugs. *Anthocoris nemorum* preys on aphids, scale insects, gall-midge larvae, small caterpillars, thrips, and mites. Adults consume around 50 fruit-tree red spider mites per day, or 500–600 aphids during the lifetime of one individual. *A. nemorum* and *A. nemoralis* are important predators of the aphid *Pemphigus bursarius*, which lives during the spring in galls on the petioles of poplar leaves before migrating to the roots of lettuce. Anthocorids enter the galls and a single nymph can rapidly kill the whole aphid colony, which averages 100 individuals.

anthocyanins pigments frequently found in cell sap, and responsible for red, blue and intermediate colors in flowers, foliage and stems.

anthracnose A group of fungal diseases usually caused by *Colletotrichum* species, characterized by black, sunken lesions on which pustules of mucilaginous spores are produced.

ANTIRRHINUM ANTHRACNOSE (*Colletotrichum coccodes*) affects greenhouse-grown antirrhinums under damp growing conditions; it also occurs on plants outdoors at the end of summer. Leaf and stem lesions can result in the collapse of plants.

BEAN ANTHRACNOSE (*C. lindemuthianum*) is a major disease of haricot beans that can also affect scarlet runners, lima beans, cowpeas, broad beans, and other legumes. Particularly damaging in wet conditions and under protected cultivation, it is readily spread by rain-splash, overhead irrigation, and cultural operations. Symptoms are circular brown to black spots on pods developing a pinkish ooze of spores in damp weather, which leads to seedborne infection, the usual route for introduction into gardens.

BRASSICA ANTHRACNOSE (*C. higginsianum*) is a seedborne disease which can damage Chinese cabbage, mustard greens, turnips, and other brassicas in warmer areas of the US.

CLIVIA ANTHRACNOSE (*C. gloeosporioides*) may be the fungus responsible for the reddish spots commonly seen on *Clivia* foliage. No control is usually needed.

CUCURBIT ANTHRACNOSE (*C. lagenarium* or *C.orbiculare*) attacks all above-ground parts of cucurbits; it is particularly serious on protected cucumbers and on watermelons. Cucumber seedlings may suffer from damping-off. Pale green leaf spots occur later; they enlarge, dry up, and may kill whole leaves. Sunken lesions are produced on stems and on developing fruits, causing cracking. Poorly ventilated conditions encourage spread of the disease. On watermelons, leaves develop small black spots that spread until the foliage becomes black and shriveled. Fruits may be covered with numerous sunken lesions and also suffer sunburn as a side effect of defoliation. The disease can become epidemic in conditions of high rainfall

and temperatures of 75°F (24°C) and over, and is a widespread problem on the Pacific Coast of the US, but rare in regions of low rainfall.

DIGITALIS ANTHRACNOSE (*C. fuscum*) causes damping-off of seedlings on foxgloves and other Scrophulariaceae. It may also cause serious damage to older plants as small purple-brown spots on leaves, and lesions on stems and petioles. It is seed-borne and may be prevented by hot-water treatment of seed.

HOLLYHOCK ANTHRACNOSE (*C. malvarum*) is a serious disease in North America, but less damaging in Europe. Seedlings are blighted and older leaves and stems show black spotting and blotching. *Abutilon*, *Lavatera* and *Malva* can also be infected.

STEM ANTHRACNOSE (*C.truncatum*) is a serious seedborne disease of soybeans in the southern US. Reddish lesions occur on stems, leaves and pods, and if infection is heavy, plants are stunted or killed.

Anthracnose of many plants is caused by *Glomerella cingulata* (anamorph *Colletotrichum gloeosporioides*). In tropical and subtropical areas, it has an extremely wide host range as a pathogen, as a secondary fungus following other infections, injury, or stress, and as a saprophyte. It is a common cause of leaf lesions, shoot dieback (withertip), and fruit spotting. In addition to anthracnose, the fungus causes cankers and fruit rots. The following are among the many anthracnose-type diseases caused by *G.cingulata*.

Fruit spotting of avocado, banana, guava, loquat, mango, and papaya is a serious problem for which control measures include hot fungicidal dips, fruit wrapping on the tree, treatment with fungicidal wax, and gamma radiation. The natural microflora on fruit inhibit germination and penetration of spores, and encouraging these flora may lead to development of a biological control.

MANGO ANTHRACNOSE may infect fruits so badly that they drop before ripening or degenerate on the tree. It remains quiescent until fruit ripening after harvest, when it can cause serious losses during shipment and at the point of sale. Fruit set may also be badly affected by earlier blossom blight. There is varietal resistance. Control with fungicide needs to be combined

with hygiene measures, including the collection and destruction of diseased fruit and foliage.

In the US, PRIVET ANTHRACNOSE and TWIG BLIGHT are widespread and serious diseases on *Ligustrum* and the dogwoods. They are controlled by the use of resistant species and the destruction of diseased foliage.

Since spores are produced in a mucilaginous mass and dispersed by water, anthracnose diseases are encouraged by wet conditions and are particularly common in rainy climates, where control by spraying is difficult. Where chemical treatments can be used, copper-based and other general fungicides are usually effective. The level of disease can be reduced by crop rotation, the use of healthy seed, and careful disposal of crop residues, on which the fungus is able to continue growing at the end of the season.

Anthriscus (from Greek, *anthriskos*, chervil). Umbelliferae. Europe; N Africa; Asia. 12 species, hardy annual, biennial and perennial herbs with fine, ternately divided leaves and in spring and summer, small, white to cream flowers in compound umbels. *A. cereifolium* is the herb CHERVIL, (q.v.). *A. sylvestris* is a beautiful addition to the wild garden, where it will naturalize, making banks of soft, foamy flower. It will grow in most soils in sun or part shade. Increase by seed sown *in situ*.

A. cereifolium CHERVIL; annual to 24 in (60 cm) tall; leaves bright green, delicately scented of aniseed; *A. sylvestris* COW PARSLEY, QUEEN ANNE'S LACE; inedible biennial or perennial to 3¼ ft (1 m) tall with spreading, ferny foliage and lacy flower heads borne in spring; 'Moonlit Night': foliage solidly deep bronze-purple, flowers white; 'Ravenswing': foliage purple-black, flowers off-white—both cultivars come more or less true from seed.

Anthurium (from Greek, *anthos*, flower, and *oura*, tail, referring to the tail-like spadix). Araceae. Tropical Americas. FLAMINGO FLOWER; TAIL FLOWER. Perhaps 900 species, tender, evergreen, perennial herbs, many epiphytic, with climbing stems or, as is the case of those below, a short, rooting stem bearing a clump of long-stalked, leathery leaves. Produced throughout the year, the flowers are very small and packed in a slender spadix backed by a showy, shieldlike spathe. Grow in dappled sun or shade with a minimum temperature of 59°F (15°C) and medium to high humidity. Plant in small pots containing an open, neutral to acidic, soilless mix high in coarse bark and leaf mold. Keep moist at all times, never waterlogged. Apply a weak liquid fertilizer monthly. Propagate by rooted offsets.

A. andraeanum Colombia and Ecuador; to 24 in (60 cm) tall; spadix white to yellow, tapering, pointing downward toward the tip of a 2½–6 in (6–15 cm)-long, heart-shaped, puckered spathe in bright waxy red; cultivars with white, flamingo pink, golden, vermilion and scarlet spathes are available; *A. crystallinum* Panama to Peru; leaves 12–20 in (30–50 cm)-long, broadly heart-shaped, soft, bronze-pink at first becoming deep, satiny emerald green overlaid with glistening, silverwhite veins; spadix purple-brown backed by a narrow, purple-red spathe; *A. scherzerianum* Costa Rica; to 12 in (30 cm); spathe elliptic to ovate, glossy scarlet to orange-red; spadix to 4¾ in (12 cm) long, orange-red, spiraling; 'Atrosanguineum': spathe deepest blood red 'Rothschildianum': spathe red spotted: white, spadix yellow; 'Wardii': spathe large, deep burgundy.

Anthyllis (the classical name). Leguminosae. Mediterranean. 25 species, annual and perennial herbs or shrubs with pinnate leaves and heads of pealike flowers in spring and summer. Hardy to at least 14°F (–10°C), but resentful of cold *and* wet. Plant in full sun. Propagate by semiripe cuttings, or by detaching rooted branches.

A. hermanniae domed, bushy perennial to 3¼ ft (1 m) tall with a tangle of spreading, spiny-tipped, gray-hairy branches; leaves trefoil-like or reduced to a single, bright green leaflet; flowers yellow; *A. montana* (spreading, woody-

based perennial to 12 in (30 cm) tall with gray-green to mid-green leaves composed of many leaflets; flowers pale pink marked red, in dense heads; 'Rubra': leaves gray, flowers crimson.

tail-like spadix

Anthurium andreanum

antibiotics substances produced by microorganisms, especially fungi and actinomycetes, that are toxic to other microorganisms. As a spinoff from medical research, streptomycin and terramycin have been used to control bacterial disease and downy mildew in plants, but this practice is questionable on public health grounds. Antibiotics specifically developed to control plant diseases include actidione (against powdery mildews, leaf spots and some rusts) and kasugamycin (against bacterial and fungal disease).

The use of antibiotics for the control of plant pathogens requires a thorough understanding of the implications for human health.

antidesiccant see *antitranspirant*.

Antigonon (from Greek, *anti*, against, and *gonia*, an angle, referring to the flexuous stems). Polygonaceae. Central America. 3 species, rampant perennial vines, usually tuberous-rooted, with axillary, tendril-tipped racemes of small flowers with colorful papery sepals. A vivid, fast-growing climber which, in frost-free gardens, will quickly cover any support or structure. Elsewhere, it should be grown in a cool greenhouse or conservatory or, in mild regions, outdoors in very sheltered positions as a deciduous perennial with a thick mulch in winter. Grow in full sun. Increase by division or seed. *A. leptopus* CONFEDERATE VINE, MEXICAN CREEPER, CORAL VINE, CHAIN OF LOVE, ROSA DE MONTANA, QUEEN'S WREATH; Mexico; to 40 ft (12 m); flowers coral pink, white in 'Album', hot pink to crimson in 'Baja Red', produced chiefly in summer.

antipetalous opposite to or superposed on a petal, i.e., not alternate.

Antirrhinum (from Greek *anti*, opposite, and *rhis*, snout, referring to the corolla shape). Scrophulariaceae. SNAPDRAGON. Temperate regions. 40 species annual and perennial herbs and subshrubs with tubular, 2-lipped flowers solitary in the leaf axils or in terminal racemes; these have a billowing upper lip and a tonguelike lower lip with a conspicuous, bearded palate. The typical *A. majus* is short-lived with a woody base and rather ragged habit. Most cultivars, however, are treated as annuals or biennials and retain their vigor and bushiness; they range in height from tall (to 3¼ ft/1 m), to intermediate (to 18 in/45 cm) and dwarf (to 12 in/30 cm). The larger cultivars are suitable for cutting. In addition to these more conventional snapdragons, new races of pendulous hybrids are becoming popular. These have gray-green foliage and a loose, cascading habit ideal for hanging baskets and containers. Examples include the deep rose and yellow 'Rose Pink' and 'Primrose Vein', white flushed yellow and rose, combed with red. Grow in full sun in fertile, well-drained soil. Deadhead regularly. Sow seed *in situ* in late spring, or take cuttings in spring or early fall.

A. majus SNAPDRAGON; SW Europe, Mediterranean; erect, shrubby perennial to 3¼ ft (1 m); flowers in narrow, terminal racemes, tubular some 2 in (5 cm) long with two distinct lips and an enlarged palate; typically purple or pink, but the many seed races now available encompass plants with white, yellow, apricot, orange, flame, rose, red and purple flowers, some with mixtures of color and differently toned lips or palates; flower forms range from small (1¼ in/3 cm) to large (2¾ in/7 cm), single and straight-tubed to penstemon- and trumpet-shaped, peloric and double).

antisepalous opposite to or superposed on a sepal, i.e., not alternate.

antitranspirant a chemical preparation applied to aerial parts of plants to reduce water loss from foliage and shoots by sealing stomatal pores. Emulsions of plastic polymers are commonly used on newly transplanted evergreen woody plants to aid establishment. Some contribute a protective effect against pests and diseases. Also known as an antidesiccant.

antrorse turned, curved or bent upward or forward, toward the apex; cf. *retrorse*.

ants (Hymenoptera: Formicidae) a very large family of small social insects, which live in nests containing wingless infertile females and at least one fertile female or queen. During summer, usually in hot, humid weather, winged males and females swarm in mating flights; fertilized females shed their wings and choose a suitable site to establish a new nest. Some queens are capable of living for over 15 years. Ants feed on sugary substances such as nectar, as well as on oil-rich seeds, other ants, and small invertebrates. Many species have a close association with aphids, scale insects, and mealybugs, imbibing their excreted honeydew; for some sap-feeding insects, this is an essential service. Ants assist aphids by warding off predators and parasites, and there is evidence that they are capable of transporting aphids to better feeding sites.

Plants are seldom attacked directly by temperate species of garden ants, but seed collecting is common, particularly oil-rich seeds such as *Buddleja*, *Meconopsis*, *Primula*, *Rhododendron*, and *Viola*. Worker ants move along defined pathways between the nest and food source, laying down trail pheromones to mark the route. When nests are built under plants, extensive tunneling and loosening of the soil around roots can cause plants to wilt, especially those growing in free-draining soil and in pots. Excavated soil is usually deposited on the surface, so that low-growing plants may become partially buried; this can be especially troublesome on lawns.

The COMMON BLACK ANT (*Lasius niger*), with workers about $\frac{1}{8}$ in (4 mm) long, is prevalent in gardens throughout Europe, and strains occur in North America. Nests are found beneath plants, stones, pavement, and masonry, and in banks and old tree stumps. The MOUND ANT (*L. flavus*) has similar-sized workers that are mostly pale yellow. This species produces ant hills that can reach the size of mole hills. PHARAOH'S ANT (*Monomorium pharaonis*) is a ubiquitous species, having been spread throughout the world by shipping. Workers are red-yellow and about $\frac{1}{16}$ in (2 mm) long. *Pheidole* species are of comparable size, but workers are darker brown and the genus is notable in having a soldier caste, equipped with enlarged mandibles. RED ANTS (*Myrmica* species) are common in gardens; the workers are larger than those of *Lasius* and able to sting. LEAF-CUTTING ANTS (*Atta* species) occur in South America and the southern states of the US, where they are sometimes serious pests of tree crops and ornamentals; they cut leaf pieces from a wide range of plants and carry them back to their nests, sometimes virtually defoliating individual trees. A fungus on the decaying leaf fragments provides food for the ants.

Ants are best controlled by destroying the nest with boiling water or appropriate residual insecticides. Where nests are inaccessible, insecticides should be applied around the entrance holes and along pathways; commercial baits may also be used, but these may need frequent renewal.

apetalous lacking petals.

apex the growing point of a stem or root; the tip of a plant organ or structure, most commonly used of a leaf tip.

Aphelandra (from Greek, *apheles*, simple, and *aner, andros*, man: the anthers are one-celled). Acanthaceae. Tropical America. 170 species, tender evergreen shrubs and subshrubs with tough, ovate to elliptic leaves and terminal spikes of tubular 2-lipped flowers amid overlapping bracts. Grow in bright, filtered light or light shade with a minimum temperature of 55°F (13°C). Pot in a soilless, free-draining mix; keep moist throughout the year and fertilize semiweekly when in growth. Both species flower at various times of year. *A. squarrosa* bracts are a long-lasting attraction. Cut back and repot after flowering. Root tip cuttings in a sandy mix in humid conditions.

A. aurantiaca Mexico, Colombia; shrub to $3\frac{1}{4}$ ft (1 m), the finest form is 'Roezlii' (FIERY SPIKE) with leaden, puckered leaves marked with silver veins; flowers brilliant scarlet, emerging from overlapping purple-tinted bracts in 4-sided spikes to 7 in (18 cm) long; *A. squarrosa* SAFFRON SPIKE, ZEBRA PLANT; Brazil; shrub to $6\frac{1}{2}$ ft (2 m) tall but usually sold and kept small, newly propagated, bushy plants; stems purple-tinted; leaves to 10 in (25 cm) long, glossy dark green with sunken herringbone veins heavily outlined in white or gold; flowers maroon-flecked yellow, peeping from overlapping, waxy, yellow bracts of 8 in (20 cm)-long 4-sided spikes: 'Leopoldii': leaves dark green, veined pure white, flowers yellow amid maroon bracts.

aphids (Hemiptera: Aphididae and other families) small, soft-bodied, sap-feeding insects, about $\frac{1}{16}$–$\frac{1}{4}$ in (1–5 mm) long, with relatively long legs and antennae and a pair of hornlike structures (the siphunculi) on the back of the abdomen; GREENFLY, BLACKFLY, PLANT LICE, and BLIGHT are other descriptions for aphids. They may be black, green, yellow, pink or gray; in some, such as the WOOLLY APHID, the body is obscured by a covering of white waxy filaments.

Aphids feed by inserting sucking mouthparts into the phloem of plants: the resulting injury takes various forms, including leaf curling, stem distortion, galling, malformed fruits, defoliation, and, with root-feeding aphids. wilting and root splitting. Indirect damage is caused by the copious excretion of honeydew, which coats underlying foliage and becomes infected by fungal sooty molds, so that affected leaves carry out their normal functions less efficiently.

Most aphids have a single host or a narrow range of host plants. Summer

mouthparts pierce plant surfaces to suck sap

Aphids on rose

colonies usually consist of winged and wingless females that produce live young without fertilization. Winged aphids are weak fliers, but can be carried by air currents for long distances. Migratory species can find alternate hosts in this way and although mainly a minority group, are significant plant pests. They include the BLACK BEAN APHID (*Aphis fabae*), which overwinters as eggs on *Euonymus* and *Viburnum opulus* and migrates in late spring to beans and other hosts, and the LETTUCE ROOT APHID (*Pemphigus bursarius*), which migrates from poplar to the roots of lettuces and sow thistle. Like many other aphids, they produce sexual forms in fall, and fertilized females lay shiny black eggs on the stems of woody plants. Some aphids overwinter as active stages.

Many aphids, particularly the PEACH-POTATO APHID (*Myzus persicae*), are vectors of viruses such as bean yellow mosaic, cauliflower mosaic, dahlia mosaic, lettuce mosaic, pea leafroll, plum pox, potato leaf-roll, tomato aspermy, and tulip-breaking virus. *M. persicae* overwinters either as eggs on peaches or nectarines, or as active stages under glass or outdoors in warmer countries. In summer, sparse colonies occur on a wide range of ornamentals and vegetables both outdoors and under glass. Two other *Myzus* species, the SHALLOT APHID (*M. ascalonicus*) and the VIOLET APHID (*M. ornatus*) also attack a wide range of host plants. Other common polyphagous species include the MOTTLED ARUM APHID (*Aulacorthum circumflexum*), a yellow aphid with a dark horseshoe-shaped mark on the abdomen, which is widespread on greenhouse and house plants; the green-yellow greenhouse and POTATO APHID (*A. solani*), which occurs in Europe, Kenya, Japan, New Zealand, Peru, and the US and attacks vegetables and ornamentals both outdoors and under glass; and the POTATO APHID (*Macrosiphum euphorbiae*), which is green or pink and attacks vegetables and ornamentals in Europe, Asia, Australia and the Americas.

Aphids that overwinter in the egg stage on deciduous trees and shrubs, especially fruit plants, can be controlled by the application of a winter wash when growth is dormant. In spring and summer, aphids are readily susceptible to a number of contact and systemic insecticides, and early and repeated treatment is necessary. The instructions provided with commercial products must be followed, especially with regard to approval for use on and persistence in edible crops. The choice and application of chemical sprays should take into account useful predators and parasites. Aphids have many natural enemies including ladybugs, lacewing and hoverfly larvae, and braconid and chalcid wasps, some of which can be purchased for biological control. Aphids may be attacked by insect-feeding fungi, and one of these, *Verticillium lecanii*, has been used to control certain species on greenhouse plants. See *blackfly*, *root aphids*, *woolly aphid*.

Aphyllanthes (from Greek, *aphyllos*, leafless, and *anthos*, flower, referring to the rushlike stems). Liliaceae (Aphyllanthaceae). SW Europe; Morocco. 1 species, *A. monspeliensis*, a perennial herb with a mop of wiry and chalky, leafless stems to 12 in (30 cm) long picked out in late spring and summer with ¾ in (2 cm)-wide, 6-parted, lilac to bright blue flowers. Hardy to 23°F (−5°C). Plant in sheltered sunny niches on the rock garden in well-drained, humusrich, sandy soil. Propagate by division.

aphyllous lacking leaves.

apical borne at the apex of an organ, farthest from the point of attachment; pertaining to the apex.

apical dominance suppression of the growth of lateral buds by a shoot tip, or apex. The dominance of the apical meristem accounts for the upward growth of most plants, which may be suppressed by natural plant growth processes or by stopping or pruning to produce branched, bushy or low growth. An apical bud is the terminal or topmost bud on a stem.

apicule a short, sharp but not rigid point terminating a leaf, bract, or perianth segment.

Apium (Classical Latin name for this plant). Umbelliferae. Europe; temperate Asia. 20 species, annual, biennial and perennial herbs. See *celeriac*, *celery*.

apogeotropic see *ageotropic*.

apomixis, apomict generally used to describe the process of reproducing without the fusion of gametes (asexually), which is also sometimes referred to as parthenocarpy. A plant in which seeds or seedlike structures develop from such unfertilized cells is termed an apomict, and its offspring are usually uniform. The phenomenon is common in plants such as *Rubus*, *Hieracium*, and *Taraxacum*.

The term "apomict" is sometimes used to describe the product of other asexual (vegetative) means of increase, as an alternative to the term *clone*.

Aponogeton (from Aquae Aponi, the Latin name for the healing springs of Bagni d'Abano, plus Greek *geiton*, a neighbor. This name was originally applied to another aquatic, *Zannichellia*). Aponogetonaceae. Old World Tropics and Subtropics. 44 species, aquatic perennial herbs with bottom-rooting, tuberous rhizomes and submerged or floating, long-stalked, oblong to oval leaves. Small, often fragrant flowers are produced in summer on forked, spikelike racemes held just clear of the water. *A. disachyos* will tolerate lows to 23°F (−5°C) and needs fairly deep, still water in full sun. Plant in spring into the pond floor or in baskets of sticky loam plunged to a depth of 10–24 in (25–60 cm). Grow *A. madagascariensis* in warm greenhouse ponds and aquariums that do not fall below 75°F (24°C). Plant in a mix of loam, sand, and leaf mold with a deep top-dressing of fine gravel. Propagate both species by division in spring.

A. distachyos CAPE PONDWEED, WATER HAWTHORN; South African; leaves floating, bright green to 10 in (25 cm) long; flowers sweetly scented and with purple-brown to black anthers in two rows, one along each 4 in (10 cm) branch of a pinnately lobed, waxy white, forked raceme; *A. madagascariensis* Madagascar; leaves 4–20 in (10–50 cm) long, lanceolate to oblong, fully submerged, leaf veins prominent, closely woven—the tissue that would normally connect them is absent or transparently thin, leaving a beautiful emerald latticework.

appendage secondary part or process attached to or developed from any larger plant organ—for example, the leafy appendages terminating the lower inflorescence bracts of some *Heliconia* species or the whiskerlike appendages of a *Tacca* inflorescence.

appendiculate furnished with appendages.

appendix a long, narrowed development of the spadix in Araceae.

applanate of plant parts, flattened.

apple (*Malus domestica*) The many cultivated forms are derived from hybridization between *Malus sylvestris* and *M. pumila*, both widespread in Southwest Asia, *M. sylvestris* (WILD CRAB) being common in Western Europe, including Britain. There is evidence that apples were a human foodstuff as early as 6500 BC, and of their progressive introduction through the Middle East, Egypt, Greece, and Western Europe, whence their cultivation spread throughout the world during the colonial period.

Good quality fruit production requires high summer temperature together with moderate, evenly distributed rainfall of 24–31½ in (600–800 mm) per year. Trees must be afforded relative freedom from frost, and shelter from strong wind. Fertile soil to a depth of 24 in (60 cm) is ideal, and free drainage essential. Natural hybridization has been an important source of good cultivars: the widely grown dessert apples 'Cox's Orange Pippin' and 'Golden Delicious' originated as chance seedlings. Many introductions result from the efforts of amateur selectors and breeders, but there are scientifically based breeding programs throughout the world which continue to produce new cultivars by traditional methods and by relatively new techniques such as the irradiation of propagating material to induce genetic change. *Malus baccata* features in breeding schemes to improve hardiness and disease resistance.

Propagation is by budding or grafting; the choice of rootstock influences the ultimate size of a tree. Commonly used are M27 (extremely dwarfing; an excellent choice for vigorous cultivars and container-grown trees; requires very good soil and permanent staking); M9 (very dwarfing and widely used; trees usually come into bearing within 3 or 4 years to produce a high percentage of good-sized fruit; requires permanent staking); M26 (dwarfing; a good choice for average soil conditions; trees usually come into bearing within 4 years); MM106 (semidwarfing; suitable in most soils; often used for espalier and fan forms); and MM111 (vigorous, making large trees in good soil and moderately sized trees in poor soil).

Apples may be trained in various forms to suit garden size and layout; the most common choice is the dwarf bush and cordon, but dwarf pyramid, spindle bush, fan, and pole are all suitable. Vertically trained cordons, with one or two stems, are known as minarettes; the Ballerina series, bred to be trained as vertical stems, has compact fruiting spurs and few long sideshoots; the limited number of available cultivars require little summer pruning. Standard and half standard trees are more challenging to manage in small gardens. Apple cultivars are not consistently self-fertile and depend on cross-pollination by insects and local advice should be sought on compatibility and flowering time prior to selection.

Plant in early winter at distances depending on rootstock, cultivar, and local conditions. The following range is a general guide for garden purposes: bushes, 10–15 ft (3–5 m) stations in rows 15–20 ft (5–6 m) apart; cordons, 30 in (75 cm) apart in rows 6 ft (1.8 m) apart; dwarf pyramids 4 ft (1.2 m) apart in rows 6½ ft (2 m) apart; spindle bushes, 6½ ft (2 m) apart in rows 12 ft (4 m) apart; fans and espaliers, 11½ ft (3.5 m) apart on dwarfing rootstocks and 15 ft (4.5 m) apart on more vigorous ones.

Flowers and fruits are produced on shoots two or more years old and on short spurs on the older wood; fruit thinning is essential where heavy crops are likely. Established trees of trained forms such as cordons, espaliers, and dwarf pyramids require pruning during late summer, cutting back laterals of the current season's growth to three leaves above the basal cluster where they arise direct from the main stem, or to one leaf in the case of shoots arising from existing side shoots or spurs. Secondary growth from later in the season is pruned in the winter, together with essential thinning and training. Free-growing forms such as bushes, spindle bushes, and half-standards are winter-pruned to stimulate growth the following season, and to remove dead and crossing shoots and maintain shape. Vigorously growing

Apple espalier
Apple trees trained in restricted forms, especially as cordons, fans, or espaliers (pictured here) make attractive garden features.

trees should be pruned more lightly than weak ones, which will benefit from tip pruning of branch leaders by up to a quarter of their length and the shortening of selected laterals. Successful pruning requires practice, and a basic understanding of growth habit and performance: continual hard pruning usually results in limited fruiting. Notable cultivars include: *Dessert, early*, 'Discovery', 'Laxton's Epicure'; *midseason*, 'Ellison's Orange', 'James Grieve'; *late* 'Ashmead's Kernel', 'Pixie'. Culinary, *early*, 'Emmeth Early', 'Grenadier'; *midseason*, 'Golden Noble', 'Peasgood's Nonsuch'; *late*, 'Bramley's Seedling', 'Lane's Prince Albert'.

Possible problems: aphids, capsid bug, codling moth, sawfly, tortix moth, winter moth; brown rot, canker, crown gall, fireblight, powdery mildew, scab; bitter pit.

appressed see *adpressed*.

approximate of plant parts drawn very closely together, sometimes confused with proximate.

apricot (*Prunus armeniaca*). Found in the wild throughout Central Asia but probably originating in China. Apricot cultivation in England is documented from around the mid-16th century, and trees were distributed during the 18th and 19th centuries to flourish in warmer climates, including southern Europe, Australia, and the US, where there are now considerable areas of commercial plantation. Apricots need a warm, sunny, sheltered position and in cool temperate areas do best where fan-trained against a tall, south-facing wall. They may be similarly trained under greenhouse protection, and this is the most promising method for gardens in northerly latitudes. Since apricots are one of the earliest flowering fruits, protection from frost damage with temporary wall covers is desirable in cool areas.

Propagation is effected by grafting onto 'St. Julien A' plum rootstock or seedling apricot or peach. The dwarfing rootstock 'Pixy' is a possibility, but double working with 'St. Julien A' is necessary to overcome incompatibility. Apricots are self-fertile but benefit from hand pollination by lightly touching the open flowers with a camel-hair brush or rabbit's tail around midday. Flowers and fruit are borne on shoots of the previous year and on spurs on older wood. To encourage spur formation, developing laterals should be pinched back to 3 in (7.5 cm), or where growth is vigorous to 5½ in (14 cm); subsequent sublaterals should be shortened back to one leaf. Shoots needed to fill spaces must be tied in while still pliable.

Possible problems: birds, scale insects; bacterial canker (see *bacterial diseases*), Eutypa canker (see *canker*), peach leaf curl, rust, silverleaf.

Aptenia (*Greek apten*, wingless; the valves of the seed capsules lack wings). Aizoaceae. South Africa. 2 species, dwarf succulents with bushy, trailing stems and fleshy leaves. Small, daisylike flowers are produced during warm and sunny spells throughout the year. Useful for edging, groundcover, and baskets in frost-free gardens and, elsewhere, for outdoor summer display, and for the cool greenhouse. Pot in a sandy, loam-based mix; water moderately in spring and summer, very sparingly in winter. Position in full sun or light shade. Propagate by stem tip cuttings at any time of year. *A. cordifolia* (syn. *Mesembryanthemum cordifolium*) dwarf bush or cushion to 4¾ × 16 in (12 × 40 cm); leaves mid- to bright green, oval to heart-shaped, ¼–⅝ in (0.5–1.5 cm) long; flowers ½ in (1 cm) across, purple-red; 'Variegata': leaves bordered cream.

aquatic a plant growing in water. Aquatics are often divided into floating plants, submerged or oxygenating plants, and marginals.

Aquilegia (from Latin *aquila*, eagle, alluding to the aquiline spurs). Ranunculaceae. COLUMBINE, MEETING HOUSES, GRANNY'S BONNETS, HONEYSUCKLE. N Hemisphere. 70 species, short-lived, evergreen perennial herbs, with a short, erect rhizome becoming woody, and a clump of rather ferny, ternately divided leaves, basically triangular in outline with wedge-shaped to rounded leaflets, their margins often cleft or cut. The flowers appear in summer, one to several atop a slender stem. They consist of five petal-like sepals, often spreading to reflexed, and five petals pointing forward in a cup and projecting behind as slender, nectar-filled spurs. They are fully hardy, but species from the southwest US prefer a warm and sheltered situation and are intolerant of wet winter conditions—as are *A. alpina*, *A. jonesii*, and *A. viridiflora*, which are smaller plants suited to protected niches in the rock garden or pots in the alpine house. Grow in full sun in fertile, free-draining soil. Sow seed *in situ* in spring or fall. These plants hybridize freely and are in any case highly variable. Unless kept far apart or painstakingly pollinated, seed races and cultivars are unlikely to come true from seed, although a few, like *A. vulgaris* 'Nora Barlow', are reliable. Susceptible to mildew.

A. alpina ALPINE COLUMBINE; Alps;6–32 in (15–80 cm) tall; flowers nodding, sepals bright blue to violet, to 1½ in (4 cm) long, petals shorter and paler, sometimes white, spurs straight or curved, to ¾ in (2 cm); *A. alrata* Alps, Apennines; to 32 in (80 cm) tall; flowers nodding, rich purple-violet to darkest maroon, sepals to 1½ in (4 cm), petals shorter, spurs to ½ in (1 cm), hooked; *A. coerulea* ROCKY MOUNTAINS COLUMBINE; W US; to 24 in (60 cm) tall; flowers erect, sepals to 1½ in (4 cm), blue, pink or white, petals shorter, white or cream, spurs to 2 in (5 cm), straight or curved; includes the snow-white 'Candidissima', long-spurred blue and white 'Heavenly Blue', 'Helenae', a vivid blue cross with *A. flabellata*, the pale pink 'Coral', and 'Rostern' with carmine and cream flowers; *A. canadensis* CANADIAN COLUMBINE, MEETING HOUSES, HONEYSUCKLE; eastern N America; 12–24 in (30–60 cm) tall; flowers nodding; sepals to ⅝ in (1.5 cm), not reflexed, red, petals to ½ in (1 cm), yellow, spurs to 1 in (2.5 cm), straight, red; *A. chrysantha* YELLOW COLUMBINE; SW US; 12–40 in (30–100 cm) tall; flowers held horizontally, sepals to 1¼ in (3 cm), yellow sometimes tinged pink, petals shorter, yellow, spurs 1¼–2¾ in (3–7 cm), curving outward; includes the creamy white 'Alba', the double-flowered 'Florepleno', large, primrose yellow 'Grandiflora Sulphurea', and large, golden 'Yellow Queen'; *A. flabellata* E Asia; 8–20 in

(20–50 cm) tall; flowers nodding, sepals to 1 in (2.5 cm), blue-purple to lilac or white, petals shorter, white or pale lilac tipped yellow-white, spurs to ¾ in (2 cm), curving; var. *pumila* 'Alba' is dwarf and white-flowered; *A. formosa* WESTERN COLUMBINE; western N America; 20–40 in (50–100 cm) tall; flowers nodding, sepals to 1 in (2.5 cm), red, petals shorter, yellow, spurs stout, straight, red; includes dwarf forms with paler, or white flowers, the double, red 'Rubraplena', and var. *truncata* (syn. *A. californica*), a tall plant with flame-colored sepals and very short golden petals. *A. jonesii* Rocky Mountains; to 4 in (10 cm) tall, flowers erect on short, slender stems, sepals to ⅝ in (1.5 cm), blue to purple, petals shorter, blue, broad, spur to ½ in (1 cm), incurved; *A. longissima* SW US, to 40 in (100 cm); flowers erect, sepals 1 in (2.5 cm), yellow sometimes tinged red, petals same length as sepals, yellow, spurs to 6 in (15 cm) long, very slender, straight to drooping; *A. scopulorum* W US; 4–8 in (10–20 cm) tall; flowers erect, sepals to ¾ in (2 cm), blue to white, sometimes red, petals shorter, white to pale yellow, spur 1¼–2 in (3–5 cm), straight, blue to red; *A. viridiflora* Siberia, China; 6–12 in (15–30 cm); flowers to 1¼ in (3 cm) nodding, fragrant, sepals to ¾ in (2 cm), green, petals shorter, chocolate to maroon; *A. vulgaris* GRANNY'S BONNETS, COLUMBINE; Europe, naturalized N America; 12–28 in (30–70 cm) tall; flowers nodding, blue to purple, red or white, sepals to 1 in (2.5 cm), petals shorter usually white to yellow, petals shorter, spurs to ¾ in (2 cm), strongly hooked; many cultivars and seed races developed with yellow, white, pink, rose, red-purple, lilac, mauve, sky blue and dark blue flowers, some bicolored, double, or lacking spurs; one of the most intriguing cultivars is 'Nora Barlow' × pompon flowers with ragged sepals and petals in pale red or pink edged lime green and fading to cream;

Reflexed sepals and spurs give impression of bird in flight

Aquilegia 'Crimson Star'

another group of cultivars, variously called 'Woodside' or Vervaeneana Group, has leaves that are variegated lime and gold.

Arabis (from Greek *arabia*, Arabia). Cruciferae. North America, Europe, Asia. ROCK CRESS. 120 species, small, hardy, annual to perennial herbs with spathulate to obovate leaves, often toothed and hairy, and 4-petaled flowers in racemes in spring and summer. Suitable for the rock garden, dry walls, and the alpine house. Grow in full sun in fast-draining, loamy soil with added grit. Propagate by softwood cuttings in summer in a sandy mix in a shaded frame, or by division or seed in spring and fall. Attacked by arabis midge: affected parts should be destroyed.

A. alpina Europe; 2–16 in (5–40 cm); flowers white or, rarely, pink; includes small, large, white, rose and variegated cultivars; subsp. *caucasica* (syn. *A. albida*) South Europe; similar to *A. alpina*, with gray-green leaves; flowers white to pink; includes cultivars with variegated leaves and double flowers; *A.* × *arendsii* (a garden hybrid between *A. aubretioides* and *A. alpina* subsp. *caucasica* with rose-red flowers; includes several cultivars with flowers ranging through pink, red, lilac and maroon; *A. blepharophylla* California; to 4 in (10 cm); flowers rose-purple; includes white and carmine cultivars; *A. ferdinandi-coburgi* Bulgaria; to 8 in (20 cm) tall; flowers white; includes cultivars with ivory-, lime- and gold-variegated leaves.

arabis mosaic virus a disease that affects many different plants but is actually insignificant on *Arabis*. It causes raspberry yellow dwarf disease, where leaves show yellow spots and yellow vein clearing; affected plants are stunted and produce few fruits. It is one of several viruses that affect rhubarb and strawberry with a yellow

leaf mosaic and general stunting. Among susceptible ornamentals are *Forsythia*, jasmine, privet, *Sambucus*, and *Syringa*. Most strains of the virus are spread by the root feeding of *Xiphenema diversicaudatum*, a free-living, plant-parasitic soil nematode. Nematodes acquire and transmit the virus very rapidly: they survive in soil for a long time, remaining infectious, and cannot be eradicated easily. Infected plants must be removed; where appropriate, plant virus-free stocks, on new sites. See *virus*.

Arachnis (from Greek *arachnis*, spider, referring to the appearance of the flowers). Orchidaceae. SE Asia. SCORPION ORCHID. 7 species, tender evergreen orchids with tall, slender scrambling stems clothed with strap-shaped leaves. Carried in slender racemes and panicles throughout the year, the flowers are waxy and consist of five, narrowly oblanceolate, curving tepals and a small, tonguelike lip. The flowers are long-lived, last very well when cut, and are common in floristry. Cultivation as for *Vanda* but with a minimum temperature of 59°F (15°C), full sun and high humidity. *A. flos-aeris* flowers to 2¾ in (7 cm) across, dark green, cream, pale rust or dull, fiery orange with broad, maroon to fox red or chocolate bands.

arachnoid interlaced with a cobweb of fine white hair, as in the leaves of some tightly growing succulent rosette plants.

Aralia (from the French-Canadian name *aralie*). Araliaceae. Asia; Americas. 40 species, evergreen or deciduous trees, shrubs, climbers and suckering herbs, often with prickly stems and leafstalks and 1–3 × pinnately compound leaves. The flowers are small, green-white and produced in abundant umbels on large panicles in spring and summer. Plant in full sun or light shade in a sheltered position on a freely draining but moist and fertile loam. The following species is hardy but will produce taller stems and more luxuriant foliage in warm, protected locations. Old or cold-damaged stems will die and should be cut out cleanly at the base. They will be replaced by new suckers. Propagate by division of clumps, removal of rooted suckers and root cuttings potted in early spring and rooted in heat. *A. elata* (syn. *A. chinensis*) JAPANESE ANGELICA TREE E Russia, China, Korea, Japan; clump-forming suckering, deciduous shrub to 30 ft (10 m); stems narrow, pithy, sparsely branched, erect and spiny; leaves to 5 ft (1.5 m) long, triangular in outline, bipinnate with toothed mid- to gray-green leaflets to 4¾ in (12 cm) long; inflorescence creamy-white, to 3¼ ft (1 m), assuming a pink tint as the summer advances; fruit glossy, purple-black; 'Albovariegata': syn.. 'Variegata', leaflets edged white; 'Aureomarginata': leaflets edged yellow.

araneous see *arachnoid*.

Araucaria (from the Arauco Indians of Central Chile, to whose territory *A. araucana* is native). Araucariaceae. SW Pacific; S America. 20 species, evergreen, coniferous trees with erect stems, resinous bark and whorled branches in a candelabra-like head, each branch with pinnately arranged, drooping to ascending branchlets clothed with scale- or needlelike, overlapping leaves. The following are widely grown and will withstand harsh winds, full sun, and all but the wettest or driest soils. Only *A. araucana* is fully hardy. Young plants of *A. heterophylla* make attractive house and conservatory plants. Increase by seed.

A. araucana (syn. *A. imbricata*) CHILE PINE, MONKEY PUZZLE TREE; Chile, Patagonia; trunk columnar, dark, to 100 ft (30 m) tall with a head of drooping then ascending branches with rope-like branchlets densely covered in ¾–2¾-in- (2–7-cm-) long, triangular, dark green, tough and sharp-tipped leaves; *A. bidwillii* BUNYA BUNYA; Queensland; narrow to broadly domed tree to 150 ft (45 m) tall with whorls of spreading branches hung with weeping branchlets; juvenile leaves ¾–2 in (2–5 cm) long, oblong to lanceolate, sharp-tipped glossy and arranged in a spiral, adult leaves shorter, ovate, sharp-tipped, very tough and overlapping; *A. cunninghamii* Northern Australia, New Guinea; HOOP or MORETON BAY PINE; to 200 ft (60 m) tall with spreading to upswept branches bare at their bases

and tufted with drooping twigs at the tips, ½–¾-in- (1–2-cm-) long leaves needle- to scalelike, olive to gray-green; *A. heterophylla* (syn. *A. excelsa*) NORFOLK ISLAND or HOUSE PINE; Norfolk Islands; to 200 ft (60 m) tall, strongly pyramidal; branches outspread, whorled, clothed with scalelike leaves to ¼ in (0.6 cm) long; juvenile plants have soft, slender branches covered in needlelike, gray-green leaves. These are marked silver-white in 'Albospica', golden-striped in 'Aureovariegata' and blue-green in 'Glauca'.

Araujia (from the Brazilian vernacular name for this plant). Asclepiadaceae. South America. 4 species, evergreen, woody-based perennial climbers grown for their flowers produced in summer. Provide a minimum temperature of 50°F (10°C). Plant in moist, fertile soil; provide ample humidity and bright, filtered light. Propagate by tip cuttings. *A. sericifera* (syn. *A. sericofera*) CRUEL PLANT; climbing to 30 ft (10 m); flowers to 1¼ in (3 cm) diam., fragrant, salverform, white sometimes striped maroon within.

arborescent with the habit or stature of a tree.

arboretum a garden or park that is devoted to a collection of trees and shrubs. Planted since ancient times, arboretums became popular in Europe in the late 18th century and have since served scientific as well as amenity purposes.

arbor a shady enclosure or retreat surrounded by trees or shrubs or trellis clad with climbing plants, often at the end of, or in conjunction with, a pergola. Known in the Middle Ages as herbers, they were then often extended to form long tunnel arbors. In 16th-century usage, the term also meant an herb or flower garden, grassy sward, or orchard, and in the 18th century included garden-houses.

arboriculture the science and practice of tree-growing, especially the establishment and maintenance of trees and shrubs in amenity and ornamental areas.

Arbutus (the Classical Latin name). Ericaceae. N and C America, Europe, Asia Minor. MADRONE, MANZANITA, STRAWBERRY TREE. 14 species, evergreen trees and shrubs with flaking to peeling bark, tough-textured, dark green leaves and small, lily-of-the-valley-like flowers in racemes and panicles. The fruits are globose and fleshy, usually warm, glowing red and textured with small, prismatic bumps. *A. unedo* and *A. × andrachnoides* are hardy to 5°F (−15°C); *A. andrachne* and *A. menziesii* to 14°F (−10°C). All prefer full sun, acidic to neutral soil, and shelter from cold, drying winds. Propagate by basal cuttings taken in late winter, or by simple layering. Seed sown with the flesh removed and stratified for 4–6 weeks at or just above freezing point will usually germinate when brought under glass.

A. andrachne GRECIAN STRAWBERRY TREE; SE Europe, Asia Minor; spreading tree or large shrub to 40 ft (12 m) tall with peeling, red-brown bark; leaves to 4 in (10 cm) long, oval to oblong, entire, dark green above, paler beneath; flowers in late spring, dull white in erect panicles to 4 in (10 cm) long; fruit orange, granular, ⅝ in (1.5 cm) diam.; many plants cultivated under this name are *A. × andrachnoides*; *A. × andrachnoides* (naturally occurring hybrid between the last species and *A. unedo*) spreading tree or large shrub to 30 ft (10 m) with rusty red, peeling bark; leaves to 4 in (10 cm) long, oval to elliptic, finely serrate, dark green above, paler beneath; flowers in late fall or spring, ivory to white in nodding panicles; fruit to ½ in (1 cm) diam., smoother than in *A. unedo*; *A. menziesii* STRAWBERRY TREE; W US; tree to 100 ft (30 m) with peeling red bark; leaves to 6 in (15 cm) long, elliptic to ovate, blunt, entire or sometimes serrate on young plants, dark green above, glaucous beneath; flowers in late spring, white in erect, pyramidal panicles to 6 in (15 cm) long; fruit to ⅝ in (1.5 cm) diam.; *A. unedo* STRAWBERRY TREE; S Europe to Asia Minor, Eire; shrub or small, broad-crowned tree to 30 ft (10 m) tall, with coarse, flaking, red-brown bark; leaves to 2¾ in (7 cm) long, elliptic to obovate, serrate, glossy dark green above, paler beneath; flowers appear in late fall, cream to white, pink or red-stained (f. *rubra*) in drooping panicles to 2¾ in (7 cm) long; fruit to ¾ in (2 cm) diam., surface rough and granular, edible).

arcade a series of trained-plant arches forming a decorative garden feature; a pergola walk. Arcades are often constructed by training tree fruits to meet at the top.

Arctostaphylos (from Greek *arktos*, bear, and *staphule*, fruit: bears are said to eat the berries). Ericaceae. Northern Hemisphere. BEARBERRY; MANZANITA. 50 species, evergreen or semievergreen shrubs and small trees with small, urn- to bell-shaped flowers in terminal racemes and panicles and spherical, red to purple-black or brown berrylike fruit. The following are hardy and prefer full sun in moist, acidic soil. Propagate by simple layering in spring, severing rooted stems of trailing species, or semiripe cuttings in summer.

A. alpina (syn. *Arctous alpinus*) ALPINE BEARBERRY, BLACK BEARBERRY Circumpolar regions; dwarf, creeping shrub to 6 in (15 cm) tall; leaves to 1¼ in (3 cm), oblanceolate, finely serrate, fresh green in summer, red in fall; flowers white flushed pink; *A. diversifolia* (syn. *Comarostaphylis diversifolia*) SUMMER HOLLY; California; erect shrub to 12 ft (4 m) tall; leaves 1¼–3 in (3–8 cm), oblong to broadly elliptic, toothed to entire, glossy; flowers white; *A. manzanita* MANZANITA; California; shrub or tree, erect, to 20 ft (6 m), with purple-red bark and a gnarled habit; leaves to 2 in (5 cm), broadly ovate, pale to gray-green; flowers white to pink in drooping panicles; *A. nevadensis* PINEMAT MANZANITA; W US; mat-forming, to 16 in (40 cm) tall; leaves to 1¼ in (3 cm), lanceolate to obovate with a short, distinct tip, light green; flowers white to pink; *A. nummularia* FORT BRAGG MANZANITA; California; mat-forming or rounded shrub; leaves to ⅝ in (1.5 cm), elliptic to ovate, shiny; flowers white; *A. patula* GREEN LEAF MAN; California; erect shrub to 6½ ft (2 m) tall; leaves to 2 in (5 cm), broadly oval to oblong, blunt and rounded, thick-textured; flowers pink, in broad panicles; *A. uva-ursi* COMMON BEARBERRY, KINNI KINICK, MOUNTAIN BOX; N America, N Europe, N Asia; mat-

forming shrub with creeping and rooting stems; leaves to 1¼ in (3 cm), obovate, dark green above, paler beneath, often turning red in winter; flowers white tinted pink; includes several ground-smothering cultivars with bright, glossy foliage and pink to white flowers, e.g., 'Point Reyes', 'Radiant', 'Vancouver Jade'; the California native, *A. hookeri*, MONTEREY MANZANITA, is sometimes treated as a subspecies of *A. uva-ursi*; it forms a dense mound 4–40 in (10–100 cm) high with shining bright green leaves to ¾ in (2 cm); white or pink flowers, one of the best groundcover cultivars is 'Monterey Carpet'.

Arctotheca (from Greek *arktos*, bear, and *theke*, chest). Compositae. South Africa. 5 species, stemless to creeping perennial herbs with lyrate to pinnately lobed leaves and daisylike flower heads. In frost-free regions, the following species is used for covering dry, sunny banks and rock gardens; in cooler zones, it is treated as an annual. Sow seed *in situ* in spring. *A. calendula* CAPE WEED; fast-spreading groundcover; flower heads to 2 in (5 cm) diam., bright yellow, on stalks to 20 in (50 cm) tall.

Arctotis (from Greek, *arktos*, bear, and *ous*, ear). Compositae. South Africa. AFRICAN DAISY. 50 species, annual or perennial herbs with low rosettes of gray-scurfy, pinnately lobed leaves and bright, daisylike flower heads in summer. Use as half-hardy bedding plants, repropagated annually by stem cuttings taken in late summer and overwintered in a heated greenhouse, or raised from seed in spring. Grow in full sun in light, fast-draining soil.

A. fastuosa (syn. *Venidium fastuosum*) CAPE DAISY, MONARCH OF THE VELDT; leaves gray-white-hairy; flower heads to 3 in (8 cm) diam., ray florets orange, purple-brown at base, disk florets maroon to black; *A.* × *hybrida* (syn. × *Venidioarctotis hybrida*) garden hybrids between *A. fastuosa* and *A. venusta*; leaves covered with thin, gray-white felt; flower heads to 4 in (10 cm) diam., on stalks to 8 in (20 cm) tall, ranging in color from gray-blue to white, cream, apricot, peach, yellow, orange, bronze, carmine and wine red, usually with darker centers; *A. venusta* (syn. *A.*

stoechadifolia) BLUE-EYED AFRICAN DAISY; to 24 in (60 cm) tall; leaves with gray-white hair especially beneath; flower heads to 2¾ in (7 cm) diam., white to purple-red with a blue to blue-red center.

arcuate curved downward, bow-shaped, usually applied to a smaller, more rigid structure than would be described as arching—for example, the column of an orchid.

arcure an unusual and decorative system of training fruit trees, used especially for apples and pears, and involving bending branches to form tiers of spur-bearing loops.

Ardisia (from Latin, *ardis*, a point, referring to the acutely pointed anthers). Myrsinaceae. Asia, Australasia, Americas. 250 species, evergreen trees, shrubs and subshrubs with whorled, tough leaves, small 5-parted flowers in stalked, axillary clusters and berrylike fruit. *A. crenata* is grown as a potted plant in the cool greenhouse, conservatory, or home. It needs bright, filtered light. Grown as a standard, up to 3 ft (1 m) tall with a clear stem, this species tends naturally to display its fruit in a ring of trusses below a mop of deep green growth, making a beautiful houseplant, particularly at Christmas. *A. japonica* will tolerate mild frosts and makes handsome groundcover for lightly shaded, moist and fertile sites in mild climates. Trim in spring. Can be propagated by seed sown in spring, or by semiripe cuttings in summer.

A. crenata (syn. *A. crenulata*, *A. crispa*) Asia CORALBERRY, SPICEBERRY; shrub to 6½ ft (2 m) tall; leaves 2½–8 in (6–20 cm) long, elliptic to narrowly obovate, deep, glossy green with finely wavy-toothed margins, edged creamy-white in 'Variegata'; flowers white to pink in clusters at the end of slender stalks among and beneath the leaves; berries coral-pink to scarlet; *A. japonica* MARLBERRY; China, Japan; low, spreading shrub with creeping and rooting stems and erect shoots to 16 in (40 cm) high; leaves 2–2¾ in (5–7 cm)-long, oval to ovate, glossy dark green, sharply toothed; flowers white to pale pink on short racemes; cultivars exist with leaves variously toothed and frilled and marked white, cream, gold, and pink).

Arenaria (from Latin *arena*, sand—the plants grow in sandy places). Caryophyllaceae. Widespread, especially in northern temperate regions. SANDWORT. 160 species, low-growing, hardy perennial herbs with white, usually 5-petaled flowers. Suitable for sunny positions in fast-draining soil. Propagate by division, seed or (larger species) by softwood cuttings of basal shoots in early summer.

A. balearica W Mediterranean Islands; mat-forming; flowers to ½ in (1 cm) diam., white; *A. montana* SW Europe; gray-green and downy with prostrate shoots; flowers ¾–1½ in (2–4 cm) diam., white, similar to *Cerastium*, but with entire, not cleft petals; *A. purpurascens* Pyrenees, N Spain; loosely tufted with branching stems ascending to 4 in (10 cm); flowers to ¾ in (2 cm) diam., pale purple, pink or white; *A. tetraquetra* Pyrenees, N Spain; small, gray-green cushion-forming; flowers very short-stalked, to ½ in (1 cm) across, white, with four petals.

areole a small area or space, often between anastomosing veins; also a depression or elevation on a cactus stem, bearing spines.

Argemone (from Latin, *argema*, eye cataract: the genus was once used as a treatment for this condition). Papaveraceae. Americas. PRICKLY POPPY; ARGEMONY. 28 species, annual or perennial herbs and one shrub; the prickly stems contain yellow or orange latex. The leaves are glaucous and lobed with fiercely prickly margins. Poppylike flowers are composed of usually six, broadly wedge-shaped petals and appear in summer. The seed pods are fiercely prickly. Sow under glass in early spring and plant out after the last frost in a sunny, well-drained position. Seed may also be sown *in situ* in late spring. *A. mexicana* DEVIL'S FIG, MEXICAN POPPY, PRICKLY POPPY; SW US, C America, W Indies; annual to 3¼ ft (1 m); leaves glaucous blue-green with silvery white flashes on the veins and spiny-lobed margins; flowers 2–2¾ in (5–7 cm)-wide bright to pale yellow, white or pale tangerine.

Argyranthemum (from Greek, *argyros*, silver, and *anthemos*, flower). Compositae. Canary Islands. Some 23 species, perennial, half-hardy subshrubs or shrubs with entire to dissected leaves and slender-stalked, daisylike flower heads from late spring to fall. Marguerites are bright and trouble-free perennials for frost-free gardens or cool greenhouses and conservatories. They are equally among the finest half-hardy summer bedding or container plants in cooler regions. Grow in full sun in well-drained soil. Deadhead regularly. Take stem cuttings in fall and overwinter them in a frost-free greenhouse where temperatures drop below 10°F (−12°C). Unless growing them to achieve height for training as standards, pinch out young plants to promote bushiness and plant them out in midspring.

A. frutescens (syn. *Chrysanthemum frutescens*) MARGUERITE; Canary Islands; a subshrub or shrub to 6½ ft (2 m) tall with finely pinnatisect, gray-green leaves to 4 in (10 cm) long and white flower heads to 2½ in (6 cm) across with bright yellow center. *Cultivars*: 'Chelsea Girl' to 28 in (70 cm), leaves very fine, flower heads white, single, 'Jamaica Primrose' to 3¼ ft (1 m), leaves gray-green, coarsely cut, flower heads large, single, golden, 'Levada Cream' flower heads single, long-stalked, primrose to cream, 'Mary Cheek' to 16 in (40 cm), leaves fine, flower heads double, pink, 'Mrs. E. Sander' compact, leaves blue-gray, flower heads small, double, pompom-like, pure white, 'Peach Cheeks' low and spreading, flower heads single to double, peach pink to white with a yellow center, 'Petite Pink' to 16 in (40 cm), compact, leaves fine and slightly fleshy; flower heads single, pale pink with a golden center, 'Powder Puff' miniature with fine foliage and double, rather ragged-looking pink flower heads, 'Rollason's Red' to 16 in (40 cm), leaves coarse, flower heads single, ray florets crimson to scarlet, gold at the base, forming a bright ring around the dark red disk.

Argyreia (from Greek, *argyreios*, silvery, referring to the silver-hairy under-surfaces of the leaves of some species). Convolvulaceae. Tropical Asia to Australia. 90 species, perennial, evergreen, woody or woody-based climbers with large, rounded to heart-shaped leaves and showy funnel-shaped flowers. Provide a minimum temperature of 55°F (13°C), and full sun or bright, filtered light. Propagate by seed sown in spring in a heated case, or by softwood cuttings with bottom heat in spring. *A. nervosa* (syn. *A. speciosa*) WOOLLY MORNING GLORY, India, Bangladesh; to 30 ft (10 m); leaves coated beneath in silver hairs; flowers 2¾ in (7 cm)-long flowers tubular to funnel-shaped, lavender with a deep mauve throat and silkily hairy.

Argyroderma (from Greek, *argyros*, silver, and *derma*, skin, referring to the silvery leaf surface). Aizoaceae. South Africa. 10 species, evergreen perennial herbs with very succulent, smooth, gray-green leaves in pairs with their bases fused. These leaf pairs may be borne on dwarf shrubs or in stemless clusters or be solitary, and are often partially buried. Daisylike flowers appear in the cleft between the leaves. The following should be cultivated as for *Conophytum*.

A. delaetii (syn. *A. blandum*) stem largely subterranean; leaves semiovoid; flowers white, purple or yellow; *A. fissum* (syn. *A. brevipes*) mat-forming; leaves to 4¾ in (12 cm) long, yellow-green, finger-shaped; flowers with outer petals purple or yellow, inner petals white; *A. pearsonii* (syn. *A. schlechteri*) leaves semiglobose with a narrow fissure; flowers with outer petals purple, white or, rarely, white, inner petals yellow or white.

Ariocarpus (from *Aria*, a genus now included in *Sorbus*, and Greek, *karpos*, fruit, from a supposed resemblance between the fruits of these genera). Cactaceae. Texas, Mexico. 6 species, slow-growing cacti with thick rootstocks and unbranched, usually hemispherical to broadly conical stems. They are covered in large tubercles, usually spineless and bear openly funnelform flowers in fall and winter. Grow in full sun with a dry, airy atmosphere and a minimum temperature of 41°F (5°C). Plant in a gritty medium with a pH of 6–7.5; water liberally but intermittently in spring and summer; keep dry from midfall to early spring except for a light misting on warm days. Propagate by seed. Faster growth rates can be achieved by grafting of young plants. *A. fissuratus* (stem to 4 in (10 cm) diam., with prominent triangular tubercles, gray-green to gray-brown, each deeply fissured so as to resemble scales, and wrinkled with a woolly groove above; flowers to 1½ in (4 cm) diam., magenta.

aril a generally fleshy appendage of the funiculus or hilum, partially or entirely enveloping the seed.

arillate possessing an aril; more loosely, any outgrowth or appendage on the testa.

Arisaema (from *Arum* and Greek *haima*, blood red, a reference to the red-blotched petioles of some species). Araceae. N America, Africa, Asia. 150 species, tuberous or thickly rhizomatous deciduous perennial herbs with trifoliate to palmately or pedately compound, long-stalked leaves. Produced in spring and early summer, the small flowers are packed on a spadix which bears a terminal appendage and is enclosed in a showy, pitcherlike spathe with a hooded to erect, ovate to lanceolate blade. They favor light shade and moist (but never wet), acidic to neutral soil rich in sand and leaf mold. Those described here are hardy to 0°F (−18°C) but may deteriorate when planted in regions with prolonged hard frost and wet winters. Mulch thickly in winter. Propagate by seed sown when fresh in the cold frame, or by separating offsets and cormels produced by long-established plants.

A. candidissimum China; spathe 3–6 in (8–15 cm) long, tube pale green striped white, limb white striped or zoned cool, candy pink, ovate to orbicular and slightly hooded with a tapered tip; *A. griffithii* Himalaya; spathe blade large, broad, in pearly gray with deep purple interior and green, netted veins, arching forward and curving over itself,

Fleshy yew fruits are correctly named "arils"

Taxus baccata

undersurface dull purple overlaid with an intricate network of green veins; spadix largely hidden, but ending in long, slender appendage; *A. sikokianum* Japan; spathe 8 in (20 cm) long, tube dark, satiny maroon to black outside and snow white within, blade erect, ovate, acuminate, purple-green striped green-white within, far darker beneath and striped silvery white; spadix terminates just above the rim of the spathe in a bright white knob; *A. triphyllum* JACK-IN-THE-PULPIT, INDIAN TURNIP; Eastern North America; spathe to 6 in (15 cm) long and yellow-green to purple, striped green or white with an erect to arching, tapering limb, the spadix narrowly club-shaped, green to purple and protruding from the tube.

Arisarum (from Greek *aris-aron*, the name for *A. vulgare*). Araceae. Mediterranean; Southwest Europe; Atlantic Islands 3 species, tuberous or rhizomatous perennial herbs, deciduous or semievergreen with slender-stalked, arrow-shaped, dark green leaves borne close to the ground, and low-lying inflorescences produced in spring. These consist of a spathe, tubular below and hooded above, with a finely tapering tip, the whole surrounding a slender spadix. They tend to lie beneath or just above the dense cover of foliage. Hardy to 14°F (−10°C), or lower if mulched. *A. proboscideum* requires moist soil in dappled sunlight or full shade. *A. vulgare* prefers a sunnier, slightly drier location in gritty soil. Propagate by division when dormant (for *A. proboscideum* this is late summer; for *A. vulgare*, late spring).

A. proboscideum MOUSE PLANT; Italy and Spain; rhizomatous; spathes 2½–4 in (6–10 cm) long; white and bulbous at the base, chocolate-brown to maroon-black above where a hooded blade narrows sharply to a long and upturned tip (the mouse's "tail"); spadix purple-brown, white-tipped, fully enclosed; *A. vulgare* FRIAR'S COWL;

Mediterranean, Canaries, Azores; tuberous; spathes 1½–2½ in (4–6 cm)-long, silver-white striped purple-brown at base, solid metallic maroon to violet-black above where the hooded blade expands and curves over like a cowl; spadix purple-green, protruding.

aristate of a leaf apex abruptly terminated in a very slender, pointed continuation of the midrib. It may also mean awned.

Aristea (from Greek *arista*, a point, referring to the leaves). Iridaceae. Africa; Madagascar (those below from South Africa). 50 species, rhizomatous, evergreen perennial herbs, clump-forming with erect, grassy to swordlike leaves and, in summer, tall, narrow panicles bearing spikes of short-lived, 6-parted flowers. Grow in a well-drained, acidic medium. Position in part shade or bright, filtered light; provide a minimum temperature of 45°F (7°C), good ventilation and plentiful water when in growth. In mild locations, they may survive frosts, especially if dry and mulched. Propagate by division after flowering, or by seed in sown spring at 68°F (20°C).

A. ecklonii to 36 in (90 cm) tall with lax clusters of blue flowers to 1¼ in (3 cm) across; *A. major* (syn. *A. thyrsiflora*) to 3¼ ft (1 m) tall with dense clusters of mauve to pale blue flowers to 2 in (5 cm) across.

Aristolochia (from Greek *aristos*, best, and *lochia*, childbirth—because of its fetus-shaped flowers, *A. clematitis* was used in medieval times as an abortifacient and birth-inducer. Aristolochiaceae. Cosmopolitan. BIRTHWORT; DUTCHMAN'S PIPE. 300 species, evergreen or deciduous woody or herbaceous, twining climbers and erect herbaceous perennials. Produced in spring and summer, the flowers are axillary and pitcherlike with a swollen, inflated base that narrows to a slender tube curving upward to an expanded limb. The hardy species are deciduous or semievergreen. Grow *A. clematitis* in full sun in well-drained, fertile, and free-draining soil. In exposed positions, the stems may require some support. Propagate by division or cuttings in early spring. *A. macrophylla* and

A. sempervirens favor a sheltered position in rich, moist soil, the first in dappled sun or semishade, the second in full sun. Support on trellis, walls, pergolas or tree trunks. The tender species are evergreen or briefly deciduous. *A. fimbriata* and *A. littoralis* require moist, fertile soil in bright, filtered light with a minimum temperature of 50°F (10°C). Train on wires or pergola; cut back hard in early spring. The remaining species need a minimum temperature of 59°F (15°C), bright, filtered light and high humidity. Grow in moist and fertile, loamy soil and prune back hard after flowering. Most Aristolochias have malodorous flowers; although magnificent, the larger-flowered species can make a confined space almost unbearable. Propagate climbers by softwood cuttings—hardy species in midsummer, tender species in early spring using a rooting hormone and bottom heat. Multistemmed plants can also be divided. Seed needs three months of stratification at 41°F (5°C), or may be sown when ripe in fall after soaking in warm water for 48 hours. Surface sow under cover at 77°F (25°C).

A. clematitis BIRTHWORT; Europe; E N America; hardy, erect herb to 3¼ ft (1 m) tall; flowers to 1½ in (4 cm) long, yellow-green, slender with an erect, triangular limb; *A. cymbifera* Brazil; tender, woody climber to 30 ft (10 m); flowers to 8 in (20 cm) long, basically dirty white, base flasklike heavily mottled maroon, tube short and erect, limb divided into two lips, lower short and beaklike, marked maroon to violet, upper far longer and ruffled, hanging over the lower and expanding to a broad, blunt lobe intricately veined in purple or maroon; *A. fimbriata* Brazil; tender, herbaceous or woody-based climber to 6½ ft (2 m); leaves bright green veined yellow or silver; flowers to 2½ in (6 cm) long, base swollen and rounded, tube olive, short, erect, expanding to a round or reniform limb with a deeply fringed margin and velvety maroon veined gold; *A. gigantea* (syn. *A. clypeata*) Panama; tender woody climber to 30 ft (10 m); flowers to 12 in (30 cm) long, base buff, flask-shaped and prominently veined, tube short and curving upward to an inflated flesh-colored sac, limb very broadly ovate to triangular with a shortly taper-ing, ribbonlike tip, held upward and open like a scoop, white to ivory or yellow-orange, very heavily veined or blotched maroon to blood-red; *A. grandiflora* (syn. *A. gigas*) PELICAN FLOWER; Central America; tender woody climber to 50 ft (15 m); flowers to 10 ft (300 cm) long (including tail), base flask-shaped, heavily veined, white to buff or yellow-green, curving upward in a short, erect tube which becomes saclike then expands into a broadly heart-shaped, downward-pointing limb to 20 in (50 cm) across and tipped with a spiraling, ribbonlike tail to 6½ ft (2 m) long; the limb is white to olive, buff or rust heavily veined in dark brown-red, maroon or purple; *A.* × *kewensis* (*A. labiata* × *A. trilobata*) garden hybrid intermediate between parents; *A. labiata* (syn. *A. brasiliensis*) ROOSTER FLOWER; South America; tender woody climber to 30 ft (10 m) tall; flowers to 8 in (20 cm) long, cream to buff or brick red, mottled olive and yellow and veined red-brown to chestnut, base flask-shaped, tube short, slender, erect expanding in 2-lipped blade, lower lip beaklike, lanceolate and forward-pointing with the margins almost touching and rimmed, upper lip equal in length or slightly longer, broadly spathulate with margins ruffled and hanging downward; *A. littoralis* (syn. *A. elegans*) CALICO FLOWER; South America, naturalized Central America and Southern US; tender, woody-based climber to 20 ft (6 m) tall; flowers to 4 in (10 cm) long, base flask-shaped, white, narrowing and curving to white tube supporting a broad, heart-shaped to reniform limb which points upward and is golden-throated and white overlaid with rich, velvety purple mottling; *A. macrophylla* (syn. *A. durior*) DUTCHMAN'S PIPE; E US; hardy, woody-based climber to 28 ft (9 m) tall; flowers to 1½ in (4 cm) long, green spotted purple-brown and yellow, base swollen, tube curving upward like a pipe, limb with three spreading, rounded to acute lobes stained maroon; *A. ringens* (C America; tender woody climber; flowers to 11 in (28 cm) long, mottled red, yellow and green heavily veined red-brown to purple, base swollen and flask-shaped, tube slender, short and curving upward, limb divided into two lips, upper erect and forward-pointing,

spathulate with a frilled margin, lower longer and forward-pointing, chutelike, shaped like a tongue with its margins slightly inrolled; *A. sempervirens* Mediterranean to Aegean; hardy, woody-based climber to 15 ft (5 m); flowers yellow-green striped purple, to 2 in (5 cm) long, base swollen, tube slender, erect, expanding to a short, acute, erect limb; *A. trilobata* (syn. *A. macroura*) Central America; tender woody climber; flowers to 10 in (25 cm) long including tail, olive green veined and tipped brown to maroon, base swollen then narrowing and curving upward to an erect tube with a distinct rim and erect lid tipped with a long, downward-spiraling tail.

Aristotelia (for Aristotle). Elaeocarpaceae. Australasia; S America. 5 species, evergreen or deciduous trees and shrubs with small flowers in axillary clusters or panicles followed by glossy berries. Hardy to 14°F (−10°C). Plant in slightly acidic soil in sun; protect from winds. Propagate by ripewood cuttings, seed, or simple layers.

A. chilensis Chile; evergreen shrub or tree to 15 ft (5 m); leaves to 4 in (10 cm) long, ovate, toothed, glossy dark green, marked white in 'Variegata'; flowers green-white; fruit purple-black; *A. fruticosa* New Zealand; MOUNTAIN WINEBERRY; small evergreen shrub with intricate, wiry branches, narrow leaves, very small flowers and red to purple-black fruit; *A. serrata* New Zealand; NEW ZEALAND WINEBERRY; deciduous shrub or tree to 25 ft (8 m) tall; leaves to 4 in (10 cm) long, ovate, deeply serrate; flowers pale pink in crowded panicles; fruit dark red, ripening black.

aristulate bearing a small awn.

Armeria (a Latinized form of the old French vernacular name for sweet William, *armoires*, to which this genus was thought to bear some resemblance). Plumbaginaceae. Europe; Asia Minor; North Africa; Americas (Pacific coast). SEA PINK; THRIFT. Some 80 species, low-growing, tufted, evergreen perennial herbs or subshrubs with short-branching, cushion- to hummock-forming stems terminating in packed rosettes of very narrow, dark green leaves. Produced throughout the year but chiefly in spring and summer, the flowers are small, pink to white and 5-parted and carried amid chaffy bracts in dense heads atop slender, erect stalks. The most commonly grown species are *A. alpina*, *A. arenaria*, *A. juniperifola* (syn. *A. caespitosa*), *A. maritima*, and *A. pseudarmeria*. The flower stalks range in height from 2½ to 12 in (6 to 30 cm). They prefer fast-draining sandy soil in full sun, and are suitable for exposed positions in the rock garden, on dry banks and walls, especially in coastal regions. Although fully hardy, they dislike cold, wet conditions, but need ample moisture in spring. Propagate by seed or division in early spring.

armillaria root rot HONEY FUNGUS; BOOTLACE FUNGUS, a notorious, lethal root rot of trees, shrubs, and some herbaceous plants. *Armillaria mellea* is mostly responsible for infections of broad-leaved trees and shrubs in gardens; *A. ostoyae* is the main cause of death from this disease in conifers. First signs of infection may be a discoloration of foliage and progressive dieback of shoots, but symptoms only become visible when the fungus has invaded a significant part of the root system, and death can then follow rapidly. Other signs of infection may be an exceptional show of flowers, premature fall color, leaf-fall, and splitting of bark at or just above ground level, sometimes accompanied by a gummy exudate. If bark is lifted away from the collar and main roots, flat, often fan-shaped sheets of white fungal growth and/or flat black-brown strands may be present. The fungus also penetrates and decays the wood, in which narrow black "zone lines" occur.

In late summer or fall, toadstools may emerge in dense clusters around the base of dead tree stumps or other infected plants. These are extremely variable in size and color, but the cap and stalk are typically honey-colored at some stage of growth. The cap may be up to 9 in (23 cm) in diameter, the gills are white and there is a whitish ring attached to the upper part of the stalk. The fungus can spread by contact between diseased

and healthy roots; it also survives in dead tree stumps and roots, from which it sends out long black rhizomorphs resembling bootlaces, which grow through the topsoil to infect new host plants. A large dead tree or stump can be a source of rhizomorphs for many years, possibly having died from other causes and later been colonized by honey fungus. Spores from toadstools can theoretically infect newly exposed stumps, but this means of spread is unimportant. Trees and shrubs growing in gardens developed in or near woodland, orchards, or hedgerows are more likely to be attacked, particularly if growth is weakened for any reason.

The disease is incurable. In woodland, control is neither practicable nor necessary. In parkland or arboreta, trees should not be planted within 28 ft (9 m) of an infection site, and removal of the stump and root system of diseased trees is worthwhile. In gardens, orchards, and other closely-planted areas, disease control depends on the removal of all infected material. Measures need to be taken to prevent the disease from spreading by removing all infected root and stump material. Dead, dying, and adjacent plants should be removed with as much of the root system and surrounding soil as possible and the site refilled with soil from a non-woodland source. The use of chipping as a means of stump disposal goes some way toward eliminating the food source. Any chips that may be contaminated with fungus should be destroyed and not used as mulch. There is no risk of infection resulting from the use of commercial wood and bark mulches. Composted bark used for soil mixes is considered

black/brown strands on bark underside

Armillaria mellea
Honey fungus produces distinctive black "bootlace" growths that spread through the soil to new hosts.

to be quite safe.

If a neighboring source of infection cannot be removed, it may be possible to prevent the spread of rhizomorphs through the soil by means of a barrier made by burying heavy-gauge plastic sheeting, vertically, at least 20 in (0.5 m) deep in light soil or 3¼ ft (1 m) deep in clay soil. A narrow ditch, the bottom of which is cultivated, or a strip of ground that can be deeply cultivated, are other means of isolation.

The following lists of plants more susceptible or resistant to the disease are based on records kept at Wisley by the Royal Horticultural Society. More susceptible: *Acer* (except *A. negundo*) *Araucaria araucana*, *Betula*, *Buddleja*, *Ceanothus*, *Cedrus*, *Chamaecyparis*, *Cotoneaster*, *Crataegus*, × *Cupressocyparis leylandii*, *Cupressus*, *Forsythia*, *Hamamelis*, *Hydrangea*, *Juglans regia*, *Laburnum*, *Ligustrum*, *Malus*, *Paeonia*, *Picea omorika*, *Pinus* (except *P.patula*), *Prunus* (except *P.spinosa*), *Rhododendron*, *Ribes*, *Rosa*, *Rubus*, *Salix*, *Sequoiadendron giganteum*, *Syringa*, *Thuja plicata*, *Ulmus*, *Viburnum*, *Vitis*, *Wisteria*.

More resistant: *Abelia*, *Abeliophyllum*, *Abies alba*, *A. grandis*, *A. procera*, *Abutilon*, *Acer negundo*, *Actinidia*, *Ailanthus altissima*, *Akebia*, *Albizia*, *Aloysia*, *Arbutus menziesii*, *Aristolochia*, *Aronia*, *Artemisia*, *Aucuba*, bamboos, *Buxus sempervirens*, *Callicarpa*, *Callistemon*, *Calycanthus*, *Caragana*, *Carpenteria*, *Carya*, *Castanea*, *Catalpa*, *Celastrus*, *Celtis*, *Ceratostigma*, *Cercidiphyllum*, *Cercis*, *Cestrum*, *Chaenomeles*, *Chionanthus*, *Clematis*, *Clethra*, *Colutea*, *Corokia*, *Coronilla*, *Cotinus coggygria*, *Cunninghamia*, *Daboecia*, *Deutzia*, *Diervilla*, *Drimys*, *Elaeagnus*, *Embothrium*, *Enkianthus*, *Erica*, *Exochorda*, *Fabiana imbricata*, *Fagus sylvatica*, *Fothergilla*, *Fraxinus excelsior*, *Fremontodendron*, *Gaultheria*, *Gleditsia*, *Grevillea*, *Griselinia*, *Hakea*, *Halesia*, *Halimium*, *Hebe*, *Hedera*, *Helianthemum*, *Hippophae*, *Hoheria*, *Hypericum*, *Indigofera*, *Itea*, *Jasminum*, *Juniperus*, *Juglans hindsii*, *Kerria*, *Koelreuteria*, *Lagerstroemia*, *Larix*, *Laurus nobilis*, *Lavatera*, *Leptospermum*, *Leucothoe*, *Lindera*, *Lithospermum*, *Lomatia*, *Lonicera nitida*, *Maackia*, *Maclura*, *Mahonia aquifolium*, *Menziesia*, *Morus*, *Myrica*, *Myrtus*, *Nandina*, *Nothofagus*, *Nyssa*, *Oemleria*, *Ostrya*, *Paliurus*, *Parahebe*, *Parrotia*, *Passiflora*, *Paulownia*, *Phillyrea*,

Phlomis, Photinia, Phygelius, Phyllodoce, Physocarpus, Pieris, Pileostegia, Pinus patula, Pittosporum, Plagianthus, Podocarpus, Polygonum baldschuanicum, Prunus spinosa, Pseudotsuga menziesii, Ptelea, Pterocarya, Pterostyrax, Punica, Pyrus, Pyracantha, Quercus, Rhamnus, Rhus, Robinia, Romneya, Ruscus, Ruta, Sambucus, Santolina, Sarcococca, Sciadopitys, Shepherdia, Sophora, Stachyurus, Staphylea, Stephanandra, Stewartia, Styrax, Symphoricarpos, Symplocos, Tamarix, Taxus, Teucrium, Tilia, Ulex, Vaccinium, Yucca, Zelkova, Zenobia.

In the US, the following other trees and shrubs are reported to show resistance: French pear, fig, persimmon and the rootstock Myrobalan 29; *Acacia decurrens* var. *mollis, A. verticillata, Berberis darwinii, B.thunbergii, B.wilsoniae, Euonymus japonicus, Ilex aquifolium, Ligustrum japonicum, Prunus ilicifolia, P. lyonii, Pyracantha coccinea* 'Lalandei' and *Spiraea prunifolia*. The grading of plants as resistant or susceptible depends on disease records which are continually being added to, and these lists should not be regarded as definitive.

Armoracia (Classical name for horseradish). Cruciferae. Europe; Asia. 3 species, fully hardy perennial herbs with deep taproots, coarse, basal leaves and small, white flowers in racemes and panicles. *A. rusticana* is HORSERADISH (q.v.). The cultivar 'Variegata', with leaves splashed cream and white, is sometimes grown as an ornamental.

Arnebia (from the Arabian name). Boraginaceae. Europe; North Africa; Asia. PROPHET FLOWER; ARABIAN PRIMROSE. 25 species, bristly-hairy hardy annual or perennial herbs with 5-lobed, cup- to funnel-shaped flowers in simple or branched cymes in spring and summer. Plant in full sun or part shade in a sheltered position in cool, moist, but well-drained soil rich in humus and high in grit. Propagate by seed sown *in situ*.

A. densiflora Greece, Turkey; perennial to 16 in (40 cm) tall, velvety and bristly with yellow flowers to 1¾ in (4.5 cm) long; *A. pulchra* Caucasus, Iran, Asia Minor; a perennial to 16 in (40 cm) tall with flowers to 1 in (2.5 cm) long, rich yellow with purple-black spots on the lobes.

aroid A plant belonging to the family Araceae, characterized by an inflorescence made up of a spadix and spathe—for example, *Arum* and *Zantedeschia*.

Aronia (from *aria*, the Classical Greek name for whitebeam, *Sorbus aria*). Rosaceae. North America. CHOKEBERRY. 2 species, hardy deciduous shrubs with elliptic to oblong or oblanceolate, wavy-toothed leaves, corymbs of small, white to pink flowers in summer, and red, purple or black berrylike fruit. Cultivate as for the smaller *Amelanchier* species.

A. arbutifolia to 6½ ft (2 m) tall; leaves dull, turning scarlet in fall; flowers in gray-hairy corymbs; fruit bright red; 'Brilliant': scarlet fall color and fruit; *A. melanocarpa* differs from the last species in its shiny leaves turning red-brown in fall, its glabrous corymbs of and its black fruit.

Arrhenatherum (from Greek *arren*, male, and *ather*, bristle, a reference to the awned male flowers). Gramineae. Europe; Africa; Asia. OAT GRASS 6 species, perennial grasses with slender, erect to spreading culms and narrow leaves, bearing airy panicles of papery, long-awned florets in summer. Somewhat invasive and not entirely ornamental, the typical *A. elatius* is seldom cultivated, although the panicles are attractive if cut and dried. *A.* 'Variegatum' is, however, one of the purest-white of the variegated grasses. It requires regular division and replanting to maintain quality and vigor. It will grow in any moderately fertile soil in sun or part shade. It suffers in regions with long, hot summers and may enter dormancy. *A. elatius (Avena elatior* is the FALSE OAT) FRENCH RYE; tussock-forming and to 3¼ ft (1 m) tall with loose, purple-tinted and lustrous panicles; 'Variegatum': leaves edged and striped pure white.

Artemisia (for Artemis, Greek goddess of chastity). Compositae. Northern Hemisphere; South America; South Africa. MUGWORT; SAGEBRUSH; WORMWOOD; LAD'S LOVE; OLD MAN. 300 species, aromatic annual, biennial and perennial herbs and subshrubs (those here usually perennial subshrubs

and shrubs), with entire to toothed or lobed leaves often covered in short, silvery hair, and buttonlike, yellow and gray flower heads carried in terminal racemes and panicles. The larger species and cultivars will grace any mixed border, but work especially well in warm sunny places, often in poor soil. They prefer full sun and fast-draining, gritty, neutral to alkaline soil. Clump-formers can be cut back in early spring; more shrubby types should be pruned only sparingly and then to remove frost-damaged or exhausted growth. Mulch at the limits of hardiness. Low-growing and truly prostrate plants, such as *A. caucasica, A. schmidtiana*, and *A. stelleriana* 'Mori' grow well on sunny rock gardens, dry banks and walls. Propagate by division in spring or fall, or (shrubby species) by softwood or heeled, semiripe cuttings in summer. The following are hardy to 0°F (–18°C), or lower still if mulched in winter.

A. abrotanum LAD'S LOVE, OLD MAN, SOUTHERNWOOD; origin uncertain, naturalized in South and Central Europe; erect to 3¼ ft (1 m), stems clumped, more or less woody; leaves olive to dull gray-green, very finely cut into many slender lobes; *A. absinthium* ABSINTH, WORMWOOD, OLD MAN, LAD'S LOVE; Europe, Asia; bushy erect, woody-based, to 3¼ ft (1 m) tall; leaves finely 2–3-pinnately cut, silver-hairy; the cultivar 'Lambrook Silver' is massed with very fine, silver-gray foliage; *A. arborescens* Mediterranean; erect to sprawling shrub to 3¼ ft (1 m) tall with gray-green, finely cut foliage; 'Faith Raven': somewhat hardier with silver-white leaves; *A. armeniaca* (syn. *A. canescens*) Russia, Caucasus, Iran; erect, bushy, 12–39 in (30–100 cm) tall with silver-hairy, gray leaves cut into many filigree-like lobes; *A. caucasica* (syn. *A. assoana, A. pedemontana*) Spain to Ukraine; tufted, prostrate subshrub to 12 in (30 cm) tall with silver-white, ferny foliage; *A. frigida* Russia; woody-based, tufted and mat-forming, to 20 in (50 cm) tall with finely pinnately to palmately cut leaves, gray-white with linear lobes; *A. lactiflora* WHITE MUGWORT; China; vigorous, erect perennial with clumped, usually herbaceous stems and large, jaggedly cut dark green leaves; the flower heads are gray-white and carried in massive panicles; 'Guizhou' is strongly flushed purple to maroon with white flower heads; 'Variegata' has gray-cream variegated leaves; *A. ludoviciana* WESTERN MUGWORT, WHITE SAGE, CUDWEED; western US, Mexico; erect and bushy, woody-based perennial herb to 3¼ ft (1 m) tall with clumped stems and gray-silver, lanceolate leaves entire to jaggedly toothed or divided; includes the finely cut 'Silver Frost' and 'Silver King', the jagged 'Silver Queen' and 'Valerie Finnis'; var. *albula* has virtually white leaves, while var. *latiloba* has silver leaves with broad, sharp lobes; *A. pontica* ROMAN WORMWOOD; Europe; erect, bushy perennial to 32 in (80 cm) tall with clumped stems and feathery, sage green to pewter gray leaves; 'Old Warrior': to 20 in (50 cm). densely bushy and neat with very finely cut sage green to hoary gray foliage; *A.* 'Powis Castle' (garden origin, probably *A. arborescens* × *A. absinthium*) vigorous, erect to spreading shrub or subshrub to 3¼ ft (1 m) with silver filigree leaves: *A. schmidtiana* Japan; prostrate, carpet- or mound-forming subshrub to 24 in (60 cm) tall with silver-gray, finely cut, downy leaves; the dwarf, cushion-forming 'Nana' is an excellent rock or sink garden plant, likewise the low, hardy and bright gray-white 'Silver Mound'; *A. stelleriana* BEACH WORMWOOD, OLD WOMAN, DUSTY MILLER; NE Asia, E US; erect to arching, bushy, woody-based perennial to 24 in (60 cm) tall with silver-white-hairy leaves, deeply lobed, toothed or entire; 'Boughton Silver': compact, hardy and prostrate with off-white to silver-white leaves cut into fairly broad, dissected lobes, may be deciduous.

Arthropodium (from Greek *arthron*, joint, and *pous*, foot: the pedicels are jointed). Liliaceae (Asphodelaceae). Australasia. 12 species, evergreen or deciduous perennial herbs with narrow leaves in clumps or rosettes and starry, 6-parted flowers in racemes or panicles. Min. temp. 0°F (–18°C). Plant in full sun or part-shade in fast-draining but permanently damp soil high in leaf mold and grit. Mulch *A. cirrhatum* in cold winters. Increase by division.

A. candidum deciduous; small clumps of finely grassy dull green leaves to 8 in (20 cm) long; flowers white, to ½ in (1 cm) wide, on threadlike stalks in a loose, erect panicle; 'Maculatum': smaller, leaves dull flesh pink mottled and spotted olive to bronze; *A. cirratum* RIENGA LILY; ROCK LILY; evergreen; leaves narrowly lanceolate, to 24 in (60 cm), white to glaucous beneath; flowers white, ¾–1½ in (2–4 cm) wide, on panicles to 12 in (30 cm) across, standing on stout scapes to 3¼ ft (1 m).

artichokes a group of three types of perennial vegetable plant. The GLOBE ARTICHOKE (*Cynara cardunculus* Scolymus Group) is not known in the wild and probably derived from the cardoon (*C. cardunculus*). It is a herbaceous perennial grown in the vegetable garden mainly for the fleshy basal portions of the scales and the "heart" or base of the flower, all of which are boiled. The young shoots, blanched by covering for six weeks with black polythene, may be used in salads. Globe artichokes are best replanted every three years by suckers taken from well-performing mother plants in spring; plant 36 in (90 cm) apart each way. Safeguard from frost damage by covering with a 12 in (30 cm) layer of straw.

JERUSALEM ARTICHOKE (*Helianthus tuberosus*), native to North America, is a herbaceous perennial 6½–10 ft (2–3 m) high, related to the sunflower (*H. annuus*). It is grown mainly for its edible tubers, harvested in fall; they have the appearance of knobby potatoes, 2¾–4 in (7–10 cm) long and 1¼–2½ in (3–6 cm) in diameter, which are peeled and boiled. Rich in inulin rather than starch, the tubers are a suitable source of carbohydrates for diabetics. They are best replanted annually in spring, 3 in (8 cm) deep, at 16–20 in (40–50 cm) stations in rows 36 in (90 cm) apart. Plants are also grown in gardens to form temporary shelter screens.

CHINESE ARTICHOKE *Stachys affinis*), a native of the Far East, is a herbaceous perennial 12–18 in (30–45 cm)

high, grown for its small edible tubers produced on a creeping root system, with a flavor similar to Jerusalem artichoke. Plant tubers in spring 2¾–3 in (7–8 cm) deep and 12 in (30 cm) apart each way. They may be overwintered in the ground in all but the severest winters.

articulate, articulated of stems and stalks; jointed; possessing distinct nodes or joints, sometimes swollen at their attachment and breaking easily.

Arum (Latinized form of the Greek name for these plants, *aron*). Araceae. Europe: Asia. 26 species, hardy, tuberous perennial herbs with hastate to sagittate leaves and inconspicuous flowers arranged on a spadix terminating in a cylindric, club- shaped or tapering appendix and surrounded by a cup- or hoodlike spathe. Most of the following species will tolerate cold to 23°F (–5°C); *A. italicum* and *A. maculatum* are fully hardy. *A. pictum* and *A. rupicola* fare better in the cold greenhouse, alpine house or bulb frame. Most prefer a sheltered, warm position in full or dappled sun. Keep moist during the growing season (usually early fall to late spring), but drier during the summer resting period. *A. italicum* and *A. maculatum* are easier to please and will grow in shade and permanent moisture. The first is an invaluable foliage plant for the winter garden, its brilliant fruiting heads giving way to tufts of marbled leaves. Sow ripe seed, cleansed of pulp, in a gritty medium in fall, or divide plants after flowing. The berries are toxic.

A. creticum Crete; spathe produced in spring, to 8 in (20 cm), bright yellow to yellow-green or white, recurved, spadix tapering, yellow or, rarely, purple; *A. dioscoridis* Cyprus to Turkey, Middle East; spathe produced in spring, to 16 in (40 cm), green suffused and blotched deep, satiny maroon, more or less erect, spadix cylindric, purple-black; *A. italicum* S and W Europe; leaves appearing in fall and winter, to 14 in (35 cm), glossy mid- to dark green, often heavily marbled cream to white

hoodlike spathe

flower-bearing spadix

Arum maculatum

or yellow on veins–plants described as 'Marmoratum', or, erroneously, 'Pictum'—spathe produced in spring, to 16 in (40 cm), yellow-green or green-white, faintly edged purple-red, erect, hooded, spadix club-shaped, yellow; fruiting head an oblong mass of showy orange-red berries; *A. maculatum* LORDS-AND-LADIES, CUCKOO-PINT, JACK-IN-THE- PULPIT; Europe; leaves often spotted purple-black; spathe produced in early spring, to 10 in (25 cm), pale, pearly green-white, often tinted purple-red especially on margins and with faint purple-red blotches, erect, hooded, spadix club-shaped, purple-red or, rarely, yellow; berries orange-red; *A. pictum* W Mediterranean Is; leaves appearing in fall, shimmering dark green with fine silver-green veins; spathe produced in fall, to 10 in (25 cm), dark, satiny purple-red, erect, hooded and stout, spadix club-shaped, maroon-black; *A. rupicola* W Asia, SW Mediterranean; spathe produced in spring and early summer, to 16 in (40 cm), green to purple-red or maroon, paler with at base, very narrow and erect, spadix tapering, green-white at base and maroon above. For *A. dracunculus*, see *Dracunculus vulgaris*; the white arum lily is *Zantedeschia aethiopica*.

Aruncus (Classical name for these herbs). Rosaceae. Northern Temperate Regions. GOAT'S BEARD. 2 species, hardy perennial herbs, clump-forming with slender-stalked, pinnate to ternately compound, ferny leaves composed of dark green, ovate and coarsely toothed leaflets. Small, off-white flowers are borne in frothy, plumelike panicles in summer. Hardy to 5°F (–15°C), grow in moist soil in filtered sun or light shade. Propagate by division in fall or early spring, or by seed in fall. *A. dioicus* (*A. sylvester*) Europe to S Russia; to 6½ ft (2 m) tall smaller forms include the Japanese var. *astilboides*, and 'Kneiffii', a vigorous plant with narrow and gracefully cut leaflets, and delicately branched, creamy panicles, growing up to 3¼ ft (1 m) in height.

Arundinaria (from Latin *arundo*, reed). Gramineae. SE US. 1 species. See *Bamboos*.

Arundo (from Latin *arundo*, reed).

Gramineae. Warm regions of the Old World. GIANT REED. 3 species, very large, rhizomatous perennial grasses, evergreen in mild climates, more or less deciduous elsewhere. Tall and canelike, the stems bear two alternate ranks of sword-shaped leaves. Flowers are produced after long, hot summers in terminal, silky plumes. Plant in fertile, moist but well-drained loamy soil in full sun. In frost-free regions, growth is fast, continuous and spreading. Elsewhere, the canes are usually killed or at least stripped by hard frosts—protect the crowns with a thick, dry mulch and sacking. Cut out dead or damaged canes in spring. Increase by division. *A. donax* Mediterranean; canes to 20 ft (6 m), stout; leaves 24 in (60 cm), rough-edged, gray-green, arching; flower spikes pearly pink becoming gray-white; 'Macrophylla' larger with purple-tinted stems and broader, blue-green leaves; var. *versicolor*. syn. 'Variegata', leaves striped and edged off-white.

Asarina (from a Spanish vernacular name for *Antirrhinum*, which it resembles). Scrophulariaceae. Mexico; SW US; S Europe. CLIMBING SNAPDRAGON. 16 species, sprawling or twining perennial herbs sometimes grown as annuals. Flowers produced in spring and summer, axillary, tubular to funnel-shaped with two lips and a distinct palate. Essentially tender, with a minimum temperature requirement of 41°F (5°C). In favored locations, they may, however, survive outdoors to 10°F (–12°C) as herbaceous perennials—this is certainly true of *A. procumbens*, which overwinters successfully on sheltered rock gardens. Otherwise, grow outdoors as half-hardy annuals. Provide support in the form of pea sticks, canes, or surrounding vegetation. In the cool greenhouse or conservatory, grow in pots and train on a trellis or a wigwam of bamboo canes. Grow in full sun or part shade; ventilate, water and feed freely in summer; keep barely moist in winter; cut back in early spring. Increase by seed grown under glass in spring.

A. filipes (*Antirrhinum filipes*) YELLOW TWINING SNAPDRAGON; SW US; glabrous, sometimes glaucous twiner; flowers to ⅝ in (1.5 cm) long, yellow spotted black on palate; *A. procumbens*

(*Antirrhinum asarina*) SW Europe; woody-based, glandular hairy trailer; flowers to 1½ in (3.5 cm), white veined purple-rose, lips pale yellow or pale pink, palate yellow.

Asarum (from Classical Greek name *asaron*). Aristolochiaceae. Asia; N America; Europe. 70 species, low-growing, evergreen perennial herbs with spicily aromatic rhizomes and heart- to kidney- or arrow-shaped leaves borne close to the ground. The purple-brown flowers appear in spring. Solitary and short-stalked, they lie between the leaves and consist of a fleshy cup with three, tail-like lobes at its rim. The following are hardy to –10°F (–23°C). Grow in the wild or woodland garden, or as a groundcover among shrubs. Plant in moist but porous soil rich in leaf mold in dappled sunlight to deep shade. Increase by division of well-established clumps in spring.

A. arifolium SE US; leaves 6–8 in (16–20 cm), triangular to sagittate, blunt, marked light green or silver between veins; *A. asaroides* Japan; leaves 3–4¾ in (8–12 cm), broadly ovate, blunt, spotted; *A. blumei* Japan; leaves 2½–4 in (6–10 cm), hastate to ovate, acute to blunt, dark green with white veins; *A. canadense* WILD GINGER, eastern N America; leaves 2½–4 in (6–10 cm), broadly reniform, apex acuminate, dark green, usually lost in winter; *A. europaeum* ASARABACCA, W Europe; leaves 1–4 in (2.5–10 cm), reniform to cordate, blunt, dark glossy green; *A. hartwegii* W US; leaves to 4 in (10 cm), cordate to ovate, acute, dark green to bronze, mottled silver; *A. shuttleworthii* SE US; leaves 2–4 in (5–10 cm), orbicular to cordate, mid-green marked silver; *A. virginicum* SE US; leaves 2–4¾ in (5–12 cm), orbicular to cordate, dark green with purple or silver mottling.

Asclepias (from the Greek god of medicine, Asklepios, referring to the medicinal properties of some species). Asclepiadaceae. Americas; South Africa. MILKWEED; SILKWEED. 108 species, annuals and perennials, herbs, subshrubs and shrubs, exuding milky sap if damaged, some tuberous-rooted. Carried in spring and summer in dense, flat-topped, umbel-like cymes, the flowers are small and starry with five, spreading and pointed lobes and a central corona—a crown of five hooded lobes often differently colored. The pods are slender and caselike or resemble a balloon; they disperse silk-tasseled seeds. *A. curassavica* and *A. physocarpa* should be grown in full sun with a minimum temperature of 45°F (7°C). Keep almost dry in winter. Short-lived and fast-growing, these shrubs are best replaced every two to three years with new plants grown from seed sown in late winter in a heated case. They are plagued by whitefly under glass. The remaining, hardy perennial species are handsome additions to the herbaceous border and the wild garden where they attract bees and butterflies. Plant in full sun. Increase by division in early spring.

A. curassavica BLOOD FLOWER, SWALLOW WORT; S America; annual or short-lived perennial subshrub to 5 ft (1.5 m) tall; flowers bright orange red with yellow centers; *A. hallii* W US; tuberous perennial to 3¼ ft (1 m) tall; flowers deep pink; *A. physocarpa* (syn. *Gomphocarpus physocarpus*) SWAN PLANT; S Africa; willowy, erect short-lived shrub to 6½ ft (2 m) tall; flowers cream to green-white; fruit to 2½ in (6 cm) wide, rounded and inflated, pale, translucent green covered in soft spines and hanging from a curving stalk that resembles a swan's neck; *A. syriaca* North America; tuberous perennial, 3¼–6½ ft (1–2 m) tall; flowers pink to mauve or white; *A. tuberosa* BUTTERFLY WEED; INDIAN PAINTBRUSH; US; tuberous perennial, 3¼–6½ ft (1–2 m) tall; flowers flame red, vermilion, orange or gold, sometimes scented, sometimes pink or bicolored.

aseptate of fruit; lacking partitions or divisions.

asexual lacking sexual characteristics or (of reproductive processes) occurring without the fusion of gametes. The description includes apomixis and mechanical methods of propagation such as grafting, cuttings and division.

ashes coke or coal ash is sometimes used to lighten heavy soil but may contain impurities; it is also used for surfacing standing ground or in plunge beds for pots. Fresh dry wood ash is a useful fertilizer. See *wood ash*.

Asparagus (Classical name for this plant). Liliaceae (Asparagaceae). Old World. 300 species, perennial herbs, sometimes shrubby or climbing, with thick rhizomes or root tubers and clumped, tough and slender stems. These are clothed with needle- or leaflike cladophylls, subtended by the sharp, scalelike true leaves. With the exception of the two hardy species, all listed here are evergreen and hail from Africa. Small, green-white flowers are followed by glossy red to black berries.

EDIBLE ASPARAGUS (*A. officinalis*) has been used for over 2,000 years, first as a medicine and then as a food. Grown for its edible shoots or "spears." This species and the ornamental *A. verticillatus* are hardy, requiring full sun and freely draining, deep soil; *A. verticillatus* needs the support of surrounding vegetation or trellis.

Plant edible asparagus in spring as one-year old crowns, raised from seed; set 4 in (10 cm) deep at 12–16 in (30–40 cm) stations, in rows 24 in (60 cm) apart. Plants may be grown on the flat or, preferably, in ridges to aid drainage and weed control; earth up in fall after planting. Plants are dioecious; males produce higher yield and do not give rise to troublesome seedlings; male plants can be selected in the second year in the seed bed, and there are all-male clones available through micropropagation. Close planting gives higher yield. Cutting can take place one year after planting, over a 3–4-week period; but it is better to leave beds uncut for at least two years from planting to build up strong crowns, after which harvest can be made over an 8–10 week period. Spears are cut about 8 in (20 cm) long; green when allowed to develop above the surface or mostly white when cut from more deeply earthed crowns. In fall cut the tall stems of fernlike foliage down to within ¾ in (2 cm) of ground level; mulch the rows with rotted organic matter. Beds can remain productive for many years.

The remaining species are tender. During the colder months, when growth virtually ceases, reduce water and withhold fertilizer. Bright, filtered light is ideal, but most will tolerate light or even heavy shade. Provide a minimum temperature of 45°F (7°C). Propagate by division.

A. asparagoides (syn. *A. medeoloides*, *Medeola asparagoides*) stems erect to gently twining, 24–60 in (60–150 cm) tall; cladophylls to 1¼ in (3 cm) long, narrowly ovate with tapering tips, glossy green and long-lasting; foliage offered by florists under the name SMILAX; *A. densiflorus* tuberous, making a clump of erect to sprawling stems to 3¼ ft (1 m) tall, with whorled branches dense with linear cladophylls to ½ in (1 cm) long and bright emerald green; 'Myersii': syn.. *A. meyeri*, *A. myersii*, FOXTAIL FERN, erect with short, compact lateral branches dense with cladophylls and creating soft, ferny cylinders; Sprengeri Group: syn.. *A. sprengeri*, EMERALD FERN, looser, airy, emerald green foliage on gracefully arching stems; *A. drepanophyllus* tuberous, making a dense clump of sprawling to arching, thinly woody stems 3¼–30 ft (1–10 m) long; cladophylls tough, narrowly oblong, ¾–2¾ in (2–7 cm) long and dark green; *A. falcatus* SICKLE THORN; differs from the last species in its longer, slightly curving cladophylls with a distinct midrib; *A. officinalis* EDIBLE ASPARAGUS; Europe, C Asia, N Africa; fleshy-rooted herbaceous perennial to 5 ft (1.5 m) tall making a clump of finely branched, plumelike stems clothed with very fine, threadlike cladophylls; *A. setaceus* (syn. *A. plumosus*) erect to climbing evergreen with very slender stems ranked with horizontal branches of very fine, short, dark green cladophylls—the asparagus fern of florists; *A. verticillatus* SE Europe to Siberia; differs from *A. officinalis* in its very long stems (scrambling to 6½ ft/2 m) and black, not red berries.

Pests: asparagus beetle.

asperous, asperulous of plant surfaces; rough, coarse, sharp.

Asperula (from Latin, *asper*, rough). Rubiaceae. Europe; Asia; Australia. WOODRUFF. 100 species, annual and perennial herbs or dwarf shrublets with narrow leaves and terminal clusters of small, 4-parted flowers in summer. Fully hardy but intolerant of damp winter conditions, it should be grown in fast-draining soil in full sun on the rock garden, in sink gardens or in the alpine house. Increase by division, by seed or by soft cuttings in early summer. *A. arcadiensis* (syn. *A. suberosa* of gardens) Bulgaria. Greece; perennial, making a tufted clump of frosted growth to 4 in (10 cm) tall; flowers bright pink clustered on an elongated spike to 2 in (5 cm) long. For *A. odorata* see *Galium odoratum*.

Asphodeline (related to *Asphodelus*). Liliaceae. (Asphodelaceae). Mediterranean to Caucasus. JACOB'S ROD. 20 species, more or less deciduous, rhizomatous perennial or biennial herbs producing an erect stem in spring and summer, clothed with slender leaves and terminating in a tall spike of 6-parted flowers among thin-textured bracts. Hardy to 5°F (−15°C). Grow in full sun or dappled shade in low- to medium-fertility, freely draining soil. Propagate by division or by seed sown in a sandy mix in the cold frame.

A. liburnica C Europe, Balkans; perennial to 24 in (60 cm) tall; stem leafy below; flowers 1¼ in (3 cm) long and yellow striped green; *A. lutea* KING'S SPEAR, YELLOW ASPHODEL; Mediterranean; perennial to 3¼ ft (1 m) tall; stem clothed throughout in fine, gray-green leaves and ending in a spike of fragrant flowers each to 1¼ in (3 cm) long and golden yellow.

Asphodelus (from the Greek name for these plants, *asphodelos*). Liliaceae (Asphodelaceae). Mediterranean to Himalaya. 12 species, thickly rhizomatous hardy herbs, perennial or annual with slender, grassy leaves and spikes of starry, 6-parted flowers in late spring and summer. Of the following, the first is suited to scree or rock gardens, or to the alpine house, the others to the herbaceous border. Grow in full sun. Increase by seed.

A. acaulis N Africa; low-growing perennial with a stemless spike of green-striped, white or pale pink flowers held low in the leaf rosette; *A. aestivus* (syn. *A. microcarpus*) Canaries, Mediterranean, Turkey; branching perennial to 6½ ft (2 m) tall with tan striped, white flowers; *A. albus* C and S Europe; erect perennial, sometimes branched, to 3¼ ft (1 m) tall with white or pale rose flowers that have

deeper pink stripes.

Aspidistra (from Greek *aspidion*, a small, rounded shield, referring to the shape of the stigma). Liliaceae (Convallariaceae). E Asia. 8 species, tender, evergreen perennial herbs with thick, creeping rhizomes and erect, long-stalked, lanceolate to elliptic leaves. Cuplike and 6–8-lobed, the fleshy flowers arise along the rhizome and open at soil level. Grow in filtered sunlight to deep shade. Keep moist throughout the year; apply weak fertilizer semiweekly in spring and summer. Maintain a minimum winter temperature of 41°F (5°C). Propagate by division in spring. *A. elatior* CAST IRON PLANT; BAR ROOM PLANT; BEER PLANT; China; leaves smooth, deep green, to 24 in (60 cm) tall; flowers ¾–1¼ in (2–3 cm)-wide, cream mottled purple-red. 'Variegata': leaves long, striped creamy yellow; 'Variegata Exotica' leaves boldly streaked white.

Asplenium (from the Greek name, *asplenon*, derived from *a-*, without, and *splen*, spleen; these ferns were thought effective against complaints of the liver and spleen). Aspleniaceae. Cosmopolitan. SPLEENWORT. 700 species, evergreen ferns with short rhizomes and fronds in rosettes or tufts. Hardy species include *A. scolopendrium* and *A. trichomanes*, both of which will grow in a wide range of garden situations, although the former prefers some shade and moisture and the latter dislikes wetness. Among tender *Asplenium* species are two very popular and resilient house plants, *A. bulbiferum* and *A. nidus*. The first will thrive in cool, airy and shaded conditions; the second prefers warmth and humidity, but will cope with minimum temperatures of 45–50°F (7–10°C) and dry air. Both need a porous, soil-free potting mix, permanently damp but never wet, and protection from strong sunlight. Propagate all species by division; *A. bulbiferum* by plantlets; *A. scolopendrium* from spores.

A. bulbiferum HEN-AND-CHICKENS FERN, MOTHER SPLEENWORT; fronds to 24 in (60 cm), olive to jade green, very finely cut and bearing plantlets; *A. nidus* BIRD'S-NEST FERN; fronds 12–32 in (30–80 cm) long, broadly oblanceolate, thin-textured, uncut and glossy light

green with black midribs; *A. scolopendrium* (syn. *Phyllitis scolopendrium*) HART'S-TONGUE FERN; fronds 8–16 in (20–40 cm), lanceolate to narrowly spear-shaped, undivided and tough, light olive to dark green with a smooth, glossy texture; cultivars are available with fronds short or long, broad or narrow and with margins wavy, toothed, crested, crisped or cut, and sometimes forking at the tips; *A. trichomanes* MAIDENHAIR SPLEENWORT; fronds 2½–12 in (6–30 cm)-long, with dark, wiry stalks ranked with small, broad and leathery, dark green leaflets.

Astelia (from Greek *a-*, without, and *stele*, a pillar: some species are epiphytic and thus unable to prop themselves up). Liliaceae (Asteliaceae). Australasia, Polynesia, Réunion, Mauritius, Falkland Islands. 25 species, evergreen perennial herbs with clumps of sword-like, ribbed leaves and inconspicuous flowers crowded in long-stalked panicles. Hardy to 0°F (−18°C) if grown in a sheltered position and mulched in winter. Otherwise, grow in containers and overwinter in a frost-free greenhouse. Plant in gritty, acidic soil. Position in full sun. Keep moist but avoid wet winter conditions. Increase by seed or division. *A. nervosa* New Zealand; leaves 20–80 in (50–200 cm) long linear to lanceolate, covered in brilliant silvery chaff; flowers green to purple-bronze; fruit orange to red.

Aster (from Greek *aster*, a star, referring to the shape of the flowers). Compositae. Americas; Europe; Asia; Africa. Some 250 species, mostly perennial herbs and subshrubs, rhizomatous or fibrous-rooted with erect, clumped stems and white to pink, red, lilac, mauve or blue, daisylike flower heads in summer and fall. A large genus that includes low-growing montane natives for the rock garden to tall back border perennials, with a large number of the North American species, such as *A. acuminatus*, *A. cordifolius*, and *A. divaricatus*, suited to naturalizing in the wild and woodland garden and other informal situations. Most asters thrive in sun or semishade in any moderately fertile, well-drained soil that retains sufficient moisture throughout the growing season. The rock garden species, generally flowering in early summer, include the very low-growing types such as *A. alpigenus*, *A. himalaicus*, *A. tongolensis*, and *A. bellidiastrum*, together with taller species such as *A. farreri*, *A. souliei*, and *A. yunnanensis*. The many varieties of *A. alpinus*, with *A. × alpellus*, are also suited in scale to the larger rock garden and can be useful in smaller gardens. Where space is limited, the European and Asiatic species are slower growing and less rampant than their American counterparts. Selections from the *A. amellus* cultivars, in a height range of about 20–24 in (50–60 cm), suit the front of sunny borders with well-drained, moderately fertile soil; plants benefit from division every third or fourth year in spring to avoid overcrowding and reduce losses from verticillium wilt. Hybrids of *A. × frikartii* and *A. sedifolius* are slightly taller. *A. thomsonii* 'Nanus' is more compact and is floriferous over exceptionally long periods; these plants appreciate similar treatment and conditions as for *A. amellus*.

The huge range of tall, clump-forming, late summer and fall flowering asters, derived largely from the NEW ENGLAND ASTER, *A. novae-angliae* and the MICHAELMAS DAISY, *A. novi-belgii*, thrive in rich, fertile and moisture-retentive soil, in full sun or part shade. Top-dress with garden compost after cutting back in later fall after flowering. Flower quality and good health are maintained by frequent division and replanting of the more vigorous growth at the outside of the clumps, every second or third year in fall or spring. Tall cultivars need staking in more carefully tended areas of the garden and this must be done early in the season, using pea sticks or other grow-through support which will be obscured by the subsequent growth. *A. ericoides* and its cultivars, with slender-branched stems of small, starry flower heads, bring light effects to the sunny border with drier soil and have the advantage of being largely self supporting and rarely needing division.

A. divaricatus can be used to similar airy effect and is best left to flop gracefully over lower plants at the front of the border. *A. lateriflorus*, holding its minute flower heads in horizontally branching sprays, suits similar soils and situations. *A. macrophyllus*, though its small flowers are not in the first order of merit, is particularly useful for naturalistic plantings in dry soil in shade, where the heart-shaped leaves and running root form good groundcover.

Propagation is usually by division, but also possible by soft cuttings in spring. A number of cultivars come approximately true from seed; most species can be raised from seed but *Aster* hybridizes freely and seedlings may not come true.

Aster may be affected by gray mold, leaf spots, sclerotinia rots, and aster wilt; powdery mildew may strike, especially in hot dry summers; modern varieties of *A. novi-belgii* are particularly susceptible. Selection of resistant cultivars is the preferred means of control, followed by treatment with appropriate fungicide at the first signs of infection, and regular treatment at semiweekly intervals thereafter as necessary. Remove and burn affected foliage in fall.

Asteranthera (from Greek *aster*, star, and *anthos*, flower, referring to the flower shape). Gesneriaceae. 1 species, *A. ovata*, an evergreen, woody-based scrambler native to Chile and climbing to 12 ft (4 m). The stems are slender and picked out with small, downy leaves. The flowers appear singly or in pairs in summer and are bright red, to 2½ in (6 cm) long, with a narrow tube widening to a 2-lipped limb to 1¼ in (3 cm) across, the lower lip marked yellow. Plant outdoors in in a sheltered, sunny position in acidic soil (min. temp. 0°F/−18°C). Keep moist but never waterlogged. Mulch in winter. Propagation is by semiripe cuttings, simple layering, or by division.

Astilbe (from Greek, *a-*, without, and *stilbe*, brightness, a reference to the dullness of the leaves of the type species). Saxifragaceae. E Asia; N America. 12 species, hardy, deciduous perennial herbs, rhizomatous and forming dense clumps, with slender-stalked, 1–3-ternately compound leaves composed of elliptic to ovate, toothed leaflets. Small, white, cream, pink, or deep red, the flowers are crowded in dense, plumelike panicles. For woodland and water garden or moist borders. In some, the young, coppery foliage is handsome; flowering begins in early summer with *A. japonica* and hybrids, extending to late summer flowerers like *A. chinensis*. The many commonly available cultivars are usually grouped as *A. × arendsii* and range in height from 20 to 39 in (50 to 100 cm), in color, from white to darkest red, flowering from midspring to late summer. Smaller species and forms like *A. chinensis* 'Pumila' and *A. simplicifolia* may be used in alpine troughs, beside rock garden pools or in pans. Plant in spring or fall in rich, moisture-retentive soil (pH 5–7) and part-shade. Mulch with dry bracken or straw in winter, and with leaf mold and garden compost in early spring. Cut to ground level in late winter; lift and divide every three to four years in spring.

Astilboides (from *Astilbe* and Greek *-eides*, resembling) Saxifragaceae. N China. 1 species *A. tabularis*; fully hardy, clump-forming perennial. Leaves peltate, broadly-lobed, dentate, softly hairy on slender petioles to 3 ft (90 cm). Flowers numerous, small white, in plumelike panicles to 5 ft (1.5 m); early/midsummer. Grow in cool moist, humus-rich soil, in partial shade. Increase by seed or division.

Astrantia (this name has two possible derivations—from Greek *aster*, referring to the starry flower heads, or from the Mediaeval Latin *magistrantia*, "masterwort," from *magister*, master). Umbelliferae. Europe to Asia. MASTERWORT, HALTIC'S PINCUSHION. 10 species, fully hardy evergreen or semideciduous perennial herbs, with palmate or palmately lobed, toothed leaves arising from a short, woody rhizome. Produced in spring and summer, the flowers are small, white to green and carried on long-stalked umbels. These are surrounded by a collar of papery, green-white bracts with toothed margins, the whole resembling a larger flower. Grow in full sun or part shade. Increase by seed or division in early spring.

A. major MASTERWORT; C and E Europe; 10 to 32 in (25 to 80 cm); umbels to 1½ in (3.5 cm) across, bracts lanceolate, white netted olive green or pale pink and coarsely toothed; subsp. *involucrata*: bracts larger, deeply cut; 'Shaggy': syn. 'Margery Fish', bracts deeply cut, pink-white; 'Sunningdale Variegated': leaves yellow-cream-variegated; *A. maxima* S Europe, Caucasus; to 36 in (90 cm) tall; bracts pink-tinted, elliptic—white in the cultivar 'Alba', dark pink in 'Hadspen Blood', a very showy hybrid with *A. major*.

Astrophytum (from Greek *aster*, star, and *phyton*, plant). Cactaceae. US (Texas); Mexico. 4 species, tender, perennial cacti with an unbranched, dome- to ball-shaped stem, ribbed and sometimes spiny and marked with a pattern of chalky white scales. Provide a minimum temperature of 41°F (5°C) and a dry, buoyant atmosphere in full sun. Plant in a gritty, low- to medium-fertility mix. Keep dry from midfall to early spring except for a light misting on warm, sunny days. Water moderately in summer. Propagate by seed.

A. asterias SEA URCHIN, SILVER DOLLAR CACTUS; stem circular, flattened to hemispherical, to 6 in (15 cm) wide with broad low, spineless ribs; flowers yellow sometimes tinted red; *A. myriostigma* BISHOP'S CAP, BISHOP'S MITER; stem rounded to domed, to 8 in (20 cm) wide with prominent and faceted, spineless ribs, the whole covered in minute, chalky scales; flowers gold with a yellow-orange heart; *A. ornatum* stems spherical to column-shaped, 6–40 in (15–100 cm) tall with six to eight deep, winglike and spiny ribs, dark green and lined with silvery white, dotlike scales; flowers, brilliant yellow.

asymmetric, asymmetrical (1) of a leaf margin or the shape of an inflorescence that is irregular or unequal in outline or shape, (2) of a flower incapable of being cut in any vertical plane into similar halves.

Atherosperma (from Greek, *ather*, bristle, and *sperma*, seed). Monimiaceae. Australia. 1 species, *A. moschatum* (AUSTRALIAN SASSAFRAS, TASMANIAN SASSAFRAS), a spreading, evergreen tree to

80 ft (25 m) tall with nutmeg-scented, lanceolate leaves to 4 in (10 cm) long, glaucous to glossy above and white-downy beneath with toothed or entire margins. Creamy white, cup-shaped flowers to 1 in (2.5 cm) across appear in summer. Grow in nonalkaline soil in full sun or part shade. Provide good ventilation and a minimum winter temperature of 37–41°F (3–5°C). Propagate by seed or semiripe cuttings in summer.

star-shaped profile

Astrophytum myriostigma

Athrotaxis (from Greek *athroos*, crowded, and *taxis*, arrangement, referring to the disposition of the leaves and cone scales). Cupressaceae. Tasmania. 3 species, evergreen conifers with fissured, flaking bark and small, subulate or scalelike leaves overlapping or spreading on erect branchlets. The cones are small and spherical. The following favor equable, rainy areas in mild climates. Plant in moist, humus-rich soil in full sun or part shade with shelter from harsh winds. Propagate by cuttings.

A. selaginoides KING WILLIAM PINE; to 100 ft (30 m) tall with a broadly conical crown and red-brown bark falling away in shreds; leaves to 1/2 in (1 cm), spreading and subulate, the outer surface bright green, the inner marked with two white lines; *A. cupressoides* SMOOTH TASMANIAN CEDAR; to 52 ft (16 m); leaves scalelike; the hybrid offspring of these two is *A.* × *laxifolia*, SUMMIT CEDAR, hardier than either parent and with fresh, yellow-green new growth.

Athyrium (from Greek *athoros*, good at breeding, referring to the diverse forms of the sori). Athyriaceae. Cosmopolitan. 100 species, evergreen or semideciduous ferns with 2–3-pinnately divided fronds. *A. filix-femina* and *A. nipponicum* are popular garden plants. Both species prefer light shade and humus-rich, moist, and slightly acidic soil; they will, however, tolerate some chalk and full sun, provided the roots are cool and damp. Fully hardy, they nonetheless benefit from a dry winter mulch. Increase by division in early spring.

A. filix-femina LADY FERN; northern temperate regions; fronds 8–40 in (20–100 cm) long, light-textured and a soft, pale green; numerous cultivars are available with fronds variously forked, bunched, crested, crisped and fringed—one of the most remarkable is 'Frizelliae' (TATTING FERN), with long, narrow fronds in which the segments are reduced to widely spaced balls of parsleylike growth; *A. niponicum* (syn. *A. goeringianum*) E Asia; fronds 4–12 in (10–30 cm)-long, broader than in *A. filix-femina*, of a heavier texture and dark green with a bronze-purple tint, especially when young; var. *pictum*: JAPANESE PAINTED FERN, PAINTED LADY FERN, fronds emerging purple-bronze, turning dull aquamarine with silver-gray flush along purple-tinted veins.

Atriplex (from the Greek name for these plants). Chenopodiaceae. Cosmopolitan. ORACH; SALT BUSH. 100 species, evergreen shrubs or annual herbs, often with a gray or silver-white mealy coating, and small flowers in dense panicles. *A. hortensis* is a fast-growing hardy annual with edible, spinachlike foliage. The red-flushed forms are very decorative. Sow seed *in situ* in spring. Unattended, these plants will seed themselves. *A. halimus* is fully hardy and tolerates saline conditions, drought, and fierce winds. The remaining species are fine, silver shrubs for very dry, windy, saline or alkaline situations and are useful fire-retardants and windbreaks. All need a warm, dry and sheltered position in sharply draining soil. Increase by softwood cuttings in summer.

A. canescens FOUR-WING SALTBUSH; to 6 1/2 ft (2 m) tall, broadly spreading; leaves to 5/8 in (1.5 cm) long, linear to narrowly oblong, silvery gray; *A. halimus* SEA ORACHE, TREE PURSLANE; S Europe; semievergreen, bushy perennial shrub to 6 1/2 ft (2 m) tall; leaves tough, ovate-rhombic to hastate, pewter gray to silvery white; *A. hortensis* MOUNTAIN SPINACH, ORACH; Asia, widely naturalized elsewhere; annual herb to 6 1/2 ft (2 m) tall with arrow-shaped, leaves; var. *rubra*: leaves strongly purple-red-tinted, selections include 'Cupreatorosea' with red-tinted leaves burnished with copper, and 'Rosea' with pale rose leaves veined dark purple-red; *A. hymenelytra* DESERT HOLLY; low, compact to 3¼ ft (1 m) tall; leaves rhombic to oblong or bluntly hastate, coarsely toothed, silver-white, tough and hollylike; *A. lentiformis* QUAIL BUSH; WHITE THISTLE; broadly spreading, to 10 ft (3 m) tall, spiny; leaves oblong to ovate-deltoid, silver-gray; subsp. *breweri* lacks spines and is virtually evergreen.

attapulgite a clay mineral, which after calcining and crushing can be used as an ingredient of potting media. Its physical properties are similar to sand, but it has a higher buffering capacity.

attenuate of the apex or base of a leaf, sepal, petal, stem or bulb; tapering finely and concavely to a long drawn out point.

aubergine (*Solanum melongena*). EGG-PLANT, a short-lived perennial treated as an annual, it is 24–28 in (60–70 cm) high and is grown for its two-locular fruits. Of various shape and size, these are 2–6 in (5–15 cm) long and 1¼–2½ in (3–6 cm) in diameter, yellow, black, white, or purple in color, and may be fried or roasted. Probably originating in India, but also found in Southeast Asia and China, the eggplant was introduced into Europe in the 13th century.

In warm climates, sow seeds in a sheltered place; transplant seedlings to ridges or raised beds either 20–24 in (50–60 cm) apart each way or spaced 24–30 in (60–75 cm) stations in rows 30–36 in (75–90 cm) apart. In temperate areas, raise seedlings in a greenhouse at a minimum temperature of 59°F (15°C); grow to maturity under protection in beds, growing bags or 10–12 in (25–30 cm)-diam. pots at a maintained temperature of 77–86°F (25–30°C). Stop to encourage bushy growth, and stake; fruit is harvested when fully colored, 80–120 days from transplanting.

Possible problems: aphids, red spider mite, whiteflies; gray mold.

Aubrieta (for Claude Aubriet [1668–1743], French botanical artist). Cruciferae. Europe to Central Asia. AUBRETIA. 12 species, cushion- or mat-forming, evergreen, hardy perennial herbs with small leaves and clusters or short racemes of 4-petaled flowers throughout the year, but chiefly in spring and summer. Plant in a sunny, well-drained position, e.g., walls, dry banks, paving, edging, and the rock gardens. Shear off flowered growth. Increase by semiripe cuttings in early fall or seed sown *in situ* in late spring.

A. deltoidea Aegean; sprawling cushions of bristly, mid-green, rhomboid to ovate leaves, the margins entire or sparsely toothed; flowers to ⅝ in (1.5 cm) across, mauve to lilac, pink or purple-red; this species has silver-white- and gold-edged cultivars, some with minute leaves; *A. × cultorum* includes garden hybrids close to *A. deltoidea*, but ranging in flower shape and size from the small and single to the large and semidouble, and in color through deep violet to royal purple, mauve, lilac, magenta, carmine and rose pink.

auctoris, auctorum (abbrev. auct., auctt.) Latin "of an author," "of authors." A formula used in full botanical citations to show when a name has been applied by authors to the wrong entity. It is used usually with the "non" formula to contrast it with the true type of the plant as would be embodied by the correct author citation. For example, by *Betula platyphylla* auct. non Sukachev, we indicate that some authors call what is in fact *B. mandschurica* by a valid name belonging to a wholly different plant (the type named by Sukachev). This formula is sometimes used interchangeably with "hort." and "misapplied."

Aucuba (from the Japanese name for this plant). Cornaceae (Aucubaceae). East Asia. 3 species, evergreen shrubs and small trees with green branches, star-shaped maroon-green flowers and attractive berries. Plant in part-sun or shade in most soils. Male *and* female plants are needed for berrying. Once established, *Aucuba* will withstand hard frost, some drought, and heavy atmospheric pollution. Prune to size in spring. Propagate from seed and suckers in spring or from basal cuttings of the current year's growth in fall.

A. japonica JAPANESE LAUREL; China, Japan; broad, rounded shrub to 12 ft (4 m) tall; leaves 4–10 in (10–25 cm) long, elliptic to narrowly ovate, more or less toothed, thick and deep glossy green, unmarked in the cultivars 'Viridis', the narrow-leaved 'Salicifolia', and the dwarf 'Nana'; cultivars include 'Bicolor' (leaves with a central yellow blotch and large teeth), 'Crotonifolia' (female, leaves finely speckled and blotched gold), 'Gold Dust' (female, leaves speckled gold), 'Sulphurea' (leaves edged pale yellow), and 'Variegata' (female, leaves spotted and blotched yellow. The berries last from late summer to early spring, sometimes longer. Typically bright scarlet and about ½ in (1 cm) wide, they are also known in white and yellow forms (f. *leucocarpa*, f. *luteocarpa*), while the variegated selection 'Fructualbo' has yellow-white to pale buff fruit.

auger a T-shaped metal hand tool about 3 ft (1 m) long with the lower 6 in (15 cm) of the main stem twisted into a wide thread. It is used to collect cores or twists of soil from various depths for inspection or analysis.

aural screen a planting of trees and shrubs designed to reduce noise, especially traffic noise; the best effect is obtained with tall evergreen species planted more than one row deep.

auricle an earlike lobe or outgrowth, often at the base of an organ (e.g., a leaf), or the junction of leaf sheath and blade in some Gramineae.

auriculas a group of distinctive primulas believed to arise from the natural hybrid *Primula × pubescens*, the progeny of two variable high-alpine crevice plants *P. auricula* and *P. rubra*. The two pigments, flavone and hirsutin, produce a wide range of colors in the progeny, only true blue being absent. Auriculas have been documented since the mid-16th century, when they were valued for medicinal purposes and were introduced into northern England by Huguenot silk-weavers. Auricula societies flourished in England in the late 18th century, running shows with strict rules and displays of "stage auriculas" shown in tiny theaters against a black velvet backdrop, often with mirrors. They are now divided into four

Auricula primula 'Adrian'
Striking petal patterning and, often, a mealy white farina (q.v.) characterize this attractive, if demanding, group of primulas.

classes, Shows, Alpines, Doubles and Borders, and are much grown for exhibition, from unheated greenhouses or frames. Hardy to 7°F (–14°C), they require good drainage and a dry atmosphere in winter. Cultivars are propagated by offsets between spring and late summer and are hybridized by hand pollination. Fresh seed germinates best and most flower by the second spring from sowing. Grow outdoor types in raised beds rich in humus, tender cultivars singly in pots, protecting buds from frost and strong sunshine. Repot annually after flowering.

Possible problems: aphids, root aphids, woolly aphids, fungus gnats, red spider mite, slugs, vine weevil; root rots.

auriculate, auricled of the base of a leaf blade or perianth segment possessing two rounded, ear-shaped lobes that project beyond the general outline of the organ.

Aurinia (from Latin, *aureus*, golden, referring to the flowers of *A. saxatilis*). Cruciferae. Central Europe east to Ukraine and Turkey. 7 species, woody-based biennial and perennial herbs with sprawling to mound-forming branches, oblanceolate leaves and racemes or panicles of small, 4-parted flowers in spring and early summer. Fully hardy and ideal for rock gardens, dry walls and banks. Grow in full sun in well-drained, poor to medium-fertility soil. Increase by greenwood cuttings

in early summer in a shaded cold frame, or from seed in fall. Cut back after flowering. *A. saxatilis* (syn. *Alyssum saxatile*) evergreen perennial to 16 × 12 in (40 × 30 cm) with downy, gray-green leaves and broad panicles of pale yellow flowers; 'Citrina': lemon yellow; 'Dudley Nevill': rich cream tinted apricot; 'Gold Dust': deep gold; 'Variegata': gray-green leaves with yellow-white margins.

Austrocedrus (from Latin *auster*, the south wind, and *Cedrus*, cedar). Cupressaceae. Chile; Argentina. 1 species, *A. chilensis* (syn. *Libocedrus chilensis*), CHILEAN INCENSE CEDAR, an evergreen coniferous tree to 50 ft (15 m) tall. The crown is loosely ovoid to narrowly conical or columnar. Dark brown to orange-gray, the bark falls away in narrow shreds. Scalelike dark green leaves with white undersides overlap in four ranks along flattened, feathery branches. The cones are small, ovoid to oblong and mid-brown. Hardy to 0°F (–18°C), the Chilean cedar prefers a cool, humid and sheltered location in moist, sandy and humus-rich soil. It suffers in hot weather and drying winds. Increase by seed and cuttings.

author in taxonomy, the first worker validly to publish a new name or combination for a taxon. The author name, usually abbreviated, follows that of the taxon in a botanical citation: for example, *Physalis alkekengi* L., where L. stands for Linnaeus. The author citation can be qualified to denote a misapplied name (e.g., *Physalis alkekengi* hort, non L., which describes a name wrongly used by some growers for a plant more correctly named *P.alkekengi* var. *franchetii*), or used in a double citation to indicate that a name first described at one rank (here a species) has been relegated to the status of variety within another species, for example *Physalis alkekengi* var. *franchetii* (Mast.) Mak. In this case Makino, has reduced Masters's species *P.franchetii* to a variety of *P.alkekengi*. The convention is also used when a name is transferred to a different genus entirely.

autoecious completing the entire life cycle on one kind of host; cf. *heteroecious*.

autogamous self-fertilizing.

autopolyploid a polyploid with multiple chromosome sets derived from a single individual or species; cf. *allopolyploid*.

fall color Prior to discarding their foliage in fall, deciduous trees and shrubs and most herbaceous perennials of temperate regions set in motion a process of transferring from their leaves useful materials such as carbohydrates for storage in stems or underground parts. To assist this function, accessory materials contained in the sap are called into use. Some of these materials are colorless, but anthocyanin, which often features, is red where sap is very acidic, blue in the absence of acidity, and violet in the intermediate condition. As chlorophyll degenerates, it gives rise to yellow grains. Combinations of these and other materials impart a range of color to the leaves of plants approaching dormancy.

The timing and habit of fall color depends upon the species; its intensity and duration is influenced by soil and atmospheric moisture (for example, colors are rarely strong following a dry period), by temperature (early frost hastens leaf fall) and by light (transmission of color is greatest in bright sunshine). Good fall coloring species can be found among *Acer*, *Amelanchier*, *Berberis*, *Betula*, *Carpinus*, *Cornus*, *Euonymus*, *Liquidambar*, *Liriodendron*, *Parrotia*, *Sorbus* and *Viburnum*.

auxins a group of plant growth substances (hormones) naturally synthesized in meristematic tissues, concerned with root and shoot elongation, apical dominance and root initiation in cuttings, etc. The main naturally occurring auxin is beta indole acetic acid (IAA).

available water capacity a measure of the water in soil available to plants; expressed as a percentage of the volume of soil; that which is held between field capacity and permanent wilting point.

avocado pear see *Persea*.

awl-shaped of plant features; narrowly wedge-shaped and tapering finely to a point, subulate.

awn a slender sharp point or bristle-like appendage found particularly on the glumes of grasses.

awned see *aristate*.

axial relating to the axis of a plant.

axil the upper angle between an axis and any offshoot or lateral organ arising from it, especially a leaf.

axillary situated in, or arising from, or pertaining to an axil. For example, an axillary inflorescence arises from the junction of a petiole and the stem, whereas a terminal inflorescence grows directly from the apex of the stem.

axis a notional point or line around or along which organs are developed or arranged, whether a stem, stalk or clump; thus the vegetative or growth axis and the floral axis describe the configuration and development of buds and shoots and flowers respectively, and any stem or point of origination on which they are found.

axillary buds
in leaf axils

Quercus petraea

AYR abbreviation for "all year round"; applied to the continuous flower production of greenhouse chrysanthemums, especially by the manipulation of day length.

Azara (for J. N. Azara [1731–1804], Spanish patron of botany). Flacourtiaceae. South America (those below from Chile). 10 species of evergreen trees and shrubs grown for their attractive habit and foliage (usually neat, dark glossy green and gracefully disposed on arching or fanlike branches) and axillary clusters of small flowers with crowded yellow stamens. Freestanding, they nonetheless benefit from the protection of a south-facing wall or fence: this will show their habit to best advantage and encourage free flowering and the production of attractive small berries. *A. petiolaris* and *A. microphylla* withstand temperatures to 5°F

(–15°C); *A. serrata* to 14°F (–10°C); *A. lanceolata* to 23°F (–5°C). Other species will not tolerate heavy frosts, and the leaves of all species will scorch and drop if exposed to harsh, cold winds. Plant in sun or light shade in deep, humus-rich soil. Prune after flowering only to remove any overcrowded, exhausted, or badly placed branches. Propagate by semiripe cuttings in a closed case with bottom heat, or by simple layering of the past season's growth.

A. dentala small tree to 6½ ft (2 m); leaves elliptic, toothed, dark glossy to 1½ in (3.5 cm) long; fruit yellow; *A. integrifolia* treelike shrub, usually to 15 ft (5 m) tall with 1½ in (4 cm)- long oval leaves more or less untoothed; flowers yellow; fruit glaucous black; var. *browneae*: leaves larger, obovate with a few apical teeth; 'Variegata': leaves smaller variegated with pale pink and creamy white) *A. lanceolata*: shrub or small tree to 20 ft (6 m) tall; leaves toothed, glossy dark green, lanceolate, on slender arching branches; flowers ocher-yellow, fragrant; fruit violet-black; *A. microphylla* tree to 25 ft (8 m) tall with fanlike sprays of branchlets densely ranked with very small, rounded, dark green leaves—edged pale yellow in the cultivar 'Variegata'—flowers yellow-green, strongly scented of vanilla; fruit blood red; *A. petiolaris* tree to 15 ft (5 m) tall with glossy, 1½-in-(4-cm-) long, ovate to elliptic, toothed leaves on distinct stalks; flowers pale yellow, richly scented, carried on short cylindrical spikes in late winter and early spring; fruit purple-black with a plumlike bloom; *A. serrata* shrub to 12 ft (4 m) high with 2½-in- (6-cm-) long oblong to elliptic, toothed leaves of a deep, shining green; flowers small, golden, clustered, in each leaf axil; fruits black or white.

Azolla (from Greek, *azo*, to dry up, *ollymi*, to kill: these plants are killed by

drought). Azollaceae. Cosmopolitan. MOSQUITO FERN; WATER FERN; FAIRY MOSS. 8 species, aquatic ferns. They are usually perennial, surviving cold periods as submerged fragments. At other times they float on the surface of standing water or colonize saturated mud. Their small bodies consist of forked or feather-shaped rhizomes from which hang threadlike roots. The "fronds" are reduced to minute scales that overlap closely in two ranks along the rhizome branches. *A. filiculoides* (syn. *A. caroliniana*) is often grown in ponds and freshwater aquariums. Native to the warm Americas, it is now widely naturalized in the waterways, lakes, and ditches of most temperate, subtropical and tropical regions in the Northern Hemisphere. Each plant body is some ½ × ¾ in (1.5 × 1.8 cm) with water-repellent "fronds" to ¹⁄₁₆ in (1 mm) long of a soft pea green. It will proliferate with remarkable speed, forming a velvety emerald skin that may become a nuisance. In hot sunshine, times of drought, and with the onset of fall, the fronds take on a rusty tint before becoming a deep fox- or blood red. *Azolla* can be grown outdoors in ponds (min. temp. 0°F/ –18°C). Where frosts occur, it will sink into winter dormancy, resurfacing in spring. By midsummer, it may be necessary to skim off surplus growth if other aquatics are not to be choked and the pond life below sealed in darkness.

Azorella (diminutive of Azores, application uncertain). Umbelliferae. South America; Antarctic Is; New Zealand. 70 species, dwarf, carpeting or hummock-forming perennial evergreen herbs with tufted rosettes of small leaves and, in summer, stalkless umbels of small flowers. Hardy to 1°F (–17°C), and suitable for perfectly drained but moist, sunny positions on the rock garden, scree, raised bed or sink garden. Propagate by division or seed. The following plant is sometimes confused with *Bolax gummifera* (syn. *Azorella glebaria*). *A. trifurcata* Chile, Argentina; forming dense cushions or mats; leaves ¼–½ in (0.6–1 cm) long, leathery and dark glossy green to gray-green with three distinct teeth at their tips; flowers yellow.

B

Babiana (Latinized form of the Afrikaans *bobbejaan*, baboon: baboons are said to eat the corms). Iridaceae. Africa (those below from South Africa). BABOON FLOWER. Some 60 species, cormous perennials grown for brilliantly colored flowers produced in spring and summer. They seldom exceed 8 in (20 cm) in height and produce a flattened fan of plicately ribbed, often hairy, lance-shaped leaves in spring. This gives rise to an erect, simple or branched spike of up to ten flowers, dish-shaped with six broadly elliptic tepals in the majority of species, irregular and tubular with narrow tepals in species formerly included in *Antholyza*.

Baboon flowers are usually described as frost-tender, requiring container treatment much like that for *Freesia* and a minimum temperature of 50°F (10°C). They certainly respond well in such conditions and make attractive spring-flowering potted plants for the cool greenhouse, conservatory, and home. Most can equally be grown outside where winter temperatures do not fall much below 23°F (–5°C), in a warm, sunny position in free-draining, light but fertile soil. Outdoors, plant deeply (i.e., to 4 in/10 cm) and give a thick winter mulch of bracken litter or leaf mold. Alternatively, lift corms in fall and overwinter, cleaned and dry, in frost-free conditions. Replant or pot in early spring in equal parts loam, leaf mold, and sand. Feed pot-grown plants prior to flower formation. Propagate by offsets.

B. plicaia to 8 in (20 cm), flowers slightly irregular, fragrant, funnel-shaped, to 1½ in (4 cm) diam., in shades of pale blue, violet, and white with mauve and yellow blotches at the base of the lower tepals; *B. ringens* (syn. *Antholyza ringens*) to 8 in (20 cm), flowers 2 in (5 cm) long in shades of

Babiana rubrocyanea
The baboon flowers require winter protection in frost-prone climates. Corms may be lifted and stored, or plants given a thick mulch.

red or maroon, closely 2-ranked on unbranched spikes to 8 in (20 cm) tall in summer; *B. rubrocyanea* to 8 in (20 cm), flowers 1½ in (4 cm)-diam. funnel- to dish-shaped flowers with spreading tepals, royal blue in their upper half, deep wine red below; *B. stricta* to 8 in (20 cm), flowers funnel- to disk-shaped with broad tepals in shades of purple, mauve, blue and yellow, sometimes mixtures thereof; *B. thunbergii* (syn. *Antholyza plicata*) to 24 in (60 cm), flowers 2–2½ in (5–6 cm), tubular, curving in shades of bright red or deep pink stained green.

baccate of fruit; berrylike, with a juicy, pulpy rind.

Baccharis (for Bacchus, god of wine). Compositae. GROUNDSEL BUSH. Americas. Some 350 species, hardy evergreen or deciduous shrubs adapted to dry exposed conditions with tough, small, toothed leaves, or few or no leaves and photosynthetic stems instead. Large clusters of small discoid flower heads are followed by copious quantities of downy pappus. Grow in full sun in well-drained soil (minimum temperature 5°F [–15°C]). *B. halimifolia* will tolerate dry soils and saline, windy exposures; an excellent coastal shrub, it can be pruned to a hedge. *B. pilularis* is a fine open groundcover for binding impoverished soils in dry, sunny exposures, especially the cultivar 'Twin Peaks'. An annual shearing will improve its density. *B. sarothroides* is ideal for xeriscapes and for screening and erosion control in even the driest

locations. Prune all species where necessary in early spring. Propagate by softwood or semiripe cuttings.

B. halimifolia GROUNDSEL BUSH or SEA MYRTLE; Eastern US to the West Indies; fast-growing, deciduous shrub to 10 × 10 ft (3 × 3 m); branches angled, scurfy; leaves 1¼–2¾ in (3–7 cm), obovate, coarsely toothed; in fall, flower heads give way to masses of silver-white down; *B. pilularis* COYOTE BUSH, DWARF CHAPARRAL-BROOM; California; fast-spreading groundcover shrub to 20 in (50 cm) tall by 6½ ft (2 m) across; branches resinous, tangled; leaves ½–1½ in (1–4 cm)-long obovate, sawtoothed, bright green and tough-textured; 'Centennial': a cross with *B. sarothroides*, heat-resistant and narrow-leaved; 'Pigeon Point': to 3¼ × 12 ft (1 × 4 m) fast-growing with larger, light green leaves; 'Twin Peaks': a small leaved, slow-growing selection, male and thus free from the cotton down which can in this species become a nuisance; *B. sarothroides* DESERT BROOM; to 6½ ft (2 m), with no or very few leaves and bright green branches covered in snow-white pappus in winter.

Bacillus thuringiensis a bacterium used for biological control, mainly of caterpillars.

backbulb a dormant pseudobulb retained after active growth of usually only one season.

backcross a cross made between a hybrid plant and a plant genetically identical to one of the hybrid's parents. This procedure is used in breeding programs for a number of seed-raised generations with the object of concentrating desirable characters into an individual line.

backyard garden in the US a garden at the rear of a dwelling, usually enclosed with direct access from the living quarters. Also known as a yard garden.

Bacopa (from the South American name). Scrophulariaceae. WATER HYSSOP. 56 species, aquatic or semi-aquatic perennials with creeping to erect stems. Small, campanulate flowers are produced singly in the axils of thinly fleshy leaves. Plant in aquariums or at the margins of ponds and lakes. Cuttings of stem tips will root in warm water or wet loam, at a temperature of 68°F (20°C) or over.

B. caroliniana N America; leaves 1 in (2.5 cm), entire, ovate, scented of lemon; flowers blue; *B. monnieri* tropics; succulent, with obovate to spathulate leaves to ¾ in (2 cm) long sometimes notched at the tips; flowers white to pale blue.

bacteria single-celled, microscopic organisms lacking a true nucleus and chlorophyll. Most bacteria are saprophytic and beneficial, breaking down organic matter in soil or fixing nitrogen, but some are pathogens.

bacterial diseases bacterial infections cause many different symptoms in plants, including seedling blights, leaf spots or blotches, shoot blight, wilting, scabs, galls, cankers and rots. The same pathogen may cause different symptoms on its host, depending on climatic conditions or the stage in the host's development at which infection takes place. In warm, moist conditions bacterial cells can multiply extremely rapidly and this accounts for the destructiveness of many bacterial diseases and their common occurrence in warm climates especially. Among the hundreds of kinds of bacteria known to cause plant diseases, some have a wide host range, for example the CROWN GALL bacterium (*Agrobacterium tumefaciens*), while others, such as that causing HYACINTH YELLOWS (*Xanthomonas campestris* pv. *hyacinthi*), are restricted to a narrow range of host species.

The local spread of bacteria over short distances is effected principally by rain and wind. Bacteria on the surface of an infected plant disperse in rainwater, which is broken up into droplets and carried by the wind to other plants. Storms provide ideal conditions for the epidemic spread of bacterial diseases, as potential hosts will be likely to have waterlogged and wounded tissues which are highly susceptible to infection. Some diseases are transmitted by insects and other animals, including humans, and longer-distance spread is effected in this way.

Many bacterial diseases are dispersed through infected plants and propagating material; many are seed borne or in accompanying debris; others are soilborne but generally do not survive long in the absence of plant debris.

Bacterial blight is the common name for a bacterial disease causing widespread blackening of leaves and shoots. Examples include LILAC BLIGHT (*Pseudomonas syringae* pv. *syringae*), which also affects *Forsythia* and can cause blossom blight of pears. A number of plants can be attacked by other pathovars (pv.) of *P.syringae*, the diseases usually being referred to as bacterial leaf spots, such as blight of mulberries (*Morus* species) caused by *Pseudomonas syringae* pv. *mori*, and PEA BLIGHT (*P.syringae* pv. *pisi*), a serious seed-borne disease which has only recently become established in Britain. HALO BLIGHT (*Pseudomonas syringae* pv. *phaseolicola*) is a seed-borne disease of French and sometimes runner beans causing pale areas on leaves, stems and pods. Bacterial blight of walnuts (*Juglans regia*) is caused by *Xanthomonas campestris* pv. *juglandis*, which in the UK is mainly a disease of nursery stock but can also affect the fruits. An important bacterial blight affecting many rosaceous trees is FIREBLIGHT (*Erwinia amylovora*).

Bacterial canker manifests itself as sunken necrotic lesions of stem tissue. Cankers are often limited in size by a host reaction so there may be some malformation and outgrowth of the surrounding bark. *Pseudomonas syringae* pv. *mors-prunorum* is the cause of bacterial canker of *Prunus* species, especially cherries and plums, although almonds, apricots, peaches, nectarines and ornamental species are also susceptible. During fall or winter, bacteria from the leaves infect stem tissue through wounds or leaf scars. Unfolding leaves are yellow, often narrow and curled, and may wither and die during the summer. Infection spreads in spring to produce shallow, depressed cankers; branches usually show a characteristic flattening on one side. Affected branches may be killed and gum may exude from the lesions. No new cankers are formed in summer, but by then the leaves have been attacked and develop circular brown spots. The centers of these spots often drop out to

give a "shot hole" symptom.

Bacterial canker of poinsettia (*Curtobacterium flaccumfaciens* pv. *poinsettiae*) is a serious disease in which water-soaked streaks occur on stems and petioles, often extending to cause leaf-blotching and complete defoliation. BACTERIAL CANKER OF TOMATO (*Clavibacter michiganensis* subsp. *michiganensis*) is a vascular wilt disease in which deep cankers may be produced on the stems. The bacteria are seed- and soilborne, and outdoor crops are most seriously affected. CITRUS CANKER (*Xanthomonas campestris* pv. *citri*) is a major disease thought to have originated in Asia, and has been subject to strict quarantine measures for many years. Eradication campaigns have been successful following outbreaks in Australia, New Zealand, South Africa and the US, but the disease has become established in several South American countries. Affected plants show branch cankering and the smaller shoots, foliage and fruit are also attacked. There are several strains of different pathogenicity to citrus cultivars. BACTERIAL CANKER OF POPLARS (*Xanthomonas populi*) produces a cream-colored bacterial slime which oozes from cracks in young shoots in spring; large cankers may develop on branches and stems. Black poplars, including the Lombardy poplar (*Populus nigra* var. *italica*), are resistant to the disease.

Bacterial leaf and stem rot (*Erwinia chrysanthemi* pv. *dieffenbachiae*) is a widespread cause of brown leaf spotting and stem rot of *Dieffenbachia* species.

Bacterial leaf spot is caused by *Pseudomonas* and *Xanthomonas* species, and can give rise to leaf spots and other symptoms on various plants. LEAF SPOT OF ANTIRRHINUMS (*Pseudomonas syringae* pv. *antirrhini*) causes pale green leaf spots on seedling leaves which become brown and sunken in the center and may coalesce, leading to total collapse. It is seedborne and similar to diseases caused by *Pseudomonas* species on *Lobelia*, *Primula*, *Tagetes* and *Viola*; LEAF SPOT OF DELPHINIUMS (*P.syringae* pv. *delphinii*) results in large black blotches on the leaves, stems and flower buds of some cultivars. ANGULAR LEAF SPOT OF CUCURBITS (*P.syringae* pv. *lachrymans*) results in small, irregular, water-soaked spots which enlarge to become angular in shape between leaf veins. The affected tissue, which may exude drops of liquid containing bacteria, dries out, causing holes in the leaves. Small spots may also develop on the fruit and cause it to rot. LEAF BLOTCH OF MAGNOLIAS may be caused by *P.syringae*. LEAF SPOT OF BERBERIS is caused by *P.syringae* pv. *berberidis*. LEAF SPOT OF BEGONIAS (*Xanthomonas campestris* pv. *begoniae*) gives rise to small translucent spots on the underside of leaves and the spots may enlarge and merge so that the leaves turn brown and die. LEAF SPOT OF IVY (*Xanthomonas campestris* pv. *hederae*) may be troublesome in greenhouses and during propagation, when humidity is high and moisture persists on foliage.

Apart from copper preparations, most fungicides are ineffective against bacteria and control is best effected by an integrated program of measures intended to break the cycle of disease, involving: (a) the exclusion of the disease by the use of healthy seed and planting material, the destruction of infected tissue, plant debris and volunteer plants, general cleanliness and measures to ensure that contaminated tools, implements, and containers are not brought onto the site; (b) the prevention of damage to plants by cultural or harvesting operations, particularly during wet weather; (c) the use of resistant selections if available; (d) the control of possible insect or other animal vectors.

bacteriophage a virus that infects bacteria.

bagasse the fibrous residue of sugar cane processing, used as a ground mulch or as an ingredient of potting media.

bagging hook a sickle-shaped grass-cutting tool with a short handle.

bagworm (*Thyridopteryx ephemerae-formis*) a destructive garden insect familiar in N America, where its larvae devour the leaves of many trees and shrubs, especially conifers. They feed within spindle-shaped cases up to 2 in (50 mm) long, composed of plant foliage tied together with silk, in which

the fully fed larvae pupate in late summer. Adult males, mostly black with almost transparent wings, fly to cocoons containing wingless females, which die within the cocoons after egg-laying. The larvae emerge in spring. Remove and destroy the bags containing eggs in winter or apply contact insecticide in spring just after the young larvae hatch.

Baileya (for L.H. Bailey [1858–1954], US botanist and horticulturist). Compositae. Western North America. 3 species, hairy annual or perennial herbs with daisylike flower heads carried from spring until early fall. Grow in full sun. Sow seed *in situ* in late spring or, in cool climates, under glass in late winter for planting out in late spring. *B. multiradiata* DESERT MARIGOLD; annual to 14 in (35 cm) tall with entire or pinnately divided gray leaves and bright yellow flower heads to 2 in (5 cm) diam.

ball (1) the mass of roots and growing medium at the base of plants lifted from the open ground or removed from pots; (2) a condition of rose flowers in which the expanded bud decays before opening; (3) a class of dahlias with rounded flower heads larger than pompons.

ballbarrow a wheelbarrow with a large, usually pneumatic ball for the wheel.

balled and wrapped a description of plants lifted from the open ground where the root ball is wrapped in fabric for protection during transportation. Also known as burlapped.

Ballota (from *ballote*, the Greek name for black horehound, *B. nigra*). Labiatae. Europe, Mediterranean (chiefly), West Asia. 35 species, perennial herbs, sub-

shrubs and shrubs, mostly with paired leaves and whorled, two-lipped tubular flowers cupped by enlarged calyces in summer. Grow in sunny, sheltered situations in well drained soils (min. 0°F (−18°C)). *Ballota* may require some protection where the temperature frequently falls below 14°F (−10°C): frosts tends to kill off the soft top growth. Cut back or thin out dead wood in spring before new growth commences. Propagate by softwood or semiripe cuttings in spring and early summer.

B. acetabulosa Eastern Mediterranean, Greece; stems woolly, erect, ranked with crenate, rounded to heart-shaped leaves to 2 in (5 cm) long; flowers lilac-pink, backed by a white-felted dish-like calyx to ¾ in (2 cm) diameter; *B. pseudodictamnus* S Aegean; smaller, more rounded than the last species, with ovate to cordate, virtually entire leaves and far smaller calyces; 'All Hallow's Green': smaller still, with finely downy foliage in soft lime green.

bamboos A group of long-lived grasses of the subfamily Bambusoidae, comprising about 90 genera and 1000 species; with natural habitats ranging from 50°N in Japan to 47°S in Chile, at altitudes from sea level to 13,000 ft (4,000 m) and therefore variously hardy in gardens. Bamboos differ from other grasses in having silica-rich culms and stalked leaves joining the leaf sheaths. They vary in height from a few inches to 130 ft (40 m). Flowering is uncommon. When it does occur, the plants may be seriously weakened. Seed production is correspondingly rare and propagation is best done by division. Outside the cool, temperate West, bamboos are an important source of construction material, food and medicine. In gardens throughout the world many bamboo species are grown to provide ornamental screens and groundcover. The ripened culms make excellent plant supports. (*See table overleaf.*)

root ball lifted with surrounding soil

Balled and wrapped

B

BAMBOOS

Name	Distribution	Habit	Culms	Leaves
Bambusa multiplex *B. glaucescens; B. nana;* *B. argentea;* HEDGE BAMBOO	S China	10–50 ft (3–15 m), densely clump-forming	½–1¾ in (1–4.5 cm) diam., arching with prominent nodes and many branches	1–6 × ¼–⅝ in (2.5–15 × 0.5–1.5 cm), in two rows, rather silvery beneath
Comments: Much used in subtropical and tropical Asia for hedging. Good bonsai. 'Alphonso Karrii': culms and branches striped orange- yellow and green, tinged pink when young 'Golden Goddess': small,			culms golden, leaves larger. 'Riviereorum' (CHINESE GOODDESS BAMBOO): culms delicate, somewhat sinuous, leaves small. 'Silver Stripe': large, culms and leaves striped yellow or white.	
Bambusa oldhamii *Sinocalamus oldhamii* CLUMPING GIANT TIMBER BAMBOO; OLDHAM BAMBOO	China, Taiwan	20–50 ft (6–15 m), thickly clump-forming, erect with dense foliage	stout, 1¼–5 in (3–13 cm) diam., with white powder below nodes and short branches	6–12 × 1¼–2½ in (15–30 × 3–6 cm), tough and broad
		Comments: Much used in warm places for screening.		
Bambusa ventricosa BUDDHA'S BELLY BAMBOO	S China	25–70 ft (8–20 m), densely clump-forming	1¼–2¼ in (3–5.5 cm) diam., smooth and green to yellow-green	4–8 × ⅝–1¼ in (10–20 × 1.5–3 cm)
Comments: In containers or on poor soils, culms seldom exceed 6½ ft (2 m) and develop swollen internodes, considered ornamental.				
Bambusa vulgaris COMMON BAMBOO	so widely cultivated in S Asia that its natural habitat is obscure	15–80 ft (5–25 m), densely clump-forming	2–10 in (5–25 cm) diam., smooth with prominent nodes	4–10 × ¾–1½ in (10–25 × 1.8–4 cm)
		Comments: Used for light timber, paper pulp, and edible young shoots. 'Vittata': culms and leaves striped green and yellow.		
Chimonobambusa marmorea *Arundinaria marmorea*	long cultivated in Japan, native country uncertain	6½–10 ft (2–3 m), running rhizomes making large, sometimes invasive stands of widely spaced culms	½–¾ in (1–2 cm) diam., round in sec- tion, sheaths marbled purple or pink- brown with white spots when young, densely leafy with many branches	3–6½ × ¼–⅝ in (7.5–16 × 0.5–1.5 cm)
Chimonobambusa quadrangularis *Arundinaria quadrangularis* SQUARE BAMBOO	SE China, Taiwan, natu- ralized Japan	6½–30 ft (2–10 m), run- ning rhizomes with well- spaced, strongly erect culms and soft tiers of branches	½–1¼ in (1–3 cm) diam., green, square in section with 4 angles and thornlike root protuberances at nodes	4–11 × ¾–2¾ in (10–29 × 2–7 cm), dark green.
Chimonobambusa tumidissinoda *Quiongzhuea tumidinoda*	China (Yunnan, Sichuan)	6½–20 ft (2–6 m), running, erect to spreading above with outspread branches and graceful foliage	½–1¼ in (1–3 cm) diam., dull to glossy olive to sap green, basically narrow but bulging like a spinning top at each node; branches slender	2–6 × ¼–1 in (5–15 × 0.5–2.5 cm), finely tapering and thin-textured, mid- green above, gray-green beneath
Comments: A very elegant bamboo valued for its unusual culms; requires moist, fertile soil in a sheltered situation.				
Chusquea coronalis	C America	to 20 ft (6 m), forms clumps; culms arch or sprawl	¼–¾ in (0.5–2 cm) diam., slender with rings of fine branches	1–2¾ × ⅛–⅜ in (2.3–7 × 0.3–0.8 cm)

Comments: Distinguished from *C.culeou* by the branches, which completely encircle the culms, and the leaves without tessellate veins.

Bambusa multiplex

Chimonobambusa
quadrangularis

Chimonobambusa
tumidissinoda

BAMBOOS

Name	Distribution	Habit	Culms	Leaves
Chusquea culeou	Chile	12–20 ft (4–6 m), stately, large clumps with distinctively "whorled" branches	⅜–1¼ in (1.5–3 cm) diam., with solid pith, pale papery sheaths and slender, rather short branches crowded in alternating semicircles	2½–5 × ¼–⅝ in (6–13 × 0.5–1.5 cm)

Comments: Differs from *C. coronalis* in the branches on one side of each node only and the leaves with tessellate veins. 'Tenuis' (var. *tenuis*; *C. breviglumis*) grows to 6½ ft (2 m) with narrower culms spreading outward at 45° from a narrow-based clump.

Dendrocalamus giganteus *Sinocalamus giganteus* GIANT BAMBOO	SE Asia	50–130 ft (15–40 m), giant clump-former with a strong V-shaped outline from base and arching upper reaches hung with light branches	6–14 in (15–35 cm) diam., green to yellow-green, very stout with prominent nodes and large sheaths	8–22 × 1¼–4¾ in (20–55 × 3–12 cm)

Comments: A spectacular giant for subtropical and tropical gardens, large warm greenhouses, and the atriums of public buildings.

Drepanostachyum falcatum *Arundinaria falcata;* *Chimonobambusa falcata;* *Sinarundinaria falcata;* *Thamnocalamus falcatus*	E Himalaya	6½–20 ft (2–6 m), densely clump-forming and slow-growing	⅜–1 in (1.5–2.5 cm) diam., slender, white-powdery at first becoming glossy yellow with bushy branches at nodes	4½–14 × ½–1 in (11–35 × 1–2.5 cm)

Comments: Intolerant of wet/cold conditions and temperatures below 21°F (–6°C). Best grown in large tubs of fertile, sandy loam kept evenly moist in the cool conservatory. **D. khasianum** differs in its culms colored a rich, polished coppery red.

Fargesia dracocephala	China (Sichuan)	10–15 ft (3–5 m), makes a neat, fountainlike clump with arching top and branches	⅛–⅜ in (0.4–0.8 cm) diam., with numerous branches at first growing close to internodes, then spreading or drooping	2–6½ × ¼–¾ in (5–17 × 0.5–2 cm), held horizontally in a frond-like arrangement

Fargesia murieliae *Arundinaria murieliae;* *Arundinaria spathacea;* *Fargesia spathacea;* *Sinarundinaria murieliae;* *Thamnocalamus spathaceus* UMBRELLA BAMBOO	C China	10–12 ft (3–4 m), clump-forming with culms gently arching outward from a narrow base and making a light, airy, arching top	⅛–½ in (0.4–1 cm) diam., white-powdery at first, soon yellow-green, then yellow with pale brown sheaths gradually standing away from culms	2½–6 × ¼–¾ in (6–15 × 0.5–1.8 cm), apple green, tip finely tapering

Fargesia nitida *Arundinaria nitida;* *Sinarundinaria nitida* FOUNTAIN BAMBOO	C China	10–12 ft (3–4 m), clump-forming with graceful, slender culms bowed outward from a narrow base and weighted with airy, drooping branches	⅛–⅜ in (0.4–0.8 cm) diam., gray-powdery at first then lined or tinted purple-brown with purple-green sheaths	1½–4½ × ¼–½ in (4–11 × 0.5–1.1 cm) dark green, flickering in the breeze

Comments: Includes 'Eisenach', to 6½ ft (2 m), culms strongly erect, black-tinted with prominent nodes; 'Ems River', to 12 ft (4 m), culms almost black, very hardy; 'Maclureana', to 20 ft (6 m), culms strongly arching, pearly gray-powdery; 'Nymphenburg', culms dull gray-green, weeping).

Chusquea culeou

Fargesia nitida

Phyllostachys aureosulcata var. **aureocaulis**

B

BAMBOOS

Name	Distribution	Habit	Culms	Leaves
× **Hibanobambusa tranquillans** *Phyllostachys tranquillans;* *Semiarundinaria tranquillans* INYOU-CHIKUZOKU	Japan	6½–15 ft (2–5 m), rhizomes running in warm, wet and fertile conditions, otherwise making open clumps with rather sparse branches	½–1¼ in (1–3 cm) diam., erect to arching at apex	6–10 × 1½–2 in (15–25 × 3.5–5 cm), dark green, tough, glossy

Comments: Possibly a hybrid between *Phyllostachys* and *Sasa*. Includes 'Shiroshima' with culms, sheaths and leaves striped white and yellow.

Name	Distribution	Habit	Culms	Leaves
Himalayacalamus falconeri *Arundinaria falconeri;* *Drepanostachyum falconeri;* *Sinarundinaria falconeri;* *Thamnocalamus falconeri*	C Himalaya	15–30 ft (5–10 m), makes a V-shaped clump of elegant slender culms and abundant feathery foliage	¾–1¼ in (2–3 cm) diam., yellow-green with a purple ring below the nodes	2¾–6 × ⅜–1 in (7–16 × 0.8–2.7 cm)

Comments: 'Damarapa': (syn. *Arundinaria hookeriana* of gardens; *Sinarundinaria hookeriana* of gardens); culms emerging pink striped lime green then turning deep amber or red-brown with irregular, dark olive stripes. Requires a sheltered, warm site in moist, fertile, sandy soil rich in leaf mold. In cold regions, grow in tubs in a cool conservatory.

Name	Distribution	Habit	Culms	Leaves
Himalayacalamus hookerianus *Arundinaria hookeriana;* *Chimonobambusa hookeriana;* *Drepanostachyum hookerianum;* *Sinarundinaria hookeriana* BLUE-STEMMED BAMBOO	E Himalaya	20–28 ft (6–9 m), tall, V-shaped clump-former	⅝–1¼ in (1.5–3 cm) diam., blue-green, thickly white-powdered at first with a blue-gray ring below nodes, later yellow-green or purple-red	to 7 × ¾ in (18 × 2 cm), very graceful, appearing misty blue en masse and at a distance

Comments: The name *Arundinaria hookeriana*, properly a synonym of this species, is often misapplied to *Himalayacalamus falconeri* 'Damarapa' (q.v.).

Name	Distribution	Habit	Culms	Leaves
Indocalamus latifolius *Arundinaria latifolia*	E China	1½–3¼ ft (0.5–1 m), rhizome running in warm, wet conditions, otherwise slowly building a spreading, moundlike clump	to ¼ in (0.5 cm) diam., slender and sparsely branched	4–16 × ⅝–3 in (10–40 × 1.5–8 cm), spreading, mid- to deep green; veins not tessellated

Name	Distribution	Habit	Culms	Leaves
Indocalamus tessellatus *Arundinaria ragamowskii;* *Sasa tessellata; Sasamorpha tessellata*	C China, Japan	3¼–8 ft (1–2.5 m), rhizomes running or growing slowly to make spreading, rather untidy, mounded clumps	¼–⅝ in (0.5–1.5 cm) diam., slender and sparsely branched	to 24 × 4 in (60 × 10 cm), spreading to drooping, mid- to dark green with tessellated veins

Comments: The largest leaves of any bamboo listed here — an exotic and luxuriant screen or mounded, tall groundcover; also good for containers.

Name	Distribution	Habit	Culms	Leaves
Otatea acuminata *O. acuminata ssp. aztecorum;* *Arthrostylidium longifolium;* *Yushania aztecorum* MEXICAN WEEPING BAMBOO	Mexico to Nicaragua	6½–25 ft (2–8 m), clump-forming with very graceful foliage on slender culms that arch almost to the ground	¾–1½ in (2–4 cm) diam., ultimately weeping	2¾–6 × ⅛–¼ in (7–16 × 0.3–0.5 cm), numerous, pendulous

Comments: Plant outdoors only in regions with short-lived frosts; otherwise suitable for the cool greenhouse or conservatory. Once established, will cope with drier conditions than most bamboos.

Phyllostachys bambusoides

Phyllostachys bambusoides 'Allgold'

Phyllostachys flexuosa

BAMBOOS

Name	Distribution	Habit	Culms	Leaves
Phyllostachys aurea FISHPOLE BAMBOO; GOLDEN BAMBOO;	SE China, Japan	6½–30 ft (2–10 m), strongly erect runner with dense foliage; may remain a clump-former in cold climates	¾–2 in (2–5 cm) diam., smooth, green then brown-yellow with short, crowded internodes at base	2–6 × ¼–¾ in (5–15 × 0.5–2 cm)

Comments: Makes a good screen or hedge and will tolerate some drought. 'Albovariegata': culms slender, leaves striped white; 'Holochrysa': culms yellow sometimes striped green, leaves sometimes striped; 'Violascens' (_Phyllostachys violascens_): to 20 ft (6 m) tall, culms stout, green-striped purple, ultimately stained gray-purple to violet, leaves large, rather glaucous beneath.

Name	Distribution	Habit	Culms	Leaves
Phyllostachys aureosulcata YELLOW GROOVE BAMBOO	NE China	10–30 ft (3–10 m), vigorous, erect runner with dense foliage (may remain in clump in colder climates)	½–1½ in (1–4 cm) diam., yellow-green with a distinct yellow groove, often flexuous below	2–6½ × ½–1 in (5–17 × 1–2.5 cm)

Comments: Good hedging bamboo. f. _aureocaulis_, syn. f. _spectabilis_: culms yellow marked with a green groove.

Name	Distribution	Habit	Culms	Leaves
Phyllostachys bambusoides _P. mazellii; P. reticulata_ GIANT TIMBER BAMBOO; JAPANESE TIMBER BAMBOO	China, Japan, widely grown elsewhere	10–100 ft (3–30 m), strongly erect and running, forming large groves of well-spaced culms decked with airy foliage. In colder climates it will remain in a clump	6–8 in (15–20 cm) diam., stout, green, with heavily marked sheaths	3½–8 × ¾–1¾ in (9–20 × 2–4.5 cm)

Comments: Includes 'Albovariegata' (leaves marked white), 'Castillonis' (culms yellow with a green stripe), 'Castillonis Inversa' (culms green with a yellow stripe), 'Holochrysa' ('Allgold') (smaller and more open with golden-yellow culms sometimes striped green), 'Marliacea' (culms green, internodes strangely wrinkled).

Name	Distribution	Habit	Culms	Leaves
Phyllostachys edulis _P. heterocycla f. pubescens;_ _P. pubescens; P. mitis of gardens_ MOSO BAMBOO	China, intro- duced Japan	10–81 ft (3–27 m), rhizomes running, forming large groves of stout, erect, gray-green culms with small feathery leaves; in colder climates, will remain in a clump	1½–12 in (4–30 cm) diam., very thick, gray and velvety when young, ultimately green or almost orange with white powder below nodes, curved near base; sheaths heavily mottled brown	2–4¾ × ¼–¾ in (5–12 × 0.5–2 cm)

Comments: 'Bicolor': culms striped yellow; f. **_heterocycla:_** syn. _P. heterocycla,_ TORTOISESHELL BAMBOO, lowest culm internodes short, distorted and bulging to one side.

Name	Distribution	Habit	Culms	Leaves
Phyllostachys flexuosa Comments:	China	6½–30 ft (2–10 m), rhizomes running, making open groves of erect to arching culms with feathery foliage; remains clump-forming in colder climates	¾–2¾ in (2–7 cm) diam., erect then arching, green-yellow becoming darker (almost black) with age, smooth with white powder below nodes	2–6 × ⅝–¾ in (5–15 × 1.5–2 cm)

Name	Distribution	Habit	Culms	Leaves
Phyllostachys nigra BLACK BAMBOO	E & C China	10–30 ft (3–10 m), running with fairly dense culms erect then arching above; remains in a tight clump in colder climates	½–1½ in (1–4 cm) diam., green at first, typically turning glossy black in the second year with some gray-white powder below nodes	1½–5 × ⅜–¾ in (4–13 × 0.8–1.8 cm), bright green, thin-textured

Comments: A beautiful and popular bamboo for sheltered borders and large containers. The blackest form is f. **_nigra_** with glossy, pure black culms; it includes the cultivar 'Othello' with tightly clumped culms that are jet black even in their first year. In f. **_henonis_** the culms are green to yellow-green. The culms are variably marked dark purple-brown on green in f. **_punctata;_** in 'Boryana' they are green-blotched brown.

Phyllostachys nigra

Phyllostachys nigra f. _henonis_

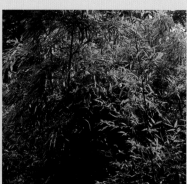

Phyllostachys viridiglaucescens

BAMBOOS

Name	Distribution	Habit	Culms	Leaves
Phyllostachys sulphurea	E China	12–40 ft (4–12 m), running, making groves of erect culms; remains clumped in colder climates	¼–3½ in (0.5–9 cm) diam.., ultimately yellow, sometimes striped green, sheaths thick, spotted and blotched brown	2½–6 × ⅜–1 in (6–16 × 1.5–2.5 cm)
Comments: f. ***viridis*** (*P. mitis; P.* 'Robert Young'; *P.viridis*) is a larger plant with green culms; it seldom thrives in cold climates.				
Phyllostachys viridiglaucescens *P.elegans*	E China	12–40 ft (4–12 m), running, forming a dense stand of erect to arching culms; often remains clumped in cooler climates	½–2 in (1–5 cm) diam.., smooth, with white waxy powder below nodes, often curved at base; sheaths large, with dark spots and blotches	1½–8 × ¼–¾ in (4–20 × 0.6–2 cm)
Pleioblastus argenteostriatus *P.chino var. argenteostriatus; Arundinaria argenteostriata; Nippocalamus argenteostriatus; Sasa argenteostriata*	origin unknown, long cultivated in Japan	to 3¼ ft (1 m), running, forming erect stands of dense slender culms	¼–½ in (0.5–1 cm) diam., thin, sparsely branched	5½–9 × ½–¾ in (14–22 × 1–2 cm), pale to mid- green striped creamy white
Comments: Attractive medium-height groundcover, best cut back every 1–2 years in spring.				
Pleioblastus chino *P. maximowiczii; Arundinaria chino; Nippocalamus chino*	C Japan	6½–12 ft (2–4 m), running and somewhat invasive making dense stands of lax, reedy stems	¼–½ in (0.5–1 cm) diam., slender and sparsely branched	4¾–10 × ½–1¼ in (12–25 × 1–3 cm)
Comments: Includes the narrow-leaved, erratically white-striped f. **angustifolius** (*P.angustifolius*) and f. **gracilis** (*P.chino* 'Elegantissimus') which differs in its reliably white-striped, slender leaves, not hairy beneath.				
Pleioblastus gramineus *Arundinaria graminea*	Japan, E China	6½–15 ft (2–5 m), running, making dense stands of slender culms	¼–¾ in (0.5–2 cm) diam., freely branches	6–12 × ⅜–¾ in (15–30 × 0.8–2 cm), narrow and finely tapering
Comments: A graceful, medium-sized bamboo with long narrow leaves.				
Pleioblastus humilis *Arundinaria humilis; Nippocalamus humilis; Sasa humilis*	C Japan	3¼–6½ ft (1–2 m), running makes a dense stand of erect slender stems	1⁄16–⅛ in (0.2–0.3 cm) diam., reedy, branching throughout	4–10 × ⅜–¾ in (10–25 × 1.5–2 cm)
Comments: Useful medium-height groundcover. Responds well to clipping or even mowing in spring and early summer. var. **pumilis** (*Sasa pumila; Arundinaria pumilia; Arundinaria gauntlettii*) is more sturdy and compact with very fresh green foliage.				
Pleioblastus pygmaeus *Arundinaria pygmaea; Nippocalamus pygmaeus; Sasa pygmaea* DWARF FERN-LEAF BAMBOO	origin obscure, long cultivated in Japan	4–8 in (10–20 cm), running, making dense, short thickets of soft, slender culms	1⁄32–1⁄16 in (0.1–0.2 cm) diam.	¾–1½ × 1⁄16–¼ in (2–4 × 0.2–0.5 cm), arranged in two ranks, the tips sometimes withering and becoming papery white in hard winters

Comments: A charming miniature bamboo useful for containers, the margins of small ponds and for groundcover. The cultivar most often grown is 'Distichus', somewhat taller and very vigorous with leaves arranged in two distinct ranks at the culm tips. Both respond well to trimming or mowing.

Pleioblastus pygmaeus 'Distichus'   *Pleioblastus variegatus*

Pleioblastus viridistriatus

BAMBOOS

Name	Distribution	Habit	Culms	Leaves
Pleioblastus simonii *Arundinaria simonii; Nippocalamus simonii* SIMON BAMBOO	C & S Japan	10–25 ft (3–8 m), running, but usually remaining confined to a clump of erect, elegant culms with arching branches and airy foliage	½–1¼ in (1.2–3 cm) diam., stout but thin-walled with white waxy powder below nodes and persistent sheaths that stand away from the culms as branches develop	5–11 × ½–1 in (13–27 × 1.2–2.5 cm), tapering finely, somewhat glaucous beneath

Comments: Includes 'Variegatus' (*P. simonii* var. *heterophyllus*; *Arundinaria simonii* var. *albostriata*; *Arundinaria simonii* var. *striata*), less robust, with variable leaves, some narrow, some broad and many white-striped.

Name	Distribution	Habit	Culms	Leaves
Pleioblastus variegatus *P.fortunei; Arundinaria fortunei; Arundinaria variegata; Nippocalamus fortunei; Sasa variegata* DWARF WHITE-STRIPED BAMBOO	probably a selection of the green-leaved var. *viridis*, itself of unknown origin but widely cultivated in Japan	8–30 in (20–75 cm), running, but usually making loose clumps of slender culms	¹⁄₁₆–½ in (0.2–1 cm), typically very thin with a few erect branches	4–8 × ¼–¾ in (10–20 × 0.7–1.8 cm), tapering finely, dark green to sea green with white to cream stripes of varying breadth

Comments: One of the finest and most widely grown variegated bamboos, a semidwarf making miniature stands of bright foliage. Once established, it responds well to trimming. Also suitable for bonsai treatment and use in cut flower arrangements.

Name	Distribution	Habit	Culms	Leaves
Pleioblastus viridistriatus *P. auricomus; Arundinaria auricoma; Arundinaria viridistriata; Sasa auricoma*	origin obscure, naturalized in Japan	3¼–10 ft (1–3 m), running but usually making a loose, moundlike clump of graceful stems	¹⁄₁₆–⅛ in (0.2–0.4 cm) diam., slender, reedy and sparsely branched	4¾–9 × ⅝–1½ in (12–22 × 1.5–3.5 cm), softly hairy, emerald green with brilliant yellow stripes

Comments: Very colorful small bamboo for ground cover or specimen planting. Cut hard back in spring every year. The leaves of 'Chrysophyllus' are a striking pure gold.

Name	Distribution	Habit	Culms	Leaves
Pseudosasa amabilis *Arundinaria amabilis* LOVELY BAMBOO; TONKIN CANE	S China, widely cultivated throughout SE Asia	15–43 ft (5–13 m), running, making dense thickets of tall, erect then arching culms; in colder climates, more likely to remain in a clump	¾–2¾ in (2–7 cm) diam., thick-walled with hairy, persistent sheaths and usually 3 branches per nodes	4–14 × ½–1½ in (10–35 × 1.2–3.5 cm)

Comments: A very handsome bamboo producing long, rigid culms widely used for canes. It suffers in cold and windy conditions and favors moist, fertile and sheltered locations to 10°F (–12°C).

Name	Distribution	Habit	Culms	Leaves
Pseudosasa japonica *Arundinaria japonica; Sasa japonica* ARROW BAMBOO	Japan, Korea	10–20 ft (3–6 m), running, making dense stands of erect then arching culms with resilient foliage, clump-forming in colder climates	½–¾ in (1–2 cm) diam., thin-walled with persistent, thick sheaths and, usually, one branch per node	8–14 × 1–1½in (20–36 × 2.5–3.5 cm), tapering finely, tough, two-thirds of undersurface glaucous (thus distinguished from *Sasamorpha borealis*)

Comments: One of the most commonly grown bamboos, excellent for large gardens and for screening; it resists high winds and will tolerate poor soils, dry or saturated.

Pseudosasa japonica

Sasa veitchii

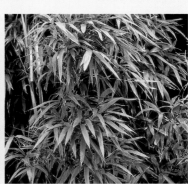

Semiarundinaria fastuosa

BAMBOOS

Name	Distribution	Habit	Culms	Leaves
Sasa nipponica	Japan	20–32 in (50–80 cm), running, forming loose stands or clumps of graceful culms	$^1/_{16}$–$^1/_8$ in (0.2–0.4 cm) diam.., tinted purple, nodes glabrous, prominent, not branched	3–8 × $^1/_2$–1$^1/_4$ in (8–20 × 1.4–3 cm), thin-textured
Comments: A handsome medium-sized bamboo with a distinctive habit: a handlike arrangement of broad leaves atop narrow, crowded culms. A rampant spreader.				
Sasa palmata *S.paniculata; S. cernua; S. senanensis*	Japan	5–13 ft (1.5–4 m), running, forming a thicket of slender culms topped with a canopy of luxuriant foliage	$^1/_{16}$–$^1/_8$ in (0.2–0.5 cm) diam.., often streaked purple, branches few	10–16 × 2–3$^3/_4$ in (25–40 × 5–9.5 cm), tapering finely, tough, bright shinning green with a yellow-green midrib
Comments: A handsome medium-sized bamboo with a distinctive habit: a handlike arrangement of broad leaves atop narrow, crowed culms. A rampant spreader.				
Sasa veitchii *S.albomarginata*	Japan	32–60 in (80–150 cm), gently running, forming low thickets of outspread foliage	to $^1/_4$ in (0.5 cm) diam.., purple-lined, glaucous, more or less glabrous	6–10 × 1$^1/_4$–2$^1/_2$ in (15–25 × 3.2–6 cm), lanceolate-ovate, dark green with a yellow-green midrib, the margin withering and becoming papery-white
Comments: Excellent medium-height groundcover or a low, loose hedge. The broad, ribbed leaves are especially attractive in winter, when they develop ivory, parchmentlike margins.				
Sasaella masumuneana *Arundinaria atropurpurea; Sasa masumuneana*	Japan	1$^1/_2$–6$^1/_2$ ft (0.5–2 m), running, forming low thickets of slender, branching culms topped with a graceful, nodding canopy	$^1/_8$–$^1/_6$ in (0.3–0.4 cm) diam.., sheaths sparsely bristly	4–7$^1/_2$ × $^5/_8$–2 in (10–19 × 1.5–3.5 cm), glabrous, sheaths lined purple
Comments: Includes 'Albostriata' with leaves striped white turning to yellow, and f. ***aureostriata*** with leaves striped yellow.				
Sasaella ramosa *Arundinaria vagans; Sasa ramosa* **Comments:**	Japan	3$^1/_4$–5 ft (1–1.5 m), running and rampant, forming low thickets of broadly branching, slender culms topped with narrow, nodding leaves	$^1/_8$–$^1/_6$ in (0.3–0.4 cm) diam.., sometimes purple, sheaths lacking bristles	4–8 × $^1/_2$–1$^1/_4$ in (10–20 × 1.4–3 cm), hairy beneath, margins withering, becoming white and parchmentlike
Semiarundinaria fastuosa *Arundinaria fastuosa; Arundinaria narihira; Phyllostachys fastuosa*	S Japan	10–40 ft (3–12 m), clump-forming with plum-colored new growth and tall erect culms	$^3/_4$–2$^3/_4$ in (2–7 cm) diam.., hollow, lined purple-brown, glabrous with white powder below nodes; sheaths thick with shining, wine-colored insides	3$^1/_2$–8 × $^5/_8$–1 in (9–21 × 1.5–2.7 cm)
Comments: Survives lows of –8°F (–22°C). Plant on moist rich soils in a sheltered position. Only the upper reaches of the culms are furnished with foliage, making this bamboo especially suitable for underplanting with low shrubs and perennials.				
Shibataea kumasasa *Phyllostachys kumasasa; Phyllostachys ruscifolia*	China, Japan	1$^1/_2$–6 ft (0.5–1.8 m), running but appearing clumped and making a compact 'bush' of broad, bright green foliage	$^1/_{16}$–$^1/_4$ in (0.2–0.5 cm) diam.., slender, green, with very short branches throughout	2–4$^1/_2$ × $^1/_2$–1 in (5–11 × 1.3–2.5 cm), elliptic-ovate, dark to bright glossy green, borne along culms

Comments: Dwarf to medium-sized shrubby bamboo, not unlike *Ruscus*. Excellent high groundcover or low hedging; responds well to clipping over in spring and is even trimmed into rounded shapes in some Japanese gardens. Requires a moist, fertile, sheltered position.

Shibataea kumasasa

Thamnocalamus tessellatus

Yushania anceps

BAMBOOS

Name	Distribution	Habit	Culms	Leaves
Sinobambusa tootsik	China	15–40 ft (5–12 m), running, and sometimes rampant, forming light, elegant groves	$^3/_4$–$2^1/_2$ in (2–6 cm) diam.., smooth, with hairy sheaths	3–8 × $^1/_2$–$1^1/_4$ in (8–20 × 1.3–3 cm), tapering finely

Comments: A graceful bamboo requiring moist fertile soil, dappled sun and a humid atmosphere. Will not tolerate hard frosts and harsh winds.

Name	Distribution	Habit	Culms	Leaves
Thamnocalamus aristatus *T.spathiflorus ssp. aristatus;* *Arundinaria aristata*	NE Himalaya	10–30 ft (3–10 m), vigorously clump-forming, erect	$^1/_2$–$2^1/_2$ in (1–6 cm) diam.., yellow-green speckled brown with age, nodes with white waxy bloom below; branches red-lined, sheaths sometimes with dark markings	$2^1/_2$–$5^1/_4$ × $^1/_4$–$^3/_4$ in (6.5–13.5 × 0.6–1.8 cm), with hairy callus at base of stalk

Comments: An excellent hardy bamboo for screening or waterside plantings.

Name	Distribution	Habit	Culms	Leaves
Thamnocalamus crassinodus *Fargesia crassinoda*	Tibet	10–12 ft (3–4 m), erect, forming a V-shaped clump with very graceful, feathery foliage on spreading, fine branches	$^1/_2$–$^3/_4$ in (1–2 cm) diam.., blue-green with thick white- or blue-gray bloom at first, later smooth, purple- or yellow-green, nodes swollen; sheaths large, parchmentlike	$1^3/_4$–$3^1/_2$ × $^1/_4$–$^1/_2$ in (4.5–9 × 0.5–1 cm), gray-green

Comments: 'Kew Beauty', with very slender branches and small narrow leaves is one of the most elegant hardy bamboos.

Name	Distribution	Habit		
Thamnocalamus spathiflorus *Arundinaria spathiflora*	NW Himalaya	**Comments:** Differs from *T. aristatus* in its slightly flexuous gray culms bloomed white at first and later flushed pink in strong sunlight; the leaves are gray-green with no callus at the base of the stalk.		

Name	Distribution	Habit	Culms	Leaves
Thamnocalamus tessellatus *Arundinaria tessallata*	S Africa	8–22 ft (2.5–7 m), clump-forming or (in warm climates) running and invasive; pink-streaked shoots become tall, erect culms with dense whorls of short branches	$^1/_2$–$2^1/_2$ in (1–6 cm) diam.., pale green, nodes tinted purple-pink; sheaths large, papery, white; branches short, red-tinted, many per node	2–8 × $^1/_4$–$^3/_4$ in (5–21 × 0.5–2 cm), finely tapered, dark green

Comments: A striking and robust bamboo for mild climates or cool greenhouses.

Name	Distribution	Habit	Culms	Leaves
Yushania anceps *Arundinaria anceps;* *Arundinaria jaunsarensis;* *Chimonobambusa jaunsarensis;* *Sinarundinaria anceps*	C & NW Himalaya	$6^1/_2$–15 ft (2–5 m), forms an erect to spreading clump with arching branches above	$^1/_4$–$^1/_2$ in (0.5–1.2 cm) diam.., smooth; branches pendulous, not developing in first year; sheaths soon falling	$2^1/_2$–$5^1/_2$ × $^1/_4$–$^3/_4$ in (6–14 × 0.5–1.8 cm), mid-green, smooth, stalks sometimes purple-tinted

Comments: Popular medium-sized bamboo, resembles a larger, clump-forming *Fargesia*. 'Pitt White' (*Arundinaria nitikayamensis*) grows to twice the height of the type and is exceptionally graceful, if less hardy.

Name	Distribution	Habit	Culms	Leaves
Yushania maling *Arundinaria maling; Fargesia maling; Sinarundinaria maling*	NE Himalaya	10–30 ft (3–10 m), erect, clump-forming	$^3/_4$–2 in (2–5 cm) diam.., rough when young, sheaths persistent	$3^1/_3$–$^3/_4$ × $^1/_3$–$^3/_5$ in (8.5–1.8 × 0.8–1.6 cm), slightly rough-textured

Bambusa (from the Malay vernacular name). Gramineae. Tropical and subtropical Asia. 120 species, tender, clump-forming bamboos. See *bamboos*.

Banksia (for Sir Joseph Banks [1743–1800], British botanist who first collected these plants). Proteaceae. AUSTRALIAN HONEYSUCKLE. Australia. 50 species, tender trees and shrubs, evergreens with leathery leaves and, in spring and summer, long-styled flowers in dense terminal spikes which resemble brilliantly colored, whiskery cones. Also decorative, the seeds ripen in flat-tened, woody capsules which gape like duck bills or oysters amid the bristly remnants of the flower cone. They thrive in sheltered locations (min. 20°F/–7°C) but will tolerate short-lived frosts to 19°F (–7°C) if quite dry. In less favored locations, they need a minimum temperature of 45°F (7°C) and the protection of a greenhouse or conservatory. Grow in full sun in free-draining sandy, slightly acidic soil low in nutrients (especially nitrates and phosphates). Under glass ventilate liberally. Use slow-release fertilizer devoid of superphosphate. Application of sulfate of iron may wean shy-flowering plants. Water moderately in growth, scarcely at all in winter. Prune only to remove dead growth or to cut flowers and seed heads for decoration. Increase by seed. See table overleaf.

Banksia seed head
In the wild, the flattened, bill-like seeds of *Banksia* may open following a bush fire; an environmental adaptation.

BANKSIA

Name	Habit	Leaves	Inflorescence
B. ashbyi ASHBY'S BANKSIA	spreading tall shrub or tree to 25 × 10 ft (8 × 3 m)	4–12 in (10–30 cm), linear, wavy-serrate	bright orange, 6–8 in (15–20 cm) long
B. baueri WOOLLY BANKSIA	compact, low shrub to 6½ ft (2 m)	1½–5 in (4–13 cm), oblong cuneate, serrate, brown-green at first	orange-brown to gray, to 8 × 5 in (20 × 13 cm), woolly
B. baxteri BAXTER'S BANKSIA	spreading shrub to 12 × 12 ft (4 × 4 m)	2¾–6½ in (7–17 cm), rusty brown then bright green, divided into triangular lobes	globose 2–3 in (5–8 cm) diam.., red-brown to green with yellow styles
B. blechnifolia	prostrate, spreading shrub to 20 in (50 cm) tall	10–18 in (25–45 cm), erect, long-stalked and fernlike, appearing basal, deeply 8–22-pinnately lobed	cylindrical, to 6 in (16 cm), red-pink, borne at ground level
B. brownii FEATHER-LEAVED BANKSIA	tall shrub to 12 × 6½ ft (4 × 2 m)	to 4½ in (11 cm), featherlike, soft-textured, whorled, white beneath with narrow, curving segments	6–8 in (15–20 cm), oblong-cylindrical, flowers cream below, gray-brown above
B. coccinea SCARLET BANKSIA	shrub to small tree, 6½–15 × 3¼–50 ft (2–5 × 1–15.5 m)	to 3½ in (9 cm), oblong, dentate, velvety pink brown at first, then dark green above, silver beneath	to 8 in (20 cm), globose, gray with scarlet styles
B. dryandroides DRYANDRA-LEAVED BANKSIA	dense, spreading shrub, to 3¼ × 5 ft (1 × 1.5 m)	to 6½ in (17 cm), broadly linear with pinnate triangular segments	to 1¼ in (3 cm) diam.., spherical, pale brown to dull orange
B. ericifolia HEATH BANKSIA	compact shrub to 15 ft (5 m) tall	to ¾ in (2 cm), narrowly linear	to 12 in (30 cm), cylindrical, orange-red to russet or gray with orange styles
B. 'Giant Candles' (B. ericifolia × B. spinulosa) BULL BANKSIA	compact shrub to 12 ft (4 m)	to 1¾ in (4.5 cm), linear, revolute, slightly toothed	to 16 in (40 cm), deep orange
B. grandis	tall, robust tree to 30 ft (10 m)	to 18 in (45 cm), deeply lobed, pink-brown at first, then bright green	to 16 in (40 cm), yellow, cylindrical
B. hookeriana HOOKER'S BANKSIA	multi-stemmed bushy shrub to 4 ft (1.2 m)	to 8 in (20 cm), narrow-linear, finely toothed, rusty brown at first	to 6 in (15 cm), cylindrical, woolly white becoming orange
B. integrifolia COAST BANKSIA	low shrub to large tree, up to 80 ft (25 m)	to 4 in (10 cm), whorled, elliptic to obovate, entire, velvety, green with white reverse or light brown	cylindrical, 4–4¾ in (10–12 cm) long, pale yellow in late summer to winter
B. laevigata TENNIS BALL BANKSIA	bushy shrub to 11 ft (3.5 m)	to 5½ in (14 cm), broadly linear or narrowly obovate, toothed, rusty brown at first	tightly spherical, yellow and brown
B. laricina ROSE BANKSIA	rounded shrub to 4 ft (1.2 m)	to ⅝ in (1.5 cm), narrowly linear	spherical, yellow to red-brown

B. baxteri

B. ericifolia

B. serrata

B

BANKSIA

Name	Habit	Leaves	Inflorescence
B. marginata SILVER BANKSIA	low shrub or tree to 40 ft (12 m)	⅝–2½ in (1.5–6 cm), linear to cuneate, entire or serrate	2–4 in (5–10 cm), cylindrical, yellow
B. media SOUTHERN PLAINS BANKSIA	dense shrub 6½–15(–30) ft (2–5(–10) m)	2–4¾ in (5–12 cm), cuneate, toothed, pale brown at first	4–6 in (10–15 cm), cylindrical, forming a bright yellow dome
B. nutans NODDING BANKSIA	compact, rounded shrub to 3¼ ft (1 m)	½–¾ in (1.2–2 cm), linear, blue-green, revolute	cylindrical, nodding, green aging pink-purple then rusty brown and onion-scented
B. occidentalis RED SWAMP BANKSIA	erect, bushy shrub to 10 × 10 ft (3 × 3 m)	4–5 in (10–13 cm), linear, whorled, silver beneath	to 5½ in (14 cm), cylindrical, red
B. pulchella TEASEL BANKSIA	small, spreading shrub to 3¼ ft (1 m)	½ in (1 cm), linear	to 1 in (2.5 cm), cylindrical, orange-brown
B. quercifolia OAK-LEAVED BANKSIA	erect shrub to 10 × 6½ ft (3 × 2 m)	1¼–6 in (3–15 cm), cuneate, serrate	to 4 in (10 cm), narrowly cylindrical, red and green opening rusty brown
B. repens CREEPING BANKSIA	prostrate, creeping	to 12 in (30 cm), erect, irregularly lobed, rusty brown at first	to 4 in (10 cm), cylindrical, pink brown
B. serrata SAW BANKSIA	small tree, 6½–50 ft (2–15 m)	to 6 in (15 cm), narrowly obovate, strongly serrate	to 6 in (15 cm), cylindrical, green-yellow to cream, sometimes blue-gray in bud
B. speciosa SHOWY BANKSIA	large shrub or tree to 20 ft (6 m)	to 16 in (40 cm), linear, gray-green, silver beneath, deeply incised	to 4¾ in (12 cm), squat, rounded, white opening yellow-green
B. verticillata GRANITE BANKSIA	spreading shrub or small tree to 12 ft (4 m)	to 3½ in (9 cm), oblong, dark green, silver beneath	to 8 in (20 cm), cylindrical, yellow
B. victoriae WOOLLY ORANGE BANKSIA	tall, rounded shrub to 15 ft (5 m)	8–12 in (20–30 cm), broadly linear with deep, sharply pointed lobes opening orange	to 4¾ in (12 cm), cylindrical, white and hairy in bud
B. violacea VIOLET BANKSIA	low shrub to 5 ft (1.5 m)	to ¾ in (2 cm), linear	to 2½ in (6 cm) diam.., spherical, purple

Baptisia (from Greek, *bapto*, to dye, some species yield an indigo substitute). Leguminosae. US. PLAINS FALSE INDIGO, WILD INDIGO. 17 species, hardy tap-rooted perennial herbs usually with three-parted leaves and erect, terminal racemes of pealike flowers. Plant in deep, well-drained, neutral to acidic soil in full sun. Propagate from seed sown ripe in the cold frame, or by careful division in late winter (plants resent disturbance). *B. australis* BLUE FALSE INDIGO; summer-flowering perennial, 30–60 in (75–150 cm) tall; flowers pale violet to indigo marked white, to ⅝ in (1.5 cm) diam.; seed pods inflated gray, attractive in dried flower arrangements.

barb a hooked semirigid hair.

barbate bearded, with hairs in long weak tufts.

barbed of bristles or awns with short, stiff lateral or terminal hairs which are hooked sharply backward or downward.

barbellae short, stiff hairs, for example, those of the pappus in Compositae.

bare-root applied to plants which are lifted with little or no soil around their roots; as from nursery rows, where the specimens may be referred to as bare-root transplants.

bark the outermost protective tissue of woody plants. Shredded bark can be used as a soil conditioner, as a surface mulch, and as the sole or a constituent ingredient of growing media.

bark beetles (Coleoptera: Scolytidae). Small, dark-colored, cylindrical beetles, up to ¼ in (6 mm) long, adapted for burrowing in wood. Adults excavate tunnels, usually in the sapwood just beneath the bark, especially that of trees that are sickly or dying. Typically, a large number of beetles invade simultaneously in response to an aggregation pheromone.
The FRUIT BARK BEETLES (*Scolytus rugulosus* and *S. mali*) are

Adult bark beetle

sometimes found in gardens, infesting fruit trees and hawthorn (*Crataegus monogyna*). *Ips* species are pests of forest conifers throughout the Northern Hemisphere. In Europe and North America the ELM BARK BEETLES (*S. scolytus* and *S. multistriatus*) are serious pests of elm (*Ulmus* species), since they are vectors of Dutch elm disease. The SHOT-HOLE BORER (*Xyleborus dispar*), a European species, infests many trees and, in contrast to *Scolytus* species, tunnels extensively into the heartwood. The only feasible way of controlling bark beetles in gardens is to cut and burn infested trees and branches. In forests, traps containing aggregation pheromones may be used.

bark-bound trees with hard bark that prevents girth expansion. See *slitting*.

bark house a rustic garden house made of timber with bark still attached, featured in some Victorian gardens.

Bark ringing
Continuous parallel cuts are made through bark and cambium. The wound is protected with tape after removing the band of tissue.

bark ringing excising with a sharp knife a narrow ring of bark around the trunk or limb of, usually, a fruit tree, to arrest vegetative growth.

Barleria (for Jacques Barrelier [1606–1673], French botanist). Acanthaceae. Old World Tropics and Subtropics. 250 species, tender evergreen herbs and shrubs grown for their tubular, 5-lobed flowers. These plants grow well in full sun or part shade planted in moist, fertile, loamy soil. Under glass, provide a minimum temperature of

45°F (7°C). Propagate from semiripe or softwood cuttings in a closed case with bottom heat.

B. cristata PHILIPPINE VIOLET; SE Asia; bristly shrublet to 3¼ ft (1 m); flowers 1¼–2 in (3–5 cm), violet-blue to pink, borne amid spiny sepals; *B. lupulina* HOP-HEADED BARLERIA; Mauritius; leaves with a white or pink midvein and hop-like spikes of yellow flowers; *B. obtusa* S. Africa; spreading unarmed shrublet with elliptic leaves to 2¾ in (7 cm) long and loosely arranged axillary clusters of 1¼ in (3 cm)-long mauve flowers.

barrier banding see *grease banding*

basal plate the compressed stem within a bulb from which the leaves arise as scales.

basal rot (*Fusarium oxysporum* f.sp. *narcissi*) a progressive rotting of narcissus bulbs after flowering caused by a specialized form of the widespread soil fungus *F.oxysporum*. The rot can be detected by softness, usually at the base of a bulb, and the dark coloration of the fleshy scales seen when the bulb is cut transversely. It should be distinguished from damage by stem and bulb eelworm (*Ditylenchus dipsaci*), where the rotted tissue is in concentric rings. Cultivars vary in susceptibility. The fungus is capable of surviving in soil for many years in the absence of a narcissus crop. Infection can occur at any time but particularly via dying roots as temperatures rise in spring. Its progress is greatly influenced by temperature during growth, harvesting and storage, the most severe attacks occurring at about 77°F (25°C). Control measures in gardens should include rejecting diseased bulbs, rotating the planting site, lifting early and avoiding long exposure to sunshine, and storage at no more than 63°F (17°C). Post harvest dipping of bulbs in fungicide may be beneficial, subject to local pesticide approvals.

basal stem rot (*Pythium* species) a soilborne pathogen of chrysanthemums, also transmitted by contaminated water and tools. Control is by strict hygiene, use of city or well water, sterilization of soil and compost, and use of soil drench fungicide, subject to local pesticide approvals.

base dressing an application of organic manure or processed fertilizer incorporated into the soil prior to sowing or planting, with the aim of improving its fertility.

base exchange a process of importance in fertilizer application whereby a soil retains bases available as a salt solution in soil water while giving up an equivalent amount of bases which form new salts in solution. For example, the application of lime sets free insoluble potassium occurring naturally in clay soil in exchange for insoluble calcium which is retained. See *cation exchange capacity*.

base fertilizer see *base dressing*

basic slag a waste product from the lining of blast furnaces. Once an important insoluble phosphate fertilizer, containing between 7% and 22% phosphoric acid with calcium, magnesium, and some trace elements.

basifixed of a plant organ; attached by its base rather than its side or top, as in an anther joined to the filament by its base.

basil (*Ocimum basilicum*) an aromatic annual or short-lived perennial used as an herb, for its clovelike flavor, in salads, sauces and liqueurs. It reaches 8–24 in (20–60 cm) in height, and is suitable for container growing. In cool temperate climates basil is best treated as a tender annual, raised under protection in spring. Plant out after frost risk into a sheltered, sunny position, 6 in (15 cm) apart. For winter use indoors sow in early summer and pot up; and after light trimming bring indoors in late summer.

basing up building up a low ridge of soil in a complete circle around the base of a plant in order to retain applied water.

basionym a taxonomic term; the 'base name' of a taxon that has been transferred by a later author from one rank to another within a species, or to a new species or genus altogether. For example, in 1964 Cullen and Heywood judged that *Paeonia arietina* (published by Anderson 146 years earlier) was in fact a subsp. of *Paeonia mascula*. *P.arietina* Anderson became *P.mascula* subsp. *arietina* (Anderson) Cullen and Heywood. The original name is now the basionym or base name of the new combination and synonymous with it. To make this change clear and to indicate that the type of Cullen's and Heywood's *arietina* is one and the same as Anderson's, the basionym author is cited in parentheses.

basipetalous developing from apex to base, as in an inflorescence where the terminal flowers open first, cf. *acropetalous*.

basiscopic of ferns; directed toward the base of a frond; the first lateral vein or leaflet on a pinna branching off in a downward direction.

bass, bast the strong inner fibrous bark of lime trees and similar fibers, once widely used as a horticultural tying material.

Bassia (for Ferdinando Bassi [1710–1774], Italian botanist). Chenopodiaceae. Warm temperate regions. 26 species, annual herbs or herbaceous perennials. *Bassia* quickly makes a dense miniature 'tree' ideal for bedding schemes as a dot or background plant or the centerpiece of container plantings. Sow seed under glass in early spring; plant out in sun after the last frost. Alternatively, sow seed *in situ* in late spring. *B. scoparia* (syn. *Kochia scoparia*); SUMMER CYPRESS, BURNING BUSH; annual 24 in (60 cm), with a bushy spire of linear leaves turning from apple green to purple-red in late summer; f. *trichophylla*: particularly fine foliage, flushing deep blood red.

Bauhinia (for Johann Bauhin [1541–1613] and Caspar Bauhin [1560–1624], Swiss botanists. The two-lobed leaves characteristic of this genus symbolize the brothers' relationship). Leguminosae. Tropics and Subtropics. ORCHID TREE. 250–300 species, evergreen or deciduous shrubs, lianes and trees, often thorny and with large, rounded, 2-lobed leaves and showy, 5-petalled flowers with long stamens. The following are commonly grown

outdoors in subtropical and tropical gardens and elsewhere under glass (minimum temperature 45°F/7°C). They flower at various times of year, depending on location; flowers are most often seen, however, from late fall to spring. Use *B. corymbosa*, *B. galpinii*, and *B. vahlii* as climbers or wall shrubs; the others as freestanding specimen shrubs and trees. Under glass, pot in tubs or beds and avoid wet conditions in winter. *B. vahlii* may require some shading to protect its large leaves from fading and scorching. Prune to restrict size or to thin out congested growth after flowering. Propagate by seed, simple layering, or grafting. Insert semiripe cuttings with the leaves removed in moist sand in a closed case with bottom heat.

B. × blakeana (*B. purpurea × B. variegata*); HONG HONG ORCHID TREE; S China; deciduous or evergreen umbrella-shaped shrub or tree to 40 ft (12 m); flowers narrow-petalled mauve, rose or bright red, to 6 in (15 cm) across; *B. corymbosa* (syn. *B. glauca* of gardens; *B. scandens* of gardens); PHANERA VINE; S China; liane, climbing by tendrils; flowers fragrant, white to pink; *B. forficata* (syn. *B. candicans*); S. America; evergreen to deciduous shrub or small tree to 30 ft (10 m) tall with gnarled, leaning trunk and thorny branches; flowers narrow-petalled, 6 in (15 cm)-diam., cream to snow-white; will withstand some frost; *B. galpinii* (syn. *B. punctata*); PRIDE OF THE CAPE, CAMEL'S FOOT or RED BAUHINIA; Africa; evergreen or semideciduous, spreading or climbing shrub to 10 ft (3 m); flowers orange or fiery red with ruffled petals; *B. purpurea* SE Asia, confused with *B. variegata*, from which it differs in its oblanceolate, rosy purple petals which do not overlap one another; *B. vahlii* MALU CREEPER; India; a robust liane, climbing to 120 ft (35 m); leaves 12 in (30 cm). diam., kidney-shaped, downy; flowers ruffled, cream or white, to 2 in (5 cm) diam.; *B. variegata* (syn. *B. purpurea*); MOUNTAIN EBONY, BUTTER-FLY or ORCHID TREE; E Africa; broadly spreading more or less deciduous shrub or tree to 40 ft (12 m); flowers pale pink to magenta or indigo or white.

beak a long, pointed, hornlike projection; particularly applied to the terminal points of fruits and pistils.

bean seed fly (*Delia platura*) a small fly similar to the cabbage root fly. The white, legless maggots, which are up to 3/8 in (9 mm) long, eat germinating French and runner bean seeds and seedlings. Crops may fail to emerge or be distorted and/or blind shoots are produced. Conditions unsuitable for rapid germination increase the risk of damage. There may be three or four generations of maggots during the summer but damage is usually confined to the spring period. Control by raising plants in cell modules.

beans a variable group of plants in the family Leguminosae, grown in most cases for their edible seeds and/or seed pods.

The BROAD BEAN (ENGLISH BEAN, EUROPEAN BEAN) (*Vicia faba*) is an erect hardy annual. The seeds, which may be eaten when immature, are produced in large fleshy green pods which may also be consumed whole at an early stage of development when 2–3 in (5–7.5 cm) long. Sow selected cultivars in fall for earliest cropping in the following year or successively from spring throughout summer. Sow direct to a depth of 2–3 in (5–7.5 cm) or in containers under protection for planting out. Rows should be 18 in (45 cm) apart with plants at 6 in (15 cm) final stations.

The FRENCH BEAN (HARICOT, DWARF, COMMON, KIDNEY, SNAP, STRING AND FLAGEOLET BEAN) (*Phaseolus vulgaris*) is a tender annual including bushy or climbing cultivars, mostly grown for their round or flat fleshy pods or their semimature (flageolet) or mature (haricot) seeds. Sow *in situ* to a depth of 2 in (5 cm) successively from late spring when soil temperature has reached 50°F (10°C) and the risk of frost has passed. Alternatively, sow in containers under protection for planting out in rows 18 in (45 cm) apart with plants at 12 in (30 cm) final stations. The optimum temperature range for growth is 61–86°F (16–30°C).

The RUNNER BEAN (SCARLET RUNNER, CASE KNIFE BEAN) (*Phaseolus coccineus*) is a tender climbing perennial treated as an annual in gardens and grown for its seed pods, which are edible when young. Sow *in situ* 2–3 in (5–7.5 cm) deep from late spring when the risk of frost has passed. Alternatively, sow in containers under protection for planting out in rows 24 in (60 cm) apart, with plants at 6 in (15 cm) stations. Plants can be trained up support structures such as 8 ft (2.5 m) poles or canes erected in parallel rows and tied in pairs at the top or in groups of four to form wigwams. Strings or net may also be used. Non-climbing or dwarf cultivars are available, and climbing cultivars may be kept dwarf by pinching off developing shoots to produce an early low-yield crop.

Other cultivated beans include: COWPEA, CHERRY BEAN (*Vigna unguiculata*); YARD-LONG BEAN, ASPARAGUS BEAN, PERU BEAN, SNAKE BEAN (*V. unguiculata* ssp. *sesquipedalis*); CATJANG (*V.u.* ssp. *cylindrica*). The MUNG BEAN (*Phaseolus aureus*) is grown for its edible shoots. The BUTTERBEAN (*Phaseolus lunatus*) is similar to the LIMA BEAN (*P. lunatus* syn. *P. limensis*) but smaller and more heat-resistant. The WINGED BEAN (*Psophocarpus tetragonolobus*) has edible pods and, in some cultivars, roots rich in protein. The DOLICHOS BEAN, HYACINTH BEAN (*Lablab purpureus*) requires a temperature range of 64–86°F (18–30°C) and high humidity to produce crops of bean sprouts, edible pods and mature seeds. Cultivation is described under the entries for these plants. Possible problems: aphids, root aphids, bean seed fly, slugs, thrips, weevils; halo blight, chocolate spot (see *botrytis*).

beard (l) an awn; (2) a tuft or zone of hair as on the falls of bearded irises.

Beaumontia (for Diana Beaumont [*d.* 1831] of Bretton Hall, Yorkshire, England). Apocynaceae. East Asia. 9 species, evergreen twining shrubs with funnel- to bell-shaped, five-lobed flowers. *Beaumontia* requires hot, moist conditions in summer and cool, dry conditions in winter (minimum temperature 45°F/7°C). Grow in full light in a fertile but well drained medium. Root heeled, semiripe cuttings in a heated case in late summer. *B. grandiflora* (HERALD'S TRUMPET, NEPAL TRUMPET FLOWER; EASTER LILY VINE, MOONFLOWER; to 15 ft (5 m); flowers fragrant, waxy white, produced in spring

and summer, 3–5 in (8–13 cm) long and broadly funnel-shaped with wavy-margined lobes).

bedding the planting in outdoor beds of mostly greenhouse-raised flowering and foliage ornamentals for display. Half-hardy annuals are widely used as summer bedding plants, but also perennials; spring and winter bedding displays are possible using hardy plants. Carpet or tapestry bedding is a specialized form made popular in Victorian gardens. It involves high density planting of low growing species to create often intricate patterns. Such beds may be raised and sloped and growth is contained by shearing or pinching.

bedeguar a mosslike gall of roses, also known as Robin's pincushion, caused by the larvae of the gall wasp *Rhoditis rosae*.

bed system the arrangement of usually closely-spaced plant rows, especially of vegetables, in narrow beds most conveniently 4 ft (1.2 m) wide. For temperature and drainage advantage beds may be of raised construction, contained by timber or brick walls to a height up to 12 in (30 cm) and slightly wider at the base than at the surface.

bee plant a plant particularly attractive to bees, such as *Buddleja davidii*, *Cotoneaster horizontalis* and *Alcea rosea*, the hollyhock.

beetle mites (Acarina: Cryptostigmata) red-brown or black mites important in the breakdown of woodland litter. Several species feed on algae and lichen, and some are arboreal, such as *Humerobates rostrolamellatus*. They congregate on bark and may be mistaken for red spider mite eggs, but are larger and paler red. *Perlohmannia dissimilis* can damage the underground parts of potatoes, tulips and strawberries.

abnormal mossy growth

Bedeguar

beetles (Coleoptera) Beetles constitute the largest order of the animal kingdom. They have forewings modified to form hardened wing cases (elytra), which are held flat over the body when the beetle is not in flight, protecting the membranous hindwings and abdomen. The immature larvae are generally soft-bodied grubs of very different appearance and habit to adults, and pass through a nonfeeding pupal stage before becoming adults. Many beetles are major agricultural or horticultural pests, feeding on plants or on stored seeds; some are scavengers (e.g., dung beetles); others are useful predators on other pests; many more, including the fire-flies, are of no economic importance. See *bark beetles*; *blister beetles*; *chafer beetles*; *Colorado beetle*; *flea beetles*; *ground beetles*; *Japanese beetle*; *ladybirds*; *leaf beetles*; *lily beetle*; *longhorn beetles*; *pollen beetles*; *rove beetles*; *sap beetles*; *wireworms*.

beet (*Beta vulgaris* subsp. *vulgaris*) a biennial grown as an annual vegetable for its edible swollen hypocotyl or 'root', which is typically bright red throughout. It is sometimes included in ornamental borders. Harvested 'seed' consists of a dried flower head or cluster which contains two or three true seeds; single-seeded or monogerm cultivars reduce the need for thinning. Sow seed ¾ in (2 cm) deep. For the earliest crops, choose bolt-resistant cultivars, sown in rows 7 in (18 cm) apart with plants at 4 in (10 cm) final stations. Sow main crops in rows 8 in (20 cm) apart with plants at 2 in (5 cm) final stations. To advance the first harvest date, plants may be raised under protection in cells for transplanting or sown under cloches or plastic film. Mature roots may be stored in clamps or in boxes of sand, free from frost, for extended season use.

Begonia (for Michel Begon [1638–1710], Governor of French Canada, patron of botany). Begoniaceae. Tropics and Subtropics, especially the Americas. Some 900 species, perennial herbs grown for their foliage and flowers. They may be fibrous- or tuberous-rooted, with thick, creeping rhizomes or low to trailing or erect, fleshy stems and a more or less bushy habit. Most are evergreen, although the tuberous species dieback in winter. The leaves range widely in shape, but are commonly asymmetric with one side slightly larger or more oblique than the other, especially at the base. They are thinly succulent, sometimes hairy, and often marked. Borne in axillary clusters and cymes or showy panicles, the flowers too are slightly fleshy; the males consist of two sets of two sepals, while female flowers comprise sets of two to six.

For the most part, begonias are highly susceptible to frost and, indeed, to any sudden drop in temperature. Members of the Semperflorens and Tuberous groups are, however, familiar sights in cool temperate gardens, where they are used as half-hardy annuals in bedding, baskets and windowboxes. *B. grandis* subsp. *evansiana* has proved hardy to 0°F (–18°C), given a thick winter mulch and a sheltered position. All favor a fertile, porous medium, moist but never wet, and rich in leaf mold, composted bark and sand. Feed actively growing plants fortnightly with a high-potash fertilizer. Avoid wetting the foliage and try to prevent sun scorch. In cultural terms, the genus can be divided into six main groups as follows:

1. *Cane-stemmed* Tall evergreens with fibrous roots and erect, branching stems, slender and canelike with prominent nodes, and fleshy becoming thinly woody. The leaves are usually large and lanceolate to ovate with an obliquely heart-shaped base. Small but cheery flowers are carried in drooping, slender-stalked panicles. These are excellent greenhouse and house plants — a common sight in office buildings.

Provide a minimum temperature of 50°F (10°C) and bright light, not direct sunlight. New canes arise from the base of the plant and may require staking and some pinching to promote bushiness — they tend to last for two to three years and should then be cut out cleanly at the base. Propagate by tip cuttings in spring or by division of large clumps.

2. *Rex and rhizomatous* Low evergreens with thick, creeping to ascending rhizomes. The leaves are usually lanceolate to broadly ovate and often brilliantly colored. Popular house plants. Provide a minimum temperature of 55°F (13°C) with ample humidity during warm weather and light to heavy shade. Water carefully, especially in cool weather, and never allow water to rest on the crown or leaves. Propagate by division of rhizomes or leaf cuttings.

3. *Semperflorens* A group of hybrids with fibrous roots, low, clumped and bushy stems, rounded waxy leaves and clusters of small, brightly colored flowers. These are the bedding begonias, essentially perennial but commonly treated as half-hardy annuals. Sow seed under glass in early spring at a temperature of 77°F (25°C); plant out in sunny or lightly shaded positions after the last frosts. Plants may be reused if they are lifted in fall, overwintered in dry, frost-free conditions, and pruned, divided and restarted in a moist, fertile medium at 59°F (15°C) in spring. Especially vigorous or attractive examples might equally be potted up in fall and brought into the home for winter display. Propagate by seed, division or stem cuttings.

4. *Shrublike* Evergreens with fibrous roots and clumped, bushy stems that tend to remain rather succulent. Some, for example *B. metallica* and *B. scharfii*, make fine house plants. Grown for their foliage and flowers, the members of this group range widely in origin and appearance. Their requirements are basically the same as for the Cane-stemmed begonias, but with rather higher temperatures and humidity.

5. *Tuberous* Deciduous with a large, rounded tuber and annual, succulent stems, thick or slender, erect or pendulous. Grown mostly for their showy flowers. Grown under glass or treated as half-hardy "annuals" (*B*. Tuberhybrida hybrids) planted out in late spring in dappled sun or light shade. Start tubers into growth in early spring on trays of moist coir in a shaded greenhouse at a temperature of 59°F (15°C). Once growth has begun, pot into the normal medium, potting on and staking as required. Flower

buds develop three per axil — pinch out all until a strong head of foliage has been achieved. With large-flowered cultivars, pinch out the two outer buds in each truss of three: these are female and seldom so large and showy as the central male which should be encouraged to develop to its full potential. Foliage fades and flowering ceases in fall, when plants should be dried off. Once the dead top growth has fallen away, store the tubers dry in their pots or in boxes of sawdust at 45°F (7°C). Propagate in spring by detaching and rooting unwanted sideshoots, or by division of tubers (bisect longitudinally with a sharp, clean knife; dust the cut surfaces with flowers of sulfur); also by seed.

Not all tuberous begonias produce the distinctive, cormlike tubers of the type whose cultural regimen is outlined above. These are described as semi-tuberous. In some, for example, *B. dregei* and *B. sutherlandii*, the tuber is a thickened stem and not all of the top growth is lost in winter. These plants and their hybrids (e.g., *B*. 'Weltoniensis') are usually grown year-round under glass or in the home. They require a dry winter rest in their pots and should be repotted in spring into a rather gritty medium. Propagate by stem cuttings and by bulbils, which sometimes form in the growth axils.

6. *Winter-flowering* Evergreen and low-growing with slender stems and showy flowers produced from late fall to early spring. This group is sometimes included among the Tuberous begonias, but can itself be split into Hiemalis types (with single to fully double flowers in a wide range of colors), Rieger begonias (improved plants of the Hiemalis type, widely grown as winter-flowering potted plants for the home), and Cheimantha types with single, white or pink flowers and derived from *B. dregei* and *B. socotrana*. Provide a minimum temperature of 59°F (15°C) (not much higher in winter), with bright, indirect light, low humidity and a well-ventilated atmosphere. Ensure that these plants are consistently moist, but never wet. Cut back flowered stems. Increase by stem cuttings or by rooted stems detached during repotting.

See table overleaf.

B

BEGONIA

Name	Distribution	Habit	Leaves	Flowers
B. albopicta GUINEA-WING BEGONIA **Comments:** Group 1.	Brazil	fibrous-rooted with clumped, erect, canelike stems to 3¼ ft (1 m) tall, succulent and simple at first, becoming much-branched and slightly woody	to 3 in (8 cm) long, obliquely ovate-lanceolate, tip acuminate, margins somewhat toothed and wavy, glossy dark green spotted silver-white above	small, green-white (pale rose in the cultivar 'Rosea')
B. bowerae EYELASH BEGONIA **Comments:** Group 2. Includes 'Major' with larger, rather faintly marked leaves, and var. *nigromarga* with emerald leaves marked dark brown, and pale marginal hairs.	Mexico	creeping-rhizomatous, low and bushy	1–2 in (2.5–5 cm) long, oval, light emerald to lime green with irregular green-brown marginal markings and eyelashlike marginal hairs	small, palest pink
Cane-stemmed group ANGELWING BEGONIAS	garden origin	fibrous-rooted with tall woody, canelike stems, erect and branching with prominent nodes	4–12 in (10–30 cm) long, but usually large, obliquely ovate to lanceolate, base rounded to heart-shaped, apex acuminate, margins wavy to toothed, waxy, variously colored and marked	small, pink to white in nodding panicles

Comments: Group 1. A large and varied group of hybrids, mostly large, sturdy and long-lived plants excellent for interiors and attractive in leaf and flower. Some of the finer cultivars include **B.** 'Edinburgh Brevimosa' (leaves large, very shiny, deep cerise with broad zones of maroon-black along impressed veins); **B.** 'Good 'n' Plenty' (leaves large, satiny purple-black with lilac-pink spots and wavy margins); **B.** 'Lucerna' (leaves large, olive green spotted silver, flowers deep pink); **B.** 'Orpha C. Fox' (leaves medium-sized, dark silky green with zones of silver-gray between veins); **B.** 'Papillon' (leaves small to medium-sized, satiny maroon-black with wavy margins, contrasting beautifully with small, shell pink flowers); **B.** 'Pinafore' (leaves small to medium-sized, dark green and glossy above, red-tinted beneath, margins wavy, flowers deep salmon pink); **B.** 'Pink Spot Lucerne' (leaves medium-sized, slightly angled, deep olive with cerise spots and a pale margin); **B.** 'President Carnot' (leaves large, green with paler spots, flowers pink in large panicles); **B.** 'Snowcap' (leaves small, very dark olive green with dense silver-white spots).

Name	Distribution	Habit	Leaves	Flowers
B. carolineifolia **Comments:** Group 2.	Mexico; Guatemala	ascending to erect with very stout, fleshy and thin-barked cylindrical stems covered in prominent leaf scars	to 12 in (30 cm) across, palmately compound with 5–9 lanceolate to obovate leaflets in a circular arrangement, these with toothed or slashed, wavy margins, smooth, mid- to deep green	small, pale fleshy pink in branching cymes
B. × cheimantha BLOOMING FOOL BEGONIA; CHRISTMAS BEGONIA; LORRAINE BEGONIA	garden origin (*B. dregei* × *B. socotrana*)	fibrous-rooted with robust, branching stems to 14 in (35 cm) long	rounded with a cordate base and toothed margins, smooth bright green	large, pink in loose, pink-stalked cymes in winter

Comments: Group 6. Cultivars include 'Gloire de Lorraine' with rounded bright green leaves and white to pale pink flowers, the lilac-pink 'Love Me', 'Marjorie Gibbs' with a profusion of pale pink bloom offset by dark green, rounded leaves, and 'White Marina' with pale green leaves and large white flowers edged soft pink.

Name	Distribution	Habit	Leaves	Flowers
B. coccinea ANGEL-WING BEGONIA **Comments:** Group 1.	Brazil	fibrous-rooted with robust, erect, canelike stems	to 6 in (15 cm) long, obliquely oblong to ovate, serrate, deep, glossy green and somewhat glaucous above, red-tinted beneath	small, pink with a large, coral-red ovary, profuse, in spring

B. bowerae

B. 'Orpha C. Fox' (Cane-stemmed)

B. dregei

BEGONIA

Name	Distribution	Habit	Leaves	Flowers
B. corallina	Brazil	fibrous-rooted with canelike stems erect to 10 ft (3 m)	to 8 in (20 cm) long, lanceolate, glossy green with white spots above, red beneath	many, large, coral red, pendent
Comments: Group 1. Includes two cultivars with sweetly scented flowers, the white 'Fragrans', and the pale rose 'Odorata'.				
B. cubensis CUBAN HOLLY; HOLLY-LEAF BEGONIA	Cuba	stems erect, branched, brown-hairy **Comments:** Group 4.	to 2 in (5 cm) long, obliquely ovate, acuminate, toothed, glossy dark green above, veins brown-hairy beneath	small, white
B. dichroa **Comments:** Group 1.	Brazil	roots fibrous; stems canelike, erect to spreading, woody, branched, to 14 in (35 cm) long	6–12 in (15–30 cm) long, obliquely ovate-oblong, base cordate, apex acuminate, margins somewhat undulate, smooth, bright green with silver-white spots	orange to salmon pink with white ovaries in nodding umbels
B. dregei GRAPE-LEAF BEGONIA; MAPLE-LEAF BEGONIA **Comments:** Group 5. In var. *macbethii*, the leaves are smaller, much incised with deep green veins.	S Africa	tuberous or semituberous with succulent stems to 3¼ ft (1 m) tall	to 3 in (8 cm) long, maplelike, i.e., ovate-rhombic and shallowly palmately lobed, toothed, pale green with purple veins and pewter spots above, purple-bronze beneath	small, white, pendent
B. × erythrophylla B. × *feastii* BEEFSTEAK BEGONIA; KIDNEY BEGONIA	creeping, rhizomatous, to 8 in (20 cm) tall	creeping, rhizomatous, to 8 in (20 cm) tall	to 6 in (15 cm) long, almost round, base cordate but appearing peltate, thick, olive green above, purple-red beneath, margins and petiole with white hairs	small, pink, many in panicles held clear of foliage
Comments: Group 2. Includes 'Bunchii' (LETTUCE-LEAF BEGONIA) with bright green leaves with ragged and crested margins, and 'Helix' (WHIRLPOOL BEGONIA; POND-LILY BEGONIA) with the basal leaf lobes spiraled.				
B. foliosa FERN-LEAVED BEGONIA; FERN BEGONIA	Colombia; Venezuela	fibrous-rooted, stems to 3¼ ft (1 m) tall, slender, canelike, branching, erect to arching	½–1¼ in (1–3 cm) long, ovate-oblong, slightly toothed, glossy dark green, many in 2, close ranks	small, white **Comments:** Group 1.
B. fuchsioides B. *foliosa* var. *miniata*; FUCHSIA BEGONIA; CORAZON-DE-JESUS **Comments:** Group 1.	Venezuela	fibrous-rooted, stems to 5 ft (1.5 m) tall, slender, canelike, branching, erect to arching	¾–2 in (2–5 cm) long, oblong, toothed, tinted pink at first later dark green, in 2 ranks	to 1¼ in (3 cm) across, bright rosy pink to coral red, hanging on pink stalks
B. gracilis var. **martiana** B. *martiana* HOLLYHOCK BEGONIA	Mexico; Guatemala	tuberous, stem erect to 40 in (100 cm), succulent, usually unbranched	small, orbicular to lanceolate, base cordate, succulent, crenate, pale green, with bulbils borne in axils	large, pink, fragrant **Comments:** Group 5.

B. foliosa

B. grandis subsp. *evansiana*

B. listada

B

BEGONIA

Name	Distribution	Habit	Leaves	Flowers
B. grandis ssp. **evansiana** B. evansiana HARDY BEGONIA	E Asia	tuberous with erect to arching stems to 3¼ ft (1 m) tall, these produced annually, red-tinted and lightly branched	to 6 in (15 cm) long, obliquely ovate, base cordate, apex acuminate, veins prominent, the upper surface rather corrugated and pale bronzy olive to lime green, the lower surface red-tinted	to 1¼ in (3 cm) wide, fragrant, white or pink, nodding in branching cymes

Comments: Group 5. Hardy outdoors to 0°F (−18°C)—plant in a sheltered, sunny or semishaded position in fertile, humus-rich, moist but well-drained soil. In late summer and fall, bulbils form at leaf axils and may be detached and grown on in the cool greenhouse. Mulch crowns thickly before the first frosts.

B. heracleifolia STAR-LEAF BEGONIA; STAR BEGONIA;	Mexico to Belize	rhizome stout, succulent, creeping	to 12 in (30 cm) across, orbicular in outline, base cordate, deeply palmately lobed, lobes 7–9, lanceolate, margins wavy, toothed and hairy, bronze-green above, red beneath with green blotches along veins and tufts of hair; petiole blotched red, hairy	pink, packed atop an erect, hairy stalk

Comments: Group 2. 'Sonderbruchii' has deeply cut leaves streaked bronze; var. **nigricans** has leaves edged dark olive to black; var. **punctata** has leaden, black-green leaves blotched black.

B. × hiemalis WINTER-FLOWERING BEGONIAS	garden origin (B. socotrana × B. Tuberhybrida hybrids)	fibrous-rooted to semituberous with fleshy stems	obliquely oval	single or double, white to pink, yellow, orange or red, in winter or year-round

Comments: Group 6. Rots off easily—water from below. 'Krefeld' has mid-green leaves and profuse orange to crimson flowers in winter.

B. listada	Brazil	fibrous-rooted with erect, branching stems to 12 in (30 cm)	to 2½ in (6 cm) long, obliquely ovate-lanceolate, base unequally cordate, toothed, downy, velvety olive green with a lime to gold zone along midrib and red hairs beneath	few, white, to 2 in (5 cm) across, red-hairy

Comments: Group 4.

B. manicata	Mexico	rhizomatous with fleshy, erect to decumbent stems to 24 in (60 cm)	obliquely ovate-cordate, to 6 in (16 cm) long, toothed and ciliate, glossy light green above, red-tinted and weakly hairy on veins beneath; leaf stalk with a stiff collar of red hairs at its summit	small, pale pink with winged, pink ovaries, many together in panicles in early spring

Comments: Group 2. 'Aureomaculata' (LEOPARD BEGONIA; leaves blotched white or flushed red); 'Aureomaculata Crispa' (leaves pale green marbled yellow, margin ruffled, becoming pink in sun); 'Crispa' (leaves pale green with crisped and ruffled, hairy margins).

B. masoniana IRON GROSS BEGONIA	New Guinea	low-growing with a creeping, fleshy rhizome	to 8 in (20 cm) long, obliquely ovate-cordate, margins toothed and hairy, surface covered in bumpy bristles, pale green with a broad, dark brown to black areas along the main veins forming a crosslike marking	small, green-white many together on an erect stalk in spring and summer

Comments: Group 2. A popular houseplant.

B. manicata   *B. masoniana*   *B. metallica*   *B. nelumbiifolia*

BEGONIA

Name	Distribution	Habit	Leaves	Flowers
B. mazae	Mexico	fibrous-rooted with trailing, fleshy stems	to 4¾ in (12 cm), often smaller, rounded to heart-shaped, toothed, shiny green with red-bronze markings or veins above, red beneath	to ⅝ in (1.5 cm) across, white spotted red, fragrant, many together in winter and spring
Comments: Group 2. A good basket plant. Includes cultivars 'Nigricans' with dark and burnished leaves, and 'Stitchleaf' with pale green, heart-shaped leaves with dark purple 'stitches' along the margins.				
B. metallica METALLIC-LEAF BEGONIA	Brazil	fibrous-rooted, silver-hairy, erect and branching, to 5 ft (1.5 m) tall	to 6 in (15 cm) long, obliquely ovate, apex acuminate, base cordate, margins wavy and toothed, bronze-green with silver hairs and metallic purple veins	to 1½ in (3.5 cm) across, pale pink to rose, many together from summer to fall
Comments: Group 4.				
B. nelumbiifolia LILY PAD BEGONIA	Mexico to Colombia	rhizome short and stout, decumbent to ascending	to 12 in (30 cm) across, rounded, peltate, margin toothed and hairy, bright green, on long, hairy stalks	to ⅝ in (1.5 cm) across, white or pale pink in long-stalked clusters in winter and spring
Comments: Group 2.				
B. olsoniae	Brazil	fibrous-rooted, compact and shrubby, to 6 in (15 cm) tall	to 8 in (20 cm) across, obliquely rounded to heart-shaped, silky, bronze-green with pale green, white or pink veins	white to pale rose, one to a few together on long, arching stalks in winter
Comments: Group 4. A good basket plant.				
B. partita	S Africa	shrubby, to 8 in (20 cm) tall from a swollen base	to 2½ in (6 cm) long, variably 3-lobed, usually with small lateral lobes and a far longer, finely tapering midlobe, smooth pewter gray	small, white
Comments: Group 5. Requires free-draining, rather gritty soil, full sun and good ventilation; can be given a dry winter rest.				
B. paulensis	Brazil	rhizome creeping to ascending, fleshy, downy	to 8 in (20 cm), oblong, acuminate, peltate, margin toothed, surface puckered, glossy mid-green with a network of white veins	1½–2 in (3.5–5 cm) across, white with red hairs, many together on a tall stalk
Comments: Group 2.				
B. 'Phyllomaniaca' CRAZY-PLANT BEGONIA	a Brazilian hybrid (*B. incarnata* × *B. manicata*)	stem erect to 24 in (60 cm) tall, branched and hairy with many buds and leafy outgrowths	to 8 in (20 cm) long, obliquely cordate, margin slightly lobed, toothed and hairy, upper surface glossy with many leafy outgrowths	to 1 in (2.5 cm) across, pink on erect stalks in winter
Comments: Group 4. Well-grown plants assume a remarkable, "ragged" appearance, as if strewn with leaf fragments.				
B. prismatocarpa	Guinea	rhizomatous, stems creeping and rooting	to 2 in (5 cm) long, very obliquely ovate-cordate to rounded, margin wavy-toothed and 2–3-lobed, hairy	bright yellow, produced throughout the year
Comments: Group 2. 'Variegation' has leaves marked yellow-green and clear yellow flowers produced in great abundance.				

B. olsoniae

B. prismatocarpa

B. pustulata 'Argentea'

B. 'Princess of Hanover' (Rex)

B

BEGONIA

Name	Distribution	Habit	Leaves	Flowers
B. pustulata	Mexico; Guatemala	rhizomatous, low-growing	to 6 in (15 cm) long, often shorter, obliquely and broadly ovate, base cordate, apex acuminate, margin finely toothed, upper surface velvety with a dense pattern of small blisters, dark green faintly veined silver above, red-tinted beneath	small, rose pink, in summer

Comments: Group 2. '**Argentea**' has very dark green leaves with a heavy pattern of silver flashes along the veins.

B. radicans *B. undulata* of gardens SHRIMP BEGONIA	Brazil	rhizomatous with scrambling, erect to pendulous, white-spotted stems to 6½ ft (2 m) long	to 2¾ in (7 cm) long, obliquely ovate to oblong, apex acuminate, margins wavy, red-tinted at first, becoming gray-green with white spots	to 1 in (2.5 cm) across, coral pink to brick red in dense, nodding clusters, usually in winter

Comments: Group 1. 'Purpurea' has persistently bronze-red-tinted leaves.

B. rex KING BEGONIA; PAINTED LEAF BEGONIA	Assam	rhizome thick and fleshy, buried to creeping	to 10 in (25 cm) long, obliquely ovate, apex acute, base cordate, margins wavy with small, hairy teeth, surface puckered and sparsely hairy, rich metallic green with a broad silver zone above, purple-red beneath	to 2 in (5 cm) across, pale pink, a few together in winter and early spring

Comments: Group 2. A popular houseplant and the parent of many hybrids, most of which are sold as *B. rex*, but strictly belong to the *B. Rex Cultorum* hybrids.

B. Rex Cultorum hybrids *B. rex* of gardens BEEFSTEAK GERANIUM; REX BEGONIA	garden origin (*B. rex* crossed with related Asiatic species)	rhizomes thick, fleshy, creeping to erect	4–12 in (10–30 cm) long, obliquely ovate to oblong-lanceolate, base cordate to rounded, apex acute to acuminate, margins toothed to jaggedly lobed, smooth to hairy, dark green to wine red or bronze patterned or zoned silver-white, leaden gray, red, purple or black	white to pink or red in small clusters, seldom seen

Comments: Group 2. A large and popular group of hybrids widely grown as houseplants, includes 'Black Knight' (leaves large, black-red with rows of pink dots), 'Duartei' (leaves large with spiraling basal lobes, darkest green edged purple-black with silver streaks), 'Helen Lewis' (leaves medium-sized to large, silken dark purple with silver bands), 'Fireworks' (leaves large, maroon marked white blending to purple between veins), 'Merry Christmas' (syn. *B. ruhrtal*, leaves large, deep green flecked pink with a large central cherry red zone fading to silver at its edges and deepening to burgundy at its center, margins burgundy), 'Princess of Hanover' (leaves large with spiraling basal lobes, emerald green with silver bands edged dark red and covered in fine, pink hairs), 'Raspberry Swirl' (leaves medium-sized, rounded with overlapping basal lobes and jagged margins, silver edged purple-red with a purple-red center radiating along veins as a raspberry red blotch), 'Roi des Roses' (leaves medium-sized, pale pink mottled silver), and 'Wood Nymph' (small, leaves rounded, rich brown speckled silver).

Rhizomatous group	garden origin	low-growing plants with fleshy, creeping to erect rhizomes	1¼–10 in (3–25 cm) long, ranging widely in shape, color and texture	white, pink, or red

Comments: Group 2. Large and disparate group of hybrids, making good houseplants. Includes 'Aries' (leaves medium-sized to large, broad and shallowly palmately lobed, maplelike, downy emerald green with chocolate markings toward margins), 'Beatrice Haddrell' (leaves medium-sized to large, incised, dark green with paler veins, flowers pale pink), 'Bethlehem Star' (leaves small, black with a fine cream, central star, flowers cream spotted pink), 'Bokit' (leaves ovate, spirally twisted, yellow-green striped brown, flowers white flecked pink), 'China Doll' (compact, leaves cool green with red-brown mottling, flowers light pink), 'Little Darling' (leaves very small, ovate, acute, toothed and lobed, deep jade green patterned with darkest olive), 'Mac's Gold' (leaves small to medium-sized, star-shaped, yellow with chocolate brown marks), 'Munchkin' (leaves medium-sized, rounded, deep bronze, smooth, margins much-toothed, ruffled, crested and densely ciliate), 'Norah Bedson' (leaves medium-sized, rounded, bright green with dark brown markings, flowers pink), 'Oliver Twist' (leaves medium-sized, rounded, twisted and puckered, olive green, margins crested and covered in massed, red-tinted hairs), 'Scherzo' (leaves small, soft lime green with dark brown, stitchlike marks along margins), 'Silver Jewel' (leaves blistered, rich green streaked silver, flowers white).

B. 'Bethlehem Star' (Rhizomatous)

B. scharffii

B. Cocktail Series (Semperflorens)

BEGONIA

Name	Distribution	Habit	Leaves	Flowers
B. 'Ricinifolia' BRONZE-LEAF BEGONIA; CASTOR-BEAN BEGONIA; STAR BEGONIA	garden origin (*B. heracleifolia* × *B. peponifolia*)	rhizome thickly succulent and creeping to ascending **Comments:** Group 2.	to 12 in (30 cm) long, round in outline with 5–7 lobes, dark bronze-green above, purple-red beneath	small, white to pale rose, many together on tall stalks
B. scharffii *B. haageana* **Comments:** Group 4.	Brazil	fibrous-rooted, shrubby, stems erect, white-hairy, to 3¼ ft (1 m) tall	to 10 in (25 cm) long, obliquely ovate, apex acuminate, base cordate, margin shallowly lobed, bronze-green with red veins above, red-tinted beneath	to 2 in (5 cm) across, pale pink with pink hairs in large, nodding clusters throughout the year
B. Semperflorens-Cultorum hybrids *B. semperflorens* of gardens; *B.* × *semperflorens-cultorum*; BEDDING BEGONIA; WAX BEGONIA	garden origin, hybrids derived from *B. cucullata* var. *hookeri B. schmidtiana*, *B. fuchsioides*, *B. gracilis*, *B. minor* and *B. roezlii*	roots fibrous, stems clumped, fleshy and brittle, bushy, 6–16 in (15–40 cm) tall	2–4 in (5–10 cm) long, rounded, smooth and glossy, thinly fleshy, bright green to red-tinted or purple-bronze, (variegated in the Calla-lily begonias)	½–1½ in (1–3.5 cm) across, single or double, white, pink or red, a few together in axillary clusters throughout year but chiefly in summer

Comments: Group 3. Large group of small, bushy and free-flowering perennials usually called *B. semperflorens* and used as half-hardy bedding. Single-flowered selections include the green-leaved 'Derby' (flowers profuse, pale coral), Frilly Dilly Mixed (leaves bright green, flowers white, pink and red with frilly tepals), 'Red Ascot' (leaves emerald green, flowers dark crimson), and 'Viva' (flowers pure white). Bronze-leaved and single-flowered selections include the Cocktail Series. Double-flowered cultivars include 'Bo Peep' (leaves bronze, flowers dark pink, very double), 'Curly Locks' (leaves bronze, flowers yellow and pink), 'Dainty Maid' (leaves green, flowers white edged salmon), 'Old Lace' (leaves bronze, flowers rosy red, very double and lacy), and 'Pink Wonder' (leaves green, flowers pink and rounded, abundant). One of the best variegated cultivars is 'Charm' (leaves bright green blotched gold and cream, flowers single, pale pink, everblooming).

Name	Distribution	Habit	Leaves	Flowers
B. serratipetala **Comments:** Group 4.	New Guinea	fibrous-rooted and shrubby with arching stems to 24 in (60 cm) long	to 1½ in (4 cm) long, obliquely ovate, apex acuminate, margins lobed, sharply toothed and crisped, deep olive to metallic bronze-red with raised pink spots	rose pink to purple-red, sometimes with toothed tepals, throughout the year
Shrublike group		fibrous-rooted and bushy with erect to pendulous, branching, fleshy stems	4–12 in (10–30 cm) long, of various shapes and hues, hairy or smooth	white, pink or red

Comments: Group 4. Large and varied group making good houseplants, including 'Dancing Girl' (leaves variously shaped, spotted and streaked silver), 'Gloire de Sceaux' (leaves small, rounded, deep metallic bronze, flowers dark to pale pink, scented), 'Ingramii' (leaves small to medium-sized, mid-green, flowers candy pink, produced in abundance), 'Midnight Sun' (outer, older leaves moss green, inner and younger leaves glowing pink to peach with green veins, flowers white), 'Thurstonii' (leaves medium-sized to large, obliquely ovate-lanceolate, metallic bronze-green with darker impressed veins), 'Tiny Gem' (leaves very small, crinkle-edged, deep green, flowers candy pink), 'Withlacoochee' (leaves small, oblong-ovate, very velvety, dark emerald to gray-green with white hairs, flowers pearly white).

Name	Distribution	Habit	Leaves	Flowers
B. solananthera	Brazil	rhizomatous, stems trailing to scrambling, to 32 in (80 cm) long	to 3 in (8 cm) long, broadly ovate, apex acuminate, margins angled, glossy deep green, paler beneath	to ¾ in (2 cm) across, white tinted rose, fragrant, in short, nodding clusters in winter and early spring

Comments: Group 6. A beautiful, winter-flowering basket plant for the warm greenhouse or home.

B. serratipetala

B. 'Ingramii' (Shrublike)

B. 'Roy Hartley' (Tuberhybrida)

BEGONIA

Name	Distribution	Habit	Leaves	Flowers
B. stipulacea B. angularis; B. zebrina **Comments:** Group 1.	Brazil	fibrous-rooted, stems canelike, erect to spreading or pendulous, to 8 ft (2.5 m) long	to 6 in (15 cm) long, obliquely ovate, apex acuminate, glossy with gray-white veins above, dull red beneath	to ⅝ in (1.5 cm) across, many, white or pink in winter or early spring
B. sutherlandii **Comments:** Group 5. An excellent basket plant. Somewhat hardier than many Begonias, it will overwinter in frost-free conditions if dry. 'Bulbils' may form in the axils of old stems and can be potted and grown.	S Africa	tuberous, stems red, slender, trailing	to 6 in (15 cm) long, obliquely lanceolate, margin toothed to lobed, bright green or sometimes olive with a red tint to veins and petiole	to 1 in (2.5 cm) across, orange to orange-red in pendulous bunches in summer
B. Tuberhybrida hybrids B. × tuberhybrida; B. tuberosa of gardens TUBEROUS BEGONIAS	garden origin, hybrids between the Andean species, B. boliviensis, B. clarkei, B. davisii, B. pearcei, B. veitchii and, possibly, B. frobelii and B. gracilis	tubers usually large and circular, compressed with a central depression above, stems fleshy and branching, erect to arching or pendulous	2½–8 in (6–20 cm) long, obliquely ovate to lanceolate, base rounded to cordate, apex acute to acuminate, margins toothed to cut, veins usually prominent, smooth to lightly hairy, pale green to dark green	1½–8 in (4–20 cm) across, single to semidouble or double, tepals smoothly rounded to fringed, frilled, cut-edged or ragged, many colors

Comments: Group 5. A very wide range of hybrids grown in pots under glass or in the home, and outdoors in containers and borders for summer display; the pendulous cultivars and some members of the Multiflora Group are excellent plants for hanging baskets. Cultivars include the pendulous 'Apricot Cascade' (flowers double, deep apricot), 'Bridal Cascade' (flowers white edged pink), 'Crimson Cascade', 'Gold Cascade' and 'Orange Cascade'. The largest-flowered selections include 'Billie Langdon' (double and roselike, pure white), 'Can-Can' (double, peach to apricot, edged warm red), 'City of Ballarat' (double, deep orange), 'Masquerade' (double and ruffled, white edged rosy red), 'Midas' (double, pale gold), and 'Roy Hartley' (double, salmon pink to deep rose). The Multiflora Group covers smaller, bushy plants with numerous small to medium-sized flowers, among them 'Flamboyant' (leaves narrow, bright green, flowers single, scarlet), 'Helene Harms' (flowers bright yellow, semidouble), and 'Madame Richard Galle' (flowers small, double, apricot).

Name	Distribution	Habit	Leaves	Flowers
B. versicolor FAIRY-CARPET BEGONIA **Comments:** Group 2.	China	rhizome short, creeping	2¾–4¾ in (7–12 cm) across, obliquely ovate to broadly oblong, margins finely toothed and hairy, emerald to apple green with silver-white markings and red veins above, red beneath	salmon pink or red in clusters on long, white-hairy stalks throughout the year
B. vitifolia B. palmifolia **Comments:** Group 1.	Brazil	fibrous-rooted, stems fleshy, smooth, erect to 4 ft (1.2 m) tall	to 12 in (30 cm), ovate to rounded in outline, hairy, margins toothed and broadly lobed, bright to deep green and shining	small, white on erect stalks
B. 'Weltoniensis' MAPLE-LEAF BEGONIA; GRAPEVINE BEGONIA	garden origins (B. dregei x B. sutherlandii)	tuberous or semituberous with fleshy, branching stems, erect to 3¼ ft (1 m)	to 3 in (8 cm) across, ovate, apex acuminate, margins toothed to shallowly lobed, dark glossy green tinted or veined purple-red	many, pink or white, in summer **Comments:** Group 5.

Belamcanda (Latinized form of this plant's vernacular names, *balamtandam* [Malayalam] and *malakanda* [Sanskrit]). Iridaceae. E Europe; Asia. 2 species, rhizomatous perennial herbs very similar to *Iris* and grown for their flowers and attractive seeds. The leopard lily is hardy to 5°F (−15°C), or lower still if given a dry winter mulch. Plant in sun or light shade. Propagate by seed sown in spring, or by division in spring or early fall. *B. chinensis* LEOPARD LILY; BLACKBERRY LILY; Russia to Japan; hardy, deciduous perennial to 3¼ ft (1 m); flowers short-lived, 1½ in (4 cm)-wide, produced in succession from midsummer to fall, ranging in color from tawny yellow to deep orange spotted or blotched red, maroon or purple; seed capsules split open to reveal blackberry-like clusters of glossy black seeds.

Bellevalia (for Pierre Richer de Belleval [1564–1632], who founded the Montpellier botanic garden in 1593). Liliaceae (Hyacinthaceae). Mediterranean to W and C Asia. 45 species, spring-flowering hardy bulbous perennials similar to *Muscari*, but often larger with looser racemes of tubular to campanulate rather than squatly urceolate flowers. Cultivate as for *Muscari*.

B. atroviolacea; Russia and Afghanistan; spike conical, 3–12 in (8–30 cm) tall packed with nodding, violet-black flowers; *B. hyacinthoides* (syn. *Strangweja spicata*); Greece; raceme cylindric to 6 in (15 cm) tall; flowers pale blue, veined with darker blue; *B. paradoxa* (syn. *B. pycnantha*; *Muscari paradoxum*; *Muscari pycnanthum*); Russia and Turkey; to 16 in (40 cm); raceme conical crowded with nodding, dark blue flowers.

bell glass a bell-shaped thick-glass cloche placed over plants to advance growth or sometimes as an aid to propagation. Developed in France in the 17th century, bell glasses are usually about 15 in (38 cm) high and 17 in (43 cm) wide. Versions manufactured in molded plastic are available.

Bellis (from the Latin *bellus*, pretty). Compositae. Europe; Mediterranean; W Africa. DAISY. 7 species, small, hardy annual or perennial herbs grown for their flower heads. Although hardy to at least 5°F (–15°C), the perennial cultivars of *Bellis perennis* are mostly grown as biennials. They are used in carpet bedding, for border and path edging and in containers, especially where winter color is wanted. Plant in sun or part shade in soil that does not dry out in summer. Dead head often to prolong flowering. Sow seed in early summer to plant out in late summer or fall. For winter flowers in pots, grow on in a low-fertility, loam-based mix in a cold frame and bring under glass in fall; provide a winter temperature of 39–45°F (4–7°C) and brisk ventilation.

Bellis perennis

B. perennis ENGLISH DAISY; perennial often treated as a biennial; leaves $^1/_2$–$2^1/_2$ in (1–6 cm), obovate to spathulate; scapes to 2 in (5 cm) tall; flower heads $^1/_2$–$1^1/_4$ in (1–3 cm) wide with yellow disk florets and white ray florets, often stained rose pink or red; a wide range of cultivars is available with flower color pure white to deep cherry red. There are double-flowered and variegated-leaf selections; flower heads may be up to $2^3/_4$ in (7 cm) wide and stem length up to $4^3/_4$ in (12 cm).

belvedere see *gazebo*.

bench, benching a narrow tablelike structure of wood or metal upon which plants in containers are set out within a greenhouse. It may have a solid or slatted surface and is also referred to as staging. A potting bench may be of similar construction, with a solid sur-

face used as a work table for potting and propagating operations.

beneficial insects Many species of insects are beneficial as predators, parasites or pollinators.

Most predatory insects are general feeders, preying as adults or larvae on several different types of insect and other small organisms, thereby contributing to natural pest control. They usually have fast-moving hunting skills and their mouthparts are adapted for biting and chewing or lacerating prey. Although most capsid bugs are plant feeders, some (especially the BLACK-KNEED CAPSID *Blepharidopterus angulatus*) are predacious, feeding significantly on fruit tree red spider mite. The related ANTHOCORID BUGS are also important predators. DRAGONFLIES (Odonata) take their prey on the wing, including mosquitoes, beetles and wasps. LACEWINGS (Neuroptera), some GALL MIDGE LARVAE (Diptera: Cecidomyiidae) and HOVERFLY LARVAE (Diptera: Syrphidae) are important predators of aphids. Most of the remaining predators are beetles (Coleoptera), including carabid or GROUND BEETLES, and the staphylinid, or ROVE BEETLES, which are general predators of small insects and other small invertebrates. The GLOWWORM (*Lampyris noctiluca*) has larvae which feed on snails. Various species of LADYBUG BEETLES are important predators of aphids, mealybugs, scale insects and spider mites, both as adults and larvae.

Most parasitic insects with plant-feeding hosts are more correctly called parasitoids. They are found in several families of Hymenoptera, and include ICHNEUMON WASPS, CHALCID WASPS and BRACONID WASPS. Only the larvae are parasitic, and they tend to be more host specific than predators.

Another beneficial function carried out by insects is pollination. Bees are the most valuable and abundant pollinators; other contributors include hoverflies and blowflies.

Berberidopsis (*Berberis* and Greek *opsis*, resemblance; the leaves of this

plant were thought similar to those of *Berberis*). Flacourtiaceae. Chile. CORAL PLANT. 2 species. *B. corallina*, an evergreen woody-based perennial climber to 15 ft (5 m), with hollylike leaves. From midsummer to fall, rounded, $^1/_2$–$^3/_4$ in (1–2 cm)-wide coral-red flowers hang on slender stalks. Although hardy to 14°F (–10°C), it suffers badly from wind scorch and prolonged frosts and may require protection in the form of a burlap drape and a thick mulch. Plant in a cool, semishaded and sheltered position in moist but porous, neutral to acidic soil rich in decayed vegetable matter. Propagate by semiripe cuttings in a closed case with bottom heat, or by simple layering.

Berberis (from *berberys*, the Arabic name for the fruit). Berberidaceae. Europe, Asia, Africa, Americas. BARBERRY. 450 species, hardy evergreen or deciduous shrubs grown for foliage, flowers and fruit. The stems have thin gray-brown bark and yellow wood and are armed with sharp spines. The leaves are small, thin to tough and sometimes sharply toothed. Some deciduous species and cultivars color brilliantly in fall. Small, cream to yellow or fiery orange flowers are produced in axillary clusters, racemes or panicles, usually in spring and summer. Berries range in color from creamy yellow to pink, red, purple or blue-black.

Berberis species are widely used in gardens for hedging and specimen planting in lawns, borders and the rock garden. Plant in well-drained soil in full sun or light shade. Prune out exhausted or congested stems in late winter; trim evergreen hedges after flowering, deciduous hedges in late winter. Propagate by seed cleansed of flesh and sown in a seedbed outdoors in late winter (offspring may be variable); or by heeled nodal and basal cuttings treated with a rooting hormone in a cold frame in early fall. Treated with a rooting hormone, mallet cuttings will root under mist in summer. Multi-stemmed plants can be earthed-up and encouraged to produce rooting stems which may be detached and grown on in fall or spring. Sometimes affected by bacterial leaf spot. Some species are alternate hosts for rusts (*See table overleaf.*)

B

BERBERIS

Name	Distribution	Habit	Leaves	Flowers	Fruit
B. aggregata *B. geraldii*	W China	densely branched, spiny, deciduous shrub to 6½ ft (2 m) tall	to 1 in (2.5 cm) long, oblong-ovate, base cuneate, apex obtuse, margin toothed, olive above, glaucous beneath, fiery red to crimson in fall blue-white	pale yellow in erect, rounded panicles to 1¼ in (3 cm) long in late spring	to ¼ in (0.7 cm) long, ovoid, pale red
Comments: Parent of many hybrids including 'Crimson Bead' with dark carmine fruit in pendulous trusses, and 'Sibbertoft Coral' with coral red bloomed fruit.					
B. buxifolia *B. dulcis; B. micro-phylla*	Chile	spiny, dense, evergreen or semievergreen shrub to 10 ft (3 m) tall	to 1 in (2.5 cm) long, obovate, blunt, mucronate, tough, dark green above, glaucous beneath	deep orange-yellow, 1–2 per axil in late spring	to ⅜ in (0.8 cm), globose, dark purple, gray-pruinose
Comments: Includes 'Aureomarginata' with leaves edged gold, and 'Nana', a sparsely flowered dwarf form.					
B. calliantha	Tibet	spiny evergreen shrub to 28 in (70 cm) tall; young stems red-tinted	hollylike, to 2½ in (6 cm) long, oblong-elliptic, sharply toothed, deep, glossy green above, pale and glaucous beneath	relatively large, yellow, 2–3 per axil in late spring	to ½ in (1 cm) long, ovoid, purple-black, glaucous
Comments:					
B. candidula *B. hypoleuca* of gardens; *B. wallichiana* var. *pallida*	W China	evergreen, dense rounded shrub 20–39 in (50–100 cm) tall	to 1¼ in (3 cm), elliptic-ovate, sparsely toothed, shiny dark green above, pale beneath	small, yellow stained red, 1 per axil in late spring	to ½ in (1 cm) long, ovoid, gray-pruinose **Comments:**
B.× carminea (*B. aggregata* × *B. wilsoniae*)	garden origin	deciduous shrubs, erect to domed, seldom exceeding 6½ ft (2 m)	to 1¼ in (3 cm) long, obovate, more or less toothed, pale beneath	yellow, in panicles to 2 in (5 cm) long in spring and early summer	to ⅜ in (0.8 cm) long, oblong-ovoid, pink to scarlet
Comments: Vigorous garden hybrids valued for their colorful fruits borne in profusion in fall; they include the cultivars 'Barbarossa' (stems to 6½ ft (2 m) tall, twigs red-tinted, leaves entire, fruit abundant, scarlet), 'Buccaneer' (leaves narrow, entire, more or less persistent, fruit		large, rounded, cloudy white turning shiny red), 'Pirate King' (vigorous, branches pendulous, fruit bright orange), and 'Sparkler' (fruit conic, tinted tangerine).		
B. coxii	E Himalaya	spiny evergreen shrub to 5 ft (1.5 m) tall	to 2½ in (6 cm) long, elliptic-ovate with incurved teeth, glossy dark green above, white and pruinose beneath	pale yellow, relatively large, to 6 per axillary cluster in late spring	to ½ in (1 cm) long, obovoid, glaucous blue-black
Comments:					
B. darwinii	Chile; Patagonia	spreading and suckering, evergreen, spiny shrub to 6½ ft (2 m) tall	hollylike, to ¾ in (2 cm) long, obovate, tough, with 1–3 spiny teeth per side, glossy dark green above, paler beneath	orange-gold often tinted red in pendulous racemes to 4 in (10 cm) long in spring	to ¼ in (0.7 cm) long, globose, blue-pruinose

Comments: Includes cultivars 'Flame' (flowers vivid dark orange), and 'Gold' (flowers vivid gold). The hybrid between *B. darwinii* and *B. valdiviana* is 'Goldilocks' (see below), a large, vigorous shrub with erect to arching branches, large, spiny, glossy dark green leaves and golden flowers in pendulous, red-stalked clusters. The cultivars 'Nana' (dwarf with small leaves and sparse flowers), and 'Prostrata' (dwarf and semi-prostrate with dull green leaves, red flower buds and profuse flowers) strictly belong to *B.* × *stenophylla*.

B. buxifolia

B. × *carminea* 'Buccaneer'

B. 'Goldilocks'

B. empetrifolia

BERBERIS

B

Name	Distribution	Habit	Leaves	Flowers	Fruit
B. empetrifolia *B. revoluta*	Chile; Argentina	evergreen, spiny, arching to semi- prostrate shrub to 12 in (30 cm) tall	to ¹⁄₂ in (1 cm) long, elliptic but strongly revolute, thus appearing narrow, mucronate, dark green above, pruinose beneath	small, deep yellow, paired, in late spring	to ¹⁄₄ in (0.7 cm) long, globose, glau- cous blue-black
Comments:					
B. gagnepainii	W China	evergreen, spiny shrub with sucker- ing, slender stems erect to 5 ft (1.5 m) tall	to 1¹⁄₂ in (4 cm) long, lanceo- late, apex tapering finely, undulate with to 10 teeth per side, matt gray-green above, yellow-green beneath	bright yellow, to 7 per cluster in early summer	to ¹⁄₂ in (1 cm) long, ovoid, purple-black, pruinose

Comments: Includes var. *lanceifolia* 'Fernspray' compact with long, narrow and undulate, pale green leaves, and 'Robin Hood', low-growing and rounded, to 3¹⁄₄ in (1 m) tall, leaves tinted dark red with age.

Name	Distribution	Habit	Leaves	Flowers	Fruit
B. × hybridogagnepainii *B. × media; B. × wokingensis;* (*B. verruculosa* × *B. gagnepainii*)	garden origin	varied range of evergreen spiny shrubs	more or less ovate with spiny margins	close to *B. gag- nepainii*	purple-black, gray-pruinose

Comments: A large complex of hybrids including 'Chenaultii' (*B. chenaultii*, to 8 ft (2.5 m) tall, leaves to 1¹⁄₄ in (3 cm) long, lanceolate, undulate, spiny shining above, pruinose beneath, flowers golden yellow), 'Park Juweel' (small, low, dense and thorny with more or less untoothed leaves coloring brilliantly in fall and sometimes persistent), and 'Red Jewel' (differs from 'Park Juweel' in its broader leaves assuming deep, purple-red tints.

Name	Distribution	Habit	Leaves	Flowers	Fruit
B. jamesiana	SW China	erect, deciduous, spiny shrub to 6¹⁄₂ ft (2 m) tall	obovate, entire or slightly toothed toward apex, thick, olive green above, gray-green beneath, coloring vividly in fall	pale orange in pendulous racemes to 4 in (10 cm) long	globose, opaque white ripening translucent pink
Comments:					
B. julianae	W China	evergreen, fiercely spiny, bushy shrub erect to 12 ft (4 m)	to 4 in (10 cm), obovate, ser- rate, tough, dark green above, paler beneath, tinted bronze- red when young	yellow, faintly fragrant in axil- lary clusters in early summer	to ³⁄₈ in (0.8 cm) long, oblong, black, glaucous

Comments: Good hedging shrub; includes 'Dart's Superb' (spreading, leaves small), 'Lombart's Red' (leaves red beneath), and 'Nana' (dwarf).

Name	Distribution	Habit	Leaves	Flowers	Fruit
B. linearifolia	Chilean Andes	evergreen, erect to arching and rather spiny, rangy, shrub to 5 ft (1.5 m) tall	to 2 in (5 cm) long, narrowly obovate-oblanceolate, entire with strongly revolute margins and a sharp tip, dark green above, pale beneath	orange in clus- ters in late spring and late summer	to ¹⁄₂ in (1 cm) long, ellipsoid, black, glaucous

Comments: Includes the large-and free-flowering red-yellow 'Jewel' and the large-and orange-flowered 'Orange King'.

Name	Distribution	Habit	Leaves	Flowers	Fruit
B. × lologensis (*B. darwinii* × *B. linearifolia*)	garden origin	evergreen, spiny, medium-sized shrub	to 1¹⁄₄ in (3 cm) long, obovate- spathulate, entire and/or toothed, tough, dark green	orange-yellow in umbel-like clusters	to ¹⁄₄ in (0.7 cm) long, ovoid, glaucous purple-blue

Comments: Includes 'Apricot Queen' (growth erect, flowers orange) and 'Stapehill' (flowers orange-yellow tinted fiery red).

B. gagnepainii **var.** *lanceifolia*   *B. julianae*   *B. linearifolia* 'Jewel'

B

BERBERIS

Name	Distribution	Habit	Leaves	Flowers	Fruit
B. × ***ottawensis*** (*B. thunbergii* × *B. vulgaris*)	garden origin	deciduous, erect shrub, very vigorous and suckering with large spines and (sometimes) expanded spiny stipules	³/₄–2¹/₂ in (2–6 cm), obovate to elliptic-ovate, blunt to acute, soft, mid-green with slightly paler undersides, coloring well in fall	pale yellow to golden to drooping racemes	red

Comments: Very robust and fast-growing, includes two purple-leaved forms often confused with each other—f. *purpurea*, to 6¹/₂ ft (2 m) tall with deep and solid purple-red leaves, obovate-elliptic, entire and to 1¹/₂ in (4 cm) long; 'Superba', to 10 ft (3 m) tall with wine-red tinted, pea green leaves, spathulate-orbicular, very finely serrate to entire and to 2¹/₂ in (6 cm) long, subtended by large 3-parted thorns and spiny stipules.

Name	Distribution	Habit	Leaves	Flowers	Fruit
B. poiretii **Comments:**	N China	deciduous or semievergreen shrub to 3¹/₄ ft (1 m) tall with angular, more or less spiny branches	to 1¹/₂ in (4 cm), narrowly oblanceolate, acuminate, with wavy margins and fine teeth	yellow flushed red in pendent racemes in late spring	narrowly oblong, pale red
B. prattii **Comments:**	W China	deciduous, spiny shrub to 10 ft (3 m) tall	to 1¹/₂ in (4 cm) long, whorled, obovate, obtuse, entire to sparsely serrate, glossy olive green above, gray-pruinose beneath	yellow in erect or drooping panicles	to ¹/₄ in (0.6 cm) long, ovoid, coral pink
B. × ***rubrostilla*** B. 'Rubrostilla'; (*B. aggregata* × *B. wilsoniae*)	garden origin	deciduous, spiny, erect to arching shrub to 5 ft (1.5 m) tall	to ³/₄ in (2 cm) long, oblanceolate with to 6 teeth per side, gray-pruinose beneath	pale yellow in umbel-like clusters in late spring and early summer	to ⁵/₈ in (1.5 cm) long, ovoid, scarlet, glossy

Comments: Large-fruited and showy especially in fall. Includes 'Chealii' (fruit garnet red), 'Cherry Ripe' (fruit pink-white ripening scarlet), 'Crawleyensis' (leaves larger, fruit large, scarlet.

Name	Distribution	Habit	Leaves	Flowers	Fruit
B. sargentiana **Comments:**	W China	evergreen, spiny shrub to 6¹/₂ ft (2 m) tall	to 4 in (10 cm) long, elliptic, acute with to 25 teeth per side, thick, dark glossy green above with impressed veins, yellow-green beneath	pale yellow in clusters in early summer	to ¹/₄ in (0.6 cm) long, purple-black, oblong, glossy
B. × ***stenophylla*** (*B. darwinii* × *B. empetrifolia*)	garden origin	evergreen shrub to 10 ft (3 m) tall with slender, arching branches	to ³/₄ in (2 cm) long, linear-lanceolate, mucronate, entire, tough, margin revolute, dark green above, pale and glaucous beneath	golden, solitary, in clusters, or in racemes in late spring and often again later in the year	to ¹/₄ in (0.7 cm) long, globose, purple-black

Comments: A resilient and varied group of hybrids used for specimen plantings, hedging, screening, and high, impenetrable ground cover; popular cultivars include 'Compacta' (dwarf, compact), 'Corallina Compacta' (dwarf, compact, flower buds coral-tinted opening burnt orange), 'Crawley Gem' (low-growing with many slender and arching stems and red-tinted orange-yellow flowers), 'Cream Showers' (flowers cream-white), 'Etna' (stems many, arching, covered in dense, dark green leaves and clusters of brilliant, orange-red flowers), 'Irwinii' (syn. *B.* × *irwinii*, small and compact with golden yellow flowers), 'Pink Pearl' (leaves splashed ivory and rose, flowers ivory, coral and orange), 'Semperflorens' (flowers red-orange to tangerine, long-lasting and produced late in season). For 'Nana' and 'Prostrata' see *B. darwinii*.

B. × *lologensis* 'Stapehill'

B. × *stenophylla* 'Corallina Compacta'

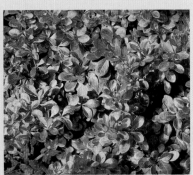
B. thunbergii 'Atropurpurea Nana'

BERBERIS

Name	Distribution	Habit	Leaves	Flowers	Fruit
B. thunbergii	Japan	deciduous, spiny suckering, bushy shrub to 3¼ ft (1 m) tall	to ¾ in (2 cm) long, ovate to obovate, blunt, olive-green above, gray-tinted beneath, scarlet to fiery red in fall	yellow tinted red, clustered in umbel-like racemes	to ⅜ in (0.8 cm) long, ellipsoid, glossy red

Comments: Compact shrub with superb fall color, excellent for low hedging. Includes cultivars 'Atropurpurea' (medium-sized shrub, foliage purple to purple-red), 'Atropurpurea Nana' (dwarf, foliage purple-red), 'Aurea' (leaves yellow, becoming lime green), 'Golden Ring' (leaves purple-red edged gold), 'Green Carpet' (low and spreading, leaves green turning red in fall), 'Harlequin' (compact, leaves small, mottled pink), 'Helmond Pillar' (narrowly upright, leaves dark purple), 'Kel-leriis' (leaves mottled silvery white, this color flushing pink to dark rose in fall; 'Silver Beauty' is similar but smaller), 'Kobold' (dwarf, dense and domed with green leaves and bright red fruit), 'Pink Queen' (leaves red-purple flecked gray and white), 'Red Pillar' (densely branched dwarf, erect shrub with purple-red leaves), 'Rose Glow' (small with new foliage purple mottled silver-white and rose pink).

Name	Distribution	Habit	Leaves	Flowers	Fruit
B. verruculosa	W China	evergreen spiny shrub to 5 ft (1.5 m) tall with arching, warty stems	to ¾ in (2 cm) long, obo-vate-elliptic, more or less toothed, glossy dark green above, white beneath	golden, solitary or paired to ½ in (1 cm) long, ovoid or pyriform, purple-black, frosted	neat and slow-growing.

Comments:

Name	Distribution	Habit	Leaves	Flowers	Fruit
B. vulgaris COMMON BARBERRY	North America; Europe; W Asia	deciduous, spiny suckering shrub to 6½ ft (2 m) tall	to 2½ in (6 cm) long, obovate-elliptic, serrulate, matt green	small, yellow-white in pendent racemes to 2½ in (6 cm) long	to ½ in (1 cm) long, oblong, bright to dull red, translucent

Comments: Wood once harvested for tooth picks and, being bright yellow, held to be a cure for jaundice. The fruits are edible and especially sweet in the cultivar 'Dulcis'; 'Asperma' is seedless. 'Alba' is white-fruited, 'Lutea' yellow-fruited. Selections for leaf color include 'Atropurpurea' with wine-red leaves and the silver-edged 'Marginata'.

Name	Distribution	Habit	Leaves	Flowers	Fruit
B. wilsoniae	W China	deciduous, thorny mound-forming shrub to 3¼ ft (1 m) tall	to 1¼ in (3 cm) long, obovate to linear-oblong, entire, mucronate, gray-green turning scarlet in fall	small, pale yellow, to 6 per cluster	to ¼ in (0.6 cm) diam.., coral pink, globose

Comments: var. **stapfiana** has spathulate leaves with gray undersides and vivid scarlet fruit. Among the finest cultivars are 'Joke' (hardy and vigorous with a profusion of large, red-flushed pink fruit), and 'Orangeade' (semiprostrate, spreading, fruit orange and pink). Wisley hybrids closest to B. wilsoniae include 'Comet' (fruit rounded, scarlet), 'Coral' (fruit conic, scarlet), 'Ferax' (fruit oblong-ovoid, scarlet), 'Fireball' (fruit conic, vermilion), 'Stonefield Surprise' (shoots red-tinted, flowers and fruit small), and 'Tom Thumb' (small, shoots yellow leaves broad, persisting).

berceau a trellis arch covered by climbing plants.

Berchemia (for M. Berchem, 17th-century French botanist). Rhamnaceae. Asia; Africa; Americas. 20 species, mostly deciduous, woody climbers with twining stems and very small, white flowers in short panicles and racemes, followed by fleshy fruits in fall. Hardy to 5°F (–15°C). Grow in sun or light shade. Provide support or allow to scramble through trees and shrubs. Propagate from seed sown in fall or spring, by semiripe stem cuttings or root cuttings in winter; also by simple layering.

B. racemosa Japan and Taiwan; to 12 ft (4 m); leaves 2½ in (6 cm)-long, ovate to cordate, splashed creamy white in 'Variegata'; fruit red to black; B. scan-dens (syn. B. volubilis); RATTAN VINE, SUPPLEJACK; US, Mexico, Guatemala; differs from the last species in its slightly larger, elliptic leaves marked cream to white in 'Variegata'; oblong fruit turns from plum blue to black in fall.

Bergenia (for Carl von Bergen [1704–1759], author of *Flora Francofurtana* [1750]). Saxifragaceae. East Asia. SOW'S EARS. 8 species, hardy evergreen rhizomatous perennial herbs with broad and leathery leaves, and scapose cymes of 5-parted, cup-shaped flowers from late winter to spring. Once established, they will thrive in damp or rather dry situations, in light shade or full sun. Mulch annually in late winter with well-rotted garden compost mixed with a little slow-release garden fertilizer. Divide in fall or spring.

B. ciliata W Pakistan to Nepal; leaves to 14 in (35 cm), hairy with ciliate margins, flushing deep red-bronze in cold weather; flowers nodding, rose-tinted white, on stalks to 12 in (30 cm); B. cordifolia Siberia and Mongolia; leaves to 16 in (40 cm), smooth with sunken veins and wavy, toothed margins; flowers rose or magenta on 12–18 in (30–45 cm) stalks; B. purpurascens E Himalaya; leaves to 10 in (25 cm), dark, shining green turning deep purple-red in fall and winter; flowers deep, rosy red on stalks to 16 in (40 cm) high; B. stracheyi Afghanistan to Tibet; leaves to 8 in (20 cm), smooth except for downy margins, flushing dark garnet in winter; flowers fragrant, pale rose to white in nodding clusters. Cultivars — 'Abendglut': to 16 in (40 cm), with leaves large, tinted red; flowers dark red; 'Ballawley': glossy, purple-flushed in winter; flowers purple-crimson; 'Morgenröte': small; flowers large, cherry pink, produced twice a year; *B.* × *schmidtii* (*B. ciliata* × *B. crassifolia*); leaves smooth, bluntly toothed flowers, rose pink; 'Silberlicht': leaves large; flowers white, later tinted palest pink; 'Sunningdale': rounded, bronze-red leaves in fall and winter; flowers deep lilac pink.

Berkheya (for M.J.L. de Berkhey, Dutch botanist). Compositae. South Africa. Some 80 species, perennial herbs, subshrubs and shrubs with daisylike flower heads. Plant Berkheya on fertile, well-drained soils in a sheltered, sunny position (min. 10°F /−12°C). Propagate by division in spring. *B. macrocephala* Natal; erect perennial to 3¼ ft (1 m); leaves are deeply lobed, spiny; flower heads to 2½ in (6 cm), ray florets rich yellow, disk florets orange-yellow, produced during summer in branched inflorescences.

berry a baccate, indehiscent fruit, one- to many-seeded; the product of a single pistil. Frequently applied to any pulpy or fleshy fruit.

Berries of
Sorbus aucuparia

Bertolonia (for A. Bertoloni [1775–1869], Italian botanist). Melastomataceae. South America. 14 species, tender perennial herbs with decorative, thinly succulent leaves and one-sided cymes of rosy-purple flowers. Plant in shallow pots, terraria or bottle gardens in a porous, soilless mix. Keep moist and humid in shade or filtered light; minimum temperature, 59°F (15°C). Draughts, cold and damp, and exposure of wet foliage to sun are all deleterious. Propagate by stem or leaf cuttings in a sandy propagating mix in a closed case. *B. marmorata* Brazil; evergreen to 8 in (20 cm); leaves ovate to

oblong, upper surfaces downy and vivid green with streaks of silver-white, or overlaid with a copper luster, or, again, satiny bottle green veined silver; their undersides are deep purple-red: flowers magenta.

Berzelia (for Berzelius, a Swedish chemist of the early 19th century). Bruniaceae. South Africa. 12 species, evergreen shrubs grown in the cool greenhouse or conservatory for their heatherlike habit and small flowers in globose heads. Plant in a well-drained, neutral to acidic medium rich in organic matter. Position in full sun; ventilate freely. Keep the roots cool and moist in summer, drier in winter, maintaining a minimum temperature of 45°F (7°C). Sow seed in spring or root semiripe cuttings during late summer. *B. lanuginosa* to 6½ ft (2 m); the leaves are downy, needlelike; flowers minute, white in summer.

Beschorneria (for Friedrich Beschorner [1806–1873], German botanist). Agavaceae. Mexico. 10 species, very large, evergreen, perennial herbs with tough, sword-shaped leaves far exceeded by scapose panicles of 6-parted, tubular flowers in late spring and summer. The following species is hardy to 0°F (−18°C) if planted in well-drained soil in a sheltered, sun-baked position. Propagate by division, or by rooted offsets in spring. *B. yuccoides* leaves gray-green, to 3¼ ft (1 m) long in an open rosette; panicle to 6½ ft (2 m), stalk and bracts glaucous, coral to sealing wax red, flowers pendulous, 2¾ in (7 cm)-long, yellow-green.

Bessera (for W.S.J.G. von Besser [1784–842], Austrian-Polish botanist). Liliaceae (Alliaceae). Mexico. 1 species, *B. elegans* (CORAL DROPS), a frost-tender, cormous perennial herb with narrow leaves. In summer, a loose umbel of 10–30 pendulous flowers is carried atop a slender scape, 39 in (100 cm) tall. The flowers are campanulate, to 1½ in (4 cm) long, bright red to purple-red veined green on the exterior, ivory veined or edged scarlet on the interior. Plant in full sun in a sheltered position. Where frosts are hard, mulch thickly in winter, or lift and store dry in a cool place. Alternatively, grow in a cool

greenhouse or conservatory. Increase by seed or division in spring.

Beta (from Celtic *bett*, red) Chenopodiaceae; Europe and Mediterranean. 6 species of perennial or biennial, hardy, glabrous herbs. Roots often swollen. Leaves flat, usually entire, often glossy, long petioles, green or reddish purple. Flowers small, hermaphrodite cymes. Several seeds form a seed ball giving more than one seedling on germination. Of food crop or ornamental interest are *B. vulgaris* ssp. *vulgaris* BEET (q.v), grown for its edible roots, *B. v.* ssp. *cicla* var. *flavescens*, SWISS CHARD (q.v), grown for its edible leaves and midribs and ornamental value. *B. v.* ssp. *cicla* var. *cicla*, SPINACH BEET (q.v), syn. PERPETUAL SPINACH, also has edible leaves.

betanin pigment responsible for color in red beets.

Betula (the Classical Latin name). Betulaceae. Temperate and Arctic N Hemisphere. BIRCH. Some 60 species, hardy deciduous trees and shrubs grown for their graceful habit, bark, foliage and catkins. The habit ranges from erect and conical or pyramidal to slender and weeping. The bark is usually papery, the thin older bark peeling to expose chalky white to glossy red new bark; the oldest bark (i.e., that on bole) becomes sooty gray and riven. The leaves are mostly ovate and thin-textured with toothed margins. Small tightly packed in male or female catkins and, the flowers appear in late fall but do not open until spring (in the following descriptions, the catkins of the species below are female and measured at fruiting unless otherwise stated; produced in late winter and spring, the ornamental male catkins tend to be longer, narrower and pendulous with green-gold anthers).

Plant in full sun in fertile, moist, but well-drained soil. Propagate by ripe seed; by side-veneer grafts in late winter in a cold greenhouse; by greenwood cuttings in early to midsummer; or by semiripe cuttings in late summer under mist or in a closed case. Attacked by bracket fungi (entering by bark wounds and resulting in older stems' snapping in their upper reaches); also by mildew and birch rust.

BETULA

Name	Distribution	Habit	Bark	Leaves	Catkins
(in the following descriptions, the catkins are female and measured at fruiting unless otherwise stated; produced in late winter and spring, the ornamental male catkins tend to be longer, narrower and pendulous with green-gold anthers)					
B. albosinensis CHINESE PAPER BIRCH	China	open-crowned, clear stemmed, medium-sized tree, 60–80 ft (18–25 m) tall	glaucous gray-white at first then peeling, thin and coppery pink to orange-red	1½–2¾ in (4–7 cm) long, narrowly ovate, acuminate, biserrate, glossy light green	1¼–1½ in (3–4 cm) long, ovoid-cylindric, pendulous
Comments: var. ***septentrionalis*** differs in its orange-pink to red bark bloomed violet-white and peeling in shaggy rolls; the leaves are longer and narrower, dull green and drooping.					
B. alleghaniensis *B. lutea* YELLOW BIRCH	Eastern North America	open-branched tree, 70–100 ft (20–30 m) tall, often multistemmed	thin, crisped or curled, tinged yellow or gray, peeling in translucent sheets and yellow-brown where exposed	2½–4¾ in (6–12 cm), ovate to ovate-oblong, acute, coarsely biserrate, dull green, silky hairy beneath, turning yellow in fall	1–1¼ in (2.5–3 cm) long, thickly cylindrical, erect
B. dahurica *B. davurica* ASIAN BLACK BIRCH **Comments:**	NE Asia	medium-sized tree, 50–100 ft (15–30 m) tall	thick, peeling in curling flakes, brown tinged gray, becoming silver-gray and rugged with age; twigs hairy at first, dark gray, resinous with white glands	2–4 in (5–10 cm) long, ovate-rhombic, serrate, acute, dark green and glabrous above, glandular-punctate beneath	¾–1 in (2–2.5 cm) long, narrowly oblong, drooping
B. ermanii ERMAN'S BIRCH; GOLD BIRCH; RUSSIAN ROCK BIRCH	NE Asia	graceful, vigorous tree or large shrub to 80 ft (25 m) tall, usually widely spreading	peeling, creamy yellow to white with pale brown lenticels, or red-brown, orange-brown to purple-brown on young branches; twigs hairless, glandular-warty when young	2–4 in (5–10 cm), deltoid-cordate, coarsely serrate, apex cuspidate, with scattered glands	¾–1¼ in (2–3 cm) long, ovate-ellipsoid, erect
Comments: 'Grayswood Hill' is a selected form of this species, sometimes offered under the name *B. costata*.					
B. 'Fetisowii'	C Asia (hybrid origin)	graceful, narrow-crowned tree	chalky white, peeling, colorful on trunk and branches		
B. fontinalis *B. occidentalis* AMERICAN RED BIRCH; WATER BIRCH	W N America	shrub to 20 ft (6 m) tall, or tree to 40 ft (12 m) tall	smooth, lustrous dark bronze	1–2 in (2.5–5 cm) long, rhomboid-ovate, apex acute, biserrate, dark dull green above, paler beneath, slightly hairy above, soon hairless beneath, turning yellow in fall	to 1¼ in (3 cm) long
Comments: Needs moist but not saturated conditions.					
B. lenta CHERRY BIRCH; SWEET BIRCH **Comments:**	E N America	shrub or narrowly upright tree to 80 ft (25 m) tall	polished red-brown to purple-black, fissured, not peeling, aromatic	2½–4¾ in (6–12 cm) long, ovate-oblong, biserrate, acute to acuminate, glossy green above, paler beneath, gold in fall	¾–1½ in (2–3.5 cm) long, oblong-ovoid, erect

B. albosinensis

B. alleghaniensis

B. ermanii

B. lenta

B

BETULA

Name	Distribution	Habit	Leaves	Flowers	Fruit
B. maximowicziana MONARCH BIRCH	Japan	fast-growing tree to 100 ft (30 m) tall with an open crown	thin, peeling in strips, tinged orange-brown, gray and pink-white; branches and twigs dark red-brown, shiny	3–5½ in (8–14 cm), broadly ovate, base cordate, apex acute to acuminate, dark green turning clear yellow in fall sometimes with red veins	1¼–2¾ in (3–7 cm), pendulous

Comments: Resistant to bronze birch borer.

Name	Distribution	Habit	Leaves	Flowers	Fruit
B. nana ARCTIC BIRCH; DWARF BIRCH	subarctic regions	prostrate to ascending shrub or dwarf tree 1½–3¼ ft (0.5–1 m) tall	dull brown, rather hairy at first	1½–5 ft (0.5–1.5 m) long, suborbicular to reniform, apex rounded, crenate, dark green tinged yellow or red in fall	to ½ in (1 cm) long, ovoid, erect

Comments: Charming dwarf, treelike shrub, especially attractive in early spring when the twigs are bright with fresh new leaves and squat, yellow-brown catkins. Prefers moisture and will tolerate extreme cold; suitable for rock and bog gardens, acidic borders, light woodland, and wild gardens.

Name	Distribution	Habit	Leaves	Flowers	Fruit
B. nigra BLACK BIRCH; RIVER BIRCH; RED BIRCH	E US	fast-growing tree to 70 ft (20 m) tall, with a pyramidal crown or multi-stemmed	thick, peeling in shaggy scales, pink-brown on young trees, on older trees very dark red tinged black	2¾–3½ in (7–9 cm) long, ovate-rhombic, biserrate, glossy green above, pale and glaucous beneath, yellow in fall	1–1½ in (2.5–4 cm) long, cylindric, erect

Comments: Prefers moist soil; resistant to bronze birch borer. 'Heritage' is a vigorous selection with peeling, light brown to cream bark and glossy, dark green leaves.

Name	Distribution	Habit	Leaves	Flowers	Fruit
B. papyrifera CANOE BIRCH; PAPER BIRCH; WHITE BIRCH	N America; Greenland	open-branched, round-headed tree to 100 ft (30 m) tall	bright white, dull white or dull gray-brown, smooth, peeling in papery layers; branchlets red-brown	1½–3½ in (4–9 cm), broadly ovate, apex acute, biserrate, ciliate, with dark, glandular spots beneath	1¼–1½ in (3–4 cm) long, cylindric, pendulous

Comments: Similar to *B. pendula* but taller with a more open and less weeping crown.

Name	Distribution	Habit	Leaves	Flowers	Fruit
B. pendula EUROPEAN WHITE BIRCH; COMMON BIRCH; SILVER BIRCH; WARTY BIRCH	Europe to W Asia	tree to 100 ft (30 m) with a slender, open crown weeping branches and very slender, pendulous branchlets	thin, peeling and silvery white when young, thick, fissured and ashy black with age, especially at base of trunk; twigs bumpy with glands	1¼–2¾ in (3–7 cm) long, broadly ovate-deltoid to rhombic, biserrate, thin viscid when young, smooth	⅝–1¼ in (1.5–3 cm), cylindric, pendulous

Comments: Very widely planted and naturalized tree; popular cultivars include 'Dalecarlica' (SWEDISH BIRCH; tall, slender tree, branches weeping; leaves deeply cut); 'Fastigiata' (erect, medium-sized tree with closely upright branches; 'Obelisk' is similar but narrower still); 'Golden Cloud' (small tree with arching branches and golden leaves, requires shelter, light shade, and good water supply); 'Purpurea' (slow-growing, slender and weeping tree with white bark, purple-black twigs and purple-red leaves; favors cooler climates); 'Laciniata' (similar to 'Dalecarlica' and often grown under that name but more markedly weeping and with less deeply cut leaves); 'Tristis' (tall and graceful with a narrow crown and weeping branches); 'Trost's Dwarf' (dwarf shrub or tree seldom exceeding 3¼ ft (1 m), with arching branches and small, dissected leaves, good for bonsai, alpine troughs, and rock garden); 'Youngii' (small, weeping tree with a dome-shaped crown).

B. nana

B. papyrifera

B. pendula 'Youngii'

B. utilis var. jacquemontii

BETULA

Name	Distribution	Habit	Leaves	Flowers	Fruit
B. platyphylla B. mandshurica ASIAN WHITE BIRCH	Siberia to Manchuria, Korea, Japan	open-crowned tree to 70 ft (20 m) tall	pure chalky white, not fissuring at base; twigs brown, warty and resinous	1½–2¾ in (4–7 cm) long, triangular-ovate, apex shortly acuminate, coarsely serrate, hairless	to 1¼ in (3 cm) long, pendulous

Comments: Differs from typical *B. pendula* in its unfissured, white bark and larger leaves, and from the solidly white-barked *B. pendula* var. *lapponica* in its acutely, not bluntly, toothed leaves. var. *japonica* (syn. *B. mandshurica* var. *japonica*, JAPANESE WHITE BIRCH), has larger leaves, sometimes finely hairy beneath and catkins to 2 in (5 cm) long.

Name	Distribution	Habit	Leaves	Flowers	Fruit
B. szechuanica B. mandshurica var. szechuanica; B. platyphylla var. szechuanica	W China	tree to 80 ft (25 m) tall	thin, peeling, chalky pure white; twigs shortly acuminate, dark gray to red brown with pale resinous warts	2–4¾ in (5–12 cm) long, ovate-cordate to deltoid, apex serrate, blue-green above, glaucous beneath	1¼–2 in (3–5 cm) long, pendulous
		Comments:			

Name	Distribution	Habit	Leaves	Flowers	Fruit
B. utilis HIMALAYAN BIRCH	Himalaya	tree to 70 ft (20 m) tall, usually single-stemmed with a broad, open crown	thin, peeling in horizontal papery flakes, pink to orange-brown, bloomed white; twigs red-brown in fall	2–4¾ in (5–12 cm) long, ovate-acuminate, serrate, dark green above, paler beneath, tough, smooth above, somewhat hairy beneath, yellow in fall	to 1½ in (3.5 cm) long, cylindric, spreading to nodding

Comments: var. *jacquemontii* (syn. *B. jacquemontii*) differs in its pure, startling white bark; the shoots and buds lack resin (thus distinguished from var. *occidentalis*). It includes some of the finest silver-bark birches, medium-sized, relatively slow-growing and long-lived trees with clear trunks, ellipsoid to conical crowns and handsome leaves—'Jermyns' has brilliant white bark and showy male catkins to 6 in (15 cm) long; 'Silver Shadow' has the brightest white bark and large, deep green and rather drooping leaves.

Biarum (name used by Dioscorides for a similar aroid). Araceae. Mediterranean; W Asia. 15 species, hardy or slightly frost-tender tuberous, perennial herbs with spathes in subtle or sinister tones, and foul-smelling, similarly colored spadices. The inflorescence usually emerges in spring or fall, unaccompanied by leaves and sitting directly on the soil. Plant in light, fertile, and very well drained soil in full sun (minimum winter temperature 23°F/–5°C). Wet winter conditions are usually lethal to this plant. Flowering is unlikely unless a dry, warm summer dormancy can be ensured. Propagate Biarum by seed sown under cover during fall, or by division when dormant.

B. davisii Crete, S Turkey; spathe squat, pitcherlike, to 3 in (8 cm) long, cream flecked pink-brown or dull mauve; *B. eximium* S Turkey; spathe 4 in (10 cm), recurved, oblong to ovate in velvety purple-black; *B. tenuifolium* Portugal to Turkey; spathe lanceolate, recurved to 12 in (30 cm) long, dark purple.

Bidens (from Latin *bi-*, twice, and *dens*, tooth, referring to the biaristate fruit). Compositae. Cosmopolitan. TICKSEED; BEGGAR'S TICKS; STICK-TIGHT; BUR-MARIGOLD; PITCHFORKS; SPANISH NEEDLES. 200 species, hardy annual and perennial herbs and shrubs with simple or pinnate leaves and daisy-like flower heads. Grow in moderately fertile, moisture-retentive soil in sun. Propagate by seed sown *in situ* in spring, or (perennial clones and 'Golden Goddess') by division in early spring. *B. ferulifolia* (syn. *B. procera*); Southern United States to Guatemala; bushy, annual or perennial herb to 3¼ ft (1 m) tall; foliage is finely divided; flower heads are yellow, to 2 in (5 cm) across, especially large and golden in the cultivar 'Golden Goddess', produced from midsummer to late fall.

biennial a plant that flowers and seeds in the second season following germination, such as Canterbury bells (*Campanula medium*). Some biennials are treated as annuals, for example carrot (*Daucus carota* subsp. *sativus*).

biennial bearing relating to fruit plants which produce little or no fruit in alternate years, as a result of a natural characteristic or an inducing factor.

bifid of deeply cleft leaves, bracts, sepals and petals that form two points or lobes.

Bifrenaria (from the Latin *bi-*, twice, and *frenum*, bridle, a reference to the double band by which the two pollinia are connected). Orchidaceae. South America. 16 species, tender epiphytic orchids with fragrant and long-lasting flowers in spring and summer. Pot in a very open, bark-based mix. Grow in full sunlight and with high humidity. Water and feed copiously while in growth. Once pseudobulbs have developed fully, impose a cooler, drier atmosphere (minimum temperature 45°F/7°C) and reduce water to a daily misting. Begin watering again when new growth appears. Increase by division. *B. harrisoniae* Brazil; flowers thickly waxy, 2¾ in (7 cm) across; tepals oval, ivory or rich cream cupping a frilled and hairy, dark rose or blood red lip.

big bud a condition of black currants in which the buds become swollen and fail to develop, caused by the BLACK CURRANT GALL MITE (*Cecidophyopsis ribis*), which also transmits reversion disease.

bigeneric hybrid, bigener a plant that results or is created from cross-pollination between parents of different genera.

B

Bignonia (for the Abbé Bignon [1662–1743], Librarian to Louis XIV). Bignoniaceae. Southeastern US. 1 species, *B. capreolata*, the CROSS VINE, QUARTER VINE or TRUMPET FLOWER, a woody, evergreen climber grown for its flowers, produced in summer. The leaves consist of a pair of leaflets sometimes separated by a coiling tendril. The flowers are 1½–2 in (4–5 cm) long, funnel- to trumpet-shaped, deep orange to scarlet (rich purple-brown to blood red in the cultivar 'Atrosanguinea'). Grow in a well-drained, fertile medium in full sun; minimum temperature 23°F (–5°C). Water and feed generously when in growth and spray and ventilate freely under glass. Tub cultivation will restrict the roots and encourage flowering. Cut back the previous season's growth in spring. Propagate by layering, or by leaf bud cuttings rooted in a closed case with bottom heat.

bilabiate a flower possessing two lips, as in the corolla of Labiatae and Acanthaceae.

Billardiera (for J.J.H. de Labillardiere [1755–1834], French explorer and botanist). Pittosporaceae. Australia. 8 species, perennial, woody-based evergreen climbers grown for their pendulous flowers and glossy, oblong to globose berries in late summer and fall. Plant in a moist neutral to acidic medium with a cool root run and protection from scorching sunlight. Hardy in mild areas if planted on a sheltered, sunny wall and mulched thickly in winter. Train on wires or trellis. In colder regions, grow in a cool greenhouse or conservatory. Propagate by seed sown when fresh or stem cuttings in early summer; also by simple layering. *B. longiflora* CLIMBING BLUE-BERRY, PURPLE APPLE BERRY; to 6½ ft (2 m); leaves narrow, dark green; flowers slender, to 1¼ in (3 cm) long in shades of green-yellow, later dull pink to pale mauve; berries cobalt blue to indigo, pink, mauve or white.

Billbergia (for J.G. Billberg [1772–1884], Swedish botanist). Bromeliaceae. C and S America. 54 species, epiphytic, evergreen, perennial herbs with narrow, tough and saw-toothed leaves in a funnel-based rosette and tubular flowers in an erect or arching, terminal raceme or panicle clothed with colorful bracts. Position in bright, filtered light or light shade; minimum temperature 45°F (7°C). Water and feed generously during warm weather; keep barely moist at other times. Increase by division or offsets.

B. chlorosticta RAINBOW PLANT; Brazil; to 20 in (50 cm) tall with white-marked, red-brown leaves and an arching to nodding raceme of blue-tipped, sulfur flowers amid broad, lobster red bracts; *B. nutans* FRIENDSHIP PLANT, QUEEN'S TEARS; Brazil to Northern Argentina; freely clump-forming, to 16 in (40 cm) tall with narrow, plain green leaves and an arching to nodding raceme of yellow-green flowers tipped slate-blue amid narrow, flamingo pink bracts; *B. pyramidalis*; E Brazil; to 24 in (60 cm) tall with lanceolate, purple-flushed leaves banded white beneath and an erect, pyramidal inflorescence with red or orange-pink, violet-tipped flowers amid bright rose bracts); *B. sanderiana* Brazil; to 24 in (60 cm) tall with green leaves clouded with gray-white and a compound, nodding inflorescence of indigo-tipped, lime green flowers between bright rose bracts; *B.* × *windii* ANGEL'S TEARS; *B. decora* × *B. nutans*; differing from the latter in its broader, spreading leaves obscurely banded gray beneath and larger floral bracts; *B. zebrina* S Brazil to N Argentina; to 3¼ ft (1 m) tall with an open rosette of bronze-tinted and silver-banded leaves and an arching to nodding raceme of sulfur flowers clothed with large, papery, pink bracts.

billhook, bill a heavy-duty trimming implement of variable design; basically a wide blade fashioned into a hook at the top. A long-handled version is called a slasher.

bindweed the popular name for two climbing perennials with funnel-shaped flowers that occur as invasive weeds in gardens. HEDGE BINDWEED (*Calystegia sepium*) is the stronger stemmed of the two producing large white, occasionally pink, flowers. FIELD BINDWEED (*Convolvulus arvensis*) bears small white and pink flowers and is more productive of seed. Bindweed is difficult to control because of its depth of rooting, and frequent and careful forking out and hoeing off is necessary to weaken and eradicate it. Glyphosate and glyphosate trimesium are effective as foliage-applied total weed killers.

bine a term sometimes used to describe climbing stems, especially of beans, peas and hops.

binomial a taxonomic term for the basic unit of naming in botany comprising a generic name and a species, cultivar, group or hybrid epithet describing and distinguishing the individual belonging to that genus. *Buddleja alternifolia*, *Buddleja* 'Petite Indigo', *Buddleja* Davidii Group and *Buddleja* × *weyeriana* are all examples of binomials.

biodynamic gardening a system akin to organic gardening, first advocated in the 1920s by Rudolph Steiner. The philosophy perceives plant life as essentially self-sustaining. It places emphasis on skilful handling of manures through composting, and on symbiotic relationships between plants and insects. The plant is considered as a whole and there is a holistic approach to its well-being. The concept of biodynamic gardening incorporates a theory of interplanetary influence on plant life.

biological controls strictly, the control of pests and weeds by the use of other living organisms such as parasites, predators or pathogens. More generally, the term includes specially devised cultural practices and host resistance. It embraces both the encouragement of natural pest control and the introduction of artificially bred beneficial organisms, including insects such as parasitoids and predators, predacious mites, insect-feeding fungi, bacteria, and insect viruses. Selected plant-feeding insects are being used increasingly for weed control. In refined biological control natural enemies are introduced from a pest's center of origin and only relatively small numbers need to be released because, providing the environment is favorable, they should multiply and be self-perpetuating and reduce the pest to a nondamaging level. In common practice, biological control always requires repetitive action by humans; it involves the release of natural enemies at times when pest numbers rise to critical levels, or any method that avoids destroying natural enemies or provides more favorable conditions for them to flourish.

Biological control agents available to gardeners include a chalcid wasp (*Encarsia formosa*) for the control of whitefly under glass; the lady-bird beetle (*Cryptolaemus montrouzieri*), which is used against mealybugs; the gall-midge (*Aphidoletes aphidimyza*) whose larvae attack aphids; the predatory mite *Phytoseiulus persimilis*, which controls red spider mites under glass; the nematode *Phasmarhabditis hermaphrodita* against slugs; and the bacterium *Bacillus thuringiensis*, used for controlling moth and butterfly caterpillars. Other biological controls of pests are the fungus *Verticillium lecanii*, if permitted for use, against greenhouse whitefly and aphids, and the parasitic nematodes *Steinernema krausei* and *Heterorhabditis megidis*, used against vine weevil grubs. Some diseases of plants can be controlled biologically by the introduction of fungi; for example, *Phlebia* (*Peniophora*) can be used as a competitive invader of cut tree stumps, and protects against later invasion by destructive decay fungi such as *Fomes* bracket fungi – a technique now well-established in forestry practice. *Trichoderma viride*, if permitted for use, works both as a parasite of the silver leaf pathogen (*Chondrostereum*) of plums and also as an 'antagonist' producing antibiotics which protect the host tree against infection. Trichoderma shows promise for controlling other tree diseases such as Dutch elm disease.

Most gardens, with a mixed flora of trees, shrubs, flowers, vegetables and fruit, encourage the establishment of natural pest enemies by providing a variety of food, shelter and reproductive sites, particularly if spraying with chemicals is restricted. Gardeners should be aware of the presence of natural predators in their gardens and take measures to encourage them. Sometimes it is possible to augment resources such as food, shelter and reproductive sites: hoverflies feed on

the nectar of flowers; mulching with organic materials provides shelter for useful predators such as rove and ground beetles; and insectivorous birds such as tits can be encouraged with nest boxes. See *cultural controls*; *integrated pest management*.

biorational pesticides pathogens and parasites of pest species, naturally occurring chemicals, and pest growth regulators used in biological control or integrated pest management systems.

biotic disease a parasitic disorder caused by a living organism such as a virus, bacterium or fungus.

each leaflet in turn divided (bipinnate)

first division into leaflets (pinnate)

Single leaf of Gleditsia triacanthos

bipinnate of compound leaves where both primary and secondary divisions are pinnate.

birds Most birds are welcome in gardens but some cause a considerable amount of damage. The BULLFINCH (*Pyrrhula pyrrhula*) which for most of the year feeds on seeds from weeds and trees, often attacks the flower buds of top and bush fruits. Plum, pear, cherry and gooseberry are attacked from late fall to early spring when the buds are dormant; apple and black currant are at risk in spring after the buds have opened. Ornamental cherry, crab apple, almond, *Forsythia* and *Amelanchier* are also subject to attack. Barren shoots with flowers at the tip indicate that bullfinches have been at work. The HOUSE SPARROW (*Passer domesticus*) is usually more destructive in urban areas: plums, currants and gooseberries may be disbudded in late

spring; and flowers of many plants damaged in spring and summer. *Crocus*, *Primula*, polyanthus, lettuce, peas, runner beans and freshly sown lawn seed are particularly vulnerable. WOOD PIGEONS and FERAL PIGEONS eat seeds of beans, peas and other crops and strip bush fruits. Brassicas are particularly subject to attack, both as young plants and during winter, when they may be completely defoliated. Other birds causing damage in gardens, especially to fruits, include TITS, BLACKBIRDS, STARLINGS and JAYS.

The only certain way to protect vulnerable crops is to cover them with ³⁄₄ in (2 cm)-mesh netting or purpose-built fruit cages. Black cotton can be strung along seed rows or strands crisscrossed above new-sown lawns, crocuses and primulas in flower; it can also be wound among the branches of fruit trees to deter bullfinches. Nylon thread, which does not decay and can readily trap birds, must not be used. Strips of narrow plastic ribbon made taut above crops to vibrate in the wind may deter birds by the ultrasonic sounds produced. Scaring devices such as traditional scarecrows, glitter strips, windmills and imitations of predators can be effective initially; however, they need to be changed or repositioned frequently. Techniques such as distress-call transmissions are unsuitable in built-up areas; trapping, shooting or nest destruction are also not applicable to most gardens. Chemical repellents are restrictive, usually erratic in performance and subject to weathering.

biserial arranged in two rows.

biserrate doubly serrate, i.e., with toothed teeth.

bisexual of flowers, with both stamens and pistils; of plants, with perfect (hermaphrodite) flowers.

biternate with compound leaves ternately divided but with each division itself ternately compound.

bitter pit a disorder of apple and pear fruits, expressed as sunken spots in the skin with small brown areas below the lesions and scattered throughout

111

the flesh. It results from induced calcium deficiency probably connected with water shortage, and may only become apparent in store. Its incidence can be reduced by spraying calcium nitrate, timely watering and mulching.

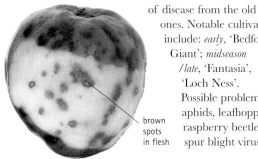

brown spots in flesh

Bitter pit in apple

bitter rot most commonly used to refer to the round, brown, sunken lesions occurring on fruits of apple, pear and quince late in the season and after harvest; caused by the fungi *Glomerella cingulata* or *Pezicula* species. Concentric rings of white to pink pustules of spores develop on the lesions. The fungi are present in the small cankers which appear on branches. Spores from these are washed on to fruits and enter the lenticels, eventually causing rot as the fruits mature. Damaged fruits should not be stored; fruits in store should be frequently examined.

G.cingulata also causes similar rot on cherries, cranberries, grapes (RIPE ROT), and peaches.

bizarre a type of carnation with patches of two or more colors on a differently colored background.

blackberry (*Rubus fruticosus*) the true blackberry of Europe, as distinct from the North American dewberry (q.v.) (which describes trailing *Rubus* species native of the eastern states) and the upright-growing highbush or erect blackberries. They are grown for their glossy black aggregate fruits, picked with the plug intact. Most are self fertile and flowering is usually late enough in spring to avoid frost damage. Plant one- or two-year-old plants shallowly, 8–10 ft (2.5–3 m) apart for erect cultivars, 11–15 ft (3.5–4.5 m) apart for trailers; cut back to a bud 8–12 in (20–30 cm) above soil level after planting. Trailing blackberries require support, such as a line of upright posts bearing four parallel wires spaced 12–18 in (30–45 cm) apart, with the lowest 3¼ ft (1 m) from ground level. Fruit is produced on second-year canes. New canes should be tied in away from the fruiting canes to reduce the spread

of disease from the old ones. Notable cultivars include: *early*, 'Bedford Giant'; *midseason /late*, 'Fantasia', 'Loch Ness'. Possible problems: aphids, leafhopper, raspberry beetle; spur blight virus.

black currant (*Ribes nigrum*) a deciduous shrub 4 ft (1.2 m) high, grown for the juicy, many-seeded berries that develop in bunches from pendent racemes. It grows wild in central and eastern Europe and in northern and central Asia as far as the Himalayas. Most cultivars are self fertile.

The black currant grows most satisfactorily in the cool moist climates of Europe, Canada and New Zealand, where the requirement of low temperature to break dormancy is best met, though the flowers are susceptible to spring frost. It is rarely grown in the US because the plant is an alternative host to white-pine blister-fungus.

Plant two-year-old certified bushes 5–6 ft (1.5–1.8 m) apart each way depending on potential vigor, and cut down all shoots to one bud above ground level after planting. The best quality fruit is borne on one-year-old wood: the structure of established bushes should be thinned by about one third each year, pruning out two-and three-year-old shoots as near as possible to the base of the stool. Propagate from hardwood cuttings. Notable cultivars include: *early*, 'Boskoop Giant'; *midseason*, 'Ben Lomond', Ben Sarek'; *late*, 'Jet'.

Possible problems: aphids, big bud mite, capsid bug; American gooseberry mildew (see *powdery mildew*), gray mold, leaf spot, reversion.

blackfly any species of *aphid* (q.v.) characterized by black coloring. It commonly refers to the BLACK BEAN APHID (*Aphis fabae*).

black knot (*Apiosporina morbosa*) a serious disease of *Prunus* species especially plum in North America. Black masses of fungus tissue form on infected stems, and knots up to four times the diameter of the host twigs produce

spores. Control by cutting out knotted stems before spring; spray trees with copper or lime-sulfur just before bud break.

black leg a term used for certain plant diseases in which the base of the stem turns black. In black leg of potatoes, caused by the bacterium *Erwinia carotovora* subsp. *atroseptica*, inward curling and yellowing of leaflets is followed by wet black decay at the base of stems. Only healthy tubers should be saved as seed. Black leg of beet and sugar beet (*Pleospora bjöerlingii*) causes stems of young seedlings to become blackened and shrivelled; it is seed-borne but not usually a problem in gardens. Black leg of pelargoniums, in which cuttings or plants die from root and stem decay, is typically caused by *Pythium* species, but other fungi such as *Rhizoctonia solani* and *Thielaviopsis basicola*, like the bacterium *Xanthomonas campestris* pv. *pelargonii*, cause similar symptoms. Cuttings should be taken from healthy stock and plants grown in sterilized medium; fungicide soil drenches may be effective, subject to local pesticide approvals. BRASSICA CANKER (*Leptosphaeria maculans*) is also referred to as black leg.

black mildew parasitic fungi, mostly of warm climates, which form dark superficial mycelium on foliage. See *sooty mold*.

black root rot (*Thielaviopsis basicola*). a disease that attacks many different vegetables and ornamentals causing blackening of roots and often stem base infection. Affected seedlings are stunted and chlorotic, and may be killed outright. Drenches of systemic fungicide can give some control. Because the fungus is soilborne, it can best be avoided by growing seeds in sterilized medium and by careful hygiene. The fungus is also the cause of specific cherry replant disease, which results in poor growth and cropping; it can be overcome through soil fumigation. In black root rot of cucurbits the fungus *Phomopsis sclerotioides* causes black spots on roots which eventually rot, causing plants to wilt. It can be controlled by soil fumigation and systemic fungicide drenches, subject to local pesticide approvals.

black rot a term for several diseases including black rot of brassicas (*Xanthomonas campestris* pv. *campestris*). The latter is uncommon in the UK, but can occur in warm conditions if the seed is infected. Young plants may be killed in the seedbed following blackening of the cotyledons. On older plants, V-shaped yellow areas with dark veins develop at leaf margins and leaves may become desiccated. The petioles and stems, when cut, may show a black ring of vascular tissue. The disease is seed-borne and can also survive on crop debris. It is spread mainly by rain splash. Control by crop rotation, destruction of crop residues, and use of healthy seed. The same bacterium causes a similar disease of wallflowers. Black rot of carrots (*Alternaria radicina*) commonly causes damping-off of seedlings, leaf and stalk spots and a slow developing dry rot of stored roots. Celery, dill and parsley can also be affected by the same seed-borne fungus. GRAPE BLACK ROT (*Guignardia bidwellii*) causes shrivelled and blackened fruit. It overwinters on mummified berries from which spores are produced in spring, when they start to infect new growth. Red-brown dead spots, up to $^1/_4$ in (5 mm) in diameter with minute black fruiting bodies develop on the foliage, purple-black lesions on shoots and tendrils. The rot can be of major importance particularly in humid regions. Control measures include the disposal of fallen mummified grapes and fungicide treatment.

black spot (*Diplocarpon rosae*) a common disease of roses. Black spots appear on leaves and radiating strands of mycelium beneath the cuticle give the characteristic fringed border to young spots. Spots may coalesce until large areas of the leaf are blackened and the rest turns yellow, resulting in premature leaf-fall. Warm moist conditions favor the disease and the spores overwinter on stem and bud scale lesions and fallen leaves. The ascospore-producing stage develops on fallen leaves in the US, but does not usually occur in Britain. Rose cultivars vary in susceptibility but because there are many races of the fungus none is immune, although among rose species,

R.bracteata seems to be resistant to all races of the pathogen. Severe spring pruning to remove infected shoots is of more practical control value than leaf collection; fungicide sprays are effective if applied regularly throughout the growing season.

blade the thin, expanded part of a leaf or petal, also known as the lamina, excluding the petiole, stipe or claw; (in the strap-shaped leaves of certain monocots, i.e., grasses, orchids and bromeliads) the part of a leaf above the sheath.

blanching the practice of excluding light from parts of plants, so as to make vegetables, such as celery, leeks, chicory and endive more palatable. It is also practiced to induce root formation from shoots, for example in propagating plum and cherry rootstocks. Resultant growth is devoid of chlorophyll, and white or cream in color.

blanketweed filamentous algae which form dense masses in ornamental pools. Their development is encouraged where water is shallow, rich in nutrients or supports imbalanced plant and animal life. Control measures include constant removal by hand, and the immersion of loose bundles of barley straw at $^2/_3$ ounce per 35 cubic feet (10 g per cubic meter).

Blechnum (from Greek *blechnon*, a fern). Blechnaceae. Cosmopolitan. 200

species, ferns with rather leathery, pinnate leaves in a rosette. The spore-bearing (fertile) fronds arise in midsummer and create a strong contrast with the sterile foliage, being longer and rigidly erect with modified, rust-brown pinnae. *B. penna-marina* is hardy to –10°F (–23°C) and a charming groundcover for damp rock gardens and the drier fringes of the bog garden. *B. spicant* is hardy to –30°F (–34°C), a superb strong green accent for stone walls and banks and the woodland garden, especially in winter; propagate by division in early spring. *B. tabulare* is rather frost-tender: below 0°F (–18°C), it needs a protected position and a deep mulch in winter. Plant all three in a sheltered situation in shade or diffused light; the soil should be damp and cool, neutral to acidic and rich in garden compost, leaf mold and grit. The tender *B. brasiliense* and *B. gibbum* need a minimum temperature of 50°F (10°C). Plant them in an open medium rich in bark and leaf mold; keep away from drafts and bright sunlight; water and syringe throughout the year (the trunks especially). Propagate all species by offsets or division.

B. brasiliense Brazil and Peru; trunk stout, erect, to 12 in (30 cm) tall crowned with a shuttlecock of oblong to lanceolate fronds to 36 in (90 cm) long with many linear to lanceolate pinnae to 6 in (15 cm) long, wavy, finely toothed, emerging a deep, burnished bronze, hardening glossy, dark green; *B. gibbum* (syn. *Lomaria gibba*);

BLANCHING CURLY ENDIVE

1 To partially blanch the heart of an endive plant, lay a dinner plate over the center, first making sure the leaves are dry. For total blanching, invert a bucket over the whole plant.

2 After about 10 days, the central leaves should have turned white, and have a sweet taste in contrast to the more bitter, greener leaves. Harvest them when ready; once blanched, they soon deteriorate.

MINIATURE TREE FERN; Fiji; trunk narrow, black-fibrous; to 3¼ ft (1 m) tall topped with rosettes of 12–36 in (30–90 cm)-long fronds, pinnae closely ranked, linear to oblong, undulate, to 4 in (10 cm) long, lime to mid-green; *B. penna-marina* cool regions of S America and Australasia; dwarf fern seldom exceeding 6 in (15 cm) tall with loose and suckering rosettes of spreading, linear fronds with many bluntly ovate to oblong pinnae ¼–½ in (0.5–1 cm) long; *B. spicant* DEER FERN, HARD FERN; Northern Hemisphere; dense clumps of arching, dark emerald fronds to 24 in (60 cm) long, with slightly curving, lanceolate to oblong pinnae to ¾ in (2 cm) long; *B. tabulare* (syn. *B. chilense, B. cordatum, B. magellanicum*); Southern Hemisphere; rhizomes thick, almost trunklike, loose rosettes of lanceolate fronds to 3¼ ft (1 m) long, these emerge pink-bronze and harden sea green with lanceolate, undulate and serrate pinnae.

bleeding the continuous flow of sap from the cut surface of a plant, as occurs in grapevines (*Vitis* species) pruned in late winter.

bleeding canker a bark disease of nonconiferous trees, especially apple, beech, horse chestnut, lime and maple. It is usually caused by *Phytophthora cactorum* but also by *P.citricola* and *P.syringae*. The same fungi also cause phytophthora root rot. A gummy liquid, which dries to form a black shiny crust, oozes from lesions on the collar, trunk or branches; dieback occurs if stems are girdled. Affected tissue should be cut away down to healthy wood using a cutting tool sterilized with sodium hypochlorite (diluted to give 1% available chlorine), and a strip of healthy bark should be removed from around the edge of the original lesion. Resulting wounds can be treated with a recommended fungicide, and later with wound sealant.

Bletilla (diminutive form of the name *Bletia*, a related genus, named for Luis Blet [fl. 1794], a Spanish apothecary who kept a botanic garden at Algeciras). Orchidaceae. E Asia. 10 species, deciduous, near-hardy terrestrial orchids with subterranean, cormlike pseudobulbs and narrowly lanceolate, pleated leaves. Produced in summer in slender loose racemes, the flowers consist of five oblong to oblanceolate tepals and a frilly lip. Hardy to 0°F (–18°C). Plant in early spring in soil rich in leaf mold and garden compost. Keep moist and sheltered in sun or light shade. In winter protect the crowns with a thick mulch of coir and bracken or leaf litter, or lift the 'corms' and store frost-free in slightly damp sawdust. Propagate by division. *B. striata* (syn. *B. hyacinthina*; China, Tibet and Japan; to 24 in (60 cm); flowers ¾–1¼ in (2–3 cm) across, candy pink, rose, magenta or pale mauve, lip lined with pure white, frilly crests; white-flowered and variegated forms also occur).

bletting the process of over-ripening fruits such as medlars and figs to a preferred condition for harvest.

blight a term used loosely of plant disease or severe pest infestation causing withering and rapid death of plant parts. It is more correctly applied to disease infections such as POTATO BLIGHT caused by *Phytophthora infestans*; POTATO AND TOMATO EARLY BLIGHT (*Alternaria solani*); RASPBERRY CANE BLIGHT (*Leptosphaeria coniothyrium*); HALO BLIGHT of beans (*Pseudomonas syringae* pv. *phaseolicola*); FIRE-BLIGHT of pear and other rosaceous trees (*Erwinia amylovora*); and SPINACH BLIGHT, which is caused by the cucumber mosaic virus. See *bacterial blight*.

blind, blindness used to describe a plant where growing points or flowers fail to develop. Blindness may be due to growth or environmental factors, or physical damage including pest or disease attack.

blister beetles (Coleoptera: Meloidae) soft-bodied beetles up to ¾ in (20 mm) long with long legs and antennae; they range in color from red-yellow to blue- or green-black, some with white stripes or spots, and the head is wider than the thorax. Their name derives from the blister-forming fluid excretion containing cantharidin. They are not a problem in Europe, but in North America large numbers can defoliate vegetables and ornamentals over a short period in late summer. Examples include the STRIPED BLISTER BEETLE (*Epicauta vittata*), the SPOTTED BLISTER BEETLE (*E. maculata*) and the BLACK BLISTER BEETLE (*E. pennsylvanica*). Numbers can be reduced by spraying with locally approved contact insecticides.

blocking the technique of compressing growing media into variously shaped blocks in which to raise plants.

bloom (1) pertaining to flower or blossom; (2) the white or blue powdery or waxy coating on some leaves and fruits; (3) the rapid proliferation of algae in still water.

Bloomeria (for H.G. Bloomer [1821–1874], Californian botanist). Liliaceae (Alliaceae). SW US; Mexico. 3 species, hardy, bulbous, perennial herbs grown for their long-stemmed heads of star-shaped flowers produced in late spring. Plant in well-drained soil in a sheltered, sunny place. *Bloomeria* becomes dormant in summer. Propagate by seed or division in late summer and fall. *B. crocea* (syn. *B. aurea*); to 12 in (30 cm) tall; flowers 1 in (2.5 cm)-wide, dark-striped, golden.

blossom-end rot a common non-parasitic disorder of tomatoes and peppers. On tomato fruit it first shows as a small water-soaked bruise at the blossom end; as ripening progresses, the lesion darkens and becomes leathery and sunken, but not soft. The rest of the fruit is lighter colored than normal at the stem end. In peppers, lesions are liable to develop fungal or bacterial rots. Blossom-end rot is caused by calcium deficiency in fruits but can be brought on by irregular watering. Plants most susceptible are those grown with ammonium rather than nitrate

leathery sunken patch at blossom end

Blossom-end rot

fertilizer, or grown in an acidic medium, or subjected to periods of drought or waterlogging when fruit is starting to develop.

blossom fall also known as petal fall. See *bud stages*.

blossom wilt see *wilt*.

blown refers to a flower beginning to wither.

blueberry (*Vaccinium* species) The most important in gardens is the HIGH-BUSH BLUEBERRY developed from *Vaccinium corymbosum* and *V. australe*, natives to eastern North America. A deciduous shrub usually 5–6 ft (1.5–1.8 m) high in cultivation, the highbush blueberry is grown for the blue-black, wax-covered, globose berries which may be up to ³⁄₄ in (2 cm) across; they are borne in clusters and selectively picked. Plants are self-fertile and decorative both in flower and in fall foliage, but the minimum cold requirement of 800 hours below 45°F (7.2°C) limits the climatic range for successful growing. Acidic soil is essential, the optimum pH range being 4.3–4.8. Their shallow rooting habit calls for regular watering during fruit development and for surface mulching, and fruit must be protected from birds. Highbush blueberries are grown as stooled bushes planted 5 ft (1.5 m) apart each way. The best fruits are produced on two- or three-year-old shoots. Pruning in the first three years should be light; thereafter, cut out the oldest unproductive wood, removing about one quarter of the bush annually. Propagate from summer softwood cuttings. Notable cultivars include: *early*, 'Earliblue', *midseason*, 'Berkeley', *late*, 'Coville'.

Possible problems: aphids, birds; gray mold.

blueing the process of making red or pink hydrangeas turn blue; achieved by lowering soil pH level to facilitate the uptake of aluminum or by applying aluminum sulfate or a commercial product.

blue mold the visible growth of blue or blue-green fungus spores of those *Penicillium* species responsible for stor-

Blueberries
Blueberries will only thrive in acidic soil. Fruits are particularly attractive to birds, so netting is essential.

age rots. *Penicillium corymbiferum* and other species affect many ornamental bulb species; infection occurs through small wounds while bulbs are in the soil. The rot develops rapidly in storage, especially under conditions of high humidity and lower temperature. Careful handling and the provision of adequate storage conditions, as well as dipping in a systemic fungicide are preventive measures. *Penicillium expansum* causes rotting of apples in storage. The store should be cool and well-ventilated, contact between individual fruits avoided, and damaged fruit removed. Citrus fruits are commonly affected by the post-harvest rots GREEN MOLD (*P. digitatum*) and the less serious BLUE MOLD (*P.italicum*). A devastating downy mildew disease of tobacco (*Peronospora tabacina*) is also referred to as blue mold.

bog garden an area in which the damp, often acidic conditions of natural wetlands is recreated, and where plants native to such places may be cultivated.

Bolax (from Greek *bolax*, clod). Umbelliferae. S America. 2 species, evergreen, cushion-forming perennials grown in rock gardens, alpine sinks, tufa and pans in the alpine house for their massed rosettes of very small, dark green leaves. They require moist, gritty soil in full sun. Propagate by detaching rooted rosettes. *B. gummifera* (syn. *Azorella glebaria*; South America

and the Falklands; forms a dense cushion ultimately to 3¼ ft (1 m) across, with jade green, 3-lobed leaves ¹⁄₁₆–¹⁄₄ in (2–6 mm) long.

bole the main stem of a tree or other arborescent plant.

bolting the premature production of flowers, especially of vegetables; usually triggered by environmental or cultivation factors.

Boltonia (for James Bolton [*c* 1758–1799], British botanist). Compositae. N America; Asia. FALSE CHAMOMILE. 8 species, hardy, perennial herbs with panicles of daisylike flower heads in fall. Plant in moderately fertile soil in full sun or dappled shade. Stake in exposed positions. Divide and replant regularly. *B. asteroides* to 6½ ft (2 m) tall; flower heads ³⁄₄ in (2 cm)-wide with white, rosy mauve or purple ray florets and yellow disk florets; var. *latisquama*: flower heads larger, darker; 'Nana' and 'Snowbank': white, the former a dwarf selection, the latter attaining 6½ ft (2 m).

Bomarea (for Jacques Christophe Valmont de Bomare [1731–1807], French patron of science). Liliaceae (Alstroemeriaceae). S America. 100 species, tender or near-hardy tuberous-rooted, twining perennial herbs with terminal umbels of brightly colored, tubular to campanulate flowers to 2½ in (6 cm) long. Grow with the support of wire or trellis, in a light, fertile, loam-based mix. Provide good ventilation, a minimum temperature of 41°F (5°C) and bright, filtered light. Water and feed plentifully when in growth; keep almost dry in winter. Propagate by division in late winter, or by seed germinated at 73°F (23°C). Several species have proved hardy in sheltered sites in to 0°F (−18°C), especially when thickly mulched in winter.

B. caldasii (syn. *B. caldasiana*, *B. kalbreyeri*); flowers orange-red to bright yellow flecked green, brown or red; *B. cardieri* flowers with mauve to pink tepals tipped bright green and spotted darker mauve or green; *B. edulis* flowers pink with the inner tepals yellow-green flecked purple-pink; *B. patacocensis* flowers with orange to crimson outer tepals and

B

inner tepals yellow to crimson tipped orange and flecked chocolate or violet; *B. racemosa* flowers with brown-spotted, yellow to scarlet inner tepals; *B. shuttleworthii* flowers with orange-red outer tepals spotted at their tips, and yellow inner tepals tipped green with a red midrib and dark spots above.

bone manure an additive used to improve soil fertility, made from crushed animal bones, that typically contain 25% phosphate and 1–5% nitrogen, with some calcium. It should be sterilized to eliminate pathogens and handled with suitable precautions to avoid inhalation and other personal contact. Bone meal is a finely ground form.

Bongardia (for Heinrich Gustav Bongard [1786–1839], German botanist). Berberidaceae. W Asia. 1 species, *B. chrysogonum*, a tuberous, perennial herb. Pinnate leaves to 10 in (25 cm) long arise in early spring from a large, tuber; the gray-green leaflets are themselves lobed and marked purple-red. In late spring, a red-tinted panicle arches over the leaves, bearing golden flowers. Hardy to 10°F (–12°C). Plant deeply in very free-draining, sandy and gritty soil in full sun. Keep moist from winter to early summer; dry at other times. Sow seed in fall: a minute tuber develops at first, pulling itself deep into the soil.

boning rods T-shaped wooden devices, typically 36 in (90 cm) long, used in land levelling. Sightings are made across three rods in a straight line, maneuvered to establish a level.

bonsai the ancient Japanese art of container cultivation incorporating miniaturization. 'Bonsai' means a plant in a pot, and originally described the practice of taking specimens from the wild and maintaining them in the home or garden with the essence of their wildness preserved or recreated. Gradually potting, pruning, pinching and wiring became the rule and led to the cult of the miniaturized tree.

The aim of bonsai is to create on a miniature scale a picture of what one sees in nature using living plants with the container a key element. Most people identify woody plants most readily as bonsai, but some perennial herbs are of importance and may appear in advanced Western collections, among them terrestrial orchids, grasses, the smaller bamboos, ferns and mosses.

Among woody subjects many conifers are grown, and *Juniperus* is especially prized. Other trees and shrubs commonly chosen are *Acer palmatum*, *Pinus*, *Ulmus* and *Zelkova*, *Ginkgo*, *Lespedeza*, *Prunus* and *Wisteria*.

Woody bonsai are trained to one of the traditional styles. These imitate the growth forms of trees and shrubs in nature. Bonsai can be created from large well-established trees and shrubs cut down to the appropriate height and regrown and shaped into the desired style or young grown from seeds and cuttings and trained to the size required. To reduce a container-grown plant to a bonsai style can be achieved in two or three hours but take years of training to become good bonsai. Growing from seed gives maximum control but is slow. It will be 2–3 years before

restricted growth miniaturizes leaves

Bonsai silver birch

most young plants are large enough to be repotted and trained; usually the young tree will begin to look like a bonsai when it is five years old. Bonsai can be started from rooted cuttings which is quicker than seed and ensures that new plants will have the same characteristics as the parent. Aerial and ground layering are also suitable methods.

Pots and repotting Pots used for bonsai are usually made from frost-proof ceramic materials such as stoneware. They must always have drainage holes. Dark containers complement a mass of foliage, a light color a more delicate, open branch structure. A rugged tree looks good in a simple, angular container; an elegant bonsai may look better in a rounded and more elaborate pot. Shallow pots are usually used for trees with slender trunks, and deeper ones for trees with thicker and older trunks and for a bonsai that has part of its foliage falling below the line of the container. Tall pots are used for trees that hang downward in the cascade style.

Young conifers usually need repotting every 2–3 years and older conifers every 3–5 years; young deciduous trees should be repotted annually and older deciduous bonsai every 1–2 years. Spring is generally the best time to repot, although it may also be done in midfall.

Potting media A suitable medium is made from one part leaf mold or well-rotted garden compost, one part loam, and one part sharp sand. Most bonsai prefer slightly acidic soil of pH 6.0 to 6.5. For *Juniperus* species and *Pinus* species the medium may contain as much as 75% sharp sand, and for fruiting and flowering plants and most of the deciduous trees up to 50% loam may be used. For deciduous trees, start feeding when buds open in spring right through to fall. Evergreens should be lightly fed from midwinter, increasing the rate from summer until midfall. Liquid fertilizers can be used: a high-nitrogen product during the early part of the growing season and a high-potash one during the latter half. Fruiting and flowering trees should be fed extra potash, but hold back any feeding when the trees are in flower or fruit. Adding slow-release fertilizer into the potting medium is a suitable method choosing the long-acting (8–9 months) and lower-nitrogen formulations.

Pruning is done to reduce the size of the trunk and branches, to obtain proportion and shape and to clean out congested growth. Special bonsai tools make pruning and trimming easy; always make a clean cut a little above a bud, and make large cuts at the rear of the tree so that the wound will not be visible. Pinching back, or soft pruning, encourages denser growth and foliage. Cutting the first flush of leaves will reduce the size of leaves in successive flushes and is often done for deciduous species. Vigorously growing species may need annual root pruning, and mature, old bonsai may require root pruning occasionally for re-invigoration. The best time to root-prune most trees is in early spring. About one third of the soil is removed from the outside of the root-ball and roots cut back with scissors before replanting in fresh soil in the same container.

Training generally involves wrapping wire around the trunk or branches to hold a position for several months. Copper wire is firmer, holds the shapes of branches better and is used for conifers and evergreen shrubs where it may take slightly longer for the position to set. Aluminum wire is more pliable and is more suitable for deciduous trees. Plastic-covered wire is available, also bare metal wire wrapped in thin paper. Wire conifers and evergreen shrubs in winter and deciduous trees in late spring. Hold back on watering prior to wiring and feed well for several weeks thereafter.

Ageing or Jin is an attempt to mimic storm damage or extreme old age by killing certain sections of branches or trunks and stripping them of bark. Select a branch, strip it of foliage and bark. A variation on *Jin* is *sharimiki*, in which only a strip of bark is removed from live wood on a branch or a trunk, leaving the bonsai with a dramatic slash of silver-white on healthy wood.

General care Traditional bonsai are outdoor subjects and may be brought indoors for display but only for two days followed by six days outside. Indoors, protect from any heating source, mist regularly and provide

good natural lighting. During winter bonsai may be protected in sheds or greenhouses just above freezing point. Alternatively, the pots may be planted in sheltered parts of the open garden. Where neither is practicable, take precautions to protect the pots from frost-damage and the plants from physiological drought.

Chrysanthemum bonsai A fully mature chrysanthemum bonsai can be achieved in 12 to 14 months, shaped into one of the traditional bonsai styles, especially informal upright and cascade. There should be many small flowers of the same size, one per stalk, blooming simultaneously. The bonsai may be kept for many years but is most commonly repropagated annually.

Cuttings are taken from the mature stems of very compact, small-flowered cultivars in early September and will root in two to three weeks. These are potted up in 4 in (10 cm) pots. In midwinter select the two most vigorous shoots and prune back all others to the main stem. Prune back the original stem, ⅝ in (1.5 cm) at a time for the next month. Pot on about every 45 days, until the final 12 in (30 cm) diameter size is reached in late summer; root-prune as necessary. Top dress in late winter-early spring with a solid fertilizer and begin liquid feeding as the growing season progresses until color can be seen on buds.

Training by wiring can begin in late winter using copper wire wrapped in paper to protect the delicate growth. In midspring and every 25 days or so thereafter pinch the tips of the shoots to control overall growth and shape the plant. A final overall pinching is done in late summer. Select one bud from each of the clusters and remove all others. Blooms open in midfall.

Boophone (from Greek *bous*, ox, and *phone*, murder, a reference to the toxic foliage). Amaryllidaceae. S and E Africa. 6 species, deciduous, perennial herbs with large bulbs, strap-shaped

leaves in two ranks and spherical umbels of slender-stalked flowers. The pedicels are long, becoming longer still in fruit, when the whole, globelike inflorescence breaks free and is blown across the plains. Dried, these flower heads make attractive decorations. Plant in early spring with the bulb's shoulders and neck exposed. Maintain a minimum winter temperature of 45°F (7°C) with full sunlight and a dry, airy atmosphere. Water liberally from the emergence to the withering of the leaves; thereafter, keep dry in a hot, sunny place. Propagate by offsets or from ripe seed sown in sand at 68°F (20°C). *B. disticha* CAPE POISON BULB; South African; leaves 12 in (30 cm) long, blue-green and wavy-margined; inflorescence short-stemmed, 12 in (30 cm) wide, composed of 2 in (5 cm) wide, pink flowers on rigid, raylike pedicels to 4 in (10 cm).

edible flowers

Stem of borage

Borago (perhaps from Latin, *burra*, a hairy garment, referring to the bristly-hairy leaves). Boraginaceae. Europe. 3 species, annual or perennial herbs. BORAGE has a long history in herbalism. The 16th-century herbalist Gerard claimed a syrup of its flowers 'purgeth melancholy and quieteth the phreneticke and lunaticke person.' The cucumber-flavored leaves are eaten raw in salads, added to cool drinks and cooked as for spinach. The flowers are also used in salads, or frozen in ice cubes for summer drinks. Sow seed *in situ* in spring in full sun. *B. officinalis* BORAGE; annual to 24 in (60 cm) tall, densely bristly-hairy; flowers star-shaped, sky blue or cobalt with a cone of purple-black scales at the center.

Borassus (from Greek *borassos*, the immature spadix of the date palm). Palmae. Africa; SE Asia to New Guinea. 7 species, tall palms with stout, ringed, solitary stems and rounded to wedge-shaped, palmate leaves with spiny petioles and rigid, blue-green blades divided to at least half their depth into narrow segments. Provide a minimum temperature of 50°F (10°C).

B

Sow seed in moist, sandy mix at high temperatures. *B. flabellifer* PALMYRA PALM, WINE PALM, TODDY PALM, DOUB PALM, LONTAR PALM; to 70 ft (20 m); trunk swollen at the base or middle; leaf blades to 10 ft (3 m) long, divided into some 80 segments.

borax a salt containing boron and sodium; used for the correction of boron deficiency and sometimes as an insecticide or to kill persistent weeds.

Bordeaux mixture the first universal fungicide, the result of a serendipitous discovery by Pierre Millardet, a professor of botany at Bordeaux University. In 1882, while walking in the vineyards of the Medoc, where the newly introduced vine downy mildew (*Plasmopara viticola*) was devastating the crop, he noticed that vines near the path were free from disease. He found that it was the practice for growers to sprinkle a mixture of copper sulfate and lime (calcium hydroxide) on plants to discourage pilfering; those which had been so treated had escaped infection. Bordeaux mixture is a suspension of a flocculent precipitate of insoluble copper hydroxide and calcium sulfate. It can be useful against a wide range of pathogens, including bacteria and fungi, but it is not generally effective against powdery mildews or all rusts. However, its use is no longer permitted in the UK. Legality of use elsewhere is subject to local approvals. Containers used for preparing the mixture and the spraying equipment must be able to resist its corrosive effect, and brass and plastic are suitable. Commercial formulations of Bordeaux mixture are available with appropriate recommendations for use.

border a strip of cultivated ground, often backed by a wall or hedge, in which plants are grown. Commonly used of such an area containing herbaceous plants, but by no means exclusively so.

borecole an alternative name for curly or Scotch forms of kale (*Brassica oleracea* Acephala Group). See *kale*.

boron an essential trace element. Its deficiency is predisposed by high pH,

and the development of hollow stems in brassicas is the symptom most commonly met with in gardens.

Boronia (for Francesco Borone, 18th-century Italian botanist). Rutaceae. Australia. Some 95 species, winter- and spring-flowering aromatic evergreen shrubs with small, 4-petalled, star- or bell-shaped flowers usually solitary and nodding from the axils of fine, simple or compound leaves. Plant in a free-draining, lime-free medium. Keep just moist in winter and maintain a minimum temperature of 45°F (7°C). Cut flowered stems hard back. Root semiripe cuttings in late summer under mist or in a case with bottom heat.

B. heterophylla RED BORONIA, KALGAN; densely twiggy shrub to 6½ ft (2 m) tall, leaves needle- and feather-shaped; flowers fragrant cup-shaped, pink or scarlet; *B. megastigma* BROWN or SCENTED BORONIA; slender, cypresslike shrub, 5–10 ft (1.5–3 m) tall; leaves strongly aromatic, needlelike; flowers bell-shaped, chocolate brown on the exterior, primrose yellow on the interior, sweetly scented.

bosket, boskage a plantation or thicket of trees in a park or garden; sometimes containing walks and garden features. Often a backdrop to a parterre.

bossed see *umbonate*.

bostryx a uniparous helicoid cyme, i.e., a cyme producing one axis with each branching; often used interchangeably with helicoid cyme.

botrytis fungi of the genus *Botrytis* are responsible for many diseases of field crops, fruits, vegetables and ornamentals worldwide, mainly in cool temperate regions. They cause many and varied diseases including damping-off and rots of flowers, fruit, stems, roots, and storage organs. The most common disease is the ubiquitous GRAY MOLD (q.v.) caused by *B. cinerea*. Other diseases are CHOCOLATE

SPOT (*B. fabae*) of broad bean, SNOW-DROP GRAY MOLD (*B. galanthina*), HYACINTH FIRE (*B. hyacinthi*), LILY LEAF SPOT (*B. elliptica*), NARCISSUS SMOULDER (*B. narcissicola*), ONION NECK ROT (*B. allii*), PEONY BLIGHT (*B. paeoniae*) and TULIP FIRE (*B. tulipae*).

The relationships between the asexual fungal states classified as *Botrytis* and *Monilia*, their sexual states in the fungal genera *Botryotinia* and *Monilinia*, and the related genus *Sclerotinia*, are incompletely known. Many are important plant pathogens known predominantly or exclusively from their asexual or sclerotial states. The genus *Sclerotium* also contains sclerotium-producing plant pathogenic fungi, whose relationships are diverse and sometimes unknown. See *chocolate spot*, *neck rot*. Fungicides can give effective control, subject to local pesticide approvals. Botrytis fungi produce tough, seed-like resting structures in diseased plant tissue; avoid contaminating the soil with these.

bottle garden a garden, usually of small slow-growing plants, made in a bottle, carboy or other glass container.

bottom heat warmth applied from below, in a frame or propagator, to advance growth or aid rooting and germination. Traditionally produced from decomposing organic matter but today usually provided through special electrically heated cables. See *hotbed*.

bottom-worked see *low-worked*.

botuliform sausage-shaped.

Bougainvillea (for L.A. de Bougainville [1729–1811], French navigator. He embarked on a voyage of discovery to the South Seas in 1768). Nyctaginaceae. South America. 14 species, mostly woody climbers, evergreen or briefly deciduous, many with stout thorns. The leaves are ovate to elliptic. Small, tubular, yellow-white flowers are produced amid clusters of brilliant, papery, leaf-shaped bracts. Although frost-tender, these spectacular climbers have become a common feature of

decayed petals of pelargonium

Botrytis

gardens in the Mediterranean and in California where, once established in a sunny, sheltered spot, they survive freezing temperatures. In these and warmer regions, *Bougainvillea* is unsurpassed for covering trellis and pergolas; it can also be trained as a standard and, in the more shrubby cultivars derived from *B. glabra*, be planted as an informal hedge. In warm, wet climates, it remains evergreen.

B. glabra and its offspring tend to flower continuously and are best grown where they experience virtually no dry season, or can be watered and fed throughout the year. Within this group, very young plants will flower and are ideal for container cultivation. *B. spectabilis* and its hybrids require a dry season to induce flowering. Under glass, water and feed plentifully at first to produce strong growth, then reduce supplies to promote flowering. In an open garden, grow in full sun in rich, well-drained soil. Plants of the *B. spectabilis* alliance will hook themselves to trees, beams and rafters; otherwise, they require regular tying to a strong support frame-work. Under glass, they need a minimum night temperature of 45°F (7°C). Plant in a moderately fertile gritty, loam-based medium in pots, tubs or beds with a confined root run. Provide support. In early spring, spur prune established specimens (not *B. peruviana* which resents pruning) and remove any dead or exhausted wood. Pot-grown plants may be moved outside in warm summers. Root greenwood cuttings in late summer with bottom heat at 68°F (20°C). Air layer in spring.

B. glabra (PAPER FLOWER; The Brazil; thick-stemmed climber to 50 ft (15 m); inflorescence bracts white to deep magenta, sometimes outliving the flowers; perianth tube five-angled and covered in short hairs); *B. peruviana* (Peru; stoutly thorny with smaller bracts than *B. glabra* (to 4 in (10 cm) long), and the perianth tube, smooth and only obscurely five-angled; the hybrid between these two species, *B.* × *buttiana*, produces smaller bracts (to 2 in (5 cm)) in shades of rose, magenta and fiery orange; the perianth tube is angled, hairy and waisted below the middle); *B. spectabilis* (syn. *B. brasiliensis*; Brazil; robust climber with large, hooked

thorns; inflorescence bracts purple-pink, to 2½ in (6 cm) long; perianth tube obscurely angled, hairy); *B.* Spectoglabra group (*B. spectabilis* × *B. glabra*, cultivars ranging in habit from low and spreading to bushy and erect, to tall and arching, leaves small, gray-green and downy or large, dark green and glossy, some cream-, white- and yellow-variegated forms; inflorescence bracts range from the small, persistent and densely clustered ('double') to large, crêpelike and short-lived, in color from white to lilac, shell pink, rose, deep cerise, garnet, purple-red, crimson, magenta, to bronze-red, brick red, coral, flame, vermilion, orange, apricot and pale yellow).

boulingrin a sunken grassed area at the center of a bosket or dell.

bourse in apples and pears, the swollen stem at the base of a flower cluster, which may carry wood or fruit buds. Also known as a cluster base or knob.

Bouteloua (named for the brothers Boutelou, Claudio [1774–1842] and Esteban [1776–1813], Spanish botanists). Gramineae. US; Central America; West Indies. 39 species, annual or perennial grasses with one-sided panicles, the branches short, spicate and closely aligned along the underside of the summit, thus resembling the teeth of a comb. The flower heads are suitable for drying. Easily grown in full sun (min. –20°F/–29°C). Propagate by seed sown *in situ* or in pots under glass in spring, or by division. *B. gracilis* (syn. *B. oligostachya*); BLUE GRAMA GRASS, MOSQUITO GRASS; perennial; flowering stems to 24 in (60 cm), the inflorescence occupying the topmost 2 in (5 cm) and angled at 45°, florets hanging (or seeming to hover) below the spikelets that clothe the 'comb' of branches.

Bouvardia (for Charles Bouvard [1572–1658], physician to Louis XIII and Keeper of the Jardin du Roi, Paris). Rubiaceae. Subtropical and tropical Americas. 30 species, perennial herbs or shrubs, frost-tender and grown for their clusters of narrowly tubular flowers, each with a limb of four

spreading lobes, produced throughout the year. Provide a minimum winter temperature of 45°F (7°C), medium humidity and filtered sunlight. Propagate by softwood cuttings in spring, or by semiripe cuttings in summer.

B. longiflora (syn. *B. humboldtii*); to 3¼ ft (1 m) tall, with fragrant, pure white flowers to 3½ in (9 cm) long; *B. ternifolia* (syn. *B. jacquinii*); weak-stemmed shrub to 3¼ ft (1 m) tall with 1¼ in (3 cm) long flowers in red, pink, rose and coral; *B. triphylla* to 3¼ ft (1 m); flowers orange-red, to 1¼ in (3 cm), very close to *B. ternifolia*.

bower a shady recess in a garden. See *arbor*.

Bowiea (for James Bowie [*c.* 1789–1869], a Kew gardener who collected plants in South Africa and Brazil). Liliaceae (Hyacinthaceae). Southern and tropical Africa. 3 species, tender, bulbous herbs. The following species is a bizarre addition to the succulent collection, grown either in the cool greenhouse (minimum temperature 45°F/7°C) or indoors on a bright, draft-free windowsill. Plant in a very sandy and gritty, loam-based medium with the upper half to three quarters of the bulb exposed. Position in full sunlight in a dry, airy atmosphere. Water sparingly to encourage sprouting. As the new stem emerges, provide support in the form of a small trellis, wire mesh, or dead twigs. Water while the stem develops. Once growth and fruiting are finished, reduce the water, allowing the stem to die off. Keep virtually dry until the next growth flush begins, watering only to prevent excessive shrivelling of the bulb. Increase by seed. *B. volubilis* CLIMBING ONION; bulb wide, fleshy, green; leaves narrow, dark green, usually present only in young plants; stem to 3¼ ft (1 m), slender, succulent, translucent green, twining and branching freely and intricately; flowers green-yellow, malodorous.

Boykinia (for Samuel Boykin [1786–1848], planter, physician and naturalist from Georgia, US). Saxifragaceae. North America; Japan (those below from Western N America). 9 species, hardy perennial herbs, mostly rhizomatous and hairy with rounded, long-stalked leaves and panicles of small, five-parted flowers in summer. Plant in damp, acidic soils in light shade. Divide in late winter.

B. aconitifolia leaves 1½–3 in (4–8 cm) long, rounded to kidney-shaped, lobed and toothed; stalks to 7 in (18 cm) long; flowers white in 6–32 in (15–80 cm)-tall panicles); *B. jamesii* (syn. *Telesonix jamesii*); differs from the last species in its smaller, toothed rather than lobed leaves and crimson flowers.

boysenberry see *hybrid berries*.

Brachycereus (from Greek *brachys*, short and *Cereus*). Cactaceae. Galapagos Islands LAVA CACTUS. 1 species, *B. nesioticus*, a shrubby cactus to 24 in (60 cm) tall and spreading to 6½ ft (2 m) across in clumps of erect, ribbed and cylindrical, 1¼–2 in (3–5 cm)-wide stems covered in yellow spines. The large flowers are creamy-white and narrowly funnel-shaped. Plant in an acidic, gritty and sandy, loam-based medium. Grow in full sun in a dry, airy environment, minimum temperature 50°F (10°C); water very sparingly in winter. Propagate by stem cuttings.

Brachychiton (from Greek *brachys*, short, and *chiton*, outer garment, a reference to the seed coat). Sterculiaceae. Australia; Papua New Guinea. 31 species, tender, evergreen or deciduous trees and tall shrubs, often with swollen trunks, grown for their large panicles of small cup-shaped to tubular flowers produced in spring and summer. Large and woody, the beaked fruits are used in dried flower arrangements. Grow in acidic soil in full sun; minimum temperature 45°F /7°C, or cooler (25°F/–4°C) for short periods if well-established and dry. Propagate by seed or ripewood cuttings.

B. acerifolius (syn. *Sterculia acerifolia*); FLAME KURRAJONG, FLAME TREE; deciduous tree to 100 ft (30 m); leaves to 10 in (25 cm), ovate to palmately lobed; flowers bright red or orange, on bare branches; *B. populneus* (syn. *Sterculia diversifolia*); KURRAJONG, BOTTLE TREE; evergreen tree to 70 ft (20 m) with a swollen trunk, poplarlike leaves to 4¾ in (12 cm) long, and clusters of small, green-white flowers.

Brachyglottis (from Greek *brachys*, short, and *glottis*, tongue, referring to the short ray florets). Compositae. New Zealand; Chatham Is; Tasmania. 30 species, evergreen trees, shrubs, climbers and perennial herbs, usually with gray-woolly foliage and panicles of yellow to cream, daisylike flower heads. Most were formerly included in the genus *Senecio*. Many *Brachyglottis* species are adapted to thrive in exposed, coastal situations, notably *B. buchananii*, *B.* 'Leonard Cockayne', *B. monroi*, *B. rotundifolia* and *B.* 'Sunshine'. The last is one of the most widely planted silver-leaved shrubs and seems tolerant of all but the wettest darkest spots. Smaller species, such as *B. bidwillii* and *B. compacta*, suit the large rock garden or silver border in a sheltered position. *B. hectoris* favors protected, semiwooded places. All prefer full sunlight. Hardiness varies: *B.* 'Sunshine' withstands lows to 5°F (–5°C) with little damage. *B. monroi* will take 14°F (–0°C) and *B. compacta* and *B. rotundifolia* 23°F (5°C). *B. kirkii*, *B. perdicioides* and *B. repanda* are frost-tender (minimum 37°F/3°C). Dead-head regularly. Propagate by seed or semiripe cuttings.

B. bidwillii (syn. *Senecio bidwillii*); compact, to 24 in (60 cm); leaves to ¾ in (2 cm), elliptic to oblong, smooth above, silver-or buff-hairy beneath; flower heads inconspicuous; *B. buchananii* (syn. *Senecio buchananii*); robust, to 5 ft (1.5 m); leaves 1–2 in (2.5–5 cm), broadly oblong, smooth above, silver-hairy beneath; flower heads yellow to cream; *B. compacta* (syn. *Senecio compactus*); to 3¼ ft (1 m); leaves ¾–1½ in (2–4 cm), obovate to oblong, wavy-edged, white-hairy beneath; flower heads yellow; *B.* Dunedin Group (hybrids between *B. compacta*, *B. grayi* and *B. laxifolia* shrubs to 6½ ft (2 m) tall with elliptic to oblong leaves to 2 in (5 cm) long, emerging silvery or white, hardening dull to lustrous sea or gray-green above, white-scurfy beneath; flower heads bright yellow; the most commonly grown selection is 'Sunshine', syn. *Senecio grayi* of gardens, described above; 'Moira Read' has variegated leaves; *B. grayi* to 6½ ft (2 m); leaves 1½–3 in (4–8 cm), ovate to oblong, tough, silver-scurfy beneath; flower heads bright yellow — the true

plant is rare in gardens and the name is often misapplied to *B.* 'Sunshine'; *B. hectoris* (syn. *Senecio hectoris*); to 12 ft (4 m); leaves to 8 in (20 cm), oblanceolate, coarsely toothed and pinnately cut at base, thinly white-hairy beneath; flower heads white; *B. huntii* (syn. *Senecio huntii*), RAUTINI; compact shrub or tree to 20 ft (6 m); leaves to 4 in (10 cm), lanceolate to oblong, tawny-hairy at first: flower heads yellow; *B. kirkii* (syn. *Senecio kirkii*; *Senecio glastifolius*); KOHURANGI; to 10 ft (3 m); leaves 1½–4 in (4–10 cm) long, obovate to oblong, wavy-toothed to entire, fleshy; flower heads white; *B. laxifolia* (syn. *Senecio laxifolius*); resembles *B. grayi*, but with smaller, pointed leaves; *B.* 'Leonard Cockayne' (*B. grayi* × *B. rotundifolia*); spreading with wavy-edged, gray-green leaves to 6 in (15 cm) long, silver beneath; flower heads yellow; *B. monroi* (syn. *Senecio monroi*); to 3¼ ft (1 m); leaves to 1½ in (4 cm), obovate to oblong, wavy and crenate, silver-felted beneath; flower heads bright yellow; *B. perdicioides* (syn. *Senecio perdicioides*); RAUKUMARA; to 6½ ft (2 m); leaves 1–2 in (2.5–5 cm), oblong to elliptic, finely crenate, thin-textured, smooth, dull green; flower heads to ½ in (1 cm) diam., yellow; *B. repanda* (syn. *B. rangiora*; *Senecio repanda*); PUKAPUKA; RANGIORA; to 20 ft (6 m); leaves to 10 in (25 cm), broadly oblong to elliptic, with large, wavy teeth, mid- to sea green above, silver-scurfy beneath; flower heads inconspicuous, mignonette-scented; 'Purpurea': leaves purple above; 'Variegata': leaves stippled yellow, gray-green and cream; *B. rotundifolia* (syn. *Senecio reinoldii*; *Senecio rotundifolius*); MUTTONBIRD SCRUB; to 20 ft (6 m), dense, rounded; leaves to 4 in (10 cm), broadly ovate to rounded, tough, white-felted beneath; flower heads yellow. For *B.* 'Sunshine' see above under *B.* Dunedin group.

Brachyscome (from Greek *brachys*, short, and *kome*, hair, referring to the short pappus hairs). Compositae. Australasia. 70 species, annual and perennial herbs or shrublets with slender-stalked, daisylike flower heads in spring and summer. A tender perennial useful for edging, bedding and baskets and often treated as a half-hardy annual. Sow seed under glass in fall, or *in situ* in spring; alternatively, take stem cuttings in early spring from stock plants cut back hard, potted up and overwintered in frost-free conditions. *B. iberidifolia* SWAN RIVER DAISY; bushy, to 16 in (40 cm) with very finely cut foliage; flower heads fragrant, ½ in (1 cm)-wide, sky to deep blue with a yellow center, also white, pink, lilac and deep mauve.

Brachysema (from Greek *brachys*, short, and *sema*, standard, referring to the very short standard of the flower). Leguminosae. Australia. 15 species, shrubs with clusters of pealike flowers in spring and summer. Plant in free-draining, loamy and sandy soil in full sun; minimum temperature 45°F (7°C); water moderately in spring and summer, scarcely at all in winter. Avoid fertilizers containing phosphorus. Propagate by seed in spring, or from semiripe cuttings in a closed case; also by layering. *B. celsianum* (syn. *B. lanceolatum*); SWAN RIVER PEA, SCIMITAR FLOWER; spreading to prostrate evergreen shrub to 6½ ft (2 m), stems flattened, green, ribbonlike; leaves lanceolate; flowers scarlet to 2½ in (6 cm)-long with a sharply curved keel.

Brachystelma (from Greek *brachys*, short, and *stelma*, garland, referring to the dense inflorescence). Asclepiadaceae. Tropical and South Africa. 100 species, perennial herbs usually with swollen, turniplike roots or caudices bearing short-stalked clusters of five-parted flowers. Many species are grown in succulent collections; the best-known is probably the South African *B. barbariae* with a flattened caudex to 4 in (10 cm) wide. The flowers are produced before the leaves in a dense, hemispherical umbel to 4¾ in (12 cm) wide. They are malodorous and a dirty purple-brown with yellow centers and tawny spots. Very slender, the 1 in (3 cm)-long petals stand erect and joined at the tips in a cage- or lanternlike structure. Plant in a gritty medium; do not bury the caudex. Place in full sunlight in dry, airy conditions with a minimum temperature of 46°F (8 °C). Water sparingly when in growth; keep dry when dormant. Propagate by seed.

bracing The provision of artificial support to tree branches, using cables or metal rods.

bracken (*Pteridium aquilinum*) an invasive fern which spreads as a weed by means of its thick, fleshy, brown underground stems. Persistent removal of frond growth will weaken the stand, and is best done by cutting in early summer and again as regrowth emerges a few weeks later. Glyphosate and glyphosate trimesium are effective herbicides against bracken. Fronds can be composted, used as a surface mulch or for insulating tender plants against winter cold.

bracket fungi (Aphyllophorales: Basidiomycetes). The fruiting bodies of various saprophytic or parasitic fungi, which form bracketlike projections on infected trees or on deadwood. The structures may be annual (and usually produced in fall) or perennial.

braconid wasps (Hymenoptera: Braconidae). Small wasps with relatively long antennae and wings, and a distinct dark area about half-way along the front margin of the forewing. Closely related to ichneumon flies. Females parasitize many insects, particularly caterpillars of butterflies and moths, and lay eggs in their bodies. *Cotesia glomerata* is a familiar parasitoid of caterpillars of the large cabbage white butterfly (*Pieris brassicae*), and up to 150 fully fed larvae emerge from the collapsed skin of the host and pupate together in conspicuous sulfur-yellow cocoons. Several braconids species are used for biological control of pests, for example, some *Aphidius* and *Praon* species infest aphids.

bract a modified protective leaf associated with the inflorescence (clothing the stalk and subtending the flowers), with buds, and with newly emerging shoots and stems. Bracts exhibit varying degrees of reduction, from the leafy inflorescence bracts of *Euphorbia pulcherrima* to the navicular bracts of

Heliconia, or the thin scalelike stem bracts of many herbaceous species. In the developing shoots of members of the last category, a progression from bract to true leaf can be seen as the shoot develops.

bracteate possessing or bearing bracts.

bracteole a secondary or miniature bract, often borne on a petiole or subtending a flower or inflorescence.

bract scale in conifers, the scale of a female cone that subtends the seed-bearing scale.

Brahea (for Tycho Brahe [1546–1601], Danish astronomer and pioneer of science). Palmae. Central America (those listed below are from Mexico and Baja California). 12 species, slow-growing palms with stout, columnar trunks clothed in fibers and large, fan-shaped leaves cut into many, narrow segments. The inflorescences are large, drooping and much-branched, bearing many small cream flowers. The following two species thrive on parched, rocky soils in full sunlight and will tolerate several degrees of frost if dry and well-established. Increase by seed.

B. armata BLUE FAN PALM, BLUE HESPER PALM, GRAY GODDESS PALM, MEXICAN BLUE PALM, SHORT BLUE PALM; to 30 ft (10 m); foliage silver-

true leaves

petal-like bracts are modified leaves

Bracts on *Cornus kousa* var. *chinensis*

blue; inflorescence to 12 ft (4 m) long, very showy; *B. brandegeei* SAN JOSÉ HESPER PALM; to 100 ft (30 m) with pale, gray-green leaves to 5 ft (1.5 m) long.

Brassavola (for A.M. Brasavola [1500–1555], Venetian botanist. His name is spelt with one 'S', that of the genus with two). Orchidaceae. Central and South America; West Indies. 30 species, evergreen, epiphytic and lithophytic orchids with more or less pendulous, pencil-thin pseudobulbs terminating in a single, tough, narrow leaf and solitary or clustered flowers, often nocturnally scented and in shades of white, cream and pale green; the tepals are slender, the lip is funnel-shaped. Provide a minimum temperature of 45°F (7°C), with bright light and a buoyant, humid atmosphere. Plant in baskets or small pots containing a very open, bark-based medium, or attach to rafts and bark slabs against pads of moss and leaf mold. While in growth, water and feed frequently, allowing the medium to dry between drenchings; syringe daily in hot weather. Except for misting to prevent the shrivelling of leaves and pseudobulbs, withhold water for one to two months on completion of new pseudobulbs. Recommence watering when root and shoot activity resumes. Propagate by division.

B. cordata flowers 1¾ in (4.5 cm)-wide, vanilla-scented, tepals lime green to ivory, lip bright white; *B. cucullata* flowers fragrant with long and drooping tepals, to 2¾ in (7 cm), very narrow and ivory, lip cream, fringed at its base, tapering narrowly at the tip; *B. flagellaris* leaves and pseudobulbs pendulous, long and whiplike, picked out with 2½ in (6 cm)-wide flowers, the tepals spreading and pale cream, the lip white stained lime green in the throat; *B. nodosa* LADY OF THE NIGHT; flowers to 3 in (7.5 cm) wide with nodding, green, ivory or white tepals and a white lip stained green and spotted maroon at the throat. For *B. digbyana* and *B. glauca* see *Rhyncholaelia*.

Brassia (for William Brass, 18th-century botanist who collected in Guinea and South Africa). Orchidaceae. Central and South America. SPIDER ORCHID. 25 species, tender epiphytic orchids with ovoid to cylindrical pseudobulbs, strap-shaped leaves and racemes of flowers with very long, slender tepals and a shorter, trowel-shaped lip. Pot in a very open, bark-based mix. Grow in cool to intermediate conditions (minimum winter temperature 45°F/7°C) with high humidity. Admit full sunlight except in the hottest months, when the plants should be shaded, freely syringed and ventilated. Water and feed liberally when in growth; reduce temperatures and keep almost dry once the new pseudobulbs are developed. Increase by division.

B. caudata tepals to 7 in (18 cm), pale yellow-green to yellow-orange marked red-brown, lip paler and spotted red-brown; *B. lawrenceana* tepals to 2¾ in (7 cm), green-yellow, spotted maroon at the base, lip white to pale lime; *B. verrucosa* tepals to 4¾ in (12 cm), pale lime green spotted chocolate or black at the base, lip white, spotted red-brown at the base and scattered with green warts.

Brassica (a name used by Pliny). Cruciferae. Mediterranean to temperate Asia. 30 species of annual or biennial glabrous herbs, occasionally perennial, rarely subshrubs. Most erect, branching and tap-rooted. Leaves simple oblong ovate-rounded, glaucous. Flowers yellow, yellow-white, rarely white, borne in terminal racemes. The following species are of particular horticultural interest and there is reference to their cultivation under the various main brassica crop entries. *B. carinata* (TEXSEL GREENS, ABYSSINIAN CABBAGE, ETHIOPIAN CABBAGE, see *cabbage*); *B. napus* (RAPE) which, densely sown, produces fast-establishing seedlings for soil incorporation as a green manure (see *green manuring*); *B. n.* Napobrassica Group (SWEDE [rutabaga] q.v.); *B. juncea* (MUSTARD CABBAGE see *oriental greens*); *B. oleracea* (WILD CABBAGE) has evolved numerous selections, grown mainly as vegetable crops, classified in Groups, including: Acephala Group (KALE, COLLARD, see *kale*), Alboglabra Group (CHINESE BROCCOLI CHINESE KALE, see

broccoli), Botrytis Group (CAULIFLOWER, PERENNIAL BROCCOLI, see *cauliflower*), Capitata Group (CABBAGE q.v), Gemmifera Group (BRUSSELS SPROUTS q.v), Gongylodes Group (KOHLRABI q.v), Italica Group (CALABRESE, SPROUTING BROCCOLI, ASPARAGUS BROCCOLI, CAPE BROCCOLI, see *broccoli*); *B. r.* Periviridis Group (MUSTARD SPINACH, KOMATSUMA, SPINACH MUSTARD, TENDERGREEN) see *oriental greens*; Tronchuda Group (PORTUGUESE CABBAGE, see *cabbage*). Ornamental cultivars of *B. oleracea* are grown as annual bedding plants, for their rosettes of green, cream, red or pink foliage; *B. r.* var. *nipposinica* (MIZUNA GREENS, KYONA see *oriental greens*). *B. rapa* Chinensis Group (CHINESE WHITE CABBAGE, PAK CHOI, see *cabbage*); *B. r.* Pekinensis Group (CHINESE CABBAGE, CHINESE LEAVES, see *cabbage*); *B. r.* Rapifera Group (TURNIP q.v).

brassicas a term commonly used as a collective description for edible plants within the genus *Brassica* (q.v).

cruciform flower

Brassica oleracea

× **Brassocattleya** (*Brassavola* (or *Rhyncholaelia*) × *Cattleya*). Orchidaceae. Garden hybrids ranging widely in habit and size from the dwarf and tufted to the tall and rangy, with the ellipsoid to cylindrical pseudobulbs and tough oblong to elliptic leaves characteristic of *Cattleya*. The flowers are *Cattleya*-like, but have very ruffled lips; they vary from small and neat to exceptionally large and frilly, in shades of white, pink, magenta, purple, red, orange, apricot, yellow and lime green. Many grexes are available. Cultivation as for *Cattleya*.

× **Brassolaeliocattleya** (*Brassavola* (or *Rhyncholaelia*) × *Laelia* × *Cattleya*). Orchidaceae. Garden hybrids ranging in habit from dwarf to medium-sized or large, squat, robust or reedy. Flowers slender and starry to buxom and lacy in shades of white, rose, magenta, mauve, red, orange, apricot, yellow, green or cream, often flushed, veined or marked a different color. Many grexes are available. Cultivation is the same as for *Cattleya*.

break, breaking (1) the growth made from an axillary bud, especially in chrysanthemums and carnations, as a result of pinching out the growing point or as a natural occurrence; (2) a stage in the opening of buds; see *bud stages*; (3) a mutation or sport seen in flowers, often characterized by streaks or flecks, and possibly virus induced.

breastwood shoots growing outward from espalier or other wall-trained trees.

Breynia (for. J.P. Breyn, 17th-century German botanist). Euphorbiaceae. Tropical Asia; Pacific Islands; Australia. 25 species, evergreen shrubs and trees with small, usually 2-ranked leaves and inconspicuous flowers. Plant in moderately fertile, soilless or loam-based mix; position in dappled sunlight or light shade; minimum temperature 45°F (7°C). Propagate by soft cuttings in early summer. *B. nivosa* (syn. *B. disticha*); SNOW BUSH; shrub to 5 ft (1.5 m); leaves ⅝–¾ in (1.5–2 cm) long in two ranks giving the branches a ferny appearance, densely mottled, spattered and zoned white, most often with veins picked out in emerald green; 'Atropurpurea': leaves rich purple-red; 'Roseapicta': leaves mottled pink and red.

Briggsia (for Munro Briggs Scott [1889–1917], botanist) Gesneriaceae. India to China. 23 species, rhizomatous, near-hardy perennial herbs grown for their stalked cymes of tubular, two-lipped flowers produced in summer. Suitable for an alpine house or frame, or for very sheltered positions in a rock garden. Plant in pans, raised beds, or rock crevices in neutral to acidic soil rich in leaf mold. Keep moist from spring to fall. Provide full sun except where likely to scorch or dry the plants excessively (i.e., under glass in summer). Propagate from seed. *B. muscicola* China, Bhutan and Tibet; leaves woolly in a stemless rosette; flowers pale yellow, the interior orange-yellow marked purple).

Brimeura (for Maria de Brimeur, a 16th-century Dutch aristocrat who loved flowers). Liliaceae (Hyacinthaceae). Mediterranean; SE Europe; Aegean. 2 small, perennial,

Color break in tulip
Petal color variation in this Parrot Group tulip 'Estella Rijnveld' is referred to as a break. Breaking may arise from breeding, natural mutation, or virus infection.

bulbous herbs grown for their flowers which are produced in spring and resemble miniature bluebells (*Hyacinthoides*). Plant in full sun or light shade in well drained soil; minimum temperature 5°F (–15°C). Propagate by division of established clumps as the foliage withers in early summer. *B. amethystina* flowers bright blue, indigo or white; *B. fastigiata* flowers, lilac, lilac-pink or white.

brindille a thin lateral shoot of a fruit tree, 3–12 in (7.5–30 cm) long and usually terminating in a fruit bud.

Briza (Classical Greek name for a grass, probably rye). Gramineae. Cosmopolitan (mainly northern temperate regions). QUAKING GRASS. 12 species, annual or perennial hardy grasses with erect, open panicles, their branches very fine and hung with ovate spikelets, the lemmas large, papery and overlapping in two ranks giving the spikelet the appearance of a rattlesnake's tail. Among the most graceful of ornamental grasses, *Briza* has a pearly, translucent quality. The parchment flower heads are used in dried flower arrangements. Grow in full sun in moderately fertile soil; ample moisture is required until the flower heads are developed, drier conditions thereafter. Sow seed *in situ* in early spring, or divide *B. media*.

B. maxima (syn. *B. major*); GREAT QUAKING GRASS, PUFFED WHEAT; annual to 24 in (60 cm); spikelets on threadlike branches, each to 1 in (2.5 cm) and olive to straw-colored tinged red-brown or purple; *B. media* COMMON QUAKING GRASS, COW QUAKES, DODDERING DICKIES, LADY'S HAIR GRASS, PEARL GRASS and TOTTER; perennial to 3¼ ft (1 m) tall; spikelets to ½ in (1 cm), ovate to deltoid, often tinted purple, in erect panicles to 7 in (18 cm); *B. minor* LESSER QUAKING GRASS; annual to 24 in (60 cm) with spikelets to ¼ in (0.5 cm) long, remarkably airy and delicate in the cultivar 'Minima'.

broadcasting the scattering of seeds evenly over a seed bed rather than sowing in drills.

broadleaf, broad-leaved a tree or shrub with broad flat leaves as opposed to needles. Commonly used to mean a nonconiferous tree.

broad mite see *tarsonemid mites*.

broccoli (*Brassica oleracea* Italica Group); a name used in the UK to describe purple and white sprouting broccoli; the more dwarf, green sprouting broccoli is usually known as calabrese. In parts of Britain the term broccoli is often used incorrectly to refer to large-headed white cauliflower (Botrytis Group) maturing in winter. In N America the term broccoli refers to all sprouting types in the Italica Group and to large-headed, winter maturing white cauliflower (Botrytis Group) which can only be grown in climatically favorable areas. Sprouting broccolis, including calabrese, differ from cauliflower in their more divided leaves, and the developing terminal and axillary flower-buds — the primary edible parts — form less dense heads.

Raise PURPLE and WHITE SPROUTING BROCCOLI (ASPARAGUS BROCCOLI, CAPE BROCCOLI) in a seedbed or in modules under protection, from mid-April/late-May sowings; plant out June or July, 24 in (60 cm) apart each way. Plants grow to 36 in (90 cm) tall and may require staking. The main season is from February to late May. Purple forms tend to be hardier, larger and more prolific than white forms.

CALABRESE makes a smaller, compact plant to 24 in (60 cm) tall and is not reliably hardy. For summer to fall harvesting sow successively *in situ* from late March to early July; thin to 6 in (15 cm) stations in rows 12 in (30 cm) apart; raising in modules for transplanting is possible but less reliable.

Late summer sowings may be overwintered for spring maturing under protection, or grown outdoors in mild winter areas.

Following cutting of the central head subsequent side shoots are regularly snapped off in tight bud.

CHINESE BROCCOLI, CHINESE KALE closely resembles sprouting broccoli. An oriental brassica grown for its flavorous, leafy, flowering shoots. Sow late spring to early fall in rows 12 in (30 cm) apart (for large plants) or 4 in (10 cm) apart (for small plants) or raise in modules. Thin to or plant out 12 in (30 cm) or 5 in (13 cm) apart depending on size of plants required. Harvest within 10 weeks, as for calabrese. Can be raised similarly under cover for winter use.

PERENNIAL BROCCOLI is a form of cauliflower (q.v) in the Botrytis Group of *Brassica oleraceae* (*B. o.*) Alboglabra Group.

Possible problems: aphids, cabbage caterpillars, cabbage root fly, flea beetle, turnip gall weevil (see *weevils*); clubroot, leaf spot.

Brodiaea (for James Brodie, Scottish botanist). Liliaceae (Alliaceae). W US. 15 species, deciduous, cormous perennial herbs with narrow leaves often withering before the inflorescence expands in early summer. The flowers are funnel- or bell-shaped and carried on slender stalks in lax, scapose umbels. Hardy to 10°F (−12°C). Grow in sun on light, fertile, sandy loams. Keep moist when in growth; dry and warm after flowering. Propagate by division of established colonies, removal of offsets or seed sown when ripe. The HARVEST BRODIAEAS, *B. coronaria* (syn. *B. grandiflora*, *B. howellii*) and *B. elegans* produce 2–12, ¾–1½ in (2–4 cm)-long, purple-blue to deep mauve flowers, the first on a scape to 12 in (30 cm), the second to 20 in (50 cm). *B. minor* produces pink to deep violet

blue flowers to 1 in (2.5 cm) long on 2¾–12 in (7–30 cm)-tall scapes. See also *Dichelostemma* and *Triteleia*.

bromeliads members of the family Bromeliaceae, e.g., *Aechmea*, *Ananas*, *Billbergia*, *Bromelia*, *Cryptanthus*, × *Cryptbergia*, *Dyckia*, *Fascicularia*, *Guzmania*, *Neoregelia*, *Nidularium* (*see right*), *Pitcairnia*, *Puya*, *Tillandsia*, *Vriesea*.

Bromelia (for Olaf Bromel [1639–1705], Swedish botanist). Bromeliaceae. Central and South America. 47 species, perennial herbs, usually terrestrials with spreading rosettes of rigid and spiny, swordlike leaves and showy flower spikes in spring and summer. Grow in full sun, minimum temperature 45°F (7°C), in a very open medium. Water, feed and syringe liberally in warm weather; keep virtually dry in winter. Propagate by offsets. *B. balansae* (HEART OF FLAME; leaves flushing brilliant scarlet at the heart of the rosette in the flowering season; inflorescence torchlike, densely branched, to 3¼ ft (1 m), with white-edged, rosy flowers guarded by outward-curving, scarlet bracts).

Bromus (from Greek *bromos*, oat). Gramineae. BROME, CHESS. N Temperate Regions. 100 species, annual, biennial or perennial grasses with loose erect culms, narrow leaves and long-awned spikelets in graceful panicles in summer. The following are hardy. With the exception of the shade-loving *B. ramosus*, they will grow in most situations but prefer sun and free-draining soil. Increase by seed or by division. The flower heads of all except *B. madritensis* are suitable for drying.

B. briziformis Europe, Temperate Asia; annual or biennial to 24 in (60 cm), with loosely pyramidal panicles hung with *Briza*-like spikelets; *B. inermis* Europe, Temperate Asia; creeping perennial erect to 3¼ ft (1 m); panicles drooping; 'Skinner's Gold': leaves striped gold, seed heads golden; *B. madritensis* COMPACT BROME, STIFF BROME, WALL BROME; Mediterranean; annual erect to 24 in (60 cm) with very fine, feathery arching panicles tinted pink to wine-red; *B. ramosus* WOOD BROME, HAIRY BROME; Europe, N

Nidularium regeliodes
The name of this classic bromeliad genus refers to the "nest" of leaves formed around the vibrant flower spikes.

Africa, SW Asia; clump-forming perennial, 3¼–10 ft (1–3 m) tall with sea green foliage and fine, purple-tinted spikelets in gracefully arching panicles.

Broussonetia (for Pierre Marie August Broussonet [1761–1807], Professor of Botany at Montpellier). Moraceae. East Asia; Polynesia. 8 species, deciduous trees or large shrubs with large, entire to lobed leaves, small, male flowers in catkins and female flowers in globose heads. Tolerant of dry, poor soils, heat and pollution, *Broussonetia* will thrive where temperatures do not often fall below 23°F (−5°C); elsewhere it will need a sunny, sheltered site and may be killed to the ground by frost (it suckers freely). Propagate by semiripe, heeled cuttings in late summer under mist or in a closed case, or from hardwood and root cuttings in winter, or by layering in spring.

B. papyrifera PAPER MULBERRY; China and Japan; broad-crowned tree to 50 ft (15 m) tall, or, a spreading shrub to 10 ft (3 m); leaves 2¾–8 in (7–20 cm) long, ovate, often toothed, 'tattered' or 3–lobed and variably so on the same plant; female plants produce orange-red ball-like fruits; 'Billardii': leaves are much dissected; 'Laciniata': leaves reduced sometimes to small remnants of blade hanging on the tip of the midvein; 'Variegata': leaves are splashed white or yellow; 'Leucocarpa': fruit white.

Browallia (for Johan Browall [1705–1755], Bishop of Abo, Sweden, a defender of Linnaeus' system of plant classification). Solanaceae. South America. AMETHYST FLOWER; BUSH VIOLET. 3 species, tender annual and perennial herbs or shrubs with trumpet-shaped flowers. Grow in a shaded, humid environment (minimum temperature 50°F/10°C). For summer flowers, sow seed in early spring; for winter display, sow seed in late summer or cut back, repot and feed the strongest, existing plants. Take short, soft cuttings of cultivars in spring or late summer. *Browallia* is usually treated as an annual, but may persist for some years if regularly pruned, fed and repotted, *B. speciosa* especially.

B. americana (syn. *B. elata*); bushy, annual or short-lived perennial to 24 in (60 cm) tall; flowers blue to violet or white to 1 in (2.5 cm); includes the cultivars 'Caerulea' (flowers sky blue), 'Compacta' (habit small, compact), 'Grandiflora' (*B. grandiflora*) and 'Major' (flowers larger), and the dwarf 'Nana'; *B. speciosa* (syn. *B. gigantea*); shrubby perennial to 3¼ ft (1 m); flowers to 1½ in (4 cm) in shades of blue and violet with a white eye; many cultivars developed in shades of white, pale blue, royal blue, indigo, violet and lilac; 'Major': SAPPHIRE FLOWER, flowers large, purple-blue; *B. viscosa* (annual to 24 in (60 cm) tall; flowers to 1¼ in (3 cm) violet-blue with a white eye; 'Alba': flowers white; 'Sapphire': sapphire blue.

Browningia (for W.E. Browning, Director of the Instituto Ingles at Santiago, Chile). Cactaceae. South America. 7 species, shrubby to treelike cacti with spiny, strongly ribbed, cylindric stems and nocturnal, tubular to funnelform flowers. Large but slow-growing, this cactus is usually offered as an unbranched stem to 3¼ ft (1 m) tall. Provide a minimum temperature of 50°F (10°C). Plant in a neutral to slightly acidic medium high in grit and sand. Shade in hot weather and maintain low humidity. Keep cool and dry

from midfall to early spring except for occasional mistings on warm days. Propagate by seed or cuttings of detached branches. *B. hertlingiana* (syn. *Azureocereus hertlingianus*); Peru; erect and treelike, ultimately to 25 ft (8 m); stems to 12 in (30 cm) wide, glaucous blue with 18 wavy ribs; spines 2 in (5 cm), tawny; flowers white to pink.

brown coal see *lignite*.

brown rot a fungal disease of tree fruits especially, caused by species of *Monilinia*, which also attacks flower spurs causing blossom wilt. There are differences in biology and world distribution of these fungi, but the general pattern of disease development is the same. Most damage is caused to fruit while it is still on the tree, although post-harvest rotting can also be a serious problem. Blossoms of fruit trees may also be attacked by the disease, which subsequently causes cankers on fruit spurs and smaller branches, resulting in crop loss and providing a source of inoculum for further infection. Symptoms of

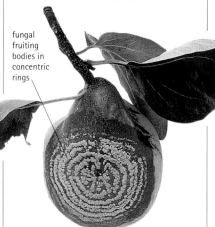

fungal fruiting bodies in concentric rings

Brown rot in pear

infection on fruit are soft brown rotten areas which spread quickly, and on blossom, brown spotting of petals followed by shrivelling of the whole flower.

M. fructicola, which is native to North America and is particularly damaging to peaches and other stone fruit, is the most important of the brown rots; it now occurs also in South America, Australia and New Zealand. Infected fruits form abundant tufts of powdery ashy-gray spores, sometimes in concentric rings. European stone fruit growing

could be at risk from this disease. *M. fructigena*, primarily a disease of apples and pears, is of Eurasian origin and is still mainly restricted to the Old World. It sporulates abundantly on affected fruit, forming raised masses of fungal tissue in concentric rings covered with buff-colored spores. There is a danger of introducing this species into American and Australian orchards.

M.laxa is thought to have originated in Eurasia but now has a worldwide distribution. Its fawn-gray spores form less luxuriantly and it is mainly a disease of *Prunus*, causing BLOSSOM BLIGHT and canker rather than fruit rot; a form of this species is particularly pathogenic to apples and pears. Fruits infected before maturity shrivel on the tree and are the principal means whereby the brown rot fungus, having overwintered in them, is able to infect blossom in spring. Mummified fruits infected by *M. fructicola* give rise to the ascospore-producing sexual stage of the fungus in spring; this provides an additional opportunity for dispersal of the disease, as well as the possibility of genetic change in virulence and fungicide tolerance. The sexual stage of the life cycle is rare in the other two species of *Monilinia*.

Control measures include: (a) reducing the over-wintered inoculum by disposing of mummified fruits, dead spurs and branches; (b) a fungicidal spray program from blossom time where the disease is established, especially on peaches; (c) the prevention of fruit damage by insects; (d) avoiding harvesting in wet weather; (e) careful handling of fruits.

Other brown rot fungi are *M. aucupariae*, which causes a fruit rot and foliage blight of *Sorbus commixta* in Europe and Japan; *M. johnsonii*, CRATAEGUS LEAF BLOTCH and BLOSSOM BLIGHT, which is widespread; *M. kusanoi*, blight of flowering cherry in Japan; *M. linhartiana*, QUINCE FRUIT ROT in Turkey; *M. oxycocci*, CRANBERRY HARD ROT; and *M. vaccinii-corymbosi*, BLUEBERRY BROWN ROT or MUMMY BERRY, in North America. Other diseases also referred to as brown rot are (*Pseudomonas solanaceanum*) bacterial wilt of potatoes; ORCHID LEAF SPOT disease such as *Erwinia cypripedi*; and decay caused by certain wood-rotting fungi.

B

Brugmansia (for Sebald Justin Brugmans [1763–1819], Professor of Natural History at Leiden). Solanaceae. South America. ANGEL'S TRUMPET. 5 species of shrubs or small trees. Produced in summer, the large, pendulous, trumpet-shaped flowers widen to a pleated, 5-pointed limb. The following species were formerly included in the genus *Datura*, a genus now limited to short-lived or annual shrubby herbs with very similar but less markedly pendulous flowers. Grow in full sun or light shade in a fertile, loamy medium. Water and feed generously when in growth. In winter, they should be kept frost-free and almost dry. Prune hard in early spring. Propagate by semiripe, heeled cuttings in late summer.

B. arborea (syn. *Datura cornigera*); to 12 ft (4 m); flowers to 6 in (15 cm), white, only slightly pendent; this name is often misapplied to *B.* × *Candida*, which has far larger, pendulous flowers; *B. aurea* to 30 ft (10 m); flowers to 10 in (24 cm), nocturnally fragrant, white to golden yellow; *B.* × *Candida* (*B. aurea* × *B. versicolor*), fast-growing to 15 ft (5 m); flowers to 12¹/₂ in (32 cm) fragrant, creamy yellow becoming pure white, rarely pink; double-flowered, pure white forms include 'Double White' and 'Knightii'; *B.* × *insignis* (*B. suaveolens* × *B. versicolor*), resembles *B. suaveolens* but with longer flowers (to 15 in (38 cm) in white, pink, salmon or apricot with narrower corolla lobes); *B.* × *rubella* (*B. arborea* × *B. sanguinea*); to 10 ft (3 m); flowers to 6 in (15 cm), red-flushed; *B. sanguinea* RED ANGEL'S TRUMPET; to 30 ft (10 m); flowers to 10 in (25 cm), yellow-green at base, then yellow deepening to scarlet or orange-red at limb); *B. suaveolens* to 15 ft (5 m); flowers to 12 in (30 cm), strongly nocturnally fragrant, white to pale yellow or pink; *B. versicolor* to 15 ft (5 m); flowers to 20 in (50 cm), white sometimes becoming orange or peach; often mislabelled *B. arborea*; the popular 'Grand Marnier' with soft apricot flowers is derived from this species, as are the salmon 'Charles Grimaldi' and the cream to pink 'Frosty Pink'.

Brunfelsia (for Otto Brunfels, 16th-century botanist and physician). Solanaceae. Tropical America. 40 species, shrubs and small trees. Borne in summer, the flowers are fragrant, tubular with five broad lobes. Grow in a humid, lightly shaded environment with a minimum temperature of 55°F (13°C). Plant in a slightly acidic mix; water and feed generously during periods of warm weather and active growth, sparingly at other times. Propagate from greenwood cuttings in a case with bottom heat in spring and summer.

B. lactea JAZMIN DEL MONTE; Peru; shrub to 10 ft (3 m) tall with intensely fragrant, waxy ivory flowers to 3 in (7.5 cm) across; *B. pauciflora* (syn. *B. calycina*); Brazil; bushy shrub to 10 ft (3 m) tall; flowers purple with a white eye ringed in lavender blue to 2³/₄ in (7 cm) across; 'Floribunda': YESTERDAY TODAY AND TOMORROW; flowers violet with small white center, fading to lavender then white over a period of three days; 'Macrantha': probably synonymous with *B. grandiflora*, a more luxuriant shrub, with flowers to 2 × 3 in (5 × 8 cm) in deep purple with a white to lavender throat and also fading through lilac to white over a period of days.

Brunnera (for Samuel Brunner [1790–1844], Swiss botanist). Boraginaceae. Eastern Europe to Siberia. 3 species, hardy, rhizomatous perennial herbs with broad, coarsely hairy leaves and, in spring and early summer, erect, terminal panicles of small forget-me-not-like flowers. Plant in humus-rich, moist soil in dappled sun or full shade with some protection from harsh winds. Propagate by division in fall or root cuttings in early spring. *B. macrophylla* to 20 in (50 cm); leaves ovate to cordate to 6 in (15 cm) long; flowers clear blue; 'Dawson's White' and 'Variegata': leaves variegated white; 'Hadspen Cream': leaves splashed cream; 'Aluminum Spot' and 'Langtrees': leaves spotted silver; 'Betsy Bowring': flowers white.

Brunsvigia (for Karl Wilhelm Ferdinand, Duke of Brunswick-Luneburg [1713–1780], patron of the arts and sciences). Amaryllidaceae. South Africa. 20 species, deciduous perennial herbs with large bulbs and broadly strap-shaped leaves to 36 in (90 cm) long emerging after the flowers. Produced in late summer, the flowers are funnel-shaped and carried in spherical umbels on stout, red-tinted scapes. After flowering, the individual flower stalks extend after the fashion of *Boophone*. Cultivation as for *Boophone*, although these bulbs have proved slightly more hardy, sometimes surviving in very sunny, sheltered positions (min. 10°F/−12°C), protected in winter with a deep mulch or framelights.

B. josephinae (syn. *B. gigantea*); JOSEPHINE'S LILY; scape to 36 in (90 cm) tall with many, 2¹/₂ in (6 cm)-long, crimson flowers each on slender, ray-like stalk; *B. orientalis* (syn. *B. multiflora*); differs in its hairy rather than glabrous leaves, its shorter scape and flower stalks and the flowers to 2³/₄ in (7 cm) long and pink or scarlet.

brushwood killer a herbicide used on woody perennial weeds.

Brussels sprouts (*Brassica oleracea* Gemmifera Group) a tall biennial grown mostly as a winter vegetable for its small cabbagelike axillary buds. It has a loose head of large leaves which may also be harvested like cabbage. It is widely grown in Britain, and mainly in California within the US.

Sow ¹/₂–³/₄ in (1–2 cm) deep in a seedbed from mid-March to mid-April, transplanting to 24 in (60 cm) each way from mid-May to the end of June. Stopping the plants by removing the growing tip was once recommended for advancing maturity and improving sprout quality but is no longer necessary because of the improvement in cultivars, particularly F1 hybrids.

Possible problems: aphids, cabbage caterpillars, cabbage root fly, flea beetle, turnip gall weevil (see *weevils*), whiteflies; clubroot, leaf spot.

brutting a partial breaking of hazelnut or fruit tree shoots, leaving the ends hanging, to prevent late summer growth. See *hazelnuts*.

bryobia mite see *red spider mites*.

bryophytes small multicellular lowly plants, belonging to the division Bryophyta; mostly living on land and represented by mosses and liverworts.

bubbler a water-feature device propelling a low pressure jet of water through the center of a millstone, cobblestones etc. to create a gentle flow.

buccae the lateral sepals (wings) in the flowers of *Aconitum* and allies.

bud blast (*Pycnostysanus azaleae*) a fungal disease of *Rhododendron* species characterized by drying and silvering of buds. It is associated with the rhododendron leafhopper. The removal of infected buds is a useful control measure, but only practicable on a small scale. The incidence of the disease can be limited by the use of recommended insecticides, applied at 10–14 day intervals from early August, to control the leafhopper.

bud burst see *bud stages*.

bud drop the shedding of flower buds, particularly by tuberous begonias, lupines, sweet peas, runner beans and tomatoes. It is most often caused by low night temperature or waterlogging, or draft under glass.

budding a technique of *grafting* (q.v.) using a single bud, for propagating a wide range of woody plants.

budding knife a knife designed for bud-grafting, commonly termed budding. It is usually made with a part of the blade or handle modified for lifting bark.

Buddleja (for Adam Buddle [1600–1715], amateur botanist and cleric). Loganiaceae. Asia; America; Africa. 100 species, evergreen or deciduous shrubs and trees, usually downy or felty, with narrow, pith-filled branches, lanceolate to ovate leaves and panicles of 4-lobed, tubular flowers from late spring to fall.

B. alternifolia, *B. davidii*, *B. globosa*, *B.* 'Lochinch', *B.* 'West Hill' and *B.* × *weyeriana* are hardy to 5°F (−15°C) and, if cut to the ground, will usually regenerate. *B. colvilei*, *B. crispa*, *B. fallowiana* and *B. lindleyana* are usually damaged by temperatures below 14°F (−10°C) and grow best against a sheltered, south-facing wall (min. 0°F (−18°C). *B. asiatica*, *B.* × *lewisiana* and *B. madagascariensis* are frost-tender and should be grown in cool greenhouses and conser-

Bud blast of rhododendrons
Symptoms are blackened buds with a silvery coating. The condition is caused by a combination of fungus and insect attack.

vatories. Grow all in fertile, well-drained soils in full sun and with protection from strong winds. Plant tender species in tubs or borders, ideally near a wall to provide support for their wandlike branches and with good ventilation and abundant water supplies except in cool weather.

Much is made of the differing pruning requirements of buddlejas. If the plants are growing and flowering well, there is really little need to prune them; since they do, however, produce a good deal of short-lived wood and are easily damaged by freezing weather, the following guidelines may be of use — prune *B. asiatica*, *B. crispa*, *B. davidii*, *B. fallowiana*, *B.* × *lewisiana*, *B. lindleyana*, *B.* 'Lochinch', *B. madagascariensis* and *B.* 'West Hill' in spring, cutting back either to near ground level or to within 2 in (5 cm) of a permanent woody framework established in the first few years after planting by cutting back selected stems to half their length. *B. alternifolia* and *B. colvilei* flower on the previous season's growth and should be pruned after flowering: cut back old, flowered shoots to the desired shape and remove dead, diseased and congested branches. *B. globosa* and *B.* × *weyeriana* flower on growth which emerges from terminal buds on the previous year's wood: unless a major assault is needed, remove only weak or exhausted branches in early spring. Propagate by heeled, semiripe cuttings in the cold

frame, or, *B. alternifolia*, hardwood cuttings in fall. Pinch out new plants to encourage branching.

B. alternifolia China; deciduous shrub or small tree to 28 ft (9 m); branches slender, weeping; leaves narrow, dark green, to 2¾ in (7 cm) long, silvery in the cultivar 'Argentea'; flowers fragrant, lilac-purple flowers to ½ in (1 cm) long, in dense clusters on the previous year's wood; *B. asiatica* E Asia; evergreen, winter-flowering shrub or small tree; branches long, spreading and woolly; leaves narrowly lanceolate, with white-felted undersides; flowers white, fragrant, to ¼ in (0.6 cm) long, in dense, drooping, narrow panicles; *B. colvilei* Himalayas; summer-flowering evergreen, shrub or small tree to 20 ft (6 m) tall with large, dark green leaves; flowers 1 in (2.5 cm) wide, showy, bell-shaped, gathered in lax, drooping trusses to 8 in (20 cm) long, rose-purple to crimson or maroon or deep red in the cultivar 'Kewensis'; *B. crispa* Northern India; bushy, deciduous shrub to 10 ft (3 m) tall with thickly white-felted branches and gray-woolly, wavy-toothed, triangular to ovate-lanceolate leaves; flowers fragrant, lilac with orange or white throats are in bluntly pyramidal panicles; *B. davidii* BUTTERFLY BUSH, SUMMER LILAC; China, Japan; evergreen, spreading shrub or tree to 12 ft (4 m) tall; leaves lanceolate, dull to dark green above and felty beneath; flowers fragrant, ½ in (1 cm)-long, in dense, narrowly conical panicles; typically deep lilac with an orange-yellow throat, there are many cultivars ranging in color through white ('Peace', 'White Bouquet', 'White Cloud', 'White Profusion') to pink ('Charming', 'Pink Delight', 'Pink Pearl'), magenta, ('Dartmoor'), lilac ('Fascinating', 'Fortune'), mauve ('Amplissima', 'Veitchiana'), darkest purple ('Black Knight', 'Dubonnet'), violet ('Empire Blue', 'Fromow's Purple', 'Ile de France', 'Magnifica') and purple-red ('Border Beauty', 'Royal Red'), usually with an orange-yellow throat; in 'Harlequin', the leaves are variegated ivory and the flowers a deep purple-red; variety *nanhoensis*: low-growing, elegant shrub with slender branches, smaller and narrower leaves and panicles of fine blue-mauve flowers (white in 'Alba') includes 'Nanho Blue' with powder blue flowers and 'Nanho Purple' with orange-eyed, violet flowers; *B. fallowiana* Burma, Western China; robust, deciduous shrub to 15 ft (5 m) tall with stout, white-woolly branches and crenate, ovate to lanceolate leaves gray above with white-woolly undersides; flowers fragrant, 1/2 in (1 cm)-long, lavender or white with orange throats; crossed with *B. davidii*, producing 'Lochinch', a gray-downy, vigorous, bushy shrub with fragrant, violet flowers with a deep orange eye, and 'West Hill' with narrow, arching panicles of pale lilac flowers with a gold to bronze eye, both flowering in late summer and fall; *B. globosa* ORANGE BALL TREE; Chile, Argentina, Peru; semievergreen erect shrub or tree to 20 ft (6 m); leaves wrinkled, glossy, dark green; flowers honey-scented, yellow-orange in tight, 3/4 in (2 cm)-wide balls; *B. × lewisiana* (*B. asiatica × B. madagascariensis*; includes 'Margaret Pike', a large shrub with long, felty branches and dense racemes of pale yellow flowers in winter; *B. lindleyana* evergreen shrub to 6½ ft (2 m) with slender, arching branches, pale green, elliptic to lanceolate leaves to 4¾ in (12 cm) long and narrow spikes of curving, 5/8 in (1.5 cm)-long, purple-violet flowers in summer; *B. madagascariensis* Madagascar; evergreen sprawling to semiscandent shrub producing 10 in (25 cm)-long panicles of orange-yellow flowers in winter; *B. × weyeriana* (*B. globosa × B. davidii*); intermediate between parents; includes 'Golden Glow', orange-yellow flushed lilac, and 'Sungold', deep orange.

bud scales the coverings of a bud.

bud stages the phases through which flower buds and flowers progress. These have established descriptions in fruit plants, for example, breaking, bud burst, and have relevance to the timing of sprays or other treatment for control of pests and diseases. Bud stages on various fruits are illustrated on p.854.

budwood, bud stick a plant shoot from which buds are obtained for budding.

Buglossoides (*Buglossum* and *-oides*, 'resembling'). Boraginaceae. Europe; Asia. 15 species, hardy, bristly annual or perennial herbs with erect to decumbent stems and cymes of 5-lobed, blue or white flowers in spring and summer. Grow in moist but well-drained, neutral to alkaline soil in part-shade. Mulch in very cold areas. Propagate by division. *B. purpureo-caerulea* (syn. *Lithospermum purpureo-caeruleum*); W Europe to Iran; rhizomatous perennial, 10–28 in (25–70 cm) tall with narrow leaves to 3 in (8 cm) long; flowers to 5/8 in (1.5 cm), emerging red-purple, becoming bright blue.

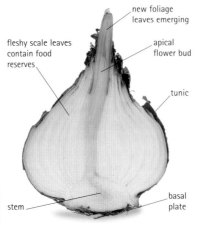

Cross-section through Hippeastrum bulb

bulb a modified bud, usually subterranean, consisting of a short thickened stem, serving as a storage organ. There are two principal kinds, (1) naked, composed of free, overlapping scaly modified leaves, all of them fleshy, for example, *Lilium*; (2) tunicated, with thin, membranous, fibrous or reticulated outer and fleshy concentric inner layers, for example, *Allium*. The "solid bulb" is a corm.

bulb fiber a growing medium for bulbs in containers, with 6 parts peat, 2 parts crushed oyster shell, and 1 part crushed charcoal, by volume.

bulb flies (Diptera: Syrphidae) species of plant-feeding hoverflies, of which the most injurious is the LARGE NARCISSUS FLY (*Merodon equestris*). First recorded in England in 1869, thought to have originated in southern Europe and has now spread to many parts of the world, including America. Its principal host is *Narcissus*, but it also attacks other members of Amaryllidaceae, and some bulbs of other families. The adult is a stout hairy fly, about 5/8 in (15 mm) long, resembling a small bumble bee, but with one pair of wings and short antennae. Fertilized females produce about 40 eggs, normally deposited singly on the neck of host plants. The legless grub crawls down the outside of the bulb, enters through the basal plate and eats out the central portion of the bulb. When fully fed, the cream-white maggots are up to 3/4 in (18 mm) long. The bulbs are usually killed, although daughter bulbs often remain unharmed and produce thin leaves known as "grass."

SMALL NARCISSUS FLIES (*Eumerus* species) are widespread in Europe and North America. They are smaller, about 1/4 in (6 mm) long, with three pairs of crescent-shaped, white markings on a black, hairless abdomen. The legless larvae are 3/8 in (8 mm) long when fully fed, and there are usually several per bulb. In most cases damage by *Eumerus* species is secondary.

Infested bulbs should be removed and burned. Fill in the holes left at the soil surface as the foliage begins to die down to deter flies from reaching the necks of the bulbs. Dusting the soil surface with contact insecticide at the same time is helpful. Covering bulbs in June-early July with a fine-mesh floating mulch will exclude egg-laying females.

bulb frame an all-glass frame used by specialist growers to provide a dry environment for bulbs in their resting period.

bulbiferous bearing bulbs or bulbils.

bulbiform in the shape of, or resembling, a bulb.

bulbil, bulblet a small bulb or bulb-like growth, arising from a leaf axil or in place of flowers in an inflorescence.

bulbiliferous bearing bulbils.

Bulbocodium (from Greek *bolbos*, bulb, and *kodya*, capsule). Liliaceae (Colchicaceae). S and E Europe. 2 species, hardy, perennial, cormous herbs. Apparently stemless flowers with 6, erect to spreading oblong to lanceolate tepals emerge in early spring before or with narrow leaves. Cultivate as for the smaller *Colchicum* species. *B. vernum* flowers 1–3, 2 in (5 cm)-wide with spreading, rose to magenta tepals; *B. versicolor* differs in its smaller flowers.

Bulbophyllum (from Greek *bylbos*, bulb, and *phyllon*, leaf, referring to the pseudobulbs which usually bear a single leaf). Orchidaceae. Tropics and subtropics. 1,200+ species, evergreen, epiphytic and lithophytic orchids, small plants with creeping rhizomes carrying rounded to ovoid pseudobulbs each terminating in single or paired, oblong to elliptic, thinly fleshy leaves. Produced throughout the year, the flowers vary greatly in size, color and shape — they may be solitary or borne on racemes or slender-stalked umbels. The dorsal sepal and petals are usually short, ovate to lanceolate and can be fringed or tufted with hairs and ribbons, the lateral sepals longer, linear to lanceolate and often twisted downward and together; the lip is small, fleshy and sometimes hinged.

Grow in an open, bark-based mix in small, shallow pots or baskets, or attach to rafts, branches and cork slabs against pads of moss. Provide bright, humid conditions (minimum temperature 50°F/10°C). Water and mist freely when in growth; at other times, merely mist to prevent shrivelling of pseudobulbs. Propagate by division.

B. barbigerum W and C Africa; flowers to ¾ in (2 cm) across, several in erect racemes, tepals red-green, lip deep burgundy, long and projecting forward with a dense beard of glossy hairs; *B. guttulatum* India; flowers to 1½ in (4 cm) across, several in an umbel, tepals broad, yellow or pale green speckled purple, lip short, pale purple; *B. umbellatum* differs in larger flowers in cream or ivory overlaid with fine lines of rose-purple spots, lip rose-purple; *B. lobbii* India to Philippines; flowers solitary, to 4 in (10 cm) across, waxy, red to dull ocher or pale yellow sometimes speckled or veined red-brown, lateral sepals large and curving outward like horns. *B. longiflorum* Africa, Asia, Australasia, Polynesia; flowers produced freely, to ¾ in (2 cm) long in a semicircular umbel, dorsal sepal and petals small, pink to brown or olive speckled deep red, tipped with maroon hairs, lateral sepals larger, cream to olive, striped or speckled rose, wine red or maroon, curving forward and together in a shoelike form, lip very small, maroon; *B. longissimum* SE Asia; flowers large in an umbel, dorsal sepal and petals short, cream lined purple-red, lateral sepals to 8 in (20 cm) long, white to cream striped rosy purple, curving inward and together, tapering finely, lip short, tonguelike; *B. medusae* Southeast Asia; flowers in a dense umbel, white to ivory lightly spotted rose or maroon at the center with very long (to 6 in (15 cm)), finely tapering lateral sepals drooping in a ghostly mop.

bulb planter a tool consisting of a hollow cylinder on a handle; used to remove plugs of soil prior to planting bulbs. It is sometimes called a transplanter or, in the US, a turf plugger.

bulb scale a component of a bulb.

bulb scale mite see *tarsonemid mites*.

bulb scaling a method of propagating bulbs, such as lilies, from the outer scales of a mother bulb; see *cuttings*.

bulky organic matter high-volume animal or plant waste, usually low in nutrient content, used to maintain or improve fertility and moisture holding in soils through incorporation or surface mulching.

bullace (*Prunus institia*) a type of plum producing small rounded fruits varying in color from almost black through red to pale green-yellow. Native to Britain and across Europe to Asia Minor; closely allied to the damson but with more rounded fruits that are not as distinctively purple. Plums and damsons have so evolved that they have surpassed the bullace in cultivation, and it is now most widely represented by its near relative the small-fruited Mirabelle plum of France. Notable cultivars are 'White Bullace' and 'Mirabelle de Nancy'.

Possible problems: aphids, bacterial canker; silver leaf.

bullate where the surface of an organ (usually a leaf) is 'blistered' or puckered (i.e., with many superficial interveinal convexities).

bumble bees (*Bombus* species) widely distributed, fat-bodied, hairy insects up to 1 in (25 mm) long, with membranous wings and waisted abdomens. Females have heavily fringed hind tibiae for carrying pollen. They are basically dark in color, with horizontal bands or patches of yellow or orange, and sometimes white hairs. They are social insects, building annual colonies in underground cavities, and are valuable pollinators. Unlike hive bees, they are able to forage in less favorable weather conditions. All bumble bees are able to pollinate flowers with a short corolla but only those with long tongues, such as *Bombus hortorum*, can pollinate flowers with long corolla tubes. Short-tongued bumble bees often bite a hole at the base of the corolla of such plants as beans, sweet peas, antirrhinums and aquilegias to obtain nectar. The timing of pesticide sprays should take account of bumble bee activity.

Buphthalmum salicifolium
The flowers of the yellow ox-eye daisy can be more than 2 in (5 cm) in diameter, borne on tall, slender stems. It makes an excellent cut flower.

Buphthalmum (from Greek *bous*, ox, and *opthalmos*, eye, referring to the wide, eyelike flower heads). Compositae. Europe; W Asia. 2 species, hardy, perennial herbs grown for their daisylike flower heads produced in summer. Plant in medium- or low-fertility soils in full sun in the herbaceous border or wild garden. Stake in exposed or over-fertile conditions. Propagate by division. *B. salicifolium* OX EYE DAISY, YELLOW OX EYE; forming a clump of yard-tall willowy stems with slender, 4 in (10 cm)-long, oblong to lanceolate leaves; flower heads 2–2¾ in (5–7 cm) wide, typically golden yellow.

Bupleurum (from Greek *boupleuros*, 'ox-rib', a name given to another plant). Umbelliferae. Europe; Asia; Northern US; Canary Islands; South Africa. HARE'S EAR; THOROW-WAX. 100 species, annual and perennial herbs and shrubs with entire, leathery leaves and, in summer, small yellow flowers in slender-rayed, compound umbels. Sow seed of herbaceous species in spring on well-drained soils in sunny borders, meadow gardens and the fringes of woodlands and shrubberies. Thorow-wax will naturalize itself in favorable locations. *B. falcatum* and *B. petraeum* are suitable for sunny banks, large rock gardens and dry borders on very well-drained soils. They suffer in cold, damp conditions. Propagate by division or seed in early spring. In a sheltered, sunny position, the shrubby *B. fruticosum* will survive temperatures as low as 5°F (–15°C). It tolerates poor, rather dry soils and is an excellent evergreen for training on walls and allowing to trail over walls and banks. It grows well on the coast. Prune out exhausted or frost-damaged growth in spring. Propagate by semi-ripe cuttings in summer.

B. falcatum SICKLE-LEAVED HARE'S EAR; woody-based, yard-tall perennial with scimitar-like leaves to 4 in (10 cm) long; *B. fruticosum* SHRUBBY HARE'S EAR; slender-branched, evergreen shrub, to 6½ × 6½ ft (2 × 2 m), with erect to sprawling branches clothed with dull or sea green, oblanceolate leaves to 3 in (8 cm) long with gray undersides; *B. petraeum* ROCK HARE'S EAR; woody-based perennial to 12 in (30 cm) tall, making low rosettes of narrow, glaucous, 8 in (20 cm)-long leaves; *B. rotundifolium* THOROW-WAX; annual or short-lived perennial to 24 in (60 cm) tall; leaves rounded, clasping to perfoliate and pink-tinted at first becoming glaucous sage

green; flower heads lime green to gold; 'Green Gold': bright green leaves, bracts lime, flowers golden yellow.

Burgundy mixture a fungicide similar to Bordeaux mixture, except that sodium carbonate is used instead of calcium hydroxide, giving a precipitate of basic copper carbonate. Its use is of historic interest only.

burlap see *burlap*.

burlapped see *balled and wrapped*.

burr, bur a prickly fruit, usually adapted for distribution on the coats or feet of animals.

bush (1) a low shrub with branches arising initially from ground level or from a short leg; (2) refers to tomatoes that have a determinate habit.

bushel an outmoded measure of volume equivalent to approximately 1.5 cu ft (0.04 m³). Horticulturally significant in the formulae of John Innes seed and potting mixes. A bulk of about one bushel is contained in a box of dimensions 10 in × 10 in × 22 in (25 cm × 25 cm × 55 cm).

bush fruit a group description of currants, gooseberries and blueberries. c.f. *cane fruit*.

bush tree a trained form of top fruits, usually having a stem 24–36 in (60–90 cm) high with the main branches arising fairly close together to form the head.

Butia (the vernacular name in Brazil). Palmae. S America. YATAY PALM; JELLY PALM; PINDO PALM. 12 species, palms with short to columnar trunks, large pinnate leaves and spikes of small yellow flowers followed by egg-shaped, edible fruit. Plant in well-drained soil in full sun or light shade with plentiful water. Once established, it will take periods of drought and low temperatures to 28°F (–2°C). Propagate by seed. *B. capitata* to 20 ft (6 m) tall with a stout trunk armored with husky petiole bases; leaves 3¼–6½ ft (1–2 m) long and erect to strongly arching, segments

30 in (75 cm)-long, glaucous, gray-green; fruit yellow to bright red.

Butomus (from Greek *bous*, ox, and *temno*, to cut, a reference to the sharp leaf margins which render this plant unusable as cattle fodder). Butomaceae. Europe; Asia. 1 species, *B. umbellatus* FLOWERING RUSH, WATER GLADIOLUS, GRASSY RUSH, a hardy, summer-flowering deciduous, aquatic perennial to 3¼ ft (1 m) tall with rushlike leaves and scapose, umbels of slender-stalked, rosy pink flowers each to 1¼ in (3 cm) diam. Pot in a rich, sandy and loamy mix and cover with up to 10 in (25 cm) depth of water in an open, sunny pond, lake or a half barrel. Propagate by division in spring.

butterflies (Lepidoptera). Butterflies generally differ from moths in having clubbed antennae and slender bodies, and in their diurnal activity, although these distinctions are not definitive. Most are welcome visitors to gardens with the exception of CABBAGE WHITE BUTTERFLIES (*Pieris* species), the larvae of which cause extensive damage to the foliage of brassicas and garden nasturtiums (*Tropaeolum* species) (See *cabbage caterpillars*). Butterflies contribute to pollination while visiting flowers as nectar feeders and find *Buddleja* species and *Sedum spectabile* particularly attractive. Caterpillars of the RED ADMIRAL (*Vanessa atalanta*) and TORTOISESHELL (*Aglais urticae*) feed upon stinging nettle (*Urtica dioica*).

buttoning a disorder of cauliflower in which underdeveloped curds form flowers on immature plants. It is usually caused by a temperature or water associated growth check.

buttress the supporting outgrowths of the bole of certain trees; produced as a result of fused, flangelike aerial roots or a fluted or swollen trunk. Produced usually to contend with saturated or shallow-rooting conditions.

Buxus (the Classical Latin name for the box tree). Buxaceae. Europe; Asia; Africa; C and S America. BOX; BOXWOOD. 70 species, slow-growing, evergreen shrubs and small trees, usually with small, tough, deep green leaves and inconspicuous clusters of yellow-green to cream flowers. The most important species is *B. sempervirens*, used for hedges, edging, screens and topiary and, in its pendulous or prostrate forms, for specimen plantings. The varieties and cultivars of *B. microphylla* with distinctively thin-textured leaves and compact habit can be put to similar uses. *B. balearica* and *B. wallichiana* are subject to injury below 10°F (−12°C). Shade-tolerant, *Buxus* nonetheless prefers sunlight for at least part of the day, although the foliage can be scorched by long exposure to bright sun and harsh winds. Prune in spring to remove dead or unwanted growth or to stimulate new shoots. Clip hedges and topiary to shape in summer. Propagate by heel cuttings in fall or by nodal cuttings in spring.

B. balearica BALEARIC BOXWOOD; Balearics, Spain, North Africa; an erect shrub or small tree ultimately attaining 30 ft (10 m); leaves to 1½ × ¾ in (4 × 2 cm), broadly oblong to oval, leathery, bright to deep green above, paler beneath; *B. harlandii* a tender shrub native to Hong Kong and South China and rare in cultivation; this name is applied in gardens to a dwarf, compact and domed selection of *B. sinica* var. *insularis* with bright green, oblanceolate

Clipped box
The small, closely spaced leaves of *Buxus* and its slow, compact growth make it ideal for clipping into both geometric and novel shapes.

leaves; *B. microphylla* long grown in Japan, this plant has never been found in the wild; compact, rounded or semi-prostrate shrub to 3¼ ft (1 m) tall with thin-textured, obovate or bluntly lanceolate leaves, ¼–¾ in (1–1.75 cm) long; var. *japonica*: habit open, spreading; branches thicker, 4-angled, leaves ovate to elliptic, leathery; var. *koreana*: lax, spreading small, leaves deep green, sometimes bronze in winter; *B. sempervirens* COMMON BOX; Europe, W Asia, N Africa; shrub or tree to 25 ft (8 m) tall, often multi-stemmed with age and developing attractively snaking trunks and tiered, weeping branches if grown in sheltered conditions; leaves ½–1¼ in (1–3 cm) long, oval to oblong bluntly elliptic, tough, dark, glossy to leaden green above and paler beneath; *cultivars* 'Agram': columnar, leaves elliptic, notched, medium-sized, dark, glossy green; 'Arborescens': large shrub or small tree with large, deep green leaves; 'Argenteovariegata': habit spreading, leaves tinted gray, edged cream; 'Aureovariegata': bushy, medium to large shrub, leaves marked pale gold; 'Elegantissima': slow-growing, compact dome, leaves small, somewhat misshapen, edged cream; 'Notata': topmost leaves of new shoots tipped-golden yellow; 'Handsworthiensis': erect to spreading, large, leaves rounded to oblong, tough, dark green; 'Bullata': large, dense and spreading, leaves large, puckered; 'Latifolia Maculata': dense, mound-forming, leaves large, blotched yellow, especially on new shoots; 'Longifolia': large shrub or small tree of elegant habit with sprays of large, narrow leaves, 'Angustifolia' is very similar; 'Marginata': large, erect, leaves medium-sized, puckered, green splashed and edged yellow; 'Myosotidifolia': erect, slow-growing, compact and twiggy with small, dark leaves; 'Pendula': large, open shrub or small tree with pendulous branches; 'Prostrata': vigorous, medium-sized shrub with strongly spreading branches; 'Rosmarinifolia': dwarf, compact, leaves narrow, small, deep sage green; 'Rotundifolia': small and slow-growing with rounded leaves; 'Salicifolia': differs from 'Longifolia' in weeping branches and narrower leaves; 'Suffruticosa': dwarf or small, compact shrub with medium-sized, ovate, glossy, bright

green leaves; the cultivar most commonly used for formal edging; *B. sinica* var. *insularis* CHINESE BOX, China, Japan, Taiwan, spreading and lax shrub or small tree to 20 ft (6 m), leaves to 1¼ in (3 cm) long, obovate to oblong, blunt to retuse and revolute, leathery, olive green; *cultivars* 'Compacta': dwarf, slow-growing, rounded with very small leaves, good for rock garden or alpine trough; 'Curly Locks': like 'Compacta' but with many, tiny accessory leaves; 'Filigree': procumbent, leaves round, pale sea green; 'Green Gem': very hardy, dwarf, rounded, with bright green, narrow leaves; 'Green Pillow': like 'Compacta', dome-forming with dark green leaves; 'Kingsville Dwarf': very slow-growing with minute leaves; 'Richard': low, bushy, leaves oblong, notched, thick, wavy-edged, bright green; 'Tide Hill': low and broad with glossy lanceolate leaves; 'Winter Gem': compact with oval, deep green leaves that keep their color well in winter); *B. wallichiana* HIMALAYAN BOX; shrub or small tree to 30 ft (10 m) tall; lax and open in habit, its long branches bearing dark green, narrowly oblong to lanceolate leaves to 2½ in (6 cm) long.

Byblis (named after Byblis, granddaughter of Apollo, who fell in love with her twin brother and, on his desertion, wept so profusely she was turned into a fountain — these plants glisten as if drenched with dew). Byblidaceae. Australia; New Guinea. 2 species, carnivorous herbs with slender, woody-based stems, long, threadlike leaves covered with sticky glands and solitary, 5-petalled, flaxlike flowers. Plant in a sandy, peat- and sphagnum-based mix in summer; keep damp in winter and wet (the pot base immersed) in summer. Always use rainwater. Provide full sunlight, a humid, well-ventilated atmosphere and a minimum temperature of 50°F (10°C). Propagate *B. gigantea* by root and stem cuttings. Surface-sow seed of *B. liniflora* thinly in spring into the final container — it is best allowed to grow *en masse*.

B. gigantea perennial to 24 in (60 cm); flowers sky blue, lilac, mauve or pink flowers; *B. liniflora* annual, to 10 in (25 cm); flowers bright blue or pink.

C

C3 plants, C4 plants plants in which the first products of photosynthesis contain three or four carbon atoms respectively.

C:N ratio see *carbon/nitrogen ratio*.

cabbage a collective name for several types of plant within the genus *Brassica* grown as vegetables for their edible leaves.

CABBAGE (*Brassica oleracea* Capitata Group) probably originated along the Mediterranean coast, where wild forms still occur, and was known to the ancient Greeks for its medicinal properties. A biennial grown as an annual, it forms round or pointed compact heads; the leaves are green or red, smooth or wrinkled. Cabbage is the most widely cultivated of the brassicas in the US, but selection and breeding have led to types suited to conditions worldwide. In temperate climates, fresh harvest is possible year round by growing cultivars of different maturity groups and with successional sowing.

Cultivars are conveniently grouped according to season of maturity, but there is great overlap: spring cabbage (April–May, often harvested before heading as greens); summer cabbage (June–August, including red cabbage); fall cabbage (September–October); winter cabbage (November–March, including January King type, very hardy savoys with crinkly leaves, and Dutch winter white. All have similar cultivation requirements and are usually sown ½–¾ in (1–2 cm) deep (in July–August for spring cabbage, March–May for the other crops) in rows 6 in (15 cm) apart. Transplant to 4–16 in (10–40 cm) final spacings in rows 12–24 in (30–60 cm) apart, as recommended for the chosen cultivar. Raising in modules under protection

maximizes use of a growing site and allows for manipulation of harvest date.

CHINESE CABBAGE (CHINESE LEAVES) (*Brassica rapa* Pekinensis Group) is a biennial grown as an annual. It has large, deeply veined leaves with a prominent, edible midrib, forming a dense, compact head. The typical barrel type is 8–10 in (20–25 cm) high, with tight heads; the cylindrical type is 15–18 in (38–45 cm) high, and greener, with a loose habit; used mainly as an excellent cut-and-come-again salad vegetable. Most cultivars are best sown *in situ* in early summer for maturing in early fall, or raised earlier in modules under protection for planting out. They can be grown under cover to extend the season. Space 12–16 in (30–40 cm) apart each way. Chinese cabbage tends to bolt when raised at low temperature, and when transplanted or deprived of water.

CHINESE WHITE CABBAGE (PAK-CHOI) (*Brassica rapa* Chinensis Group) is a biennial grown as an annual, closely related to Chinese cabbage. It is upright and does not form a compact head; the leaves are spoon-shaped with thick, broad, white stems. There are numerous cultivars, some 4–6 in (10–15 cm) high, which should be closely planted. They are tolerant of a wide range of climatic conditions, but must have a regular supply of water.

PORTUGUESE CABBAGE (*Brassica oleracea* Tronchuda Group) is an annual nonheading, transitional type between kale and ordinary cabbage; the leaves are large with prominent white midribs. Grow as for cabbage, raising from a seedbed in spring; plant 20–24 in (50–60 cm) square.

TEXSEL GREENS (ABYSSINIAN or ETHIOPIAN CABBAGE) (*Brassica carinata*), is fast-growing, with shiny leaves that have a flavor reminiscent of spinach. The young leaves and stems can be used as a cooked vegetable, the flower buds and young leaves eaten raw, and the seeds crushed for use as a condi-

ment. Sow *in situ* ½ in (13 mm) deep, successively from spring to late summer, in rows 12 in (30 cm) apart; thin to stand 1 in (2.5 cm) apart. Alternatively, seed may be broadcast, or sown for transplanting in rows 12 in (30 cm) apart, 3–12 in (8–30 cm) apart, depending on the size of plant required. Plants will regenerate if cut, and may be grown under cover to extend the season. See *oriental greens*.

Possible problems: aphids, cabbage caterpillars, cabbage root fly, whiteflies, flea beetle, turnip gall weevil (see *weevils*), clubroot, downy mildew.

cabbage caterpillars the larvae of various pests that commonly attack all leafy brassicas. The CABBAGE MOTH (*Mamestra brassicae*) has green or brown larvae up to 1½ in (35 mm) long; there is one generation, active from July to September. The caterpillars often bore into cabbage hearts, but also feed on other vegetable and ornamental plant foliage. They pupate in the soil. The LARGE CABBAGE WHITE BUTTERFLY (*Pieris brassicae*) has hairy yellow larvae up to 1¾ in (45 mm) long, with black markings; there are two generations, active from June to July and August to October. They feed in groups on outer leaves at first, but later tend to separate. The SMALL CABBAGE WHITE BUTTERFLY (*Pieris rapae*) has green larvae up to 1¼ in (30 mm) long, with a velvety covering of hairs. There are two generations, active from May to June and from July to September, and the caterpillars often bore into cabbage hearts. Butterflies of both species also attack other Cruciferae, and pupate on plant stems, fences and in sheltered places. Caterpillars of the DIAMOND-BACK MOTH (*Plutella xylostella*) are often troublesome.

Inspect plants regularly for infestation. Control by hand-picking. Alternatively, use a bacterial spray of *Bacillus thuringiensis*, or an approved chemical insecticide. Caterpillars of *P. brassicae* are sometimes parasitized by the braconid wasp (*Cotesia glomerata*).

caterpillars feed in colonies at first

Large cabbage white caterpillars

cabbage maggot (*Delia radicum*) a widely distributed fly, similar in size to a house fly, the larvae are destructive pests of cabbage, calabrese, cauliflower, Brussels sprouts, radish, turnip, rutabaga and kohlrabi, the ornamentals *Matthiola*, *Alyssum*, *Arabis*, *Draba* and *Lunaria*, and cruciferous weeds. The legless white larvae grow up to ⅜ in (8 mm) long and feed on roots near the taproot, causing collapse; they may tunnel through leaf midribs and the buttons of Brussels sprouts. There are two or three generations per year in temperate regions, four in warmer zones. The off-white, oval eggs are laid at the base of the plant, just below the soil surface; they hatch in 3–7 days.

Control by placing 4 in- (10 cm)-diameter disks of thin, durable material or special mats around stem bases. Growing under horticultural fleece stops adult flies from laying eggs near the plants.

Cabomba (native name in Guyana). Cabombaceae. Tropical and subtropical America. 7 species, aquatic perennial herbs with clumps of long, submerged to floating stems and cleft to finely divided leaves in whorls or pairs. Grow in pools or freshwater aquariums where the temperature does not fall below 41°F (5°C). Propagate by stem cuttings inserted into the pool or tank bed in spring and summer. *C. caroliniana* CAROLINA WATERSHIELD, FANWORT, FISH GRASS; SE US; leaves ¾–2¾ in (2–7 cm), bright green, fan-shaped, divided into threadlike segments.

cactus (1) any member of the family Cactaceae, which is the best known of over 40 families belonging to the range of plants known as succulents. Cacti are natives of hot, dry regions of the Western Hemisphere, with the one exception of *Rhipsalis baccata*, which also occurs spontaneously in Africa, Madagascar, and Sri Lanka. They are predominantly of cylindrical or globose

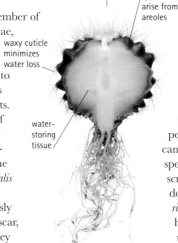

spines arise from areoles

waxy cuticle minimizes water loss

water-storing tissue

Cross-section, golden barrel cactus (Echinocactus grusonii)

habit and bear spines, but a few genera, such as *Schlumbergera*, have spineless leaflike stems while the genus *Pereskia* has barely succulent stems and large, "leafy" leaves. Apart from flower characters, they most are reliably distinguished from other succulent plants by cushionlike growths called areoles, from which branches, small, succulent leaves, spines and flowers emerge. Possible problems: fungus gnats, mealybug, red spider mite, scale insects, vine weevil; rots. (2) a class of dahlias. See *dahlia*.

Caesalpinia (for Andrea Cesalpini [1519–1603], Italian botanist, philosopher and physician to Pope Clement VIII, author of *De Plantis* [1583] and other botanical works). Leguminosae. Tropics and subtropics. 70 species, trees, shrubs and perennial herbs, some climbing, some thorny. The bipinnate leaves are composed of many small leaflets; they persist in warm, humid conditions, but usually fall in cool, dry winters. In spring, summer or year-round, the showy flowers are borne in terminal racemes and panicles and consist of five, rounded petals and a cluster of long, protruding stamens.

With the exception of *C. decapetala* var. *japonica*, these shrubs are tender. Killed to the ground by frost, they may regenerate if dry, mulched and sheltered, and might be attempted outdoors in very favorable locations in mild climates. Otherwise, grow under glass in large tubs or borders with a minimum winter temperature of 45°F (7°C). Water and feed generously in spring and summer; keep almost dry in winter. Outdoors, plant in well-drained soil in full sun and away from strong winds. *C. decapetala* needs to be trained against a wall or pergola; the other species can be used as freestanding specimens, wall shrubs, screens or stooled back. Cut down in spring, *C. pulcherrima* responds quickly in hot summers, with several, unbranched and free-flowering shoots from a single rootstock. Propagate by

seed, pre-soaked in warm water for 24 hours, or by softwood cuttings in a case with bottom heat.

C. decapetala MYSORE THORN; prickly climber or shrub to 10 ft (3 m) tall; flowers pale yellow, red-spotted; stamens slender, downy, pink or red; includes var. *japonica*, with 1½ in (4 cm)-wide, golden flowers and bright scarlet stamens; *C. gilliesii* (syn. *Poinciana gilliesii*); POINCIANA, BIRD-OF-PARADISE SHRUB; angular shrub or small tree to 13 ft (4 m); flowers bright yellow; stamens scarlet, 2¾ in (7 cm) long; *C. mexicana* MEXICAN BIRD-OF-PARADISE; thornless shrub or small tree to 33 ft (10 m); flowers in dense clusters 1¼ in (3 cm) wide, petals pale gold marked orange-red at the base; stamens yellow; *C. pulcherrima* BARBADOS PRIDE, FLAMBOYANT TREE, PARADISE FLOWER, PEACOCK FLOWER BARBADOS FLOWER FENCE; shrub/small tree to 33 × 33 ft (10 × 10 m); flowers 1½ in (4 cm) wide in apricot, orange and flame; stamens bright red, to 3 in (8 cm) long. Royal poinciana is *Delonix regia*.

caespitose, cespitose tufted, growing in small, dense clumps.

caisse de Versailles a large wooden container for a tender tree, for overwintering in an orangery and then moving outside in summer.

caked see *cap*.

calabrese see *broccoli*.

Caladium (Latinized form of the Malay name *kaladi*). Araceae. ANGEL'S WINGS, ELEPHANT'S-EAR. Tropical S America. 7 species, tuberous perennial herbs with large, slender-stalked leaves, often beautifully veined and patterned, and dull green, *Arum*-like inflorescences. Used in frost-free climates for year-round bedding, elsewhere for summer bedding and for display in a greenhouse and home. It is usually bought as a pot plant in full leaf and will remain in glory for six to eight months after which the foliage tends to die back. Store dormant tubers almost dry in their pots or sawdust at a minimum temperature of 55°F (13°C). Check for signs of decay; if necessary, dust with fungicide. Bring the tubers

C

into growth in early spring at 73°F (23°C), having repotted them into a porous but moisture-retentive soilless medium (that said, *Caladium* seems to thrive in wet and heavy soil in hot climates or hot seasons such as the New York summer). Grow in bright, indirect light with high humidity and a minimum temperature of 64°F (18°C). Water, syringe and feed frequently in warm weather. For summer bedding, place outdoors in early summer. Reduce water as the leaves begin to fade. Propagate prior to repotting by separation of small tubers or by cutting the parent tubers into sections (dust cut surfaces with a fungicide).

C. bicolor to 36 in (90 cm) tall with 8–20 in (20–50 cm)-long, heart- to arrow-shaped leaves of a soft, slightly quilted and chalky in texture, oriented downward on the petioles and variably spotted, veined, blotched, zoned or solidly stained white, rose pink or blood red on a lime or gray-green background; now incorporated in this species are *C. marmoratum*, with leaves marbled white, ivory and gray, and *C. picturatum*, with rather narrow, spotted leaves. The many hybrids between these former species were grouped under the names *C. × hortulanum* and *C. × candidum*, now also synonyms of *C. bicolor*. They range in height from 6 to 39 in (15 to 100 cm); in leaf size from 3 to 12 in (8 to 30 cm); in leaf shape from narrowly lance-shaped to broadly heart-shaped; and in color from almost pure white through cream and gray to pink and red to the deepest burgundy, and combinations thereof in washes, spots, veins, tints and suffusions.

Calamagrostis (from Greek *kalamos*, a reed, and *agrostis*, a kind of grass). Gramineae. REED GRASS. Temperate Northern Hemisphere. 250 species, clump-forming, perennial grasses with reedlike stems, slender leaves and silky flowers in plumelike panicles in summer. Grow in full sun or light shade in moist but well-drained soil. The flower heads can be used in dried-flower arrangements. Increase by division. *C. × acutiflora* (*C. arundinacea* × *C. epigejos*) FEATHER REED GRASS; erect to 6½ ft (2 m) with lax, arching foliage and soft, silvery to pearly pink or

purple-bronze panicles; 'Karl Foerster': tall erect, with upright, red-bronze to buff panicles; 'Overdam': to 3¼ ft (1 m), arching, leaves white-striped.

Calathea (from Greek *kalathos*, basket: the flowers are surrounded by bracts, as if in a basket). Marantaceae. Tropical America. Some 300 species, evergreen perennial herbs with long-stalked, ovate to oblong-lanceolate and often colorful leaves, mostly 8–14 in (20–35 cm) long. The flowers are small, usually white to cream with a pink to mauve tint, and carried among bracts on a spike or raceme. Provide a minimum temperature of 59°F (15°C) and light to deep shade in a humid, draft-free environment. Plant in a soilless mix high in bark, leaf mold and sand. Keep evenly moist, never wet, throughout the year. Increase by division.

C. crocata ETERNAL FLAME; Brazil; leaves dark green with a gray feathered pattern above, purple beneath; flowers orange-red in spikes with showy orange bracts; *C. ecuadoriana* RED ZEBRINA, TIGRINA; Ecuador; leaves dark green with midrib and veins pale lime to yellow above, purple-red beneath; flowers yellow-orange amid green bracts; *C. lancifolia* RATTLESNAKE PLANT; Brazil; leaves narrow, wavy, pale yellow-green with a dark midrib and margins and alternating, small and large, dark blotches along veins above, purple-tinted beneath; *C. lindeniana* Brazil, Peru; leaves dark green with olive, feathered zones along the midrib and on margins above, purple-tinted beneath; *C. makoyana* CATHEDRAL WINDOWS, PEACOCK PLANT, BRAIN PLANT; Brazil; leaves pale green, feathered cream with dark, oblong blotches along veins and a dark border above, purple beneath; *C. majestica* (syn. *C. ornata*); Brazil; leaves glossy green above, dull purple beneath; includes 'Albolineata', with fine white lines along lateral veins, 'Roscolineata', with fine pink lines along veins, and 'Sanderiana', with broader, glossy leaves, olive green with white and pink markings; *C. zebrina* (ZEBRA PLANT; Brazil; leaves deep velvety green with broad chartreuse stripes along lateral veins above, purple-tinted beneath; includes several cultivars with silver-gray markings.

calcarate furnished with a spur.

calcareous used to describe alkaline soil that contains either chalk or limestone.

Calceolaria (from Latin *calceolus*, a slipper, referring to the shape of the flower). Scrophulariaceae. SLIPPER FLOWER, SLIPPERWORT, POCKETBOOK FLOWER, POUCH FLOWER. C and S America. 300 species, annual, biennial and perennial herbs, subshrubs and shrubs, generally with hairy stems and leaves. The slipperlike flowers are usually borne in stalked cymes in spring and summer (winter if grown under glass). They consist of a rounded and inflated corolla with a short, rimlike upper lip and a larger, puffy and pouch-shaped lower lip.

The low-growing, alpine species need full sun, a cool, airy atmosphere and sharply draining acidic soil high in grit. Although frost-hardy, they are intolerant of wet, cold conditions and are usually short-lived outdoors unless planted in a sheltered rock garden niche or sink and given cloche protection in winter. Alternatively, grow in an alpine house or cold greenhouse. The larger perennial species (*C. integrifolia*, *C. pavonii*) require a fertile, nonalkaline medium in a cool greenhouse or conservatory with good light and ventilation; keep almost dry in winter. Sow seed of the showy garden hybrids (*C.* Fruticohybrida Group, *C.* Herbeohybrida Group) under glass in summer or spring and grow on with a minimum temperature of 50°F (10°C). For bedding and window box displays, plant out in late spring. Propagate *Calceolaria* by seed, basal cuttings or division.

C. arachnoidea Chile; rhizomatous, tufted perennial herb to 24 in (60 cm) tall, covered in silver down; flowers to ½ in (1 cm) in diameter, dull violet-purple, very rounded, clustered on slender stalks; *C. biflora* Chile, Argentina; perennial herb with low-lying rosettes of hairy leaves; flowers ¾ in (2 cm) in diameter, bright yellow spotted red within and carried two or more together on stalks to 8 in (20 cm) tall; *C. darwinii* S Patagonia, Tierra del Fuego; dwarf perennial herb with low-lying tufts of small, glossy leaves; flowers solitary to 1¼ in (3 cm) long and basically yellow-ocher, the upper lip short and hooded, the lower lip large, triangular and with a white band on its inner rim and stained and spotted ruby red; *C.* 'Walter Shrimpton' is a hybrid between this species and *C. fothergillii*, of greater vigor and with rather longer, saclike flowers in rich ocher, extensively spotted red-brown with a broad white band like a clerical collar; *C. fothergillii* Falkland Islands, Patagonia; dwarf perennial herb with low-lying leaf rosettes; flowers solitary, to 1½ in (3.5 cm) long sulfur yellow spotted or streaked ruby red below; *C.* Fruticohybrida Group a popular group of rather shrubby hybrids, usually grown under glass or treated as half-hardy annuals and differing from the next group in their smaller, less puffy flowers, which are usually carried in dense, stalked clusters; many cultivars and seed races are available, ranging in color from yellow to orange and bronzy red, often spotted or stained; *C.* Herbeohybrida Group (a group of popular hybrids grown under glass and often treated as annuals or biennials; they have a soft and bushy growth habit with broad leaves and large heads of showy, strongly inflated flowers in tones of pale yellow, gold, tangerine, scarlet ruby red, maroon and bronze, which are often spotted or stained in a darker shade and sometimes scented; *C. integrifolia* Chile; erect to sprawling perennial subshrub to 5 ft (1.5 m), covered in clammy hairs; flowers small, yellow, clustered in short, branched cymes; var. *viscosissima*: larger, with very sticky leaves; *C. pavonii* Ecuador, Peru; scandent, buff-hairy, perennial subshrub to 5 ft (1.5 m); leaf bases broadly winged and connate; flowers yellow sometimes marked purple-red in large cymes; *C. polyrhiza* Chile, Patagonia; prostrate perennial herb with small, rounded, hairy leaves, long-stalked flowers solitary, to 1¼ in (3 cm) long and yellow with purple spots; *C. tenella* Chile; creeping to mat-forming perennial herb; leaves small; flowers relatively large, rounded and open, golden yellow with a few orange-brown flecks, in short-stalked clusters.

calceolate slipper-shaped; resembling a round-toed shoe in form.

calcicole a plant that favors or tolerates very alkaline soil—for example, *Syringa*; also sometimes called a calciphile.

Calcifuge plants
Rhododendrons (here *R.* 'Berryrose') are the classic calcifuge, or lime-hating, plants; others include heaths and heathers and *Pieris* spp.

calcifuge a plant that will not grow normally in very alkaline soil—for example, *Rhododendron*; commonly called a lime-hater or sometimes a calciphobe.

calcium a macronutrient that is essential for plant growth. Calcium is found in, or applied to, soil mainly as chalk, limestone, magnesian limestone or gypsum. Its concentration in soil determines acidity or alkalinity, which is measured on the pH scale.

calcium carbonate the chemical constituent of chalk and limestone. See *lime*.

calcium hydroxide hydrated or slaked lime, a relatively expensive but quick-acting form of lime.

calcium nitrate an inorganic fertilizer combining calcium and ammonium nitrate (15.5% nitrogen). A nonacidifying source of nitrogen, it is recommended for the treatment of bitterpit of apples and pears.

calcium oxide quicklime, made by heating limestone. It is caustic and dangerous to handle. See *lime*.

Calendula (from Latin, *calendae*, the first day of each month—a reference to the long flowering period of these plants). Compositae. Mediterranean, Macaronesia. MARIGOLD. 20 species, annual and perennial herbs, often glandular and aromatic, with flat, wide flower heads with strap-shaped ray florets. Treated as a hardy annual, *Calendula* is used for bedding, borders and window boxes. Sow *in situ* in spring or fall in a sunny position in free-draining soil. For prolonged blooming, deadhead or sow successively.

C. officinalis ENGLISH MARIGOLD, POT MARIGOLD, RUDDLES, SCOTCH MARIGOLD; hardy, muskily scented annual or perennial of obscure origin, now widespread through cultivation, to 28 × 16 in (70 × 40 cm), with flower heads to 2¾ in (7 cm) wide in shades of orange and yellow, produced from late spring to fall; many seed races are available—dwarf races to 12 in (30 cm) include Bon Bon (early-flowering, vivid orange), Dwarf Gem and Fiesta; among the taller races to 24 in (60 cm) are the pompon-centered Kablouna and the quilled, "cactus-bloomed" Radio; color ranges from the bright yellows of Sun Glow and Lemon to the vivid orange Orange Prince and the red-tinted Indian Prince; larger-flowered seed races include the rich orange, 18 in (45 cm)-tall Mandarin Flower Hybrids and the mixed orange, yellow and apricot of Pacific Beauty Mixed and Art Shade Mixed; in Japan, the marigold has been developed as a cut flower, giving rise to tall, strong-stemmed and fully "double" selections like 'Early Nakayasu'; three old and dependable cultivars are 'Chrysantha', with 'double' bright gold flower heads, 'Prolifera', with proliferous flower heads, and 'Variegata', with leaves variegated yellow.

Calla (from Greek *kallos*, beauty). Araceae. Temperate regions. 1 species, *C. palustris* (BOG ARUM, WATER ARUM), a perennial, marginal to aquatic herb with creeping, green rhizomes and smooth, heart-shaped leaves to 3 in (8 cm) across. Minute, green flowers are carried in spring on a creamy, club-shaped spadix. This is loosely surrounded by a white spathe to 2½ in (6 cm) long. Decorative, red berries follow in late summer. Hardy to −30°F (−34°C). Plant in full sun at the muddy margins of ponds and lakes. Allow the rhizomes to creep toward the water. Propagate by division in early spring.

Calliandra (from Greek *kalos*, beautiful, and *aner*, man, a reference to the beautiful stamens). Leguminosae. POWDERPUFF TREE. Tropics and subtropics. 200 species, trees, shrubs and perennial herbs with bipinnate leaves and stalked, terminal and axillary flower heads. The corolla is small and scarcely distinguishable, but the stamens are many, colorful and slender, making, *en masse*, a powder-puff-like ball. The following species are evergreen and fall- to spring-flowering, although they may become at least semideciduous in arid seasons outdoors and may flower sporadically throughout the year under glass. Grow in full sun in a loamy medium with extra sand and grit. Provide a minimum winter temperature of 41°F (5°C). Water and syringe freely in summer. Keep rather dry in winter. Prune if necessary, after flowering. An excellent choice for indoor bonsai. Propagate from seed soaked in warm water for 24 hours then sown in a moist, sandy mix at 73°F (23°C).

C. eriophylla MOCK MESQUITE, MESQUITILLA, FAIRY DUSTER; California to Mexico; spreading shrub to 3¼ to 5 ft (1 × 1.5 m) with 1-in- (2.5-cm-) long leaves composed of many tiny leaflets; flower heads ¾–1½ in (2–3.5 cm) wide, with red to rosy pink or white stamens; *C. haematocephala* PINK POWDER PUFF; S America; flat-topped, spreading shrub or tree to 20 ft (6 m), usually less in cultivation; leaflets to 2¾ in (7 cm), emerging bronze-pink and hardening mid-green; flower heads 2½–3½ in (6–9 cm) wide, white at the base of the stamens deepening through pink to vivid red at their tips; *C. tweedii* TRINIDAD, MEXICAN or BRAZILIAN FLAMEBUSH; warm Americas; spreading, shrub to 6½ ft (2 m) tall with fine, ferny foliage; flower heads 2¾ in (7 cm) wide, with bright crimson stamens.

Callicarpa (from Greek *kalos*, beautiful, and *karpos*, fruit). Verbenaceae. Subtropics and tropics. 140 species, trees and shrubs, usually deciduous and covered with felty or scurfy hair. The leaves are oblong to elliptic-lanceolate and the flowers small and dull, borne in compact, axillary cymes. They are followed in late summer by clusters of brilliantly colored, beadlike berries; these last well into early winter. Hardy to 0°F (–18°C), they will usually resprout if cut down by hard frosts. Plant in full sun, away from strong winds, in fertile, well-drained soil, with ample moisture in spring and summer. Propagate by seed or short, heeled cuttings taken in early spring.

Callicarpa bodinieri var. giraldii 'Profusion'

C. americana southern N America, West Indies; much-branched shrub to 10 ft (3 m) tall with red-purple, hairy twigs; leaves coloring bronze, pink and flame in fall; fruit ¼ in (6 mm)-wide in shades of rose-pink, red-violet and blue-mauve—off-white in 'Lactea'; *C. bodinieri* var. *giraldii* BEAUTYBERRY; China; 10 ft (3 m)-tall shrub with slender, spreading branches clothed in tawny hair; leaves turning purple-red to amber in fall; fruit ¹⁄₁₆–¹⁄₈ in (2–3 mm)-wide, shining amethyst purple or deep mauve—abundant and violet in 'Profusion'.

Callisia (from Greek *kallos*, beauty). Commelinaceae. Subtropical and tropical America. 20 species, tender perennial and annual herbs (those listed here are perennial). Trailing and rooting, thinly succulent stems are clothed in slightly fleshy, ovate to lanceolate leaves. Small, white to pink and three-petalled flowers are produced throughout the year. *C. elegans* and *C. repens* are fine plants for baskets and hanging pots and should be treated as for tender *Tradescantia* species. The remaining two species prefer a gritty, loamy medium with full sun and cool, dry winters (minimum temperature 45°F/7°C). Propagate by detaching

rooted lengths of stem or plantlets formed on stolons; can also be increased by stem cuttings.

C. elegans stems to 12 in (30 cm) long; leaves loosely 2-ranked, 1–4 in (2.5–10 cm) long and dull green, finely striped silver-white above, purple-tinted beneath; *C. fragrans* bold rosette of 12 in (30 cm)-long, mid-green leaves—striped in the cultivar 'Melnickoff'—giving rise to leafy stolons bearing miniature plants; *C. navicularis* growth of two types—succulent, keel-shaped leaves to 1¼ in (3 cm) long overlapping in short, bulblike shoots, or more remotely disposed along creeping stolons, leaves smooth, mid-green above and striped or stained purple beneath; *C. repens* (syn. *Tradescantia* 'Little Jewel'; mat-forming trailer with dense, glossy, deep green, ovate leaves to 1 in (2.5 cm) long.

Callistemon (from Greek *kallos*, beauty, and *stemon*, stamen). Myrtaceae. Australia. BOTTLEBRUSH BUSH. 25 species, shrubs and small trees, evergreen with slender, arching branches and narrow leaves; these emerge pink and silky and harden leathery, smooth and dark green. Produced in summer, the flowers consist of bundles of long and spreading stamens. They are held flush with the branch on one- to two-year-old wood in a cylindrical arrangement—the whole resembling a bottlebrush. The following are hardy to 0°F (–18°C), or in favored locations to –10°F (–23°C). *C. sieberi* will thrive in most regions to –10°F (–23°C). Plant in full sun in fast-draining soil, ideally with the shelter of a south-facing wall. Avoid pruning if possible. Propagate by semiripe cuttings in summer.

C. citrinus CRIMSON BOTTLEBRUSH; medium shrub to small tree; leaves lemon-scented if crushed; flowers bright crimson with dark anthers; 'Splendens': dense spikes of carmine flowers; *C. linearis* NARROW-LEAVED BOTTLEBRUSH; medium-sized shrub; leaves narrow; flowers dull red with gold anthers; *C. pallidus* LEMON BOTTLEBRUSH; medium to tall shrub; flowers cream to yellow-green with yellow anthers; *C. rigidus* STIFF BOTTLEBRUSH; small- to medium-sized shrub with hard-edged leaves; flowers deep red;

C. salignus PINK TIPS, WILLOW BOTTLE-BRUSH, WHITE BOTTLEBRUSH; tall shrub to medium-sized tree with papery white bark and narrow leaves; flowers green-white, pink, red or rosy mauve; *C. sieberi* ALPINE BOTTLEBRUSH; erect to spreading, tall to dwarf shrub, with dense, short, pointed leaves; flowers cream to yellow; *C. speciosus* ALBANY BOTTLEBRUSH; erect, medium-sized shrub with prominently veined, rigid and spreading leaves; flowers deep red or white with golden anthers; *C. subulatus* arching shrub to 5 ft (1.5 m) with hard-pointed, narrow leaves; flowers crimson; *C. viminalis* WEEPING BOTTLE-BRUSH; small shrub or tree with cascading branches; flowers bright red; ' Red Cascade': strongly weeping, flowers rose-red.

Callistephus (from Greek *kallos*, beauty and *stephos*, crown, referring to the fruit appendages). Compositae. China. 1 species, *C. chinensis* (CHINA ASTER), an erect and bushy annual herb to 32 in (80 cm) tall with coarsely toothed, ovate leaves to 3 in (8 cm) long. Produced in summer and fall, the flower heads resemble large daisies or chrysanthemums. To 4¾ in (12 cm) across, they are typically white to pale mauve or violet with a central disk of yellow. Seed races range in flower form from single to double, anemone-centered to quilled, in color from white to cream, palest pink, flamingo pink, deep rose, magenta, apricot, peach, salmon, scarlet, crimson, lilac and deep purple, and in habit from dwarf and compact to tall and long-stalked. Sow seed under glass in early spring or outdoors in late spring. Plant out after the last frosts in full sun in well-drained, fertile soil. Stake taller cultivars. Deadhead regularly.

Calluna (from Greek *kallunein*, to beautify, referring to its use as a brush or broom). Ericaceae. N America, Azores, N and W Europe to Siberia. 1 species, *C. vulgaris* LING, SCOTS HEATHER, a low and bushy evergreen shrub to 24 in (60 cm) tall with many, tiny, scalelike leaves overlapping on the narrow, upright branches. Produced in summer and fall, the flowers are shortly tubular to bell-shaped, to ¼ in (0.5 cm) long and borne at the leaf axils, forming long and slender racemes on the branch tips. They differ from the flowers of *Erica* in the calyx, which is typically pink and virtually conceals the corolla. This plant is immensely variable, with over a thousand cultivars recorded. These cultivars range in height and habit from low and creeping, to compact and domed to tall and cypresslike, in flower color from pure white to pale pink, rose, lilac-pink, magenta, salmon, crimson and mixtures thereof. Many are excellent foliage plants, coloring especially well in winter and early spring, with leaves ranging through deep emerald green to yellow, gold, orange, flame, bronze, rusty red and purple-red. Fully hardy. Plant in sandy, well-drained, acidic soil in full sun. Further requirements as for hardy *Erica* species.

Callused pruning wound
Callus tissue forms across wounds to prevent entry by harmful pathogens. Careful pruning helps this process occur as quickly as possible.

callus an abnormal or isolated thickening of tissue, either produced in response to wounding or abscission or as a surface feature of leaves and perianth segments. It is important in propagation by cuttings and in one method of tissue culture (see *micropropagation*). Callus tissue may also occur as protuberances on the lips of many orchid flowers.

Calocedrus (from Greek *kalos*, beautiful, and *kedros*, cedar). Cupressaceae. Western N America, E Asia. 3 species, large evergreen, coniferous trees with flattened sprays of small, scalelike leaves and rounded to oblong, red-brown cones. Fully hardy. Plant in any but the wettest and heaviest soils in full sun. Water young plants in dry climates. Once established, this a remarkably drought-tolerant conifer. It will also survive harsh winds and poor soil. Propagate as for *Chamaecyparis*. The genus is Armillaria-resistant.

C. decurrens (syn. *Libocedrus decurrens*; INCENSE CEDAR); western N America; broadly conical to pyramidal tree to 150 ft (45 m) tall with deeply fissured red-brown bark and fans of rich green foliage; cones 1 in (2.5 cm) long, oblong, carried erect on pendulous shoots; size and habit vary according to climate—dense and fastigiate in warm, moderately dry summers and cool or cold winters, dense and broadly ovoid in cool, wet summers and mild winters, broadly conic and open with level branches in cold wet winters and hot, dry summers; 'Aureovariegata': medium-sized, foliage spattered with yellow-cream; 'Compacta': habit globose to columnar, densely branched; 'Depressa': dense, globose, dwarf, tinted bronze in winter; 'Glauca': foliage glaucous, tinted blue-gray; 'Intricata': dwarf, compact, with tortuous branches, foliage tinted brown in winter; 'Riet': globose, dwarf, seldom exceeding 30 in (75 cm).

Calochortus (from Greek *kalos*, beautiful, and *chortos*, grass, referring to the grassy leaves). Liliaceae (Calochortaceae). N America to Guatemala (those listed here are from the SW US, principally California). 60 species, bulbous perennial herbs with grassy leaves and erect, branched stems bearing showy flowers in spring and summer. They fall into three groups: GLOBE TULIPS or FAIRY LANTERNS with several, nodding, globose to campanulate flowers; STAR TULIPS, with erect, campanulate to cup-shaped flowers, usually with the petal margins rolled outward and (in *C. tolmiei*) covered in hairs; and MARIPOSA LILIES, with large, cup-shaped flowers on tall stems. *Calochortus* flowers consist of three, narrow sepals and three broad petals with a semicircular zone in their lower half that may be differently colored, hairy and marked with a dark, glandular patch.

Although happiest above 20°F (−7°C), *Calochortus* may survive outdoors in favored locations to 0°F (−18°C). Plant in deep, freely draining, sandy soil in a sheltered position in full sun. Keep just damp in fall and winter, moist in late winter and spring. After flowering, keep dry until midfall, allowing the foliage to wither and the soil to bake. In many places, these conditions are more easily achieved in a raised bed with covers, or in pots and pans in an alpine house or bulb frame. Leave the bulbs in the ground or in their containers during dormancy. Propagate by ripe seed in a cool greenhouse or frame, by offsets when dormant, or from bulbils which sometimes form in the leaf axils.

C. albus FAIRY LANTERN, WHITE GLOBE LILY; 8–32 in (20–80 cm); flowers to 2½ in (6 cm) in diameter, petals broad, white, bearded with a deep red-brown spot; *C. amabilis* GOLDEN FAIRY LANTERN; 4–12 in (10–30 cm); flowers to 2 in (5 cm) in diameter, petals golden yellow, fringed, bearded; *C. amoenus* PURPLE GLOBE TULIP; like a shorter *C. albus*, with nodding, deep rose or mauve flowers; *C. barbatus* (to 24 in (60 cm); flowers nodding, campanulate, to 2 in (5 cm) in diameter, petals yellow, often tinted rose or mauve, bearded and fringed; *C. clavatus* (20–39 in (50–100 cm); flowers erect, cup-shaped, 3–4 in (8–10 cm) in diameter, bright yellow, lower half of petals covered in hairs and bounded by a dark brown arc; *C. kennedyi* to 20 in (50 cm); flowers campanulate, erect, 2–4 in (5–10 cm) in diameter, petals rich orange to vermilion with a glossy, black gland and hairs toward the base; *C. luteus* (similar to *C. venustus* with erect, campanulate dark yellow flowers with dark brown markings and hairs toward base of petals; *C. splendens* LILAC MARIPOSA; 8–24 in (20–60 cm); flowers erect, campanulate, 2–4 in (5–10 cm) in diameter, petals pale pink with fine teeth and hairs; *C. superbus* (similar to *C. venustus*, flowers campanulate, petals white, cream or yellow, streaked purple at base usually with a brown or maroon spot surrounded with yellow; *C. tolmiei* (syn. *C. maweanus*; CAT'S EARS, PUSSY EARS); 2–12 in (5–30 cm); flowers open-campanulate, erect or spreading, ¾–2 in (2–5 cm) in diameter, white or cream often tinged rose or purple, petals hairy and fringed; *C. uniflorus* (syn. *C. lilacinus*); STAR TULIP; stem very short, flowers 1¼–2½ in (3–6 cm) in diameter, petals pale lilac, sometimes toothed

and bearded; *C. venustus* WHITE MARIPOSA TULIP; 8–24 in (20–60 cm); flowers 2–4 in (5–10 cm) in diameter, white to yellow or purple or dark red, petals bearded below, with a dark red-brown spot; *C. vestae* similar to *C. venustus*, petals white to purple-tinged streaked with red to purple near base and each with a central brown spot edged with yellow; *C. weedii* 12–24 in (30–60 cm); flowers erect, campanulate, petals to 1¼ in (3 cm), deep yellow with purple dots or margins, bearded and fringed.

Calomeria (from Greek, *kalos*, beautiful, and *meris*, part, in reference to the capitula). Compositae. Africa, Madagascar, Australia. 14 species, annual to perennial herbs with small, buttonlike flower heads in large, much-branched panicles in summer. A spectacular biennial grown in a cool greenhouse (minimum temperature 45°F/7°C) or in subtropical bedding schemes. Sow seed in summer under glass. Grow on in individual pots in a fertile, loam-based mix in a well-ventilated, sunny greenhouse. Water moderately when in growth, scarcely at all in winter. Pot on to flower in large containers, or plant outdoors in a warm and sunny position in late spring. Support with canes. *C. amaranthoides* (syn. *Humea elegans*); INCENSE PLANT, PLUME BUSH; Australia; robust and intensely aromatic biennial or perennial to 6½ ft (2 m) or taller; flower heads small, red-brown to pink, massed on the cascading branches of a broad panicle.

Calothamnus (from Greek *kalos*, beautiful, and *thamnos*, bush or shrub). Myrtaceae. Western Australia. ONE-SIDED BOTTLE BRUSH. 25 species, small to large evergreen shrubs with wand-like branches clothed in papery bark and rigid, narrow, terete or flat leaves. The flowers grow directly from the old wood and below the new growth, forming a stemless, crowded spike or cluster composed of long, brilliantly colored stamens, the whole resembling a one-sided *Callistemon* inflorescence. The following species should be cultivated as for *Callistemon* but kept rather dry and frost-free in winter.

C. quadrifidus COMMON NET BUSH, 6½–10 ft (2–3 m), upright to spreading; flower spikes to 8 in (20 cm) long,

stamens to 1 in (2.5 cm), of equal length, deep red with golden anthers; *C. sanguineus* BLOOD RED NET BUSH; much-branched, dwarf to medium-sized shrub; inflorescence to 4 in (10 cm), stamens to 1 in (2.5 cm), not equal, deep red with golden anthers; *C. validus* BARRENS CLAW FLOWER; erect, rounded, medium-sized shrub (i.e. to 6½ ft (2 m); inflorescence to 2 in (5 cm) long, stamens to 1½ in (4 cm) long, of equal length, rich red with golden anthers; *C. villosus* SILKY NET BUSH; downy, upright to spreading, small to medium-sized shrub; branches hairy; inflorescence to 4 in (10 cm), stamens equal, bright red with golden anthers.

Caltha (name of a yellow flower, used by Virgil and Pliny). Ranunculaceae. Temperate regions. 10 species, perennial herbs with long-stalked, rounded to reniform leaves and cymes of buttercup-like flowers composed of broad, petal-like sepals in yellow or white. Fully hardy and spring flowering, they will grow in sun or part shade in moist or saturated soil (neutral to acidic for *C. leptosepala*). They thrive at the margins of ponds, streams and lakes and may even be partially submerged. The smaller cultivars are suitable for damp positions in the rock garden. Propagate by division in spring, or from fresh seed sown in late summer in a cold frame.

C. leptosepala N America; to 12 in (30 cm) tall; flowers white with a golden boss of stamens; *C. palustris* KINGCUP, MARSH MARIGOLD, MEADOW BRIGHT; northern temperate regions; variable, from 4–32 in (10–80 cm) tall, low and compact to tall and rangy; flowers rich golden yellow sepals; includes creeping, alpine and very large forms; 'Florepleno' has fully double flowers.

Calycanthus (from Greek *kalyx*, calyx and *anthos*, flower—the sepals and petals are alike). Calycanthaceae. China, US. ALLSPICE, SPICE BUSH. 6 species, spicily aromatic, deciduous shrubs, to 12 ft (4 m) tall, with dull to glossy dark green, elliptic to obovate leaves and solitary flowers in summer. These are composed of numerous, similar sepals and petals, oblong to oblanceolate and spreading. Fully hardy, they will thrive in most fertile, moist, but well-drained soils in sun or part shade.

Increase by seed harvested from the distinctive, goblet-shaped capsules in fall, or by softwood cuttings in summer.

C. fertilis SE US; leaves more or less smooth beneath; flowers to 2 in (5 cm) in diameter, purple-red to maroon, slightly fragrant; includes the dwarf 'Nanus', and 'Purpureus', with leaves tinted purple beneath; *C. floridus* (syn. *C. sterilis*); CAROLINA ALLSPICE, STRAWBERRY SHRUB; SE US; leaves hairy beneath; flowers to 2 in (5 cm) in diameter, dark maroon, strawberry-scented; *C. occidentalis* CALIFORNIA ALLSPICE, SPICE BUSH; distinguished from *C. fertilis* by the summer buds that are concealed by petiole bases; flowers to 2¾ in (7 cm) in diameter, maroon fading to yellow, fragrant.

calyptra a hood or caplike structure ending a circumscissile calyx or pyxis.

calyx a collective term for the sepals, (separate or united) that form the outer whorl of the perianth or floral envelope.

sepals that protected bud remain once petals drop

Calyx

Camassia (from *quamash*, so-named by Native Americans for whom the bulbs of *C. quamash* were an important foodstuff). Liliaceae (Hyacinthaceae). Americas (those listed here are from western N America). QUAMASH, CAMASS, CAMOSH. 6 species, deciduous, bulbous perennial herbs with narrow leaves and, in late spring and early summer, tall spikes of white, blue or violet, starlike flowers with six, linear to oblong tepals. Plant in deep, moisture-retentive and fertile soil in full sun or light shade. Where temperatures fall below 5°F (−15°C) for long periods, mulch the crowns thickly. Propagate by seed, by offsets or by division of established clumps in fall or early spring.

C. cusickii raceme dense, standing to 3¼ ft (1 m); flowers 2 in (5 cm) wide, pale blue, larger and deep blue in the

cultivar 'Zwanenburg'; *C. leichtlinii* flowers 1½–3 in (4–8 cm) across, creamy white, blue or violet, carried on a raceme to 48 in (120 cm) tall; in this species, the tepals always twist together as they wither: this never happens in *C. cusickii* and only sometimes in *C. quamash*; includes 'Plena' and 'Semiplena', with creamy white flowers, double and semidouble respectively; subsp. *suksdorfii* 'Blauwe Donau', with dark blue flowers, and subsp. *suksdorfii* 'Electra', with rich blue flowers to 4 in (10 cm) across; *C. quamash* (syn. *C. esculenta*); flowers ¾–2¾ in (2–7 cm) wide, white to pale violet or blue, carried loosely on racemes to 24 in (60 cm) tall; includes 'Orion', with a denser raceme and flowers that are deep purple in bud, opening dark, steely blue.

cambium secondary or inner meristem that increases the girth of a plant stem or root by adding vascular tissue.

Camellia (for Georg Kamel [Camellus] [1661–1706], Moravian Jesuit who traveled in Asia and wrote a history of the plants of Luzon published in 1704 by John Ray). Theaceae. Asia. About 250 species, evergreen shrubs or trees with elliptic to lanceolate, tough and shiny leaves. The flowers are solitary or clustered, bowl-shaped and composed of 5–12, broad, silky petals and a central boss of golden stamens. Camellias need cool winters and many will tolerate moderate frosts but they must have good drainage, plenty of organic matter in the soil, and a pH between 5 and 7. *C. japonica* prefers the more acidic end of this range, most other species nearer to neutral. They need warmth and some sunlight in late summer to form flower buds which open during the following fall, winter or spring. In cold climates, the flowers and young growth may be damaged by cold winds and late frosts. Partial shade tempers late frosts and hot sun; this is especially important for young plants. If their roots are cool, established bushes of many cultivars of *C. japonica* and most of *C. reticulata* and *C. sasanqua* will flourish in full sun in all but very hot climates. *C. japonica* is the hardiest species. Damage can occur in some forms of *C. japonica* at 9°F (−13°C). At a temperature of −8°F

(−22°C), considerable damage can be expected to established plants; smaller ones are liable to "bark-split" and can be cut to the ground; such plants should be pruned back to just above ground level; most will regrow. If severe frost persists, and especially if it is accompanied by strong winds, even large plants will be killed. As the term "camellia house" would suggest, most will thrive in an unheated glasshouse, given a cool root-run, excellent ventilation and protection from scorching sun. Free drainage is very important. Where soil is impermeable or very alkaline, raised beds can be made of slightly acidic sand, sandy potting mix or light topsoil, topped up with a moderately acidic mulch. If necessary, prune in spring after flowering and before growth starts. Neglected large plants can be rejuvenated by hard pruning, although a season's flowering will be lost. Increase by semiripe cuttings of the current season's growth. Insert them into a moist, fine mix under mist, glass or polyethylene, after being wounded and dipped into a hormone rooting powder. Some cultivars, particularly those of *C. reticulata*, dislike root disturbance and are best rooted directly into small individual pots. Side or cleft grafting is also used for these and especially for promising new cultivars. Most new cultivars are raised from seed. Fresh seed germinates easily, especially with bottom heat.

Camellias are affected by a number of pests. Scale insects are often the most important and the sooty mold they engender is a serious disfigurement. Diseases include the soilborne *Phytophthora cinnamomi*. Plants grafted onto *C. sasanqua* are virtually immune. Camellia dieback, *Glomerella cingulata*, is chiefly a problem with *C. sasanqua* and *C. × williamsii* in very acidic soil. In areas where dieback is endemic, spray after pruning and treat cuttings and grafts before use by soaking in a fungicidal solution. Widespread in the Far East and North America, flower blight, *Ciborinia camelliae*, is spread by affected flowers. The recommended treatment is to remove lower branches, clear all vegetation beneath the bushes, apply a dry mulch and spray with fungicide.

See table overleaf.

CAMELLIA

Name	Distribution	Habit	Leaves	Flowers	Flowering time
C. chrysantha	S China	open shrub or tree to 16½ ft (5 m)	4–6¾ in (10–17 cm), oblong-lanceolate, acuminate, dark green, tough	cup-shaped, single; petals ¾–2 in (2–5 cm), 9–11, pure yellow	spring
C. cuspidata	W China	bushy shrub, erect to 10 ft (3 m)	2–3 in (5–7.5 cm), elliptic to lanceolate, acuminate to caudate, serrulate, bronze at first, later dark, glossy green	cup-shaped, single; petals 6–7, to 1¼ in (3 cm), white	early spring
C. granthamiana	Hong Kong	open shrub to 10 ft (3 m)	to 4 in (10 cm), elliptic to oblong-elliptic, bluntly acuminate, bluntly toothed, glossy deep green with impressed veins	fragrant, saucer-shaped, single; petals 8, to 2¾ in (7 cm), white, broad and cleft at tips	late fall
C. hiemalis (*C. japonica* × *C. sasanqua*)		erect, bushy shrub or tree to 10 ft (3 m)	2½–3½ in (6–9 cm), oblong-lanceolate, serrulate	fragrant, cup-shaped, semidouble; petals 7, to 1½ in (3.5 cm), white, pink or red	late fall to winter
C. honkongensis	Hong Kong	bushy shrub or tree to 33 ft (10 m)	to 4¾ in (12 cm), oblong-elliptic, tip shortly tapered, iridescent bronze at first, hardening dark, glossy green	cup-shaped, single; petals 6–7, 1¼ in (3 cm), broad and blunt or cleft, deep crimson with velvety undersides	late spring
C. japonica *C. hozanensis*	Japan	shrub or small tree to 33 ft (10 m), usually less in gardens	2–4 in (5–10 cm), broadly elliptic to elliptic-oblong, apex briefly acuminate, finely toothed, rigid and glossy dark green	saucer-shaped, single to double; petals typically 5–6, to 1½ in (4 cm), red, broad and rounded to cleft	late winter to early spring

Comments: The common camellia of gardens, with over 2000 cultivars varying greatly in habit, hardiness, leaf shape and color. The flowers range in type from formal to semidoubles, peony-, rose- and anemone-forms, and in color from pure white to pale pink, deep rose, crimson and velvety scarlet, including bicolors, striped and picotee forms. The stamens are typically golden and showy, but may be replaced to varying degrees by petaloid growths. The Higo Japonicas are an ancient group of cultivars developed in Japan and characterized by large and single, flat flowers with bosses of golden anthers or petaloids.

Name	Distribution	Habit	Leaves	Flowers	Flowering time
C. × maliflora (parentage obscure)		erect, bushy and densely leafy shrub to 8 ft (2.5 m)	1½–2 in (3.5–5 cm), oblong-elliptic to broadly lanceolate, apex bluntly acute to acuminate, finely toothed, thin-textured, mid-green	dish to cup-shaped, semidouble; petals and petaloids numerous, to ¾ in (2 cm) across, blush rose, often white at center with deeper rose margins	spring
C. oleifera	China, Indochina	bushy shrub or small tree to 23 ft (7 m)	1½–3½ in (4–9 cm), elliptic to oblong-acuminate, apex acute or acuminate, finely toothed, dark green	fragrant, cup-shaped, single; petals 5–7, to 1½ in (3.5 cm), obovate with rounded, cleft tips, white, sometimes flushed pink	early spring

Comments: FORTUNE'S YELLOW CAMELLIA is the cultivar 'Jaune', with white petals and a dense boss of yellow petaloids.

C. japonica 'Alexander Hunter'

C. reticulata 'Miss Tulare'

C. saluenensis

CAMELLIA

Name	Distribution	Habit	Leaves	Flowers	Flowering time
C. reticulata	China	loose-branched shrub or tree to 50 ft (15 m)	3–4³⁄₄ in (8–12 cm), broadly elliptic to oblong-elliptic, apex acute to shortly acuminate, finely toothed, tough, dark green	saucer-shaped, single; petals 5–6, to 2 in (5 cm), broad and often cleft, crimson to rose pink or white (in the typical plant, now known as 'Captain Rawes', the flowers were semidouble, very large and carmine)	spring

Comments: Over 400 cultivars and hybrids, ranging in flower form from cupped to bowl-shaped, single to double, some with wavy petals and petaloids. Colors from white to pale rose, deep pink, crimson and dark cherry red.

Name	Distribution	Habit	Leaves	Flowers	Flowering time
C. rosiflora	China	spreading shrub to 3¹⁄₄ ft (1 m)	1¹⁄₂–3 in (4–8 cm), elliptic, bluntly acuminate, finely toothed, dark green	saucer-shaped, single; petals 6–9, to ³⁄₄ in (1.8 cm), sometimes notched, pale rose	spring
C. saluenensis	W China	bushy shrub to 16¹⁄₂ ft (5 m)	1¹⁄₄–2¹⁄₂ in (3–6 cm), oblong-elliptic, apex acute to blunt, finely toothed, glossy dark green with conspicuous veins	cup-shaped, single; petals 6–7, to 1¹⁄₄ in (3 cm), broadly oval, notched, shell pink to deep rose, or white	early spring

Comments: Includes cultivars with semidouble and rosebudlike flowers, some with ruffled or irregular petals, in shades of white and pale pink tinted or veined with darker rose, also solid pale pink and coral.

Name	Distribution	Habit	Leaves	Flowers	Flowering time
C. sasanqua	Japan	erect, bushy shrub or small tree to 16¹⁄₂ ft (5 m)	1¹⁄₄–3 in (3–8 cm), elliptic to oblong, acute to cuspidate, finely toothed, bright glossy green	fragrant, dish- to cup-shaped, single to semidouble; petals 6–8, to 1¹⁄₂ in (3.5 cm), rounded to notched, white to rose	fall

Comments: Many cultivars are available including plants with a compact and densely bushy habit and handsome foliage, especially when newly emerged. The flowers range from small to large, tightly cupped to spreading, single to double, in tones of white, pink, salmon, cerise and red, often with one of these colors tinting, edging or overlaying a paler background.

Name	Distribution	Habit	Leaves	Flowers	Flowering time
C. tsaii	Burma, N Vietnam, W China	shrub to 10 ft (3 m)	2¹⁄₂–3¹⁄₂ in (6–9 cm), oblong-lanceolate, apex acuminate or caudate, finely toothed and somewhat undulate, dark glossy green, bronze-tinted with age	cup-shaped, single; petals 5, ³⁄₄ in (2 cm), broad, entire to cleft, white	spring
C. × *vernalis* (*C. japonica* × *C. sasanqua*)		erect shrub to 10 ft (3 m)	1¹⁄₂–3 in (3.5–7.5 cm), elliptic-oblanceolate, apex bluntly tapered, finely toothed, bright, glossy green	fragrant, dish- to cup-shaped, single to semidouble, white sometimes suffused pink or solid rose to red	late winter
C. × *williamsii* (*C. saluenensis* × *C. japonica*)		erect to spreading shrub to 13 ft (4 m)	2³⁄₄–4 in (7–10 cm), elliptic to oblong-lanceolate, shallowly and finely toothed, bright, shining green	cup-shaped, single, 2 in–4³⁄₄ in (5–12 cm) diam., white flushed rose or pale rose with deeper centers	early spring

Comments: Many cultivars are available, including singles, semidoubles and doubles, anemone- and peony-forms, in shades of white, pink, rose and red, sometimes tinted with a deeper shade. 'Golden Spangles' has deep pink flowers and yellow-green-variegated leaves.

C. sasanqua 'Narumigata'

C. tsaii

C. × *williamsii* 'Anticipation'

C

Campanula (diminutive form of the Latin *campana*, a bell, alluding to the shape of the flower). Campanulaceae. BELLFLOWER. Temperate N Hemisphere. Some 300 species, annual, biennial or perennial herbs varying greatly in habit and size. The flowers are typically bell-shaped and produced in spring and summer. With very few exceptions, *C. isophylla*, *C. pyramidalis* and *C. vidalii* among them, most are reliably hardy to between 5 and –4°F (–15 and –20°C), although several alpine species dislike a combination of winter cold and wet. The larger perennials are invaluable in the herbaceous and mixed border. These include lower-growing species for the foreground of borders, such as *C. carpatica* and the slightly taller and invasive *C. glomerata*. *C. persicifolia*, reaching almost 3¼ ft (1 m) in height, is especially elegant. The clump-forming, deeply rooting *C. latifolia*, and the undemanding *C. lactiflora* are among the tallest hardy species. They may need staking in exposed positions, but otherwise need only moderately fertile and well-drained soil in sun or light shade. Many of the long-stemmed perennials make beautiful cut flowers. Magnificent but slightly frost-tender, *C. pyramidalis* is more safely grown in a cool greenhouse or conservatory in cool temperate regions, and may be moved out of doors for the summer months. This species, *C. isophylla* and *C. vidalii* need a moist but freely draining, medium-fertility, loam-based potting mix, bright indirect light and good ventilation with a winter minimum of 45°F (7°C). *C. medium* is a biennial, usually sown in summer for early summer bloom in the following season; plants are overwintered *in situ* or lifted and overwintered in a cool greenhouse. Alternatively, seed sown under glass in late winter or early spring will flower in its first year.

Many of the smaller species suit rock gardens, troughs and dry stone walls. Most make few demands other than gritty, well-drained, moisture-retentive, neutral or limy soil, in sun or light shade. *C. morettiana* is suitable for tufa rock plantings and deserves protected cultivation in an alpine house. Other delicate species requiring protection from winter wet include *C. betulifolia*, *C. raineri* and *C. zoysii*. These need a lean and gritty alpine mix with plentiful water in spring and summer, and to be kept dry but not arid in winter. Propagate biennials by seed, perennials by seed, division and basal cuttings; smaller alpines can also be propagated by the removal of rooted offsets. (*See table opposite.*)

campanulate of a corolla; bell-shaped; a broad tube terminating in a flared limb or lobes.

Campsis (from Greek *kampsis*, bending: the stamens are curved). Bignoniaceae. E Asia, N America. TRUMPET CREEPER, TRUMPET VINE. 2 species, deciduous vines clinging by means of aerial roots. The leaves are pinnate with saw-toothed, ovate to lanceolate leaflets. Borne in summer in terminal cymes or panicles, the flowers are large and funnel-shaped with five short, spreading lobes. Plant in full sun or light shade in a warm, sheltered position in medium- to high-fertility, loam-based soil with plentiful water in spring and summer. *C. grandiflora* is hardy to 14°F (–10°C), *C. radicans* to –4°F (–20°C). Hardiness is improved in places where summers are long and hot enough to ripen new wood fully. Train on walls, fences, trellis and trees. Propagate *Campsis* by simple layering or by semiripe to hardwood cuttings in a cold frame in fall.

C. grandiflora (syn. *C. chinensis*); China, Japan; to 20 ft (6 m) tall with few or no aerial roots; flowers to 2 × 2½ in (5 × 6 cm), orange outside and deep yellow inside; includes the hardier 'Thunbergii', with orange flowers produced later in the season; *C. radicans* SE US; differs from the last species in its abundant aerial roots and larger flowers, pale orange with a yellow interior and flame to scarlet lobes; includes f.*flava*, with large flowers of a solid rich yellow, 'Praecox', with scarlet flowers, and 'Speciosa', shrubby and weakly climbing, with small, flaming orange flowers; *C.* × *tagliabuana* (hybrid offspring of *C. grandiflora* and *C. radicans*); the best-known is 'Madame Galen', with deep apricot to salmon flowers to 3 in (8 cm) across and dark green foliage.

camptodromous describing venation of a leaf in which the secondary veins curve toward the margin without forming loops.

canal a narrow, rectilinear stretch of water. Canals are a feature of western and Mogul formal gardens and are often associated with fountains.

canaliculate channeled with a long, concave groove, like a gutter.

Canarina (from the habitat of *C. canariensis*). Campanulaceae. Canary Islands, tropical E Africa. 3 species, fleshy-rooted, scrambling, perennial herbs differing from *Campanula* in their 6-parted flowers and berrylike fruit. Provide a minimum temperature of 45°F (7°C), full sun and an airy atmosphere. Water moderately during the growing and flowering period (late fall to midspring) and provide support. Keep just dry during summer dormancy and remove faded growth. Increase by seed, division or basal cuttings. *C. canariensis* (syn. *C. campanula*); CANARY BELLFLOWER; to 5 ft (1.5 m); leaves hastate, serrate to sinuate; flowers large, pendulous, waxy, orange-yellow striped blood red to maroon, bell-shaped, with an upturned rim.

candelabriform of branching patterns and stellate hairs; candelabra-like, with tiered whorls or ranks of radiating or divergent branches.

cane the slender stem of a clump-forming perennial, produced annually and usually completing its development within a year or two. Canes are typically rather hard and jointed and may be hollow and silica-rich as in bamboos, woody as in *Rubus*, or fleshy as in *Dendrobium*.

cane fruit a collective term for raspberry, blackberry and hybrid berries, cf. *bush fruit*.

canescent hoary, or becoming so; densely covered with short, gray-white pubescence.

cane spot (*Elsinoe veneta*) a fungus causing spotting of the main stems, leaves and flower stalks of cane fruits, especially in wet seasons. The spots are

CAMPANULA

Name	Distribution	Habit	Leaves	Flowers
C. alliariifolia	Caucasus, Asia Minor	hairy, erect perennial to 28 in (70 cm)	to 3 in (8 cm), cordate, hairy	campanulate, blue or white with bearded lobes, nodding in erect racemes
C. barbata BEARDED BELL-FLOWER	Norway, Alps	tufted, short-lived perennial or biennial to 20 in (50 cm)	lanceolate to strap-shaped, hairy	campanulate with ciliate lobes, lavender to white, nodding in one-sided racemes
C. betulifolia	Armenia	perennial with erect, then arching, purple-tinted stems to 12 in (30 cm)	ovate to lanceolate, toothed	tubular-campanulate, erect to nodding, white to pink with a deep pink flush on the exterior
C. carpatica CARPATHIAN BELLFLOWER	Carpathian Mountains	clump-forming perennial to 16 in (40 cm)	heart-shaped to ovate, crenate	broadly campanulate, blue or white, large, erect, solitary and long-stalked

Comments: Includes cultivars with flowers in shades of white, pearl, lilac, lavender and blue.

Name	Distribution	Habit	Leaves	Flowers
C. cochleariifolia *C. pusilla* FAIRIES' THIMBLES	Europe	tufted and creeping dwarf perennial	small, broadly heart-shaped to ovate, toothed	campanulate, solitary, nodding, blue to pearl or white

Comments: Includes cultivars ranging in flower color from pale to deep blue, silver-blue to pure white, some double.

Name	Distribution	Habit	Leaves	Flowers
C. elatines ADRIATIC BELLFLOWER	Adriatic Coast	tufted, compact perennial to 6 in (15 cm)	rounded to heart-shaped, finely toothed	campanulate to rotate and starry, with deflexed lobes, blue or white in loose spikes or panicles
C. garganica	Italy	close to *C. elatines*	ovate to cordate	star- to bell-shaped, in shades of lavender blue

Comments: Includes cultivars with white, pale lilac, lavender and deep mauve blue flowers; 'Dickson's Gold' has golden leaves and blue, star-shaped flowers; 'W.H. Paine' has erect, starry flowers, strong lavender blue with white centers.

Name	Distribution	Habit	Leaves	Flowers
C. glomerata CLUSTERED BELLFLOWER	Europe, Temperate Asia	bristly-hairy perennial erect to 30 in (75 cm)	oblong to ovate or lanceolate, wavy-toothed	violet-blue to white, broadly tubular, in dense, terminal heads subtended by bracts
C. × ***haylodgensis*** *C. carpatica* × *C. cochleariifolia*	garden origin	sprawling, tufted perennial to 6 in (15 cm)	rounded to ovate or heart-shaped, toothed	campanulate, large, pale blue or white

Comments: Includes double-flowered cultivars.

Name	Distribution	Habit	Leaves	Flowers
C. isophylla STAR OF JERUSALEM ITALIAN BELLFLOWER	N Italy	dwarf, trailing or creeping perennial	broadly ovate to cordate, toothed	campanulate to star-shaped, violet to pearly gray or white, large, in erect, loose clusters

Comments: Includes cultivars with white-variegated and gray-downy leaves and flowers in shades of blue and white.

C. carpatica 'Jewel'

C. glomerata 'Superba'

C. isophylla

C. latiloba 'Hidcote Amethyst'

CAMPANULA

Name	Distribution	Habit	Leaves	Flowers
C. lactiflora	Caucasus	erect perennial with branching stems to 5 ft (1.5 m)	ovate to oblong, toothed	broadly campanulate, milky blue fading to a white center, erect in a broad, leafy panicle
Comments: Includes cultivars with white, lilac and violet flowers.				
C. latifolia	Europe to Asia	erect, unbranched, finely hairy perennial to 3¼ ft (1 m)	ovate to oblong with a heart-shaped base, toothed, hairy	cup- to bell-shaped, pale blue to lavender, in axils or terminal clusters
Comments: Includes cultivars with white, indigo, purple and lilac flowers.				
C. latiloba	Siberia	differs from *C. persicifolia* in its broadly lanceolate leaves on narrowly winged stalks		deep blue, lavender or white
C. medium CANTERBURY BELLS, CUP AND SAUCER	S Europe	hairy, erect, much-branched biennial to 36 in (90 cm) tall	elliptic, hairy more or less toothed	campanulate to urceolate with the lobes forming a curved-back rim, blue, lavender, mauve, pink, pale rose, cream or white, sometimes with an enlarged calyx - the 'saucer' to the corolla 'cup', borne in terminal racemes and panicles
Comments: Many seed races and cultivars.				
C. morettiana	N Italy, Alps	dwarf, tufted, hairy perennial	heart-shaped, crenate, more or less smooth	campanulate to funnel-shaped, violet-blue to white, solitary, erect
C. persicifolia WILLOW BELL, PEACH-LEAVED BELLFLOWER	Europe, N Africa, W Asia	erect, glabrous perennial to 28 in (70 cm)	lanceolate to narrowly oblong, crenate, dark green	broadly campanulate, blue or white, nodding in a slender, terminal raceme
Comments: Includes many cultivars—among them plants with flowers ranging from pure white to pink, lilac, indigo and darkest blue, some double.				
C. portenschlagiana	Europe	tufted, downy perennial with sprawling to ascending stems to 10 in (25 cm) long	cordate to rounded, toothed	funnel-shaped to campanulate with short, deflexed lobes, deep lavender in loose panicles
Comments: Includes cultivars with white, pale violet and vivid blue flowers.				
C. poscharskyana	Balkans	similar to *C. portenschlagiana* but less coarse with more finely tapering and toothed leaves	funnelform to star-shaped, lavender to violet	**Comments:** Includes cultivars with white, pink, lavender and deep violet flowers.
C. pulla	E Europe	short-lived, tufted perennial to 4¾ in (12 cm) tall, spreading by underground runners	very small, rounded to spathulate, toothed, glossy, in rosettes	funnelform to campanulate, dark violet, solitary, nodding on slender stalks

C. poscharskyana *C. raineri* *C. takesimana* 'Elizabeth' *C. zoysii*

CAMPANULA

Name	Distribution	Habit	Leaves	Flowers
C. pyramidalis CHIMNEY BELLFLOWER	Europe	biennial or short-lived perennial attaining 6½ ft (2 m) in flower with a stout base and a spirelike or narrowly pyramidal heavily branched inflorescence	heart-shaped	broadly campanulate, fragrant, pale blue to white **Comments:** A spectacular half-hardy plant best grown under glass or moved outdoors in summer to a very sheltered location.
C. raineri	Switzerland, Italy	tufted perennial to 3 in (8 cm), spreading by underground runners	obovate, toothed, gray	broadly campanulate, large, erect, solitary, pale lavender blue
C. rotundifolia BLUEBELL, HAREBELL	N Hemisphere	tufted perennial erect to 18 in (45 cm)	rounded to cordate, wavy-edged	campanulate, white to deep blue or indigo, slender-stalked, solitary or few
C. takesimana	Korea	erect perennial to 24 in (60 cm)	ovate to cordate, toothed	tubular to campanulate, large, pendulous and lanternlike, lilac to white spotted dark mauve-pink within, on an arching, branched inflorescence
C. trachelium BATS-IN-THE-BELFRY, NETTLE LEAVED BELLFLOWER, THROATWORT	Europe, N Africa, Siberia	erect, bristly-hairy red-tinted perennial to 3¼ ft (1 m)	ovate to cordate, crenate, bristly	tubular to campanulate, blue-purple to lilac in dense panicles **Comments:** Includes white and blue, double-flowered cultivars.
C. vidalii *Azorina vidalii* **Comments:** Tender.	Azores	evergreen subshrub to 20 in (50 cm) tall	narrow, glossy dark green	campanulate to urceolate, waxy, dusky pink to white, hanging in arching panicles
C. zoysii	Italian Alps	tufted perennial to 4 in (10 cm)	obovate to rounded	cylindric to urceolate, pendulous, clear blue to pale mauve

purple, later turning gray with purple margins, becoming sunken with the outer tissue cracked. Die-back of canes and fruit infection may occur. Severely infected canes should be cut out and burned; where regularly a serious problem a recommended fungicide spray should be applied repeatedly, commencing when the buds are early developed.

canker a general term for a sunken necrotic lesion of a root or stem, usually of a woody plant, often with malformation and outgrowth of the surrounding bark. It is caused by a variety of fungi and bacteria.

APPLE AND PEAR CANKER (*Nectria galligena*) is a fungus that kills twigs and fruit spurs and often forms deep cankers on older branches. The cankers elongate and become elliptical in shape as they grow, the bark shrinks in concentric rings, and the branch usually swells; the stem may become girdled and die back. Spores infect bark through leaf scars or wounds caused by frost, pruning, or pests and diseases. Fruits are sometimes infected: the rot starts around the eye and extends. Cut off and burn small affected branches and spurs; on larger branches, pare back to healthy tissue using a knife sterilized in sodium hypochlorite; burn the parings and protect the wounds with canker paint. A systemic fungicide program for the control of scab and mildew should also keep canker in check. Wet, heavy soil aggravates canker, especially on susceptible apple cultivars such as 'Cox's Orange Pippin', 'James Grieve',

sunken lesion

Canker

'Worcester Pearmain' and 'Spartan'. *N.galligena* can also affect ash, beech, hawthorn, poplar and *Sorbus* species.

Gibberella baccata f.sp. *mori* causes die-back of young shoots on mulberry; cut out affected parts.

GARDENIA CANKER (*Phomopsis gardeniae*) enters through small wounds. Swollen brown lesions occur near soil level and may girdle the stem, resulting in death. Obtain cuttings from healthy plants and raise in a sterile medium.

ROSE CANKER is commonly caused by *Leptosphaeria coniothyrium*, but *Cryptosporella umbrina*, *Clethridium corticola* and *Coniothyrium wernsdorffiae* can be involved. They enter through pruning wounds. Protect larger cuts with canker paint, and spray with an approved fungicide at pruning time.

CYPRESS CANKER (mainly *Seiridium cardinale*) is recorded throughout the world, and is usually referred to as CORYNEUM CANKER. Members of the Cupressaceae vary in susceptibility: the

Monterey cypress (*Cupressus macrocarpa*), Italian cypress (*Cupressus sempervirens*) and Leyland cypress (× *Cupressocyparis leylandii*) are highly susceptible; the Lawson cypress (*Chamaecyparis lawsoniana*) and *Thuja plicata* are relatively resistant; *Juniperus sabina* and *Thuja occidentalis* are resistant. In Britain, the disease is most severe on the Monterey and Italian cypresses. The first symptoms are fading and death of old foliage at branch ends in spring, followed by the death of new growth and dying back of branches. Infection of bark and sapwood results from injury to twigs, branches or the main stem. Cankers may be 4–6 in (10–15 cm) long and 1 in (25 mm) wide; they become sunken as the rest of the stem continues to grow. On young, vigorous trees, resin exudes from the margins of lesions. Young trees with main-stem cankers can be killed within a year; multiple cankers on older trees can result in death within 5–10 years. The canker is spread locally by water splash or during cultural operations. All infected branches should be cut out well below the cankers, and badly affected trees removed.

CANKER STAIN of *Platanus* (*Ceratocystis fimbriata* f.sp. *platani*) is a lethal disease of the London plane (*P. acerifolia*) in North America. It is spreading in Europe, but is not recorded in the UK. Infection enters through wounds in the bark or sapwood, and can also be introduced from diseased trees on saws, ropes and even wood-protection paints. Several species of Nitidulid sap beetles have been reported as carriers. Symptoms are darkly stained lesions in underlying layers of bark and sapwood. Infected sapwood dies and bark develops cankers. Vertical spread is rapid, up to 10 ft (3 m) a year. External symptoms are long, shrunken, often cracked cankers following the grain of the wood. Infected tissues are killed and rapidly invaded by secondary wood-rotting fungi. Fully grown trees decline following infection, with thinning and yellowing of foliage over a period of years, resulting in dieback and eventual death. Young trees of pole size may die within two years. There is no cure for infected trees. Remove diseased trees as soon as they are identified; protect healthy trees from injury; and disinfect pruning tools.

EUTYPA CANKER and die-back (*Eutypa lata*), also known as DEAD ARM or DYING ARM, is a serious disease of the grapevine (*Vitis* species) and of apricot (*Prunus armeniaca*) in Europe, Australia, North America and South Africa. *Phomopsis viticola* is a common secondary invader of dead arm infection. Several strains of *E.lata* occur, all pathogenic to the grapevine but of different degrees of virulence to apricot. The fungus is widespread as a secondary organism on the dead twigs of woody plants such as apple, ash, hawthorn and ivy, which act as a constant source of infection. The fungus is not usually seen on vines less than seven years old. First symptoms are weak growth of the new season's shoots in midspring; the leaves are small and distorted and may become yellowed and spotted. The vascular tissue of dying branches shows dead areas beneath pruning wounds; death of these branches (dead arm) occurs the following year. Symptoms on apricots are cankers on branches, usually with gumming, resulting in dead foliage that remains attached to the tree until winter; death of the branch follows. Remove and burn dead wood during dry spells; treat pruning wounds with fungicide or antagonistic fungus immediately after pruning. Pneumatic pruners with a spraying attachment combine pruning and treatment operations.

BOX CANKER and BLIGHT is caused by *Pseudonectria rousseliana* and *Cylindrocladium buxicola*. Affected plants are slow to start into growth in the spring, and foliage becomes straw-colored; diseased leaves and branches are covered with pink fungal spore pustules. Cankers develop on main stems and branches, often following winter injury. Remove all cankered stems and dead foliage, and apply an approved garden fungicide.

ELAEAGNUS CANKER (*Phomopsis elaeagni*) is a serious fungal disease of *Elaeagnus angustifolia*, which is widely planted in North America. It is prevalent on nursery plants. Other species of fungi also cause cankers of *Elaeagnus* in the US.

CANKER OF BRASSICAS (also known as BLACK LEG) is caused by *Leptosphaeria maculan*. Symptoms include damping-off as well as stem canker. It is very common on oilseed rape (*Brassica napus*) and often affects broccoli (*B.oleracea* Italica Group) and Brussels sprouts (*B.oleracea* Gemmifera Group), especially when grown from home-saved seed. Elongated, sunken lesions dotted with black fungal bodies occur at ground level, and small, circular brown spots on leaves. On rutabagas (*B.napus* Napobrassica Group) and turnips (*B.rapa* Rapifera Group), the canker causes a dry rot on roots. The fungus is seed-borne; commercial seed will normally be derived from healthy crops and treated with fungicide.

BLACK CANKER of parsnips is caused by *Itersonilia pastinacae* and *Phoma* species. Lesions on roots spread and develop into black rot around the shoulder and crown. On black fen soil, canker may also be caused by *Mycocentrospora acerina*, where the rot is purple rather than black. An orange-brown canker with roughened skin is caused by other weakly parasitic soil-inhabiting fungi. Spores of *Itersonilia* arise from leaf spots and are washed into the soil to cause original infection. Earthing up roots, rotation and close spacing are useful control measures. The cultivar 'Avonresister' is resistant to all three types of canker. See *bleeding canker*.

cankerworm see *winter moths*.

Canna (a Classical name for a type of reed). Cannaceae. New World subtropics and tropics. 9 species, tender or semihardy perennial herbs, deciduous to evergreen with fleshy rhizomes, broad leaves, and, in late spring and summer, erect to arching, terminal racemes and panicles of showy flowers with three sepals, three petals, and one to four staminodes, some of them petal-like.

Cultivars of *C. × generalis* are excellent plants for a cool greenhouse or, outdoors, in tubs and bedding displays, massed or as dot plants. Plant in rich, loamy, moist soil in full sun. Where frosts are common and hard, lift the rhizomes once the top growth has withered and overwinter them, cool but frost-free, in barely damp wood shavings or vermiculite. In early spring, start the rhizomes into growth in pots in warm, humid conditions. Plant out in late spring. In favored areas (min. 0°F/−18°C), plants might be risked outside all year in a sunny, sheltered position with a thick mulch in winter. *C. indica* can be similarly treated, but prefers a warmer and damper site and will take some shade. It seldom survives heavy frosts. Under glass, it is an attractive plant for large containers and beds, remaining in leaf and flower throughout the year if encouraged to form large clumps and given a minimum temperature of 50°F (10°C). *C. iridifolia* grows best in a humid greenhouse with a minimum temperature of 64°F (18°C). It needs plenty of head-room and a moist, fertile, loamy medium. At high temperatures, this species thrives in saturated conditions and associates well with other large, tropical and subtropical marginals, e.g. *Cyperus* and *Thalia*. Propagate all by division in spring. Soak seed of species in warm water for 24 hours or make a small nick in the seed coat prior to sowing in a soilless medium at 68°F (20°C).

C. × generalis (syn. *C. × orchioides*); CANNA LILY; garden hybrids derived from a number of species and much interbred, ranging from 12–54 in (30–130 cm) and from low and clump-forming to tall and single-stemmed; leaves 12–32 in (30–80 cm) long, broadly ovate to narrowly oblong, blue-green to jade striped gold, from bronze to purple-red to chocolate veined fiery orange; flowers large and ruffled (to 3 in (8 cm) in diameter) or small and spidery, white, cream, yellow, orange, peach, coral pink, vermilion, scarlet, blood red, or combinations thereof in patches, spots and streaks; *C. indica* (syn. *C. musifolia*); INDIAN SHOT; C and S America; 1²/₃–6¹/₂ ft (0.5–2 m); smooth, mid-green leaves to 20 in (50 cm) long, usually with red-purple stained sheaths or midribs; flowers, to 2¹/₂ in (6 cm) across, with narrow segments in shades of scarlet and orange, marked yellow and held among purple-red bracts; includes 'Purpurea', to 6¹/₂ ft (2 m) tall, with large, paddlelike purple-bronze leaves and small, scarlet flowers; *C. iridifolia* Peru; 3¹/₄–10 ft (1–3 m) leaves to 3¹/₄ ft (1 m) broadly oblong, blue-green; flowers to 2¹/₂ in (6 cm), with curving, narrowly lanceolate segments in shades of deep pink or orange.

Cantua ("cantua" is the Quechua name for *C. buxifolia*). Polemoniaceae. Temperate S America. 6 species, evergreen shrubs with tubular, 5-lobed flowers in pendulous, terminal corymbs in late spring and summer. In Mediterranean-type climates, *Cantua* will grow in the open border or year-round in tubs. Below 10°F (−12°C), it requires the protection of a sheltered, south-facing wall; alternatively, grow in borders and tubs in a cool greenhouse greenhouse or conservatory. Under glass grow in sun, water plentifully in spring and summer, sparingly in winter. Root semiripe cuttings in a closed case with bottom heat. *C. buxifolia* SACRED or MAGIC FLOWER OF THE INCAS; Peru, Bolivia, Chile; erect to spreading shrub 3¹/₄–15 ft (1–5 m) tall, flowers 2¹/₂–3 in (6–8 cm) long, narrowly trumpet-shaped, the tube pink to purple with yellow stripes, the spreading lobes cerise to crimson or scarlet.

cap, capping (1) the formation of an impermeable crust on a soil surface, usually due to the impact of rain drops on weakly structured, fine-textured soil. Capping can reduce water infiltration and aeration and form a barrier to emerging seedlings. A capped surface may alternatively be referred to as caked. (2) a layer of soil or plastic sheeting placed over a compost pile.

cape gooseberry (*Physalis peruviana*) a half-hardy perennial up to 3¹/₄ ft (1 m) in height, native to Tropical South America; grown as an annual for its edible, golden, cherry-sized fruits that are borne within persistent lantern-shaped calyces. It may be grown in sheltered sites outdoors, or under greenhouse protection in border soil or pots. Sow seeds ¹/₄ in (6 mm) deep, in pots or trays, in gentle heat during spring. Seedlings are pricked out into small pots or other modules, and planted out when established, 30 in (75 cm) apart in ground beds or into 10 in (25 cm) pots. Support individual plants with canes 30 in (75 cm) out of the ground. Plants may

Cape gooseberry

be pinched when 12 in (30 cm) high to induce branching. Water sparingly and apply liquid fertilizer as for tomatoes after the first flowers are set. Fruits on plants outdoors may be slow to ripen; they are ready to harvest when golden yellow, and the sweet, distinctive flavor improves where left for a week or two on the plant. The cultivar 'Golden-berry' produces large fruits.

capillarity the movement of liquid as a result of surface tension. Capillarity is of horticultural relevance to the availability of soil moisture and the functioning of certain watering systems.

capillary (1) slender and hairlike; much as filiform, but even more delicate; (2) pertaining to capillarity (see above). *Capillary watering* applies to the irrigation of container-grown plants, utilizing the property of upward movement of water from a wetted mat or sand bed. A *capillary bed* is a specially constructed ground-level bed, usually of fine sand, used especially for the capillary watering of container-grown ornamentals. A *capillary bench* is a carefully levelled greenhouse bench covered by a capillary mat (usually made of synthetic fiber or wool) or sand, used for capillary watering of pot plants.

capitate (1) arranged in heads, as in the inflorescence of Compositae; (2) terminating in a knob or somewhat spherical tip.

capitulum a head of densely clustered and sessile or subsessile flowers or florets on a compressed axis, characteristically found in members of the daisy family, Compositae.

caprification cross-pollination in the fig (*Ficus carica*), accomplished by the FIG WASP (*Blastophaga psenes*), which breeds inside the wild form or caprifig. On emergence, with pollen adhering to its body, the wasp is attracted to the inflorescences of female figs and transfers pollen on contact. Caprification is a necessary process for certain cultivated figs, such as the ancient 'Smyrna' that is grown for drying, but modern cultivars are self-fertile.

Capsicum (from Greek *kapto*, to bite, referring to the bitingly hot taste of chili). Solanaceae. Tropical America. CHILI PEPPER, PEPPER, GREEN PEPPER, BELL PEPPER. 10 species, shrubby, annual to perennial herbs grown for their edible fruits—these are large, chambered berries with thick, sweet to bitingly pungent rinds. The two principal crop species are *C. annuum* (CHILI PEPPER, PAPRIKA, CAPISCUM, RED PEPPER), and *C. frutescens* (HOT PEPPER, SPUR PEPPER, TABASCO PEPPER), both much-developed and highly varied. See *peppers*. Some ornamental (and inedible) cultivars are grown, usually as annuals for container display in the home and cool greenhouse, and for summer bedding. They are listed below. Sow seed in spring with a minimum temperature of 50°F (10°C). Grow in a fertile, loamy medium with plentiful water in full sun. Syringe in summer to promote fruit set and discourage red spider mite. *C. annuum*—'Holiday Cheer' (bushy with a dense head of round fruits turning from green to cream, yellow and red), 'Holiday Time' (bushy with a dense head of conical fruits turning from green to yellow, red, and, sometimes, purple), 'Piccolo' (slender and treelike in outline, with small leaves variegated cream, dark and pale green and purple, small, mauve flowers and round, purple-black fruits; *C. frutescens*—'Chameleon' (low and bushy with fruits turning from yellow to purple, then red), 'Long Gold Spike' (fruits conical, gold to brick red, erect in a spire-like, branching head to 3¼ ft (1 m) long; a fine plant for cut displays in fall)

capsid bugs (Hemiptera: Miridae) insects up to ¼ in (6 mm) long, with relatively long probosci, legs and antennae. Adults have hardened forewings that lie flat and cover the membranous hindwings and they vary in color from green to red-brown. All are elusive and deceptively common. The cylindrical curved eggs are either deposited on the surface of plants or inserted into plant tissue. Some species overwinter in the egg stage on woody plants, others pass the winter as adults in sheltered situations. Emergent nymphs resemble the adults but are smaller, sexually immature and wingless. Most capsids are plant feeders; some are largely predacious, including the BLACK-KNEED CAPSID (*Blepharidopterus angulatus*) and FLOWER BUGS (*Anthocoris* species). Plant-feeding species infest a wide range of fruit, vegetable, woody and herbaceous plants. Shoots become distorted or blind; leaves become puckered with irregular-shaped holes developing around the punctures; blooms may be malformed or aborted; and fruits of apples and pears develop raised corky patches.

The principal European species are the TARNISHED PLANT BUG (*Lygus rugulipennis*), which is green mottled with red-brown, and mostly attacks ornamentals; the COMMON GREEN CAPSID (*Lygocoris pabulinus*), which is bright green with darker markings, and is particularly injurious to soft and top fruit, but also attacks ornamentals; the POTATO CAPSID (*Calacoris norwegicus*), which is similar to the common green capsid in color and found chiefly on potatoes and a range of Compositae; and the APPLE CAPSID (*Plesiocoris rugicollis*), which is similar to the common green capsid in color, and mainly attacks apples and soft fruits.

In North America, the name tarnished plant bug is applied to *Lygus lineolaris*, a capsid similar in biology and appearance to the European species but which has 3–5 generations each year, depending on latitude. It attacks a range of garden plants, particularly apples, peaches and strawberries, which become misshapen. The FOUR-LINED PLANT BUG (*Poecilocapsus lineatus*) is yellow-green with four dark stripes running lengthwise down the back. There is one generation each year, and it overwinters in the egg stage. It attacks woody and herbaceous plants, especially currants. Weeds serve as alternative hosts to capsids and should be destroyed. Using a recommended insecticide, apples and pears should be sprayed at petal fall, and susceptible ornamental plants at the first sign of capsid presence. The level of damage to vegetables does not usually warrant control.

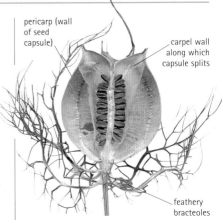

pericarp (wall of seed capsule)

carpel wall along which capsule splits

feathery bracteoles

Capsule, *Nigella damascena*

capsule a dry, dehiscent seed vessel.

Caragana (Latinized form of *karaghan*, Mongolian name for *C. arborescens*). Leguminosae. E Europe, C Asia. PEA SHRUB, PEA TREE. 80 species, very hardy deciduous shrubs and small trees, with neat, pinnate leaves; the leafstalks are often sharply tipped and persist as spines. Small, pealike flowers are borne singly or in clusters during spring. These plants will survive a wide range of conditions, except wet and shade. Top-grafted on stocks of the typical plant, the weeping filigree-leaved cultivars of *C. arborescens* are beautiful small trees, although they are more prone to damage by cold and wind. Propagate from seed sown when ripe or after being pre-soaked in warm water. *Caragana* can also be propagated by taking softwood and semiripe cuttings during summer.

C. arborescens SIBERIAN PEA TREE; treelike shrub to 20 ft (6 m) tall with dark green leaves composed of eight to twelve leaflets; flowers pale yellow; includes 'Lorbergii', with very slender, ribbonlike leaflets; *C. frutex* RUSSIAN PEA SHRUB; upright, suckering shrub to 10 ft (3 m) tall; leaves with four leaflets; flowers yellow; includes 'Globosa', more rounded and compact.

Caralluma (from *carallum*, name given to *C. adscendens* by the Telugas of Coromandel, India). Asclepiadaceae. Spain, Africa, India, Burma. Some 80 species, clump-forming, leafless perennial herbs with erect to sprawling, succulent stems, angled and with rows of teeth or tubercles. Often malodorous, the flowers are fleshy and star- to cup-shaped with five, acute lobes in spring and summer. Cultivation as for *Stapelia*.

C. adscendens India, Burma, Sri Lanka; stems to 24 in (60 cm); flowers outspread to bell-shaped, erect to pendulous, to ¾ in (2 cm) wide, green to tawny or chestnut, spotted or striped purple, often hairy; *C. europaea* N Africa, S Europe; stems to 6 in (15 cm); flowers to ¾ in (2 cm) wide, spreading to campanulate, yellow to red-brown with purple bands, more or less hairy; *C. joannis* Morocco; stems to 4 in (10 cm); flowers to 1 in (2.5 cm), bell- to star-shaped, olive-yellow, spotted red, lobes marked purple with small hairs on margins.

carbon/nitrogen ratio the ratio of the weight of carbon (C) to the weight of nitrogen (N) in plant material (variably 10–100:1 depending on age and type) and in soil (typically 10–15:1). The C/N ratio influences the respective rates of decomposition of carbon and nitrogen in compost piles. Where the ratio is high, as in woody debris or straw, decomposition is slow, nitrogen is depleted and a supplementary dressing is advisable.

carbonate of lime see *calcium carbonate*.

Cardamine (diminutive form of Greek *kardamomon*, a name used by Dioscorides for cress). Cruciferae. N Hemisphere. BITTERCRESS. 150 species, perennial or annual herbs (those listed here are hardy perennials) with racemes or panicles of 4-parted flowers in spring and early summer. Plant in semiwooded locations and herbaceous borders (*C. enneaphylla*, *C. pentaphylla*), or in shaded rock gardens, borders and woodland (*C. trifolia*), or naturalize in long, damp turf (*C. pratensis*). They favor cool, moist, fertile soil. Increase by division or seed in fall; *C. pratensis* also by leaf cuttings.

C. enneaphylla (syn. *Dentaria enneaphylla*); W Carpathians, E Alps, S Italy; 4–14 in (10–35 cm) tall, with a scaly, fleshy rhizome; leaves pinnately lobed, each leaflet ovate to lanceolate, toothed; flowers to 1¼ in (3 cm) across, white to cream, nodding in a congested raceme; *C. pentaphylla* (syn. *Dentaria pentaphylla*); mountains of W and C Europe; 6–24 in (15–60 cm) tall, with a

scaly, creeping rhizome; leaves digitately lobed with five, lanceolate to ovate, toothed leaflets; flowers to 1¼ in (3 cm) across, rose to pale lilac or white in congested racemes; *C. pratensis* CUCKOO FLOWER, LADY'S SMOCK; widespread in Europe; 2½–12 in (6–30 cm) tall, clump-forming; leaves in a loose rosette, pinnate with small, broad leaflets; flowers to ¾ in (2 cm) in diameter, white veined to flushed pale rose to lilac, in slender, erect racemes; includes the double-flowered 'Florepleno'; *C. trifolia* C and S Europe; 4–12 in (10–30 cm) tall, with a creeping rhizome; leaves neat, composed of three, broad and toothed, dark green leaflets; flowers to ¾ in (2 cm) in diameter, white or pink, in racemes atop slender, bare stalks.

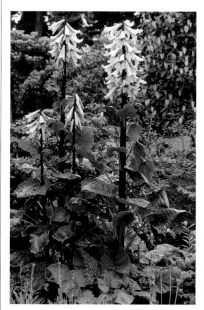

Cardiocrinum giganteum var. yunnanense
The spectacular giant or Himalayan lily must have deep, rich soil and a shaded position.

Cardiocrinum (from Greek *kardia*, heart, and *krinon*, lily). Liliaceae (Liliaceae). E Asia. GIANT LILY. 3 species, spectacular perennial herbs, with single, stout stems arising from annually produced bulbs, glossy, deep green heart-shaped leaves and, in summer, large, funnel-shaped, white flowers with six tepals. Suited to a woodland garden or a shady, moist border among shrubs, the giant lily is hardy to 14°F (−10°C), but fares better if thickly mulched in winter. Plant in deep,

nutrient- and humus-rich soil that remains cool and moist. The bulbs perish after flowering but are replaced by daughter bulbs that take three to five years to reach flowering size. The seed capsules are large and attractive, bursting in fall to release many papery seeds that germinate where they fall or in a cool, shaded frame. Seed-grown plants may take seven years to flower, but tend to be taller and more robust than vegetatively propagated plants.

The most popular species is *C. giganteum* from Himalaya, Burma and China. It grows to 12 ft (4 m) tall with a clump of basal leaves to 18 in (45 cm) long, and stem leaves diminishing in size toward its summit. The fragrant flowers are regularly funnelform, to 8 in (20 cm) long and marked maroon inside. The Chinese *C. cathayanum* is shorter than *C. giganteum*, to 5 ft (1.5 m), and also differs in having leaves absent from the lower part of the stem, but scattered in its upper two thirds. The flowers are 4 in (10 cm) long, irregularly funnelform and cream tipped and spotted purple. The Japanese *C. cordatum* grows to 6½ ft (2 m) tall, with leaves arranged in a loose whorl in the lower half of the stem and 6 in (15 cm)-long, irregularly funnelform, cream flowers blotched yellow and spotted red-brown at the base within.

Cardiospermum (from Greek *kardia*, heart, and *sperma*, seed: the seed is marked with a heart-shaped white spot). Sapindaceae. Tropical Africa, America, India. 14 species, slender-stemmed herbs or shrubs climbing by tendrils. The leaves are usually biternately compound with toothed or pinnately cut leaflets. In summer, small, 4-petalled flowers are followed by inflated capsules. They require frost-free conditions, although *C. halicacabum* is often grown as a half-hardy annual, the seed sown under glass in early spring or *in situ* in early summer. Grow in full sun or shade in a fertile, loam-based medium with ample moisture; provide support. Both species can also be propagated by softwood cuttings in spring.

C. grandiflorum HEARTSEED; tropical America and Africa; perennial, herbaceous vine climbing to 25 ft (8 m); leaves to 8 in (20 cm) long, hairy beneath; flowers fragrant, cream, to ½ in (1 cm) wide; fruit smooth, triangular-ovoid, to 2¾×1½ in (7 × 4 cm); (*C. halicacabum*); BALLOON VINE, HEART SEED, LOVE-IN-A-PUFF; tropical Asia, Africa and America, naturalized southern US, Australia; vine to 10 ft (3 m); differs from the first species in its smooth leaves to 4¾ in (12 cm), smaller, white and scentless flowers and very inflated capsules, bladderlike, bristly and to 1 × 1 in (2.5 × 2.5 cm).

Cardoon
Grown particularly for its edible blanched stems. A worthy border perennial on account of its deep blue flowers and dark foliage.

cardoon (*Cynara cardunculus*) a herbaceous perennial, to 6½ ft (2 m) high, closely related to the GLOBE ARTICHOKE (*Cynara cardunculus* Scolymus Group) and grown for its edible hearts and fleshy petioles which are sometimes blanched. Serve raw or boiled. Sow seed 1¼–1½ in (3–4 cm) deep in rows 5 ft (1.5 m) apart; thin to final spacings of 20 in (50 cm).

Possible problems: aphids, slugs.

Carex (from Greek *keiro*, to cut, alluding to the sharp leaf margins). Cyperaceae. Cosmopolitan. SEDGE. Some 1,000 species, evergreen, rhizomatous or tufted, perennial herbs with short or distinct and slender stems, usually long, narrow and grasslike leaves and very small, grainlike flowers in male or female spikes arranged together in a panicle. All prefer moist, neutral to slightly acidic soil with a high organic content. The very hardy weeping sedges, *C. pendula* and *C. pseudocyperus*, grow well at the waterside or even partially submerged, and will soon self-sow. *C. atrata*, *C. grayi* and *C. riparia* can be used to colonize the margins of water and bog gardens. The broad-leaved sedges, *C. plantaginea* and *C. siderosticha*, are handsome groundcover for damp and shaded borders. The narrow-leaved Japanese sedge grasses (*C. hachijoensis*, *C. morrowii* and *C. oshimensis*) thrive in similar conditions, but will also take more light and less water. *C. fraseri* naturalizes well in light, acidic woodland and the bog garden, making a carpet of white, buttonlike flower heads in early spring. The bronze and copper New Zealand sedges favor a sheltered position with full sunlight, in acidic, gritty, moist soil. *C. atrata* and the more tender *C. baccans* produce attractive fruiting heads (jet black and brick red respectively). The palm sedges, *C. muskingumensis* and *C. phyllocephala*, make dense stands of reedy stems, hardy to 0°F (−18°C) and ideal for stark modern landscapes. The variegated *C. phyllocephala* 'Sparkler' is an excellent container plant for a cool greenhouse, likewise *C. brunnea* 'Variegata'. Propagate all by division in early spring.

C. atrata BLACK SEDGE, JET SEDGE; Europe; clump-forming, to 24 in (60 cm) tall; stems dark below; leaves slender, pale blue-green; female spikes to 2 in (5 cm), rounded to oblong, purple-black; *C. baccans* CRIMSON-SEEDED SEDGE; India to China; loosely tufted to 3¼ ft (1 m) tall; leaves to ½ in (1 cm) wide, leathery, flat, deep green; in fruit, female spikes resemble tight clusters of orange-red berries; *C. berggrenii* New Zealand; broad, low and tufted with short, linear leaves that may be metallic gray-brown, bronze, glaucous and, in some selections, distinctively narrow; *C. brunnea* Japan, Australia; stems slender, tufted, 12–36 in (30–90 cm) tall; leaves to ¼ in (0.5 cm) wide, yellow- to bright green, robust; spikes nodding; includes 'Variegata', small, with leaves broadly edged yellow; *C. buchananii* LEATHERLEAF SEDGE; New Zealand; densely tufted, 4–28 in (10–70 cm) tall; leaves very slender, straight and erect to outward-leaning and arching, often curling and whiplike at tips, pink-orange to red-green below to copper or bronze above; *C. comans* NEW ZEALAND HAIRY SEDGE; New Zealand; densely tufted, 2½–16 in (6–40 cm) tall; leaves very slender, arching to drooping in a pale green mophead, sometimes taking on red-bronze tints in cold weather; includes forms with deep bronze leaves, and 'Frosted Curls', with very narrow, hairlike, curling and tangled leaves, bronze-green to bleached gray-green at tips in winter; *C. conica* Japan, S Korea; tufted, to 20 in (50 cm) tall; leaves to ⅛ in (0.4 cm) wide, dark green, rigid, flat, rough; includes 'Snowline', small, neat, with arching leaves dark green edged white, and 'Variegata', with leaves variegated white; *C. elata* BOWLE'S GOLDEN SEDGE; Europe; tussock-forming, 8–39 in (20–100 cm) tall; leaves fine, to ¼ in (0.6 cm) wide, folded in section, glaucous; includes 'Aurea', with leaves edged yellow, 'Bowles Golden', with golden yellow leaves edged green, and 'Knightshayes', with yellow leaves; *C. firma* Europe; to 8 in (20 cm) tall, densely tufted, mat-forming; leaves to 4 in (10 cm), narrow, rigid, pointed, blue-green; includes 'Variegata', with leaves striped creamy yellow; *C. flagellifera* (New Zealand; resembles a taller, coarser *C. buchananii*; leaves whiplike, pale bronze to tawny brown, arching to form a low dome; *C. grayi* GRAY'S SEDGE, MACE SEDGE; N America; clump-forming, 12–39 in (30–100 cm) tall; leaves flat, to ½ in (1 cm) wide, pale green, margins rough; female spikes to 1¼ in (3 cm) wide, round and spiky, resembling a mace; *C. hachijoensis* Japan; differs from *C. morrowii* in narrower, softer leaves; for the cultivars 'Evergold' and 'Variegata', see under *C. oshimensis* and *C. morrowii* respectively; *C. morrowii* Japan; resembles *C. oshimensis* but with slightly wider leaves with rough margins; includes 'Fisher's Form', large, with leaves striped cream, and 'Variegata', with leaves narrowly striped white near margins—this cultivar is often included in *C. hachijoensis*; *C. muskingumensis* PALM SEDGE; N America; stems narrowly canelike, erect, tufted, to 3¼ ft (1 m) tall, ranked with spreading to arching, slender, bright green leaves; includes 'Wachtposten' syn. 'Sentry Tower', a particularly fine form, with long stems and shining, deep green leaves; *C. oshimensis* JAPANESE SEDGE GRASS; Japan; to 12 in (30 cm) tall, densely tufted, making a spilling, hairlike tussock; leaves fine and narrow, smooth, deep, glossy green, typically with narrow white margins; includes 'Aureavariegata', with leaves with a broad, central, golden stripe, 'Evergold', with leaves with a creamy yellow central stripe—this cultivar is often included in *C. hachijoensis*—and 'Variegata', with leaves with a central white stripe; *C. pendula* WEEPING SEDGE, PENDULOUS SEDGE; Europe; clump-forming, to 5 ft (1.5 m) tall; leaves to ³/₄ in (2 cm) wide, long and finely tapering, coarse; spikes to 3 in (8 cm) long, cylindrical, pendulous on slender-branched, arching panicles; *C. petriei* New Zealand; resembles a smaller *C. buchananii*, with narrower, pinker leaves and stouter spikes; *C. phyllocephala* Japan; stems tufted, cane-like, to 18 in (45 cm) tall, with long, narrowly strap-shaped leaves at their summit; includes 'Sparkler', with lime to dark green leaves striped and edged white; *C. pilulifera* PILL SEDGE; dwarf, tufted, to 12 in (30 cm) tall; leaves very fine; spikes in a small head; includes 'Tinney's Princess', with very small leaves striped creamy yellow; *C. plantaginea* N America; tufted, to 14 in (35 cm) tall; leaves broadly strap-shaped, ribbed; spikes purple; *C. pseudocyperus* CYPERUS SEDGE; temperate regions; resembles a smaller, softer *C. pendula* with coarser spikes; to 32 in (80 cm) tall; leaves flat, to ¹/₂ in (1 cm) across, bright green; spikes to 2 in (5 cm) long, green-brown pendulous on arching stems; *C. riparia* Northern Hemisphere; to 3¹/₄ ft (1 m) tall, fast-spreading; leaves flat, to ⁵/₈ in (1.5 cm)

wide; spikes to 4 in (10 cm), cylindrical; includes 'Variegata', with striped or almost wholly white tufted leaves; *C. siderosticha* to 4 in (10 cm) tall, with smooth, lax, strap-shaped leaves in clumps, emerging pink turning bright green; includes 'Variegata', with leaves edged and striped white; *C. uncifolia* New Zealand; spreading or loosely tufted, to 4 in (10 cm) tall; leaves very narrow, curving, with curly tips, pink to red-brown.

carina keel, (1) the anterior petals of a papilionaceous flower; (2) the keel of the glume in flowers of Gramineae; (3) the midvein of a leaf, petal or sepal, prominent to ridged beneath.

carinate of a leaf, bract or perianth segment; boat-shaped or, more usually, keeled, with a line or ridge along the center of its dorsal surface.

Carissa (based on an Indian name). Apocynaceae. Old World tropics and subtropics. 20 species, evergreen shrubs and small trees with intricate, often spiny branches, glossy, ovate to oblong leaves and clusters of star-shaped, fragrant flowers. These have a slender corolla tube expanding to a spreading limb of five, oblong to obovate lobes; they are followed by colorful, succulent fruit. Grow in most well-drained, moderately fertile soils in full sun or light shade. Tolerant of light frost, wind, salt spray and short-lived drought, it makes an excellent specimen planting, screen, hedge or groundcover. Below 0°F

(–18°C), grow in a cool greenhouse or conservatory. It responds well to frequent clipping and hard pruning. Propagate by heeled, semiripe cuttings of side shoots rooted in a warm case.

C. macrocarpa (syn. *C. grandiflora*); NATAL PLUM; S Africa; shrub or tree to 28 ft (9 m) tall; branches tipped with formidable forked spines and clothed with glossy green leaves to 2¹/₂ in (6 cm) long; flowers to 2 in (5 cm) wide, white and jasmine-scented; fruits plum-shaped and bright red to purple-black, ³/₄–2 in (2–5 cm)-long, edible; 'Horizontalis': NATAL CREEPER, dense and trailing, leaves very small, fruit vivid scarlet.

carnation (*Dianthus caryophyllus*) The wild ancestor of the border and perpetual flowering carnations originated in the Pyrenees and has been cultivated in western Europe since the 15th century. The modern classification of show carnations includes Selfs (all colors except blue; White-, Yellow- and Apricot-ground Fancies; Other Fancies; White- and Yellow-ground Picotees; Other Picotees; Cloves. Fancies are striped, flaked, or suffused with one or more contrasting or blended colors. Cloves may be of any color but must possess a strong clove scent.

Border carnations are grown as annuals or perennials for cutting or garden decoration and are 16–24 in (40–60 cm) high; they flower prolifically in midsummer and prefer a cool temperature climate. Grow unstopped but staked. Propagate perennial beds

CARNATION PETAL PATTERNING

Self
"Self"-colored carnations such as 'Golden Cross' have completely plain, unmarked petals.

Fancy
Streaking and mottling characterizes the petals of fancies such as 'Forest Treasure'.

Picotee
Picotees (here 'Eva Humphries') have a delicate but well-defined band on the petal margins.

C

by layering every three or four years, soon after flowering. Plant out in fall or early spring 15–18 in (38–45 cm) apart each way. When grown as annuals, sow seed in early spring under protection at 61°F (16°C).

Perpetual flowering carnations are grown primarily as fragrant cut flowers. They require light, airy, greenhouse protection for good quality and a winter minimum temperature of 40–45°F (4–7°C). They are raised from cuttings, potted into 3 in (8 cm)-diameter containers and stopped at eight or nine pairs of leaves. Selected side shoots are stopped thereafter. Grow on in 6 in (15 cm)-diameter pots for the first year, then pot up into 8 in (21 cm)-diameter pots and stand on a deep gravel base. Support with 4 ft (1.2 m) canes and wire hoops. Disbud for large blooms, leaving only the crown bud; for sprays, remove only the crown bud.

American spray carnations are grown for commercial cut flower production and originate in Connecticut from selected crosses. Culture is as for perpetual flowering carnations except that the crown buds are always removed to induce sprays.

Malmaison carnations The name alludes to the resemblance of the blooms to the Bourbon rose 'Souvenir de la Malmaison'. They were first raised in France in 1857 from a seed mutant, and bud sports followed. Cultivation is as for perpetual flowering carnations but they require more shade in summer. Disbud to leave 3–4

buds per stem. Propagate by cuttings in winter or by layers in summer. See *pinks*.

Possible problems: aphids, carnation tortrix moth, scale insects, thrips; gray mold, rust, wilt, virus.

Carnegiea (for Andrew Carnegie [1835–1919], philanthropist, steel magnate and patron of science). Cactaceae. 1 species, *C. gigantea* (SAGUARO), from the southwestern US and northern Mexico. This giant cactus grows to 52 ft (16 m) tall with a trunk some 30 in (75 cm) thick. For many years it remains unbranched, as a deeply ribbed column with gray-brown spines to 2¾ in (7 cm) long. Produced at the column's summit in spring and summer, the white, funnel-shaped flowers are some 4 in (10 cm) long and open at night. Edible, red-green fruit split jaggedly from top to bottom, revealing bright red pulp. When they finally appear, the branches are few and erect, resembling the main stem. Grow in a frost-free garden or a heated greenhouse (minimum temperature 50°F/10°C) in a gritty and sandy, loam-based medium, pH 6–7.5. Under glass, admit full sunlight except in very hot weather and maintain low humidity and good air circulation. Keep dry from midfall to early spring, except for a light misting on warm days in late winter. Branch cuttings will root but are seldom available. Being endangered in the wild, saguaro is best raised from seed sown on a fine, sandy medium in a heated case. It is very slow-growing.

carnivorous plant a plant adapted to attract, capture and digest small creatures for its own nutritional benefit. Recognized in 450–500 species within the families Sarraceniaceae, Nepenthaceae, Cephalotaceae, Droseraceae, Byblidaceae, Lentibulariaceae, Dioncophyllaceae, Roridulaceae and Bromeliaceae, carnivorous plants thrive in moist acidic conditions. The adaptation serves to provide a protein source of nitrogen in habitats where the nutrient is otherwise deficient. Their prey is predominantly insects (hence the common description, insectivorous plant) but may include protozoa, spiders, crustaceae, amphibians and even small mammals.

There are four trapping mechanisms: (1) the snap-trap, with hinged leaves resembling an open jaw, as in VENUS' FLY TRAP (*Dionaea muscipula*), to which the prey are attracted by pigment and secretion; (2) suction, as in *Utricularia* species, where the trap is a small bladder with appendages and mouth covered by a trap door; a partial vacuum arising in the closed bladder keeps the trap shut. The finely balanced mechanism is disrupted by the prey, which is then drawn into the open receptacle in a flow of air or water; (3) pitfall traps, as in *Sarracenia*, where modified leaves form pitchers into which insects are lured and then trapped by surface hairs and wax; (4) flypaper traps, as in the SUNDEWS (*Drosera* species), in which insects are attracted to glistening glands on leaf

CARNIVOROUS PLANT TYPES

Snap-trap (Dionaea muscipula)
Highly specialized hinged leaves snap shut when an insect's presence is detected.

Pitfall (Sarracenia sp.)
Prey lured to the pitchers falls into a "well" filled with a solution of digestive enzymes.

Flypaper (Drosera capensis)
Lured by a sweet, glistening secretion, prey is held fast in its stickiness and engulfed.

and stem surfaces; they are overwhelmed by copious secretions of sticky fluid and then digested. For cultivation details refer to the above genera and *Byblis, Cephalotus, Darlingtonia, Drosophyllum, Heliamphora, Nepenthes, Pinguicula.*

carotenoids yellow, orange, or red pigments, including carotene and xanthophyll, that are associated with chlorophyll and responsible for these colors in many plant parts.

carpel a female sporophyll, a simple pistil or one element of a compound pistil bearing an ovule.

Carpenteria (for Professor William Carpenter [1811–1848], Louisiana physician). Hydrangeaceae. California. 1 species, *C. californica* (TREE ANEMONE), an evergreen shrub to 6½ ft (2 m) tall with glossy, elliptic to oblong leaves to 4 in (10 cm) long. Produced in summer, the fragrant flowers are 2–2¾ in (5–7 cm) across, pure white, with five to seven, spreading petals and a central boss of golden stamens. Plant in full sun with shelter from strong winds in well-drained soil. It will tolerate occasional lows to 5°F (–15°C) if grown on a warm, south-facing wall and mulched in winter. It withstands dry conditions. Propagate by seed in spring and fall, or by basal ripewood cuttings in spring and greenwood cuttings in summer (both rooted in a case with bottom heat).

carpet bedding see *bedding.*

Carpinus (Classical Latin name). Betulaceae. Europe, E Asia, N and C America. HORNBEAM. 35 species, mostly deciduous trees with slender branchlets and ovate to cordate leaves, usually toothed and with ribbed veins. Inconspicuous female flowers are carried in pendulous, hoplike catkins clustered with narrow, leafy bracts; these persist and are an attractive feature of the tree. *C. betulus* can be used for formal hedging, informal screening, and for pleaching. It and the remaining species are fine specimen trees, flourishing in most soils, especially chalk. Although all are fully hardy, late frosts may damage the new growth. Leave newly planted hornbeam hedges to

grow for two seasons, pruning hard thereafter in late winter and trimming in late summer. Sown in fall in an open bed, ripe seed will germinate the following spring. Taken in late summer, wounded and treated with a rooting agent, cuttings will root in a closed case or under mist.

C. betulus HORNBEAM; Europe, Asia Minor; broad, pyramidal- to irregular-crowned tree to 70 ft (20 m) with a fluted trunk and gray bark; leaves 2½–4¾ in (6–12 cm) long, dentate and bright to mid-green, becoming amber to clear yellow in fall; 'Columnaris': similar to 'Fastigiata', but slow-growing, dense, compact and columnar; 'Fastigiata': medium-sized, narrowly pyramidal and erect, becoming broader with age; 'Frans Fontaine': similar to the last but retaining narrow, fastigiate habit; 'Incisa': with small, narrow leaves with one or a few deep indentations; 'Pendula': dwarf and domed with strongly weeping branches; 'Purpurea': leaves tinted purple at first; 'Variegata': leaves sporadically marked creamy white; *C. caroliniana* (syn. *C. americana*); AMERICAN HORNBEAM, BLUE BEECH, IRONWOOD; eastern N America and C America; gray-barked, spreading tree to 43 ft (13 m) tall with arching branches; leaves to 8 in (20 cm) long, toothed and dark to glaucous blue-green, assuming red-orange tints in fall; *C. japonica* JAPANESE HORNBEAM; widely spreading tree or small shrub to 50 ft (15 m) tall with scaly, gray bark; leaves 2–4 in (5–10 cm) long, downy, with small teeth and deeply impressed veins giving a corrugated appearance, emerging with a red tint and opening deep green; *C. turczaninovii* China, Japan, Korea; small, shrubby tree to 40 ft (12 m) tall with slender branches and red-tinted new growth; leaves, to 2½ in (6 cm) long, and serrate.

Carpobrotus (from Greek *karpos,* fruit, and *brota,* 'edibles': some species have fleshy edible fruit). Aizoaceae. South Africa, Australia, Mexico, Chile, widely naturalized elsewhere. ICE PLANT. 30 species, mat-forming succulents with creeping, slightly woody stems, narrow, cylindrical to 3-sided, thickly fleshy leaves, and flushes of short-stalked, daisylike flowers opening *en masse* and for a short time in hot,

bright weather. These succulents will thrive in most well-drained soils (sand included) in full sun. They withstand drought, mild frost, high temperatures and salt spray and are excellent groundcover for dry and impoverished areas in Mediterranean and subtropical gardens. Their fleshy, carpeting growth has made them an invaluable fire break in some dry regions. In cold-winter regions, grow in beds, tubs or large pots in a greenhouse and move outdoors for the summer months; avoid cool, wet conditions. Propagate by detaching rooted lengths of stem.

C. chilensis (syn. *Mesembryanthemum aequilaterale*); western US to Mexico and Chile; leaves 2 in (5 cm)-long, straight and 3-sided; flowers faintly fragrant, 2½ in (6 cm) wide, rosy purple; *C. edulis* (syn. *Mesembryanthemum edule*); HOTTENTOT FIG, KAFFIR FIG; South Africa; leaves to 3 in (8 cm), dull, dark green, tapering and curving toward tip; flowers 2¾–3½ in (7–9 cm) wide, pale yellow, becoming flesh-colored then bright pink; fruit fleshy, edible, top-shaped.

carrier an inert material that is used to facilitate the application of a pesticide.

carrot (*Daucus carota* subsp. *sativus*) a biennial, widely grown in temperate and tropical regions as an annual for its edible root. Widely distributed through cultivation, it probably originated in Afghanistan from a dark-rooted type, spreading to China by the 13th or 14th century, and to Western Europe by the 15th century. Yellow and white mutants arose; the familiar orange, due to the presence of beta carotene, derives from selections made in the Netherlands around 1600.

Carrot is a cool-season crop, best grown at a mean temperature range of 61–64°F (16–18°C); temperatures above 84°F (29°C) give rise to reduced top growth and increased root flavor, while below 61°F (16°C) roots become long, tapered and of poor color. Sow successively *in situ* from March, ¾ in (2 cm) deep in rows 12–14½ in (30–37 cm) apart with roots thinned to ¾–2 in (2–5 cm) apart; early crops can be sown in rows 6 in (15 cm) apart.

Earliest maturity is achieved from sowings made under glass, plastic cloches or fleecy or perforated polyethylene film; remove covering at six true leaves. Late supplies can be maintained by storing in the sown site, which must be well-drained and covered with straw in severe winter weather; alternatively, store in clamps outdoors or cover with sand in boxes kept in a cool dry place.

Cultivars are grouped on the basis of maturity date, size, and root shape, as follows: Amsterdam Forcing (early, small to medium size, slender, cylindrical; Nantes (midseason, medium size, broader and longer than Amsterdam Forcing, cylindrical; Chantenay (maincrop, medium size, broader and shorter than Nantes, conical; Berlicum (late, large, cylindrical; Autumn King (very late, very large and long, conical.

Possible problems: aphids, carrot fly; virus.

carrot fly (in the US, CARROT RUST FLY) (*Psila rosae*) a shiny-black fly, up to ¹/₂ in (1 cm) long, with yellow legs; its larvae are a pest of the carrot, principally, but also of celery, parsnip and parsley. Taproots and lateral roots are damaged, foliage yellows, and plants wilt and may die; there are often extensive rust-colored tunnels in the taproot.

grubs bore into root

Carrot fly damage

There are two generations per year, three in a favorable climate. Oval white eggs are laid in the soil surface around the host plant and hatch within seven days. The colorless larvae become creamy white and up to ¹/₂ in (1 cm) long when fully fed.

Avoid damage from the first generation by sowing after mid-May; damage by the second generation can be avoided by lifting an early-sown crop before late August. Other preventive measures include the use of less susceptible cultivars, such as 'Flyaway', 'Resistafly' and 'Sytan', open sites, avoidance of the need to thin, growing under horticultural fleece, or planting in blocks surrounded by a 24 in (60 cm)-high polyethylene barrier to deflect egg-laying females. There are no pesticides approved for the control of this pest in gardens of the UK.

Carthamus (from Arabic, *qurtom*, and Hebrew, *qarthami*, to paint, referring to the dye extracted from the florets of *C. tinctorius*). Compositae. Mediterranean, Asia. 14 species, annual and perennial herbs with spiny to pinnately cut leaves and terminal heads of small florets surrounded by spiny bracts. *C. tinctorius*, SAFFLOWER or FALSE SAFFRON, is a W Asian annual with erect, spiny-leaved stems to 3¹/₄ ft (1 m) tall. Produced in late summer and fall, the flower heads are 1¹/₄–1¹/₂ in (3–4 cm) wide and composed of bright orange-yellow florets in a thistle-like involucre surrounded by leafy, spiny bracts. The flower heads are good for cutting and dry well if taken when still in bud. Sow seed *in situ* after the last frosts.

cartilaginous hard and tough in texture, but flexible.

Carum (Latin form of the Greek name, *karon*: *C. carvi* was extensively grown in Caria, a district in Asia Minor). Umbelliferae. Temperate and subtropical regions. 30 species, perennial and biennial, taprooted herbs with finely 2–3-pinnately divided leaves and compound umbels of small flowers in summer. CARAWAY, *C. carvi*, is a Eurasian biennial to 24 in (60 cm) tall, cultivated in the herb garden for its aromatic leaves, its roots (sometimes prepared as for parsnip) and, principally, for its small, narrow, licorice-flavored seeds. It will grow in full sun in any well-drained, deep and moderately fertile soil, including heavy clay. Harvest seed in mid- to late summer as the flower heads begin to dry off and the seed darkens. Sow seed *in situ* when ripe or in early spring.

Carya (from Greek *karya*, a nut-bearing tree). Juglandaceae. HICKORY, PECAN. US, China. 25 species, large deciduous trees, with smooth, brown to gray twigs and pinnate leaves. Produced in spring, the flowers are inconspicuous—the males borne in branched, drooping catkins; the females in a terminal spike. The fruit is a thick-skinned, green drupe, ovoid to rounded and splitting into four valves containing sometimes edible nuts. The following species are fully hardy and valued for their majestic habit, fall color and fruit (which needs long, hot summers to ripen). Plant in full sun or light shade, in deep, moist and fertile soil. All but the youngest saplings will suffer if transplanted. Propagate by seed sown ripe or stratified over winter for spring-sowing. Increase edible nut-bearing cultivars by splice or veneer grafting on stocks of *C. cordiformis*.

C. cordiformis BITTERNUT, BITTERNUT HICKORY, SWAMP HICKORY; NE US; to 92 ft (28 m) tall; bark smooth then fissured, young branches rusty-hairy; leaflets 2³/₄–5 in (7–13 cm), 5–9, ovate to lanceolate, mid-green turning bright yellow in fall; fruit rounded, to 1¹/₄ in (3 cm), nuts bitter; *C. glabra* HOGNUT, PIGNUT, PIGNUT HICKORY; NE US; to 100 ft (30 m) tall; bark gray, furrowed; leaflets to 6 in (15 cm), 3–7, ovate to lanceolate, dark green turning yellow and orange in fall; fruit rounded to pear-shaped, to ³/₄ in (2 cm), nuts bitter; *C. illinoinensis* PECAN; E US and Midwest to Texas and Mexico; to 160 ft (50 m); leaflets to 6 in (15 cm), 11–17, oblong to lanceolate; fruit to 2³/₄ in (7 cm), oblong with a thin, brown shell and edible nuts; many commercial cultivars are available, bred for fruit, suitability as pollinators, and disease- and climate-tolerance; *C. ovata* SHAGBARK HICKORY; E US; to 130 ft (40 m); bark gray, shaggy; leaflets to 6 in (15 cm), 5, oblong to obovate, acuminate, dark green turning golden-yellow in fall; fruit to 2 in (5 cm), thin-shelled, nuts edible; numerous cropping cultivars are available.

caryopsis of Gramineae; a one-celled, one-seeded, superior fruit in which the pericarp and seed wall are adherent.

Caryopteris (from Greek *karyon*, nut, and *pteron*, wing, referring to the winged fruit). Verbenaceae. E Asia. BLUE BEARD. 6 species, deciduous herbs and shrubs with aromatic leaves and clusters of small flowers in late summer and fall. Grow in full sun in light, well-drained and moderately fertile soil. Where temperatures fall below 14°F

(−10°C) for prolonged periods, provide a deep winter mulch and the protection of a sheltered, south-facing wall. Cut back hard to a woody framework in spring (plants growing in areas with severe winters are often killed to the ground and should be pruned that low, effectively becoming 'herbaceous' perennials). Propagate by semiripe or green wood cuttings rooted in a sandy mix in a case with bottom heat.

C. × *clandonensis* (syn. *C. incana, C. mongholica*); slender-branched, bushy shrub, to 5 × 3¼ ft (1.5 × 1 m); leaves to 4 in (10 cm), toothed, sage- to gray-green above, silver to white beneath; flowers lavender to deep blue; cultivars include: 'Arthur Simmonds', very widely grown, resilient, with compact spikes of bright blue flowers; 'Dark Knight', of low and spreading habit, with silvery leaves and deep blue flowers; 'Ferndown', with very deep blue-violet flowers; 'Heavenly Blue', with deep blue flowers; 'Kew Blue', with silvery leaves and flowers of a deep Cambridge to lavender blue; 'Longwood Blue', to 24 in (60 cm) tall, with silvery leaves and sky blue flowers; 'Worcester Gold', with golden leaves and deep lavender flowers; *C. incana* (syn. *C. mastacanthus*); COMMON BLUE BEARD, BLUE SPIRAEA; China, Japan; to 5 ft (1.5 m) tall, gray-felted shrub; leaves toothed; flowers blue to mauve, white in the cultivar 'Candida'; *C. mongolica* N China, Mongolia; smaller than *C. incana* and weaker in appearance; flowers deep blue.

Caryota (from Greek *karyon*, nut). Palmae. SE Asia to the Pacific Islands and Australia (both species listed here are from SE Asia). FISHTAIL PALM. 12 species, medium-sized to large palms with single or clump-forming trunks and large, bipinnate leaves; these are triangular in outline and consist of many wedge- to diamond-shaped leaflets that have a distinctive ragged or cleft edge (hence 'fishtail'). Large, branched inflorescences ultimately bear plum-shaped, irritant fruit. Provide a humid environment, protection from scorching sunlight and a minimum temperature of 50°F (10°C). Plant in a medium containing composted bark, leaf mold, and clay or polystyrene granules and well-rotted manure; keep moist and regularly syringed, except in

cool weather. Propagate by seed surface-sown on damp sand in a heated case, or, for *C. mitis*, by offsets.

C. mitis BURMESE FISHTAIL PALM, CLUSTERED FISHTAIL PALM, TUFTED FISHTAIL PALM; clumped stems, 10–40 ft (3–12 m) tall; leaves 3¼–12 ft (1–4 m) long, erect to spreading, with 4–12 in (10–30 cm)-long, deltoid, light green segments; *C. urens* JAGGERY PALM, JAGO PALM, WINE PALM, TODDY PALM; differs in its taller and stouter, solitary stem to 40 ft (12 m), outspread to arching leaves and drooping, dark green segments.

cascade (1) a small waterfall, especially one of a series. Cascades are important artificial features in formal gardens, often in the form of a long series of steps and usually in combination with fountains and other waterworks; (2) a form of chrysanthemum; (3) a training style in bonsai.

Cassia (from Greek *kasia* in Dioscorides). Leguminosae. Tropics. SHOWER TREE. 535 species, semideciduous or evergreen trees, shrubs and herbs with pinnate leaves and broadly 5-petalled flowers with long stamens in racemes or panicles principally in spring and summer. Tender. Plant in full sun or light shade in free-draining, moderately fertile, sandy loam. They prefer infrequent but deep watering and will tolerate some drought. Under glass, these are attractive flowering shrubs, blooming when young and responding well to hard pruning in early spring. Provide a minimum temperature of 50°F (10°C), filtered sunlight and a fertile, sandy medium. Water and feed generously in warm weather; keep almost dry in winter. Propagate by seed or by semiripe cuttings in sand in a closed case with gentle bottom heat.

C. fistula (syn. *C. excelsa*); GOLDEN SHOWER TREE, PURGING CASSIA, INDIAN LABURNUM, PUDDING PIPE TREE; Asia, the warm Americas, Australia and the Pacific; tree to 70 ft (20 m); flowers 1¼–2½ in (3–6 cm) wide, vivid yellow, sweetly scented, carried in dense drooping racemes to 16 in (40 cm) long; *C. grandis*(PINK SHOWER, HORSE CASSIA, APPLEBLOSSOM CASSIA; tropical Americas; to 100 ft (30 m); flowers to 1 in (2.5 cm) wide, pink fading to orange-

pink, peach or light yellow, white or cream, in erect racemes to 10 in (25 cm) long; *C. javanica* APPLEBLOSSOM SENNA, RAINBOW SHOWER, PINK SHOWER; SE Asia; to 80 ft (25 m) tall; flowers to 2¾ in (7 cm) wide, crimson to pale pink or buff, in rigid, corymbose racemes to 4 in (10 cm) long; *C. leptophylla* GOLD MEDALLION TREE; Brazil; to 50 ft (15 m); flowers deep yellow, 1¼ in (3 cm) wide, carried in densely packed, terminal racemes to 10 in (25 cm) long; *C. moschata* BRONZE SHOWER; tropical Americas; to 70 ft (20 m); flowers to 1¼ in (3 cm) wide, bronze or golden yellow, often veined red in loose racemes to 12 in (30 cm) long. Many ornamental *Cassia* species are now included in the genus *Senna*.

Cassiope (for Cassiope, wife of Cepheus, King of Aethiopia, and mother of Andromeda). Ericaceae. Europe, Asia, N America. 12 species, hardy, dwarf evergreen shrubs, having slender, creeping to erect stems clothed with small overlapping, scalelike leaves, thus appearing heath- or club-mosslike. In spring, the small solitary flowers, bell- to urn-shaped with four to six pointed lobes, nod on threadlike stalks. Plant in moist, acidic soil, rich in sand and leaf mold. They prefer full sunlight but will suffer in scorching conditions. A shallow winter mulch of ground leaf mold and garden compost will encourage the sprawling stems to layer and rejuvenate themselves and will protect young shoots. Propagate by semiripe cuttings in summer; also by detaching rooted stems.

C. fastigiata Himalaya; to 8 × 12 in (30 × 20 cm); flowers bell-shaped, white ⅜ in (8 mm) across with curving lobes, on red or green stalks; *C. lycopodioides* NE Asia to Alaska; to 4 in (10 cm) tall; flowers ⅜ in (8 mm) long, white or pink and bell-shaped with slightly curving lobes on threadlike, red-tinted stalks; *C. mertensiana* WHITE HEATHER; N America; 6–12 in (15–30 cm) tall; flowers ¼ in (6 mm)-wide, bell-shaped, white, on slender, red-tinted stalks; *C. selaginoides* Himalaya; to 10 × 6 in (25 × 15 cm); flowers bell-shaped, white or pink-tinged to ½ in (1 cm) wide with 5, curving lobes; *C. tetragona* Arctic Circle, and N Europe; to 12 in (30 cm); flowers pendulous, bell-shaped, ¼–⅜ in

C

(6–8 mm) across, white or pink-tinged and 4–5-lobed; *C. wardii* Tibet; flowers white, urn-shaped, some ⅜ in (8 mm) long with five lobes, tinted red inside at the base, on short stalks.

Castanea (the Classical Latin name for these trees, after Castania, a town in Thessaly famous for them). Fagaceae. North America, Europe, Asia. CHEST-NUT, CHINKAPIN. 12 species, hardy, deciduous trees and shrubs with gray to black, smooth to furrowed bark, oblong to lanceolate or oval, usually toothed leaves and small, white to yellow-green, muskily scented flowers in long catkins in summer. The fruit are ovoid to triangular, glossy brown, edible nuts, one to several enclosed in a spiny case (burr) that splits open in late summer.

The genus divides into two groups on the basis of habit—true chestnuts are large trees, usually single-stemmed unless damaged by the elements or grazing animals or coppiced by man or chestnut blight; chinkapins (chinquap-ins) are smaller and shrubby. *C. crenata*, *C. dentata*, *C. mollissima* and *C. sativa* belong to the first group, while chinkapins include *C. alnifolia*, *C. pumila* and *C. ozarkensis*.

Chestnuts are attractive, drought-tol-erant and hardy trees, grown for their large, bright green leaves (yellow-brown in fall), their pleasing, if rather rank-smelling, catkins, their nuts, eaten roasted or candied, and for timber. Where fruit is the main objective, only *C. crenata* and *C. sativa* are well-adapted to cool-summer regions, but all grow and fruit well in climates such as those of the eastern US. Individual trees are usually self-sterile and two or more clones should be near each other to ensure a good seed set. Grow in well-drained, neutral to slightly acidic deep loam (dry and highly acidic, sandy soil included). Propagate by seed in fall (most species hybridize freely), or by budding in summer or grafting in winter on to stocks of *C. crenata* and *C. sativa*.

The greatest threat to chestnuts is the chestnut blight. Introduced acci-dentally to the US at the turn of the century, it has devastated the native *C. dentata*, a species now often to be seen only in the form of suckering stands that have arisen from infected mature

trees and that in turn await death through reinfection. *C. sativa* is also susceptible but survives in the cooler summers of northern Europe and has yet to be affected in the British Isles. Species from E Asia (the blight's place of origin) are largely resistant, as are hybrids between them and the western species (e.g. Dunstan Hybrid Chest-nuts). Fruit are sometimes affected by chestnut weevils, which lay their eggs on the developing fruit in summer. Having bored into the burr and fed on the developing kernel, the weevils pupate in the soil beneath the trees and it is at this stage that they are most easily treated. The two-lined chestnut borer tunnels under the bark and may cause severe damage to small or weak trees.

Chinkapins are hardy and useful in large gardens, grown for their foliage and spreading habit. They are able to withstand wet and acidic conditions, adapting well to the wild or woodland garden and to lakesides, and are an excellent, soil-enriching understory for impoverished and sandy coniferous woodland.

C. alnifolia BUSH or TRAILING CHINKAPIN; SE US; a suckering, spreading shrub to 3¼ ft (1 m) tall; leaves oblong to elliptic, toothed, 4¾ in (12 cm) long, glossy dark green above, tawny-hairy beneath with short-spiny burrs; *C. crenata* JAPANESE CHESTNUT; Japan; spreading, short-trunked, to 70 ft (20 m) tall; leaves to 6 in (15 cm), oblong, glabrous above, gray-downy beneath with small, bristly teeth; fruit to 1½ in (4 cm), 1–4 per 1½–3 in (4–8 cm)-wide, slender-spiny burr; crossed with *C. dentata* to produce blight-resistant clones such as 'Essate-Jap' and 'Sleeping Giant'; *C. dentata* (syn. *C. americana*); AMERICAN SWEET CHESTNUT; eastern US; to 150 ft (45 m) tall, but often smaller and multi-stemmed due to chestnut blight; leaves to 8 in (20 cm) long, oblong to lanceo-late, dull green, glabrous throughout with large, glandular teeth on margins; fruit to 1¼ in (3 cm), 2–3 per long-spiny, 2–2¾ in (5–7 cm) burr; *C. mollis-sima* CHINESE CHESTNUT; China, Korea; to 70 ft (20 m) tall, broad-crowned and stout-trunked; leaves to 8 in (20 cm), oblong to lanceolate to elliptic, downy beneath at first, with bristly teeth; fruit to 1¼ in (3 cm), 1–4

per 2–3 in (5–8 cm), slender-spiny burr; large-fruited selections include 'Nanking', and the small, sweet-fruited 'Kelsey', which is resistant to chestnut-blight; *C. ozarkensis* OZARK CHINKAPIN; differs from *C. pumila* in its smooth, not hairy shoots and its larger leaves—to 9 in (23 cm) long; *C. pumila* CHIN-QUAPIN; eastern US; a suckering shrub or small tree, 12–30 ft (4–10 m) tall; leaves oblong to ovate, to 6 in (15 cm) long, smooth above and pale-hairy beneath with short teeth and 1½ in (4 cm), slender-spiny burrs; var. *ashei*: COASTAL CHINKAPIN, leaves densely hairy beneath, burrs with short spines; *C. sativa* SPANISH CHESTNUT, SWEET CHESTNUT; Europe, N Africa, W Asia; broad to columnar, to 130 ft (40 m) tall; leaves to 10 in (25 cm), oblong to lanceolate, deep, glossy green, smooth above, initially hairy beneath, with remote, bristly teeth; fruit to 1¼ in (3 cm) long, 1–5 per 1½–2¾ in (4–7 cm), slender-spiny burr; includes the ornamental cultivars 'Asplenifolia' and 'Laciniata', with finely cut leaves, 'Albomarginata', with white-edged leaves, 'Variegata', with yellow-edged leaves, 'Heterophylla' with leaves of varying shapes, sizes, teeth and lobing, and 'Holtii', with a narrowly conic crown; the finest fruit-ing clone is generally thought to be 'Marron de Lyon', bearing large, sweet fruit even when young.

Castanopsis (*Castanea*, and Greek, *opsis*, resemblance). Fagaceae. E Asia. Some 110 species, evergreen trees and shrubs with scaly bark and leathery leaves. Inconspicuous flowers are borne in catkins and followed by nuts con-tained by prickly cupules. Hardy to 0°F (–18°C), but thriving in regions with long, hot and humid summers; else-where, plant it in a sheltered and warm location. Grow in full sun in fertile, moist and acidic to neutral soil. Increase by seed. *C. cuspidata* SE China, S Japan; tree to 80 ft (25 m) with spreading to pendent branches and dark gray bark; leaves to 3½ in (9 cm), ovate to oblong with a long, drawn-out apex, thick, tough, entire, glossy dark green above, bronze beneath.

castor meal a by-product of the manufacture of castor oil, used as an organic fertilizer with an analysis of 5–6% nitrogen, 1–2% phosphate and 1% potash.

Casuarina (the long, drooping branchlets were thought to resemble the tail feathers of the cassowary [*Casuarius*]). Casuarinaceae. Australia, Pacific. AUSTRALIAN PINE, SHE OAK, BEEFWOOD, BULL OAK, WHISTLING PINE. Some 70 species, trees and shrubs, usually with slender, weeping branches and many, jointed and whiplike branchlets. These give young plants the look of a tamarisk or a broom; in older trees, they hang from the branches like very long, fine pine needles. The true leaves are reduced to tiny withered scales. Fruit is woody and conelike, adding to the pinelike appearance. Grown in regions that experience little or no frost, where they make fast-growing and elegant street and specimen trees and are well-suited to dry, windy and saline conditions. Elsewhere, they are grown in borders and tubs in a cool greenhouse or conservatory. Plant in full sun in moisture-retentive but free-draining soil with a high sand or grit content. Provide a minimum temperature of 41°F (5°C) and avoid cold, wet conditions. Propagate from seed or by semiripe cuttings in a closed case with bottom heat.

C. cunninghamiana RIVER SHE OAK; to 120 ft (35 m) tall; branchlets 2¾–10 in (7–25 cm) × $^1/_{64}$–$^1/_{32}$ in (0.4–0.7 mm) 6–9-ridged, glabrous, dark green; cones to ⅝ in (1.5 cm), dull gray; *C. equisetifolia* HORSE-TAIL TREE, SOUTHSEA IRONWOOD; to 120 ft (35 m) tall; branchlets 2¾–8 in (7–20 cm) × $^1/_{50}$–$^1/_{25}$ in (0.5–1 mm), 6–8-ridged, hairy, gray-green; cones to 1¼ in (3 cm), gray-brown; *C. torulosa* (to 70 ft (20 m) tall, usually less; branchlets 2–6 in (5–15 cm) × ⅛–¼ in (0.4–0.5 cm), 4–5-ridged, bronze green; cones to 1¼ in (3 cm), glossy mahogany to black-brown; forms are grown with very fine, purple-bronze foliage; *C. verticillata* (syn. *C. stricta*); MOUNTAIN SHE-OAK, DROOPING SHE-OAK, COAST BEEFWOOD; to 30 ft (10 m) tall; branchlets to 4 in (10 cm) × $^1/_{16}$ in (1.5 mm) 9–13-ridged, somewhat hairy, dark

green; cones ¾–1½ in (2–4 cm), glossy dark brown to black.

Catalpa (from "catawba," the vernacular name of this plant among the American Indians of Carolina and Georgia). Bignoniaceae. N America, Cuba, E Asia. 11 species, hardy deciduous trees with large, ovate to cordate leaves, and, in midsummer, pyramidal panicles of showy, trumpet-shaped flowers edged with five, wavy lobes. Long, inedible fruit resemble narrow beans and hang, blackened and thinly woody, through the winter and spring. Hardy to 5°F (–15°C), or lower where long, hot summers ensure wood ripening. Grow in deep, fertile, moisture-retentive soil in an open, sunny site with shelter from strong winds. Sow seed outdoors in fall or in cold frames in spring after stratification for three weeks at 34°F (1°C). Taken in late spring before the leaves are fully developed, softwood cuttings will root in a closed case with bottom heat.

C. bignonioides INDIAN BEAN TREE, SOUTHERN CATALPA, COMMON CATALPA, INDIAN CIGAR, EASTERN CATALPA; SE US; broad-crowned tree to 50 ft (15 m) tall; leaves 4–8 in (10–20 cm)-long, thinly hairy, pale to deep green, usually unlobed and malodorous when crushed; flowers 1¼–2 in (3–5 cm) long, white with purple spots and yellow stains in the throat; includes

flowers best after a previous long hot summer

long seed pods or "beans"

Catalpa bignonioides

'Aurea', with large, yellow to lime leaves, and 'Nana', UMBRELLA CATALPA, often misnamed *C. bungei*, with a dense, broad mop of small leaves, usually top grafted for use as a closely pruned, ball-headed standard; *C. bungei* (N China; differs from *C. bignonioides* in its more triangular, 6 in (15 cm)-long leaves that taper to narrowly pointed lobes; flowers fewer, and white to pale rose with dark maroon spots and yellow streaks; *C. × erubescens* (*C. bignonioides* × *C. ovata*); intermediate between the parents with entire and lobed leaves together on the same tree; includes 'Purpurea', with purple-black shoots and leaves to 12 in (30 cm), bruised purple to faintly violet-tinted dark green; *C. fargesii* W China; broad-crowned tree to 70 ft (20 m) tall; leaves 3–5½ in (8–14 cm) long; flowers 1¼ in (3 cm) long, rose to mauve with yellow and maroon markings; includes f. *duclouxii*, with 3-lobed leaves and purple-rose flowers; *C. ovata* China; to 30 ft (10 m) tall with 4–8 in (10–20 cm)-long leaves that taper finely and have one to five lateral lobes; flowers to 1 in (2.5 cm), white stained yellow and marked purple within; includes 'Flavescens', with paler green leaves and flowers stained dull, pale yellow; *C. speciosa* NORTHERN, WESTERN CATALPA, HARDY CATALPA, SHAWNEE WOOD; differs from *C. bignonioides* in its height, to 100 ft (30 m), its leaves, to 12 in (30 cm) long and unscented when crushed, and in having fewer and more heavily marked flowers; it occupies a more westerly range, from southern Illinois to Arkansas, and flowers some two to three weeks before *C. bignonioides*.

Catananche (from Greek *katanangke*, a strong incentive—this plant was used in love philtres). Compositae. Mediterranean. 5 species, annual and perennial herbs with long-stalked, daisylike flower heads in summer. *C. caerulea* (CUPID'S DART or BLUE CUPIDONE) is a perennial herb to 36 in (90 cm) tall with grassy, gray-green foliage. The flower heads are 2 in (5 cm) wide and carried on slender stalks to 12 in (30 cm) long, each consisting of strap-shaped florets in a deep lavender blue and encased by shining, papery bracts. In the cultivars 'Alba' and 'Perry's White', the flower heads are white; in

C

'Bicolor', they are white with a deep blue center; in 'Blue Giant' and 'Major', they are large, profuse and cornflower blue. A hardy perennial suitable for flower borders and for drying—air-dried, the flower heads tend to close up, making a silvery 'bud'; dried in silica or borax, the florets retain their open attitude and color. Grow in full sun in well-drained soil. Sometimes short-lived, especially on wet and heavy soil. Propagate by root cuttings or by seed sown under glass in early spring.

cataphyll any of the several types of reduced or scarcely developed leaves produced either at the start of a plant's life (i.e. cotyledons) or in the early stages of shoot, leaf or flower development (e.g. the bractlike rhizome scales of some monocots—those subtending and enveloping pseudobulbs, those found in the crowns of cycads alternating with whorls of developed leaves, and the imperfect leaf forms found, progressing up the stem from the most reduced scales, in the basal portions of the stems of many herbs.

catch crop a quickly maturing crop grown in the interval between harvesting one main crop and sowing or planting another.

catenary an ornamental support for climbing or rambling plants, especially roses. It consists of chains or ropes hanging loosely, but evenly, from the tops of vertical posts set out in a continuous line.

caterpillars (Lepidoptera) the larvae of butterflies and moths. They have biting mouthparts and pairs of stumpy abdominal legs (prolegs) bearing hook-like crotchets. Most lepidopterous larvae have five pairs of prolegs. Those of the family Geometridae have only two pairs and because of this they progress in a series of looping movements, hence the common name LOOPER (in North America they are called inchworms, cankerworms and spanworms). The larvae of SAWFLIES (Hymenoptera) have six to eight pairs of prolegs devoid of crotchets.

All parts of plants are subject to attack by lepidopterous caterpillars: the roots and underground organs on herbaceous plants may be damaged by the caterpillars of SWIFT MOTHS (Hepialus species); stems may be girdled or severed at ground level, especially on young vegetables, by CUTWORMS (Noctua and Agrotis species); leaves may be tied together or rolled by the caterpillars of TORTRIX MOTHS (e.g. the FRUIT TREE TORTRIX MOTH, Archips podana); foliage may be eaten on deciduous trees and shrubs by gregarious web-formers, such as the LACKEY MOTH (Malacosoma neustria), and by gregarious non web-formers, such as the BUFFTIP MOTH (Phalera bucephala); foliage may also be eaten by solitary larvae, such as those of the DIAMOND BACK MOTH (Plutella xylostella) on the cabbage tribe, those of the ELEPHANT HAWK MOTH (Deilephila elpenor) on Fuchsia and Impatiens especially, and those of the MAGPIE MOTH (Abraxus grossulariata), a looper caterpillar, on Ribes species. Caterpillars that bore into stems include the LEOPARD MOTH (Zeuzera pyrina) on fruit and ornamental woody plants; those that damage fruit include the CODLING MOTH (Cydia pomonella) on Malus species; those that mine leaves include the AZALEA LEAF MINER (Caloptilia azaleella).

Various residual contact insecticides, many of which also act as stomach poisons, are available for caterpillar control, particularly for those feeding openly on foliage. Infestations by tunnelers and borers may be prevented or reduced by timely application. Pheromone traps can be used to monitor the presence of some pest species and ensure optimum timing for insecticide application. A bacterial spray containing Bacillus thuringiensis is effective against most caterpillars and harmless to other types of animals.

See *bagworm, butterflies, cabbage caterpillars, clearwing moths, codling moth, cutworms, larvae, leaf roller, moths, swift moth, tent caterpillar, tortrix moth, winter moth.*

Catharanthus (from Greek *katharos*, pure, or unblemished, and *anthos*, flower). Apocynaceae. Madagascar. 8 species, bushy annual or perennial herbs with *Vinca*-like flowers chiefly in summer. In frost-free regions, this species can be grown year round outdoors and is a colorful bedding and tub plant, tolerating a wide range of

Catharanthus roseus 'Parasol'
The genus name means "unblemished flower"—attested to by these pure white petals surrounding a clear pink eye.

conditions once established, drought included. In areas with hard frosts, *Catharanthus* is used for summer bedding or grown under glass and in the home as a bright and free-flowering perennial. Grow in full sun or part shade in a fertile, moisture-retentive but freely draining medium. Water and feed liberally in spring and summer, sparingly in winter; maintain a minimum temperature of 45°F (7°C). Cut back in early spring to promote fresh, bushy growth. Sow seed in late winter or early spring at 68°F (20°C). Root greenwood or semiripe cuttings in summer in a closed case with bottom heat. *C. roseus* (syn. *Vinca rosea*); MADAGASCAR PERIWINKLE, VINRA, ROSE PERIWINKLE, CAYENNE JASMINE; evergreen to 24 in (60 cm) tall, perennial sometimes treated as an annual, with glossy leaves and white to candy pink to rose-purple 2 in (5 cm)-wide flowers with a dark purple-red or pink eye.

cation exchange capacity (**CEC**) the ability of a soil to adsorb positively charged ions (cations), on the surface of clay particles and organic matter. It is a measure of the retention of such nutrients as potassium, magnesium, calcium and ammonium. See *base exchange*.

catkin a cylindrical, bracteate spike or spikelike inflorescence composed of single flowers or cymules, the flowers usually apetalous and unisexual. It is also known as an *ament*.

cats (*Felis catus*) Cats foul newly cultivated soil and thereby disturb seedbeds and newly sown lawns. They are attracted to the extra warmth provided by cloches and greenhouses and prefer dry soil. Keep vulnerable areas well-watered and exclude cats by covering sites and access with wire or plastic netting. Pepper dust and other repellents have some deterrent effect but are not long-lasting. Cats will eat certain plants for therapeutic reasons; as well as catmint, *Actinidia kolomikta*, and similarly pungent plants, they will chew *Chlorophytum* and *Cyperus* leaves indoors. Repellent substances give, at best, only temporary protection to small areas. Ultrasonic sound devices are effective in scaring away some cats.

Cattleya (for William Cattley [died 1832], English horticulturist and patron of botany). Orchidaceae. C and S America. 45 species, tender, evergreen, perennial herbs grown for their spectacular flowers. Epiphytes and lithophytes, they produce club- to cane-like pseudobulbs, 4–20 in (10–50 cm) tall, along a creeping rhizome. The pseudobulbs terminate in one or two, tough, oblong to elliptic leaves, from the base of which a papery sheath emerges and splits to free a stem of one to ten thickly textured flowers. These consist of three, lanceolate to oblong sepals, two, usually broader and larger petals and a funnel-shaped lip with a spreading, colorful midlobe.

The many *Cattleya* hybrids are among the most popular orchids. They include miniatures, medium-sized and large plants. Flowers range in shape and size from the small and starlike to the very large (to 7 in (18 cm) in diameter), lush and lacy; in color, through white, pale rose, magenta, mauve, burgundy, velvety red, scarlet, vermilion, orange, gold, lemon yellow, bronze and green, often with a differently colored lip or blotches or veins. The range is greatly extended by intergeneric hybrids with *Brassavola*, *Epidendrum*, *Laelia*, *Rhyncholaelia* and *Sophronitis*. Some are languorously scented; some last well when cut. The species generally possess more character than the hybrids and are regaining popularity. The principal flowering time is winter to spring, but this may vary from year to year with the same plant and even a small collection should provide some color at all times. Most of the species

are grown by orchid specialists, and several at least are easy and reliable plants for a greenhouse (minimum temperature 50°F/10°C) or the home. Grow in very bright, humid and buoyant conditions with some protection from full, midday sun. Plant in an open, bark-based medium in small pots, pans or baskets. Water, syringe and feed frequently when in growth. Once the new growth is fully developed, water only to prevent shrivelling of pseudobulbs and impose cooler, drier conditions. As temperatures rise in spring, mist over with increasing frequency; return to a full watering regimen when the new shoots and roots appear. Propagate by division, taking one active growth and two to three backbulbs per division. *Cattleya* resents disturbance and is quite happy to grow over the edge of the pot for a season or two.

C. aurantiaca tall plants with clusters of 1¼ in (3 cm)-wide, starry flowers in scarlet, vermillion or pale orange; *C. bicolor* (small to medium-sized plants with several flowers to 4 in (10 cm) wide, tepals bronze, lip tonguelike, bright purple-red; *C. bowringiana* medium to tall, gray-green plants with clusters of 2 in (5 cm)-wide, spreading flowers, tepals rose to magenta, lip stained deep mauve or rosy purple; *C. dowiana* medium-sized plants with one to three, 6 in (15 cm)-wide flowers, tepals golden yellow, petals broad and frilly, lip large stained deep, velvety red; *C. forbesii* small plants with a few, 3 in (8 cm)-wide, delicately scented flowers, tepals pale olive to buff or bronze, lip cream stained yellow and flesh pink; *C. guttata* tall plants with clusters of 2¾ in (7 cm) wide flowers, tepals olive to lime green spotted rosy purple to maroon, lip white with a bright magenta or deep garnet midlobe; *C. labiata* medium-sized plants with one or few broad and frilly, fragrant flowers to 7 in (18 cm) wide, tepals white to pale rose, magenta or mauve, lip very large and showy, rose-mauve stained yellow and overlaid with mauve or red-purple; *C. loddigesii* medium-sized to tall plants with clusters of spreading, fragrant flowers to 4 in (10 cm) wide, tepals palest rose to lilac, lip shell-like, white to cream tinted yellow and stained rose to magenta; *C. mossiae* medium-sized plants, flowers one or few, to 7 in

(18 cm) wide, very broad and lacy, fragrant, tepals white to pale rose or magenta or lilac, lip white to rose or lilac with a central orange patch and purple-red veins and tip; *C. schilleriana* medium-sized plants with a few, fragrant flowers to 4 in (10 cm) wide, tepals narrow and wavy, deep olive to bronze spotted chocolate to maroon, lip white densely combed with rosy purple; *C. skinneri* medium-sized to tall plants with clusters of spreading, rounded flowers to 4¾ in (12 cm) wide, rose to deep magenta, lip with a white or cream throat; *C. walkeriana* small plants, flowers to 4 in (10 cm) wide, one or few, fragrant, tepals pale pink-lilac to bright rose-purple, petals rounded and spreading, lip with lateral lobes held flat and open and midlobe kidney-shaped, stained white to yellow at base, deep magenta to mauve at tip.

caudate of a leaf or perianth segment apex, tapering gradually into a fine tail-shaped point, tip or appendage.

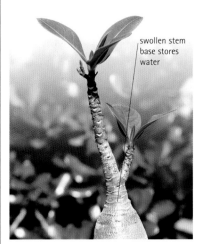

swollen stem base stores water

Adenium obesum
Adeniums fall into a group of succulents characterized by a swollen, bottlelike stem base commonly known as a caudex.

caudex strictly, the basal axis of a plant, comprising both stem and root; sometimes applied to the aerial stems of palms and superficially palmlike plants. The term is most often used in connection with plants with stout, swollen or succulent unbranched stems, usually crowned with narrower branches, leaves or inflorescences.

caudiciform resembling or possessing a caudex, encountered in the phrase 'caudiciform succulents', a disparate group of succulent and semi-succulent plants of horticultural importance and defined by its members' exhibiting a caudex.

caulescent producing a well-developed stem above ground.

cauliflory the production of flowers directly from older wood, i.e. springing from the trunk or branches as in the Judas tree (*Cercis*), cocoa (*Theobroma*), and *Goethea*. Such plants are termed cauliflorous.

cauliflower (*Brassica oleracea* Botrytis Group) Closely related to cabbage, cauliflower is grown for its edible inflorescence made up of thick, fleshy flower stalks compacted to form a spherical head of edible curd, usually white. Most are annual but some biennial and perennial forms also exist. A native of the Mediterranean region, cauliflower has been widely cultivated since the 18th century and is an important crop in France, Italy and the UK.

Curd development is governed by temperature; with annual cultivars in temperate zones, it occurs after the formation of a prerequisite number of leaves, at around 63°F (17°C); above this temperature, curds may not form or be of poor quality. With biennial and perennial cultivars, curds are formed after exposure to 50°F (10°C) or below, depending partly on plant size. In situations where the temperature fluctuates around a threshold at critical times, vegetative growth may take place, resulting in curds with leafy bracts. Cultivars vary in winter hardiness, and may be grouped according to maturity time: early summer; summer; fall; winter-heading; spring-heading overwintered.

For early summer-heading curds, sow in October ½ in (1 cm) deep under protection, into a seedbed or, for best results, in pots. Overwinter with careful ventilation and plant out in March or as soon as suitable conditions prevail. For summer- and fall-heading curds, sow from mid-March to mid-May under a cold frame or cloches, or in a sheltered outdoor seedbed. For winter-

and spring-heading cultivars, sow in late May in an outdoor seedbed. Plant out summer-heading cultivars from early March to mid-May 22 in, (55 cm) square or at 18 in (45 cm) spacings in rows 24 in (60 cm) apart; plant out fall-heading cultivars in mid- to late June, 22–25 in (55–63 cm) each way or at 20–24 in (50–60 cm) spacings in rows 24–26 in (60–65 cm) apart; winter- and spring-heading cultivars should be planted in mid- to late July, 28 in (70 cm) each way. Mini cauliflowers can be produced over 13–18 weeks during summer months from sowings made from April onward, with the plants spaced 6 in (15 cm) each way. There is interest in green curd cultivars, grown for fall maturity, and in the perennial cultivar 'Nine Star Perennial', sown in spring and planted 3¼ ft (1 m) square. See *broccoli, calabrese.*

Possible problems: aphids, cabbage caterpillars, cabbage root fly, flea beetle; clubroot, leaf spot.

cauline attached to or arising from the stem.

Ceanothus (from Greek *keanothos*, name used by Theophrastus for spiny plants). Rhamnaceae. W N America, Mexico. CALIFORNIA LILAC. Some 60 species, hardy evergreen or deciduous shrubs and small trees, often with tough, small dark green leaves and grown for their dense panicles of small, blue, mauve, pink or white flowers produced in spring and summer. The following are hardy to –10°F (–23°C), but should be planted against a south-facing wall in areas that experience prolonged hard frosts and cold winds. Many have a spreading habit, which benefits from some support and is shown to best advantage on a wall; an exception is *C. thyrsiflorus* var. *repens*, an excellent groundcover. Plant in full sun in free-draining, light soil. Prune deadwood from evergreen species in spring; trim over after flowering. Reduce long, flowered shoots of deciduous species and hybrids to within a few buds of the main framework in spring. Increase by softwood or semiripe cuttings in summer.

C. arboreus FELTLEAF CEANOTHUS, CATALINA MOUNTAIN LILAC; evergreen shrub or tree 10–22 ft (3–7 m); leaves 1¼–3 in (3–8 cm), broadly ovate to

rounded, densely white-tomentose beneath; inflorescence to 4¾ in (12 cm), pyramidal; flowers pale blue, fragrant; includes 'Trewithen Blue', spreading, with dark green, broadly oval leaves and deep blue flowers; *C.* 'Burkwoodii' (*C. dentatus* var. *floribundus* × *C.* × *delilianus* 'Indigo'); dense, evergreen, spreading shrub to 5 ft (1.5 m); leaves ⅜–1¼ in (1.5–3 cm), elliptic, toothed, dark green and glossy above, pale-hairy beneath; inflorescence 1¼–2½ in (3–6 cm), flowers bright blue with darker stamens; *C.* 'Burtonensis' (*C. impressus* × *C. thyrsiflorus*); spreading evergreen shrub to 6½ ft (2 m); leaves small, circular, dark green and glossy, appearing crinkled; inflorescence to ¾ in (2 cm) in diameter, dense, rounded; flowers dark blue; *C.* 'Concha' evergreen, to 6½ ft (2 m), spreading; leaves to 1 in (2.5 cm); flowers dark blue, red-tinted in bud; *C.* 'Delight' (*C. papillosus* × *C. rigidus*); evergreen shrub to 15 ft (5 m); leaves glossy pale green; inflorescence a long panicle; flowers deep blue; *C.* × *delileanus* FRENCH HYBRID CEANOTHUS; *C. coeruleus* × *C. americanus*); evergreen shrub to 15 ft (5 m); leaves 1½–3 in (4–8 cm), elliptic to oblong, dark green above, paler and downy beneath; flowers blue in large panicles; includes the popular 'Gloire de Versailles', a large, semideciduous and free-flowering form, with a rangy habit, pale to mid-green leaves and fragrant, powder blue flowers; *C.* 'Dark Star' evergreen, arching to 6½ × 10 ft (2 × 3 m); leaves ovate, toothed, dark green; flowers dark purple-blue, honey-scented; *C. dentatus* CROPLEAF CEANOTHUS; dense, evergreen shrub to 5 ft (1.5 m); leaves ¼–¾ in (0.5–2 cm), elliptic to narrowly oblong or linear, dark green above, paler beneath, margins revolute and glandular-papillate; flowers dark blue in short, dense clusters; *C. gloriosus* POINT REYES CREEPER; prostrate to decumbent, evergreen shrub, 6½–10 ft (2–3 m) across; leaves ¾–2 in (2–5 cm), broadly oblong to rounded, toothed, tough, dark green; inflorescence umbel-like; flowers dark blue to violet to purple; *C. impressus* SANTA BARBARA CEANOTHUS; low, evergreen shrub to 5 ft (1.5 m); leaves ¼–½ in (0.6–1.2 cm) elliptic to suborbicular, veins sunken above, margins wavy, dark glossy green; flowers dark blue in a narrow inflorescence to 1 in (2.5 cm) long; *C. incanus* COAST WHITETHORN; erect evergreen shrub to 12 ft (4 m), twigs thorny, bloomed white; leaves ³⁄₄–2¹⁄₂ in (2–6 cm), broadly ovate to elliptic, gray-green above, paler beneath; flowers white in 1¹⁄₄–2³⁄₄ in (3–7 cm)-long, dense panicles; *C.* 'Italian Skies' (a hybrid with *C. foliosus*); evergreen shrub to 5 ft (1.5 m) tall, spreading, densely branched; leaves to ⁵⁄₈ in (1.5 cm), oval to oblong, glossy dark green with small teeth; inflorescence to 2³⁄₄ in (7 cm), conical; flowers intense blue; *C.* × *lobbianus* (*C. dentatus* × *C. griseus*); erect, evergreen shrub to 3¹⁄₄ ft (1 m); leaves to 1 in (2.5 cm), elliptic, leathery, dark green, toothed; flowers bright blue in rounded, axillary clusters with blue-haired stalks; *C.* × *pallidus* 'Marie Simon' (*C.* × *delilianus* × *C. ovatus*); much-branched, deciduous shrub to 5 ft (1.5 m) tall; leaves broadly oval; flowers soft pink in conical, dense and terminal panicles; *C. papillosus* WART LEAF CEANOTHUS; evergreen shrub to 15 ft (5 m); leaves ¹⁄₂–2 in (1–5 cm), oblong to elliptic, margins revolute with glandular teeth, dark green and hairy, upper surface strongly papillose to pustular; flowers pale to deep blue or lilac-mauve in short, narrow spikes; *C. prostratus* SQUAW CARPET; prostrate evergreen shrub forming dense mats; leaves ¹⁄₂–³⁄₄ in (1–2 cm), cuneate to obovate, margins undulate, tough, pale, glossy green; flowers pale lavender to dark blue or white in umbel-like, terminal panicles; *C.* 'Puget Blue' evergreen, to 10 ft (3 m), dense; leaves elliptic to oblong, glandular-toothed; flowers pale to dark blue; *C. rigidus* MONTEREY CEANOTHUS; evergreen tree to 6¹⁄₂ ft (2 m), or low and spreading; leaves ¹⁄₄–⁵⁄₈ in (0.6–1.5 cm), cuneate to broadly obovate, leathery, sometimes toothed, tough, glossy dark green; flowers fragrant, lilac to dark blue or white in sparse, umbel-like clusters; *C.* 'Southmead' a hybrid involving *C.* × *lobbianus*; evergreen dense, bushy shrub to 5 ft (1.5 m) tall; leaves small, oblong, glossy dark green; flowers very dark, rich blue, in rounded inflorescences; *C. thyrsiflorus* BLUEBLOSSOM, BLUE BRUSH; large, evergreen shrub or small tree to 20 ft (6 m); leaves ¹⁄₂–⁵⁄₈ in (1–1.5 cm), oblong-ovate to broadly

elliptic, toothed, dark, glossy green; flowers pale to dark blue or white in rounded, short panicles; includes var. *repens* CREEPING BLUE BLOSSOM), prostrate, giving dense cover, with small, dark, glossy leaves and dark blue flowers—the best selection is 'Blue Mound'; *C.* × *veitchianus* (*C. griseus* × *C. rigidus*); robust evergreen shrub to 1¹⁄₄ in (3 cm); leaves to ³⁄₄ in (2 cm), obovate to ovate, toothed, glossy green; inflorescence ³⁄₄–2 in (2–5 cm), dense, oblong to capitate; flowers intense, dark blue.

CEC see *cation exchange capacity*.

Cedrus (from the Greek name, *kedros*). Pinaceae. E Mediterranean, N Africa, W Himalaya. CEDAR. 2 species, hardy evergreen coniferous trees with a pyramidal to tiered habit and needle-like foliage. Oblong to cylindric cones stand erect on outspread branches. These stately conifers thrive in most well-drained soils and will tolerate some drought once established. Plant young trees in midspring; feed and stake them in the early years and prune to remove any forked leaders and weak lower branches. Propagate by seed, except in the case of cultivars, which must be grafted (*C. atlantica* Glauca Group will, however, come more or less true from seed).

C. atlantica, ATLAS CEDAR, to 160 ft (50 m) tall, crown ovoid to conic at first, ultimately flat-topped, with roughly 4-sided, ¹⁄₂–1¹⁄₄ in (1–3 cm)-long, blue-green to blue-gray leaves (Glauca Group) and gray-bloomed cones; includes fastigiate, weeping, pyramidal, white-variegated, blue-gray and silver cultivars; *C. deodara* DEODAR CEDAR, HIMALAYAN CEDAR; W Himalaya; 120–200 ft (35–60 m) tall; crown broadly conic, leader nodding, branches tiered with drooping tips; leaves 1¹⁄₄–2¹⁄₂ in (3–6 cm), rich green to gray-green, somewhat 4-sided; cones 3–5¹⁄₂ in (8–14 cm), glaucous blue-gray to brown, composed of

scales with ridged apices; includes dwarf, bushy, fastigiate, blue-green, yellow and very hardy cultivars; *C. libani* CEDAR OF LEBANON; Lebanon, Syria, Turkey; to 150 ft (45 m); crown conic, becomes flat-topped and irregular with age, branches tiered and horizontal to slightly ascending; leaves ¹⁄₂–1¹⁄₄ in (1–3 cm), mid-green, often blue-tinted, 4-sided; cones 3–4³⁄₄ in (8–12 cm), dull green becoming brown, composed of scales without ridged apices; includes dwarf, spreading, weeping, gold and variegated cultivars.

Celastrus (from *kelastros*, Greek name for *Phillyrea*). Celastraceae. Widespread. BITTERSWEET, STAFF VINE. 30 species, evergreen or deciduous shrubs. Those listed here are deciduous vines with ovate to elliptic, toothed leaves and bright, orange to red seeds held in woody, 3-valved and spherical capsules in fall and winter. Rampant vines thrive in most soils in sun or semi-shade. They are best left to make dense tangles and luxuriant cascades of growth among trees or along walls and fences in the wilder parts of the garden. Cut back hard in spring to remove dead stems and keep within bounds. Root cuttings in late winter in a cold frame. Plants of both sexes are usually required for fertile seed.

C. orbiculatus (syn. *C. articulatus*); ORIENTAL BITTERSWEET, STAFF VINE; NE Asia, naturalized N America; to 40 ft (12 m); fruit interior yellow, seeds coral pink to red; *C. scandens* AMERICAN BITTERSWEET, CLIMBING BITTERSWEET WAXWORK, STAFF TREE; N America; to 22 ft (7 m); fruit interior orange-yellow, seeds carmine to scarlet.

celeriac (*Apium graveolens* var. *rapaceum*) a biennial, usually grown as an annual for its edible celery-flavored root, which is swollen and knobbly and is shredded for use in salads, or boiled. Celeriac requires a long season of uninterrupted

celery-like leaves

edible root

Celeriac

C

growth. Sow in February/March under protection, at around 59°F (15°C), in seed boxes or modules, or in a cold frame in March/April. Pot up and harden off for planting outside in late May, 12–15 in (30–38 cm) square; keep well-watered. Harvest from October. The crop is best left *in situ* and covered with straw during severe winter weather.

Possible problems: carrot fly.

celery (*Apium graveolens* var. *dulce*) a biennial, grown as an annual for its crisp, edible, fleshy petioles. Native to damp sites in Europe and Asia, and cultivated for more than 2000 years, it does best in temperate zones with a mean monthly temperature of 61–70°F (16–21°C). Above this temperature range, leaf growth is poor, below it, plants may bolt. Celery matures in fall/winter until the first frosts, but the season can be extended by greenhouse protection or by covering plants outdoors.

Two main divisions may be distinguished by cultivation method. Trench celery, with white-, pink- or red stemmed cultivars, is traditionally blanched by planting in a trench for gradual earthing up; the same result can more easily be achieved with thick paper collars. For self-blanching celery, with its white- or cream-stemmed cultivars, close planting and straw packing are used to produce good-quality plants. Sow trench celery under protection in February/March at about 59°F (15°C). Pot up and harden off, then plant out in late May, 12–18 in (30–45 cm) square as double rows in a prepared trench, or as single rows 36 in (90 cm) apart, with 10 in (25 cm) between plants. Self-blanching celery should be raised similarly and planted out 10 in (25 cm) square in block formation. American green-stemmed cultivars should be treated in the same way. Leaf celery is grown for flavoring salads and for soup. The small, very hardy plants can be cut over frequently from four weeks after planting out from modules, at 5 in (13 cm) stations in rows 12 in (30 cm) apart. Late summer sowings can provide supplies from under protection throughout the winter. All celery requires an uninterrupted growing season, with generous watering.

Possible problems: carrot fly, celery fly, leaf miner, slugs; heart rot, leaf spot.

celery fly CELERY LEAF MINER (*Euleia heracleii*) a small fly, about ¼ in (5 mm) long, brown with a dark zig-zag banding on its wings. The legless maggots are up to ⅜ in (8 mm) long, white or very pale green. Celery, celeriac, and parsnips are subject to attack, the maggots mining within the leaves and giving rise to blotchlike blisters, eventually causing shriveling. There are two or three generations per season, and early summer attacks are most damaging. Pick off affected parts of leaves or squeeze to crush the larvae within. There are currently no pesticides approved for use in UK gardens.

cell (1) the primary unit of plant tissue, microscopic in size, consisting of cytoplasm and usually a single nucleus, which contains the code of plant characteristics, and is bounded by a thin wall of cellulose; (2) the lobe of an anther or locule of an ovary or pericarp; (3) a small individual container for raising plants, manufactured of plastic or polystyrene in the form of a multicelled tray; it is often called a module. See *module*.

cellulose a polymer of glucose molecules, the major constituent of plant cell walls.

Celmisia (for Celmisius, son of the nymph Alciope, after whom a related genus was named). Compositae. Australasia (those listed here from New Zealand). 60 species, more or less hardy perennial herbs and subshrubs with silvery-hairy leaves and slender-stalked, white, daisylike flower heads produced in spring and summer. Hardy to 0°F (–18°C), they are suited to the rock garden, scree, raised beds, alpine troughs and peat terrace. Small and cushion-forming species grow best in pans in an alpine house. Grow in sun, with shelter from cold, drying winds, in a gritty, humus-rich, nonalkaline soil. Water freely when in growth and keep roots cool. Keep just moist in winter. Propagate by cuttings and division in early summer, or by fresh seed germinated in cool, moist conditions in a mix high in silver sand and leaf mold.

C. bellidioides creeping, mat-forming herb; leaves to ⅝ in (1.5 cm), oblong-ovate to spathulate, dark green above, gray-floccose beneath; flower heads to ¾ in (2 cm) in diameter; *C. coriacea* clump-forming herb with lanceolate to oblong leaves to 24 in (60 cm) long, tough and ribbed, very lustrous and silvery; flower heads to 3 in (8 cm) in diameter; *C. ramulosa* small procumbent to ascending shrub or subshrub to 8 in (20 cm); leaves to ½ in (1 cm), tough, linear to oblong, gray-tomentose; flower heads to 1 in (2.5 cm) in diameter; *C. traversii* clump-forming herb with oblong to lanceolate leaves to 16 in (40 cm), dark green with cream-felted undersides and red-purple margins and midrib; flower heads to 2 in (5 cm) in diameter, on a scape to 20 in (50 cm) tall; *C. walkeri* sprawling, much-branched shrub or shrublet to 6½ ft (2 m); leaves to 2 in (5 cm), narrowly oblong, leathery, white-hairy beneath; flower heads to 1½ in (4 cm) in diameter.

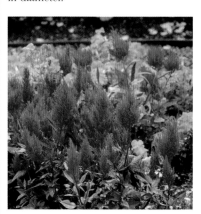

Celosia 'Forest Fire'
These flamelike flower spikes in a burning scarlet are typical of the Plumosa Group of *Celosia* cultivars.

Celosia (from Greek *keleos*, burning: the inflorescence of some species is flamelike). Amaranthaceae. Asia, Africa, Americas. COCKSCOMB, WOOLFLOWER. 50 species, annual and perennial herbs with rather fleshy stems and small, pearly flowers packed in showy terminal, plume-, spire- or coral-like heads. Sow seed under glass at 65°F (18°C) in late winter. Grow on in a fertile, loamy mix at 59°F (15°C) in direct or filtered sunlight, watering and feeding freely. Reduce water and feed to induce and prolong flowering. For half-hardy bedding, harden off carefully and plant out after the last frosts in a well-drained, fertile soil in full sun.

C. argentea (RED FOX; widespread, intensively developed annual, ³/₄–6½ ft (0.25–2 m) tall with lanceolate to ovate, mid-green to maroon leaves and flowers in shades of red, crimson, purple, magenta, pink, scarlet, salmon, apricot, orange and yellow; inflorescence types range from the broad, terminal cockscomb with brainlike folds of the Cristata Group (syn. *C. cristata*) to the tapering, torchlike spikes of the Plumosa Group.

Celtis (from *keltis*, a Greek name applied to another tree). Ulmaceae. Tropics, Europe, N America. HACKBERRY, NETTLE TREE. 70 species, trees or shrubs, deciduous or evergreen. Those listed here are deciduous, hardy trees grown for their broad-headed, spreading habit, ovate to lanceolate, toothed leaves and small, berrylike fruits which hang on slender stalks and follow inconspicuous green flowers in summer. Although tolerant of harsh winters, these trees require long, hot summers for good growth and fruit. Plant in fertile, deep soil in full sun. Propagate by fresh seed collected in fall and stratified in moist sand for two to three months with the flesh removed.

C. australis EUROPEAN NETTLE TREE, MEDITERRANEAN HACKBERRY, LOTE TREE; Mediterranean, Middle East; to 70 ft (20 m); leaves to 6 in (15 cm), roughly hairy and dark green above, paler and downy beneath; fruit red ripening brown; *C. occidentalis* HACKBERRY; N America; to 80 ft (25 m); leaves to 4³/₄ in (12 cm), smooth, glossy green above, slightly hairy beneath; fruit yellow or red ripening deep purple; *C. sinensis* JAPANESE HACKBERRY; E Asia; to 50 ft (15 m); leaves to 3 in (8 cm), tough, smooth, glossy dark green above, duller beneath; fruit dark orange.

celtuce see *lettuce*.

Centaurea (from Greek *kentauros*, centaur). Compositae. Mediterranean, Asia, N America, Australia. HARDHEADS, KNAPWEED. 450 species, annual and perennial herbs, fully hardy and grown for their thistlelike flower heads. Produced from late spring through summer, these consist of a scaly, ovoid involucre crowned

with showy outspread florets, tubular and deeply lobed. Grow in full sun in well-drained soil. Annual species, such as *C. cyanus* and its cultivars, are excellent seasonal fillers; their bright blooms are also suitable for cutting and drying. Sow seed *in situ* in spring. Successional sowings will give flowers throughout the summer. Perennial species are fine plants for the herbaceous or mixed border; propagate by seed or division in fall or spring (*C. montana* may also be increased by root cuttings).

C. cyanus BACHELOR'S BUTTONS, CORNFLOWER, BLUE-BOTTLE; northern temperate regions; annual to biennial to 36 in (90 cm) tall; leaves lanceolate, entire to toothed, pale-floccose beneath; flower heads deep violet-blue to azure, sky blue, mauve, pink, red and white; *C. dealbata* Caucasus; perennial to 3¼ ft (1 m) tall; leaves pinnatisect, long-stalked, gray-hairy; flower heads bright pink to lilac-mauve; *C. hypoleuca* W Transcaucasia, Turkey, Iran; perennial to 20 in (50 cm) tall; leaves lyrate to pinnatisect, gray-hairy beneath; flower heads pink to bright magenta-rose in the cultivar 'John Coutts'; *C. macrocephala* Caucasus; perennial to 3¼ ft (1 m); leaves lanceolate, entire to deeply cut, green; florets yellow to yellow-orange; *C. montana* MOUNTAIN BLUET; European mountains; perennial to 32 in (80 cm); leaves ovate to lanceolate, entire to lobed, floccose beneath; outer florets typically blue, inner florets violet to mauve; *C. pulcherrima* Transcaucasia; perennial to 16 in (40 cm); leaves lanceolate, entire to lyrate or pinnatisect, gray-hairy beneath; outer florets bright rose-purple, inner florets paler) *C. margaritae*, *C. moschata* and *C. suaveolens* are now treated as *Amberboa moschata*.

centipedes (Chilopoda) small soil inhabiting animals with segmented bodies, They have one pair of legs on each trunk segment, in contrast to

millipedes which have two pairs; and, depending on species, they may have 15 to over 100 pairs of legs. The legs on the first segment behind the head are modified into a pair of clawlike appendages, each with a poison gland used to seize and immobilize prey. Centipedes are mostly carnivorous, feeding on small slugs, worms and insects and they are generally beneficial in the garden.

The most common species belong to the orders Geophilomorpha and Lithobiomorpha. Geophilomorphs, which are adapted to subterranean life, are very long and slender, and have 31–177 pairs of legs. They are often brought to the surface during cultivation and writhe and twist with little progress. The most common species is *Necrophlaoephagus longicornis*, which is yellow, and 3 in (8 cm) long. Lithobiomorphs are surface dwellers. They are found under stones and in other sheltered places. They have flattened bodies and adults have 15 leg-bearing segments and relatively long and stout legs, allowing for rapid progress over the soil surface. Another species often encountered is *Lithobius forficulatus*, which is chestnut brown and about 1 in (2.5 cm) long.

central cell a binucleate cell in the center of the embryo sac from which the endosperm develops. See *polar nuclei*.

central leader a central stem carrying branches and/or fruiting spurs.

Centranthus (from Greek *kentron*, spur, and *anthos*, a flower, from the spurred flower). Valerianaceae. Europe, Mediterranean. 12 species, hardy annual and perennial herbs, with clumps of erect stems decked with broad, packed cymes of small flowers in late spring and summer. Hardy to –10°F (–23°C). Grow in full sun in fast-draining, poor and preferably alkaline soil in the herbaceous or mixed border, or in the crevices of old walls. Shear over after flowering. Propagate from seed in fall or spring. *C. ruber* JUPITER'S BEARD, KEYS OF HEAVEN, RED VALERIAN, FOX'S BRUSH; perennial to 32 in (80 cm) tall; flowers crimson to pale red, held above foliage in branched

one pair of legs per segment

Centipede

C

heads from late spring to early fall; white, pink and deep red forms are common in cultivation.

centrifugal progressing or extending from the center toward the margin.

centripetal developing or progressing toward the center from the margin.

cephalanthium the capitulum or flower head of Compositae.

Cephalaria (from Greek *kephale*, head: the flowers are in round heads). Dipsacaceae. 65 species, annual and perennial herbs with pinnately toothed to lobed leaves and, in summer, small flowers in rounded heads surrounded by bracts and carried on slender stalks. Fully hardy, plant in a sunny, well-drained position in a large herbaceous border or the wild garden. Increase by division in spring, or by seed in fall. *C. gigantea* (syn. *C. tatarica*); GIANT SCABIOUS, YELLOW SCABIOUS; Caucasus, Siberia; stately perennial to 6½ ft (2 m) tall with long-stalked, 2 in (5 cm)-wide heads of ivory to yellow flowers.

cephalium a woolly growth bearing flowers, terminating the stem of certain Cactaceae.

Cephalocereus (from Greek *kephale*, head, and Latin, *Cereus*, referring to the headlike, differentiated flowering zone). Cactaceae. Mexico. 3 species, tender cacti with tall, usually unbranched columnlike stems that are ribbed and spiny. Tubular to campanulate flowers open at night amid wool and bristles. Provide a minimum temperature of 50°F (10°C), low humidity and shade from the hottest summer sun. Plant in an acidic to neutral soil high in grit and sand. Keep dry from midfall until early spring, except for a light misting over on warm days in late winter. *C. senilis* (OLD MAN CACTUS; stem gray-green, growing extremely slowly to 40 ft × 16 in (12 × 0.4 m), usually grown as far smaller, narrower plants, covered in a mass of white, shaggy hairs; flowers off-white marked pink.

Cephalophyllum (from Greek *kephalos*, head, and *phyllon*, leaf, referring to the dense, headlike clumps

formed by the leaves of some species. Aizoaceae. Namibia, South Africa. 30 species, low-growing, tender perennials with succulent, cylindric to triangular leaves and large, daisylike flowers opening on warm, sunny days. Cultivate as for *Conophytum*.

C. alstonii has leaves to 2¾ in (7 cm), gray-green; flowers dark red; *C. pillansii* has leaves 1–8 in (2.5–20 cm), dark green; flowers yellow with a red center.

Cephalotaxus (from Greek *kephale*, head, and Latin *taxus*, yew, referring to the headlike inflorescences of these yewlike trees). Cephalotaxaceae. N India, China, Taiwan, Japan. PLUM YEW. 9 species, evergreen coniferous trees with 2-ranked, yewlike leaves and fleshy, egg-shaped fruits. Hardy to −20°F (−29°C), but better in milder regions. It favors moist, sandy soil, a cool, humid atmosphere and semi-shade, and may be grown as a specimen, an understory shrub, or as a screen or hedge. Propagate by greenwood cuttings of terminal shoots, under mist or in a cold frame, in late summer or early fall. Sow seed in a cold frame when ripe; alternatively, stratify seed and sow in spring (germination may be delayed until the second spring). *C. harringtonia* COW TAIL PINE, PLUM YEW; Japan; shrub or small tree to 15 ft (5 m) tall; leaves to 2½ in (6 cm), linear to falcate, dark green above, with two gray bands beneath; fruit ¾–1¼ in (2–3 cm), ripening purple-brown; dwarf, shrubby, fastigiate, procumbent and semiweeping forms exist.

Cephalotus (from Greek *kephalotos*, with a head: the stamens are capitate). Cephalotaceae. W Australia. AUSTRALIAN PITCHER PLANT. 1 species, *C. follicularis*, a small, tender perennial herb, carnivorous with leaves of two types: the first ovate to spathulate in a central tuft, and the second (the traps) pitcherlike and low-borne. The pitchers are some ½–2 in (1–5 cm) long, squat and green with bristly wings, the rim heavily ribbed, waxy and tinted blood red and the lid veined purple-red and zoned with paler, semilucent patches. Small, green-white flowers are produced in slender-stalked spikes in

summer. Plant in deep clay pots containing a mix of silver sand, peat and live sphagnum; maintain a minimum temperature of 50°F (10°C) and position in full sun with high humidity. From midspring to fall, stand the pot to one third of its depth in rain water; during the winter months, reduce the water depth keeping the medium constantly moist but not sodden. Propagate by division or leaf cuttings in late spring.

Cerastium (from Greek *keras*, horn, alluding to the shape of the fruit). Caryophyllaceae. Wide-spread. MOUSE-EAR CHICKWEED. Some 100 species, hardy annual or perennial herbs, often tufted or mat-forming with small, hairy leaves. Produced in summer, the flowers are white and consist of five, obovate petals with notched tips; they are carried one or a few together on slender stalks. Grow *C. alpinum* in the rock garden or in an alpine house and *C. tomentosum* as groundcover to the fore of borders, in the interstices of paving, or on dry walls. Both are hardy to −30°F (−34°C) and prefer full sun, minimal winter wet and a rather dry, poor and neutral to alkaline soil. Shear off dead flower heads. Increase by division or by seed in spring.

C. alpinum ALPINE MOUSE EAR; Arctic, European mountains; mat-forming perennial with very small, gray-white hairy and obovate to elliptic leaves; flowers to ¾ in (2 cm) in diameter, on stalks to 3 in (8 cm); *C. tomentosum* SNOW-IN-SUMMER; mountains of Europe and W Asia; mat-forming perennial with gray to white-hairy, linear to lanceolate to elliptic leaves, to ¾ in (2 cm) long; flowers to 1 in (2.5 cm) in diameter, on stalks to 6 in (15 cm).

Ceratophyllum (from Greek *keras*, horn, and *phyllon*, leaf). Ceratophyllaceae. Europe, Africa, Asia, US. HORNWORT. 30 species, submerged aquatic herbs with slender floating stems whorled with brittle, threadlike leaves. Grow the following species in unheated freshwater aquariums or ponds, pushing the stem bases into the substrate. Increase by stem cuttings or by spontaneously offsetting winter buds. *C. demersum* Africa, Mediterranean, Eastern Europe; fully hardy with stems to 3¼ ft (1 m) long encircled by forked, dark green leaves.

Ceratostigma (from Greek *keras*, horn and *stigma*, alluding to the horn-like excrescences on the stigmas). Plumbaginaceae. Asia, Africa. PLUMBAGO. 8 species, hardy, woody-based perennial herbs or small shrubs with ovate to obovate, more or less bristly leaves and terminal heads of blue flowers in late summer and fall. Plant in a sheltered position in full sun in well-drained soil. Where temperatures fall below 5°F (−15°C) for prolonged periods, these plants benefit from a dry winter mulch and may perform as herbaceous perennials. Propagate by removal of rooted suckers or spontaneous layers in spring, or by softwood or semiripe cuttings.

C. griffithii (Himalaya; evergreen, procumbent to creeping, evergreen shrub forming mats to 12 in × 5 ft (0.3 × 1.5 m); leaves ½–1¼ in (1–3 cm), tough and bristly, becoming red-tinted in hard weather; flowers bright blue; *C. plumbaginoides* (W China; multi-stemmed, more or less erect and semideciduous woody-based herb or subshrub to 20 in (50 cm); leaves to 3½ in (9 cm), undulate, thin-textured, bright green slightly bristly, flushing rusty red in fall; flowers dark to brilliant blue; *C. willmottianum* (CHINESE PLUMBAGO; W China to Tibet; deciduous shrub, broad, bushy and erect to 3¼ ft (1 m), with ribbed and bristly, twiggy branches; leaves ¾–2 in (2–5 cm), bristly, tinted red in fall; flowers pale to deep sky blue amid red-brown calyx lobes.

Cercidiphyllum (from *Cercis*, and Greek *phyllon*, leaf). Cercidiphyllaceae. W China, Japan. KADSURA, KATSURA TREE. 2 species. *C. japonicum* is a hardy deciduous tree to 100 ft (30 m) tall, with an erect, sometimes multistemmed habit, gray, furrowed bark and slender, glossy shoots. The winter buds are small, red and clawlike, often appearing on short spurs. Broadly ovate to kidney- or heart-shaped, the leaves are 2–4 in (5–10 cm) long and finely crenate. Soft pea-green at first, they shift in fall through shades of amber, yellow and scarlet, becoming candy-scented. The small red flowers are inconspicu-

ous. A form with pendulous branches is sometimes grown. Plant in sun or part shade in moist, humus-rich and preferably acidic soil. Propagate by seed cuttings taken in late spring and rooted in humid, heated case.

Cercis (from Greek *kerkis*, a weaver's shuttle: a name given by Theophrastus to describe the large, woody, flattened fruits). Leguminosae. Asia, Europe. 6 species, hardy deciduous trees and shrubs with broadly heart- to kidney-shaped leaves and small, pea flowers in clusters or short racemes, often sprouting directly from the older wood in spring. Plant in full sun in fertile, well-drained soil. Most are grown for their flowers, but *C.* 'Forest Pansy' is an exceptional foliage plant, especially when young, or if stooled back in late winter. Propagate by seed or (cultivars), by semiripe cuttings in a closed case with bottom heat; increase also by budding.

C. canadensis (EASTERN REDBUD, REDBUD; N America; spreading tree to 46 ft (14 m); leaves 1¼–4¾ in (3–12 cm), smooth to shining above, puberulent beneath; flowers to ½ in (1 cm), crimson, lilac or white; 'Forest Pansy': leaves darkest wine red at first, ultimately purple-red; *C. siliquastrum* JUDAS TREE, LOVE TREE; E Mediterranean; spreading tree or shrub to 30 ft (10 m), usually smaller; leaves 2½–4 in (6–10 cm), matt gray- to mid-green, glabrous; flowers ½–¾ in (1–2 cm), pale rose to magenta; includes white and dark-flowered forms.

Cereus (from Latin *cereus*, a wax torch taper, referring to the shape of some species). Cactaceae. West Indies, S America. 40 species, tender, shrubby or treelike cacti with erect, ribbed and spiny, columnar stems and large, funnel-shaped flowers composed of many tepals and usually opening at night. Grow in full sun with low humidity and a minimum temperature

of 50°F (10°C). Plant in an acidic to neutral medium that is high in grit and sand. Water moderately in summer, very sparingly in winter. Increase by rooting sections of stem.

C. uruguayensis (syn. *C. peruvianus*; Brazil to Argentina; tree to 20 ft (6 m); stems 3–4¾ in (8–12 cm) in diameter, glaucous, with 8 deep, rounded ribs and spines to ¾ in (2 cm) long; flowers to 7 in (18 cm), white with green outer tepals edged in red; 'Monstrosus': stems distorted, compressed to fan-shaped; *C. validus* (syn. *C. forbesii*); Argentina; tree to 20 ft (6 m); stems to 4¾ in (12 cm) in diameter, blue- to gray-green, with 4–7 deep, thin ribs and spines to 1¾ in (4.5 cm) long; flowers to 8 in (20 cm), white with red-tinted outer tepals.

ceriferous wax-producing.

Cerinthe (from Greek *kerinos*, waxy, bees were thought to obtain wax from the flowers). Boraginaceae. HONEY-WORT. Europe. 10 species, annual, biennial or perennial herbs (those here annual or, rarely, biennial). They are loosely branching and erect to spreading with oblong to broadly obovate, sessile leaves. Produced in spring and summer, the tubular flowers nod amid colorful bracts in arching, terminal cymes. The following species are among the most striking of all hardy annuals. They prefer a well-drained, sandy or gritty soil, full sun and shelter, consorting brilliantly with blue-gray grasses and Mediterranean-type plants. As the season progresses, they tend to become bare and leggy and may need support from pea sticks or dead twigs. Sow seed under glass in early spring for planting out after the last frosts, or sow *in situ* in late spring. In the right situation, they will self-sow; otherwise, collect the black, shotlike seed from late summer onward. Pinch out new plants to establish a bushy, free-flowering habit. Any shoots so removed make good cuttings, and will root quickly under glass.

C. major S Europe; to 24 in (60 cm); leaves blue-green with irregular gray spots; bracts sea green tinted bronze-purple, becoming violet then black-

Cercis
siliquastrum

shuttle-shaped seedpods

blue with age; flowers gold at base, progressing through copper, wine red and violet to the indigo tip; 'Purpurascens': a robust plant with especially fine coloring—maroon then blue-purple; *C. retorta* S Europe; to 20 in (50 cm); leaves pale to mid-green with two rows of dull silver blotches and a purple-brown stain near the apex; bracts yellow-green suffused maroon to violet; flowers yellow tipped dark maroon or violet.

cernuous nodding, usually applied to flowers with curved or drooping pedicels attached to a straight or erect inflorescence axis.

Ceropegia (from Greek *keros*, wax, and *pege*, fountain, alluding to the appearance of the waxy flowers). Asclepiadaceae. Old World tropics and subtropics. 200 species, tender perennials, tuberous or caudiciform with slender, twining to cascading stems and small, succulent leaves, or erect and shrubby with candelabra-like, succulent and virtually leafless stems. The flowers are short-stalked and solitary or clustered; they consist of a bladderlike base, a narrow, upward-curving tube and a 5-lobed limb, the lobes narrow, hairy and outspread or (more characteristically) directed inward in a lantern or cage. Provide a minimum temperature of 50°F (10°C) with low to medium humidity and full sun. Plant in a gritty, loam-based medium; water moderately in spring and summer, very sparingly in winter. Increase by tip cuttings of mature shoots with two to three nodes or, for *C. linearis*, by detaching lengths of stem on which tubers have developed. *C. linearis* subsp. *woodii* is a popular houseplant, an excellent choice for baskets and hanging pots.

C. haygarthii South Africa; stem stout, slightly succulent, twining, to 6½ ft (2 m); flowers ½–1¼ in (1–3 cm) long, white to buff, tube pitcher-shaped, widening above and spotted purple, the lobes narrowing greatly and joining across aperture of pitcher, then twisting together to form an erect tail tipped with rounded, hairy appendage; *C. linearis* subsp. *woodii* (syn. *C. woodii*); HEARTS ON A STRING, ROSARY VINE, SWEETHEART VINE; South Africa; tuberous with many slender, pendulous stems and small, thinly succulent heart-

shaped leaves, tinted maroon beneath and marbled gray-green above; flowers with flesh pink tube and dark 'cage' covered in black hairs; *C. sandersonii* PARACHUTE PLANT, FOUNTAIN PLANT; Mozambique, South Africa; stems to 6½ ft (2 m), thickly succulent, twining; flowers 1¼–2 in (3–5 cm) long, green marked dark green and covered with white hairs above, the tube flaring from a narrow base, the lobes fusing above in a lanternlike canopy—the "umbrella"—to 1 in (2.5 cm) in diameter.

certified stock plants that have been examined by an officially authorized inspector and found to conform to the standards of a certification program designed to ensure freedom from pathogens (especially viruses), vigor, and trueness to type. Certified stock is the best-quality planting material available to gardeners, and particularly important as regards new stocks of strawberries, raspberries and black currants.

cespitose see *caespitose*.

Cestrum (from the Ancient Greek name *kestron*, for similar but unrelated plants). Solanaceae. S America. BASTARD JASMINE, JESSAMINE. Some 175 species, evergreen or deciduous trees and shrubs, many frost-tender with spreading to semiscandent branches and lanceolate to elliptic leaves. Borne in panicles or corymbs, tubular to funnel-shaped flowers appear from early summer to fall. *C. elegans*, *C. fasciculatum*, *C. parqui* and *C. roseum* will survive mild frosts, especially if planted on a sheltered, south-facing wall, as suits their semiclimbing habit. Plants cut down by frost will usually resprout if thickly mulched in winter. The remaining species need a minimum temperature of 45°F (7°C). Grow in full or filtered sun in fertile, well-drained soil. Feed and water container-grown plants freely when in growth, sparingly at other times. Provide support for scandent species. Prune in spring to remove weak or dead growth. Increase by semiripe or greenwood cuttings in summer.

C. aurantiacum Guatemala; evergreen shrub to 6½ ft (2 m), sometimes climb-

ing; flowers bright orange; *C. elegans* Mexico; evergreen shrub to 10 ft (3 m), bushy with arching branches; flowers deep pink to purple-red; *C. fasciculatum* Mexico; evergreen shrub to 6½ ft (2 m) with arching branches; flowers carmine to purple-red; *C.* 'Newellii' (a possible hybrid with *C. elegans*, with crimson flowers and dark green leaves; *C. nocturnum* LADY OF THE NIGHT, NIGHT JESSAMINE; West Indies; evergreen shrub to 12 ft (4 m) with spreading to scandent branches; flowers pale green to ivory, deliciously scented at night; *C. parqui* WILLOW-LEAVED JESSAMINE; Chile; deciduous shrub to 10 ft (3 m); flowers yellow-green to yellow, or violet in the cultivar 'Cretian Blue'; *C. roseum* Mexico; evergreen shrub to 6½ ft (2 m); flowers rose to purple, rosy pink in the cultivar 'Illnacullin'.

Chaenomeles (from Greek *chainein*, to gape, and *melon*, apple, referring to the incorrect belief that the fruit is split). Rosaceae. E Asia. FLOWERING QUINCE, JAPANESE QUINCE, JAPONICA. 3 species, deciduous, fully hardy shrubs or small trees with spiny, slender branches, toothed, oval to lanceolate leaves and, from late winter to early summer, showy flowers composed of five, broad petals. Dull yellow and aromatic, the quincelike fruits are used to make jellies and conserves, often combined with apple and pear. Plant in well-drained soil in full sun. These shrubs are grown to best advantage on walls, tied to trellis, wires or wall nails, with their lateral shoots reduced to spurs of two or three buds after flowering (or fruiting) and any weak shoots that grow outward removed over the spring and summer. Increase by softwood or greenwood cuttings in summer.

C. cathayensis China; shrub or small tree to 20 ft (6 m), with tortuous branches armed with spiny spurs; flowers to 1½ in (4 cm) in diameter, white, sometimes flushed pink; *C. japonica* JAPANESE QUINCE; Japan; spreading, thorny shrub to 3¼ ft (1 m); flowers 1½ in (4 cm) in diameter, orange-red, scarlet or crimson; includes white, dwarf and brilliant orange-red forms; *C. speciosa* China; spreading, thorny shrub to 10 ft (3 m); flowers to 1¾ in (4.5 cm) in diameter, scarlet to crimson;

includes cultivars with single, semidouble and double flowers in tones of blood red, scarlet, salmon pink, crimson, rose, palest pink and pure white—for example, the shell pink-tinted cream 'Apple Blossom'; *C.* × *superba* (*C. speciosa* × *C. japonica*); erect to spreading, spiny shrub to 5 ft (1.5 m); leaves close to *C. japonica*; flowers white, pink, crimson to orange and orange-scarlet; includes 'Crimson and Gold', with crimson petals and golden anthers, 'Etna', small with deep fiery red flowers, the pink 'Hever Castle', orange-scarlet 'Knap Hill Scarlet' and the large, dark crimson 'Rowallane'.

chafer beetles (Coleoptera: Scarabaeidae) stout, medium to large beetles with antennae terminating in a club consisting of 3–7 flat, leaflike segments. The larvae live in soil or decaying wood and are white or gray and C-shaped, with a heavily sclerotized yellow or brown head. They have three pairs of thoracic legs, and the last abdominal segment is enlarged.

Chafer beetle larva

The larvae of many species feed on plant roots. They are abundant in grassland, particularly on light soil, and attack lawns and the roots of a wide range of fruit, vegetable and ornamental plants. Adults feed on leaves, buds, flowers and fruits of deciduous trees and shrubs. Chafer beetles are on the wing in summer and the females deposit eggs in the soil. The life cycle varies: larger species, such as the COCKCHAFER, have larvae that live for two-and-a half years before pupating in the soil; smaller species, such as the GARDEN CHAFER and the JAPANESE BEETLE, complete the cycle in one year.

The COCKCHAFER (*Melolontha melolontha*) is up to 1¼ in (3 cm) long, with a black head and thorax and red-brown wing cases. In both sexes the abdomen terminates in a spadelike point. Males are much attracted to light during the early summer flight period. The larvae measure up to 2½ in (6 cm) long and take two-and-a-half years to become fully fed.

The GARDEN CHAFER (*Phyllopertha horticola*) is up to ½ in (1.1 cm) long,

with a metallic green head and thorax and brown wing cases. The larvae, up to ¾ in (1.8 cm) long, complete their development in one year.

The SUMMER CHAFER (*Amphimallon solstitialis*) is uniformly brown and up to ¾ in (1.8 cm) long. It is seldom injurious in gardens, although it swarms occasionally on elms and poplars.

The ROSE CHAFER (*Cetonia aurata*) is metallic golden-green, up to ¾ in (2 cm) long; it is locally common and may feed on flowers, buds and leaves of roses from June to August.

Chafer beetles are not easy to control. Apply a pathogenic nematode (*Heterorhabditis megidis*) to moist soil in midsummer to control the young larvae. There are no suitable insecticides approved for use in the UK.

See *Japanese beetle*.

chalcid wasps (Hymenoptera: Chalcidoidea) an important group of beneficial insects. They are no more than ¹⁄₁₆ or ¹⁄₁₆ in (1 or 2 mm) in length and although abundant in gardens, are usually overlooked. They have elbowed antennae and the wings are held flat when at rest. Many have a metallic green or blue body sheen. Some larvae feed on seeds or within galls (e.g. *Megastigmus* species, and *Torynus varians*, which can damage apple fruits in North America).

Several chalcid wasps are utilized in biological control and many are potential candidates. The majority are parasites of insects, mites and spiders; a few parasitize parasites and should be excluded from the breeding phase of biological-control organisms. *Encarsia formosa* is widely used for the biological control of greenhouse whitefly (*Trialeurodes vaporariorum*); *Aphelinus* species parasitize aphids and scale insects; and the apple woolly aphid parasite (*A.mali*) occurs widely throughout the world. Several other cosmopolitan genera, including *Aphycus*, *Aphytis*, *Physcus*, *Aspidiotiphagus* and *Prospantella*, parasitize scale insects. *Pteromalus* species parasitize the pupae of cabbage white butterflies and related insects. *Trichogramma* species are bred in large numbers in many countries for mass-

release programs to attack the eggs of various injurious species of moth. Unlike many parasitoids, they have a wide range of hosts; as many as 20 individuals may develop in a single host egg.

chalk a soft white form of limestone, composed of calcium carbonate. It is incorporated in loam-based seed and potting mixes.

Chamaecyparis (from Greek *chamai*, lowly, dwarf, and *kuparissos*, cypress). Cupressaceae. E Asia, N America. FALSE CYPRESS. 8 species, fully hardy, evergreen coniferous trees and shrubs with small, awl- to scalelike leaves, aromatic and covering finely branched sprays or fans of growth; the cones are small and usually globose. Pollution-tolerant, moderate- to fast-growing conifers suitable for screening, hedging and lawn specimens; dwarf cultivars are used for rock gardens, island beds and containers. They fare best in full sun in moist, well-drained, acidic to neutral soil. Propagate by seed or, for cultivars, by heeled greenwood cuttings in late summer in a humid cold frame or by softwood cuttings under mist in summer. All species are susceptible to phytophthora root rot (*Phytophthora cinnamomi*). *Phytophthora lateralis* is a serious problem on *C. lawsoniana*, especially in parts of the western US, where this popular and versatile conifer is now gravely threatened.

C. lawsoniana LAWSON'S FALSE CYPRESS, OREGON CEDAR, PORT ORFORD CEDAR; W US; to 200 ft (60 m) in the wild, crown narrowly conic then columnar; branches level, branchlets pendulous; leaves to ¹⁄₁₆ in (2 mm), keeled, bright green or tinted blue-gray with pale lines beneath; includes many cultivars ranging in habit from dwarf and rounded to columnar in tones of green, blue-green, gray, blue, lime and yellow; there are also some white-variegated forms and others with threadlike or feathered foliage; the most popular cultivar is 'Ellwoodii', erect to 10 × 5 ft (3 × 1.5 m) with blue-gray leaves; *C. nootkatensis* (ALASKA CEDAR, FALSE NOOTKA CYPRESS, YELLOW CYPRESS; western N America; to 130 ft (40 m), slender or broadly conic, becoming domed with age; branches upswept,

167

**Chamaecyparis lawsoniana
'Green Pillar'**
The Lawson cypresses include numerous
forms of different habit, color and height.
Many are suitable for small gardens.

branchlets pendulous; leaves to ⅛ in (4 mm), deep green; includes cultivars with yellow to moss green or blue-gray foliage and dwarf, compact or tall and weeping habit; *C. obtusa* HINOKI CYPRESS; Japan; to 130 ft (40 m), slow-growing with a broadly conic crown becoming columnar; branchlets in flattened, layered fans; leaves to 1/16 in (2 mm), blunt and closely overlapping, dark green above, silver-white beneath; includes dwarf, tiered, congested, filiform and rounded cultivars with very deep green, cream to gold or gray foliage—one of the most popular is the dwarf, dark green 'Nana'; *C. pisifera* SAWARA CYPRESS; Japan; to 130 ft (40 m), broadly conic to irregularly conic; bark rusty brown and peeling; leaves to ⅛ in (3 mm), mossy green above, silvery beneath, tapered and pointed; cultivars range in size from the dwarf and slow-growing to medium-sized trees, in habit from flat-topped to rounded and bushy and in foliage color from steel blue (e.g. 'Boulevard', 'Squarrosa') to yellow-green or white-variegated; *C. thyoides* WHITE CYPRESS, WHITE CEDAR; E US; to 100 ft (30 m), slow-growing, crown narrowly conic to irregularly ovoid; leaves to ⅛ in (3 mm), dark gray-green or glaucous, in fan-shaped sprays; includes dwarf forms with blue-gray, gold and bronze foliage, the leaves sometimes needlelike; the most popular is 'Andelyensis', a bluntly conic shrub to 10 ft (3 m) with fanlike branchlets of linear, blue-green leaves.

Chamaecytisus (from Greek *chamai*, lowly, dwarf, and *Cytisus*). Leguminosae. Europe, Canary Islands. 30 species, more or less evergreen trees, shrubs and subshrubs, usually with small, trifoliolate leaves and pealike flowers in spring and summer. The following species are hardy to −10°F (−23°C). Cultivate *Chamaecystisus* like *Cytisus*.

C. albus (syn. *Cytisus albus*); PORTUGUESE BROOM; SE and C Europe; erect to 32 in (80 cm); leaflets often hairy; flowers white or yellow in terminal clusters; *C. purpureus* (syn. *Cytisus purpureus*); SE Europe; to 24 in (60 cm), bushy and low-growing; leaflets dark green, smooth; flowers pale pink to lilac flushed ruby or crimson; white, opal, pink and dark red cultivars are grown; *C. supinus* (syn. *Cytisus supinus*); S and C Europe to Ukraine; to 3¼ ft (1 m), ascending to prostrate; leaflets smooth or thinly hairy; flowers yellow in short, terminal racemes; *C.* × *versicolor* (*C. purpureus* × *C. hirsutus*); to 20 in (50 cm), erect to diffuse with long, slender branches; leaflets hairy beneath; flowers pale yellow with a pink-violet keel; includes 'Hillieri', a low-growing plant with arching branches and large yellow flowers later becoming bronze- to pink-tinted.

Chamaedaphne (from Greek *chamai*, lowly, dwarf, and *Daphne*). Ericaceae. Northern temperate regions. LEATHERLEAF, CASSANDRA. 1 species, *C. calyculata*, a spreading evergreen shrub, fully hardy and seldom exceeding 3¼ × 5 ft (1 × 1.5 m). To 2 in (5 cm) long, the leaves are oval to lanceolate, tough and rusty-scaly beneath. Pure white, urn-shaped flowers appear in short racemes in spring. Grow as for *Andromeda*.

Chamaedorea (from Greek *chamai*, lowly, near the ground, and *dorea*, a gift: the fruits are easily reached). Palmae. C and S America. 100 species, small, tender palms, often with canelike stems and pinnate to fishtail-shaped leaves. Small, golden to creamy flowers are carried in freely branched. Provide a minimum temperature of 59°F (15°C), with filtered sun to light shade and medium to high humidity. Grow in a porous, soilless mix kept consistently moist. Feed and syringe frequently in summer. Increase by careful division of stems when repotting. These conditions are ideal, but *C. elegans* has proved itself capable of surviving (and often receives) far harsher treatment. *C. elatior* may need some support with age.

C. elatior stems solitary or clumped, slender, canelike, green, to 12 ft (4 m), ultimately weakly climbing; leaves to 10 ft (3 m), pinnate, with narrow drooping leaflets; *C. elegans* (syn. *Neanthe bella*); PARLOR PALM; stems solitary or clumped, to 6½ ft × 1¼ in (2 m × 3 cm) erect; leaves to 12 in (30 cm), pinnate; a very popular pot plant, especially when young; *C. microspadix* (syn. *C. metallica* of gardens); stems to 3¼ ft (1 m), canelike; leaves to 10 in (25 cm), fishtail-shaped, ribbed and puckered, metallic sea green.

Chamaemelum (from Greek *chamai*, lowly, and *melon*, apple). Compositae. Europe, Mediterranean. CHAMOMILE. 4 species, annual or perennial frost-hardy herbs with finely and pinnately cut foliage and yellow-centered, white, daisylike flower heads. Plant in full sun in loamy soil with a high sand content and ample moisture, but avoid sites where there is risk of waterlogging. Flower heads of the typical plant are used to make chamomile tea. The non-flowering cultivar, 'Treneague', is used in lawns and walks and on seats and banks. Chamomile lawns become bare and patchy unless regularly sheared and diligently replanted wherever thin. Increase by seed in fall or, for 'Treneague', by division or rooted stem cuttings in spring. *C. nobile* W Europe; strongly aromatic, decumbent perennial with finely 2–3-pinnatisect mid- to gray-green leaves and small flower heads; 'Treneague': non-flowering, carpeting cultivar suitable for lawns.

chamaephyte a low-growing plant with growth buds above the soil surface; that is usually bushy and of mountainous or arid origin.

Chamaerops (from Greek *chamai*, lowly, dwarf, and *rhops*, a bush). Palmae. Mediterranean. 1 species, *C. humilis*, a palm with shaggy, solitary to clumped trunks 10 in–10 ft (0.25–3 m) tall. To 3¼ ft (1 m) long, the palmately divided leaves consist of a coarsely toothed petiole and a fan of linear to lanceolate, scurfy gray segments. This palm will tolerate short frosts, especially if grown in a sunny, sheltered position and kept dry in winter with its upper trunk and crown wrapped in sacking. Elsewhere, grow in full sun in a frost-free greenhouse or conservatory. Plant in a fast-draining, gritty and low- to medium-fertility soil. Keep moist in summer, virtually dry in winter. Increase by offsets or seed.

Chamelaucium (name derivation obscure). Myrtaceae. SW Australia. WAXFLOWER. 21 species, strongly aromatic, evergreen, tender shrubs with soft, needle-shaped foliage and bright flowers composed of five, broad and spreading petals. Grow in full sun with low to medium humidity and a minimum winter temperature of 45°F (7°C). Plant in tubs or borders of sandy, acidic soil. Water, feed and ventilate liberally in spring and summer; keep almost dry in winter. The following species usually flowers in late winter and spring and is a popular cut flower. Increase by seed or by semiripe cuttings. *C. uncinatum* WAXFLOWER; shrub to 10 ft (3 m) tall; leaves strongly lemon-scented; flowers to 1 in (2.5 cm) in diameter, red, purple, mauve, pink or white.

charcoal the black, porous residue from wood burned slowly under conditions of limited air supply. Charcoal is of no nutrient value, consisting wholly of carbon. It is used in crushed form to lighten texture and absorb surplus moisture in potting mixtures, or powdered to reduce bleeding from cuttings of latex-bearing plants, such as *Ficus*.

chards see *swiss chard*.

charmille a smoothly-clipped hedge, usually of HORNBEAM (*Carpinus betulus*).

Charmilles are used in the French garden to line allées.

chartaceous used to describe leaf and bract texture; thin and papery.

Chasmanthe (from Greek *chasma*, chasm, and *anthos*, flower: the perianth is gaping). Iridaceae. South Africa. 3 species, cormous perennial herbs with 2-ranked linear to lanceolate leaves and, from fall to spring, spikes of showy flowers with curving perianth tubes and six, unequal segments. Cultivate as for *Babiana*.

C. aethiopica 16–28 in (40–70 cm); spike unbranched, flowers to 3 in (8 cm), red, maroon in throat, tube with yellow stripes; *C. floribunda* 20–60 in (50–150 cm); spike branched, flowers to 3¼ in (8.5 cm) orange-red or yellow.

Chasmanthium (from Greek *chasma*, chasm, and *anthos*, flower: the spikelets gape widely). Gramineae. US, Mexico. 6 species, hardy perennial grasses with linear to lanceolate leaves and loosely clumped, slender culms that terminate in arching panicles of large, flattened spikelets. Hardy to –20°F (–29°C). Grow in sun or dappled shade in rich, moisture-retentive soil with shelter from strong winds. Increase by division in spring. The inflorescences are suitable for drying. *C. latifolium* (syn. *Uniola latifolia*); NORTHERN SEA OATS, SPANGLE GRASS, WILD OATS; to 3¼ ft (1 m) tall; panicle weeping; spikelets ¾–1½ in (2–4 cm), oblong to lanceolate to broadly ovate, with overlapping lemmas, like a large, flat *Briza* and changing by late summer from olive-bronze to straw yellow.

Cheilanthes (from Greek *cheilos*, lip, and *anthos*, flower, referring to the clustered marginal sori). Adiantaceae. Cosmopolitan. LIP FERN. Some 180 species of ferns; those described below are small, half-hardy and evergreen with short to creeping rhizomes and pinnately compound fronds. Grow in a cold greenhouse or frame in pans containing a humus-rich medium with a little added dolomitic limestone. Water sparingly in summer, avoiding foliage; keep almost dry in winter. Provide a dry, cool and buoyant atmosphere. Admit bright, dappled light in summer,

full sun in winter. Increase by spores or by careful division.

C. lanosa N America; fronds 6–12 in (15–30 cm), blades broadly ovate to lanceolate, tripinnatifid, pinnules oblong, soft green, on black, hairy stipes; *C. pteridioides* (syn. *C. fragrans*); S Europe; fronds 1¼–6 in (3–15 cm), blades subtriangular to linear to lanceolate, bipinnate, pinnules oblong to suborbicular, toothed, dark green and sweetly scented, on shiny, chestnut-colored stipes.

Cheiridopsis (from Greek *cheiris*, sleeve, and *opsis*, resemblance: the older leaf bases enclose the new growth in a dried sheath). Aizoaceae. South Africa. 80 species, tender perennial herbs forming low clumps of thickly succulent, semicylindrical leaves usually with flat tops. Daisylike flowers open on bright days in summer. Cultivate as for *Conophytum*.

C. denticulata (syn. *C. candidissima*); leaves 3–4 in (8–10 cm), erect, more or less 3-sided, white-gray or blue-green sometimes with a reddened tip; flowers 2¾ in (7 cm) in diameter, yellow to white; *C. purpurea* (syn. *C. purpurata*); leaves to 2½ in (6 cm), bluntly 3-sided, gray to blue-gray, becoming purple-red-tinted; flowers to 1¾ in (4.5 cm) in diameter, yellow; the name *C. purpurea* is sometimes applied in horticulture to a plant with rose-magenta flowers.

chelate see *sequestrol*.

Chelidonium (from Greek *chelidon*, swallow: the flowers were said to appear with the swallows in spring, and to die on their departure). Papaveraceae. Europe, W Asia, naturalized E US. 1 species, *C. majus*, GREATER CELANDINE or SWALLOW WORT, a hardy biennial or perennial with irritant, orange sap. The leaves are more or less lanceolate with rounded tips and wavy to toothed, or lobed. Measuring up to 1 in (2.5 cm) in diameter, the flowers consist of four orange to yellow petals (more in 'Florepleno') and are carried on branching stems up to 3¼ ft (1 m) tall in summer. Hardy to –10°F (–23°C) and suitable for the wild or woodland garden on most soils in sun or shade. Sow seed *in situ* in spring.

Chelone obliqua
The aptly named turtlehead is a North American native that thrives in partial shade or in sun, provided that the soil is moist.

Chelone (from Greek *chelone*, tortoise: the flower is said to resemble a turtle's head). Scrophulariaceae. N America. TURTLEHEAD, SHELLFLOWER. 6 species, hardy erect perennial herbs with tubular, hooded and 2-lipped flowers in dense, terminal spikes in summer and early fall. Hardy to −10°F (−23°C). Plant in moist, fertile soil in full sun or part-shade. Increase by division, or by soft tip cuttings in summer. *C. obliqua* to 24 in (60 cm); flowers to ¾ in (2 cm), deep rose pink to lilac or purple-red, with a sparse yellow beard.

chemical controls see *pesticides*.

chemotropism, chemonasty growth or bending toward a chemical stimulus, particularly seen in fungi and in the pollen tubes of flowers.

cherry The edible fruit of selected *Prunus* species. Three types are grown in gardens: SWEET CHERRY, derived from *P. avium*, which is widespread from Europe, including Britain, to western Asia (its seedlings are often known as GEANS or MAZZARDS); SOUR CHERRY, derived from *P. cerasus*, which has a distribution similar to *P. avium*; and the DUKE CHERRY, a hybrid of the two. Edible fruits are also produced by *P. pseudocerasus*, *P. tomentosa*, and *P. besseyi*. There is evidence that cherries were a Bronze Age and Iron Age food in Britain, and trade in cultivated forms flourished from the 16th century. Much breeding work was undertaken in England during the 19th century, including significant introductions from British Columbia.

For gardens, sour cherries, especially in the form of fans or bushes, are the most suitable choice because they are the smallest of the three types. The self-fertile 'Morello' is the most successful, and is suitable for north- or east-facing walls. It is propagated by bud grafting on to semivigorous 'Colt' rootstock, although in the US selected seedlings of *P. avium* are preferred. The wide choice of cherry cultivars includes those with fruit ranging in color from creamy white to purple-black; many are self-incompatible and require a cross pollinator.

Prune all cherries in summer. Since sour cherries carry fruit almost exclusively on young shoots of the previous year, aim for replacement, thinning new shoots 2–3 in (5–7.5 cm) apart along the ribs of the fan; after cropping, cut fruited laterals back to a trained replacement shoot. Sweet cherries form fruit buds at the base of young laterals of the previous year and on older wood: all shoots except those required as replacement shoots should be pinched at 5–6 leaves, and then to three leaves in late summer. The cherry flowers later than other stone fruits and is therefore less vulnerable to frost damage, but all types require protection from birds. Harvest with scissors.

Possible problems: aphids, birds, slugworm, winter moth; bacterial canker, shot-hole, silver leaf.

chervil (*Anthriscus cereifolium*) a rapidly growing annual, up to 24 in (60 cm) high and parsleylike in appearance; it is used as a herb for its aniseed flavor. Sow *in situ* in a sheltered but unshaded site outdoors or under protection, or raise in containers for transplanting. Sow from February to April for a summer crop, or in August for cropping between fall and spring. Seed may take 2–3 weeks to germinate.

Cheshunt compound a chemical preparation for the prevention and treatment of damping-off diseases (especially *Pythium* species) in seedlings. It was devised at the former Cheshunt Experimental Station, England, and is a powdered mixture consisting of two parts by weight of copper sulfate and eleven parts of ammonium carbonate. It is dissolved in warm water at the rate of ½ oz per gallon (3 g per liter) and is used to water seed boxes and seedbeds at the time of sowing. Repeat treatment when pricking out or transplanting seedlings.

Chiastophyllum (from Greek *chiastos*, arranged diagonally or crosswise, and *phyllon*, leaf). Crassulaceae. Caucasus. 1 species, *C. oppositifolium*, a hardy perennial herb with creeping stems and low rosettes of rounded and toothed, succulent leaves, each to 3 in (8 cm) long. In spring and summer, arching panicles to 6 in (15 cm) tall bear numerous small, golden flowers. In the cultivar 'Frosted Jade', the leaves are marked white to cream and tinted pink in winter. Hardy to 5°F (−15°C). Grow in cool crevices in the rock garden in well-drained but moisture-retentive soil. Increase by side-shoot cuttings in early summer.

chicory (*Cichorium intybus*) WITLOOF CHICORY a native of Europe including Britain, where it grows wild, and used for centuries as a cooked or salad vegetable of distinctive slightly bitter flavor. Chicory may be grown similarly to lettuce or more suitably forced in darkness to produce tight clusters of mild-flavored, folded leaves known as chicons. The taproot is roasted and ground as a coffee substitute or flavoring. Sow from May to early June ½ in (1 cm) deep in rows 12 in (30 cm) apart; thin to 8 in (20 cm) spacings. Summer and fall leaves may be eaten but are bitter. Lift the roots, which should be 2–3½ in (5–9 cm) in diameter, in late October to December; trim the leaves hard and the thongs to 8 in (20 cm). Close pack in deep boxes or large pots, in light soil or sand, to crown level. Place in a dark cellar or shed, or cover potted roots with an upturned pot, with light totally excluded. The optimum temperature range for forcing is 50–64°F (10–18°C). Harvest 3–4 weeks from housing. On light or sandy soil, forcing can be done outside *in situ* by earthing up trimmed plants to 6–7 in (15–18 cm) depth.

RED CHICORY (RADICCHIO) has red, sometimes variegated leaves; it forms a small crisp heart, the inner leaves part white and part colored. It is grown and used as lettuce, though rather more bitter. Sow from April through to August, thinning plants to 8–14 in (20–35 cm) apart each way.

SUGAR LOAF CHICORY resembles cos lettuce; the inner leaves are tightly packed, white and sweetened, but of sharper flavor than lettuce. It is mainly grown for fall maturity as a salad ingredient, from June–July sowings, as for witloof chicory. Alternatively, grow as a cut-and-come-again salad crop from early-season sowings onward.

Chilean potash nitrate see *potassium nitrate*.

chilling the exposure of plants to low temperature, usually during dormancy. It is necessary to initiate growth or flowering in certain plants, for example, rhubarb (*Rheum* × *cultorum*).

chimaera, chimera a plant in which two genetically different sorts of tissue coexist. Outer and inner tissues may be different in character, causing variegation or no obvious difference. Chimaeras may arise as a result of a natural mutation, or through grafting as in the case of + *Laburnocytisus* 'Adamii', which bears parts characteristic of both *Laburnum anagyroides* and *Chamaecytisus purpureus*.

Chimonanthus (from Greek *cheimon*, winter, and *anthos*, flower). Calycanthaceae. China. 6 species, deciduous

chimaera
(+ Laburnocytisus)

flowers show traits of both parents

shrubs to 10 ft (3 m) tall with dull green, ovate to lanceolate leaves to 4 in (10 cm) long. Waxy and bell-shaped, the flowers consist of numerous sepals and petals, are deliciously scented and appear in short-stalked clusters in late winter on bare twigs. The following species is one of the finest winter-flowering shrubs. Hardy to 0°F (–18°C), it nonetheless performs better if grown against a sheltered, sun-soaked wall. Plant in fertile, moist but well-drained soil in full sun. Prune only to limit size or to remove weak or damaged growth. Propagate by seed, grafting, layers or semiripe cuttings in summer. New plants may take some years to reach flowering size. Grafted plants come into flower more quickly. *C. praecox* (syn. *C. fragrans*); WINTERSWEET; flowers to 1 in (2.5 cm) long, nodding, dull yellow to buff with the inner petals marked maroon to blood red; cultivars with pure yellow, large, small and more heavily marked flowers are available.

Chimonobambusa (from Greek *cheimon*, winter, and Latin *Bambusa*: referring to the late appearance of the new shoots in some areas). Gramineae. S and E Asia. Some 20 species, small to medium-sized bamboos with running rhizomes. See *bamboos*.

Chinese broccoli see *broccoli*.

Chinese cabbage see *cabbage*.

Chinese gooseberry see *kiwi fruit*.

Chinese leaves *see cabbage*.

chinoiserie a European interpretation of the Chinese style of garden design, favoring an irregular and asymmetrical layout and incorporating pagodas, bridges and ornaments. It has been a major influence in English landscape gardening; surviving examples of chinoiserie garden buildings include the Pagoda at Kew Gardens, which was built in 1761.

Chionanthus (from Greek *chion*, snow, and *anthos*, flower). Oleaceae. E Asia, Pacific, E US. FRINGE TREE. 100 species, hardy deciduous trees and shrubs with elliptic to ovate leaves and, in summer, lacy panicles of flowers composed of four, white, oblong petals. These are followed by purple-blue, fleshy fruits. Hardy to –20°F (–29°C). Plant in full sun in moist but

FORCING WITLOOF CHICORY

1 Allow plants a full season to grow and mature. In late fall, lift the taproots carefully, trim to 8 in (20 cm) (removing any side roots) and trim the leaves to 1 in (2.5 cm) of the crown.

trim the root tips

2 A 9 in (22 cm) pot is adequate to force three roots. Use moist potting potting mix or garden soil, and firm the roots in so that they stand upright, with the crown exposed.

crown exposed

3 Line a second pot with foil or black plastic to prevent light entering the holes at the base, and invert it over the pot containing the roots. Keep in a warm place (50–64°F/10–18°C).

4 After 3–4 weeks, provided that no light has reached them, the pale, sweet "chicons" of new growth will be ready to cut. Stumps may resprout if recovered for a second, smaller crop.

C

free-draining, fertile soil (acidic to neutral for *C. virginicus*). Propagate by seed sown when ripe, or by layering in fall or spring.

C. retusus CHINESE FRINGE TREE; Taiwan; to 10 ft (3 m); leaves to 4 in (10 cm), pale green above; panicles erect; *C. virginicus* E US; leaves to 8 in (20 cm), dark green above, turning pale gold in fall; panicles drooping.

Chionodoxa (from Greek *chion*, snow, and *doxa*, glory: these plants flower amid the melting snows). Liliaceae (Hyacinthaceae). W Turkey, Cyprus, Crete. GLORY OF THE SNOW. 6 species, bulbous perennial herbs, usually small or dwarf with linear leaves and erect racemes of shortly tubular, 6-tepaled flowers in spring. Cultivation as for hardy *Scilla*.

C. forbesii (syn. *C. luciliae* of gardens); W Turkey; raceme 3–12 in (8–30 cm) tall with 4–12 slightly drooping flowers, deep blue with white centers, or snow white or pink; includes Siehei Group, syn. *C. siehei* and 'Tmoli', syn. *C. tmolusii*; *C. luciliae* W Turkey; raceme 2–5½ in (5–14 cm), with 1–2(–3), erect flowers, soft violet blue with white centers, or pure white or pink; includes Gigantea Group, syn. *C. gigantea*; *C. sardensis* W Turkey; raceme 4–16 in (10–40 cm) with 4–12 slightly drooping or outward-facing flowers, of pure rich blue.

× **Chionoscilla** (*Chionodoxa* × *Scilla*). Liliaceae (Hyacinthaceae). 1 species, × *C. allenii*, a natural hybrid between *Chionodoxa forbesii* and *Scilla bifolia*, a hardy, spring-flowering bulb to 3 in (8 cm) tall, with oblanceolate leaves and erect racemes of starry blue or lilac-pink flowers with paler or white centers. Cultivate as for hardy *Scilla*.

chip budding a modified form of bud grafting, which is used for propagating a wide range of woody plants. See *grafting*.

chipping (1) the puncturing of a hard seed coat before sowing by nicking with a knife, or filing; it is a form of scarification; see *seeds and seed sowing*; (2) a method of propagating tunicate bulbs, especially *Narcissus* species, by slicing them into portions. See *cuttings*; *bulb scaling*.

Chirita (from Hindustani *cheryta*, name for the gentian) Gesneriaceae. Tropical Asia. 100 species, mat-forming annual or perennial herbs with fleshy stems, frost tender. Leaves in unequal, opposite pairs or in whorls, rarely alternate, densely downy. Flowers axillary, solitary to clustered, tubular or funnel-shaped, summer–fall. Under glass, grow in loamless medium in bright, filtered light. Very high humidity essential but without waterlogging; good ventilation is essential. Propagate from seed or leaf cuttings. *C. sinensis* (Himalaya Evergreen perennial, leaves crowded at base, elliptic or ovate-lanceolate, dark green or variegated with silver gray pubescence, 6–8 in (15–20 cm) long. Flowers 1-4, to 6 in (15 cm), white marked with yellow, lobes pink-purple.

chitting (1) the sprouting of potato tubers before planting; (2) the germination of seeds before sowing, especially as practiced in fluid drilling.

chive (*Allium schoenoprasum*) a hardy perennial about 10 in (25 cm) high, grown primarily as a herb for its onion-flavored leaves, which are used chopped in salads. Sow in modules under protection in spring; plant out clusters of 4 or 5 seedlings 10 in (25 cm) apart. Established clumps can be divided in fall or spring.

chlamydia (1) bud scales; (2) perianth envelopes.

Chlidanthus (from Greek *chlide*, a costly ornament, and *anthos*, flower).

use a small, sharp knife

Chipping
Nicking a hard seed coat (here of *Paeonia lutea*) speeds germination by aiding water penetration and the swelling of the seed.

Amaryllidaceae. Peru. 1 species, *C. fragrans*, a tender or half-hardy, bulbous perennial herb with linear, gray-green leaves. It bears fragrant, trumpet-shaped flowers, to 2¾ in (7 cm) across and in shades of yellow, red, cinnabar and green striped red atop 12 in (30 cm)-tall scapes. Grow in a sandy, loam-based medium in full sun. Water liberally from spring until flowering occurs in mid- to late summer; thereafter, keep frost-free and dry. Increase by seed or by offsets in spring.

chlorenchyma parenchymatous tissue containing chloroplasts; the type of tissue in which photosynthesis occurs.

chlorine a micronutrient or trace element rarely deficient in plants due to its almost universal occurrence in soil.

Chlorogalum (from Greek *chloros*, green, and *gala*, milk, an allusion to the color of the sap). Liliaceae (Hyacinthaceae). Western N America. SOAP PLANT, AMOLE. 5 species, hardy bulbous perennial herbs with linear leaves and, in summer, erect panicles of small, 6-parted flowers that open in the afternoon. Cultivate as for *Camassia*. *C. pomeridianum* SOAP PLANT, WILD POTATO; 24–60 in (60–150 cm); flowers with purple- or green-striped, white tepals to ¾ in (2 cm) long.

chlorophyll a mixture of two green pigments occurring in most plants, mainly in leaves but also in some stems; it is largely responsible for the conversion of light energy to sugars in the process of photosynthesis.

Chlorophytum (from Greek *chloros*, green, and *phyton*, plant). Liliaceae (Anthericaceae). Widespread in tropics and subtropics. 215 species, more or less tender, evergreen perennial herbs with fleshy roots. Linear to strap-shaped or ovate to lanceolate, the leaves are smooth and borne in basal rosettes or clumps. Throughout the year, slender-stalked panicles bear small, white flowers and sometimes plantlets. The following species is one of the most ubiquitous and long-suffering of foliage house plants. Notwithstanding, it prefers a minimum temperature of 45°F (7°C), bright indirect light, a fertile, free-draining, loam-based medium and ample supplies of water and feed throughout the year. Increase by division or plantlets. *C. comosum* SPIDER PLANT, RIBBON PLANT; South Africa; clumped or rosette-forming with linear, arching leaves, green usually boldly striped white or cream; panicles loose-branched, bearing small, white flowers and numerous plantlets.

pale patches between veins

Chlorosis

chloroplasts usually spherical or discoid bodies found in the cells of leaves and young stems; they contain the chlorophyll of green plants.

chlorosis a condition in which plants become abnormally pale green or yellow due to a partial or complete loss of chlorophyll. It may be caused by inadequate light, mineral deficiency (especially in very alkaline soil), or diseases such as those caused by viruses and mycoplasma-like organisms.

chocolate spot (*Botrytis fabae*) a fungal disease of the broad bean (*Vicia faba*); numerous small brown spots appear on leaves. The disease may become aggressive in wet seasons, causing plant death. Control by optimizing growing conditions and by the use of fungicide spray.

Choisya (for Jacques Denis Choisy [1799–1854], Swiss botanist). Rutaceae. SW US, Mexico. 9 species, evergreen, hardy aromatic shrubs with digitately compound, glossy leaves and, in summer and late fall to winter, terminal clusters of fragrant white flowers composed of 4 or 5, spreading, obovate petals, each to ⁵⁄₈ in (1.5 cm) long. *C. ternata* is hardy to –10°F (–23°C) but benefits from a sheltered position; the remaining two species are less tolerant, thriving only in very favored locations in mild areas. Something of their finesse is, however, shared by the hardy *C.* 'Aztec Pearl'. All prefer fertile, moist but fast-draining soil and full sun. Increase by semiripe cuttings in late summer.

C. dumosa var. *arizonica* Arizona; bushy shrub to 3¼ ft (1 m) tall; leaves with 3 or 5, linear, crenulate leaflets to 2 in (5 cm) long; *C. dumosa* SW US, Mexico; bushy shrub to 6½ ft (2 m); leaves with 8–13, linear to oblong, crenulate leaflets to 1¾ in (4.5 cm) long; *C. ternata* (syn. *C. grandiflora*); MEXICAN ORANGE BLOSSOM; Mexico; bushy shrub to 6½ ft (2 m); leaves with 3 oblong to obovate, entire leaflets to 3 in (8 cm) long; 'Lich': syn. 'Sundance', pale gold to lime green foliage; 'Aztec Pearl': hybrid with *C. arizonica*, with slender leaflets.

choripetalous see *polypetalous*.

Chorizema (from Greek *choros*, a dance for joy, and *zema*, a drinking vessel: the botanist Labillardière was close to exhaustion and dehydration when he came across this plant and water in the same place). Leguminosae. Australia. FLAME PEA. 18 species, tender, evergreen shrubs, sometimes climbing, with entire to sharply toothed leaves and racemes of colorful, pealike flowers in spring and summer. Provide a minimum temperature of 45°F (7°C), full sun and a rather dry, buoyant atmosphere. Plant in a sandy, acidic to neutral mix; water and feed moderately in spring and summer, sparingly in winter. Provide support. Sow seed in spring after immersing it in hot water and allowing it to cool and soak for 24 hours; root semiripe cuttings in summer.

C. cordatum HEART-LEAVED FLAME PEA, AUSTRALIA FLAME PEA, FLOWERING OAK; dense upright shrub to 10 ft (3 m), sometimes climbing; leaves sometimes minutely spiny-toothed or lobed; flowers with red, orange and yellow standard and magenta or mauve keel; *C. ilicifolium* HOLLY FLAME PEA; scrambling herb or shrub to 3¼ ft (1 m); leaves sinuously toothed and hollylike, tough, dark; flowers with orange-red and yellow standard and rose-mauve keel.

chromatid one of the two strands of a replicated chromosome, prior to their separation in mitosis or meiosis.

chromoplast, chromoplastid microscopic granules in plant cells containing other coloring than chlorophyll.

chromosome a microscopic body made up of DNA and protein, found in the nucleus of a plant cell; it contains the genes, or units of inheritance, that transmit a plant's characteristics to its offspring. Each species has its own distinctive shape of chromosomes, and there is a characteristic number which is always even.

chrysalis the pupa or transitional nonfeeding stage between larva and adult that is represented in all advanced orders of insects. It is usually concealed in a cell or cocoon. There are variations in form, for example, the appendages and rudimentary wings are free from the body in Coleoptera and Hymenoptera, whereas in Lepidoptera they are tightly fixed to it.

Chrysanthemum (from Greek *chrysos*, gold, and *anthemon*, flower). Compositae. Europe, N Africa. 5 species, hardy annual herbs with entire to pinnately lobed and toothed leaves and large, daisylike flower heads. Sow seed *in situ* in spring in well-drained, fertile soil in full sun. *C. segetum* is often sold in wildflower mixtures and will naturalize.

C. carinatum (Morocco; to 3¼ ft (1 m); flower heads to 4 in (10 cm) in diameter, ray florets white, yellow, often tinged red or with a very dark red-brown basal stripe and white zone, disk florets purple; includes red, pink, orange, yellow, maroon, bronze and white zoned red or orange cultivars; *C. coronarium* CROWN DAISY; Mediterranean, Portugal; to 32 in (80 cm); flower heads to 2 in (5 cm) in diameter, yellow; includes 'double' and deep yellow cultivars; *C. segetum* CORN MARIGOLD; E Mediterranean, W Africa, naturalized throughout Europe; to 32 in (80 cm); flower heads to 2½ in (6.5 cm) in diameter, primrose to golden yellow. For the florists' chrysanthemum see *chrysanthemums* and *Dendranthema*.

Possible problems: aphids, capsid bug, earwigs, eelworm, leaf miner, red spider mite, whiteflies, thrips; powdery mildew, rust.

C

173

CHRYSANTHEMUM FLOWER FORMS

Single ('Bill Wade')
Single flower heads have up to 5 rows of flat ray-florets surrounding a central yellow, or often green-centered disk.

Incurved ('Salmon Fairweather')
These have fully double, spherical flower heads with ray-florets opening from the bases and curving upward.

Intermediate ('Beacon')
Fully double, loose, spherical flower heads with the ray-florets mainly incurving, but some lower ones reflexing.

Reflexed ('Primrose West Bromwich')
Fully double, spherical flower heads with ray-florets opening from the crown, curving downward and inward to touch the stem.

Anemone-centered ('Sally Ball')
Single flower heads with enlarged disk florets that form dome-shaped centers, up to half the width or more of the flower head.

Pompon ('Salmon Faerie')
Fully double, spherical flower heads with tubular florets regularly and tightly packed, growing outward from the crown.

chrysanthemums FLORISTS' CHRYSANTHEMUM: a perennial grown for cut flowers, garden decoration and exhibition. The origin of the florists' chrysanthemum has been variously credited to China, Japan and Tibet. It probably derived from *Dendranthema indicum*, and has been grown in Britain since the late 18th century; many thousands of cultivars have been progressively introduced.

Chrysanthemums are classified into 30 sections according to form, flowering time, color and size. The six major exhibition forms are Incurved, Reflexed, Intermediate, Anemone-centered, Single and Pompon. Charms are dwarf, bushy plants bearing hundreds of small, single flowers; they are grown in pots and form spherical or hemispherical plants up to 36 in (90 cm) in diameter. Cascades have similar flowers, up to 1 in (2.5 cm) in diameter, and are usually trained as pillars, fans and pyramids, and, especially, in cascading forms.

Chrysanthemums may be disbudded, with one bloom per stem or lateral, or grown as sprays with many blooms per stem. Propagate from 2 in (5 cm) spring cuttings taken from boxed stools, which should be overwintered in a well-ventilated, frost-free cold frame or cold greenhouse and moved to a warm greenhouse five weeks before cuttings are taken. Cuttings should be taken 14–15 weeks before the recommended stopping date for a particular cultivar and rooted in small pots or seed trays at an optimum temperature of 61°F (16°C). Pot up rooted plants, using a loam-based medium, individually into 3½ in (9 cm) pots or box into deep trays, and protect from frost. Plants should be watered regularly, and liquid fertilizer applied at 7–10 day intervals between bud appearance and first coloring. For garden decoration or cut flowers, plant singly in groups in the border, supporting with 4 ft (1.2 m) canes. For late flowering, from earlier rooting dates, pot on successively through 6 in (15 cm), 8 in (20 cm) and 9–10 in (23–25 cm) sizes of pot.

The purchase of healthy stock plants is of great importance and vigilance to allow for timely chemical sprays.

The stopping date for individual cultivars needs to be established. Stop plants by removing the growing tips; the resulting laterals, or breaks, are further stopped and the flower buds removed according to choice of single large blooms or sprays per stem. Charms, cascades and exhibition plants require special training. For quality blooms, protection is needed from fall onward. Chrysanthemum blooms can be produced year round by manipulating day length with the aid of artificial lighting and shading.

chrysanthemum stool miner
(*Psila nigricornis*). An insect pest, related
to the carrot fly, which attacks the roots
and stem bases of chrysanthemums. It
is particularly damaging to stools of
chrysanthemums brought into a heated
greenhouse to produce cuttings, and
the new shoots may be killed. There
are no recommended insecticides for
this pest. Hot water treatment of dormant chrysanthemum stools, as used to
control eelworm, will also kill the
larvae of the stool miners.

Chrysogonum (from Greek *chrysos*,
gold, and *gone*, joints: the golden flowers are borne at the nodes). Compositae. E US. GOLDEN STAR 4 species, *C.
virginianum*, a hardy perennial herb to
8 in (20 cm) tall with downy, ovate to
lanceolate and toothed leaves, and a
succession of 1¼ in (3 cm)-wide, starry
yellow flowers from late spring to fall.
Hardy to 5°F (–15°C) or lower; use as
groundcover in dappled shade in moist,
humus-rich soil. Propagate by ripe seed
sown when fresh, or by division in spring.

Chrysosplenium (from Greek,
chrysos, gold, and *splen*, spleen, hence
splenium, a herb with medicinal
properties). Saxifragaceae. GOLDEN
SAXIFRAGE. Temperate regions. 55
species, low perennial herbs with creeping stems, round leaves and small yellow
flowers in terminal heads surrounded
by yellow-tinted, leafy bracts in spring.
Both species listed here are suited to
damp, shady positions in acidic soil
rich in leaf mold. They thrive in a
woodland garden and as groundcover
in the bog garden and fern border. The
first is hardy to 0°F (–18°C) (but may be
damaged by late frosts), the second to
–20°F (–29°C). Increase by division or
cuttings of new shoots.
    C. davidianum Himalaya; creeping,
hairy; leaves to 2 in (5 cm), dark green,
toothed to lobed; flower heads to 2¾ in
(7 cm) diam., rich gold to lime green;
C. oppositifolium Europe; tufted to creeping, sparsely hairy; leaves to ¾ in
(2 cm), bright, pale green, lobed; flower
heads to 1¼ in (3 cm) diam., pale gold
to lime green.

Chusquea (from the vernacular
name used in NE S America).
Gramineae. Mexico to Chile. Some

Copiapoa cinerea
This succulent species takes its name from
its ashy gray, or "cinerous" coloring

120 species, clump-forming bamboos
with pith-filled culms. See *bamboos*.

Cicerbita (Italian name of Medieval
origin for the sow thistle). Compositae.
Northern temperate regions. 18 species,
hardy perennial herbs with milky sap,
runcinate to lyrate-pinnatisect leaves
and thistlelike flower heads on branching stems in summer. Hardy to at least
5°F (–15°C), and suitable for naturalizing in the wild garden. Grow in moist
but well-drained, humus-rich, neutral
to acidic soil. Deadhead to prevent
seeding (conversely, propagate by seed).
    C. alpina (syn. *Lactuca alpina*); MOUN-
TAIN SOW THISTLE; Arctic and Alpine
Europe; 20 in–8 ft (0.5–2.5 m); flower
heads pale blue; *C. bourgaei* (syn. *Lactuca
bourgaei*); Asia Minor; 5–10 ft (1.5–
3 m); flower heads lavender or lilac.

Cichorium (Latinized form of the
Arabic name). Compositae. Europe,
Africa, Asia, naturalized elsewhere. 8
species, hardy annual or perennial herbs
with milky latex, runcinately to pinnately
lobed leaves and short-lived, daisylike
flower heads on slender, erect stems in
summer. *C. endivia* is ENDIVE, grown for
its edible leaves, as is *C. intybus*, CHICORY.
The latter is also ornamental, hardy to
–30°F (–34°C), and a superb summer
meadow plant, contrasting brilliantly
with ripe grasses and wild poppies.
Grow in full sun in free-draining soil.
Once established, this plant will withstand drought. Increase by seed in fall
or spring. *C. intybus* CHICORY, WITLOOF;
Europe, W Asia, N Africa, naturalized
N America; perennial to 3¼ ft (1 m) tall
with a long, thick taproot; flower heads
sky blue. See *chicory, endive*.

ciliate bearing a marginal fringe of
fine hairs.

cinereous ashy gray.

circinate of an unexpanded leaflet,
frond or frond segment, rolled up in a
close coil with the tip at its center, like
a crozier.

circumscissile a form of dehiscence in which a pod opens along a
line parallel with its circumference,
allowing the top to come off like a lid.
See *calyptra*.

cirrhous, (cirrose) of the apex;
terminating in a curled, coiled or spiraling continuation of the midrib.

Cirsium (from Greek *kirsos*, a swollen
vein) PLUME THISTLE. Compositae. About
200 species of hardy biennial or perennial herbs. Leaves alternate, pubescent
above, with spiny margins. Tubular flower
heads usually large, discoid, spiny,
purple, red, yellow, sometimes white.
Many are invasive through rhizomes or
self-seeding. Grow selected species in
borders or woodland, in moist, well-
drained, sunny positions. Deadhead to
avoid self-seeding. *C. arvense* CREEPING
THISTLE; Europe, NE US. Perennial to
5 ft (1.5 m). Leaves lanceolate to oblong
with apical spines, glabrous to slightly
hairy above, tomentose beneath. Capitulum to 1¼ in (3 cm) diam., 1–5 terminal. Florets lilac or pink. An invasive
garden weed, propagating from brittle,
lateral roots. Can be weakened by
repeatedly cutting top growth just
before flowering or by meticulous
forking, both over a number of years.
Glyphosate nonselective herbicide is
effective: apply just before the flower
heads color; *C. japonicum* Japan. Clump-
forming biennial or perennial to 6½ ft
(2 m). Leaves oblong-obovate, pointed,
deeply lobed to pinnate, dark green, 1 ft
(30 cm). Flowers in thistlelike capitulum
heads solitary or few to 2 in (5 cm) diam.,
late summer– fall; *C. rivulare* C and SW
Europe. Clump-forming perennial to 5 ft
(1.5 m). Leaves elliptic to oblong-lanceolate, dark green to 18 in (45 cm), soft
hairs beneath, spines to ¼ in (4 mm).
Capitulum to 1½ in (3.5 cm) diam., solitary or in clusters of 2–5, deep crimson-
purple to purple, late summer-early fall.

C

C

Cissus (from Greek *kissos*, ivy). Vitaceae. Tropics and subtropics. GRAPE IVY, TREEBINE. 350 species, herbs, shrubs and vines. Those listed here are shrubby with handsome, evergreen foliage on slender stems climbing by tendrils. The flowers are small and followed by inedible, dry berries. *C. antarctica* and *C. rhombifolia* are popular pot plants, especially in offices and other public buildings where, grown on trellis and canes, they withstand years of abuse. They prefer a minimum temperature of 50°F (10°C), light shade and moderate humidity. *C. discolor* is suited to hanging baskets and trellis. It requires a minimum temperature of 59°F (15°C), shade and high humidity. *C. striata* will tolerate light frosts and bright light. Propagate all by stem cuttings in late spring rooted in a heated case; increase also by layering.

C. antarctica KANGAROO VINE; Australasia; leaves 2¾–4 in (7–10 cm), ovate to oblong, apex long-acuminate, margins entire to sinuate or irregularly dentate, glossy, dark green, smooth, tough; *C. discolor* REX BEGONIA VINE; SE Asia to Australia; leaves 2½–10 in (6–25 cm), ovate-oblong to lanceolate, quilted dark velvety green above with a double row of gray-green, silvery-white or pale pink blotches, dark wine red beneath; *C. rhombifolia* GRAPE VINE TREEBINE; tropical America; leaves composed of 3 leaflets, each 1–4 in (2.5–10 cm) long, rhombic to ovate, glossy dark green above, remotely and sharply toothed; 'Ellen Danica': leaflets deeply incised; *C. striata* IVY OF URUGUAY, MINIATURE GRAPE IVY; Chile, Brazil; leaves composed of 5 palmately arranged, obovate to oblanceolate leaflets, each ⅜–1¼ in (1.5–3 cm) long, smooth and thin-textured and with gland-tipped teeth at their apices; leaves usually dropped in cold weather. For *C. bainesii*, see *Cyphostemma bainesii*; for *C. juttae* see *Cyphostemma juttae*; for *C. voinieriana*, see *Tetrastigma voinierianum*.

Cistus (from *kistos*, the Greek name for this plant). Cistaceae. S Europe, N Africa. ROCK ROSE, SUN ROSE. 20 species, small to medium-sized, more or less hardy evergreen shrubs with gummy to downy lanceolate to ovate leaves. Produced in abundance on bright summer days, the flowers are short-lived and composed of five, broadly obovate and crêpelike petals. The following species are hardy to 10°F (−12°C), especially if planted in a sheltered position and given a thick, dry mulch (or complete covering) in exceptionally hard winters. They need a fast-draining, light soil, full sun and protection from strong winds. Increase by softwood or heeled cuttings taken in late summer and rooted in a sandy mix at 59°F (15°C). Overwinter newly rooted plants in frost-free conditions.

C. × *aguilarii* (*C. ladanifer* × *C. populifolius*); leaves to 4 in (10 cm), lanceolate, undulate, bright green above, paler beneath; flowers to 1½ in (3.5 cm) in diameter, white; bases of petals purple-blotched in 'Maculatus'; *C. albidus* to 6½ ft (2 m); leaves to 2 in (5 cm), oblong to ovate, covered in white down; flowers to 1½ in (4 cm) in diameter, rosy pink to lilac with yellow basal spots; *C.* × *cyprius* (*C. ladanifer* × *C. laurifolius*); to 6½ ft (2 m); leaves to 4 in (10 cm), viscid, aromatic, oblong to lanceolate, undulate, dark gray-green and glabrous above, gray-hairy beneath; flowers to 2¾ in (7 cm) in diameter, white, often with bold, carmine basal spots; *C.* × *dansereaui* (syn. *C.* × *lusitanicus*; *C. ladanifer* × *C. hirsutus*); to 24 in (60 cm); leaves to 2½ in (6 cm), oblong to lanceolate, dull green; flowers to 2¾ in (7 cm) in diameter, white with crimson basal spots; *C.* × *hybridus* (syn. *C.* × *corbariensis*; *C. populifolius* × *C. salviifolius*); spreading, to 3¼ ft (1 m) tall; leaves to 2 in (5 cm), ovate, undulate, dark green above, paler and hairy beneath; flowers to 1½ in (3.5 cm) in diameter, white, usually with yellow basal spots; *C. creticus*, leaves undulate-crispate, flowers rose pink to purple, to 2½ in (6 cm) in diameter, with yellow basal spots; *C. creticus* subsp. *incanus* to 3¼ ft (1 m); leaves ⅜–2¾ in (1.5–7 cm), ovate to elliptic, green or silver-hairy with sunken veins; flowers to 2½ in (6 cm) in diameter, pink-purple; *C. ladanifer* COMMON GUM CISTUS, LADANUM; viscid, aromatic, to 6½ ft (2 m); leaves 1½–4 in (4–10 cm), linear to lanceolate, dark leaden green above, paler beneath; flowers to 2¾–4 in (7–10 cm) in diameter, white, usually with deep maroon basal spots; *C. laurifolius* to 5 ft (1.5 m); leaves 1¼–3½ in (3–9 cm), ovate to lanceolate, undulate, dark green and smooth above, white-hairy beneath; flowers to 2½ in (6 cm) in diameter, white with yellow basal spots; *C. monspeliensis* MONTPELIER ROCK ROSE; to 5 ft (1.5 m); leaves ⅜–2 in (1.5–5 cm), linear to lanceolate, rugose, dark green above, thinly gray-hairy beneath; flowers to 1 in (2.5 cm) in diameter, white; *C. parvifolius* to 5 ft (1.5 m); leaves to 1¼ in (3 cm), ovate, gray-hairy; flowers to 1¼ in (3 cm) in diameter, pink; *C.* 'Peggy Sammons' (*C. albidus* × *C. laurifolius*); to 3¼ ft (1 m); leaves to 2½ in (6 cm), oval, soft sage green; flowers to 2 in (5 cm) in diameter, pink; *C. populifolius* to 6½ ft (2 m); leaves 2–3½ in (5–9 cm), ovate to cordate, glabrous, mid-green, clammy; flowers to 2 in (5 cm) in diameter, white, often with yellow basal spots; *C.* × *purpureus* (*C. ladanifer* × *C. incanus* subsp. *creticus*); to 3¼ ft (1 m); leaves to 2 in (5 cm), oblong to lanceolate, gray-hairy beneath; flowers to 2¾ in (7 cm) in diameter, pink with dark red basal spots; *C. salviifolius* to 24 in (60 cm), spreading; leaves ⅜–1½ in (1.5–4 cm), ovate to oblong, gray-green and rugose above, paler beneath; flowers to 1½ in (4 cm) in diameter, white with yellow basal spots; *C.* 'Silver Pink' to 20 in (50 cm), low, spreading, bushy; leaves to 2¾ in (7 cm), ovate to lanceolate, pale sage green to gray above, silvery beneath; flowers to 2¾ in (7 cm) in diameter, pale, silky rose; *C.* × *skanbergii* (*C. monspeliensis* × *C. parviflorus*); to 3¼ ft (1 m); leaves to 2 in (5 cm), oblong to lanceolate, downy beneath; flowers pale pink).

Galanthus rizehensis
Wild snowdrops are threatened by overcollection; all have protection under CITES.

CITES an acronym for the Convention on International Trade in Endangered Species, established in 1972 to monitor and control international trade in species actually or possibly threatened with extinction from their natural habitat. About 126 countries throughout the world are signatories to the Convention, which is concerned with the movement of animals and plants across international boundaries and rather than internal trade within countries. The Convention operates through a system of export and import licenses with regard to three lists of species which comprise CITES Appendices I, II and III.

× **Citrofortunella** Rutaceae. Garden hybrids between *Citrus* and *Fortunella*, these are small, tender, evergreen trees or shrubs with intensely citrus-scented foliage, fragrant, waxy white flowers and small and tart, orangelike fruit. The following hybrid is commonly offered as the dwarf ornamental orange. Largely decorative, the fruit is painfully sharp, but will add something to marmalade, duck and cocktails. Grow in full sun with a minimum temperature of 45°F (7°C) and ample ventilation. Keep barely moist in cool weather; water, feed and syringe freely in the growing season. Hand-pollination with a fine brush is sometimes helpful for plants grown indoors and flowering in winter. Sudden fluctuations of temperature and water supplies will cause fruit drop. Prune only to remove exhausted, bare growth. Propagate by seed or by greenwood or semiripe cuttings in summer; increase also by grafting. × *C. microcarpa* (syn. *Citrus mitis; Citrus reticulata* × *Fortunella margarita*); CALAMONDIN ORANGE; small shrub or miniature tree to 6½ ft (2 m) with a rounded crown; leaves, elliptic to broadly ovate, dark glossy green; fruit 1–1½ in (2.5–3.5 cm), globose, bright orange, peel loose, strongly orange-scented, pulp sour; includes 'Tiger', with leaves streaked white, and 'Variegata', with white and gray leaves.

Citrus (from *Mala citrea*, ancient name of *Citrus medica*). Rutaceae. Asia, Pacific Islands, widely cultivated and naturalized elsewhere. 16 species, small, aromatic evergreen trees and shrubs with thorny branches, ovate to elliptic leaves and fragrant waxy white flowers. The edible fruit (hesperidium) is composed

of juicy pulp encased in a thick rind dotted with oil glands. The genus includes the following important fruit crops, some (e.g. *C. meyeri*) grown as ornamentals under the same regimen as × *Citrofortunella*, but requiring rather more room: *C. aurantifolia* (LIME); *C. aurantium* (SEVILLE ORANGE); *C. bergamia* (BERGAMOT); *C. limon* (LEMON); *C.* × *meyeri* (DWARF LEMON, MEYER LEMON); *C.* × *paradisi* (GRAPEFRUIT); *C. reticulata* (MANDARIN ORANGE, TANGERINE, CLEMENTINE, SATSUMA); *C. sinensis* (ORANGE, SWEET ORANGE); *C.* × *tangelo* (TANGELO, UGLI FRUIT).

cladophyll, cladode a flattened or acicular branch that takes on the form and function of a leaf, arising from the axil of a minute, bractlike, and usually caducous true leaf, for example in

Cladode
In this example (*Ruscus hypoglossum*) the larger leaflike growth is a cladode. *Ruscus* (see below).

Cladrastis (from Greek *klados*, branch and *thraustos*, fragile, referring to the brittle twigs). Leguminosae. E Asia, N America. 5 species, hardy deciduous trees with large pinnate leaves and pealike flowers in terminal racemes and panicles in summer. Hardy to –22°F (–30°C), the following will grow in most, fertile, well-drained soil in full sun, thriving on chalk. Prune young plants in late summer to encourage a strong, clear leader—the branches of this tree are brittle and easily brought down by strong winds. Propagate by seed, scarified and stratified at 41°F (5°C) for two to three months; increase also by root cuttings in winter. *C. kentuckea* KENTUCKY YELLOW-WOOD; round-headed tree to 50 ft (15 m); leaves dark green turning yellow in fall; flowers white, fragrant, in drooping panicles.

clair-voyée an aperture cut into a garden wall to allow a view beyond; typically at the end of a walk or allée.

clamp in vegetable growing, a conical pile of root vegetables covered with layers of straw and soil to enable outdoor storage over the winter.

Clarkia (for Captain William Clark [1770–1838], explorer in North America). Onagraceae. Western N America, S America. FAREWELL TO SPRING, GODETIA. 33 species, annual herbs with linear to lanceolate or elliptic leaves and spikes or racemes of flowers with four, obovate and clawed, silky petals. Sow *in situ* in spring (also in fall in more or less frost-free climates) in well-drained soil of low to moderate fertility in full sun. Pinch young plants to encourage bushiness. Larger cultivars may need some support. *C. amoena* SATIN FLOWER; California; fast-growing, slender-stemmed, erect or decumbent, 8–39 in (20–100 cm) tall; flowers 1½–2½ in (4–6 cm) in diameter, cupped to outspread, single or double with smooth or ruffled petals in shades of deep crimson, magenta, pink, lavender, scarlet, apricot, salmon and white, sometimes with paler margins or bases or darker basal blotches; many cultivars and seed races are available.

clasping partially or wholly surrounding an organ, as for example, in the case of a leaf base which clasps a stem; such leaves are termed *amplexicaul*

class the principal category of taxa intermediate in rank between Division and Order, e.g. Monocotyledonae.

clathrate latticed, pierced with holes and windows, as for example, in the leaves *Aponogeton madagascariensis*.

clavate, claviform shaped like a club or a baseball bat; thickening to the apex from a tapered base.

claviculate bearing hooks or tendrils.

claw the narrowed petiole-like base of some sepals and petals.

clay the finest texture of soil, with particles of less than 0.002 mm diam.

C

C

and consisting mainly of alumino-silicate minerals. See *soil*.

Claytonia (for John Clayton [1686–1773], American botanist). Portulacaceae. Americas, Australasia, New Zealand. SPRING BEAUTY, PURSLANE. 15 species, small, rosette-forming herbs with thinly succulent, smooth leaves and cup-shaped, 5-petaled flowers in spring. Both of the following are hardy to –10°F (–23°C). *C. megarhiza* requires deep, sharply draining soil, high in grit and leaf mold and moist in spring and summer, but almost dry in winter. It thrives in full sun in airy conditions and is perhaps best-suited to culture in long clay pots in an alpine house or frame. *C. virginica* occurs in damp and cool, humus-rich soil in wooded or semiwooded places. It is suited to similar conditions in the garden. Propagate by seed, offsets, or division.

C. megarhiza western N America; taprooted; leaves 2–6 in (5–15 cm), spathulate to obovate; flowers white to pink, white to deep pink; *C. virginica* SPRING BEAUTY; eastern N America; cormous; leaves 2½–4¾ in (6–12 cm), linear to oblanceolate; flowers white tinted pink, some forms yellow veined red.

clearwing moths (Lepidoptera: Sesiidae) moths differing from most other Lepidoptera in having wings largely devoid of scales. They fly in the daytime and resemble wasps or ichneumon flies. The CURRANT CLEARWING MOTH (*Synanthedon tipuliformis*) is a destructive pest of black currants and, to a lesser extent, red- and white currants and gooseberries. It occurs widely over Europe and parts of Asia and has been introduced into North America, Australia and New Zealand. The moths have a wingspan of up to ¾ in (20 mm), and a black abdomen with three or four yellow bands, terminating in a prominent tuft of black hairs. The larvae tunnel into shoots, causing wilting and death or weakness of the stems. Any affected shoots must be removed and burned..

In North America, the crown and main roots of peach may be attacked by the PEACH TREE BORER (*Synanthedon exitiosa*), whose adults, up to 1 in (25 mm) long, are steel blue with yellow

markings. In addition, flowering dogwoods may be attacked by the DOGWOOD BORER (*S. scinula*); raspberries by the RASPBERRY CROWN BORER (*Pennitsetia marginata*), which hollows out the crowns; and grapes by the GRAPE WOOD BORER (*Vitacea polistiformis*), whose larvae bore into the roots, reducing vigor.

cleft of a flat organ (e.g. a leaf or perianth segment); cut almost to the middle.

Cleistocactus (from Greek, *kleistos*, closed, and *cactus*, referring to the unexpanded perianth). Cactaceae. S America. Some 30 species, shrubby or treelike cacti with cylindric stems and narrowly tubular flowers in summer. Provide a minimum temperature of 41°F (5°C), full sun and low humidity. Plant in a fast-draining mix high in grit and with a pH of 6–7.5. Keep these plants dry from midfall to early spring, except for light misting on warm days during late winter. At all other times, water sparingly. *C. strausii* SILVER TORCH; Bolivia; stems 3¼–10 ft (1–3 m) × 1½–3 in (4–8 cm), erect and branching below, with many ribs and dense, fine, white spines; flowers to 3 in (8 cm), dark red.

cleistogamy, cleistogamous self-pollination and self-fertilization within an unopened flower. The process often follows unsuccessful insect pollination on a plant and occurs late in the season, as in sweet violet (*Viola odorata*).

Clematis (from Greek *clema*, a tendril; name used by Dioscorides for several climbing plants). Ranunculaceae. OLD MAN'S BEARD, TRAVELERS JOY, VIRGIN'S BOWER, VASE VINE, LEATHER FLOWER. N and S Temperate regions, mountains of Tropical Africa. Over 200 species, deciduous or evergreen, semiwoody to woody climbers or woody-based, erect to sprawling perennials. The flowers are campanulate to bowl-shaped, solitary, clustered or borne in panicles, and composed of petal-like sepals and numerous stamens. In some species, petal-like staminodes are also present. The fruit consists of numerous achenes with long, persistent, often plumose styles.

Clematis have long been cultivated in Japan, and have been cultivated in Europe since the 16th century. Japanese cultivars, mainly those of the Patens Group, were introduced into European gardens in the mid-19th century. Nurserymen and plant breeders took the opportunity of using these earlier-flowering cultivars in a vast breeding program, crossing them with European species and cultivars and other large-flowered clematis introduced from China, mainly during the period 1855–80. Many of those cultivars are still popular today.

Clematis species and cultivars have many uses in the modern garden. The vigorous species such as *C. montana* are ideal for growing over buildings and through large trees. The herbaceous species are suitable for borders. Less vigorous climbers, like *C. alpina* and *C. macropetala*, are superb against north- or east-facing walls or fences. *C. viticella* and its colorful cultivars are best-suited for growing over shrubs or small trees and even over medium-height groundcover plants. The winter-flowering evergreen species like *C. cirrhosa* are more suited to the sheltered garden or, in cold districts, the conservatory or cool greenhouse. The spectacular evergreen *C. armandii* is far hardier in cool temperate areas than is often believed and will thrive on a north-facing wall to 0°F (–18°C).

The large-flowered clematis cultivars fall into two basic groups: those that flower on ripened stems of the previous season and those that flower on the current season's growth from midsummer onward. Compact and free-flowering, the early large-flowered types can, for purposes of cultivation, be split again into sections. The very early flowering types (typical of the *C.* Patens Group) such as *C.* 'Miss Bateman', are ideal for growing in containers or small gardens. The double and semi-double, large-flowered cultivars, such as *C.* 'Vyvyan Pennell', are more suited to growing through wall-trained shrubs such as *Pyracantha* because of the weight of their flowers. The later, early summer-flowering cultivars with large flowers and vigorous habit, such as *C.* 'Marie Boisselot', fare better grown through large freestanding shrubs or small trees. The second group of large-flowered cultivars, such as the popular *C. × jackmanii*, which flowers on the current season's growth, will grow well through wall-trained shrubs, climbing or rambler roses or freestanding species roses.

In addition to the climbing species and cultivars, there are several herbaceous species which are particularly useful for the border. These include *C. heracleifolia*, *C. integrifolia*, *C. recta* and *C. stans*. The slender-stemmed taller species, such as *C. recta* may need the support of twigs or sticks. The herbaceous species and their cultivars flower on the current season's stems. *C. × jouiniana* might be termed semiherbaceous, producing a sprawling mass of vigorous stems. It is best used for covering paving, breaking up the outlines of borders and over tree-stumps and drain-covers.

The New Zealand species and their cultivars are fine plants for the conservatory or frost-free greenhouse in cool temperate areas; they may also be grown successfully in virtually frost-free gardens in a sunny well drained site. When grown in containers, the potting medium should be gritty, well-drained and never wet during the winter months. Some cultivars make ideal plants for an alpine house, such as *C. × cartmanii* 'Joe'. All are evergreen and flower on the previous season's ripened stems. They therefore require only the removal of dead and weak stems after flowering each year.

In the garden, *Clematis* will grow in most well-drained, fertile soils in sun or part-shade. To avoid damage by animals and total infection by clematis wilt, all climbing clematis should be planted with the top of the root ball buried some 3 in (8 cm) below the soil surface. This will help to build up a good root crown of growth buds. Newly planted clematis should be

seed heads with fluffy plumes

Clematis vitalba

pruned hard the first spring after planting, especially those planted in containers. All growth should be removed down to a strong pair of leaf axil buds 12 in (30 cm) above soil level. Most clematis climb by their leaf petioles, which twist themselves around the support, whether it be wire, trellis or another plant. They may also be tied on to supports.

For the purpose of pruning, climbing clematis fit into three basic groups according to whether they flower on old or previous season's wood or that of the current year. Of species it can, however, be remarked that pruning can be limited to the removal of excess, exhausted or congested growth after flowering.

GROUP 1. The plants in this group produce short flower-stalks direct from the previous season's leaf axil buds. Group 1 includes including the spring-flowering species *C. alpina*, *C. macropetala* and *C. montana*. Remove any dead or damaged stems after flowering and, as the growing season progresses into summer and fall, train new growth into the support if it can be reached, keeping stems within their allocated space.

GROUP 2. This group consists of the early large-flowered cultivars, the double and semidouble and the large-flowered types which flower before midsummer (i.e. Florida, Lanuginosa and Patens Groups). These plants produce stems of varying lengths with a single flower at the end. The stems grow away from axillary buds which will have ripened the previous season. Remove any dead or damaged stems down to a strong pair of buds during late winter or very early spring. Leave all healthy growth untouched. Tie in the old and new growth so that it can support the large flowers.

GROUP 3. These produce all their flowers in clusters or panicles at the

end of the current season's growth (i.e. Jackmanii, Texensis and Viticella Groups). Remove all top growth down to just above the base of the previous season's stems during late winter and very early spring. New growth may be visible at this time; prune to just above where it commences. All top growth should be trained and tied in to its support during the growing season.

In addition to these three groups, evergreen clematis like *C. armandii*, *C. cirrhosa* and some New Zealand species may be divested of old and exhausted stems after flowering. Herbaceous species can be cut near the ground between late fall and early spring.

Species can be successfully propagated from seed sown soon after harvesting in a cold frame. Cultivars should be reproduced by layering, cuttings or grafting. Layering can be carried out during late winter or early spring with old stems, or in early summer using the current season's growth. Herbaceous clematis can be increased by division. *C. heracleifolia* and its cultivars increase easily by layering. Take cuttings before flowering during late spring or, from the very early spring-flowering types, in early summer. Internodal cuttings of soft to semiripe wood are best; one of the pair of leaves should be removed. Insert the cuttings in a light, sandy potting mixture in a cold frame; alternatively, a propagation unit can be used. Nodal cuttings of *C. armandii* will root in a cool mist unit. Graft large-flowered cultivars on to rootstocks of *C. viticella* or *C. vitalba* during early spring. A propagation unit or cold frame can be used; a cleft-graft is generally preferred. Pot grafted plants with the union well below soil level.

Clematis wilt causes the plant to collapse while in full growth and the growing tips to turn black. If a plant is infected, all its top growth should be removed down to soil level and burnt. If the clematis was planted deeply enough, it should start to grow again from below soil level. The wilt is caused by a fungus and can be controlled by spraying with a fungicide at intervals.

See table overleaf.

CLEMATIS

Name	Distribution	Habit	Leaves	Flowers
C. afoliata *C. aphylla*	New Zealand	sprawling to climbing, almost leafless shrub to 6½ ft (2 m)	where present, trifoliolate with minute leaflets	1 in (2.5 cm) diam., sepals green-white, 4ate, spreading

Comments: Spring.

| **C. alpina**
Atragene alpina | N Europe & mts of C & S Europe, N Asia | deciduous climber to 8 ft (2.5 m) | biternate, leaflets 9, to 2 in (5 cm), ovate-lanceolate, serrate | pendulous, star- to bell-shaped, sepals 4, to 1½ in (4 cm), blue or mauve, oblong-lanceolate, staminodes petaloid, pale blue to white, spoon-shaped |

Comments: Spring. (*C. macropetala*, which is more showy, is also of the Atragene range, which is characterized by petal-like staminodes in the center of each flower. Cultivars are often attributed alternatively to either species.) *C. alpina* 'Pamela Jackman', blue. 'Burford White': large, clear white; 'Columbine': pale lavender, campanulate sepals long and acute; 'Frances Rivis' ('Blue Giant'), sepals up to 2 in (5 cm) long, sky blue; 'Pink Flamingo': white, blushed pale rose; 'Ruby': soft rosy red, staminodes cream.

| **C. armandii** | C & W China | evergreen climber to 28 ft (9 m) | trifoliolate, leaflets to 6 in (15 cm), oblong-lanceolate to ovate, entire, emerging bronze-pink, soon becoming rich glossy green, tough and prominently veined | to 2½ in (6 cm) diam., fragrant, sepals 4, pure white or cream-white, later rose |

Comments: Spring. 'Apple Blossom': leaves strongly tinted bronze when young; flowers cup-shaped, pink in bud, fading to white. 'Snowdrift': leaves large, new foliage tinted copper; flowers large, white, waxy, very fragrant.

| **C. barbellata** | W Himalaya | climber to 12 ft (4 m), differing from *C. montana* in flower color | | campanulate, sepals 4, ovate, to 1½ in (4 cm), downy, dull purple to brown-violet |

Comments: Spring. 'Plum Beauty' (*C.* 'Pruinina'): flowers plum, lantern-shaped, stamens petaloid, white.

| **C. campaniflora** | Portugal | deciduous climber to 20 ft (6 m) | 5- or 7-ternate, leaflets to 3 in (7.5 cm), narrowly lanceolate, ovate or oval, simple or sometimes lobed | bowl-shaped, pendulous, sepals white tinged violet-blue, 4, to ¾ in (2 cm), oblong, recurved, downy |

Comments: Summer.

| **C. × cartmanii**
(*C. marmoraria* × *C. paniculata*.) | garden origin | bushy dwarf evergreen with finely dissected dark green leaves and large panicles of white flowers | **Comments:** 'Joe': tufted to mat-forming, branches purple-tinted, flowers to 1½ in (4 cm) diam., white, profuse. | |

| **C. chrysocoma** | China | deciduous climber to 8 ft (2.5 m) | trifoliolate, tawny-hairy, leaflets to 1¾ in (4.5 cm), broadly ovate or rhomboid, trilobed, coarsely toothed | 1¾ in (4.5 cm) diam., solitary, sepals white tinged pink, 4, broadly oblong, downy beneath |

Comments: Summer-fall.

| **C. cirrhosa** | S Europe, Mediterranean | evergreen climber to 12 ft (4 m) | to 2 in (5 cm), simple and toothed, jaggedly cut or trilobed, or ternate or biternate with toothed or lobed leaflets, glossy dark green | pendulous, campanulate, to 2¾ in (7 cm) diam., each long-staked and subtended by a small cuplike pair of bracteoles, sepals ovate, to 1 in (2.5 cm), cream, sometimes spotted red |

Comments: Winter. 'Wisley Cream': flowers cream; var. **balearica**: sepals pale cream, always spotted and flecked red-maroon within. var. **purpurascens** 'Freckles': flowers large, cream, intensely flecked and spotted maroon to violet within, on very long, slender pedicles.

C. alpina 'Columbine'

C. armandii

C. barbellata 'Plum Beauty'

C. cirrhosa

CLEMATIS

Name	Distribution	Habit	Leaves	Flowers
C. colensoi	New Zealand	evergreen climber, much-branched	2¾ in (7 cm), triangular, trifoliolate and pinnately cut	sepals green, 6, narrowly lanceolate, downy
Comments: Spring–summer.				
C. County Park Hybrids (*C. petriei* × *C. marmoraria*)	garden origin	dwarf, usually evergreen shrubs, trailing and bushy or weakly climbing, with dark, much-dissected foliage and dense panicles of pale flowers	**Comments:** Spring-summer. 'Pixie': trailing, flowers pale yellow-green in a congested panicle, male selection. 'Fairy': a female selection with silky golden styles and showy fruiting heads where pollinated.	
C. crispa BLUE JASMINE, MARSH CLEMATIS, CURLY CLEMATIS, CURLFLOWER	SE US	climbing deciduous shrub to 8 ft (2.5 m)	pinnately 3-, 5- or 7-foliolate, leaflets to 2¾ in (7 cm), often trifoliolate or lobed, thin, lanceolate to ovate	campanulate, pendulous, sepals to 2 in (5 cm), fused below, distinct and spreading at tips, lavender, almost white at margins, thin and wavy
Comments: Summer.				
C. × diversifolia (*C. integrifolia* × *C. viticella*)	garden origin	sprawling subshrub to 10 ft (3 m)	pinnately divided, leaflets usually 7, elliptic, deep green, entire or slightly lobed	sepals 4, dark violet to lavender, spathulate, 1½ in (4 cm), reflexed
Comments: Summer.				
C. douglasii	W N America	herbaceous, nonclimbing perennial to 24 in (60 cm)	simple below, 2-pinnate above, leaflets oblong, lanceolate or ovate, downy	tubular or campanulate, nodding on long, swan-necked stalks, sepals 4, deep mauve to violet, exterior paler, to 1¼ in (3 cm), oblong with reflexed, tapered tips
Comments: Spring–summer. var. **scottii**: leaves gray-green, flowers urceolate, lavender to pale magenta, downy; includes 'Rosea' with rose pink flowers.				
C. × durandii (*C. × jackmanii* × *C. integrifolia*)	garden origin	robust, erect to weakly climbing shrub to 71 in (180 cm)	to 6 in (15 cm), simple, ovate, glossy green **Comments:** Summer–fall.	to 4¾ in (12 cm) diam., sepals deep violet-blue, usually 4, to 6, outspread or reflexed, obovate, slightly wavy
C. flammula	S Europe, N Africa, W Syria, Iran, Turkey	deciduous subshrub climbing to 15 ft (5 m)	3- or 5-foliolate, leaflets narrowly lanceolate to rounded, bright green, smooth, rather tough	very fragrant, to 1 in (2.5 cm) diam., sepals pure white, 4, to ½ in (1.2 cm), oblong, obtuse
Comments: Summer–fall.				
C. florida	China, Japan	deciduous or semievergreen climber to 12 ft (4 m)	to 5 in (12.5 cm), ternate, each division trifoliolate, leaflets to 2 in (5 cm), ovate to lanceolate, entire or toothed, shiny, downy beneath	to 3 in (7.5 cm) diam., sepals white or cream, sometimes lined or tinted green, 4, deep violet, to 1 in (2.5 cm)

Comments: Summer. 'Albaplena': flowers double, staminodes and sepals white flushed green, exterior with central green stripe. var. **sieboldiana** ('Bicolor'): flowers white with many purple staminodes forming a roselike center.

C. flammula

C. florida var. *sieboldiana*

C. 'Proteus' (Florida Group)

C. integrifolia

CLEMATIS

Name	Distribution	Habit	Leaves	Flowers
C. Florida Group. Woody climbers, 8–10 ft (2.5–3 m), flowering spring to summer on previous year's wood; flowers usually semidouble or double, or single later in season, 6–9 in (15–22 cm) across, white to lilac or deep violet.				
C. forsteri	New Zealand	evergreen climber	trifoliolate, leaflets to 2¾ in (7 cm), lanceolate to broadly ovate, smooth, entire to toothed or pinnately cut, tough, bright green	sepals 5, white to yellow
Comments: Summer. 'Tempo': male selection, very vigorous; flowers to 1½ in (4 cm) diam., pale green becoming white.				
C. fusca	NE Asia	climber to 10 ft (3 m)	pinnate, leaflets to 2½ in (6 cm), ovate, smooth or downy beneath	urn-shaped, nodding, sepals 4, to 1 in (2.5 cm), dull purple to violet inside, densely hairy outside
Comments: Summer. var. ***violacea***: flowers violet.				
C. graveolens	Himalaya	climber to 12 ft (4 m); close to *C. orientalis* but with more finely divided glaucous leaves, and heavily scented flowers with spreading sepals		fragrant, sepals 4, yellow, ovate to obovate, often notched at apex, 1¼ in (3 cm)
Comments: Summer.				
C. heracleifolia	C & N China	woody-based perennial herb, erect to 5 ft (1.5 m)	trifoliolate, leaflets to 2½ in (6.5 cm), rounded to ovate, coarsely toothed, with pale hairs	tubular to narrowly campanulate, to 1 in (2.5 cm), sepals 4, deep blue, tips recurved, exterior hairy
Comments: Summer–fall. 'Cote d'Azur': hyacinth blue. 'Jaggards': deep blue.				
C. hookeriana	New Zealand	differs from *C. paniculata* in leaflets deeply lobed and green-yellow to light yellow flowers		
C. integrifolia	C Europe, SW Russia, W & C Asia	erect, nonclimbing herbaceous perennial or subshrub to 3¼ ft (1 m)	to 3½ in (9 cm), simple, ovate to lanceolate, entire, glabrous above, downy beneath, prominently veined	bell- to star-shaped, nodding on long, erect stalks, sepals dark violet or blue, rarely white, usually 4, lanceolate, to 2 in (5 cm), spreading with recurved tips and slightly wavy margins
Comments: Summer. 'Pastel Pink': flowers soft light pink. 'Rosea': flowers sugar pink, underside darker, scented.				
C. intricata	W China to Siberia	climber to 12 ft (4 m)	pinnate or bipinnate, leaflets to 2 in (5 cm), elliptic to lanceolate, 2–3-lobed, blue-green	sepals to ¾ in (2 cm), yellow
Comments: Summer				
C. × jackmanii (*C. lanuginosa* × *C. viticella*)	garden origin	climber to 12 ft (4 m)	simple to trifoliolate, leaflets to 4¾ in (12 cm), broadly ovate, deep green and glabrous above, paler and downy beneath	rich velvety violet-purple, numerous, to 4¾ in (12 cm) diam., sepals 4-6, broadly ovate
Comments: Summer. 'Alba': flowers gray-white; 'Purpurea Superba': flowers deep violet. 'Rubra': flowers red to plum, double, or single later in season.				

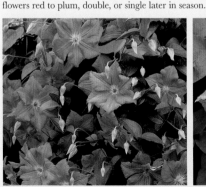

C. 'Perle d'Azur' (Jackmanii Group)

C. 'Henryi' (Lanuginosa Group)

C. *macropetala* 'Markham's Pink'

CLEMATIS

Name	Distribution	Habit	Leaves	Flowers
C. Jackmanii Group. 6½–20 ft (2–6 m), flowering summer to fall on new shoots; flowers 4¾–8 in (12–20 cm) diam.; sepals usually 4, wide to narrow and pointed, shell pink, red or blue to purple.				
C. × jouiniana (*C. tubulosa* × *C. vitalba*)	garden origin	vigorous, sprawling, semievergreen, woody-based perennial or semiscandent shrub to 12 ft (4 m)	leaflets 3 or 5, to 4 in (10 cm), ovate, coarsely toothed, weakly hairy	fragrant, sepals 4, white to ivory deepening to opal then lilac or sky blue toward tips, strap-shaped, ¾ in (2 cm), tip expanded and somewhat recurved
Comments: Fall. 'Mrs. Robert Brydon': small, off-white, somewhat tinted blue. 'Praecox': pale blue flushed silver.				
C. ladakhiana	India, Tibet	deciduous or semievergreen climber to 10 ft (3 m), stems tinged brown-purple	pinnate to bipinnate, leaflets narrow	sepals spreading, narrowly elliptic, yellow to orange-yellow, usually with darker markings or staminodes
Comments: Summer.				
C. Lanuginosa Group. Woody climbers, 8–15 ft (2.5–5 m), flowering on short side-shoots on current year's growth; flowers very large, loosely arranged, summer to fall, appearing consecutively, single or double, 15.				
C. macropetala	N China, E Siberia, Mongolia	deciduous climber, to 3¼ ft (1 m)	biternate, leaflets to 1½ in (4 cm), ovate to lanceolate, coarsely toothed and lobed	to 4 in (10 cm) diam., pendulous, sepals blue or violet-blue, 4, oblong to lanceolate, to 2 in (5 cm), exterior downy, staminodes numerous, outer violet-blue, inner blue-white
Comments: Spring–summer. See also *C. alpina*. 'Blue Bird' (*C. macropetala* × *C. alpina* var. *sibirica*): semidouble, large, deep lavender. 'Jan Lindmark': pale purple, 'Maidwell Hall': semidouble, to 2 in (5 cm) diam., deep blue. 'Markham's Pink': strawberry pink, nodding. 'Rosy O'Grady' (*C. macropetala* × *C. alpina*): to 2¾ in (7 cm) diam., semidouble, deep bright pink, sepals long and pointed. 'White Swan' (*C. macropetala* × *C. alpina* var. *sibirica*): to 4¾ in (12 cm) diam., pure white.				
C. marmoraria	New Zealand	prostrate, suckering evergreen shrub to 2½ in (6 cm) tall, the smallest *Clematis* species, loosely resembling a rigid clump of parsley	leaflets deeply and closely divided, glossy green, thick	to ¾ in (2 cm) diam., sepals 5 green-white becoming creamy white; stamens many, filaments green, anthers cream
C. montana	C & W China, Himalaya	vigorous, climber, to 25 ft (8 m)	trifoliolate, leaflets to 4 in (10 cm), ovate to lanceolate, toothed to trilobed	to 2 in (5 cm) diam., lantern- to star-shaped, sepals white or pink, 4, rarely 5, elliptic, exterior downy
Comments: Spring-summer. 'Alexander': flowers large, perfumed, creamy white with yellow stamens; 'Peveril': to 3 in (8 cm) diam., pure white, stamens long and shimmering. var. **grandiflora**: very vigorous, flowers white, abundant. var. **rubens**: young leaves tinged purple-bronze, flowers pink-red. 'Pink Perfection': vigorous; flowers profuse, small, deep pink, sepals round. 'Lilacina' : flowers pale mauve.				
C. orientalis	Aegean, Ukraine, SE Russia, Iran, W Himalaya, W China, Korea	deciduous vine or scrambler to 25 ft (8 m)	pinnately 5, trilobed, entire or toothed, gray-green **Comments:** Summer–fall.	to 2 in (5 cm) diam., sepals yellow or green-yellow, 4, oblong or elliptic, outspread, later recurved, thick and fleshy, stamens maroon

C. marmoraria

C. montana

C. 'Barbara Dibley' (Patens Group)

CLEMATIS

Name	Distribution	Habit	Leaves	Flowers
C. patens	Japan, China	deciduous climber	pinnately 3-5-lobed	to 6 in (15 cm) diam., sepals 6, cream white, violet or bright blue, elliptic to obovate, to 3 in (8 cm), anthers purple-brown

Comments: Spring–summer. 'Standishii': flowers to 5½ in (14 cm) diam., pale lilac with a metallic luster, center lilac-rose.

C. Patens Group. Woody climbers, 6½–11 ft (2–3.5 m), flowering in spring on old wood; flowers with pointed sepals, normally single, 6–10 in (15–25 cm) across, sepals wide and overlapping to pointed, flat to wavy, white to purple, often with a darker midstripe.

Name	Distribution	Habit	Leaves	Flowers
C. petriei	New Zealand	sprawling woody vine to 12 ft (4 m)	bipinnate or tripinnate, leaflets to 1¼ in (3 cm), tough, ovate to oblong, entire or bluntly toothed	yellow-green, sepals 6, to oblong, ¾ in (2 cm), downy

Comments: Summer. 'Limelight': male selection, leaves purple, flowers lime. 'Princess': female selection, similar to 'Limelight' but with smaller flowers and showy seed heads.

Name	Distribution	Habit	Leaves	Flowers
C. phlebantha	W Nepal	erect to trailing or sprawling bush to 5 ft (1.5 m)	to 3 in (7.5 cm), pinnate, leaflets ⅝ in (1.5 cm), white-woolly beneath, lobed	to 1¾ in (4.5 cm) diam., sepals white, 5-veined, elliptic to obovate, cupped to spreading, exterior densely woolly, anthers yellow

Comments: Spring–summer.

Name	Distribution	Habit	Leaves	Flowers
C. × pseudococcinea (*C. × jackmanii × C. texensis*)	garden origin			

Comments: Similar to *C. texensis* but with campanulate flowers. 'Duchess of Albany': deep pink, erect, center tinted brown, ventral side striped white. See also *C. Texensis Group*.

Name	Distribution	Habit	Leaves	Flowers
C. ranunculoides	China	erect, nonclimbing perennial herb to 20 in (50 cm) or climber to 6½ ft (2 m)	trifoliolate or pinnately 5-foliolate, or simple and trilobed, leaflets rounded to obovate or ovate, to 2 in (5 cm), coarsely toothed, hairy	pendulous, sepals purple to pink, 4, oblong, ⅝ in (1.5 cm), spreading, reflexed, downy

Comments: Spring–fall.

Name	Distribution	Habit	Leaves	Flowers
C. recta	S & C Europe	erect, nonclimbing perennial to 5 ft (1.5 m), densely branched	to 6 in (15 cm), pinnate, leaflets to 3½ in (9 cm), oval to lanceolate, entire, glabrous and deep blue-green above, paler beneath	to ¾ in (2 cm) diam., erect, in many-flowered panicles, sepals milky white, 4, narrowly ovate or oblong, spreading

Comments: Summer. 'Grandiflora': flowers large, very abundant. 'Plena': flowers double. 'Purpurea': branches and leaves flushed deep purple-bronze, becoming green in time.

Name	Distribution	Habit	Leaves	Flowers
C. rehderiana	W China	deciduous, woody-stemmed climber to 25 ft (7.5 m)	pinnate, leaflets to 2¾ in (7 cm), broadly ovate, often trilobed, coarsely toothed, hairy	campanulate, pendulous, sepals soft primrose yellow or pale green, 4, to ¾ in (2 cm), reflexed, downy outside

Comments: Summer.

Name	Distribution	Habit	Leaves	Flowers
C. spooneri *C. chrysocoma* var. *sericea*	China	deciduous climber to 20 ft (6 m)	trifoliolate, leaflets to 2¾ in (7 cm), oval or ovate, coarsely toothed, yellow-silky beneath	to 2½ in (6 cm) diam., sepals pure white, 4, rounded to oval or obovate, to 1 in (2.5 cm) diam., silky-hairy outside

Comments: Spring.

C. recta

C. rehderiana

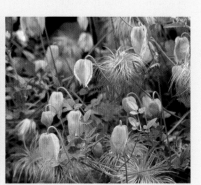

C. tangutica

CLEMATIS

Name	Distribution	Habit	Leaves	Flowers
C. stans *C. heracleifolia* var. *stans* **Comments:** Summer–fall.	Japan	deciduous erect shrub or subshrub or climber to 71 in (180 cm)	trifoliolate, leaflets to 6 in (15 cm), broadly ovate, coarsely toothed, with distinct, hairy veins	tubular, sepals white, ½ in (1 cm), recurved, blue inside, white and tomentose outside
C. tangutica *C. orientalis* var. *tangutica*	Mongolia, NW China **Comments:** Summer–late fall.	climber to 10 ft (3 m)	pinnate or bipinnate, leaflets to 3 in (8 cm), oblong to lanceolate, lobed and toothed, bright green	campanulate to lantern-shaped, pendulous, sepals golden yellow, 4, oval to lanceolate, to 1½ in (4 cm), apex tapering to spreading, exterior hairy
C. texensis	SW US (Texas)	climbing subshrub or erect to scrambling perennial to 6½ ft (2 m)	soft gray-green, pinnate, leaflets to 3 in (8 cm), ovate to rounded	to 1¼ in (3 cm), much narrowed toward mouth, pendulous, sepals scarlet-red or carmine, thick, narrowly ovate, somewhat reflexed

Comments: Summer. 'Major': flowers scarlet with white or yellow interior; 'Passiflora': flowers to ¾ in (2 cm), scarlet throughout.

C. Texensis Group. Nonclimbing, erect to sprawling or weakly climbing shrubs or woody-based semiherbaceous perennials, flowering abundantly on young shoots over a long summer period; flowers urceolate to narrowly campanulate.

Name	Distribution	Habit	Leaves	Flowers
C. tibetana	N India	differs from *C. orientalis* in the finely cut, smooth and glaucous foliage and thickly textured pale yellow flowers	**Comments:** ssp. ***vernayi***: leaves glaucous; flowers to 2 in (5 cm), solitary or in threes, nodding, narrowly campanulate then outspread, sepals green-yellow to burnt orange, thickly fleshy, somewhat wrinkled, stamens dark purple—easily distinguished by its remarkably thick sepals—these have led to its being given the popular name 'Orange Peel Clematis', which has also been applied as a cultivar name to a selection of this subspecies with thick sepals of a rich yellow-orange.	
C. × triternata *(C. flammula × C. viticella)*	garden origin	climber to 12 ft (4 m) **Comments:** 'Rubromarginata': flowers white, edged wine red, profuse.	simple or bipinnate, leaflets entire	1¼ in (3 cm) diam., in terminal panicles; sepals lilac, 6
C. × vedrariensis *(C. chrysocoma × C. montana* var. *rubens)* **Comments:** Spring–summer.	garden origin	closely resembles *C. montana* var. *rubens*, vigorous evergreen climber to 20 ft (6 m)	leaflets to 2½ in (6 cm), ovate, often 3, trilobed, coarsely toothed, dull purple-green and pale-hairy above, paler and more densely so beneath	to 2½ in (6.5 cm), sepals rose, lilac or pink, 4–6, occasionally rounded to oval, outspread, stamens yellow
C. viticella	S Europe	deciduous semiwoody climber to 11 ft (3.5 m)	to 5 in (12.5 cm), pinnately trifoliolate, leaflets to 2½ in (6.5 cm), lanceolate to broad-ovate, often 2–3-lobed	nodding, sepals blue, purple or rose-purple, 4, oblong to obovate, apex acuminate, to 1½ in (4 cm), undulate, exterior silky

Comments: Summer-fall. 'Plena': flowers double, violet. 'Purpurea': flowers plum. 'Purpurea Plena Elegans': flowers to 3 in (8 cm) diam., very double, deep violet. 'Rubra': flowers deep carmine. 'Rubra Grandiflora': flowers large, carmine red. f. ***albiflora***: flowers pure white.

C. Viticella Group. Woody climbers, 8–20 ft (2.5–6 m), flowers abundant, appearing consecutively over a short season, to 6 in (15 cm) diam., single to double, white to red and deep purple with colored midstripe or veins.

C. tibetana

C. viticella 'Purpurea Plena Elegans'

C. 'Mme Julia Correvon' (Viticella Group)

C

Cleome (name used by Theophrastus). Capparidaceae. Tropics and subtropics. 150 species, annual and perennial herbs with palmately lobed leaves and dense, terminal racemes of flowers in spring and summer. These consist of four, narrowly ovate and clawed petals and a bundle of very long, slender stamens. Sow under glass some two months before the last frosts or *in situ* in late spring. Grow in a warm, sunny position in light, fertile and preferably sandy soil. Propagate by seed. *C. hassleriana* (syn. *C. spinosa* of gardens); SPIDER FLOWER; S America; annual, 20–60 in (50–150 cm) tall; flowers white to pink or purple with petals to 1¼ in (3 cm) long and stamens to 4 in (10 cm).

Clerodendrum (from Greek *kleros*, chance, and *dendron*, tree, alluding to the variable medicinal properties of some species). Verbenaceae. Tropics and subtropics. Some 400 species, trees and shrubs, mostly tender and many climbing, with ovate to elliptic or obovate leaves and, in summer, panicles or corymbs of flowers composed of a campanulate to tubular calyx, a salverform 5-lobed corolla and exserted stamens. *C. bungei* and *C. trichotomum* will tolerate temperatures as low as 5°F (–15°C); the former may be killed to the ground, but will resprout from the roots if thickly mulched. Both require a sheltered, sunny site in well-drained, deep and fertile soil. Remove deadwood in spring. The remaining species need a minimum temperature of 50°F (10°C), full sun except on the hottest summer days and moderate to high humidity. Water and feed freely in spring and summer; keep barely moist in winter. Support climbing species. Cut back after flowering and then only if it is necessary to alleviate overcrowding, remove weak or dead growth or keep the plant within bounds. Long-established specimens of climbing species may, however, need hard rejuvenation pruning from time to time, and this should be done during early spring. Propagate by seed in spring or by softwood and semiripe cuttings rooted in a sandy mix in a heated case; increase also by root cuttings in spring and by removal of rooted suckers.

C. bungei GLORY FLOWER; E Asia;

suckering, semievergreen erect shrub to 8 ft (2.5 m) tall; leaves foetid; flowers white to rose or purple-red, sweetly scented in rounded terminal heads to 6 in (15 cm) long; *C. paniculatum* PAGODA FLOWER; SE Asia; erect evergreen shrub to 5 ft (1.5 m); flowers scarlet in a terminal, much-branched panicle to 12 in (30 cm) tall; *C. philippinum* (syn. *C. fragrans*); GLORY BOWER; E Asia; semievergreen, erect shrub to 10 ft (3 m); flowers pink, white, or sometimes tinged lilac, often double, sweetly fragrant, in dense, domed heads; *C. speciosissimum* (syn. *C. fallax*); erect, evergreen shrub to 12 ft (4 m), often grown as a smaller, pot plant; flowers bright scarlet in erect, conical panicles to 18 in (45 cm); *C. × speciosum C. splendens × C. thomsoniae*; JAVA GLORY BEAN, PAGODA FLOWER; differs from *C. thomsoniae* in its pale red or pink calyx and deep purple-rose corolla. *C. splendens* tropical Africa; evergreen climber to 10 ft (3 m); flowers bright red to scarlet in crowded, terminal panicles; *C. thomsoniae* BAG FLOWER, BLEEDING HEART VINE; tropical W Africa; evergreen climber to 12 ft (4 m) tall; flowers in drooping, terminal panicles, calyx large, white, corolla deep red; *C. trichotomum* Japan; deciduous, broad-crowned shrub or tree to 22 ft (7 m) tall; leaves foetid; flowers fragrant in broad, nodding cymes, calyx red-tinted, corolla white; fruit turquoise to black-blue, among persistent, red calyces; includes var. *fargesii*, a hardy and free-fruiting form; *C. ugandense* BUTTERFLY BUSH; tropical Africa; erect to sprawling, evergreen shrub to 11 ft (3.5 m) tall; flowers in terminal panicles to 6 in (15 cm), calyx crimson-tinted, corolla pale blue to violet.

Clethra (from Greek *klethra*, alder). Clethraceae. Asia, Americas, Madeira. WHITE ALDER, SUMMER-SWEET, SWEET PEPPERBUSH. Some 30 species, trees and shrubs, usually deciduous with obovate to lanceolate, serrate leaves and fragrant, 5-petaled flowers, small, bell-shaped and white, in racemes from summer to fall. *C. alnifolia* is the hardiest, surviving to –30°F (–34°C); the Asian species will suffer below –10°F (–23°C), while *C. arborea* is tender and should be grown in a cool greenhouse or conservatory where hard frosts occur. All *Clethra* species prefer a humus-rich,

acidic soil, moist but well-drained, and light shade to dappled sunlight. Propagate by seed in spring or by heeled cuttings of lateral shoots in mid- to late summer in a heated frame. *C. alnifolia* produces suckers that may be detached and grown on once rooted.

C. alnifolia SWEET PEPPER BUSH, SUMMER SWEET, BUSHPEPPER; eastern N America; tree or shrub to 12 ft (4 m); flowers in erect, cylindrical panicles; includes pink-flowered forms; *C. arborea* LILY-OF-THE-VALLEY TREE; Madeira; evergreen shrub or tree to 25 ft (8 m); young stems tinged red; flowers nodding in slender racemes; *C. barbinervis* China to Japan; shrub to 30 ft (10 m) with peeling bark; leaves turning red and yellow in fall; flowers with fringed petals in hairy, spreading racemose panicles to 6 in (15 cm); *C. delavayi* W China; tree to 43 ft (13 m); flowers nodding in a raceme to 10 in (25 cm) long, white to cream emerging from pink sepals.

Cleyera (for Dr. Cleyer, 18th-century Dutch botanist). Theaceae. E Asia, C America. 17 species, evergreen or deciduous trees and shrubs with flowers composed of five, obovate, white to creamy yellow petals produced in summer. Hardy in favored locations to 0°F (–18°C). Plant in sun or part shade with protection from strong winds, in moist, fertile and acidic soil. Increase by semiripe cuttings in summer. *C. japonica* SAKAKI; China, Korea, Japan; evergreen, glabrous shrub to 12 ft (4 m); leaves 2¾–4 in (7–10 cm), narrowly oblong to ovate, blunt, glossy, dark green above, paler beneath; flowers to ¾ in (2 cm) in diameter, cream, fragrant, produced in early summer; includes two very similar cultivars, 'Fortunei' (syn. *C. fortunei*), with pointed leaves variegated cream and rose toward margins, and 'Tricolor', with pointed leaves tinged pink at first, marbled gray and cream and edged cream to yellow-green—both are sometimes confused with *Eurya japonica* 'Variegata'.

Clianthus (from Greek *kleos*, glory, and *anthos*, flower). Leguminosae. Australia, New Zealand. 2 species, evergreen trailing to clambering shrubs and subshrubs with pinnate leaves and pealike flowers characterized by a billowing, reflexed standard to 2 in (5 cm) long and a finely tapered, clawlike keel to 2¾ in (7 cm) long. *C. formosus* requires a minimum temperature of 41°F (5°C), full sunlight and a dry, buoyant atmosphere. Grow in baskets or pots of a loam-based mix high in sand and grit; keep just moist in spring and summer, virtually dry in winter. This species is best watered from below and should not be syringed. Propagate from seed sown in spring at 65°F (18°C). The life of this often short-lived perennial can be prolonged in cultivation by grafting scions of 6–12-month-old seedlings on to stocks of *Colutea arborescens* of the same age; use an apical wedge graft. *C. puniceus* will survive outdoors on sunny and sheltered walls in mild regions. Plant in full sun on fast-draining, gritty soil. Tie in to a wall, if necessary, and remove dead or exhausted growth in spring. Propagate by seed or by semiripe cuttings in summer in a heated case.

C. formosus (syn. *C. dampieri*, *C. speciosus*); DESERT PEA, GLORY PEA, STURT'S DESERT PEA; Australia; silky-hairy, prostrate subshrub; flowers in erect, long-stalked, umbel-like racemes, vivid scarlet, the standard with a glossy black, bulging blotch; *C. puniceus* GLORY PEA, PARROT'S BEAK, LOBSTER CLAW; New Zealand; erect to clambering shrub to 15 ft (5 m) with spreading to arching branches; flowers in drooping racemes, satiny scarlet, vermilion, coral-pink or white.

click beetles see *wireworms*.

climacteric in fruit cultivation, the point of maximum rate of respiration in stored fruit, such as apples, which coincides with the attainment of ripeness.

climatic zone see *hardiness*.

climber any plant that climbs, or has a tendency to do so, by means of various adaptations of stems, leaves or roots.

clinandrium in orchids, the part of the column containing the anther.

cline a population of plants exhibiting continuous morphological variation

therefore presenting problems in plant classification, for example the orchid genus *Ophrys*.

Clitoria (the keel of these flowers resembles the clitoris). Leguminosae. Tropics. 70 species, tender herbs and shrubs, many climbing, with trifoliolate or pinnate leaves and pealike flowers. These are usually carried with the large and showy standard held downward and the small, incurved keel uppermost. Provide a minimum winter temperature of 59°F (15°C), medium to high humidity and bright, filtered light. Grow in a fertile, loam-based medium. Water, feed and syringe generously in summer; keep barely moist in winter. Train on wires, trellis or canes. Increase by seed in spring, or by spontaneous layers and softwood cuttings in summer.

C. amazonum Brazil; woody climber to 12 ft (4 m); flowers to 3 in (8 cm), white or pale pink lined with dark rose veins; *C. ternatea* BLUE PEA, BUTTERFLY PEA; tropical Asia; soft-stemmed, woody-based climber to 10 ft (3 m); flowers to 2 in (5 cm), bright blue fading to white at center with a yellow stain.

Clivia (for Charlotte Florentina, Duchess of Northumberland, née Clive, d. 1866, who was first to flower the type species). Amaryllidaceae. KAFFIR LILY. S Africa. 4 species, tender perennial, evergreen herbs with glossy, dark green, strap-shaped leaves in two ranks, their bases overlapping and bulb- or stemlike. Appearing throughout the year, the flowers are waxy, funnel-shaped, composed of six, oblong to obovate segments and carried in umbels atop stout scapes. Provide a minimum winter temperature of 45°F (7°C) and bright indirect light. Grow in a fertile, free-draining mix. Water and feed freely in spring and summer; keep barely moist in winter. *C. miniata* is an excellent house plant. It benefits from occasional leaf sponging. Propagate by seed in late winter, or by division after flowering.

C. miniata (leaves to 24 × 2¾ in (60 × 7 cm); scape to 12 in (30 cm), flowers erect to spreading, each to 2¾ in (7 cm) long, and scarlet to orange with a yellow throat; includes flame-, peach-,

yellow-, and large-flowered cultivars, and forms with leaves striped white, yellow or cream; *C. nobilis* more drooping, narrower flowers than *C. miniata*, to 2 in (5 cm) long, red edged yellow, and tipped green.

Tunnel cloche
The wire hoops, normally clad with polyethylene film, can be covered with horticultural fleece to exclude flying insect pests.

cloche a low portable unit constructed of glass or rigid-plastic panes on a wire frame; used for the protection of plants and to advance growth. The term is also applied to plastic film stretched over wire hoops, a construction alternatively known as a low continuous polyethylene tunnel.

clod a consolidated mass of soil particles, which can form at the surface of heavy soil after inappropriate cultivation.

clone the genetically identical offspring of a single parent, produced by asexual reproduction or vegetative propagation.

close case, closed case see *propagation frame*.

clubroot (*Plasmodiophora brassicae*) FINGER AND TOE, CLUBBING, CLUB FOOT ANBURY, a fungal disease affecting most crucifers, including weeds such as charlock and shepherd's purse, and ornamentals such as candytuft, stocks and wallflowers; it is especially severe on brassicas. Radish and certain cultivars of calabrese, Chinese cabbage

stem of brassica

grossly distorted roots

Clubroot
Brassicas are highly susceptible to this persistent soilborne fungal disease, which can destroy crops. Bought-in plants are a common means of establishing infected land.

and kale have been found to be resistant to clubroot.

Affected plants become stunted with discolored leaves, wilt in dry weather, and roots become abnormally swollen. Symptoms vary according to the habit of the host plant: on plants with a slender taproot and numerous laterals, such as cabbage, there may be clusters of small galls or a single large club-shaped swelling; on rutabagas and turnips, warty outgrowths occur mainly at the base of the naturally swollen roots. Symptoms can be confused with those caused by the turnip gall weevil, but such galls either contain the maggots or have conspicuous exit holes.

Plasmodiophora is a slime mold; it survives in soil as minute resting spores which can remain viable for at least 20 years. In the presence of susceptible roots, spores germinate to form swimming zoospores which eventually penetrate root hairs.

Clubroot is most damaging in acidic soil and can be much reduced by liming to bring the soil up to pH7. Rotation is advisable, but alone is not effective because of the longevity of the resting spores. Avoid brought-in brassica plants, which are a common source of infection. On infected sites, raise plants in pots of sterilized medium. In the early stages of infection, a foliar feed may help plants to become established.

cluster cups a descriptive term for the fruiting bodies of rust fungi.

Clytostoma (from Greek *klytos*, glorious, and *stoma*, mouth, referring to the flowers). Bignoniaceae. Tropical America. 9 species, tender, summer-flowering evergreen vines. The leaves are composed of two or three leaflets and terminate in a tendril. Produced in late spring and summer, the 5-lobed flowers are funnel-shaped and borne in pairs or short panicles. Cultivate as for *Bignonia* but with a minimum temperature of 50°F (10°C). *C. callistegioides* (syn. *Bignonia callistegioides*, *B. speciosa*, *B. violacea*, ARGENTINE TRUMPET VINE, LOVE CHARM; Brazil, Argentina; fast-growing woody climber to 15 ft (5 m); flowers to 2¾ in (7 cm) long, throat creamy yellow veined lilac, lobes mauve-pink fading to rose.

CO_2 enrichment the introduction of extra carbon dioxide into a greenhouse to maintain a maximum rate of photosynthesis in intensively cultivated crops, especially tomatoes. It may be generated by burning propane, natural gas, or paraffin or derived from liquid CO_2.

Coade stone an artificial stone made of fired clay with added ingredients; invented and manufactured by Eleanor Coade in the late 18th century and used for a range of garden and architectural ornaments.

Cobaea (for B. Cobo [1572–1659]. Jesuit priest and naturalist active in Mexico and Peru). Polemoniaceae (Cobaeaceae). C and S America. 20 species, herbaceous or shrubby perennial, evergreen climbers, tender and sometimes treated as annuals. The leaves are pinnate and tendril-tipped. Solitary flowers are produced in great abundance from late spring to fall. They are usually fragrant and composed of a leafy, spreading calyx and a 5-lobed, campanulate corolla. In frost-free regions, the following species will thrive in fertile, moist soil in full sun, soon covering its support. Cut back and feed plants grown as perennials in spring. Elsewhere, grow year round in a cool greenhouse or use as a half-hardy annual, sowing seed in early spring at

68°F (20°C) for planting out in warm and sheltered locations in early summer. *C. scandens* CATHEDRAL BELLS, CUP AND SAUCER VINE; MEXICAN IVY; VIOLET IVY; Mexico; rampant, woody-based climber to 30 ft (10 m), usually treated as a half-hardy annual; flowers with campanulate corolla (the "cup") to 2 × 1½ in (5 × 4 cm), green-cream and muskily fragrant at first, later violet, then deep purple and sweetly scented; the corolla sits on a leafy pale green calyx, the "saucer."

cobnut see *hazelnuts*.

Coccoloba (from Greek *kokkos*, a berry, and *lobos*, a pod, referring to the fruits). Polygonaceae. Americas. 150 species, trees, shrubs and lianes, tender and evergreen with large, leathery leaves, small, green-white flowers and fleshy, grapelike fruit. Young specimens make good pot plants grown in sun or part shade with a minimum temperature of 50°F (10°C). Plant in a fertile, sandy mix. Keep moist throughout the year, and syringe and feed in summer. In the tropics and subtropics, this species is often to be seen as a large shrub, tree or hedge, showing remarkable tolerance of scorching sun, poor soil and saline winds; it is an excellent coastal plant. Propagate by greenwood cuttings. *C. uvifera* SEA GRAPE; coastal tropical America; stoutly branched, erect shrub or tree to 30 ft (10 m), usually smaller; leaves to 8 in (20 cm) wide, broadly oblong to obovate, base more or less cordate, apex rounded, glossy olive to dark green, often with bronze to yellow or red veins and wavy margins.

Cocculus (diminutive form of the Greek *kokkos*, berry, referring to the small fruits). Menispermaceae. Asia, Africa, America. 11 species, deciduous or evergreen trees, shrubs and lianes with small, green-white flowers and globose fruits containing horseshoe-shaped seeds. Hardy to 5°F (–15°C) and suited to woodland gardens, trellises and pergolas in light shade or dappled sun. Plant in moist, humus-rich soil. Prune in early spring to keep within bounds and remove dead or congested growth. Propagate by seed, semiripe cuttings and root cuttings.

C. carolinus CAROLINA MOONSEED, CORAL BEADS, SNAILSEED; E US; deciduous twiner to 12 ft (4 m); leaves to 4 in (10 cm), ovate to cordate, sometimes obscurely 3–5-lobed with 3–7 principal veins; fruit bright red; *C. orbiculatus* E Asia; differs from *C. carolinus* in having leaves sometimes shallowly 3-lobed with 3–5 principal veins, and pruinose black fruits.

coccus part of a schizocarp or lobed fruit.

cochlea a tightly coiled legume.

cochleate coiled like a snail's shell.

cochlear, cochleariform spoon-shaped.

Cochlioda (from Greek *kochlion*, a little snail, referring to the curiously shaped callus). Orchidaceae. Peru. 6 species, compact, tender, evergreen perennial herbs with clumped pseudobulbs and strap-shaped leaves. They are grown for their flowers composed of five, lanceolate to elliptic tepals and a showy, 3-lobed lip. Provide a minimum temperature of 45°F (7°C) with full sun in winter, and bright, indirect light and high humidity when in growth. Plant in an open, bark-based mix. Water and feed freely in spring and summer; keep almost dry in winter, apart from occasional mistings on warm days. Increase by division.

C. noezliana (flowers vivid scarlet, lateral lobes of lip rounded; *C. rosea* (flowers deep rose to crimson, lateral lobes of lip rhombic.

cockroaches (Dictyoptera: Blattidae) active insects up to 1½ in (40 mm) in length, with long, many-jointed antennae and thickened forewings lying horizontally and overlapping the hindwings on a flattened body. The indigenous European species are small and of no economic significance; injurious species have, however, become widespread, mainly by shipping from warmer regions. They can breed throughout the year in a heated greenhouse. Eggs are laid in batches of about 15 in a tough purse-shaped capsule which may be carried around by the female for some days before being deposited in soil or in a crevice. Over a period of 3–12 months, a female may produce as many as 30 capsules. After 4–12 weeks (or more, depending on temperature), the young hatch inside the capsule, which then splits open. The nymphs resemble the adults but are wingless; they moult 6–12 times, according to species, before attaining their adult form.

The largest of the four cosmopolitan species is the AMERICAN COCKROACH (*Periplaneta americana*), which is up to 1½ in (38 mm) long, and has red-brown wings extending beyond the abdomen. The AUSTRALIAN COCKROACH (*P. australasiae*) is similar, but about 1¼ in (30 mm) long, with a narrow yellow band behind the head. The ORIENTAL COCKROACH (*Blatta orientalis*) is up to 1 in (25 mm) long and dark brown, almost black. The wings of the male do not reach the end of the abdomen and those of the female are rudimentary. The GERMAN COCKROACH (*Blattella germanica*) is up to ½ in (12 mm) long, and is dull yellow with two dark stripes on top of the thorax; the wings extend beyond the abdomen. The adults and nymphs of these four species are omnivorous. Greenhouse plants constitute only a small part of their diet, and all plant parts are subject to attack. Cinerarias, chrysanthemums, pot cyclamen, nicotianas, *Schizanthus* and the flowers and aerial roots of orchids are especially vulnerable. Cockroaches are mostly active at night and are more prevalent in old greenhouses, which provide suitable hiding places.

Control by attention to hygiene and the elimination of daytime resting sites. Apply contact insecticides to floors, walls and heating pipes, or use commercial baits. This treatment should be a continual process, because the cockroach eggs may take a year to hatch, especially at lower temperatures. Where resistance to chemicals is suspected, pitfall traps may be used.

cocoa husks the husks of cacao nuts (*Theobroma cacao*), used as a ground mulch, soil conditioner or occasionally as a potting medium ingredient. The husks should be aged before use to reduce nitrogen and salt levels.

coconut fiber see *coir*.

Cocos (from Portuguese and Spanish *coco*, a grinning face, referring to the facelike marks on the base of the nut). Palmae. 1 species, *C. nucifera*, the COCONUT, a palm widespread throughout the tropics, especially in coastal regions. It grows to 100 ft (30 m) tall with an unbranched trunk, often gray, fissured and ringed and tapering upward from a swollen base. The leaves are pinnate and spreading to arching, mid-green and to 20 ft (6 m) long. The fruits are rounded, to 14 in (35 cm) long and covered in a smooth, green to orange coat; the "coconut" is the endocarp, woody and fibrous and lined with white, oily endosperm. Widely grown and naturalized in the tropics, especially in coastal regions. Elsewhere, grow in beds, large pots or tubs in a fertile and free-draining, sandy medium rich in lime and potash. Water plentifully, and maintain high humidity and a minimum temperature of 64°F (18°C). Shade this plant from full summer sun. Fresh seed will germinate readily at 81–86°F (27–30°C), and it is as a seedling, with the "nut" still attached, that this palm is usually offered for sale.

Codiaeum (from the native Ternatean name, *kodiho*). Euphorbiaceae. SE Asia, Pacific Islands. 6 species, tender evergreen trees and shrubs grown for their leathery, often brightly colored leaves. Small, creamy white flowers are carried in slender racemes. Provide a minimum temperature of 55°F (13°C) during winter, with medium to high humidity and protection from strong direct sunlight, drafts and temperature fluctuations. Grow in moist, fertile and nonalkaline potting mix; water, feed and mist freely when in full growth. Prune leggy plants hard in late winter, then dress the wounds with charcoal. Propagate by air layering or root greenwood stem tip cuttings in a heated case—control bleeding by dipping in charcoal. *C. variegatum* (syn. *Croton pictum*); CROTON; SE Asia; shrub to 6½ ft (2 m); leaves 12 in (30 cm), obovate to elliptic to oblong or lanceolate, tough, glossy dark green; many cultivars of this shrub are grown, and they have become particularly popular as house plants: their leaves range in shape from entire to jaggedly lobed,

189

C

near-round to ribbonlike, blade- to cup-shaped, and in color from deep emerald to lime or gold, variously stained, spotted and veined yellow, orange, pink, red, maroon and purple-black.

Codling moth caterpillar damage
The "frass" or excrement of the tunnelling larvae at the eye end of fruits is the most readily identifiable sign of this pest.

codling moth (*Cydia pomonella*) a small moth with a wingspan of ³/₄–1 in (19–22 mm) and gray-brown forewings with a copper-colored patch at the tips. Its larvae are a serious pest of mature apple fruits (dessert cultivars are particularly susceptible) and also attack pear, quince, walnut and some ornamental *Malus* species. In northern Europe, there is normally only one generation during summer, but sometimes a second; in hot countries, there are regularly three. Eggs are laid on fruits and foliage, and after hatching, the caterpillars tunnel toward the core of the fruit. Damage often goes unnoticed until the fruit is mature; damaged fruits may ripen prematurely and drop early. The fully fed white-pink caterpillar leaves the fruit either through the eye end or by tunnelling through the side of the apple. The skin around the exit hole may be dark red and the tunnel is filled with caterpillar excrement.

The caterpillar overwinters under loose bark and pupates in the following spring, so that bands of sacking or corrugated cardboard fitted around the trunk or larger branches of a tree can serve as artificial over-wintering sites; these may be removed and destroyed during winter. Many overwintering caterpillars are eaten by birds. Fruit can be protected by spraying with an insecticide at egg-hatching times in early summer. Placing a pheromone trap in a tree can help to indicate flight periods, and thus the most effective time for spraying. On isolated trees, such traps may give some direct control by depleting the male moth population.

Codonopsis (from Greek *kodon*, bell, and *opsis*, appearance, alluding to the shape of the corolla). Campanulaceae. Asia. 30 species, hardy perennial herbs, often muskily scented and scandent, grown for their 5-lobed, campanulate flowers produced in spring and summer. Hardy to 14°F (–10°C). Grow in a light, fertile, humus-rich and well-drained soil in sun or dappled shade. Keep roots cool and moist in summer; mulch in winter. Allow climbers to twine through pea sticks or surrounding shrubs. Propagate by division or by seed in spring.

C. clematidea Russia to Himalaya; erect scrambler to 32 in (80 cm); flowers to 1 in (2.5 cm), bell-shaped, pale blue with tangerine and black markings at base within; *C. convolvulacea* Himalaya to SW China; twiner to 10 ft (3 m); flowers to 1½ in (4 cm) in diameter, azure to violet-blue with distinct, spreading, ovate lobes; *C. vinciflora* is similar; *C. ovata* W Himalaya; erect to 12 in (30 cm), rarely twining; flowers funnelform to campanulate, pale blue with darker veins and a near-black base within.

Coelogyne (from Greek *koilos*, hollow, and *gyne*, woman, referring to the deep stigmatic cavity). Orchidaceae. Asia. 200 species, tender perennial herbs with globose to flask-shaped pseudobulbs crowned with paired, lanceolate to elliptic leaves. Produced in spring and summer, the flowers consist of five linear to elliptic tepals and a showy lip and are carried in terminal clusters or racemes. Maintain a minimum winter temperature of 50°F (10°C) for all species except *C. pandurata* and *C. speciosa*, which require a minimum of 59°F (15°C). Grow in a humid, buoyant atmosphere with filtered light in summer and full sun in winter. Pot in an open, bark-based mix. Water, feed and syringe freely from midspring to early fall; in winter, water and syringe only to prevent severe shriveling of pseudobulbs and then only on warm days. Coelogyne should be propagated by division after the plant has flowered.

C. cristata India; flowers to 2½ in (6 cm) in diameter, often fragrant, lacy, snow white marked yellow on crested lip, in nodding racemes to 6 in (15 cm) long; *C. dayana* Borneo; similar to *C. tomentosa*, but flowers slightly larger and a deep parchment color, heavily edged and blotched chocolate brown on the white-veined lip; *C. nitida* (syn. *C. ochracea*); India to Laos; flowers to 1½ in (4 cm) in diameter, sweetly fragrant, sparkling white marked orange-yellow and red on lip, in erect to nodding racemes to 8 in (20 cm) long; *C. ovalis* India to Thailand; flowers to 1½ in (4 cm) in diameter, pale tan marked dark brown on fringed lip, solitary or a few together on a very short, erect raceme; *C. pandurata* SE Asia; flowers to 3 in (8 cm) in diameter, sometimes fragrant, jade to lime green, veined black on lip, on an erect to arching raceme to 12 in (30 cm) tall; *C. speciosa* SE Asia; flowers to 3 in (8 cm) in diameter, olive to buff or pale salmon, marked brown to buff on the white-tipped, fringed lip, solitary or a few and nodding on an erect raceme to 4¾ in (12 cm) tall; *C. tomentosa* (syn. *C. massangeana*); SE Asia; flowers to 1½ in (4 cm) in diameter, pale yellow, ivory or tan, veined brown and white on pale yellow lip, many together in strongly pendulous racemes to 18 in (45 cm) long.

berries contain coffee seeds or "beans"

Coffea arabica

Coffea (from the Arabic name). Rubiaceae. Asia and Africa, widespread in tropics through cultivation.

COFFEE. 40 species, tender evergreen shrubs and small trees with leathery, ovate to elliptic leaves and clusters of fragrant, creamy white flowers. These give rise to green-red berries; the seeds are roasted as coffee beans. Grow in neutral to slightly acidic, loam-based mix. Provide bright filtered light, high humidity and a minimum temperature of 59°F (15°C). Water and feed freely when in growth. Prune in spring to encourage the formation of several erect leaders in young plants, and to limit the flower-bearing lateral branches to one per node in established plants. When grown under glass, hand-pollination may be needed for fruit set. Propagate by seed sown in spring or by cuttings of upright shoots with a snag of old wood. *C. arabica* COFFEE, ARABIAN COFFEE; Ethiopia, Sudan; shrub to 10 ft (3 m); berries to ⅝ in (1.5 cm) long and green ripening red, yellow or purple; dwarf forms are sometimes grown as ornamentals.

coherent of parts usually free or separate, fused together, as in a corolla tube. The term is sometimes used to describe the adhesion of similar parts; cf. *adherent*.

coir fiber from the outer husk of the coconut (*Cocos nucifera*), once widely used in plunge beds and as a rooting medium; of interest as a peat alternative in growing medium. Special care is required in the watering of coir; nutrient replenishment is also essential.

Coix (from Greek *koix*, a reedy plant). Gramineae. Tropical Asia. 6 species, annual and perennial herbs with slender leaves and gracefully arching panicles in summer, the female flowers are enclosed in distinctive, beadlike utricles which hang like tear drops. Where temperatures drop below 10°F (−12°C), sow seed in late winter under glass (minimum temperature 59°F/15°C) and pot several plants together in a rich loamy mix. Protect from fierce summer sun. Alternatively, grow outdoors as half-hardy annuals; raise under glass and plant out in a warm, sunny position in moist but well-drained, fertile soil in late spring. In frost-free regions with long, hot summers, sow seed *in situ* in spring. *C.*

lacryma-jobi JOB'S TEARS; SE Asia; annual to 5 ft (1.5 m) tall; utricles to ⅝ in (1.5 cm) in diameter, white to gray tinged blue or brown.

seeds will yield colchicine

colchicine an alkaloid derived from the FALL CROCUS (*Colchicum fallale*); used in plant breeding to produce growths with more than the normal number of chromosomes.

Colchicum (of Colchis). Liliaceae (Colchicaceae). E Europe to Asia, N Africa. AUTUMN CROCUS, FALL CROCUS, MEADOW SAFFRON. 45 species, hardy perennial herbs with large corms and linear to elliptic leaves. Produced mostly in late summer and fall, the flowers appear before the leaves. Virtually stalkless, they are campanulate to funnelform or star-shaped and consist of six, lanceolate to oblong lobes. Plant in full sun in fertile, well-drained soil. The larger species and cultivars are suitable for naturalizing in turf; the smaller species suffer in dull and wet conditions and may need to be grown in a bulb frame or in a sheltered rock garden. Increase by seed or by division in fall.

C. agrippinum Greece to SW Turkey; flowers funnel-shaped, segments to 2 in (5 cm), checkered rose-purple and white; *C. fallale* FALL CROCUS, MEADOW SAFFRON; W and C Europe; flowers funnel-shaped to campanulate, segments to 2½ in (6 cm), purple-pink to pale pink or white; *C. bivonae* (syn. *C. bowlesianum*, *C. sibthorpii*); S Europe to Turkey; flowers campanulate, segments 1½–3 in (4–8 cm), rosy purple, checkered; *C. byzantinum* Turkey, Syria, Lebanon; flowers funnel-shaped, segments to 2 in (5 cm), pale mauve-pink; *C. cilicicum* Turkey, Syria, Lebanon; flowers funnel-shaped to campanulate, segments 1½–2¾ in (4–7 cm), pale lilac to deep rose-purple, sometimes obscurely checkered; *C. luteum* C. Asia to China; flowers funnel-shaped to narrowly campanulate, segments to 1¼ in (3 cm), pale to deep yellow; *C. speciosum* Turkey, Iran, Caucasus; flowers funnel-shaped to campanulate, segments to 3 in (8 cm), pale pink to deep rose-purple or white, sometimes white in throat; *C.* 'The Giant' flowers large, lilac pink

and faintly checkered with a white throat; *C. variegatum* Greece, SW Turkey; flowers broadly funnel-shaped, segments to 2 in (5 cm), purple-red, strongly checkered, white in throat; *C.* 'Waterlily' flowers large, double, deep rose-pink with a white throat.

Fall crocus

cold frame an unheated frame.

cold house an unheated greenhouse.

cold store a refrigerated room or container used to store plants, propagating material or produce at low temperature.

coleoptile a sheath protecting the plumule of a germinating grass seedling.

coleorhiza a sheath protecting the radicle of a germinating grass seedling.

collar sometimes used to describe the junction point of the stem and roots of a plant.

collar rot rotting of the stem at, or just above, soil level. The original damage may be caused by careless weeding, animals, insects, waterlogging or heating up under densely packed basal mulch. It provides an entry for bacteria and fungi. Collar rot sometimes refers to the post-emergence damping-off of seedlings and may be applied to the black-leg symptoms caused by the bacterium *Erwinia carotovora* on potato, the fungi *Leptosphaeria maculans* on brassicas and *Pythium* species on pelargonium cuttings. When the rot extends below soil level, the symptom may be described as foot rot. See *black leg*.

collenchyma a strengthening tissue of young plant organs, composed of living cells with irregularly thickened walls.

Colletia (for Philibert Collet [1643–1718], French botanist). Rhamnaceae. Temperate S America. 17 species, hardy shrubs, leafless or with very small and short-lived leaves, and green, photosynthesizing stems and

191

branches. These are covered in ferocious spines. White to cream or pale flesh pink and scented, small flowers cluster along the spines in winter and spring. They give rise to fleshy berries. Hardy to 23°F (–5°C), or lower if planted against a warm and sheltered wall. Grow in full sun, preferably in fast-draining, lean soil. Increase by heeled semiripe cuttings of short side shoots in a heated case.

C. hystrix (syn. *C. armata*) S Chile; to 6½ ft (2 m); spines dark green, to 1 in (2.5 cm), thinly hairy; *C. paradoxa* (syn. *C. cruciata*) Uruguay, S Brazil; to 6½ ft (2 m); spines chalky blue-green, thickly glaucous, to 2 in (5 cm), tapering from a broad, flattened base; *C. spinosissima* (syn. *C. infausta*) S Chile; to 8 ft (2.5 m); spines olive green, to 1 in (2.5 cm), smooth.

Collinsia (for Zaccheus Collins [1764–1831], vice president of the Philadelphia Academy of Natural Sciences). Scrophulariaceae. N and C America. 25 species, half-hardy annual herbs with racemes of tubular, 2-lipped flowers in summer. Cultivate as for *Alonsoa*.

C. bicolor CHINESE HOUSES, INNOCENCE; California; to 24 in (60 cm); flowers to ¾ in (2 cm), upper lip white, lower lip rose-purple; white and multicolored forms are available; *C. grandiflora* BLUE LIPS; western N America; to 14 in (35 cm); flowers to ¾ in (2 cm), upper lip pale purple to white, lower lip dark blue or violet.

colloid a substance in a colloidal state, in which particles or droplets are held in suspension because of their very small size. Colloids have a high ratio of surface area to volume, are very reactive chemically and physically and usually possess electrical charge; they attract oppositely-charged ions and water. Some clay particles and fractions of humus are colloidal. Emulsions, aerosols and smokes are other colloids important in horticulture.

Colocasia (from Arabic *kolkas* or *kulcas*). Araceae. Tropical Asia (some widespread through cultivation). 6 species, large, tender, evergreen, perennial herbs. Long-stalked, sagittate to cordate leaves arise from a turnip-shaped tuber, massive and edible in *C. esculenta*. The inflorescences resemble those of *Arum* and are usually dull yellow-green. Cultivate as for *Alocasia*.

C. esculenta TARO, COCOYAM, DASHEEN; leaves to 24 in (60 cm), mid-green and smooth, on stalks to 3¼ ft (1 m) tall; includes the cultivars 'Fontanesii', with dark purple-red to violet-black leafstalks and leaf blades veined and stained violet-black, and 'Illustris', the IMPERIAL TARO or BLACK CALADIUM, with purple-brown leafstalks and bright green leaf blades stained violet-black between the veins.

colonnade a row of columns or sometimes trees, either forming part of a loggia or leading from one group of buildings to another. Colonnades are a feature of formal gardens.

Colorado beetle

Colorado beetle (*Leptinotarsa decemlineata*) (Coleoptera: Chrysomelidae) a beetle with a stout, oval, convex body up to ½ in (10 mm) long and yellow wing cases with five black stripes. Adults overwinter in soil and orange-yellow eggs are laid in masses, mainly on potato leaves, but also on tomato and tobacco. Up to two generations per year; larvae are soft and red-orange, with three pairs of short, stumpy thoracic legs. Both stages feed openly on foliage with devastating effects. The Colorado beetle is a native of the western US but widespread in North America. Recorded in Europe since 1876, it was established in France by 1920 and thereafter in most European countries except Britain and Ireland. Control with contact insecticide. In the UK, suspected incidences of Colorado beetle must be reported to the Plant Health and Seeds Inspectorate.

Colquhounia (for Sir Robert Colquhoun [d. 1838], a patron of the Calcutta Botanic Garden who collected plants in Kumaon). Labiatae. Asia. 3 species, hardy or slightly frost-tender evergreen shrubs covered in felty white down. The leaves are ovate to lanceolate with toothed margins. Showy, tubular and two-lipped, the flowers appear in whorls in late summer. Hardy to 19°F (–7°C) or lower if grown against a warm and sheltered wall and thickly mulched in winter. Plant in full sun in fast-draining but fertile soil. Prune hard in spring to remove frosted top growth and to establish a low, woody framework from which tall and free-flowering shoots will arise by summer. Root softwood cuttings in late summer in low humidity. *C. coccinea* Himalaya to China; to 10 ft (3 m); flowers to ¾ in (2 cm), flame to scarlet marked yellow within.

columella the central axis of a multicarpeled fruit.

column (1) a solid ornamental upright or pillar, as used in a formal garden feature; (2) an upright form of fruit tree producing tightly packed spurs on a central trunk. Also known as a pole tree. In apples columnar trees may be genetically induced. The term is occasionally used for weak-growing pears; (3) a feature of orchids in which the style and stamens are fused; (4) the tubelike configuration formed by the fusion of staminal filaments in some Malvaceae.

Columnea (for Fabio Colonna [1567–1640], author of the first botanical book with copperplate illustrations). Gesneriaceae. Tropical Americas. 160 species, tender perennial, evergreen herbs and subshrubs, usually with long stems cascading from a low crown, small, paired, downy leaves and tubular flowers with a hoodlike upper lip, two spreading lateral lobes and an entire lower lip. Cultivate as for *Aeschynanthus*.

C. × *banksii* (*C. schiedeana* × *C. oerstediana*); stems to 32 in (80 cm), pendent; leaves to 1½ in (4 cm), ovate to oblong, smooth above, dark green, tinted purple-red beneath; flowers to 3 in (8 cm), bright red marked yellow within; *C. crassifolia* Guatemala, Mexico; stems to 12 in (30 cm), ascending; leaves to 4 in (10 cm), narrowly elliptic, smooth above, mid-green; flowers to 4 in

(10 cm), brilliant scarlet; *C. gloriosa* GOLDFISH PLANT; C America; stems to 3¼ ft (1 m), cascading; leaves to 1¼ in (3 cm), ovate, hairy; flowers to 3 in (8 cm), scarlet with a yellow throat; *C. microphylla* Costa Rica; stems to 24 in (60 cm), cascading; leaves to ½ in (1 cm), ovate to orbicular, covered in soft, purple-red hairs; flowers to 3 in (8 cm), scarlet with a yellow blotch in throat; includes dwarf forms with very small leaves, and 'Variegata', with gray-green leaves edged with cream.

column foot a basal platform found in the column of some Orchidaceae, to which the lip is attached.

Colutea (name used by Theophrastus). Leguminosae. Europe, Africa, Asia. 26 species, hardy deciduous shrubs or small trees, sometimes spiny, with pinnate or trifoliolate leaves, pealike flowers in summer and strongly inflated, translucent, bladderlike pods. Hardy to –4°F (–20°C). Grow in full sun in well-drained soil, with protection from fierce winds. Prune in spring to keep within bounds and remove exhausted growth. Propagate by seed sown in gentle heat in early spring, or by semiripe, heeled cuttings rooted in a sandy mix in midsummer.

C. arborescens BLADDER SENNA; S Europe; shrub to 15 ft (5 m); flowers to ¾ in (2 cm), yellow faintly marked red on standard; pods to 3 in (8 cm), bladder-like, pale green becoming red-tinted, then pearly gray-green; *C. × media* (*C. arborescens × C. orientalis*); shrub to 10 ft (3 m); flowers to 1¼ in (3 cm), yellow to coppery orange stained bronze-red or orange; *C. orientalis* S Russia, N Iran; shrub to 10 ft (3 m); flowers to ⅝ in (1.5 cm), orange-red with coppery veins and yellow markings.

coma (1) a tuft of hairs projecting from a seed, as in Asclepiadaceae; (2) a tuft of leaves or bracts ending in an inflorescence or syncarp, for example the crown of a pineapple; (3) a leafy head in the crown of a tree or shrub.

Combretum (name used by Pliny for a climbing plant). Combretaceae. Tropics. 250 species, tender trees and shrubs, many of them climbers. The showy flowers have long stamens and appear in dense racemes and panicles in summer. Cultivate as for *Petrea*.

C. grandiflorum N Africa; evergreen, twining shrub to 20 ft (6 m); flowers relatively large and red in one-sided spikes to 4 in (10 cm) long; *C. microphyllum* FLAME CREEPER, BURNING BUSH; small deciduous or semievergreen tree or scrambler to 25 ft (8 m); flowers bright red and downy in short racemes.

comfrey *Symphytum officinale*, a robust, coarsely hairy and large-leaved perennial herb in the Family Boraginaceae. Native to Europe and Western Asia, it has a long history of medicinal use (hence such vernacular names as BONE-SET). Today it is grown for ornamental purposes (see *Symphytum*) and for its mineral-rich foliage which makes an excellent liquid manure if harvested fresh and added in bulk to water.

Commelina (for Jan Commelin [1629–1692] and Caspar Commelin [1667–1731], Dutch botanists). Commelinaceae. Mostly tropics and subtropics. DAYFLOWER, WIDOW'S TEARS. Some 100 species, annual and perennial herbs (those listed here are usually treated as annuals), sometimes tuberous, with slender stems, ovate to lance-olate leaves and clusters of 3-, but apparently 2-petalled flowers enclosed in a boatlike spathe. *C. tuberosa* Coelestis Group is treated as half-hardy in cold winter regions, its tuberous roots lifted in fall, stored in frost-free conditions, brought into growth in gentle heat in late winter and replanted outdoors in late spring. *C. benghalensis* will thrive in sun or shade in moist, frost-free conditions; a fast-growing and dependable groundcover, it can be useful under staging. *C. communis* is similar but will grow outdoors in cold-winter areas with long, hot summers (e.g. the east coast of the US). Propagate *C. tuberosa* Coelestis Group by division; the others by spontaneous layers or stem tip cuttings.

C. benghalensis tropical Asia, Africa; stems to 12 in (30 cm), creeping and rooting; flowers to ⅝ in (1.5 cm), deep blue to violet; 'Variegata': leaves creamy white-edged; *C. communis* China, Japan, naturalized S Europe, E US; stems sprawling and rooting, to 28 in (70 cm) long; flowers pale to bright, deep blue; 'Aureostriata': leaves cream-striped; *C. tuberosa* Coelestis Group C and S America; erect to 3¼ ft (1 m); flowers bright blue to indigo; includes cultivars with white flowers and variegated leaves.

common name a popular or vernacular name for a plant, as opposed to a botanical name, for example, daisy for *Bellis perennis*.

community plot, community garden see *allotment*.

compaction the loss of pore spaces in soil caused by excessive cultivation or surface traffic. Wet soil of heavy texture is particularly susceptible, and results in deterioration of structure.

Companion planting
The admixing of suggested ornamental and vegetable companion plants can be an attractive as well as a productive feature.

companion, companionate planting the practice of growing plants reputed to have beneficial effects on their neighbors in close proximity to other species. Such plants may be held to have growth-enhancing or pest-suppressing properties, for example, *Tagetes patula* is claimed to be an insect pest deterrent.

compatibility (1) the ability of one plant to fertilize another; of particular relevance in top fruit growing; (2) the ability of a stock and scion to be combined successfully in a graft; (3) the suitability of two or more pesticides for mixing together.

complanate flattened, compressed.

complete used to describe flowers that possessing all four whorls (sepals, petals, stamens and carpels).

compost (1) rotted organic matter (usually plant refuse) that is absorbent, humus-rich, and, where well-made, friable; it is added to soil to improve fertility, structure and water-holding capacity; low in nutrients; (2) in the UK, the term is also used to describe seed and potting mixtures or media.

compost pile a stack or bin of organic waste kept moist and, ideally, aerated to encourage its breakdown by microorganisms.

A compost pile should be established either on a soil base, which encourages worm activity, or with a floor of widely spaced bricks covered with strong wire mesh to aid air flow. The containing walls should be constructed of concrete blocks, straw bales or thick timber, and a composting unit should preferably comprise two or more compartments, each about 3¼–5 ft (1–1.5 m) square. The front wall of each bin should be made from removable boards, added as the height of the pile increases, with a detachable waterproof cover provided where rainfall is high. To ensure good drainage, the soil base should be forked over and a 2 in (5 cm) layer of brush-wood put down. Organic matter is added in layers about 6 in (15 cm) deep, with different sorts mixed together; thickened material should be cut or shredded. Layers of chopped, damp straw incorporated throughout the pile will aid aeration. Where practicable, filling the bin in one operation gives the best results.

For good microbial activity, the carbon/nitrogen ratio should be 30:1, carbon occurring mostly in roots and stems, and nitrogen in green leaves. During fall and winter, the application of an activator is beneficial. The compost pile is filled to near the top of the bin and the waterproof covering insulated with straw, sacks, or other similar heavy fabric.

High temperature is necessary to ensure decomposition and destruction of weed seeds; in a well-prepared pile, up to 176°F (80°C) can soon be attained. The compost pile can be kept active by regularly turning the contents of one compartment into another, moving the outermost material to the center. See *activator*.

compound made up of two of more similar parts. For example, the compound leaves of clover (*Trifolium* species), the compound inflorescences of dandelion (*Taraxacum* species) and the compound fruits of mulberry (*Morus* species).

compound fertilizer a manufactured fertilizer providing more than one nutrient.

compressed flattened, usually applied to bulbs, tubers and fruit and qualified by "laterally," "dorsally" and "ventrally".

concatenate linked like a chain.

conceit any fanciful, grotesque, or exaggerated garden feature, such as a folly, grotto, ruin or elaborate waterworks. The term is sometimes applied to a whole garden or landscape having a conglomeration of these features.

concolorous of a uniform color.

conductivity a measure of the electrical conductivity of soil or liquid feed, which determines the salinity or concentration of dissolved mineral salts, some of which are plant nutrients. The higher the salt concentration the lower the resistance to electrical flow will be, which means the conductivity will also be higher. High salt concentration may inhibit water uptake by roots.

conduplicate refers to leaves; folded once lengthwise, so that the sides are parallel or applied; refers to cotyledons, folded in this manner, with one cotyledon enclosed within the other, and enclosing the radicle in its fold.

cone (1) in gymnosperms, an assemblage of bracts and sporophylls, usually densely crowded and overlapping in an ovoid, spherical or cylindrical structure on a single axis and (in the female cone) persisting to the seed-bearing stage. In the families Gnetaceae and Podocarpaceae the bracts or scales may be very few so that the whole scarcely resembles a cone; but the term is retained here, as is strobilus, to avoid the misleading use of 'inflorescence'; (2) in flowering plants, a compact spike or raceme with conspicuous and congested bracts suggesting a true cone, as found in Zingiberaceae.

conferted closely packed or crowded.

conglomerate tightly clustered, usually into a ball.

Conifers
Not all conifers bear the familiar cones of the group. Some have fleshy fruits or arils (q.v.), as in *Podocarpus nivalis* (above) and yew, or *Taxus* species.

conifer a tree or shrub, usually evergreen and many with needlelike leaves, belonging to the Division Gymnospermae which is characterized by the production of ovules not enclosed in an ovary. The seeds are often aggregated in woody cones, for example, *Pinus*, *Sequoia*, *Cupressus* or with fleshy coats as in the drupes of *Cephalotaxus*, or with fleshy arils as in *Taxus*, or swollen receptacles as in *Podocarpus*. Deciduous conifers include *Larix*, *Metasequoia* and *Taxodium*. "Softwood" is a loose alternative term for conifers.

conifer spinning mite see *red spider mites*.

conjugate coupled, a linked pair, as in the leaflets of a pinnate leaf.

conk the hard fruiting body of a wood-rotting fungus, found on the branches, trunks and stumps of trees. It is also called a bracket fungus.

connate united, usually applied to similar features when fused in a single structure.

connate-perfoliate where opposite sessile leaves are joined by their bases, through which the axis appears to pass.

connective the part in a stamen that connects the lobes of an anther at the point of attachment to the filament.

connivent converging, and even coming into contact, but not fused; of petals, gradually inclining toward the center of their flower.

conoid resembling or shaped like a cone.

Conophytum (from Greek *konos*, cone, and *phyton*, plant, referring to the conical plant bodies). Aizoaceae. South Africa. Some 80 species, tender, succulent perennials, dwarf with the fleshy leaves more or less fused in pairs; these form the plant "bodies," low-lying, solitary or clumped, globose to cylindric, round- to flat- or sunken-topped, and notched to deeply cleft. Daisylike flowers open at their cleavages in bright sunlight. Provide a minimum temperature of 45°F (7°C), full sunlight and a dry atmosphere. Grow in shallow pots or pans containing a loam-based medium very high in sand and grit and top-dressed with gravel or pebbles. Water sparingly from late summer to early fall, very occasionally during sunny spells from midfall to early winter; give a few waterings again during early spring, then withhold water from late spring to midsummer, when the old plant bodies dry up completely and the new leaves form within them. Propagate by seed germinated and grown on for a year in warm, moist and lightly shaded conditions, prior to gradual acclimatization to the harsher, adult regimen. Increase also by careful division of clumps when repotting in late summer. *Conophytum* will soon be killed by wet and drafty conditions.

C. bilobum (clump-forming, plant bodies to 2¾ in (7 cm), sea green to blue-gray, narrowly wedge-shaped with a rounded apex and a deep, wide cleavage making 2, long and distinct lobes sometimes spotted or edged red-brown; flowers golden yellow; *C. meyeri* (clump-forming, plant bodies to ¾ in (2 cm), obovoid, apex slightly bilobed and keeled, dull green to pale white-green, smooth to somewhat velvety and sometimes edged or marked red-brown; flowers white to yellow; *C. notabile* plant bodies to 1¼ in (3 cm), clumped, obovoid, with a rounded apex and slight fissure, gray-green and faintly spotted; flowers orange-red; *C. obcordellum* (syn. *C. nevillei*); plant bodies to ¾ in (2 cm), clumped, squatly top-shaped with a flattened or dimpled apex, more or less circular if viewed from above, silvery pale green to sea green, dotted and sometimes stained red-brown; flowers scented, white, yellow or pink; *C. truncatum* plant bodies to 1¼ in (3 cm), squatly top-shaped to rounded with a round-edged, flattened upper surface, dimpled and kidney-shaped if viewed from above, sea-green with fine, darker dots; flowers creamy yellow and spidery.

conservation measures taken to safeguard species from extinction, and to protect or restore natural habitats and gardens. Considerations of the topic are wide ranging and have important relevance to all forms of practical horticulture. Gardeners need to be aware and supportive of the Convention on International Trade in Endangered Species of Wild Fauna and Flora (CITES q.v.). Laudable interest in wildlife gardening must be governed by an appreciation of acceptable means of acquiring suitable plants. Gardeners have many opportunities to contribute also to the preservation of animal species as well. In direct connection with conservation there is a need for discretion in choosing garden products originating from nonrenewable sources; also attention should be given to energy and water saving and to opportunities for recycling plant and other materials. See also NCCPG.

conservatory originally synonymous with greenhouse, now usually a glassed structure attached to a house; used for relaxation in planted surroundings.

Consolida (Latin name for a wound-healing herb). Ranunculaceae. Mediterranean to C Asia. LARKSPUR. Some 40 species, annual herbs related to *Delphinium*, with slender, erect stems, finely and palmately cut leaves and showy, spurred flowers in summer. Sow in spring *in situ* in fertile, moist but well-drained soil in full sun. Many cultivars and hybrids of the following species provide excellent cut flowers, harvested just as the lowermost buds open. To retain their form and color as *dried* flowers, cut when almost fully open and hang in bundles in a cool, dry place. Taller cultivars may need staking. *C. ajacis* (syn. *C. ambigua*, *Delphinium consolida*; Mediterranean; stems to 32 in (80 cm) tall, branching above; flowers to 1 in (2.5 cm) in diameter, in racemes terminating branches, sky blue to azure, violet, lilac, pink or white, or white freaked and splashed with pink and blue, sometimes semi or fully double and with toothed to cut petals.

conspecific belonging to the same species; often describes highly similar populations scarcely worthy of recognition as separate species.

contact in horticulture, applied to (1) insecticides that enter insects through the intact cuticle; (2) herbicides that damage plant tissue by direct contact.

container-grown applied to plants established in containers, from which they can be planted out with minimal root disturbance.

continuous an uninterrupted symmetrical arrangement. Sometimes used as a synonym of decurrent.

contractile roots roots that contract in length and pull parts of a plant farther into the soil—for example, the corms of *Crocus*.

controlled release see *slow release*.

Convallaria (from Latin, *convallis*, a valley, alluding to the habitat). Liliaceae

(Convallariaceae). Northern temperate regions. 3 species. *C. majalis* is LILY OF THE VALLEY, a hardy, rhizomatous herbaceous perennial to 8 in (20 cm) tall, with one to four, ovate to elliptic leaves on a short shoot and, in spring, an arching raceme of fragrant white to ivory flowers. These are $\frac{1}{4}$–$\frac{1}{2}$ in (0.5–1 cm) deep and spherical to urceolate to campanulate, edged with six, short reflexed segments. They give rise to glossy, scarlet berries. Hardy to at least –4°F (–20°C). Grow in a moderately fertile, humus-rich and moisture-retentive soil in part shade, ideally in a woodland garden or under shrubs, where the creeping rhizomes will build up extensive colonies. For forced blooms, lift strong, 2–3-year-old 'crowns' (lengths of rhizome terminating in a bud) in the fall and pot into a fertile, loamy mix with sand and leaf mold; overwinter in the cold greenhouse or frame, increasing water and heat as growth proceeds. Propagate by division.

convolute rolled or twisted together longitudinally, with the margins overlapping, as leaves or petals in a bud.

Convolvulus (from Latin *convolvere*, to twine). Convolvulaceae. Cosmopolitan. 250 species, annual and perennial herbs and subshrubs, bushy or vigorously twining, with short-lived funnel-shaped flowers. The perennial species listed below are hardy to 23°F (–5°C). They need a warm and sunny, sheltered position in well-drained, low to medium fertility soil. Most benefit from a dry winter mulch, and some, like *C. althaeoides*, may be killed to the ground by cold. *C. sabatius* is often used as a half-hardy annual. Support climbing species, or allow them to sprawl and trail. Propagate by softwood cuttings in early summer. In warm regions, the annual *C. tricolor* should be sown *in situ* in fall or spring; elsewhere, sow in early spring under

heated glass and plant out in a sunny, warm position after the last frosts.

C. althaeoides S Europe; slender-stemmed, sprawling or climbing perennial to 3$\frac{1}{4}$ ft (1 m) tall; leaves gray-green, sagittate to ovate-cordate, often deeply and finely palmately to pinnately cut; flowers to 1$\frac{1}{2}$ in (4 cm) in diameter, pink to purple-pink; *C. cneorum* SILVERBUSH; Italy and Balkans to N Africa; erect or spreading bushy shrub or woody-based perennial to 20 in (50 cm); leaves oblanceolate to linear, covered in bright, silver, silky hairs; flowers to 1 in (2.5 cm) in diameter, palest shell pink with darker zones along folds; *C. sabatius* (syn. *C. mauritanicus*); Italy, N Africa; woody-based perennial to 20 in (50 cm) with bushy to trailing habit and slender stems; leaves oblong to rounded, mid- to dark green, sometimes silvery; flowers to 1 in (2.5 cm) in diameter, pale to deep blue, lilac or pink; *C. tricolor* (syn. *C. minor*), Portugal to Greece and N Africa; erect and bushy annual to 24 in (60 cm); leaves oblanceolate to ovate, mid-green; flowers to 2 in (5 cm) in diameter, pale to deep blue with a white throat and golden eye; includes low and very deep blue cultivars, e.g. 'Blue Flash' and 'Royal Ensign', and some with paler flowers, e.g. 'Cambridge Blue'; because of its name, this species is commonly confused with *Ipomoea tricolor*, the climbing morning glory, another popular annual.

cool house a greenhouse where heating is maintained to provide frost protection or, more usually, a minimum winter temperature of 45°F (7°C).

coping the top course of masonry in a wall; usually sloping and sometimes providing an overhang to protect wall-trained fruit trees.

copper a micronutrient or trace element. Copper deficiency occurs in soil high in organic content and lime, and is manifest in arrested growth or dieback of shoot tips.

twining stems

funnelform flowers

Convolvulus althaeoides

copper sulfate a compound that is (1) applied to soil for the correction of copper deficiency, (2) an ingredient of the fungicide known as Bordeaux mixture.

coppicing the practice of regularly cutting down young growth arising from the base of a tree or shrub, thereby giving rise to numerous vertical shoots. It is mainly a forestry practice but is also used on certain ornamentals to obtain colorful bark (e.g. *Cornus* species), juvenile foliage (e.g. *Eucalyptus* species) or very large foliage (e.g. *Paulownia* species). It is also known as stooling.

Coprosma (from Greek *kopros*, dung, and *osme*, odor, the plants are often malodorous when crushed). Rubiaceae. SE Asia, Australasia, Pacific Islands. 90 species, dioecious, evergreen shrubs and small trees, erect to prostrate or scrambling with leaves ranging from small and narrow to large, broad and glossy. Inconspicuous flowers give rise to fleshy berries. The hardiest species listed here is *C. brunnea*, which will tolerate lows to 23°F (–5°C) if planted in fast-draining, acidic soil in full sun, with shelter from winter wet and harsh winds. The others are essentially frost-tender, growing best in cool greenhouse conditions, in moist, acidic to neutral, fertile soil and with good ventilation and protection from the hottest summer sun. Increase by ripe wood cuttings in fall, or by seed sown in spring in a cold frame with the berry pulp removed.

C. brunnea (syn. *C. acerosa*; SAND COPROSMA; New Zealand; stems wiry, creeping to ascending; leaves to $\frac{5}{8}$ in (1.5 cm), linear; fruit translucent pale blue; includes forms with bronze foliage and cobalt blue to violet fruit, some of them hybrids with *C. petriei*; *C. × kirkii* (*C. brunnea* × *C. repens*); prostrate to spreading or ascending shrub to 5 ft (1.5 m); leaves to 1$\frac{1}{4}$ in (3 cm), linear-oblong to narrowly obovate, leathery and dark green; fruit white faintly flecked red; includes cultivars with bronze, white-edged and yellow-splashed leaves; *C. repens* LOOKING-GLASS PLANT, MIRROR PLANT; New Zealand; spreading to erect shrub to 25 ft (8 m); leaves to 3 in (8 cm), broadly oblong to obovate, apex blunt, base tapered, glossy dark green; fruit yellow-orange to red; includes cultivars with leaves splashed or edged white or gold and some with coppery tones.

Coral spot
Dead wood is a prime site for infection with this fungal disease, which should be pruned out as soon as seen. Burn affected prunings.

coral spot (*Nectria cinnabarina*) a fungal disease producing pink to orange pustules and groups of red fruiting bodies scattered over bark, dead twigs and branches. It grows commonly as a saprophyte on woody debris, but can also enter living tissue through wounds to become parasitic, and cause dieback. Although generally regarded as a secondary fungus causing minor diseases, coral spot can be serious, especially where infection follows grafting operations. *Acer*, *Aesculus*, apple, beech, *Cercis*, currants, *Elaeagnus*, elm, fig, gooseberry, hornbeam, lime, *Magnolia*, mulberry, *Pyracantha*, *Ribes* and walnut are particularly affected. Trained forms of trees and shrubs requiring frequent pruning are vulnerable. Prune off dead shoots and branches to a point well below the diseased area; burn prunings and affected woody debris. Treat posts, fences and other wooden structures with wood preservative. Badly affected soft fruit bushes should be dug up and burned.

coralloid resembling coral in structure. It refers to certain types of root adapted to house blue-green algae or saprophytic fungi. It is also applied to

the heavily cristate inflorescence of some *Celosia* cultivars, the body shapes of some cacti and to the calli and stigmatic surfaces of some monocots.

cordate heart-shaped; applied to leaves and leafy stipules that are usually ovate-acute in outline, with a rounded base and a deep basal sinus or notch where the petiole is inserted.

cordon (1) a trained form of tree or bush fruit, comprising one stem, usually planted obliquely, or two or three stems in the form of a vertical U or double U shape. Step-over cordon refers to forms with one or two shoots trained horizontally along a low level wire; (2) a system of growing sweet peas where each plant is restricted to one shoot in order to produce large flowers for exhibition.

Cordyline (from Greek *kordyle*, club, referring to the thickened roots). Agavaceae. SE Asia, Australasia, Polynesia. 15 species, evergreen shrubs and small trees, at first with simple, canelike stems, later more treelike and branched above. Leaves oblong to broadly lanceolate to linear, in dense mops and rosettes at branch ends. Flowers small, cream, massed in very large, dense panicles. *C. australis* is hardy outdoors in favored locations to 0°F (–18°C); *C. indivisa* to 10°F (–12°C). Much can be done to aid their survival in terms of siting, selection of cultivar, tying up of leaves and wrapping of crown base in winter. When very hard winters threaten, they are perhaps best brought into a frost-free greenhouse. Plant both in a warm, sunny position in fertile, fast-draining soil. *C. australis* is a good coastal and city plant for milder regions. Younger specimens of colored cultivars are among the most popular pot and patio container plants. The TI TREE, *C. fruticosa*, is equally well-loved in the tropics and subtropics and, elsewhere, as a house plant. It needs a minimum winter temperature of 50°F (10°C), bright, indirect light and moist, fertile, potting mix. Propagate all species by seed or suckers in spring. Increase *C. fruticosa* also by 2–3 in (5–8 cm) cuttings of mature stem laid flat on sand in a heated frame; pot on as the new shoots appear.

C. australis GIANT DRACENA, NEW ZEALAND CABBAGE PALM; New Zealand; to 70 ft (20 m), becoming branched above with age; leaves to 39 × ¾ in (100 × 2 cm), arching, linear, light green to olive; includes cultivars with leaves flushed deep purple-bronze to copper and ruby red, some striped white, cream, yellow or pink, or with a red midvein; *C. fruticosa* (syn. *C. terminalis*); GOOD LUCK TREE, TI TREE; SE Asia, Australia, Polynesia; to 12 ft (4 m), shrubby; leaves to 24 × 4 in (60 × 10 cm), oblong to lanceolate, narrowing to a grooved petiole, glossy green, often tinged red; widely grown with many cultivars available, ranging from dwarf to tall, and with leaves brightly stained, striped and zoned in shades of scarlet, crimson, pink, purple, bronze, copper, lime, yellow, cream and white; *C. indivisa* (syn. *Dracaena indivisa*); New Zealand; to 25 ft (8 m), scarcely branched above; leaves to 79 × 4 in (200 × 10 cm), narrowly lanceolate, somewhat glaucous with the midvein often tinted red; purple- and bronze-leaved cultivars are grown.

core flush a physiological disorder of apples stored for long periods. It is more serious at low temperature, high carbon dioxide levels, and when water loss from the fruit is excessive. The discoloration of the core between the seed cavities often extends into the flesh.

Coreopsis (from Greek *koris*, a bug, and *opsis*, like, alluding to the appearance of the fruit). Compositae. Americas. TICKSEED. 80 species, annual or perennial herbs with entire to toothed to finely pinnately lobed leaves and bright, daisylike flower heads in summer. Fully hardy, *Coreopsis* species prefer full sun and fertile, moist but free-draining soil. Propagate by seed, or perennials by division in spring or from softwood cuttings in summer.

C. auriculata SE US; erect perennial to 5 ft (1.5 m); leaves entire or 1–2-lobed; flower heads to 2 in (5 cm) in diameter, long-stalked, yellow; includes the vivid gold 'Cutting Gold', the dwarf 'Nana', with orange-yellow flower heads, and 'Superba', with bright yellow flower heads tinted purple; *C. grandiflora* C and SE US; erect annual or perennial to 24 in (60 cm); leaves entire to 3–5-parted; flower heads to 2½ in (6 cm) in diameter, long-stalked, ray florets yellow, disk florets tinted orange; includes 'Badengold', a short-lived perennial to 39 in (100 cm) tall with golden flower heads, 'Ruby Throat', with a red-stained center, and the deep yellow, "double" 'Sunray'; *C. lanceolata* C and SE US; perennial to 24 in (60 cm); leaves usually entire; flower heads to 2½ in (6 cm) in diameter, golden, long-stalked, ray florets usually with jagged margins; includes the dwarf 'Goldfink', and cultivars with double and red-tinted flower heads; *C. tinctoria* N America; erect, bushy annual up to 4 ft (1.2 m); leaves 1–2-pinnate; flower heads to 1¼ in (3 cm) in diameter, long-stalked and borne several together, ray florets yellow marked brown-red at base, disk florets dark red; *C. verticillata* SE US; bushy perennial, erect, 8–36 in (20–90 cm) tall; leaves very finely bipinnate; flower heads up to 2 in (5 cm) in diameter, golden yellow or pale lemon yellow in 'Moonbeam'.

coriaceous leathery or tough but smooth and pliable in texture.

Cilantro (coriander)
Sow cilantro at intervals of three to four weeks from spring to late summer for a succession of foliage for harvesting over a long season. Later sowings will need protection.

coriander, cilantro (*Coriandrum sativum*) a hardy annual to 18 in (45 cm) high, grown as a culinary herb for its seed (coriander) and aromatic leaves (cilantro), which are used especially in Asian cooking. Sow successively from spring to late summer *in situ*, ½ in (1 cm) deep in rows 12–18 in (30–45 cm) apart, thinning to 6 in (15 cm) final spacings. For winter supply, late fall sowings can be made under cover.

Coriaria (from Latin *corium*, hide or leather: some species are used in tanning). Coriariaceae. Europe, Asia, Americas, New Zealand, Pacific Islands. 30 species, herbs, shrubs and small trees with angular stems and arching, frondlike branches ranked with small, ovate leaves. At first the flowers are small, dull and green, but as the fruits mature, the petals persist, becoming enlarged, fleshy and colorful. Hardy to 0°F (–18°C) if grown against a warm, sheltered wall and mulched in winter. Plant in full sun in moist, fertile soil. Prune back exhausted or frost-damaged growth in spring. Increase by seed sown in fall, by semiripe cuttings or by rooted suckers. *C. terminalis* Himalaya to W China; deciduous suckering subshrub or shrub to 5 ft (1.5 m); leaves red in fall; fruiting raceme to 6 in (15 cm) long, cylindrical with enlarged corollas to ½ in (1 cm) across and glossy black; includes f. *fructorubro*, with translucent red corolla, and var. *xanthocarpa*, with translucent yellow corolla.

cork a layer of protective tissue, usually elastic and spongy, that replaces the epidermis in the older superficial parts of some plants. It is also known as phellem.

cork bark the thick corky bark of trees, such as *Quercus suber*, which is often used by gardeners to sustain epiphytic bromeliads, ferns and orchids. The round sections can be filled with sphagnum moss or other substrate and the plant established through a hole in the bark.

cork cambium a layer of meristematic tissue from which cork is derived. It is also known as phellogen.

corm a solid, swollen, subterranean, bulblike stem or stem-base. Corms are produced by annuals; the next year's corm developing from the terminal bud or, in its absence, one of the lateral buds.

cormel, cormlet a small corm developing from and around the mother corm.

cormous bearing corms.

Cornell mixes soilless growing media based on peat and vermiculite or perlite, developed by Cornell University, New York.

corniculate horned, shaped like a new moon, bearing or terminating in a small hornlike protuberance.

Cornus (Latin name for *C. mas*). Cornaceae. CORNEL, DOGWOOD. Temperate regions of the N Hemisphere; also S America and Africa. Some 45 species, perennial, semiwoody herbs, or, more usually, shrubs and small trees, mostly deciduous. They bear small, pale flowers in flat-topped cymes, panicles or heads, often subtended by bracts. These give rise to small, colorful drupes. *C. alba* and *C. sericea* are prized for their winter beauty, having brilliant fall foliage, handsome fruits and colorful stems which range from yellow through brilliant crimson to black-purple. The "flowering dogwoods," such as *C. florida*, *C. kousa* and *C. nuttallii*, also have stunning fall color, but it is for their large, white or pink floral bracts, produced in spring and early summer, that they are celebrated. *C. mas* is valued as an early spring-flowering shrub. The only nonwoody species commonly grown is *C. canadensis*, which forms an attractive carpet of creeping stems, with white-bracted flowers in summer and red fruits in fall. Most are hardy to between 14–13°F (–10°C and –25°C), although *C. capitata* is only hardy to 23°F (–5°C). *C. florida* and *C. nuttallii* will tolerate low temperatures, but need long, hot humid summers to ripen their wood. Late frosts may damage their decorative bracts. Dogwoods thrive in range of soil types, from acidic through to thin chalky soil. Many colored-stemmed dogwoods will grow in poorly drained soil and are ideal for waterside plantings. For the best winter color, cut back *C. alba* and *C. sericea* to near ground level in spring, or grow them as a low pollard or stub. This promotes fresh, rodlike growths that will color brilliantly the following fall and winter. Most other species have gracefully tiered habits that should be left untouched. Increase by seed or cuttings; also, *C. canadensis* by detaching rooted lengths of stem.

CORNUS

Name	Distribution	Habit	Bark	Leaves	Inflorescence	Fruit
C. alba REDTWIG DOGWOOD, TARTARIAN DOGWOOD	Siberia to Korea	deciduous, erect to spreading, suckering shrub to 10 ft (3 m)	new shoots turn sealing wax red in winter	1½–3 in (4–8 cm), ovate-elliptic with short, pointed tip, mid- to dark green above, slightly glaucous beneath	flowers small, cream in flattened, 2 in (5 cm)-wide cymes in late spring	small, white to blue

Comments: Cultivars with variegated leaves include 'Variegata' (edged white), 'Aurea' (soft yellow-green), 'Elegantissima' (gray-green edged white to cream), 'Gouchaltii' (pink-flushed, edged yellow) and 'Spaethii' (edged yellow, bronze-flushed at first). Cultivars with exceptional winter stem color include 'Atrosanguinea' (dwarf with crimson stems), 'Kesselringii' (stems purple-black), and 'Sibirica' (stems bright coral red).

Name	Distribution	Habit	Bark	Leaves	Inflorescence	Fruit
C. alternifolia GREEN OSIER, PAGODA DOGWOOD,	E N America	deciduous shrub or tree to 25 ft (8 m) with a flat-topped crown and tiered branches		2½–4¾ in (6–12 cm), ovate-elliptic, dark green above, somewhat glaucous beneath	flowers small, yellow-white in 2 in (5 cm)-wide cymes in early summer	small, black, rarely yellow

Comments: Includes 'Argentea' with white-marked leaves, 'Corallina' with dull red stems, the yellow-fruited 'Ochrocarpa' and the strongly tiered 'Umbraculifera'.

Name	Distribution	Habit	Bark	Leaves	Inflorescence	Fruit
C. canadensis *Chamaepericlymenum canadense* BUNCHBERRY, CREEPING DOGWOOD, DWARF CORNEL, CRACKERBERRY	Greenland to Alaska	creeping perennial with rooting, ground-smothering stems to 3 in (8 cm) tall		¾–1½ in (2–4 cm), ovate-lanceolate, in a whorl at the summit of erect stems	green to red-violet, clustered in a tight umbel surrounded by 4–6, ovate, white bracts each to ¾ in (2 cm) long in early summer	bright red berries
C. capitata *Dendrobenthamia capitata* BENTHAM'S CORNEL	Himalaya, China	evergreen or semievergreen, spreading tree to 52 ft (16 m)		2–4¾ in (5–12 cm), ovate to lanceolate, dark above, pale beneath	flowers small, white in clusters to ¾ in (2 cm) across, subtended by obovate, cream to white bracts to 3 in (8 cm) long in early summer	a fleshy, strawberry-shaped, scarlet aggregate to 1 in (2.5 cm) diam.
C. controversa GIANT DOGWOOD	Himalaya, China, Japan	deciduous tree to 56 ft (17 m) tall with horizontal, tiered branches		2¾–6 in (7–15 cm), ovate to broadly elliptic, cuspidate, dark green above, paler beneath, flushed red in fall	small, white in flat-topped cymes to 4 in (10 cm) diam.	

Comments: 'Variegata' (WEDDING CAKE TREE) has an uneven white-yellow margin.

Name	Distribution	Habit	Bark	Leaves	Inflorescence	Fruit
C. 'Eddie's White Wonder' (*C. florida* × *C. nuttallii*)	garden origin	deciduous tree, erect and pyramidal to 20 ft (6 m) tall with drooping branches		to 6 in (15 cm), ovate-elliptic, mid-green turning orange-brown and purple-red in fall	small and green, surrounded by 4 (–6) large, rounded, white bracts in late spring	

C. alba

C. alternifolia 'Argentea'

C. capitata

C. controversa 'Variegata'

CORNUS

Name	Distribution	Habit	Bark	Leaves	Inflorescence	Fruit
C. florida FLOWERING DOGWOOD, COMMON WHITE DOGWOOD	E N America	deciduous tree or shrub to 30 ft (10 m) tall with many, spreading then ascending branches		2¾–6 in (7–15 cm), oval to ovate, dull green above, pale beneath, turning orange-red in fall	small, green in a buttonlike head surrounded by 4 bracts each to 1½ in (4 cm) long, obovate with curled margins and white to cream or pink, in late spring	scarlet

Comments: Includes many cultivars with bracts ranging in size, number and in color from pure white to bright flamingo pink and deep rose.

Name	Distribution	Habit	Bark	Leaves	Inflorescence	Fruit
C. kousa KOUSA DOGWOOD	China, Korea, Japan	deciduous, erect tree or shrub to 22 ft (7 m) tall		2–3½ in (5–9 cm), ovate-acuminate, undulate, dark green above, paler beneath, turning red in fall	small, green in rounded heads surrounded by 4, large, lanceolate, creamy white bracts in summer	a fleshy, scarlet, strawberry-like aggregate to ¾ in (2 cm) diam.

Comments: Includes the larger var. *chinensis* with longer, more pointed bracts turning from green to white and assuming pink tints.

Name	Distribution	Habit	Bark	Leaves	Inflorescence	Fruit
C. mas CORNELIAN CHERRY	Europe, W Asia	deciduous, spreading and bushy shrub or tree to 15 ft (5 m) tall		1½–4 in (4–10 cm), ovate-elliptic, mid- to dark green	small, bright yellow in rounded cymes to ¾ in (2 cm) diam., produced before leaves in late winter and early spring	small, oblong, bright red

Comments: Includes cultivars with variegated leaves and white, yellow and violet-blue fruit.

Name	Distribution	Habit	Bark	Leaves	Inflorescence	Fruit
C. 'Norman Hadden' (*C. kousa* × *C. capitata*)	garden origin	deciduous, erect to spreading tree to 25 ft (8 m)			small and green surrounded by showy white bracts that assume pink tints with age	a bright red, large, strawberry-like aggregate

Name	Distribution	Habit	Bark	Leaves	Inflorescence	Fruit
C. nuttallii PACIFIC DOGWOOD, MOUNTAIN DOGWOOD,	W N America	deciduous tree to 100 ft (30 m) tall with a broadly conical crown		3–4¾ in (8–12 cm), oval to obovate, mid- to dark green, downy at first	small, green in tight heads surrounded by 4–8, broadly oval to obovate bracts, each to 3 in (8 cm) long and green-white turning pure white, later assuming a pink flush	

Name	Distribution	Habit	Bark	Leaves	Inflorescence	Fruit
C. sanguinea BLOODTWIG, COMMON DOGWOOD, DOGBERRY	Europe	deciduous, erect and freely suckering shrub to 12 ft (4 m) tall	new shoots green flushed purple-red especially in winter	1½–4 in (4–10 cm), broadly elliptic to ovate, dull green flushed purple-red in fall	small, off-white, muskily scented in dense cymes to 2 in (5 cm) diam. in summer	small, purple-black

Name	Distribution	Habit	Bark	Leaves	Inflorescence	Fruit
C. sericea RED OSIER DOGWOOD, AMERICAN DOGWOOD,	E N America	deciduous shrub to 10 ft (3 m), freely suckering with spreading to erect, slender branches	young branches purple-red to deep red especially in winter	2–4 in (5–10 cm), oval to oval-lanceolate with a finely tapering tip, dark green above, glaucous beneath	small, dull white in cymes to 2 in (5 cm) across in late spring	small, white

Comments: Includes 'Flaviramea' with yellow shoots in winter, and 'Kelseyi', dense and dwarf with red-tipped, yellow-green winter shoots.

C. florida 'Cherokee Chief'

C. kousa 'China Girl'

C. 'Norman Hadden'

C. sanguinea 'Winter Beauty'

Corokia (from the Maori vernacular name *korokiataranga*). Cornaceae. New Zealand. 3 species, evergreen shrubs and small trees with slender, twiggy branches, often spiraling or zig-zagging and becoming congested. These are silver to ash gray at first and ultimately covered in thin, black-brown bark. The leaves are tough and lanceolate to spathulate, bronze to olive above, silvery beneath. Clusters of small yellow flowers in late spring are followed by orange-red berries. Hardy to 0°F (−18°C). Plant in full sun in fertile, well-drained soil that is moist in spring and summer, but somewhat dry in winter. For best results, place within the shelter of a south-facing wall. Root short, heeled cuttings of the previous season's growth in a sandy mix in a frame or case in fall.

C. buddlejoides to 12 ft (4 m); branching pattern fairly straightforward; leaves to 4 in (10 cm), lanceolate; *C. cotoneaster* WIRE NETTING BUSH; to 6½ ft (2 m); branching pattern intricate and tortuous; leaves ¼–¾ in (0.5–2 cm), orbicular to spathulate, sometimes shallowly and sparsely toothed; *C.* × *virgata* (*C. buddlejoides* × *C. cotoneaster*, to 10 ft (3 m); branching pattern somewhat twisted and intricate to erect and straightforward; leaves ½–1½ in (1–4 cm), spathulate to oblanceolate.

corolla the interior perianth whorl; a floral envelope composed of free or fused petals. When the petals are separate, a corolla is termed choripetalous or polypetalous; when fused, the corolla is termed gamopetalous or sympetalous—in such cases, the petals may be discernible only as lobes or teeth on the rim of a corolla tube, cup or disk.

corona a crown- or cuplike appendage or ring of appendages. It may be a development of the perianth (as in *Narcissus*), of the staminal circle (as in *Asclepias*), or located between perianth and stamens (as in *Passiflora*).

Coronilla (from Latin *coronilla*, a little crown, alluding to the radiating golden umbels of most species). Leguminosae. Europe, Asia, Africa. CROWN VETCH. 20 species, evergreen herbs and small shrubs with pinnate or trifoliolate leaves and pealike flowers in stalked,

circular umbels at various times of year, including winter (*C. valentina*). Hardy to 0°F (−18°C), but best given the shelter of a south-facing wall. Grow in full sun in light, fast-draining soil. Support or tie-in to walls if necessary. Prune after flowering to remove any weak growth. Older plants may need harder, rejuvenative pruning at this time. Root greenwood cuttings in summer.

C. emerus (syn. *Hippocrepis emerus*); SCORPION SENNA; C and S Europe; shrub to 6½ ft (2 m); leaves to 2½ in (6 cm), pinnate, dark green; flowers fragrant, yellow; *C. valentina* S Portugal, Mediterranean, N Africa, Aegean; shrub to 5 ft (1.5 m); leaves to 2 in (5 cm), pinnate, leaflets bright green above, glaucous beneath; flowers golden yellow, fragrant; subsp. *glauca*: syn. *C. glauca*, leaves glaucous, blue-green, flowers lemon to golden; 'Variegata': foliage and young shoots striped and zoned creamy yellow to white.

Correa (for Jose Francesco Correa de Serra [1750–1823], Portuguese botanist). Rutaceae. Australia. AUSTRALIAN FUCHSIA. 11 species, evergreen shrubs and trees with small, leathery leaves and pendulous tubular to campanulate flowers year-round,

usually waxy and with four, short, reflexed lobes. Most species tolerate short-lived frosts to about 23°F (−5°C) (*C. decumbens* lower still), but in colder zones need greenhouse protection. Plant in a fast-draining, gritty and sandy, acidic medium. Position in full or dappled sun in an airy, rather dry atmosphere. Water moderately when in growth, sparingly in winter. Root softwood or semiripe cuttings in a closed case with bottom heat.

C. backhouseana dense, spreading shrub to 6½ ft (2 m); flowers to 1 in (2.5 cm), creamy yellow to pale green; *C. decumbens* prostrate shrub to 3¼ ft (1 m); flowers to 1 in (2.5 cm), red tipped green; *C.* × *harrisii* (*C. pulchella* × *C. reflexa*√; flowers to 1¼ in (3 cm), scarlet; *C. pulchella* (more or less prostrate shrub to 5 ft (1.5 m); flowers to 1 in (2.5 cm), orange to pink-red or, rarely, white; *C. reflexa* (syn. *C. speciosa*); erect or prostrate shrub to 10 ft (3 m); flowers to 1½ in (4 cm), white to green, pink or red, sometimes bright red tipped green.

corrugate crumpled or wrinkled but more loosely so than in rugose. Corrugate aestivation describes the irregular and apparently crumpled folding of a

Corona in Passiflora caerulea
The passion flower displays perhaps the most spectacular coronas, with a ring or several rings of fringelike, brightly colored appendages surrounding a stalk bearing the pistil and stamens.

stamens (male flower parts)

pistil (female flower parts)

ring or corona of fleshy filaments

perianth in bud, as for example happens with the petals of many members of the poppy family, Papaveraceae.

Cortaderia (from *cortadera*, Argentine name for these plants). Gramineae. S America, New Zealand, New Guinea. 24 species, large, evergreen perennial grasses with very long and slender, sharp-edged leaves making dense tussocks. The flowers are carried in tall, plumelike panicles in late summer and fall. Hardy to –20°F (–29°C). Plant in full sun in well-drained but moisture-retentive soil. These grasses accumulate a good deal of dry, dead material within their dense and massive crowns—this should be cleared each spring, along with spoiled plumes and any damaged leaves (great care being taken to avoid their razorlike margins). The short cut of setting light to the whole clump and incinerating growth dead or alive is a little harsh and possibly dangerous. Increase by division in late spring. *C. selloana* PAMPAS GRASS, TUSSOCK GRASS; temperate S America; leaves arching, making tussocks to 5 × 6½ ft (1.5 × 2 m); panicles to 48 in (120 cm), oblong to pyramidal, pearly white or cream, sometimes flushed purple, red or rose; cultivars range from dwarf to very tall (i.e. 10 ft (3 m) and include selections with white- or yellow-striped foliage and panicles in tones of silver-white, pale violet and rose.

cortex bark or rind; stem tissue situated between the stele and epidermis.

corticate covered with thick bark, with a hard coating, but softer center; corky.

Cortusa (for J.A. Cortusi, 16th-century Italian botanist). Primulaceae. C Europe to N Asia. 8 species, hardy perennial herbs with rosettes of long-stalked, rounded to heart-shaped, toothed and hairy leaves, and funnel-shaped, 5-lobed flowers in long-stalked umbels in summer. Hardy to 0°F (–18°C) and suitable for lightly shaded areas of the rock garden and for planting beneath shrubs. It favors moist, humus-rich soil and a mulch of leaf mold and garden compost in fall. Propagate by seed sown as soon as ripe, by division in early spring or fall, or by

cuttings of thick, mature roots in late summer. *C. matthioli* (flowers pink to magenta, nodding, on scapes to 12 in (30 cm) tall.

Corydalis (from Greek *korydalis*, crested lark: the flowers resemble the head of this bird). Fumariaceae. Northern temperate regions, South Africa. Some 300 species, annual or deciduous perennial herbs with ferny, biternately compound foliage and racemes of flowers in spring and summer; these are tubular and angled horizontally, the outer petals recurved at the tip and spurred at the base, the inner petals beaklike. Hardy to –10°F (–23°C). Plant in full sun or light shade in a humus-rich, well-drained soil that is cool and moist in spring and summer. Propagate the perennial species by division when dormant, or—if tuberous—by detaching offsets. Sow seed of annual species *in situ* in spring.

C. cashmeriana Himalaya; fibrous-rooted perennial to 8 in (20 cm); leaves bright green; flowers bright blue with darker tips; *C. cava* (syn. *C. bulbosa*; C Europe; tuberous perennial to 6 in (15 cm); leaves pea-green; flowers dull purple or white; *C. cheilanthifolia* China; fleshy-rooted perennial to 12 in (30 cm) with very fernlike, soft olive green leaves; flowers bright yellow; *C. claviculata* CLIMBING CORYDALIS; Europe; slender, climbing annual to 5 ft (1.5 m) tall with sea green, tendril-tipped leaves; flowers cream to pink, tipped dark red; *C. diphylla* Himalaya; tuberous perennial to 6 in (15 cm); leaves gray-green; flowers lilac-white, tipped purple; *C. flexuosa* Himalaya; fleshy-rooted perennial to 8 in (20 cm); leaves bright green to gray-green; flowers sky blue to deep cobalt; includes various cultivars with flowers in a range of blues and foliage marked or tinted bronze to deep maroon; *C. fumariifolia* (syn. *C. ambigua* of gardens); Japan; tuberous perennial to 4 in (10 cm); leaves glaucous; flowers azure; *C. lutea* Europe; bushy perennial to 12 in (30 cm) with mid-green leaves, their undersides glaucous; flowers bright yellow; *C. nobilis* Siberia; fleshy-rooted perennial to 20 in (50 cm) with glaucous leaves; flowers yellow, tipped purple-brown; *C. ochroleuca* SE Europe; similar to *C. lutea* but with white to

cream flowers tipped pale yellow; *C. popovii* C Asia; tuberous perennial to 6 in (15 cm) with blue-green leaves and maroon-lipped, white flowers; *C. solida* FUMEWORT; N Europe, Asia; tuberous perennial to 8 in (20 cm) with dark-tipped, pale mauve-pink to light red flowers; includes 'George Baker', with deep, rosy red flowers; *C. wilsonii* China; fleshy-rooted perennial to 12 in (30 cm); leaves glaucous, blue-green; flowers bright yellow, tipped green.

Corylopsis (from Greek *korylos*, hazel, and *opsis*, appearance, the leaves resemble those of *Corylus*). Hamamelidaceae. Asia. WINTER HAZEL. 30 species, hardy, deciduous shrubs and small trees with slender branches, and broadly ovate leaves with impressed veins. Small, fragrant and yellow, the bell-shaped flowers appear before or alongside the leaves and hang in narrow racemes amid translucent green bracts. Hardy to 5°F (–15°C). Grow in a sheltered, partially shaded position in well-drained but moisture-retentive, acidic to neutral soil. Mulch in dry summers. Allow space for the strongly spreading habit that is characteristic of *C. pauciflora* and *C. spicata*. Propagate by seed in fall, by softwood or greenwood cuttings rooted in a closed case in late spring, or by simple layering.

C. glabrescens Japan, Korea; to 15 ft (5 m); leaves glaucous beneath, veins in up to 12 pairs; inflorescence to 1 in (2.5 cm), flowers very pale yellow, anthers yellow or purple; *C. pauciflora* BUTTERCUP WITCH-HAZEL; Japan, Taiwan; to 10 ft (3 m); leaves to 1¼ in (6.5 cm) glaucous beneath, veins in up to 9 pairs; inflorescence to 1¼ in (3 cm), flowers relatively large (i.e. to ¾ in (1.8 cm) across), sweetly fragrant, primrose yellow, anthers yellow; *C. sinensis* (syn. *C. willmottiae*; China; to 15 ft (5 m); leaves glaucous and downy beneath with veins in 7–12 pairs, deep purple-bronze-tinted in 'Spring Purple'; inflorescence to 3 in (8 cm) with lemon yellow flowers with yellow anthers; *C. spicata* SPIKE WITCH-HAZEL; Japan; to 10 ft (3 m); leaves glaucous and downy beneath with veins in 6–7 pairs; inflorescence to 2½ in (6 cm), flowers bright yellow, anthers red-brown.

Corylus (Classical Latin name). Betulaceae. N Temperate regions. HAZEL, FILBERT. 15 species, hardy deciduous shrubs or small trees with large and coarse, ovate leaves, their veins impressed and margins toothed. The tiny, yellow male flowers hang in catkins in early spring; the female flowers resemble small buds with protruding red styles. The fruits are woody nuts enclosed by two, leafy, lobed bracts. For habit and foliage color respectively, *C. avellana* 'Contorta' and *C. maxima* 'Purpurea' are exceptional shrubs, while *C. colurna* proves to be a tough but distinguished street tree. All are hardy to at least −22°F (−30°C). Plant in full or dappled sun in fertile, free-draining soil. Prune to restrict size and remove suckers from grafted plants. Propagate by seed sown immediately upon ripening, or, for cultivars by simple layering and grafting. Hazel is attacked by several leaf-eating moths, and also by the hazel sawfly, nut gall mite, nut weevil, hazelnut aphids and gray squirrels.

C. avellana AMERICAN FILBERT; Europe; multistemmed shrub to 20 ft (6 m), or tree to 30 ft (10 m); leaves to 4 in (10 cm), with short, stiff hairs; fruit edible, to ¾ in (2 cm), amid jagged bracts to ½ in (1 cm); includes 'Contorta', CORKSCREW HAZEL, HARRY LAUDER'S WALKING STICK, a slow-growing shrub to 10 ft (3 m) with strongly spiraling shoots and contorted leaves;

Corylus avellana
The familiar hazelnut, or cobnut, may be grown as a tree or as a multistemmed shrub for easy harvesting.

C. colurna TURKISH HAZEL; SE Europe, Asia Minor; tree to 100 ft (30 m) with a pyramidal crown; leaves to 4¾ in (12 cm), lustrous deep green; fruit to ¾ in (2 cm) amid thickened, glandular and deeply cut bracts to 1¼ in (3 cm); *C. maxima* FILBERT; SE Europe, Asia Minor; differs from *C. avellana* in its larger leaves, usually biserrate, and in bracts, to twice the length of the fruit, deeply lobed and forming a loose tube; includes 'Purpurea' (syn. 'Atropurpurea'), with dark purple-red foliage.

corymb an indeterminate flat-topped or convex inflorescence, where the outer flowers open first; cf. *umbel*.

corymbose, corymbiform resembling or forming a corymb.

Coryphantha (Greek, *koryphe*, summit, and *anthos*, flower—the flowers arise near the stem apex). Cactaceae. SW Mexico, US. 45 species, cacti with single or clustered globose to cylindric stems, usually spiny, and funnel- to bell-shaped flowers. Provide a minimum temperature of 41°F (5°C), with full sun and low humidity. Plant in a mix containing at least 50% grit. Keep dry from midfall until early spring, except for a light misting on warm days in late winter. Water thoroughly in spring and summer, but allow the soil to become dry between waterings. Increase by seed.

C. cornifera stem to 4¾ in (12 cm), pale green with pyramidal tubercles and spines in flattened circles covering stem; flowers yellow; *C. radians* (differs from *C. cornifera* in its woolly tubercles and flowers with red-tinged outer tepals. For *C. vivipara*, see *Escobaria vivipara*.

Cosmos (Greek *kosmos*, ornament). Compositae. Tropical and warm Americas. 26 species, annual and perennial herbs and subshrubs with simple to lobed or pinnate leaves and long-stalked, daisylike flower heads in summer. *C. atrosanguineus* is a perennial, developing root tubers much like those of *Dahlia*. Once established, it will survive frosts provided that the crown is thickly mulched in winter. Alternatively, lift the tubers in late fall and store as for *Dahlia*, or root basal cuttings in late

Corymb
Verbena species, such as this *Verbena corymbosa*, bear the characteristic flat-topped flower clusters of a corymb.

spring and summer—these can be overwintered under glass and treated as half-hardy annuals. Sow seed of the annual *C. bipinnatus* and cultivars in a cool greenhouse in fall or early spring for planting out in a sunny position in fertile, well-drained soil after the last frosts. In areas with hot, humid summers, sow *in situ* in late spring.

C. atrosanguineus CHOCOLATE COSMOS; Mexico; perennial, 12–39 in (30–100 cm) tall, ultimately tuberous-rooted; leaves pinnate; flower heads to 2 in (5 cm) in diameter, deep velvety black-red to darkest maroon, chocolate-scented; *C. bipinnatus* Mexico, S US; annual, 12–79 in (30–200 cm) tall; leaves finely bipinnate; flower heads to 4 in (10 cm) in diameter, carmine to rose-pink or lilac with a yellow center; many seed races and F_1 hybrids have been developed, including plants dwarf and tall, with single, semidouble and double flower heads in shades of red, pink, orange, yellow and white, sometimes marked and usually with contrasting centers.

costa a single pronounced midvein or midrib; the term is sometimes used to describe the rachis of a pinnately compound leaf.

costapalmate refers to (1) a pinnate leaf where the pinnae are congested in a radial, fanlike order and perhaps to

C

some degree united, the whole therefore appearing palmate; (2) a palmate leaf when the petiole continues through the blade as a distinct midrib.

Costus (name used by Theophrastus and Pliny). Zingiberaceae. Tropics. 90 species, tender perennial herbs, mostly evergreen with creeping, aromatic rhizomes and clumped, canelike stems. Showy flowers with ruffled, crepelike lips appear in cone-shaped, terminal heads. Cultivate as for *Alpinia*. *C. afer* SPIRAL GINGER; W Africa; 3¼–12 ft (1–4 m); leaves lanceolate, smooth, spirally arranged; flowers white marked yellow; *C. malortieanus* (syn. *C. zebrinus*, *C. rumphii*); SPIRAL GINGER PLANT; Brazil, Costa Rica; to 3¼ ft (1 m); leaves broadly obovate to obcordate, thick, hairy, striped or mottled dark green to purple-brown; flowers yellow marked red-brown; *C. speciosus* CREPE GINGER, MALAY GINGER; SE Asia to New Guinea; to 10 ft (3 m); leaves elliptic to lanceolate, striped creamy white in 'Variegatus'; flowers white to pink stained yellow-orange, amid red-tinted bracts; *C. spiralis* SPIRAL FLAG; West Indies, Ecuador; to 5 ft (1.5 m); leaves obovate to oblong, spirally arranged; flowers rose to flesh pink or red, bracts sometimes red-tinted.

cot split a bud stage of plums, when the yellow calyx splits off small green fruitlets. See *bud stages*.

Cotinus (from Greek *kotinos*, wild olive). Anacardiaceae. Northern temperate regions. SMOKEWOOD, SMOKE TREE. 3 species, deciduous trees and shrubs with elliptic to obovate leaves and very small flowers in large, finely branched and feathery panicles in summer, many of these abort, resulting in bare panicle branches that assume a ghostly or smokelike appearance. Fully hardy. Plant in sun in well-drained, low to medium-fertility soil. Prune in late winter to remove deadwood and straggling growth—contact may cause dermatitis. Root heeled, ripewood cuttings in early fall in a cold frame.

C. coggygria (syn. *Rhus cotinus*); SMOKE BUSH, VENETIAN SUMAC; S Europe to C China; shrub to 15 ft (5 m); leaves to 3 in (7.5 cm), soft mid-green, often tinted pink to bronze at first; inflorescences to

Cotinus coggygria 'Notcutt's Variety'
Many good cultivars have been developed that bear dark, richly colored leaves, set off here by the "smokelike" plumes of flowers.

8 in (20 cm), purple-buff becoming smoky gray; cultivars and hybrids with the next species include plants with a fog of pink to wine red flowers and purple or maroon leaves, sometimes edged scarlet and usually coloring richly in fall; *C. obovatus* AMERICAN SMOKE TREE, CHITTAMWOOD; S US; tree or shrub to 30 ft (10 m), differs from *C. coggygria* in its leaves with cuneate (not rounded or truncate) bases, sea green often tinted purple when young, turning gold, amber and scarlet in fall.

Cotoneaster (from Latin *cotoneum*, quince and *-aster*, a suffix indicating incomplete resemblance; the name refers to the loose resemblance of some species to the quince, *Cydonia*). Rosaceae. Europe, N Africa, E Asia, Siberia, Himalaya. Over 70 species, deciduous or evergreen shrubs or small trees. Produced in spring and summer, the flowers are small, solitary, clustered or carried in flat-topped corymbs. White or pink-tinted, they consist of five spreading, rounded petals and numerous stamens. They are followed by small, red or black pomes; these are highly ornamental and often persist on the shrub long into the winter.

Cotoneasters are grown for their profuse flowers, which are particularly attractive to bees, and for the rich colors of their fall foliage and berries; these are most attractive in fall

and winter, and a useful food source for birds.

Low-growing and spreading species of *Cotoneaster* and cultivars are excellent groundcover on banks. They are also useful for underplanting large shrubs and trees, or for trailing over rocks and walls.

The evergreen *C. franchetii*, *C. conspicuus* and *C. lacteus* and the deciduous *C. bullatus* and *C. hupehensis* can be used in the shrub border or for woodland edge plantings; the evergreens also making good windbreaks. *C. simonsii*, *C. franchetii*, *C. lacteus*, *C. divaricatus* and *C. frigidus* are often used in informal hedging. A number of dwarf species, such as the ground-hugging *C. adpressus* and *C. microphyllus* var. *thymifolius* are well-suited to the rock garden. *C. horizontalis* and *C. microphyllus* can be wall-trained with little or no support and will thrive even on north- and east-facing walls, when they will provide bright flowers, rich fall color and vivid fruit.

Cotoneasters will tolerate atmospheric pollution, and all except the boggiest soil. Most are hardy to –4°F (–20°C), although the foliage of evergreen species and cultivars may be scorched or killed at very low temperatures. Grow in full sun or semishade. For hedging, use young plants of *C. franchetii* or *C. simonsii* set 12–14 in (30–35 cm) apart; or plants of *C. frigidus*, *C. lacteus* and *C.* × *watereri* 24–36 in (60–90 cm) apart.

Pruning is usually necessary only to restrict size and promote bushy growth; it should be undertaken in late winter. Remove outward-facing growths on wall-grown plants and tie in new growth. Trim informal hedges selectively, taking out badly placed branches. Propagate evergreen species and cultivars by semiripe heel cuttings in early fall. Increase deciduous species by cuttings in mid- to late summer, in a closed case with bottom heat. Sow seed outdoors in fall or stratify in damp sand over winter and sow under glass in spring. They hybridize freely, and seed may not come true.

Cotoneasters are susceptible to fireblight, armillaria root rot and silver leaf. Many of the apple pests also attack this genus. They may also become infested with the hawthorn webber moth.

COTONEASTER

Name	Distribution	Habit	Leaves	Flowers	Fruits
C. adpressus	China	scandent, spreading or prostrate deciduous shrub	to ⁵⁄₈ in (1.5 cm), broadly ovate or obovate, dull green, scarlet in fall	red with some white, solitary or paired	red

Comments: 'Little Gem': growth weaker, cushion-forming with little fall color and no fruit.

Name	Distribution	Habit	Leaves	Flowers	Fruits
C. bullatus	China	deciduous shrub to 12 ft (4 m)	to 2³⁄₄ in (7 cm), ovate to oblong or elliptic, apex tapering, dark green and bullate with fiery tints in fall	white tinted red in clusters to 2 in (5 cm) across	currant red

Comments: 'Firebird': spreading shrub to 10 ft (3 m), fruit dark orange or red in dense clusters.

Name	Distribution	Habit	Leaves	Flowers	Fruits
C. cochleatus C. cashmiriensis, C. microphyllus var. cochleatus	Kashmir	slow-growing, low, dense, dwarf shrub close to *C. microphyllus*	¹⁄₄–¹⁄₂ in (0.5–1 cm), ovate to elliptic, usually notched, deep glossy green	white	small, bright red
C. congestus	Himalaya	congested, spreading, scandent or prostrate, evergreen or semievergreen shrub or subshrub	to ¹⁄₂ in (1 cm), often in two rows, obovate to elliptic or oblong, tough, dull green	white	carmine
C. conspicuus	Tibet	spreading scandent or prostrate evergreen or semievergreen shrub to 3¹⁄₄ ft (1 m)	to ³⁄₄ in (2 cm), oblong or lanceolate, tough	white, solitary	shiny, scarlet

Comments: 'Decorus': spreading and low-growing with abundant flowers and fruit; 'Tiny Tim': mat-forming, fruit orange washed red.

Name	Distribution	Habit	Leaves	Flowers	Fruits
C. dammeri	China	scandent to prostrate evergreen shrub with long shoots	to 1¹⁄₄ in (3 cm), elliptic to obovate or oblong, dark glossy green	white, usually solitary	red
C. dielsianus	China	arching to pendulous, semievergreen shrub to 10 ft (3 m)	to 1 in (2.5 cm), rounded to oval or obovate, tough, yellow- to gray-hairy beneath	pink, clustered	blood red to currant red (coral in the round-leaved var. *elegans*)
C. divaricatus	China	spreading deciduous shrub to 6¹⁄₂ ft (2 m) with distinctly divaricating branches	to ³⁄₄ in (2 cm), ovate to elliptic, glossy dark green, red in fall	white tinted red, clustered	deep red
C. franchetii	China, Tibet, Burma	evergreen slender shrub to 10 ft (3 m) with arching branches	to 1¹⁄₄ in (3 cm), oval, gray-green above, felted with gray-white or mustard-colored hairs beneath	white tinged rose pink, clustered	orange-scarlet
C. frigidus	Himalaya	spreading, deciduous shrub or tree to 60 ft (18 m)	to 4³⁄₄ in (12 cm), elliptic to oblong or obovate, dull green, woolly at first beneath	white, clustered	light red

Comments: includes 'Cornubia', with large, drooping clusters of red berries; other cultivars, e.g. 'Fructo Luteo', have pendulous branches and creamy yellow fruit.

C. adpressus

C. cochleatus

C. divaricatus

C. frigidus 'Fructu Luteo'

COTONEASTER

Name	Distribution	Habit	Leaves	Flowers	Fruits
C. glaucophyllus	China	evergreen shrub to 12 ft (4 m)	oval, glaucous white beneath, with conspicuous veins, covered in tawny hairs when young	white, in clusters	orange to deep red
C. horizontalis	China	deciduous shrub to 5¾ ft (1.75 m) with arching branches and branchlets 2-ranked and flattened in a distinctive herring bone pattern	¼–⅝ in (0.5–1.5 cm), rounded to elliptic, glossy dark green, usually tinted deep bronze to fiery red in fall	solitary or in pairs, white tinted pink or red	orange-red to blood red
Comments: Includes cultivars with white or cream-variegated leaves and of dwarf, low and spreading habits.					
C. hupehensis	China	deciduous shrub to 6½ ft (2 m) with arching branches	to 1½ in (3.5 cm), elliptic to ovate, dark green above, gray and somewhat hairy beneath	white, clustered	large, bright crimson
C. 'Hybridus Pendulus'	Garden origin	evergreen shrub, with narrow, spreading to creeping branches, but usually grown as a standard with a domed and weeping crown	oblong to lanceolate, dark green	white, clustered	bright red, abundant
C. lacteus	China	evergreen shrub to 12 ft (4 m)	oblong to obovate or elliptic, tough, mid- to dark green above with impressed veins, gray-green beneath	milky white in broad clusters	dull scarlet to deep brick red, persistent
C. linearifolius C. microphyllus f. thymifolius	Nepal	dwarf, evergreen shrub with prostrate branches	very small, narrow, glossy dark green	white, in small clusters	deep pink to red
C. microphyllus	Himalaya	low, spreading, evergreen shrub to 3¼ × 6½ ft (1 × 2 m) with short, stiff branches and neat foliage	¼–½ in (0.5–1 cm), oval, dark, glossy green	white, solitary or in small clusters	carmine red
Comments: See also C. cashmiriensis and C. linearifolius.					
C. prostratus	Himalaya	evergreen, arching to prostrate shrub	½–⅝ in (1–1.5 cm), broadly oval to rounded, dark green, glossy above, pale beneath	white, solitary	crimson to deep ruby red
C. salicifolius	China	evergreen shrub to 15 ft (5 m) with a graceful, arching habit	oblong to lanceolate, tapering narrowly, dark green	white in clusters	bright red

Comments: Includes numerous cultivars and involved in hybrids with erect and strongly arching to low or prostrate habits, most with narrow, dark foliage and fruits in shades of orange, flame, scarlet and brick red. 'Exburiensis' may be semievergreen, with large, rugose leaves and apricot-yellow fruits, tinged pink in winter; 'Gnom' is prostrate, widely spreading, fruits light red; 'Rothschildianus' has creamy white flowers and creamy yellow to gold fruits.

C. horizontalis

C. lacteus

C. salicifolius 'Gnom'

C. sternianus

COTONEASTER

Name	Distribution	Habit	Leaves	Flowers	Fruits
C. simonsii	Himalaya, Nepal, Sikkim	erect, twiggy, deciduous or semievergreen shrub to 12 ft (4 m)	½–1¼ in (1–3 cm), ovate to broadly elliptic, dark, shiny green turning red-bronze in fall	solitary or in small clusters, white tinted pink-red	orange-red to scarlet, persistent
Comments: An excellent hedging plant.					
C. sternianus *C. franchetii* var. *sternianus; C. wardii* of gardens	Tibet, Burma	evergreen or semievergreen shrub to 10 ft (3 m), with spreading to stiffly arching branches	to 1½ in (3.5 cm), elliptic, sage green above, with white, downy undersides	white tinted red in small clusters	orange-red, abundant
C. ✕ watereri varied group of hybrids between *C. frigidus, C. henryanus, C. rugosus* and *C. salicifolius*	garden origin	large shrubs or small trees, evergreen or semievergreen, often with arching branches	usually large, narrow and dark green	white in broad clusters	red, abundant in large, showy clusters
Comments: Covers many clones—low and near-prostrate to tall and arching with fruit in shades of scarlet, brick red, flame, orange, salmon, yellow-pink, yellow and cream; among them some of the most popular cotoneasters, including *C.* 'John Waterer', a strong-growing shrub to 15 ft (5 m) with arching branches, large, dark green lanceolate leaves and abundant red fruit.					

cottage garden a small, country garden, traditionally planted with flowers such as sweet Williams (*Dianthus barbatus*), hollyhocks (*Alcea rosea*), pinks (*Dianthus plumarius* derivatives) and pansies (*Viola* species), all growing in a colorful jumble. The flowers are often interspersed with vegetables, and fences, walls and porches are clothed with honeysuckle (*Lonicera* species) and rambler roses (*Rosa* species).

Cotula (from Greek *kotyle*, a small cup). Compositae. Cosmopolitan. 80 species, hardy annual or perennial herbs, rhizomatous, with pinnately compound leaves and stalked, buttonlike flower heads in spring and summer. The first species is hardy to 0°F (–18°C) and will grow in full sun at the water's edge or in the bog garden. The second needs full sun, a fast-draining, gritty medium on the rock garden or in an alpine trough, and protection from wet, cold conditions. Propagate by division or by seed in spring.

C. coronopifolia BRASS BUTTONS; South Africa; annual or perennial with fleshy, ascending to decumbent stems to 12 in (30 cm) long; leaves to ½ in (1.2 cm), linear, entire, toothed or pinnately lobed; flower heads to ½ in (1 cm) in diam., yellow or cream; *C. hispida* S. Africa; perennial with dense, tufted stems to 1½ in (4 cm); leaves very finely cut, covered in silver hair; flower heads small, golden on slender stalks.

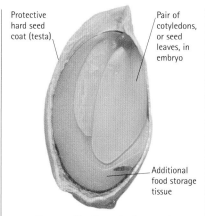

Cross-section through citrus seed

Protective hard seed coat (testa)

Pair of cotyledons, or seed leaves, in embryo

Additional food storage tissue

cotyledon the primary, storage leaves (see above), either solitary (in monocots), paired (in dicots) or whorled as in some conifers. They may remain within the seed coat or emerge and become green during germination.

Cotyledon (from Greek *kotyle*, a small cup or cavity, referring to the leaves of some species). Crassulaceae. Africa. 9 species, small, tender evergreen shrubs and subshrubs with large and thickly succulent leaves and nodding, bell-shaped to tubular flowers in dense panicles. Cultivate as for the tender *Crassula* species.

C. orbiculata South Africa; to 3¼ ft (1 m); leaves to 6 in (16 cm), obovate to linear, terete to flattened, gray-green often edged red; flowers orange to red;

C. tomentosa subsp. *ladysmithiensis* (South Africa; to 12 in (30 cm); leaves to 2½ in (6 cm), oblong-obovate, rounded, toothed, thickly fleshy and covered in short, yellow-brown hairs; flowers red-brown; *C. undulata* SILVER CROWN, SILVER RUFFLES; South Africa; to 3¼ ft (1 m); leaves to 6 in (15 cm), broadly obovate and gray-green with a strongly wavy apical margin; flowers orange.

couch grass (*Elymus repens*) TWITCH, SCUTCH a perennial, invasive grass-weed of gardens, which spreads rapidly by means of underground stems. Control by forking out. Glyphosate and glyphosate trimesium are effective as foliage-applied total weedkillers; apply when growth is active, especially in spring, at 4–6 in (10–15 cm) high.

courgette (*Cucurbita pepo*) ZUCCHINI the immature fruit of some cultivars of marrow (mainly hybrids), grown as a vegetable throughout the summer in temperate regions; the fruits are pale or dark green or yellow, sometimes striped. Sow 1 in (2.5 cm) deep in small pots under protection at 55°F (13°C) minimum; transplant 4–5 weeks later after hardening off, and only when danger of frost is passed. Space 36 in (90 cm) apart each way. Seedlings can be advanced outdoors under cloches or film. In mild climates, zucchini may be sown direct outdoors. Plants produce

C

separate male and female flowers and are insect-pollinated; under cool conditions, hand-pollinate (see right) by removing male flowers and dabbing pollen into female flowers, which can be recognized by the immature ovary below the perianth. Harvest fruits regularly, when 4 in (10 cm) long. Possible problems: aphids, red spider mite, whiteflies; virus, downy mildew, gray mold.

coursonne a small fruiting lateral of apples or pears.

cover cropping see *green manuring*.

crab apple (*Malus* species) hardy, deciduous trees bearing pome fruits, found throughout temperate zones of the Northern Hemisphere. *M.sylvestris* is native of Europe. The fruits of most species and cultivars are small and too sour for eating, but some are suitable for jam. *M. floribunda* and *M.* × *purpurea* 'Aldenhamensis', *M.* × *zumi* var. *calocarpa* 'Golden Hornet' and *M.* 'John Downie' are very effective as pollinators of apple. Ornamental species are grown for blossom (white in *M.hupehensis*, *M.florentina* and *M.sargentii*, pink in *M. floribunda* and *M.spectabilis*, deep rose in *M.* × *purpurea*); for fragrance (violet-scented in *M.angustifolia* and *M.coronaria* var. *dasycalyx* 'Charlottae'); for decorative fruits, ranging from yellow to deep red/purple; and for fall color (e.g. *M.coronaria*, *M.glaucescens* and *M. kansuensis*. Prune, as for apples, in winter to remove congested and diseased growth. Propagate species by seed, cultivars by budding or grafting on to seedling rootstocks. For ornamental species, see *Malus*.

Crab apple
Crabs such as *Malus* 'John Downie' are not only decorative but may serve as pollinators for certain apple varieties.

HAND-POLLINATING ZUCCHINI

1 Tear the petals from a male flower. This will have a smaller central boss and lack the "bump" behind the flower that the female flowers possess.

2 Brush the pollen from the stamens of the male flower onto the stigma of the female flower. Alternatively, use a fine paint brush to transfer the pollen.

3 For the best chance of fertilization and fruit set, tie the petals of the female flower together. The swelling of the bump behind the flower will indicate success.

Crambe (Greek name for cabbage). Cruciferae. C Europe to Asia, Africa. 20 species, annual or perennial herbs (those listed here are perennial), evergreen to deciduous, with a stout, woody rootstock and leaves that are tough, broadly elliptic to ovate, puckered and wavy. Appearing in late spring and summer, the flowers are small, fragrant, four-petalled, white and in large panicles. *C. cordifolia* is a magnificent perennial for the large herbaceous border. It prefers a fast-draining, alkaline soil in full sun. In areas with very hard or dull, wet winters, mulch the crowns once the foliage has died away. *C. maritima*, needs a sandy and stony, free-draining soil, again in full sun, and is at home in coastal regions. It is also cultivated for its edible stems, blanched and harvested in late winter and early spring. Both species are hardy to –20°F (–29°C). Propagate by seed sown in spring or fall in a cold frame or cold greenhouse; alternatively, increase by root cuttings or division in spring.

C. cordifolia Caucasus; leaves to 12 in (30 cm), dark glossy green, much puckered; panicle to 5 ft (1.5 m) tall, pyramidal, with many fine, spreading branches and a mass of flower; *C. maritima* SEA KALE; coastal N Europe, Baltic Sea and Black Sea; leaves to 12 in (30 cm), fleshy, wavy and crisped to lobed, blue-gray to purple-tinted, glaucous; panicle to 20 in (50 cm) tall, dense and corymbose. See also *sea kale*.

cranberry a dwarf shrub producing small, dark red acidic berries of culinary use. The AMERICAN CRANBERRY (*Vaccinium macrocarpon*) is a dwarf, evergreen shrub, native to eastern North America. It has been cultivated since the early 18th century but is seldom grown in gardens. The fruits are rich in vitamin C, and are harvested for cooking in fall, picked over several times. The native BRITISH CRANBERRY (*V. oxycoccus*) is not grown commercially; the related LINGEN or LINGBERRY (*V. vitis-idaea*) is grown on a small scale in Europe.

American cranberries require a very acidic soil (pH4–5) and a controlled soil-water level in order to produce bog conditions and afford frost protection. Plant from cuttings in late spring, 6–18 in (15–45 cm) apart each way, according to local practice; fruits are produced in the second or third year. No pruning is necessary.

crane flies see *leatherjackets*.

Crassula (diminutive of Latin *crassus*, thick or swollen). Crassulaceae. Some cosmopolitan, most restricted to South Africa. 300 species, annual, biennial and perennial herbs and small shrubs (those listed here are perennials from South Africa) with succulent leaves and small, usually white, starlike flowers in clusters or panicles. All except *C. sarcocaulis*, (which is hardy to 0°F (–18°C), need a minimum winter temperature of 45°F (7°C) and a dry atmosphere. Most need full sun, although some species with thinner-textured leaves prefer bright, indirect light. Grow in a free-draining, gritty, loam-based medium. Water frequently in summer, but allow the soil to become almost dry between times. From late fall to midspring, water only to prevent shrivelling of leaves. Propagate by stem or leaf cuttings.

C. atropurpurea var. *arborescens* SILVER JADE PLANT, SILVER DOLLAR, CHINESE JADE; 3¼–6½ ft (1–2 m) tall, shrubby and treelike with stout branches; leaves ¾–2 in (2–5 cm), obovate to round, tip rounded, base tapering, blue-green and gray-bloomed with a red-brown tinted margin; *C. deceptor* (syn. *C. deceptrix*; to 6 in (15 cm) tall, branches covered in compressed, 4-ranked leaves forming a squat column, each leaf to ½ in (1 cm) long, ovate to wedge-shaped, thickly fleshy, gray and covered in dots; *C. falcata* PROPELLER PLANT, AIRPLANE PLANT, SCARLET PAINT BRUSH, SICKLE PLANT; stout-stemmed and erect to 20 in (50 cm); leaves thick, gray, broadly lanceolate, paired and twisted in opposite directions from their fused bases; flowers fragrant, bright red, in large clusters; *C. lactea* FLOWERING CRASSULA, TAILOR'S PATCH; to 8 in (20 cm), stems horizontal to scrambling, thick; leaves ¾–2¾ in (2–7 cm), terete, oblanceolate, base tapering, apex pointed, dull, deep green; flowers cream tinted pink, produced in great abundance; *C. multicava* to 16 in (40 cm) tall, shrubby; leaves 2 in (5 cm), oblong to ovate, mid- to gray- green; flowers cream tinted rose, massed in stalked panicles, sometimes giving rise to plantlets; *C. muscosa* (syn. *C. lycopodioides*); RATTAIL MOSS CYPRESS, PRINCESS PINE, TOY CYPRESS, WATCH-CHAIN CYPRESS; to 24 in (60 cm), resembling a miniature cypress or club moss; stems slender, concealed by very small, olive green, scalelike leaves which overlap in four ranks; *C. ovata* JADE PLANT, JADE TREE, DOLLAR PLANT; differs from *C. arborescens* in glossy mid- to dark green leaves sometimes edged with red-brown—one of the most popular *Crassula* species, and widely grown as a house plant; *C. sarcocaulis* shrubby, to 20 in (50 cm) tall with a broad, dense and twiggy crown; leaves ¼–¾ in (0.5–2 cm), semiterete, elliptic to lanceolate, pointed, red-tinted; flowers pink, malodorous, in massed clusters; *C.*

schmidtii tufted, mat-forming, to 6 in (15 cm) tall; leaves to 1¼ in (3 cm), linear to lanceolate, green with dark spots, tinged red-brown, ciliate; flowers pink to magenta; *C. socialis* cushion-forming, to 4 in (10 cm); stems densely clothed in 4-ranked leaves, these small, triangular, thickly fleshy, mid-green; flowers white in long-stalked clusters.

+Crataegomespilus Rosaceae. Garden origin. Graft hybrids between *Crataegus* and *Mespilus*, differing from *Mespilus* in the smaller flowers clustered at the branch tips, and from *Crataegus* in the *Mespilus*-type fruit. Cultivate as for *Mespilus*. Increase by grafting. +*C. dardarii* (*Crataegus monogyna* × *Mespilus germanica*; BRONVAUX MEDLAR; deciduous tree to 20 ft (6 m) with spiny branchlets; leaves to 6 in (15 cm), narrowly oblong to elliptic, dark green above, woolly beneath; flowers to ⅝ in (1.5 cm) in diameter, white; fruit to ¾ in (2 cm) in diameter; includes 'Jules d'Asnières', with flowers tinted rose.

× *Crataemespilus* is a naturally occurring inter-generic hybrid between *Crataegus* and *Mespilus*. There are two hybrids, × *C. gillotii* (*Crataegus monogyna* × *Mespilus germanica*) and × *C. grandiflora* (*Crataegus laevigata* × *Mespilus germanica*). The graft hybrid and the natural hybrids may be propagated by grafting onto *C. monogyna*.

Crataegus (from Greek *kratos*,

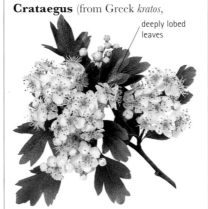

deeply lobed leaves

Crataegus monogyna

strength, referring to the wood). Rosaceae. N Hemisphere. HAWTHORN. Some 200 species, hardy deciduous trees and shrubs, often thorny, with entire, toothed, lobed or pinnatisect leaves and corymbs of flowers in late spring, usually white and headily scented. The fruits are small, red to

orange or brown pomes and often persist in decorative clusters late into fall and winter. The following species are fully hardy and will grow on all but the wettest soil. They prefer full sun, but will tolerate light shade. Several make excellent hedges and windbreaks, and most cope with harsh winds, coastal exposures and urban pollution. Sow seed of species in fall; increase cultivars by budding.

C. coccinea SCARLET HAW; E US; slender-branched, thorny tree to 22 ft (7 m); leaves 2–4 in (5–10 cm), broadly ovate with 4–5 pairs of shallow, biserrate lobes, dark green and rugose, turning fiery red in fall; flowers with pink-red anthers; fruit to ½ in (1 cm), pyriform, bright red; *C. crus-galli* COCK-SPUR HAWTHORN; E US; wide-spreading, flat-topped tree to 30 ft (10 m) with vicious, ultimately branching thorns; leaves 1–4 in (2.5–10 cm), obovate, toothed, dark glossy green becoming orange-red in fall; flowers with pink anthers; fruit to ½ in (1 cm), subglobose, deep red; *C. ellwangeriana* E US; tree to 20 ft (6 m) tall with sparse spines; leaves to 3 in (8 cm), ovate to oval, shallowly lobed, serrate, dark green and rugose above, hairy beneath; flowers with pink anthers; fruit ⅝ in (1.5 cm), oblong, red; *C. flava* YELLOW HAWTHORN, YELLOW-FRUITED HAW; N America; tree to 20 ft (6 m) with spines to 1 in (2.5 cm); leaves to 2 in (5 cm), obovate to oblong, apex with 3, biserrate lobes, tough, pale green; flowers with purple anthers; fruit to ½ in (1 cm), rounded to pyriform, green-yellow, edible; *C. laevigata* (syn. *C. oxyacantha*); ENGLISH HAWTHORN, QUICK-SET THORN, WHITE THORN, MAY; thorny shrub or small tree, 8–20 ft (2.5–6 m) tall; leaves to 2 in (5 cm), obovate with 3–5, shallow and blunt, serrate lobes; flowers white to pink or crimson with pink-purple anthers; fruit to ½ in (1 cm), ovoid to globose, deep red; there are many cultivars including forms with semi and fully double flowers, pure white to deep crimson, variegated leaves and dark blood red to yellow fruit; *C.* × *lavallei* (*C. stipulacea* × *C. crus-galli*); the most popular cultivar is 'Carrierei', a spreading tree to 22 ft (7 m) tall with elliptic to oblong and irregularly toothed leaves that turn from dark green to deep red in fall; the flowers have pink anthers and the long-lasting fruit are orange-red, ellipsoid and to ³/₄ in (1.8 cm); *C. macrosperma* N America; thorny tree to 25 ft (8 m) tall; leaves ovate to elliptic with five, broadly triangular and sharply toothed lobes; flowers with red anthers; fruit to ⅝ in (1.5 cm), obovoid to oblong, red; includes 'Acutiloba', with broad and jaggedly serrate leaves; *C. mollis* RED HAW; C US; spreading tree to 43 ft (13 m) with thorny, white-hairy shoots; leaves to 4 in (10 cm), broadly ovate, with 4–7 pairs of shallow, glandular-toothed lobes, hairy becoming rugose; flowers with yellow anthers; fruit to 1 in (2.5 cm), globose-pyriform, red, downy; *C. monogyna* SLINGSEED HAWTHORN, ENGLISH HAWTHORN, MAY; W Europe; thorny shrub or tree to 15 ft (5 m) tall; leaves to 2½ in (6 cm), broadly ovate to rhombic with 3–7 lobes, glossy dark green; fruit to ½ in (1 cm), ovoid to ellipsoid, red; widely grown as a hedge; there are many cultivars including forms with tightly compact to low and spreading or narrowly erect habits, pendulous to twisted branches, variegated leaves, pink flowers and yellow fruits; one of the most celebrated is 'Biflora', the GLASTONBURY THORN, which produces flowers and a few leaves in winter as well as spring; *C. orientalis* SE Europe, W Asia; tree to 22 ft (7 m) tall with sparse thorns and downy shoots; leaves to 2 in (5 cm), triangular to rhombic with 5–9, deep, toothed lobes, deep green with ashy gray down; flowers large with maroon anthers; fruit to ⅝ in (1.5 cm), globose, downy, orange-red; *C. phaenopyrum* WASHINGTON HAWTHORN; SE US; broad-crowned tree to 30 ft (10 m) with slender branchlets and long, sometimes branched thorns; leaves to 2¾ in (7 cm), triangular to broadly ovate, 3–5-lobed toward base, toothed, bright glossy green turning orange-red in fall; flowers with pink anthers; fruit to ¼ in (0.5 cm), subglobose, bright red, lasting well; *C. × prunifolia* (*C. crus-galli* × *C. succulenta* var. *macracantha*); tree to 20 ft (6 m) with a dense, spreading crown and large, stout thorns; leaves to 3 in (8 cm), broadly ovate to oval, coarsely serrate, dark green turning rich purple-red in fall; flowers with pink anthers; fruit to ⅜ in

(1.5 cm), globose, bright red; *C. tanacetifolia* TANSY-LEAVED THORN; W Asia; erect shrub or tree to 30 ft (10 m), branchlets felty at first and often thornless; leaves 1–2½ in (2.5–6 cm), oval to rhombic with 5–7, narrow, pinnately cut and toothed lobes, hairy at first; flowers with red anthers; fruit to 1 in (2.5 cm), globose, yellow-red, reminiscent of apples in scent and flavor.

crateriform shaped like a bowl or goblet, in the form of a concave hemisphere slightly contracted at the base.

crazy paving paths or terraces made of broken paving slabs fitted closely together in a random arrangement.

creeper specifically, a plant that spreads over the soil surface, rooting as it grows, for example, *Vinca* species. The term is often loosely applied to climbers and other wall plants, for example, *Vitis* species.

cremocarp a dry, seedlike fruit consisting of two one-seeded carpels with an epigynous calyx. The carpels separate into mericarps on ripening.

crenate scalloped, with shallow, rounded teeth. Where the teeth themselves have crenate teeth, the term used is bicrenate.

crenulate minutely crenate.

Crepis (from Greek *krepis*, name of a plant in Theophrastus). Compositae. N Hemisphere. HAWK'S BEARD. 200 species, annual or perennial herbs with rosettes of entire to pinnatifid leaves and long-stalked, dandelion-like flower heads in summer and fall. Fully hardy. Grow in full sun or part shade in well-drained soil. Increase perennials by root cuttings or division, annuals and biennials by seed in fall. All will self-sow.

C. aurea Alps; glabrous perennial to 12 in (30 cm); flower heads orange to deep yellow, tinted maroon beneath; *C. incana* PINK DANDELION; Greece; gray-hairy perennial to 6 in (15 cm); flower heads bright pink to magenta; *C. rubra* more or less hairy annual or short-lived perennial to 24 in (60 cm); flower heads usually rose, sometimes red or white.

American land cress
Very hardy and evergreen through winter, this little grown, biennial salad leaf makes a good substitute for watercress.

cress a group name for several low-growing salad herbs, including AMERICAN LAND CRESS (*Barbarea verna*), ITALIAN CRESS (*Eruca sativa*) and GARDEN CRESS (*Lepidium sativum*), all members of the Cruciferae. Garden cress is the most commonly grown, the young seedlings being cut and used as a salad garnish. Sow seed in succession thickly on to a water-soaked, fibrous mat lining a shallow dish, or in trays or pots; maintain a temperature of 50°F (10°C) and harvest after 10–14 days. For salad greens, all three may be sown outdoors in early spring in rows 12 in (30 cm) apart at 2–3 week intervals. Indoor cress is often grown with milder flavored MUSTARD (*Sinapis alba*), raised similarly.

crest an irregular or dentate elevation or ridge; generally applied to an outgrowth of the funiculus in seeds but also found on the summit of some organs and on the lip of some orchids.

crickets (Saltatoria: Gryllidae and other families) insects related to grasshoppers with long thin antennae and two pairs of wings folded horizontally over a broad flat abdomen in the pest species. Adult males produce a characteristic chirping sound by rubbing forewings against hindwings. Most lay eggs in the soil, but some bush crickets place them on plants. The eggs hatch into wormlike larvae; these molt almost immediately to form the first nymphal stage, which resembles the adult, and gradually increase in size with subsequent moults. They are mostly omnivorous, and are common in hot, dry places. Plants are attacked occasionally, but only in frames and heated greenhouses in temperate countries.

The HOUSE CRICKET (*Acheta domesticus*) may eat the tops of young seedlings and attack older plants at ground level. Reduce infestations by eliminating daytime hiding places. Alternatively, apply contact insecticide or employ baits: pitfall traps may also be used. The MOLE CRICKET (*Gryllotalpa gryllotalpa*) is robust, up to 1¾ in (45 mm) long; it has expanded forelegs armed with teeth modified for digging. It is rare and protected legally in Britain, but common in southern Europe, and has been introduced into North America. It burrows in soil to eat the roots and stems of many plants, especially potatoes, carrots, tomatoes and sweet corn. Control by applying a locally approved soil insecticide in countries where it is a pest.

BUSH CRICKETS (Tettigoniidae) mostly frequent trees and shrubs, and some feed mainly on small insects. Other species feed on foliage but rarely cause enough damage to be pests. Females can be recognized by their prominent sword-shaped ovipositor.

important. Grow in partial shade or dappled sun in moist but well-drained, fertile, humus-rich and acidic soil. Propagate by softwood or semiripe cuttings in a closed case with gentle bottom heat.

C. hookerianum (syn. *Tricuspidaria hookeriana*; CHILE LANTERN TREE; tree to 28 ft (9 m), or shrub to 12 ft (4 m); flowers scarlet to carmine, to 1¼ in (3 cm), lantern- or urnlike, fleshy; *C. patagua* (tree to 46 ft (14 m) or shrub to 12 ft (4 m); flowers white, to 1 in (2.5 cm), resembling a fringed bell.

Crinum (Greek *krinon*, lily). Amaryllidaceae. Tropics and subtropics. 130 species, perennial bulbous herbs, evergreen or deciduous, the bulb often with an elongated, stemlike neck. The leaves are strap- or sword-shaped. Large, funnel-shaped and 6-lobed, the flowers are often fragrant and arise in scapose umbels in summer and fall. More or less hardy, the South African species and hybrids prefer rich but well-drained soil in full sun, that is moist in spring and

fragrant flowers

Crinum x powellii

(13°C). Grow these in large pots or beds of moisture-retentive, humus-rich soil. All species resent disturbance. Propagate by offsets in spring, or from ripe seed sown in spring at 68°F (20°C).

C. americanum SOUTHERN SWAMP LILY, SOUTHERN SWAMP CRINUM; S US; scape to 30 in (75 cm); flowers to 4 in (10 cm), creamy white; *C. asiaticum* POISON BULB; tropical Asia; scape to 24 in (60 cm); flowers to 6 in (15 cm), white, fragrant; *C. bulbispermum* (syn. *C. longifolium*); S Africa; scape to 36 in (90 cm); flowers to 8 in (20 cm) green-white tinted or streaked pink to red; *C. macowanii* PAJAMA LILY; South Africa; scape to 36 in (90 cm); flowers to 8 in (20 cm), pink or white striped deep pink along lobes; *C. moorei* South Africa; scape to 36 in (90 cm); flowers to 4¾ in (12 cm), fragrant, pale to deep pink or white; *C. × powellii* (*C. bulbispermum* × *C. moorei*); garden origin; leaves to 3¼ ft (1 m); scape to 48 in (120 cm); flowers to 7 in (18 cm), fragrant, pale to candy pink to soft rose or white.

crispate curled and twisted extremely irregularly, refers either to a leaf blade or, more often, to hairs.

crispy-hairy of hairs; wavy and curved, in dense short ringlets.

cristate crested or, less commonly, crestlike. The term is sometimes used to denote the presence of crests (cristae), e.g. *Coelogyne cristata*, but more often to describe a perceived abnormality of growth (e.g. closely sculpted brain- or coral-like ridges, as found in *Celosia*, or the ruffled and usually forked tips of fern fronds).

crocks fragments of broken clay pots placed in the base of a growing container to prevent loss of the growing medium through the drainage hole, and to create an area of free drainage and air circulation at the base of the rootball. Crocking is beneficial for soil-based and soilless potting mixes and essential for the finer bark and leaf mold mixes used for certain orchids, ferns and aroids. Also known as shards.

Crinodendron hookerianum
The Chilean lantern tree, although not completely hardy, is a beautiful shrub for sheltered woodland or a warm wall in cold-winter areas; in mild regions it tolerates an exposed site.

Crinodendron (from Greek *krinon*, a kind of lily, and *dendron*, tree). Elaeocarpaceae. Chile. 2 species, hardy evergreen shrubs or small trees with leathery leaves and solitary, pendulous flowers in late spring. Hardy to 14°F (−10°C), especially if given the shelter of a wall or surrounding trees and shrubs; a cool root-run is, however,

summer, but rather dry in winter; *C. × powellii*, for example, will thrive at the foot of a south-facing wall to 0°F (−18°C). *C. americanum* requires virtually frost-free conditions and a permanently moist, acidic soil. It will tolerate part shade. Tropical Asiatic species need light shade, medium to high humidity and a minimum temperature of 55°F

Crocosmia (from Greek *krokos*, saffron, and *osme*, smell, referring to the smell of saffron given off by the dried flowers when immersed in water). Iridaceae. South Africa. MONTBRETIA. 7 species, deciduous perennial herbs, cormous with narrow, sword-shaped and ribbed leaves. The flowers are red, orange or yellow, tubular and curving and produced in summer on slender-stalked, erect to angled racemes or sparsely branched panicles. Hardy to –10°F (–23°C). Grow in full sun in fertile, well-drained soil. In areas with very hard winters, plant in a warm and sheltered site, or lift the corms and store them over winter in dry and frost-free conditions. Increase by division of corms in spring.

C. aurea to 3¼ ft (1 m) tall; flowers pale to burnt orange, straight-sided, to 2 in (5 cm) long, opening to broad lobes; *C.* × *crocosmiiflora* (*C. aurea* × *C. pottsii*); a garden hybrid differing from *C. aurea* in the curved and slightly inflated upper part of the perianth tube and the narrower lobes; *C. masoniorum* to 3¼ ft (1 m); flowers vermilion, to 2 in (5 cm), narrowed to base, widening above to outspread lobes; includes 'Firebird', with fiery orange-red flowers tinted green in the throat; *C. paniculata* to 3¼ ft (1 m); flowers to 2½ in (6 cm), deep orange, curving downward, somewhat inflated with lobes spreading; *C. pottsii* to 36 in (90 cm); flowers to 1¼ in (3 cm), widening sharply from a narrow base, orange flushed red, lobes to ½ × ¼ in (1 × 0.5 cm). Cultivars: 'Bressingham Blaze', with widely funnel-shaped, fiery orange-red flowers; 'Citronella', with yellow flowers with red-brown markings at center; 'Emberglow', with glowing orange-brown flowers, arching upward; 'Jackanapes', with small flowers, bicolored yellow and deep orange-red; 'Lucifer', with large, flame flowers; 'Solfatare', with apricot-yellow flowers and smoky bronze leaves; and 'Star of the East', with large, soft apricot-yellow flowers with a paler throat and darker lobes.

Crocus (Greek *krokos*, saffron, an ancient plant name that shares its derivation with the Hebrew *karkom* and Arabic *kurkum*). Iridaceae. Europe, N Africa, Middle East, Central Asia. Some 80 species, small, cormous perennial herbs. The leaves are grassy, often with a pale green or silver-white central stripe. The leaf bases dilate to form a caplike corm tunic, which is papery or composed of parallel or reticulate fibers. Produced in fall, late winter and spring, the flowers are funnel- to goblet-shaped, narrowing below into stemlike tube and expanding above into 6 lobes. The style is divided at the tip into 3 or more branches.

Most are hardy to –4°F (–20°C), if the ground does not freeze for long periods. They are suitable for a range of garden situations, with the most vigorous species, such as *C. speciosus* and *C. vernus*, used to great effect in the wild garden, naturalized beneath deciduous trees and shrubs, or in grass where the first cut does not occur until the crocus foliage has died back. On light, freely draining soil where turf is sufficiently fine, *C. tommasinianus*, *C. flavus*, *C. nudiflorus*, *C. serotinus*, *C. sieberi* and the more robust cultivars of *C. chrysanthus* can be used for similar effect. These species also suit beds and borders, and will tolerate low groundcover that will mask the fading foliage.

Cultivars of *C. vernus* are useful for indoor decoration in spring, gently forced in pots plunged beneath 6 in (15 cm) of sand for 6–8 weeks in a cold frame and then brought indoors to a temperature of 50–54°F (10–12°C). The smaller species are suited to the rock garden, raised bed, or for troughs and tubs, planted in a gritty loam-based mix. More delicate species, and those whose perfection may be marred by rain and wind in winter, can be grown in an alpine house.

Although most will thrive in a sunny position, sheltered from wind, in moderately fertile well-drained soil, in cultural terms, crocuses may be split into three groups. Members of the first group need moisture to complete their growth cycle, but

stamens of this species supply saffron

Crocus sativus

undergo a baking during dormancy in the long hot summer. They need a sheltered, sunny situation and a fast-draining soil. Although hardy, in some regions, these species are generally more safely grown with cloche protection, or in the bulb frame or alpine house, where they can be protected from excessive rainfall in summer. They include *C. aerius*, *C. biflorus*, *C. cartwrightianus*, *C. dalmaticus*, *C. minimus*, *C. niveus*, *C. olivieri* and *C. tournefortii*.

The second group is more tolerant of damp and can be grown in the open garden, given a warm, sunny position and good drainage. They include *C. ancyrensis*, *C. angustifolius*, *C. chrysanthus*, *C. etruscus*, *C. flavus*, *C. gargaricus*, *C. imperati*, *C. malyi*, *C. medius*, *C. pulchellus*, *C. sativus*, *C. serotinus*, and, if given the perfect drainage of a raised bed, *C. cancellatus*, *C. goulimyi*, *C. laevigatus* and *C. longiflorus*. The third group includes plants from climates that experience intermittent rainfall throughout the year, with a peak in fall and winter. This group does not share the requirement for a warm dry dormancy and needs at least some moisture to prevent the dormant corms from shrivelling. They also prefer some shade from the hottest sun in summer. They include *C. banaticus*, *C. cvijicii*, *C. nudiflorus*, *C. tommasinianus* and *C. vernus*, and, given a sheltered situation in well-drained but retentive soil, *C. kotschyanus* and *C. speciosus*.

Plant corms 2–3 in (5–8 cm) deep. Propagate by removal of cormlets, by division of established colonies or by seed sown when ripe in a sandy propagating mix. Plants raised from seed will bloom in their third or fourth year. A number of species, notably *C. imperati* and *C. tommasinianus*, will self-seed freely when conditions are suitable. Rodents and pheasants may dig up and eat the corms, while squirrels often feed on the emerging shoots. Planting under fine mesh may reduce losses. Birds may damage the flowers. Tulip-bulb aphids sometimes infest corms in storage and persist to form colonies that damage young shoots. *Crocus* may be affected by blue mold, gladiolus dry rot, hard rot, scab, hyacinth black slime, narcissus basal rot, tulip gray bulb rot and the rust fungus, *Uromyces croci*.

CROCUS

Name	Distribution	Flowers
C. aerius C. biliottii	N Turkey	tube to 3½ in (9 cm), deep blue, often flushed, royal blue from base of lobes, overlaid with darker feather veins; style trifid, vermilion to scarlet
Comments: Mid–late spring. For C. aerius of gardens, see C. biflorus ssp. pulchricolor.		
C. ancyrensis	Turkey	tube yellow or mauve; throat yellow, glabrous, lobes ½–1¼ in (1–3 cm), vivid yellow to pale orange; style trifid, deep orange
Comments: Spring. 'Golden Bunch': up to 7 flowers per corm.		
C. angustifolius C. susianus CLOTH OF GOLD CROCUS	SW Russia **Comments:** Spring.	throat yellow, glabrous or minutely hairy, lobes yellow, exterior flushed or veined maroon; style trifid, deep yellow to vermilion
C. banaticus C. byzantinus; C. iridiflorus	N Romania, former Yugoslavia, SW Russia	lilac-mauve, inner lobes to 1¼ in (3 cm), erect, outer lobes to 2 in (5 cm), spreading or deflexed, darker; style slender, multifid, feathery, violet
Comments: Fall.		
C. biflorus	S Europe, Asia Minor	throat white to golden yellow, glabrous, lobes to 1¼ in (3 cm), white, lilac or pale blue with dark mauve veins on exterior; style trifid, deep yellow
Comments: Spring and fall. ssp. **alexandri**: white, exterior suffused deep violet. ssp. **melantherus**: flecked white and feathered gray-purple on exterior; throat pale yellow, anthers damson purple to black. ssp. **pulchricolor**: syn. C. aerius of gardens, flowers indigo throughout,		color most intense at base of lobes, throat bright yellow. ssp. **weldenii**: white flushed pale lilac at base or, rarely, throughout undersides of lobes, throat white or pale blue.
C. boryi C. ionicus, C. cretensis	W & S Greece, Crete **Comments:** Fall.	tube 2–6 in (5–15 cm), ivory, exterior sometimes veined or flushed mauve, lobes to 2 in (5 cm), often smaller, obovate; style multifid, burnt orange
C. cancellatus	former Yugoslavia, Greece, Turkey, W Syria, Lebanon, N Israel	white to opal or lilac with purple veins, throat yellow, sometimes hairy, lobes to 2¼ in (5.5 cm); style multifid, deep orange
Comments: Fall. ssp. **mazziaricus**: flowers white to lilac sometimes stained yellow at base, usually veined violet and more cupped.		
C. candidus C. kirkii	NW Turkey	tube to 2¾ in (7 cm), white, tube stained purple-maroon, throat yellow, glabrous, outer lobes flushed and spotted violet-gray or blue; style 6-branched, deep yellow
Comments: Late winter, early spring.		
C. carpetanus C. lusitanicus	C & NW Spain, N Portugal **Comments:** Spring	tube 2½–4½ in (6–11 cm), white flushing to lilac usually with fine mauve veins, throat white with yellow tint; style ivory or lilac, trifid, flattened and ruffled at tips
C. cartwrightianus C. sativus var. cartwrightianus WILD SAFFRON	Greece **Comments:** Fall–early winter.	fragrant, throat hairy, lobes ⅝–1¼ in (1.5–3 cm), white, lilac or mauve with darker veins and a stronger purple flush at base, albino forms also occur; style trifid, vermilion, branches club-shaped

C. ancyrensis *C. banaticus* *C. cartwrightianus* *C. chrysanthus* 'Gipsy Girl'

C

CROCUS

Name	Distribution	Flowers
C. chrysanthus *C. annulatus* var. *chrysanthus;* *C. croceus*	Balkans, Turkey	tube 1¾ in (4.5 cm), occasionally striped or stained bronze-maroon; style trifid, deep yellow
Comments: Late winter: large and rounded, pure white, exterior gray-blue. 'Blue Pearl': pearly blue, base bronze, interior silver-blue with a rich orange stigmata. 'Blue Peter': soft blue inside with a golden throat, exterior rich purple-blue. 'Brass Band': apricot yellow outside with a bronze green-veined blotch, inside straw-yellow with a tawny glow. 'Cream Beauty': rounded, on short stalks, creamy yellow. 'E.A. Bowles': rounded, old gold, throat dark bronze. 'Elegance': violet outside, edges paler, inner tepals with a deep blue blotch, inside pale		violet with a bronze center. 'Gipsy Girl': large, golden yellow, outer tepals striped and feathered purple-brown. 'Ladykiller': outer tepals rich blue, narrowly edge white, inner tepals white, blotched with inky blue, silver-white inside. 'Snow Bunting': pure white with golden throat, exterior feathered purple. 'Snow White': pointed, frost-white with a gold base. 'Zenith': glossy violet-blue, inside silver-blue, contrasting with gold anthers and prominent gold throat. 'Zwanenburg Bronze': flowers golden yellow, exterior dark bronze.
C. cvijicii **Comments:** Late spring.	S former Yugoslavia, N Greece, E Albania	solitary, tube 1½–3 in (3.5–7.5 cm), delicate yellow-golden, rarely white, tube to 1½ in (3.5 cm), white or pale yellow, sometimes tinted purple, throat white, sometimes stained yellow, hairy; style trifid, yellow-orange, branches widened at tips
C. cyprius **Comments:** Late winter.	Cyprus	1–2, tube, 1¾–3½ in (4.5–9 cm), scented, white-lilac, exterior flushed mauve, darkest at base of lobes and on tube, throat yellow; style trifid, orange, tips enlarged
C. dalmaticus **Comments:** Late winter–early spring.	SW former Yugoslavia, N Albania	differs from *C. sieberi* in its single flowers, their exteriors pearly gray-mauve to biscuit and faintly striped purple
C. etruscus **Comments:** Late winter–spring. 'Zwanenburg': flowers pale blue, but appearing a stronger, almost pure blue if planted *en masse*.	N Italy	delicate lilac, tube white, 1¾–2¾ in (4.5–7 cm), throat hairy, sulfur yellow, lobes 1¼–1½ in (3–4 cm), the outer whorl ivory, pearly or tawny, feathered with purple below
C. flavus *C. luteus; C. aureus* **Comments:** Spring.	S former Yugoslavia, C & N Greece, Bulgaria, Romania, NW Turkey	tube 2¾–7 in (7–18 cm), scented, light golden yellow to apricot-yellow, tube exterior and base of lobes sometimes striped or stained brown; style trifid, yellow
C. gargaricus **Comments:** Spring.	NW Turkey	tube 2¼–4¼ in (5.6–10.5 cm), yellow-orange, lobes yellow, style deep yellow, trifid and widening, fimbriate at tips
C. goulimyi **Comments:** Fall. 'Albus': pure white.	S Greece	3–8 in (8–20 cm), throat hairy, white, lobes ⅝–1½ in (1.5–4 cm), rounded, lilac-pale mauve, inner whorl paler than outer; style trifid, white deepening to orange
C. hadriaticus *C. peloponnesiacus* **Comments:** Fall.	W & S Greece	tube 1¼–3½ in (3–9 cm), white, yellow, maroon or mauve, throat hairy, yellow, sometimes white, lobes ¾–1¾ in (2–4.5 cm), elliptic, white suffused yellow, buff or lavender at base, occasionally tinted lilac throughout; style trifid, orange

C. cvijicii

C. dalmaticus

C. etruscus 'Zwanenburg'

C. gargaricus ssp. *herbertii*

CROCUS

Name	Distribution	Flowers
C. imperati *C. neapolitanus*	W Italy, Capri	tube 1¼–4 in (3–10 cm), white, occasionally expanding yellow or mauve, throat deep yellow, lobes 1¼–1¾ in (3–4.5 cm), bright purple within, exterior tawny with to 5, feathered violet stripes; style orange to coral red, trifid
Comments: Late winter–early spring. 'De Jager': lilac inside, with buff and purple stripes on the exterior. ssp. **suaveolens**: flowers smaller, each outer lobe marked with 3 purple stripes.		
C. korolkowii	Afghanistan, N Pakistan, Russia	scented, tube 1¼–4 in (3–10 cm), golden, sometimes marked bronze or maroon, throat yellow to metallic buff, lobes to 1¼ in (3 cm), elliptic, golden yellow, outer lobes marked dark brown or maroon below; style trifid, orange, tips widened, papillose
Comments: Late winter–early spring.		
C. kotschyanus *C. zonatus*	C & S Turkey, NW Syria, C & N Lebanon	scented, tube to 5 in (13 cm), white, throat hairy, white tinted yellow with 2 golden splashes at base of each lobe, sometimes fusing, lobes 1¼–1¾ in (3–4.5 cm), pale lavender with darker, parallel veins running almost to apex; style trifid, ivory to pale yellow, tips expanded and subdivided
Comments: Fall. var. **leucopharynx**: blue-lavender, veined blue, with central white zone, yellow markings absent; style pale cream. ssp. **suworowianus**: unscented, throat glabrous with pale yellow markings, lobes held nearly erect, cream with mauve veins, tone suffusing where veins converge.		
C. laevigatus *C. fontenayi*	Greece, Crete	fragrant, tube ¾–3 in (2–8 cm), white tinted yellow or mauve toward throat, throat yellow, lobes ½–1¼ in (1–3 cm), obovate to elliptic, white or pale rose-lilac above, outer lobes white, mauve, bronze or yellow, with up to 3 broad dark purple or maroon feathered lines below, markings sometimes absent or exterior wholly purple; style multifid, orange
Comments: Fall–early spring.		
C. longiflorus *C. odorus*	SW Italy, Sicily, Malta	scented, tube 2–4 in (5–10 cm), pale yellow, striped violet; throat yellow, glabrous or thinly hairy lobes ¾–1¾ in (2–4.5 cm), lilac, exterior with darker veins, sometimes shaded bronze; style trifid, vermilion, tips widened, crenate, sometimes subdivided
Comments: Fall.		
C. malyi	W former Yugoslavia	tube 1½–3½ in (4–9 cm), white, occasionally flushed yellow, bronze or mauve, throat hairy, yellow, lobes ¾–1½ in (2–4 cm), white, often with gray-blue or bronze stain at base; style trifid, orange, tips widening, notched
Comments: Spring.		
C. medius	NW Italy, SE France	tube 3–8 in (8–20 cm), white to mauve at apex, throat white veined violet, lobes 1–2 in (2.5–5 cm), obovate, pale blue-mauve, veined darker at base; style multifid, vermilion, branches notched and recurving
Comments: Fall.		
C. minimus *C. insularis*	Sardinia, Corsica, Isles Sanguinaires	tube 1½–4½ in (4–11 cm), white flushed mauve at apex, throat white sometimes tinted pale yellow; lobes ¾–1¼ in (2–3 cm), oblanceolate, light rosy mauve to deep purple, the undersides of the outer tepals striped, veined or shaded darker purple to brown on a bronze background; style trifid, orange, tips, flattened, crenate-lobed
Comments: Late winter–early spring.		

C. kotschyanus   *C. longiflorus*   *C. malyi*   *C. medius*

CROCUS

Name	Distribution	Flowers
C. niveus	S Greece	tube 3¹/₂–7 in (9–18 cm), ivory to dull yellow, throat golden, hairy, lobes 1¹/₄–2¹/₂ in (3–6 cm), obovate, white, sometimes stained lilac; style trifid, scarlet, tips flattened,
C. nudiflorus *C. multifidus; C. aphyllus; C. fimbriatus; C. pyrenaeus*	SW France, N & E Spain **Comments:** Fall.	tube 4–9 in (10–22 cm), white flushed mauve toward apex, throat white-mauve, lobes 1¹/₄–2¹/₂ in (3–6 cm), pale mauve to amethyst; style multifid, orange
C. ochroleucus **Comments:** Fall–winter.		tube 2–3 in (5–8 cm), white, throat hairy, pale yellow-golden, spreading to base of lobes, lobes ³/₄–1¹/₄ in (2–3 cm), elliptic, ivory; style trifid, golden yellow
C. olivieri **Comments:** Late winter–spring. ssp. **balansae**: flowers striped or stained brown-bronze or maroon below.	Balkans, Turkey	tube 2–2³/₄ in (5–7 cm), yellow or maroon, throat yellow; lobes ⁵/₈–1¹/₂ in (1.5–3.5 cm), yellow-orange, or striped bronze-maroon below and on tube; style divided × 6, pale orange
C. pulchellus **Comments:** Fall–early winter. Turkey. 'Zephyr': flowers very large, pale, pearly blue.		differs from *C. speciosus* in its golden yellow throat, gracefully incurving, opal-blue lobes with lilac veins
C. sativus *C. officinalis* SAFFRON CROCUS	widespread through cultivation	ancient sterile cultigen derived from *C. cartwrightianus*, from which it differs chiefly in perianth lobes to 2 in (5 cm), and style branches to 1¹/₄ in (3 cm)
C. serotinus **Comments:** Fall to winter. ssp. **salzmannii** has lilac-blue flowers to 4 in (10 cm) long, sometimes with yellow throats.	Portugal, Spain, Gibraltar, N Africa	scented, tube ³/₄–2 in (2–5 cm), white to mauve; throat hairy, white or ivory; lobes 1–1¹/₂ in (2.5–4 cm), obtuse, pale mauve to lilac blue, sometimes veined purple; style multifid, burned orange
C. sieberi	Greece, Crete	scented, tube 1–2 in (2.5–5 cm), white or mauve, usually deep yellow toward throat; throat glabrous, golden yellow or orange; lobes ³/₄–1¹/₄ in (2–3 cm), obtuse, white within, tinted purple, exterior of outer whorl striped, barred or suffused mauve; style trifid, yellow-orange, branches short, the tips divided or ruffled

Comments: Spring–early summer. 'Albus': pure white with an orange throat; stigma scarlet. 'Firefly': outer tepals nearly white, inner violet, base yellow. 'Hubert Edelsten': deep purple, blotched white at tip. 'Violet Queen': rounded, violet-blue. ssp. **atticus**: pale lilac to violet with an orange style. ssp. **nivalis**: lilac, throat yellow. ssp. **sublimis**: throat yellow, tepals blue-mauve, darker at tips, sometimes white at base. ssp. **sublimis** 'Tricolor': flowers with 3 distinct bands of color: lilac, pure white and golden yellow.

C. speciosus **Comments:** Fall. 'Aitchisonii': large, pale lilac with feather venation; 'Albus': white; 'Artabir': pale lilac with strong venation; 'Cassiope': large, pale violet with yellow throat; 'Oxonian': indigo.	Russia, Iran, Turkey	scented, tube 2–8 in (5–20 cm), white or pale mauve; throat glabrous, off-white, rarely, tinted yellow, lobes 1¹/₄–2¹/₂ in (3–6 cm), mauve-blue above, exterior veined or spattered purple, sometimes on a paler, opal ground; style multifid, orange

C. minimus

C. ochroleucus

C. sieberi 'Hubert Edelsten'

C. vernus 'Purpureus Grandiflorus'

CROCUS

Name	Distribution	Flowers
C. tommasinianus	Balkans, Hungary, Bulgaria	tube 1½–4 in (3.5–10 cm), white, throat white, thinly hairy, lobes ¾–1¾ in (2–4.5 cm), pale mauve to violet, occasionally white or rose, darker at apex, sometimes with silver or bronze hue below; style trifid, orange, flattened and fimbriate at tips

Comments: Late winter. 'Barr's Purple': outer lobes tinged gray, inner lobes rich purple-lilac. var. *pictus*: outer lobes marked mauve or purple at apex. var. *roseus*: pink-purple. 'Ruby Giant': probably a hybrid with *C. vernus*; dark red-purple, especially in upper part and base of lobes. 'Whitewell Purple': exterior purple-mauve, interior silver-mauve.

Name	Distribution	Flowers
C. tournefortii *C. orphanidis*	S Greece, Crete, Cyclades	sometimes scented, tube 1¼–4 in (3–10 cm), white, rarely suffused purple, throat glabrous or downy, yellow to ivory, lobes ⅝–1½ in (1.5–3.5 cm), pale lilac, often veined darker at base of lobes, rarely white throughout; style multifid, orange-crimson

Comments: Fall–winter.

Name	Distribution	Flowers
C. vernus DUTCH CROCUS	Italy, Austria, E Europe	tube 2–6 in (5–15 cm), mauve or white, throat white, often suffused mauve, lobes 1¼–2¼ in (3–5.5 cm), white, violet or blue-mauve, sometimes striped white or violet, usually with a darker, v-shaped marking near tips; style trifid, yellow-orange, widened and fimbriate at tips

Comments: Spring–early summer. 'Early Perfection': violet-purple to blue with dark edges. 'Enchantress': light amethyst with silvery floss, dark base. 'Pickwick': white with deep lilac stripes, base deep purple. 'Remembrance': large, rounded, silver-purple, base flushed purple. 'Vanguard': light blue, exterior gray; blooms more than 2 weeks in advance of other cultivars. 'Glory of Limmen': very large, rounded, white with short purple stripes at base. 'Haarlem Gem': small, silvery-lilac externally, pale lilac-mauve within. 'Jeanne d'Arc': large, white, with 3 thin purple stripes, tinged violet at base. 'Kathleen Parlow': large, white, base and tube purple. 'Little Dorrit': very large, rounded, pale silver-lilac. 'Paulus Potter': large, glossy red-purple. 'Purpureus Grandiflorus': large, deep glossy rich purple. 'Queen of the Blues': flowers large, lavender-blue. 'Striped Beauty': pale silver-gray, striped deep mauve, base violet-purple. ssp. **albiflorus**: usually white, sometimes marked purple.

Name	Distribution	Flowers
C. versicolor	S France to W Italy, Morocco	tube 2½–4 in (6–10 cm), white or purple-striped, throat lemon yellow or ivory, lobes 1–1½ in (2.5–3.5 cm), white-mauve, exterior usually with darker stripes, sometimes with bronze-yellow hue; style trifid, pale orange, tips widened, indented

Comments: Late winter–spring. 'Picturatus': flowers white on the exterior, feathered violet.

crome, cromb a dragfork. See *fork*.

crop rotation see *rotation*.

cross a naturally occurring or induced hybrid between two plants.

cross-fertilization fertilization resulting from cross-pollination; cf. *self-fertilization*.

cross-pollination the transfer of pollen from one flower to another flower on a different plant; often used to imply cross-fertilization; cf. *self-pollination*.

Crossandra (from Greek *krossoi*, fringe, and *aner*, male, referring to the fringed stamens). Acanthaceae. Africa, Madagascar,

Indian subcontinent. 50 species, tender evergreen shrubs and subshrubs with 5-lobed, narrowly tubular flowers in terminal spikes clothed in green, overlapping bracts. Cultivate as for *Aphelandra*.

C. infundibuliformis FIRECRACKER FLOWER; S India, Sri Lanka; to 3¼ ft (1 m) tall; flowers to 1½ in (3.5 cm) across, bright orange to salmon pink with fan-shaped lobes, in spikes to 4 in (10 cm) long; *C. nilotica* tropical Africa; to 20 in (50 cm); flowers to 1 in (2.5 cm) across, brick-red to orange or apricot with obovate lobes, in spikes to 2¾ in (7 cm) long.

Crotalaria (from Greek *krotalon*, rattle: the seeds rattle in the dried pods). Leguminosae. Widespread in tropics and subtropics. RATTLEBOX. 600 species, herbs

bee carries pollen from plant to plant

Cross-pollination

or shrubs with simple to trifoliolate leaves and pealike flowers. The following species will survive mild frosts if thickly mulched in winter. Grow in full sun in free-draining, fertile soil. Cut back stems after flowering. Increase by semiripe cuttings in summer, or by seed in spring. *C. agatiflora* CANARY BUSH; E Africa; shrub to 20 ft (6 m); leaves trifoliolate, gray-green; flowers to 2¾ in (7 cm) across, pale lemon yellow tinted olive green, in erect terminal racemes to 16 in (40 cm) long.

crotch the junction of primary branches with the center stem or trunk of a tree.

crown (1) a corona; (2) a collective term for the main stem divisions and foliage of a tree or shrub and the branching pattern and overall habit that they assume (i.e. domed, spreading, narrowly conical); (3) the basal portions of a herbaceous plant, usually where root or rhizome and aerial stems or resting buds meet; (4) a length of rhizome with a strong terminal bud, used for propagation as, for example, with *Convallaria*; (5) the head of a single-stemmed treelike plant or shrub bearing a distinct apical whorl, rosette or flush of foliage; (6) the leaves and terminal buds of a low-growing plant when arranged in a fashion resembling that of the larger plants mentioned under (5), for example, many ferns.

crown bud a flower bud at a shoot tip, surrounded by other usually smaller buds. It is of special importance in the training of carnations and chrysanthemums.

crown gall (*Agrobacterium tumefaciens*) a widespread bacterial disease. It is an important problem in woody plant nurseries, especially in warm climates, but is not of major importance in temperate gardens. Tumorlike galls are usually found at ground level or on roots, and occasionally on stems well above ground, as soft, white, rounded swellings with uneven surfaces that become brown with age; they vary in size from that of a pea to a huge ball. On woody plants, the galls become hard and persist; on herbaceous plants, they are soft and disintegrate.

Crown gall affects monocot and dicot woody and herbaceous plants. Common hosts among fruits and nuts are apple, particularly the rootstocks M9 and M2, almond, apricot, blackberry, cherry, fig, grape, gooseberry, loganberry and other *Rubus* fruit, nectarine, pecan, plum, peach, pear, raspberry and walnut. Other hosts include *Begonia*, chrysanthemums, *Dahlia*, *Daphne*, elm, *Euonymus*, *Gladiolus*, hollyhock, honeysuckle, hawthorn, *Libocedrus*, juniper, lupine, marigold, marrow, *Phlox*, poplar, privet, *Rhododendron*, rhubarb, rose, runner bean, rutabaga, sweet pea, tomato, wallflower and willow. Several strains affect only certain host plants.

Crown gall is soilborne and capable of living saprophytically in soil for long periods. A wound parasite, it can only enter injured roots and stems. On entry, it stimulates the cells of the host plant to grow and multiply abnormally. While infection takes place during rapid growth, galls develop within days or weeks, depending on the host plant. When a perennial plant is infected late in the growing season, the bacterium may not produce galls until the following spring. Secondary galls remote from the original gall are sometimes formed as chains along roots or on stems. Aerial galls are most frequently found on roses, *Daphne* species and raspberry and blackberry canes. The bacterium is more likely to persist and spread in wet soil.

Preventive measures include the provision of good drainage; the inspection of new stocks to avoid infecting the soil; a long rotation plan of nonsusceptible crops on affected sites; and avoidance of injury to roots. Where shrubs and fruit show aerial galls, the affected parts should be cut out.

crown lifting the removal of the lower branches of, usually, ornamental trees, carried out mainly to admit light or prevent obstruction of passage or a view.

crown rot refers to an infection at soil level girdling and killing the host.

crown shaft a characteristic of some palms in which the overlapping leaf bases form a tight cylindrical or vase-shaped shaft distinct from the (usually) bare stem below.

crown thinning the selective removal of tree branches to reduce crowding and admit more light and air into the crown.

cruciate, cruciform cross-shaped.

crumb a small rounded, porous aggregate of soil particles found in top soil where the level of organic matter is high. Also generally called a ped.

Cryptanthus (from Greek *kryptos*, hidden, and *anthos*, flower). Bromeliaceae. Brazil. EARTH STAR, STARFISH PLANT. 20 species, tender, evergreen perennial herbs, stemless with narrowly triangular to lanceolate, tough and finely saw-edged leaves in a low-lying rosette. Small, white flowers appear at the rosette's center. Grow in small containers in a coir and bark mix with added sand and polystyrene granules; provide a minimum temperature of 55°F (13°C) and bright, indirect light or dappled sun. Water freely in summer, avoiding foliage; keep barely moist in winter. Propagate by removal of rooted offsets after flowering. Small and colorful, these bromeliads make resilient house plants and are commonly used in mixed container plantings, bottle gardens and Wardian cases.

C. acaulis GREEN EARTH STAR, STARFISH PLANT; leaves to 4 in (10 cm), undulate, in a small, low, flat rosette, typically gray-green, but cream-striped to red-flushed or bronze in some cultivars and hybrids; *C. bivittatus* leaves to 10 in (25 cm), in a dense, low, spreading rosette, dark green with 2 broad, longitudinal, white or pink bands above; red-flushed and banded red in var. *atropurpureus*; *C. bromelioides* RAINBOW STAR; stoloniferous with stalked rosettes; leaves 4–8 in (10–20 cm), lanceolate, base narrowed, olive green or variously striped white, cream, pale green and rose; *C. zonatus* ZEBRA PLANT; leaves to 8 in (20 cm) in a spreading rosette, undulate, dark olive to chocolate, irregularly banded silver-gray to cream or white; chocolate banded silver in the more robust and erect 'Zebrinus'.

× **Cryptbergia** Bromeliaceae. Garden origin. Hybrids between *Cryptanthus* and *Billbergia* with linear-lanceolate, sharply pointed leaves to 12 in (30 cm) long in freely suckering, narrow, funnel-shaped rosettes; the small, white flowers are rarely produced. Cultivate as for *Billbergia*. × *C. meadii* (*Cryptanthus beuckeri* × *Billbergia nutans*; leaves mottled pink; × *C. rubra* (*Cryptanthus bahianus* × *Billbergia nutans*; leaves dark bronze-red to brilliant blood red).

cryptogams flowerless and seedless plants that nonetheless increase by means of sexual fusion, producing spores. (i.e. neither angiosperms nor gymnosperms, but pteridophytes, bryophytes.)

Cryptogramma (from Greek *kryptos*, hidden, and *gramme*, a line, referring to the lines of sori concealed before maturity). Cryptogrammataceae. Widespread in temperate and subtropical regions. ROCK BRAKE, PARS-LEY FERN. 4 species, dwarf, deciduous ferns with dense tufts of deeply and much-divided fronds that are said to resemble parsley. The following species are fully hardy and suitable for the rock garden, scree, wall crevices and small pans in an alpine house. Grow in an acidic, gritty mix in full sun. Keep moist until established. Increase by division.

C. acrostichoides AMERICAN ROCK-BRAKE; N America; fronds to 4¾ in (12 cm), stipes green, blades bright green, 2–3-pinnate with crowded, ovate to oblong, crenate pinnules; *C. crispa* EUROPEAN or MOUNTAIN PARSLEY FERN; fronds to 8 in (20 cm), stipes straw yellow to pale green, blades bright pale green, 2-pinnate with cuneate to elliptic, dentate pinnules, thick-textured.

Cryptomeria (from Greek *kryptos*, hidden, and *meris*, a part, referring to the hidden floral parts). Cupressaceae. Japan, China. JAPANESE CEDAR, SUGI. 1 species, *C. japonica*, a hardy, ever-green, coniferous tree to 200 ft (60 m) tall with a conical crown and a thick bole covered in fibrous, peeling, red-brown bark. The leaves are soft, awl-shaped and some ½–⅝ in (1–1.5 cm) long, turning from sea green to deep, glossy green, sometimes purple-bronze or rust in cold weather. They clothe crowded, drooping branchlets on tiered boughs. Many cultivars are available including dwarf, rounded, conical, pen-dulous and contorted types and forms with cristate, filamentous, persistently juvenile, variegated, purple-flushed and sea green growth. *C. japonica* is hardy to –10°F (–23°C). Plant in full sun with shelter from harsh, drying winds. Deep, moisture-retentive and acidic to neutral soil is preferred, as is a mild and humid climate. Propagate as for *Chamaecyparis*.

cryptophyte a plant whose growth buds are located below the soil surface; cf. *chamaephyte*.

Cryptotaenia (from Greek, *cryptos*, hidden, and *tainia*, a fillet or band). Umbelliferae. Temperate Regions. 4 species, perennial herbs with short clumped stems bearing lobed leaves, and forked sprays of small flowers in summer. Hardy to –10°F (–23°C), *C.*

japonica f. *atropurpurea* is likely to become one of the most desirable, purple-leaved foliage plants. It prefers moist, rich soil, and will grow well either in full sun or part shade. Increase by divi-sion in early spring. *C. japonica* (E. Asia; to 20 in (50 cm); leaves to 4¾ in (12 cm) diam., smooth, divided into 3 broad, shallowly toothed lobes; flowers pink; *C. japonica* f. *atropurpurea*: foliage maroon to chocolate brown.

Ctenanthe (from Greek *kteis*, comb and *anthos*, flower, referring to the arrangement of the bracts). Maran-taceae. Costa Rica, Brazil. 15 species, tender, evergreen perennial herbs, clump-forming with long-stalked, oblong to lanceolate leaves, often beautifully marked and colored, and small, white and purple flowers in racemose cymes. Cultivate as for *Calathea*.

C. lubbersiana Brazil; to 16 in (40 cm); leaves to 7 in (18 cm), deep green with yellow-green variegation above, pale green beneath); *C. oppen-heimiana* Brazil; to 3¼ ft (1 m); leaves to 16 in (40 cm), green with silvery-gray feathering above, wine-red to purple beneath; includes 'Tricolor', NEVER-NEVER PLANT, with leaves blotched cream.

cubiform dice-shaped, cubic.

cuckoo spit the frothy mass sur-rounding the larvae of *froghoppers* (q.v.) or spittlebugs.

cucullate furnished with or shaped like a hood.

cucumber (*Cucumis sativus*) a frost-sus-ceptible annual, native of Sino-Himalaya, with a vigorous trailing habit; it is grown as a salad vegetable for the immature, edible fruits. Grown in the open in tropical and subtropical areas; in temperate areas selections giving the best quality and yield require protection for all of the life cycle.

In frost-prone zones, sow singly in pots under protection at 68°F (20°C), reducing to 61°F (15°C) on germina-tion. Transplant into well-manured beds, growing bags or 9–10 in (22–25 cm) pots, spaced 24 in (60 cm) apart; maintain a temperature of 68°F

(20°C), with high humidity, and support with canes. Train the main shoot vertically and stop at 4¼ ft (1.3 m). All-female cultivars bear fruits on the main stem, so remove laterals; other cultivars require hori-zontal wire supports, and laterals are stopped two leaves beyond a female flower.

RIDGE CUCUMBERS are hardier and can be transplanted outdoors in early summer. Space 24 in (60 cm) apart each way on ridged beds and stop at 6–7 leaves; where trained up trellis or netting, space 18 in (45 cm) apart and stop when at top of support.

Possible problems: aphids, red spider mite, whiteflies; virus, downy mildew, gray mold, gummosis, wilt.

culm the stems of Gramineae.

cultigen a plant found only in cul-tivation or in the wild having escaped from cultivation. Cultigens include many hybrids and cultivars, some exotic ornamentals whose wild origins have become lost or were never recorded, and several ancient and important crops that have undergone development and distrib-ution at man's hands for so long that, although they may have 'wild' distributions, details of their original forms and native places are lost or confused.

cultivar (abbreviation cv.) a 'culti-vated variety'; a distinctive plant or plants arising and/or maintained in cultivation. This can happen either as a result of hybridization, or through some type of mutation, or within the natural variation of a species. When reproduced (whether by sexual or asexual means accord-ing to the particular type of plant and cultivar), such plants retain their distinguishing characteristics. A cultivar is named with a cultivar (or fancy) epithet, a word or words in a vernacular language (unless published prior to 1959), or a botanical (Latin) epithet already established for a taxon, like a variety or forma that has since been judged to be a cultivar). The epithet is printed in roman characters, takes a capital first letter and is either enclosed in single quotation marks or prefixed by the abbreviation cv. Many of the most popular garden plants are cultivars. These include plants selected for their foliage (often named 'Argentea', 'Aurea', 'Dissecta', 'Variegata' and so forth), and for their flowers ('Alba', 'Florepleno', etc.). Examples of cultivars with more recent, vernacular names include *Mahonia* 'Charity' and *Rosa* 'Peace'.

Three-pronged cultivator
This is an ideal tool for first cultivation after digging. Versions are available with more tines for better effectiveness.

cultivator an implement for cultivating soil. The term is applied in particular to machines powered with electricity or gasoline and having rotating blades or tines, but is also used for various hand tools, especially those with recurved prongs, and also sometimes for those with blades fixed behind a wheel.

cultrate, cultriform knife-shaped, resembling the blade of a knife.

cultural controls the suppression of plant pests and diseases through good husbandry methods. These include careful management of the soil; the production of healthy well-grown plants; the use of resistant cultivars, for example root-aphid resistant lettuces; general hygiene, including careful disposal of infected debris; the use of healthy seed and planting stock; frequent inspection and roguing; rigorous elimination of weeds; crop rotation which is especially useful in deterring eelworms; cultivation of the soil to expose soil pests such as leather-jackets and wireworms to predation by birds; and manipulation of sowing or planting dates of vegetable crops to avoid

times when adult pests (e.g. the carrot fly) are egg-laying, cf. *pesticides*. See *biological controls*.

Cuminum (from the Greek name for this plant, *kyminon*). Umbelliferae. Mediterranean to C Asia. 2 species, annual herbs with fine, biternately divided foliage and small white to pink flowers in compound umbels. *C. cyminum* is grown for its aromatic seeds, harvested when dry and ground to make the spice cumin, which is a key ingredient in the cuisine of the Middle East and Indian subcontinent. Cultivate as for *dill* (q.v.).

cuneate, cuneiform inversely triangular, wedge-shaped.

Cunninghamia (for James Cunningham, who collected *C. lanceolata* in China about 1701). Taxodiaceae. China, Taiwan. 2 species, hardy, coniferous evergreen trees to 160 ft (50 m) tall. The crown is conical, the bark red-brown, fibrous and deeply fissured and the branches whorled. Narrowly ovate to lanceolate, sharp-pointed, glossy and pliable, the leaves are arranged in two ranks along drooping, 2-ranked branches. Hardy to −13°F (−25°C), although shelter from harsh winds and a mild, humid climate are preferred. Plant in rich, moist and acidic to neutral soil in sun or part shade. Propagate as for *Chamaecyparis*. *C. lanceolata* (syn. *C. sinensis*); CHINA FIR; C China; leaves 1¼–2¾ in (3–7 cm) long, lanceolate, lustrous bright green above with 2 broad, white bands beneath.

cup the corona of *Narcissus*, where it is shorter than the perianth segments. A large cup is more than one third of the length of the perianth segments, a small cup less than one third their length. See *trumpet*.

Cuphea (from Greek *kyphos*, curved, referring to the curved capsule. Lythraceae. SE US to Brazil. 260 species, small, bushy, tender annual or short-lived, evergreen perennial herbs and subshrubs with neat foliage and brightly colored tubular flowers in summer. The following species need a minimum temperature of 45°F (7°C), full sun and a fertile, free-draining

medium that is moist in spring and summer and only barely so in winter. *C. ignea* is often grown as a half-hardy annual, raised from cuttings taken in late summer and overwintered under glass or as house plants. Pinch new plants to promote bushiness and set out in a warm, sunny position in late spring. Increase all by greenwood cuttings in spring or summer.

C. cyanea Mexico; glandular-hairy subshrub to 6½ ft (2 m); flowers to 1 in (2.5 cm), orange-red with yellow-green apex bearing purple-black petals; *C. hyssopifolia* ELFIN HERB, FALSE HEATHER, HAWAIIAN HEATHER; Mexico, Guatemala; downy subshrub to 24 in (60 cm); flowers to ½ in (1 cm), silky, pale lilac veined lavender, or pink, or white; *C. ignea* CIGAR FLOWER, FIRE-CRACKER PLANT; Mexico, Jamaica; more or less glabrous shrublet to 24 in (60 cm); flowers to 1¼ in (3 cm), scarlet, apex black edged white; includes 'Variegata', with leaves flecked lime and gold.

× **Cupressocyparis** Cupressaceae. Garden hybrids between Cupressus and Chamaecyparis, fast-growing, coniferous evergreen trees with dense, pinnate or plumose sprays of growth covered in small, overlapping, scalelike leaves. The intergeneric hybrid × *C. leylandii* is fully hardy and, with provisos, it is a good choice for a rapidly establishing, attractive hedge in large gardens. Its thick, heavy top growth makes it an effective windbreak tree on moderately exposed sites if care is taken to ensure strong root growth from planting time. To produce a secure boundary and appealing garden feature plants in hedge lines must be clipped tightly several times each season and the top growth restricted to a manageable height. Forethought must be given to the particular capacity of × *C. leylandii* plants to deplete surrounding soil of moisture and nutrients on account of exceptional vigor; similarly, to the potential for disputes with neighboring properties where inability to manage hedges or specimen trees continuously into the future may result in over growth or the obstruction of sunlight. Increase by cuttings. *C. × leylandii* (*Cupressus macrocarpa × Chamaecyparis nootkatensis*); LEYLAND CYPRESS; a vigorous, fast-growing tree to 120 ft (35 m) or more with a dense, columnar to pyramidal crown, smooth to fissured green-brown bark and pendent branchlets; the leaves are dark green tinged gray and carried in flat sprays; cultivars include: 'Castlewellan Gold', slower-growing with plumose sprays of yellow-green leaves, tinted bronze in winter; 'Harlequin', with gray-green leaves in plumose sprays broken with patches and flashes of white to ivory; the fast-growing, dense and narrowly columnar 'Leighton Green'; and the compact and conical 'Robinson's Gold', which has lime green to golden foliage with bronze tints during winter and early spring.

cupressoid with *Cupressus*-like foliage, i.e. narrow branchlets clothed with scalelike leaves, for example *Hebe armstrongii*, *Tamarix*.

Cupressus (from Greek *kuparissos*, a word taken from an unknown near Eastern language, allied to the Hebrew *gopher*, the name of *C. sempervirens*). Cupressaceae. N and C America, N Africa to China. CYPRESS. 20 species, evergreen, coniferous trees with peeling or flaking bark, sprays of aromatic growth covered in overlapping, scale-like leaves, and spherical cones composed of resinous, peltate scales. Most species are from mountains, some are from in or around desert. All are good for low rainfall areas on hot sites except *C. torulosa*, which prefers cooler, wetter areas. *C. arizonica* var. *glabra* thrives in any soil, from chalk to highly acidic sand; *C. macrocarpa* and *C. sempervirens* are less happy on chalk but thrive on limestones; others prefer soil at pH6 or below. All but *C. arizonica* var. *glabra* have been killed by temperatures of −13°F (−25°C) or below, and *C. lusitanica* by −4°F (−20°C). Winds of 14°F (−10°C) will scorch most species. *C. torulosa* 'Cashmeriana' is not hardy and should be grown in a cool greenhouse or conservatory where temperture drop below 10°F (−12°C). For propagation and pests, see *Chamaecyparis*.

C. arizonica SMOOTH CYPRESS, ARIZONA CYPRESS; Arizona to Texas and N Mexico; to 80 ft (25 m), crown broadly ovoid-conic; shoots dense, branching angular, leaves very finely serrate;

includes var. *glabra* (syn. *C. glabra*) with smooth, purple to red bark exfoliating in papery layers and bright blue-green leaves with white resin glands—dwarf, globose, fastigiate, blue-, silver- and gold-leaved cultivars are available, one of the best is 'Blue Ice', narrow and erect with cool, blue-gray foliage; *C. cashmeriana*; KASHMIR CYPRESS; Bhutan; to 130 ft (40 m) tall, crown broadly pyra-midal with an open, tiered habit, rusty red bark exfoli-ating in strips, and long, weep-ing feathery branchlets of a vivid blue-gray; *C. lusitanica* CEDAR OF GOA, MEXICAN CYPRESS, PORTUGUESE CYPRESS; to 150 ft (45 m), crown coni-cal, bark brown, furrowed, exfoliating in strips; leaves aromatic, dark to blue-green, spirally arranged; includes culti-vars with whiplike and pendulous branchlets and gray and variegated foliage; *C. macrocarpa* MONTEREY CYPRESS; California; to 150 ft (45 m), bark purple-brown or gray, thick, ridged; crown columnar to conical becoming flat-topped with age with tiered branches; leaves slightly fleshy, bright green to yellow-green with paler margins; includes dwarf, globose, narrowly columnar, prostrate and golden cultivars; *C. sempervirens* ITALIAN CYPRESS, MEDITERRANEAN CYPRESS; Crete, Rhodes, Turkey to Iran, naturalized elsewhere in Mediter-ranean; to 130 ft (40 m), bark gray-brown, shallowly ridged, scaly; crown narrowly conical with dense more or less ascending branchlets; leaves dark green, aromatic; dwarf, open and tiered and very tightly columnar culti-vars are grown, as are golden and steely blue-gray forms; *C. torulosa* KASHMIR CYPRESS; Himalaya; to 130 ft (40 m), bark brown, furrowed, curled, peeling in long ribbons; crown conical; branches horizontal, branch-lets whiplike and more or less pendu-lous, young shoots maroon; leaves pale yellow-green, incurved; includes cultivars with congested foliage, leaves turning brown in winter, and open, bushy habit.

loosely scaled cup or cupule

Quercus alnifolia

cupule a cup-shaped involucre of hardened, coherent bracts, subtending a fruit or group of fruits, as in the acorn. See *cyathium*.

Curcuma (from Arabic *kurkum*, yellow: *C. longa* is turmeric). Zingiberaceae. Tropical Asia. 40 species, tender perennial herbs, ever-green or deciduous with reedlike stems clothed with lanceolate to oblong leaves; these arise from a thick and aromatic rhizome and clumped, swollen roots. The small, thin flowers, textured with a conspicuous, tubular lip, protrude from colorful, overlapping bracts of a scapose or terminal, conelike inflorescence. Cultivate as for *Brachychilum*.

C. petiolata QUEEN LILY; Malaysia; to 24 in (60 cm) tall; inflorescence to 6 in (15 cm), terminal, bracts violet to magenta, flowers yellow and white; *C. roscoeana* HIDDEN LILY; Malaysia; to 36 in (90 cm) tall; inflorescence to 8 in (20 cm), terminal, bracts orange-red, flowers yellow.

curd the tight, unexpanded flowering head of cauliflowers and broccoli.

currants a collective name for BLACK CURRANT (*Ribes nigrum*), RED CURRANT (*Ribes rubrum* Red-currant Group), WHITE CURRANT (*Ribes rubrum* white currant Group), and PINK CURRANT (*Ribes rubrum* pink currant Group).

cushion the enlarged area of tissue above, beneath or on either side of an insertion or at the axis of two branches or a stem and a branch; also known as a pulvinus.

cushion plant a plant with a low, dense and rounded habit; for example many high alpines.

cuspidate refers to apices, ending in a sharp, inflexible point, or cusp.

cuticle the outermost, multilayered skin of waxy tissues covering the epi-dermis and containing cutin, fatty acids and cellulose.

cutin a polymer of fatty acids forming a major part of the cuticle.

cuttings the most widely used technique of vegetative propagation by which identical characteristics of plants are replicated. It involves selecting and detaching portions of root, stem, leaf or buds and inserting them in a growing medium, within a suitable environment, in order to induce the production of roots and eventually an independent plant. The ease of regenerating from cuttings varies widely and is influenced by genetic potential, stock plant conditioning through nutrition, hard pruning, manipulation of temperature and light, and time of taking.

Stem cuttings Successful rooting by this method depends on stage of shoot maturity, and stem cuttings may be considered as follows:

SOFTWOOD CUTTINGS are generally taken from spring into summer, selecting from the first flush of new growth and continuing until it becomes lignified, but cuttings may be available all the year round from greenhouse plants such a *Fittonia*, *Pilea*, chrysanthemums and *Fuchsia*. Cuttings should be prepared with a sharp knife and the cut made usually below a node. Nodal *or* internodal tip cuttings are perfectly satisfactory for easy-rooting plants, including shrubby subjects such as *Buddleja davidii*, *Forsythia* × *intermedia*, *Fuchsia* species and *Spiraea* × *bumalda*; leaf-bud stem sections are suitable for climbers such as *Lonicera* and *Vitis* species.

For plants that are more difficult to root, softwood heel cuttings may be obtained by using a light downward pressure to carefully pull the shoot from the parent plant so that it breaks away from the main stem with a basal plate or "heel" of tissue attached. Plants that benefit from this treatment include cultivars of *Cotinus coggygria*, *Acer palmatum*, deciduous azaleas and plants that produce bulky leafy growth or long vigorous internodal shoots, for example, cultivars of *Actinidia chinensis*, *Sambucus nigra*, *Jasminum officinalis* and climbing *Lonicera*.

The rooting medium should be sterile and open, as can be achieved with peat or coir and sand mixes. Whether mist, fog, a glass frame or a plastic film cover is used as the propagating system, the aim must be to minimize water and energy loss from the time of taking cuttings through to rooting. This can be achieved by ensuring adequate humidity and temperature around the tops of cuttings; a good air/water ratio at the rooting zone; the appropriate pH for the rooting media (a pH of 7 and over may encourage hard callus tissue, thus restricting root emergence; uniform basal heat, which may be between 59°F (15°C) and 77°F (25°C); and sufficient light. Rooting time varies

Tip cutting (Fuchsia)

lower leaves removed

with species and rooting environment. Root initials will develop on some chrysanthemums after four days, with root emergence taking between 7–10 days; for deciduous azaleas, emergence of significant roots may take up to 6 weeks.

GREENWOOD CUTTINGS are a transitional condition of stem cutting, between softwoods and semiripe or semihardwoods.

A 'firming up' of shoots or a change in stem and foliage coloration can be taken as an indication that shoots are of a suitable maturity, for example, stems of some cultivars of hybrid *Clematis* will change from a light green to a reddish-purple color, and the leaves will become deep green. A second category of greenwood cuttings may be found, for example, in *Acer palmatum* cultivars, where extension growth is usually produced in three distinct flushes, each punctuated by a short period of bud dormancy lasting 2–3 weeks.

Observation of these growth patterns is important for judging correctly the appropriate time for taking cuttings. The speed of root development from greenwood cuttings is slower than from softwoods, and problems sometimes occur in overwintering late-struck cuttings. The method is suitable where the softwood stage has been missed

Internodal cutting (Clematis montana)

single leaf node

SOFTWOOD CUTTINGS

leaves removed from leaf node

Stem tip cuttings
Using a sharp knife, cut straight across the stem just below a leaf node.

next cut can be made here

Leaf bud cuttings
A stem cut straight across just above each leaf node may provide several cuttings.

Heel cutting
A side shoot is carefully pulled, not cut, from the parent stem with a sliver of its bark.

"heel" exposes greater area of active cambium layer

lower leaves removed

and it may be more effective with some plants, for example, *Magnolia × soulangeana* and its cultivars.

SEMIRIPE CUTTINGS As the season's growth slows down and there is development of terminal and axillary buds, stems become firmer and may be described as being in a semiripe or semihardwood condition. This stage is important for the propagation of broad-leaved evergreens and conifers.

Semiripe cuttings can be used for easy-to-root deciduous plants, such as *Forsythia*, *Weigela* and *Berberis thunbergii* cultivars. Judge the timing of taking so as to achieve rooting well before the onset of winter, and if cold frames are used, winter covering should be provided. For the propagation of evergreens, systems under protection with basal heat are normally used, although cold frames or low plastic tunnels are suitable and desirable for some plants, including *Berberis × stenophylla*, *Lavandula spica* cultivars, *Salvia officinalis* cultivars and *Santolina chamaecyparissus*. Such plants are best propagated from late August to early October and root initiation should take place before December. *Ceanothus*, *Cistus*, *Elaeagnus* and *Pyracantha* will generally root best in August to October, followed by *Camellia*, *Ilex* and *Mahonia* in October to November. *Osmanthus*, *Phillyrea* and *Ulex* often root best after a cold spell, bringing the program to December and possibly into February.

The procedure for making these cuttings is similar to that used for softwood cuttings, but a variation is the mallet cutting, which is especially useful for woody plants with hollow or pithy stems, and for those producing very short sideshoots. Mallet cuttings are made by cutting a detached stem of the previous year's growth into sections each containing a vigorous side shoot, with a portion of the mother stem, about 1 in (2.5 cm) in length, retained as the base of the new cutting. Thick mallets are best slit lengthwise.

CONIFER CUTTINGS Most conifers are propagated by semiripe cuttings, although some species, including *Picea glauca* var. *albertiana* 'Conica' and the deciduous *Metasequoia glyptostroboides*, can be increased from softwood and greenwood cuttings. Selected forms of *Abies*, *Cedrus*, *Larix*, *Picea* and *Pinus* are

Ripening growth
A change in bark color from green to brown, plus increased resistance when a shoot is gently bent, indicates ripening.

difficult to root from stem cuttings and are normally raised by grafting. Semiripe propagation of evergreen conifers can be undertaken from August right through to March, commencing with Cupressus in August/September and *Chamaecyparis* and *Thuja* from September through to November. *Juniperus* and *Taxus* forms root best after a period of low temperature and propagation of these may be delayed until January. Selection of cutting material is important: three-dimensional terminal shoots should be selected that are neither weak nor taken from sublateral branches low down. Conifers with a normal upright habit can be made to produce horizontal growth where rooted from horizontal terminal cuttings, for example, *Sequoia sempervirens* 'Adpressa'.

Suitable cutting length varies according to the vigor of the plant. Cuttings of *Chamaecyparis pisifera* 'Boulevard' may be no longer than 2 in (5 cm), contrasting with those from *C. lawsoniana* 'Stewartii' at 6½ in (170 mm).

Effective propagation facilities range from enclosed environments with basal heat, such as intermittent mist, fog or plastic-covered frames, to basic cold frames out-of-doors.

WINTER HARDWOOD CUTTINGS This technique is generally reserved for deciduous woody plants, with cuttings taken during the dormant season when material is fully mature and may be cut into lengths using pruners, a guillotine or a power-driven bandsaw. In most cases, it is a cheap reproduction

method requiring modest facilities. Plants normally considered include *Clematis montana*, *Cornus alba*, *Deutzia scabra*, *Forsythia × intermedia*, *Kerria japonica*, *Ligustrum ovalifolium*, *Lonicera fragrantissima*, *Philadelphus* species, *Physocarpus opulifolius*, *Platanus × hispanica*, *Populus* species, *Ribes* species, *Salix* species, *Spiraea thunbergii*, *Stephanandra incisa*, *Symphoricarpos orbiculatus*, *Tamarix* species, *Viburnum × bodnantense* and *Weigela* species. To provide sufficient suitable cutting material in quantity, the establishment of stock plants as hedges or stools is appropriate, established preferably from an approved Clonal Selection Scheme to ensure trueness to type, health and vigor.

Taking hardwood cuttings at leaf fall will improve rooting, although with easy-rooting plants, such as willows and poplars, they may be taken any time during the dormant period. Hardwood cuttings may vary from a short stem 1½ in (3.5 cm) long with one bud at the apex (a vine eye cutting), to a branched stem 8 ft (2.5 m) long (e.g. willow "sets" planted direct into the final position). For the majority of species, lengths of 6–8 in (15–20 cm) are suitable. Cut the base horizontally and the top slanting away from the apex bud; it is not necessary to cut just below a node except with hollow- or pithy-stemmed plants such as *Forsythia* and *Sambucus*.

Some cuttings need to be modified to encourage a "leg" (e.g. red currants) or to discourage basal suckering (e.g. *Rosa rugosa* and *R. multiflora* selections for rootstocks; this is achieved by cutting out the lower buds on the stem, retaining just two or three at the top.

To improve rooting performance, hardwood cuttings may be subjected to basal stem wounding, dipping in rooting hormones, and pre-callusing techniques. Basal heat treatment between 64°F (18°C) and 68°F (20°) for no more than three months will speed up rooting in some subjects, such as *Malus* clonal rootstocks, *Tilia*, *Platanus*, *Ailanthus* and *Laburnum*.

The open ground is suitable for easily rooted hardwood cuttings and those pre-treated with basal heat. Plant vertically in well-defined rows, with the apical bud just showing above the surface. Cold frames are useful for rooting

C

ROOTED CUTTINGS

cut leaves reduce wilting

soft green stem

nodal area sends out fibrous roots

Softwood cuttings
The stem of the cutting usually ripens as the roots and fresh top-growth develop.

trimmed below node

new shoots from original leaf axils

Semiripe cuttings
With a firmer stem, woodier at the base, the cutting will be less prone to wilting.

slanting cut on upmost end

length of woody stem

roots slow to develop but substantial

Hardwood cuttings
The length of stem contains sufficient food reserves to enable sturdy root growth.

---

hardwood cuttings in exposed localities, with the bed prepared by blending equal parts of granulated pine bark and crushed washed grit; slow-release fertilizer may also be added. Greenhouse protection is a convenient additional facility but there may be difficulties in preventing shoot growth advancing too quickly before root development.

Rooting enhancement techniques WOUNDING the base of stem cuttings can enhance rooting, especially in semiripe and hardwood types.

SLICE WOUNDING is a speedy and effective method, where a sliver of wood ¾–2 in (2–5 cm) long is removed at the base of the cutting, just exposing the cambium. With conifers, stripping the lower foliage by hand so that a rough scar is left exposing the cambium can be effective.

SPLIT WOUNDING hardwood cuttings with a pair of pruners encourages well-distributed root formation. Cut through the center of the base of the cutting to leave a split 1¼–2 in (3–5 cm) long.

SLIT OR INCISION WOUNDING is suitable for cuttings prone to basal rots or those that are too thin or soft to make an effective slice wound. Normally, two or three slits are made by carefully drawing the point of a knife along the base of the stem for ¾–2 in (2–5 cm) to penetrate the cambium layer. Roots appear from new cambium formed along the slits.

SCRAPING the base of the stem for ¾–2 in (2–5 cm) with a knife

exposed cambium layer

Slice wounding

blade is sometimes advocated for cuttings that are thin-stemmed or have a thin epidermal layer, for example, *Ceanothus impressus*.

SYNTHETIC HORMONES Dip treatments increase the chances of successful rooting, promoting quicker root initiation and general improvement in quality and quantity of roots. The substances are often synthetic relatives of natural auxins. Most used are IBA (4-indole-3-butyric acid), which has stable qualities and wide effectiveness. NAA (2-(1-napthyl)acetic acid) is often blended with IBA, and certain plants, such as large-flowered hybrid rhododendrons, are considered more responsive to it. Fungicides are often incorporated, as is boron, which seems to further aid root development. The most appropriate concentration of powder preparations for softwood and easy-rooting greenwood cuttings is 0.1% IBA; for other greenwood and easy-rooting semiripe cuttings, 0.3% IBA is suitable; for difficult semiripe and hardwood cuttings, 0.8% IBA is recommended. Powders are applied to the base of the cutting to a depth of ½ in (1 cm). After use, the product should be re-sealed and stored in a refrigerator at between 37°F (3°C) and 41°F (5°C); contamination from plant debris, water, long exposure to air, light and warmth will accelerate the breakdown of the active ingredient. Liquid preparations are more effective than powders, but less widely available.

The concentrations used for a quick dip are 500–1,000 ppm for softwood cuttings; 1,000–2,500 ppm for greenwood, semiripe and easy-rooting hardwood cuttings; and 2,500 ppm–5,000 ppm for difficult semiripe and hardwood cuttings. The use of correct concentrations for dipping is important; too much rooting hormone will cause distortion, leaf drop and basal rots. An alternative, safer option is a long-soak method from two to 24 hours, using low concentrations ranging from 20 ppm for softwood cuttings to up to 250 ppm for more lignified material. Recommendations come with the product, which may be supplied in tablet form for dissolving.

Root cuttings Among the limited range of plants that have the capacity to be increased by this means are those that naturally produce adventitious shoots from the root zone, for example, *Aesculus parviflora, Acanthus mollis, Ailanthus altissima* and *Aralia elata*.

Most root cuttings need to be taken during late winter; healthy stock plants between three- and five-years-old provide the most suitable material. The roots should be washed free of soil and one-year-old roots of uniform size severed from the stock plant as close to the crown as possible.

Vigorous hardy plants producing long fleshy roots can be planted vertically, direct in the open ground. Cuttings should be 4–6 in (10–15 cm) long with a minimum diameter of ¼ in (5 mm), and regeneration may take up to 16 weeks. Where greenhouse or cold

C

frame protection is available, cuttings 2–2½ in (5–6 cm) long may be used and the regeneration period reduced to 8–10 weeks; if basal heat is available at 64°F (18°C), the cutting size can be reduced to 1–1¼ in (2.5–3 cm) long, and the regeneration period may be as short as 4–6 weeks.

Plants with roots that regenerate easily, for example *Geranium sanguineum* and *Primula denticulata*, can be placed horizontally in the planting situation and covered; difficult ones, such as *Koelreuteria paniculata* and *Romneya coulteri*, respond more favorably when planted vertically. Open ground beds are suitable for root cuttings of vigorously rooting plants that are capable of tolerating adverse weather, such as *Ailanthus altissima, Cochlearia armoracia* and *Rhus typhina*.

Cold frames provide a suitable protected environment for root cuttings taken from alpines (e.g. *Anchusa, Erodium, Geranium, Primula denticulata*); herbaceous perennials (e.g. *Acanthus, Eryngium, Limonium, Papaver, Phlox, Verbascum*); subshrubs (e.g. *Romneya*); shrubs (e.g. *Aesculus parviflora, Aralia chinensis, Chaenomeles speciosa, Clerodendrum trichotomum, Rhus glabra, R.typhina, Rubus biflorus, R.thibetanus*) and trees (e.g. *Ailanthus altissima, Catalpa bignonioides, C. bungei, C. ovata, Paulownia tomentosa, Populus alba, P. tremula*). The frame can consist of a raised bed covered with plastic film supported by hoops, or one constructed with fixed surrounds and

covered with glazed lights. A base dressing of a general fertilizer should be applied and the pH maintained at between 5.5–6.5. The prepared cuttings should be planted vertically in rows, with the tops just below the soil surface, or spaced horizontally in a shallow drill 2 in (50 mm) deep and covered with the frame soil and a ½ in (12 mm) layer of ¼ in (5 mm) washed nonalkaline crushed grit.

Alternatively, root cuttings may be planted in trays or pots, and placed in a cold frame. A rooting mixture of equal parts peat, ⅛ in (3 mm) washed nonalkaline crushed grit and sterilized loam is suitable, with the container filled to within ½ in (12 mm) of the rim. Cuttings planted vertically should be placed so that the top ends are flush with the surface of the mixture, while horizontally planted cuttings should be spaced over the surface. To help aeration, the container is topped off with a covering, such as ¼ in (5 mm) washed nonalkaline crushed grit.

Greenhouse facilities extend the attributes of a cold frame, especially where basal heat is available. In addition to the plants listed under cold-frame propagation, the following can be propagated in such an environment: climbing plants (e.g. *Bignonia capreolata, Campsis radicans, Eccremocarpus scabra, Passiflora caerulea*); trees and shrubs (e.g. *Albizia julibrissin, Daphne genkwa, Embothrium coccineum, Kalopanax pictus, Koelreuteria paniculata, Lagerstroemia indica,*

Paulownia tomentosa, Phellodendron amurense, Zanthoxylum piperitum). It is important to keep the air temperature in a greenhouse cool but above freezing, while the basal temperature should not exceed 64°F (18°C). Potting-up can usually be done during early summer, and with further protective growing-on facilities, substantial plants can be produced by the end of the growing season.

Using root cuttings as a source of stem cutting material is a technique that greatly enhances the rooting capabilities of plants such as *Albizia julibrissin* and *Populus* and *Alnus* species, when compared to conventional stem cuttings.

Leaf cuttings Some plants can be induced to regenerate from appropriately treated leaves, in particular species of the families Begoniaceae, Crassulaceae, Gesneriaceae and Melastomataceae. Leaves of *Paulownia tomentosa* will differentiate and produce buds and roots; and leaf rooting is possible with *Clematis, Cyclamen, Hedera, Jasminum* and *Mahonia*, although these will not develop into fully composite plants. A range of monocotyledonous plants will also regenerate from leaf cuttings, including *Endymion, Galanthus, Heloniopsis, Hyacinthus, Lachenalia, Leucojum* and *Sansevieria*.

The most suitable rooting environment is a closed case shaded from direct sunlight, with high humidity maintained and a basal heat between

ROOT CUTTINGS

1 Lift the plant (here an acanthus) when dormant and wash the soil from the roots. Select strong roots of medium thickness and sever them as close to the crown as possible.

cut a slanting sliver from base

2 With a sharp knife, cut each root into sections that are 2–4 in (5–10 cm) long. Make an additional diagonal cut at the "bottom" end of each section of root. Discard the thin root tips.

3 The slanting cuts at the base of the cuttings will serve as a reminder of which way up they should go in the pot—that is, oriented in the same way as when attached to the parent.

use a dibber to make deep holes

4 Make holes as deep as the cuttings in moist standard cuttings potting mix and insert them, diagonally cut end downward, so only the cut surface is exposed. Top-dress with grit.

C

64–68°F (18–20°C). Plants responsive to leaf propagation can usually be propagated at any time of the year. Leaves selected should be fully expanded and healthy, with no signs of aging. Succulent leaves are prone to rotting, so the propagation facilities, potting medium and leaves should be kept as clean as possible.

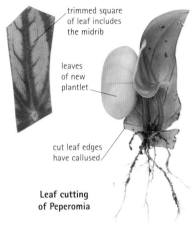

trimmed square of leaf includes the midrib

leaves of new plantlet

cut leaf edges have callused

Leaf cutting of Peperomia

LEAF-PETIOLE CUTTINGS This is a suitable technique for plants that produce small leaves, for example, *Begonia* 'Gloire de Lorraine', *Peperomia*, *Ramonda* and *Saintpaulia*. The leaf petiole should be trimmed to leave a stalk about 1½ in (4 cm) long; this is then inserted into a soft, open rooting medium, for example, of equal parts moss peat and perlite—a suitable mix for all leaf cutting systems.

MIDRIB LEAF CUTTINGS Plants such as *Gesneria*, *Sinningia*, and in particular *Streptocarpus*, will produce plantlets from veins severed along the length of their leaves. Detached leaves should be placed upside down on a clean piece of glass and the central midrib cut out. The two remaining leaf pieces are then placed in the surface of the rooting medium, with the cut tissue horizontal and all cut ends of the lateral veins just buried. Plantlets should develop from each lateral vein within 6–8 weeks.

LATERAL VEIN-LEAF CUTTINGS The narrow, straplike leaves of *Streptocarpus*, *Sansevieria* and *Helonipsis* can be cut into a series of 1–1½ in (2.5–3.5 cm)-wide sections across their width, and the cuttings planted vertically with the basal ends inserted into the rooting medium. When propagating *Lachenalia*, *Galanthus* and *Leucojum* by this method, extra care must be taken to keep the leaf sections turgid and, since foliage dies down after flowering, timing of propagation is critical.

LEAF SLASHING Plants with large broad leaves with reticulated veining, such as *Begonia rex*, can be induced to produce plantlets by slashing the reverse side of selected leaves. Cuts about ½ in (10 mm) long are made across the main veins and repeated every 1 in (2.5 cm) or so. The leaf is then pegged down, top side up, on the soil surface. Buds will form at the incisions to produce roots and plantlets.

LEAF SQUARES are a means of rapid multiplication of any plant that will regenerate from leaves, but are generally reserved for large-leaved plants, such as some *Begonia* species. Selected leaves are placed upside down on a clean piece of glass, and cut up into approximately ¾ in (2 cm) squares. Sound leaf pieces are then laid on the rooting medium face upward, each secured by a small clean stone resting on its surface. Alternatively, they may be inserted vertically, with care taken to ensure that the end originally nearest the leaf stalk is buried.

Bulb scaling The scaly and fleshy specialized leaves that form the bulbs of *Lilium* and *Fritillaria* species will readily form bulblets. Firm clean scales are snapped off the base of the bulb. These are mixed with moist sharp sand, perlite or vermiculite to avoid dehydration and placed in trays or sealed in polyethylene bags. Callus tissue forms at the base of the scale and in a few weeks one or more bulblets develop from it; these are prised off to be grown on in a sterilized medium. With broad scales, the number of progeny can be increased by nicking the base edge to a depth of ¼ in (5 mm) every ¼ in (5 mm) of its width. Outermost scales are the best choice and dipping in rooting hormone increases yield.

Asiatic, Oriental, Caucasian, Martagon, European and Eastern North American lilies should be scaled between flowering time and spring. They benefit from being stored in a dark place at 64–75°F (18–24°C) and usually produce bulblets within 12 weeks. Most Asiatic sorts will grow away freely, but others first require a period of 6–8 weeks cool storage in a refrigerator. Western American lilies should be scaled in the fall/early

TWIN-SCALING BULBS

dormant daffodil bulb

cut down through basal plate

pair of scales

new bulblet

1 Select a healthy dormant bulb and, with a clean, sharp knife, trim off the old roots and the outer papery scales. Slice off the nose of the bulb.

2 Turn the bulb upside down and slice it vertically in half, then into quarters. Each segment should have an equal portion of the bulb's basal plate.

3 With a craft knife or scalpel, very carefully separate and cut free pairs of scale segments, making sure each retains its own small piece of the basal plate.

4 Pot the scales up (see also Bulb scaling, above) and keep in a dark warm place. After about 12 weeks, new bulblets should have formed between the scales.

winter and stored in a dark place at 37–50°F (3–10°C). The bulblet-bearing scales are potted up ½ in (1 cm) apart in 6 in (15 cm) pots to grow on.

TWIN-SCALING is a variation used for bulbs such as daffodils, snowdrops, hippeastrums, nerines and hyacinths. Here, the outer brown scales are removed, the roots trimmed without damaging the basal plate, and the nose sliced off. The bulb is up-ended and divided into up to 16 segments, each with a section of basal plate attached. The segments are then separated into pairs of scales, each retaining a fragment of basal plate. From a bulb cut into eight segments, up to 40 twin-scales can be produced.

CHIPPING is an alternative system where the mother bulb is prepared similarly, but the portions are not divided into pairs of scales. Large bulbs may be divided into 16 chips, small bulbs into 4 or 8 chips.

Good hygiene is vital and at all stages equipment must be kept scrupulously clean. Twin-scales and chips should be treated with fungicide, then mixed with moist vermiculite, in 30 micron sealed polyethylene bags, and stored in a dark place at 68°F (20°C) for about 12 weeks. Bulblets should be hardened off before planting in a cool, frost-free environment. Flowering size is usually reached in three years. See *scooping*, *foliar embryos*.

cutworms (Lepidoptera: Noctuidae) the larvae of various noctuid moths, so-called because they attack plants at ground level, severing young plants completely and often girdling the stems of older plants. Roots, corms, tubers and leaves are also eaten. Most damage occurs on light soil during a dry summer. Young vegetables, especially lettuces, onions and brassicas, are particularly susceptible; carrots, celery, beet, potatoes and strawberries are also vulnerable, as are China asters, chrysanthemums, dahlias, marigolds, primulas and zinnias.

The principal European species are the YELLOW UNDER-WING MOTH (*Noctua pronuba*), which has brown forewings, yellow hindwings and a wingspan of up to 2½ in (60 mm); the

TURNIP MOTH (*Agrotis segetum*), which varies in the color of its forewings from gray or brown to almost black, with a wingspan of up to 1½ in (40 mm); and the HEART AND DART MOTH (*A.exclamationis*), which is similar to *A.segetum* but with forewings bearing characteristic dark markings. The habit of North American species is similar, but in warmer areas the number of generations increases.

The moths are on the wing from June until August depending on species. Up to 1000 eggs are deposited in clusters on stems or leaves of plants. The newly hatched caterpillars feed on the foliage, but within a week or so descend to the soil. The plump larvae are various shades or brown yellow or green and up to 2 in (50 mm) long. They live most of their lives in the soil near the surface.

Control weeds that encourage egg-laying, and cultivate soil in fall and winter to expose the larvae to predators such as birds. In susceptible areas, treat the bases of young plants with insecticide. Small infestations can be controlled by locating and destroying caterpillars in the soil near recently damaged plants.

Cyananthus (Greek *kyanos*, blue and *anthos*, flower). Campanulaceae. Himalaya, China. TRAILING BELL-FLOWER. 30 species, evergreen, tufted and carpet-forming perennial herbs with small leaves and solitary flowers in late summer. Fully hardy, the following species thrive in pockets of moist, humus-rich soil in light shade or dappled sun in the rock garden. Propagate by softwood cuttings in spring.

C. lobatus Himalaya; a mat of ½ in (1 cm)-long, obovate, toothed to lobed leaves; flowers purple, blue or white, 1¼ in (3 cm), narrowly funnelform with five broad lobes; *C. microphyllus* differs in its smaller, oblong to elliptic leaves and more broadly funnelform, violet-blue flowers with ovate to lanceolate, not obovate lobes.

Cyanotis (Greek *kyanos*, blue and *ous*, ear). Commelinaceae. Old World tropics. 30 species,

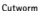
Cutworm

tender perennial herbs, usually with hairy, thinly succulent leaves overlapping in two ranks along creeping stems that radiate from initial rosettes. The flowers are small and three-petalled. Cultivate as for the tender *Tradescantia* species but with less water in winter.

C. kewensis TEDDY BEAR VINE; India; stems to 6 in (15 cm) long; leaves lanceolate, ¾–2 in (2–5 cm)-long, dark green above, purple beneath and velvety; flowers purple-pink; *C. somaliensis* PUSSY EARS; Somalia; stems to 10 in (25 cm) long; leaves oblong to linear, densely white-hairy, ¾–4 in (2–10 cm) long; flowers purple-blue.

Cyathea (from Greek *kyatheion*, little cup, a reference to the appearance of the sori). Cyatheaceae. Tropics. TREE FERN, SAGO FERN. 600 species, evergreen tree ferns with erect, rather slender, smooth stems marked with the scars of fallen frond bases (thus easily distinguished from *Dicksonia*). The large fronds form a spreading or shuttlecock-like crown; they are basically triangular in outline and finely bipinnately divided. *C. australis* and *C. cooperi* will survive lows of 19°F (–7°C) with some foliage loss: they might be attempted outdoors in favored, maritime climates to 10°F (–12°C). Elsewhere, grow in a frost-free conservatory or greenhouse. *C. arborea* and *C. medullaris* need a minimum temperature of 50°F (10°C). All prefer a porous planting medium, ideally soilless, and rich in garden compost, bark and charcoal. Position in dappled sunlight or shade, sheltered from strong winds and in a humid, buoyant atmosphere. Water and syringe freely in warm weather, less in winter but never allow to dry out.

C. arborea WEST INDIAN TREE FERN reaches a height of 30 ft (10 m). Its canopy consists of fronds to 11 ft (3.5 m) long, divided into fresh green pinnules that are themselves divided into 25–32 pairs of ⅛ in (3 mm)-wide, serrate, oblong-falcate segments. The stipes arch strongly, are tinged yellow and clothed below with creamy scales. The AUSTRALIAN or ROUGH TREE FERN, *C. australis*, and the very similar *C. cooperi*, attain heights between 10 and 60 ft (3 and 18 m). The 3¼–12 ft (1–4 m) fronds spread gracefully and are lime to mid-green with entire, serrulate or

227

C

crenate, 4 in (10 cm)-long pinnules. The stipes are covered with brown scales which become darker as they descend toward the stem. *C. medullaris* BLACK TREE FERN, SAGOFERN is native to Australia, New Zealand and the Pacific Islands. The largest species listed here, its black stem may be over 50 ft (15 m) tall. It is crowned with arching fronds to 20 ft (6 m) long, dark, glossy green above, paler beneath. The stipes are stained black and covered below with black scales.

cyathiform shaped like a cup, similar to urceolate but without the marginal contraction.

cyathium an inflorescence-type characteristic of *Euphorbia*, consisting of a cupule (an involucre of small bracts sometimes furnished with glands and subtended by petaloid bracts or appendages) enclosing several "stamens," each equivalent to a single male flower, and a stalked trilocular "ovary" (a 3-carpeled pistil equivalent to the female flower). In dioecious species, the male or female is lacking according to the sex of the individual.

cycad a primitive gymnosperm belonging to any one of the families Cycadaceae, Zamiaceae or Stangeriaceae. Although allied to conifers, cycads very superficially resemble ferns and palms. Having dominated the world's flora 200 million years ago, they now survive, more or less unchanged, scattered throughout the tropics and subtropics. See *Cycas*, *Dioon*, *Encephalartos*, *Macrozamia*, *Zamia*.

Cycas (from *koikos*, the Greek name for the doum palm, *Hyphaene*). Cycadaceae. Old World tropics and subtropics. FERN PALM, SAGO PALM, CYCAD, FALSE SAGO. Some 20 species, tender, evergreen perennials. The trunks are stout and columnlike, usually unbranched and covered with scars and the remains of leaf bases. They terminate in a crown of large, pinnate leaves with many tough-textured, narrow segments. Male plants produce large, yellow cones composed of closely packed, diamond-shaped scales; the female cones are looser with egg-

Cyathium (Euphorbia paralias)

shaped seeds borne on much reduced, felty, leaves. Handsome foliage plants for subtropical and tropical gardens and for interiors. The most commonly cultivated species, C. *revoluta*, is a resilient pot or landscape plant, tolerating neglect and even mild frosts provided the leaf rosette is tied upward and wrapped with sacking in winter. The remaining two species require a minimum winter temperature of 50°F (10°C). Plant in large pots, tubs or borders in a loamy mixture rich in garden compost, bark and sand. Provide C. *circinalis* and C. *rumphii* with a shady, humid environment. C. *revoluta* will accept brighter, drier conditions. Water, feed and syringe frequently in spring and summer, but keep barely moist at cooler, duller times of year. Propagate by seed, surface-sown on a moist, sandy mixture at temperatures of 59–84°F (15–29°C), or by detaching the budlike offsets that sometimes develop at the base and along the trunks of older plants.

C. *circinalis* FALSE SAGO is native to southeast India. It makes a trunk to 15 ft (5 m) tall, some 12 in (30 cm) wide. The leaves are 5–10 ft (1.5–3 m) long; the segments to 12 × ⅜ in (30 × 1.5 cm), linear to lanceolate and somewhat curved, smooth, mid- to pea green and of a rather supple, leathery texture. C. *rumphii* may be synonymous with this species, differing only in its larger and more luxuriant habit, its softer and broader leaf segments, sometimes a deep sea green, and certain cone

details. It is widespread in coastal southeast Asia, and extends to East Africa, Madagascar and the Pacific Islands. The Japanese C. *revoluta* is a smaller and stockier plant, to 10 ft (3 m) tall. Its 3¼–6½ ft (1–2 m)-long leaves are held erect to spreading and are crowded with narrow, linear segments, each to 6 × ¼ in (15 × 0.5 cm), rigid, and glossy dark green with a distinct midrib and revolute margins.

Cyclamen (from the Greek *kyklos*, circle, referring to the rounded tubers). Primulaceae. SOWBREAD, PERSIAN VIOLET. Europe, Mediterranean to Iran, Somalia. 19 species, tuberous perennial herbs. The tubers are usually circular and somewhat flattened. They bear tufts of stalked, circular to heart-shaped leaves. The flowers are solitary and nod on curving stalks. The five petals are rounded and twist upward.

With the exception of *C. persicum* and its cultivars, the following are hardy. *C. hederifolium*, *C. coum* and *C. alpinum* will survive to –10°F (–23°C). The remainder prefer rather higher temperatures and protection from wet winter conditions. They should be grown outdoors in very sheltered positions in mild climates and over, and elsewhere in an alpine house or frame. Plant in sun or part-shade in gritty, fertile and humus-rich soil. Keep moist when in growth, drier when at rest (i.e. summer except for *C. purpurascens*). Pot-grown plants can be dried out completely during dormancy. The hardiest species, however, cope well with conditions in the open garden and may be naturalized under trees and shrubs and even in short grass without suffering. Grow *C. persicum* and its cultivars in a cool greenhouse or in the home (minimum temperature 41°F/5°C). Plant the tubers in a fertile, porous, soilless medium with their upper surface exposed. Position in bright, filtered light in well-ventilated conditions. Water and feed when in growth. Dry off after flowering, when the leaves will wither. Tubers may be started into growth at any time of year. Increase by seed. Old tubers may develop short, woody 'stems' at their growing points. These may be removed and rooted. *C. persicum* and its cultivars are affected by black root rot.

CYCLAMEN

Name	Distribution	Leaves	Flowers
C. alpinum *C. trochopteranthum*	SW Turkey, Cilician Taurus	1–2 in (2.5–5 cm), reniform to broadly ovate, base cordate, apex blunt, dark green zoned silver above, tinted purple-red beneath	to ¾ in (2 cm), scented, petals broadly obovate, twisted and spreading, propeller-like, pale pink to magenta or deep carmine with a dark basal blotch
C. africanum	Algeria	to 4 in (10 cm), circular to reniform or cordate, crenate to serrate, dark green lightly marked silver-gray, lustrous, pale green beneath	to 1 in (2.5 cm), violet-scented, petals slightly reflexed, ovate-lanceolate to lanceolate, pale pink to deep rose with a deep red patch at base; fall
C. cilicium **Comments:** Includes the white-flowered f. *album*.	SW Turkey	to 1½ in (4 cm), suborbicular, serrate to crenate, gray-green to dark green with silver-gray and dark blotches, purple-red beneath	to ¾ in (2 cm), petals obovate-acute, twisted, strongly reflexed, white to deep pink with a dark crimson blotch at the base suffusing petals; fall
C. coum *C. hiemale, C. orbiculatum, C. vernale*	Caucasus, Turkey, Lebanon, Israel	1–2½ in (2.5–6 cm) diam., orbicular-reniform, dark to mid-green marked with lighter spots or silver-gray zone or band above, purple-red-tinted beneath	to ¾ in (2 cm), petals ovate-elliptic, strongly reflexed, somewhat twisted or folded, white to pale rose or deep carmine with a dark crimson to maroon blotch at base; late winter-early spring

Comments: Includes many cultivars ranging in color from pure white to deepest magenta; members of the Pewter Group have leaves almost wholly overlaid with solid, dull silver to pewter; ssp. ***caucasicum*** (syn. *C. caucasicum*) differs in its cordate leaves with silver markings, and flowers with a pale mauve rim and acute petals.

Name	Distribution	Leaves	Flowers
C. creticum	Crete	to 1½ in (4 cm) diam., cordate, dentate, dark gray-green, usually spotted or patterned silver-gray above, purple-red beneath	to 1 in (2.5 cm), fragrant, petals lanceolate, white to pale pink; spring
C. cyprium	Cyprus	to 1½ in (3.5 cm) diam., broadly cordate to ovate-lanceolate, apex tapered, toothed to shallowly lobed, olive green blotched light green near margin with a hastate inner pattern marked with gray-green, stained red beneath	to 1 in (2.5 cm), petals sharply reflexed, folded near base, twisting and toothed toward apex, pure white or pale pink with a V-shaped, purple-pink marking near base; fall-early winter
C. graecum	Greece, S Aegean Is, S Turkey, Cyprus	to 2½ in (6 cm) diam., cordate-acute, toothed, velvety dark green with a moss green to silver-gray zone at center, veined lime green or silver gray above, purple-red-tinted beneath	to ¾ in (2 cm), petals strongly reflexed, oblong-elliptic, pale pink to deep carmine with a darker stain at base; fall-early winter
C. hederifolium *C. neapolitanum* **Comments:** Many cultivars available covering the range of variation described here.	S Europe to Turkey	ivylike, 1½–3 in (4–8 cm), rounded to cordate, bluntly hastate or lanceolate-oblong, entire to toothed or lobed, very variable in color—dark to pale green or gray-green above, variously mottled, veined or zoned pale green to silver-gray	to 1 in (2.5 cm), petals ovate-lanceolate, acute, reflexed, constricted at base, pale to deep pink, usually with a dark carmine stain at base, sometimes pure white, rarely fragrant; late summer to early winter
C. libanoticum	Syria, Lebanon	to 3 in (8 cm) diam., rounded to cordate, dull blue-green with darker blotches, red-tinted beneath	to 2 in (5 cm), petals oblong-elliptic, white to palest pink in lower half with a dark carmine blotch at base, clear pink in upper half; winter-early spring

C. africanum

C. cilicium

C. coum **Pewter Group**   *C. pseudibericum*

CYCLAMEN

Name	Distribution	Habit	Leaves
C. mirabile	SW Turkey	to 1½ in (3.5 cm) diam., suborbicular to reniform, minutely toothed, blunt, dark green, zoned or marbled gray, pink or red above, purple beneath	to 1¼ in (3 cm), petals oblong to obovate, more or less toothed toward apex, pale pink with a dark carmine blotch at base; fall
C. parviflorum	E Turkey	to 1 in (2.5 cm), suborbicular, base cordate, margins entire, dull dark green	to ½ in (1 cm), very short-stalked, petals broad, spreading then abruptly reflexed and slightly twisted, mauve-pink with a dark purple blotch at base; winter
C. persicum	E Mediterranean, Rhodes, Crete, Libya	2–4¾ in (5–12 cm) diam., ovate-cordate, finely toothed, dark green variably veined, mottled, spotted or zoned pale green or silver-gray, often red-tinted beneath	¾–3 in (2–8 cm), often fragrant, petals oblong-lanceolate to obovate, strongly reflexed and twisted, white to pale rose, deep pink, magenta or cerise with a darker blotch at base; winter to spring, but bred and grown to flower throughout year

Comments: This is the florist's cyclamen with many cultivars ranging in habit from the large and robust to the dwarf and compact, in leaf from the large, dark and fleshy to the small and exquisitely marked, and in flower from small, fragrant and "species-like" to very large, in tones of white, pink, salmon, cerise, scarlet and red, the petals small and slender to broad and heavy, ruffled and "double."

Name	Distribution	Habit	Leaves
C. pseudibericum	S Asia Minor	to 2½ in (6.5 cm), obcordate, toothed, dark green marbled silver-gray above, red-maroon beneath	to 1 in (2.5 cm), fragrant, petals broadly lanceolate to elliptic, mauve to bright magenta or pink with a purple-brown blotch at the base streaking across the white rim; winter-spring
C. purpurascens C. europaeum, C. fatrense	C & E Europe	to 3 in (8 cm), circular-ovate, base cordate, finely toothed, dark green veined or marbled silver-gray above, tinted red beneath	to 1¼ in (3 cm), very fragrant, petals oblong-elliptic, reflexed and slightly twisted, lilac-pink to deep magenta or purple-red, darker at base; late summer-fall
C. repandum	C & E Mediterranean	2½–4 in (6–10 cm), broadly cordate, shallowly lobed and toothed, dark green with a paler inner pattern bordered silver-gray, sometimes with paler or silver spots	to 1¼ in (3 cm), fragrant, petals linear-oblong, white to deep carmine with a darker stain at rim; spring
C. rohlfsianum	Libya	to 4 in (10 cm), reniform to orbicular, margins shallowly lobed, toothed, deep green with a darker central zone bordered with a jagged region of gray-green to silver	to 1¼ in (3 cm), usually fragrant, petals lanceolate-obovate, strongly reflexed and twisted, pale rose to lilac pink, darker toward base; fall

cyclic bearing the production of fruit or seed crops at intervals of longer than one year. It commonly occurs in some apple cultivars as biennial bearing.

Cydonia (for the town of Cydon in Crete). Rosaceae. W Asia, naturalized throughout temperate Europe, Mediterranean, Middle East, S America. QUINCE. 1 species, *C. oblonga*, a deciduous shrub or small tree with a spreading crown, to 20 ft (6 m) tall. The leaves are 4 in (10 cm) long, ovate to elliptic, deep green above and woolly gray beneath. The solitary flowers appear in spring and early summer. Some 2 in (5 cm) wide, they consist of five, rounded, white or pale pink petals and are followed in late summer and fall by broadly pyriform fruits to 4 in (10 cm) long. These are golden-yellow, downy, scented like a spicy pear with a bouquet of pine; they are used for jellies, preserves, added to pies and souffles, stewed with spirits and spices, served with meat and game and put to many herbal uses. The seeds are toxic.

Hardy to –30°F (–34°C), quince nonetheless needs a long, warm summer to ripen its fruit. When grown for fruit, it is treated as a bush or standard tree with an open center, or, in less favored districts, as a fan or espalier against a south-facing wall. *C. oblonga* provides a dwarfing rootstock for pears. *C.* 'Vranja' and *C.* 'Bereczki' are vigorous plants and generous bearers of well-flavored fruit, suited to fan training. The fruits of *C.* 'Champion', also a heavy cropper, are milder in flavor. The apple-shaped fruit of *C.* 'Maliformis' ripens well in colder climates. The Portuguese quince, *C. oblonga* 'Lusitanica', produces an abundance of large, pale rose flowers.

Grow in full sun, in deep, moist, fertile loam; in light soil, apply an organic mulch to conserve water. Prune in winter to establish a fruiting framework, cutting back leaders by one third of the previous season's growth to an outward-facing bud. Fruit is borne on spurs and on the tips of the previous summer's growth: once a framework is established, little pruning is required save to relieve overcrowding and to remove badly placed branches. Unless frosts are heavy, wait until fruit is fully ripe for harvest in mid- to late fall. In a

C

cool place, fruit will keep for 2–3 months. For propagation, see *apples*. For the Japanese or flowering quince, see *Chaenomeles*, several species of which were once included in *Cydonia*. See also *quince*.

Cymbalaria (from Greek *kymbalon*, cymbal, referring to the leaf shape of some species). Scrophulariaceae. W Europe. 10 species, perennial herbs, often short-lived with slender, trailing and rooting stems and small, shallowly lobed, reniform to rounded leaves. From late winter to early fall, many solitary, 2-lipped flowers appear; these resemble a miniature snapdragon or *Linaria*. Use the following species for baskets, cracks in walls and paving, and small-scale carpeting effects in sun or shade on damp or (once established) rather dry and impoverished soil. *C. aequitriloba* may not survive temperatures below 1°F (–17°C); *C. muralis* is hardy to –10°F (–23°C) and becomes invasive if given any encouragement. Sow seed *in situ* in spring or in a frame in late winter; otherwise, take rooted sections of stem in spring or summer.

C. aequitriloba dense, mossy mat of entire or bluntly 3–5-lobed leaves; flowers $1/4$–$1/2$ in (8–13 mm) long, purple; *C. muralis* KENILWORTH IVY, COLISEUM IVY, PENNYWORT, IVY-LEAVED TOADFLAX rampant short-lived trailer, often infesting old walls; leaves reniform to semicircular with five to nine, blunt to acute lobes; flowers lilac to mauve, white or violet and with a yellow palate, $3/8$–$5/8$ in (9–15 mm) long.

Cymbidium (diminutive form of the Greek *kymbe*, boat—a reference to the hollow recess in the lip). Orchidaceae. Asia to Australia. 50 species, epiphytic, lithophytic and terrestrial orchids with clustered, small to large pseudobulbs sheathed by long, narrow leaves. Produced in basal racemes usually in winter and spring, the flowers are long-lasting and waxy with similar, ovate to lanceolate tepals and a showy lip with two, incurved lateral lobes and a projecting, platformlike midlobe.

Cymbidium is the most popular orchid genus, once widely sold as a cut flower, today so easily produced that it is simpler to sell whole plants in full bloom. These are likely to be hybrids,

hundreds of which have been registered. They range in habit from the miniature (i.e. 32 in (80 cm) tall with many, 2 in (5 cm)-wide flowers) to very large (i.e. to 5 ft (1.5 m) tall with up to 30, $4 3/4$ in (12 cm)-wide flowers. The foliage is generally grassy and the flower spikes may be erect, arching or pendulous. The flowers are in shades of white, rose, bright pink, wine red, chestnut brown, amber, ocher, yellow and green, often marked with red or brown, especially on the lip, which may be a different ground color altogether with a ruffled margin, prominent, sometimes golden crests and hairy.

The following species are also grown. They need a minimum winter temperature of 41°F (5°C). Pot in a bark-based mix with added slow-release fertilizer and a moisture-retentive medium such as rock wool or coir. Water and feed frequently when in growth and provide a humid, bright and warm environment. By midsummer, the new growth should be well-developed and will benefit from a ripening period of hot, sunny days and cool nights—easily achieved by placing the plants outdoors until fall. Once the new pseudobulbs are plump and fully formed, place in a cool, airy situation and reduce water to a minimum (*C. ensifolium* and *C. goeringii* are exceptions, requiring a permanently moist medium and cool, shaded conditions). The flower spikes should now begin to form and may require staking and training. Those of *C. devonianum* and *C. elegans* may bury themselves in the pot unless guided over the edge. Grown in too consistently warm an atmosphere, *Cymbidium* will usually fail to flower, producing luxuriant foliage instead—the most common problem with plants bought in flower and grown in the home.

Increase by division or from back-bulbs taken when repotting (best carried out after flowering and as seldom as possible—these plants flower better if pot-bound). *Cymbidium* is affected by fungal rots and cymbidium mosaic virus. Plants infected by the latter should be discarded, and care taken to sterilize blades used in division, to avoid its transmission.

C. aloifolium India, China, Java; leaves fleshy; inflorescence to 36 in

(90 cm), pendulous; flowers to 2 in (5 cm) wide, tepals cream-yellow streaked red-brown, lip cream or white stained yellow, veined maroon; spring- to summer-flowering; *C. atropurpureum* Thailand; Malaysia, Philippines; differs from last species in flowers that are more solid maroon and coconut-scented; *C. bicolor* Indochina to Malaysia; inflorescence to 30 in (75 cm), strongly arching; flowers to $1 3/4$ in (4.5 cm) wide, fragrant, tepals yellow-cream striped maroon, lip white stained yellow dotted or blotched maroon; spring- to summer-flowering; *C. canaliculatum* Australia; inflorescence to 18 in (45 cm), arching; flowers to $1 1/2$ in (4 cm) wide, tepals green to pale bronze streaked red-brown, lip ivory spotted purple-red; fall- and winter-flowering; *C. dayanum* N India to Japan, Malaysia; inflorescence to 14 in (35 cm); flowers to 2 in (5 cm) wide, fragrant, tepals white with a central maroon stripe, lip white stained yellow, marked maroon; summer-flowering; *C. devonianum* N India to Thailand; inflorescence to 16 in (40 cm), strongly pendulous; flowers to $1 1/2$ in (3.5 cm) wide, tepals olive streaked blood red, lip garnet to deep maroon; spring-flowering; *C. eburneum* India to China; inflorescence to $14 1/4$ in (36 cm), few-flowered; flowers to $4 3/4$ in (12 cm) wide, fragrant, tepals white, sometimes tinged pink, lip ivory stained yellow; winter- to spring-flowering; *C. elegans* (syn. *Cyperorchis elegans*); N India to China; inflorescence to 24 in (60 cm), pendulous; flowers ivory, crowded, narrowly campanulate; fall- to winter-flowering; *C. ensifolium* India, China, Philippines; habit grassy; inflorescence to 28 in (70 cm), few-flowered; flowers to 2 in (5 cm) wide; tepals slender, straw yellow to olive green streaked red-brown, lip cream to white spotted red; spring- and summer-flowering; *C. erythrostylum* Vietnam; inflorescence to 24 in (60 cm), few-flowered; flowers to $4 3/4$ in (12 cm) wide, tepals white to palest pink, lip cream veined and blotched deep red; summer-flowering; *C. finlaysonianum* SE Asia; inflorescence to $3 1/4$ ft (1 m), pendent; flowers to $2 1/2$ in (6 cm) wide, tepals olive to yellow-green tinted pink, lip white marked red; summer- to fall-flowering; *C. flori-bundum* (syn. *C. pumilum*); S China,

Taiwan; inflorescence to 16 in (40 cm), arching; flowers 1¼–1½ in (3–4 cm) wide, tepals rusty brown or yellow green, lip white marked red to maroon; winter- to spring-flowering; *C. goeringii* China, Japan; plants small, grassy; flowers solitary on stalks to 4 in (10 cm), 2 in (5 cm) wide, tepals slender, curving, olive, yellow green, or rusty red, lip white marked red; winter- to spring-flowering; *C. hookerianum* N India, China; inflorescence to 28 in (70 cm), arching; flowers to 5½ in (14 cm) wide, fragrant, tepals apple green spotted red below, lip cream edged green, spotted maroon; winter- to early spring-flowering; *C. insigne* Thailand, Vietnam, China; inflorescence to 5 ft (1.5 m) arching, flowers to 3½ in (9 cm) wide, tepals white to pale pink sometimes spotted red, lip white stained yellow spotted and veined red; late fall- to spring-flowering; *C. iridioides* (syn. *C. giganteum*); N India, Burma, S China; inflorescence to 3¼ ft (1 m); flowers to 4 in (10 cm) wide, scented, tepals olive green with broken stripes of rusty red, lip yellow marked red; summer-flowering; *C. lowianum* Burma, China, Thailand; inflorescence to 3¼ ft (1 m), arching; flowers to 4 in (10 cm) wide, tepals olive to lime green irregularly veined rust to blood red, lip white to yellow spotted red brown; winter- to summer-flowering; flowers unmarked in 'Concolor'; *C. madidum* (syn. *C. iridifolium*); Australia; inflorescence to 24 in (60 cm), pendent; flowers to 1¼ in (3 cm) wide, tepals pale bronze to yellow-green, lip primrose blotched red-brown; summer- to winter-flowering; *C. parishii* Burma; resembles a larger *C. eburneum* with highly scented flowers with the callus not velvety on midlobe; summer-flowering; *C. sanderae* Vietnam; inflorescence to 16 in (40 cm), few-flowered; flowers to 3 in (8 cm) wide, tepals white flushed pink and spotted red at base, lip cream stained yellow, marked maroon; winter- to late spring-flowering; *C. tigrinum* NE India, Burma; flowers to 2 in (5 cm) wide, fragrant, tepals olive to yellow, faintly lined or dotted purple-red, lip white lined, spotted and edged purple-red; spring- to summer-flowering; *C. tracyanum* China, Burma, Thailand; inflorescence to 4 ft (1.2 m); flowers to 5 in (12.5 cm) wide, tepals olive to tawny yellow, heavily streaked chestnut to rusty brown, lip cream to yellow lined brown or maroon; fall- to summer-flowering.

cymbiform boat-shaped, attenuated and upturned at both ends with an external dorsal ridge, as in the keel of many papilionaceous flowers.

Cymbopogon (from Greek *kymbe*, boat, and *pogon*, beard). Gramineae. Old World tropics and subtropics. 56 species, largely tender, perennial grasses, many with aromatic foliage. All parts of the following species are strongly scented of lemon. Sections of culm and lengths of leaf are cut and used fresh, whole, grated or chopped as a flavoring in southeast Asian cooking. Grow in moisture-retentive, loamy soil in full sun; maintain a moderately humid atmosphere with a minimum temperature of 50°F (10°C). Water plentifully when in growth. Propagate by division. *C. citratus* INDIAN LEMON GRASS; southern India, Sri Lanka, widely naturalized elsewhere in Asia; to 5 ft (1.5 m) tall; culms canelike leaves slender, gray-green.

Cyme
Sedum spectabile bears its flowers in cymes: flattish to slightly domed clusters, the central flowers of which are first to open.

cyme a more or less flat-topped and determinate inflorescence, the central or terminal flower opening first.

cymose arranged in or resembling a cyme or bearing cymes.

cymule a small and generally few-flowered cyme.

Cynara (from Greek *kyon*, dog—the phyllaries are shaped like dog's teeth). Compositae. Mediterranean, NW Africa, Canary Islands. 10 species, hardy perennial herbs with bold, pinnately cut leaves and discoid, thistlelike flower heads in summer; these are large and goblet-shaped and composed of thick and densely overlapping phyllaries that surround a boss of purple-blue florets. The following are grown for the kitchen (blanched young leaves of *C. cardunculus*, flower heads of *C. cardunculus* Scolymus Group), but are equally ornamental. *C. cardunculus* is a magnificent foliage plant for any large border, but especially valuable in the white and silver garden. If the globe artichoke lacks the stately, frosted appearance of the cardoon, its flower heads nonetheless have a *Protea*-like quality welcome in late summer. Although tolerant of impoverished, stony soil and heavy clay, both species prefer moist but well-drained, loamy soil in full sun with some protection from strong winds. Where hard frosts or cold, wet weather are common, mulch *C. cardunculus* in winter. Propagate by seed or by division in spring, or by root cuttings in sandy soil in a cold frame in early spring.

C. cardunculus CARDOON; Mediterranean, N Africa; to 5¾ ft (1.75 m); leaves 20–39 in (50–100 cm), arching, deeply and jaggedly cut and densely overlaid with fine silver wool; flower heads spiny, 2½ in (6 cm) wide and packed with purple florets; Scolymus Group: syn. *C. scolymus*; GLOBE ARTICHOKE; Mediterranean; to 6½ ft (2 m); differs from *C. cardunculus* in its duller and less spiny foliage and flower heads broader and clothed with thickly leathery to fleshy phyllaries; the florets are lilac to mauve. See *artichoke, cardoon*.

Cynoglossum (from Greek *kyon*, dog and *glossa*, tongue, referring to the shape of the leaves). Boraginaceae. Temperate regions. HOUND'S TONGUE. 55 species, annual, biennial and perennial herbs with coarse, hairy foliage and cymes of forget-me-not-like flowers in spring and summer. Fully hardy, hound's-tongue prefers fertile, well-drained soil with ample moisture in spring and early summer. Annual and biennial species grow well in full sun in the flower border. The perennials will also thrive in semiwooded locations. Sow seed of annual and biennial species *in situ* in fall or spring. Divide perennials in early spring.

CHINESE FORGET-ME-NOT, *C. amabile*, is an east Asian biennial to 24 in (60 cm) tall with ¼ in (0.5 cm)-wide flowers in blue, pink and white. The cultivar 'Firmament' has gray-tinted leaves and azure flowers. *C. cheirifolium* from southwest Europe is biennial, to 16 in (40 cm) tall, with white-hairy leaves and ⅜ in (0.8 cm)-wide flowers which turn form pale mauve to indigo. WESTERN HOUND'S TONGUE, *C. grande*, attains a height of 24 in (60 cm), with trusses of ½ in (1 cm)-wide, deep blue flowers. This North American native usually dies back to a stout rhizome after flowering. HIMALAYAN HOUND'S TONGUE, *C. nervosum*, is a perennial growing to 32 in (80 cm) with sprays of intense blue flowers held over narrow leaves. From North America, *C. virginaticum* is an unbranched perennial to 36 in (90 cm) tall with ovate, 8 in (20 cm)-long leaves and ½ in (1 cm)-wide flowers in shades of white, mauve and pale blue.

Cypella (from Greek *kypellon*, a goblet or cup, referring to the shape of the flowers). Iridaceae. C and S America. 15 species, small, summer-flowering bulbous perennials resembling *Iris*. Planted in a free-draining soil at the base of a sunny, sheltered wall, *C. herbertii* may survive frosts, especially if given a thick, dry mulch in winter and watered well in late spring and summer. Otherwise, lift the bulbs and store cool and dry in winter. Under glass, maintain a minimum temperature of 50°F (10°C); water carefully but plentifully when in growth. Store in sand and keep dry and frost-free when dormant. Sow ripe seed into a sandy potting mix, or detach bulbils and off-sets, growing them on in moist, cool conditions until near flowering size. *C. herbertii* Brazil, Uruguay, Argentina; panicle to 12 in (30 cm) high; flowers 1½–2½ in (4–6 cm)-wide, short-lived but produced in succession, three large outer segments are tawny yellow to golden, often with a purple-brown central stripe, ovate and waisted at the middle, the inner segments far smaller, pale yellow heavily marked purple to maroon.

Cyperus (the classical name for this plant, from the Greek for sedge). Cyperaceae. Warm and temperate regions worldwide. 600 species, mostly perennial, rhizomatous, evergreen herbs from marshy places. Where present, the basal leaves are grassy. Inconspicuous, the flowers are packed in small spikelets at the tips of slender rays that form spreading umbels atop tall, clumped stems; a collar of leaflike bracts subtends the umbel in some species. All of the following are grown for their graceful inflorescences, produced or persisting throughout most of the year. The first two species are attractive greenhouse or house plants, the variegated cultivars especially. Plant in a fertile, loamy mix; keep constantly moist or even stand or submerge in water. *C. papyrus* requires a large tub *in* or a saturated bed *beside* ponds under glass. Inflorescences of this species and *C. alternifolius* are used as cut flowers. Growth is rapid and rhizomes may need to be reduced or rejuvenated every few years. Propagate by division in spring, or by stem cuttings of the umbels cut just below the bracts and rooted in water.

C. albostriatus (syn. *C. diffusus*, *C. elegans*) is a South African native, 12–20 in (30–50 cm) tall. Its leaves and inflorescence bracts can be distinguished by their prominent veins (boldly striped white in the cultivar 'Variegatus'. The umbel rays are 1–4 in (2.5–10 cm) long, shorter than the 6–9, spreading bracts. From Madagascar, the UMBRELLA PLANT, *C. alternifolius* is taller than the last species 16–60 in/40–150 cm) and leafless. The leafy inflorescence bracts are longer than the 2½ in (6 cm) umbel rays. The cultivar 'Variegatus' is heavily striped or zoned white. *C. papyrus* is the PAPYRUS or EGYPTIAN PAPER REED, a majestic African native 6½–15 ft (2–5 m) tall with thick, pithy stems which carry mops of countless, nodding rays. It lacks leaves and the umbel bracts are reduced to papery spathes. A dwarf (i.e. 3¼ ft / 1 m tall) form of this species is grown under the names 'Nanus' and *C. prolifer*.

Cyphomandra (from Greek *kyphos*, a tumor or swelling, and *aner*, man, referring to the humped shape formed by the anthers). Solanaceae. S America.

30 species, herbs, shrubs, vines and trees similar to *Solanum*, but differing in their large, juicy fruit. *C. betacea* is the TREE TOMATO or TAMARILLO, a hairy, sparsely branched shrub, 3¼–10 ft (1–3 m) tall. It is grown for its dull red, ovoid to ellipsoid, 3 in (8 cm)-long fruit, in the subtropics, tropics and elsewhere under glass (minimum temperature 50°F/10°C). In flavor, the fruit resembles a tart tomato and is good stewed with a little sugar. Plant in a fertile, loamy medium; position in part shade or full sun in a sheltered, humid environment. Water and feed liberally when in growth and fruiting, then scarcely at all after fruiting when growth will pause and much of the foliage may drop. Raise from seed.

Cyphostemma (from Greek *kyphos*, curved or swollen, and *stemma*, wreath). Vitaceae. Africa, Madagascar (both species listed here are from Namibia). 150 species, tender, deciduous shrubs usually with greatly swollen, succulent trunks covered in peeling, papery bark and forking into short, thick branches or producing soft, climbing stems. The leaves are large and fleshy. Packed in flat-topped cymes, the small, yellow-green flowers are followed by colorful berries. These splendid caudiciform succulents require a minimum temperature of 50°F (10°C), full sunlight, a dry, buoyant atmosphere and a loam-based potting medium high in sand and grit. Water only when in growth and then sparingly, and avoid wetting the foliage and stems. They deteriorate quickly in cool, damp conditions. Propagate by stem cuttings or by seed.

C. bainesii (syn. *Cissus bainesii*) makes a flask-shaped trunk to 24 in (60 cm) tall with few, if any, short branches at its summit. The leaves are downy and divided into 3 leaflets, these are ovate to elliptic, some 4¾ in (12 cm) long and coarsely toothed. *C. juttae* (syn. *Cissus juttae*) develops a massive bole to 6½ ft (2 m) tall, often with several thick, short limbs. The leaves are simple to 3-parted, with each segment 4–14 in (10–35 cm) long, oval, coarsely toothed, smooth and waxy blue-green.

Cypripedium (from Greek *Kypris*, Venus, and *pous*, foot). Orchidaceae. Northern temperate regions. LADY'S

SLIPPER ORCHID, SLIPPER ORCHID, MOC-CASIN FLOWER. 45 species, deciduous hardy or near-hardy orchids, rhizomatous with broad, ovate to elliptic leaves and one to many flowers produced in spring and early summer. The flowers consist of an ovate dorsal sepal, two narrower and spreading petals and a showy, inflated, slipperlike lip backed by the fused lateral sepals. With the exception of *C. calceolus* which tolerates lime (although not the variety *parviflorum*), the following species require a slightly acidic soil rich in decayed leaf matter. They associate well with ferns, trilliums and dwarf, bog-loving Ericaceae in damp, semiwooded locations and the drier reaches of the bog garden. They are frost-hardy but benefit from a thick dry winter mulch. In very exposed locations, they fare better in pots in an alpine house, *C. japonicum*, *C. macranthos* and the otherwise scarcely visible *C. debile* especially. *Cypripedium* resents disturbance and is slow to increase; it may, however, be divided in early spring, taking some of the old soil with the new plants.

C. acaule from eastern North America produces a pair of basal leaves between which arises a 4–12 in (10–30 cm)-high stalk carrying a single flower to 3 in (8 cm) across. The drooping tepals are deep olive to chocolate brown, the lip rose pink. The European *C. calceolus* carries two to four leaves on a 6–20 in (15–50 cm) stem which terminates usually in a single, 2–3 in (5–8 cm)-wide flower. The tepals are olive to chocolate or maroon, the lip clear yellow. Its variety *parviflorum* from eastern North America has smaller flowers with spiraling petals; those of the Asian var. *pubescens* are larger and a uniform yellow flecked purple-brown. The largest species listed here, *C. californicum* from the western US produces yard-high stems hung with up to twelve, 1½ in (4 cm)-wide flowers, their tepals yellow-green, the lip snowy white. The oriental *C. debile* seldom exceeds 4 in (10 cm), a dwarf species with glossy green, heart-shaped leaves paired midway on the stem and a single, nodding flower to 1¼ in (3 cm) wide, pale green with blood red stippling on the lip. Also from Japan and China, *C. japonicum* (syn. *C. formosanum*) can be readily identified by its large, pleated

Cypripedium calceolus
This European species has fused and twisted tepals in a rich purply-brown, and a very pronounced pouched lip, or "slipper."

and fan-shaped leaves. The single flower is 4 in (10 cm) wide with green-white, spotted tepals and a rosy pink lip which is bowl-shaped and puffy. *C. macranthos* extends from eastern Russia to Japan. It bears three to four large leaves and a solitary, purple-red-stained, 3 in (8 cm)-wide flower. From North America, *C. reginae* (syn. *C. album*) is a robust species with broad, ribbed leaves and two to four, 2½–3½ in (6–9 cm)-wide flowers toward the summit of its yard-high stems; the tepals white, the lip pink or white. Several hybrids are available and are proving hardy and vigorous. One of the best is *C.* Gisela Frosch, a cross between *C. calceolus* var. *parviflorum* and *C. macranthos*, with chocolate tepals and a puffy rose-purple lip. Many species of *Paphiopedilum* were formerly included in this genus.

cypsela an achene invested with an adnate calyx, as in the fruit of Compositae.

Cyrilla (for Dominico Cirillo [1734–1790], physician and professor of botany at Naples, executed by the Bourbons for his radical views). Cyrillaceae. SE US to Brazil. LEATHERWOOD, BLACK TITI, MYRTLE. 1 species, *C. racemiflora* (syn. *C. parviflorda*), a highly variable tree or shrub, 3¼–28 ft (1–9 m) tall, deciduous or evergreen

and fully frost-hardy or slightly tender according to provenance. Leatherwood is grown for its 1½–4 in (4–10 cm)-long, elliptic to oblong leaves which are glossy dark green turning deep red in fall, and for its small, white flowers. These appear in late summer, crowded in whorled and slender racemes to 6 in (15 cm) long. Plant in full sun in damp, acidic soil rich in leaf mold. Propagate by semiripe cuttings.

Cyrtanthus (from Greek *kyrtos*, curved, and *anthos*, flower, referring to the curved perianth tube). Amaryllidaceae. Tropical Africa, South Africa (those listed here are from South Africa). FIRE LILY. 47 species, bulbous perennial herbs with linear or strap-shaped leaves and tubular to funnel-shaped flowers borne on scapes.

C. angustifolius FIRE LILY, to 16 in (40 cm) tall, with four to ten, nodding, 2 in (5 cm)-long, scarlet flowers), *C. brachyscyphus* DOBO LILY, to 10 in (25 cm) tall, with six to eight, narrow, 1 in (2.5 cm)-long flowers in coral red, flame or scarlet) and *C. mackenii* IFAFA LILY, to 12 in (30 cm) tall, with four to ten, 1 in (2.5 cm)-long, slender, white to cream flowers with a sweet fragrance) will take the mildest of frosts, growing well outdoors in southern Europe and California. *C. breviflorus* (syn. *Anoiganthus breviflorus*), with two to ten, yellow or white, 1¼ in (3 cm)-long, open flowers on a scape to 12 in (30 cm) tall) is hardy to 23°F (−5°C) in warm, sheltered positions in well drained soil. *C. falcatus* (with six to fifteen, 2½ in (6 cm)-long, flesh and yellow-green flowers narrow and nodding atop a 12 in (30 cm)-tall scape) will withstand light frosts if perfectly dry when dormant and mulched with its own dead foliage.

Most other species are not hardy but are well suited to pot cultivation under glass (minimum temperature 41°F/5°C). Some species, notably the SCARBOROUGH or GEORGE LILY, *C. elatus* (syn. *C. purpureus*, *Vallota purpurea*, *Vallota speciosa*), to 3¼ ft (1 m) with six to nine, 4 in (10 cm)-long, broadly funnel-shaped

Cypsela (Tragopogon pratensis)

flowers in scarlet, pink or white), and *C. sanguineus* (syn. *Gastronema sanguineum*), to 10 in (25 cm) tall, with one to three, 4 in (10 cm)-long, broadly funnelform, scarlet flowers) make excellent house plants. Grow in a fibrous, loam-based mix with added leaf mold and sharp sand in full sun or bright indirect light. Water plentifully and apply dilute liquid feed weekly when in growth. Dry off deciduous species gradually after flowering; water evergreen species very sparingly in winter. Top-dress with fresh growing medium as growth recommences; repot as seldom as possible. Propagate by seed or offsets in spring.

Cyrtomium (from Greek *kyrtos*, curved or arched, referring to the growth habit). Dryopteridaceae. Cosmopolitan. 20 species, evergreen ferns with loose rosettes of pinnate leaves, the segments usually large and firm-textured. Grow the following species in the home, or under glass (just frost-free or warmer), or in very sheltered positions outdoors, where it will tolerate lows of 14°F (–10°C) for short periods if mulched. Plant in a neutral medium, soilless for containers, humus-rich for borders. Provide a cool, humid environment in light to deep shade and keep moist throughout the year; feed in late spring and summer. Spores soon give rise to fast-growing new plants. *C. falcatum* JAPANESE HOLLY FERN, FISH-TAIL FERN; Far East, South Africa, Hawaii; fronds 8–24 in (20–60 cm) long, semierect to spreading, broadly lanceolate in outline, segments in three to eleven pairs, each 2¾–5 in (7–13 cm) long, deep, glossy green, ovate to oblong, tapering and curving above, broad and rounded below toothed or shallowly lobed.

cyst nematodes see *eelworms*.

Cystopteris (from Greek *kystis*, bladder, and *pteris*, fern, alluding to the shape of the indusium). Woodsiaceae. Cosmopolitan. BLADDER FERN. 18 species, small, deciduous ferns with creeping rhizomes and lacy, fresh green, 2–3-pinnate fronds. Fully hardy, the following species will colonize gullies and crevices in the rock garden or stony ledges by ponds, favoring neutral,

porous soil that never dries out, light shade and shelter from strong winds. Remove faded foliage in late winter and mulch the rhizomes thinly with a mixture of garden compost, leaf mold and a little bonemeal. Propagate by division in early spring or, *C. bulbifera*, by bulbils.

The North American *C. bulbifera* BERRY BLADDER FERN, BULBLET BLADDER FERN produces 6–28 in (15–70 cm)-long fronds, broadly lance-olate in outline with small bulbils in the axils of the upper pinnae. *C. fragilis* BRITTLE FERN, BRITTLE BLADDER FERN is found throughout the temperate Northern Hemisphere and extends south to Chile. Its 2½–18 in (6–45 cm)-long fronds lack bulbils (although the sori are characteristically bladderlike), are very finely divided and cut, and a pale emerald which contrasts well with the brittle, dark stipes.

Cytisus (from *kytisos*, a name applied by the Ancient Greeks to woody Leguminosae). Leguminosae. N Africa, W Asia, Europe, Canary Islands. BROOM. 33 species, evergreen or deciduous trees and shrubs, usually with slender, ribbed green branches and small, simple to trifoliolate leaves. Pealike flowers are borne on short axillary shoots or terminal racemes in spring and summer. Most will tolerate temperatures as low as 5°F (–15°C), often far lower given perfect drainage and a sheltered location. *Cytisus* resents root disturbance. Prune lightly to remove dead or exhausted growth. Hard pruning seldom succeeds. In prostrate and decumbent species, pruning is rarely necessary, although deadheading is beneficial. Propagate by heeled semi-ripe cuttings of lateral shoots in summer; treat these with a hormone rooting compound and root in a sandy propagating mix in a case with gentle bottom heat. Increase also from ripewood cuttings in late summer in a cold frame. *C. battandieri* may be propagated from seed.

C. ardoinoi SW Alps, S France; dwarf, prostrate, deciduous shrub to 16 in (40 cm) tall with ridged and winged young branches; flowers rich yellow, solitary or a few together in clusters; *C. battandieri* PINEAPPLE BROOM, MOROC-CAN BROOM; Morocco; open-branched,

semievergreen or deciduous shrub to 12 ft (4 m) tall; large trefoil-like leaves covered in silvery down and tightly packed cone-shaped racemes of golden pealike and pineapple-scented flowers carried through the summer; includes 'Yellow Tail', particularly fine, with chrome yellow racemes to 6 in (15 cm) long or more; propagate from scarified or pre-soaked seed in a warm greenhouse in spring; also by semiripe cuttings; *C.* × *beanii* (*C. ardoinoi* × *C. purgans*); low-grow-ing, deciduous shrub to 16 in (40 cm) with many, slender erect to arching branches; flowers golden yellow, borne in profusion along branches; *C.* × *dallimorei* (*C. multiflorus* × *C. scoparius*; erect shrub to 8 ft (2.5 m); flowers solitary or clustered, yellow stained ruby red to purple-red or lilac-pink; *C.* × *kewensis* (*C. ardoinii* × *C. mul-tiflorus*); arching to prostrate shrub to 12 in (30 cm) with very small, 3-foliolate leaves; flowers solitary or clustered, pale yellow or cream; *C. multiflorus* PORTUGESE BROOM, WHITE SPANISH BROOM; Portugal, Spain; erect, much-branched shrub to 8 ft (2.5 m); flowers white, solitary or in clus-ters; includes cultivars with pale yellow-cream, pure white and pink-tinted flowers; *C. nigricans* SE and C Europe; erect shrub to 3¼ (1 m); flowers yellow in terminal racemes; *C.* × *praecox* (*C. multiflorus* × *C. purgans*); WARMINSTER BROOM; to 3¼ ft (1 m) tall, similar to *C. multiflorus* but with denser branchlets; flowers pale yellow to deep gold, massed along ascend-ing branches; includes gold-, cream- and white-flowered cultivars; *C. scoparius* COMMON BROOM, SCOTCH BROOM; Europe; erect, many-branched shrub to 6½ ft (2 m) tall with yellow flowers; includes the dwarf, low-growing subsp. *maritimus* with large golden flowers, the showy, red-blotched f. *andreanus*, the ivory and gold 'Diana', and the large, rich red 'Windlesham Ruby'. The following popu-lar *Cytisus* species have been transferred to other genera: *C. albus* (= *Chamaecytisus albus*); *C. canariensis* (= *Genista canariensis*); *C. purpureus* (= *Chamaecytisus purpureus*); *C.* × *spachianus* (= *Genista* × *spachiana*).

cytokinins a class of plant hormones involved in cell division and organ differ-entiation and causing delay in senescence.

cytology the branch of biology that concerns itself with the structure, func-tions, generation and life history of cells.

Daboecia (named after St. Dabeoc). Ericaceae. W Europe to the Azores. 2 species, summer-flowering low-growing and compact evergreen shrubs differing from *Erica* in their broader leaves and relatively large, glandular flowers, which fall away rather than wither and persist on the plant. For cultivation, see *heaths and heathers*.

D. azorica Azores; leaves dark above and silvery beneath; flowers ruby red, bell-shaped; *D. cantabrica* (CANTABRIAN HEATH, ST. DABEOC'S HEATH; W Europe; taller than the last species, forming a straggling bush to 20 in (50 cm) high; flowers urn-shaped, rose-purple; selections available in a range of colors including white ('Alba', 'Snowdrift'), pale pink ('Donard Pink'), dark pink ('Praegerae', dwarf and spreading with narrow flowers), magenta ('Porter's Variety'), dwarf and narrow-flowered), deep rose-purple ('Atropurpurea') and 'Bicolor', with pink, white, and striped flowers on the same raceme; hybrids between the two species are *D. cantabrica* subsp. *scotica*, including the ruby-flowered 'Jack Drake' and free-flowering crimson 'William Buchanan', combining the color and compactness of *D. azorica* with the hardiness of *D. cantabrica*.

Dacrydium (from Greek *dakrudion*, small tear, referring to the resin drops these trees exude). Podocarpaceae. SE Asia, W Pacific Islands, New Zealand. Some 30 species, evergreen, coniferous trees or shrubs, with scalelike, dark green leaves closely overlapping on narrow branchlets and inconspicuous cones. RED PINE or RIMU, *D. cupressinum*, is a New Zealand native to 130 ft (40 m) tall with a narrowly conic to rounded crown hung with long, slender, weeping branchlets. This exceptionally graceful, slow-growing conifer

is hardy to 20°F (–7°C). In colder regions, grow as a container specimen in the unheated greenhouse or conservatory. It requires moist, acidic soil, full sun, warm humid summers and mild winters. Propagate by seed or cuttings of stem tips under mist.

dactyloid, dactylose fingerlike.

Dactylorhiza (from Greek *daktylos*, finger, and *rhiza*, root, referring to the fingerlike tuber lobes). Orchidaceae. Europe, Asia, N Africa, N America. 30 species, deciduous, terrestrial orchids with lobed tubers and lanceolate to strap-shaped leaves sometimes spotted maroon. Produced in spring and summer in dense, terminal racemes, the flowers consist of five ovate tepals and a broadly wedge-shaped to rounded, shallowly 3-lobed lip. Hardy to –10°F (–23°C). The southern species may be damaged by prolonged frosts, frost-heave, and cold, wet conditions, but will usually survive if mulched in winter. In very cold regions, grow them in pans in an alpine house. Plant in sun or part-shade in cool, moist soil that is rich in sand and leaf mold. Several species will thrive in damp conditions and are suited to the bog garden: *D. elata, D. incarnata, D. majalis, D. praetermissa, D. purpurella,* and *D. traunsteineri. D. fuchsii* and *D. maculata* will naturalize in grassland. Most species prefer neutral soil, although *D. maculata* favors acidic conditions while *D. fuchsii* and *D. traunsteineri* are alkaline-loving. Increase by division in early spring, or by seed allowed to self-sow in areas unlikely to be disturbed (hybrids may arise).

D. aristata Japan, Korea, N America; 4–16 in (10–40 cm) tall; leaves sometimes spotted; flowers in a loose spike, purple-pink to maroon, lip spotted dark purple; *D. elata* ROBUST MARSH ORCHID; S Europe, Mediterranean, especially Algeria; 12–39 in (30–100 cm) tall; leaves unspotted; flowers large, in a dense, long spike, deep rose to rich magenta with darker stippling on lip; clones with yellow variegated leaves are sometimes offered; *D. fuchsii* COMMON SPOTTED ORCHID; N, W, C and E Europe, east to Mongolia; 8–24 in (20–60 cm) tall; leaves spotted, tips rather broad and blunt, thus

differing from *D. maculata*; flowers in a dense spike, white to pale pink or pale lilac-mauve, spotted or streaked blood red or maroon, especially on lip; *D. incarnata* EARLY MARSH ORCHID; Mediterranean; 6–32 in (15–80 cm) tall; leaves unspotted; flowers in a short spike, pale rose, lilac, pink, cream or rich rosy mauve, lip spotted red; *D. maculata* SPOTTED ORCHID; N, W and C Europe east to Asia; 6–24 in (15–60 cm) tall; leaves usually spotted, tips tapering, thus differing from *D. fuchsii*; flowers in a dense spike, white, pale lilac or rose to mauve, with dark red or magenta spots and lines especially on lip; *D. majalis* BROAD-LEAVED MARSH ORCHID; S and C Europe east to Russia and W Asia; 8–30 in (20–75 cm) tall; leaves plain green or spotted, broad; flowers in a dense spike with leafy bracts, lilac to magenta, lip blotched white and patterned with dark purple-red; *D. praetermissa* SOUTHERN MARSH ORCHID; W Europe including S UK; 8–28 in (20–70 cm) tall; leaves unspotted; flowers in a dense spike, deep magenta to rosy purple, lip spotted and streaked purple; *D. purpurella* NORTHERN MARSH ORCHID; NW Europe including N UK; similar to *D. praetermissa*; to 16 in (40 cm) tall; leaves sometimes spotted purple; flowers in a dense spike, dark rosy purple to wine red, spotted or ringed dark purple on lip; *D. traunsteineri* IRISH MARSH ORCHID; N and C Europe; 6–20 in (15–50 cm) tall; leaves sometimes spotted; flowers in a loose spike, bright magenta, lip spotted purple.

daffodil a popular name for *Narcissus* (q.v.), especially used of cultivars. Confusingly, in the cut-flower trade and some bulb catalogs, the term is reserved for cultivars with long trumpets (coronas), while those with short cups (coronas) are referred to as narcissi.

The Royal Horticultural Society is the International Registration Authority for the genus *Narcissus*, and the current (1998) system identifies 13 divisions. (1) *Trumpet*, one flower per stem; trumpet at least as long as the petals (perianth segments). (2) *Large cup*, one flower per stem; cup more than one-third but less than equal to the length of the petals. (3) *Small cup*, one flower per stem; cup not more than one-third the length of the petals. (4) *Double*, one

D

DAFFODIL DIVISIONS

The Royal Horticultural Society is the International Registration Authority for the genus *Narcissus*, and their current system identifies 13 divisions, based largely on the differences in their flower forms. In addition to those shown below, there are two other more diverse divisions not represented here: Division 12 (Miscellaneous), which includes all daffodils not falling into one of the other divisions; and Division 13, which includes daffodils distinguished solely by their botanical name.

TRUMPET ('BRAVOURE')
Division one

One flower per stem; trumpet at least as long as the petals (perianth segments).

LARGE CUP ('CANISP')
Division two

One flower per stem; cup more than one-third but less than equal to the length of the petals.

SMALL CUP ('WOODLAND STAR')
Division three

One flower per stem; cup not more than one third of the length of the petals.

DOUBLE ('YELLOW CHEERFULNESS')
Division four

One or more flowers per stem; with doubling of the petals or cup or both.

TRIANDRUS ('HAWERA')
Division five

Characteristics of *N. triandrus* clearly evident; usually two or more pendent flowers per stem; petals reflexed.

CYCLAMINEUS ('LITTLE WITCH')
Division six

Characteristics of *N. cyclamineus* clearly evident; usually one flower per stem; petals reflexed; the flower at an acute angle to the stem with a very short neck.

JONQUILLA ('STRATOSPHERE')
Division seven

Characteristics of *N. jonquilla* group clearly evident; usually 1–3 flowers per rounded stem; leaves narrow, dark green; petals spreading and not reflexed; flowers fragrant.

TAZETTA ('MINNOW')
Division eight

Characteristics of *N. tazetta* group clearly evident; usually 3–20 flowers per stout stem; leaves broad; petals spreading and not reflexed; flowers fragrant.

POETICUS ('CANTABILE')
Division nine

Characteristics of *N. poeticus* group; usually one flower per stem; petals pure white; cup usually disk-shaped, with green or yellow center and red rim.

BULBOCODIUM (*N. BULBOCODIUM*)
Division ten

Characteristics of Section Bulbocodium evident; usually one flower per stem; perianth segments insignificant compared with the dominant corona.

SPLIT-CORONA ('BELCANTO')
Division eleven

Corona split rather than lobed, usually for more than half its length.

or more flowers per stem; with doubling of the petals or cup or both. (5) *Triandrus*, characteristics of *N. triandrus* clearly evident; usually two or more pendent flowers per stem; petals reflexed. (6) *Cyclamineus*, characteristics of *N. cyclamineus* clearly evident; usually one flower per stem; petals reflexed; the flower at an acute angle to the stem with a very short neck. (7) *Jonquilla*, characteristics of *N. jonquilla* group clearly evident; usually 1–3 flowers per rounded stem; leaves narrow, dark green; petals spreading, not reflexed; flowers fragrant. (8) *Tazetta*, characteristics of *N.tazetta* group clearly evident; usually 3–20 flowers per stout stem; leaves broad, petals spreading and not reflexed; flowers fragrant. (9) *Poeticus*, characteristics of *N. poeticus* group without admixture of any other; usually one flower per stem; petals pure white; cup usually disk-shaped, with a green or yellow center and a red rim; flowers fragrant. (10) *Bulbocodium*, characteristics of Section Bulbocodium clearly evident; usually one flower per stem; perianth segments insignificant compared with the dominant corona; anthers attached more or less centrally to the filament; filament and style usually incurved. (11) *Split corona*, corona split rather than lobed, usually for more than half its length. (12) *Miscellaneous*, all daffodils not falling into one of the other divisions. (13) Daffodils distinguished solely by botanical name.

Within each division, daffodils are further distinguished by code letters for colors: white or whitish = W; green = G; yellow = Y; pink = P; orange = O; red = R. The color code consists of two letters or groups of letters separated by a hyphen, letters before the hyphen describing petals (perianth segments) and letters after the hyphen describing the trumpet or cup (corona). For purposes of color-coding, the petals and trumpets or cups are divided

crenate (scalloped) margin

perianth tube

perianth (consisting of six petals)

trumpet-shaped corona

Typical daffodil

into three zones, none of which need to be in specific proportions. When petals are substantially of one color, one letter is used; when of more than one color, two or three letters are used, the outer zone being described before the mid-zone and/or base. When the trumpet or cup is of one color, one letter is again used; otherwise, three letters are always used, the eye-zone described before the mid-zone and rim. In double daffodils, the code letter(s) before the hyphen describe not only the outer whorl of petals but also any extra petals of the same color interspersed with the trumpet or cup segments. The full classification consists of the division followed by the color code; for example, a large cup cultivar with flowers of mainly yellow petals, white at the base, and with the cup having a white eye-zone, white mid-zone, and yellow rim would be coded 2YW-WWY.

The leaves and flowers are tolerant of severe frost, except those of division 8. Generally, plant bulbs one and a half times their depth, but deeper in light-textured soils. Shallow planting results in greater increase and smaller bulbs. Plant in late summer or early fall, in random groups, with bulbs 2 in (5 cm) apart; planting should be earliest for plants in division 9, which have virtually no resting period.

Daffodils may be grown for decoration or exhibition in deep, 9–10-in-(22–25-cm-) diameter pots; a mass of flowers can be obtained by planting one layer halfway down the pot and another layer immediately above. Daffodils are particularly attractive where established in grass; remove turf temporarily to allow planting, or use a bulb-planting tool. Turf plantings will usually thrive for many years, but both the grass and the daffodil foliage should be left uncut for four to six weeks after the flowers have faded. In borders, lift bulbs after three years to maintain vigor in the stock, but only

after the leaves turn yellow. Dry the bulbs, clean off old tunics, discard defective bulbs and, when not replanted immediately, store in a cool dark place. Daffodils are usually propagated from offsets or, for rapid multiplication, by chipping or twin-scaling; see *cuttings*; they are sometimes increased by micropropagation (q.v.). Seed is used for hybridizing and for increasing many species.

The development stages or forms of daffodil bulbs are variously described. Mother bulbs have two or three new bulbs attached at the base and can be expected to produce one or two flower stems in the first year and to increase. Offsets are new bulbs developed to the stage of detachment from the mother bulb, either naturally or by being pulled apart when loose enough; they are usually flattened on one side and produce leaves in the first year, but rarely flower until at least the second year. Chips are very small offsets (the term should not be confused with that used to describe a system of propagation; see *chipping*). Rounds are evenly rounded bulbs with a single growing point or "nose" at the top, developed from offsets, chips, or seed and usually producing one flower when of suitable size. Double-nosed bulbs consist of a round bulb with a large offset still attached, so that there are two associated growing points or "noses" at the top, each of which will produce a flower.

Possible problems: bulb scale mite, bulb flies, eelworm; basal rot, virus.

Dahlia (for Anders Dahl (1751–1789), Swedish botanist). Compositae. C America. 30 species, perennial, tuberous-rooted herbs and subshrubs with pinnately compound leaves and long-stalked radiate flower heads produced in summer and fall. In cultivars, the disk florets are often replaced by ray florets, giving a "double" (sometimes spherical) effect. The florets of cultivars range from strap-shaped, to rolled and quill-like, to broadly petal-like. The species are undeservedly rare in cultivation. They are fine plants for the cool glasshouse and conservatory, and for subtropical bedding schemes. The taller species should be encouraged to climb, supported on wires and trellis.

Garden dahlias derive especially from *Dahlia coccinea* and *D. pinnata*, and cultivation of the genus dates from at least the 16th century. Dahlias were introduced into England in 1789, and their popularity spread throughout Europe and the US in the mid-19th century. 20,000 cultivars are now listed in the International Register of Dahlia Names maintained by the Royal Horticultural Society. Dahlias are frost-tender but prolific and long-flowering with strongly fragrant sap. Seed-raised types include dwarf forms, suitable for bedding and containers. Border types, which are perpetuated by tubers, require staking, and they are often disbudded.

Ten groups are classified: (1) *Single-flowered*: open-centered blooms with one or two complete rows of outer florets surrounding a disk; blooms usually about 4 in (10 cm) diameter; most

plants to 12 in (0.3 m) high. (2) *Anemone-flowered*: one or more rows of ray florets surrounding a dense group of upward-pointing tubular florets; blooms 3 in (7.5 cm) diameter; plants 2–3 ft (0.6–0.9 m) high. This group consists of very few cultivars. (3) *Collerette* (US Collarette), open center blooms, surrounded by an inner ring of short florets, known as the "collar" and one or two complete outer rows of usually flat ray florets; blooms 4–6 in (10–15 cm) diameter; plants 3½ ft (1 m) high. (4) *Water lily or Nymphaea-flowered*, fully double blooms with generally sparse flat ray florets, with slightly incurved or recurved margins; blooms 4–4¾ in (10–12 cm) diameter; plants 3–4 ft (0.9–1.2 m) high. (5) *Decorative*, fully double blooms with no central disk, and broad, flat, or slightly involute ray florets, sometimes slightly twisted with the apex obtuse; plants

3–5 ft (0.9–1.5 m) high. (6) *Ball*, ball-shaped or globose blooms, sometimes slightly flattened at the top with ray florets blunt or rounded at their tips and cupped for more than half their length; blooms 2–6 in (5–15 cm) diameter; plants 3–3½ ft (0.9–1.1 m) high. (7) *Pompon*, sometimes referred to as drumstick dahlias, and similar to Ball group cultivars but more globose with florets involute for their entire length; miniature-sized blooms up to 2 in (5 cm) diameter; plants up to 3 ft (0.9 m) high. (8) *Cactus-flowered*, blooms fully double with no central disk, and long pointed ray florets, finely quilled for more than half the length; plants 3–3½ ft (0.9–1.1 m) high. In the US, this group is subdivided into *straight cactus types*, with straight, slightly incurved or recurved rays, and *incurved types*, where pointed rays turn toward the center of the bloom. (9) *Semi-cactus-*

Dahlia flower forms

SINGLE ('PRESTON PARK')
Open-centered blooms with one or two complete rows of outer florets surrounding a central cluster of tiny disk florets.

COLLERETTE ('CLAIR DE LUNE')
Open-centered blooms surrounded by an inner ring of short florets and one or two complete outer rows of usually flat ray florets.

WATERLILY ('ABRIDGE NATALIE')
Fully double blooms with relatively few broad ray florets that have slightly incurved or recurved margins.

DECORATIVE ('AUDACITY')
Fully double blooms with no central disk, and broad, flat or slightly involute ray florets, sometimes slightly twisted.

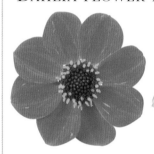

BALL ('BARBERRY CAROUSEL')
Ball-shaped or globose blooms, with ray florets blunt or rounded at their tips and cupped for more than half their length.

POMPON ('NOREEN')
Also known as drumstick dahlias; similar to Ball cultivars, but more spherical, with florets incurved for the whole of their length.

CACTUS ('SHIRLEY ALLIANCE')
Fully double blooms with no central disk; long, pointed ray florets, strongly recurved for more than half their length.

MISCELLAENEOUS ('JESCOT JULIE')
A grouping of relatively small disparate classes, including Orchid (as above), Star, Chrysanthemum, and Peony.

Dahlia 'Wootton Impact'
This is a classic exhibition or show dahlia, of the semi-cactus-flower type, with blooms of medium size held well above the foliage on strong, straight stems.

flowered, blooms fully double with slightly pointed ray florets broad at their base and revolute for more than half their length, either straight or incurving; plants 4 ft (1.2 m) high. (10) *Miscellaneous*, a grouping of relatively small disparate classes, including Orchid, Star, Chrysanthemum, and Peony cultivars, the latter considered a distinct group in the US, all growing to 1–3½ ft (0.3–1 m) high. Decorative and Cactus-Flowered groups are further divided in the US to give twelve groups. Subdivisions of groups are made according to bloom diameter and color. Those made according to size are the prerogative of national societies on account of the effect of varying cultural conditions.

In the UK, five subdivisions of bloom size apply: giant, 10 in (254 mm) or more; large, 8–10 in (203–254 mm); medium, 6–8 in (152–203 mm); small, 4–6 in (102–152 mm); miniatures, up to 4 in (102 mm). Subdivisions according to color are: white; yellow; orange; bronze; flame; red; dark red; light pink; dark pink; lilac, lavender, or mauve; purple, wine, or violet; blends, two or more colors intermingled; bicolored, ground color tipped with another color; variegated, several colors striped or splashed in one bloom. A cultivar annotated 5a Lt.Pk is a light pink giant-flowered decorative type.

Sow bedding types during late winter/early spring at 61°F (16°C), and harden off, planting out after any risk of frost. Propagate border types from tubers or rooted cuttings. In frost-prone areas, lift tubers in mid- to late fall, or immediately after the first frost, and place upside down until the stems are dry. Treat with fungicide and store in dry sand at 41°F (5°C) min. Overwintered tubers may be planted out directly, six weeks before the last frost is expected, 6 in (15 cm) deep. Alternatively, raise plants from 3-in- (7.5-cm-) long cuttings taken from tubers forced at 59–64°F (15–18°C) in late winter. Pot and harden off to plant out after any risk of frost, 24–36 in (60–90 cm) apart, according to ultimate height. Stop plants from rooted cuttings at

15 in (38 cm) high. On all plants, restrict the number of side shoots according to the size of blooms required: 4–6 for giant/large, 7–10 for medium/small. Support each plant with three canes, placed 6 in (15 cm) apart, and surrounding string ties. For high-quality blooms, remove the pairs of buds from axils behind the terminal bud.

D. coccinea Mexico to Guatemala; to 10 ft (3 m), usually tinged purple; ray florets scarlet, orange or deep maroon; *D. excelsa* Mexico; to 20 ft (6 m); ray florets lilac, solitary or a few clustered together; *D. imperialis* Guatemala to Colombia; to 30 ft (9 m); ray florets yellow sometimes tipped red; *D. pinnata* Mexico; to 6½ ft (2 m), tinged purple; ray florets pale purple stained yellow or pink at base; *D. tenuicaulis* Mexico; to 13 ft (4 m); ray florets lilac, many clustered together.

Possible problems: aphids, capsid bug, earwigs, red spider mite, slugs and snails, thrips; crown gall (see *gall*), gray mold, virus.

Dais (from Greek *dais*, a torch, referring to the shape of the inflorescence). Thymelaeaceae. South Africa, Madagascar. 2 species, deciduous or semievergreen shrubs with small leaves and fragrant, tubular to star-shaped flowers in terminal heads. Provide a minimum winter temperature of 41°F (5°C) in full sun. Plant in a sandy mix; water

OVERWINTERING DAHLIA TUBERS

1 Once the first frost blackens the stems, cut back top growth to about 6 in (15 cm); lift, clean, and label the tubers, and stand them upside down in a tray in a frost-free place to dry thoroughly.

2 After about 3 weeks, turn the tubers the right way up and cover with a thick dry material— for example, a chipped bark mulch. Keep them dry and frost-free until spring.

3 In spring, the first shoots that grow from the tubers can be taken as basal cuttings, with a thin sliver or heel from the tuber. Pot them in moist potting mix and place in a propagator.

4 Once the parent tuber is once again showing signs of new growth, trim off any wizened portions of tuber and replant in a generous hole. Use the label to mark the plant's position.

plentifully when in growth, very sparingly when dormant. Propagate by semiripe cuttings, alternatively by seed sown in spring. *D. cotinifolia* leaves to 2¾ in (7 cm), obovate to oblong, blue-green; flowers fragrant, to ⅝ in (1.5 cm) in diameter, pale lilac.

daisy grubber a short-handled tool designed for extracting thick-rooted weeds, especially from lawns. It consists of a narrow forked blade, bent into a U-shape at a point along its length to facilitate leverage.

damping DAMPING DOWN is the wetting of greenhouse floors and staging in order to increase humidity, especially when temperatures are high. Damping down is important as an aid to pollinating tomatoes. DAMPING OVERHEAD is the spraying of greenhouse plants with water to reduce water loss via transpiration loss. Damping overhead is usually performed only in warm greenhouses, and out of bright sunlight.

damping-off a soilborne fungal disease that destroys sprouting seeds, or causes stem rotting of young seedlings at soil level. It commonly affects bedding plants, herbaceous perennials, newly sown grass, vegetables, and tree seedlings. Several fungi may be involved, including *Pythium* species, (which thrive in wet conditions and in soils with a high pH), *Rhizoctonia solani* (especially in drier and more acidic conditions), *Thielaviopsis*, *Botrytis*, *Fusarium*, and *Phytophthora*. Preemergence damping-off is encouraged by overwatering or poor drainage, and by temperatures that are too low for quick germination. In post-emergence damping-off, there will often be spreading patches of disease. The latter condition is prevalent in wet, warm conditions where seed is sown too thickly and ventilation is poor.

The disease is difficult to control. To prevent its occurrence, avoid the conditions mentioned above and use sterilized or otherwise pathogen-free growing media. Disinfect containers prior to use and employ clean water in raising. Post-emergence, damping-off spreads rapidly, but early treatment with fungicide can help to check its progress. Cheshunt compound and copper oxychloride have been successfully used in the UK. Seed treatment and the application of chemicals to the soil prior to planting are recommended in some cases.

Damsons

bloom on skin of fruits

damson a type of plum derived from *Prunus instita*. The fruits are small with a pronounced neck, oval, purple, and initially acid sour. The dwarf compact trees have leaves much smaller than plums; closely allied to the bullace. Probably known in Syria in pre-Roman times; the name damson or "damascene" derives from "Damascus." The trees succeed in wet and harsh conditions; notable self-fertile cultivars are 'Prune Damson' for flavor, 'Merryweather Damson' for good size, and 'Farleigh Damson' for flavor and compact habit.

Possible problems: aphids, birds, plum moth (see *moths*), red spider mite; bacterial canker (see *bacterial diseases*), brown rot, silver leaf.

Danaë (for Danaë, daughter of King Acrisius of Argos). Liliaceae (Ruscaceae). W Asia. ALEXANDRIAN LAUREL. 1 species, *D. racemosa*, an evergreen perennial herb, related to *Ruscus* but with flowers in short terminal racemes. The stems grow from 20 to 39 in (50 to 100 cm) tall in shrubby clumps, emerging as asparagus-like shoots and hardening in one year. The true leaves are scalelike and are replaced by luxuriant, dark, glossy green cladophylls. These are 1¼–2¾ in (3–7 cm) long, ovate to lanceolate, and taper finely to the tip. The small, green flowers are sometimes followed by orange-red berries. It is hardy to 0°F (–18°C). Grow in sun or part shade on moist, fertile soil. Propagate by division, or by seed in fall, although growth from seed is slow.

Daphne (for Daphne, the nymph changed by Apollo into *Laurus nobilis*, the bay tree). Thymelaeaceae. Europe, Asia, N Africa. Some 50 species, small evergreen and deciduous shrubs, with heads or clusters of flowers usually in late winter and spring. These are tubular with four spreading lobes. In some species, they are followed by berries.

These shrubs are grown for their beautiful and intensely fragrant blooms, sometimes followed by brightly colored fruits. In some, the foliage is also handsome, laurel-like (*D. odora*, *D. laureola*) or variegated, as in cultivars of *D. odora*, or the gold-edged *D.* 'Carol Mackie'. Most are hardy to at least 5°F (–15°C). *D. mezereum*, *D. petraea*, and *D. cneorum* withstand temperatures down to –22°F (–30°C). Evergreen species may become semideciduous in less favored climates. Plant in well-drained but moisture-retentive soil. For woodland species, incorporate additional organic matter, and provide shade during the hottest part of the day. *D. arbuscula*, *D. bholua*, *D. blagayana*, *D. genkwa*, *D.* × *hybrida*, *D. mezereum*, and *D. pontica* tolerate partial shade, *D. laureola* will grow in deep shade. Most thrive in soils ranging from slightly acidic to alkaline, but *D. arbuscula*, *D. blagayana*, *D. genkwa*, *D. pontica* and *D. tangutica* demand nonalkaline soil.

Propagate species from seed sown ripe, after removal of the fleshy exterior. Stand in cool, shaded position (heat inhibits germination). Retain the seed pan for a second flush of seedlings in the following year. Progeny may be variable, but is more likely to be virus-free, and for this reason seed is the most sensible means of increase for *D. mezereum*. Select seed from a free-flowering parent with good flower color when possible. Propagate cultivars by semiripe heel cuttings, in a closed case. With trailing plants, propagate by simple layering in summer. Increase also by whip-grafting in late winter: deciduous species on to *D. mezereum*, and evergreens on to *D. laureola* understock. Plants suffering sudden dieback may be under stress or infected with virus diseases. Cucumber mosaic and other viruses cause mottling and distortion of the leaves. The fungus *Marssonina daphnes* causes spotting at the base of the leaves and on the petioles that may result in defoliation. (*See table overleaf.*)

DAPHNE

Name	Distribution	Habit	Leaves	Flowers	Fruit
D. alpina	S & C Europe	deciduous, erect or prostrate to 18 in (45 cm)	$\frac{1}{2}$–$1\frac{1}{2}$ in (1–4 cm), lanceolate to oblanceolate, gray-green, hairy	fragrant, white in terminal heads in spring or early summer	red to orange-yellow, downy
D. arbuscula	Hungary	evergreen, procumbent, to 8 in (20 cm)	to $\frac{3}{4}$ in (2 cm), linear to oblanceolate, obtuse, glossy, tough	very fragrant, rose pink, in terminal clusters in summer	gray-white, not fleshy
D. bholua	E Himalaya	evergreen or deciduous, erect or spreading, to 12 ft (4 m)	2–4 in (5–10 cm), elliptic to oblanceolate, undulate to obscurely toothed, dull, deep green, leathery	very fragrant, white to purple-pink, in terminal clusters in winter	black

Comments: Includes the hardy, deciduous var. *glacialis* 'Gurkha', and the hardy, evergreen 'Jacqueline Postill' with large, deep pink flowers.

Name	Distribution	Habit	Leaves	Flowers	Fruit
D. blagayana	E Europe, Balkans, Greece	evergreen, procumbent, to 12 in (30 cm)	$1\frac{1}{4}$–2 in (3–5 cm), oblong to obovate, blunt, smooth	fragrant, creamy white in dense terminal heads in spring	pink-white
D. × burkwoodii (*D. caucasica* × *D. cneorum*)	garden origin	vigorous, erect, semievergreen to deciduous, to $5\frac{1}{2}$ ft (1.7 m)	$\frac{3}{4}$–$1\frac{1}{2}$ in (2–4 cm), oblanceolate, bluntly apiculate, dull green, more or less smooth	fragrant, white flushing rose pink to mauve-red in terminal clusters in spring	

Comments: Includes the vigorous 'Albert Burkwood', with white flowers aging pink then rose-mauve, and 'Carol Mackie' with leaves edged bright, pale gold.

Name	Distribution	Habit	Leaves	Flowers	Fruit
D. cneorum GARLAND FLOWER	C & S Europe	low-growing, evergreen, to 16 in (40 cm)	$\frac{1}{2}$–1 in (1–2.5 cm), oblanceolate, deep green above, blue-green beneath	fragrant, pale to deep rose in dense terminal clusters in spring and sometimes again in late summer	yellow to brown

Comments: 'Eximia' has dark green leaves and, in late spring, white flowers with pink to red exteriors and throat, opening from rosy buds.

Name	Distribution	Habit	Leaves	Flowers	Fruit
D. genkwa	China	deciduous, erect, slender, sparsely twiggy, to $3\frac{1}{4}$ ft (1 m)	$1\frac{1}{4}$–$2\frac{1}{2}$ in (3–6 cm), lanceolate to ovate, thinly downy at first	subtly fragrant, amethyst, lilac, rose-purple or white, in sparse clusters before leaves in spring	
D. giraldii	China	erect, deciduous, to 4 ft (1.2 m)	$1\frac{1}{4}$–$2\frac{1}{2}$ in (3–6 cm), oblanceolate	fragrant, golden yellow, sometimes tinted purple in bud, in terminal clusters in early summer	red

D. alpina   *D. bholua*   *D. × burkwoodii* 'Somerset'   *D. genkwa*

DAPHNE

Name	Distribution	Habit	Leaves	Flowers	Fruit
D. × houtteana (*D. laureola* × *D. mezereum*)	garden origin	erect, bushy, semievergreen, to 3¼ ft (1 m)	to 3½ in (9 cm), oblanceolate to elliptic, glossy dark green strongly flushed purple-red or maroon at first	deep to pale lilac-rose, in clusters below leaves in spring	
D. × hybrida (*D. sericea* × *D. odora*)	garden origin	bushy, evergreen to 5 ft (1.5 m)	1¼–2¾ in (3–7 cm), oblong to ovate, glossy, leathery	very fragrant, deep purple-pink in terminal clusters throughout the year	
D. jasminea	SE Greece	erect or semiprostrate evergreen to 12 in (30 cm)	to ½ in (1 cm), oblong to lanceolate, blue-gray, smooth	highly fragrant, white sometimes with a red-purple exterior, in sparse terminal clusters in spring	
D. laureola SPURGE LAUREL	Europe, W Asia	evergreen, erect to 5 ft (1.5 m)	2–3 in (5–8 cm), obovate to lanceolate or oblong, leathery, glossy	fragrant, yellow-green, in clusters below leaves in late winter and early spring	black

Comments: ssp. **philippi** is semiprostrate and compact, the flowers smaller, lime green and sometimes tinted purple.

Name	Distribution	Habit	Leaves	Flowers	Fruit
D. × manteniana (*D. × burkwoodii* × *D. retusa*)	garden origin	evergreen, dwarf and rounded habit	to 1½ in (3.5 cm), glossy dark green	very fragrant, deep rose-purple to lilac in terminal clusters in spring, summer and fall	

Comments: 'Manten', the clone usually seen, is described here.

Name	Distribution	Habit	Leaves	Flowers	Fruit
D. mezereum FEBRUARY DAPHNE, MEZEREON	Europe	deciduous shrub to 5 ft (1.5 m) with numerous, erect, rodlike branches arising from a short trunklike stem	1¼–3 in (3–8 cm), oblanceolate, soft sea green, thinly downy at first	fragrant, rose to deep purple-red in clusters below leaf buds or leaves in winter and early spring	bright red, persistent

Comments: Includes selections with white, palest pink, and deep crimson flowers, also with variegated leaves.

Name	Distribution	Habit	Leaves	Flowers	Fruit
D. × napolitana (*D. sericea* × *D. cneorum*)	garden origin	bushy erect evergreen to 30 in (75 cm)	¾–1½ in (2–3.5 cm), oblanceolate to narrowly ovate, shiny above, glaucous beneath	very fragrant, rose-lilac, in terminal clusters in spring with further flushes in summer and fall	
D. odora WINTER DAPHNE	China, Japan	evergreen, erect to procumbent to 6½ ft (2 m)	2–3 in (5–8 cm) narrowly ovate to lanceolate or elliptic, leathery, glossy	sweetly fragrant, rose tinted purple-red or white with a rosy purple exterior, in terminal clusters in late winter and spring	red

Comments: 'Aureomarginata' : leaves deeply edged creamy yellow to pale gold.

D. jasminea

D. mezereum 'Bowles' Variety' *D. odora* 'Aureomarginata' *D. sericea* Collina Group

DAPHNE

Name	Distribution	Habit	Leaves	Flowers	Fruit
D. petraea **Comments:** 'Grandiflora': flowers larger, deeper rose to magenta.	N Italy	evergreen, mat-forming, to 12 in (30 cm)	½ in (1 cm), narrowly oblanceolate to spathulate, tough, dark green	fragrant, rose pink in terminal clusters in spring and summer	green-brown, downy
D. pontica	SE Europe, Caucasus, Asia Minor	evergreen to 5 ft (1.5 m)	1¼–4 in (3–10 cm), obovate to oblong, pointed, deep, glossy green	fragrant, pale yellow-white or yellow-green in pairs usually below new growth in spring and summer	black
D. sericea *D. collina*	E Mediterranean	small, many-branched evergreen to 3¼ ft (1 m)	½–2 in (1–5 cm), oblanceolate to obovate or narrowly elliptic, glossy above, downy beneath	strongly scented, dark rose aging buff in clusters in spring, sometimes with a second flush in fall	red or orange-brown
Comments: The name Collina Group applies in gardens to very hardy forms with dense, dark green leaves and small, purple-pink flowers.					
D. tangutica **Comments:** *D. tangutica* Retusa Group differ in their slow-growing, dwarf and rather stiff habit and shorter, retuse leaves.	NW China	evergreen, erect and open or rounded and densely branched to 5¾ ft (1.75 m)	1½–2½ in (3.5–6 cm), oblanceolate to oblong or elliptic, more or less acute glossy, leathery, deep green	fragrant, exterior rose-purple, interior white flushed rose-purple in tube, in dense, terminal clusters in spring and again in late summer	red
D. 'Valerie Hillier' (*D. cneorum* × *D. longilobata*)	garden origin	dwarf, spreading evergreen	to 2 in (5 cm), narrowly oblong to elliptic, glossy green	fragrant, pink-purple fading to white edged pink from spring to fall	

Daphniphyllum (from *Daphne* and Greek *phyllon*, leaf.) Daphniphyllaceae. Asia. 15 species, evergreen shrubs or trees with stout branches, tough leaves and small flowers in dense clusters in early summer—these are green in female plants, purple-red in male plants. The following species is hardy to −4°F (−20°C), but must be sheltered from cold, drying winds. Grow in cool, humid borders or light open woodland, preferably in neutral, humus-rich, and moisture-retentive soil. Propagate from seed in spring, or by greenwood cuttings under mist or in a closed case with gentle bottom heat. *D. himalense* var. *macropodum* (syn. *D. macropodum*) Japan, Korea, China; shrub or tree to 50 ft (15 m); young branches red-brown; leaves 3–8 in (8–20 cm), oblong, somewhat deflexed, leathery, dark glossy green above, glaucous beneath, petiole and midrib usually tinted red.

dard a short lateral shoot of a fruit tree, not more than 3 in (7.5 cm) long and usually terminating in a fruit bud.

dark dominant describing plants where flowering is dependent on the exceeding of a critical duration of darkness; typically short-day plants. See *photoperiodism*.

Darlingtonia (for Dr. William Darlington of Philadelphia, botanist). Sarraceniaceae. US (N California, S Oregon). 1 species, *D. californica*, the COBRA LILY or CALIFORNIA PITCHER PLANT, an evergreen, carnivorous perennial herb. It forms a clump of insect-trapping leaves, each to 14 in (35 cm) long. These are pitcherlike (i.e., tubular and filled with a digestive brew of water and bacteria). They spiral gently upward from a narrow base to a broader, bulbous apex, which resembles a hooded cobra. The pitcher mouth is small and opens on the underside of the hood, guarded by a forked tongue-like appendage. The pitchers are usually bright green laced with translucent white windows; with age and bright sunlight, the traps assume purple-red tints. White flowers nod on tall stalks in summer. Grow in full sunlight in a breezy but humid environment, with a minimum winter temperature of 41°F (5°C). Plant in a mix of live sphagnum moss, peat, and sand. In spring and summer, stand the pot in rainwater or distilled water to half its depth and water or mist overhead daily with the same. In winter, keep permanently moist, not sodden. In the home, *Darlingtonia* can be grown in large terrariums. Propagate by division in spring.

Darmera (for Karl Darmer, 19th-century Berlin horticulturist). Saxifragaceae. W US. UMBRELLA PLANT, INDIAN RHUBARB. 1 species, *D. peltata* (syn. *Peltiphyllum peltatum*), a perennial herb with fleshy, creeping and flattened rhizomes. The rounded leaves are 12–24 in (30–60 cm) across, with toothed to lobed margins and attached to hairy stalks 3¼–6½ ft (1–2 m) tall. Produced in spring, flowers are small, white to pink, and borne in domed cymes on stout and hairy, purple-tinted scapes to 16 in (40 cm) tall. It is an excellent perennial for damp gardens and the margins of ponds, lakes, and streams. Plant in full sun or part shade on a humus-rich medium that never dries out. Once established, *Darmera* will tolerate saturated soils when in growth. Mulch the networks of stout, exposed rhizomes in winter. Propagate by division in spring.

Darwinia (for Erasmus Darwin [1731–1802], naturalist and writer). Myrtaceae. W Australia. 60 species, dwarf to medium-sized shrubs with aromatic leaves. Produced in spring, the flowers are small and arranged in terminal heads surrounded by a pair of conspicuous bracts. Provide a minimum temperature of 45°F (7°C) with full sun and a breezy, rather dry atmosphere. Grow in a perfectly drained, sandy, acidic to neutral medium low in nitrogen. Water moderately when in growth, at other times sparingly. Trim back after flowering to maintain compactness. Propagate by seed in spring or by semiripe cuttings in summer. *D. citriodora* LEMON-SCENTED MYRTLE; dwarf to small shrub; leaves to ¾ in (2 cm), glaucous, lemon-scented; flower heads to 1¼ in (3 cm) across, erect to nodding, bracts orange-red and green, flowers orange-red).

Dasylirion (from Greek *dasys*, thick, and *leirion*, lily, owing to the thickness of the stem). Agavaceae (Dracaenaceae). S US to Mexico. SOTOL, BEAR GRASS. 18 species, evergreen perennials, sometimes with a short, stout trunk at whose summit the linear, spiny-edged leaves emerge in a fountainlike rosette. Off-white, bell-shaped flowers are borne in large, narrow panicles in summer. Grow in full sun with a minimum temperature of 41°F (5°C) and in a dry, airy atmosphere. Plant in a fast-draining, loam-based medium high in sand and grit. Water moderately in spring and summer, very sparingly in winter. Propagate by seed in spring. The following may prove hardy to 0°F (−18°C) in very sheltered locations. Plant in sandy soil near a sun-baked wall. Provide a dry mulch in winter.
  D. acrotrichum Mexico; trunk to 5 ft (1.5 m); leaves to 39 (100 cm) × ½–¾ in (1–2 cm), pale green, finely toothed with hooked, pale yellow spines with fibrous tips; inflorescence to 13 ft (4 m); *D. glaucophyllum* (Mexico; trunk absent or to 12 in (30 cm); leaves to 48 in (120 cm) × ½–¾ in (1–2 cm), glaucous, margins finely toothed and bearing hooked, yellow spines; inflorescence to 20 ft (6 m); *D. texanum* (TEXAS SOTOL;

Texas, N Mexico; trunk to 16 ft (5 m), often buried; leaves to 39 in (100 cm) × ½–⅝ in (1–1.5 cm), glossy green, marginal spines yellow becoming brown and with fibrous tips; includes the glaucous-leaved 'Glaucum').

Datura (from an Indian vernacular name). Solanaceae. N and C America, naturalized elsewhere. THORN APPLE. 8 species, annual or short-lived perennial shrubby herbs with entire or sinuately toothed leaves and large flowers in summer. These are broadly funnel-shaped with five pointed folds. The fruit is a spiny, 2-chambered capsule. Woody perennial species with pendulous, not erect flowers, are now included in *Brugmansia*. Grow in full sun in moisture-retentive but well-drained, fertile and preferably calcareous soil. Propagate by seed sown *in situ* in spring or earlier under glass. Set out seedlings after danger of frost has passed. The foliage is extremely susceptible to viruses affecting other solanaceous plants and may act as a host; do not grow in close proximity to potato crops. All parts are extremely toxic.
  D. ceratocaula C and S America; purple-tinted annual to 36 in (90 cm); flowers fragrant, to 7 in (18 cm), white, marked or flushed red-mauve; *D. inoxia* DOWNY THORN APPLE, INDIAN APPLE, ANGEL'S TRUMPET; C America, naturalized Old World; hairy annual to 3¼ ft (1 m) tall; flowers to 4 in (10 cm), white to pink or lavender; *D. metel* HORN OF PLENTY, DOWNY THORN APPLE; S China, widely naturalized in the tropics; glabrous annual to 5 ft (1.5 m), stems sometimes purple-tinted; flowers to 8 in (20 cm), white to creamy yellow or deep purple, sometimes bicolored, often double; *D. stramonium* JIMSON WEED, JAMESTOWN WEED, COMMON THORN APPLE; Americas, naturalized Europe; glabrous to short-hairy annual to 6½ ft (2 m); flowers to 4 in (10 cm), white or purple.

Daucus (from *daukos*, ancient Greek name). Umbelliferae. Cosmopolitan. 22 species, taprooted annual and biennial herbs with finely cut, 2–3-pinnate leaves and small, white to cream or mauve flowers in compound umbels. A native of Europe and Central Asia, *D. carota*, WILD CARROT, is a summer-

flowering, hardy biennial, useful in cultivation for meadow areas of the wild garden. It is a food plant for the caterpillars of the swallowtail butterfly, and a source of nectar and pollen for bees. Sow seed *in situ* in fall or early spring. Subspecies *sativus*, with a fleshy, orange taproot, is the edible *carrot* (q.v.).

Daucus carota
The wild carrot makes a statuesque plant for the wild garden, and is particularly attractive to both useful and beautiful insects.

Davallia (for E. Davall [1763–98], Swiss botanist). Davalliaceae. Warm temperate, subtropical and tropical Old World. HARE'S FOOT FERN. Some 40 species, deciduous or semideciduous frost-tender ferns with finely pinnate or pinnatifid fronds, deltoid to ovate in outline and delicately cut into lacy segments. The genus is most readily recognized by the tough, creeping rhizomes. Covered in chestnut scales, they branch and ramble freely, cascading from pots, encasing baskets and sometimes forming impenetrable tangles. Grow in bright indirect light or shade, with a minimum winter temperature of 45°F (7°C). Provide an airy, humid atmosphere. Water and syringe generously when in full growth, but scarcely at all during dormancy and cold weather. Well-established plants will withstand periods of drought and extremes of temperature, but may drop all their fronds. Plant the rhizome bases in an open, soilless medium with added bark; thereafter, allow the rhizomes to follow their own path—often through the air and outside the pot. Repot as seldom as possible. These ferns were often grown as "balls"—apparently self-supporting spheres of dense foliage hung in lightly shaded, humid places. To create such a "ball," make a globe of wire mesh, then line it with moss and fill with potting mix.

Poke rooted lengths of rhizome into the holes or pin them to the surface. Keep moist, warm, and shaded until established. Water large "balls" by plunging. Push fresh potting mix among the tangle of rhizomes at least once a year. The best species for this treatment are *D. bullata* and *D. canariensis*. Increase all by detaching rooted pieces of rhizome.

D. bullata HARE'S FOOT FERN tropical Asia; fronds to 12 in (30 cm) long, 3–4-pinnate, long-stalked and rather soft-textured, bronze at first becoming dark olive to jade green, fertile fronds distinctly bullate above, segments linear, acute; *D. canariensis* DEER'S FOOT FERN, CANARY ISLAND, HARE'S FOOT FERN; W Mediterranean to Atlantic Islands; fronds to 18 in (45 cm), 4-pinnate, emerald to dark green, rather tough, fertile fronds bullate above, segments ovate to rhomboid; *D. fejeensis* (RABBIT'S FOOT FERN; Fiji; fronds to 18 in (45 cm). 4-pinnate, fine and feathery, segments linear, sometimes cleft at apex; *D. mariesii* SQUIRREL'S FOOT FERN, BALL FERN; E Asia; fronds to 8 in (20 cm), 3–4-pinnate, finely cut, bright green, segments lanceolate to oblong, entire to lobed; *D. trichomanoides* SQUIRREL'S FOOT FERN, BALL FERN; S E Asia; fronds to 12 in (30 cm), 3–4-pinnate, very finely cut, dark green, segments cleft to toothed and horned.

Davidia (for the French missionary Armand David, who introduced the tree from China in the 1890s). Nyssaceae (Davidiaceae). SW China. DOVE TREE, GHOST TREE, HANDKERCHIEF TREE. 1 species, *D. involucrata*, a deciduous tree to 66 ft (20 m), with flaking gray-brown bark and a broadly pyramidal crown. The leaves are broadly ovate, to 6 in (16 cm), sharply serrate, with a cordate base and an acuminate apex. The small purple flowers appear in spring and summer, forming a ¾-in-(2-cm-) wide ball-like head that hangs on a slender stalk. The head is subtended by two, drooping and fluttering, pure white bracts, the larger to 8 in (20 cm). Hardy to –10°F (–23°C). Plant on deep, moist loam in a sheltered site. In cold areas, protect when young with burlap or sacking during the winter. Propagate by semiripe cuttings under mist in summer or from heeled cuttings

in a cold frame; alternatively, propagate by seed sown in a cold frame in spring while still moist from fruit (drying may inhibit germination).

day-degrees a measure of accumulated heat units; calculated by progressively adding the difference between the daily mean temperature and a prescribed base temperature. The measure is used to determine optimum sowing or harvest dates for certain vegetable or fruit crops.

day length, day-neutral see *photoperiodism*.

deadheading the removal of faded blooms from flowering plants. It is carried out to improve the plant's appearance and to prevent seed from setting, thereby in many cases encouraging further flowering.

dealbate whitened, covered with a white powder.

deblossoming the removal of flowers from fruit trees, and sometimes from late-planted strawberries, in the first season after planting, as an aid to establishment. It is also a means of discouraging biennial bearing in tree fruits.

Decaisnea (for Joseph Decaisne [1807–82], Director of the Jardin des Plantes, Paris.) Lardizabalaceae. E Asia. 2 species, deciduous shrubs with pinnate leaves and, in early summer, flowers composed of six narrow sepals hanging in slender, pendulous racemes. These are followed by large, beanlike fruits containing black seeds embedded in white pulp. Hardy to at least 5°F (–15°C), but often hit by late frosts. Grow in moist, fertile, loamy soil in sun or partial shade. Propagate from seed sown fresh in the cold frame in fall, or under glass in early spring, although germination may be slow and irregular by the latter method. *D. fargesii* W China; erect to 10 ft (3 m) with several rodlike stems; leaves to 32 in (80 cm), composed of up to 25 leaflets, each to 5½ in (14 cm) long, ovate to elliptic and glaucous beneath; flowers to 1½ in (4 cm), yellow-green in panicles to 16 in (40 cm) long; fruit to 4 in (10 cm)

long, thickly cylindrical, pendulous, leaden blue.

deciduous (1) falling off when no longer functional, as with nonevergreen leaves, also as with the petals of many flowers; (2) of a plant that sheds its leaves annually, or at certain periods; cf. *evergreen*.

deck, decking a terrace made of wood boarding, common in the US. Popular as an alternative to stone or concrete paving, decking is also suitable for raised viewing platforms and linking across water, to provide an effective contrast of form. However, deck surfaces can be treacherous if wet or icy.

declinate bent or curved downward or forward.

decompound a compound leaf with two or more orders of division, e.g., bipinnate, tripinnate, triternate.

Decumaria (from Latin *decimus*, tenth, referring to the number of flower parts). Hydrangeaceae. W China, S US. 2 species, climbing deciduous or semievergreen shrubs, similar to *Hydrangea anomala* and *Schizophragma*, but differing in their inflorescences, which are wholly composed of small, fertile florets. Fully hardy; cultivate as for *Schizophragma*.

D. barbara CLIMBING HYDRANGEA, WOOD VAMP; SE US; to 33 ft (10 m); leaves to 4 in (10 cm), ovate-oblong, apex tapering, margin toothed; flowers creamy white, sweetly fragrant, in broad panicles to 4 in (10 cm); *D. sinensis* leaves to 2¾ in (7 cm), broader than in *D. barbara* and often persistent; flowers muskily scented.

decumbent of a stem, lying horizontally along the ground, but with the apex ascending and almost erect.

decurrent of a leaf blade, where the base extends down and is adnate to the petiole (if any) and the stem.

decurved curved downward.

decussate of leaves, arranged in opposite pairs with adjacent pairs at right angles to each other, thus forming four longitudinal rows.

deep bed method a method of cultivation in beds constructed above soil level, usually to a height of about 12 in (30 cm). Ideally, the beds should be 4 ft (1.2 m) wide so that all necessary work can be carried out from the pathways, avoiding compaction from foot traffic. The method is frequently associated with deeply dug beds and high organic-matter input, and is sometimes referred to as the French intensive method. See *bed, raised bed*.

deer any mammal of the family *Cervidae*, of which two species, the ROE DEER (*Capreolus capreolus*) and FALLOW DEER (*Cervus dama*), are most likely to invade gardens in Europe; other species such as SIKA and MUNTJAC may do so in some areas. Deer attack trees and shrubs by browsing foliage and stripping bark. They may also fray bark by rubbing their newly formed antlers against it to remove the velvet covering. Low-growing plants are eaten to ground level. Deer mostly feed at dusk and dawn so they are seldom seen, but hoof marks will usually be apparent in soft soil. Since deer lack incisor teeth in their upper jaw, the shoots of damaged trees and shrubs are cleanly cut on one side with a characteristic frayed edge on the other. A wide range of plants is subject to attack by deer, but the extent to which a particular garden is affected will depend on alternative sources of food in local woodland, the size of the deer population, and weather conditions. Control is best achieved by erecting strong fencing around the garden to a height of at least 6½ ft (2 m), or by protecting trees with trunk guards. Deer repellents and scaring devices are best avoided, since they seldom prove effective in the long term.

deficiency a condition in plants, soil, or growing media in which essential nutrients are absent or insufficient to sustain healthy growth. Symptoms of deficiency—variously expressed in leaves, shoots, and fruits, according to species and the nutrient concerned—commonly arise as a result of the inability of plants to absorb or transport available nutrients. This may be due to soil acidity or alkalinity, waterlogging, or drought. See *nutrients*.

deflexed bent downward and outward; cf. *reflexed*.

deflocculation the disintegration of aggregated clay particles, as may occur in soils low in calcium and high in sodium. It leads to the loss of soil structure.

defoliant a chemical substance that, when applied to a plant, induces abscission, causing the leaves to fall.

defoliation the removal of leaves from plants. It may occur as a natural response to seasonal change in the case of deciduous species, or as a result of pest or disease attack, drought, waterlogging, or other disorder in the case of evergreen species. Defoliation may be a deliberate operation for cultural advantage, especially in the case of tomatoes, where the lower leaves are progressively removed as a means of improving air circulation and also of extracting moribund tissue.

defruiting see *fruit thinning*.

degree-days see *day-degrees*.

dehiscence the mode and process of opening (e.g., by valves, slits, pores, or splitting) of a seed capsule or anther to release seed or pollen.

dehiscent of a seed capsule; splitting open along definite lines to release seeds when ripe; cf. *indehiscent*.

dehorning the severe cutting back of a selection of large branches in an established tree, especially a fruit tree, to invigorate, contain, or improve shape. The process is less drastic than heading back.

Deinanthe (from Greek *deinos*, strange, and *anthos*, flower, which refers to the exceptionally large flowers). Hydrangeaceae. E Asia. 2 species, robust, erect perennial herbs with ovate to elliptic, toothed or lobed leaves, borne toward the stem apex. Produced in summer in terminal clusters or panicles, the

Hydrangea-like flowers are numerous, large and nodding. Hardy to about 5°F (–15°C). Grow in sheltered shade in cool, humus-rich, moisture-retentive but freely draining nonalkaline soil. Propagate by division or by ripe seed sown when fresh. *D. caerulea* (China; to 20 in (50 cm); flowers pale mauve to lilac-blue with blue stamens).

delayed open-center a form of fruit tree where the lower main branches arise from a central trunk over a distance of 4–6 ft (1.2–1.8 m), above which the head opens out to produce a goblet shape.

Delonix (from Greek *delos*, conspicuous, and *onyx*, claw, referring to the showy, clawed petals). Leguminosae. Old World tropics. 10 species, evergreen or deciduous trees with bipinnate leaves and racemes of showy flowers, each composed of five clawed petals and a bundle of long stamens. The following species is widely planted in tropical and subtropical regions as a fast-growing and long-flowering street tree. In temperate zones, it will grow in large tubs in the greenhouse or conservatory, with a minimum temperature of 50°F (10°C). In frost-free zones, grow in deep, well-drained soil with full sun and shelter from cold winds. Propagate as for *Caesalpinia*. *D. regia* (syn. *Poinciana regia*) FLAMBOYANT, FLAME TREE, ROYAL POINCIANA, PEACOCK FLOWER; Madagascar; to 33 ft (10 m) with spreading crown; flowers to 4 in (10 cm) across, scarlet to flame or orange, variably marked or striped gold to cream or pure gold).

dehiscent seed capsule (larkspur)

Delosperma (from Greek *delos*, visible, and *sperma*, seed, referring to the lidless seed capsules). Aizoaceae. Africa. Over 150 species, perennials or, rarely, annuals or biennials, with succulent leaves and daisylike flowers. Cultivate as for *Lampranthus*. *D. tradescantioides* (South Africa; dwarf and creeping perennial with ovate to cylindrical, 3-angled leaves to 1¼ in (3 cm) long and white flowers to 1 in (2.5 cm) wide).

Delphinium (from Greek *delphis*, dolphin; *delphinion* was a name used by Dioscorides). Ranunculaceae. North temperate regions. 250 species, annual, biennial, or perennial herbs with palmately or digitately lobed and cut leaves in basal clumps and on tall, erect stems. Produced in summer in narrow, sometimes branching racemes, the flowers are spurred and consist of five petal-like sepals and two pairs of smaller petals. When the latter are distinctively colored and downy, they are termed the "bee." The smaller species are suited to the rock garden and sunny borders on free-draining, gritty soils. Those from the western United States may need winter protection in cold areas. There is a wide choice of hybrid cultivars.

The tall spectacular hybrids of gardens, which are available in varying shades of blue, and purple, mauve, pink, cream, and white, are derived mainly from *D. elatum*, *D. grandiflorum*, and *D × belladonna*.

Cultivars may be considered in three groups. The Belladonna Group are perennials, upright and branching with palmately lobed leaves. Cap-shaped single flowers are borne in abundance on strong stems of loose branches; each flower $^3/_4$ in (2 cm) or more in diameter, with spurs up to $1^1/_4$ in (3 cm) long. Plant height is up to 4 ft (1.2 m); flowering early to late summer; suitable as cut flower as well as garden decoration. The Elatum Group are clump-forming perennials with flowering spikes bearing numerous single, semi-double or double flowers, at least $2^1/_2$ in (6 cm) in diameter; each with five large outer sepals and eight inner sepals. Stems bear lateral shoots that produce smaller flowers after those on the main stem. Plant height is up to $6^1/_2$ ft (2 m); flowering early to midsummer, repeat flush in fall if cut back. The Pacific Hybrids include annual, biennial, or perennial cultivars, similar to the Elatum Group. Flowers up to $2^3/_4$ in (7 cm) in diameter, semidouble, borne in dense, erect inflorescences up to 8 ft (2.5 m) high; early to mid-summer.

Delphiniums thrive in any fertile soil that is not waterlogged in winter. Perennial types can be planted from spring to early fall and annual types in the spring; adequate watering is essential. Hybrids and cultivars do not come true from seed. They may be propagated by division in early fall or early spring or, preferably, from 2–4-in (5–10-cm) shoot cuttings, with solid stems, taken in the spring. Rooting can be achieved in a mixture of peat and sand, or in perlite or in water. Where appropriate, seed should be packaged and refrigerated to preserve viability, before sowing during late winter or early spring under protection at 59°F (15°C). In the US, delphiniums are not usually grown as perennials.

Tall garden hybrids require staking; for high-quality flower spikes, shoots should be thinned to 5–7 per established plant. Watering is essential in dry spells, and cutting the stems to ground level immediately after flowering will produce a second flush, but supplementary feeding should be applied.

D. × belladonna (*D. elatum × D. grandiflorum*) garden hybrids with tall, branching stems to $5^3/_4$ ft (1.75 m) with single or semidouble flowers in shades of sky blue, dark blue, gentian, and indigo, often with a white "eye"); *D. brunonianum* Himalaya; perennial to 20 in (50 cm) tall with pale purple-blue, dark-spurred flowers; *D. cardinale* California; short-lived perennial to 24 in (60 cm) with spikes of scarlet flowers with yellow "eyes"; *D. elatum* Southern and Central Europe to Siberia; perennial to $6^1/_2$ ft (2 m) tall with dense spikes of single, semidouble, or double flowers in shades of blue, purple and white and with contrasting "eyes"); *D. grandiflorum* (syn. *D. chinense*) Siberia, E Asia; perennial often treated as an annual, to $3^1/_4$ ft (1 m) tall with blue, purple, or white flowers in loose racemes, usually with contrasting dark and white "eyes"); *D. nudicaule* California; short-lived perennial, 8–24 in (20–60 cm) tall with loose racemes of yellow-eyed, orange to fiery red flowers; *D. tatsienense* China, Tibet; short-lived perennial, 8–24 in (20–60 cm) tall with loose spikes of bright blue or white flowers. For *D. ajacis* and *D. consolida* see *Consolida ambigua*.

Possible problems: aphids, slugs and snails; powdery mildew, virus.

deltoid, deltate resembling an equilateral triangle attached by the broad end rather than the point; shaped like the capital form of the Greek letter, delta Δ.

demersed of a part constantly submersed under water.

Dendranthema (from Greek *dendron*, tree, and *anthemon*, flower). Compositae. Europe, C and E Asia. About 20 species, muskily aromatic perennial herbs, sometimes woody at base, with pinnatifid or entire leaves and daisy-like flower heads in loose corymbs produced in late summer and fall. The florist's chrysanthemum is *D. grandiflorum*, an ancient cultigen probably raised in gardens from the yellow-flowered, Japanese *D. indicum* (see *chrysanthemum*).

dendritic, dendroid branching finely at the apex of a stem, in the manner of the head of a tree.

dendrology the botanical science concerned with the natural history of trees.

Dendrocalamus (from Greek, *dendron*, tree and *kalamos*, reed). Gramineae. SE Asia. 30 species of giant, clump-forming bamboos, separated from *Bambusa* mainly by floral characters and size. See *bamboos*.

Dendrobium (from Greek *dendron*, tree, and *bios*, life, referring to the epiphytic habit of most species). Orchidaceae. Asia, Polynesia, Australia. At least 1000 species, mostly epiphytic, perennial herbs. They range widely in habit from dwarf plants with clumps of fleshy leaves to tall species with cane-like pseudobulbs. The flowers consist of five spreading tepals and a showy lip. They are produced at various times of year, singly or in clusters, racemes or panicles. Plant in small containers, preferably clay pots or baskets, containing a very open, bark-based mix. In very humid conditions, plants can be mounted on slabs of bark or dead branches. Grow in bright, filtered sun with a breezy, humid atmosphere. Provide a minimum temperature of 50°F (10°C). Water, mist, and fertilize generously when in growth.

DENDROBIUM

Name	Distribution	Flowering time	Hardiness	Habit	Flowers
D. aggregatum	India	spring	cool-growing	evergreen with squat, spindle-shaped pseudobulbs	to 1½ in (4 cm) diam., often scented, in arching racemes, golden yellow, throat orange
Comments: Grow in pans; give cool dry rest in winter.					
D. aphyllum *D. pierardii*	India	late winter	cool-growing	deciduous with narrow pendulous canes	to 2 in (5 cm) diam., in clusters along canes, translucent white to pink, lip cream-yellow marked purple at base
Comments: Mount on bark or raft to allow for pendulous habit.					
D. bigibbum COOKTOWN ORCHID	Australia	year-round	intermediate- to warm-growing	evergreen with erect canes and leathery dark green leaves	to 2½ in (6 cm) diam., in long-stalked sprays, pink, purple, magenta, or white, lip spurred, often with a white throat
Comments: Includes var. ***phalaenopsis*** with broader petals and strong color. A common cut flower with many hybrids and cultivars.					
D. chrysanthum	India	spring	cool-growing	deciduous, canes long, slender, pendulous	to 1½ in (4 cm) diam., fragrant, in short clusters, golden yellow, lip fringed, with a dark red-brown blotch
Comments: Grow in a basket to allow for pendulous habit.					
D. densiflorum	India	spring	cool-growing	evergreen, medium-sized; canes club-shaped	to 2 in (5 cm) diam, fragrant in dense pendulous racemes, yellow, lip orange in throat, finely fringed
D. fimbriatum	India, Burma, Thailand, China, Malaysia	spring	cool-growing	deciduous, canes long, narrowly spindle-shaped	to 2 in (5 cm) diam., in pendulous racemes, deep orange-yellow, lip golden with maroon blotch, margin intricately fringed
D. infundibulum	Burma, Thailand	late spring	intermediate-growing	evergreen; canes erect, with sparse black felt	to 3 in (8 cm) diam., in clusters, sparkling white, lip funnel-shaped, frilled with yellow stain at base
D. kingianum	Australia	year-round	cool-growing	medium-sized evergreen with dense clumps of tapering pseudobulbs and tough leaves	to 1¼ in (3 cm) diam., in erect terminal racemes, white cream, pink or purple-red
Comments: Very vigorous plant flowering profusely if left to form large pot-bound clumps.					
D. loddigesii	Laos, China	spring	intermediate-growing	semievergreen; short sprawling canes with fleshy leaves	to 2 in (5 cm) diam. solitary along stems, lilac-purple, lip orange banded white, edge purple, fringed
Comments: Grow in pans.					

D. aphyllum

D. chrysanthum

D. infundibulum

D. nobile

DENDROBIUM

Name	Distribution	Flowering time	Hardiness	Habit	Flowers
D. moschatum	India to Thailand	summer	cool-growing	evergreen; canes erect	to 2¾ in (7 cm) diam., in drooping racemes, pale yellow tinted or veined pale rose, lip hairy, slipper-shaped with 2 dark purple blotches
D. nobile	India, China, Thailand	winter-spring	cool-growing	deciduous or semievergreen; canes tall, erect	to 3 in (8 cm) diam., scented, in short clusters, white flushed mauve to pink lip white edged rosy-pink, blotched velvety crimson to maroon in throat
Comments: Very resilient, popular plant with many color forms including whites, purples, and yellow-marked. Parent of many hybrids.					
D. speciosum	Australia	year-round	intermediate-growing	evergreen; pseudobulbs stoutly club-shaped; leaves leathery	to 1½ in (4 cm) diam., fragrant, waxy, in dense terminal racemes, narrow, not opening fully, white to cream, lip marked purple
Comments: Highly floriferous if allowed to become potbound and placed outdoors in full sun from mid- to late summer.					
D. spectabile	New Guinea	summer	warm-growing	evergreen; pseudobulbs tall, canelike; leaves fleshy	to 3 in (8 cm) diam., in erect racemes, tepals narrow, wavy and twisted yellow-green striped purple, lip paler veined purple-red narrowing to a beaklike tip
D. strebloceras	Molucca	summer	warm-growing	evergreen; pseudobulbs tall, canelike; leaves fleshy	to 3 in (8 cm) diam., fragrant in lax racemes, green-yellow marked purple, petals narrow, erect and strongly twisted
D. wardianum	Assam, Burma, Thailand	spring	cool-growing	semievergreen; canes long, narrow, arching	to 4 in (10 cm) diam., fragrant, solitary or clustered, white tipped magenta, lip with orange stain and dark crimson blotches in throat
Comments: Requires high temperatures and plentiful water and fertilizer in growth, cool dry conditions at rest.					

When resting, they should be watered only to prevent the pseudobulbs from shriveling. *D. nobile*, *D. bigibbum*, and their respective hybrids make excellent houseplants. Increase by division; also by detaching and growing on the plantlets that sometimes develop along the canelike pseudobulbs.

Dendromecon (from Greek *dendron*, tree, and *mekon*, poppy). Papaveraceae. SW US, Mexico. TREE POPPY, BUSH POPPY. 1 species, *D. rigida*, a summer-flowering, evergreen shrub or small tree, 10–20 ft (3–6 m) tall, with tough, ovate to lanceolate leaves to 4 in (10 cm) long. The solitary flowers are ¾–2¾ in (2–7 cm) in diameter, fragrant, and composed of four yellow petals and numerous stamens. It is hardy to 10°F (–12°C) if planted near a sunny, south-facing wall and in well-drained loamy soil, with added sharp sand and rubble. Protect in winter with a dry mulch. Propagate by ripe-wood cuttings in summer, with moderate heat, in a very sandy mix.

denitrification the reduction of nitrates to nitrites, ammonium and gaseous ammonia through microbial activity in anaerobic conditions. See *nitrogen*.

Dennstaedtia (for August Wilhelm Dennstedt [1776–1826], German botanist and physician). Dennstaedtiaceae. Tropics and subtropics, eastern N America. Some 70 species, evergreen or deciduous ferns with creeping rhizomes and more or less deltoid, 1–4-pinnate or -pinnatifid fronds. The following species is hardy to at least –22°F (–30°C). Plant in the woodland garden in full or part shade in moist and acidic, humus-rich soil. Propagate by division or spores. *D. punctiloba* HAY-SCENTED FERN; eastern N America; deciduous, fronds to 30 × 8 in (75 × 20 cm), bright green, deltoid to lanceolate, finely 2–3-pinnate; pinnules ovate to rhomboid, acute, notched to lobed; scented of hay when dried.

toothed ("dentate") leaves

Castanea dentata

dentate toothed; of the margins of leaf blades and other flattened organs, cut with teeth. Strictly, dentate describes teeth that are shallow and represent two sides of a roughly equilateral triangle, in contrast to serrate (saw-toothed), where the teeth are sharper and curved forward, and crenate, where the teeth are blunt and rounded. Less precisely, the term is used to cover any type of toothed margin.

denticulate minutely dentate.

depauperate reduced in stature, number, or function, as if starved and ill-formed. Species with organs described thus are, however, usually perfectly healthy but adapted to cope with a particular ecological factor.

dependent hanging downward as a result of its weight, as in a flower- or fruit-laden branch.

deplanate flattened or expanded.

depressed sunken or flattened, as if pressed from above.

descending tending gradually downward.

Deschampsia (for Louis Deschamps [1765–1842], French naturalist). Gramineae. HAIR GRASS. Temperate Regions. 50 species, perennial or, rarely, annual grasses forming dense tussocks. They flower in summer, bearing many small spikelets in finely branched, long-stalked panicles. Both species described below are perennial, hardy, and will grow in sun or light shade. They prefer moist (not wet) conditions, but will tolerate some drought, especially from late summer onward. *D. cespitosa* will grow in heavy, poorly drained soils. *D. flexuosa* needs a neutral to acidic soil, ideally rich in leaf mold and sand. Clumps of *D. lexuosa* may become tired and bald within a few years. Increase both species by division or seed.

D. cespitosa syn. *D. caespitosa*; TUFTED HAIR GRASS, TUSSOCK GRASS, HASSOCKS; northern temperate regions; evergreen to semideciduous, densely tufted, forming large, erect to spreading clumps; leaves 4–12 (10–30 cm) × $^{1}/_{12}$–$^{1}/_4$ in (0.25–0.5 cm), linear, glossy dark green, ridged and channeled above, rough to touch; inflorescence

8–39 in (20–100 cm), loosely pyramidal to cylindrical, branches occupying up to half length of inflorescence, sometimes weeping to one side, spikelets small, green, or golden suffused silver to bronze or purple, pale blonde when dry and persisting well into fall; var. *parviflora*: a small, rare and rather fine variety; var. *vivipara*: spikelets develop into plantlets instead of seed; 'Bronzeschleier': syn. 'Bronze Veil', inflorescence large, tinted bronze; 'Goldhaenge': syn. 'Golden Showers', late-flowering, tall with golden inflorescences; 'Tautraeger': syn. 'Dew Carrier': small, compact, inflorescence tinted blue; *D. flexuosa* CRINKLED HAIR GRASS, COMMON HAIR GRASS; northern temperate regions; deciduous to semievergreen, densely tufted forming low, moplike clumps; leaves to 6 × $^{1}/_{16}$ in (15 × 0.1 cm), threadlike, terete, bright green, smooth; inflorescence 8–39 in (20–100 cm), loosely pyramidal, branches occupying uppermost quarter of inflorescence, very fine, somewhat wavy, glistening, copper-red to bronze-green, spikelets small, shimmering, bronze to copper-red, silver or yellow-green; 'Tatra Gold': leaves pale gold to lime green, inflorescence soft bronze, comes true from seed.

Desfontainia (for René Louiche Desfontaines [1752–1833], French botanist). Loganiaceae. Chile, Peru. 1 species, *D. spinosa*, a bushy, evergreen shrub to 10 ft (3 m) with hollylike leaves. Produced in late summer and fall, the solitary flowers are $^{5}/_8$–$3^{1}/_2$ in (1.5–9 cm) long, tubular to funnelform, crimson to scarlet-orange and edged with five yellow, shallow lobes. With shelter from cold, drying winds, it is hardy to 14°F (–10°C), but may also be grown in the cold greenhouse or conservatory. Plant in humus-rich, moisture-retentive, acidic soil in partial shade. Mulch established plants and water plentifully during dry weather. Propagate from seed surface-sown on a soilless propagating mix, or in summer by semiripe cuttings rooted under mist or in a closed case with bottom heat.

deshooting the removal of soft young shoots from trained fruit trees, especially those growing toward or out from the wall on wall-trained trees.

desiccant a chemical substance that causes the aerial parts of plants to dry out. It is used to facilitate the harvesting of commercially grown potatoes. In gardens, lawn sand has such an effect on some plants growing in turf.

Desmodium (from Greek *desmos*, band, referring to the stamens which are united in a band). Leguminosae. Widespread. BEGGARWEED, TICK-TREFOIL. Over 300 species of deciduous shrubs, subshrubs, herbs or perennials with 3-lobed to trifoliolate or pinnate leaves and pealike flowers in racemes or panicles in late summer. The genus is hardy to –10°F (–23°C). Cultivate as for *Indigofera*. *D. elegans* (syn. *D. tiliifolium*) shrub to 5 ft (1.5 m); leaves with three leaflets, each to $2^{1}/_2$ in (6 cm) long, obovate to rounded, dark green above, gray-downy beneath; flowers rose to carmine or pale lilac, in racemes to 8 in (20 cm) long.

determinate (1) of inflorescences such as cymes where a central or terminal flower opens first, thus ending extension of the main axis; (2) of tomato cultivars of bush habit, where side branches develop instead of a continuous main stem (cf. *determinate*).

Deutzia (for Johann van der Deutz [1743–88], friend and patron of Thunberg, the namer of this genus). Hydrangeaceae. Asia, C America. 60 species, usually deciduous shrubs with pith-filled branches and peeling bark. The leaves are ovate to lanceolate or elliptic, sometimes toothed and more or less hairy. Often fragrant and in tones of white, cream, and rose to purple-red, the flowers appear in spring and summer in racemes, cymes, panicles, or corymbs. They consist of five elliptic to lanceolate or rounded petals and ten stamens. Most species will tolerate cold to at least 5°F (–15°C), although a number, including *D. gracilis*, *D. grandiflora*, *D.* × *lemoinei*, and *D.* × *rosea*, are susceptible to damage by late frosts. They perform best in moist but well-drained, fertile and humus-rich loamy soil, with shade from early morning sun in regions that suffer late spring frosts, and with protection from hot afternoon sun. After flowering, remove old and overcrowded growth at

D

the base. Flowers are carried on the short laterals produced by the previous season's growth and are produced more generously on young wood. Propagate species by seed, cultivars and hybrids by soft nodal cuttings in late spring; treat cuttings with 0.4% IBA and root in a sandy mix in a closed case with bottom heat. Alternatively, propagate by semiripe cuttings and hardwood cuttings in a cold frame, by removal of suckers or by layering for low-growing plants such as *D. compacta*, *D. scabra*, *D.* × *rosea*.

D. compacta China; to 3¼ ft (1 m); leaves to 2¾ in (7 cm), lanceolate, finely toothed; flowers to ½ in (1.2 cm) across, white, in small, compact corymbose panicles; *D.* × *elegantissima* (garden origin; to 5 ft (1.5 m); leaves ovate to oblong-ovate, sharply toothed above; flowers to ¾ in (2 cm) across, pink, in loose cymes; includes 'Elegantissima', with upright growth, dark green leaves, and pale pink flowers edged carmine, 'Fasciculata', an erect, rounded shrub with mid-green leaves and pale pink flowers, and 'Rosealind', with deep carmine flowers; *D. gracilis* Japan; erect to 6½ ft (2 m); leaves lanceolate to ovate, serrulate; flowers pure white, to ¾ in (2 cm) across, in racemes or narrow panicles to 3 in (8 cm) long; includes 'Grandiflora', a hybrid with *D. scabra* that is larger in all respects, and forms with yellow-mottled leaves and pink flowers; *D. longifolia* China; to 6½ ft (2 m); leaves lanceolate, finely tapering, serrulate; flowers to 1 in (2.5 cm) across, white, tinted purple-pink outside, in broad cymes to 3 in (8 cm); includes 'Elegans', with drooping branches and purple-pink-tinted flowers, and 'Veitchii', with narrow leaves and purple-tinted flowers; *D.* × *magnifica* (garden origin; to 6½ ft (2 m), robust and upright; leaves ovate to oblong, sharply and finely toothed; flowers white, single or double, in dense panicles to 2½ in (6 cm) long; includes 'Staphyleoides', with large, drooping panicles of white, fragrant flowers with reflexed petals; *D. monbeigii* (China; to 5 ft (1.5 m), with slender branches; leaves ovate to lanceolate, serrate; flowers to ½ in (1.4 cm) across, white, in corymbose inflorescences to 2½ in (6 cm); *D. pulchra* Philippines, Taiwan; to 12 ft (4 m); leaves lanceolate

to narrowly ovate, entire to toothed, thick-textured, very hairy beneath; flowers white, sometimes tinted pink, in a slender and sparse, nodding panicle to 4¾ in (12 cm); *D.* × *rosea* garden origin; dwarf and arching to 3¼ ft (1 m); leaves elliptic to oblong or lanceolate, serrate; flowers white, tinted pink, in short, broad panicles; includes 'Carminea', with red-pink flowers; *D. scabra* Japan; to 8 ft (2.5 m); leaves broadly ovate, coarsely serrate; flowers to ⅝ in (1.5 cm) across, white, honey-scented, in loose, broadly pyramidal panicles; 'Plena': flowers double, pale pink; *D. setchuenensis* China; to 6½ ft (2 m); leaves ovate, finely tapering, serrulate; flowers white, to ½ in (1 cm) across in loose, broad corymbs.

dewberry, various *Rubus* spp,. especially *R. almus* DEWBERRY, *R. caesius* EUROPEAN DEWBERRY, *R. canadensis* AMERICAN DEWBERRY, *R. flagellaris* AMERICAN DEWBERRY, NORTHERN DEWBERRY, *R. hispidus* SWAMP DEWBERRY *R. minus* SWAMP DEWBERRY, *R. trivialis* SOUTHERN DEWBERRY.

dewpoint as temperature falls during calm, clear nights, the capacity of air to hold moisture is reduced until saturation is reached, and this is known as the dewpoint. Condensation and the formation of dew consequently occurs on the cool surfaces of plants.

diammonium phosphate see *ammonium phosphate*.

diadelphous of stamens, borne in two distinct bundles, or with several stamens united and a further solitary stamen set apart from the others, as in many Leguminosae.

dialypetalous see *polypetalous*.

diandrous possessing two perfect stamens.

Dianella (diminutive of Diana). Liliaceae (Phormiaceae). Tropical Africa, Asia, Australasia, flax lily. 25–30 species, evergreen, fibrous-rooted, perennial herbs with erect, slender stems, each bearing a terminal fan of grasslike to narrowly sword-shaped leaves. To ¾ in (2 cm) across, the starlike flowers con-

sist of six tepals and nod in spreading, loose panicles. The flowers are followed by deep purple-blue berries. Grow *Daniella* in the cool greenhouse or conservatory, and provide a minimum temperature of 41–45°F (5–7°C). These plants will also survive outdoors in sheltered sites where temperatures do not drop far below freezing for long periods. Grow in any moderately fertile soil in sun or dappled shade. Water plentifully and fertilize when in full growth; keep just moist in winter. Propagate by seed sown under glass in spring, alternatively by division.
D. caerulea stem to 24 in (60 cm) tall; flowers to ⅝ in (1.5 cm) across, blue to white with pale yellow anthers, in panicles to 12 in (30 cm); *D. tasmanica* stem to 48 in (120 cm) tall; flowers to ¾ in (2 cm) across, pale blue with brown anthers, in panicles to 24 in (60 cm).

Dianthus 'La Bourboule'
Alpine pinks are much smaller and daintier than modern pinks and border carnations.

Dianthus (from Greek *dios*, and *anthos* ["flower of the gods"]). Caryophyllaceae. CARNATION, PINK. Mostly Europe and Asia. 300 species, perennial, biennial and, rarely, annual herbs. They range in habit from woody-based mat-formers to erect herbs. Produced in spring and summer, the flowers are solitary or borne in terminal clusters. They consist of a cylindric calyx and five, spreading, clawed petals. These are usually obovate, toothed to cut at the outer margin and sometimes bearded below. Many are perfumed, most characteristically of cloves.

The perennial species listed here are hardy and suited to well-drained, sunny positions—for example, border edges, cracks in paving, wall crevices, and the rock garden. The smaller species generally fare better in alpine sinks or in raised beds. All *Dianthus* need sandy soil, neutral to alkaline, with the exception of the acid-loving *D. pavonius*. They will deteriorate in wet conditions. Increase by cuttings or rooted offsets in spring and summer. *D. barbatus* and *D. chinensis* are usually treated as annuals or biennials, sown under glass in spring and planted out in fall or (in severe climates) the following spring, having been overwintered in a cold frame. They need well-drained soil and full sun. See also *carnation* and *pinks*.

D. alpinus Alps; tufted perennial, 2–6 in (5–15 cm); leaves linear to oblong-lanceolate, shiny; flowers solitary, deep pink with crimson purple spots on a white "eye," petals ½–¾ in (1–2 cm), toothed and bearded; includes white- and salmon-flowered cultivars; *D. armeria* DEPTFORD PINK; Europe, W Asia; hairy biennial or annual, 8–16 in (20–40 cm); leaves narrowly oblong; flowers in dense, involucrate heads, pink with pale dots, petals to ¼ in (0.5 cm), toothed and bearded; *D. barbatus* SWEET WILLIAM; S Europe, widely naturalized; glabrous, short-lived perennial, 12–28 in (30–70 cm); leaves lanceolate-elliptic; flowers in dense, broad, involucrate heads, red-purple with pale dots or a white band at center, petals to ½ in (1 cm), bearded; the parent of numerous cultivars, hybrids, and seed races including short and tall plants, some bushy, others willowy, with dense heads of flowers in shades of white, pale rose, bright pink, cerise, crimson, and blood red, many of them bicolored—for example, a white-fringed flower with a bold red center); *D. carthusianorum* S and C Europe; glabrous perennial, 8–24 in (20–60 cm); leaves linear, grassy; flowers in slender-stalked heads, red-purple, pink or white, petals to ⅝ in (1.5 cm), toothed, bearded; *D. chinensis* INDIAN PINK; China; biennial or short-lived perennial, 8–28 in (20–70 cm), usually somewhat hairy; leaves lanceolate; flowers in loose clusters, lilac-pink with a purple "eye," petals to ⅝ in (1.5 cm), deeply toothed

or cut; includes cultivars with flowers in shades of pink, red, and white, many treated as annuals, among them 'Heddewigii'—compact, very free-flowering plants in a range of colors; *D. deltoides* MAIDEN PINK; Europe, Asia; tufted, mat-forming perennial, 6–18 in (15–45 cm), sometimes hairy, often glaucous; leaves narrowly oblanceolate to linear; flowers solitary, pale to deep pink with pale spots in a dark "eye," petals to ⅜ in (0.8 cm), toothed and bearded; *D. gratianopolitanus* (syn. *D. aesius*) CHEDDAR PINK W and C Europe; compact, mat-forming perennial, 2–8 in (5–20 cm); leaves linear, glaucous; flowers solitary, pink or red, very fragrant, petals ½ in (1 cm), toothed, sometimes bearded; *D. haematocalyx* Balkans; tufted perennial, 4–12 in (10–30 cm); leaves linear, glaucous, with thickened margins; flowers solitary or a few per cluster, deep purple-pink with buff exteriors and a purple-red calyx, petals ¼–½ in (0.5–1 cm), toothed, sparsely bearded; *D. microlepis* Bulgaria; dwarf, cushion-forming perennial to 2 in (5 cm); leaves linear, glaucous; flowers solitary, clear pink or white, petals to ¼ in (0.7 cm), toothed and bearded; *D. monspessulanus* S and C Europe; loosely tufted, mat-forming perennial, 12–24 in (30–60 cm); leaves linear, grassy, sometimes glaucous; flowers solitary or a few grouped together, strongly fragrant, pink, pale lilac or white, petals ½–¾ in (1–2 cm), finely cut into narrow segments; *D. myrtinervius* Balkans, Macedonian border of Greece; densely mat-forming perennial to 2 in (5 cm); leaves very small, elliptic to narrowly oblong; flowers solitary, very short-stalked, bright pink, sometimes with a dark-bordered white "eye," petals ¼ in (0.5 cm), toothed, sparsely bearded); *D. pavonius* (syn. *D. neglectus*) SW Alps; densely tufted, mat-forming perennial, 2–6 in (5–15 cm); leaves linear, usually gray-green; flowers solitary, pale pink to crimson, buff on exterior, petals ½ in (1 cm), toothed and bearded; *D. superbus* Europe, Asia; mat-forming perennial, 8–24 in (20–60 cm); leaves linear to narrowly lanceolate, pale green; flowers solitary, very fragrant, pink to pale lilac or purple-pink, petals ½–1¼ in (1–3 cm), finely and deeply cut into many narrow lobes.

diapause the state of reduced metabolic activity in which insects may overwinter in temperate climates.

Diapensia (ancient Greek name). Diapensiaceae. Circumboreal. 4 species, low-growing, tufted, evergreen subshrubs with glabrous, entire leaves and solitary, terminal flowers in early summer—these are tubular with five, spreading lobes. In cool, damp climates, *D. lapponica* is suited to north-facing crevices in a rock garden, shady scree beds, or troughs. Plant in part shade or good indirect light in moist, nonalkaline sandy soil, enriched with leaf mold. Increase by careful division in spring; alternatively, propagate by soft tip cuttings taken after flowering. *D. lapponica* Alaska, N Asia; creeping subshrub to 3 in (7.5 cm); leaves to ½ in (1 cm), spathulate to linear, leathery turning red in winter; flowers solitary, white, to ¾ in (2 cm) across.

Diascia (from Greek *dis-*, two, and *askos*, sac, referring to the two sacs marked by yellow and maroon patches on the corolla and known as "windows"). Scrophulariaceae. South Africa. 50 species, erect to decumbent annual and perennial herbs (those listed here are perennial). The leaves are small, elliptic to ovate or heart-shaped, serrate and often glandular. Bright flowers, carried from late spring to fall in terminal racemes, have rounded petals and lateral spurs containing dark glands. Most *Diascia* species can survive temperatures down to 23°F (–5°C) in very well-drained soil. Take cuttings as a precaution against winter losses, planting out in a sunny, sheltered site when all danger of frost is past. These plants may also be treated as half-hardy annuals, and are especially suited to baskets and containers. Deadhead plants to prolong the flowering period. Under glass, grow in pots of low-fertility loam-based medium; water plentifully in summer, and feed semiweekly with a diluted liquid fertilizer when in active growth. Propagate *Diascia* by softwood cuttings in summer, and from lightly covered seed sown in cold frames or under glass, at 59°F (15°C) in fall or early spring; overwinter fall-sown plants at

50°F (10°C). Alternatively, increase by division in spring.

D. barberae (syn. *D. cordata*) TWINSPUR stems erect or sprawling, to 12 in (30 cm), glandular-hairy above; flowers in loose racemes, rose-pink with a yellow blotch and maroon-black glands; includes 'Ruby Field', with profuse, salmon-pink flowers; *D. rigescens* stems erect or sprawling, to 20 in (50 cm); leaves becoming tinted red-brown with age; flowers in dense racemes, rose-pink with dark glands; *D. vigilis* sprawling, to 20 in (50 cm) with small, rounded, fleshy leaves; flowers in loose racemes, pale pink with dark glands.

Pricking out with a dibber
This pencil-shaped tool is invaluable for both making holes in soil and guiding in the delicate roots of seedlings, avoiding the need to touch and possibly damage them.

dibber, dibble a tool used to make holes in soil or containerized growing media for planting or for inserting seed, seedlings, or cuttings. Dibbers for outdoor use take the form of a wooden implement about 10 in (25 cm) long, as thick as a standard spade handle, with a T- or D-shaped hand grip and sometimes a steel tip. Dibbers for greenhouse use are pen-sized and made of wood or plastic. Both forms have tapered ends.

Dicentra (from Greek *dis*, two, and *kentron*, spur, referring to the 2-spurred flowers). Fumariaceae. Asia, N America. 19 species, annual or perennial deciduous herbs (those listed here are perennial), with ferny, ternately decompound leaves. Borne in spring and summer in panicles, racemes, or corymbs, the pendulous flowers are heart-shaped in outline and consist of four petals in two pairs, the outer pair spurred at the base and usually pouched, the inner pair tongue-shaped,

with convex inner faces and crested apices forming a hood covering the anthers. The genus is fully hardy. Grow in humus-rich, moist, acidic to neutral soil, ideally with light shade. *D. formosa*, *D. peregrina* and *D. spectabilis* will grow in a sunny border in cool, moist soil. *D. cucullaria* naturalizes well in woodland and shrubbery. Propagate from seed sown in spring at 59°F (15°C) also, divide in spring or after foliage dieback. Root cuttings of *D. spectabilis* will succeed in a sandy mix, placed in a cold frame.

D. cucullaria DUTCHMAN'S BREECHES; N America; to 12 in (30 cm); leaves soft, ferny, blue-green; flowers white to palest pink, tipped yellow; *D. eximia* TURKEY CORN, STAGGERWEED; US; to 24 in (60 cm); leaves finely cut, mid-green above, glaucous beneath; flowers magenta to pink, rarely white; *D. formosa* WILD BLEEDING HEART; western N America; to 16 in (40 cm); leaves finely cut, blue-green to silver gray with a purple-pink cast; flowers red to coral, salmon, rose, or pure white; very glaucous plants are sometimes named subsp. *oregana*, one of the best silver-leaved white-flowered cultivars is 'Langtrees'; *D. peregrina* E Asia; to 6 in (15 cm); leaves glaucous, finely and deeply cut; flowers white to magenta or purple, tipped purple; *D. spectabilis* BLEEDING HEART; to 40 in (100 cm); leaves mid- to dark green, loosely but deeply divided; flowers large, with heart-shaped, deep red to pink outer petals and white inner petals; includes pure white forms).

dichasium a type of determinate inflorescence; the basic structure has three flowers (members), one terminating the primary axis, the other two carried on more or less equal secondary branches arising from beneath the primary member in a false dichotomy. The secondary members may themselves be dichasia. Such a structure is known as a dichasial cyme or a compound dichasial cyme, although the former term has been applied by some authors to the basic dichasium itself.

dichogamy the maturing of a flower's anthers and stigmas at different times, preventing self-pollination. See *protandry*, *protogyny*.

Dichorisandra (from Greek *dis*, two, *choris*, apart, and *aner*, man, referring to the way two stamens stand apart from the others in some species). Commelinaceae. Tropical America. 25 species, evergreen perennial herbs, with erect, stout stems and large, smooth, lanceolate to elliptic leaves. Produced in clusters in summer, the flowers consist of three, showy, rounded petals. Provide humid conditions, with a minimum winter temperature of 54°F (12°C) and shade from direct sunlight. Grow in a well-drained, fertile and moist medium. Propagate by division or cuttings.

D. reginae Peru; stem to 12 in (30 cm); leaves to 7 in (18 cm), striped or flecked silver above, flushed purple beneath; flowers white edged violet-blue; *D. thyrsiflora* (SE Brazil; stem to 80 in (200 cm) are below; leaves to 12 in (30 cm), deep green above, faintly purple-tinted beneath; flowers violet, white at base).

dichotomous branching regularly by forking repeatedly in two, the two branches of each division are basically equal.

Dicksonia (for James Dickson [1738–1822], British botanist). Dicksoniaceae. America, SE Asia, Australasia, Polynesia. Some 25 species, large tree ferns with erect, columnlike trunks—these are clothed with dead frond bases, shaggy hairs, and fibrous roots and crowned with spreading rosettes of 1–4-pinnately compound, lanceolate to deltoid fronds. *D. antarctica* is hardy to 23°F (–5°C) and may be grown outside in (min. 0°F/–18°C). Water copiously during the summer growing months. Plants growing outside should have their trunks hosed down daily during hot, dry weather to encourage rooting through the stem. Under glass, provide bright indirect light, plentiful water, and frequent dampening down during hot weather (temperatures greater than 90°F/32°C are harmful). Grow in a slightly acidic medium, moist but porous and rich in leaf mold. Specimens in large containers or those planted out should be top-dressed or mulched with fresh compost or organic matter annually. During the winter, water moderately and ensure that maximum light reaches plants growing under glass.

Those growing outside need to be protected with bracken or burlap if severe weather threatens. Propagate by spores. Although slow-growing, young plants so raised are usually quick to establish and will cope better with life in the garden than the ancient, wild-collected trunks recently exported in such numbers. *D. antarctica* MAN FERN, TASMANIAN TREE FERN, WOOLY TREE FERN; Australia, Tasmania; trunk to 4 ft × 16 in (3 m × 40 cm), densely fibrous, fox red to dark brown, with large scars and remnants left by fallen fronds; fronds 5–8 ft (1.5–2.5 m) lanceolate-triangular, light to dark green and coarsely textured; pinnae to 18 in (45 cm), lanceolate; pinnules linear; segments oblong, toothed or lobed.

dicotyledons (abbreviation: dicot[s]) one of the two major divisions of the angiosperms, the other being the monocotyledons. Dicots are usually characterized by having two cotyledons, the presence of cambium in many species and floral parts commonly occurring in fours and fives.

Dictamnus (from Greek *diktamnon*, dittany). Rutaceae. SW Europe to E Asia. DITTANY, BURNING BUSH. 2 species. *D. albus*, a woody-based, perennial herb to 32 in (80 cm) tall with glandular, trifoliolate to pinnate leaves. Borne in summer in erect, terminal racemes, the flowers are some 1½ in (4 cm) across and consist of five elliptic to lanceolate white, pink, red, or lilac petals, sometimes streaked or dotted with red. Hardy to –30°F (–34°C). Plant in a sunny or partly shaded position in well-drained, fertile soil. Propagate from seed sown in a cold frame in spring (seedlings may take several years to attain flowering size), or by division of large, mature clumps in spring or fall.

didymous twinned; (in pairs) the two parts similar and attached by a short portion of the inner surface.

didynamous possessing two pairs of stamens, the two pairs are of unequal lengths.

dieback (1) a general term for a disorder in which shoots or branches die from the tip backward, usually relatively slowly when compared to a wilt; (2) a nonspecific symptom of a number of diseases or disorders, particularly affecting woody plants.

Dieffenbachia (for Herr Dieffenbach, gardener in 1830 at Schonbrünn, Austria). Araceaea. Tropical America. DUMB CANE, MOTHER-IN-LAW'S TONGUE, TUFTROOT. Some 25 species, evergreen, erect, perennial herbs with stout, rather fleshy green stems and oblong or lanceolate to elliptic leaves. These are smooth and commonly variegated in tones of gray, white, cream, and yellow-green. The flowers are inconspicuous—packed in a club-shaped spadix and surrounded by a dull, green-white spathe. Popular foliage plants for tropical and subtropical gardens; elsewhere, they are suited to the home, interior landscapes and the intermediate to warm greenhouse (minimum winter temperature 50°F/10°C). Grow in bright, indirect light to shade, ideally with medium to high humidity. Pot in a porous, fertile, soil-less medium. Water and fertilize freely in warm weather and when in full growth, sparingly at other times. Propagate by tip cuttings, air layering, division of basal shoots, and slightly dried 2–3 in (5–8 cm) stem cuttings, in warm, humid conditions. Note: the sap of *Dieffenbachia* is poisonous.
D. amoena to 6½ ft (2 m), very robust with thick stems; leaf blades to 20 in (50 cm), elliptic to oblong, dark green with creamy white zones along lateral veins; *D. maculata* to 3¼ ft (1 m); leaves to 10 in (25 cm), oblong to lanceolate, acuminate, often heavily spotted white; includes many cultivars and

seed casings are twinned or "didymous"

Biscutella didyma

hybrids, among them, 'Exotica', compact, with ovate dark green heavily zoned leaves veined white or green-white and to 10 in (25 cm) long, and 'Rudolph Roehrs' with broad leaves heavily spattered or almost wholly zoned lime green to yellow and edged and veined dark jade green; *D.* × *memoria-corsii* leaves to 12 in (30 cm), elliptic to oblong, dark green heavily blotched silver-gray and spotted white; *D. seguine* to 4 ft (1.2 m); leaves to 18 in (45 cm), oblong to elliptic or lanceolate, glossy deep green; several cultivars and hybrids variously spotted, blotched, zoned, and veined white, cream or emerald green.

Dierama pulcherrimum
With its graceful habit and arching stems, angel's fishing rod is ideal placed by the side of a garden pond or stream.

Dierama (from Greek *dierama*, funnel, referring to the shape of the flowers). Iridaceae. Tropical and South Africa. ANGEL'S FISHING ROD, WAND FLOWER, AFRICAN HAREBELL. Iridaceae. 44 species evergreen, cormous, perennial herbs, with clumps of narrow, gray-green grassy leaves. The flowers are bell- to funnel-shaped and composed of six silken tepals; they hang on the threadlike, weeping branches of tall, slender, arching panicles in summer. All species are reliably hardy to between 23–14°F (–5°C and 10°C), although established clumps of *D. pulcherrimum* have survived temperatures of 1°F (–17°C). Grow in a sunny, sheltered site in deep, rich, moist but free-draining soil. Propagate by division in spring or by seed in fall or spring.
D. dracomontanum syn. *D. pumilum*; 12–39 in (30–100 cm) tall; flowers ¾–1¼ in (2–3 cm), pale to deep rose

pink, mauve, purple-pink, or coral; *D. pendulum* (39–79 in (100–200 cm); flowers 1¼–2 in (3–5 cm), widely bell-shaped, pale rose to magenta; includes dwarf forms with rose flowers; *D. pulcherrimum* 36–70 in (90–180 cm); flowers 1¼–2 in (3–5 cm), narrowly bell-shaped, pale pink to deep magenta or purple-red, rarely white.

Diervilla (for M. Dierville, a French surgeon who traveled in Canada 1699–1700, and introduced *D. lonicera*). Caprifoliaceae. N America, bush honeysuckle. 3 species, low, often suckering, deciduous shrubs with ovate to lanceolate leaves and, in summer, tubular, honeysuckle-like flowers in small clusters. Hardy to −22°F (−30°C). Plant in sun or part shade in well-drained soil. Prune in spring before growth begins. Propagate from suckers in spring, or from seed.

D. lonicera eastern N America; to 3¼ ft (1 m); branches smooth; flowers green-yellow, 3 per axil or 5 per terminal cyme); *D. sessilifolia* (SE US; to 3¼ ft (1 m); branches hairy; leaves tinted red at first, coloring well in fall; flowers sulfur yellow, 2 per terminal cyme; has been crossed with *D. lonicera* to produce *D.* × *splendens*.

Dietes Iridaceae. Africa (1 species, Lord Howe Island). 6 species, rhizomatous perennial herbs with fans of sword-shaped leaves and short-lived flowers on branching stems in summer. The flowers are composed of six segments, the outer three larger and outspread. Even the hardiest species, *D. bicolor*, will not tolerate temperatures much below 23°F (−5°C) and should be kept dry as temperatures fall and given a dry mulch in winter. Other species will not stand prolonged freezing. Grow in full sun or light dappled shade in open but moisture-retentive, humus-rich soil; apply liquid fertilizer and water if necessary during full growth, but reduce both water and fertilizer during the summer months after flowering. Propagate by seed or by division after flowering (divisions may not reestablish readily and should be given a period of protected cultivation).

D. bicolor South Africa; 24–39 in (60–100 cm); flowers 2½–3 in (6–8 cm) in diameter, yellow, blotched brown

and orange at center; *D. iridioides* (syn. *D. vegeta* of gardens) tropical E Africa to South Africa; 12–24 in (30–60 cm); flowers 1½–2¾ in (4–7 cm) in diameter, white stained yellow, mauve, or blue and spotted deep yellow or brown at center.

diffuse spreading widely outward.

diffusion the movement of a substance toward equilibrium from a high to low concentration. It is an important function in plant nutrient uptake and also relevant to soil aeration.

digamous with two sexes in the same flower cluster.

Double digging
Once the base of the first trench is forked over, the spoil from the second trench is turned into it, and so on up the strip.

digging the process of turning over soil with a spade or fork in preparation for sowing or planting crops. Digging can improve soil structure and fertility by breaking down clods, either directly or as a result of exposure to weathering, and by facilitating the incorporation of organic matter and lime. It can also improve drainage and aeration, bury weeds, and expose pests to predators. Some exponents of organic gardening are satisfied that equal or better results can be obtained by not digging soils of naturally good structure. During digging, the spade or fork is forced vertically into the soil to the full blade or prong depth and the handle pressed down and backward to lift the soil and turn it upside down, thereby burying weeds and crop residue.

Single digging cultivates down to blade or prong depth, which is referred

to as the top spit. A trench about 12 in (30 cm) wide is taken out at one end of the plot and the soil removed by wheelbarrow to the other end and dumped evenly just outside the boundary. Large plots may be equally divided down the longest dimension and a starting trench taken out across just half the width, the resultant soil being placed off the plot, along the adjacent untrenched boundary. Digging proceeds by turning the soil into the first trench, thereby creating a new trench. This operation is repeated progressively, the last trench being filled with soil originally barrowed to the far end. Where a large plot has been divided, the end trench is filled with soil taken from a new trench started across the undug half. The digging of the second half then proceeds in the opposite direction to the first half until the last trench is filled with soil originally dumped off the plot boundary.

Ridging is a variation aimed at exposing more surface area. Strips of ground are dug three spade widths at a time, following the single digging method described above. The left and right spadesful are thrown forward onto the central spadeful, and in this manner wide ridges are formed down the plot. These are leveled out by forking prior to sowing or planting.

Double digging (double spading, bastard trenching) follows the same principle of operating as single digging, except that the working trench is 24–30 in (60–75 cm) wide and more definitely maintained. As digging progresses, the base of the trench is forked to one spit depth.

Trenching involves cultivating to three spits deep, and requires a working trench 3¼ ft (1 m) wide. The top and second spits are turned over and the trench base forked to one spit depth. This more complex operation requires the trench to be divided along its length and each half to be dug in sequence to avoid mixing of the layers. The full-width top spit of the first trench and the second spit of one half width of the trench are initially removed in the manner described for single digging.

It is best to dig heavy, textured soils in late fall to benefit from the action of frost in breaking up clods. Light-textured soils are best left until spring to preserve their structure. Annual digging is usually necessary, but on most sites double-digging should only be required every three years and trenching only where serious compaction is identified. Organic manure can be worked in during any of the digging operations, and there are advantages in applying it so that it becomes mixed throughout the top spit. On lighter-textured soil, the manure may be spread over the ground in fall—earthworm activity will draw much of it into the surface layer before spring digging. If lime is needed, apply it over the soil surface in the fall, before digging, and always fork in several weeks ahead of any dressing of animal manure.

Digitalis (from Latin *digitus*, finger, referring to the shape of the flower). Scrophulariaceae. Europe, NW Africa, to C Asia. FOXGLOVE. Some 20 species, biennial or perennial herbs, with leaves occurring in a basal rosette and on the erect flowering stems. Tubular to deeply bell-shaped and weakly 2-lipped, the flowers are carried in a one-sided spike in summer. Grow in freely draining, humus-rich soil in partial or dappled shade, or in sun where soil is reliably moisture-retentive throughout the growing season. Propagate by seed, which requires light for germination; perennials may also by increased by division.

D. *ferruginea* RUSTY FOXGLOVE; S Europe, W Asia; biennial or perennial to 3¼ ft (1 m); flowers to 1¼ in (3 cm), golden brown tinted rusty red with darker veins inside; D. *grandiflora* LARGE YELLOW FOXGLOVE; Europe; biennial or perennial to 3¼ ft (1 m); flowers to 2 in (5 cm), cream to pale yellow or apricot, with darker veins or spots within, broadly funnel-shaped; D. *lanata* GRECIAN FOXGLOVE; E Europe, Aegean, Turkey, Siberia; biennial or short-lived perennial to 5 ft (1.5 m); flowers to ¾ in (2 cm), white with nutmeg spots and maroon veins; D. *lutea* (STRAW FOXGLOVE; Europe, NW Africa; perennial to 39 in (100 cm); flowers to ¾ in (2 cm), creamy white to pale yellow, narrow; D. × *mertonensis* (D. *grandiflora* × D. *purpurea*) garden origin; perennial to 30 in (75 cm); flowers to 2 in (5 cm) rose-mauve to strawberry pink or cop-

pery red; D. *purpurea* COMMON FOXGLOVE; W Europe; biennial or perennial, 32–70 in (80–180 cm) tall; flowers to 2 in (5 cm), purple, red, pink or white, the interior usually paler, hairy and heavily marked with white-edged, deep maroon spots; many cultivars and seed races are offered, including short or tall plants, with "double" and otherwise distorted flowers, ranging in color from the deepest purple-red to bronzy gold and pure white).

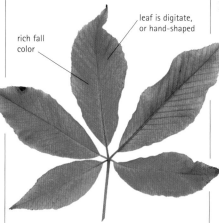

rich fall color

leaf is digitate, or hand-shaped

Aesculus flava

digitate with leaflets palmately arranged resembling the fingers of an outspread hand.

digonous two-angled, as in the stems of some cacti.

digynous with two separated styles or carpels.

dill (*Anethum graveolens*) a strongly aromatic annual up to 24 in (60 cm) high, grown for its distinctively flavored leaves and seeds, which are used in salads, fish cooking, sauerkraut, and pickling-spice mixtures. The leaves are best used fresh, but may be dried or frozen. Sow successively *in situ* from spring to midsummer. Seeds are harvested on turning brown and the seed heads dried between single layers of paper at low temperature.

diluent an inert material used to reduce the concentration of active ingredient in a pesticide formula.

dilutor a device used in liquid-fertilizer systems for dispensing a concen-

trated solution of fertilizer into a water pipeline. It usually functions on a diaphragm or water displacement principle. Dilutors are particularly identified with commercial nurseries, where they may also be used to distribute certain pesticides.

Dimorphotheca (from Greek *dis*, two, *morphe*, form, and *theke*, case: the fruits of the ray and disk florets differ in shape). Compositae. South and tropical Africa. AFRICAN DAISY. 7 species, herbs or subshrubs, with entire to pinnately lobed leaves and long-stalked, daisylike flower heads in summer. Cultivate as for *Arctotis*. D. *pluvialis* (syn. D. *annua*) WEATHER PROPHET; South Africa; aromatic annual to 16 in (40 cm); leaves to 4 in (10 cm), obovate to oblanceolate, toothed to pinnately lobed, deep green, hairy; flower heads to 2½ in (6 cm) in diameter, ray florets white above with dark purple bases, blue-violet beneath, disk florets purple-brown.

dioecious having male and female flowers on separate plants.

Dionaea (from Dione, mother of Aphrodite, alluding to the plant's beauty). Droseraceae. SE US (coastal N and S Carolina). VENUS' FLYTRAP, VENUS' MOUSETRAP. 1 species, D. *muscipula*, a low-growing, carnivorous, perennial herb. To 4 in (10 cm) long, the leaves are semierect or lie close to the ground in a basal rosette. They consist of a winged, spathulate petiole, bearing at its tip a blade of two semicircular lobes that are hinged at the middle and edged with lashlike teeth. The inner surface of these lobes is glossy, glandular, and turns a deep, meaty red in bright sunlight. Each lobe bears three fine trigger hairs. When alighting insects touch these hairs, they cause the lobes to snap shut. The blade then becomes a digestive purse, leaching the imprisoned prey of its vital juices. In spring and summer, white, 5-petaled flowers are carried in umbel-like cymes atop slender scapes. Plant the bulblike rosette bases in a porous mixture of vermiculite, peat, and sphagnum moss, either singly in fairly deep pots or massed in pans or trays. Keep constantly moist by standing con-

tainers in soft water and/or by frequent overhead watering with a fine
spray. Tolerant of temperatures just
above freezing, at which point growth
will cease and even die back to resting
bulbs: water should be reduced accord-
ingly. Temperatures between 55°F
(13°C) and 81°F (27°C) will ensure
continuous growth. Fresh air and full
sunlight will promote a low-growing
rosette habit and the most highly colored traps. Propagate by seed (sown
under cover on damp sphagnum and
bottom-watered), division, or by leaf
cuttings of the petiole.

Dionysia (for Dionysos, Greek god of
wine). Primulaceae. W and C Asia. 41
species, tufted or cushion-forming alpine
subshrubs. The stems are branched and
in old plants become woody and covered
by withered leaf remains. The leaves
form rosettes and are highly variable in
shape and size, from large and *Primula*-
like to minute and scalelike; they are
usually hairy and glandular on one or
both surfaces, and farinose beneath.
Narrowly tubular with a limb of five,
spreading lobes, the flowers are virtually
stalkless and solitary, or carried in scapose
and sometimes tiered umbels. Alpine-
house conditions are essential, and
plants grow best if double-potted or if
single-potted and placed in a plunge bed.
Plant cushions may be wedged between
small pieces of rock on the pot surface
or grown in tufa to ensure that the neck
zone remains dry. Use a gritty, loam-
based potting mix. Keep just moist,
never wet, and position in sun. Propagate by softwood cuttings in summer.

D. aretioides N Iran; leaves to ¼ in
(0.7 cm), oblong to narrowly spathulate,
hairy, farinose, bluntly toothed, forming
low, dense, gray cushions; flowers to
⅝ in (1.5 cm) in diameter, bright yellow,
solitary, stemless, scented, the petals
more or less toothed; *D. lamingtonii* Iran;
leaves to ⅛ in (0.3 cm), oblong to
spathulate, entire, hairy, forming dense,
compact cushions; flowers to ¼ in
(0.5 cm) across, bright yellow, stemless,
the petals shallowly cleft; *D. tapetodes* W
Asia; leaves to ⅛ in (0.4 cm), obovate to
spathulate, entire to crenulate, minutely
glandular, farinose, in tight cushions;
flowers to ½ in (1 cm) in diameter, solitary, stalkless, bright yellow, the petals
more or less rounded.

Dioon (from Greek *dis*, two, and *oon*,
egg—the seeds are borne in pairs).
Zamiaceae. C America. 10 species,
long-lived and slow-growing evergreen
cycads, superficially resembling tree
ferns or palms. The stems are erect,
usually unbranched, stoutly columnar,
and clothed with the scars or remains
of leaf petioles. Tough, pinnate leaves
are produced in terminal rosettes.
Massive, ovoid cones are borne in the
woolly crowns on plants of separate
sex. Grow *D. edule* in full sun in a
medium high in sand and grit, rather
dry and airy conditions, and a minimum temperature of 45°F (7°C).
D. spinulosum prefers part shade, humidity, moist, humus-rich soil, and a minimum temperature of 59°F (15°C).
Propagate by seed.

D. edule Mexico; stem to 6 ft (1.8 m),
stoutly columnar; leaves to 5 ft (1.5 m),
semierect; pinnae closely set, to 5 ×
⅝ in (13 × 1.5 cm), linear to lanceolate,
tip narrowly acuminate and sharply
pointed, base decurrent, rigid, gray-
green, margins usually entire but
spiny-toothed in some juveniles and
varieties; *D. spinulosum* Mexico; stem
to 33 ft (10 m), narrowly columnar;
leaves to 6½ ft (2 m), arching; pinnae
well-spaced, to 6 × 1½ in (15 × 4 cm),
lanceolate, tip broadly acuminate with
a soft but distinct point, base decurrent, rigid but more flexible than in
D. edule, glaucous sea-green at first,
hardening mid- to dark green, margins
always spiny-toothed.

Dioscorea (for Dioscorides, 1st-cen-
tury Greek physician and herbalist,
author of *Materia Medico*). Dioscore-
aceae. Tropics and subtropics. YAM.
Some 600 species, twining perennial
herbs, often with tuberous roots. The
flowers are yellow-green and inconspicuous. *D. discolor* needs part to full shade,
high humidity, and a minimum winter
temperature of 55°F (13°C). Plant in a
rich, coir-based mix with added leaf
mold and sand. Water and fertilize
liberally when in growth and during
warm weather; at other times, keep just
moist. Grow *D. elephantipes* in full sun
with a dry, breezy atmosphere and a
minimum winter temperature of 45°F
(7°C). Plant in a deep, fertile, loam-
based mix high in grit. Leave the
caudex two-thirds exposed. Water and

fertilize generously once the new shoots
appear at the summit of the caudex;
provide support as they develop. Withhold water when the growth turns
yellow and dies off, except for very
occasional soakings to prevent the
caudex from withering. Dormancy
may last for up to six months; after two
or three, it may be deliberately broken
by raising the temperature and by
watering. Propagate by seed.

D. discolor tropical South America;
stems vigorously climbing to 13 ft
(4 m); leaves to 12 in (30 cm), ovate to
cordate with a finely tapering tip, velvety emerald above with broken zones
of deep chocolate-maroon and irregular flashes of silver along midrib and
principal veins, maroon beneath);
D. elephantipes (syn. *Testudinaria elephantipes*) ELEPHANT'S FOOT, HOTTENTOT
BREAD; South Africa; caudex to 3¼ ft
(1 m) in diameter, woody, fissured and
faceted; stems to 6½ ft (2 m), of annual
duration; leaves ¾–2½ in (2–6 cm) in
diameter, broadly heart-shaped to reniform, smooth, bright green.

Diosma (from Greek *dios*, divine, and
osme, smell, referring to the pleasant
fragrance of the crushed leaves).
Rutaceae. South Africa. Some 28
species, evergreen shrubs with aromatic, glandular leaves and small,
5-petaled flowers in winter and spring;
these are usually fragrant and white or
red-tinted. Grow in full sun, with a
minimum winter temperature of 41°F
(5°C). Plant in a well-drained acidic
mix; reduce water in winter. Prune
after flowering. Increase by seed in
spring or semiripe cuttings. *D. ericoides*
BREATH OF HEAVEN; to 32 in (80 cm)
tall, rounded and many-stemmed;
leaves to ¼ in (0.6 cm), aromatic,
oblong, crowded; flowers white,
very fragrant.

Diospyros (from Greek *dios*, divine,
and *pyros*, wheat or grain, alluding to
the edible fruits). Ebenaceae. Europe,
Americas, Africa, Asia. Around 475
species, deciduous or evergreen trees or
shrubs (those listed below are deciduous trees) with hard, often black wood.
Small flowers in summer give rise to
large, fleshy berries. Plant all species in
deep, fertile and loamy soil, in sun or
light shade. The following species are

Diospyros kaki 'Hachiya'
Persimmons (or kaki fruit) need long,
hot summers to ripen, rarely provided in
cool temperate or maritime climates.

hardy to –10°F (–23°C), but are susceptible to frost, especially when young.
D. kaki, which is grown for its fruit,
should be protected from wind. For
commercial production, *D. kaki* is generally restricted warm regions,
although as a garden fruit, where high
yields may not be as important, it
shows more adaptability. In cooler
temperate areas (min. –20°F/–29°C),
provide the protection of a warm
south-facing wall, where the fruit may
ripen over long hot summers. Plants of
both sexes are needed for fruit to set.
Propagate from seed sown when ripe
and stratified, by layers in spring, or
from semiripe cuttings in a closed case/
under mist in summer. Commercial
cultivars are whip-grafted just below
soil level, or shield-budded just before
dormancy, on to seedling rootstock.

D. kaki CHINESE PERSIMMON, KAKI,
JAPANESE PERSIMMON; wild origin
unknown; to 45 ft (14 m); leaves to 8 in
(20 cm), ovate to obovate, deep, glossy
green above, turning orange-red in
fall; flowers pale yellow; fruit to 3 in
(7.5 cm) in diameter, globose to oblong,
waxy yellow to orange or red with a
persistent, accrescent calyx; *D. lotus*
DATE PLUM; temperate Asia; to 80 ft
(25 m); leaves to 4¾ in (12 cm), lanceolate to elliptic, tough, falling when
green; flowers yellow-buff to brown;
fruit to ¾ in (2 cm) in diameter, globose
to ovoid, yellow, red or blue-black,

pruinose; *D. virginiana* AMERICAN
PERSIMMON, POSSUMWOOD; E US; to
66 ft (20 m); leaves to 4¾ in (12 cm),
elliptic to ovate or oblong, deep glossy
green turning red in fall; flowers
yellow-white; fruit 1 in (2.5 cm) in
diameter, orange.

Dipelta (from Greek *di-*, two, and
pelte, shield, referring to the form of
the bracts). Caprifoliaceae. C and W
China. 4 species, deciduous shrubs
allied to *Weigela*. The flowers are tubular to campanulate, large and solitary
or clustered; they hang on slender
stalks, encircled by two to four shieldlike bracts which become larger after
fertilization of the flower. The following species will withstand winter temperatures down to –4°F (–20°C).
Cultivate as for *Weigela*.

D. floribunda to 15 ft (4.5 m) flowers
fragrant, to 1¼ in (3 cm), white sometimes flushed shell pink at base, marked
or stained deep yellow in throat, subtended by shieldlike, green-white
bracts; *D. yunnanensis* 6½–12 ft (2–4 m);
flowers to 1 in (2.5 cm), fragrant,
cream stained pale pink, throat marked
orange, subtended by cordate, thin-
textured bracts.

Diphylleia (from Greek *dis*, double,
and *phyllon*, leaf, alluding to the deeply
lobed leaf). Berberidaceae. Eastern N
America, Japan. 3 species, perennial,
rhizomatous herbs with large, peltate,
and long-stalked leaves, their blades
rounded and deeply 2-lobed. Small,
white flowers appear in spring in terminal cymes. These are followed by
colorful berries. Grow in damp,
humus-rich soil in part shade.
Propagate by division in spring or by
seed. *D. cymosa* UMBRELLA LEAF; E
US; to 3¼ ft (1 m); leaves 12–24 in
(30–60 cm) across, cleft, each segment
5–7-lobed and toothed; flower stalks
becoming red in fruit; berries to ½ in
(1.2 cm) across, blue.

Diplarrhena (from Greek *diploos*,
double, and *arrhen*, male—the flowers
have two perfect stamens). Iridaceae.
SE Australia, Tasmania. 2 species, rhizomatous perennial herbs with swordlike leaves in tufts or fans. The fragrant
flowers are carried in slender-stalked
clusters in summer and consist of six

segments, the outer three broad
and rounded, the inner three smaller.
In frost-free zones or areas where
temperatures only occasionally fall
to 15°F (–10°C), *Diplarrhena* is suitable
for the herbaceous border or rock
garden. In colder regions, plant in
pots or large tubs in the cool greenhouse or conservatory. Grow in full
sun in freely draining, sandy, humus-
rich and acidic soil. Propagate by seed,
division, or by plantlets. *D. moraea*
flowering stem to 26 in (65 cm);
flowers to 1½ in (4 cm) in diameter,
fragrant, white, the inner segments
suffused or veined mauve-blue or
yellow toward apex.

diploid of a plant, having the normal
number of chromosomes for the
species, i.e., twice the number borne in
the pollen and ovule cells; commonly
annotated $2 \times$; cf. *haploid*, *polyploid*,
triploid, *tetraploid*.

Dipsacus (name used by
Dioscorides). Dipsacaceae. Europe,
Asia, Africa. TEASEL. 15 species, biennial or short-lived perennial herbs, with
tall, erect stems and toothed to pinnately cut lanceolate to oblong leaves
in pairs, with their bases more or less
fused in a cup. The small flowers are
packed in heads that resemble finely
textured, prickly cones. These are surrounded by erect and rigid, spinelike
bracts. The flowers may be dried and
used in everlasting arrangements. Harvest for drying when in bloom. *Dipsacus*
is hardy. Grow in sun in moderately
fertile soil. Allow to self-sow, or sow
seed *in situ* in fall or spring.

D. fullonum FULLER'S TEASEL; Europe,
Asia, naturalized N America; biennial
to 6½ ft (2 m); basal leaves oblanceolate, crenately toothed, spiny-pustular;
flowers lilac in an oblong to ovoid
inflorescence with unhooked bracts; *D.
sativus* FULLER'S TEASEL; Europe, Asia,
N Africa, naturalized N America; differs from *D. fullonum* in its entire basal
leaves and cylindrical
inflorescence with hooked bracts.

Dipteronia (from Greek *di-*, double,
and *pteron*, wing, referring to the fruit).
Aceraceae. C and S China. 2 species,
deciduous trees and large shrubs with
pinnate leaves, small, 5-parted green-

D

white flowers in erect panicles, and clusters of paired, winged fruits—these turn red as they mature in late summer. Cultivate as for the smaller *Acer* species. *D. sinensis* tree or bushy shrub to 33 ft (10 m); leaves to 10 in (25 cm); leaflets 7–11, to 3½ in (9 cm), ovate to lanceolate, serrate.

Disa (alluding to the mythical Queen Disa of Sweden who came to the King of the Sveas wrapped in a fishing net: the dorsal sepal of *D. uniflora* is net-veined). Orchidaceae. Africa, Madagascar. About 130 species, terrestrial orchids with tuberous roots and linear to lanceolate leaves in basal rosettes and on the erect flowering stems. The flowers are borne in slender racemes or a few together. Each consists of a large, erect and hoodlike dorsal sepal with a basal spur, small petals and lip, and two larger, outspread lateral sepals. Grow in the cool greenhouse or conservatory (minimum temperature 45°F/7°C) in pans of neutral to acidic fibrous mix, enriched with leaf mold; protect from scorching sunlight and avoid wetting foliage. Keep plants moist throughout the growing season, watering with rainwater. Decrease water supplies slightly after flowering. Repot every two years. Propagate by division or seed.

   D. uniflora South Africa; 6–24 in (15–60 cm); flowers ¾–2½ in (2–6 cm) long, lateral sepals and lip usually carmine red, hood orange within, veined red, petals light carmine at base, the blade yellow with red spots; yellow and pink forms also occur. *Disa* grexes (q.v.) include 'Betty's Bay' (tall plants with bright orange flowers), 'Diores' (tall plants with many flowers in shades of pink, red and orange), 'Kewensis' (small flowers in shades of pink and orange), 'Kirstenbosch Pride' (tall spikes with many small, bright orange-red flowers), 'Langleyensis' (tall spikes of pale pink flowers), and 'Veitchii' (tall spikes of bright orange flowers).

Disanthus (from Greek *dis*, twice, and *anthos*, flower: the flowers are paired). Hamamelidaceae. China, Japan. 1 species, *D. cercidifolius*, a

deciduous, bushy shrub to 13 × 6½ ft (4 × 2 m). To 4 in (10 cm) wide, the leaves are ovate to orbicular with a cordate base. Blue-green above and paler beneath, they turn a rich wine red in fall, finally assuming fiery tints. Small and spidery, the flowers are dark purple-red and appear in fall and winter. Hardy to 0°F (–18°C). Plant in a sheltered position in dappled shade in acidic soil. Cultivate otherwise as for *Hamamelis*.

disbudding (1) the removal of buds, carried out to allow those remaining to develop top-quality flowers, especially where intended for exhibition. It is of special relevance in the cultivation of carnations, chrysanthemums, dahlias, and roses; (2) a technique for restricting side growths on vines and on wall-trained fruits, although in the latter case the technique is more accurately described as deshooting.

petal-like ray florets

tubular disk florets cover the disk

Flower of Compositae (Helianthus)

disc, disk (1) a fleshy or raised development of the torus that may occur within the calyx, within the corolla and stamens, or surrounding the pistil, in which case it is composed of coalesced nectaries or staminodes; (2) (in Compositae) the central part, or sometimes whole, of the capitulum bearing short tubular florets as opposed to peripheral ray florets; (3) the central part of the lip in Orchidaceae, often elevated and callused or crested; (4) a circular flattened organ—for example, the disklike tendril tips of some plants climbing by adhesion; (5) the basal plate of a bulb around which scales are arranged.

Discaria (from Greek *diskos*, disk, referring to the fleshy nectariferous disk

of flowers). Rhamnaceae. Temperate S America, Australia, New Zealand. 12 species, deciduous shrubs or small trees, with long, slender, green thorns, small and often obsolete leaves, and dense clusters of minute 4-parted flowers in spring. The following species is suitable for sunny, south-facing walls in well-drained soil. It is capable of surviving winter temperatures as low as 5°F (–15°C). Prune, if necessary, after flowering. Propagate by seed or by semiripe cuttings. *D. toumatou* WILD IRISHMAN; New Zealand; shrub or small tree to 16 ft (5 m) with green, flexuous twigs and many spines to 2 in (5 cm) long; flowers green-white.

disc floret, disk floret a flower with a tubular corolla, often toothed, found in the center of a radiate capitulum or occupying the whole of a discoid capitulum. Found in the family Compositae. See *ray floret*.

discoid (1) of a leaf, with a round fleshy blade and thickened margins; (2) more commonly, pertaining to the capitula of some Compositae, composed entirely of disk florets.

disease any plant ailment caused by pathogenic organisms, such as fungi, bacteria, or viruses, affecting the viability, quality, or economic value of a plant. The term is occasionally used more loosely to denote any ailment of a plant, including malfunctions caused by faulty cultivation or unsatisfactory growing conditions, which are more accurately termed disorders.

Disocactus (from Greek *dis*, twice; *isos*, equal; cactus). Cactaceae. Mexico. 2 species, epiphytic or lithophytic cacti with trailing or cascading, succulent, cylindrical stems and tubular flowers with a spreading limb. Plant in an open, acidic mix rich in coarse bark, sand, and grit. Choose a container or situation where the stems can cascade freely. Position in full sunlight with a minimum temperature of 41°F (5°C). Water freely in hot weather, scarcely at all in winter. Propagate by rooting detached segments of stem. *D. flagelliformis* RAT'S TAIL CACTUS; stems up to

3¼ ft (1 m) × ⅜ in (5 cm) long, with many short, yellow-tinted spines; flowers 2–3 in (5–8 cm) and scarlet to dark magenta).

Disporum (from Greek *di-*, twice, and *spora*, seed, referring to the usually 2-seeded fruits). Liliaceae (Colchicaceae). US, E Asia. 10–20 species, perennial, rhizomatous herbs, with leafy, sparingly branched stems and ovate to lanceolate leaves. Nodding, bell-shaped to tubular flowers appear in spring and are followed by orange to red berries. Cultivate as for *Tricyrtis*. Propagate by division in spring or by seed.

D. *hookeri* NW US; 12–39 in (30–100 cm); leaves 1¼–5½ in (3–14 cm), lanceolate to ovate, apex acuminate, base cordate, stem-clasping; flowers to ¾ in (2 cm), green-white; fruit scarlet; D. *sessile* Japan; to 24 in (60 cm); leaves 2–6 in (5–15 cm), oblong to lanceolate; flowers to 1¼ in (3 cm), white tipped green; fruit blueblack; includes 'Variegatum', with leaves striped cream.

Acer palmatum 'Dissectum Atropurpureum'
The finely cut or dissected foliage of this Japanese maple gives it its great charm.

dissected cutin any way; a general term applicable to leaf blades or other flattened organs that are incised, lacerate, laciniate, pinnatisect, or palmatisect.

distal the part farthest from the axis— for example, the tip of a leaf is distal; cf. *proximal*.

distant of leaves on a stem, stipes on a rhizome, or flowers on a floral axis,

widely spaced, synonymous with remote; cf. *proximate*.

distichous of leaves, distinctly arranged in two opposite ranks along a stem or branch.

Distictis (from Greek *di-*, twice, and *stiktos*, spotted: the seeds are very flat and resemble two rows of spots in the fruit). Bignoniaceae. Central America, W Indies. 9 species, slender shrubs climbing by tendril-tipped leaves. Produced in spring and summer, the flowers are tubular to funnel-shaped. Cultivate as for *Bignonia* but with slightly higher temperatures and ample heat and light to ripen the new growth.

D. *buccinatoria* Mexico; flowers to 3 in (8 cm), rich purple-red, throat golden yellow; D. *lactiflora* W Indies, Puerto Rico, St. Domingo; flowers to 1¼ in (3 cm), white, throat yellow; D. *laxiflora* (Mexico, Nicaragua; flowers to 3 in (8 cm), rich purple in bud, opening magenta, fading to lilac-white; D. 'Rivers' flowers dark mauve with a golden throat.

distinct with similar parts that are not united.

Distylium (from Greek *dis*, twice, and *stylos*, style). Hamamelidaceae. E Asia. 12 species, small, evergreen trees and shrubs with leathery, dark green foliage and, in spring and early summer, short racemes of flowers with tinted calyces, no petals, and colorful anthers. Cultivate as for *Hamamelis*. D. *racemosum* ISU TREE; Japan; broadly spreading shrub or small tree to 80 ft (25 m) in wild; leaves to 2¾ in (7 cm), elliptic to obovate; flowers in racemes to 3 in (7.5 cm) long, stamens red.

diurnal of activity taking place only during daylight.

divaricate broadly divergent and spreading, a term usually applied to branching patterns where the branches spread 70° to 90° outward from the main axis.

divergent broadly spreading from the center.

Division the highest rank of the prin-

cipal categories in the plant kingdom. The names of Divisions end in *phyta* ("plants").

division a method of increasing plants, suitable for those that produce a mass of closely knit shoots or buds in a clump or crown of growth which can be separated into pieces. Many herbaceous perennials can be readily propagated in this way. The best time for division is when roots and shoots have started to form in the spring. It is best to use portions from the periphery of the crown, and depending on species these may be pulled off by hand or pried off by inserting two border forks back to back and levering the handles. Plants with tough compacted crowns are most easily divided by cutting through lifted, washed crowns.

Many alpines can be divided to produce new plantlets annually. These divisions should be made about ten days after main flowering ceases, when new root and shoot growth commences. However, in the case of latesummer- and fall-flowering plants, division should be delayed until the spring.

Herbaceous plants with tough, grassy, or swordlike leaves crowded in dense clusters should be divided with a spade or hatchet, in time to establish well before winter. Some shrubs produce a suckering base or crown or layer themselves, providing young shoots that may then be separated.

DNA abbreviation for deoxyribonucleic acid; a complex molecule found in chromosomes, and the chemical basis of genes.

Docynia (the name is an anagram of *Cydonia*, a close relation). Rosaceae. E Asia. 2 species, evergreen or deciduous shrubs or small trees with clusters of fragrant, 5-petaled flowers; these are white, opening from pink-tinted buds in spring, and are followed by downy, ovoid, quincelike fruit in fall. *Docynia* species are not reliably frost-hardy and in areas at the limits of their hardiness (min. 10°F/−12°C), are best positioned against a south-facing wall. Plant in full sun in well-drained soil. Propagate by budding in summer, grafting in winter, or by seed in fall. D. *delavayi* S China; tree to 33 ft (10 m);

leaves persistent, oblong, entire, white-hairy beneath; fruit yellow, 1½ in (4 cm) in diameter.

Dodecatheon (from Greek *dodeka*, twelve, and *theos*, god—Pliny applied the name to a spring flower, probably the primrose, protected by the twelve gods). Primulaceae. N America, Bering Straits. SHOOTING STAR, AMERICAN COWSLIP. 14 species, perennial herbs forming clumps or tufts of oblanceo-late to obovate leaves. Produced in spring and summer, the *Cyclamen*-like flowers nod in slender-stalked umbels. Hardy to −10°F (−23°C) and suitable for the woodland or damp rock garden. Grow in full sun or part shade in cool, moist but well-drained soil rich in sand and leaf mold. Propagate from ripe seed or by division.

D. dentatum W US; to 4 in (10 cm); flowers white, anthers yellow, tinted black; *D. hendersonii* MOSQUITO-BILLS, SAILOR-CAPS; California; to 16 in (40 cm); flowers mauve-pink with a cream and yellow basal rim, anthers violet-black; *D. meadia* SHOOTING STAR, AMERICAN COWSLIP; E US; to 20 in (50 cm); flowers purple-pink or pink or white, with a cream and yellow basal rim and purple-red anthers; *D. pulchellum* (western N America, Mexico, natu-ralized E US; to 14 in (35 cm); flowers deep carmine to rose-purple or lilac, with a cream to gold basal rim and purple-black anthers.

Dodonaea (for Rembert Dodoens [1516–85], Dutch physician and herbalist). Sapindaceae. Tropics and subtropics, especially Australia. Some 50 species, evergreen shrubs and trees with tough, glossy foliage and showy winged fruits. In a sheltered, warm and sunny spot. *D. viscosa* will tolerate brief, mild frosts and withstand drought, salt, wind, and pollution. In hot, arid zones, it makes a good wind-break or hedging plant, responding well to light clipping. Plant in well-drained soil in full sun. Propagate from seed sown in spring or by greenwood cuttings in summer. *D. viscosa* HOP BUSH; South Africa, Australia, Mexico; light-textured, treelike shrub to 6½ ft (2 m) with erect, resinous foliage; leaves to 5 in (13 cm), narrowly elliptic to oblanceolate, wavy, glossy pale green;

seed capsules clustered, to ¾ in (2 cm) in diameter, flushed purple-red; 'Pur-purea': leaves strongly flushed red-bronze to purple.

dolabriform hatchet-shaped.

doleiform barrel-shaped.

dollar spot (*Sclerotinia homoeocarpa*) a fungal disease of turf causing round discolored patches. In the US, it occurs on a wide range of grasses including *Agrostis*, *Poa*, and *Stenotaphrum*. In the UK, it is common only on CREEPING RED FESCUE (*Festuca rubra*) in some locations. Infected leaves are white or straw-colored, arising in patches up to 2 in (5 cm) in diameter (hence "dollar spot"), which may merge to form larger areas of infec-tion. The disease is associated with poor fertility, especially nitrogen defi-ciency, which should be rectified. Other control measures are selection of resistant types and spraying with a rec-ommended fungicide.

Dombeya (for Joseph Dombey [d. 1794], French botanist). Sterculiaceae. Africa and Madagascar to Mascarene Islands. About 200 species, deciduous or evergreen shrubs or small trees, with large and hairy, ovate to cordate leaves. The flowers consist of five petals and are candy- or toffee-scented. They hang in pompon-like umbels on slen-der, drooping stalks in spring and summer. Grow in bright light or partial shade, providing protection from the hottest sun in summer, in a well-drained, fibrous loam-based medium, with additional leaf mold and sharp sand. Water plentifully when in growth, reducing supplies as light levels and temperatures fall in winter; maintain a minimum temperature of 50°F (10°C). Prune after flowering to confine to allotted space. Propagate by seed or semiripe cuttings in a closed case with gentle bottom heat. *D. burgessiae* (syn. *D. mastersii*) central and South Africa; shrub or tree to 12 ft (4 m); leaves to 9 × 7 in (22 × 18 cm); flowers to 2 in (5 cm) in diameter, white to candy pink, sometimes with darker veins.

dominant describing one of the forms taken by components of a single

gene, which preferentially exhibits its characteristics when paired with another form in cross-pollination; cf. *recessive*.

Doritis (from Greek *dory*, spear, refer-ring to the spear-shaped lip). Orchi-daceae. SE Asia. 2 species, epiphytic, evergreen orchids with abundant aerial roots and short-stemmed growths of 2-ranked, leathery leaves. The flowers are borne at various times in rigidly erect and sometimes branching racemes. The tepals are obovate to elliptic and the lip 3-lobed, with the lateral lobes rounded and erect and the midlobe arrowlike and forward-pointing. Cultivate as for *Phalaenopsis*. *D. pulcherrima* flower spikes 8–24 in (20–60 cm), flowers to 1½ in (4 cm) in diameter, deep magenta with lip midlobe mauve, lateral lobes red, disk lined white.

dormancy a condition in living plants where vegetative activity ceases (true dormancy) or is brought to an absolute minimum (quiescence) for a prolonged period. It may be due to physiological factors or seasonal rhythm, especially temperature, or it may be a response to environmental conditions unfavorable to growth. Dormancy is exhibited in deciduous species during winter, when plants rest in a leafless condition, and in bulbs, corms, tubers, and seeds, which are a means of succession from one season to another, or over a number of years. In many species a period of dormancy is a suitable time for transplanting. Dormancy can be artificially broken through special techniques, most com-monly through exposure to controlled temperature.

dormant oil see *winter wash*.

Doronicum (from the Arabic name for this plant, *Doronigi*). Compositae. Europe, Asia. LEOPARD'S BANE. 35 species, perennial tuberous or rhizoma-tous herbs with clumps of ovate to cordate leaves and yellow, daisylike flower heads on slender stalks in spring and summer. Grow in moderately fertile, well-drained but moisture-retentive soil in part shade or in good light, with protection from the strongest sun in summer. Propagate by division in fall.

D. × *excelsum* 'Harpur Crewe' to 24 in (60 cm); 3–4 golden flower heads per stem, to 5 in (10 cm) diameter, in spring; *D. orientale* SE Europe, Caucasus, Lebanon; to 24 in (60 cm); flower heads ¾–2½ in (2–6 cm) in diameter; includes 'Finesse', with long-stalked flower heads and slender, bright yellow florets, 'Frühlingspracht', with double, golden yellow flower heads, 'Gerhard', with lemon yellow flower heads and a green disk, 'Goldenkranz', with large deep yellow, double flower heads, the dwarf, golden 'Goldzwerg', and 'Magnificum', with large flower heads; *D. pardalianches* (syn. *D. cordatum*) GREAT LEOPARD'S BANE; W Europe to SE Germany; to 36 in (90 cm); flower heads 1¼–2 in (3–5 cm) in diameter; *D. plantagineum* W Europe; to 32 in (80 cm); flower heads to 2 in (5 cm) in diameter; cultivars derived from this species include the free-flowering, mildew-resistant 'Strahlengold'.

Dorotheanthus (for Dorothea, the mother of G. F. Schwantes, the botanist who named this plant, and Greek *anthos*, flower). Aizoaceae. South Africa. 6 species, succulent annuals, with fleshy leaves more or less covered with crystalline papillae. Brightly colored, daisylike flowers open on warm, sunny days. Sow seeds thinly during late winter and early spring. Grow under glass with a temperature of 59–68°F (15–20°C); shade from direct sunlight. Prick out seedlings into trays or small unit containers. Grow on in full sunlight at a temperature of 50–59°F (10–15°C), and with plenty of ventilation. Harden the plants off gradually during late spring, ready for planting outside in full sun in well-drained soil in early summer. *D. bellidiformis* (syn. *Mesembryanthemum criniflorum*) LIVINGSTONE DAISY; leaves 1–2¾ in (2.5–7 cm), tonguelike, thinly fleshy, glistening; flowers to 1½ in (4 cm) in diameter, white, pale pink, magenta, red, orange, apricot or white edged red; many seed races available.

dorsal pertaining to the back of an organ, or to the surface that is turned away from the axis, thus abaxial; cf. *ventral*.

dorsifixed of an organ, attached by its dorsal surface to another.

dorsiventral flattened, and having separate dorsal and ventral surfaces, as with most leaves and leaf-blades.

Doryanthes (from Greek *dory*, spear, and *anthos*, flower, in reference to the tall flowering stems). Agavaceae. E Australia. SPEAR LILY. 3 species, very large, evergreen perennial herbs, with sword-shaped leaves. The flowers are carried in short spikes compressed into a large terminal globose head or oblong thyrsus and held aloft on a tall scape. They are commonly replaced by bulbil-like plantlets. Grow in humus-rich, well-drained soil in full sun with a minimum temperature of 50°F (10°C). Water plentifully when in growth; keep just moist in winter. Propagate by seed, suckers or by bulbils. *D. palmeri* basal leaves to 6½ ft (2 m); scape to 8 ft (2.5 m); flowers to 2 in (5 cm), rich orange-red, paler within, among red-flushed bracts.

dot plant a bold specimen plant used to give contrast of foliage color, form, and height in a bedding scheme—for example, *Eucalyptus globulus* or standard fuchsias.

double, semidouble any flower with many more than the basic number of petals, sepals, florets, or colored bracts. Fully double blooms have densely packed rounded heads

in which stamens are totally obscured or absent and the flower usually sterile. Semidouble blooms have two or three times the basic number of petals, sepals, or florets, arranged in several rows with stamens conspicuous. A double form may be designated "flore pleno" (abbreviation fl.pl.), "plenus," or "pleniflorus." The form of doubling in tubular flowers—where one perfect corolla develops within another—and frequently found in primulas and rhododendrons, is often described as hose-in-hose.

double digging, double spading see *digging*.

double working the grafting of an intermediate cultivar or interstock between scion and rootstock to overcome incompatibility, to confer disease or cold resistance, or to control vigor.

dovecote a pigeon house. Originally substantial, functional buildings, dovecotes later became popular as decorative garden features, often in the form of a small wooden house on top of a long pole.

downy mildew diseases caused by fungal parasites belonging to the family Peronosporaceae, including *Bremia*, *Peronospora*, *Plasmopara*, and *Pseudoperonospora*. The fungi penetrate deeply into plant tissue and their aerial growth can be seen as a glistening downy white or purple growth, usually on the

Single and double kingcups
The normal form of *Caltha palustris* (left) has a single ring of petals, while the double cultivar 'Flore Pleno' has tightly packed petals and petaloid stamens, forming dense, golden heads.

D

undersurface of leaves. Yellow patches develop beneath the visible fungus growth and affected leaves turn brown and eventually die. In some downy mildews, there is marked distortion of the host due to swelling and curling of the infected tissues. Spread is by spores during the growing season, but a resistant sexual stage may overwinter inside plant tissues. Downy mildews are favored by damp conditions. The following plants are common sufferers: crucifers (affected by *Peronospora parasitica*), onions (*P. destructor*), pea (*P. viciae*), rose (*P. sparsa*, mainly on greenhouse plants), spinach and beet (*P. farinosa*), umbellifers (*Plasmopara nivea*), grapevine (*P. viticola*) and cucurbits (*Pseudoperonospora cubensis*). Other plants sometimes affected include *Anemone*, *Antirrhinum*, *Campanula*, chrysanthemums, *Clarkia*, *Digitalis*, *Geum*, *Hebe*, *Helleborus*, *Laburnum*, *Mesembryanthemum*, *Myosotis*, *Papaver*, *Primula*, and *Viola*.

Control downy mildew with proper ventilation, removing infected plant debris and, where essential, fungicide application. Copper-containing chemicals and many broad-spectrum organic fungicides, including the di-thiocarbamates mancozeb and zineb, will give good protection against these diseases. The use of such chemicals is subject to local pesticide approvals.

downy see *pubescent*.

Draba (name used by Dioscorides for another crucifer, *Lepidium draba*). Cruciferae. N Hemisphere, mountains of S America. 300 species, dwarf, annual or perennial, cushion-forming herbs with tiny leaves in tight rosettes and 4-petaled, usually yellow flowers in short racemes in late spring and summer. Grow in the rock garden, in troughs or raised beds, or in the alpine house. All *Draba* species dislike winter moisture, especially those with woolly foliage—these, if grown in the open, should be protected with a cloche or a propped pane of glass and given a top-dressing of gravel or small stones. Grow in sandy, well-drained and moderately fertile soil in full sun. In the alpine house, grow the plants in pans of a mix of equal parts loam, leaf mold, and sharp sand, with a wedge of tufa or layer of limestone

chips around the neck of the plant. Water moderately during growth and flowering, avoiding the cushions; otherwise, water very sparingly. Remove dead or dying material from the rosettes to avoid rot. Propagate from seed sown fresh in early spring. Alternatively, increase by careful division, by small offsets in spring or by soft cuttings in summer.

D. aizoides C and S Europe, Great Britain; leaves to ½ in (1 cm), linear, sparsely ciliate, incurved in dense, compacted cushions; flowers bright yellow, 4–18 on smooth flowering stems to 4 in (10 cm) tall; *D. hispanica* Spain; differs from the first species in having slightly broader, roughly hairy leaves, shorter, bristly flowering stems and pale yellow flowers; *D. mollissima* Caucasus; leaves to ¼ in (0.6 cm), oblong, blunt, white-hairy, in tight cushions; flowers golden yellow in tight, short racemes; *D. polytricha* Armenia, Turkey; leaves to ¼ in (0.5 cm), oblong to spathulate, with long white hairs, in tight cushions; flowers bright yellow on hairy stems; *D. rigida* Armenia, Turkey; leaves to ¼ in (0.6 cm), broadly linear, ciliate, dark green in tight, mossy rosettes; flowers bright yellow on smooth stalks; includes var. *bryoides* with very small, incurved dark green leaves and more or less stemless flowers.

Dracaena (from Greek *drakaina*, a female dragon, referring to the resinous red gum exuded from the stems of *D. draco*). Agavaceae (Dracaenaceae). Old World, 1 species America. Some 40 species, evergreen shrubs or trees, sparingly to much-branched, the bark smooth and ringed to rough and fissured. The leaves vary in shape from narrow and swordlike to lanceolate or elliptic, smooth and tough. Creamy, star-shaped and nocturnally fragrant flowers are borne in large panicles at various times of year. *D. draco* prefers full sun, rather dry, lean soil, and a minimum winter temperature of 41°F (5°C). In Mediterranean-type climates, it becomes a large, much-branched tree. The other species listed here are often grown in the home, or in interior landscapes, and are valued for their resilience and decorative foliage. Grow them in a fertile, porous medium in light shade or dappled

sun, with a minimum winter temperature of 55°F (13°C). Water, fertilize, and syringe liberally in warm weather; keep barely moist at other times. Sponge over leaves of plants grown indoors. Propagate by seed, stem-tip cuttings, or air-layering.

D. cincta origin obscure; shrub to 6 ft (1.8 m), stem slender, usually unbranched; leaves to 15 × ⅝ in (38 × 1.5 cm), linear, mid- to deep green, edged red to brown; some plants cultivated as *D. marginata* may belong here; 'Tricolor': leaves striped cream and edged red; *D. concinna* Mauritius; shrub to 6 ft (1.8 m), stem slender, red-tinted; leaves to 36 × 3 in (90 × 7.5 cm), linear to ensiform, dull green edged purple-red; some plants cultivated as *D. marginata* may belong here; *D. draco* DRAGON TREE; Canary Islands; tree to 33 ft (10 m), ultimately with a very thick, gray-barked trunk exuding red resin if wounded and developing a massively branched, broad crown; leaves to 24 × 1½ in (60 × 4 cm), linear to lanceolate, glaucous, tough; *D. fragrans* Sierra Leone to Malawi; shrub or tree to 50 ft (15 m), branching above, stems thick; leaves to 39 × 4 in (100 × 10 cm), lanceolate, narrowing below, outspread with tips curving, glossy pale to dark green; includes the popular 'Massangeana', CORN PLANT, with pale green leaves broadly striped yellow; *D. fragrans* Deremensis Group tropical E Africa; shrub to 13 ft (4 m), stem slender, sparsely branched; leaves to 28 × 2 in (70 × 5 cm), linear to lanceolate, narrowing toward base, spreading and clothing much of stem, dark to gray green; includes several popular variegated cultivars—for example 'Bausei' with a central white band, 'Lemon Lime', lime green with a yellow central band and margins, 'Roehrs Gold', with a pale gold central band and margins, and 'Warneckii', gray-green with a pure white central stripe and margins; *D. hookeriana* SE Africa; shrub to 6 ft (1.8 m), sometimes branched; leaves to 30 × 4½ in (75 × 11 cm), lanceolate, semierect with curving tips and narrow base, margins translucent white or red-tinted; includes 'Gertrude Manda', with broad and thick leaves with translucent edges, and 'Variegata', with white-striped leaves; *D. reflexa* (syn. *Pleomele reflexa*) SONG OF INDIA;

Madagascar, Mauritius; graceful shrub to 16 ft (5 m), freely branching with slender, rather sprawling stems; leaves to 8 in (20 cm) × ¾–2 in (2–5 cm), linear to lanceolate or narrowly elliptic, tapering finely at both ends, dark green; includes forms with narrow, white-edged and yellow-striped leaves; *D. sanderiana* RIBBON PLANT, BELGIAN EVERGREEN; Cameroon; erect, sparingly branched shrub to 5 ft (1.5 m); stems slender; leaves to 8 in (20 cm) × ⅝–1½ in (1.5–4 cm), lanceolate, base and apex tapering, spreading and somewhat wavy, clothing stems, pale to gray-green broadly edged or striped cream-white; *D. surculosa* (syn. *D. godseffiana*) GOLD DUST DRACAENA, SPOTTED DRACAENA; shrub, 3¼–12 ft (1–4 m) with slender, twiggy branches; leaves to 8 in (20 cm), elliptic, apex acute, base shortly tapered, deep glossy green, spotted to flecked or blotched gold to cream). For *D. indivisa*, see *Cordyline indivisa*; for *D. godseffiana*, see *D. surculosa*; for *D. marginata*, see *D. cincta* or *D. concinna*; for *D. terminalis*, see *Cordyline terminalis*.

Dracocephalum (from Latin *draco*, dragon, and Greek, *kephale*, head, referring to the shape of the flowers). Labiatae. Europe, Africa, Asia, N America. About 45 species, annual or perennial herbs and dwarf shrubs with whorls of tubular, 2-lipped flowers in terminal or axillary spikes or racemes. The following species is perennial and hardy to 5°F (–15°C). Grow in a sunny position in fertile well-drained soil. Propagate by division in spring or fall, or from basal cuttings of young growth in spring. *D. ruyschianum* C Europe to Japan; erect to 24 in (60 cm); flowers to 1¼ in (3 cm), violet-blue, rarely pink or white.

Dracula (from the diminutive form of Latin, *draco*—the name does not commemorate the Transylvanian count, although both names mean "little dragon"; one of the most splendidly undead-looking species also rejoices in the name *D. vampira*). Orchidaceae. Central and South America. About 100 species, evergreen perennial herbs. They are similar to *Masdevallia*, with the flowers consisting of 3 sepal-segments more or less fused in a triangular or 3-pointed shield or cup, each

segment drawn out to a long, tail-like tip (the descriptions below measure the flowers from tip to tip). Unlike *Masdevallia*, the flowers hang on slender stalks and have a distinctly clawed, usually pouch-shaped lip. They are produced in abundance during spring and summer.

Small orchids with spectacular, if rather sinister flowers, they need a temperature range of 50–75°F (10–24°C), shade, high humidity, and an airy atmosphere. Plant in small baskets or perforated pots (flower stalks often burrow through the medium before finding an outlet) in a fine, bark- or perlite-based mix with chopped sphagnum moss. Keep moist and syringe frequently. Feed while the new growth develops. Increase by division after flowering.

D. bella (syn. *Masdevallia bella*) Colombia; flowers to 8 in (20 cm) across, basically triangular with fused segments and long, slender tips, buff or dull olive densely spotted oxblood with darker tips and a white or pale lip; *D. chestertonii* (syn. *Masdevallia chestertonii*) Colombia; flowers to 2¾ in (7 cm) across with three distinct segments, each with a slender tip, sulfur green or gray-white, dotted and edged with purple to gray-black warts, lip ocher lined with red radiating gills, resembling an upturned mushroom; *D. chimaera* (syn. *Masdevallia chimaera*) Colombia; flowers to 12 in (30 cm) across, segments triangular to ovate with very long, slender tips, buff to olive flecked and stained maroon to violet-black, hairy and warty, lip cream to flesh pink, buff to orange at base; *D. erythrochaete* (syn. *Masdevallia erythrochaete*) Guatemala, Nicaragua, Costa Rica, Panama; flowers to 4¾ in (12 cm) across, segments more or less fused, forming a broad cup with long, slender tips, cream to gray-pink densely spotted flesh pink to maroon and hairy, with maroon tails, lip white or buff; *D. platycrater* (syn. *Masdevallia platycrater*) Colombia; flowers to 10 in (25 cm) across with distinct and outspread, narrow segments and slender tips, white to rose dotted purple-red, lip pink; *D. vampira* Ecuador; flowers to 12 in (30 cm) across with ovate to triangular segments and very slender, long tips, white to yellow green densely overlaid and veined purple-black, with golden sun-

burst-like markings at center, tips maroon-black, lip white flecked violet.

Dracunculus (name used by Pliny for a plant with a curved rhizome, from Latin diminutive of *draco*, a dragon). Araceae. Mediterranean, Madeira, Canary Islands. 3 species, tuberous herbaceous perennials with pedately compound leaves—their mottled sheaths and stalks forming a pseudo-stem—and, in spring and summer, large and malodorous, *Arum*-like inflorescences. The following species will establish itself in most sheltered, well-drained positions (min. 0°F/–18°C), tolerating full sun or dappled shade. It becomes dormant in summer, when the soil should be warm and dry. In very wet or cold areas, protect the corms with a dry mulch in winter. Increase by offsets in late summer, or seed in fall. *D. vulgaris* (syn. *Arum dracunculus*) DRAGON ARUM; C and E Mediterranean; stem 16–39 in (40–100 cm), mottled maroon; spathe to 39 × 8 in (100 × 20 cm), wavy, deep red-purple, spadix black-red.

drag brush a wide-headed brush-like hand tool, designed to be pulled across turf to work in top-dressings.

drag, dragfork see *fork*.

Drainage trench
A strip of sod separates the gravel-filled trench from the topsoil above. Within it, water percolates into a porous tile pipe.

drainage the removal by gravity of excess surface or soil water to a lower level. Good soil drainage is very important in gardens, providing or improving conditions for healthy plant growth and preventing flooding of surfaces. Imperfect drainage may be indicated by surface puddling after rain, and by the presence of moss in lawns. It may be due to a high water table, or more often to compacted layers that arise naturally on some soils or as a result of treading or cultivating in unfavorable conditions.

Drainage status can be assessed by digging 12-in- (30-cm-) deep holes across a site shortly after heavy rain and examining them a few hours later for water presence. Drainage defects are more apparent in soils of heavy texture, and on sites where a problem is identified it is advisable to dig inspection holes to at least 24 in (60 cm) depth. Where these are kept covered from rainfall for 24 hours and are then found to have an accumulation of water, the existence of a high water table is indicated and skillful site management will be needed. Alternatively, close examination of the side walls of the inspection holes will reveal whether compaction is a problem.

Soil drainage can be improved by careful cultivation, and, where compaction is a problem, double digging or trenching (see *digging*) may be desirable. Incorporation of lime and rotted organic matter serves to improve soil structure, and in some situations grit or sand additives can aid drainage.

Where fundamental site characteristics cause impeded drainage, it may be worth laying down a drainage system. However, such a project is expensive, in terms of both labor and materials and must be carefully surveyed and executed. The first essential is to plan for disposal of collected water from the lowest point of the site. Ideally, the water should be directed to a ditch or other authorized outlet or, alternatively, to a soakaway pit, constructed at least 6 ft (1.8 m) square and filled with rubble. Specially made drainpipes of earthenware or plastic, 2–3 in (5–7.5 cm) in diameter, should be laid on a firmed 2-in (5-cm) bed of coarse gravel in trenches 14–16 in (35–40 cm) deep. The trenches must follow a natural slope or a constructed one with an ideal fall of 1:40. A herringbone design is appropriate, with the feeders meeting main lines at an angle of 45 degrees. The drain pipes should be overlaid

with a shallow layer of coarse gravel. As an alternative to drainpipes, trenches may be filled with a 4–6 in (10–15 cm) layer of coarse gravel, or for a shorter serviceable period with tight bundles of brushwood, all conforming to the same principles of depth, layout, and outfall. On heavy clay soils, narrow drainage tunnels, known as mole drains, may be formed at intervals across a site by using a flat-bladed plow to draw a metal cylinder through the soil in such a way that it penetrates below cultivation depth. Mole drains are usually constructed in conjunction with a pipe system and will remain functional for a number of seasons.

The term "top draining" describes the use of shallow channels or ditches to drain off surface water.

lack of light causes pale color

stems are weak and prone to collapse

Drawn seedlings

drawn describing seedlings or plants that become abnormally tall and thin as a result of poor light or crowding.

Dregea (for Johann Franz Drege [1794–1881], botanist). Asclepiadaceae. Old World (warm regions). 3 species, woody-based, evergreen climbers with large leaves and umbels of starry and fragrant, *Hoya*-like flowers in summer. The following species is hardy to 10°F (−12°C). Plant in well-drained, moist and fertile soil in sun or part shade. Provide support. Increase by seed in spring or stem cuttings in summer. *D. sinensis* (syn. *Wattakaka sinensis*) China; evergreen climber to 10 ft (3 m) tall; leaves to 4 in (10 cm), broadly ovate to cordate, gray-felted beneath;

flowers to ⅝ in (1.5 cm) in diameter, white marked pink, in long-stalked, downy umbels to 4 in (10 cm) across.

drench, drenching the liberal application of a pesticide solution to the soil around the roots of a plant; usually to control a soilborne pest or disease by contact, but also for systemic action, where the pesticide is taken up by roots and transported throughout the plant to destroy pests feeding on aerial parts.

drepanium a sickle-shaped cyme.

Drepanostachyum (from Greek *drepanon*, sickle, and *stachys*, spike, for the sickle-shaped inflorescence.) Gramineae. Himalaya. A genus of clumping bamboos; see *bamboos*.

dressing (1) any bulky organic manure or fertilizer applied to the soil in a solid as opposed to a liquid state, in preparation for cropping or as an application around established plants (see *base dressing*, *side dressing*, *top dressing*); (2) any fungicidal or insecticidal substance applied to seeds, bulbs, corms, or tubers to prevent disease or pest attack.

dribble bar a perforated metal or plastic bar fitted to a watering can or sprayer for the application of insecticide, fungicide or weedkiller. Also known as a sprinkler bar.

dried blood a quick-acting organic fertilizer containing 10–12% nitrogen, used either as a dry, base- or top-dressing or as a liquid fertilizer when mixed with water. The sterilized product should be handled with suitable precautions to avoid inhalation and other personal contact.

drift (1) any part of a pesticide spray that has been carried beyond its intended target. Drift may cause damage to neighboring plants with which it comes into contact. Particularly at risk are tomatoes, in which even very low concentrations of hormone-type weedkillers, carried as drift over long distances, can cause serious distortion of growth; (2) a block planting of young trees.

drill a shallow furrow or groove made in soil for the sowing of seeds, or for transplants.

Drimys (from Greek *drimys*, acrid, sharp). Winteraceae. S America, Malaysia, Australasia. Some 30 species, evergreen trees or shrubs with leathery, aromatic leaves and clusters of star-shaped flowers in late spring. *Drimys* is hardy to 10°F (–12°C), and in sheltered areas. Plant in semishade on light, non-alkaline soils that are well drained but moisture-retentive. Propagate by green-wood cuttings in late summer, on a mist bench or in a closed case, by soft-wood basal cuttings in spring, or by simple layering.

D. lanceolata Australia; PEPPER TREE; shrub or small tree to 10 ft (3 m); branchlets dull red to purple-red; leaves to 4¾ in (12 cm), lanceolate to oblong, subcoriaceous; flowers pale brown to green-white; fruit black); *D. winteri* (Chile, Argentina; tree or shrub to 66 ft (20 m), often multi-stemmed; bark aromatic; leaves 1¼–8 in (3–20 cm), elliptic to oblong or lanceolate, coriaceous, glaucous and pale beneath; flowers white to cream, fragrant; fruit glossy black.

drip irrigation see *trickle irrigation*.

drip line (1) the actual or predicted line on the soil surface below a tree canopy where its leaves shed raindrops. It is used as a guide for fertilizer application; (2) a term used to describe a small-bore irrigation pipe in trickle systems.

drip-point, drip-tip a leaf tip, either acuminate, caudate or aristate, from which water readily drips in wet conditions.

drop layering, dropping see *layering*.

dropsy see *oedema*.

Drosanthemum (from Greek *drosos*, dew, and *anthemon*, flower, referring to the glistening, dewdrop appearance of the papillae). Aizoaceae. South Africa. 90 species, succulent perennial shrubs with fleshy, usually papillose leaves and bright, daisylike flowers opening on warm and sunny days. Cultivate as for *Lampranthus*.

D. hispidum freely branching shrub to 24 in (60 cm) tall and over 3¼ ft (1 m) across, stems rooting, with rough white hairs; leaves ⅜–1 in (1.5–2.5 cm), cylindric, obtuse, light green to red-tinged with large, transparent papillae; flowers to 1¼ in (3 cm) in diameter, deep purple-red; *D. speciosum* shrub to 24 in (60 cm), stem papillose, with rough spots; leaves ½–⅝ in (1–1.6 cm), semi-cylindric, curved, obtuse, covered in crystal-like papillae; flowers to 2 in (5 cm) in diameter, deep orange-red with a green center.

Drosera (from Greek *droseros*, dewy, from the glands on the leaf surface). Droseraceae. Cosmopolitan. SUNDEW, DAILY DEW. Some 100 species, highly varied carnivorous herbs, mostly perennial and all trapping their prey by sweet and glistening, red-tinted tentacles. These cover the leaf surfaces and bend slowly inward to ensnare victims. The leaf itself may roll inward, enclosing the prey and forming a pocket in which the digestive process takes place. The dish-shaped flowers have five (sometimes four or eight) rounded petals and may be solitary, racemose or paniculate.

All *Drosera* species require full sun and a humid atmosphere. The hardy species will endure hard frosts, dying back to resting winter buds. These include *D. anglica*, *D. intermedia*, and *D. rotundifolia*. Since, however, it is almost impossible to recreate the sphagnum bog they inhabit in the open garden, these sundews tend to be grown in the cool greenhouse or in the home. The tender (remaining) species need a minimum temperature of 45°F (7°C). Plant all species in small clay pots containing a mix of coarse peat, sharp sand, and fresh sphagnum. In spring and summer, stand the pots in rainwater up to one-third of their depth. In fall and winter, keep just moist. Tuberous species will die back during this period. In hot, dry weather, syringing with soft water can be beneficial, together with light shading to prevent scorching. In the home, it may be necessary to grow these plants in a case, or at least to stand them in large bowls or trays of water. Propagate by seed or leaf and

Drosera rotundifolia
The common sundew, popular with amateur growers, is hardy but may need protection to provide the humid atmosphere it requires.

root cuttings. Alternatively, increase by division or by gemmae (tiny budlike propagules produced during the resting period) sown on damp potting mix.

D. adelae Australia; leaves 4–10 in (10–25 cm), narrow-lanceolate, thin-textured with a distinct midrib, pale green to olive, sparsely red-glandular; flowers to ⅛ in (0.3 cm) in diameter, cream to beige or red-brown; *D. anglica* GREAT SUNDEW, ENGLISH SUNDEW; N Europe, N Asia, N America; leaves to ½ in (1.3 cm), linear-oblanceolate, pale green, glands bright red; flowers to ¼ in (0.5 cm) in diameter, white; *D. binata* (Australia, New Zealand; leaves to 12 in (30 cm), the blade deeply forked into 2–14 linear to filiform spreading lobes with long, red tentacles; flowers to ¾ in (2 cm) in diameter, white to pink; *D. capensis* S Africa; leaves 1¼–2½ in (3–6 cm), narrowly oblong to spathulate-linear, with red tentacles; flowers to ¾ in (2 cm) in diameter, rosy pink; *D. capillaris* PINK SUNDEW; subtropical and tropical Americas; leaves to ¼ in (0.6 cm), broadly spathulate to orbicular; flowers to ½ in (1 cm) in diameter, pink or white; *D. cistiflora* (South Africa; leaves to 4 in (10 cm), linear; flowers 2 in (5 cm) in diameter, scarlet, violet or white); *D. filiformis* DEW-THREAD SUNDEW, THREAD-LEAVED SUNDEW; US; leaves 4–10 in (10–25 cm), filiform with purple-red tentacles; flowers to 1¼ in (3 cm) in diameter, rose-pink);

D

D. gigantea W Australia; leaves to ¼ in (0.6 cm) diam., cup-shaped, peltate, with red tentacles, on slender scrambling stems; flowers to ⅝ in (1.5 cm) diam., white; *D. glandulifera* COMMON SCARLET SUNDEW; Australia; leaves to ¼ in (0.5 cm) in diameter, transversely oval, concave, with red tentacles; flowers to ⅜ in (0.8 cm) in diameter, red with black centers; *D. intermedia* LOVE NEST SUNDEW; N Europe and Asia, N and C America; leaves to ¼ in (0.5 cm), obovate, covered in red tentacles; flowers ½ in (1 cm) in diameter, white; *D. prolifera* Australia; leaves to ⅝ in (1.5 cm), reniform with pale tentacles; flowers small, pink to red, on scapes which in time bend over and bear plantlets, coming to resemble proliferous stolons; *D. pygmaea* Australia, New Zealand; leaves to ¹⁄₁₆ in (0.2 cm) in diameter, round, concave; flowers to ⅛ in (0.3 cm) in diameter, white; *D. regia* GIANT SUNDEW; S Africa; leaves to 28 in (70 cm), linear to lanceolate; flowers to 1½ in (3.5 cm) in diameter, pale pink to purple; *D. rotundifolia* ROUND-LEAVED SUNDEW; northern temperate regions; leaves ¼–½ in (0.5–1 cm) in diameter, round with bright red tentacles; flowers to ¼ in (0.6 cm) in diameter, white to pink; *D. spathulata* (SPOON-LEAF SUNDEW; NE Asia to New Zealand; leaves ½–¾ in (1–2 cm), oblong to spathulate; flowers to ⅜ in (0.8 cm) in diameter, white to pink; *D. whittakeri* Australia; leaves 1½ in (3.5 cm), spathulate to obovate, pale green with bright red tentacles; flowers to 1¼ in (3 cm) in diameter, white, fragrant.

Drosophyllum (from Greek *drosos*, dew, and *phyllon*, leaf, alluding to the glistening appearance of the glandular leaves). Droseraceae. Portugal, S Spain, Morocco. 1 species, *D. lusitanicum*, a carnivorous perennial to 12 in (30 cm). It resembles *Drosera*, but its sticky leaf tentacles are shorter and do not move to enmesh prey. The plant develops a slender, usually trailing, woody stem bearing a terminal rosette of threadlike leaves. These are some 8 in (20 cm) long and densely covered on their undersides by glandular hairs that secrete adhesive and digestive fluid. Withered leaves persist in a shaggy, gray-brown ruff. The flowers consist of five broad, bright yellow petals, and are carried in a corymbose cyme in spring and summer. Provide a minimum winter temperature of 45°F (7°C), full sun and an airy, rather dry atmosphere. *Drosophyllum* resents disturbance and is best grown from seed in a small clay pot containing a mix of two parts moss peat, two parts loam-based mix, and one-and-a-half parts sand. As the plant increases in size, plunge the smaller pot within a larger pot of the same mix. The medium in the larger pot should be moist at all times (use rainwater) but that in the smaller pot (i.e., around the crown of the plant) should be kept dry. The roots will descend into the large pot below. Good results have also been achieved by drilling through a piece of pumice stone on tufa. This is placed on a pan containing the medium described above. A young plant may then be established in the hole in the stone (also containing the medium). This will eventually root into the pan, which should be kept just moist by watering from beneath.

drought the depletion of soil moisture due to lack of rainfall or insufficient watering. Physiological drought occurs when soil salinity is so high that it restricts the absorption of water by plant roots. Either form of drought causes flagging and various degrees of damage in plants not adapted to grow in such conditions.

single seed or "pit"

Drupe (plum)

drupaceous resembling, or pertaining to a drupe; with a juicy seed coat.

drupe an indehiscent, one- to several-seeded fruit, in which the endocarp is osseous or cartilaginous, and is contained within a soft, fleshy pericarp. Stone fruits, such as mangoes or plums, are drupes.

drupelet a small drupe, generally a part of an aggregate fruit such as a blackberry (*Rubus*).

dry rot a general term for diseases that cause a dry decay, with discoloration and shriveling of tissue, of various plant parts including fruits and underground storage organs—for example, *Fusarium solani* rot of potatoes.

dry set a condition in which fruits appear to set but fail to swell. It is especially common in greenhouse tomatoes grown in hot dry conditions, and is largely preventable by regular dampening down.

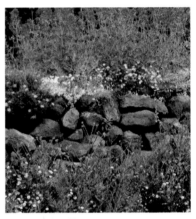

Dry stone wall
A mortar-free retaining wall provides ample opportunity to grow trailing and crevice plants, softening hard edges.

dry wall a stone wall built without mortar, used in gardens to stabilize vertical banks and terrace edges. Dry walls are suitable for planting vigorous alpines and trailing plants.

Dryandra (for Jonas Dryander [1748–1810], Swedish botanist.) Proteaceae. W Australia. Some 60 species, evergreen shrubs or small trees with leathery, toothed to lobed leaves, often white-downy beneath. Small, tubular flowers are carried in dense, terminal heads subtended by persistent bracts during spring and summer. Cultivate as for *Banksia*. Chlorosis may be treated with chelated iron. *D. formosa* SHOWY DRYANDRA; W Australia; shrub to 6½ ft (2 m); leaves 4–8 in (10–20 cm), soft, triangular-lobed, tomentose beneath; flower heads large, golden-orange.

Dryas (after Dryas, a wood nymph to whom the oak was sacred—the leaves of *D. octopetala* resemble those of the oak). Rosaceae. Arctic and alpine regions. MOUNTAIN AVENS. 5 species, evergreen, creeping shrublets, forming extensive, loose mats of slender, woody branches clothed with tough, rugose leaves. Produced in early summer, the flowers are solitary, borne on long stalks and consist of 7–10 rounded petals and numerous stamens. They give rise to snow white, feathery seed heads. The following species are suitable for the rock garden, making good light cover for spring bulbs, and for planting in paving joints. Hardy to 5°F (–15°C). Plant in sandy, well-drained, neutral to slightly alkaline soils. Grow in an open position in sun. Propagate by ripe seed sown fresh, by semiripe, heeled cuttings rooted in sharp sand; also by division of rooted stems.

D. drummondii N America; leaves to 1½ in (4 cm), elliptic to obovate, pale green above, white-tomentose beneath or throughout, margins coarsely crenate; flowers cream or white tinted yellow, nodding *D. octopetala* MOUNTAIN AVENS; northern temperate regions; leaves to 1½ in (4 cm), oblong to ovate, dull green and glabrous above, white-tomentose beneath, margins crenate; flowers white, erect); *D.* × *suendermanii* (a vigorous hybrid between the two preceding species; flowers slightly nodding, cream in bud, opening white.

Dryopteris (from Greek *dryas*, oak, and *pteris*, fern—some species are found in oak woods). Dryopteridaceae. Cosmopolitan. BUCKLER FERN, WOOD FERN, SHIELD FERN, MALE FERN. 150 species, ferns with erect to creeping rhizomes and shuttlecock-like to loose and spreading crowns of fronds—these are triangular to oblong-lanceolate in outline and 1–3-pinnate. The following species are hardy down to –22°F (–30°C) if well-established and mulched during cold periods. Most are tolerant of a wide range of pH. Grow in part to full shade or dappled sun (some species, such as *D. erythrosora*, will tolerate full sun if cool and moist at the roots, but their fronds will be of poorer quality). Plant in moist but porous soil, rich in leaf mold and well-rotted garden compost. Water generously

during the first spring and summer. Propagate by spores or by division of mature plants with multiple crowns.

D. affinis GOLDEN SHIELD FERN; Europe, Asia; stipes covered with golden to orange-brown scales; frond blades 12–48 in (30–125 cm) elliptic to narrowly elliptic, pinnules oblong, lobed, toothed, deep, glossy green; includes dwarf, congested and crested forms; *D. carthusiana* NARROW BUCKLER FERN; Europe; stipes covered with pale brown scales; frond blades 2½–12 in (6–30 cm), stiffly erect, lanceolate to ovate-lanceolate, pinnules pinnate or pinnately lobed, lime green, glandular-hairy beneath; *D. dilatata* BROAD BUCKLER FERN; Europe; stipes covered with pale brown scales; frond blades 2¾–39 in (7–100 cm), triangular-ovate, pinnules ovate to oblong, dentate or pinnately lobed, dark green, sparsely glandular beneath; includes cultivars with crisped pinnules or crested fronds; *D. erythrosora* JAPANESE SHIELD FERN, COPPER SHIELD FERN; E Asia; stipes red-brown to deep copper with brown or black scales; frond blades 12–28 in (30–70 cm), broadly ovate-triangular to oblong, pinnules narrowly oblong to linear-lanceolate, dentate or pinnately lobed, emerging deep copper-pink, turning gold to lime with a bronze tint, ultimately deep olive flushed copper; *D. filix-mas* MALE FERN; N America, Europe, N Asia; stipes with brown scales; frond blades 12–36 in (30–90 cm), lanceolate-triangular, apex finely acuminate; pinnae oblong-lanceolate, finely tapering with oblong, serrate segments, dull mid- to deep green, more or less hairy; includes cultivars with crested, crisped, and much-reduced fronds; *D. goldieana* GIANT WOOD FERN, GOLDIE'S WOOD FERN; E N America; stipes covered with dark, glossy brown scales; frond blades to 3¼ ft (1 m) cm, ovate, abruptly acuminate, pinnae oblong-lanceolate, acuminate, segments oblong, serrate; *D. intermedia* FANCY FERN; N America; stipes straw-colored, covered in dense scales; frond blades to 28 × 12 in (70 × 30 cm), ovate-lanceolate, abruptly acuminate, pinnules with segments oblong, obtuse, minutely spiny-toothed, bright green, glandular; *D. marginalis* N America; stipes covered in pale brown scales; frond blades 10–30 in

(25–75 cm), lanceolate, pinnae oblong-lanceolate, segments oblong, blunt, entire to crenate, coriaceous; *D. oreades* MOUNTAIN MALE FERN; Caucasus; stipes with pale brown scales; blades 12–32 in (30–80 cm), oblong-lanceolate to narrowly lanceolate, pinnae linear-lanceolate, attenuate, pinnules oblong, bluntly toothed; includes wavy to crested forms.

Duchesnea (for Antoine Nicolas Duchesne [1747–1827], French horticulturist, who published in 1766 *Histoire naturelle des fraisiers*, an account of the history of the strawberry). Rosaceae. Asia. INDIAN STRAWBERRY, MOCK STRAWBERRY. 2 species, stoloniferous perennial herbs. They closely resemble strawberries (*Fragaria*), differing in their yellow flowers and small, rather dry and inedible fruit. Hardy to –4°F (–20°C), *D. indica* is a vigorous and fast-growing carpeting plant. It favors a moist, sandy but fertile soil in dappled sun. Increase by offsets freely produced on runners. *D. indica* (syn. *Fragaria indica*) India to Japan, naturalized N America; leaflets to 2¾ in (7 cm), obovate, crenate, silky-hairy beneath; flowers to ¾ in (2 cm) in diameter; fruit bright red.

Dudleya (for William Russel Dudley [1849–1911], first professor of botany at Stanford University, California). Crassulaceae. Western N America. 40 species, succulent perennials with fleshy, ovate to linear leaves in basal rosettes. The flowers are tubular or star-shaped with five, acute lobes; they are borne in spring and summer in panicles. Grow in full sun, in a perfectly drained, sandy medium, with a minimum winter temperature of 45°F (7°C). Water very sparingly when plants are dormant. Increase by stem cuttings.

D. brittonii leaves 2¾–10 in (7–25 cm), crowded, finely pointed, dusted white, in a solitary rosette; flowers yellow to green; *D. lanceolata* (leaves 4–6 in (10–15 cm), lanceolate, tip tapering narrowly, crowded in a solitary rosette, glaucous; flowers red-yellow; *D. pulverulenta* CHALK LETTUCE; leaves 2¾–12 in (7–30 cm), oblong to spathulate, apex tapering and pointed, thickly white-glaucous in a large, solitary rosette; flowers red); *D. saxosa* (leaves 2–6 in (5–15 cm), pointed, semi-terete, glaucous, in few or solitary rosettes; flowers yellow to red; *D. virens* ALABASTER PLANT; leaves 1½–10 in (4–25 cm), linear, pointed, glaucous; flowers white.

Duranta (for Castor Durantes, early-18th-century physician and botanist in Rome). Verbenaceae. Tropical America. Some 30 species, trees or shrubs with 5-lobed, salverform flowers in slender racemes or panicles in summer and fleshy, globose fruit. Cultivate as for *Lantana*. *D. erecta* (syn. *D. plumieri*, *D. repens*) GOLDEN DEWDROP, PIGEON BERRY, SKY FLOWER; tropical America; shrub or small tree to 20 ft (6 m), sometimes spiny; racemes to 6 in (15 cm), flowers white, lilac, blue or purple; fruit to ½ in (1 cm) diameter, yellow.

dust, dusting the application to plants or soil of a pesticide formulated as a fine powder. Dusts have good adherence to plants but can be unsightly. They are best administered by means of a special applicator.

Dutch elm disease
The beetles bore characteristic networks of tunnels, or "galleries," beneath the bark.

Dutch elm disease (*Ophiostoma novo-ulmi* [syn. *Cyratocystis ulmi*]; *O. ulmi*) a serious disease of *Ulmus* and *Zelkova* species, first detected in the Netherlands in 1918 and in the eastern US in the 1920's. The major epidemic in the UK resulted from the introduction of *O. novo-ulmi* from the US on infested elm wood. This more virulent species has largely replaced *O. ulmi*, which causes a less serious form of the disease. Dutch elm disease has been responsible for devastating losses to the

elm population throughout the British and American countryside. Trees of all ages are vulnerable to infection. Leaves in the crown wilt, become yellow and die during summer months; notching appears in twig crotches and the twigs may become crook-shaped. Longitudinal streaks can be seen under the bark. Symptoms recur and spread in succeeding seasons, and the tree is killed within a few years, although growth may regenerate from the base.

The disease is mainly spread by bark beetles, especially the ELM BARK BEETLE (*Scolytus scolytus*), which emerge from brood galleries in dead elm bark and transmit fungal spores as they feed in the crotches of twigs and bore into older bark. Transmission through root contact also occurs. The only practical means of control is to fell and burn affected trees.

Dutch gardening in Britain, a style of gardening broadly dating from the reign of William and Mary and reflecting a combination of French and contemporary Dutch influence. It is characterized by an elaborate layout with statuary, topiary, and low boxwood hedges, orangeries, trees in tubs, and the use of bulb flowers.

Dutch light a single sheet of glass, usually 56 × 29 in (1422 × 730 mm), fitted into a wooden framework. Dutch lights are used to cover garden frames and sometimes mounted to form a Dutch-light greenhouse, with sloping sides and a pitched roof.

Duvalia (for H. A. Duval [1777–1814], author of *Plantae succulentae in horto alenconio* [1809]). Asclepiadaceae. Arabia, Africa. 19 species, small, succulent, perennial herbs with fleshy, 4–6-angled and toothed stems. The short-lived leaves are minute and scalelike. The fleshy flowers are deeply bell-shaped with five, recurved lobes. Cultivate as for *Stapelia*. *D. corderoyi* South Africa; stems to 2 in (5 cm) tall, usually prostrate, purple-tinted, thick; flowers to 2 in (5 cm) in diameter, olive green edged red-brown with deep purple hairs.

dwarf pyramid a trained form of fruit tree, with tiers of successively shorter horizontal branches forming a conical shape. Also known as a fuseau.

dwarf, dwarfing a small or slow-growing form of a plant, which may arise by mutation, breeding or, as in the case of many dwarf conifers, by the propagation of witches' brooms. Dwarfing rootstocks are particularly valued for predicting the ultimate size of fruit trees. Dwarfing can also be achieved by cultural methods, as in bonsai, or by the use of growth inhibitors on potted plants.

Dyckia (for Count Salm-Dyck [1773–1861], German botanist). Bromeliaceae. C and S America. 104 species, stemless, rosette-forming perennial herbs with rigid, sword-shaped leaves covered with gray scales and edged with spiny teeth. Small flowers are crowded in erect, branching, scapose inflorescences. Grow in full sun in a dry, airy atmosphere (minimum temperature 45°F/7°C); pot in a very sandy, open medium. Keep virtually dry in winter. *D. remotiflora* will tolerate several degrees of frost if dry. Propagate by rooted offsets.

D. brevifolia S Brazil; leaves to 8 in (20 cm); flowers yellow; *D.* 'Lad Cutak' (*D. brevifolia* × *D. leptostachya*) leaves 6–10 in (15–25 cm), maroon-flushed; flowers orange-yellow in a spike to 3¼ ft (1 m); *D. leptostachya* throughout range; leaves 16–39 in (40–100 cm), bulbous below, covered in ash-gray scales; flowers red-orange; *D. remotiflora* S Brazil, Uruguay; leaves 4–10 in (10–25 cm), dark green; flowers dark orange.

Dypsis Palmae. Madagascar, Comoros Islands. 20 species, tender palms, often multistemmed with smooth, erect trunks, and graceful pinnate leaves. Grow in a moisture-retentive, coir-based mix, in bright, indirect light, with a minimum temperature of 59°F (15°C) in winter, and plentiful supplies of water and liquid fertilizer in summer. Propagate by detaching rooted suckers. *C. lutescens* (syn. *Areca lutescens*) YELLOW PALM, ARECA PALM, BUTTERFLY PALM, CANE PALM stems to 30 ft × 6¾ in (9 m × 12 cm), clumped, resembling giant canes; leaves to 6½ ft (2 m), pinnae bright green, erect to arching, narrow, rachis, petioles, and leaf sheaths yellow-green to golden covered in wax; young plants— 12–40 in (30–100 cm) tall, stemless or multistemmed and light-textured—are commonly grown as potted plants).

E

e-, ex- prefix meaning "without," or "deprived of"—for example, estipellate, without stipels.

ear (1) an auricle; (2) the spikelet of some grasses.

earthing up drawing up of soil around plants, usually with a draw hoe or drag fork. It is carried out on potato crops to prevent tuber-greening and infection from blight; on brassicas to prevent wind-rocking; on leeks and celery to blanch stems; and in layering and stooling fruit-tree rootstocks to encourage the formation of rooted shoots.

earthworms (Annelida: Oligochaeta) worms characterized by long, soft, multiringed or segmented cylindrical bodies, which have pairs of bristles on the underside to aid movement. They are widely distributed in soil. Mature worms have a swollen glandular area about halfway along the body which, depending on species, is either saddle-shaped or completely encircling; its main function is to produce a yellow, lemon-shaped cocoon in which 20–30 eggs are deposited. Young worms emerge after 4–24 weeks, and take 35–70 weeks to reach maturity. Unless the weather is extremely cold or dry, earthworms are active within 20 in (50 cm) of the surface.

The earthworms' burrowing improves drainage and aerates the soil, and bacterial decomposition of organic matter is hastened by their digestion processes. The small earthworms known as BRANDLING or MANURE WORMS, particularly *Eisenia foetida*, are useful in compost piles, where they accelerate the decomposition of vegetable matter.

Worms feed by pulling organic matter lying on the surface into their burrows and by extracting the organic matter content from soil ingested during burrowing activities. This soil is ejected in a semiliquid state and used for lining burrows. Excess excreted soil is deposited as worm casts above or below the surface, where it can be a problem on lawns.

Since earthworms cannot thrive in very acidic soil, any measures taken to reduce pH will lower their numbers. Where control of earthworms is necessary, recommended chemical treatments can be used.

Earwig trap
Fill a pot with hay and invert it on a cane. Earwigs will creep inside, and can then be taken away from prize blooms.

earwigs (Dermaptera: Forficulidae) insects up to 1 in (25 mm) long, with large semicircular membranous hindwings folded under shortened leathery wing sheaths, leaving most of the abdomen exposed. The end of the abdomen is characterized by a pair of horny pincers, curved in males and almost straight in females. Of most importance to gardeners is the COMMON EARWIG (*Forficula auricularia*), which occurs in Europe, North America, northern Africa, western Asia, Japan, Australia and New Zealand. The female lays eggs in a soil cavity and remains with them until they hatch in early spring; the nymphs resemble adults but are smaller. A second brood of young may be produced in midsummer. Adults and nymphs feed on small insects such as aphids and attack plant tissue, preferring multipetaled flowers such as chrysanthemums and dahlias. They also make irregularly shaped holes in leaves and attack young buds, causing distorted shoots, and often create secondary damage in cavities in fruits, especially peaches and apples.

Disposing of garbage and fallen leaves helps to reduce the earwig population by limiting shelter, as does cutting bamboo stakes close to a node. Pieces of sacking, corrugated cardboard, or flower pots stuffed with straw and inverted on canes attract earwigs, and these serve as traps that can be removed and destroyed at intervals. Susceptible plants may be sprayed with residual contact insecticides, applied at dusk on warm evenings.

Ecballium (from Greek *ekballein*, to throw out, alluding to powerful projection of dehiscing fruits). Cucurbitaceae. Mediterranean to S Russia. SQUIRTING CUCUMBER; EXPLODING CUCUMBER. 1 species of monoecious, trailing or bushy, tender herbaceous perennial. *E. elaterium*: stems stout, hispid, to 100 ft (30 m). Leaves palmately lobed, ovate, triangular, gray to dark green, $1\frac{1}{2}$–2 in × $1\frac{1}{2}$–6 in (4–5 cm × 4–15 cm). Male inflorescence a raceme, $1\frac{1}{2}$–16 in (4–40 cm); female flowers solitary, flowers pale yellow. Fruits $1\frac{1}{4}$–2 in × $\frac{3}{4}$–$1\frac{1}{4}$ in (3–5 × 2–3 cm), ovoid, blue green, detaching violently if touched at base in fall. Seeds to $\frac{1}{6}$ in (4 mm), expelled en masse in astringent mucilage to distance of $6\frac{1}{2}$ ft (2 m) or more. Raise from spring-sown seed at 64°F (18°C). Plant out in full sun in well-drained soil after risk of frost.

Eccremocarpus (from Greek *ekkremes*, pendent, and *karpos*, fruit). Bignoniaceae. Chile and Peru. GLORY FLOWER. 5 species, evergreen or herbaceous perennial vines, the bases and older branches sometimes thinly woody. The leaves are bipinnate or twice pinnatisect, with terminal tendrils. Produced in summer in terminal racemes, the flowers are tubular, swelling toward the tip, then abruptly contracting at the mouth before expanding again in a small, entire or 2-lipped limb. The following species is a valuable climber for walls, fences, and arbors, and will scramble through shrubs, bearing a succession of exotic and brightly colored blooms throughout the summer until the first frosts. In a warm, sheltered position with good drainage, it will resprout from the base, even where temperatures have fallen to 23°F (–5°C) and below. In colder zones, grow in a cool greenhouse or conservatory. Remove overcrowded growth and frost-damaged stems in spring. Propagate from seed under glass in late winter, or by soft tip cuttings in early summer. *E. scaber* Chile; to 13 ft (4 m); flowers to 1¼ in (3 cm), typically scarlet to orange-yellow, also pink and deep crimson in cultivars and hybrids.

Echeveria (for Atanasio Echeverria, one of the botanical draftsmen employed on *Flora Mexicana* [1858]). Crassulaceae. C and S America. Around 150 species, succulent, evergreen perennial herbs and subshrubs with short, usually unbranched stems and fleshy leaves in terminal rosettes. Small and urn-shaped, the 5-lobed flowers are carried on slender, erect to arching racemes. Grown for their attractive foliage, as house or greenhouse plants, most will withstand temperatures down to 41°F (5°C). Some are used in carpet bedding and may tolerate light frosts if dry. Grow in full sun, with good ventilation, in a gritty medium. Water generously in summer; keep dry but not arid in winter. Propagate by leaf cuttings, seed, division, and offsets.

E. agavoides Mexico; leaves 1¼–3 in (3–8 cm), ovate-triangular, sharply pointed, waxy, with transparent margins, sea green with a red tip; flowers orange-pink outside, yellow within; *E. derenbergii* Mexico; leaves ¾–1½ in (2–4 cm), cuneate to obovate, thick, bristle-tipped, pale green with a red margin; flowers yellow tipped red; *E. elegans* MEXICAN GEM, MEXICAN SNOW BALL, WHITE MEXICAN ROSE; Mexico; leaves 1¼–2½ in (3–6 cm), thickly spathulate-oblong, bristle-tipped, icy blue-gray in rounded rosettes; flowers pink outside, yellow-orange within; *E. gibbiflora* Mexico; leaves 6–12 in (15–30 cm), obovate to spathulate, pointed, tinted purple with wavy margins; flowers red outside, buff within; *E. harmsii* Mexico; hairy throughout; leaves ¾–2 in (2–5 cm), oblanceolate, pointed, downy pale green with red margins; flowers red

with yellow interiors; *E. pulvinata* PLUSH PLANT, CHENILLE PLANT; Mexico; leaves ¾–2½ in (2–6 cm), spathulate-obovate, finely pointed, minutely hairy, gray- to mid-green with red margins; flowers yellow marked red; *E. secunda* Mexico; leaves 1–3 in (2.5–7.5 cm), spathulate-cuneate, blunt, bristle-tipped, glaucous, margin often red; flowers red outside, yellow within; *E. setosa* MEXICAN FIRE-CRACKER; Mexico; leaves 1½–2 in (4–5 cm), oblanceolate, pointed, white-hairy, bristle-tipped; flowers yellow with red markings.

Echinacea (from Greek *echinos*, hedgehog or sea-urchin, referring to the prickly phyllaries). Compositae. E US. CONE FLOWER. 9 species, tall perennial herbs producing large daisy-like flower heads in summer and fall, the disk florets usually raised in a cone-like mass. Grown in herbaceous and cut-flower borders and in native plant collections, they will withstand heat with high humidity, as well as drought, partial shade and temperatures as low as 5 to –4°F (–15 to –20°C). Give a deep dry mulch of bracken litter in zones at the limits of their hardiness. Cut back and feed plants that have flowered in midsummer for a second flowering. Propagate by seed, division or root cuttings. *E. purpurea* (syn. *Rudbeckia purpurea*) to 5 ft (1.5 m) tall; ray florets to 3 in (8 cm), magenta to red-purple, disk florets orange and dark red-brown; includes cultivars with pale pink, deep carmine and burnt orange and pure white flower heads.

echinate covered with many stiff hairs or bristles, or thick, blunt prickles.

Echinocactus (from Greek *echinos*, hedgehog, and Latin, *cactus*). Cactaceae. SW US, Mexico. 5 species, disk-shaped, globose or shortly columnar cacti with strongly ribbed stems, broad woolly crowns and stout spines. The flowers are shortly funnel-shaped to campanulate. Grow in full sun in a cool frost-free greenhouse (minimum temperature 36–45°F/2–7°C) with low humidity. Plant in a very gritty, acidic to neutral medium. Keep dry from midfall until early spring, except for light misting on warm days in late winter. Propagate by seed or offsets.

E. grusonii GOLDEN BARREL CACTUS; C Mexico; stem to 54 in (130 cm), globose, green with many raised ribs with golden to pale yellow spines; flowers to 2½ in (6 cm), yellow; *E. platyacanthus* (syn. *E. ingens*) C and N Mexico; stem to 10 ft (3 m), glaucous and sometimes banded purple when young with many distinct ribs, spines, yellow or brown; flowers 1¼–2½ in (3–6 cm), yellow.

Echinocereus (from Greek *echinos*, hedgehog, and Latin, *Cereus*). Cactaceae. SW US, Mexico. 45 species, low-growing shrubby cacti with simple or clustering stems—these are self-supporting, procumbent or rarely clambering, globose to cylindric and ribbed. The flowers are funnel-shaped. Some can withstand freezing temperatures when dry and may be hardy outdoors in fairly mild climates. *E. reichenbachii* for example may be grown in a cold greenhouse or out-of-doors with winter protection from rain. The remaining species need a cool greenhouse (minimum temperature 41°F/5°C). Grow all species in a gritty, neutral medium in full sun with low humidity. Withhold water from midfall until early spring, except for light misting on warm days in late winter. Propagate by stem cuttings, seed or offsets.

E. cinerascens E Mexico; sprawling stems, cylindric, 4–12 in (10–30 cm) × ⅝–4¾ in (1.5–12 cm), spines to 1¾ in (4.5 cm); flowers to 4 in (10 cm), pink to magenta with paler throat; *E. leucanthus* (syn. *Wilcoxia albiflora*) NW Mexico; stems ascending, cylindric, to 12 × ¼ in (30 × 0.6 cm), spines minute; flowers ¾–1½ in (2–4 cm), white with darker throat and sometimes pale pink stripes; *E. pectinalus* SW US, N Mexico; 3–14 in (8–35 cm) × 5 in (13 cm), globose to cylindric, spines to ¾ in (2 cm); flowers 2–6 in (5–16 cm) diameter, white to yellow or pink to lavender; *E. pentalophus* E Mexico, S Texas; stems cylindric, sprawling to erect, 8–24 in (20–60 cm) × ½–2½ in (1–6 cm), spines very short or to 2½ in (6 cm); flowers 3–4¾ in (8–12 cm), bright pink or magenta with white or yellow throat, rarely pure white; *E. reichenbachii* NE Mexico, SW US; globose to cylindric, erect, to 16 × 4 in (40 × 10 cm), short spines; flowers 2–4¾ in (5–12 cm), pale pink to purple or crimson; *E. schmollii* (syn. *Wilcoxia schmollii*) E Mexico; stem ascending, cylindric, to 10 × ½ in (25 × 1 cm), spines to ¼ in (0.7 cm), hairlike, giving the whole a woolly appearance; flowers to 2 in (5 cm), bright pink; *E. triglochidiatus* SW US, N Mexico; stems ovoid to cylindric, 2–12 (5–30 cm) × 2–6 in (5–15 cm), woolly, spines ½–2¾ in (1–7 cm); flowers 1¼–3½ in (3–9 cm), brilliant scarlet or pink.

Echinops (from Greek *echinos*, sea-urchin or hedgehog, and *opsis*, resemblance). Compositae. Europe to Asia. GLOBE THISTLE. About 120 species, perennial, biennial or rarely annual herbs (those listed below perennial) with entire to pinnately cut leaves, the margins spiny-toothed, the undersides white-felted. The flower heads are globe-like and composed of many, spiky tubular florets, gray to blue or white and with blue to gray anthers. They stand above foliage on slender stalks in summer. Fully hardy. Grow in full sun in any well-drained soil of low to moderate fertility. Propagate by seed sown under glass or *in situ*, division or by root cuttings in winter.

E. bannaticus E Europe; 20–48 in (50–120 cm); flower heads to 2 in (5 cm) diameter, gray-blue or deep blue; *E. ritro* C and E Europe to C Asia; 8–24 in (20–60 cm); flower heads 1¼–2 in (3–5 cm) diameter, pale to deep blue or, rarely, white; *E. sphaerocephalus* S and C Europe to Russia; 20–79 in (50–200 cm); flower heads gray-blue or white.

Echinopsis (from Greek *echinos*, hedgehog, and *opsis*, appearance). Cactaceae. Central S America. 50–100 species, shrubby, treelike or columnar cacti with simple, branched or clustering, cylindric to globose, ribbed stems with few to many spines. Produced in spring and summer, the flowers are large and bell- to funnel-shaped. Provide a minimum temperature of 36–45°F (2–7°C). Grow in full sun with low humidity in a gritty, neutral medium. Keep dry from midfall until early spring, except for light misting on warm days in late winter. Increase by seed, stem cuttings and offsets.

E. aurea (syn. *Lobivia aurea*) Argentina; stem globose to elongate, 4–16 (10–40

cm) × 1½–4¾ in (4–12 cm), spines to 1¼ in (3 cm); flowers 2–3½ in (5–9 cm), yellow; *E. eyriesii* S Brazil to N Argentina; stem globose to shortly cylindric, to 6 × 4 in (15 × 10 cm), spines very short and dark; flowers 8–10 in (20–25 cm), white; *E. oxygona* (syn. *E. multiplex*) S Brazil, N Argentina; stem globose, to 12 × 6 in (30 × 15 cm), spines to 1 in (2.5 cm), yellow-brown; flowers to 10 × 4 in (25 × 10 cm), pink; *E. rhodotricha* Paraguay, NE Argentina; stem globose to shortly columnar, to 32 × 3½ in (80 × 9 cm), spines to 1 in (2.5 cm) pale yellow tipped brown; flowers to 6 in (15 cm) diameter, white.

Echium (name used by Dioscorides). Boraginaceae. Canary Islands, Europe, Africa, W Asia. Some 40 species, bristly annual, biennial or perennial herbs or shrubs. The flowers are produced in summer in terminal cymes which usually form a panicle. In zones that are frost-free or almost so, the giant, spirelike and monocarpic species (*E. candicans E. simplex*, *E. wildpretii*, *E. pininana* and *E. giganteum*) are impressive and beautiful focal plants for the large mixed or herbaceous border; in cooler climates, grow in the cool greenhouse or conservatory. Since they are easily raised from seed, it is worth attempting these noble plants outdoors even where frosts are

Echium candicans
These impressive blue spires are a magnet for butterflies; echiums are ideal for a sunny planting designed for wildlife.

expected: they can always be given light protection at the harshest times. Hybrids between *E. pininana* and *E. wildpretii* have shown cold tolerance to temperatures of at least 14°F (–10°C): overwinter seedlings from summer sowings in a cool greenhouse at 45°F (7°C) and plant out in spring to flower in the following season. Under glass, provide direct sunlight and water plentifully when in growth. Keep fairly dry in winter and maintain a minimum temperature of 41°F (5°C), with good ventilation. The hardy *E. vulgare* is well-suited to the wild garden and is attractive to bees and butterflies; it also serves as a fast-growing annual filler for the mixed border or for bedding. Grow in an open position in sun in well-drained, low to moderately fertile soil. Propagate by seed. Sow seed under glass or (*E. vulgare*) *in situ*.

E. candicans PRIDE OF MADEIRA; Madeira; biennial shrub to 8 ft (2.5 m); leaves lanceolate, silvery; flowers red-purple in bud, opening blue-white in cylinder-shaped panicles to 12 in (30 cm); *E. giganteum* Canary Islands; giant, monocarpic herb with a single, spire-like stem to 8 ft (2.5 m) tall, bearing many flowering branches; leaves to 8 in (20 cm), lance-shaped, bristly; flowers white; *E. pininana* Canary Islands; as for *E. giganteum*, but to 13 ft (4 m) tall with slender, silvery-hairy leaves and blue and rose flowers; *E. simplex* PRIDE OF TENERIFE; Canary Islands; as for *E. giganteum*, but leaves densely silver-hairy; *E. vulgare* VIPER'S BUGLOSS; Europe; biennial, bristly herb, 10–24 in (25–60 cm); leaves to 6 in (15 cm), oblong to lance-shaped; flowers blue to violet, or rosy pink or white in a loosely branching panicle; *E. wildpretii* (syn. *E. bourgaeanum*) Canary Islands; as for *E. giganteum*, but with many overlapping and downward-pointing, narrow leaves covered in white hairs; flowers pale red.

ecology the study of the relationships between organisms and their environment.

ecosystem the unit composed of a community and its environment.

ecotype a variant of a species adapted to a particular environment.

edaphic pertaining to soil.

edema see *oedema*.

Edgeworthia (for M.P. Edgeworth [1812–81], an English botanist employed by the East India Company). Thymelaeaceae. Nepal to China, introduced Japan. PAPER BUSH. 3 species, deciduous or semievergreen shrubs to 6½ ft (2 m), with thick branches covered with papery bark and tough, lanceolate to oblong leaves to 4 in (10 cm) long. Fragrant silky-hairy flowers are borne in dense, stalked, axillary heads in spring. They each consist of a white to yellow calyx with a golden or pale orange stain at the base of the shortly cylindrical tube; the limb is divided into four lobes. With shelter from cold winds and in well-drained soil, they will survive temperatures to 5°F (–15°C) without injury. Grow in full sun or part shade. In areas at the limits of hardiness, grow against a south-facing wall, or in the cool greenhouse. Propagate from semiripe cuttings in summer, or from seed in fall.

E. chrysantha (syn. *E. papyrifera*) PAPER BUSH; China; flowers yellow to orange-red; *E. gardneri* Nepal, Sikkim; flowers white stained yellow.

edging (1) the practice of trimming lawn edges; (2) the use of solid materials, such as long narrow strips of plastic or thin metal, paving slabs or edging tiles, to demarcate lawn edges and prevent grass growing into beds and borders; (3) a continuous planting along the boundaries of beds or borders, often employing low, shrubby species, such as box or lavender.

edging iron, edging knife a long-handled tool, consisting of a half-moon-shaped blade fixed in the same plane as the handle, used for slicing lawn edges or turf. Wheeled versions are known as turf racers.

edging shears long-handled shears designed for trimming the edges of lawns. The blades may be fashioned to lie in the same plane as the handles or at right angles to them.

Edraianthus (from Greek *hedraios*, sitting, and *anthos* flower—the flowers are sessile). Campanulaceae. Mediterranean to Caucasus. GRASSY BELLS. Some 24 species of tufted perennial herbs, similar to *Campanula*, with bell-shaped, 5-lobed flowers in late spring and early summer. Suited to the sunny rock garden, troughs and dry stone walls. Grow in light, freely draining, humus-rich, calcareous soil, in sun or with some shade at the hottest parts of the day. They are hardy to about 5°F (–15°C), but the resting buds are susceptible to winter wet. They may perform better in an alpine house, watered plentifully when in growth and kept almost dry in winter. Propagate by seed sown in a cold frame in spring or by softwood cuttings of side shoots in late spring/early summer.

E. dalmaticus Balkans; to 2¾ in (7 cm); leaves linear; flowers several together, blue to violet or white; *E. pumilio* Balkans; dwarf with very slender, gray-hairy leaves and solitary, violet to blue flowers; *E. serpyllifolius* Balkans; to 2 in (5 cm); leaves spathulate; flowers solitary, deep violet, exceeding blunt bracts.

EDTA ethylene diamine tetra-acetic acid; an organic substance used in the chelating of trace elements to maintain their availability in soil. See *sequestrol*.

eelworms NEMATODES wormlike animals, some of which are predators or parasites; many feed on bacteria or fungi. Those that are plant pests are usually less than $\frac{1}{16}$ in (1 mm) long and have pin-shaped mouthparts with which they pierce plant cells in order to feed. Their flexible bodies enable them to swim in an eel-like manner in thin water films between plant cells or soil particles. At least two species, *Steinernema bibionis* and *Heterorhabditis heliothis*, have been used for the biological control of insect pests, such as vine weevil grubs. Eelworms reproduce by laying eggs which hatch and pass through four immature stages, each of which resembles the adult form. The following are the principal types of eelworm that damage plants.

CYST EELWORMS (*Heterodera* species, *Globodera* species) develop inside the roots of their host plants; when fully mature, the females' bodies swell and burst through the root surface, where they can be seen as tiny spherical or lemon-shaped brown cysts. These are packed with eggs which can remain viable in the soil for many years; when host plants are grown the eggs are stimulated to hatch by chemicals secreted from the roots. Heavy infestations disrupt the uptake of water and nutrients, resulting in poor growth and the early death of plants. In gardens, only potatoes and tomatoes are commonly damaged by cyst eelworms.

ROOT KNOT EELWORMS (*Meloidogyne* species) are mainly pests of tropical and subtropical areas but elsewhere can be troublesome in greenhouses. They develop inside the roots of many plants causing swellings; heavy infestations can result in plant death through disruption of water and nutrient uptake.

STEM AND BULB EELWORM (*Ditylenchus dipsaci*) appears to be a single species, occurring in a number of biological races capable of attacking different plants. The races commonly found in gardens typically attack *Narcissus*, onion and *Phlox*, and sometimes tulip. This nematode lives within stems, bulbs and foliage; symptoms are distinctive forms of distorted growth. See *stem and bulb eelworm*.

LEAF AND BUD EELWORMS (*Aphelenchoides* species) live within the leaf tissues and/or between the embryonic leaves in buds. Two species are common in gardens and attack an extremely wide range of plants, including chrysanthemums, ferns, *Begonia*, *Anemone* and strawberry. Typical damage consists of brown infested areas within the leaf, sharply separated from healthy tissue by the larger leaf veins.

Eelworms on phlox

Various types of virus vectors such as *Trichodorus* species and *Longidorus* species live in the soil and feed on plant roots. They are particularly associated with virus diseases, including arabis mosaic, cherry leaf-roll and tobacco rattle, which affect strawberry, cane fruits and some ornamentals.

Infestations can be limited by burning affected plants and by crop rotation. Care should be taken to acquire only healthy plant material. Some potato cultivars have resistance to, or are tolerant of, cyst eelworms. *Narcissus* bulbs and chrysanthemum stools can be essentially freed of eelworms by immersion in hot water for set periods (see *hot water treatment*). Effective chemical treatment against eelworms is too toxic for garden use.

Egeria (Egeria, a water nymph of Roman mythology who married Numa). Hydrocharitaceae. S America, naturalized elsewhere. 2 species, evergreen, perennial aquatic herbs. The submerged stems are long and densely furnished with opposite or whorled, linear to oblong leaves. Cymes of small, white to yellow flowers are subtended by a tubular spathe and held clear of the water in summer. The following species is an excellent oxygenator for the cold or tropical aquarium, and offers cover for spawning and young fish. Provide good light and a minimum temperature of 45°F (7°C). Trim regularly to keep fresh appearance. Propagate by stem cuttings in spring. *E. densa* (syn. *Anacharis densa*, *Elodea densa*) S America, widely naturalized elsewhere; leaves to ¾ × ⅛ in (2 × 0.3 cm), dark green.

Ehretia (for Georg Dionysus Ehret [1708–1770], German botanical artist who worked in England). Boraginaceae. Africa, Asia, Americas. 50 species, deciduous or evergreen trees or shrubs with oblong to elliptic leaves. Borne in summer in terminal panicles, the flowers are small, star-shaped and sometimes fragrant. The corolla is tubular-campanulate with five spreading or reflexed lobes. The fruits are subglobose, glabrous drupes, to ¾ in (2 cm) and yellow or orange to red. Given a sheltered position with good drainage, *E dicksonii* will tolerate temperatures to about 14°F (–10°C). Grow

in full sun. Propagate by softwood or semiripe cuttings. *E. dicksonii* China, Taiwan, Ryukyu Islands; deciduous tree to 39 ft (12 m); leaves to 7 in (18 cm), oblong to elliptic, serrate, leathery and shiny, bristly above, velvety beneath; flowers to ¼ in (0.6 cm), white tinted yellow, fragrant.

Eichhornia (for J.A.F. Eichhorn [1779–1856], Prussian politician). Pontederiaceae. Tropical S America, widely naturalized in other tropical and subtropical waterways. WATER HYACINTH, WATER ORCHID. 7 species, perennial, aquatic herbs. The leaves are borne in stoloniferous, floating rosettes. They consist of a swollen, spindle-shaped petiole filled with spongy, buoyant tissue, and a glossy, rounded to heart- or kidney-shaped blade. Composed of six, broad petals, the flowers are produced in summer in dense, erect spikes. Grow on still freshwater in sun with shelter from wind. Where frosts occur, collect the strongest-looking plants in fall and overwinter them on trays of wet loam, leaf mold and sand, with a minimum temperature of 50°F (10°C) and good light. Propagate by detaching young plants produced freely on runners. *E. crassipes* leaves 2–6 in (5–15 cm), shining pale to dark green; flowers to 1½ in (4 cm), pale lilac to violet blue, often with paler or deeper feathering and a central violet and yellow blotch.

Elaeagnus (from Greek *elaia*, olive, and *agnos*, the Greek name for *Vitex agnus-castus*. The name was applied by Theophrastus to a willow). Elaeagnaceae. Asia, S Europe, N America. OLEASTER. About 45 species, deciduous or evergreen shrubs or trees, often spiny. The leaves are lanceolate to ovate or oblong and often covered with minute silvery or brown scales, especially beneath. Small and often fragrant, the tubular to campanulate flowers are carried in clusters in late winter and spring. They are followed by small, fleshy fruits. These shrubs will thrive in a range of soil types provided they are free-draining (the deciduous species are particularly tolerant of poor soil). They are useful in coastal gardens or as shelter belts in exposed areas. They respond well to hard prun-

ing where required, quickly producing young shoots from the old wood. Propagate from fresh seed sown in a cold frame—a stratification period of three months at 39°F (4°C) is otherwise required. *E. commutata* can be propagated easily from suckers. Root cuttings, hardwood cuttings (*E. angustifolia*) and leafy summer cuttings (*E. pungens*) are also successful.

E. angustifolia OLEASTER, RUSSIAN OLIVE, WILD OLIVE, SILVERBERRY; W Asia; deciduous shrub or small tree to 23 ft (7 m); leaves 2–3½ in (5–9 cm), narrow, covered in pale bronze to silver scales at first; flowers yellow to silver, fragrant; fruit yellow covered in silvery scales; *E. commutata* SILVERBERRY; N America; deciduous suckering shrub to 16 ft (5 m); leaves to 2½ in (6 cm), broad, lustrous, silvery; flowers fragrant, silvery yellow; fruit yellow, covered in silvery scales; *E.* × *ebbingei* (*E. macrophylla* × *E. pungens*); shrub to 10 ft (3 m), usually evergreen; leaves to 4 in (10 cm), broad dark, glossy green or metallic sea-green above, silvery beneath; flowers intensely fragrant, white to cream; includes cultivars with gold-edged and yellow-green variegated leaves; *E. macrophylla* Japan, Korea; evergreen shrub to 10 ft (3 m); leaves 2–4¾ in (5–12 cm), broad, glossy deep green above, silver-scaly beneath; flowers cream, scaly, highly fragrant; fruit red, scaly; *E. pungens* Japan; evergreen shrub to 13 ft (4 m); leaves 1½–3 in (4–8 cm), broad, wavy, deep smooth green above, dull silvery white and brown-scaly beneath; flowers fragrant, silvery white; fruit brown becoming red; includes several popular cultivars with leaves edged, splashed or zoned yellow, gray-green, pale green and darkest emerald, the most popular being 'Maculata'; *E.* 'Quicksilver' (*E. angustifolia* × *E. commutata*); tall, deciduous suckering, more or less pyramidal shrub with narrow, gray leaves overlaid with silver scales; *E. umbellata* Himalayas, China, Japan; deciduous shrub or small tree to 33 ft (10 m); leaves to 4 in (10 cm), wavy, bright green above with silver and some brown scales beneath; flowers yellow-white, scented; fruit silver-bronze, ripening red; includes cultivars with pale lime and silvered foliage, and amber or deep red fruit.

Elaeocarpus (from Greek *elaia*, olive, and *karpos*, fruit: the fruit resembles an olive.) Elaeocarpaceae. E Asia, Indomalaysia, Australasia, Pacific. 60 species, evergreen trees or shrubs with small, fragrant flowers with 3–5 fringed petals, in axillary racemes in summer, followed by small, spherical fruits. Where frosts are light and short-lived, provide a sheltered position; otherwise, grow in the cool greenhouse or conservatory with a minimum temperature of 41–45°F (5–7°C). Under glass, admit full light but ensure shade from the hottest summer sun; water plentifully when in full growth, less in winter. Cut back previous season's growth in late winter. Propagate by seed sown under glass in spring or by semiripe cuttings in a sandy propagating medium with gentle bottom heat. *E. cyaneus* (syn. *E. reticulatus*) Australia; tree to 60 ft (18 m) tall, often a shrub in cultivation; leaves to 6 in (15 cm), oblong, toothed; flowers small, ivory; fruit blue.

Elatostemma (from Greek *elatos*, driving, striking, and *stema*, stem). Urticaceae. Tropical and subtropical Asia. Some 50 species, perennial herbs or subshrubs, sometimes with succulent stems. The leaves are alternate, 2-ranked, and entire or dentate. Inconspicuous flowers are borne in dense cymes. Cultivation as for *Pilea*.

E. pulchra RAINBOW VINE; Vietnam; low spreading to creeping herb, stems fleshy, tinged purple; leaves ³/₄–2 in (2–5 cm), obliquely oblong to elliptic, marked dull black-green along midrib and veins above, purple beneath; *E. repens* TRAILING WATERMELON BEGONIA; SE Asia; creeping herb to 24 in (60 cm), stems succulent, tinged pink; leaves ¹/₂–2¹/₂ in (1–6 cm), oblong to orbicular, scalloped, bronze-green above, tinged violet with a central band of pale gray-green, tinged pink beneath.

electronic leaf a device for controlling the frequency of water droplet application in a mist propagation unit. It comprises a plastic sensor, in which two electrodes are implanted. When a film of moisture connects the two electrodes, an electric current flows and the unit is programmed "off." When the current is interrupted as a result of the "leaf" drying out, a switch is activated and a fine water mist is emitted over the bench.

Eleocharis (Greek, *helodes*, marshy or of marshy places, and *charis*, grace). Cyperaceae. More or less cosmopolitan. SPIKE RUSH. Around 150 species, annual or perennial grasslike herbs with very narrow leaves and 3–4-angled stems. Borne in summer, the flowers are minute and arranged in solitary, brown and bristly spikelets. *Eleocharis* is fully hardy. Cultivate as for *Carex* in bog gardens and at pond margins with a slightly acidic pH. *E. acicularis* NEEDLE SPIKE RUSH, SLENDER SPIKE RUSH, HAIR GRASS; widespread in N America, Europe, Asia; perennial, 2–12 in (5–30 cm) tall.

Eleutherococcus (from Greek *eleutheros*, free, and *kokkos*, pip, here referring to the fruit structure). Araliaceae. S and E Asia, Japan, the Ryukyu Islands, Taiwan and the Philippines (Luzon); most diverse in C and W China. About 30 species, generally deciduous and often bristly or prickly shrubs or trees some more or less scandent or sprawling with digitately compound leaves. Small, 5-parted flowers are carried in umbels or heads in terminal, simple or compound inflorescences. They are followed by small, drupaceous fruits that turn black or purple-black at maturity. In positions sheltered from north and east winds, *E. sieboldianus* will usually survive temperatures from 14°F (–10°) to 5°F (–15°C) and withstands poor soil and pollution. Often used for hedging in cool and warm temperate areas, it seems to thrive on urban pollution, and one or two heavy trimmings per year. That said, for best results, grow in well-drained, humus-rich soil in full sun. Specimen shrubs may be pruned to thin crowded wood and to shorten ungainly growth in late winter. Propagate by ripe seed in fall or by root cuttings in late winter; alternatively, increase by suckers and semiripe cuttings, with bottom heat, in summer. *E. sieboldianus* (syn. *Acanthopanax sieboldianus*) E China, Japan (introduced); arching to scandent shrub to 10 ft (3 m) with slender, canelike stems, often spiny; leaflets usually five per leaf, toothed; flowers green-white; fruit black; 'Variegatus': leaves edged creamy-white.

ellipsoid elliptic, but 3-dimensional.

elliptic, elliptical ellipse-shaped; midway between oblong and ovate but with equally rounded or narrowed ends, with two planes of symmetry and widest across the middle.

Elodea (from Greek *helodes*, of the marshes). Hydrocharitaceae. N America to subtropical S America. PONDWEED, WATERWEED, DITCHMOSS. 12 species of submerged freshwater perennials, usually dioecious. Stems to 13 ft (4 m), erect or creeping, slender, rhizomatous. Leaves cauline to ovate, in whorls of 3, transparent to pale green. Inflorescence subtended by spathe comprising 2 united, acute bracts; male flowers open at water surface. *E. canadensis* CANADIAN PONDWEED; N America. Hardy, submerged perennial, with branching, brittle stems up to 13 ft (4 m) long; flat, translucent dark green leaves ¹/₄–¹/₂ in (0.5–1 cm) long. Floating petal-less purple flowers, tinged green, ¹/₃ in (8 mm) wide, on long, thin stalks, pollinated by water movement. Widely naturalized in Europe. Must be confined to large, easily managed areas of water because of its vigor and invasiveness.

elongate lengthened, as if stretched or extended.

Elsholtzia (for John Sigismund Elsholtz [1623–1688], Prussian horticulturist and physician). Labiatae. C and E Asia, NE Africa. 38 species, aromatic shrubs or perennial and annual herbs with small, tubular and 2-lipped flowers in dense, whorled spikes in late summer and fall. Shrubby growth is usually hardy to 14°F (–10°C) but may be killed by prolonged frosts and is in any case best cut hard back each year in spring. Mulch in winter. Propagate from seed sown under glass in spring or by cuttings of new growth, under mist or a warm cloche, in early summer. *E. stauntonii* China; subshrub 5³/₄ ft (1.75 m); leaves to 6 in (15 cm), ovate, toothed flowers dark pink or white.

Elymus (from Greek *elymos*, classical name for millet). WILD RYE; LYME GRASS. Gramineae. Northern temperate Asia. Some 150 species of tufted or rhizomatous perennial grasses valued

E

for the often bright blue-greens of the foliage clumps, topped by flowering spikes in shades of buff and parchment. *E. magellanicus* is one of the most intensely blue of all grasses. They are tolerant of temperatures to at least 14°F (–10°C). They will thrive in any gritty, moisture-retentive soil in sun. Propagate by division.

E. hispidus (syn. *Agropyron glaucum*) Europe, Asia; to 20 in (50 cm), erect, tightly clump-forming; leaves intense gray-blue, hispid; *E. magellanicus* (syn. *A. magellanicum*) S America; to 12 in (30 cm), loosely clump-forming; leaves arching, brilliant blue-gray, smooth or finely grooved.

emarginate the apex of a leaf or other organ shallowly notched, the indentation (sinus) being acute.

emasculation the removal of anthers from a flower before the pollen is ripe; carried out by plant breeders to prevent self-fertilization.

Embothrium (from Greek *en*, in, and *bothrion*, a little pit, in reference to the sunken anthers). Proteaceae. C and S Andes. 8 species, evergreen shrubs or trees with leathery leaves. Produced in clusters or racemes in late spring and early summer, the flowers are narrowly tubular and split into four, narrow and twisted lobes, parted by a slender style. Hardy to 5°F (–15°C), given a warm and sheltered site with protection from cold drying winds. Plant in well-drained, moist, neutral or acidic soil in sun, against a south-facing wall or in light, open woodland. Propagate by seed sown under glass in spring, from suckers and from root cuttings in the cold frame; also by nodal cuttings of the current season's growth, under mist or in a closed case with gentle bottom-heat, in summer. *E. coccineum* CHILEAN FIREBUSH, CHILEAN FLAME-FLOWER; Chile; shrub or tree to 33 ft (10 m) with clumped, stems; leaves to 4¾ in (12 cm), oblong; flowers to 1¾ in (4.5 cm), sealing-wax red to bright scarlet.

embryo the rudimentary plant within the seed.

embryo culture a form of micro-propagation using excised plant embryos.

emersed raised out of and above the water.

Emilia (probably a commemorative name, but for whom it is unknown). Compositae. India, Polynesia, tropical Africa. About 24 species, annual herbs with lanceolate to oblong or lyrate leaves. Small, pomponlike flower heads are carried in summer in long, branching sprays. Grown for its brightly colored blooms suitable for mixed bedding, cutting and drying. Treatment as for *Acroclinium*. *E. coccinea* (syn. *E. flammea*, *E. javanica*) TASSEL FLOWER; tropical Africa, Asia; to 24 in (60 cm); flower heads scarlet, fiery orange or rich yellow.

EMLA an acronym for two eminent British horticultural research stations (East Malling in Kent and Long Ashton in Somerset), both formerly concerned mainly with fruit research. Their collaboration was particularly important in the re-selection of *Malus* clonal rootstocks. See *apple*.

Emmenopterys (from Greek *emmenes*, enduring, and *pteryx*, wing— one of the calyx lobes becomes enlarged and winglike). Rubiaceae. China, SE Asia. 2 species, deciduous trees with entire, somewhat leathery, elliptic to oblong leaves. Produced during hot summers in terminal panicles, the flowers are funnel- or bell-shaped with five, spreading, ovate and downy lobes. Of the five calyx lobes, one is sometimes enlarged, ovate to oblong and white. Hardy to –13°F (–25°C); grow in a sunny site sheltered from cold winds, in a deep, fertile and moisture-retentive loam. Propagate from softwood cuttings in early summer. *E. henryi* to 85 ft (26 m) young growth red-bronze; leaves to 8 in (20 cm) dark green above, pale beneath, petioles red to purple; panicles to 7 in (18 cm), corolla white, to 1¼ in (3 cm), enlarged calyx lobe white, to 2 in (5 cm) with a claw to 2 in (5 cm).

Encephalartos (from Greek *en-*, within, *kephale*, the head, and *artos*, bread—the inner tissues of the upper trunk are starchy and, with much careful preparation, edible). Zami-

aceae. South and C Africa (those listed below are from South Africa). Some 25 species, evergreen cycads, stemless or with short and squat to tall and columnar trunks. Long and leathery, the leaves are pinnate and borne in terminal flushes or rosettes. The leaflets are tough and two-ranked. Large cones are carried on plants of separate sex. Species with glaucous, woolly or narrow pinnae will tolerate low temperatures (minimum 41°F/5°C), full sunlight and dry conditions: these include (leaflets glaucous) *E. horridus*, *E. lehmannii* and *E. trispinosus*, and (leaflets woolly or very narrow) *E. ghellinckii*, *E. friderici-guilielmi*. Grow in a gritty, sandy, neutral to slightly acidic mixture; water freely when in growth

Encephalartos horridus
The cycads are an ancient group; plants similar to this are known to have existed among prehistoric vegetation.

(i.e., when bract, leaf or cone activity is visible in the crown) and apply a weak, semiweekly feed. Water very sparingly in winter. The remaining species require a minimum temperature of 55°F (13°C), at least partial shade, high humidity, plentiful water supplies throughout the year and a more open, bark-based mix rich in garden compost and leaf mold. Propagate by seed sown under glass in warmth, or by offsets.

E. altensteinii 12–22 ft (4–7 m); leaves to 11½ ft (3.5 m), leaflets to 6 in (15 cm), linear to oblong, rigid, fresh green, with 1–3 spiny teeth along each margin; *E. ferox* to 3¼ ft (1 m); leaves to 6 ft (1.8 m); leaflets to 4¾ in (12 cm), oblong to ovate, glossy dark green with 2–4 broad, sharp and spiny teeth along each marg in; *E. friderici-guilielmi* to 13 ft (4 m); leaves to 5 ft (1.5 m), leaflets to 7 in (18 cm), narrowly linear, entire, tip sharply pointed, densely woolly at first, later dark green; *E. ghellinckii* to 10 ft (3 m); leaves to 3¼ ft (1 m), spirally twisted, leaflets to 5½ in (14 cm), linear but with strongly revolute margins thus appearing needlelike, covered in gray wool at first, later rigid bright green; *E. horridus* stem very short; leaves to 3¼ ft (1 m), leaflets to 4 in (10 cm), broad and deeply cut with 2–3 large, spine-tipped and revolute lobes, rigid, bright glaucous blue-gray; *E. lebomboensis* to 13 ft (4 m); leaves 3¼–10 ft (1–3 m), leaflets to 6½ in (17 cm), lanceolate, bright green with 2–4 teeth along each marg in; *E. lehmannii* to 6½ ft (2 m); leaves to 5 ft (1.5 m), leaflets to 7 in (18 cm), oblong to lanceolate, usually entire, glaucous blue-gray; *E. longifolius* to 13 ft (4 m); leaves to 6½ ft (2 m), leaflets to 8 in (20 cm), lanceolate, dark glossy green, entire or with 1–4 teeth along lower marg in; *E. natalensis* to 13 ft (4 m); leaves to 11½ ft (3.5 m), leaflets to 10 in (25 cm), broadly lance-olate, dark green, entire or with 1–4 teeth along one or both margins; *E. transvenosus* to 43 ft (13 m); leaves to 8 ft (2.5 m), leaflets to 10 in (25 cm), broadly lanceolate, with 2–5 small teeth along upper margin, 1–3 along lower margin, glossy, dark green; *E. trispinosus* differs from *E. horridus* in the narrower, less strikingly glaucous leaflets with one or two strongly recurved and spine-tipped lobes on lower margin only.

enchytraeid worms (Annelida: Oligochaeta) many-segmented, small, threadlike worms, up to ¹⁄₁₆ in (2 mm) long, translucent white in color and often abundant in leaf mold, compost and manure, where they feed on decay-ing organic matter. They are com-monly known as POT WORMS, ASTER WORMS, ROOT WORMS or WHITE WORMS. Although frequently found near plant roots, they do not feed on living plant tissue and are harmless.

Encyclia (from Greek *enkyklo*, to encircle, referring to the characteristic of the lateral lobes of the lip which encir-cle the column). Orchidaceae. Florida, West Indies, C and S America. Some

Encyclia cochleata
The encyclias mainly dwell in trees, taking in nourishment via their aerial roots from rainwater and from canopy debris.

150 species, epiphytic and lithophytic orchids, closely allied to and formerly included in *Epidendrum*. They vary greatly in size and habit, but generally have clumped, rounded to flask- or spindle-shaped pseudobulbs topped with oblong-lanceolate to linear leaves. The flowers consist of five, obovate to linear tepals and a showy lip; they are borne usually in spring and summer in terminal racemes or panicles.

Grow in pans or baskets of very open bark-based mix in sunny, cool to intermediate conditions (minimum temperature 45°F/7°C). Water and feed freely in spring and summer and maintain high humidity. Once the new pseudobulbs are complete and ripened, water and syringe only to prevent their shrivelling. Resume watering when new growth starts. These guidelines apply to most species, with the following excep-tions—the dwarf *E. tripunctata* should be mounted on fiber blocks on pads of moss and kept just moist and in filtered sunlight throughout the year. *E. vitellina* requires cool, buoyant, rather dry con-ditions in full sunlight with a decided dry winter rest. *E. mariae* and *E. citrina* must be mounted "upside-down" on cork or bark slabs and suspended in a cool, bright, dry environment. Plunge often and syringe daily when in growth. Once growths are complete, lower temperatures (to near-freezing, if possible) and withhold water com-pletely. With lengthening days, start

back into growth by raising tempera-tures slightly and misting roots—this will encourage development of flower spikes for spring blooming. Increase all by division when repotting in spring.

E. adenocaula (syn. *E. nemoralis, Epi-dendrum adenocaulum, Epidendrum nemorale*) Mexico; flowers to 3½ in (9 cm) diame-ter, slender, nodding, pale rose-pink to magenta, the lip with darker markings, several together on an arching, warty panicle to 39 in (100 cm); *E. alata* (syn. *Epidendrum alatum*) Mexico to Nicaragua; flowers to 2½ in (6 cm) diameter, tepals pale green or yellow-green marked purple-bronze or red-brown, the lip white veined maroon, many together on a minutely warty panicle to 32 in (80 cm); *E. brassavolae* (syn. *Epidendrum brassavolae*) Mexico to Panama; flowers to 2¾ in (7 cm) diam-eter, slender, spreading, tepals green to olive or pale tan, lip cream tipped rose-purple, many on an erect raceme to 12 in (30 cm); *E. citrina* (syn. *Cattleya citrina, Epidendrum citrinum*) Mexico; flowers fra-grant, to 3 in (8 cm) long, strongly pen-dulous and not opening widely, waxy lemon yellow, the lip veined deep gold, solitary or paired on a short, hanging stalk; *E. cochleata* (syn. *Epidendrum cochleatum*) CLAMSHELL ORCHID, COCKLE ORCHID; widespread in C America; flowers to 2½ in (6 cm) diameter, tepals slender, lime to olive, lip held upper-most, shell-like, white, tipped and veined dark purple to purple-black, many in an erect raceme to 12 in (30 cm); *E. cordigera* C America; flowers to 2¾ in (7 cm) diameter, tepals chocolate brown to maroon or bronze-green, lip large, wavy, cream streaked or flushed rose to magenta; *E. fragrans* (syn. *Epi-dendrum fragrans*) C America, northern S America, West Indies; flowers highly fragrant, to 1½ in (4 cm) diameter, tepals white to ivory, lip held upper-most, striped maroon; *E. mariae* (syn. *Epidendrum mariae*) Mexico; similar to *E. citrina*, but with narrower, lime to olive tepals and a white lip; *E. prismatocarpa* (syn. *Epidendrum prismatocarpum*) Costa Rica to Brazil; flowers to 2 in (5 cm) diameter, fragrant, tepals yellow-green spotted or banded dark maroon to black, lip lilac-purple, base olive, mar-gins white, in tall racemes; *E. radiata* (syn. *Epidendrum radiatum*) Guatemala, Honduras, Mexico; similar to *E. fra-*

grans but with smaller flowers, the lip rounded rather than heart-shaped, with a cleft and wavy, not smooth and pointed tip; *E. tripunctata* (syn. *Epidendrum tripunctatum*) Mexico; flowers to ⅝ in (1.5 cm) diameter, a few borne together in short racemes, tepals lime to olive green, lip white, column dark purple with yellow teeth; *E. vespa* (syn. *Epidendrum vespa*) tropical America; flowers to ¾ in (2 cm) diameter, tepals olive to yellow or cream blotched purple to maroon or dark chocolate, lip white or yellow marked pink, many in a raceme to 14 in (35 cm); *E. vitellina* (syn. *Epidendrum vitellinum*) Mexico, Guatemala; flowers to 2 in (5 cm) diameter, tepals vermilion to scarlet, lip orange to deep gold, several in an erect raceme to 16 in (40 cm).

endemic occurring naturally in one locality only.

endive (*Cichorium endivia*) an annual, native of Asia and Europe, of similar appearance to lettuce, forming a rosette of leaves with a loose heart. It is used in salads or braised, the green outer leaves being sharper flavored than the light-colored, sweeter inner leaves. The curled or staghorn-leaf endive is better adapted to higher temperatures than the broad or Batavian forms. The main season is fall to early winter outdoors, later under protection. Sow in cell modules for transplanting or *in situ* for thinning to a final spacing of 15 × 15 in (38 × 38 cm) for broad-leaf types and 12 × 12 in (30 × 30 cm) for curled-leaf types. Sow during April in heat for early summer cropping and successionally outdoors from May to July for summer to fall maturity. Latest crops of broad-leaf cultivars are best raised under glass or cloches from an August sowing. Endive is useful for cut-and-come again harvest, and leaves of broad-leaf types especially can be made sweeter by blanching. Either bunch and tie the rosettes together or cover with an upturned container or dinner plate to exclude light, for about 10 days in summer and twice as long in winter.

endo- prefix meaning "within," "inner"—for example, endodermis, the inner layer of skin in a periderm.

endocarp the innermost layer or wall of a pericarp, which encloses the seed, and either membranous or bony or cartilaginous.

endosperm a nutritive tissue of developing seed.

Enkianthus (from Greek *enkyos*, swollen or pregnant, and *anthos*, flower— the type species has basal swellings on the flowers). Ericaceae. Himalaya to Japan. 10 species, usually deciduous shrubs with whorled branches and obovate to elliptic, toothed to entire leaves. Carried in spring in drooping, terminal umbels or racemes, the flowers are waxy, campanulate to urceolate, and 5-lobed. Suitable for the peat terrace and shrub border, for open situations in the woodland garden and for moist and peaty pockets in the rock garden. Hardy to 5°F (−15°C). Grow in moisture-retentive, nonalkaline soil, enriched with leaf mold, in full sun or dappled shade; mulch in hot, dry weather. Propagate from ripe seed, by semiripe cuttings in summer, alternatively by simple layering.

E. campanulatus Japan; variable, deciduous shrub to 15 ft (5 m) tall; leaves becoming vivid red in fall; flowers pale cream to pale pink with faint salmon, peach or rust veins, deeper and more solid red in some forms, campanulate, in drooping racemes; *E. cernuus* Japan; deciduous shrub to 10 ft (3 m); flowers white or deep red, broadly campanulate with jagged, unequal lobes, in drooping, hairy racemes; *E. perulatus* Japan; deciduous shrub to 6½ ft (2 m); leaves becoming yellow and red in fall; flowers white, urceolate, in drooping umbels.

Ensete (from the African Amharic name *anset*) Musaceae. Old World tropics. 7 species, massive evergreen perennial herbs, close to *Musa*, but with a more shuttlecock-like growth habit and unpalatable fruit. They are august foliage plants for subtropical and tropical gardens and, elsewhere, for tubs and borders in large greenhouses and interiors. Fast-growing, young plants can be overwintered under glass and planted out in late spring to make striking foci for "tropical" bedding schemes in temperate gardens. Grow in full sun or shade in a humid, sheltered environment with a minimum temperature of 50°F (10°C). A free-draining, highly fertile medium is essential, as are plentiful supplies of water and feed in the growing season. Stems will deteriorate after flowering and should be cut down once the replacement suckers are well-established. Increase by rooted suckers and by seed (see *Musa*).

E. ventricosum (syn. *Musa arnoldiana*, *Musa ensete*) ABYSSINIAN BANANA, ETHIOPIAN BANANA; Africa; pseudostem 3¼–40 ft (1–12 m); leaves 6½–20 (2–6 m) × 3¼–5 ft (1–1.5 m), olive green with a maroon midrib; *E. gilletii* (syn. *Musa gilletii*) differs from *E. ventricosum* in its narrower leaves with sealing-wax red midribs.

ensiform sword-shaped, straighter than lorate, and with an acute point.

entire continuous; uninterrupted by divisions, teeth or lobes. Thus, "leaves entire" describes leaves with margins that are neither toothed nor lobed.

entomophily the transfer of pollen by insects.

Eomecon (from Greek *eos*, the dawn or east, and *mekon*, poppy, referring to its distribution). Papaveraceae. E China. SNOW POPPY. 1 species, *E. chionantha*, a perennial, rhizomatous herb to 16 in (40 cm) tall with branched stems containing orange sap. To 4 in (10 cm) across, the leaves are heart-shaped to arrow-shaped, leathery, slightly succulent, gray-green and wavy-edged. Produced in summer, the pure white flowers are 2 in (5 cm) across with four, broad petals and many stamens. With good drainage *Eomecon* will tolerate temperatures to 14°F (−10°C). Plant in shade or sun in well-drained, humus-rich, fertile soil that remains cool and moist in summer. The rhizomes resent disturbance but may spread extensively and become a nuisance. Propagate in spring from seed sown *in situ*, or by division.

Epacris (from Greek *epi*, upon, and *akris*, a summit; alluding to the high-altitude habitat of some species). Epacridaceae. E and SE Australia, Tasmania, New Zealand and New Caledonia. AUSTRALIAN HEATH. 35 species, heathlike, evergreen shrubs with small leaves and cylindric to campanulate, 5-lobed flowers in erect, terminal racemes. Grow in moist and cool, humus-rich but minerally poor neutral to acidic soil in dappled shade or sun. Under glass, maintain good ventilation; water moderately when in full growth, less in fall and winter. Overwinter at about 41°F (5°C). Propagate by seed in spring under glass, or by semiripe cuttings. *E. impressa* COMMON AUSTRALIAN HEATH; S Australia, Tasmania; spindly erect shrub to 5 ft (1.5 m); leaves to ⅝ in (1.5 cm), narrow, pointed; flowers to ¾ in (1.8 cm), white to rose or purple-red, nodding in erect terminal racemes.

Ephedra (from a Greek name used by Pliny for the mare's tail, *Hippuris*, which *Ephedra* very loosely resembles). Ephedraceae. S Europe, N Africa, Asia, subtropical America. JOINT FIR. Some 40 species, erect to scrambling shrubs with slender, green and jointed stems, the leaves reduced to small and withered scales. The "inflorescences" of these primitive conifer allies are inconspicuous, yellow-green cones. Where male and female plants are grown together, the female may bear fleshy, berrylike fruit. Those named here are very similar in general appearance and grow to about 6½ × 10 ft (2 × 3 m). They are drought- and lime-tolerant and good for groundcover in dry soil, for rock gardens, dry walls and raised beds. Some have proved useful in stabilizing sand. Of those most commonly seen in temperate gardens, *E. distachya* and *E. gerardiana* are hardy to 5°F (−15°C), while *E. americana*, *E. fragilis* and *E. viridis* are frost-tender. Plant in porous, freely draining soil in full sun. Propagate by seed sown under cool glass in fall, by division or by simple layering.

ephemeral short-lived; strictly, of flowers lasting for one day only, but also used to describe plants that survive for only a few weeks and may have several generations in one season.

epi- prefix meaning "upon," "uppermost"—as in epigynous, growing upon or arising from the ovary.

epicalyx an involucre of bracts surrounding a calyx; a false calyx.

epicarp see *exocarp*.

epicormic of branches or buds, developing on or from the trunk of a tree. The growth can be latent or adventitious.

epicotyl the portion of the stem of an embryo or seedling above the cotyledons.

Epidendrum (from Gk *epi*, upon, and *dendron*, tree, referring to the epiphytic habit of most species). Orchidaceae. Tropical Americas. Some 500 species, perennial herbs: the tall cane-growing species are often, at least initially, terrestrial; the smaller caned species and pseudobulbous plants are epiphytic and lithophytic. Pseudobulbous species (e.g., *E. ciliare*) should be cultivated as for *Laelia* or *Rhyncholaelia*, potted tightly into an open bark-based mix and grown in cool to intermediate conditions with full sun and a cool dry winter rest. The tall-growing cane species (e.g., *E. ibaguense*) are among the most flexible of all orchids: in frost-free sunny conditions, they will scramble freely and flower throughout the year. Provide a foothold in a bark mix with plenty of well-rotted farmyard manure. Syringe and foliar-feed regularly. Propagate by adventitious plantlets. The smaller cane-type species (e.g., *E. pseudepidendrum*) require intermediate conditions, high humidity, dappled sunlight and only a semidry winter rest. The magnificent *E. parkinsonianum* should be treated as a large *Brassavola*, but mounted on bark or a raft and suspended in full sunlight.

E. ciliare widespread in C and S America; pseudobulbous; flowers in erect racemes to 12 in (30 cm), fragrant, white to cool green or pale yellow with a white lip, each to 6 in (15 cm) across with slender tepals and a 3-parted lip, the midlobe narrow, the outer lobes broader and finely cut and fringed; *E. oerstedii* differs in its lip with entire, not fringed lateral lobes; *E. conopseum* GREENFLY ORCHID; SE US; stems short, slender, clumped; flowers in loose, erect racemes to 6 in (16 cm), fragrant, lime green to gray green, usually tinted maroon or bronze, each to ¾ in (2 cm) across; *E. ibaguense* widespread in C and S America; stems erect, canelike, to 6½ ft (2 m), rooting only at or near base; flowers in erect, long-lasting racemes to 12 in (30 cm), each to 1¼ in (3 cm) across, vermilion to fiery scarlet, rarely rose to magenta, lip cross-shaped and fringed, often held uppermost; cf. *E. radicans*; *E. nocturnum* Tropical Americas; habit variable, stems stout or reedy, short or tall; flowers in short racemes, fragrant, to 2¾ in (7 cm) across, tepals very slender, white to parchment or yellow-green, lip white, resembling that of *E. ciliare* but with entire lateral lobes; *E. parkinsonianum* C America; stems short, on creeping rhizomes; leaves large, thick, tough, sickle-shaped and pendulous; flowers similar to those of *E. nocturnum*; *E. falcatum* differs in its pink-tinted flowers with a yellow throat; *E. peperomia* S America; dwarf, forming mats of creeping, bright green growth; flowers to 1 in (2.5 cm) across, solitary, short-stalked, insectlike, tepals lime green, narrow, lip large and broad, glossy chestnut brown; *E. pseudepidendrum* Costa Rica, Panama; stems erect, canelike; flowers in loose, erect to arching racemes to 6 in (15 cm), each to 2½ in (6 cm) across, tepals narrow, apple green, lip large, glossy orange to orange-red; *E. radicans* widespread in C and S America; differs from *E. ibaguense* in its scrambling stems, which root freely throughout their length, the column is also longer and arching; *E. stamfordianum* Mexico to Colombia; pseudobulbs are narrowly spindle-shaped; many flowers are produced, in erect to arching racemes or panicles to 24 in (60 cm) long, fragrant, each to 1½ in (4 cm) across, tepals yellow-green spotted red-brown or purple, lip white with a yellow-green midlobe, often spotted or stained purple to rose.

Each cistus flower is short-lived

Ephemeral flower

epidermis the outermost layer of plant cells, which serves to protect interior tissues.

Epigaea (from Gk *epi*, on, and *gaia*, earth, referring to the lowly habit). Ericaceae. N America, W Asia, Japan. 3 species, small, creeping, evergreen shrubs with bristly branches and tough, ovate to oblong or elliptic, hairy leaves. Produced in spring in short clusters or racemes, the scented flowers are funnel- to bell-shaped with five, rounded lobes. Suitable for shaded pockets in a rock garden, peat terrace or woodland garden, or for pot cultivation in a shaded alpine frame. Hardy to at least –22°F (–30°C). The flower buds need a period of chilling before they will open. Grow in acidic moist but well-drained soil. Protect young plants from prolonged frost with bracken litter or evergreen branches. Germinate ripe seed in shade, watering with nonalkaline water from below. Overwinter seedlings in their first year at 55–59°F (13–15°C). Increase also by semiripe cuttings rooted in a closed case, or by layers.

E. asiatica Japan; leaves 1½–4 in (3.5–10 cm); flowers to ½ in (1 cm) long, white tinted pale rose; *E. gaultherioides* (syn. *Orphanidesia gaultherioides*) NE Turkey; leaves 3–4¾ in (8–12 cm); flowers to 2 in (5 cm) diameter, soft pink; *E. repens* TRAILING ARBUTUS, MAYFLOWER; N America; leaves ¾–3 in (2–8 cm); flowers fragrant, to ⅜ in (1.5 cm) long, white to pale pink or deep rose.

epigeal describing a type of germination where the cotyledons emerge from the ground to form the first green foliage leaves of the plant, as occurs, for example, in French beans; cf. *hypogeal*.

epilithic growing on rocks.

Epilobium (from Greek *epi*, upon and *lobos*, pod: the petals surmount the podlike ovary). Onagraceae. Temperate regions. 200 species, perennial, rarely annual herbs and subshrubs, with shortly tubular to funnelform, 4-petalled flowers. Spreading by running white stolons and prolific airborne seed, *E. angustifolium* is usually considered a weed. Its white form is less rampant, and an attractive plant for an herbaceous border. In a rock garden, the lower-growing species make carpets of color. These small plants should be given shade part of the day in hot climates; they require a cool, moist and gritty root-run. Propagate from seed sown in spring, or by division from fall to spring; low-growing species can also be propagated by softwood cuttings taken from fall to spring.

E. angustifolium (syn. *Chamaenerion angustifolium*) GREAT WILLOWHERB, FRENCH WILLOW, ROSEBAY WILLOWHERB, FIREWEED, WICKUP; northern Hemisphere; perennial with erect, clumped stems to 6½ ft (2 m) tall; leaves long, narrow; flowers pale pink to purple-pink, rarely white; *E. chloraefolium* New Zealand; branching, clump-forming and bushy perennial to 16 in (40 cm) tall; leaves small, often tinted bronze at first; flowers white to pink; *E. glabellum* New Zealand; similar to *E. chloraefolium* but larger, the leaves not tinted bronze; flowers white to rose violet, pink or pale yellow.

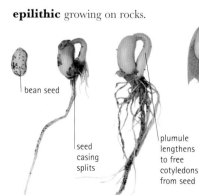

first true leaves

cotyledons rise up above ground

growing tip emerges from within cotyledons

bean seed

seed casing splits

plumule lengthens to free cotyledons from seed

Epigeal germination

For *E. canum* see *Zauschneria*.

Epimedium (from *epimedion*, the ancient Greek name for a wholly unrelated perennial). Berberidaceae. Mediterranean to E Asia. BARRENWORT, BISHOP'S HAT; BISHOP'S MITER. Around 25 species, more or less evergreen perennial herbs. They make dense mats of creeping, thin but tough rhizomes, which give rise to slender-stalked, ternately compound leaves, the leaflets rhombic or lanceolate, thinly leathery and sometimes finely toothed. Produced in spring, the delicate flowers nod on slender stalks along erect to arching racemes. They consist of two sets of four sepals, the inner set petal-like and spreading, and four, spurred petals. Hardy to 14°F (–10°C), or lower. Grow in partial shade in fertile, humus-rich, moist soil. Carefully remove faded foliage in early spring to show flowers to best advantage. Propagate by division in spring or by fresh, ripe seed in late summer in a cold frame.

E. alpinum S Europe; leaflets to 5 in (13 cm), bright green, at first tinged red; flowers with dull red inner sepals and yellow petals to ⅛ in (0.4 cm); *E. grandiflorum* NE Asia; leaflets to 5 in (13 cm), light green tinted bronze at first; flowers white, violet or deep rosy red, the inner petals usually darker than the petals; *E. × perralchicum* (*E. perralderianum × E. pinnatum*); similar to *E. pinnatum* except leaves occasionally simple, bronze when young; flowers large bright golden yellow; *E. perralderianum* N Africa; similar to *E. pinnatum* except leaves bronze when young, sepals green not brown; *E. pinnatum* subsp. *colchicum* N Iran; leaflets to 3 in (8 cm); flowers yellow sometimes veined red; *E. pubigerum* Turkey, SE Europe; leaf undersides hairy; flowers with inner sepals pale rose or white and petals bright yellow; *E. × rubrum* (*E. alpinum × E. grandiflorum*); leaflets to 5½ in (14 cm), bright red-tinted at first; flowers with bright crimson inner sepals and yellow petals; *E. × versicolor* (*E. grandiflorum × E. pinnatum*) subsp. *colchicum*; differs from *E. grandiflorum* in the smaller flowers with the petals only just exceeding or shorter than the sepals; includes several cultivars with copper- or red-mottled or tinted young growth and flowers in various shades of yellow; *E.* × *warleyense* (*E. alpinum* × *E. pinnatum*) subsp. *colchicum*; leaflets to 5 in (13 cm), hairy beneath, sparsely spiny-toothed; flowers with yellow to brick red inner sepals and yellow petals; *E.* × *youngianum* (*E. diphyllum* × *E. grandiflorum*); flowers white or rose to purple-red.

epinasty usually on leaves; when more rapid growth on the upper leaf surface results in a downward rolling; often induced by the presence of ethylene.

Epipactis (the Greek name for this genus). Orchidaceae. Northern temperate zone, tropical Africa, Thailand, Mexico. Some 24 species, terrestrial herbaceous orchids with mat-forming rhizomes and clumps of erect stems. The leaves are linear to elliptic and often pleated. Borne in summer in lax terminal racemes, the flowers consist of five, ovate to elliptic tepals and a showy, boat-shaped lip. The following species is fully hardy and may be grown in full sun or light shade. It needs fertile soil, rich in leaf mold and fast-draining but never dry. Increase by careful division of the rhizomes in fall or spring when the new growing points are just visible. *E. gigantea* N America; 8–36 in (20–90 cm); flowers to 1¼ in (3 cm) diameter, tepals green, tinted or veined rose-purple, lip cream to yellow with purple-red to brown veins and spots and an orange-yellow midlobe.

epipetalous growing on or arising from the petals.

Epiphyllum (from Greek *epi*, upon, *phyllon*, leaf: the flowers are borne on leaflike stems.) Cactaceae. Warm Americas. ORCHID CACTUS. About 15 species, mostly epiphytic cacti with green and succulent, laterally flattened stems, their margins wavy to notched or deeply lobed. The flowers are tubular to funnel-shaped and consist of numerous, spreading, silky tepals. Provide a minimum temperature of 59°F (15°C), plentiful water, humidity in warm weather and protection from burning sun. Plant in a fast-draining and acidic bark-based mix. Water less in winter and rest winter-flowering species in late summer. Orchid cacti are popular in cultivation and have

spawned numerous cultivars, mostly with large, broadly funnel-shaped flowers in shades of white, cream, pink, rose, red and orange-red.

E. anguliger FISHBONE CACTUS; S Mexico; stems flattened, to 100 (39 cm) × 1½–3 in (4–8 cm), deeply pinnately lobed; flowers 15–18, scented, outer tepals lemon or golden, inner tepals white; *E. crenatum* S Mexico to Honduras; stems flattened to 20 × 1½ in (50 × 3.5 cm), rather thick, crenate; flowers 20–29 × 4–8 in (10–20 cm), outer tepals pale yellow, inner tepals white; *E. oxypetalum* S Mexico to Honduras, widely cultivated in the tropics and subtropics; stems flattened, to 12 (30 cm) × 4–4¾ in (10–12 cm), undulate-crenate; flowers 10–12 in (25–30 cm), outer tepals red, inner tepals white.

epiphyte a plant that grows on another plant, but is not parasitic and does not depend on it for nourishment.

Epipremnum (from Greek *epi*, upon, and *premnon*, a trunk, referring to the climbing and epiphytic habit) Araceae. SE Asia to W Pacific. 8 evergreen perennial lianes, climbing by adventitious, adhesive roots. The leaves are leathery, smooth, and entire to pinnately lobed, or occasionally perforated. They tend to occur in markedly different juvenile and adult phases, the juveniles usually smaller, more heart-shaped and entire than the adults. (Plants in cultivation are generally juveniles.) Inconspicuous flowers are carried in club-shaped spadices surrounded by cowel-like spathes. The following species favors a minimum winter temperature of 50°F (10°C), semishade, moderate to high humidity and an open, bark-based mix with plentiful water and feed. That said, *E. aureum* and its cultivars are often seen in the home, in offices and in public buildings, contending bravely with dehydrated moss-poles and neglected hydroponic planters. Propagate by rooted lengths of stem. *E. aureum* (syn. *Pothos aureus, Rhaphidophora aurea, Scindapsus aureus*) DEVIL'S IVY, GOLDEN POTHOS, HUNTER'S ROBE; Solomon Islands; stem climbing or sprawling to cascading, green striped yellow or white; juvenile leaves 2½–12 in (6–30 cm), bright green, variegated

yellow or white; adult leaves to 32 in (80 cm), pinnately cut, marked yellow or cream; includes 'Marble Queen', with moss green leaves boldly streaked bright white on white petioles, and white-streaked stems; *E. pinnatum* Malaysia to New Guinea; stems ½–1½ in (1–4 cm) diam., up to 66 ft (20 m) long; adult leaves to 39 × 17 in (100 × 44 cm), elliptic oblong, perforate or with translucent spots along midrib, irregularly pinnatifid; spathe to 9 in (23 cm), green.

Episcia (from Greek *episkios*, shaded referring to the natural habitat of these plants). Gesneriaceae. S America. 6 species, evergreen, creeping herbs with hairy ovate leaves and bell- to funnel-shaped, 5-lobed flowers at various times of year. Of cascading habit, they are suited to hanging baskets. Grow in an open, bark-based mix. Keep moist and humid in spring and summer with bright, indirect light to shade; in winter, keep barely moist, position in full sun and maintain a minimum temperature of 59°F (15°C). Increase by stem cuttings and offsets.

E. cupreata Colombia, Venezuela, Brazil; leaves to 3 in (8 cm), puckered with fine, impressed veins, dark emerald green to purple-green, bronze or dark chocolate brown above, often with a metallic tint or silver blotches, purple-red beneath; flowers scarlet often marked or ringed yellow or purple; *E. dianthiflora* (syn. *Alsobia dianthiflora*) LACE FLOWER VINE; Costa Rica, Mexico; leaves to 1½ in (4 cm), thinly fleshy, green, downy; flowers sparkling white, lobes deeply fringed; *E. lilacina* Costa Rica; leaves to 2 in (5 cm), dark green, purple-tinted beneath; flowers lilac.

Epithelantha (from Greek *epi*, upon, *thele*, nipple, and *anthos*, flower, referring to the position of the flowers). Cactaceae. SW US, N Mexico. 1 species, *E. micromeris* (syn. *Mammillaria micromeris*), a dwarf cactus with globose to obovoid stems, ½–3 in (1–7.5 cm) in diameter. These are covered in radiating, white to pale gray or pale yellow spines. The flowers, ⅛–½ in (3–12 mm) in diameter, arise in the woolly stem apex. They are campanulate, almost white or pale orange to pink, and are followed by red and juicy, club-shaped fruit. Grow in full sun with low humidity and a minimum temperature of 45°F (7°C). Plant in a gritty, neutral medium. Keep dry from midfall until early spring, except for light misting on warm days in late winter. Increase by offsets.

epithet any word in a binomial which is neither the generic name nor a term denoting rank. The epithet qualifies a generic name or a name of lower rank, for example, *Primula vulgaris* subsp. *sibthorpii*, where *Primula* is the genus name, *vulgaris* the specific epithet, and *sibthorpii* the subspecific epithet.

Epsom salts see *magnesium sulfate*.

equitant when conduplicate leaves overlap or stand inside each other in two ranks in a strongly compressed fan, as in many Iridaceae.

erect of habit, organ or arrangement of parts, upright, perpendicular to the ground or point of attachment.

Eranthemum (from Greek *eros*, love, and *anthemon*, flower). Acanthaceae. Tropical Asia. Some 30 species, perennial shrubby herbs and shrubs with tubular, 5-lobed flowers amid bracts in spikes or panicles. Grow in bright filtered light or with part-day shade. Water plentifully but carefully when in full growth, allowing the surface of the medium to dry out between waterings, and maintain a moderately humid but buoyant atmosphere. Ensure that the winter temperature is no lower than 55°F (13°C). Propagate by softwood cuttings in a closed case with bottom heat in late spring/early summer. Cut back the flower stems of mature specimens by about half their length after flowering. *E. pulchellum* (syn. *E. nervosum*) BLUE SAGE; evergreen shrub to 4 ft (1.25 m) flower spikes to 2³⁄₄ in (7 cm); bracts green feathered with white; flowers to 1¹⁄₄ in (3 cm), deep blue.

Eranthis (from Greek *er*, spring, and *anthos*, flower). Ranunculaceae. S Europe (also naturalized W and N Europe and N America), Asia (Turkey to Japan). WINTER ACONITE. 7 species, perennial herbs with small, rounded tubers. The basal leaves are petiolate and deeply palmately lobed. The three stem leaves form a ruff below the flower. Solitary, terminal and yellow to white, the flowers are cupped, short-stalked and consist of two whorls of ovate to elliptic perianth segments. *Eranthis* are valued for the bright carpet of flower color they provide in late winter and early spring. They may be naturalized under deciduous trees or shrubs or in light grassland. Plant in summer or early fall in humus-rich, heavy soil. Propagate by division in spring after flowering. Like *Cyclamen* and *Galanthus*, *Eranthis* can be difficult to establish from dry tubers: try to purchase plants that are "in the green" (i.e., bareroot but in leaf) where possible. Sow seed as soon as ripe (hybrids are sterile).

E. hyemalis S France to Bulgaria; to 3 in (8 cm); flowers ³⁄₄–1¹⁄₄ in (2–3 cm) diameter, bright yellow, produced in late winter; Cilicica Group: to 2 in (5 cm); leaves tinged bronze at first; flowers shiny golden yellow, larger and emerging later; Tubergenii Group: leaves tinged bronze at first; flowers large, golden, appearing later; includes 'Guinea Gold', which has deeply and narrowly cut bracts and fragrant, long-lasting, deep golden flowers.

Ercilla (for Don Alonso de Ercilla [1533–95], of Madrid). Phytolaccaceae. Americas, South Africa. 2 species, evergreen climbers attaching themselves by disklike holdfasts. The leaves are leathery and entire, and the flowers small and borne in spring in dense spikelike racemes. These are sometimes followed by glossy berries.Tolerant of temperatures to between 23–14°F (–5 and –10°C). Grow in well-drained nonalkaline soil in sun to part shade. Provide support. Propagate by nodal stem cuttings in midsummer. *E. volubilis* (syn. *E. spicata*) Peru, Chile; to 20 ft (6 m); leaves to 2 in (5 cm), ovate to oblong, fleshy, glossy dark green; flowers purple or green with white stamens; fruit dark purple.

Eremurus (from Greek *eremia*, desert, and *oura*, tail, referring to the appearance of the flower spikes in their desert or semidesert habitats). Liliaceae (Asphodelaceae). W and C Asia. DESERT CANDLE, FOXTAIL LILY. 40–50 species, fleshy-rooted perennial herbs with strap-shaped leaves forming tufts or rosettes. Small, starry and 6-parted, the flowers are packed in summer in long, tapering racemes atop erect scapes. *Eremurus* produces a fleshy rooted crown with a central growing-point, which may rot if too wet in winter. Where possible, grow *Eremurus* on raised beds or banks where water drains away quickly; alternatively, set the crown on sharp sand and cover it with same when planting. These plants require cold in winter to flower well, and are unsuited to cultivation in completely frost-free zones. Grow in rich, well-drained, sandy soil in full sun. Without shelter from wind, taller species and hybrids may require staking. Protect from winter wet with a mulch of sharp sand or ashes. In regions that experience late frosts, give young shoots the protection of dry bracken litter or straw. Propagate *Eremurus* from ripe seed in fall, alternatively by careful division when the foliage dies back during late summer. *E. himalaicus* to 8 ft (2.5 m) tall, flowers white; *E.* × *isabellinus* (*E. stenophyllus* × *E. olgae*) to 5 ft (1.5 m) tall, flowers orange, pale yellow, gold, pink, white to copper; includes the Shelford Hybrids and Highdown Hybrids; *E. robustus* to 3¹⁄₄ ft (1 m); flowers pink; *E. spectabilis* (to 3¹⁄₄ ft (1 m); flowers pale yellow suffused green; *E. stenophyllus* to 5 ft (1.5 m) tall; flowers orange-yellow to clear yellow aging topaz.

erianthous woolly flowered.

Erica (from the Greek name *ereike*). Ericaceae. HEATH, HEATHER. Africa, Madagascar, Middle East, Europe, Atlantic Is. Some 735 species, evergreen shrubs and shrublets with small, narrow leaves. Tubular to urn- or bell-shaped, the flowers are carried in heads at the branch tips or disposed along the branches in a raceme- or panicle-like arrangement. For cultivation, see *heaths and heathers*. (See *table overleaf.*)

E

283

ERICA

Name	Distribution	Habit	Leaves	Flowers
E. arborea TREE HEATH	SW Europe, Mediterranean, N Africa	treelike, to 13 ft (4 m)	to ¼ in (5 mm), dark green, in whorls of 4	to ⅛ in (4 mm), white tinged gray or cream, campanulate, fragrant in large, pyramidal panicles
Comments: Late spring. Lime-tolerant. Includes clones with bright gold to lime green foliage.				
E. australis SPANISH HEATH	W Iberian Peninsula, Tangier	erect to 6½ ft (2 m)	to ¼ in (5 mm), dark green, in whorls of 4 or 3	to ⅜ in (9 mm), red-pink, tubular to campanulate with reflexed lobes; on short branches
		Comments: Spring-summer.		
E. canaliculata	S Africa	erect to 6½ ft (2 m)	⅛–½ in (4–10 mm), bright to dark green, in whorls of 3	to ⅜ in (3.5 mm), cup-shaped, purple-pink to pale rosy pink with conspicuous dark purple-red to black anthers; in whorls at ends of branchlets
Comments: Year-round.				
E. carnea *E. herbacea* SPRING HEATH	C & E Europe	dwarf, with procumbent to ascending stems to 10 in (25 cm)	to ⅜ in (8 mm), dark green in whorls of 4	to ¼ in (6 mm), purple-pink, cylindric, often with dark anthers; in terminal, somewhat 1-sided racemes
Comments: Late winter-early spring. Lime-tolerant. Many cultivars, ranging in habit from the tall and open to the dwarf and dense; in foliage color from dark green to emerald, sea-green, gold and lime to			copper and bronze; in flower color from pure white to palest shell pink, rose, purple-pink, deep magenta and carmine.	
E. ciliaris DORSET HEATH	SW Europe	spreading, to 32 in (80 cm)	to ⅛ in (4 mm), ovate to lanceolate, ciliate	to ½ in (12 mm), deep pink-red, swollen-tubular to urn-shaped; in terminal racemes
Comments: Late summer-fall. Includes cultivars with foliage turning red-bronze in winter, and flowers in tones of white, pink and rose, also bicolors—*E.* 'David McClintock', for example, has white to blush flowers tipped with purple-pink.				
E. cinerea BELL HEATHER	W Europe	low, bushy, to 24 in (60 cm) with hairy young twigs	to ¼ in (5 mm), dark green, revolute, in whorls of 3	to ¼ in (7 mm), pink, purple-red or white, urn-shaped; in terminal racemes or umbels
Comments: Summer. Many cultivars—in habit, prostrate to low and spreading, dome-shaped or rounded to erect and narrow, densely bushy to loose and open; in foliage color, dark green to bronze-red or gold,			some changing from yellow to deep rusty orange in winter, or with bright copper new growth; in flower color, pure white, pale rose, pink, magenta, crimson and deep ruby.	
E. × **darleyensis** (*E. erigena* × *E. carnea*)	garden origin	as for *E. carnea*, but more vigorous and bushy, to 24 in (60 cm)	to ½ in (13 mm)	white to rosy pink with dark anthers
Comments: Winter-spring. Lime-tolerant. Cultivars range in foliage from dark green to lime or golden yellow, some with cream- or red-tipped new growth, or turning bronze-red in winter; in flower color from silvery white to rose, pink, magenta and lilac.				

E. canaliculata   *E. carnea* 'December Red'   *E. ciliaris* 'David McClintock'   *E. cinerea* 'C.D. Eason'

E

ERICA

Name	Distribution	Habit	Leaves	Flowers
E. erigena E. hibernica; E. mediterranea of gardens IRISH HEATH	Tangier, Iberian Peninsula, SW France, Eire	as for *E. carnea*, but erect to 6½ ft (2 m)	**Comments:** Late winter-early spring. Cultivars range in habit from low, slow-growing and compact to erect and rangy; in leaf color from deep green to gray-green and gold, some tinted purple-red or copper in winter or when new; in flower color from white to shell pink, rose, deep crimson, magenta and lilac, some becoming darker with age, some scented.

| **E. gracilis** | S Africa | compact, to 20 in (50 cm) tall | ¹/₁₆–¹/₈ in (2–4 mm), in whorls of 4 | to ¹/₈ in (4 mm), pale to deep pink, ovoid to rounded, in terminal whorls of 4 |

Comments: Summer. Includes cultivars with glowing deep red flowers.

| **E. × hiemalis**
FRENCH HEATHER;
WHITE WINTER
HEATHER | origins and
parentage
obscure | to 24 in (60 cm) | to ¹/₄ in (5 mm), bright green, in whorls of 4 | to ⅝ in (15 mm), white suffused pink with dark anthers, tubular; in short, terminal racemes |

Comments: Winter. Includes cultivars with long, tubular flowers in shades or purple-pink and rose, often with paler or white lobes and opening.

| **E. lusitanica**
PORTUGUESE HEATH | W Iberian
Peninsula to
SW France,
naturalized
SW England | close to *E. arborea*, but
to 10 ft (3 m) tall and
not so dense and
treelike | to ¹/₄ in (7 mm) | to ¹/₄ in (5 mm), pink in bud, opening white, narrowly campanulate

Comments: Spring to early summer. Requires shelter. 'George Hunt': leaves yellow, flowers white. |

| **E. mackayana** | Spain, Ireland | low and spreading to
erect, to 20 in (50
cm) | to ¹/₄ in (6 mm), oblong to lanceolate, revolute, glandular, in whorls of 4 | to ¹/₄ in (7 mm), pink, squatly urn-shaped, in terminal umbels |

Comments: Midsummer to early fall. Includes clones with white, rose and deep purple-pink flowers, some semidouble or double.

| **E. pageana**

Comments: Spring. | S Africa | erect to 20 in (50
cm), downy | ¹/₄–⅜ in (5–8 mm), closely packed, in whorls of 4 | ¹/₄–⅜ in (6–8 mm), yellow, downy, tubular to campanulate with a green calyx; in terminal clusters of 3–4 |

| **E. scoparia**
BESOM HEATH | SW Europe,
N Africa,
Canary Is | slender and erect, to
20 ft (6 m) | to ¹/₄ in (7 mm), glossy, in whorls of 3–4 | to ¹/₈ in (3 mm), green tinged red-brown, campanulate; in narrow leafy racemes |

Comments: Late spring to early summer. Includes small, neat clones with bright green, shiny leaves.

| **E. spiculifolia**
SPIKE HEATH | SE Europe,
Asia Minor | Mat-forming, to 10 in (25 cm) tall | Very small, narrow, dark | small, magenta to candy pink; in erect, bell-shaped racemes, 1¼ in (3 cm) long |

Comments: Late spring to summer.

E. × darleyensis 'White Glow'   *E. mackayana* 'Plena'   *E. × stuartii* 'Irish Lemon'   *E. tetralix* 'Con Underwood'

ERICA

Name	Distribution	Habit	Leaves	Flowers
E. × stuartii *E. × praegeri*; (*E. mackayana × E. tetralix*)	W Ireland	close to *E. mackayana*, distinguished by hairy ovary and calyx	**Comments:** Summer to fall. Includes clones with pink to pale mauve flowers, some tipped with a deeper tone, maroon, for example. Several have new foliage tinted yellow, orange or coral.	
E. terminalis CORSICAN HEATH	SW Mediterranean	to 8 ft (2.5 m), erect and treelike	dark green, in whorls of 4	to ¼ in (7 mm), rosy pink to deep mauve-pink fading to rusty red, urceolate; in umbel-like clusters
Comments: Summer to early fall. Lime-tolerant.				
E. tetralix CROSS-LEAVED HEATH	Iberian Peninsula, France, UK	dwarf and spreading, to 10 in (25 cm)	to ¼ in (6 mm), lanceolate to narrowly oblong, gray-green, ciliate, in whorls of 4	to ⅜ in (9 mm), pale pink, swollen tubular to urceolate; in terminal umbels
Comments: Summer to early fall. Includes clones with white to pale pink and dark rosy red flowers, sometimes arranged in a tight, radiating cluster; some have very fine silvery gray foliage.				
E. umbellata PORTUGESE HEATH	W Iberian Peninsula, Tangier	dwarf, to 32 in (80 cm) **Comments:** Late spring to early summer.	to ⅛ in (4 mm), in whorls of 3	to ¼ in (6 mm), rose pink to purple with dark brown anthers, campanulate to ovoid; in umbels
E. vagans CORNISH HEATH	W France, Spain, Cornwall, Ireland	decumbent to erect, to 32 in (80 cm)	to ½ in (10 mm), mid-green, in whorls of 4 or 5	to ⅛ in (4 mm), cylindric to campanulate, lilac pink to white, with dark maroon to brown anthers; in leafy racemes
Comments: Midsummer to late fall. Somewhat lime-tolerant. Includes clones with white, cream, pink, cerise, deep ruby and purple flowers; some with yellow foliage, or foliage taking on colorful tints in winter. In 'Viridiflora', the flowers are replaced by green bracts.				
E. × veitchii (*E. arborea × E. lusitanica*)	garden origin	resembles a more vigorous *E. arborea*	similar to *E. lusitanica*	cylindric to near-spherical, white to cream with pink stamens, fragrant
Comments: Spring. 'Gold Tips': young shoots golden, fading to lime or pale green.				
E. × watsonii (*E. ciliaris × E. tetralix*)	garden origin	compact, hairy, to 12 in (30 cm)	mid-green, often colorful in spring	broadly campanulate to urceolate, pink
Comments: Summer. Includes clones with white, rose and deep crimson flowers; some with new foliage flushed gold, yellow-orange, copper or red-bronze.				
E. × williamsii (*E. vagans × E. tetralix*)	garden origin	resembles *E. vagans* but usually with yellow to rich gold new growth		campanulate, rose pink with dark brown anthers
Comments: Spring.				

E. vagans 'Valerie Proudley'   *E. × veitchii* 'Exeter'   *E. × watsonii* 'Dawn'   *E. × williamsii* 'P.D. Williams'

ericaceous (1) a plant belonging to the family Ericaceae; (2) planting media with low pH suitable for growing calcifuge plants; (3) resembling the genus *Erica* in general habit.

Erigeron (from Greek, *eri*, early, and *geron*, an old man, either alluding to the hairy pappus, or to the hoary appearance of the leaves of some species in spring). Compositae. Cosmopolitan, especially N America. FLEABANE. Some 200 species, annual or, more commonly, perennial herbs with daisylike flower heads in spring and summer—the ray florets range widely in color, the disk florets are yellow. The following species are fully hardy and suitable for an herbaceous border or rock garden; *E. karvinskianus* is an exquisite colonizer of damp old walls and paving. Grow the others in sun in moderately fertile, freely draining soil that remains moist in the growing season. Provide the support of pea-sticks for taller perennials and deadhead to produce a second flush of bloom later in the season. Cut back the plants during fall. Propagate Erigeron by seed sown *in situ*, also by division and by basal softwood cuttings in spring.

E. alpinus Europe; hairy perennial herb to 16 in (40 cm) tall; flower heads to 1½ in (3.5 cm) diameter, ray florets lilac; *E. aurantiacus* ORANGE DAISY; Turkestan; mat-forming, downy perennial herb to 12 in (30 cm); flower heads to 2 in (5 cm) diameter, ray florets bright orange-yellow; *E. aureus* N America; hairy perennial herb to 8 in (20 cm); flower heads to 1¼ in (3 cm) diameter, ray florets yellow; *E. glaucus* BEACH ASTER, SEASIDE DAISY; W US; tufted perennial herb to 20 in (50 cm), stems sprawling; leaves gray-green; flower heads with lilac to violet ray florets; includes the white-flowered 'Albus', and 'Elstead Pink' with deep lilac-pink flower heads; *E. karvinskianus* (syn. *E. mucronatus*) C America; woody-based perennial with slender, sprawling stems to 12 in (30 cm); leaves small; flower heads to ¾ in (2 cm) diameter, slender-stalked, white or pink, becoming red-purple with age; *E. speciosus* NW US; perennial herb to 32 in (80 cm); flower heads to 2 in (5 cm) across, ray florets violet to blue or white.

Erinacea (from Latin *erinaceus*, resembling a hedgehog, referring to the overall appearance of the plant). Leguminosae. W Mediterranean to E Pyrenees. 1 species, *E. anthyllis* (syn. *E. pungens*) HEDGEHOG BROOM, BRANCH THORN, BLUE BROOM, an evergreen, clump-forming shrublet, to 12 in (30 cm) tall with thornlike branchlets. The leaves are small and short-lived. Pale blue, indigo or mauve, pealike flowers appear in clusters in summer. Hardy to 5°F (−15°C). Grow in a hot position in a rock garden, at the base of a sunny wall or on raised beds or low walls. Plant in gritty free-draining soil, with shelter from cold, drying winds. Propagate from seed: cold-stratify overwinter and germinate in warmth in early spring. Alternatively, increase by heel cuttings in early fall.

erinous prickly, coarsely textured with sharp points.

Erinus (Greek name *erinos*, used by Dioscorides for a basil-like plant). Scrophulariaceae. N Africa, S and C Europe. 2 species, tufted perennial herbs with tubular, broadly 5-lobed flowers in erect racemes in late spring and summer. A hardy perennial alpine, although shortlived, it seeds itself freely and will carpet large areas. Grow in light, well-drained soil in sun or part-shade on rock gardens, walls, raised beds, scree, troughs or in tufa; it is also useful for sowing in spring directly into paving joints. A mulch of shingle or grit provides a good seedbed and protection against winter rots around the neck. Keep moist but never waterlogged. Propagate from seed sown as soon as ripe in cold frames or *in situ*. Small softwood cuttings will also succeed. *E. alpinus* FAIRY FOXGLOVE, ALPINE BALSAM, LIVER BALSAM; S and C Europe; to 12 in (30 cm), carpet-forming small leaves; flowers ¼–½ in (0.6–1 cm), typically purple, white in var. *albus*, red in 'Carmineus', crimson in 'Dr. Hähnle', pink in 'Roseus', violet in 'Lilacinus'.

Eriobotrya (from Greek *erion*, wool, and *botrys*, a cluster of grapes, referring to the woolly, clustered panicles). Rosaceae. E Asia. Some 10 species of evergreen shrubs or trees with stout

Eriobotrya japonica
The loquat will not fruit in temperate zones, but makes a handsome foliage plant.

branches and large, leathery leaves. Small, white flowers are produced in late winter and spring in broad and often densely woolly panicles. The fruit is an obovoid to globose pome, with persistent calyx teeth at the apex and a few large seeds. *E. japonica* is extensively cultivated in subtropical and warm-temperate climates for its edible fruits—these are eaten raw, poached, stewed as preserves or pickled with sweet spices. In Japan over 800 cultivars are known. The fruit, which resembles an apricot, has a firm flesh and slightly acidic, sweet aromatic flavor; the seeds are slightly poisonous. In temperate zones, it makes a handsome ornamental, with bold and luxuriant foliage. The flowers, borne intermittently from early winter to spring, are produced in quantity only after hot summers. The fruit ripens in spring, but is likely to be rendered inedible by hard frosts in cold areas. It will survive temperatures as low as 1°F (−17°C), and tolerates dry soil and maritime exposures. Plant in fertile, well-drained soil, in full sun or light shade with shelter from cold winds, which will scorch the foliage. In regions at the limits of its hardiness, grow against a south-facing wall. Propagate by seed sown under glass when ripe, by semiripe cuttings with a heel, or by air layering. *E. japonica* LOQUAT, JAPANESE LOQUAT, JAPANESE MEDLAR, NISPERO; China, Japan; large and spreading shrub or tree to 23 ft (7 m) tall; branches stout, covered in tawny hairs at first; leaves to 12 in (30 cm), broadly oblanceolate to elliptic, leathery and corrugated; fruit to 1½ in (4 cm) diameter, globose to pyriform, yellow to apricot.

Eriogonum (from Greek *erion*, wool, and *gonia*, a joint or knee, referring to the downy nodes). Polygonaceae. N US, mostly western. ST. CATHERINE'S LACE; WILD BUCKWHEAT; UMBRELLA PLANT. 150 species, herbs and subshrubs (those listed below are perennial), usually with woolly leaves and small, pale flowers in terminal heads or umbels. Hardy to between 14–5°F (–10 and –15°C). Most are also tolerant of exposed sites, although those with woolly leaves need protection from winter wet. Grow in gritty, perfectly drained soil in full sun. Water sparingly in spring and fall, moderately when in full growth and keep almost dry in winter. These plants resent disturbance once established. Propagate *Eriogunum* by ripe seed sown in a cool greenhouse during fall or spring; alternatively, increase by heeled greenwood cuttings in midsummer or by division during early spring.

E. arborescens California; shrub to 5 ft (1.5 m); leaves ¾–1¼ in (2–3 cm), linear to oblong, white-hairy beneath; flowers white to pale rose; *E. crocatum* SAFFRON BUCK-WHEAT; California; herb or subshrub to 8 in (20 cm); leaves ⅝–1¼ in (1.5–3 cm), ovate to elliptic, white-felted; flowers sulfur yellow; *E. giganteum* ST. CATHERINE'S LACE; S California; shrub to 8 ft (2.5 m); leaves 1¼–4 in (3–10 cm), oblong to ovate, gray- to white-hairy; flowers white fading to rusty red; *E. ovalifolium* W US; silver-hairy, mat-forming and small to dwarf; leaves ¼–⅝ in (0.5–1.5 cm), broadly oblanceolate to elliptic; flowers white to pink or rose-purple; *E. umbellatum* SULFUR FLOWER; western N America; herb or subshrub, low and spreading, rarely exceeding 12 in (30 cm); leaves to ¾ in (2 cm), spathulate to obovate, tomentose, in rosettes; flowers cream to sulfur yellow, sometimes tinted red with age.

Eriophorum (from Greek *erion*, wool and *phoreo*, to bear, alluding to hairy fruits). Cyperaceae. Europe, N America,

S Africa. COTTON GRASS. 20 species of hardy bog, marsh or marginal aquatic grasslike, evergreen perennials. Tufted clumps or slender rhizomes. Leaves slender, flat, tough. Inflorescence an umbel of multiflowered spikelets or a single erect terminal spikelet. Sepals and petals represented by soft, pale, cottonlike hairs. *E. angustifolium* COMMON COTTON GRASS, N Europe (incl. Arctic), N America. 6–30 in (15–75 cm), stem 3-angled at apex. Leaves grooved, ⅛–¼ in (3–7 mm) wide, tapering to 3-sided tip. Inflorescence an umbel of 3–7 pendent, downy, white spikelets 1¼–2 in (3–5 cm) across. Effective feature beside wildlife pool and in a bog garden. Grow in acidic soil. Propagate by division of clumps in spring.

Eriophyllum (from Greek *erion*, wool, and *phyllon*, leaf). Compositae. Western N America. WOOLLY SUNFLOWER. About 12 species, hairy, annual to perennial herbs and shrubs, with entire to toothed or pinnatifid leaves and daisylike flower heads in late spring and summer. Grow in full sunlight on a well-drained, preferably sandy soil. Clip over after flowering. Propagate by seed sown under glass in fall, or by division in spring. *E. lanatum* hairy herb, 8–24 in (20–60 cm) tall; leaves to 6 in (15 cm), spathulate to narrowly oblanceolate, entire to pinnately lobed; flower heads ¾–2 in (2–5 cm) in diameter, yellow.

Eritrichium (from Greek *erion*, wool, and *trichos*, hair, the plants are woolly). Boraginaceae. Temperate northern Hemisphere. ALPINE FORGET-ME-NOT. Some 30 species, low-growing, tufted, alpine perennial herbs, with small, downy leaves and forget-me-not-like flowers in short cymes in early summer. Hardy to about 5°F (–15°C), but intolerant of winter wet and perhaps best grown in the alpine house in a lean

and gritty alpine mix. Provide a deep collar of grit around the neck and/or a prop of small stones to keep foliage clear of the soil surface. Alternatively, grow in tufa rock half-buried in the pot. Water plentifully when in growth, avoiding the foliage, and keep just moist in winter. Sow seed in a mix of loam, leaf mold and sharp sand, with additional parts of crushed slate and tufa dust; expose to frost but protect from rain, and germinate in a cold greenhouse; increase also by softwood cuttings in summer.

E. elongatum W US; to 3 in (7.5 cm), densely tufted, mat-forming; leaves to ¼ in (0.7 cm), oblanceolate, woolly; flowers to ¼ in (0.7 cm) diameter, blue with yellow crests; *E. nanum* Alps; to 2 in (5 cm); densely tufted; leaves to ½ in (1 cm), elliptic to linear, silver-hairy; flowers to ⅜ in (0.8 cm) diameter, sky blue with yellow crests.

Erodium (from Greek *erodios*, heron, the carpels resemble the head and beak of a heron). Geraniaceae. Europe, C Asia, temperate Australia, tropical S America. HERON'S BILL, STORKSBILL. 60 species, mostly perennial, but some annual herbs and subshrubs (those listed below are small, compact perennial herbs). *Erodium* differs from *Geranium* in having only 5 fertile stamens (*Geranium* has 10). The leaves are usually lobed or pinnately divided with toothed margins. Produced from spring to late summer, the flowers are 5-petaled, and are carried in stalked umbels or rarely solitary. The fruit resembles a slender, bird's bill and, when ripe, splits lengthwise into five 1-seeded parts. Plant the smaller species on the rock garden, in a sunny, well-drained spot with humus-rich, preferably alkaline, soil. The taller species are less demanding as to soil type (although drainage must be good). The following are hardy to 0°F (–18°C), but the more southern natives will suffer from winter

distinctive "storkbill" fruits

Erodium cicutarium

damp and are best protected with a propped pane of glass in an open garden during the winter months. Alternatively grow in pans in an alpine house. Propagate from seed sown under glass, or by division in spring.

E. cheilanthifolium (syn. *E. petraeum* subsp. *crispum*) S Spain, Morocco; leaves to 2 in (5 cm), white-hairy, ferny; flowers, white to pale pink veined red and with dark stains; *E. chrysanthum* Greece; leaves to 1½ in (3.5 cm), ferny, silver-hairy; flowers creamy yellow to pale sulfur; *E. corsicum* Corsica, Sardinia; leaves silvery-downy ovate, crumpled, crenate; flowers rose pink or white veined red; *E. foetidum* (syn. *E. petraeum*) Pyrenees, S France; leaves ferny, softly hairy; flowers veined red; *E. glandulosum* (syn. *E. petraeum* subsp. *glandulosum*) Pyrenees; leaves ferny, hairy, aromatic; flowers lilac with dark stains or rose stained purple; *E. manescaui* Pyrenees; leaves to 12 in (30 cm), ovate to lanceolate, pinnate; flowers purple-red with darker patches; *E. reichardii* (syn. *E. chamaedryoides*) ALPINE GERANIUM; Majorca, Corsica; leaves cordate, crenate, dark green; flowers white with rose veins; *E.* × *variabile* (*E. corsicum* × *E. reichardii*); intermediate between parents; includes white, bright pink and double-flowered cultivars.

erose irregularly dentate, as if gnawed or eroded.

Eryngium (from Greek *eyringion*, name used by Theophrastus). Umbelliferae. Cosmopolitan. ERYNGO, ERINGOE, SEA HOLLY. 230 species, perennial, biennial and annual herbs (those listed below are perennial unless otherwise stated) with mostly basal leaves ranging in shape from swordlike to heart-shaped, the margins toothed to intricately cut, lobed and spiny. Produced in late spring and summer, the flowers are small, generally blue-gray or white and packed in a conelike, hemispherical to cylindrical head, subtended by a ruff of spiny to lacerate, decorative bracts. Most are hardy to 5°F (–15°C); South American species such as *E. agavifolium* and *E. bromeliifolium* are less reliable where temperatures fall far below freezing point, but have been successfully cultivated in sheltered

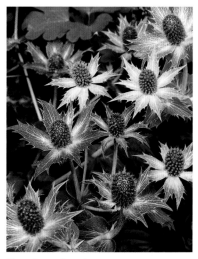

Eryngium giganteum
"Miss Willmott's ghost" is so named because the eponymous plantswoman liked to scatter seed in gardens that she visited.

niches with perfect drainage. Grow in full sun in moderately fertile, well-drained soil. Propagate by seed in fall in the cold frame; also by root cuttings in winter or by careful division in fall or spring.

E. agavifolium Argentina; to 3¼ ft (1 m) tall; leaves sword-shaped, spiny-toothed; flower heads to 2 in (5 cm), green-blue with entire to spiny-toothed bracts to ½ in (1 cm) long; often confused with *E. bromeliifolium*; *E. alpinum* Europe; to 24 in (60 cm); leaves ovate to heart-shaped, spiny-toothed; flower heads to 1½ in (4 cm), steel blue to sky blue, violet, lilac or white with softly spiny, pinnately lobed bracts to 2½ in (6 cm); *E. amethystinum* Italy, Sicily, Balkans; to 28 in (70 cm); leaves obovate to finely palmately divided, the segments pinnately lobed and spiny; flower heads to ¾ in (2 cm), electric blue to amethyst on silver stems, with spiny bracts to 2 in (5 cm); *E. bourgatii* Spain, E Mediterranean; to 16 in (40 cm); leaves 3-parted, each segment narrowly pinnately lobed, spiny and silver-veined; flower heads to 1¼ in (3 cm), sky blue with electric blue and silver, toothed bracts to 2 in (5 cm); *E. bromeliifolium* Mexico; differs from *E. agavifolium* in the white-blue flower heads to 1 in (2.5 cm) exceeded by many rigid, sharp bracts; *E. campestre* C and E Europe; leaves pinnately divided; flower heads small, massed, blue-gray; *E. eburneum* S America; differs from

E. agavifolium in the entire but spiny-margined leaves and taller flowering stems to 6½ ft (2 m), with ivory flower heads to ¾ in (2 cm) and spiny-tipped bracts; *E. giganteum* MISS WILLMOTT'S GHOST; Caucasus; biennial to ⅝ in (1.5 cm); leaves heart-shaped to triangular, crenate to spiny and incised; flower heads to 1½ in (4 cm), electric blue to pale green or white, with spiny bracts to 2½ in (6 cm) tinted gray-white or silver-blue; *E. maritimum* SEA HOLLY; coasts of Europe, naturalized east coast of US; short lived perennial 8–24 in (20–60 cm) tall with tough, spiny, glaucous blue-gray foliage; flower heads to 2 in (5 cm), pale blue to lilac with bracts to 1½ in (4 cm) resembling leaves; *E.* × *oliverianum* (*E. alpinum* × *E. giganteum*); to 39 in (100 cm); lower leaves heart-shaped to ovate, slightly 3-lobed, spiny-toothed with conspicuous veins; flower heads to 1½ in (4 cm), vivid blue with linear, spiny-toothed and purple bracts; *E. planum* C and SE Europe; to 30 in (75 cm); leaves ovate to oblong, toothed to palmately lobed, spiny and tinted blue; flower heads to 1¼ in (3 cm), iridescent azure; lilac to pink forms are also grown; *E.* × *tripartitum* parentage unknown; to 3¼ ft (1 m); leaves are 3-lobed and spiny-toothed; flower heads to ½ in (1 cm) metallic blue, exceeded by narrow, blue-tinted bracts; *E. variifolium* N Africa; to 18 in (45 cm); leaves rounded to heart-shaped, margins toothed, dark green marbled white; flower heads to ¾ in (2 cm) diameter, silver-blue exceeded by spiny, white-blue to steel gray bracts; *E. yuccifolium* SW US; similar to *E. agavifolium*, although usually deciduous, with blue-green glaucous leaves and green-white flower heads.

Erysimum (name used by Hippocrates, from Greek *eryo*, to draw out: some species produce blisters). Cruciferae. Europe to W and C Asia, N Africa and N America. Around 80 species, annual, biennial or perennial, evergreen herbs, usually bushy with clumped, woody-based stems and oblong to linear leaves. Carried in terminal racemes, the flowers are more or less fragrant and consist of four, spreading, obovate petals.

Derived from *E. cheiri*, most wallflowers are grown for spring and early

E

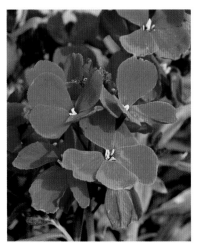

Erysimum cheiri 'Blood Red'
Wallflowers were formerly placed in the genus *Cheiranthus* before being included in *Erysimum*—hence the species name.

summer flowering and most commonly used for bedding, cutting and for containers. Selection has yielded dwarf, intermediate and tall forms, and colors that include pastels and range from white and pale lemon yellows through orange-yellow to deep crimson, brown and purple; many are scented. They are short-lived perennials, treated as biennials. Fully hardy, they need moist but well-drained, neutral to slightly alkaline soil in full sun. *E.* × *allionii*, the SIBERIAN WALLFLOWER, is used similarly but is less commonly grown, with a color range restricted to orange, golds and apricots. Nevertheless, it has a number of advantages, being denser in habit than *E. cheiri*, spicier of scent, more tolerant of cold, and flowering slightly later.

The genus includes several perennials, some of them shrubby, including the bushy, two-tone *E. bicolor*, the shrubby, silver and mauve *E.* 'Bowles Mauve', the low and tufted *E. kotschyanum*, found on high scree, the violet, bushy *E. linifolium* and *E. purpureum* with beautiful ash-gray leaves and purple flowers. These are hardy to −10°F (−23°C) given sharply draining, rather poor soil in full sun, with protection from harsh winds and prolonged cold. Repropagate and replace regularly; overwinter small, new plants in a cold greenhouse.

Biennials should be sown in late spring/early summer; grow on in a nursery bed, and transfer to their

flowering positions in early fall. In places where winter temperatures fall consistently below 5°F (−15°C) to −4°F (−20°C), overwinter in the cold frame and plant out in early spring. Propagate perennials from seed in spring and early summer, or from heel cuttings in summer, rooted in a sandy propagating medium in a cold frame; alternatively, increase by division.

E. × *allionii* (syn. *Cheiranthus* × *allionii*) SIBERIAN WALLFLOWER; perennial grown as a biennial; flowers large, bright orange; *E. bicolor* Madeira, Canary Islands; subshrub or shrub to 36 in (90 cm); flowers lightly fragrant, cream to pale yellow or bronze turning pale lilac; *E. mutabile* differs in its mauve-pink flowers turning orange-bronze; *E.* 'Bowles Mauve' shrub or subshrub to 30 in (75 cm); leaves gray-green; flowers small, rich mauve; *E. cheiri* (syn. *Cheiranthus cheiri*) WALL-FLOWER; S Europe; perennial subshrub cultivated as a biennial, 10–32 in (25–80 cm) tall; flowers bright orange-yellow, usually striped or spotted purple-red; *E. helveticum* (syn. *E. pumilum*) C and E Europe; clump-forming, tufted perennial to 4 in (10 cm); flowers small, fragrant, bright yellow in flat heads opening from purple-tinted buds; *E. hieraciifolium* (syn. *E. alpinum*) biennial or perennial, 12–48 in (30–120 cm) tall; flowers yellow with hairy undersides to petals; sometimes treated as a synonym of *E.* × *allionii*; *E. kotschyanum* Turkey; densely tufted perennial to 4 in (10 cm); flowers orange-yellow to yellow; *E. linifolium* (syn. *Cheiranthus linifolius*) Spain, Portugal; woody-based perennial 4¾–28 in (12–70 cm) tall with numerous slender stems; flowers mauve or violet; *E. purpureum* Turkey, Syria; erect, woody-based perennial to 12 in (30 cm); leaves gray-green; flowers violet-mauve.

Erythrina (from Greek *erythros*, red, referring to the color of the flowers). Leguminosae. Pantropical. CORAL TREE. 108 species, deciduous or evergreen shrubs, trees and perennial herbs, usually with blunt, conical thorns or recurved prickles, and trifoliolate to pinnate leaves. Produced in late summer in erect racemes, the flowers are large, pealike and usually red with a large, cowl- or boatlike standard petal.

E. crista-galli is usually grown in a cool greenhouse or conservatory in temperate zones. It will, however, grow outdoors with the shelter of a south-facing wall, and will tolerate temperatures as low as 14°F (−10°C) provided the stem bases are thickly mulched with leaf litter or sawdust and covered with bracken. In harsh climates, the stems are usually killed by frost to ground level. They are best left until mid- to late spring when they can be cut down and removed along with the bracken cover. By this time new shoots should be in evidence; these will develop quickly, flowering by late summer.

E. × *bidwillii* has a thick woody rootstock and shows similar tolerances. The roots of this species are sometimes lifted and stored in frost-free conditions over winter. In warm temperate zones, grow in full sun in moderately fertile, well-drained soil. Under glass, grow in direct sun in a freely draining, high-fertility, loam-based mix; water plentifully when in growth, gradually withdrawing water in fall to overwinter in cool, dry conditions with a minimum temperature of 41–45°F (5–7°C). Propagate from seed sown in gentle heat in spring; seed-grown plants usually flower in their third or fourth year. Alternatively, increase by semiripe cuttings in summer, or by heeled cuttings of young growth in spring.

E. × *bidwillii E. crista-galli* × *E. herbacea*; woody-based perennial herb or shrub to 13 ft (4 m) with dark red flowers to 2 in (5 cm) long; *E. crista-galli* CORAL TREE, COCKSPUR CORAL TREE; S America; prickly erect shrub or small tree to 30 ft (9 m); flowers to 2¾ in (7 cm) long, bright scarlet, in large, leafy terminal racemes.

Erythronium (from Greek *erythros*, red, more or less the color of *E. dens-canis*). Liliaceae (Liliaceae). N US, Europe and Asia. DOG'S-TOOTH VIOLET, ADDER'S TONGUE, TROUT LILY, FAWN LILY. Some 20 species, perennial herbs with yellow-white bulbs, which are elongated and toothlike. The leaves are basal, ovate to elliptic, and mottled white, pink, chocolate or maroon, or plain. Produced in spring, the nodding flowers are borne singly or several together on an erect scape. Deeply bell-to hat-shaped, they consist of six, ovate to lanceolate perianth segments, their tips sometimes strongly reflexed. Hardy to 5°F (–15°C) and below. Most species are suited to shady pockets in the rock garden and for naturalizing in the shrub and mixed border, but are perhaps seen at their best in the dappled sunlight of the woodland garden. Grow in partial shade in well-drained, humus-rich and moisture-retentive soil. *E. dens-canis* is sturdy enough to naturalize in thin grass. Mulch established clumps annually with leaf mold. Propagate by division of established clumps as leaves fade, and replant immediately to avoid desiccation of the bulbs. Increase also by ripe seed sown fresh in a moist and humus-rich propagating soil mix.

E. americanum YELLOW ADDER'S TONGUE, TROUT LILY, AMBERBELL; eastern N America; leaves mottled brown and white; flowers solitary, yellow, exterior marked brown or purple, interior spotted; *E. californicum* FAWN LILY; California; leaves mottled brown-green; flowers 1–3, creamy white with a central ring of orange-brown; *E. dens-canis* DOG'S TOOTH VIOLET; Europe, Asia; leaves mottled pink and chocolate; flowers solitary, rose to mauve, sometimes pale pink, lilac, plum purple or pure white; *E. grandiflorum* AVALANCHE LILY; W US; leaves plain green; flowers 1–3, yellow; *E. hendersonii* SW Oregon, NW California; leaves dark green, mottled, margins crisped; flowers to 10, lilac-pink with a purple center; *E. oregonum* Oregon to British Columbia; differs from *E. californicum* in its flowers with yellow centers; *E. revolutum* N California, Vancouver Island; leaves mottled, margins crisped; flowers 1–3 per stem, deep pink with a yellow center; *E.* 'Pagoda' has bronze-marbled leaves and pale sulfur flowers with brown centers.

Escallonia (for Señor Escallon, a Spaniard who traveled in South America in the late 18th century). Grossulariaceae (Escalloniaceae). S America. Some 50 species, aromatic and more or less viscid, evergreen shrubs and small trees with glossy, dark green leaves and racemes or panicles of shortly funnel-shaped flowers, each with five, spreading lobes, from late spring to early fall. In cool and exposed maritime gardens,

many of the taller species are useful screens and windbreaks, and in milder regions can be clipped as hedging for more formal situations. Most are valuable additions to a shrub border, grown for their small, usually dark glossy leaves and for their flowers—these are often carried late in the season, from summer into early fall. Where temperatures fall much below 14°F (–10°C), most species need the protection of a south-facing wall. If cut back by frost they will usually regenerate from the base or from older wood if thickly mulched at the roots. The Donard Hybrids (*E.* × *langleyensis*), especially 'Slieve Donard' and 'Apple Blossom', and *E. rubra* cultivars are among the hardiest, surviving temperatures to –4°F (–20°C). *E.* 'Iveyi' is almost as hardy, being cut back at temperatures at about 5°F (–15°C). Grow in full sun to light shade in deep, moisture-retentive and well-drained soil. Summer-flowering species bloom on wood made in the previous season and can be cut back after flowering to remove old, weak and overcrowded growth; those that flower late in the season are best cut back in spring. Propagate species by seed. For cultivars and hybrids, increase by softwood cuttings in early summer, by nodal, basal or heeled semiripe cuttings in summer, or by hardwood cuttings in fall or early winter.

E. 'Apple Blossom' erect to 4 ft (1.2 m); flowers profuse, pale pink with white 'eyes'; *E.* 'Donard Scarlet' erect and narrow to 6½ ft (2 m), with scarlet flowers; *E.* 'Edinensis' arching shrub to 6½ ft (2 m) tall; flowers deep pink; *E.* 'Iveyi' erect shrub to 10 ft (3 m); flowers fragrant, white opening from pink buds; *E.* 'Langleyensis' semievergreen, to 6½ ft (2 m), with rose-red flowers; *E. leucantha* Chile, Argentina; large shrub or small tree to 40 ft (12 m); flowers white in racemes to 2 in (5 cm) long; *E. rubra* Chile; shrub to 13 ft (4 m) tall; flowers pink to red; includes var. *macrantha*, a dense and vigorous shrub to 13 ft (4 m) tall with darker flowers, and its cultivars 'Crimson Spire', erect to 6½ ft (2 m), with very dark, glossy leaves and crimson-red flowers, and 'Woodside', dense, dwarf and spreading with intense red flowers; *E.* 'Slieve Donard' compact to

5 ft (1.5 m), with rose flowers; *E. virgata* Chile, Argentina; deciduous shrub to 6½ ft (2 m), with slender, arching branches; flowers small, white or palest pink.

escape (1) a garden plant that has become established in the wild; (2) a plant capable of surviving in adverse environmental conditions through adaptation of its life cycle; (3) a susceptible plant which fails to succumb to a prevalent disease.

Eschscholzia (for Johann Friedrich Eschscholz [1793–1831], German physician and naturalist). Papaveraceae. Western N America, naturalized in Europe. Some 10 species, annual or perennial herbs with glaucous and deeply dissected leaves. Solitary and long-stalked, the flowers are broadly funnel-shaped and consist of four to eight petals that fold together in parasol-fashion in dull weather. They are brilliantly colorful, the best blooms and strongest colors obtained in poor, well-drained soil, where the plants may self-sow and overwinter after blooming. Sow seed *in situ*. Removing faded blooms will prolong flowering.

E. caespitosa TUFTED CALIFORNIA POPPY; C California; tufted annual to 10 in (25 cm), branching freely below; leaves more finely and narrowly divided than in *E. californica*, blue-gray; flowers to 2 in (5 cm) across, bright yellow; *E. californica* CALIFORNIA POPPY; W US, naturalized elsewhere; annual or short-lived perennial to 24 in (60 cm) tall; leaves glaucous gray-green; flowers to 2¾ in (7 cm) across, typically yellow to orange; cultivars and seed races include dwarf and large plants, with single, semidouble or double flowers in shades of white, cream, yellow, orange, vermilion, flame, scarlet, salmon, rose, cerise, carmine and purple-bronze.

Escobaria (for the Mexican brothers Romulo and Numa Escobar, early 20th century). Cactaceae. W US, S Canada, N Mexico and Cuba. About 17 species of low-growing cacti, the stems simple or clustering, squatly globose to cylindric, tuberculate and spiny; the flowers are short and tubular. Provide a minimum temperature of 41–45°F (5–7°C).

Grow in a gritty medium of low to neutral pH, in full sun and low humidity; keep dry from midfall until early spring, except for an occasional light misting on warm days during late winter. Increase by seeds, alternatively by offsets. *E. vivipara* (syn. *Coryphantha vivipara*) S Canada, US, N Mexico; stems 2½–6 in (6–15 cm), densely gray-spiny; flowers ¾–2½ in (2–6 cm), pink, purple or yellow.

esculent suitable for human consumption.

Espaliered apple
Both apples and pears make fine espaliers. They take years to train, but the result is a very long-lasting garden feature.

espalier strictly, a system of supports for training plants, especially fruit trees, consisting of horizontal wires stretched along a wall, or between upright posts (a variation correctly described as *contre espalier*). The wires are spaced 16–20 in (40–50 cm) apart. Conventionally, "espalier" refers to the trained woody plant structure itself, which usually consists of a vertical stem with three or more horizontal tiers of branches, all in the same plane.

Espostoa (for Nicholas E. Esposto, Peruvian botanist, early 20th century). Cactaceae. S America (S Ecuador, Peru, Bolivia). 10 species, shrubs or small trees, the stems are succulent, columnar, many-ribbed and spiny; the flowers are tubular to campanulate, usually nocturnal, and develop at a distinct cap or patch of wool at the stem apex (cephalium). Grow in a gritty,

slightly acidic to neutral medium, providing a minimum temperature of 50–59°F (10–15°C). Shade in hot weather and maintain low humidity. Keep dry from midfall until early spring, except for light misting on warm days in late winter. Seedlings are readily raised, and young plants of all species are valued for their attractive, very dense covering of fine spines and/or hairs. *E. lanata* Ecuador, Peru; stems 13–23 (4–7 m) × 6 in (15 cm) with 20–30 ribs, covered in long, silky hairs, spines yellow to black; flowers 1½–3 in (4–8 cm) in diameter, white to purple, from a white to tawny cephalium.

estrade a type of trained tree in which the branches form successive horizontal tiers around the trunk.

ethnobotany the study of man's use of and relationships with plants, especially within a given community or race.

ethylene a colorless flammable gas (C_2H_4), of horticultural relevance because of its association with ripening fruits. For example, stored apples emit ethylene as their respiration rate increases, encouraging other fruits in store to ripen prematurely.

etiolated describing pale and/or spindly, elongated plant growths which are due to the exclusion of light. Etiolation is employed to advantage in the process of blanching.

etiology (aetiology) the study of the causes of disease.

Etlingera (for the botanist A.E. Etlinger, [fl. 1774]. Zingiberaceae. Sri Lanka to New Guinea. 57 species, rhizomatous, perennial herbs with cane-like stems. Scapose inflorescences arise from the rhizome: they consist of many, waxy, overlapping bracts, the lowermost spreading to reflexed like the tepals of a water lily or an overblown *Magnolia*, the uppermost forming a dense and torchlike cone. These bracts virtually conceal small flowers, each with a tubular, frilly lip and three petals. Grow as for *Alpinia*. *E. elatior* TORCH GINGER, PHILIPPINE WAXFLOWER; (syn. *Alpinia elatior, Alpinia magnifica, Nicolaia elatior, Nicolaia speciosa,*

Phaeomeria magnifica) to 16 ft (5 m) tall; inflorescence to 12 in (30 cm) across, standing 3¼ ft (1 m) tall, bracts pale coral to deep flamingo pink; flowers white or yellow with a dark crimson lip.

Euanthe (from Greek *euanthes*, blooming well, referring to the spectacular inflorescence). Orchidaceae. Philippines. 1 species, *E. sanderiana* (syn. *Vanda sanderiana*), a robust epiphytic orchid to 3¼ ft (1 m) tall. It resembles *Vanda*, with two ranks of strap-shaped leaves along an erect stem. Borne in an axillary raceme, the flowers are 2½–4 in (6–10 cm) in diameter and flat with broad sepals: the dorsal sepal is rose, tinged white and variably spotted blood red; the lateral sepals are tawny-yellow, net-veined or flushed brick-red to rose; the petals are ovate to rhombic and dotted red; the short, fleshy lip is honey-colored, and streaked, veined or stained purple-red. Cultivate as for *Vanda*.

Eucalyptus (from the Greek, *eu*, well, and *kalypto*, to cover, referring to the calyptra or lid that covers the flowers before opening). Myrtaceae. GUM. Australia, Malesia, Philippines. Over 500 species, evergreen trees and shrubs, usually oily and intensely aromatic. The bark flakes or peels, exposing the pale new surface beneath. Often tough and glaucous, the leaves vary greatly in form, from the circular to the narrow and willowy. Moreover, many have distinct juvenile phases where the leaves are quite different from those of the adult plant. The flowers consist of numerous stamens set on a top-shaped or cuplike hypanthium. Prior to opening, this is sealed by a lid or *calyptra*, derived from the calyx and corolla. The fruits are cylindrical to squatly spherical, woody, and may persist for many years. The following need full sun, shelter from harsh winds and freely draining soil. They cope well with drought. *E. globulus, E. gunnii* and *E. pauciflora* ssp. *niphophila* are hardy in sheltered places to −10°F (−23°C), and will usually regenerate if cut down by hard frosts. *E. coccifera, E. dalrympleana* and *E. perriniana* will survive outdoors to 10°F (−12°C), or in favored positions to 0°F (−18°C). The remaining species need a cool greenhouse or conservatory. Increase by seed.

EUCALYPTUS

Name	Habit	Bark	Juvenile leaves	Adult leaves	Flowers
E. camaldulensis MURRAY RED GUM	tree to 150 ft (45 m)	smooth, white, gray, brown or red	ovate to broadly lanceolate, gray- to blue-green	3–12 in (8–30 cm), narrowly lanceolate, thick, gray-green	cream, small
E. citriodora LEMON-SCENTED GUM	tree, 80–160 ft (25–50 m)	white, powdery, sometimes pink, red or blue-gray	narrowly to broadly lanceolate	3–6 in (8–16 cm), lanceolate, lemon-scented when crushed	white
E. coccifera TASMANIAN SNOW GUM	shrub or tree to 33 ft (10 m)	smooth, white-gray, yellow or pink when fresh and peeling	broadly elliptic to rounded. somewhat glaucous	2–4 in (5–10 cm), elliptic or lanceolate, pointed to scimitar-like, thick, gray-green, peppermint-scented	white
E. dalrympleana BROAD LEAVED KINDLING BARK	tree to 130 ft (40 m)	blotched white and gray to yellow-white, peeling to expose pink, green to olive patches	sometimes stem-clasping, rounded to ovate, light green to glaucous	4–8 in (10–20 cm), narrowly lanceolate, tapering finely, shiny	white
E. eremophila TALL SAND MALLEE	shrub to 15 ft (4.5 m)	smooth, light brown or yellow-brown to gray-white	alternate, ovate	to 3 in (8 cm), narrowly lanceolate, acuminate	white
E. ficifolia RED-FLOWERING GUM; FLOWERING GUM	tree to 33 ft (10 m)	rough, fibrous, shaggy	ovate to broadly lanceolate, bristly	3–6 in (8–15 cm), broadly lanceolate to ovate, tapering, thick, glossy, dark green	showy, crimson
E. forrestiana FUCHSIA EUCALYPTUS	tree or shrub to 16 ft (5 m)	rough, gray, flaky to smooth and gray, exposed new bark gray-brown	alternate, ovate	to 3½ ft (9 cm), lanceolate, tapering finely, shining deep green	white or red giving rise to red pear-shaped fruit
E. globulus TASMANIAN BLUE GUM; BLUE GUM	tree to 230 ft (70 m)	white to cream, yellow or gray, smooth then peeling in ribbons	ovate to lanceolate, gray-green, glaucous to resinous, opposed in stem-clasping pairs	4¾–10 in (12–25 cm), lanceolate to falcate, glossy to dull mid-green	white

Comments: The most popular gum in British gardens after *E. gunnii*—very fast-growing with bolder, duller, rather rank foliage. Young plants are often used in subtropical bedding schemes.

E. camaldulensis

E. citriodora

E. dalrympleana

E. ficifolia

EUCALYPTUS

Name	Habit	Bark	Juvenile leaves	Adult leaves	Flowers
E. gunnii CIDER GUM	tree to 80 ft (25 m)	smooth, brown gray-green, peeling to expose pink to gray-white areas	neat, ovate to rounded, blue-gray to gray-green, glaucous, perfoliate or opposed in stem-clasping pairs	to 3 in (8 cm), broadly elliptic to ovate, gray-green, glaucous	white

Comments: The most hardy and popular gum in British gardens; pruned hard or even stooled in spring, it produces a mop of fresh blue, juvenile growth—an ideal complement for silver-gray or purple foliage and pastel flowers in shrubberies and mixed borders.

Name	Habit	Bark	Juvenile leaves	Adult leaves	Flowers
E. macrocarpa	shrub to 16 ft (5 m), spreading or sprawling	smooth, gray	opposite, broadly elliptic to rounded, gray-green, glaucous	to 4¾ in (12 cm), opposite, broadly ovate, glaucous	showy, red, pink or cream
E. nicholii NARROW-LEAVED PEPPERMINT	tree to 50 ft (15 m), willowy with a light, airy crown	rough, fibrous, yellow-brown	small, linear, gray-green, crowded	2½–5 in (6–13 cm), narrowly lanceolate and tapering finely, blue- to gray-green, peppermint-scented	white
E. pauciflora CABBAGE GUM	tree or suckering shrub to 66 ft (20 m)	smooth, white to ghostly gray or brown-red, falling away in patches and strips giving a mottled appearance	large, ovate to elliptic, thick, gray-green with a white bloom	to 8 in (20 cm), lanceolate to falcate, blue-green	white

Comments: More common in gardens is the SNOW GUM, ssp. **niphophila** (syn. *E. niphophila*), to 20 ft (6 m) tall with silvery gray, tough, ovate juvenile leaves and ovate to lanceolate, blue-green adult leaves, often with red margins and stalks. Hardier than the type, this gum has striking bark—a patchwork of white, ivory and pale rusty pink.

Name	Habit	Bark	Juvenile leaves	Adult leaves	Flowers
E. perriniana ROUND LEAVED SNOW GUM; SPINNING GUM	tree or multistemmed shrub to 26 ft (8 m)	white to gray with brown patches	circular, perfoliate, bright silver-gray	to 6 in (15 cm), lanceolate to scimitar-shaped, pendulous, blue-gray	white

Comments: Especially showy when juvenile; sometimes hardy in sheltered areas.

Name	Habit	Bark	Juvenile leaves	Adult leaves	Flowers
E. pyriformis DOWERIN ROSE; PEAR-FRUITED MALLEE	shrub to 16 ft (5 m)	smooth, gray to light brown	alternate, ovate-lanceolate to rounded	to 3 in (8 cm), ovate to lanceolate, light green	red, pink, yellow or ivory from large pear-shaped buds
E. viminalis MANNA GUM; RIBBON GUM	tree to 160 ft (50 m)	smooth, gray, white or yellow-white and rough, peeling on upper branches	lanceolate to cordate, sometimes stem-clasping	to 8 in (20 cm), narrowly lanceolate, tapering finely, dark green	white

E. gunnii

E. nicholii

E. pauciflora ssp. *niphophila*

Eucharis (from Greek *eu*, good, and *charis*, attraction, in reference to the blooms). Amaryllidaceae. W Amazon and adjacent E Andes (Guatemala to Bolivia). 17 species and 2 natural hybrids, summer-flowering, bulbous evergreen perennial herbs, with dark green, shiny, ovate to broadly lanceolate stalked leaves. The flowers are carried in a scapose umbel; they are usually white and highly fragrant with six, spreading, ovate tepals. The six stamens are broadened at their bases and fused to form a cup. Grow in dappled sunlight or shade, with a minimum temperature of 50°F (10°C), in a fibrous loam-based medium, with added leaf mold and sharp sand. Keep dry but not arid until growth commences early in the year, then water moderately, applying a balanced liquid fertilizer weekly when in full growth. Propagate by offsets.

E. amazonica Ecuador, N Peru, S Colombia; scape to 28 in (70 cm); flowers to 4 in (10 cm) diameter, white; *E.* × *grandiflora* AMAZON LILY, EUCHARIST LILY, STAR OF BETHLEHEM; a natural hybrid from Colombia involving *E. amazonica* and very similar to it, usually differing in its slightly smaller flowers.

Eucomis (from Greek *eukomos*, lovely-haired, referring to the crown of bracts at the apex of the inflorescence). Liliaceae (Hyacinthaceae). PINEAPPLE LILY. Africa (those listed below are from South Africa). Some 15 species, robust, bulbous perennials with strap-shaped to broadly lanceolate, smooth leaves. The flowers are small, usually green, and star-shaped. They appear in late summer, packed in dense, cylindrical spikes; these are carried atop stout scapes and crowned with a tuft of leaflike bracts. The following species favor a minimum temperature of 39–50°F (4–10°C), but may be tried outdoors in mild regions, and either lifted in winter or grown in a very sheltered site and protected with a heavy dry mulch. Plant about 6 in (15 cm) deep in fall, in a sunny position, in rich, well-drained soil. In pots, grow one bulb to a 5 in (12.5 cm) pot or three bulbs to a larger-sized pot, with bulb tips just showing. Give bright, filtered light and good ventilation. Water sparingly when dormant, plentifully while in growth. Propagate from seed

sown in spring, or by offsets.

E. fallalis (syn. *E. undulata*) to 20 in (50 cm); leaves with wavy margins; flowers white or pale olive at first becoming deeper green, bracts wavy; *E. bicolor* to 24 in (60 cm); leaves with wavy margins; scape flecked maroon, flowers edged purple, bracts wavy, edged purple; *E. comosa* to 28 in (70 cm); leaves with wavy margins, spotted to striped purple beneath; scape spotted purple; flowers purple-tinted, bracts sometimes edged or spotted purple; *E. pallidiflora* to 30 in (75 cm); leaves with crispate margins; flowers green-white, bracts crispate.

Eucommia (from the Greek *eu*, well, and *kommi*, gum, from the rubberlike latex produced by this tree). Eucommiaceae. C China. 1 species, *E. ulmoides*, the HARDY RUBBER TREE, a deciduous tree to 66 ft (20 m) tall. The leaves are 2¾–6 in (7–15 cm) long, narrowly ovate to elliptic and finely toothed. Hairy at first, they soon become glossy, dark green and will exude threads of latex if broken. The flowers lack petals and are borne in axillary clusters with or before leaves; the males with numerous red-brown anthers. Hardy to 5°F (–15°C) or lower. Grow in full sun; shelter from cold winds. Propagate from seed sown in fall, or from softwood cuttings.

Eucryphia (from Greek *eu*, well, and *kryphios*, covered; the sepals form a cap over the flower bud). Eucryphiaceae. Chile, SE Australia (Tasmania, New South Wales, Victoria). 6 species, evergreen trees or shrubs (*E. glutinosa* is deciduous in cultivation), with tough and often glossy, simple or pinnate, finely toothed leaves. Often fragrant, the solitary flowers are white and appear in summer and early fall. Generally, they consist of four broad petals and numerous fine stamens with pink anthers. They are best grown in moist, but well-drained acidic soil; *E. cordifolia* and *E.* × *nymansensis* will grow in alkaline soil. Ideally, site among other trees and shrubs that will shade the base from hot sun and keep the soil cool and moist, but allow the crown to grow into the light. Most species are hardy to 0°F (–18°C), although protection from cold winds is essential. Pruning is generally not required. Propagate by

semiripe cuttings in late summer, by seed sown when ripe or by layers or suckers.

E. cordifolia ULMO, ROBLE DE CHILE; C and S Chile; columnar tree to 66 ft (20 m); leaves to 2¾ in (7 cm), simple oblong; flowers to 2 in (5 cm) diameter; *E. glutinosa* NIRRHE; C Chile; upright tree or shrub to 33 ft (10 m); leaves to 2 in (5 cm), leaflets 3–5, elliptic to oblong, coloring well in fall if deciduous; flowers to 2½ in (6 cm) diameter; *E. lucida* LEATHERWOOD, PINKWOOD; Tasmania; erect shrub or tree to 26 ft (8 m); leaves to 2 in (5 cm), juveniles with 3 leaflets, adults simple, oblong to lanceolate; flowers 1¼–2 in (3–5 cm) diameter, nodding; includes pink- and cream-flowered cultivars; *E. milliganii* Tasmania; differs from *E. lucida* in its narrowly columnar habit, smaller leaves and cup-shaped flowers to ¾ in (2 cm) diameter; *E.* × *nymansensis* (*E. cordifolia* × *E. glutinosa*); dense, vigorous, columnar tree to 50 ft (15 m) tall; leaves simple or with 3 leaflets to 3 in (8 cm) long; flowers to 3 in (7.5 cm) diameter.

Euonymus (from the ancient Greek name *euonymon dendron*, hence to Latin meaning 'of good name'—an ironic allusion to its toxicity). Celastraceae. Asia, Europe, N and C America, Madagascar, Australia. Over 170 species, deciduous or evergreen shrubs or trees with inconspicuous, green-white to yellow flowers. These give rise to clusters of 3–5-valved, shell- or envelope-like fruit, splitting to reveal beadlike, white to coral or orange-yellow seeds, enclosed in fleshy, colorful arils. Evergreen species are hardy in to –10°F (–23°C), deciduous species to –30°F (–34°C). Plant in well-drained, moist and fertile soil in full sun or light shade. Evergreens used for hedging or edging may be trimmed in spring. Support climbing cultivars where required. Increase by nodal cuttings between summer and fall or by fresh seed sown under glass or in the cold frame.

E. alatus SPINDLE TREE; N Asia; much-branched, deciduous shrub to 10 ft (3 m); branches with 4, deep and corky wings; leaves ¾–2¾ in (2–7 cm), ovate to elliptic, serrate, pale green turning crimson to brilliant scarlet in fall; fruit pale red with orange arils; *E. americanus* strawberry bush; E US;

erect, deciduous shrub to 10 ft (3 m); branches 4-angled; leaves to 3 in (8 cm), narrowly ovate to lanceolate, tough, persisting well into fall; fruit pink, warty, aril bright red; *E. europaeus* COMMON SPINDLE TREE; Europe to W Asia; deciduous shrub or small tree to 23 ft (7 m); branches with corky stripes; leaves to 3 in (8 cm), ovate to oblong, mid-green, finely toothed, turning scarlet in fall; fruit pink to bright red, arils orange; includes dwarf and large cultivars, some with leaves pale yellow-green, variegated or turning very deep purple-red in fall, some with orange-red fruit; *E. fortunei* China; evergreen, slender-stemmed shrub, procumbent or climbing to 15 ft (5 m); leaves to 2½ in (6 cm), ovate to elliptic, finely toothed, leathery and glossy dark green; fruit ivory to yellow, arils orange to pink; a variable and much-developed species including selections with erect and bushy, vigorously climbing, dwarf and compact or densely ground-smothering habits, the leaves ranging in size from ½ to 2½ in (1 to 6 cm), in color from dark green assuming purple-red fall tints, to white-, cream-, or yellow-variegated; *E. hamiltonianus* Himalayas to Japan; deciduous shrub or small tree, similar to *E. europaeus* but with smooth branches and longer, narrower and thicker leaves; fruit pink, arils red; includes cultivars with good fall color and bright coral fruit; *E. japonicus* China, Korea, Japan; erect, evergreen shrub or small tree to 26 ft (8 m);

Euphorbia pulcherrimum
In hot countries (here, Egypt) the poinsettia makes a tall shrub or multistemmed tree, its upper branches bearing these bright bracts.

leaves to 2¾ in (7 cm), elliptic to oblong, bluntly and finely toothed, tough, smooth, glossy deep green; fruit pink, arils orange; a popular and much-developed species often used for hedging and edging, it includes many cultivars ranging in habit from the dwarf and boxlike to the tall and shrubby, in leaf form from very small and narrow to large and broad, in color from gray-green to deep emerald, edged, zoned or splashed white, cream or yellow; *E. obovatus* RUNNING STRAWBERRY BUSH; N America; slender-stemmed, deciduous shrub, prostrate and rooting, or climbing if supported; leaves to 2½ in (6 cm), obovate to elliptic, crenate, pale green; fruit carmine, warty, aril red.

Eupatorium (for Eupator, King of Pontus, who used one species as an antidote for poison). Compositae. E US, Eurasia. HEMP AGRIMONY, JOE PYE WEED, THOROUGHWORT. About 40 perennial herbs, subshrubs or shrubs with many, buttonlike flower heads packed in terminal panicles or corymbs in late summer and fall. Fully hardy. Grow in any moderately fertile, well-drained but moisture-retentive soil in sun or part shade. Propagate by seed or division. *E. purpureum* BONESET, THOROUGHWORT; E US; purple-tinged, perennial herb 3¼–10 ft (1–3 m) tall; leaves whorled, to 10 in (25 cm), ovate to lanceolate, vanilla-scented when bruised; flower heads pale pink to green-yellow or rose-purple.

Euphorbia (named for Euphorbus, physician to the King of Mauretania). Euphorbiaceae. MILKWEED. Cosmopolitan. At least 2000 species, ranging greatly in habit, from small, weedy annuals, to herbaceous perennials, shrubs and succulents. All have milky, toxic sap and bear small flowers in cyathia. A cyathium is a small cup composed of bracts. It is sometimes furnished with glands and subtended by other, larger bracts. Inside the cyathium are found several "stamens," each equivalent to a male flower, and a stalked ovary equivalent to the female. The cyathia themselves are often disposed on radiating branches and surrounded by showy bracts.

The succulent species need a mini-

mum temperature of 50°F (10°C), full sun and low humidity. Grow in a gritty and sandy, loam-based medium. Water and feed moderately in warm weather; keep fairly dry at other times, watering only to prevent shrivelling of the stems.

The herbaceous perennial species are hardy to –10°F (–23°C). Evergreens and semievergreens with glaucous, fleshy leaves need a sunny, sheltered site in fast-draining, gritty soil. They are excellent plants for rock, gravel and silver gardens. Other perennials will grow in a range of situations, from sun to light shade, and prefer damp and fertile, humus-rich soil. *E. amygdaloides* var. *robbiae* and *E. cyparissias* will tolerate full sun and impoverished, drought-stricken clay, often spreading to the point of nuisance. The semishrubby *E. characias* is fully hardy and will grow in sun or shade. The shrub *E. mellifera* will be tender unless grown in a sheltered position.

Annuals and biennials should be sown *in situ* in spring in well-drained soil in full sun. *E. lathyris* is unlikely to be welcome, but *E. marginata* is highly desirable, a fine cut flower and an excellent filler for white borders.

E. fulgens and *E. pulcherrima* (poinsettia) need a minimum temperature of 41°F (5°C), full sun and a dry, buoyant environment. Both will become sizeable, if rather sparse, shrubs in time, but they are usually grown as pot plants, repropagated every few years. Keep poinsettias moist and well-fed during growth and flowering. After flowering (which usually occurs in late winter), reduce the water until the leaves and bracts drop. Cut back the stems. Keep the plants more or less dry and in a cool, shaded place. Repot in midsummer. Increase light, temperature, water and feed as the nights grow longer. The plants should be in flower by Christmas.

Increase succulents, glaucous-leaved perennials and shrubs by stem cuttings; herbaceous perennials by division in early spring; annuals and biennials by seed. The milky sap is toxic and irritant: care should be taken when handling all species.

Euptelea (from Greek *eu*, well, and *ptelea*, elm, referring to the edible fruit). Eupteleaceae. E Asia. 3 species, deciduous trees and shrubs, usually with

EUPHORBIA

Name	Distribution	Habit	Leaves	Inflorescences
E. abyssinica	Ethiopia, Eritrea, Somalia	tree to 33 ft (10 m) tall with candelabra-like branches thickly succulent with several deep, wavy and spiny wings	absent	dense, inconspicuous
E. amygdaloides WOOD SPURGE	Europe, W Asia	evergreen perennial herb to 20 in (50 cm) with clumped and suckering stems	2–4¾ in (5–12 cm), spathulate to narrowly obovate, dark green, hairy at first, then smooth	lime green to bright yellow in an erect to nodding, terminal spike amid leaflike bracts in early spring

Comments: Includes 'Purpurea', a compact and bushy plant with stems and foliage flushed ruby red to deep purple-red, especially in winter and early spring, and bright lime green flowers; also, the popular var. *robbiae* (syn. *E. robbiae*), a freely spreading plant with broader, smooth and dark green leaves in a rufflike arrangement and tall, loose spikes of lime to pale gold flowers.

Name	Distribution	Habit	Leaves	Inflorescences
E. candelabrum	NE Africa to S Africa	tree to 66 ft (20 m) with candelabra-like branches, each succulent and with deep, spiny and dark-toothed wings	small, short-lived	yellow-green
E. caput-medusae MEDUSA'S HEAD	S Africa	succulent perennial to 12 × 32 in (30 × 80 cm) with a stout, more or less buried base from which radiate numerous low-lying branches, each cylindrical, snaking and covered in cone-shaped tubercles	narrow, small, short-lived	each with a white fringe, packed in terminal heads
E. characias	W Mediterranean, Portugal	evergreen perennial herb to 5 ft (1.5 m) with numerous clumped stems arising from a woody base	4–9 in (10–22 cm), linear to oblong or narrowly oblanceolate, sea green to gray-blue, softly and minutely downy	small, bell-shaped, yellow-green with deep maroon, eyelike glands and sometimes rims, in a dense and branching terminal head from spring to summer

Comments: Includes the taller ssp. *wulfenii* with gray-green leaves and bright lime flower heads with yellow glands; ssp. *characias* 'Burrow Silver', smaller with white-variegated leaves and creamy flower heads and 'Portuguese Velvet', compact with crowded, short and broad, velvety leaves.

Name	Distribution	Habit	Leaves	Inflorescences
E. cyparissias CYPRESS SPURGE	Europe, naturalized N America	perennial herb, fast spreading with erect and branching annual stems to 12 in (30 cm)	⅝–1¼ in (1.5–3 cm), linear to oblong, soft sea green or bright green, giving the branches the appearance of feathery cylinders; fall color yellow to fox red	small, lime green to bright gold in frothy, branching heads in spring **Comments:** 'Fens Ruby': small, bushy plant with new growth tinted copper red to soft bronze.

E. amygdaloides

E. candelabrum

E. characias

E. cyparissias

EUPHORBIA

Name	Distribution	Habit	Leaves	Inflorescences
E. dulcis	Europe	perennial herb to 16 in (40 cm) tall, with erect, branching annual stems arising from a thick rootstock	1¼–3 in (3–8 cm), oblong to oblanceolate, mid-green, smooth, soft-textured	yellow in broad, branching heads, glands and bracts sometimes tinted red or purple, in early summer

Comments: 'Chameleon': leaves and stems flushed solid dark chocolate to purple-red; self-seeds freely and comes true from seed.

Name	Distribution	Habit	Leaves	Inflorescences
E. fulgens SCARLET PLUME	Mexico	evergreen shrub to 6½ ft (2 m) with slender, arching branches	to 6 in (16 cm), narrowly lanceolate, dark green	small, flowerlike with rounded "petals," bright scarlet in dense axillary clusters throughout the year

Comments: Includes forms with white, cream, yellow, orange and pink flowers. A popular cut flower.

Name	Distribution	Habit	Leaves	Inflorescences
E. griffithii	E Himalaya	clump-forming perennial herb with erect, branching stems to 3¼ ft (1 m)	3–7 in (8–18 cm), narrowly oblong to lanceolate, dark green with a paler midrib often tinted pink, upper leaves and bracts flushed pink to glowing orange-red	copper to fiery red or orange, in dense terminal heads in spring

Comments: Includes 'Dixter', a compact plant with luxuriant, dark foliage tinted bronze and pink and orange inflorescences, and 'Fireglow', a tall plant with bronze-pink new foliage and bright fiery red inflorescences.

Name	Distribution	Habit	Leaves	Inflorescences
E. lathyris CAPER SPURGE, MOLE PLANT, MYRTLE SPURGE	cosmopolitan	biennial herb to 5 ft (1.5 m) tall; stem erect, unbranched below, extensively branched above in a broad inflorescence	2½–7 in (6–18 cm), oblong to lanceolate, sea green with paler midribs, smooth, angled downward in four distinct ranks along stem	yellow-green with triangular bracts on the forking stems of a large, terminal head in summer

Comments: A widespread weed, sometimes encouraged for the striking regularity of its growth habit and its curious inflorescences. Also said to deter moles. The fruits resemble capers (but are poisonous).

Name	Distribution	Habit	Leaves	Inflorescences
E. mammillaris CORN COB, CORKSCREW	S Africa	succulent shrub or shrublet to 12 in (30 cm) with 5-sided, dense and erect branches to 2½ in (6 cm) thick and covered in tubercles and spines	absent	small and green-maroon, the stalks of dead flower heads persisting as spines to ½ in (1 cm) long

Comments: 'Variegata': stems marbled green-white, bright green and tinted pink when young.

Name	Distribution	Habit	Leaves	Inflorescences
E. marginata GHOST WEED, SNOW ON THE MOUNTAIN	N America	softly and minutely hairy annual, erect to 3¼ ft (1 m) tall	to 3 in (8 cm), ovate to oblong, gray-green, upper leaves and inflorescence bracts edged bright white	white, surrounded by wholly white or white-edged bracts in terminal heads from spring to fall

Comments: A good cut flower.

E. dulcis 'Chameleon'   *E. griffithii* 'Fireglow'   *E. lathyris*   *E. marginata*

EUPHORBIA

Name	Distribution	Habit	Leaves	Inflorescences
E. × martinii (*E. amygdaloides* × *E. characias*)	**Comments:** A natural hybrid including plants intermediate between both or favoring either of the parents. The plants are usually compact with ruffs of narrow leaves and columns of flower heads; these tend to be cupped as per *E. characias*, but smaller and bright yellow or lime, often with dark wine-red glands and margins.			
E. mellifera	Madeira, N Tenerife, La Palma	evergreen shrub to 6½ ft (2 m) or tree to 10 ft (3 m) with stout, olive, candelabra-like branches and a dense, broad crown	3–7 in (8–18 cm), oblong to bluntly lanceolate, smooth, mid- to deep green with a white to pale green midrib	honey-scented, yellow-green with maroon glands in crowded heads in early summer

Comments: A handsome if rather tender shrub almost extinct in the wild and richly deserving a sheltered, sunny position in the garden.

Name	Distribution	Habit	Leaves	Inflorescences
E. meloformis MELON SPURGE	S Africa	dwarf succulent to 4 in (10 cm) tall with a more or less spherical stem with 8 to 12 facets; dark olive with obscure transecting bands of deep green and purple-green	inconspicuous and soon lost	small, yellow-green, borne on very short stalks at the sunken stem apex

Comments: An easy succulent, often confused with *E. obesa*, from which it differs in its persistently spherical stem with a sunken top.

Name	Distribution	Habit	Leaves	Inflorescences
E. milii *E. splendens* CROWN OF THORNS	Madagascar	erect to scrambling shrub to 3¼ ft (1 m) tall with gray, viciously spiny branches	¾–2½ in (2–6 cm), obovate to oblong, dark green	slender-stalked with cupped, scarlet bracts and yellow glands, produced throughout the year

Comments: A popular pot plant with numerous cultivars, the inflorescences in shades of scarlet, flame, peach, pink, yellow, ivory and white.

Name	Distribution	Habit	Leaves	Inflorescences
E. myrsinites	S Europe, Asia Minor	evergreen perennial herb with a stout stock from which arises a crown of succulent trailing stems, each to 12 in (30 cm) long	to 1¼ in (3 cm), obovate with a short, pointed tip, fleshy, blue-gray, glaucous, densely and spirally arranged	sulfur-yellow, on branching stems in dense terminal heads from late winter to midspring

Comments: A superb plant for sunny situations on the rock and dry garden. *E. rigida* and *E. seguieriana* are similar but have narrower leaves.

Name	Distribution	Habit	Leaves	Inflorescences
E. nicaeensis	S, C, E Europe	evergreen perennial to 32 in (80 cm) with clumped, red-tinted stems arising to 32 in (80 cm) from a woody stock	to 3 in (8 cm), oblong to lanceolate, gray-green, tough to thinly fleshy, blunt	yellow-green in broad heads in summer
E. obesa LIVING BASEBALL	S Africa	succulent perennial to 12 in (30 cm); 6-facetted stem, spherical at first, then stoutly cylindrical with a pointed apex, dull green with bands of pale olive, gray or dull purple	inconspicuous, short-lived or absent	small, more or less stalkless, yellow-green

Comments: A popular succulent; cf. *E. meloformis*.

E. × *martinii*

E. *mellifera*

E. *milii*

E. *myrsinites*

EUPHORBIA

Name	Distribution	Habit	Leaves	Inflorescences
E. palustris **Comments:** A robust, handsome spurge suitable for damp, even waterlogged sites.	Europe	deciduous perennial resembling a taller, smoother, cleaner *E. polychroma*, with clumped stems sparsely branching above and erect to 4 ft (1.25 m)	to 3 in (8 cm), elliptic to oblong or lanceolate, mid-green with a paler midrib, upper leaves sometimes turning rusty red or orange in fall	bright sulfur yellow or pale gold in large, domed heads in spring
E. polychroma *E. epithymoides*	C & SE Europe, Asia Minor	deciduous perennial herb with a bushy clump of erect, unbranched or sparsely branched stems to 16 in (40 cm) tall	1¼–2½ in (3–6 cm), obovate to elliptic or oblong, soft and minutely hairy at first, bright green often with a purple blush, becoming mid-green	sulfur yellow to bright gold in broad, caplike heads **Comments:** Includes cultivars with bright gold and purple-tinted inflorescences.
E. portlandica PORTLAND SPURGE **Comments:** Provide full sun and well-drained soil.	W Europe	neat, deciduous or evergreen biennial or perennial herb with clumped, bushy stems erect to 12 in (30 cm)	¼–¾ in (0.5–2 cm), oblong to oblanceolate, bluntly pointed, thinly fleshy, sea green to blue-green sometimes flushed red	in loose terminal clusters with triangular, sea-green bracts and yellow-orange glands
E. pulcherrima POINSETTIA **Comments:** A popular houseplant, grown for display at Christmas and available in a range of colors and sizes.	Mexico	deciduous shrub to 10 ft (3 m), typically gaunt and flowering on bare branches, but usually seen as a pot plant, short, leafy and bushy	4–8 in (10–20 cm), ovate to elliptic with jagged or sinuate, pointed lobes or teeth	small and green-yellow in terminal clusters surrounded by very showy, leaflike bracts to 8 in (20 cm) long and ranging in color from dark scarlet to flamingo pink, peach, cream or white
E. rigida *E. biglandulosa* **Comments:** Plant in full sun in sharply drained soil.	S Europe to Caucasus	evergreen perennial herb resembling an erect *E. myrsinites* to 16 in (40 cm) tall	to 2 in (5 cm), lanceolate, tapering to a sharp point, tough, fleshy, pale gray-blue, glaucous, sometimes tinted rose	golden yellow sometimes with maroon glands, in broad terminal heads at various times of year; in full sun and with age, the bracts become amber or scarlet with glowing orange-red tints
E. schillingii	Nepal	deciduous, erect, clump-forming perennial to 3¼ ft (1 m) tall	to 5 in (13 cm), oblong to bluntly lanceolate, fresh emerald green with a white midrib, pale veins and a thin, clear red margin	bright yellow in broad, rounded terminal heads in spring and summer
E. seguieriana	SW to C and E Europe, W Asia	evergreen perennial herb resembling *E. myrsinites* but with looser, narrower and less rigid foliage	to 2¾ in (7 cm), narrowly linear to oblong, finely tapering, thinly fleshy, blue green, glaucous, forward-pointing	bright sulfur yellow in broad, branching terminal heads, usually from midsummer

E. obesa

E. polychroma

E. pulcherrima 'Lilo White'

E. schillingii

EUPHORBIA

Name	Distribution	Habit	Leaves	Inflorescences
E. sikkimensis	E Himalaya	differs from *E. griffithii* in its coral pink, ruby-veined new growth and the inflorescence bracts, which are yellow, not orange or red		
E. wallichii	Himalaya	deciduous perennial herb with erect, clumped stems to 20 in (50 cm)	to 4¾ in (12 cm), narrowly elliptic to oblong, dark jade green with a white midrib and fine, purple-tinted margins	terminal, yellow-green with large, green glands

broadly pyramidal crowns. The leaves are toothed and often tinted red on emergence. Small and lacking sepals and petals, the flowers are produced before the leaves in clusters along shoots and consist of numerous stamens with red anthers. Hardy to –10°F (–23°C) and suitable for open situations in the woodland garden or shrub border. Propagate by fresh seed sown as soon as it becomes ripe, or by layers.

E. pleiosperma W China; to 33 ft (10 m); leaves to 4¾ in (12 cm), broadly ovate, apex tapering, with shallow, regular teeth, coloring red in fall; *E. polyandra* Japan; to 22 ft (7 m); leaves to 4¾ in (12 cm), broadly ovate with deep, irregular teeth, coloring red and yellow in fall.

Eurya (from Greek, *eury*, broad, perhaps referring to the broad petals). Theaceae. S and E Asia, Pacific Islands. Some 70 species, mostly evergreen trees and shrubs, usually with a herringbone branch pattern and tough, dark green and crenately toothed leaves. Small, 5-petalled flowers with many stamens appear in summer. These are sometimes followed by small berries. Hardy to 10°F (–12°C), given a protected site. Where winters are more harsh, grow *Eurya* in a cool greenhouse or conservatory. Plant in sun or part shade, with shelter from cold, drying winds. Protect from frost when young. Under glass, water the plants plentifully when in full growth. Keep just moist in winter, ensuring a minimum temperature of 41°F (5°C). Propagate by seed sown fresh or in spring, alternatively by semiripe cuttings in late summer.

E. emarginata Japan; shrub or small tree; leaves ¾–1½ in (2–3.5 cm), obo-vate to oblong, emarginate; flowers yellow-green; fruit purple-black; *E. japonica* E Asia; shrub or tree to 33 ft (10 m); leaves 1¼–3 in (3–8 cm), oval to obovate, apex bluntly acute; flowers white; fruit black.

Euryops (from Greek *euryops*, having large or wide eyes, referring to the broad disks of some species). Compositae. Arabia, Africa (those listed below are from South Africa). About 100 species, evergreen shrubs and subshrubs to perennial or annual herbs with yellow daisylike flower heads in summer.

The following species are suitable for rock gardens, containers and raised beds. They need excellent drainage and some shelter (for example, a south-facing wall). They are able to withstand temperatures as low as 9°F (–13°C). Grow in full sun in gritty, neutral to slightly acidic soil. Trim over after flowering if necessary. Propagate by

Euryops acraeus
This dense, rounded shrub with its evergreen gray foliage and bright flowers is suited to the larger rock garden or raised bed.

seed or by greenwood or semiripe cuttings with a heel.

E. acraeus (syn. *E. evansii* of gardens) dense rounded shrub to 3¼ ft (1 m) tall; leaves to 1¼ in (3 cm), narrowly oblong, tip 3-toothed, blue-green, glaucous; *E. pectinatus* vigorous shrub 3¼–6½ ft (1–2 m) tall, often gray-hairy; leaves to 4 in (10 cm), pinnately lobed, silvery.

Eustoma (from Greek *eu*, good, and *stoma*, mouth, referring to the beautiful corolla throat). Gentianaceae. Southern N America to northern S America. 3 species, annual, biennial or perennial herbs usually with glaucous, ovate to linear or lanceolate leaves in opposite pairs. The long-stalked flowers are solitary or in loose, erect panicles. The corolla is funnel-shaped to campanulate with five to six, oblong or obovate and satiny lobes. Beautiful plants for the cool greenhouse or conservatory, where they need a minimum winter temperature of 41°F (5°C). Treat as biennials. Raise from seed in fall and prick out into a sandy, soilless mixture. Grow on in bright, well-ventilated conditions. Cool temperatures with good light and fresh air are vital; overheating at the roots is disastrous. The slender stalks may require support. Protect blooms from strong sunlight.

E. exaltatum S US, Mexico, West Indies; glaucous annual or short-lived perennial to 24 in (60 cm); flowers to 1½ in (4 cm) deep, white, blue, pink or purple; *E. grandiflorum* (syn. *Lisianthius russellianus*) PRAIRIE GENTIAN; US, Mexico; erect, glaucous annual or perennial to 24 in (60 cm); flowers to 4 in (10 cm) deep; a popular cut flower available in shades of white, cream, pale yellow, peach, pink, deep rose, purple, indigo and blue, often with a darker or far paler central patch or margins.

eutrophication the increase of algal and bacterial growth in a pond or other receptacle of water, which occurs as a result of nutrient enrichment.

evapotranspiration the combined loss of water from evaporation and transpiration.

evergreen a plant that retains green leaves through more than one growing season, as opposed to a deciduous plant.

everlasting flowers that retain their form for a very long period after cutting, especially if they are carefully dried—for example, *Helichrysum* species. Many everlastings belong to the Compositae, and have papery petals or bracts; grasses and prepared foliage such as beech are also included in the description. Everlasting flowers are also referred to as immortelle.

evolute unfolded.

Exacum (from Latin *ex*, out, and *agere*, to drive, which refers to the purgative properties of members of the genus). Gentianaceae. Old World tropics and subtropics. 25 species, annual, biennial or perennial herbs with small, salverform to rotate flowers in cymes. Exacum is a free-flowering pot plant for the home or conservatory, where it requires a minimum temperature of 50°F (10°C) in winter. Sow seed in late summer, at 59°F (15°C), and prick out into a soilless mix. Keep moist but never wet; provide good light and a weak liquid feed. Increase also by cuttings in fall. *E. affine* PERSIAN VIOLET, GERMAN VIOLET; S Yemen, naturalized elsewhere; densely bushy annual or short-lived perennial, 8–24 in (20–60 cm); leaves small and neat; flowers ³⁄₈–³⁄₄ in (0.8–2 cm) diameter, fragrant, sky blue to pale violet or rich purple with yellow anthers; includes dwarf and large cultivars and flowers in various shades of mauve, blue, pink and white.

excrescence an outgrowth or abnormal development.

excurrent (1) projecting beyond the margin or apex of its organ, for example a midvein terminating in an awn; (2) a growth habit where the primary axis remains dominant and recognizable throughout life, with the branches secondary to it—as in a strongly single-stemmed tree with a remote, tiered branching pattern.

exfoliating peeling off in thin layers, shreds or plates.

exo- prefix meaning outward.

exocarp the outermost wall of a pericarp.

Exochorda (from Greek *exo*, outside, and *chorde*, a cord, referring to the fibers outside the placenta). Rosaceae. China. PEARLBUSH. 4 species, deciduous shrubs with entire or serrate, pale green, and usually softly hairy leaves. Showy, white flowers are produced in spring in erect to spreading racemes; they consist of five, obovate petals and numerous stamens. Fully hardy. Grow in sun or dappled shade. Prune after flowering if necessary, to reduce overcrowding or to remove weak growths. Propagate by simple layering, by removal of rooted suckers, or by seed sown in fall. Alternatively, increase by semiripe cuttings in a closed case, or basal softwood cuttings in spring—these should be wounded and treated with hormone rooting preparation, and grown under mist or in a closed case with bottom heat.

E. giraldii China; to 10 ft (3 m), spreading; flowers to 1 in (2.5 cm) diameter in racemes to 3 in (8 cm); *E.* × *macrantha* (*E. korolkowii* × *E. racemosa*); erect to 6½ ft (2 m); flowers to 1¼ in (3 cm) diameter; includes the popular cultivars 'Irish Pearl' (syn. 'The Pearl'), with very long, spreading flowering shoots, leaves pale green above and tinted blue-gray beneath, and 'The Bride', compact with arching to spreading branches, pea green leaves and large flowers produced in great abundance; *E. racemosa* China; to 10 ft (3 m); flowers to 1½ in (4 cm) diameter, in racemes to 4 in (10 cm) long.

exotic a plant that has been introduced from its natural habitat into a different habitat. The term is often loosely used for showy tropical specimens, but it is not necessarily linked to hardiness.

explanate spread out, flat.

explant in micropropagation, a tiny portion of a plant which is inserted in an aseptic growing medium.

exserted obviously projecting or extending beyond the organs or parts that surround it—for example, stamens that stick out from the corolla; cf. *included*.

extension shoot, extension growth a shoot, especially on a fruit tree, which has been selected to extend the branch framework. It is more often called a leader.

extra- prefix meaning outside; for example extra-floral, outside the flower proper.

extrorse turned or facing outward, often indicating the dehiscence of an anther; cf. *introrse*.

Chitting seed potatoes
The "eyes" or latent buds on a potato may be invisible until the stimulus of light causes them to develop and sprout.

eye (1) a latent growth bud, especially on tubers such as potatoes; (2) the center of a flower when it is colored differently from the rest, as in many pinks, pansies, auriculas and delphiniums; (3) the center of primula flowers, which may be described as pin-eyed or thrum-eyed according to whether the stigma or stamens are visible at the top of the corolla tube. See *heterostyly*.

F

F1 the first-generation progeny of a cross. The F1 hybrid relates to seed derived from two highly selected, inbred parent lines and is of particular value in vegetables and flowers, for the desirable characteristics of uniformity, vigor, and high yield. F1 hybrids will not breed true from their own seed.

F2 the progeny from self- or cross-pollinated F1 plants. They are less uniform and vigorous than their parents, but often have desirable characteristics.

Fabiana (for Francisco Fabian y Fuero [1719–1801], Spanish botanist). Solanaceae. Warm temperate S America. Some 25 species, heathlike, evergreen shrubs. Borne in early summer, the flowers are tubular with a limb of five short lobes. Hardy to about 23°F (–5°C) if given a sheltered position at the base of a warm, south-facing wall. Plant in sun in light, well-drained soil. Prune in spring to shape straggly older plants. Propagate from seed sown in a sandy medium in spring, or by greenwood cuttings rooted with gentle bottom heat in summer. *F. imbricata* Chile; erect to 6½ ft (2 m) with many short, downy lateral branches and minute, dark green, overlapping leaves; flowers to ⅝ in (1.5 cm) long, white to rose, pale mauve to blue-violet in f. *violacea*.

facultative saprophyte a pathogen that can grow on dead organic matter as well as on living hosts; cf. *obligate parasite*.

Fagus (the Classical name for this tree). Fagaceae. Northern temperate regions. BEECH. 10 species, deciduous trees, usually with smooth, gray bark, slender young shoots, and narrowly ellipsoid buds. Oblong to elliptic or ovate, the leaves are alternate, 2-ranked, entire to dentate and shiny. Small, male flowers are borne in slen-der-stalked heads. The female flowers give rise to cuplike, thinly woody casings, often covered in soft spines and splitting open in four sections to release small, chestnut-brown triangular nuts.

The following species are hardy and tolerant of most fertile, well-drained soils and sites. However, they perform poorly in coastal exposures and drought-stricken areas. They make fine specimen trees for large gardens; *F. sylvatica* is also an excellent hedge plant, and will retain its withered foliage in winter if juvenility is simulated by pruning. The US and Chinese species may grow only slowly in the cool summers of Britain while doing well in the eastern US. Propagate as for *Quercus*, although the seeds are a little more tolerant of drying, and seedlings do not produce a taproot. Plant out at 2–4 years old and 12–24 in (30–60 cm) tall. Seed should be from extensive single-species stands or wild-collected if identity is to be guaranteed. Cultivars are grafted on seedlings of *F. sylvatica*. Young trees are shade-tolerant and need shelter for the first few years; on open ground, they may be damaged by frost.

F. grandifolia (syn. *F. americana*) AMERICAN BEECH; eastern N America; to 120 ft (35 m) tall; leaves 2½–6 in (6–15 cm), obovate to oblong, serrate, blue-green above, paler beneath, turning golden in fall; *F. orientalis* ORIENTAL BEECH; SE Europe to W Asia; to 130 ft (40 m); leaves 3–6½ in (8–17 cm), elliptic-oblong to obovate, dentate, dark green turning yellow in fall; *F. sylvatica* EUROPEAN BEECH; Europe; to 160 ft (48 m) leaves 2–4½ in (5–11 cm), elliptic-ovate, wavy-edged, pale and softly downy at first, becoming deep, glossy green and turning yellow to rusty brown in fall; includes var. *heterophylla* f. *laciniata*, CUT- OR FERN-LEAF BEECH, with deeply cut leaves; 'Pendula', WEEPING BEECH, with strongly weeping branches, and Atropurpurea Group, COPPER BEECH, with purple-bronze leaves; cultivars are available which display these traits in combination—for example, 'Rohanii' with deeply cut, purple leaves; two further important trends in variation are represented by clones with yellow new foliage—for example. 'Aurea Pendula', 'Zlatia', GOLDEN BEECH—and by clones with strongly fastigiate habit, such as 'Dawyck', DAWYCK BEECH, the purple-leaved 'Dawyck Purple' and the purple-, cut-leaved 'Rohan Obelisk').

fairy ring a ring of toadstools formed in lawns by fruiting bodies of a number of fungi. In the UK, fairy rings are most commonly formed by *Marasmius oreades*. The ring of dead grass at the edge of the circle is usually surrounded by rings of darker green grass, which benefit from nutrients produced by fungal activity. Fungicides may be applied after spiking and dethatching the turf, subject to local pesticide regulations. Removal of infected soil is also effective.

falcate strongly curved sideways, resembling a scythe or sickle.

fall in irises, the outer petaloid perianth segments, which may be pendulous or horizontal in presentation. It is a prominent feature of bearded irises.

Fallopia (for Gabriele Fallopi [1523–62], Italian anatomist) Polygonaceae. W China, Tadzhikistan. 7 species of hardy, woody-based, climbing or scrambling perennials. Leaves simple, entire, alternate, triangular or ovate; inflorescences large panicles of small, funnel shaped, white tinged-pink flowers, in summer. *F. baldschuanicum* MILE-A-MINUTE VINE, SILVER FLEA VINE. E. Europe, Iran; rampant twining woody vine to 50 ft (15 m); leaves 1¼–4 in (3-10 cm), ovate to ovate oblong, apex acute, slightly cordate at base; flower 6-8 mm across in broad drooping panicles, white tinged pink in time; late summer—fall, followed by small, angled pinkish-white fruits. Rampant grower, challenging to control. Successful on most sites in sun or part shade. Require sturdy support. Propagate from seed in spring or semi-ripe heel or hardwood cuttings. Various forms occur; a quite common less woody variant, with smaller flowers, frequently cataloged as *F. aubertii* , is now regarded as botanically synonymous. *F. japonica* JAPANESE KNOTWEED, MEXICAN BAMBOO; Japan, massive, freely suckering rhizomatous perennial to 6 ft (2 m); stems stout, canelike, branched above; leaves broadly ovate, acuminate, base truncate, 2½–4¾ in (6–12 cm); panicles axillary; flowers cream-white; 'Spectabile': leaves red later marbled with yellow. See also *Japanese knotweed*.)

fallow the practice of leaving ground clear of crops for a period, either short-term in the course of natural rotation, or long-term in preparing a site. A fallow period benefits soil structure by allowing weathering. It can reduce soilborne pests because the lack of cover gives predators easier access to prey; it is also a good opportunity for weed removal.

false fruit a fruit in which the receptacle, and not the ovary, forms the most conspicuous part, e.g., a strawberry.

family the principal category of taxa between order and genus, e.g., Rosaceae, the rose family. The names of most families derive from that of the type genus (in the above example, *Rosa*) and are plural nouns ending in *aceae*. Exceptions to this include Palmae, Gramineae, Leguminosae, Umbelliferae; these have modern equivalents in Arecaceae, Poaceae, Fabaceae and Apiaceae, respectively.

family tree in fruit cultivation, a tree comprising two or more cultivars grafted onto a common framework. The concept is of ancient origin and depicted in Greek and Roman records. Besides providing garden interest as a novelty feature, a family tree offers one possible solution where growing space is limited. The occurrence of cross-compatible, simultaneous flowering of more than one cultivar on the same tree facilitates successful pollination and good fruit set. Family trees of apples and pears are formed by multiple grafting dormant scion shoots, of different cultivars of the same fruit, onto a very young tree raised preferably on a dwarfing rootstock. For open-ground family apples, suitable rootstocks are the semidwarfing M26 and dwarfing M9. The very dwarfing M27 is suitable for trees grown in large containers. For pears, the semidwarfing Quince C rootstock is an acceptable choice for grafting more than one cultivar.

fan a form of trained tree with branches radiating from a short stem like the ribs of a fan. This method of training is most often used for peaches, nectarines, and apricots, and sometimes for plums, cherries, and bush fruits suitable for planting against a wall.

fancy (1) flowers, especially carnations, that have variegated markings, as opposed to those of a single color known as selfs; (2) a 19th-century term denoting a particular pursuit, especially the art of breeding and showing specific plants—the specialist being called a fancier; (3) a term used of names published in accordance with the *International Code of Nomenclature for Cultivated Plants* and applied to cultivars, grexes and hybrids. It is invariably formed in a vernacular language, not Latin—for example, *Lupinus* 'Loveliness', *Heuchera* 'Palace Purple'.

Farfugium (name used by Pliny). Compositae. E Asia. 2 species, rhizomatous, evergreen perennial herbs with long-stalked leaves in clumps, their blades rounded to fan-shaped and broad. Daisylike flower heads are borne in loose corymbs. Hardy to 14°F (−10°C), and a fine foliage plant for pond and stream margins, Japanese gardens, and partly shaded terraces. Plant in full or dappled sun on a moist, fertile soil. Increase by division in early spring. *F. japonicum* (syn. *Ligularia kaempferi*, *Ligularia tussilaginea*, *Tussilago japonica*) Japan; leaves to 12 in (30 cm) across, long-stalked and rounded to kidney-shaped, toothed to entire, thick-textured, dark green; flower heads yellow, to 2½ in (6 cm) across, inflorescences to 30 in (75 cm) tall; includes 'Argenteum' with leaves stippled and blotched gray-green and cream on deep green, and 'Aureomaculatum', with leaves spotted yellow.

Fargesia (for Paul Guillame Farges [1844–1912], French missionary and naturalist in Central China). Gramineae. China, Himalaya. Some 40 species of clumping bamboos; see *bamboos*.

farina a powdery or mealy coating on the stems, leaves, and sometimes flowers of certain plants.

farinose, farinaceous floury, having a mealy, granular texture.

fasciation see *malformation*.

Distorted, flattened flower stem

Fasciation

fascicle a cluster or bundle of flowers, racemes, leaves, stems, or roots, almost always independent but appearing to arise from a common point.

Fascicularia (from Latin *fasciculus*, a small bundle, alluding to the growth habit). Bromeliaceae. Chile. 5 species, low, evergreen, perennial herbs with rigid, narrow, and spiny-toothed leaves in a dense, flat, and stemless rosette. In summer and fall, small flowers are carried in a dense, headlike spike—these are embedded in the rosette center and surrounded by spiny and often colorful bracts. Hardy to 10°F (−12°C), with full sun and a warm, perfectly drained position such as in raised borders on south-facing walls, dry, sheltered rock gardens, and xeriscapes. Plant in slightly acidic soil rich in sand and grit. Increase by rooted offsets in late spring. *F. bicolor* (leaves to 20 in (50 cm), deep green covered with silver scales, those at the center of the rosette turning bright scarlet at flowering time; flowers small, blue, amid red to white bracts.

fastigiate describing the habit of trees and shrubs that have a strongly erect, narrow crown, and branches virtually parallel with the main stem.

father plant the pollen parent of a hybrid.

× **Fatshedera** (*Fatsia japonica* 'Moseri' × *Hedera hibernica*). Araliaceae. Garden origin. × *F. lizei* is an evergreen shrub of loose sprawling habit, to 4 ft (1.2 m) tall with palmately and deeply 5-lobed, dark lustrous green leaves to 8 in (20 cm) across. Small and sterile, the green-white flowers are borne in umbellate panicles in late summer and fall. Cultivars include 'Annemieke' with yellow-variegated leaves, 'Pia', with wavy leaves, and the cream-marked 'Variegata'. Hardy to about 5°F (−15°C). Grow in sun or shade. Although not self-clinging like its *Hedera*

X Fatshedera lizei
Characteristics of both parents, one *Fatsia* and the other *Hedera*, or ivy, can clearly be seen in both the foliage and the habit of this hybrid evergreen shrub.

parent, it does show a slight tendency to climb and may be tied to a trellis, pillars, or other supports; it is also useful as a conservatory or houseplant. Specimens with single, straight, clean stems make excellent stocks for standard ivy "trees"—take an upright, 16–40-in- (40–100-cm-) tall × *Fatshedera* and remove leaves, branches, and apex before cutting deeply and cleanly crosswise into the tip; then insert two or four scions of *Hedera*, bind the wound, and grow in warm, sheltered conditions. Increase by greenwood cuttings in summer.

Fatsia (from the Japanese name of *F. japonica*, *Fatsi*). Araliaceae. E Asia (Japan, Taiwan, Bonin Islands), introduced Hawaii. 3 species, evergreen shrubs or small trees with stout, usually sparsely branched stems and foliage crowded toward branch tips. The leaves are large, leathery, and palmately lobed. Small, 5-petaled flowers are borne in umbels on the branches of a large panicle, and are followed by small, drupaceous fruits. Hardy to 23°F (−5°C), although in cold areas it should be given the protection of a south- or west-facing wall. It is an excellent choice for sheltered city gardens. The more compact and variegated cultivars are slightly less frost-hardy and demand richer soil and part shade in the garden. In colder areas, it is also grown in the home or conservatory, where it prefers cool, humid

conditions. Grow in sun or part shade. Prune to remove lax growth or leggy stems. Propagate from seed sown at 59–68°F (15–20°C) in fall, by air-layering or by greenwood cuttings (with all but one leaf removed) rooted with bottom heat in summer. Root cuttings will also succeed. *F. japonica* (syn. *Aralia japonica*) JAPANESE ARALIA; Japan; shrub to 16 ft (5 m), with widely spreading, sparsely branched stems becoming bare below; leaves to 20 × 16 in (50 × 40 cm), with 7–11, oblong-elliptic, toothed lobes, dark glossy green above, long-stalked; flowers creamy white in rounded umbels along the branches of a loosely pyramidal panicle to 32 in (80 cm) long, produced in fall; fruits small, black; includes 'Aurea', with gold-variegated leaves, 'Marginata', with gray-green leaves edged off-white, 'Moseri', compact and vigorous, and the white-edged 'Variegata'.

Faucaria (from Latin *fauces*, jaw: the toothed leaves resemble gaping jaws). Aizoaceae. TIGER JAWS. South Africa. 30 species, succulent, almost stemless perennials. The fleshy leaves are decussate and spread outward; in outline they are rhombic, spathulate, or broadly lanceolate, often with a flattened upper surface fringed with ferocious-looking marginal teeth. The underside is deeper, resembling the keel and prow of a ship. Large, daisy-like flowers open during the afternoon from late summer to late fall. Cultivate as for *Conophytum*, although these plants are more robust and will take sporadic and sparing waterings throughout the spring and summer; the leaves usually persist for several seasons. *F. tigrina* leaves 1¼–2 in (3–5 cm), margins with 10 hair-tipped teeth, gray-green with numerous, small dots; flowers yellow.

faveolate, favose honey-combed.

feathered (1) a maiden or first-year tree with a slender upright trunk bearing a number of lateral growths or feathers; hence "feathered maiden"; (2) in flowers, especially tulips, referring to featherlike markings of one color upon a different ground color; (3) leaf surfaces where the veins or color markings spring from a central rib; hence feather-veined.

feather-veined describing leaves whose veins all arise pinnately from a single midrib.

fedge a composite word from fence and hedge, denoting a garden feature that consists of a fence or net-clad structure up which mostly climbing or scrambling plants are grown to form a screen.

Felicia (for Herr Felix [d. 1846], German official). Compositae. Tropical & South Africa, Arabia. BLUE MARGUERITE, BLUE DAISY, KINGFISHER DAISY. 83 species, annual to perennial herbs, dwarf subshrubs and shrubs with long-stalked, daisylike flower heads in summer, the ray florets blue, mauve, pink, or white, and the disk florets yellow. Suitable for bedding, baskets, containers, and rock gardens. Plant in full sun in well-drained soil. Both species listed here are killed by hard frost and wet conditions. Remove dead flower heads and trim back any weak growth. Increase by seed sown under glass in spring, or, for *F. amelloides*, by cuttings taken in late summer or fall and overwintered under glass.

F. amelloides BLUE DAISY, BLUE MARGUERITE; South Africa; bright green, perennial subshrub to 24 in (60 cm); stems slender, trailing to erect; flower heads to 1½ in (4 cm) diameter, long-stalked, ray florets pale blue; includes 'Santa Anita', with large, clear blue flower heads, and the cream-blotched 'Santa Anita Variegata'; *F. bergeriana* KINGFISHER DAISY; South Africa; hairy, gray-green annual herb to 10 in (25 cm) tall, forming bushy mats; flower heads to 1¼ in (3 cm) diameter, short-stalked, ray florets bright blue.

felted-tomentose tomentose, but more woolly and matted, the hairs curling and closely adpressed to the surface.

fence a barrier constructed of wood, or sometimes plastic, in contrast to walls of brick or stone. There is a wide choice of fence designs including close-boarded, interwoven, weather-boarded, split chestnut, and planed paling, rustic, wattle and trellis. Some are

F

available as prefabricated panels 6 ft (1.8 m) wide.

Fenestraria (from Latin *fenestra*, window, referring to the translucent leaf tips of this genus). Aizoaceae. Namibia. 2 species, succulent, evergreen perennial herbs. Smooth and fleshy, the leaves are ¾–1½ in (2–4 cm) long, mid- to dark green and stand erect in stemless clusters. Each leaf is club-shaped, expanding upward to a flattened or domed tip with a translucent zone, or "window." Daisy-like flowers appear in late summer and fall. Cultivation as for *Conophytum*. In habitat, these plants grow with only their leaf tips showing, but they are best cultivated with their leaves largely exposed.

F. aurantiaca flowers 1¼–2¾ in (3–7 cm) in diameter, golden yellow; *F. rhopalophylla* BABY'S TOES; flowers ¾ in–1¼ in (1.8–3 cm) in diameter, white.

fenestrate irregularly perforated by numerous openings or translucent zones (windows).

aniseed-scented foliage

edible "bulb" (swollen leaf bases)

Florence fennel

fennel (*Foeniculum vulgare*) a native of Europe, including coastal parts of Britain. COMMON FENNEL (*F. vulgare*) is a perennial grown for its aniseed-flavored leaves and leaf sheaths, which are used in salads, meat, and fish dishes, and for its seeds, which are used in baking, fish dishes, and herbal tea. Sow *in situ* outdoors after the risk of frost has passed, or divide existing plants in spring and set out at final spacings of 12–14 in (30–35 cm). *F.* 'Purpureum' is an attractive border

plant. *F. vulgare* var. *azoricum*, FLORENCE FENNEL or FINNOCHIO, is cultivated as an annual. It is smaller than *F. vulgare* and is grown for the succulent, swollen, aniseed-flavored bases of the leaf stalks, which are served fresh in salads or cooked; the foliage can be used as flavoring. Sow May–June *in situ* for thinning, or raise in cell modules for transplanting no later than the 3–4-leaf stage to final spacings of 12 in (30 cm), in rows 20 in (50 cm) apart. For transplanting under glass to extend the cropping season, choose bolt-resistant cultivars and sow in mid-July–early August.

ferns any of a group of plants belonging to the division Pteridophyta, prominent in the Earth's vegetation for millions of years; their fossilized form is the origin of the vast coal deposits that were laid down in the Carboniferous period. Ferns are established widely in temperate zones, are prolific and dominant in the tropics and are absent only in extremely cold or dry regions. They occur at altitudes from sea level up to 14,500 ft (4,400 m), the majority in wet climates from humid lowland jungle to highland cloud forests. Their lightweight spores are carried very long distances on air currents, and local adaptations arise. Ferns have long been used for medicinal purposes including disorders of the spleen, hence the common name spleenwort.

Exotic ferns have been grown in England for display since 1628, when specimens were imported by John Tradescant from Virginia to his garden in Lambeth, London. Interest in their cultivation increased in the late 18th century with the development of reliable techniques for raising fresh spores, giving rise to a spectacular popularity which peaked in the Victorian "Pteridomania." This in turn gave rise to widespread plundering of native habitats, particularly in Britain. The fashion for fern cultivation diminished from the late 19th century, and between the two world wars, collections declined, with an estimated 60% loss of old collected variants.

There exist between 230 and 250 genera, including 10–12,000 species, from greatly diverse environments. Ferns are grown for the elegant and

delicate symmetry of their fronds, for textural contrasts, and for color—for example, the beautifully colored emerging croziers of *Adiantum* and *Blechnum* species, the fall color of *Osmunda regalis*, and the metallic sheen on the emergent fronds of *Pityrogramma*, and *Cheilanthes* species. Variegated sports are established in cultivation (e.g., *Pteris* cultivars), as are cristate forms. Aromatic fronds are produced in some *Pityrogramma* and *Dryopteris* species. Hardy ferns are valuable for shady areas and are undemanding except for requiring moisture; some, like *Dryopteris filix-mas* and *Blechnum penna-marina*, are useful groundcover plants. In New Zealand, *Dicksonia squarrosa* is used to stabilize roadside banks. They have few culinary uses since many ferns contain carcinogens, but the steamed croziers of *Matteuccia struthiopteris* and *Osmunda cinnamomea* are eaten for their asparagus-like flavor, and the soft pith of *Cyathea* species may be baked or roasted.

Successful fern cultivation requires an understanding of the three types of natural habitat. (1) Woodland or rainforest ferns are native to the herbaceous understory and will grow in dappled, sometimes total shade with medium to high levels of humidity. Rooting is usually shallow. These include taller forest plants such as the tree ferns *Dicksonia* and *Cyathea* and epiphytes such as *Platycerium*, as well as climbers (e.g., *Lygodium* species), hemiepiphytes, and many of the hardy, woodland species familiar to gardeners. (2) Ferns of rocky, more exposed conditions or of subalpine meadows, such as *Cryptogramma* and *Woodsia* species, may be treated as alpine subjects, either in an alpine house or on walls and dry rockeries. The group includes high-altitude species naturally subject to snow cover and long periods of freezing, and subjects that encounter scree, rock crevice, wet rocky grassland, or stream and waterfall overhangs. Their light requirements may be higher but a moist, shaded root run is essential. (3) Natives of arid or semiarid zones with limited seasonal rainfall include the 'Resurrection Ferns' of the New World, such as *Cheilanthes* species, which regenerate from shriveled growth. Such species may grow on exposed ground,

Osmunda regalis
The magnificent royal fern is especially striking in spring when its crook-shaped young fronds first begin to uncoil.

rock ledges, scree, gullies and crevices; in cultivation, they require alpine house or rock garden conditions.

Growing regimens reflect these different habitats. In cool temperate zones, tropical ferns should be treated as greenhouse or indoor subjects, requiring a minimum temperature of 64°F (18°C), high humidity with frequent dampening in the summer months, indirect sunlight from midspring to midfall, and direct sunlight at other times. Warm-temperate ferns should be grown indoors or in a glasshouse, with a minimum temperature of 55°F (13°C), medium humidity and bright filtered sunlight. Cool temperates should be grown in cool greenhouses (minimum temperature 45°F/7°C), indoors or in a sunless position outdoors, with medium humidity. Alpine, nonhardy ferns require cold, frost-free greenhouse conditions: dampen down and ventilate when the temperature exceeds 68°F (20°C), and shade and water plentifully in summer. Moderate watering and frequent misting are essential if grown indoors. In centrally heated rooms, tropical and subtropical species are the best choice. For a cool room, choose cool temperate types, mist occasionally, and water moderately in summer and sparingly in winter. Ferns are well adapted to thrive indoors in low light levels placed away from drafts. Repot every other year and feed at 14-day intervals during the growing season with an organically based fertilizer.

Potting media for ferns should be free-draining and enriched with organic matter. Most species prefer a slightly acidic medium of pH 6–6.5, though there are other preferences, such as a very alkaline mix for the limestone polypody, *Gynnocarpium robertianum*. For terrestrial temperate and tropical ferns, a suitable mix is 1 part loam: 2 parts sharp sand: 3 parts leaf mold: 1 part medium grade forest bark, with hoof-and-horn added. For epiphytic ferns, use 1 part fine-grade bark: 1 part charcoal: 1 part perlite, and mount to establish on slabs of cork or tree-fern fiber with a pad of sphagnum moss. Aquatic ferns are grown in ponds, aquariums, or slow-moving water, where potted plants should be in a medium that is low in organic matter to avoid fermentation. Hardy ferns for the garden include *Adiantum, Asplenium, Athyrium, Blechnum, Dicksonia, Dryopteris, Gymnocarpium, Matteuccia, Onoclea, Osmunda, Polypodium, Polystichum* and *Woodsia*.

Some ferns are propagated from active or dormant bulbils and plantlets (e.g., *Asplenium bulbiferum*), or from offsets (e.g., *Dicksonia* species); others by air-layering (e.g., *Davallia* species) and by stem propagation (e.g., *Lycopodium* species).

Most ferns, however, are propagated by division or from spores. Division of plants should take place in spring. Ensure that basal roots are included, shallowly potted and kept in warm, moist conditions. Reproduction by spores entails a cycle in which two generations (sporophyte and gametophyte) lead an independent existence, each requiring different cultural conditions. The mature fern plant (sporophyte) develops specialized spore-producing structures on the underside of its leaves. Spores germinate under damp shady conditions to produce a flattened plate of cells called a prothallus (gametophyte), on the underside of which male and female structures arise to facilitate fertilization. Cross-fertilization of these organs results in the development of new sporophytes—the "ferns" we know and grow.

Spores of temperate and hardy ferns are generally long-lasting and those of tropical habitats short-lived. Successful raising from spores requires the careful sterilization of the sowing area before the spores are sown. Use a sterile mixture of equal parts peat and sharp sand, and surface sow in sterilized clay pots covered with a sheet of glass. Hardy and temperate species are maintained at 59–61°F (15–16°C) and tropical species at 70°F (21°C). The pots should be stood in shade in ½ in (1 cm) depth of water to maintain a moist medium for the prothalli—these will usually form after a few weeks. They resemble fragile liverworts or mosses. If very crowded, they may be separated into small blocks using a sterile scalpel and replanted with space around them in larger pans. Again, keep moist and covered and grow on in shade. Young sporophytes will develop within a period ranging from two weeks to several months. Once they fill the pot, they may be carefully moved on to a fine, soilless medium and raised in shade with humidity.

Possible problems: aphids, scale insects; rust.

fern-case a glazed container, sometimes of bellglass form, used to protect ferns grown indoors from dry air and drafts. It is akin to a *Wardian case* (q.v.).

fernery a place devoted to the cultivation of ferns. It may be a greenhouse, fern-case or, as featured in Victorian gardens, an outdoor area where ferns are placed among rocks, tree stumps, and roots.

fern-leaf a descriptive term for the narrow and elongated leaves of tomatoes infected with tobacco or cucumber mosaic viruses.

Ferocactus (from Latin *ferox*, fierce, and Cactus). Cactaceae. SW US, Mexico. BARREL CACTUS. 23 species, large cacti with simple or clustered, squat and rounded to barrel-shaped or cylindric stems covered in ribs and fierce spines. The flowers are bell- to funnel-shaped. Provide a minimum temperature of 36–40°F (2–5°C). Grow in a gritty, slightly acidic to neutral medium in full sun with low humidity. Keep dry from midfall until early spring, except for light misting on warm days in late winter. Propagate by seed. *F. chrysacanthus* NW Mexico; stem globose to shortly cylindric, to 40 × 12 in (100 × 30 cm), spines to 2 in (5 cm), yellow or red, flattened and twisted; flowers yellow to orange with red-tinted midveins to tepals; *F. cylindraceus* (syn. *F. acanthodes* of gardens) NW Mexico, SW US; stem to 10 ft × 20 in (3 m × 50 cm), cylindric or barrel-shaped, spines 2¾–6½ in (7–16 cm) long, red, orange or yellow, sometimes hooked; flowers tinged green yellow or red; *F. hamatacanthus* (syn. *Hamatocactus hamatacanthus*) N Mexico, SW US; stems to 24 × 12 in (60 × 30 cm), hemispheric to cylindric, spines to 3 in (8 cm), some hooked; flowers to 4 in (10 cm), yellow; *F. latispinus* C & S Mexico; stems 4–16 in × 6–16 in (10–40 cm × 16–40 cm), squatly globose or flattened; spines flattened; flowers purple-pink or yellow; *F. wislizeni* SW US, NW Mexico; stem 5½–10 ft (1.6–3 m) × 18–32 in (45–80 cm), globose to barrel-shaped or cylindric, tapering above, spines to 4 in (10 cm), brown to gray, the lowermost usually flattened and hooked; flowers to yellow, orange or red.

Ferraria (for Giovanni Battista Ferrari [1584–1655], Italian botanist). Iridaceae. Tropical and South Africa. 10 species, small, cormous perennial herbs with sword-shaped leaves. Produced in spring and summer, the flowers are short-lived, often malodorous and composed of six, radiating and ovate to lanceolate segments. Hardy to about 23°F (–5°C). Plant 6 in (15 cm) deep in a warm, sunny and sheltered site with a protective mulch of bracken litter in winter. Where grown under glass, they are best planted directly into the greenhouse border, or else in deep pots. Grow in direct sunlight in a well-drained potting mix with additional sharp sand; maintain a minimum temperature of 50°F (10°C) in spring and summer. Reduce watering after flowering until leaves wither; keep completely dry and frost-free when dormant. Propagate by seed sown in late summer or fall, or by offsets in fall. *F. crispa* (syn. *F. undulata*) South Africa; to 18 in (45 cm); flowers to 2 in (5 cm) diam., deep, velvety chestnut with cream to white markings at center, spotted and lined in a paler shade, or yellow to tan spotted and lined dark maroon, margins wavy to crisped.

ferrous sulfate a constituent of lawn sand and other moss-killer products. It is sometimes recommended as a corrective treatment for iron deficiency in plants.

Digitalis ferruginea
This foxglove takes its species name from the rusty, or ferruginous, hue to its flowers, quite unlike the usual pinks and purples.

ferruginous brown-red, rust-colored.

fertile (1) producing viable seed; describes anthers containing functional pollen, flowers with active pistils, fruit bearing seeds and of spore-bearing fern fronds; (2) used to describe a flower-bearing shoot.

fertility (1) of soil; its suitability to support good plant growth. Soil fertility is influenced by drainage, physical structure and the presence of organic matter, lime, and nutrients; (2) of plants; the capacity to produce viable seeds, in which an important factor is self- or cross-compatibility of pollen.

fertilization (1) the union of male and female sexual cells (gametes), resulting in a unicellular zygote from which an embryo develops; see *cross-fertilization*, *pollination*, *self-fertilization*; (2) (in the US) the use of fertilizers.

fertilizer correctly, any material that provides plant nutrients in relatively concentrated form, as opposed to bulky manure, although the terms fertilizer and manure are often used loosely and interchangeably. Fertilizers can be of organic or inorganic origin, produced naturally or synthetically, and may be formulated as powder, granules, or liquid. The concentration of nutrients is stated on containers as a percentage; for compounded products containing the three primary nutrients, this will be expressed in code form, thus 7–7–10 indicates 7% nitrogen, 7% phosphate and 10% potassium. The higher the percentage, the greater the concentration of nutrient per unit of weight; see *compound fertilizer*; *slow-release*; *straight fertilizer*.

Ferula (Latin name for fennel). Umbelliferae. Mediterranean to C Asia. GIANT FENNEL. 172 species, robust perennial herbs arising from a thick rootstock. The leaves are finely divided into very narrow segments. Small, yellow or yellow-white flowers are carried in large, compound umbels in late spring and summer. Suitable for a large herbaceous and mixed border, or for waterside plantings and hardy to at least 23°F (–5°C). Grow in moist, deep and fertile soils in sun. They do not transplant well and should be given permanent positions when young. Mulch thickly in winter. Propagate by fresh seed in late summer, or by careful division. This is not the edible fennel, for which see *Foeniculum*. *F. communis* GIANT FENNEL; Mediterranean; 6½–10 ft (2–3 m) tall; leaves mid-green with threadlike segments; flowers yellow; giant, bronze- and purple-leaved forms are sometimes grown.

festooning the bending of shoots or branches of fruit trees into a more horizontal position by means of weights or ties; it is also practiced on some ornamentals. Festooning is done to control vigor or stimulate flowering, and is employed especially in the arcure form of training.

Festuca (from Latin *festuca*, stalk or stem; in Pliny, the wild oat growing among barley). Gramineae. Cosmopolitan (mainly cold and temperate regions). FESCUE. Some 300 species, rhizomatous or tufted perennial grasses up to 6½ ft (2 m), usually very much shorter, with flat, folded or involute leaves. The species described below are ornamental, valued for the attractive, often brilliant blue-greens of the low, hairlike foliage tussocks. Most are tolerant of cold to at least 5°F (–15°C), although many do not tolerate heavy snow cover or prolonged winter rain. Plant in light, well-drained soil in full sun. Clip over in spring to encourage dense fresh foliage; divide and replant older plants. Propagate by division or seed, although species hybridize readily and may not come true from seed.

F. eskia Europe; densely tufted, forming a low tussock or thatch of very slender dark green leaves to 3 in (8 cm) long; *F. glauca* BLUE FESCUE, GRAY FESCUE; Europe; densely tufted, forming a tussock, cushion or mop of very slender leaves to 4¾ in (12 cm) long; these are typically glaucous blue-green; a varied and confused group with many cultivars, some of which doubtless belong to other species, for example, *F. cinerea*, *F. ovina*, its blue-gray subspecies *coxii*, and *F. rubra*—they range in habit from relatively tall, loose and spilling to dense and compact, and in color from deep green to bronze-red-tinted, sea green, and blue-green to silver-gray.

fibrillate finely striated or fibrous.

fibrillose with threadlike fibers or scales.

fibrous (1) a threadlike, woody texture; (2) refers to plant roots produced as a mass of fine growth, in contrast to fewer coarse or fleshy roots; (3) describes loam with a high content of fiber derived from dead grass roots and rotted turf.

Ficus (Latin name for the edible fig). Moraceae. Tropics and subtropics. FIG. About 800 species, deciduous or evergreen trees, shrubs and woody root-climbing vines (those listed below are usually evergreen in cultivation, except *F. carica*). Their growth habits and foliage vary enormously from species to species, although all show the characteristic protective stipule which encloses the new growth in a rolled, pointed tube. This falls away as the leaves emerge, leaving a ringlike scar. The minute flowers are embedded on the inner surface of a fleshy receptacle (the "fig," or syconium). This may be large or small, rounded, pear-shaped or oblong, but is usually—if tautologously—"fig-shaped." Pollination is effected by various genera of wasps, which are specially adapted to enter the syconium through the tight aperture at its apex and lay their eggs within.

With the exception of *F. carica*, the following species require a minimum temperature of 50°F (10°C), bright, indirect light and medium to high humidity. Some, however, survive in less than ideal conditions and show remarkable tolerance of drought, dry air and harsh light, especially when pressed into service as houseplants and staples of the interior landscaper's art; most notable among these are *F. benjamina*, *F. binnendykii* 'Amstelveen', *F. deltoidea*, the ubiquitous rubber plant, *F. elastica*, and *F. lyrata*. The climbing species listed below make excellent houseplants when young and still creeping—small specimens of *F. pumila* are very commonly used to cascade over the rims of mixed planters. Plant in a fertile, porous, soil-free medium. Water, syringe and feed generously during summer or when temperatures are high. At other times, keep just moist and protect from drafts. Propagate by stem cuttings, air-layering, or, for climbing species, by detaching rooted lengths of stem. For cultivation of *F. carica*, see FIG below.

F. benghalensis BANYAN TREE; S Asia; evergreen tree to 100 ft (30 m), ultimately with many stem buttresses and massive aerial roots; leaves to 10 in (25 cm), broadly ovate, base rounded to cordate, apex blunt or briefly tapered, leathery, mid- to dark green; 'Krishnae': leaves cuplike with inrolled, fused margins; *F. benjamina* WEEPING FIG; S Asia to Australia and Pacific; graceful evergreen shrub or tree to 100 ft (3 m), branches weeping; leaves to 5 in (13 cm), ovate-lanceolate, cuspidate, thinly leathery, dark green; includes dwarf, strongly weeping and bushy clones with foliage ranging from large and long to short and tufted, some variegated white, cream, gray or gold; *F. binnendykii* (NARROW-LEAF FIG; SE Asia; evergreen shrub or tree to 65 ft (20 m), branches somewhat weeping; leaves to 8 in (20 cm), pendulous, narrowly lanceolate, tip finely pointed, tough; the cultivar usually grown is 'Amstelveen' with narrow, glossy dark green leaves hanging daggerlike; *F. carica* COMMON FIG, BROWN TURKEY FIG; Cyprus, Turkey, Middle East, W Asia; deciduous shrub or tree to 33 ft (10 m); leaves to 12 in (30 cm) with three to five broad lobes, coarsely textured and somewhat downy; fruit to 2 in (5 cm) diam., dull green to brown or deep, glaucous maroon, edible; for cultivars see FIG below; *F. deltoidea* MISTLETOE FIG; SE Asia; evergreen shrub or small tree to 23 ft (7 m); leaves to 3 in (8 cm), broadly spathulate to deltoid, apex rounded, base cuneate, tough, olive to dark green, dull or somewhat glossy; fruits small, inedible, abundant even on young plants; *F. elastica* INDIA RUBBER TREE, RUBBER PLANT; evergreen tree to 200 ft (60 m) with many buttresses and aerial roots, usually seen as a smaller, sparsely unbranched shrub; stipules large, dull coral pink to scarlet; leaves to 16 in (40 cm), oblong to elliptic, tip acuminate or apiculate, tough, somewhat rigid, glossy dark green with a prominent, pale or red midrib; a very popular houseplant, it includes tall, dwarf, rarely branched and bushy clones with leaves ranging from small and broad to long and narrow, some variegated white, gray or creamy yellow or flushed wine red; *F. lyrata* BANJO FIG; Tropical Africa; evergreen tree to 40 ft (12 m); leaves to 20 in (50 cm), obovate to lyrate or pandurate, apex rounded, very tough but flexible, glossy mid-green with corrugated upper surface; *F. macrophylla* AUSTRALIAN BANYAN, MORETON BAY FIG; Australia; evergreen tree to 180 ft (55 m), sometimes developing massive buttresses and aerial roots; leaves to 10 in (25 cm), oblong to elliptic or ovate, tough, glossy dark green above, paler beneath; young plants superficially similar to *F. elastica* but with leaves less leathery; *F. microcarpa* (syn. *F. retusa* of gardens, *F. nitida* of gardens) INDIAN LAUREL, CURTAIN FIG, GLOSSY-LEAF FIG; E Asia to Australia and Pacific; evergreen tree to 100 ft (30 m), ultimately producing many buttresses and festoons of aerial

F

F

roots; leaves to 4¾ in (12 cm), elliptic to obovate, tough, glossy dark green; includes var. *crassifolia* with broad, thickly textured leaves, and dwarf clones with variegated leaves; *F. pumila* CLIMBING FIG, CREEPING FIG; E Asia; evergreen or semideciduous creeping or climbing shrub with matted, slender branches clinging by dense, short aerial roots; leaves ½–2 in (1–5 cm), broadly oblong to elliptic or ovate, thinly leathery with a puckered, papery texture, dark green to bright mid-green; a very popular potted plant with numerous cultivars, the leaves ranging from very small and rounded to broadly toothed or strongly wavy, some variegated white or gold; *F. religiosa* BO TREE, PEEPUL, SACRED FIG; fast-growing, deciduous or semideciduous tree to 33 ft (10 m), sometimes producing buttresses and aerial roots; leaves to 7 in (18 cm), broadly triangular with a finely tapering tip, thinly leathery, rather papery, dull to deep green; *F. rubiginosa* PORT JACKSON; Australia; evergreen tree to 40 ft (12 m); leaves to 7 in (18 cm), oblong to elliptic or ovate, tough, flushed red at first and with rusty hairs beneath, later dark green and smooth; includes cultivars with variegated leaves; *F. sagittata* E Asia; similar in habit to *F. pumila*, but more robust and with larger, cordate to sagittate leaves, the surface not puckered; includes variegated clones; *F. sarmentosa* E Asia; differs from *F. pumila* in its larger leaves, lobed in juvenile plants, lanceolate in adults; includes variegated cultivars.

field capacity the maximum amount of water a freely drained soil will hold before it is lost to drainage by the force of gravity.

field heat heat held by a crop at the time of harvest.

field-immune plants that are not infected by a pathogen under normal growing conditions despite being experimentally susceptible.

fig (*Ficus carica*) a deciduous bush or tree, with large, lobed leaves, grown for its small, rounded, green, maroon or brown colored fruits. One of the

Previous year's fruit, now ripening

Current year's fruit (may not ripen in cool climates)

Stages in fig fruit development

oldest fruits known in cultivation, the fig is believed to originate in the Tajik mountains of Transcaucasia, but has long been native to southwest Asia and the eastern Mediterranean, growing wild in southern Europe and northern Africa. Its cultivation is recorded from 2700 BC. It is valued for its nutritious fruits, which can be dried and stored, and for its use as a shade tree.

The fig was introduced into Britain by the Romans, but there is little evidence of its later cultivation until the 16th century. In the 18th century, new cultivars were introduced from Europe, including 'Brown Naples', later known as 'Brown Turkey' and still the most widely grown cultivar in the UK. By the late 18th century 75 cultivars were grown by the Horticultural Society at Chiswick, the fruit being found to thrive against relatively warm walls and in glasshouses, some with heat. Fig cultivation increased progressively into the 20th century but declined with the great country estates after World War II. Today the fig is grown widely in commercial plantings in California, Turkey, southern Europe and northern Africa, principally for its dried fruit. The ancient cultivar 'Smyrna' is most famous because of its high quality and suitability for drying; in common with older selections, it relies on cross-polli

nation by the small fig wasp (*Blastophaga psenes*) in the process known as caprification. Modern cultivars are self-fertile. In warm climates, goblet-shaped bushes are successful, spaced 20–30 ft (6–9 m) apart with five or six branches quite severely pruned and thinned. In cooler climates, trees are best planted against a south-facing wall as fan-trained specimens: wall protection aids fruit ripening, shields the plant from rain, and provides some safeguard against severe winter weather. Roots should be restricted by constructing a sealed brick-, concrete block- or slab-lined bed, 30 in (75 cm) long and 24 in (60 cm) wide and deep, with the soil base covered by a 12 in (30 cm) layer of rubble. Propagate from suckers, by cuttings or layering. One- or two-year-old specimens are best planted in March or April, when there is no longer a risk of severe frost; position 9 in (22 cm) from the wall with 12 ft (3.6 m) between plants. Train the main ribs so that they are no less than 12 in (30 cm) apart.

Figs can also be grown successfully in 10–14½ in (25–37 cm) pots, provided the base is well-crocked and firmly filled with a soil-based medium. Small bushy trees up to 4¼ ft (1.3 m) should be trained and repotted every second year when dormant, with the old potting mix carefully replaced with a fertile mix. Renew the surface mix in the intervening year, and apply high-potash liquid fertilizer every ten days during summer.

In cooler climates, only one harvest is possible per season outdoors; the crop arises from small pea-sized fruitlets formed toward the end of short laterals from late summer. Frost damage to young fruitlets can be prevented by covering the plants with bracken or some other insulating material after leaf fall, or by moving pot-grown figs under glass. Fruits ripen in late summer or early fall; those fruitlets formed early on new shoots of the current year will not ripen but turn yellow, and should be removed. Regular light pruning and thinning is necessary to contain growth. In late spring, cut out old, damaged wood and any shoots that do not lie on the same plane as the wall; a proportion of the remainder should be cut back near to the main branch to stimulate new growth. Encourage suitable short growths from around midsummer by pinching shoots at the fourth or fifth leaf no later than late June. Water in dry summers, particularly pot- or bed-grown trees, but not near ripening time. Fruit thinning may be necessary in warm climates where a crop may be produced from both overwintered fruits and those initiated early in the current year. Every other fruit may be removed at swelling for improved quality. Fruits are best picked warm, fully ripe, and hanging downward, particularly where showing a longitudinal split and a drop of nectar at the eye. Netting to protect against birds is usually necessary.

Possible problems: scale insects; gray mold, virus.

filament (1) a stalk bearing an anther at its tip, the two forming a stamen; (2) a threadlike or filiform organ, hair or appendage.

filamentous composed of or bearing filaments.

filbert see *hazelnut*.

filial generation a cross-bred generation; hybrid offspring, that of the first crossing being denoted by the symbol F1, the second by F2.

filiform of leaves, branches, etc., filament-like, i.e., long and very slender, rounded in cross-section.

Filipendula (from Latin *filum*, thread, and *pendulus*, drooping, referring to the root tubers of some species, which hang together with threads. Rosaceae. Northern temperate regions. MEADOWSWEET; DROPWORT. 10 species, rhizomatous perennial herbs, sometimes tuberous. The leaves are basal or alternate on erect stems and pinnate, with pairs of large leaflets alternating with smaller ones. The terminal leaflet is largest and coarsely toothed to palmately cut. White or pink and often with contrasting stamens, the small, 5-petaled flowers are borne in great abundance in frothy, cymose corymbs

in spring and summer. They are suitable for streamside and bog garden plantings, for the herbaceous and mixed border, and for moist, cool woodland or other naturalistic plantings. Plant in well-drained but moisture-retentive soils in sun or semishade. With variegated cultivars, removal of young flower shoots will result in successive flushes of fresh, colorful foliage. Propagate by division in fall or winter, or by seed in fall or spring.

F. camtschatica Kamchatka, Korea, Japan; to 10 ft (3 m) tall, hairy; flowers white to pale pink; *F. palmata* Siberia to China and Japan; to 3¼ ft (1 m) tall; flowers white with red anthers; includes cultivars with pure white, pink, red and purple-red flowers; *F. purpurea* Japan; to 4¼ ft (1.3 m) tall, more or less glabrous and purple-tinted; flowers purple-red or pink; includes cultivars with white flowers and with strongly purple-tinted foliage; *F. rubra* QUEEN OF THE PRAIRIE; US; to 8 ft (2.5 m) tall; flowers deep peach to rose; *F. ulmaria* MEADOWSWEET, QUEEN OF THE MEADOWS; Europe, W Asia; 3¼–6½ ft (1–2 m) tall, more or less hairy; flowers creamy white in frothy corymbs; includes double- and pink-flowered cultivars and plants with leaves flushed gold or consistently striped or zoned creamy-yellow—'Aurea' is one of the finest pure gold foliage plants; *F. vulgaris* DROPWORT; Europe, N & C Asia; to 32 in (80 cm) tall; flowers white, sometimes tinted red or purple; includes cultivars with large, double and pale pink flowers.

fillis a strong soft string of various ply, usually colored brown or green. It is specially made for tying plants.

fimbriate bordered with a fringe of slender outgrowths, usually derived from the lamina rather than attached as hairs.

fir a common name applied to trees of the genus *Abies*, but also used of the genera *Pseudotsuga* and *Cunninghamia*.

fireblight (*Erwinia amylovora*) a bacterial disease principally affecting pome fruits in the family Rosaceae, including apple, *Amelanchier*, *Chaenomeles*, *Cotoneaster*, hawthorn, loquat, *Photinia*, *Pyracantha*, *Sorbus* and especially pear.

It has been known in North America since 1780, where it has occasionally also infected other rosaceous plants, including apricot, cherry, *Kerria*, plum, and rose. Identified in New Zealand in 1920 and in England 1956–57, it has spread to other parts of western Europe, the eastern Mediterranean and the Far East.

Fireblight was the first plant disease shown to be caused by a bacterium, and the name refers to the fact that the flowers, leaves, and twigs are blackened as if burnt by fire. It overwinters in cankers, from which it exudes as a slime at about the same time as the flowers open in spring. The bacteria are disseminated by wind, rain, or insects and infect the shoots of blossoms (especially in pears), from where they spread down the branches. In pears, the disease can spread rapidly and kill the trees, but in apple and other hosts, the main branches and trunk are not usually affected. In gardens and orchards, hawthorn hedges are often a source of infection.

Badly affected trees must be removed completely; in other cases, branches may be cut back to a point at least 24 in (60 cm) below where there is any sign of the disease beneath the bark. Pruning tools should be immersed in strong disinfectant after each cut, and the severed surfaces treated with a wound sealant and all infected tissues burned. Some restrictions remain on the movement of susceptible plants within the nursery trade.

Using a firmer
Applying diffuse pressure over the surface of potting mix results in an even-textured medium more conducive to root growth.

firmer an oblong or round implement, usually consisting of a flat piece of wood with an additional smaller piece fixed to one surface as a handle; used for leveling and firming soil in a seed box or pot.

Firmiana (for Karl Josef von Firmian [d. 1782], governor of Lombardy and patron of the Padua botanic garden). Sterculiaceae. E Asia, 1 species E Africa. 9 species, trees or shrubs with entire or palmately lobed leaves. The flowers are borne in axillary and terminal panicles or racemes. Usually yellow, they lack petals but consist of a showy, bell-shaped and 5-lobed calyx with a prominent, stamen bearing pistil. Suitable for outdoor cultivation in sheltered gardens where temperatures seldom fall below freezing. Otherwise, grow in the cool greenhouse in full light or part-shade. Water plentifully when in growth. Maintain good ventilation, with a winter minimum temperature of 36–41°F (2–5°C). Prune only when necessary to confine to allotted space. Propagate by seed sown under glass as soon as it ripens. *F. simplex* (syn. *F. platanifolia*, *Sterculia platanifolia*) CHINESE PARASOL TREE, CHINESE BOTTLETREE, JAPANESE VARNISH TREE, PHOENIX TREE; E Asia; deciduous tree to 65 ft (20 m); leaves 12–16 in (30–40 cm) across, with 3–7 deep lobes, deep green; flowers to 1½ in (4 cm) across, lemon yellow; 'Variegata': leaves white-mottled.

fish manure, fish meal, fish guano an organic compound fertilizer made by drying and pulverizing fish waste. It contains 7–10% nitrogen, 5–15% phosphate, and 2–3% potash.

fistulose, fistular hollow and cylindrical like a pipe.

Fittonia (for Elizabeth and Sarah May Fitton, authors of *Conversations on Botany* [1823]). Acanthaceae. NERVE PLANT. S America. 2 species, downy evergreen perennial herbs with low or creeping and rooting stems. The leaves are oblong to broadly and bluntly elliptic, soft-textured and overlaid with a network of metallic or brightly colored veins. Small, white and two-lipped, the tubular flowers are carried in slender spikes clothed with overlapping, green bracts. Striking, small foliage plants for

the home and greenhouse (minimum temperature 59°F/15°C). Plant in shallow pots or pans containing a porous, soilless mix. Water and fertilize freely during warm weather; keep barely moist at other times. Position in light shade, with moderate to high humidity and protection from drafts. The flower spikes are often pinched out to encourage bushy and luxuriant growth. Propagate by stem cuttings or spontaneous layers. *F. albivenis* Argyroneura Group: syn. *F. argyroneura*, SILVER NET-LEAF, SILVER THREADS, with silver-white-veined, emerald green leaves; 'Pearcei': SNAKESKIN PLANT, with larger and thinner-textured leaves in sage green, net-veined carmine; Verschaffeltii Group; syn. *F. verschaffeltii* MOSAIC PLANT; to 3 in (8 cm); leaves 2–4 in (5–10 cm), soft-textured and finely downy, olive green to purple-bronze with an intricate network of ruby to scarlet veins.

Fitzroya (for Robert FitzRoy [1809–65], Captain of HMS *Beagle*). Cupressaceae. C Chile, N Patagonia. 1 species, *F. cupressoides* (syn. *F. patagonica*) PATAGONIAN CYPRESS, an evergreen, coniferous tree to 150 ft (45 m) or shrubby at high altitude in the wild. The thick trunk is clothed with fissured and peeling, rusty red bark. Slender and pendulous, the branchlets bear overlapping leaves, each to ¼ in (0.5 cm) long, oblong and dark green with a paler midrib. An enormous and very long-lived but slow-growing tree in the hills of Chile and Argentina. It favors mild, damp maritime climates, growing well on the Pacific coast of North America from central California to Vancouver. Its needs are similar to those of *Abies*, although it requires extra shelter, humidity and moist, acidic soil. Propagate by seed sown in a cold frame or by cuttings.

flabellate, flabelliform fan-shaped, with a wedge-shaped outline and sometimes conspicuously pleated or nerved.

flag, flagstone a flat slab of stone used for paving. Various simulated products are available in concrete.

flagellate with whiplike runners; sarmentose.

flaked describing bicolored flowers, especially carnations and tulips, where one color overlies a ground color in large splashes.

flamed describing flowers, especially tulips, where in the center of each petal there is a band of solid color in combination with fine feathering.

flame gun a large, hand-held or wheel-mounted blowtorch, used principally to destroy surface weeds. It produces a long flame with intense local heat from the ignition of paraffin vaporized under pressure.

flat a shallow tray with open-jointed base strips, often used for plant raising. See *seed box*, *seed tray*.

flatworms (*Platyhelminthes: Turbellaria*) Many flatworms live in ponds, lakes, and waterways, where they prey on small animals or feed on detritus. Some live on land, especially in tropical and subtropical areas. They have flat, ribbonlike unsegmented bodies and some species are up to 8 in (20 cm) long when extended. The New Zealand flatworm (*Artioposthia triangulata*) and the Australian flatworm (*Australasion sanguinea*) have become established in the UK and Ireland. Both feed on earthworms and in some areas they have reduced earthworms to a very low level. They reproduce by laying egg capsules that contain 6–10 eggs. There are no suitable means of controlling flatworms.

Flea beetle

flea beetle (Coleoptera: Chrysomelidae) small beetles, up to about ⅛ in (3 mm) long and mostly black, although some species have a broad yellow stripe on their wing cases. The common name refers to their ability to jump when disturbed. In North America, the GRAPE FLEA BEETLE (*Altica chalybea*), with metallic blue-green adults up to ¼ in (5 mm) long, attacks the buds and unfolding leaves of grape; the larvae skeletonize the leaves. Other plants subject to attack include Virginia creeper, plum, apple, pear, quince, beech and elm. Infestation can be controlled with appropriate contact insecticides, subject to local pesticide regulations.

Five species of *Phyllotreta* are of most concern in Europe: the SMALL STRIPED FLEA BEETLE (*P. undulata*), the LARGE STRIPED FLEA BEETLE (*P. nemorum*), and the TURNIP FLEA BEETLES (*P. atra, P. cruciferae* and *P. nigripes*). Other *Phyllotreta* species occur in North America and their habits are similar.

Adults overwinter in such places as hedge bottoms, under loose bark, or in grass tussocks; on emergence in spring, they are attracted to brassicas and related plants. Eggs are deposited on or near the plants and the resulting larvae feed on the roots or (in the case of *P. nemorum*) tunnel the leaves, but resulting injury is seldom serious. The adult beetles attack emerging seedlings, biting small holes in leaves and stems causing severe damage, especially in dry seasons when seedling establishment is slow. Cruciferous plants are particularly susceptible; other plants attacked by other species of flea beetle include beet, anemones, fuchsias, *Solanum* spp., godetias, and irises.

Damage may be reduced by keeping seedlings well-watered to hasten growth and by clearing away plant debris from beneath hedge bottoms to reduce adult hibernation sites. Seed dressings and recommended contact insecticides are effective as control measures, subject to local pesticide controls.

Another flea beetle, the CABBAGE STEM BEETLE (*Psylliodes chrysocephala*), occurs in Europe and has been recorded in Canada. The adults are metallic green or blue and up to ¼ in (5 mm) long with reddish legs. The larvae tunnel inside the stems and leaf veins of brassica plants causing a growth check and, in many cases, death. The pest can be controlled with contact insecticide applied at setting out, subject to local pesticide approvals.

fleecy film a soft fibrous material of spun plastic, used to cover the soil surface to advance warming, or placed over plants to extend their season of

Fleecy film
Carefully anchored horticultural fleece can be used to protect maturing crops from pest attack while allowing in light, air, and water.

maturing and to provide frost protection. The film allows air and rain to penetrate and is best laid over shallow V-shaped drills of sown crops such as carrot, or over cell-raised plants, such as lettuce, after they have been set out. Cover for no more than four weeks in the spring, longer in fall. Where carefully anchored, the film provides a barrier against aphids, root flies, bulb flies, moths and butterflies. Fleecy film can also be used for greenhouse insulation and shading.

flexible paving paving slabs that are bedded close together on sand, without mortar.

flexuous used to describe an axis that is zigzag, bending, or curving in alternate and opposite directions.

flies one of the largest groups of insects, classified in the order Diptera. They are widely distributed and include many serious pests of cultivated plants. True flies are easily recognized: the adult insects have only one pair of wings, the hind pair being modified into clublike structures used as sensory and balancing organs. The larval stages are legless maggots that often have no obvious head or other external features. Damage to plants is usually caused by the larvae, which in most species are concealed in the soil, in galls, or in other plant tissue. See *bean seed fly*; *bulb flies*; *cabbage-root fly*; *carrot fly*; *celery fly*; *chrysanthemum stool miner*; *frit fly*; *fruit flies*; *fungus gnat*; *gall midge*; *hoverfly*; *leaf miners*; *leatherjacket*; *onion fly*; *sawfly*.

floating mulch a temporary ground or crop covering made of plastic fabric, described as "floating" on account of its loose but secure fastenings. It is used to advance soil temperature, extend the season of vegetable crops, and, in some cases, provide protection against frost and insects. The most usual kinds are perforated polythene sheet film, close-woven net, and fleecy film.

floccose possessing dense, woolly hairs that fall away easily in tufts.

flocculation the process whereby fine soil particles join together into larger aggregates as a result of the neutralizing of clay colloids. Lime, gypsum, humus, and other soil conditioners are used for the flocculation of clay soils to improve structure and, hence, drainage, aeration and root penetration.

flocculent, flocculose slightly floccose, woolly.

flood bench a level, water-tight bench that is periodically flooded and then pumped dry. It is one form of irrigation for potted plants.

floral diagram a diagram providing a condensed and simplified view of the flower from above, with the parts of the flower shown in one plane and symbols representing each part. The organs of a flower displayed in a floral diagram (starting from the center) are the ovary, stamens, corolla, and calyx, with the bracts and bracteoles, if present, shown beyond, in relation to their position beside the flower. The ovary in cross-section shows the arrangement of carpels, and the side on which the anthers open to release pollen is indicated. An absent organ, in terms of expected symmetry, is indicated by a dot or an asterisk. If one part is attached to another, lines are drawn between them, and the separation or linkage of petals and sepals is also made clear.

To supplement a diagram and section a floral formula can be used, in which K = calyx, C = corolla, A = androecium, G = gynoecium. To these

313

F

symbols are appended figures showing the numbers of each part, brackets around a number showing that the parts are united. Where the number of a part is large and indefinite, the symbol ∞ is used; if a part is absent, a zero (0). Where perianth whorls are linked, a bridging line or square brackets indicate this. A bar above or below the number for the gynoecium indicates an inferior or superior ovary, a feature visible in the flower section. It should be noted that the floral diagram does not indicate the overall shape of the flower. This can be rectified by accompanying it with a realistic half-flower section which at once indicates its actual form.

flore pleno (abbrev. fl.pl.) see *double*.

floret (1) a very small flower, generally part of a congested inflorescence; (2) in grasses, a collective term embracing various structures of the flower head.

floricane a biennial stem that fruits and flowers in its second year, as found in, for example, *Rubus* species.

floriferous bearing flowers freely.

florigen a hypothetical plant hormone, responsible for initiating flowering.

florilegium a collection or selection

of flowers; occasionally, also used to describe a book or a list of plants.

flower a structure bearing one or more pistils or stamens, or both, usually with some floral envelope. If surrounded by a perianth of calyx and corolla, it is termed perfect.

flower bud see *fruit bud*.

flower gatherer a pair of pruners or scissors specially designed to hold a flower stem as it is cut.

fluid drilling, fluid sowing the process of sowing pregerminated seeds mixed with a specially prepared gelatinous carrier. It was developed to advance the establishment of plants in instances where soil is too cold for direct sowing, and also to economize on seed.

In fluid drilling, seeds are sown under protection on damp absorbent paper at a suitable temperature, and when the roots are no more than ¼ in (5 mm) long the germinated seeds are mixed throughout the gel. The mixture is transferred to a polythene bag; one corner of the bag is then cut off, and the gel mixture "piped" along prepared soil drills, which must be kept moist.

flush a surge in the production of flowers, fruits, or fruiting bodies, espe-

cially roses and mushrooms.

fluted of a trunk with long, deep, rounded grooves running vertically.

fly speck a superficial growth of the fungus *Schizothyrium pomi* on apple, citrus, pear, plum, and possibly other fruits. It is often associated with sooty blotch and occurs as groups of tiny, black, circular dots, the individual dots just $\frac{1}{128}$–$\frac{1}{64}$ in (0.2–0.4 mm) in diameter. No damage is caused.

Fockea (for Gustav Woldemar Focke, early-19th-century German physician and plant physiologist). Asclepiadaceae. Southern Africa (Angola to the Karroo). 10 species, perennial succulent shrubs, developing a massive, woody, turniplike caudex crowned with slender, twining to sprawling branches. The leaves are oblong to ovate. Up to 1½ in (4 cm) diameter, the starfishlike flowers are borne singly or several together in leaf axils. Plant in deep pots or large pans containing a fast-draining, gritty, loam-based medium. Maintain a minimum winter temperature of 50°F (10°C) in full sun with low humidity. Water and fertilize generously during the spring and summer growing season, but ensure that the plants are allowed to dry out between waterings. Keep dry from midfall to early spring except for occasional mistings or drenchings to

FLUID SOWING

1 Pregerminate the seed on moist absorbent paper such as paper towels. Place a sheet on the base of a plastic container, wet it, and then spread on the seeds in a single layer.

2 As soon as the seeds show signs of germination, very carefully wash them off the paper. A plastic sieve and a slow-running stream of water risks the least damage.

3 Mix up some wallpaper paste (without fungicide) in a container. Make about 8 fl oz (250 ml) of paste for 100 seeds. Put the seeds in and stir until they are evenly distributed.

4 Transfer the mixture to a plastic bag, knot it firmly, and snip off a corner. Use the bag to "pipe" an even line of paste and seeds into a prepared, wetted seed drill. Cover the mixture lightly.

prevent withering and collapse of caudex. Propagate by
seed sown under glass or by
stem cuttings in spring
(plants that are obtained
from cuttings seldom
develop the
attractive caudex).

F. crispa (syn.
F. capensis) grows to
13 ft (4 m); leaves to
1¼ in (3 cm), finely
hairy, oval with wavy
margins; flowers
gray-green, blotched
brown; *F. edulis* dif-
fers from *F. crispa* in
that its smooth, dark
green leaves lack the
wavy margins.

foliar
embryos
form
around
margin

single leaf

**Kalanchoe
daigremontiana**

Foeniculum (the Latin name
for fennel). Umbelliferae.
Europe, Mediterranean. 1 species, *F. vulgare*, FENNEL, an aromatic, glaucescent
perennial or biennial herb to 6½ ft (2 m).
Leaves are to 20 in (50 cm) long, triangular in outline, 3–4-pinnate, and very
finely cut, with threadlike segments to 2
in (5 cm) long. Small, yellow flowers are
borne in compound umbels in summer.
The cultivar 'Purpureum' (syn. 'Purpurascens') has especially fine, purple-
bronze-flushed leaves and is beautiful
with pastel flowers and silvery foliage in
an herbaceous border. Hardy to −10°F
(−23°C). Grow in a well-drained site in a
warm sunny position. Propagate by seed,
or by dividing established plants in the
spring as soon as fresh growth appears;
seeds may be sown outside once the risk
of frost has passed. See *fennel*.

fogger, fogging nozzle a device for
producing very small droplets of water
or pesticide solution.

fogging the application of a pesticide
carried in droplets so fine that visibility
in an enclosed treated area is reduced.
The pesticide particles slowly settle,
well distributed mainly on the upper
surfaces of leaves. Formulations are
usually oil-based and are applied
with special equipment to produce
an aerosol.

foliaceous resembling a leaf, in
appearance or texture.

foliage plant a plant that is
grown predominantly for the
color, markings, shape, or texture of its leaves.

foliar embryo an embryonic plant that arises on the
leaves of mature specimens
of a species, and provides
a means of increasing a
stock. This may be a nat-
ural occurrence in the
case of plants such as
*Tolmiea menziesii, Bryophyl-
lum pinnatum*, and the ferns
Asplenium bulbiferum
and *Cystopteris bulbifera*.
The production of foliar
embryos at specific locations on
a leaf can be stimulated in certain plants. Sedums will produce
small plantlets only at the point
where the leaf was detached
from its parent and these may be
encouraged to root by pressing the leaf
base lightly into the surface of a sandy
potting mix, which should be kept dry.
Tiarella species, *Mitella* species, and *Cardamine trifoliata* produce plantlets at the
junction of the leaf petiole and leaf
blade. In these species, fully expanded
leaves are removed, retaining about
¾ in (20 mm) of petiole, and inserted
into a rooting medium with the leaves
lying flat on the surface; these are then
placed in a humid, shaded environment at 68°F (20°C) until plantlets
develop. *Kalanchoe* species, including
K. daigremortana shown above as well
as K. *blossfeldiana*, will produce plantlets
only around the indented leaf-margin;
suitable leaves may be removed,
anchored on the surface of a sandy
medium and kept dry until plantlets
have formed. Also known as proliferation and vivipary.

foliar feeding the application of a
diluted solution of fertilizer to the
leaves of plants; useful as an emer-
gency treatment for correcting deficient
trace elements, and of value for supplementary feeding. The absorption of
liquid fertilizer is greatest where leaf
cuticles are thin, as on the undersides
of leaves or where they are just
expanding. Liquid fertilizer should not
be applied in bright sun, because
foliage may be scorched.

foliate bearing leaves.

foliolate bearing leaflets.

follicle a dry, dehiscent, one- to
many-seeded fruit, derived from a
single carpel and dehiscing by a single
suture along its ventral side.

folly a garden structure designed to
catch the eye, but with no functional
purpose, often taking the form of a
pyramid, pinnacle, tower or mock ruin.

Fontanesia (for R. L. Desfontaines
[1750–1833], French botanist).
Oleaceae. Near East, China. 1 species,
F. phillyreoides, a deciduous shrub to
10 ft (3 m). The leaves are ¾–4 in
(2–10 cm) long, ovate to lanceolate,
glossy, glabrous and serrulate to entire.
In early summer, small, 4-petaled flowers are borne in dense axillary racemes
or terminal panicles. It is fully hardy.
Grow in well-drained soil in sun
or partial shade. Propagate by semihardwood cuttings in late summer in
a cold frame, or by hardwood cuttings
outside in fall; sow seed in a cold frame
in spring.

Fontinalis (from Latin *fontalis*, meaning of or belonging to a spring or fountain). Fontinalaceae. Cosmopolitan.
WATER MOSS. Some 55 species, aquatic
mosses forming clumps of long and
slender, submerged stems covered in
small, dark green leaves. The following
species grows rooted to rocks and tree
roots submerged in cold, fast-flowing
rivers and streams, in ditches and
ponds and on cliff faces in water seepage. It will grow as an oxygenator in
ponds or cold-water aquariums, providing useful cover for spawning fish
and acting as host to the small invertebrates they feed upon. Grow in nonalkaline water in indirect light. Propagate
by division of large clumps in spring.
Take stems with part of the anchorage
attached or tie gently to new anchorage in the form of rough stone or
brick. *F. antipyretica* Northern Hemisphere; stems to 32 in (80 cm), slender,
mossy and feathery, dark emerald to
olive green.

foot rot a rot of the lower part of the
stem-root axis. Where used generally to

315

F

describe a base rot disease symptom, it often overlaps with the terms collar rot, damping-off and root rot. Foot rot is also used more specifically to refer to particular diseases, such as those caused by the soilborne fungi *Fusarium solani* on peas and beans, *Mycosphaerella pinodes* on peas and *Phytophthora cryptogea* on tomatoes.

forcing the acceleration of vegetative growth and especially flowering or fruiting, usually by temperature and light manipulation. Rhubarb, sea kale, chicory, daffodils, and hyacinths are commonly forced. Commercial forcing is carried out in specially designed greenhouses or sheds, often with additional bottom heat; but in the domestic garden it is usually improvised in greenhouses and frames or achieved with the use of forcing pots.

Forestiera (for Charles le Forestier, French physician and naturalist). Oleaceae. N & C America. 20 species, usually deciduous trees or shrubs. The leaves resemble those of *Ligustrum*. Small, cream, or green-white flowers are borne on axillary clusters or in racemes. They are followed by small, black, fleshy fruits. Hardy to –10°F (–23°C). Plant on a well-drained soil in a sunny site. Propagate by half-ripe cuttings in summer or by seed when ripe in a cold frame.

F. acuminata US; shrub or small tree to 6½ ft (2 m) with smooth branches; leaves 1¼–4 in (3–10 cm), ovate-oblong to lanceolate, tip serrate; flowers green-white; fruit to ½ in (1.2 cm), purple; *F. neomexicana* SW US; shrub to 10 ft (3 m) with somewhat armed branches; leaves to 2 in (5 cm), ovate to lanceolate, crenulate; flowers yellow-white; fruit to ¼ in (0.5 cm), purple, pruinose.

forest transplant a young tree, usually of forestry or native species, that is raised from seed and especially suitable for planting on a large scale or in difficult sites. A three-year-old transplant described as 2+1 indicates two years in a seed bed and one year in a nursery row.

fork (1) a hand implement comprising a steel shaft with a head of three or four narrow prongs; the shaft is attached to a handle usually made of wood. Handgrips may be D-, T- or Y-shaped, or occasionally absent. A standard digging fork has four tines about 12 in (30 cm) long, which are round or square in section, with the shaft mounted on a handle about 24 in (60 cm) long; there are curved-tine and long-handled versions for various purposes. A border or lady's fork differs in its shorter tines and narrower head. A flat-tined, spading, or potato fork has broad flat tines, suitable for digging heavy-textured soil.

A drag fork is a long-handled fork without a handgrip, the tines bent at right angles to the shaft. Drag forks come in various sizes and designs, and are used as cultivating tools or for pulling garden refuse or manure. A hollow-tine fork has tubular tines, designed to remove cores of soil from lawns to aid drainage, aeration, and top-dressing. A pitchfork has only two tines, which are slightly curved upward and fixed to a straight handle. It is suitable for handling straw or very long cut grass. A hand-fork has three or four flat tines about 4 in (10 cm) long on a handle about 5 in (12 cm) long or longer, without a handgrip; it is used for cultivating small areas.

(2) a point on a tree where two branches of similar size meet.

form, forma (abbrev. f.) an infraspecific taxon, subordinate to subspecies and variety. The lowest rank in the taxonomic hierarchy, forms are usually distinguished only by minor characteristics. These characteristics may be of importance to the gardener, however, and include such features as habit and leaf and flower color, e.g., *Hosta crispula* f. *viridis*.

formaldehyde a chemical substance (H-HCO) effective as a fungicide, formerly widely used for sterilizing bulbs, soil, containers and tools, and for greenhouse hygiene. Formaldehyde volatilizes rapidly and is toxic to plants in active growth. It is a severe irritant to the eyes and nose.

formal garden a garden of geometric, usually symmetrical design, typically incorporating architectural features, clipped trees and water.

Forsythia (for William Forsyth [1737–1804], superintendent of the Royal Gardens, Kensington). Oleaceae. E Asia, C Europe. 6 species, deciduous shrubs with golden-green branches covered with lenticels. The leaves are simple or three-parted with entire to toothed margins. The short-stalked, yellow flowers are borne before the leaves, singly or in clusters and usually nodding; tubular to bell-shaped, they consist of four, oblong lobes. Among the most colorful and floriferous of early spring-flowering shrubs, they are fully hardy. They will tolerate part shade but bloom more prolifically in sun. Cut back after flowering to within

FORCING RHUBARB

1 Early, tender stems of rhubarb are one of the first crops of the year in the kitchen garden. Watch the crowns in late winter for signs of growth.

2 Invert a lightproof container over the crown. These custom-made, lidded terra-cotta forcers can be expensive to buy—a small plastic bin works just as well.

3 The blanched stems with their brilliant yellow leaves should be ready in about four weeks (these need a little longer). Uncover the crown for a second, normal crop.

an inch or two of the old wood. Older plants may be rejuvenated by thinning by one third to one half every two to three years. The slender branches of *F. suspensa* should be allowed to develop in weeping profusion, given some support but otherwise unhindered. For hedging, choose vigorous, erect cultivars. Propagate by half-ripe cuttings in summer in a case or cold frame, or by hardwood cuttings outside in fall. Susceptible to leaf spot fungi, forsythia gall (which may disfigure but not damage) and bacterial blight.

F. × *intermedia* (*F. suspensa* × *F. viridissima*) garden origin; to 10 ft (3 m), erect to spreading; flowers in clusters, deep yellow; includes 'Arnold Giant', with large, nodding, golden flowers, 'Beatrix Farrand', large, with deep gold flowers with broad lobes, 'Karl Sax', vigorous and free-flowering, with deep yellow flowers marked orange in the throat and foliage turning purple-red in fall, 'Lynwood Variety', free-flowering, vigorous and erect, and the erect and vigorous 'Spectabilis', with densely packed, deep yellow flowers with 4–5–6, twisted lobes; *F. ovata* EARLY FORSYTHIA; Korea; to 3¼ ft (1 m), domed, compact; flowers small, bright yellow, sparse, solitary or paired; includes the hardy, erect and profusely flowering 'Ottawa'; *F. suspensa* China; semiscandent to erect shrub to 10 ft (3 m) tall; leaves often 3-parted; flowers clustered, nodding, pale to deep yellow with somewhat twisted lobes; includes var. *fortunei*, erect to arching with deep yellow flowers, and var. *sieboldii*, slender-stemmed and weeping to semiscandent with clear, pale yellow flowers, f. *atrocaulis*, with maroon-tinted branchlets and pale flowers, and 'Nymans', which is similar to f. *atrocaulis* but produces larger, brighter flowers later in the season, i.e., mid- to late spring; *F. viridissima* (China; erect to 10 ft (3 m) with persistently green, 4-angled branches; leaves flushing claret to plum-purple in fall; flowers bright yellow stained green with narrow lobes.

Fothergilla (for Dr. John Fothergill [1712–80], who cultivated many American plants at Stratford-le-Bow, Essex). Hamamelidaceae. E US. 2 species, deciduous, low-growing shrubs, to 10 ft (3 m) tall with widely spreading branches. Obovate to oval and coarsely toothed, the leaves are pale green when first opening, mature to mid-green in summer, and turn a glorious crimson or orange-yellow in fall. The fragrant flowers open before the leaves in bottle-brush-like, terminal heads or spikes. They lack petals, but are made up of about 24 stamens with white filaments, each to 1 in (2.5 cm) long. Among the finest shrubs for fall color, they are fairly low-growing and need a cool, moist, acidic soil in sun. Otherwise, cultivation as for *Hamamelis*.

F. gardenii (syn. *F. alnifolia, F. carolina, F. parvifolia*) SE US; leaves to 2½ in (6.5 cm), toothed in upper half; flowers with white filaments to 1 in (2.5 cm) long; includes compact, blue-green-leaved cultivars and forms with pink flowers, possibly hybrids with the next species; *F. major F. monticola*; Allegheny Mountains; leaves to 4 in (10 cm), more or less entire or sparsely toothed in upper half; flowers with pink-tinged, white filaments to ¾ in (2 cm) long.

foundation planting in garden design, the basic structural planting of trees and hedges.

fountain a jet or spout of water, produced artificially by pumping and/or gravity. Fountains are an important feature of formal gardens.

foveolate with shallow small pits or precise indentations.

fractiflex intermittent zigzag lines.

Fragaria (the Latin name for the strawberry, from *fragrans*, fragrant, referring to the aroma of the fruit). Rosaceae. Northern temperate zones, Chile. STRAWBERRY. Some 12 species, stoloniferous, perennial herbs with 3-parted, toothed leaflets. Made up of five, rounded to obovate petals and numerous stamens, the flowers are carried in cymes in spring and summer. The fruit consists of many small achenes scattered on the surface of an enlarged, conical, fleshy, red receptacle. Grow in fertile, well-drained, moisture-retentive soil in sun. When grown in very rich soil, variegated cultivars may produce green crowns. Propagate from seed in early spring, or by removal of runners (plant-bearing stolons). Among the edible strawberries, several ornamental cultivars can be found. *F.* × *ananassa* (*F. chiloensis* × *F. virginiana*), the GARDEN or CULTIVATED STRAWBERRY, the WILD STRAWBERRY, *F. vesca* and its variant 'Semperflorens', the ALPINE STRAWBERRY or FRAISE DU BOIS; all have variegated cultivars. *Fragaria* 'Pink Panda' is a pleasing, pale-tomentose plant with large, candy pink flowers. For *F. indica*, see *Duchesnea indica*. See also *strawberry*.

Frailea (for Manuel Fraile, [b. 1850 in Salamanca, Spain], curator of cacti at the US Department of Agriculture, Washington, DC). Cactaceae. E Bolivia, S Brazil, Paraguay, Uruguay and N Argentina. About 15 species, dwarf cacti with tufted or solitary, squatly globose to cylindric stems, usually weakly ribbed or tuberculate. Produced amid wool and bristles, the yellow, shortly funnelform flowers open only briefly, if at all. Provide a minimum temperature of 50–59°F (10–15°C), full sun, and low humidity. Plant in an acidic medium, high in grit. Water very sparingly in winter (to avoid shriveling). Most species of *Frailea* can be raised to maturity from seed in less than three years. They need ample watering during the warmer months and may flower intermittently over the summer and fall; except in the brightest weather, the flowers often fail to develop fully or to open, but fruits will still be formed, *F. pygmaea* (syn. *F. pulcherrima*) Argentina, S Brazil, Uruguay; stems 1–7 (½–2¾) × ½–1 in (1–2.5 cm), globose to squatly cylindric, dark green to purple-red, with small tubercles, woolly areoles and short yellow to white spines; flowers small, yellow.

frame a structure with a removable or hinged glass or plastic cover resting on a low framework of masonry, wood or metal; it is used for propagation, forcing, hardening off, or winter protection. It is usually unheated, when it is known as a cold frame, but is sometimes provided with a source of bottom heat. See *hotbed, soil warming*.

frameworking a form of grafting fruit trees in which scions of a different cultivar are inserted on the prepared framework of an established tree. See *grafting*.

Francoa (for F. Franco, who encouraged the study of botany in 16th-century Spain). Saxifragaceae. Chile. BRIDAL WREATH. 5 species, perennial evergreen herbs with a clump of obovate to broadly lanceolate leaves pinnately cut into blunt lobes. Abundant small flowers are produced in summer in long-stalked racemes; they consist of four, oblong petals, usually white and with a dark pink spot at the base of the claw. Plant in a well-drained, fairly moist, sunny position. In colder areas, overwinter in frost-free conditions and plant outdoors the following spring. Although frost-hardy, these plants are commonly grown indoors in cool, bright conditions. Propagate from seed in early spring or by division.

F. appendiculata inflorescence to 27 in (68 cm), sparingly branched, compact; flowers shell pink, sometimes spotted; *F. ramosa* inflorescence to 36 in (90 cm), much-branched; flowers white; *F. sonchifolia* leaves with broadly winged petioles; inflorescence to 24 in (60 cm), simple to sparingly branched; flowers pink with red spots.

Franklinia (for Benjamin Franklin [1706–90], US statesman). Theaceae. SE US (Georgia, now extinct in the wild). 1 species, *F. alatamaha* (syn. *Gordonia alatamaha*), a deciduous tree or shrub, erect to 33 ft (10 m) tall with smooth bark. To 6 in (15 cm) long, the leaves are obovate to oblong, sparsely toothed and dark glossy green, turning bright red in fall. Produced in late summer, the cup-shaped, solitary flowers are fragrant, 3 in (8 cm) across and composed of five, rounded, white petals and a boss of golden stamens. This tree needs long hot summers to flower well and for wood to ripen—specimens perform exceptionally only in continental climates, where they prove hardy to at least 5°F (−15°C). In less favored climates, plant in a sheltered south-facing niche with good drainage and full sun. Grow in moisture-retentive but well-drained, neutral to slightly acidic soils. Propagate by fresh seed sown ripe, by softwood cuttings or by semiripe cuttings in mid-summer; alternatively, increase by simple layering of low branches.

Fraxinus (the Latin name for the ash). Oleaceae. Temperate Europe, Asia, N America, a few in tropics. ASH. 65 species, medium-sized to large trees, mostly deciduous (those listed below are deciduous) with pinnate leaves and panicles of small flowers borne before or alongside the leaves. The fruits are 1-seeded samaras, each with a long, flattened wing. Fully hardy, the following species should be planted in moist but well-drained soils in full sun. Propagate from stratified seed in spring. Graft cultivars in spring or bud in summer on seedling stock of the same species under glass. Susceptible to ash heart rot and ash bark beetle.

F. americana (syn. *F. alba*, *F. juglandifolia*) WHITE ASH; NE US; tree to 130 ft (40 m) tall, crown spreading; leaflets to 9, to 6 in (15 cm), oblong to lanceolate, entire or serrate, slightly downy beneath; fruit wing oblong, 1¼–2 in (3–5 cm); includes 'Acuminata', with long-tapering, entire leaflets, dark green above and almost white beneath, turning purple-red in fall, 'Autumn Applause', with a rounded, dense crown and deep red to mahogany fall color, and 'Autumn Purple', with leaves persisting late into fall and turning purple to chocolate mottled mauve and bronze; *F. angustifolia* (syn. *F. oxycarpa*) NARROW-LEAVED ASH; S Europe, N Africa; tree to 80 ft (25 m); leaflets to 13, to 2¾ in (7 cm), oblong to lanceolate, finely serrate, dark green above, paler beneath, glabrous; fruit wing elliptic-oblong, to 1½ in (4 cm); includes the striking 'Raywood', with an elegant, feathery crown, the leaflets narrow and dark green, assuming a hazy, metallic appearance toward summer's end and turning deep plum to claret in fall—an exceptional street tree; *F. excelsior* COMMON EUROPEAN ASH; Europe to Caucasus; tree to 130 ft (40 m); leaflets to 11, to 4¾ in (12 cm), obovate, serrate, dark green above, paler beneath, glabrous; fruit wing oblong, to 1½ in (4 cm); includes f. *diversifolia*, with only one or three leaflets per leaf, 'Jaspidea', with yellow new growth turning gold in fall, and 'Pendula' with a gnarled, spreading crown and branches weeping to the ground; *F. mandshurica*, MANCHURIAN ASH, differs in its more distinctly toothed leaflets with veins sunken beneath; *F. nigra* BLACK ASH; N America; tree to 80 ft (25 m); leaflets to 11, to 4¾ in (12 cm), oblanceolate, serrulate, veins brown and downy beneath; fruit wing bluntly oblong, to 1½ in (4 cm); includes 'Fallgold', with leaves turning gold in fall; *F. ornus* FLOWERING ASH, MANNA ASH; S Europe, Asia Minor; broad-crowned tree to 26 ft (8 m); leaflets to 7, to 2¾ in (7 cm), obovate, serrulate, dark green above, paler beneath with a somewhat downy midrib; flowers white and fragrant in showy, lacy panicles; fruit wing narrow-oblong, to 1 in (2.5 cm); *F. pennsylvanica* RED ASH; N America; tree to 60 ft (18 m); leaflets to 9, 2¾–6 in (7–15 cm), lanceolate, entire or serrulate toward tip, olive green; fruit wings spathulate to lanceolate; includes 'Patmore', vigorous and strongly erect with good pest-resistance and dark green foliage lasting well into fall, 'Summit', with a broadly pyramidal crown and gold fall tints, and 'Urbanite', tolerant of city pollution and sun scorch, with a broadly pyramidal crown and thick, glossy leaves becoming bronze in fall; *F. sieboldiana* (syn. *F. mariesii*) Japan, China; compact-crowned tree to 26 ft (8 m); leaflets to 7, to 2¾ in (7 cm), ovate, serrate or entire, dark green, glabrous except for downy midrib; flowers cream, fragrant in panicles to 6 in (15 cm); *F. velutina* ARIZONA ASH; SW US; shrub or small tree; leaflets 3–5–7, lanceolate to elliptic, coarsely serrate, dull green above, more or less hairy beneath, tough-textured; includes 'Fan-Tex', fast-growing and well-proportioned with large, deep green and leathery leaves.

Freesia (for Friedrich Heinrich Theodore Freese [d. 1876], a pupil of the botanist Ecklon). Iridaceae. South Africa. 11 species, cormous perennial herbs with a fan of lightly pleated, narrow leaves and erect to horizontal, simple or branched flowering stems in winter and spring. Often fragrant, the flowers are more or less funnel- or goblet-shaped, sometimes 2-lipped, and consist of six tepals.

Frost-tender bulbs, grown in a cool glasshouse for winter and early spring flowers, or, using prepared bulbs, in an open garden for flowers in summer. Grow indoor bulbs in a medium-fertility sandy mix, at 2–3-in (5–8-cm) spacings in prepared beds, boxes, or pots; plant in succession from late summer through to winter. Water and keep in a frame or cold greenhouse (41°F/5°C) and cover with a 1¼-in (3-cm) layer of coir and a top-dressing of grit. Gradually increase water as growth resumes, and raise the temperature to 50°F (10°C); provide full light and good ventilation, and feed semiweekly with a diluted liquid fertilizer as flower buds show. Provide support. Temperatures above 59°F (15°C) will result in spindly plants with quickly fading blooms. Reduce water as plants die back, and keep completely dry when dormant; lift and store cool and dry until the following season. In mild, essentially frost-free areas, corms may be planted directly into open ground in late summer/early fall into fertile sandy soils in a sunny and sheltered position. Propagate by presoaked seed in a cool greenhouse or cold frame, alternatively by offsets during fall.

F. caryophyllacea stem 4¾–16 in (12–40 cm); flowers 1–2½ in (2.5–6 cm) long, sweetly scented, white, sometimes flushed purple outside and lined with purple in throat, lowest tepals sometimes marked with yellow; *F. corymbosa* (syn. *F. armstrongii*) stem to 20 in (50 cm) with several branches, spikes 3–10-flowered; flowers 1–1½ in (2.5–3.5 cm), scented or not, ivory or pale yellow with the lower tepals marked bright yellow, or pink with a yellow throat; *F. leichtlinii* stem 3–8 in (8–20 cm); flowers 1–1½ in (2.5–4 cm) long, scented, cream or pale yellow, the lower tepals orange-yellow, the upper tepals sometimes flushed with purple-brown on the outside; *F. refracta* close to *F. caryophyllacea* and *F. leichtlinii*, but with spicily scented, two-lipped flowers in pale yellow, sometimes flushed green or purple, the lower tepals marked orange and the throat veined purple. The florist's freesias are complex hybrids involving the above species; they have been grouped under various names—*F. × hybrida*, *F. × kewensis*, *F. × ragioneri*, and *F. × tubergenii*. They range in height from 4 in (10 cm) to 12 in (30 cm). The flowers may be single or "double," scarcely to sweetly scented, and vary in color from silvery white to ivory, yellow, or bronze and from soft pink to red and mauve, blue, and indigo. These colors are frequently combined—for example, as bronze, pearly or lavender flushing on the exterior, or as a pale yellow or white throat.

Fremontodendron (for Major-General John Charles Frémont [d. 1890], US explorer, botanist and horticulturist). Sterculiaceae. Southwest N America. FLANNEL BUSH; CALIFORNIA BEAUTY. 2 species, evergreen shrubs and trees covered in short, felty hair. The leaves are unlobed or palmately 3-, 5-, or 7-lobed. Produced from late spring to early fall, the solitary, short-stalked flowers consist of a cupped, showy calyx with five, ovate to elliptic, petal-like lobes and a staminal tube divided into 5 parts toward the tip and ending in a filiform style. Hardy to 5°F (−15°C). Grow in full sun against a sheltered, south-facing wall. They prefer poor, dry soil. It may be necessary to tie in branches to a framework of trellis or wire. Cut out any frost-damaged growth in spring. Pruning is otherwise inadvisable (the countless short hairs are extremely irritating). Propagate by seed or by softwood or semiripe cuttings in a sandy propagating mix with gentle bottom heat.

F. californicum (syn. *Fremontia californica*) shrub to 23 ft (7 m); leaves unlobed to 3-lobed, sparsely hairy above, densely so beneath; flowers opening all at once, 1½–2½ in (3.5–6 cm) in diameter, shining golden yellow; *F. mexicanum* (syn. *Fremontia mexicana*) differs from the first species in its 5–7-lobed leaves and flowers opening in succession, 2½–3½ in (6–9 cm) in diameter, deep gold to orange yellow, becoming stained brick-red at the base; this species has crossed with the first, producing *F.* 'California Glory', a vigorous and free-flowering plant hardier than either parent with lemon yellow flowers tinged red on the exterior.

French garden the grand garden style developed by Le Nôtre during the reign of Louis XIV in which a garden was centered on the house and designed along a series of axes, often combined with water features in the form of canals. Also incorporated were elaborate parterres, formal lakes, clipped trees and hedges along straight walks, geometric woods, and circular open spaces from which avenues radiated in a fan pattern.

French intensive method see *deep bed method.*

friable used to describe soil that is of good crumb structure, and suitable for working down to a seed bed or tilth.

frill girdling the formation of downward-sloping overlapping cuts around the trunk of a tree, near soil level, using a light ax or billhook. Frill girdling is done in preparation for the application of brushwood killer or ammonium sulfamate, either of which is deposited in the cuts as a treatment to kill the tree.

frit a formulation of fertilizer that is incorporated into a melted glass matrix, which is then shattered into "frits" and ground up to produce an insoluble nutrient additive. Frits are often used to supply trace elements, particularly in potting mixes.

frit fly (*Oscinella frit*) a very small fly, the maggots of which are about ⅛ in (3 mm) long and may attack sweet corn during May and June. The growing points of seedlings are bored into and there is distortion, wilting, and death. Seedlings are most susceptible up to the five- to six-leaf stage. Where the fly is a troublesome pest, raise the sweet corn in cell modules in a greenhouse, or spray emerging shoots outdoors with a recommended insecticide, subject to local pesticide approvals.

Fritillaria (from Latin *fritillus*, a dice-box, referring to the shape of the capsules, or to the checkered pattern on the flowers of some species, reminiscent of the traditional decoration on a dice-box). Liliaceae (Liliaceae). Temperate regions of Northern Hemisphere, particularly Mediterranean, SW Asia (mountainous regions), western N America. FRITILLARY. Some 100 species, bulbous perennial herbs with alternate to whorled, oblanceolate to linear leaves. The flowers are usually nodding and broadly bell-shaped. The six tepals are commonly marked with

FRITILLARIA

Name	Distribution	Height and foliage	Flowers
F. acmopetala	W Asia, E Mediterranean	6–18 in (15–45 cm) tall; leaves linear	1–3, broadly campanulate, tepals 1–1½ in (2.5–4 cm), lanceolate to oblanceolate, green stained brown
F. aurea syn. *F. bornmuelleri*	Turkey	1½–6 in (4–15 cm) tall; leaves lanceolate to ovate-lanceolate, glaucous	solitary, broadly and deeply campanulate, tepals ¾–2 in (2–5 cm), ovate-oblong, yellow with orange or red-brown tessellations
F. bucharica	C Asia, NW Afghanistan	4–14 in (10–35 cm) tall; leaves lanceolate to ovate	1–10, cup-shaped, tepals ⅝–¾ in (1.5–2 cm), lanceolate, white or off-white with green veins
F. camschatcensis BLACK SARANA	NE Asia to NW N America	6–30 in (15–75 cm) tall; leaves broadly lanceolate, whorled below	1–8, broadly campanulate to cup-shaped, tepals ¾–1⅛ in (2–3 cm), oblong-ovate, shining purple-brown to black with finely grooved and ridged inner surfaces
F. cirrhosa	E Himalaya, China	8–24 in (20–60 cm) tall; leaves linear, whorled below, the upper leaves or bracts very slender with coiling, tendril-like tips	1–4, broadly campanulate, tepals 1⅜–2 in (3.5–5 cm), narrowly elliptic, basically green or yellow-green, often tinted or tessellated purple-brown
F. crassifolia	Anatolia	2½–8 in (6–20 cm) tall; leaves lanceolate	1–3, broadly campanulate, tepals ¾–1 in (1.8–2.5 cm), ovate, green with brown tessellations

Comments: ssp. *kurdica* has yellow-green tepals heavily suffused with maroon and a central yellow stripe.

Name	Distribution	Height and foliage	Flowers
F. imperialis CROWN IMPERIAL	S Turkey to Kashmir	20–60 in (50–150 cm) tall, muskily scented; leaves lanceolate, whorled, bright green	3–5, campanulate, nodding in a terminal umbel crowned with leafy bracts, tepals 1½–2 in (4–5 cm), ovate-oblong, orange to red

Comments: Includes cultivars with yellow, tangerine, deep orange and red flowers.

Name	Distribution	Height and foliage	Flowers
F. meleagris CHECKERED LILY, SNAKE'S HEAD FRITILLARY, GUINEA-HEN FLOWER, LEPER LILY	Europe	4¾–12 in (12–30 cm) tall; leaves linear	solitary or paired, broadly campanulate, nodding, tepals 1⅛–1¾ in (3–4.5 cm), oblong-elliptic, white or pink heavily checkered purple-red

Comments: A variable species, checkered to varying degrees, some flowers pure white, some with the faintest tessellations, others darkest purple-red with a leaden cast.

Name	Distribution	Height and foliage	Flowers
F. michailovskyi	NE Turkey	2½–10 in (6–24 cm) tall; leaves lanceolate	1–4, broadly campanulate, clustered together, tepals ¾–1⅛ in (2–3 cm), ovate-elliptic, purple-brown to green with yellow tips
F. pallidiflora	E Siberia, NW China	4–32 in (10–80 cm) tall; leaves broadly lanceolate, glaucous	2–5, campanulate, tepals 1–1¾ in (2.5–4.5 cm), oblong-elliptic, pale buttery yellow, sometimes tinted green or faintly checkered

F. camschatcensis

F. imperialis

F. meleagris

F. pallidiflora

FRITILLARIA

Name	Distribution	Height and foliage	Flowers
F. persica *F. eggeri, F. libanotica* **Comments:** 'Adiyaman': to 3¼ ft (1 m) tall with many dark maroon flowers.	Middle East, W Asia	8–36 in (20–90 cm) tall; leaves lanceolate, glaucous gray-green, many alternating on stems	7–20, nodding in an erect, terminal raceme, narrowly campanulate; tepals ⅝–1 in (1.5–2.5 cm), dull purple-black to chalky maroon or green
F. pontica	Balkans, N Greece, NW Turkey	3–12 in (8–30 cm) tall; leaves linear-lanceolate	solitary or paired, broadly campanulate, nodding, tepals 1–1¾ in (2.5–4.5 cm), oblong-obovate, green faintly marbled and edged brown within and with dark, visible nectaries
F. pudica YELLOW FRITILLARY	W N America	3–12 in (8–30 cm) tall; leaves linear to narrowly lanceolate	1–6, campanulate, nodding, tepals ⅜–1 in (1–2.5 cm), elliptic-obovate, deep yellow sometimes suffused with warm orange or red
F. pyrenaica	SW France, NW Spain	6–12 in (15–30 cm) tall; leaves linear to lanceolate	solitary or paired, broadly campanulate, nodding; tepals 1–1⅜ in (2.5–3.5 cm), oblong-elliptic, the tips recurved, yellow checkered brown and heavily suffused dark purple-brown on exterior
F. raddeana	NW Iran, Turkmenia	20–60 in (50–150 cm) tall; leaves lanceolate, whorled and alternate, dark green	6–20, broadly campanulate in a terminal umbel crowned with leafy bracts, tepals 1½–2 in (4–5 cm), oblong to rhombic, white to palest yellow suffused green
F. recurva SCARLET FRITILLARY	California, S Oregon	8–36 in (20–90 cm) tall; leaves linear-lanceolate, gray-green, whorled	3–12, narrowly campanulate, nodding in a raceme, tepals ⅜–1⅛ in (2–3 cm), ovate to oblong-lanceolate, the tips recurved, orange-red to scarlet with yellow tessellations
F. sewerzowii *Korolkowia sewerzowii*	C Asia, NW China	6–8 in (15–20 cm) tall; leaves lanceolate	4–12 in a raceme or solitary, narrowly campanulate with a broadly flared mouth, tepals 1–1⅛ in (2.5–3 cm), oblong-obovate, green to livid purple without and yellow to brick red at base and within
F. stenanthera	E Russia	4–12 in (10–30 cm) tall; leaves linear to ovate-lanceolate	1–10 in a raceme, narrowly campanulate and flared at mouth, tepals ⅝–¾ in (1.5–2 cm), obovate-lanceolate, pale pink
F. verticillata	C Asia, W Siberia	8–24 in (20–60 cm) tall; leaves narrowly lanceolate to linear, whorled, the upper leaves or bracts with tendril-like tips	1–5, broadly campanulate, nodding, tepals to 1¾ in (4.5 cm), oblong-obovate, white, suffused and faintly checkered green to brown

F. pudica　　*F. raddeana*　　*F. sewerzowii*　　*F. verticillata*

tessellations or have dark nectaries at the base on their inner surfaces.

The species described here are spring-flowering and fully hardy unless otherwise specified. The smaller species will, however, suffer in cold, wet winters and dull damp summers. For this reason, they tend to be grown in the alpine house, bulb frame or raised bed, with cloche protection in winter. Most of the smaller species require sharply draining, fertile soil, full sun, ample moisture during the growing and flowering season, and a dry (but not arid) rest in summer. *F. meleagris* prefers permanently damp sites and is suitable for naturalizing in long grass, provided that the first lawn cut does not occur until the leaves have died back in summer. *F. camschatcensis* needs a lightly-shaded position in cool, damp and humus-rich soil. The larger *F. imperialis* and *F. persica* are suited in scale to the mixed border, and will thrive in full sun in well-drained, fertile loams. Above −10°F (−23°C), they require no additional winter protection. Increase by seed sown when ripe or in spring, in a loam-based propagating mix with additional sharp sand; germination may take six months. Propagate also by bulbils. *Fritillaria* is attacked by lily beetle and, in the case of *F. meleagris*, greedy pheasants.

froghoppers (Hemiptera: Cercopidae) sap-sucking insects, up to ¼ in (6 mm) long, which are so named because of the adults' froglike shape and ability to jump. The US common name of SPITTLEBUG refers to the characteristic white froth or "cuckoo spit" which surrounds the pale-colored nymphs when they feed. The COMMON FROGHOPPER (*Philaenus spumarius*) varies in color from yellow through shades of brown to almost black; in the US, it is known as the MEADOW SPITTLEBUG. The adult female lays eggs in the fall, and nymphs hatch in spring, feeding on plants until reaching maturity in midsummer. A wide range of plants may be attacked, including blackberries, raspberries, perennial asters, campanulas, chrysanthemums, *Coreopsis*, geums, lavender, *Lychnis*, *Phlox*, roses, rudbeckias, solidagos, and willows, but insecticides are seldom necessary and a powerful jet of water will normally remove cuckoo spit and nymphs.

frost the condition occurring when air temperature falls below 32°F (0°C), the freezing point of water. When atmospheric moisture freezes to produce ice crystals on the ground or on other surfaces, the condition is known as white or hoar frost. Temperatures between 32 and 7°F (0° and −3°C) are generally referred to as slight frost, between 25°F and 21°F (−4°C and −6°C) as keen frost, between 19°F and 14°F (−7°C and −10°C) as hard frost, and below 14°F (−10°C) as severe frost. The susceptibility of plant tissues to frost damage varies according to species, provenance, acclimatization, and site exposure. Some parts of a plant may be more susceptible than others: in fruit trees, for example, the blossom more so than the bark. The effects of frost may depend on its duration as well as its severity: repeated freezing and thawing or very rapid thawing can be particularly damaging.

The effects of frost can be lessened by choosing frost-resistant plants, by protecting plants with insulating materials including glass, and by artificial heating. Protection from freezing wind is desirable, and for frost-tender species, sites likely to accumulate cold air behind barriers or in hollows should be avoided. Frost can benefit soil structure, especially that of clay soils, where the freezing of soil water causes the shattering of large clods.

frost heave the lifting upward of soil and plants resulting from expansion when ice forms in the soil.

frost pocket a site where cold air accumulates behind a barrier or in a hollow, giving rise to frequent frosts.

fruit a fertilized and ripened plant ovary, together with any adnate parts.

fruit bud, blossom bud, flower bud a bud which on opening gives rise to flowers (or flowers and leaves), with potential for fruit production. It is distinguished from a vegetative bud by its larger size and more rounded shape.

fruit cage a wood or metal framework, to about 6 ft (1.8 m) high, clad with plastic or wire netting, and used especially to protect soft fruits such as berries from birds.

fruit flies (Diptera: Tephritidae) small, grayish-yellow flies often with mottled wings, which are distributed worldwide but mostly in the tropics. Their white maggots feed on fleshy fruits and the flower heads of Compositae, but some mine leaves or make galls. The CHERRY FRUIT FLY (*Rhagoletis cerasi*), which is found in North America and in parts of Asia, in Europe but not the UK, attacks cherries, honeysuckle and *Prunus* species; as many as six larvae may invade a single fruit. The APPLE FRUIT FLY (*R. pomonella*) is a major pest of apples in North America; the maggots make winding tunnels in the flesh of the fruit and also attack plum, pear, cherry, blueberry, huckleberry, and hawthorn. In North America, currant and gooseberry fruits may be attacked by the CURRANT FRUIT FLY (*Epochra canadensis*). WALNUT HUSK FLIES (*Rhagoletis species*) occur throughout the US; the larvae burrow into the green husks of walnuts, turning them black and slimy. The MEDITERRANEAN FRUIT FLY (*Ceratitis capitata*) attacks peach, citrus, plum, apple and various other fruits in the subtropics. European species include the BERBERIS SEED FLY (*Anomoia purmunda*), which damages berries of *Berberis*, *Pyracantha*, and *Cotoneaster*, and the ROSE HIP FLY (*Rhagoletis alternata*), which feeds on the flesh and seed of rose hips.

Chemical control methods must be aimed at the adults. In North America, pheromone traps and biological controls are used. The name "fruit fly" is normally given to *Drosophila* species, which are not pests of cultivated plants.

fruit house a greenhouse designed for growing fruit. Typically a tall, narrow lean-to structure with fruit trees trained on the back wall. Also known as an orchard house.

fruitlet an immature fruit. See *bud stages*.

fruit set the open flower condition in gooseberry fruit development. See *bud stages*.

fruit setting the development of fruit following the pollination and fertilization of flowers, especially with tree and soft fruits, tomatoes, and cucurbits. Fruit setting can be artificially induced by certain plant hormones. See *dry set*.

fruit swelling an early development stage of tree and soft fruits. See *bud stages*.

fruit thinning the removal of a proportion of immature fruitlets from fruit plants in order to improve the size and color of those remaining, or to prevent overcropping, or as a means of discouraging biennial bearing. It is also referred to as defruiting.

Fuchsia (for Leonhart Fuchs [1501–66], German herbalist and botanical illustrator). Onagraceae. C & S America including Mexico and Tierra del Fuego, also New Zealand, Tahiti. LADY'S EARDROPS. 105 species, evergreen to deciduous shrubs and trees. Often drooping on slender pedicels, the flowers consist of a tubular to bell-shaped calyx with four, ovate to lanceolate, outspread lobes and four or no petals—these are often shorter and broader than the sepals, differently colored and rolled together or spreading. The stamens and long stigma are usually exserted. Globose to oblong, berrylike fruit follow in late summer and fall.

Most fuchsia cultivars are the result of breeding between many species, much of it undocumented. *F. magellanica* and possibly *F. coccinea* arrived at Kew around 1788. *F. magellanica* and *F. fulgens* appear to be the original parents of plants resembling modern cultivars, though perhaps 10 other species may have been involved later. *F. magellanica* has a few variants and hybrids, and *F. triphylla* probably crossed with *F. boliviana* and then with *F. fulgens* and *F. splendens*, giving rise to several cultivars grouped as Triphylla Hybrids, which typically have flowers in clusters with very long tubes and very short sepals. There are also some cultivars and hybrids among the small-flowered species.

Fuchsias are of great value for summer bedding, windowboxes, hanging baskets, and containers on decks; they will grow in any light except deep shade. Hardy species and cultivars are useful in permanent shrub borders and as ornamental hedges up to 6½ ft (2 m) tall, flowering from midsummer until late fall. The tender cultivars and species are lifted in late fall and stored in a frost-free environment during the winter months. Garden plants will grow in any fertile, free-draining soil. Some protection from frost should be given in winter, either by earthing up the crowns or by covering them with sand or leaf litter.

Plant outdoor fuchsias in late spring and early summer; they are best planted deeply to afford the rootstock some protection and a chance of regeneration in areas where frosts are severe. Summer bedding fuchsias are planted out in early summer. Garden plants should be watered during hot, dry weather. Prune in spring once new growth has started, cutting away all old, flowered wood.

All fuchsias may be grown in a greenhouse, either in pots or planted directly in the ground. A minimum winter temperature of 45°F (7°C) is required for species and Triphylla types, but cultivars can be successfully overwintered at 34°F (1°C). Maintain humidity during the summer months by dampening down and misting, except when plants are in bud or flower. Water moderately in spring and plentifully in summer. Shade from direct sun. Under glass, pot in either a medium fertility loam-based potting mix (high-fertility for baskets) or a soil-less medium with added grit (this will need more frequent fertilizing). Repot when growth starts in spring. Feed with a high-nitrogen fertilizer in spring to encourage growth, changing to a high-potash fertilizer in midseason to encourage flowering and ripen growth. Greenhouse plants may be set outside in fall to ripen the wood before they are overwintered in frost-free conditions. They must not be allowed to dry out completely during this period.

For plants grown under glass, little pruning is needed other than in spring, when the previous season's plants are started into growth and are cut back to 2–3 nodes from the main branch, primarily to shape the plant. During the early part of the growing season, pinch out the growing tips to encourage the plant to bush out. When training standards, leave the leading shoot intact and pinch out the side shoots until the main stem has reached two-thirds of the desired height of the finished standard. The next five or six pairs of side shoots are left and the growing tip then removed. Side shoots are pinched out at every 2–3 pairs of leaves until the head of the standard is formed. For weeping standards, train laterals downward to a wire framework.

Propagate from seed or by cuttings. (*See table on following page.*)

full blossom an early development stage of top fruits. See *bud stages*.

fumigation the application of a pesticide to an enclosed growing area in the form of vapor or smoke. On a large scale—for example, in warehouses or commercial greenhouses—volatile substances are vaporized to produce toxic gases. Similar formulations may be injected into the soil or applied under plastic sheeting for soil sterilization.

fungicide a substance used to control diseases caused by fungi. Fungicides may eradicate established infections, prevent spread, or both. Most have contact action, a few are systemic. Fungicides are usually applied as sprays or dips, but seed dressings can be very effective. The term "fungistat" may be used to describe a substance capable of preventing growth of a fungus without killing it.

Commonly used fungicides are derived from a wide range of chemicals, and their effectiveness may depend on environmental conditions, and always on timely application. Approved products should only be used where essential. Careful husbandry and good management of the growing environment, including rotation, attention to drainage, and general crop hygiene, will all mitigate against fungal attack. Overuse may lead to the build-up of resistant fungus strains.

fungus an organism belonging to a group distinct from plants and animals. They are incapable of photosynthesis, and obtain sustenance either as

323

FUCHSIA

Name	Distribution	Habit	Leaves	Flowers
F. arborescens LILAC FUCHSIA	Mexico	shrub or small tree, 10–26 ft (3–8 m) tall	4–8 in (10–20 cm), oblong-elliptic to obovate-lanceolate, entire, dark green above, paler beneath	to ½ in (1 cm), pink to pale purple with contrasting stamens, in dense, erect panicles
F. × bacillaris _F. cinnabarina;_ (_F. microphylla_ × _F. thymifolia_)	garden origin	erect or spreading, twiggy, small shrub, 12–80 in (30–200 cm) tall	¼–¾ in (0.5–2 cm), ovate to broadly lanceolate, entire to serrate, bright green	to ⅝ in (1.5 cm), rose-pink to red, solitary

Comments: Includes 'Reflexa' with minute leaves and very small, cerise flowers.

Name	Distribution	Habit	Leaves	Flowers
F. boliviana syn. _F. cuspidata_	N Argentina to Peru	erect shrub or small tree, 6½–13 ft (2–4 m) tall	2–8 in (2–4 m), narrowly elliptic to broadly ovate, finely toothed, upper surface deep green and smooth to downy, often with red-tinted veins, undersurface paler and downy	2–3 in (5–8 cm), pale pink to vermilion with a scarlet limb, narrowly tubular, pendulous in short racemes or panicles

Comments: 'Alba' has pale green leaves and pure white flowers.

Name	Distribution	Habit	Leaves	Flowers
F. denticulata	Peru and Bolivia	erect to scrambling or sprawling shrub, 13–33 ft (4–10 m) tall	1½–6½ in (4–17 cm), elliptic to lanceolate, denticulate, firm, dark green and smooth above, paler or red-tinted beneath	2–2¾ in (5–7 cm), pink to pale red tipped green-white, petals orange to vermilion, tubular, clustered toward branch tips
F. excorticata	New Zealand	shrub or small tree 3¼–6½ ft (1–2 m), with peeling and papery, rust-colored bark	2–4 in (5–10 cm), ovate-lanceolate, more or less entire	¾–1¼ in (2–3 cm), green marked maroon with blue anthers, solitary, long-stalked
F. fulgens	Mexico	tuberous-rooted shrub, 20 in–10 ft (0.5–3 m) tall	3½–6 in (9–15 cm), ovate-cordate with fine red teeth, glandular, pale green above, flushed red beneath	2–3 in (5–8 cm), pink to orange or fiery scarlet, tubular, pendulous, in racemes
F. magellanica _F. globosa, F. gracilis_	Chile, Argentina, widely naturalized elsewhere	erect shrub to 10 ft (3 m) tall	⅝–2 in (1.5–5 cm), ovate-elliptic, wavy-toothed, mid-green, sometimes tinted red	¾–1½ in (2–4 cm), deep crimson to pink or white with purple to pink or white petals, solitary or paired, pendent

Comments: A variable and hardy species; includes var. **_eburnea_** ('Alba'), with white flowers, var. **_gracilis,_** a slender and highly floriferous shrub with small, scarlet and violet flowers, and var. **_molinae,_** with the palest shell pink flowers. Variegated cultivars include 'Variegata', with leaves edged cream, and 'Versicolor' ('Tricolor') with foliage tinted red or pink at first, becoming gray-green tinted silver and pink and irregularly edged creamy white. One of the most commonly grown cultivars is 'Riccartonii', a robust, suckering and hardy shrub with dark calyx and broader sepals.

| _F. arborescens_ | _F. boliviana_ **var. alba** | _F. fulgens_ | _F._ **Triphylla Group 'Thalia'** |

FUCHSIA

Name	Distribution	Habit	Leaves	Flowers
F. microphylla *F. minutiflora*	Mexico to Costa Rica and Panama	bushy or scrambling, densely twiggy small shrub, 20 in–16 ft (0.5–5 m) tall	¼–1½ in (0.6–4 cm), broadly lanceolate to oblanceolate, entire or toothed, bright green	¼–½ in (0.5–1 cm), white to pink, magenta, cerise or deep red with similarly colored, or paler, or purple petals, solitary
F. procumbens	New Zealand	wiry-stemmed, prostrate to climbing or cascading shrub to 3¼ ft (1 m) tall	¼–¾ in (0.6–2 cm), more or less rounded with a cordate base	½–¾ in (1–1.8 cm), gold to pale orange suffused green and tipped with maroon, with blue anthers, erect, solitary
F. splendens	Mexico to Costa Rica	erect shrub, 20 in–8 ft (0.5–2.5 m) tall	1½–5 in (3.5–13 cm), ovate to cordate, serrate, smooth or hairy, often flushed red and hairy beneath	1¼–2½ in (3–6 cm), rose pink to orange-red tipped green, solitary, pendent to spreading
F. thymifolia	Mexico to Guatemala	erect to spreading, twiggy shrub, 20 in–10 ft (0.5–3 m) tall	⅜–2½ in (0.8–6 cm), elliptic to ovate, entire or toothed, pale, bright green	¼–½ in (0.5–1 cm), green-white to pale pink, the color deepening with age, solitary, pendent
F. triphylla	Hispaniola	erect shrub or subshrub, 12 in–6½ ft (0.3–2 m) tall	1–4 in (2.5–10 cm), elliptic to oblanceolate, entire to finely toothed, mid- to deep green, hairy and often tinted bronze above, flushed purple beneath	1½–2½ in (4–6 cm), orange-red to coral pink, narrowly tubular with a bulbous base, in erect to nodding racemes

parasites of other living organisms or as saprophytes of dead organic material. Fungi reproduce by spores and include such diverse types as yeasts, lichen fungi, molds, mushrooms, and pathogens of plants and animals.

fungus gnats (Diptera: Sciaridae) midgelike flies, up to ⅛ in (4 mm) long, mostly black or dark gray with relatively long legs. Also known as SCIARID FLIES. They are often seen moving rapidly over the soil surface on pot plants and in cucumber crops, occasionally making short slow flights. Fungus gnats occur in fungi, leaf mold, rotting wood, manure and compost piles, and soils containing any of these are readily infested; they are often abundant in peat-based medium. Under favorable conditions, such as in greenhouses where temperatures are high and on moist media with high organic content, breeding continues throughout most of the year.

Most are harmless, but some may damage seedlings, cuttings, and young plants. *Lycoriella auripila* and *L.solani* are important pests of mushrooms. The larvae burrow into small buttons, and the stalk and cap of mature specimens. In greenhouses, avoid accumulations of the plant debris on which flies breed; where the gnats are troublesome, insec-

ticides can be used, either premixed with the growing medium or watered as a drench. Nonchemical control is possible with sticky traps and with the pathogenic eelworm *Steinernema feltiae* or the predatory mite *Hypoaspis miles*.

In North America, the POTATO SCAB GNAT (*Pnyxia scabiei*) can be a serious pest of potatoes. The larvae invade tubers and continue to develop after harvest. Clean seed and crop rotation provide good control.

funicle, funiculus the stalk or thread bearing the ovule or seed and attaching it to the placenta.

funnelform funnel-shaped, e.g., a corolla tube that widens gradually from its base.

furcate forked; the terminal lobes pronglike.

Furcraea (for Antoine François de Fourcroy [1755–1809], French chemist). Agavaceae. Mexico, C America. Some 20 species, evergreen, perennial herbs with large rosettes of swordlike, succulent leaves. Tubular, fragrant flowers composed of six, oblong tepals are carried in very tall, scapose panicles. Cultivate as for *Agave*, with a minimum

temperature of about 43°F (6°C). *Furcraea* rarely sets seed but frequently produces large numbers of bulbils. *F. foetida* (syn. *F. gigantea*) MAURITIUS HEMP, GREEN ALOE; C America; leaves to 70 in (180 cm), sword-shaped, in a basal rosette, with entire to spiny-toothed margins; inflorescence to 23 ft (7 m) tall; flowers strongly scented, milky white inside; var. *mediopicta*: spineless, dark green leaves, striped cream and brushed with pale to blue-green.

fusarium patch disease (*Monographella nivalis*) a common and damaging fungal disease of lawns and sports turf, especially *Poa* species. It causes patches of dead grass, edged dark brown or orange, and wet and slimy, with white or pink fungal bodies matting dead leaves. It is favored by wet conditions, high nitrogen, and dense thatch. Control by good management or by applying a recommended fungicide in the growing season.

fuseau see *dwarf pyramid*.

fusiform spindle-shaped; swollen in the middle and tapering to both ends.

FYM farmyard manure; cow, horse or pig dung, usually mixed with straw; good for improving soil fertility. See *manure*.

G

Gagea (for amateur botanist Sir Thomas Gage [1761–1820], of Hengrave Hall, Suffolk). Liliaceae. Europe, C Asia, N Africa. About 50 species, small, bulbous perennial herbs with linear leaves. Borne singly or in umbels or racemes in spring, the flowers are cylindric to campanulate or rotate and consist of six segments. The following species need shallow soil and hot, dry conditions in summer for bulb ripening. They are best grown in shallow pans in a sunny bulb frame, watered copiously when growing, and dried out when dormant, with just sufficient moisture left to prevent shriveling. Outdoors (min. temp 0°F/−18°C), grow them in well-drained, sandy soil in full sun, in situations that are dry but not completely arid in summer. Provide adequate moisture when in growth. Propagate by division of bulbils or by seed in spring, under glass.

G. graeca (syn. *Lloydia graeca*) E Mediterranean, Greece, Crete; flowers ½–⅝ in (1–1.5 cm) across, white with purple stripes; *G. peduncularis* (N Africa, Balkans, Aegean; flowers ½–¾ in (1–2 cm) across, yellow.

Gaillardia (for M. Gaillard de Charentoneau, French patron of botany). Compositae. S US, Mexico, S America. BLANKET FLOWER. About 30 species, annual, biennial and perennial herbs with entire, toothed or pinnatifid, hairy leaves. Daisylike flower heads are produced in summer, the ray florets yellow to red, tipped with yellow or red-purple, the disk florets purple to red-bronze. Grow in sun in moderately fertile, well-drained soil; they are hardy but generally perform best in poor soil and in hot dry conditions. Cut back after flowering. In zones experiencing heavy snows, protect the crowns of perennial species with a dry mulch

covered with pea sticks or brushwood. Propagate by seed, cultivars by root cuttings in winter also by division.

G. aristata N America; perennial to 28 in (70 cm); flower heads to 4 in (10 cm) across, ray florets yellow or yellow stained red, especially at base; *G. × grandiflora* (*G. aristata* × *G. pulchella*) like *G. aristata* but larger and more vigorous; includes many cultivars with flower heads ranging from pure yellow to burnished gold, dark orange, bronze-red or blood red, in pure shades or bicolors; *G. pulchella* INDIAN BLANKET, FIRE FLOWER, FIRE WHEELS; US, Mexico; annual or short-lived perennial to 24 in (60 cm); flower heads to 2½ in (6 cm) across, ray florets red with yellow tips or bands, or entirely yellow or red; largely represented in cultivation by 'Lorenziana', with many enlarged and tubular disk florets in red, yellow or bicolors.

Galanthus (from Greek *gala*, milk, and *anthos*, flower). Amaryllidaceae. W Europe to Iranian Caucasus and Caspian Sea. SNOWDROP. About 15 species, dwarf to small bulbous perennials ultimately forming clumps. Strap-shaped to elliptic, the leaves emerge from a slender, tubular sheath alongside the flowers. Solitary flowers appear in fall, winter and early spring, nodding atop slender scapes. They are bell-shaped with three larger outer petals, usually oblong to obovate and white, and three smaller, inner petals that form a cup and are marked green.

Grow in dappled sun in moist but well-drained, humus-rich soil that does not dry out excessively in summer; a mulch of leaf mold is beneficial. Dried snowdrop bulbs do not establish easily. Plants are better if bought and planted "in the green"—that is, after flowering and with fully developed leaves. *G. reginae-olgae* requires more sun and greater protection from cold winds than other species. In pots, grow in a mix of equal parts loam, leaf mold, and sharp sand, in a cool shaded frame in summer, bringing into the alpine house in early winter. Most species are reliably hardy to at least 5°F (−15°C). *G. ikariae* is more tender and will suffer below 23°F (−5°C). To bring into bloom in midwinter, pot in spring after flowering and move from the frame to cold green-

house in early fall when bulbs are dormant. Increase by division of clumps after flowering or sow ripe seed sown in a cool shaded frame.

Gray mold is indicated when infected shoots first appear above the ground covered with gray mycelium and spores of the fungus; the rot extends into the bulbs. Small black sclerotia develop on affected bulbs and contaminate the soil, so that any bulbs bearing these resting stages of the fungus should be discarded.

G. elwesii Balkans, W Turkey; winter-flowering; leaves broadly oblong to elliptic, glaucous, hooded at tip; scape to 4 in (10 cm), flowers honey-scented, outer segments broadly obovate to rounded, usually flared, to 1¼ in (3 cm), inner segments marked green at tip and base; var. *monostichus* (syn. *G. caucasicus* hort.): Caucasus; winter-flowering; leaves oblong, glaucous; scape to 5½ in (14 cm), outer flower segments obovate, ¾–1¼ in (2–3 cm), inner segments marked green at tips; Hiemalis Group: smaller, flowering in late fall and early winter; *G. gracilis* (syn. *G. graecus*) Bulgaria, Greece, Turkey; winter-flowering; leaves narrow, twisted, glaucous; scape to 4 in (10 cm), flowers sometimes violet-scented, outer segments broadly obovate and rounded, to 1 in (2.5 cm), inner segments marked green at apex and base; *G. ikariae* (syn. *G. latifolius*) Aegean Is., Turkey, Caucasus; winter-flowering; leaves strap-shaped to broadly oblong, bright, glossy green; scape 2¾–6 in (7–15 cm), outer flower segments oblong to spathulate to 1¼ in (3 cm), inner segments notched and marked green at tips; *G. nivalis* COMMON SNOWDROP; Europe; winter- and early spring-flowering; leaves linear to narrowly strap-shaped, more or less glaucous; scape to 4 in (10 cm); flowers sometimes faintly scented, outer segments oblong, to ¾ in (2 cm), inner segments marked green at tip; f. *pleniflorus* 'Flore Pleno': flowers double with many, sometimes ruffled inner segments; f. *pleniflorus* 'Pusey Green Tips': flowers with a long, earlike bracteole, long, arching, green-tipped outer segments and numerous ruffled inner segments; Sandersii Group: small and delicate with a yellow-green scape, yellow ovary and yellow markings on the inner segments; Scharlockii Group: flowers with two long, earlike bracteoles and outer segments marked green at tips; *G. plicatus* E Europe; winter-flowering; leaves broadly strap-shaped with recurved margins and loosely folded upper surface, glaucous; scape 4–8 in (10–20 cm), outer flower segments oblong to narrowly elliptic, to 1 in (2.5 cm), inner segments marked green at tips; subsp. *byzantinus*: inner segments marked green at tips and base; *G. reginae-olgae* Sicily, Greece, SW Turkey; typically fall-flowering; leaves linear with a glaucous stripe, produced after flowers; scape to 4 in (10 cm), flowers faintly scented, outer segments to 1 in (2.5 cm), inner segments marked green at tips; subsp. *reginae-olgae*: plants flowering in late fall with leaves developed; subsp. *vernalis*: plants flowering in spring with leaves developed; *G. rizehensis* Turkey; late-winter- and early-spring-flowering; leaves linear, dull deep green; scape 4–8 in (10–20 cm), outer flower segments oblong to oval, to ¾ in (2 cm), inner segments marked green at tips.

Galax (from Greek *gala*, milk; meaning obscure). Diapensiaceae. SE US. WANDFLOWER, WAND PLANT, BEETLE WEED, GALAXY, COLTSFOOT. 1 species, *G. urceolata* (syn. *G. aphylla*), a tufted, evergreen perennial herb with a matted, creeping rootstock. The leaves are basal and slender-stalked with blades 1–3 in (2.5–7.5 cm) in diameter, circular to cordate and toothed. Glossy dark green, they often become bronze in cold weather or bright sunlight. Small, white flowers are carried in spikelike racemes to 18 in (45 cm) tall in late spring and early summer. Fully hardy and suitable for the woodland garden and for underplanting in shrubberies. Excellent groundcover, the foliage also lasts well when cut. Grow in moist, leafy, nonalkaline soil with part shade, and mulch annually in spring with acidic organic matter, such as pine needles. Propagate by division in early spring, or by seed sown in early spring or in fall and kept moist in the shaded cold frame.

Galega (from Greek *gala*, milk; once thought to increase milk flow). Leguminosae. S Europe to Asia Minor, tropical E Africa. Some 6 species, erect, perennial herbs with pinnate leaves. The pealike flowers are carried in axillary racemes in summer. *Galega* is a vigorous perennial for the large herbaceous and mixed border and for more informal plantings in the wild garden. It is hardy at least to 5°F (–15°C). Grow in sun or light shade in moisture-retentive soil. Propagate by division or by seed soaked for 12 hours before sowing. *G. officinalis* GOAT'S RUE; C and S Europe, Asia Minor; to 5 ft (1.5 m); flowers to ½ in (1 cm) long, white to lavender; includes the Hartlandii Group, syn. *G. × hartlandii*, with flowers in shades of white, palest lavender, lilac blue and mauve-pink, also combinations thereof.

Galium (from Greek *gala*, milk; referring to former use of *G. verum* in curdling milk for cheese manufacture). Rubiaceae. Subcosmopolitan (temperate). BEDSTRAW, CLEAVERS. Some 400 species, annual or perennial herbs with clumped, erect to climbing stems and whorled leaves. Starry, 4-parted flowers are borne in cymes in summer.

G. odoratum develops its persistent, sweet coumarin fragrance on drying and is an ingredient of potpourri and sachets traditionally used as a moth deterrent. It has been collected and cultivated since the Middle Ages at least, to flavor wines, brandy, apple jellies, sherbets, creams, and fruit salads. As a tisane (allow to wilt slightly before infusing), it has a fresh grassy flavor and a gently sedative effect. Harvest before flowering, and dry in a cool dry and shaded place. As an ornamental, it provides useful groundcover for cool shade, under shrubs or in the woodland garden. It is hardy to at least 5°F (–15°C). Propagate from seed sown fresh in late summer. Divide in spring or at any later time during the growing season.

G. odoratum (syn. *Asperula odorata*) WOODRUFF, SWEET WOODRUFF; Europe, N Africa; creeping to ascending perennial to 18 in (45 cm) with slender, 4-angled stems, the dried shoots strongly scented of hay; leaves whorled, ½–2 in (1–5 cm), dark to bright green; flowers white in terminal clusters.

gall a localized swelling or outgrowth resulting from an abnormal increase in

Marble gall
Pithy "oak apples" or woody marble galls are familiar and benign, spherical outgrowths formed on many *Quercus* species by chemicals secreted by tiny wasps as they feed.

the number of plant cells or from individual cells becoming enlarged. Galls can be caused by bacteria (for example, the beneficial nitrogen-fixing root nodules on legumes caused by *Rhizobium* species, or the damaging CROWN GALL, *Agrobacterium tumefaciens*); by fungi (for example, CLUBROOT of brassicas, caused by *Plasmodiophora brassicae*); by eelworms (for example, ROOT KNOT EELWORM, *Meloidogyne* species, on tomatoes); by viruses, which may cause LEAFY OUTGROWTHS referred to as enations; by mites (for example, BIG BUD of black currants, caused by *Cecidophyopsis ribis*); or by insects (for example, RED LEAF BLISTER of red and white currants caused by the aphid *Cryptomyzus ribis*, OAK APPLES caused by the gall wasp *Biorhiza pallida* and ROOT GALLS on brassicas caused by the TURNIP GALL WEEVIL, *Ceutorhynchus pleurostigma*).

gall midges (Diptera: Cecidomyiidae) small fragile flies, up to ⅛ in (3 mm) in length, mostly with delicate hairy wings. The legless larvae, up to ⅛ in (4 mm) long, have diverse feeding habits depending on the species to which they belong. Some are predators, mainly of aphids or, sometimes, mites; others feed on decaying organic matter; some feed on fungi, especially rusts and mildew; many are plant parasites, sometimes inducing plant galls.

Several gall midges are pests of tree and soft fruit, including two common in both Europe and North America. The PEAR MIDGE (*Contarinia pyrivora*) has yellow or white larvae that infest pear fruitlets, causing them to become blackened and fall prematurely; the PEAR LEAF MIDGE (*Dasineura pyri*) has white larvae that live and feed within the upward-rolled margins of pear leaves. Other species that attack fruit in Europe include the BLACK-CURRANT LEAF MIDGE (*D. tetensi*), the RASPBERRY CANE MIDGE (*Resseliella theobaldi*), and a related species, the RED BUD BORER (*R. occuliperda*), which is a pest of newly budded fruit trees and roses.

European species responsible for damage to vegetables include the RUTABAGA MIDGE (*Contarinia nasturtii*), whose yellow-white larvae feed on young leaves and shoots of various brassicas, often causing blindness (where growing points fail to develop), and the PEA MIDGE (*C. pisi*), whose larvae feed on the flowers, leaves, and pods of peas.

Gall midges common on ornamental plants in both Europe and North America include the honey locust or GLEDITSIA GALL MIDGE (*Dasineura gleditchiae*), which converts leaflets into podlike structures. European species targeting ornamentals include the HEMEROCALLIS GALL MIDGE (*Contarinia quinenotata*), which enlarges and destroys the flower buds, and the VIOLET GALL MIDGE (*Dasineura affinis*), which causes swollen and rolled leaves on violets. The ROSE MIDGE (*Dasineura rhodophaga*) is an important pest of roses in North America, its white to light orange larvae deforming shoot tips with malformation and death of flower buds.

Control by hand-picking and destruction of the galls. Residual contact insecticides can be effective if applied when gall midges are likely to be laying eggs.

gall mites (Acarina: Eriophyidae) very small mites, up to $1/100$ in (0.25 mm) long, with white or yellow, elongated, maggotlike bodies; they differ from other mites in having two pairs of legs rather than four. Gall mites are capable of moving only short distances and are mainly dispersed by wind. All are plant-feeders and most attack a single plant species or closely related plants. Often there is no discernible damage, but some mites are associated with characteristic galls on

the leaves of woody plants, such as the NAIL GALL MITE of Europe (*Eriophyes tiliae*), which makes small, pointed red galls on the upper surface of linden (*Tilia* species) leaves. Several species common to Europe and parts of North America live in leaf buds causing them to swell, including the YEW GALL MITE (*Cecidophyopsis psilaspis*). Among the rust mite species that feed openly on leaves, the APPLE RUST MITE (*Aculus schlechtendali*) is widespread in Europe and North America; it causes severe russeting of leaves and fruitlets.

The BROOM GALL MITE (*Aceria genistae*) invades the vegetative buds of *Cytisus*, which as a result develop into cauliflower-like growths. Several species of gall mite been associated with witches' brooms, which commonly occur on birch and willows, although the implication of the mites has never been confirmed.

Gall mites are difficult to control in gardens due to the restricted availability of effective chemicals. Most damage is only cosmetic and can be tolerated; where damage is more severe, it may be necessary to replace plants.

gall wasps (Hymenoptera: Cynipidae) small, inconspicuous insects, up to $3/8$ in (8 mm) long, with brown or black bodies and two pairs of wings, or sometimes wingless. They lay eggs in plant tissue, the majority infesting oaks and others living mostly on wild roses. As the eggs hatch, the larvae feed on the plant tissue that swells up around them to form galls. Within the life cycle of oak gall wasps, two different types of gall may be produced on different parts of the host plant to accommodate alternate sexual and asexual generations. Gall wasps seldom cause sufficient damage to warrant control measures; see *bedeguar*.

Galtonia (for Sir Francis Galton [1822–1911], geneticist, anthropologist and explorer). Liliaceae (Hyacinthaceae). Eastern South Africa. 3 species, bulbous perennial herbs. The leaves are rather fleshy and narrowly lanceolate to strap-shaped. Long-stalked and cylindric to conical, the flower spikes arise in late summer and fall. White or green, the flowers are showy, funnel- to bell-shaped and nodding. *G. candicans* is the hardiest species. With deep mulch

protection, it may be grown where winter temperatures fall to 5°F (–15°C); the remaining species are slightly less cold-tolerant, suffering at temperatures between 23° and 14°F (–5° and –10°C). Grow in a sunny, sheltered position in well-drained soil that does not dry out when plants are in leaf. In harsh climates, lift the bulbs in winter and store them in dry, frost-free conditions prior to replanting in spring. Propagate by ripe seed sown in spring, or by offsets.

G. candicans SUMMER HYACINTH; to $3 1/4$ ft (1 m) tall; leaves 20–40 in (50–100 cm) × 2 in (5 cm); flowers fragrant, to $1 1/4$ in (3 cm), white faintly tinted green at base; *G. princeps* differs from *G. candicans* in its flowers, strongly tinted green at base and on lobes, these are carried in shorter, broader spikes; *G. viridiflora* to $3 1/4$ ft (1 m); flowers $3/4$–2 in (2–5 cm), pale green with white-edged lobes.

gamete a fertile reproductive cell of either sex, which unites with another gamete at fertilization to form a zygote.

gametophyte the sexual, or haploid, stage in the life-cycle of a plant showing alternation of generations, when the gametes are produced on a specially developed form of the plant.

gamopetalous with petals united by their margins, in the form of a tubular or funnelform corolla, at least at their bases.

gamophyllous with leaves or leaflike organs united by their margins.

gamosepalous with sepals united by their margins.

garden line a length of thin cord or string wound directly or by a spool onto a stout wooden or metal pin, with the free end tied to a second pin. Pulled taut between two marker stakes, it is used to lay out straight lines for seed drills or planting rows.

gardenesque a style of gardening promoted by J. C. Loudon in the mid-19th century and based on the principle of attributing equal importance to carefully cultivated exotic plants and their setting. It aimed to make the garden appear as a work of art rather than of nature. Later writers used the term derogatorily when referring to Victorian gardens, which they felt lacked a sense of design.

Gardenia (for Dr. Alexander Garden [1735–91], botanist of South Carolina and correspondent of Linnaeus). Rubiaceae. Tropical Old World. Some 250 species, shrubs or trees with leathery leaves and axillary or terminal flowers. Typically white to cream and produced at various times of year, the flowers are either solitary or in few-flowered cymes and usually fragrant. They consist of a cylindric to campanulate corolla tube and a spreading limb of 5–12 lobes. Grow in a humus-rich, acidic, soilless medium, with high humidity and bright indirect light. Water freely when growing and moderately at other times. Maintain a minimum temperature of 59°F (15°C) in winter. In areas where tap water is alkaline, use rainwater or apply sequestered iron at approximately semiweekly intervals. Propagate in spring by greenwood cuttings. Alternatively, take ripewood cuttings, with a heel, in late summer or fall, and root these in a sandy mix in a closed case with a bottom heat.

G. jasminoides (syn. *G. augusta*) CAPE JASMINE, COMMON GARDENIA; E Asia; evergreen shrub or tree to 40 ft (12 m) tall, usually far smaller in cultivation; leaves glossy dark green; flowers 2–4 in (5–10 cm) across, white to ivory,

Garden line and measure
Twine pulled taut between two marker stakes establishes straight rows along which planting or sowing distances can be marked out.

intensely fragrant, roselike in shape and usually double with a shortly cylindric corolla tube to 1¼ in (3 cm) long; includes several cultivars, among them 'Fortuniana', with large, heavily perfumed flowers turning from pure white to ivory; *G. thunbergia* WHITE GARDENIA; South Africa; evergreen shrub or tree to 16 ft (5 m); leaves glossy; flowers white to cream, fragrant, with a limb of overlapping segments each to 1¼ in (3 cm) long, and a narrow corolla tube to 2¾ in (7 cm) long.

garlic (*Allium sativum*) a hardy onion-like perennial, probably of Central Asian origin but cultivated in Egypt before 2000 BC; grown for its strongly aromatic oily bulbs, consisting typically of a number of offsets, or cloves. The cloves are used, either raw or cooked, as a savory flavoring, and the young green leaves may be finely chopped in salads; also for medicinal purposes.

Bulb formation is encouraged by increased day-length and higher temperatures, but garlic is hardier and more easily grown than often thought. Cool storage of dormant cloves at 32–50°F (0–10°C) hastens bulbing; high temperature delays or prevents it.

Plant only healthy individual cloves, of at least ½ in (13 mm) diam. or about ⅓ oz (10 g) in weight, in early spring (from cold store) or in fall. Space 6 in (15 cm) apart in rows 12 in (30 cm) apart, and cover with soil to a depth of 1 in (25 mm) above the clove tip. Garlic can be raised in small pots or cell modules prior to setting out, although a cold period outdoors is necessary. Bulbs become dormant in summer, and should be lifted when the leaves die down. After drying, they can be stored as ropes through to spring, or for longer in cold storage. Pink and white forms exist, and some store better than others.

Garlic chives (*Allium tuberosum*) is a perennial grown for the mild garlic flavor of its flat leaves and flowers. Cultivate as chives (q.v.).

garotting a method of restricting growth and improving the yield of fruit trees by twisting a metal wire tightly around a branch or the main trunk. It is similar in principle to bark ringing but less drastic in effect.

Garrya (for Nicholas Garry [d. 1830] of the Hudson Bay Company, who helped David Douglas on his plant collecting expeditions in western North America). Garryaceae. W US, Mexico, West Indies. Some 18 species, dioecious, evergreen trees or shrubs with leathery leaves. Inconspicuous flowers are carried amid overlapping, paired bracts along pendulous, tassel-like catkins—these are more showy on male plants. Hardy to 0°F (−18°C), especially if grown as a wall shrub. Plant in spring in well-drained soil, in sun or shade. Propagate in late summer by cuttings of semiripe side shoots with a heel, or, in late winter, by hardwood basal cuttings rooted under mist, or in a case. Prune only to establish shape or to remove deadwood; do this immediately after flowering, since catkins are borne at the tips of the previous season's wood. Purple blotches or blackening of the leaves are symptoms of frost damage and wind scorch.

G. elliptica SILK TASSEL BUSH, TASSEL TREE; W US; shrub or small tree to 13 ft (4 m) tall; leaves to 3 in (8 cm), oblong to elliptic, wavy-edged, tough, glossy gray-green to matt dark green; male catkins to 8 in (20 cm) long, gray narrow, hanging in clusters in winter and spring; includes 'James Roof', with deep sea green leaves and silver-gray to mushroom-colored catkins, to 8 in (20 cm) long and in abundant clusters.

Gasteria (from Greek *gaster*, belly, alluding to the inflated base of the perianth tube). Liliaceae (Aloeaceae). South Africa. 14 species, compact, more or less stemless perennial succulents. The fleshy leaves are strap-shaped and distichous or spirally arranged in compact rosettes. Nodding on a lax, simple or sparingly branched raceme, the flowers are tubular and pink to vermilion tipped green. Cultivate as for the smaller *Aloe* species.

G. bicolor (syn. *G. caespitosa*) leaves 1¼–9 in (3–22 cm), dark green spotted white in obscure crossbands, tip pointed; *G. liliputana* miniature with leaves to 2½ in (6 cm) long, blotched white; *G. carinata* leaves 1¼–4¾ in (3–12 cm), keeled beneath, dark green covered in pale tubercles; *G. verrucosa* leaves not keeled but densely covered in white tubercles).

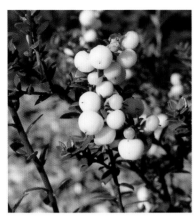

Gaultheria mucronata 'Wintertime'
The shrubby genus *Gaultheria* now encompasses several species formerly known to gardeners as *Pernettya*.

Gaultheria (for Dr. Gaultier, a mid-18th-century physician and botanist from Quebec). Ericaceae. Americas, Japan to Australasia. (Including *Pernettya*.) Around 170 species, evergreen shrubs and shrublets with tough-textured leaves and small, urn-shaped flowers in spring and early summer. These are followed by spherical fruits, often vividly colored, lasting well and with a scent of winter-green. Fully hardy. Grow in sun or semishade in moist, humus-rich, nonalkaline soil. Prune only when necessary to remove deadwood and weak growth. Vigorous species such as *G. shallon* will withstand close clipping. Species previously included in *Pernettya* are particularly useful when mass-planted as medium-height groundcover. Species such as *G. mucronata* and *G. pumila* may require one male pollinator to 5–10 fruiting plants to fruit well. Propagate by greenwood cuttings in summer, by division in early spring or fall, or by seed sown in early spring.

G. cuneata W China; dwarf, compact shrub to 12 in (30 cm); leaves ½–1¼ in (1–3 cm), ovate to obovate, glandular-serrate, leathery; flowers white; fruit to ¼ in (0.6 cm), white; *G. forrestii* SW China; rounded bush to 3¼ ft (1 m); leaves 2–3½ in (5–9 cm), narrowly ovate to oblong or oblanceolate, bristly-serrate, leathery; flowers to ¼ in (0.5 cm), fragrant, milky white; fruit to ¼ in (0.6 cm), blue); *G. miqueliana* (Japan; shrub to 12 in (30 cm); leaves ¾–1½ in (2–4 cm), ovate to bluntly obovate, glandular-serrate; flowers to

⅛ in (0.4 cm), white; fruit to ½ in (1 cm), white or pale pink; *G. mucronata* (syn. *Pernettya mucronata*) Chile, Argentina; rigidly branched, suckering shrub to 5 ft (1.5 m); leaves ⅜–¾ in (0.8–1.8 cm), oval to elliptic, sharply pointed, entire to toothed, rigid, dark green; flowers to ¼ in (0.6 cm), white to pink; fruit to ½ in (1.2 cm) white, rose or lilac to crimson or purple-black; includes numerous cultivars; *G. nummularioides* (Himalaya; prostrate shrublet; leaves ¼–⅝ in (0.6–1.5 cm), ovate to elliptic, rounded, bristly-serrate, rugose, dull green; flowers to ¼ in (0.6 cm), white to pink or red-brown; fruit to ⅜ in (0.8 cm), blue-black; *G. procumbens* CHECKERBERRY, WINTERGREEN, TEA BERRY, MOUNTAIN BERRY; eastern N America; creeping shrublet to 12 in (30 cm); leaves ¾–2 in (2–5 cm), elliptic to obovate, finely crenate to bristly serrate, otherwise smooth, mid- to deep green; flowers to ¼ in (0.7 cm), white to pale pink; fruit to ⅜ in (1.5 cm), dark pink to deep red, flesh white to pink, strongly scented of wintergreen; *G. pumila* (syn. *Pernettya pumila*) southern S America, Falkland Islands; prostrate shrub; leaves to ¼ in (0.6 cm), ovate to lanceolate, blunt to rounded, leathery, glossy, smooth; flowers to ¼ in (0.6 cm), white; fruit to ¾ in (2 cm), white or red-tinted; 'Harold Comber': fruit large, deep pink; *G. shallon* SALAL, SHALLON; Alaska to California; low-growing, suckering and spreading shrub to 24 in (60 cm); leaves 2–4 in (5–10 cm), broadly ovate, apex acute, bristly serrate; flowers to ¼ in (0.5 cm), white tinged pink, in drooping racemes; fruit to ½ in (1 cm), red ripening with a black tinge); *G. tasmanica* (syn. *Pernettya tasmanica*) Tasmania; mat-forming shrub; leaves to ⅜ in (0.8 cm), oblong, acute, more or less crenate, leathery and glossy; flowers to ¼ in (0.6 cm), white; fruit to ½ in (1 cm) with a vivid red, enlarged fleshy calyx; *G. trichophylla* W China, Himalaya; wiry-stemmed, cushion-forming shrub; leaves to ½ in (1 cm), elliptic or ovate to narrowly oblong, bristly-serrate; flowers to ⅛ in (0.4 cm), red to pink or white; fruit to ½ in (1 cm), pale blue; *G.* × *wisleyensis* (*G. shallon* × *G. mucronata*; syn. × *Gaulnettya wisleyensis*; vigorous, suckering shrubs to 3¼ ft (1 m), forming dense thickets of small, tough, dark green

leaves, the flowers white to pink or red-tinted, the fruit showy and white to purple-red or ruby; includes numerous cultivars).

Gaura (from Greek *gauros*, superb, referring to the flowers). Onagraceae. N America. 21 species, annual, biennial or perennial herbs. Borne in spikes in summer and fall, the short-lived flowers are tubular to funnel-shaped and consist of four, clawed petals. A graceful hardy plant for herbaceous borders, the wild garden or collections of native plants. Plant in sun in well-drained soil. Propagate from seed in spring or early summer. *G. lindheimeri* Texas, Louisiana; willowy perennial to 5 ft (1.5 m) tall; flowers to 1¼ in (3 cm) across, white suffused with pink in loose, erect spikes.

Gaylussacia (for J. L. Gay-Lussac [1778–1850], French chemist). Ericaceae. Americas. Some 40 species, deciduous or evergreen shrubs. The flowers are small and tubular, urceolate or campanulate with five lobes. They are carried in axillary racemes in late spring and give rise to berrylike fruit. Plant in moist, sandy, acidic soil in the shrub border, open woodland or rock garden, in part shade or full sun. Propagate by softwood cuttings in summer, by division of rooted suckers or by seed in fall. *G. baccata* HUCKLEBERRY; E US; erect, deciduous shrub to 3¼ ft (1 m) tall; leaves pale green turning red in fall, resinous; flowers dull red; fruit black, glossy, edible.

Gazania (perhaps named for Theodore of Gaza [1398–1478], who translated the botanical works of Theophrastus into Latin). Compositae. Tropical and southern Africa. TREASURE FLOWER. About 16 species, perennial or annual herbs. They produce showy, daisylike flower heads on slender stalks in summer. In dry climates that are frost-free or almost so, the following are grown as annuals or perennials in flower borders and rockeries. In cool temperate gardens, they are grown as half-hardy annuals, but, in warm sunny positions with good drainage, they may overwinter successfully. They are drought-tolerant and will withstand salt-laden winds. Propagate by seed in early spring under glass or *in situ* after the last frost. Root heeled cuttings in summer; in sand in a closed case with bottom heat; overwinter new plants at 50°F (10°C). *G. rigens* TREASURE FLOWER; S Africa; decumbent perennial to 12 in (30 cm) tall; leaves oblong to spathulate, entire to pinnately lobed, dark green above, silvery beneath with margins incurved; flower heads to 3 in (8 cm) across, ray florets orange with black basal spots, disk florets orange-brown; var. *uniflora*: syn. *G. uniflora*, smaller flower heads with bright yellow ray florets; many cultivars and hybrids have been developed, including plants with very silvery, or yellow-variegated leaves, and flower heads in tones of white, yellow, tangerine, orange, red, pink, and purple-bronze.

gazebo a roofed structure designed to command a view. A gazebo may take the form of a turret or lantern on a housetop or, often, a separate garden house. It is also known as a belvedere. The term gazebo is sometimes used of a projecting window or balcony.

gazon coupe a form of parterre in which shapes are cut from turf and filled with colored sand or gravel.

Gelsemium (from Italian, *gelsomino*, jasmine). Loganiaceae. Americas, SE Asia. CAROLINA JASMINE, YELLOW JASMINE. 3 species, perennial, evergreen, twining shrubs with clusters of sweetly fragrant flowers in late spring and summer—these are funnel-shaped and five-lobed. In zones that are more or less frost-free, the following species is suitable for training on trellis and pergolas or for growing on steep banks. Elsewhere, it will need the shelter of a warm, south-facing wall. In such conditions and where long, hot summers ensure ripening, it may tolerate temperatures to 14°F (−10°C) or below. Otherwise, grow in the cool greenhouse or conservatory. Plant in full sun or light shade. Under glass, this climber flowers more profusely if restricted at the roots. Prune hard after flowering. Propagate by seed in spring at 64–68°F (18–20°C), or by semiripe cuttings in a closed case with gentle bottom heat. *G. sempervirens* FALSE JASMINE, EVENING TRUMPET FLOWER;

S US, C America; to 20 ft (6 m) tall; leaves glossy; flowers sweetly scented, to 1¼ in (3 cm), yellow with an orange center.

gel sowing see *fluid drilling*.

geminate paired.

gemma an asexual reproductive body, budlike and detaching itself from the parent plant.

gemmation a form of secondary growth in potato tubers, occurring especially after spasmodic development as a result of a drought period. Characteristically, areas near the eyes swell into smooth knoblike protuberances.

gemmiparous bearing vegetative buds.

gene a segment of chromosome which encodes for a specific characteristic; a unit of inheritance in plants.

genetic modification (GM), genetic engineering a laboratory process whereby particular genes are identified, extracted and transferred from one plant cell to another, including to a cell of a different species. By this means, desirable characteristics can be implanted and perpetuated by propagation.

genetics the study of heredity and variation; sometimes loosely used to describe the practice of plant breeding.

geniculum a kneelike joint or node where an organ or axis is sharply bent.

Genista (name used by Virgil). Leguminosae. Europe, Mediterranean to W Asia. BROOM, WOAD WAXEN. Some 90 species, shrubs, or small trees, sometimes spiny, mostly deciduous, but appearing evergreen due to green, flattened branchlets. Pealike, yellow flowers are carried in terminal racemes or heads in spring and summer. Grow in full sun in well-drained and not-too-fertile soil. The low-growing and compact species are suited to warm, sunny ledges in the rock garden. *G. sagittalis* thrives on the tops of dry-stone walls, or trailing over the edges of

raised beds. *G. hispanica* is hardy to about −4°F (−20°C) and one of the best shrubs for clothing dry sunny banks. Most *Genista* species are cold-tolerant to at least 5°F (−15°C), including the graceful weeping tree broom, *G. aetnensis*. *G. tinctoria* can show cold tolerance to −31°F (−35°C) and below. *Genista* does not shoot freely if cut hard back. Increase by softwood or semiripe cuttings or by seed in fall.

G. aetnensis MOUNT ETNA BROOM; Sardinia, Sicily; slender shrub or tree to 20 ft (6 m) with fine, weeping branches; leaves linear, sparse or absent; flowers golden yellow) *G. canariensis* (syn. *Cytisus canariensis*) Canary Islands; bushy shrub to 6½ ft (2 m); leaves trifoliolate, downy, each leaflet to ½ in (1 cm); flowers bright yellow, fragrant; *G. cinerea* SW Europe, NW Africa; erect shrub to 10 ft (3 m) with long, slender branches; leaves to ½ in (1 cm), narrowly elliptic, downy beneath; flowers bright yellow; *G. hispanica* SPANISH BROOM; S France, N Spain; spiny, erect shrub to 28 in (70 cm); leaves to ½ in (1 cm), ovate-oblong, downy beneath, present only on flowering branches; flowers golden yellow; *G. lydia* E Balkans, Syria; prostrate shrub to 12 in (30 cm), the branches ascending with prickly tips, gray-green; leaves to ½ in (1 cm), linear to elliptic; flowers golden yellow; *G. pilosa* W and C Europe; prostrate to erect shrub to 18 in (45 cm), branches ascending, downy; leaves to ⅝ in (1.5 cm), oblanceolate, silky beneath, dark green above; flowers golden yellow; includes prostrate and mound-forming cultivars; *G. sagittalis* (syn. *G. delphinensis*) S and C Europe; prostrate shrub to 6 in (15 cm), branches green with broad wings, giving the whole a leafy, evergreen appearance; leaves to ¾ in (2 cm), lanceolate; flowers golden yellow; *G.* × *spachiana* (*G. stenopetala* × *G. canariensis*; syn. *Cytisus* × *spachianus*, *G. fragrans*); evergreen shrub 10–20 ft (3–6 m) tall; leaves trifoliolate, leaflets to ⅝ in (1.5 cm), obovate, rounded, dark green above, silky beneath; flowers yellow; *G. tenera* Madeira, Tenerife; resembles *G. cinerea*, but with shorter, stouter branches, becoming twiggy; leaves gray-green; flowers yellow; 'Golden Shower': flowers bright gold in profusion; *G. tinctoria* DYER'S GREENWEED; Europe, Asia

Minor, Ukraine; variable, more or less erect shrub to 6½ ft (2 m); leaves to 2 in (5 cm), elliptic to oblanceolate, bright green, glabrous; flowers golden yellow; 'Royal Gold': profuse, conical panicles of rich yellow flowers.

genotype the genetic constitution of an organism; cf. *phenotype*.

Gentiana (named for Gentius, ancient King of Illyria, said to be the discoverer of medicinal properties of gentian roots). Gentianaceae. Cosmopolitan except Africa, usually in mountainous regions. GENTIAN. About 400 species, annual, biennial or perennial herbs (the following are perennial). The flowers are rotate to funnel-shaped, the corolla tube sometimes pleated, and the limb divided into five to seven short and pointed lobes.

The smaller alpine species do well on scree beds with underlying moisture, especially *G. verna*. Dwarf gentians (*G. ornata*, *G. sino-ornata*, and *G. acaulis*) are well suited to moist sites in the rock garden. Although they should not be planted where they will suffer tree drip, they do appreciate some protection from fierce sunlight. *G. saxosa* is best cultivated in the alpine house, in a 2:2:1 mix of loam, sand, and leaf mold or coir, with a collar of sharp grit around the neck. *G. acaulis*, *G. farreri*, *G. verna* and their hybrids may also be accommodated in the alpine house, where their flowers will not be damaged by rain and their winter requirements (for cool and relatively dry conditions) can be met more easily.

Some species lend themselves to pocket plantings in paving where, given a gritty substrate, they will appreciate the coolness at their roots. These include *G. acaulis*, *G. septemfida* and *G. sino-ornata*. For border plantings, two types are useful: those forming low-growing mats, such as *G. sino-ornata*, *G. acaulis*, *G. farreri* and *G. septemfida*, suitable for drifts and groups at the border's edge, and taller-growing subjects, such as *G. asclepiadea* and *G. lutea*. These last two are shade-tolerant and may naturalize in wild, woodland and bog gardens, in moist, acidic soil. All require perfect drainage and ample moisture at the roots during their growing season.

Gentiana septemfida
This spreading, low-growing plant is suitable for both the front of the border and the rock garden, and is more tolerant of full sun than some of the other smaller gentians.

Sow seed as soon as ripe, thinly and combined with fine, dry sand into a light, porous, sandy mix, and plunge pots in the cold frame. All species require light for germination. Take 1½–2½-in (4–6-cm) cuttings of those species that do not form a central rosette and taproot; cut cleanly with a sharp knife, close to the crown, and insert firmly into a sandy sterilized mix. Place in a cool, shaded frame and keep moist. Mat-forming species with fibrous root systems may be divided in early spring. Layering, which often occurs naturally, can be induced by pegging down shoots in spring; these may be detached in the following season. Rust fungus gives rise to brown pustules on the leaves and stems.

G. acaulis (syn. *G. excisa*, *G. kochiana*) Europe, Spain to Balkans; tufted; leaves in a basal rosette; flowers solitary, to 2 in (5 cm), campanulate, dark blue, spotted green within tube; *G. angustifolia* Europe, particularly SW Alps, Jura, Pyrenees; tufted; leaves in a rosette; flowers solitary to 2 in (5 cm), funnel-shaped, deep sky blue, paler and spotted green within tube; *G. asclepiadea* WILLOW GENTIAN; Europe, Asia Minor; clump-forming with erect to arching stems to 12 in (30 cm); flowers in clusters, to 1½ in (3.5 cm), narrowly campanulate, azure, spotted purple within white-striped throat; sky blue and white-flowered forms are also grown; *G. clusii* C and S Europe; tufted; leaves in rosettes; flowers solitary, to 2 in (5 cm), funnelform or campanulate, deep azure, paler and spotted olive green within; *G. farreri* NW China; stems slender, branched, trailing; leaves tufted or paired; flowers solitary, to 2½ in (6 cm), narrowly funnel-shaped, Cambridge blue tinged green, tube white within, striped deep violet-blue and white on exterior; *G. gracilipes* (NW China; stem to 10 in (25 cm), branched, decumbent; flowers solitary, long-stalked, 1½ in (3.5 cm), narrowly campanulate, deep purple-blue, exterior green; *G. lutea* BITTERWORT; Europe; robust, erect to 6½ ft (2 m), stems thick; leaves paired and opposite; flowers yellow in axillary clusters, to 1 in (2.5 cm), rotate to campanulate; *G. × macaulayi* (*G. sino-ornata* × *G. farreri*) vigorous with low, branching and rooting stems; flowers solitary, to 2½ in (6.5 cm), widely funnel-shaped, deep blue, striped violet and paneled green-white outside; includes the mid-blue, late-flowering 'Edinburgh', the large, deep blue 'Kidbrooke Seedling', and the pale blue 'Wells Variety'); *G. ornata* C Nepal to SW China; prostrate, to 4 in (10 cm); flowers solitary, to 1½ in (3.5 cm), broadly campanulate, pale blue striped purple-blue with white panels outside; *G. saxosa* New Zealand; tufted, stems prostrate then ascending; leaves fleshy; flowers solitary or two to five per cyme, to ¾ in (2 cm), white veined purple-brown, campanulate, with blunt, oblong lobes; *G. septemfida* W and C Asia; erect or ascending, 6–12 in (15–30 cm), clumped; leaves paired; flowers in terminal clusters, to 1½ in (3.5 cm), narrowly campanulate, deep blue with pale spots, paler within; *G. sino-ornata* W China, Tibet; prostrate with sprawling and rooting stems; leaves paired; flowers solitary, to 2¼ in (5.5 cm) funnel-shaped, deep blue, paler within, exterior with stripes of purple-blue, paneled green-white; *G. verna* (SPRING GENTIAN; low, tufted, flowering stems to 4 in (10 cm); flowers solitary, ½–1¼ in (1–3 cm) in diameter, rotate, brilliant blue, sometimes pale blue, or pink to purple-red, throat white).

genus (pl. genera) the principal rank in the taxonomic hierarchy between

G

family and species. The genus represents a single highly distinctive species (monotypic or monospecific genus) such as *Ginkgo* or, more often, a number of species united by a common suite of distinctive characters. The genus or generic name is italicized and takes a capital letter.

geocarpy the subterranean ripening of fruits developed from flowers borne above ground, as in the peanut (*Arachis hypogaea*).

geophyte a plant growing with a stem or tuber below ground; usually applied to tuberous or bulbous species from arid or semiarid lands.

geotropism directional growth of a plant in response to gravity. Positive geotropism is demonstrated by roots growing downward, negative geotropism by shoots growing upward. See *stimulus movements*.

Geranium (from Greek, *geranos*, crane, referring to the long beak of the fruit; the name *geranion* was used by Discorides). Geraniaceae. Temperate regions. CRANESBILL. Some 300 species of mostly perennial, but also annual herbs and some subshrubs, not to be confused with *Pelargonium*, which is popularly known as geranium. Those here are perennial herbs, often hairy and to varying degrees glandular. Their leaves are typically rounded in outline and palmately divided, the segments themselves may be lobed, forked and toothed. Produced in spring and summer, the flowers have 5, usually obovate petals.

G. canariense, G. incanum, G. maderense, and *G. traversii* var. *elegans* are not fully hardy. Below 10°F (–12°C), they need a warm and sheltered site, fast-draining soil, and protection from wet winter conditions. They might equally be grown in the cold greenhouse or conservatory. These species are, however,

easily propagated from seed and wellworth risking outdoors. The remaining species are hardy.

Several of the smaller plants thrive on the rock garden, old walls, among paving stones and in raised beds and sinks, including *G. cinereum, G. dalmaticum, G. orientalitibeticum, G. pylzowianum,* and *G. sanguineum* var. *striatum.* They prefer full sun and freedraining soil. Increase by division, rooted lengths of stem and runners. Two of the smaller species, *G. renardii* and *G. sessiliflorum*, have differing needs—the first seems happier in the dry garden among pinks, artemisias, and silver sages; the second favors cool, moist but gritty soil, still in full sun.

The others described here are superb hardy perennials for the herbaceous and mixed border, woodland garden and for underplanting shrubberies. They tolerate a wide range of conditions, from full sun to shade, and will usually withstand periods of drought. Some, like *G. endressii* and *G. macrorrhizum* are near-invincible groundcover. *G. pratense* is a lovely plant for the wild or meadow garden. *G. phaeum* and *G. sinense* are among the most richly and subtly colored of all hardy plants; while the vibrant lime and magenta of the scrambling *G.* 'Anne Folkard' is almost too bright to behold. All of these should be propagated by division in early spring.

G. 'Ann Folkard' (*G. procurrens* × *G. psilostemon*) garden origin; leaves emerging pale gold, later lime green; inflorescence to 3¼ ft (1 m), sprawling and scrambling, much-branched, flowers produced in succession over a long period, to 1¼ in (3 cm) across, deepest magenta veined black; *G. cinereum* Pyrenees; rosette-forming, to 6 in (15 cm); leaves to 2 in (5 cm) across, round, cut into 5–7 wedge-shaped, lobed segments, gray-green, softly hairy; flowers to 1 in (2.5 cm) across, white to pink with purple or

"cranesbill" fruits

Geranium phaeum

white veins; *G. clarkei* Kashmir; to 20 in (50 cm); leaves with 7 pinnately lobed and toothed segments; flowers to 1½ in (4 cm) across, deep purple, pink or white with purple-pink veins; *G. dalmaticum* Balkans, Albania; trailing dwarf to 6 in (15 cm); leaves to 1½ in (4 cm) across, round, glossy green with 5–7 toothed to lobed segments; flowers to 1¼ in (3 cm) across, bright pink; *G. endressii* (Pyrenees; hairy, clump-forming, to 20 in (50 cm); leaves to 6 in (15 cm) across, with 5 lobed and toothed segments; flowers ¾–1½ in (2–4 cm) across, pale rose becoming candy pink with darker veins; 'Wargrave's Pink': a popular cultivar with pale salmon flowers, good weed-smothering groundcover; *G. farreri* China; dwarf, tap-rooted, rosette-forming; leaves to 2 in (5 cm) across, round to reniform, cut into 7 segments, each 3-lobed and toothed, stalks and margins tinted red; flowers to 1½ in (3.5 cm) across, pale mauve-pink with blue-black anthers; *G. himalayense* (syn. *G. grandiflorum*) Himalaya; carpet-forming, hairy, to 12 in (30 cm); leaves to 8 in (20 cm) across, cut into 7 lobed and toothed segments; flowers to 2½ in (6 cm) across, deep violet-blue, fading to magenta then white at center; *G. ibericum* Caucasus, Turkey, Iran; clump-forming, to 24 in (60 cm); leaves to 4 in (10 cm) across, hairy, cut into 9–10, overlapping, lobed and toothed segments; flowers to 2 in (5 cm) across, rich lavender blue with feathered purple veins; *G. incanum* S Africa; bushy, branching, to 3¼ ft (1 m); leaves aromatic, cut into 5 narrow, toothed and lobed segments, gray- to white-hairy; flowers to ¾ in (2 cm) across, deep magenta with a white "V" at the base of each petal and darker veins; *G.* 'Johnson's Blue' (*G. himalayense* × *G. pratense*) garden origin; clump-forming, to 12 in (30 cm); leaves to 6 in (15 cm) across, cut into 5–7 segments each deeply lobed and toothed; flowers to 2 in (5 cm) across, deep lavender blue; *G. macrorrhizum* S Europe; clump-forming and carpeting, to 16 in (40 cm), muskily scented and clammy; leaves to 8 in (20 cm) across with 5–7 broad, lobed and toothed segments, coloring well in fall; flower stalks and calyces tinted purple-red to brown, flowers to 1¼ in (3 cm) across, magenta to pale pink or white; an excellent, weed-smothering groundcover; *G. maculatum* NE US;

G

clump-forming, hairy, to 30 in (75 cm); leaves to 8 in (20 cm) across, deeply cut into 5–7 widely spaced and deeply toothed segments, coloring well in fall; flowers to 1½ in (4 cm) across, pink or white; *G. maderense* Madeira; to 5 ft (1.5 m); leaves to 24 in (60 cm) across, deeply lobed and finely cut and toothed, dark green, in a rosette atop a short, stout "trunk," stalks tinted red-brown; flowers to 1½ in (4 cm) across, deep magenta with paler veins; *G.* × *magnificum* (*G. ibericum* × *G. platypetalum*) garden origin; flowers rich violet-purple with darker veins; *G. nodosum* Pyrenees to Balkans; clump-forming and spreading, to 20 in (50 cm); leaves 2–8 in (5–20 cm) across, glossy, broadly and sparsely lobed and shallowly toothed; flowers to 1½ in (4 cm) across, lilac-pink with darker markings at center; *G. orientalitibeticum* (syn. *G. stapfianum* 'Roseum') China; dwarf tuberous carpeter to 8 in (20 cm), differs from *G. pylzowianum* in its larger, marbled leaves and petals lacking claws, these are bright purple-pink with a white base; *G.* × *oxonianum* (*G. endressii* × *G. versicolor*) garden origin; vigorous clump-forming and carpeting, to 26 in (65 cm); leaves sometimes marked; flowers pink with notched petals and dark veins; 'Claridge Druce': leaves dark and rather glossy, flowers rose pink with darker veins; 'Walter's Gift': new growth brown tinted orange, later bronze-green, flowers pale pink, heavily veined; *G. palmatum* Madeira; differs from *G. reuteri* in developing a trunk only with age, in its stalked, central leaf segments, and in its purple-pink flowers with cream, not red, anthers; *G. phaeum* DUSTY CRANESBILL; Europe; clump-forming, to 28 in (70 cm); leaves to 8 in (20 cm) across, rounded, shallowly lobed and toothed, usually with maroon markings near the base; flowers to ¾ in (2 cm) across, silky purple-black to maroon, deep mauve-pink, lilac or white; includes numerous cultivars, one of the finest is var. *phaeum* 'Samobor', with broad rounded leaves clearly marked with a chocolate horseshoe, and flowers fading from maroon to cloudy mauve; *G. pratense* MEADOW CRANESBILL; Europe, Asia; clump-forming, to 28 in (70 cm); leaves to 8 in (20 cm) across, with 7–9 deeply cut, lobed and toothed segments; flowers to

1¾ in (4.5 cm) across, violet to blue or white, sometimes with paler, or pink veins; includes cultivars with white, opalescent, sky blue, deep blue, violet, pink and mauve flowers; *G. procurrens* Himalaya; clump-forming, glandular-hairy with trailing and rooting stems; leaves to 4 in (10 cm) across with 5 segments, each 3-lobed and toothed; flowers to 1¼ in (3 cm) across, deep purple-pink with black veins and markings at the center; *G. psilostemon* Turkey; clump-forming, erect, to 40 in (100 cm); leaves to 10 in (25 cm) across with 7 segments and deep, sharp lobes and teeth, coloring well in fall; flowers to 1½ in (3.5 cm) across, intense magenta, veined and stained black at center; *G. pylzowianum* China; 2–8 in (5–20 cm), tuberous, carpeting and spreading by runners; leaves to 2 in (5 cm) across, cut into toothed and lobed, wedge-shaped segments, dark green; flowers to 1¾ in (4.5 cm) across, pink, center white to green, veins darker; *G. renardii* Caucasus; clump-forming, to 8 in (20 cm); leaves 2–4 in (5–10 cm) across, rounded, shallowly and bluntly lobed, dull gray to sage green with fine, pale down and impressed wrinkled veins; flowers to 1½ in (3.5 cm) across, white to palest lavender with dark purple, branching veins; *G. reuteri* Canary Is; short-lived, to 16 in (40 cm) tall; leaves to 12 in (30 cm) across in a spreading rosette atop a short "trunk," stalks stained purple-red, blades cut into 5 pinnately lobed and toothed segments; flowers to 2 in (5 cm) across, deep pink; *G. sanguineum* BLOODY CRANESBILL; Europe; spreading, hummock-forming, to 10 in (25 cm); leaves 2–4 in (5–10 cm) across, rounded, deeply cut into 5–7, toothed and lobed segments; flowers to 1½ in (4 cm) across, deep purple-red to bright carmine, pink, or white, the center white and the veins usually darker; includes numerous cultivars; var. *striatum*: syn. var. *lancastriense*, a low-growing plant suitable for the rock garden with clear pink flowers marked with darker veins; *G. sessiliflorum* New Zealand; dwarf, clump-forming, to 3 in (8 cm); leaves to 1 in (2.5 cm) across, rounded, shallowly lobed; flowers to ½ in (1 cm) across, white to dull cream; selections such as subsp. *novae-zealandiae* 'Nigricans' and 'Porter's Pass' have pale bronze to deep chocolate leaves

turning orange to coral red as they die; *G. sinense* China; clump-forming, to 16 in (40 cm); leaves to 8 in (20 cm) across, deep green, with 5–7 deep, toothed segments; flowers to 1¼ in (3 cm) across, velvety dark maroon to chocolate brown with a pink center and red anther filaments; *G. sylvaticum* Europe; clump-forming, glandular-hairy, to 28 in (70 cm); leaves to 8 in (20 cm) across, deeply cut with 7–9, toothed and lobed segments; flowers to 1¼ in (3 cm) across, blue to violet with a white base, sometimes lilac, white or rose; 'Mayflower': flowers rich violet-blue with a white center; *G. traversii* var. *elegans* Chatham Is.; low-growing and spreading, silvery throughout; leaves to 4 in (10 cm) across, with 5–7 lobed and toothed segments; flowers to 1¼ in (3 cm) across, cloudy pink with darker veins; *G. wallichianum* Himalaya; clump-forming, low-growing, to 18 in (45 cm); leaves with 3–5, deep, sharply lobed and toothed segments; flowers to 1½ in (3.5 cm) across, purple-pink with a white center; 'Buxton's Variety': syn. 'Buxton's Blue', dense, carpeting, leaves emerald green flecked with pale green or silvery white, flowers porcelain blue with a bright white center; *G. wlassovianum* E Russia to China; clump-forming, bushy, softly hairy, to 16 in (40 cm); leaves to 6 in (15 cm) across, rounded, shallowly cut into 7 pinnately lobed segments; flowers to 1¾ in (4.5 cm) across, dark to pale purple-violet with a white center and feathered, deep violet veins.

Gerbera (for German naturalist Traugott Gerber [d. 1743], who traveled in Russia). Compositae. Africa, Madagascar, Asia, Indonesia. BURBERTON DAISY, TRANSVAAL DAISY. About 40 species, hairy, stemless, perennial herbs with entire to toothed or pinnately lobed leaves and showy, long-stalked, daisylike flower heads. The following species and its hybrids provide very long-lasting cut flowers, notable for their range of radiant colors, from softer pastels to deep shades of red and orange. Scald the bases of the flower stalks and stand them in cool deep water before arranging. In essentially frost-free zones, grow permanently in the open garden in full sun in free-draining soil; otherwise, grow in the cool, well-ventilated greenhouse, in the border or in pots. Dwarf hybrids such as 'Happipot' are particularly well-suited to pot cultivation and may be brought into the house for temporary display when in bloom. Under glass, provide a freely draining, medium-fertility, loam-based mix and ensure some shade from the hottest summer sun; water plentifully and liquid-fertilize semiweekly when in growth. Overwinter at a temperature of 41–45°F (5–7°C), and keep just moist. Divide and repot in spring. *G. jamesonii* BARBERTON DAISY, TRANSVAAL DAISY; flower heads to 6 in (15 cm) across, on stalks to 28 in (70 cm) tall; many cultivars and seed races are available with single or double flower heads, some very large, and in shades of yellow, orange, vermilion, deep scarlet, brick red, salmon, crimson, pale pink, magenta and white.

germination a complex sequence of physiological and structural changes that occurs as a seed starts growing.

Percentage of successful seed is calculated

Germination test

germination test any of various methods for determining the viability of seeds, including germinating a seed sample under optimum conditions, studying a sample's reaction to chemical treatment, or germinating excised embryos. Viability is expressed as a percentage of seeds successfully tested.

Gesneriads a group name for plants of the family Gesneriaceae, including *Achimenes, Aeschynanthus, Alloplectus, Asteranthera, Briggsia, Chirita, Codonanthe, Columnea, Conandron, Episcia, Eucodonia, Gesneria, Gloxinia, Haberlea, Jankaea, Kohleria, Lysionotus, Mitraria, Nautilocalyx, Nematanthus, Niphaea, Paraboea, Petrocosmea, Phinaea, Ramonda, Rehmannia,*

Saintpaulia, Sinningia, and *Streptocarpus.*

The family includes small shrubs and trees, epiphytic vines and almost stemless rosette-forming plants, of tropical, subtropical, Asian, and European origin. The majority have fine, fibrous root systems (for example, *Columnea, Ramonda*), in some cases producing rhizomes bearing scales of modified leaves (for example, *Achimenes, Gloxinia*). Others form tubers with fine roots arising on the upper surface (for example, *Sinningia*). Fibrous rooters grow continuously, while rhizome and tuber formers have a period of dormancy which varies according to species.

Cool-temperate genera are native to high altitudes in Europe, Asia, and the Americas and can be grown in the rock garden or alpine house. For outdoor cultivation in temperate zones, well-drained positions such as rocky crevices are necessary to avoid excess winter wetness. Plant rosette-forming genera such as *Haberlea* and *Ramonda* in vertical crevices; provide support for shrubby/climbing genera such as *Asteranthera* and *Mitraria* to keep the plants above wet ground. For outdoor cultivation in warmer zones, plant in moisture-retentive soil. It is important to identify soil pH requirements; for example, *Conandron* and *Ramonda serbica* are acid-lovers, while *Haberlea, Jankaea,* and *Ramonda myconi* are lime-lovers. Protect from prolonged hard frost and hot sunshine. In the alpine house, pot in shallow containers of well-drained, soil-based medium. Water sparingly during the winter resting phase; water moderately and position in bright, filtered light in summer.

Subtropical and tropical genera can be grown indoors in temperate areas at 45–86°F (7–30°C), with shrubs and terrestrial species (e.g., *Lysionotus, Petrocosmea*) at the lower end of the range, epiphytes (e.g., *Aeschynanthus, Columnea*) at the higher end, and others (e.g., *Saintpaulia* and *Streptocarpus*) in the range of 59–68°F (15–20°C). In temperate zones, position plants in bright filtered light during summer. They are day-length responsive, so, for optimum results, supplement by artificial means to provide 12–14 hours of light. Outdoors in long-day warmer zones, provide shade, especially for *Episcia*

and *Aeschynanthus*. Water plentifully but carefully, avoiding wetting the leaves. Store dormant rhizomes and tubers free of frost and repot each season.

In their active growth stage, all gesneriads prefer medium to high humidity and, in high-temperature areas, outdoor misting twice a day is beneficial. Some genera (e.g., *Episcia, Gesneria,* and *Phinaea*) require high humidity to grow well in temperate zones, as can be obtained in a closed case. Plants benefit from modest, balanced supplementary feeding during their growing period; nitrogen should be omitted during flowering. Pot into shallow containers of peat-based medium or equal parts sterilized loam, sphagnum peat, perlite and vermiculite; ensure a pH range of 6.5–7.0, except for *Phinaea,* which requires 7.5. Grow large vining and epiphytic sorts in hanging mesh baskets or pots, and humidity-lovers in terraria.

Gesneriads may be propagated from seed or cuttings. Sow freshly harvested seed, without covering, at a temperature of 68–77°F (20–25°C) to achieve germination in 4 weeks. Some genera (e.g., *Streptocarpus*) suspend development and should be pricked out very early. Leaf cuttings should be set into 2–2½-in (5–6.5-cm) pots, and placed in a propagator, at 68–77°F (20–25°C), or in a warm position under a polythene-bag cover. Increase large-leafed types, (e.g., *Streptocarpus*), by leaf cuttings made as 2-in- (5-cm-) long, wedge-shaped segments. Stem cuttings, with or without growing tips, may be taken, cutting below leaf nodes, into portions 2–4 in (5–10 cm) long; the lowest leaves should be removed. This method can be used for shoots arising from tubers.

Scaly rhizomes can be broken into segments ½ in (1 cm) long and several inserted into individual 3½ in (9 cm) pots to a depth of ½ in (1 cm). Tubers may be increased by cutting into individual segments, each possessing a bud; dust cut surfaces with fungicide and allow to dry for a while before potting with the bud eye standing just above the surface.

Geum (name used by Pliny). Rosaceae. Europe, Asia, New Zealand, N and S America, Africa. AVENS. Some 50 species, perennial herbs and subshrubs (those listed below are perennial herbs). The leaves are lyrate or pinnate, usually hairy, in basal clumps and on the erect flowering stems. The bell- to bowl-shaped flowers, produced in spring and summer in stalked cymes, consist of five persistent calyx lobes and five broad petals. The following species are hardy to at least 5°F (–15°C), but in areas of prolonged low temperatures, should be protected in winter with evergreen branches or a dry mulch of bracken litter or leaf mold. Grow in well-drained, moisture-retentive soil rich in organic matter. Propagate cultivars by division in fall or spring and divide plants every three to four years to maintain vigor. Species may be propagated by seed, sown in fall or spring, although species hybridize freely and seed may not come true.

G. 'Borisii' clump-forming, to 20 in (50 cm); flowers bright yellow or, in the forms usually cultivated, orange-scarlet; *G. chiloense* Chile; to 24 in (60 cm); flowers scarlet to yellow, washed deep fiery orange, in erect cymes; *G. coccineum* Balkans; to 18 in (45 cm); flowers to 1¼ in (3 cm) in diameter, cupped to outspread, deep fiery red to orange or apricot; *G.* × *heldreichii* (*G. coccineum* × *G. montanum*) to 12 in (30 cm); flowers large, orange-red; *G. montanum* ALPINE AVENS; C and S Europe; to 12 in (30 cm); flowers to 1¼ in (3 cm) in diameter, pale yellow; *G. rivale* INDIAN CHOCOLATE, PURPLE AVENS, WATER AVENS, CHOCOLATE ROOT; Europe; to 14 in (35 cm); flowers to 1 in (2.5 cm) in diameter, nodding, calyx dark purple-brown, corolla campanulate, cream to dusky pink or brick red to pale orange streaked purple-red.

Gevuina (the native name). Proteaceae. Chile. CHILEAN HAZELNUT, CHILE NUT. 1 species, *G. avellana*, an evergreen shrub or tree to 40 ft (12 m), with rusty-tomentose new growth. The leaves are pinnate or bipinnate, 8–16¼ in (20–42 cm) long, coriaceous, sap-green, and coarsely toothed. Appearing in late summer in narrow racemes, the flowers are spidery and cream to pale buff. These are followed by fleshy-coated fruits that turn from red to black. Usually considered tender, *G. avellana* is nevertheless known to tolerate temperatures to 14°F (–10°C) in a sheltered woodland environment.

It may also be grown in tubs in the cool greenhouse or conservatory. Grow in semishade in cool, moist soil rich in sand and leaf mold. Shield from harsh winds. Propagate by semiripe cuttings or by seed.

Gibbaeum (from Latin *gibba*, hump, referring to the hump-shaped plant bodies of many species). Aizoaceae. S Africa (W Cape). 20 species, highly succulent, more or less stemless, clump-forming perennial herbs, with paired and fleshy leaves united at their base to a greater or lesser extent. Daisylike flowers open at the junction of the leaves on bright days. Provide a minimum winter temperature of 45°F (7°C), with full sun and a dry, draft-free environment. Water sparingly during periods of sunny weather when in growth and not at all when dormant. Plant in a perfectly drained, gritty medium. Feed during periods of active growth in sunny weather, using a very weak, low-nitrogen, liquid fertilizer. Propagate as for *Conophytum*.

G. petrense leaves to ½ in (1 cm), triangular, smooth, pale gray-green; flowers pink to red; *G. velutinum* leaves to 2½ in (6 cm), narrowly triangular, pale gray-green, velvety; flowers white or pink.

gibberellins a group of naturally occurring plant hormones that influence growth, especially as stimulators. They are synthesized as gibberellic acid. See *growth regulators*.

gibbous swollen on one side or at the base.

Gilia (for Filippo Gilii [1756–1821], an astronomer in Rome and author, with Caspar Xuarez, of *Osservazioni fitologiche*). Polemoniaceae. SW US, southern S America. 25 species, annual, rarely perennial herbs. The leaves are usually pinnately lobed, rarely entire, and often downy or glandular. Carried in summer and fall in panicles or clusters atop slender stems, the flowers are tubular to funnelform. Suitable for annual and cut-flower borders, or for pots in the cool greenhouse where late winter/early spring blooms are required. Grow in full sun in very well-drained, fertile soil; provide support in exposed situations. Sow seed *in situ* in

spring or early fall. For late-winter flowering under glass, sow in late summer and overwinter in well-ventilated conditions with a minimum night temperature of 45°F (7°C).

G. achilleifolia S California; glandular-hairy annual to 28 in (70 cm); flowers ½–¾ in (1–2 cm), violet-blue in a dense, fanlike cluster of cymes; *G. capitata* western N America; smooth to glandular-hairy annual to 32 in (80 cm); flowers to ⅜ in (0.8 cm), lavender, in small, crowded terminal heads.

Gillenia (for Arnold Gille, 17th-century German botanist, who had a garden at Cassel). Rosaceae. N America. 2 species, rhizomatous perennial herbs with erect to arching, branching stems and trifoliolate leaves. Five-petaled flowers are carried in loose panicles in summer. Hardy to at least 5°F (–15°C). Grow in sun or semishade in nonalkaline, moist but porous soil. Provide support by staking. Propagate by division, or by seed sown in fall or spring. *G. trifoliata* BOWMAN'S ROOT, INDIAN PHYSIC; NE US, Canada; erect, slender, finely branched; flowers to ¾ in (2 cm) across with narrow, white petals.

ginger *Zingiber officinale*. Zingiberaceae. Tropical Asia. A tender, deciduous perennial, to 5 ft (1.5 m) with lanceolate leaves; grown for its highly aromatic, thick, branching rhizomes and for stem ginger. Requires a minimum temperature of 59°F (15°C), plentiful water and high humidity, and space to accommodate lax growth. Propagate by division of rhizomes in spring or by seed, sown at 64°F (18°C).

Ginkgo (from Chinese *yin-kuo*, silver apricot, via Japanese pronunciation, *ginko*.) Ginkgoaceae. China. 1 species, *G. biloba* MAIDENHAIR TREE; a deciduous, dioecious tree to 130 ft (40 m). The trunk is erect, and the crown basically open and conical with several, large and upswept stems from a low fork. The branches are spreading with weeping tips. The leaves are fan-shaped with an irregular upper margin often shallowly cut into two lobes. They are 2–4¾ in (5–12 cm) across, tough, yellow-green above and paler beneath, turning pale gold to rich

Ginkgo biloba
Ginkgo is what is termed a monospecific genus, comprising only a single species from which several cultivars have been developed.

butter yellow in fall. Male flowers are carried in short, yellow-green catkins in spring. The female inflorescences consist of two cap-shaped ovules at the head of a short, drooping stalk. The fruit matures the following fall, and is fleshy-coated, spherical and to 1 in (2.5 cm) long. Pale olive at first, it ripens to purple-black and smells of rancid butter. A remarkable tree, the *Gingko* is grown for its beautiful maiden-hair-like foliage, elegant crown, and its curiosity value as a "living fossil." It resists many pests, diseases, and urban pollution, and is particularly suitable as a street tree (especially the cultivar 'Fastigiata' and similar clones); the fall color is brief but spectacular. It does best in climates with hot summers. Male clones are often grown in the US and Europe, for the fruit is malodorous and messy when ripe. Female plants are more often seen in Japan and China, where ginkgo nuts are eaten and used in medicine. Plant in well-drained soil in a fairly sheltered site. Hard pruning will result in the production of long, soft watershoots, and felled trees will coppice. Old specimens may become hollow-trunked. Propagate from seed stratified and sown in fall. Take half-ripe cuttings in summer or hardwood cuttings in winter. Graft scions of desirable clones and males (side-veneer) onto seedling stock in spring, providing intermediate greenhouse conditions, medium light and occasional syringing.

girdling (1) the removal of a circle of bark around a tree trunk or branch, often the result of the activity of rabbits or deer but sometimes due to other mechanical damage. It usually results in the death of the tree or limb; see *bark ringing*; (2) (US) the growth of roots around a tree trunk, or other larger roots, so tightly that it prevents normal expansion.

glabrate, glabrescent (1) nearly glabrous, or becoming glabrous with age; (2) minutely and almost invisibly pubescent.

glabrous smooth, hairless.

gladiate swordlike.

Gladiolus (from Latin *gladiolus*, diminutive of *gladius*, a sword, referring to the leaf shape). Iridaceae. Africa, mainly South Africa, Madagascar, Europe, Arabia, W Asia. About 180 species, cormous perennial herbs with linear to sword-shaped leaves. Produced in spring and summer in narrow spikes, the flowers consist of six equal or unequal perianth lobes. These may be broad or narrow, ruffled or pointed, and closed or spreading, their bases forming a long or short, usually curved tube.

The species will flower in late winter or spring if grown under glass. In the open garden, they flower in summer and early fall, as do the hybrids. The species are generally rather tender and may not survive below −10°F (−23°C). *Gladiolus communis* subsp. *byzantinus* and *G. italicus* are, however, reliably hardy to 0°F (−18°C), while *G. atroviolaceus*, *G. callianthus*, and *G. papilio* may last for many years in a sheltered, sunny position. The remaining species should be planted outdoors in spring and lifted for dry, frost-free storage in fall. Otherwise, keep them under glass, planted in fall for spring flowering—in which case, dry the corms off when the new growth is complete and store them dry in their pots until repotting in the fall. All need full sun and sandy or gritty soil that dries out thoroughly once the foliage has withered. The hybrids should be planted out in spring, 4–6 in (10–15 cm) apart and deep, in fertile, well-drained soil in full sun. Water in dry weather and stake taller cultivars if necessary. Although many of the hybrids will survive the winter outdoors if protected from slugs and rain, it is safe practice to lift the corms in the fall and store them in dry, frost-free conditions. Increase by cormlets removed from the dormant parent corms. Affected by rots when in storage (dust with fungicide). Gladiolus scab produces lesions and blotches on the foliage. Foliage streaked with yellow and dying prematurely probably indicates gladiolus yellows. Destroy infected plants.

G. atroviolaceus Greece, Turkey, Iraq, Iran; 14–28 in (35–70 cm); flowers deep violet-purple, almost black; *G. callianthus* (syn. *Acidanthera bicolor*) E Tropical Africa; 20–40 in (50–100 cm); flowers scented, white with dark purple-red marks or staining in throat; *G. cardinalis* WATERFALL GLADIOLUS, NEW YEAR LILY; S Africa; 24–40 in (60–100 cm); flowers crimson or scarlet with a white or cream, mauve-edged marking on each of the lower perianth lobes; *G. carneus* (syn. *G. blandus*) PAINTED LADY; S Africa; 8–40 in (20–100 cm); flowers white, cream, mauve or pink, usually with yellow, red or purple markings on the lower perianth lobes or with dark blotches in throat; *G. × colvillii* (*G. tristis × G. cardinalis*; syn. *G. nanus*) a garden hybrid and parent of the Nanus or Miniature Hybrids; *G. communis* subsp. *byzantinus* (syn. *G. byzantinus*) BYZANTINE GLADIOLUS; S Spain, Sicily; 20–40 in (50–100 cm); flowers deep purple-red with narrow, paler marks bordered with purple on the lower perianth lobes; white, pink and vivid cerise forms are also grown; *G. dalenii* (syn. *G. natalensis*, *G. primulinus*, *G. psittacinus*) Tropical Africa, S Africa; 20–40 in (50–100 cm); flowers green, yellow, orange, red, pink or purple, sometimes striped or mottled with another color; *G. italicus* (syn. *G. segetum*) FIELD GLADIOLUS; S Europe; 16–40 in (40–100 cm); flowers purple-pink to magenta, lower perianth lobes with a narrow pink blotch outlined in purple; *G. papilio* (syn. *G. purpureoauratus*) S Africa; 20–36 in (50–90 cm); flowers off-white to dull yellow suffused cloudy purple to dove gray especially on exterior, lower lobes with buff to golden, wedge-shaped patches outlined with mauve; *G. tristis* MARSH AFRIKAANER; S Africa; 16–40 in (40–100 cm); flowers

GLADIOLUS TYPES

Grandiflorus group ('Tesoro')
This group produces one showy spike per corm, ideal for show and for cutting, and is further classified by flower diameter.

Nanus group ('Amanda Mahy')
The Nanus and Primulinus groups are shorter in stature, and produce several slender and more delicate flower spikes per corm.

Species (Gladiolus papilio)
Some species, including this and the popular *G. communis*, are hardy enough to overwinter in the ground in all but the coldest areas.

white, pale cream or yellow, often tinged with green, usually dotted, lined or flushed dark green, brown or purple.

The following informal horticultural classification of *Gladiolus* is used: Butterfly (B), Exotic (E), Giant (G), Large (L), Medium (M), Miniature (Min), Nanus (N), Primulinus (P), Small (S), Tubergenii (Tub). A great number of garden hybrids and cultivars exist with wide variation in form, size, and flower color, except true blue. These are divided into groups, of which three are most widely representative. Grandiflorus Group: large flowered hybrids in bloom mid- to late summer; spikes to 36 in (90 cm) bearing up to 28 closely-arranged buds with half open simultaneously. Flowers 2½–5½ in (6–14 cm) across; tepals may be plain (Dutch origin) or ruffled (American origin); Nanus Group: miniature hybrids, flowering early summer; two or three slender spikes per corm, to 14 in (36 cm) bearing up to seven loosely arranged buds with three to five open at the same time. Flowers up to 2 in (5 cm) across, often frilled; Primulinus Group: flowering mid- to late summer; one single, slender spike per corm, to 24 in (60 cm), bearing 20 + loosely-arranged buds with up to seven open at the same time. Flowers up to 3 in (7.5 cm) across, with the upper most perianth lobe hooded and arching over stigma and anthers.

gland any cell or group of cells that is able to secrete a substance or substances, such as oil, calcium or sugar—for example, nectaries.

glandspine in some Cactaceae, a short spine borne in the upper part of an areole, which is nectariferous in its first year.

glandular-pubescent either covered with intermixed glands and hairs, or possessing hairs terminated by glands.

glass a widely used material for greenhouses, frames, and cloches, which has the advantages of being long-lasting, with very high levels of sunlight transmission and good heat retention. Its disadvantages are fragility, and weight and cost compared with substitutes such as acrylic, polycarbonate, polyester, polyethylene, or polyvinyl chloride. For garden purposes, horticultural glass at least ⅛ in (3 mm) thick should be chosen; the most common pane size is 24 in (60 cm) square. For conservatory glazing, thicker toughened glass is essential, often in double-layered sheets for improved heat retention.

glass case any of a wide range of glazed structures for protecting plants. Long wall cases were formerly a common feature of large gardens, used for protecting trained forms of peaches, pears, and cherries. Within greenhouses, glass cases may be used to contain ferns or orchids, and to house cuttings and germinating seeds; such units are sometimes referred to as close cases. Occasionally, the term is used to refer to a bell glass, which is a type of cloche.

glaucescent slightly glaucous.

Glaucidium ("resembles *Glaucium*"—the general shape of the flowers is similar). Paeoniaceae. Japan. 1 species, *G. palmatum*, a perennial, rhizomatous herb to 16 in (40 cm) tall, and white-pubescent when young. Rigid stems bear 2 leaves at their summits, each to 8 in (20 cm), kidney-shaped to rounded, palmately lobed and toothed to incised. Produced in late spring, the solitary, terminal flowers are to 3 in (8 cm) wide and consist of four broad, petal-like sepals; these are mauve to pale lilac, (rarely white), with a boss of yellow stamens. Hardy to 5°F (−15°C) and below. It requires shelter from cold drying winds, protection from summer heat and drought and is well suited to the woodland garden, peat terrace or north-facing herbaceous border. Grow in cool, moisture-retentive, humus-rich soil in partial shade. Propagate by seed or careful division in spring.

Glaucium (from Greek *glaukos*, gray-green, referring to the leaf color). Papaveraceae. Europe, N. Africa, C and SW Asia. HORNED POPPY. Some 25 species, annual, biennial, or perennial herbs with orange latex. The oblong to oblanceolate leaves are pinnately lobed or dissected and toothed. Produced in summer in loosely and broadly branched terminal panicles, the flowers are cup-shaped, short-lived, and consist of four petals. They are followed by long, narrowly cylindric and sharply tapered (hornlike) seed pods. Hardy to −10°F (−23°C) and an excellent plant for silver, dry and coastal gardens. Grow in a warm, sunny position in fast-draining soil. Sow seed *in situ* in spring, or in the cold frame in summer.

G. flavum YELLOW HORNED POPPY; Europe, N Africa, W Asia; biennial or short-lived perennial to 3¼ ft (1 m) tall, usually shorter; leaves bright gray-green to cool blue-green; flowers to 2 in (5 cm) across, deep golden yellow; fruit to 12 in (30 cm); *G. corniculatum* has darker flowers, from deep orange to scarlet).

Glaucium flavum
Often seen growing wild along shorelines, the yellow horned poppy is tolerant of salt-laden winds and is ideal for coastal gardens.

glaucous coated with a fine bloom, whitish, or blue-green or gray, and easily rubbed off.

Glechoma (from Greek *glechon*, name for a plant in PseudoDioscorides). Labiatae. Europe, naturalized N America. Some 12 species, evergreen perennial herbs, most with creeping and rooting stems. Small, two-lipped, tubular flowers are carried in whorls in summer. Fully hardy and tolerant of sun, shade and most soils, the following perennial species is usually cultivated in its variegated form and is a very useful trailing plant for hanging baskets and containers. It makes equally dependable, if invasive, groundcover. Increase by detaching rooted lengths of stem. *G. hederacea* GROUND IVY, ALEHOOF, FIELD BALM, GILL-OVER-THE-GROUND, RUNAWAY ROBIN; Europe to Caucasus, naturalized N America; flowering stems ascending, 2–12 in (5–30 cm) tall, nonflowering stems creeping to trailing, mat-forming and rooting; leaves to 1¼ in (3 cm), broadly ovate, toothed; flowers to ¾ in (2 cm), violet to mauve or lilac, sometimes white or pink; includes the pink-flowered 'Rosea', and 'Variegata', with leaves with broken edges and zones of silver-gray and white.

Gleditsia (for Johann Gottlieb Gleditsch [1714–1786], German botanist, director of Berlin Botanical Garden, and friend of Linnaeus). Leguminosae. C and E Asia, N and S America, Iran, tropical Africa. HONEYLOCUST. 14 species, deciduous trees, usually with stout, simple or branched thorns on the trunks and branches. The leaves are pinnate and/or bipinnate. Small, green-white flowers are carried in spring and summer in axillary racemes and may give rise to large seed pods. Honey locusts are widely used in landscaping and frequently grown in parks and gardens. Some species are used as hedges, and some for fences and as resilient street trees—in the US, most notably *G. triacanthos*, which tolerates large-scale container cultivation in northeastern cities. Where fallen pods would cause litter problems, the sterile and unarmed *G. triacanthos* 'Moraine' may prove useful. They are able to withstand temperatures down to at least −22°F (−30°C). Grow in full sun. Propagate species by scarified seed, cultivars by grafting or by budding onto seedling stocks of *G. triacanthos*. In the US, *Gleditsia* is affected by mimosa webworm. The *G. triacanthos* cultivars, 'Green Glory' and 'Moraine', show some resistance.

G. caspica CASPIAN HONEYLOCUST; N Iran, Transcaucasia; to 40 ft (12 m), trunk thorns to 6 in (15 cm), branched, slightly flattened; leaves to 10 in (25 cm) long, pinnate, with shining green leaflets, each to 2 in (5 cm), ovate to oval and finely crenate; *G. japonica* Japan, China, introduced E US, California; to 65 ft (20 m), trunk thorns to 3 in (8 cm), branched, slightly flattened; leaves to 12 in (30 cm), bipinnate or pinnate with oblong to lanceolate leaflets to 1½ in (4 cm), glossy, entire to sparsely crenate; *G. triacanthos* (HONEY LOCUST; N America, introduced temperate Old World; to 150 ft (45 m), trunk and branches armed with stout, sharp, simple or branched, flat thorns; leaves to 8 in (20 cm), bipinnate or pinnate with oblong to lanceolate, crenulate, deep green leaflets to 1½ in (4 cm) long; includes thornless cultivars and others with golden to lime green foliage (e.g., 'Sunburst'), or dark bronze red foliage (e.g. 'Rubylace'), some weeping, and some with dark green foliage persisting well into fall—for example, 'Shademaster'.

gley used of soil that has developed under impeded drainage conditions. Typically, the soil has a comparatively shallow surface horizon and gray coloring, with a thin coating to granular components and frequently rust-colored discoloration from ferric oxide deposits.

Globba (from *galoba*, native name in Amboina, Indonesia). Zingiberaceae. SE Asia. Some 70 species, rhizomatous perennial herbs with clumped, reedlike stems. Produced in late spring and summer, the inflorescence is a pendulous raceme with showy, reflexed bracts. The delicate flowers consist of three petals, petal-like staminodes and one fertile stamen with a slender, curling filament. The lower flowers are sometimes replaced by bulbils. During growth, maintain a minimum temperature of 64°F (18°C), with high humidity, plentiful water and bright indirect light. In the winter months, keep virtually dry, provide full sun and a minimum temperature of 50°F (10°C). Propagate by division in spring, or by removing bulbils. *G. winitii* Thailand; to 3¼ ft (1 m); inflorescence to 6 in (15 cm), with pink to magenta or mauve bracts and yellow flowers).

globose spherical, sometimes used to mean near spherical.

G

globular composed of globose forms, as in the aggregate fruits of *Rubus*.

Globularia (from Latin *globulus*, a small round head, from the form of the flower head). Globulariaceae. Cape Verde Islands, Canary Islands, Europe and Asia Minor. GLOBE DAISY. 22 species, usually evergreen perennial herbs or shrublets. They form low hummocks or mats of neat foliage, giving rise in spring and early summer to fluffy, ball- or buttonlike flower heads. Hardy to −10°F (−23°C) and well-suited to the rock garden. Grow in gritty, well-drained, neutral or slightly alkaline soil in full sun. Propagate by division, by softwood or semiripe cuttings, or by seed sown when ripe.
    G. cordifolia Europe; dwarf, creeping and mat-forming shrublet with spathulate, notched leaves and buttonlike, sky blue to lavender (rarely white or pink) flower heads; *G. meridionalis* Europe; more robust than *G. cordifolia* with oblanceolate, rarely notched leaves and mauve-blue to lilac-pink flower heads.

glochid a barbed spine or bristle, often tufted, on the areoles of cacti.

glomerate aggregated in one or more dense or compact clusters.

glomerule a cluster of capitula or grouped flowers, usually subtended by a single involucre.

gloriet in Spanish gardens, a pavilion or arbor placed in a central open space from which paths may radiate.

gloriette a hilltop focal point in a landscape garden.

Gloriosa (Latin *gloriosus*, glorious). Liliaceae (Colchicaceae). Tropical Africa and Asia. GLORY LILY, CLIMBING LILY, CREEPING LILY. 1 species, *G. superba*, a tuberous, perennial herb. Its slender stems climb to 6½ ft (2 m) by means of tendrils at the leaf tips. Solitary flowers are produced in summer and fall on long pedicels in the leaf axils. The flowers are usually angled downward and consist of six spreading tepals, each 1½–4 in (4–10 cm) long, lanceolate, bowed at center and gently but distinctly reflexed at tip. They range in color from yellow to red or purple or bicolored, with the margins often incurved, undulate or crisped. The most popular named variants are the lemon yellow-flowered 'Citrina', 'Rothschildiana', to 6½ ft (2 m) tall, with wavy flowers to 7 in (18 cm) across in scarlet or ruby stained and edged golden yellow, and 'Simplex', a shorter plant with broader, if smaller, tepals in deep orange and yellow.
    Beautiful climbers for the warm greenhouse or home. Grow in full sun in a freely draining, fertile mix. Support the climbing stems on pea sticks, a cane frame, or a wire hoop. Water plentifully and feed semiweekly with diluted liquid fertilizer when in full growth. Withhold water as growth dies back in late summer/early fall; store the long, narrow tubers dry in their pots at a minimum temperature of 50°F (10°C). Repot every one or two years in early spring. Propagate by seed sown in a sandy propagating mix in late winter, with gentle bottom heat, by careful division in spring, or by offsets.

Glottiphyllum (from Greek *glotta*, tongue, and *phyllon*, leaf, referring to the thick, fleshy, tonguelike leaves). Aizoaceae. South Africa. More than 50 species, highly succulent perennials with low, branching stems giving rise to clumps of thickly fleshy leaves. Solitary and virtually stalkless, the daisylike flowers open on bright days in spring and summer. Provide a minimum winter temperature of 45°F (7°C), low humidity and full sun. Grow in a low-fertility potting mix with high proportions of sand and grit. Water very sparingly during periods of very warm weather. Keep dry from fall to spring. Propagation as for *Conophytum*.
    G. nelii leaves to 2 × ¾ × ½ in (5 × 2 × 1 cm), upper surface flat, lower surface obscurely carinate, light green with translucent angles; flowers golden-yellow; *G. semi-cylindricum* leaves to 2 × ¼ × ¼ in (5 × 0.6 × 0.6 cm), semi-cylindric, fresh glossy green with faint dots and small, toothlike projections on margins; flowers yellow.

glume a small, dry, membranous bract found in the inflorescences of Gramineae and Cyperaceae and usually disposed in two ranks.

glutinose, glutinous see *viscid*.

Glyceria (from Greek *glykys*, sweet, referring to the flavor of the seeds). Gramineae. Northern temperate regions, Australia, New Zealand, S America. MANNA GRASS, SWEET GRASS. 16 species, perennial grasses, often found in wet and marshy places. They form extensive colonies of pithy, reed-like stems with narrowly strap-shaped leaves. The flowers are borne in summer in plumelike, terminal panicles. Fully hardy, the following species thrives in fertile, moisture-retentive soil in the herbaceous and mixed border, but is more often used as an aquatic or marginal. Grow in full sun. *Glyceria* spreads vigorously in watery places and should be confined in a tub or basket in smaller pools. Propagate by division in early spring. *G. maxima* (syn. *G. aquatica*) REED SWEET GRASS, REED MEADOW GRASS; Europe, Asia; to 8 ft (2.5 m) tall in flower; includes var. *variegata*, with leaves striped green and cream, flushed pink on emergence, and 'Pallida', with leaves boldly striped off-white).

goblet a form of fruit tree or bush in which the main branches are trained to encircle an open center.

Gomphrena (name used by Pliny for a kind of amaranth). Amaranthaceae. Tropical America, Australia. 90 species, annual, rarely perennial herbs. Produced in spring and summer, the individual flowers are inconspicuous, but are carried in dense ball- or buttonlike heads amid highly colored, chaffy bracts. In cool temperate zones, *Gomphrena* is treated as a frost-tender annual in beds and borders, for cutting and drying, and as a pot plant for the greenhouse or conservatory. It is grown for its cloverlike flower heads in strong colors that are retained on drying. Grow in full sun, in a sheltered sunny position in deep, fertile, well-drained soil. Sow *in situ* in spring in warm temperate areas; elsewhere, sow under glass in early spring, hardening off before planting out after the last frosts. *G. globosa* GLOBE AMARANTH, BACHELOR'S BUTTONS; Panama, Guatemala; annual, usually erect, to 24 in (60 cm) tall; flower heads ¾–2½ in (2–6 cm), globose to broadly cylindric, in shades of white, pink, scarlet, deep crimson, purple-red or mauve; includes dwarf, compact and rounded, and decumbent cultivars).

gooseberry (*Ribes uva-crispa*) a hardy, deciduous, spiny shrub, grown for its ovoid berries. The many hundreds of European cultivars derive from *R. uva-crispa*, which is a native of the Mediterranean region, North Africa, the Caucasus, and northern China. North American cultivars, which have smaller fruits on less compact or upright bushes, derive from the native *R. hirtellum*, which is often crossed with European hybrids and shows resistance to mildew. Recently introduced into Europe, genes of the American species *R. divaricatum* confer resistance to American gooseberry mildew fungus.

The first recorded date of cultivation in England is 1276, but there was no general development until the introduction of gooseberries and other fruits from the Continent in the early 16th century. Much hybridizing followed throughout the 18th and 19th centuries, and gooseberry clubs flourished in the north of England during the 19th century; a few of these still survive, members competing to produce heavy fruits.

Fruits are available green for cooking from late spring through to summer when ripe for dessert. The cool, moist climates of northern Europe, the northern US, and Canada favor fruit development, although frost can damage flowers and young fruits. Wind shelter is desirable.

In gardens, the gooseberry is usually grown as a bush on a 6-in (15-cm) leg, or trained as a cordon or fan; commercially, often as a suckering bush or hedgerow. Bushes of European cultivars should be planted 5–6½ ft (1.5–2 m) apart, and American cultivars 10 ft (3 m) apart. Plant single cordons 20 in (0.5 m) apart, double ones 3¼ ft (1 m) apart. Select two- or three-year-old plants for bushes, and one-year-olds to train against canes as cordons. In all cases, remove stem suckers.

Propagate from 12–16 in (30–40 cm) long hardwood cuttings, made from the

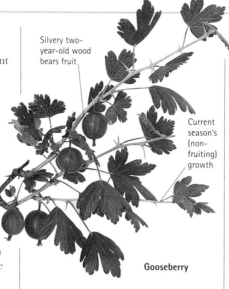

Silvery two-year-old wood bears fruit

Current season's (non-fruiting) growth

Gooseberry

current year's growth; taken just before leaf fall, with all but the topmost four buds removed. Leaving some basal buds will improve rooting, but it then becomes necessary to remove the consequent shoots at planting time. In North America and Germany, mound layering is practiced. After planting, cut main branches by one half and lateral shoots to one bud. Prune in the early years to establish a bush framework of six to eight branches radiating from the top of the stem. Fruit is borne on one- and two-year-old shoots. Annual pruning aims at maintaining a supply of new shoots and removing congestion: basically, shorten leaders by half, cutting to an upward bud on spreading cultivars, and reduce laterals to 3 in (8 cm). Cordons are treated as a branch of a bush, where old spurs require thinning with age. Summer pruning of laterals to five buds at green-fruit stage encourages spur formation, light and air penetration, and removes mildew-infected tips. Gooseberries require netting as protection from birds that depredate buds in winter. Of the American gooseberries, 'Captivator', 'Josselyn', 'Oregon Champion' and 'Welcome' are notable. Successful cultivars for the UK include the earlies 'Careless' (green), 'May Duke' (red) and 'Golden Drop' (yellow); midseason, 'Invicta' (green) and 'Leveller' (yellow-green); lates, 'Lancashire Lad' (red) and 'Lancer' (green).

Possible problems: aphids, birds, capsid bug, caterpillars, sawflies; American gooseberry mildew (see *powdery mildew*), gray mold, leaf spot.

gootee see *layering*.

gopher a small burrowing rodent that, like other ground squirrels, is occasional garden pests in western North America, burrowing into garden areas with resultant damage to plants. The usual control is to place poisoned bait in the burrows, but this causes painful death and is not permitted in some states. Trapping is an alternative method. Advice from local pest-control officials should be sought.

Gordonia (for James Gordon, London nurseryman [d. 1781]). Theaceae. SE Asia, warm N America. 70 species, evergreen trees and shrubs with saucer-shaped, solitary flowers composed of broad petals and a showy boss of stamens. Cultivation requirements are mainly as for *Franklinia*, although it requires higher temperatures (ideally frost-free conditions) and hot humid summers.

G. axillaris (syn. *G. anomala*) China, Taiwan; shrub or tree to 40 ft (12 m); leaves to 6½ in (17 cm), oblong, leathery, dark glossy green; flowers to 6 in (15 cm) across, with five to six, creamy white petals and orange yellow stamens from early winter to spring; *G. lasianthus* LOBLOLLY BAY; SE US; shrub or tree to 65 ft (20 m); leaves to 8 in (20 cm), obovate to lanceolate, deep glossy green; flowers 2½–3 in (6–8 cm) across, with five white petals and yellow stamens in summer.

gourds hard-shelled fruits of the family Cucurbitaceae, some of which are grown for ornament or utensils, others primarily as edible crops. Often the immature fruit is edible and the mature fruit hard-shelled, as in *Lagenaria siceraria*. Some species provide both hard-shelled, inedible fruits and distinct edible ones whose shells are not durable—for example, *Cucurbita pepo*, which includes summer squashes. All gourds are frost-sensitive and in temperate climates should be raised in a greenhouse at 64–68°F (18–20°C). Sow in containers for transplanting outside when the plants are 4–6 in (10–15 cm) tall, and have been hardened off. In warm areas seeds may be sown direct into the open ground. A spacing of 8 × 8 ft (2.5 × 2.5 m) is

G

appropriate for most cultivars, and 3¼ ft (1 m) apart for small-fruited kinds. Rich, well-drained soil is needed, with liberal amounts of water applied throughout the growing season. Supports are necessary for some gourds, while others naturally trail on the ground. Pruning the vines of most species is recommended, reducing the main shoots to 8 ft (2.5 m) and the laterals to 4–6 leaves.

Ornamental gourds In Africa and South and Central America, the shells of gourds are traditionally carved, decorated, used as kitchen utensils, and made into musical instruments and ceremonial masks

In the garden, ornamental gourd plants may be trained on poles, fences, or trellises to form screens, and they provide decorative display over arbors and pergolas. Plants may be allowed to trail over terraces or steep banks as a decorative feature, and in some situations to help stabilize soil.

Ornamental gourds include attractive cultivars of: *Benincasa hispida* (BOTTLE GOURD, CHINESE MELON) which in temperate climates requires warm greenhouse conditions and produces 10 in (25 cm) long fruits, covered in fine hairs and a waxy secretion; *Cucurbita ficifolia* (MALABAR MELON, FIG-LEAVED or SIAMESE GOURD), is the hardiest of the ornamental gourds suitable for training over pergolas and producing large, green fruits resembling a watermelon. *C. maxima* (TURK'S-CAP

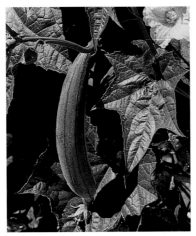

Luffa cylindrica
The loofah or dishcloth gourds make unusual, ornamental climbers for the warm greenhouse or conservatory. They may be grown outdoors in subtropical climates.

and large yellow forms) which produces exceptionally large fruits and requires stout supports. *C. moschata*, which has red, green, white, and butternut forms, and is adapted for training, shows resistance to virus diseases and vine borer. *C. pepo* (CUSTARD, CROOKNECK, and ORANGE GOURDS) and *C. pepo* var. *ovifera* (YELLOW-FLOWERED GOURD) are popular ornamental gourds; *Lagenaria siceraria* (WHITE-FLOWERED CALABASH or BOTTLE GOURD) includes the MINIATURE BOTTLE GOURD, WARTED BOTTLE GOURD, POWDER HORN, CLUB, and DOLPHIN types, but does not readily fruit in temperate areas; *Luffa cylindrica* (SMOOTH LOOFAH, DISHCLOTH GOURD) and *L. acutangula* (ANGLED LOOFAH, RIDGED GOURD) can be grown outdoors in subtropical areas or under greenhouse conditions in temperate climates. The bathroom loofah is the bleached, fibrous interior of *L. aegyptiaca*; When grown under warm greenhouse conditions *Momordica charantia* (BITTER GOURD) produces highly decorative fruits, light green, ripening to bright red, and covered with prominent warts that burst open when ripe; *Trichosanthes cucumerina* produces gourds up to 24 in (60 cm) long, which are bright green when young, becoming bright orange when mature, and often twisted and curled in shape.

After harvest, gourd fruits are usually washed with a mild disinfectant, dried for 4–6 weeks, and waxed to ensure preservation. Fruit shape can be modified by tying plastic-coated wires around the young developing fruits, or confining them in a rigid container. They may be stored for weeks or months if hung in a dry, well-ventilated room.

Edible gourds In tropical and subtropical climates, *Benincasa, Coccinia, Lagenaria, Luffa, Momordica, Telfairia* and *Trichosanthes* are fairly widely grown, and in temperate zones many of these can be grown successfully under greenhouse conditions.

The most important species of edible gourds cultivated in warm-temperate areas are *Cucumis anguria* (WEST INDIAN GOURD or GHERKIN); *C. melo* (CANTALOUPE, HONEYDEW, MUSK or SWEET MELON); *Cucurbita moschata*, which includes the WINTER SQUASHES; *C. pepo*, which includes

PUMPKINS, SUMMER SQUASHES, and VEGETABLE MARROWS; also vegetable spaghetti, with flesh that separates into spaghetti-like strands when boiled; *C. maxima*, which includes WINTER SQUASHES and the SQUASH GOURD; *C. mixta*, the WINTER SQUASH and pumpkin. See *cucumber, melons; pumpkins and squashes*.

gourmand see *water shoot*.

graft (1) a plant resulting from grafting; (2) loosely, a plant shoot, or scion, suitable for grafting; (3) an old word for a spade-depth of soil; (4) a type of spade with a long slightly concave blade, used for digging drains; it is also called a grafting tool.

graft hybrid see *chimera*.

grafting a method of vegetative propagation which normally involves joining together two separate plants in such a way that they eventually function as one. Grafts may arise naturally or be purposely made. Closely clipped hedges such as BEECH (*Fagus sylvatica*) and FIELD MAPLE (*Acer campestre*) will often form an interconnecting network of natural grafts. Similarly, where trees with thin bark, such as *Eucalyptus, Fagus, Fraxinus, Pinus, Platanus* and *Populus*, are growing close together, natural bridge grafts may form between individuals of the same species.

Grafting is a means of replicating selected plants that do not come true from seed or are difficult to propagate by other vegetative methods. Bench grafting refers to any grafting method performed at a bench, where the rootstocks may be bare-root plants, unrooted cuttings, or young plants established in pots.

Grafted plants often produce a larger plant in a shorter period of time, and the selection of an appropriate rootstock can improve the plant's tolerance of soil type, pH, and temperature, and provide resistance to certain pests and diseases. Specified rootstocks can induce vigorous or dwarfing growth response, as exploited in the propagation of most tree fruits. To overcome incompatibility, preserve cold or disease resistance, or control vigor, it is sometimes necessary to graft an intermediate variety or interstock, a technique known as double-working.

Grafting may also be used to produce curiosities, such as a prostrate form grafted onto an upright stock, or family fruit trees, with different cultivars grafted on to a single plant. Grafting can promote the early development of features that would take many years if plants were raised from seed; for instance, the distinctive bark of *Betula ermanii* or the flowering of *Wisteria*. Dioecious plants such as *Ilex aquifolium* may be grafted with a scion of the opposite sex, to improve the probability of fruiting, while bridge grafting can be used to to overcome an incompatible graft union or to combat the results of the girdling of stems by vandalism, machinery, or rodents.

Grafted plants of the same species will generally form a compatible union, although occasionally (especially with conifers) the graft may fail to form a union or the union may fail after ten years or so. Some species will form compatible unions with a different species belonging to the same genus, as with *Sorbus hupehensis* on *S. aucuparia*. Two different genera can form compatible unions—for instance *Amelanchier* on *Crataegus*; such successful intergeneric grafts will invariably be between members of the same family. Long-term compatibility of scions of one genus upon a rootstock of another is, however, unreliable.

There are two main grafting techniques.

Approach grafting (inarching)
This technique is a means of propagating plants that are difficult to graft by other methods, and also of saving valued dying trees. Here, the scion continues to grow on its own roots until the union with the rootstock is made. The plant providing the scion may be grown in a container, and sometimes the stock plant also. The plants are arranged so that the stems are alongside each other, and, in the simplest method, a sliver of bark and wood about 2 in (50 mm) long is taken off each stem, on the facing sides; other methods include the use of tongues and inlays. The two cut surfaces are then bound together with plastic wrap, rubber strips, or wax tape; in some cases, the whole area may need to be covered with grafting wax to form a waterproof seal.

When the two cut surfaces have grown together, the scion plant is cut just below the point of union and the upper part of the stock is removed.

A similar method may be used for providing disease-resistant rootstocks for the production of tomatoes and cucumbers in infected border soil. One type of inarching can be used to change the rootstock of an established orchard tree, and involves planting at least three plants of the new choice of rootstock close to the trunk of the tree and grafting the top of each into the trunk.

Detached scion grafting
This is the most widely used grafting method and involves removing a scion from a stock plant and working it onto a rootstock. The timing of the operation is crucial, and so is the physiological condition of both rootstock and scion: the rootstock should preferably be more advanced in growth than the scion, thus ensuring that the healing of the union occurs well before the scion breaks into growth. Water loss from the scion and graft union must be kept to a minimum, and for this reason the graft should be made quickly, and then firmly secured and covered with wax or another waterproofing substance. Detached scion grafting may be carried out in the open field or under protection, usually between the time the sap begins to rise in the spring and before it ceases in fall; except in the case of bud grafting, it is advisable to avoid midsummer. Evergreen and tender plants should be grafted under cold frames or in cool or heated greenhouses with high humidity and shade.

The two principal methods of detached scion grafting are apical grafting and side grafting.

APICAL GRAFTING, where the top of the rootstock is decapitated and replaced by a scion.

Splice grafting (whip grafting), a simple method suitable for bench grafting, which is the process of joining a root stock with a scion before potting. The rootstock and scion are held together by hand when tying and must be of similar diameter. The scion cut should overhang the top of the rootstock by about $1/8$–$1/4$ in (3–5 mm) to ensure that the developing callus forms a bridge between the two components.

Whip and tongue grafting is widely used to produce young plants in the field, notably where bud grafts have failed to take. The rootstock is trimmed of all side growth and the top cut to within 4 in (10 cm) of the ground. The scion is prepared from a stout one-year-old shoot and a piece selected that contains at least three or four buds, the lowest being about $1 1/4$–$1 1/2$ in (3–4 cm) above the bottom end. The tip should be neatly trimmed back just above the adjacent top bud. The tongue is made in the top half of the slanting cut surface, pointing downward. The slanting cut on the rootstock must match the dimensions of that on the scion, allowing for the scion cut to overshoot the top of the rootstock by $1/8$–$1/4$ in (3–5 mm). An equivalent facing tongue is made near the top of the rootstock cut, allowing the scion to be fitted. The graft is tied and made watertight.

Saddle grafting is a more difficult apical graft, traditionally used for large-flowered hybrid rhododendrons. Rootstock and scion must be of the same diameter. The cut rootstock is prepared by removing the top to leave a clear stem of about 4 in (10 cm), the top end of which is cut on both sides to form a central apex about $1 1/4$–$1 1/2$ in (3–4 cm) long. The base of the scion is cut by removing a wedge of tissue matching the shape of the cut rootstock, so that the scion may neatly straddle it. The cambium layers should exactly match. The graft is securely tied and sealed.

Wedge or cleft grafting is a simplified inverted saddle graft, achieved by splitting the top of the rootstock through the center. It is normally practiced on easy subjects like *Hibiscus syriacus* cultivars and evergreen azaleas. The base of the scion is cut in a V-shape and pushed into the split rootstock. The union may be secured with a simple clip like a small plastic clothespin.

Rind or crown grafting is a method of overcoming the problem of oversized rootstocks, and is also used for topworking mature fruit trees to change them from one cultivar to another. A slanting cut is made at the base of the scion, and a further incision, about $1/2$–$3/4$ in (1–2 cm) long, made through the rind of the decapitated rootstock, allowing the rind to be peeled back.

G

DETACHED SCION GRAFTING (WHIP GRAFT)

1 Using a very sharp knife and with arms held close to the body, pare a 1¼-in (3-cm) diagonal sliver from the base of the scion, opposite a healthy bud.

2 Cut the rootstock diagonally across, and from the high side, cut gently down the stock until you have an exposed area that corresponds to that on the scion.

3 The two cuts, when aligned, bring together the exposed cambium layers of the stock and the scion, which will be active in uniting them.

4 Bind the stock and scion together with grafting tape. On thin stocks, the tape may cover the cut surface; otherwise, paint with grafting wax to seal.

The scion is pushed behind the rind to the required depth, leaving an arch of a fraction of an inch visible on the cut face of the scion at the top of the rootstock to allow the callus to form a bridge between the two components. Since the scions are held firmly under the rind, tying is not required, but the unions must be made waterproof with a suitable sealant.

SIDE GRAFTING involves inserting scions without beheading the rootstock. This method of grafting is useful for propagating and for supplying an extra branch in any part of a tree; a spliced side graft (veneer side graft) is used for a wide range of evergreen and deciduous trees and shrubs where one- or two-year-old rootstocks have been established in pots. *Betula*, *Fagus*, and *Rhododendron* are best grafted in late winter, and *Acer palmatum*, *Hamamelis* and *Cedrus* in summer. The foliage should be retained on evergreens, but removed on summer-grafted deciduous plants to reduce water loss, with the leaf petioles retained to allow for natural abscission and to prevent bleeding. The scion should be prepared by making a 45° cut at the bottom, followed by a slice-cut down the stem, about 1–1½ in (2.5–3.5 cm) long, which meets the sharp end of the 45° basal cut. The stem of the rootstock should be thoroughly cleaned of shoots, and then a matching cut made as low down as is practical. Various modifications of this graft are used.

Side cleft grafting is where two slanting cuts are made on opposite sides of the base of the scion to form a wedge about ¹⁄₁₆–⅛ in (2–3 mm) long; one of the cuts should be slightly longer than the other. An angled incision of about 20° is made in the side of the rootstock, of sufficient depth to accommodate the scion. The incision is sprung open and the scion pushed home, ensuring that the longer cut is opposite the inner face of the rootstock and in line with the cambium. The graft is tied and sealed.

FRAMEWORKING AND TOP GRAFTING or topworking are procedures for changing the cultivar in mature trees, especially apples. In frameworking, the main structure is retained and branches headed back ("dehorned") by about 3 ft (1 m); only strong healthy laterals are retained and these are cut back to about 2 in (5 cm). The remaining shoots are grafted by whip and tongue or rind methods and the framework supplemented with side grafts set into the branches. Topworking involves cutting the main branches right back to near the crotch and inserting a number of scions, usually as rind grafts, around each cut. Topworked trees take longer to come into bearing and may be more prone to infection from diseases such as silverleaf.

The term "topworking" is also commonly used to describe the nursery practice of bud grafting high up on rootstock whips.

ROOT GRAFTING covers any method of grafting shoots on pieces of root. It can be used for a wide range of woody and herbaceous perennials, including *Clematis*, *Gypsophila*, *Hibiscus syriacus*, *Wisteria*, and *Campsis*, and is recorded as successful with apples and rhododendrons. When there are large fleshy roots and thin scion wood, as in tree peonies, an inlay-type graft is normally used. Where the root and scion are of approximately the same diameter, splice, wedge, or saddle grafts are suitable. Nurse grafting is a form of root grafting useful for propagating difficult stem cuttings or for plants where other sorts of grafting are likely to produce excessive rootstock suckers. Normal root grafting methods are used except that the scion/cutting is encouraged to root and the nurse root is removed once this has occurred. Plants that are nurse grafted include *Clematis* cultivars, using a tailed-scion graft onto roots of *C. vitalba* or *C. viticella*.

CUTTING GRAFTING is practiced on plants that are difficult to root: the graft is made on to a stem or root cutting, which is easily regenerated. The method is used commercially on a limited range of plants, including *Salix caprea* 'Pendula', large-flowered hybrid rhododendrons, and grape vines.

BUDDING is a detached side grafting technique, which employs a single bud to propagate fruit and ornamental trees and shrubs. The methods most widely used are shield-budding (T-budding) and

G

chip budding, normally carried out between midsummer and early fall; also practiced is patch budding of walnuts. In all cases, the rootstock should be well-established and actively growing, with selected buds dormant, uniform in size, well-developed and vegetative.

In *shield* or *T-budding* the scion buds, which occur in the axils of leaves, are removed from shoots of the current year's growth by means of a shallow slicing cut. This commences about ½ in (12 mm) below the bud, passing well under it and being completed some distance above it, so that there is a tail of rind that is convenient for handling. The removal of a sliver of wood at the back of the bud is generally required, especially for roses. The prepared bud forms the shield, and this is inserted beneath the rind of the rootstock, which is prepared with a T-shaped cut made down to the wood. The bud graft is tied with a suitable binding to secure the components in close contact, to minimize dessication and to make a watertight seal.

Chip budding
A chip of bark bearing a single bud is bound onto an equivalent cut in the stem of the rootstock, so that the cambium layers meet and unite. The stock is then headed back.

Chip budding is used extensively and involves a single bud graft that does not rely on lifting the rootstock bark. It is essentially a cleft graft, with the bud fitting exactly onto the chip of stem tissue removed from the rootstock. Both cambiums should be in line with each other to produce a neat, speedy union with minimal callus tissue. Chip buds need to be tied more securely than T-buds. Plastic tape, 1 in (25 mm)

wide, is used to completely cover the stem tissue, with pressure points above and below the bud, which may itself be covered. Union will take 5–8 weeks, depending on the plant, time of budding, and weather conditions. Hot, dry weather encourages speedy unions. The bud-take can be assessed the following February and the rootstock headed back to the top of the live bud. A slanting cut of about 22°, away from the bud, should be made. Clip and stake devices can be used initially to support the extension growth and keep it straight.

Grafting and sealing materials For tying grafts, raffia has been largely superseded by plastic materials, but it is still used for delicate operations, such as the split scion on *Clematis*, and rind grafts on miniature roses. For bench grafts, suitable tying materials are waxed cotton (or waxed fillis for large-diameter scions), 6-in (15-cm) strips of ¼-in- (5-mm-) wide rubber bands, or paraffin wax tape, which is self-sealing and gradually disintegrates. Paper and cotton tapes may be used for outdoor grafts, but the union must be made rainproof with a sealant. Plastic grafting tapes are available in widths of ½ in or 1 in (12 mm or 25 mm), and unions can usually be made watertight without sealant.

Sealants include bitumastic emulsions, applied cold to cut ends of scions and rootstocks where the union has been made rainproof by tying. Resin-based mastics, formulated with grease, mineral oil, synthetic wax or ethyl alcohol, are good alternatives to hot resin-based sealants, which need a portable heat source when used outdoors. Paraffin wax is widely used for bench grafting; rubberized latex compounds are suitable for both bench and outdoor grafts, applied cold to set and forming a flexible rainproof covering.

grafting knife a strong folding knife designed for grafting, comprising a blade about 3 in (7.5 cm) long, with an angled point at its end, set in a handle 4–5 in (10–12.5 cm) long.

grafting tool see *graft*.

graft union the point on a grafted plant where the scion and stock join.

graminaceous grassy, resembling grass in texture or habit.

granules a pesticide formulation, in which a chemical substance is combined with a carrier to form small pellets, usually for application to the soil. Granules facilitate even distribution through special applicators. They are suitable for the continuous release of an active chemical and for band treatment of insecticide along crop rows, and for broadcasting herbicide substances.

grape any of several species of *Vitis*, cultivated for their fruit. The grape grown in Europe and Asia is derived from *Vitis vinifera*, the EUROPEAN WILD GRAPE. Several *Vitis* species indigenous to N America (in particular the SUMMER GRAPE, *V. aestivalis*, the MUSCADINE, *V. rotundifolia*, and the FOX GRAPE, *V. labrusca*) have also been the sources of a range of cultivars.

Ancient vine growing is indicated by grape seeds found in Early Bronze Age sites at Jericho and Lachish. It spread west and north and also into Egypt, and figures prominently in Greek and Roman literature and in the Bible. Viticulture was introduced to Britain by the Romans, and by the time of the Domesday Book, 38 vineyards were recorded in southern England from Kent to Gloucestershire. Imports of superior wine gradually undermined the importance of the home-grown product, and grapevine-growing in Britain has ebbed and flowed with changing climatic conditions.

In North America, early efforts to cultivate grapevines in the eastern states foundered through the ravages of *Phylloxera vastatrix*, but this pest was not present in California, and vineyards flourished there. Resistant Californian grapevines became the rootstocks onto which *Phylloxera*-susceptible European vines were grafted in the late 19th century, thereby saving the great vineyards from extinction. At about the same time, European vines were cross-pollinated with American cultivars, producing *Phylloxera*-resistant hybrids that are widely grown today.

Grapes under glass A greenhouse needs to provide adequate space and ventilation and sufficient root run into a good growing medium, with surface access to it for routine top-dressing and watering. A lean-to structure is most suitable, the back wall offering residual heat. The soil must be fertile and well-drained, and the vine can be planted inside or outside the greenhouse; if outside, the stem or rod is led through an opening in the supporting wall of the structure. Grapes for greenhouse cultivation are classified as (1) Sweetwater: early-ripening cultivars, which are the best choice for unheated houses; for example, 'Black Hamburgh' and 'Foster's Seedling'. (2) Muscats: the finest-flavored grapes, normally requiring heat; for example, 'Muscat of Alexandria' and 'Madresfield Court'. (3) Vinous: the latest to ripen, requiring adequate heat; for example, 'Alicante' and 'Gros Colmar'.

PLANTING AND TRAINING. Planting of bareroot plants is carried out in November or December, but container-grown specimens may be planted at any time. In small houses, planting at one end and training the vine up and along the ridge is suitable, with fixtures inserted to support wires that should hold the vine 14 in (35 cm) away from the glass, although in a small greenhouse 10 in (25 cm) will suffice. Where there is space, suitable extra main shoots are trained along wires spaced 4 ft (1.2 m) apart.

The simple rod and spur training method is commonly used in greenhouse culture. After planting, shorten the stem to about 3 in (7.5 cm) above soil level or the graft union; always prune by January 1 to prevent bleeding of sap. One leading shoot (also called rod or stem) should be allowed to grow up and tied loosely to the wire during the first summer. Laterals (also called rods or canes) growing out from the leading shoot are shortened to five leaves and any sublaterals to one leaf. Competing leaders should be removed in the first winter, the leading shoot reduced by two-thirds of its length, and the laterals pruned to one bud from the leading shoot stem.

In the second summer, the leading shoot extends and is tied to the wires, and the treatment of laterals and sublaterals repeated. Any flower trusses must be pruned off to prevent fruiting before the third year.

In subsequent winters, the leading shoot is shortened and restricted to the available space; laterals are repeatedly shortened to one bud, and with annual cuts, spurs are formed that eventually require thinning out with a pruning saw. Where laterals are trained at an upward angle, they should be cut loose in winter and allowed to hang, or retied horizontally, until growth begins, to ensure even growth at each spur; the laterals are then returned to their normal positions.

As growth starts in spring, only two fruiting laterals must be retained at each spur. The weaker of the two is pinched to two leaves and is kept as insurance against any accident to the lateral which will normally carry the crop. As this develops, flower trusses and usually also vine leaves will appear up to 24 in (60 cm) along its length. The tip of the fruiting lateral should be pinched out two leaves beyond the best flower truss, other trusses being cut out. If no flower truss appears, such shoots should be pinched at six to eight leaves. Any sublaterals are pruned to one leaf and tendrils removed.

In the third summer, just one or two bunches of grapes are allowed to develop, gradually increasing the number of bunches in subsequent summers. In general, at least 12 in (30 cm) of stem should be left between each bunch.

MANAGEMENT. Most vines are self-fertile, but tapping the laterals around midday to distribute pollen will assist setting in many cultivars. The Muscats, especially, benefit from cupping hands gently and passing them over the flower truss from one vine to another; lightly dusting flower trusses with a soft brush is an alternative procedure.

Greenhouse ventilators must be opened to provide a cold environment until late winter, after which they should be progressively closed to maintain a uniform temperature for the encouragement of early growth. Ventilation should be restricted during pollination but given freely after fruit set to reduce risk of disease. Ventilators may need to be equipped with covers of fruit netting if birds are troublesome.

Dampening down is advantageous on sunny days except during flowering and fruit ripening, and mist spraying of

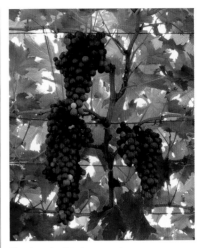

Cordon–trained grapevine
A single cordon, with fruiting stems radiating horizontally from a single vertical main stem, may be trained across the roof of a greenhouse on a system of wires.

the foliage in early morning is recommended, until the first sign of fruit ripening.

Fruit thinning is essential, and special grape-thinning scissors are used to remove smaller, crowded fruits within the bunch, a forked stick being used to manipulate the bunch.

Winter treatment involves pricking the soil over lightly with a fork in order to remove the top $1\frac{1}{2}$–2 in (4–5 cm) layer, which is replaced with fresh, rich, soil-based mixture. Following the first waterings, a mulch of well-rotted farmyard manure or compost should be applied. Once active growth is evident, feeding at two- to three-week intervals with a high-potash fertilizer should be given, until the fruits show color.

Bunches of grapes should be harvested with a small piece of the spur attached to act as a handle to avoid damaging the bloom on the surface of the fruit.

Grapes in containers. If space is limited, grapes can be grown in pots, tubs or other containers with a minimum diameter of 12 in (30 cm). Drainage holes are essential, and should be covered with a layer of broken crocks and fibrous turf. The container is filled with a fertile soil-based medium in preference to a peat-based mix.

Where practical, a containerized vine should be moved in and out of a greenhouse or conservatory on to a sheltered terrace to aid growth and ripening. Cultivation requirements are similar to those of greenhouse vines, involving development of a permanent rod, which is spur-pruned each winter. A suitable support for the rod is essential to a height of about 6 ft (1.75 m), and only five or six bunches should be retained per plant. A mulch of rotted farmyard manure and regular feeding as for greenhouse crops is beneficial. Thorough daily watering is essential once growth begins, being reduced as the grapes begin to color. Repot in midwinter every two or three years.

Grapes on outdoor walls. Sheltered, warm sunny walls are suitable for grape-growing, the vines being trained and pruned as for greenhouse culture. Control of dense growth by thinning and pinching and by annual pruning in winter is essential for success. The soil should be thoroughly and deeply prepared and only where the soil is poor should small amounts of rotted manure or compost be incorporated; otherwise, excessive growth and delayed cropping will result. A 1–2-year-old vine should be planted 8–10 in (20–25 cm) away from the wall, in winter in milder climates and in early spring in regions with cold winters. Feed, renew the topsoil, and mulch as for the greenhouse crop. Early-ripening cultivars are the best choice.

Where phylloxera or nematodes are a problem, grapes must be propagated onto resistant rootstocks. For other situations, most vines can be propagated from hardwood cuttings taken in early winter and rooted outdoors. Muscadine cultivars do not root readily from cuttings and are usually layered. For other cultivars, green softwood cuttings also provide a suitable means of increase.

Possible problems: birds, mealy bug, phylloxerids, red spider mite, scale insects, wasps; black rot, downy mildew, gray mold, powdery mildew; shanking.

grape marc the seed, skin and stem residue from grape pressing, which can be composted and used in growing media. The compost is saline, with a high potassium content, and the residual seeds have properties similar to very coarse sand.

grape scissors scissors with long narrow tapering blades, specially designed for thinning bunches of grapes. Also known as vine scissors.

grape stage see *bud stages.*

Graptopetalum (from Greek *graptos,* painted or written upon, and *petalon,* petal). Crassulaceae. Paraguay, Mexico to Arizona. Around 12 species, succulent perennial herbs and shrubs. The fleshy leaves are usually borne in rosettes. Small, 5-petaled flowers are carried in spring and summer in lax cymes. Cultivate as for *Echeveria.*

G. amethystinum JEWEL-LEAF PLANT; Mexico; subshrub to 12 in (30 cm) tall; leaves 1¼–2¾ in (3–7 cm) in loose rosettes, oblong to ovate, blunt, margin rounded, blue-green to lavender or purple-red; *G. paraguayense* GHOST PLANT, MOTHER OF PEARL PLANT; Mexico; decumbent herb to 12 in (30 cm); leaves 1¼–2 in (3–5 cm) in open rosettes, obovate to spathulate, thick, short-pointed, emerging pale mauve, becoming thickly gray-white-glaucous.

Graptophyllum (from Greek *graptos* to write, and *phyllon,* leaf, alluding to the beautifully marked leaves). Acanthaceae. Australasia, SW Pacific. 10 species, evergreen shrubs, often with colorfully marked leaves and producing racemes of two-lipped, tubular flowers in summer. The following species is grown primarily for its handsome foliage. It will tolerate poor light levels and drier atmospheres in the office and home. Provide a minimum temperature of 50°F (10°), with protection from drafts, and full sun. Water and feed freely when in growth, but keep barely moist in winter. *G. pictum* CARICATURE PLANT; habitat obscure, widespread as an escape in SE Asia; to 6½ ft (2 m); leaves to 6 in (15 cm), oval, glossy dark green blotched or marbled cream in central zone; flowers crimson to purple.

grass hook see *scythe*

grasshoppers (Orthoptera: Acrididae) mostly large insects, up to 2 in (50 mm) long or more, usually brown or green, with biting mouthparts and hind legs modified for jumping. Most feed predominantly on grasses but some have a wide range of host plants. Locusts are grasshoppers that have both a solitary phase in their life cycle and a gregarious one when they swarm. Grasshoppers and locusts lay their eggs in the soil.

Locusts are important pests in Africa and Asia. In Australia, the AUSTRALIAN PLAGUE LOCUST (*Chortoicetes terminifera*) damages pastures, field crops and vegetables. The SPUR-THROATED LOCUST (*Austacris guttulosa*) and the SMALL PLAGUE LOCUST (*Austroicetes cruciata*) are less serious pests. In North America, grasshoppers are more important pests than locusts. The CLEARWING GRASSHOPPER (*Camnula pellucida*) attacks cereals and other crops and several *Melanoplus* species are pests of a wide range of plants. Control of locusts often requires national or international action on a concerted scale; like grasshoppers, they are susceptible to nonpersistent insecticides, often applied aerially at ultra-low volume rates. Baits are used for grasshopper control, but not for locusts.

grassing down the sowing of grass; especially around fruit trees to slow down the rate of growth through competition for water and nutrients, and thereby encourage fruiting.

grease banding a technique used mainly on fruit and ornamental trees to control winter moths and related species; it involves encircling the trunk with a 4-in (100-mm) band of grease-proof paper smeared with grease. Female WINTER MOTHS are wingless and gain access to trees by climbing the trunk, where they become trapped in the greaseband. The device should be applied in midfall and regularly maintained throughout the winter. A band of petroleum jelly around the stems of chrysanthemums can help to prevent CHRYSANTHEMUM EELWORM (*Aphelenchoides ritzema-bosi*) from ascending the stems in humid weather. Grease banding is also referred to as barrier banding or tree-banding.

grecian saw a pruning saw with a narrow curved blade, with the teeth set for pulling action.

greenback a condition of tomato fruits in which an area around the stalk

G

remains hard and green while other parts ripen. It is associated with hot sunshine and an inadequate supply of potash. There are differences in susceptibility between cultivars. Prevention is by greenhouse shading and careful feeding and watering.

green bud see *bud stages*.

green cluster see *bud stages*.

greenfly see *aphids*.

greenhouse a structure in which plants are cultivated for the production of a crop or for display. It may be covered with glass, rigid plastic sheeting or plastic film. The terms "greenhouse" and "glasshouse" are interchangeable but to avoid confusion arising from the introduction of plastic alternatives to glass, there is international agreement to use the term "greenhouse" in all technical and scientific publications.

Glass-clad greenhouses, regardless of design, are often described according to the temperature level normally maintained: COLD HOUSE, without heating; COOL HOUSE, heated to maintain frost protection only or a minimum of about 45°F (7°C); TEMPERATE HOUSE, heated to maintain about 55°F (13°C) minimum; HOT HOUSE (also warm house or stove house), heated to maintain about 64°F (18°C) minimum.

The design of greenhouses must take into account five main requirements:maximum light transmission, minimum obstruction of the growing area, structural integrity, energy efficiency, and cost. Light transmission is affected by the proportion of opaque structural material, orientation and roof shape. The use of steel and aluminum extrusions gives increased strength for size and reduces the amount of opaque material. An east-west orientation increases light transmission as does a high south-facing eave, with the side wall inclined.

Cladding materials Glass is the best choice in terms of light transmission, heat retention, durability, and cost-effectiveness. Panes usually measure 24 × 24 in (600 × 600 mm), but may be smaller for some wooden greenhouses; Dutch-light panes are 56 × 29 in (1,422 × 730 mm). A thick-

ness of ⅛ in (3 mm) is adequate for panes up to 24 in (600 mm) wide, except in situations where there are particular safety risks; special types are available for double glazing.

Where timber glazing bars are used, the glass is normally bedded on putty and secured by brass pins; the bars may be capped with aluminum strip and soft mastic. With aluminum bars, the glass is bedded on mastic or into profiled polyvinyl chloride (PVC) or neoprene extrusion and secured with stainless-steel clips. Dutch-light panes are normally dry glazed, each sheet being held in grooves machined along the frame members.

Glass alternatives are available in the form of rigid plastic sheeting and plastic film. Acrylic and acrylic-coated polycarbonate are the most satisfactory sheet plastics, having optical properties similar to glass and being available in twin-walled form for improved insulation; acrylic can be formed into curved profiles. Very tough and durable film plastics can also be used to manufacture tensioned glazing panels.

Polythene film cannot be regarded as a direct replacement for glass, but it provides suitable covering for low-cost tunnel greenhouses. The risk of its degrading in sunlight is greatly reduced where the product contains an ultraviolet light inhibitor, and the incorporation of the copolymer, EVA, improves heat retention characteristics. The film is stretched over galvanized-steel tubular arches anchored in the soil, to form walk-in tunnels. Single-span structures are available in widths of 14–33 ft (4.3–10 m), and multi-span forms, up to 9 ft (2.4 m) high, with connecting gutters, in spans of 21–33 ft (6.5–10 m). These structures are more susceptible to wind than glasshouses, so the arches must be well-secured, the structure braced and the cover applied as a single sheet secured to a base or dug into the ground. Polythene tunnels are mainly used for production of salad crops, celery, peppers, and strawberries, and for protection of container-grown nursery stock.

Heating and ventilation Where supplementary heating is provided, the range and season of plants can be extended. However, it must be remembered that the cost of heating escalates dramatically as the minimum tempera-

ture requirement is raised. Commercial greenhouses are usually heated either by hot water circulated through fixed pipes, or by fan-propelled hot air distributed through large-diameter polythene tubes. More common and convenient for garden greenhouses are portable units fueled by electricity, kerosene, or gas.

Electric fan heaters are a suitable choice for the small greenhouse, circulating air quickly and providing cool air in summer. Electric tubular heaters, fixed about 4 in (10 cm) from the walls, can maintain a higher temperature in large greenhouses, and they give more even distribution of heat. Both types must be thermostatically controlled for efficiency.

Kerosene heaters are relatively cheap to buy and operate, although they cannot be thermostatically controlled. They emit water vapor, which can encourage disease, and at high settings or where inadequately maintained may produce harmful gases; they are best regarded as a standby where only frost protection is required.

Flueless gas-fired heaters employing natural or bottled gas are available, and these may be thermostatically controlled and will enhance atmospheric carbon dioxide levels. Both types of fuel-burning heaters require regular maintenance, and a little ventilation should be provided.

The required output capacity of greenhouse heaters can be calculated, each based on temperature lift, which is the degree difference between the required minimum inside the glasshouse and the likely minimum outside. Another factor to take into account is the coefficient of heat loss through the cladding, which necessitates calculating the area of all exposed surfaces and dividing that for brick walling by two because of its better insulating properties. A suitable formula for calculating required electric-heater capacity in kilowatts is then:

$$\frac{28 \times \text{equiv. surface area (sq yd)} \times \text{temp. increase (°F)}}{1{,}000}$$

Greenhouse ventilation limits the rise of air temperature, provides cooling, controls the rise of humidity, and maintains the ambient level of carbon dioxide. Ventilators built into the ridge and low down on the sides of the structure are recommended for good air circulation; and their total area when fully open should be equivalent to at least one-sixth of the greenhouse floor area. Extractor fans give positive air movement but result in uneven temperature distribution. They should be fitted high in the gable-end away from the door, and can be thermostatically controlled. See *bench, shading*.

green manuring the practice of growing certain quick-maturing plants and subsequently digging them in to improve soil fertility. Examples of green manures are RAPE (*Brassica napus*), WHITE MUSTARD (*Sinapis alba*), CLOVER (*Trifolium* species), WINTER FIELD BEANS (*Vicia faba*), and GRAZING RYE GRASS (*Secale cereale*). Usually sown broadcast in close rows, green manures must be dug in while lush.

Green manuring provides a source of humus, thereby improving soil structure; where leguminous nitrogen-fixing species are grown, it is also a means of adding nitrogen to the soil. However, green manuring is essentially a technique supplementary to manuring and fertilizing and should not be solely relied upon for poor soil. On light-textured soil, it provides protection from winter erosion. Also known as cover cropping, sheet composting.

green tip see *bud stages*.

greenwaste collected plant residues, which following composting are a valuable source of organic matter for soil amelioration and mulching.

Grevillea (for Charles F. Greville [1749–1809], a founder of the Royal Horticultural Society, once vice president of the Royal Society). Proteaceae. Australia, New Caledonia. SPIDER FLOWER. Some 250 species, evergreen trees or shrubs. The leaves range in shape from small, rigid, and needlelike to broad, soft, and pinnately lobed. Tubular, curving flowers are borne in racemes or panicles, usually in spring and summer. Many species are known to tolerate frost to about 23°F (−5°C), if given perfectly drained soil and a sheltered position against a south-facing wall. Many of the cultivars show a greater tolerance than their parents.

G. alpina, G. juniperina, and *G. rosmarinifolia* are among the hardiest species, the last having survived temperatures to 50°F (10°C). The genus is grown primarily for its nectar-rich flowers, although some species also have very attractive foliage—for example, *G. robusta*, a popular plant for the home or office, grown either as a compact, rooted stem cutting or as a specimen shrub. Most thrive given full sun and good drainage in neutral or slightly acidic soil. Propagate from fresh seed in spring, or by semiripe cuttings. *G. robusta* is resistant to root-rotting fungus and is used as a rootstock for grafting western Australian species and as a stock for standard and weeping specimens.

G. alpina E Australia; prostrate to erect shrub to 6½ ft (2 m); leaves ½–1¼ in (1–3 cm), linear to rounded; flowers red, pink, green, yellow, and white, crowded in short, spidery racemes; *G. banksii* RED-FLOWERED SILKY OAK; E Australia; shrub to 13 ft (4 m); leaves to 10 in (25 cm), pinnatifid, lobes linear, silky gray beneath; flowers red or white in cylindrical racemes to 4 in (10 cm); *G.* 'Canberra Gem' (*G. juniperina* × *G. rosmarinifolia*) vigorous, rounded shrub to 8 ft (2.5 m); leaves to 1¼ in (3 cm), linear, sharply pointed; flowers bright pink, waxy, in clusters sometimes throughout the year; *G. juniperina* E Australia; dense rounded shrub to 6½ ft (2 m) tall; leaves ½–¾ in (1–2 cm), narrowly lanceolate to linear; flowers green to yellow pink or red; *G.* Poorinda Hybrids: a group of garden hybrids including 'Poorinda Constance', a large, rounded shrub to 13 ft (4 m) with sharply pointed, oblong leaves to 1¼ in (3 cm) and red flowers in spidery clusters, the purple-red 'Poorinda Peter', with bronze-tinted, pinnate leaves, and the apricot-flowered 'Poorinda Queen'; *G. robusta* SILK OAK; E Australia; fast-growing tree to 115 ft (35 m); leaves to 12 in (30 cm), bronze at first, becoming olive, broadly oblong, pinnatifid, segments deeply cut, silky; flowers orange; *G. rosmarinifolia* E Australia; dense shrub to 6½ ft (2 m) tall; leaves to 1¼ in (3 cm), linear, rigid, bright to gray-green; flowers pink to red with cream, sometimes pure creamy yellow.

Paphiopedilum Buckhurst 'Mont Millais'
The grex (here "Buckhurst") is a group name peculiar to orchids, indicating hybrids with the same, established parentage.

grex a group name for all plants derived from the crossing of the same two or more species. The grex (herd or hybrid swarm) is close in some senses to the *group*, but relates more specifically to an established parentage or lineage. The term has become limited to orchid hybrids. It is printed in roman with a capital initial. The grex may be combined with a cultivar or clonal name which is printed within single quotation marks—for example, *Paphiopedilum* Maudiae 'The Queen'.

grey (gray) bulb rot (*Rhizoctonia tuliparum*) a soilborne disease of ornamental bulbs in cool temperate regions. Poor emergence is an early indication of the disease, and lifted plants have rotted shoots with soil adhering even though the roots may appear healthy. The fungus shows as grayish mycelia around rotted bulbs and between bulb scales, with numerous large flattened white or black fruiting bodies on the bulbs and in the surrounding soil; by means of these fruiting bodies, the fungus can survive for several years. It is most serious on tulips, but *Colchicum, Crocus*, hyacinths, *Iris, Ixia*, lilies, and *Narcissus* can also be infected. Control by removing all affected bulbs and the surrounding soil as soon as symptoms are noticed. The affected area should not be used for bulb growing for at least five years.

349

Greyia (for Sir George Grey [1812–1898], governor general of Cape Colony). Greyiaceae. South Africa. NATAL BOTTLEBRUSH. Some 3 species, shrubs or small trees. The toothed leaves are white-woolly when young. Produced in spring and summer, the small flowers have showy stamens and are carried in dense, bottlebrush-like spikes. Plant in a well-drained, sandy medium in full sun. Under glass, provide good ventilation, maintain a minimum temperature of 45–50°F (7–10°C), and water moderately when in growth. Keep almost dry in winter. Propagate by seed in spring, by basal cuttings of new growth, by semiripe cuttings, or by removal of rooted suckers. *G. sutherlandii* to 15 ft (4.5 m); leaves up to 2¾ in (7 cm), rounded to heart-shaped, toothed; flower spikes up to 4 × 2 in (10 × 5 cm), red.

grey (gray) mold the visible growth of the ubiquitous fungus *Botrytis cinerea*. It is found on many different hosts and causes leaf, flower and bud rots, dieback of woody plants, and rots of fruits and vegetables. Affected organs are covered with a fluffy gray mold from which clouds of spores are released, rapidly spreading the disease. The fungus is common on decaying plant material and is a weak parasite that mainly attacks damaged or stressed plants growing under cool, damp, overcrowded conditions.

Control depends on good hygiene, involving the removal of crop debris and damaged or affected tissues, good ventilation, especially in greenhouses, and the avoidance of damp or overcrowded conditions. Chemical control is possible with recommended systemic and protectant fungicides. However, control by the continual use of systemic fungicides alone may lead to the buildup of resistant strains of the fungus, or development of infection by other fungi, such as *Alternaria* and *Stemphylium*, which are not controlled by the group of fungicides in use.

Although a major disease of vines, requiring costly control measures during the growing season, gray mold can also be beneficial to certain wine-producers. *Botrytis* is the agent causing "noble rot" (*pourriture noble*) of ripe grapes, the condition in which the berries lose moisture and thereby yield juice of a higher sugar content. The infection is essential to the production of some wines, such as Sauternes and Tokay.

greywater, graywater see *irrigation*.

Grindelia (for David Hieronymus Grindel [1776–1836], Russian botanist). Compositae. Western N and S America. GUM PLANT, ROSIN-WEED, TARWEED. About 60 species, resinous annual or perennial herbs, rarely shrubs. They produce large, daisylike flower heads in summer. Suitable for the larger rock garden, for the warm sunny border, and for dry, sunny banks, especially in poor, dry soil. Hardy to 5°F (–15°C). Grow in well-drained soil in full sun. Propagate by seed, or by semiripe cuttings in late summer. *G. chiloensis* (syn. *G. speciosa*) Patagonia; clammy, shrubby perennial to 3¼ ft (1 m); flower heads deep golden yellow.

Griselinia (for F. Griselini [1717–1783], Italian botanist). Cornaceae (Griseliniaceae). New Zealand, Brazil, Chile. 6 species, evergreen trees and shrubs with leathery leaves and inconspicuous flowers in racemes or panicles. Where temperatures do not fall below 23°F (–5°C), *G. littoralis* may be grown in the open garden; it will thrive in colder areas still (to 10°F/ –12°C) if given a sheltered, south-facing niche and excellent drainage; it is suitable for screens and hedging in coastal areas. *G. lucida* is frost-tender, but may be grown in the conservatory in cold areas. Grow in sun or part shade. Trim hedges in summer. Propagate from nodal cuttings in late summer/ early fall, in a sandy propagating mix in the cold frame.

G. littoralis New Zealand; shrub or tree to 26 ft (8 m); leaves to 3½ in (9 cm), ovate to oblong, olive to apple green, glossy, slightly fleshy, more or less undulate; includes 'Dixon's Cream', with leaves splashed creamy white, and 'Variegata', with leaves blotched or zoned white; *G. lucida* New Zealand; shrub to 13 ft (4 m); leaves to 18, mid-green, glossy; includes the large- and round-leaved var. *macrophylla* and the yellow-cream-marked 'Variegata'.

grit very small stone fragments, larger than sharp sand, that are used as an ingredient of certain growing media, or on the surfaces of pots and sinks for alpines, especially.

grotto an artificial garden feature made to resemble a small, picturesque cave. Grottos have been known since Roman times and have been either excavated or constructed, often from tufa rock, and ornamented with stones, shells, or attractive minerals. They sometimes incorporate waterworks.

ground bed usually a temporary cold frame, comprising low board or block walls covered by glass lights or film plastic.

ground beetles (Coleoptera: Carabidae) a very large and widely distributed family of small to medium-large beetles. Most are black, with long beadlike antennae, biting mouthparts, and slender legs adapted for running. Many species are flightless. Normally, ground beetles are active at night and spend the day under stones, leaves, logs, etc., especially in damp places. Adults and larvae feed on small worms, slugs, snails and a wide range of insects, and the species *Bembidion lampros* and *Trechus quadristriatus* are predators of the eggs and larvae of the cabbage root fly (*Delia radicum*). Some ground beetles, including the strawberry seed beetle (*Harpalus rufipes*) and the strawberry ground beetles (*Pterostichus madidus* and *P. melanarius*), may damage the ripening fruits of strawberries.

Ground beetle

groundcover selected species planted between shrubs to cover the ground and conceal all signs of the soil beneath. Provided that perennial weeds are removed before planting, groundcover will smother other weeds and can provide an attractive garden feature in itself, as well as enhancing plants beneath which it grows. Groundcover may also be useful as a mulch for conserving moisture, but where well-established it can compete with main plantings for moisture and nutrients.

Plants used as groundcover are usually less than 12 in (30 cm) high, although in large areas some shrubs can be grown for the purpose. Species should not be so vigorous as to become weeds, and the majority of plants should be evergreen. However, individual species that spread over an area of about 24 in (60 cm) diameter and die back in the fall are useful for under-planting spring-flowering dwarf bulbs. For groundcover, flower qualities are secondary to foliage effect.

Herbaceous perennials are valuable groundcover plants, and among these are the evergreen "carpeters" *Saxifraga umbrosa* (London Pride), *Ajuga reptans*, (bugle), *Potentilla alba*, and *Waldsteinia ternata*, all of which will spread over a wide area from a single plant. Larger plants, making clumps which eventually join together, include *Alchemilla mollis*, *Geranium endressii* and *G. × magnificum*, *Tellima grandiflora*, *Brunnera macrophylla*, *Bergenia* species, *Pachyphragma macrophyllum*, and *Pulmonaria* species. Suitable taller hardy perennials that are effective in expansive colonies are *Hosta*, *Hemerocallis*, *Helleborus orientalis*, and *Nepeta*. Effective small-scale ground-cover of dense spreading growth is provided by the alpine campanulas and phloxes, *Dryas octopetala*, *Polygonum vacciniifolium*, *Asarum europaeum*, and the smaller cultivars of *Geranium sanguineum*.

Low-growing shrubs, such as *Cornus canadensis*, *Cotoneaster dammeri*, *Euonymus fortunei*, *Lonicera pileata*, *Mahonia repens*, *Pachysandra terminalis*, *Rubus pentalobus*, and *Vinca* species can be effective. Suitable taller shrubs include lavender, hydrangeas, *Prunus laurocerasus* 'Otto Luyken', *Sarcococca* species, *Viburnum davidii*, and, for acidic soil, *Arctostaphylos*, *Gaultheria*, and *Vaccinium* species. Heaths and heathers are some of the most valuable of all groundcover. *Erica carnea* and *E. erigena* hybrids flourish in alkaline soil, *E. vagans* on neutral ground, and all other species of *Erica* and *Calluna* in nonalkaline soil.

Some climbing plants make effective groundcover, eventually covering large areas and being therefore relatively inexpensive in outlay. These include the less rampant forms of *Hedera*, *Hydrangea petiolaris*, and *Lonicera japonica* 'Halliana'. Certain ferns can be used, two British natives, the male fern, *Dryopteris filix-mas*, and the hart's tongue, *Asplenium scolopendrium*, being among the most valuable. Others are *Athyrium filix-femina*, *Blechnum chilense*, *Cystopteris bulbifera*, *Matteuccia struthiopteris*, and *Polypodium vulgare*.

Prostrate and semiprostrate conifers are worth consideration, especially those with colored foliage—for example, the procumbent, gray selections of *Juniperus*. Ornamental grasses and sedges, among them *Festuca glauca*, *Luzula* species, *Phalaris arundinacea*, *Stipa calamagrostis*, and *Carex* species, can also be used.

All of the foregoing are satisfactory in most gardens in eastern North America and in the UK. In temperate regions like the Mediterranean and the western seaboard of North America, where frost in winter is unlikely and the summer is characterized by long dry periods, dense-growing low shrubs can be selected from the natural range of *maquis* and *garrigue* plants, while low creepers can be found among such plants as *Acaena* species, *Armeria*, dwarf *Ceratostigma* species, *Convolvulus cneorum*, spreading *Chamaecytisus* and *Genista*, *Liriope*, mesembryanthemums, *Osteomeles*, the dwarf saxifrages, *Sedum* species, and *Teucrium* species.

Subtropical areas, such as parts of Florida, can support perennials that are often grown as tender summer bedding in northern states—for example *Chlorophytum*, coleus, *Iresine*, *Helichrysum petiolare* and *Tradescantia*. Other plants for full sun include *Asystasia gangetica*, *Hemigraphis alternata*, and *Lantana montevidensis*. Ferns provide important groundcover plants for shade in such climates, together with species such as *Episcia*, *Fittonia*, *Peperomia*, and *Pilea nummularifolia*. *Asparagus sprengeri* grows in sun or shade. See *mulch*.

ground elder (*Aegopodium podagraria*) an invasive perennial weed of uncultivated ground, borders, and sometimes lawns. It occasionally establishes itself from seed but is mainly transported by fleshy underground stems. These form a dense network in the top layer of soil and give rise to thick leaf cover that can stifle all but the most vigorous plants. Left unchecked, ground elder can spread 3 ft (1 m) per year. Control by forking is difficult because of the need to remove all root portions, which readily become established among roots of garden plants. The best recourse is to lift infested plants for renewal while the site is thoroughly cleared by meticulous forking out of the fleshy underground stems, or by applying a total weedkiller if possible. Where practicable, smother with a light-excluding fabric such as thick polyethylene sheeting, left down for several growing seasons. Glyphosate and glyphosate trimesium are effective as total weedkillers.

groundkeeper used particularly of a potato tuber that is unharvested and gives rise to a plant in the following season. It may be of significance as a source of disease infection in the new season. Also known as a volunteer.

groundwork the ground level of a bedding scheme composed of low growing plants.

group a category intermediate between species and cultivar, used to distinguish: (1) an assemblage of two or more similar cultivars and/or individuals within a species or hybrid; (2) plants derived from a hybrid of uncertain parentage. Group names are written in roman script, take a capital initial letter, no quotation marks, and are always followed by the word "Group," with an upper case initial.

growing bag a sealed, plastic bag, about 12½ in (32 cm) wide and 3¼ ft (1 m) long, filled with 1¾–2¼ cu ft (50–60 liters) of compressed soilless growing medium, usually fertilized peat or composted bark. Growing bags are used for the cultivation of tomatoes and other plants where it is beneficial to avoid rooting into greenhouse border soil, and for growing on concrete surfaces. Two or three planting holes are cut into the top of the module and 2-in (5-cm) drainage slits made in the sides, about 1 in (2.5 cm) from the base. Regular watering and supplementary feeding are essential.

G

growing point the tip of a stem.

growing room, growth chamber a windowless room in which light, temperature, and humidity are controlled. Commonly used for raising bedding plants, tomatoes, cucumbers, and lettuce in winter and early spring, and for research purposes. Typically, lighting is provided by static or mobile rigs of 8-ft- (2.5-m-) long 125W fluorescent tubes, giving a visible irradiance of roughly 40W per sq yd (m²) or 20W per sq yd (m²) depending on 12- or 24-hour cycles of operating.

Growmore a standard, compound, balanced fertilizer, made to a formula first recommended by the UK Ministry of Agriculture during World War II, and marketed as National Growmore. It contains 7% nitrogen: 7% phosphate: 7% potash.

growth cycle periods of active growth in plants alternating with dormancy or slowed growth brought about by low rainfall or changed levels of temperature or day length. In temperate zones, it is illustrated by deciduous trees losing their leaves in fall and by evergreen growth slowing during cold spells and in poor light conditions.

Growth regulator
Auxin-containing hormone rooting powders or talcs are widely used by gardeners to promote rooting in cuttings.

growth regulators chemicals that influence plant growth. They either occur naturally in association with plant tissue or are manufactured and applied to achieve a desired effect.

Ethylene gas is produced by ripening apples and hastens maturity in unripened fruits and wilting in cut flowers. Various complex chemicals, often referred to as hormones, occur within plants. Among these are auxins, which cause stem elongation and root formation on cuttings; gibberellins, which break dormancy and induce flowering and stem elongation; cytokinins, which stimulate cell division; and abscisic acid, which inhibits growth.

Synthetic imitations of plant hormones are developed to produce abnormal growth, as in the weed-killers 2,4-D and mecoprop. Other manufactured growth regulators include maleic hydrazide, which suppresses sprout development in potatoes and sucker growth in trees and shrubs, dikegulac, which retards growth of hedges, chlormequat, which restricts stem growth in ornamentals, and IBA (4-indole-3-butyric acid), which promotes the rooting of cuttings.

growth rings see *annual rings*.

grubber see *mattock*; *daisy grubber*.

grubs a popular term for the larvae of beetles (Coleoptera); also sometimes applied to those of bees, wasps, and ants (Hymenoptera). Beetle larvae have biting mouthparts, a well-developed, hardened head capsule, and usually three pairs of thoracic legs. The larvae of ants, wasps and bees are legless with the head only slightly hardened and less prominent.

guano originally, seabird droppings used as a rich natural fertilizer. The term is now loosely applied to other concentrated organic fertilizers, especially those that are made from fish and known as fish guano.

guard cells two cells that surround each stoma (which are the porelike openings distributed over the epidermis of the aerial parts of plants), and serve to open and close it.

guavas *Psidium guajava*. Myrtaceae. Tropical America. A tender evergreen tree or small shrub to 23 ft (7 m). Guavas are grown for their ovoid to pear-shaped edible fruits, which are 1–4 in (2.5–10 cm) in diameter, with white or pink flesh. Requires a minimum temperature of 50°F (10°C), thriving above 72°F (22°C), with high humidity. Can be grown in large containers. Propagate by cuttings of ripe shoots at 75°F (24°C) in summer.

gumming the exudation of gumlike resins by plants, particularly *Prunus* species and conifers, often in response to injury or disease, but sometimes as a reaction to poor soil conditions or insect attack. In stone-fruit trees, gumming is a physiological condition triggered by stress; plum fruits may form gum around the stone.

gummosis the exudation of gum from sunken spots on fungus-infected cucumber fruits, upon which dark mold may develop. The condition is encouraged in a wet, cool environment with limited ventilation.

Gunnera (for Ernst Gunnerus [1718–1773], Norwegian bishop and botanist). Gunneraceae (Haloragidaceae). Australasia, South Africa, S America, Pacific region north to Hawaii. Some 50 species, dwarf or giant rhizomatous, perennial herbs. The small species form interlacing mats, the large ones, clumps or colonies. In either case, the leaves are broadly ovate to rounded, basal and long-stalked. In spring and summer, inconspicuous flowers are borne massed in panicles and give rise to dry or fleshy fruit. The two giants described here (*G. manicata* and *G. tinctoria*) are magnificent foliage plants for the waterside, wet ditches, and bog gardens. They thrive in moist or wet, rich soil in sun or part shade (min. temp. –10°F/–23°C). In fall, protect them from frost by covering crowns with the current season's foliage (break the leafstalks and bend the leaves down to cover the growing point), or with straw or bracken. *G. magellanica* is suitable for moist areas in the rock garden or peat bed, and for pans in the alpine or cool greenhouse. Grow in full sunlight or partial shade in a moist medium, rich in organic content. Increase all species by division in spring.

G. magellanica southern S America, Falkland Islands; dwarf, mat-forming; leaves ¾–3½ in (2–9 cm) in diameter, blades reniform, somewhat cupped, deep green, crenate, stalks ¾–6 in (2–15 cm); fruit a cluster of orange-red berries; *G. manicata* GIANT RHUBARB; S Brazil, Colombia; rhizomes massive and shaggy; leaves 3¼–6½ ft (1–2 m) in diameter, blades rounded to reniform, margins broadly lobed and jaggedly toothed, upper surface dull green and bullate, lower surface with very prominent, prickly veins, stalks 5–8 ft (1.5–2.5 m) tall, stout, prickly; flowers minute, rust to fox red, massed in a conical to cylindrical panicle to 5 ft (1.5 m) tall; *G. tinctoria* (syn. *G. chilensis*, *G. scabra*) Chile; differs from *G. manicata* in forming smaller clumps with shorter leafstalks and blades to 5 ft (1.5 m) wide, these more sharply toothed and lobed; the flowers and fruit, and sometimes the leaf veins, have a strong wine red tint.

guttation the exudation of drops of water, mostly from the margins or tips of leaves, seen for example in *Tropaeolum majus*, *Alchemilla mollis*, and lawn grass. It usually takes place under humid atmospheric conditions, which give rise to low transpiration when water absorption is occurring freely and root pressure develops.

guying the use of guy wires to support trees. The wires are fixed high up around the trunk, and attached to pegs driven into the ground.

Guzmania (for Anastasio Guzman [d. 1802], Spanish naturalist and apothecary). Bromeliaceae. C and S America. 126 species, perennial, epiphytic herbs. The leaves are strap-shaped and smooth and arranged in a basal rosette, their bases forming a cup or vase. From its center, the flower spike emerges at various times of year, branched or unbranched and usually covered in waxy, colorful bracts. The flowers are small and broadly tubular. Cultivate as for *Aechmea*.

G. lingulata C and S America; to 18 in (45 cm); leaves pale to mid-green; flowers white to yellow amid orange to red or yellow bracts; *G. monostachya* (syn. *G. tricolor*) C and S America; to 16 in (40 cm); leaves pale green, often with brown stripes or tint at base; flowers white, lower bracts green striped brown-black, upper bracts bright scarlet; *G. sanguinea* (C and S America; to 12 in (30 cm); leaves mid- to dark green, flushing red at center when in flower; flowers yellow amid red to orange-yellow bracts; *G. vittata* Brazil, Colombia; to 24 in (60 cm); leaves dark green with paler bands and sometimes banded purple beneath; flowers white amid purple-spotted, green bracts.

Gymnocalycium (from Greek *gymnos*, naked, and *kalyx*, bud). Cactaceae. Brazil, Paraguay, Bolivia, Uruguay, Argentina. Perhaps 50 species of low-growing cacti. Their stems are globose and mostly unbranched with prominent ribs and spines. The flowers are funnelform to campanulate. Provide a minimum winter temperature of 45°F (7°C). Grow in a neutral medium containing more than 50% grit. Maintain low humidity; keep dry from fall until early spring, except for light misting on warm days in late winter. Slight shading during the summer months is desirable in greenhouses exposed to full sun. The flowering season is spring to early summer, although a few species may produce a few flowers well into fall. Increase by seed, stem cuttings, or grafting.

G. andreae N Argentina; stems to 1¾ in (4.5 cm) in diameter, globose, lustrous dark blue- or black-green, spines dull white or dark brown, needlelike, often curved; flowers to 1¼ in (3 cm), yellow; *G. gibbosum* Argentina; stems to 8 × 6 in (20 × 15 cm), glaucous, globose becoming club-shaped, brown-green, spines brown to gray, straight or slightly curved; flowers to 2½ in (6 cm), pure white or outer tepals tinted pale pink; *G. mihanovichii* N Paraguay; stems to 3 in (8 cm) in diameter or more, squatly globose to shortly cylindric, dark olive green with cross banding, spines dull yellow tipped brown; flowers to 1¾ in (4.5 cm), yellow-green tipped red; cultivars exist that lack chlorophyll, having stems wholly and brightly colored yellow, red or pink; to survive, these clones must be grafted; *G. quehlianum* N Argentina; stem to 1½ × 2¾ in (3.5 × 7 cm), flattened to globose, turning bronze in full sun, spines adpressed, somewhat bristly, horn-colored, red-brown toward base; flowers to 1½ in (4 cm), white with a red throat; *G. schickendantzii* N Argentina; stem, to 6 × 12 in (15 × 30 cm), broadly flattened to globose, turning bronze in full sun, ribs somewhat spiraled, spines flattened and recurved, gray-red to horn-colored, often darker-tipped; flowers white tinged pink or red-green.

Gymnocladus (from Greek *gymnos*, naked, and *klados*, a branch). Leguminosae. US, China. Some 5 species, deciduous trees with bipinnate leaves. The flowers are small, green-white and borne in short terminal panicles or racemes in early summer. The fruit is a large, woody pod. Hardy to –22°F (–30°C) and tolerant of salt, drought, and alkaline soil. Propagate from seed sown fresh or in spring, after chipping or soaking in hot water. Alternatively, take root cuttings in winter. *G. dioica* KENTUCKY COFFEE TREE; central and eastern N America; to 80 ft (25 m), bark coarsely fissured, branchlets thick; leaves 12–32 in (30–80 cm), emerging pale pink, turning dark green, yellow in fall; flowers dull green-white, downy, in racemes; fruit to 6 × 1½ in (15 × 4 cm), brown or maroon, thick, succulent becoming woody.

gymnosperm a plant in which seeds are borne naked on a sporophyll, rather than enclosed in an ovary, as in angiosperms; the ovules develop without the enclosing pericarp found in angiosperms. Gymnosperms include conifers, cycads, *Welwitschia*, *Ephedra*, and *Gnetum*.

Gymnospermium (from Greek *gymnos*, naked, and *sperma*, seed). Berberidaceae. Europe to C Asia. 4 species, deciduous perennial herbs with tuberous rhizomes. The ferny leaves are ternately divided into pinnately lobed leaflets. The flowers loosely resemble those of *Berberis* but are borne in slender-stalked, terminal racemes. Cultivate as for *Bongardia*.

G. albertii C Asia; to 10 in (25 cm); flowers to ¾ in (2 cm) across, yellow with red-brown veins on sepals and a stalked ovary; *G. altaicum* Black Sea; differs from *G. alberti* in having plain yellow sepals and an ovary that is not stalked.

Gynandriris (from Greek *gyne*, female, *andros*, male, and *Iris*—referring to the united stamens and pistil). Iridaceae. Southern Africa, Mediterranean, east to Pakistan. 9 species, cormous perennial herbs. Short-lived, *Iris*-like flowers are produced in spring. Hardy to about 23°F (–5°C), the following species needs plentiful moisture when in growth but requires a dry summer baking to ensure flowering. Plant deeply, at about 6 in (15 cm), in well-drained, gritty soil in a warm sunny position. Sow seed in a sandy propagating mix in early spring at about 50°F (10°C); increase also by offsets. *G. sisyrinchium* Portugal, Mediterranean to SW Asia; 4–16 in (10–40 cm); leaves slender, usually prostrate and curling; flowers produced in succession, 1–6 per cyme, faintly scented, violet-blue to lavender, the falls with a white or white and orange patch.

gynodioecious having female and hermaphrodite flowers on separate plants of the same species, as in, for example, ground ivy (*Glechoma hederacea*).

gynoecium the female element of a flower, comprising the pistil or pistils.

pistil (female parts or gynoecium)

stamens (male parts)

Gynoecium prominent in tulip

gynomonoecious having female and hermaphrodite flowers on the same plant, as occurs in, for example, *Syringa* × *persica*.

gynophore the stalk of a pistil, which raises it above the receptacle.

gynostegium the staminal crown in Asclepiadaceae.

gynostemium a single structure combining androecium and

gynoecium, as in the column of Orchidaceae.

Gynura (from Greek *gyne*, woman, and *oura*, a tail: the stigma is long and rough). Compositae. Old World tropics. VELVET PLANT. About 50 species, perennial herbs and subshrubs with entire to pinnately dissected leaves and orange-yellow buttonlike flower heads. The following are striking foliage plants suitable for pot or basket cultivation in the greenhouse or home. Grow in a fertile and well-drained potting mix in bright indirect light, ensuring shade from strong summer sun. Maintain a minimum temperature of 59°F (15°C). Keep evenly moist. Propagate by softwood or semiripe cuttings in a shaded, closed case with gentle bottom heat. *G. aurantiaca* PURPLE VELVET PLANT, VELVET PLANT, ROYAL VELVET PLANT; perennial herb, erect to sprawling or clambering, to 24 in (60 cm), all parts covered in short purple hairs; leaves coarsely toothed, dark green with a velvety purple sheen from the hairs; includes the popular 'Purple Passion', syn. *G. sarmentosa* of gardens, a decumbent plant, the leaves narrow with wavy-lobed and toothed margins and thickly covered in velvety purple hairs.

Gypsophila (from Greek *gypsos*, chalk, and *philos*, loving, referring to the preference of some species for alkaline soil). Caryophyllaceae. Eurasia, particularly common in SE Europe. BABY'S BREATH. About 100 species, annual or perennial herbs of varying habit. The leaves are often somewhat fleshy and glaucous. Usually numerous and small in spreading panicles, rarely large and solitary, the flowers are borne in spring and summer. They are broadly funnel-shaped and consist of five, obovate petals.

Gypsophila is represented in cultivation by the small montane species, such as *G. repens*, and larger species, such as *G. paniculata*, from dry, stony or sandy habitats. The perennial *G. paniculata* and the fast-growing annual *G. elegans* are particularly useful in the flower border. They are grown for the light, airy masses of tiny flowers, carried in summer on slender, much-branched stems. Both species are excellent cut flowers. The following are fully hardy,

but favor a warm and sheltered position with protection from excessive winter wetness. Grow in full sun in well-drained soil—sandy, poor, and stony for the alpine species, deep and fertile for the larger species. Avoid disturbing established plants. Cut back or trim over after flowering. Propagate perennials by softwood cuttings in summer, by seed in spring, or (*G. paniculata* cultivars) by grafting in winter. Sow seed of *G. elegans* under glass in early spring for planting out after the last frosts, or *in situ* in midspring.

G. cerastioides Himalaya; loose, gray-hairy, mat-forming perennial; flowers to ¾ in (2 cm) diam., white or lilac veined pink, in loose corymbs; *G. elegans* Asia Minor, Caucasus, S Ukraine; glabrous annual to 20 in (50 cm), branching above; flowers up to 1¼ in (3 cm) in diameter, white veined pink or purple, on long, slender stalks in a finely but loosely branched panicle; a popular cut flower, rather coarser and larger than the *G. paniculata*; cultivars include the large, pure white 'Covent Garden' and 'Giant White', the pale pink 'Rosea', the vinous 'Purpurea' and the carmine 'Red Cloud'; *G. paniculata* BABY'S BREATH; C and E Europe, C Asia; stoutly rhizomatous, diffusely branched perennial to 48 in (120 cm), usually smooth and glaucous; flowers up to ⅜ in (0.8 cm) in diameter, white or pink, many in a finely branched, cloudlike panicle; includes cultivars with large or dwarf habit, and single or double flowers; *G. repens* C and S Europe; mat-forming, gray-glaucous perennial with flowering stems ascending to 8 in (20 cm); flowers up to ⅝ in (1.5 cm) in diameter, white, pink or purple-pink in loose panicles; cultivars include pale to deep rose-flowered plants and forms with single or double flowers, one of the finest being 'Dorothy Teacher', a neat, compact, blue-green plant with profuse flowers turning from white to soft pink.

gypsum hydrated calcium sulfate (sulfate of lime), used to improve the structure of clay soil without affecting their alkalinity. It is valuable for land reclamation after flooding by sea water.

gyrate curving in a circular or spiral fashion.

H

ha-ha a deep, wide ditch separating a garden or park from the surrounding countryside, designed to exclude animals without creating a visual barrier. Originating in the early 18th century, the device became a characteristic of the English Landscape style of garden designer Capability Brown [1716–83] and his followers.

Haageocereus (for F. Haage, and *Cereus*). Cactaceae. Peru, N Chile. To 10 species, shrubby or arborescent cacti with ribbed and spiny stems. Mostly white or dull red, the tubular to funnelform flowers bloom at night and often remain open through the following morning. Grow in a cool frost-free greenhouse (minimum temperature 36–45°F/2–7°C). Use "standard" cactus mix, with a moderate to high inorganic content (more than 50% grit) and a pH of 6–7.5. Provide full sun and low air humidity. Keep dry from midfall until early spring, except for light misting on warm days in late winter. Increase by stem cuttings.

H. decumbens S Peru; stems to about 3¼ ft (1 m) × 1½–3 in (4–8 cm), decumbent or pendent, spines very stout, dark; flowers white; *H. multangularis* (syn. *H. chosicensis*) C Peru; stems to 5 ft (1.5 m) × 2½–4 in (6–10 cm), erect or ascending, spines very stout; flowers red, pink or white; *H. versicolor* N Peru; stems slender, erect, to 5 ft (1.5 m) × 2 in (5 cm), spines variable in color; flowers white.

Haberlea (for Karl Konstantin Haberle [1764–1832], Professor of Botany at Budapest). Gesneriaceae. Balkans. 2 species, tufted perennial herbs. Borne in low rosettes, the leaves are obovate to broadly oblong, coarsely crenate and more or less hairy. Produced in late spring and summer in loose scapose umbels, the flowers are broadly tubular with five rounded lobes. Cultivate as for *Ramonda*.

H. ferdinandi-coburgi C Bulgaria; similar to *H. rhodopensis*, except that the leaves are more or less glabrous above; flowers lilac, tube darker above, throat yellow-spotted; *H. rhodopensis* C and S Bulgaria, NE Greece; leaves softly hairy; flowers ⅝–1 in (1.5–2.5 cm) pale blue-violet; includes the white-flowered 'Virginalis'.

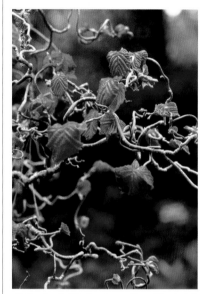

Distinctive habit: *Corylus avellana* 'Contorta'

habit (1) the characteristic growth form of a plant; for example, the spreading, columnar or weeping habit of trees; (2) loosely used to describe plant type; for example, herb, shrub, or tree.

habitat the natural environment in which a species lives, characterized by climate, elevation, soil type, and association with other organisms.

Habranthus (from Greek *habros*, graceful, and *anthos*, a flower). Amaryllidaceae. Temperate S America, especially Argentina, Uruguay, and adjacent regions of Brazil and Paraguay. 10 species, perennial bulbous herbs with narrowly strap-shaped leaves and solitary, scapose flowers—these are funnel-shaped and 6-lobed. Somewhat tender bulbs grown for their flowers. *H. brachyandrus* may be grown at the base of a south- or southwest-facing wall in sheltered gardens with little or no frost. *H. tubispathus* is reliably hardy to 10°F (–12°C), especially if established in a dry, sheltered, and sunny position. Grow in a fibrous loam-based mix with additional leaf mold, planting firmly with neck and shoulders above soil level. Propagate by offsets and also from fresh ripe seed.

H. brachyandrus S Brazil; to 12 in (30 cm), flowers to 3½ in (9 cm), brilliant or pale pink, tube red-black at base; *H. tubispathus* (syn. *H. andersonii*) S Chile, Argentina, S Brazil, Uruguay; to 6 in (15 cm), tinged red, flowers to 2¾ in (7 cm), burnt orange, yellow, or golden-bronze above, gray-pink with darker stripes beneath.

Hacquetia (for Balthasar Hacquet [1740–1815], author of *Plantae Alpinae Carniolicae*). Umbelliferae. Europe. 1 species, *H. epipactis*, a clump-forming, perennial herb to 2¾ in (7 cm) tall (usually shorter). The emerald green leaves are near circular in outline and palmately cleft and toothed. Small yellow flowers are produced in early spring in a dense, rounded umbel, subtended by a ruff of leaflike bracts—the whole arrangement gives the impression of a single, green-petaled flower with a boss of golden stamens. A slowly spreading perennial for the rock and woodland garden and underplanting among winter- and spring-flowering shrubs. Hardy to 5°F (–15°C). Grow in moist, humus-rich soil in part shade. Propagate by sowing fresh seed, by careful division of well-established plants in early spring, and by root cuttings.

Haemanthus (from Greek *haima*, blood, and *anthos*, flower, referring to the color of the flowers.) Amaryllidaceae. BLOOD LILY. South Africa, Namibia. 21 species, deciduous or evergreen bulbous herbs with broadly strap-shaped 2-ranked leaves and small flowers packed in scapose umbels and subtended by several bracts. The fruits are colored berries. Plant with the bulb neck at or just above soil level, in well-crocked pots of humus-rich, loam-based potting medium, with added coarse grit and well-rotted manure. Maintain a winter minimum temperature of 50°F (10°C); grow in bright filtered light, but move into part shade as the

355

flower buds develop to preserve color and prolong flowering. Dry off deciduous species as leaves yellow; keep evergreen species dry but not arid during rest. The plants flower better when underpotted and resent disturbance. Propagate by offsets, removed as new growth begins and grown on in a closed case until established; or from ripe seed.

H. albiflos South Africa; leaves sometimes spotted white, usually downy; scape to 14 in (35 cm), green, glabrous or pubescent, spathe white veined green, ciliate, flowers white; fruit white, orange or red; *H. coccineus* CAPE TULIP; South Africa; leaves sometimes barred maroon, green, or white, glabrous or downy; scape to 14½ in (37 cm), cream to pale red streaked dark red, umbel to 4 in (10 cm) across, spathe 6–9-valved, coral, vermilion, or scarlet, flowers coral to scarlet with white markings; fruit white to deep pink; *H. sanguineus* South Africa; leaves scabrid above, glossy beneath, margin red or transparent; scape to 11 in (27 cm), claret red, spathe red-pink, flowers red to salmon pink marked white; fruit glassy white to claret.

haft the base of an organ when narrow or constricted; most often applied to the haft of the falls in *Iris* flowers.

hair an outgrowth of the epidermis; unicellular or comprising a row of cells, and conforming to one of several types (e.g., dendritic, stellate, scale-like, peltate) according to branching, form, grouping, and attachment.

Hakea (for Baron Christian Ludwig von Hake [1745–1818], German patron of botany). Proteaceae. PINCUSHION TREE. W Australia. Some 110 species, shrubs or small trees, usually hairy with leathery to rigid leaves. Borne in short axillary racemes or clusters, the flowers are tubular with slender lobes and a protruding style. Cultivate as for *Banksia*.

H. lissosperma (syn. *H. sericea* of gardens) MOUNTAIN HAKEA; E Australia; shrub or small tree to 20 ft (6 m) tall; leaves to 4 in (10 cm), terete, sharply pointed, curved upward; flowers white

in clusters) *H. suaveolens* West Australia; erect shrub, 5–6½ ft (1.5–2 m); leaves 2¾–8 in (7–20 cm), pinnate, segments erect, sharply pointed; flowers cream in dense racemes.

Hakonechloa (from Hakone in Honshu, Japan). Gramineae. Japan. 1 species, *H. macra*, a perennial grass 12–30 in (30–75 cm) tall. The stems are slender and clumped, bending outward in a graceful "shaggy" crown. The leaves are narrowly lance-shaped and fresh green, becoming rust- and orange-tinted in fall. In the cultivar 'Aureola', the leaves are striped lime and creamy yellow to gold; in 'Alboaurea', they are lime green, gold, and cream, acquiring pink to maroon stripes and tints in bright sun and in fall. Given shelter from cold drying winds, they are hardy to between 5° and –4°F (–15° and –20°C) and easily grown in moderately fertile, moisture-retentive soil with additional leaf mold. Light shade will enhance leaf color. Plants spread slowly once established to form substantial clumps; also excellent for container cultivation. Propagate by division in spring.

"silverbell" or snowdrop-like flowers

Halesia carolina

Halesia (for Dr. S. H. Hales [1677–1761], author of *Vegetable Staticks* [1727]). Styracaceae. SILVERBELL TREE, SNOWDROP TREE. China, eastern N America. 5 species, deciduous trees or shrubs. In late spring and early summer, the flowers hang in clusters from the previous year's wood. White or pale rose, they are broadly bell-shaped and four-lobed, and are followed by winged fruit. Plant in deep, humus-rich, nonalkaline soil that is moist but well-drained, in sun with shelter from wind. Propagate by simple

layering in spring, or, in the same season, by softwood basal cuttings, treated with hormone-rooting powder, under mist or in a closed case. Overwinter young plants in the cold frame. Seed exhibits a complex dormancy: sow fresh in fall, and maintain at 57–77°F (14–25°C) for 60–100 days, followed by cold stratification at 32–41°F (0–5°C) for a further 2–3 months. Bring into equable conditions when germination starts.

H. carolina (syn. *H. tetraptera*) S US; small tree or shrub, to 20 ft (6 m); leaves 2–2½ in (5–6 cm), ovate to lanceolate, serrulate, glabrous above, gray-downy beneath; flowers white, ½–⅝ in (1–1.5 cm); includes 'Meehanii', with broader, wrinkled leaves and smaller flowers with more deeply cut lobes, and var. *mollis*, with broader, downy leaves and larger flowers; *H. monticola* (syn. *H. carolina* var. *monticola*) SE US; tree to 90 ft (28 m) leaves 3–6 in (8–16 cm), elliptic to obovate, serrate, soon glabrous except veins beneath; flowers white, ⅝–1 in (1.5–2.5 cm); f. *rosea*, with pale rose flowers, and var. *vestita*, with leaves white-tomentose beneath when young and sometimes a rose tint to the flowers.

half hardy applied to plants which, in a given climatic zone, may be grown outdoors after the risk of frost has passed. Used particularly of bedding plants, and other annuals. See *hardiness*.

half-pot see *pots and potting*.

× **Halimiocistus** Cistaceae. S Europe. Hybrids between *Cistus* and *Halimium*, small to medium-sized evergreen shrubs with small, narrow, and downy leaves and lax cymes of five-petaled flowers in summer. Cultivate as for *Cistus*.

H. 'Ingwersenii' (*Halimium umbellatum* × *Cistus hirsutus*;) Portugal; to 20 in (50 cm); flowers white in sparse, long-stalked branching cymes; *H. sahucii* (*Halimium umbellatum* × *Cistus salviifolius*) S France; to 3¼ ft (1 m); flowers 3–5 per cyme, white; *H. wintonensis* (*Halimium ocymoides* × *Cistus salviifolius*) garden origin; to 24 in (60 cm); flowers white, often yellow at center with maroon blotches in long-stalked, 2–4-flowered cymes; includes 'Merrist Wood

Cream', with flowers deep cream to primrose blotched dark maroon.

Halimium (from Greek *halimos* belonging to the sea). Cistaceae. Mediterranean, SW Europe, N Africa, Asia Minor. Some 12 species, evergreen shrubs and subshrubs, differing from the closely related *Cistus* in their predominantly yellow flowers. Gray-leaved summer-flowering plants, hardy to 0°F (−18°C) and suited to areas with mild winters and warm dry summers. Cultivate as for *Cistus*.

H. lasianthum SW Europe; to 28 in (70 cm); flowers to 1½ in (4 cm) in diameter, petals golden with a dark basal spot; includes 'Concolor', with unspotted flowers, 'Sandling', with the flowers conspicuously blotched maroon, and subsp. *formosum*, with larger flowers and the basal spot higher up each petal; *H. ocymoides* SW Europe; to 3¼ ft (1 m); flowers golden, typically with a wide maroon spot at the base of each petal, in erect, terminal panicles forming a broad inflorescence; includes the compact, broad-leaved 'Susan'; *H. umbellatum* Mediterranean; to 16 in (40 cm); flowers white stained yellow at base of petals, to ¾ in (2 cm) in diameter, 3–6 per umbel-like panicle.

halo blight a bacterial disease of beans. See *bacterial diseases*.

halophyte a plant adapted to, or tolerant of, saline soil, such as the glassworts (*Salicornia* species) found on salt marshes.

Hamamelis (from Greek for a pear-shaped fruit). Hamamelidaceae. WITCH HAZEL. N America, Europe, E Asia. 5 species, deciduous shrubs or small trees with tomentose branches and buds and ovate to obovate, toothed leaves, most turning yellow in fall but also showing tints of orange and red. Produced in late winter in axillary clusters, the scented, spidery flowers consist of four slender petals arising from the cup of a glossy, chestnut-colored calyx.

Most *Hamamelis* species are hardy to −4°F (−20°C). Grow with shelter from cold drying wind, in fertile, neutral or preferably slightly acidic, well-drained and humus-rich soil; incorporate

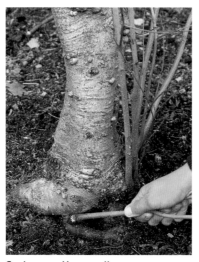

Suckers on Hamamelis
Many witch hazels are grafted, and this may lead to suckering at the base. Shoots from the rootstock should be torn away cleanly at their point of origin.

additional organic matter, such as leaf mold or well-rotted compost, at planting time. Deep soil overlying chalk is acceptable; lime-induced chlorosis may be treated with sequestered iron. All species prefer moisture-retentive soil. Pruning is necessary only to remove deadwood. Grafted specimens may produce suckers which should be removed at the base as they appear. Cultivars may be propagated by side-grafting in gentle heat in late winter/early spring, or by budding in late summer on to seedling understock of *H. virginiana*. Layering in fall is useful where small numbers are required. Take softwood cuttings in summer, treat with 0.8% IBA, and root under mist or in a closed case with bottom heat; overwinter in the first year in the cold greenhouse or frame. Propagate species by ripe seed sown fresh in the open cold frame; some germination may occur in the first spring, but seed usually requires a second winter in the cold frame before germinating. Dormancy may be broken by warm treatment, for a period of nine weeks at 68°F (20°C), followed by 14 weeks at 41°F (5°C).

H. × *intermedia* (*H. japonica* × *H. mollis*) garden origin; shrub to 13 ft (4 m); flowers to 1¼ in (3 cm) in diameter, petals crumpled; cultivars include: 'Advent', the earliest flowering, with bright yellow flowers; the medium-

sized 'Allgold', with ascending branches, leaves that are yellow in fall, and butter-yellow flowers with narrow, twisted petals and red calyces; 'Arnold Promise', with densely clustered, deep sulfur-yellow flowers, with red-green calyces; the late-flowering 'Carmine Red', with narrow, twisted, pale bronze petals to ¾ in (2 cm), with tips suffused copper; 'Diane', with yellow and scarlet foliage during fall and coppery carmine flowers with purple-bronze calyces; 'Hiltingbury', with large, rounded leaves turning red, orange and copper in fall, and pale copper-red flowers with maroon calyces; the large ascending shrub 'Jelena'—also known as 'Copper Beauty'—with leaves turning bronze, red, and orange in fall and densely clustered, yellow flowers suffused deep copper-red, with twisted petals and burgundy calyces; the erect medium-sized shrub 'Feuerzauber'—also known as 'Magic Fire' or 'Fire Charm'—with leaves turning yellow in fall and copper-orange petals, suffused red and twisted; the medium to large shrub 'Moonlight', with circular leaves turning yellow in fall, and highly fragrant, densely clustered, pale sulfur-yellow flowers, with a burgundy basal blotch; 'Nana', with deep yellow petals to 1¼ in (3 cm); 'Orange Beauty', with golden yellow to orange-yellow flowers; 'Pallida', with flowers covering branches, sulfur yellow; 'Primavera', with flowers densely clustered and sickle-shaped, primrose yellow petals to ¾ in (2 cm); 'Ruby Glow'—also known as 'Rubra Superba' or 'Adonis'—with leaves turning orange, bronze, and scarlet in fall, and copper-red petals to ¾ in (2 cm); the early flowering 'Sunburst', with sulfur yellow flowers; the late-flowering 'Westerstede', with pale yellow flowers; and 'Winter Beauty', with flowers similar to 'Orange Beauty' but larger, and petals brown-red at base; *H. japonica* JAPANESE WITCH HAZEL; Japan; shrub or tree to 10 ft (3 m); flowers yellow with petals to ¾ in (2 cm) and calyces green or purple within; cultivars include: the vigorous 'Arborea', to 16 ft (5 m), with yellow, wavy petals and maroon calyces; 'Sulphurea', with sulfur yellow petals to ⅜ in (1.5 cm); 'Zuccariniana', with erect to spreading branches, leaves yellow in fall, flowers with twisted, wavy,

H

sulfur yellow petals to ½ in (1.2 cm; *H. mollis* CHINESE WITCH HAZEL; W China; shrub or small tree to 16 ft (5 m); flowers sweetly fragrant, with calyces red-purple within and straight petals to ¾ in (1.7 cm), golden yellow and tinged red at base; cultivars include the early flowering 'Brevipetala' with orange-yellow petals to ½ in (1 cm); 'Coombe Wood', with golden yellow flowers, suffused red at base; the large shrub 'Goldcrest', with golden petals to ¾ in (2 cm), each with a wavy tip and a burgundy basal blotch, and calyces with a purple-red interior; *H. vernalis* Southern Central US; upright suckering shrub to 6½ ft (2 m), similar to *H. virginiana*, except calyx interior red, petals yellow to red; cultivars include 'Carnea', with pale fleshy pink flowers; 'Lombart's Weeping', with pendulous branches, blue-green, leaves and pale red flowers; 'Red Imp', with claret petal bases and copper tips; 'Sandra', with violet-purple young foliage, becoming green, flushed purple beneath, turning red, scarlet, and orange in fall, with cadmium yellow flowers; and 'Squib', with cadmium yellow petals and green calyces; *H. virginiana* COMMON WITCH HAZEL; E US; shrub or small tree, to 16 ft (5 m); leaves yellow during fall, calyces green or brown inside, petals ¾ in (17 mm), crinkled, golden yellow; includes 'Rubescens', with petal bases suffused red; *H. macrophylla* from the SE US has larger leaves with superb fall color and small, crinkled, pale yellow flowers, opening in late fall and winter.

hamate hooked at the tip.

handbarrow a wooden platform, about 48 in (120 cm) long and 28 in (70 cm) wide, with the side bearers extended to form handles, and usually having a short leg at each corner of the platform. It is used mostly to transport plants in containers, with one person standing between each pair of handles for holding and lifting.

handlight see *bellglass*; *cloche*.

hanging basket a hemispherical container of galvanized or plastic-coated wire suspended on chains to display ornamental plants or, sometimes, for growing pendulous dwarf tomatoes. Square baskets made of wooden slats are used for orchid-growing. Hanging baskets are commonly used for summer decoration outdoors but make valuable additions to the large greenhouse or conservatory.

To retain the growing medium, the basket needs to be lined with moss (if it can be obtained from an approved source), plastic sheeting or netting, coconut fiber, foam plastic, impregnated cardboard, or wool waste. Soilless mixes are suitable, and the incorporation of moisture-absorbing polymers and slow-release fertilizer is advantageous. Dead-heading flowers, regular watering, and supplementary feeding are essential practices for the maintenance of a good display.

hapaxanthic with only a single flowering period.

haploid describing the basic number of chromosomes borne in the unpaired pollen and ovule cells of a diploid plant. It is commonly annotated **x**; c.f. *polyploid*.

haptonasty, haptotropism the response of plants to contact or touch, as demonstrated by the tendrils of climbing plants and by some carnivorous plants. See *stimulus movements*.

Hardenbergia (for Countess von Hardenberg, sister of the celebrated traveler Baron von Hügel, who collected plants in western Australia in 1833). Leguminosae. Australia, Tasmania. CORAL PEA. 3 species, evergreen vines. The leaves consist of one to five, ovate to lanceolate leaflets. Small, pealike flowers are produced in spring and summer in long, axillary racemes. Where winter temperatures do not fall much below 23°F (–5°C), they are well-suited to growing over arches, fences, or pergolas, or trailing over a retaining wall. In cooler zones, they may be pot-grown in a cool greenhouse or conservatory, with a minimum winter temperature of 45–50°F (7–10°C). Grow in moist, well-drained, nonalkaline soil in sun or light dappled shade. Water moderately and feed monthly with diluted liquid feed when in growth; keep just moist in winter. Container-grown plants with integral support may be plunged outdoors in summer. Propagate by seed sown in spring; presoak for 24 hours prior to sowing at 68°F (20°C) and cover with fine grit. Alternatively, root tip cuttings in late spring in moist sand or vermiculite, in a closed case with bottom heat.

H. comptoniana WESTERN AUSTRALIA CORAL PEA; W Australia; evergreen vine to 10 ft (3 m); leaves with 3–5 leaflets; flowers blue to purple, standard with a green-spotted, white blotch at base; *H. violacea* (syn. *H. monophylla*) PURPLE CORAL PEA, VINE LILAC, FALSE SARSAPARILLA; E Australia, Tasmania; evergreen vine to 6½ ft (2 m)+; leaves with only one leaflet; flowers purple, white, pink, or lilac, standard spotted yellow or green at center.

Hardening off
Seed-raised plants of half-hardy bedding such as *Tagetes* must be gradually acclimatized to outdoor temperatures.

hardening off the process of acclimatizing plants to more rigorous conditions. Hardening off is achieved by gradually increasing exposure to lower temperature and air movement, often by transferring containerized plants to unheated frames. It is usually practiced with half-hardy or tender plants raised under glass and intended for planting outside.

hardiness a complex quality attributed to plants that are capable of withstanding climatic rigors without greenhouse protection. In tropical and subtropical climates, the term may extend to drought tolerance. Natural adaptations among plants to ensure hardiness include a reduced surface area, a deciduous or herbaceous habit, seed dormancy, an accelerated life cycle, hairiness, thickened cell walls, thick bark, procumbent growth, and a lack of fleshy parts (except in xerophytes).

Within cells, special oils and crystals are effective against freezing.

Hardiness may be much affected by macroclimate. For example, plants overwintering with their metabolic processes naturally at a near standstill may succumb to periods of unusually persistent rainfall. A seasonal rise in the temperature of a locality promotes rapid growth and full ripening of wood and flower buds, which are therefore more tolerant of wind and very low winter temperatures. These factors are influenced by the prevailing climate, which in turn may be affected by topography. Whereas little can be done to alter the effect of macroclimate on plant hardiness, there are opportunities for improving the microclimate in the garden: drainage may be improved by building raised beds; soil structure can be ameliorated; shelter and surface insulation can be provided with layered mulches and by wrapping up frost-susceptible plants and protecting them with glass or plastic. Natural selection and hybridization can contribute to plant hardiness, and seeds and plants should be chosen with their provenance in mind.

Low-temperature hardiness

In the Northern Hemisphere, injury to plants from wind frosts and sustained low temperatures is usually associated with bursts of cold air from the north, most likely during the winter months from December to March. The precise cause and effect of low temperature damage is variable and, besides species, provenance, and growing locality, includes the influence of mineral nutrition, sugar content, shoot ripeness, and frequency and duration of exposure. A period of subzero temperatures often causes the ground to freeze to some depth, and evergreen trees and shrubs may suffer particularly, since water from the soil is difficult to extract and they cannot transpire; severe wind chill can "burn" or kill green shoots and stems. There may be bark splitting in trees and shrubs and physical "lifting" disturbance of plants in the soil; also death of plant cells following the formation of ice crystals on freezing, or following rapid temperature rise at thawing when water flow is replenished suddenly and forcefully, causing protoplast to swell and rupture cell walls.

Many plants develop a hardier constitution as they mature, and stock grown in containers under protection must be hardened off. Where this is not done, it is advisable to delay planting out until the spring, or to protect evergreens from severe weather. Most slightly tender species may rejuvenate if cut hard back after frost injury.

Radiation frost injury is more common and can be sudden, the most serious damage occurring in late spring or early summer. Soft growth of trees and shrubs as well as fruit crops is very vulnerable, as are half-hardy or tender bedding display plants. Damage is severe after a mild spell has stimulated new growths or early flowers. Cell sap expands on freezing, and this may destroy plant cell walls, thus killing tender plants or parts of plants. Severe cold may cause the bark of some woody plants to split. Repeated hard freezing followed by rapid thawing causes the greatest damage to roots. Remedial measures include locating frost pockets and draining off cold air from behind walls and hedges by creating suitable openings with permeable fences; tender plants should not be planted out until the main risk of frost is past.

Hardiness zones

Hardiness zones based on winter isotherms are a means of expressing the cold tolerance of garden plants. The isotherm is a line on a map connecting places with the same mean temperature at a given time. In his *Manual for Cultivated Trees and Shrubs* (1972), Alfred Rehder developed a system using eight zones to cover the cold-temperate areas of the US, with five-degree-Fahrenheit bands based on the lowest mean temperatures of the coldest months. In 1960 the US Department of Agriculture (USDA), in cooperation with the American Horticultural Society, published a map based on ten-degree-Fahrenheit differences in the annual minimum temperature, on which the US state boundaries were superimposed. The map was revised in 1990, using data from 124,500 weather stations, to include Alaska, Canada, Mexico, and Hawaii and has 11 zones (*see table*). The next revision of the USDA map will have 15 zones to help gardeners in subtropical and tropical areas. The new breakdown will be: zone 11, 40–50°F (4–10°C); zone 12, 50–60°F (10–16°C);

zone 13, 60–70°F (16–21°C); zone 14, 70–80°F (21–27°C); zone 15, ≥80°F (≥27°C). A new zoning system modeled on that of the USDA was introduced for western Europe in *The New Royal Horticultural Society Dictionary of Gardening* (1992). Zone maps have been published for South Africa, Australia, New Zealand, Japan, China, and Canada. The Plant Hardiness Zones of Canada 2000 map was developed by Natural Resources Canada and Agricultural and Agri-Foods Canada.

Maps based on isotherms represent meteorological patterns, not hardiness zones. Hardiness is a complex phenomenon, a highly relative quality of the individual plant—not of its projected site—and is affected by various linked factors, of which cold is only one.

The European Garden Flora defines seven hardiness zones as follows—G2: requires a heated greenhouse even in south Europe; G1: requires a cool greenhouse even in south Europe; H5: hardy in favorable areas, can withstand 32–41°F (0–5°C) minimum; H4: hardy in mild areas, can withstand 23°–14°F (–5° to –10°C) minimum; H3: hardy in cool areas, can withstand 14°–5°F (–10° to –15°C) minimum; H2: hardy almost everywhere, can withstand 5° to –4°F (–15° to –20°C) minimum; H1: hardy everywhere, can withstand –4°F (–20°C) and below.

These guides to plant hardiness must be regarded as flexible and therefore of general use only.

The climatic zone numbers as adopted by the *New RHS Dictionary of Gardening* and the USDA can be summarized as follows:

Zone	°F	°C
1	<–50	<–45.5
2	–50 to –40	–45.5 to –40.0
3	–40 to –30	–40.0 to –34.4
4	–30 to –20	–34.4 to –28.9
5	–20 to –10	–28.9 to –23.3
6	–10 to 0	–23.3 to –17.8
7	0 to +10	–17.8 to –12.2
8	+10 to +20	–12.2 to –6.7
9	+20 to +30	–6.7 to –1.1
10	+30 to +40	–1.1 to +4.4
11	≥+40	≥+4.4

hardwood (1) a common name for a broad-leaved tree, and descriptive of its timber; cf. *softwood*; (2) used to describe cuttings made from mature shoots of woody plants.

hastate arrow-shaped; triangular, with two equal and approximately triangular basal lobes, pointing laterally outward rather than toward the stalk; cf. *sagittate*.

Hatiora (anagram of *Hariota*, an earlier generic name commemorating Thomas Hariot [1560–1621], English scientist and historian, mentor to Sir Walter Raleigh). Cactaceae. SE Brazil. 4 species, epiphytic or lithophytic cacti with freely branching, cylindric, angled, winged or flat stems composed of short segments. These are unarmed or bear soft, bristly spines. The flowers are campanulate with a short tube and a spreading perianth of intense yellow, pink or red. Small, obovoid fruits follow. Grow in an intermediate greenhouse (minimum temperature 50–59°F/10–15°C) in "epiphyte" mix, consisting of equal parts organic/inorganic matter and a pH below 6. Provide shade in summer and maintain high humidity. Reduce watering in fall/winter until flowerbuds begin to develop. *H. gaertneri*, often incorrectly called *Schlumbergera gaertneri*, and the hybrid *H.* × *graeseri* (*H. gaertneri* × *H. rosea*) are floriferous and popular house plants, flowering in the Northern Hemisphere at about Easter time. Increase by stem cuttings.

H. gaertneri EASTER CACTUS; E Brazil; stem segments mostly flat, oblong or elliptic, truncate, 1½–2¾ in (4–7 cm), shallowly crenate; flowers to 1¾ in (4.5 cm), intense scarlet, rose, magenta, ruby, and orange to gold in some cultivars and hybrids; fruit oblong, red; *H. salicornioides* DRUNKARD'S DREAM, BOTTLE CACTUS, BOTTLE PLANT; SE Brazil; small shrub, much-branched, erect or pendent, stem-segments whorled, bottle-shaped, ⅝–2 in (1.5–5 cm); flowers to ½ in (1.3 cm), yellow to orange; fruit globose, white.

haulm the stems of potatoes, peas, and beans.

haustorium (plural haustoria) a sucker attachment in parasitic plants penetrating the host.

haw (1) fruit of the hawthorn (*Crataegus monogyna*); (2) an archaic term for a hedged enclosure or a hedge.

Haworthia (for Adrian Hardy Haworth [1765–1833], English plantsman, amateur botanist, and entomologist, author of books on succulent plants and bulbs). Liliaceae (Aloeaceae). South Africa, extending to Namibia, Swaziland and Mozambique. Over 70 species, dwarf, perennial, evergreen, rosette-forming succulents, distinguished from *Aloe* by their smaller, usually tufted habit and 2-lipped white or off-white flowers. They require a winter minimum of

hastate leaf
(Alocasia)

39–45°F (4–7°C), porous, well-drained but nutritious soil, and good ventilation and lighting, although the softer-leaved species appreciate partial shade. As houseplants, they are among the few succulents to accept a sunless, north-facing windowsill. Annual repotting is recommended, as the thick fleshy roots die back and are renewed each growing season. During the colder winter months, impose a dry rest; water freely during warm, bright spring and summer days. Increase by offsets and division of clumps.

H. arachnoidea COBWEB ALOE; Cape Province; stemless, clustering; rosettes ¾–5 in (2–13 cm) in diameter, leaves arachnoid, ascending to incurved to 2¾ in (7 cm), oblong to lanceolate, green, soft and juicy, semitranslucent flecked, aristate, longitudinally lined, margins and upper part of keel with white to pale brown teeth; *H. attenuata* Cape Province; stemless or short-stemmed with basal offsets; leaves erect or slightly curving, to 3 in (8 cm), dark green, flexible, narrowly triangular, acuminate, rough from white tubercles in bands on underside; includes 'Variegata', with variegated leaves; *H. clariperla*, a widely grown plant with

orange, pearl-dotted leaves, is a variant of this species; *H. fasciata* ZEBRA HAWORTHIA; South East Cape; similar to *H. attenuate* but with shorter leaves that are smooth on the upper side and with bands of white tubercles beneath; *H. maughanii* Western Cape; plant body below soil level with only the flat, translucent window tip of each leaf exposed; *H. truncata* Western Cape; similar to *H. maughanii* but with flatter, broader leaves in two series like the pages of an open book.

hazelnuts the fruits of the hazel (*Corylus*), of which the most important are the COBNUT (*C. avellana*) and the FILBERT (*C. maxima*) both of which are natives of Europe; in the US, the name "filbert" is commonly applied to both these species. The widespread use of *C. avellana* dates back to prehistoric times, since the hardened shoots were suitable for road-building and for thatching, wattle, stakes, and utensils. Selected forms of hazelnuts were grown by the Greeks and Romans, and by the 16th-century the distinction between cobs and filberts was recognized in cultivation. Named cultivars resulting from breeding programs were introduced in the early 19th century, and the twin-shelled cobnut 'Cosford Cob' remains famous, together with the filberts 'Lambert's Filbert' and 'Kentish Cob'.

Hazelnuts are unsuitable for small gardens because trees may reach 15 ft (4.5 m) in width, and ensuring good pollination requires more than one cultivar. The male flowers produce attractive yellow catkins in late winter on the same plant as the inconspicuous red female flowers. Unlike cobnuts, filbert fruits bear a husk longer than the nut and usually completely enclosing it. Selections with frilled and twisted husks are known as frizzled filberts; others produce ornamental purple leaves.

Plant bushes about 15 ft (4.5 m) apart with 8–12 main branches trained to form an open center. Pruning should restrict height to 6½ ft (2 m), with the leading shoot of a one-year-old specimen pruned at 18 in (45 cm) to induce branch leaders from the top 6 in (15 cm), and any below this level removed. In the following winters,

H

"Brutting" hazelnut
The traditional practice of brutting hazelnut bushes—breaking long, vigorous shoots part-way through and leaving them on the plant—is widely held to improve yields by stimulating the production of female flowers.

branch leaders are shortened by about one-third and side-shoots crowding the center of the tree are removed together with basal shoots; any suckers must be cut out with a spade to avoid proliferation. Once the desired height has been reached, branch leaders should be cut back to a weak side-shoot and any strong upright shoots removed.

On an established bush, summer pruning is important, using a technique known as "brutting." This consists of breaking by hand stronger side shoots at about half their length in August and allowing the broken part to hang by the rind, the shoot not being completely severed. This reduces vigor and encourages the formation of female flowers, as well as allowing greater light and air penetration to improve the quality of the maturing crop. The brutted shoots are cut back to 3–4 buds in winter, the pruning best timed to coincide with flowering so that the disturbance of shoots assists pollination.

The nuts are harvested as the husks yellow, laid out in trays in an airy room and turned to ensure even drying. For prolonged storage, they may be packed in layers in earthenware jars, intermingled with coconut fiber mixed with a little salt.

Artificial hybrids include the TRAZEL, *C. × colurnoides* (*C. avellana × C. colurna*),

with large long nuts; the HAZELBERT or MILDRED FILBERT (*C. avellana × C. americana*), with large nuts resistant to Eastern filbert blight; and the FILAZEL (*C. avellana × C. cornuta*), which is hardy to –30°F (–34°C).

Possible problems: sawflies, squirrels.

head (1) a dense cluster or spike of flowers; (2) the part of a tree above the clear trunk; (3) the harvestable part of hearted leaf and stem vegetables, such as lettuce, cabbage, and celery, when alternatively it may be referred to as a heart. It is also used for the edible part of a cauliflower.

heading back drastic cutting back of trees or shrubs by shortening for all or most of the main branches. It is done in preparation for topwork grafting of fruit trees, for reshaping, and for inducing vigor in ornamentals.

heart (1) see *head*; (2) used to describe soil, which is said to be in "good heart" when it is adequately aerated, irrigated, and otherwise fertile.

heart rot (1) a general term describing rot of the heartwood of trees, usually caused by bracket fungi. These mostly enter through wounds, and rotting may not be evident until a tree is blown over or felled. Pruning and treating wounds with a fungicidal sealant may help prevent the spread of such fungi, but little can be done once the main trunk heartwood is infected. (2) used to describe celery heart rot, a wet, slimy brown rot at the center of plants, caused by the bacterium *Erwinia carotovora*; heart rot of rutabaga results from boron deficiency.

heartwood the inner, nonfunctional xylem layers of a woody stem, which are harder and usually darker than the outer sap wood.

heaths and heathers a common group name for species of *Erica*, *Daboecia*, and *Calluna* (q.v.) that are native to Europe and Africa. For most of the group, a maximum soil pH of 4.5–5.0 is required for good growth, although *E. erigena*, *E.terminalis*, and cultivars of *E.carnea* and *E. × darleyensis* will tolerate alkaline soil. The term "heath" strictly

describes species of *Erica* and *Daboecia*, and these occur in poor soil with little shelter, and, in Europe, where rainfall is high. Cape heaths are southern African species, which do not survive winter temperatures below 19°F (–7°C). Heather refers to the great number of cultivars of *Calluna vulgaris*, also called ling, which thrive on moor and mountain. Grow in full sun in moist but free-draining soil. Some will tolerate drought once established.

Propagate from cuttings of semiripe shoots, 1¼–1½ in (3–4 cm) long, taken in summer and inserted in a peat/sand mixture under plastic film. Layering in September/October is possible and especially useful for certain dwarf cultivars of *Calluna*. Trimming keeps plants in good shape. Summer-flowering types should be trimmed in March to just below the old flower heads but not into old wood. Winter and spring flowerers are treated similarly, immediately after flowering. The tree heaths should be pruned only when there is a need for rejuvenation or containment, in April or May. Spring planting is generally preferable; choose well-hardened plants and apply an annual mulch of pulverized bark or similar material.

heavy used of soils containing a high proportion of clay, which therefore need careful and timely management. See *soil*.

Hebe (from *Hebe*, goddess of youth and cup-bearer to the gods). Scrophulariaceae. New Zealand, Australia, temperate S America (those here are from New Zealand unless otherwise stated). Some 75 species, small to medium-sized evergreen shrubs ranging in habit from dwarf and procumbent to erect and bushy, to treelike. The leaves vary from needle- or scalelike and overlapping on whip-cord- or cypresslike branchlets, to rounded or lanceolate and more openly arranged on stouter shoots. Small, four-lobed flowers are carried in axillary or subterminal racemes or heads usually in spring and summer. Hardy to 5°F (–15°C). Plant in a position sheltered from cold winds, in full sun and well-drained soil. Propagate by heeled, semiripe cuttings in a gritty medium in the cold frame in late

361

summer; whipcord types are more prone to rotting off and need careful and judicious watering.

H. albicans compact spreading or rounded shrub to 24 in (60 cm); leaves to ³/₄ × ⁵/₈ in (2 × 1.5 cm), spreading to imbricate, ovate to oblong, glaucous, fleshy; racemes to 2¹/₂ in (6 cm), flowers white, anthers purple; cultivars include the low, domed shrub 'Cranleigh Gem', to 24 in (60 cm), with gray leaves, flowers in short broad racemes, and dark anthers; 'Red Edge', with leaves edged red and mauve flowers; and the hardy 'Sussex Carpet', to 12 in (30 cm), spreading, with glaucous leaves and a short inflorescence; *H.* 'Alicia Amherst' robust with deep green, lustrous leaves and showy racemes of strong purple flowers; *H.* × *andersonii* (*H. salicifolia* × *H. speciosa*) spreading shrub to 5¹/₂ ft (1.6 m); leaves to 4 × 1¹/₄ in (10 × 3 cm), ovate to lanceolate, obtuse, deep green; flowers crowded on spikes to 4 in (10 cm), violet; includes the vigorous 'Variegata', with dark green leaves, mottled or graded with gray-green and irregularly edged white to ivory, and lilac flowers; *H. armstrongii* (erect shrub to 3¹/₄ ft (1 m); branches whipcord, spreading then ascending, terete, yellow-green particularly in winter; leaves to ¹/₁₆ in (1.8 mm), closely adpressed; flowers white, in erect terminal clusters; differs from *H. ochracea* in its yellow-green (not ocher) branches and less arching habit; *H.* 'Autumn Glory' (to 32 in (80 cm); stems flushed dark red; leaves to 1¹/₄ in (3 cm), broadly obovate, dark green edged red when young; flowers violet-blue in long racemes; *H. buchananii* shrub to 8 in (20 cm), forming clumps to 36 in (90 cm) across; branches tortuous, black; leaves to ¹/₄ in (0.7 cm), spreading, ovate and concave, dull dark green; flowers white, crowded; includes the smaller and more compact 'Minor', forming a hummock of minute green leaves; *H. canterburiensis* low shrub to

3¹/₄ ft (1 m); leaves to ³/₄ in (1.7 cm), loosely overlapping, distichous, elliptic to obovate, subcoriaceous, margins pubescent, apex acute; inflorescence to 1 in (2.5 cm), crowded, flowers white; includes the procumbent 'Prostrata', with internodes flushed red and bright green leaves, twisted back and overlapping; *H.* 'Carnea' dense, glabrous, to 3¹/₄ ft (1 m); leaves to 2¹/₂ in (6 cm), narrowly oblong to lanceolate, green faintly tinted red at margins and midrib; racemes 2¹/₂–3 in (6–8 cm), flowers pink fading to white, giving a 2-tone appearance to inflorescence; *H. carnosula* shrub to 16 in (40 cm), forming leafy tufts of erect shoots; leaves to ³/₄ in (2 cm), closely overlapping, decussate, obovate, concave, thick, somewhat glaucous; flowers white, in terminal rounded inflorescence to ⁵/₈ in (1.5 cm) diameter, anthers purple; commonly mistaken for *H. pinguifolia*, from which it can be distinguished by its less glaucous leaves; *H.* 'County Park' as *H. pimelioides*, to 8 × 20 in (20 × 50 cm), decumbent with gray-green leaves edged red, flushed red-purple in cold weather, and violet flowers; *H. cupressoides* cypresslike whipcord, with dense, rounded or open habit, to 5 × 6¹/₂ ft (1.5 × 2 m); branchlets sometimes glutinous and aromatic; juvenile leaves are linear, occasionally lobed, mature leaves up to ¹/₁₆ in (0.15 cm), scalelike, closely adpressed but not hiding stems, narrow-ovate to triangular, ciliate; flowers very pale blue, anthers red-brown; includes 'Boughton Dome', to 12 × 20 in (30 × 50 cm), forming a broad and densely branched dome of fine gray-green branchlets clothed with both juvenile and adult leaves; *H. elliptica* New Zealand, Tierra del Fuego, Falkland Islands; shrub to small tree to 16 ft (5 m), usually about 5 ft (1.5 m); leaves to 1 in (2.4 cm), spreading, often oriented in one direction, elliptic to oblong, coriaceous, lustrous dark green, ciliate; flowers clustered at branch tips,

white to violet or pink; *H.* 'Fairfieldii' compact, upright to 24 in (60 cm), close to *H. hulkeana* but with branches rigidly erect, duller leaves, shorter, stout inflorescence and larger lilac flowers; *H.* × *franciscana* (*H. elliptica* × *H. speciosa*) shrub to 4¹/₄ ft (1.3 m), habit rounded, dense; leaves to 2¹/₂ × 1 in (6 × 2.5 cm), larger, duller than *H. elliptica*, distichous, obovate to elliptic, fleshy, dark green, apiculate; inflorescence to 3 in (7.5 cm), cylindrical; flowers purple tinged pink; includes 'Blue Gem', with red-violet flowers and violet anthers, and 'Variegata', with leaves mottled and margined yellow at beginning of season; *H.* 'Great Orme' similar to *H.* 'Carnea', although more robust, with dark internodes, leaves to 3¹/₂ in (9 cm), oblong-lanceolate, somewhat falcate; *H.* 'Hagley Park' to 16 × 24 in (40 × 60 cm); leaves obovate to spathulate, serrate; flowers in terminal panicles to 12 in (30 cm), similar to *H. hulkeana* but a stronger lilac-pink; *H. hectorii* whipcord to 30 in (75 cm); branches crowded, or spreading to decumbent with age, yellow-green; leaves to ¹/₈ in (0.4 cm), scalelike, overlapping, closely adpressed, concealing stems, glossy, yellow-green; flowers white to pink in congested terminal heads; *H. hulkeana* NEW ZEALAND LILAC; sprawling shrub to 3¹/₄ ft (1 m), usually slender, habit loose, internodes tinted purple-red; leaves to 2 × 1¹/₄ in (5 × 3 cm), spreading, elliptic to rounded, subcoriaceous, glabrous, deep lustrous green above, pale beneath, margin often flushed red, serrate; flowers lavender to white in panicles to 12 in (30 cm); includes 'Averil', with pale green leaves not edged red and more compact inflorescences; *H.* 'La Séduisante' young leaves lustrous, tinted purple; flowers red-purple in long showy racemes in late summer; *H. lycopodioides* rigid and narrowly erect whipcord to 24 in (60 cm); resembles *H. hectoris* but branchlets tetragonal; juvenile leaves linear-subulate, mature leaves to ¹/₈ in (3 mm), scalelike, adpressed, ribbed or striped yellow, margins yellow; flowers white with lilac-blue anthers; *H.* 'Midsummer Beauty' robust, soon attaining 6¹/₂ ft (2 m) or more; leaves oblong to lanceolate or broadly elliptic, deep green tinted purple-red when young; flowers

paired leaves and flower clusters

Hebe x franciscana 'Blue Gem'

pale blue to lilac or magenta, often fading to pale rose, in long slender racemes; *H. ochracea* (whipcord to 24 in (60 cm); branches spreading, rigid, dark, bowed outward; branchlets olive green to ocher, arising from upper side of branches; leaves to ¹⁄₁₆ in (1.5 mm), ocher to olive, tightly adpressed; flowers small, white, in short spikes; often confused with *H. armstrongii*, this species is the more commonly cultivated and can be distinguished by its ocher branches and strongly outspread to arching habit; includes the very compact 'James Stirling'; *H.* 'Pewter Dome' as *H. albicans* with small, dull gray-silver leaves, very compact; *H. pimeleoides* densely branched low-growing shrub to 18 in (45 cm); leaves ¹⁄₄–⁵⁄₈ in (6–15 mm), elliptic to broadly obovate, sometimes concave, spreading to recurved, glaucous, blue-gray, margins occasionally red; flowers white flushed pale lilac to pale violet; cultivars and varieties include: the very small, creeping 'Minor', with flowers tinted lilac blue; 'Quicksilver', with small, recurved, especially glaucous leaves; var. *glaucocaerulea*, erect to 14 in (35 cm) becoming decumbent, with larger, broadly elliptic, concave, strongly glaucous leaves, edged red in summer, and violet-blue flowers; *H. pinguifolia* procumbent or ascending to 3¼ ft (1 m); leaves to ⁵⁄₈ in (1.5 cm), overlapping to spreading, obovate to elliptic, concave, thick, glaucous, blue-green, often edged red, obtuse to subacute; flowers white, anthers blue; often confused with *H. carnosula*, which has broader leaves and a glabrous ovary and style; includes the popular cultivar 'Pagei', with gray, oblong to obovate, scarcely concave leaves, and white flowers in dense short spikes; *H. rakaiensis* shrub to 36 in (90 cm); branchlets slender with rough leaf scars; leaves to ³⁄₄ in (2 cm), spreading, obovate to oblong, entire, subcoriaceous, glossy, bright green; racemes to 1¹⁄₂ in (4 cm), simple, covering plant, flowers white; often labeled *H. subalpina* or *H. buxifolia* in gardens; *H. recurva* spreading shrub to 3¼ ft (1 m); leaves to 2 in (5 cm), spreading to deflexed, narrowly lanceolate, glabrous, gray-green; flowers white (often pink in bud) in spikes to 2¹⁄₂ in (6 cm) long; selections of *H. recurva* are available with longer, plain green leaves, or particularly strong

gray tones, and in some cases, mauve flowers fading to white; *H. salicifolia* New Zealand, Chile; shrub to 16 ft (5 m), usually shorter; branchlets green; leaves to 6 in (15 cm), suberect to spreading, lanceolate to oblong, apex acuminate, entire or denticulate, glossy dark green; racemes to 8 in (20 cm), narrowly conical to cylindric, flowers white, usually tinted pale lilac; *H. speciosa* strong-growing shrub to 6¹⁄₂ ft (2 m); branches stout, somewhat angular; leaves to 4 in (10 cm), broadly elliptic to obovate, glossy, margin cartilaginous; flowers dark red to magenta, crowded in conic-cylindric racemes to 2³⁄₄ in (7 cm) long; a highly variable species giving rise to many cultivars and hybrids; *H. tetragona* erect whipcord to 3¼ ft (1 m), much-branched; branchlets distinctly tetragonal, yellow-green; leaves to ¹⁄₈ in (3.5 mm), decussate, adpressed, deltoid to subulate; *H.* 'Trixie' as *H. albicans* with green leaves and white flowers; *H.* 'Wingletye' close to 'County Park' but lower-growing, with strongly glaucous leaves that do not flush red in cold weather, and lilac blue flowers; *H.* 'Youngii' to 6 in (15 cm), procumbent, compact; leaves to ³⁄₈ in (0.75 cm), elliptic, dark green, faintly edged red at times; flowers deep violet fading to white in short racemes.

Hedera (Latin name for the plant.) Araliaceae. Europe, Asia, N Africa. IVY. 11 species of evergreen, woody, climbing or creeping plants with distinct sterile, juvenile and fertile, arborescent stages. The stems of the juvenile stage climb by means of aerial rootlets. Juvenile leaves are conspicuously lobed or cordate, those of arborescent stage are more nearly entire; all are glabrous and often waxy and shining above, stellate-hairy or scaly beneath. Small, cream to yellow-green flowers are carried in globose umbels. They are followed by small, spherical drupes; these are usually black, sometimes orange, yellow or cream.

Ivies are valued as coverage for walls, garages, and even unsightly tree stumps; ivy-clad buildings have considerable charm. For large expanses of wall, the larger-leaved kinds such as *H. colchica* and *H. hibernica* are the most suitable; for smaller areas, the diversity of leaf shape and variegation of the many cultivars of *H. helix* can be used

to good effect. Variegated ivies look particularly fine against red-brick backgrounds and add immensely to the winter beauty of a garden. The yellow-green leaved clones, such as *H. helix* 'Buttercup', associate well with purple-leaved shrubs or blue-flowered plants, while against white walls the winter purple of the leaves of *H. helix* 'Atropurpurea' can make a dramatic contrast.

Its creeping habit and preference for shade make ivy an excellent ground-cover plant and one whose variegated cultivars can be used with great effect to brighten dark corners. The sulfur-cream *H. hibernica* 'Sulphurea' underplanted with fall crocus (*Colchicum* species) makes an attractive color combination and will guard the flowers against mud splash.

Concern is sometimes expressed as to the effects of ivy on trees or buildings. Ivy is not parasitic and, while the growth of ivy on trees of value or beauty is to be avoided, an unloved tree may be given up to it. When such a tree becomes ivy-laden, it makes a pleasing winter picture and a refuge for birds. On sturdy buildings and walls, ivy is harmless but can become unwieldy and harbor insects. To obviate this, it should be clipped over in late spring every other year or so. Walls and fences that are very weak may fall if a mass of ivy becomes heavy with snow or rain; clipping will prevent this. (*Continued on p.365.*)

Trimming back Hedera
Ivies that encroach on house eaves and gutters should be trimmed back periodically or they will cause damage, either with their prying aerial roots or by their weight.

HEDERA

Name	Distribution	Leaves
H. azorica	Azores	3½–4½ × 4–4¾ in (9–11 × 10–12 cm), with 5–7 bluntly acute lobes, center lobe only slightly longer than laterals, sinuses shallow, light matt green, hairs stellate, 3–5-rayed, white and so extensive as to give young stems and leaves a felted appearance
H. canariensis *H. algeriensis* CANARY ISLAND IVY	Canary Is., N Africa	juvenile leaves unlobed or 3-lobed, 4–6 × 3–4¾ in (10–15 × 8–12 cm), bluntly acute, base cordate, margin entire, mid-green and glossy, stems purple-red; adult leaves elliptic-lanceolate, hairs scalelike, with 1–15 rays

Comments: 'Gloire de Marengo': leaves with areas of silvery-gray and creamy yellow; a popular houseplant but an outdoor climber in favored areas. 'Marginomaculata': leaves extensively mottled creamy yellow. 'Montgomery': leaves 3-lobed, stems and petioles wine-red 'Ravensholst': with large, mostly 3-lobed leaves, center lobe acute and broad, some leaves unlobed and elliptical; dark glossy green.

H. colchica COLCHIS IVY; PERSIAN IVY; BULLOCK'S HEART IVY	Caucasus to Asiatic Turkey	ovate, generally unlobed, 2½–4¾ × 2½–3 in (6–12 × 6–8 cm), apex acute, base cordate, margin entire, dark green, resin-scented when crushed; adult leaves lanceolate; hairs scalelike, with 12–20 rays

Comments: 'Dentata' (ELEPHANT'S EARS): leaves pendent, larger than the type, 6–8 × 6–7 in (15–20 × 15–18 cm), base auriculate, the margins carrying widely spaced fine teeth, light green. 'Dentata Variegata': similar to 'Dentata' but leaves smaller, light green variegated with areas of gray-green and irregular marginal areas of cream-yellow. 'Sulphur Heart' ('Paddy's Pride'): similar to 'Dentata Variegata' but leaves a deeper green with an irregular central splash of yellow.

H. helix COMMON IVY; ENGLISH IVY	Europe and E Russia	juvenile leaves 3–5-lobed, 2–3 in (5–8 cm), leathery, entire with cordate base and pale venation, young stems and leaves with white-stellate, 4–6-rayed hairs; leaves of arborescent stage elliptic, entire, less than 2 in (5 cm) wide

Comments: 'Angularis': leaves 5-lobed, center lobe prolonged and acuminate, laterals bluntly acute, dark green in summer, coloring purple in winter. 'Atropurpurea': leaves 3-lobed, center lobe prolonged and acuminate, laterals bluntly acute, dark green in summer, purple in winter. 'Buttercup': leaves 5-lobed, apex acute, base cordate, light green, butter yellow in sunlight. 'Chrysophylla' ('Spectabilis Aurea'; 'Aurea Spectabilis'): leaves 3-lobed, lobes acute, leaf base truncate, mid- to deep green, slightly suffused yellow. 'Congesta': nonclimbing, erect; leaves 3-lobed, dark green, in a distichous arrangement. 'Conglomerata': creeping but producing short upright shoots; leaves unlobed, margins undulate and waved. 'Dealbata' ('Discolor'): leaves 3-lobed, dark green mottled cream-white. 'Erecta': nonclimbing, erect; leaves 3-lobed; stems green; larger in all parts than 'Congesta'. 'Eva': leaves small with gray-green center, splashed deep green, margined cream. 'Fantasia': leaves 5-lobed, bright green heavily mottled cream-yellow. 'Goldchild': leaves 3–5-lobed, base cordate, mid-green with bright yellow, mostly marginal variegation. 'Glacier': leaves 3-lobed, apex acute, mid-green overlaid gray-green with occasional cream variegation. 'Glymii': leaves unlobed, ovate-acuminate, glossy, becoming deep purple in winter. 'Ivalace': leaves 5-lobed, margins strongly undulate, convolute at the sinus giving a crimped and laced effect, dark green and glossy. 'Kolibri': leaves 3–5-lobed, light green with flecks of gray-green and areas of cream variegation. 'Little Diamond': leaves unlobed, diamond-shaped, gray-green, white variegation slight and mainly at the edge. 'Manda's Crested': leaves 3–5-lobed, lobes convolute with blunt, downward-pointing apices giving a curly effect. 'Maple Leaf': leaves 5-lobed, apex acuminate, center lobe 1.5 times length of laters, edges irregularly indented, mid-green. 'Midas Touch': leaves unlobed, deltoid or triangular, apex bluntly acute, base cordate, dark green, irregularly variegated bright yellow. 'Minor Marmorata' (SALT AND PEPPER IVY): leaves 3-lobed, small dark green, spotted and splashed cream-white. 'Oro di Bogliasco' ('Goldheart'): leaves 3-lobed, dark green with prominent yellow splash in center. 'Parsley Crested': leaves unlobed, ovate to almost circular, margins crimped and crested, light green. 'Pedata' (BIRD'S FOOT IVY): leaves 5-lobed, center lobe prolonged and narrow, basal lobes back-pointing, dark green, veins gray-white. 'Shamrock': leaves 3-lobed, center lobe broad, lateral lobes sometimes folded in pleated fashion alongside center lobe, dark green. 'Spetchley': leaves 3-lobed, very small, center lobe prolonged, dark green. 'Tricolor': leaves unlobed, triangular, small, gray-green with cream-yellow edge that is slightly pink in summer, intensifying to purple in winter. 'William Kennedy': leaves 3-lobed but laterals often reduced to give a single lobed small (⅝–1¼ in / 1.5–3 cm), leaf. f. ***poetarum*** (syn. var. *poetica*): POET'S IVY; ITALIAN IVY; leaves 5-lobed, the two basal lobes much reduced giving a somewhat "square" appearance to the light green leaf; grown for the novelty of its dull orange berries.

H. canariensis 'Ravensholst' *H. colchica* 'Dentata' *H. helix* 'Oro di Bogliasco' *H. pastuchovii* var. *cypria*

HEDERA

Name	Distribution	Leaves
H. hibernica H. helix subsp. hibernica ATLANTIC IVY	Atlantic coast of GB, Ireland, W France, Spain, Portugal	juvenile leaves 5-lobed, 2–3½ × 3–5½ in (5–9 × 8–14 cm), lobes triangular and bluntly acute, central lobe larger, base cordate, dark green, with stellate hairs tending to lie in parallel fashion rather than the haphazard fashion of H. helix; adult leaves ovate-elliptic

Comments: 'Deltoidea' (SWEETHEART IVY): leaves sometimes 3-lobed but more often deltoid and unlobed, base strongly cordate with overlapping lobes giving an almost heart-shaped leaf, dark green. 'Hamilton': leaves 5-lobed, center lobe only slightly longer than laterals, mid-green, edge thickened. 'Helford River': leaves 5-lobed, center lobe prolonged and acuminate, mid-green with gray-white veins. 'Lobata Major': leaves 3-lobed, lateral lobes at right angles to the long-acuminate central lobe. 'Rona': leaves 5-lobed, mid-green with freckled and diffused yellow variegation; less green leaf intrusion than with 'Variegata'. 'Rottingdean': leaves 5-lobed, digitate, center lobe slightly longer than laterals, sinuses narrow and convolute at the clefts, dark green. 'Sulphurea': leaves edged and splashed sulfur yellow. 'Variegata': some leaves entirely yellow or part-colored.

Name	Distribution	Leaves
H. maderensis	Madeira	juvenile leaves 3-lobed, occasionally unlobed, 1½–2 × 2½–2¾ in (4–5 × 6–7 cm), sinuses very shallow or absent, lobes obtuse, base truncate or slightly cordate, mid- to dark green, very glossy at first; hairs scalelike with 10–16 rays
H. maroccana MOROCCAN IVY	Morocco	3-lobed, 2¾–3½ × 2¾ in (7–9 × 7 cm), center lobe twice as long as laterals, sinuses shallow, apex acute, base cuneate or truncate, dark green; hairs scalelike, rays 6–8; petioles purple-red

Comments: 'Spanish Canary': leaves very large; hardy and fast growing.

Name	Distribution	Leaves
H. nepalensis H. himalaica, H. cinerea HIMALAYAN IVY	Himalaya to Kashmir	juvenile leaves ovate to lanceolate, 2½–4 × 1½–2 in (6–10 × 4–5 cm), obscurely lobed, lobes often little more than 3–6 marginal indentations, apex acute, base truncate, matt olive-green, hairs scalelike, 12–15-rayed; adult leaves elliptic-lanceolate, unlobed

Comments: Readily identified by the dull orange berries. var. nepalensis 'Suzanne': differs from type in 5-lobed leaves, the short basal lobes back-pointing to give a "bird's foot" effect, dark green. In var. sinensis from Northern China, the juvenile leaves are usually unlobed and ovate-acuminate with a cuneate base, they emerge maroon, rapidly maturing to matt mid-green.

Name	Distribution	Leaves
H. pastuchovii	Russia, Iran	juvenile leaves narrowly ovate, 1½–3½ × 1¼–1½ in (4–9 × 3–4 cm), unlobed, apex acuminate, base slightly cordate, dark green, glossy, slightly leathery, hairs scalelike with 8–12 rays, sparse
H. rhombea H. japonica JAPANESE IVY	Japan	juvenile leave ovate to triangular, unlobed, ¾–1½ × 1½–2 in (2–4 × 4–5 cm), apex acute, mid-green, leathery, stems green, hairs scalelike, rays 10–18

Comments: 'Pierrot': leaves smaller, stems thin and wiry. var. rhombea 'Variegata': leaves slightly smaller, finely edged with white.

The nonclimbing forms of *H. helix*, 'Congesta' and 'Erecta', and the slow-growing, rock-hugging 'Conglomerata' make good feature plants for rock garden or patio. In completely shaded town gardens, ivy will grow perfectly well, and here the variegated kinds can be used to brighten a dark site. "Standard" ivies can be produced through grafting small-leaved, trailing kinds on the single stems of × *Fatshedera*.

Increase by nodal cuttings of juvenile growth with one or two leaves. Woody shoots of the adult stage are less easy and may require mist facilities. Cuttings are best taken between June and October when the young growth has hardened sufficiently. Inserted in sharp sand in lightly shaded frames, these root rapidly and may then be potted into a medium-fertility soil-based mix. When well rooted and growing, plant out or, if specimen or conservatory plants are required, pot into larger pots and then train either to canes in the form of a trellis or on moss poles. In the conservatory or home, ivies should never be placed in direct sunlight or be allowed to dry out. During summer, a balanced liquid fertilizer every 14 days is beneficial.

Soil preparation for ivies growing outside should be generous, as for any permanent planting. In nonalkaline areas, the inclusion of lime or concrete rubble can be advantageous but is not essential. Plants intended to climb need to be guided by being tied to a cane leading to their support. If this is not done, the ivy will initially creep along the ground, possibly ascending at a point not intended by the planter.

hedge a continuous row of trees or shrubs, usually low-growing and closely planted to provide a boundary line, screen, or ornamental feature. There is no hard and fast definition of a hedge by height, but living barriers more than 16 ft (5 m) tall are usually referred to as shelter belts, and continuous plantings less than 20 in (50 cm) high as edging. Hedges may be formally clipped or informal, and a very wide range of species are suitable subjects, for example: FORMAL EVERGREEN *Aucuba*, *Berberis*, *Cotoneaster*, *Escallonia*, *Ilex*, *Lonicera nitida*, *Quercus ilex*, *Taxus baccata*; FORMAL DECIDUOUS *Alnus glutinosa*, *Carpinus betulus*, *Crataegus monogyna*,

Fagus sylvatica, Prunus cerasifera, Salix, Sambucus nigra, Sorbus intermedia; INFORMAL EVERGREEN *Brachyglottis, Camellia japonica, Choisya ternata, Cotoneaster, Mahonia aquifolium, Rhododendron ponticum, Rosmarinus, Viburnum tinus*; INFORMAL DECIDUOUS *Amelanchier lamarckii, Cornus stolonifera, Deutzia scabra, Forsythia*; *Fuchsia magellanica*; *Hydrangea macrophylla, Kerria*; *Rosa* species.

Hedychium (from Greek *hedys*, sweet, and *chion*, snow: *H. coronarium* has fragrant white flowers). Zingiberaceae. Tropical Asia, Himalaya and Madagascar. GARLAND LILY, GINGER LILY. About 40 species, perennial herbs with stout rhizomes and reedlike stems bearing two-ranked, oblong to lanceolate leaves. Fragrant flowers are carried in dense, terminal spikes in summer. They consist of three petals, a showy lip, petal-like staminodes and long, slender filaments. The Himalayan species, particularly *H. coccineum* and *H. densiforum* and its cultivars, are hardy to 28°F (−2°C) if grown at the foot of a south-facing wall or given a mulch as winter protection. *H. gardnerianum* is a fine plant for the cool conservatory or subtropical bedding scheme. *H. coronarium* and *H. flavescens* need a minimum of 65°F (18°C) with high humidity, and plentiful water. Liquid-fertilize plants in pots throughout growth. Reduce water considerably in winter and allow plants to become dormant, cutting out old spikes. Propagate by division in spring or by seeds sown fresh at 64°F (18°C).

H. coccineum RED GINGER LILY, SCARLET GINGER LILY; Himalaya; to 10 ft (3 m); flowers pale to deep red or orange, lip ½–¾ in (1–2 cm) across, red and yellow to mauve; includes 'Tara', with bold spikes of orange flowers, and var. *angustifolium*, with narrower leaves and orange flowers; *H. coronarium* GARLAND FLOWER, WHITE GINGER LILY, BUTTERFLY LILY; India; to 10 ft (3 m); flowers very fragrant, white, lip 2 in (5 cm) across, white with yellow-green center; 'F. W. Moore': *H. coronarium* × *H. coccineum*, showy spikes and fragrant, amber yellow flowers, with a base of segment blotched orange-yellow; var. *maximum*: larger flowers and filaments tinged pink; *H. densiflorum* Himalaya; 3¼–16 ft (1–5 m); flowers vermilion, in dense, cylindric spikes; lip ¼ in (0.7 cm)

across; filaments red; includes 'Assam Orange', with shorter stems and very fragrant, vivid burnt orange flowers; *H. flavescens* YELLOW GINGER; Bengal; to 10 ft (3 m); flowers in dense 8-in (20-cm) spike; corolla pale yellow with linear, green lobes, lip red-yellow at base, staminodes yellow, filaments yellow; *H. gardnerianum* KAHILI GINGER; N India, Himalaya; 3¼–6½ ft (1–2 m)+; flowers fragrant, white and yellow, in dense 10–14 in (25–35 cm) spike, lip ½–¾ in (1–2 cm) across, yellow, filaments bright red.

Hedysarum (the Greek name *hedysaron*, from *hedys*, sweet). Leguminosae. Northern temperate regions. Some 100 species, perennial herbs, subshrubs or shrubs with racemes of pealike flowers in summer. Suitable for the herbaceous border; the flowers also last well when cut. Grow *Hedysarum* in full sun, in moderately deep and fertile, well-drained soil. Hardy to 5°F (−15°C). Propagate by seed, alternatively by careful division in spring. *H. coronarium* FRENCH HONEYSUCKLE; S Europe; herb, 12–39 in (30–100 cm); leaflets ⅝–1½ in (1.5–3.5 cm), 7–15, elliptic to orbicular; flowers intensely fragrant, bright red to purple-red; 'Album': flowers white.

heel a small strip of wood and bark retained at the base of a cutting at the time of removal from the main shoot. The presence of a heel often improves rooting potential.

heeling in the temporary insertion of plants in soil, usually prior to permanent planting, in order to prevent deterioration due to drying out.

Helenium (from Greek *helenion*, for an Old World plant (perhaps *Inula helenium*), said to have been named for Helen of Troy). Compositae. Americas. SNEEZEWEED. About 40 species, annual, biennial or perennial herbs with linear to lanceolate leaves and daisylike flower heads with a prominent, domed disk produced from midsummer to fall. Grow in full sun in fertile and moisture-retentive soil, enriched with well-rotted organic matter; apply balanced fertilizer in spring and provide support for taller plants. Lift and divide every

second or third year, and discard less vigorous portions of the clump. Provide a winter mulch where low temperatures are prolonged. Propagate also by seed or basal cuttings.

H. fallale SNEEZEWEED; N America; perennial to 5 ft (1.5 m); flower heads to 2 in (5 cm) diameter, clustered in a corymb, ray florets yellow to bright yellow; includes 'Grandicephalum', to 60 in (150 cm), with large, yellow flower heads, the dwarf 'Nanum Praecox', with yellow flower heads produced early, 'Praecox', with yellow, brown and red flower heads, produced early, 'Rubrum', with dark red flower heads, and 'Superbum', to 60 in (150 cm) tall, with large, bright yellow flower heads with wavy ray florets; see below for further cultivars; *H. bigelovii* California, Oregon; perennial, to 36 in (90 cm); flower heads long-stalked, to 2½ in (6 cm) diameter; ray florets yellow; includes 'Aurantiacum', with gold ray florets. *Cultivars* Taller selections include the 60 in (150 cm) yellow 'Sonnenwunder', the gold, brown-centered 'Goldrausch', 'Zimbelstern', with wavy ray florets, and the brown-red, 48 in (120 cm)-tall 'Wonnadonga' and 'Margot', and the 48 in (120 cm) 'Flammenrad' and 'Riverton Beauty', yellow with red edges and eyes; medium cultivars include the gold 'Butterpat', 'Waltraut', 'Bressingham Gold' and the bronze to velvety wine red 'Moerheim Beauty', 'Goldlackzwerg', 'Baudirektor Linne' and 'Bruno'. Smaller clones include the yellow 'Aurantiacum', the gold and copper 'Wyndley', the red-brown 'Kupferzwerg' and the soft mahogany 'Crimson Beauty'.

Heliamphora (either from Greek *helios* the sun, or from *helos* a marsh, and *amphora*, a jug or pitcher, referring to its appearance and habitat). Sarraceniaceae. Guyana Highlands, Guyana and Venezuela. SUN PITCHER. 6 species, carnivorous perennial herbs. Borne in a basal clump, the leaves are pitcher-shaped and bright green, assuming a red tint in full sun. Stoutly tubular in the lower half, they then narrow in a short bottle-neck before expanding above in a flattened blade; this terminates in a spoon-shaped cap. White flowers nod in loose, arching racemes in spring and summer. *Heliamphora* requires a very open but absorbent growing medium, such as perlite and living sphagnum, and perfect drainage (that said, these plants sometimes thrive in terrariums). Under glass, air should circulate freely and high humidity be maintained by regular overhead spraying. Provide bright light but shade from fierce sun. Maintain winter temperatures of between 42–68°F (5.5–20°C), and summer temperatures that do not exceed 77°F (25°C). In the open greenhouse, drench with rainwater once or twice daily in warm weather; keep moist and humid at all times. Diluted foliar or slow-release fertilizers are beneficial but must be carefully applied.

H. heterodoxa pitchers cauline, to 12 in (30 cm), upper part of pitcher interior with velvety hairs or glabrous, cap large; *H. minor* pitchers constricted above and below middle, usually not exceeding 3 × ½ in (7.5 × 1 cm) in cultivation, pubescent in upper portion of interior, cap very small, or absent; *H. nutans* pitchers basal, constricted above and below middle, to 8 in (20 cm), green with red margins, hairy in upper portion of interior, cap medium-sized, i.e. to ⅝ in (1.5 cm) across.

Helianthemum (from Greek *helios*, sun, and *anthemon*, flower—the flowers open only in bright sunshine). Cistaceae. Americas, Europe, Mediterranean, N Africa, Asia Minor to C Asia. ROCK ROSE, SUN ROSE. 110 species, evergreen or semievergreen shrublets with small, more or less graydowny, oblong to linear leaves. Borne on one-sided, racemose cymes in spring and summer, the short-lived flowers are dish-shaped and consist of five, crêpe-like petals and numerous golden stamens. Suitable for rock gardens (in company with similarly tough and fast-growing species), for the front of sunny borders and for wall crevices or gravel beds. All are hardy to at least 14°F (–10°C) and may be overwintered with a covering of bracken or sacking in colder areas. Provide a sunny, open site and light, well-drained soil. Trim back after flowering for a second flush of flowers in late summer. Plants are short-lived, and may require replacement when too leggy and sparse. Propagate by softwood or heeled cuttings in late summer, rooted in a sandy mix;

Helianthemum 'Wisley White'
Most of the helianthemums found in gardens are hybrids, grown for their long, free-flowering season and drought tolerance.

overwinter in a cold frame for planting out in spring.

H. apenninum Europe, Asia Minor; to 20 in (50 cm); flowers to 1⅛ in (2.8 cm) in diameter, petals white, yellow at base; var. *roseum*: flowers pink; *H. nummularium* Europe, Asia Minor; to 20 in (50 cm); flowers ¾–2 in (2–5 cm) in diameter, golden yellow, pale yellow, pink, white or orange, rarely cream; *H. oelandicum* Europe; to 8 in (20 cm); flowers to ⅜ in (0.8 cm) in diameter, yellow.

Cultivars The rock roses most frequently encountered in gardens tend to be hybrids with *H. apenninum*, *H. nummularium*, and *H. croceum* involved in their parentage. They range in flower color from white to cream, pale yellow, gold, orange, tangerine, flame, scarlet, wine red, crimson, rose pink, and blush and have gray, sage green, or silvery foliage.

Helianthus (from Greek *helios*, sun, and *anthos*, flower). Compositae. N and S America. SUNFLOWER. About 70 species, annual to perennial herbs with showy daisylike flower heads in summer. *H. tuberosus* is the JERUSALEM ARTICHOKE (see *artichoke*). *H. salicifolius* is a hardy, spreading perennial, well-adapted to dry, sunny situations in the garden. The annual *H. annuus* is available in a wide range of cultivars,

including dwarf (12–24 in/30–60 cm), intermediate (39–48 in/100–120 cm) and tall forms (10 ft/3 m and more). Smaller cultivars make fine cut flowers. Sow seed under glass in early spring for planting out in early summer, or sow *in situ* in late spring. Grow in full sun in fertile, well drained soil. Mulch perennials annually in spring with well-rotted farmyard manure. Stake tall cultivars and provide a deep winter mulch where prolonged low winter temperatures are not accompanied by snow cover. Lift and divide perennials every third or fourth year to maintain vigor. Propagate by seed and (perennials) by division or basal cuttings.

H. annuus COMMON SUNFLOWER; US; stout, often giant, annual with an erect, more or less unbranched stem to 16 ft (5 m); leaves to 16 in (40 cm), broadovate to cordate, acute, coarsely toothed, roughly hairy or bristly, dark green to silver; flower heads terminal, one or few, to 24 in (60 cm) across, ray florets yellow, occasionally tinged red, bronze or purple, disk florets red or purple; includes numerous cultivars and seed races—dwarf (20 in/50 cm) to giant (20 ft/6 m), flower heads 6–24 in (15–60 cm) in diameter, "single" or "double," with florets in pale primrose to deep gold or copper red or with purple-bronze tints; *H.* × *multiflorus* (*H. annuus* × *H. decapetalus*; perennial, to 6½ ft (2 m), with flower heads to 4¾ in (12 cm) in diameter, florets golden yellow, disk florets occasionally replaced by ray florets; includes numerous cultivars, to 72 in (180 cm) tall, "single" or "double," pale primrose to deep gold; *H. salicifolius* southern central US; perennial, to 10 ft (3 m); leaves to 8 in (20 cm), narrowly linear to lanceolate, slightly hairy, arching; flower heads numerous, to 3 in (8 cm) in diameter, ray florets golden yellow, disk florets purple, rarely yellow.

Helichrysum (from Greek *helios*, sun, and *chrysos*, golden). Compositae. Warm Old World, especially South Africa and Australia. EVERLASTING FLOWER. About 500 species, annual, biennial and perennial herbs, subshrubs and shrubs, often hairy and glandular and producing button- or daisylike flower heads, usually in summer. Almost without exception

367

Helichrysum species require a sheltered position in sun with well-drained soil, although they are suited to a diversity of situations in the garden depending on size and habit; some also have flowers that are suitable for drying. The low-growing perennials and dwarf shrublets (for example, *H. bellidioides*), are suitable for a sunny position in gritty, freely draining soil in the rock garden, but will require at least some protection from excessive wet in winter. Cushion-forming types, such as *H. milfordiae*, are more reliable when given the protection from winter rain afforded by the alpine house; *H. milfordiae* is also suited to tufa plantings. Many species have beautiful foliage, extremely useful for color and textural contrast in the herbaceous border and invaluable in the silver border; these include taller aromatic species, such as *H. italicum*, var. *serotinum*. In regions where winters are severe, protect with a mulch of bracken litter and cut back damaged growth in spring. *H. petiolare* is frequently grown as a half-hardy annual in cool temperatures zone for edging, groundcover and hanging baskets. The species most often grown for cutting and drying, *H. bracteatum* comes in a wide range of heights and colors. It is easily grown in moderately fertile and moisture-retentive soil in full sun and may be sown *in situ* in spring, but better harvests are obtained by starting earlier under glass, especially in regions where summers are short. Cut the flowers before they are fully open; dry upside down and away from direct light in small bunches; strip foliage from stems to avoid rotting. This species is usually treated as an annual, but may live for several years if protected from cold, wet conditions. Propagate shrubby species by heeled semiripe cuttings in summer; perennials by division or seed in spring. Remove rosettes of *H. milfordiae* and root in a sandy propagating mix in the cold frame.

Helichrysum bracteatum
King Size Series

H. bellidioides New Zealand; perennial herb to 8 in (20 cm), stems prostrate; leaves to ¼ in (6 mm), orbicular, silvery-arachnoid; flower heads to 1¼ in (3 cm) in diameter, solitary, phyllaries linear, papery white; *H. bracteatum* (syn. *Xerochrysum bracteatum*, *Bracteantha bracteata*) STRAWFLOWER, GOLDEN EVERLASTING, YELLOW PAPER DAISY; Australia; annual or perennial herb to 5 ft (1.5 m); leaves to 4¾ in (12 cm), oblong to lanceolate, acuminate, glabrous or subglabrous, sometimes downy and silver-gray; flower heads solitary, to 2¾ in (7 cm) in diameter; seed races include dwarf to tall plants with large or small flower heads in shades of sulfur, golden yellow, orange, bronze, copper, red, rose, purple and white; *H. italicum* (syn. *H. angustifolium*) S Europe; bushy aromatic subshrub or small shrub to 3¼ ft (1 m); leaves to 2½ in (6 cm), narrowly linear, pale-tomentose to glabrescent, revolute; flower heads yellow, 1/16–⅛ in (2–4 mm) in diameter in a cluster to 3 in (8 cm) across; includes subsp. *serotinum*, the CURRY PLANT, to 24 in (60 cm), with silver, slender, strongly curry-scented foliage; *H. milfordiae* (syn. *H. marginatum*) South Africa; subshrub to 6 in (15 cm), cushion-forming, prostrate; leaves to ⅝ in (1.5 cm), obovate to subspathulate, densely tomentose, apex scarious; flower heads 1½ in (4 cm) in diameter, solitary, phyllaries glossy white, usually crimson- or brown-tipped; *H. petiolare* (syn. *H. petiolatum*) LICORICE PLANT; South Africa; climbing or sprawling subshrub or shrub to 3¼ ft (1 m); stems slender, branched, thinly gray-tomentose; leaves to 1½ in (3.5 cm), rounded to broadly ovate, silver-gray-tomentose; flower heads to ¼ in (7 mm) in diameter, in loose corymbs; includes 'Limelight' with gold to lime-green leaves, 'Roundabout', dwarf and compact to 6 in (15 cm), with variegated leaves, and 'Variegatum', with variegated gray and cream leaves; *H. splendidum* E and South Africa; shrub to 5 ft (1.5 m); stems

branched, leafy, thinly tomentose; leaves to 2½ in (6 cm), linear to lanceolate, tomentose beneath, revolute; flower heads to ¼ in (5 mm) in diameter, in crowded or loose, terminal corymbs, bright yellow, rarely orange. For *H. coralloides*, see *Ozothamnus coralloides*; for *H. rosmarinifolium*, see *Ozothamnus rosmarinifolius*; for *H. selago*, see *Ozothamnus selago*.

Heliconia (for Mount Helicon in Greece, the home of Muses, a pun reflecting the closeness of this genus to *Musa*). Heliconiaceae. C and S America, S Pacific Islands, to Indonesia. FALSE BIRD OF PARADISE, WILD PLANTAIN. About 100 species, large, evergreen perennial herbs with clumped pseudostems and paddle-shaped leaves. Borne amid waxy, brilliantly colored boat-shaped bracts in erect to pendulous spikes, the flowers are white to yellow or orange, often tipped or striped with blue-black. Magnificent perennials for the warm greenhouse or moist, semishaded positions in subtropical and tropical gardens, *Heliconia* species are grown for their stately, banana-like habit (sometimes to 20 ft/6 m tall), handsome foliage (beautifully marked in *H. indica*) and their superb waxy inflorescences. These may be erect or pendulous, flat or spiraling, and range in color from yellow to pink to sealing-wax red and combinations thereof. All are suitable for cutting. They need a moisture-retentive open bark mix, rich in leaf mold and well-rotted manure. Plant in tubs or borders (dwarf cultivars of *H. stricta* are excellent potted plants) in semishaded, humid conditions (minimum temperature 59°F/15°C); syringe and foliar-feed frequently, except during flowering period and at the coolest times of the year. Cut away flowered growths once new suckers have formed. Propagate by division.

H. acuminata Brazil to S Venezuela and SE Peru; stem ¼–1¼ in (0.5–3 cm); leaves 6–28 in (15–70 cm); inflorescence erect, 20–39 in (50–100 cm), bracts distichous, 2½–10 in (6–25 cm), 4–6, red, orange or yellow, glabrous to hairy, flowers white, orange or yellow, usually with dark green "eye-spots" toward apex, or olive-green with white or pale orange tips; *H. bihai* FIREBIRD, MACAW FLOWER, BALISIER; C and S America; stem 20–15 ft (0.5–5 m); leaves 10

Heliconia psittacorum
The black flower tips, reminiscent of a parrot's beak, give this colorful exotic the common name of parrot or parakeet flower.

in–6½ ft (25 cm–2 m); inflorescence erect, 18–42 in (45–110 cm), bracts 3–15, distichous or alternate, sides red, keel yellow, margins green and/or yellow, more or less glabrous, flowers white, apex pale green; *H. caribaea* WILD PLANTAIN, BALISIER; Jamaica and E Cuba to St. Vincent; stems 6½–18 ft (2–5.5 m); leaves 24–54 in (60–130 cm); inflorescence 8–16 in (20–40 cm), erect, bracts to 10 in (25 cm), 6–15 in 2 overlapping rows, broadly triangular, red or yellow, keels and apices sometimes green or yellow, flowers white, apex green; *H. chartacea* Amazon Basin; stems to 13 ft (4 m); leaves to 4 ft (1.2 m); inflorescence to 3¼ ft (1 m), pendent, bracts to 16 in (40 cm), 4–28, slender, loosely spiraling, carmine to blush pink edged lime green, somewhat glaucous, flowers dark green; includes the candy pink and deep rose-magenta 'Sexy Pink' and 'Sexy Scarlet'; *H. hirsuta* Antilles and Belize to Bolivia, N Paraguay and E Brazil; stems 20–15 ft (0.5–5 m); leaves 6–20 in (15–50 cm); inflorescence 8–28 in (20–70 cm), erect, often hairy or cobwebby, bracts 3–9 slender, upcurved, loosely 2-ranked, orange to red, flowers yellow to orange or red, with dark green eyespots near apex; *H. indica* Papua New Guinea; stems to 16 ft (5 m), stout; leaves to 8 ft (2.5 m); inflorescence to 3¼ ft (1 m), erect, bracts to 14 in (35 cm), distichous, tough, carinate,

spreading, often with leafy appendages, green, flowers green; includes 'Spectabilis', with leaves green above, purple-bronze beneath or purple-green throughout, often with fine rose to white markings, and 'Striata', with green leaves with green-yellow or white markings; *H. metallica* Honduras to NW Colombia and Bolivia; stems 1½–13 ft (0.5–4 m); leaves 10 in–4½ ft (25 cm–1.4 m), emerald green above, metallic purple beneath; inflorescence 12–36 in (30–90 cm), erect, bracts 2–5½ in (5–14 cm), 3–8, distichous, linear to lanceolate, green to red, cobwebby, flowers rose pink to purple tipped white; *H. psittacorum* PARROT'S FLOWER, PARAKEET FLOWER, PARROT'S PLANTAIN; E Brazil to Lesser Antilles; stems 1½–6½ ft (0.5–2 m); leaves 4–20 in (10–50 cm); inflorescence 4¾–28 in (12–70 cm), erect, bracts 1½–6 in (4–16 cm), 2–7, pink, orange or red, sometimes edged yellow or green, upcurved, glabrous, waxy, not overlapping, slender, flowers yellow-green, orange or red with a dark green apical band and tipped white; *H. stricta* S Venezuela and Surinam to Bolivia and Ecuador; stems 1½–13 ft (0.5–4 m); leaves 16–60 in (40–150 cm); inflorescence 8–12 in (20–30 cm), erect, bracts 2¾–4½ in (7–11 cm), distichous, overlapping, broadly carinate, slightly inflated, red or orange, keel and margins yellow, tipped green, flowers white or pale yellow at base and apex, with a bright green band toward apex; *H. zebrina* Central E Peru; stems 3¼–6½ ft (1–2 m); leaves to 30 in (75 cm), dark green, often with dark green or purple bands and blotches, purple beneath; inflorescence 8–20 in (20–50 cm), erect, bracts 2½–8 in (6–21 cm), 6–9 distichous, narrow, spreading, red, glabrous, flowers pale yellow-green.

helicoid spirally clustered, in the shape of a spring or a snail shell.

helicoid-cyme see *bostryx*.

Helictotrichon (from Greek *heliktos*, twisted, and *thrix, trichos*, hair or bristle, referring to the shape of the awn). Gramineae. OATGRASS. Temperate Northern Hemisphere, South Africa. 60 species of perennial grasses with

slender, clump-forming culms and fine, arching foliage. *H. sempervirens* grows to 3¼ ft (1 m) tall and is one of the finest of the blue and silver grasses, making a fountain of blue-gray foliage topped by weeping, ash-blond flower spikes. Grow in well-drained soil in sun; give mulch protection where winter temperatures fall below 5°F (–15°C). Remove dead foliage regularly to retain form. Propagate by division or seed in spring.

Heliopsis (from Greek *helios*, sun, and *opsis*, appearance, referring to the showy flower heads). Compositae. N America. OX-EYE. About 13 species, loosely branched, erect perennial herbs with daisylike flower heads in late summer. Noted for ease of cultivation, extreme cold-hardiness, longevity, vigor and the warm colors of the large daisy flowers that appear from mid- to late summer and fall. Best grown in moisture-retentive, fertile soil in full sun. Propagate by division. *H. helianthoides* eastern N America; to 5 ft (1.5 m); flower heads to 3 in (7.5 cm) in diameter, ray florets pale to deep yellow, apex toothed, disk florets yellow; cultivars range from 3¼–16 ft (1–5 m) high with 1- or many-ranked ray florets ranging in color from light to dark gold.

heliotropism see *phototropism*.

Heliotropium (from Greek *helios*, sun, and *trope*, turning, from the long-disproved idea that the inflorescence turned with the sun). Boraginaceae. Tropical and temperate regions. HELIOTROPE; TURNSOLE. Some 250 species, annual or perennial herbs, subshrubs or shrubs with small, 5-lobed flowers in scorpioid spikes or racemes in summer. The most commonly cultivated plants are those hybrids derived from *H. arborescens*; when treated as frost-tender annuals, these are suitable for borders, pots and window boxes. When container-grown, they may be trained as pyramids or standards, for summer bedding or for permanent positions in the cool greenhouse or conservatory, where their delightful perfume may be more easily appreciated. Grow in moist but well-drained, moderately fertile soil in full sun. For potted plants, use a medium-fertility, loam-based mix and water plentifully

369

when in growth. Maintain a winter minimum temperature of 41–45°F (5–7°C) and ventilate freely as temperatures rise to 55°F (13°C). Propagate from seed sown in early spring at 61–64°F (16–18°C). Many cultivars are available. Propagate these by greenwood cuttings in summer or by semiripe cuttings in late summer or fall. Alternatively, take soft tip cuttings in late winter from stock plants grown on under glass over winter at 55°F (13°C). Standards are usually grown on through the winter at 50–61°F (10–16°C) from late summer semiripe cuttings; training for standards and pyramids follows procedures similar to those used for *Fuchsia*.

H. arborescens (syn. *H. peruvianum*; CHERRY PIE, HELIOTROPE) Peru; hairy, perennial shrub to 6½ ft (2 m); flowers sweetly scented, violet or purple to white; cultivars include 'Chatsworth', with rich purple-blue, very fragrant flowers; 'Florence Nightingale', with pale mauve flowers; 'Grandiflorum', with large flowers; 'Iowa', bushy and erect, with dark green leaves, lightly tinted purple, and dark purple, fragrant flowers in large clusters; 'Lemoine', to 24 in (60 cm), with deep purple, fragrant flowers; 'Lord Roberts', small, with soft violet flowers; 'Princess Marina', with deep violet flowers; 'Marine', bushy and compact, to 18 in (45 cm) high, with dark green, wrinkled leaves and deep violet, fragrant flowers in large clusters; 'Regal Dwarf', dwarf, with dark blue, fragrant flowers in large clusters; 'Spectabile', compact, to 4 ft (1.2 m) high, with pale violet, scented flowers; and 'White Lady', small and shrubby, with white flowers, tinged pink in bud.

Helleborus (name used by Theophrastus for medicinal herbs, probably not of this genus, but later always associated with it and with *Veratrum*). Ranunculaceae. Europe, especially Italy and Balkans, Turkey to Caucasus, W China. HELLEBORE. 15 species, rhizomatous perennial herbs for the most part evergreen. The leaves are trifoliolate to palmate or pedately compound. They may be basal, or, in caulescent species, borne on the flowering stem. The flowers may be solitary or, more commonly, produced a few

together in loose cymes subtended by leaflike bracts; in some (caulescent) species, many flowers will be carried in a paniculate cyme. Usually nodding, they are dish- to bell-shaped and consist of five broadly ovate to elliptic segments, numerous shortly tubular nectaries and many stamens.

Except for *H. argutifolius*, *H. lividus*, their offspring, and *H. thibetanus*, the following are hardy to –20°F (–29°C). They should be planted in moist but well-drained and fertile soil—heavy clay is tolerated but wet conditions may encourage leaf spot. Site in sun or part-shade with protection from harsh winds. Fertilize in spring and summer. Most flower from late winter to mid-spring. With stemless species bearing all-basal leaves (e.g., *H. orientalis*), it is advisable to remove the old foliage once the flower buds are visible, the better to display the flowers. *H. argutifolius*, *H. lividus*, and their hybrid offspring need full sun, shelter, and fast-draining gritty soil (min. temp. –10°F/–23°C). Where cold, wet weather threatens, protect *H. lividus* with a dry mulch, a cloche, or grow in a cold greenhouse. *H. thibetanus* is still quite new to gardens, but it seems likely to need a shaded, humid position in cool, permanently moist soil rich in leaf mold. It may die back by midsummer, is somewhat tender and should be mulched in cold winters.

Division is possible for most species (not *H. foetidus*). Fresh seed sown in cold frames in early summer is also worthwhile and seedlings grow quickly into good plants, flowering in 2–3 years and often producing attractive color forms. In suitable conditions, they will seed freely; the self-sown seedlings may be carefully transplanted in early spring. *H. argutifolius*, *H. foetidus* and *H. lividus* may also be propagated using cuttings of young vegetative shoots. All (especially those with softer leaves such as *H. niger*) are susceptible to leaf spot.

H. argutifolius (syn. *H. corsicus*) Corsica, Sardinia; stems to 3¼ ft (1 m), erect or sprawling, soon becoming naked below; leaves cauline, trifoliate, coriaceous, leaflets to 10 in (25 cm), elliptic to lanceolate, glabrous, olive to gray-green, spiny-toothed; inflorescence terminal, many-flowered, flowers pale green, cup or bowl-shaped, to 2 in

Self-seeding in Helleborus
Hellebores readily hybridize and self-seed, giving rise to offspring that may not resemble the parent, but may have subtle and often attractive flower color variations.

(5 cm) across; *H. atrorubens* NW Balkans; to 14 in (35 cm); leaves basal, deciduous, dark green, pedate, glabrous, central leaflet, 4–8 in (10–20 cm), lateral leaflets divided into 3–5 lobes (to 7 segments in all), coarsely serrate; inflorescence to 12 in (30 cm), flowers produced before leaves, 2–3, deep purple suffused green within, pendent, flat or shallowly saucer-shaped, 1½–2 in (4–5 cm) across; *H. foetidus* BEAR'S FOOT, DUNGWORT, STINKING HELLEBORE, STINKWORT; W and C Europe; stems to 32 in (80 cm), erect, hard, dying after fruiting; leaves cauline, coriaceous, dark green or gray-green, pedate; segments 7–10, linear to lanceolate or narrowly-elliptic, tapering finely, to 8 in (20 cm), coarsely serrate or nearly entire; inflorescence terminal, to 12 in (30 cm), branches many-flowered, flowers pendent, green, usually flushed red-purple at apex, campanulate, to ¾ × 1 in (2 × 2.5 cm), sometimes fragrant; includes Wester Flisk Group, with stems, petioles and inflorescence branches tinted red and flowers yellow-green edged maroon; *H. lividus* Majorca; to 18 in (45 cm)+; stems erect or sprawling, dying after fruiting; leaves cauline, trifoliolate, coriaceous, leaflets 4–8 in (10–20 cm), obliquely elliptic, deep green to gray-green with silvery white veins above, suffused pink-purple beneath, serrate or entire; inflorescence terminal, flowers to 10, creamy-green

suffused pink-purple, flat to bowl-shaped, 1¼–2 in (3–5 cm) across; *H. multifidus* C Balkans; leaves basal, usually deciduous, coriaceous, pedate, leaflets deep green much-divided, segments 20–45, linear to narrowly lanceolate, to 5 in (13 cm), serrate; inflorescence exceeding leaves, branched, flowers 3–8, conic to cup-shaped, nodding, green, to 1¾ in (4.5 cm) diameter, scented; *H. niger* CHRISTMAS ROSE; C Europe; to 12 in (30 cm), evergreen; leaves basal, leathery, dark green, pedate, segments 7–9, oblong or oblanceolate, to 8 in (20 cm), toothed toward apex; flowers solitary or 2–3 on stout peduncle, waxy white, tinged green at center, flushed pink, peach or dull purple with age, saucer- to bowl-shaped, to 3 in (8 cm) across; includes numerous cultivars with large and well-rounded flowers, often in very pure tones of white, but some ivory or near-yellow, others assuming rose, tawny or apricot tints, especially as the flowers age, or when the plants are grown on very lean soil in full sun; clones with variegated leaves are sometimes offered; *H. niger* × *H. lividus* leaves pedate to trifoliate, deep green with pale veins; flowers large, flat, white suffused pink-brown or pink-purple, turning dull purple with age; *H. niger* × *H.* × *sternii* very variable; leaves somewhat pedate with some of the attractive veining of *H. lividus*; flowers large, white, tinged pink-brown or green outside, coloring more deeply with age; *H.* × *nigercors* (*H. niger* × *H. argutifolius*) stem short, leafy, with terminal clusters of flowers, but some leaves and flowers basal; leaves large, gray- to dark green, semirigid, trifoliate to pedate with 7 segments, dentate or spinulose; flowers large, saucer-shaped, waxy white sometimes tinged green; *H. odorus* Balkans, S Hungary, S Romania; to 12 in (30 cm); leaves basal, coriaceous, pedate, central leaflet undivided, laterals with 3–5 lobes, elliptic or oblanceolate, to 8 in (20 cm), hairy beneath, coarsely serrate; inflorescence branched, short at first; flowers fragrant, usually 3–5, saucer- shaped, facing outward, to 2½ in (6 cm) in diameter, green to yellow; *H. orientalis* LENTEN ROSE; NE Greece, N and NE Turkey, Caucasian Russia; to 18 in (45 cm); leaves basal, coriaceous, deep green, pedate with central leaflet entire, laterals divided giving 7–9 elliptic or oblanceolate seg-

ments, to 10 in (25 cm), serrate; inflorescence to 14 in (35 cm), branched, flowers 1–4, saucer-shaped, 2½–2¾ in (6–7 cm) across, white to cream or cream tinged green, flushed purple or pink particularly below and at center, green or purple-green following fertilization; includes subsp. *abchasicus*, syn. *H. abchasicus*, with flowers suffused red-purple, often finely spotted, and subsp. *guttatus*, syn. *H. guttatus*, with white or cream flowers, spotted red-purple. Members of the *H. orientalis* complex will hybridize freely, producing plants with flowers in shades of white, pale pink, rose, plum and deep purple, often flushed with another of these tones or spotted or streaked purple-red. Hybridization also occurs between *H. orientalis* and other species. The influence of *H. purpurascens* will produce dark pruinose purple shades—for example, *H.* × *hybridus* 'Queen of the Night'. Crossing with *H. torquatus* introduces strong, glaucous, purple-black tones, such as *H.* × *hybridus* 'Pluto', wine-purple outside, green and slaty purple inside, with purple nectaries. Hybrids involving *H. odorus*, *H. cyclophyllus* or *H. multifidus* exhibit shades of yellow and green, e.g., *H.* × *hybridus* 'Citron', clear pale yellow, and *H.* × *hybridus* 'Orion', cream tinged green, purple stain in center and purple nectaries; *H. purpurascens* east central Europe; to 8 in (20 cm) at flowering; leaves basal, deciduous, coriaceous, palmate with 5 leaflets, each divided into 2–6 lanceolate segments, to 8 in (20 cm), hairy beneath, coarsely serrate; inflorescence appearing before leaves, branched or simple, flowers 2–4, nodding, cup-shaped, to 2¾ in (7 cm) across, externally purple-violet or red-purple to brown or green, glaucous, internally sometimes green; *H.* × *sternii* (*H. argutifolius* × *H. lividus*) leaves pewter to dark gray-green, obscurely veined green-white or silver, suffused purple to pale rose, entire or spiny-toothed; flowers lime green to green flushed pink or purple-brown; includes 'Ashwood Strain' with silver, jagged leaves, the compact 'Boughton Beauty', with gray-green leaves marked and sometimes tinted rose-purple and flowers and floral axis suffused rose; Blackthorn Group, with leaves leaden gray-green, conspicuously veined, and flowers

slightly flushed with pink, and 'Bulmer's Strain' with neat gray foliage, marbled as in *H. lividus*; *H. thibetanus* SW China; to 12 in (30 cm); leaves similar to *H. orientalis*, but softer-textured, more finely toothed, emerging bronze-green turning pea green; flowers nodding, bowl- to bell-shaped, to 1¼ in (3 cm) diam., palest rose with textured veins, or white with pale pink veins; *H. torquatus* Balkans; to 16 in (40 cm); leaves basal, deciduous, emerging with or after flowers, coriaceous, pedate with 10–30 narrow segments to 7 in (18 cm), tapered, dark green above, puberulent beneath, coarsely serrate; inflorescence with apical leafy bracts, flowers 1–10, nodding or facing outward, saucer- to cup-shaped, to 5¼ in (5.5 cm) across, externally dark plum purple, pruinose, internally same color or blue-green; includes 'Aeneas', with double, predominantly green flowers, with exterior shaded maroon, and 'Dido', with double flowers, with a lime green interior and dark purple exterior; *H. vesicarius* S Turkey, N Syria; to 24 in (60 cm), becoming dormant in summer; leaves basal, thin, bright green, pedate, with 3 primary divisions each to 7 in (18 cm), the leaflets lobed and toothed; inflorescence loosely cymose with leafy bracts, flowers bell-shaped, green tipped maroon or chocolate; fruit to 3 in (7.5 cm), pale yellow-green, inflated with distinct wings; *H. viridis* W Europe; to 16 in (40 cm); leaves deciduous, thin, glossy, pedate, segments 7–13, oblong-lanceolate to narrow-elliptic, to 4 in (10 cm), pubescent beneath, serrate; inflorescence emerging with leaves, long-branched; flowers 2–4, nodding, saucer-shaped or rather flat, to 2 in (5 cm) across, green.

helminthoid worm-shaped.

Helonias (from Greek *helos*, swamp, the natural habitat of the plant). Liliaceae (Melanthiaceae). N America. SWAMP PINK. 1 species, *H. bullata*, an evergreen tuberous perennial. Bright green and glossy, the leaves are to 18 in (45 cm) long, oblong to lanceolate and form a basal rosette. Starry and scented, the flowers are pink, with pale blue anthers, and appear in spring in dense, conical racemes atop scapes to 18 in (45 cm) tall. Suited to bog garden and waterside plantings. Hardy at least to 5°F (–15°C). Grow in moist, fertile, humus-rich, acidic soil in sun or light, dappled shade. Propagate by division after flowering.

Heloniopsis (from *Helonias* and Greek *opsis*, resemblance). Liliaceae (Melanthiaceae). Japan, Korea, Taiwan. 4 species, rhizomatous, perennial, evergreen herbs with oblong or lanceolate leaves in a basal rosette. In spring, one or a few flowers nod in a loose, scapose, umbellate raceme; these differ from those of *Helonias* in the larger and broader perianth segments and the purple-blue to dark violet anthers. Hardy to between 14 and 5°F (–10 and –15°C). Grow in moisture-retentive, humus-rich soil in light shade, with some protection from cold winds. Propagate by division of established clumps or by seed sown when ripe or in spring.

   H. orientalis (syn. *H. japonica*) Japan, Korea, Sakhalin Islands; leaves 3–4 in (8–10 cm), tinged red-brown toward apex; scape to 8 in (20 cm); flowers to 1½ in (4 cm) diameter, tepals pink or violet; anthers blue-violet.

helophyte a plant that grows in permanent or seasonal mud, under water or around the water's edge.

Hemerocallis (from Gk *hemere*, day, and *kallos*, beauty; the flowers only live for one day.) Liliaceae (Hemerocallidaceae). E Asia, Japan, China. DAYLILY. Some 15 species, rhizomatous, clump-forming, perennial herbs with linear, arching leaves and short-lived flowers in summer; these are produced in succession on tall, more or less branching stems, and are funnel-shaped with 6 ovate to lanceolate, spreading segments. They will grow in most fertile garden soils, including sand and heavy clay, but do best at a pH of 6–7. Abundant blooms will be produced if they are planted in soil liberally enriched with well-rotted manure. Copious water is required to maximize both the size and number of blooms, but the ground must be free-draining. If grown in waterlogged ground or rough grass, daylilies produce more foliage and fewer flowers. Most daylilies require long periods of full sun. Some species and

MODERN HEMEROCALLIS FLOWER FORMS

Circular ('Moonlight Mist')

Triangular ('Jason Salter')

Star-shaped ('Red Rum')

Spiderlike ('Cat's Cradle')

older hybrids (*H.* 'Corky', *H.* 'Golden Chimes', *H.* 'Lemon Bells') will tolerate part shade, but the palest, pastel forms, especially pink-toned cultivars, may not open fully unless exposed to long periods of strong sunlight. Some dark red and deep purple cultivars benefit from part shade in tropical and subtropical climates. Unless naturalized, plants should be lifted and divided every three years to maintain vigor and promote flowering. Divide cultivars in spring, or after flowering. Most species, except some forms of *H. fulva*, produce fertile seed, although the seedlings may not resemble the parent.

   Young foliage is particularly susceptible to slug and snail damage, but daylilies are also prone to attack by the gall midge, which is indicated by the presence of small white maggots in the flower bud, and the daylily aphid, which leaves white flecks on the foliage in spring. Daylilies can be affected by 'spring sickness', which rots the new inner leaves. This is more likely to be a problem in temperate climates and will prevent flowering for a least a year. It is seldom a problem where continental winters are the norm. Crown rot is also

a problem in temperate regions. It is encouraged by the ground's heaving at times of alternate freezing and thawing. It can be prevented by thick winter mulching.

   Daylilies hybridize readily and some 20,000 cultivars are now registered with the International Registration Authority; this figure is being increased by some 400–800 each year. The American Hemerocallis Society has categorized daylily cultivars in several useful ways. Plants are classed as evergreen, semievergreen or dormant. Evergreen types prefer temperatures above –10°F (–23°C); many will not thrive in cold climates, especially if there is no snow cover. Dormant types are suited to cooler regions and may not perform well in warmer climates. semievergreen sorts are best suited to temperate climates but some can do well in hotter or colder regions. Some evergreens will acclimatize to colder conditions as they mature. It is a matter of trial and error. Leaves vary from graceful and grasslike (*H. minor*) to coarse and straplike (*H. fulva*) and range from 12 in (30 cm) (*H.* 'Eenie Weenie') to 5 ft (1.5 m) (*H. altissima*).

Mature foliage color ranges from blue-green to mid- or dark green, sometimes yellowish, although excessive yellowness can denote an unhealthy plant. A few cultivars have leaves with unstable longitudinal variegation. Daylilies are further categorized according to height of flower stems which, for garden value, should be proportional to height of leaf-mound. Dwarf: below 12 in (30 cm); low: 12–24 in (30–60 cm); medium: 24–36 in (60–90 cm); tall: over 3¼ ft (1 m). Daylilies are also categorized by flower size, expressed as a diameter. Miniature: less than 3 in (7.5 cm); small-flowered: 3–4½ in (7.5–11.5 cm); large-flowered: over 4½ in (11.5 cm). They are further classified by flower color and pattern as selfs, blends, polychrome, bi-tone, reverse bi-tone, bicolor, reverse bicolor, banded, eye-zoned, edged, haloed, tipped or watermarked. Throat and eye color can be an attractive contrast. The perianth consists of six segments arranged in threes, the outer, narrower sepals lying below the petals. The midribs of the segments may differ in color from the segments; the stamens may also differ in color from the segments, giving added garden value. Flowers of heaviest substance are found in tetraploid cultivars, where the colors are usually brighter and the blooms more prolific. Some of the species' characteristic gracefulness can be lost in tetraploid cultivars. Bloom texture varies from smooth, satiny to velvety and creped, and may have an overlay known as diamond dusting. The edges may be ruffled. Natural flower form is trumpet-shaped but the flowers of modern hybrids may be circular, triangular, star-shaped, flat or spiderlike. Those with more than six segments are known as doubles or camellia forms. Flower color in the species ranges from lemon-chrome to tawny-orange. Hybridizers have raised cultivars in almost every color except true blue and pure white, although some daylilies appear virtually white if exposed to strong sunlight. All daylilies have a yellow undertone to a greater or lesser degree and the color range usually encountered runs from pale citron yellow to glowing orange and gold overlaid with darkest blood red. Heavy rain can cause the pigment to scatter in some rich red cultivars.

Most species are diurnal. Nocturnal species (e.g., *H. citrina*) open their flowers in late afternoon and remain open all night. *H. lilioasphodelus* is an extended bloomer, the flower sometimes remaining open up to 16 hours. Both diurnal and nocturnal types can also have this characteristic. *H. lilioasphodelus* and *H. citrina* are very strongly fragrant, a characteristic inherited by some of their offspring. The season of blooming is categorized as extra early, early, early-midseason, midseason, late-midseason, late and very late. Some are remontant, either flowering early and repeating in fall, or flowering over a quick succession of bloom periods. Repeat blooming is often influenced by growing conditions.

H. citrina China; flowering stems erect, branched above, taller than foliage; flowers 20–65, 3½–4¾ in (9–12 cm), fragrant, pale lemon, tinged brown beneath, opening at night, perianth tube to 1½ in (4 cm), tepals narrow; *H. fulva* (origin uncertain, perhaps Japan or China; flowering stems taller than foliage, forked; flowers 10–20, 2¾–4 in (7–10 cm), widely funnelform, rusty orange-red, usually with darker median zones and stripes, perianth tube ¾–2 in (2–5 cm); *H. lilioasphodelus* (syn. *H. flava*) flowering stems branched above, weak, ascending, taller than foliage; flowers 8–12, 2¾–3 in (7–8 cm), fragrant, shortly funnelform, yellow, perianth tube to 1 in (2.5 cm); *H. minor* (Japan, China; flowering stems taller than foliage, forked or shortly branched above; flowers 2–5, 2–2¾ in (5–7 cm), shortly funnelform, lemon yellow, tinged brown outside, tepals narrow, perianth tube less than ¾ in (2 cm).

hemicryptophyte a plant whose latent buds are located at or just above the soil surface, and which is shallow rooted and poorly anchored.

Hemigraphis (from Greek *hemi*, half, and *graphis*, brush—a reference to the hairy outer filaments). Acanthaceae. Tropical Asia. Some 90 species, annual or perennial herbs and subshrubs, usually with toothed or crenate leaves. Slender and 5-lobed, the tubular, usually white flowers appear intermittently in terminal spikes with conspicuous bracts. Suited to hanging baskets,

terrariums, and as groundcover in a tropical greenhouse or in gardens in the humid tropics and subtropics. Grow in bright filtered or indirect light. Otherwise cultivate as for *Eranthemum*.

H. alternata (syn. *H. colorata*) RED FLAME IVY, RED IVY; India, Java; evergreen, downy, prostate perennial herb; leaves to 3½ in (9 cm), cordate to ovate, crenate, bullate, silver-gray above, flushed purple beneath; *H. repanda* Malaysia; evergreen, prostrate, perennial herb, more or less hairless, flushed red or maroon; leaves to 2 in (5 cm), linear to lanceolate, bluntly toothed to lobed, satiny leaden-gray, deeply flushed red or purple.

hen and chickens see *malformations*.

Hepatica (from Greek *hepar*, liver: the leaves were thought to resemble the liver in outline and color and thus, by the doctrine of signatures, to cure liver disease). Ranunculaceae. Northern Temperate Regions. Some 10 species, small perennials. The leaves are basal, 3–5-lobed, entire to crenately toothed and often dull gray-green flushed purple, particularly beneath and during dormant season, when they usually persist. Solitary, scapose flowers appear before the new growth in spring. A calyx-like involucre of three reduced leaves subtends a bowl-shaped flower of 5–12 petaloid sepals. Grow in cool, moist, but well-drained humus-rich soil in part shade. Apply a mulch of organic matter in fall or late spring; annual dressings of slow-release fertilizer will improve flowering. Propagate by division in late spring or fall. Fresh seed sown in early summer will germinate the following spring.

H. × *media* (*H. transsilvanica* × *H. nobilis*; intermediate between parents; includes 'Ballardii', with deep blue flowers and many sepals, and 'Millstream Merlin', with semidouble, deep blue flowers; *H. nobilis* (syn. *H. triloba*) Europe; leaf lobes 3, ovate, tinged purple and hairy beneath, petioles 2–6 in (5–15 cm); flowers ⅝–1 in (1.5–2.5 cm) in diameter, blue-purple to white or pink; *H. transsilvanica* (syn. *H. angulosa*) Romania; similar to *H. nobilis* but leaf lobes crenately toothed, flowers 1–1¾ in (2.5–4.5 cm) in diameter, pale blue or opal-white, rarely tinted pink.

H

herb (1) a plant grown for its medicinal or flavoring properties, or for its scented foliage (see *herbs*). The term *pot herb* refers to those grown for culinary purposes (2) strictly, a plant without persistent stems above ground, often confined to perennials with annual stems or leaves arising from a persistent subterranean stem or rootstock. More generally, any nonwoody plant.

herbaceous (1) describing a plant without persistent stems above ground; (2) pertaining to soft green leaves.

herbaceous border a garden planting primarily devoted to the cultivation of herbaceous perennials. It was first introduced in the early 1800s and significantly developed around the end of the century under the influence of Gertrude Jekyll and William Robinson, when it became an essential feature of British gardens. Today, herbaceous perennials are often grown with annuals and bedding plants, bulbs and shrubs, in what is correctly referred to as a mixed border.

herbal originally, a book describing plants in general; now referring to one that covers only plants grown for medicinal or culinary purposes.

herbarium a collection of preserved plant specimens used for identification and classification, and typically maintained in a botanic garden. Originally, a herbarium was a small garden or lawn; it later became synonymous with an arbor.

herber see *arbor*.

Herbertia (for Dr. William Herbert [1778–1847] a dean of Manchester and expert on bulbous plants). Iridaceae. Temperate S America. 6 species of perennial cormous herbs, allied to *Tigridia* and bearing 1–2 short-lived flowers, each composed of 6 segments, the 3 outer broadly triangular to ovate and spreading or reflexed, and the 3 inner segments, smaller rounded and erect. In zones that are frost-free or almost so, they are suited to the warm and well-drained sunny border; where temperatures only occasionally fall to about 23°F (−5°C), they can be

grown outside with a deep protective mulch of bracken litter. Otherwise, cultivate as for *Homeria*.

H. amoena Argentina, Uruguay; scapes to 12 in (30 cm), flowers violet, outer perianth segments to ¾ in (2 cm); *H. lahue* S Chile, Argentina; scape 3–6 in (8–15 cm); outer perianth segments ½–⅝ in (1–1.5 cm), violet stained blue near base, inner perianth segments violet; *H. pulchella* southern S America to S Brazil; scape 3–6 in (8–15 cm); outer perianth segments 1–1¹⁄₈ in (2.5–2.8 cm), blue to lilac or purple tinted pink, often with a central white stripe, claw white and bearded, flecked or flushed violet, inner segments mauve.

herbicide a chemical substance that destroys plants. Herbicides are used especially to control those plants regarded as weeds and are usually applied in spray or granular form.

herbs plants grown primarily for their culinary or medicinal properties or aromatic foliage, and often planted in combination for ornamental effect.

A herb garden can be an attractive garden feature, with simple designs being the most effective, for example, those based upon circles, squares or rectangles surrounding a central feature, such as a statue, sundial, fountain or beehive. Cultivation in raised beds can be both practical and decorative, and for further labor-saving, herbs may be grown successfully in gravel. When planted in a border in groups of three or five individual plants herbs make an effective contribution of contrasting color, texture and leaf shape. Herbs are ideal for patios, balconies, window boxes, troughs and other containers; those especially suitable for containers include basil (*Ocimum basilicum*), borage (*Borago officinalis*), chamomile (*Chamaemelum nobile*), lemon balm (*Melissa officinalis*), rosemary (*Rosmarinus officinalis*), rue (*Ruta graveolens*), sage (*Salvia officinalis*), great burnet (*Sanguisorba officinalis*), tarragon (*Artemisia dracunculus*), parsley (*Petroselinum crispum*), mint (*Mentha* species), thyme (*Thymus* species), chives (*Allium schoenoprasum*) and marjoram (*Origanum* species).

Herbs often produce a better essential oil when grown in poor or dry soil, and it is best to mulch annually with garden compost, rather than to apply manures or fertilizers.

Herbs must be harvested when the oils are at their most concentrated, usually just as the flowers reach maturity. Dry, clean material should be selected. Plants with roots containing essential oils should be harvested during early fall, then rubbed or washed free of soil and dried off. Examples include horseradish (*Armoracia rusticana*), licorice (*Glycyrrhiza glabra*), and orris (*Iris florentina*). For seed crops, such as anise (*Pimpinella anisum*), caraway (*Carum carvi*) and coriander (*Coriandrum sativum*), enfold the seed heads in paper bags and suspend these in a dry, warm,

Golden leaves add to ornamental value

Melissa officinalis 'Aurea'

shaded place for at least three weeks to facilitate shedding.

Drying may be carried out in a constantly warm airing cupboard, with the herbs spread out on trays to allow air to circulate and turned occasionally. Alternatively, the herbs can be dried on racks in an oven at a temperature of not more than 90°F (32°C); for really fast drying, they may be heated in small quantities in a microwave oven for about one-and-a-half minutes. Some herbs, such as parsley (*Petroselinum crispum*), dill (*Anethum graveolens*) and fennel (*Foeniculum vulgare*), do not dry well and are better frozen without blanching soon after picking.

Hermannia (for Paul Hermann [d. 1695], German botanist and professor of Botany at Leiden). Sterculiaceae. Tropical and South Africa. HONEYBELLS. Over 100 species, herbs and subshrubs, generally hairy. Solitary or in cymes, the flowers are campanulate to rounded and consist of five obovate to oblong petals, their bases often narrowed into a claw and more or less spirally twisted. Suited to sunny banks and rock gardens in essentially frost-free Mediterranean-type climates. In cooler zones, grow *Hermannia* in the cool to intermediate greenhouse. Plant in sun, with some shade during the hottest parts of the day, in well-drained soil. Under glass, water moderately when in growth, less at other times, and maintain a minimum temperature of 45–50°F (7–10°C) during winter. Repot and prune leggy specimens before growth resumes in late winter/early spring. Propagate by seed or softwood cuttings in spring. *H. incana* (syn. *H. candicans*) South Africa; gray-hairy perennial herb to 6½ ft (2 m); flowers to ¾ in (2 cm) diam., honey-scented, yellow, petals broadly rounded or truncate, hairy.

hermaphroditic bisexual, having both pistils and stamens in the same flower.

Hermodactylus (variant of old Greek name for *Colchicum*, from *Hermes*, Mercury, and *dactylos*, finger). Iridaceae. S Europe, from France through the Balkans, to Greece, Turkey, and Israel. 1 species, *H. tuberosus*, (syn. *Iris tuberosa*), MOURNING WIDOW IRIS, a winter- to spring-flowering tuberous-rooted perennial herb. It grows to 12 in (30 cm) and resembles a large Reticulata iris. The flowers are scented, to 2 in (5 cm) diameter, and pale olive to apple green with velvety brown-black falls. It is undemanding in cultivation, well-suited to dry chalky soil, and will form large clumps where conditions suit. Although hardy to 5°F (−15°C), *Hermodactylus* is sometimes given cold greenhouse protection in regions where early spring weather may spoil the flowers. Grow in sun in well-drained soil. The flowers last fairly well when cut and kept in a cool room. Propagate by division during late summer.

Hesperaloe (from Greek *hesperos*, western, and *Aloe*, from the plant's habitat and appearance). Agavaceae. SW US, Mexico. 3 species, evergreen perennial herbs, forming grassy clumps of linear leaves with white marginal fibers. Short-lived, the narrowly campanulate flowers are carried in sparsely branched racemes in summer and fall. Cultivate as for *Nolina*. *H. parviflora* (syn. *H. yuccifolia*) SW Texas; leaves to 4¼ ft (1.3 m), leathery, margins with fine white threads; panicle slender, to 4 ft (1.2 m); flowers dark to light red, golden yellow within, not opening fully; 'Rubra': flowers bright red.

Hesperantha (from Greek *hespera*, evening, and *anthos*, flower). Iridaceae. sub-Saharan Africa, with most species in South Africa. 55 species, cormous perennial herbs with linear leaves and spikes of starry to saucer-shaped flowers opening after dusk in spring and summer. Cultivate as for *Ixia*. *H. cucullata* (syn. *H. buhrii*) South Africa; to 12 in (30 cm); flowers scented, to 1½ in (4 cm) diameter, white with outer tepals stained red.

hesperidium a berry, pulpy within with a tough rind, for example the fruits of *Citrus*.

Hesperis (from Greek *hespera*, evening, when the flowers are most fragrant). Cruciferae. Europe, N and W Asia. 60 species, biennial or perennial, erect herbs with lax racemes of 4-petalled flowers in late spring and summer—these are especially fragrant in the evening. A plant for the herbaceous border and wild garden. It tends to become woody, tired and less floriferous with age: new stock should be propagated every 2–3 years. Double-flowered cultivars are especially good for cutting. Hardy to at least 5°F (−15°C). Plant in moist but well-drained neutral to alkaline soil, in full sun or light shade. Propagate cultivars from basal cuttings in spring. Sow seed *in situ* in fall or spring; the white-flowered cultivars come approximately true, some individuals being tinted pale pink. *H. matronalis* DAME'S VIOLET, SWEET ROCKET, WILD PHLOX; S Europe to Siberia; biennial or perennial, 24–39 in (60–100 cm); flowers scented, especially at evening, petals ½–¾ in (1–2 cm), white to lilac; includes cultivars with single and double flowers in shades of white, pink, rose, purple and lilac.

Hesperocallis (from Greek *hesperos*, western, and *kallos*, beauty). Liliaceae (Agavaceae). SW US (S California, W Arizona). 1 species, *H. undulata*, the DESERT LILY, a bulbous perennial herb to 12 in (30 cm) tall, with wavy-edged linear leaves and terminal racemes of fragrant, funnelform flowers, to 2¾ in (7 cm) long and white striped with green. Native to desert and semidesert, where the bulbs are often found at great depth, *Hesperocallis* is especially useful for dry, frost-free gardens. In cool temperate zones, it may be grown in the cool greenhouse or conservatory. Plant in a sandy and gritty medium. Position in full sun with a dry, buoyant atmosphere. Water moderately when in growth, but keep dry when dormant. Propagate by seed and offsets.

hessian a strong, coarse cloth, also known as burlap, used in gardens to insulate frames or cloches from frost, to form windbreaks and to wrap root balls after lifting trees or shrubs.

Heterocentron (from Greek *heteros*, different or variable, and *kentron*, spur). Melastomataceae. C and S America. Some 27 species, tender perennial herbs and low-growing shrubs with 4-petalled, bowl-shaped flowers borne singly or in small panicles from late summer to winter. In frost-free regions, grow in sun in fertile and well-drained soil. Under glass, admit full sun and use a medium-fertility loam-based mix. Water plentifully and feed weekly with dilute liquid fertilizer when in full growth; maintain a winter minimum temperature of 45°F (7°C). Propagate by seed, by softwood or stem tip cuttings and by division. *H. elegans* SPANISH SHAWL; Mexico, Guatemala, Honduras; carpet-forming subshrub; flowers solitary; petals to 1 in (2.5 cm), magenta to mauve.

heteroecious requiring two unrelated plant hosts in order to complete a life cycle, as in many rust fungi; cf. *autoecious*.

heterogamous (1) bearing two types of flower, as in the ray and disk florets of Compositae; (2) with sexual organs abnormally arranged or developed, or with the sexual function transferred from flowers of one sex to another.

Heteromeles (from Greek *heteros*, different, and *mela*, the apple tree). Rosaceae. US (California). CHRISTMAS BERRY, TOLLON. 1 species, *H. salicifolia* (syn. *Photinia arbutifolia*), an evergreen, treelike shrub to 30 ft (9 m) tall. To 4 in (10 cm) long, the leathery leaves are lanceolate to obovate, thick-textured and sharply toothed. Small and 5-petalled, the flowers are white and borne in large, flattened panicles in summer. They give rise to bright-red, berrylike fruit. Its general requirements are as for *Photinia*, but with a warm and sheltered site if grown where temperatures drop below 20°F (–7°C).

heteromorphic describing a plant that assumes different forms or shapes at different stages in its life history cf. *polymorphic*.

heterophyllous a plant bearing two or more different forms of leaf on the same plant.

heterosis the improvement in vigor, fertility or yield potential exhibited by F1 hybrids. It is also known as hybrid vigor.

heterosporous producing spores of two sexes, which develop into male and female gametophytes.

heterostylous of species whose flowers differ in the existence or number of styles.

heterostyly condition in which the styles and stamens of flowers are of different lengths in individual plants of the same species. Heterostyly is a natural adaptation to ensure cross-pollination, found, for example, in species of *Primula* and *Linum*. In dimorphic heterostyly, there are two types of flower: 'thrum-eyed', where the style is short and the stamens long, and 'pin-eyed', where the opposite condition exists. In some plants, such as *Oxalis* and *Lythrum*

Heterostyly in primrose

salicaria, trimorphic heterostyly exists, with three variations of style and stamen length.

heterozygous describing a plant that bears both dominant and recessive genetic components for a particular character, giving rise to a hybrid. It is used of cross-pollinated species or cultivars; cf. *homozygous*.

Heuchera (for Johann Heinrich Heucher [1677–1747], a professor of medicine at Wittenberg). Saxifragaceae. N America. CORAL FLOWER, ALUM ROOT. Some 55 species, evergreen perennial herbs with a semi-woody rootstock and basal clumps of slender-stalked rounded to heart-shaped leaves. Small, bell-shaped flowers are produced in spirelike panicles or racemes in spring and summer. Evergreen groundcover for the woodland garden and damp, sunny, border edges, valued for foliage and graceful flowering spikes in subtle shades of coral pink and green. *H.* 'Palace Purple Select' is one of the most striking small herbaceous perennials: its dark maroon foliage and delicate white flowers commend it as a contrast plant for mixed borders, preferably in slightly damp soil; it has also been used in bedding schemes, propagated from seed in the year prior to display. A new generation of smaller cultivars offers still more exciting foliage color—for example, *H.* 'Stormy Seas', with cloudy pewter leaves, shot with silver and ruby, or the satiny, liver red *H.* 'Cascade Dawn', a marvelous companion for *Millium effusum* 'Aureum'. Plant in well-drained but moisture-retentive soil, in sun or part shade, with the crowns just above soil level. Mulch well against soil heave in areas with cold winters. Reduce and replant or mulch if the crowns lift in subsequent years. Propagate in fall by

division or from seed in spring.

H. × *brizoides* (a range of hybrids with *H. sanguinea* as part of the parentage; the precise application of this name is obscure, but it is also likely to embrace hybrids involving *H. micrantha* and *H. americana*; H. *cylindrica* (flowers cream, tinged green or red; includes 'Greenfinch', vigorous with sulfur-green flowers, 'Hyperion', with coral pink flowers on 2½ in (6 cm) spikes, 'Siskiyou Mountains', dwarf with scalloped leaves and cream flowers in a 4 in (10 cm) raceme; H. *micrantha* stem and petioles white-pilose at base, leaves shallowly lobed; often assigned to this species but likely to be of hybrid origin is the popular *H.* 'Palace Purple Select', all parts of which are deep glossy purple-bronze except for its small white flowers; H. *sanguinea* New Mexico, Arizona; to 24 in (60 cm); leaves ¾–2¼ in (2–5.5 cm), broadly reniform to ovate, near pentagonal in outline, glandular, veins hairy beneath; flowers bright red, ¼–½ in (6–12 mm); includes 'Alba', with white flowers, 'Maxima', with burgundy flowers, 'Splendens', with rich red flowers, 'Variegata', with variegated leaves, and 'Virginalis', with white flowers. Other notable *Heuchera* hybrids are Bressingham Hybrids, with graceful inflorescences and flowers ranging in color from pink through rose, carmine and red with some whites, 'Green Ivory', with a robust inflorescence and green and white flowers, 'Scintillation', with silver marbled leaves and flowers tipped vivid pink, 'Snowflake', to 24 in (60 cm) with white flowers in a lax panicle, and 'Taff's Joy', with leaves variegated cream and tinted pink.

× **Heucherella** (*Heuchera* × *Tiarella*.) Saxifragaceae. Garden origin. Evergreen, perennial herbs to 18 in (45 cm) tall with rounded leaves to 5 in (13 cm) in diameter, the margins shallowly lobed and toothed, the surfaces bristly-hairy and light green (mottled brown when young, becoming dark green with age and turning bronze in fall). In spring and summer, small pink flowers are carried in loose, slender panicles to 16 in (40 cm) tall. Cultivate as for *Heuchera*. Propagate by division.
× *H. alba*. (*Heuchera* × *brizoides* × *Tiarella wherryi*) close to × *H. tiarelloides*, but lacks stolons and is normally white-

flowered; includes 'Bridget Bloom', with shell pink flowers in dense spikes); × *H. tiarelloides* (*Heuchera* × *brizoides* × *Tiarella cordifolia*; stoloniferous; leaves cordate to suborbicular, coarsely toothed and lobed, crenate; scapes tinted brown, flowers pink.

× **Hibanobambusa** (Bamboo of Mount Hiba). Gramineae. Japan. 1 species. See *bamboos*.

Hibbertia (for George Hibbert [d. 1838], a patron of botany). Dilleniaceae. Madagascar, Australasia, Polynesia. BUTTON FLOWER, GUINEA GOLD VINE. Some 125 species, evergreen shrubs, many of them climbers. Chiefly produced in summer, the flowers are large, solitary and terminal, consisting of five, broad and spreading petals and numerous stamens. Given the shelter of a warm south- or southwest-facing wall, the following may tolerate light and short-lived frosts. In cooler regions, grow in the cool greenhouse or conservatory. Plant in sun or part shade. Provide support. Under glass, admit bright filtered light, but provide shade from the hottest summer sun. Water plentifully and feed fortnightly when in full growth, reducing water as light levels and temperatures fall. Maintain a minimum winter temperature of 50°F (10°C). Prune to thin out congested growth in early spring. Propagate by semiripe cuttings in a sandy propagating mix, or by layers. *H. scandens* SNAKE VINE, GOLD GUINEA PLANT; Australia; shrub to 40 ft (12 m), procumbent or twining; leaves 2–4 in (5–10 cm), obovate to lanceolate, silky-hairy; flowers to 2 in (5 cm) diameter, malodorous, petals golden yellow, obovate to triangular, with ragged tips.

hibernaculum the winter-resting body of some plants; usually a budlike arrangement of reduced leaves.

Hibiscus (Greek name for mallow). Malvaceae. Warm temperate, subtropical and tropical regions. MALLOW, ROSE MALLOW, GIANT MALLOW. About 220 species, annual or perennial herbs, shrubs, subshrubs and trees. Bowl- to funnel-shaped, the showy flowers consist of five, more or less obovate petals with, at their center, a long, and pro-

truding staminal column. The hardiest here include *H. sinosyriacus*, tolerant of temperatures to 5°F (–15°C), and *H. syriacus*, with many exceptional cultivars, most tolerating cold to –4°F (–20°C). *H. mutabilis* is frost tender, but will regenerate from the woody base if cut back by light frost. In subtropical and warm temperate, essentially frost-free zones, *H. rosa-sinensis* is used for hedging and screening and, as with *H. schizopetalus*, makes a fine specimen for large containers. Species from moist habitats, such as *H. coccineus* are suited to waterside plantings. *H. moscheutos* is a vigorous perennial for similar situations where winter temperatures do not fall much below 23°F (–5°C). Several are grown as frost-tender annuals in cool temperate regions, including *H. acetosella* and *H. sabdariffa*. *H. trionum* has naturalized as a weed in parts of North America. The F1 hybrids *H.* Southern Belle Group and 'Dixie Belle' are treated as annuals but may survive several degrees of frost, especially if protected with bracken litter.

Grow hardy species in well-drained, humus-rich, fertile soil in full sun, with mulch protection at the roots and the shelter of a warm south-facing wall in zones at the limits of hardiness. Little regular pruning is necessary; long shoots may be tipped back immediately after flowering and overgrown specimens may be cut hard back and thinned out in spring. Grow tender species in a medium- to high-fertility loam-based mix or soilless medium. Water plentifully when in growth and, unless high winter temperatures of about 61°F (16°C) can be maintained, reduce water in winter to keep almost dry until growth resumes in spring. Maintain a minimum temperature of 45–50°F (7–10°C) for *H. rosa-sinensis*, *H. mutabilis* and *H. coccineus*; tropical species such as *H. schizopetalus* need higher temperatures 61°F (16°C). Ventilate at 68°F (20°C) and above. Tip prune young plants to encourage bushiness, and cut hard back in spring.

distinctive staminal column

Hibiscus rosa-sinensis

Propagate annuals from seed sown under glass in early spring or *in situ* in late spring. Propagate shrubs by greenwood or semiripe cuttings in a shaded case with bottom heat, or by simple layering in midsummer/early fall. Increase perennials by division.

H. acetosella E and C Africa; annual or woody-based perennial herb to 5 ft (1.5 m), usually smooth, tinted red; leaves unlobed or 3- or 5-lobed; flowers solitary, petals purple-red or yellow, deep purple at base; includes 'Red Shield' with brilliant maroon leaves; *H.* × *archeri.* (*H. rosa-sinensis* × *H. schizopetalus*); similar to *H. rosa-sinensis*, but leaves more coarsely toothed, petals red, laciniate or crenate; *H. cannabinus* INDIAN HEMP, BIMIL, DECCAN HEMP; origin unknown, probably East Indies; annual or short-lived woody-based perennial to 11½ ft (3.5 m); leaves 3-, 5-, or 7-lobed; flowers axillary, forming racemes, petals 1½–3 in (4–8 cm), pale yellow or less commonly pale purple, with red-purple spot at the base; *H. coccineus* (SE US; tall, hemplike, woody based, perennial herb to 10 ft (3 m); leaves glaucous, palmately lobed; flowers solitary, petals to 3 in (8 cm), deep red; *H. moscheutos* (COMMON ROSE MALLOW, SWAMP ROSE MALLOW; S US; robust, woody-based perennial herb to 8 ft (2.5 m); leaves 3–9 in (8–22 cm), broadly ovate to lanceolate, unlobed or 3- or 5-lobed, downy; flowers solitary, petals 3–4 in (8–10 cm), white, pink, rose, base sometimes banded crimson, or petals wholly or edged crimson; *H. mutabilis* COTTON ROSE, CONFEDERATE ROSE MALLOW; China; shrub to 10 ft (3 m) or small tree to 16 ft (5 m); leaves 3–6½ in (8–17 cm), palmately 3-, 5- or 7-lobed, hairy beneath; flowers solitary or in clusters, petals 2–2¾ in (5–7 cm), white, pink or scarlet, with darker base; *H. rosa-sinensis* CHINESE HIBISCUS, HAWAIIAN HIBISCUS, ROSE-OF-CHINA, CHINA ROSE, SHOE BLACK; probably Asian tropics; shrub to 8 ft (2.5 m) or tree to 16 ft (5 m), sparsely puberulent to glabrate; leaves to 6 in (15 cm), ovate to broadly lanceolate, toothed; flowers solitary, petals 2½–4¾ in (6–12 cm), very variable in color, but commonly red to deep red, darker toward the base. Cultivars selected for foliage include: 'Cooperi', leaves narrowly lanceolate, olive green marbled red, pink and white, flowers rose; 'Lateritia Variegata', leaves pointed and irregularly lobed, heavily variegated off-white, flowers gold; 'Snow Queen', leaves broadly ovate, marbled white, and gray-green. Those selected for flower color and form include 'Aurora', flowers, pom-pon shape, blushing pink; 'Bridal Veil', flowers large, single, crêpe-textured, pure white; 'Crown of Bohemia', flowers fully double, gold with flaming orange throat; 'Fiesta', flowers large, single, crinkled, deep apricot orange with pink-red eye; 'Kissed', petals reflexed, vivid red; 'Percy Lancaster', flowers single, petals narrow, palest pink washed apricot, eye russet; 'Ruby Brown', flowers single, large, brown tinted orange with dark red throat; 'Sunny Delight', flowers single, large, brilliant yellow, throat white; H. *sabdariffa* ROSELLE, JAMAICA SORREL, RED SORREL, SORREL; Old World tropics, widely cultivated; annual or robust, woody-based perennial herb or subshrub to 8 ft (2.5 m); leaves 3–6 in (8–15 cm), ovate, undivided or palmately 3- or 5-divided; flowers solitary or in short leafy raceme; petals 1½–2 in (4–5 cm), light yellow, purple-red at base; H. *schizopetalus* JAPANESE HIBISCUS, JAPANESE LANTERN; Kenya, Tanzania and N Mozambique; shrub to 10 ft (3 m); leaves to 4¾ in (12 cm), ovate, serrate; flowers on long slender pedicels; petals to 2¾ in (7 cm), deeply and irregularly laciniate, pink or red; staminal column long-exserted; H. *sinosyriacus* C China; similar to H. *syriacus*, but leaves large; includes 'Autumn Surprise', flowers white, base feathered cherry, 'Lilac Queen', flowers white, lightly tinted mauve, base clear burgundy, profuse, 'Red Center', stem with silver sheen when mature, flowers white, center red, 'Ruby Glow', flowers white, base clear burgundy; H. *syriacus* Old World, widely cultivated; shrub or small tree to 10 ft (3 m); leaves 1¼–2¾ in (3–7 cm), 3-lobed, coarsely toothed; flowers solitary or paired, petals 1½–2¾ in (3.5–7 cm), white, red-

purple or blue-lavender, with rose base. Cultivars selected for foliage include 'Meehanii': habit low, leaves edged yellow, flowers single, lavender; 'Purpureus Variegatus': leaves variegated white. Those selected for flower color and form include 'Admiral Dewey': flowers double, wide, snow white, abundant; 'Ardens', habit broad, flowers densely double, purple tinted blue; 'Coelestis': pale violet, rose at base, single; 'Diana': habit upright, leaves trilobed, flowers single, white, very wide, crinkled edges, profuse; 'Duc de Brabant': deep rosy purple, double; 'Hamabo': flowers single, light pink, crimson markings and eye; 'Hélène': flowers single, large, white with dark red edge and surrounding veins, abundant; 'Jeanne d'Arc': white, semidouble; 'Lady Stanley': white suffused shell pink, maroon at base, semidouble; 'Lucy': flowers double red; 'Monstrosus': white with maroon eye, single; 'Oiseau Bleu ('Blue Bird'): habit erect, flowers wide, very large, sky blue with small red eye; 'Snowdrift': white, large, single; 'Violet Clair Double': vinous purple, red-purple at center, double; 'William R. Smith': pure white, single, very large; 'Woodbridge': flowers single, large, rich pink to carmine at center; H. *trionum* FLOWER-OF-AN-HOUR, BLADDER KETMIA; arid Old World tropics; erect or ascending hispid annual or short-lived perennial herb to 4 ft (1.2 m); leaves to 2¾ in (7 cm), deeply 3- or 5-lobed or -parted, incised or entire; flowers solitary, calyx with purple veins, becoming inflated, petals to 1½ in (4 cm), white, cream or yellow, with red base.

Hieracium (from the classical Greek name *hierakion*, used for a range of yellow-flowered Compositae). Compositae. Europe, to N and W Asia, NW Africa and N America HAWKWEED. Some 10,000 species, perennial, more or less hairy herbs, with milky sap. The leaves are arranged in basal rosettes or on the flowering stems. Yellow, daisy-like flower heads are carried in long-stalked and slender-branched panicles in spring and summer. The following are hardy to −10°F (−23°C) and suitable for the large rock garden or the foreground of well-drained borders.

Easily grown in low-fertility, gritty neutral or alkaline soil in sun. Propagate by seed, alternatively by division.

H. *lanatum* SE France, W Switzerland, NW Italy; 4–6 in (10–15 cm); leaves covered with dense, white, woolly hairs, to 4 in (10 cm), elliptic to lanceolate; H. *maculatum* W and C Europe, only sporadically elsewhere; 8–32 in (20–80 cm); leaves spotted or blotched brown-purple, to 1¾ in (4.5 cm), ovate to lanceolate.

hilum the scar on a seed at the point at which the funicle was attached.

scar at attachment point

Hilum

hip, hep the fleshy developed floral cup, with enclosed achenes, that forms the fruit of a rose.

Hippeastrum (from Greek *hippeus*, a rider, and *astron*, a star; reference unclear). Amaryllidaceae. Americas. AMARYLLIS; KNIGHT'S STAR LILY. About 80 species, bulbous perennial herbs with strap-shaped leaves and flowers atop a hollow scape. These consist of a tubular to funnelform perianth tube often, dilating at the throat, and six, spreading lobes, the inner 3 sometimes narrower than the others.

Grow under glass in bright filtered light, in a free-draining, loam-based mix of medium-fertility (e.g., 3:1:1 loam, leaf mold, sharp sand). Plant firmly with the neck and shoulders of the bulb above soil level. Winter-flowering species and cultivars should be planted in late summer/early fall, and summer-flowering species in early spring. Maintain a minimum temperature of 55–61°F (13–16°C) and water sparingly until growth commences; at this point, temperatures may be increased to 61–64°F (16–18°C) for earlier flowers, although flowering is prolonged at lower temperatures. When in active growth, water plentifully, syringe the leaves with soft water, and feed weekly with a dilute liquid fertilizer. Leaves continue their development after flowering, and feeding and watering should be continued until growth ceases and leaves yellow—usually by midsummer. Reduce water gradually and withhold completely when dormant, keeping bulbs dry and warm (not below 41–45°F/5–7°C) until growth resumes. *Hippeastrum* dislikes root disturbance: repot only once every three of four years, before the new cycle of growth begins.

Propagate by offsets, and by seed sown when ripe at 61–64°F (16–18°C); if grown on without dry rest during their first year, seedlings mature and flower more quickly, and may flower in their second or third year from sowing. Red spot disease, caused by the fungus *Stagonospora curtisii*, produces watery red lesions on the bulbs, leaves and flower stalks, while red scabs form on the outer scales of the bulbs. The emerging foliage and flower buds may be sprayed with a copper-based or dithiocarbamate fungicide.

H. aulicum LILY OF THE PALACE; Brazil, Paraguay; flowers usually 2, crimson, to 6 in (15 cm), throat green, lobes obovate, pointed, the 2 upper inner ones much broader than the others; H. *papilio* S Brazil; flowers 2, pale green streaked and stained dark red, perianth segments oblanceolate, to 5½ × 2 in (14 × 5 cm; H. *reginae* MEXICAN LILY; Mexico to Peru and Brazil, West Indies, W Africa; flowers 2–4, drooping red, perianth tube to 1 in (2.5 cm), lobes to 5 in (13 cm), obovate, bright red with a large green-white star in the throat; H. *striatum* Brazil; flowers 2–4, to 4 in (10 cm), crimson, keeled green to halfway up the lobes; H. *vittatum* Peruvian Andes; flowers 3–6, to 4¾ in (12 cm) diameter, perianth tube to 1 in (2.5 cm), lobes obovate to oblong, to 1½ in (4 cm) across, keel white, margins irregular and white, striped red in between. *Cultivars* 'Apple-Blossom', white suffused soft pink; 'Beautiful Lady', pale mandarin red; 'Bestseller', scape short, flowers cerise; 'Bouquet', salmon; 'Byjou', soft burnt apricot; 'Cantate', milky deep red; 'Christmas Gift', white; 'Dazzler', pure white; 'Dutch Belle', opal rose; 'Ludwig's Goliath', large, bright scarlet; 'Lydia', pale salmon; 'Oskar', rich deep red; 'Orange Sovereign', pure orange; 'Picotee', white rimmed red; 'White Dazzler', pure white.

hippocrepiform shaped like a horseshoe.

Hippophaë (from Greek *hippophaes*, a kind of spurge). Elaeagnaceae. Europe, Asia. SEA BUCKTHORN. 3 species, thorny, deciduous, dioecious trees or shrubs. Lanceolate to linear, the leaves are more or less covered in somewhat metallic, scale- or chafflike hairs, as is the newgrowth. Inconspicuous flowers appear before the leaves and, where male and female plants are grown together, give rise to long-lasting and brightly colored berries. The genus is primarily used for its ornamental qualities, especially in maritime plantings, although *H. rhamnoides* is also used in shelterbelts and in soil stabilization, especially on coastal dunes, and may subsequently naturalize. Plant in full sun or part shade. Prune only to remove straggling shoots in later summer. Propagate by layering in fall, from suckers, by semiripe cuttings in summer, or by hardwood cuttings in late fall. Alternatively, sow seed fresh during fall, or in spring following stratification at 39°F (4°C) over three months. *H. rhamnoides* (W Europe to China; thorny shrub, 3¼–29 ft (1–9 m); twigs rigid, metallic-scaly then gray, thorny; leaves to 2½ in (6 cm), linear to lanceolate, silver; fruit to ¼ in (6 mm) diameter, orange, clothing bare branchlets in winter.

hirsute with long hairs, usually rather coarse and distinct.

hirsutullous slightly hirsute.

hispid with stiff, bristly hairs; not so distinct or sharp as when *setose*.

hispidulous minutely hispid.

hoary densely covered with white or gray hairs.

hoe a hand implement used for surface cultivation and destroying weeds, typically consisting of a flat, usually oblong, metal plate, or blade, attached to a handle about 5 ft (1.5 m) long. The

two most common types are the Dutch hoe (also known as the push hoe or scuffle hoe), primarily used for surface hoeing, and the more versatile draw hoe, which is useful for cultivation, drill drawing, thinning seedlings and earthing up. The Dutch hoe has the blade set on the same plane as the handle, with the operator walking backward to leave the cultivated ground untrodden. The draw hoe has the blade set at right angles to the handle, with the operator adopting a more stooping posture and walking forward over the cultivated ground. An onion hoe is a type of draw hoe, fixed to a handle about 12 in (30 cm) long, and used for cultivating among closely spaced plants.

hoggin a fine gritty aggregate, often with clay content, used for bedding paving slabs and providing a firm undersurface for gravel.

Dutch hoe   Draw hoe

Hoheria (Latinized form of the Maori name for these plants). Malvaceae. New Zealand. LACEBARK. 5 species of evergreen or deciduous shrubs and small trees with thinly leathery leaves. Solitary or clustered, the flowers are produced in the leaf axils in summer. They consist of five, obovate, white, cream or ivory petals and a boss of many stamens. Given shelter from cold, drying winds, most species tolerate temperatures to 5°F (−15°C). Deciduous species will regenerate freely from the base if cut back by frost. *H. populnea* is more tender and prone to damage at 23°F (−5°C); in severe conditions, *H. sexstylosa* may defoliate, but usually recovers in spring. The soft growth generated on over-rich soil is more prone to frost damage and, in addition, may suffer sudden die-back for other, physiological reasons. Grow in sun or light dappled shade, in deep, well-drained, humus-rich and moderately fertile soil. In regions at the limits of hardiness, provide the shelter of a warm south- or southwest-facing wall,

379

and a protective mulch of organic matter in winter. Prune in spring: removing deadwood and weak or over-crowded growth. Propagate by semi-ripe cuttings or by layers. Ripe seed sown in fall germinates freely; *H. sexstylosa* in particular self-seeds in profusion. Seed-raised specimens will pass through a juvenile stage.

H. angustifolia evergreen tree to 30 ft (10 m) with slender flexible branches; leaves ³⁄₄–2 in (2–5 cm), narrowly obovate, oblanceolate to lanceolate, coarsely spinulose, dentate to serrate; flowers to ³⁄₄ in (2 cm) diameter, petals snow white, narrowly oblong, notched; *H. glabrata* deciduous tree to 30 ft (10 m); leaves 2–5¹⁄₂ in (5–14 cm), glabrate, broadly ovate to ovate-lanceolate, acuminate, crenate to dentate; flowers to 1¹⁄₂ in (4 cm) diameter; petals white to cream, obovate, anthers purple; *H.* 'Glory of Amlwich' (*H. glabrate* × *H. sexstylosa*); small tree; leaves to 3¹⁄₂ in (9 cm), ovate and slender-pointed, serrate, pale green; flowers to 1¹⁄₂ in (4 cm) diameter, snow white, profuse; *H. lyallii* LACEBARK; deciduous tree to 20 ft (6 m); leaves 2–4 in (5–10 cm), cordate to ovate, gray-green, white-pubescent and felty; flowers ³⁄₄–1¹⁄₄ in (2–3 cm) in diameter, snow white, petals obovate, anthers purple; *H. populnea* LACEBARK; evergreen tree to 30 ft (10 m), branchlets slender, bark exfoliating in fine ash-gray strips; leaves 2³⁄₄–5¹⁄₂ in (7–14 cm), broadly ovate to elliptic, acuminate, serrate; flowers 1–1¹⁄₄ in (2.5–3 cm) in diameter, pure white; includes 'Alba Variegata', with leaves broadly edged white, 'Purpurea', with leaves flushed and veined maroon beneath, and 'Variegata', with pale yellow-green leaves edged dark green; *H. sexstylosa* RIBBONWOOD; evergreen tree to 20 ft (6 m); bark glossy red-brown, overlaid with gray exfoliating strips; leaves 2–6 in (5–15 cm), lanceolate to ovate, glossy; flowers ³⁄₄–1 in (2–2.5 cm) in diameter, pure white, fragrant, petals oblong, notched, anthers white; includes 'Crataegifolia', with small, coarsely toothed juvenile leaves.

Holboellia (for Frederik Ludvig Holboell [fl. 1847], a superintendent at the Copenhagen Botanic Garden). Lardizabalaceae. N India to China.

About 5 species, evergreen, twining shrubs with palmately compound leaves and unisexual flowers in spring and summer. These are small, waxy and bell-like. They are grown for their handsome, evergreen foliage and small, delicately colored flowers, and may be used to drape a wall or cover a tree stump, or to climb small trees, a trellis or a tripod system in a border. The cream to shell-pink *H. coriacea* is considered to be the hardiest species, but may suffer damage during prolonged spells below 23°F (–5°C). Cut back weaker growths and dead wood during spring. *Holboellia* succeeds in most garden soils, either in sun or shade. Increase by seeds and cuttings, alternatively by layering.

Holcus (from Greek *holkos*, a kind of cereal). Gramineae. Europe, temperate Asia, N and South Africa. 8 species, annual or perennial grasses with flimsy, tufted culms and linear leaves. The flowers are borne in spikelike, dense or open panicles in summer. Grow in sun in well-drained but moisture-retentive soil. Clip over *H.* 'Albovariegatus' after flowering. Propagate by division, and, for species, also by seed. *H. mollis* CREEPING SOFT GRASS; Europe; perennial to 18 in (45 cm); leaves to ¹⁄₂ in (1 cm) wide, gray-green, glabrous to slightly hairy; flowers in narrowly oblong to ovate, dense to loosely branched panicles to 4³⁄₄ in (12 cm); 'Albovariegatus': with leaves broadly edged white with a narrow green stripe).

hollow heart a disordered condition of potatoes, most usually found in large tubers, where a sound cavity is apparent when the potato is cut across. It is the result of checked development, most likely due to a drought period being followed by abundant rain, which causes rupturing of the central tissue.

Holmskioldia (for Theodor Holmskiold [1732–94], Danish botanist). Verbenaceae. Tropical Africa, Asia. Some 10 species, evergreen climbing shrubs. Produced in fall and winter in panicles or racemes, the flowers consist of a bowl- to bell-shaped calyx with a short tube and a circular, spreading rim, and a tubular, two-lipped corolla. Once established, *Holmskioldia* is highly drought-tolerant and extremely useful for plantings in poor sandy soil in tropical and subtropical gardens. In cooler climates, it needs warm greenhouse protection (minimum temperature 59°F/15°C), and treatment as for climbing *Clerodendrum*. *H. sanguinea* CHINESE HAT PLANT, CUP AND SAUCER PLANT, MANDARIN'S HAT; Himalaya; calyx to 1 in (2.5 cm) diameter, brick red to orange, net-veined, corolla scarlet.

Holodiscus (from Greek *holos* entire, and *diskos*, disk, referring to the entire disk of the flower). Rosaceae. Western N America to Colombia. 8 species, deciduous shrubs with pinnately lobed and toothed leaves and small, creamy white flowers massed in cascading sprays in summer. *Holodiscus* is hardy to 5°F (–15°C). Grow in full sun or light shade in moist, fertile soil that does not dry out in summer. Prune after flowering or in early spring, only to remove old or overcrowded branches. Increase by layering; also, by semiripe heeled cuttings. *H. discolor* OCEAN SPRAY, CREAMBUSH; western N America; to 16 ft (5 m); flowers in a 12 in (30 cm) plumelike panicle.

Homeria (from Greek *homereo*, to meet together: the filaments are united in a sheath around the style). Iridaceae. South Africa. 31 species, cormous perennial herbs with linear to sword-shaped leaves. The flowers are short-lived but produced in long succession over the summer. They consist of six perianth segments in a broadly cup-shaped arrangement. Grow in the cool greenhouse in a medium-fertility, loam-based mix with additional leaf mold and sharp sand; maintain good ventilation and a minimum temperature of 41–45°F (5–7°C). Water plentifully when in growth and dry off gradually as flowers fade. Store dormant corms in a cool dry place. Propagate by seed in fall, or by division or offsets. *H. ochroleuca* to 32 in (80 cm); flowers to 3 in (8 cm) diameter, pale yellow, occasionally stained orange at center, muskily scented.

homogamous having hermaphrodite flowers, or flowers of the same sex.

homologous of organs or parts that resemble each other in form or function.

homomorphic having the same shape.

homonym the same scientific name given to two or more distinct plants. Under the rules of nomenclature, only one plant may assume the *f*. name, and this is usually the first plant to have received it.

homosporous (1) producing only one kind of seed; (2) developed from only one kind of spore.

homozygous describing a plant bearing the same genetic components at a given position on a chromosome, so that there can be no genetic segregation. It is used for self-pollinated species or cultivars; cf. *heterozygous*.

honey bee (Hymenoptera: Apidae) (*Apis mellifera*) a widely distributed social insect of benefit to gardening. Thought to be of tropical origin, it has been introduced into most countries of the world for its honey. A colony consists of three well-defined castes: a queen, worker bees (sterile females) and drones (males). In summer, large colonies may contain up to 80,000 workers and several hundred drones. Workers leave the hive to forage for water, nectar, pollen or propolis (a resinous plant exudate collected from buds and other parts of trees, used to fill unwanted gaps in the hive). Nectar is the main substance collected, and this is imbibed by the bees; pollen and propolis are collected in the pollen baskets on the hind legs.

When visiting flowers, honey bees are of great value as pollinators; most fruits, vegetables and ornamental plants relying on insect pollination. To avoid harming honey bees, careful timing of pesticide application is crucial, choosing to spray during their periods of least activity.

Ants "herd" the pests

Treehoppers excrete sugary fluid

Ants "farming" treehoppers for honeydew

honeydew a sugary fluid excreted by sap-feeding insects such as aphids, whiteflies, mealybugs and scale insects, which creates a sticky coating on leaves and stems.

It is most markedly seen under *Tilia* species in urban areas, where paving is often covered with the sticky residue. Honeydew, which is sweet, is eagerly sought and imbibed by ants; it is often colonized by the sooty mold fungus. Any sign of stickiness on a plant indicates the possibility of attack by one of these sap-feeding pests, either of the plant or one nearby.

honey fungus see *armillaria root rot*.

hooded cucullate or, more loosely, referring to inarching parts enclosing others.

Hoodia (for Mr. Hood [fl. 1830], a grower of succulent plants). Asclepiadaceae. South Africa, Namibia. Some 17 species, succulent, perennial, leafless herbs. The stems are gray-green, angled and covered in conical tubercles and hard, thornlike teeth. Saucer- or cup-shaped with five, short and pointed lobes, the large flowers appear near the stem apex at various times of year. Cultivate as for *Stapelia*. *H. bainii* Cape Province; stem to 15-angled, tubercles compressed, spiraled, spines pale brown; flowers ¾–2¾ in (2–7 cm) in diameter, deeply cup-shaped to flat, pale yellow to buff, veins darker, with a dark red-brown corona.

hoof-and-horn a slow-release organic fertilizer made from the ground-up hooves and horns of cattle; it contains 7–15% nitrogen and 1–10% phosphate, with some calcium. It should be sterilized to eliminate pathogens, and handled with suitable precautions to avoid inhalation and other personal contact.

hops, hop manure matured spent hops from breweries, which can be used to improve soil structure, although the nutrient content is low. Hop manure is made by adding fertilizers to matured hops, and the analysis varies considerably according to the manufacturer. Spent hops can be applied at any time, but hop manure is best applied in spring.

Hordeum (Latin *hordeum*, barley, a corruption of *horridus*, bearded with bristles, referring to the bristlelike, long-awned glumes and vestigial spikelets). Gramineae. Temperate northern Hemisphere and S America BARLEY. Some 20 species of annual or perennial grasses. Grown for graceful, feathery flower heads, which dry and dye well. *H. jubatum* is a highly ornamental barley, with delicate, long, straight and silky awns faintly tinged crimson. Pick immature heads and air dry. Sow seed *in situ* in fall or spring, in light, well-drained soil in full sun. *H. jubatum* SQUIRRELTAIL BARLEY, FOXTAIL BARLEY; N America, NE Asia; annual or perennial to 24 in (60 cm); flowers in dense, finely bristly, silky, nodding, pale green to purple-tinged spikes to 4¾ in (12 cm).

Horminum (from Greek *hormao*, I excite, referring to the use of the plant as an aphrodisiac). Labiatae. Pyrenees, Alps. DRAGON'S MOUTH, PYRENEAN DEAD-NETTLE. 1 species, *H. pyrenaicum*, a rhizomatous perennial herb to 18 in (45 cm). Borne in basal rosettes, the dark green leaves are to 2¾ × 2 in (7 × 5 cm), ovate to cordate and toothed. Tubular, 2-lipped and violet, the flowers nod in whorls held clear of the foliage in summer. Hardy to −4°F (−20°C) and suitable for the front of the border or for cultivation in the rock garden. Grow in moderately fertile, well-drained soil in full sun. Propagate by division in spring or fall, or from seed sown in a cold frame in winter for germination in spring.

hormone see *growth regulators*.

hornet see *wasps*.

horny hard and brittle, but with a fine texture and easily cut.

horseradish (*Armoracia rusticana*) a fleshy-rooted perennial, also known as

Horseradish
The large leaves of horseradish form impressive clumps, but plants are extremely invasive, with stout, spreading, thonglike roots.

red cole, which is native to temperate regions of Europe and Asia and naturalized in North America. It has been used since ancient times as a medicinal and condiment herb. The grated root is used in a traditional English sauce to accompany meat or fish, or (in small quantities) as a salad garnish; young leaves may be added to salads.

Since horseradish regenerates from its spreading roots, it is potentially a pernicious weed and in gardens its territory must be contained and all portions of root removed on lifting. Propagate by pencil-thick roots, or thongs, 6–8 in (15–20 cm) long, taken from mother-plants to overwinter; store in bundles buried in sand under cool conditions. Plant sprouted thongs in spring 2–2¾ in (5–7 cm) deep at 18 in (45 cm) spacings in rows 24 in (60 cm) apart. Harvest roots in fall and store in darkness. Quality can be improved by removing the topsoil when plant growth reaches 8 in (20 cm) high and rubbing off side roots. Replant in beds annually, or at intervals of no more than three years, to maintain quality.

horsetail *Equisetum arvense* is the COMMON HORSETAIL, a flowerless perennial with leafless, branching rough-textured stems. Unchecked, it can be a serious weed spreading by tuber-bearing underground stems which may penetrate to a depth of 6½ ft (2 m). Stalked shoots bearing fruiting bodies appear in early spring, but propagation by spores is less common.
Complete eradication of dense

established stands is unlikely. Repeated application of approved herbicides will at least weaken plants, and glyphosate and glyphosate trimesium are effective foliage-applied total weedkillers, suitable for use on uncropped ground. Vigilance is needed to avoid the introduction of horsetail; light infestations should be tackled early with meticulous cultivation of the ground to remove all parts of the plants. Where horsetail is established in neglected lawns, it can usually be suppressed by regular mowing.

hort., horti, of the garden; **hortorum** of gardens; **hortulanorum,** of gardeners; all three are abbreviated hort.; never capitalized. The use of hort. after a plant name indicates either the misapplication of a name by gardeners or denotes a name of confused authorship or of no standing. The citation hort. or horti. preceding a surname indicates a plant name published in a nursery catalog, for example hort. Lemoine.

horticulture the art, practice and science of garden cultivation; in common parlance, it includes the commercial production of fruit, vegetables and ornamentals.

hortus conclusus 'enclosed garden'—a mediaeval garden within a garden, enclosed by a hedge, fence, or wall, and containing a lawn and often a fountain, roses, arbors, and turf seats.

hortus siccus 'dried garden'—a collection of dried specimens comprising a herbarium.

hose-in-hose see *double*; *malformations*.

hose reel a device for rolling up a garden watering hose. The through-feed type is the most convenient, with a special valve enabling the hose to be wound or unwound while the water supply remains connected.

host an organism upon which another lives and may feed.

Hosta (for Nicolaus Tomas Host [1761–1834], physician to the Austrian Emperor). Liliaceae (Hostaceae, Funki-

aceae). Japan, China, Korea. PLANTAIN LILY. 40 species, clump-forming herbaceous perennials, fleshy-rooted with thick, short rhizomes and stout resting buds. Emerging in midspring, the leaves form a basal mound or rosette. They are broadly heart-shaped to narrowly lanceolate in outline, glossy to glaucous, thin and pliable to thick and tough, smooth to ruggedly textured. Produced in summer and fall, the funnel-shaped flowers are ranked along one side of a slender raceme, or gathered among bracts at the top of a scape. The following are among the most valuable hardy foliage plants. Their flowers and papery, wind-swept seed heads are also beautiful. *Hostas* may be grown as single specimens, massed for dense groundcover, or used in containers. All listed here will grow in full sun given adequate moisture, but leaf quality is usually better in dappled sun or shade and especially so in the case of plants with blue-gray, lime green and golden leaves. *Hostas* are hardy to –20°F (–29°C) if thickly mulched in winter. Plant in fertile, open soil rich in leaf mold and compost. Keep moist throughout the year; avoid freezing, waterlogged conditions in winter and early spring. Increase by division in spring. Martyrs to slugs and snails.

H. crispula Japan; leaves to 10 × 6 in (25 × 15 cm), ovate-lanceolate, undulate, dull olive green, deeply and irregularly edged white; flowers pale mauve; *H. decorata* Japan; leaves to 6 × 4¾ in (16 × 12 cm), ovate to rounded, dull dark green, leathery, narrowly edged white; flowers rich violet or white; *H. fortunei* garden origin; leaves to 12 × 8 in (30 × 20 cm), heart-shaped to rounded or broadly lanceolate, heavy-textured, mid- to deep green, sometimes glaucous and rugose above; flowers mauve to pale violet; var. *albopicta*: leaves unfurling pale creamy yellow with a green margin, ultimately pale green with a hint of variegation; var. *aureomarginata*: leaves edged gold; 'Marginato-alba': leaves edged white; *H. hypoleuca* Japan; leaves to 18 × 12 in (45 × 30 cm), broadly ovate-cordate, somewhat leathery, pale green, glossy or glaucous above, powdery white beneath; flowers pale lavender to milky white; *H. lancifolia* garden origin; leaves to 6½ × 1¼ in (17 × 3 cm), lanceolate, finely tapering, thin-textured, glossy, deep olive green; flowers deep mauve; H. *montana* Japan; leaves to 12 × 7 in (30 × 18 cm), broadly ovate to heart-shaped, dull or shiny mid- to deep green or glaucous, veins deeply impressed; flowers gray-mauve to white; 'Aureomarginata': leaves narrower, broadly and irregularly edged gold, undulate; H. *plantaginea* AUGUST LILY; China; leaves to 11 × 8 in (28 × 20 cm), ovate-cordate, glossy olive green with sunken veins; flowers white, fragrant, opening at dusk; sometimes confused with H. 'Thomas Hogg'; H. *rectifolia* Japan; leaves to 6 × 2 in (15 × 5 cm), ovate to elliptic, erect, margins somewhat inrolled, dull mid- to dark green; flowers violet; H. *sieboldiana* Japan; leaves to 20 × 12 in (50 × 30 cm), ovate to cordate or rounded, heavily textured, puckered, matt glaucous gray-blue to blue-green or olive above, paler beneath; flowers pale lilac-gray fading to white clouded with pale lilac; var. *elegans*: leaves heavily textured, strongly puckered, thickly glaucous blue-gray, flowers pale pearly lilac; 'Frances Williams': leaves yellow-edged; H. *sieboldii* Japan, Sakhalin Is; leaves to 6 × 2½ in (15 × 6 cm), lanceolate to elliptic, sometimes wavy, somewhat puckered, matt mid-green above edged pure white; flowers pale mauve, striped violet and lined white; H. *tardiflora* garden origin; leaves to 6 × 2¾ in (15 × 7 cm), erect, lanceolate to narrowly elliptic, semirigid, thick-textured, glossy deep olive green above; flowers clear mauve, produced in fall; H. *tokudama* garden origin; leaves to 12 × 6 in (30 × 15 cm), cordate to rounded, heavily textured, puckered, glaucous blue-gray, flat to concave above; flowers pale gray-mauve to off-white; 'Aureonebulosa': leaves clouded yellow at center; 'Flavocircinalis': leaves edged bright yellow; H. *undulata* garden origin; leaves to 6 × 2½ in (15 × 6 cm), ovate to lanceolate-elliptic, very wavy and twisted, glossy mid-green with a creamy white center, later breaking into white streaks; flowers pale purple; var. *erromena*: leaves wholly mid-green; var. *univittata*: leaves large, twisted with narrow, white centers; H. *ventricosa* China; leaves to 10 × 7 in (24 × 18 cm), broadly ovate to cordate, slightly wavy, thin-textured, glossy

dark green; flowers deep mauve; var. *aureomaculata*: leaves bright yellow in center, fading by midsummer; H. *venusta* Korea, Japan; leaves to 1¼ × ¾ in (3 × 2 cm), lanceolate-elliptic to ovate-cordate, dull to glossy olive to dark green; flowers pale violet). *Cultivars* There are many hosta cultivars and hybrids, ranging in size from the very large and robust to dwarf plants suitable for rock and container gardens. The leaves vary in shape from the narrowly lanceolate to almost round, in texture from thick and puckered to thin and smooth, glossy to glaucous. Leaf color runs through frosty blue-gray to aquamarine, olive and dark jade green, including some solid golds and limes. Variegation may be marginal, central or throughout, and take the form of white, cream, gold or lime flashes, stripes, patches and clouding. There follows a selection of popular cultivars—'August Moon' (leaves large, ovate, pale golden yellow, faintly glaucous, corrugated, flowers near-white); 'Big Daddy' (leaves very large, round, thickly textured, puckered, glaucous blue, flowers near-white); 'Blue Moon' (leaves small, heart-shaped, glaucous blue, flowers mauve-gray); 'Ginko Craig' (leaves small, low, dark green edged clear white, flowers violet); 'Gold Edger' (small, low, neat, leaves ovate-cordate, cool lime turning soft gold, flowers pale mauve); 'Gold Standard' (leaves large, ovate-cordate, chartreuse green turning pale yellow, edged dark green, flowers lavender); 'Halcyon' (leaves medium-sized, heart-shaped, glaucous blue-gray, flowers lavender-gray); 'Popo' (dwarf, leaves very small, cordate, blue-gray); 'Royal Standard' (leaves large, ovate, bright green, flowers white); 'Shining Tot' (dwarf, leaves very small, dark, glossy green, flowers lilac); 'Sum and Substance' (leaves very large, smooth, thickly textured, pale lime green to yellow, flowers pale lavender); 'Tiny Tears' (dwarf, leaves very small, narrow, dark green, flowers violet); 'Wide Brim' (leaves large, heavily puckered, dark green with a wide, irregular cream margin, flowers mauve); 'Zounds' (leaves very large, heavy-textured and puckered, gold with a metallic sheen, flowers pale lavender).

host plant any plant that provides sustenance, or other support, for another organism, such as a plant, virus, bacterium, fungus or insect.

hotbed a specially prepared growing bed producing a warm-growing medium to advance the growth or maturity of plants and crops. A hotbed is particularly valuable for growing cucumbers and melons, advancing certain root and salad vegetables, and for rooting cuttings or providing bottom-heat for seed germination. It may be constructed in a frame or greenhouse or freestanding outdoors.

Traditionally, hotbeds were based on fermenting horse manure, although tanning bark was also used, either alone or with animal manure. A common practice involved mixing equal parts fresh stable litter and fallen leaves into a well-watered heap, which was turned several times within a week. The substrate was then stacked on to a well-drained growing site, and up to 6 in (15 cm) of growing medium added. As a result of the relative scarcity of stable manure, hotbeds were bottom-heated through hot water pipe systems, a method now generally superseded by electric warming cables.

hot house see *greenhouse*.

hot water treatment a pest-control treatment that involves immersing plants in warm water, exploiting the difference between the thermal death point of certain pests (especially eelworms) and plants. It is usually carried out when the plants are dormant. Temperature and immersion time are critical and vary with the subjects; a few degrees temperature variation may kill or seriously damage plants or, alternatively, leave pests unharmed. Pre-warming of some stock improves safety or efficacy. Home-improvised tanks may be used, but sensitive thermostatic control and a means of water circulation are essential for success.

STEM EELWORM (*Ditylenchus dipsaci*), BULB FLIES (*Merodon equestris* and *Eumerus* species) and the TARSONEMID BULB SCALE MITE (*Steneotarsonemus laticeps*) in narcissus can be controlled by immersion of dormant bulbs for three hours at 111–113°F (44–45°C).

Dormant forms of stem eelworm, known as 'eelworm wool', may survive unless a wetting agent is added to the water. Hyacinths may be similarly treated but should be immersed for four hours, and tulips, which are easily damaged, must first be dry stored at 93°F (34°C) for three days, followed by a three-hour pre-soak in cold water. Iris bulbs infested with POTATO TUBER EELWORM (*Ditylenchus destructor*) require immersion in water for three hours at 111–113°F (44–45°C), preceded by 10–14 days' dry storage at 86°F (30°C).

Lilies are subject to attack by the LEAF EELWORM (*Aphelenchoides fragariae*) and those with white bulbs may be disinfested by treating at 106°F (41°C) for two hours, following storage for 8–10 weeks at 36°F (2°C) to prevent sprouting; cultivars with darker bulbs for example, *Lilium speciosum* and *L. regale* should be similarly pre-treated, followed by hot water treatment at 102°F (39°C) for two hours. Ferns and other plants, such as gloxinias and begonias, that are infested with the same eelworm can be treated after soil removal at 120°F (49°C) for five minutes. Chrysanthemum stools, trimmed and washed clean of soil, can be disinfested by immersion in water for five minutes at 115°F (46°C) or 20–30 minutes at 110°F (43.5°C). Phlox can be prepared in a similar way and treated at 110°F (43.5°C) for one hour to rid the stools of STEM EELWORM (*Ditylenchus dipsaci*). Strawberry runners attacked by *D. dipsaci* and *Aphelenchoides fragariae* may be disinfested by immersion at 115°F (46°C) for 10 minutes, a treatment which also controls tarsonemid mites.

Hot water treatment can be used to treat mint runners infected with RUST, and also to protect chrysanthemum stools against WHITE RUST.

Hottonia (for P. Hotton, Dublin botanist). Primulaceae. Northern Hemisphere. 2 species, aquatic, perennial herbs, rooting in mud or floating. The leaves are submerged and finely dissected. Salverform with five, spreading lobes, the flowers stand clear of the water in whorled racemes in summer. Vigorous aquatics for ponds and slow-moving streams, where their ferny leaves are submerged below water level while the spikes of white to lilac flowers rise in spring above the surface. They are also useful as shallow-water oxygenators, especially if fish are present. They produce winter-resting buds which sink to the bottom until the following spring. Plant in spring by throwing divisions/cuttings into water or by rooting into submerged marginal mud. Propagate also from seed sown in spring in pans standing in water.

H. inflata AMERICAN FEATHERFOIL; E Europe; leaves ½–2 in (1–5 cm), ovate or oblong, lobes narrow-linear; flowers ¼–⅜ in (0.5–0.8 cm), white; *H. palustris* WATER VIOLET; Europe, W Asia; leaves ¾–5 in (2–13 cm), lobes linear, sometimes further divided; flowers to 1 in (2.5 cm) diameter, violet, throat yellow.

house plant a plant that will grow satisfactorily in the temperature, humidity and light of a house. Suitable subjects include a range of evergreen foliage plants, such as *Monstera*, *Sansevieria* and *Peperomia*, as well as flowering plants such as *Cyclamen*, *Hippeastrum*, and chrysanthemums. The greatest success with houseplants is achieved where the recommended environment is maintained without wide fluctuation, with careful attention to watering and feeding.

Houstonia (for Dr. William Houston [1695–1733], British botanist and writer on American plants). Rubiaceae. N America, Mexico. Some 50 species, hardy perennial herbs or, rarely, subshrubs with small, broadly funnel-shaped and 4-parted flowers in spring and summer. Low-growing, stem-rooting, perennials, grown for their loose mats of small shining leaves and for their dainty flowers in clear blue, white or blue-violet. They are suitable for crevices in the rock garden, for the alpine house or frame, and for other shady situations in the garden. Hardy to –4°F (–20°C). Grow in a cool, sheltered site, in moist, well-drained, leafy soil. Propagate by division in fall or spring, or from seed sown in a soilless propagating mix in the cold frame in spring.

H. michauxii BLUETS, INNOCENCE, QUAKER-LADIES; N America; perennial herb to 8 in (20 cm), mat-forming; leaves small; flowers few, solitary on slender stalks to 2½ in (6 cm), corolla salver-shaped, to ½ in (1 cm), pale blue to lilac or violet, or white, and yellow-eyed; includes 'Fred Millard', mat-forming with deep blue flowers; *H. longifolia* LONGLEAF BLUETS; E US; erect perennial herb to 12 in (30 cm); flowers numerous in cymes, corolla white or purple, funnel-shaped to ⅜ in (8 mm); *H. purpurea* MOUNTAIN HOUSTONIA; C and S US; erect perennial herb to 20 in (50 cm); flowers in dense cymes or clusters, corolla pale purple, lilac or white, funnel-shaped, to ⅜ in (8 mm); *H. serpyllifolia* SE US; perennial herb to 3 in (8 cm), stem prostrate; leaves very small; flowers on erect stalks to 1½ in (4 cm), corolla violet-blue or white, salver-shaped, to ½ in (1 cm).

Houttuynia (for Martin Houttuyn, 18th-century Dutch naturalist). Saururaceae. E Asia. 1 species, *H. cordata*, a semievergreen perennial herb of damp places. All parts of this plant have a peppery aroma. The clumped stems are 6–16 in (15–40 cm) tall and spread widely and often somewhat unpredictably by means of subterranean suckers. The leaves are to 2½ × 1¼ in (6 × 3 cm), heart-shaped, smooth and dark green (brilliantly painted red and cream in the cultivar 'Chameleon'). Small, green flowers are carried in small, squat, conelike spikes subtended by white bracts. An attractive groundcover in the bog garden or damp border, *Houttuynia* can also be grown as a pond marginal in up to 4 in (10 cm) of water. It can be invasive but is less vigorous in drier soil. Hardy to at least 5°F (–15°C), it should be grown in moist soil in full sun to light shade. Propagate by division in spring.

Hovenia (for David Hoven, an Amsterdam senator). Rhamnaceae. E and S Asia. 2 species, deciduous shrubs or trees, usually with large leaves. Small, fragrant and 5-petalled, the flowers are borne in cymes in summer. With age, the fleshy flower stalks become red and edible. Grow in fertile, sandy loam soil in full sun. *Hovenia* is hardy to at least 5°F (–15°C). Propagate by softwood cuttings in summer, by hardwood cuttings or by seed. Seed germinates freely if sown fresh; stored seed may need acid scarification before sowing. Poorly

H

ripened wood is likely to be more susceptible to coral spot; application of high-potash fertilizer in midsummer may help. *H. dulcis* RAISIN TREE, CHINESE/JAPANESE RAISIN TREE; E Asia; tree to 66 ft (20 m); leaves 4–8 in (10–20 cm) broadly ovate, apex acuminate, base cordate, coarsely toothed, downy beneath; flowers to ¼ in (6 mm) in diameter, green-yellow, pedicels fleshy becoming red and edible after frost.

hoverflies (Diptera: Syrphidae) flies that are easily recognizable by their habit of remaining stationary in flight before darting to another position; they frequent flowers to feed on nectar or, sometimes, pollen. Many are brightly colored with black and yellow stripes, resembling wasps; their legless larvae may be scavengers, living in decaying organic matter, dung or stagnant water. A few other species are injurious to plants, including the bulb flies (see *bulb flies*). A third group, including *Syrphus ribesii* and many other species, are beneficial in gardens because their larvae feed upon aphids.

Hoverfly

Howea (native to Lord Howe Island, in the S Pacific). Palmae. Lord Howe Island. 2 species, large palms, ultimately with solitary, erect stems. The leaves are pinnately compound with fibrous sheaths, unarmed petioles and linear to lanceolate leaflets. *Howea* species are among the most elegant of feather palms, and are suitable for outdoor cultivation in frost-free temperate climates. Elsewhere, they show remarkable tolerance of neglect, low light, low temperatures and of the dry atmospheres that generally pertain in the home. Among the most widely used palms for interior decoration, they are slow-growing and exceptionally beautiful as juveniles, and require infrequent repotting. Propagate by seed.

H. belmoreana BELMORE SENTRY PALM, CURLY PALM; up to 23 ft (7 m); trunk markedly ringed, usually swollen at base; pinnae up to 1 in (2.5 cm) across; *H. forsteriana* SENTRY PALM, FORSTERSENTRY PALM, KENTIA PALM, THATCH LEAF PALM; to 59 ft (18 m) but grown as a stemless juvenile; trunk obliquely ringed, straight; pinnae to 3¼ ft (1 m) long, 1¼–1½ in (3–4 cm) across, dark green.

Hoya (for Thomas Hoy, head gardener to the Duke of Northumberland at Syon House in the late 18th Century). Asclepiadaceae. WAX FLOWER, PORCELAIN FLOWER. Asia, Polynesia, Australia. Some 200 species, evergreen shrubs and subshrubs, some climbing with slender, rooting stems, others bushy. The leaves are tough, leathery and, in some cases, thinly succulent. Borne at various times of year in long-lasting pendulous umbels, the flowers are waxy and star-shaped. They consist of five, pointed lobes surrounding a fleshy and often differently colored corona. The flowers are sometimes sweetly fragrant and dripping with nectar.

Provide a minimum temperature of 50°F (10°C). Grow in dappled sun or light shade. Plant in an open mix rich in organic matter (that suitable for the orchids *Paphiopedilum* will suit). Water, syringe and feed freely in warm weather; water sparingly in cool conditions. Train climbing species on wires, trellis and moss poles. Shrubby species, such as *H. lanceolata*, are excellent plants for baskets. Increase by semiripe cuttings (allow the wound to dry) in a heated case, alternatively by layering.

H. carnosa WAX PLANT; India, Burma, S China; climber to 20 ft (6 m); leaves to 4 in (10 cm), elliptic-ovate, smooth, thick; flowers to ⅝ in (1.5 cm) across, white to fleshy pink with a glistening, papillose texture, corona purple-pink to pale red; includes cultivars with leaves variegated cream and yellow, or splashed with silver; 'Hindu Rope' differs in having leaves tightly folded together with only their lower surfaces exposed; *H. imperialis* SE Asia; climber to 26 ft (8 m); leaves to 8 in (20 cm), elliptic-oblong, smooth, thick; flowers to 2¾ in (7 cm) across, chocolate to wine red or magenta, corona creamy white; *H. lanceolata* (including *H. bella* and *H. sikkimensis* of gardens); MINIATURE WAX PLANT; Himalaya to N Burma; shrubby, to 18 in (45 cm), with arching branches; leaves to 1¼ in (3

cm), ovate-lanceolate, very thinly fleshy, often pale green; flowers highly fragrant, to ½ in (1 cm) across, sparkling white, corona purple-red; *H. linearis* Himalaya; stems drooping to trailing; leaves ¾–2 in (2–5 cm), linear, more or less narrowly cylindric to terete, grooved, downy; flowers to ½ in (1 cm) across, faintly scented, ivory, corona yellow tinged pink; *H. longifolia* STRING BEAN PLANT; Himalaya, SE Asia; stems trailing or weakly climbing; leaves to 4 in (10 cm), angled downward, linear to narrowly lanceolate, thick, dark green, smooth, with a sunken midvein; flowers ½–1½ in (1–4 cm) across, white sometimes flushed pink, corona rose pink to red; *H. polyneura* FISHTAIL HOYA; Himalaya, S China; shrubby to 3¼ ft (1 m), branches arching; leaves to 4 in (10 cm), broadly ovate-rhombic, smooth, glossy deep green with darker veins; flowers to ⅝ in (1.5 cm) across, white to cream, corona purple-red.

Huernia (for Justus Huernius [1587–1652], a Dutch missionary and the first collector of plants from the Cape of Good Hope). Asclepiadaceae. DRAGON FLOWER. South Africa to Ethiopia and Arabia (1 species), W Africa. Some 70 species, succulent, perennial herbs. *Huernia's* stems are clumped, fleshy, and gray-green with toothed angles. The leaves are rudimentary and short-lived. Malodorous and fleshy, the flowers are bell-shaped with five short, pointed lobes. Cultivate as for *Stapelia*.

H. boleana Ethiopia; stem to 3 × ⅝ in (8 × 1.5 cm), 5 angled, teeth soft to ¼ in (6 mm), gray-green to green mottled purple; corolla ¾ in (17 mm) in diameter, lobes deltoid, inner surface blood-red, covered with large yellow papillae; *H. macrocarpa* Eritrea, SW Saudi Arabia, S Yemen; stem to 3½ in (9 cm), 4-angled, thick, ridges sinuate, teeth to ⅜ in (8 mm); corolla ½–¾ in (11–20 mm) in diameter, papillose to smooth, exterior yellow green, interior pale yellow with concentric maroon bands or wholly purple to crimson, lobes broadly triangular, attenuate; *H. pillansii* COCKLEBUR; Cape Province; stem to 1½ in (4 cm), subglobose when young, with conical tubercles in many rows, apices softly setose; corolla to ⅛ in (4 mm) in diameter, cream to pink with

H

Huernia pillansii
These bizarre succulents with their muddy-hued, malodorous flowers tend to appeal only to specialist collectors.

red spots, lobes recurved, attenuate, interior pale yellow with crimson spots, densely red-papillose; H. *primulina* Cape Province; stem to 3 in (8 cm), sometimes spotted red, ridges sinuate, with dark, hooked teeth; corolla 1 in (2.5 cm) in diameter, pale to sulfur-yellow, smooth, fleshy and waxy, sometimes tinged with red, lobes triangular-attenuate; H. *zebrina*. OWL-EYES, LITTLE OWL; N Transvaal, Botswana, Namibia; stem to 3 in (8 cm), 5-angled, teeth ⅛–¼ in (4–5 mm), conical; corolla 1½–1½ in (3.5–4 cm) in diameter, yellow blotched red-brown, lobes triangular, lime or sulfur-yellow, interior downy, banded red-brown.

humidity the amount of water vapor in the atmosphere, measured on a scale of relative humidity (RH): RH 0% = totally dry air, RH 100% = saturated air, at a given temperature. Excepting the extremes of xerophytes and hygrophytes, most species grow satisfactorily within the range of 65–80% RH. Below 65%, growth is progressively and adversely affected; above 80%, there are increasing problems with fungal and bacterial diseases. Above 90%, transpiration begins to be restricted and the movement of nutrients, particularly calcium, is reduced to the extent that deficiency symptoms may appear.

Humidity can be reduced by applying heat and ventilation or, on a large scale, with dehumidification systems that employ heat exchangers or refrigerant cooling. Damping down, manually with a hose, watering can or overhead sprinkler, will raise humidity. "Fogging" systems are available for expansive greenhouses; these produce free-floating droplets of less than 5 microns with no excess water.

humification the breakdown of organic matter in soil leading to the formation of humus.

Humulus (from Latin *humus*, soil, referring to the creeping habit). Cannabidaceae. Temperate Europe, N America, C and E Asia. HOP. 2 species, twining, herbaceous perennials with more or less palmately lobed leaves and pendulous, conelike inflorescences with papery bracts. Rapidly growing twiners, *Humulus* species are especially useful as summer screening plants on trellis or wires, and for scrambling through hedging and large open shrubs; they are valued for their foliage. In fall, *H. lupulus* also produces fragrant straw-colored inflorescences, used in brewing and, when air-dried, to make swags and garlands. The young shoots are edible in salads or cooked as for spinach. *H. lupulus* is hardy at least to 5°F (–15°C). *H. japonicus* is usually grown as annual in cool temperate climates, rapidly forming a green screen that makes an admirable backdrop for more brightly colored flowers. Grow in moderately fertile, well-drained soil in sun or part shade; *H. lupulus* 'Aureus' colors best in sun, when few foliage climbers can rival the beauty of its fresh gold to lime leaves. Propagate cultivars of *H. lupulus* by greenwood leaf-bud cuttings in midsummer, taken from material on which leaves have fully expanded. Apply 0.2% IBA and root in a closed case with bottom heat at 68°F (20°C). Progeny from seed is highly variable. Sow *H. japonicus in situ* in spring, or earlier under glass at 59–64°F (15–18°C). Lower the temperature on germination, and plant out in late spring.

H. japonicus JAPANESE HOP; temperate E Asia; stem very rough; leaves to 8 in (20 cm), 5–7-lobed, strongly serrate, petioles longer than blades; includes 'Lutescens', with pale gold to lime green foliage, and 'Variegatus', with foliage blotched and streaked white; H. *lupulus* COMMON HOP, EUROPEAN HOP, BINE; northern temperate regions, widely naturalized; stem rough; leaves 3–5-lobed, coarsely toothed, petioles usually shorter than blades; 'Aureus': leaves golden yellow.

humus a complex mixture of compounds resulting from the microbiological decomposition of organic matter in soil; it forms a black or dark brown amorphous colloid. Humus affects the retention and availability of nutrients by increasing cation exchange capacity, and slowly releases nitrogen and phosphate. Humus influences soil structure and, in clay soil, will assist in bonding particles; on sandy soil especially, it increases available water.

Hunnemannia (for John Hunneman [d. 1839], botanist and plant collector). Papaveraceae. MEXICAN TULIP POPPY, GOLDEN CUP. Mexico. 1 species, *H. fumariifolia*, a perennial, glaucous herb to 3¼ ft (1 m) tall with finely, ternately divided leaves. Produced in summer, the yellow flowers are solitary, to 3 in (8 cm) in diameter and composed of four, rounded petals. Usually grown as an annual, although perennial in frost-free climates. Sow *in situ* in spring, or in late winter in the greenhouse at 55–59°F (13–15°C), in a sandy medium. Plant out in late spring, taking care not to disturb roots, in a sunny, well-drained site.

hurdle see *wattle*.

husk the outer layer of certain fruits—for example *Juglans*, *Physalis*—generally originating from the perianth or the involucre.

Hyacinthella (diminutive of *Hyacinthus*). Liliaceae (Hyacinthaceae). E Europe to W Asia and Israel. Some 20 species of small, bulbous, perennial herbs with slender leaves and bell-shaped flowers in scapose racemes in spring. Grow in a well-drained, sunny position in the rock garden. They may also be grown in the alpine house or bulb frame where they can be given protection from wet weather when dormant in summer. Otherwise, cultivate as for *Muscari*.

H. glabrescens central S Turkey; flowers to ¼ in (6 mm), tubular to campanulate, deep violet-blue, borne on distinct pedicels; *H. nervosa* SE Turkey, through Syria, Jordan and Iraq to Israel; flowers ½ in (1 cm), tubular to narrowly campanulate, sessile, pale blue.

Hyacinthoides (from *Hyacinthus* and Greek *-oides*, resembling). Liliaceae (Hyacinthaceae). BLUEBELL. W Europe, N Africa. Some 4 species, perennial, bulbous herbs with narrowly strap-shaped leaves and scapose racemes of bell-shaped flowers with spreading perianth lobes in spring. Grow in humus-rich, moisture-retentive soil in semishade; flower color will bleach in sun and these are, in any case, bulbs associated by most with woodland carpets and dappled glades. They tolerate a range of in types, but prefer heavier soil. Propagate by division of established colonies (bulbs will be found quite deep in the soil), or by seed sown *in situ* when ripe or in spring in the shaded cold frame.

H. hispanica (syn. *Endymion hispanicus*) SPANISH BLUEBELL SW Europe, N Africa; close to *H. non-scripta*; flowers 6–8, unscented, widely campanulate, borne in a rather loose, not 1-sided raceme, tepals spreading, not curved at tips, anthers blue; plants cultivated as *H. hispanica* are often hybrids between this species and *H. non-scripta*. Cultivars include: 'Alba', with white flowers; 'Danube', with abundant, dark blue flowers; 'Excelsior', tall, with large, blue-violet flowers, with a marine blue stripe; 'La Grandesse', with pure white flowers; 'Mount Everest', with white flowers, in a broad spike; 'Myosotis', with porcelain blue flowers, with a sky blue stripe; 'Queen of the Pinks', with deep pink flowers; 'Rosabella', with soft pink flowers; 'Rose', with violet pink flowers, in a large spike; and 'White City', with white flowers; *H. italica* (SE France, NW Italy, Spain, Portugal; scape 4–16 in (10–40 cm); flowers 6–30, borne in dense, conical, erect, not 1-sided raceme, tepals ¼–¼ in (5–7 mm), spreading widely, blue-violet, occasionally white, anthers blue; *H. non-scripta* (syn. *Endymion non-scriptus*) BLUEBELL; W Europe; scape 8–12 in (20–30 cm), flowers 6–12, fragrant, tubular with tepals curved at tips in

loose, 1-sided, drooping raceme, tepals ⅝–¾ in (1.5–2 cm), oblong to lanceolate, violet-blue, occasionally pink or white, anthers cream; includes 'Alba', with white flowers, and 'Rosa', with pink flowers).

Hyacinthus (an ancient Greek name used by Homer, the flowers being said to spring from the blood of the dead Hyakinthos). Liliaceae (Hyacinthaceae). HYACINTH. W and C Asia. 3 species, bulbous perennial herbs with linear-lanceolate to broadly strap-shaped leaves and cylindrical, scapose racemes of tubular to campanulate flowers with spreading to recurved perianth lobes in spring.

Smaller species, such as *H. orientalis* and *H. litwinowii*, are suited to the sunny rock garden or bulb frame and to sandy, well-drained soil. Most commonly grown are those highly fragrant and showy cultivars derived from *H. orientalis*, the Dutch hyacinths, and the looser-flowered Roman hyacinths, from *H. orientalis* var. *albulus*, which, with successional planting and selection may be had in bloom from Christmas until late spring. The Multiflora Group, producing several slender stems with individual blooms more loosely set, are also suitable for indoor and outdoor use. These cultivars are available in a wide color range and are used in traditional spring bedding, in beds and borders and in tubs and other containers.

Outdoor bulbs are planted in fall in an open and sunny position in well-drained, moderately fertile soil. Prepared bulbs for forcing are potted in fall, usually into a commercial bulb mix, and require a period of about 8–10 weeks, in cool, dark, moist conditions, to develop a good root system; at this stage, temperatures should not exceed 45–50°F (7–10°C). When necessary to apply water, avoid wetting the shoot, as this may cause the bulb to rot. On emergence of the shoot tips, increase temperatures to 50°F (10°C); thereafter, increase light and temperature as growth progresses. Alternatively,

on shoot emergence, place pots in a dark cupboard, at 64–68°F (18–20°C), and water plentifully. Bring into subdued light as the bud emerges (usually when the shoot is between 2½–3 in (6–8 cm) high) and increase light levels as growth progresses and the stem elongates. Forced hyacinths may be planted out after blooming in the open garden, and will flower in subsequent years, although the blooms will decline in quality. Bulbs forced in a bulb glass are best discarded after flowering.

Propagate species by ripe seed sown thinly in a loam-based propagating mix in the cold frame, so that seedlings may remain *in situ* during their first season's dormancy.

Increase cultivars by cutting out a cone of tissue from the bulb base, or by cutting crosswise slits through the base—both treatments result in the formation of large numbers of bulbils.

Hyacinth fire, caused by the fungus *Botrytis hyacinthi*, was so-called by Dutch growers because it could spread through the fields "like fire." Beginning at the tips, the leaves become brown and shrivelled; in damp conditions, a gray mold develops on affected parts and the flowers may be destroyed. If detected early enough, the disease can be controlled by fungicide sprays. In the disease known as black slime, the leaves turn yellow and fall over just after flowering; they can be pulled away easily because they are rotten at the base. The bulb scales are dry and dark gray but, under moist conditions, a white, fluffy mycelial growth develops on them. Black sclerotia, sometimes up to half an inch across, are formed between and within the scales and can remain in the soil to perpetuate the fungus. The aphid-transmitted virus diseases, hyacinth mosaic and ornithogalum mosaic, can cause a conspicuous yellow or gray leaf mottling; affected plants should be destroyed to prevent the diseases from spreading.

H. litwinowii Central Asia, E Iran; 4–10 in (10–25 cm); flowers 3–13, not

Bulbs may be forced in special, water-filled glass

Hyacinth

H

fragrant, perianth ¾–1 in (1.8–2.5 cm), green-blue, tube constricted above ovary, lobes longer than tube, spreading and recurved above, filaments longer than anthers; H. *orientalis* COMMON HYACINTH; C and S Turkey, NW Syria, Lebanon; to 12 in (30 cm); flowers 2–40, waxy, heavily scented, perianth ¾–1½ in (2–3.5 cm), pale blue to deep violet, pink, white or cream, tube as long as or exceeding lobes, constricted above ovary, lobes spreading or recurved, anthers longer than filaments. Cultivars and subspecies include: 'Amethyst', with lilac flowers; 'Anna Marie', with light pink flowers; 'Appleblossom', miniature, with shell pink flowers; 'Ben Nevis', with double, large, ivory white, compact flowers; 'Blue Jacket', with navy flowers, striped purple; the late-flowering 'City of Haarlem', with primrose flowers; 'Delft Blue', with soft blue flowers; 'Distinction', with deep burgundy to purple flowers; 'Gipsy Queen', with pale salmon orange flowers; 'Hollyhock', with double, crimson, compact flowers; 'Jan Bos', with cerise flowers; 'Lord Balfour', miniature, with claret flowers tinted violet; 'Multiflora White', with multiple stems and sparse, white flowers; 'Myosotis', with palest blue flowers; 'Ostara', with large, purple-blue flowers; 'Pink Pearl', with deep pink flowers, with paler edges; 'Sunflower', miniature, with bright yellow flowers; subsp. *orientalis*, with 2–12 flowers and a ¾–1¼ in (2–3 cm) perianth, pale violet-blue at base shading to white above, with lobes to four-fifths the length of tube.

hyaline transparent, translucent; usually applied to the margins of leaves and bracts.

hybrid a plant produced by the cross-breeding of two or more genetically dissimilar parents which generally belong to distinct taxa. A natural hybrid is one arising in nature; a spontaneous hybrid is one arising without the direct intervention of man, usually in gardens; an artificial hybrid is a cross deliberately made by man. Specific or interspecific hybrids arise between species of the same genus; intergeneric hybrids arise between taxa of different genera—the number of

genera involved being usually denoted by a prefix, for example bigeneric and trigeneric.

hybrid berries the large group of hybrids produced by crossing a wide range of *Rubus* species; often the species crossed are far apart botanically. The cultivation and propagation of hybrid berries should follow the same practices for the blackberry.

The LOGANBERRY was raised at the end of the 19th century in California by Judge Logan, reportedly from *Rubus ursinus* 'Auginbaugh' × 'Red Antwerp' raspberry. The PHENOMENAL BERRY was raised in 1905 in California by Luther Burbank as a second-generation selection from a cross between the 'Auginbaugh' and 'Cuthbert' raspberries. The VEITCHBERRY was introduced in England in 1902 as a cross between *Rubus rusticanus* × raspberry 'November Abundance', and is important as a parent of the earliest-fruiting blackberry 'Bedford Giant'. The YOUNGBERRY, introduced in 1926 as a cross between the phenomenal berry and a dewberry ('Austin Mayes'), has sweeter and better-colored fruits than loganberry and is widely grown in South Africa as South African loganberry.

BOYSENBERRY was introduced in 1935 and is similar to the youngberry, but of unknown origin. Grown widely in New Zealand and the north western states of the US, it has red-purple fruits and is moderately vigorous. The NECTARBERRY is probably a sport of boysenberry, and another selection is 'Riwaka', grown in New Zealand. MARIONBERRY resembles boysenberry though its origin is unrecorded. It has large, black, well-flavored fruit on vigorous plants, and yields over a longer period than boysenberry.

NESSBERRY was introduced in 1921 in Texas, from breeding work at the Texas Experimental Station. It combines the raspberry flavor of the fruit with the drought resistance of the dewberry, and has been important in breeding several erect blackberries, suited to commercial cultivation in the southern US.

TAYBERRY and TUMMELBERRY were introduced by the Scottish Crop Research Institute in 1979 and 1983 respectively. The parentage of tayberry

is 'Aurora' blackberry and a tetraploid raspberry; tummelberry, which ripens a week later than tayberry, results from a cross between tayberry and a sister seedling. Both have larger fruits than loganberry and are less acidic.

SUNBERRY is a loganberry-type fruit with good flavor, introduced from the East Malling Research Station, Kent, in 1981 as a cross between *Rubus ursinus* × raspberry 'Malling Jewel' seedling; SILVANBERRY is an Australian raised hybrid of very mixed parentage; it is very vigorous and produces large, dark red, sweet fruits; JAPANESE WINEBERRY (*R. phoenicolasius*) has red bristly stems and produces bright red conical fruits. See *jostaberry*, *Worcesterberry*.

hybrid vigor see *heterosis*.

hydathode a water-secreting gland on the surface or margin of a leaf, usually situated at the end of a vein and often surrounded by a concretion of white salts. It is similar to a stoma but with functionless guard cells, and is sometimes termed a lime-dot.

Hydrangea (from Greek *hydor*, water, and *aggeion*, vessel: an allusion to the cup-shaped fruit). Hydrangeaceae. China, Japan, the Himalaya, Philippines, Indonesia and N and S America. 100 species, deciduous or evergreen shrubs, small trees or climbers. Numerous small flowers are borne in panicles or corymbs. Many species bear larger, sterile flowers, usually at the outer edges of the corymbs; in these flowers, the conspicuous, colored part is the enlarged calyx.

Hydrangea species are grown primarily for their flowers, although a number of species also have handsome foliage, including *H. quercifolia* and *H. aspera*; those with foliage coloring well in fall include *H. serrata*, *H. quercifolia* and *H. heteromalla*. Flowers show two characteristic forms: the large, conspicuous and round-headed form composed of sterile ray florets, exemplified by the Hortensia group of garden hybrids, and the "lacecap" type, comprising the majority of species, where a central boss of small, insignificant, fertile florets is accompanied or surrounded by larger sterile ray florets. In *H. paniculata* and its clones, the flowers are carried in elegant, densely flowered, conical panicles.

Hydrangea species make most attractive specimens for the shrub or mixed border. Many, such as *H. quercifolia* and *H. aspera*, are effective in more informal situations in the open woodland garden (in general, large-leaved species require a position in semishade). *H. paniculata* is amenable to training as a single-stemmed standard; with hard pruning, it makes a multistemmed shrub, noted for its generosity in bloom.

The many named garden hybrids, largely derived from *H. macrophylla* and *H. serrata*, fall into two (horticultural) groups—the round-headed 'Hortensia' types, and the slightly hardier "lacecaps." These two groups are well-suited to seaside gardens. Although tolerant of alkaline soil, they may become chlorotic on shallow chalk. They include several cultivars suitable for tub cultivation or for use as house plants (usually for a single season). As with some of the species, the flowers are often dried for winter decoration. Tub cultivation has the additional advantage of permitting greater control over flower color than in open ground. Color is dependent on cultivar and on the availability of aluminum, which is largely determined by soil pH. In acidic soil at pH 4.5–5.5, flowers may achieve an intense deep blue ('Marechal Foch', 'Nikko Blue'), this changing to shades of pink as soil pH rises; with careful selection of cultivars, blooms may become a clear warm rose pink ('Queen Elizabeth', 'King George') or deeper shade (as in 'Hamburg' and 'Ami Pasquier') in soil at pH 7.4. In containers and in near-neutral soil, blue coloration may be maintained or enhanced by a weekly or semiweekly application of bluing compound (aluminum sulfate) at 3 oz per 3½ gallons (85 g per 13.5 liters) of water.

The climbing species, such as *H. anomala* and *H. serratifolia*, will climb up and through trees, although they may need initial support until they develop their aerial roots. *H. petiolaris* is particularly useful for shaded walls, usually showing good tolerance of atmospheric pollution.

Some hydrangeas are extremely hardy, such as *H. paniculata* and *H. arborescens* subsp. *discolor* and their

Lacecap hydrangea
H. villosa is a typical lacecap, with a central boss of inconspicuous, fertile florets and a few outer showy but infertile ray florets.

Mophead hydrangea
'Bouquet Rose' is one of the Hortensia group of garden hybrids, with large, tightly packed heads of conspicuous, infertile ray florets.

forms. *H. aspera* and its allies and the Hortensia and "lacecap" cultivars are generally winter hardy; in Europe, most appear to tolerate temperatures down to –4°F to –13°F (–20°C to –25°C). An undeserved reputation for a lack of hardiness is due to their long growing season, which makes early shoots and unripened fall growth particularly vulnerable to late spring and early fall frosts.

Grow in fertile, moist but well-drained soil, if necessary incorporating well-rotted organic matter to improve fertility; an annual mulch of the same in spring, with a top dressing of balanced fertilizer, is beneficial. Site in sun or part shade and, when in flower, provide some protection from cold winds and from full sun to preserve color. *H. involucrata* and *H. paniculata* will tolerate full sun, provided there is sufficient moisture in the growing season. In containers, use a medium-fertility, loam-based mix (omitting lime for blue flowers). For early flowers in pots, take leaf bud or stem cuttings in early spring, root in a closed case with bottom heat, pot on individually and pinch out in early summer. Overwinter under glass, at 41–50°F (5–10°C), watering sparingly; in late winter/early spring, gradually raise the temperature to 55°F (13°C), growing on in full sun with plentiful water.

A minimum of pruning is generally required. Vigorous species that flower at the tips of the current season's growth (e.g., *H. paniculata*, *H. arborescens*)

may have the previous season's growth cut back in late winter/early spring to 2–3 pairs of buds, in order to obtain extra large panicles of flowers for a more formal effect. Without pruning, such species will make large shrubs with a larger number of smaller flowers, a result which may be preferred. With clump-flowering types that produce shoots from the base (e.g., *H. serrata* and *H. macrophylla* cultivars), flowers are carried occasionally on these shoots but in the main are formed terminally on the previous season's wood. Pruning of these types should be confined to the removal of old flower heads (leave this until spring to help frost protection) and weak, congested or exhausted growth at the base; this allows light and air to the center of the bush, encouraging good ripening and flowers. Shoots should not be simply shortened back since, in most cases, the removal of the terminal bud will cause the flowers to be lost for that season.

Plants may, after many years, be rejuvenated by cutting hard back to the base. The crowded sheaf of shoots that results must be thinned as it grows to allow a few strong shoots to ripen fully. Climbing species, which flower on lateral shoots, require minimal pruning, other than the removal of unwanted extension growth in summer and the restriction of the outward spread of wall-grown plants. Cut back outward-growing laterals to a suitable bud in spring; this may best be done over several seasons to minimize loss of bloom.

H

Propagate species by seed sown under glass in early spring (offspring may be variable). Increase climbing species by basal softwood cuttings of non-flowering shoots; treat these with 0.8% IBA and root in a closed case with bottom heat at 68°F (20°C), or use the warm bench with plastic method. Propagate other species by hardwood stem or tip cuttings, or from leaf bud cuttings of the current season's growth; root these in a closed case with bottom heat at 55–59°F (13–15°C).

H. anomala Himalaya, China; deciduous climber to 39 ft (12 m); shoots becoming rough and peeling; leaves 3–5 in (7.5–13 cm), ovate, apex shortly acuminate, cordate at base, coarsely toothed, downy tufts in the vein axils beneath; corymbs fairly flat 6–8 in (15–20 cm) across, with few white, peripheral sterile flowers, each ⅝–1½ in (1.5–3.7 cm) across, and numerous, small, cream fertile flowers; *H. arborescens* E US; loose, open, deciduous shrub, 3¼–10 ft (1–3 m); shoots downy at first; leaves 3–6¾ in (7.5–17.5 cm), broadly ovate, acuminate, with coarse, teeth, shiny, dark green above, paler and downy beneath on veins; corymbs fairly flat, much-branched, 2–6 in (5–15 cm) across, with 0–8 long-stalked, creamy white sterile flowers, each ½–¾ in (1–1.8 cm) across, and numerous, small, dull white fertile flowers; *H. aspera* Himalaya, W and C China, Taiwan, Java, Sumatra; spreading deciduous shrub, or small tree, to 13 ft (4 m); shoots at first with spreading hairs, later hairless and peeling; leaves 3½–10 in (9–25 cm), lanceolate to narrowly ovate, acute or acuminate, rounded or tapered to the base, serrate, densely downy beneath, sparsely hairy above; corymbs fairly flattened, to 10 in (25 cm) across, with few to many white to pale pink or purple, darker-veined, sterile flowers with 4 rounded sepals, each to 1 in (2.5 cm) across, fertile flowers small, numerous, white-purple or pink; includes subsp. *strigosa*, with short, stiff hairs beneath leaves, and subsp. *sargentiana*, from China, a loose, spreading, deciduous shrub to 10 ft (3 m); shoots with small, erect hairs and translucent bristles; leaves 4–10 in (10–25 cm), broadly ovate, rounded at the base, velvety above, densely bristly beneath; corymb

fairly flattened, 5–8¾ in (12.5–22.5 cm) across, with a few, pink-white peripheral sterile flowers to 1¼ in (3 cm) across, and numerous, small, pale purple fertile flowers; *H. heteromalla* Himalaya, W and N China; deciduous shrub to 10 ft (3 m); shoots hairy at first later glabrous; leaves 3½–8 in (9–20 cm), narrowly ovate, rounded, crenate or sometimes cordate at base, toothed and bristly at the margins, pubescent beneath; corymbs flattened, 6 in (15 cm) across, with few white or ivory sterile flowers, each 1–2 in (2.5–5 cm) across, and numerous, small, white fertile flowers; includes Bretschneideri Group, with peeling bark, leaves white beneath, and white "lacecap" flowers; *H. involucrata* Japan, Taiwan; open, deciduous shrub to 6½ ft (2 m); shoots bristly at first; leaves 3–6 in (7.5–15 cm), broadly ovate to oblong, acuminate, finely toothed, bristly; corymbs irregular, 3–5 in (7.5–12.5 cm) across, enclosed by broadly ovate bracts covered with flattened white hairs, with few, long-stalked, pale blue or faintly pink sterile flowers, each ¾–1 in (1.8–2.5 cm) across, and numerous, small, blue fertile flowers; includes 'Hortensis', with more numerous, double, pink-white, sterile flowers; *H. longipes* C and W China; loose, spreading, deciduous, shrub, 6½–8 ft (2–2.5 m); shoots loosely downy at first; leaves 3–6½ in (7.5–17 cm), rounded to ovate, apex abruptly acuminate, cordate at base, sharply toothed, bristly; corymbs fairly flat, 4–6 in (10–15 cm) across, sterile flowers 8–9, white or faintly purple, to ¾ in (2 cm) across, fertile flowers small, white, numerous; *H. macrophylla* Japan; spreading deciduous shrub to 10 ft (3 m); shoots ± glabrous; leaves 4–8 in (10–20 cm), broadly ovate, acute or acuminate, coarsely toothed, glabrous; corymbs flattened, much-branched, with few pink lilac or blue sterile flowers, each 1¼–2 in (3–5 cm) across, and numerous small blue or pink fertile flowers; the wild type, sometimes called *H. macrophylla* var. *normalis* (syn. *H. maritima*) is a maritime plant with a corymb of the "lacecap" type; it is thought to be the ancestor of many cultivars of both "lacecap" and "mop-head" types; *H. paniculata* E and S China, Japan, Sakhalin; large decidu-

ous shrub or small tree to 13 ft (4 m); shoots at first pubescent; leaves 3–6 in (7.5–15 cm), ovate, acuminate, toothed, sparsely bristly; panicle conical or pyramidal, 6–8 in (15–20 cm), with few white-pink sterile flowers, each ¾–1¼ in (1.75–3 cm) across, and numerous yellow-white fertile flowers. Cultivars include: 'Everest', with dark green leaves and all-sterile, white to pink florets in large heads; 'Floribunda', with a long, narrow inflorescence and largely sterile, packed flowers; 'Grandiflora', with small, sterile, white flowers, turning pink-red, in very large panicles; 'Greenspire', with sterile, green flowers, becoming red-tinged; 'Kyushu', erect, with dark, shining, tapering leaves and many sterile flowers; 'Pink Diamond', with sterile flowers becoming pink in large panicles; 'Praecox', early-flowering, with toothed sterile flowers in small panicles; 'Tardiva', late-flowering; and 'Unique', with a very large inflorescence with many white sterile flowers; *H. petiolaris* Japan, Sakhalin, Korea, Taiwan; deciduous climber to 66 ft (20 m); shoots becoming rough and peeling; leaves 1½–4½ in (3.5–11 cm), ovate to rounded, shortly acuminate, ± cordate at base, finely toothed, sometimes pubescent beneath; corymbs flat, 6–10 in (15–25 cm) across, with to 12 white, peripheral sterile flowers, each 1–1¾ in (2.5–4.5 cm) across, and numerous, small, off-white fertile flowers; *H. quercifolia* SE US; loose, rounded, deciduous shrub, 3¼–8 ft (1–2.5 m); shoots thick, red-downy, then hairless and flaky; leaves 3–8 in (7.5–20 cm), ovate to rounded and deeply 5–7-lobed, minutely toothed, bristly, turning red-bronze in winter; panicles conical-pyramidal, 4–10 in (10–25 cm), with numerous long-stalked, white sterile flowers, each 1–1½ in (2.5–3.5 cm) across, and numerous, small, white fertile flowers; includes 'Snow Flake', with predominant, double, green sterile florets, turning white as they mature; *H. scandens* S Japan, E Asia; spreading or almost pendulous shrub to 3¼ ft (1 m); shoots glabrous or very finely pubescent; leaves 2–3½ in (5–9 cm), lanceolate or oblong to ovate, shortly toothed, finely pubescent on the veins beneath; corymbs fairly flattened, to 3 in (7.5 cm) across, with a few white-blue sterile flowers, each $3/4$–$1\frac{1}{2}$ in (1.75–3.75 cm) across, fertile flowers numerous, white, with small, clawed petals; H. *seemanii* Mexico; evergreen climber or creeper with dark green, leathery, elliptic, acuminate leaves and white flowers; differs from *H. serratifolia* in its inflorescence—a single terminal corymb (not many)—and the presence of large, sterile flowers; H. *serrata* Japan and Korea; spreading deciduous shrub to $6\frac{1}{2}$ ft (2 m); shoots at first finely pubescent; leaves 2–6 in (5–15 cm), lanceolate, acuminate, glabrous above, veins beneath with short hairs; corymbs flattened, 2–4 in (5–10 cm) across, with to 12 pink or blue sterile flowers, each $\frac{1}{2}$–$5/8$ in (1–1.5 cm) across, and numerous, small, pink or blue fertile flowers; "lacecap" cultivars derived from *H. serrata* include 'Bluebird', 'Blue Deckle', 'Diadem' and 'Miranda', blue, compact, tending to be hardier than those of *H. macrophylla* origin and some of the best for general garden use; H. *serratifolia* Chile, Argentina; evergreen climber, to 100 ft (30 m); shoots at first finely pubescent; leaves 2–6 in (5–15 cm), elliptic, acuminate, base often cordate, usually entire, leathery; inflorescence to 6 × $3\frac{1}{2}$ in (15 × 9 cm), composed of numerous small corymbs arranged one above the other, each at first enclosed by 4 papery bracts, flowers small, fertile, white, some variants exist with 1 or few white sterile flowers). *Cultivars* In most cultivars, the color of the corymbs is influenced by the presence of aluminum in the soil. Some "lacecap" cultivars, such as 'Bluebird', are often associated with *H. macrophylla*; they belong, however, to *H. serrata*, which some authorities treat as a subspecies of *H. macrophylla*.

Mophead hydrangeas (Hortensias) These bear predominantly sterile flowers, which may be single or double and produced throughout the flower head; the inflorescences are compact to loose, usually rounded. They include: the semidwarf 'Ami Pasquier', with crimson to plum, nonfading flowers; 'Ayesha'—also known as 'Silver Slipper'—with glossy green leaves and cupped lilaclike florets in misty lilac to pink flattened heads; 'Générale Vicomtesse de Vibraye', tall, with light aqua blue flowers in dense heads; 'Hamburg', large, with long-lasting,

deep vivid pink to purple flowers and deeply serrated sepals; 'Heinrich Seidel', of stiff growth, with cherry red to purple flowers in dense heads; 'Holstein', with abundant, pink to sky blue flowers and serrate sepals; 'Joseph Banks'—also known as 'Hortensis'— $7\frac{1}{4}$ ft (2.25 m), with flowers opening green, aging pink to blue; the original introduction from China; 'Madame Emile Mouillère—also known as 'Sedgwick's White'—stem unspotted, with white flowers with a pink to blue eye; the compact, late 'Mathilde Gutges', with intense blue to purple flowers; 'Niedersachsen', tall, with very pale blue or pink flowers, reliable; 'Nigra', with an almost black stem and rose to blue flowers; 'Nikko Blue', with pink to bright blue flowers; 'Otaksa', with rounded leaves and pink to blue flowers; an early 'Hortensia' from Japan; 'Pia', dwarf, to 12 in (30 cm), with pink to red flowers in an irregular inflorescence; 'Preziosa', a hybrid with *H. serrata*, tinged purple-red throughout, with rose to purple red flowers; 'Vulcain', dwarf, with deep pink-purple or orange and green flowers; and 'Westfalen', with red to purple flowers, nearest to crimson in alkaline soil.

Lacecap hydrangeas These bear sterile flowers that are largely peripheral to the flower head with pedicels to 2 in (5 cm); the inflorescences are flattened. "Lacecaps" include 'Lanarth White', compact, with pink to blue fertile flowers and white ray florets; 'Lilacina', strong growing, with pink through lilac to blue flowers and serrate florets; 'Mariesii', with pale pink flowers, reluctantly blue, the inflorescence including both large and small ray florets; 'Quadricolor', with leaves mottled cream, yellow, pale and dark green; 'Sea Foam', with blue flowers edged by white ray florets; arose as a branchsport on a plant of 'Joseph Banks'; 'Tricolor', with leaves mottled cream, yellow, pale and dark green; 'Veitchii', with dark green leaves and white flowers aging pink; and 'White Wave', with pink to blue fertile flowers, surrounded by pearly white ray florets.

Hydrocharis (from Greek *hydor*, water, and *charis*, graceful, referring to the appearance of these aquatic plants). Hydrocharitaceae. Europe,

W Asia, N Africa. FROGBIT. 2 species, aquatic, perennial herbs with slender, stolonlike stems, usually floating and rooting, and rosettes of small, stalked leaves with smooth, rounded to reniform leaves. Produced in spring and summer, the flowers are solitary or clustered and consist of three, broad petals. For sunny garden ponds. In cold areas, a sufficient depth of water must be given to prevent freezing in winter. Plants are free-floating; alkaline water is preferred. Resting buds are formed in fall each year and sink to overwinter at the bottom, rising with increasing light levels in early summer to produce young plants. Increase in spring by the introduction of runners thrown on to the water surface. Alternatively, propagate from seed sown in pots of a loambased medium; stand these in shallow trays of water. H. *morsus-ranae* FROGBIT; Europe, W Asia; leaves small, rounded to heart-shaped, bright green, flowers to $3/4$ in (2 cm) across, white stained yellow.

hydroculture a synonym of hydroponics, but often reserved for the cultivation of plants in nutrient-enriched water using sterile aggregate to support plant roots. As such it is a valuable technique for interior landscaping, where ornamental plants are grown in shallow tanks. See *hydroponics*.

hydroleca see *clay granules*.

hydrophyte a plant that grows partly or wholly submerged in water.

hydroponics, hydroponic culture the cultivation of plants in nutrient-enriched water. The Nutrient Film Technique (N ft), which was devised in the UK for commercial production in 1975, overcomes the constraints of poor aeration. Plants are raised in small blocks of rock wool and stood in polythene-film troughs containing a circulated solution less than $1/4$ in (5 mm) deep. A prepared slope of 1:75 is required from one end of a greenhouse to the other for the continuous troughs, the edges of which are clipped together between plants. Dilute nutrient solution is pumped from a catchment tank to the feeder end of the troughs, from where there is a flow rate along the troughs of about $3\frac{1}{2}$

H

pints (2 liters) per minute. Electronic devices monitor pH and conductivity of the solution and inject nutrients and acid. Typical nutrient concentrations in parts per million for tomatoes would be 150–300 calcium, 40–50 magnesium, 3–6 iron, 0.5–1.0 manganese, 0.1 copper, 0.1 zinc, 0.3–0.4 boron and 0.05 molybdenum. See *hydroculture*.

hydroseeding the sowing of imbibed seed in a stream of water, practiced with grass seed for large areas or on steep slopes.

hydrotropism growth in the direction of moisture, demonstrated especially by the roots of seedlings. See *stimulus movements*.

hygrometer an instrument for measuring atmospheric humidity, such as a wet-and-dry bulb thermometer, or electrolytic or dial gauge.

Hygrophila (from Greek *hygros*, wet, and *-philos*, loving, referring to the aquatic habitats of some species). Acanthaceae. Tropics. Some 100 species, aquatic or marginal perennial herbs. The leaves may range in form from entire to finely dissected, according to the degree of submersion. The flowers are small, tubular and 2-lipped, and arranged in whorl-like clusters in terminal racemes. Suited to the pool margin in the tropical greenhouse or aquarium; the submerged foliage is almost invariably more attractive. Leaf form in *H. difformis* is extremely variable, the more desirable, finely pinnate forms depending on high light intensity for their development; maintain a minimum water temperature of 68°F (20°C). In similar well-illuminated conditions, the undemanding *H. polysperma* may develop a red cast to the leaves and, where water temperatures remain at or above 59°F (15°C), will remain evergreen. Detached leaves will root if allowed to float freely. *Hygrophila* does not show marked preferences for substrates.

H. difformis WATER WISTERIA; SE Asia; evergreen; stem to 24 in (60 cm),

slender, soft, rooting; immersed leaves to 4 in (10 cm), pinnatifid, translucent, brittle, emersed leaves smaller, thicker, lanceolate to ovate, crenate; flowers to ¾ in (2 cm), lilac or violet marked purple on lower lip; H. *polysperma* India, Bhutan; deciduous; stem to 20 in (50 cm), submerged, rather woody; leaves to 1½ in (4 cm), oblong to lanceolate, pale green; flowers to ⅜ in (0.8 cm), white to sky blue or pale lilac, downy.

hygrophyte a plant that grows under permanently moist conditions.

hygroscopic expanding when water is present, contracting in its absence; hygroscopic water is water retained in essentially dry soil and unavailable to plants because of high surface tension forces.

Wet-dry thermometer (see hygrometer)

Hylocereus (from Greek *hyle*, wood, and *Cereus*). Cactaceae. C America, West Indies, Colombia and Venezuela. Some 16 species, epiphytic, climbing or scrambling cacti. Segmented and slender, the stems are usually 3-winged or angled, with short spines and aerial roots. Large, funnel-shaped flowers open at twilight and last for one night only. Provide a minimum temperature of 50°F (10°C). Grow in an acidic mix rich in bark. Shade in summer, and maintain high humidity. Reduce watering in winter. *H. undatus* epiphytic or climbing to 16 ft (5 m) or more; flowers 10 × 12 (25–30 cm) × 6–10 in (15–25 cm), white; fruit to 6 in (15 cm) in diameter, globose, edible.

Hylomecon (from Greek *hyle*, wood, and *mekon*, poppy). Papaveraceae. Japan, Korea, E China. 1 species, *H. japonica*, a deciduous, perennial herb, to 12 in (30 cm). To 10 in (25 cm) long, the leaves are pinnately divided, toothed and bright green. Produced in spring and summer, the long-stalked, solitary flowers are 2 in (5 cm) across with four, rounded, golden yellow petals. Hardy and suitable for damp, cool, and humus-rich soil in the wild garden, especially in light woodland,

and for the shady rock garden. Propagate from seed sown in spring, or by careful division in early spring.

Hymenocallis (from Greek *hymen*, membrane, and *kalos*, beauty, referring to the attractive corona). Amaryllidaceae. Subtropical and tropical Americas. SPIDER LILY. 30–40 species, bulbous perennial herbs with elliptic to strap-shaped leaves, their bases stalklike or sheathing. In spring and summer, stout scapes are topped with umbels of fragrant white or ivory flowers. The perianth is tubular to funnel-shaped, with six spreading lobes. The six stamens are fused at their bases into a showy cup (corona) inserted into the top of the perianth tube. Provide a minimum temperature of 50°F (10°C). Grow in a light, well-drained potting mix of equal parts loam, leaf mold and sharp sand, in bright filtered light. Water plentifully when in growth and continue watering and liquid-feeding after flowering, as for *Hippeastrum*. Keep just moist when resting. Propagate from offsets or by seed.

H. × *festalis* (*H. longipetala* × *H. narcissiflora*); scape 4 in (10 cm), flowers pure white; perianth tube curved, 1½ in (4 cm), lobes to 4½–1½ in (11.5 × 1.3 cm), curved: staminal cup to 2 × 2½ in (5 × 6.5 cm), with reflexed teeth, free ends of filaments to 1½ in (4 cm); style far exserted; H. *latiflora* CAYMAN ISLANDS SPIDER-LILY, CHRYSOLITE LILY; flowers 2½–4¾ in (6–12 cm), perianth tube to 6 in (16 cm), lobes to 4 in (10 cm), linear, arching; H. × *macrostephana* (*H. narcissiflora* × *H. speciosa*); scape 12–18 in (30–45 cm); perianth tube to 3¼ in (8.5 cm), green below, white above, segments linear to lanceolate, 3½–4½ in (9–11 cm), white to pale green-yellow, outer whorl with thickened green tips; corona funnel-shaped, to 2½ × 3 in (6 × 7.5 cm), bluntly toothed, white; free part of filaments 1 in (2.5 cm), style far exserted; H. *narcissiflora* PERUVIAN DAFFODIL, BASKET FLOWER; scape equalling leaves; perianth tube funnelform above, to 4 in (10 cm), spreading, green, lobes to 4 × ½ in (10 × 1.2 cm), lanceolate; staminal cup, to 2 in (5 cm) long and more than 2 in (5 cm) in diameter, striped green, with rounded spreading toothed processes, filaments to ½ in (12 mm), pointing inward; style exceeding limb; H. *palmeri* ALLIGATOR LILY; scape to 10 in

(25 cm); perianth tube 3 in (8 cm), yellow-green, lobes to 4 in (10 cm), filiform, linear, spreading from base; staminal cup funnelform, with erect dentate margins, to 1¼–2 in (3–5 cm), filaments 1½ in (4 cm); H. *speciosa* scape to 16 in (40 cm); flowers 7–12, green tinged; perianth tube to 3½ in (9 cm), lobes to 6 in (15 cm); staminal cup funnelform, to 2 in (5 cm), margin toothed, filaments nearly erect to 2 in (5 cm).

Hymenosporum (from Greek *hymen*, a membrane, and *sporos*, seed, the seed has a membranous wing). Pittosporaceae. Australia. 1 species, *H. flavum*, AUSTRALIAN FRANGIPANI, an evergreen, narrow-crowned tree or large shrub, to 39 ft (12 m) tall. The glossy, deep green leaves are 2¾–6 in (7–15 cm) long, oval to oblong and entire with a narrowly tapering apex. Produced in spring and summer in lax panicles to 8 in (20 cm) across, the flowers are intensely fragrant and creamy white, aging golden-yellow. To 1 in (2.5 cm) in diameter, they consist of five, obovate petals, united in a short tube below and spreading above. Grown for its fragrant creamy flowers and dark glossy foliage, *Hymenosporum* makes an attractive lawn specimen in frost-free climates. It is also suited to tub cultivation in the cool greenhouse or conservatory. Propagation as for *Pittosporum*.

Hyophorbe (from Greek *hys*, pig, and *phorbe*, food: the fruits are eaten by pigs). Palmae. Mascarene Islands. BOTTLE PALM, PIGNUT PALM. 5 species, medium-sized to large palms with a single trunk often strongly swollen at the base or middle, then tapering to a slender neck. The leaves are pinnate and arching with linear-lanceolate leaflets and smooth petiole bases forming a distinct crown shaft. Beautiful feather palms from the coastal forests of the Mascarene Islands, where they are threatened with extinction. In the coastal gardens of the low-altitude tropics and subtropics, they make curious and elegant specimens, with arching foliage emerging from the prominent crown shaft above a more or less swollen stem; they are sometimes used there in avenue plantings. When available, they are fine palms for large pots in the warm greenhouse or conservatory. Propagate by seed.

H. lagenicaulis BOTTLE PALM; Round Island; trunk to 20 ft (6 m), closely ringed, gray, with vertical cracks, flask-shaped, expanded base to 28 in (70 cm) in diameter; leaves to 6½ ft (2 m), pinnae to 70 each side of rachis, 6½–24 in (17–60 cm), with 2 pairs of lateral veins prominent above and beneath; H. *verschaffeltii* SPINDLE PALM; Rodrigues Island; trunk to 16 ft (5 m), gray, markedly ringed, to 10 in (25 cm) in diameter, straight becoming tapered; leaves to 5¾ ft (1.75 m), pinnae to 80 each side of rachis, glossy green above, dull green beneath, midrib prominent above, no veins prominent beneath.

hypanthium cup-, ring- or tubelike structure formed by the enlargement and fusion of the basal portions of calyx, corolla and stamens, together with the receptacle on which these parts are borne, as in Rosaceae. It is sometimes termed the floral cup or, inaccurately, the calyx tube.

Hypericum (Greek name for this plant, used by Dioscorides and earlier authors, from *hyper*, above, and *eikon*, image). Guttiferae. Cosmopolitan except for tropical lowlands, arctic, high altitude and desert regions. Over 400 species, small trees, shrubs or herbs, evergreen or deciduous and dotted with pale and dark glands. The stems are often ridged or angled at first, and the rounded to oblong to ovate leaves are paired or sometimes whorled. Solitary or cymose flowers are produced usually in summer. They are typically dish- or bowl-shaped with five (rarely four) yellow petals and numerous stamens in distinct bundles or a single boss. The fruit is a fleshy, spherical to ellipsoid capsule sometimes ripening from dull red to purple-black.

In general terms, the following are hardy to −10°F (−23°C), possibly lower. They favor full sun or part shade and fertile, well-drained soil. H. *calycinum* is rampant and resilient groundcover in shade or sun, but may become a nuisance in smaller gardens. H. 'Rowallane' and H. 'Hidcote' are useful additions to informal shrub and mixed borders. The colorful fruits of H. 'Elstead' extends the season of interest into fall; they are also used by flower arrangers, lasting well in water.

Grown in a sunny, sheltered spot, *H. hookerianum*, its hybrids and cultivars are among the most attractive free-standing shrubs in the genus. Many of the alpine, Mediterranean and Southwest Asian shrublets are found on chalk or limestone soils and will benefit from neutral to alkaline soil in the garden. These include H. *cerastioides*, H. *coris*, H. *olympicum* and H. *reptans*. They require open, well-drained sites in full sun on the rock garden, gravel garden, on scree or between paving stones. H. *empetrifolium* may succumb to wet and cold unless grown in the alpine house. The more choice, Asiatic shrubs and the alpine shrublets may be cut to the ground at temperatures below 14°F (−10°C), but will usually regenerate from the base if the rootstock has been mulched. H. *calycinum* is hardy to at least −4°F (−20°C).

Prune H. *calycinum* by shearing back almost to ground level every second year. Cut out deadwood for other species in spring or stool them back annually to within an inch or two of the previous season's growth. Plants with long, gracefully arching stems should be pruned only by removal of old shoots at the base. Propagate from seed sown in spring; by heeled, semi-ripe cuttings in a cold frame, or (alpine species) by basal softwood cuttings in early summer. Where creeping rhizomes or rooting stems are produced, propagate by division of layers. Affected by the rust fungus *Melampsora hypericorum*, which produces pustules on the undersurfaces of leaves. Leaves may also be tied together by the caterpillars of the carnation tortrix moth.

H. acmosepalum China; shrub, 2–6½ ft (0.6–2 m), branches erect, gradually outcurving; leaves ¾–2½ in (1.8–6 cm) oblong to elliptic, apex obtuse to rounded, paler or glaucous beneath, thinly coriaceous to thickly papery; flowers 1¼–2 in (3–5 cm), diameter, 1–3, terminal, star-shaped, deep yellow, sometimes red-tinged; H. *balearicum* Balearic Islands; evergreen shrub or tree, 2–6½ ft (0.6–2 m), spreading; stem and leaves glandular; leaves ¼–⅝ in (0.6–1.5 cm), ovate to oblong, apex rounded, somewhat undulate; flowers ⅝–1½ in (1.5–4 cm) in diameter, solitary, star-shaped, golden, exterior faintly red-tinged; H. *beanii* China;

shrub 2–6½ ft (0.6–2 m), bushy, robust, erect or arching; leaves 1–2½ in (2.5–6.5 cm), narrowly elliptic or oblong to lanceolate or ovate, paler to glaucous below, thickly papery to thinly coriaceous; flowers 1¼–1¾ in (3–4.5 cm) in diameter, 1–14, terminal, star-shaped to cupped, golden yellow; H. *bellum* N India, China, Burma; shrub 1–5 ft (0.3–1.5 m), erect to arching; leaves ⅝–3 in (1.5–7.8 cm), oblong-lanceolate to subcircular, apex obtuse to rounded or indented, often apiculate, paler or glaucous beneath, thickly papery; flowers 1–2½ in (2.5–6 cm) in diameter, 1–7, terminal, cupped, golden to butter-yellow or pale yellow; H. *calycinum* Bulgaria, Turkey; shrub 8–24 in (0.2–0.6 m) tall, evergreen, with creeping branching stolons and erect stem; leaves 1¾–4 in (4.5–10.4 cm), oblong to elliptic or narrowly ovate, apex obtuse or apiculate, pale beneath, leathery; flowers 1 (rarely 2–3), star-shaped, bright yellow; H. *cerastioides* Bulgaria, Greece, Turkey; perennial herb, 2¾–11 in (7–27 cm), often shrubby at base, decumbent or ascending; leaves ½–1¼ in (1–3 cm), oblong to elliptic or ovate, apex rounded, downy, slightly paler beneath, thickly papery; flowers ¾–1¾ in (2–4.5 cm) in diameter, star-shaped, 1–5, bright yellow; H. *coris* SE France, Switzerland, N and C Italy; dwarf subshrub or perennial herb, 4–18 in (10–45 cm); leaves ¼–¾ in (0.5–1.8 cm), in whorls, linear, apex shortly apiculate to rounded, revolute, glaucous beneath, coriaceous; flowers ⅝–¾ in (1.5–2 cm) in diameter, star-shaped, 1 to 20, in a broadly pyramidal to shortly cylindric inflorescence, golden yellow, sometimes veined red; H. × *cyathiflorum* (probably H. *addingtonii* × H. *hookerianum*); shrub to about 5 ft (1.5 m), widely spreading; leaves 1¼–3 in (3–7.5 cm), lanceolate, apex acute to apiculate, paler beneath, thickly papery; flowers 1½–2 in (4–5 cm) in diameter, cupped, golden yellow; introduced as H. *patulum* 'Gold Cup'. H. *empetrifolium* Albania, Greece, Crete, Turkey, Cyprus, Libya; shrublet to 24 in (60 cm) erect, tufted and narrowly branched, or cushionlike, sometimes procumbent, rooting at nodes; leaves ¹⁄₁₆–½ in (0.2–1.2 cm), in whorls, linear or narrowly elliptic, revolute, paler beneath, coriaceous; flowers ½–¾

Hypericum 'Hidcote'
This garden hybrid forms a large, dense, and bushy shrub, with dark green foliage and flowers from midsummer to early fall.

in (1–2 cm) diameter, star-shaped, 1–40 in (2.5–101 cm) cylindric to slender pyramidal inflorescence, golden yellow; H. *forrestii* SW China, NE Burma; shrub, 1–5 ft (0.3–1.5 m), bushy ± erect; leaves ¾–2½ in (2–6 cm), lanceolate or triangular-ovate to broadly ovate, apex obtuse to rounded, paler beneath, thickly papery; flowers 1–2½ in (2.5–6 cm) in diameter, 1–20, usually deeply cupular, golden; H. 'Hidcote' (probably H. × *cyathiflorum* 'Gold Cup' × H. *calycinum*); shrub to 5¾ ft (1.75 m), bushy; branches arching to spreading; leaves 1¼–2½ in (3–6 cm), triangular to lanceolate, apex acute to obtuse or slightly mucronate, thickly papery; flowers 1½–2½ in (3.5–6.5 cm) in diameter, produced over a long time, forming subcorymbiform inflorescence, cupped, golden yellow; H. *hookerianum* India, N Thailand, Bangladesh; shrub 1–6½ ft (0.3–2 m), bushy, round-topped erect to spreading; leaves 1–3 in (2.5–8 cm), narrowly lanceolate to oblong, apex acute to rounded, paler or glaucous beneath, thickly papery; flowers 1¼–2½ in (3–6 cm) in diameter, 1–5, terminal, deeply cupped, deep to pale yellow; H. × *inodorum* (H. *androsaemum* × H. *hircinum*); deciduous shrub 2–6½ ft (0.6–2 m), bushy, erect; leaves 1½–4½ in (3.5–11 cm), oblong-lanceolate to broadly ovate, apex acute to rounded, somewhat paler beneath papery; flowers ⅝–1¼ in (1.5–3 cm) in diameter, star-shaped or cupped, golden yellow; widely naturalized; yellow-leaved and variously variegated cultivars include 'Summergold', 'Ysella', 'Goudelsje', 'Hysan' and 'Beattie's Variety';

'Elstead' is a selection (or back-cross to H. *androsaemum*) with large fruit that flush rosy-red, not the usual cerise, during ripening; H. *kouytchense* China; shrub 3¼–6 ft (1–1.8 m), bushy; branches arching or pendulous; leaves ¾–2¼ in (2–5.8 cm), elliptic to ovate or lanceolate, apex acute to obtuse or rounded to apiculate, paler beneath, thickly papery; flowers 1½–2½ in (4–6.5 cm) in diameter, star-shaped, bright golden yellow; H. × *moserianum* (H. *patulum* × H. *calycinum*); shrub 12–28 in (30–70 cm), semievergreen, spreading or arching; leaves ¾–2½ in (2.2–6 cm), oblong to lanceolate or ovate, acute to apiculate, paler beneath, thickly leathery; flowers 1¾–2½ in (4.5–6 cm) in diameter, 1–8, forming subcorymbiform inflorescence star-shaped or slightly cupped, bright yellow; 'Tricolor': leaves variegated cream, pink and green; H. *olympicum* Greece, Balkans, Turkey; dwarf shrub, ¼–1½ in (0.5–4 cm) erect to creeping; leaves ¼–1½ in (5–38 mm), oblong to elliptic or ovate to linear, apex acute to obtuse, thinly glaucous, thinly coriaceous; flowers ¾–2½ in (2–6 cm) in diameter, star-shaped, golden to lemon yellow, sometimes tinted red; 'Sunburst': robust, flowers large; 'Citrinum': flowers lemon yellow. 'Sulphureum': leaves narrow, flowers pale yellow; H. *patulum* China, introduced Taiwan, Japan, shrub 12–5 ft (0.3–1.5 m), bushy, arching to spreading, sometimes weakly frondose; leaves ⅝–2½ in (1.5–6 cm), lanceolate or oblong-lanceolate to ovate, glaucous beneath, thickly papery; flowers 1–1½ in (2.5–4 cm) in diameter, forming subcorymbiform inflorescence, cupped, golden yellow; H. *reptans* Himalaya; shrublet, prostrate or ascending to 12 in (0.3 m), forming clumps or mats; leaves ¼–¾ in (0.7–2.2 cm), elliptic to obovate, obtuse to rounded, paler beneath, leathery; flowers ¾–1¼ in (2–3 cm) in diameter, solitary, ± deeply cupped; petals, deep golden yellow, sometimes tinged red; H. 'Rowallane' (probably H. *leschenaultii* × H. *hookerianum* 'Charles Rogers'); shrub to 10 ft (3 m); branches erect, gradually outcurving; leaves 1–2¾ in (2.7–6.7 cm), ovate to oblong-lanceolate, paler or glaucous beneath, thinly coriaceous to thickly papery. Flowers

2–3 in (5–7.5 cm) in diameter, 1–3, terminal, shallowly cupped.

hypertrophy abnormal development of plant tissue due to an increase in cell size which may result from various causes including disease infection.

hypertufa an artificial material with water absorbent properties similar to tufa, made by mixing one part cement, one part sand, and one or two parts finely granulated peat, or a similar material, with water. It is used for the cultivation of alpines, and for coating glazed sinks to resemble troughs of natural stone.

hypha, hyphae the branching filament that is the basic form of most fungi.

hypocotyl the axis of an embryo lying beneath the cotyledons and, on germination, developing into the radicle.

Hypoestes (from Greek *hypo*, under, and *estia*, house: the calyx is enclosed by bracts). Acanthaceae. South Africa, Madagascar, SE Asia. Some 40 species, evergreen perennial herbs, subshrubs and shrubs with clustered or solitary, tubular, two-lipped flowers. The following species is a popular houseplant, much valued for its colorful foliage. Cultivation as for *Justicia*. *H. phyllostachya* POLKA DOT PLANT, MEASLES PLANT; evergreen subshrub to 3¼ ft (1 m); leaves to 2 in (5 cm), oval, dark green flecked or blotched white to pink or purple-red; flowers magenta to lilac.

hypogeal describing a type of germination where the cotyledons remain underground, gradually giving up their stored food reserves to the developing plumule and radicle, for example broadbean cf. epigeal.

hypogynous borne beneath the ovary, generally on the receptacle; used of the calyx, corolla and stamens of a superior ovary.

Hypoxis (from Greek *hypo*, beneath, and *oxys*, sharp, referring to the base of the capsule). Hypoxidaceae. N America, Africa, Australia, tropical Asia. STAR GRASS. About 150 species,

perennial cormous herbs. The clumped, basal leaves are narrowly sword- or strap-shaped, sometimes ridged beneath and often hairy. Produced singly or in sparse racemes in spring and summer, the flowers are starry and consist of six, outspread, ovate to oblong tepals. Grow in light, freely draining soil in full sun or in light dappled shade with a minimum temperature of 45°F (7°C). Keep well-ventilated as the shoots appear; water sparingly until the roots are growing well, and thereafter moderately. Keep plants moist when in full growth and then gradually dry off and store dry in a shaded and frost-free position. Propagate by seed and offsets.

H. angustifolia South Africa; leaves 4–6 in (10–15 cm), weakly hairy or smooth; flowers to ¾ in (2 cm) across, bright yellow, usually paired; *H. capensis* WHITE STAR GRASS; South Africa; leaves 4–12 in (10–30 cm), smooth; flowers ¾–2½ in (2–6 cm) across, white or yellow with purple basal spots, solitary.

Hypsela (from Greek *hypselos*, high, referring to the occurrence of the type species in the Andes). Campanulaceae. S America, New Zealand, Australia. 4 species, prostrate perennial herbs, with small, solitary flowers tubular below and spreading above in a 5-lobed, 2-lipped limb. Creeping

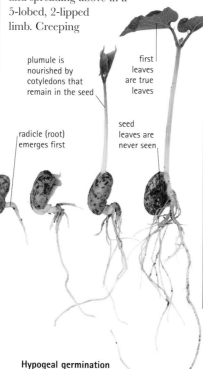

plumule is nourished by cotyledons that remain in the seed

first leaves are true leaves

radicle (root) emerges first

seed leaves are never seen

Hypogeal germination

plants forming dense low mats of ground cover, with a mass of tiny flowers in spring and summer. Well-suited to humus-rich and moisture-retentive gritty soil in the rock garden, in part to full shade. Hardy to between 23–14°F (−5 to −10°C). Propagate by division in spring. *H. reniformis* (syn. *H. longiflora*) S America; stem to 2 in (5 cm), creeping; leaves to ½ in (1 cm), elliptic to reniform; flowers small, white suffused pink, veined carmine, dotted yellow at base; includes 'Greencourt White', with bright green leaves and white flowers.

Hyssopus (identified, possibly mistakenly, with a plant described by Dioscorides). Labiatae. S Europe to C Asia. Some 10 species, strongly aromatic perennial herbs or dwarf shrubs with narrow leaves and spikes of tubular and 2-lipped flowers in summer. Grow individually in borders or pots; alternatively, use *H. officinalis* as a low hedge in the herb garden. Plant in well-drained soil on sunny sites. Pinch to give bushy plants. Propagate from seed or by softwood cuttings in spring or early summer. *H. officinalis* HYSSOP; S and E Europe, widely naturalized in Europe and US; erect to 24 in (60 cm); flowers violet or blue, occasionally white; includes 'Albus', with white flowers, 'Grandiflorus', with large flowers, 'Purpurascens', with deep red flowers, 'Roseus', with rose pink flowers, and 'Sissinghurst', dwarf and compact.

hysteranthous with leaves developing after the flowers; cf. *precocious* and *synanthous*.

Hystrix (from Greek *hystrix*, porcupine, referring to the spiky panicles). Gramineae. N America, N India, China, New Zealand. BOTTLEBRUSH GRASS. 6 species of perennial grasses. Grown for its flower heads, *H. patula* produces slender gray stems and swaying heads of long-awned, horizontally spreading spikelets. The flower heads should be picked when immature for air drying. Hardy to −10°F (−23°C), it grows best in moisture-retentive but well-drained soil in sun or light dappled shade, but also tolerates dry shade, and is therefore ideal for naturalistic woodland gardens. Propagate by division or by seed in spring.

I

IAA indole-3-acetic acid; an auxin capable of producing a wide range of growth effects in plants. Where synthesized as a product to aid the rooting of cuttings, it has the disadvantage of breaking down quickly before use in the presence of sunlight and where contaminated with plant or soil debris.

IBA indole-3-butyric acid; an auxin widely used in synthesized form as an aid to rooting cuttings. It is more extensively used than IAA because of its relative stability and effectiveness on many different plants.

Iberis (from Iberia, where most of the species are found). Cruciferae. S Europe, W Asia. CANDYTUFT. Some 30 species, annual or perennial herbs and subshrubs bearing small, white or mauve, 4-petaled flowers in racemes or corymbs in spring and summer. Hardy to 5°F (–15°C). Grow in well-drained and rather poor, neutral to alkaline soil in full sun. Propagate annuals by seed sown *in situ* from early spring to summer. For greenhouse blooms, sow during fall and midwinter at 59°F (15°C), growing in light, well-ventilated conditions, with a maximum temperature of 50°F (10°C). Perennials can be propagated by semiripe cuttings.

I. amara W Europe; annual; erect, bushy, 6–16 in (15–40 cm) tall; leaves lanceolate, entire to toothed; flowers white or purple-white, fragrant *I. saxatilis* SW Europe; evergreen perennial subshrub to 6 in (15 cm) tall; leaves subcylindrical, fleshy, linear to needle-like; flowers white, often tinged purple with age; *I. sempervirens* S Europe; spreading evergreen, perennial subshrub to 12 in (30 cm); leaves oblong to spathulate; flowers white; 'Snowflake': mound-forming, dark green leaves, flowers sparkling white; *I. umbellata*

S Europe; bushy annual to 12 in (30 cm) tall; leaves linear to lanceolate; flowers white, pale purple-pink or mauve, sometimes bicolored, in umbels.

ichneumon wasps (Hymenoptera: Ichneumonidae) small to medium-sized insects that are potentially beneficial to the gardener as a biological control of pests. They have two pairs of membraneous wings. The first segment of the abdomen is constricted to form a narrow waist. The adults are active in warm, sunny weather, frequenting flowers such as umbellifers. Their larvae are all parasitic, especially of butterfly and moth caterpillars, while some parasitize sawfly larvae. Others show a preference for beetles and to a lesser extent fly larvae, and a few parasitize spiders, aphids, and lacewings. The red-brown *Ophion* species are familiar, being often attracted to light at dusk, and these parasitize various noctuid moths. *Rhyssa persuasoria* is about 1 in (25 mm) long and the female has an ovipositor twice this length, with which it parasitizes the larvae of wood-boring wood wasps (*Urocerus* species) in conifer trunks.

Ichneumon wasp

Idesia (for Eberhard Ysbrant Ides [fl. 1720], Dutch traveler in Asia). Flacourtiaceae. S Japan, Taiwan, C and W China, Korea. 1 species, *I. polycarpa*, a dioecious, deciduous tree to 39 ft (12 m) tall with stout and spreading branches. The leaves are to 8 in (20 cm) long and cordate to ovate with toothed margins, dark green above and glaucous beneath. The petioles are red and to 8 in (20 cm) long. Small, fragrant, and yellow-green, the flowers are produced in summer in a pendulous panicle to 12 in (30 cm) long. Orange-red berries persist in crowded trusses after leaf fall. *Idesia* is hardy to 5°F (–15°C). Grow in free-draining but moist, neutral to slightly acidic soil in sun or light shade. Plants of both sexes are needed for fruit-set. Propagate by seed, or by softwood or semiripe cuttings in summer.

Ilex (from its resemblance to the leaves of *Quercus ilex*, the evergreen oak). Aquifoliaceae. Cosmopolitan, temperate and tropical. HOLLY. Over 400 species, evergreen and deciduous trees, shrubs and climbers with tough, entire, toothed to spiny-margined leaves. Small and yellow-green to white, the flowers are borne in the axils singly, in clusters, or in cymes. They are followed by shiny and sometimes highly colored berries.

Hollies are excellent, hardy plants for woodland or specimen planting, while some make fine hedges and windbreaks They will tolerate all but waterlogged soils.

Propagate by grafting in spring on seedlings of the species. Alternatively, increase by cuttings in late summer; reduce the number of leaves, dip in fungicide, put in a sandy mix, and place in mild heat. Cuttings will also root in an outside frame. Seed can take 2–3 years to germinate.

I. × *altaclarensis* (*I. aquifolium* × *I. perado*) large evergreen trees and shrubs to 65 ft (20 m), differing from *I. aquifolium* in their more vigorous growth, larger, broader and more variable leaves and larger fruit; includes numerous cultivars, among them selections with broad and dense to narrow, erect habits, leaves ranging in form from large, broad and spineless to puckered and prickly, in color from darkest green to lime and pure gold, some variegated yellow, white and gray-green, some female clones are very free-fruiting, with fruit ranging in color from scarlet to deep brick red; *I. aquifolium* ENGLISH HOLLY, COMMON HOLLY; S & W Europe, N Africa, W Asia; evergreen shrub or tree to 80 ft (25 m); leaves 2–4 in (5–10 cm), elliptic to ovate, dark glossy green, undulate, entire or spiny; fruit red; many cultivars, broadly conforming to the range described for *I.* × *altaclarensis*, but embracing a far greater variety of habit, from low and dense to tall and columnar; the berries may be dark blood red, scarlet, orange-red or yellow; the leaves range from small to large, narrow to broad, entire to viciously spiny; leaf coloration can include gold, lime, white and silvery gray splashes, tints and variegation, as well as bright pink flushes when young; *I.* × *aquipernyi* (*I. aquifolium* × *I. pernyi*) evergreen shrub or small tree to 20 ft (6 m); leaves similar to *I. pernyi*, to 1½ in (4 cm), apex prolonged, margins wavy-spiny; *I. ciliospinosa* W China; evergreen shrub to 20 ft (6 m); leaves elliptic to ovate, to 2 in (5 cm), acute, weakly spined, dull dark green; fruit red; *I. cornuta* CHINESE HOLLY, HORNED HOLLY; China, Korea; dense, rounded evergreen shrub to 13 ft (4 m); leaves rectangular, 2–3 in (5–8 cm), dull green, spines variable; fruit red; includes cultivars with dense, compact habits, leaves spiny to more or less spineless, some variegated yellow, others narrow and twisted; *I. crenata* JAPANESE HOLLY, BOX-LEAVED HOLLY; Japan, Korea, Sakhalin Is.; evergreen shrub or small tree to 16 ft (5 m); leaves ovate to elliptic, ⅝–1¼ in (1.5–3 cm), acute, crenate, dark green; fruit glossy black; includes many cultivars, ranging in habit from near-prostrate to dwarf and compact, some densely bushy, taller and suitable for low hedging; the leaves range from small to miniature broad to narrow, toothed to spineless, flat to puckered, and may be bright green, golden, variegated, dark green, purple-flushed or almost black; the best female clones produce glossy black berries in abundance; *I. dipyrena* HIMALAYAN HOLLY; W China, E Himalaya; evergreen tree to 50 ft (15 m); leaves 2–4½ in (5–11 cm), oblong or elliptic, acute or briefly tapering, entire or spiny in juveniles, dull mid-green; fruit red; *I. fargesii* China; evergreen shrub or small tree to 39 ft (12 m); leaves 2½–4¾ in (6–12 cm), oblanceolate to oblong-elliptic, apex tapering, serrate or entire near base, leathery, dull dark green; *I. georgei* Burma, Yunnan; wide-spreading, dense shrub to 16 ft (5 m); leaves 1½–2 in (3.5–5 cm), lanceolate to ovate, apex acuminate, weakly spined, leathery, dark glossy green; fruit red; *I. glabra* GALLBERRY, INKBERRY; E N America; evergreen, erect shrub to 10 ft (3 m); leaves ¾–2 in (2–5 cm), narrowly obovate to oblanceolate, entire or with a few teeth near the apex, glossy green; fruit black; includes cultivars with white berries,

Male and female hollies
Ilex cultivars may be male or female; the female plants, such as *I. aquifolium* 'Madame Briot' (left), bear the berries, but will not fruit unless a male, nonfruiting cultivar, such as *I. aquifolium* 'Ferox Argentea' (right), is planted within pollinating distance.

also dwarf and slow-growing, hardy selections, some with foliage flushed dark wine red during winter; *I. integra* Japan, Korea, Taiwan; evergreen shrub to 23 ft (7 m); leaves 2–3 in (5–8 cm), obovate to elliptic, blunt, entire, dark glossy green; fruit dark red; *I. kingiana* (syn. *I. insignis*) E Himalaya, Yunnan; evergreen tree to 18 ft (5.5 m); leaves 4½–9 in (11–22 cm), oblong, narrowly tapering, very spiny when juvenile, adults slightly serrate or entire, leathery, glossy green; fruit bright red; *I.* × *koehneana* (*I. aquifolium* × *I. latifolia*) evergreen tree to 23 ft (7 m); leaves 3–6 in (8–15 cm), oblong to elliptic, acute, glossy mid-green; fruit bright red; cultivars include free-fruiting, lime-green, bright green and black-green-leaved clones; *I. laevigata* SMOOTH WINTERBERRY; E US; differs from *I. verticillata* in its glabrous leaves and longer-stalked, orange-red to yellow fruit; *I. latifolia* TARAJO; Japan, China; erect, evergreen shrub to 23 ft (7 m); leaves 3–7 in (8–18 cm), oblong to oblong-ovate, blunt or briefly tapered, serrate, leathery, dark glossy green; fruit orange-red; *I. macrocarpa* S China; deciduous tree to 56 ft (17 m); branchlets short, spurlike; leaves 2¾–4½ in (7–11 cm), ovate to elliptic, tapered, finely toothed; fruit very large, black; *I.* × *meserveae* (*I. aquifolium* × *I. rugosa*) evergreen shrub to 6½ ft (2 m), resembling a small-leaved *I. aquifolium*; leaves glossy, often bluegreen, spiny; fruit red; cultivars include clones with improved hardiness, slow-

growing, compact habit, purple-tinted stems and new growth, foliage ranging from mid-green to dark, glossy bluegreen; *I. opaca* AMERICAN HOLLY; E & C US; evergreen tree to 50 ft (15 m); leaves 2–4¾ in (5–12 cm), oblong to elliptic, entire or spiny, usually tipped with a spine, dull matt green above, yellow-green beneath; fruit crimson; many cultivars varying in hardiness and rate of growth, some tall and open or conical to densely columnar, others small and compact to near-dwarf; there are also clones with exceptionally fine foliage and fruit, some yellow-berried; some, like 'Mrs. Santa' are suitable for hedging; 'St. Mary' is offered as a Christmas potted plant in N America; *I. pedunculosa* Japan, China, Taiwan; evergreen tree to 33 ft (10 m); leaves 1½–3 in (4–8 cm), ovate, acuminate, entire, dark glossy green; fruit bright red, long-stalked; *I. pernyi* C & W China; evergreen shrub or small tree to 28 ft (8.5 m); leaves ⅝–1¼ in (1.5–3 cm), triangular, margins 5-spined, apex tapered, base square, dark glossy green; fruit dark red; 'Jermyns Dwarf': habit low, arching; *I. serrata* JAPANESE WINTERBERRY; Japan, China; deciduous shrub to 13 ft (4 m); leaves 1½–3 in (4–8 cm), elliptic, apex acute to narrowly tapered, finely toothed, somewhat downy at first; fruit red; includes yellow- and whitefruited cultivars; *I. verticillata* BLACK ALDER, WINTERBERRY; E N America; deciduous, suckering shrub to 6½ ft (2 m); leaves 1½–4 in (4–10 cm), obovate to lanceolate, acuminate, serrate, bright green, hairy beneath; fruit red; includes cultivars with foliage that turns rich bronze in fall and berries ranging from bright scarlet to orange-red and yellow; the leafless, fruiting branches of some cultivars are sold in the cut-flower trade; *I. yunnanensis* Burma, China; evergreen shrub to 13 ft (4 m); leaves ¾–1½ in (2–3.5 cm), ovate to lanceolate, crenate to serrulate, glossy dark green; fruit red.

Illicium (from Latin *illicium*, allure, alluding to the attractive odor of these plants). Illiciaceae. SE Asia, SE US, West Indies. ANISE TREE. Some 40 species, evergreen, aromatic shrubs and small trees with thick-textured, glossy leaves. Produced during late spring and summer, the solitary flowers are borne in the leaf axils and consist of numerous, oblong, petal-like segments. Strongly anise-scented, the fruit is star-shaped with thinly woody 1-seeded carpels. The following are hardy to 0°F (–18°C), but prefer a sheltered situation, or wall protection. Grow in sun or part shade, in nonalkaline, humus-rich soil that is well-drained but never dry. Propagate from simple layers, alternatively by semiripe cuttings.

I. anisatum CHINESE ANISE; Japan, Taiwan; highly aromatic shrub or small tree to 26 ft (8 m); flowers to 1¼ in (3 cm) in diameter, segments to 30, yellow-green to white; *I. floridanum* PURPLE ANISE; SE US; shrub or small tree to 10 ft (3 m); flowers to 2 in (5 cm) in diameter, nodding, segments to 30, dark red, purple or maroon; *I. henryi* C and W China; shrub or small tree to 23 ft (7 m); flowers to ¾ in (2 cm) in diameter, cupped, segments 10–14, copper to dark red.

imago the adult form of an insect.

imbibition the absorption of water by seeds in preparation for germination.

imbricate of such organs as leaves or bracts, overlapping.

immersed (1) entirely submerged in water; cf. *emersed*; (2) features embedded and sunken below the surface of a leaf blade.

immortelle see *everlasting*.

immunity absolute and specific resistance of plants to disease or, less commonly, to pest infestation. Immunity is due to metabolic or morphological factors; it should not be confused with resistance or tolerance (two terms often used interchangeably). Immunity is a possible aim of plant breeders, and successful products are known as immune cultivars. The advantages of immune cultivars should be seen against one potential disadvantage: unlike resistant cultivars, they present fungal, bacterial and viral pathogens with a threat to their existence, and this encourages genetic variation in the attacking organism. A consequent breakdown in immunity of the host species can have catastrophic effects.

imparipinnate a pinnately compound leaf that terminates in a single leaflet, pinna or tendril; cf. *paripinnate*.

fleshy stems

copious seeds

Impatiens glandulifera

Impatiens (from Latin *impatiens*, impatient, referring to the elastic valves of the seed pod, which violently discharge the ripe seed). Balsaminaceae. Cosmopolitan except S America, Australia and New Zealand. BALSAM, BUSY LIZZIE, PATIENCE PLANT, SULTANA. 850 species, annual or perennial herbs or subshrubs with more or less succulent

stems. Borne in spring and summer, the flowers consist of five petals and a curving spur. The fruit is an explosive capsule which, when touched, suddenly splits and rolls inward, flinging the seeds in all directions. *I. walleriana*, *I. hawkeri*, and *I. balsamina* make good houseplants, but are more usually grown as summer-flowering bedding for borders and containers; they are particularly useful in shady sites. Grow species like *I. niamniamensis* and *I. repens* in the intermediate to hot greenhouse—keep the larger perennials fairly dry during winter dormancy, when leaf loss may occur. *I. glandulifera* and *I. capensis* will survive and self-sow in the open when winter temperatures fall to 5°F (–15°C) and below. They are suitable for naturalizing in the cool, shady wild garden, but may become invasive. Sow seed of these hardy species *in situ* in late spring.

For frost-tender species, sow seed under glass in spring and prick out into individual pots of a loamless or medium-fertility loam-based mix; grow on in sunny, airy but frost-free conditions, and pinch and turn frequently to create bushy plants. For bedding, plant out after the last frosts, and keep well-watered. Regular pinching of the succulent stems is necessary to obtain compact, attractive specimens. For the greenhouse or home, grow on in a low-fertility loam-based mix and give cool conditions and filtered light in summer, with direct light and a minimum temperature of 50°F (10°C) in winter. If the sideshoots and first flower buds of *I. balsamina* are removed, tall flowering spikes result. Propagate good color forms by softwood cuttings in spring; root in a soilless propagating mix in a closed case with gentle bottom heat. Seed of many of the warmer-growing species is short-lived. This is not the case, however, with *I. balsamina*, *I. hawkeri*, and *I. walleriana* and their cultivars.

I. balsamina ROSE BALSAM, TOUCH-ME-NOT; SE Asia; more or less unbranched annual, erect to 30 in (75 cm); flowers 1–2 in (2.5–5 cm) in diameter, saccate, white, creamy yellow, pink, lilac, deep crimson, scarlet or purple, some bicolored, some double or semidouble; *I. capensis* JEWELWEED, LADY'S EARRINGS, ORANGE BALSAM; N US, naturalized Europe; annual to 3¼ ft (1 m), erect to spreading; flowers to 1 in (2.5 cm), saccate, orange-yellow with red-brown spots; *I. glandulifera* HIMALAYAN BALSAM, POLICEMAN'S HELMET; Himalaya, naturalized Europe, N America; stout annual erect to 6½ ft (2 m); flowers to 1½ in (4 cm), fragrant, deeply saccate, pink to rose-purple, to lavender or white with a yellow-spotted interior; *I. niamniamensis* E tropical Africa; perennial to 36 in (90 cm), more or less erect and unbranched; flowers to 2 in (5 cm), deeply saccate and compressed, sepals red, petals yellow-green; 'Congo Cockatoo': flowers large, red and bright yellow-green; *I. repens* India, Sri Lanka; creeping and freely branching perennial; flowers to 1½ in (4 cm), saccate, yellow, spur downy; *I. schlechteri* New Guinea to Solomon Islands; branched perennial herb to 4 in (10 cm); stems thick, red-tinted; leaves tinged bronze; flowers 2½–3 in (6–8 cm) in diameter, red, crimson, purple, pink or white; includes cultivars with large, double and frilled flowers, some with very deep bronze-red leaves, or variegated emerald, yellow and red; *I. walleriana* (syn. *I. sultanii*) BUSY LIZZIE, PATIENCE PLANT, SULTANA; perennial treated as an annual, 6–24 in (15–60 cm) tall, bushy with translucent, succulent branches; flowers 1–2 in (2.5–5 cm) diameter, flat, bright red, crimson, orange, pink, white or multicolored; numerous cultivars and seed races include dwarf and large plants, with single and double flowers in a wide color range, and leaves variegated yellow or tinted red or purple-bronze.

Imperata Gramineae. Cosmopolitan. 8 species, clump-forming to running perennial grasses with linear to lanceolate leaves. Silky flowers are carried in spikelike panicles from late summer to fall. Grow in damp but well-drained, fertile soil, preferably in full sunlight. Hard frosts and winter rain may cause young plants to deteriorate or perish—their crowns may need a dry mulch below −10°F (−23°C). Increase by division in early spring. *I. cylindrica* (Japan; leaves to 20 in (50 cm) erect to arching, bright green;

the plant usually grown is 'Red Baron', (syn. 'Rubra'), JAPANESE BLOOD GRASS; it seldom exceeds 12 in (30 cm), with new growth flushed bright ruby red at first, becoming brilliant blood red to deep garnet in fall.

imperfect when certain parts usually present are not developed. Imperfect flowers are unisexual.

impressed a feature sunken into the surface of, for example, a leaf or stem.

inarching see *grafting*.

inbreeder a genetically uniform cultivar that reproduces uniformly by self-pollination and self-fertilization.

inbreeding the process of fertilizing the flowers of a plant with its own pollen; resultant plants may be referred to as an inbred line.

inbreeding depression the loss of vigor, fertility, yield, or other desirable characteristics that may result from inbreeding.

Incarvillea (for Pierre d'Incarville [1706–57], French missionary in China, and botanical correspondent of the botanist Bernard de Jussieu). Bignoniaceae. C and E Asia, Himalaya. 14 species, annual or perennial herbs (those listed below are perennials), usually with basal clumps of pinnate or pinnatisect leaves. Produced in summer in terminal racemes or panicles, the flowers are tubular to campanulate with a limb of five broad and spreading lobes. The following species are hardy to 5°F (−15°C), but where the ground is likely to be frozen for long periods, protect the crowns with a deep, dry mulch. Grow them in deep, fertile soil, neither waterlogged in winter nor dry in summer. Position in full sun but with some protection in the hottest part of the day. Propagate by seed in fall or spring, and prick out into individual pots. Division is possible but difficult: established plants resent disturbance.
I. delavayi China; to 24 in (60 cm); corolla tube to 2½ in (6 cm), purple-pink and yellow outside, yellow lined purple inside, lobes to 1¼ in (3 cm), rounded, wavy, purple-pink; *I. mairei*

SW China; to 12 in (30 cm); corolla tube 1¼–2½ in (3–6.5 cm), deep rose outside, white to gray or yellow inside, lobes to 1¼ in (3 cm), rounded, wavy, crimson to deep carmine.

inchworm see *caterpillars*.

incised dissected, but cut deeply and irregularly with the segments joined by broad lamina.

included enclosed within; as of a grass floret by its glume, or stamens within a corolla.

Compatibility in tree fruits
Good crops of tree fruits, especially apples, pears, and plums, are dependent on the ability of certain cultivars to fertilize others—for example, by flowering simultaneously.

incompatibility (1) the inability of one plant to fertilize another, a factor that is of particular relevance in tree-fruit growing; (2) the inability of a given rootstock to form a long-term union with a scion.

incomplete flowers lacking one or more of the four whorls of the complete flower.

incrassate thickened.

incumbent folded inward and lying on or leaning against another organ. It is used to describe a cotyledon with the radicle lying on one side instead of along the edge, and an anther when it lies against the inner face of its filament.

incurved, incurving applied to one of the major exhibition forms of chrysanthemums in which the florets turn upward and inward, either tightly to form a compact globose flower (incurved), or loosely (incurving).

indehiscent not splitting open to release its pollen or, more usually, seeds or spores. It is generally applied to fruit types, such as achenes, berries, drupes and pomes; cf. *dehiscent*.

indeterminate (1) an inflorescence that does not terminate in a single flower, and in which the spike continues to grow as lower flowers open; (2) tomato cultivars with main stems that continue to grow to great length unless stopped; cf. *determinate*; *bush*.

Indianesque a garden style reflecting elements of Indian gardening, particularly in its use of ornaments and architectural detail. Occasionally practiced in England by Humphry Repton and his followers in the late 18th and early 19th centuries.

indigenous strictly native; not exotic, naturalized or introduced.

Indigofera (from Latin *indigus* indigo, and *-ferus*, bearing). Leguminosae. Widespread in tropical and subtropical regions. Some 700 species, small trees, shrubs, or annual or perennial herbs with pealike flowers in racemes or spikes. Although liable to be cut back to the ground in cold winters, they will tolerate temperatures to about 5°F (−15°C). Grow in full sun, with the shelter of a warm wall and a deep winter mulch in zones at the limits of hardiness. Prune out dead and frosted growth and rejuvenate old, leggy specimens by cutting back to ground level in spring. When growth above ground survives several winters, cut the latest season's growth back to a framework of older wood in spring. Propagate by semiripe cuttings of lateral shoots rooted in the cold frame; alternatively, increase by root cuttings or by removal of suckers.
   I. decora Japan, C China; shrub to 32 in (80 cm); racemes erect, to 8 in (20 cm), flowers to ¾ in (2 cm), standard white suffused pale crimson at base, wings pink; *I. dielsiana* SW China; shrub to 60 in (150 cm); racemes to 6 in (15 cm), erect, flowers to ⅝ in (1.5 cm), pale red-pink, downy; *I. heterantha* (syn. *I. gerardiana*) NW Himalaya; shrub to 8 ft (2.5 m); leaves gray-downy; racemes dense, erect, 2¾–6 in (7–15 cm); flowers to ⅝ in (1.5 cm), pale pink, rosy purple or crimson; *I. pseudotinctoria* Taiwan, Japan, C China; subshrub to 36 in (90 cm); racemes 1½–4 in (4–10 cm), packed; flowers to ¼ in (0.5 cm), pale red to pale pink or white tinted rose; *I. tinctoria* SE Asia; racemes slender, shorter than leaves, standard pale red to rose, wings and keel of a somewhat deeper hue.

Indocalamus (from *indo*, Indian, and Greek *kalamos*, reed). Gramineae. China, Japan, Malaysia. Some 25 species of relatively small, running bamboos; see *bamboos*.

indumentum a covering of hair, scurf, or scales, most often used in the general sense of hair.

induplicate of a leaf, sheath, sepal or petal, folded inward.

indurate hardened and toughened.

indusium the epidermal tissue that covers or surrounds the spore-bearing region of a fern frond.

Gleditsia inermis
Inerm or "unarmed" species and cultivars of plants such as this gleditsia and the rose *R. canina* 'Inermis' lack spines or thorns, and are good choices for family gardens.

inerm, inermous unarmed; without spines, prickles, or teeth.

inferior beneath.

infertile (1) a plant unable to produce viable gametes (or seed) and fruit; (2) sometimes describes soils that are acidic or low in nutrients, with poor structure, or impeded drainage.

infiltration the passage of rain or irrigation water into the soil.

inflexed bent inward toward the main plant axis.

inflorescence the arrangement of flowers and their accessory parts on an axis.

infra- as a prefix, denotes below, as in infrastipular, meaning below the stipules.

infrageneric describing a taxon below the rank of genus, i.e., subgenus, species, subspecies, variety, forma, cultivar.

infraspecific describing a taxon below the rank of species, i.e., subspecies, variety, forma, cultivar.

infructescence fruiting stage of the inflorescence.

infundibular, infundibuliform funnel-shaped.

injection the placement of a pesticide beneath the soil surface—for example, as a possible control for eelworm—or, occasionally, into the branches, trunks, or roots of trees. In most cases, special equipment is necessary to ensure correct dosage.

inoculum (1) potentially infective material present in the garden environment, for example fruiting bodies of black spot (*Diplocarpon rosae*) overwintering on fallen rose leaves; (2) material containing microorganisms used to inoculate a plant or substrate.

inorganic denoting a substance devoid of carbon; of neither plant nor animal origin. Inorganic fertilizers, whether in natural or synthesized form, are of mineral origin. The identification of organic/inorganic origins is of particular relevance in considerations of organic gardening.

insects an extremely diverse class of animals represented by more than 800,000 described species, which constitute about 70 percent of all known animal species. Adult insects have a hard external skeleton with three pairs of jointed legs; the body consists of a head, thorax, and abdomen. The head has compound eyes, a pair of antennae, and mouthparts, which may be adapted for biting and chewing or for sucking liquids. The thorax consists of three segments, each of which has a pair of legs, and in most insects there is a pair of wings on each of the front two segments. Some insects, such as worker ants, have no wings, while others, such as female winter moths, have tiny nonfunctional wings. The abdomen is made up of 11 segments, although some may be very small and modified to form part of the genitalia.

Most insects reproduce by laying eggs, but some groups, such as the aphids, can give birth to live young. The immature stages in the life cycle may be very different in appearance from the adult form and often have entirely different dietary requirements. A typical example is the cabbage white butterfly, with caterpillar larvae that feed on brassica leaves; the larval stage is followed by a nonfeeding resting stage called a pupa, from which the adult butterfly emerges to suck nectar from various flowers. Lacewings, moths, flies, beetles, ants, bees, wasps, and sawflies also go through this form of development, known as complete metamorphosis. Other insects, including earwigs, termites, aphids, scale insects, mealybugs, whiteflies, capsid bugs, and thrips, go through incomplete metamorphosis, producing immature stages that are similar in appearance to the adult form. The length of life cycle may be as little as two to three weeks, as shown by aphids breeding under warm conditions, while the larvae of some wood-boring insects need several years to reach maturity.

Virtually all cultivated plants are attacked by at least one insect pest. Thrips and the various insects that belong to the Hemiptera have needle-like mouthparts used to suck sap. Most

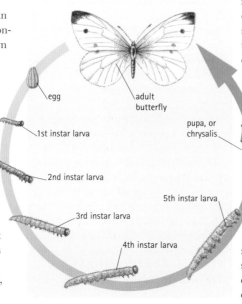

egg

adult butterfly

1st instar larva

pupa, or chrysalis

2nd instar larva

5th instar larva

3rd instar larva

4th instar larva

Complete metamorphosis, small cabbage white butterfly
The more advanced types of insect undergo a complete transformation in appearance and often in feeding habits during their lives. While adult butterflies feed on nectar, their larvae will feast on brassica crops.

feed on foliage and stems, but some species of aphids and mealybugs take sap from roots. Many aphids, whiteflies, scale insects, suckers, and mealybugs excrete a sugary liquid called honeydew. This makes the foliage sticky and allows the growth of black sooty molds. Some aphids, leafhoppers, and thrips are efficient vectors of plant virus diseases, carrying viral particles on their mouthparts or in their saliva when they transfer to a new plant. The remaining plant pests have mouthparts used for biting and chewing plant tissues and may be root feeders, stem borers, defoliators, leaf miners, leaf rollers, gall formers, flower feeders, or fruit borers. Some moth caterpillars and beetle larvae specialize in feeding on dry plant material such as seeds and stored food.

Not all insects are pests. The vast majority are of no practical importance, and some are of definite benefit in gardens. Predators and parasites help to keep pest numbers down (see *beneficial insects, biological control*), and the inconsiderate use of pesticides can lead to a resurgence of some pests once their natural enemies are eliminated.

insecticide a chemical used to kill or control insect pests. Insecticides are sometimes given names that describe the type of pest or stage of its life cycle controlled—for example, acaricide (mites), nematicide (nematodes or eelworms), molluscicide (slugs and snails) and ovicide (eggs).

Most insecticides work by contact action, i.e., it is necessary for the pest either to be covered by the chemical or to walk over a treated surface in order for it to be affected. Some insecticides are absorbed into the plant and are effective against sap-feeding pests such as aphids. Others are stomach poisons deposited on plant surfaces to be eaten by pests such as caterpillars and beetles; a few insecticides are volatile and work by vapor action. In practice, many chemicals act on pests in more than one way. Insecticides are usually applied as sprays, but also as dusts, granules, smokes, baits, and aerosols.

The availability of insecticides for garden use is governed primarily by a system of statutory approval. This is driven by considerations of health and safety risk to humans and identified harmful effects within the natural environment. The chemical substances referred to in the following paragraphs are not necessarily available or approved for use in horticulture. Their inclusion is provided to indicate types or examples of substances formerly or currently in use as insecticides.

Plant-derived insecticides
Plant-derived insecticides are naturally occurring, chemically unrelated substances, which include some of the earliest pesticide discoveries. Pyrethrum, derived from the flower head of *Tanacetum cinerariifolium*, was used as early as the 18th century in Persia. Derris, or rotenone, is produced from the roots of *Derris* and *Lonchocarpus* species; its insecticidal properties were developed in the 1920s from the practice of South American native peoples using crushed roots to paralyze fish. Nicotine is extracted from tobacco waste, which emanates from *Nicotiana* species. Soft soaps are derived from palm oil as well as other natural fats. All of these substances provide some control of pests, but they have very short persistence.

I

Their harmful effects on beneficial insects are limited, and when diluted they are of low toxicity to humans and most other vertebrate animals, except fish.

Synthesized insecticides

ORGANOCHLORINES This group of insecticides, developed during the period 1939–60, combine relatively low mammalian toxicity with a high degree of insecticidal activity. Those such as DDT, aldrin, dieldrin and chlordane have been banned in many countries because of their persistence and accumulation within the environment and harmful effects on birds and animals. Lindane, also known as gamma-HCH or BHC, is of moderate persistence. Dicofol is an acaricide effective against tarsonemid and red spider mites, although resistance to it is now widespread among the latter.

ORGANOPHOSPHATES A group of insecticides, developed from 1950 onward, containing many compounds of short to medium persistence and that break down to harmless chemicals, and are therefore less damaging to the environment than organochlorines. The contact insecticides malathion, fenitrothion, trichlorfon, dichlorvos, diazinon, and pirimiphos-methyl, and systemics, including dimethoate, heptenophos, and oxydemeton-methyl, are organophosphates effective against sap-feeding pests and leaf miners.

CARBAMATES Among carbamates, developed in the mid-1950s for use as insecticides, were carbaryl and pirimicarb; the latter used as a selective insecticide for the control of aphids while leaving most other pests and beneficial insects unharmed.

PYRETHROIDS A series of synthetic pyrethroid compounds arising as a result of changes made to the molecular structure of natural pyrethrum. Some of the early products introduced during the 1970s, such as resmethrin and bioresmethrin, have the low mammalian toxicity and short persistence of natural pyrethrum, but greater insecticidal activity. Permethrin is a pyrethroid of moderate persistence, which has low toxicity to mammals and birds. Some of the later pyrethroids, such as deltamethrin and cypermethrin, are more toxic and have greater persistence.

Resistance to insecticides

Various pests of fruit, vegetables, and greenhouse crops have developed resistance to at least one group of pesticides; these include red spider mites, whiteflies, aphids, some root flies of vegetables, Colorado beetle, diamond back moth, codling moth, and pear psyllids. There is no evidence that pesticides induce mutations, but rather that they act as a selective agent, killing only individuals with susceptible genetic characteristics and leaving those possessing genes that provide them with immunity.

Three factors are conducive to the development of resistance. First, the frequency of the occurrence of resistant genes in the original population: some resistant strains are very localized, indicating, in such cases, that the resistant genes are not universally distributed. Second, the intensity of selection, which is dependent upon the magnitude of the population exposed to the pesticide and the proportion killed. Third, the number of generations passed through each year.

In the development of resistance, there are essentially two types of mechanisms involved. In one, enzymes undergo genetically-based changes that enhance their ability to break down the pesticide to a nontoxic product; the other, also under genetic control, makes the organisms insensitive to the pesticide. Although such mechanisms usually develop in response to the selective pressure of a single pesticide, the system, when established, is invariably capable of affording protection against a group of related pesticides. Once resistance has been established, effective chemical pest control can only be obtained by switching to a chemically unrelated group of insecticides. However, this practice often proves of short-lived value, because many insects and mites have the capacity to develop additional mechanisms that provide them with multiple resistance.

Resistance develops through intensive and widespread use of insecticides. Where appropriate, nonchemical methods are valuable in helping to avoid the problem. See *beneficial insects, biological control, integrated pest management, organic gardening.*

insectivorous plant see *carnivorous plant.*

inserted attached to or placed on.

insertion the point or mode of attachment for a body to its support.

instar any stage between moltings in the growth of an insect larva or nymph.

insulation a means of conserving heat in greenhouses, frames, and garden buildings, and around plants, in order to maintain a required growing temperature and/or to protect tender plants from frost. Insulation of heated garden structures results in economy of fuel usage.

On greenhouse structures, insulated glass and double-skin cladding with rigid or film plastic are effective forms of insulation. Polythene sheet added to the inside surfaces of a greenhouse provides useful insulation, while products made by fusing two sheets of film to enclose air bubbles are very efficient in heat retention. In large greenhouses, mechanized installations for drawing an insulating sheet horizontally across the width of the greenhouse at about the height of the eaves are worthwhile; these systems are known as thermal screens. During cold spells, frames may be insulated by covering with a polythene sheet, burlap, old carpet or similar materials. All of these methods of insulation involve some loss of light.

Covering plants with glass or plastic cloches, or horticultural fleece, provides varying degrees of protection from heat loss. Bracken or straw wrapped around tender plants outdoors is a valuable means of insulation, but some form of outer cover is necessary in order to prevent waterlogging. Polythene screens are suitable for some wall plants. Mounding with soil or any organic mulching material will conserve heat in vegetable clamps and around the roots of plants that are not reliably hardy.

integrated pest management (IPM) The term IPM initially referred to the control of insects and other pests, but has been extended to encompass disease and weed control. The

Integrated pest management
Preventive measures such as the use of brassica collars as a barrier to root fly are the key to minimizing the need to use chemicals.

description "integrated control" was first used in the US in 1956, and in 1967 the Food and Agriculture Organization defined the concept as "a pest management system that utilizes all suitable techniques and methods, in as compatible a manner as possible, to maintain the pest population at levels below those causing economic damage." Although in its conceptual sense IPM involves the scientific study of targeted organisms, in practice its implementation is usually concerned with supervisory control. Its broad objectives are an increase in biological control and conservation of natural enemies present, together with a reduction in the use of pesticides and utilization of any secondary measures of control that are available.

Gardeners may not be in a position to practice full IPM, but some of its principles can be followed by increasing the use of nonchemical control methods. For example, the use of greasebands on tree trunks against winter moths reduces the need to use insecticides, as does the placing of disks around the base of brassicas to protect them against root fly (*Delia brassicae*). Correct timing often means that a single application of a nonchemical control method can replace several protective sprays; this would apply, for example, when using pheromone traps for codling moth (*Cydia pomonella*).

Available pesticides can often be applied as spot treatments to individual plants or in band treatments along plant rows; also as seed dressings, granules, and baits. Not only are such methods less wasteful and therefore more economic but, most important, they target the application effectively,

with reduced risk to beneficial insects. Pesticides with a narrow spectrum and a short period of persistence should be preferred.

The garden is an ideal environment for both plants and pests, and gardening skills are needed to tip the balance in favor of plant health. Healthy plants produced by sound husbandry are less likely to fall prey to pests and diseases. See *beneficial insects*, *biological control*.

inter- as a prefix, denotes between or among, as in interstaminal, meaning between the stamens.

intercropping, intersowing growing a relatively rapid maturing crop between rows of a slower-growing one in order to make maximum use of available ground. For example, lettuce or radishes can be sown and harvested between widely spaced rows of establishing Brussels sprouts.

intergeneric hybrid the offspring of a cross between plants of different genera. It is designated in written descriptions by a multiplication sign before the hybrid genus name—for example, the common conifer × *Cupressocyparis leylandii*, which originates from the hybridization of *Cupressus macrocarpa* with *Chamaecyparis nootkatensis*.

intermediate (1) applied to one of the major exhibition forms of chrysanthemums in which flowers are intermediate in form between Incurved and Reflexed; (2) a hybrid plant showing characteristics intermediate between both parents.

internal rust spot a condition of potatoes which only becomes apparent when affected tubers are sectioned. It is typically visible as small rust-colored patchy spots distributed across the tuber; these are often more concentrated toward the surface. The condition is most prevalent in potatoes grown in sandy, infertile soils, especially those low in organic matter, and where plants encounter drought stress. There are differences in cultivar susceptibility.

internode the length of plant stem between nodes.

interspecific hybrid the offspring of a cross between two species of the same genus. It is designated in written descriptions by a multiplication sign between the genus name and the hybrid epithet—for example, *Forsythia* × *intermedia*, the hybrid offspring of *F. suspensa* and *F. viridissima*.

interstock the intermediate portion of stem that is grafted to the scion and rootstock of a double-worked tree. Interstocks are used as a means of overcoming incompatibility. For example, the pear cultivar 'Beurré Hardy' is commonly used as an interstock between a quince rootstock and some scion cultivars such as 'Packham's Triumph' and most clones of 'William's Bon Chrétien'. See *grafting*.

intra- as a prefix, denotes within or inside, as in intrastaminal, meaning inside the stamens or the circle of stamens.

intraspecific describes hybrids that have occurred between two distinct varieties of the same species.

introduction a nonindigenous plant, usually purposefully introduced.

introrse turned or facing inward, toward the axis, as with an anther that opens toward the center of its flower.

intumescence a small, localized proliferation of plant tissue, on leaves and fruit especially, caused by a humid growing environment or other situation where water uptake is greater than the rate of loss by aerial parts. Similar lesions which are more widespread, and often larger, are referred to as *oedema* (q.v.).

Inula (name used by Pliny for a plant similar to *Helenium* (Greek *helenion*), perhaps *I. helenium*). Compositae. Temperate and warm Old World. About 90 species, mostly perennial herbs or subshrubs, rarely annual or biennial (those listed below are herbaceous perennials), usually hairy, with daisylike flower heads composed of slender, golden-yellow ray florets, in summer. Grow in sun in moderately fertile, well-drained soil. Propagate by seed or division.

I. *acaulis* Asia Minor; to 8 in (20 cm), stem tinted purple; leaves 1¼–2½ in (3–6 cm), oblanceolate to spathulate, entire, ciliate, minutely glandular; ray florets to ⅝ in (1.5 cm); *I. ensifolia* E Europe; to 24 in (60 cm); leaves to 3½ in (9 cm), linear to lanceolate, entire, ciliate, glabrous; ray florets to ¾ in (2.2 cm *I. hookeri* Himalaya; to 24 in (60 cm); leaves to 5 in (13 cm), oblong to lanceolate, minutely toothed, hairy; ray florets 1 in (2.5 cm); *I. magnifica* Caucasus; to 6½ ft (2 m), stem tinted purple-black; leaves to 10 in (25 cm), elliptic to ovate, dentate, dark green, glabrous above, villous beneath; ray florets to ¾ in (2 cm); *I. loculus-christi* E Europe, Caucasus, Turkey, Iraq, Iran; to 6 in (15 cm); leaves to 5½ in (14 cm), oblong to lanceolate or elliptic, entire or denticulate; ray florets to ¾ in (2 cm).

invalid applied to botanical names published without, for example, the necessary formalities of description, diagnosis, type designation, or not published in a valid (i.e., botanically acceptable) publication.

involucel a secondary or diminutive involucre.

involucre a single, highly conspicuous bract, a bract pair, or a whorl of small bracts or leaves subtending a flower or inflorescence.

involute rolled inward, toward the uppermost side.

Iochroma (from Greek *ion*, violet, and *chroma*, color, referring to the flowers of some species). Solanaceae. Tropical America. Some 20 species, shrubs or small trees with clusters of tubular to narrowly trumpet-shaped, 5-lobed flowers in summer. Provide a minimum temperature of 50°F (10°C), full or bright indirect light and a buoyant atmosphere. Grow in a well-drained, medium-fertility, loam-based mixture;

water plentifully in summer, sparingly in winter. In cool temperate zones, pot-grown specimens may be moved outside for the summer. Prune in spring to restrict or rejuvenate. Propagate by greenwood cuttings, rooted with bottom heat in a case in summer, or by seed sown in spring. *I. cyaneum* (syn. *I. tubulosum*) northwestern S America; shrub to 10 ft (3 m); flowers to 1½ in (3.5 cm), deep purple-blue.

Ipheion (from *iphyon*, a Classical Greek name used in a number of different forms for an assortment of plants, including bulbous genera). Liliaceae (Alliaceae). S America. 10 species, tufted, bulbous perennials, most parts smelling of garlic if bruised, the leaves especially. The bulbs are small and clumped and the leaves narrow and smooth, arising in loose tussocks. Produced in spring and summer, the flowers are salverform with a spreading limb of six, ovate-oblong tepals; they are carried singly or in pairs on slender scapes. *I. uniflorum* is hardy to −10°F (−23°C), but may need mulch protection in areas with prolonged frosts. Plant in well-drained, sandy soil in dappled or full sun in a sheltered position. Propagate by seed during spring or by offsets in late summer when foliage dies back. *I. uniflorum* (syn. *Triteleia uniflora, Milla uniflora, Brodiaea uniflora, Beauverdia uniflora*) SPRING STAR-FLOWER; Argentina, Uruguay; leaves to 10 in (25 cm), narrowly strap-shaped, glaucescent; scapes 2–8 in (5–20 cm), numerous, flowers to 1½ in (4 cm) in diameter, pale blue to deeper lilac, with a white or cream suffusion in throat and darker stripes along the midvein of each segment; includes the pure white 'Album', 'Froyle Mill' with deep violet flowers, the clear blue 'Rolf Fiedler', and 'Wisley Blue' with pale blue flowers with deeper tips.

whorl of bracts

Involucre (Bougainvillea)

Ipomoea (from Greek *ips*, a worm, and *homoios*, resembling). Convolvulaceae. Widely distributed in tropical and subtropical regions. MORNING GLORY. 450–500 species, annual to perennial herbs, shrubs, or small trees, woody to herbaceous and usually climbing. The leaves are entire to lobed. Solitary to cymose or paniculate, the flowers are deeply funnel-shaped to tubular with a circular, entire rim or a limb of five lobes.

Apart from *I. tricolor*, the ubiquitous morning glory, other popular species include *I. alba*, the spectacular moonflower, a woody-based perennial with huge white blooms, and *I. coccinea, I. quamoclit*, and *I. × multifida*—vigorous vines, though delicate in appearance, with small flowers in brilliant tones of crimson and scarlet. The last two, with finely divided leaves, are especially attractive. The Spanish flag, *I. lobata*, is a weakly twining annual or short-lived perennial with erect spikes of flowers that pass with age through scarlet, yellow, and cream. Subtropical gardens and large heated conservatories might accommodate the two robust, semiwoody species, *I. mauritiana* and *I. horsfalliae*, the first with narrowly funnel-shaped deep red or purple-pink flowers, the second with wider blooms in shades of pink with a darker "eye."

In cool-temperate areas, grow *Ipomoea* under glass (minimum temperature 45–50°F/7–10°C) in pots and tubs. Grow vigorous species in borders where space allows, or treat the fast-growing, soft-stemmed twiners as frost-tender annuals. Plant in fertile, well-drained loam in a warm, sunny site and provide support. In frost-free areas, sow *in situ*. Under glass, give a high-fertility, loam-based mix and medium to high humidity; water plentifully during the growing season. Prune semiwoody species in late winter or spring to thin out old congested growth. Propagate from seed sown singly in pots in spring at 64°F (18°C): nick seeds or soak for 12 hours in tepid water to promote rapid germination. Perennials may also be propagated by softwood or semiripe cuttings in summer.

I. alba (syn. *I. bona-nox, Calonyction aculeatum*); BELLE DE NUIT, MOONFLOWER; Pantropical; woody-

I

based, herbaceous perennial climber, 16–100 ft (5–30 m); leaves to 6 in (15 cm), ovate to heart-shaped, entire to 3-lobed, smooth; flowers to 6 × 5½ in (15 × 14 cm), trumpet-shaped, white faintly striped green, fragrant at night; *I. coccinea* (syn. *Quamoclit coccinea*) RED MORNING GLORY, STAR IPOMOEA; US; annual herb climbing to 13 ft (4 m); leaves to 4 in (10 cm), ovate to heart-shaped, entire or toothed; flowers to 1 × ¾ in (2.5 × 2 cm), tubular, scarlet with a golden throat, fragrant; *I. hederacea* (syn. *Pharbitis hederacea*) S US to Argentina; hairy, annual herb climbing to 10 ft (3 m); leaves broadly ovate to heart-shaped, usually 3-lobed; flowers to 1½ × 1¼ in (4 × 3 cm), funnel-shaped, blue, purple or cerise with a white tube); *I. horsfalliae* (W Indies; perennial, woody climber to 25 ft (8 m); leaves to 8 in (20 cm), palmately 3–5-lobed, smooth; flowers to 1½ × 2 in (4 × 5 cm), trumpet-shaped, cerise to deep purple-red; *I. lobata* (syn. *I. versicolor*, *Mina lobata*, *Quamoclit lobata*) SPANISH FLAG; Mexico; annual or short-lived perennial herb climbing to 16 ft (5 m); leaves ovate to heart-shaped, toothed to deeply cut or lobed; flowers in 1-sided racemes, each to 1½ × ⅜ in (4 × 1.5 cm), broadly tubular, curving and narrowing toward tip and appearing closed, scarlet in bud, opening yellow tipped scarlet, fading to cream; *I. mauritiana* Pantropical; woody, perennial climber to 15 ft (5 m); leaves to 6 in (15 cm), palmately lobed; flowers to 2½ × 2½ in (6 × 6 cm), funnel-shaped, pink to deep rosy red with a darker stain in throat); *I.* × *multifida* (syn. *I.* × *sloteri*, *Quamoclit* × *sloteri*; *I. coccinea* × *I. quamoclit*) CARDINAL CLIMBER; garden origin; annual climber to 3¼ ft (1 m); leaves finely pinnately cut; flowers to 2 × 1 in (5 × 2.5 cm), trumpet-shaped, scarlet to crimson; *I. nil* (syn. *Pharbitis nil*) Pantropical; hairy annual herb climbing to 16 ft (5 m); leaves to 6 in (15 cm), broadly ovate, entire or 3-lobed; flowers to 2½ × 2 in (6 × 5 cm), funnel-shaped, blue, purple or red; includes numerous cultivars with flowers large to small, single or semidouble, in shades or combinations of white, blue, cerise, scarlet, mauve, violet and maroon, some nonclimbing, others with variegated foliage; *I.* × *imperialis*, IMPERIAL JAPANESE MORNING GLORY, differs in its larger, double flowers often

with fringed or fluted limbs; *I. purpurea* (syn. *Convolvulus major* of gardens, *Pharbitis purpurea*) COMMON MORNING GLORY; Mexico, widely naturalized elsewhere in Tropics; annual herb, usually hairy, climbing to 8 ft (2.5 m); leaves to 4 in (10 cm), ovate to rounded, entire or 3-lobed; flowers to 2 × 2 in (5 × 5 cm), funnel-shaped, blue, purple, pink, red, white, or with stripes of these colors on a white background; includes cultivars with silver-variegated leaves and deep violet, double flowers; *I. quamoclit* (syn. *Quamoclit vulgaris*, *Quamoclit pennata*) STAR GLORY, CYPRESS VINE, INDIAN PINK; Tropical America; annual climber to 10 ft (3 m); leaves ½–3½ in (1–9 cm), finely pinnately cut; flowers to 1¼ in (3 cm), narrowly trumpet-shaped with a small, starlike limb, scarlet; includes cultivars with very fine, ferny foliage and flowers in shades of plum, scarlet, flame, crimson, pink and white, some doubles; *I. tricolor* (syn. *I. rubrocaerulea*) MORNING GLORY; Central America, widely naturalized elsewhere; glabrous annual or perennial climbing herb to 13 ft (4 m); leaves ovate to heart-shaped, tip pointed; flowers to 2½ × 2¾ in (6 × 7 cm), funnel-shaped, bright sky blue, often with faint lavender-pink stripes at least at first, tube white, golden at base within; includes cultivars with very large flowers in shades and combinations of white, sky blue, cobalt, lavender, pink and carmine; the most famous selection is probably the large, sky blue 'Heavenly Blue'; this species should not be confused with *Convolvulus tricolor*.

Ipomopsis (from Greek *ipo*, to impress, and *opsis*, appearance, due to the showiness of many species of this genus). Polemoniaceae. US (Pacific coast to Florida and South Carolina), S Argentina (1 species). 24 species, annual to perennial herbs with entire to pinnately lobed leaves in basal rosettes and on stems. The flowers are tubular or hypocrateriform and appear in spring and summer in terminal, cymose racemes. Grow in a sandy, fertile medium in the conservatory or cool greenhouse in full sun with good ventilation. Keep moist but never wet. Sow seed under glass in early spring.

I. aggregata SCARLET GILIA, SKY-ROCKET; western N America; glandular-

hairy biennial, erect to 32 in (80 cm); leaves finely pinnate; flowers to 1½ in (4 cm), pink to magenta or bright red mottled yellow, rarely pure yellow or white; *I. rubra* STANDING CYPRESS; SE US; more or less glabrous, unbranched biennial or perennial erect to 6½ ft (2 m); leaves finely pinnate; flowers to 1 in (2.5 cm), scarlet, interior yellow spotted red.

Iresine (from Greek *eiros*, wool, referring to a harvest garland bound with wool). Amaranthaceae. Americas, Australia. BLOOD LEAF. 80 species, annual to perennial herbs or subshrubs with entire, often brilliantly marked or colored leaves and spikes of inconspicuous, white or green flowers. Frost-tender plants, valued for their colorful foliage. The following species are grown outdoors in the tropics and subtropics, and used for summer bedding or as pot plants elsewhere. They need a minimum temperature of 50°F (10°C). Grow in sun or light shade. Water and feed freely in summer; keep just moist in winter. Pinch out young plants to promote a bushy habit. Increase by seed sown under glass in early spring at a minimum temperature of 59°F (15°C), or by stem cuttings in spring.

I. herbstii (syn. *I. reticulata*) BEEF PLANT, CHICKEN GIZZARD, BEEFSTEAK PLANT; Brazil; annual erect to 3¼ ft (1 m) with glossy and thinly succulent, purple- or red-tinted stems; leaves ¾–2½ in (2–6 cm), ovate with variegation ranging from green with yellow veins or mottling to deep purple-red with pink veins; includes 'Aureoreticulata', with red-tinted leaves netted with yellow veins, 'Brilliantissima', with rich crimson leaves, and 'Wallisii', dwarf with purple-black veins; *I. lindenii* Ecuador; erect perennial to 3¼ ft (1 m); leaves 1½–4 in (4–10 cm), ovate to lanceolate, glossy deep blood red with prominent red veins; includes 'Formosa', with yellow leaves veined with crimson.

Iris (from the Greek messenger Iris who came to earth via a rainbow). Iridaceae. North temperate zones. FLAG, FLEUR-DE-LIS, SWORD LILY. About 300 species, rhizomatous, fleshy-rooted or bulbous perennial herbs with grassy to sword-shaped leaves. The flowers consist of a tubular perianth with six segments. Each of the three outer segments ("falls") is narrowed toward the base into a "haft," sometimes with a beard of colored hairs or crested or ridged, and often with a patch of different color (the "signal"); the apex of the fall is expanded, showy and hangs downward. Each of the inner three segments ("standards") is narrowed toward the base into a claw and usually expanded toward the tip; they tend to stand erect between the falls, but are sometimes much-reduced or bristlelike. The style has three petal-like arms, which arch over the falls. The fruit is a leathery capsule. Irises fall into several, natural groups with distinctive characteristics and cultural requirements.

Rhizomatous irises

(1) BEARDED OR POGON IRISES (sub-genus Iris, section Iris). Several species are good plants for a mixed border and of these *I. germanica* and its white-flowered cultivar 'Florentina' and *I. pallida*, with its two variegated-leaf forms 'Argentea Variegata' and 'Variegata', are well known. Some of the smaller species such as *I. lutescens* and *I. pumila* are suitable for rock gardens. There is,

Iris flower parts

Labels: standard; petal-like style ("stigma flap"); fall; signal

in addition, a vast number of named hybrid cultivars of bearded iris. These are classified as follows: Miniature Dwarf Bearded (MDB) up to 8 in (20 cm), the first to flower; Standard Dwarf Bearded (SDB), 8–16 in (21–40 cm); Intermediate Bearded (IB), 16–28 in (40–70 cm); Miniature Tall Bearded (MTB), 16–28 in (40–70 cm); Border Bearded (BB), also 16–28 in (40–70 cm), and the Tall Bearded (TB), over 28 in (70 cm). The MTB and BB cultivars flower with the TBs. Many iris species will occasionally flower for a second time later in the year, and this trait has been developed by the hybridizers, particularly of the bearded cultivars, to create cultivars that bloom again, often repeatedly, until the first frost. To sustain this additional growth in one season, remontant irises may require a further application of fertilizer after the first flowering and should be watered in dry summers. To flower well, bearded irises require a sunny situation and well-drained soil. The soil should ideally be in the pH range 6.0–7.5; they do not require lime, but ground limestone should be worked in if the soil is acidic. They will

tolerate a higher pH and can grow well in chalky soil. Some humus should be incorporated, but avoid fresh manure or green compost, which may cause rhizome rot. Raise the soil level in wet places or if the soil is heavy. Although iris rhizomes can be transplanted at any time, for the best results move only when absolutely necessary and then after flowering during summer dormancy. For planting in sandy soil, dig a hole allowing the roots to fall straight down, push the nose of the rhizome into the side of the hole and fill in with soil, ensuring that no space is left beneath the rhizome. In heavy soil, place the rhizome on a mound or ridge within the planting hole, with the roots spread out, cover with soil and pat down. Under most conditions leave the top surface of the rhizome exposed, but cover thinly in hot areas, to avoid sun scorch. Shorten the leaf fan to prevent wind-rocking. Water and keep moist until new growth is seen. Apply low-nitrogen compound fertilizers during soil preparation and subsequently in early spring and fall. Do not trim off leaves of established plants in summer. After 3–4 years, when the clump becomes crowded, dig up and separate it into single rhizomes; discard the oldest, leafless and exhausted portions. Replant in groups with noses together, in fresh soil. Propagate species by seed or by detached rhizomes. Sow seeds thinly in a soil-based medium with a quarter extra grit; cover with coarse grit and leaves exposed to the

DIVIDING RHIZOMATOUS IRIS

1 Lift the plant to be divided, inserting a garden fork well away from the rhizomes to avoid damaging them. Shake excess soil from the roots.

2 With your hands, or using two handforks back to back with a levering action, split the clump into individual fans of leaves with a portion of rhizome attached.

3 Trim off and discard any shriveled or weak parts. Dust cut surfaces of rhizomes with fungicide, and trim the leaves by two-thirds of their length.

4 Replant 6 in (15 cm) apart, with the rhizomes half-buried in the soil. The reduced leaf area will minimize wind-rock, helping new roots establish.

weather. Cultivars are propagated by vegetative means only. Principal diseases of bearded iris are rhizome soft rot and scorch. With rot, remove infected tissue, cutting back to firm rhizome, and allow to dry, then dust the new surface with a fungicide. If the infection is grave (affecting more than half the rhizome), discard altogether. With scorch, the leaves suddenly turn red-brown as if burned; the rhizome remains firm, but roots wither and the plant dies. This can occur at any time; it is not believed to be contagious, but affected rhizomes should be removed and destroyed. Leaf spots are either bacterial or fungal, usually occurring after flowering.

(**2**) ONCOCYCLUS IRISES (subgenus Iris, section Oncocyclus) occur in areas of dry, often hot summers and dry, cool or cold winters. The winter months may be spent under snow or in desert conditions; next comes a period of growth and flowering in spring. This is followed by a long summer dormancy. The flowers are large, often in vivid colors with striking patterns. Except in places where the climatic conditions resemble their habitat, these irises cannot be grown in the open garden. Instead, they are grown either in raised beds outdoors and covered with glass or plastic to protect them from winter and summer rain, or in the cold greenhouse in deep pots. Soil should be gritty, free-draining and with pH above 6.5, with a low-nitrogen fertilizer added. Allow full sun and ventilation at all times. Water moderately to initiate growth between late winter and early spring; continue to water and feed until the foliage begins to die down after flowering. Thereafter keep dry. Germination of seed is often slow and erratic. Oncocyclus irises are very susceptible to virus diseases.

(**3**) REGELIA IRISES (subgenus Iris, section Regelia) differ from the last group by having a beard on the standards *and* the falls. They grow on open rocky hillsides and also have a long summer dormancy. They are best suited to bulb frame culture like the Oncocyclus irises, but are easier to grow; some species, such as *I. hoogiana*, can be grown outside in temperate climates in a well-drained sunny site if protected from heavy winter rain.

Many crosses have been made between Oncocyclus and Regelia irises; classified as Regeliocyclus Hybrids, these are easier to grow than either parent yet retain their strange beauty. They are good plants for an alpine house. Hybrids between Oncocyclus or Regelia irises with bearded iris species or cultivars are called Arilbred Irises and are suitable for garden use in temperate areas with low rainfall.

(**4**) EVANSIA IRISES (subgenus Limniris, section Lophiris) are mostly creeping to spreading plants with branched rhizomes and fans of foliage. *I. confusa* is frost-tender. Where temperatures drop below 0°F (−18°C), it should be grown in large pots of a fertile, neutral to acidic and gritty medium. Keep moist throughout the year; feed in summer and place outside in full sun. Bring under cover in fall. The remaining species are more or less hardy to −10°F (−23°C). *I. cristata* is suitable for the rock garden or peat bed. *I. gracilipes* enjoys cool, peaty soil in dappled shade. *I. japonica* will grow in semishade in most good soils but needs a warm and sheltered spot. *I. tectorum* prefers gritty but moist soil against a sunny wall. Increase by division.

(**5**) SIBERIAN IRISES (subgenus Limniris, series Sibiricae) are easy garden plants, hardy to −30°F (−34°C) and requiring fertile soil that does not dry out during the spring and early summer growth period. Although often grown beside streams and pools, they are not true waterside plants and will do equally well in a mixed border. Hybrids between Siberian and Pacific Coast Irises (Cal Sibs) are also known. Many selected hybrids are available, both diploid and tetraploid, the latter having stouter, more upright foliage and larger flowers of heavier substance with broad flaring falls in clear rich colors. Increase by division or seed. In the US, Siberian irises are attacked by the iris borer and the iris weevil.

(**6**) PACIFIC COAST IRISES (subgenus Limniris, series Californicae) occur in California, Oregon, and Washington, growing in neutral or slightly acidic well-drained soil in lightly wooded areas. All are very variable in color and hybridize freely. They are easy to grow as garden plants, but they develop chlorosis and lose vitality in

alkaline soil. They are usually hardy to −10°F (−23°C) and prefer a sunny to lightly shaded position in moist but porous, humus-rich soil. They resent disturbance. Propagate by careful division when the plant is showing renewed growth some months after flowering, and keep moist and shaded until established. They are readily raised from seed in a soil-based medium, but the offspring are likely to be hybrids. There are many cultivars available in a wide range of colors.

(**7**) WATER IRISES (subgenus Limniris, series Laevigatae) are plants of wet places, ditches and swamps and are excellent candidates for the margins of ponds or streams. They are hardy to −30°F (−34°C). Included in this group are *I. pseudacorus* and *I. versicolor*. *I. laevigata* is often grown in containers set on shelves in garden ponds. Propagation is by division of clumps and is best carried out in early fall. *I. ensata* has been cultivated in Japan for centuries and many new forms, including tetraploids, are now being raised in the US and Europe. The flowers are large, sometimes double, with spreading standards, in a wide range of colors. They flower late in the iris season, often into midsummer. Japanese irises are often grown as marginal plants in containers, and are probably best removed from the water and kept drier in winter. Japanese irises will develop chlorosis if grown in alkaline soil, but some of the Higo strain or the CaRe (calcium-resistant) cultivars will survive up to pH 7.4. Members of this group are occasionally attacked by the larvae of the iris sawfly. If the plants are in or near a pond be sure to use a chemical control that is not harmful to pond life.

(**8**) LOUISIANA IRISES (subgenus Limniris, series Hexagonae) are showy, late-flowering waterside irises from the swamps of the southern US. They are robust plants with branched flower stems, often in a zigzag form, and are popular garden plants in the southern US and Western Australia, where the high summer temperatures necessary for successful growth can be attained. Many superb hybrids have been raised. Although hardy to −30°F (−34°C), they seldom thrive in cool-temperate regions, needing long, hot and humid

I

I

summers. That said, the bright blue *I. brevicaulis* and coppery red *I. fulva* will flower in Western Europe if planted in sun in humus-rich, neutral to acidic soil and kept moist and well-fed while in growth. The hybrid between them, *I.* × *fulvala*, will also grow under the same conditions.

(**9**) THE TRIPETALAE SERIES (subgenus Limniris, series Tripetalae) includes the iris with the widest distribution, *I. setosa*. In this series the standards are tiny and the flower appears to have only three petals. Ranging from Japan to Alaska and eastern Canada, *I. setosa* exists in many variants, the smaller of which are good for the rock garden. Increase by seed or division.

(**10**) SPURIA IRISES (subgenus Limniris, series Spuriae) are very diverse in habit and size, ranging from 10–60 in (25–150 cm) tall. The taller species are herbaceous and good plants for the back of a mixed border in deep soil with ample humus. Some of the smaller species, such as the yellow *I. kerneriana*, are rock-garden plants requiring good drainage, while the plum-scented *I. graminea* is happy in humus-rich soil in part shade. There are two general groups, one typified by *I. orientalis*, which becomes dormant after flowering, and the other including *I. spuria* itself, which retains its leaves until winter. Many excellent hybrid plants have been raised in a range of bright colors, both self- and multicolored. Propagation is by division in fall or early spring, planting the rhizome below the surface in rich deep soil and keeping moist until established. New plantings may be slow to flower but can remain undisturbed for many years.

(**11**) IRIS FOETIDISSIMA (subgenus Limniris, series Foetidissimae) is a widespread native of Western Europe and North Africa that will grow almost anywhere or in any soil. It seems most at home in semiwooded or lightly shaded situations in humus-rich soil above −10°F (−23°C). This hardy, evergreen iris is much prized by flower arrangers for the scarlet seeds that are displayed when the capsules split in fall; forms with white or yellow seeds are known. Slow-growing white- and cream-variegated forms occur. *I. foe-*

tidissima var. *citrina* produces larger, clear topaz-yellow flowers. This species is susceptible to virus disease.

(**12**) THE ALGERIAN OR CRETAN IRIS, *I. unguicularis* (subgenus Limniris, series Unguiculares) flowers from early fall to midspring. Hardy to −10°F (−23°C), it needs a warm sunny position, ideally against a south-facing wall in sharply draining, neutral to alkaline soil. In summer, it should become dry and baked. A top dressing of potash or bone meal in early fall and spring will promote growth and flowering. Propagate by division in spring and keep watered until established. This species is, however, better left undisturbed for many years; indeed, new plants may take years to flower, preferring cramped, impoverished conditions. Seed capsules will sometimes be found in the clumps at ground level; seed will germinate if sown in a soil-based medium by the following fall. Larvae of the angleshades moth may eat the ends of flower buds while still at ground level.

Bulbous irises (13) XIPHIUM IRISES (Subgenus Xiphium) occur in Western Europe and North Africa, usually in alkaline soil. Since there is a dormant period after flowering, several of the species need bulb frame culture in wet summer areas. *I. xiphium* occurs over a wide range of habitats. Both the typical plant and the many named color forms called Spanish irises are reliable garden plants. Their leaves appear in fall. Hybrids between *I. xiphium* and *I. tingitana*, known collectively as Dutch irises, are good garden plants, and are widely used for the cut-flower market throughout the year; colors range from white and yellow to deep purple. *I. latifolia*, erroneously named the English iris in the 16th century and still so called, is an exception, growing in damp grassy places in the Pyrenees. An easy plant for the border, it prefers a soil that does not dry out. Many color forms are available in blue, violet, purple, and white.

(**14**) JUNO IRISES (Subgenus Scorpiris) comprise a group of over 55 species. Most of them are difficult in temperate areas. They occur in western Asia ranging from Turkey to central Russian Asia and south to Jordan, with the one exception of *I. planifolia*, found

in Southwest Europe and North Africa. They are fleshy-rooted, bulbous plants with channeled leaves in one plane. The flowers are attractive, the falls large and brightly colored, the standards very small, often reduced to bristles. The majority of the Junos grow in areas of hot dry summers and cold winters with snow cover, and unless this can be achieved naturally, then overhead protection from summer and winter rain is essential. Grow in deep pots in an unheated, well-ventilated alpine house or plant out in a bulb frame. Free-draining soil with added dolomitic limestone is recommended; feed with balanced fertilizer in the growing period from midfall until the leaves turn yellow after flowering. Never wet the foliage, as water trapped in the channeled leaves may cause rot. Some Junos are more tolerant of damp; for example, *I. aucheri*, *I. bucharica* and *I. magnifica* will thrive in the open garden in cool-temperate areas in well-drained loam. The smaller forms of *I. bucharica* are excellent plants for the rock garden, flowering in early spring. Propagate from small young bulbs carefully separated when replanting, or from seed. Artificial cross-pollination may be necessary—many species are self-sterile.

(**15**) RETICULATA IRISES (subgenus Hermodactyloides) are dwarf irises, their bulbs covered in netted (reticulate) tunics. Reticulata irises occur in Turkey, Iran, Central Asia and south to Jordan. In temperate gardens, both *I. histrioides* and *I. reticulata* will flourish in a sunny position in well-drained soil, and can be left undisturbed for years. There are many color forms available, as well as some named hybrids. The yellow *I. winogradowii* is a high mountain plant that likes plenty of moisture during the growing season and, unlike the other reticulatas, does not require a summer dry period. A hybrid with *I. histrioides* named *I.* 'Katharine Hodgkin' is a hardy bulb that increases rapidly in the open garden or a raised bed. *I. danfordiae* will flower well in the first season but then breaks up into many tiny bulblets and should be replaced annually (flowering colonies only seem to develop when this species is planted deeply in a bulb frame). Increase by bulb offsets or from seed, which germinates freely. Affected by ink disease.

IRIS

Name	Distribution	Group	Habit	Leaves	Flowers
I. aphylla	C & E Europe to W Russia and N Caucasus	[1]	to 12 in (30 cm), deciduous; flowering stems branched from middle or near base, bracts 1¼–2½ in (3–6 cm), inflated, sometimes purple-tipped	arranged in fans, outer leaves curved, inner leaves upright, ¼–¾ in (0.5–2 cm) wide	flowers 1–5, 2½–2¾ in (6–7 cm) diam., pale to deep purple to blue-violet, beard hairs blue-white, tips yellow
Comments: Spring.					

Aril Irises: [group 3]. Regeliocyclus Hybrids. 'Ancilla': flowers white veined purple, falls flaked and netted purple. 'Chione': standards white veined lilac blue, falls veined gray, blotched black-brown. 'Clotho': standards deep violet with black beard, falls brown, veins and blotch black. 'Dardanus': standards tinged lilac, falls cream blotched matt purple. 'Theseus': standards violet with darker veins, falls ivory marked deep violet. 'Thor': flowers gray veined purple, blotch bright purple. 'Vera': flowers chocolate-brown tinged purple with blue beard. Aril-Median Irises: (Aril × Miniature Tall Bearded irises). 'Canasta': to 11 in (28 cm); standards pale violet, falls rich beige with deep red signal and veining, the latter paler at edges, beard brown-bronze. 'Little Orchid Annie': to 12 in (30 cm); standards pale amethyst veined and shaded green-gold, ruffled, midrib green, falls orchid edged yellow-green, signal and veining red, beard dark yellow. Arilbred Irises (Aril × Tall Bearded irises). 'Lady Mohr': to 30 in (75 cm); standards light mauve-blue, falls yellow and green with deep red markings, beard brown. 'Loudmouth': to 10 in (25 cm); fls deep red, falls with black signal. 'Nineveh': standards purple shaded pink, falls violet-red, beard dark brown. 'Saffron Charm': fls in blend of deep yellow, gray and lavender.

Name	Distribution	Group	Habit	Leaves	Flowers
I. aucheri	SE Turkey, N Iraq, N Syria, Jordan, NW Iran	[14]	to 16 in (40 cm); roots fleshy	10 × 1–1¾ in (25 × 2.5–4.5 cm), completely concealing stem until fruiting	3–6, blue, rarely almost white; tube to 2½ in (6 cm); fall blade with central yellow ridge, margin wavy, haft broadly winged; standards ¾–1½ in (2–3.5 cm), horizontal to deflexed, obovate
Comments: Late winter–spring. Crossed with *I. persica* to produce *I.* 'Sindpers'.					
I. bakeriana	SE Turkey, N Iraq, W Iran	[15]	to 6 in (15 cm); bulb tunics netted	cylindric, 8-ribbed, otherwise close to *I. reticulata*	solitary, white, tipped violet on falls with a cream ridge surrounded by violet spots and veins, haft spotted and veined violet, standards and style branches lilac

Bearded (Pogon) Irises: [group 1]. (1) *Border Bearded* (steins to 28 in (70 cm); fls large). 'Brown Lasso': standards butterscotch, falls pale violet and brown. 'Carnival Glass': red-brown, occasionally tinged blue or red. 'Impelling': bright pink and yellow with an orange beard. 'Impetuous': sky-blue, ruffled, beard white. 'Marmalade Skies': apricot-orange. 'Whoop Em Up': vivid golden-yellow, falls clear chestnut-red, rimmed with bright yellow. (2) *Intermediate Bearded* (stems to 28 in (70 cm); abundant). 'Annikins': deep violet blue. 'Black Watch': very dark velvety black-purple. 'Golden Muffin': standards ruffled, yellow, falls amber-brown edged yellow. 'Indeed': standards clear lemon-yellow, falls translucent white edged bright yellow with a white beard. 'Silent Strings': clear blue. 'Why Not': bright apricot-orange with darker beard. (3) *Miniature Dwarf Bearded* (stems to 8 in (20 cm), to 2 flowers per stem). 'April Ballet': standards light blue with a violet-blue spot. 'Egret Snow': standards pure while, falls occasionally flecked blue. 'Jasper Gem': rust-red bicolor. 'Orchid Flare': pink with white beard. (4) *Miniature Tall Bearded* (stems to 28 in (70 cm); flowers 8 or more). 'Carolyn Rose': cream-white lined rose-pink. 'Dappled Pony': standards dark blue, falls white heavily flecked violet. 'Smarty Pants': yellow with red stripes on falls. 'Surprise Blue': lavender blue with white hafts. (5) *Standard Dwarf Bearded* (stems to 16 in (40 cm); flowers 3 or 4 per stem). 'Austrian Sky': blue with darker markings on falls. 'Blue Denim': blue, flaring with a white beard. 'Gingerbread Man': deep brown with a bright blue beard. 'Green Halo': pale olive-green with a darker 'halo'. 'Melon Honey': melon-orange with a white beard. 'Toots': velvet burgundy with a yellow beard. (6) *Tall Bearded* (over 28 in (70 cm) high; flowers large, usually ruffled). 'Broadway': standards golden-yellow, beard orange, falls white. 'Going My Way': white striped violet-purple, 'Jane Phillips': large, pale blue. 'Love's Allure': standards gray-lilac flecked purple, falls edged sandy gold. 'Red Lion': deep brown-burgundy. 'Vanity': light pink flashed white with a pink-red beard.

I. 'Vanity' (Bearded)   *I.* 'Brown Lasso' (Bearded)

I. 'Jasper Gem' (Bearded)   *I.* 'Toots' (Bearded)

IRIS

Name	Distribution	Group	Habit	Leaves	Flowers
I. bucharica I. orchioides of gardens	Russia, NE Afghanistan	[14]	to 16 in (40 cm)	to 8 × 1½ in (20 × 3.5 cm) at flowering, later elongated on expanded stem, shiny green, channeled, margins white	2–6 in upper leaf axils; perianth tube to 1¾ in (4.5 cm), golden yellow to white, fall with central ridge yellow surrounded by green to dull purple suffusion or markings, standards spreading, trilobed or lanceolate
Comments: Spring.					
I. chrysographes	W China, NE Burma	[5]	to 20 in (50 cm); rhizome stout	20–⅝ in (50–1.5 cm)	1–4 on hollow, branched or unbranched stems, fragrant, 2–4 in (5–10 cm) diam., dark red-purple streaked gold on falls; falls deflexed; standards spreading
Comments: Late spring–summer. Hybridizes with *I. forrestii* and *I. sibirica*. 'Black Night': flowers indigo-violet, 'Inshriach': flowers almost black. 'Margot Holmes': flowers purple-crimson lined yellow at throat. 'Rubella': flowers burgundy.					
I. clarkei	E Himalaya	[5]	rhizome stout; stems to 24 in (60 cm), 1–3-branched	to ¾ in (2 cm) wide, glossy green above, glaucous beneath	2 per branch, 2–4 in (5–10 cm) diam., blue-violet to red-purple; falls with large, white, central signal patch, veined violet; haft slightly yellow; standards bent to horizontal
Comments: Late spring–early summer.					
I. confusa	W China	[4]	vigorous, clump-forming, to 5 ft (1.5 m); stems green, canelike, procumbent and branching, then ascending, with an apical fan of foliage	bright green, sword-shaped, to 2 in (5 cm) across	to 2 in (5 cm) diam., many borne on branching stems to 36 in (90 cm) long, short-lived, white spotted yellow or mauve; falls 1 × 2 in (2.5 × 5 cm), crest yellow, signal patch yellow
Comments: Spring.					
I. cristata	NE US	[4]	rhizome small, much-branched	to 6 × ½–1¼ in (15 × 1–3 cm) at flowering, linear	1–2 per spathe, subsessile, 1¼–1½ in (3–4 cm) diam., pale lilac to purple; tube to 4 in (10 cm); falls obovate, blunt, reflexed, ½ × ½ in (1 × 1 cm), central patch white, crest of 3 crisped yellow ridges; standards erect, oblanceolate, shorter and narrower than falls
Comments: Early summer. 'Alba': fls white. 'Caerulea': fls blue.					
I. crocea	Kashmir	[10]	rhizome woody, roots wiry	to 30 × ⅝–¾ in (75 × 1.5–2 cm), sword-shaped, leathery	flowers 4¾–7 in (12–18 cm) diam., in terminal clusters on branched stems to 3¼ ft (1 m), dark golden yellow; falls oblong, margins crisped; standards oblanceolate, erect, margins slightly crisped; style branch lobes narrow-triangular

I. bucharica

I. chrysographes

I. confusa

I. danfordiae

IRIS

Name	Distribution	Group	Habit	Leaves	Flowers
I. danfordiae	Turkey	[15]	to 6 in (15 cm); bulb tunic netted, tiny, producing offset bulblets	½–6 in (1–15 cm), taller than flowers, quadrangular	solitary, to 2 in (5 cm) diam., yellow; tube to 3 in (7.5 cm); falls lightly spotted green in center and lower part, ridge deeper yellow-orange; standards reduced, bristlelike, ⅛–¼ in (3–5 mm)
Comments: Early spring.					
I. douglasiana	W US (S Oregon, California)	[6]		to 39 × ¾ in (100 × 2 cm), dark green, base stained red, ribbed	2–3, 2¾–4 in (7–10 cm) diam. on branching 6–28 in (15–70 cm) stems, lavender to purple, veins darker; tube to 1¼ in (3 cm); falls yellow in center; standards erect, lanceolate, clawed
Comments: Summer. 'Alba': flowers white. 'Southcombe Velvet': flowers deep violet.					
I. ensata *I. kaempferi* JAPANESE WATER IRIS	Japan, N China, E Russia	[7]	stoutly rhizomatous, aquatic or marginal	8–24 × ⅛–½ in (20–60 × 0.4–1.2 cm), leathery, midrib prominent	3 or 4 per branch on flowering stems to 36 in (90 cm), 3–6 in (8–15 cm) diam., purple to red-purple; tube ½–¾ in (1–2 cm); fall haft yellow, blade elliptic-ovate, also suffused yellow; standards smaller, erect

Comments: Summer. A large number of cultivars, many of which originate from Japan, with a few (such as some of the Higo Hybrids) beginning to enter western gardens; flowers to 8 in (20 cm) in shades of white, pink, blue and violet often mottled or flecked; single to double; often with spreading standards. 'Alba': flowers pure white. 'Blauer Berg' ('Blue Mountain'): flowers bright sky blue, abundant; middle to late season. 'Gei Sho Ne': habit unusually short; flowers violet; middle to late season. 'Good Omen': growth strong; flowers double, violet tinged red, abundant; early season. 'Major': habit tall to 18 in (46 cm); flowers darker. 'Moonlight Waves': flowers white with lime-green center. 'Peacock Dance': falls white, veins red-violet, signal patch yellow; standards dark red-purple; style branches purple. 'Prairie Love Song': flowers white, signal patch yellow. 'Raspberry Rimmed': flowers white, margins red-pink, signal patch yellow. 'Returning Tide': flowers pale blue, signal yellow. 'Sorcerer's Triumph': flowers double, white, veins red-purple, signal orange. 'Stranger in Paradise': flowers white, margins pink, signal patch yellow. 'Summer Storm': flowers to 7 in (18 cm) diam., violet tinged red, veined blue; late flowering. 'The Great Moghul': flowers black-purple. 'Unschuld' ('Innocence'): flowers clear white, perianth seg. undulate; early flowering. 'Variegata': leaves striped white; flowers purple. 'Aichi-no-Kagayaki' (*I. ensata* × *I. pseudacorus*): flowers large, bright yellow, veins brown. 'Chance Beauty' (*I. ensata* × *I. pseudacorus*): flowers large, bright yellow, veins red-brown.

Name	Distribution	Group	Habit	Leaves	Flowers
I. foetidissima STINKING GLADWYN; STINKING IRIS; ROAST BEEF PLANT; GLADWYN	S & W Europe, N Africa, Atlantic Is.	[11]		evergreen, sword-shaped, in basal fans, deep green, to 1 in (2.5 cm) wide	to 5 per branch, 2–2¾ in (5–7 cm) diam., malodorous, short-lived, on short-branching stems to 32 in (80 cm); falls obovate, ¾ in (2 cm) wide, blade blue-lilac to topaz or yellow, veins purple, center fading to white, haft bronze to brown, winged; standards smaller, oblanceolate, erect, flushed lilac

Comments: Summer-flowering. Grown chiefly for its handsome foliage and scarlet, beadlike seeds persisting in the capsules from late summer through winter. 'Fructo Alba': seeds white. 'Variegata': leaves striped cream. var. ***citrina***: flowers pale yellow and mauve. var. ***lutescens***: flowers pure clear yellow.

Name	Distribution	Group	Habit	Leaves	Flowers
I. forrestii	W China, N Burma	[5]		narrow-linear, shiny above, glaucous below, shorter stem	2, on an unbranched stem to 18 in (45 cm), scented, 2–2½ in (5–6 cm) diam., yellow lined purple-brown on fall haft; falls oblong-ovate, blade 2 in (5 cm); standards erect, oblanceolate
Comments: Summer.					

I. douglasiana   *I. ensata*   *I. foetidissima* var. *citrina*   *I. forrestii*

IRIS

Name	Distribution	Group	Habit	Leaves	Flowers
I. fulva	C US (Mississippi Valley)	[8]	to 36 in (90 cm); rhizome slender, green	$^5/_8$–1 in (1.5–2.5 cm) wide, green, ensiform	to 2½ in (6.5 cm) diam., bright red to rust, orange or rarely deep yellow; tube to 1 in (2.5 cm); falls and standards hanging downward, falls oblanceolate, to 1 in (2.5 cm) wide, blunt, narrowed to a claw, standards broad, truncate, notched, to 2 × ¾ in (5 × 2 cm)

Comments: Summer.

Name	Distribution	Group	Habit	Leaves	Flowers
I. × ***fulvala*** (*I. fulva* × *I. brevicaulis*)	garden origin	[8]			purple-red

Name	Distribution	Group	Habit	Leaves	Flowers
I. germanica	widely naturalized; either a Mediterranean native or an ancient fertile hybrid	[1]	rhizome stout, horizontal, branching; flowering stem 24–48 in (60–120 cm), with 1–2 short branches and thick, purple-tinted bracts	2-ranked, equitant, 12–16 × 1–1¾ in (30–40 × 2.5–4.5 cm), gray-green	3½–4 in (9–10 cm) diam., in shades of blue, violet, white, beard yellow, standards sometimes paler than falls

Comments: Late spring. 'Amas': falls deep blue-purple, standards paler blue, prominent blue-white beard tipped orange. 'Askabadensis': tall, flowering later; falls red-purple, veins on hafts yellow-brown, beard tipped yellow, standards paler blue. 'Karput': leaves edged red-purple; falls narrow, black-purple, standards paler red-purple. 'Nepalensis': falls and standards both dark purple-red tipped orange; beard blue-white grading to white. 'Sivias': blue; beard white, hairs scarcely tipped yellow. 'Florentina': smaller; flowers scented, palest blue-white; veins on haft of falls yellow, beard yellow.

Name	Distribution	Group	Habit	Leaves	Flowers
I. gracilipes	China, Japan	[4]	4–6 in (10–15 cm); dwarf, clump-forming, stoloniferous; stems slender, branching	grassy, ensiform, to 12 × ¼–½ in (30 × 0.5–1 cm)	1¼–1½ in (3–4 cm) diam., pink to blue-lilac veined violet; tube $^5/_8$ in (1.5 cm), falls obovate, to 1 × $^5/_8$ in (2.5 × 1.5 cm), notched, center white, crest wavy, yellow and white

Comments: Early summer. 'Alba': fls white.

Name	Distribution	Group	Habit	Leaves	Flowers
I. graeberiana	Russia	[14]	to 16 in (40 cm)	2-ranked, shiny green above, gray-green beneath, margins white	4–6, 2¾ in (7 cm)+ diam., blue sometimes tinged violet; tube to 2½ in (6 cm), fall blade deeper blue, center ridge white on veined, white ground, standards obovate, to 1 in (2.5 cm), tips pointed

Comments: Spring.

Name	Distribution	Group	Habit	Leaves	Flowers
I. graminea *I. colchica*	NE Spain to W Russia, N & W Caucasus	[10]	stem 8–16 in (20–40 cm), strongly flattened or 2-winged	borne on stem, uppermost leaves taller than flowers	1–2, fruit-scented, 2¾–3 in (7–8 cm) diam.; falls rounded, ½ in (1.2 cm) wide, violet, blade white at center veined violet, haft winged, occasionally tinged green or yellow; standards erect, purple, ¼ in (0.5 cm) wide; style branches purple, base tinged green or brown

Comments: Summer.

I. germanica

I. germanica 'Florentina'

I. graminea

I. histrioides 'Major'

IRIS

Name	Distribution	Group	Habit	Leaves	Flowers
I. histrio	S Turkey, Syria, Lebanon	[15]	bulb offsetting, tunic netted	12–24 in (30–60 cm), 4-angled	1 per spathe, 2½–3 in (6–8 cm) diam., falls lilac, streaked and spotted, ridge yellow surrounded by a pale, bluer spotted area, standards lilac, oblanceolate, unmarked

Comments: Winter-early spring.

Name	Distribution	Group	Habit	Leaves	Flowers
I. histrioides	Central N Turkey	[15]		4-angled in section, not or scarcely developed at flowering time, later extending to 20 in (50 cm)	2½–2¾ in (6–7 cm) diam., blue, fall blade pale spotted blue with a yellow ridge

Comments: Early spring. 'Golden Harvest': yellow. 'Imperior': dark blue. 'Major': purple-blue, spotted white on falls. A plant with much larger, dark violet blue flowers with almost horizontal falls has also been offered as *I. histrioides* 'Major'. 'White Excelsior': large white. 'White Perfection': large, white var. **sophenensis:** flower segments narrower, dark violet-blue, lightly spotted; fall ridge yellow. See also under *I. winogradowiI*.

I. × *hollandica*—The Dutch Irises—*I. xiphium* × *I. tingitana*, possibly with the influence of *I. latifolia*. See *I. xiphium*.

Name	Distribution	Group	Habit	Leaves	Flowers
I. hoogiana	Russia	[3]	16–24 in (40–60 cm); rhizome stout, producing long stolons	erect, almost straight, tinged purple, to 20 × ⅝ in (50 × 1.5 cm) - 2–3 per pair of bracts, 2¾–4 in (7–10 cm) diam., scented, plain gray-blue; tube to 1 in (2.5 cm); falls and standards bearded yellow	late spring. 'Alba': white, with a faint overlay of pale lavender-blue. 'Bronze Beauty': gray-violet, falls deep rich violet, edged cinnamon-brown. 'Noblense': blue-violet, crest golden yellow. 'Purpurea': deep purple.

Name	Distribution	Group	Habit	Leaves	Flowers
I. iberica	SW Asia	[2]	to 8 in (20 cm), rhizome compact	to ¼ in (6 mm) diam., gray-green, linear, curving	solitary, to 2½ in (6.5 cm) diam., tube to 1½ in (3.5 cm), falls reflexed from base, white densely veined brown and spotted, signal patch black-brown, velvety, beard hair purple-brown, standards to 3¼ in (8.5 cm), erect, white to pale lilac, obscurely veined

Comments: Late spring. ssp. **elegantissima**: falls cream to ivory spotted and veined maroon, blade deflexed almost vertically, standards white, sometimes veined brown at base.

Name	Distribution	Group	Habit	Leaves	Flowers
I. innominata	W US	[6]	to 10 in (25 cm)	slender, 1/16–⅛ in (2–4 mm) wide, dark green, base tinged purple	1–2 per stem, 2½–3 in (6.5–7.5 cm) diam., cream-yellow to orange or pink-lilac to dark purple, veins darker; tube to 1¼ in (3 cm); falls to 2½ in (6.5 mm), margins of falls and standards frilly, standards shorter, style lobes broad, margins toothed

Comments: Summer. Used in hybridizing, see Pacific Coast hybrids. 'Lilacina': lavender. 'Lutea': yellow. 'Spinners': soft brown-yellow, veined and marked rich brown.

Japanese Irises: See *I. ensata*, *I. laevigata*

I. iberica   *I. innominata*   *I. japonica*   *I. kerneriana*

IRIS

Name	Distribution	Group	Habit	Leaves	Flowers
I. japonica	C China, Japan	[4]	18–32 in (45–80 cm), rhizome stoloniferous; stems erect, branched	to 18 in (45 cm), in fans, ensiform, shiny green	3–4 per branch, 1½–2 in (4–5 cm) diam., appearing flattened due to spreading perianth lobes, margins fringed, white to light blue-lilac; falls ¾ in (2 cm) wide, blade with orange frilly crest on purple blotched area; standards lilac

Comments: Spring. 'Ledger': frilled, white, marked purple, crest orange. 'Rudolph Spring': pale purple-blue marked orange. 'Variegata' ('Aphrodite'): leaves striped white and marked purple.

Name	Distribution	Group	Habit	Leaves	Flowers
I. kerneriana	N & C Turkey.	[10]	rhizome slender, with fibrous remains of old leaf bases	linear, to ¼ in (5 mm) wide, slightly shorter than flowering stems	2–4 per branch, 2¾–4 in (7–10 cm) diam., deep cream to pale yellow; fall blade elliptic, to ¾ in (2 cm) wide, with deep yellow central blotch, strongly recurved, tip almost touching stem, haft narrow, ¼ in (5 mm); standards erect, margins wavy, notched

Comments: Summer.

Name	Distribution	Group	Habit	Leaves	Flowers
I. korolkowii	Russia, NE Afghanistan	[3]	16–24 in (40–60 cm); rhizome thick, stoloniferous, with fibrous leaf base remains	linear, ¼–½ in (0.5–1 cm) wide, base tinged purple	2–3 per spathe, 2½–3 in (6–8 cm) diam., appearing elongated, cream-white lightly veined deep maroon, falls oblong, to 1½× 1 in (4 × 2.5 cm), acute, deflexed, signal patch dark green to black-brown, beards inconspicuous, standards acute, erect

Comments: Early summer. 'Concolor': bright blue-purple. 'Violacea': cream veined red-violet.

Name	Distribution	Group	Habit	Leaves	Flowers
I. laevigata	E Asia	[7]	aquatic or marginal, to 18 in (45 cm); similar to *I. ensata* but stouter	⅝–1½ in (1.5–4 cm), without prominent midrib	2–4, 3–4 in (8–10 cm) diam., blue-violet, tube to ¾ in (2 cm); fall haft pale yellow, standard erect, smaller than falls

Comments: Summer–fall. var. *alba*: flowers white, style branches mauve. 'Albopurpurea': falls purple, mottled white around edges, standards white. 'Atropurpurea': red-purple. 'Colchesterensis': flowers white, fall center dark blue. 'Lilacina': light blue. 'Midnight': very deep blue lined white. 'Montrosa': very large, deep blue, white at center. 'Mottled Beauty': white, falls spotted pale blue. 'Regal': red-purple. 'Snowdrift': double, white, style branches light violet. 'Variegata': leaves striped green and white; flowers pale blue.

Name	Distribution	Group	Habit	Leaves	Flowers
I. latifolia *I. xiphioides* ENGLISH IRIS	Spain and Pyrenees	[13]	to 32 in (80 cm).	appearing in spring, to 26 × ⅜ in (65 × 0.8 cm), channeled, gray-white above	1–2 per bract pair, 3–4 in (8–10 cm) diam., violet-blue, tube ¼ in (5 mm), falls with central yellow blotch, broad, ovate-oblong, to 3 in (7.5 cm), haft winged, standards to 2½ in (6 cm), oblanceolate

Comments: Late spring-summer. 'Almona': flowers light blue-lavender. 'Blue Giant': Standards blue-purple, speckled darker, falls deep blue. 'Isabella': flowers pink-mauve. 'La Nuit': flowers dark purple-red. 'Mansfield': flowers magenta-purple. 'Montblanc': flowers white. 'Queen of the Blues': flowers rich purple-blue.

Louisiana Hybrids: [group 8]. Hybrids of the Series *Hexagonae* (including *I. fulva*) are becoming increasingly popular in the US. They are mostly tender, and bear flowers in a wide range of colors including shades of yellow, pink, red, brown, purple and blue. 'Black Gamecock': flowers blue-black with line signal. 'Mme. Dorothea K. Williamson' (*I. fulva* × *I. brevicaulis*): hardy; flowers very large, plum-purple. 'Gold Reserve': flowers golden-orange veined red. 'May Roy': Standards pale pink, falls pink tinged purple. 'Roll Call': to 36 in (90 cm); flowers violet with green styles. 'Sea Wisp': to 42 in (110 cm); flowers blue with yellow line signal.

I. laevigata

I. laevigata 'Variegata'

I. latifolia

I. magnifica

IRIS

Name	Distribution	Group	Habit	Leaves	Flowers
I. lutescens *I. chamaeiris*	NE Spain, S France and Italy	[1]	fast-growing, to 12 in (30 cm); rhizome stout	12 × ¼–1 in (30 × 0.5–2.5 cm), equitant, straight to curved	1–2, 2½–3 in (6–8 cm) diam., yellow, violet, purple, white or bicolored, tube to 1½ in (3.5 cm), falls oblong-spathulate, to 3 × ¾ in (7.5 × 2 cm), beard yellow, standards oblong, erect or converging, to 3 × 1 in (7.5 × 2.5 cm), margins crisped

Comments: Early to mid-spring 'Campbellii': dwarf; flowers bright violet-blue, falls darker. 'Jackanapes': flowers blue and white. 'Nancy Lindsay': dwarf; flowers pale yellow.

Name	Distribution	Group	Habit	Leaves	Flowers
I. magnifica	Russia	[14]	12–24 in (30–60 cm); bulb tunics papery	many, remote, 1¼–2 in (3–5 cm) wide, channeled, pale green, lustrous	3–7, to 3 in (8 cm) diam., pink-lilac, tube 1½–1¾ in (4–4.5 cm), falls yellow at center, crest white, fall haft widely winged, to 1 in (2.5 cm) wide, standards obovate, to 1¼ in (3 cm), horizontal to deflexed

Comments: Late spring.

Name	Distribution	Group	Habit	Leaves	Flowers
I. missouriensis	W US	[7]	to 30 in (75 cm)	leaves to ¼ in (7 mm) wide, absent in winter, usually taller than flowers	2–3 per bract pair, 2–3 in (5–8 cm) diam., on pedicels to 8 in (20 cm), white, lilac, or blue; falls obovate, deflexed, veined, signal patch yellow; standards oblanceolate, upright

Comments: Late spring-summer. 'Alba': flowers white.

Name	Distribution	Group	Habit	Leaves	Flowers
I. orchioides	Russia	[14]	bulb tunics papery; roots fleshy	7 × ½–1¼ in (18 × 1–3 cm), straight to curved, pale green, concealing stem until after flowering	3–4, 2 in (5 cm) diam., light yellow suffused mauve, tube 1¼–2½ in (3–6 cm), fall haft broadly winged, ¾ in (2 cm) wide, crest gold on dark yellow ground, veined green or mauve, standards trilobed or linear

Comments: *I. orchioides* of gardens is usually *I. bucharica*.

Name	Distribution	Group	Habit	Leaves	Flowers
I. orientalis	NE Greece, W Turkey	[10]	to 36 in (90 cm), branched	to 36 × ½–¾ in (90 × 1–2 cm)	2–3 per pair of papery bracts, 4 in (10 cm) diam., white; fall blade rounded, signal area large, yellow, haft narrow, slightly pubesc., standards to 3¼ in (8.5 cm), erect

Comments: Summer. For *I. orientalis* of gardens, see *I. sanguinea*.

Pacific Coast or **Californian Irises:** [6]. (*I. douglasiana* × *I. innominata*, etc.). 'Arnold Sunrise': flowers white flushed blue, fall marked with orange. 'Blue Ballerina': flowers white, falls marked with purple. 'Broadleigh Rose': flowers marked with shades of pink.

Name	Distribution	Group	Habit	Leaves	Flowers
I. pallida DALMATIAN IRIS	former Yugoslavia	[1]	stems branched, to 48 in (120 cm)	glaucous, 8–24 × ½–1½ in (20–60 × 1–4 cm), usually evergreen	2–6, fragrant, 3–4¾ in (8–12 cm) diam., soft lilac-blue, bracts silvery, papery; beard yellow

Comments: Late spring-early summer. 'Argentea Variegata': leaves striped blue-green and white. 'Variegata': leaves striped yellow.

Name	Distribution	Group	Habit	Leaves	Flowers
I. pseudacorus YELLOW FLAG	Europe to W Siberia, Caucasus, Turkey, Iran, N Africa	[7]	marginal or aquatic; stems branched, to 6½ ft (2 m); rhizome stout	to 36 × 1¼ in (90 × 3 cm), gray-green, midrib prominent	4–12, 2–4¾ in (5–12 cm) diam., bright yellow veined brown or violet; tube to ⅝ in (1.5 cm), falls rounded, to 1½ in (4 cm) wide, blotched deeper yellow; standards oblanceolate, erect, to 1¼ in (3 cm)

Comments: Early–midsummer. 'Alba': creamy white, with brown veins near tips. 'Golden Fleece': deep yellow without darker veins. 'Variegata': leaves striped yellow at first. var. ***bastardii:*** flowers pale yellow; fall blade not blotched deeper yellow.

I. missouriensis

I. orientalis

I. pallida 'Variegata'

I. pseudacorus

IRIS

Name	Distribution	Group	Habit	Leaves	Flowers
I. pumila *I. aequiloba,* *I. taurica*	SE & EC Europe to Urals	[1]	dwarf, to 6 in (15 cm)	almost straight, gray-green, to 6 × ⅝ in (15 × 1.5 cm), dying away in winter	usually solitary, rarely 3 in some forms, mostly purple-violet, some white yellow or blue; tube 2–4 in (5–10 cm), beard blue or yellow

Comments: Spring. A parent of the dwarf bearded cultivars.

Name	Distribution	Group	Habit	Leaves	Flowers
I. reticulata	N & S Turkey, NE Iraq, N & W Iran, Russia.	[15]	bulb pear-shaped with netted tunic and producing bulblets after flowers	4-angled, very narrow, to 12 × 1/16 in (30 × 0.2 cm), synanthous or hysteranthous	solitary, dark violet blue to paler blue to red-purple; tube 1½–2¾ in (4–7 cm); falls 2 in (5 cm), often yellow-ridged, haft 1 in (2.5 cm); standards erect, oblanceolate, 2½ in (6 cm)

Comments: Early spring.

Reticulata Hybrids [group 15]. (derived from *I. histrioides* and *I. reticulata* and hybrids between them). 'Alba': flowers white. 'Cantab': flowers very pale Cambridge blue, crested yellow. 'Clairette': Standards sky-blue, falls deep blue marked white. 'Edward': flowers dark blue marked orange. 'Gordon': flowers light blue with orange blotch on white ground lightly striped blue. 'Harmony': Standards blue, falls royal blue blotched yellow and white. 'Ida': Standards light blue, falls paler, blotch pale yellow on white ground slightly spotted blue. 'Jeannine': flowers violet, falls blotched orange with white-and-violet striped patches; fragrant. 'Joyce': Standard lavender-blue, falls deep sky-blue with yellow markings and gray-brown stripes. 'J.S. Dijt': flowers dark red-purple; fragrant. 'Natascha': flowers white tinged blue, falls veined green with golden-yellow blotch. 'Pauline': flowers purple-violet with dark purple falls blotched blue and white. 'Purple Gem': flowers violet, falls black-purple blotched purple and white. 'Royal Blue': Standard deep velvet blue, falls blotched yellow. 'Springtime': Standards pale blue, falls dark blue tipped white, with purple spots and yellow midrib. 'Violet Beauty': Standards velvet-purple, falls deep violet with orange crest.

Name	Distribution	Group	Habit	Leaves	Flowers
I. rosenbachiana	C Asia	[14]		bright glossy green, to 2 in (5 cm) at flowering, later to 10 in (25 cm), tips curving outward	1–3, light purple; falls blotched deep purple, crest orange

Comments: Winter–early spring. var. **baldschuanica** is smaller, with pale primrose flowers veined and blotched brown-purple.

Name	Distribution	Group	Habit	Leaves	Flowers
I. sanguinea *I. orientalis* of gardens	SE Russia, Korea, Japan	[5]		similar to *I. sibirica* but leaves as tall as or taller than the 30 in (75 cm), unbranched flowering stems	2, blue-purple marked white

Comments: Early summer. 'Alba': white. 'Kobana': narrow, white. 'Snow Queen': ivory.

Name	Distribution	Group	Habit	Leaves	Flowers
I. serotina	SE Spain	[13]	16–24 in (40–60 cm)	narrow, channeled, appearing in fall, dying before flowering	1–2 on an unbranched stem, violet-blue, tube to ½ in (1 cm), fall center yellow, standard reduced, to ½ in (1 cm), extremely narrow

Comments: Late summer.

I. reticulata

I. 'Harmony' (Reticulata hybrid)

I. setosa

I. 'Butter and Sugar' (Siberian)

IRIS

Name	Distribution	Group	Habit	Leaves	Flowers
I. setosa	Northeastern N America, E Russia, N Korea, Japan	[9]	6–36 in (15–90 cm)	rhizome stout, clad with old leaf bases; stems usually 2–3-branched to 20 × 1 in (50 × 2.5 cm), deciduous, base suffused red	to 15, 2–3½ in (5–9 cm) diam., tube to ½ in (1 cm), falls orbicular, 1 in (2.5 cm) diam., light blue-purple to purple, haft narrow, palest yellow, veins blue-purple, standards greatly reduced so that flowers appear to have only 3 petals, bristlelike, erect

Comments: Late spring–early summer. 'Kasho En': white. f. **serotina:** flowers solitary, sessile.

Name	Distribution	Group	Habit	Leaves	Flowers
I. sibirica	C & E Europe, NE Turkey, Russia	[5]	stems 1–2-branched, 20–48 in (50–120 cm), taller than leaves	to ⅛ in (4 mm) wide	to 5, to 2¾ in (7 cm) diam.; falls blue-purple, veined and marked white and gold, haft paler but darker-veined

Comments: Late spring–summer. 'Alba': white. 'Ann Dasch': flowers dark blue, falls marked yellow. 'Anniversary': flowers white with yellow hafts. 'Butter and Sugar': flowers white and yellow. 'Caesar's Brother': flowers dark pansy purple. 'Ego': flowers rich blue. 'Ewen': flowers burgundy, tetraploid. 'Helen Astor': flowers dark plum tinged rosy red, conspicuous white veins near throat. 'Mrs. Rowe': flowers small, gray-pink. 'Papillon': flowers pale blue. 'Ruffled Velvet': flowers red-purple marked yellow. 'Sparkling Rosé': flowers rose-mauve, falls flecked blue. 'Tropic Night': flowers blue-violet. 'Wisley White': flowers white.

Name	Distribution	Group	Habit	Leaves	Flowers
I. spuria	Europe, Asia, Algeria	[10]	to 20 in (50 cm)	12 × ½ in (30 × 1.2 cm)	violet-blue, yellow or white, fall blades rounded, to 1 in (2.5 cm) diam., standards oblanceolate

Comments: Summer. ssp. **spuria**: to 32 in (80 cm); flowers 2½–3 in (6–8 cm) diam., lilac or blue-violet, veins violet; falls to 2½ in (6 cm), striped yellow in center, haft exceeding blade. ssp. **carthaliniae**: to 38 in (95 cm); flowers 4–5, sky blue or white, veined deeper blue. ssp. **halophila**: 16–34 in (40–85 cm); flowers 4–8, 2½–2¾ in (6–7 cm) diam., white, dull light yellow to bright yellow, veined deeper, falls to 2½ in (6 cm), haft longer than blade. ssp. **maritima**: 12–20 in (30–50 cm); flowers to 4, bract green, falls to 1¾ in (4.5 cm) diam., veins dense, purple, blade deep purple, haft longer than blade, centrally striped green, ssp. **musulmanica**: syn. *I. klattii*, *I. musulmanica*, *I. violacea*; 16–36 in (40–90 cm); flowers light violet to dark lavender-violet, veins darker, falls to 3 in (8 cm), blade striped yellow, base tinged yellow, haft equalling or exceeding blade, ssp. **notha**: 28–36 in (70–90 cm); flowers violet-blue, fall haft striped yellow, exceeding blade.

Spuria Group. [group 10]. Many cultivars with flowers in shades and combinations of white and yellow through orange, red and brown to blue. 'Connoisseur': lavender blue. 'Elixir': saffron. 'Imperial Bronze': deep yellow veined brown. 'Protégé': Standards blue, falls white veined blue. 'Red Oak': brown-purple. 'Shelford Hybrid': blue.

Name	Distribution	Group	Habit	Leaves	Flowers
I. susiana MOURNING IRIS	Origin unknown, possibly Lebanon	[2]			to 4¾ in (12 cm) diam., pale lilac-gray heavily veined deep purple, falls and standards similarly sized and shaped, blade round, to 3 in (8 cm) wide, signal patch velvety purple-black, beard deep brown-purple

Comments: Late spring.

Name	Distribution	Group	Habit	Leaves	Flowers
I. tectorum ROOF IRIS	C & SW China, possibly Burma, naturalized Japan	[4]	rhizome stout; stems sometimes branched, to 16 in (40 cm)	thin, ribbed, glossy dark green to 12 × ¾–1 in (30 × 2–2.5 cm)	2–3 per spathe, to 4 in (10 cm) diam., somewhat flat, blue-lilac, veined and patched darker, falls 1 in (2.5 cm) wide, crest well-divided, frilly, white, spotted darker; standards and falls spreading, margins wavy

Comments: Early summer. 'Alba': white, veined yellow. 'Variegata': leaves streaked cream.

I. 'Wisley White' (Siberian)

I. tectorum

I. tenax

I. unguicularis

IRIS

Name	Distribution	Group	Habit	Leaves	Flowers
I. tenax	NW US	[6]	to 12 in (30 cm)	tinged pink at base	1–2, 2³/₄–3¹/₂ in (7–9 cm) diam., palest yellow to lavender or red-purple; tube short, to ¹/₂ in (1 cm), falls lanceolate, 1 in (2.5 cm) wide, reflexed, with a white or yellow central patch of purple, standards lanceolate, ¹/₄ in (0.6 cm) wide

Comments: Early summer. Used in hybridizing; see Pacific Coast hybrids.

Name	Distribution	Group	Habit	Leaves	Flowers
I. unguicularis *I. stylosa*	Algeria, Tunisia, W Syria, S & W Turkey	[12]	stemless; rhizome tough, branching	evergreen, in tufts, linear-ensiform, to 24 × ¹/₂ in (60 × 1 cm)	solitary short-stalked, fragrant, tube very long, to 8 in (20 cm), falls obovate, reflexed, 1 in (2.5 cm) wide, white veined lavender, central band yellow, haft linear, veins dark, standards size and shape as falls, erect, lilac; style branches yellow-glandular above

Comments: Winter-spring. ssp. cretensis (syn. *I. cretensis*, *I. cretica*): dwarf; leaves very narrow and grassy; flower segments to 2¹/₄ in (5.5 cm), purple-blue, fall blades and hafts white veined violet, blade striped orange in center. 'Alba': flowers white, falls with central green-yellow line. 'Ellis's Variety': leaves narrow; flowers bright violet-blue. 'Marginata': flowers lilac, margins white. 'Mary Barnard': flowers violet-blue. 'Oxford Dwarf': flowers deep blue, falls white veined purple, with central orange line, tips lavender. 'Speciosa': leaves short, narrow; flowers fragrant, deep violet, central yellow stripe. 'Starker's Pink': dwarf: leaves shorter, narrower; flowers pink-lavender. 'Variegata': flowers mottled and streaked purple on lavender ground. 'Walter Butt': flowers large, fragrant, pale silver-lilac; late fall-winter.

Name	Distribution	Group	Habit	Leaves	Flowers
I. variegata	C & SE Europe	[1]	8–20 in (20–50 cm), stems branched	dark green, sword-shaped, ribbed, to 12 × 1¹/₄ in (30 × 3 cm)	3–6, 2–3 in (5–8 cm) diam., bright yellow to white, tube to 1 in (2.5 cm), falls obovate, ³/₄ in (2 cm) wide, reflexed, veined red-brown, standards oblong, erect

Comments: Spring-summer. Forms with brown-red falls occur. Used in hybridizing; parent plant of the miniature tall bearded hybrids.

Name	Distribution	Group	Habit	Leaves	Flowers
I. verna	SE US	[8]	to 2¹/₂ in (6 cm) at flowering	equitant, sword-shaped, to 6 × ¹/₂ in (15 × 1 cm) after flowering, glaucous, purple at base	to 2 in (5 cm) diam., bright blue-lilac, tube ³/₄–2 in (2–5 cm), falls obovate, 1¹/₂ × ¹/₂ in (4 × 1 cm), center striped orange with brown spots, standard obovate, erect

Comments: Spring.

Name	Distribution	Group	Habit	Leaves	Flowers
I. versicolor	E US	[7]	marginal; rhizome stout, creeping; stems 8–32 in (20–80 cm), branched	14–24 × ¹/₂–³/₄ in (35–60 × 1–2 cm)	several per branch, 2¹/₂–3 in (6–8 cm) diam., violet to red-purple, falls wide-spreading, blade oval, 3–1 in (8–2.5 cm), blotched green-yellow, surrounded by white veined purple, haft white, purple-veined, standards oblanceolate, smaller, 1¹/₂ in (4 cm), paler, erect

Comments: Summer. 'Kermesina': flowers red-purple. var. *rosea*: flowers pink. *I. × robusta* 'Gerald Darby' (*I. versicolor × I. virginica*): flowers large, purple-blue.

I. variegata

I. versicolor

I. warleyensis

I. winogradowii

IRIS

Name	Distribution	Group	Habit	Leaves	Flowers
I. virginica SOUTHERN BLUE FLAG	E US	[7]	similar to *I. versicolor* but flowering stems usually unbranched, often curved	½–1¼ in (1–3 cm) wide, soft, tips drooping	1–4, blue, fall center yellow-hairy (not bearded)
Comments: Summer. 'Alba': flowers white. 'Giant Blue': flowers large, blue. 'Wide Blue': leaves blue-green; flowers blue.					
I. warleyensis	Russia	[14]	8–18 in (20–45 cm); roots slightly thickened	channeled, spaced along stem, to 8 × 1¼ in (20 × 3 cm)	to 5, 2–2¾ in (5–7 cm) diam., pale to dark violet to blue-purple, tube 2 in (5 cm), fall blade orbicular, margins white, crest white to yellow, on yellow ground, dissected, haft unwinged, standard deflexed, linear to trilobed, to ¾ in (2 cm)
Comments: Spring. 'Warl-sind' (*I. warleyensis* × *I. aucheri*): to 10 in (25 cm); falls yellow, blade blotched purple-blue, ridge yellow, standards and styles white.					
I. wendelboi	SW Afghanistan	[14]	dwarf, to 4 in (10 cm); bulb tunics papery	well-developed at flowering, to 8 × ½ in (20 × 1 cm), glaucous, arching, concealing stem until after flowering	1–2, to 2¼ in (5.5 cm) diam., deep violet, tube 1¼ in (3 cm); falls not winged, crest bright golden yellow, frilly, standards much reduced, to ¼ in (0.5 cm)
Comments: Spring.					
I. winogradowii	Russia	[15]	to 6 in (15 cm); differs from *I. histrioides* in producing rice-grain-like bulblets and pale primrose fls spotted green on the fall haft and center of blade	**Comments:** Early spring. 'Frank Elder' (*I. winogradowii* × *I. histrioides*): flowers pale blue slightly shaded yellow. 'Katharine Hodgkin' (*I. winogradowii* × *I. histrioides*): flowers yellow veined blue and faintly tinged pale blue.		
I. xiphium *I. hispanica* SPANISH IRIS	Iberian peninsula, Mediterranean	[13]	stems to 16–24 in (40–60 cm)	8–28 × ⅛–¼ in (20–70 × 0.3–0.5 cm), channeled, appearing in fall	1–2, usually blue or violet, sometimes white, yellow or mauve, tube ¹⁄₁₆–⅛ in (1-3mm), fall blade center usually orange or yellow
Comments: Spring-early summer. Hybridized with *I. tigitana* to produce Dutch irises. 'Battandieri' (syn. *I. battandieri*): flowers white, ridge on fall blades orange-yellow. 'Blue Angel': flowers bright blue, central falls marked yellow. 'Bronze Queen': flowers golden brown, suffused purple and bronze. 'Cajanus': flowers yellow. 'King of the Blues': flowers blue. 'Lusitanica' (syn. *I. lusitanica*): flowers yellow. 'Praecox' (syn. *I. xiphium* var. *praecox*): flowering earlier; flowers large blue. 'Professor Blaauw': flowers bright violet-blue. 'Queen Wilhelmina': flowers white. 'Taitii' (syn. *I. taitii*): flowers pale blue. 'Thunderbolt': falls bronze-brown, blotched yellow, standards purple-brown.					

Irishman's cutting
When small plants grow in gravel, it is often especially easy to tease up a small portion of root attached to a shoot in this simple form of propagation.

Irishman's cutting a portion of a plant with pre-formed roots, which has been detached from the mother-plant to establish as an individual. Commonly, the term is used to refer to any very small piece of a plant taken as a division, or to a naturally rooted layer.

iron an essential trace element in plants necessary for the formation of chlorophyll. Plants are especially susceptible to iron deficiency in alkaline soil, but also through waterlogging, low temperature, excessive phosphate in soil or, occasionally, heavy metal contamination. Iron deficiency is expressed as interveinal or overall yellowing of young leaves, which progresses down the shoots; the condition is referred to as chlorosis. The application of iron sequestrol (chelate) and mulching with organic matter will successfully alleviate iron deficiency.

irregular zygomorphic; asymmetrical.

irrigation the application of water, sometimes containing nutrients in solution, to support plant growth. The frequency of need and most effective timing and rate of application vary with species, growing media and situation, as well as with levels of rainfall and atmospheric conditions, which are in turn affected by climate and season. Careful consideration must be given to these factors to ensure that irrigation is

419

Targeted watering
Creating a saucer-shaped depression in the soil when young plants are planted out helps water pool around the root area, enabling water resources to be used efficiently.

I

of maximum benefit, to conserve water as a valuable natural reserve, and to avoid harmful waterlogging.

Incorporating organic matter into the soil improves water availability, and the application of mulch to the surface of moist soil reduces water loss through evaporation. Damping down or misting around growing plants cools leaves and reduces transpiration, and similar benefits can be obtained by careful ventilation and shading in greenhouses, and by providing wind-shelter for outdoor plants. Many ornamental plants desirable in gardens are adapted to conditions of low water availability; most established trees and shrubs have a great capacity to extract water from deep down in the soil; and many fruit and vegetable crops have different water requirements at particular stages of growth. All of these considerations are important in assessing the real need for irrigation, which can be a laborious, expensive, and potentially wasteful undertaking.

Methods of irrigation

WATERING CANS are convenient for irrigating small areas outdoors and for plants grown under protection; a capacity of 2 gallons (9 liters) is suitable. Galvanized cans are durable but heavier than plastic ones and, whatever the type, a long spout is advisable to allow careful placement between plants. A fine oval-shaped rose is necessary for watering seedlings, while the round, coarser type of rose is a good choice for irrigating established plants because of the larger droplet size and faster delivery.

HOSES provide a convenient means of continuously delivering water over a distance from the faucet source, but distribution is imprecise without special fittings. Most hoses are available in PVC, commonly 1/2-in- (13-mm-) bore, and may be reinforced to reduce kinking and interruption of the flow. Control of water output, distribution pattern, and droplet size can be effected with a control nozzle or hand-gun, or by squeezing the hose by hand at or near its outlet. Flat hoses are available, reducing storage space required, and all types are best stowed on a reel, some designs of which allow the water to flow evenly when the hose is only partly unwound.

SPRINKLERS automatically deliver a spray of coarse droplets over a broadly defined area. In large greenhouses, these may be mounted overhead, but in gardens they are most commonly used as single static, rotating or oscillating units, placed on the ground and fed through a hose. Traveling sprinklers are available for large lawns, and in some circumstances it may be appropriate to have a permanent grid of distribution pipes below ground level into which sprinklers can be connected. Irrigation by sprinkler can be wasteful because much water may be lost to evaporation or blown off target, and puddling may occur where plant foliage obstructs distribution. Most sprinklers work efficiently only above 30 psi, and a low trajectory is preferable. On average a sprinkler may discharge 200 gallons (900 liters) of water per hour.

TRICKLE SYSTEMS are especially useful for plants suited to individual watering, such as potted plants and tomatoes; they can also be used in outdoor borders and on a capillary bench, which is an effective means of irrigating pot plants. Trickle irrigation will work at lower flow pressure than sprinklers, but output needs to be closely monitored and outlets kept unblocked and clean. Water distribution may be via nozzles fitted directly into the line, or through spurs of flexible tubing of 1/16–1/4 in (2–5 mm) diameter, which can be fitted singly or in multiples at each regularly spaced outlet.

SEEP-HOSES, or soak-hoses, are an excellent means of low-level watering because they dispense water exactly where it is required. Such lines may consist of small-bore plastic delivery pipes, continuously stitched along their length, or of compressed rubber with micropores 5–8 microns in diameter; with both systems water oozes along the length of run. Some types of seep-hoses are recommended for burying below the surface, thereby further reducing evaporation loss. Flat polythene tube, which swells under water pressure, is another form similar to seep-hose, with water emitted through small regularly spaced perforations. As the water pressure is increased, the water is discharged in thin sprays. Seep-hose systems of garden irrigation are both effective and economic in water use.

AUTOMATIC DEVICES are available to control water flow for indoor and outdoor irrigation systems and these make an excellent contribution to economies.

Water sources and supply

Irrigation water must be free of sand or biological matter, including algae, which can block small outlets. Filtration and the covering of stagnant storage vessels are important. Care must be taken to keep water sources from becoming infected with plant disease organisms, which can happen when plant debris or soil drainage water contaminates a low-level tank. High concentration of dissolved mineral salts can affect plant growth and block irrigation nozzles; over 300 ppm calcium can cause lime-crusting. Gardeners do not have recourse to acidifying treatments, such as nitric acid used

Seep-hose
Porous or finely perforated hose delivers a gentle, continuous water supply, ideal for young plants whose fine roots may be disturbed by splashing water.

by commercial growers, and domestic water softeners are unsuitable in view of phytotoxic residues. The use of ionized water is rarely a practical proposition, and the best means of avoiding high-lime content is to collect rainwater.

Rain barrels with lids and low-level faucets are useful for collecting roof water, although small debris will usually be washed down; the volume of storage is also limited and quickly used up during periods of little rainfall.

Supply from wells, boreholes, rivers, and streams has relevance to a limited number of sites, and for most gardeners, city or well water is the norm. City water is filtered at the supply source and biological and chemical content is controlled to within limits suitable for plant growth. Its availability may be subject to metering, or surcharge for certain garden uses, and also to restrictions during times of drought. Irrigation systems adapted for special uses, such as automatic injection of liquid fertilizer, must have devices to ensure that back-siphonage into the main supply is not possible; $^3/_4$-in (20-mm) faucets usually discharge about 200 gallons (900 liters) per hour.

Domestic waste water from washing, sometimes called gray water, is often suggested for irrigation use during drought. The problem is the variability of content, and while it is unlikely that moderate use of domestic waste water will have a damaging effect on soil structure, soil organisms or plant growth, heavy applications loaded with soap detergent and other household cleaners, or water softening additives, can give rise to an increase in soil pH, phosphate content and the total salinity of soil. The safest course is to avoid repeated irrigation of the same site with waste water and to reserve its use for established plants.

Need, timing, and quantity

Soil moisture loss from a growing medium arises through evaporation from the surface and transpiration from the aerial parts of plants, collectively referred to as evapotranspiration. Plant requirements are met from soil reserves, which are replenished by rainfall or irrigation. By the end of March in most years outdoor soil will be fully charged with water from snow or winter rain. At this time the soil is at field capacity, the level at which any added water passes to drainage. As the season progresses, evaporation and transpiration result in water loss from the soil and where the loss is greater than rainfall or irrigation, a soil moisture deficit (SMD) arises.

Calculation of irrigation requirements for outdoor crops balances input of water from rainfall with losses through evapotranspiration. Rainfall can be measured with a rain gauge and weekly evapotranspiration rates can be predicted from tables of local averages, or more accurately through adjusted data from weather centers.

Average monthly values for SMD in southern and central England are April 2 in (50 mm); May 3 in (75 mm); June 4 in (100 mm); July 4 in (100 mm); August 3 in (75 mm) and September 2 in (50 mm). In the north of England, the SMD is about one third less. A reasonable target is to apply 1 in (25 mm) of water each time the SMD reaches 1 in (25 mm), but woody plants in general may tolerate a SMD of 2–3 in (50–75 mm). Note: 25 mm (1 in) of rainfall is equivalent to an application rate of 1 gallon of water per square foot (20 liters per square meter).

Whether or not irrigation is practiced with reference to collected or provided data, it is important to ensure that high SMD levels do not build up. Water shortage in soils should be anticipated in order to maintain steady growth.

In terms of irrigation needs, garden plants that should be given priority are seedlings and transplanted crops and specimen plants, together with leafy vegetables and those with swelling edible parts such as peas, beans, corn, zucchini, and tomatoes. Raspberries and strawberries benefit from irrigation as the fruits color and begin to swell respectively. A good yield of early potato tubers depends on moisture availability, whereas established leeks, carrots, parsnips, and onions are less responsive.

Irrigation techniques should be selected with the aim of ensuring that plants are thoroughly watered. Light sprinkling is wasteful and ineffective. Crops growing under greenhouse protection need special care to meet water requirements, particularly those in containers. Irrigation need can be assessed by handling the surface of the soil, or by making a judgment based on the weight of those containers that are small enough to be easily lifted. Tapping clay pots to test for a hollow "ring" is effective. Moisture deficit indicators are available; saucers to provide reservoirs of water, and capillary benching are useful aids to greenhouse irrigation.

Isatis (Greek name for woad). Cruciferae. Europe, Mediterranean to C Asia. WOAD. Around 30 species, annual to perennial herbs with loose racemes of 4-petalled flowers in summer. The following species is hardy to 5°F (–15°C). Grow in a sunny position, in well-drained fertile soil. Sow seed *in situ* in fall or spring. *I. tinctoria* WOAD, DYER'S WOAD; Europe; biennial to 3$^1/_4$ ft (1 m); flowers yellow.

island bed a large bed usually devoted to herbaceous perennials, heathers or dwarf conifers, in which the display can be seen from all sides. It may be irregular in outline and often deep and curving, and may be set into a lawn or surrounded by pavement.

Isoplexis (from Greek *isos*, equal, and *plexis*, braid, as the upper corolla segment and the lip are of equal length). Scrophulariaceae. Canary Islands, Madeira. 3 species, evergreen subshrubs with toothed leaves and erect, terminal racemes of tubular, 5-lobed and 2-lipped flowers in summer. Grow in full sun in a medium-fertility loam-based mix, to which sand and leaf mold have been added. Maintain a minimum temperature of 45°F (7°C) and ventilate freely whenever possible; water plentifully in summer, moderately in winter. Propagate from seed in a sandy seed mixture in spring or by greenwood cuttings in late summer. *I. canariensis* (syn. *Digitalis canariensis*) Canary Islands; to 3$^1/_4$ ft (1 m); raceme to 12 in (30 cm), flowers to 1$^1/_4$ in (3 cm), orange-yellow to brick red or orange-brown.

Isopyrum (from Greek *isos*, equal, and *pyros*, grain: the fruit resembles grains of wheat). Ranunculaceae. Northern Hemisphere. FALSE RUE ANEMONE. 30 species, tufted perennial herbs with ferny, ternately lobed leaves and small, cup-shaped flowers, each composed of five petal-like sepals, nodding on fragile stalks in spring. Suitable for woodland, peat beds and the cool, shaded rock garden. Cultivate as for *Anemonella*. *I. thalictroides* Europe; to 10 in (25 cm); flowers white.

Italian garden, Italianate the style of the great medieval and Renaissance formal gardens of Italy, where stonework, statuary, and waterworks played the most important role. Plants were treated formally as hedges, topiary, knots, and parterres and trimmed in pots. It was actively copied in Britain between 1830 and 1860.

Itea (from Greek *itea*, willow, after the pendulous catkins). Grossulariaceae (Iteaceae). NE Asia, eastern N America. 10 species, evergreen or deciduous shrubs and trees with toothed leaves and small, green to white flowers in racemes or panicles in summer. *I. ilicifolia* is a fine small shrub suitable for well-drained, fertile soil in warm and sunny positions. Below 0°F (–18°C), it will succumb to hard frosts, wet soil, and cold winds, and tends therefore to be planted on south-facing walls and, at first, protected with dry bracken or evergreen clippings. *I. virginica* is altogether hardier. It favors semishade or full sun and moist, slightly acidic positions where it can spread freely—lake or pond margins and islands, for example. It is excellent as tall groundcover. *Itea* can be propagated either by soft stem-tip cuttings in late spring, inserted in mist or under polythene, or by heeled semihard cuttings in a sandy mix in the cold frame during late winter. Air-layering will also succeed.

    I. ilicifolia W China; erect, evergreen shrub to 16 ft (5 m); shoots smooth, slender; leaves 2–4¾ in (5–12 cm), elliptic, spiny-toothed, glossy olive to dark green, tough; raceme slender, pendulous with cream to gold or pale lime flowers; *I. virginica* SWEETSPIRE, VIRGINIA WILLOW, TASSEL-WHITE; E US; arching deciduous shrub to 10 ft (3 m); leaves 1¼–4 in (3–10 cm), narrowly elliptic to oblong, rich red in fall; racemes erect, to 6 in (15 cm), with cream flowers.

Ixia viridiflora
This cormous perennial bears flowers of a striking color. Although not frost-hardy, it makes an unusual container plant for the patio.

Ixia (from Greek *ixia*, the name of a plant noted for the variability of its flower color). Iridaceae. South Africa (Cape Province). 45–50 species, perennial herbs with small corms, grassy foliage, and, in summer, slender spikes of tubular flowers with six, spreading, ovate to lanceolate segments. Where temperatures seldom fall below freezing, *Ixia* can be planted in a sunny, south-facing border or under a south wall, about 4–6 in (10–15 cm) deep, with a winter covering of bracken litter or leaf mold. Plant in fall to bloom in spring and summer, or in spring for summer blooms. For potted specimens, set 6–8 corms firmly in a 4¾ in (12 cm) pot in a mix of sandy loam and leaf mold. Plunge in a cool frame and water very sparingly during winter until the flower spikes appear, then give full light and good ventilation. Continue to water until foliage begins to die back, then dry off gradually and store dry in cool but frost-free conditions. Offsets usually flower in their second year. Sow seed in fall, and let seedlings remain in the same pans for their first year. Seed-raised plants will usually flower in their third or fourth year.

    I. maculata 7–20 in (18–50 cm); flowers 1–2 in (2.5–5 cm) in diameter, orange, yellow-orange or white with a dark brown, black or purple center; *I. monadelpha* (6–16 in (15–40 cm); flowers 1¼–1½ in (3–4 cm) in diameter, white, pale pink, lilac, mauve, purple, violet, blue, or claret, usually with a brown or red-brown central marking;

I. viridiflora (20–39 in (50–100 cm); flowers 1–2 in (2.5–5 cm) diam., pale aquamarine with purple-black center).

Ixiolirion (from *Ixia* and Greek *lirion*, lily, for its resemblance to *Ixia*). Amaryllidaceae. SW and C Asia. 4 species, bulbous perennial herbs. Produced in a rosette, the leaves are linear to lanceolate, and usually persist in winter. Carried in spring and summer in umbels or loose racemes, the starry flowers consist of six segments, either free or united toward the base in a short tube. Hardy to 5°F (–15°C), they need a warm and sheltered position in rich and perfectly drained soil, where they can be baked in summer and protected from excessive moisture in winter. They are sometimes grown in the cool conservatory or greenhouse. Plant 6 in (15 cm) deep in late summer/early fall. A winter mulch of bracken litter or leaf mold is beneficial. Propagate by removal of offsets after flowering, or by seed in fall. *I. tataricum* (syn. *I. montanum*) SW and C Asia, Kashmir; to 16 in (40 cm); flowers in a loose umbel, ¾–2 in (2–5 cm), pale to mid-blue or violet.

Ixora (from the name of a Malabar deity to whom the flowers were offered). Rubiaceae. Tropics (Old and New World). Some 400 species, evergreen shrubs or trees bearing paniculate or corymbose cymes of small, narrowly tubular flowers in summer, each with four spreading lobes. Grow in warm greenhouse conditions (minimum temperature 59–64°F/15–18°C), with high humidity and bright indirect light, in a fibrous, soilless medium. Water plentifully. Prune as necessary after flowering. Propagate from short-jointed semiripe cuttings of nonflowering shoots, potted singly and plunged in a shaded closed case with bottom heat.

    I. coccinea FLAME OF THE WOODS, JUNGLE GERANIUM, RED IXORA, JUNGLE FLAME; tropical Asia; shrub to 8 ft (2.5 m); flowers red, orange, apricot, pink or yellow; *I. javanica* COMMON RED IXORA, JAVANESE IXORA; Java; shrub or tree to 13 ft (4 m); flowers red or, rarely, pink to orange; *I. thwaitesii* WHITE IXORA; Sri Lanka; shrub or tree to 20 ft (6 m); flowers white to cream.

J

Jaborosa (from the Arabic *jaborose*, referring to the closely related *Mandragora*). S America. Solanaceae. 20 species, low-growing, perennial herbs with clumped, elliptic leaves and low-borne, solitary flowers in summer—these are tubular to campanulate with a starry limb of five, narrow lobes. Plant in a sandy, well-drained soil in full sun or part shade. Although hardy to 0°F (−18°C), when hard frosts are common and prolonged, the following species should be grown in a warm, sunny position at the base of a south-facing wall. Propagate by division in spring. *J. integrifolia* S Brazil, Uruguay, Argentina; leaves to 6 in (16 cm), dark green; flowers green to white, to 2½ in (6 cm) diameter.

Jacaranda (from the vernacular Brazilian name for these plants). Bignoniaceae. Tropical America: Belize, Guatemala, West Indies to Argentina. Some species, deciduous or evergreen trees, usually with bipinnate leaves. Tubular to campanulate and 5-lobed, the flowers are carried in terminal or axillary panicles in spring and summer. *J. mimosifolia* is widely planted in the subtropics and warm temperate regions as a specimen or street tree. Where temperatures drop below 10°F (−12°C), it is grown in the cool greenhouse or conservatory, predominantly as a foliage plant, although it may begin to bloom at about 5 ft (1.5 m) in a large tub. It is also used, when young, as a foliage plant in summer bedding. Grow in a well-drained, high-fertility, loam-based mix in full sun. Water plentifully when in growth, sparingly at other times. Maintain a minimum temperature of 45°F (7°C), with good ventilation. Prune plants grown for their foliage hard back in late winter and repot or topdress at the same time. Propagate by seed, alternatively by heeled semiripe cuttings. *J. mimosifolia* (syn. *J. ovalifolia*); Argentina, Bolivia, widely cultivated elsewhere; tree to 50 ft (15 m) tall with a rounded crown; leaves deep green, ferny; flowers 1–2 in (2.4–5 cm), blue-purple with a white throat; 'Alba' is white-flowered.

Jamesia (for Dr. Edwin James [1797–1861], who discovered the plant on Major Long's expedition to the Rocky Mountains in 1820). Hydrangeaceae. W US. CLIFFBUSH, WAXFLOWER. 1 species, *J. americana*, a deciduous, rounded shrub to 5 ft (1.5 m) tall, with peeling, papery bark. The downy leaves are 1¼–2¾ in (3–7 cm) long, ovate, toothed and prominently veined. To ½ in (1 cm) across, the 5-petaled flowers are white (pink in 'Rosea') and carried in terminal panicles to 2½ in (6 cm) in early summer. Hardy to −30°F (−34°C). Grow in free-draining, moderately fertile soil in full sun. Prune after flowering to remove old, weak, or overcrowded growth. Propagate by ripe seed, semiripe cuttings, or layering in spring.

Jankaea (for Victor Janka von Bulc [1837–1900], Austrian soldier and botanist). Gesneriaceae. C Greece (Mount Olympus). 1 species, *J. heldreichii*, a perennial, evergreen herb. The leaves are ¾–1½ in (2–4 cm) long, bluntly obovate, hairy, and carried in low rosettes. Bell-shaped with four to five rounded lobes, the flowers are lilac and carried in small clusters atop stalks to 2 in (5 cm) tall. This plant resents wet conditions, and especially water on its foliage or around the crown. For this reason, it is often grown in the alpine house, in tufa, or with a collar of stones. It will survive outdoors to 0°F (−18°C), but needs the enhanced drainage of a scree or sink garden, and cloche protection in winter. Plant in a fast-draining, sandy, alkaline medium that is rich in leaf mold. Grow *Jankaea* in a dry, buoyant (well-ventilated) atmosphere, such as an alpine house, vents open to allow circulation. Full sun. Water moderately during spring and summer, hardly at all in winter. Propagate by division.

Japanese beetle (*Popillia japonica*) (Coleoptera: Scarabaeidae) a beetle that is bluntly ovoid in shape and about ½ in (11 mm) long, with the head, thorax, and legs metallic green and the hardened wing cases dull coppery brown. The larvae have creamy-white C-shaped bodies with a swollen last segment and well-developed brown heads, legs, and biting mouthparts. When fully fed, they are about 1 in (25 mm) long. The larval stage lasts about 10 months, but may be longer in colder areas where the complete life cycle can extend to two years.

The Japanese beetle is native to the Far East but is widespread in North America since its introduction in 1916, and now poses a threat to other areas including Europe, Africa, and western Asia. It is mainly a pest of permanent pasture and ornamental grasses, but its larvae also feed widely on plant roots, often causing serious damage to nursery stock. The adults fly in sunny weather, attacking mostly apple, cherry, plum, elm, horse chestnut, linden, Lombardy poplar, willow, raspberry, strawberry, dahlia, hollyhock, rose, Virginia creeper, and zinnia. Japanese beetles eat holes in leaves and flowers, and in severe attacks may cause complete defoliation. Deep holes are made in ripe fruits. In North America, biological control organisms have been used successfully, including the eelworm *Neoplectana hoptha*, two hymenopterous parasites, and the bacterium *Bacillus popilliae* which causes "milky spore disease" of the grubs.

The Japanese beetle is very similar in appearance to the garden chafer (*Phyllopertha horticola*), which is especially common in Europe, but the former may be readily distinguished by its green legs.

Japanese gardening an ancient art originating around 300 AD with elaborate landscape creations. It evolved to reflect aspects of Japanese traditions, symbolism, and faith. Gardens became places for contemplation, sometimes with plantings reduced to a minimum and shaped trees, moss, rocks, water, or raked sand predominating.

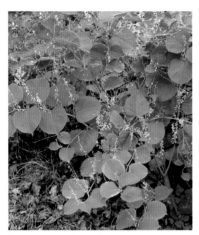

Japanese knotweed
This most pernicious of weeds was originally introduced as an ornamental garden plant. Once established, its vigorous root system makes it extremely difficult to eradicate.

Japanese knotweed (*Fallopia japonica*) an invasive perennial with stout annual stems to 6½ ft (2 m). Clump-forming, but spreading by means of strong, deep-penetrating rhizomes. Thrives in all soil conditions, including wasteland. Difficult to control. Where conditions allow, a program of continual careful forking out, over several seasons, is effective if all rhizomes are removed and regrowth is quickly attacked. This approach is more practicable in recently invaded areas. Glyphosate and glyphosate trimesium will destroy Japanese knotweed. The herbicide is nonselective and must not come into contact with valued plants. Although the weed is most susceptible at flowering time, access is easiest when the shoots are about 3¼ in (8 cm) high in spring. Regrowth should be treated on further occasions in the same year as well as in the following spring.

jardin anglais "English garden"; a European name for the landscape garden, the fashion for which resulted in the destruction of formal gardens around Florence and elsewhere in Europe during the late 18th and 19th centuries.

jardinière an ornamental plant stand or container, normally used indoors.

Jasione (name given by Theophrastus to *Convolvulus*). Campanulaceae. Tem-perate Europe, Mediterranean. SHEEP'S BIT. Some 20 species, annual, biennial, or perennial herbs, usually with clumped, oblong to lanceolate leaves, and 5-parted flowers in terminal heads or panicles, surrounded by one or more rows of spiky involucral bracts. The following species is hardy and suitable for the rock garden. Grow in well-drained sandy soils in sun. Propagate by division or seed. *J. laevis* (syn. *J. perennis*); SHEPHERD'S SCABIOUS, SHEEP'S BIT; tufted perennial, to 6 in (15 cm) tall; inflorescence bracts ovate to deltoid, toothed; flowers blue.

Jasminum (Latinized form of Persian *yasmin*). Oleaceae. Old World tropics, subtropics and temperate regions. JASMINE, JESSAMINE. About 200 evergreen or deciduous shrubs and small trees, many sprawling, scandent, or twining. The leaves are pinnate, trifoliolate or with only one leaflet, thus "simple." Often fragrant, the flowers are solitary or clustered in axils, or in cymes or cymose panicles—they consist of a tubular corolla with 4 or more spreading lobes. Grown for their often heavily fragrant flowers, the genus *Jasminum* comprises species for a number of garden situations, from *J. parkeri*, with tiny yellow flowers in early summer, which forms low, dense, and evergreen hummocks suitable in scale for the rock garden, to the free-standing semi-evergreen *J. humile*, a fine wall shrub, bearing large and fragrant flowers from early spring to late fall. The twining climbers, such as *J. officinale*, and the tropical species, *J. rex*, will scramble over trellises, shrubs, trees, or other supports.

The rambling or scandent shrubby species, which require tying with shoots carefully trained and spaced, can be used as wall shrubs, or trained over pergolas, arches, arbors, and fences. *J. nudiflorum* is also useful as a soil stabilizer on steep banks; it will cascade over a retaining wall and is tolerant of urban pollution. A sunny site is best but *J. officinale* and *J. nudiflorum* will tolerate the shade of a north-facing wall. *J. mesnyi*, with spectacular semi-double flowers, and *J. polyanthum*, vigorous and intensely fragrant, for south- or southwest-facing walls in areas with little or no frost, make excellent conservatory plants in colder zones. *J. polyanthum* may also be grown as a houseplant trained on wire hoops or canes.

Cultivate frost-tender species in a cool greenhouse or conservatory border (minimum temperature 41°F/5°C) or in a medium-fertility loam-based mix, with wires or other support. (*J. polyanthum* requires a temperature drop to induce flowering.) Water plentifully during summer, sparingly in winter, and ventilate freely when possible. *J. rex* requires a minimum temperature of 64°F (18°C), and succeeds best with part-day shade. Tie in leaders of scandent species in a fan formation after planting. Cut back flowered growth of *J. nudiflorum* immediately after flowering; remove any weak growth and tie in as necessary. Thin, but do not shorten, shoots of *J. officinale* after flowering. Other species require no regular pruning, other than thinning overgrown plants. Propagate by semiripe cuttings in late summer, and overwinter at a temperature of 45–50°F (7–10°C). Take cuttings of *J. mesnyi* and *J. polyanthum* with a heel, and root with bottom heat of 59°F (15°C). Also propagated by layers and ripe seed.

Jasminum officinale

Jatropha (from Greek *iatros*, physician, and *trophe*, food, alluding to the medicinal qualities). Euphorbiaceae. Tropics and warm temperate regions, mainly S America. TARTOGO, GOUT PLANT, BARBADOS NUT, PHYSIC NUT, CORAL PLANT, PEREGRINA, JICAMILLA. 170 species, perennial herbs and shrubs, with poisonous sap. The leaves are simple or palmately lobed or

JASMINUM

Name	Distribution	Habit	Leaves	Flowers
J. azoricum *J. fluminense*	Azores	evergreen climbing shrub	leaflets 3, ovate, acute, undulate, cordate at base, terminal leaflet larger	fragrant, long-stalked, borne in terminal panicles, corolla white, tube to ¼ in (0.5 cm), lobes to 6, ½ in (1 cm) long
	Comments: Late summer.			
J. beesianum	China	deciduous or semi-evergreen, sprawling shrub	simple, ovate-lanceolate, ¾–2 in (2–5 cm), olive green, slightly downy	1–3 per axil, small, fragrant, pale pink to deep rose
Comments: Early summer. Produces abundant shining black berries which persist in winter. A form of *J. beesianum* with longer leaves and larger, pale pink flowers is often seen; this may be a backcross with *J.* × *stephanense*. True *J. beesianum* has smaller, darker flowers.				
J. floridum	China	erect to arching, semi-evergreen shrub	leaflets 3–5, ½–1½ in (1–3.5 cm), oval to ovate, acuminate, glabrous, shining green above, pale beneath	yellow, profuse, in cymes
Comments: Late summer.				
J. fruticans	Mediterranean, Asia Minor.	erect, evergreen or semi-evergreen shrub to 4 ft (1.25 m)	leaflets ½–¾ in (1–2 cm), 3, tough, narrow-oblong, obtuse, dark green, glabrous, minutely ciliate	to 5 per terminal cyme; corolla yellow, tube to ½ in (1.25 cm), lobes 5, obtuse, to half length tube
Comments: Summer.				
J. grandiflorum CATALONIAN JASMINE; ROYAL JASMINE; SPANISH JASMINE	S Arabia, NE Africa, widely grown in warm and temperate regions elsewhere	semievergreen or evergreen climbing shrub	leaflets 5–7, to ¾ in (2 cm) (terminal leaflet longer), ovate	in terminal, branching cymes, intensely fragrant; corolla white, exterior sometimes tinted red, tube to ¾ in (2 cm), lobes 5–6, oblong
		Comments: Source of jasmine oil.		
J. humile ITALIAN JASMINE	Middle East, Burma, China	evergreen or semi-evergreen shrub to 20 ft (6 m), erect, occasionally treelike	leaflets to 7, to 1½ in (4 cm), ovate-lanceolate	sometimes scented, in umbel-like clusters; corolla yellow, tube to ¾ in (2 cm), lobes to ½ in (1 cm), rounded, spreading
Comments: Summer. Includes 'Revolutum' (syn. *J. revolutum*, *J. reevesii*, *J. triumphans*): semievergreen, robust shrub, leaflets 3–7, terminal leaflet to 2½ in (6 cm), laterals to 1½ in (4 cm), flowers 1 in (2.5 cm) wide, yellow, fragrant, 6–12 together, stamens slightly protruding; f. **farreri**		(syn. *J. farreri*, *J. giraldii*): evergreen, spreading shrub to 5 ft (1.5 m), leaflets 3, oval-lanceolate, distinctly tapering, terminal leaflet to 4 in (10 cm), dull green, coarse above, hairy beneath, inflorescence hairy, flowers yellow, to 12 per cyme.	
J. laurifolium	Assam, Bangladesh	evergreen slender climber	narrowly elliptic-lanceolate	starry, white
Comments: Summer. Includes f. **nitidum** (syn. *J. nitidum*, *J. gracile* var. *magnificum*): ANGEL HAIR JASMINE; ANGEL WING JASMINE; WINDMILL JASMINE; STAR JASMINE; CONFEDERATE JASMINE, leaves to 3 in (8 cm),		simple, elliptic-lanceolate to ovate-lanceolate, glossy bright green above, flowers fragrant, corolla white, often tinted red in bud and on exterior, tube to ¾ in (2 cm), slender, lobes to ⅜ in (1.5 cm), 9–11, linear-lanceolate.	
J. mesnyi *J. primulinum* PRIMROSE JASMINE	W China	evergreen rambling to cascading shrub to 10 ft (3 m)	leaflets 3, 1–2¾ in (2.5–7 cm), lanceolate, dark glossy green	1¼–2 in (3–5 cm) wide, solitary in axils, corolla usually semidouble, bright yellow, lobes to ½ in (1 cm) across, obtuse
Comments: Summer.				

J

J. grandiflorum

J. humile

J. mesnyi

JASMINUM

Name	Distribution	Habit	Leaves	Flowers
J. multiflorum *J. pubescens* STAR JASMINE	India	evergreen pubescent climber	to 2 in (5 cm), simple, ovate, base rounded to cordate	large, fragrant, in sparse to crowded clusters; corolla white, lobes oblong-lanceolate, 5–8, to half length of tube
Comments: Summer.				
J. nudiflorum WINTER JASMINE	N China	deciduous, rambling to cascading shrub, to 10 x 10 ft (3 x 3 m), with long, slender branches	leaflets 3, ½–1¼ in (1–3 cm), oval-oblong, dark green, glabrous, ciliate	borne before leaves, singly in axils of previous year's growth; corolla to 1¼ in (3 cm) wide, yellow, 6-lobed
Comments: Winter–early spring.				
J. officinale COMMON JASMINE; TRUE JASMINE; JESSAMINE	Asia Minor, Himalaya, China.	deciduous climbing shrub to 33 ft (10 m), shoots twining, slender	leaflets 5–9, ½–2½ in (1–6 cm), elliptic, acuminate	highly fragrant, in branched cymes; corolla white, tube to ¾ in (2 cm), lobes 4–5, shorter than tube, +/− triangular-ovate
Comments: Summer–early fall. f. *affine*: flowers larger, more profuse, exterior pink; corolla lobes broader; 'Aureum': leaves blotched golden yellow; 'Inverleith': leaves ¾–2 in (2–5 cm); leaflets 3–7, lanceolate,			terminal leaflet often lobed, flowers to ⅝ in (1.5 cm) long, cylindrical-funnelform, exterior strongly tinted pink-red, lobes 5, to ½ in (1 cm), broadly ovate, apiculate, white above, tinted red beneath.	
J. parkeri	NW India	evergreen twiggy dwarf shrub, to 12 in (30 cm), forming a dense mat or mound	leaflets 3–5, ⅛–¼ in (0.3–0.6 cm), ovate-acuminate	usually borne singly, yellow, ⅝ in (1.5 cm) wide
Comments: Summer.				
J. polyanthum *J. blinii*	China	deciduous or evergreen climbing and twining shrub to 26 ft (8 m)	leaflets 5–7, lanceolate, narrow-acuminate at apex, terminal leaflet to 3 in (8 cm), coriaceous, 3-nerved	in axillary panicles, highly fragrant; corolla to ¾ in (2 cm), white within, exterior flushed pink, lobes obovate
Comments: Summer.				
J. rex	Thailand	glabrous climber	simple, to 6 in (16 cm), dark glossy green, broadly ovate, acuminate	on slender, drooping stalks, 2–3 per axillary cyme, unscented; corolla white, salverform, tube to 1 in (2.5 cm), lobes 8(–9), ovate-oblong
Comments: Summer.				
J. sambac ARABIAN JASMINE	widespread through long cultivation; may originate in India	evergreen twiner, shoots pubescent, angular	simple, semirigid, shiny, glabrous or hairy, broad-ovate to 3 in (8 cm), acute, conspicuously veined	in clusters, highly fragrant; corolla waxy white, pink with age, tube ½ in (1.2 cm), lobes to ⅝ in (1.5 cm), 6–9, oblong
Comments: Flowers continuously. 'Grand Duke of Tuscany' : flowers double, lobes rounded, resembling a small *Gardenia*.				
J. x stephanense (*J. beesianum* x *J. officinale*)	garden origin, also said to occur wild in W China	fast-growing climber, twining, to 16 ft (5 m), stems often yellow-green or cream at first	simple or 3–5-lobed, leaflets pale olive green, pubescent beneath	pale pink, small, in sparse cymes
Comments: Summer.				

J. nudiflorum

J. officinale **'Argenteovariegatum'**

J. sambac

cut. Small flowers are produced in dense, flat-topped, thick-stalked and many-branched cymes. Grow in a minimum temperature of 50°F (10°C), with full sun and a dry atmosphere. Plant in a well-drained, loam-based mix with additional leaf mold and sharp sand. Water moderately when in full growth. Keep virtually dry during the winter rest period, when the plants may become leafless. Propagate by seed or by semiripe cuttings. All parts of this plant are poisonous.

J. multifida CORAL PLANT, PHYSIC NUT; tropical America; shrub or tree to 23 ft (7 m); leaves to 12 in (30 cm) diameter, dark green, palmately and deeply 7–11-lobed, lobes finely dissected and toothed, petioles sometimes finely spotted purple-brown, as are stems of young plants: flowers scarlet; *J. podagrica* GOUT PLANT, TARTOGO; Guatemala, Panama; stem to 8 ft (2.5 m), usually thickly gouty with branches only at its summit and a large central swelling; leaves to 12 in (30 cm) diameter, ovate to orbicular, with 3–5, broad and shallow lobes; flowers coral red.

Jeffersonia (for Thomas Jefferson [1743–1826], third president of the United States, author, architect and horticulturist). Berberidaceae. N America, E Asia. TWIN LEAF. 2 species, perennial herbs with radical, 2-lobed, rounded and toothed leaves peltately attached to long stalks. Carried on slender scapes in spring, the solitary flowers are cup-shaped with five to eight, oblong petals. Hardy. Grow in light shade or dappled sun, in an acidic to neutral humus-rich soil. Keep the root run cool and moist. Sow fresh ripe seed in the cold frame or cool greenhouse, or divide well-established plants in early spring.

J. diphylla RHEUMATISM ROOT; N America; leaves to 6 in (15 cm) across, glaucous beneath; scapes exceeding petioles; flowers white); *J. dubia* (NE Asia; leaves to 4 in (10 cm) across, glaucous, tinged mauve-gray; scapes shorter than petioles; flowers lavender to pale blue.

John Innes base a compound fertilizer containing 2 parts hoof and horn (73% nitrogen), 2 parts superphosphate (18–21% phosphate), and 1 part potas-

sium sulfate (48% potash) by weight. It is formulated for use in John Innes potting mixes.

John Innes composts see *potting media*.

jostaberry (*Ribes* × *culverwellii*) a bush fruit hybrid between black currant and gooseberry, bearing small clusters of dull berries that resemble black currants. The plant is vigorous, upright, spineless, and self-fertile. Its flowers are frost-susceptible and carried on old and young wood. It may be cultivated and propagated as a black currant and grown either as a stooled bush or as a half-standard, in which case it will require staking. Jostaberry is resistant to American gooseberry mildew, black-currant leaf spot, and gall mite. Also known as yostaberry.

Jovellana (for Dr. C.M. de Jovellanos [1744–1811], student of the Peruvian flora). Scrophulariaceae. Chile, New Zealand. Some 6 species, tender herbs, subshrubs and shrubs, resembling *Calceolaria* in the strongly saccate corolla, but having two almost equal corolla lobes (lips) with the margins flat or involute. The following species is usually grown in the cool greenhouse or conservatory, but will tolerate mild frosts if planted in a warm, sheltered position and mulched in winter. Grow in full sun in a free-draining loam-based medium. Avoid excessive moisture in winter. Propagate by seed or by semiripe cuttings. *J. violacea* Chile; puberulent shrub to 6½ ft (2 m); flowers to ⅝ in (1.5 cm) diameter, pale violet spotted purple, throat blotched yellow.

Jovibarba (from Latin *Ioves*, of Jupiter, and *barba*, beard). Crassulaceae. Europe. 5 species, perennial herbs with monocarpic leaf rosettes. They are close to and sometimes included in *Sempervivum* but distinguished from that genus by their secondary leaf rosettes and campanulate flowers. Cultivate as for *Sempervivum*.

J. hirta (syn. *Sempervivum hirtum*); C and SE Europe; rosettes 2–2¾ in (5–7 cm) across; leaves lanceolate to obovate, ciliate, green tipped brown to red-brown or flushed deep red; flowers pale

Jovibarba hirta
Similar to sempervivums in both appearance and requirements, jovibarbas make attractive plants for a rock garden or trough.

yellow-brown; *J. sobolifera* (syn. *Sempervivum soboliferum*); C and SE Europe; rosettes ¾–1½ in (2–4 cm) across; leaves obovate to oblong, bright green tipped red with age, ciliate; flowers yellow.

Juanulloa (for Jorge Juan [1713–73] and Antonio Ulloa [1716–95], Spanish travelers in S America). Solanaceae. C and S America. Some 10 species, epiphytic or climbing and stem-rooting shrubs. Produced in either clusters or racemes, the flowers consist of a large, campanulate calyx, often fleshy and ridged, with oblong to lanceolate lobes, and a tubular, 5-lobed corolla. Grow in a freely draining, medium-fertility loam-based mix in an intermediate greenhouse (minimum temperature 55°F/13°C). Keep moist, humid, and well-fed in spring and summer with some protection from full sunlight; position in full sun in winter and keep fairly dry. Propagate by seed or cuttings. *J. mexicana* (syn. *J. aurantiaca*); Peru, Colombia, C America; stems to 6½ ft (2 m), arching; calyx to ⅝ in (1.5 cm) diameter, waxy, pale orange, corolla to 1½ in (4 cm), waxy, brilliant orange.

Jubaea (for King Juba of the ancient African kingdom of Numidia). CHILEAN WINE PALM, HONEY PALM, SYRUP PALM, COQUITO PALM, LITTLE COKERNUT. Palmae. Chile. 1 species, *J. chilensis*, a palm to 80 ft (25 m) tall, stem to 4¼ ft (1.3 m) diameter at base, occasionally swollen in middle, becoming bare, with oblique scars and vertical cracks. The

J

leaves are 3¼–16 ft (1–5 m) long and pinnate, with linear, rigid, gray-green segments to 20 in (50 cm) long. A large but slow-growing and elegant feather palm, *Jubaea* is notable for its tolerance of relatively cool conditions. It is suitable for outdoor cultivation as a specimen or in avenue plantings in dry, Mediterranean-type climates and may tolerate several degrees of short-lived frost. In colder climates, it may be grown in the cool to intermediate greenhouse or conservatory and is particularly handsome as a juvenile specimen. Plant in a loamy mix high in grit and sand; keep moist in warm weather, rather dry in winter. Admit full sun and ventilate freely. Propagate *Jubaea* by fresh seed, which may take up to six months to germinate.

Juglans (from Latin *Jovis glans*, "Jove's acorn"). Juglandaceae. N and S America, SE Europe, Asia. WALNUT (q.v.). About 15 species, deciduous trees with furrowed bark and pinnate leaves. Inconspicuous male flowers are borne in axillary catkins; the female flowers in terminal spikes. The females give rise to 2–4-celled drupes with thick, furrowed pericarps and 2–4-lobed seed.

The young growth of many species is prone to damage by late spring frosts, although in the genus as a whole, spring flushing is relatively late. Substances produced by the roots and fallen leaves of many species, notably *J. regia* and *J. nigra*, appear to have toxic effects (a form of allelopathy) on a variety of plants.

All species produce edible nuts but quality is highest in cultivars of *J. regia*. Bearing commences between 5 and 15 years of age, and may be irregular due to a number of factors. It seems likely that flower initiation depends on suitable conditions the previous summer, and flowers and young growth are destroyed by even short periods (hours) with temperatures of between 28°F/–2°C and 27°F/–3°C. Although walnuts are self-fertile, in some individuals male and female flowers mature at different times and pollination may not

occur in solitary trees. When ripening is poor in cool damp climates, walnuts can nevertheless yield a good harvest of nuts for pickling, provided the nuts are gathered before the development of the hard shell. However, walnuts are cultivated as far north as Warsaw, and in recent years Polish cultivars (e.g., the *J. regia* Carpathian Group) have yielded promising results for cold temperate zones. Increased interest is being shown in Australia, where 'Franquette', a comparatively old French cultivar (on *J. nigra* rootstock), which is reliable, late-flowering, and of excellent quality, is widely planted.

Plant in deep, well-drained but moderately moist, fertile, and slightly alkaline soils. Prune only when absolutely necessary, during late summer/early fall when the tree is in full leaf, or else when it is completely dormant, otherwise wounds bleed profusely. For fruit production, *J. regia* may be pruned into a vase or cup-shaped framework when young, and, in the smaller garden, trees may be kept relatively dwarfed by judicious light pruning.

Propagate *Juglans* from seed sown ripe, or stratified in fall and then sown in spring, in a sandy, humus-rich propagating medium. The seeds' dormancy is broken at temperatures of 41–43°F (5–6°C). Protect from rodents and, since walnuts develop deep taproots that make transplanting difficult, move seedlings as soon as possible to nursery beds and then on to final positions. Cultivars will not come true from seed; propagate by splice or veneer grafting onto seedling stock

of *J. regia* under glass in winter, or by budding onto nursery-grown seedling stock in summer. For heavier soils, *J. nigra* is the preferred rootstock.

Bacterial leaf blight causes small angular black spots on the leaves and can also attack fruit. Trees may be attacked by two species of walnut aphids. Blisterlike growths on the leaves are caused by the walnut blister mite, which is widespread in Europe and Asia and has been introduced into Australia. North American pests include the walnut caterpillar, walnut husk fly, a fruit fly with larvae that tunnel into the green husks, turning them black and slimy; and two species of weevils, the black walnut curculio and the butternut curculio, which have larvae that burrow into the nuts.

J. ailanthifolia HEARTNUT, JAPANESE WALNUT; Japan; tree to 50 ft (15 m); leaves to 20 in (50 cm), leaflets 11–17, to 6 × 2 in (15 × 5 cm), oblong to elliptic, acuminate, serrate, gray-tomentose to glabrous above, glandular-hairy beneath; fruit globose to ovoid, sticky-hairy; includes var. *cordiformis*, syn. *J. cordiformis*, with narrower leaflets; *J. cathayensis* CHINESE WALNUT, CHINESE BUTTERNUT; shrub or tree to 75 ft (23 m); leaves to 32 in (80 cm), viscid; leaflets 11–19, to 6 × 3 in (15 × 8 cm), oblong to lanceolate, finely dentate, hairy; fruit ovoid to 1¾ in (4.5 cm); *J. cinerea* BUTTERNUT, WHITE WALNUT; NE US; to 100 ft (30 m); young branches glandular-glutinose; leaves 10–20 in (25–50 cm), leaflets 11–19, 2½–4¾ in (6–12 cm), oblong to lanceolate, acuminate, serrate, hairy, glandular beneath; fruit to 4 in (10 cm), glandular-glutinose; *J. microcarpa* (syn. *J. rupestris*); SW US, Mexico; shrub or small tree to 23 ft (7 m); young shoots gray to brown; leaves with 15–23 leaflets, finely serrate; *J. nigra* BLACK WALNUT; E US, naturalized C Europe; to 150 ft (45 m); leaflets 15–23, to 4½ in (11 cm), ovate to oblong, pubescent beneath; fruit globose, about 1½ in (4 cm) diameter, hairy; *J. regia* ENGLISH WALNUT, PERSIAN WALNUT, MADEIRA WALNUT; SE Europe to Himalaya and China, C Russia, naturalized US; to 100 ft (30 m); leaflets 5–9, rarely more, 2½–4¾ in (6–12 cm), elliptic to obo-

glossy leaves
fleshy fruit casing

Juglans regia

vate, entire to serrate, with tufted hairs in vein axils beneath; fruit subglobose, smooth, green, 1½–2 in (4–5 cm) across.

Juncus (from Latin *iuncus*, a rush, derived from *iugere*, to join, from the use of the stems in tying). Juncaceae. Cosmopolitan, but rare in the tropics. RUSH. About 225 species, rhizomatous grassy herbs growing in wet places. The stems and leaves are clumped and terete to narrowly swordlike and folded. The flowers are small, chaffy, green or brown, and carried in dense, rounded, terminal, or lateral cymes. Hardy and suitable for ponds and boggy ground. In smaller ponds, they can be grown in plunged containers. Propagate by division in spring.

J. effusus COMMON RUSH, SOFT RUSH; virtually cosmopolitan; stems and leaves indistinguishable, to 3¼ ft (1 m), dark green, slender, smooth, terete; inflorescence a dull brown lateral cyme near apex of stem; includes f. *spiralis*, CORKSCREW RUSH, with spirally twisted leaves and stems, 'Vittatus' with stems and leaves banded ivory, and 'Zebrinus' with leaves banded white; similar to *J. effusus* but smaller and finer is *J. decipiens*, whose cultivar 'Curly Wurly' has tightly spiraling foliage; *J. ensifolius* western N America; 8–32 in (20–80 cm), stems clumped, clothed with sea green, overlapping, sword-shaped leaves that resemble a miniature flag iris; flowers purple-black, glossy, in small, spherical heads.

June drop the natural shedding in early summer of a proportion of the immature fruits of apple, pear, plum, cherry, and citrus. Fruits fall over a short period, and the extent of the occurrence appears to be affected by soil moisture status. Planned fruit thinning should be done immediately after June drop.

Juniperus (Latin name for the tree). Cupressaceae. Northern Hemisphere from Arctic to C America, Himalaya, Taiwan; to 20°S in E Africa. JUNIPER. Perhaps 60 species, evergreen, coniferous trees or shrubs. The older bark is usually gray-brown and stringy, exfoliating in flakes or long vertical strips and exposing smooth red-brown bark beneath. The leaves are sharp and

needlelike or small, scalelike, and overlapping. The cones are globose, ovoid, or lumpy, bloomed with glaucous wax, fleshy and indehiscent, with the scales marked only by the finest lines; in color they are green, ripening to orange, red, brown, purple, or black.

The following are hardy and will adapt to most garden situations, although full sun and well-drained soil are important. *J. drupacea* prefers lime. *J. recurva* favors a humid, sheltered, cool, and damp site. Many of the glaucous species will tolerate poor, chalky, and stony soils, drought and sun. Both *J. conferta* and *J. horizontalis* (especially its selection 'Bar Harbor') endure salt spray and residue from salt-treated roads. Many species abound in cultivars, and one at least can usually be fitted to a particular garden need. The prostrate cultivars of several species, for example, are resilient, impenetrable groundcover. Dwarf cultivars are excellent rock garden and heather/conifer bed subjects. *J. chinensis* and *J. chinensis* var. *sargentii* are among the best conifers for bonsai treatment. Propagation as for *Chamaecyparis*. Affected by needle blight and stem dieback. The causal fungi enter through wounds or weakened tissue, especially in wet weather. Control by fungicidal spray. Junipers can be attacked by rusts; these cause the branches to swell and erupt with yellow-brown bodies. They are also attacked by phytophthora root rot. Pests include tent caterpillar and the juniper webber, which feeds *en masse* amid a complex of webbing. Infested foliage turns brown and dies, usually in early summer. Approved insecticides are effective if applied during late summer or early fall, when the caterpillars are young. Also afflicted by juniper scale, the conifer spinning mite, and the bagworm.

J. chinensis CHINESE JUNIPER; China, Mongolia, Japan; tree or shrub to 66 ft (20 m); crown conic; bark peeling in strips; foliage pungently scented, juvenile leaves subulate, dark green with 2 pale bands beneath, adult leaves rhombic, blunt, scalelike, overlapping; fruits violet to brown with a white bloom; includes golden, gray-blue and narrowly columnar to pyramidal cultivars; var. *sargentii* from Japan,

China is a prostrate shrub to 3¼ × 10 ft (1 × 3 m); branches layered to sweeping; bark red-brown; leaves needlelike to scalelike, gray-green or dark green, camphor-scented; fruit blue-black; *J. communis* COMMON JUNIPER; Europe, Asia; dense shrub or tree, 3¼–66 ft (1–20 m) tall; crown erect to spreading, typically bushy and erect; bark flaking or peeling; leaves subulate to needlelike, deep green with a single pale band on inner surface; fruit blue-gray to purple-black, glaucous; includes very dwarf to tall cultivars ranging in habit from tightly erect to pendulous and prostrate; *J. davurica* DAHURIAN JUNIPER; Siberia, Mongolia, China; semiprostrate shrub; bark gray, flaking; juvenile leaves needlelike, adult leaves scalelike, diamond-shaped, pointed, sage green; fruit purple-brown; includes cultivars with foliage variegated or stained golden yellow; *J. drupacea* SYRIAN JUNIPER; Greece, Syria, Turkey; columnar tree to 50 ft (15 m) in the wild, bark red-brown, peeling in long strips; leaves to 1 in (2.5 cm), needlelike, whorled, hard, sharply pointed, shiny green; fruit red-brown, violet-bloomed; *J. horizontalis* CREEPING JUNIPER; N America; low to prostrate, spreading shrub to 2 × 10 ft (0.6 × 3 m); leaves needle- or scalelike, gray-green or gray-blue; fruit dark blue with a pale bloom; includes cultivars with very low, feathery, or dense foliage, some very resistant to salt spray, others ranging in color from dull green to bright steely blue, the best turning purple-bronze in winter; *J.* × *pfitzeriana* (*J. sabina* × *J. chinensis*); spreading shrub to 6½ ft (2 m), differs from *J. sabina* in its thicker shoots and spiky crown with long, horizontal shoot tips; bark scaly, red-brown; leaves yellow- to gray-green, needle- or scalelike; fruit dark purple bloomed pale blue; cultivars include compact and low to robust and loosely tiered clones, some sports juvenile, they range in color from dull olive green to blue-gray and gold, some are yellow-variegated; one of the best-known is 'Wilhelm Pfitzer' (syn. 'Pfitzeriana'), a spreading, gray-green flat-topped shrub to 10 × 16 ft (3 × 5 m); *J. procumbens* BONIN ISLES JUNIPER; S Japan; to 30 in (75 cm), procumbent; bark maroon-brown, smooth; leaves in whorls of 3, linear, sharply pointed, pale green, the inner face with 2 gray-green bands; fruit dark brown; includes dwarf, prostrate and compact cultivars, some with gold-tipped foliage; *J. recurva* DROOPING JUNIPER, HIMALAYAN WEEPING JUNIPER; SW China, E Himalaya; tree or shrub to 66 ft (20 m), crown conical, branches weeping at least at tips; bark red-brown, peeling in strips; leaves subulate to lanceolate, sharply pointed, rigid, rather dry to touch, gray-green with a pale gray inner surface; fruit dark green-brown to black; var. *coxii*: COFFIN JUNIPER; small tree or large shrub, crown spreading, branches distinctly weeping; *J. rigida* TEMPLE JUNIPER; Japan, Korea, N China; tree to 50 ft (15 m), or shrub with an open crown and pendulous branches; bark brown to yellow-brown, peeling; leaves in whorls of 3, needlelike, sharply pointed, rigid, bright green, inner face with a single, blue-gray band; fruit dark maroon to purple-black; subsp. *conferta* SHORE JUNIPER; Japan, Sakhalin; prostrate to ascending shrub; bark red-brown; leaves needlelike, dark green, inner surface with a pale, glaucous band; fruit shiny dark purple; includes cultivars with blue-green and emerald green foliage, some turning yellow-green to bronze in winter; all are tolerant of coastal conditions; *J. sabina* SAVIN; C & S Europe, C Asia, NW China; spreading shrub or tree to 13 ft (4 m); bark rust-brown, flaking; leaves very aromatic, needlelike to scalelike, gray-green to blue-green; fruit very dark blue with a white bloom; cultivars include dwarf to robust clones of prostrate to tiered habit with compact to loosely feathered, dark green, gray, or blue-gray foliage, sometimes tipped yellow; *J. scopulorum* ROCKY MOUNTAIN JUNIPER; Rocky Mts; shrub or tree to 50 ft (15 m); crown open; bark red-brown, fissured; leaves scalelike, sharply pointed, yellow-green to dark green; fruit blue-black covered in a pale bloom; includes cultivars with dense or lax foliage in shades of gray-green and bright blue-gray, short or tall with procumbent, conical and very narrow habits; one of the best-known is 'Skyrocket', a very slender, columnar tree to 20 ft (6 m) tall with feathery, strongly ascending blue-gray foliage, sometimes listed under *J. virginiana*; *J. squamata* FLAKY JUNIPER; NW Asia to

China; prostrate to sprawling or erect shrub to 26 ft (8 m); bark rusty brown, flaky; leaves in whorls of 3, subulate, rigid, aromatic, deep gray-green to silvery blue-gray with a bright, blue-white band; fruit glossy black; cultivars include dwarf, prostrate, columnar, and bushy plants, many with bright silver-blue leaves, some assuming lilac tints in winter; one of the best-known is 'Meyeri', a broadly spreading shrub with dense, spiky boughs of steely blue foliage and old, dead growth rusty and persistent; *J. virginiana* PENCIL CEDAR, EASTERN RED CEDAR; E N America; tree to 66 ft (20 m), crown conic to columnar, branches spreading; bark rusty brown, peeling in shreds; leaves needle- and scalelike, gray-green marked with white, scented weakly of soap or mineral spirits; purple-maroon, thickly bloomed fruit; includes numerous cultivars—tall to low, narrowly erect to tiered and prostrate, pale to deep green or gray-green, sometimes turning purple-bronze in winter; this species is one of the parents of *J.* 'Gray Owl', a shrub to 6½ × 10 ft (2 × 3 m) with spreading branches and feathery, silver-gray foliage.

Justicia (for J. Justice, 18th-century Scottish gardener). Acanthaceae. Tropical and subtropical Northern and Southern hemispheres, and temperate N America. WATER WILLOW. Some 420 species, perennial herbs, subshrubs or shrubs with jointed stems and oblong to ovate leaves. The flowers are borne in axillary or terminal spikes, cymes or panicles, usually subtended by bracts; they are tubular and curving, with two lips, the uppermost narrowly hoodlike. Grow in a well-drained, medium- to high-fertility, loam-based mix in full sun or bright filtered light, with protection from hot summer sun and good ventilation. Water plentifully and feed weekly when in full growth. Keep just moist in winter, with a minimum temperature of 45°F (7°C). Propagate by semiripe stem cuttings in spring.

J. adhatoda India, Sri Lanka; shrub to 10 ft (3 m); flowers to 1¼ in (3 cm), white veined red or purple on lower lip); *J. brandegeeana* (syn. *Beloperone guttata*, *Drejerella guttata*); SHRIMP PLANT, FALSE HOP; Mexico; downy shrub to 6½ ft (2 m); flowers to 1¼ in (3 cm), white marked purple-red in shrimp- or hoplike, arching spikes to 3 in (8 cm) long, clothed with overlapping, downy, yellow, or more usually dusty pink to brick red or dull brown bracts; *J. californica* CHUPAROSA HONEYSUCKLE; southern N America; subshrub to 5 ft (1.5 m); branches downy, arching; flowers red; *J. carnea* (syn. *Jacobinia carnea*); BRAZILIAN PLUME, FLAMINGO PLANT, PARADISE PLANT; northern S America; shrub to 6½ ft (2 m); flowers to 2 in (5 cm), fleshy pink to magenta or purple-red in dense, erect, plume-shaped spikes to 6 in (15 cm) with green bracts; *J. rizzinii* (syn. *J. floribunda*, *J. pauciflora*); Brazil; small, rounded, downy shrub; flowers to ¾ in (2 cm), scarlet tipped yellow in nodding clusters; *J. spicigera* (syn. *J. ghiesbreghtiana*, *Jacobinia spicigera*); Mexico to Colombia; shrub to 6 ft (1.8 m); flowers to 1½ in (4 cm), orange or red in a secund raceme.

juvenile (1) used of the sexually immature stage of a plant; (2) used of the immature foliage of those plants that bear leaves of a distinctly different shape when young, such as *Cryptomeria* and *Eucalyptus*; cf. *adult*.

narrow adult foliage

characteristic disk or penny shape of young leaves

mature stems bear flowers

juvenile foliage

Juvenile and adult leaves of eucalyptus

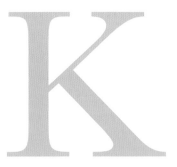

Kadsura (Japanese name for *K. japonica*). Schisandraceae. E and SE Asia. 22 species twining, evergreen shrubs with entire or obscurely toothed leaves and small flowers usually borne singly at the leaf axils in summer. These are followed by fleshy berries. Hardy to 0°F (−18°C). In colder areas, grow in the greenhouse or conservatory. Outdoors, plant in a sheltered position, in sun or part shade, on moderately fertile, well-drained neutral to acidic soils. Plants of both sexes are required for fruit set. Increase by semiripe stem cuttings. *K. japonica* Japan, Korea; climbing to 13 ft (4 m); flowers to ⅝ in (1.5 cm) wide, ivory; fruit scarlet.

Kaempferia (for Engelbert Kaempfer [1651–1716], German physician). Zingiberaceae. Tropical Asia. About 50 species, rhizomatous perennial herbs with aromatic tubers and foliage. Those here are low-growing plants with clumps of broad leaves. Produced in spring and summer in short spikes, the flowers consist of three petals, large, petal-like staminodes, and a showy, deeply lobed lip. Grow in semishade with a minimum temperature of 59°F (15°C). Plant in a porous, fertile medium rich in leaf mold. Keep warm, humid, and moist when in growth; in the winter resting period, keep cool and dry. Propagate by division of tubers.

K. atrovirens PEACOCK PLANT; Borneo; leaves bronze with a metallic sheen above; flowers white and lavender, pink, or violet; *K. pulchra* Thailand, Malaysia; leaves pale green suffused and feathered with dark purple-green or bronze-green feathered silver-green; flowers lilac; *K. roscoeana* PEACOCK LILY, DWARF GINGER LILY; Burma; leaves deep green marked paler green above, flushed red beneath; flowers white;

K. rotunda RESURRECTION LILY; SE Asia, widely cultivated; leaves green marked silver above, tinted purple beneath; flowers white with a lilac lip.

kainit a natural mineral containing potassium chloride together with sodium chloride, magnesium sulfate, and impurities. Formerly an orchard fertilizer, it is now rarely used on account of its variability and the risk of phytotoxicity caused by its impurities.

Kalanchoe (from the obscure native name for a Chinese species). Crassulaceae. Tropics, especially Old World. 125 species, perennial, occasionally annual or biennial, succulent shrubs, herbs, and climbers (those below perennials). The leaves are fleshy and the flowers, which are bell-shaped to tubular, are carried in racemes and panicles at various times of year. Many of the smaller species, notably *K. bloss-feldiana* and its hybrids, carry exotic and vibrantly colored flowers in late winter and spring. They are commonly grown as houseplants. The trailing to weeping cultivars are useful for hanging pots and baskets. Grow in a medium-fertility loam-based mix with added grit, in sun or light shade, with a minimum temperature of 50°F (10°C). Water plentifully from spring to fall, sparingly and occasionally in winter. Propagate from stem or leaf cuttings. For large-leaved species such as *K. beharensis*, the midrib is cut across in several places, and pinned to the surface of a sandy propagating mix. New plants should form within a month. A few species, such as *K. daigremontiana*, produce large numbers of tiny plantlets at the tips and margins of mature leaves; these are easily detached and root quickly when placed on the soil surface. Surface-sow seed of all species in early spring at 68°F (20°C).

LEAF CUTTINGS OF KALANCHOE

shriveled leaf

plantlets form at stalk base

1 Remove healthy leaves with stalks (here of *K. beharensis*) and thread onto wire, hanging them in a warm, airy place out of direct sun. Leaves must not touch.

2 After 3–6 months, plantlets should form from buds at the leaf stalk base. Once large enough to handle, they may be potted, using a mix formulated for cacti.

PROPAGATING KALANCHOE FROM PLANTLETS

1 Plantlets (adventitious buds) that form at leaf margins (here on *K. delagoensis*) may be gently detached at any time between spring and fall.

2 Fill a small pot with cactus mix and cover with sand. Set six plantlets on top, and keep moist in a bright, airy place, out of direct sun. They should soon root.

K.beharensis Madagascar; densely felty shrub to 20 ft (6 m); leaves to 14 in (35 cm), spear-shaped to triangular, toothed, stained brown, and silvery beneath; flowers green-yellow marked violet within; *K. blossfeldiana* FLAMING KATY; Madagascar; bushy herb to 24 in (60 cm); leaves to 2¾ in (7 cm), oblong to ovate, glossy green, tip blunt, base rounded, crenate; flowers orange, red, pink, or yellow in erect, crowded, domed to flat-topped bunches; *K. daigremontiana* DEVIL'S BACKBONE; Madagascar; robust, erect perennial to 3¼ ft (1 m); leaves to 8 in (20 cm), lanceolate, fleshy, smooth, marbled brown-purple beneath, margins toothed, bearing plantlets; flowers violet-gray; *K. delagonensis* (syn. *K. tubiflora*); Madagascar; perennial shrublet to 6½ ft (2 m); leaves ¾–4¾ in (2–12 cm), narrow, terete, gray-green, tip toothed, and bearing plantlets; flowers magenta to orange; *K. fedtschenkoi* Madagascar; dense shrublet to 20 in (50 cm); leaves ¾–2½ in (2–6 cm), oblong to ovate, glaucous blue, toothed near apex; flowers purple-red; includes 'Variegata', with cream-marked leaves; *K. pumila* Madagascar; sprawling shrublet to 12 in (30 cm); leaves to 1¼ in (3 cm), chalky, gray-white, obovate, toothed toward tip; flowers pink with purple lines; *K.* 'Tessa' bushy, sprawling to cascading perennial with neat, elliptic, smooth and deep green leaves and large, nodding, tubular flowers in deep orange-red; *K. tomentosa* PANDA PLANT; Madagascar; erect perennial to 3¼ ft (1 m), sparingly branched; leaves ¾–3½ in (2–9 cm), oblong to obovate, gray-green and covered in dense, felty, pale hairs except for the red-brown-stained tip; flowers yellow-green stained purple and covered in red-brown hairs; *K. uniflora* Madagascar; creeping perennial; leaves ¼–1½ in (0.5–4 cm), oblong to rounded, convex, sparsely crenate; flowers pendent, purple-red; *K.* 'Wendy' more or less erect, bushy perennial to 16 in (40 cm); leaves elliptic to obovate, smooth, bluntly toothed; flowers large, urn-shaped, nodding, magenta with yellow lobes.

kale (*Brassica oleracea*, Acephala Group) a biennial member of the Cruciferae, closely related to cabbage; it is grown as an annual for its edible shoots

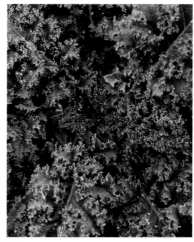

Kale

Kale is a nonheading member of the cabbage family, grown for leaves that have a mild flavor. They are frilly in the so-called curly or Scotch kales (borecole).

and young leaves, which are harvested through the winter until spring. One of the hardiest brassicas, it is capable of withstanding winter temperatures as low as 5°F (–15°C), but is also tolerant of high summer temperatures. It is widely distributed in both temperate and tropical regions.

Transplants may be raised from a spring sowing and within 6–8 weeks will be large enough to plant firmly, at 18–30-in (45–75-cm) spacings according to cultivar. For an early crop of spring greens, grow at closer spacings, sowing seed broadcast under cloches during the latter part of the winter, or in the open during early spring. Thin to 2¾–4-in (7–10-cm) spacings. Plants may be harvested as spring greens when no more than 6 in (15 cm) high, and the remaining stems allowed to resprout for a further harvest.

Kale forms may be classified into the curly or Scotch kales (borecole) and the broader smooth-leaved types. A number of kales grow extremely tall, including the so-called Jersey kale (also known as tree cabbage, walking-stick cabbage, Jersey longjacks, and *chou cavalier*). Though normally reaching around 60 in (150 cm), Jersey kale has been recorded at 18 ft (5.4 m). The straight, relatively slender stems are strong enough to dry and make into walking sticks; the 30-in (75-cm) leaves are decorative and can be cooked when young.

RAPE or SIBERIAN KALE is similar in appearance to the curly kales but is a different species (*Brassica napus*). It will not withstand transplanting and must be sown *in situ*.

CHINESE KALE, CHINESE BROCCOLI see *broccoli*.

Possible problems: cabbage root fly, flea beetle; clubroot.

Kalmia (for Peter Kalm [1716–1779], Swedish botanist and student of Linnaeus). Ericaceae. US, Cuba. 7 species, evergreen shrubs with oblong to elliptic, entire, leathery leaves and small flowers in corymbs, umbels, or fascicles in summer. The flowers are bell-shaped to broadly tubular, with five lobes. Suitable for planting in open woodland or at the woodland edge and in association with *Rhododendron* and other large Ericaceae. Hardy to –22°F (–30°C). Grow in full sun or dappled shade, in moisture-retentive, sandy soils that are nonalkaline and rich in organic matter. Sow seed in late winter, lightly covered, in a warm greenhouse. Propagate from wounded hardwood cuttings in late winter, in a closed case with bottom heat, or by layering. Alternatively, propagate by softwood cuttings in summer.

K. angustifolia LAMBKILL, SHEEP LAUREL, WICKY; E US; to 5 ft (1.5 m); flowers ¼–½ in (0.7–1.2 cm) in diameter, scarlet-pink, pink, deep rosy purple or white in axillary corymbs; *K. latifolia* CALICO BUSH, MOUNTAIN LAUREL; E US; 10–33 ft (3–10 m); flowers ¾–1 in (2–2.5 cm) in diameter, white to pale pink, deep rose or crimson, in large terminal corymbs.

Kalmiopsis ("resembling *Kalmia*"). Ericaceae. US (Oregon). 1 species, *K. leachiana*, an evergreen dwarf shrub to 12 in (30 cm). To 1¼ in (3 cm) long, the leaves are oval or obovate, bright green with large, yellow glands beneath. Produced in spring in terminal racemes, the bell-shaped flowers are ½–¾ in (1–2 cm) across, rose-purple and 5-lobed. A choice shrub, suitable for the rock garden or alpine house and frame; hardy to 5°F (–15°C). Grow in moist, peaty, acidic soil, in semishade or in sun, with some protection during the hottest part of the day. Propagate by surface sown seed, by layering, or by semiripe cuttings.

Kalopanax (from Greek *kalos*, beautiful, and *Panax*). Araliaceae. China, Korea, Sakhalin, Kuriles, Japan, Ryukyu Islands. 1 species, *K. septemlobus* (syn. *K. pictus*, *K. ricinifolius*, *Acanthopanax ricinifolius*), the TREE ARALIA, a round-headed, sparingly branched tree to 100 ft (30 m). The branches and trunk are prickly, especially in young growth. To 14 in (35 cm) across, the leaves are palmately lobed, finely toothed, dark green above and paler beneath. They are divided into 5 to 7, triangular to ovate lobes and carried on petioles to 20 in (50 cm) long. Small white flowers are borne in paniculate umbels in summer and followed by small, blue-black drupes. Hardy to −10°F (−23°C). Plant *Kalopanax* in deep, fertile, moisture-retentive soil. Give sun or semishade. On young plants, unripened wood is susceptible to frost damage. Propagate from seed in fall or semiripe cuttings under mist or with bottom heat in summer. Young plants are particularly slow-growing.

kaolinite a clay mineral with relatively low cation exchange and water-holding capacities.

keel (1) a prominent ridge, like the keel of a boat, running longitudinally down the center of the undersurface of a leaf, petiole, bracts, petal, or sepal; (2) the two lower united petals of a papilionaceous flower.

kelp any of various types of very large seaweed, especially *Laminaria* species. The term is sometimes used more generally to describe any seaweed harvested as bulky organic manure.

Kennedia (for Lewis Kennedy [1775–1818], a founding partner of Lee and Kennedy, nurserymen of Hammersmith, London). Leguminosae. Australia, Tasmania, New Guinea. CORAL PEA. Some 16 species, woody or herbaceous perennial climbers. The leaves are usually trifoliolate. Showy, pealike flowers are produced in trusses or racemes in late spring and summer. In frost-free regions, *Kennedia* species are grown as climbers or for ground-cover. They are ideal for covering dry, sunny banks and warm walls. In cooler regions, they are suited to the cool

greenhouse or conservatory, trained up pillars and along rafters or scrambling through shrubs. Grow in a sandy soil in full sun in a warm, sheltered position. Maintain a winter minimum temperature of 41–50°F (5–10°C). Water moderately when in growth, and keep virtually dry in winter. Prune after flowering to remove overcrowded growth. Propagate by seed sown in spring at 68°F (20°C). Immerse seed briefly in boiling water and soak in tepid water for 12 hours before sowing. Take semiripe cuttings in summer.

K. nigricans BLACK CORAL PEA, BLACK BEAN; W Australia; woody climber to 20 ft (6 m); flowers violet-purple to true black blotched golden yellow; *K. rubicunda* DUSKY CORAL PEA; New South Wales, Victoria; woody-based climber to 10 ft (3 m); flowers deep coral to scarlet with a paler blotch at base of standard.

kernel the inner part of a seed or the whole body within the seed coat.

Kerria (for William Kerr [d. 1814], Kew gardener who collected in China, Java, and the Philippines). Rosaceae. China, Japan; widely cultivated in Japan. JEW'S MALLOW; JAPANESE ROSE. 1 species, *K. japonica*, a deciduous shrub to 8 ft (2.25 m). The branches are green and rodlike, branching in their second season and suckering freely. To 2¾ in (7 cm) long, the leaves are oval and sawtoothed. They are usually mid- to dark green, but are edged and splashed white to cream in the cultivar 'Picta' ('Variegata'). The buttercup-like flowers, borne in spring, to 2 in (5 cm) in diameter, pale to deep golden yellow, with five ('Simplex') or more ('Pleniflora') ovate to orbicular petals and numerous stamens. *Kerria* is hardy to −4°F (−20°C). Grow in a sunny position. Prune after flowering to remove old and overcrowded stems. Propagate by semiripe cuttings or by suckers.

key a device for identifying plants, often by means of a series of couplets of mutually exclusive statements, each leading either to a further pair of statements or to the identification (a dichotomous key).

kieserite see *magnesium sulfate*.

Kirengeshoma (from Japanese *ki*, yellow, and *rengeshoma*, native name for *Anemopsis*, which this plant is held to resemble). Hydrangeaceae. Japan, Korea. 1 species, *K. palmata*, a graceful perennial herb. The stems of this plant are 24–48 in (60–120 cm) tall, erect to arching and purple- or red-tinted. The pale green leaves are 4–8 in (10–20 cm) long, broadly ovate, toothed to palmately incised, and with a tapering tip and a heart-shaped base. Borne in late summer, the flowers are narrowly bell-shaped, to 1¼ in (3 cm) long, and slender-stalked. They consist of five, overlapping, pale yellow to apricot petals. Hardy to −10°F (−23°C). Grow in deep, moist, humus-rich, non-alkaline soils, in semishade or with part-day sun. Mulch in winter. Propagate by division or by seed, which may take up to 10 months to germinate.

Kitaibela (for Paul Kitaibel [d. 1817], Hungarian botanist). Malvaceae. Balkans. 1 species, *K. vitifolia*, a perennial herb to 8 ft (2.5 m) tall. To 7 in (18 cm) long, the long-stalked leaves are rhombic to rounded, with five to seven triangular and coarsely toothed lobes. Produced in summer, the broadly funnel-shaped flowers are solitary or carried in axillary cymes; they consist of five cuneate petals, to 1 in (2.5 cm) long and white or rose. Hardy to −10°F (−23°C), *Kitaibela* will grow in any fertile, moisture-retentive but well-drained soil in sun. Propagate by seed in fall or spring, or by division or cuttings.

kitchen garden a plot of ground predominantly devoted to edible produce but often including flowers for cutting, and commonly greenhouses for growing crops out of season. Traditionally, large kitchen gardens were entirely walled in, the walls themselves being used for training fruit trees.

kiwi fruit (*Actinidia deliciosa*) CHINESE GOOSEBERRY a hardy perennial climber, very vigorous with shoots up to 33 ft (10 m) in length, bearing large heart-shaped leaves. It is native to China, and grown for its edible, hispid fruits that are up to 4 in (10 cm) long and 1¾ in (4.5 cm) across. This rampant climber can become highly invasive if not pruned with care. The young blossom-

K

433

K

bearing shoots are susceptible to frost damage so fruiting plants require a sheltered site. Propagate from seed or preferably from cuttings. The plants should be spaced 10–15 ft (3–4.5 m) apart, with a support system provided as for blackberries and hybrid berries, or by means of a pergola. Under greenhouse protection they may be trained in a manner similar to grapes. After planting, the plants should be cut back to 12 in (30 cm) height. One male plant is required for up to 6 female plants, and pollination by hand is beneficial under greenhouse conditions. Young plants are tip-pruned on reaching the top wire to encourage lateral growths, which should be trained along the support wires, pinching out the growing tips when the shoots reach the end posts. Thereafter, any fruiting sublaterals should be pinched back to six or seven leaves beyond the last fruit; nonflowering shoots should be pinched back to five leaves throughout the growing season. Three-year-old fruiting laterals are best pruned hard back to encourage replacement growth. The fruit is fall-ripening and should be stored in an airy shed or greenhouse for up to 6 weeks after picking.

Knautia (for Christian Knaut [1654–1716], German botanist at Halle). Dipsacaceae. Europe, Caucasus, Siberia, Mediterranean. 60 species, annual and perennial herbs with small flowers borne in summer in long-stalked, flat-topped heads subtended by leafy bracts. Suited to wildflower gardens, meadows, and small gardens. Both species listed below are hardy −20°F (−29°C) if grown in a warm sunny site in well-drained soil. Propagate by seed or basal cuttings.

K. arvensis BLUE BUTTONS, FIELD SCABIOUS, SCABIOUS; Europe, Mediterranean, Caucasus, naturalized N America; perennial to 5 ft (1.5 m); flowers pale purple-blue; *K. macedonica* (syn. *Scabiosa rumelica*); C Europe; perennial to 32 in (0.8 m); flowers deep purple.

knee a spongy outgrowth from a horizontal subterranean root projecting above the soil surface in saturated conditions, as in *Taxodium*.

knife-ringing see *bark-ringing*.

Kniphofia (for J. H. Kniphof [1704–1756], German botanist). Liliaceae (Aloeaceae). RED-HOT POKER. Africa (those species listed below are from South Africa). 68 species, evergreen perennial herbs forming clumps of grasslike to strap-shaped leaves. The flowers are tubular to narrowly funnel-shaped and point downward in dense, cylindric to conical, long-stalked spikes in summer and fall. Unopened or recently opened flower buds may be of a far deeper or wholly different color, giving the spike a bicolored appearance.

Red-hot pokers are best known for their range of hot reds and oranges, although numerous cultivars are available in softer colors—for example, the creamy 'Snow Maiden', the glowing yellows of 'Maid of Orleans', and the cool green of 'Green Jade'. Most species are cold-tolerant to temperatures of −5°F (−15°C), although at these low temperatures, plants require a warm and sheltered position and should be mulched deeply with leaf mold or bracken litter. In the northern US, plants are sometimes lifted and overwintered in a moist soilless medium in frost-free conditions. However, most resent root disturbance and mulch protection is preferable wherever possible. Grow in full sun in deep, fertile and freely draining, preferably sandy soil, with sufficient organic matter to ensure an adequate supply of moisture when in growth. Propagate by seed or division; increase cultivars by division only. Thrips occasionally cause mottling of the foliage.

K. angustifolia to 24 in (60 cm); leaves grasslike; flower spike graceful, loose, flowers to 1¼ in (3 cm), white to yellow, orange, and coral; *K. caulescens* 5–6½ ft (1.5–2 m); robust, forming clumps of short, stout stems; leaves thick, keeled, glaucous gray-green; flower spike dense, broadly cylindric, flowers to 1 in (2.5 cm), creamy white tinted peach, flushed flame in bud; *K. galpinii* to 32 in (80 cm); leaves slender; flower spike small, dense, red at apex shading to orange-yellow as flowers open

below, flowers to 1½ in (3.5 cm); sometimes confused with *K. triangularis*; *K. triangularis* to 3¼ ft (1 m); leaves slender; flower spike small, dense, flowers to 1½ in (3.5 cm), coral to orange with flared perianth lobes; *K. uvaria* 3¼–6½ ft (1–2 m); leaves narrowly strap-shaped; flower spike oblong to ovoid-conical, dense, flowers 1¼–1½ in (3–4 cm), brilliant red to green-yellow. *Cultivars* dwarf to 32 in (80 cm): 'Ada' (primrose yellow), 'Bressingham Comet' (orange tipped red), 'Bressingham Glow' (deep orange to flame, late-flowering), 'Canary Bird' (yellow), 'Candlelight' (clear yellow to cream, spikes slender and graceful), 'Little Maid' (ivory tipped soft yellow), 'Tubergeniana' (soft primrose), 'White Fairy' (white); medium to tall (32–60 in (80–150 cm)): 'Atlanta' (orange-yellow), 'Green Jade' (bright green), 'Nobilis' (deep, fiery orange), 'Percy's Pride' (green-yellow), 'Royal Standard' (bright yellow below, vermilion above), 'Samuel's Sensation' (deep flame shading to yellow at base, late-flowering with very long spikes), 'Spanish Gold' (rich dark yellow).

knock-down a term sometimes applied to contact insecticides that kill only those pests actually covered during the application of the material. Such substances are quick-acting and usually nonpersistent.

knot, knot garden a bed laid out in an intricate pattern, sometimes resembling a maze, using low-growing, clipped plants such as dwarf boxwood (*Buxus*), cotton lavender (*Santolina*), and thrift (*Armeria*). The area around and between the lining plants may be filled with flowering plants, which are replaced in season. In Tudor times especially, such areas were often left bare or covered with colorful materials, such as sand, chalk, or coal. Knots were especially popular in the 16th and 17th centuries, and were originally designed to be seen mainly from above, from terraces or windows. The name was derived from the resemblance of the pattern to a knot of rope arranged on the ground.

Kniphofia
'Green Jade'

Koeleria (for G. L. Koeler, [1765–1806], botanist specializing in grasses). Gramineae. Temperate regions, tropical Africa. Some 25 species, annual and perennial grasses with clumped, erect stems and narrow leaf blades. The flowers appear in summer in narrowly cylindric panicles held over the foliage. These dry to a parchment tone and can be used in dried arrangements. Fully hardy. Grow in full sun in any not too-fertile, well-drained soil, including calcareous soils and shallow soils over chalk. Propagate by seed or division in fall or spring.

K. glauca C Europe, Siberia; perennial to 24 in (60 cm); leaves slender, strongly glaucous blue-green to gray; *K. vallesiana* W Europe; perennial to 16 in (40 cm); leaves to 4 in (10 cm), very narrow, blue-green to silver.

Koelreuteria (for Joseph G. Koelreuter [1733–1806], professor of Natural History at Karlsruhe). Sapindaceae. China, Taiwan. GOLDEN RAIN TREE, SHRIMP TREE, CHINESE RAIN TREE. 3 species, flat-topped, deciduous shrubs or trees. The leaves are simple or bipinnate. Yellow, 4-petaled flowers are borne in large terminal panicles in summer. They are followed by conspicuous, bladderlike seed pods. *K. paniculata* remains of interest throughout the season, with red-flushed young growth, yellow fall tints, and inflated fruits in warm, earthy colors. It will withstand winter temperatures of at least 14°F (–10°C), but flowering and fall color are much improved where a long, hot growing season, dry fall, and cold winter are common. Plant in sun. It is tolerant of poor, dry soils, pollution and exposure to wind (not salt-laden), growing quickly to a specimen of reasonable size; it resents severe pruning. Young plants should be kept well-watered until they are 3 or 4 years old. Propagate from seed, sown in fall or stratified and sown in spring. Alternatively, increase by root cuttings in winter. *K. paniculata* GOLDEN RAIN TREE, PRIDE OF INDIA, VARNISH TREE; N China, Korea; tree to 50 ft (15 m); leaves to 16 in (40 cm), ferny, emerging pink-red, falling bright yellow; flowers in large, pyramidal panicles; fruit to 2 in (5 cm), oblong to ovoid, splitting into three brown, papery segments

and persisting well after leaf fall.

Kohleria (for Michael Kohler, 19th-century teacher of natural history at Zurich). Gesneriaceae. Tropical America. 50 species, perennial herbs and shrubs with ovate to elliptic, hairy leaves. Nodding in summer on stalked cymes, the flowers are tubular and somewhat swollen, with a narrowed throat and a limb of five, small, spreading lobes. Provide a minimum temperature of 59°F (15°C) with light shade, medium to high humidity, and protection from drafts. Grow in a porous, soilless medium; keep moist when in growth, virtually dry during the winter resting period. Increase by division of rhizomes.

K. amabilis Colombia; to 24 in (60 cm) tall, white-hairy; leaves sometimes with silver markings, often flushed red; flowers to 1 in (2.5 cm), deep rose with brick red bars and stripes, limb rose with maroon bars and spots; *K. bella* Costa Rica; to 16 in (40 cm) tall, pale red-hairy; flowers to 1½ in (4 cm), red tinged yellow below, limb yellow with purple spots; *K. bogotensis* Colombia; to 24 in (60 cm) tall, hairy; leaves with pale green or white markings; flowers to 1 in (2.5 cm), red fading to yellow at base, limb yellow spotted red; *K. eriantha* shrubby perennial herb to 3¼ ft (1 m), red-hairy; flowers to 2 in (5 cm), orange to scarlet or cinnabar red, yellow-white with red spots; *K. warscewiczii* (syn. *K. digitaliflora*);Colombia; to 24 in (60 cm) tall, covered in white hairs; flowers to 1¼ in (3 cm) long, deep rose to magenta, white below, limb green with deep purple spots.

kohlrabi (*Brassica oleracea*, Gongylodes Group) TURNIP CABBAGE a biennial member of the Cruciferae, grown as an annual for its spherical, swollen stem which is trimmed of leaves and boiled. It has a flavor similar to turnip, for which it is often used as a substitute, being better able to withstand drought and high temperature.

Kohlrabi is most suited to temperate regions but can be grown in warmer climates. It is sensitive to low temperature and a week at 50°F (10°C) will

"Sputnik"-shaped swollen stem base

Kohlrabi

cause plants to bolt: the recommended range is 64–77°F (18–25°C) with an optimum of 72°F (22°C). For continuity, sow at regular intervals from early spring to late summer in drills 12 in (30 cm) apart, later thinning seedlings to 10 in (25 cm) apart. Alternatively, seedlings may be transplanted when no more than 2 in (5 cm) tall. Kohlrabi is best harvested when young because the swollen stems become woody; it can be stored for winter use either *in situ* or in boxes of sand.

Possible problems: cabbage root fly, flea beetle; clubroot.

Kolkwitzia (for Richard Kolkwitz [b. 1873], professor of botany in Berlin). Caprifoliaceae. BEAUTY BUSH. C China. 1 species, *K. amabilis*, a deciduous shrub to 11½ ft (3.5 m). Produced in spring and early summer, the flowers are paired in terminal corymbs. The slender sepals are densely hairy to bristly. Up to ¾ in (2 cm) long, the bell-shaped corolla is white stained rose pink outside (strongly so in the cultivars 'Pink Cloud' and 'Rosea'), with deep yellow to orange markings in the throat and a limb of five, rounded lobes. Grown for its masses of beautiful bell-shaped flowers, which resemble those of the closely allied *Abelia*, *Kolkwitzia* makes a valuable addition to the shrub border. Its exfoliating bark is attractive in winter. It thrives in chalk soils and is hardy to –22°F (–30°C), although it may suffer dieback of shoot tips in very cold weather. Plant in full sun. Prune out old, damaged or weak shoots from the base after flowering. Propagate by softwood cuttings or from suckers, which are freely produced.

L

labellum a lip, especially the enlarged or otherwise distinctive third petal of an orchid.

labiate possessing a lip or lips; describing corollas of the sort found in many Labiatae.

labium one of the liplike divisions of a labiate corolla or calyx.

Lablab beans
There are both long- and short-podded cultivars of these warm-climate legumes. Most are climbing, but there are some dwarf cultivars that can be grown without support.

Lablab (from a Hindu plant name). Leguminosae. Tropical Africa, widely cultivated in India, SE Asia, Egypt, Sudan. 1 species, *L. purpureus* (syn. *Dolichos lablab*); EGYPTIAN BEAN, HYACINTH BEAN, INDIAN BEAN, LABLAB, DOLICHOS BEAN, BONAVIST, LUBIA BEAN, a perennial twining herb, to 20 ft (6 m). The leaves are trifoliolate, composed of ovate to triangular or rhombic leaflets to 6 in (15 cm), tinted purple and coloring well in fall. White, purple or bright rose, the pealike flowers are carried in erect racemes to 16 in (40 cm) long in summer. Grow in well-drained soil in full sun; maintain a minimum winter temperature of 45–50°F (7–10°C); water plentifully when in growth. Train on canes or trellis. Apply liquid feed weekly when growing strongly. Alternatively, treat as half-hardy annuals grown as for runner beans (see *beans*). Increase by seed in spring.

+ Laburnocytisus (*Laburnum* combined with *Cytisus*). Leguminosae. Garden origin. + *L* 'Adamii' a graft hybrid between *Laburnum anagyroides* and *Chamaecytisus purpureus*, is a tree to 25 ft (7.5 m) tall, resembling *Laburnum* in overall habit, but with a mixture of sporadic, true growths and flowers of both *Laburnum anagyroides* and *Chamaecytisus purpureus* where the chimaera breaks down. Otherwise, the growth is intermediate between the parents, thus the racemes are *Laburnum*-like but with smaller flowers in dull yellow tinged purple, appearing fleshy pink or pale bronze. Cultivate as for *Laburnum*. Propagate by grafting carefully chosen scions of the intermediate form on to *Laburnum anagyroides*.

Laburnum (classical Latin name). Leguminosae. SC and SE Europe, W Asia. GOLDEN CHAIN TREE. 2 species, small to medium-sized deciduous shrubs or trees with trifoliolate leaves. Produced in spring and early summer, the flowers are pealike, yellow, and packed in graceful, pendulous racemes. All parts are poisonous, the legumelike seeds especially. Fully hardy, laburnums are used as lawn and border specimens, and may be fan-trained as screens and living fences. They are perhaps at their most beautiful when grown in walkways over arches and pergolas. Plant in moderately fertile, well-drained soil in sun. Pruning of freestanding specimens is rarely necessary, but may best be done in late summer. To make a laburnum arch, support young plants with wooden stakes—these will eventually rot by which time trunks will be self-supporting. Space plants at about 6½ ft (2 m) and train side branches along rigid wires between the stakes and arched over the top. As branches meet at the top of the structure, they can be grafted together. Propagate species from seed sown ripe under glass or in the frame. Take hardwood cuttings of the past season's growth in late winter; treat with rooting hormone and insert into open ground, with sharp sand around the base. Propagate hybrids by budding on to seedling stock of *L. anagyroides* in summer. A leaf miner, *Leucoptera laburnella*, makes spiral mines within the leaves; although rarely fatal, heavy infestations disfigure small plants.

L. alpinum SCOTCH LABURNUM, ALPINE GOLDEN CHAIN; south central Europe; twigs glabrous; inflorescence to 14 in (35 cm)+, denser than in *L. anagyroides*; pedicels equaling flowers; corolla ⅝ in (1.5 cm)+, bright yellow; includes the low-crowned, weeping 'Pendulum' and the erect 'Pyramidale'; *L. anagyroides* COMMON LABURNUM, GOLDEN CHAIN; C and S Europe; twigs gray-green, weakly hairy; inflorescence to 8 in (20 cm); pedicels shorter than flowers; corolla ¾ in (2 cm), lemon to golden yellow; includes the weeping 'Pendulum', the yellow-leaved 'Aureum', and 'Autumnale' ('Semperflorens'), which produces a second flush of flowers in fall; *L.* × *watereri* (*L. alpinum* × *L. anagyroides*; Tyrol, S Switzerland; closer to *L. anagyroides* but only shoot tips hairy; inflorescence to 20 in (50 cm); flowers fragrant; includes 'Alford's Weeping', with a widely spreading, weeping crown, and 'Vossii', exceptionally floriferous, with long racemes.

lacebugs (*Stephanitis* and other species.) (Hemiptera: Tingidae). Small, flattened, sap-sucking insects, up to ¼ in (6 mm) in length, with lacelike forewings. Of some 700 recorded species, only a few are of garden importance. They include *Stephanitis rhododendri*, the RHODODENDRON LACEBUG of Europe and North America, which inserts eggs into the midrib of rhododendron leaves in late summer and fall. These hatch in spring to produce gray-black, spiny-bodied nymphs, which feed on the underside of leaves; adults appear four weeks later. Lower leaf surfaces become fouled with brown excrement and pale yellow spots appear on the upper surfaces, giving a mottled appearance. Pieris lacebugs, *Stephanitis* *takeyai*, cause similar damage on *Pieris* plants. Small infestations are best controlled by pruning and destroying affected branches, otherwise contact or systemic insecticides should be applied from midsummer onward.

lacecap a flat-topped inflorescence in which the outer flowers are sterile and enlarged, as in, for example many *Hydrangea* cultivars.

laced used to describe flowers of certain cultivars of garden pinks, which have a patch of contrasting color at the edge of each petal forming a continuous, narrow, scalloped band around the flower, thereby bearing a resemblance to lace-work.

lacerate irregularly, and more or less broadly, shallowly and sharply cut, as if torn.

lacewing flies (Neuroptera) insects up to about 1 in (25 mm) long, with long threadlike antennae and two pairs of similar sized transparent lacelike wings, held like a roof over their back when at rest; they are useful predators in gardens.

The familiar GREEN LACEWINGS (Chrysopidae) are often attracted to artificial light and have yellow-green bodies and wings, and iridescent eyes. Eggs are laid on stalks, separately or in bundles, and the bristly larvae are mostly pale green or yellow with darker markings. They feed on aphids, other small insects and sometimes mites, and typically cover their backs with the empty skins of their prey. Most overwinter in a spun cocoon before pupating in the spring.

The BROWN LACEWINGS (Hemerobiidae) are mostly smaller, with brown or gray-brown wings; their eggs are not laid on stalks. Many appear on conifers where the larvae attack aphids, and some also attack thrips and mites on other trees and herbaceous plants.

The POWDERY LACEWINGS (Coniopterygidae) are small fragile insects, their body and wings covered with white powdery wax; they resemble whiteflies except that the wings are not held flat. Their larvae have plump

bodies tapering at the hind end with relatively long legs; they feed on small aphids and mites. Of these *Conwentzia* species feed on the fruit tree red spider mite, *Panonychus ulmi*—the larvae have been recorded as consuming up to 35 of these mites a day and the adults 30 mature female mites in an hour.

Lachenalia (for Werner von Lachenal, late-18th-century Swiss botanist). Liliaceae (Hyacinthaceae). South Africa. Some 90 species, bulbous perennial herbs with strap-shaped to circular leaves and erect spikes of tubular to urn-shaped flowers. These consist of six perianth segments in two whorls: the outer whorl shorter, forming a fleshy tube or cup, each segment often with a marked apical swelling; the inner whorl protruding, usually broader and more showy, with lips colored and recurved. Most flower in winter and spring. Grow in a medium-fertility, sandy loam-based mix, in full sun; maintain a minimum temperature of 45°F (7°C). Plant in late fall. Water sparingly as growth commences, plentifully when in full growth. Dry off as leaves wither and keep almost completely dry when dormant. Propagate by ripe seed when available; seedlings may flower in the season following first dormancy. Offsets and bulbils are also produced.

L. aloides (syn. *L. tricolor*); leaves strap-shaped, blotched green or purple; raceme to 11 in (28 cm), scape often mottled and tinted red-brown; flowers pendulous, tubular to funnelform, outer segments fleshy, lemon yellow to apricot or white, sometimes flushed orange, scarlet or blue-green from the base, apical swellings bright green, inner segment ¾–1½ in (2–3.5 cm), tipped cinnabar red, magenta, scarlet or green; includes 'Pearsonii', with leaves spotted red-brown above and scape to 7 in (18 cm), mottled red-brown, outer segments to ⅝ in (1.5 cm), apricot, apical swelling lime green, inner segments to 1¼ in (3 cm), apricot to gold, tips stained red to maroon, and 'Nelsonii', with leaves spotted purple and bright yellow flowers tipped green; *L. contaminata* WILD HYACINTH; leaves, grasslike; scape mottled; inflorescence

2½–10 in (6–25 cm), flowers campanulate, white, apical swelling on outer segments maroon, inner segments striped maroon near tips; *L. mutabilis* leaf solitary, sometimes spotted or banded maroon, often crispate; inflorescence 4–18 in (10–45 cm), outer perianth segments pale blue to white, apical swelling dark brown, inner segments yellow with brown markings near tip; *L. orchioides* leaves strap-shaped, sometimes spotted; inflorescence 3–16 in (8–40 cm), flowers fragrant, oblong to cylindrical, outer segments pale blue at base shading to green-yellow or cream, apical swellings green; includes var. *glaucina*, with outer perianth segments blue at base, shading to purple, and apical swelling dark purple, sometimes entirely blue with dark blue swelling; *L. rubida* leaves strap-shaped, often spotted; inflorescence 2½–10 in (6–25 cm), flowers pendulous, cylindrical, outer segments bright pink to ruby red, or pale yellow spotted red, apical swelling yellow-green or pink-red, inner segments tipped purple, marked white.

laciniate irregularly and finely cut, as if slashed.

lacrimiform, lachrymaeform tear-shaped.

Lactuca (from Latin *lac*, milk). Compositae. Cosmopolitan, esp. N Temperate. LETTUCE. About 100 species of annual or perennial plants with milky sap. Stems usually solitary, erect, branched. Leaves alternate, often prickly. Capitulate flower heads few to many, ligulate, yellow or blue, rarely cream. Fruit is a flattened, beaked, usually ribbed, cypsela. Of special garden interest is *L. sativa* (ICEBERG, ROMAINE, BOSTON, BIBB), grown for the succulent leaves of its many forms. See *lettuce*.

lacuna a cavity or depression, especially an air hole in plant tissue.

lacunose pitted with many deep depressions or holes.

ladybugs (Coleoptera: Coccinellidae) the common species are ⅛–¼ in- (3–7 mm-) long beetles with oval or

Adult lacewing

L

rounded bodies and bright coloration. Most adults and larvae feed principally on aphids, scale insects, mealybugs, thrips or mites, but some, such as the 22-spot and 16-spot ladybugs, feed on fungal spores, especially those of powdery mildews. Typically, the adults hibernate in sheltered situations beneath leaves, loose bark or in buildings, and in spring the females deposit clusters of pale yellow spindle-shaped eggs, usually on leaves. The resulting larvae, mostly leaden gray or gray-blue spotted with yellow orange or white, wander at random in search of prey. When fully fed, after about three weeks, they attach themselves to a leaf or other support to change into pupae. Adult ladybugs appear about ten days later.

Common species include the TWO-SPOT (*Adalia bipunctata*), which usually has red wing cases with two black spots but very variable; the red and black SEVEN-SPOT (*Coccinella septempunctata*); the red and black TEN-SPOT (*Adalia decempunctata*), which is very variable in color; and the 14-spot (*Propylea 14-punctata*) and 22-spot (*Psyllobora 22-punctata*), which are both yellow with black spots. Common North American species include the CONVERGENT LADYBUG (*Hippodamia convergens*) and the SINUATE LADYBUG (*H. sinuata*), as well as *Adalia bipunctata*.

These and many other ladybugs provide natural methods of controlling various pests and some feature in biological control programs, including the VEDALIA LADYBUG (*Rodolia cardinalis*), which was introduced from Australia at the end of the last century to control the fluted scale insect (*Icerya purchasi*) in California and Florida. *Cryptolaemus montrouzieri*, also from Australia, has been used to control mealybugs (*Pseudococcus* species) under glass in temperate countries, and *Coccinella septempunctata* is released annually in Maine, US, to control aphids on potatoes.

A small number of ladybugs are plant feeders. These include the MEXICAN BEAN BEETLE (*Epilachna varivestis*), which is up to ³/₈ in (8 mm) long, has yellow, coppery or bronze wing cases with 16 black spots, and is principally a pest of soy beans in North America;

and the SQUASH BEETLE (*E. borealis*), which mainly infests squash and pumpkins. Both adults and larvae skeletonize the leaves of plants; however, they can be controlled by appropriate contact insecticides.

Laelia (for Laelia, one of the vestal virgins). Orchidaceae. C and S America, from West Indies south to Brazil. About 70 species, evergreen epiphytic or lithophytic herbs with globose to pear- or spindle-shaped pseudobulbs and leathery, ovate to linear leaves. The flowers basically resemble those of *Cattleya*, but range widely in size and shape from the small and spidery to the large and lacy. Cultivate as for *Cattleya*.

L. anceps Mexico, Honduras; flowers 3–6, fragrant, 3–4 in (8–10 cm) in diameter, rose-lilac or magenta, lip deep purple tinged with pink and yellow in the throat, sometimes wholly white; *L. autumnalis* Mexico; flower 3–6, scented, to 4 in (10 cm) in diameter, rose-purple, lip rose-white with purple apex and yellow center; *L. gouldiana* is a stouter plant with broader, solid magenta blooms, possibly a cross between *L. anceps* and *L. autumnalis*; *L. cinnabarina* Brazil; flowers 5–15, about 2 in (5 cm) in diameter, deep orange-red, slender; *L. crispa* Brazil; flowers 4–7, to 4³/₄ in (12 cm) in diameter, white, lip usually mainly purple with some yellow marks; *L. flava* Brazil; flowers 3–10, canary yellow, about 2¹/₂ in (6 cm) in diameter; *L. harpophylla* Brazil; flowers 3–7, 2–3 in (5–8 cm) in diameter, vermilion, lip with a paler margin and yellow in center; *L. milleri* Brazil; flowers 2¹/₂ in (6 cm) in diameter, few, orange-red, tinged with yellow in throat; *L. pumila* Brazil; flowers solitary, to 4 in (10 cm) in diameter, flat, slightly drooping, rose-purple, rarely white, lip deep purple with yellow throat, sometimes edged and veined amethyst; *L. purpurata* Brazil; flowers 6–8 in (15–20 cm) in diameter, 3–7, tepals white tinged with pink, sometimes pure white, lip white at apex, purple toward base, yellow with purple veins in throat, rarely deep violet; *L. speciosa* (syn. *L. majalis*); Mexico; flowers

Ladybug larva

4³/₄–7 in (12–18 cm) in diameter, 1–2, tepals rose-lilac, rarely white, lip white spotted with deep lilac, margin pale lilac; *L. tenebrosa* Brazil; flowers about 6 in (16 cm) in diameter, 4, tepals copper-bronze, lip purple, darker in throat. There are many cultivars and grexes of *Laelia*, either slender or stout in habit and with large or small flowers in shades of pink, mauve, yellow, orange, red and white.

× **Laeliocattleya** (*Laelia* × *Cattleya*). Orchidaceae. A wide range of colorful hybrids. The plants are usually robust, upright, with one or two leaves at the apex of each pseudobulb. The inflorescence is terminal, with few to many flowers of various sizes, always brightly colored and conspicuous. Cultivate as for *Cattleya*.

laevigate appearing smoothly polished.

Lagarosiphon (from Greek *lagaros*, narrow, and *siphon*, tube, alluding to the female perianth). Hydrocharitaceae. Africa, introduced to Europe and New Zealand. CURLY WATER THYME. 9 species, perennial, aquatic herbs with submerged long, branching stems and linear to lanceolate, spiraling to opposite or whorled leaves. The genus is fully hardy, but also a good aquarium oxygenator. *L. major* South Africa, introduced to Europe and New Zealand; stem to ¹/₈ in (3 mm) in diameter; leaves ¹/₄–1 × ¹/₁₆–¹/₆ in (6.5–25 × 2–4.5 mm), thick, opaque.

lageniform flask-shaped.

Lagerstroemia (for Swedish merchant Magnus von Lagerstrom [1691–1759] of Göteborg, friend of Linnaeus). Lythraceae. Tropical Asia to Australia. 53 species, deciduous shrubs or trees, usually with peeling bark and leathery elliptic to obovate leaves. The flowers have six or more, crumpled and clawed, silken petals and many stamens; they are carried in summer in pyramidal to cylindric panicles. These are shrubs for warm subtropical climates or temperate regions with hot summers. They are frequently used in Mediterranean areas and in southern California and Florida for specimen,

L

hedge, screen and avenue plantings. They have the additional interest of muted fall colors and a smooth, fluted, and shredding bark. In colder areas (with winter temperatures down of about 10°F/−12°C), *L. indica* will succeed given the shelter of a warm south-facing wall. It will tolerate still harsher winters where hot, humid summers promote rapid new growth from bases cut back by hard frosts. *L. speciosa* is tender and requires a minimum temperature of 50°F (10°C).

Grow in well-drained soil in a sheltered, sunny spot. Unless pollarding or coppicing is to be carried out, prune annually in late winter only to remove congested older wood and to open up the plant center; tip back long shoots as required. *Lagerstroemia* does not transplant well and must be moved with a large root-ball in late spring. Overwinter container-grown specimens at a minimum temperature of 55°F (13°C) and water very sparingly. Propagate by semiripe cuttings rooted under mist or with bottom heat in summer; alternatively, increase by hardwood cuttings in winter or from seed sown in spring, although the flower color of seedlings is often inferior.

L. indica CRAPE MYRTLE, CREPE FLOWER; China, Indochina, Himalaya, Japan; tree or shrub to 20 ft (6 m) panicles to 8 in (20 cm), petals suborbicular, to ½ in (1 cm), pink, purple or white; includes numerous cultivars ranging from dwarf shrubs to trees some 33 ft (10 m) tall and varying widely in hardiness, bark quality and fall color; the flowers may be small or large, smooth-petaled or ruffled, and in tones of white, cream, pink, lavender, deep rose, pale red and darkest crimson; *L. speciosa* GIANT CREPE MYRTLE, PRIDE OF INDIA; tropical Asia; tree to 79 ft (24 m); panicles to 16 in (40 cm), petals suborbicular, to 1¼ × ¾ in (3 × 2 cm), purple or white.

Lagunaria (for Andres de Laguna [d. 1560], Spanish botanist.) Malvaceae. Australasia (Queensland, Norfolk Island, Lord Howe Island). 1 species, *L. patersonii* (NORFOLK ISLAND HIBISCUS, QUEENSLAND PYRAMID TREE, COW ITCH TREE), a columnar to pyramidal evergreen tree or shrub to 50 ft (15 m). Somewhat leathery and scurfy

beneath, the leaves are to 4 in (10 cm) long, ovate to broadly lanceolate and entire with a cuneate base and blunt apex. *Hibiscus*-like, pale pink to magenta flowers, to 2½ in (6 cm) in diameter, appear in the upper leaf axils in summer. Cultivate as for tender *Hibiscus*.

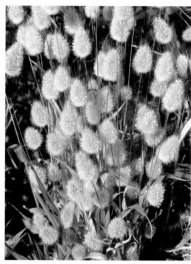

Lagurus ovatus
Native to maritime sands of the Mediterranean coast, this annual grass thrives in dry sites, bearing these attractive fluffy flower heads all summer.

Lagurus (from Greek *lagos*, hare, and *oura*, tail, referring to the fluffy panicles). Gramineae. Mediterranean. HARE'S TAIL. 1 species, *L. ovatus*, an annual grass to 24 in (60 cm). During spring and summer, it produces a spikelike, ovoid to oblong panicle, to 2½ × ¾ in (6 × 2 cm), densely and softly hairy and light green or tinged mauve. These may be the hare's-tail flowerheads that are used either fresh or dried in floral arrangements. Grow in light, sandy, freely draining soil in sun; cut or pull flower heads for drying before maturity. Seed may be sown either *in situ* in spring, or in pots in fall and overwintered in well-ventilated frost-free conditions for planting out in spring.

lambourde sometimes used to describe a fruit spur.

lamellate composed of one or more thin, flat scales or plates.

lamina see *blade*.

Lamium (Latin name used by Pliny). Labiatae. Mediterranean. DEADNETTLE. Some 50 species, perennial or annual herbs, with stoloniferous, creeping stems. Produced in spring and summer in whorls, the flowers are tubular, two-lipped and hooded. Useful, fully hardy groundcover, tolerant of a wide range of soil types, climates and light conditions. Generally, cultivars with pale foliage (e.g *L.* 'Cannon's Gold' and 'White Nancy') prefer shade, or, if grown in sun, a cool, moist root run. *L. orvala* is sometimes damaged by late frosts. Propagate by removal of rooted running stems of most species, by division of clumps.

L. galeobdolon (syn. *Galeobdolon argentatum*; *Lamiastrum variegatum*; *L. luteum*); YELLOW ARCH-ANGEL; Europe to W Asia; vigorous perennial to 24 in (60 cm), erect to widely creeping, occasionally stoloniferous; leaves toothed; flowers yellow, flecked brown; cultivars include: 'Florentinum', with large leaves, splashed silver, and, in winter, purple; 'Hermann's Pride', mat-forming, with narrow, toothed leaves, streaked and spotted silver; 'Silberteppich' (syn. 'Silver Carpet'), slow growing clump-forming, with silver leaves; 'Silver Angel', prostrate, fast-growing, with leaves marked silver; and 'Variegatum', with smaller, oval leaves, mid-green marked silver; *L. maculatum* Europe and N Africa to W Asia; perennial to 32 in (80 cm), ascending to trailing, stoloniferous, pubescent; leaves toothed white-mottled or -striped; flowers pink to red or purple, rarely white; cultivars include: 'Album', with leaves blotched silver and white flowers; 'Aureum' ('Golden Nuggetts'), with gold leaves with a white center, and pink flowers; 'Beacon Silver', habit low, with silver leaves, with a thin green edge, and pink flowers; 'Cannon's Gold', with pure gold leaves and purple flowers; 'Pink Pewter', with leaves tinted silver and rich pink flowers; 'Sterling Silver', with pure silver leaves and purple flowers; and 'White Nancy', with silver leaves with a thin green edge, and white flowers; *L. orvala* GIANT DEAD NETTLE; S C Europe; perennial to 40 in (100 cm), erect to spreading; flowers large, purple-pink with a mottled lip and throat; 'Album': flowers white.

L

L

Lammas growth a term usually applied to fruit trees to describe the growth of shoots occurring in late summer i.e., around Lammas, the first day of August.

Lampranthus (from Greek *lampros*, bright, brilliant, and *anthos*, flower, referring to the brilliant flowers). Aizoaceae. South Africa. 200 species, subshrubs with succulent, terete or 3-angled leaves and bright, daisylike flowers. Most make excellent summer bedding or container plants in temperate regions; a few are frost hardy to 30°F (–1°C) or 28°F (–2°C) and thus can be grown outside year-round in sheltered favorable sites in temperate regions. They require a position in full sun and low-fertility, well-drained soil. Plant as soon as frosts are over and leave outside until the first fall frosts; the plants should then be dug up and potted, or cuttings taken and kept frost-free over the winter. Under glass, grow in full sun with low humidity and a minimum temperature of 45°F (7°C); plant in a loam-based medium rich in grit and sand. Water sparingly in summer, scarcely at all in winter.

L. aurantiacus leaves ¾–1¼ in (2–3 cm), gray-pruinose; flowers orange; *L. haworthii* (leaves light green, densely light gray-pruinose; flowers light purple; *L. multiradiatus* (syn. *L. roseus*); leaves 1–1¼ in (2.5–3 cm), green to gray-green, glaucous with translucent dots; flowers pale pink to rose-red; *L. spectabilis* leaves flushed red; flowers purple-red to magenta.

Salix lanata
The woolly willow, *S. lanata*, takes its species and common names from the silvery gray wool that covers both shoots and leaves.

lanate, lanose woolly, possessing long, densely matted and curling hairs.

lanceolate lance-shaped; 3–6 times as long as broad, and with the broadest point below the middle; tapering to a spearlike apex.

land drain purpose-made drainpipes of earthenware or plastic, usually 3 in (7.5 cm) in diameter and 18 in (45 cm) long, although plastic types often come in longer lengths. Land drains are used to improve water drainage from soil. See *drainage*.

landscape gardening the art of laying out an estate to blend with the surrounding countryside, dating from the early 18th century when there was a move against formality and enclosure in gardening. Landscape gardening declined in the 19th century as the number of privately owned large properties contracted but the principles of landscaping have persisted. The term landscape gardening is now commonly used to cover garden design, construction and maintenance on a small scale and of variable standards.

lanuginose as lanate, but with the hairs shorter; somewhat woolly or cottony.

Lantana (from the superficial similarity to *Viburnum lantana*). Verbenaceae. Tropical Americas and Africa, a widespread weed elsewhere in the tropics and subtropics. SHRUB VERBENA. Some 150 species, aromatic shrubs, subshrubs and perennial herbs with small, salverform, 4–5-lobed flowers in compact terminal heads in spring and summer. Suitable for hedging and specimen plantings in frost-free zones, and for bedding out or for a greenhouse or conservatory in cool temperate climates. *L. camara* is easily trained as a standard. The trailing *L. montevidensis* is suited to groundcover in the conservatory border or to hanging baskets. Grow in full sun. Water plentifully when in full growth; keep just moist in winter with a minimum temperature of 50°F (10°C). Propagate by seed in spring or by semiripe cuttings in summer.

L. camara (tropical America, widespread weed in tropics and subtropics; shrub to 6½ ft (2 m); flowers yellow to orange or red often with a brighter eye;

many cultivars ranging in habit from dwarf to tall, with flowers mostly bicolors, in shades ranging from white through to yellow and salmon to red; *L. montevidensis* (syn. *L. sellowiana*; S America; herb or shrub to 3¼ ft (1 m), trailing or scandent; flowers rose-lilac to violet).

Lapageria (for Joséphine Tascher de la Pagérie [1763–1814], wife of Napoleon Bonaparte and an enthusiastic patron of gardening). Liliaceae (Philesiaceae). Chile. CHILEAN BELL-FLOWER, CHILE BELLS, COPIHUE. 1 species, *L. rosea*, an evergreen climber to 33 ft (10 m) with wiry stems clothed with sharp scalelike bracts. The leathery leaves are ovate or ovate to lanceolate and glossy dark green. Campanulate flowers hang from the axils of upper leaves in summer. They consist of six waxy tepals, 2½–3½ in (6–9 cm) long, oblong to elliptic and luminous rose to pale salmon, often stained, spotted or streaked deeper crimson. Given the protection of a partially shaded and sheltered wall, *L. rosea* will grow outside where temperatures seldom fall below 23°F (–5°C); otherwise, it makes a fine specimen for the borders of the cold greenhouse or conservatory. Grow *Lapageria* in cool, well-drained but moist soil, humus-rich and nonalkaline, in light shade or where direct sunlight penetrates for short periods only. Propagate by layering during spring or fall, alternatively by seed, pre-soaked for about 48 hours before sowing.

Lardizabala (for Miguel de Lardizabel y Uribe, 18th-century Spanish naturalist). Lardizabalaceae. Chile. 2 species, evergreen climbers with compound leaves and, in winter, slender spikes of small, curiously colored flowers followed by attractive berries. Hardy to 14°F (–10°C); plant in a shady protected site in well-drained soil rich in decayed matter. Propagate by seed in spring or by stem cuttings in spring or fall. *L. funaria* Chile; twining to 13 ft (4 m); leave ternate to biternate, dark green, leaflets 2–4 in (5–10 cm), ovate; male inflorescence to 4 in (10 cm), flowers green edged dark brown-purple; fruit 2½ in (6 cm), dark purple.

Larix (Classical Latin name). Pinaceae. Northern Hemisphere. LARCH. Some 14 species, deciduous, coniferous trees. The crown is usually conic in young trees, becoming domed or irregular with age. The branches are horizontal or somewhat drooping. Soft, needlelike leaves are arranged in loose spirals on long shoots and in dense, whorl-like spirals on short shoots.

In cool temperate maritime climates, only two species, *L. decidua* and *L. kaempferi* (and *L.* × *marschlinsii*, the hybrid between them), are wholly successful, making healthy trees, 80–165 ft (25–50 m) high, in most areas. All tolerate acidic and infertile soil; *L. decidua* will also grow in chalk. Dead branches should be removed since they are very brittle and can be dangerous. *L. decidua* is the best choice for specimen planting, although *L.* × *marschlinsii* may be preferred in less fertile sites for more rapid growth. They and *L. kaempferi* make fine shelterbelts, summer screening and copse groups, and are covered in small purple-pink cones in early spring, leafing out bright green, then turning gold to russet in fall. Pests common in Europe and North America include the larch sawfly, with defoliating olive-green larvae up to 1 in (25 mm) long, and larch adelgids made conspicuous by a covering of white woolly wax. Caterpillars of the larch casebearer make holes and mines in the foliage and cover themselves with a cigar-shaped case made from pieces of needles. A needle cast disease can cause serious damage to young larch trees in the nursery. The needles turn brown from the tips and fall off prematurely.

L. decidua EUROPEAN LARCH; Alps, Carpathians; to 165 ft (50 m); crown slender, conic, branches horizontal, branchlets drooping; leaves ³⁄₄–1¹⁄₂ (–2¹⁄₂) in (2–4 (–6.5) cm), soft, flat or slightly keeled beneath, pale green; cones ⅝ to 2 in (1.5 to 5 cm), conic to cylindric, brown, scales 40–50, straight or incurved, sometimes short-hairy on outer surface; about 20 cultivars are

described, mostly varying in habit, from dwarf ('Compacta', 'Corley', 'Repens'), erect ('Fastigiata'), pendulous ('Pendula', 'Viminalis') to twisted ('Cervicornis', 'Tortuosa') and sparsely branched ('Virgata'); in 'Alba', the immature cones are pale green, almost white; subsp. *polonica*: POLISH LARCH, W Poland and Ukraine, to 100 ft (30 m), with a very slender crown, drooping branchlets, and smaller, blunter cones, ¹⁄₂–1¹⁄₈ in (1–2.8 cm), with concave scales; *L. kaempferi* JAPANESE LARCH; Japan; to 150 ft (45 m); crown broadly conic, branches and shoots horizontal or slightly ascending; leaves ³⁄₄–1¹⁄₂ in (2–3.5 cm), slightly keeled beneath, gray-green, with stomatal bands throughout; cones 2–3, rarely 1¹⁄₂ in (4 cm), ovoid, scales truncate to emarginate, apex reflexed; about 20 cultivars are described, mainly varying in habit, and mostly dwarf ('Blue Dwarf', 'Nana', 'Varley', 'Wehlen') or with pendulous branchlets ('Georgengarten', 'Inversa', 'Pendula'), or both ('Hanan'); in 'Blue Haze' the leaves are brightly glaucous, likewise the semi-fastigiate 'Pyramidalis Argentea'; *L. laricina* TAMARACK, AMERICAN LARCH; northern N America; to 66–100 ft (20–30 m); crown conic, branches horizontal, branchlets drooping; leaves ³⁄₄–1¹⁄₄ in (2–3 cm), keeled, pale green with 2 stomatal bands beneath; cones ovoid, ¹⁄₂–1 in (12–24 mm), green or purple, becoming straw-brown, scales 15–20, nearly circular, margins slightly incurved; includes 'Arethusa Bog', dwarf, with short, narrow shoots and arching branches, 'Aurea', with leaves gold when young, later light green, and 'Glauca', with metallic blue leaves.

L. × *marschlinsii* (*L. decidua* × *L. kaempferi*); DUNKELD LARCH, HYBRID LARCH; vigorous; similar to *L. decidua* but with shoots and leaves faintly glaucous; cones conic, scale tips slightly reflexed; *L. occidentalis* WESTERN LARCH; western N America; to 165 ft (50 m); branches horizontal; leaves 1–2 in

(2.5–5 cm), keeled beneath, slightly convex above, acute, blue-green to gray-green, with 2 stomatal bands beneath; cones 1–1³⁄₄ (2.5–4.5 cm) × ¹⁄₂ in (1 cm) ovoid, scales rounded, to ¹⁄₂ in (12 mm) broad, reflexed on opening, to 1 in (2.5 cm) broad; *L.* × *pendula* (*L. decidua* × *L. laricina*); WEEPING LARCH; to 100 ft (30 m); branchlets pendent; leaves similar to *L. decidua* but blunter; cones ³⁄₄–1¹⁄₄ in (2–3.3 cm), ovoid, scales 20–30, exterior base downy; includes 'Contorta', with shoots twisted when young, and 'Repens', with horizontally creeping branches; *L. sibirica* (syn. *L. russica*); SIBERIAN LARCH; Russia; to 100 ft (30 m); crown narrowly conic; branches horizontal to upswept; leaves 1–1¹⁄₂ in (2.5–4 cm), clustered, very narrow, soft, bright green above, with 2 stomatal bands beneath and scattered stomata above; cones 1–1¹⁄₂ in (2.5–3.5 cm), rarely 1¹⁄₂ in (4 cm), scales thick, pubescent, margins incurved; includes the columnar and compact 'Fastigiata', 'Glauca', with glaucous needles, 'Longifolia', with longer needles, 'Pendula', with weeping branches, and the more vigorous 'Robusta'.

larva the immature stage in advanced insects, which does not resemble the adult form and which needs to pass through a chrysalis or pupal stage, undergoing complete metamorphosis, before developing into an adult. Larvae vary in form and habits. See *caterpillars, grubs, maggots.*

latent bud a bud that remains inactive and concealed until stimulated into growth by the removal of adjacent shoots through natural damage or pruning. It may also be referred to as dormant.

lateral on a tree or shrub, a side shoot or branch as distinct from a leader. On woody fruit plants, laterals bear fruit buds, and may be described as one-year-old or maiden laterals, or two- or three-year-old laterals. The identification and understanding of types of laterals is important to successful pruning.

latex a milky fluid or sap, usually colorless, white or pale yellow, found in plants such as *Asclepias* and *Euphorbia*.

needles drop in winter

cones age from green to tan

Larix laricina

lath house a structure clad with spaced wooden or plastic laths or trelliswork to provide plants with shelter from strong sunlight, wind and light frost. Probably originating in the southern US, lath houses are used for the acclimatization of nursery stock and by some growers of bonsai and orchids.

lath light a frame covered by laths, having the same uses as a lath house.

Lathraea (from Greek *lathraios*, hidden.) Scrophulariaceae. Temperate Europe, Asia. 7 species of parasitic, rarely saprophytic, herbs lacking chlorophyll. Leaves in 4 rows on largely subterranean rhizomes, ivory to mauve. Inflorescence a racemelike extension of the stem, flowers axillary among scales; corolla 2-lipped, upper lip hooded, lower lip entire or 3-lobed; calyx erect, campanulate, 4-lobed. Summer. Fruit a bi-valved capsule. *L. squamaria* PURPLE TOOTHWORT. Most commonly grown. Perennial, white or pale yellow rhizomes below ground, pale lilac above. Stems to 12 in (30 cm), erect, appearing above ground to flower. Raceme spikelike; pedicels short; bracts broadly ovate; calyx glabrous, to ¹/₂ in (1 cm); corolla ⁵/₈–³/₄ in (15–20 mm), white tinted rose or lilac. Parasitic especially on *Alnus, Corylus* and *Fagus*. Best naturalized in damp, dark woodland; *L. clandestina* Perennial stems partly or completely subterranean, freely branching to form pale yellow clumps. Scale leaves alternate or opposite: Raceme 4–8 flowered, subterranean except tip and flowers; pedicels to 1¹/₄ in (3 cm); calyx ⁵/₈–³/₄ in (16–20 mm), glabrous, pale lilac. Corolla to 2 in (5 cm), amethyst, lower lip shorter than upper. Parasitic on Salicaceae, flourishing in open sites provided never dry. Propagate by seed mixed with surface soil containing fibrous roots of host plant, or by the transplantation of clumps.

lath screen a portable wooden unit, usually 10 ft (3 m) long and 3¹/₄ ft (1 m) high, clad with 1 in (2.5 cm)-wide laths, nailed vertically and spaced 1 in (2.5 cm) apart; plastic variants are available. It is used for wind protection around low-growing plants.

Lathyrus (name used by Theophrastus, from the Ancient Greek name for the pea or legume, combining *la-*, very, and *thoures*, a stimulant: the seeds were said to have excitant or irritant properties.) Leguminosae. Eurasia, N America, mountains of E Africa and temperate S America. VETCHLING, WILD PEA. 110+ species, annual or perennial herbs, often climbing by leaf tendrils, with pinnate leaves and racemes of showy pealike flowers.

The species described below have handsome flowers, are often fragrant and most will tolerate temperatures below 5°F (–15°C). Those climbing by means of tendrils are useful for clothing trellis and pergola or for trailing unsupported over walls, slopes and embankments. *L. nervosus*, with periwinkle blue flowers, may be grown outdoors where winter temperatures do not fall much below zero for prolonged periods; it thrives best in zones with cool moist summers. The nonclimbing, clump-forming *L. vernus* is especially delightful in late winter when its light bunches of emerging stems, packed with rose, blue and mauve blooms, bring relief to the woodland garden and the foreground of herbaceous borders. *L. sylvestris* is eminently suited to wild gardens and native plant collections. *L. latifolius*, the everlasting sweet pea, is a favorite plant for cottage gardens. *L. odoratus* is the SWEET PEA (q.v.).

Grow in moderately fertile, well-drained soil in sun, or light dappled shade. Provide appropriate support (i.e., stakes, trellis or host-shrubs for climbers; for semiscandent or erect perennials, a few birch twigs pushed into the ground around the crowns should suffice). Dead-head throughout the season and cut back perennials in fall to ground level. Feed yearly in very poor soil.

keeled flowers

leaves terminate in tendrils

Propagate from presoaked seed sown under glass in early spring or *in situ* in spring; alternatively, increase perennials by division in early spring. This last method is most successful with *L. vernus* and the nonclimbing species; many of the climbing perennials do not transplant well and even seed-grown specimens are best planted out when young and then left undisturbed. See also *Sweet pea*.

L. grandiflorus EVERLASTING PEA, TWO-FLOWERED PEA; S Italy, Sicily, S Balkans; perennial climbing to 6¹/₂ ft (2 m); stems angled; leaves terminating in a 3-branched tendril, leaflets to 2 in (5 cm), 1 pair (rarely 3 pairs), ovate; flowers to 1¹/₄ in (3 cm), standard violet, keel pink, wings mauve; *L. latifolius* BROAD-LEAVED EVERLASTING PEA, PERENNIAL PEA; C and S Europe, naturalized N America; perennial climbing to 10 ft (3 m); stem winged; leaves terminating in a 3-branched tendril, leaflets to 6 in (15 cm), 1 pair, linear to elliptic, somewhat blue-green; flowers to 1¹/₄ in (3 cm) in diameter, magenta-purple, pink, or white; 'Albus': white; 'Blushing Bride': white flushed pink; 'Pink Beauty': dark-purple and red; 'Red Pearl': carmine red; 'Rosa Perle': 'Pink Pearl', vigorous, pink, long-lasting; 'Splendens': deep-pink flowers; *L. nervosus* BLUE PEA; S America; perennial climbing to 24 in (60 cm); leaves terminating in a 3-branched tendril, leaflets to 1¹/₂ in (4 cm), 1 pair, ovate to oblong; flowers to ³/₄ in (2.2 cm) indigo; *L. odoratus* SWEET PEA; Crete, Italy, Sicily; annual climbing to 6¹/₂ ft (2 m); leaflets to 2¹/₂ in (6 cm), 1 pair, oval to oblong; flowers to 1¹/₂ in (3.5 cm), typically purple; now highly developed resulting in a vast range of cultivars with flowers clustered or on long racemes, large or small, sometimes ruffled or 'double', sweetly to heavily scented, in shades of red, rose, mauve, purple, purple-black, white, opal, blue, lilac, peach, cream, pale yellow and variously mottled or veined; *L. rotundifolius* PERSIAN EVERLASTING PEA; E Europe, W Asia; perennial climbing to 3¹/₄ ft (1 m), stem angular; leaves

Lathyrus japonicus

terminating in a 3-branched tendril, leaflets to 2½ in (6 cm), 1 pair, ovate to orbicular; flowers to ¾ in (2 cm), deep pink; *L. sylvestris* FLAT PEA, NARROW-LEAVED EVERLASTING PEA; Europe; perennial climbing to 6½ ft (2 m); stem angular, winged; leaves with a branched tendril, leaflets to 6 in (15 cm), 1 pair, linear to lanceolate; flowers to ¾ in (2 cm), purple-pink mottled purple and green; 'Wagneri': deep red; *L. vernus* SPRING VETCH; Europe except extreme N; bushy, nonclimbing perennial to 24 in (60 cm), usually shorter; leaves terminating in a point, not a tendril, leaflets 1¼–4 in (3–10 cm), in 2–4 pairs, oval to lanceolate, acuminate, dark green; flowers ½–¾ in (1–2 cm), pink to red-violet turning green-blue; includes 'Albiflorus', with blue-white flowers, 'Alboroseus', with rose-white flowers, and 'Roseus' with rose to lavender blue flowers; also included here are very graceful forms with narrow leaflets and lilac to opal blue flowers, these may belong to other, lesser-known species.

lattice another word for trelliswork; often referring to that made of metal.

Laurelia (from Spanish *laurel*, local name for *L. sempervirens*). Monimiaceae. New Zealand, Chile, Peru. 2 species, evergreen, aromatic trees and shrubs with leathery, dark green leaves and inconspicuous flowers in panicles or racemes in summer. Hardy to about 23°F (–5°C) but susceptible to cold winds, the following species needs a warm sheltered position in zones at the limits of its hardiness. Grow in sun or part shade in moderately fertile soil that does not dry out in summer. Propagate by seed, by semiripe cuttings in a closed case, or by layering. *L. sempervirens* (syn. *L. serrata*); CHILEAN LAUREL; Chile, Peru; to 100 ft (30 m); leaves 2½–3½ in (6–9 cm), elliptic to ovate, serrate, glossy green.

Laurus (Latin name for these plants). Lauraceae. S Europe, Canary Islands, Azores. 2 species, aromatic evergreen trees or shrubs with tough, ovate to elliptic or oblong to lanceolate leaves and small, 4-parted, white to creamy buff flowers in axillary clusters. *L. nobilis* is widely grown for its foliage both as an ornamental and culinary herb. Tolerant of clipping, it is used for screening and hedging and for tubs and large pots, trained as a standard or pyramid. Given perfect drainage and a warm, sheltered site it will withstand occasional lows to 5°F (–15°C). *L. azorica* has similar requirements but prefers a warm wall and responds badly to pruning and shearing. Grow in a moisture-retentive but well-drained fertile soil in full sun. In containers, use a high-fertility loam-based mix and liquid feed semiweekly when in full growth. Trim formal shapes in summer, using pruners rather than shears to avoid unsightly damage to the foliage. Propagate by semiripe cuttings in summer or by basal hardwood cuttings of the previous season's growth in mid- to late winter; root in a closed case with bottom heat.

L. azorica CANARY LAUREL; Canary Islands, Azores; tree to 33 ft (10 m); young branchlets downy; leaves 2–4¾ in (5–12 cm), broadly lanceolate to elliptic, dark green, glabrous above, paler and pubescent, especially on midrib beneath; *L. nobilis* TRUE LAUREL, BAY LAUREL, SWEET BAY, BAY TREE; Mediterranean; small tree or shrub 10–16 ft (3–5 m); young branchlets glabrous; leaves 2–4 in (5–10 cm), narrowly elliptic to oblong to ovate, often undulate, dark green, glabrous beneath; includes 'Aurea', with leaves tinged yellow, f. *angustifolia* (syn. 'Salicifolia'), with narrow leaves, and 'Crispa' (syn. 'Undulata'), with wavy leaf margins.

Lavandula (from Latin *lavo*, I wash, referring to lavender water, made from oil of lavender). Labiatae. Atlantic Islands, Mediterranean, N tropical Africa, W Asia, Arabia, India. LAVENDER. 28 species, aromatic, evergreen shrubs and subshrubs with linear to oblong, entire to toothed or pinnate leaves. Small, shortly tubular and 2-lipped flowers crowd the upper portions of long-stalked spikes during summer. Aromatic shrubs grown for ornament and perfume. A few (*L. angustifolia* and cultivars), are frost-tolerant to 14°F (–10°C). Others (*L. stoechas* and *L. dentata*), are hardy to at least 23°F (–5°C). These slightly tender species are nonetheless worth attempting in slightly colder areas in sheltered, sunny sites in well-drained soil. Trim back after flowering. Propagate from seed sown under glass during spring, from cuttings of new growth in early summer, or from semiripe cuttings put into a cold frame in late summer.

L. angustifolia (syn. *L. spica*); ENGLISH LAVENDER; Mediterranean; shrub, 3¼–6½ ft (1–2 m); leaves ¾–2½ in (2–6 cm), entire, lanceolate, oblong or linear, revolute, tomentose, gray when young, green with age; spike ¾–3 in (2–8 cm), flowers dark purple or blue; 'Alba': flowers white; 'Rosea': flowers pink; 'Atropurpurea': flowers very dark purple; 'Dutch White': tall, with profuse white flowers in small heads; 'Hidcote': to 12 in (30 cm), dense, with lanceolate, gray leaves, lilac flowers, deep purple calyx in dense spikes; 'Hidcote Giant': very tall, with deep purple flowers; 'Hidcote Pink': as 'Hidcote' but with pale pink flowers; 'Loddon Pink': to 18 in (45 cm), with soft pink flowers; 'Munstead': to 18 in (45 cm), with small leaves, large blue-lilac flowers; 'Nana Alba': dwarf, white-flowered; Old English Group: to 20 in (50 cm), with leaves to 2¾ in (7 cm), branching flowering spikes, to 42 in (115 cm), and pale lavender to violet flowers; 'Vera': DUTCH LAVENDER, tall, robust, with rather broad gray leaves and lavender flowers; *L. dentata* Spain, N Africa; shrub to 3¼ ft (1 m); leaves ⅝–1¼ in (1.5–3 cm), oblong, linear or lanceolate, wavy-toothed to pinnatifid, gray-tomentose; spikes 1–2 in (2.5–5 cm), bracts usually tinged purple, apical bracts sometimes in a coma, flowers powder-blue to dark purple; var. *candicans*: with most parts white-tomentose; 'Silver Form': leaves soft, silver, flowers large, blue; *L. lanata* (S Spain; shrub to 3¼ ft (1 m), white-woolly throughout; leaves 1¼–2 in (3–5 cm), linear to spathulate or oblong, scarcely revolute; spike 1½–4 in (4–10 cm), flowers lilac to deep indigo; *L. stoechas* FRENCH LAVENDER; Mediterranean region; shrub 12–39 in (30–100 cm); leaves ½–1½ in (1–4 cm), linear to oblong or lanceolate, entire, usually gray-tomentose; spike ¾–1¼ in (2–3 cm), sterile bracts along spike or in a coma, ½–2 in (1–5 cm), oblong-obovate, erect, petal-like, red-purple, rarely white, flowers purple, white or pale pink; 'Alba': flowers white; subsp. *pedunculata*: inflorescences long-stalked with rich mauve sterile bracts tinged red, rarely white, long and erect, and forming a showy coma; 'James Compton': flowers deep purple in a spike with large, pale purple bracts.

Lavatera (for J. R. Lavater, 16th-century physician and naturalist in Zurich). Malvaceae. Macaronesia, Mediterranean to NW Himalaya, C Asia, E Siberia, Australia, California and Baja California. TREE MALLOW. 25 species, annual, biennial and perennial herbs or softwooded shrubs, usually downy to thickly hairy, with palmately angled or lobed leaves, and, in summer, broadly dish- or funnel-shaped flowers composed of five obovate to cordate petals. The following species are hardy to −10°F (−23°C). Grow all species in full sun in light, well-drained, moderately fertile soil. Give shrubby perennials protection from cold drying winds and a winter mulch. *L. oblongifolia* needs a warm, sheltered site, and a rather dry, gritty soil. Propagate annuals and biennials by seed sown *in situ*: annuals in spring, biennials in late summer. Increase perennials by cuttings of basal shoots in spring, and shrubs and perennials also by softwood cuttings in spring and early summer.

L. arborea TREE MALLOW; Europe, Mediterranean, Macaronesia, naturalized California and Baja California; treelike biennial or perennial to 10 ft (3 m); leaves 3–7 in (8–18 cm), orbicular-cordate, 5-, 7- or 9-lobed, pilose, crenate; flowers with petals ⅝–1 in (1.5–2.5 cm), lilac or purple-red, with darker veins at the base; includes 'Ile d'Hyéres', to 11½ ft (3.5 m), with large, palmate leaves and small, magenta flowers, in leaf axils, in early summer, and 'Variegata', of vigorous habit, with large, marbled white leaves; *L. assurgentiflora* MALVA ROSA; SW US; deciduous shrub to 20 ft (6 m); leaves 3–6 in (8–15 cm), 5- or 7-lobed, lobes triangular, coarsely toothed, white-pubescent; flowers with petals 1½ in (4 cm), red-purple, with darker veins; *L. cachemiriana* Kashmir; annual or short-lived perennial herb to 8 ft (2.5 m), downy; leaves downy beneath, cordate-orbicular, crenate, 3- or 5-lobed; flowers with petals to 1½ in (4 cm), pink, deeply bifid; *L. oblongifolia* Spain; erect, evergreen shrub to 5 ft (1.5 m), branches twiggy, covered in tawny hairs; leaves ovate to lanceolate, silky white-hairy; flowers small, sometimes not opening, rose pink with mauve markings; *L. thuringiaca* (syn. *L. olbia* of gardens); TREE LAVATERA; C and SE Europe; perennial herb, subshrub or shrub to 6 ft (1.8 m), softly gray-tomentose; leaves to 3½ in (9 cm), cordate to rounded, 3- or 5-lobed; flowers with petals ⅝–1¾ in (1.5–4.5 cm), purple-pink; × *clementii* 'Barnsley': to 6½ ft (2 m), with lobed leaves and flowers opening white with red eye, fading to pale pink with a rose eye; 'Candy Floss': with leaves softly tinted gray and bright pink flowers, with white stamens; 'Rosea': to 6½ ft (2 m), with downy leaves, tinted gray, and pale rose-mauve flowers; *L. trimestris* Mediterranean; annual herb to 4 ft (1.2 m), sparsely hairy; leaves 1¼–2½ in (3–6 cm), rounded to cordate, slightly 3-, 5- or 7-lobed; flowers with petals 1–1¾ in (2.5–4.5 cm), white, rose, pink or red; 'Loveliness': to 4 ft (1.2 m), with large, trumpet-shaped flowers, of a striking deep rose; 'Mont Blanc': dwarf and compact with dark green leaves and pure white flowers; 'Pink Beauty': dwarf and bushy habit, to 24 in (60 cm), with large, delicate pale pink flowers with violet veins and eye; 'Silver Cup': dwarf and bushy habit, to 24 in (60 cm), with large, glowing pink flowers, to 4¾ in (12 cm) in diameter; 'Splendens': flowers large, white or red.

lawn an area densely covered with grass or certain other low-growing plants, and usually closely mown. As a meadow spangled with flowers, it was first widely known in medieval Europe, although the word 'lawn' is not recorded until 1674, and its contemporary meaning, as a closely mown cover, not until 1733.

Lawns serve as decorative features in themselves, or to enhance plantings and other facets of garden design. They provide a stable surface for access and recreation.

Suitable species Turfgrasses may be divided into two main groups according to their temperature tolerance.

COOL-SEASON TURFGRASSES Cool-season or temperate grass species with a temperature optimum of 59–75°F (15–24°C) are employed for lawns in parts of North America, Britain, northern Europe, and other temperate regions. Most commonly used are FESCUES (*Festuca rubra* subsp. *rubra* and *F. rubra* subsp. *commutata*), BENTS (*Agrostis tenuis*, *A. castellana*, *A. stolonifera*), meadow grasses, which are also known as BLUE GRASSES (*Poa pratensis*, *P. trivialis*, *P. nemoralis*), and PERENNIAL RYEGRASS (*Lolium perenne*. ANNUAL MEADOWGRASS (*Poa annua*) is a widely found invasive weed-grass of temperate lawns and may often make up the greatest proportion of a lawn, although it is never intentionally sown.

These grasses are usually sown as mixtures, although in temperate areas of the US smooth-stalked meadow-grass or KENTUCKY BLUEGRASS (*Poa pratensis*) and its cultivars is sometimes sown as a single species.

Lavatera thuringiaca 'Rosea' (left) and L. trimestris 'Loveliness' (right)
Members of the genus *Lavatera*, from the tall, shrubby "tree mallows" (left) to the vigorous annuals (right) share similar, rather coarse foliage and these showy trumpet-shaped blooms.

SOWING LAWN SEED BY HAND

1 Use a simple, movable system—here, twine, pegs and canes—for marking the site out into equal areas. Weigh out enough seed for a single area, and scatter evenly.

2 After sowing, lightly rake over the surface. Netting or scaring devices may be required to protect the seed from birds. In dry conditions, water regularly.

For the finest lawns, a mixture of bents and fescues is used. BROWNTOP and HIGHLAND BENT (*Agrostis tenuis* and *A.castellana*) are mixed with CHEWINGS FESCUE and slender CREEPING RED FESCUE (*Festuca rubra* subsp. *commutata* and *F.r* subsp. *litoralis*) in a ratio of 20–30% bent to 70–80% fescue by weight.

In Britain, the major wear-resistant species is perennial ryegrass (*Lolium perenne*), usually mixed with red fescue, smooth-stalked meadowgrass/Kentucky bluegrass, and browntop or highland bent. Pure swards of smooth-stalked meadowgrass/Kentucky bluegrass (*Poa pratensis*) are extensively used in the Northeast, Midwest and other temperate regions of the US.

For lawns subjected to shade, WOOD MEADOWGRASS (*Poa nemoralis*) is often sown along with ROUGH-STALKED MEADOWGRASS (*Poa trivialis*). TURF TIMOTHY (*Phleum bertolonii*) may be used in place of perennial ryegrass in moist areas.

WARM-SEASON TURFGRASSES Warm-season species come from tropical and subtropical areas including Asia, South America, Africa and southern China, and these have a temperature optimum of 79–95°F (26.5–35°C). The major species used for lawns are BERMUDA GRASS (*Cynodon* species), *Zoysia* species and ST. AUGUSTINE GRASS (*Stenotaphrum secundatum*).

Bermuda grass forms a dense, uniform, high-quality turf which tolerates heavy wear. Three of the zoysia grasses are used for lawns: JAPANESE LAWN GRASS (*Zoysia japonica*), MANILA GRASS (*Z. matrella*) and MASCARENE GRASS (*Z.tenuifolia*). Zoysias are often used in warm humid regions and areas where the climate is subtropical only in the summer months; they form a fine if rather slow-growing turf. St. Augustine grass is by nature a coarse-textured, invasive species. Despite this, it is an acceptable species for general-purpose lawns which do not receive heavy wear. Other grass species for low-maintenance coarser lawns include CENTIPEDE GRASS (*Eremochloa ophiuroides*), CARPET GRASS (*Axonopus* species), and BAHIA GRASS (*Paspalum notatum*). Their coarse-textured leaves restrict their use to low-quality lawns.

Warm-season grasses are not usually mixed because they have a strong creeping habit and do not integrate well. They become dormant and lose their color at temperatures below 50°F (10°C).

OTHER LAWN PLANTS Broad-leaved species are sometimes used for special effect but they are unsuitable for lawns subjected to heavy wear. These include fragrant CHAMOMILE (*Chamaemelum nobile*), DICHONDRA (*Dichondra micrantha*), PENNYWORT (*Hydrocotyle novae-zealandiae*) and even various species of moss, as in some Japanese gardens. BRASS BUTTONS (*Cotula dioica*, *C.pulchella* and *C. maniototo*) makes a fine, feathery, close-knit surface of some durability. It will tolerate drought and damp and has been used for bowling greens. Historically, CLOVER (*Trifolium* species), MEDICK (*Medicago* species) and SAINFOIN (*Onobrychis* species) were used for lawns in Europe.

Site preparation The site of a lawn should be cleared of all perennial and annual weeds and, where necessary, improvements made to soil drainage.

A base dressing of fertilizer should be applied to the prepared surface. For most soils, a compound containing 10% nitrogen, 15% phosphate and 10% potash, applied at $3–4^1/_2$ oz/yd² (100–150 g/m²) and lightly raked into the soil surface, will be suitable.

For most grasses, satisfactory growth can be achieved at pH levels between 5.5 and 7.0. Fine fescues and bents have an optimum range of 5.5–6.5, while perennial ryegrass, the meadow grasses and many of the warm-season grasses grow better at pH levels between 6.0 and 7.0.

Lawn establishment Lawns can be established from seed, turf (sod in the North America), or by vegetative propagation. Most cool-season lawns are produced from seed or turf, while those using warm-season species are generally produced by vegetative means.

SEED Establishing a lawn from seed is by far the cheapest method and enables the gardener to sow specific grass species and cultivars; however, seed takes much longer to establish than turf. It is only possible to sow seed during warm moist periods unless irrigation is available. Ideally, cool-season species are best sown in late summer or early fall, with spring the second-best option. Grass seed should be sown at a rate of $^3/_4–^7/_8$ oz/yd² (25–30 g/m²) for most seed mixtures. Pure bent lawns should be sown at a rate of $^1/_4–^1/_3$ oz/yd² (8–10 g/m²), while pure perennial ryegrass and smooth-stalked meadowgrass will require higher seed rates. Sowing too thickly may encourage seedling diseases such as damping-off.

After sowing, the seed should be lightly raked into the surface and sandy soil rolled with a light (100–200-lb/ 50–100-kg) roller to consolidate the surface. Heavy soil should not be rolled until after germination, at which time a second rolling should be carried out on sandy soil. The grass seedlings will take

AERATING A LAWN

1 In fall, spike the lawn at closely spaced intervals. On small lawns a garden fork can be used; insert it straight down, then lean it back a little to open up the hole.

2 After spiking, whether with a fork or a mechanical or powered aerator, top-dress the lawn with a mix of sand, sieved soil and peat or peat substitute, and brush it in.

7–14 days to emerge depending on species, temperature, and water availability. The lawn should be regularly irrigated in dry weather. When seedlings are 1–1½ in (2.5–3.8 cm) high, they should be mown using a rotary mower and any excess clippings raked up and removed. If sown in the late summer or fall, the lawn should be mown as necessary through the late fall period, before gradually lowering the height of cut the following spring to that required for summer use. Lawns from seed should be subjected to as little wear as possible during their first season.

TURF Turf comes from established grass sward which is lifted intact and transplanted to a new site. It gives an immediate visual effect and can usually be walked on within a short period of laying. Turf is much more expensive than seed, and may carry pests, diseases and weeds.

Many different types of turf are available, including meadow turf, treated meadow turf, sea-marsh turf, custom-grown turf and seedling turf, and careful inspection of the offered product is essential.

Meadow-turf, grown initially for agricultural purposes, is likely to contain coarse grasses, including annual meadowgrass and broad-leaved weed species such as the daisy (*Bellis perennis*). Treated meadowgrass has had selective herbicide applied to eliminate broad-leaved weed species.

Sea-marsh turf was once considered the finest turf in the UK, because it contains fine fescues and bents. However, it often grows in estuaries where silt and clay are deposited, and care must be taken not to cover a free-draining soil with a silty impermeable barrier.

Seedling-turf, 6–15 weeks old, is raised in a shallow soilless medium and can be quickly grown to order. It is light and easy to transport but does not have the maturity of older turf and needs protection from heavy use until established.

Traditionally in the UK, high-quality turf was sold in 12 in (30 cm) squares and lesser-quality turf in 36 × 12 in (90 × 30 cm) strips. Most turf sold by large producers is lifted by tractor-mounted machines and cut into one square yard (meter) pieces.

Turf should be laid with an alternate bond, brick fashion, so that each piece tightly meets the next. Moist soil encourages rapid rooting and, after laying, turf should be lightly rolled to eliminate air pockets between the turf and the soil. In wet conditions, the rolling should be left until the turf has knitted together. Finally a light top-dressing of sand or sandy loam is applied over the surface and brushed into any gaps. Regular irrigation that penetrates the turf and soil beneath to a depth of 4–6 in (10–15 cm) will be needed in dry conditions.

Turf can be laid almost year round in Britain, although in the more extreme climates of continental Europe and North America the operation will be restricted by very hot or very cold conditions.

Vegetative propagation Vegetatively propagated lawns require less material than turf for a given area, but there is no instant cover and about two months is required for rooting and spread. Species commonly propagated by this method are the strong, creeping, warm-season grasses, together with cool-season creeping bent in North America. Vegetative propagation is not often practiced in Britain.

For stolonizing, the soil is prepared as for seeding and the stolons spread at a rate of around ½–1 gallon/yd² (2.25–5 liters/m²) and pressed into the soil surface.

Mowing Ideally no more than one third of the leaf growth should be removed at one mowing to prevent growth damage. For all lawns, infrequent heavy mowing will cause the greatest damage to the grasses.

Fine fescues and bents used in high-quality lawns can be cut as low as ¼ in (6 mm) in the summer and ½ in (12 mm) in winter, and these will need cutting every other day in summer so as not to remove more than one-third of the growth.

Ryegrasses and other species used in utility lawns grow better at heights between ½–1 in (1.2–2.5 cm) in summer and 1–1½ in (2.5–3.7 cm) in winter. In addition, the greater amount of grass will protect the surface against wear. These lawns will only need cutting once or twice a week in summer if no more than a third of the grass will be removed.

Grass mowing will be least frequent in the cold of winter and during summer drought conditions.

The two most commonly used types of mower are the cylinder or reel mower, and the rotary mower, which includes the hover-type. The cylinder mower gives the best finish, although the rotary type gives perfectly acceptable finishes for utility lawns.

For high-quality lawns, grass clippings should be removed (boxed off) to discourage earthworms, lessen the spread of annual meadowgrass and other seeding weeds, reduce the

L

accumulation of organic matter and leave a better surface finish.

Fertilizers On heavy-textured soil, where clippings are returned and rainfall or irrigation rates are low, only small amounts of fertilizer will be required; $^7/_8$ oz/yd² (30 g/m²) of a fertilizer containing 10% nitrogen will be a suitable annual dressing. This may be applied as one application in mid- to late spring, or in split applications in early summer and after fall renovations. Phosphorus and potassium are likely to be needed only every 3–5 years.

On light-textured soil where the clippings are removed and high rainfall or irrigation is plentiful, as much as $4^1/_2$ oz/yd² (150 g/m²) of a fertilizer containing 10% nitrogen per annum may be needed. Such a large amount of fertilizer should be applied in at least three applications, in late spring, in summer and after fall renovations. Phosphorus and potassium will also be required at a quarter and three-quarters the annual rate of nitrogen, respectively.

Iron is included in some compound fertilizers, and also widely applied as a constituent of lawn sand, which is used to control moss and encourage grass growth. Lawn sand usually contains 3 parts by weight ammonium sulfate, 1 part ferrous sulfate and 20 parts fine sand. It should be applied at 4 oz/yd² (136 g/m²) in spring or summer outside of hot dry spells.

Fertilizer must be applied evenly over the entire surface and, unless heavy rain is expected, it should be watered in to prevent scorch.

Irrigation Where ornamental effect is essential and water usage can be afforded, enough water should be applied at times of drought to ensure that the soil is moistened to a depth of 4–6 in (100–150 mm). Shallow watering encourages detrimental surface rooting, and heavy infrequent irrigation is in general better than light frequent applications. Well-established lawns are better able to recover from drought conditions that cannot be offset due to unavailability of irrigation water or restrictions in supply.

Maintenance and weed control Soil compaction and thatch accumulation are problems on well-used lawns.

Compaction restricts root growth and prevents rapid drainage, while lawns that have become acidic and from which earthworms have been eliminated can build up surface thatch (organic debris).

The techniques of scarification, hollow tining or coring, spiking and slitting are used to remove thatch and relieve soil compaction.

Scarifying
A spring-tined lawn rake is the ideal tool for removing moss and debris (thatch) from congested and compacted lawn grass.

A powered scarifier has vertical blades that rotate at a high speed and penetrate the lawn up to $^1/_2$ in (1.2 cm) in depth. Light scarification can be undertaken using a wire rake. It is advisable to scarify in two directions, one at 30 degrees to the other.

Hollow tining or coring removes cores of grass, thatch, and soil $^1/_4$–$^3/_4$ in (6–18 mm) in diameter and 3–4 in (7.5–10 cm) in depth. It can be undertaken with a special hand tool or by machine. The resulting holes may be left open or filled with a suitable sandy topdressing, which will prevent the hole from closing and improve the soil.

Spiking with a purpose-made tool or hand fork relieves soil compaction and allows air and water into the soil. For maximum effect, the spikes are pulled back after entering the soil, thereby lifting the turf and creating cracks and fissures

Slitting involves penetration of the soil with flat, knifelike blades to a depth of 3–4 in (7.5–10 cm).

Heavy scarification and hollow tining should be undertaken in early fall when warm, moist conditions permit rapid recovery. Light scarification, spiking

and slitting can be undertaken throughout the season except in dry conditions.

Bulky topdressing is also beneficial after fall work since it can aid thatch breakdown, fill core holes, and correct surface irregularities. A top-dressing containing medium/fine sand, sieved soil and peat or well-rotted compost, in a ratio of 6:3:1, is suitable for most lawns; apply at $^1/_{10}$ oz/yd² (1–3 g/m²) on a dry day and lute or brush well into the surface and core holes.

Rolling the lawn in spring resettles the surface but excessive rolling can cause compaction.

Brushing dew from grass, especially in the fall, helps prevent fungal disease spread.

Soil excreted by earthworms and deposited as worm casts on the surface of lawns can be a problem in making mowing difficult or unsightly, damaging the cutting edges of cylinder mowers. When flattened, worm casts smother grass, provide sites for weed germination and make a lawn slippery. Treatments to raise acidity, such as the application of sulfate of ammonia or sulfate of iron, discourage earthworms. Brushing with a birch broom will disperse worm casts.

Broad-leaved weeds should be treated with hormonal herbicide or weed-and-feed fertilizer. Small infestations of plants, such as daisy, dandelion and plantain, can be removed with a daisy grubber or knife, or killed by herbicide applied with a "spot-weeder."

Moss thrives in poorly drained lawns with low fertility and high acidity. It should be treated by cultural improvements and chemical moss killer or lawn sand. See *chafer beetles, dollar spot, earthworms, fairy ring, fusarium patch disease, leather-jacket, ophiobolus patch, red thread, snow mold.*

lax loose, for example flowers widely spaced in an open inflorescence.

laxpendent hanging loosely.

layering (1) a training technique used in the cordon system of growing sweet peas, and in large-scale tomato growing; (2) a method of vegetative propagation whereby stems are induced to form adventitious roots while still attached to the parent plant, to be eventually severed and grown on as separate individuals.

Plants, such as *Campsis*, *Hedera* and *Rubus*, have a natural propensity to layer themselves. Artificial methods of layering have been devised, utilizing inherent growth characteristics of plants together with varying degrees of shoot manipulation, including pruning, blanching, etiolation and constriction. Such strategies, besides providing shoots with a high capacity to produce roots, also cause natural hormones and carbohydrates to accumulate, thus encouraging quick rooting at specific locations on the stem. Layering is less widely used than formerly, mainly because of the advances made in rooting clonal material from cuttings. However, on certain plants, such as *Corylus maxima* 'Purpurea', clonal *Malus* rootstocks and certain rhododendrons, all of which are difficult to root by cuttings, layering is still a prime technique of production. For best results, the soil should be light textured, deep, well-drained, moisture-retentive, stone-free and of a pH appropriate to the species.

Simple layering Simple layering provides a means of propagating a wide range of woody plants. Vigorous one-year old shoots are encouraged to develop close to the soil, mainly by hard pruning, and are buried in such a way that the tip of the shoot is exposed well above soil level.

Many woody plants respond to this treatment, such as *Carpenteria californica*, *Chimonanthus praecox*, *Corylopsis pauciflora*, *Corylus avellana* cultivars, *C.maxima*

cultivars, *Cornus florida*, *Daphne cneorum*, *Disanthus cercidifolius*, *Kalmia latifolia* cultivars, *Magnolia* species and cultivars, *Rhododendron* species and cultivars and *Syringa vulgaris* cultivars. The time of year can influence the success rate; thus, late spring is recommended for *Disanthus cercidifolius*, when shoot growth has started, and midsummer for *Chimonanthus praecox*, when shoots are supple but not easily bruised.

Rooting is stimulated in stems blanched by covering them with soil and by constriction. A shoot is selected and pulled down to the soil to ascertain the position where the stem needs to be buried and constricted. There are a number of ways of constricting stems: by bending, twisting to rupture the tissue, cutting a tongue about 1¼ in (3 cm) long and exposing the cambium, girdling by removing a ring of bark about ¼ in (5 mm) wide, or by twisting copper wire into the stem tissue. A trench about 6 in (15 cm) deep is made with one side sloping toward the parent plant and a vertical side opposite. The constricted shoot is then bent down into the trench with the shoot tip placed against the vertical side. The tip should be exposed above the soil surface by 4–6 in (10–15 cm), secured with a peg and covered with soil; it may need to be tied to a small cane to ensure vertical growth. Layers will take one or two years to root and when sufficiently established, they can be severed from the parent plant, lifted during the dormant season and subsequently grown on. Layering is also the preferred method for increasing border

carnations; a tongue is made near the leafy end of the shoot and pegged down into a depression that is later refilled with soil.

Compound or serpentine layering This method is a modification of simple layering, utilizing the trailing shoots of climbing plants; it is suitable for subjects that do not root easily from stem cuttings, such as *Wisteria*, *Clematis armandii*, *Lapageria rosea* and *Vitis davidii*. Stem blanching and constriction techniques are applied at intervals along the trailing stems, and to avoid restricting the flow of sufficient sap, cutting a shallow tongue in the stem is probably the safest method.

During early spring, vigorous shoots are positioned on the soil surface in a circular pattern. Starting at the basal end, the first constriction is made and the shoot carefully bent into a hole about 4 in (10 cm) deep and secured with a peg before filling back with soil. This procedure is repeated along the stem, ensuring that vegetative buds are looped above the soil between each layer. New growth developing from the buds should be pinched back once or twice during the growing season to avoid excessive extension growth at the expense of root development. When sufficiently rooted, layers are severed close to the base of the parent plant. During the dormant season, these may be lifted and sectioned into separate plants.

Tip layering This method of layering is suitable for rooting plants of the genus *Rubus*, including blackberry, loganberry, boysenberry and tayberry.

METHODS OF LAYERING

Simple layering

Compound (serpentine) layering

Tip layering

Air (Chinese) layering

Healthy parent plants are established for one growing season, and in the spring of the second season are cut back to about 6–8 in (15–20 cm) above ground level. When new growth is 24 in (60 cm) in length, each shoot should be tipped to stimulate side laterals. Once side laterals have produced 3¼–5 ft (1–1.5 m) of growth, shoots may be pulled down into a 6 in (15 cm) deep trench, made with a sloping side toward the parent plant and a vertical side opposite; this will encourage the shoot to grow vertically. The shoot tip is placed so that the tip is bent upward at the vertical side and fixed with a wire staple before being covered with soil. Rooting takes place within three weeks and rooted layers can be lifted during December.

Air or Chinese layering This layering method is valuable in creating new plants from the upper growth of specimens. It is especially useful for plants that have become too tall, as often occurs with house plants, such as *Ficus elastica* cultivars, or with *Mahonia aquifolium* cultivars. Marcottage, gootee, and circumposition are other names for this method.

A woody shoot, preferably not more than two years old is selected, and either cut to remove a ring of bark about ½ in (1 cm) wide, or slit shallowly upward for about 1 in (2.5 cm) length of stem and a sliver of wood pushed in to keep the wound open. A rooting hormone should be applied over a ¾ in (2 cm) area around the wound. A handful of moist sphagnum moss is bound in and around the cut with a few turns of thread, and the area wrapped in a sleeve of black plastic film (30 microns), which should overlap and be tied firmly top and bottom. To avoid potentially lethal temperatures (95–104°F/35–40°C) building up inside the black plastic through radiation, the use of co-extruded plastic film (black with white reverse) is advised, with the white side outward-facing. Alternatively, aluminum foil or aluminized plastic may be used. When roots have developed sufficiently, cut the stem below the moss ball and grow the plant on. The old stem should be cut back to vegetative buds to prevent stem die-back and to encourage new growth.

Stooling or mound layering

This is a widely used commercial method, especially for the production of clonal rootstocks. Roots are stimulated by blanching developing shoots; this is done by heaping soil around their bases. Plants suitable for this technique must be able to tolerate hard annual pruning down to ground level, and be able to root effectively from blanched stems only; they include clonal apple root-stocks such as M9, MM106, rootstocks for plums like 'St. Julien A' and ornamentals such as *Prunus cerasifera* 'Nigra', *P. tenella* 'Fire Hill' and *Tilia* × *euchlora*.

New stool beds are established by obtaining young parent plants that are free from viruses and true to name. Planting should be done during the dormant period and the young plants grown on over one season to become well-established. During March of the following year, the stems should be cut back (stooled) about 1–2 in (2.5–5 cm) above soil level. Each stool should produce 2–6 new shoots, and once the shoots attain 4¾–6 in (12–15 cm) in height, moist, finely cultivated soil is carefully mounded up around them leaving the shoot tips visible. This procedure is normally carried out three times during the growing season, the final mounding up done soon after midsummer. Maintenance work required during the growing season will include irrigation and weed, pest and disease control. By late fall, layers will be well-rooted, and they should be harvested when fully dormant. The soil mounds are broken down to expose the rooted layers, which are gathered by cutting back to the original stool. There will be an annual increase in production up to about five years, but a well-maintained stool bed will last at least fifteen years.

French or continuous layering

The technique used here is similar to stooling, except that selected shoots are pegged down so that their buds produce new vertical shoots and these are then stimulated to root by blanching. Plants most suitable for this method should be capable of rooting effectively after blanching, produce long unfeathered shoots and be tolerant of hard pruning; they include *Cornus alba* cultivars, *Cotinus coggygria* cultivars, *Hydrangea paniculata* and *Viburnum plicatum*.

Mother plants are established for one growing season in well-prepared soil at 6½–10-ft- (2–3-m-) square pacings depending on vigor. In the following spring, the plants are cut back to 1–2 in (2.5–5 cm) above soil level and will produce 2–6 shoots, which should be left to develop fully.

During late winter in the third season after planting, long, healthy and ideally unfeathered shoots are pegged down onto the surface of the soil, arranged like the spokes of a wheel. Thin, weak shoots and any surplus to requirements should be cut hard back. In spring, growth will develop at right angles to the pegged shoots and from the center of the mother plant. The center shoots should be encouraged to develop fully as replacement layers for next season. Growths from the pegged shoots are mounded to a depth of 6 in (15 cm).

Rooted layers should be ready by early winter, and the layered shoots are severed close to the mother plant, lifted, sectioned and grown on.

Etiolation or trench layering

This method is generally reserved for plants that need to be propagated on their own roots, such as *Prunus avium* F12/1 rootstocks and walnuts. Etiolation layering differs from stooling because buds are encouraged to develop and extend on layered shoots in darkness, without foliage and virtually devoid of pigmentation. Such shoots, in which the cells of the buried sections become elongated, have a remarkable capacity to produce adventitious roots.

Mother plants are established from single shoots about 24 in (60 cm) long; these are planted at a 45-degree angle, at 24 in (60 cm) spacings, in rows 5–10 ft (1.5–3 m) apart. Plants are allowed to establish for one growing season, and during the early spring of the second year, a trench about 2 in (5 cm) deep and 12 in (30 cm) wide is taken out along the row. A little soil is removed just beside the base of each angled stem, allowing the stem to be easily bent horizontally into the trench, where it is held firmly in place with stout pegs.

Before the buds have begun to swell, the shoots are covered with soil 1 in (2.5 cm) deep and just as shoots appear above ground level a further covering of the same depth is made. This is repeated up to three times, after which the shoots are allowed to attain about 6 in (15 cm) in height and then mounded up with the tips visible.

Rooted layers will be ready for harvesting by early winter. One strong shoot is retained every 12 in (30 cm) along the row to continue the sequence of production.

Dropping This relatively simple layering technique involves disposing of the parent plant once rooted layers are removed. It is normally carried out on small bushy woody plants, such as *Berberis × stenophylla* 'Irwinii', *Calluna* and *Erica* species and cultivars, and dwarf *Rhododendron* species and cultivars.

Young bushy plants are selected during spring and lower leaves removed where rooting is expected to take place. A deep trench is dug into which the plants are placed with their shoots evenly spaced out. The soil is replaced, ensuring that the shoot tips are above the soil level. When the shoots have rooted, between one to two years later, the parent plants are lifted and the rooted layers removed and grown on.

layer planting used to describe groups of plants in a floral bed that are arranged to provide successional flowering or to achieve variable height for improved display.

Layia (for George Tradescant Lay [d. *c.* 1845], botanist to Captain Beechey's voyage in the *Blossom*, which visited California in 1827). Compositae. W US. About 15 species, annual herbs with daisylike flower heads from summer to early fall. They are frost-tender annuals for dry, sunny banks, and do not thrive where summers are hot and humid. Sow seed *in situ* in spring (or earlier under glass), in well-drained soil in sun. *L. platyglossa* (syn. *L. elegans*); TIDY TIPS; California; to 12 in (30 cm), glandular, hairy; leaves linear to narrowly oblong, dentate to pinnatifid; ray florets yellow with white tips, anthers black.

laying a traditional and effective method of training hedges by bending partially severed shoots to an angle of about 45 degrees and weaving them around wooden stakes driven into the hedge line at intervals. Hedges can be laid at any time between October and May but the work is easiest if done in spring when the sap is rising.

laying-in the process of tying in young shoots against a wall, carried out during the training of a fruit tree.

lazy-bed a system of growing potatoes, in which tubers are placed on the soil surface and covered with soil from trenches dug between the rows or bed.

leaching the drainage of water through soil or other growing media, removing soluble chemicals, especially nitrogen. It has the deleterious effects of potential waste and/or pollution of watercourses. It can be beneficial in diluting the buildup of soil salts that often follows regular supplementary feeding, as for tomatoes; and leaching is induced in such situations by flooding the soil. See *nutrients* and *plant nutrition*.

leader the main shoot of a woody plant, often referred to as the central leader; also, the dominant terminal shoot that extends the growth of a branch. In pruning, leaders are usually cut lightly (tipped) in comparison to laterals.

leaf a lateral member borne on the shoot or stem of a plant, generally differing from the stem in form and structure.

leaf beetles (Coleoptera: Chrysomelidae) one of the largest families of beetles, the adults of which are mostly oval-shaped, drab to brightly colored and ranging in size from $\frac{1}{16}$ to $\frac{1}{2}$ in (1–12 mm) long. The larvae are soft, fleshy grubs with three pairs of short, stumpy thoracic legs. Adults and larvae often feed openly on the foliage of plants, or the larvae mine leaves or feed on the roots. Species attacking vegetables include the FLEA BEETLES (*Phyllotreta* species) and related species in North America; the COLORADO BEETLE (*Leptinotarsa decemlineata*) on potatoes in North America and Europe (not the UK or Ireland; the ASPARAGUS BEETLE (*Crioceris asparagi*), with conspicuous yellow and black adults up to $\frac{1}{4}$ in (6 mm) long and gray black humped larvae, both of which feed on the foliage of edible asparagus; and, in North America, the BEAN LEAF BEETLE (*Ceratoma trifurcata*), a yellow and black marked beetle up to $\frac{1}{4}$ in (7 mm) long, which feeds on the foliage of beans and other legumes and has root-feeding larvae. In North and South America, cucurbits can be severely attacked by CUCUMBER BEETLES (*Acalymma* and *Diabrotica* species), with pale yellow green adults, marked with spots and bands of black and up to $\frac{3}{8}$ in (8 mm) long, which feed on foliage and whose larvae tunnel into roots; some of these larvae are known as CORN ROOTWORMS because they can seriously damage the roots of corn.

Fruit in North America is attacked by rootworms, particularly the GRAPE ROOTWORM (*Fidia viticida*), with chestnut brown hairy adults up to $\frac{1}{4}$ in (6 mm) long and root-feeding larvae that damage the roots of grape vines, and the STRAWBERRY ROOTWORM (*Paria fragariae*), a glistening brown beetle with black markings, up to $\frac{1}{8}$ in (3 mm) long, that feeds on foliage and whose larvae infest the roots and crowns of strawberries, raspberries, blackberries and some other plants, such as rose.

The WATER LILY BEETLE (*Galerucella nymphaeae*) is small and brown, up to $\frac{1}{4}$ in (6 mm) long, and has soft-bodied brown-black larvae that feed on the upper surface of leaves, making furrows and holes. The SUNFLOWER BEETLE (*Zygogramma exclamationis*) has adults resembling the Colorado beetle that feed, along with their humpbacked larvae, on the foliage of sunflowers in North America.

The adults and larvae of several species feed openly on the foliage of trees. These include the ELM LEAF BEETLE (*Pyrrhalta luteola*), with yellow or green adults up to $\frac{1}{4}$ in (6 mm) long, which together with their larvae cause defoliation of elm trees in North America and Europe, but not the UK; various small, metallic blue, red or green beetles, mostly *Phyllodecta* species up to $\frac{1}{4}$ in (5 mm) long, attack the foliage of willows and poplars; the EUROPEAN VIBURNUM BEETLE (*Pyrrhalta viburni*), is a dun brown beetle, up to $\frac{1}{4}$ in

(6 mm) long, with creamy yellow larvae with black markings.

Leaf beetles that feed openly at both adult and larval stages can be controlled with recommended contact insecticides. Where larvae are root feeders, measures must be aimed at eliminating the adults before egg-laying commences. See *Colorado beetle, flea beetle, lily beetle*.

leaf blister a descriptive term for foliage diseases caused by species of the fungus *Taphrina*, where limited infected leaf areas become swollen. The effect is similar to, but less severe than, that caused by PEACH LEAF CURL (*Taphrina deformans*) (q.v.). *T.bullata* causes brown blisters on pears, similar to those caused by leaf blister mites; *T. caerulescens* causes gray-pink blisters on oaks, sometimes resulting in severe defoliation; *T. populina* causes blisters on poplars, which are bright yellow on the underside of leaves when the fungus is sporulating; *T. sadebeckii* forms yellow blisters on alder; and *T.ulmi* forms small green blisters on elm, which turn brown. *T. caerulescens* can be damaging in the US and fungicide treatment of the dormant buds is recommended, as for peach leaf curl. Blister blight, *Exobasidium vexans*, is an important disease of tea plants in south and southeast Asia. Leaf blisters of various ferns are also caused by *Taphrina* species, but these are not of significance in Britain. Some gall mites cause leaf blisters on plants such as pear and walnut.

leaf-cutter bees (*Megachile* species) (Hymenoptera: Megachilidae) small solitary bees, up to ½ in (13 mm) long, which resemble honey bees but have a stouter build and are more hairy. The females use their mandibles to remove uniform oval or circular portions of leaves to construct thimble-shaped cells; these are filled with a mixture of pollen and nectar before an egg is deposited and the cell capped with a circular piece of leaf. Up to around 20 cells are built end on end in situations such as tunnels made in decaying wood, old brickwork or dry soil. Larvae feed within the cells during the summer and overwinter there, pupating in the spring and emerging as adults in early summer. Commonly

Leaf-cutter bee
These solitary bees damage leaves, but also have a valuable role as pollinators, so they should not be harmed. The damage they cause is rarely more than superficial.

found in gardens is *Megachile centunculars*, which attacks the foliage of roses, and other species cause similar injury to many ornamental plants. Control measures are seldom necessary.

leafhoppers (Hemiptera: Cicadellidae) sap-feeding insects, mostly up to ¼ in (5 mm) long, similar to froghoppers (Cercopidae) but generally less robust, and with a slender tapering body and 1–3 rows of spines on part of the hind legs. Adults are widespread on plants in summer, jumping, flying briefly and then resettling on leaves. Some species transmit plant diseases. Typically, they feed on the underside of leaves, causing small white spots to appear on the upper surface. In severe attacks, the spots coalesce and the whole leaf becomes chlorotic. The underside of infested leaves is invariably littered with discarded white molt-skins.

In gardens, the ROSE LEAFHOPPER (*Edwardsiana rosae*) is common in both North America and Europe on roses and apples; similar species attack hornbeam and beech hedges. The GLASSHOUSE LEAFHOPPER (*Hauptidia maroccana*) is commonly found in greenhouses and gardens in temperate countries, attacking a wide range of plants. The RHODODENDRON LEAFHOPPER (*Graphocephala fennahi*), common in North America and Europe, does no direct damage but by depositing eggs in the flower buds facilitates spread of

coarse, pale spotting

Leafhopper damage

the fungal disease known as bud blast. This leafhopper is conspicuous, up to ⅜ in (9 mm) in length with red oblique stripes on the green wing cases. Apples and potatoes are subject to attack by several different species of leafhopper; grapes by *Erythroneura* species; *Rubus* by *Macropsis* species; and strawberry by *Aphrodes* and *Euscelis* species, which transmit the virus causing green petal disease. Recommended contact or systemic insecticides are effective, where control is necessary.

leaflet one of the leaf- or bladelike ultimate units of a compound leaf.

leaf miners the leaf-mining larvae of several different groups of insects, including the Lepidoptera (moths), Coleoptera (beetles), Diptera (flies) and Hymenoptera (some sawflies). Apple is attacked by some species, including the SPOTTED TENTIFORM LEAF MINER (*Phyllonorycter* species), which is a more serious pest in North America than in Europe; the larvae live in raised blister-like mines. In Europe, the APPLE LEAF MINER (*Lyonetia clerkella*) is more widespread on apple, and also occurs on cherry, ornamental *Prunus*, hawthorn and birch, but the serpentine mines mostly become numerous in late summer and fall, when it is too late for the tree to be adversely affected. Other moths in Europe and North America with leaf-mining larvae include the AZALEA LEAF MINER (*Caloptilia azaleella*), which causes blotch mines on evergreen and some deciduous azaleas, and the LILAC MINER (*C. syringella*), which causes blotch mines on lilac and privet; the larvae of both these species vacate the mines when they are about half-grown to feed within a turned-over leaf margin, which is held in place by silk threads.

The CHRYSANTHEMUM LEAF MINER (*Phytomyza syngenesiae*) causes serpentine mines on the leaves of chrysanthemums, cinerarias, lettuces and some other cultivated plants; the HOLLY LEAF MINER (*P.*) causes blotch mines on *Ilex* species; the columbine leaf miners

P. aquilegiae and *P. miniscula* cause blotch and serpentine mines respectively on *Aquilegia* species; and the TOMATO LEAF MINER (*Liriomyza solani*) is responsible for serpentine mines on the leaves of tomatoes. Other *Liriomyza* species also attack chrysanthemums, peas and other vegetables in both North America and Europe. The CELERY FLY (*Euleia heraclei*), a serious pest of celery in the Northern Hemisphere, has larvae that live in communal blotch mines, which subsequently become desiccated, brown and papery, giving the foliage a scorched appearance. In Europe, the larvae of the ARNATION FLY (*Delia cardui*) cause extensive mining of carnations, pinks and sweet Williams. The larvae of the BEET LEAF MINER (*Pegomya hyoscyami*), common to both continents, cause blotch mines on beets, spinach beet and related plants.

Light infestations of leaf miners can be controlled by hand-picking and destroying affected leaves; once larvae become established in mines, they are not easily killed by spraying, although systemic insecticides have proved effective against several species.

Planting corm in leaf mold
Well-rotted fallen leaves make a fine, humus-rich soil improver that suits woodland plants such as cyclamen very well.

leaf mold the residue of decayed leaves, which forms a dark brown, friable material, rich in humus but low in nutrients. It is valuable as a soil improver and surface mulch; also as a compost ingredient, for which it was formerly widely used until superseded by peat but it remains a candidate alternative. Leaf mold occurs naturally in woodland, and can be prepared by collecting fallen leaves and depositing them in a compost bin or small

wire-mesh compound. Leaves decay more slowly than mixed garden waste, but with turning a suitable leaf mold should be available for use after 18 months. Oak, beech and hornbeam yield the best quality leaf mold. Thick leaves, such as sycamore and horse chestnut, take longer to decay, and hard leaves, such as holly and laurel, are best mixed with general plant waste for composting. Pine needles decay over a long period to produce a useful medium for acid-loving plants.

leaf mold (*Fulvia fulva*) a serious worldwide disease of tomato plants grown under conditions of high humidity; it is rare on outdoor plants. Pale yellow patches appear on the upper surface of older leaves as a result of velvety green-gray fungal growth produced on the undersides. The disease spreads up the plant and affected leaves progressively turn brown and shrivel; flowers and fruit may also be infected. Plant vigor and yield can be seriously affected, and the fungus can carry over from one crop to the next as spores or fruiting bodies on debris or seed.

Many cultivars of tomato have resistance to leaf mold, although different races of the fungus may overcome resistance. Preventative measures include close attention to ventilation, aiming to keep the greenhouse relative humidity level below 85%. Avoidance of prolonged wetness of foliage is also beneficial. Weekly sprays of a recommended fungicide will check the spread of leaf mold. All infected plant debris should be removed and empty greenhouses disinfected by burning sulfur.

leaf rollers the larvae of several groups of insects, and some mites, are associated with partial or complete leaf rolling. The rolling may be tight or loose, and directed downward or upward, but damage is always unsightly and reduces the normal functions of affected leaves.

The larvae of tortricid moths typically feed within a rolled or folded-over portion of a leaf, which is held in place by silk strands. Common in Europe and North America are the FRUIT TREE TOR-TRIX MOTH (*Archips podana*), which attacks various deciduous trees and shrubs, conifers, and especially apple, raspberry and blackberry; the STRAWBERRY

TORTRIX (*Acleris comariana*) on strawberry, geums, potentillas and azaleas; the LEAF TIER (*Cnephasia longana*) on chrysanthemums, irises, strawberry, fruit trees, shrubs, the new growth of conifers and various vegetables; and the STRAWBERRY LEAF ROLLER (*Ancylis comptana*) on strawberry, potentillas, thymes and *Dryas octopetala*. In Europe, the carnation tortrix (*Cacoecimorpha pronubana*) and the light-brown apple moth (*Epiphyas postvittana*) attack a wide range of ornamental plants in gardens and greenhouses.

Several adult weevils roll one or both sides of a leaf to form a tube in which the larvae live and feed; they include the HAZEL LEAF ROLLER WEEVIL (*Byctiscus betulae*) on hazel, birch and other deciduous trees, and the POPLAR LEAF ROLLER (*B. populi*) on poplars and aspens. The leaf-rolling habit also occurs among gall midges: the orange larvae of the VIOLET GALL MIDGE (*Dasineura affinis*) live in the upward-rolled, swollen leaves of violets, and the white larvae of the PEAR LEAF MIDGE (*D. pyri*) infest the upward-rolled margins of pear leaves. One common European sawfly, the LEAF-ROLLING ROSE SAWFLY (*Blennocampa phyllocolpa*), causes a tight downward roll of both leaf margins of roses. Hand-picking and crushing the larvae is usually an effective control measure control, as is burning affected leaves. Some gall mites are associated with leaf rolling on plants such as beech and lime trees. See *gall mites, tortrix moths.*

leaf scar scar tissue on a shoot indicating the site of leaf abscission.

leaf scorch see *scorch.*

leafsoil a soil containing a high proportion of leaf mold.

leaf spot spots on plants usually caused by fungal pathogens, affecting a range of plants, particularly when the foliage is aging. Leaf spots can be conspicuous and unsightly on ornamentals, but the majority cause only slight damage in garden plants. However, leaf-spot diseases of crops, such as banana and celery, can seriously reduce yield.

Typical leaf spots are scattered randomly and have definite edges, often with darker margins. On net-veined leaves, they are usually circular, while on leaves with parallel veins, they are elongated along the direction of the veins. The dead centers of spots are often lighter in color and may show the spore-bearing structures. Some leaf-spot fungi, such as *Alternaria* and *Cercospora*, have spores which are dispersed in dry conditions, but the majority, including *Ascochyta* and *Septoria*, have sticky spores that are adapted to spread in water.

Leaf spots may also be caused by bacterial pathogens (see *bacterial leaf spot*), and some virus diseases produce (usually) chlorotic spots. Air pollution, pesticide injury, nutrient or water deficiency, pest attack and physical damage by hail, can all produce leaf spots.

Since many fungal leaf-spot diseases are spread by spores produced on the spots, a degree of control can be obtained by picking off affected leaves as soon as symptoms appear and destroying fallen ones. Avoiding overhead watering and the handling of plants when they are wet are other practical means of control. Chemical control with copper-based and other fungicides can be effective, subject to local pesticide approvals, and celery leaf spot can be controlled by seed treatment. See *anthracnose, black spot, chocolate spot*.

leaf trace a vascular bundle supplying a leaf.

leaf weevils (*Phyllobius* species) (Coleoptera: Curculionidae) small weevils, up to ½ in (10 mm) long, dark brown to black and covered with dense scales which often appear metallic gold or green-bronze. Mostly present in early summer, the adults bite small holes in leaves and occasionally the blossom of trees and shrubs, including top fruits, birch, lime, flowering cherry, crab apples, poplars and mountain ash. The larvae live in the soil and feed on roots without causing significant damage.

The principal species are the BROWN LEAF WEEVIL (*Phyllobius oblongus*), the SILVER-GREEN LEAF WEEVIL (*P. argentatus*) and the COMMON LEAF WEEVIL (*P. pyri*). Control is seldom necessary but can be achieved by spraying with a recommended contact insecticide.

leafy gall (*Corynebacterium fascians*) a bacterial disease causing leafy galls around the collar of infected plants,

blindness, absence of flower buds, and fasciation. Susceptible plants include carnations, chrysanthemums, *Dahlia*, *Gladiolus*, *Heuchera*, nasturtiums, *Pelargonium*, *Petunia*, *Phlox*, *Schizanthus*, sweet peas, sweet Williams, and *Verbascum*. When associated with the eelworms *Aphelenchoides ritzemabosi* or *A. fragariae*, the bacterium causes cauliflower disease of strawberry, a severe stunting and swelling of the leaf and flower stalks, but the condition is very uncommon. Leafy gall is not usually serious but affected plants should be destroyed and contaminated land kept free of susceptible plants.

lean used loosely to denote soil that is free-draining and low in organic matter and nutrients.

lean-to a greenhouse or conservatory with a single pitch roof, usually built against a wall and often used to accommodate trained fruits. Lean-tos are usually economic to heat and, if well sited, readily trap solar heat. See *greenhouse*.

leatherjackets (Diptera: Tipulidae) larvae of the large, fragile, spindly-legged daddy-long-legs, or crane flies. The legless, gray-brown larvae are up to 1¾ in (45 mm) long, with leathery skins and inconspicuous heads. Adult females lay up to 300 eggs, singly or in clusters depending upon species, just below the soil surface in grassland, including lawns, or in cereal crops, where the resulting larvae feed upon roots.

Leatherjackets can be serious lawn pests, causing brown patches usually in midsummer, but earlier following a mild winter; their presence can be confirmed by soaking the area with water and covering it with black polyethylene, under which they will emerge within 24 hours. Affected lawns may be further damaged by birds searching for leatherjackets. The underground portions of plants such as young brassicas, lettuces, strawberries and various ornamentals, may be damaged by leatherjackets, especially in newly cultivated gardens.

One of the most injurious species is *Tipula paludosa*, a native of Europe but also established in North America, particularly in British Columbia and

Washington. Other common species are *T. oleracea* and the spotted crane fly (*Nephrotoma maculata*).

To reduce leatherjackets on lawns, attract them to the surface in the manner described above and then remove by hand-picking. Soil insecticides are more effective if used in late fall when the larvae are young, subject to local pesticide approvals. An alternative treatment is to apply the pathogenic nematode *Steinernema feltiae* in late summer or early fall, when the soil is moist and at least 54°F (12°C).

Ledebouria (for Carl Friedrich von Ledebour [1785–1851], German botanist). Liliaceae (Hyacinthaceae). South Africa. Some 16 species, bulbous, perennial herbs with thinly fleshy, narrowly lanceolate leaves, often striped or spotted red or green. They produce spikes of small, bell-shaped flowers with recurved perianth segments. Grow in full sun with low humidity, good ventilation and a minimum temperature of 45°F (7°C). Pot in pans containing a gritty, loam-based medium and with the bulbs for the most part exposed. Water moderately in spring and summer, very sparingly in winter. These bulbs associate well with succulents and cacti. Propagate by offsets.

L. cooperi (syn. *Scilla cooperi*; leaves to 10 in (25 cm), somewhat fleshy, oblong to ovate or linear, sometimes striped brown; flowers pale purple sometimes with green keels; *L. socialis* (syn. *Scilla socialis*; leaves to 4 in (10 cm), slightly fleshy, lanceolate, pearly gray-green with some dark green blotches above, green or deep pink-purple beneath; flowers pale purple with green keels.

Ledum (from Greek *ledon*, mastic, a name used for *Cistus*). Ericaceae. Northern temperate regions. 3–4 species of erect or diffuse evergreen shrubs with aromatic foliage and small, white, 5-petaled flowers in umbel-like corymbs in spring and summer. Fully hardy and suited to the bog or damp woodland garden in shade or semishade and to moist, humus-rich, acidic soil. Propagate by semiripe cuttings in a closed case with bottom heat, by simple

Leatherjacket

L

layering or by seed. *L. groenlandicum* LABRADOR TEA; northern North America, Greenland; 1½–6½ ft (0.5–2 m); leaves ¾–2½ in (2–6 cm), linear to oblong, revolute, dark green and somewhat hirsute above, rusty-woolly beneath; flowers white in clusters to 2 in (5 cm) in diameter; 'Compactum': dwarf.

Leea (for James Lee [1715–1795], London nurseryman). Leeaceae. Old World tropics. 34 species, shrubs and small trees with simple or 1–3-pinnate leaves, small flowers in umbels and berrylike fruit. Provide bright filtered light or shade from direct sun in high summer, and grow in a high-fertility loam-based medium. Maintain high humidity, water plentifully, and feed semiweekly with a dilute liquid feed when in full growth; reduce water in winter when a minimum temperature of 61°F (16°C) is appropriate. Propagate by stem cuttings, air-layering.

L. amabilis Borneo; evergreen shrub to 6½ ft (2 m); leaves 1–3-pinnate, leaflets to 2½ in (6 cm), lanceolate, sparsely toothed, lustrous bronze above with a broad white central stripe, claret beneath with a translucent, central, green stripe; includes 'Splendens', the whole of which is flushed dark bronzered; *L. guineensis* WEST INDIAN HOLLY; Burma; evergreen shrub to 6½ ft (2 m); leaves 2–3 pinnate, leaflets 2–4 in (5–10 cm), elliptic to obovate, revolute, sometimes toothed; flowers pink.

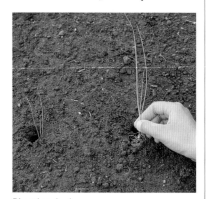

Planting leeks
In order to encourage a good length of blanched white stem, young leeks should be planted in holes to at least half their depth.

leek (*Allium porrum*) a monocotyledonous biennial with long green flat leaves, white at the base, which form a tight cylinder and normally not a distinct bulb. Wild relatives occur in the eastern Mediterranean region and into western and southern Russia.

The leek is adapted to a temperate climate and is more cold-tolerant than the onion, although it also is vernalized by low temperature and consequently bolts to become unusable. Cool conditions favor growth, and day temperatures greater than 75°F (24°C) may reduce yields.

Leeks are mostly grown as a hardy winter vegetable but they can be harvested from late summer until late spring; they are used as a cooked vegetable and in soups. They grow best in a deep soil worked with well-rotted organic manure and with a pH of 6.5–7.5. Germination is optimum at soil temperatures of 52–73°F (11–23°C), but is drastically reduced at temperatures below 45°F (7°C) and above 81°F (27°C).

Earliest crops are raised in gentle heat under protection during early spring, either direct sown into cell modules or pricked out, and hardened off before planting. Early outdoor sowings can be made under cloches or in unprotected seedbeds from March to early May, in drills approximately ¾ in (2 cm) deep. Plant out seedlings when 10–15 weeks old and about 8 in (20 cm) tall, in rows 12 in (30 cm) apart, with 6 in (15 cm) between plants. Higher-density plantings will give similar yields of small, more slender leeks. Seed can be sown *in situ* but weed control is more difficult and the plants are likely to have a reduced portion of blanched stem. Leaves and roots can be trimmed slightly to facilitate planting, with some loss of yield.

The length of blanched leaf base is influenced by cultivar and planting method. The simplest procedure is to drop individual plants into 6 in (15 cm)-deep holes made with a dibber, and water immediately. The holes will gradually fill up as the season progresses, increasing the proportion of leaf excluded from light. Alternatively, plants can be set into V-shaped drills 3 in (7.5 cm) deep which are later filled in, or they may be established on the flat and subsequently earthed up several times during growth. Leeks should be kept well-watered and lifted as required. Later cultivars can remain outside during the winter until late spring. Cultivars with short, thick stems are known as pot leeks and are of particular interest to exhibitors.

Possible problems: *eelworm, onion fly; rust, white rot.*

Heeling in leeks
Leeks are hardy enough to overwinter in situ, but if the ground they are growing in is needed, they may be lifted and heeled into the soil in a spot that is free.

leg a short stem from which the branches of a shrub are trained, as on a gooseberry bush.

legume (1) the one-celled seed pod of plants of the pea family Leguminosae; (2) more generally, used to describe any plant of that family, especially peas and beans. Leguminous plants support nitrogen-fixing bacteria that give rise to root nodules, thus harnessing atmospheric nitrogen for the benefit of the host.

Lemboglossum (from Greek *lembos*, boat or canoe, and *glossa*, tongue, referring to the boat-shaped lip). Orchidaceae. C America, Mexico. Some 14 species, evergreen, epiphytic perennials formerly included in *Odontoglossum* Showy flowers are borne in racemes or panicles at various times of year. Provide cool to intermediate conditions (minimum temperature 50°F/10°C), in light shade with humid, buoyant air. Water frequently when in growth, less so at other times. See also *Odontoglossum.*

L. bictoniense Mexico, Guatemala, El Salvador; raceme erect, to 32 in (80 cm), flowers often fragrant, tepals usually pale green or yellow-green banded or spotted red-brown, sepals to 1 in (2.5 cm), elliptic to oblanceolate, petals smaller, lip to ¾ in (2 cm), subcordate, crisped or crenulate, white to rose or magenta-tinted; white, golden and lime-green self-colored forms occur; *L. cervantesii* (syn. *Odontoglossum cervantesii*; Mexico, Guatemala; raceme 2–13 in (5–32 cm), flowers fragrant, tepals white to rose irregularly banded brown-red in basal half, sepals to 1½ in (3.5 cm), narrowly ovate to oblong, petals broader, lip white to rose, striped purple at base, to 1 in (2.5 cm), lateral lobes erect, midlobe broadly cordate, toothed, callus yellow; *L. cordatum* (syn. *Odontoglossum cordatum*; Mexico, Guatemala, Honduras, Costa Rica, Venezuela; raceme or panicle to 24 in (60 cm), tepals yellow blotched and barred deep red-brown, sepals to 2 in (5 cm), elliptic to lanceolate, petals shorter, lip to 1 in (2.5 cm), usually white spotted red-brown, cordate, margins slightly erose; *L. rossii* (syn. *Odontoglossum rossii*); Guatemala, Mexico, Honduras, Nicaragua; raceme to 8 in (20 cm), tepals white, pale yellow or pale pink, the sepals and lower portions of petals mottled and spotted chocolate to rust, sepals to 1¾ in (4.5 cm), oblong to elliptic or lanceolate, broader, crisped to undulate, lip to 1¼ in (3 cm), rounded to cordate, undulate, callus deep yellow spotted red-brown; *L. stellatum* (syn. *Odontoglossum stellatum*; Mexico, Guatemala, El Salvador; raceme to 3¼ in (8.5 cm) tepals yellow-bronze barred brown, to 1¼ in (3 cm), linear to lanceolate, petals sometimes yellow-white, lip white or pink marked mauve, to ¾ in (2 cm), ovate to triangular or suborbicular, lacerate to dentate.

lemma the lower and stouter of the two glumes that immediately enclose the floret in most Gramineae; also referred to as the flowering glume.

lenticel an elliptical and raised cellular pore on the surface of bark, or the suberous tissue of fruit, through which gases can penetrate.

lenticellate possessing lenticels.

lenticular, lenticulate lens-shaped; almost flattened and elliptical, but with both sides convex.

lentiginous minutely dotted, as if with dust.

Leonotis (from Greek *leon*, lion, and *ous*, ear, alluding to the appearance of the hair-fringed corolla lip). Labiatae. 1 species pantropical, the others Southern Africa. LION'S EAR. 30 species, aromatic, annual or perennial herbs and subshrubs with tetragonal stems, toothed leaves and bearded, tubular and 2-lipped flowers in terminal whorls from late summer to early winter. *L. leonurus* tolerates temperatures down to freezing. In cool climates, it is cultivated as a conservatory specimen or treated as a tender biennial; plants in their second year make striking specimens for the summer border. Grow in full sun, in a high-fertility loam-based mix. Water pot-grown plants plentifully when in full growth, sparingly at other times. Overwinter in bright, cool but frost-free conditions. Cut back in early spring. Propagate by seed sown in early spring under glass, or from greenwood cuttings in late spring. *L. leonurus* South Africa; downy, evergreen shrub to 6½ ft (2 m); flowers to 2½ in (6 cm), orange-red to scarlet; includes 'Harrismith White', with white flowers.

Leontopodium (from Greek *leon*, lion, and *pous*, foot, in reference to the shape of the flower heads). Compositae. Eurasia (especially mountains), possibly also Andes. EDELWEISS. About 35 species, perennial herbs, usually low-growing and forming clumps of narrow, gray-hairy leaves. In spring and summer, they produce erect, slender-stalked cymes of felty, buttonlike flower heads surrounded by a star-shaped arrangement of lanceolate, usually white-woolly bracts. Hardy alpines, suitable for the rock garden, trough and raised bed. Grow in full sun in gritty, perfectly drained, not too fertile, circumneutral or alkaline soil; in areas with damp winters, provide shelter from wet and winds. Propagate by seed sown fresh or by division.

L. alpinum EDELWEISS; mountains of Europe; loosely mat-forming perennial; inflorescence stalks to 8 in (20 cm) tall, crowned with an irregular star of spreading, linear-oblong, densely white-woolly bracts, the whole to 4 in (10 cm) diam.; *L. stracheyi* Himalaya; inflorescence stalks to 20 in (50 cm) tall, crowned with one or two irregular stars to 2½ in (6.5 cm) in diameter, with many, gray-hairy, or green and glandular bracts.

lepidote covered with tiny, scurfy, peltate scales.

Leptospermum (Greek *leptos*, slender, *sperma*, seed). Myrtaceae. Mostly S Australia; 1 species common in Tasmania is widespread in New Zealand, 2 are found in SE Asia. TEA TREE, TI-TREE. 79 species, evergreen shrubs or trees with smooth and flaking, fibrous or papery bark, tough and sometimes aromatic leaves and axillary flowers with five, rounded, spreading and silken petals. Hardy to about 14°F (−10°C) but best grown in a sunny, sheltered position in freely draining, humus-rich, neutral or acidic soil. Where prolonged and hard frosts are common, grow under glass in a fertile, well-drained but moisture-retentive ericaceous medium. Water moderately when in growth, reducing as temperatures and light levels fall to keep just moist in winter with a minimum temperature of 41°F (5°C). Maintain good ventilation in winter; plunge pot-grown specimens outdoors in a sunny, warm place in summer months. Propagate by semiripe or softwood cuttings in summer.

L. lanigerum Tasmania, S Australia, N, S and W Victoria; shrub or tree to 16 ft (5 m); leaves ¹⁄₁₆–⅝ in (0.2–1.5 cm), oblong, to narrowly oblanceolate, usually gray-downy; flowers white, ⅝ in (1.5 cm) in diameter; 'Silver Sheen': leaves silver-gray, later flowering than *L. lanigerum*, i.e., summer, not spring, hardy to 0°F (−18°C), probably attributable to *L. myrtifolium*; *L. scoparium* MANUKA, TEA TREE; N, S and W Victoria, Tasmania, New Zealand; shrub 6½–13 ft (2–4 m); leaves ¼–¾ in (0.7–2 cm), elliptic, or broadly lanceolate or oblanceolate, often silvery-hairy at first; flowers white or, rarely, pink or red, ⅜–½ in (0.8–1.2 cm) in diameter; numerous cultivars are grown with single or double flowers in shades of white, cream, pink, rose, red or cerise; these vary in habit from dwarf and bushy to tall and spirelike, and from tender to frost-hardy, with foliage ranging in shape from needlelike to broad and glossy, and in color from darkest blood red to emerald green.

Leschenaultia (for Leschenault de la Tour, botanist of the voyage of

L

discovery under Captain Nicolas Baudin in 1802). Goodeniaceae. Australia. Some 24 species, herbs, subshrubs or shrubs with a heathlike habit and linear leaves. Produced in small clusters in spring and summer, the flowers consist of a short tube and five, erect or spreading lobes, often winged and with 2-lobed tips. Grow in full light but with some protection from the strongest summer sun, in an acidic, soilless mix low in phosphates and nitrates. A topdressing of grit or gravel is beneficial in pots or in the open garden. Water carefully and moderately in growth, sparingly at other times. Maintain good ventilation and a winter minimum of 45–50°F (7–10°C). Trim after flowering. Propagate by seed, or by greenwood or semiripe cuttings in sand, in a closed case with gentle bottom heat. *L. floribunda* W Australia; shrubby erect, annual to 3¼ ft (1 m); flowers to ⅝ in (1.6 cm) blue or white.

lesion a defined area of diseased tissue such as is caused by a leaf spot or canker.

Lespedeza (for Vincente Manuel de Cespedes, the Spanish governor of eastern Florida during the late 18th century at the time of the botanist Michaux's travels in that region; the name of the governor was rendered Lespedez in Michaux's *Flora*). Leguminosae. E US, E and tropical Asia, Australia. BUSH CLOVER. Some 40 species, shrubs or herbs with tri-foliolate leaves and pealike flowers in racemes, axillary fascicles or panicles in summer. Cultivate as for *Indigofera*.

L. bicolor EZO-YAMA-HAGI; E Asia, naturalized E US; to 10 ft (3 m), woody-based perennial; flowers ½–4¾ in (1–12 cm), purple-rose or rose-violet, loosely packed in axillary racemes or in 'Yakushima', dwarf, to 12 in (30 cm) tall, with small leaves and flowers; *L. thunbergii* MIYAGINO-HAGI; Japan, China; perennial herb or subshrub, 3¼–6½ ft (1–2 m); flowers to ¾ in (2 cm), rose-purple, in numerous pendulous racemes to 6 in (15 cm) grouped in terminal panicles to 32 in (80 cm); includes 'Alba', with white flowers and terminal clusters, and 'Summer Beauty', of spreading habit, to 5½ ft (1.6 m) tall, with long-lasting flowers.

Varieties of lettuce
Lettuces may by hearting (foreground), and harvested whole, or nonhearting, forming a loose rosette of leaves to pick individually.

lettuce (*Lactuca sativa*) A cultigen possibly derived from *Lactuca serriola*, it originated in the region encompassing Asia Minor, Transcaucasia, Iran and Turkestan. It was first used as a medicinal plant and treated as a food plant as early as 4500 BC. Headed types did not appear until the 16th-century. Lettuce is widely cultivated in both temperate and tropical regions as an annual salad vegetable; in cooler regions, it is important as a greenhouse crop. It is successfully grown where mean temperature is in the range of 50–68°F (10–20°C); higher temperatures prevent heading, cause bolting and also produce a bitter leaf flavor.

The ideal site is an open area with light, well-drained and fertile soil of around 6.0 pH. The range of cultivars enables lettuce to be produced in the open throughout most of the year, and some are hardy enough to overwinter unprotected in mild areas. Cultivars can be divided into hearting and nonhearting groups. Hearting types include LOOSEHEADS (BUTTERHEADS), which have soft-textured, flat leaves forming a dense firm head, and CRISPHEADS, which are usually larger, later maturing, with less tendency to bolt, and crisp-textured, wrinkled leaves. The term 'Iceberg' lettuce refers to crisphead cultivars producing large heads, from which the outer leaves are removed after harvest to leave the white solid hearts, which have good keeping quality. 'Webbs' lettuce refers to some crisphead cultivars with a less

dense heart and more usable outer leaves. Loosehead and crisphead cultivars may be referred to as cabbage lettuce. A third type of hearting lettuce is the COS lettuce with upright, long thick leaves usually forming a loose heart and taking longer to mature than the cabbage types. Some cultivars are described as "semi-Cos," producing compact, crunchy hearts of sweet flavor.

Nonhearting lettuces are mainly the so-called SALAD BOWL types, which form a rosette of leaves suitable for picking individually; alternatively, the head may be cut for use, with resprouting usually occurring from the stump. These cultivars are the least prone to bolting, and include highly decorative sorts with deeply indented or frilly leaves, which may be in various shades of green or red according to cultivar. CUT-AND-COME-AGAIN cultivars are sometimes referred to separately in the nonhearting category. They include old European, looseleaf types which may be smooth or curly leaved.

It is possible to modify the growth habit of lettuce by planting it at high density to encourage the formation of leaves and inhibit head formation. The leaves can then be cut ¾–1¼ in (2–3 cm) above soil level; the remaining stumps will produce a second crop that will be ready to harvest between 4 and 7 weeks later. Cos lettuce is best suited for leaf production.

Lettuce may be sown direct, or in seed trays or cell modules under protection for subsequent transplanting. They do not establish well in hot weather so summer raisings are best direct-sown. Seed should be sown in drills ¾ in (2 cm) deep at two-week intervals for continuity of supply. Sowing may take place from early spring until fall, but germination, particularly of the loosehead types, is often erratic when soil temperatures are greater than 77°F (25°C). Watering will reduce the soil temperature and improve germination; other helpful devices include covering the seedbed with a reflective white material after sowing, or sowing after the heat of daytime has passed. Except during midsummer, thinnings from direct sowings can be used to provide a further crop, which will mature approximately 10 days later.

Later crops will benefit from protection under cloches during the fall; for a protected winter crop, fall sowings can either be made in the open or under glass for transplanting to unheated frames or greenhouses. Cold-hardy cultivars can be overwintered outdoors to provide an early crop during late spring; these should be sown *in situ* during late summer and thinned to approximately 3 in (8 cm) apart in the fall. A final thinning should be done when growth recommences in spring to leave 12 in (30 cm) between plants. Overwintered crops benefit from a top-dressing of nitrogen fertilizer during early spring.

Spacing of lettuce plants varies according to cultivar, but for general guidance, standard looseheads can be grown at 10 in (25 cm) spacings in rows 12 in (30 cm) apart; crispheads 12–15 in (30–38 cm) × 15 in (38 cm) apart; and cos and 'salad-bowl' types 14 × 14 in (35 × 35 cm) apart. 'Cut-and-come-again' types may be spaced as close as 1 in (2.5 cm), in rows 4¾ in (12 cm) apart.

For heading lettuce, the time from planting to maturity varies from 60–80 days during the summer to 90–145 days during the cooler period of the year. Plants should be kept well-watered, particularly during the later stages of growth.

INDIAN LETTUCE (*Lactuca indica*) is an erect perennial up to 4¼ ft (1.3 m), grown for its edible leaves; it is of Chinese origin but now grown in India, Malaysia, Indonesia, the Philippines and Japan. In warm climates, seeds are sown in nursery beds or containers and transplanted at 12 × 12 in (30 × 30 cm) spacings. Propagation by root cuttings

Cut-and-come-again lettuce
These loose-leaved lettuces, which resprout from a cut stump, may be sold as seed mixtures for a varied supply of salad leaves.

is possible and axillary buds may develop from the base to produce edible shoots. In temperate areas, seeds may be sown early in the year under greenhouse conditions, at temperatures ranging from 68–77°F (20–25°C); seedlings are transferred to 10–12 in (25–30 cm) pots when 4–6 in (10–15 cm) high. The first leaves may be harvested about 60 days from sowing or planting. The term Indian lettuce is also used as the popular name for *Montia perfoliata* (winter purslane), which is grown as a salad crop.

STEM LETTUCE (CELTUCE, ASPARAGUS LETTUCE, CHINESE LETTUCE) (*Lactuca sativa* var. *asparagina*) is widely grown in its native China, and cultivated in tropical southeast Asia. It is a nonheading form of lettuce whose immature stems and leaves are used as a cooked vegetable. The mature leaves are large, coarse and inedible and the thickened stems may grow to 3¼ ft (1 m) high. In temperate climates, the crop can be grown under greenhouse conditions, with a temperature range of 68–77°F (20–25°C), or outdoors in warm sheltered sites. Seeds may be sown early in the year and seedlings transferred to 10–12 in (25–30 cm) pots, or spaced 12–14 in (30–35 cm) apart in the border, when at the 3–4-leaf stage. Harvest at 3–4 months, when the stems are 1 in (2.5 cm) in diameter and the plants 12 in (30 cm) high.

Possible problems: *aphids, root aphids, cutworms, leatherjackets, slugs and snails; downy mildew, gray mold, virus; tipburn.*

Leucadendron (from Greek *leukos*, white, and *dendron*, tree, alluding to the best-known species, *L. argenteum*, the silver tree). Proteaceae. South Africa. Some 80 species, shrubs or trees with tough foliage and conelike, terminal inflorescences surrounded by showy, leaflike bracts. Cultivate as for *Protea.*

L. argenteum SILVER TREE; tree to 33 ft (10 m); leaves to 6 in (15 cm), lanceolate with adpressed brilliant silvery hairs; inflorescence 4¾–8 in (12–20 cm) in diameter, bracts silver-gray, downy without, shining within; *L.* 'Safari Sunset' (*L. salignum* × *L. laureolum*; vigorous shrub to 8 ft (2.5 m); leaves to 3½ in (9 cm), deep green, flushed red particularly toward branch tips; inflorescence 4–8 in (10–20 cm) in

diameter, bracts light copper red becoming deep wine red fading to golden yellow, smooth, glossy; foliage used in floristry.

Leucanthemella (diminutive of Greek *leukos*, white, and *anthemon*, flower). Compositae. SE Europe, E Asia. 2 species, perennial herbs with branched stems and daisylike flower heads in summer. Cultivate as for *Tanacetum. L. serotina* SE Europe; to 5 ft (1.5 m), branched above; leaves to 4¾ in (12 cm), lanceolate to oblong, base 2–4-lobed, toothed; ray florets white or red; includes 'Herbstern', with clear white ray florets and tinted yellow disk florets.

Leucanthemopsis (from *Leucanthemum*, and Greek *opsis*, appearance). Compositae. European mountains and N Africa. 6 species of dwarf, tufted perennials with pinnately lobed or dissected leaves and daisylike flower heads. Grow in sun in free-draining soil. Protect from cold, wet conditions. Increase by stem tip cuttings or seed. *L. alpina* (Europe; tufted or mat-forming to 6 in (15 cm); leaves to 1½ in (4 cm), ovate to spathulate, crenate to pinnatifid or palmatifid, gray-hairy or glabrous; flower heads to 1½ in (4 cm) in diameter, ray florets white, sometimes becoming pink, disk florets orange-yellow; includes subsp. *tomentosa*, dwarf, tomentose.

Leucanthemum (from Greek *leukos*, white, and *anthemon*, flower). Compositae. Europe, N Asia. About 25 species, annual or perennial herbs with daisylike flower heads in summer. The hardy border perennials grouped under *L.* × *superbum* are greatly valued for the profusion of blooms carried over long periods in summer; they are good for cutting. Grow in full sun, in moderately fertile, well-drained and moisture-retentive soil; division of clumps every second or third year will maintain flower quality, although a number of the cultivars are easily raised from seed and flower abundantly in their first year.

L. × *superbum* (*L. maximum* × *L. lacustre*); SHASTA DAISY; garden origin; perennial erect to 3¼ ft (1 m)+; flower heads to 4 in (10 cm) in diameter, ray florets pure white, disk florets yellow; over 50 cultivars, mostly white; the original single flowers are now mostly superseded by fringed, semidouble and double cultivars; notable single-flowered cultivars include the old 'Phyllis Smith' and the feathery 'Bishopstone'; notable semidoubles include 'Aglaia' and the 36 in (90 cm) 'Esther Read'; anemone-centered doubles include 'Wirral Supreme' and 'T.E. Killin'; fully double flowers include 'Cobham Gold', with yellow central florets, and the tall, to 40 in (100 cm), 'Fiona Coghill' and 'Starburst'; dwarf cultivars include 'Powis Castle' and the 18 in (45 cm) 'Little Silver Princess'; *L. vulgare* MARGUERITE, OX-EYE DAISY, MOON DAISY; temperate Europe and Asia; perennial herb; to $3\frac{1}{4}$ ft (1 m), simple or branched; flower heads $1–3\frac{1}{2}$ in (2.5–9 cm) in diameter, solitary or clustered, ray florets white, occasionally short or absent, disk florets yellow; includes 'Hofenkröne', erect to 24 in (60 cm), with 'double', white flower heads, and 'Hullavington', with stem and leaves blotched yellow.

Leucocoryne (from Greek *leukos*, white, and *koryne*, club, referring to the white staminodes). Liliaceae (Alliaceae). Chile. 12 species, bulbous perennial herbs, many with the characteristic smell of garlic. The grasslike leaves often wither before flowering. Funnel-shaped flowers with six segments are carried in scapose umbels in spring and early summer. Grow in direct sun, in a medium-fertility loam-based mix containing plentiful sharp sand. Provide a minimum winter temperature of 41°F (5°C). Water sparingly in spring when growth resumes. After flowering impose a dry rest period. Propagate from seed sown when ripe, or under glass in spring. Alternatively, increase by offsets. *L. ixioides* GLORY OF THE SUN; to 18 in (45 cm); flowers fragrant, tepals to $\frac{5}{8}$ in (1.5 cm), free portions white or deeply edged lilac to violet-blue, tube white, stamens and staminodes yellow-white.

Leucogenes (from Greek *leukos*, white, and *genea*, race). Compositae. New Zealand. 2–3 species, woody-based, tomentose perennial herbs with dense, overlapping leaves and button-like flower heads in a dense cluster, subtended by a collar of leaves. Both

species are extremely desirable for the alpine house and rock garden, with densely silver-white woolly foliage, and each flower head surrounded by a ray of white felted bracts. They suffer in cold, wet conditions, but may survive outdoors in protected locations to 10°F (−12°C). Plant in crevices in the rock garden in a lean, gritty and moisture-retentive medium, in bright light but with shade from hot sun. In the alpine house, grow in well-crocked pots in a mix of equal parts loam, leaf mold and coarse sand. Keep in cool and well-ventilated conditions, avoiding hot sun. Water plentifully and carefully when in growth; keep only just moist in winter. Repot as growth recommences in spring. Propagate by softwood cuttings in moist sand in early summer, or from fresh seed sown ripe.

L. grandiceps (SOUTH ISLAND EDELWEISS; leaves to $4 \times 1\frac{1}{2}$ in (10 × 4 cm), obovate to cuneate, blunt, tomentose; flower heads subtended by a collar of some 15, silvery-white tomentose leaves; *L. leontopodium* (NORTH ISLAND EDELWEISS; leaves to $\frac{3}{4} \times \frac{1}{4}$ in (2 × 0.5 cm), linear to oblong, acute, silver-white- to yellow-tomentose; flower heads subtended by a collar of some 20, white leaves.

Leucojum (from Greek *leukos*, white, and *ion*, violet, a name first applied by Theophrastus to *Matthiola* and a white-flowered bulbous plant). Amaryllidaceae. W Europe to Middle East, N Africa. SNOWFLAKE. About 10 species, bulbous perennials, resembling and related to *Galanthus*. In fall or spring, they bear clusters of nodding, bell-shaped flowers on slender scapes. The following are fully hardy. *L. vernum* and *L. aestivum* are suited to naturalizing in damp rough grass, or for growing in damp pockets in the rock garden; the latter thrives in moist, rich, heavy soil, especially by ponds or streams, and tolerates waterlogged conditions. Grow in partial shade, or in sun where soil remains permanently moist. *L. autumnale* is suitable for the sunny border front, path edging and for warm sunny locations on the rock garden; it is one of the least demanding of the smaller species for growing in the open, given a well-drained sandy soil. Although sometimes grown in the open in warm

and perfectly drained situations, *L. roseum* is also suited to cultivation in the alpine house or bulb frame, where its delicate beauty can be appreciated at close quarters, and where its requirements for hot, dry dormancy during summer and protection from winter wet will be more easily met. Propagate by division in spring or fall, after flowering, alternatively by seed sown when ripe.

L. aestivum SUMMER SNOWFLAKE, LODDON LILY; Eurasia; scape to 24 in (60 cm), flowers produced in spring, 2–7 per scape, faintly chocolate-scented, perianth segments broadly oblong, to $\frac{3}{4}$ in (2 cm), white, marked green just below apex; *L. autumnale* SW Europe, N Africa; scape slender, green- to red-brown, usually about 6 in (15 cm), flowers produced in late summer and fall, 1–4 per scape, perianth segments oblong, $\frac{1}{2}$ in (1 cm), crystalline white, often flushed pink at base; *L. nicaeense* S France; scape to 6 in (15 cm), usually less, flowers 1–3 per scape, produced in spring, perianth segments oblanceolate, to $\frac{1}{2}$ in (12 mm), white, spreading; *L. roseum* Corsica, Sardinia; scape to 6 in (15 cm), flowers 1 per scape produced in late summer and fall, perianth segments oblanceolate, to $\frac{1}{2}$ in (1 cm), pale pink, darker along median line; *L. trichophyllum* S Portugal, SW Spain, Morocco; scape slender, to 10 in (25 cm), flowers 2–4 per scape produced in winter and spring, perianth segments oblanceolate to oblong, white or flushed pink to purple; *L. vernum* SPRING-SNOWFLAKE; France to east central Europe, naturalized Great Britain; scape stout, to 8 in (20 cm), deep green, flowers 1(–2) per scape, appearing in late winter, perianth segments broadly oblong, to $\frac{3}{4}$ in (2 cm), white, variably marked green or yellow just below apex.

Leucophyta (from Greek *leucos*, white, and *phyton*, plant). Compositae. Australia. 18 species, annual and perennial herbs and small evergreen shrubs, usually densely covered in white wool, with entire leaves and florets packed in small, globose heads. In cool temperate gardens, *Leucophyta* is often damaged or killed by cold, wet winters. For this reason, it tends to be seen in the form of young, rather sparse plants, used for silver effects in bedding, baskets and patio pots and repropagated annually. In milder climates or in very sheltered positions to 10°F (–12°C), it will survive, forming broad, impenetrable hummocks; these thrive in gravelly, dry places, and are able to withstand severe buffeting and salt spray. Plant in a very free-draining soil in full sun. Propagate by semiripe cuttings in late summer, and overwinter in a cool, well-ventilated greenhouse. Plant out after frosts have passed. *L. brownii* (shrublet to 20 × 32 in (50 × 80 cm); branches wiry and intricate, clothed with scalelike leaves and in silvery white to gray scurf; flower heads resembling silver buttons.

Leucospermum cordifolium
These South African shrubs may be grown outdoors only in areas where temperatures do not fall below 41°F (5°C).

Leucospermum (from Greek *leukos*, white, and *sperma*, seed). Proteaceae. South Africa, Zimbabwe. 46 species, small, evergreen trees or shrubs with tough leaves and showy, terminal flower heads. These are conelike and composed of tubular flowers with reflexed segments and long, deflexed styles. Cultivate as for *Protea*.

L. catherinae CATHERINE'S PINCUSHION, CATHERINE-WHEEL LEUCOSPERMUM; shrub to 8 ft (2.5 m); inflorescence to 6 in (15 cm) in diameter, flowers pale orange, deepening to red-gold; *L. cordifolium* (syn. *L. nutans*; shrub to 6½ ft (2 m); inflorescence spherical, to 4¾ in (12 cm) in diameter, flowers yellow, orange or crimson; *L. reflexum* (small erect shrub to 6½ ft (2 m); inflorescence 1¾–2½ in (4.5–6 cm) in diameter, flowers crimson.

Leucothoë (for the daughter of Orchamur, King of Babylon and beloved of Apollo). Ericaceae. US,

S America, Himalaya, E Asia, Madagascar. Some 44 species, deciduous or evergreen shrubs with leathery leaves and small, white, tubular to ovoid flowers in terminal or axillary racemes or panicles in spring. Hardy to –10°F (–23°C), *Leucothoë* is suitable for the peat terrace, for open situations in the woodland garden and other naturalistic areas, and for moist sites in the rock garden. *L. keiskei* makes attractive groundcover, and is also amenable to pot cultivation in the alpine house. Grow in dappled shade in moist, humus-rich, nonalkaline soil, and mulch annually with leaf mold. Prune when necessary to restrict growth after flowering, cutting out old and weak growth at ground level. Propagate by semiripe cuttings during late summer in a closed case with bottom heat. Alternatively, increase by division of suckering species, or by layering.

L. axillaris SE US; evergreen shrub about 5 ft (1.5 m); leaves 2–4½ in (5–11 cm), ovate to oblong, dentate in apical half, lustrous green, glabrous above, paler and sparsely hirsute beneath; 'Compacta': compact; *L. fontanesiana* DROOPING LAUREL, DOG-HOBBLE, SWITCH IVY; SE US; evergreen shrub to 6½ ft (2 m); branches arching, tinged red; leaves 2½–6 in (6–16 cm), oblong to lanceolate tapering finely, glabrous, ciliate, dentate, dark green, lustrous above; 'Nana', compact, low-growing; 'Rainbow', young growth crimson, leaf variegation pink and cream, later white and green; this species was treated by many as *L. walteri*; *L. keiskei* Japan; evergreen shrub; branches erect or prostrate, slender, young shoots red, glabrous; leaves 1½–3½ in (4–9 cm), narrowly ovate to broadly lanceolate, apex long and slender, margins shallowly dentate, sparsely setose beneath; *L. racemosa* FETTER BUSH, SWEET BELLS; E US; deciduous shrub, 3¼–8 ft (1–2.5 m); leaves 1–2½ in (2.5–6 cm), oblong to ovate or elliptic, acute, shallowly round-toothed and finely serrate.

leveling (US: grading) a technique for producing level surfaces on a garden site by excavating banks and ridges and filling hollows; also, a method of determining heights, often for the same purpose, using a surveyor's level. Leveling

land is a demanding operation that should only be undertaken where essential for the siting of an amenity, and where the slope cannot be exploited as a design feature. Terracing is a compromise option in some situations, but if the gradient is steep expensive retaining walls will be required.

Much of the leveling necessary in the course of gardening can be assessed and verified by eye, but there may sometimes be a need to use leveling devices. On sites where the variation is only slight, a spirit level, wooden pegs and a long plank are sufficient. The pegs are driven in progressively across the plot to depths that allow the bridging plank to lie dead level, when checked with a spirit level. When all of the peg tops are in position, the soil is moved until level with the tops or with predetermined regularly spaced marks on each peg.

On steeper sites, the same principle is employed using boning rods. These are wooden stakes, each about 36 in (90 cm) long, with a pointed end and a short horizontal crosspiece fixed at the top to form a T-shape. The first rod is driven into the soil at the lowest point of the slope, and the second a few feet away and manipulated in such a way that its top is level with that of the first rod when checked with a bridging plank and spirit level. More boning rods can then be sighted into level positions by eyeing across three horizontal members. On the steepest gradients trenching will be necessary to accommodate insertion of the rods to the desired level. Working datum points for soil-moving can be fixed by marking the individual boning rods at equal distances from the top.

Steps should be taken to avoid burying topsoil and exposing subsoil. To this end, wherever possible, temporarily remove topsoil and carry out leveling on the subsoil.

Lewisia (for Captain Meriwether Lewis [1774–1809] of the Lewis and Clark expedition across North America). Portulacaceae. Western N America. 19 species glabrous, low-growing, perennial herbs with rosettes of thinly succulent leaves and, in spring and summer, cymes or panicles of broadly funnel-shaped flowers with five or more petals. Fully hardy and suitable for the rock garden, scree, alpine house and frame. Although cold-tolerant, they will rot away in wet winter conditions and may need to be grown in the alpine house or frame. Outdoors, grow deciduous species in perfectly draining, gritty and humus-rich soil on sloping sites in sun. Site evergreen species in a north- or northeast-facing niche, ensuring shade from the hottest sun, in a circumneutral or slightly acidic medium; provide a collar of grit at the neck, or grow in a vertical crevice where excess moisture will not accumulate in the rosette. Despite their alpine origins, *Lewisia* species need a fairly fertile soil to perform well and the addition of bonemeal or finely graded, well-rotted manure to the medium is recommended. In the alpine house, use an open mix of equal parts loam, leaf mold and sharp sand; top-dress with a collar of grit. Ensure that pots have good drainage. Water moderately and carefully when in growth, allowing the medium to become almost dry between waterings; withhold water from deciduous species as they enter dormancy and keep them warm and dry. Water evergreens until late summer, then reduce water to keep almost dry in winter. Propagate by fresh seed sown in the shaded cold frame. Propagate evergreen species also by offsets in summer; establish these in a shaded frame in a gritty propagating mix before potting on.

L. columbiana evergreen; leaves ¾–4 in (2–10 cm), narrowly oblanceolate or linear, fleshy; flowers ½–1 in (1–2.5 cm) in diameter, off-white veined pink to pink or deep pink-magenta; *L. cotyledon* evergreen; leaves 1¼–1½ in (3–4 cm), spathulate, oblanceolate or obovate, slightly glaucous, fleshy; flowers ¾–1½ in (2–4 cm) in diameter, pink-purple with pale and dark stripes, sometimes white, cream with pink-orange stripes, apricot or yellow; *L. nevadensis* deciduous; leaves 1½–6 in (4–15 cm), narrowly linear or linear-oblanceolate, fleshy; flowers ¾–1½ in (2–3.5 cm) in diameter, white or rarely pink-white; *L. rediviva* BITTERROOT; deciduous; leaves many, ⅝–2 in (1.5–5 cm), linear or clavate, subterete, withered at flowering; flowers 2–2¾ in (5–7 cm) in diameter, rose-pink, purple-pink or

white; *L. tweedyi* (evergreen; leaves 1½–3 in (4–8 cm), loosely tufted, green, often with purple suffusion, broadly oblanceolate or obovate; flowers 1½–2¾ in (4–7 cm) in diameter, pink-peach to yellow or rarely white.

Leycesteria (for William Leycester, chief justice of Bengal *c.* 1820). Caprifoliaceae. W Himalaya to SW China. 6 species, deciduous or semievergreen suckering shrubs with erect, clumped stems. Five-lobed, funnelform flowers are produced in pendent racemes in late spring and summer and followed by berries. *L. formosa* tolerates urban and maritime conditions, alkaline soil, and windswept locations, and is hardy to about 5°F (–15°C). *L. crocothyrsos* will tolerate temperatures to 23°F (–5°C) with protection from cold winds. Plant both in rich moisture-retentive soil in sun or part shade. Sow fresh seed in fall in the cold frame, or store in damp peat and sand for sowing in early spring. Divide established clumps of *L. formosa* in fall. Propagate *L. crocothyrsos* by semiripe cuttings of lateral shoots with a heel. The hollow stems of *L. formosa* are liable to be cut back by frost. It benefits from being cut to the ground in spring.

L. crocothyrsos Himalaya (Assam), N Burma; to 8 ft (2.5 m); flowers rich yellow in whorls of 6 on arching racemes to 4 in (10 cm); fruit translucent, yellow-green); *L. formosa* HIMALAYAN HONEYSUCKLE; Himalaya, W China, E Tibet; to 6½ ft (2 m); flowers white tinted red-purple, whorled on pendulous racemes to 4 in (10 cm) with wine red bracts; fruit beadlike, sea-green becoming maroon then purple-black, ripening at different speeds giving a multicolored effect.

Leymus (from Greek *elymos*, a kind of millet). Gramineae. Northern temperate regions, 1 species Argentina. Some 40 species, rhizomatous, perennial grasses with slender, sharply pointed, glaucous leaves and narrow, straw-colored inflorescences in summer. *L. arenarius* is often used as a sand-binder with marram grass, *Ammophila arenaria*, but is valuable in gardens as (invasive) groundcover, especially in association with other coastal natives and blue-gray and silver-leaved plants. Shear

over in spring for a flush of fresh blue-green growth. Fully hardy, it needs full sun and a sandy or gritty, free-draining soil. Remove unwanted shoots to prevent its rapid spread. Increase by division or rooted offsets. *L. arenarius* (syn. *Elymus arenarius*); BLUE LYME GRASS, BUNCH GRASS, SAND WILD RYE, LYME GRASS, SEA LYME GRASS, EUROPEAN DUNE GRASS; N and W Europe, Eurasia; culms to 5 ft (1.5 m) clumped and spreading by stolons; leaf blades linear, flat, to 24 × ⅝ in (60 × 1.5 cm), tough-textured, glaucous blue-gray, margins becoming rolled in dry conditions; spikes to 10 in (25 cm), slender, becoming parchment-colored.

liana, liane a woody climbing vine.

Liatris (derivation of name obscure). Compositae. N America. BLAZING STAR, GAYFEATHER, BUTTON SNAKE ROOT, SNAKE ROOT. About 35 species, cormous or tuberous perennial herbs with clumped, narrow leaves and many, small and feathery flower heads arranged in erect and leafy-stemmed, narrowly cylindrical spikes in summer. Fully hardy and suited to the herbaceous and cut-flower border and to more informal situations. Flowering is prolonged by removing spent blooms at the tip of the spike (they flower from the top down). Most species are tolerant of poor, dry soil in cultivation but perform best in fertile, well-drained and moist soil. Tubers are prone to rot in soil that is excessively wet in winter and they also are attractive to various rodents, for which they make a desirable food source. Propagate by division or seed sown ripe in fall.

L. pycnostachya KANSAS GAYFEATHER; SE US; to 5 ft (1.5 m); flower heads red-purple, rarely white, crowded in very dense spikes to 12 × 1¼ in (30 × 3 cm); *L. scariosa* SE US; to 32 in (80 cm); flower heads purple, few to many, in spikes; includes 'Alba', with white flower heads, 'Magnifica', with very large, white flower heads, 'September Glory', to 50 in (125 cm), with deep purple flowers, and 'White Spire', with flowers in long white spikes; *L. spicata* (BLAZING STAR; E US; to 5 ft (1.5 m); flower heads red-purple, clustered in a dense spike, to 28 in (70 cm); includes 'Alba', with white flower heads, 'Blue

Bird', with vivid mauve-blue flowers, 'Kabold' (syn. 'Goblin'), dwarf to 16 in (40 cm), with bright violet flower heads, and 'Snow Queen', to 30 in (75 cm), with snow-white flower heads.

Libertia (for Marie A. Libert [1782–1865], Belgian student of liverworts). Iridaceae. Australia, temperate S America. 20 species, rhizomatous perennial herbs, with grassy to swordlike leaves in basal tufts or fans and panicles of small, saucer-shaped flowers in summer. Hardy to 14°F (−10°C). Grow in sun or dappled shade in moist but well-drained, slightly acidic soil. In regions at the limits of its hardiness, mulch in winter with bracken litter or other organic matter. Propagate by division in spring or by seed.

L. grandiflora New Zealand; differs from *L. ixioides* in its outer perianth segments with an olive to bronze keel, and inner segments to ⅗ in (1.5 cm); *L. ixioides* New Zealand, Chatham Islands; leaves 8–16 in (20–40 cm), linear, rigid; inflorescence a broad panicle composed of umbellate 2–10-flowered clusters, outer perianth segments white tinted brown or green, inner segments to ½ in (1 cm), white; *L. peregrinans* New Zealand; leaves to 28 in (70 cm), olive-bronze to dull orange with red-tinted veins and margins; flowers to ¾ in (2 cm), white.

lichen a composite organism formed from the symbiotic relationship of a fungus and an alga, the green cells of the latter establishing among threadlike growths of the fungus. Lichens take on many forms and are commonly found as colored crusty growths on rocks, stone walls, roofs, tree trunks and soil. In moist rural climates, they may develop abundantly on the branches of trees, but rarely thrive in industrial areas. Their presence in an area therefore provides some indication of freedom from pollution.

Lichens are slow-growing and persistent. Although attractive on stonework, they are horticulturally

pale, crusty growth

Lichen

undesirable where occurring on lawns as gelatinous patches or as dog lichens, and where dense colonies develop on fruit trees. Lichens can be controlled by spraying cresylic acid on paths and tar oil on dormant deciduous trees and woody shrubs; infested lawns should be aerated and treated with lawn sand containing dichlorophen. All of these treatments should be carried out according to the manufacturer's recommendations.

lifting (1) the removal of a plant from the ground, prior to transplanting, division, or winter storage; (2) used of the harvesting of root and tuber vegetable crops where the use of a fork is required; (3) the heaving up of plants out of the ground following severe frost.

light (1) an essential requirement of green plants, providing energy for the manufacture of organic compounds through the process of photosynthesis. Plants vary in their need and tolerance of light intensity, and growth and especially flowering in some is influenced by the duration of daylight; see *photoperiodism, supplementary lighting*; (2) a movable glazed cover of a frame. The traditional English light is multipaned and usually measures 6 × 4 ft (1.8 × 1.2 m); the Dutch light measures approximately 4½ × 2⅓ ft (1.4 × 0.75 m) and is formed of one sheet of glass; (3) describing soil containing a high proportion of sand. Such soil is naturally prone to drying out and early exhaustion of nutrients, but has the advantages of being early-warming and relatively easy to cultivate.

ligneous, lignose woody in texture.

lignin a deposition within cell walls of woody plants that is formed from phenolic polymers and which give rise to thickening and strengthening; the basis of woody plant structure.

lignite a kind of coal which retains abundant traces of fibrous vegetation, representing a

middle stage in the conversion of peat to bituminous coal. It is sometimes added in crushed form to potting media to increase the cation exchange capacity. Lignite has the physical characteristics of sand, and its effectiveness is influenced by particle size, fine grades leading to reduced drainage and aeration. Problems may arise from its use, due to salinity. Also known as brown coal.

lignotuber the swollen woody base of some shrubs adapted to withstand fire and drought.

Ligularia (from Latin *ligula*, a little tongue, referring to the tongue-shaped ray florets). Compositae. Temperate Eurasia. LEOPARD PLANT. About 180 species, perennial herbs with long-stalked, basal leaves and, in late summer, small, button- or daisylike flowers in tall spikes or scapose clusters. Fully hardy, *Ligularia* species demand deep, moist, fertile and humus-rich soil in full sun or dappled shade. Propagate by division.

L. dentata (syn. *L. clivorum*; China, Japan; to 3¼ ft (1 m); leaves to 12 × 16 in (30 × 40 cm), reniform to orbicular, deeply cordate, dentate; flower heads few to many, in broad, scapose heads, ray florets bright orange; includes 'Desdemona', to 48 in (120 cm), with purple-bronze leaves and deep orange flower heads, 'Othello', to 48 in (120 cm), with rounded, long-stemmed, dark purple to maroon-black leaves and deep orange flower heads, and 'Sommergold', with rich gold flowers; *L. przewalskii* N China; to 6½ ft (2 m); stems dark purple; leaves to 16 in (40 cm) in diameter, deeply palmately lobed, segments lobed or toothed; flower heads yellow, many, small, in long, narrow racemes; *L. stenocephala* China, Japan, Taiwan; to 5 ft (1.5 m); stems dark purple; leaves to 14 × 12 in (35 × 30 cm), hastate to cordate or triangular, apex tapering; flower heads yellow, many, in a long, slender raceme; includes 'The Rocket', to 70 in (180 cm), with near-black stems and leafstalks, and 'Weihenstephan', to 70 in (180 cm), with large, gold flower heads.

ligulate (1) possessing a ligule; (2) strap-shaped, usually more narrowly so than in lorate.

L

461

ligule (1) a strap-shaped body, such as the limb of ray florets in Compositae; (2) the thin, scarious, sometimes hairy projection from the top of the leaf sheath in Gramineae and some other families, for example Palmae, Zingiberaceae; (3) any strap-shaped appendage; (4) an envelope sheathing the emerging foliage of Palmae.

Ligustrum (Latin name for privet). Oleaceae. Europe, N Africa, E and SE Asia, Australia. PRIVET. Some 50 species, shrubs and small trees, deciduous or evergreen, with smooth oblong or ovate leaves, panicles of small, white to cream flowers in summer and dark, fleshy fruit. The genus includes tough shrubs or small trees useful for hedging or informal screens, even in part shade and on city sites. *L. ovalifolium* and its cultivar 'Aureum' have largely replaced *L. vulgare* as a popular hedging plant since they are more likely to remain evergreen, although very severe winters may kill hedges back to ground level. More choice species, such as *L. lucidum* and *L. sinense*, are grown as specimen shrubs or trees in sunny, sheltered sites; they are valued for their foliage, soft, plumelike spires of cream or white, late-summer flowers and attractive fruits. Although drought- and shade-tolerant, hedges of *L. ovalifolium* and *L. vulgare* will make a healthier backdrop given sufficient moisture, sun and an annual application of fertilizer. Prune vigorous, well-established hedge plants two to three times annually. Old, straggly hedges may be rejuvenated by pruning hard back and watering and feeding thoroughly. Propagate evergreens from greenwood cuttings in spring or summer in a closed case or under mist, and deciduous species from hardwood cuttings in winter. Alternatively, sow seed in spring. Privet is susceptible to privet thrips, privet aphid, leaf spot, and lilac leaf miner.

L. japonicum Japan, Korea; evergreen shrub to 13 ft (4 m); leaves to 4 in (10 cm), glabrous, dark green, broadly ovate, often with red-green margins and midrib; flowers scented, in pyramidal panicle to 6 in (15 cm); 'Revolutum': narrow, erect, to 3¼ ft (1 m), with small, narrow leaves; 'Rotundifolium': leaves round or broadly ovate, to 1½ in (4 cm); 'Variegatum': leaves stippled

and edged white; *L. lucidum* CHINESE PRIVET, WHITE WAX TREE; China, Korea, Japan; evergreen shrub or small tree to 33 ft (10 m); leaves to 4 in (10 cm), ovate to elliptic, apex tapering; panicle 4–8 in (10–20 cm); fruit blue-black; 'Aureovariegatum': leaves yellow-variegated; 'Compactum': dense, with waxy, dark green leaves; 'Latifolium': leaves very large, glossy dark green; 'Macrophyllum': leaves large; 'Tricolor': leaves marked white and yellow, flushed pink when young; *L. ovalifolium* (CALIFORNIA PRIVET, OVAL-LEAVED PRIVET; Japan; semievergreen shrub to 13 ft (4 m), upright; leaves 1¼–2¾ in (3–7 cm), elliptic to ovate, blunt to acute, glossy, dark above, yellow-green beneath; flowers off-white, malodorous, many, in panicle to 4 in (10 cm); 'Albomarginatum': leaves edged white; 'Argenteum': leaves margined silver; 'Aureum': leaves yellow with broad, golden margins; 'Compactum': dense and slow-growing; 'Tricolor': new growth flushed pink and leaves ultimately variegated yellow-white; and 'Variegatum', with leaves stippled pale yellow; *L. sinense* China; deciduous shrub to 13 ft (4 m); leaves to 2¾ in (7 cm), elliptic to oblong, olive green above, paler beneath, midrib downy; flowers off-white, fragrant, in panicles to 4 in (10 cm); fruit claret-colored; 'Variegatum': leaves variegated soft gray-green and white; *L.* × *vicaryi* (*L. ovalifolium* × *L. vulgare*; golden origin; deciduous, spreading; leaves golden; *L. vulgare* COMMON PRIVET; N Europe, Mediterranean, N Africa, Asia Minor; distribution enlarged and confused by cultivation; deciduous shrub to 16 ft (5 m), upright, dense; leaves oblong to ovate or lanceolate, glabrous, dark green; flowers off-white in dense, erect panicles to 2 in (5 cm), malodorous; fruit black, glossy; 'Argenteovariegatum': leaves speckled white; 'Aureovariegatum': leaves marked golden yellow; 'Aureum': leaves golden; 'Buxifolium': leaves persistent, small, ovate; 'Leucocarpum': fruit white-green; 'Xanthocarpum': fruit bright yellow; var. *italicum*: syn. 'Sempervirens', leaves evergreen.

Lilium (Latin form of Greek *leirion*) Liliaceae (Liliaceae). LILY. Temperate Northern Hemisphere. About 100

Stem bulbils on lily
The tiny bulbils that grow in leaf axils may be harvested and "sown" in moist medium with a covering of coarse sand or fine grit.

species, bulbous perennials. The bulbs are composed of fleshy scales and produce erect stems clothed with narrow leaves. The flowers are carried toward the summit of these stems in late spring and summer. They consist of 6 tepals and are erect and cup-shaped, horizontal and funnel- or bowl-shaped, or pendulous and shaped like a bell or "turk's-cap" (i.e., tepals outspread with recurved tips).

In general terms, the following are hardy and will grow in sun or dappled shade in a well-drained, humus-rich soil. Most lilies grow in acidic soil, but some grow on alkaline substrates. The following are considered to be lime-loving or lime-tolerant: *L. amabile, L. bulbiferum, L. canadense, L. candidum, L. cernuum, L. chalcedonicum, L. davidii, L. hansonii, L. henryi, L. lankongense, L. longiflorum, L. martagon, L. monadelphum, L. pardalinum, L. pyrenaicum, L. regale.* Hybrids derived from these species are most probably lime-tolerant. Only a few lime-loving species, such as *L. henryi* and *L. candidum,* actually appear to deteriorate when grown in acidic soil. With the exception of *L. candidum,* lilies like to be planted at a depth of about 3–4 in (8–10 cm) and in deep, fertile soil. Bulbs may be planted on a layer of sharp sand where the subsoil is heavy. Moisture should be plentiful in late winter and spring, easing gradually in summer so that, following flowering, the soil is still moist enough for the bulb to replenish itself. The soil should never be wet. In cool-temperate areas, plant bulbs outdoors in fall. If this is not possible, planting should be delayed until spring, the bulbs having

LILIUM

Name	Distribution	Height	Leaves	Flowers
L. amabile *L. fauriei*	Korea	to 36 in (90 cm)	to 3½ in (9 cm), scattered, lanceolate, 3-veined, absent on lower part of stem, numerous toward top	1–5, turk's-cap, in a raceme, malodorous; tepals 2¼ in (5.5 cm), red with dark purple spots, 2–3 fleshy papillae on upper surface; pollen red; stigma red-brown

Comments: Summer. 'Luteum': flowers yellow.

Name	Distribution	Height	Leaves	Flowers
L. auratum GOLDEN-RAYED LILY OF JAPAN, MOUNTAIN LILY	Japan	24–79 in (60–200 cm)	to 9 × 1½ in (22 × 4 cm), numerous, scattered, lanceolate, dark green, 5–7-veined, petiolate	6–30, 12 in (30 cm) wide, bowl-shaped, horizontal or slightly pendulous, in a raceme, very fragrant; tepals 4¾–7 × 1½–2 in (12–18 × 4–5 cm), white with yellow or crimson central streaks and crimson-spotted, fleshy papillae on basal part; pollen chocolate to red

Comments: Short-lived, requiring nonalkaline soil in full sun with root shade provided by low-growing plants. Summer–fall. Crossed with *L. speciosum*, *L. japonicum* and *L. rubellum* to give rise to a wide range of cultivars—'Apollo': central band and spots ruby-red. 'Crimson Beauty': cherry red, margin white. 'Praecox': heavily spotted; early flowering. 'Rubrum': tepals banded crimson. 'Tom Thumb': dwarf. var. *platyphyllum:* to 7½ ft (2.3 m); leaves broadly lanceolate; flowers larger with fewer spots on tepals. var. *rubrovittatum:* tepals banded yellow at base, deep crimson at apex. var. *virginale:* to 6½ ft (2 m); flowers white, streaked yellow, spotted pale yellow or pink; includes 'Album': flowers pure white.

Name	Distribution	Height	Leaves	Flowers
L. bakerianum *L. lowii*	N Burma, SW China	24–36 in (60–90 cm)	4 × ⅝ in (10 × 1.5 cm), scattered on upper part of stem, linear to lanceolate, 1–3-veined	1–6, bell-shaped, pendulous; tepals white, interior spotted red-brown, exterior tinged green, 2¾ × ⅝ in (7 × 1.5 cm); anthers orange

Comments: Summer.

Name	Distribution	Height	Leaves	Flowers
L. bulbiferum *L. chaixii* ORANGE LILY	S Europe	16–60 in (40–150 cm)	4 × ¾ in (10 × 2 cm), lanceolate, scattered, 3–7-veined	to 5, occasionally to 50, erect, cup-shaped, tepals 2½–3¼ × ¾–1¼ in (6–8.5 × 2–3 cm), bright orange, tips darker, interior spotted maroon; anthers brown; pollen orange

Comments: Grows in well-drained soil in summer shade. Summer. var. *croceum:* syn. *L. croceum;* tepals orange.

Name	Distribution	Height	Leaves	Flowers
L. canadense MEADOW LILY, WILD MEADOW LILY	Eastern N America	to 5 ft (1.5 m)	6 × ¾ in (15 × 2 cm), lanceolate to oblanceolate, mostly in whorls, veins 5–7	10–12, bell-shaped, pendulous, in an umbel; tepals 2–3 × ½–1 in (5–7.5 × 1–2.5 cm), yellow, basally spotted maroon; pollen yellow to red-brown

Comments: Plant in moist but well-drained soil. Summer. 'Chocolate Chips': tepal exteriors and tips crimson, fading to orange then yellow toward the interior base, spots large. 'Fire Engine': tepals slightly recurved, exterior and interior tips crimson, fading to orange then yellow near the base; pollen burnt-orange. 'Melted Spots': flowers yellow-orange, spots dense on the basal two-thirds. 'Peaches and Pepper': flowers peach-orange, finely spotted. var. *coccineum:* syn. *L. canadense* var. *rubrum;* flowers red, throat yellow.

Name	Distribution	Height	Leaves	Flowers
L. candidum MADONNA LILY, WHITE LILY	Balkans, E Mediterranean	3¼–6½ ft (1–2 m)	basal Leaves 9 × 2 in (22 × 5 cm), 3–5-veined, produced in fall, retained in winter, stem leaves scattered, 3 × ½ in (7.5 × 1 cm), lanceolate	5–20, funnel-shaped, fragrant, in a raceme; tepals 2–3 × ½–1½ in (5–8 × 1–4 cm) white, interior base yellow; pollen yellow

Comments: Summer.

L. auratum var. *platyphyllum*   *L.* 'Apollo'   *L. bulbiferum* var. *croceum*   *L. canadense*

LILIUM

Name	Distribution	Height	Leaves	Flowers
L. cernuum NODDING LILY **Comments:** Summer.	Korea, NE Manchuria, Russia	to 24 in (60 cm)	3–6 × ¹⁄₁₆–¹⁄₄ in (8–15 × 0.1–0.5 cm), scattered, mostly crowded on center third of stem, 1–3-veined, sessile	1–14, turk's-cap, 1½ in (3.5 cm) wide, fragrant, in a pendent raceme; tepals lilac, purple, pink or occasionally white, spotted purple; pollen lilac
L. chalcedonicum *L. heldreichii* SCARLET TURK'S-CAP LILY, RED MARTAGON OF CONSTANTINOPLE	Greece, S Albania	18–60 in (45–150 cm)	to 4½ × ⅝ in (11.5 × 1.5 cm), edged silver, spirally arranged, sessile, 3–5-veined	to 12, pendulous turk's-cap, 3 in (7.5 cm) wide, slightly scented; tepals scarlet, without spots; pollen scarlet

Comments: Summer. 'Maculatum': scarlet, spotted black.

L. × dalhansonii (*L. hansonii* × *L. martagon* var. *cattaniae*)	garden origin	5–6½ ft (1.5–2 m)		turk's-cap, 1¼ in (3 cm), malodorous; tepals, dark maroon, to pink, white or yellow, spotted darker; style purple

Comments: Summer. 'Backhouse hybrids': cream, yellow, pink to maroon with darker spots. 'Damson': plum-purple. 'Destiny': yellow, spotted brown. 'Discovery': rose-lilac, base white, tinged pink, spotted deep crimson, tips darker, exterior pink with a silvery sheen.

L. davidii *L. thayerae*	W China	3¼–4½ ft (1–1.4 m)	2½–4 × ¹⁄₁₆–⅛ in (6–10 × 0.2–0.4 cm), linear, acute, dark green, 1-veined, margins finely toothed and inrolled	5–20, turk's-cap, unscented, pendulous, in a raceme, buds hairy; tepals to 3 in (8 cm), vermilion spotted purple; pollen orange or scarlet

Comments: Summer. var. **unicolor:** syn. (*L. biondii*; stems shorter, to 3¼ ft (1 m); bulbs not stoloniferous; leaves more numerous and longer, very crowded; flowers paler, spots red, mauve or absent. var. **willmottiae:** syn. *L. sutchuenense, L. chinense*; stems to 6½ ft (2 m), arching; bulbs stoloniferous; Preston Hybrids, Patterson Hybrids, Fiesta Strain and North Hybrids developed from *L. davidii*.

L. duchartrei *L. farreri* MARBLE MARTAGON **Comments:** Summer.	W China	24–39 in (60–100 cm)	4¼ × ⅝ in (10.5 × 1.5 cm), dark green above, pale green beneath, lanceolate, scattered, sessile, margins rough, veins 3–5	to 12, turk's-cap, pendulous, fragrant, in an umbel; tepals white, spotted deep purple, tube green at base, exterior white flushed purple; pollen orange
L. formosanum	Taiwan	12–60 in (30–150 cm)	3–8 × ½ in (7.5–20 × 1 cm), scattered, dark green, oblong-lanceolate, margins revolute, 3–7-veined	1–2, sometimes to 10, fragrant, funnel-shaped, horizontal; tepals 4¾–8 in (12–20 cm), white, exterior flushed purple, tips recurved; anthers yellow to purple; pollen brown or yellow

Comments: Sometimes treated as a biennial. Summer–fall. var. **pricei:** stems 12–24 in (30–60 cm); flowers 1–2, more deeply colored.

L. grayi **Comments:** Summer. 'Gulliver's Thimble': bright crimson.	E US	to 5¾ ft (1.75 m)	to 2–4¾ × ⅝–1¼ in (5–12 × 1.5–3 cm), lanceolate or oblong-lanceolate, sessile, in whorls	1–8, bell-shaped; tepals 2½ × ¼ in (6.25 × 0.5 cm), interior light red with yellow base, spotted purple, exterior crimson, darker toward base; anthers yellow; pollen orange-brown

L. candidum

L. chalcedonicum

L. × dalhansonii

L. duchartrei

LILIUM

Name	Distribution	Height	Leaves	Flowers
L. hansonii	E Russia, Korea, Japan	to 48 in (120 cm)	7 × 1½ in (18 × 4 cm), dark green, oblanceolate to elliptic, 3–5-veined	3–12, turk's-cap, fragrant, pendulous; tepals 1¼–1½ × ⅜ in (3–4 × 1.5 cm), thick, oblanceolate, deep orange-yellow, spotted purple-brown toward base; anthers purple; pollen yellow
Comments: Summer.				
L. henryi	China	3¼–10 ft (1–3 m)	3–6 × ¾–1¼ in (8–15 × 2–3 cm), shiny, scattered, upper leaves ovate, sessile, basal leaves lanceolate, petiolate, 3–5-veined, crowded below flowers	4–20, turk's-cap, pendulous, in a raceme; tepals 2½–3 × ½–¾ in (6–8 × 1–2 cm), orange, spotted black, lanceolate; anthers deep red
Comments: Summer. var. *citrinum*: fls pale lemon-yellow, spotted brown.				
L. japonicum BAMBOO LILY, SASA-YURI	Japan	16–36 in (40–90 cm)	6 × 1 in (15 × 2.5 cm), scattered, lanceolate, 3–5-veined, margins rough; petiole to ½ in (1 cm)	1–5, fragrant, funnel-shaped, horizontal; tepals 4–6 × ¾–1½ in (10–15 × 2–3.5 cm), oblanceolate to oblong, pink, occasionally white; anthers brown; pollen red or brown
Comments: Summer. 'Albomarginatum': leaves edged creamy-white. 'Album': flowers white.				
L. kelloggii	W US	12–50 in (30–125 cm)	to 4 × ¾ in (10 × 2 cm), in whorls of 12 or more, sessile, lanceolate or oblanceolate, acute, 1–3-veined	to 20, pendulous, turk's-cap, fragrant, in a raceme; tepals 2¼ × ½ in (5.5 × 1 cm), mauve-pink or white with dark purple spots and central yellow stripe; anthers and pollen orange
Comments: Summer.				
L. lancifolium *L. tigrinum* TIGER LILY, DEVIL LILY, KENTAN	E China, Japan, Korea	24–60 in (60–150 cm)	4¾–8 × ½–¾ in (12–20 × 1–2 cm), numerous, lanceolate, scattered, 5–7-veined, margins rough	to 40, in a raceme, pendulous, turk's-cap, to 5 in (12.5 cm) wide; tepals 2¾–4 × ½–1 in (7–10 × 1–2.5 cm), lanceolate, interior orange, spotted deep purple; anthers orange-red to purple; pollen brown
Comments: Summer–early fall. 'Flore Pleno': flowers double. var. **flaviflorum:** flowers yellow. var. **fortunei:** stems to 6½ ft (2 m), densely woolly; flowers 30–50, orange-red. var. **splendens:** flowers larger, bright orange-red, spotted black.				
L. lankongense *L. forrestii*	W China	to 48 in (120 cm)	4 × ⅜ in (10 × 0.8 cm), numerous, sessile, scattered, crowded near base, oblong-lanceolate, acute, 3–7-veined, margins rough	to 15, 2 in (5 cm) wide, in a raceme, pendulous, turk's-cap, fragrant; tepals 1½–2½ × ½–1 in (4–6.5 × 1–2.5 cm), rose-pink, spotted purple, green central stripe; anthers purple; pollen brown
Comments: Summer.				
L. leichtlinii	Japan	to 48 in (120 cm)	6 × ½ in (15 × 1 cm), numerous, scattered, linear-lanceolate, 1–3-veined, margins rough	1–6, in a raceme, unscented, turk's-cap, buds white-hairy; tepals to 3 × ¾ in (8 × 2 cm), lemon yellow spotted maroon, lanceolate; anthers and pollen red-brown
Comments: Summer. var. **maximowiczii:** to 1 in (2.5 cm); flowers 1–12; tepals orange-red, spotted purple-brown; anthers and pollen red.				

L. formosanum var. *pricei*

L. grayi

L. hansonii

L. henryi

LILIUM

Name	Distribution	Height	Leaves	Flowers
L. longiflorum EASTER LILY	S Japan, Taiwan	to 3¼ ft (1 m)	to 7 × ⅝ in (18 × 1.5 cm), scattered, lanceolate or oblong-lanceolate	to 6, funnel-shaped, scented, in an umbel; tepals to 7 in (18 cm), white; pollen yellow; stigma green

Comments: Summer. 'Albomarginatum': leaves edged white. 'Gelria': flowers white; tepals slightly recurved at apex; pollen yellow. 'Holland's Glory': flowers white, to 8 in (20 cm). 'White American': flowers white, tips and nectaries green, pollen deep yellow. 'White Europe': flowers white; tepals strongly recurved, throat veined green, exterior green-white below, venation cream above, pollen lemon-yellow. var. **takeshima:** stems taller, purple-brown, flowers flushed purple outside, pollen orange.

Name	Distribution	Height	Leaves	Flowers
L. mackliniae	NE India	to 16 in (40 cm)	1¼–2½ × ⅛–½ in (3–6 × 0.4–1 cm), spiral, horizontal, linear-lanceolate or elliptic-lanceolate	1–6, in a raceme, pendulous, bell-shaped; tepals 2 × ¾ in (5 × 2 cm), interior rose-pink, exterior purple-pink; anthers purple; pollen yellow-orange or brown

Comments: Late spring–summer.

Name	Distribution	Height	Leaves	Flowers
L. × maculatum	Japan	to 24 in (60 cm)	2–6 × ⅝ in (5–15 × 1.5 cm), lanceolate to elliptic, scattered, 3–7-veined	cup-shaped, erect; tepals 3–4 in (8–10 cm), yellow, orange or red, variably spotted

Comments: Summer. Considered by some to be *L. dauricum × L. concolor*. 'Alutaceum': deep apricot, spotted purple-black. 'Aureum': orange-yellow, spotted black. 'Bicolor': brilliant orange, margins bright red, spots few, faint. 'Biligulatum': deep chestnut-red. 'Sanguineum': orange-red. 'Wallacei': apricot with raised maroon spots.

Name	Distribution	Height	Leaves	Flowers
L. × marhan (*L. hansonii × L. martagon* var. *album*)	garden origin	to 5 ft (1.5 m)		pendulous, turk's-cap, 2–2½ in (5–6 cm) wide; tepals thick, orange-yellow, spotted red-brown

Comments: Summer.

Name	Distribution	Height	Leaves	Flowers
L. martagon MARTAGON, COMMON TURK'S-CAP	NW Europe, NW Asia	to 6½ ft (2 m)	to 6 × 2½ in (16 × 6.5 cm), oblanceolate, 7–9-veined, in whorls of 8–14	to 50, in racemes, pendulous, turk's-cap, 2 in (5 cm) wide, fragrant; tepals 1¼–1¾ × ¼–½ in (3–4.5 × 0.6–1 cm), dull pink, spotted maroon; pollen yellow

Comments: Summer. var. **albiflorum:** white with pink spotting. var. **album:** white, not spotted. var. **cattaniae:** maroon, unspotted. var. **caucasicum:** lilac-pink. var. **sanguineopurpureum:** dark maroon, spotted.

Name	Distribution	Height	Leaves	Flowers
L. monadelphum *L. szovitsianum, L. colchicum* CAUCASIAN LILY	NE Turkey, Caucasus	39–60 in (100–150 cm)	5 × 1 in (12.5 × 2.5 cm), lanceolate or oblanceolate, spirally arranged, 9–13-veined	1–5, occasionally to 30, fragrant, pendulous, turk's-cap; tepals 2½–4 × ½–¾ in (6–10 × 1–2 cm), yellow, interior spotted purple or maroon, exterior flushed purple-brown; pollen orange-yellow

Comments: Summer.

Name	Distribution	Height	Leaves	Flowers
L. nanum	Himalaya, W China	2½–18 in (6–45 cm)	to 4¾ × ¼ in (12 × 0.5 cm), linear, scattered, 3–5-veined	solitary, pendulous, bell-shaped, scented; tepals to ½–1½ × ⅛–⅝ in (1–4 × 0.3–1.6 cm), pale pink to purple with fine dark purple or brown mottling; anthers yellow-brown

Comments: Summer. var. **flavidum:** flowers pale yellow.

L. lancifolium var. *splendens*

L. longiflorum

L. mackliniae

L. martagon

LILIUM

Name	Distribution	Height	Leaves	Flowers
L. nepalense	Bhutan, Nepal, N India	to 3¼ ft (1 m)	to 5½ × 1¼ in (14 × 3 cm), oblong-lanceolate, 5–7-veined	1–3, slightly pendulous, funnel-shaped, with a musky nocturnal scent; tepals to 6 in (15 cm), tips twisting, green-white to green-yellow, base red-purple to dark maroon; anthers purple; pollen orange-brown
Comments: Summer. Stoloniferous and requiring a large, cool and moist root run in mild, shady conditions.				
L. occidentale EUREKA LILY	W US	28–79 in (70–200 cm)	to 5 × ⅝ in (13 × 1.5 cm), in whorls, linear-lanceolate to lanceolate, 7-veined	1–5, occasionally 20, in a raceme, pendulous, turk's-cap, to 2¾ in (7 cm) wide; tepals 1½–2½ × ⅝ in (3.5–6 × 1.5 cm), crimson with green-yellow throat, or vermilion with orange throat and brown spots; anthers purple; pollen orange-red
Comments: Summer.				
L. pardalinum LEOPARD LILY, PANTHER LILY	W US	6½–10 ft (2–3 m)	to 7 × 2 in (18 × 5 cm), in whorls of to 16, elliptic or oblanceolate, glabrous, to 3-veined	to 10 in a raceme, unscented, pendulous, turk's-cap, to 3½ × 3½ in (9 × 9 cm); tepals lanceolate, orange-red to crimson, spotted deep maroon toward base, some spots outlined yellow; anthers red-brown; pollen orange
Comments: Summer. 'Californicum': deep orange, spotted maroon, tips scarlet. 'Johnsonii': tall; flowers finely spotted. var. **giganteum:** to 8 ft (2.5 m); flowers crimson and yellow, densely spotted.				
L. parryi LEMON LILY	SW US	to 6½ ft (2 m)	to 6 in (15 cm), oblanceolate, 3-veined, margins slightly rough	to 15, sometimes many more, fragrant, horizontal, funnel-shaped; tepals to 2¾–4 × ⅜–½ in (7–10 × 0.8–1.2 cm), oblanceolate, tips recurved, lemon-yellow, base sparsely spotted maroon; anthers orange-brown; pollen red
Comments: Summer.				
L. philadelphicum L. montanum RED LILY	Eastern N America	to 4 ft (1.25 m) **Comments:** Summer.	2–4 × ⅝ in (5–10 × 1.5 cm), mostly in whorls of 6–8, oblanceolate, margins sometimes rough, 3–5-veined	1–5, cup-shaped, erect, in an umbel; tepals to 3 in (7.5 cm), oblanceolate, orange to vivid orange-red, spotted purple, edges revolute; pollen deep red
L. primulinum OCHER LILY	W China, N Burma, Thailand	to 8 ft (2.4 m)	to 6 × 1½ in (15 × 4 cm), scattered, lanceolate, 1–3-veined	2–8, occasionally 18, fragrant, funnel-shaped, pendulous; tepals 2½–6 × ½–2 in (6–15 × 1–5 cm), oblong-lanceolate, yellow, sometimes marked purple-red; pollen brown
Comments: Summer–fall. var. **ochraceum:** flowers red-purple toward base.				
L. pumilum L. tenuifolium, L. linifolium CORAL LILY	N E Asia	6–36 in (15–90 cm)	to 4 × ⅛ in (10 × 0.3 cm), scattered, sessile, linear, 1-veined	to 7–20, scented, pendulous, turk's-cap, in a raceme; buds woolly; tepals 2 × 2 in (5 × 5 cm), oblong-lanceolate, scarlet, base sometimes dotted black; pollen scarlet
Comments: Summer. 'Golden Gleam': apricot yellow.				

L. nepalense   *L. pardalinum*   *L. pumilum*   *L. regale*

LILIUM

Name	Distribution	Height	Leaves	Flowers
L. pyrenaicum	Europe to NE Turkey and Georgia	6–53 in (15–135 cm)	to 5 × ¾ in (12.5 × 2 cm), linear-lanceolate, acute, margins sometimes silver or ciliate	to 12, pendulous, turk's-cap, 2 in (5 cm) wide, in a raceme; tepals green-yellow, streaked and spotted dark maroon; pollen orange-red

Comments: Summer. 'Aureum': deep yellow. ssp. ***pyrenaicum:*** flowers yellow, interior lined and spotted dark purple; var. ***rubrum:*** orange red. ssp. ***carniolicum:*** to 48 in (120 cm); flowers yellow, orange or red, sometimes spotted purple. ssp. *carniolicum* var. ***albanicum:*** to 16 in (40 cm); flowers yellow. var. ***jankae:*** to 32 in (80 cm); flowers yellow. ssp. ***ponticum:*** 6–36 in (15–90 cm); flowers deep yellow or deep orange, interior red-brown, spotted purple toward base. var. ***artvinense:*** flowers deep orange.

Name	Distribution	Height	Leaves	Flowers
L. regale REGAL LILY	W China	20–79 in (50–200 cm)	2–5 × ⅛–¼ in (5–13 × 0.4–0.6 cm), scattered, sessile, linear, 1-veined	1–25, fragrant, horizontal, funnel-shaped, in an umbel; tepals 4¾–6 × ¾–1½ in (12–15 × 2–4 cm), white, interior of tube yellow, exterior tinted purple; anthers and pollen golden

Comments: Summer. 'Album': flowers almost pure white; anthers orange. 'Royal Gold': flowers yellow.

Name	Distribution	Height	Leaves	Flowers
L. rubellum	Japan	12–32 in (30–80 cm)	4 × 1½ in (10 × 3.5 cm), scattered, petiolate, ovate-lanceolate to oblong-elliptic, 5–7-veined	1–9, very fragrant, horizontal, funnel-shaped; tepals 3 in (7.5 cm), oblanceolate to oblong, rose-pink, base sometimes spotted maroon; pollen orange-yellow

Comments: Summer.

Name	Distribution	Height	Leaves	Flowers
L. speciosum	China, Japan, Taiwan	stems 48–67 in (120–170 cm)	to 7 × 2½ in (18 × 6 cm), scattered, lanceolate, petiolate, 7–9-veined	to 12, fragrant, pendulous, broadly turk's-cap, 6 in (15 cm) wide, in a raceme; tepals to 4 × 1¾ in (10 × 4.5 cm), white, base flushed carmine, spotted pink or crimson, ovate-lanceolate, margins wavy; pollen dark red

Comments: Late summer. 'Grand Commander': deep pink tinted lilac, edged white, spotted red. 'Krätzeri': white, exterior with central green stripe. 'Melpomene': deep carmine, segments edged white. 'Uchida': brilliant crimson, spotted green, tips white. var. ***album:*** white. var. ***magnificum:*** rose, spotted deep crimson, margins paler; pollen red. var. ***roseum:*** rose. var. ***rubrum:*** carmine.

Name	Distribution	Height	Leaves	Flowers
L. superbum AMERICAN TURK'S-CAP LILY **Comments:** Summer.	E US	5–10 ft (1.5–3 m)	1½–4½ × ⅜–1⅛ in (3.5–11 × 0.8–2.8 cm), lanceolate or elliptic, 3–7-veined, in whorls of 4–20 and scattered	to 40, pendulous, turk's-cap, in a raceme; tepals orange flushed red, spotted maroon toward green base; anthers red; pollen orange-brown

Name	Distribution	Height	Leaves	Flowers
L. × testaceum *L. isabellinum, L. excelsum* (*L. candidum* × *L. chalcedonicum*) NANKEEN LILY	garden origin	39–60 in (100–150 cm)	2–4 in (5–10 cm), scattered, linear, margins ciliate, veins pubesc. beneath	6–12, scented, pendulous, turk's-cap; tepals to 3 in (8 cm), yellow to pale orange, interior spotted red; anthers red; pollen orange

Comments: Summer.

Name	Distribution	Height	Leaves	Flowers
L. tsingtauense	NE China, Korea	to 48 in (120 cm)	to 6 × 1½ in (15 × 4 cm), glabrous, oblanceolate, petiolate, often in 2 whorls	2–7, in a raceme, unscented, erect, bowl-shaped; tepals to 2 × ⅝ in (5 × 1.5 cm), orange or vermilion with purple spotting; anthers and pollen orange

Comments: Summer. var. ***carneum:*** flowers red, unspotted. var. ***flavum:*** flowers yellow, spotted red.

L. rubellum

L. speciosum **var.** *rubrum*

L. superbum

L. tsingtauense

LILIUM

Name	Distribution	Height	Leaves	Flowers
L. wallichianum	Himalaya	to 6½ ft (2 m)	10 × ½ in (25 × 1.2 cm), scattered, linear or lanceolate	1–4, scented, horizontal, funnel-shaped, 8 in (20 cm) wide with basal tube to 4 in (10 cm); tepals 6–12 in (15–30 cm), interior creamy white, exterior tinged green; pollen yellow
Comments: Summer–fall.				
L. washingtonianum	W US	to 6½ ft (2 m)	to 6 × 1½ in (15 × 3.5 cm), in whorls, oblanceolate, margins wavy	to 20, scented, to 4½ in (11 cm) wide, bowl-shaped, horizontal to ascending, in a raceme; tepals 3 × 1 in (8 × 2.5 cm), oblanceolate, white, spotted purple at base; pollen yellow
Comments: Summer. var. **purpurascens:** flowers opening white, becoming pink then purple.				

been potted up and kept cool and moist. If the bulbs show signs of rot or other molds, they should be washed clean and then immersed in a fungicide solution for 20 minutes.

The often-quoted advice to keep the roots in the shade while allowing the heads to be in the sun is generally sound. Many of the Asiatic species, like *L. pumilum*, will accept full sun. Most of the Oriental species and hybrids will appreciate dappled shade for some of the day; this applies also to forms of *L. martagon* and western American species. The Caucasian lilies will take full sun as in the wild but must have adequate moisture, and as will *L. candidum* and other southern European species used to the heat of sun at lower latitudes. Most lilies, other than those which are stoloniferous or stoloniform (e.g., *L. nepalense*), may be grown in pots—the Asiatic and Oriental and hybrid trumpet lilies are particularly suitable. Space the bulbs at least ¾ in (2 cm) apart and ½ in (1 cm) away from the sides of the pot. The deeper the pot, the better. Loam-based mediums with good aeration, drainage and a high humus level are best, but soilless mediums can be used if compaction is avoided, adequate moisture is always provided, and the appropriate liquid feeding carried out.

In regions with prolonged, hard winters with temperatures below 10°F (–12°C), certain lilies should be grown under glass. These include *L. candidum*, *L. formosanum*, *L. longiflorum*, *L. nepalense**, *L. speciosum* and *L. wallichianum**. Those marked with an asterisk are stoloniferous and prefer to be grown in greenhouse borders or large tubs and boxes so that their stolons can wander. Lilies may be increased by seed, from bulbils formed in the leaf axils and bulblets formed below ground. Bulbs can also be increased by division and scaling (see *cuttings*). Affected by botrytis, basal rots and viruses. Attacked by lily beetle.

lily beetle (*Lilioceris lilii*) 3/8 in (8 mm)-long beetle with bright red thorax and wing cases, and black head and legs; its larvae are rounded, humped and covered in wet black excrement, reaching 3/8 in (8 mm) long when fully fed. It is widely distributed in North America, Britain and Europe. All *Lilium* species are susceptible, also *Fritillaria imperialis, F. meleagris* and other *Fritillaria* species; other plants attacked by the adults but not the larvae are *Polygonatum* species, *Convallaria* species and *Nomocharis saluenensis*. Adults and larvae cause defoliation and, in heavy infestations, also feed on flowers, seed capsules and stems. The larvae normally feed in groups from the leaf tips, while the adults create irregular holes at random.

Adults overwinter in the soil, emerging mainly in March/April to lay red eggs in clusters on the undersides of leaves. All stages can be found in summer due to progressive emergence from the soil and a long egg-laying period. Control limited infestations by hand-picking adults, eggs and larvae; otherwise, spray recommended contact or systemic insecticides, subject to local pesticide approvals, applied repeatedly when necessary.

limb (1) one of the larger branches of a tree; (2) (bot.) a broadened, flattened part of a plant organ extending from a narrower base, as in the flared upper part of a tubular or funnelform corolla.

Lily beetle

lime any of several substances containing calcium which are used in the garden to improve fertility and reduce acidity. Strictly, the term refers to calcium oxide or quicklime, produced by heating limestone or chalk in a kiln, but this form is caustic and dangerous to handle and unsuitable for garden use. Calcium hydroxide, available as slaked or hydrated lime, is quicker-acting and safer to handle, although it can damage plant foliage. Calcium carbonate, in the form of crushed chalk or ground limestone, is widely used, and is the bulkiest and cheapest of the three forms. One pound of calcium oxide is as effective as 3⅓ lb (1.5 kg) of calcium hydroxide or 4⅖ lb (2 kg) of calcium carbonate, depending on the size of particles. Magnesian or dolomitic limestone provides both calcium and magnesium nutrients. Some fertilizers, such as calcium nitrate, contain lime.

Lime is important in plant nutrition as a source of calcium, and also as a means of neutralizing soil acidity, or producing an alkaline condition where this is desirable. It improves the structure of clay soil by a chemical process known as flocculation, which gives rise to the aggregation of soil particles into large, stable crumbs providing good aeration. By neutralizing soil acidity, lime dressing facilitates the activity of those soil-inhabiting bacteria that convert ammonium salts into nitrates, and also increases the availability of important plant nutrients. The beneficial activities of earthworms and nitrogen-fixing bacteria are encouraged, while clubroot disease and some soil-inhabiting plant pests are discouraged.

L

Most vegetable crops actually do best in slightly acidic soil, although for large groups of ornamentals within the family Ericaceae acidic conditions are essential, and these have little or no requirement for calcium. Some plants, for example, many alpines, thrive in very alkaline soil, but generally, overliming can lead to nutrient deficiency in plants, especially of phosphorus, iron, manganese and other trace elements.

The degree of soil acidity is indicated by the pH level, and this should be regularly checked, particularly in vegetable gardens. Most crops do best at a pH of 6.5 on mineral soil and a pH of 5.8 on peat soil. Clay soil has a high buffering capacity and requires large quantities of lime to affect pH, whereas sandy soil requires less but the effect may be short-lived.

Indications of lime requirement gained from soil-testing need adjustment with respect to soil texture, organic matter content, the degree of acidity, rainfall and the evenness of incorporation; precise recommendations require expert consideration of numerous factors. However, for garden purposes, the following general guidelines are suggested for using hydrated lime to reduce acidity to around 6.5 pH on three different soil types.

	ounce/ft² of hydrated lime		
Original pH	*Sandy or gravely*	*Medium loam*	*Peat or Clay*
4.5	14	20	25
5.0	9	14	17
5.5	5	8	10
6.0	3	4	9
6.5	0	0	0

Where there is a need for lime dressing in excess of 9 oz/yd² (300 g/m²) it should be applied over several seasons. Even then, split dressings are advisable for best effect, with each incorporated to a depth of 6 in (15 cm). Fall or winter dressing is recommended, and there should ideally be an interval of at least several weeks between applications of animal manure and lime to avoid strong release of ammonia, with lime always being applied after manure. See *pH*.

lime-dot see *hydathode*.

lime-induced chlorosis interveinal or uniform chlorosis of young leaves, often followed by stunting, caused by deficiency, unavailability, or immobility of nutrients such as manganese and especially iron in soil that is very alkaline.

limestone a sedimentary rock that consists chiefly of calcium carbonate, although other constituents such as magnesium carbonate and silica may also be present. It is a source of lime for application to garden soil. In water-worn form, it has been used in the making of rock gardens, a practice now condemned on the grounds of conserving the natural environment.

lime-sulfur a complex mixture of calcium polysulfides, prepared by boiling together sulfur and calcium hydroxide. It was first produced at Versailles in 1851, and was an important fungicide and acaricide for many years. It has been replaced by nonphytotoxic forms of sulfur, and other fungicides.

Limnanthes (from Greek *limne*, marsh, and *anthos*, flower, referring to the habitat). Limnanthaceae. W US. POACHED EGG PLANT. 7 species, annual herbs with pinnately divided, leaves and dish-shaped, 5-petaled flowers in summer. A hardy annual, sowing itself in profusion where conditions suit. It is suitable for path and border edging, for the interstices of paving, for the base of walls and for other situations offering a

Limnanthes douglasii
Poached egg flowers are attractive to bees and also to hoverflies, beneficial insects whose larvae consume a number of pests.

cool, moist root run. The lightly scented flowers, carried over long periods in summer, are a good nectar source for bees. It is easily grown in sun in moderately fertile, moisture-retentive soil. Sow seed *in situ* in spring or, in mild winter areas, in fall. *L. douglasii* (POACHED EGG FLOWER; California, S Oregon; to 12 in (30 cm); leaves pinnately cut, thinly succulent, bright green; flowers fragrant, to 1 in (2.5 cm) in diameter, petals shiny yellow with white margins, or entirely white; includes var. *sulphurea*, with yellow petals.

Limonium (from Greek *leimon*, meadow—salt meadows are a common habitat of these plants). Plumbaginaceae. Cosmopolitan. SEA LAVENDER, STATICE, MARSH ROSEMARY. About 150 species, perennial herbs or shrubs, rarely annuals, usually with rosettes of entire or pinnatifid leaves. The flowers are small and papery with a shortly tubular, 5-lobed corolla; they are carried in summer and fall in spreading panicles composed of short spikelets. *L. bellidifolium* is hardy to 0°F (–18°C) and suited to sunny, perfectly drained sites in alpine sinks and the rock garden. More robust perennials, such as *L. platyphyllum*, are hardy to –4°F (–20°C). As with many members of this genus, it is well-adapted to coastal gardens and dry soil. Grow in deep, well-drained soil in full sun. Good textural contrasts may be achieved by naturalizing in gravel or shingle. The flowers of most species can be dried for decoration; they range in form and color from the subtle and delicate sprays on fine sinuous stems, as found in *L. platyphyllum*, to the more extravagant and densely flowered panicles of cultivars of *L. sinuatum*, frequently seen as a florist's flower. All species are easily raised from seed. Division is possible but difficult and re-establishment may be slow. *L. platyphyllum* and other large perennials may be increased by root cuttings in a sandy propagating mix in late winter/early spring.

L. bellidifolium Mediterranean and Black Sea to E England; perennial herb, 4–12 in (10–30 cm), woody at base; flowering stem branching from base, tuberculate; flowers about ¼ in (5 mm), blue-violet; includes 'Filigree', with purple-blue flowers, and 'Spangle', to 3¼ ft (1 m), with small, pale blue flowers, in loose sprays; *L. perezii* Canary Islands; perennial subshrub to 28 in (70 cm); panicle downy; flowers with a purple to blue, downy calyx and yellow corolla; *L. platyphyllum* SE and C Europe; woody-based perennial herb to 32 in (80 cm); panicle to 24 in (60 cm), domed; flowers about ¼ in (6 mm), pale violet; includes 'Violetta', with violet-blue flowers; *L. sinuatum* Mediterranean; hairy perennial to 16 in (40 cm), often treated as an annual; flowering stem winged, inflorescence dense; flowers with downy, white or pale violet calyx and papery, white or pink corolla, becoming purple; includes many cultivars and seed races with flowers in shades of white, yellow, gold, apricot, rose, deep pink, red, carmine, purple, lilac, sky blue and deep blue.

Linaria (from Latin *linum*, flax, referring to the flaxlike habit and foliage of some species). Scrophulariaceae. Northern temperate regions, especially Europe. TOADFLAX, SPURRED SNAPDRAGON. About 100 species, annual to perennial herbs with more or less erect and clumped stems clothed with narrow leaves. Tubular, 2-lipped, spurred, snapdragon-like flowers are carried in terminal racemes in summer. Hardy to −10°F (−23°C). Grow in full sun in well-drained, rather poor and sandy soil. *L. purpurea*, with long-lived and graceful spires of delicate flowers, is suitable for the flower border, *L. alpina* for scree, rock gardens, raised beds and wall crevices. The taller species such as *L. maroccana* make good cut flowers. Mediterranean species such as *L. triornithophora* and *L. tristis* are slightly more tender, tolerating temperatures to 23°F (−5°C), but may be treated as annuals or protected in winter with a mulch of bracken or evergreen prunings. Perennial species tend to be short-lived, but will self-seed, proving most persistent in perfectly drained, sunny sites. To flower *L. maroccana* in pots, overwinter fall-sown plants in a low fertility, loam-based medium, in sunny, well-ventilated, frost-free conditions. Propagate annuals and *L. alpina* from seed sown *in situ* in spring or, in mild climates, in fall. Sow perennials in

early spring under glass or in the cold frame; some cultivars, notably *L. purpurea* 'Canon Went', come true from seed. Alternatively, increase perennials by division, or from basal or softwood cuttings in spring in the cold frame.

L. alpina ALPINE TOADFLAX; C and S Europe; glaucous, dwarf annual, biennial or perennial; stem 2–10 in (5–25 cm), decumbent or ascending; inflorescence short; flowers violet with yellow palate, rarely wholly yellow, white or pink; includes 'Alba', with white flowers, 'Rosea', with rose-pink flowers with an orange-yellow palate; *L. bipartita* CLOVEN-LIP TOADFLAX; NW Africa, Portugal; annual; stem to 16 in (40 cm), slender; inflorescence lax; flowers violet, lips widely diverging, palate orange; includes 'Alba', with white flowers, 'Queen of Roses', with pink flowers, and 'Splendida', with deep purple flowers; *L. genistifolia* SE and C Europe, Asia Minor; perennial, 12–39 in (30–100 cm), erect, branched above; leaves rigid; flowers lemon-yellow to orange, palate orange-bearded; 'Nymph': flowers cream; *L. maroccana* Morocco, naturalized NE US; annual to 18 in (45 cm), erect, branched; flowers brilliant violet-purple, palate orange to yellow with smaller paler patch; 'Carminea': bright rosy carmine; 'Diadem': large, rich violet with a white eye; Excelsior Hybrids: from white to yellow and beige, to salmon, rose-carmine and crimson, to purple and blue; 'Fairy Bride': white; 'Ruby King': deep blood red; *L. purpurea* C Italy to Sicily, naturalized elsewhere including Great Britain; glaucous perennial; stem 8–24 in (20–60 cm), ascending to erect, often branched above; inflorescence slender; flowers violet tinged purple; includes 'Canon J. Went', tall, with tiny, pale pink flowers, and 'Springside White', with gray-green leaves and white flowers; *L. reticulata* PURPLE-NET TOADFLAX; Portugal, N Africa; glaucous annual: stem 24–48 in (60–120 cm); inflorescence short, downy; flowers deep purple, palate coppery orange or yellow with purple striations; 'Aureopurpurea': rich purple with orange or yellow palate; 'Crown Jewels': small, maroon, red, gold and orange; *L. triornithophora* THREE BIRDS FLYING; W

Spain, N and C Portugal; perennial glabrous and somewhat glaucous; stem 20–54 in (50–130 cm), erect or diffuse; inflorescence lax with flowers 3(–4) per whorl, pale lavender striped purple in tube with yellow palate, tube inflated; 'Rosea': pink flowers; *L. tristis* (DULL-COLORED LINARIA, SAD-COLORED LINARIA; S Spain and S Portugal, NW Africa, Canary Islands; glaucous perennial; stem 4–36 in (10–90 cm), decumbent to ascending; flowers olive to yellow tinged dull purple to brown; *L. vulgaris* (BUTTER-AND-EGGS, TOADFLAX, WILD SNAP-DRAGON; Europe except for extreme N and much of Mediterranean; perennial; stem 6–36 in (15–90 cm), erect, simple or branched, glandular-pubescent above; inflorescence dense; flowers pale to bright yellow, palate coppery.

Lindera (for Johann Linder [1676–1723], Swedish botanist). Lauraceae. Temperate and tropical E Asia (Himalayas to Malaysia, China, Japan), N America. 80 species, aromatic, evergreen or deciduous shrubs or trees grown principally for their foliage. In spring, they produce small, yellow flowers. Where plants of both sexes are present, small drupes are produced. Grow in part shade or dappled sunlight in a moisture-retentive, fertile, nonalkaline soil enriched with leaf mold. *L. benzoin* tolerates temperatures as low as −13°F (−25°C), and *L. obtusiloba* as low as 5°F (−15°C). Position plants where they have some protection from late spring frosts. Prune to remove deadwood in spring; old leggy specimens may be rejuvenated by cutting hard back to the base if necessary, although this is best carried out over several seasons. Propagate by fresh seed sown when ripe—seed has short viability and should not be allowed to dry out before sowing. Alternatively, increase by semiripe cuttings in a closed case or by layering.

L. benzoin SPICE BUSH, BENJAMIN BUSH; E US; deciduous, highly aromatic shrub to 13 ft (4 m); leaves 2½–6 in (6–15 cm), obovate, thin, glabrous above, entire, ciliate; fruit bright red; 'Xanthocarpa': fruit yellow; *L. obtusiloba* Korea, China, Japan; deciduous shrub or small tree to 33 ft (10 m); leaves 2½–4¾ in (6–12 cm), ovate, apex often

471

bluntly 3-lobed, glaucous beneath, pale gold in fall; fruit black.

Lindheimera (for Ferdinand Jacob Lindheim [1801–1879], German botanist). Compositae. S US. 1 species, *L. texana*, TEXAS STAR, an annual herb to 26 in (65 cm) with pinnatifid to entire leaves. To 1½ in (4 cm) across, the daisylike flower heads are clustered in corymbs in late summer and fall; they consist of white ray florets and yellow disk florets. An undemanding, hardy annual for the cut-flower border and for native plant collections. Grow in sun in well-drained soil. Sow *in situ* in spring or earlier under glass.

line a term used by plant breeders to describe a more or less uniform assemblage of individuals; equivalent to a cultivar.

linear slender, elongated, the margins parallel or virtually so.

lineate see *striated*.

line out to plant out young plants or hardwood cuttings in straight rows to be grown on for sale.

liner a young hardy nursery-stock plant in its first pot.

lingulate resembling a tongue.

Linnaea (for Carl Linnaeus [1707–1778], botanist). Caprifoliaceae. Circumpolar regions. TWIN-FLOWER. 1 species, *L. borealis*, a creeping, dwarf, evergreen shrub with slender, trailing and rooting branches and glossy green, rounded leaves, seldom more than ¼ in (0.5 cm) long. Fragrant flowers appear in summer, paired and nodding, atop a delicate, red-flushed stalk to 3 in (8 cm) tall. They are campanulate to funnelform, ½–¾ in (1–2 cm) long and white or pale candy-pink with deeper markings within the five, rounded lobes. A charming and fully hardy, if rather fragile-seeming groundcover for alpine sinks, peat beds, and the rock or woodland garden. Plant in a cool, moist but well-drained acidic soil in dappled sun. Propagate by rooted runners in spring.

Linum (Latin for flax). Linaceae. Temperate northern Hemisphere. FLAX. Some 200 species, annual, biennial or perennial herbs or subshrubs with short-lived, dish-shaped, 5-petaled flowers in terminal racemes in summer. Grow in a sheltered position in sun in light, well-drained, moderately fertile and humus-rich soil. Sow seed of annual species *in situ* in early spring, or in fall for early flowers in pots under glass. Overwinter at 50°F (10°C), watering carefully and sparingly until light levels and temperatures rise in spring; as roots fill their pots, water moderately and liquid feed until flower buds form. Propagate perennials by seed, cultivars by cuttings of basal shoots in spring. Perennials tend to be short-lived and should be propagated frequently. Increase shrubby species by semiripe cuttings in a shaded cold frame.

L. arboreum S Aegean; glabrous perennial shrub to 3¼ ft (1 m); flowers yellow; *L. flavum* GOLDEN FLAX; C and S Europe; erect, woody-based perennial, 12–16 in (30–40 cm); flowers golden yellow; *L.* 'Gemmels Hybrid' (*L. campanulatum* × *L. elegans*); to 6 in (15 cm); flowers rich yellow; *L. grandiflorum* FLOWERING FLAX; N Africa; erect glabrous annual to 30 in (75 cm); leaves narrow; flowers rose with a dark center; 'Bright Eyes': ivory with a deep brown center, 'Caeruleum': blue-purple; 'Coccineum': scarlet; 'Roseum': rose pink; and 'Rubrum': bright red; *L. narbonense* Mediterranean; glaucous perennial to 24 in (60 cm); leaves narrow; flowers azure with white eye; 'Heavenly Blue': clear vivid blue; 'Six Hills': bright blue; *L. perenne* PERENNIAL FLAX; Europe; erect perennial, to 24 in (60 cm); leaves narrow; flowers pale blue; 'Album': white; 'Caeruleum': sky blue; subsp. *alpinum*: to 12 in (30 cm), with smaller flowers; *L. suffruticosum* Spain to N Italy; woody-based perennial, 10–16 in (25–40 cm), flowering stem procumbent; leaves narrow; flowers white, veined purple with a violet or pink center; subsp. *salsoloides*: leaves narrower, flowers pearly-white; 'Nanum': low-growing; *L. usitatissimum* (FLAX; Asia, widespread as long-established escape in Europe and N America; erect annual, to 48 in (120 cm); leaves narrow; flowers blue.

lip (1) in, for example, Labiatae, one of the two distinct corolla divisions, one, the upper, often hooded, the other, lower, often forming a flattened landing platform for pollinators; (2) a staminode or petal modified or differentiated from the others.

Liquidambar (from Latin *liquidus*, liquid, and *ambar*, amber, referring to the fragrant resin). Hamamelidaceae. N America, Eurasia, China. SWEETGUM. 4 species, medium-sized to large deciduous trees with palmately lobed leaves superficially similar to *Acer* but in alternate, not opposite, arrangement. They are shiny dark green, turning maroon, bright orange and red in fall. The flowers are inconspicuous. *L. styraciflua*, the most commonly cultivated species, is a stately tree with a conical head and handsome, maplelike foliage; it is suitable for planting in parks, avenues and large gardens, and is hardy to at least 5°F (−15°C). The best selections produce brilliant fall tints. Other species are often not hardy below 23°F (−5°C). *L. formosana* Monticola Group is slightly more cold-tolerant and shows attractive purple-hued foliage in spring. Plant in deep, fertile, well-drained but moisture-retentive soil in full sun, giving plenty of room for development. *Liquidambar* resents transplanting and, if this is essential, prepare by root pruning a year in advance. Propagate from seed sown in fall into outdoor seed beds or from stratified seed in spring; the latter may take up to two years to germinate. Increase also by softwood cuttings in summer and by layering. Protect young plants from frost and plant out after the second year.

L. formosana FORMOSAN GUM; S China, Taiwan; straight-trunked tree to 130 ft (40 m); leaves to 6 in (15 cm) in diameter, 3-lobed, sometimes with subsidiary lobes at base, base cordate to truncate, finely serrate, glabrous above, usually downy beneath; includes Monticola Group, cold-hardy, with large, glabrous, 3-lobed leaves, coloring beautifully in fall; *L. orientalis* ORIENTAL SWEET GUM; Asia Minor; slow-growing, bushy-headed, small tree to 100 ft (30 m) in the wild; leaves usually 5-lobed, 2–2¾ in (5–7 cm) in diameter, lobes oblong, deep, glabrous, coarsely toothed and glandular; *L. styraciflua*

L

(SWEET GUM, AMERICAN SWEET GUM, RED GUM; E US; tall, narrowly pyramidal tree, to 150 ft (45 m) in the wild; leaves 5- or 7-lobed, 6 in (15 cm) in diameter, lobes triangular, shining and glabrous above, hairy in vein axils beneath; 'Aurea': leaves mottled and striped yellow; 'Burgundy': deep wine red fall color, turning later and persisting longer than in other forms; 'Festival': erect with fall leaf tints of yellow, peach, pink; 'Golden Treasure': with golden yellow leaf margins; 'Lane Roberts': fall color deep black crimsonred; 'Moonbeam': leaves variegated cream and vivid fall color; 'Palo Alto': fiery orange-red fall color; 'Pendula': branches more or less weeping from an upright bole; 'Rotundiloba': leaf lobes rounded; 'Variegata': leaves mottled yellow.

liquid feeding the use of a dilute solution of fertilizers in water for feeding plants, used especially for those grown in containers. The solution may be applied by watering can or through an irrigation system using a dilutor. Liquid feeding allows for the composition and concentration of nutrients, and the frequency of feeds, to be readily changed.

Concentrated liquid fertilizers are available as products containing various percentages of nitrogen and potassium to suit the condition of crops. Alternatively, they can be obtained by collecting liquid seeping from cowsheds or manure heaps, or by steeping a permeable sack of animal manure in a container of water. Infusions of comfrey serve a similar purpose. Liquid feeds are readily absorbed by plants and therefore quick-acting.

Liriodendron (from Greek *leirion* lily, and *dendron* tree). Magnoliaceae. Eastern N America, China, Indochina. 2 species, large deciduous trees with broadly oblong leaves, the apex cleft, truncate or retuse, the base broadly 1–2-lobed on each side. Produced in summer, the vase-shaped, solitary flowers consist of nine tepals, the outer three sepal-like, the inner six petal-like and in 2 whorls of 3, surrounding numerous, spirally arranged stamens. A graceful, upswept branch system and foliage that turns butter yellow in fall, place *Liriodendron* in the first rank of specimen and avenue trees for parks, open spaces and larger gardens. The delicately scented, pale green flowers are usually obvious only at close quarters, but are beautiful when cut and displayed where their elegant form and bright internal markings may be appreciated. Although tolerant of temperatures to at least 5°F (−15°C), flowering is more profuse in hot summer climates. Plant in a sunny, open position in deep, moisture-retentive, fertile soil. Limit young trees to a single leader—two or more are likely to incur structural weakness. Trees planted in woodland, as they would grow in habitat, tend to attain considerable heights with very straight and virtually clear trunks. Propagate from seed (a large proportion of which may be infertile) in the fall, or, in spring, by grafting.

L. chinense CHINESE TULIP TREE; C China, Indochina; similar to *L. tulipifera*, but to 52 ft (16 m); leaves more deeply lobed; flowers smaller, inner tepals to 1½ in (4 cm), green, veined yellow; *L. tulipifera* TULIP TREE, YELLOW POPLAR, TULIP POPLAR, CANARY WHITE-WOOD; eastern N America; tree to 165 ft (50 m)+; leaves to 4¾ in (12 cm), bright green, paler beneath; flowers pale yellow-green, banded orange near base, inner tepals 2½ × 1¼ in (6 × 3 cm); includes 'Aureomarginatum', with yellow or greenyellow leaf margins, 'Contortum', with contorted leaves and twiglets, 'Fastigiatum', of narrow, pyramidal habit, with fastigiate branches, and 'Integrifolium', with leaves lacking side lobes.

Liriope (after the wood nymph Liriope). Liliaceae (Convallariaceae). Japan, China, Vietnam. LILY TURF. Some 5 species, perennial, evergreen, tufted herbs with grassy leaves and small, grapelike flowers in elongated spikes or racemes from late summer to late fall; these are followed by black, berrylike fruits. Fairly drought-tolerant evergreen groundcover, hardy to 5°F (−15°C), possibly lower with shelter from cold drying winds. Cultivation as for *Ophiopogon*.

L. muscari China, Taiwan, Japan; to 18 in (45 cm), tufted, tuberous; leaves to 24 in (60 cm), narrowly strapshaped, glossy dark green; flowers dark mauve, densely clustered on a spikelike raceme; includes numerous cultivars, tall or short, compact and clumped or freely spreading, with pale to dark green, narrow to straplike leaves, some striped or edged silvery white to cream or gold, and with white to lilac, violet or dark mauve flowers, the racemes long and slender or congested and resembling a bunch of grapes; *L. spicata* China, Vietnam; to 10 in (25 cm), rhizomatous; leaves to 14 in (35 cm), grasslike, minutely serrate; flowers pale mauve to nearly white, more distinctly tubular than in *L. muscari* and on a mauve to brown stem; includes cultivars with white and pale mauve flowers, dark green or white-striped leaves and white-marbled fruit.

Lithocarpus (from Greek *lithos*, stone, and *carpos*, fruit, alluding to the hard-shelled fruit). Fagaceae. SE Asia and Indonesia, 2 in Japan and 1 in western N America. TANBARK OAK. 300 species, oaklike evergreen trees with leathery, mostly entire leaves and hard-shelled, acornlike nuts in calyx cupules. *Lithocarpus* is similar to *Quercus* but differs in the male flowers being in erect spikes (pendulous in *Quercus*) and the acorns being borne few to many, often densely, on stout, stiff spikes. Cultivate as for the smaller, evergreen *Quercus* species.

L. densiflorus TANBARK OAK; N America; tree to 100 ft (30 m), leaves 2–5 in (5–13 cm), elliptic to oblong, acute, stiff and leathery, toothed, initially downy above, white-to mentose beneath; *L. henryi* C China; tree to 66 ft (20 m)+; leaves 4–10 in (10–25 cm), elliptic to oblong, finely tapering, entire, glossy above, paler beneath.

Lithodora (from Greek *lithos*, stone, and *doron*, gift). Boraginaceae. SW Europe to Asia Minor. Some 7 species, perennial shrublets and subshrubs, usually with bristly leaves and 5-lobed, funnel- to bowl-shaped flowers in cymes in spring and summer. Given good drainage in a raised bed, *L. diffusa* will survive temperatures to about 5°F (−15°C); the remaining species will tolerate cold to between 23–14°F (−5 and −10°C). Grow in full sun in perfectly drained but moisture-retentive soil (acidic to neutral for *L. diffusa*). Trim over after flowering to maintain compactness. In the alpine house, use clay pots that have good drainage with a mix of equal parts loam, leaf mold and coarse sand. Water moderately when in growth and keep almost dry in winter. Propagate by seed in fall, by soft stem cuttings, rooted in a closed case with bottom heat, or by semiripe cuttings.

L. diffusa (syn. *Lithospermum diffusum*); NW France to SW Europe; stem to 24 in (60 cm), procumbent or straggling, bristly; flowers to ³/₄ in (2 cm), blue, sometimes purple, exterior pubescent, throat with a dense ring of long white hairs; includes white, pale blue and low-growing, deep azure cultivars, for example 'Heavenly Blue'; *L. oleifolia* (syn. *Lithospermum oleifolium*); E Pyrenees; stem to 18 in (45 cm), slender, diffuse, ascending; flowers to ⁵/₈ in (1.5 cm), pink becoming blue, or sky blue, exterior silky, interior glabrous; *L. zahnii* (syn. *Lithospermum zahnii*; S Greece; stem to 24 in (60 cm), tufted, much-branched, erect or ascending, silky-hairy; flowers to ¹/₂ in (1.2 cm), white or blue, interior glabrous.

Lithophragma (from Greek *lithos* stone and *phragma*, fence or screen, referring to its habitat). Saxifragaceae. Western N America. WOODLAND STAR. 9 species, perennial herbs with rosettes of long-stalked, rounded to trifoliolate leaves arising from subterranean bulbils. Carried in erect racemes in spring, the flowers consist of five spreading petals that are basically obovate, clawed and entire to 5-lobed. Hardy woodland natives for well-drained peaty soil in light shade. They may also be grown in the alpine house: keep them moist while in growth, but rather dry at other times. The foliage is visible only for a short growing season, withering during summer. Propagate in early spring by division, bulbils or from seed. *L. parviflorum* (leaves 3-lobed to trifoliate; flowering stem to 20 in (50 cm), petals white-pink ¹/₄–⁵/₈ in (7–16 mm), 3-cleft.

lithophyte a plant that grows on rocks or stony soil, deriving nourishment from the atmosphere rather than the soil.

Lithops schwantesii
These succulents have evolved a camouflage mechanism that serves to protect their water-rich tissues from grazing animals.

Lithops (from Greek *lithos*, stone, and *opsis*, appearance). Aizoaceae. South Africa, Namibia. LIVING STONES, STONE PLANT, FLOWERING STONE. 35 species, small, succulent, stemless perennials. They consist of solitary or clumping plant bodies each formed by the fusion of two, fleshy lobes with a marked central fissure. The upper surface of each lobe, (the face), may be elliptic to reniform, concave, flat or convex, with a remarkable range of stonelike characters—cracks, pitting, wrinkles, dots, mossy hieroglyphs—or with a central panel of a different color and usually semitranslucent, either clear or occluded to varying degrees by islandlike markings or incursions of marginal coloration and veining. Solitary, daisylike flowers are produced in summer and fall.

Provide a minimum temperature of 50°F (10°C), full sun and a dry atmosphere at all times, possibly with light shading in the height of summer if ventilation is at all inadequate. Plant in pans or half pots containing a low-fertility, loam-based medium with large proportions of sand and fine grit. A top dressing of pea gravel and pebbles flush with the upper leaf surfaces will help maintain soil temperature and moisture, and, of course, draw attention to the plants' powers of mimicry. Water very sparingly from early summer to late fall; keep dry during the winter and merely spray over lightly on warm spring days. Watering should only begin in the summer when

the old pair of leaves is almost totally shrivelled. In the fall, water only during periods of dry sunny weather—plants that remain too wet for too long at this time of year can split their bodies or rot. Repotting is done when growth starts in late spring. A weak low-nitrogen fertilizer can be given to well-established plants. Propagation as for *Conophytum*.

L. aucampiae body ³/₄–1¹/₄ in (20–32 mm), face elliptic to reniform, brick to sandy brown or ocher with sienna to green-brown dots, often joined by slender fissures, sometimes forming a semilucent green-brown panel with blotches and a broken margin; flowers yellow; *L. bromfieldii* body ³/₈–1¹/₄ in (15–32 mm), lobes equal, face elliptic to reniform, buff to gray with wrinkles sunken, irregular, dark red edged gray-green, brainlike; flowers yellow; *L. dorotheae* body ³/₄–1¹/₄ in (20–30 mm), convex, face rounded, dark beige or buff, panel translucent gray-green or olive with jagged to lobed edges and large blotches, sometimes reducing it to a pattern of hieroglyphs, with red dots; flowers yellow; *L. hookeri* body to ³/₄–1¹/₄ in (20–30 mm), face flat, reniform to elliptic, buff to pale glaucous brown, panel rich brown, filled by interlocking fleshy figures with deep dark grooves, forming a vermiculate pattern; flowers yellow; includes var. *susannae*, body ⁵/₈–³/₄ in (15–20 mm), face pale gray, sometimes with an obscure, darker panel, markings dark, sunken, forming a broken network; *L. julii* body ³/₄–1¹/₄ in (20–30 mm), face reniform, flat to slightly concave, dove to dark gray, panel dark brown to olive with red dots, eroded edges and broad blotches, leaving a pattern of loose reticulation, often with a brown stain on the inner lip of each lobe; flowers white; subsp. *fulleri*: body ¹/₂ in (12–14 mm), face buff to dull gray, panel translucent gray, sometimes with pale blotches, edges eroded and lobed, with dark brown or red spots or dashes in sinuses; var. *brunnea*: body ¹/₂ in (12–14 mm), face slightly convex, buff, panel olive to chocolate-brown with few, minute or many, distinct markings, edges shallowly to deeply eroded with red-brown flecks in sinuses; *L. karasmontana* body 1¹/₄–1¹/₂ in (30–40 mm), face elliptic to reniform, flat, concave or convex,

L

rugose, dull gray or beige, panel dark brown, with an impressed pattern of faint dendritic lines, or, in some variants, pale beige with face rugose and entirely suffused pale brick-red; flowers white; var. *lericheana*: body ⁵⁄₈–³⁄₄ in (15–20 mm), lobes near equal, buff, face rounded, rugose, pink-tinted, pale olive to dull jade-green, markings few, large, edges eroded with lobes irregular; var. *tischeri*: body ³⁄₄–1 in (20–25 mm), face broadly reniform, flat, rugose, capped pale ginger, panel dark olive to chocolate, so obscured by markings and irregular marginal incursions as to be an open pattern of dull, impressed 'veins'; subsp. *bella*: body 1–1¼ in (25–30 mm), face convex, gray to buff, panel dull olive reduced to an open, jagged-edged network by broad markings and marginal incursions; *L. lesliei* body ³⁄₄–1¼ in (20–45 mm), face elliptic to reniform, flat to convex, gray-green to buff to pale terra cotta, sometimes capped pale gold, panel pale to dark olive, with eroded edges and dense, dotted, irregular markings forming a fine, mossy, dendritic pattern; flowers yellow; var. *mariae*: body ³⁄₄–1¼ in (20–30 mm), lobes gray-buff, face sandy gold, panel olive, finely and densely marked appearing minutely green-gold-speckled; subsp. *burchellii*: body pale gray or buff, panel charcoal-gray with many fine markings creating an intricate, spreading network, or virtually unmarked, characterized by radiating marginal lines with expanded tips; *L. marmorata* body 1⅛–1¼ in (28–30 mm), face narrowly reniform, flat to convex, pale gray or beige sometimes tinted green or lilac, panel translucent, dark gray or gray-green, spreading outward from an arch on inner lip, closely and deeply marked with jagged edges, resembling a gray fissured stone; flowers white; *L. olivacea* body to ³⁄₄ in (20 mm), face flat, reniform with a straight inner margin, pale gray or beige, panel translucent, olive, edge slightly eroded, clear or with a few, scattered, raised markings; flowers yellow with white center; *L. otzeniana* body 1–1¼ in (25–30 mm), face reniform to elliptic, convex, buff, panel dull olive-brown, semitranslucent with edges appearing deeply eroded and a few broad, intramarginal markings; flowers yellow with white center; *L.*

pseudotruncatella (body 1–1¼ in (25–30 mm), face broadly reniform, flat to slightly concave, gray to buff, panel olive-brown, obscured and appearing as a fine network of dots and mossy "veins," terminating in dull red dashes, sometimes staining edges pale copper; flowers yellow; var. *elisabethae*: slightly smaller, body gray tinted lilac-blue or pink, markings dark gray, marginal dashes bright red; subsp. *archerae*: face reniform, pale gray with a slightly darker central zone, faint, delicate radial fissures, obscure spotting and, sometimes, marginal red dots and dashes; subsp. *dendritica*: face gray with a regular network of fine, dark hiero-glyph-like markings, radiating from a distinct, straight line of color at inner margin; *L. schwantesii* body 1¼–1½ in (30–40 mm), face oblong to reniform, rugose, gray or buff capped pale ginger, panel olive-gray with a network of cinnamon lines; flowers yellow; subsp. *gesneri*: body ³⁄₄–1 in (20–25 mm), lobes apex, gray-tan, capped pale brown with a network of red-brown lines; subsp. *steineckeana*: body ⁵⁄₈ in (15 mm), face semicircular, convex, gray-white suffused dirty cream, usually with a few gray-green dots, panel small, opaque, seldom present, possibly a garden hybrid; subsp. *terricolor*: body ³⁄₄–1 in (20–25 mm), oblong-reniform face, slightly convex, buff to tan, closely spotted olive or mid-green, flowers yellow, occasionally with a white center.

Littonia (For Dr. S. Litton, professor of Botany in Dublin in the mid-19th century). Liliaceae (Colchicaceae). South Africa, Arabia. 8 species tuberous, perennial climbing herbs with slender stems, tendril-tipped leaves and orange, campanulate, nodding flowers in summer. Cultivate as for *Gloriosa*. *L. modesta* (South Africa; stem to 39 ft (12 m), slender; leaves linear to lanceolate; tepals to 2 in (5 cm), orange-yellow, lanceolate.

littoral, litoral growing on the sea-shore.

liverwort common name for a primitive, flowerless land plant belonging to the group Hepatophyta. Species of *Pellia* and *Marchantia* can be a nuisance in gardens, where their flattened, overlapping

succulent forms are frequently found on the surface of potted-plant growing media; also in borders or standing ground. The stem or leaf structures are often branching, deeply lobed and undulating, rooting from the undersides with long hairlike rhizoids. Reproduction is by spores. Liverworts thrive and quickly multiply in conditions of plentiful moisture.

Development is discouraged where the soil pH is 7 or higher; also where organic fertility is maintained and there is regular cultivation including hoeing. They can be smothered by the application of a deep mulch to borders. Replacing the surface of pot plants with fresh growing media is the best course of action with container infestations.

The application of herbicide products containing benzalkonium chloride, dichlorophen or fatty acids are effective where use is acceptable and officially approved.

Livistona (for Patrick Murray, 17th-century Baron of Livingston, whose collection became the basis of the Edinburgh Botanic Garden). Palmae. Asia, Australasia. 28 species, shrubby or arborescent palms. The stems are solitary, erect and clothed with leaf sheaths, becoming bare and ringed or covered with leaf bases; the leaves are palmate. Elegant fan palms, they are grown outdoors as specimens in frost-free gardens or in deep pots in the greenhouse or conservatory (minimum temperature 45°F/7°C). Plant in full sun or light shade in a fertile, well-drained, acidic to neutral soil. Water pot-grown specimens only sparingly in winter. Propagate by seed sown in deep containers.

L. australis AUSTRALIAN FAN PALM, CABBAGE PALM, GIPPSLAND PALM, AUS-TRALIAN PALM; east coastal Australia; stem to 80 ft (25 m) × 12 in (30 cm), spiny-fibrous at first, becoming bare; leaf blades to 5¾ ft (1.75 m), glossy, segments to 70, with drooping, cleft tips; fruit to ¾ in (2 cm), red-brown to black, waxy; *L. chinensis* CHINESE FAN PALM; S Japan, Ryukyu Islands, Bonin Island, S Taiwan; stem to 39 ft (12 m) × 12 in (30 cm), swollen at base; leaf blades dull; fruit to 1 in (2.5 cm), deep blue-green to gray-pink, glossy.

Lloydia (for Edward Lloyd [1660–1709], Welsh antiquary and naturalist, and keeper of the Ashmolean Museum, Oxford). Liliaceae (Liliaceae). Temperate Northern Hemisphere. About 12 species, bulbous perennials with narrowly linear leaves. Produced in summer on slender stalks, the flowers consist of six spreading perianth segments. Fully hardy. Grow in light shade or bright indirect light, in a gritty, perfectly drained but moisture-retentive soil. Propagate by seed sown when ripe in the cold frame or in spring. *L. serotina* ALPLILY; temperate Northern Hemisphere; to 6 in (15 cm); flowers to 5/8 in (1.5 cm), white, pale yellow at base, veined red-purple.

loam a term widely used imprecisely in horticultural literature to describe soil considered of excellent quality for plant growth; "medium loam" generally refers to a fertile soil that is rich in fibrous organic matter, moisture retentive, easily worked, and without predominant proportions of silt, clay, sand or stones.

The term "loam" is used more specifically in classification systems of soil texture, where it does not imply fertility but serves to describe soils with conspicuous physical characteristics, such as silt-loam, clay-loam, sandy-loam and fibrous loam.

Formulae for soil-based growing media, such as the John Innes seed and potting composts, prescribe loam as an ingredient. In this instance, it refers ideally to fibrous clay-loam soil taken, after obtaining the necessary permission, from the top 16–24 in (40–60 cm) of long-term grass sward. The turf is lifted intact and stacked, grass side down, to mature in a heap about 10 ft (3 m) square and 6½ ft (2 m) high.

loamless mix see *soilless media*.

lobed divided into segments; the segments separated from each other by sinuses that do not reach to the base of the organ.

Lobelia (for Matthias de l'Obel [1538–1616], botanist and physician to James I of England). Campanulaceae. Tropical to temperate climates, particularly America. Some 365 species, annual or perennial herbs, shrubs and treelets. Produced in summer, usually in racemes, the flowers are tubular and bilabiate, with the lower three lobes large and spreading, and the upper 2 lobes small and recurved.

The "annual" lobelias are small, tender and half-hardy perennials commonly grown as edging and in window boxes, with trailing kinds well-suited to hanging baskets. Valued for their (typically) rich, deep blue flowers, modern selections have extended the color range to include pure white (*L. erinus* 'White Lady'), carmine pink (*L.* 'Rosamond') and pale lilacs, as in *L.* 'Lilac Fountain'. The hardy *L. siphilitica*, *L. cardinalis*, the more tender *L. fulgens*, and the hybrids derived from them, (*L. × speciosa*), include some of the most beautiful of garden perennials, bearing tall strong spikes of bloom in luminous colors in late summer. They are suited to the herbaceous border and to moist soil at stream- and pond-side. Although sometimes grown as marginal water plants, they are generally short-lived when submerged. The hardy *L. dortmanna* needs to grow in small, fairly shallow ponds, or at lake margins. *L. tupa* is a spectacular perennial. Hardy to 0°F (–18°C), it needs a sunny, warm and sheltered situation, a moist but free-draining soil and mulch protection in winter. Increase annuals by seed in spring, perennials by seed or division in spring.

L. cardinalis (CARDINAL FLOWER, INDIAN PINK; N America; short-lived perennial herb, to 36 in (90 cm), strongly tinged purple-bronze; leaves to 4 in (10 cm), glossy, often purple-red, narrowly ovate to oblong or lanceolate, toothed; flowers to 2 in (5 cm), bright scarlet, in narrow spikes; includes 'Alba', with white flowers, and 'Rosea', with pink flowers; *L. dortmanna* (WATER LOBELIA; N America, W Europe; aquatic, glabrous, perennial herb to 24 in (60 cm); leaves oblong; flowers to ³⁄₄ in (2 cm), pale mauve, few, pendulous, in a raceme standing clear of the water; *L. erinus* (EDGING LOBELIA, TRAILING LOBELIA; South Africa; small perennial herb, branches slender, sprawling then ascending or cascading; leaves small, dark green, glabrous, ovate to linear, toothed; flowers to ³⁄₄ in (2 cm), throat yellow to white, tube and limb blue to violet, in short, lax spikes; there are many cultivars and seed races including dwarf and vigorous plants, some bushy, some trailing, with single or double flowers ranging in color from violet through blue to pink and white; *L. fulgens* (syn. *L. splendens*; Texas, Mexico; close to *L. cardinalis* but slightly hairy; leaves to 6 in (15 cm), linear to lanceolate; inflorescence usually one-sided, flowers scarlet, exterior more or less downy; 'Illumination': flowers scarlet in large spikes; *L. × gerardii* (*L. cardinalis × L. siphilitica*; robust perennial, to 5 ft (1.5 m); flowers violet tinged with pink, to purple, lower lip with two white marks, in large racemes; 'Rosenkavalier': pure pink; 'Vedrariensis': dark violet; *L. siphilitica* (GREAT LOBELIA, BLUE CARDINAL FLOWER; E US; perennial herb to 24 in (60 cm); stem erect, very leafy; leaves to 4 in (10 cm), ovate to lanceolate, somewhat downy, toothed; flowers to 1 in (2.5 cm), blue, in dense spikes; 'Alba': white flowers; 'Nana': compact; *L. × speciosa* (*L. cardinalis × L. fulgens × L. siphilitica*); erect, smooth to hispid perennial; flowers to 1¼ in (3 cm), red or mauve tinged with purple or violet, in tall spikes; cultivars include 'Bees Flame', with bronze-red leaves and scarlet flowers, 'Brightness', with brilliant red flowers, 'Dark Crusader', with green to dark bronze leaves and blood-red flowers, 'Queen Victoria', with beet-red leaves and vivid red flowers, and 'Russian Princess', with tinged red leaves and bright purple flowers. *L. tupa* Chile; perennial to 6½ ft (2 m); stem upright, robust; leaves to 12 in (30 cm), lanceolate, pale sea green, finely downy; flowers large, brick red to blood red, in terminal spikes.

lobulate possessing or bearing lobules.

Lobularia (Latin *lobulus*, referring to the small fruit). Cruciferae. North temperate regions. 5 species, annual or perennial hairy herbs with narrow leaves and small, scented, 4-petaled flowers in compact terminal racemes, in spring and summer. Hardy, low-growing, bushy annuals and short-lived perennials, commonly used in bedding and edging, as temporary groundcover, and on dry walls. They are tolerant of maritime conditions. Grow in full sun, in well-drained soil. Sow seed under glass in later winter/early spring, and harden off in the cold frame before planting out in spring. Alternatively sow thinly *in situ* in spring. Deadheading, by trimming with scissors, prolongs flowering. Plants may be attacked by crucifer downy mildew, crucifer white blister and club root. *L. maritima* SWEET ALYSSUM, SWEET ALISON; S Europe, widely naturalized; low-growing bushy annual or short-lived perennial, 4–22 in (10–55 cm); leaves ½–1¼ in (1–3 cm), linear to ligulate, somewhat silvery-gray; flowers fragrant in compact heads, petals to ⅛ in (3 mm), rounded, usually white; many cultivars and seed races available, including compact and taller forms and plants with small or large flowers in tones of white, pink, purple-red and mauve.

locular, loculate furnished with locules; divided into separate chambers or compartments.

locule a cavity or chamber within an ovary, anther or fruit.

loculicidal a form of dehiscence, where the capsule splits longitudinally and dorsally, directly through the capsule wall.

locus the position of a gene on a chromosome.

locusts see *grasshoppers*.

lodicule one of two, or sometimes three, minute extrastaminal scales, adpressed to the base of the ovary in most Gramineae.

loganberry see *hybrid berries*.

loggia a covered sitting or walking place attached to a building, with one side open to the air. The term is often applied to garden rooms or house extensions, even those that are completely enclosed by glass.

Lomatia (from Greek *loma*, edge, referring to the winged edge of the seeds). Proteaceae. Australasia, S America. 12 species, evergreen shrubs with entire, toothed, pinnatifid or pinnately compound leaves. Produced in summer in racemes, the flowers are obliquely tubular, with a limb splitting into 4 narrow twisted lobes. Cultivate as for *Embothrium*, but with rather more shelter—for example, at the fringes or in clearings of woodland gardens and mature shrubberies, in moist, acidic soil. *L. ferruginea* (Chile, Patagonia; to 23 ft (7 m)); leaves to 8 in (20 cm), leathery, olive-green above, tomentose beneath, initially rusty-tomentose; flowers scarlet fading to olive green at tips.

loment a leguminous pod that contracts between the seeds it contains, drying and splitting transversely into one-seeded segments at maturity.

long-arm pruner a pruning tool consisting of cutting blades mounted on a long pole and operated by a lever attached as a handle at the opposite end; it is used for pruning parts inaccessible from ground level. It is often fitted with a saw or fruit-picking attachment, and is sometimes called a lopper.

long-day plant see *photoperiodism*.

longhorn beetles (Coleoptera: Cerambycidae) family of beetles with antennae often longer than the body. Many species are brightly colored, and some up to 4 in (100 mm) long, though most are between ½–2½ in (10–60 mm) in length. The larvae are soft white or yellow grubs with very small or absent legs, mostly tunnelers into dead or decaying wood.

Longhorn beetles are more common in the tropics than elsewhere but two species that are pests occur in gardens in North America. Larvae of the APPLE-TREE BORER (*Saperda candida*) tunnel the cambium and heartwood of trees such as apple, pear, quince, plums, cherry, mountain ash and hawthorn at ground level; the adults are up to ¾ in (20 mm) long and olive-brown with conspicuous white stripes. The pest can be controlled by routine orchard sprays. Larvae of the RASPBERRY CANE BORER (*Oberea bimaculata*) first invade shoot tips of plants, such as raspberry, blackberry and sometimes roses, but later burrow downward to ground level. The adults are slender, up to ½ in (12 mm) long, with two black spots on the yellow thorax. Damage can be reduced by cutting out and burning affected canes or shoots. None of the British longhorn beetles causes damage to growing garden plants.

long tom see *pots and potting*.

Lonicera (for Adam Lonitzer [1528–86], German naturalist, author of a herbal (*Kreuterbüch*) much reprinted between 1557 and 1783). Caprifoliaceae. HONEYSUCKLE, WOODBINE. N Hemisphere. About 180 species, deciduous or evergreen shrubs, some bushy, others twining vigorously. Borne in clusters in leaf axils or in terminal heads, the flowers are tubular to campanulate; the 5-lobed corolla limb may be bilabiate (with a 4-lobed upper lip) or regular. The fruit is a many-seeded berry.

Lonicera has a wide range of uses in the garden. The climbing and twining species are used for covering trelliswork, walls, fences, pergolas and old tree stumps. Although they will grow in sun or part shade, in habitat the climbers tend to grow with their roots in shade and their shoots reaching up to the sun. The shrubby honeysuckles will grow in full sun or light shade. Deciduous shrubby honeysuckles include several sweetly fragrant winter-flowering species and some colorful shrubs such as *L. tatarica*. Among the evergreen shrubby species, *L. pileata* makes good, loose groundcover, while *L. nitida* is familiar as a hedging plant. Those listed below are fully hardy except for the showy climber *L. hildebrandtiana*, which needs a minimum temperature of 45°F (7°C). Honeysuckles like a fertile, well-drained soil. Prune young plants to encourage a good frame-work of branches. Thereafter prune after flowering to keep within bounds and thin out old wood. *L. nitida* may be sheared throughout the growing season. Propagate by semi-ripe cuttings in summer, or by hardwood cuttings in late fall, also by simple layering in late fall. Attacked by aphids, mildew. (*See table overleaf.*)

Lonicera aphid

L

LONICERA

Name	Distribution	Habit	Leaves	Flowers	Fruit
L. × *americana* (*L. caprifolium* × *L. etrusca*)	S & SE Europe, Balkans	climber resembling *L. caprifolium*		fragrant, yellow, tinted maroon, in crowded whorls from axils of connate leaves, to 2 in (5 cm), tube slender	red

Comments: Summer. 'Atrosanguinea': flowers deep red outside. 'Quereifolia': leaves lobed, sometimes with yellow margin or red striped. 'Rubella': flowers light purple outside, buds more deeply colored.

| *L.* × *brownii* (*L. sempervirens* × *L. hirsuta*) SCARLET TRUMPET HONEYSUCKLE | garden origin | deciduous climber to 10 ft (3 m) | elliptic, blue-green, somewhat hairy beneath, uppermost leaf pairs connate | orange-scarlet in heads | |

Comments: Spring–summer. 'Dropmore Scarlet': vigorous; flowers long trumpet-shaped, bright scarlet, midsummer/early fall, long lasting. 'Fuchsioides': flowers orange-scarlet.

| *L. caprifolium* ITALIAN WOODBINE; ITALIAN HONEYSUCKLE | Europe, W Asia | deciduous climber to 20 ft (6 m) | to 4 in (10 cm), obovate or oval, glaucous, especially beneath, terminal pair fused | yellow-white, pink-tinged, to 2 in (5 cm), fragrant, in 4–10-flowered whorls | orange-red |

Comments: Spring–summer. 'Praecox': leaves gray-green; flowers cream, often tinted light red, later turning yellow, early-flowering.

| *L. etrusca* | Mediterranean region | semievergreen climber to 13 ft (4 m) | to 3 in (8 cm), oval or obovate, glaucous, blue-green, upper leaves connate | closely packed in whorls, yellow tinted red, becoming deep yellow, to 2 in (5 cm) | red |

Comments: Summer. 'Donald Waterer': flowers red and white, yellowing with age, fragrant. 'Michael Rosse': flowers cream and pale yellow, later darkening, slightly fragrant. 'Superba': shoots flushed red; flowers cream, later orange, in large terminal panicles; strong-growing.

| *L. fragrantissima* WINTER-FLOWERING HONEYSUCKLE | China | erect to spreading, evergreen to deciduous shrub to 10 ft (3 m) tall | to 3 in (7.5 cm), oval-elliptic, dull green above, somewhat glaucous beneath | to ¾ in (2 cm), cream to white, intensely fragrant, paired in axils | dull red |

Comments: Winter–early spring.

| *L.* × *heckrottii* (*L. sempervirens* × *L.* × *americana*) | garden origin | loosely climbing to sprawling deciduous shrub | to 2½ in (6 cm), oblong or elliptic, glaucous beneath, uppermost pairs connate | fragrant, rich pink outside, yellow inside, 1½ in (4 cm), in whorls on terminal spikes | |

Comments: Summer. Sometimes called *L.* 'American Beauty'. 'Gold Flame': leaves dark green; flowers yellow inside, flushed strong purple.

| *L. henryi* | W China | evergreen or semideciduous climber | to 3½ in (9 cm), oblong to lanceolate, deep, shiny green | ¾ in (2 cm), maroon or yellow, usually paired | purple-black |

Comments: Summer.

L. × *americana*

L. × *brownii* 'Dropmore Scarlet'

L. caprifolium

L. × *heckrottii*

LONICERA

Name	Distribution	Habit	Leaves	Flowers	Fruit
L. hildebrandiana GIANT BURMESE HONEYSUCKLE; GIANT HONEYSUCKLE	China, SE Asia	evergreen climber, sometimes semideciduous, to 80 ft (25 m)	to 4¾ in (12 cm), oval or rounded, deep green above **Comments:** Summer.	to 6 in (16 cm), cream, changing to gold then amber, fragrant	
L. japonica JAPANESE HONEYSUCKLE; GOLD-AND-SILVER FLOWER	Japan, Korea, China; naturalized SE US	evergreen or semievergreen climber to 30 ft (9 m)	to 3 in (8 cm), usually smaller, oblong to elliptic, incised or lobed on juvenile or very vigorous shoots	white, becoming yellow, paired, intensely fragrant, to 1½ in (4 cm)	blue-black

Comments: Spring–summer. 'Aureoreticulata' ('Reticulata'): leaves small, bright green, with golden netted veins, sometimes lobed. 'Halliana': leaves rich green; flowers white, sometimes tinted red, later yellow. 'Hall's Prolific': habit climbing, to 20 ft (6 m) high, to 10 ft (3 m) wide; leaves ovate; flowers white, later cream to yellow. 'Variegata': leaves variegated yellow.

Name	Distribution	Habit	Leaves	Flowers	Fruit
L. maackii	E Asia	deciduous, erect shrub to 16 ft (5 m)	to 3 in (8 cm), narrowly obovate to broadly lanceolate, dark green	to ¾ in (2 cm), white then yellow, paired	dark red or black

Comments: Spring-summer. 'Erubescens': flowers suffused pink, fruit red.

Name	Distribution	Habit	Leaves	Flowers	Fruit
L. morrowii	Japan	deciduous shrub to 6½ ft (2 m)	to 2 in (5 cm), oblong to elliptic	to ½ in (1.3 cm), downy, white turning yellow, paired	dark red, shiny

Comments: Spring-summer.

Name	Distribution	Habit	Leaves	Flowers	Fruit
L. nitida	SW China	twiggy evergreen shrub to 11½ ft (3.5 m)	¼–⅝ in (0.5–1.5 cm), ovate to elliptic or rounded, dark, glossy green	to ½ in (1 cm), cream to white, paired	glossy blue-purple

Comments: Spring-summer. Commonly used for hedging and ground cover, with many cultivars, ranging in habit from tall, erect and dense to low and arching, with very small leaves in tones of dark jade, emerald, lime and gold.

Name	Distribution	Habit	Leaves	Flowers	Fruit
L. periclymenum WOODBINE; HONEYSUCKLE	Europe, Asia Minor, Caucasus, W Asia	deciduous climber to 13 ft (4 m)	to 2½ in (6.5 cm), ovate, oval or obovate, uppermost pair separate	fragrant, red and yellow-white, to 2 in (5 cm), in 3–5-whorled terminal spikes	bright red

Comments: Summer. 'Belgica': flowers white, flushed purple outside, later yellow, scented, in large clusters; fruit large, red, abundant. 'Graham Thomas': flowers large, white, later yellow tinted copper, long-lasting. 'Quercina': leaves "oaklike," sinuately toothed to lobed sometimes variegated white. 'Serotina', LATE DUTCH HONEYSUCKLE: leaves narrow; flowers dark purple outside, later fading, yellow inside, profuse; fruit red.

Name	Distribution	Habit	Leaves	Flowers	Fruit
L. pileata	China	evergreen or semievergreen shrub to 5 ft (1.5 m)	to 1¼ in (3 cm), oblong, dark green, glossy	to ⅜ in (0.8 cm), yellow-white, paired	translucent purple-blue

Comments: Spring-summer. Includes cultivars with bright emerald foliage, some very low-growing and excellent groundcover.

L. hildebrandiana

L. japonica 'Halliana'

L. nitida 'Baggesen's Gold'

L periclymenum 'GrahamThomas'

LONICERA

Name	Distribution	Habit	Leaves	Flowers	Fruit
L. × **purpusii** (*L. fragrantissima* × *L. standishii*) WINTER-FLOWERING HONEYSUCKLE	garden origin	erect, semideciduous shrub to 10 ft (3 m) with arching, smooth to bristly branchlets	to 4 in (10 cm), ovate to elliptic, dark green above, paler beneath	creamy white, to 1 in (2.5 cm), paired or clustered, highly fragrant	red
Comments: Winter to early spring.					
L. sempervirens CORAL HONEYSUCKLE, TRUMPET HONEYSUCKLE	E & S US	vigorous evergreen climber	to 3 in (8 cm), oval, deep green above, blue-green beneath, uppermost pair of leaves connate	to 2 in (5 cm), rich scarlet-orange outside, more yellow inside, in whorls	bright red
Comments: Spring–fall. 'Magnifica': red outside, interior yellow. f. *sulphurea*: bright yellow, long- and late-flowering.					
L. standishii WINTER-FLOWERING HONEYSUCKLE	China	erect, deciduous or semievergreen shrub to 6½ ft (2 m) with warty and bristly branchlets	to 4 in (10 cm), broadly oblong-lanceolate, downy	to 1 in (2.5 cm), creamy-white to palest pink, intensely fragrant, paired	red
Comments: Winter–spring.					
L. tatarica	Russia, C Asia	erect, deciduous shrub to 13 ft (4 m)	to 2½ in (6 cm), ovate to lanceolate, glaucous beneath	to 1 in (2.5 cm), pink, paired	scarlet to yellow-orange
Comments: Spring-summer. Includes cultivars of tall to dwarf and compact habit, with flowers in shades of deep rosy red, pink and white, and scarlet to golden fruit.					
L. × **tellmanniana** (*L. sempervirens* × *L. tragophylla*)	garden origin	vigorous, deciduous climber	to 4 in (10 cm), ovate to oblong, deep green above, pruinose beneath, upper pair fused	to 1¾ in (4.5 cm), rich orange to coppery gold, whorled **Comments:** Summer.	
L. tragophylla **Comments:** Summer.	China	deciduous climber	to 5½ in (14 cm), oblong, glaucous, uppermost 1–3 pairs fused	to 3 in (8 cm), orange to yellow, often tinted red above, whorled	red
L. × **xylosteoides** (*L. tatarica* × *L. xylosteum*)	garden origin	erect, deciduous shrub to 6½ ft (2 m)	to 2½ in (6 cm), broadly elliptic to obovate, blue-green, hairy	small, light red, hairy with a swollen base	yellow to red
Comments: Spring-summer. Includes low-growing and compact cultivars, some with white flowers.					
L. xylosteum FLY HONEYSUCKLE **Comments:** Summer.	Europe, NE Asia	erect, deciduous shrub to 10 ft (3 m)	1¼–2¾ in (3–7 cm), oblong-ovate to obovate, downy	to ½ in (1 cm), white often tinted red or pink, carried on middle or lower half of branches	red or yellow

L. pileata

L. tatarica

L. × tellmanniana

L. xylosteum

Lopezia (for Tomas Lopez [*c.* 1540], Spanish botanist who studied South American plants). Onagraceae. C America. 21 species, annual or perennial herbs with terminal racemes of zygomorphic, 4-petaled flowers likened to colorful insects in flight. In frost-free areas, plant in well-drained soil in a sunny site or in part-day shade. In cold areas, plant in a medium-fertility loam-based mix and grow under glass, maintaining a minimum night temperature of 50°F (10°C); water moderately, and pinch tips for bushier specimens. Propagate from seed, sown with a little bottom heat, and by cuttings in spring. *L. racemosa* (MOSQUITO FLOWER; Mexico, El Salvador; variable annual or perennial to 5 ft (1.5 m); petals to ½ in (1 cm), white to palest lilac, or purple, pink to red or vermilion, lowermost obovate to rounded, uppermost linear to oblong.

Lophomyrtus (Greek *lophos*, crested, and *Myrtus*). Myrtaceae. New Zealand. 2 species, evergreen shrubs or small trees with leathery leaves and white, axillary flowers with four spreading petals. Cultivate as for *Myrtus*.

L. bullata RAMA RAMA; to 18 ft (5.4 m); leaves to 2 in (5 cm), broadly ovate to suborbicular, strongly bullate, glossy, often tinged purple-red; *L. obcordata* ROHUTU; to 15 ft (4.5 m); leaves to ½ in (1.25 cm), obcordate, cuneate, emarginate; *L.* × *ralphii* (*L. bullata* × *L. obcordata*; intermediate between parents; leaves puckered; flowers white tinted pink: 'Purpurea': leaves deep purple-red.

lopper see *long-arm pruner*.

lopping shears a pruning tool with short stout blades on medium length handles, used for cutting stout branches. They are sometimes called loppers.

lorate strap-shaped.

Lorette pruning a method of pruning fruit trees, especially pears, developed by Louis Lorette in the early 19th century. All pruning is carried out from spring to late summer by severe cutting of side laterals to stimulate a maximum amount of fruit bud from the base of shoots. The system was developed as relevant to vigorous seedling rootstocks,

and it has little advantage on selected types which are best pruned by the renewal method.

Loropetalum (from Greek *loron* strap, and *petalon*, petal: the petals are long and narrow). Hamamelidaceae. Himalaya, China, Japan. 2 species, evergreen, downy shrubs or small trees, to 10 ft (3 m) tall, with ovate to elliptic leaves and terminal clusters of spidery, 4-petaled flowers in winter and spring. Although tolerant of temperatures down to 23°F (–5°C), *Loropetalum* flowers well only where temperatures seldom drop below 41°F (5°C). In colder regions, it may be grown in the intermediate greenhouse in a well-drained but moisture-retentive, high-fertility, loam-based medium to which additional organic matter has been added. Propagation as for *Hamamelis*. *L. chinense* (syn. *L. indicum*; India, China, Japan; shrub to 10 ft (3 m); leaves to 1½ in (4 cm), dark green, bristly white, downy; petals ¾ in (2 cm), white, strap-shaped and wavy, giving a feathery appearance to whole inflorescence; 'Roseum': flowers pink.

Lotus (from the Greek name *lotos*, used by Dioscorides and Theophrastus for certain Leguminosae). Leguminosae. Mediterranean Europe, south to Sahara Desert, W Asia; W US; Australia; South Africa. Some 100 species, annual or perennial herbs and subshrubs with palmate or pinnate leaves and axillary racemes of pealike flowers in spring and summer. The shrubby *L. hirsutus* is hardy to 5°F (–15°C). Grow in full sun in fast-draining soil. Prune in spring. The herbaceous *L. jacobaeus* and the softly shrubby, scrambling *L. maculatus* and *L. berthelotii* are suitable for planting outdoors in gardens that are frost-free or almost so. Where temperatures fall below 10°F (–12°C), these species make beautiful specimens for the cool greenhouse or conservatory (minimum temperature 41°F/5°C). Alternatively, they can be used as half-hardy bedding plants, planted out after the last frosts, and overwintered in frost-free conditions as stock plants or newly rooted cuttings. With cascading stems of filigree foliage and fiery flowers, *L. maculatus* and *L. berthelotii* are among the finest plants for hanging baskets,

patio containers and groundcover planting in silver and gray gardens. Grow in full sun in a sheltered site in a fast-draining soil. Keep moist when in full growth, but rather dry and in cool, airy conditions in winter. Trim after flowering. Propagate by scarified seed in spring, or by semiripe cuttings in summer.

L. berthelotii CORAL GEM, PARROT'S BEAK, PELICAN'S BEAK; Canary Islands, Cape Verde Islands, Tenerife, naturalized US; cascading, climbing or prostrate perennial subshrub, to 3¼ ft (1 m); branches slender, ash-gray; leaves very short-stalked, leaflets ½ in (1 cm), linear, silver-gray; flowers ¾–1½ in (2–4 cm), typically scarlet but also orange-red or maroon-black, keel long, slender, beak- or clawlike; includes 'Kew Form', with silver leaves and red flowers; *L. maculatus* differs in its burnished bronze-gold and fiery red flowers; *L. hirsutus* (syn. *Dorycnium hirsutum*); HAIRY CANARY CLOVER; Mediterranean, S Portugal; densely silver-downy subshrub to 20 in (50 cm); leaflets to ¾ in (2 cm), obovate; flowers cream flushed shell pink in umbels to 2½ in (6 cm); seed heads dark, attractive; *L. jacobaeus* Cape Verde Islands; erect perennial, 12–36 in (30–90 cm), more or less gray-downy; flowers in clusters, dark maroon-black to velvety brown except for olive-yellow standard.

low-worked used of plants grafted at a point near ground level. Also known as bottom-worked.

Luma (native Chilean name). Myrtaceae. Argentina, Chile. 4 species, evergreen shrubs or small trees with leathery leaves, white, 4-petaled flowers and dark-purple berries. Hardy in sheltered locations to 0°F (–18°C). Cultivate as for *Myrtus* but with protection from strong winds and in moist but gritty, acidic to neutral soil.

L. apiculata Argentina, Chile; shrub or small tree to 33 ft (10 m); bark cinnamon, peeling to expose ash-gray wood; leaves ½–1¾ in (1–4.5 cm), elliptic to suborbicular, apiculate; 'Glanleam Gold': leaves deeply edged creamy yellow, tinged pink at first; 'Penwith': leaves gray-green edged cream-white, tinted red-pink in winter; *L. chequen* Chile; shrub or small tree to

30 ft (9 m); bark gray-brown; leaves ¼–1 in (0.5–2.5 cm), elliptic, ovate or lanceolate, rarely suborbicular, acute.

Lunaria (from Latin *luna*, moon, alluding to the shape of the pod and the moonlightlike quality of the septum). Cruciferae. C and S Europe. 3 species, biennial or perennial herbs with erect, branching stems, toothed, ovate to cordate leaves and terminal racemes of 4-petaled flowers in spring and summer. The fruit is a silique, very compressed and oblong or elliptic to nearly circular in outline. Stripped of its casing and seeds, all that is left of the fruit is a translucent, pearly white septum. These persist on the bleached branches of the inflorescence, and are popular with dried flower arrangers. Hardy to 5°F (−15°C). Grow in moist fertile soil, in part shade or sun. Propagate from seed sown in fall or spring; *L. rediviva* may also be increased by division. Both will naturalize. For dried arrangements, harvest as pods turn brown; hang to dry and allow the casings and seed to fall away.

L. annua (syn. *L. biennis*); HONESTY, SILVER DOLLAR, PENNY FLOWER; biennial to 3¼ ft (1 m); flowers unscented, to 1¼ in (3 cm) across, purple to white, sometimes white streaked or flecked purple; fruit ¾–2¾ in (2–7 cm), oblong to round, apiculate; includes 'Alba', with white flowers, 'Haslemere', with leaves variegated off-white and purple flowers, and 'Variegata', with leaves variegated and edged cream; *L. rediviva* PERENNIAL HONESTY; similar to *L. annua* except perennial, flowers fragrant, fruit tapering at base and apex.

lunate crescent-shaped.

Lupinus (from Latin *lupus*, wolf, referring to the belief that these plants ravage the land, exhausting the fertility of the soil). Leguminosae. Western N America, Mediterranean, S America, S Europe, N Africa. LUPINE. Some 200 species, annual or perennial herbs or shrubs with palmate leaves and pealike flowers in long, erect and cylindrical racemes in late spring and summer.

The most commonly cultivated perennials are those derived mainly from *L. polyphyllus* and its crosses with *L. arboreus* and several annual species. Some of the finest of these are the Russell Lupins, raised by George Russell of York over a period of 25 years and introduced in 1937. Named selections are chosen for color and height, from dwarf races such as Garden Gnome, Minarette and Dwarf Gallery, which seldom exceed 18–24 in (45–60 cm), to *L.* 'Band of Nobles', which may achieve 60 in (150 cm). Colors range from cream and white shades through yellows in *L.* 'Chandelier', orange reds in *L.* 'Flaming June', carmine in *L.* 'The Page' to rich violets in *L.* 'Thundercloud'; they include strong primary colors and bicolors, as in *L.* 'The Châtelaine' and *L.* 'The Governor'. More subtle shades are found in *L.* 'Blushing Bride' (ivory white), *L.* 'George Russell' (creamy pink), and *L.* 'Wheatsheaf' (golden-yellow flushed pink. Hybrids sold as mixed shades are at their most splendid when planted in groups of five or more, where fine contrasts can be achieved. Most hybrids and species are not long-lasting when cut, but survive longer if the cut stem is filled with water before arranging. *L. polyphyllus* and hybrids are hardy to −20°F (−29°C). Grow in full sun, in deep, moderately fertile, well-drained soil that is slightly acidic to neutral.

L. arboreus and the rather finer *L. chamissonis* are useful in the shrub border, herbaceous border and for naturalizing in poor, dry soil and in maritime areas. Given good drainage and shelter from cold winds, they will tolerate temperatures to 5°F (−15°C).

Sow seed in spring in pots and plant out when small. Lupins are generally intolerant of root disturbance. Germination is quicker if seeds are pre-soaked for 24 hours in warm water. Increase also by basal cuttings, taken with a small part of the rootstock attached, and rooted in sand in the cold frame.

The fungus *Pleiochaeta setosa* causes small black-purple spots which may enlarge so that the leaves shrivel and die; spots may also occur on stems and pods.

The disease can be controlled by copper-based fungicides. Lupins can also be affected by black root rot, crown gall, powdery mildew and sclerotina rot. Lupins may become severely infested with the lupine aphid. In North America, it may be attacked by the capsid bug.

L. arboreus TREE LUPINE; W US; evergreen shrub to 10 ft (3 m); leaflets lanuginose beneath, gray-green; flowers sulfur-yellow, sometimes blue or lavender, in erect, lax, terminal raceme to 10 in (25.5 cm); *L. chamissonis* SW US; evergreen, slender-branched shrub to 5 ft (1.5 m), leaflets narrow, silver-hairy; flowers blue and cream to yellow in racemes to 4 in (10 cm)); *L. polyphyllus* California to British Columbia; stout perennial to 5 ft (1.5 m), usually unbranched; flowers blue, purple, pink or white, verticillate, in a somewhat dense raceme to 24 in (60 cm); includes 'Moerheimii', with white and rose flowers; *L. subcarnosus* TEXAS BLUEBONNET; SW US; decumbent annual to 16 in (40 cm), branched at base; flowers bright blue, standard white at center, turning purple, crowded, in several-flowered raceme to 4¾ in (12 cm) long. For hybrid lupins and cultivars, see above under Russell Lupines.

lute an implement used for working in top-dressings, for filling hollows in lawns, and for levelling soil. Usually made in one of two forms: a length of wood about 3¼ ft (1 m) wide, fixed to a handle in the fashion of a rake, or a series of shorter crosspieces, made into a frame, and fixed by a hinged bracket to the handle.

Luzula (from Italian *lucciola*). Juncaceae. Cosmopolitan, especially temperate Eurasia. WOODRUSH. 80 species, perennial or, rarely, annual herbs (those here perennial) with basal clumps and rosettes of grassy or sedgelike leaves, sometimes with long wavy white hairs. Brown, green or white, the inconspicuous flowers are borne in spring amid small, chaffy bracts in stalked umbel-like corymbs. Fully hardy groundcover for moist and shaded conditions. Cultivars of *L. sylvatica* will brighten the darkest places; they are also useful for stabilizing banks of heavy soil. The graceful *L. nivea* is less invasive and appreciates a

silvery casing

Lunaria seedpod

sunny aspect. Propagate by division between fall and spring, alternatively by seed sown in spring and summer.

L. nivea SNOW RUSH; Alps, C Europe; to 24 in (60 cm), loosely tufted; leaves linear, to 12 × ⅛ in (300 × 4 mm), flat, dark green, hairy; inflorescence loose with up to 20 clusters of off-white flowers; includes 'Little Snow Hare', with fine, bright white flower heads with long hairs, and 'Snow Bird', with snow white flower heads; *L. sylvatica* (syn. *L. maxima*); GREATER WOODRUSH; S, W and C Europe; to 32 in (80 cm), loosely tufted, in large tussocks; basal leaves to 12 × ¾ in (30 × 2 cm), channeled, smooth or with silky hairs; inflorescence spreading, with many red-brown flowers in groups of two to five; includes 'Aurea', with broad, golden-yellow leaves, 'Hohe Tatra', with smooth, golden to lime green leaves, the color especially bright in winter, 'Marginata', with deep green leaves, edged white and brown, 'Tauernpass', with very broad, low-lying leaves, and 'Woodsman', with bright sap green leaves.

Lycaste (possibly named for Lycaste, daughter of King Priam). Orchidaceae. Mexico, C America, W Indies, S America. Some 45 species, perennial, epiphytic, terrestrial or lithophytic herbs with large, ovoid pseudobulbs bearing bold, plicate, lanceolate leaves. The flowers appear with or shortly before the new growth and are borne singly on sheathed stalks arising from the base of the pseudobulbs. They are large, waxy and fragrant, with cupped to spreading lanceolate to elliptic tepals; the lip is trilobed and the midlobe spreading to decurved, pubescent, entire to fimbriate or undulate. Pot in a mix of coarse bark, charcoal, perlite, sphagnum and leaf mold. When in growth, water and feed freely and maintain humid, buoyant conditions with light shade (avoid leaf scorch); aim to promote the largest and firmest possible pseudobulbs. Once growth is complete, reduce temperature (minimum 50°F/10°C) and watering, and increase light. Increase by division.

L. aromatica Mexico, Honduras, Guatemala; flowers scented, sepals to 1½ × ¾ in (4 × 2 cm), green-yellow, petals to 1½ × ¾ in (3.5 × 2 cm), deep yellow, lip to 1¼ in (3 cm), golden yellow, dotted orange; *L. cochleata* Guatemala, Honduras; similar to *L. aromatica*; flowers to 2 in (5 cm) in diameter, sepals green-yellow, petals deep orange, lip fimbriate; *L. cruenta* Mexico, Guatemala, Costa Rica, El Salvador; flowers spicily scented, sepals to 2 × 1 in (5 × 2.5 cm), yellow-green, petals to 1½ × 1 in (4 × 2.5 cm), bright yellow to yellow-orange, lip yellow, dotted maroon, spotted or zoned crimson at base, saccate, midlobe pubescent; *L. deppei* Mexico, Guatemala; sepals to 2½ × 1 in (6 × 2.5 cm), pale green flecked or faintly lined oxblood to red, petals to 1¾ × ¾ in (4.5 × 2 cm), white, flecked red at base, lip bright yellow with red dots, base striped red, strongly veined, crenate; *L. longipetala* (Ecuador, Peru, Colombia, Venezuela; tepals yellow-green, tinged brown, sepals to 3¼ × 1¼ in (8.5 × 3 cm), petals smaller, lip red-brown to violet-purple, denticulate or fimbriate; *L. macrophylla* Costa Rica, Panama, Colombia, Venezuela, Peru, Bolivia; sepals olive green, edged pink-brown, to 1½ × ¾ in (4 × 2 cm), petals white, spotted rose-pink, to 1½ × ¾ in (3.5 × 2 cm), lip white, margins dotted rose, midlobe spreading, ciliate; *L. skinneri* (syn. *L. virginalis*); Guatemala, Mexico, Honduras, El Salvador; sepals white to pink to violet-rose, to 3 × 1½ in (8 × 3.5 cm), petals pink to red-violet, often marked crimson, to 3 × 1½ in (7.5 × 4 cm), lip white to pale rose, flecked red-violet, to 2 in (5 cm), disk pubescent, fleshy.

Lychnis (From Greek *lychnos*, lamp; the name *Lychnis* was used for these plants by Theophrastus, and refers to the use of the gray-felted leaves of *L. coronaria* as lamp-wicks). Caryophyllaceae. Widespread in the northern temperate zone; several species grown in gardens. CAMPION, CATCHFLY. About 20 species, mostly perennial herbs, differing from *Silene* only in the combination of 5 styles and a capsule opening with 5 teeth (most *Silene* species have 3 styles and a capsule opening with 6 teeth. *Lychnis* species range through northern temperate regions in diverse habitats, from fenland, damp meadow and moist woodlands (*L. flos-cuculi*) to rocky or alpine meadow habitats (*L. alpina*). Woolly or downy-leaved species such as *L. flos-jovis*, *L. coronaria* and *L. viscaria* are suited to dry borders or raised beds. *L. coronaria* self-seeds freely in gravelly soil. *L. × haageana* and *L. chalcedonica* require more moisture to thrive; the latter is sometimes used in bog garden or stream-side plantings with the roots above water level. *L. × haageana* flowers in its first year from seed and may be grown as an annual. *L. alpina* is a dwarf, mat-forming plant for the rock garden. Most species tolerate temperatures below 5°F (−15°C), although *L. flos-jovis* and *L. × haageana* may not survive where temperatures fall below 5–14°F (−10°C to −15°C). Propagate perennials by division in fall or spring, or from seed sown when ripe or in spring.

L. alpina subarctic regions and mountains of Northern Hemisphere; glabrous, tufted perennial to 6 in (15 cm); inflorescence dense, more or less capitate, of 6–20 flowers, petals usually pale purple, deeply bifid; includes cultivars with white to rose flowers; *L. chalcedonica* MALTESE CROSS; Europe, Russia; erect, hispid perennial to 20 in (50 cm); inflorescence capitate, 10–50-flowered, petals to ⅝ in (1.5 cm), bifid, bright scarlet; includes cultivars with white to rose, salmon and deep red flowers, some double; *L. coronaria* DUSTY MILLER, ROSE CAMPION; SE Europe, but naturalized locally elsewhere from widespread cultivation; biennial or short-lived perennial to 32 in (80 cm), covered in silver-white to gray, felty hairs; inflorescence few-flowered, flowers long-stalked, petals to ½ in (1.2 cm), entire or shallowly 2-toothed, purple-red; includes cultivars with white, rose, deep carmine and double flowers; *L. flos-cuculi* FLOWER OF JOVE; Europe, also Caucasus and Siberia; sparsely hairy perennial with erect flowering stems to 30 in (75 cm); flowers on slender stalks in loose cymes, petals to ⅝ in (1.5 cm), pale purple, deeply and narrowly 4-lobed; a dwarf variant is sometimes grown in rock gardens; includes cultivars with white, pink, red and double flowers; *L. flos-jovis* European Alps, naturalized locally elsewhere; white-tomentose perennial with erect, usually unbranched stem to 32 in (80 cm); inflorescence more or less capitate 4–10-flowered, petals to ⅜ in (0.8 cm),

L

scarlet, bifid with broad, often cut lobes; includes 'Alba', with white flowers, and 'Nana' ('Minor'), dwarf, to 10 in (25 cm), with red flowers; *L.* × *haageana* short-lived, glandular-hairy perennial to 24 in (60 cm); few-flowered inflorescence, petals to ¾ in (2 cm), broadly obovate, bifid, with a narrow tooth on each side and toothed on margins, scarlet or rich orange-red; name applied to a group of garden hybrids of uncertain parentage but clearly involving Far Eastern species, especially *L. fulgens* and *L. sieboldii*; selections from crosses between these hybrids and *L. chalcedonica*, known as *L.* × *arkwrightii*, include 'Vesuvius' with dark foliage and very large orange-scarlet flowers; these hybrids are best treated as summer annuals; they include 'Grandiflora', with large, red flowers, 'Hybrida', with red flowers, and 'Salmonea', with salmon pink flowers; *L. viscaria* (Europe, W Asia; glabrous or sparsely hairy perennial with stiff stem to 24 in (60 cm), simple or slightly branched above, sticky below upper nodes; panicle narrow, interrupted, spikelike, petals to ½ in (1 cm), entire or shallowly bifid, usually purple-red; includes cultivars with white, rose, magenta and bright red flowers, some double; subsp. *atropurpurea*: flowers deep purple.

Lycium (from Greek *lykion*, from Lycia, Asia Minor; name of a species of *Rhamnus* transferred to this genus by Linnaeus). Solanaceae. Cosmopolitan, temperate and subtropical regions. BOXTHORN, MATRIMONY VINE. About 100 species, deciduous and evergreen shrubs, often spiny with slender branches, erect, spreading or scrambling. Small, dull white, green or purple flowers are borne in the leaf axils in spring and followed by bright red berries. Tolerant of maritime conditions and hardy to −10°F (−23°C). They will often succeed trained as wall plants or espaliers against a framework of wire. They also make good informal hedges, responding well to shearing, and providing a thorny and impenetrable barrier. Other garden uses include shrub plantings for stabilizing banks and clothing of unsightly tree stumps and retaining walls with their tangled and cascading stems. Prune in late

winter or early spring to confine to the space allocated, or to thin old, crowded or weak wood; shear hedging plants two to three times in the growing season. Espaliers should be pruned after fruiting in winter or early spring. Propagate from seed sown in spring and by rooted suckers. Alternatively, increase by hardwood cuttings in fall or spring, layering, or by semiripe cuttings rooted with gentle bottom heat in summer. *L. barbarum* (syn. *L. chinense*, *L. europaeum*, *L. halimiifolium*); COMMON MATRIMONY VINE, DUKE OF ARGYLL'S TEA TREE; SE Europe to China; deciduous, erect or spreading, to 11½ ft (3.5 m), usually spiny; leaves to 2 in (5 cm), narrowly oblong to lanceolate, gray-green to dull mid-green; flowers to ½ in (1 cm), in clusters of 1–4, dull lilac; fruit to ¾ in (2 cm), orange-red or yellow.

Lycopersicon *see* tomato.

Lycoris (for a beautiful Roman actress, the mistress of Mark Anthony). Amaryllidaceae. China, Japan. 10–12 species, bulbous perennial herbs with strap-shaped leaves. The flowers are produced in late summer and fall in scapose umbels; they have six, slender, reflexed and wavy tepals and prominent stamens. *Lycoris* species will tolerate temperatures to at least 5°F (−15°C), but need a period of dry warmth during their summer dormancy and minimal winter wet. They are also amenable to pot cultivation in the cool greenhouse or conservatory. They resent root disturbance, and may take several years to become well-established; top-dressing is preferable to repotting, and plants may remain in the same pot for up to 4–5 years. Propagate by offsets or from ripe seed.

L. aurea GOLDEN SPIDER LILY, GOLDEN HURRICANE LILY; China, Japan; scape to 24 in (60 cm), flowers 3¾–4 in (9.5–10 cm), golden-yellow, funnelform, lobes recurved, wavy; *L. radiata* RED SPIDER LILY, SPIDER LILY; Japan; scape to 20 in (50 cm), flowers 1½–2 in (4–5 cm), rose-red to deep red, lobes strongly reflexed, wavy; includes 'Alba', with white flowers tinged yellow at base, and 'Variegata', with crimson flowers, edged white as they fade; *L. squamigera* RESURRECTION LILY, MAGIC LILY; Japan; scape to 28 in

(70 cm), flowers fragrant, 3½–4 in (9–10 cm), pale rose-pink flushed or veined lilac or purple, funnelform, lobes recurved, slightly wavy.

Lygodium (from Greek *lygodes*, flexible, twining, referring to the climbing habit). Schizaeaceae. Cosmopolitan. CLIMBING FERN. About 40 species, climbing ferns. The roots and rhizomes form a dense clump from which arise long and slender vining fronds with twining, wiry rachises, clasping rachillae and 2–3-pinnately or palmately compound pinnae. Both species listed here prefer a minimum winter temperature of 45°F (7°C), although *L. palmatum* may survive outdoors to −10°F (−23°C), losing its fronds in winter. They need a moist, porous and fertile medium rich in leaf mold and garden compost (pH 5 or lower for *L. palmatum*). Provide a cool, buoyant and humid atmosphere in light shade with support from wires, trellis, canes or surrounding vegetation. Water copiously throughout the growing season, and feed at two week intervals. Water moderately in winter. Cut out faded fronds and mulch in early winter. Propagate from spores or by division. Serpentine layering is also a possibility: an actively growing frond is pinned to the soil surface at each node.

L. japonicum Japan to Australia; fronds bright green, divisions finely pinnately divided and 'ferny', to 8 in (20 cm) long; *L. palmatum* E US; fronds dark green, divisions palmately lobed, to 4 in (10 cm).

Lyonia (for John Lyon [died before 1818], enthusiastic collector of American plants, who introduced many into England). Ericaceae. US, E Asia, Himalayas, Antilles. Some 35 species, evergreen or deciduous shrubs or small trees with leathery leaves, conspicuously angled branches and campanulate to urceolate flowers densely packed in axillary clusters or short racemes in summer. Cultivate as for *Leucothoë*.

L. ligustrina MALE BERRY, HE HUCKLEBERRY, MALE BLUEBERRY, BIG BOY; E US; deciduous shrub to 13 ft (4 m); leaves 1¼–2¾ in (3–7 cm), oblong to elliptic or lanceolate, entire or finely serrate; flowers densely packed in downy, terminal panicles 3–6 in

(8–15 cm) long, oval-urceolate to sub-spherical, off-white, downy; *L. ovalifolia* Himalaya, W China, Japan, Taiwan; deciduous shrub or small tree to 39 ft (12 m); leaves 2½–4 in (6–10 cm), ovate to elliptic, or oblong, finely downy, somewhat setose beneath; flowers in downy racemes 1¼–2½ in (3–6 cm) long, white, tubular to urceolate, downy.

lyrate pinnatifid, but with a large, rounded terminal lobe and smaller lateral lobes diminishing in size toward the base of the whole.

Lysichiton (from Greek *lysis*, a loosening, and *chiton*, cloak, referring to the way in which the spathe opens as the fruit ripens). Araceae. NE Asia, western N America. SKUNK CABBAGE. 2 species, robust, clump-forming, deciduous, perennial herbs of marshy places, with thick rhizomes and very large leaves, ovate to oblong, muskily scented and usually appearing with or after the inflorescence. In early spring, minute, green flowers are packed on a thick clublike spadix enclosed within a large, cowl-like spathe. Both species will tolerate cold to at least 5°F (–15°C). They are ideal for the bog garden, streams and the pond- or lake-side; grow in wet or damp, deep humus-rich soil in sun or part shade. They may be slow to establish and flower. When used as a waterside marginal, prepare the planting site with rich loam to a depth of at least 12 in (30 cm), built up to water level. Propagate by division in late winter.

L. americanus western N America; leaves 20–50 × 12–32 in (50–125 × 30–80 cm); spathe to 16 in (40 cm), bright yellow; *L. camtschatcensis* NE Asia; close to *L. americanus*, but more compact in all parts, spathe white, not yellow.

Lysimachia (from Greek *lysis*, releasing, and *mache*, strife: supposed to possess soothing qualities). Primulaceae. N America, Eurasia, S Africa. LOOSE-STRIFE. 150 species, erect or procum-

bent herbs, rarely dwarf shrubs (those listed here are perennial herbs), with 5-parted, rotate flowers in spring and summer. Fully hardy and easily grown in moist borders in sun or part shade or at the waterside and in bog gardens. Rampant *L. nummularia* is a rapidly spreading, evergreen groundcover. *L. clethroides* makes a graceful show of curving white racemes in late summer and does well in the semiwild garden or in woodland. The glaucous-leaved *L. atropurpurea* and *L. ephemerum* are noninvasive perennials for damper parts of the gray border. *L. ciliata* is a handsome, erect and free-flowering hardy perennial for damp borders; its chocolate and bronze-leaved cultivars providing outstanding foils for copper, bronze, gold and lime ferns, grasses and sedges. Propagate by division or, *L. nummularia*, by rooted stem lengths. *L. atropurpurea* can be short-lived and may need to be propagated from seed collected every two to three years.

L. atropurpurea Balkans; erect; clump-forming, to 32 in (80 cm); leaves narrow, gray-green, wavy; flowers small, darkest wine red to purple-black in tight, narrow spikes; *L. ciliata* N America, naturalized Europe; stem to 3¼ ft (1 m), erect, glabrous; leaves to 5½ in (14 cm), ovate to lanceolate, ciliate, strongly flushed chocolate to bronze in 'Firecracker'; flowers solitary or paired, in axils of upper leaves, to ½ in (1 cm) in diameter, yellow with red blotches; *L. clethroides* GOOSENECK LOOSESTRIFE; China, Japan; stem to 3¼ ft (1 m), simple, erect; leaves to 5 in (13 cm), ovate to lanceolate, sparsely hairy, glandular-punctate; flowers crowded in slender, nodding, terminal racemes, to ½ in (1 cm) in diameter, white; *L. ephemerum* SW Europe; stem to 3¼ ft (1 m), simple, erect; leaves to 6 in (15 cm), linear or lanceolate to spathulate, glaucous gray-green; flowers in narrow terminal racemes, to ½ in (1 cm) in diameter, white with purple-tinted calyces; *L. nummularia* CREEPING

JENNY, MONEYWORT; Europe, naturalized eastern N America; evergreen, glabrous, stem to 20 in (50 cm), prostrate, fast-creeping and rooting; leaves to ¾ in (2 cm), broadly ovate or cordate to circular; flowers solitary, rarely in pairs in leaf axils, ½–¾ in (1–2 cm) in diameter, yellow; 'Aurea': leaves golden yellow; *L. punctata* C Europe, Asia Minor, naturalized N America; stem to 36 in (90 cm), erect; leaves to 2¾ in (7 cm), lanceolate to elliptic, ciliate, puberulent, dotted with glands beneath; flowers whorled, to ⅝ in (1.5 cm) in diameter, yellow.

Lythrum (from Greek *lythron*, blood, referring to the color of the flowers). Lythraceae. N America, Europe, Old World. LOOSESTRIFE. 38 species, perennial or annual herbs or small shrubs with 4-angled stems (those listed here are clump-forming hardy herbaceous perennials). In summer, flowers with four to eight spreading, obovate petals are borne in slender, erect, terminal spikes. Fully hardy perennials for the bog garden, water margin or sunny, moisture-retentive borders. The long, upright wands of crumpled magenta flowers last for weeks in late summer. Propagate by seed or division in spring.

L. salicaria PURPLE LOOSESTRIFE; Old World, NE US; erect, downy perennial to 48 in (120 cm); flowers in whorled clusters; petals to ½ in (1 cm), pink-purple; 'Atropurpureum': flowers dark purple; 'Brightness': to 36 in (90 cm), with deep rose-pink flowers; 'Feuerkerze' (syn. 'Firecandle'): to 36 in (90 cm), with slender, rose-pink spires; 'Happy': dwarf to 24 in (60 cm), with small leaves and red flowers; 'Lady Sackville': to 40 in (100 cm), with deep pink spires; 'Morden Pink': magenta; 'Purple Spires': vigorous, with abundant, rosy-purple flowers; 'Red Gem': to 40 in (100 cm), with long, red spikes; 'Robert': to 36 in (90 cm), of neat habit, with bright pink spikes; *L. virgatum* Europe and Asia, naturalized New England; similar to *L. salicaria* but leaves glabrous; 'Dropmore Purple': flowers purple; 'Modern Rose': compact, with rose-red flowers; 'Rose Queen': to 36 in (90 cm), with pink flowers from purple buds; 'The Rocket': to 30 in (75 cm), with vivid rose-pink flowers.

creeping habit

Lysimachia nummularia

M

Maackia (for Richard Maack [1825–86], Russian naturalist). Leguminosae. E Asia. 8 species, deciduous shrubs or trees with pinnate leaves and pealike flowers in erect, dense and branching racemes in summer. Hardy to 5°F (–15°C). Grow in a warm, sunny position in fertile well-drained soil. Restrict pruning to young plants or to the removal of small branches; large wounds do not heal quickly. Sow seed in fall after presoaking in hot water for 24 hours. Propagate also by root cuttings. *M. amurensis* E Asia; tree to 65 ft (20 m), often a shrub in cool climates; leaves to 8 in (20 cm), leaflets to 3 in (8 cm), 7–11, ovate; flowers to ½ in (1.2 cm), white or cream to yellow, then brown; fruit to 2 in (5 cm), winged.

Macfadyena (for James MacFadyen [1795–1850], Scottish botanist, author of *Flora Jamaica* [1837]). Bignoniaceae. Mexico, West Indies to Uruguay. 4 species, woody climbers. The leaves consist of two leaflets with a tendril between them. Yellow, tubular to campanulate and flared flowers are produced in spring and summer. Plant outdoors in regions that are frost-free or almost so. Elsewhere, a handsome plant for the cool greenhouse or conservatory. Cultivate as for *Bignonia*. *M. unguis-cati* flowers 2–4¾ in (5–12 cm) long, yellow striped orange in throat.

Mackaya (for James Townsend Mackay [1775–1862], Scottish-born botanist and gardener). Acanthaceae. South Africa. 1 species, *M. bella*, an evergreen, erect shrub to 5¾ ft (1.75 m), with glossy green, elliptic leaves. Borne throughout the year in terminal, loose spikes, the flowers are 2½ in (6 cm) long, tubular to campanulate and pale violet with five, purple-veined and flared lobes. Cultivate as for *Justicia*.

Macleania (for Mr. John Maclean of Lima, an English merchant and patron of botany). Ericaceae. Tropical C and S America. Some 40 species, evergreen shrubs with slender, often pendulous branches, sometimes scrambling. The leathery leaves are tinged red when young. Tubular, 5-lobed flowers hang in clusters or racemes in summer. Grow in a freely draining, humus-rich, neutral to acidic medium, in bright filtered light or part shade. Water moderately when in full growth; reduce water supplies as light levels and temperatures fall, keeping plants just moist in winter, with a minimum temperature of 50°F (10°C). Provide support. Cut back in winter or after flowering to shape and restrict shoot length as necessary. Propagate by seed, by semi-ripe cuttings or by simple layering. *M. insignis* S Mexico, Honduras, Guatemala; to 6 ft (1.8 m); flowers to 1¼ in (3 cm), orange to scarlet.

Macleaya (for Alexander Macleay [1767–1848], colonial secretary for New South Wales). Papaveraceae. E Asia. 3 species, perennial herbs with creeping, sometimes invasive rhizomes, glaucous foliage and yellow sap. The leaves are broad and rounded, toothed and palmately lobed. Small, feathery flowers are carried in terminal, plumelike inflorescences in summer. Hardy and easily established in most soils in sun or part shade. They are especially attractive at the rear of herbaceous borders, complementing soft pinks, blues or mauves with their fine, bronze-gray foliage and smoky flowers. They will, however, become invasive. Remove flower heads after blooming and cut plants down to ground level in fall. Propagate by division, in the dormant season, or by transplanting suckers in spring.

M. cordata PLUME POPPY, TREE CELANDINE; China, Japan; to 8 ft (2.5 m); leaves to 8 in (20 cm) across, rounded to cordate, obtusely toothed and lobed, gray to olive-green above, downy white beneath; flowers beige to cream-white, in plumed racemes to 3¼ ft (1 m), stamens 25–30; 'Alba': flowers white, 'Flamingo': foliage gray-green, flowers buff pink; var. *thunbergii*: leaves distinctly glaucous beneath; *M. microcarpa* C China; as for *M. cordata*

except flowers beige, flushed pink below with 8–12 stamens; 'Coral Plume': flowers pinker; 'Kelway's Coral Plume': flowers deep coral.

Maclura (for William Maclure [d. 1840], American geologist). Moraceae. America, Asia, Africa (mostly warmer regions). OSAGE ORANGE, BOW WOOD. 12 species, spiny, dioecious shrubs, treelets or climbers. The small, yellow-green flowers are followed (where plants of both sexes are grown) by large, wrinkled and fleshy fruits. The primary horticultural interest of *M. pomifera* lies in its unusual but inedible fruits, about the size of an orange. It also has attractive, ridged, deep orange-brown bark, clear yellow fall color, and, given space, develops an open and rounded head. It is valued as a thorny and impenetrable hedge, able to withstand hard shearing and harsh wind. It fares best in areas with hot, dry summers. Plant in well-drained soil, in full sun. It is hardy to –6°F (–21°C), although young growth may be cut by frost. When necessary, prune in winter; the milky sap may cause dermatitis. Sow fresh seed in an open seed bed in fall, or stored seed, stratified for two months at 39°F (4°C). Increase also from semiripe cuttings in a closed frame under mist in summer. *M. pomifera* E US; tree to 60 ft (18 m), deciduous; branchlets green, thorns to 1 in (2.5 cm)+; leaves 2–6 in (5–15 cm), ovate, shiny above, tomentose beneath, turning yellow in fall; fruit 3–4¾ in (8–12 cm) in diameter, globose, with a deeply wrinkled, shiny surface, initially green, orange-yellow when ripe, inedible; includes the thornless 'Inermis', 'Pulverulenta' with powdery, white leaves, and the hardy 'Fan d'Arc' with large, dark leaves.

macronutrients see *nutrients* and *plant nutrition*.

Macrozamia (from Greek *makros*, great, plus *Zamia*). Zamiaceae. Australia. 12 species, cycads, large, "palmlike" evergreens with stout, buried to exposed and columnlike trunks and tough, finely pinnate leaves in a terminal rosette. They are dioecious and produce massive cones. If pollinated, the female cones develop large, egg-shaped seeds encased in a fleshy, brightly colored coating. Suitable for tubs or landscaping outdoors in subtropical and tropical regions; elsewhere, they are subjects for containers and beds in the cool or intermediate greenhouse (minimum temperature 50°F (10°C), in the home and for interior landscaping. Cultivation requirements are as for *Cycas circinalis*, although *Macrozamia* thrives in full sunlight and tolerates some drought.

M. communis BURRAWONG; New South Wales; to 10 ft (3 m) stem largely subterranean; leaves to 6½ ft (2 m), pinnae to 130, to 10 × ½ in (25 × 1 cm), rigid, widely spaced, linear, pungent, pale beneath; *M. moorei* Queensland, New South Wales; to 30 ft (9 m); stem columnar, exposed to 23 ft (7 m) tall; leaves to 10 ft (3 m), many, smooth, semi-erect, pinnae to 50 pairs, linear-lanceolate to 12 × ½ in (30 × 1 cm), pungent, somewhat glaucous; *M. pauli-guilielmi* Queensland; stem swollen, ovoid, often subterranean; leaves to 3¼ ft (1 m), few, woolly then smooth, gray-green, spiraling, pinnae to 120, erect, narrow-linear to filiform, to 8 × ¼ in (20 × 0.5 cm), rachis flattened, very twisted, woolly at base; *M. spiralis* New South Wales; stem subterranean; leaves to 6½ ft (2 m), slightly twisted, pinnae to 10 × ½ in (25 × 1 cm), linear-falcate to narrowly lanceolate, dark, glossy green, often with a small, orange-pink callus at base.

maggots the common name given to the legless larvae of flies (Diptera). Some garden pest maggots have a well-developed head, such as those of fungus gnats. In others, including leatherjackets and gall midge larvae, the head is reduced and partly retracted into the thorax. Maggots of more advanced flies, such as hoverflies, fruit flies, leaf miners and vegetable root flies, have vestigial heads. Garden pest maggots cause damage by burrowing into and feeding on plant tissues.

magnesian limestone see *lime*.

magnesium a major (macro-) nutrient; an essential constituent of chlorophyll and of importance in the transport of phosphate. Deficiency can occur on acidic sandy soils, and may be induced by unbalanced fertilizer application, for example, very high dressings of potassium; soil compaction, waterlogging and water stress aggravate the disorder. Symptoms of deficiency are interveinal chlorosis on older leaves where the margins may remain green; in severe cases, the affected tissue dies. Mature plants are more susceptible. On acidic soils, dressings of magnesian limestone (9–11% Mg) may be applied, otherwise kieserite (16–17% Mg). Foliar sprays of magnesium sulfate (10% Mg) are beneficial, applied every 14 days as Epsom salts at 9 oz to 3 gallons (210 g to 10 liters) of water.

magnesium carbonate the chemical constituent of magnesian or dolomitic limestone.

magnesium sulfate a magnesium fertilizer, obtainable in two forms: kieserite (16–17% Mg), which is relatively insoluble and suitable for soil application; and Epsom salts (10% Mg), which is soluble and more expensive and therefore used mainly for liquid and foliar fertilizing.

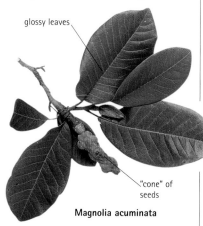

glossy leaves

"cone" of seeds

Magnolia acuminata

Magnolia (for Pierre Magnol [1638–1715], Professor of Botany and Director of Montpellier Botanic Gardens, France). Magnoliaceae. Japan, Himalaya, W Malaysia (to Java), eastern N America to Tropical America. Some 125 species, evergreen or deciduous shrubs or trees with large, solitary flowers in spring and summer. These are starlike to vase-shaped, and consist of numerous ovate to straplike segments. The seeds have colorful coats and are borne in curiously-shaped cones.

The following species are hardy. Given adequate moisture at the roots, most magnolias enjoy full sun. However, the late spring- and summer-flowering species, such as *M. wilsonii*, *M. sieboldii*, and *M. sieboldii* subsp. *sinensis*, prefer light dappled shade or some shade for at least part of the day. All prefer a sheltered position. *M. grandiflora* and *M. delavayi* grow best on a warm wall in colder regions. Magnolias are tolerant of urban pollution and make excellent choices for town gardens and street plantings.

They thrive in a wide variety of soil types. Provided there is an adequate supply of moisture and drainage is good, most will at least tolerate alkaline conditions, given adequate reserves of humus in the soil. The ideal soil is a neutral to acidic loam, with plenty of organic matter. *M. virginiana* will grow in damp or waterlogged conditions.

Pruning is generally a matter of shaping the plant at planting time by removing weak and badly placed growth and tipping back long shoots. Routine pruning is usually restricted to removing deadwood and water shoots. Where a specimen outgrows its allotted space, it can be pruned hard back immediately after flowering for deciduous species and in early spring for evergreens. It is important when removing larger branches to preserve the branch/bark ridge, leaving the branch collar intact.

The early-flowering species and hybrids can be grown from softwood cuttings with mist and bottom heat at 68–75°F (20–24°C) or, with careful management, from semi-ripe cuttings using the warm bench and polyethylene system or a closed case with bottom heat. Light wounding and treatment with 0.8% IBA are advantageous. Cuttings will take 6–8 weeks to root in trays or pots and should be overwintered *in situ*, leaving potting on until growth has started in the following spring. They should be kept barely moist over winter and cool but frost-free. Simple layering in early spring is often a good alternative using standard procedures, although shrubby species like *M. stellata* may not produce suitable material and, where specimens are large and high-branching, it may be awkward to

M

MAGNOLIA

Name	Distribution	Habit	Leaves	Flowers
M. acuminata CUCUMBER TREE	EN America	deciduous tree to 100 ft (30 m), crown conical, later candelabriform	to 10 in (24 cm), ovate to elliptic or oblong-ovate, apex acute, base cuneate, dark green above, downy or glaucescent beneath	cup-shaped, erect, segments to 3½ × 1¼ in (9 × 3 cm), 9, gray-green tinged green to yellow-green, sometimes flushed maroon, oblanceolate to oblong-spathulate

Comments: Spring-summer. 'Variegata': leaves stippled bright gold. f. **aurea**: inner segments golden yellow. var. **subcordata**: YELLOW CUCUMBER TREE, flowers faintly scented, lime-green to clear yellow. 'Elizabeth' (*M. acuminata* × *M. denudata*): flowers precocious, yellow fading to cream.

Name	Distribution	Habit	Leaves	Flowers
M. campbellii	Himalaya to China	robust, deciduous tree to 100 ft (30 m)	to 9 in (23 cm), elliptic-ovate to oblong-lanceolate, acute, base rounded, unequal, coriaceous, dark sea green above, paler, sometimes silky beneath	precocious, segments to 16, to 5½ × 2½ in (14 × 6 cm), broad, fleshy, concave, white or crimson to rose-pink, paler above, inner whorls erect, outer whorls often reflexed

Comments: Early spring. Alba Group: flowers white. 'Maharaja': flowers large, white, purple at base. ssp. **mollicomata**: flowers produced earlier, usually bright pink beneath, white above. var. *mollicomata* 'Lanarth': habit fastigiate, flowers opening deep red.

Raffillii Group includes 'Charles Raffill': flower buds stained claret, segments purple-pink beneath, white stained pink at margin above, and 'Kew's Surprise': flowers darker pink than in 'Charles Raffill'.

Name	Distribution	Habit	Leaves	Flowers
M. delavayi	SW China	evergreen tree, to 33 ft (10 m), often cut back by hard winters	to 20 × 8 in (50 × 20 cm), ovate to oblong, sinuate, base round to cordate, coriaceous, glabrous, deep sea-green above, gray-green, glaucescent beneath	to 8 in (20 cm) across, slightly fragrant, inner segments 6–7, to 4 × 2 in (10 × 5 cm) in 2 whorls, fleshy, ivory to topaz, cupped

Comments: Late summer.

Name	Distribution	Habit	Leaves	Flowers
M. denudata *M. heptapeta, M. yulan* YULAN, LILY TREE	E and W China	deciduous tree to 50 ft (15 m), crown broadly pyramidal	to 6 in (15 cm), obovate to ovate, softly pubescent beneath	to 6 in (15 cm) diameter citrus-scented, precocious, goblet-shaped, erect, segments 9, to 3 in (7.5 cm), white to ivory, sometimes stained purple-pink at base

Name	Distribution	Habit	Leaves	Flowers
M. fraseri EAR-LEAVED UMBRELLA TREE	SE US	erect deciduous tree to 53 ft (16 m)	to 11 × 7 in (27 × 18 cm), whorled at branch tips, obovate, base deeply cordate or auriculate, glabrous light green, sometimes glaucous beneath	fragrant, tulip-shaped, expanding to 8 in (20 cm) diameter; segments 9, to 4¾ × 2 in (12 × 5 cm), white tinted yellow at first, later ivory, spathulate to obovate

Comments: Spring.

Name	Distribution	Habit	Leaves	Flowers
M. grandiflora BULL BAY, SOUTHERN MAGNOLIA, LARGE-FLOWERED MAGNOLIA	SE US	evergreen tree to 100 ft (30 m)	to 8 in (20 cm), elliptic to ovate, stiffly coriaceous, glossy dark green above, rust-red pubescent beneath	to 10 in (25 cm) diameter, fragrant, erect, segments 9–12 to 4¾ × 3½ in (12 × 9 cm), creamy white, obovate or spathulate, fleshy, cupped

Comments: Summer–fall. 'Exmouth': habit conic; leaves narrow, acuminate, finely pubescent beneath, margins recurved; flowers to 10 in (25 cm) diameter. 'Ferruginea': erect and compact, leaves rust-brown tomentose beneath, glossy dark green above. 'Goliath': habit bushy; leaves short, broad, obtuse, blistered, glabrous beneath. 'Praecox': early- and long-flowering. 'Praecox Fastigiata': early and long-flowering, narrow and erect in habit.

M. acuminata

M. campbellii subsp. *mollicomata*

M. delavayi

M. denudata

Magnolia

Name	Distribution	Habit	Leaves	Flowers
M. hypoleuca **Comments:** Summer. fruiting cones red, showy.	Japan	deciduous to 100 ft (30 m), crown pyramidal	to 16 in (40 cm), obovate, gray-green, in spreading whorls	to 8 in (20 cm) diameter, fragrant, cup-shaped or spreading, segments to 12, ivory flushed yellow-pink with age, fleshy, stamens crimson to blood-red
M. kobus *M. praecocissima* **Comments:** Winter–spring.	Japan	deciduous shrub or tree to 100 ft (30 m), spreading, conical or domed	to 7½ in (19 cm), oblong-elliptic, pubescent beneath	to 4 in (10 cm) diameter, precocious, erect, segments usually 6, 2¾ × 1½ in (7 × 3.5 cm), creamy white, often stained wine-red or pink, spathulate to obovate
M. liliiflora *M. quinquepeta* LILY-FLOWERED MAGNOLIA **Comments:** Spring. 'Nigra': flowers claret to amethyst above, paler below.	China	deciduous shrub to 13 ft (4 m)	to 8 in (20 cm), elliptic to obovate, acute, sparsely pubescent, sap-green above, paler beneath	erect, goblet-shaped, segments 9, inner 2½–3 in (6 to 7.5 cm), obovate-oblong, obtuse, concave tip, thick, white often flushed pink to claret
M. × loebneri (*M. kobus* × *M. stellata*)	garden origin	shrub or small tree, habit as for *M. stellata* but twigs velutinous not silky	6 in (15 cm), narrow-obovate	with 12 spathulate segments each to 3 × 1¼ in (8 × 3 cm), white, occasionally tinged pink
Comments: 'Leonard Messel': flowers to 5 in (13 cm) diameter, lilac-pink. 'Merrill': flowers larger than in *M. stellata*, semi-double.				
M. macrophylla LARGE-LEAVED CUCUMBER TREE, UMBRELLA TREE, GREAT-LEAVED MACROPHYLLA **Comments:** Fruiting cones rose-pink with red seeds.	SE US	large deciduous shrub or tree to 65 ft (20 m)	to 38 in (95 cm), in dense whorls, elliptic, oblanceolate to oblong-ovate, base cordate to auriculate, pale green, glabrous above, downy white beneath	fragrant, to 12 in (30 cm) diameter, segments 6–9, 8 × 5½ in (20 × 14 cm), thick, ivory or cream, inner 3 spotted or tinged purple toward base, outer segments narrow-spathulate, tinged green
M. rostrata **Comments:** Summer. Fruiting cone long, pink, showy.	China, Burma	medium-sized rather skeletal deciduous tree	to 20 in (50 cm), broadly obovate, prominently veined, covered at first in tawny velvetlike hair	fleshy, cream to pink
M. salicifolia ANISE MAGNOLIA, WILLOW-LEAFED MAGNOLIA	Japan	tree or shrub to 40 ft (12 m); twigs scented of lemon or anise	to 4¾ in (12 cm), narrow-oval to lanceolate, glabrous, dull green above, paler beneath, sometimes downy	precocious, inner 6 segments to 3½ × 1½ in (9 × 4 cm), lanceolate to spathulate, white, occasionally tinged green or flushed pink at base

Comments: 'Wada's Memory' (*M. kobus* × *M. salicifolia?*): small tree, habit upright, compact, leaves elliptic, flushed red-brown at first; flowers to 6½ in (17 cm) diameter, fragrant, white, segments 6, at first borne horizontally, then drooping and fluttering.

M

M. grandiflora 'Goliath'

M. hypoleuca

M. liliiflora

M. × loebneri 'Leonard Messel'

MAGNOLIA

Name	Distribution	Habit	Leaves	Flowers
M. sargentiana	W China	deciduous tree to 80 ft (25 m)	to 7 in (18 cm), elliptic to obovate, occasionally oblong or suborbicular, deep glossy green above, paler, gray-pubescent beneath	fragrant, precocious, pendent, segments 10–14, to $3\frac{1}{2} \times 1\frac{1}{2}$ in (9 × 3.5 cm), spathulate or oblong-oblanceolate, white to pale purple-pink above, purple-pink below

Comments: Spring. 'Caerhays Belle' (*M. s.* var. *robusta* × *M. sprengeri* var. *diva*): segments 12, broad, large, pale carmine to salmon pink.

Name	Distribution	Habit	Leaves	Flowers
M. sieboldii	E Asia	deciduous shrub or tree to 33 ft (10 m)	$4\frac{3}{4}$ in (12 cm), oblong to ovate-elliptic, deep green, subglabrous above, glaucescent, pubescent beneath	to 4 in (10 cm), fragrant, cup- then dish-shaped, held horizontally, not nodding as in ssp. *sinensis*, segments to 12, white, obovate to spathulate, to $2\frac{1}{2} \times 1\frac{3}{4}$ in (6 × 4.5 cm), stamens crimson

Comments: Spring–summer. ssp. ***sinensis*** (syn. *M. sinensis*): CHINESE MAGNOLIA; broadly branching shrub or tree to 20 ft (6 m); young shoots silky; leaves 3–8 in (7.5–21 cm), oval to oblong, obovate or suborbicular, glabrous above, glaucescent and, at first, velutinous beneath; flowers to 5 in (13 cm) diameter, nodding, segments 1–2 in (2.5–5 cm) across, white obovate, to oblong-spathulate, stamens bright crimson.

Name	Distribution	Habit	Leaves	Flowers
M.* × *soulangeana (*M. denudata* × *M. liliiflora*) SAUCER MAGNOLIA, CHINESE MAGNOLIA	garden origin	deciduous shrub or tree to 33 ft (10 m); habit of *M. denudata* but more slender	to $6\frac{1}{2}$ in (16.5 cm), broadly elliptic to suborbicular, shiny green above, often puberulent beneath	precocious, erect, segments 9, cupped, oblong-obovate, concave at tip, white, marked rose-pink to violet-purple beneath to $4\frac{1}{2} \times 2\frac{3}{4}$ in (11 × 7 cm)

Comments: Spring. The most widely grown magnolia, cultivars ranging in flower color from white to claret, may be early- or late-flowering.

Name	Distribution	Habit	Leaves	Flowers
M. sprengeri	China	deciduous tree to 65 ft (20 m); young shoots yellow-green, glabrous	to $5\frac{1}{4}$ in (13.5 cm), obovate to lanceolate-elliptic, glabrous, above, pale, glabrous to villous beneath	precocious, fragrant, dish-shaped, segments 12–14, $4\frac{3}{4} \times 2\frac{1}{4}$ in (12 × 5.5 cm), spathulate to oblong-ovate, white, occasionally tinged red to pale pink

Comments: Spring. var. *diva* (rosy red) includes 'Burncoose': rose-purple, and 'Claret Cup': claret beneath, fading to white above.

Name	Distribution	Habit	Leaves	Flowers
M. stellata *M. tomentosa* STAR MAGNOLIA	Japan	same as for *M. kobus* but smaller, to $24\frac{1}{2}$ ft (7.5 m); twigs silky-pubescent, bark muskily scented at first	$5\frac{1}{4}$ in (13.5 cm), narrow-oblong to obovate	starlike, segments 12–33, spreading, $2\frac{1}{2} \times \frac{5}{8}$ in (6.5 × 1.5 cm), snow white, sometimes faintly flushed pink

Comments: Spring–summer. Includes cultivars with semi-double to double flowers in pure white to rose flowering early to late in season.

Name	Distribution	Habit	Leaves	Flowers
M. tripetala UMBRELLA TREE, ELKWOOD; UMBRELLA MAGNOLIA	EN America	deciduous tree, to 40 ft (12 m); crown broadly spreading	20 × $10\frac{1}{4}$ in+ (50 × 26 cm+), in whorls at ends of branch, oblanceolate, conspicuously veined, pale pubescent beneath at first	creamy-white, erect, vase-shaped, muskily scented, segments 9–12, oblong-spathulate, fleshy

Comments: Spring–summer. Fruiting cones to 4 in (10 cm), red-pink; seeds red. 'Silver Parasol' (*M. tripetala* × *M. hypoleuca*): leaves large, in showy, umbrella-like whorls, silver beneath; flowers like *M. hypoleuca*.

M. × *soulangeana* 'Lennei Alba'   *M. sprengeri*   *M. virginiana*   *M.* × *wieseneri*

M

MAGNOLIA

Name	Distribution	Habit	Leaves	Flowers
M. × **veitchii** (*M. denudata* × *M. campbellii*)	garden origin	deciduous tree, to 100 ft (30 m)	9 in (22 cm), oblong to obovate, dark green veins pubescent above, often tinted purple at first	precocious, vase-shaped, erect, segments 7–10, obovate to spathulate, 5 × 2½ in (12.5 × 6 cm), white tinged violet to pink beneath, pale pink above
M. virginiana SWEET BAY, SWAMP BAY, SWAMP LAUREL **Comments:** Summer–fall.	E US	evergreen or semi-deciduous shrub or tree, to 100 ft (30 m+) often multi-stemmed and straggling	4½ in (11 cm), narrow-oblong to suborbicular, shiny green above, glaucous to silver-velvety beneath	rounded to cup-shaped, 6 cm diameter, white to ivory, highly fragrant, segments 6–15, 2 × ¾ in (5 × 2 cm), obovate or suborbicular
M. × **wieseneri** (*M. hypoleuca* × *M. sieboldii*) **Comments:** Distinguished from *M. sieboldii* by its larger flowers and broader, tougher leaves.	garden origin	tree or shrub to 23 ft + (7 m+)	appearing whorled, obovate, undulate, veins pubescent above, green, glaucous beneath with velvety midvein	spicily fragrant, cup-shaped, erect, segments 9, 2½ × 1½ in (6 × 3.5 cm), obovate, creamy white, stamens crimson
M. wilsonii **Comments:** Closely related to *M. sieboldii*.	W China	deciduous shrub or tree to 26 ft + (8 m+)	to 6 in (16 cm), lanceolate to oblong-ovate, matt green above, velvety beneath	fragrant, nodding, cup-shaped becoming saucer-shaped, segments 9–12, inner segments 2½ × 1¾ in (6.5 × 4.5 cm), white, spathulate to narrow-lanceolate, incurved, stamens rose-purple

effect. In commercial nurseries, it is common practice to stool stock specimens grown on good fertile soil to force them to produce long flexible growth from the base; stems tongued and pegged in spring will be ready to sever in the following spring, to be lined out during late fall/early winter. Fall layers of the current season's wood with the leaves removed are treated in a similar fashion, but will take two years to root. An alternative for the amateur gardener —although not for the timid—involves cutting a single stem hard back in early spring to force new growth suitable for layering in the following spring. Magnolias generally show good regeneration and often produce strong growth even from old wood.

When available, seed is an excellent method of propagation for the species and will yield strong young plants that grow away very quickly, although they will show a range of variation and may take several years after first flowering to achieve good quality blooms. Seed should be sown fresh, or vernalized for spring sowing: store cleaned seed for about 100 days at 36–39°F (2–4°C). Dried seed may germinate after a year's dormancy, but frequently fails to do so.

Chlorosis can be caused by excessive alkalinity, and by an excess or deficit of potash. It should not be confused with the natural pallor seen on the young leaves of many *Magnolia* species. Lime-induced chlorosis is quickly remedied by foliar applications of iron chelates (sequestered iron). On alkaline soils, care must be taken to ensure that mulching materials such as leaf mold and garden compost are nonalkaline. A black bacterial leaf spot is probably caused by *Pseudomonas syringae*; it can be controlled by copper-based fungicidal sprays. Pale irregular spots on the leaves of *M. grandiflora* are caused by the fungus *Phyllosticta magnoliae* but its effects are usually cosmetic. In the US, magnolias are sometimes attacked by magnolia scale.

Mahonia (for Bernard McMahon [d. 1816], American horticulturist,). Berberidaceae. Asia, N and C America. OREGON GRAPE, HOLLY GRAPE. 70 species of evergreen shrubs and small trees closely related to *Berberis* but lacking stem thorns and with tough, sharply toothed pinnate or trifoliolate leaves. Small, sometimes fragrant flowers are borne in slender racemes, clusters or congested panicles near or at the stem summit from late fall to spring. The fruits are berrylike and plum-red to pruinose purple-black.

The robust, taller-growing Asian species are usually native to damp woodlands, while the shorter, spreading, American species are plants of forest edges or dry scrub. Most are tolerant of a wide range of sites, given a free-draining soil. The larger Asiatics, notably *M. japonica*, M. Bealei Group, *M. napaulensis*, *M. lomariifolia* and *M.* × *media*, are particularly valued for their bold foliage and winter blooming. They are best used as specimen plants in a semi-shaded position in a woodland garden or mixed shrubbery. Provide damp, slightly acidic to neutral soil with a high humus content. Prolonged exposure to harsh winds and temperatures below 5°F (–15°C) is liable to cause leaf scorch and flower damage. *M. lomariifolia* requires a slightly sheltered site although its hybrids, *M.* × *media*, are more resilient; *M. napaulensis* suffers in gardens where temperatures fall regularly below 14°F (–10°C). *M. japonica* will tolerate –4°F (–20°C). Thin out only leggy, exhausted stems in spring.

Most North American species tolerate a wider range of soils and conditions than members of the first group. They may sometimes become invasive, and should be held in check by the removal of unwanted offshoots. Older portions of these species may lose vigor and become bare, in which case it may be necessary to reduce and replant them. *M. nervosa* is unusual in its very short or absent stems and suckering, ground-smothering habit. It favors neutral to acidic, humus-rich soil in full sun or light shade. Glaucous-leaved species from the southern US and Central America require dry, perfectly drained sites in full sun. They will suffer from wind scorch, winter wet and exposure to temperatures below 14°F (−10°C). Plant in gritty, slightly acidic soil, preferably against a south-facing wall.

Propagate by fresh seed; clean off the fleshy exterior and surface sow on a sandy propagating mix under glass. Division of most species is possible where offshoots or basal branches have rooted; to this effect, stooling may be advantageous. Take stem section cuttings of members of the first group in late winter. The suckering species may be readily divided in spring. Mallet cuttings of the warmer-growing American species, taken in late winter may root in a cold frame; alternatively, they may be grafted on to stocks of *Berberis thunbergii*. For diseases and pests, see *Berberis*.

M. acanthifolia Himalaya; erect shrub to 16 ft (5 m); leaves to 24 in (60 cm), leaflets 17–27, 2–4 in (5–10 cm), oblongovate to oblong-lanceolate, apex acute to acuminate, base truncate, thinly leathery, dull to slightly glossy above with veins impressed, sinuately toothed, teeth 3–7 on lower margin, 2–5 on upper margin; raceme to 12 in (30 cm), spreading, rather thick and crowded, flowers deep yellow; 'Maharajah': fine form, with deep yellow flowers; *M. aquifolium* OREGON GRAPE; western N America; shrub to 6½ ft (2 m), sparingly branched, suckering freely; leaflets 5–13, to 3 × 1½ in (8 × 4 cm), ovate, with to 12 spiny teeth per side, glossy, dark green turning purple-red in winter; flowers golden, on dense, erect racemes to 3 in (8 cm); cultivars include: 'Apollo', low-growing, expansive, to 24 in (60 cm), with larger, dull leaves and good winter color; 'Atropurpurea', with red-purple leaves in winter; 'Orange Flame', low-growing, to 24 in (60 cm), with leaves becoming bronze, tinted with orange-red after first season, dark red in winter; and 'Smaragd', spreading, with red-bronze winter color and profuse flowers; *M. confusa* China; small shrub;

leaflets to 20, narrow-lanceolate, spinose, sea-green to leaden gray above, silvery beneath, rachis purple-tinted; flowers pale yellow in erect, slender racemes; *M. fremontii* SW US; to 13 ft (4 m), leaves to 4 in (10 cm), leaflets 3–7, to 2½ in (6 cm), oblong to lanceolate, sinuately spiny, bright glaucous blue; flowers in clusters, pale yellow; *M. gracilipes* China; erect, loosely branching, to 5 ft (1.5 m); leaves to 20 in (50 cm), leaflets 5–13, 3–8 in (8–20 cm), oblong to obovate, apex acute to acuminate, spiny, sea green above, silver beneath; flowers maroon and white; *M. japonica* Japan, in cultivation only—possibly originating in China or Taiwan; to 10 ft (3 m) leaves 12–16 in (30–40 cm), leaflets 7–19, 2–4½ in (5–11 cm), obliquely ovate-lanceolate to oblong-lanceolate, apex acuminate, base rounded with 4–6 sinuate, spiny teeth per side, very leathery, dull dark green to sea green; raceme 4–8 in (10–20 cm), slender, spreading to ascending or pendulous, flowers sulfur yellow, scented of lily of the valley; Bealei Group: W China; erect, scarcely branching shrub to 6½ ft (2 m); leaves to 20 in (50 cm); leaflets to 4 × 2½ in (10 × 6 cm), terminal leaflet larger and broader, 9–15, obliquely and broadly ovate acuminate, coarsely and sinuately spiny-toothed (3–4 teeth per side), rigid, sea green to olive green; flowers scented, pale yellow in short, crowded, more or less erect racemes; a hybrid between this Group and *M. napaulensis* has been offered under the name *M. japonica* 'Trifurca', an upright shrub with bold ruffs of outspread leaves, the leaflets broad and very sharply and coarsely toothed, the flowers pale yellow in short, erect, clustered racemes; *M.* × *lindsayae* (*M. japonica* × *M. siamensis*); includes 'Cantab', a medium-sized, spreading shrub, with long, arching leaves, leaflets to 15, remote, with to 6 spines per side, petiole tinted red in cold weather, and large, fragrant, lemon yellow flowers on spreading or drooping racemes; *M. lomariifolia* Burma, W China; stems erect to 13 ft (4 m), seldom branching above base; leaves to 24 in (60 cm), outspread, leaflets to 2¾ × ½ in (7 × 1 cm), 18–41, crowded, overlapping toward apex, oblong-ovate to oblong-lanceolate, with to 7 spines per side,

sharply acuminate, subfalcate, dark green; flowers pale yellow, crowded on erect spikes to 6 in (15 cm); *M.* × *media* (*M. japonica* × *M. lomariifolia*); tall, vigorous hybrids with spreading ruffs of rigid dark green leaves and long racemes of yellow flowers; includes 'Buckland', with an inflorescence to 26 in (65 cm) in diameter composed of some 14 racemes, and fragrant, pale yellow flowers; 'Charity', erect to 16 ft (5 m), with ovate-lanceolate, acuminate leaflets, with to 3 teeth on upper margin and to 4 on lower, and deep yellow flowers in erect racemes to 14 in (35 cm); 'Faith', similar to *M. lomariiflora*, but with broader leaflets and paler flowers; 'Hope', with dense, bright pale yellow flowers; 'Lionel Fortescue', with a fragrant, erect inflorescence; 'Underway', of branching, bushy habit, with flowers in fall; and 'Winter Sun', with horizontal racemes and topaz-yellow flowers opening in fall and winter; *M. napaulensis* Nepal, Sikkim, Assam; differs from *M. acanthifolia* in having shorter leaves with fewer, rather narrower leaflets, usually more closely toothed and glossy, and faintly scented flowers produced in later winter; *M. nervosa* NW US; dwarf, more or less stemless shrub to 10 in (25 cm), suckering and forming dense, leafy colonies; leaves to 10 in (25 cm), resembling a miniature *M. japonica* in shape, sea green turning a rich bronze to maroon in cold weather; flowers pale gold in racemes to 3 in (8 cm) long; *M. nevinii* California; erect to 7½ ft (2.25 m); leaflets to 1¼ in (3 cm), 3–7, narrow-lanceolate, with to 6 spiny teeth per side, gray-blue, glaucous; flowers in loose, broad racemes; *M. pinnata* California; distinguished from *M. aquifolium* by its more erect, rigid habit, and more finely serrate leaflets; to 8 ft (2.5 m); leaflets 5–9, to 2½ in (6 cm), ovate-lanceolate, sinuate with to 13 slender, forward-pointing spines per side, dull sea green above, tinted red in winter, pruinose beneath; racemes to 2½ in (6 cm), flowers primrose yellow; plants grown under this name are often *M.* × *wagneri*, particularly the clone 'Pinnacle'; *M. repens* western N America; suckering, semi-prostrate shrub to 20 in (0.5 m); leaves to 10 in (25 cm), leaflets usually 5, ovate, dull green above, papillose

M

beneath, glaucous at first, with 9–18 spiny teeth per side; flowers deep yellow, in racemes to 3 in (8 cm); includes the very low-growing 'Rotundifolia', with larger, broadly ovate, entire or serrulate leaves; *M. siamensis* N Thailand to Burma, China; to 13 ft (4 m); leaves to 28 in (70 cm), leaflets 11–17, obliquely lanceolate to ovate, 5½–6½ in (14–17 cm), sinuately toothed, dull green very leathery with veins impressed; raceme 4¾–10 in (12–25 cm), 6–10-fascicled, ascending to erect, flowers deep yellow, very fragrant; *M. trifoliolata* Mexico; erect to 7½ ft (2.25 m); leaflets 3, to 2¾ in (6.8 cm), narrowly lanceolate, rigid, undulate with 1–4 lobelike marginal spines per side, gray to blue-green, glaucous; flowers pale yellow in short corymbs; *M.* × *wagneri* (*M. pinnata* × *M. aquifolium*) cultivars include 'Aldenhamensis', vigorous and erect to 5 ft (1.5 m), with large, sea green leaves, tinted blue beneath, bronze young leaves and yellow flowers; 'Fireflame', to 4 ft (1.25 m), with 7 leaflets, green or glaucous blue above, gray-green beneath, blood red to bronze in winter; 'Moseri', erect to 32 in (80 cm), with young leaves tinged bronze-red, later dark green, and yellow flowers; 'Pinnacle', syn. 'Pinnata', erect to 5 ft (1.5 m), vigorous, with young foliage and winter leaves tinted copper, otherwise bright green; 'Undulata', erect to 5 ft (1.5 m), vigorous, with very glossy leaves with undulate margins, young and winter leaves tinted red-bronze; and 'Vicaryi', broadly erect to 3¼ ft (1 m), with small leaves, some tinted red in fall, and yellow flowers in small dense racemes.

Maianthemum (from Greek *maios*, the month of May, and *anthemon*, blossom). Liliaceae (Convallariaceae). Northern temperate regions. MAY LILY. 3 species, low-growing perennial herbs with creeping rhizomes. They produce slender stems bearing two to three, smooth, heart-shaped leaves and, in late spring, small white flowers in terminal racemes. These are followed by red berries. Plant in humus-rich, slightly acidic soils in moist and shaded locations in the wild and woodland garden where they may soon form large colonies. They suffer in hot, dry summers. Propagate by division.

M. bifolium FALSE LILY OF THE VALLEY; W Europe to Japan; stem 2–4 in (5–10 cm); leaves 1¼–3 in (3–8 cm), broadly cordate-ovate, thinly-textured, short-stalked with a deep, open sinus; *M. canadense* TWO-LEAVED SOLOMON'S SEAL; N America; stem 2–4 in (5–10 cm); leaves 2–4 in (5–10 cm), broadly ovate-cordate, more or less sessile with a narrow sinus.

unbranched stem known as "whip"

graft union

Maiden apple

maiden mainly used to describe a tree or shrub, especially a fruit tree, in its first year after grafting or budding and before any pruning has taken place. A feathered maiden has lateral growths. It is often also used to describe newly rooted strawberry plants, and sometimes other plants in their first year after propagation.

Maihuenia (from *maihuen*, a local name for the plant). Cactaceae. Argentina and Chile. 2 species, low, shrubby cacti with clumped, cylindrical stems bearing small, terete leaves at their summits and slender spines. Funnel-shaped, yellow flowers appear in summer. Grow in an unheated greenhouse, or outdoors (min. temp. 0°F/−18°C) with winter protection from rain. Provide gritty, more or less

neutral medium and full sun. Keep dry from late fall until early spring. *M. poeppigii* S Argentina, S Chile; dwarf shrub, forming low mounds; stem segments shortly cylindric, ½–1¼ in (1.2–3 cm); leaves ⅛–¼ in (4–6 mm), central spine ½–⅝ in (1–1.5 cm); flowers 1¼–1¾ in (3–4.5 cm), yellow.

maincrop used to distinguish those vegetable crops that do not mature particularly early or late in the season; applied particularly to potatoes and carrots.

Malcolmia (for William Malcolm, late 18th-century London nurseryman). Cruciferae. Mediterranean to Afghanistan. MALCOLM STOCK. 35 species, annual to perennial herbs with branching, often prostrate stems and entire or pinnately lobed, downy leaves. Produced from spring to fall in loose racemes, the flowers consist of four, linear or obovate petals. A hardy annual, grow in well-drained, medium- to low-fertility neutral to alkaline soils, in sun or part-day shade. Plants suffer in hot, humid summers. Sow seed thinly *in situ*, from early spring until fall. *M. maritima* VIRGINIA STOCK; Mediterranean; annual to 14 in (35 cm); flowers fragrant, petals ½–1 in (12–25 mm), red-purple, rarely violet, notched, long-clawed; Compacta Mixed: compact, to 16 in (40 cm), with small, fragrant, pink, white and red flowers.

Malephora (from Greek *male*, armpit, and *phorein*, to bear). Aizoaceae. South Africa, Namibia. 15 species, erect or creeping shrubby perennials with succulent, semi-cylindric leaves and daisylike flowers, golden, yellow or pink and to 2 in (5 cm) in diameter. Cultivate as for *Lampranthus*. *M. crocea* stem stout, gnarled; leaves 1–1¾ in (2.5–4.5 cm), more or less 3-sided, pruinose; flowers 1¼ in (3 cm) in diameter, golden yellow inside, tinted red outside; var. *purpureocrocea*: flowers brilliant red.

male sterility the failure of flowers to form fertile pollen.

malformations to a greater or lesser extent, all plant species show variation from the condition usually

Malformation
This top-grafted *Prunus* shows abnormal tissue growth at the graft points. Never cut or pare such growth.

accepted as normal. Adaptation to habitat is held to account for many such variations. Frequently, however, malformations or monstrosities in plants arise from other factors and may be seen as excessive or arrested growth, or other abnormal development in form or position of parts.

Imbalance of auxin and other non-specific hormones accounts for many instances of malformation. Parasitism by mites or viruses can influence the production of hormones and stimulate the formation of galls or witches' broom growths. Occasionally, an abundant supply of mineral nutrients, particularly nitrogen, can lead to malformation.

Genetic change is also a potential cause of abnormal growth, and minor variations brought about in this way or through environmental influence are held by some to account for reversion to an ancestral condition. Chromosome changes and abnormality can produce unusual growth forms, for example, autote-traploids are frequently larger than diploids of the same species, for example the grape cultivar 'Perlette', *Clematis montana* 'Tetrarose' and the majority of *Narcissus* cultivars. The growing points (apical meristems) of a plant contain immature tissue and physical or chemical damage can influence their future behavior. The accidental division of the apex into two independent meristems can lead to two shoots developing from one region. Breakdown in growth coordination can take place in the apex, often induced by hormonal imbalance and bringing about abnormal multiplication of shoots and bushy development, or unusual leaf

arrangement (phyllotaxy), or clusters of leaves produced instead of flowers. Plant parts sometimes develop out of place and inflorescences can revert to vegetative shoots; such malformations may be of hormonal origin or due to changes in temperature or day length at critical times in the plant's growth cycle.

One of the most striking abnormalities is FASCIATION, which results from unusual activity in the apical meristem. Familiar examples occur in *Ranunculus*, *Delphinium* and *Forsythia* with wide, laterally branching stems giving the impression of several normal stems fused together (*see p.304*). Sometimes, an abnormal number of flowers is produced on fasciated stems, as may be seen in lilies. In "ring fasciation," a ring of subsidiary flower heads is produced around a normal central flower. This occurs, for instance, in members of the Compositae, such as the daisy, where the abnormality is referred to as "hen-and-chickens." Sometimes lateral buds develop on a thickened stem, and branches of normal dimension and appearance grow from it.

Some fasciated forms are cultivated, for example, *Salix udensis* 'Sekka', whose flattened, recurving stems are encouraged to form by hard pruning. Another example is *Celosia argentea* var. *cristata*, the cock's comb, a tetraploid cultigen derived from *C.argentea*, which can be seed-propagated; and there are cristate forms among cacti, forming fan-shaped or densely convoluted growths. Many fern cultivars have crested ends of fronds and are given names like 'Cristata' or 'Monstrosa'.

In some plants, leaves may fail to separate properly from stems, or parts of flowers may appear to be stuck together. In double flowers, it is quite common to find PETALOID STAMENS.

Another interesting variation is the rearrangement of flower parts, probably the outcome of a small genetic change and well-documented in *Antirrhinum*. This phenomenon is known as PELORY or PELORIA and a frequently met example is the foxglove *Digitalis purpurea* 'Monstrosa', in which a large, open, regular flower tops the spike of normal 2-lipped, bell-shaped flowers; this is heritable from seed. In the abnormality of flowers known as HOSE-IN-HOSE, one perfect corolla develops

within another, in some cases giving the appearance of a double bloom and in others clearly separated. This condition is found particularly in primulas, but also in rhododendrons and *Mimulus*.

Freak plants produced artificially by grafting are often regarded as teratological, but this is not strictly so. Unusual color mutants, lacking chlorophyll, can sometimes be perpetuated by grafting, for example, *Gymnocalycium* in the Cactaceae. Unsuitable matching of stock and scion may bring about peculiar forms, for example, the selection of a vigorous scion for a restricting rootstock in *Fraxinus* can lead to the scion bulging above the graft. The reverse condition is commonly seen in *Prunus*.

mallet cutting see *cuttings, semi-ripe*

Malope (name of Greek origin, used by Pliny for a mallow). Malvaceae. Mediterranean to W Asia. 4 species, annual and perennial herbs with unlobed or palmately lobed leaves. Produced in summer, the flowers are funnelform and consist of five, obovate petals. *Malope* performs best in regions with cooler summers and may fail in very hot, humid conditions. Grow in moderately fertile and humus-rich, sandy soils in full sun. Deadhead regularly. Propagate from seed sown under glass in early spring, or, later, *in situ*. *M. trifida* W Mediterranean; annual to 4 ft (1.2 m); flowers 1½–2½ in (4–6 cm), purple-red; 'Alba': white; 'Grandiflora': large, dark rose; 'Rosea': rose-red; 'Vulcan': large, bright red.

Malus (Latin for "apple tree"). Rosaceae. Europe, Asia, US. APPLE, CRAB APPLE. Some 35 species, deciduous trees and shrubs, many with thorny or short, spurlike lateral shoots. Produced in corymbs in spring and summer, the flowers consist of five, outspread, rounded to obovate petals and numerous stamens. They are followed by pomes, often highly colored, and ranging from small "crabs" to large apples. *Malus* provides ornamental interest throughout the year, especially in spring when in blossom. The decorative fruit, with a color range from clear yellow through bright reds to deep red-purple, often persists well into winter. The foliage of some colors well in fall. Taller species, such as *M. floribunda*, *M. hupehensis* and *M. prattii*,

MALUS

Name	Distribution	Habit	Leaves	Flowers	Fruit
M. × arnoldiana (*M. baccata* × *M. floribunda*)	garden origin	shrub to 6½ ft (2 m), resembling *floribunda*: shoots arching, soon glabrous	2–3 in (5–8 cm), elliptic to ovate, long-tapered, biserrate, ultimately glabrous except for veins beneath	carmine-red in bud, later pink becoming white	⅝ in (1.5 cm), globose, yellow-green

Comments: 'Linda': flowers single, carmine becoming light pink; fruit to 1¼ in (3 cm) diameter, carmine.

Name	Distribution	Habit	Leaves	Flowers	Fruit
M. × atrosanguinea (*M. halliana* × *M. toringo*)	garden origin	spreading, with slightly pendulous shoots	ovate, serrate, lobed at base on strong shoots, waxy	single, deep carmine	½ in (1 cm), globose, red or yellow flushed red
M. baccata SIBERIAN CRABAPPLE	NE Asia	tree or shrub to 16 ft (5 m), often confused with *M. robusta*; shoots slender, glabrous	1¼–3 in (3–8 cm), ovate, long-tapered, serrate, glabrous	1¼–1½ in (3–3.5 cm) diameter, white	½ in (1 cm), globose, yellow and red

Comments: 'Columnaris': habit narrowly upright to 25 ft (8 m); flowers snow white; fruit yellow with red cheek. 'Gracilis': habit shrub-like, slow-growing, branches slender, dense; leaves small, narrow; buds pink, flowers white, stellate; fruit small, red. 'Jackii': crown broader, branches stout; leaves broadly elliptic; flowers 1¼ in (3 cm) diameter, white; fruit ½ in (1 cm), red, waxy. 'Lady Northcliffe': buds light pink, flowers profuse, white; fruit to ⅝ in (1.5 cm) diameter, dark orange. 'Macrocarpa': fruit large, to 1¼ in (3 cm), diameter, glossy yellow stained red. 'Orange': habit large, shrublike; buds light pink, flowers white; fruit large, to 1½ in (4 cm) diameter; red washed orange. 'Spring Snow': habit upright: flowers large, white; fruitless; seedling of 'Dolgo'. var. **himalaica**: leaves wide, elliptic, roughly serrate, glabrous, veins on lower leaf surfaces downy; flowers 1¼ in (3 cm) diameter, pink in bud; fruit ½–⅝ in (1–1.5 cm), yellow flushed red. var. **mandschurica**: leaves broadly elliptic, margins with few serrations, lower surface downy at first; flowers to 1½ in (4 cm) diameter, white, scented: fruit ½ in (12 mm), ellipsoid, bright red, ripening early.

Name	Distribution	Habit	Leaves	Flowers	Fruit
M. bhutanica	W China	shrub or small tree to 25 ft (8 m), soon glabrous	1¼–3 in (3–8 cm), ovate and crenately lobed or simple, veins downy beneath	¾ in (2 cm) diameter, white	⅝ in (1.5 cm), globose to pyriform, yellow flushed red, persistent
M. coronaria	NE United States	small tree to 23 ft (7 m) wide, spreading, shoots with numerous short-thorned laterals, becoming glabrous	2–4 in (5–10 cm), ovate-oblong, pointed, serrate, slightly lobed, becoming glabrous and scarlet-orange in fall	to 1½ in (4 cm) diameter, pink	1½ in (4 cm), depressed-globose, green, base slightly ribbed

Comments: 'Charlottae': leaves red stained orange in fall; flowers double, soft pink, fragrant. 'Nieuwlandiana': habit shrublike, to 10 ft (3 m) flowers in large hanging clusters, vivid pink, very fragrant, fruit blue pruinose. var. **dasycalyx**: leaves paler green beneath; flowers smaller, pink, highly fragrant; fruit 1½ in (4 cm), yellow-green.

Name	Distribution	Habit	Leaves	Flowers	Fruit
M. floribunda JAPANESE FLOWERING CRABAPPLE	Japan	shrub to 13 ft (4 m), or tree to 33 ft (10 m), crown dense, shoot tips slightly pendulous, downy	1½–3 in (4–8 cm), long-tapered, deeply serrate, sometimes lightly lobed	1–1¼ in (2.5–3 cm), diameter, deep pink in bud, opening pale pink, white inside	¼ in (0.5 cm), yellow

Comments: 'Peachblow': habit upright; buds dark pink, flowers white; fruit to ½ in (1 cm) diameter, red.

M. × *arnoldiana* *M. baccata* **var.** *mandschurica* *M. floribunda* *M. hupehensis*

MALUS

Name	Distribution	Habit	Leaves	Flowers	Fruit
M. hupehensis	India	tree or shrub, 16–23 ft (5–7 m), shoots spreading, soon glabrous	2–4 in (5–10 cm), ovate to oblong, long-tapered, deeply incised, slightly downy beneath	1½ in (4 cm) diameter, pink fading to white	½ in (1 cm), rounded, yellow-green, flushed red

Comments: 'Rosea': flowers profuse, cherry blossom pink; fruit yellow, sometimes tinted red.

Name	Distribution	Habit	Leaves	Flowers	Fruit
M. × magdeburgensis (*M. pumila* × *M. spectabilis*)	garden origin	shrub or small tree, resembling *M. spectabilis*; crown globose	2½–3 in (6–8 cm), elliptic, acuminate, downy beneath	1¾ in (4.5 cm) diameter, bright red in bud, opening deep pink	1¼ in (3 cm), rounded, green-yellow flushed red
M. prattii	W China	erect shrub or small tree to 23 ft (7 m), shoots downy at first	2½–6 in (6–15 cm), elliptic-oblong, long-tapered, finely biserrate, veins downy beneath, turning red and orange in fall	¾ in (2 cm) diameter, white	½–⅝ in (1–1.5 cm), rounded-ovate, red to yellow, white-pitted
M. prunifolia	NE Asia	small tree to 33 ft (10 m), shoots downy at first	2–4 in (5–10 cm), elliptic or ovate, sinuate, downy beneath	1¼ in (3 cm) diameter, pink in bud opening white	¾ in (2 cm), ovoid-conical, yellow-green to red

Comments: 'Cheal's Crimson': habit upright to broad, to 16 ft (5 m); buds pink, flowers single, white; fruit prolific, to 1 in (2.5 cm) diameter, light orange with scarlet cheek. 'Cheal's Golden Gem': flowers single, white; fruit rounded, gold. 'Fastigiata': habit narrow upright, later spreading; flowers white; fruit yellow and red. 'Hyslop': habit upright to spreading; crown broad; fruit globose, to 1½ in (4 cm) diameter, yellow stippled and blotched light red, edible. 'Pendula': branches weeping.

Name	Distribution	Habit	Leaves	Flowers	Fruit
M. × purpurea (*M. atrosanguinea* × *M. pumila* 'Niedzwetzkyana')	garden origin	large shrub or small tree, bark red-black	3–3½ in (8–9 cm), ovate, scalloped, occasionally lobed, brown-red at first, shiny	1¼–1½ in (3–4 cm) diameter, purple-red, soon fading	⅝–1 in (1.5–2.5 cm), rounded, purple-red

Comments: 'Aldenhamensis': habit shrublike, low-growing, to 11½ ft (3.5 m); leaves bronze red; buds deep red, flowers profuse, maroon; fruit red tinted brown. 'Eleyi': habit shrublike, slightly spreading; leaves darker; flowers single, maroon; fruit ovoid, purple. 'Eleyi Compacta': habit compact, shrublike; branches short; leaves, flowers and fruit purple. 'Hoser': buds dark purple; flowers pink; fruit pruinose purple. 'Jadwiga': habit pendulous; crown broad; buds maroon, flowers pink; fruit conic, to 2 in (5 cm) diameter, black currant purple. 'Lemoinei': habit shrublike, upright, vigorous; leaves dark purple, later bronzed or dark green; flowers single to semi-double, maroon; fruit to ⅝ in (1.5 cm) diameter, dark purple.

Name	Distribution	Habit	Leaves	Flowers	Fruit
M. × robusta *M. baccata* × *M. prunifolia*	garden origin	vigorous, conical shrub or small tree	3–4½ in (8–11 cm), elliptic, margins scalloped, bright green	1¼–1½ in (3–4 cm) diameter, white, occasionally pink.	½–1¼ in (1–3 cm), ellipsoid to rounded, yellow or red, long-stalked, sometimes pruinose

Comments: 'Alexis': buds light pink, flowers single, white; fruit to 1¼ in (3 cm) diameter, vivid pink-red, pruinose. 'Beauty': habit narrowly upright; flowers single, white; fruit to 1¼ in (3 cm) diameter, scarlet. 'Erecta': habit narrowly upright when young, later spreading; flowers single to semi-double, white stained light pink; fruit small, to ¾ in (2 cm) diameter, yellow with red cheeks, pruinose. 'Red Sentinel': flowers single, white, early, fruit glossy scarlet, persistent. 'Red Siberian': fruit bright red. 'Yellow Siberian': fruit yellow, var. **persicifolia**: large shrub, branches slender; leaves 2–4 in (5–10 cm), oval-lanceolate, finely scalloped; flowers 1½ in (4 cm) diameter, numerous, pink in bud opening white; fruit ¾ in (2 cm), abundant, rounded or oblong, red.

M. prunifolia

M. × robusta 'Red Sentinel'

M. toringo

M. toringo subsp. *sargentii*

MALUS

Name	Distribution	Habit	Leaves	Flowers	Fruit
M. spectabilis CHINESE FLOWERING CRABAPPLE	China	large shrub or small tree to 25 ft (8 m), pyramidal at first, later spreading; shoots becoming red-brown	2–3 in (5–8 cm), elliptic-oblong, short-tapered, dentate, downy beneath	1½–2 in (4–5 cm) diameter, single or semi-double, dark pink in bud, opening pale pink	¾–1¼ in (2–3 cm), rounded, yellow

Comments: 'Blanche Amis': habit shrublike, upright; buds carmine, flowers semi-double, white inside, carmine outside; fruit globose, small, yellow. 'Plena': flowers profuse, double, pink, soon fading; fruit globose, to ¾ in (2 cm) diameter, yellow. 'Riversii': flowers double, pink, fruit large, to 1½ in (3.5 cm) diameter, yellow.

Name	Distribution	Habit	Leaves	Flowers	Fruit
M. sylvestris EUROPEAN APPLE, WILD CRAB	C Europe	tree or shrub to 23 ft (7 m), slightly thorny	1½–3 in (4–8 cm), oval to rounded, scalloped or incised, subglabrous	to 1½ in (4 cm) diameter, pink-white outside, pinker within	¾–1½ in (2–4 cm), rounded, yellow-green flushed red

Comments: 'Plena': flowers double, soft pink, fading to snow white; fruit scarlet, sometimes blotched yellow; often listed as *M. spectabilis alba plena.* var. **domestica**: ORCHARD APPLE; the variety gives rise to edible apples.

Name	Distribution	Habit	Leaves	Flowers	Fruit
M. toringo *M. sieboldii*	Japan	shrub to 13 ft (4 m), shoots arched, black-brown	1¼–2½ in (3–6 cm), ovate-elliptic, tapered, dentate and 3–5-lobed, downy, red or yellow in fall	¾ in (2 cm) diameter, deep pink in bud, eventually white	small, globose, red to yellow-brown, persistent

Comments: 'Fuji': habit low, spreading; flowers anemone-centered, white stained green or purple; fruit small, orange. 'Seafoam': somewhat pendulous; flowers carmine, fading to white flushed with pink. 'White Angel': upright, later nodding; flowers in clusters, snow-white; fruit prolific, small, scarlet. 'Wintergold': shrublike, upright to spreading; flowers pink in bud fading to white; fruit gold, persistent. subsp. *sargentii* (*M. sargentii*): shrub to 6½ ft (2 m), thorny, leaves orange in fall; flowers along whole length of shoot, buds pale pink, opening white; fruits dark red.

Name	Distribution	Habit	Leaves	Flowers	Fruit
M. transitoria	NW China	closely resembles *M. toringoides,* smaller, crown narrower; shoots felted when young	¾–1¼ in (2–3 cm), broadly ovate, deeply narrow-lobed, downy	to ¾ in (2 cm) diameter, white	⅝ in (1.5 cm), red
M. trilobata	W Asia	erect shrub or small tree	2–3 in (5–8 cm), 3-lobed, shiny, soon glabrous, intense red in fall	1½ in (3.5 cm) diameter, white	¾ in (2 cm), ellipsoid, red
M. tschonoskii	Japan	tree to 40 ft (12 m), pyramidal then spreading; shoots felted	2¾–4¾ in (7–12 cm), ovate-elliptic, serrate to slightly lobed, white-felted at first, orange-red in fall	1¼ in (3 cm) diameter, white.	¾–1¼ in (2–3 cm), rounded, yellow-green flushed red
M. yunnanensis	W China	compact, erect tree to 33 ft (10 m), shoots felted at first	2½–4¾ in (6–12 cm), broadly ovate, roughly biserrate, occasionally with 3–5 pairs of broad lobes, felted beneath, red-orange in fall	⅝ in (1.5 cm) diameter, usually in crowded corymbs to 2 in (5 cm), white	½–⅝ in (1–1.5 cm), red, pitted

Comments: var. *veitchii*: leaves slightly lobed, soon glabrous; flowers to ½ in (1.2 cm) diameter; fruit to ½ in (1.3 cm), red with white pits

M **M**

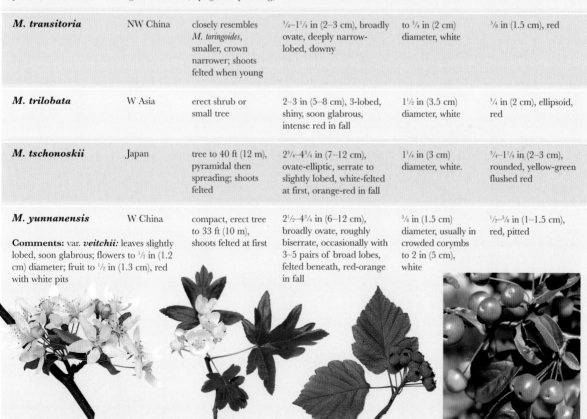

| *M. transitoria* | *M. trilobata* | *M. yunnanensis* **var.** *veitchii* | *M.* × *zumi* 'Professor Sprenger' |

MALUS

Name	Distribution	Habit	Leaves	Flowers	Fruit
M. × **zumi** (*M. baccata* var. *mandshurica* × *M. toringo*)	Japan	small pyramidal tree, shoots more or less downy	2–3½ in (5–9 cm), ovate, long tapered, scalloped to lobed, downy beneath at first	1¼ in (3 cm) diameter, pink in bud, fading to white	½ in (1 cm), rounded, red

Comments: var. *calocarpa*: more spreading; leaves smaller, always entire on fruiting wood, distinctly lobed on strong shoots; flowers smaller, white; fruit ½ in (1–1.3 cm), crowded bunches, scarlet. 'Golden Hornet': flowers white; fruit gold. 'Professor Sprenger': fruit orange.

when grown as standards, are suitable as lawn specimens, at the woodland edge, or in large borders. Smaller species or those grown as half-standards can be selected for the smaller garden or border. *M. tschonoskii* is a small conical tree, bearing few fruits but with brilliant fall colors in orange, purple and scarlet, and is well-suited to planting in public areas.

Malus tolerates light, dappled shade, but fall color and fruiting are better in sun. All are hardy to at least 5°F (−15°C) and most tolerate a range of fertile soils. Grow in a sunny position, in moisture-retentive but not boggy soil. Prune in winter, to remove dead, diseased, damaged or crossing wood. On grafted specimens, it may be necessary to remove suckers. Standard and half-standard trees grown for ornamental purposes are often nursery trained, and have an open, wide-branching crown; for fruiting purposes, it may be preferable to obtain a feathered maiden to form a central leader (spindlebush) tree, with a well-spaced framework of laterals.

Propagate species by seed, although this may not come true. *M. hupehensis* produces seed apomictically, and seedlings of this species will come true. Sow seed in spring, following three months of cold stratification in a damp medium at 34°F (1°C). Temperatures above 59–68°F (15–20°C) in the sowing medium may induce secondary dormancy. Cultivars are T-budded, or whip and tongue grafted on to clonal rootstocks. Pests and diseases of crab apples are similar to those affecting orchard apples. See *apples*.

Malva (from Latin *malva*, mallow, from the Greek *malache*, probably derived from Greek *malachos*, soothing, referring to its medicinal properties). Malvaceae. Europe, Asia, Africa; widely introduced into temperate and tropical regions.

MALLOW. 30 species, annual or perennial herbs and subshrubs, with rounded to reniform or cordate leaves, often toothed or lobed. The flowers are broadly funnel- to bowl-shaped with five obovate petals and are carried in loose terminal spikes in summer. The following are hardy to 5°F (−15°C). Grow in reasonably drained and moderately fertile soil, in full sun. Staking with twiggy sticks may be necessary, especially on moist rich soils. Cut down flowered stems in fall. Sow seed in early spring in the cold frame or under glass at 59°F (15°C); alternatively, increase also by softwood cuttings in spring. *Malva* is prone to rust: collect and burn all affected material in fall and spring.

M. moschata MUSK MALLOW; Europe, NW Africa, naturalized US; aromatic perennial erect to 3¼ ft (1 m); leaves shallowly 3-lobed to deeply divided; petals ¾–1¼ in (2–3 cm), white or pink; includes 'Alba', to 24 in (60 cm), with deeply cut leaves and silky white flowers, and 'Rosea', with rose flowers tinted purple; *M. sylvestris* TALL MALLOW, HIGH MALLOW, CHEESES; Europe, N Africa, SW Asia, US as garden escape; perennial to 3¼ ft (1 m); leaves broadly cordate or suborbicular, lobed; petals ⅝–¾ in (1.5–2 cm), mauve, paler and hairy at base, notched at apex; includes 'Alba', with pure white flowers, 'Brave Heart', upright, to 36 in (90 cm), with large, pale purple flowers with a dark eye, 'Cottenham Blue', to 30 in (75 cm), with pale mauve-blue flowers with darker veins, and 'Primley Blue', low-growing, with soft violet flowers with darker veins.

Malvaviscus (from Latin *malva*, mallow, and *viscum*, glue, referring to the sticky seeds). C and S America. 3 species slender-stemmed, evergreen shrubs, sometimes vinelike, with

unlobed or palmately lobed, toothed leaves. Produced in summer, the flowers resemble those of *Abutilon*, with the petals often incurved in a bell- or turbanlike arrangement. From the center protrudes a long, staminal column. In frost-free, warm temperate regions, grow outdoors in full sun in well-drained soil. In cool temperate zones, grow under glass with a minimum winter temperature of 50°F (10°C), in direct sunlight, in a loam-based mix. Water plentifully when in growth; keep just moist during the winter months. Cut flowered stems hard back in winter to maintain shape. Propagate by softwood or semi-ripe cuttings or by seed in spring. *M. arboreus* WAX MALLOW; Mexico to Peru and Brazil; to 13 ft (4 m); leaves lobed, downy; flowers long-stalked, petals 1–2 in (2.5–5 cm), rich red; var. *mexicanus*: TURK'S CAP, leaves almost glabrous, more or less unlobed.

mamillate, mammillate furnished with nipplelike prominences.

Mammillaria (from Latin *mammilla*, little nipple, referring to the tubercles). Cactaceae. SW US, Mexico, C America, Caribbean region, Colombia, Venezuela. Some 150 species, low-growing cacti with globose to squatly cylindrical stems covered in prominent, spiny tubercles. Campanulate to funnelform flowers are borne freely at various times of year. The fruit is berrylike, oblong or clavate, and often bright red. These small, undemanding cacti are popular as houseplants, producing an abundance of small, colorful flowers. Provide a minimum temperature of 45°F (7°C), full sun and low humidity. Plant in a gritty and sandy, loam-based mix. Water moderately in spring and summer. Keep dry from midfall until early spring, except for light misting on warm days during late winter. Increase

M

by seed, alternatively by offsets.

M. bocasana C Mexico; freely clustering; stem more or less globose, almost hidden by spines; axils naked or with fine hairs or bristles; central spines 1(–5), ¼–½ in (5–10 mm), 1–2 hooked, red or brown, radial spines 25–50, ⅜–½(–¾) in (8–10(–20) mm), hairlike, white; flowers creamy white, outer tepals with pale pink stripe; *M. candida* NE Mexico; simple or clustering; stems to 5½ in (14 cm) in diameter, globose to stoutly cylindric; tubercles cylindric; areoles with scant wool; axils with fine white bristles; central spines 8–12, to ½ in (1 cm), white or tipped pink or brown, radial spines numerous, to ⅝ in (1.5 cm), white; flowers rose pink; *M. densispina* C Mexico; usually simple; stem to 4½ (12 cm) × 2½(–4) in (6(–10) cm), globose to short-cylindric; central spines 5–6, ½ (–⅝) in (10–12(–15) mm), straight, black-tipped, radial spines about 25, unequal, ⅜–½ in (8–10 mm), yellow; flowers pale yellow; *M. elongata* C Mexico; clustering; stem ½–1¼ in (1–3 cm) in diameter, cylindric, elongate; tubercles short, central spines 0–3, to ⅝ in (5 mm), pale yellow to brown, radial spines 14–25, ⅛–⅜ in (4–9 mm), yellow; flowers pale yellow or tinged pink; *M. geminispina* C Mexico; soon clustering and forming mounds; individual stem 2½–3 in (6–8 cm) in diameter, becoming cylindric; axils with wool and short bristles; central spines 2 or 4, uppermost ⅝–1½ in (15–40 mm), white, dark-tipped, radial spines 16–20, ⅛–¼ in (5–7 mm), chalky white; flowers deep pink; *M. gracilis* east C Mexico; offsetting very freely, stem to 5 (13 cm) × ½–1¼ in (1–3 cm), cylindric; tubercles short, obtusely conic; central spines 0–2(–5), up to ½ in (12 mm), white or dark brown, radial spines 11–17, ⅛–⅜ in (3–8 mm), bristly, white; flowers pale yellow with pink or brown midline; *M. haageana* (syn. *M. elegans*); SE Mexico; stem usually simple, reaching 6 (15 cm) × 2–4 in (5–10 cm) in larger variants: tubercles small, crowded; axils often woolly and sometimes with bristles; central spines usually 2, sometimes 1 or 4, to ⅝ in (15 mm), brown, radial spines 15–25, ⅛–¼ in (3–6 mm), white; flowers small, deep purple-pink; *M. hahniana* C Mexico; simple or clustering; individual stem to 8 × 4¾ in (20

Mammillaria bocasana var. rubrifolia
This form of the snowball cactus has pinker flowers than the species, forming a more conspicuous ring around the crown.

× 12 cm); tubercles very numerous, triangular-conic, small; axils with long white bristles; central spines 1(–4), up to ⅛ in (4 mm), white tipped brown, radial spines 20–30, ¼–⅜ in (5–15 mm), hairlike, white; flowers deep purple-pink; *M. magnimamma* C Mexico; usually clustering and forming mounds 20 in (50 cm) or more in diameter; individual heads to 4–4¾ in (10–12 cm) in diameter; tubercles pyramidal-conic; axils woolly in flowering zone; spines 3–6, usually 1 longer and stronger than the others and curved; flowers pale yellow to deep purple-pink; *M. microhelia* C Mexico; simple or clustering; stem to 10 (25 cm) × 1½–2½ in (3.5–6 cm), cylindric; tubercles shortly conic; axils soon naked; central spines 0–4(–8), to ½ in (11 mm), dark red-brown, radial spines (30–)50, ⅛–¼ in (4–6 mm); yellow, often slightly recurved; flowers creamy white to red or purple; *M. plumosa* NE Mexico; clustering to form mounds to 16 in (40 cm) or more in diameter; stem to 2½–2¾ in (6–7 cm) in diameter, globose, hidden by spines; tubercles cylindric; axils woolly; spines up to 40, ⅛–¼ in (3–7 mm), feathery, white; flowers small, creamy white or tinged brown-pink; *M. prolifera* NE Mexico, SW US, Cuba, Hispaniola; forming dense clumps; stem to about 3½ × 1¾ in (9 × 4.5 cm), globose, to cylindric-clavate; tubercles terete; axils naked or with fine white hairs; central spines 5–12, ⅛–⅜ in (4–9 mm), straight, puberulent, white to red-brown, some-

times dark-tipped, radial spines 25–40, ⅛–½ in (3–12 mm), fine, straight to tortuous, white; flowers creamy yellow, or tinged pink, outer tepals brown-striped; *M. rhodantha* C Mexico; usually simple, occasionally offsetting or branching; stem to 16 × 4¾ in (40 × 12 cm), cylindric; tubercles obtuse-conic to cylindric, axils woolly at first and with a few bristles; central spines 4–9, to ¾(–1) in (18(–25) mm), usually recurved, typically red-brown, radial spines typically 17–24, ⅛–⅜ in (4–9 mm), glassy white to pale yellow; flowers purple-red; *M. schiedeana* clustering; stem to 4 × 2½ in (10 × 6 cm), depressed-globose; tubercles tapering, cylindric, terete; axils with long white woolly hairs; central spines 0, radial spines very numerous, ¹⁄₁₆–¼ in (2–5 mm), adpressed, minutely pubescent, white, pale yellow toward base, golden yellow at base, the tip usually hairlike; flowers creamy white; *M. sempervivi* east central Mexico; simple at first, sometimes later dividing apically or offsetting; stem to 4 in (10 cm) in diameter, depressed-globose; tubercles angled-conic, dark blue-green, axils woolly; central spines usually 2, sometimes 4, to ⅛ in (4 mm), brown or black, later gray, radial spines rudimentary, on juvenile stem only; flowers nearly white or pale pink; *M. zeilmanniana* C Mexico; freely clustering; stem to 2½ × 1¾ in (6 × 4.5 cm); tubercles subcylindric, central spines 4, the upper 3 straight, the lowest hooked, slightly longer, all red-brown, radial spines about 15–18, finely bristly, pubescent, white; flowers violet-pink or purple, rarely white.

Mandevilla (for H. J. Mandeville, British Minister in Buenos Aires, who introduced *M. laxa*). Apocynaceae. C and S America. Some 120 species, woody, evergreen lianes with funnelform to salverform, 5-lobed flowers at various times of year. Grow in a coarse, well-drained but moisture-retentive medium rich in organic matter, with shade from the strongest summer sun. Provide a minimum temperature of 45–50°F (7–10°C). Young plants grow well and flower freely in well-lit, warm rooms in the home and are often offered for sale as houseplants trained on wire hoops. Water plentifully and liquid-fertilize occasionally

M

when in growth and flower. Provide support and mist over frequently, especially in warm bright weather or if grown in the home. Reduce water as light levels and temperatures drop in fall; keep just moist in winter. Prune in late winter/early spring to thin old and crowded growth and cut back remaining branches to short spurs. Propagate by semi-ripe or softwood nodal cuttings.

M. × *amabilis.* (*M. splendens* × *?*); climber to 13 ft (4 m); flowers 3½–4¾ in (9–12 cm) in diameter, rose pink, rosy crimson at center, throat yellow; *M.* × *amoena* (*M.* × *amabilis* × *M. splendens*); a backcross with more abundantly produced, darker flowers to 4 in (10 cm) in diameter; includes *M.* 'Alice du Pont' and *M.* 'Splendens Hybrid'; *M. boliviensis* Bolivia, Ecuador; WHITE DIPLADENIA; slender climber to 13 ft (4 m); flowers to 2 × 3 in (5 × 8 cm), white, throat golden yellow; *M. laxa* (syn. *M. suaveolens*); CHILEAN JASMINE; Argentina; climber to 13 ft (4 m); flowers highly fragrant, to 2 in (5 cm) in diameter, white to ivory; *M. sanderi* Brazil; climber to 2 in (5 cm); flowers rose-pink, throat to 1¾ in (4.5 cm); 'Rosea': BRAZILIAN JASMINE, flowers to 3 in (8 cm), salmon pink with throat and tube yellow within; *M. splendens* SE Brazil; climber to 20 ft (6 m); flowers 3–4 in (7.5–10 cm) in diameter, rose pink; includes 'Rosacea', with rose-pink flowers, flushed and edged deeper rose and with a tube ringed bright rose at throat and yellow within.

Mandragora (Classical Greek name used by Hippocrates). Solanaceae. Mediterranean to Himalaya. 6 species, perennial herbs with stout, forked taproots and oblong to lanceolate leaves in a basal rosette. The short-stalked, solitary flowers are bell-shaped, 5-lobed and appear in spring. They are followed by toxic, tomato-like fruit. Hardy to 0°F (−18°C). Grow in a warm, sheltered position, in deep, light, well-drained but moisture-retentive, circumneutral soil; it will tolerate some shade. Propagate by seed sown ripe or in spring, or by root cuttings in winter. *M. officinarum* MANDRAKE, DEVIL'S APPLES; N Italy,

W Balkans; leaves to 12 in (30 cm), somewhat puckered and wavy; flowers to 1 in (2.5 cm), blue to purple, lobes triangular; fruit to 1¼ in (3 cm) in diameter, yellow.

Manettia (For X. Manetti [b. 1723], keeper of the botanic garden at Florence). Rubiaceae. Tropical America. Some 80 species, soft-stemmed or woody-based, evergreen twiners with brightly colored, tubular to funnel-shaped flowers at various times of year. Grow in bright, indirect light, on trellis or other support, in the greenhouse or conservatory, with a minimum temperature of 50°F (10°C). Water plentifully when in growth; reduce watering as temperatures fall in fall. Avoid persistent wetting of foliage, especially in bright sunlight or cold weather. Cut back if necessary in spring. *Manettia* species can also be grown as half-hardy annuals, planted outside for summer display, in humus-rich soils with part shade. Most plants will degenerate after a few years, making frequent repropagation desirable: take softwood cuttings of new growth in spring or semi-ripe cuttings in summer.

M. cordifolia FIRECRACKER VINE; Bolivia to Argentina, Peru; twining herb, to 13 ft (4 m); leaves heart-shaped, smooth; flowers to 2 in (5 cm), vivid red or dark orange fading to yellow at lobes, tube distended above; *M. luteorubra* (syn. *M. bicolor*, *M. inflata*); BRAZILIAN FIRECRACKER, TWINING FIRECRACKER, FIRECRACKER VINE; Paraguay, Uruguay; perennial, twining herb or shrub to 13 ft (4 m); leaves ovate to elliptic, roughly but minutely hairy; flowers to 2 in (5 cm), tube cylindric, bright red, downy, lobes yellow.

manganese an essential minor (micro-) nutrient, required as a constituent of enzymes that are important in respiration and protein synthesis. Symptoms of deficiency occur in plants grown on high lime soils, especially those rich in organic content; however, symptoms may be due to the element being unavailable rather than absent. Deficiency is commonly

Mandrake root

expressed as leaf chlorosis, commencing at the margins with color left in the finest veins, thus giving a distinct netted appearance. Although commencing in shoot tips, older leaves appear more affected as new leaves grow out of the symptoms. Characteristic spotting occurs on potatoes and beet; and also on the cotyledons of peas and some beans where it causes the condition known as marsh spot, found when the seeds are split open. The avoidance of overliming will prevent deficiency and sprays of manganese sulfate are an effective treatment. Manganese toxicity can occur on soils of a pH below 5.0.

Manglietia (from the Malay name for one of the species). Magnoliaceae. Malaysia to S China, E Himalaya. Some 25 species, shrubs or trees, resembling *Magnolia*, but with leaf petiole bases appearing swollen, 9 flower segments in 2 whorls, occasionally more, and ovules to 6 per carpel (*Magnolia* has 2 ovules per carpel). Cultivate as for *Michelia*. *M. insignis* W China, Himalaya, Burma; tree to 40 ft (12 m); young shoots gray-downy; leaves to 8 in (20 cm), oblong to elliptic, glossy above, glaucous beneath, tough; flowers to 3 in (7.5 cm) in diameter, white tinged pink or carmine.

mangos tropical evergreen trees up to 100 ft (30 m) tall, of the family Anacardiaceae, native from India to S China and the Solomon Islands, and naturalized in N Australia. *Mangifera indica* is of ancient origin in cultivation, producing fleshy, resinous edible fruits, colored green to red depending on the cultivar. Fruit size varies greatly from 1½–9¾ in (4–25 cm) in length, weighing up to 4½ lb (2 kg). Optimal climate range is from monsoon tropics to frost free subtropics; some cultivars are adapted to growing in minimum outdoor temperature range of 70–77°F (21–25°C), with high humidity. In temperate regions, specimen plants can be grown only in lofty greenhouses maintaining a minimum temperature of 59°F (15°C).

manure is a term often used to refer to any substance added to soil as a source of plant nutrients, although it is most appropriately used as a description

Manuring a trench
Manure added to any hole or trench for young plants (here for a hedge) must be well-rotted; fresh dung will burn the roots.

of bulky organic material derived from animals or plants. Manure provides nutrients and humus that benefit soil structure. The type most commonly referred to is farmyard manure (FYM), which is cow, pig, or horse dung mixed with straw or litter. The nutrient content varies according to the type of animal and its feeding, the proportion of litter and the duration and method of storage. Exposure to the elements rapidly lowers nutrient levels, especially of nitrogen. The average analysis of FYM is 0.5% nitrogen (N), 0.25% phosphate (P) and 0.5% potash (K).

Horse dung is usually the richest and driest, and has the best effect on soil structure. It is also very suitable for hot beds and mushroom beds. Pig and cow manure have a close texture and are better used on light soils than on heavy ones. Cow manure will dry rapidly and can be crumbled for use in potting mixtures.

FYM is a possible source of weed seeds and occasionally plant pests and diseases. It should be composted for six months before use, preferably stacked on a concrete surface under cover.

Poultry manure has a higher nitrogen and phosphate content than farmyard manure at about 2.5% N and 1% P, which rises on drying. Pigeon manure has the highest nutrient content of all, at about 14% N, 11% P and 3% K. Both can be used fresh as long as care is taken not to exceed the nitrogen requirements of a crop, but they are best added in small quantities

to a compost pile, or dried and mixed with soil or sand for top-dressing.

Sewage sludge provides organic matter for the improvement of soil structure but it is of variable nutritional content and it is important to assure freedom from heavy metal contamination. It is more suitable for use on agricultural land than in gardens. Organic manures can be worked into the soil at fall or spring digging or alternatively spread over the surface, 3–4¾ in (8–12 cm) deep, during fall or winter, for incorporation by earthworms prior to spring digging; incorporate throughout the top 7 in (18 cm) at rates of not less than 10 lb/yd². (5.5 kg/m²). See *compost, green manuring, guano, fish manure, leaf mold, liquid feeding.*

Maranta (for B. Maranti [fl. 1559], Venetian botanist). Marantaceae. Tropical C and S America. Some 32 species, evergreen herbaceous perennials with short, clumped stems arising from a starchy rhizome. The leaves are long-stalked with obovate to elliptic blades and exhibit sleep movements—standing erect as if in prayer at night. Small flowers are carried in sparsely branched, bracteate spikes throughout the year. Cultivate as for *Calathea.* The following species is one of the most widely grown foliage houseplants. *M. leuconeura* PRAYER PLANT, TEN COMMANDMENTS; Brazil; low-growing; leaves to 4¾ in (12 cm), elliptic, lustrous dark green, zoned gray or maroon, veined silver, red or purple above, gray-green or maroon beneath; flowers white stained or spotted violet; var. *erythroneura*: HERRINGBONE PLANT, leaves velvety black-green with prominent red veins and a lime green zone along midvein; 'Massangeana': leaves blue-tinted, dull rusty-brown toward center with a jagged silver band along midrib and silver lines along lateral veins; var. *leuconeura*: leaves broadly elliptic, dark green above with a pale, comblike central zone and silver feather veins; and var. *kerchoviana*: RABBIT'S FOOT, leaves gray-green with a row of

Golden marjoram

purple-brown to dark olive blotches on each side of midrib.

marcescent withered but persisting, for example, the leaves of young beech plants or those trimmed as hedges in late summer.

marcottage, marcotting see *air layering.*

marginal plant a plant grown either in shallow water or in moist soil around pool edges and banks of watercourses.

Margyricarpus (from Greek *margaron*, pearl, and *karpos*, fruit, referring to the white fruit). Rosaceae. S America (Andes). 1 species, *M. pinnatus*, PEARL FRUIT, an evergreen, densely branched subshrub to 24 in (60 cm) with pinnate leaves to ¾ in (2 cm) long divided into many fine and silky leaflets. Inconspicuous flowers are followed in summer by fleshy, rounded fruits to ¼ in (0.7 cm) in diameter and white with purple tints. Grow in well-drained, moisture-retentive, preferably lime-free soils in an open position, but with some shade during the hottest part of the day. Hardy to 23°F (–5°C)—protect from prolonged winter frosts. In the alpine house, grow in pans and water freely when in growth, keeping dry but not arid in winter. Propagate by softwood cuttings in early summer, by simple layering, or from seed sown in fall.

marionberry see *hybrid berries.*

marjoram (*Origanum* species) a culinary herb native of mountainous Mediterranean areas and known to have been cultivated in Ancient Egypt. SWEET or KNOTTED MARJORAM (*O. majorana*) is grown as an annual, and reaches a height of 24 in (60 cm). Sow under protection in March or a little later outdoors, planting or thinning to 8 in (20 cm) stations. POT MARJORAM or OREGANO (*O.vulgare*) is hardier and grown as a bushy perennial, up to 36 in (90 cm) high. Raise from seed, cuttings or division, and trim regularly. There are attractive variegated forms of marjoram, usually less distinctly flavored. The leaves can be dried satisfactorily, and specimens potted to overwinter productively under protection.

marl a calcareous clay soil. Marl is sometimes applied to sandy soils to improve structure, fertility and water retention.

marrow (*Cucurbita pepo*) VEGETABLE MARROW a bush or trailing annual producing large, cylindrical, edible fruits; immature marrows of some cultivars are known as zucchini (or "courgettes" in the UK). Originating in northern Mexico and the southern US, the marrow is now widely distributed in many tropical and subtropical regions and can be cultivated outdoors in temperate regions during the summer.

Marrows require fertile, moisture-retentive soil achieved by incorporating well-rotted organic matter. A soil temperature of a least 55°F (13°C) is necessary for germination, and plants are best sown in small pots under protection in the spring; set out 4–5 weeks later, after hardening off and when risk of frost has passed. Later direct sowings can be made in the open or under cloches, placing two or three seeds per site at a depth of 1 in (2.5 cm); thin later to leave only the strongest seedling. Space 36 in (90 cm) apart each way for bush types and 4 ft (1.2 m) for trailing types. Marrows must be kept well-watered, particularly during flowering, and mulching of the soil surface is beneficial.

Separate male and female flowers are produced and these are insect-pollinated; under cool conditions, hand-pollinate by removing male flowers and dabbing pollen into the female flowers—these can be recognized by the immature ovary below the perianth. Regular harvesting extends the production period and increases total yield. Zucchini should be cut when about 4 in (10 cm) long and marrows when between 6–8 in (15–20 cm) long. Marrows developed to their full size can be stored for winter use. Possible problems: aphids, red spider mite, whiteflies; virus, downy mildew, gray mold, gummosis, powdery mildew.

See also *courgette*, *pumpkins*, *squashes*.

Mary garden a medieval enclosed garden with features of religious significance, including flower-spangled turf and plants having Christian symbolism, especially the Madonna lily.

Masdevallia (for José Masdevall [d. 1801], Spanish botanist and physician). Orchidaceae. Mexico to Brazil and Bolivia. Some 350 species, small evergreen perennial herbs with clumps of obovate to oblanceolate leaves borne on short stalks. The flowers are solitary or racemose, thinly fleshy and essentially triangular in outline due to the showy, expanded sepals. These are ovate to triangular, fused below in a narrow or cup-shaped tube, then spreading and terminating in a tail. The petals and lip are far smaller and virtually hidden within the sepaline cup. Pot in a mix of fine bark, charcoal and sphagnum in small pots. Position in light shade in a buoyant, humid, cool environment—growth will deteriorate where temperatures exceed a day maximum of 77°F (25°C) or a night range of 41–50°F (5–10°C). Although these plants should never be allowed to dry out, they are susceptible to damping off, and should therefore be watered carefully. Propagate by division.

M. barleana Peru; inflorescence to 10 in (25 cm), 1-flowered; sepaline tube narrow, scarlet, campanulate-cylindric, slightly decurved, dorsal sepal to 1½ in (4 cm), red-orange with red lines, ovate-triangular to subquadrate, lateral sepal connate for two-thirds, bright carmine shaded scarlet, with scarlet lines, tails to ½ in (14 mm), sometimes crossing; *M. caudata* Colombia, Venezuela, Ecuador; inflorescence 1-flowered, flowers slightly fragrant, to 6 in (15 cm) across, usually smaller; sepaline tube short, cuplike, dorsal sepal lime to buff, spotted and lined lilac, free portion to 1 in (2.5 cm), obovate, concave, tails to 2½ in (6.5 cm), slender, yellow, lateral sepal buff flushed or spotted lilac or rose, free portion to ⅜ in (1.5 cm), ovate, tails to 2 in (5 cm), pale green, deflexed; *M. coccinea* Colombia, Peru; inflorescence to 16 in (40 cm), 1-flowered; flowers waxy, variable in color, sepals deep magenta, crimson, scarlet, pale yellow or cream-white, sepaline tube to ¾ in (2 cm), campanulate to cylindric, dorsal

sepal to 3 in (8 cm), triangular or linear, tail slender, erect or recurved, lateral sepals ovate-triangular, large, fused, with ridges and short tails; *M. ignea* (syn. *M. militaris*); Colombia; inflorescence to 16 in (40 cm), 1-flowered; flowers to 3 in (8 cm) across; sepals scarlet to orange, often tinged crimson, sepaline tube to ¾ in (2 cm), cylindrical, hooded, curved, dorsal sepal free portion to ½ in (1 cm), triangular, tail to 1½ in (4 cm), lateral sepals broadly falcate-ovate, tails short; *M. macrura* Colombia, Ecuador; inflorescence usually equalling leaves, 1-flowered; flowers to 10 in (25 cm) across; sepals red to dull brown-yellow, with maroon warts, sepaline tube to ⅝ in (1.5 cm), cylindrical or flattened, ribbed, dorsal sepal free portion to 6 in (15 cm), lanceolate to triangular, tail long, yellow-green, lateral sepals to 5 in (12.5 cm), ovate to oblong, connate for basal 1½ in (4 cm), tails long, strongly decurved; *M. mooreana* (syn. *M. elephanticeps*); Colombia, Venezuela; inflorescence to 4 in (10 cm), 1-flowered; flowers to 3½ in (9 cm) across; sepaline tube broadly cylindrical, sepals long, tapering, forward-pointing, dorsal sepal yellow-white streaked purple at base, triangular, tail yellow, to 2 in (5 cm), lateral sepals crimson to purple, interior with black-purple papillae, triangular, tail yellow toward apex; *M. schroederiana* Peru; inflorescence to 8 in (21 cm), 1-flowered to 3 in (8 cm) across; sepaline tube short-campanulate, white, ribbed, expanding as a flattened oblong platform formed by fusion of the lateral sepals, pearly white flushed ruby red in upper portions and at dorsal sepal, tails long, yellow, lateral tails held horizontally, dorsal tails erect; *M. tovarensis* (syn. *M. candida*); Venezuela; inflorescence to 7 in (18 cm), 1–4-flowered; flowers to 1½ in (3.5 cm) across, pure white, with tails cream or pale jade; sepaline tube cylindrical, to ¼ in (6 mm), dorsal sepal free portion to 1½ × ¼ in (4 × 0.6 cm), filiform, erect, lateral sepals to 1½ × ½ in (4 × 1 cm), shaped like a lyre, connate for half of length, ribbed, tails short, often, crossing; *M. veitchiana* Peru; inflorescence to 18 in (45 cm), 1-flowered; flowers to 3 in (8 cm) across, sepal interior shining vermilion covered with many iridescent purple papillae, sepaline tube to 1¼ in (3 cm), campanulate-cylindrical, dorsal sepal free portion to 1¼ in (3 cm), triangular-ovate, tail, to 1½ in (3.5 cm), lateral sepals larger than dorsal sepal, broadly ovate or triangular, acuminate, curving downward, connate for 1¼ in (3 cm), tails short, often forward-pointing or overlapping; *M. wageneriana* Venezuela; inflorescence 1-flowered to 2 in (5 cm), slender; flowers to 2½ in (6 cm) light green-yellow or cream, orange-yellow toward base, spotted and streaked violet, sepaline tube short, dorsal sepal free portion broadly ovate-oblong, to ½ in (1 cm), concave, tail slender, to 2 in (5 cm), sharply recurved, lateral sepals similar to dorsal sepal, connate for more than half of length. For *M. bella*, see *Dracula bella*; for *M. chimaera*, see *Dracula chimaera*; for *M. erythrochaete*, see *Dracula erythrochaete*; for *M. vampira*, see *Dracula vampira*.

mat (1) the layer of dead grass and debris accumulating near soil level in turf; (2) a thick cover of fabric used to protect frames against frost; (3) a coir or chain mat used to work top-dressings into turf. See *capillary mat*.

Matteuccia (for C. Matteucci [1800–1868], Italian physicist). Dry-opteridaceae (Athyriaceae). Temperate N America, Europe, E Asia. OSTRICH FERN. 4 species, deciduous perennial ferns with erect, stout stocks and fast-spreading rhizomes. The sterile fronds are lanceolate to oblong in outline and 2–3 × pinnately compound; they stand semi-erect in shuttlecock-like rosettes. The fertile fronds are erect and smaller with darker, much-reduced pinnae. Hardy and ideal for damp situations, *Matteuccia* spreads by underground rhizomes to form colonies of fresh lime "shuttlecocks." The foliage is a delightful feature in the garden in spring but can become rather ragged late in a dry season. The fertile fronds persist throughout the following winter. Plant in moist or wet soils rich in decayed vegetable matter, in shade or dappled sun. *M. struthiopteris* can be invasive. Propagate by offsets,—these may surface at some distance from the mother plant. *M. struthiopteris* OSTRICH FERN, SHUTTLECOCK FERN; Europe, E Asia, eastern N America; usually deciduous, spreading by buried runners; sterile fronds 12–100, soft, bright green, pinnae 30–70, narrowly lanceolate, pinnatifid.

Matthiola (for Pierandrea Mattioli [1500–77], Italian physicist and botanist). Cruciferae. W Europe, C Asia, South Africa. STOCK, GILLYFLOWER. 55 species, annual or perennial herbs, occasionally subshrubs, with terminal racemes of 4-petalled flowers in summer. These are highly fragrant, especially at night, and are excellent for cutting.

Grow in sun in fertile, well-drained, neutral or slightly alkaline soil. Sow seeds of annuals in early spring under glass, at 59°F (15°C). Grow on in well-ventilated conditions at 50°F (10°C); water moderately, allowing the plants to become almost dry between waterings. Harden off and plant out after the last frost; stake tall cultivars. In areas that do not experience hot humid summers, seed may be sown *in situ* in spring. To ensure double flowers, seed stock must be from a selected race and germinated in warmth. On emergence of the first pair of leaves, the temperature is dropped to at least below 50°F (10°C). The genetic difference expressed in cotyledon color should then be quite distinct: those with yellow green or pale colored cotyledons will be double-flowered, and dark green seedlings may be discarded. With the Trisomic seven-week strains, after pricking out and growing on in the usual way, doubles should beapparent at four-leaf stage, although the difference is less obvious—the sturdier seedlings are likely to be double. Stocks of the Stockpot type, a dwarf strain grown for bedding, cutting and pot plants, exhibit notched seed leaves in double-flowered plants. For greenhouse flowers, sow from late summer in succession until midwinter, spaced 6–8 in (15–20 cm) in the greenhouse border or given a final pot size of 4–6 in (10–15 cm). Use a porous, medium-fertility, loam-based propagating mix. Maintain a temperature of about 50°F (10°C), and ventilate well. Liquid-fertilize weekly, as the roots fill their pots. Sow biennials in summer in a seedbed or lightly shaded frame; overwinter in a cold greenhouse or frost-free frame, and plant out in early spring. Provide cloche protection if overwintering outdoors in all but the mildest areas. A bacterial leaf spot, leaf rot and stem rot, canker, black root rot, club root, downy mildew and the cabbage root fly can affect stocks.

Bedding stocks

Matthiola incana Cinderella Series

Matthiola 'Giant Excelsior'

Matthiola 'Giant Imperial'

M

M. incana brompton stock; S and W Europe; woody-based biennial, 12–32 in (30–80 cm); leaves lanceolate, gray-green, hairy; flowers purple, sometimes pink or white; includes 'Annua', the fast-growing TEN-WEEK STOCK, grown as an annual; *M. longipetala* NIGHT-SCENTED STOCK; Greece to SW Asia, S Ukraine; annual, 3–20 in (8–50 cm); leaves oblong to linear, simple or pinnatisect, entire or toothed; flowers yellow, green-white or pink. *Cultivars.* Modern selections of garden stocks are available in a wide range of sizes, from the 8 in (20 cm) dwarf Stockpots to the Column types up to 3¼ ft (1 m) tall, in colors from pastel pinks to mauve-blues and carmines, and shades of yellow, copper and gold. The annuals are the largest group, and include the Ten-week and dwarf, bushy Trisomic seven-week races. Annuals fall into the following groups—(a) *Ten-week Dwarf Large-flowering*: compact, free flowering, to 12 in (30 cm), excellent for bedding purposes. (b) *Ten-week Excelsior (Column)*: of upright habit, to 32 in (80 cm), producing the single columnar densely flowered spike valued by florists; for the greenhouse or outdoors and excellent for cutting. The Pacific seed race is also of this columnar type, and better suited to outdoor cultivation. (c) *Ten-week Giant Imperial*: of bushy, branching habit, to 24 in (60 cm), with long well-shaped spikes; for cutting and bedding. (d) *Ten-week Giant Perfection*: of erect and bushy habit, to 28 in (70 cm), with long spikes of large flowers; for bedding and cutting and exhibition. (e) *Ten-week Mammoth* or *Beauty*: erect, bushy and compact, to 18 in (45 cm), producing several spikes of large flowers; for bedding, cutting and for greenhouse cultivation for winter bloom. (f) *Perpetual-flowering*, or *All the Year Round*: dwarf, vigorous plants, with large spikes of pure white flowers, excellent for cutting and pot culture. Other major divisions are Brompton stocks, erect and bushy biennials, to 18 in (45 cm), used for bedding, and Intermediate or East Lothian stocks that, treated as annuals, flower to follow on from the Ten-week stocks, and are also grown as biennials flowering in spring and early summer. Virginia stock is *Malcolmia maritima*.

mattock a short-handled tool for breaking up hard ground and grubbing up trees; similar to a pickaxe, with one side of the head pointed and the other fashioned into a broader chisel-like blade. In the *grubbing ax*, one blade is made in the same plane as the handle for use as an ax. The *grubber* or *grubbing mattock* has a broad blade at right angles to the handle, and the other blade pointed or chisel-like.

Maurandella (for Catalina Pancratia Maurandy, 18th-century Spanish botanist). Scrophulariaceae. SW US and Mexico. 1 species, *M. antirrhiniflora* (syn. *Asarina antirrhiniflora*) VIOLET TWINING SNAPDRAGON. Herbaceous, half-hardy perennial climber. Hairless, slender, multi-branched stems to 7¼ ft (2.2 m). Leaves ovate-triangular, lobed, 1–4 in (2.5–10 cm) long. Flowers singular, tubular, axillary, up to 1¾ in (4.5 cm) long with white tubes and usually violet or purple, occasionally pink lobes, similar to snapdragon; summer–fall. In temperate climates, grow under frost protection or as an annual in the open; propagated from seed or softwood cuttings in late spring.

Maurandya (for Catalina Pancratia Maurandy, 18th-century Spanish botanist). Scrophulariaceae. C US and Mexico. 2 species of twining, herbaceous, half-hardy perennials. *M. barclayana* (syn. *Asarina barclayana*) Medium-sized erect climber to 16½ ft (5 m); leaves angular to shallowly lobed, ovate, 1–1¾ in (2.5–4.5 cm) long, with heart-shaped bases. Flowers 1½–2¾ in (4–7 cm) long, white or green-tinted white tubes and white, pink or deep purple lobes. Cultivation and propagation as for *Maurandella*.

Maxillaria (from Latin *maxilla*, jaw, referring to the supposed resemblance of the column and lip to the jaws of an insect). Orchidaceae. Tropical America from West Indies and Mexico to Brazil, with 1 species in Florida. Over 600 species, evergreen, epiphytic perennial herbs. Those listed here have pseudobulbs and slender leaves. Produced in spring and summer, the flowers are solitary with petals similar to sepals but usually smaller; the lip is fleshy, concave and entire or trilobed. Cool or intermediate-growing (minimum temperature 50°F/10°C), *Maxillaria* species require an open bark mix, a brief winter rest and plentiful water, high humidity and light shade in spring and summer.

M. cucullata Mexico; flowers dingy dark brown, tepals 1–1⅕ in (25–28 mm), lanceolate, lip ⅘ in (23 mm) dark purple-red; *M. grandiflora* Ecuador, Colombia, Peru, Venezuela, Guyana; flowers nodding, milk-white, scented, fleshy, dorsal sepals 1½–1¾ in (35–45 mm), ovate to oblong, lateral sepals slightly longer and wider, petals shorter and narrower; lip to 1 in (25 mm), ovate; *M. lepidota* Venezuela, Colombia, Ecuador; tepals yellow, marked red at base, lip creamy yellow with maroon marks, sepals to 2½ in (60 mm), lanceolate, petals to 1¾ in (45 mm), curved-lanceolate, lip ¾ in (20 mm), fleshy, midlobe covered with yellow-green farina; *M. meleagris* Mexico, Guatemala, Panama; flowers scented of coconut, buff-orange, buff-olive or flesh-colored, marked with dark red, lip dark blood red, sepals ½–1¼ in (12–30 mm), elliptic, petals shorter, lip ¼–⅝ in (7–16 mm), trilobed, recurved, midlobe fleshy, tonguelike; *M. picta* Brazil; flowers large, golden yellow inside, cream-yellow outside, banded and flecked purple-brown, lip yellow-white or cream spotted red, sepals about 1¼ in (30 mm), oblong, petals slightly shorter and narrower; midlobe tongue-shaped; *M. sanderiana* Peru, Ecuador; flowers large, fleshy, tepals white flecked violet-purple, lip dull yellow with red markings, dark purple on outer surface, dorsal sepal 2½–3 in (60–75 mm), oblong to lanceolate, lateral sepals wider and longer, petals somewhat shorter, lip 1¼ in (30 mm), ovate, obscurely trilobed, margin crisped; *M. tenuifolia* Mexico to Honduras and Nicaragua; flowers with a strong coconut scent, deep red mottled with yellow toward base of tepals, lip yellow, marked dark red, sepals spreading ¾–1 in (20–25 mm), lanceolate or ovate, petals shorter, projecting forward, lip about ⅝ in (16 mm), obscurely trilobed, midlobe tongue-shaped, fleshy; *M. venusta* Colombia; flowers nodding, tepals milk-white, lip yellow with 2 red spots, margins of lateral lobes red, sepals to 3 in (75 mm), lanceolate, dorsal sepal concave, lateral sepals curved, petals slightly shorter, lip fleshy, trilobed, midlobe triangular, recurved.

maypoling the practice of supporting heavily laden branches of a fruit tree with strong ties in order to avoid breakage of limbs. Ties may be attached to the top of a pole which is lashed to the trunk of the tree or to a central stake.

central cane — supporting ties

Maypoling
A stout bamboo cane lashed to the tree's stake is used as an anchor for ties that support the fruit-laden branches of this young apple tree. Soft twine or ribbons of plastic netting can be used as the ties.

Maytenus (from Chilean vernacular name). Celastraceae. Tropical and subtropical regions. Some 255 species, evergreen shrubs or small trees. Produced in spring, the flowers are inconspicuous, but the fruits split to reveal seeds with colorful arils. *M. boaria* will tolerate temperatures to 14°F (–10°C), but needs a warm and sheltered site in sun or semishade. The soil should be well-drained, but never dry. Root semi-ripe cuttings under mist and with gentle bottom heat. *M. boaria* (syn. *M. chilensis*); MAYTEN; Chile; evergreen shrub or tree to 79 ft (24 m) with a broad, weeping crown; leaves 1–2 in (2.5–5 cm), lanceolate to narrowly elliptic, finely serrate; fruit yellow; seeds 2, aril scarlet.

maze a layout of paths with numerous alternatives, dead ends, and confusing turnings. The earliest garden mazes were two-dimensional, made up of paths cut in turf to form a knot garden. The hedge-maze, properly a labyrinth, is the later more popular concept formed with evergreens, such as box, holly or yew, designed to confuse the user, with the hedges usually trained to a height that is impossible to see over.

Mazus (from Greek *mazos*, breast, referring to the protuberances in the corolla throat). Scrophulariaceae. SE Asia, China, Taiwan, Malay Archipelago, Australasia. Some 30 species, annual or perennial herbs, usually creeping or prostrate, with tubular flowers in spring. These are 2-lipped, the upper lip shorter and hooded, the lower lip large, 3-lobed and colorfully marked in the throat. A charming dwarf groundcover for sheltered, slightly acidic positions in the rock garden, *Mazus* is hardy to 10°F (–12°C). Protect in winter with evergreen branches or overwinter stock plants in frost-free conditions. Increase by division in spring. *M. reptans* Himalaya; creeping perennial; leaves to ½ in (1 cm); flowers purple-blue, lower lip blotched white, yellow and red-purple; 'Albus': flowers white.

meadow gardening see *alpine meadow*.

meal (1) a powdered fertilizer produced by drying and grinding organic materials, such as bones or fish; it is easy to apply and the nutritional content is quickly available to plants; (2) a natural surface covering of the leaves of some plants, known as farina.

mealybugs (Hemiptera: Pseudococcidae) sap-feeding insects, up to ¼ in (5 mm) long, with soft, flesh-colored bodies fringed with fine waxy filaments and covered with a powdery white secretion known as "meal." The male mealybugs are winged and resemble very small flies, but some species have females only and reproduce by parthenogenesis. Mealybugs congregate in leaf axils, sheaths and under loose bark, covering themselves and their eggs with a fluffy, white wax, which is often the first sign of infestation. Established colonies debilitate plants and deposit honeydew on the foliage; this acts as a substrate for unsightly sooty mold growth.

ROOT MEALYBUGS seldom exceed ⅛ in (3 mm) in length and are plainly visible in pockets and dry patches in the root balls of infested plants knocked out of their pots. Poor growth followed by wilting is the most obvious symptom above the soil.

Most mealybugs are natives of tropical and subtropical regions. In temperate zones, they are mainly a problem on species grown under protection, particularly *Bougainvillea, Codiaeum, Cycas, Ficus, Gardenia, Hippeastrum, Hoya, Passiflora, Plumbago, Saintpaulia*, citrus plants, palms, and cacti and succulents. Because of their hidden feeding sites and waxy covering, mealybugs are difficult to control but approved insecticides may be applied by immersion, by the use of a drenching spray, or by direct application with a fine brush. Biological control may be achieved using a ladybug (*Cryptolaemus montrouzieri*) and/or certain parasitic wasps (*Leptomastix dactylopii, Leptomastidea abnormis* and *Anagrus pseudococci*).

meat meal, meat guano an organic fertilizer made by processing meat refuse into powdered form. Where made only from meat, it is purely nitrogenous, providing up to 10% nitrogen. The inclusion of ground bone gives an analysis of around 6% nitrogen and 20% phosphate, and also adds trace elements. Both products are relatively slow-acting. Where available they should be sterilized to eliminate pathogens, and handled with suitable precautions to avoid inhalation and other personal contact.

Meconopsis (from Greek *mekon*, poppy, and *opsis*, appearance). Papaveraceae. Himalaya to W China, W Europe. ASIATIC POPPY, BLUE POPPY. 43 species, annual, biennial or perennial herbs, often monocarpic, with hairy to bristly leaves in basal rosettes and, in spring and summer, poppylike flowers on erect, simple or branching stems.

Hardy and semi-hardy biennials and perennials which, with one exception (*M. cambrica*), are native to the Himalayas and mountains of China and Tibet. Many are monocarpic, although they may take between two and four years before flowering. They are cultivated for their beautiful nodding poppylike flowers, although the basal leaf rosettes of some species are also very handsome. These plants are ideal for the woodland garden, peat terrace and shady herbaceous border. Although tall, many are suitable for a rock garden if planted in moist crevices

M

with perfect drainage out of direct sun. They are hardy to 0°F (–18°C), but need cool, moist summers and relatively mild winters. Nearly all grow best in part shade, and this is important to ensure and preserve good flower color. They require shelter from summer heat and strong winds, and a moist but not stagnant root run in soil that is fast-draining. Even the hardiest species will rot if water accumulates around the collar. In very wet areas, protect evergreen species with open cloches or panes of glass. The exception is *M. cambrica*, which will grow in virtually any soil, in any position. Plant in spring in humus-rich, lime-free soil. Deadhead to prolong flowering and cut down perennial species in fall. Lift and divide perennial species every three years to prevent deterioration. Some, including *M. grandis*, *M. × sheldonii*, *M. quintuplinervia*, can be divided in spring or fall. All species can be seed-propagated. Sow ripe seed in late summer in equal parts peat and sand. Prick out into boxes and overwinter in a well-ventilated cool greenhouse or frame. Plants may suffer from downy mildew (*Peronospora*), which is grave at seedling stage and should be treated with appropriate fungicide. The perennial species are thought to be longer-lived if they develop several crowns before being allowed to flower—for example, *M. betonicifolia* will be monocarpic if flowered as a biennial but may flower over several seasons if raised slowly (in cool conditions) and stopped in the first two years to induce offsetting.

M. betonicifolia BLUE POPPY; China; short-lived perennial, 12–79 in (30–200 cm); leaves up to 14 in (35 cm), stalked, oblong to ovate, serrate, sparsely bristly; flowers to 6, in somewhat drooping cymes, petals to 2 in (5 cm), mauve-pink to bright sky blue; var. *alba*: white; *M. cambrica* WELSH POPPY; W Europe; perennial to 24 in (60 cm); leaves pinnately lobed, to 8 in (20 cm), glabrous to hairy; flowers solitary, in axils of upper stem leaves; petals to 1¼ in (3 cm), yellow; includes var. *aurantiaca*, with orange flowers, 'Frances Perry', with scarlet flowers, and 'Florepleno', with semi-double, yellow or orange flowers; *M. grandis* Himalaya; perennial to 48 in (120 cm); leaves to

12 in (30 cm), narrowly oblanceolate to elliptic to oblong, serrate, rusty-bristly; petals to 2½ in (6 cm), purple or deep blue; *M. horridula* Himalaya to W China; short-lived perennial, to 32 in (80 cm); leaves elliptic to narrowly obovate, to 10 × 1¼ in (25 × 3 cm), gray-green with purple or yellow warty and spiny bristles; petals to 1½ in (4 cm), cobalt blue to violet or white; *M. integrifolia* Tibet, Upper Burma, W China; short-lived perennial, to 36 in (90 cm), covered with downy, orange-red hairs; leaves entire, oblanceolate to obovate or linear, to 15½ in (37 cm), densely hairy; petals to 1¼ in (3 cm), yellow or white; *M. napaulensis* SATIN POPPY; C Nepal to SW China; perennial, to 8½ ft (2.6 m); leaves to 20 in (50 cm), pinnately cut, with dirty gold to brown or tawny hairs and bristles; petals to 1½ × 1¼ in (4 × 3 cm), red or pink to purple or blue, rarely white; *M. paniculata* E Nepal to NE Assam; short-lived perennial, to 6½ ft (2 m); leaves pinnately cut, white- to tawny-shaggy and bristly; petals to 2 in (5 cm), yellow; *M. quintuplinervia* NE Tibet, China; perennial, to 12 in (30 cm); leaves to 10 in (25 cm), golden to rusty-bristly, obovate to narrowly oblanceolate; petals to 1¼ in (3 cm), pale mauve-blue or light violet, rarely white; *M. × sheldonii* *M. betonicifolia* × *M. grandis*; leaves oblong to lanceolate, bristly, serrate; petals to 1¼ in (3 cm), blue; includes 'Slieve Donard', to 3¼ ft (1 m), with aquamarine flowers.

Medicago (from *Medike*, name given by Dioscorides to a grass). Leguminosae. Europe, Mediterranean, Africa, Asia. ALFALFA, MEDICK. 56 species, annual or perennial herbs or small shrubs with trifoliolate leaves and racemes of small, pealike flowers, usually in summer. The fruit is a legume, but often spiny and spiraling like a snail's shell. The shrubby *M. arborea* is hardy to about 14°F (–10°C). In regions at the limits of its hardiness, it requires the protection of a south wall, but is resistant to salt spray and wind. Plant in full sun in fast-draining soil. Prune out dead or weak growth in spring. Sow seed in fall or spring (stratification or scarification may improve germination); increase also by division of softwood or semi-ripe

cuttings in summer. *M. arborea* MOON TREFOIL; S Europe; gray-downy shrub 3¼–6½ ft (1–2 m); flowers ½–⅝ in (12–15 mm), yellow; fruit in spiral of 1–2 turns.

Medinilla (for J. de Medinilla de Pineda, Governor of the Marianne Islands in 1820). Melastomataceae. Tropical Africa, SE Asia, Pacific. Some 150 species, evergreen shrubs, usually with bold, leathery leaves and small flowers whorled amid large waxy bracts in showy panicles. Provide a minimum temperature of between 59 and 68°F (15 and 20°C). Grow in bright filtered light, ensuring shade from the hottest summer sun, in a fertile, open and porous medium with leaf mold and bark. Provide high humidity, syringe frequently, water plentifully and feed semiweekly when in full growth. During the winter months, water only to prevent wilting and lower temperatures slightly; this will help promote flowering. Propagate by semi-ripe cuttings in a sandy propagating mix in a humid closed case with bottom heat; pinch out young plants to encourage branching. *M. magnifica* Philippines; robust epiphytic shrub to 10 ft (3 m) branches stout, tetragonal to winged, jointed; leaves 8–12 in (20–30 cm), broadly ovate, deep glossy green; panicle to 20 in (50 cm), strongly pendulous, bracts very large, candy pink, paired, concave, flowers to 1 in (2.5 cm) in diameter, pink to coral-red.

medium a seed or potting mixture or other material in which plants may be grown or propagated.

medlar (*Mespilus germanica*) a hardy deciduous tree or shrub to 16 ft (5 m) high, grown for its small flattened apple-shaped fruits, which have a wide, open eye and horny calyces. The MEDLAR is indigenous throughout Europe and probably originated in Transcaucasia; although recorded in Ancient Greece, Rome and Asia Minor, it has never been of great horticultural importance. It is occasionally found growing wild in southern England, and was introduced by the French into North America in the 17th-century; it is sometimes found as a hedging subject in Florida.

Medlar

Medlars have limited culinary appeal, but to use the fruits, pick and store when ripe, stalk upward, in a cool dark place until the flesh turns soft and yellowish brown. The "bletted" fruits can then be made into preserves.

The MEDLAR forms a decorative tree with arching branches, large pink and white flowers, and orange-gold tinted foliage in fall. Its fruits have a characteristic flavor which only develops when they are partially decayed (bletted) after late fall harvest and storage with calyces downward, on slatted trays; they are also used to make preserves.

MEDLARS are grown as bushes or half standards; they are self fertile and have a chilling requirement of between 100–450 hours below 45°F (7°C). Trees are usually grafted onto QUINCE A rootstocks, or for half standards onto SEEDLING PEAR. Pruning and training is similar to that employed for apple.

Possible problems: *brown rot, powdery mildew.*

medulla parenchymatous tissue in the center of stems of many dicotyledonous plants. It is also called pith.

medullary consisting of pith; spongy.

Meehania (for Thomas Meehan [1826–1901], writer and nurseryman). Labiatae. Asia, N America. JAPANESE DEAD NETTLE. 6 species, creeping stoloniferous perennial herbs with toothed leaves and small, tubular and 2-lipped flowers whorled in leafy spikes in spring and summer. *Meehania* species form large patches of groundcover in dappled shade or in exposed but sun-

less areas, and are hardy to 5°F (–15°C). They flower from mid- to late summer, giving a display of lilac or blue flowers on rather untidy running stems which may form dense clumps. Propagate by rooted stolons, or by seed sown in a cold frame in spring. *M. urticifolia* Japan, NE China, Korea; hairy; 6–12 in (15–30 cm); leaves ovate to cordate, coarsely toothed; flowers 1½–2 in (4–5 cm), blue-purple, lower lip spotted dark purple.

megaspore the larger of the two types of spore produced by heterosporous plants; they develop into female gametophytes.

megasporophyll in non-flowering plants, a sporophyll bearing megaspores; in angiosperms, a carpel.

Melaleuca (from Greek *melas*, black, and *leukos*, white, in allusion to the often black trunk and white branches). Myrtaceae. Mainly Australia; also New Caledonia, New Guinea and Malaysia. PAPER BARK, HONEY MYRTLE, BOTTLE-BRUSH. Over 150 species, evergreen trees and shrubs, usually with papery bark, tough leaves dotted with aromatic oil glands and rounded, 5-petalled flowers with showy stamens. Provide a minimum temperature of 41°F (5°C), full sun and a dry, buoyant atmosphere. Plant in a fast-draining, nitrogen-poor medium. Water moderately throughout spring and summer, but only sparingly in winter. Increase by seed during spring, alternatively by semi-ripe cuttings in summer.

M. armillaris BRACELET; New South Wales, Victoria, South Australia; to 25 ft (8 m); leaves ½–1⅓ in (1.4–2.8 cm), linear or narrowly elliptic to compressed or semi-terete; inflorescence 20–70-flowered, stamens white to mauve; *M. elliptica* W Australia; to 10 ft (3 m) leaves to ¼ in (0.6 cm), opposite, ovate to suborbicular, close, leathery; inflorescence in oblong or cylindrical spikes, stamens red; *M. hypericifolia* New South Wales; to 20 ft (6 m); leaves ½–1½ in (1–4 cm), opposite, elliptic to obovate; inflorescence a many-flowered, dense axillary spike, stamens crimson-red; *M. leucadendra* RIVER TEATREE, WEEPING TEATREE, BROAD-LEAVED PAPERBARK, PAPERBARK, BROAD-LEAVED

TEATREE; N Australia, W Australia, Queensland, also in Malaysia and New Caledonia; tree to 100 ft (30 m); leaves scattered, 3–9 in (8–23 cm), narrowly ovate to elliptic, thinly leathery; inflorescence a many-flowered, open spike, stamens white; *M. nesophila* WESTERN TEA MYRTLE; W Australia; to 23 ft (7 m)+; leaves to ⅘ in (2.3 cm), alternate, obovate-oblong to oblong-cuneate; inflorescence in terminal dense heads, stamens lavender or rose-pink; *M. squarrosa* South Australia, SE Australia; to 50 ft (15 m); leaves ¼–⅝ in (0.5–1.5 cm), decussate, ovate, pointed; inflorescence a dense terminal spike, stamens white or pale yellow; *M. viridiflora* New Guinea, New Caledonia, Australia; to 80 ft (25 m); leaves 2–9 in (5–22 cm), scattered, obovate, elliptic or broadly ovate; inflorescence a many-flowered spike, stamens white, yellow, green, pink or red; var. *rubriflora*: leaves thinner, shorter, stamens red.

Melasphaerula (from Greek *melas*, black, and *sphaerula*, a Latinized diminutive of a sphere, referring to the corms). Iridaceae. South Africa. 1 species, *M. ramosa*, a perennial, cormous herb to 24 in (60 cm) with lanceolate, grasslike leaves and small, white to cream, purple-veined flowers nodding on wiry panicle branches. Cultivate as for *Ixia*.

Melastoma (from Greek *melas*, black, and *stoma*, mouth; the mouth is stained black by the berries). Melastomataceae. SE Asia. Some 70 species, evergreen shrubs with broad, distinctly veined and tough-textured leaves and 5-petalled flowers in cymes in summer. Cultivate as for *Medinilla*. *M. candidum* Taiwan and Ryukyu Islands to SE Asia and Philippines; 4–8 ft (1.2–2.5 m), hairy; flowers 2–3 in (5–8 cm) in diameter, fragrant, pink or white.

Melia (Greek name for ash). Meliaceae. Old World tropics, Australia. 5 species, deciduous or semi-evergreen trees or shrubs with pinnate or 2-pinnate leaves. The flowers appear in spring and summer in loose, axillary panicles; they consist of five to six, spreading, oblong petals with the stamens united in a tube. Drupaceous fruits follow in fall. Hardy to 10°F

M

(–12°C) or below where summers are long and hot, *M. azederach* is a rapidly growing tree, often used in its native regions for reforestation. It is valued for its dense, rounded crown and fragrant blooms; the yellow berries are toxic. It tolerates a range of well-drained soils and hot, dry conditions, self-seeding in profusion where conditions suit. Propagate by seed. *M. azederach* BEAD TREE, CHINA-BERRY, PERSIAN LILAC, PRIDE OF INDIA; N India, China; deciduous tree to 50 ft (15 m); leaves to 32 in (80 cm), leaflets to 2 in (5 cm), ovate to elliptic, serrate; flowers ¾ in (2 cm) in diameter, lilac, in panicle 4–8 in (10–20 cm) long, staminal tube violet; fruit ½–2 in (1–5 cm) in diameter, yellow; 'Umbraculiformis': TEXAS UMBRELLA TREE, branches radiating in a spreading head.

Melianthus (from Greek *meli*, honey, and *anthos*, flower—the calyces are filled with nectar). Melianthaceae. South Africa; *M. major* naturalized in India. 6 species, shrubs with robust,

Melianthus major
Although *M. major* must be lifted and protected over winter in frost-prone areas, it grows vigorously once planted out, making a superb foliage plant over a single season.

sparsely branched stems, often following a semi-herbaceous habit in colder locations, otherwise evergreen, becoming woody, especially the basal portions, and scented in all parts. The leaves are pinnately compound with winged petioles, conspicuous stipules and large, jaggedly toothed leaflets. Tubular, hooded and richly nectariferous flowers are borne in erect racemes in

summer. *M. major* is a magnificent plant grown for its blue-green, architectural foliage in sheltered locations (min. temp. 0°F/–18°C). It is also used as a temporary dot plant in bedding schemes, overwintered in a cold greenhouse. Grow in full sun or light shade in moisture-retentive but freely draining soils; fertile soils give good foliage effects, although flowering is better on poor soils. Mulch with a thick layer of coir or bracken litter in fall in areas where frosts are prolonged—the top growth will be cut back by frost, but the base will resprout in spring. When siting young plants, bury the older, slightly woody stem portion to protect the rootstock and promote offsetting. Propagate by seed in spring, by greenwood stem tip cuttings in summer, or by removal of rooted suckers in spring. Red spider mite may be a problem under glass. *M. major* HONEY BUSH; to 7½ ft (2.25 m); stem sea-green and thickly glaucous at first, becoming woody below; leaves to 20 in (50 cm), glaucous, sea green to gray-blue, leaflets 2–5 in (5–13 cm), 9–11, ovate-oblong, coarsely serrate; raceme to 32 in (80 cm), flowers brown-red.

Melica (from *melike*, the Greek name for a grass). Gramineae. Temperate regions (except Australia). MELICK. 70 species, perennial grasses with clumped culms, linear to lanceolate leaves and small but ornamental spikelets hanging from the delicate branches of slender, arching panicles in spring and summer. These are followed by ricelike grains, pearly in most species but jetlike in *M. altissima* 'Atropurpurea'. Hardy to –10°F (–23°C). Grow in sun or shade in light, moisture-retentive, loamy soil. Most species perform well on calcareous soils. Propagate by seed or division. *M. altissima* SIBERIAN MELICK; C and E Europe; to 60 in (150 cm); leaf blades to 10 in (25 cm), scabrous; panicle erect, 1-sided, dense, to 10 × 1 in (25 × 2.5 cm); spikelets oblong, to ½ in (1 cm); includes 'Alba', with very pale green spikelets, and 'Atropurpurea', with deep purple-black spikelets, sweeping downward and overlapping.

Melicytus (from Greek *meli*, honey, and *kytos*, a hollow vessel, referring to

the staminal nectaries). Violaceae. New Zealand, Norfolk Island, Fiji, Solomon Islands. 4 species, dioecious shrubs or trees with small flowers and showy berries. Hardy to about 23°F (–5°) given wall protection and shelter from cold drying winds. Grow outdoors or in a cool, well-ventilated greenhouse, in a moderately fertile, loam-based mix, with direct sun or bright filtered light. Water moderately when in growth, sparingly in winter. Propagate by seed sown when ripe or in spring. *M. ramiflorus* WHITEY WOOD; tree, to 33 ft (10 m)+; bark gray-white; leaves to 6 in (15 cm), toothed; flowers to ⅛ in (4 mm) in diameter, yellow-green; fruit glossy, lavender to violet, dark blue or purple.

Meliosma (from Greek *meli*, honey, and *osme*, scent, alluding to the honey-scented flowers). Sabiaceae. Tropical America, tropical and temperate Asia. 25 species, deciduous or evergreen trees or shrubs with pinnate leaves and small, starry and fragrant flowers in large, pyramidal panicles in spring and summer. Hardy to 0°F (–18°C). Grow in sun in deep, moisture-retentive, moderately fertile, circumneutral soils. Propagate by seed or layers, alternatively from softwood cuttings under mist.

M. pinnata (syn. *M. oldhamii*); Korea, China; deciduous, 66–130 ft (20–40 m); leaves 6¾–14 in (17.5–35 cm), leaflets 5–13, lowermost 1 × ¾ in (2.5 × 2 cm), orbicular to obovate, terminal leaflet 3–5½ in (7.5–14 cm), dentate, pubescent above when young; panicle 6–12 in (15–30 cm); flowers pure white; *M. veitchiorum* W China; deciduous to 165 ft (50 m); leaves 18–30 in (45–75 cm), leaflets 3¼–6¾ in (8.5–17.5 cm), 7–9, ovate or oblong, entire or sparsely toothed, midrib pubescent beneath; panicle to 18 in (45 cm); flowers cream-white.

Melittis (from Greek *melissa* or *melitta*, bee: the plant is attractive to bees). Labiatae. BASTARD BALM. Western central and southern Europe to Ukraine. 1 species, *M. melissophyllum*, a perennial herb to 20 in (50 cm) with erect, hairy stems. The leaves are oval, to 3 in (8 cm), crenate, hispid, and honey-scented when fresh. Tubular and 2-lipped, the flowers are white, pink, or purple or with a large purple blotch on the lower lip. They appear in whorls in early summer. Found in open woodlands, *Melittis* is useful for the front of an herbaceous border and for an herb garden. Plant in moisture-retentive soil with added leaf mold, preferably in light, woodland shade. Propagate by division in spring. When dried, *Melittis* retains its fragrance for a long time.

Melocactus (from Latin *melo*, melon, and *cactus*, referring to the shape). Cactaceae. Tropical America. About 30 species, cacti with globose, strongly ribbed, and spiny stems. The flowers are small, tubular, red to pink, and sunken in a woolly apical cephalium. The fruit is a juicy berry, usually clavate and red, pink, or white. Grow in full sun with low humidity and a minimum temperature of 50°F (10°C). Plant in a gritty, acidic medium. Water very sparingly in winter (i.e. only to avoid shrivelling). Increase by seed or offsets.

M. bahiensis E Brazil; stem 3¾–8 (9.5–21 cm) × 4½–8 in (11–21 cm), depressed-globose to conic; ribs 8–14, acute to rounded; central spines 1–4, ¾–2 in (1.7–5 cm), radial spines 7–12, ¾–2½ in (2–6 cm); fruit red to crimson; *M. curvispinus* (syn. *M. oaxacensis*); widespread in C and S America, Cuba; stem 2½–12 (6–30 cm) × 3–11 in (8–27 cm), depressed-globose, globose or ovoid; ribs 10–16, acute; central spines 1–5, to 1 in (5.2 cm), radial spines 7–11(–15), ⅝–1½ in (1.6–4.2 cm), curved, rarely straight; fruit bright red; *M. intortus* (syn. *M. communis*); West Indies; stem to 24(–36) × 12 in (60(–90) × 30 cm), globose to tapered-cylindric; ribs (9–) 14–27, rounded, thick; central spines 1–3, radial spines 10–14, ¾–2¾ in (2–7 cm), stout, straight; cephalium growing tall; fruit pink to red); *M. matanzanus* (N Cuba; resembling *M. violaceus* and *M. neryi*, but with 8–9 ribs and a cephalium with dense orange-red bristles; *M. neryi* Venezuela to N Brazil; resembling *M. violaceus*, but with a dark blue-green stem and curved, sometimes longer spines; *M. violaceus* E Brazil; stem 16–60 ft (5–18 m) × 20–56 ft (6–17 m), depressed-globose to subpyramidal; ribs 8–15, acute; central spine 0–1, ascending, shorter than radials, radials 5–9(–11), to ½ in–1 in (1–2.4 cm), straight; fruit pink or white.

Greenhouse melon
To hold the weight of melons on vines trained vertically, the net must be attached to the supporting wires, not to the plant's stem.

melon, sweet (*Cucumis melo* subsp. *melo*) an annual, prostrate herb grown for its edible fruits, which are usually consumed fresh. Assumed to have originated in Africa, melons were known to the Romans, and in the 15th century were brought from Turkish Armenia to the papal estate of Cantaluppe near Rome, and distributed from there to the rest of the Mediterranean area, western Europe, and on to North America by Columbus on his second voyage.

Melons are a warm-season crop and, according to cultivar, need 85–125 days without frost from sowing to when the fruits reach maturity. In colder climates, with a shorter frost-free period, melons need protection for all or part of the growing season: they take 3–4 months to reach maturity, and warm dry conditions are essential for ripening.

There are many cultivars, grouped according to fruit character. The Cantalupensis group, the cantaloupes, including Charentais types, have ovoid or round fruits with a ridged rind; they include the well-known 'Ogen'. The Reticulatus group, the musk melons, have net markings on the rind, orange flesh and are widely grown in the US, in the Mediterranean area and under glass in the north. The Inodorus group, winter melons, includes honeydew melons with a harder rind which facilitates longer storage.

Cultivars either have all male or all female flowers on the same plant or they may have male and hermaphrodite flowers on the same plant, as is the case with most American cultivars. Assisted pollination is recommended on a garden scale (see *marrow*).

The most suitable soil is a well-drained fertile loam (pH 5.5–7.0), with a minimum depth of 16 in (40 cm). Where grown outdoors, soil preparation is started in the fall before planting, with organic manure thoroughly incorporated to maintain soil structure and improve moisture retention. In some areas, melons are grown on ridges. Before sowing in rows or ridges, the planting site may be covered with a plastic mulch to raise soil temperature.

Plants are best raised in pots under protection for transplanting when two or three true leaves have formed, after hardening off and when risk of frost has passed. They may also be direct-sown outdoors, up to 1½ in (3.7 cm) deep. Plants should be spaced 24 in–3¼ ft (0.6–1.0 m) apart in rows on flat ground, or 4–6½ ft (1.2–2.0 m) apart on ridges. The minimum soil temperature for germination is 59°F (15°C) and the optimum for seedling growth about 86°F (30°C). In cooler climates, young plants grown outdoors may be protected by glass cloches, translucent paper or low polyethylene-clad tunnels.

Water demand is high when the plants are growing fast and fruits are swelling, but should be reduced just before the fruits start to mature; trickle or seep-hose irrigation is the most efficient system. Fruits that are allowed to ripen develop the best flavor and picking should be carried out at regular intervals. In most musk melon cultivars, fruit is ready for picking when it separates easily from the stem; in cantaloupes, ripeness is indicated by a change in rind color or, in certain cultivars, by the development of scent and fine circular cracks at the base of the stem. Melons can only be stored for relatively short periods. Musk melons can be kept for 6–12 days at 37–39°F (3–4°C) (relative humidity 85–90%), and honeydew melons for 14–90 days at 50–60°F (10–15°C).

In greenhouses, melons may be grown in beds or in raised troughs and boxes (12 in (30 cm) deep, 18 in (46 cm) wide) in a loam soil rendered highly fertile with well-rotted manure.

M

The usual time for sowing is spring. Seeds are sown singly in pots or in soil blocks at a temperature of 61–64°F (16–18°C); after seedlings have emerged, the temperature is reduced to 55–59°F (13–15°C). When true leaves appear, melons are transplanted into a greenhouse bed, 18–24 in (45–60 cm) apart, along the side walls. When about 4–6 in (10–15 cm) tall, the growing point is pinched out, stimulating the production of two shoots to be trained up wires on the side walls. A temperature of 61–81°F (16–27°C) is maintained, and ventilation provided when the temperature rises above this. When each shoot has produced five leaves, the growing tip is again removed to stimulate side shoots, on which the flowers are produced. When three leaves are produced on each of these side shoots, the tips are pinched out. Six to eight flowers are selected per plant and hand-pollinated; once set, four fruits of uniform size are selected (not more than one per lateral) for growing on, and the others removed.

Plants should be kept well-watered, and given a weekly liquid fertilizer from the stage when the fruits are about the size of a walnut. Stop the fruit-bearing laterals at the first joint beyond the fruit when it begins to swell. As the fruits grow, support with nets tied to the wires. Leaves and laterals are thinned out as necessary. When the fruit has reached full size, humidity levels are lowered for ripening, feeding is stopped, and watering is reduced so that the medium is kept just moist enough to avoid rind splitting.

For early crops grown on hot beds in frames, the growing medium must be of sufficient depth to maintain a temperature of about 64°F (18°C). Two plants should be positioned in the center of each frame, and two shoots from each led to the corners of the frame. When each shoot has produced 6–8 leaves, the growing tips must be cut back to four leaves. The side shoots thus stimulated are next stopped at three leaves, and the flowers hand-pollinated, eventually allowing two fruits to develop per plant for main crops, and one fruit per plant for early and late crops. A flat stone may be placed under each fruit to keep it clean and to aid uniform ripening.

Possible problems: collar rot, gray mold, root rot, virus.

membranous (membraneous), membranaceous thin-textured, soft and flexible.

Menispermum (from Latin *menis*, a tiny half-moon-like device inscribed at the opening of books, and *spermum*, seed, referring to the shape of the seed). Menispermaceae. Eastern N America, E Asia. MOONSEED. 2 species, woody-based, dioecious twiners with slender stems and rounded, obscurely lobed leaves. Inconspicuous, yellow-green flowers are borne in axillary, stalked racemes or panicles in summer. When plants of both sexes are grown together, the female bears small dark berries, toxic and hanging in grapelike bunches. Hardy to 14°F (–10°C); plants will resprout from the base in spring if cut down. Grow in partial shade or full sun in moist moderately fertile soil. Provide trellis, fence or tree support. Propagate by seed, by the removal of rooted suckers, or by ripewood cuttings in the cold frame or cool greenhouse in fall. *M. canadense* CANADA MOONSEED; eastern N America; stem to 20 ft (6 m); leaves 2–8 in (5–20 cm), ovate to cordate or rounded, entire or obscurely 5–7-lobed, dark green above, paler beneath; fruit pruinose purple-red to blue-black.

Mentha (the classical Latin name, from Greek *minthe*). Labiatae. Eurasia, Africa. MINT. 25 species, aromatic herbaceous perennials or, occasionally, annuals with creeping rhizomes and small, 2-lipped, tubular or campanulate flowers in dense whorls. Nearly all mints are invasive creeping plants. They are grown for their aromatic foliage and have long been cultivated for their culinary, antiseptic and aromatic qualities. They will tolerate a wide range of soils and habitats, thriving in hot, well-drained places where plenty of moisture is available to them. Commonly grown for culinary use are spearmint (*M. spicata*) and

applemint (*M. suaveolens*), also *M.* × *villosa*. See **mint**. These and all others listed here are hardy, except the slightly tender *M. requienii*, a tiny mat-forming plant requiring cool, damp shade. Propagate by division in early spring.

M. aquatica WATERMINT; Eurasia; subglabrous to tomentose perennial; stem 6–36 in (15–90 cm), often red-purple; leaves ¾–2½ in (2–6 cm), ovate to ovate-lanceolate, serrate; flowers lilac in terminal heads comprising 2–3 verticillasters; *M.* × *gracilis* (*M. arvensis* × *M. spicata*); GINGERMINT, RED-MINT; N Europe, including Great Britain, widely cultivated; variable perennial, 12–36 in (30–90 cm); stems erect, usually glabrous, often tinged red; leaves 1¼–2¾ in (3–7 cm), ovate to lanceolate, oblong or elliptic, entire or remotely serrate, glabrous or sparsely pubescent; flowers lilac in distant verticillasters; includes 'Aurea', to 12 in (30 cm), with gold, strongly fragrant leaves, and 'Variegata', with leaves flecked gold, with a fruity scent and ginger flavor; *M.* × *piperita* (*M. aquatica* × *M. spicata*); PEPPERMINT; Europe; perennial, 12–36 in (30–90 cm), usually glabrous, often tinged red-purple; leaves 1½–3½ in (4–9 cm), ovate to lanceolate, petiolate, serrate, apex acute, usually glabrous or thinly hairy; flowers lilac-pink in congested verticillasters forming a terminal oblong spike; cultivars include 'Candymint', with sweetly fragrant leaves; 'Citrata', LEMON MINT, with lemon-scented leaves; 'Crispa', with crinkled leaves; 'Lime Mint', with leaves scented of lime; and 'Variegata', with leaves deep green mottled cream with a peppermint flavor; *M. pulegium* PENNYROYAL; SW and central Europe to Great Britain; glabrous to tomentose perennial, 4–16 in (10–40 cm); stem procumbent or upright; leaves ¼–1¼ in (5–30 mm), narrowly elliptic to oval entire or toothed, usually glabrous above, pubescent beneath; flowers lilac in distant verticillasters; 'Cunningham Mint': low, with oval, light green leaves; *M. requienii* CORSICAN MINT; Corsica, Italy, Sardinia; glabrous or sparsely hairy procumbent perennial;

whorls of flowers

Mentha pulegium

stems 1¼–4 in (3–10 cm), threadlike, creeping, forming cushions or mats; leaves ¹⁄₁₆–¼ in (2–7 mm), ovate orbicular, entire or sinuate; flowers lilac; *M. spicata* SPEARMINT; S and C Europe; perennial, 12–39 in (30–100 cm); leaves 2–3½ in (5–9 cm), lanceolate to ovate, smooth or rugose, serrate, glabrous to hairy; flowers lilac, pink or white in cylindrical spikes; includes 'Chewing Gum', with deep mahogany leaves scented of bubble gum, 'Crispa', with strongly curled leaves, and 'Kentucky Colonel', with large, ruffled, richly scented leaves; *M. suaveolens* APPLE MINT; S and W Europe; perennial, 16–39 in (40–100 cm); stem white-tomentose, apple-scented; leaves 1¼–1¾ in (3–4.5 cm), rugose, downy, serrate; flowers white or pink in congested verticillasters forming a terminal spike 1½–3½ in (4–9 cm), often interrupted and branched; often found under the name of *M. rotundifolia*; 'Variegata': PINEAPPLE MINT: leaves streaked white, with a pineapple arom; *M. × villosa* (*M. spicata* × *M. suaveolens*); garden origin; a variable hybrid; leaves 1½–3 in (4–8 cm), broadly ovate or orbicular, softly hairy, serrate; flowers pink.

mentum a chinlike extension of the flower, formed by the association of the bases of the lateral sepals with the foot of the column in many orchids.

Menyanthes (possibly derived from *menanthos*, "moonflower," a name used by Theophrastus for a plant growing on lake Orchomenos, or a reference to the month-long flowering period of this plant). Menyanthaceae. BOG BEAN, MARSH TREFOIL, BUCK BEAN. 1 species, *M. trifoliata*, a perennial aquatic or marginal herb, often rooting at water margins and with rhizomes spreading across the water surface. The leaves are glabrous and trifoliolate with oblong to obovate leaflets. Produced in spring and summer in erect racemes to 8 in (20 cm) tall, the flowers are some 1 in (2.5 cm) across, white flushed pink, with five, heavily fringed and bearded petals. *M. trifoliata* is hardy. Plant in submerged pots and baskets in ponds or establish at the margins where the rhizomes can spread freely across the water surface. Increase by division.

Menziesia (for Archibald Menzies [1754–1842], naval surgeon and botanist). Ericaceae. US, E Asia. 7 species, deciduous shrubs with drooping, bell- to urn-shaped flowers in terminal umbels or racemes. Hardy to –4°F (–20°C). Grow in dappled shade in moist but free-draining soil that is lime-free and humus-rich; maintain an acidic organic mulch and protect from cold dry winds and late frosts. Remove fading flower heads, but prune only to remove dead-wood after flowering. *Menziesia* blooms on the previous season's wood. Propagate from greenwood cuttings in summer in a closed case with bottom heat, or from seed sown in fall at about 55°F (13°C). *M. ciliicalyx* Japan; erect shrub, 12 in –3¼ ft (30 cm–1 m); flowers to ¾ in (1.7 cm), yellow or green-white, purple-tipped, tubular to urceolate, white downy inside, lobes 4 or 5, small; var. *multiflora*: flowers many, purple-tinted; van *purpurea*: flowers purple.

Merendera (from *quita meriendas*, Spanish for Colchicum.) Liliaceae (Colchicaceae). Mediterranean, N Africa, W Asia, outliers in Middle East and NE Africa. Some 10 species, perennial, cormous herbs with linear to lanceolate leaves partially developed at flowering. Produced in fall, the stalkless flowers are funnelform to spreading with six linear to narrowly obovate tepals. Hardy outdoors to 0°F (–18°C), but perhaps more safely grown in a bulb frame or in pans in an alpine house where the flowers and dormant bulbs can be protected from rain. Grow in full sun in gritty soil. Propagate by seed and offsets.

M. montana (syn. *M. bulbocodium*); Iberian Peninsula, central Pyrenees; flowers pale magenta to rosy purple, tepals to 10¼ × ⅛–½ in (26 × 3–11 mm), narrowly elliptic to narrow oblong-oblanceolate; *M. robusta* C Iran, S Russia, N India; flowers deep pink to pale lilac or white, fragrant, tepals ¾–½ × ¹⁄₁₆–⅜ in (18–14 × 2–9 mm), oblong to narrowly elliptic.

mericarp a one-seeded carpel; one of a pair split apart at maturity from a syncarpous or schizocarpous ovary.

mericlone a clone produced by meristem culture.

meristem undifferentiated plant tissue found at sites of active cell division and from which new cells are produced.

meristem culture a form of micropropagation using meristematic tissue. It is valuable for the production of virus-free plants.

-merous a suffix denoting number and disposition of parts; often combined simply with an arabic number, thus a 3-merous or trimerous flower has parts arranged in threes.

Merremia (for German naturalist Blasius Merrem [d. 1824]). Convolvulaceae. Pantropical. 600 species, perennial, herbaceous or woody climbers similar to *Ipomoea*, with showy, campanulate or funnel-shaped flowers. Cultivation requirements are as for the tender, perennial species of *Ipomoea*, although *Merremia* is tolerant of full sun and thrives in fairly dry situations. Maintain a minimum winter temperature of 45°F (7°C), and water very sparingly at this time. *M. tuberosa* SPANISH WOODBINE, YELLOW MORNING GLORY, WOOD ROSE; Mexico to tropical S America, introduced in many other tropical regions; woody, tuberous climber to 65 ft (20 m); leaves to 6 in (15 cm), 7-lobed; flowers 2–2½ in (5–6 cm), campanulate, bright yellow.

Mertensia (for Francis Karl Mertens, [1764–1831], Professor of Botany, Bremen). Boraginaceae. Northern temperate regions. Some 50 species, perennial herbs with tubular to campanulate, 5-lobed flowers nodding in scorpioid cymes in spring. *M. echioides* is suited to cool, moisture-retentive places in the rock garden; plant in light, neutral to slightly acidic soils with good light but shade from hot sun. *M. maritima* and *M. simplicissima* thrive in sun on nutritionally poor, gravelly or sandy soils and are best-suited to maritime gardens or perfectly drained sites in the dry and silver garden. From moist woodland, *M. pulmonarioides* prefers deep, moist but well-drained soils rich in organic matter. It is well-suited to naturalizing in open woodland in shade or semi-shade. Its foliage dies back in summer. All are hardy to at least 5°F (−15°C). Propagate from seed sown ripe in the cold frame. Increase also by careful division in early fall or spring; *M. maritima* and allies resent root disturbance and are more reliably propagated by seed.

M. echioides Pakistan, Kashmir, Tibet; stem to 12 in (30 cm), erect or decumbent, pubescent; leaves to 3½ in (9 cm), lanceolate to elliptic; flowers deep blue to blue-purple; *M. maritima* OYSTER PLANT; Alaska to Massachusetts, Greenland, Eurasia; stem to 39 in (100 cm), decumbent or spreading; leaves to 4 in (10 cm), fleshy, spathulate to oblong-ovate, glaucous sea green; flowers pink becoming blue; similar but superior to this species is *M.simplicissima*, syn. *M. asiatica*, a sprawling herb with thinly fleshy silver-blue chalky leaves and small blue flowers; *M. virginica* (syn. *M. pulmonarioides*); VIRGINIA BLUEBELLS, VIRGINIA COWSLIP, BLUEBELLS, ROANOKE BELLS; N America; stem to 28 in (70 cm), erect; leaves to 8 in (20 cm), elliptic to ovate, soft blue-green; flowers blue, sometimes pink or white; includes 'Alba', with white flowers, and 'Rubra', with pink flowers.

Meryta (from an artificial Greek word *merytos*, meaning growing together—the male flowers in some species form a knob or head). Araliaceae. Pacific Islands (Micronesia through Vanuatu to New Zealand and SE Polynesia). 250 species, small to medium evergreen trees with large and leathery, spirally arranged leaves, inconspicuous, umbellate flowers in compound inflorescences and small drupes. Provide a minimum temperature of 50°F (10°C). Plant in beds or large tubs in a medium fertility, loam-based mix with additional organic matter. Give strong, filtered to indirect light and water moderately. Propagate from seed in fall, by semi-ripe cuttings rooted with bottom heat, or by air layering. *M. sinclairii* PUKA; New Zealand; round-headed tree to 25 ft (8 m); leaves oblong to obovate, to 20 in (50 cm); inflorescence to 18 in (45 cm); flowers green-white, in dense umbels; fruit black, fleshy, to ½ in (13 mm).

mesh pot a plastic pot with sides consisting mainly of large rectangular perforations, used in orchid culture.

mesocarp the middle layer of a pericarp, often fleshy, occasionally fibrous, rarely membranaceous or spongy.

mesophyte a plant that grows in a habitat where the soil is not continuously waterlogged and where extreme drought is not regularly experienced.

Mespilus (the Latin name for this fruit). Rosaceae. Europe, Asia Minor. MEDLAR. 1 species, *M. germanica*, a deciduous tree or shrub, to 16 ft (5 m), usually shorter. The bark is gray-brown and fissured to flaking, the branches arching and divaricate. To 4¾ in (12 cm) long, the oblong to lanceolate leaves are dull green above, tomentose beneath, with serrate margins. They turn yellow, amber and rusty brown in fall. To 2 in (5 cm) wide, the white flowers are usually solitary with 5, rounded petals and numerous stamens. The fruit is turbinate, to 1 in (2.5 cm), brown when ripe, and crowned with 5 narrow calyx lobes around the transecting ends of the bony seed vessels. See *medlar*.

metamorphosis the change in appearance, life style, and/or feeding habits that distinguishes the juvenile and adult forms of insects and amphibians, such as frogs. It may be radical (complete metamorphosis) or slight (incomplete metamorphosis).

Metasequoia (from Greek *meta*, with or beside (i.e. 'related to'), and *Sequoia*). Cupressaceae. W China (E Sichuan, W Hubei). 1 species, *M. glyptostroboides*, DAWN REDWOOD, a deciduous conifer, fast-growing, to 150 ft (45 m)+. The bole is up to 6½ ft (2 m) in diameter, deeply ridged and buttressed at base with fox red, furrowed and fibrous bark flaking in long shreds. The crown is conic, becoming columnar. Bright green, linear-oblong leaves to 1½ in (4 cm) long are borne in two ranks on the feathery shoots; they turn yellow, red and finally rusty brown in fall. Hardy. Avoid dry sites and frost pockets where first growth will be scorched. Like *Taxodium*, it can be planted beside or even in shallow standing water. Warm summers are needed for good growth. Pruning basal branches is said to decrease irregularities in the trunk,

although for some, these flutes, ridges and pockets lend the tree its unique character.

Metrosideros (from Greek *metra*, middle, and *sideros*, iron, in reference to the hard wood of the genus). Myrtaceae. South Africa, Malaysia, Australasia, Pacific Islands. 50 species, aromatic evergreen shrubs, trees or woody climbers with tough foliage. The flowers are showy with five, spreading petals and a central boss of long, colorful stamens. In favored maritime climates that are frost-free or almost so, they make beautiful specimens and may also be used as hedging. Blooming even when young, they are excellent shrubs for large pots and tubs in a cool greenhouse or conservatory in cooler temperate zones, and may be moved outdoors for the summer months. Plant in a free-draining but moisture-retentive, medium- to high-fertility potting mix with additional leaf mold. Water plentifully when in growth, less at other times. Under glass, provide a winter minimum temperature of 45°F (7°C), protect from the hottest summer sun and maintain good ventilation with moderate humidity. Prune immediately after flowering to restrict size and to remove old weak and overcrowded growths. Propagate by seed sown in spring, or root semi-ripe cuttings in summer in a heated case.

M. diffusa SMALL RATA VINE; New Zealand; slender liane to 20 ft (6 m)+; leaves ¼–⅜ in (7–8 mm), oblong to ovate-lanceolate, somewhat downy when young; flowers white to pink with white to pink stamens; *M. excelsa* CHRISTMAS TREE, POHUTUKAWA; New Zealand; tree to 65 ft (20 m); leaves 2–4 in (5–10 cm), elliptic to oblong, coriaceous, thick, white-tomentose beneath; flowers crimson with crimson stamens; *M. perforata* FLOWERY RATA VINE; New Zealand; liane to 50 ft (15 m)+; leaves ¼–½ in (6–12 mm), broadly ovate to oblong or rounded, glabrous above, pale beneath and more or less bristly; flowers white or pink with white or pink stamens; *M. robusta* NORTHERN RATA; New Zealand; tree to 80 ft (25 m)+; leaves 1–2 in (2.5–5 cm), elliptic to ovate-oblong, glabrous, coriaceous; flowers red with red stamens.

mice small, widely distributed mammals that damage bulbs and corms, especially lilies, crocuses and tulips, and dig up and eat seeds, particularly peas and beans. The main culprit is the WOOD- or LONG-TAILED FIELD MOUSE (*Apodemus sylvaticus*), which measures up to 4 in (100 mm) from nose to base of tail, which is about as long again. Adults are brown with white underparts and have relatively large ears. They live in burrows in hedgerows, fields and banks, and, especially in winter, they may enter greenhouses and other buildings. Spring traps, baited with carrot, apple or chocolate and set during fall or early winter, help to control mice before damage occurs. Seedbeds and bulbs may be protected with ½ in (10 mm)-mesh netting. Bulbs and corms are more vulnerable when newly planted. Pesticide-treated seeds are unpalatable to mice, but such treatment is subject to local pesticide approvals. Mouse poisons are effective, but special care must be taken to prevent other animals from gaining access to them.

Michelia (for P.A. Michel [1679–1737], Florentine botanist). Magnoliaceae. SE Asia, India, Sri Lanka. Some 45 species, evergreen or deciduous shrubs or trees, resembling *Magnolia* but with axillary flowers. *Michelia* species thrive best in frost-free gardens (although *M. doltsopa* and *M. figo* have survived outdoors in sheltered situations in southern Britain). Elsewhere, grow in a cool greenhouse or conservatory. Plant in humus-rich, well-drained, neutral to alkaline soils, in direct light or partial shade. Water pot-grown specimens plentifully during the growing season, but only sparingly in winter. Prune only if necessary to restrict growth. Propagate from seed sown ripe during fall or spring, or by greenwood cuttings in summer, either under mist or with bottom heat in a closed case.

M. doltsopa SW China, E Himalaya, E Tibet; tree, to 40 ft (12 m); leaves to 7 in (18 cm), oblong to lanceolate, glossy above, gray-silky beneath; flowers to 2 × 1½ in (5 × 4 cm), ovoid to globose, fragrant, white; *M. figo* BANANA SHRUB; China; evergreen shrub to 14¾ ft (4.5 m), densely branched; leaves 2–4 in (5–10 cm), elliptic to oblong, dark green; flowers to 1¼ in (3 cm) in diameter, cupulate, scented of banana, ivory tinged yellow, base and margins tinged rose to purple.

Microbiota (from Greek *mikros*, small, and *Biota*, a synonym of *Platycladus*, which is the closest ally of this conifer). Cupressaceae. SE Siberia. 1 species, *M. decussata*, an evergreen, spreading, semi-prostrate coniferous shrub, 16(–28) in (40(–70) cm) high, and to 6½ ft (2 m) or more across. The leaves of *Microbiota* are small, subulate or scalelike; pale green at first, they become bronzed red or purple to dull gold in hard winters; they overlap on flat sprays. A valuable prostrate evergreen for rockeries and dwarf conifer collections, *Microbiota* is exceedingly hardy and site-tolerant. Increase by cuttings.

Microclimate
Almost every garden will have its own microclimates; this brick wall gives shelter to tall-stemmed perennials and reflects heat.

microclimate the environmental conditions of a specific locality or garden area, which may work to the advantage or disadvantage of cultivated plants. Conditions within a particular geographical area may be affected by topographical features, such as high ground, or in a garden by hedge planting or the construction of water features, raised beds or a greenhouse. Wind, rainfall, and soil and air temperature may thus be different compared to the conditions prevailing outside of the defined area.

Micromeria (from Greek *mikros*, small, and *meris*, part, referring to the usually very small flowers). Labiatae. Mediterranean, Caucasus, SW China. Some 70 species, perennial, rarely annual, herbs or dwarf shrubs, often aromatic and bearing spikes of whorled, 2-lipped, tubular flowers in summer. Hardy and suitable for rock gardens on open, sunny sites and in poor, well-drained soils. Propagate by softwood or semi-ripe heel cuttings in spring and summer. *M. juliana* SAVORY; Mediterranean; dwarf, downy shrub, to 16 in (40 cm); leaves to ½ in (1.3 cm), (ovate to narrowly lanceolate, revolute; flowers to ⅛ in (4 mm), purple.

micronutrients see *nutrients* and *plant nutrition*.

micropropagation the propagation of plants from the culture of very small portions of tissue grown *in vitro* (literally 'in glass'), under aseptic conditions, in a specially-formulated gelatinous or liquid medium.

Micropropagation, sometimes referred to by horticulturists as tissue culture, evolved from techniques conceived by research biologists in the early part of the 20th century as a means of studying the functioning and development of tissues, and ultimately cells, separately from the whole organism. The technology was first used horticulturally in the 1920s for the germination of orchid seeds; the method still forms the basis of seed-raising in the orchid industry.

The discovery that small pieces of tissue from shoot tips, approaching a meristem in size, are often free of virus infection led to the use of meristem culture for the production of virus-free individual plants, an important benefit of micropropagation. Development work on this process, including the modification of the medium in which these plantlets were grown *in vitro*, principally by the addition of plant-growth regulators, showed that axillary buds could be stimulated to give multiple-shoot plantlets. Such multiple shoots could then be divided and transferred to a fresh medium at regular intervals to achieve the rapid multiplication in plant material that is characteristic of micropropagation.

M

Micropropagation is used in horticulture for the production of a wide range of ornamental, fruit and vegetable crops, and also as a means of rescuing rare and endangered species. Variations of the technique are used to assist in plant-breeding procedures, and as a way to introduce new cultivars rapidly.

There are a number of routes to *in vitro* micropropagation, depending on species. Plantlets are commonly established from meristems or shoot tips, but leaf or stem tissue, bulb scales or even anthers and pollen are also used. Natural or artificially-induced callus tissue can be a source of shoot development, either directly or following procedures for the separation of cells. Choosing the most appropriate method of micropropagation requires a clear objective and good knowledge of the plant to be propagated.

An essential consideration for success is freedom from contamination by microorganisms, which can arise on or within the mother plant or from any part of the working environment. Plant material used for micropropagation is subjected to prescribed steps of sterilization involving washing and immersion; the growing medium, glassware and operating instruments are sterilized most effectively with the aid of an autoclave. The sterilization of plant tissue and all micropropagation operations must be carried out in a sterile environment, created by means of a laminar flow cabinet in which a non-turbulent airstream, filtered to remove contaminants, is created across the working area.

The growing medium must supply all the plant tissues' requirements for nutrients and moisture to sustain growth and development *in vitro*. Variations in nutrient levels and pH have been developed to suit particular groups of plants. In most cases, plant tissue culture *in vitro* requires the incorporation of plant growth hormones, usually cytokinins or auxins for shoot and root growth respectively. Manipulating the ingredients and levels of hormonal substances added is a means of influencing plant development.

The control of temperature and artificial light level is essential, and must be matched to the prescribed requirements of particular groups of plants. Rapidly-growing cultures require division and transfer to a fresh medium at regular intervals and the process is referred to as subculturing. Typically, many plants require subculturing on a four-week cycle, but some herbaceous plants may need processing as frequently as every two weeks, while for some woody plants every ten weeks is adequate.

Micropropagation is a specialist technique of immense current and potential value to the practice of horticulture. Successful implementation demands a knowledge of the protocols developed for specific plants, and careful attention to the provision and maintenance of aseptic working conditions and procedures.

Besides the challenges posed by cultural practice *in vitro* and the skill required to wean plantlets into growing mediums, certain limitations of the technique should be understood. There is a risk, albeit rare, of permanent off-types occurring as a result of induced change in genetic make-up. The risk is highest when callus tissue is liberally produced, and/or with high concentrations of cytokinins or auxins. Transient variation may occur in micropropagated offspring due to a change in environmental conditions, and as a quality-control measure in commercial situations, a proportion of propagules need to be grown on to test trueness to type before release.

microspore the smaller of the two types of spore produced by heterosporous plants; they develop into male gametophytes.

midrib, midvein the primary vein of a leaf or leaflet, usually running down its center as a continuation of the petiole or petiolule.

Mikania (for J. G. Mikan [1743–1814], Professor of Botany at Prague, or his son J. C. Mikan [d. 1844], plant collector in Brazil). Compositae. Tropics, especially New World. About 300 species, evergreen, perennial, woody or herbaceous lianes producing clusters of small, buttonlike flower heads in late summer and fall. Cultivate as for *Delairea*. *M. scandens* WILD CLIMBING HEMP-WEED, CLIMBING HEMP-VINE; tropical America; herbaceous; leaves to 4 in (10 cm), triangular to hastate, entire or toothed, glabrous to hairy; flower heads strongly vanilla-scented, white, tinged yellow, or lilac to purple.

mildew in horticulture and plant pathology, used to describe certain diseases in which the pathogen is visible on the plant surface. DOWNY MILDEWS are caused by fungi of the family Peronosporaceae and POWDERY MILDEWS by those of Erysiphaceae. The SOOTY MOLDS caused by fungi of the families Capnodiaceae and Meliolaceae are sometimes called dark or black mildew. The term mildew is sometimes encountered as a former name for honeydew. See *downy mildew, powdery mildew, sooty molds*.

Milium (Latin *milium*, millet). Gramineae. Eurasia, N America. 6 species, annual or perennial grasses with tussocks of short culms, linear, arching leaves and loose, airy panicles of small spikelets in spring and summer. Hardy to –4°F (–20°C) and below. Plant in fertile, moist but well-drained soil in sun or shade (ideally dappled sunlight). In hot, humid summers, these grasses may enter summer dormancy. Propagate by seed and division; *M. effusum* 'Aureum' comes true from seed and will self-sow. Often affected by mildew. *M. effusum* WOOD MILLET; loosely tussock-forming perennial to 12 in (30 cm); leaf blades to 12 × ⅝ in (30 × 1.5 cm), soft-textured, arching; panicle to 12 × 8 in (30 × 20 cm), basically pyramidal in outline, loose and airy, light green or tinged purple, branches delicate, whorled, spikelets small; includes 'Aureum' (BOWLES' GOLDEN GRASS), with pale golden yellow to lime green leaves and spikelets, and the weak-growing 'Variegatum', with bright green leaves striped white.

Milla (for Juliani Milla, gardener to the Spanish court in Madrid, 18th century). Liliaceae (Alliaceae). S US, C America. 6 species, cormous perennial herbs with linear leaves and, in summer, tubular, 6-lobed flowers in scapose umbels. Cultivate as for *Ipheion*. *M. biflora* (to 12 in (30 cm); flowers campanulate to funnelform, ⅝–1½ in (1.5–3.5 cm), white sometimes tinted lilac, usually striped or veined green on exterior). For *M. uniflora*, see *Ipheion uniflorum*.

millepedes (*Diplopoda*) elongate animals with many body segments, characterized by two pairs of legs on each trunk segment, except for the first few segments behind the head and some at the hind end; there may be as many as 50 segments. Centipedes look similar, but have only one pair of legs per body segment.

Millepedes thrive in moist soil of high organic content and feed principally on decaying or soft vegetable matter. They lay eggs in batches in the soil and the young may take several years to reach maturity. Only a few species are harmful to garden plants. The SPOTTED SNAKE MILLEPEDE (*Blaniulus guttulatus*) usually causes the most serious damage; it is creamy white, up to ¾ in (20 mm) long, with orange-red dots along each side of the body. It attacks seedlings and soft growth, such as strawberry fruits and mushrooms, as well as enlarging damage to potato tubers and bulbs that has been initiated by other pests such as slugs. The FLAT-BACKED MILLEPEDES (*Brachydesmus superus* and *Polydesmus angustatus*) may damage seedlings and other plants outdoors; in temperate countries, the TROPICAL GLASSHOUSE MILLEPEDE (*Oxidus gracilis*), which is up to 1½ in (40 mm) long and varies from white to brown, can be injurious to greenhouse plants, particularly cucumbers. Good hygiene and thorough cultivation help reduce numbers and can provide sufficient control, but for persistent attacks, dust seedlings, bulbs and corms with recommended contact insecticide, subject to local pesticide approvals.

Millepede

Miltonia (for Lord Fitzwilliam Milton [1786–1857], landowner and orchidologist). Orchidaceae. Brazil, one species in Peru. Some 20 species, epiphytic, evergreen perennial herbs with ovoid to ellipsoid pseudobulbs, strap-shaped leaves and racemes of showy flowers at various times of year. The flowers consist of ovate to oblong, spreading tepals and a larger, simple or

pandurate, oblong to rounded lip. Cultivate as for *Odontoglossum*.

M. candida Brazil; resembles *M. clowesii* except tepals oblong-obtuse, lip shorter than other segments, clasping column at base; *M. clowesii* Brazil; inflorescence to 18 in (45 cm); tepals yellow, heavily blotched and barred chestnut-brown, sepals to 1½ × ½ in (4 × 1 cm), lanceolate, acuminate, undulate, petals to 1½ × ½ in (3.5 × 1 cm), lip white at tip, deep purple at base, to 1½–¾ in (4–2 cm), subpandurate, caudate, callus white or yellow; *M. regnellii* Brazil; inflorescence to 16 in (40 cm); tepals cream suffused rose to lilac or pale amethyst, sepals to 1¼ × ½ in (3 × 1 cm), oblong-lanceolate, recurved, petals wider; lip to 1½ × 1½ in (3.5 × 3.5 cm), pale rose streaked lilac or amethyst, margins white, rotund to obovate, obscurely trilobed, callus of several radiating yellow lines; *M. spectabilis* Brazil; inflorescence to 10 in (25 cm); flowers solitary, sepals to 1½ × ⅝ in (4 × 1.5 cm), white, often tinged rose at base, lanceolate-oblong, petals similar with white patch at base, lip rose-violet, margins white or pale rose, to 2 × 1¾ in (5 × 4.5 cm), obovate-orbicular, callus yellow with pink lines. There are many cultivars and grexes in *Miltonia* (some strictly assignable to *Miltoniopsis*) with pale green foliage and flowers in shades of white, pink, red and lilac, among them the classic pansy orchids with broad blooms in deep velvety red. For *M. phalaenopsis* see *Miltoniopsis phalaenopsis*; for *M. roezlii*, see *Miltoniopsis roezlii*; for *M. superba*, see *Miltoniopsis warscewiczii*; for *M. vexillaria*, see *Miltoniopsis vexillaria*.

Miltoniopsis (Miltonia and Greek *opsis*, resemblance). Orchidaceae. Pansy orchid. Costa Rica, Panama, Venezuela, Ecuador, Colombia. 5 species of epiphytes or lithophytes closely allied to *Miltonia*, generally with larger, pansylike flowers. Cultivate as for *Odontoglossum*.

M. phalaenopsis (syn. *Miltonia phalaenopsis*); Colombia; raceme to 8 in (20 cm); tepals pure white, sepals to ¾ × ½ in (2 × 1 cm), elliptic-oblong, acute, petals wider, elliptic, obtuse, lip to 1 × 1¼ in (2.5 × 3 cm), white blotched and streaked purple-crimson or pale purple,

4-lobed, callus with yellow spots; *M. roezlii* (syn. *Miltonia roezlii*); Colombia; raceme to 12 in (30 cm); sepals to 2 × ¾ in (5 × 2 cm), white, ovate-oblong, acuminate, petals to 2 × 1 in (5 × 2.5 cm), white blotched wine-purple at base, lip to 2 × 2¼ in (5 × 5.5 cm), white, orange-yellow at base, widely obcordate; *M. vexillaria* (syn. *Miltonia vexillaria*); Colombia, Ecuador; raceme to 12 in (30 cm); tepals rose-pink or white flushed rose-pink, sepals to 1¼ × ⅝ in (3 × 1.5 cm), obovate-oblong, recurved above, petals slightly wider, margins white, lip much larger than sepals, white or pale rose, deep rose on disk, suborbicular, cleft, callus yellow; *M. warscewiczii* (syn. *Miltonia superba*); Costa Rica; raceme to 12 in (30 cm); flowers cream-white, each segment with a rose-purple blotch at base, tepals 1¼ × ⅝ in (3 × 1.5 cm), ovate-elliptic, acute, lip to 1½ × 1½ in (3.5 × 3.5 cm), widely pandurate, basal lobes 2, small, rounded, midlobe emarginate, callus yellow.

mimicry resemblance of a plant to an insect or object; a feature that serves to attract pollinators or provide camouflage, for example bee orchids (*Ophrys* species), which attract male bees because of the flowers' similarity to female bees, and pebble plants (*Lithops* species), which are not readily distinguished from the rocks and stones among which they grow.

Mimosa (from Greek *mimos*, mimic; the leaves of many species resemble animals in their ability to move). Leguminosae. C and S America, S US, Asia, tropical and E Africa. Some 400 species, usually spiny herbs, shrubs or small trees. The leaves are bipinnate with numerous, oblong to linear leaflets and a swelling at the base of the stalk. When touched, or at nightfall, or in times of drought, the leaflets fold rapidly together and the leafstalks wilt—a trick with the dual functions of alarming would-be grazers and conserving water. The flower heads are typically *Acacia*-like, rounded, stalked and packed with small, "fluffy" flowers. Grow in pots or beds, in bright filtered light with a minimum temperature of 50°F (10°C). Water plentifully and apply liquid fertilizer to established plants weekly when in growth; water

M

very moderately in winter. Although leggy plants can be pruned hard prior to repotting in spring, they are best replaced after a year or two. Propagate by seed, pre-soaked in hot water and sown uncovered in early spring at 64–68°F (18–20°C). *M. pudica* HUMBLE PLANT, SENSITIVE PLANT, TOUCH-ME-NOT, SHAME PLANT, LIVE-AND-DIE, ACTION PLANT; S Mexico to C America, West Indies, Hawaii, Fiji, Australia; prostrate to semi-erect herb, subshrub or shrub, 12–32 in (0.3–0.8 m); pinnae (1–)2 pairs, to 4 in (10 cm), leaflets 10–25 pairs, mid- to gray-green, soft-textured, oblong; flowers pale pink to lilac, in heads to ³⁄₄ in (2 cm) in diameter.

mimosiform, mimosoid possessing flower heads resembling those of the genus *Mimosa*, in which calyx and corolla are inconspicuous or reduced and the stamens are showy.

Mimulus (diminutive form of the Latin *mimus*, a mimic actor, referring to the resemblance of the markings of the corolla to a grinning face). Scrophulariaceae. Mostly America, also South Africa and Asia. MONKEY FLOWER, MUSK. 150 species, annual or perennial herbs, or rarely shrubs, with racemes of showy, tubular flowers in spring and summer. These are 2-lipped, the throat open or closed by a raised and hairy palate. The soft-stemmed perennial species are hardy to 0°F (–18°C) and thrive in full sun or light shade on moist, or saturated, fertile soils; many of these will grow in water and are excellent marginals. The shrubby species (e.g. *M. aurantiacus*) are frost-tender and should be grown under glass in cold areas or, where winters are mild, in the open garden against a warm wall in a dry, sunny spot. Where winters are severe, the herbaceous *Mimulus* are best treated as annuals for summer-bedding display or as flowering pot plants for windowsills and cool greenhouses. When grown in an open garden in hard winter areas, take cuttings in summer as an insurance policy or protect plants in the open with cloches. In late winter prune pot-grown specimens; repot them, and start into growth at 55°F (13°C), ventilating freely whenever possible. Water plentifully when growing strongly and plunge

in the open during the summer months. Fertilize established plants semiweekly with a dilute liquid fertilizer. Sow seed in early spring at 55–59°F (13–15°C) under glass and cover very lightly with grit or sieved soil. For winter/spring-flowering annuals in pots, sow in fall and overwinter under glass. Seed may also be sown *in situ* after the last frosts. Increase by division in spring or by softwood cuttings in spring and summer. Propagate shrubby species by semi-ripe cuttings in late summer, rooted in a closed propagating case.

M. aurantiacus (syn. *M. glutinosus*); BUSH MONKEY FLOWER, ORANGE BUSH MONKEY FLOWER; S Oregon to California; clammy shrub, 24–48 in (60–120 cm); flowers 1½–1¾ in (3.5–4.5 cm), orange or deep yellow; *M. guttatus* COMMON LARGE MONKEY FLOWER; Alaska to Mexico; largely glabrous annual or biennial herb; stem 16–39 in (40–100 cm), erect or decumbent; flowers ³⁄₄–1¼ in (2–3 cm), bright yellow, throat with pair of red to purple-brown-spotted hairy ridges; *M. × hybridus* (*M. luteus* × *M. guttatus*); flowers large, color variable; cultivars include 'Bee's Dazzler', with brilliant crimson-red flowers; 'Brilliant', with deep purple-crimson flowers; Calypso Hybrids, with large, burgundy, scarlet and gold flowers; 'Duplex', with enlarged, colorful calyx; 'Fireflame', with bright flame red flowers; 'Highland Pink', with rich pink flowers; 'Highland Red', with deep red flowers; 'Highland Yellow', with yellow flowers; 'Hose in Hose', with soft tan flowers, one sitting inside the other; 'Inschriach Crimson', dwarf, carpet-forming, with crimson flowers; 'Leopard', with yellow rust-spotted flowers; 'Malibu', to 10 in (25 cm), of strong growth, with orange flowers; 'Mandarin', with abundant, bright orange flowers; 'Nanus', of dwarf habit, with glossy leaves and bright orange to gold flowers with a red throat; 'Old Rose', to 6 in (15 cm), with bright red flowers; 'Queen's Prize', dwarf, with large flowers in bright colors, many spotted and blotched; 'Royal Velvet', to 8 in (20 cm), with large velvety, mahogany red flowers with gold throats speckled mahogany; 'Röter Kaiser' ('Red Emperor'), to 8 in (20 cm) high, with

crimson to scarlet flowers; 'Shep', with large, yellow flowers splashed brown; 'Whitecroft Scarlet', with vermilion flowers; and 'Wisley Red', to 6 in (15 cm), with velvety blood red flowers; *M. luteus* MONKEY MUSK, YELLOW MONKEY FLOWER; Chile, naturalized elsewhere; glabrous perennial herb; stem 4–12 in (10–30 cm), decumbent to ascending, hollow; flowers ³⁄₄–2 in (2–5 cm), yellow, with deep red or purple spots; *M. moschatus* MUSK FLOWER, MUSK PLANT; British Colombia to Newfoundland, S to W Virginia and California; perennial herb, glandular-pilose, sometimes aromatic; stem 4–16 in (10–40 cm), decumbent; flowers ³⁄₄–1 in (1.8–2.5 cm), pale yellow, throat tubular, finely brown-spotted and streaked with black.

mineralization see *nutrients*

mint (*Mentha* species) a group of creeping, invasive perennials grown as culinary herbs for their aromatic foliage; there are many types, with variation in flavor. Commonly grown are SPEARMINT (*M. spicata*) and APPLEMINT (*M. suaveolens*), natives of central, south and west Europe, and also BOWLES' MINT (*M. villosa alopecuroides*), of garden origin. Propagate in spring from division of young shoots with roots, or by 2 in (5 cm) long pieces of root planted horizontally 2 in (5 cm) deep and about 9 in (23 cm) apart. Mint beds are best reestablished every three years. For shoot and leaf production in winter and spring, roots can be lifted in fall and planted in a large container within a greenhouse. Mints may need containment with physical barriers to control their invasive habit. See *Mentha*.

Mirabilis (from Latin *mirabilis*, "wonderful"). Nyctaginaceae. UMBRELLA-WORT, MARVEL OF PERU. SW US, S America. Some 50 species, annual or perennial herbs with large tuberous roots. The stems are regularly forked, and the leaves ovate to elliptic or lanceolate. Produced in summer in axillary corymbs, the flowers are tubular with a spreading limb of five lobes. Hardy to 23°F (–5°C), given a warm, sheltered position in very well-drained soil. Alternatively, lift and overwinter tubers in a frost-free place as for *Dahlia*. Grow in full sun or part-day shade. Propagate from seed sown at 59°F (15°C) in spring, harden off young plants before planting out. Increase also by division of tubers in spring. *M. jalapa* FOUR-O'CLOCK, MARVEL OF PERU, FALSE JALAP; Peru, garden escape in N America and S Europe; erect perennial, to 3¼ ft (1 m); flowers fragrant, opening in the late afternoon or evening, 1¼–2 (3–5 cm) × ½–1 in (1–2.5 cm), purple, crimson, apricot, yellow or white, several shades often present on one plant, often striped or mottled.

Miscanthus (from Greek *mischos*, stalk, and *anthos*, flower, referring to the stalked spikelets). Gramineae. Old World tropics, South Africa, E Asia. 17 species, deciduous perennial grasses with clumped, reedlike culms clothed with slender, arching leaves. Silky-hairy spikelets are borne on the arching branches of terminal panicles in summer and fall. Hardy to –10°F (–23°C) and tolerant of a wide range of sites, these grasses prefer fertile, moist soils in full sun. Most are dry and dormant by midwinter, although the windswept skeletons of the inflorescences remain beautiful, especially when rimed with frost. The flowering time ranges from early summer to early fall. Although the flowers of some selections open with a reddish cast and others open silver, all take on a silver-white appearance upon drying. They are superb for cut or dried arrangements. Clumps eventually tend to die out in the center, and may require lifting and dividing after 5–7 years. Annual maintenance generally consists of cutting back by midspring before new growth begins, or in late fall if winter interest is not a consideration. Species are easily grown from seed. The cultivars should be propagated by division. Division is safest done in spring, but may succeed in an fall followed by a mild winter. The same holds true for transplanting times. The mealybug, *Pilococcus miscanthi,* now poses a serious threat to *Miscanthus sinensis* and possibly to other species. The eggs hatch and crawlers appear in late spring. This mealybug is big and prolific, and can reduce even the largest clump of *Miscanthus* to a stunted, chlorotic mess that will cease to flower.

By fall, the lower culms and insides of the leaf sheaths may be white-caked with mealybugs. They attack all parts of the plant. including the roots, so above-ground mechanical or chemical methods are not sufficient for control. For those not fond of using pesticides in the garden, the best strategy is probably to remove and destroy any plants that show infestation and to be cautious when purchasing new plants.

M. sacchariflorus SILVER BANNER GRASS; Asia, escaped in US; to 10 ft (3 m) leaves to 36 × 1¼ in (90 × 3 cm), flat, stiff, smooth, margins rough, midrib pale; inflorescence to 16 × 5 in (40 × 13 cm), very pale green, tinged red or purple, racemes to 12 in (30 cm), flimsy, beige, with long silky hairs; 'Aureus': to 5 ft (1.5 m), leaves striped gold; 'Robustus': vigorous, to 7 ft (2.2 m); 'Variegatus': leaves narrowly striped white; *M. sinensis* EULALIA; E Asia; to 13 ft (4 m); leaves to 48 × ½ in (120 × 1 cm), flat, glabrous to puberulous above, blue green; inflorescence to 16 × 6 in (40 × 15 cm), obpyramidal, pale gray tinted brown or mauve, racemes to 8 in (20 cm), with long silky hairs; there are many cultivars: (*habit*) 'Goliath': large, to 6½ ft (2 m); 'Gracillimus': more slender than type, leaves with a white midrib; 'Grosse Fontaine': large fountainlike, early-flowering; 'Strictus': as for 'Zebrinus', but smaller, very erect, with leaves banded yellow; 'Yaku Jima': to 34 in (85 cm), with narrow, arching leaves; (*leaves striped*) 'Goldfeder': leaves edged and striped yellow; 'Morning Light': leaves narrow, arching, neatly edged white, panicles red-bronze; 'Sarabande': leaves with a wide central silver stripe; 'Variegatus': leaves with white or cream-white stripes: (*leaves banded*) 'Tiger Tail': leaves banded cream; 'Zebrinus': ZEBRA GRASS, leaves and culms banded white and yellow; 'Graziella': leaves narrow, somewhat arching, burgundy and orange, with bronze tints in fall, panicles large, white, nodding; 'Purpureus': syn. 'Purpurascens', small, leaves with a pink-tinted central vein, turning shades of brown and orange-red in fall, panicles oatmeal flushed pink; (*flowers*) 'Flamingo': panicles tinted flamingo pink; 'Kleine Fontaine': small, with graceful, arching leaves and early flowers; 'Malepartus': robust, with

burgundy leaves in fall, and large, copper to silver panicles tinted mauve; 'Rotsilber': panicles red-tinted; 'Silberfeder': upright, with narrow, silver-veined leaves, slender stems and loose, silver panicles occasionally flushed pink; *M. tinctorius* Japan; tufted perennial to 3¼ ft (1 m); leaves flat, to 16 in × ½ in (40 × 1.2 cm), margins scabrous, mostly glabrous, pilose toward base; inflorescence erect, with a very short axis, racemes to 6 in (15 cm); 'Variegatus': to 12 in (30 cm), leaves streaked white to cream or pale yellow.

mistletoe the plant often cut for Christmas decoration is *Viscum album*, one of about 70 species of parasitic evergreens in the family Viscaceae, native of temperate zones. Plants are dioecious, of about 3¼ ft (1 m) spread; they occur on a range of deciduous trees but predominantly on *Malus* and *Populus* spp. *V.a* subsp. *abietis* occurs on conifers, especially *Abies* spp., and *V.a* subsp. *austriacum* on *Pinus* and *Larix* spp. Propagation naturally arises through seed transference by birds. For intentional cultivation, berries should be gathered in late winter or spring and the sticky seed extracted and rubbed into a bark crevice or beneath a lifted flap of bark, on the underside of a

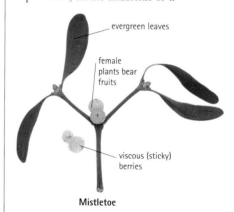

evergreen leaves

female plants bear fruits

viscous (sticky) berries

Mistletoe

branch of at least 4 in (10 cm) diameter and at least 5 ft (1.5 m) from ground level. The host plant chosen should be at least 20 years old. Numerous seedings are necessary to ensure male and female plants for berry production. Percentage germination is usually less than 50 percent. Successful parasitizing is indicated by a swelling of the seeded site; flowering is unlikely before the fifth year.

M

517

mist propagation a method of rooting cuttings under protection by means of a fine spray of water applied at frequent intervals to prevent the cuttings from wilting. A mist propagation unit consists of a bench or ground bed layered with a rooting medium, along the length of which spray nozzles are fitted on risers. The misted water application is controlled by an electronic leaf, which simulates the regularity with which cutting leaves dry out. See *electronic leaf*.

mist-sprayer, mister a small specialized sprayer used to deliver a fine mist of water around houseplants to increase humidity.

Mitella (diminutive of Latin *mitra*, a cap or mitre—thus a small cap or mitre, alluding to the shape of the fruit). Saxifragaceae. N America, NE Asia. BISHOP'S-CAP, MITERWORT. 20 species perennial, minutely hairy herbs making clumps of long-stalked, ovate-cordate, lobed and crenate leaves. Small, green or yellow flowers are carried in narrow, erect spikes in summer. An attractive, dainty groundcover for moist woodland or pockets in the rock garden. It prefers cool, damp, humus-rich soil and shade. Increase by division in spring. *M. breweri* British Colombia to California and Idaho; to 4 in (10 cm); leaves 1½–4 in (4–10 cm) broad; flowers green-yellow, petals $\frac{1}{16}$–$\frac{1}{16}$ in (1–2 mm), divided into 5–9 segments.

mites a group of very small plant pests with needlelike mouthparts which they insert into plant tissues in order to suck sap. Most have four pairs of jointed legs (gall mites have only two pairs), and bodies consisting of a head and a fused thorax and abdomen. There are three important groups of mite pests: TETRANYCHIDS or RED SPIDER MITES; TARSONEMID MITES; and ERIOPHYID or GALL MITES.

Bryobia mites (Acarina: Tetranychidae) are black with pink legs, and feed from the upper leaf surface of plants such as primulas, ivy and gooseberry.

FALSE RED SPIDER MITES (Acarina: Tenuipalpidae) are small, bright red, slow-moving mites, up to $\frac{1}{16}$ in (2 mm) long, with an oval body; they are related to the red spider mite (Tetranychidae). Most species feed on the undersides of leaves near to veins, and those which are occasionally significantly injurious are mostly in the genus *Brevipalpus*, which includes the SCARLET TEA MITE (*B. californicus*), the ORCHID MITE (*B. oncidii*), the CITRUS FLAT MITE (*B. lewisi*), the privet mite (*B. obovatus*) and the RED CREVICE TEA MITE (*B. phoenicis*). All infest hosts such as citrus, tea, coffee, peach, rubber, coconut, apple, pear, olive, fig, walnut, grape, date palm, privet, orchids, buddleias, fuchsias and many other ornamental plants. They feed by sucking the sap and cause a fine pale mottling of the upper leaf surface. These mites are more tolerant of acaricides than are red spider mites.

The FALSE RED SPIDER MITES (*Brevipalpus* species) are closely related to the tetranychids.

See *gall mites*, *red spider mites*, *tarsonemid mites*.

Mitraria (from Latin *mitra*, cap or mitre, referring to the shape of the fruit). Gesneriaceae. Chile. 1 species, *M. coccinea*, a climbing or straggling, evergreen perennial herb, eventually becoming somewhat woody, with dense, tangled branches. To ¾ in (2 cm) long, the leaves are ovate, dentate, lustrous dark green, coriaceous and hairy. In late spring and summer, solitary flowers hang from the leaf axils, each to 1¼ in (3 cm) long, tubular to goblet-shaped, downy and scarlet to orange-red. Cultivate as for *Asteranthera*.

mixed border see *herbaceous border*.

MLO see *phytoplasmas*.

module a small individual container or growing unit for plant raising, mainly used for direct single or multi-seed sowing to each unit, which removes the need for pricking out and offers the possibility of economizing on seed. Modules are of particular value in reducing the effects of growth check at planting time, and also in facilitating early establishment under protection to allow for planting out at a favorable or convenient time. Modules take the form of small pots made of various materials: molded plastic, polystyrene,

Planting out from modules
Sowing into a "cell tray" of individual modules allows each seedling to develop its own root system, which need not be disturbed on planting out.

peat or fiber cellular trays of various sizes (the smallest units of which are known as plugs), and soil blocks.

Mogul (Mughal, Mughul) gardens formal gardens of India created by Persian Mogul invaders in the 16th and 17th centuries. They are based on water and fountains, with pavilions, lawns, flower-beds and shade trees.

mole drain see *drainage*.

moles (*Talpa europaea*) small subterranean mammals, up to 6½ in (165 mm) long, with short tails, dense dark brown fur and forelegs adapted for burrowing. Moles construct a system of tunnels that may reach 3¼ ft (1 m) in depth, and their activity damages plants indirectly by undermining roots; excavated soil is thrown up into surface molehills which can disfigure lawns. Moles are territorial and live for up to 3–4 years, feeding mainly on earthworms.

Signs of activity in a small garden may be the work of an individual since moles are solitary animals except in the breeding season. The young are born usually four to a litter in spring, in an underground nest chamber or, where there is a high water table, in an unusually large molehill. They disperse above ground to new territories in early summer.

Specially designed mole traps are available for control, and fumigant smokes are effective, subject to local pesticide approvals, but the most lethal poisons may only be used by qualified pest-control contractors. Electronic repellent devices have been used with varying degrees of success. Once established, control is difficult and recolonization of vacant tunnel systems can occur from adjoining infested sites.

Molinia (for J. I. Molina [1740–1829], writer on the natural history of Chile). Gramineae. Eurasia. 2 species, perennial grasses with tufted culms and slender leaves. Small and shimmering, the florets are loosely borne on the threadlike branches of erect, spreading panicles in summer. Hardy. Grow in moisture-retentive, lime-free soils in sun. Propagate by division in early fall and spring.

M. caerulea PURPLE MOOR-GRASS; to 48 in (120 cm); leaf blades to 18 × ½ in (45 × 1 cm); panicle dense, to 16 × 4 in (40 × 10 cm), purple to olive green; spikelets to ½ in (1 cm); subsp. *arundinacea*: to 8 ft (2.5 m), with leaves to ½ in (12 mm) across and panicles with long, spreading branches; subsp. *arundinacea* cultivars: 'Altissima', to 3¼ ft (1 m), with golden-yellow leaves in fall; 'Fontane', with inclining stems, forming a fountain; 'Karl Foerster', tall, with leaves to 32 in (80 cm); 'Skyracer', tall, with leaves to 3¼ ft (1 m), clear gold in fall; 'Transparent', with sparse spikelets, giving the whole inflorescence a light, spacious, transparent quality; 'Windspiel', with slender, swaying stems and gold-brown, dense plumes; subsp. *caerulea* cultivars: 'Dauerstrahl': stems tall, yellow-tinted 'Heidebraut': stems soft straw yellow, to 5 ft (1.5 m), spikelets yellow-tinted, forming a glistening cloud; 'Moorhexe': narrowly upright, with slender stems, to 20 in (50 cm), and dark flowers in straight, narrow panicles; 'Moorflamme': leaves coloring well in fall, inflorescence dark; 'Overdam': to 24 in (60 cm), with strong stems and fine leaves; 'Variegata': to 24 in (60 cm), leaves striped dark green and cream-white.

molluscicide a pesticide active against slugs and snails (mollusks), such as metaldehyde and methio-carb.

Moltkia (for Count Joachim Gadake Moltke of Denmark [d. 1818]). Boraginaceae. N Italy to N Greece, SW Asia. Some 6 species, perennial herbs or sub-

shrubs usually coarsely hairy and with massed clusters of funnel-shaped flowers in summer. Hardy, *Moltkia* prefers neutral to alkaline soils but otherwise has garden uses and cultural requirements similar to those of *Lithodora*. Propagate also by layering.

M. × *intermedia* (*M. petraea* × *M. suffruticosa*); closely resembles *M. suffruticosa* except larger and more shrubby with broader leaves and deep bright blue flowers, in spreading heads; includes 'Froebelii', with azure-blue flowers; *M. petraea* Balkans to C Greece; white-bristly, slender shrublet to 16 in (40 cm); leaves to 2 in (5 cm), oblanceolate to linear, revolute; cymes compact, flowers to ⅜ in (8 mm), blue or violet-blue; *M. suffruticosa* N Italy; loosely branched, bristly shrublet to 10 in (25 cm); leaves to 6 in (15 cm), linear, sometimes revolute; cymes short, dense, flowers to ¾ in (17 mm), blue.

Moluccella (from the original collection region, the Moluccas). Labiatae. Mediterranean to NW India. 4 species, glabrous, annual or short-lived perennial herbs with erect, scarcely branching stems and wavy-toothed leaves. The flowers are borne in summer in whorls forming a tall, erect spike. They are remarkable for the calyx which enlarges with age becoming a green, net-veined and prickly-edged dish or funnel, far exceeding the small, tubular and two-lipped corolla. A distinguished annual for the flower border and, later, for drying. Treat as half-hardy, sowing seed under glass in early spring at 59°F (15°C), or, later, *in situ*, in sunny well-drained borders. *M. laevis* BELLS OF IRELAND; W Asia; annual, erect, 12–39 in (30–100 cm); calyx light green, with pale or white net markings, campanulate or saucer-shaped, margin more or less spiny, corolla white to pale lilac.

molybdenum an essential plant micronutrient, required for enzyme activity. Deficiency, which is predisposed by soil acidity, is rare in the UK,

but more common in Australia and New Zealand. It is seen particularly in brassicas, lettuce, tomatoes and poinsettia; in cauliflower, it produces blind plants with reduced and twisted lamina, or only the midribs persisting, in a condition known as whiptail (which may occur in soil up to pH 7). Death of growing points and chlorotic mottling and cupping or rolling of leaves are symptoms common to other molybdenum-deficient plants. Legumes may show signs of nitrogen deficiency because the function of nitrogen-fixing bacteria is dependent on the availability of molybdenum.

monadelphous stamens united by fusion of their filaments into a single group or bundle.

Monarda (for Nicholas Monardes [1493–1588], Spanish botanist and physician, author of the first medicinal flora of North America (1571) translated 1577 as *Joyfull Newes*). Labiatae. N America. BEE BALM, WILD BERGAMOT, HORSEMINT. 16 species, aromatic annual or perennial herbs, more or less hairy with clumped, erect stems. Hooded, tubular and 2-lipped, the flowers are borne in late spring and summer in dense clusters or heads or in an interrupted spike, and subtended by leafy bracts. Hardy. Plant in full sun. Propagate by division of established clumps during the dormant period. Various mildew fungi can be destructive, especially in hot dry summers.

paired leaves

nettlelike flowers

Monarda didyma

M. didyma BEE BALM, BERGAMOT, OSWEGO TEA; Canada, US; strongly aromatic perennial herb, 28–48 in (70–120 cm); flowers bright crimson, 1¼–1¾ in (3–4.5 cm); includes 'Alba', which has white flowers; *M. fistulosa* Canada, US, Mexico; perennial herb, 14–48 in (35–120 cm); flowers lavender, lilac or pink, ¾–1¼ in (2–3 cm); differs from *M. didyma* in having bluntly 4-angled stem, usually only 1 flower cluster (not 2 super-imposed) and fewer flowers with bracts tinted purple-pink, not red, and densely, not sparsely, hairy calyx throat. *Cultivars* selections or hybrids: 'Adam', to 3¼ ft (1 m), with cerise flowers; 'Beauty of Cobham', tall, with lilac-pink flowers; 'Blue Stocking', tall, with brilliant deep violet flowers; 'Burgundy', with dark purple-red flowers; 'Cambridge Scarlet', with red flowers; 'Capricorn', with purple flowers; 'Croftway Pink', with clear rose-pink flowers; 'Kardinal', tall, with red flowers tinted purple; 'Loddon Crown', with maroon flowers; 'Mahogany', tall, with deep wine red flowers; 'Morning Red', with dark salmon flowers; 'Pisces', with strong pink flowers with a green calyx; 'Prairie Night', with rich violet flowers; 'Salmonea', with salmon pink flowers, and 'Snow Queen', low, with creamy white flowers.

moniliform a regularly constricted organ, giving the appearance of a string of beads or a knotted rope.

mono-ammonium phosphate see *ammonium phosphate*.

monocarpic dying after bearing flowers and fruit only once.

monochasial cyme as a dichasial cyme, but with the branches missing from one side.

monochlamydeous with only one perianth whorl.

monocotyledons (monocots) one of the two major divisions of the angiosperms, the other being the dicotyledons. Monocots are characterized by the single cotyledon in the seed, usually the absence of cambium and thus of woody tissue and, in many cases, parallel leaf venation. The monocotyledons include Gramineae, Liliaceae, Orchidaceae, Iridaceae, Bromeliaceae, Palmae.

monoecious having separate male inconspicuous female flowers

and female or bisexual flowers on the same plant, cf. *dioecious*.

monogeneric a family or grouping of higher rank containing a single genus.

monogerm seed seed that contains single embryos and is produced mechanically or genetically. It is available for beet species, the seed of which otherwise comprises a cluster of embryos, requiring resultant seedlings to be thinned.

monopetalous strictly, with one petal; often loosely used for gamopetalous.

monopodial describes a stem or rhizome in which growth continues indefinitely from the apical or terminal bud, and which generally exhibits little or no secondary branching; cf. *sympodial*.

monotypic having only one component, for example a genus with one species.

Monstera (from Latin *monstrum*, a marvel, possibly alluding to curious shape of leaves). Araceae. Tropical America. SWISS-CHEESE PLANT, WINDOW-LEAF. 22 species, evergreen, epiphytic, perennial lianes with freely rooting, clambering stems and large, smooth, heart-shaped leaves, often pinnately lobed or perforated. Small flowers are borne on a dense, clublike spadix surrounded with a thick-textured spathe. The fruit is cone-shaped, composed of tightly packed white berries. In temperate zones, *Monstera* species are most commonly grown as houseplants or in warm greenhouses. Under such conditions, poles of sphagnum moss are often used in imitation of natural supports, dampened to improve atmospheric humidity and to provide a

moist medium for the running aerial roots. If the necessary draft-free conditions with filtered light and high humidity are not provided, the leaf perforations typical of well-grown adult specimens of many species may fail to develop. Too much or too little water will cause leaf yellowing. Plants benefit from frequent sponging of leaves. Propagate *Monstera* by internodal cuttings, or from cuttings of growing tips with one leaf attached, rooted with bottom heat in a sandy propagating mix. Alternatively, increase by air-layering.

M. deliciosa CERIMAN, SWISS-CHEESE PLANT; Mexico to Panama; robust climber with stout, green stems and copious, thick aerial roots; leaves 10–36 (25–90 cm) × 10–30 in (25–75 cm), orbicular to ovate, base cordate, margins pinnately lobed in adult foliage, segments curved, oblong, usually perforated with elliptic to oblong holes; spathe to 12 in (30 cm), spadix to 10 × 1¼ in (25 × 3 cm), swelling in fruit, becoming cream-colored and tasting of banana and pineapple when mature; includes 'Albo-variegata', with large, partly rich deep green leaves with other sections a contrasting creamy-white, and 'Variegata', with leaves and stem irregularly variegated cream or yellow; *M. dubia* C America; robust, bushy climber with thick aerial roots; adult leaves to 54 × 24 in (130 × 60 cm), oblong, pinnately cut, segments 12–20; leaves linear in juvenile forms and silver-variegated; *M. obliqua* northern S America; slender-stemmed climber; leaves to 8 × 2¾ in (20 × 7 cm), elliptic to oblong-lanceolate, entire or perforated with holes covering much of the surface area.

monstrous, monstrosity describing plants showing some abnormality of growth or flower, due to genetic makeup or pest or disease. Monstrous plants are sometimes prized by gardeners. See *malformations*.

montmorillonite a primary type of clay mineral with a high capacity for cation exchange and water-holding.

moongate a circular doorway in a wall; Chinese in origin and used in Western gardens from the 18th century.

twigs from same plant

male flowers ("catkins")

Monoecious plant (Corylus avellana)

mor a type of humus found as an unincorporated surface layer on mineral soils, typically as leaf litter on a forest floor where decomposition and incorporation are restricted by acidity; cf. *mull*.

Moraea (for Robert More, 18th-century botanist and natural historian. The name was originally spelled *Morea*, but changed to *Moraea* by Linnaeus in 1762, possibly in honor of his father-in-law Johan Moraeus, a Swedish physician). Iridaceae. Sub-Saharan Africa from Ethiopia to South Africa. About 120 species, perennial, cormous herbs with erect, simple or branched stems bearing terminal clusters of flowers with six tepals. Species which grow in winter and flower in spring need protection from frost in cool temperate climates. They are well-suited to cultivation in the cool greenhouse or conservatory. Species which flower in summer, are frost-hardy, withstanding winter temperatures between 23° and 14°F (−5° and −10°C). All need full sun and a fertile, sandy and well-drained medium. Provide plentiful moisture when in growth, but keep dry when dormant. Increase by seed.

M. huttonii to 3¼ ft (1 m); flowers scented, yellow with darker yellow marks, style crests with brown or purple blotch; outer tepals to 2 in (5 cm), inner tepals to 1½ in (4 cm), lanceolate, erect; *M. polystachya* to 32 in (80 cm); flowers pale blue or violet, outer tepals 1¼–2 in (3–5 cm) with yellow or orange nectar guides, inner tepals 1¼–1½ in (3–4 cm), erect or reflexed; *M. spathulata* to 36 in (90 cm); flowers yellow, outer tepals 1½–2 in (3.5–5 cm) with darker yellow nectar guides, inner tepals erect, 1¼–1½ in (3–4 cm).

moraine in nature, the accumulation of rocky debris, sand and silt at the snout or sides of a glacier, produced by grinding action on the bed rock. Being freely drained, it supports a specialized flora of rosette- or cushion-forming plants with long taproots. Moraine conditions can be imitated in the garden by the provision of specially constructed beds. See *rock plant gardening*.

Morina (for Louis Morin [1636–1715], French botanist). Morinaceae. E Europe to Asia. 4 species, aromatic perennial,

prickly herbs. The leaves are mostly basal, tufted, lanceolate to oblong, undulate and spiny-toothed, progressively reduced on flowering stems to whorled, leafy and spiny bracts. The flowers are borne in whorls on an erect spike in summer. They are tubular and 5-lobed, with a spreading, somewhat 2-lipped limb. Hardy to 1°F (−17°C). Grow in fertile, humus-rich, well-drained but moderately moisture-retentive, sandy or gritty soil in sun. Fresh, ripe seed germinates freely in an open, gritty propagating mix and is best sown in individual pots to avoid damage to the taproot. Overwinter young plants in a well-ventilated cold frame. Increase also by root cuttings. *M. longiflora* WHORLFLOWER; Himalaya; to 4¼ ft (1.3 m); corolla to 1 in (2.5 cm), white, flushing shell pink, then bright crimson, particularly the limb.

morphogenesis changes in shape or form of a plant during development, or in response to environmental changes.

morphology the study of the external form and relative position of plant organs; one of the most important divisions of botanical science.

Morus (from Latin *morus*, mulberry). Moraceae. Western N America and S Europe east to Japan, south to lowland tropics in C Africa. MULBERRY. About 12 species, deciduous trees and shrubs. The crown is usually dense and rounded with rugged, gnarled branches, the bark brown, rough, and often burred. Young shoots exude white latex when cut. The leaves are generally ovate to cordate and toothed, turning yellow in fall. The inflorescences are green and catkinlike, the females developing as fruits that superficially resemble a large raspberry but differ by consisting of closely packed but separate drupes. These are green at first, ripening through orange or white to red or deep purple-black by late summer to midfall of the same year.

M. alba WHITE MULBERRY; China; tree to 52 ft (16 m); fruit ½–1 in (1–2.5 cm), green-white ripening pink to dark red; cultivars include 'Aurea', with yellow leaves and bark; 'Laciniata', with leaves deeply lobed and toothed; 'Macrophylla', with large leaves; var.

multicaulis, suckering shrub, with leaves to 14 in (35 cm) and fruit that is nearly black when ripe; 'Nana', dwarf, shrubby, rounded, with regularly lobed leaves; 'Nigrobacca', with fruit ripening purple-black; 'Pendula', producing a weeping crown if grafted on tall stocks of the typical mulberry; and 'Pyramidalis', with a pyramidal crown; *M. nigra* BLACK MULBERRY; probably originating in SW Asia, but now widespread through cultivation; tree to 50 ft (15 m); fruit ¾–1 in (2–2.5 cm), green ripening through orange, and red to deep purple; *M. rubra* RED MULBERRY; E US, SE Canada; tree to 50 ft (15 m), rarely 65 ft (20 m); fruit 1–1¼ in (2.5–3 cm), green ripening through orange and red to purple; includes 'Nana', dwarf, slow-growing, with smaller, 3–5-lobed leaves. See *mulberry*.

mosaic leaf discoloration with numerous discrete lighter and darker areas, for example yellow or pale greens on darker greens, often angular and tending to be delineated by the veins. Mosaic is a characteristic virus disease symptom; cf. *mottle*. See *virus*.

moss primitive non-flowering, plants belonging to the Bryophyta. Delicate in form, they posses stems and leaves, but no true root. Mosses generally grow in damp places. Like ferns, they exhibit alternation of generations, except that with mosses the conspicuous generation is the sexual one, which can live independently.

The common peat or bog moss of the genus *Sphagnum* is of horticultural significance: harvested peat is formed in bogland from its incompletely decomposed remains, and it is used in its living form as a medium for supporting epiphytes and for lining hanging baskets and slatted containers. The use of sphagnum moss and sphagnum peat conflicts with wildlife conservation objectives. Peat and moss alternatives are available for most horticultural uses, and moss, such as Highland moss (*Pseudoscleropodium purum*), is obtainable from sustainably harvested sources.

Some species of moss may be cultivated or maintained for ornamental purposes, but naturally growing plants are most commonly met in gardens as undesirable invaders of lawns.

M

521

moss house a rustic building featured in some Victorian gardens, with interior walls formed of wooden slats into which mosses collected from the wild were pressed.

moss pole a wooden pole on to which sphagnum moss is bound, or a cylinder of wire or plastic netting filled with moss; used to provide support for climbing plants with aerial roots.

mother plant a plant from which young plantlets or propagating material are obtained; often stock plants exclusively reserved for the purpose and kept free of pathogens, especially for the production of certified stock.

M

moths Together with butterflies, moths make up the insect order Lepidoptera, none of which are pests as adult insects: some do not feed at all, others suck nectar or similar sweet liquids. They lay eggs on suitable host plants. These hatch into caterpillars with three pairs of jointed legs at the head end and up to five pairs of claspers or prolegs on the abdomen; geometrid larvae, known as loopers or inchworms, have only two pairs of prolegs. Caterpillars pass through several stages before becoming fully fed, and often leave the food plant to pupate in the soil before emerging as adults. All caterpillars have mouthparts adapted for biting and chewing, and most feed on foliage. Some feed exposed, while others, for example, many of the tortrix moths, feed hidden from view by binding two leaves together. Some moths, such as the GYPSY MOTH, BROWN TAIL MOTH, LACKEY MOTH, SMALL ERMINE (*Yponomeuta* species) and COTONEASTER WEBBER MOTHS, have larvae that feed gregariously and

Epipremnum climbing moss pole

cover infested shoots with dense silk webbing; these can defoliate shrubs and small trees completely. Some of the smallest moths have larvae that feed as leaf miners within the foliage of plants such as apple, oak, lilac and laburnum.

The roots and stem bases of many plants are damaged by soil-dwelling caterpillars, known as cutworms, which are the larvae of various species of noctuid moth. SWIFT MOTH LARVAE (*Hepialus* species) also feed in a similar manner. Annual flowers, lettuce, small herbaceous plants and root vegetables are most at risk.

The larvae of CLEARWING MOTHS are stem borers, mainly of woody plants such as currant, apple, willow and poplar. Caterpillars of the LEOPARD MOTH attack the branches and trunks of apples and other trees, and pine trees have caterpillar pests that bore into buds killing or distorting the leading shoot. A number of moths have caterpillars that feed on ripening fruits or seeds, including the CODLING MOTH, which is a worldwide pest of apples and pears, the PLUM MOTH, the PEA MOTH and the ORIENTAL FRUIT MOTH, which attacks peach and many other fruits. Some moth caterpillars can be very destructive in seed stores and granaries.

Most moth larvae cause insignificant amounts of damage and some have been used successfully in the biological control of weeds such as prickly pear and ragwort. Where control measures against caterpillars are required, the young larvae should be targeted with contact insecticides since these are more effective than systemic types. Biological control is possible for some pests, such as cabbage caterpillars, using a bacterial spray containing *Bacillus thuringiensis*. See *clearwing moths, codling moth, swift moths, tent caterpillars*.

motile hairs, appendages, lobes and spores capable of movement.

mottle leaf discoloration with small chlorotic areas of irregular shape without sharply defined edges and in a pattern that is not related to the vein network. Mottle is a common virus disease symptom; cf. *mosaic*. See *virus*.

mold the visible surface growth of fungal spores and mycelium, which is common on organic matter of plant or animal origin with a high moisture content. BLUE MOLD is the spores of *Penicillium* species, which cause storage rots of fruit and bulbs. GRAY MOLD describes the fungus *Botrytis cinerea*, which causes various forms of dieback and rots in many plants, and rots fruits and vegetables. *Rhizopus stolonifer*, which can cause fruit rot, is sometimes called PIN MOLD, while LEAF MOLD is a disease of tomatoes caused by the fungus *Fulvia fulva*. SOOTY MOLD fungi grow on plant surfaces that are covered with honeydew excreted by insects. SLIME MOLDS are organisms related to fungi which ingest bacteria, fungus spores and particles of organic matter.

mount an artificial hill within a garden. Mounts were constructed in Europe, especially Britain, from the 14th century to the early 18th, to provide a viewpoint over high garden walls. Mounts could be square or circular, with stairways or a spiral ramp leading to a flat viewing terrace, with perhaps an arbor, pleasure house, or temple on top.

mouse ear see *bud stages*.

mowing see *lawns*.

mucilage a viscous substance or solution.

mucilaginous slimy.

mucro an abrupt, sharp, terminal spur, spine or tip.

mucronate an apex terminating suddenly with an abrupt spur or spine developed from the midrib.

mucronulate diminutive of mucronate.

Mucuna (Brazilian name for these plants). Leguminosae. Widespread in the tropics and subtropics of both Hemispheres. Some 100 species, evergreen, woody climbers and erect shrubs with trifoliolate leaves and pealike flowers in axillary clusters or racemes in spring and summer. *M. bennettii* is a spectacular flame-flowered climber for tropical gardens or the warm greenhouse. Its cultural requirements are as for *Strongylodon*. *M. pruriens* and *M. sempervirens* are less showy, more intriguing, with racemes and clusters respectively of purple-black or mauve to white flowers. Where temperatures drop below 20°F (–7°C), they perform best in cool greenhouses and conservatories, but might be attempted outdoors in favored regions.

M. bennettii NEW GUINEA CREEPER; New Guinea; perennial woody climber to 65 ft (20 m); flowers to 3¼ in (8.5 cm), vivid scarlet or flame-colored, in a short inflorescence; *M. pruriens* (syn. *M. cochinchinensis*); VELVET BEAN; Asia, naturalized elsewhere; annual or perennial semi-woody, climbing herb to 13 ft (4 m); racemes to 12 in (30 cm), flowers 1¼–1½ in (3–4 cm), dark damson colored to pale purple or white; var. *utilis*: VELVET BEAN, FLORIDA BEAN, BENGHAL BEAN, flowers with a purple standard flushed green and wings of a dirty red; *M. sempervirens* China; perennial evergreen climber to 40 ft (12 m); raceme short, nodding, flowers waxy, bruised purple-black, malodorous.

Muehlenbeckia (for H. G. Muehlenbeck [1798–1845], Swiss physician and student of the flora of Alsace). Polygonaceae. S America, New Zealand, Australia, New Guinea. 15 species of largely dioecious, evergreen climbing or procumbent subshrubs and shrubs with wiry stems, small leaves, inconspicuous white flowers and fruit surrounded by the enlarged, fleshy white perianth. Grown for its intricate habit, minute foliage and small but sweetly fragrant flowers, *M. complexa* is suitable for covering tree stumps and rocky banks, or for scrambling through shrubs. It also does well in hanging-baskets,

forming a mass of intricately tangled dark wiry stems. This species is sometimes treated as a standard, grown on without support in open beds to promote a number of long stems, then potted in tubs of rich loamy soil with the stems gathered and tied to a central cane. Plants grown in this way produce a weeping crown of fine branchlets. Despite its delicate appearance, *M. complexa* can match other climbing Polygonaceae in vigor and has become a troublesome invader in warmer regions. Plant in a position sheltered from cold and drying winds (min. temp. 0°F/–18°C). Grow in well-drained soil in sun to part shade. Prune only to restrict to allotted space. Propagate by semi-ripe cuttings in summer. *M. axillaris* Australia, New Zealand; small, prostrate or straggling shrub to 3¼ × 3¼ ft (1 × 1 m); branches delicate, intricate, black; leaves ¼–½ in (0.5–1 cm) diam., oblong—pandurate to orbicular, dark green above, gray beneath; 'Nana': dwarf, leaves pandurate; *M. complexa* MAIDENHAIR VINE, WIRE VINE, MATTRESS VINE, NECKLACE VINE; New Zealand; fast-growing semi-deciduous liane, creeping or climbing to 16 ft (5 m), stems slender, dark and wiry, forming dense tangles; leaves ¼–¾ in (5–20 mm), dark green above, purple to silver beneath, oblong to circular or pandurate, rounded or cordate at base; includes var. *microphylla*, a dense shrub to 24 in (60 cm), with few, rounded, very small leaves, and var. *triloba*, with pandurate, 3-lobed leaves.

Mukdenia (from the Chinese city, Mukden). Saxifragaceae. N China, Korea. 2 species, deciduous perennial herbs. The long-stalked leaves are peltate, round to reniform, cordate at the base, palmately lobed and toothed. In spring, paniculate racemes of numerous small, white flowers stand taller than the foliage. Deciduous groundcover for woodland fringe and other shaded locations. Cultivate as for *Mitella*. *M. rossii* N China, Manchuria, Korea; to 24 in (60 cm); leaves bronze-green; flowers small, white.

mulberry (*Morus* species) Probably originating in the Caucasus or farther east, the BLACK MULBERRY (*Morus nigra*) is prized for its fruit which superficially

resembles a large raspberry. There are biblical references to the mulberry and its spread can be traced from ancient Greece and Rome across Europe to Britain and thence to other parts of the world. Mulberries are grown as either standard or half standard trees; they are slow growing but may eventually reach 33 ft (10 m) in height, forming ornamental specimens with attractive gnarled bark, and a spreading head. They may survive for several hundred years. Mulberries require a sheltered, sunny situation, and in the UK do best in southern parts. Small trees can be maintained in large tubs.

The flowers, which are borne on inconspicuous catkins, are unisexual and self-fertile; the trees have a high chilling requirement and are therefore late into leaf and flower, thus avoiding frost damage.

Mulberry (Morus nigra)
Avoid planting the black mulberry where its branches will overhang paving, or its pulpy fruits will fall and stain the surface.

Fruits ripen in late summer, changing gradually from green to deep crimson when they acquire a sweetly acidic flavor; the juice stains strongly and is persistent. Either pick the fruit from the trees or gather when fallen onto grass or a collecting sheet; use immediately for dessert, preserves or wine making, or for freezing.

Prune young trees in winter to establish a framework and minimally thereafter to maintain shape; where cut or damaged between spring and fall the wounds will bleed profusely and should be cauterized with a hot iron. Propagation may be by simple layering in fall, or by air layering, but usually by 7 in (18 cm) long hardwood cuttings

M

taken from two year-old wood, with a heel, in fall or spring.

Possible problems: *canker, powdery mildew.*

WHITE MULBERRY (*M. alba*) is not usually grown for its fruits, but in China, its leaves have provided food for silkworms for over 5000 years.

Mulch
A straw mulch over celeriac roots that are to be left in the ground for winter harvesting protects them from frost damage.

M

mulch a covering placed on the surface of cultivated soil. The benefits of a mulch include: conserving soil moisture by reducing evaporation; insulating the soil against extreme cold in winter, while keeping it relatively cool in summer; in some instances, encouraging early soil warming in spring; stimulating beneficial soil bacteria; deterring some soil-inhabiting pests; smothering weeds; keeping some fruits and vegetables off the soil surface; providing nutrients; and improving soil structure.

Mulches usually consist of bulky organic materials, such as rotted animal manure, chopped straw, spent mushroom compost, spent brewery hops, leaf mold, bark chips, and garden compost. Lawn mowings can be used provided they do not form too dense a layer, as can chopped bracken.

Unless incorporated into the surface layer, decaying organic mulches have little depleting effect on soil nitrogen. Certain types, such as farmyard manure and garden compost, may be a source of weeds if they have not been prepared or stored carefully. Some spent mushroom compost offered for sale may include lime, which will adversely affect pH where ericaceous plants are grown. Assurance should be obtained that straw for mulching does not contain residual hormone weed-killer, which might have a harmful effect upon plant growth.

Non-organic mulching materials include pea gravel and stone chips, which are visually acceptable for some garden situations, and black polyethylene sheet for weed suppression and moisture retention around fruit and vegetable crops and newly planted trees. Clear polyethylene and spun fiber fleece aid soil warming and seed germination, as well as moisture retention. Film or sheet covers are often referred to as "floating mulches," and some plants, for example, strawberries, may be planted through holes in the mulch; all such covers must be firmly buried at the edges to avoid removal by wind. Perennial weeds should be cleared from a site before mulches are put down.

The best time for mulch application is in spring, by which time winter rain or snow will have fully charged the soil with water. Organic materials should be spread to a depth of at least 4 in (10 cm). It is important to remember that, in times of prolonged drought, sufficient water must be applied to penetrate the mulch layer; sheet mulches should have irrigation lines installed beneath the covers at the time of laying down.

In very cold conditions, the temperature immediately above a mulch tends to be lower than over bare soil; where the temperature falls below freezing, shoots and flowers, for example, of strawberries, should be protected with additional straw, bracken or a cloche.

Hoeing provides some of the insulating benefits of mulching, but only if it is done to a shallow depth.

mule a sterile hybrid of two plant species.

mull a type of humus consisting of a dark-colored mixture of mineral and organic material, found in the surface layer of soil, typically on a forest floor where decomposition and incorporation of organic matter occurs freely; cf. *mor.*

multifid as bifid, but cleft more than once, forming many lobes.

multifoliate many-leaved.

multigeneric describing hybrids with more than two genera involved in their immediate ancestry, for example *Potinara* (*Brassavola* × *Cattleya* × *Laelia* × *Sophronitis*). Multigeneric hybrid names are formed either by combining the generic names of the parents, as for example with *Sophrolaeliocattleya*, or, as in the case above, by creating a commemorative personal name using the suffix *-ara.*

multiple fruit a fruit derived from an entire inflorescence, i.e. from the parts of a number of flowers.

mummified fruit dry and shrivelled fruit infected by fungi, especially that of apples, grapes, peaches and plums. Mummified fruit can often carry over disease and should be collected and burnt.

municipal waste see *town refuse.*

muriate of potash see *potassium chloride.*

muricate rough-surfaced; furnished with many short, hard, pointed projections.

muriculate slightly muricate.

Murraya (for John Andrew Murray [1740–1791], pupil of Linnaeus and Professor of Medicine and Botany at University of Gottingen). Rutaceae. Asia (India and China south to Australia). 5 species, aromatic evergreen trees and shrubs with pinnate leaves and fragrant, orange blossomlike flowers in spring and summer. Grown in their native regions as border specimens, as screens or as hedging, in cool temperate climates *Murraya* species are handsome specimens for tubs or large pots in the greenhouse or conservatory. Young plants of *M. paniculata* are also used as houseplants. Plant in a fertile, moisture-retentive but well-drained medium in full sun or part shade. Water plentifully and feed semiweekly when in full growth, moderately at other times. Maintain a winter minimum of 50°F (10°C). Prune if necessary in early spring. Propagate by seed in spring or by semi-ripe cuttings.

M. koenigii CURRY LEAF; Asia; evergreen tree, 14³/₄–20 ft (4.5–6 m); leaves pungently aromatic, leaflets 1–1½ in (2.5–4 cm), oblong-lanceolate to ovate, membranous; flowers white to ivory; fruit dark blue tinged black; *M. paniculata* ORANGE JESSAMINE, SATIN-WOOD, COSMETIC BARK TREE, CHINESE BOX; China and India south to Australia; evergreen tree or shrub, 14¾–24½ ft (4.5–7.5 m); evergreen; leaves glabrous and glossy, leaflets 1–1½ in (2.5–4 cm), cuneate-obovate to rhombic; flowers white; fruit orange to red.

Musa (from Arabic *mouz*, banana, or for Antonius Musa, physician to the Emperor Augustus). Musaceae. Old World tropics and subtropics, east to Japan, south to Queensland. BANANA, PLANTAIN, MANILA HEMP. About 40 species, giant, evergreen perennial herbs with thickened rhizomes and swollen and suckering rootstocks. The leaves are large and paddle-shaped with a distinct, sunken midrib. The sappy and fibrous petiole bases stand one within the other, forming a trunk-like pseudostem. The inflorescence is a terminal spike, pendulous or erect, with tubular flowers in clusters subtended by large and fleshy to waxy, colored bracts. The fruit is the banana, most familiarly fingerlike and gently curving, but globose to ellipsoid in some species. After flowering/fruiting, the main growth dies, but is soon replaced by offsets.

Magnificent and fast-growing foliage and flowering ornamentals for tropical and subtropical gardens and, in cooler climates, for large containers or borders in a greenhouse, conservatory or home. Careful note should be taken of eventual size when buying, although some "dwarf" selections of *M. acuminata* and *M.* × *paradisiaca* are now widely offered as houseplants and seldom make the home uninhabitable. With the exception of *M. basjoo*, those described here need a minimum temperature of 50°F (10°C), but are largely unfussy as to light and humidity, provided they are grown in a moist and richly fertile medium. Water and feed generously when in growth. Remove the blades of faded leaves and cut out flowered growths once they begin to deteriorate. The Japanese *M. basjoo* is virtually hardy in sheltered areas to 0°F (–18°C) and can certainly be used as a dot plant in bedding schemes or as a patio container plant. Overwinter it in a cold greenhouse with leaves removed and the rootstock wrapped in scarcely damp burlap or plunged in coir or sawdust. If grown outdoors year round, this banana should be sited with protection from wind which quickly shreds the leaves. Wrap the stem with sacking in fall and mulch the base thickly. Where the stems are killed by frost, replacement shoots will usually appear by early summer. Propagate all species by seed germinated in spring at 68°F (20°C), or by removing suckers with a portion of root-bearing rhizome attached. See also *Ensete*.

M. acuminata (syn. *M. cavendishii*); BANANA, PLANTAIN; SE Asia, N Queensland; pseudostems to 23 ft (7 m) or more, green blotched brown; leaves to 10 ft × 28 in (3 × 0.7 m), sometimes dark-flecked above, green or purple beneath; inflorescence pendulous, bracts bright red to purple or yellow; fruit to 8 in (20 cm), yellow, pulp white to yellow; includes the BLOOD BANANA, *M. sumatrana*, with leaves blotched wine red above, stained red beneath—coloring strong and persistent in 'Rubra'; *M. basjoo* (syn. *M. japonica*); JAPANESE BANANA; Japan, Ryukyu Islands; to 10 ft (3 m), stoloniferous; pseudostem green to red-tinted; leaves 6½ ft × 28 in (2 × 0.7 m), oblong-lanceolate, bright green, midrib sometimes red-tinted; inflorescence horizontal to pendulous, bracts yellow-green or tinged purple-brown; fruit to 2½ × 1 in (6 × 2.5 cm), yellow-green with white pulp; 'Variegata': leaves banded or flecked lime green, cream and white; *M. coccinea* (syn. *M. uranoscopus*); Indochina; pseudostem to 3¼ ft (1 m), glossy red-green; leaves to 30 × 12 in (75 × 30 cm), oval to elliptic, glossy above, somewhat waxy beneath, midrib green to rose-pink; inflorescence to 30 in (0.75 m), erect, bracts magenta to scarlet; fruit oblong to cylindric, to 2 × 1 in (5 × 2.5 cm), red-purple to pink-green; *M.* × *paradisiaca* EDIBLE BANANA, FRENCH PLANTAIN; *M. acuminata* × *M. balbisiana*; Tropics; to 25 ft (8 m); leaves to 8 ft × 28 in (2.5 × 0.7 m), oblong, green; inflorescence pendulous, to 5 ft (1.5 m), bracts purple-red; fruit usually seedless, often yellow, pulp white; there may be as many as 300 cultivars of edible banana worldwide; two ornamental cultivars are 'Koae', with leaves laterally striped white and pale green on dark green, and 'Vittata' with leaves variegated pale green and white, the

M

PROPAGATING MUSA BASJOO FROM SUCKERS

1 Clear away soil to expose the sucker's point of origin, and cut it cleanly away with its portion of root.

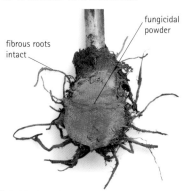

fibrous roots intact

fungicidal powder

2 Fill in the soil around the parent plant. Dust the cut surface of the sucker's root with a fungicide to ward off rots.

plant at the same depth as before

3 Pot the sucker in a container just larger than the root system, water, and grow in a warm, shaded place.

midrib white, edged red). For *M. ensete*, see *Ensete ventricosum*; for *M. superba*, see *Ensete superbum*.

Muscari (from Greek *moschos*, musk, alluding to the scent of some species). Liliaceae (Hyacinthaceae). Mediterranean, SW Asia. GRAPE HYACINTH. 30 species, bulbous perennial herbs with slender, rather fleshy leaves and erect spikes packed with small, bell- to urn-shaped flowers in spring. Hardy to 0°F (−18°C). Plant in full sun in free-draining soil. Top-dress established clumps with bonemeal in spring; lift and divide when overcrowded, incorporating fresh topsoil before replanting. Propagate by offsets after flowering or by seed sown when ripe.

M. armeniacum SE Europe to Caucasus; raceme 1–3 in (2.5–7.5 cm), flowers crowded, fertile flowers ⅛–¼ in (3.5–5.5 mm), obovoid to urceolate, azure, sometimes flushed purple, rarely white, lobes paler or white, sterile flowers few, smaller and paler; includes white-, pale blue- and white-rimmed cultivars; *M. aucheri* (syn. *M. tubergenianum*); Turkey; raceme dense, ovoid or cylindric, fertile flowers ⅛–¼ in (3–5 mm), subspherical or ovoid, bright azure, rarely white, lobes paler or white, sterile flowers paler; *M. azureum* E Turkey; raceme ⅝–1¼ in (1.5–3 cm), dense, fertile flowers ⅛–¼ in (4–5 mm), campanulate, bright blue with a darker stripe on the lobes, sterile flowers smaller and paler; includes white- and pale blue-flowered cultivars; *M. botryoides* C and SE Europe; raceme dense then loose and cylindric, fertile flowers ⅛–¼ in (2.5–5 mm), subspherical, scented, azure or white, lobes white; includes white, bright blue and pink cultivars; *M. comosum* TASSEL HYACINTH; S and C Europe, N Africa, SW Asia, naturalized Europe; raceme loose, fertile flowers ¼–⅜ in (5–9 mm), oblong-urceolate, brown-olive, lobes yellow-brown, sterile flowers subspherical or obovoid, rarely tubular, bright violet on violet, ascending pedicels; includes 'Plumosum', syn. 'Monstrosum', with a sterile, mauve-blue, densely branched inflorescence; *M. latifolium* S and W Asia; raceme dense then loose, fertile flowers ¼ in (6 mm), oblong-urceolate, tube strongly constricted, deep violet, sterile flowers

blue; *M. macrocarpum* Aegean Islands, W Turkey; raceme loose, fertile flowers ⅜–½ in (8–12 mm), fragrant, oblong-urceolate, blue-violet then yellow, expanding to form brown or yellow corona, sterile flowers tinged purple, few or none; *M. massayanum* E Turkey; raceme dense, cylindric, fertile flowers to ½ in (1 cm), pink to violet at first, later pale green- or yellow-blue, lobes dark brown, sterile flowers pink or violet on ascending pedicels, forming a dense tuft; *M. muscarimi* (syn. *M. moschatum*); SW Turkey; flowers muskily scented, fertile flowers ⅜–½ in (8–14 mm), narrowly urceolate, purple then pale green to ivory, strongly contracted then expanded to form a brown corona, sterile flowers purple-tinged, rarely present; *M. neglectum* (syn. *M. racemosum*); COMMON GRAPE HYACINTH; Europe, N Africa, SW Asia; raceme dense in flower; fertile flowers 1/16–⅛ in (1.5–3.5 mm), ovoid to oblong-urceolate, strongly constricted, deep blue-black, lobes white, sterile flowers smaller and paler blue. For *M. paradoxum*, see *Bellevalia pycnantha*.

muscariform in the shape of a broom or brush.

mushroom compost spent compost from commercial mushroom production, used as a soil improver, a mulch, or an ingredient of potting media. It is the product of composting straw with horse manure or nitrogenous fertilizers, and, depending on the type of casing ingredients used for spawning mushrooms, may be alkaline in nature; hence, regular applications can alter soil pH. Where incorporated, it improves soil structure, provides some nutrients and can enhance nutrient and water retention. Its physical properties are determined by age: for example, with decomposition, aeration decreases and moisture-holding increases.

mushrooms Edible fungi have been collected from the wild since ancient times but few species are in cultivation due to the complex microbial processes and associations involved in their growth, and to the difficulties involved in preparing substrates on which they will establish and fruit. Mushroom culti-

vation is unique because it provides the only profitable process for converting waste lignocellulose from agriculture and forestry into a useful, edible product. Mushrooms cultivated on a significant scale worldwide are *Agaricus bisporus* and *A. bitorquis*, SHIITAKE MUSHROOM (*Lentinus edodes*), CHINESE or STRAW MUSHROOM (*Volvariella volvaceae*), WINTER MUSHROOM (*Flammulina velutipes*), OYSTER MUSHROOM (*Pleurotus* species), NAMEKO or VISCID MUSHROOM (*Pholiota nameko*), JEW'S EAR (*Auricularia* species) and SNOW MUSHROOM (*Tremella fuciformis*).

Agaricus accounts for two thirds of the world production of cultivated fungi; it dominates production in the west and is the only species of significance cultivated in the British Isles.

Agaricus bisporus is cultivated on substrates prepared from cereal straw, preferably wheat. In the first phase of preparation, straw or strawy horse manure is wetted and mixed with activators, such as chicken manure or molassed malt waste; these provide a source of nitrogen and soluble carbohydrate to promote microbial breakdown of the substrate when stacked. Fermentation develops and the stack is turned at intervals of 2–4 days over a period of 7–14 days to maintain aeration and ensure uniformity. In the second phase, the fermenting compost is transferred to a facility in which it is pasteurized at 131–140°F (55–60°C) over a period of 4–8 days in a process known as "peak heating." At the end of this period, the compost is cooled at 77°F (25°C) and inoculated with a pure culture of *Agaricus* mycelium (spawn) grown on cereal grain. The spawned compost is maintained at 77°F (25°C) for 10–14 days during which it is colonized by the fungal mycelium (spawn-running). The upper surface of the colonized compost is then covered with a layer of peat/chalk (casing) and the temperature lowered to 61–64°F (16–18°C). The mycelium continues to colonize the compost and also invades the casing layer. After 18–21 days, fruit bodies are initiated (pinning) and these develop into the typical gilled caps. The crop is produced in flushes at intervals of 7–10 days over a period of 30–35 days. Production is then terminated by heating to at least 140°F (60°C) with live steam (cooking

M

out), the spent compost removed and the facility cleaned in preparation for the start of the next cycle. The production cycle takes 12–14 weeks.

Commercial crops may be cultivated in purpose-built sheds, in insulated "tunnels" covered with plastic film, or in caves. The substrate may be contained and the crop produced in ridged beds on the floor, in tiered wooden trays, on metal shelves, in deep troughs or in open-topped plastic bags. The processes involved in preparation and handling of compost, filling of trays and shelves, spawning, casing, watering and clearance of the used compost are all highly mechanized.

Cultivation requires accurate control of the environment and particularly of temperature, CO_2 level, ventilation rate and evaporative capacity of the air at different stages in the production cycle. It is therefore difficult for private gardeners to prepare composts on which mushrooms can be successfully grown, but there are mushroom-growing kits available, consisting of prepared compost already spawned, together with a bag of casing material. The packaging may be a plastic bag, a water-resistant cardboard or rigid plastic box, or a rigid plastic tub, which doubles as a growing container. The purchaser simply follows the instructions enclosed.

Possible problems: *eelworms, sciarid flies; virus, bacteria.*

Mussaenda (from the Sri Lankan name). Rubiaceae. Tropical Old World. Some 100 species, shrubs, subshrubs and herbs, often scandent. They bear 5-lobed, tubular to funnel-shaped flowers in axillary or terminal, panicles or cymes. With some flowers in each inflorescence, a calyx lobe is greatly enlarged as a highly colored, leaflike limb. Grow in a hot greenhouse (ensure a minimum temperature of 60–65°F/15–18°C), in direct sunlight, in a pH-neutral mix of equal parts loam, coir and leaf mold with added sharp sand. Water plentifully when in growth, sparingly in winter. Provide support for climbing specimens, and thin out crowded stems or prune to a framework in spring. Propagate by semi-ripe cuttings or air layering in summer, alternatively by seed in spring.

M. erythrophylla Tropical Africa; erect or climbing, evergreen or deciduous shrub to 25 ft (8 m); flowers in dense panicles or cymes, pink to red and white to yellow, many with an enlarged calyx lobe to 4 in (10 cm) long, oval and, typically, scarlet; includes 'Queen Sirikit', with deep pink to ivory inflorescences.

White mustard (Sinapsis alba)
Mustard is either harvested very young for salad leaves, or allowed to flower in order to obtain its seeds.

mustard, white (*Sinapis alba*) a cruciferous annual, native of the Mediterranean region, C Asia, and N Africa. Of horticultural importance as a salad plant and for green manuring, it is also grown for its seed, which is an ingredient of table mustard and curries, and as a fodder crop. Mustard is often grown with common garden cress (*Lepidium sativum*) for harvesting as dense young seedlings with elongated stems about 1½–2 in (4–5 cm) high. It should be sown indoors two days later than cress for even development of the two, either in a soilless medium like blotting paper or any other moisture-retentive substrate. Mustard is milder in flavor than cress and is sometimes substituted with rape (*Brassica napus* subsp. *oleifera*).

White mustard can also be grown as a cut-and-come again salad vegetable, either sown in seed trays under protection, broadcast, or in drills outdoors, especially in spring and fall. Other vegetable crops known as mustards are SPINACH MUSTARD (*Brassica rapa* Perviridis Group) and MUSTARD CABBAGE (*Brassica juncea*) see *oriental greens*.

mutation a spontaneous or induced genetic change in a plant leading to an altered phenotype with characteristics

such as leaf variegation and color change or distribution in flowers. A mutation may occur by chance or be induced by chemicals, radiation or the activity of viruses. Many mutations are perpetuated as desirable forms in gardens. A plant arising from such a change is known as a mutant, sport or break.

muticous blunt, unpointed.

Mutisia (for José Celestino Mutis of Cadiz [1732–1808], teacher of anatomy and student of South American plants). Compositae. S America. About 60 species, evergreen subshrubs or shrubs, many of them sprawling or twining, often with tendril-tipped leaves. Brightly colored daisylike flower heads are produced in late spring and summer. Given the protection of a south-facing wall and good drainage, *M. oligodon* will tolerate temperatures to about 5°F (–15°C) and *M. decurrens* to about 14°F (–10°C). Grow in deep, well-drained, moderately fertile soils, with shade at the roots but where top growth will receive full sun; a large rock or deep organic mulch placed over the roots will provide the necessary protection and help conserve moisture when in growth. Provide support by means of wire or trellis, or plant at the foot of a wall shrub in a sheltered, sunny position. Under glass, water moderately when in growth, and maintain good ventilation with a minimum winter temperature of 45–50°F (7–10°C). Prune to remove weak and overcrowded growth after flowering or in spring in cool climates. Propagate by stem cuttings in summer, by simple layering, or by removal of rooted suckers; increase also by seed in spring.

M. decurrens Chile, Argentina; much-branched, rhizomatous subshrub to 6½ ft (2 m); leaves to 4 in (10 cm), lanceolate, with a long tendril at the apex and decurrent base, margins entire or sharp-toothed; flower heads to 4¾ in (12 cm) in diameter, brilliant orange; *M. oligodon* S Chile, S Argentina; straggling shrub or liane to 3¼ ft (1 m); leaves to 1½ in (3.5 cm), oblong to elliptic, apex acute or obtuse and sparsely toothed, sometimes terminating in a tendril, base cordate;

flower heads to 2¾ in (7 cm) in diameter, bright red.

mycelium typically, the vegetative body of a fungus made up of a mass of microscopic filamentous branches, known as hyphae.

mycology the study of fungi.

mycoplasmas (MLOs) see *phytoplasmas*.

mycorrhiza a symbiotic association between the root cells of a plant and fungal mycelium, whereby the absorption of nutrients is enhanced to the benefit of both organisms. The relationship is common in plants such as orchids, trees and heaths.

Myoporum (from Greek *myo*, to close, and Latin *porum*, a pore, due to the densely glandular-punctate leaves). Myoporaceae. Australia and New Zealand to E Asia and Mauritius. About 30 species, glandular-punctate evergreen trees and shrubs, often shrubby and heathlike. Small, 5-lobed and campanulate to hypocrateriform flowers are borne singly or in clusters in summer and are followed by colorful drupes. In frost-free, Mediterranean-type climates, grow *Myoporum* species in the rockery or on sunny banks; they thrive in dry soils and maritime conditions. In colder areas, grow in a sandy loam-based mix in a cool, well-ventilated greenhouse or conservatory. Propagate by simple layers, by semi-ripe cuttings or by seed.

M. laetum New Zealand; tree to 33 ft (10 m); leaves 1½–4 in (4–10 cm), lanceolate to obovate, somewhat fleshy, crenate to sinuate; flowers to ½ in (1 cm) in diameter, campanulate, white with purple spots; fruit pale to dark maroon; *M. parvifolium* Australia; low, spreading, glabrous shrub to 20 in (50 cm); leaves ½–1 in (1–2.5 cm), linear; flowers honey-scented, to ½ in (1 cm) wide, white.

Myosotidium (from *Myosotis* and Greek *oides*, resembling—the flowers resemble those of *Myosotis*). Boraginaceae. New Zealand (Chatham Islands). 1 species, *M. hortensia*, the CHATHAM ISLANDS FORGET-ME-NOT, a

perennial or biennial herb to 3¼ ft (1 m) tall with long-stalked, thinly fleshy, reniform to broadly ovate or ovate-cordate leaves to 12 in (30 cm) in diameter and glossy above with deeply impressed veins. In summer, it produces broad, stalked heads of large, dark to sky blue forget-me-not flowers. Hardy to 0°F (–18°C). In gardens with cool summers and little frost, it is suitable for the front of borders or a rock garden. Where hard frosts occur, protect with evergreen branches or dry bracken litter, otherwise grow in the cold greenhouse. Plant in a cool position in semi-shade, sheltered from wind, in free-draining, humus-rich soils. Propagate from seed sown ripe in fall or by careful division.

Myosotis (from Greek *mys*, mouse, and *ous*, ear, referring to the appearance of the leaves). Boraginaceae. Temperate distribution, mainly Europe, New Zealand. FORGET-ME-NOT, SCORPION GRASS. Some 50 species, hairy annual, biennial or perennial herbs. They bear small, rotate or salverform flowers with five rounded lobes and distinct faucal scales (the "eye") at various times of year and usually in paired cymes. *M. sylvatica* and *M. alpestris* occur in damp woodland and meadow. Their many cultivars are grown as hardy annuals or biennials (tolerating winter temperatures of at least 5°F/–15°C); these are available as compact dwarf cultivars, such as 'Ultramarine', with deep indigo blue flowers, 'White Ball', compact with white blooms, and the taller rose-pink flowered 'Rose'. Traditionally used in spring bedding and as border edging, they are also suited to window boxes and to pot cultivation in a cold greenhouse for winter and early spring blooms. They will self-seed. *M. scorpioides* and *M. laxa*, found in wet habitats at water margins and in marshy ground, are suited to pond edge and other damp sites, in mud or very shallow water, especially in wilder areas of the garden. *M. australis* occurs at higher altitudes in exposed, moist and rocky habitats. Grow it in gritty, moderately fertile and perfectly draining soils in sun or in light, partial shade—scree plantings, for example. Propagate by seed or division in early spring.

Powdery mildew may seriously reduce flowering of annual/biennial species. *Myosotis* smut shows as off-white spots on the leaves, and often occurs on plants allowed to self-sow.

M. alpestris Europe, Asia, N America; tufted perennial to 12 in (30 cm); flowers bright or deep blue, to ⅜ in (9 mm) in diameter; *M. australis* Australia, Tasmania, New Zealand; perennial to 12 in (30 cm); corolla white or yellow; *M. caespitosa* Europe, Asia, N Africa, N America; perennial to 24 in (60 cm), sparingly covered with white hairs; flowers blue to ⅛ in (4 mm) in diameter; *M. laxa* Europe, N America; annual to perennial; stem to 20 in (50 cm), decumbent, adpressed-pubescent; flowers bright blue with a yellow eye, to ¼ in (5 mm) in diameter; *M. scorpioides* FORGET-ME-NOT; Europe; perennial; stem to 20 in (50 cm), angled, mostly glabrous; flowers bright blue, with white, yellow or pink eye, to ⅜ in (8 mm) in diameter; includes 'Sapphire', with bright blue flowers, 'Semperflorens', of dwarf habit, to 8 in (20 cm), and 'Thuringen', with sky blue flowers; *M. sylvatica* GARDEN FORGET-ME-NOT; N Africa, Europe, W Asia; biennial to perennial; stem to 20 in (50 cm), hairy; flowers bright blue, purple or white-blue, varying to pink, with a yellow eye to ⅜ in (8 mm) in diameter; cultivars include 'Blue Ball', small and compact, with rich indigo flowers; 'Blue Bird', tall, with deep blue flowers; 'Carmine King', erect, with rosy carmine flowers; 'Compacta', dense and low; 'Royal Blue', tall, early-flowering, with abundant, indigo flowers; 'Robusta Grandiflora', vigorous, with large flowers; 'Rosea', tall, with soft pink flowers; and 'White Ball', small and compact, with large, white flowers.

Myriophyllum (from Greek *myrios*, many, and *phyllon*, leaf, referring to the much-divided leaves). Haloragidaceae. Cosmopolitan. MILFOIL. Some 45 species, aquatic or terrestrial herbs (those listed here are perennial aquatics with slender, floating to emergent stems clothed with many whorled leaves, entire or slightly dentate when emergent, usually finely pinnatifid when submerged). Inconspicuous flower spikes are produced in summer. Useful oxygenators for freshwater pools and aquariums, as well as providing fish with shelter. *M. verticillatum* will survive in ponds where winter temperatures fall as low as 5°F (–15°C); *M. aquaticum* and *M. hippuroides* will not tolerate temperatures below freezing. Frost-tender species may be overwintered as rooted pieces in a moist medium in a frost-free greenhouse. Propagate by stem cuttings rooted directly into the growing medium or by division.

M. aquaticum PARROT FEATHER, DIA-MOND MILFOIL; S America, Australia, New Zealand, Java; stem to 6½ ft (2 m); leaves more or less uniform, in whorls of 4 or 5, to 1½ in (4 cm), pinnatifid, segments short, bright yellow-green or blue-green; *M. hippuroides* WESTERN MILFOIL; SW US; stem to 24 in (60 cm); leaves in whorls of 4 or 5, pale green, emergent leaves linear to lanceolate, entire to serrate, submerged leaves to ¾ in (2 cm); *M. verticillatum* MYRIAD LEAF; N America, Europe, Asia; stem to 3¼ ft (1 m); emergent leaves to ½ in (1 cm), pectinate to pinnatifid, submerged leaves to 1½ × 1½ in (4 × 4 cm), in whorls of 4–6, with 8–16 pairs of opposite segments.

myrmecophytes, myrme-cophilous plants plants that live in symbiosis with ants, forming hollow structures in which the insects nest in exchange for benefits, such as carbon dioxide enrichment and protection from predators and competition by other plants. Examples include, *Myrmecodia*, *Lecanopteris*, *Dischidia* and *Cecropia*.

Myrrhis (name used by Dioscorides.) Umbelliferae. Europe. 1 species, *M. odorata*, SWEET CICELY, an aromatic, perennial herb to 6½ ft (2 m) with bipinnate leaves, the segments ½ in (1 cm), oblong to lanceolate, pinnatifid or deeply toothed, pale beneath and often blotched white. Small, white flowers are carried in compound umbels in early summer. In an herb garden, it is valued for its culinary and medicinal virtues. It is also well-suited to naturalizing in woodland walks and for plantings in a shrub border. If cut back periodically in an herbaceous border, the fresh green foliage makes an admirable foil for other plants. It is hardy to at least 5°F (–15°C) and self-seeds freely. Propagate from ripe seed,

by careful division, or by root cuttings, in spring or fall.

Myrsine (name given by Dioscorides to the myrtle, *Myrtus communis*). Myrsinaceae. Azores to China and New Zealand. 5 species, evergreen trees and shrubs with leathery, aromatic leaves, inconspicuous flowers and, where plants of both sexes are present, small drupes. *Myrsine* species are grown for their often aromatic foliage and attractive fruits. In warm Mediterranean-type climates, they are sometimes used as hedging and as specimens for the shrub border. Given good drainage and shelter from cold drying winds, the aromatic *M. africana* may tolerate several degrees of short-lived frost and is suitable for the sunny rock garden; in cooler areas, young plants are grown as houseplants. Grow in full sun or part shade in fertile, well-drained, circumneutral soil. Propagate by seed or semi-ripe cuttings. *M. africana* AFRICAN BOXWOOD, CAPE MYRTLE; Azores, mountains of E and South Africa, Himalaya, China; shrub 20 in–5 ft (0.5–1.5 m), young shoots softly hairy; leaves ¼–¾ in (0.6–2 cm), narrowly obovate to elliptic, apex rounded or truncate, sparsely toothed; flowers pale brown, 3–6 per cluster; fruit ¼ in (6 mm) in diameter, blue-lilac.

Myrtillocactus (so-named because *Vaccinium myrtillus* has similar-looking fruits). Cactaceae. Mexico, Guatemala. 4 closely related species of arborescent or shrubby cacti with numerous, ascending, few-ribbed and spiny branches. The flowers are small and rotate, the fruit small, edible and berrylike. Plant in a circumneutral medium high in grit, with a minimum temperature of 50°F (10°C). Shade in hot weather and maintain low humidity; keep dry from mid-fall until early spring, except for light misting on warmer days during late winter. *M. geometrizans* C and S Mexico; tree 13–16 ft (4–5 m), with short trunk; branches numerous, upcurving, 2½–4 in (6–10 cm) in diameter, blue-green, ribs 5–6, central spine, 1, ½–2¾ in (1–7 cm), daggerlike, almost black, radial spines 5–9, ¹⁄₁₆–½ in (2–10 mm), red-brown then gray; flowers to ¾ × 1 in (2 × 2.5 cm), creamy white; fruit ½–¾ in (1–2 cm) in diameter, dark red or purple.

Myrtus (Greek name for this plant). Myrtaceae. Mediterranean, N Africa. 2 species, aromatic, evergreen shrubs with neat, glossy leaves and, from spring to summer, fragrant, solitary flowers with four broad and spreading petals and many showy stamens. In mild areas of (min. temp. 0°F/–18°C), *M. communis* is grown as a specimen and sometimes for hedging. In colder areas, it tends to be grown as a standard or pyramid in containers and moved into a cold greenhouse for the winter months. Given shelter from harsh winds and good drainage, it will, however, tolerate mild frosts; the smaller-leaved cultivars are hardier still. Grow in full sun in a moderately fertile, well-drained soil. In pots, use a free-draining, medium-fertility, loam-based mix. Under glass, water moderately when in growth; keep just moist in winter, and at a temperature of around 41°F (5°C). Prune during spring to maintain size and shape, and to remove any damaged growth. Semi-ripe nodal cuttings will root in a frame or a case with bottom heat.

M. communis MYRTLE; Mediterranean and SW Europe, widely cultivated since ancient times, native range uncertain; much-branched erect shrub to 16 ft (5 m); leaves to 2 in (5 cm), ovate to lanceolate, coriaceous, lustrous green, aromatic; flowers white to ivory or pink-white, to 1¼ in (3 cm) in diameter, fragrant; fruit to ½ in (1 cm), blue-black or red-black to dark purple-red: 'Albocarpa': fruit white; 'Buxifolia': leaves neat, boxlike; 'Compacta': dwarf, dense; 'Flore Pleno': flowers double, white; 'Leucocarpa': fruit white; 'Microphylla': dwarf and densely leafy, with very small and narrow leaves; 'Microphylla Variegata': leaves striped white; 'Minima': dwarf, with small leaves; 'Variegata': small, leaves with white to cream margins or blotches; var. *italica*: narrowly upright, with 1¼ × ½ in (3 × 1 cm), oval to lanceolate leaves; var. *latifolia*: leaves ¾–1¼ (2–3 cm) × ½–⅝ in (1–1.5 cm), oval to oblong, acuminate; var. *romana*: leaves 1¼–1¾ (3–4.5 cm) × ½–⅝ in (1–1.5 cm), broadly ovate, strongly acuminate, light green, in whorls of 3–4; subsp. *tarentina*: compact, rounded habit, with small, narrow, dark leaves, pink-tinted, cream flowers, and white fruit.

N

NAA 2-(1-napthyl) acetic acid; an auxin used in synthesized form as an aid to rooting cuttings, usually blended with IBA in powder form. NAA is considered to be especially useful in the rooting of large-flowered hybrid rhododendrons. NAA is also used in preparations available for the control of suckers or water shoots in raspberries and pome and stone fruits.

Nandina (from Japanese name, *nandin*). Berberidaceae. HEAVENLY BAMBOO. India to Japan. 1 species, *N. domestica*, a semideciduous or evergreen shrub to 6½ ft (2 m) with erect and clumped, slender stems. The leaves are bipinnate to tripinnate, to 36 in (90 cm) long and held semierect or horizontal. They are composed of elliptic to rhombic leaflets to 2¾ in (7 cm) long. Smooth and thinly leathery, these emerge slightly glaucous and lime green tinted rose, harden to sap-green, and turn bright red to purple in fall. Small, white flowers are borne in terminal panicles in summer and followed by red berries. Hardy to –10°F (–23°C). Plant in humus-rich, moist but well-drained soil, in a cool but sunny position, sheltered from cold winter winds. Remove damaged or exhausted shoots by cutting them right back to the base. Propagate by single node cuttings, taken in midsummer and rooted in a closed case with bottom heat in a sandy mix. Seeds do not germinate freely, but may succeed if sown when ripe.

nappe a smooth sheet of water falling over a weir or cascade.

Narcissus (Greek name derived from *narke*, numbness, torpor, from its narcotic properties: the youth Narcissus fell in love with his own reflection in a pool and was turned into a lily by the gods). Amaryllidaceae. DAFFODIL. S Europe and Mediterranean; also N Africa, W Asia, China and Japan. About 50 species, bulbous perennial herbs with grassy to strap-shaped leaves. The flowers of *Narcissus* are characteristically yellow or white, sometimes fragrant, and solitary or in an umbel borne on a leafless scape. The perianth is tubular at the base, with 6 segments and a conspicuous corona in the form of a trumpet or a smaller ring or cup. For cultivation see *daffodils*. (*See table opposite.*)

nastic movements growth movements in plants that take place in response to an environmental stimulus. Unlike tropism, the direction of growth is not influenced by the location of the stimulus. For example, the opening and closing of some flowers, induced by changes in light or temperature.

National Growmore see *Growmore*.

Naturalized Narcissus
Daffodils are popular subjects for naturalizing in long grass, which must not be mown until the leaves of the bulbs have died down.

naturalizing the practice of introducing plants into a setting where they give the appearance of having established naturally. It may involve plants generally within their native habitat or exotic ones.

Naturalizing bulbs in grass is effective in gardens, and randomly planted drifts of daffodils are popular. Crocuses, snakeshead fritillary (*Fritillaria meleagris)*, and *Chionodoxa*, *Scilla*, and *Leucojum*, together with *Dactylorhiza* orchids, combine well in grass areas, which must be mown only after leaves of the bulbous species have died down; where wild flowers are also established in grass, mowing should be left until late summer to allow seed ripening. Many plants, including *Cyclamen*, *Galanthus*, hellebores, and ferns, are well-suited to naturalizing in woodland areas, and spring-flowering bulbs established around the base of deep-rooted and lightly-shaded trees can be attractive.

Nautilocalyx (from Greek *nautilos*, sailor, and *calyx*, probably referring to the boat-shaped floral bracts). Gesneriaceae. Tropical Americas. About 38 species, perennial evergreen herbs and subshrubs with fleshy stems, elliptic to lanceolate, toothed leaves and solitary or cymose axillary flowers. These are tubular with a limb of five lobes. Provide a minimum temperature of 59°F (15°C), with moderate to high humidity and light shade. Pot in a sandy soilless mixture. Keep moist when in growth, but almost dry when at rest during the cooler, duller times of year. Increase by stem cuttings in summer.

N. bullatus Peru; to 20 ft (6 m); leaves bullate, purple beneath; flowers downy, pale yellow; *N. lynchii* Colombia; to 24 in (60 cm), erect; leaves flushed dark purple or red-brown, glossy; flowers pale yellow, exterior covered with red hairs, interior flecked purple.

navicular, naviculate shaped like the keel of a boat.

NCCPG The National Council for the Conservation of Plants and Gardens. The NCCPG is a registered charity in the UK, founded in 1978, which is committed to encouraging the propagation and conservation of endangered garden plants in the British Isles and to relevant research. The organization coordinates a network of plant collections maintained in public and private gardens, and further promotes its objectives through nationwide membership, publications, and educational events.

neck used of the upper part of a bulb, where the leaves and flower stem emerge.

NARCISSUS

Name	Distribution	Height	Leaves	Flowers
N. assoanus *N. requienii,* *N. juncifolius, N. pallens* RUSH-LEAVED JONQUIL	S France, S & E Spain	2¾–10 in (7–25 cm)	to 8 × ¹⁄₁₆ in (20 × 0.2 cm), cylindric, spreading or prostrate, green, terete, smooth	¾ in (2–3, to 2.2 cm) diam., horizontal or slightly ascending, yellow, fragrant; perianth tube ½–¾ in (1.2–1.8 cm), straight; segments obovate, ¼–½ × ¼ in (0.7–1 × 0.7 cm) spreading to incurved, corona cup-shaped, conical, ¼ × ½–¾ in (0.5 × 1.1–1.7 cm), crenate, deeper yellow than segments
N. asturiensis *N. minimus*	N Portugal, NW & NC Spain	2¾–5½ in (7–14 cm)	3 × ¼ in (8 × 0.6 cm), glaucous-green, spreading, channeled	solitary, to 1½ (3.5 cm) across, usually drooping, soft yellow; perianth tube to ⅜ in (0.8 cm), green-yellow; segments to ⅝ × ⅛ in (1.4 × 0.4 cm), usually twisted, deflexed; corona ¾ in (1.7 cm), widened below, constricted at middle, mouth spreading, fimbriate
Comments: 'Giant': larger in all parts.				
N. broussonetii	Morocco	to 16 in (40 cm)	11 × ⅜ in (28 × 0.9 cm), glaucous, erect	1–8, ascending, white, to 1½ in (3.5 cm) diam., fragrant; perianth tube to 1⅛ in (2.8 cm), funnel-shaped, white; segments ⅗–½ in (1.6 × 1.2 cm), spreading or incurved; corona rudimentary
Comments: Fall.				
N. bulbocodium HOOP PETTICOAT DAFFODIL, PETTICOAT DAFFODIL	W France, Spain, Portugal, N Africa	1–8 in (2.5–20 cm)	4–12 × ¹⁄₁₆–¼ in (10–30 cm × 1–5 mm), semi-cylindrical, erect, ascending or prostrate, dark green	solitary, horizontal, pale yellow to deep golden-yellow, often green-tinged, to 1¾ in (4.5 cm) diam.; perianth tube ¼–1 in (0.6–2.5 cm), yellow, often tinged green, especially below; segments much shorter than corona, ¼–¾ × ¹⁄₆₄–¼ in (0.6–2 cm × 0.5–5 mm), often tinged green; corona funnel-shaped, ⅜–1¼ × ¼–1¼ in (0.9–3.2 × 0.7–3.4 cm), yellow, margin of mouth spreading or incurved, entire to dentate or crenate
Comments: var. **bulbocodium:** plants usually dwarf; flowers golden-yellow. var. **conspicuus:** plant robust; flowers dark yellow to citron; var. **citrinus:** a name loosely applied to large-flowered pale yellow plants.				
N. cantabricus *N. clusii* WHITE HOOP PETTICOAT DAFFODIL	S Spain, Morocco, Algeria	2–4 in (5–10 cm)	ascending or spreading, to 6 × ¹⁄₁₆ in (15 cm × 1 mm), semicylindrical, slightly channeled	solitary, ascending, to 1½ in (40 mm) diam., pure- or milk-white, fragrant; perianth tube to 1 × ½ in (2.4 × 1.2 cm), funnel-shaped, white, green below; segments ½ × ¼ in (1.2 × 0.5 cm), white, virtually outspread; corona to ⅝ × 1½ in (1.5 × 4 cm) entire or crenate or undulate
N. cyclamineus	NW Portugal, NW Spain	to 8 in (20 cm)	4¾–12 × ⅛–¼ in (12–30 cm × 4–6 mm), bright green, spreading, keeled	solitary, drooping or pendent, deep yellow; perianth tube ¹⁄₁₆–⅛ in (2–3 mm), green; segments sharply reflexed, corona ¾ in (2 cm), slightly constricted just below flared margin, lobed or fimbriate
N. dubius	S France, SE Spain	6–10 in (15–25 cm)	20 × ¼ in (50 cm × 7 mm) at flowering, spreading, dark green, inner face flat, outer striate	2–6, ascending, white; perianth tube ⅗ × ¹⁄₁₆ in (1.6 × 0.2 cm), green below; segments ¼ × ¼ in (7 × 6 mm), spreading; corona ⅛ × ¼ in (4 × 7 mm), cup-shaped, crenate
N. elegans **Comments:** Fall.	W & S Italy, Sicily, Corsica, Sardinia, Morocco to Libya	8 in (20 cm)+	4¾–10 × ⅛–¼ in (12–25 cm × 3–5 mm), erect, glaucous, striate on outer surface	2–7, horizontal, 1–1½ in (2.5–3.5 cm) diam., fragrant; perianth tube ⅗ × ¹⁄₁₆ in (1.6 × 0.2 cm), green; segments ⅝ × ⅛–¼ in (1.5 × 0.3–0.7 cm), white, spreading, becoming twisted with age, corona ½ × ¾ in (1 × 2 cm), green, becoming dull orange

N. bulbocodium

N. cantabricus

N. cyclamineus

N. jonquilla

NARCISSUS

Name	Distribution	Height	Leaves	Flowers
N. jonquilla JONQUIL	S & C Spain, S & E Portugal, naturalized elsewhere	to 16 in (40 cm)	erect to spreading, to 18 × ³⁄₈ in (45 × 0.8 cm), channeled at base, cylindric toward apex, striate, green	1–6, to 1¼ in (3 cm) diam., ascending; perianth tube to 1¼ in (3 cm), slightly curved, pale green, segments elliptic, to ½ in (1.3 cm), spreading, yellow; corona cup-shaped, ¼–½ × ¹⁄₁₆–¹⁄₈ in (7–10 × 2–4 mm), yellow, margin shallowly lobed or somewhat crenate
N. minor N. nanus, N. provincialis	Pyrenees, N Spain	5½–8 in (14–20 cm)	erect, 3–6 × ¹⁄₈–½ in (8–15 × 0.4–1 cm), sage-green or glaucous, flat or channeled	solitary, to 1½ in (3.7 cm) diam., horizontal or ascending; perianth tube ½–¾ in (1–1.8 cm), yellow or green-yellow; segments ovate-lanceolate, ⁵⁄₈–¾ in (1.5–2.2 cm), somewhat twisted, drooping, yellow, often with deeper median streak; corona ¾ × 1 in (1.7 × 2.5 cm), plicate, dilated at mouth, margin frilled
N. × obvallaris TENBY DAFFODIL	garden origin	to 8 in (20 cm)	erect, 12 in (30 cm) long, glaucous	solitary, 1½ in (4 cm) diam., horizontal; perianth tube ½ in (1 cm), yellow with green stripes; segments to 1¼ in (3 cm), slightly twisted, yellow; corona to 1½ in (3.5 cm), margin dilated, 6-lobed, sometimes reflexed
N. × odorus N. calathinus, N. campernellii: (N. jonquilla × N. pseudonarcissus) CAMPERNELLE JONQUIL	garden origin; naturalized S Europe	to 16 in (40 cm)	to 20 × ³⁄₈ in (50 × 0.8 cm), strongly keeled, bright green	1–4, ascending, bright yellow, very fragrant, perianth tube to ¾ in (2 cm); segments to 1 × ½ in (2.5 × 1.3 cm); corona to ¾ × ¾ in (1.8 × 2 cm), lobed to more or less entire
Comments: 'Rugulosus': larger than the typical plant. 'Plenus': flowers double.				
N. papyraceus N. tazetta ssp. papyraceus PAPER-WHITE NARCISSUS	S Europe	to 16 in (40 cm)+	to 12 × ¾ in (30 × 1.7 cm), erect, keeled, glaucous	2–20, 1–1½ in (2.5–4 cm), diam., ascending, fragrant; perianth tube to ⁵⁄₈ × ¹⁄₈ in (1.5 × 0.3 cm), green below, white above, segments white, to ¾ in (1.8 cm), ovate; corona cup-shaped, ¹⁄₈–¼ × ³⁄₈–½ in (3–6 × 8–11 mm), entire or slightly notched, white

Comments: Winter–spring. ssp. **polyanthus:** syn. N. polyanthus; flowers 3–12(–20), 1–1½ in (2.5–4 cm) diam.; corona pale yellow when young, becoming white.

N. poeticus N. ornatus POET'S NARCISSUS, PHEASANT'S-EYE NARCISSUS	France to Greece	14–20 in (35–50 cm)	to 18 × ¼–½ in (45 × 0.6–1 cm), erect, channeled, green or somewhat glaucous	solitary, 1¾–2¾ in (4.5–7 cm) diam., horizontal to ascending, fragrant; perianth tube cylindric, 1 × ¹⁄₈ in (2.5 × 0.4 cm), green; segments suborbicular to cuneate, to 1¼ × ¾ in (3 × 2.2 cm), spreading white, yellow at base; corona flat, to 1 × ½ in (2.5 × 14 mm), yellow with red, frilled margin
Comments: Late spring. var. **recurvus:** PHEASANT'S EYE NARCISSUS; perianth segments strongly reflexed, pure white.				
N. pseudonarcissus LENT LILY, WILD DAFFODIL, TRUMPET NARCISSUS	W Europe	4¾–36 in (12–90 cm)	3–20 × ¼–⁵⁄₈ in (8–50 × 0.5–1.5 cm), erect, strap-shaped, usually glaucous	usually solitary, occasionally 2–4, horizontal to dropping, fragrant; perianth tube ³⁄₈–1 in (1.5–2.5 cm); segments ¾–1½ in (1.8–4 cm), spreading, sometimes twisted, white to deep yellow; corona ⁵⁄₈–1¾ in (1.5–4.5 cm), white to deep yellow, subentire to 6-lobed

N. minor   N. × odorus 'Rugulosus'   N. poeticus   N. pseudonarcissus

NARCISSUS

Name	Distribution	Height	Leaves	Flowers
N. romieuxii *N. bulbocodium* ssp. *romieuxii*	N Africa	4–8 in (10–20 cm)	to 20 × $^{1}/_{16}$ in (20 × 0.1 cm), erect or spreading, dark green, weakly striate	solitary, 1–1½ in (2.5–4 cm) diam., horizontal or ascending, yellow; perianth tube to 1 in (2.5 cm), green at base, yellow above; segments to ½ × $^{1}/_{8}$ in (1.3 × 0.4 cm), spreading; corona $^{5}/_{8}$ × 1¼ in (1.5 × 3 cm), margin 6-lobed and crenate, spreading to flattened
Comments: ssp. *albidus:* flowers white.				
N. rupicola *N. juncifolius* ssp. *rupicola*	Spain, Portugal	5½–9 in (14–23 cm)	7 × $^{1}/_{8}$ in (18 × 0.3 cm), erect, 2-keeled, glaucous	solitary, to 1¼ in (3 cm) diam., ascending; perianth tube ¾ in (2.2 cm), green or green-yellow; segments to $^{5}/_{8}$ × ½ in (1.5 × 1.1 cm), spreading, yellow; corona $^{1}/_{8}$–¼ × ¼–¾ in (3–5 × 6–18 mm), conic or reflexed, deeply 6-lobed to crenate or subentire, yellow
Comments: ssp. *watieri* : syn. *N. watieri:* flowers white.				
N. serotinus	Mediterranean	5–12 in (13–30 cm)	4–8 × $^{1}/_{16}$–¼ in (10–20 × 0.1– 0.5 cm), erect or spreading, dark green, sometimes with longitudinal white stripes	solitary or occasionally 2–3, to 1¼ in (3.4 cm) diam., ascending, fragrant; perianth tube to ¾ in (2 cm), dark green; segments oblong-lanceolate, to $^{3}/_{5}$ × ¼ in (1.6 × 0.7 cm), spreading or recurved, twisted, white; corona minute, to $^{5}/_{8}$ × $^{1}/_{8}$ in (1.5 × 4 mm), 6-lobed, dark yellow to orange
Comments: Fall.				
N. tazetta BUNCH-FLOWERED NARCISSUS, POLYANTHUS NARCISSUS	S Portugal, Mediterranean, east to Iran, probably introduced farther east, where fully naturalized in Kashmir, China and Japan	8–18 in (20–45 cm)	8–20 × ¼–1 in (20–50 × 0.5– 2.5 cm), erect twisted, keeled, glaucous	1–15, 1½ in (4 cm) diam., horizontal, fragrant; perianth tube cylindric, ¾ in (2 cm), pale green; segments broad-ovate, $^{3}/_{8}$–¾ in (0.8–2.2 cm), patent, incurving, white; corona cup-shaped, ¼ × ½ in (0.5 × 1 cm), bright to deep yellow
		Comments: ssp. *aureus*: syn. *N. aureus, N. cupularis:* perianth segments deep yellow to golden yellow; corona deep yellow to orange. ssp. *corcyrensis:* syn. *N. corcyrensis:* flowers 1–2; perianth segments narrow, sometimes reflexed, pale yellow; corona yellow. ssp. *italicus*: syn. *N. italicus:* perianth segments cream or very pale yellow; corona deeper yellow. 'Canaliculatus': syn. *N. canaliculatus* of gardens; to 8 in (20 cm); leaves narrow, erect, glaucous, striate; flowers small; segments white, corona ocher yellow; sometimes shy-flowering.		
N. triandrus ANGEL'S TEARS	Spain & Portugal, NW France	8–12 in (20–30 cm)	$^{5}/_{8}$–1¼ × $^{5}/_{8}$–¼ in (15–30 × 1.5– 5 mm), keeled or striate, flat or channeled, erect or decumbent, sometimes curled at tip, green, or slightly glaucous	1–6, pendulous, white to bright yellow; perianth tube $^{5}/_{8}$ in (1.5 cm), green below, yellow above; segments sharply reflexed, lanceolate to linear-oblong, ½–1¼ in (1–3 cm), often with deeper median streak; corona cup-shaped, ¼–$^{5}/_{8}$ × ¼–1 in (0.5–1.5 × 0.7–2.5 cm), entire, somewhat undulate
Comments: var. *concolor*: flowers deep yellow: the name is loosely applied in horticulture to any yellow-flowered example of this species.				
N. willkommii *N. jonquilloides*	S Portugal, SW Spain	to 7 in (18 cm)	to 14½–$^{1}/_{8}$ in (37 × 0.3 cm), erect, flattened at base, rounded above, glaucous dark green	usually solitary, 1¼ in (3 cm) diam., horizontal; perianth tube to $^{3}/_{5}$ in (1.6 cm), green-yellow, segments broad-elliptic, ¼–½ × ¼ in (0.6–1.3 × 0.7 cm), spreading or reflexed and curving inward, slightly imbricate, yellow; corona cup-shaped, ¼ × ½ in (0.6 × 1 cm), deeply 6-lobed, yellow

N

N. romieuxii　　　*N. rupicola*　　　*N. tazetta*　　　*N. triandrus*

neck rot generally, decay at the neck of a bulb; more specifically, an onion disease caused by the fungus *Botrytis allii*. The term also refers to a disease known as gladiolus scab and neck rot, caused by the bacterium *Pseudomonas gladioli*.

Neck rot of *Narcissus* is usually caused by *Fusarium oxysporum* f. sp. *narcissi*, better known as the agent of basal rot, but other fungi, including *Botrytis* and *Trichoderma* species, may be involved. Infection of the dying flower stalk spreads down into the bulbs and may lead to extensive rotting in store. It is usually necessary to cut across the neck of the bulb in order to see symptoms of the disease.

ONION NECK ROT, *Botrytis allii*, is very common in stored onions. A rot spreads from brown sunken lesions around the neck, and a fluffy growth of gray mycelium and small black fruiting bodies may develop on the bulb. The disease is seedborne and invades the cotyledons and leaf bases, although there may be no obvious symptoms during the growing season. Crop rotation should be practiced, crop residues removed, and onions properly ripened and dried before being stored.

GLADIOLUS SCAB and NECK ROT affects crocuses, freesias, and other members of the Iridaceace, as well as gladioli. Circular or elongated dark brown spots appear on the leaves, especially at the base, where they may coalesce and cause the leaves to turn brown and dry up. Pale yellow spots develop on the corms and in severe attacks lead to large cavities. There is a copious exudation of gum containing bacteria from the corm lesions; this may dry up, leaving a lacquerlike surface. Affected corms should be destroyed and the contaminated site kept free of Iridaceae for as long as possible.

necrosis the death of plant cells, particularly when the affected tissues become dark in color. Necrosis a common symptom of fungus infection. A necrotic reaction to tissue infection is one in which areas of plant tissue usually on leaves, die—for example, in the NECROTIC RINGSPOT of *Prunus* species. See *pedicel necrosis*.

nectar sweet, liquid secretion attractive to pollinators.

nectarberry see *hybrid berries*.

lines converge on nectaries

Nectary guides
Many insect-pollinated flowers have petal patterning that indicates to their visitors where the "reward" of nectar is.

nectary a gland, often in the form of a protuberance or depression, which secretes and sometimes absorbs nectar.

nectarine see *peaches*.

Nectaroscordum (from Greek *nektar*, nectar, and *skorodon*, garlic, referring to the large nectaries on the ovaries of these relations of the onion). Liliaceae (Alliaceae). S Europe, W Asia, Iran. 3 species, bulbous perennials closely resembling *Allium*. The leaves are linear to narrowly strap-shaped. The bell-shaped flowers nod in scapose umbels in spring and summer. The flower stalks stand erect after flowering, and remain attractive. Hardy to at least 9°F (–13°C). Grow in light, well-drained soil that is neither excessively dry nor waterlogged, in sun or part shade. Propagate by seed in early spring, or by offset bulbils. In favorable conditions, these bulbs will naturalize themselves. *N. siculum* (syn. *Allium siculum*) SICILIAN HONEY GARLIC; France, Italy; flowers 10–30, bell-shaped, pendulous; tepals to ⅝ in (1.5 cm), cream, flushed flesh-pink to caramel brown, stained dark red within, green toward base; includes subsp. *bulgaricum*, syn. *N. bulgaricum*, *N. dioscoridis*, from East Romania, Bulgaria, Turkey, and the Crimea,

with white to yellow tepals, flushed pale pink and green above, edged white, and flushed green below.

needle a linear stiff leaf; as found in conifers.

needle blight term used to describe some foliage diseases of conifers, in which the leaves are infected and die but do not fall. *Didymascella thujina* is a serious form of needle blight affecting young *Thuja plicata* in North America and Europe.

needle cast the premature shedding of conifer leaves, which may be due to diseases such as *Hypodermella laricis* on larch, *Lophodermella sulcigena*, SWEDISH PINE CAST, on pines, *Lophodermium setisiosum* on Scotch pine, *Meria laricis* on European larch, and *Rhabdocline pseudotsugae* on Douglas fir. Symptoms show as yellow spotting of needles in the spring, followed by brown discoloration before falling. In the most severe attacks, only current-year foliage remains to produce a very thin canopy. Control by fungicide sprays should be combined with collecting and burning of fallen needles to reduce disease carry-over.

Neillia (for Patrick Neill [1776–1851], Scottish naturalist, secretary of the Caledonian Horticultural Society). Rosaceae. E Himalaya to China and W Malaysia. Some 10 species, subshrubs or, more often, arching shrubs with flexuous branches and alternate leaves. These are usually 3-lobed and irregularly serrate. Produced in spring and early summer in spreading to nodding racemes, the flowers are cylindric to campanulate with five rounded lobes. Hardy to –4°F (–20°C). In areas where low temperatures are prolonged, protect the roots with a deep mulch. Grow in moist, well-aerated soil, in sun to part-shade. Prune after flowering, cutting out old stems at ground level. Propagate by semiripe cuttings in a closed case with bottom heat, by softwood cuttings in early summer, by removal of suckers in fall, or by seed.

N. sinensis C China; to 3 m (10 ft) branchlets glabrous; leaves to 3 in (8 cm), oval to oblong, incised-serrate

N

and lobed, light green; flowers white to pink in nodding racemes to 2½ in (6 cm); *N. thibetica* W China; to 6½ ft (2 m); branchlets finely downy; leaves to 3 in (8 cm), ovate, finely downy beneath; flowers pink to white in 3–6 in (8–15 cm) racemes.

Nelumbo (name used in Sri Lanka for *N. nucifera*). Nelumbonaceae. Eastern N America, warm Asia to Australia. LOTUS. 2 species, perennial aquatic herbs, evergreen in warm climates, with spreading, cylindrical, spongy rhizomes. The leaves are large and usually emergent, the circular, glaucous blades peltately attached and held aloft on tall stalks. Solitary and long-stalked, the showy flowers are chalicelike and composed of numerous oblong-ovate petals and many golden stamens. The ovaries are sunken in pits in the flat upper surface of a top-shaped receptacle. These persist long after the flowers and are handsome in dried flower arrangements.

The sacred lotus is usually treated as a tender aquatic below 20°F (–7°C). Some of its cultivars, especially those of east Asian provenance, prove perfectly hardy, however, in outdoor pools in places as far north as New York City. Deep-water cultivation, where the leaf stalks will reach their potential height of 8 ft (2.5 m), is generally practicable only in warm subtropical climates or in the tropical house pool. In cooler regions, shallow water heats up more quickly, providing the warmth necessary for good growth and flowering. Grow in tubs, baskets, or beds in heavy loam, enriched with well-rotted farmyard manure or compost; set rootstocks horizontally at about 1 in (2.5 cm) deep and gradually increase the depth of water from 2 to 16 in (5 to 40 cm) as growth proceeds. Remove any fading foliage during the growing season. In outdoor temperate cultivation, gradually reduce the water level and mulch deeply, with leaf mold or compost, as temperatures begin to fall in late summer and fall, or lift, wash, and store the rhizomes in moist sand in a cool but frost-free place for the winter.

The lotus will also grow in tubs and half barrels on terraces: establish rhizomes on a loamy rich mix in the lower two-thirds of wooden or glazed tubs, and fill the remaining space with water. As frost kills foliage, remove tubs to shelter (a cold greenhouse or garden shed) and keep just moist. Move containers outside, fertilize, and replenish water in late spring. Propagate by division of rhizomes. Chip seed before sowing in small pots of rich loamy medium in early spring; set in an aquarium or warm greenhouse, covered with water, and maintain a temperature of 77–86°F (25–30°C). Repot and gradually acclimatize to greater depths of water, setting out in late spring/early summer after the last frost. Seed-grown plants will flower in their third year.

Nelumbo 'Sharon'
Lotuses are characterized by voluptuous flowers centered on a very distinctive "pepperpot"-shaped seed vessel.

N. lutea AMERICAN LOTUS, WATER CHINQUAPIN, YANQUAPIN; eastern N America; leaves to 6½ ft (2 m) above water surface, leaf blades 20 in (50 cm) across; flowers 4–10 in (10–25 cm) across, pale yellow; includes 'Flavescens', with leaves splashed red in center and small flowers; *N. nucifera* SACRED LOTUS; Asia from Iran to Japan, south to Australia; leaves to 6½ ft (2 m) above water surface, leaf blades to 32 in (80 cm) across; flowers 4–12 in (10–30 cm) across, fragrant, single or double, palest pink to rose, salmon or cerise, or white to creamy yellow; numerous cultivars are grown.

Nematanthus (from Greek *nema*, thread, and *anthos*, flower). Gesneriaceae. S America. Some 30 species, climbing or trailing subshrubs. The leaves are usually small and thinly fleshy. Produced at various times of the year in small, compact clusters, the flowers consist of a green, orange or red- or purple-tinged calyx, enclosing a tubular, 5-lobed corolla. Cultivate as for *Aeschynanthus*, although *Nematanthus* species are generally bushier.

N. gregarius (syn. *Hypocyrta nummularia*; *N. radicans*) CLOG PLANT; eastern S America; climbing or pendent, to 32 in (80 cm); leaves glabrous; flowers to 1 in (2.5 cm), pouched, bright orange with a purple-brown stripe leading to each lobe; 'Variegatus': leaves green with yellow center; *N. strigilosus* eastern S America; climbing to 5 ft (1.5 m); leaves hairy beneath; flowers to ¾ in (2 cm), tube orange, limb yellow.

nematicide a pesticide active against nematodes.

nematodes see *eelworms*.

Nemesia (name used by Dioscorides). Scrophulariaceae. South Africa. About 65 species annual or perennial herbs or subshrubs with shortly tubular, 2-lipped flowers in terminal racemes during summer. Commonly used as frost-tender annuals for summer bedding, mixed borders, and pot-plant display in cool greenhouses. Plant out after last frost in a sunny position. After the first flush of flowers, trim back to promote a second display. Water well in dry weather. Sow seed in fall or spring at 59°F (15°C); harden off before planting out into the open garden.

N. barbata glabrous annual herb to 20 in (50 cm); flowers to ⅝ in (1.5 cm), blue, upper lip pale blue within, with white margin and purple lines, white without, with short obtuse lobes, lower lip longer than upper, entire or nearly so, deep blue, lower part white striped purple; *N. strumosa* more or less glandular-hairy annual herb, 6–24 in (15–60 cm), erect; flowers yellow or purple to white, often veined purple without, throat yellow with darker markings, lower lip ¾–1¼ in (2–3 cm) broad, notched at apex, bearded within; *N. versicolor* more or less glabrous annual herb, to 20 in (50 cm); flowers to ½ in (1.2 cm), blue, mauve, yellow or white, lips often different colors, lower lip broad, obtuse, shortly bilobed, palate broad; includes f. *compacta*, more compact, with profuse, white, rose, violet and blue flowers. *Cultivars and hybrids.* Mostly derived from *N. strumosa* and *N. versicolor*, these are the nemesias popular for summer bedding. They include: 'Blue Gem', of bushy habit, to 8 in (20 cm), with a cloud of sky-blue flowers; Carnival Hybrids, compact and bushy, to 12 in (30 cm), and very floriferous; 'Funfair', to 10 in (25 cm), with flowers in brilliant colors; 'Grandiflora', with large flowers; 'Mello Red and White', with raspberry red and white flowers; 'Mello White', with white flowers; 'Nana Compacta', of dwarf habit; 'Suttonii', to 20 in (50 cm), with irregularly shaded flowers, each with a broad lip in front and pouch at base and ranging from carmine, through yellow and pink to white; and 'Tapestry', to 10 in (25 cm), of upright habit, with flowers richly colored.

Nemopanthus (from Greek *nema*, thread, *pous*, foot, and *anthos*, a flower, referring to the very slender pedicels.) Aquifoliaceae. Eastern N America. MOUNTAIN HOLLY. 1 species, *N. mucronatus*, a deciduous, stoloniferous shrub to 11½ ft (3.5 m), differing from *Ilex* in the much reduced calyx and free petals. The leaves are oblong to ovate, to 2½ in (6 cm) long, entire or slightly serrate. Small, green-yellow flowers are followed by spherical, red fruit. Cultivate as for the smaller *Ilex* species.

Nemophila (from Greek *nemos*, grove, and *philos*, loving, in reference to the habitat of some species). Hydrophyllaceae. Western N America. 11 species of annual glabrous, downy or hispidulous herbs with spreading, brittle and slightly succulent stems and pinnately lobed leaves. Produced in summer, the flowers are campanulate, cylindrical, or rotate with 5 rounded petals. Fast-growing annuals, used for border edgings, window boxes, and other containers and suitable for north-facing sites with good light. They are sometimes grown in pots in the cool greenhouse or conservatory. Grow in moisture-retentive soil in sun or part shade with shelter from wind. Sow *in situ* in spring or fall.

N. maculata FIVE-SPOT; C California; to 12 in (30 cm), glabrous to hairy, erect to spreading; flowers to 1¾ in

Nemophila maculata
Bold blotches of violet at the petal tips give this pretty, trailing annual the common name of "five-spot."

(4.5 cm) in diameter, petals white, each with a deep violet blotch near or at the apex, sometimes faintly veined or tinted mauve-blue; *N. menziesii* (syn. *N. insignis*) BABY-BLUE-EYES; California; to 4¾ in (12 cm), hirsute, spreading-procumbent; flowers to 1½ in (4 cm) in diameter, petals white to sky-blue, often with a white or yellow-stained center, or spotted or stained darker blue or purple-black; cultivars include 'Alba', with white flowers with a black center; 'Crambeoides', with pale blue flowers veined purple, unspotted; 'Coelestis', with white flowers edged sky-blue; 'Grandiflora', with pale blue flowers with a white center; 'Insignis', with pure blue flowers; 'Marginata', with blue flowers edged white; 'Occulata', with pale blue flowers with a purple-black center; 'Penny Black', with deep purple-black petals edged bright white; 'Purpurea Rosea', with purple-pink flowers; var. *atromaria*, with white flowers spotted black-purple; and var. *discoidalis*, with bronze-purple flowers edged white.

Neolloydia (for Professor F.E. Lloyd [1868–1947], American botanist). Cactaceae. E and NE Mexico and SW Texas. 14 species, low-growing or dwarf cacti with depressed-globose to shortly cylindric, tuberculate and spiny stems. The flowers are small and shortly funnelform. Plant in a gritty mix with a pH of 6–7.5. Provide a minimum temperature of 45°F (7°C), full sun, and low humidity; keep dry from midfall until early spring, except

for light mistings on warm days in late winter. Increase by offsets. *N. conoidea* E and NE Mexico, SW Texas; stem simple or clustering, 2–9 (5–24 cm) × 1¼–2½ in (3–6 cm), globose to ovoid or shortly cylindric, gray to slightly yellow-green; flowers ¾–1¼ in (2–3 cm), magenta.

Neomarica (from Greek *neon*, new, plus *Marica*). Iridaceae. Tropical America, W Africa. 15 species, rhizomatous, herbaceous perennials with tough, sword-shaped leaves in a basal fan. The short-lived, *Iris*-like flowers are carried in clusters atop tall stems. Provide a minimum temperature of 50°F (10°C). Grow in bright filtered light or full sun, in a well-drained, fertile, loam-based mix with additional organic matter and sharp sand. Water moderately when in growth; keep almost dry in fall and winter. Propagate by division or by seed. *N. caerulea* Brazil; to 24 in (60 cm); flowers 3–4 in (8–10 cm) in diameter, outer perianth segments blue to lilac, inner segments deep blue, the claws and blade bases of all segments yellow-white banded brown and orange-yellow.

Neoporteria (for Carlos Porter, Chilean entomologist). Cactaceae. Chile, S Peru and W Argentina. Some 25 species, mostly rather small cacti with globose to short-cylindric, ribbed and tuberculate stems and felted, depressed areoles. Funnelform or campanulate flowers arise at the apex in summer. Cultivate as for *Neolloydia*.

N. chilensis Chile; stem globose to short-columnar, woolly at apex; ribs 20–21, spines glassy white; flowers pink or pale yellow; *N. napina* Chile; stem to 4 × 2 in (10 × 5 cm), globose to ovoid, gray-green or tinged red, ribs about 14, spines almost black; flowers pale yellow or tinged pink; *N. nidus* Chile; stem to 12 (30 cm) × 2–3½ in (5–9 cm), globose to short-cylindric, ribs 16–18, spines weak and tortuous, interlaced, brown, yellow or almost white; flowers pink; *N. subgibbosa* Chile; stem to 3¼ ft × 4 in (1 m × 10 cm), globose to short-cylindric at first, green to gray-green, ribs 16–20, spines yellow, brown or nearly black at first or amber-yellow; flowers pink, paler toward the throat; *N. villosa* Chile; stem to 6 × 3 in (15 ×

N

8 cm), short-cylindric, gray-green, becoming tinged purple-black, ribs 13–15, spines bristly, dark and hairlike, pale brown or off-white; flowers pink with white throat.

Neoregelia (for E. A. von Regel [1815–92], German botanist and director of the Imperial Botanic Gardens, St. Petersburg, 1875–92). Bromeliaceae. S America. 71 species, mostly terrestrial, evergreen perennial herbs with strap-shaped leaves in a dense, funnel-shaped or tubular rosette. Small flowers are borne in a low, dense head of tightly packed bracts, usually held deep with the rosette. Cultivate as for *Aechmea*.

N. carolinae BLUSHING BROMELIAD; Brazil; leaves 16–24 in (40–60 cm), innermost with scarlet bases when in flower, sparsely scaly beneath, closely toothed; inflorescence bracts bright red, papery, flowers lavender-blue; f. *tricolor*: leaves with yellow, white and green stripes; *N. concentrica* Brazil; leaves to 16 in (40 cm), mid-green often with obscure, darker spots, spiny teeth black, inner leaves flushing purple-pink at base when in flower; inflorescence bracts yellow-white flushed violet or purple, flowers white or blue; *N. fosteriana* Brazil; leaves to 12 in (30 cm), copper-red with a few green spots, pale gray-scaly, apex dark red, margins laxly toothed; inflorescence compound, red, flowers red; *N. marmorata* MARBLE PLANT; Brazil; leaves to 24 in (60 cm), laxly toothed, sheaths purple spotted pale green, blades darkly mottled or spotted, particularly at base, apex sometimes with a bright red spot; flowers white tinged pink; *N. princeps* Brazil; leaves 8–20 in (20–50 cm), laxly toothed, bases large, green, densely scaly, blades green, gray-scaly beneath, the innermost flushed bright red in flower; flowers white tipped dark blue; *N. spectabilis* FINGERNAIL PLANT, PAINTED FINGERNAIL; Brazil; leaves 16–20 in (40–50 cm), gray-scaly and banded white beneath, outer leaves green with a bright red apical spot, inner sometimes wholly red, often edged purple, subentire or denticulate; inflorescence bracts red or purple, flowers violet-blue).

Nepenthes (name used by Homer, meaning grief-assuaging, applied because of supposed medicinal properties). Nepenthaceae. Madagascar, Seychelles, tropical Asia to Australia (N Queensland). TROPICAL PITCHER, PLANTPITCHER PLANT. 70 species, climbing or scrambling, evergreen perennial shrubs. They are carnivorous with each tough, oblanceolate leaf terminating in a tendril which in turn supports a pitcherlike trap. These pitchers are cylindric to rounded, usually green with red spots or tints. The mouth of the pitcher has a thickened, ribbed and often colorful rim, and a fixed lid, standing erect or projecting over pitcher mouth. Along the front of the pitcher run two wings or ridges, usually toothed or fringed. Small, dull flowers are carried in dense spikes at various times of year. Provide a minimum winter temperature of 64°F (18°C). The growing medium must be well-drained; two parts bark, two parts perlite, and one part moss peat is a standard mix. Ample moisture and high humidity are required, but free drainage is essential; lattice or basket pots are recommended for this reason. Diluted liquid fertilizer is beneficial, applied to the roots or as a foliar spray. Old plants benefit from heavy pruning in spring. Increase by air layering.

N. alata Philippines, Malaysia, Borneo, Sumatra; pitchers weakly dimorphic—lower 3½–5 in (6.5–13 cm), cylindric above, constricted at center, inflated at base, light green with red flecks, or heavily suffused red, lip green or occasionally red, lid elliptic with glandular crest at base; wings prominent, fimbriate; upper pitchers elongate; *N. ampullaria* Malaysia, Borneo, Sumatra to New Guinea; pitchers to 2 in (5 cm), rounded, squat, produced low on plant, green spotted and blotched deep red, or entirely green or deep red, lip with narrow rim, lid to 1½ in (3.5 cm), narrow, wings broad, widely spreading, strongly toothed; *N.* × *hookeriana* (*N. rafflesiana* × *N. ampullaria*) natural hybrid, Malaysia,

rim secretes nectar to attract prey

Nepenthes (pitcher plant)

Sumatra, Borneo; pitchers dimorphic—lower to 4½ in (11 cm), ovoid, pale green with dark red spots, or sometimes heavily blotched red, lip broad, descending into pitcher, green, lid flat, obovate, wings broad, fimbriate; upper pitchers to 5 in (12.5 cm), funnel-shaped); *N. mirabilis* MONKEY CUP; Malaysia, Sumatra, Borneo, S China, SE Asia to New Guinea and Queensland; pitchers cylindric or slightly inflated at base, to 7 in (18 cm), pale green with red spots, or wholly red, lip broad, flattened, striped red, lid orbicular to ovate, wings present in lower pitchers, toothed; *N. rafflesiana* Malaysia, Sumatra, Borneo; pitchers dimorphic—lower to 5 in (12.5 cm), ventricose, rounded at base, green, heavily spotted red, lip broad, crimson, ribbed, narrowing upward to form elongate process to lid, spiny above, lid oblong-orbicular, wings to 1 in (2.5 cm) broad, teeth incurved; upper pitchers to 9 in (23 cm), funnel-shaped; *N. rajah* KING MONKEY CUP; Borneo; pitchers dimorphic—lower to 14 × 6 in (35 × 15 cm), rounded, green lightly spotted red, or entirely red to purple externally, spotted red and purple-black within, lip broad, outer margin projecting, undulate, ribbed, crimson with darker bands, lid large, wings narrow, toothed; upper pitchers funnel-shaped.

Nepeta (named used by Pliny, probably after Nepi in Italy). Labiatae. Eurasia, N Africa, Tropical Africa. About 250 species, usually perennial, aromatic herbs with toothed leaves and small, tubular, 2-lipped flowers whorled in spikes in summer. The following species are fully hardy. Grow them in well-drained, light soils in sun. Propagate by division in spring or fall, or by stem tip or softwood cuttings in spring or summer. Sow seed *in situ* in fall.

N. cataria CATNIP, CATMINT; Europe, where it is widely naturalized, SW and

C Asia; to 3¼ ft (1 m), erect; leaves 1½–3 in (3.5–8 cm), ovate, cordate at base, serrate, gray-tomentose beneath; inflorescence spikelike, flowers white spotted blue-violet; includes the lemon-scented 'Citriodora'; *N.* × *faassenii* (synonyms *N. mussinii* of gardens, *N. racemosa* of gardens; *N. racemosa* × *N. nepetella*) to 24 in (60 cm); leaves to 1¼ in (3 cm), oblong to ovate, truncate at base, crenate, silver-gray; flowers pale lavender with darker spots; 'Six Hills Giant': tall, vigorous with lavender-blue flowers in large sprays; 'Snowflake', low and spreading, with leaves tinted gray and flowers snow white; 'Superba', spreading, with leaves tinted gray and abundant, dark blue flowers; *N. govaniana* W Himalaya; erect; leaves large, ovate to oblong or elliptic, rounded at base, crenate; raceme elongated, lax, flowers yellow; *N. grandiflora* Caucasus, eastern Central Europe; erect to 16–32 in (40–80 cm); leaves to 10 cm (4 in), ovate, cordate at base, crenulate, glabrous; spikes elongate, interrupted, flowers blue; *N. nepetella* SW Europe to S Italy; stem to 32 in (80 cm); leaves to 1½ in (4 cm), oblong to lanceolate, truncate at base, crenate to dentate, pubescent to lanate, green to glaucous; inflorescence usually branched, calyx often tinged pink or blue, corolla pink or white; includes subsp. *amethystina*, from North Africa and the Iberian Peninsula, with blue-violet flowers; *N. nervosa* Kashmir; to 24 in (60 cm); leaves to 10 cm (4 in), linear to lanceolate, entire or somewhat dentate, strongly veined; raceme dense, cylindric, flowers blue or yellow.

Nephrolepis (from Greek *nephros*, kidney, and *lepis*, scale, alluding to the common form of the indusia). Oleandraceae. Pantropical. LADDER FERN, SWORD FERN, BOSTON FERN. Some 30 species, epiphytic or terrestrial ferns with spreading rhizomes and prolific, wiry stolons. The fronds are pinnate with linear to oblong blades and numerous leaflets. *N. exaltata* and *N. cordifolia* are remarkably tolerant houseplants. The many *N. exaltata* cultivars have arisen from the original "Boston fern" (*N. exaltata* 'Bostoniensis'), a 19th-century mutation with markedly drooping fronds. Many of these cultivars, particularly those with thickly layered or lacy foliage (e.g., 'Childsii' and 'Smithii'), resent very moist conditions and are more susceptible to a range of pests and diseases. Provide a minimum temperature of 45°F (7°C). Grow in a coarse, fast-draining, soilless mix with sand and bark. Give bright filtered light and a moist but airy atmosphere, ventilating whenever possible. Syringe in hot weather. Water sparingly in winter. Propagate by division in late winter or spring, and by young plantlets formed on the stolons.

N. cordifolia LADDER FERN, SWORD FERN; pantropical; frond blades to 24 × 2 in (60 × 5 cm), erect, arching or pendent, lanceolate to linear, acute or acuminate, sterile pinnae to ¾ × ⅜ in (20 × 9 mm), fertile pinnae 1¼ × ¼ in (30 × 5 mm), to 70 pairs, short-stalked, oblong to linear, apex toothed, base unequal and cordate to obtuse, entire or dentate; 'Duffii': syn. *N. duffii*, DUFF'S SWORD FERN, rachis usually forked, pinnae orbicular, crowded, attached in more than one plane; 'Plumosa': pinnae lobed; *N. exaltata* BOSTON FERN; pantropical; frond blades linear, 20–100 × 2½–6 in (50–250 × 6–15 cm), pinnae numerous, ¾–3 in × ¼–½ in (2–8 × 0.7–1.3 cm), apex acute or subacute, base subcordate with auricle overlapping rachis, bluntly serrulate to crenate; 'Bostoniensis': syn. *N. bostoniensis*, fronds erect to pendent; this is the "original" Boston fern, which has produced, among others, the following sports: 'Childsii', fronds approximate and over-lapping, to 4-pinnate, deltoid; 'Elegantissima', fronds 2-pinnate; 'Fluffy Ruffles', fronds dense, to 3-pinnate, deltoid; 'Smithii', fronds finely 3-pinnate, lacelike).

Nerine (from Greek Nereis, the name of a sea nymph, an allusion to the probably apocryphal tale that these bulbs were washed ashore on Guernsey following a shipwreck). Amaryllidaceae. South Africa, Lesotho, Botswana, Swaziland. 30 species, bulbous perennials with strap-shaped or thread-like leaves appearing with or soon after the flowers. Numerous flowers are produced, generally in fall, in scapose umbels. These consist of six slender and spreading, wavy segments and

Nerine sarniensis
While the Guernsey lily will thrive in the mild, maritime climate of the Channel Islands, it is in fact a South African native.

long, declinate stamens. In cool temperate zones, most species are cultivated in the cool greenhouse, since they do not tolerate temperatures below freezing. *N. masonorum*, a dainty species for warm sheltered pockets in the rock garden in areas with mild winters, is well-suited to cultivation in the alpine house in cooler zones. *N. bowdenii* will grow where winter temperatures drop to 5°F (–15°C), although it needs protection from winter wetness: in regions at the limits of its hardiness, grow at the base of a south-facing wall in perfectly drained soil, with a dry mulch of bracken litter or leaf mold. In northern Britain, large and well established clumps are most commonly seen at the base of south-facing house walls, in the rain shadow of the eaves. *N. sarniensis* may be treated similarly, but is rather more susceptible to cold and wet.

N. bowdenii leaves strap-shaped; scape to 18 in (45 cm), tepals to 2¾ in (7 cm), wavy, candy pink to deep rose or white; *N. filifolia* leaves very slender; scape to 12 in (30 cm), tepals to 1 in (2.5 cm), crisped, white, rose, magenta or crimson; *N. flexuosa* leaves narrowly strap-shaped; scape to 3¼ ft (1 m), flexuous, tepals to 3 cm (1¼ in), crisped, pale pink or white; *N. masonorum* (leaves threadlike; scape to 12 in (30 cm), tepals to ⅝ in (1.5 cm), wavy, pale to deep rose with a darker pink midstripe; *N. sarniensis* GUERNSEY LILY; leaves strap-shaped; scape to 18 in (45 cm), tepals to 1½ in (3.5 cm), slightly crisped, pink, pale rose, crimson, scarlet, mauve-pink, orange-red or white; *N. undulata* leaves very narrow; scape to 18 in (45 cm), tepals to ¾ in (2 cm), pale candy pink or rose, strongly crisped.

Nerium (name used by Dioscorides). Apocynaceae. Mediterranean to W China, widely naturalized. OLEANDER, ROSE BAY. 1 species, *N. oleander*; glabrous evergreen shrub to 8½ ft (2.6 m), tall with spreading to erect branches and tough, dark green, lanceolate leaves to 8 in (20 cm) long. Produced in summer in broad, terminal cymes, the flowers are white to rose, salmon, deep pink, cerise, peach or yellow, often fragrant and funnelform with a spreading, 5-lobed limb to 2 in (5 cm) across. All parts are extremely toxic. In cool climates, *Nerium* is commonly grown in tubs in the greenhouse or conservatory, to be moved outdoors for the summer months. However, in a sheltered, sunny position, it may tolerate temperatures to 14°F (−10°C) for short periods. Grow in full sun. Keep almost dry in winter. Prune established specimens in late winter to shape and restrict size. Propagate cultivars by semi-ripe cuttings of terminal shoots, or by stem sections in summer after flowering.

Nertera (from Greek *nerteros*, lowly, alluding to the habit). Rubiaceae. S China and SE Asia to Australia, New Zealand, Polynesia, Antarctic and Hawaii to C and S America, Tristan da Cunha. Some 15 species, diminutive, prostrate or creeping herbs with very small leaves, solitary and inconspicuous flowers and bright, beadlike berries. Grow in sandy/gritty, moisture-retentive and freely draining soils, with shelter from cold winds in a semi-shaded situation. Maintain a minimum temperature of 41°F (5°C). Propagate by careful division, tip cuttings, or by seed in spring in a sandy propagating mix in the shaded cool greenhouse or frame. *N. granadensis* BEAD PLANT, CORAL MOSS, ENGLISH BABYTEARS; S America, Taiwan and SE Asia, Australia and Tasmania, New Zealand; forming dense mats and mossy patches to 16 in (40 cm) wide or more; leaves to ⅜ in (0.8 cm), usually far smaller, rounded, bright green; fruit ¼ in

(0.5 cm) wide, globose or ovoid, orange to scarlet or dark red; easily confused with the unrelated *Soleirolia*, whose fruits are quite insignificant.

nervose, nerved furnished with ribs or veins.

nessberry see *hybrid berries*.

netted reticulate, net-veined.

neuter, neutral sterile, asexual; concerning flowers, lacking both pistils and stamens.

NFT Nutrient Film Technique; see *hydroponics*.

Nicandra (for Nikander of Colophon, [*c.* 150 AD], Greek botanist and medical writer). Solanaceae. Peru. 1 species, *N. physaloides* APPLE OF PERU, SHOO-FLY; a glabrous annual herb, to 54 in (130 cm) tall. The flowers are to 1½ × 1½ in (3.5 × 4 cm), bell-shaped with a white throat and 5-lobed, with a lilac-purple to blue and white limb. A sturdy, free-branching annual, grown for its bell-shaped flowers produced freely throughout late summer and fall, although opening fully for only a few hours around midday. The attractive fruits are enclosed in purple calyces and resemble those of *Physalis*. It may self-sow freely in the garden. Sow *in situ* after the last frost in rich, well-drained soil in full sun.

niche a recess in a garden wall, often at the end of a vista, in which a statue, urn, or stone vase is placed.

nicking removing a small crescent of bark, or slitting the bark on a shoot below a dormant bud, as a means of inhibiting its growth; cf. *notching*.

Nicotiana (for Jean Nicot [1530–1600], French consul in Portugal, who introduced *Nicotiana* to France). Solanaceae. Tropical America, Australia, Namibia. TOBACCO. 67 species, mostly clammy, annual or perennial herbs and shrubs. Produced in summer in terminal panicles, the flowers are tubular to funnel-shaped with a 5-lobed limb. Their fragrance becomes especially intense at evening. In cool-temperate areas, *Nicotiana*

species and cultivars are generally treated as half-hardy annuals, although some species are perennial. In sheltered gardens, *N. alata* and *N. sylvestris* may survive temperatures down to about 23°F (−5°C), shooting in spring from dormant buds on their thick rootstocks. *N. glauca* is almost as hardy. Plant out in late spring in rich, moisture-retentive, but well-drained soil. Deadhead bedding plants to prolong flowering. Surface sow the fine seed in spring at 64°F (18°C), planting out in late spring or early summer. Harden off before planting out. Prone to viruses.

N. alata (syn. *N. affinis*) FLOWERING TOBACCO, JASMINE TOBACCO; S Brazil to NE Argentina; viscid, sparsely branched perennial, to 5 ft (1.5 m); flowers green-white, interior white, tube to 4 in (10 cm), pubescent, limb to 1 in (2.5 cm) diameter; *N. glauca* TREE TOBACCO, MUSTARD TREE; S Bolivia to N Argentina, naturalized in United States; glaucous subshrub or shrub to 20 ft (6 m)+; flowers cream yellow-green, tube to 1¾ in (4.5 cm), limb to ⅛ in (0.4 cm) in diameter, lobes short, throat slightly inflated; *N. langsdorffii* Brazil; erect, branched, viscid-pubescent annual to 5 ft (1.5 m)+; flowers lime green, tube to 1 in (2.5 cm), viscid limb small, pleated); *N.* × *sanderae* (*N. alata* × *N. forgentiana*; shrubby, viscid-pubescent annuals to 24 in (60 cm)+; flower tube green-yellow at base, limb to 1½ in (4 cm)+ in diameter, red, occasionally white or green to rose or purple; includes 'Breakthrough', early-flowering, dwarf, compact, with fragrant flowers in a range of colors; 'Crimson King', with deep crimson flowers; 'Daylight Sensation', with day-blooming flowers in shades of lavender, purple, white and rose; 'Dwarf White Bedder', of low habit and bushy, with pure white, fragrant flowers; 'Fragrant Cloud', with large, pure white flowers, fragrant at night; 'Grandiflora', with large flowers, with a large, widely dilated throat; 'Lime Green', with flowers bright sulfur yellow tinged lime green; 'Nana', dwarf; Nikki Hybrids, bushy and hardy, with flowers in a range of colors including white, shades of pink, red and yellow; 'Rubella', with rose-red flowers; Sensation Hybrids, with flowers in a range of colors including pink, red and white, fragrant; 'Sutton's Scarlet', with a dark red corolla; and 'White', with heavily scented, white flowers); *N. tabacum* (TOBACCO; COMMON TOBACCO; NE Argentina, Bolivia; annual or biennial, viscid-pubescent, to 48 in (120 cm), stem sometimes becoming woody at base; flowers green-white to rose, tube inflated, to 2¼ in (5.5 cm), limb to ⅜ in (1.5 cm) in diameter; var. *macrophylla*: leaves large, flowers rose to carmine red; 'Variegata': leaves to 12 in (30 cm), variegated cream with green, flowers white tinged pink).

Nidularium (from Latin *nidulus*, a little nest, referring to the inflorescence bracts). Bromeliaceae. E Brazil. 23 species, evergreen perennial, terrestrial or epiphytic herbs. The leaves are usually strap-shaped, finely toothed, and arranged in a flat rosette with a central reservoir. Small flowers are carried in a compound inflorescence surrounded by showy bracts. Cultivate as for *Aechmea* but avoid direct sunlight and mist frequently in warm weather.

N. fulgens leaves to 16 in (40 cm), pale green with darker mottling, pointed, slightly scaly beneath, laxly toothed; inflorescence crowded, domed, on a very short scape, bracts cerise, coarsely toothed, sepals red, petals white, tipped dark blue, with white margins; *N. innocentii* leaves 8–24 in (20–60 cm), purple- to blood-red beneath or throughout, shiny, toothed; scape short; inflorescence bracts red tipped green, large, toothed, sepals white or pink, petals white with green bases; var. *lineatum*: leaves pale green with fine white lines, inflorescence bracts green with brick red tips; var. *striatum*: leaves green striped white, inflorescence bracts carmine; *N. procerum* Brazil; leaves 16in–3¼ ft (0.4–1 m), broadly acuminate, tough, finely toothed, pale waxy green tinted copper; inflorescence bracts tinted red to strong red, flowers vermilion tipped blue.

Nierembergia (for John Eusebius Nieremberg [1595–1658], Spanish naturalist). Solanaceae. S America. CUP FLOWER. Some 23 species, annual or perennial herbs or subshrubs. Produced in summer, the flowers are cupped to tubular with a spreading limb of five lobes. Hardy to 10°F (–12°C). In colder areas, they are used as bedding annuals or container plants for summer color, flowering the first year from seed. Plant out in a sunny position after the last frost. Clip back *N. linariifolia* lightly after flowering. Propagate from seed, division, or by heeled cuttings in summer. Harden off new plants in a cold frame before planting out.

N. linariifolia (Argentina; erect, white-hairy herb to 12 in (30 cm)+; flowers blue tinged violet, tube slender, yellow); *N. repens* (WHITE CUP; Andes, warm temperate S America; procumbent herb; flowers white, tinged yellow or rose-pink at base, tube slender; 'Violet Queen': flowers rich purple-blue).

Nigella (from diminutive of Latin *niger*, black, referring to the seed). Ranunculaceae. Eurasia. FENNEL FLOWER, WILD FENNEL, LOVE-IN-A-MIST, DEVIL-IN-A-BUSH. Some 14 annual herbs, with erect, usually unbranched stems. The leaves are finely pinnately cut with slender segments. Produced in spring and summer, the flowers are solitary and consist of five petal-like sepals and many smaller petals. In some species, the flowers are subtended by a ruff of conspicuously veined leaves, each terminating in hairlike divisions. The fruit is a large capsule, ultimately inflated with persistent horn-like styles. Hardy annuals, valued for their fine foliage, flowers and seed capsules, which are used in dried-flower arrangements. Sow *in situ* in fall or spring in full sun. Established plants will withstand dry, infertile conditions. Propagate by seed – self-sowing is common. *N. damascena* (DEVIL IN A BUSH; S Europe, N S Africa; to 2–20 in (5–50 cm); flowers white, rose-pink, pale blue or purple-blue, 1½–1¾ in (3.5–4.5 cm) in diameter, subtended by a finely divided, collarlike involucre; includes numerous cultivars and seed races ranging from tall to dwarf and single, semi-double and double, in shades of deep blue, sky blue, violet, lavender, lilac, mauve, purple-red, rose, and white).

Nipponanthemum (from Nippon and Greek *anthemon*, flower). Compositae. Japan. 1 species, *N. nipponicum*, a perennial herb or subshrub to 3¼ ft (1 m). The leaves are to 3½ in (9 cm) long, spathulate, crenately toothed, dark and lustrous. Produced in late summer, the long-stalked, daisylike flower heads are to 3 in (8 cm) in diameter, with white ray florets and yellow disk florets. Grow in full sun in very well-drained and moderately fertile soil. In places where winter temperatures fall much below 14°F (–10°C), protect roots with a deep mulch of leaf mold or bracken litter, and foliage with a covering of evergreen branches. Plants cut back to the ground in winter may regenerate from the roots. Propagate by seed or division.

nitrate see *nitrogen*.

nitrate of potash see *potassium nitrate*.

nitrate of soda see *sodium nitrate*.

nitrification see *nitrogen*.

Nitro chalk see *ammonium nitrate*.

nitrogen (N) a major (macro-) nutrient, essential to, and highly influential on, the rate of plant growth. As a constituent of protein, and thus all protoplasm, it is needed in great quantity by most plants. It is mainly absorbed in the form of nitrate or ammonium ions.

Nitrogen can be stored long-term in soils as organic matter. Such organic nitrogen becomes available to plants through its mineralization to inorganic ions as a result of the activity of soil-inhabiting microorganisms in the process of nitrification. Organic nitrogen is reduced to ammonia, nitrite, and then nitrate. This process depends on the presence of water, oxygen, other nutrients, temperature, and pH. Organic matter relatively high in carbon can be slow to break down, and may in fact take up free nitrogen from the soil during the process of mineralization. These considerations make it necessary to add nitrogen compounds to compost piles incorporating woody waste.

Nitrogen-fixing bacteria and blue-green algae shortcut mineralization by obtaining nitrogen directly from the air. Some of these organisms live in the soil; others, such as *Rhizobium* bacteria, form nodules on roots of leguminous plants. *Actinomyces*, a bacteria-like organism, has a similar symbiotic relationship with alders and *Elaeagnus*.

Nitrogen deficiency can occur on soils that are low in organic matter, very dry, or of low temperature; where impeded drainage or other factors create anaerobic conditions; when leaching occurs following winter rain or excessive irrigation; and where large quantities of organic matter, relatively high in carbon, are added to the soil. It also occurs as a result of exhaustion of growing media in pots, or where plants are too closely spaced. Symptoms are feeble growth, pale or yellow-green foliage, often developing red or purple tints, and premature defoliation.

Besides bulky manures, organic sources of nitrogen include dried blood, hoof and horn, shoddy, and urea. Inorganic sources include ammonium nitrate, ammonium phosphate, and ammonium sulfate, as well as calcium nitrate, potassium nitrate, and sodium nitrate.

nitrogen fixation see *nitrogen*.

noble rot see *gray mold*.

nocturnal of flowers, opening or fragrant only during the evening and night.

node the point on an axis where one or more leaves, shoots, whorls, branches, or flowers are attached.

nodose possessing many closely packed nodes; knobby.

nodule a small rounded growth on a root or other plant part. Nodules commonly occur on roots and are particularly associated with nitrogen-fixing bacteria and certain eelworm infestations.

Nolana (from Latin *nola*, a little bell, alluding to shape of corolla).

Nolanaceae. Chile to Peru, Galapagos Islands. 18 species, glandular annual or perennial herbs or subshrubs. The flowers are bell- to funnel-shaped with five lobes. Annuals, easily grown outdoors in any moderately fertile soil in sun, or as potted plants in the cool greenhouse. Sow seed *in situ* in spring.

N. humifusa (syn. *N. prostrata*) Peru; to 6 in (15 cm), often decumbent; flowers to ³/₄ in (1.7 cm), lilac with throat white, streaked violet or purple; 'Shooting Star': trailing, with lilac to lavender flowers, streaked dark purple; *N. paradoxa* Chile, Peru; to 10 in (25 cm), usually decumbent; flowers to 1¹/₂ in (3.5 cm), bright dark blue, throat yellow or white; 'Blue Bird': deep sky-blue flowers with white throats; 'Cliff Hanger': trailing with cornflower blue flowers with pale yellow throats; subsp. *atriplicifolia*: leaves spathulate to linear, flowers blue, violet or white flowers, with yellow or white tubes.

Nolina (for P. C. Nolin, 18th-century French agriculturalist). Agavaceae. S US, Mexico to Guatemala. Some 24 species, evergreen shrubs and trees. The stem is usually sparsely branched and grossly swollen at the base. Tough, linear leaves are arranged in terminal tufts and rosettes. Small, creamy white flowers are borne in great abundance in large panicles. *Nolina* is for outdoor cultivation only in frost-free desert and semidesert regions. Elsewhere, they are usually grown as part of a greenhouse succulent collection or as a feature of interior landscapes. Grow in a well-drained, gritty medium; provide a minimum temperature of 50°F (10°C). Water plentifully during summer and sparingly in winter. Propagate during spring by seed or offsets.

N. hookeri (syn. *Calibanus hookeri*) EC Mexico; caudex massive, turniplike, mostly subterranean, lacking aerial branches; leaves clumped, glaucous, grassy.

internodal stem

leaves and buds originate at nodes

Node

Nomocharis (from Greek *nomos*, meadow, and *charis*, loveliness, referring to the plant's habitat and beauty). Liliaceae (Liliaceae). W China, SE Tibet, Burma, N India. 7 species, bulbous perennial herbs, resembling small lilies (*Lilium*), with flat to bowl-shaped, white to pink or pale yellow flowers, often spotted purple or maroon. Usually carried in summer in loose terminal racemes, the flowers consist of six ovate to elliptic segments, their margins entire to toothed or fringed. Hardy to 0°F (–18°C). They require acidic, cool, and shady conditions and are well-suited to the peat terrace and woodland garden. Grow in dappled light or semishade in well-drained, moist peaty or leafy soils. Propagate by seed.

N. pardanthina China; to 36 in (90 cm); flowers 2–3¹/₂ in (5–9 cm) diameter, nodding to erect, flattened, outer segments white to pink blotched purple, dark maroon at base, inner segments more densely blotched, with fringed tips; *N. saluenensis* China, Burma; to 34 in (85 cm); flowers 2¹/₂–3¹/₂ in (6–9 cm) diameter, horizontal or drooping, saucer-shaped, outer segments rose-pink with a dark maroon patch and spots at base, inner segments entire.

nonvascular without vascular tissue; for example, algae, lichens, fungi.

Nopalxochia (from the ancient Mexican name, meaning cactus with scarlet flowers). Cactaceae. S Mexico. 3–4 species, epiphytic cacti with flattened, wavy-edged stems and funnel-shaped flowers. Provide a winter minimum temperature of 50°F (10°C), high humidity, and shade from direct sun. Plant in acidic potting mix rich in sand, leaf mold, and coarse bark. Water freely in summer, very sparingly in winter. Increase by stem cuttings.

N. ackermannii S Mexico; stem to 8–28 (20–70 cm) × 2–2³/₄ in (5–7 cm); flowers 4³/₄–5¹/₂ in (12–14 cm), orange-red; *N. phyllanthoides* S Mexico; stem to 16 × ¹/₄ in (40 × 0.6 cm); flowers 3–4 in (8–10 cm) pink.

notching removing a small crescent of bark on a shoot above a dormant bud to stimulate it into growth; cf. *nicking*.

Nothofagus (from Greek *nothos*, false, and *Fagus*, to which it is related). Fagaceae. Temperate southern S America, New Zealand, E Australia, and tropical high altitude New Caledonia and New Guinea. SOUTHERN BEECH. About 40 species, evergreen and deciduous trees and shrubs resembling beech trees (*Fagus*). The leaves are oblong to ovate with wavy to toothed margins and distinct veins. The nuts are surrounded by a thick, splitting involucre, often covered with sticky protuberances. These trees favor cool, wet summers in maritime temperate climates. *N. antarctica* is hardy to 0°F (−18°C). All other species are killed or injured at −4°F (−20°C) and some at 14°F (−10°C). They are not suitable for frost-prone, inland areas and should only be planted on sites with good air drainage. Regions with hot, humid summers should also be avoided. Plant in full sun on moist but well-drained soils with a pH of 5–7. Increase by seed.

N. alpina syn. *N. procera*; ANTARTIC BEECH; Chilean Andes; deciduous tree to 130 ft (40 m); leaves 1½–6 in (4–15 cm), ovoid to lanceolate, matt green and thinly pubescent, margin slightly scalloped, finely crenate-serrate, veins 15–22 pairs, impressed above, veins ending in a slight sinus with 4 to 5 unequal intervening teeth; *N. antarctica* NIRRE; Tierra del Fuego to Chile; deciduous tree or shrub to 56 ft (17 m); leaves ⅜–1½ in (1.5–4 cm), oblong, finely but irregularly toothed, with 4 pairs of veins, glossy rich green above, paler beneath, often sweetly aromatic, glabrous except for a few hairs on veins; 'Benmore': syn. 'Prostrata', a low-spreading form with interlacing branches in a dense mound; *N. betuloides* COIGUE DE MAGELLANES, GUINDO BEECH; Chile, W Argentina; evergreen tree to 80 ft (25 m), or shrub in exposed sites; leaves ½–1¼ in (1–3 cm), ovate, crenate, glossy dark green, slightly sticky, finely freckled with white glands beneath, veins often pink; *N. dombeyi* COIGUE; Chile, Argentina; evergreen tree to 165 ft (50 m); leaves ¾–1½ in (2–4 cm), ovoid to lanceolate, irregular-serrate, glossy dark green above, matte and pale beneath, minutely freckled black; *N. menziesii* SILVER BEECH; New Zealand; evergreen tree to 100 ft (30 m); leaves ½–⅝ in (1–1.5 cm), orbicular to broadly ovoid, margin double-crenate, silvery gray on young trees, glossy dark green on older trees, coriaceous, glabrous except for hair-filled vein axils at base of blade; *N. obliqua* ROBLE BEECH; Chile, W Argentina; deciduous tree to 130 ft (40 m); leaves 1¼–3 in (3–8 cm), ovoid to oblong, mid-green above, paler beneath, glabrous, margin double-toothed, veins 7–12 pairs, impressed above, each ending in a large lobelike tooth, itself 1–3-toothed each side.

Notholirion (from Greek *nothos*, false, and *leirion*, lily; these plants have been placed in *Lilium* and *Fritillaria* but are now considered separate from both). Liliaceae (Liliaceae). Afghanistan to W China. 4 species, bulbous perennials with linear to lanceolate leaves produced during fall and winter. Lilylike, trumpet-shaped flowers are carried in racemes in summer; they consist of six spreading segments with recurved tips. Leafing early in the season, *Notholirion* is prone to frost damage; for this reason, in cool temperate zones, it is commonly cultivated in large containers in the cool greenhouse. Use a loam-based mix with silver sand and leaf mold; grow in bright, filtered light and water plentifully when in full growth. Reduce water when dormant. Increase by seed or bulbils. *N. campanulatum* N Burma, W China; to 32 in (80 cm); flowers to 20, pendulous, to 2 in (5 cm), crimson to maroon tipped green.

Notospartium (from Greek *notos*, southern, and *spartion*, broom). Leguminosae. New Zealand (South Island). PINK BROOM, SOUTHERN BROOM. 3 species, shrubs and trees. Adult plants are mostly leafless with a mop of slender, flattened, weeping branchlets. In spring and summer, pea-like flowers are carried in pendulous lateral racemes. Hardy to about 14°F (−10°C) and suitable for a warm, sheltered border or for the base of a sunny wall. Grow in well-drained but moisture-retentive, humus-rich soil. Provide support for older plants, and protect young plants from prolonged winter frost with bracken litter or evergreen branches. Propagate from seed sown in the cold frame or greenhouse in spring, or by semiripe cuttings in summer, rooted in a closed case with bottom heat.

N. carmichaeliae shrub to 16 ft (5 m); branchlets rushlike, grooved, olive; racemes to 2 in (5 cm), sericeous, flowers light purple to pink; *N. glabrescens* round-headed tree to 30 ft (9 m); branches slightly grooved, gray-green to olive; racemes to 2 in (5 cm), glabrescent, flowers magenta with standard paler and stained dark purple-red.

novirame a flowering or fruiting shoot arising from a primocane.

NPK the combined chemical symbols for the three major plant nutrients, nitrogen, phosphorus, and potassium; commonly used to describe the make up of a basic balanced fertilizer.

nuclear stock plants propagated vegetatively from a single parent. The term is primarily used of plants grown from a mother plant that has been tested for trueness to type and freedom from viruses, other diseases, and pests, thus providing a basis for the production of certified stock.

nucleus the membrane-bound body containing the genetic material of plant and animal cells.

Nuphar (from *nufar*, Arabic name for *Nymphaea*). Nymphaeaceae. Temperature regions of northern Hemisphere, COW LILY, SPATTERDOCK, YELLOW POND LILY, WATER COLLARD. Some 25 species, perennial, aquatic herbs with floating to emerging large, ovate to orbicular leaves. Held above the water surface, the flowers are solitary and consist of a shallow cup of broad sepals and numerous smaller petals. These surround numerous stamens and a large ovary. The fruit is large, green, and flask-shaped. Grow in deep water and full sun or light shade. Plant in containers or on the bed itself in still or slow-moving water. For propagation, see *Nymphaea*.

N. advenum Europe and C US, Mexico, West Indies; leaves to 13 in (33 cm); flowers to 1½ in (4 cm) in diameter, yellow tinged red; *N. lutea* (YELLOW WATER LILY, BRANDY BOTTLE;

N

E US, West Indies, N Africa, Eurasia; leaves to 16 in (40 cm); flowers to 2½ in (6 cm) in diameter, bright yellow.

nursery, nursery garden a site devoted to the propagation and raising of young plants.

nursery bed an area reserved for the rearing of young plants, where they can remain until large enough to be transferred to more permanent positions. It is sometimes also called a reserve border.

nut (1) an indehiscent, one-celled, and one-seeded, hard, ligneous or osseous fruit, for example, the acorn of *Quercus*; (2) more loosely applied to a drupe with a thin exocarp and a large nutlet.

nutant nodding; usually applied to a whole inflorescence or stem.

nutlet a small nut or a small stone of a drupaceous fruit. It is similar to an achene, but with a harder and thicker pericarp.

"nutant" or nodding flowers

nutrient film technique (NFT) see *hydroponics*.

nutrients nutrients are mineral ions used by plants to form the proteins, fats, and other compounds needed for growth. Essential plant nutrients are divided into the macronutrients (needed in relatively large amounts of 10s or 100s of lb/acre), which are nitrogen (N), phosphorus (P), potassium (K), magnesium (Mg), calcium (Ca) and sulfur (S), and the micronutrients or trace elements (needed in relatively small amounts), which are iron (Fe), manganese (Mn), copper (Cu), zinc (Zn), boron (Bo), molybdenum (Mb) and chlorine (Cl). Other trace elements may be needed, but in such small amounts that it is effectively impossible to prove the requirement.

Nutrients are not always beneficial and problems can arise if levels are too high. There can be harmful effects of

Ornithogalum nutans

salinity from excessive concentrations; this problem is most likely to occur when soluble NPK fertilizers are used. Some micronutrients, notably zinc, copper, and boron, can prove directly toxic at very much lower levels than those producing salinity effects.

Excess nitrogen may lead to a delay in flowering and fruiting, enhanced vegetative growth, a reduced root-shoot ratio, decreased winter-hardiness, and greater pest and disease susceptibility.

With some sensitive species, it is possible to see visual signs of damage at what would normally be regarded as relatively low levels of a given nutrient. For example, many Australasian plants are adapted to soils that are extremely deficient in phosphorus, and these suffer toxicity when planted in more normal substrates.

Some trace elements are capable of improving the growth of particular plants, the most commonly encountered of which is sodium. This can usefully be applied to plants from the beet and cabbage families, which have developed from seaside habitats. However, sodium can be damaging to soil structure and should not normally be applied as a fertilizer without good reason.

Nutrients in soils Very few soils are actually deficient in total amounts of plant nutrients; deficiency symptoms more commonly arise due to a shortfall in the manner or rate in which nutrients are made available. Nutrients are taken up by plants as mineral ions dissolved in soil water, and for prolonged growth and vigor, there must be a constant supply. They originate in the following ways: WEATHERING OF SOIL MINERALS Mineral-rich rocks are broken down by the action of frost, water, and organic acids and are the ultimate source of most soil-borne nutrients, although nitrogen is an important exception. BREAKDOWN OF ORGANIC MATTER Organic matter from dead plant and animal remains is gradually broken down by soil organisms to release constituent mineral nutrients in a process known as mineralization; this is the source of a regular supply of

nitrogen ions, in particular. INPUTS FROM THE ATMOSPHERE Many nutrients fall to earth dissolved in rain, and this low input is of importance in some ecosystems; inputs are greater in areas of high atmospheric pollution. Nitrogen-fixation in plants can greatly increase soil fertility by converting nitrogen from air within the soil structure into organic form. Nutrient ions in solution are prone to leaching, and the most important mechanisms of temporary storage are: CATION EXCHANGE CAPACITY (CEC) Positively charged ions (cations) are held by electrostatic charge on the surface of clay particles and organic matter. These stored nutrients are in equilibrium with those held in the soil solution so that, within broad limits, as the concentration in solution falls, more stored ions are released. CHEMICAL COMPLEXES BETWEEN THE IONS Nutrient ions can combine with other nutrients or other soil minerals to form relatively insoluble salts. These can in turn break down to release ions if the equilibrium with the soil solution changes. The relative solubility of different mineral elements changes dramatically with soil pH, so that attention to alkaline status in a soil is very important.

Any problem that interferes with or slows the normal movement of water through the soil, such as drought or compaction, can severely limit the availability of nutrients to a plant. Water shortage can also limit nutrient uptake by restricting root growth.

Nutrient losses The most obvious means by which nutrients are lost from soil is by uptake into vegetation; they can be locked up in the biomass of large long-lived plants, especially trees, and it can be centuries before they enter the soil again. When plants are harvested, grazed, or mown, the nutrients removed can represent a loss from the system unless replaced by rotted matter.

Nutrients can be lost from a growing medium by leaching, the process of drainage water removing dissolved mineral salts and clay particles. Leaching is a natural process intensified by heavy rainfall or excessive irrigation and the effects are only serious if the mineral ions move out of the root zone. Leaching into lower soil levels can

N

actually be beneficial if it allows plants to continue nutrient uptake when there is surface drought. It is also advantageous in reducing soil salt concentrations that may arise from the continual use of supplementary fertilizers. Some elements are more mobile than others—for example, nitrogen ions are prone to leaching, whereas phosphorus moves extremely slowly in soil. Leaching is worse on coarse-textured soils where the drainage rate is high and CEC is low. Leaching rates can therefore be reduced by increasing CEC or by reducing the rate of water movement down the profile by improving structure and water retention; adding clay or organic matter helps to meet both these objectives. Vegetation restricts leaching by recovering and recycling ions and by reducing water drainage, whereas leaving land fallow can cause depletion of readily available nutrients. Reduced leaching is one of the benefits obtained by using green manures on unused land. On sandy soils, soluble fertilizers, such as ammonium nitrate, can be lost in just a few days of wet weather, making this an ineffective and uneconomic fertilizer. Slow-release fertilizers are often much better value on sands, even though they appear to be more costly. In general, thoughtful and timely application of manures and fertilizers helps to reduce waste and the risk of ground water pollution.

Fire causes nutrient loss; when vegetation is burned, certain elements, such as nitrogen and sulfur, form gases that escape into the atmosphere, although potassium remains in the ashes.

Soil nitrogen can be lost to the atmosphere by denitrification, which occurs following bacterial action in waterlogged soils. A similar loss can occur by ammonia volatilization, when fertilizers or manures rich in ammonium compounds are applied to well-aerated soils which have a high pH or have recently been limed.

Nutrient antagonisms Not only are the absolute levels of a given nutrient important, but also the relative proportions of two or more elements can affect plant growth and yield and influence the availability of other minerals. For example, adding extra nitrogen to a soil already deficient in phosphorus can increase the severity of the deficiency. Similarly, high potassium levels aggravate magnesium deficiency. Other nutrient antagonisms include N/K; K/Mg; Mg/K; P/K; P/Zn; Na/Ca; K/Ca; Mg/Ca; Ca/Mn; Cu/Fe; Zn/Fe; Co/Fe; and Ni/Fe.

The opposite phenomenon is seen when the addition of one nutrient improves the uptake or efficiency of use of another. These are called synergisms and include N/Mg and K/Fe.

Identifying nutrient deficiencies In the majority of cases, and particularly at low levels of deficiency, visual clues can vary according to the availability of other nutrients and the type of plant; confusion may also result due to problems such as virus infection, physical root damage, waterlogging, and herbicide damage, which can cause similar symptoms.

Deciding which nutrient is causing a deficiency problem can be difficult; it is important to note whether the symptoms are affecting old or young leaves and leaf margins or leaf veins. A pictorial reference book is invaluable. The major problem with using visual symptoms to identify a deficiency is that growth and yield can be affected long before there are obvious signs. Annual dressings of fertilizers provide some insurance but can be expensive and may contribute to a buildup of soil salts harmful to plant growth, and to pollution.

If more precision is required, an assessment of the current nutrient status of the soil can be made by soil analysis, achieved by laboratory tests, by the use of portable electrodes or with soil-testing kits. Most soil analysis relies on chemical extractants, which remove nutrients at levels that are roughly equivalent to the amounts taken up by plant roots. Although a broad indication of fertility can be obtained, there are drawbacks relating to the interpretation of results. A soil is only deficient when the plant in question cannot obtain enough nutrients: both the demands and the root systems of a mature tree will be very different from those of a small vegetable seedling. In addition, the more unusual the soil type to be tested, the less certainty there is with regard to the accuracy of the tests. Levels of nitrogen are particularly difficult to interpret, as the amount available in the soil after a wet winter indicates nothing about the likely levels in summer. In addition, most soil-testing kits will only give readings for nitrogen as nitrate ions. For vegetables grown at a high pH this will be adequate, but it will be of no value for plants growing on acidic ground where ammonium is important. Foliar analysis and sap testing can be more reliable techniques, but these are impracticable for most gardeners.

Assessment of the nutrient status of soil on a new site is desirable, and determining levels of phosphorus, potassium, and magnesium, as well as pH, may be worthwhile. When fertility is established, combining moderate levels of regular feeding, with an eye for possible deficiency symptoms, usually means that repeated complicated tests of garden soil are unnecessary.

The natural response of many gardeners faced with a nutrient deficiency is to add fertilizer. However, if the real problem is linked to poor nutrient availability rather than low levels, fertilizing may be of limited or no benefit and alternative feeding strategies may be needed. For example, iron is present in huge amounts in soil, yet deficiencies can result from a high pH. This can be corrected by foliar feeding, using special sequestrene compounds that remain soluble at high pH, or by adding bulky organic manures, which slightly acidify the soil and also produce their own natural by-products.

The nutrient status of crops can also be modified by various cultural practices: mulching or irrigating will reduce drought and improve nutrient movement; mulches or cloches increase soil temperature and bacterial activity early in the year; cultivation aerates the soil and increases the rate of organic matter breakdown, and also influences the rooting depth and extent of the plants. Marling a sandy soil or adding organic matter can improve structure, water retention and CEC.

The choice of fruit rootstock affects the extent of rooting and hence the

N

likelihood of nutrient deficiencies, while the presence of grass in an orchard can influence nutrient availability. Above all, modifying the soil pH is one of the most effective means of altering nutrient availability in gardens.

It is not always desirable for soils to have high nutrient levels. In nature, very fertile soils are dominated by a few aggressively competitive plants. The decline of wildflowers in rural areas can often be directly attributed to the increased use of fertilizers, particularly in species-rich grassland where the more attractive plants have been replaced by vigorous grasses.

nyctinasty the nighttime folding up of leaflets, as occurs, for example, in some *Oxalis* species.

nymph the immature stage of those more primitive insects that undergo incomplete metamorphosis; the offspring resemble the parents except that they are smaller, sexually immature, and develop wings gradually. Nymphs are usually found in much the same places as adults, and consume the same type of food. Familiar plant pests with nymphal stages include springtails, earwigs, grasshoppers, and crickets; others include leafhoppers, aphids, scale insects, mealybugs, whiteflies, and capsid bugs.

Nymphaea (from Greek *nymphe*, a water-nymph, referring to the habitat). Nymphaeaceae. Cosmopolitan distribution. WATERLILY. Some 50 species, aquatic, perennial herbs with stout rhizomes or tubers and long-stalked floating leaves, their blades usually rounded and with a deep basal sinus. The flowers are solitary, floating or emergent, and fragrant, with many oblong petals in a bowl-like arrangement around a boss of stamens.

Species from cooler regions are suitable for permanent positions in the pools and lakes of temperate gardens, one of the most important factors for success being the selection of appropriate species and cultivars for the given depth of water. Depth requirements range from 6 to 12 in (15 to 30 cm) for *N. tetragona* and its hybrids, making them suitable for

even the smallest stretches of water, including half-barrels in the patio or courtyard garden. The majority of *N.* Laydekeri Hybrids are grown at a depth of 12–16 in (30–40 cm), and the *N.* Marliacea Hybrids at 36 in (90 cm), although the tiny 'Mary Patricia' requires only 6–12 in (15–30 cm), and the more robust 'Carnea' and 'Rosea' need up to 4 ft (1.2 m) of water above the crown. Deep-water species, at depths of 6½–8 ft (2–2.5 m) for larger-scale plantings, include *N. alba* cultivars and hybrids such as 'Gladstoniana', with semidouble, starry white flowers. The tropical species and hybrids are fine plants for large pools in the heated greenhouse (minimum temperature 59°F/15°C).

Plant all in baskets or on the pond floor in a loamy medium in water with a pH of 6.0–7.0. Position in full sun away from disturbance by waterfalls, fountains or pumps. Feed when necessary with a slow-release fertilizer placed in the baskets or in the vicinity of root systems. At planting time, remove adult leaves and damaged roots and treat cut surfaces with charcoal. Plant the rhizomes or tubers vertically with the fibrous roots spread out beneath. The crown must be just at the surface of the medium. Topdress with a layer of pea gravel. Lower the container into the water slowly; gradually increase the plant's depth to the appropriate level as growth progresses. In larger expanses of water, plant roots in a packet of soil wrapped in burlap, place carefully in water, and allow to sink. Temperate species are generally cold hardy where temperatures fall to 5°F (–15°C) and below, but there must be sufficient depth of water above the crown (about 9–12 in/22–30 cm) to protect it from freezing. Alternatively, tubers can be lifted and stored in cool conditions if kept moist and protected from vermin. When plants become overcrowded, flowers are smaller and fewer and foliage stands clear of the water. It may be necessary to remove overcrowded foliage in summer by pulling away the older, outer leaves. Propagate by division or by removal of pieces of rhizome with a sprouting eye.

Increase viviparous tropical types by the removal of young plantlets borne in the leaf blade sinus.

The waterlily beetle can be a destructive pest—adults overwinter among pond-side vegetation, laying eggs on upper leaf surfaces in late spring. The emerging larvae feed on foliage, eating holes in the leaves and flowers. The water lily aphid attacks many soft-leaved aquatics during the summer, distorting foliage and flower stems and discoloring flowers. Eggs overwinter on *Prunus*, especially plum and blackthorn, but also on flowering cherries; large-scale landscape plantings with these trees at the waterside will almost certainly make it difficult to maintain a healthy population of *Nymphaea* species. Waterlily leaf spot shows as dark rotting patches on leaves that eventually disintegrate. Remove and destroy affected parts. With crown rot, the crown suffers a putrid rot and rapidly collapses.

N. alba EUROPEAN WATERLILY; Eurasia, N Africa; leaves to 12 in (30 cm) in diameter, entire, dark green above, red-green to yellow beneath; flowers to 8 in (20 cm), diameter, white, opening diurnally, floating, faintly fragrant, stamens yellow to orange; *N. caerulea* BLUE LOTUS; N and tropical Africa; leaves to 16 in (40 cm) in diameter, entire or undulate, green above, spotted purple beneath; flowers to 6 in (15 cm) in diameter, pale blue, emergent, opening diurnally, stamens yellow; *N. capensis* CAPE BLUE WATERLILY; S and E Africa, Madagascar; leaves to 16 in (40 cm) in diameter, dentate to undulate, green, spotted purple beneath when young; flowers to 8 in (20 cm) in diameter, bright blue, opening diurnally, sweetly fragrant, emergent, stamens golden; cultivars and varieties include 'Eastoniensis', with serrate leaves and steel blue flowers; var. *zanzibariensis*, with smaller leaves, tinged purple beneath, and deeper blue flowers to 12 in (30 cm) in diameter; 'Azurea', with light blue flowers; 'Jupiter', with large, scented, dark violet blue flowers; and 'Rosea', with leaves tinted red beneath and pale pink flowers flushed

Waterlily beetle

red); *N.* × *daubenyana.* (*N. caerulea* × *N. micrantha*) leaves viviparous; flowers 2–7 in (5–18 cm) in diam., emergent, azure blue, opening diurnally; *N. flavovirens* Mexico, S America; leaves to 18 in (45 cm) in diameter, subentire to deeply sinuate, sometimes red beneath; flowers to 8 in (20 cm) in diameter, white, strongly fragrant, opening diurnally, emergent, stamens deep yellow; cultivars include 'Astraea', with star-shaped, blue flowers shading to white at center, and yellow stamens; 'Mrs. C. W. Ward', with rosy red flowers and golden yellow stamens tipped pink; 'Purpurea', with vivid purple flowers and gold stamens; 'Stella Gurney', also known as 'Pink Star', with large, pale pink flowers; and 'William Stone', with large, dark blue flowers, violet at center, and stamens gold tipped blue; *N. gigantea* AUSTRALIAN WATER LILY; tropical Australia, New Guinea; leaves to 24 in (60 cm) in diameter, undulate, dentate, tinged pink to purple beneath; flowers to 12 in (30 cm) in diameter, sky blue to blue-purple, opening diurnally, emergent, stamens bright yellow; *N.* × *helvola* (syn. *N.* 'Pygmy Yellow'; *N. tetragona* × *N. mexicana*) leaves to 2½ in (6 cm), red blotched brown; flowers to 2 in (5 cm) in diameter, canary-yellow, stamens orange; *N.* Laydekeri Hybrids (syn. *N.* × *laydekeri*) hybrids involving *N. alba* var. *rubra*, *N. tetragona* and others; hardy garden hybrids lacking the vigor of the Marliacea Hybrids; usually with brown-mottled or -tinted leaves and flowers 2½–3 in (6–8 cm) in diameter; cultivars include 'Fulgens', with leaves mottled brown, and crimson-magenta flowers to 3½ in (9 cm) in diameter, with red stamens; 'Liliacea', with fragrant, lilac-pink flowers, with orange-red stamens; and 'Purpurata', with green leaves and crimson flowers, with orange-red stamens. *N. lotus* EGYPTIAN WATER LILY, LOTUS, WHITE LILY; Egypt to tropical and SE Africa; leaves to 20 in (50 cm) in diameter, undulate to serrate, dark green above, green or brown and usually hairy beneath; flowers to 10 in (25 cm) in diameter, white, sometimes tinged pink, opening diurnally or nocturnally, slightly fragrant, emergent; *N.* Marliacea Hybrids (syn. *N.* × *marliacea*) MARLIAC HYBRIDS, involving *N. alba*, *N. odorata*

var. *rosea*, *N. mexicana* and others; hardy, robust garden hybrids with large flowers held above the water; cultivars include 'Albida', with fragrant, white flowers, exterior tinted pink below, with yellow stamens; 'Carnea', with fragrant, flesh-pink to deep rose flowers; 'Chromatella', with leaves mottled purple-bronze, and chrome yellow, semidouble flowers; and 'Rosea,' with leaves flushed purple at first, and rosy red flowers; *N. odorata* FRAGRANT WATER LILY, POND LILY; E US; leaves to 10 in (25 cm) in diameter, entire, dull dark green above, usually purple and rough beneath; flowers to 6 in (15 cm) in diameter, white, usually floating, sweetly fragrant, opening diurnally, stamens gold; cultivars include 'Eugene de Land', with scented, pale orange-pink flowers held above water; 'Exquisita', with small, star-shaped, rose flowers; 'Helen Fowler', with large deep pink, very fragrant flowers held above water; 'Roswitha' with rich rose-red flowers; 'Sulphurea Grandiflora', *N. odorata* × *N. mexicana*, with dark green, marbled leaves and very large, stellate flowers of a bright rich yellow; 'William B. Shaw', with large, flat, creamy pink flowers, with an internal zone of dark red; var. *rosea*, with deep pink, strongly scented flowers to 4 in (10 cm) in diameter; and 'Prolifera', with abundant flowers; *N. tetragona* (syn. *N. pygmaea*) PYGMY WATER LILY; NE Europe, N Asia to Japan, N America; leaves to 4 in (10 cm), entire, blotched brown when young above, dull red beneath; flowers to 2 in (5 cm) in diameter, white, sometimes faintly lined purple, floating, slightly fragrant, anthers golden yellow; cultivars include 'Alba', with small, oval leaves, purple beneath, and white flowers to 1 in (2.5 cm) in diameter; 'Hyperion', with dark amaranth flowers; 'Johann Pring', with rich pink flowers—inner ring of stamens light orange, outer ring dark pink—to 2 in (5 cm) in diameter; 'Rubis', with deep red flowers, lacking white dots on outer petals; f. *rubra*, with leaves tinted purple, red beneath, and dark red flowers, with orange stamens.

nymphaeum a grotto or building usually containing statuary and waterworks, a feature of Roman and Italian Renaissance gardens.

Nymphoides (resembling *Nymphaea*). Menyanthaceae. Cosmopolitan. FLOATING HEART. 20 species, aquatic perennial herbs with creeping rhizomes and elongate stems. The leaves are floating, long-stalked and rounded to heart-shaped. The flowers are borne on slender stalks, the flowering nodes sometimes with clusters of short spur roots, and the corolla rounded with five entire or fringed lobes. A hardy, floating aquatic for smaller ponds or containers. Cultivate as for hardy *Nymphaea* in full sun. Propagate by division in spring or by separation of young plantlets in fall. Damaged, or killed, by formalin, when this is used against algae. *N. peltata* YELLOW FLOATING HEART, WATER FRINGE; Europe, Asia, naturalized US; freely stoloniferous; leaves 2–4 in (5–10 cm) in diameter, mottled; flowers to 1 in (2.5 cm) in diameter, golden yellow, fringed.

Nyssa (for Nyssa, a water nymph: *N. aquatica* grows in swamps). Nyssaceae. TUPELO. Eastern N America, E Asia. 5 species, deciduous trees having inconspicuous green flowers and leaves coloring beautifully in fall. The following are fully hardy and perform best in full sun or light shade on moist or wet, acidic to neutral soils. *N. sylvatica* is tolerant of pollution, maritime conditions, and shade. Try to avoid root disturbance. Sow seed, following stratification at 41°F (5°C) for three months; alternatively, increase by layers or semiripe cuttings during late summer.

N. sinensis CHINESE TUPELO; C China; similar to *N. sylvatica* but 33–50 ft (10–15 m) and more spreading; leaves to 8 in (20 cm), oblong to lanceolate, sparsely hairy and tinged red when young; fall color usually finer than that of *N. sylvatica*; *N. sylvatica* BLACK GUM, PEPPERIDGE, SOUR GUM; eastern N America; broadly columnar to conical, 66–100 ft (20–30 m); leaves to 6 in (15 cm), ovate to elliptic or obovate, downy on the veins beneath, flame-colored in fall; fruit ovoid, ½ in (1 cm), blue-black; var. *biflora*: SWAMP TUPELO, SE US, to 50 ft (15 m), with base of trunk swollen when growing in water, and more leathery, oblanceolate leaves.

N

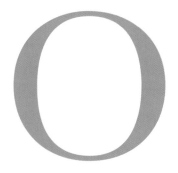

O

ob- a prefix, meaning inverted; thus, oblanceolate means lanceolate, but with the broadest part farthest from the base.

obelisk a pointed, tapering shaft of masonry, usually square in section, often used in landscape gardens as a focal point.

obligate essential; unable to exist without; for example, true parasites are said to be obligate parasites.

oblique (1) of a base, with sides of unequal angles and dimensions; (2) of direction, extending laterally, the margin upward and the apex pointed horizontally.

obtuse apex or base terminating gradually in a blunt or rounded end.

Ochna (from Greek *ochne*, name used by Homer for the wild pear, the leaves of which are said to resemble those of some species in this genus). Ochnaceae. Old World tropics. BIRD'S EYE BUSH. 86 species, deciduous or evergreen trees and shrubs with leathery, glossy, and toothed leaves. Produced in spring and summer, the flowers give rise to fruits with enlarged and fleshy calyces and glossy drupes attached to a swollen, lobed receptacle. Grow *Ochna* in full sun; water plentifully and feed semiweekly when in full growth; maintain a minimum temperature of 50°F (10°C) during winter. Prune in early spring if necessary to shape or confine to bounds. Propagate by seed, alternatively by semiripe cuttings. *O. serrulata* MICKEY-MOUSE PLANT, BIRD'S-EYE BUSH; South Africa; to 7¼ ft (2.25 m); flowers solitary or clustered, calyx lobes bright red in fruit; drupes glossy, black.

Ocimum (plant name used by Theophrastus). Labiatae. Old World tropics. 35 species of aromatic annual and perennial herbs, subshrubs, and shrubs with small, two-lipped flowers whorled in spikes. *O. basilicum* is one of the most important culinary herbs; the leaves are used in salads, casseroles, sauces, and liqueurs. Although more or less perennial, basil is best treated as a tender annual in cool temperate climates and sown under glass in a soilless mix in spring; pot under glass in a similar medium and plant after the last frost. In hotter climates, it is possible to obtain two or more crops per year— sow *in situ*. *O. basilicum* COMMON BASIL, SWEET BASIL; tropical Asia, now widespread through cultivation; annual or short-lived perennial, 8–24 in (20–60 cm); leaves ⅝–2 in (1.5–5 cm), narrowly ovate to elliptic, entire to serrate; cultivars include 'Citriodorum', with lemon-scented leaves; 'Crispum', with leaves curled around the edges; var. *purpurascens*, BUSH BASIL, GREEK BASIL, 6–12 in (15–30 cm), bushy with very small leaves, includes 'Purple Ruffles', with purple leaves, curled around the edges, and 'Dark Opal', with red-purple, clove-scented leaves.

sweet basil leaves

Ocimum basilicum

ocrea, ochrea a tubular or inflated sheath formed by a pair of coherent stipules, as in Polygonaceae.

× **Odontioda** Orchidaceae. Garden hybrids between *Odontoglossum* and *Cochlioda*. Plants consist of a group of compressed pseudobulbs with two or more straplike leaves. The flowers arise at various times of year in simple or branched racemes. Most have a rounded shape and wide sepals and petals, the lip large or small depending on the ancestry. They come in many colors, often conspicuously marked in a variety of contrasting tones; the bright red of so many of the crosses is inherited from the *Cochlioda* parent. Most of these hybrids are "cool" growers

(minimum temperature 50°F/10°C), although a few are tolerant of warmer conditions and may thrive in the home; see *Odontoglossum* for general requirements.

× **Odontocidium** Orchidaceae. Garden hybrids between *Odontoglossum* and *Oncidium*. The flowers arise on simple or branched racemes and are very varied—rounded in shape, or with long, narrow sepals and petals, the lip large or small depending on the ancestry; many colors are represented, often marked in contrasting tones. Most of these hybrids are "cool" growers (minimum temperature 50°F/10°C), although a few are tolerant of warmer conditions; see *Odontoglossum* for general requirements.

Odontoglossum (from Greek *odous*, *odontos*, tooth, and *glossa*, tongue, referring to the toothlike processes of the lip). Orchidaceae. S America. Some 60 species, evergreen perennial herbs, for the most part epiphytes or lithophytes with pseudobulbs and strap-shaped leaves. The flowers are carried in erect to arching racemes or panicles and vary greatly in size, shape and color. The sepals are more or less equal and spreading, the petals similar to the sepals but often shorter. The lip is either simple or 3-lobed, its basal portion often clawlike, the lateral lobes spreading or erect, the midlobe entire or cleft, and the disk crested, bumpy, or with keels. These plants are cool-growing (minimum temperature 50°F/10°C in winter) and demand a freely ventilated and humid atmosphere in light shade. Their roots are slender: a fine bark mix is best, containing rock wool or sphagnum. Water and syringe freely when in growth, and impose drier, cooler conditions when at rest. Never syringe in cold weather. Propagate by division.

O. cirrhosum Ecuador, Colombia, Peru; raceme or panicle to 24 in (60 cm), arching; flowers to 3 in (8 cm) across, tepals slender, wavy, with narrow, curved tips, white, more or less blotched red-brown, lip with a narrow, pointed midlobe, white stained yellow in throat and marked red-brown; *O. crispum* Colombia; raceme to 20 in (50 cm), arching; flowers to 3½ in (9 cm) across, tepals broad, spreading, toothed and lacy, pure white, sometimes tinted pale rose or with a few red spots, lip short, broad, white stained yellow at base with a few red spots; *O. cristatum* Colombia, Ecuador, Peru; raceme to 20 in (50 cm), arching; flowers to 3 in (8 cm) across, tepals ovate, tapering narrowly, creamy yellow to olive with chestnut blotches, lip finely pointed, olive blotched chestnut with a white throat; *O. harryanum* Columbia, Peru; raceme erect to 3¼ ft (1 m), sometimes branched; flowers to 4 in (10 cm) across, tepals broadly oblong, wavy, yellow to olive overlaid with chestnut to chocolate brown, lip large, heart-shaped, white heavily veined with red; *O. lindleyanum* Colombia, Venezuela, Ecuador; raceme or panicle to 12 in (30 cm); flowers to 2½ in (6 cm) across, tepals narrowly oblanceolate, golden blotched and barred chestnut brown, lip narrow, forward-pointing, white with a spear-shaped midlobe that progresses from yellow at the tip through burnt orange to fuchsia pink at the base; *O. luteopurpureum* Colombia; raceme to 3¼ ft (1 m); flowers to 4 in (10 cm) across, tepals ovate to lanceolate, pointed, wavy, creamy yellow heavily blotched and overlaid with glossy maroon, lip ax-shaped, finely fringed, white blotched maroon at base; *O. pendulum* (syn. *Cuitlauzina pendula, O. citrosmum*) Mexico; raceme to 20 in (50 cm), pendulous; flowers to 2¾ in (7 cm) across, lemon-scented, tepals broadly obovate, pure white sometimes flushed pale rose or lilac, lip broadly hatchet-shaped, mauve-pink, yellow at base; *O. pulchellum* (syn. *Osmoglossum pulchellum*) LILY OF THE VALLEY ORCHID; Mexico, Guatemala, El Salvador; raceme to 20 in (50 cm), erect to arching; flowers to 1¼ in (3 cm) across, sweetly scented, tepals obovate, cupped, sparkling white tinted rose, lip white; *O. wallisii* Colombia, Venezuela, Peru; raceme or panicle to 20 in (50 cm), arching; flowers to 2 in (5 cm) across, tepals

narrowly oblanceolate, golden blotched red-brown, lip white spotted rose-purple near apex. For *O. bictoniense, O. cervantesii, O. cordatum, O. rossii,* and *O. stellatum,* see under *Lemboglossum*; for *O. grande,* see *Rossioglossum.*

oedema, edema the formation of small blisterlike swellings on leaves or stems, which may become brown and corky. The result of increased intracellular water, oedema occurs where intake exceeds transpiration. It is favored by a humid atmosphere and heavy watering. Tomatoes and pelargoniums especially are prone to oedema. Also known as dropsy.

Oemleria (for Augustus Gottleib Oemler, 19th-century German-born pharmacist and naturalist working in Savannah, Georgia). Rosaceae. Western N America. OREGON PLUM, OSO BERRY. 1 species, *O. cerasiformis* (syn. *Osmaronia cerasiformis*), a deciduous, slender-stemmed shrub to 16 ft (5 m). The leaves are to 4 in (10 cm) long, oblong to oblanceolate, glossy dark green above, gray and downy beneath. Small, white, fragrant flowers are carried in nodding racemes in early spring and are followed by small, sloe-black fruits. Hardy to –4°F (–20°C). Grow in well-drained but moisture-retentive neutral to acidic soils in shade. Prune after flowering to thin out old shoots and to relieve overcrowding. Old plants may be rejuvenated by cutting hard back. Propagate by rooted suckers.

Oenanthe (from Greek *oinanthe,* inflorescence of the grapevine). Umbelliferae. Western N America. 30 species of glabrous perennial herbs, many of them highly toxic. The stems are procumbent to ascending and often rooting. The leaves are pinnately compound or decompound with toothed leaflets. Small, white flowers are borne in tight compound umbels. Hardy to –10°F (–23°C), *O. javanica* 'Flamingo' is a brightly variegated groundcover plant ideal for wet situations or use in containers and bedding. It will also thrive in shallow water. Propagate by stem tip cuttings, division or by simple layering.
O. javanica (syn. *O. japonica;* India to Japan, Ryukyu Islands, Taiwan,

Malaysia, N Australia; stems 8–16 in (20–40 cm), procumbent to erect; leaf segments ½–1¼ in (1–3 cm), ovate to narrowly obovate, toothed, sometimes lobed; 'Flamingo': leaves splashed and zoned pink, cream and white).

Oenothera (name used by Theophrastus for another plant). Onagraceae. N and S America, many naturalized elsewhere, usually on disturbed ground. EVENING PRIMROSE, SUNDROPS, SUNCUPS. 124 species, annual, biennial or perennial herbs. Produced in spring and summer, the flowers are usually short-lived but showy, either solitary in leaf axils or gathered into corymbose, racemose, or spicate inflorescences. Bowl- to funnel-shaped, they consist of four silky, obovate petals and open at dawn or dusk. The following species are hardy to –10°F (–23°C) and fare best in full sun on well-drained, low- to medium-fertility soils. Their longevity varies, influenced by climate and soil type: certain perennial species are better treated as annuals or biennials when gardening on heavy soils or in cold areas. The tall-growing species are prolific seeders useful for naturalizing in wild areas (gravelly banks and near-pure sand included). Low-growing species make good front-of-border or scree plants. Sow seed from spring to early summer. Propagate perennials by division, or by softwood cuttings taken in spring before flowering. *O. biennis* COMMON EVENING PRIMROSE, GERMAN RAMPION; eastern N America, naturalized Europe and elsewhere; erect, annual or biennial, 4–60 in (10–150 cm); inflorescence spicate; petals ¾–1 in (1.8–2.5 cm), yellow, aging gold; *O. deltoides* DESERT EVENING PRIMROSE; California; annual, 2–10 in (5–25 cm), branching from base; flowers solitary, white, aging pink, 1½–3 in (4–8 cm) diameter; *O. fruticosa* SUNDROPS; eastern N America; biennial or perennial, 12–32 in (30–80 cm), hairy, tinged red; petals ⅝–1 in (1.5–2.5 cm), toothed, deep yellow; cultivars include 'Fireworks', with leaves tinged purple and yellow flowers; 'Golden Moonlight', to 32 in (80 cm) high, with large, bright yellow flowers; 'Highlight', with yellow flowers; 'Illumination', with leaves tinged

O

bronze, and large, deep yellow flowers; 'Silvery Moon', to 32 in (80 cm) high, with large, pale yellow flowers; 'Yellow River', with stem brick red and bright canary yellow flowers; 'Youngii', to 20 in (50 cm), with large, bright yellow flowers; subsp. *glauca*, syn. *O. tetragona*: leaves broader, tinted red when young, includes 'Sonnenwende', to 24 in (60 cm), with leaves red in fall, and red-orange flower buds; *O. macrocarpa* (syn. *O. missouriensis*) OZARK SUNDROPS; south central US; perennial, rather short-stemmed, branched from base, decumbent to erect, pubescent; flowers yellow, up to 4 in (10 cm) in diameter; includes 'Greencourt Lemon', which has lemon yellow flowers; *O. perennis* (syn. *O. pumila*) SUNDROPS; eastern N America; perennial, 4–20 in (10–50 cm); stem slender, simple or few-branched; flowers in a loose spike, petals ¼–⅜ in (0.6–0.8 cm), yellow; *O. rosea* Texas to Peru, naturalized S Europe; erect, strigulose, perennial or annual, 6–24 in (15–60 cm); inflorescence spicate, petals ⅛–½ in (0.4–1 cm), pink to red-violet; *O. speciosa* (WHITE EVENING PRIMROSE; SW US to Mexico; rhizomatous perennial, erect, 12–24 in (30–60 cm), strigose; petals ¾–1 in (2–2.5 cm), white aging rose, sometimes pink when young; 'Rosea': to 12 in (30 cm), with pale pink flowers opening during the day; 'Siskiyou': habit neat, bushy, flowers rose-pink with white centers veined pink, the very center and anthers golden.

officinal strictly meaning "of apothecaries' shops." Pertaining to commercial value, especially as sold in shops; applied to plants with real or presumed medicinal properties, hence the specific epithet *officinalis*.

offset, offshoot a young plant that is produced naturally by vegetative means. An offset or offshoot is joined to its parent plant, but is easily detached from it. The term is commonly applied to bulbs, corms, and many rosette-forming plants, including sempervivums; it is also used of fibrous-rooted plants that produce a number of loosely joined groups of shoots, such as perennial asters. See *daffodils*.

oilstone a fine-grained sharpening stone lubricated with oil, used for sharpening knives and pruners.

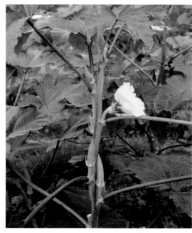

Okra
The seed pods are the edible part, harvested green for using as a cooked vegetable once the mallowlike flowers have faded.

okra (*Abelmoschus esculentus*) LADY'S FINGER A tender annual, up to 6½ ft (2 m) in height, grown for its edible pods used when immature as a cooked vegetable, or matured, dried, and finely ground for use as a flavoring. The pods are 4–10 in (10–25 cm) long, angled, beaked, and bristly and there are green-, red-, or yellow-skinned cultivars. In warm temperate and sub-tropical climates, OKRA can be grown outdoors. An ideal temperature range for good growth is 68°–86°F (20–30°C), so greenhouse protection may be required. Seed should be pre-soaked and germinated at a minimum temperature of 61°F (16°C). In suitable climates, seed can be sown *in situ* outdoors in rows 24–28 in (60–70 cm) apart at 8–12 in (20–30 cm) stations. Under protection grow in pots, growing bags or border soil allowing at least 16 in (40 cm) between plants. Plants require staking and the growing points should be pinched out at 24 in (60 cm) height. The maintenance of high humidity is beneficial. Harvest from 8–12 weeks after sowing, cutting the pods off with a knife.

Olea (from Greek *elaia*, the olive). Oleaceae. Temperate and tropical Old World. OLIVE. Some 20 species of long-lived evergreen trees and shrubs with leathery leaves, small, white or

off-white flowers in summer, and ovoid or globose drupes. Although badly damaged by temperatures lower than 14°F (–10°C), *O. europaea* is hardy to 10°F (–12°C) if given the shelter of a wall and full sunlight. However, good fruiting can be expected only in warm-temperate regions with moist winters and hot, dry summers. Plant in deep, fertile soil with perfect drainage. The weighting or arching of branches will encourage fruiting. Pruning may stimulate the overproduction of non-fruiting water shoots. Container-grown plants thrive in cool, well-lit greenhouses and conservatories and may be moved outdoors in summer. Propagate by seed sown in gentle heat in spring, or by semiripe cuttings in summer. *O. europaea* COMMON OLIVE, EDIBLE OLIVE; to 23 ft (7 m); leaves to 3 in (8 cm), elliptic to lanceolate, gray-green above, silver-scurfy beneath; fruit ripening red to purple-black, to 2 in (5 cm); widespread throughout the Mediterranean region, var. *europaea* is the fruit- and oil-yielding cultigen; it includes numerous cultivars; the fruit may range in size from ½ to 2 in (1 to 5 cm), in shape from near-spherical, to egg- to spindle-shaped, in color from purple-red to blue-black or yellow-green, in quality from firm and waxy to smooth and yielding, and from sour to sweet.

oleaginous oily, though of a fleshy nature.

Olearia (for Johann Gottfried Olschlager [1635–1711], German horticulturist—the family name was Latinized to "Olearius"). Compositae. Australasia. DAISY BUSH. About 130 species, herbs, evergreen shrubs, or small trees with leathery leaves and daisylike flower heads in spring and summer. Most are not reliably hardy where temperatures fall much below 23°F (–5°C), unless given warm wall protection. They are valuable in mild maritime gardens, showing good resistance to salt-laden winds and maintaining a dense and compact habit when grown in full sun and an exposed position. Several species of particularly dense habit are suitable for hedging, including *O. macrodonta*, *O. avicenniifolia* and *O. × haastii* (the last two also tolerate urban pollution). *O. nummularifolia*, *O. virgata*, *O. mollis*, and *O. ilicifolia*, are among the hardiest plants, tolerating temperatures to 5°F (−15°C); *O.* × *scilloniensis* and O. 'Talbot de Malahide' are almost as hardy, to about 14°F (−10°C). Grow in well-drained soil in full sun. *Olearia* responds particularly well to hard pruning, breaking freely from older wood. Propagate by semiripe cuttings in summer or by heeled ripewood cuttings of lateral shoots in the cold frame in early fall. Softer-leaved types, such as *O. phlogopappa*, can be increased by softwood cuttings.

O. avicenniifolia New Zealand; shrub or small tree to 23 ft (7 m); leaves 2–4 in (5–10 cm), ovate to lanceolate, tapered at base and apex, entire, gray-white, glabrous above, white- or pale yellow-tomentose beneath; flower heads white; *O. chathamica* New Zealand; shrub, to 6½ ft (2 m); leaves 1¼–3 in (3–8 cm), oblanceolate to elliptic, acute, tapered at base, regularly and obtusely dentate, glabrous above, midrib raised beneath; flower heads white or tinged purple, with dark purple centers; *O.* × *haastii* (*O. avicenniifolia* × *O. moschata*; New Zealand; shrub, 3¼–10 ft (1–3 m); leaves ½–1 in (1–2.5 cm), crowded, oval or ovate, entire, dark glossy green, glabrous above, white-tomentose beneath; flower heads white with centers yellow; *O.* 'Henry Travers' (*O. chathamica* × *O. semidentata*) medium-sized shrub; leaves lanceolate, gray-green, silvery beneath; flower heads large, lilac, deep mauve centers); *O. hookeri* Tasmania; shrub to 3¼ ft (1 m); leaves 1¼–2½ in (3–6 cm), narrow, grooved above, revolute; flower heads indigo, centers yellow; *O. ilicifolia* New Zealand; tree or shrub to 16 ft (5 m), with musky fragrance; leaves 2–4 in (5–10 cm), linear to oblong or lanceolate, acute to acuminate, coriaceous to glabrous above, white- to yellow-tomentose beneath, undulate, serrate-dentate; flower heads fragrant, white; *O. lacunosa* (New Zealand; shrub to 16 ft (5 m); leaves 2¾–6 in (7–16 cm), linear to oblong, acute to acuminate, coriaceous, rugose, midrib yellow above, minutely sinuate-dentate; flower heads white; *O. macrodonta* ARORANGI; New Zealand; shrub or tree to 20 ft (6 m); leaves 2–4 in (5–10 cm), ovate to

oblong, acute to acuminate, dark glossy green above, silver-tomentose beneath, musk-scented when crushed, undulate, acutely dentate-serrate; flower heads white with red-tinted centers; *O.* × *mollis* (*O. ilicifolia* × *O. lacunosa*) New Zealand; shrub to 10 ft (3 m) leaves to 4 in (10 cm), lanceolate, spinulose, rounded at base, veins sunken above, very prominent beneath, densely white- to pale yellow-tomentose beneath, revolute; white flower heads; 'Zennorensis': shrub to 6½ ft (2 m), with narrow, acute, sharply dentate leaves, 4 × ½–⅝ in (10 cm × 1–1.5 cm), dark olive green above, white-tomentose beneath; *O. nummulariifolia* New Zealand; shrub to 10 ft (3 m) leaves ¼–½ in (0.5–1 cm), dense, ovate to suborbicular, glabrous above white- to buff- or yellow-tomentose beneath, revolute; flower heads fragrant, pale yellow or cream; *O. phlogopappa* Tasmania, Victoria, New South Wales; aromatic shrub to 10 ft (3 m) leaves ⅝–2 in (1.5–5 cm), oblong or narrowly obovate, sinuous or shallowly toothed, dark dull green above, white- or gray-tomentose beneath; flower heads white, occasionally pink, mauve or blue, with centers yellow. *O.* × *scilloniensis* (*O. lirata* × *O. phlogopappa*) shrub to 10 ft (3 m) leaves to 4½ in (11 cm), elliptic to oblong, obtuse, deep green and reticulate above, pale green, tomentose beneath, sinuate; flower heads white with yellow centers; 'Master Michael': leaves tinted gray, flowers blue; *O. semidentata* Chatham Island, New Zealand; rounded shrub to 11½ ft (3.5 m); leaves 1½–2¾ in (3.5–7 cm), linear to lanceolate, serrate above, rugose, glabrous above, white-tomentose beneath; flower heads pale purple with darker violet-purple centers; for *O. semidentata* of gardens, see *O.* 'Henry Travers'; *O. solandri* New Zealand; shrub or small tree to 13 ft (4 m); leaves to ⅝ in (1.5 cm), midrib sunken, linear to spathulate or narrowly obovate, subcoriaceous, glabrous above, white- to yellow-tomentose beneath; flower heads yellow; includes 'Aurea', with leaves strongly tinged gold; *O.* 'Talbot de Malahide' (syn. *O. albida*) very similar to *O. avicenniifolia* except leaves blunter and more rounded; *O. virgata* New Zealand; shrub to 15 ft

(5 m); leaves ¼–¾ in (0.5–2 cm), narrowly obovate, glabrous above, white-tomentose beneath; flower heads yellow to white; var. *lineata*: leaves narrow, strongly revolute.

Olsynium (from Greek meaning "hardly united," referring to the stamens). Iridaceae. Americas. About 12 species, perennial herbs with fibrous roots and basal fans or tufts of linear to lanceolate leaves. Produced in summer in terminal clusters, the flowers are bell-shaped and consist of six tepals. Graceful perennials for cool, semishaded positions in acidic pockets on the rock garden or the peat bed. They will survive frosts to −4°F (−20°C) and become dormant in late spring, but nonetheless require permanent moisture. Increase by seed or division. *O. douglasii* (syn. *O. grandiflorum*, *Sisyrinchium douglasii*, *Sisyrinchium grandiflorum*) GRASS WIDOW, PURPLE-EYED GRASS; western N America; 6–12 in (15–30 cm) high; flowers pendent, wine-red, purple-pink or white.

Omphalodes (from Greek *omphalos*, navel, and *oides*, -like; the nutlets resemble a navel). Boraginaceae. Europe, N Africa, Asia, Mexico. NAVELWORT, NAVELSEED. Some 28 species, annual, biennial or perennial herbs, with long-stalked, oblong to ovate leaves. Produced in spring and summer in cymose sprays, the small, bowl-shaped flowers have five rounded lobes and, usually, a paler eye. *O. luciliae* requires a sunny position with its roots in light, moist, sharply drained soil, with additional limestone. Hardy to about 23°F (−5°C), it dislikes winter wetness and may be more safely grown in the alpine house. The annual *O. linifolia*, with white blooms that last well when cut, is sown *in situ* in spring, in sun and well-drained soil. *O. verna* is hardy to −10°F (−23°C) and suitable for cool positions in the rock garden or for naturalizing in light, open woodland. Increase by division in early spring.

O. cappadocica Asia Minor; perennial to 11 in (28 cm), erect or ascending; flowers bright blue with a white eye, to ¼ in (5 mm) in diameter; 'Bright Eyes': flowers white edged bright blue;

O

'Cherry Ingram': to 10 in (25 cm), with deep blue flowers; *O. linifolia* SW Europe; annual to 16 in (40 cm), erect; flowers up to $^1/_2$ in (12 mm) in diameter, white or blue; *O. luciliae* Greece, Asia Minor; perennial to 10 in (25 cm), tufted, glabrous; flowers up to $^3/_8$ in (8 mm) in diameter, rose becoming blue; *O. verna* CREEPING FORGET-ME-NOT; Europe; perennial to 8 in (20 cm), stoloniferous; flowers up to $^1/_2$ in (12 mm) in diameter, blue; 'Alba': flowers white.

Omphalogramma (from Greek *omphalos*, navel, and *gramma*, line). Primulaceae. Himalaya, W China. 15 species, perennial, usually rhizomatous, herbs. The solitary flowers are bell- to funnel-shaped with six to eight lobes and are produced atop glandular-hairy scapes in spring. *O. vinciflorum* is hardy to 0°F (−18°C) and suited to the shady rock garden, with gritty, moist, non-alkaline soil. Otherwise, cultivate in the alpine house or cold frame, in pans of a gritty alpine mix with added leaf mold. Propagate from seed or by division in spring. *O. vinciflorum* China; flowers or scapes to 8 in (20 cm), deep indigo-blue or purple, $1^1/_4$–2 in (3–5 cm) in diameter.

Oncidium (from Greek *onkos*, a lump or tumor, referring to the fleshy, protuberant calli on the lips of many species). Orchidaceae. Tropical and subtropical America. Some 450 species, evergreen perennial herbs, for the most part epiphytes or lithophytes. They vary greatly in habit and size, from dwarf species to "giants," many with pseudobulbs, some lacking these but with tough, overlapping leaves or merely one or two very large and fleshy leaves. Produced in racemes or panicles, the flowers are generally small and often in bright shades of yellow barred or mottled with brown. The tepals are oblong to obovate, the lip larger and entire to 3-lobed with a warty or crested callus. A large genus of cool and intermediate-growing orchids. The smaller species and those with distinct pseudobulbs need dappled sunlight and a humid, airy atmosphere in the cool house (winter minimum 50°F/10°C). In the growing season, water and feed freely; at other

times, water only enough to prevent the plants from shriveling. Pot in a fine- to medium-grade, bark-based mix. Larger species, with reduced pseudobulbs and massive, leathery, "mule's-ear" leaves, should be mounted on bark or planted in baskets and afforded maximum light and humidity throughout the year. They need less water than the first group but favor a warmer and steamier situation. Increase by division or seed.

O. bifolium Uruguay, Argentina, Brazil; plants small to medium-sized, pseudobulbous; raceme to 16 in (40 cm), flowers to $1^1/_4$ in (3 cm) across, tepals small, yellow marked brown, lip far larger with a broad, kidney-shaped midlobe, rich golden yellow with red callus; *O. cavendishianum* Mexico, Honduras, Guatemala; pseudobulbs very small or absent; leaves solitary, very large, tough and fleshy; panicles to 5 ft (1.5 m), flowers to $1^1/_2$ in (4 cm) across, tepals rounded, yellow to olive spotted chocolate or red-brown, lip larger, 3-parted with a notched, fan-shaped midlobe, rich yellow with red dots on callus; *O. crispum* Brazil; plants medium-sized, pseudobulbous; panicle to $3^1/_4$ ft (1 m), erect to arching; flowers to 3 in (8 cm) across, tepals obovate, the petals far larger and wavy, yellow to buff, heavily veined and overlaid with chocolate brown, lip with two small lateral lobes and a large, wavy, fan-shaped midlobe, yellow to tan mottled or veined brown especially near margin; *O. flexuosum* Brazil, Argentina, Paraguay, Uruguay; plants small to medium-sized, pseudobulbous; panicle wiry, to $3^1/_4$ ft (1 m), flowers to 1 in (2.5 cm) across, tepals small, recurved, yellow barred red-brown, lip far larger, broadly fan-shaped, bright gold, sometimes spotted red-brown, callus marked red-brown; *O. fuscatum* (syn. *Miltonia warscewiczii*, *Miltonioides warscewiczii*) Peru, Colombia, Costa Rica; plants are medium-sized and pseudobulbous; panicle to 20 in (50 cm), flowers to 2 in (5 cm) across, tepals oblong to oblanceolate, wavy, brown edged yellow-white, lip large, oblong to shield-shaped, purple to crimson with a deep white margin and a shiny red-brown central patch; *O. globuliferum* Colombia, Venezuela, Costa Rica, Panama; plants small to medium-sized, pseudobulbous; raceme

to $1^1/_4$ in (3 cm), flowers to $1^1/_4$ in (3 cm) across, tepals small, oblanceolate, wavy, golden yellow spotted or barred red-brown at base, lip far larger, kidney-shaped, deep gold spotted red-brown at base; *O. hastatum* (Mexico; plant medium-sized, pseudobulbous; panicle to 5 ft (1.5 m); flowers to 1 in (2.5 cm) across, tepals lanceolate to ovate, yellow to olive blotched brown, lip narrowly arrow-shaped, lateral lobes white, midlobe yellow to flame red with a crimson callus; *O. jonesianum* Brazil, Paraguay, Uruguay; plants small to medium-sized; pseudobulbs very small or absent; leaves clumped, pendulous, fleshy, narrowly cylindrical and pointed; raceme to 20 in (50 cm), flowers to 3 in (7.5 cm) across, tepals obovate, wavy, yellow to olive blotched red-brown, lip fan-shaped, white with a red-spotted, yellow base; *O. ornithorhynchum* C America; plant small to medium-sized, pseudobulbous; panicle to 20 in (50 cm), arching to pendulous, crowded; flowers to $^3/_4$ in (2 cm) across, lacy, pale lilac-pink to rich rose with a yellow callus; *O. pulchellum* (syn. *Tolumnia pulchella*) Jamaica, Guianas, Cuba, Hispaniola; plants dwarf to small, pseudobulbs absent; leaves tough, narrow, folded and keeled, in a fanlike growth; panicle to 20 in (50 cm), flowers to 1 in (2.5 cm) across, tepals small, white tinted rose to rich magenta, lip large, broadly fan-shaped, white tinted rose to deep magenta, yellow at base; *O. pusillum* (syn. *Psygmorchis pusilla*; C and S America, W Indies; plant dwarf, short-lived, pseudobulbs absent; leaves folded and keeled, in a fanlike tuft; flowers to $1^1/_4$ in (3 cm) diam., borne singly in succession on short, wiry stalks, tepals very small, yellow blotched red-brown, lip large, frilly, golden yellow with a red-spotted, white callus; *O. sphacelatum* Mexico to El Salvador; medium-sized to large plants, pseudobulbous; panicle to 5 ft (1.5 m), flowers to 1 in (2.5 cm) across, tepals ovate to lanceolate, pointed, yellow barred and blotched chestnut brown, lip large with rounded lateral lobes and a broadly kidney-shaped midlobe, golden blotched orange-yellow at base with an orange-spotted, white callus; *O. superbiens* Colombia, Venezuela, Peru; plant medium-sized to large, pseudobulbous;

O

panicle to 6½ ft (2 m), slender and snaking, flowers to 2¾ in (7 cm) across, tepals broadly obovate, long-clawed, sepals chocolate brown tipped yellow, petals yellow or white barred chocolate, lip small, purple-brown and trowel-shaped; *O. tigrinum* Mexico; plants medium-sized to large, pseudobulbous; raceme or panicle to 3¼ ft (1 m), erect, flowers to 2½ in (6 cm) across, tepals lanceolate to ovate, wavy, yellow barred dark brown, lip far larger with a broad, kidney-shaped midlobe, bright yellow; *O. varicosum* Brazil; plants medium-sized, pseudobulbous; panicle to 5 ft (1.5 m), loose, arching, flowers to 2 in (5 cm) across, tepals small, olive to yellow barred chestnut brown, lip far larger, fan-shaped, golden yellow with a red-spotted callus.

onion (*Allium cepa*) a biennial grown as an annual for its edible bulb which usually has a strong, pungent flavor; the leaves and immature bulbs are also edible. The onion probably originated in the regions of Iran and western Pakistan, and its use can be traced back to 3200 BC, when it was an important food crop for the Egyptians.

Hot, dry summers are ideal for bulb maturation, but there are many cultivars suited to a range of growing conditions, including cool-season production in tropical regions. For high yield, cool weather is desirable during the early stages of growth. The crop is tolerant of frost, but prolonged exposure to temperatures below 50°F (10°C) will cause plants to bolt. Optimum seedling growth occurs in the range 68–77°F (20–25°C) and declines rapidly at temperatures above 81°F (27°C). Bulb formation takes place in response to long-day conditions and, in temperate climates, most cultivars bulb up during early summer for late summer harvest. Some cultivars will produce bulbs over a long-day range from 12 to more than 16 hours, which makes it possible to manipulate crop supply. Bulbing is also advanced by raised temperatures and nitrogen deficiency. Bulb dormancy may be prolonged by storing at 34°F (1°C), with low relative humidity.

With choice of cultivars and by storage, onions can be continuously available from summer until the following spring. Immature salad onions can be harvested throughout most of the year. Most onion cultivars are brown- or yellow-skinned, with some red-skinned; they may be globe-shaped or flat.

Bulb onions can be propagated either from seed or vegetatively, using small bulblets referred to as sets. Maincrop onions should be sown in a well-prepared seedbed from February to April. Germination is poor in cold, wet soils and cloches should be used to warm the soil for early sowings in cold areas. Seed, preferably treated with a fungicidal dressing, should be sown thinly in ¾-in- (2-cm-) deep drills in rows 12 in (30 cm) apart, with seedlings thinned to 1½-in (4-cm) spacings for medium-sized bulbs, or up to 4-in (10-cm) spacings for large bulbs. Crops that mature in early summer can be obtained by raising transplants under protection for early planting in spring, or by sowing suitable cultivars outside in fall.

Transplants are best raised in multi-seeded cell modules or blocks of up to six seedlings; sow at 50–61°F (10–16°C) in January and, after hardening off, plant out 10–12 in (25–30 cm) apart each way. For outdoor fall sowings, specially selected cultivars should be chosen. The sowing date is critical and depends on local climatic conditions. If sown too early, plants may develop to a size where they are vernalized by low winter temperature and will bolt in spring; if sown too late, they may be too small to survive the winter. Sow seeds 1 in (2.5 cm) apart in rows spaced 12 in

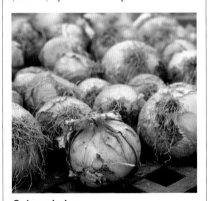

Onions drying
Once onions have been lifted, a further period in the sun, ideally (as here) on a slatted surface, ripens the skins for storage.

(30 cm) apart, at times based on local recommendations and aiming for seedlings to be 6–8 in (15–20 cm) high before the onset of winter.

Onions raised from sets have the advantages of being less prone to disease and onion fly attack; they yield reasonably in poorer soil conditions, and mature earlier than seeded crops. Cultivars are available for both spring and fall planting and should be planted firmly, 2 in (5 cm) apart, with the tips at soil level, in rows spaced 10 in (25 cm) apart. The risk of bolting is reduced with small-sized sets, and with heat-treated ones, which should not be planted before late March.

For salad use, thinnings of maincrop onions can be used; for a continuous salad supply, sow specific cultivars, usually referred to as green onions, from spring to midsummer at intervals of two to three weeks. Overwintered sowings of extra-hardy cultivars can be harvested in spring.

Weed control is important, and during dry spells watering may be necessary, but not as the crop reaches maturity. Onions are ready to harvest when the leaves start to die back and fall over; after drying in the sun or in a cool, dark shed, they may be tied in ropes and hung up or stored in net bags or shallow trays.

Pickling onions are bulb onion cultivars that tolerate poorer, drier soils than bulb or green onions. Sow in March ¼ in (6 mm) apart (competition ensures small size), in rows 12 in (30 cm) apart. Harvest in late summer.

SHALLOTS (*Allium cepa*. Aggregatum Group) have a distinct flavor, and are available in yellow- or red-skinned forms. Raise from sets, about ¾ in (2 cm) in diameter; plant December to March to tip level, 6 in (15 cm) apart, in rows 8 in (20 cm) apart. Bulb clusters are harvested in late summer.

WELSH ONION, PERENNIAL GREEN ONION, or CIBOULE (*Allium fistulosum*), is a hardy clump-forming type used as a salad onion; it grows to 24 in (60 cm) tall. Sow in spring or August in rows 12 in (30 cm) apart, thinning to 9 in (23 cm) apart. Lift and replant clumps every 2–3 years. JAPANESE BUNCHING ONIONS (*Allium fistulosum*) are a much shorter improved form, also available as a single-stemmed type; they are best sown as annuals or biennials in rows 12 in (30 cm) apart, and thinned to 3 in (7.5 cm) spacings.

The EVERLASTING ONION, a cultivar of *A. cepa*, is similar in habit to the Welsh onion but with thinner, flatter leaves and a mild flavor. It should be propagated periodically by division.

Egyptian or tree onion
These unusual onions produce aerial bulblets in place of flowers that, if left in place, eventually fall to the ground and root.

The EGYPTIAN or TREE ONION (*Allium cepa* Proliferum Group) produces clusters of very small aerial bulbs, borne on tall stems in place of flowers. They are hardy and can be used all year round. Plant 10 in (25 cm) apart in spring or fall; the plants are often self-perpetuating as the bulb-laden stems fall over.

Possible problems: *eelworm, onion fly; downy mildew, neck rot, white rot.*

onion fly (*Delia antiqua*) a small gray fly similar in appearance to a housefly, with white, legless maggots up to ⅜ in (8 mm) long, which attack the roots of seedling onions, shallots, and leeks. Early signs of attack are a yellowing and wilting of the outer leaves; symptoms are worse in hot weather on dry soils. There are two generations and damage usually occurs from June to August; second-generation maggots may tunnel inside the bulbs as well as eating roots.

Spring-sown seedlings and sets can be protected by treating the soil with a recommended insecticide at sowing or planting time, subject to local pesticide rules. Plants overwintered from a late-summer sowing require a second treatment in May/June. Growing plants under horticultural fleece is another means of protection. Heavily infested plants should be removed and burned.

Onoclea (from Greek *onos*, vessel, and *kleio*, to close, referring to the closely rolled fertile fronds). Athyriaceae. Eastern N America, E Asia. 1 species, *O. sensibilis*, the SENSITIVE FERN or BEAD FERN, a deciduous perennial fern with extensively creeping rhizomes. The fronds are 12–40 in (30–100 cm) long, more or less erect and pinnately divided with pinnae in 8–12 pairs, each pinna to 3 in (8 cm) wide, deeply lobed to sinuate or entire. The fronds emerge a soft coppery pink and become bright lime green. The rachis is broadly winged. Hardy to –20°F (–29°C), *Onoclea* is usually cultivated in bog and woodland gardens in damp leafy soils, or at the margins of ponds and lakes, where the spreading rhizomes may actually grow outward, covering the water's edge with a dense undulating blanket. Plant in part or full shade in permanently damp, acidic to neutral soils rich in organic matter. Propagate by division in early spring.

Ononis (the name for this plant used by Theophrastus). Leguminosae. Canary Islands, Mediterranean, N Africa, Iran. RESTHARROW. Some 75 species, annual or perennial herbs or dwarf shrubs. *Ononis* leaves are generally trifoliolate, and glandular-hairy. Pealike flowers are produced in panicles, spikes, or racemes during summer. The following species are hardy to 5°F (–15°C). Grow in well-drained, neutral to alkaline soils in full sun, giving *O. fruticosa* a sheltered position. Propagate by scarified seed sown during spring or when ripe in fall. Take special care not to damage the developing taproot when pricking out. Alternatively, take softwood cuttings during early summer and root in a closed case with bottom heat. *O. fruticosa* C and E Spain, central Pyrenees, SE France; dwarf shrub to 3¼ ft (1 m); pink flowers; *O. natrix* S and W Europe, N Spain; dwarf shrub, erect, many-branched, to 24 in (60 cm); flowers yellow, often veined violet or red; *O. rotundifolia* SE Spain to E Austria and C Italy; perennial dwarf shrub, to 20 in (50 cm), erect; flowers pink or white.

Onopordum (also spelled *Onopordon*, Latinized form of a Greek name, *onopordon*, from *onos*, ass, and *pordos*, flatulence, referring to its effect on the digestive system of these animals when eaten). Compositae. Europe, Mediterranean, W Asia. About 40 species, biennial herbs, usually with spiny-winged stems and pinnately lobed and toothed leaves. Erect, branching stems bear large, thistlelike flower heads in summer. Hardy to –10°F (–23°C). Grow in fertile, well-drained or heavy, preferably slightly alkaline soil, in full sun or light shade. Unless deadheaded, *Onopordum* will self-seed. Propagate by seed in fall or spring, sown *in situ* or in the cold frame. *O. acanthium* COTTON THISTLE; SCOTCH THISTLE; W Europe to C Asia; stately, giant biennial to 10 ft (3 m), covered in gray-white felt; flower heads large, scurfy, and spiny with white or purple florets.

Onosma (from Greek *onos*, ass, and *osme*, smell: the plant is said to be liked by asses). Boraginaceae. Mediterranean to E Asia. Some 150 species, bristly-hairy biennial and perennial herbs, often woody-based. The tubular to funnel-shaped flowers are carried in terminal cymes in summer. Hardy to 0°F (–18°C). Plant in the rock garden, gravel garden, or dry borders in full sun in light, fast-draining soil. Increase by softwood cuttings in summer, or by seed in fall.

O. alborosea SW Asia; perennial to 10 in (25 cm); leaves gray-green, white-bristly; flowers nodding, white to pink-purple, becoming purple or violet-blue; *O. stellulata* Balkans; perennial to 10 in (25 cm), shortly hairy and bristly; flowers light yellow.

Oophytum (from Greek *oon*, egg, and *phyton*, plant, referring to the egg-shaped plant bodies). Aizoaceae. Africa (Cape Province). 2 species, highly succulent perennials that resemble *Conophytum*, forming dense mats of closely packed, spherical to ovoid bodies. The flowers are daisylike. Cultivate as for *Conophytum*.

O. nanum (bodies ¾ × ¼ in/2 × 0.7 cm), minutely papillose; flowers white with reddened tips); *O. oviforme* (bodies to ¾ × ½ in/2 × 1 cm), olive green, often flame-colored, glossy-papillose; flowers white below, purple-pink above).

O

open-center a form of fruit tree in which the main branches are trained to form a cup or goblet shape, leaving the center clear. See *delayed open center*.

open pollination pollination by natural means; as opposed to closely controlled crossing undertaken by a plant breeder.

operculum the lid or cap of a capsule with circumscissile dehiscence.

ophiobolus patch (*Gaeumannomyces graminis*) a disease of lawn grasses, very prevalent in the northwest US. It especially affects creeping bentgrass, *Agrostis stolonifera*; rings of yellow or orange grass occur up to 3¼ ft (1 m) in diameter, with weeds and resistant grasses sometimes creating a green center. Dark brown hyphae can be found on infected roots. Wet conditions and surface alkalinity favor the disease, and management of these conditions provides more effective control than fungicide application.

Ophiopogon (from Greek *ophis*, serpent, and *pogon*, beard). Liliaceae (Convallariaceae). Asia. 4 species, evergreen, perennial herbs, with clumped, narrowly strap-shaped, grassy leaves. Small and bell-shaped, the flowers are borne in congested spikes in spring and summer. The berrylike fruits are usually dark violet blue and persist late into fall. Excellent plants for edging, groundcover, and containers. *O. planiscapus* 'Nigrescens' is a remarkable plant, creating dramatic contrasts with its purple-black foliage and ink-black fruit. All are hardy to −10°F (−23°C), although foliage may be damaged in hard winters. Grow in sun, where soils remain moist during the growing season, or in partial shade, in moderately fertile, well-drained soil. Propagate by ripe seed sown fresh in a sandy propagating mix in the cold frame, or by division.

O. intermedius China; leaves to 24 × ¼ in (60 × 0.5 cm), dark green; flowers white to lilac, numerous, in a loose raceme; 'Argenteomarginatus': leaves edged white; *O. jaburan* Japan; close to *O. japonicus*, but more robust; roots not tuberous; leaves to 24 × ¼ in (60 × 0.5 cm); flowering stem to 24 in

(60 cm), flowers tinted lilac or white in a dense 3–6 in (7.5–15 cm) raceme; fruits violet-blue; 'Aureovariegatus': leaves striped yellow; 'Crow's white': leaves variegated white; 'Vittatus': leaves pale green striped and edged creamy white; 'White Dragon': leaves boldly striped white, with almost no green; *O. japonicus* Japan; roots tuberous; leaves to 16 × ⅛ in (40 × 0.3 cm), rather rigid, dark green, somewhat curved; flowering stem 2–4 in (5–10 cm), flowers white to light lilac in a loose short raceme; fruit blue, ¼ in (0.5 cm) in diameter; 'Compactus': miniature and dense, to 2 in (5 cm); 'Minor': compact, to 3 in (8 cm), with curling, black-green leaves; 'Silver Dragon': leaves variegated white; *O. planiscapus* Japan; roots thickened; leaves to 14 in × ⅛–¼ in (35 cm × 0.3–0.5 cm), arching forward, dark green; flowers white or lilac, in 2½-in (6.5-cm) racemes; fruit dull blue; 'Nigrescens': to 6 in (15 cm), with curving, purple-black leaves, lined silver-green at base when young, flowers tinted pink to lilac, fruit black).

Ophrys (from Greek *ophrys*, meaning "eyebrow," probably alluding to the hairy lip of some species). Orchidaceae. Europe, N Africa, W Asia. 30 species, perennial herbs with paired, spherical tubers. Leaves are ovate to narrowly lanceolate, and produced in winter in low rosettes, giving rise in spring and summer to slender, erect racemes. The flowers are remarkably insectlike, with three ovate to elliptic sepals and narrow, antenna-like petals. The lip resembles the insect body, entire and rounded to slender and 3-lobed, variously covered in felt- or bristlelike hairs. In many species, the base or center of the lip is marked with a sparkling to glossy, iridescent patch— the speculum. The following species are hardy to −10°F (−23°C), although the southernmost species suffer in prolonged frosts and all dislike cold, wet winter conditions. The familiar and durable *O. apifera* will naturalize in

undisturbed grass. *O. fusca* and *O. insectifera* tolerate some shade, growing well in woodland clearings and fringes and especially among pines. The remaining species prefer alpine house conditions, or culture in raised beds where they can be covered in winter. Grow in full or dappled sun in a loamy medium that is rich in sand and fine leaf mold. Adding limestone chips to the mix will benefit most species. Keep moist when in growth and flower. After flowering, allow the plants to dry out. Repot the tubers in fall and resume watering. Increase by division when repotting, and by seed.

Ophrys bombylifera

Ophrys speculum

O. apifera BEE ORCHID; W & C Europe; 4–20 in (10–50 cm); flowers to 1 in (2.5 cm) across, sepals pink to pale lilac, lip broad, rounded, velvety chestnut brown with 2 yellow-white spots at tip, speculum red-brown with a double, horseshoe-shaped, yellow-white border; *O. ciliata* MIRROR OPHRYS; syn. *O. speculum*, *O. vernixia*; Mediterranean, N Africa; 4–20 in (10–50 cm); flowers to 1 in (2.5 cm) across, sepals green tinted pink and striped purple-brown, lip distinctly 3-lobed, olive green fringed with dense red-brown hairs, speculum covering midlobe, glossy blue thinly edged yellow; *O. fusca* Mediterranean, SW Romania; 4–16 in (10–40 cm); flowers to 1 in (2.5 cm) across, sepals green, lip obovate, shallowly 3-lobed, dark velvety brown with a narrow, yellow-green margin and a 2-lobed, purple-blue speculum; *O. holoserica* (syn. *O. arachnites*, *O. fuciflora*) LATE SPIDER ORCHID W, C & S Europe, Mediterranean, Russia; 4–20 in (10–50 cm); flowers to 1¼ in (3 cm) across; sepals broad, white to pale rose or magenta, lip broad, square, with a forward-pointing, green tip, velvety red-brown to maroon or yellow, speculum H- to W-shaped, mauve to blue bordered white; *O. insectifera* (FLY ORCHID; Europe, including Scandinavia; 4–20 in (10–50 cm); flowers to ¾ in (2 cm) across, sepals green, lip tongue-shaped with 2 shorter, distinct lateral lobes, dark, velvety brown, speculum dark blue to violet; *O. lutea* YELLOW BEE ORCHID; Mediterranean; 3–12 in (8–30 cm); flowers to 1¼ in (3 cm) across, sepals pale green, lip rounded, broad, 3-lobed, bright yellow with a central, velvety brown patch and a 2-lobed, rich blue speculum; *O. scolopax* WOODCOCK ORCHID; S Europe; 4–16 in (10–40 cm); flowers to 1 in (2.5 cm) across, sepals green to white or dusky pink, lip with 2 narrow, projecting, hairy lateral lobes, midlobe rounded with a green, forward-pointing tip, dark velvety brown, speculum H- or X-shaped, bordered white; *O. tenthredinifera* SAWFLY ORCHID; Mediterranean; 4–18 in (10–45 cm); flowers to 1¼ in (3 cm) across, sepals broad, pale rose to magenta, lip broad, rounded to square, hairy, green to yellow with a large, brown central patch, a small blue, W-shaped speculum and a tuft of brown hairs at the tip.

Oplismenus (from Greek *hoplismenos*, "armed," referring to the plant's awned spikelets). Gramineae. Tropics and subtropics. Some 6 species, trailing annual or perennial grasses, with slender, rooting stems and lanceolate, finely tapering leaves. These tender grasses are grown in temperate areas in hanging baskets and as low edging in the warm greenhouse or conservatory. Grow in bright indirect light or filtered light. Water plentifully when in growth. Maintain a minimum temperature of 59°F (15°C). Propagate by division of rooted stems.

O. burmannii tropics; annual glabrous to pubescent, to 24 in (60 cm); leaves to 2½ in (6 cm); includes 'Albidus', with white leaves with a pale green median stripe; *O. hirtellus* tropical America, Africa, Polynesia; evergreen perennial, to 36 in (90 cm)+; leaves to 2 in (5 cm), somewhat hairy; 'Variegatus': syn. 'Vittatus', leaves striped white, sometimes tinted pink.

opossum (*Procyon lotor*) a species of small marsupial animals. The adults are 24–42 in (60–110 cm) long, with a distinctive black "mask" across the eye region of the face and a long tail ringed with dark and pale fur. In parts of North America, opossums may invade gardens and feed on a wide range of fruits, vegetables, and buds. They are nocturnal, climbing animals, and shooting or trapping (subject to local regulations) are the only effective controls.

opposite used of two organs at the same level, or at the same or parallel nodes, on opposite sides of the axis.

Ophrys
scolopax

Opuntia (a pre-Linnaean name for some kind of spiny plant associated with the ancient Greek town of Opus, or the surrounding region, known as Eastern or Opuntian Locris, between Thermopylae and Thebes). Cactaceae. Throughout America, from S Canada to Patagonia. PRICKLY PEAR, TUNA. Over 200 species, stoutly succulent trees and shrubs, some low and clumped or spreading. The stem segments are cylindric, club-shaped, subglobose, or more or less flattened. Where present, the leaves are terete or subulate, usually small and short-lived. Most species have spines cushioned by tufted glochids. The flowers are broadly funnel- to bowl-shaped with numerous silky tepals and many stamens. The fruit resembles a more or less prickly pear and is edible in some species.

A few species from the central and eastern United States are frost-hardy, and some from lowland tropical areas require warm temperatures, but the great majority can be grown in a cool greenhouse (minimum temperature 45°F/7°C). Plant in a gritty, sandy, loam-based medium with a pH of 6–7.5. Provide full sun and low humidity. Keep dry from midfall until early spring, except for light misting on warm days in late winter. Avoid contact with these plants—the numerous, minutely barbed glochids are easily detached from the plant but difficult to see and remove from the skin, where they will cause irritation. When repotting, hold the plants with a collar of folded newspaper. Increase by rooting stem segments.

O. brasiliensis eastern S America; treelike, to 20–30 ft (6–9 m) or more, with cylindric, unjointed trunk and branches; stem segments flat and somewhat leaflike, obovate to oblong or lanceolate, to 6 × 2½ in (15 × 6 cm), ⅛–¼ in (4–6 mm) thick; leaves small, subulate, spines to ⅝ in (15 mm); flowers pale yellow; *O. cholla* Baja California; small tree, to 16 ft (5 m); stem segments cylindric, 2–12 in × ¾–1¼ in (5–30 × 2–3 cm), tuberculate, glochids numerous, yellow, spines ⅛–1 in (3–25 mm), yellow then gray; flowers purple-pink; *O. ficus-indica* INDIAN FIG, PRICKLY PEAR, BARBARY FIG; Mexico, widely naturalized; large shrub or small tree to 16 ft (5 m) with a trunk sometimes 3¼ ft (1 m) in diameter; stem segments obovate to oblong 8–24 in × 4–16 in (20–60 × 10–40 cm), spines to 1 in (2.5 cm), white or off-white; flowers yellow; fruit 2–4 in × 1½–2¾ in (5–10 × 4–7 cm) yellow, orange, red or purple in different cultivars; *O. humifusa* east and central US; shrub, forming clumps or mats 4–12 in × 6½ ft ((10–30 cm × 2 m) or more, stem segments elliptic to obovate to orbicular, 2–5 in × 1½–4 in (5–12.5 × 4–10 cm), often tinged purple, leaves subulate ⅛–¼ in (4–7 mm), spines absent or to 1 in (2.5 cm); flowers yellow, often with red center; *O. microdasys* C and N Mexico; shrub, forming thickets 16–24 in (40–60 cm); stem segments oblong, obovate or suborbicular, 2½–6 in (6–15 cm), green, velvety, glochids yellow, or white, spines absent or very short; flowers yellow, outer segments often tinged red; *O. robusta* central Mexico; shrub to 6½ ft (2 m) or more; stem segments orbicular or nearly so, massive, to 16 in (40 cm) or more, waxy pale blue, spines to 2 in (5 cm), white, pale brown or yellow below; flowers yellow; *O. tunicata* Mexico, SW US, and naturalized in some parts of S America; shrub, to 24 in (60 cm), densely branched; spines to 2 in (5 cm), yellow or off-white; flowers yellow; *O. verschaffeltii* Bolivia, N Argentina; low shrub, forming clumps; stem segments usually elongate in cultivars, 2½–8 in (6–20 cm), with low tubercles, leaves terete, to 1¼ in (3 cm), persistent, spines ½–1¼ in (1–3 cm) and bristlelike or absent; flowers orange to deep red).

orangery originally, a sheltered south-facing area within a garden set aside for the cultivation of orange trees. During the 16th century, such areas were enclosed by structures for winter protection, and by the 17th century the term was used more to describe the elaborate structures than the garden area. The orangery was the forerunner of the greenhouse and conservatory.

Orbea (from Latin *orbis*, a disk, referring to the thickened annulus in the flowers). Asclepiadaceae. S & E Africa. 20 species, succulents very similar to *Stapelia*, whose cultural requirements they share. *O. variegata* (syn. *Stapelia variegata*) STARFISH CACTUS, TOAD CACTUS; Cape Province; stems to 8 in (20 cm), sprawling to erect, leafless, with toothed ridges; flowers 2–3½ in (5–9 cm) across, star-shaped, flat, fleshy, wrinkled, malodorous, pale yellow to sulfur, blotched, spotted, lined and ringed maroon to dark brown.

orbicular perfectly circular, or nearly so.

orchard a garden or field area mainly devoted to fruit trees.

orchard house see *fruit house*.

orchids a large group of highly developed flowering plants belonging to the family Orchidaceae. Orchids are not difficult to cultivate if the correct environmental conditions are provided. The growing requirements of orchids are usually designated as "warm," "intermediate," "cool," or "hardy," depending on the natural habitat of the plant in question.

"Warm-growing" orchids comprise those species (and their hybrids) that occur in tropical regions at sea level or low altitude. These plants require a minimum greenhouse temperature of 68°F (20°C) at night throughout the year. Included in this group are *Phalaenopsis*, *Vanda*, *Catasetum*, the larger *Angraecum* species, some *Paphiopedilum*, and larger *Dendrobium* species.

"Intermediate-growing" orchids come from middle altitudes. They require a minimum greenhouse night

Epiphytic orchid (Gomesa planifolia)

Terrestrial orchid (Ophrys fusca subsp. iricolor)

temperature of 57°F (14°C) during winter, slightly higher during summer. A wide range of orchids can be grown under these conditions, including *Cattleya* species and their hybrids, *Laelia*, *Brassavola*, *Oncidium*, *Brassia*, some *Coelogyne* species, and many *Paphiopedilum*, *Dendrobium* and *Bulbophyllum* species.

"Cool-growing" orchids originate at middle or high altitudes in the tropics. They require a minimum greenhouse night temperature of 50°F (10°C) during winter, slightly higher in summer. The "cool-growing" group includes many kinds within *Cymbidium*, *Paphiopedilum*, *Coelogyne*, *Masdevallia*, *Odontoglossum*, *Lycaste*, *Laelia*, *Oncidium*, and *Maxillaria*, and many epiphytes from eastern Africa.

Most orchids are grown in containers that are either placed on greenhouse staging or suspended from the walls on a special framework. Clay or plastic pots are mostly used, but wire or wooden slatted baskets are suitable for some kinds with pendulous growth or inflorescences. Many epiphytes also grow well mounted on slabs of cork-oak bark or firmly attached to chunks of tree-fern fiber. At first, they need to be tied to the surface, with coarse nylon thread, plastic tape, or copper wire, but new roots will soon grow and attach the plants to the mount.

Potting Orchids need repotting when the growing medium is exhausted, or as they begin to grow over the edge of the pot, or where vigorous root growth causes the whole plant to rise out of the pot. However,

the presence of adventitious roots is quite normal in many genera, particularly *Phalaenopsis* and the *Laelia* alliance, and such overgrown plants are best left undisturbed for many seasons. Some orchids resent disturbance and take a long time to reestablish after repotting. For some of the larger orchids in the *Vanda* alliance, including *Angraecum* species, repotting is rarely necessary where plants are well-managed. Large plants of most genera will eventually need rejuvenating, but plants grown in rock wool require repotting much less frequently.

The growing medium should be well aerated, moisture-retentive, and a source of nutrients, and, since it is replaced only after long intervals, must decompose slowly. Suitable growing mediums are made from natural materials, such as conifer bark, coarse grit, fibrous peat, or chopped dried sphagnum mixed with inert materials like perlite, perlag, charcoal, and sometimes polystyrene fragments. These may have bone meal, dried blood, or hoof-and-horn meal base dressing added, or, alternatively, have liquid fertilizer applied on a regular basis.

A mix containing large particles will have large air spaces and need watering more frequently than a close mix. There are two successful basic formulas. One is for terrestrial orchids and comprises 3 parts fibrous peat: 2 parts coarse perlite: 2 parts coarse grit: 1 part horticultural-grade charcoal; the other is for epiphytic orchids and comprises 3 parts washed, medium grade bark chips: 1 part coarse perlag: 1 part horticultural grade charcoal: 1 part fibrous peat or dried leaves or chopped sphagnum. Rock wool mixed with perlite provides a substrate very similar to mossy tree branches in tropical forests. A carefully controlled system of watering and feeding is necessary with this medium, so it is inadvisable to use both rock wool and other mediums in a mixed collection. Pine bark requires soaking, and all other ingredients, including perlite and rock wool, should be moistened before use.

Choose a pot size to allow space for at least one year's growth—many orchids do best in smaller pots. In order to ensure adequate drainage, fill one-third of the container with polystyrene fragments, vertically packed pot crocks, or large stones (these are particularly useful in plastic pots, because they provide stability).

When potting, the base of the pseudobulbs, or other part from which roots will emerge, should be just below the level of the pot rim, and plants may need staking until they become established. After potting, the medium should be thoroughly watered for two or three days; newly potted plants are then kept dry for two or three weeks, during which period they must be kept in a humid place and misted frequently.

Watering Orchids variously adapt to a weekly or daily watering or misting regimen; they need to dry out periodically, some growing best with a long moist season followed by a dry

period of several months. New growers need to study a plant's natural habitat and try to imitate it in greenhouse management. Rainwater is the best choice, preferably stored in a covered tank within the greenhouse.

Once established and with new root growth visible, a regular watering regimen should be followed, with plants heavily and thoroughly watered on each occasion. The need for water can be assessed by checking the weight of the pots; as a general rule, this should be done once or twice a week. Daily watering will be necessary in summer, whereas in winter once every two to four weeks may be sufficient. Do not allow moisture to collect in leaf axils or the apex of new shoots overnight, since this can encourage waterborne disease. Misting early in the day and repeatedly during periods of sunshine helps ensure high humidity and lowers leaf temperature; however, do not wet leaves or flowers in strong sunshine.

Fertilizing It is beneficial to fertilize orchid plants regularly during their active growth season, and this is essential where they are potted in rock wool, coarse bark, or perlite only. Diluted liquid fertilizer is most convenient; commercial products are suitable but should be diluted to a quarter or half the strength recommended for other pot plants.

Resting Many terrestrial orchids have pseudobulbs or tubers that allow the plants to survive a long dormant season that may be too hot or too cold

for active growth. Similarly, many epiphytic orchids are structurally adapted with pseudobulbs or succulent rigid leaves to withstand drought. The nature of these essential resting periods must be understood so that appropriate cultural treatment can be given, especially as regards restricted watering. For example, in the Indian *Dendrobium* species, dormancy may last only a few weeks, while in many high-altitude Mexican orchids, it continues over several winter months, during which period the plants often flower.

Flowering and staking Most orchids flower once a year; however, *Phalaenopsis* hybrids flower twice a year, and some hybrids, such as *Odontoglossum* species, will flower at ten-month intervals. Many genera produce long inflorescences bearing numerous flowers, but most plants of *Lycaste* and *Paphiopedilum* species and hybrids bear flowers singly.

For attractive presentation, nearly all inflorescences need training; this is best done by placing a cane or wire support adjacent to each flower spike soon after it appears and tying the spike in when it reaches about 4–6 in (10–15 cm) in height.

Propagation Orchids can be increased by division of mature plants, by activating dormant buds on "backbulbs," by taking inflorescence or stem cuttings, and by sowing seed.

DIVISIONS AND "BACKBULBS" Large plants can be divided easily into two or more portions, and many readily fall apart when removed from their pots.

O

PROPAGATING ORCHIDS FROM BACKBULBS

1 An orchid with a healthy number of backbulbs may be divided in two in spring. Use a knife to cut through thick roots.

dormant pseudobulbs are the "backbulbs"

2 Carefully detach the backbulbs from the divided sections. Discard any that are old and shriveled.

pull backbulb to detach it

3 Pot the healthy backbulbs in orchid mix. Place in a cool, shaded position and keep moist for 2–3 months.

most of backbulb above surface

3-in (8-cm) pot

4 Trim off dead roots from the two sections of the parent plant, and repot in pots just larger than the rootball.

pseudobulbs level with medium

Other plants have pseudobulbs joined to each other by a tough rhizome, which needs to be cut with a sterilized knife or pruners. For most orchids, two or three growths should be retained in each division; *Cattleya* and its allies need at least one leafy pseudobulb on the back growth, with a prominent dormant bud at its base. For *Lycaste* and members of the *Odontoglossum* alliance, two or three pseudobulbs are usually separated as a clump. *Cymbidium* species are the easiest to propagate from old leafless pseudobulbs, which, after removal of loose sheaths and drying of the cut base, can be immersed up to one third their height in sharp sand, and kept moist and cool. Within two or three months, a new shoot will appear above the surface; after a similar period, the shoot will bear its own roots. New plants propagated by this means should reach flowering size in two or three years.

CUTTINGS Pseudobulbs, stems and inflorescence stalks of some orchids provide suitable cutting material. Each section must contain one or more dormant buds; when detached from the rest of the plant and laid on a bed of damp moss or inserted in a pan of moist grit, the buds will produce new plantlets after a few months in humid conditions. Suitable for this method are the canelike stems of *Epidendrum* and *Dendrobium*, and the inflorescence stalks of *Phalaenopsis*, *Phaius* and *Calanthe*. On many pseudobulbs, such as those of *Pleione*, dormant buds may spontaneously develop plantlets, sometimes known as "keikis."

SEEDS Orchid seeds are minute and the food reserves in the embryo are inadequate for the early development of new plants without some form of supplement. In nature, most orchid seeds develop a symbiotic partnership with a soil- or bark-inhabiting fungus: on invading the seed, the fungus is digested and nutrients obtained from it. This process can be simulated most successfully in a specialized laboratory by sowing sterilized seeds with a fungus culture on to agar, with the addition of rolled oats to sustain the fungus. An alternative method is to use a medium containing all that the germinating seed requires in terms of nutrients and thus dispense with the intermediary fungus. All these techniques must be carried out in sterile conditions, which the amateur can achieve by using a domestic pressure cooker to prepare glassware and media; a large polythene bag can be used to provide isolation for the sowing operation, which should be carried out as speedily as possible.

Orchid seedlings developing in a jar

Conical jars or sterile bottles containing the newly sown seeds are kept under controlled conditions while the embryo grows out to form a rounded protocorm, covered in rhizoids, and then a small plantlet. In some instances, the containers need to be kept in the dark for the first few months, but epiphytic orchids develop green protocorms almost immediately and are kept under artificial light for 12–16 hours per day. After a few months, transfer the plantlets to freshly prepared medium in a new container (a process that should, again, be carried out under sterile conditions). Six to twelve months after sowing, the orchid plantlets will be large enough to be removed from the flask, carefully washed, and then potted in a fine potting mix. Extra warmth and humidity should be provided for the first few weeks. Species and hybrids can grow to flowering size in 18–20 months, but four to six years is average for most orchids.

MERISTEM PROPAGATION Techniques for the culture and multiplication of the apical meristem of a young shoot, and the various forms of tissue culture, are valuable for rapid multiplication. The processes involved are similar to those used for propagation from seed, but because the starting material is already mature, the protocorms develop into new, flowering-size plants far more quickly. Once again, sterilized equipment and plant material are essential, and a warm growth chamber is also necessary. After eventual transfer to an orchid medium, the propagules grow rapidly.

USE OF COLCHICINE The poisonous alkaloid colchicine can be used to change the chromosome constituents in cells of orchid protocorms. The concentration and duration of the chemical application to plantlets must be carefully and accurately monitored or monstrosities may arise. There has been success with many of the free-flowering *Cymbidium* hybrids, and some of the *Paphiopedilum* protocorms. The resultant adult plant will usually have larger leaves and flowers of superior shape, and there may be improvements in fertility. However, plants reach flowering size more slowly and may have fewer flowers.

Registration and nomenclature of orchids The Royal Horticultural Society is the International Registration Authority for Orchid Hybrids, and publishes bimonthly lists of new registrations in its journal *The Orchid Review*. Collated lists of registrations for a given period of years are published occasionally under the title *Sander's List of Orchid Hybrids*. The complete International Register now lists over 100,000 hybrids.

Orchid hybrids are named at two or three levels—for example, in the hybrid *Cattleya* Bow Bells 'White Wings', the name of the genus is *Cattleya*, the name of the grex is *Cattleya* Bow Bells and the name of the cultivar is *Cattleya* Bow Bells 'White Wings'.

The term "grex" is unique to orchids and is the equivalent to the cultivar-group of the International Code of Nomenclature for Cultivated Plants, 1995. It denotes a group of individual plants derived from an artificial hybrid, and the grex name is applied to all progeny directly raised from the same two named parent taxa, whenever that cross is made.

A cultivar in orchids is a clone—a genetically similar assemblage of individuals derived originally from a single seedling following vegetative propagation. A grex epithet should always be used in conjunction with a generic name, and both a generic name and grex epithet should accompany the epithet of any cultivar.

Hardy species A number of orchids from the mountains of sub-tropical regions and temperate areas are amenable to cultivation. They may require frost-free conditions or a completely dry period when dormant, and are most easily accommodated in a cold frame or unheated greenhouse. Common examples are the species and hybrids of *Pleione*, which grow best in shallow pans of fast-draining but moisture-retentive medium; keep under warm, humid conditions in summer, dried off in the fall, and very cool during the winter. European orchids, such as *Orchis*, *Ophrys*, and *Dactylorhiza*, can also be grown easily in pots in an alpine house, as can some species of *Cypripedium* and *Bletilla*.

Some terrestrial orchid genera are deciduous, coming into growth in spring and flowering during late spring or midsummer. They may be grown outdoors in the garden and include some species of the lady's slipper genus, *Cypripedium*, *Dactylorhiza*, and *Orchis*.

Wild orchid plants are specially protected in most countries and should never be collected without first obtaining the required permits. CITES controls the import and export of orchid species. When purchasing terrestrial orchids, it is important to be sure that stocks have originated as nursery-propagated plants.

Orchids for the windowsill Many of the tropical orchids which in the past have been babied in greenhouses will do equally well on a windowsill if a few basic rules are observed. Of these, the most important are ensuring that there is enough light for the plants, without too much heat, and that there is adequate humidity in the immediate surroundings.

During the winter months, a south-facing windowsill or a table placed within a bay window is an ideal situation; in summer, an east-facing windowsill that receives morning sunshine is suitable. A deep windowsill is ideal, fitted with a polypropylene tray containing about ¾–1¼ in (2–3 cm) of a clean, moisture-retentive material; this should be kept moist (but not waterlogged) in order to maintain a humid atmosphere around the pots. Orchids with "intermediate" or "warm" temperature requirements do best in centrally heated homes. Many *Phalaenopsis* and *Paphiopedilum* species and hybrids give pleasure with their long-lasting flowers, and a wide variety of species can be grown successfully with patience and understanding.

Possible problems: *aphids, cockroaches, red spider mites, scale insects, vine weevil; leaf spot virus.*

Orchis (from Greek *orchis*, testicle, referring to the shape of the tubers). Orchidaceae. Temperate N Hemisphere. 35 species, herbaceous perennials with spherical tubers and lanceolate leaves. Produced in spring and summer in erect spikes, the flowers are spurred with a hood of ovate tepals and a showy, entire to 3-lobed lip. *O. mascula* and *O. purpurea* are hardy to –10°F (–23°C); *O. papilionacea* to 10°F (–12°C). All may be grown in the alpine house, the last especially. Grow in a neutral, loamy mix rich in sand and leaf mold. *O. mascula* will grow in light shade and is suited to the woodland garden; the remainder prefer full or dappled sun. Keep moist when in growth and flower; fairly dry when at rest (usually high summer to fall). Increase by division before growth recommences, or by seed.

O. mascula EARLY PURPLE ORCHID; Europe; 4–20 in (10–50 cm); leaves usually spotted maroon; raceme dense, narrow; flowers to ¾ in (2 cm) across, tepals curved upward, rosy mauve to purple-red, lip fan-shaped, shallowly 3-lobed, white-edged and spotted pink to purple-red; *O. papilionacea* BUTTERFLY ORCHID; Mediterranean; 6–16 in (15–40 cm); raceme fairly loose, somewhat pyramidal; flowers to 1¼ in (3 cm) across, tepals forward-pointing, hooded, purple-red with darker veins, lip broad, fan-shaped, rose- to purple-red with darker spots and lines; *O. purpurea* LADY ORCHID; Europe, Mediterranean; 12–32 in (30–80 cm); raceme dense, somewhat conical; flowers to 1 in (2.5 cm) across, tepals forward-pointing, hooded, purple-brown, lip white spotted purple-red, deeply 3-lobed, the lateral lobes narrow and outspread, resembling arms, the midlobe itself deeply cleft into two parts, "legs."

order, ordo the principal category of taxa intermediate in rank between class and family—for example, Commelinales, the order containing the families Rapateaceae, Xyridaceae, Mayacaceae, and Commelinaceae. Until the present century, botanists used *ordo* to denote the rank of family and *cohors* for the modern order.

organic gardening a system of cultivation that makes minimal use of manufactured chemical substances, placing emphasis on the use of manures and fertilizers of plant and animal origin to establish and maintain soil fertility; control of pests, diseases and weeds is also pursued chiefly by nonchemical methods, such as crop rotation, hygiene, ground mulching, hand-picking and trapping, cultivar resistance, and the use of natural predators and parasites. Recycling of organic residues through composting and green manuring are other important features of the system. Noncultivation or organic-surface cultivation, also known as the no-dig system, entails placing organic residues on the soil surface, from where they are drawn into the top profile by the action of earthworms and microorganisms.

These approaches stem from a broader philosophy that advocates a holistic approach to gardening and recognizes the interdependence of life forms. Considerations of conserving wildlife and natural resources, and the avoidance of pollution, are central to the concept of organic gardening.

The principles of organic agriculture were promoted by Rudolf Steiner in the 1920s. The Rodale Organization was founded in the US in the early 1940s, and in 1954 Lawrence Hills established the Henry Doubleday Research Association (HDRA) in the UK. The HDRA is the world's largest specialist organic-gardening organization for amateurs.

The pursuit of organic gardening requires understanding of garden ecology, dedication, and at least the same level of input as less stringent regimens. The incidence of pests, diseases, and other disorders is less likely where plants' requirements for steady growth are met; this applies to the choice of site, soil preparation and

O

maintenance, nutrition, and watering. In the garden situation, maximum yield and perfect quality are usually less important than in commercial growing, and the principles of organic gardening are both attainable and commendable. See *biodynamic gardening*.

Mizuna greens
These oriental greens may be sown late for a winter supply of young salad leaves, cropping best if given some protection.

organochlorines, organophosphates see *insecticides*.

oriental greens a collective name for a number of fast-growing brassicas, cultivated for eating cooked or raw. CHINESE CABBAGE, CHINESE LEAVES (*Brassica rapa* Pekinensis Group), CHINESE WHITE CABBAGE, PAK-CHOI (*Brassica rapa* Chinensis Group) and CHINESE BROCCOLI, CHINESE KALE (*Brassica oleracea* Alboglabra Group) may also be considered under this heading (see *broccoli*; *cabbage*).

LOOSE HEADED CHINESE CABBAGE (*Brassica rapa* Pekinensis Group) is a faster-growing type of Chinese cabbage that produces open heads of light green leaves which may be serrated or wavy, some cultivars having very loose tops with pale centers. It is grown in the same way as Chinese cabbage for harvesting as mature heads, or from spring sowings as a cut-and-come-again crop, first harvested five weeks after sowing.

KOMATSUNA or SPINACH MUSTARD (*Brassica rapa* Perviridis Group) is closely related to the turnip, producing large leaves on vigorous plants. The various forms are tolerant of drought and a wide temperature range; they will overwinter outdoors but yield better quality where protected. Sow in midsummer for fall/winter harvest outdoors, or in late summer where they are to be overwintered under cover; space seedlings 2–12 in (5–30 cm) apart depending on required stage of maturity. Cut-and-come-again supplies can be obtained from successional spring/early summer sowings outdoors.

MIZUNA GREENS (*Brassica rapa* var. *nipposinica*) produces highly decorative rosette heads of much-divided, glossy green leaves. Young leaves are suitable for salad use, the older ones as a cooked vegetable. Grow as komatsuna.

MUSTARD GREENS (*Brassica juncea*) are a robust, hardy group of brassicas producing coarse leaves, some cultivars being colored purple and most spice-flavored. Grow as komatsuna, spacing on average 12 in (30 cm) apart.

Possible problems: *aphids, cabbage caterpillars, cabbage root fly, whiteflies; clubroot.*

Origanum (from Greek *oros*, mountain, and *ganos*, joy). Labiatae. Mediterranean to E Asia. MARJORAM, OREGANO. Some 20 species, subshrubs or perennial herbs, often pubescent, generally aromatic. Small, 2-lipped flowers appear in summer, whorled amid conspicuous, overlapping bracts in terminal spikes. Plant in full sun on lean, fast-draining soils. *O. rotundifolium* favors nonalkaline soil; other species prefer slightly alkaline conditions. Trim back after flowering. Mulch in winter where temperatures drop below 0°F (–18°C). Harvest for freezing or drying just before flower buds open. Propagate from seed sown under glass in early spring, or later in the open ground. Alternatively, take softwood cuttings in early summer; pot individually, overwintering in frost-free conditions for planting out the following spring. Winter supplies for the kitchen may be taken as cuttings in summer and overwintered at a minimum of 50°F (10°C).

O. amanum Mediterranean, Turkey; stem to 8 in (20 cm), hirsute to scabrous; leaves to ³⁄₄ in (1.9 cm), cordate; flowers pink, bracts purple; *O. dictamnus* DITTANY OF CRETE, HOP MARJORAM; Crete; dwarf shrub to 12 in (30 cm); leaves ¹⁄₂–1 in (1.3–2.5 cm), woolly-white, ovate to round; flowers amid hoplike, rose-purple bracts; *O. laevigatum* Turkey, Cyprus; stem to 28 in (70 cm), glabrous; leaves 1¹⁄₄ in (3 cm), ovate to elliptic, smooth; flowers purple; 'Hopley's': to 30 in (75 cm), with large pink flowers and bracts; *O. majorana* KNOTTED MARJORAM, SWEET MARJORAM; originally Mediterranean and Turkey, now widespread escape in Europe; annual, biennial or perennial herb to 24 in (60 cm), stem glabrous or tomentose; leaves to ³⁄₄ in (2 cm), ovate, gray, downy; flowers white to mauve or pink; bracts gray-green; *O. onites* POT MARJORAM; Mediterranean; mound-forming shrublet to 24 in (60 cm); leaves to ³⁄₄ in (2 cm), ovate, rounded to cordate at base, bright green, aromatic; flowers mauve or white; 'Aureum': leaves gold; *O. rotundifolium* Armenia, Georgia, Turkey; subshrub to 12 in (30 cm), spreading by rhizomes; leaves to 1 in (2.5 cm), rounded or cordate, stem-clasping, blue-gray; inflorescence nodding, hoplike, bracts pale green tinged purple-pink, flowers white or pale pink; *O. vulgare* OREGANO, WILD MARJORAM, POT MARJORAM; Europe; rhizomatous, woody, branched perennial herb to 36 in (90 cm), strongly aromatic; leaves to 1¹⁄₂ in (4 cm), round to ovate, entire or slightly toothed; bracts purple or green, flowers purple; var. *album*: to 10 in (25 cm), bushy, with light green leaves and white flowers; 'Aureum': to 12 in (30 cm), spreading, with small, gold leaves and lavender flowers; 'Compactum': to 6 in (15 cm), compact and cushion-forming, with small, round, dark green leaves; 'Gold Tip': leaves tipped yellow; 'Nanum': dwarf, to 8 in (20 cm), with purple flowers; 'Roseum': flowers pink; 'Thumble's Variety': to 14 in (35 cm), with large, pale yellow leaves, later turning yellow-green, and soft white flowers.

Ornithogalum (name used by Dioscorides, from Greek *ornis*, bird, and *gala*, milk). Liliaceae (Hyacinthaceae). South Africa, Mediterranean. Some 80 species, bulbous perennial herbs with linear to lanceolate or obovate leaves, sometimes with a silver-white median stripe above. The flowers are 6-parted and starry, each with a prominent ovary; they are produced in spring and summer in long-stalked, pyramidal to subcylindric racemes or corymbs. The hardiest species, such as *O. umbellatum*, withstand temperatures to between 5°F (−15°C) and −4°F (−20°C); *O. montanum* and *O. nutans* are almost as tolerant, surviving temperatures at the warmer end of this range. *O. narbonense* and *O. oligophyllum* are hardy in places where temperatures seldom fall below 14°F (−10°C). *O. arabicum* suits warm sunny borders, or, where temperatures fall much below freezing, containers of medium-fertility, loam-based mix in the cold greenhouse. The South African species are generally frost-tender and are planted temporarily in summer borders of cool temperate gardens or grown in pots in the cool greenhouse. They include a number of species that provide long-lived cut flowers, notably *O. thyrsoides*. Grow in moderately fertile, well-drained soil in sun. Propagate by seed sown when ripe in the cold frame. Increase also by offsets when dormant.

O. arabicum Mediterranean; scape 12–32 in (30–80 cm), raceme cylindric to rounded or conical, flowers fragrant, 1¼–2 in (3–5 cm) across, white or cream with a black or purple-black ovary; free-flowering, large-flowered forms are sometimes called *O. corymbosum*; *O. dubium* S Africa; scape to 12 in (30 cm), raceme broadly and loosely pyramidal, flowers ¾–1½ in (2–4 cm) across, orange, red, yellow or white, often stained brown at center; *O. montanum* Europe, W Asia; scape 4–24 in (10–60 cm), raceme broadly cylindric, flowers drooping, ¾–2 in (2–5 cm) across, pearly translucent white striped green; *O. narbonense* Mediterranean, Caucasus, Near East; scape to 36 in (90 cm), raceme loose, many-flowered, flowers to 2 in (5 cm) across, milky white striped green; *O. nutans* Europe, W Asia, naturalized E US; scape to 24 in (60 cm), raceme cylindric, one-sided, flowers nodding, 1¼–2 in (3–5 cm) across, translucent white striped green; *O. oligophyllum* (syn. *O. balansae*) Balkans, Turkey Georgia; scape to 6 in (15 cm), raceme broadly pyramidal to rounded, flowers ¾–1¼ in (2–3 cm) across, white to ivory edged pure white, exterior striped yellow-green; *O. saundersiae* GIANT CHINCHERINCHEE; S Africa; scape 12–40 in (30–100 cm), raceme pyramidal, flowers to 1¼ in

(3 cm) across, white to cream, ovary dark green or black; *O. thyrsoides* CHINCHERINCHEE, WONDER FLOWER; S Africa; scape to 20 in (50 cm), inflorescence broadly pyramidal, flowers ¾–1½ in (2–4 cm) across, white to ivory, stained green at center; a long-lasting cut flower, it includes cultivars with snow white, topaz, and golden flowers; *O. umbellatum* STAR OF BETHLEHEM; Europe, N Africa, Middle East; scape 4–12 in (10–30 cm), raceme broadly pyramidal to rounded, flowers 1¼–1½ in (3–4 cm) across, shiny white striped green on exterior.

Orontium (from *orontion*, the Greek name for an aquatic growing in the Syrian river Orontes). Araceae. E US. GOLDEN CLUB. 1 species, *O. aquaticum*, an aquatic, perennial herb with thick rhizomes rooting into the muddy bed, pond margins, or (in cultivation) a waterlily basket. Floating or emergent, the leaves are to 10 in (25 cm), oblong to narrowly elliptic with glaucous silvering above and often purple-tinted beneath. Breaking the water's surface in spring and summer, the inflorescence consists of a white-stalked spadix to 7 in (18 cm) long; this is bright yellow and resembles a slender, upcurved club. Hardy to about 5°F (−15°C). Plant rhizomes in fertile, loamy soil and submerge in still water in full sun. Propagate by division in spring.

Orostachys (from Greek *oros*, mountain, and *stachys*, spike). Crassulaceae. N Asia to Europe. 10 species, biennial succulent herbs with fleshy, spine-tipped leaves in a dense, rounded rosette. Small, starry flowers are carried in a dense terminal raceme in the summer of the second year. Grow in a free-draining, gritty medium in full sun, with good ventilation and a minimum temperature of 47°F (8°C). Keep nearly dry in cool weather. Plants usually die after flowering but set seed freely and are easily raised by this means.

O. chanetii China; similar to *O. fimbriata* except leaves linear with a small, hard spine; flowers white to pink; *O. fimbriata* Tibet, Mongolia, Japan, China; to 6 in (15 cm); leaves 1 in (2.5 cm), oblong, tip bears a long spine; flowers are tinged red.

Oroya (after Oroya, Peru). Cactaceae. Peru. 2 species, low-growing cacti with squatly globose to shortly cylindric, many-ribbed stems bearing elongate areoles and pectinate spines. Shortly funnel- or bell-shaped, the flowers open in spring and summer. Grow in a cool greenhouse (minimum temperature 36–45°F/2–7°C) in a gritty, acidic to neutral, free-draining medium. Position in full sun with low humidity. Keep dry from midfall until early spring, except for light misting on warm days in late winter. Increase by seed or offsets. *O. peruviana* to 16 × 8 in (40 × 20 cm); spines to ¾ in (2 cm); flowers to 1¼ in (3 cm), pale to deep rosy red usually with a yellow center.

Orthrosanthus (from Greek *orthros*, morning, and *anthos*, flower; the flower opens early in the morning). Iridaceae. Tropical America, Australia. 7 species, rhizomatous, evergreen perennial herbs with basal clumps and fans of narrow, rigid or grassy leaves. The *Iris*-like flowers are short-lived but produced in succession in a slender-stalked panicle in summer. Grow in the border or in pots in the cool greenhouse or conservatory (minimum temperature 45°F/7°C). Plant in humus-rich and well-drained soil in sun. Water carefully and moderately when in growth; keep almost dry at other times. Propagate by careful division of established plants or by seed, which germinates readily, although seedlings develop slowly.

O. chimboracensis Mexico to Peru; flowers lavender-blue, to 1½ in (4 cm) in diameter; *O. violaceus* China; flowers violet, to 2½ in (6 cm) in diameter.

Oryza (from Greek *oryza*, for the rice plant and its grain). Gramineae. Tropical Asia, Africa. RICE. 19 species of annual or perennial, rhizomatous grasses. Stems flimsy to robust; leaves linear, flat. The staple food of up to 50 percent of the world's population; cultivars have been developed to suit a wide range of climates and soils, mainly for tropical and sub-tropical conditions and wetlands. Some selections have ornamental value. Propagate from seed. *O. sativa* (SE Asia. An annual to 70 in (180 cm); stems stout, upright, arching. Leaves

561

elongate up to 60 × 1 in (150 × 2.5 cm). Inflorescence a panicle to 18 in (45 cm), spikelets to ½ in (1 cm). In temperate climates, *O. sativa* can be grown as a frost-tender annual planted around pond margins; otherwise cultivated primarily as an educational/ interest feature in full sun under glass, in containers suited to flooding and drainage of water and maintained within an optimum temperature range 68–86°F (20–30°C). Sow thinly in early spring in loam-based medium; cover with ¾ in (2 cm) coarse sand and submerge in 1-in- (2.5-cm-) deep water. Matures in 90–260 days.

Osmanthus (from Greek *osme*, fragrance, and *anthos*, flower). Oleaceae. N America, Asia, Pacific. DEVILWOOD, SWEET OLIVE, CHINESE HOLLY. 30 species, evergreen shrubs or small trees with dark green, smooth, and leathery leaves, the margins entire to sharply toothed. Clustered in the leaf axils or, rarely, in terminal panicles, the flowers are small, highly fragrant and bell-shaped to tubular with four lobes. The fruit is an oval, blue-black to purple drupe. All species here will grow in sun or light shade in a range of fertile, well-drained soils, preferably neutral to acidic, although some lime is tolerated and *O.* × *burkwoodii*, *O. delavayi*, and *O. yunnanensis* thrive in chalky conditions. *O. decorus* and *O. heterophyllus* are very hardy. The remaining species are hardy to 0°F (–18°C), but need a site sheltered from freezing winds. In regions of prolonged winter frost, *O. fragrans* will need the protection of a cool, airy greenhouse in winter (minimum 39°F/4°C). Remove straggly or winter-damaged growth. Propagate in late summer by semi-ripened cuttings in a propagating case with bottom heat or root ripe growths in fall in a cold frame. Alternatively, increase by layering in fall or spring, or by seed sown in a cold frame on ripening.

    O. armatus W China; shrub, leaves 2¾–5½ in (7–14 cm), oblong to ovate, strongly toothed, spiny, sometimes entire; flowers off-white; fruit deep violet; *O.* × *burkwoodii* (syn. × *Osmarea burkwoodii*; *O. delavayi* × *O. decorus*) compact shrub to 6½ ft (2 m); leaves ¾–1½ in (2–4 cm), ovate to elliptic,

serrate; flowers white, fragrant; *O. decorus* Caucasus, Lazistan; broad shrub, to 10 ft (3 m) leaves to 4¾ in (12 cm), entire, oblong apex acuminate, yellow beneath; flowers white; fruit blue-black; 'Baki Kasapligil': slow-growing, hardy, with narrow leaves; *O. delavayi* W China; stocky shrub to 6½ ft (2 m); leaves to 1¼ in (3 cm), ovate, finely toothed; flowers white, sweetly fragrant; *O.* × *fortunei* (*O. fragrans* × *O. heterophyllus*) expansive shrub, to 10 ft (3 m) leaves to 4 in (10 cm), oval, acuminate, teeth large, triangular, or leaves entire; flowers white, fragrant; *O. fragrans* FRAGRANT OLIVE, SWEET TEA; Himalaya, Japan, China; shrub or small tree to 40 ft (12 m); leaves to 4 in (10 cm), oblong to lanceolate, entire or finely toothed; flowers white, highly fragrant; f. *aurantiacus*: flowers orange; *O. heterophyllus* (syn. *O. ilicifolius*) FALSE HOLLY, HOLLY OLIVE, CHINESE HOLLY; Japan, Taiwan; erect dense shrub, to 16 ft (5 m); leaves to 2½ in (6 cm), elliptic to oblong, entire or with large lobelike teeth—both forms found together on same branch; flowers white, fragrant; fruit purple-blue; 'Goshiki': leaves prickly, cream- and bronze-variegated, young growth rose-pink; 'Latifolius Variegatus': leaves large, variegated cream: 'Myrtifolius': leaves ovate, entire; 'Purpureus': new growth purple-red; *O. serrulatus* W China; shrub, to 10 ft (3 m) leaves resembling those of *O. yunnanensis*, but broader with finer, forward-pointing teeth or sometimes entire, flowers white; *O. yunnanensis* (syn. *O. forrestii*) W China; similar to *O. serrulatus* but leaves with longer, more spiny teeth; tall shrub to 16 ft (5 m); leaves to 8 in (20 cm), ovate to lanceolate, tip finely tapering, spotted black beneath with to 30 sharp teeth on either side, or entire; flowers waxy, off-white to light yellow, very fragrant; fruit dark purple, pruinose.

osmosis the movement of water across a semipermeable membrane from an area of low concentration of solutes (dissolved substances) to an area of greater concentration; of important relevance to the flow of water in plants, especially water intake from the soil and other growing media by root hairs.

Osmunda regalis
The conspicuous "flower" of the royal fern is in fact a dense panicle of fertile pinnae bearing clusters of spherical sporangia.

Osmunda (opinions vary as to the name derivation—possibly for the Nordic god Thor, also called Osmunder; or for Osmundus (Asmund), an 11th-century Scandinavian writer of runes and Christian apologist; or from the Latin *os*, mouth, and *mundare*, to clean). Osmundaceae. Asia, Americas. FLOWERING FERN. About 12 species, large terrestrial ferns with profuse, matted and fibrous roots and more or less erect, bipinnate or bipinnatifid fronds in large clumps or crowns. The spores are produced on specialized, narrow pinnules, either separately on entirely fertile fronds or in the middle or at the ends of more regular (i.e., "sterile"-type) fronds. The following species are hardy to –20°F (–29°C) and will grow in full sun (*O. regalis*) or dappled to deep shade (*O. cinnamomea*, *O. claytoniana*). They need a cool, acidic mix rich in leaf mold. They must never be dry; indeed, *O. regalis* will grow at the water's edge and make islands of its own dense root growth in shallow pools and streams. Propagate by spores or by division in spring.

    O. cinnamomea CINNAMON FERN, FIDDLEHEADS, BUCKHORN; N and S America, West Indies, E Asia; whole plant densely rusty-hairy at first; sterile fronds 24–36 in (60–90 cm), pinnate, pinnae 3–4 in × ¾–1 in (8–10 × 2–2.5 cm), ligulate to lanceolate, cut almost to rachis; fertile fronds distinct, much smaller, becoming cinnamon brown, pinnae lanceolate; *O. claytoniana* INTERRUPTED FERN; N America, Himalaya,

China; foliage pink-downy at first; fronds 12–24 in (30–60 cm), pinnate to pinnatifid, sterile pinnae 4–6 in × 1 in (10–15) × 2.5 cm), lanceolate, cut almost to rachis, fertile pinnae borne at center of regular fronds, far smaller with dense cylindric pinnules; *O. regalis* FLOWERING FERN, ROYAL FERN; cosmopolitan; rhizome becoming erect and moundlike, to 3¼ ft (1 m) tall, massive, with tough fibrous roots; fronds 24–70 in (60–180 cm), bipinnate, sterile pinnae 6–12 in (15–30 cm), pinnules 1–2 in × ½–¾ in (2.5–5 × 1–2 cm), oblong, blunt, minutely serrate, fertile pinnae cylindric, forming large rusty panicle at frond apex; 'Crispa': pinnules crisped; Cristata Group: pinnules finely crested; 'Purpurascens': growth purple when young, rachis purple throughout season.

osmunda fiber dried and coarsely chopped roots of the royal fern, *Osmunda regalis*, formerly an ingredient of potting media for orchids. In the interests of conserving the royal fern, it is now no longer recommended for this use, and there are satisfactory alternatives. See *orchids*.

Osteomeles (from Greek *osteon*, bone, and *melon*, apple, referring to the fruit). Rosaceae. China to Hawaii and New Zealand. 2 species, evergreen shrubs or trees with small, finely pinnate leaves and white, 5-petaled flowers in small, terminal corymbs in late spring and early summer. These are followed by small, red to blue-black pomes. Hardy to 14°F (–10°C), but best given the shelter of a south-facing wall. Grow in sun in well-drained soil. Propagate by semiripe cuttings, or by layering. Sow stratified seed in spring. *O. schwerinae* SW China; to 10 ft (3 m) branchlets slender, pendulous; leaves to 2¾ in (7 cm), gray-downy, leaflets elliptic to obovate-oblong, to ½ in (1.2 cm), cuspidate; flowers white; var. *microphylla*: leaves smaller and finer, less woolly.

Osteospermum (from Greek *osteon*, bone, and Latin *spermum*, seed). Compositae. Africa (those listed below are from South Africa). About 70 species of shrubs, subshrubs or annual to perennial herbs with entire, toothed, pinnatifid, or pinnatisect leaves and large, daisylike flower heads. Brilliantly colored perennials are grown in containers and as half-hardy summer bedding. Given a warm, sunny position with perfect drainage and shelter from cold winds, the following may survive where temperatures fall to between 23° and 14°F (–5° and –10°C). Alternatively, take cuttings during the summer and overwinter young plants under glass prior to planting out the following spring.

O. barberiae spreading, rhizomatous perennial to 20 in (50 cm), glandular-pubescent; ray florets magenta above, usually light orange-brown beneath, disk florets deep purple or yellow; 'Compactum': to 4 in (10 cm), with deep pink flower heads with a dark purple reverse; *O. ecklonis* robust subshrub to 3¼ ft (1 m); ray florets white above, indigo often with white margin beneath, disk florets bright blue; 'Deep Pink Form': to 12 in (30 cm), with numerous, narrow, dark pink florets; 'Giant Mixed'; to 14 in (35 cm), with flowers in cream, orange and salmon pastels; 'Starshine': to 30 in (75 cm), with snow-white flowers with blue eyes; 'Weetwood': to 10 in (25 cm), with white flowers, olive green below; *O. jucundum* perennial herb, to 20 in (50 cm); ray florets red on both surfaces, disk florets black-purple at apex. *Cultivars*: shorter cultivars (to 10 in/25 cm) include the white- and pink-backed 'Cannington Roy' and the pink 'Hopleys' and 'Langtrees'; taller cultivars (to 24 in/60 cm) include the white-flowered, variegated-leaved 'Silver Sparkler', the pink 'Pink Whirls' and 'Bodegas Pink' with variegated leaves, and 'Buttermilk' with pale yellow flowers. 'Whirligig' has gray-green foliage, powder-blue to chalky gray ray florets, strongly contracted with margins inrolled above midpoint, then expanded again at tip, and dark blue-gray disk florets. The Cannington Hybrids include pink-, white-, and purple-flowered forms 6–12 in (15–30 cm) tall. Seed races, such as the 10-in (25-cm) Dwarf Salmon and the 18-in (45-cm) Tetra Pole Star, are also offered.

Ostrowskia (for Michael Nicolayevich von Ostrowsky, minister of Imperial Domains and Russian patron of botany during the late 19th century). Campanulaceae. Turkestan. 1 species, *O. magnifica*, GIANT BELLFLOWER, a perennial herb erect to 6 ft (1.8 m), with whorled, gray-green, ovate leaves to 6 in (15 cm). Produced in summer in terminal racemes, the bell-shaped flowers are up to 2 in (5 cm) long with broadly ovate lobes, lilac suffused with white or opal blue with darker mauve veins. Hardy to at least 5°F (–15°C). It dies back completely in midsummer and then requires a dry rest until late fall. Grow in a warm, sunny, sheltered position in deep, fertile, freely draining but moisture-retentive soil. Mulch in winter with leaf mold or dry bracken. Propagate by seed or root cuttings. It resents disturbance.

Ostrya (from *ostrys*, the Greek name for these trees). Betulaceae (Carpinaceae). Europe, Asia, America. Some 9 species, deciduous trees with leaves alternating in 2 rows, their veins parallel and the margins dentate or serrate. The male inflorescence resembles that of *Carpinus*, but develops during fall. The female catkins are made up of leafy bracts and take on a hoplike appearance. Cultivate as for *Carpinus*. *O. carpinifolia* HOP HORNBEAM; S Europe, Asia Minor; to 65 ft (20 m); young shoots downy; leaves ovate, rounded at base, acute at apex, to 4 × 2 in (10 × 5 cm), lustrous dark green, hairy between veins above, paler beneath with sparse hairs on veins, veins in 15–20 pairs, margins double-dentate; *O. virginiana* AMERICAN HOP HORNBEAM, IRONWOOD; eastern N America; to 65 ft (20 m); young shoots glandular-hairy; leaves ovate to lanceolate, rounded to cordate at base, apex long-acuminate, 2¾–4¾ in × 1¼–2 in (7–12 × 3–5 cm), dark green, hairy on midrib and between veins above, pale, pubescent beneath, veins in 11–15 pairs.

Otatea (from the Aztec name for these bamboos). Gramineae. Mexico to Nicaragua. 2 species; see *bamboos*.

Othonna (from Greek *othone*, linen, in reference to the soft leaves—a name used by Dioscorides and Pliny for the same or similar plants). Compositae. Mostly South Africa. About 150

563

species, perennial herbs or small shrubs, usually glabrous and glaucous. The leaves are entire to variously dissected, lobed or toothed, membranous, leathery or fleshy. Daisylike flower heads appear in summer. The following species is hardy to 0°F (−18°C), given a sheltered position in full sun. Plant in lean, gritty soil and protect from winter wetness. Propagate by softwood cuttings in early summer. *O. cheirifolia* (syn. *Othonnopsis cheirifolia*) Algeria, Tunisia; spreading evergreen subshrub or shrub, to 16 in (40 cm); leaves to 3 in (8 cm), paddle-shaped, glaucous blue-gray, thinly succulent; flower heads yellow.

Ourisia (for General Ouris [d. 1773], governor of Falkland Islands). Scrophulariaceae. Andes, Antarctic, S America, New Zealand, Tasmania. Some 25 species, low, usually dwarf perennial herbs or subshrubs. Produced in late spring and early summer, the flowers are salverform to funnel-shaped with a spreading and slightly zygomorphic limb of five broad lobes. Hardy to 0°F (−18°C). Grow in raised beds or rock gardens on acidic soils that are cool and moist but contain plenty of sand and grit. Shelter from scorching sun and drying winds. Propagate from fresh seed, or by division in spring.

O. caespitosa New Zealand; creeping stems; leaves ⅛–⅜ in (0.4–0.8 cm); flowers white with a yellow throat, to ½ in (16 mm) in diameter); *O. macrocarpa* (New Zealand; stems erect, 4–24 in (10–60 cm); leaves to ⅝ in (1.5 cm); flowers ⅝–1 in (15–25 mm) in diameter, white sometimes with yellow throat; *Cultivars* include 'Loch Ewe' (*O. coccinea* × *O. macrophylla*), to 8 in (20 cm), slowly spreading in tight rosettes, with shell pink flowers, and 'Snowflake' (*O. macrocarpa* × *O. caespitosa*), to 4 in (10 cm), with dark, glossy leaves and white flowers.

outbreeder a plant that reproduces predominantly by cross-pollination.

ovate egg-shaped in outline; rounded at both ends but broadest below the middle, and 1.5–2 times as long as broad.

ovicide a pesticide used to kill the eggs of pests—for example, tar oils formerly applied to dormant fruit trees against aphid and sucker eggs.

oviparity the laying of fertilized eggs by insects; cf. *viviparity*.

ovoid egg-shaped, ovate but 3-dimensional.

Oxalis (from Greek *oxys*, acid, sharp, sour, referring to the sour taste of leaves). Oxalidaceae. Cosmopolitan but with centers of diversity in South Africa and S America. SHAMROCK, SORREL. 800 species, annual or perennial herbs and shrubs. They range greatly in habit, from succulent subshrubs to gaunt, truly woody shrubs, and from annual herbs to bulbous and tuberous perennials. The leaves are typically palmately lobed. The flowers are bowl- to funnel-shaped or salverform, with five obovate petals. Relatively few of the desirable species are reliably frost-hardy; those that are include *O. adenophylla* and *O. enneaphylla* (particularly valued for their neatly pleated glaucous foliage, suited to the sunny raised bed and large trough or to well-drained, humus-rich, sandy niches in the rock garden), *O. depressa* (for the well-drained interstices of paving or partially shaded bases of walls and rockwork), and *O. acetosella* (for naturalizing in the wild and woodland garden in moisture-retentive, humus-rich soils with shade or dappled sunlight). These can tolerate temperatures as low as 5°F (−15°C), and will thrive in temperate climates where summers are relatively cool, or where they can be given shade from the hottest sun in summer. Other species will tolerate short-lived frosts, especially in a sheltered rock garden or where their roots are protected by paving or gravel; these include *O. bowiei*, *O. hirta*, *O. laciniata*, *O. latifolia*, *O. lobata*, *O. purpurata*, and *O. tetraphylla*; otherwise, these may be easily grown in the alpine house in well-crocked pans or pots in a gritty, leafy alpine mix. The excellent purple-leaved house plant *O. triangularis* is proving hardy outdoors in sheltered regions to 0°F (−18°C), if thickly

leaves fold in at night

Oxalis deppei

mulched in winter. Tropical shrubby species, such as *O. hedysaroides*, need a fertile, moist and soil-free medium, protection from drafts and full sun, moderate to high humidity and a minimum temperature of 50°F (10°C). Propagate *Oxalis* by ripe seed, by division, or by offsets. Soft-stemmed species may be increased by cuttings in sand, in a shaded closed case with gentle bottom heat.

Oxalis spp. can become troublesome weeds in gardens as a result of their rapid spread by bulbils or by seed. *O. debilis* (syn *O. corymbosa*) bears red/purple flowers with darker veins and a white throat; it also produces numerous tiny bulbils. Control by forking out during the active growing season requires careful, laborious attention; a permanent, frequently replenished, very deep mulch will reduce spread in borders; glyphosate sprays are effective but nonselective. *O. carniculata* bears yellow flowers and spreads by seed; continual, thorough hoeing in borders can prevent seeding; where established in lawns, improving soil fertility and regular mowing and raking will reduce infestation; herbicide treatment with selective substances is effective in lawns, and glyphosate can be used in borders, as for *O. debilis*. *O. acetosella* IRISH SHAMROCK, WOOD SORREL; N Temperate regions; rhizomatous, creeping, to 3 in (8 cm); leaves to 1¼ in (3 cm) across, pale green; flowers white veined pink; var. *subpurpurascens*: flowers rose veined purple; f. *rosea*: flowers rich pink; *O. adenophylla* (Chile, Argentina; bulbous, to 3 in (8 cm); leaves to 1¼ in (3 cm) across, leaflets gray-green, folded; flowers lilac-pink, throat white veined pink, maroon at base; *O. bowiei* (syn. *O. purpurata* var. *bowiei*) S Africa; bulbous, to 12 in (30 cm); leaves to 4 in (10 cm) across, purple beneath; flowers bright rose-red to pink; *O. chrysantha* Brazil; mat-forming perennial to 2 in (5 cm) tall; leaves to ⅝ in (1.5 cm) across, green, downy; flowers golden with red marks in throat; *O. depressa* (syn. *O. inops*) S Africa; bulbous; to 4 in (10 cm) tall; leaves to ¾ in (2 cm) across, gray-green, sometimes with dark markings; flowers bright pink to rich, rosy mauve or white, throat yellow; *O. dispar* Guyana; gaunt shrub to 5 ft (1.5 m); leaves to 6 in (15 cm) across; flowers golden yellow, sweetly scented; *O. enneaphylla* SCURVY GRASS; Falkland Is, Patagonia; tufted and rhizomatous with bulbils; to 2 in (5 cm) tall; leaves to ¾ in (2 cm) across, leaflets gray-green, folded, narrow, somewhat fleshy; flowers white to deep rose or red, scented; crossed with *O. laciniata* producing *O.* 'Ione Hecker' with narrower, wavy leaflets and purple-blue flowers pale at the edges, dark in the throat; *O. hedysaroides* C America; erect, bushy subshrub to 3¼ ft (1 m) tall; leaves to 2 in (5 cm) across; flowers yellow; 'Rubra': stems and foliage strongly flushed maroon; *O. hirta* S Africa; bulbous with erect or trailing stems to 12 in (30 cm); leaves to 1¼ in (3 cm) across, leaflets narrow; flowers purple-red with a yellow throat; *O. laciniata* Patagonia; rhizomatous with chains of tiny bulbils; 2–4 in (5–10 cm) tall; leaves ½–¾ in (1–2 cm) across, leaflets gray-green, folded, with purple, wavy margins; flowers fragrant, steel blue, lilac, violet, or crimson with darker veins; *O. lobata* Chile; rootstock bulbous; to 4 in (10 cm) tall; leaves to ½ in (1 cm) across, bright green, smooth, sometimes marked with purple; flowers bright golden yellow; *O. tetraphylla* (syn. *O. deppei*) Mexico; GOOD LUCK PLANT, LUCKY CLOVER; bulbous; 4–12 in (10–30 cm) tall; leaves 1½–4¾ in (4–12 cm) across, mid-green usually with maroon bands or stains; flowers red to pink or lilac with a white-edged, yellow throat; *O. triangularis* Brazil; rootstock swollen; to 6 in (15 cm) tall; leaves to 4 in (10 cm) across, dark purple to beet red sometimes with darker or paler markings; flowers white tinted purple-pink.

Oxydendrum (from Greek *oxys*, sharp, and *dendron*, tree, for the sour taste of the foliage). Ericaceae. E US. 1 species, *O. arboreum*, SORREL TREE or SOURWOOD, a deciduous shrub to 30 ft (9 m) or tree to 65 ft (20 m), slender and sometimes multistemmed, with rusty-red to gray bark and branches forming a fine canopy in older specimens. The leaves are 3–8 in (8–20 cm) long, oval, elliptic or oblong to lanceolate, lustrous, and pale to deep green, coloring vivid red in fall. White and urn-shaped, the small flowers are produced during summer on finely branched panicles to 10 in (25 cm) long; the panicle branches persist in fall and impart a pale, rather ghostly appearance to the whole tree. Hardy to −20°F (−29°C), especially if planted in a sheltered position with the protection of surrounding trees. Grow in moist but well-drained, acidic soils, in light dappled shade or full sun. Propagate from seed sown in fall or spring, or by softwood cuttings in summer—treat these with rooting hormone and root in a closed case with bottom heat.

oxygenator a plant grown submerged in a pool or aquarium and producing oxygen for the benefit of fish and other plants and life forms—for example, Canadian pondweed, *Elodea canadensis*.

Oxygenator in garden pond
Submerged or semisubmerged oxygenating plants are essential to keep pond water clear and able to support life.

oyster shell the protective shell of sea mollusks; formerly widely used in crushed or ground form as an ingredient of potting media, especially bulb fiber, and valued for its high calcium content (50%) and water-holding property. However, it is not commonly available and has been replaced by materials such as perlite, vermiculite, and rock wool.

Ozothamnus (from Greek *ozos*, branch, and *thamnos*, shrub). Compositae. Australasia. About 50 species, evergreen shrubs and woody perennial herbs with small and often heathlike leaves. The neat, buttonlike flower heads are produced in dense, domed clusters during summer. The following species will tolerate temperatures to 14°F (−10°C), and probably lower, given good drainage and shelter from cold drying winds. They thrive in warm, sunny situations in sharply drained but moist and slightly acidic soil. Cut back leggy specimens in spring before growth commences. Propagate by semiripe cuttings in summer.

O. coralloides (syn. *Helichrysum coralloides*) New Zealand; shrub to 20 in (50 cm), branches spreading, densely tomentose; leaves closely adpressed, to ¼ in (5 mm), scalelike, thick and leathery, silver-hairy on inner surface, smooth dark green on outer surface; *O. ledifolius* (syn. *Helichrysum ledifolium*) KEROSENE WEED; Tasmania; strongly aromatic, flammable shrub to 3¼ ft (1 m), young shoots downy, older leaves and branches viscid, producing yellow gum; leaves to ⅝ in (15 mm), oblong to linear, obtuse, spreading, leathery, strongly revolute, glabrous, above, downy beneath, red-tinted at first; *O. rosmarinifolius* (syn. *Helichrysum rosmarinifolium*) New South Wales, Victoria, Tasmania; shrub to 10 ft (3 m), branches erect, woolly at first; leaves crowded, to 1½ in (4 cm), linear, mucronate, woolly beneath, revolute; 'Silver Jubilee': leaves very silvery; *O. scutellifolius* Tasmania; shrub to 6½ ft (2 m), tomentose; leaves minute, scalelike, ovate, reflexed, revolute, glabrous to tomentose above, tomentose beneath; *O. secundiflorus* CASCADE EVERLASTING New South Wales, Victoria; shrub to 6½ ft (2 m), branches white-woolly; leaves to ½ in (12 mm), oblong to linear, sparsely downy above, densely woolly beneath; *O. selago* (syn. *Helichrysum selago*) New Zealand; shrub to 16 in (40 cm) with woolly, arching to pendulous branches; leaves minute, closely overlapping, leathery, woolly above, dark green beneath; *O. thyrsoideus* SNOW IN SUMMER; New South Wales, Victoria, Tasmania; shrub to 10 ft (3 m), young shoots glutinous; leaves to 2 in (5 cm), narrowly linear, adpressed, dark green, resinous above, paler beneath with fine down.

P

Pachycereus (from Greek *pachys*, thick, and *Cereus*). Cactaceae. Mexico. 9 species, treelike or shrubby cacti, often massive with stout, erect stems and shortly tubular, funnelform or campanulate flowers. Grow in neutral, gritty medium. Provide a minimum temperature of 50–59°F (10–15°C) and shade in hot weather. Maintain low humidity. Keep dry from midfall until early spring, except for light misting on warm days in late winter. Increase by stem cuttings.

P. pecten-aboriginum W Mexico; resembles *P. pringlei*, but not glaucous when young and with fewer ribs (10–11) and spines (8–12 per areole), and less woolly flowers; *P. pringlei* NW Mexico; massive tree to 50 ft (15 m), trunk short, branches erect, 10–20 in (25–50 cm) in diameter, blue-green; ribs 11–17; spines 20 or more per areole, $\frac{1}{2}$–1$\frac{1}{4}$ in (1–3 cm), stout; flowers 2$\frac{1}{2}$–3 in (6–8 cm), densely woolly, white.

pachycaul thick-stemmed; sometimes applied to treelike herbs or shrubs with thickly swollen stems or trunk stems (e.g. *Adenium*), and to simple-stemmed trees (e.g. *Carica* species).

Pachyphytum (from Greek, *pachys*, thick, and *phyton*, plant). Crassulaceae. Mexico. 12 species, succulent perennial herbs or subshrubs. The fleshy leaves are alternate or crowded in rosettes and may be flattened to almost circular in cross-section; they are usually glaucous and tinged purple or pink-red. Campanulate to cup-shaped, 5-petalled flowers are carried in erect to nodding racemes in spring and summer. Cultivate as for *Echeveria*.

P. compactum Mexico; leaves $\frac{3}{4}$–1$\frac{1}{4}$ in (1.8–3.0 cm), fusiform, acute, glaucous, sometimes tinged red-purple; flowers orange-red with darker tips; *P. oviferum* Mexico; leaves 1$\frac{1}{4}$–2 in (3–5 cm), thickly obovoid, purple-glaucous, with dense white bloom; flowers pale green-white.

Pachypodium (from Greek *pachys*, thick, and *pous*, foot, referring to the swollen stem bases). Apocynaceae. South Africa, Madagascar. 17 species, deciduous or semi-evergreen shrubs or small trees with greatly swollen stems, (usually) spiny branches, tough leaves and funnel-shaped flowers similar to those of *Adenium*. Cultivate as for *Adenium*.

P. lamerei S Madagascar; tree to 20 ft (6 m) with a tapered or cigar-shaped trunk covered in low spiraled tubercles, grossly swollen below and forking at its summit; flowers 1$\frac{1}{4}$–2$\frac{1}{2}$ in (3–6 cm), white; *P. succulentum* C and S Cape to Orange Free State; low, spiny and twiggy shrublet arising from a turnip-like caudex; flowers $\frac{1}{2}$–1$\frac{1}{2}$ in (1–4 cm), red, pink or particolored to white.

Pachysandra (from Greek *pachys*, thick, and *aner*, man, stamen). Buxaceae. E Asia, US. 4 species, evergreen or semi-evergreen, procumbent subshrubs or perennial herbs, with fleshy, rhizomelike stems and erect branches with leathery leaves clustered at the branch tips. Small, white flowers are carried in short spikes in spring and summer. *P. terminalis* is widely used as an evergreen groundcover, thriving beneath trees and shrubs. It responds well to a close shearing over after flowering. *P. procumbens* is less rampant. Both are fully hardy. They do not thrive in dry soil or if exposed to strong sun or winds. They are ideally suited to dappled shade. Increase by division in spring or by leafy shoot cuttings taken in late summer.

P. procumbens SE US; semi-evergreen perennial herb, carpet-forming and with erect stems 2–12 in (5–30 cm); leaves 2–4 in (5–10 cm), gray-green with brown-green, mottling, ovate to round, coarsely toothed above; *P. terminalis* Japan, north central China; evergreen subshrub, carpet-forming and with erect stems 2–8 in (5–20 cm); leaves 2–4 in (5–10 cm), oblong to rhombic or obovate, apex toothed, dark green, glossy; includes 'Green Carpet', erect, low and compact, with small, finely toothed, deep green leaves,

'Silver Edge', with leaves light green, narrowly edged silver-white, and 'Variegata', slow-growing, with leaves variegated white.

Pachystachys (from Greek *pachys*, thick, and *stachys*, spike). Acanthaceae. Tropical America. 12 species, evergreen, perennial herbs and shrubs with showy, tubular and two-lipped flowers in terminal spikes clothed with colorful bracts. Cultivate as for *Eranthemum*. *P. coccinea* CARDINAL'S GUARD; West Indies, northern S America; shrub to 6$\frac{1}{2}$ ft (2 m); inflorescence to 6 in (15 cm), 4-sided, flowers scarlet; *P. lutea* Peru; shrub to 3$\frac{1}{4}$ ft (1 m); inflorescence to 4 in (10 cm), 4-sided, bracts golden to amber, flowers white.

Paeonia (from Greek *paionia*, possibly derived from Paion, the physician of the gods, who used the plant medicinally.) Paeoniaceae. Europe, temperate Asia, NW America, China. PEONY. Some 33 species, perennial herbs or shrubs ('tree peonies') with ternately compound leaves and large cup- to bowl-shaped flowers in spring and summer. These long-lived perennials are divided into two distinct groups: herbs, which include the many garden forms and hybrids derived from *P. lactiflora*, the Chinese peony; and the shrubby tree peonies.

Herbaceous peonies are hardy to below 14°F (–10°C) to –4°F (–20°C), especially if mulched with evergreen branches or bracken. Established plants are best left undisturbed. Fork in generous amounts of well-rotted manure or garden compost, with bone-meal or super-phosphate, when planting. They are lime-tolerant and may be grown in moist, fertile soil, with good drainage and a soil depth of not less than 12 in (30 cm). Plant in sun or part-shade, avoiding early morning sun on flowers in areas with late frosts. Mulch annually in spring with well-rotted manure or garden compost.

The tree peonies enjoy similar soil conditions with greater emphasis on good drainage, and a slight preference for lime. Because they start into growth earlier in spring than herbaceous peonies they are slightly more tender, needing a sheltered position. At winter temperatures below 14°F (–10°C), protect when young with a covering of bracken; if cut back by frost, plants may still shoot from the base. No pruning is necessary, except to remove dead wood in spring. Rejuvenation is possible by cutting back to ground level in fall.

Divide herbaceous peonies in early fall, each division consisting of three stout shoots 4–6 in (10–15 cm) long, with 3–5 eyes. All peonies can be raised from seed but named cultivars and hybrids do not come true. Sow firm ripe seeds in fall in a loam-based propagating medium in pots in a shaded cold frame, transplanting the seedlings to nursery bed 18 in (45 cm) apart when they are large enough to handle in the following spring. Germination is slow if dormancy is allowed to develop; with fresh seed, the root appears about six weeks after sowing, and the shoot the following spring. They will reach flowering size in 4–5 years, or slightly longer for tree peonies.

Propagation of tree peonies is usually by grafting in summer using *P. lactiflora* or *P. officinalis* as rootstock. A wedge-shaped scion, 1½ in (4 cm) long, bearing a single leaf with a vegetative bud, is pushed into a slit in the rootstock, which should be 4 in (10 cm) long and ½ in (1.2 cm) in diameter. Plant in equal parts peat/sand, with the union covered, in a closed shaded frame, and leave to callus over. Admit air gradually to harden off. They should be ready to pot on by fall; plunge the pots in a cold frame over winter, and spray against botrytis. As the pots fill with roots the following spring, plant out deeply in a frame to encourage scion rooting. Layering and 6–8 in (15–20 cm) hardwood cuttings in fall are possible but success rates are low.

The major disease of peonies is peony gray mold blight (sometimes called peony wilt). Soft brown areas develop at leaf bases causing them to wilt. This is followed by a dark brown rot in both stem and leaf bases, and gray mold can subsequently be seen on stems at ground level. Young buds may blacken and wither, and gray mold develops on all damaged tissue. *B. cineria* causes similar symptoms later in the season. Both are best prevented by good hygiene, good drainage, and good air circulation.

P. cambessedesii Balearic Islands; herb to 18 in (45 cm), tinged red; leaves gray-green, tinted purple; flowers to 4 in (10 cm) diameter rose to pale magenta; *P. delavayi* China; tree peony to 5½ ft (1.6 m) leaves deeply and gracefully dissected; flowers to 3½ in (9 cm) diameter, with very dark red to maroon golden anthers; var. *angustiloba* f. *angustiloba* (syn. *P. potaninii*); China, Tibet; TREE PEONY; as for *P. delavayi* except stoloniferous, leaf segments narrower, flowers to 21 ft (6.5 m) diameter, nodding, maroon to dark velvety red; var. *ludlowii*: TIBETAN PEONY, to 8 ft (2.5 m), flowers to 5 in (12.5 cm) diameter produced earlier; var. *lutea*: Tibet, China; as for *P. delavayi* except flowers to 3 in (7.5 cm) diameter, yellow; *P. emodi* India; herb to 30 in (75 cm) flowers to 4¾ in (12 cm) diameter, white; *P. lactiflora* Tibet, China, Siberia; herb to 24 in (60 cm); flowers to 4 in (10 cm) diameter, fragrant, white; hybrids of *P. lactiflora* Chinese Peonies) vary in flower color from white to pink, deep red, crimson or maroon, and are single, double or semi-double in form; *P.* × *lemoinei P. delavayi* var. *lutea* × *P. suffruticosa*; tree peony to 6½ ft (2 m); flowers yellow or combinations of yellow and pink; includes 'Alice Harding': flowers double, lemon yellow; 'Argosy': flowers single, to 7 in (18 cm) diameter, petals primrose yellow, basal blotch carmine; 'Chromatella': flowers double, sulfur

yellow; 'La Lorraine': flowers double, cream-yellow; 'L'Espérance': flowers 6–8 in (15–20 cm) diameter, petals pale yellow, basal blotch crimson; 'Souvenir de Maxime Cornu': flowers double, yellow to peach, tinged brown, orange and red; *P. mascula* S Europe, Asia Minor; herb, 10–24 in (25–60 cm) flowers to 5 in (13 cm) diameter, red, pink or white; subsp. *arietina*: leaves gray-green, hairy beneath, flowers pink to red; 'Mother of Pearl': flowers pale pink; 'Northern Glory': leaves gray-green, flowers single, deep magenta-carmine; 'Purple Emperor': flowers single, rose-purple; 'Rose Gem': flowers single, bright blood-red; subsp. *mascula*: leaves smooth beneath flowers to 4¾ in (12 cm) diameter, purple-red; *P. mlokosewitschii* Caucasus; herb to 3¼ ft (1 m); leaves broad, dark to silvery or blue-green above, glaucous beneath; flowers to 4¾ in (12 cm) diameter, cupped, yellow; *P. officinalis* Europe; herb to 24 in (60 cm) flowers to 5 in (13 cm) diameter, red; 'Alba Plena': flowers double, white; 'China Rose': flowers single, salmon pink, anthers orange-yellow; 'Crimson Globe': flowers single, garnet-red, petaloid stamens crimson and gold; 'Mutabilis Plena': flowers deep pink fading to blush pink; 'Roseaplena': flowers double, darker pink; 'Rosea Superba': flowers large double, pink; 'Rubra Plena': flowers double, crimson; *P. peregrina* S Europe; herb to 20 in

Paeonia mascula (left) and P. delavayi var. ludlowii (right)
Despite their space demands and brief flowering season, the attractiveness of peonies makes them deserving garden plants, whether the herbaceous types (left) or the shrubby tree peonies (right).

(50 cm); flowers to 4¾ in (12 cm) diameter, cup-shaped, deep red; 'Otto Froebel' flowers vermilion, produced early); *P. rockii* (syn. 'Joseph Rock': flowers semi-double, spreading, petals very pale flesh pink to silvery-white blotched maroon at base; *P. suffruticosa* China, Tibet, Bhutan; MOUTAN PEONY; tree peony to 6½ ft (2 m); leaves tinted purple-bronze at first; flowers to 6 in (15 cm) diameter, pink to white, each petal with a deep purple, red-bordered basal patch and finely scalloped margins; 'Banksii': flowers double, carmine; 'Godaishu': flowers semi-double, large, clear white; 'Koka-mon': flowers large, red-brown striped white; 'Reine Elizabeth': flowers fully double, large, salmon-pink tinged red, margins ruffled; 'Renkaku': flowers double, dense, white, ruffled, anthers long, deep yellow; 'Superb': flowers cherry red; *P. tenuifolia* S E Europe to Caucasus; herb to 24 in (60 cm); leaves finely divided; flowers cup-shaped, to 3 in (8 cm) diameter, deep red; 'Early Bird': flowers single, deep red; 'Plena': flowers double, longer-lasting; 'Rosea': flowers pale pink; *P. veitchii* China: herb to 20 in (50 cm); flowers nodding to 3½ in (9 cm) diameter, pale to deep magenta; 'Alba': flowers cream-white; *P. wittmanniana* Caucasus; herb to 48 in (120 cm); flowers to 5 in (12.5 cm) diameter, pale yellow.

paired usually applied to flowers or leaflets in opposite pairs; bi-, tri-, and multijugate describe compound leaves with two, three or many such pairs.

pak-choi see *cabbage*.

palate the lower lip of a corolla, apparently closing its throat.

palea specifically the upper and generally slimmer of the two glumes enclosing the floret in most Gramineae; more generally, a small, dry bract or scale.

paleaceous bearing small, chaffy bracts or scales (paleae); more generally, chaffy in texture.

palisade a fence made up of spaced upright planks or railings fixed to horizontal members. It is sometimes used to describe a closely clipped hedge, grown as edging on narrow pathways or to conceal walls.

Paliurus (name for the genus used by Dioscorides.) Rhamnaceae. S Europe to E Asia. 8 species, spiny, deciduous or evergreen trees or shrubs with small yellow flowers in axillary clusters in summer, followed by dry, woody and winged fruits. Hardy to 5°F (−15°C) and suited to planting at the base of a warm, south- or southwest-facing wall or for dry borders, especially on alkaline soil. If the top growth is cut down by frost, it will resprout from the base so long as the roots are protected from damage. Grow in full sun in well-drained fertile soil. Prune in winter to remove old and overcrowded growth. Cut overgrown specimens hard back to the base. Propagate by softwood cuttings in summer or by seed sown in a frame or under glass after a winter scarification. Alternatively, increase by root cuttings or simple layering. *P. spina-christi* CHRIST'S THORN; Spain to C Asia and N China; deciduous, 10–23 ft (3–7 m), twigs flexuous, hairy, thorns paired; leaves ¾–1½ in (2–4 cm), entire to crenate-serrate, hairy on veins beneath; fruit ¾–1¼ in (1.8–3 cm) in diameter, woody, 3-lobed, subglobose, wings undulate.

palmate of leaves, with three or more free lobes or similar segments originating in a palmlike manner from the same basal point; of venation, with three or more veins arising from the point of attachment of the petiole.

palmatifid palmately cleft rather than lobed.

palmatisect palmately cut into segments almost to the base of the leaf.

palmette a trained form of fruit tree; similar to an espalier, with the tiers staggered and inclined upward.

palms a group of monocotyledonous plants, mostly of tree and shrubby form, belonging to the family Palmae. They have special potential as garden and landscape features, and where dwarf species are used in their distinctive juvenile state, can be equally valuable as indoor container-grown specimens.

For outdoor cultivation, most palms need tropical or subtropical temperatures, besides which local climatic conditions and soils may affect their success rate. Palms suitable for outdoor planting in temperate areas are limited; those that thrive in favored areas include the CHUSAN PALMS, *Trachycarpus fortunei*, and *T. wagnerianus*, *Chamaerops humilis*, *Butia capitata*, and *Jubaea chilensis*. Where varying degrees of protection can be provided during winter, species of borderline hardiness can be grown, including the COTTON PALM, *Washingtonia filifera*, the New Zealand FEATHER DUSTER PALM, *Rhopalostylis sapida*, and the CANARY DATE PALM, *Phoenix canariensis*. Several species are extremely cold-resistant but require summer heat to grow well. They include the DWARF PALMETTO, *Sabal minor*, and the BLUE HESPER PALM, *Brahea armata*.

Care should be exercised in the choice of species. A large number are extremely fast-growing and can rapidly dominate the landscape. Many are best grown as individual specimens, whereas others look good in groups of a single species. Palms require virtually no maintenance and the predictability of their mature size and shape is an advantage in garden design. Most palms succeed in a range of soil types.

The majority of palms grown in pots under cover benefit from high air humidity. In a greenhouse, this can be provided by damping down; in conservatories and the home, it can be achieved by means of an electric humidifier or by frequent misting. Grouping plants together and standing pots on a tray of pebbles, kept permanently moist, is helpful. A kitchen or bathroom is often a good place for palms because of the usually high humidity level.

Bright indirect light benefits most species. Many

old leaf bases surround the stem

Palm (*Phoenix roebelenii*)

palms, including *Caryota*, *Phoenix roebe-linii*, *Chamaedorea*, *Howea* and *Rhapis*, grow as seedlings on the jungle floor and thus tolerate low light levels. Sunlight filtered through net curtains and a north-facing window position are ideal, but direct sunlight through glass must be avoided. Dry air and insufficient levels of light in a greenhouse, conservatory or home, cause most palms to grow slowly; this can be an advantage, as long as the plant remains healthy, for a palm can then remain in the same container for a number of years. Conservatories are ideal locations.

Palms are most easily propagated from seed, although some such as *Chamaerops*, *Rhapis*, *Caryota*, *Ptychosperma*, and *Chamaedorea* species, can be increased by division or from suckers. The more tropical the plant's origin, the more essential it is that seed is fresh. Palms from temperate or arid zones have a considerably longer seed-viability period; for example, *Washingtonia*, *Trachycarpus*, *Chamaerops* and *Phoenix*.

Seed should be planted to its own depth in a moist potting medium that both retains moisture and is free-draining. Plant in pots or trays in a seed propagator or sealed plastic bag to retain humidity. Large quantities of seed can be mixed with moistened medium and placed directly in a clear plastic bag and removed individually on germination. No light is required. Large seeds such as the COCONUT, *Cocos*, are half-buried in a seed-raising medium in individual pots.

Temperate-area palms will germinate well without additional heat but tropical species require 86–95°F (30–35°C). Fresh seed may sprout within a week or two, but most species take two or three months to germinate, and some take up to two years. During this time, the planting medium should not be allowed to dry out, and the temperature must be maintained. Germination-hastening practices include filing or cracking the hard seed coat, soaking in warm or hot water for long periods and soaking in acid.

"Sprouts" should be potted up individually as soon as the first leaf appears and placed in a warm and bright location out of direct sunlight. The seed should not be removed from the seedling at any stage and pots must be kept watered. Pot on as soon as roots fill the old pot, and feed regularly with a pot plant fertilizer.

In general, palms transplant successfully if moved when in active growth, generally in spring and early summer. Ideally, the tree should be prepared some months before being moved by trenching two or three spade-widths from its base to a depth of four or five spits, cutting through any roots encountered. The trench is then filled in for at least three months, during which time new roots will grow from the base of the trunk.

Pamianthe (for Major Albert Pam [d. 1955], English horticulturist, and Greek *anthe*, flower). Amaryllidaceae. S America. 2 or 3 species, bulbous herbs with linear leaves and scapose umbels of large, fragrant flowers in spring. These consist of a long cylindrical tube, six lobes and six stamens, their filaments short, incurved and fused at the base into a campanulate corona with six short lobes. Maintain a winter minimum temperature of 50°F (10°C). Plant in a fibrous, loam-based medium in late summer/early fall with the neck of the bulb at soil level, and water sparingly until growth commences. Grow in bright indirect light and water moderately when in growth. Propagate by offsets. Seeds take 12–15 months to mature on the plant, but germinate rapidly if sown when ripe in a warm and humid closed case. *P. peruviana* Peru; scape to 24 in (60 cm); flowers fragrant, perianth tube to 5 in (13 cm), green, lobes to 5 in (13 cm), white or flushed cream, the inner ones to 1¼ in (3 cm) wide, oblanceolate with a central green stripe; corona to 3 in (8 cm), lobes bifid or mucronate.

pan (1) a compacted layer within a soil profile that is impermeable to water and air and thus impedes drainage and also root growth. It may arise naturally in soil of high iron content where the element accumulates at depth, or it may result from mechanical cultivation or treading of medium or heavy textured soil, especially when wet. The presence of a pan can be determined by digging a narrow pit into the profile, and the layer can be broken up by

Hard pan in soil
This deep, straight-sided hole reveals a compacted layer, or pan, in the soil profile, likely to impede drainage.

deep cultivation; (2) a plant container the diameter of which measures much more than its depth; it is useful for seed sowing, for growing plants with spreading or surface roots or for small bulbs. See *pots and potting*.

Pancratium (name in Dioscorides for a bulbous plant). Amaryllidaceae. Canary Islands, Mediterranean to tropical Asia, W Africa to Namibia. About 16 species, bulbous perennial herbs with 2-ranked, linear to lorate leaves. The large, white flowers are borne in summer in scapose umbels. The perianth is more or less funnelform with six spreading, linear-lanceolate lobes; the bases of the anther filaments are united in a conspicuous corona. They are suitable for the cool greenhouse or conservatory, or for outdoor cultivation in full sun at the base of a south-facing wall. *P. illyricum* is hardy to 23°F (–5°C). *P. maritimum* is almost as hardy although the foliage is susceptible to frost, and in cool temperate gardens, the hot dry conditions necessary for bulb ripening are seldom achieved. Propagate by offsets or ripe seed.

P. illyricum Corsica, Sardinia; scape to 16 in (40 cm); flowers fragrant; perianth white, sometimes ivory or cream at base of segments and on corona, tube 3 in (8 cm), lobes 2 in (5 cm), linear-oblong to narrowly elliptic; corona much longer than perianth, teeth paired, long and narrow, alternating with stamens; *P. maritimum* SEA daffodil, sea lily; Mediterranean, SW Europe; flowers highly fragrant; perianth tube to 3 in (7.5 cm), very slender; corona two-thirds length of perianth, with short triangular teeth alternating with stamens.

Pandanus (from *pandang*, the Malayan name for these plants). Pandanaceae. SE Asia, especially Malaysia, Australia. SCREW PINE. 600 species, evergreen trees and shrubs with sparsely branching, stout stems bearing numerous stilt roots. Sword-shaped with saw-toothed margins, the leaves are inserted in three, twisted ranks, forming spirally arranged, terminal rosettes. The fruit is an oblong to globose syncarp of woody drupes, often pendulous and sometimes edible. Juveniles of *P. veitchii* and *P. sanderi* are handsome foliage plants for the home or conservatory. Grow in sun or light shade in a sandy loam-based medium with additional leaf mold and some charcoal; maintain a minimum temperature of 55°F (13°C) and a humid, buoyant atmosphere. Water plentifully and feed semiweekly with dilute liquid feed when in growth, allowing the medium to dry slightly between waterings; reduce water during winter to keep almost dry. Avoid wetting the foliage in cool weather—an accumulation of water in the leaf axils will cause rot. As pot-grown specimens mature, they tend to heave themselves out of the pots. Propagate by offsets, suckers, by cuttings of lateral shoots in summer or by seed, pre-soaked for 24 hours before sowing.

P. sanderi origin uncertain, possibly from Timor; leaves 30 × 2 in (75 × 5 cm), striped yellow or golden and green, margins minutely spiny; 'Roehrsianus': leaves deep golden-yellow, later striped pale yellow; *P. veitchii* origin uncertain, possibly from Polynesia; leaves 20–39 in (50–100 cm) × 30 in (75 cm), slightly drooping, margins spiny, dark green bordered with pure or silvery-white; 'Compactus': dwarf form.

Pandorea (for the Greek goddess *Pandora*). Bignoniaceae. Australia, Papuasia, E Malaysia, New Caledonia. 6 species, lianes with pinnate leaves. Produced in clusters between winter

and summer, the flowers are cylindrical or funnelform with five, rounded lobes. Both *P. pandorana* and *P. jasminoides* withstand light frost and are drought-tolerant. Cultivate as for *Bignonia*.

P. jasminoides BOWER PLANT, BOWER OF BEAUTY; NE Australia; to 16 ft (5 m); flowers 1½–2 in (4–5 cm), white, streaked or stained deep, rich pink within; 'Alba': flowers pure white; 'Lady Di': flowers white, with a cream throat; 'Rosea': flowers pink, with a darker throat; 'Rosea Superba': large, pink, with a darker, spotted purple throat; *P. pandorana* WONGA-WONGA VINE; Australia, New Guinea, Pacific Islands; evergreen to 20 ft (6 m); flowers fragrant, to 1½ in (4 cm), creamy yellow, streaked and splashed red or purple; 'Rosea': pale pink.

pandurate fiddle-shaped; rounded at both ends.

panicle an indeterminate branched inflorescence; the branches generally racemose or corymbose.

paniculate resembling, or in the form of a panicle.

Panicum (from a Latin name for millet). Gramineae. Pantropical to temperate N America. PANIC GRASS. Some 470 species, annual or perennial grasses with threadlike to lanceolate leaves and flowers in panicles and racemes in spring and summer. The annual *P. capillare* is grown for its large, intricately branched flower heads which are used for drying. *P. virgatum*, a hardy perennial, is noted for its generosity of bloom and the summer blue foliage colors of some cultivars, and the russet fall tones. Grow in moderately fertile well-drained soil in sun. Propagate *P. capillare* by seed sown in early spring under glass and set out after danger of frost is passed; increase *P. virgatum* by division.

P. capillare OLD WITCH GRASS, WITCH GRASS; S Canada, US; annual, to 36 in (90 cm); culms clumped, upright

to spreading, slender to robust; leaves undulate, linear to narrow-lanceolate, to 12 × ½ in (30 × 1.4 cm) hairy; panicles open, to 18 in (45 cm)+, green to purple; branches very fine, spreading, resembling a cloud; *P. virgatum* SWITCH GRASS; C America to S Canada; perennial, narrowly upright, to 70 in (180 cm); culms clumped, flimsy to robust, purple to glaucous green; leaves linear, flat, erect, to 24 in × ½ in (60 cm × 1.4 cm), usually glabrous, green, sometimes glaucous blue, becoming vivid yellow, bronze or burgundy in fall; panicle open, to 20 × 10 in (50 × 25 cm), with many fine branches and spikelets resembling a cloud or swarm lasting well into winter; branches spreading, feathery, stiff to drooping; 'Cloud Nine': to 6½ ft (2 m), with blue-green leaves; 'Hänse Herms': RED SWITCH GRASS, to 4 ft (1.25 m), weeping, with plum to rich burgundy leaves in fall and flowers suffused red; 'Heavy Metal': stiffly erect with pale metallic blue leaves, turning yellow in fall; 'Rotbraun': to 32 in (80 cm), with light brown leaves, flushed red at tips, with rich fall color; 'Rubrum': to 3¼ ft (1 m), with leaves flushed red, turning bright red in fall, and rich brown seed heads in clouds; 'Squaw': leaves tinted red in fall; 'Strictum': TALL SWITCH GRASS, narrowly upright, to 4 ft (1.2 m); 'Warrior': tall, strong-growing, with leaves tinted red-brown in fall.

pannose feltlike in texture; being densely covered in woolly hairs.

Papaver (from Latin *pappa*, food or milk, an allusion to the milky latex). Papaveraceae. Europe, Asia, South Africa, W Australia, western N America. POPPY. 50 species, annual or perennial herbs with white or yellow latex. The leaves are generally oblong to lanceolate, pinnately lobed, incised and toothed. Produced in spring and summer on slender stalks, the short-lived flowers consist of four silky, obovate to rounded petals around numerous stamens. These in turn surround a top-shaped ovary capped with

Panicle

Buddleja 'Lochinch'

P

Poppy seed heads
Papaver species, (here *P. somniferum*) form attractive seed heads which are also popular for dried flower arrangements.

a sculpted, downy stigmatic disk. Poppies are easily grown in the mixed border, herbaceous border and in rock gardens. The annuals will usually self-seed freely unless deadheaded. Sow annuals *in situ*, in spring or late summer in well-drained soil in a sunny position. Thin to 10–12 in (25–30 cm) apart and keep weed-free. Give late-sown plants cloche protection in winter. The biennial *P. triniifolium* is a superb foliage plant for silver and dry gardens. *P. nudicaule*, a short-lived perennial, can also be treated as an annual, but best results are obtained by growing it as a biennial. The blooms, 4–4¾ in (10–12 cm) across on wiry stems, make good cut flowers, lasting for up to a week if cut in bud and the stem tips scalded in boiling water before arranging. Sow thinly in late spring/early summer in a cold frame or outdoors. Transplant when large enough to handle, 6 in (15 cm) apart in rows 12 in (30 cm) apart, in a sunny well-drained bed. Transfer to the final site in full sun and fertile soil, in fall or the following spring. *P. alpinum* and its allies are short-lived perennials for the rock garden, stone walls and raised beds. They need gritty soil and full sun.

The oriental poppies, *P. orientale*, are among the loveliest hardy herbaceous perennials, although their flowering period is brief, and the leaves die back and leave gaps in the border. The seed pods are attractive when dried. Plant in deep well-drained soil, in full sun. Propagate by division in early fall or spring, or by root cuttings in late summer/early fall. Place pieces of thick roots, crown end up, in boxes of sandy medium in a cold frame. Keep moist, not wet, and protect from frost. Transfer to a nursery bed in spring for a season before planting out. Propagation from seed is possible, but cultivars do not come true.

P. alpinum Alps, Carpathians, Pyrenees; perennial to 10 in (25 cm); leaves 2–8 in (5–20 cm), 2–3-pinnate, lobes 6–8, linear to ovate-lanceolate, acute, occasionally pinnatisect, glaucous gray-green to green, glabrous to sparsely bristly, toothed; flowers solitary on scapes to 10 in (25 cm); petals white, yellow or orange, to 1 in (2.5 cm); a variable species—*P. burseri*, *P. kerneri*, *P. pyrenaicum* and *P. rhaeticum* are closely related; *P. atlanticum* Morocco; perennial to 18 in (45 cm); leaves to 6 in (15 cm), oblong to lanceolate, jagged-toothed or pinnatisect, pilose; scapes to 18 in (45 cm), simple or forked; petals to 1 in (2.5 cm), buff to orange to red; *P. burseri* C Europe; perennial to 10 in (25 cm); leaves to 8 in (20 cm), 2–3-pinnate, glaucous, segments 6–8, linear to lanceolate, acute; scapes to 10 in (25 cm), setose; flowers solitary, petals to ¾ in (2 cm), usually white; *P. commutatum* Caucasus, Asia Minor; annual to 16 in (40 cm); stem erect, branching, sparsely hairy; leaves to 6 in (15 cm), pinnatifid, downy, segments to 1¼ in (3 cm), oblong to ovate, dentate to entire; scapes long, hairy, petals to 1¼ in (3 cm), red with black basal spot; includes 'Lady Bird', with scarlet flowers splashed with black; *P. nudicaule* ARCTIC POPPY, ICELANDIC POPPY; subarctic regions; perennial; leaves 1¼–12 in (3–30 cm), pinnatifid to pinnatisect, somewhat glaucous, hairy, segments 3–4, oblong, incised; flowers to 3 in (7.5 cm) in diameter, solitary on scapes to 24 in (60 cm), white with yellow basal patch, yellow, orange, peach or pale red, ruffled; many cultivars and seed races are available, with large, long-stalked flowers in a wide range of pastel shades, bright yellows and warm oranges; *P. orientale* ORIENTAL POPPY; SW Asia; robust perennial to 36 in (90 cm); leaves to 10 in (25 cm), bristly, pinnate to pinnatisect at apex, segments lanceolate or oblong; flowers solitary, to 4 in (10 cm) in diameter, red, orange or pale pink usually with a purple to black basal blotch; includes many cultivars, ranging from dwarf and compact to tall, the flowers sometimes double, in a range of colors from white, pink and orange to deep red and purple, sometimes bicolored, some with petals fringed or ruffled; among the finest are 'Cedric Morris' with gray hairy leaves and shell-pink petals with a large violet-black basal spot, 'Glowing Embers', to 42 in (110 cm), robust, erect, with bright orange-red flowers, 4 in (10 cm) in diameter, with ruffled petals, 'Harvest Moon', to 3¼ ft (1 m), with semi-double, deep orange flowers, and 'Perry's White', to 32 in (80 cm), with gray-white flowers with a purple-black center; *P. rhoeas* CORN POPPY, FIELD POPPY, FLANDERS POPPY; temperate Old World; bristly annual to 36 in (90 cm); stem erect, branching; leaves pinnate or pinnatisect, segments lanceolate, to 6 in (15 cm); flowers solitary, to 3 in (7.5 cm) across, brilliant red sometimes with a black basal spot; includes the Shirley Poppies, with medium-sized flowers, single or double, in a wide range of colors except yellow, and 'Valerie Finnis', with gray mauve, pink and white flowers; *P. somniferum* OPIUM POPPY; SE Europe, W Asia; annual to 48 in (120 cm), glaucous, gray-green; leaves to 5 in (12.5 cm), obovate-oblong, deeply and jaggedly incised and toothed; flowers to 4 in (10 cm) across, pale white, pink, light mauve, purple or marked, frequently double, with erose petals, occasionally with a dark basal blotch; includes the Peony-flowered Hybrids, with double flowers; *P. triniifolium* Asia Minor; biennial to 16 in (40 cm); leaves silver-gray, bristly, finely divided and cut; flowers to 1½ in (4 cm) across, pale orange-red.

papayas *Carica papaya*. Caricaceae. S.America. PAWPAW. A tender tree to 33 ft (10 m) in the wild; extensively grown in tropical and frost-free subtropical regions for the medicinal and industrial uses of its unripe fruit; also for flavorful, vitamin-rich qualities when ripe. Fruits to 18 in (45 cm), elongate-globose, hanging on stout stalks. Leaves to 27½ in (70 cm) diam., deeply palmatifid. Flowers usually unisexual. For satisfactory growth requires temperature within the range 75–79°F (24–26°C) with high humidity. In temperate zones, under protection

P

with a minimum winter temperature of 59°F (15°C), makes an unusual foliage plant with palmlike clusters; fruit production is possible, but plants should be replaced after 4 years. Propagate by seed at 75–86°F (24–30°C).

papery bark a disorder occurring most frequently on trees of apple and ornamental *Malus*, where the bark peels in loose, papery and translucent sheets. In severe attacks, the affected area may be girdled, causing branch or trunk dieback. Papery bark commonly results from waterlogging, but is also a sign of infection with silver leaf (*Chondrostereum purpureum*) or apple canker (*Nectria galligena*). Where poor growing conditions persist, papery bark may recur, ultimately severely reducing fruit yield or even proving fatal. Badly damaged or dead shoots should be cut back to healthy wood. Papery bark also occurs as a nonpathogenic ornamental feature on many trees, for example *Acer griseum, Betula utilis, Prunus serrula*.

Paphiopedilum (from Greek *Paphos*, an Aegean island with a temple to Aphrodite, and *pedilon*, slipper, describing the saccate lip formed by the third petal of each flower). Orchidaceae. SE Asia, India, Indonesia, SW China, New Guinea, Philippines, Solomon Islands. SLIPPER ORCHID. About 60 species, largely terrestrial, evergreen orchids. They lack stems and pseudobulbs. Borne in loose basal fans, the leaves are leathery, more or less strap-shaped and plain green or mottled with light or dark markings. The flowers are terminal, waxy, and carried one to several on a slender stalk; the dorsal sepal is large and erect, the lateral sepals fused to form a shieldlike synsepalum behind the lip and the petals are horizontal or pendent. The lip is strongly saccate, forming a slipperlike pouch.

Compact orchids, with handsome, evergreen foliage and intriguing, long-lived flowers, usually from winter to spring. They are easy to grow in a greenhouse and conservatory or in the home, in a growing case or stood on a tray of moist gravel. All need shade and a buoyant, humid atmosphere. Most need a night-minimum temperature of 59–64°F (15–18°C) with a daytime increase of at least 9°F (5°C).

Some of the most popular species, however, hail from cooler locations and will tolerate a night-minimum of 45°F (7°C). These include *P. hirsutissimum, P. insigne, P. fairrieanum, P. spicerianum,* and *P. venustum*. With the exception of *P. venustum*, it can generally be assumed that mottled-leaved species require warmer conditions, as do species and grexes with plain leaves and multiple-flowered inflorescences. Water throughout the year, aiming to drench the medium once it begins to dry out. Plants should not be allowed to dry out completely, but waterlogged conditions are disastrous. Although overhead misting is beneficial in optimum conditions, never allow water to stand on foliage or to settle for long periods in the center of growths. Medium may be composed of a variety of mixtures using conifer-bark, perlag, perlite and charcoal with possible additions of sphagnum moss and/or coir. *P. bellatulum* benefits from the addition of broken chalk to the crocks. Feed semiweekly when the plants are growing. Propagate by division.

In addition to the species described below, there are many grexes and cultivars of *Paphiopedilum*. These vary widely in size, shape and color. Some bear single flowers of great size and substance and almost perfectly circular in outline. Others are smaller and finer, closer to the species, with slender, sometimes twisted petals, carried one to many per spike. In color, they range from white to cream, yellow, ocher, green, rose, ruby red, garnet, plum purple, violet, maroon and deep, glossy chestnut. These colors may be combined–for example, a white dorsal sepal with a maroon lip and ocher petals. All parts may be spotted, mottled, striped or veined, sometimes with hairy margins or hairy warts. One of the most popular grexes is *P.* Maudiae with attractively mottled leaves and lime green flowers with a white, green-striped dorsal sepal. In the clone *P.* Maudiae 'Coloratum', the flowers are large and wine red with a white-striped dorsal sepal and green-brown lip.

P. bellatulum W Burma, Thailand; leaves dark green mottled pale green above, spotted purple beneath, flowers 1, white or cream, heavily spotted maroon; dorsal sepal to 1½ × 1½ in

(3.5 × 4 cm); petals to 2½ × 1¾ in (6 × 4.5 cm); lip narrowly ovoid, to 1½ × ¾ in (4 × 2 cm), margins strongly incurved; *P. callosum* Thailand, Cambodia, Laos; leaves tessellated pale and dark green above; flowers 1; sepals white flushed purple in lower half, veined purple and green, dorsal sepal broadly ovate, to 2⅛ × 2½ in (5.5 × 6 cm), ciliate, recurved; petals curved downward, to 2½ × ¾ in (6.5 × 2 cm), white to yellow-green, apical third purple, maroon-spotted on upper margin and sometimes basal half; lip to 1¾ × 1 in (4.5 × 2.5 cm), incurved lateral lobes warty, green, flushed maroon; *P. delenatii* Vietnam; leaves mottled dark and pale green above, spotted purple beneath; flowers 1(–2), pale pink with red and yellow markings on staminode, hairy; dorsal sepal ovate, to 1½ × 1 in (3.5 × 2.5 cm); petals broadly elliptic, rounded at apex, 1⅔ × 2 in (4.3 × 5 cm); lip ellipsoid to subglobose, 1½ × 1¼ in (4 × 3 cm), margins incurved, minutely hairy; *P. fairrieanum* Sikkim, Bhutan, NE India; leaves very faintly mottled above; flowers 1, sepals white, veined green and purple, with a purple suffusion on dorsal sepal, petals similar; dorsal sepal elliptic, to 3 × 2¾ in (8 × 7 cm), ciliate, apical margins recurved, lateral margins undulate; petals curved downward with rising tips, 2 × ⅝ in (5 × 1.5 cm), margins ciliate, undulate; lip deep, outcurved at rim, 1½ × 1 in (4 × 2.5 cm), olive to yellow-green, veined darker; *P. haynaldianum* Philippines; flowers 3–4; dorsal sepal obovate to elliptic, apex hooded, to 2½ × 1 in (6 × 2.5 cm), basal margin recurved, creamy white, sides flushed purple, center green or yellow with basal half spotted maroon; petals arching, spathulate, half-twisted, to 3 × ½ in (8 × 1.4 cm), ciliate, green or yellow, basal half spotted maroon, purple above; lip to 1¾ × 1 in (4.5 × 2.3 cm), ocher-green, veined darker, purple-hairy with in; *P. hirsutissimum* NE India; leaves spotted purple beneath; flowers 1, sepals pale yellow to pale green with glossy dark brown suffusion almost to margins, petals pale yellow, lower half spotted purple-brown, apical half flushed rose-purple; dorsal sepal ovate to elliptic, 1¾ × 1½ in (4.5 × 4 cm), undulate, ciliate; petals horizontal to deflexed, spathulate, 2¾ × ⅞ in (7 × 2.2

cm), half-twisted toward apex, strongly undulate, hairy, ciliate; lip 1¾ × ¾ in (4.5 × 2 cm); *P. insigne* NE India, E Nepal; flowers 1; dorsal sepal obovate to elliptic, 2½ × 1½ in (6.4 × 4 cm), apical margins incurved, pale green, inner surface with raised maroon spots, margin white; petals slightly oblong to spathulate, 2½ × ¾ in (6.3 × 1.8 cm), yellow-brown veined red-brown; lip 2 × 1¼ in (5 × 3 cm), yellow, marked purple-brown; *P. niveum* N Malaysia and S Thailand; leaves mottled very dark and pale green above, dotted purple beneath; flowers 1–2, white, often dotted purple near base of segments and front of lip, hairy; dorsal sepal very broadly ovate, to 1¼ × 2 in (3 × 5 cm); petals elliptic, rounded, to 1½ × 1¼ in (4 × 3 cm), ciliate; lip ovoid to ellipsoid, to 1¼ × ⅔ in (3 × 1.7 cm), margins incurved; *P. primulinum* Sumatra; flowers many, opening in succession, pale yellow with yellow-green sepals; dorsal sepal ovate, to 1 × 1 in (2.6 × 2.6 cm), ciliate, hairy beneath; petals linear, finely tapering, spreading tip; twisted, to 1¼ × ⅜ in (3.2 × 0.8 cm); lip to 1½ × ¾ in (3.5 × 2 cm), bulbous toward apex; *P. rothschildianum* Borneo; flowers 2–4; dorsal sepal ovate, to 2⅝ × 1⅝ in (6.6 × 4.1 cm), ivory-white or yellow veined maroon; petals to 4¾ × ⅝ in (12 × 1.5 cm), narrowly tapering to a rounded apex, yellow or ivory-white marked maroon; lip to 2½ × ¾ in (6 × 2 cm), golden, heavily suffused purple; *P. spicerianum* NE India, NW Burma; flowers 1;

Paphiopedilum callosum
The saccate lower lip formed by the basal petal is the "slipper" after which these orchids are named.

dorsal sepal curving forward, obovate to transversely elliptic, to 1⅝ × 2 in (4.2 × 5 cm), sides recurved, hairy, white with central maroon stripe and green-tinged base; petals falcate, linear-oblong, to 1½ × ½ in (3.9 × 1.3 cm), yellow-green with central brown-purple vein, flecking on other veins; lip to 2 × 1¼ in (5 × 3 cm), glossy, pale green, flushed brown with darker veins; *P. sukhakulii* NE Thailand; leaves tessellated dark and yellow-green above; flowers 1; sepals white veined green, spotted purple at base, outer surface downy, dorsal sepal concave, to 1½ × 1¼ in (4 × 3 cm), ciliate; petals to 2½ × ¾ in (6.2 × 2 cm), green heavily spotted maroon, margins ciliate; lip saccate, 2 × 1 in (5 × 2.3 cm), green, veined and flushed maroon, lateral lobes warty; *P. venustum* NE India, E Nepal, Sikkim, Bhutan; leaves tessellated dark green and gray green above, densely spotted purple beneath; flowers 1, sepals white veined green, petals white veined with green, warted maroon-black, flushed purple in apical half; dorsal sepal ovate, to 1½ × 1¼ in (4 × 3 cm), outer surface hirsute; petals oblanceolate, recurved, ciliate, to 2⅛ × ⅝ in (5.5 × 1.5 cm); lip to 1½ × 1¼ in (4 × 3 cm), yellow tinged purple and veined green, lateral lobes verrucose.

papilionaceous describes the pea-type corolla characteristic of papilionoid legumes.

papilla a nipplelike projection from an epidermal cell, often swollen and covered with wax.

papillate, papillose covered with papillae.

pappus a whorl or tuft of delicate bristles or scales in the place of the calyx, found in some flowers of Compositae.

papyraceous papery.

paradise garden a description of ancient gardens of the Near and Middle East. *Paradaisos* in Greek meant a park for a king, and was derived from the old Persian *pairidaeza*, an enclosure, and the Hebrew *pardes*, an enclosed

garden or park. Its influence can be traced to India, China, Japan and into Italy and other parts of Europe.

Paradisea (for Count Giovanni Paradisi of Modena [1760–1826]). Liliaceae (Asphodelaceae). S Europe. 2 species, fleshy-rooted, perennial herbs with grassy leaves and, in spring and summer, 6-parted, funnel-form to campanulate flowers in slender, lax racemes. Cultivate as for *Anthericum*. *P. liliastrum* PARADISE LILY, ST. BRUNO'S LILY; S Europe; to 24 in (60 cm); leaves 1¼–2 in (3–5 cm); flowers white tipped green, in a secund raceme; 'Major': robust, with larger flowers.

Parahebe (from Greek *para*, beside, i.e., close to, and *Hebe*). Scrophulariaceae. New Zealand, New Guinea, Australia. Some 30 species, prostrate or decumbent subshrubs, rarely herbs, like *Hebe* but with a less shrubby habit and with flowers in short axillary racemes. Hardy to 0°F (–18°C). Grow in gritty, free-draining soil in a sunny, sheltered position. Increase by semiripe cuttings, layering, and (*P. perfoliata*) by division. Cut away flowered stems of *P. perfoliata* when new growth emerges in spring.

P. catarractae New Zealand; subshrub to 12 in (30 cm), decumbent to ascending; leaves to 1½ in (4 cm), ovate to lanceolate, dark above, paler beneath, glabrous, acute, serrate; flowers white, veined pink or purple; includes 'Alba', with white flowers, 'Delight', to 6 in (15 cm), bushy, with blue flowers, 'Miss Willmott', with rose-lilac flowers veined mauve, 'Porlock', to 10 in (25 cm), with blue and white flowers, and 'Rosea', to 8 in (20 cm), with pink flowers; var. *diffusa*: to 8 in (20 cm), with small, toothed leaves and tiny, pink-flushed flowers; *P. lyallii* New Zealand; subshrub to 8 in (20 cm), stems slender, prostrate to decumbent; leaves to ½ in (1 cm), suborbicular to narrowly obovate, coriaceous, obtuse to rounded, crenate to serrate; flowers, white to pink; 'Rosea': flowers pink; *P. perfoliata* (syn. *Veronica perfoliata*); DIGGER'S SPEEDWELL; Australia; woody-based herb, stems 8–39 in (20–100 cm), clumped, arching; leaves to 2 in (5 cm), ovate, amplexicaul to connate-perfoliate, blue-green, glaucous and thinly succulent; flowers blue to violet.

Paraquilegia (from Greek *para*, near, and *Aquilegia*, to which it is closely related). Ranunculaceae. C Asia to Himalaya. 4 species, low, tufted perennial herbs with ferny foliage and, in spring, solitary, cup-shaped flowers on delicate stalks. Hardy and with a preference for dry winters and cool climates. Grow in full sun in well-drained alkaline soil. It is perhaps best cultivated in an alpine house, or in troughs in a gritty alpine mix. Sow fresh seed in fall. *P. anemonoides* (syn. *P. grandiflora*); Himalaya; glabrous, to 7 in (18 cm); leaves finely divided, glaucous; flowers ¾–1½ in (2–4 cm) across, white to lilac.

parasite an organism dependent for the whole or part of its nutrition on another living organism. An obligate parasite is wholly dependent on its host.

parenchyma plant tissue comprising large thin-walled cells, relatively unspecialized.

paring box a device for ensuring that sod pieces are of matching thickness, consisting of a shallow wooden tray of the same dimensions and depth as that required of the sod. It has three sides, and the is sod laid grass side down into the box and pared to even depth with a sharp-bladed tool.

paripinnate where a pinnately compound leaf is not terminated by a single leaflet pinna or tendril.

Paris (from Latin *par, paris*, equal, on account of the numerical regularity of its leaves and flowers and their overall similarity). Liliaceae (Trilliaceae). Europe to E Asia. 4 species, deciduous herbaceous perennials with swollen creeping rhizomes. The stem is erect with ovate to lanceolate leaves in a whorl at its summit. Produced in spring and summer, the flowers are solitary and terminal, consisting of four to six green sepals somewhat like the leaves, and four to six linear, yellow-green sepals, often marked with purple-red. The fruit is a fleshy capsule. Suited to the woodland or wild garden, or for shaded parts of the rock garden; hardy to at least 5°F (−15°C). Plant in mois-

ture-retentive, humus soil enriched with leaf mold. Propagate by division or by seed sown ripe in fall. *P. polyphylla* (syn. *Daiswa polyphylla*); Himalaya, Burma, Thailand, China, Tibet, Taiwan; to 3¼ ft (1 m); leaves six to twelve, oblong to oblanceolate, tapering finely; sepals to 4 in (10 cm), narrowly lanceolate to linear, green, spreading, petals to 4 in (10 cm), threadlike, semi-erect, yellow.

parted, partite divided almost to the base into a determinate number of segments; a more general term for pinnate and palmate.

Parkinsonia (for John Parkinson [1567–1650], apothecary of London, court botanist and author of the great horticultural work *Paradisi in Sole Paradisus Terrestris* [1629]) Leguminosae. America, S and NE Africa. 12 or more species, shrubs or trees, usually armed, with green bark, finely pinnate or bipinnate leaves and fragrant, 5-petalled flowers in short racemes. Grow in perfectly drained soil in full sun. Provide a minimum temperature of 55°F (13°C). Water moderately when in full growth, very sparingly at other times. Under glass, maintain a dry, buoyant environment and avoid damp winter conditions. Propagate from seed in spring. *P. aculeata* JERUSALEM THORN; tropical America; shrub or tree, deciduous or evergreen, to 33 ft (10 m), armed; branchlets weeping, yellow-green to dark green, smooth; leaflets to ¼ in (0.5 cm), ovate to oblong; flowers fragrant, to ¾ in (2 cm) in diameter, dotted orange.

Parnassia (a shortened form of the ancient name *Gramen Parnassi*, grass of Mount Parnassus). Saxifragaceae. Northern temperate regions. BOG STAR, GRASS OF PARNASSUS. 15 species, small perennial, glabrous, usually evergreen herbs with slender-stalked leaves in basal rosettes and solitary, scapose, 5-petalled flowers in spring and early summer. Fully hardy. Plant in the rock or bog garden in damp but porous, alkaline soil and leave undisturbed. When grown in an alpine house, plant in pans of high-fertility loam-based medium with added grit and leaf

mold and ground limestone. Water plentifully. Propagate from seed in late fall or by division in spring. *P. palustris* northern temperate regions; to 6 in (15 cm); leaves ovate to 1¼ in (3 cm), slender-stalked; flowers white, netted green to buff, 1 in (2.5 cm) in diameter.

Parochetus (from Greek *para*, near, and *ochetos*, brook, referring to the moist habitat). Leguminosae. Mountains of tropical Africa, Asia to Java. 2 species, tolerant of temperatures to 23°F (−5°C) and well-suited to the rock garden. In cool temperature zones, however, they are more commonly and safely grown in the cold greenhouse or alpine house, in pots and hanging baskets. Grow in a moist but gritty, well-drained medium, and give a sheltered position in full sun outdoors; protect with a cloche in winter. Propagate by seed or rooted runners. *P. communis* SHAMROCK PEA, BLUE OXALIS; prostrate cloverlike herb with slender, rooting stems, trifoliolate leaves and deep blue, pealike flowers in summer.

Parodia (for Dr. Domingo Parodi [1823–90], pharmacist and student of the flora of Paraguay). Cactaceae. Southern S America. 35–50 species, low-growing cacti, mostly with small, globose to shortly cylindric, ribbed or tuberculate stems and brightly colored, funnel-shaped flowers. Grow in a cool frost-free greenhouse (minimum temperature 45°F/7°C) in a neutral to acidic gritty medium. Provide full sun and low air-humidity; keep dry from midfall until early spring, except for light misting on warm days in late winter. Increase by seed or offsets.

P. chrysacanthion N Argentina; stem globose, to 4¾ × 4 in (12 × 10 cm), apex woolly and tufted with erect spines, tubercles spiraled, spines 30–40, to 1¼ in (3 cm), golden-yellow or paler; flowers yellow; *P. microsperma* N Argentina; stem globose, sometimes elongate, 2–8 in (5–20 cm) × 2–4 in (5–10 cm), tubercles spiraled, spines ½–2 in (1–5 cm), red, brown and white; flowers yellow or red; *P. nivosa* N Argentina; stem globose to elongate, to 6 × 3 in (15 × 8 cm), tubercles spiraled, spines to ¾ in (2 cm), white or dark; flowers fiery red.

P

Paronychia (from Greek *para*, beside, and *onyx*, nail, from the ancient use of the plant as a remedy for whitlows). Caryophyllaceae. Tropical and warmer temperate regions, common in the Mediterranean area. WHITLOW-WORT About 40 species, low-growing annuals or perennials, usually with very small leaves with silvery stipules and small flowers in dense heads surrounded by conspicuous silvery bracts. Hardy to 14°F (−10°C). Grow in a warm open position in full sun, in sharply drained, sandy or gritty soil. Propagate by division in spring or from cuttings rooted in a closed case with bottom heat.

P. argentea S Europe, N Africa, SW Asia; much-branched mat-forming perennial; leaves ovate to lanceolate; inflorescence dense, partially covered by silvery, bracts; *P. capitata* Mediterranean; like *P. argentea* but with leaves linear to lanceolate and flowers in distinct, very silvery heads; *P. kapela* Mediterranean; like *P. argentea* but with flowers in distinct, very silvery heads.

parrot a class of tulip with frilled and twisted petals, usually accompanied by splashes or streaks of contrasting color.

Parrotia (for F. W. Parrot [1792–1841], German naturalist, traveler, and professor of medicine, who climbed Mount Ararat in 1829). Hamamelidaceae. N Iran. IRONWOOD, IRONTREE. 1 species, *P. persica*, a deciduous, slow-growing, shrub or tree, to 33 ft (10 m). The bark is smooth and gray, ultimately flaking to leave paler patches. In wild colonies, the habit is erect with ascending branches. Clones in cultivation tend to be lower-growing with a broad, loose crown of spreading to arching branches. To 4 in (10 cm) long, the leaves are ovate to obovate, deep green above, paler beneath. In fall, they color richly, turning from wine red to flame and amber. Clusters of small, red flowers are produced before the leaves. This tree is fully hardy and should be grown in sun or part-shade in deep, fertile, well-drained loamy soil. Acidic soil is preferable, although it shows good tolerance of alkaline and chalky soil. Propagate by seed in fall (germination may take up to 18 months), by softwood cuttings under mist in summer or by layering.

Parrotiopsis (from *Parrotia* and Greek *opsis*, appearance). Hamamelidaceae. Himalaya. 1 species, *P. jacqemontiana*, a deciduous, erect tree, to 20 ft (6 m). The leaves are ovate to orbicular, 2–3½ in (5–9 cm) long, short-toothed, and usually turn yellow in fall. Produced in spring and summer, the inflorescences are made up of densely packed heads of yellow stamens, subtended by white, petal-like bracts. Cultivate as for *Parrotia*.

parsley (*Petroselinum crispum*) a biennial herb, native of southern Europe and naturalized in many temperate countries; it is grown as an annual for garnishing and seasoning. Parsley is generally hardy but quality deteriorates without winter protection. There are two main forms, curled-leaved with thin roots, and French or flat-leaved with thicker roots; the latter is usually better flavored and often easier to grow. Parsley struggles in soil that is light, acidic or poorly drained.

For a summer crop sow *in situ* in spring, ⅝ in (15 mm) deep, in rows 8 in (20 cm) apart, thinning plants to 6 in (15 cm) apart; alternatively, raise in modules under protection. For an fall and over-wintered crop, sow in midsummer. Germination is slow and may take 5–6 weeks, with up to four months for plants to reach reasonable size. Seedlings may be potted up and grown on in large containers for convenient location indoors or outside. The crop needs to be kept well supplied with water. Plants can be cut to ground level for harvest once or twice during the year and protected with cloches to prolong quality.

Hamburg or turnip-rooted parsley (*P. crispum* var. *tuberosum*) is a dual-purpose form, producing smooth parsnip-like roots and usable leaves that are hardier than other types. Cultivate as for parsnip. Possible problems: carrot fly.

edible root

Hamburg parsley

parsnip (*Pastinaca sativa*) a biennial grown as an annual winter root vegetable, valued for its hardiness and distinctive flavor. It is a native of Siberia and Europe, including Britain, and has been cultivated at least since Roman times. Root length varies from 5–8 in (13–20 cm) and cultivars are available of squat, rounded form with tapering roots, others with long narrow roots, and some with broad-shouldered wedge-shaped roots.

Parsnips grow best in deep, well-cultivated soil free of stones. Seed rapidly loses viability so fresh seed must be used; germination is slow and erratic under cold conditions. Although the crop benefits from a long growing season, most success is achieved by April–May sowing as growing conditions improve. Sow *in situ*, ⅝–¾ in (15–20 mm) deep in rows 12 in (30 cm) apart for large roots. Place 3–4 seeds at 6 in (15 cm) stations, later thinning to one plant: closer spacings will produce smaller roots. Canker-resistant cultivars are available. In poor soil, good-quality roots may be grown from seed sown directly into planting holes, about 36 in (90 cm) deep and 6 in (15 cm) across, made with a crowbar; the planting hole is filled with a fertile loam-based mix. This technique is also used for exhibition specimens.

Parsnips are relatively slow-growing and suitable for intercropping with faster-growing species such as radish or small lettuce. Roots can be lifted from late summer onward but exposure to frost enhances flavor. They may be stored under cool conditions in boxes of sand. Possible problems: carrot fly, celery fly; canker.

parterre a level garden area of any size or shape containing ornamental flower beds. Parterres were highly developed in 16th-century France and Italy as separate garden areas set apart from the main garden by stone balustrades or hedges. The name superseded 'knot' in the 17th century, being of similar meaning. In the *parterre*

P

de broderie, the main pattern is laid out in masses of low-growing flowers edged with sand or soil, in the style of carpet bedding. A water parterre is a shallow formal pool in which a knot-like pattern is laid out in stonework.

parthenocarpy the development of fruit without fertilization of its ovules, as occurs in greenhouse cucumbers and the cultivated banana.

Parthenocissus (from Greek *parthenos*, virgin, and *kissos*, ivy, a play on 'virginia creeper'). Vitaceae. N America, E Asia, Himalaya. VIRGINIA CREEPER. 10 species, generally deciduous woody vines attaching themselves by branched, twining tendrils usually with adhesive disks. The leaves are palmately lobed or parted. Small, yellow-green flowers in cymose panicles give rise to dark blue or black berries. Attractive and vigorous, self-clinging climbers invaluable for growing through sturdy trees, over pergolas, walls and fences and for covering buildings. Cold-tolerance varies: –13°F (–25°C) for *P. quinquefolia* and at least 5°F (–15°C) for *P. tricuspidata* and its cultivars; *P. henryana* withstands cold to between 23–14°F (–5 and –10°C). Plant in moisture-retentive but well-drained fertile soil in shade or sun. Give initial support until plants produce adhesive pads. Prune annually, in fall or early winter where it is necessary to limit growth—for example, to keep it away from roof eaves. For pergola-trained specimens, cut the current season's growth back to one or two viable buds from the main framework, thus creating a spur system, from which the following season's growth can cascade.

Propagate by seed. Remove pulp and sow fresh outdoors or in a cold frame, or stratify for six weeks, at or just below 41°F (5°C), and sow under glass in spring. Alternatively, increase by 4–4¾ in (10–12 cm) basal hardwood cuttings of the current season's growth, taken immediately after leaf fall; treat with rooting hormone and root in individual pots with a bottom heat of 64–68°F (18–20°C). Increase also by simple layering.

P. henryana China; to 16 ft (5 m); leaves palmately 5-parted; leaflets 1½–4¾ in (4–12 cm), obovate to oblanceolate or narrowly ovate, acute at apex, tapered to base, coarsely dentate except near base, dark velvety red- or brown-green with pink and silvery variegations along main veins, especially at first, becoming dark green then red in fall; *P. quinquefolia* VIRGINIA CREEPER, WOODBINE; US to Mexico; to 100 ft (30 m); leaves usually 5-parted; leaflets 1–4 in (2.5–10 cm), elliptic to obovate, acutely serrate particularly toward acuminate apex, cuneate at base, bright to dull green, rich crimson in fall; *P. thomsonii* (syn. *Cayratia thomsonii*); W and C China; to 26 ft (8 m); leaves 5-parted; leaflets 1–4 in (2.5–10 cm), rather thick-textured, glossy, ovate to obovate, acute at apex, tapered to base, shallowly serrate above; bright purple-red when young, dark shining green tinged purple when mature, aging deep maroon; *P. tricuspidata* (syn. *Ampelopsis tricuspidata*); BOSTON IVY, JAPANESE CREEPER, VIRGINIA CREEPER; China, Japan; to 66 ft (20 m); leaves very variable, often so on the same plant, 2½–8 in (6–20 cm), broadly ovate and variably 3-lobed

Parthenocissus quinquefolia

with acuminate, serrate lobes or trifoliolate with stalked obovate leaflets, dull to glossy mid-green, turning crimson, scarlet or purple in fall; 'Atropurpurea': leaves large, green, tinged blue, purple-red in spring and fall; 'Lowii': MINIATURE JAPANESE IVY, smaller and more slender, with small leaves, ¾–1¼ in (2–3 cm), 3–7-lobed, bright green tinged purple when young, coloring brilliant red in fall; 'Veitchii': JAPANESE IVY, leaves small, simple or 3-foliate, and leaflets with 1–3 large teeth on each side, purple when young.

parthenogenesis the development of an embryo from an egg cell without fertilization, as occurs with dandelion (*Taraxacum officinale*) and certain aphids.

Passiflora (from Latin *passio*, passion, and *flos*, flower, hence 'passionflower'. The name was given by the early Spanish missionaries in South America,

in reference to a fancied representation in the flowers of the story of the Crucifixion; the corona represented the crown of thorns, the five anthers the five wounds, the three styles, the three nails, the five sepals and five petals the apostles (less Peter and Judas), and the handlike leaves and flagellate tendrils the hands and scourges of Christ's persecutors). Passifloraceae. Tropical Americas, Asia, Australia, Polynesia. GRANADILLA, PASSIONFLOWER. Some 500 species, those here evergreen, woody climbers with tightly spiraling tendrils. The flowers are usually solitary, with five fleshy or membranous sepals and five petals (these sometimes absent). The filaments are arranged in several series, forming a showy corona between petals and stamens. Five stamens are inserted on a gynophore and the stigma is capitate with three styles. Sometimes edible, the fruit is usually a juicy, indehiscent, many-seeded berry.

P. caerulea is hardy to –10°F (–23°C) and will thrive in moderately fertile, well-drained and adequately moisture-retentive soil, in sun or part shade. Provide the support of wire or trellis. In less favored areas, site with shelter from cold, drying winds and mulch the base, also protecting top growth with burlap or fleece if necessary. The remaining species need protected cultivation in cool temperate zones. *P. edulis*, *P. antioquiensis*, *P. × exoniensis*, *P. manicata* and *P. mollissima* need minimum temperatures of 50°F (10°C). Most of the remaining species require a minimum temperature of 59°F (15°C).

Grow all tender species in a freely draining, fibrous, loam-based mix with additional leaf mold and sharp sand. Protect from fierce sun in summer. Water plentifully when in growth, sparingly at other times. Prune to prevent overcrowding by removing the weakest shoots in spring, and again, if necessary, after flowering; pinch out unwanted growth regularly during the growing season; spur back to an established framework in spring. Propagate by heel or nodal cuttings rooted in a sandy propagating medium in a closed case, or by seed. Some frost-tender species show greater tolerance of low soil temperatures when grafted on to *P. caerulea*.

P

PASSIFLORA

Name	Distribution	Leaves	Flowers
P. alata **Comments:** Spring–summer. Fruit edible.	NE Peru, E Brazil	to 6 in (15 cm), ovate to oblong, membranous, glabrous	to 4¾ in (12 cm) diam., fragrant; sepals pale crimson; petals brilliant carmine; filaments banded purple red and white
P. antioquiensis *P. van-volxemii* BANANA PASSION FRUIT	Colombia **Comments:** Summer.	to 6 in (15 cm), ovate to lanceolate, or trilobed, serrate, hairy beneath	to 5 in (12.5 cm) diam.; sepals rose-red or magenta; petals often of a deeper shade than sepals; filaments violet
P. × belotii (*P. alata* × *P. caerulea*)	garden origin	trilobed	to 6 in (16 cm) diam., pink to purple, white outside; sepals white inside; filaments blue-violet tipped white
P. caerulea BLUE PASSIONFLOWER; PASSIONFLOWER **Comments:** Summer-fall. 'Constance Elliott': flowers ivory white. 'Grandiflora': flowers to 6 in (15 cm) diam. *P.* 'Amethyst' (*P. caerulea* × *P. kermesina*) flowers lavender/mauve.	Brazil, Argentina	to 4 in (10 cm), palmately 5–9-lobed, glabrous	to 4 in (10 cm) diam., faintly fragrant; sepals white or pink-white inside; petals of a slightly clearer color than sepals; filaments banded blue at apex, white at center, purple at base
P. capsularis **Comments:** Summer.	Nicaragua to C Brazil to Paraguay, Greater Antilles	to 2¾ in (7 cm), bilobed, lobes downward-pointing, lanceolate, 3-veined	to 2½ in (6 cm) diam.; sepals green-white; petals ivory; filaments yellow-white
P. coccinea *P. fulgens* RED GRANADILLA; RED PASSIONFLOWER **Comments:**	Guianas, S Venezuela, Peru, Bolivia, Brazil.	to 5½ in (14 cm), oblong, serrate or crenate	to 5 in (12.5 cm) diam.; sepals scarlet; petals vivid scarlet, filaments pale pink to white at base, deep purple toward apex
P. coriacea BAT-LEAF PASSIONFLOWER **Comments:**	Mexico to N Peru and N Bolivia, Guyana.	to 10 in (25 cm) across, usually lobed, broadly divergent, the whole leaf resembling a bat with outspread wings, coriaceous	to 1½ in (3.5 cm) diam.; sepals yellow-green; petals absent; filaments ivory
P. edulis PASSION FRUIT; PURPLE GRANADILLA; GRANADILLA **Comments:** Summer.	Brazil	to 4 in (10 cm), trilobed, dentate, shiny	to 3 in (7.5 cm) diam.; sepals white; petals paler; filaments white banded purple or indigo, strongly wavy toward tips
P. × exoniensis (*P. antioquiensis* × *P. mollissima*) **Comments:**	garden origin	to 4 in (10 cm), downy, trilobed	to 5 in (12.5 cm) diam., pendulous, cylindric, exterior brick red, interior rosy pink; petals bright pink with a violet tint in the throat; filaments white
P. foetida RUNNING POP; LOVE- IN-A-MIST; WILD WATER LEMON	South America, Puerto Rico, Jamaica, Lesser Antilles **Comments:** Summer–fall.	hastate, 3–5-lobed, thin-textured, hairy	to 2 in (5 cm) diam., surrounded by showy, deeply and finely fringed bracts; sepals white to ivory streaked green; petals, ivory-lilac; filaments white banded violet

P. antioquiensis   P. caerulea   P. 'Amethyst'   P. coccinea

PASSIFLORA

Name	Distribution	Leaves	Flowers
P. insignis *Tacsonia insignis* **Comments:** Summer–fall.	Bolivia, Peru.	to 10 in (25 cm), ovate to lanceolate, finely-toothed, coriaceous, shiny above, woolly beneath	pendulous to 3½ in (9 cm), tubular, sepals violet-crimson; petals rose-purple; filaments white, mottled blue
P. kermesina **Comments:**	E Brazil	to 3 in (8 cm), trilobed, lobes oblong to ovate, deep green above, somewhat glaucous and purple-tinted beneath	to 3 in (8 cm) diam.; sepals scarlet; petals similar to sepals, filaments violet-purple
P. × kewensis (*P. caerulea* × *P. kermesina*)	garden origin		3½ in (9 cm) diam., carmine, suffused blue
P. manicata *Tacsonia manicata* RED PASSION-FLOWER	Colombia to Peru	to 4 in (10 cm), trilobed, lobes ovate, serrate, downy beneath	vivid scarlet, tubular to bell-shaped, to 2 in (5 cm), long, green-white inside; filaments blue and white
P. mixta *Tacsonia mixta* **Comments:**	C Venezuela, Colombia, Ecuador, Peru, Bolivia	to 4 in (10 cm), trilobed, lobes ovate-oblong	pendulous, to 4½ in (11 cm), tubular, sepals pink to orange-red; petals same color on sepals; filaments deep lavender or purple
P. mollissima *Tacsonia mollissima* CURUBA; BANANA PASSION FRUIT	W Venezuela, Colombia, SE Peru, W Bolivia	to 4 in (10 cm), trilobed, lobes ovate, downy	pendulous, to 3 in (8 cm), tubular, sepals olive-green, soft pink; petals obtuse, same color as sepals
P. organensis *P. maculifolia*	E Brazil	to 4 in (10 cm), bilobed, shaped like a fishtail, dark green tinted purple to chocolate brown with regions of silver, cream, pink or lime green variegation	to 1¼ in (3 cm) diam., cream to dull purple
P. quadrangularis *P. macrocarpa* GRANADILLA; GIANT GRANADILLA	Tropical America **Comments:** Fruit edible. 'Variegata': leaves blotched yellow.	to 8 in (20 cm), ovate-lanceolate	to 4¾ in (12 cm) diam.; sepals pearly gray-green tinted flesh pink; petals fleshy, pale mauve-pink; filaments white, banded blue and red-purple, twisted
P. racemosa *P. princeps* RED PASSIONFLOWER	Brazil **Comments:**	to 4 in (10 cm), ovate and simple, or trilobed, coriaceous	to 4¾ in (12 cm) diam., scarlet-red or white, in pendulous racemes; filaments white banded dark purple
P. rubra	Colombia, Venezuela, Peru, Bolivia, E Brazil, W Indies	3 in (8 cm), bilobed, membranous, downy **Comments:** Autumn.	to 2 in (5 cm) diam., ivory; filaments red-purple or lavender
P. vitifolia **Comments:** Spring–summer.	C and S America	to 6 in (15 cm), trilobed, toothed, shiny above, hairy beneath	to 3½ in (9 cm) diam., scarlet, bright red or vermilion; filaments red to bright yellow

P. manicata

P. quadrangularis

P. racemosa

patching out the use of a small clump of seedlings for planting unthinned direct into a garden border. In the case of some plants which produce very delicate seedlings, such as bedding lobelia, the technique may be used at pricking-out stage instead of handling individual seedlings.

patellate, patelliform orbicular and thick, having a convex lower surface and a concave upper surface.

patent spreading.

Patersonia (for William Paterson [1755–1810], lieutenant-governor of New South Wales 1800–1810, an early botanical collector in Australia). Iridaceae. Australia, Borneo, New Guinea. About 20 species, perennial, rhizomatous herbs with a fan of linear leaves and short-lived flowers composed of three, broad and spreading outer tepals and three small, erect inner tepals. Grow in frost-free conditions in a light, fertile and well-drained medium in full sun, watering plentifully when in growth. Propagate by division or by seed in fall. *P. umbrosa* W Australia; to 20 in (50 cm); flowers blue; 'Xanthina': flowers yellow.

pathogen a microorganism that is harmful to its host and causes disease. Most are parasitic but some are primarily saprophytic and only become pathogenic if the host is injured or stressed.

pathotype a subdivision of a species of pathogen based on common pathogenicity characteristics, especially host range.

pathovar (abbrev. pv.) a strain or pathotype of a bacterial species that infects only plants in a certain genus or species.

patio originally, the inner courtyard of a house which was built in a square to form an enclosed open space. Derived from Arab architecture, patios are characteristic of Spanish gardens and are usually associated with pools, fountains, and plants in beds and containers. The term is now generally used to describe a paved area close to a

house, especially a sitting area, which may be better termed a terrace.

patio squares squares of wood used for paving.

Patrinia (from E.L.M. Patrin (1742–1814), French traveler in Siberia). Valerianaceae. Temperate Asia. Some 15 species, small, clump-forming herbaceous perennials with pinnately cut or lobed leaves. Produced in spring or summer in corymbose panicles, the small flowers consist of five spreading lobes. Hardy and suited to the herbaceous border, rock garden and woodland garden. Cultivate as for *Valeriana*. *P. triloba* Japan; to 24 in (60 cm); leaves to 2 in (5 cm), 3–5-pinnately lobed, toothed; flowers golden-yellow, fragrant.

patte d'oie used to describe a set of paths or vistas radiating from a central point.

Paulownia (for Anna Paulowna, daughter of Paul I, Czar of Russia [1795–1865]). Scrophulariaceae. E Asia. About 17 species, deciduous trees with stout shoots, large leaves and, in spring and summer, terminal panicles of showy, foxglovelike flowers. The pollution-tolerant *P. tomentosa* is grown as a street and park tree in cities of continental Europe and has become widely naturalized in the eastern states of the US, often as a roadside weed. *P. tomentosa* and its cultivar 'Lilacina' are also grown in the mixed border, for their juvenile foliage—when young plants are grown as stooled specimens, their downy heart-shaped leaves assume enormous proportions.

In temperate maritime climates, like Britain or Washington State, flowering may be poor and sporadic—the result of inadequate wood ripening and late frost. Once established, these trees are hardy to between 5 to –4°F (–15 and –20°C). Although frost-tender when young, they will usually resprout from the base if given a protective mulch at the roots in winter.

Grow in deep, moderately fertile, moisture-retentive but well-drained soil, in full sun with shelter from strong winds. For foliage effects, stool young plants back to the woody base in spring

and pinch out any sideshoots. Propagate from seed sown at 59–68°F (15–20°C) in spring, or when ripe; seed requires light for germination. Increase also from root cuttings in winter, or by semiripe, heeled cuttings in summer, in a cold frame. Overwinter under glass in the first year.

P. fortunei China, Japan; to 66 ft (20 m); leaves 5½–8 in (14–21 cm) × 2¾–4¾ in (7–12 cm), ovate to cordate, glabrous and shining above, densely hairy beneath; flowers 3–4 in (8–10 cm), cream flushed with lilac; *P. tomentosa* (syn. *P. imperialis*); C and W China; to 66 ft (20 m); leaves 8–39 in (20–100 cm) × 4¾–24 in (12–60 cm), broadly ovate, hairy above, densely so beneath; flowers 2–2½ in (5–6 cm), violet with yellow stripes inside; 'Coreana': leaves tinted yellow, woolly beneath, flowers violet, with throats speckled yellow inside; 'Lilacina': flowers pale lilac.

paver a clay or concrete paving block, used especially for patios and terraces.

pavilion a substantial garden building, more ostentatious than a garden house, usually architect-designed and often highly decorated inside and out.

paving various solid materials used for making paths, terraces, and patios, mainly of real or composition stone, but including concrete slabs, bricks, tiles and sets.

Pavonia (for Jose Antonio Pavon [d. 1840], Spanish botanist and traveler). Malvaceae. Tropics and subtropics. About 150 species, herbs, subshrubs and shrubs with *Abutilon*-like flowers. Cultivate as for tender, shrubby *Hibiscus*. *P.* × *gledhillii* (*P. makoyana* × *P. multiflora*); shrub to 6½ ft (2 m); epicalyx bright red, corolla to 1¼ in (3 cm), tubular, dark purple, anthers exserted, filaments bright red, pollen chalky lilac-blue; 'Kermesina': dwarf, with carmine flowers; 'Rosea': flowers rose.

Paxistima (from Greek *pachys*, thick, and *stigma*, stigma). Celastraceae. N America. 2 species, dwarf, evergreen, glabrous shrubs with 4-angled, corky and warted branches and leathery leaves and, in summer, very small, 4-petaled flowers. Fully hardy, evergreen groundcover for exposed situations in the rock garden. Propagate by semi-ripe cuttings, taken in late summer and given a little bottom heat. *P. canbyi* CLIFF GREEN, MOUNTAIN LOVER; N America; stem to 16 in (40 cm), decumbent, rooting; leaves to ¾ in (2 cm), linear to oblong, obtuse, revolute, entire or finely serrate; flowers green, to ⅛ in (2.5 mm); 'Compacta': hardy, dwarf, with dark green leaves later turning bronze.

peaches and nectarines the peach (*Prunus persica*) originated in China and is known to have been cultivated by at least 2000 bc; the nectarine is a smooth-skinned form of the peach, common in parts of Turkestan.

With the demise of large estate gardens and consequent loss of their beneficial wall sites, peaches and nectarines are now little grown in British gardens. A limiting factor is the widespread incidence of peach leaf curl disease which severely debilitates trees.

By contrast, they are widely grown both domestically and commercially in warmer climates, notably southern Europe, parts of the US, Australia, New Zealand, South Africa and China. The peach flowers early and requires warm spring weather, but any tendency toward a tropical climate will not provide adequate winter chilling.

Successful seedlings are often raised by amateurs, but when propagated for growing elsewhere, they are seldom successful. Established named cultivars are propagated by budding on to either seedling peach or selected clonal plum rootstocks known to be compatible with the peach and nectarine; the former produce quite large trees. Of the plum rootstocks 'Brompton' (vigorous) and 'St. Julien A' (semi-vigorous) are widely used.

A wide range of cultivars is available and since they have different chilling requirements, local advice should be sought on which are best-suited for individual localities. Peaches may be classified as: (a) white-fleshed and predominantly free-stoned; (b) yellow-fleshed, of firm texture and free-stoned; (c) yellow-fleshed and cling-stoned. In Britain, the peaches 'Peregrine' and 'Rochester' and the nectarines 'Early Rivers' and 'Lord Napier' generally perform well.

Most peaches and nectarines are self-fertile, but satisfactory pollination is encouraged by providing sheltered conditions, and since flowering is very early, hand-pollination is advisable to supplement insect activity. Using a soft camel-hair brush or cotton wool, the centers of open flowers are gently brushed, in the middle of each day, to transfer pollen from anthers to stigma.

Plant on to well-drained sites only, by midwinter to ensure good establishment before growth begins. Trees planted in the open ground should be supported with a stake for the first two seasons, and mulched. In Britain, two tree forms predominate, the bush for open-ground cultivation and the fan for wall-training. Plant bushes 16–23 ft (5–7 m) apart, and fans 11½–20 ft (3.5–6 m) apart, allowing greater distances for trees on peach seedlings and Brompton rootstocks. Shaping to achieve the desired form should be undertaken in the spring after planting.

With each form, it is important to establish a distinct branch system in order to produce annually a succession of young shoots for fruiting the following year; unlike apples and pears, peach and nectarine shoots carry fruit only once, after which they remain bare and unproductive.

Pruning is done while the tree is in active growth, not during winter when the risk of disease infection is greater. With bushes, prune a proportion of older shoots to young shoots, keeping the center of the tree open and removing branches that are too low, crowded or crossing.

With fans, select two new shoots arising from existing growths, one from the base and one half-way up; remove any others near the base, together with any growing awkwardly, and shorten the remainder to one leaf. Tie the new shoots in where possible. After the fruit has been gathered, either cut the fruit-bearing lateral back to the replacement shoot(s) or, in younger trees, tie in all new shoots to fill existing space.

Regular applications of a compound fertilizer, higher in nitrogen and potash than phosphate, should be given at about ¼ oz/sq. ft (75g/m²) in late winter, followed by a good mulch of well-rotted manure or compost when the soil is moist. A liquid feed high in potash can also be given after flowering, at three week intervals, to induce quality and disease resistance.

Irrigation in summer is likely to be essential for wall-trained trees: apply approximately 1 gallon (5 liters) around each tree every 10–14 days. Following successful pollination and fertilization, the number of fruitlets usually needs to be limited by thinning when approximately hazelnut size, reducing them to one per cluster and 3–4¾ in (8–12 cm) apart. Once at walnut size, thin again if necessary to about 9 in (22 cm) apart.

Peaches and nectarines in gardens should be picked when the flesh gives under gentle thumb pressure near the stalk end.

The use of fruit nets as bird protection is advisable against bullfinches damaging overwintering buds, and fruit damage by other birds. Frost protection of blossom on wall-trained trees can be provided by fixing burlap netting as a temporary cover.

Where climatic conditions are not conducive to regular cropping in the open, cultivation under glass is a practical although laborious alternative. A border of good deep soil is essential. A wall-trained fan tree is the best form to develop, hence a lean-to greenhouse is ideal. Heating is an advantage, and horizontal support wires fixed 2¾–3 in (7–8 cm) away from the wall will be needed. Pruning and training are as for fan-trained trees.

a greenhouse must be continuously ventilated once the crop has been cleared to allow adequate chilling. From late winter maintain a temperature of 46–50°F (8–10°C), raising this to approximately 68°F (20°C) after ten days, with a night minimum of 39–46°F (4–8°C). Careful attention to watering is essential, and on bright days the trees must be syringed with tepid water midmorning and early afternoon. Light top dressings of well-rotted manure or a compound fertilizer should be given in late winter, followed by liquid feeds high in potash every 10–14 days during summer. Peach leaf curl will not be a problem under glass, but mildew, aphids and red spider mite will require preventive measures.

Where there is no suitable greenhouse or garden space, cultivation in large containers is a possibility and trees can be moved to frost-free positions during the vulnerable periods of flowering, early fruitlet production and ripening. A miniature bush-type tree should be developed, firmly planted in a soil-based potting mix, watered regularly and fed every 10–14 days. Repotting in fall is necessary, replacing some of the medium and removing any coarse roots in favor of fibrous ones. The trees should be kept in the open through fall and winter to allow adequate chilling, with the rootball protected against freezing.

Possible problems: aphids, red spider mite, scale insects; bacterial canker (see *bacterial diseases*), brown rot, peach leaf curl, silver leaf; gumming.

peach leaf curl (*Taphrina deformans*) a fungus that affects almonds, nectarines, peaches and, rarely, apricots, becoming apparent as young leaves emerge in spring. The leaves become puckered, curled, twisted and sometimes chlorotic, and as they mature, the thickened parts change from yellow to red. A white bloom of fungus spores can sometimes be seen on the surface of swollen areas, and severely attacked leaves eventually fall off. The fungus survives on shoots or in buds, and spores infect young leaves as the buds open. Cold and wet spring weather favors the disease. Affected leaves should be removed and burnt as soon as seen, and a copper-based fungicide spray can be applied during the winter,

Controlling peach leaf curl
An open-sided screen, clad with clear plastic film from midwinter to spring, protects buds from spore-bearing rain.

at the latest just before the buds begin to swell. Infection can be reduced on wall-trained fruit by protecting the plants from rain in spring with temporary plastic shelters. Leaf curl due to severe aphid infestation can be confused with this fungal disease and close inspection is necessary. See *leaf blister*.

pea gravel small regular-shaped gravel, used especially by alpine gardeners for surface-mulching pots and sinks.

pea guard a narrow length of small-mesh wire netting formed into an inverted U-shape over wire supports to protect rows of seeds or seedlings from attack by birds.

peanuts (*Arachis hypogaea*) Leguminosae. S.America. GROUNDNUT, MONKEY NUT. Tender annual, erect or straggling herb to 24 in (60 cm) high, 12 in (30 cm) spread. A staple food crop in many tropical and subtropical zones; it is rich in oil, protein, minerals and vitamins. Leaves 4-foliate, leaflets $\frac{3}{8}$–$2\frac{3}{4}$ in (1–7 cm) × $\frac{3}{8}$–$1\frac{1}{8}$ in (1–3 cm) long, obovate or elliptic. Flowers yellow, veined red. Fruit develops below ground after shootlike structures, produced by fertilized flowers at flower drop, penetrate soil level. For optimum growth peanuts require an average temperature within the range 68–86°F (20–30°C). Can be grown in cool temperate zones for educational purposes under glass, at minimum temperature of 50–55°F (10–13°C), in full sun with good ventilation. Sow seeds in situ in spring into soil at temperature 59°F (15°C) minimum.

peanut shells the fruit husks of the peanut, (*Arachis hypogaea*), used as a soil- and potting-medium conditioner. Physical properties vary with particle size, the coarser grade improving drainage and aeration, the finer ones improving water-holding. Structural stability is reasonable, although decomposition continues during use. Nitrogen depletion, salinity, and pathogens are potential problems.

pears (*Pyrus* species) hardy deciduous trees grown for their distinctive and variably shaped fruits. Freedom from

Pear 'Conference'
A reliably cropping cultivar, regularly producing high yields of well-flavored fruits. Can produce some crop without cross pollination.

frost and high summer temperature is essential for consistent quality cropping. The European pear has developed mainly from *Pyrus communis*, which is indigenous to Europe and much of northern Asia, particularly the Caucasus and Turkestan. It is among the most long-lived of fruit trees.

The shape of pears varies greatly with cultivar, and the classification usually adopted (from Bunyard's *Handbook of Fruits—Apples and Pears*, 1920) includes six groups: (1) Flat and round (e.g. 'Passe Crassanne'); (2) Bergamotte (flat, rounded/conical, e.g. 'Winter Nelis'); (3) Conical (e.g. 'Beurré Hardy'); (4) Pyriform, or waisted (e.g. 'Doyenné du Comice', which is widely grown and accepted as the finest flavored pear); (5) Oval (e.g. 'Emile d'Heyst'); (6) Calabash, longer than pyriform (e.g. 'Conference', the most successfully grown pear in Britain).

Pears flower comparatively early and freedom from frost and summer warmth are essential for consistent cropping. Adequate shelter is necessary for cross-pollination, as is protection from cold winds, which can blacken leaves and fruitlets.

The pear usually succeeds on most soil types but calcareous sites may induce deficiencies of iron and manganese; it is intolerant of drought, so mulching and irrigation must be considered.

Most cultivars of European pear are not self-fertile and provision of suitable pollinator cultivars is imperative.

P

'Conference' is not self-fertile, as often erroneously stated, although it sometimes does produce parthenocarpic fruits under adverse conditions. Most cultivars are diploid, a few triploid or tetraploid, and flowering times vary so that it is essential to obtain detailed advice on pollination on purchase.

Propagation is by budding or grafting on to rootstocks of quince. 'Quince A' ('Angers Quince') is moderately vigorous and the most widely used; 'Quince C' is more dwarfing and having virus-free strains is useful for inducing early fruitfulness in vigorous cultivars such as 'Doyenné du Comice'. A major disadvantage of quince rootstock is that it is not compatible with some cultivars of pear, such as 'Williams Bon Chrétien', 'Jargonelle', 'Marie Louise' and 'Packham's Triumph', and double working is necessary.

Quince rootstock is insufficiently vigorous for the hot dry conditions often encountered in the fruit-growing areas of Australia, South Africa and the US, although it is used to produce small trees for gardens.

Plant in late fall or early winter while the soil is still comparatively warm. Staking, mulching and irrigation are important. Tree forms for garden trees are similar to those used for apple.

Established cropping pear trees develop more intricate spur systems than do apples. Pruning is done between leaf-fall and late winter, the degree depending on the fruit bud to growth ratio, with less pruning being required for vigorous trees than for those of more moderate or weak habit. Some laterals can be shortened to three or four buds to encourage spur formation, and a few of the most vigorous removed completely if overcrowded. Spur systems on older trees require shortening or selective removal. Branch shortening (dehorning) may be necessary when individual branches become too long, but in general tip-pruning should not be necessary. Where heavy crops develop, some fruit thinning is essential to enhance fruit size.

The harvesting of pears requires careful monitoring, particularly for earlier cultivars, which may be picked while still green yet parting readily from the spur; later cultivars must be allowed to mature fully.

Domestically, pears should be stored in cool, dark, slightly moist conditions, such as cellars or outhouses; the fruits are best not wrapped but laid out in single layers in trays. Alternatively they may be kept in a refrigerator, maintained above freezing level. They should be conditioned in normal room temperature (at 64°F/18°C) for 2–3 days before consumption, to ensure full flavor and good eating texture. In Britain, the possibility of bullfinch damage to overwintering buds should be noted. Netting the trees is the only certain protection: without it, severe damage can render a tree worthless.

ASIAN PEARS (ORIENTAL, CHINESE, JAPANESE, NASHI) are derived from *P. pyrifolia* and *P. ussuriensis*. Until recently they were generally restricted to their regions of origin in China and Japan, where they have been known and used since ancient times, but cultivation has expanded worldwide. The chilling requirement is less than that for European pears, and so the potential for extended cultivation is considerable.

In Britain the climate is not usually conducive to success, the fruit in poor seasons remaining small, and even in more favored regions the flavor is less rich and the texture crisper than that of European cultivars.

Cultivation requirements are similar to those of European pears. Rootstocks include Asian pear seedlings, *P. betulifolia* and *P. calleryana*; in Japan, *P. pyrifolia* seedlings are favored. Growth can be vigorous but trees tend to commence fruiting quite early. Fruit is borne on two-year and older wood, with some on one-year laterals. Asian pears are partially self-fertile and flowering occurs at the same time as with European pears, which are suitable as pollinators. Heavy fruit set requires judicious thinning. The trees can be decorative, with attractive white blossom, glossy green foliage and striking red fall coloring.

Possible problems: birds, aphids, capsid bug, gall midge, winter moth; brown rot, fireblight, canker, powdery mildew, scab.

peas (*Pisum sativum*) an annual, mostly grown for its edible seeds, but including

Young peas
Pea plants will make use of twiggy supports from an early stage. Prunings from coppiced shrubs such as *Cornus* are often ideal.

some cultivars in which the immature pod may be eaten. It is believed to have originated in central or southeast Asia, but is no longer found in the wild. Mature pea seeds were known as a food crop in Europe during the 15th century, and the cultivation of green peas is now widespread in temperate regions and highland areas of the tropics.

Garden peas are either round or wrinkle-seeded, the former being hardiest and the latter sweeter. Most cultivars have green pods but there are some with purple pods. Baby peas produce a very small well-flavored seed; snow or sugar types produce edible pods, some cultivars being dual purpose. Plant height varies from 18 in (45 cm) to 5 ft (1.5 m) and supports are essential or desirable. Cultivars are classified as earlies, second earlies and main crop and the earlier-maturing type are the most suitable for small gardens.

Most pea cultivars succeed in a cool, humid climate with a temperature range of 55–64°F (13–18°C). A minimum soil temperature of 50°F (10°C) is required for germination.

In mild areas, first sowings can be made in October or November, with protection from cold and mice. Otherwise, sow earlies from late February onward, preferably protecting with cloches, and follow with successional sowings at four week intervals until midsummer. Sow 1 in (2.5 cm) deep, 2 in (5 cm) apart, either in single rows or 9 in (23 cm)-wide flat-bottomed drills. Leave a distance between lines of approximately the ultimate height of the cultivar.

Emerging plants need to be protected from birds and weed competition, and peas should be rotated around the vegetable garden to deter a build up of soilborne disease. The roots produce nitrogen-fixing *Rhizobium* nodules, so that high nitrogen feeding should be avoided. Harvest regularly for prime quality and high yield.

Possible problems: aphids, birds, weevils, pea moth (see *moths*), thrips.

peat incompletely decomposed plant remains, predominantly sedges, reed and moss arising in certain wetland areas, often in vast drifts. In its formation, natural decay processes are arrested by acid waterlogging and the exclusion of oxygen; the remains of succeeding bog plants accumulate and are compacted to form peat. It is a slow process and the average growth rate of peat layers in British bogs is estimated at no more than $\frac{1}{16}$ in (1 mm) per year. Wetland peat habitat, especially raised bogs, is rich in bird, insect and plant life, including butterflies, moths, dragonflies and damselflies, the bog asphodel and insectivorous plants. Occasionally, peatland holds important information of archaeological interest.

The first extensive use of peat in horticulture stemmed from its disposal as a waste product from cattle bedding, where it formed part of a useful bulky organic soil additive. The significant development of peat as an ingredient of standardized seed and potting mixes dates back to development work at the John Innes Institute in the 1930s. The introduction of soilless potting mix in the 1960s led to the development of peat-based products, backed by intensive research and marketing to make multipurpose peat mix widely available.

Peat offers the advantages of good air- and water-holding properties, general freedom from plant pathogens and low nutrient content. It is slow to decompose, odorless, light in weight and valued for its light brown color. Its properties are however variable, depending on origin, age and processing; Sphagnum peat has excellent water-holding properties; sedge peat is more fully decomposed with less air-filled porosity and higher nitrogen content. Acidity varies with peat types

and sources and the pH range is usually between 3.5 and 5.

The harvesting of peat initially despoils the landscape, and also destroys or threatens wildlife habitat. Its use for the improvement of soil structure and as a surface mulch is unnecessary in view of the wide range of alternative, mainly bulky organic materials, many of which contribute more benefits. Incorporating peat for the purpose of acidifying soil is not advisable in view of the large quantities actually required to effect a change. For gardeners who wish to avoid the use of peat in growing media, alternatives are available, with coconut fiber, leaf mold and reduced wood products the most promising.

pectinate pinnately divided; the segments being many, slender and long, and close together, like the teeth of a comb.

ped an aggregate of soil particles; the basic unit of soil structure. A more general term than crumb.

pedate palmate except for the basal/lowest lobes on each side, which are themselves lobed.

pedicel the stalk of an individual flower or fruit.

pedicel necrosis a condition, particularly of roses or peonies, in which the pedicel just behind the flower bud shrivels and collapses. It is also known as bud disease or topple, and is usually the result of poor growth or sunscorch.

Pedilanthus (from Greek *pedilon*, a sandal or shoe, and *anthos*, flower, referring to the appearance of the flowers). Euphorbiaceae. Southern N America to tropical America. SLIPPER SPURGE, RED BIRD CACTUS, JEW BUSH. 14 species, succulent shrubs close to *Euphorbia* but with zygomorphic involucres composed of bracts resembling bird's heads. Provide a minimum temperature of 50°F (10°C). Grow in dappled sun or bright, indirect light in a dry, airy environment. Plant in a gritty, fast-draining medium. Water regularly in spring and summer, very sparingly

in winter. Increase by stem cuttings in spring. *P. tithymaloides* West Indies; evergreen or deciduous shrub, to 10 ft (3 m); leaves to 2½ in (6 cm), ovate to elliptic, keeled beneath; cyathia red above, yellow-green at base; subsp. *smallii*: DEVIL'S BACKBONE, JACOB'S LADDER, RIBBON CACTUS stems flexuous; 'Variegatus': leaves variegated white and red.

peg plant a young plant pulled from a seedbed to transplant into its growing position. It especially refers to brassica plants, the 'peg' alluding to the planting dibber.

Pelargonium (from Greek *pelargos*, stork: the fruit resembles the head and beak of a stork). Geraniaceae. Mostly from S Africa with a few from tropical Africa, Australia and Middle East; those here are S African. GERANIUM. About 250 species, subshrubs, herbaceous perennials and annuals, sometimes with tuberous roots. Most are aromatic, glandular and hairy, many have somewhat succulent or swollen stems and leaves. The flowers are borne in stalked umbels. They consist of 5 petals, the 2 upper petals usually larger than the lower 3.

Pelargonium includes many of the garden plants commonly known as 'Geraniums'. Those described here are perennials, although some of the hybrids and cultivars are treated as half-hardy 'annuals'. They usually succumb to wet cold and prolonged frost and are therefore tender in most cool temperate zones. Many have a long flowering season and are ideal for greenhouse or house decoration, for summer bedding schemes, tubs, window boxes and hanging baskets. The garden hybrids may be roughly divided into the following groups— Angel, Zonal and Regal Pelargoniums, valued for their flowers and foliage, Ivy-Leaved Pelargoniums, derived from *P. peltatum* and valued for their trailing habit, foliage and flowers, and the diverse Scented-Leaved Pelargoniums, with a range of foliage color and form, variously scented of apple, balsam, lemon, mint and spice. Under glass or in the home, they should be grown in a free-draining, gritty medium, in a brightly lit, dry and well-

P

583

PELARGONIUM

Name	Habit	Leaves	Flowers
P. abrotanifolium SOUTHERNWOOD GERANIUM	erect and bushy, to 20 in (50 cm), becoming woody	to ⅝ in (1.5 cm), aromatic, gray-green, finely divided	to ⅝ in (1.5 cm) diam., white or pink, upper 2 petals narrow, marked maroon

Comments: Scented-leaved and species category.

Angel pelargoniums
Similar to Regal pelargoniums, but seldom exceeding 12 in (30 cm) and always with single flowers. Fine examples of this group include 'Catford Belle' with rose-red flowers with darker markings, and 'Mrs. G.H. Smith', with off-white flowers marked pink.

Name	Habit	Leaves	Flowers
P. capitatum ROSE-SCENTED GERANIUM	to 3¼ ft (1 m), woody-based, decumbent or weakly erect, aromatic, softly hairy	¾–3 in (2–8 cm), 3–5-lobed, rose-scented, velvety with crinkled margins	to ¾ in (2 cm) diam., mauve-pink, upper 2 petals marked with darker veins

Comments: Scented-leaved and species category.

Name	Habit	Leaves	Flowers
P. carnosum	erect, to 12 in (30 cm) with a stout, succulent stem, gouty below, tapering above and covered in persistent leaf bases	to 6 in (15 cm), succulent, gray-green, pinnately lobed	to ½ in (1 cm) diam., white to pale yellow-green, upper 2 petals marked red

Name	Habit	Leaves	Flowers
P. crispum LEMON GERANIUM	erect, freely branched, aromatic subshrub to 28 in (70 cm)	to ⅝ in (1.5 cm), lemon-scented, rounded to reniform with crisped to obscurely lobed margins, coarsely hairy	to ¾ in (2 cm) diam., pink, upper petals marked deep pink

Comments: Scented-leaved and species category. 'Variegatum' has leaves edged with cream.

Name	Habit	Leaves	Flowers
P. Fragrans Group	erect, much-branched subshrubs to 16 in (40 cm)	usually small, cordate-ovate with three lobes and blunt teeth, gray-green, velvety, with a spicy scent	to ⅝ in (1.5 cm) diam., white, upper petals with red lines

Comments: Scented-leaved and species category. Includes 'Old Spice', compact, with gray-green, crinkled leaves, and 'Fragrans Variegatum' with leaves edged creamy yellow.

Name	Habit	Leaves	Flowers
P. graveolens ROSE GERANIUM, SWEET-SCENTED GERANIUM	erect, downy subshrub to 60 in (150 cm)	to 1½ in (4 cm), triangular, finely pinnately lobed, gray-green, rose-scented	to ⅝ in (1.5 cm) diam., palest pink, upper petals veined purple

Comments: Scented-leaved and species category.

Name	Habit	Leaves	Flowers
P. peltatum IVY GERANIUM, HANGING GERANIUM	trailing or climbing with slender stems	1¼–2¾ in (3–7 cm) diam., thinly fleshy, rounded in outline with 5 triangular lobes	to 1½ in (4 cm) diam., pale purple to pink, 2 upper petals with darker veins

Comments: This species is the parent of many excellent plants for hanging baskets, suspended pots, etc. Cultivars within the Ivy-leaved Group range from small- to large-leaved, with single to double flowers in shades of white, peach, salmon, orange-red, red, magenta and mauve. Some, such as 'Crocodile', have attractively variegated leaves.

P. 'Tip Top Duet' (Angel)

P. carnosum

P. crispum 'Variegatum'

P. graveolens

PELARGONIUM

Name	Habit	Leaves	Flowers
P. quercifolium OAK-LEAVED GERANIUM, ALMOND GERANIUM, VILLAGE OAK GERANIUM	erect, balsam-scented, clammy subshrub to 5 ft (1.5 m)	triangular, deeply pinnately or palmately divided, the lobes themselves divided and toothed, coarsely hairy	to ⅜ in (1.5 cm) diam., purple-pink, the upper petals marked darker pink

Comments: Scented-leaved and species category. 'Royal Oak': shrubby, leaves with rounded lobes, with purple-brown blotch.

Regal pelargoniums
Often grouped as *P.* × *domesticum*. A group of complex ancestry. To 20 in (50 cm) tall, the stems are usually thick and branching, giving a bushy habit well-furnished with foliage. The leaves are to 4 in (10 cm) diam., rounded to reniform, wavy and sharply toothed to obscurely 3-lobed and hairy. The flowers are large and showy (to 4 in (10 cm) diam.), carried in dense, straight-stalked umbels. Single or double, they consist of rounded and ruffled to lacy petals in a wide range of colors from white to rose, red, peach, salmon, orange, magenta, mauve and maroon-black and combinations thereof.

Scented-leaved pelargoniums
A varied group of hybrids and selections drawn largely from the scented-leaved species described here and sharing qualities of one or the other. The foliage may be scented of roses, peppermint, lemon, balsam or apple. The leaves may be small or large, rounded and ruffled to narrowly palmately lobed, mid- to gray-green and variegated white, yellow or marked chocolate brown. The flowers are generally small and white to pale pink, salmon or magenta.

Name	Habit	Leaves	Flowers
P. tomentosum	low-growing and spreading to 20 in (50 cm)	to 2½ in (6 cm), base cordate, with 3–5, rounded lobes, velvety, peppermint-scented	large, paired, cream to pale pink, upper petals marked purple

Comments: Scented-leaved and species category.

Name	Habit	Leaves	Flowers
P. triste	low-growing deciduous herb to 8 in (20 cm) with a swollen, woody caudex and rootstock	to 6 in (15 cm), ferny and very finely divided, softly downy	scented, petals narrow, cream to brown-purple overlaid with violet to maroon markings

Unique pelargoniums
Garden hybrids, these are sprawling to erect, woody-based plants with aromatic leaves, usually gray-green and palmately to pinnately lobed and toothed. The flowers are ¾–2 in (2–5 cm) diam., and range in color from white to pale pink, magenta, bright red and combinations thereof.

Zonal pelargoniums
Garden hybrids often grouped as *P.* × *hortorum*. These are the most popular members of the genus, widely grown for perennial display under glass or outdoors in favored regions, and otherwise used for summer bedding. The plants are generally tall with succulent, jointed stems, these eventually become leggy and woody. The leaves are up to 4 in (10 cm) diam., rounded to reniform and wavy to shallowly toothed; they may be plain green, variegated with white, cream, pink, purple-red and brown, or with a dark chocolate, horseshoelike marking (zoned). The flowers are freely produced in dense, long-stalked umbels. They are ¾–1½ in (2–4 cm) across, single or double, and composed, usually, of clawed obovate petals in shades of white, rose, pink, crimson, coral, peach, salmon, orange, flame and scarlet. Many cultivars have been named and further subcategories have emerged, namely *Cactus-flowered* petals furled or quilled; *Irenes* fast-growing and vigorous with large flower heads used for cutting; *Stellar* small plants with star-shaped, zoned leaves and flowers with cut and narrow petals; *Miniature* no taller than 5 in (13 cm), very free-flowering; *Rosebud* flowers double with many small petals resembling a half-opened rosebud.

P. quercifolium 'Royal Oak' *P.* 'Sefton' (Regal) *P.* 'Voodoo' (Unique) *P.* 'Freckles' (Zonal)

ventilated position. Water carefully at all times to avoid water-logging and keep nearly dry during periods of low temperatures and low light intensity.

Tuberous and succulent species like *P. triste* and *P. carnosum* lose their foliage and should be kept dry while dormant. These species should be grown permanently under glass and associate well with cacti and other succulents.

Feed container-grown plants regularly when in growth. Pinch out the tips of young plants to encourage branching and prune shrubby, vigorous types like the scented-leaved pelargoniums to avoid legginess. Many of the more robust hybrids benefit from severe pruning in fall; it also encourages growth suitable for use as cuttings. Overwinter species and hybrids in frost-free conditions. Plants used outdoors in summer need a sunny position and well-drained soil. Because their siting is not permanent, they may thrive for a season in conditions that would not suit them in the long term—for example, ivy-leaved pelargoniums in hanging baskets filled with a dense, soilless medium. Zonal pelargoniums may be overwintered as cuttings taken in mid- to late summer. Alternatively, old plants may be dug up and stored dry in a cool, frost-free place. Cut back, removing any dead growth, and repot in late winter when the plants show signs of regrowth. Regal pelargoniums need a temperature slightly above 41°F (5°C) in winter to continue growing and produce flowers for spring. Cuttings intended for bedding out should be hardened off before planting out after the last frosts. Deadheading will encourage a succession of blooms.

Increase by cuttings or (species) by seed. Small tubers and offsets of tuberous-rooted species may be detached and potted on. Whitefly is a serious pest under glass. The leaves of some species, especially the succulent types, may be scorched by insecticides. Gray mold will attack both cuttings and mature foliage. Cuttings may be killed by blackleg, a fungal disease that attacks the base of soft fleshy stems, blackening and rotting the tissue. It is encouraged by waterlogging and excess organic matter in the soil. (*See table, previous page.*)

Pellaea (from Greek *pellos*, dusky, referring to the dark stipes). Pteridaceae (Adiantaceae). Tropical and warm temperate regions. 80 species, evergreen ferns with dark-stalked, pinnate to variously compound fronds. Cultivate as for tender *Adiantum* species.

P. atropurpurea (PURPLE ROCK BRAKE; North America; fronds 4–10 in (10–25 cm) × 1½–4 in (4–10 cm), tufted, narrowly ovate-triangular to lanceolate, bipinnate, pinnules to ⅝ in (1.5 cm), ovate to elliptic-lanceolate, auriculate at base, attenuate at tip, often glaucous rusty-red when young); *P. rotundifolia* (BUTTON FERN; New Zealand, Australia; fronds 6–12 in (15–30 cm), narrowly oblong pinnate, pinnae ½–¾ in (1–2 cm), dark glossy green, narrowly oblong to suborbicular, apiculate, minutely crenate).

pelleted (pelletized) seed seed coated with an inert material, often incorporating a pesticide, to make it spherical and facilitate accurate and more economical mechanical or hand sowing.

peloria, peloric see *malformations*.

Peltate leaves
In *Darmera peltata*, the large leaves are attached centrally to their stalks; its common name is umbrella plant.

peltate a leaf whose stalk is attached inside its margin rather than at the edge, usually at the center beneath.

pendent hanging downward, more markedly than arching or nodding.

pendulous dependent.

penicillate brush-shaped, or like a tuft of hairs.

penjing the Chinese art of container cultivation, analogous to Japanese bonsai, and often a means of creating mixed miniature landscapes. In penjing, form is usually achieved by stricter pruning-based training than in bonsai.

Pennisetum (from Latin *penna*, feather, and *seta*, bristle, referring to the plumelike bristles of some species). Gramineae. Tropics, subtropics and warm temperate regions. Some 80 species, rhizomatous or stoloniferous, annual or perennial grasses with clumped, slender culms, narrow leaves and, in summer and fall, showy, foxtail- or bottle brush-like flower heads with feathery to bristly spikelets. The following are valued for their foliage and graceful flower heads produced from midsummer to fall. Some of the cultivars are among the most colorful and elegant of all ornamental grasses. They are not reliably hardy, but may be treated as half-hardy annuals or overwintered in a cool greenhouse. They are excellent candidates for mixed container plantings for patios. Grow in full sun in a fertile, gritty medium. Keep moist when in growth, rather drier in winter. Increase by division in spring, or by stem cuttings in a closed case or under mist in summer.

P. alopecuroides FOUNTAIN GRASS, CHINESE PENNISETUM, SWAMP FOX-TAIL GRASS; E Asia to W Australia; perennial to 5 ft (1.5 m); leaves to 24 × ½ in (60 × 1.2 cm), glabrous, scabrous; inflorescence cylindric to narrow-oblong, to 8 × 2 in (20 × 5 cm), yellow-green to dark purple; 'Burgundy Giant': to 4 ft (1.2 m), with broad leaves, bronze tinted claret; 'Hameln': dwarf, to 20 in (50 cm), with golden leaves in fall and white flowers tinted green; 'Moudry': low, with wide, dark green, shiny leaves and dark purple to black flower heads; 'Woodside': robust, with a dark purple inflorescence, early-flowering; var. *purpurascens*: dark purple spikelet bristles; var. *viridescens*: pale green spikelet bristles; *P. setaceum* FOUNTAIN GRASS; tropical Africa, SW Asia, Arabia; perennial to 36 in (90 cm); leaves to 12 × ⅛ in (30 × 0.3 cm), rigid, very scabrous; inflorescence erect to inclined, plumed, to 12 × 12 in (30 × 30 cm), tinged pink to purple; 'Purpureum': purple leaves and a deep crimson inflorescence; 'Rubrum': tall, with maroon leaves tinted bronze and deep burgundy plumes; *P. villosum* FEATHERTOP; NE tropical Africa; perennial, to 24 in (60 cm); leaves to 6 × ¼ in (15 cm × 0.6 cm); inflorescence cylindric to subglobose, compact, plumed, to 4½ × 2 in (11 × 5 cm), tinged tawny brown to purple.

penninerved, penniveined, penniribbed with closely arranged veins extending from the midrib in a featherlike manner.

Penstemon (from Greek *pente*, five, and *stemon*, stamen, referring to the prominent, sterile fifth stamen). Scrophulariaceae. Western N America, 1 species in Kamchatka and N Japan. About 250 species, subshrubs or perennial herbs, with terminal racemes or panicles of tubular, two-lipped flowers. Although hardy to 0°F (−18°C), the taller species and cultivars may be cut to the ground or killed by hard frosts. For this reason, they should be thickly mulched in fall and a few rooted cuttings overwintered in frost-free conditions as an insurance policy. They are otherwise colorful and undemanding perennials for the sunny herbaceous and mixed border, thriving in all well-drained, fertile soils. Low-growing small shrubs or mat-formers, such as *P. davidsonii*, *P. menziesii*, *P. newberryi*, *P. pinifolius* and *P. rupicola*, may be grown in full sun in rock gardens, alpine sinks, among paving stones or as front of border plants. They soon deteriorate in wet, cold conditions. Shear low, shrubby species back after flowering to maintain vigor, and cut back taller plants almost to ground level in spring after the last severe frosts. Propagate by semiripe cuttings of nonflowering side shoots in late summer, rooted in a sandy, free-draining medium in a closed frame and overwintered in their first year in frost-free conditions. Increase also from softwood cuttings in early summer. Herbaceous species forming basal tufts of foliage may be divided in spring.

P. barbatus New Mexico to Utah, Arizona and N Mexico; to 3¼ ft (1 m); leaves lanceolate to ovate, to linear; flowers 1¼–1½ in (3–4 cm), red tinged pink to carmine, lower lobes yellow-hirsute at base; 'Albus': white; 'Carneus': pale pink; subsp. *coccineus*: bright scarlet; 'Roseus': pink; *P. campan-*

ulatus Mexico and Guatemala; 12–24 in (30–60 cm); leaves linear-lanceolate, serrate, to 2¾ in (7 cm); flowers 1 in (2.5 cm)+, rosy purple or violet, glandular-pubescent; *P. confertus* YELLOW PENSTEMON; British Colombia to Alberta, Montana and Oregon; stem slender, ¾–2 in (2–5 cm); leaves 1¼–2¾ in (3–7 cm), lanceolate to oblanceolate, thin; flowers ⅜–½ in (8–12 mm), pale sulfur-yellow, palate brown-hirsute; 'Violaceus': violet; *P. davidsonii* Washington to California; forming creeping mats; flowering stems to 4 in (10 cm); leaves ¼–⅝ in (0.5–1.5 cm), elliptic to orbicular, minutely serrate; flowers ¾–1⅜ in (1.8–3.5 cm), violet purple; 'Broken Top Mountain': low, spreading, rich purple; 'Microphyllus': very compact, with small leaves and lavender flowers; *P. fructicosus* SHRUBBY PENSTEMON; Washington to Oregon, east to Montana and Wyoming; shrubby, to 16 in (40 cm); leaves ½–2 in (1–5 cm), lanceolate to elliptic, entire or thinly coriaceous; flowers lavender-blue to pale purple; 'Albus': white; 'Major': flowers large; *P. hartwegii* Mexico; stem 36–48 in (90–120 cm); leaves to 4 in (10 cm), lanceolate to ovate-lanceolate; flowers 2 in (5 cm), deep scarlet, minutely viscid-pubescent; *P. heterophyllus* FOOTHILL PENSTEMON; California; subshrub or shrub, 12–20 in (30–50 cm); leaves ¾–3 in (2–8 cm), linear to lanceolate green or leaden-gray; flowers 1–1½ in (2.5–3.5 cm), rosy violet below, lobes blue or opalescent lilac; 'Blue Gem': dwarf; 'Heavenly Blue': blue to mauve; *P. hirsutus* eastern N America; stem erect, 16–32 in (40–80 cm), minutely glandular-pubescent; leaves 2–4¾ in (5–12 cm), lanceolate to oblong, subentire to dentate; flowers 1 in (2.5 cm), dull purple with white lobes; 'Caeruleus': blue-tinted; 'Purpureus': clear purple; 'Pygmaeus': to 6 in (15 cm) high, violet; 'Roseus': pink; *P. isophyllus* Mexico; stem 28 in (70 cm), decumbent then erect, simple, stout, purple; leaves 1¼–1½ in (3–4 cm), lanceolate, revolute, rather thick;

Penstemon
'Andenken an
Friedrich Hahn'

flowers 1½ in (4 cm), red with a yellow throat; *P. newberryi* MOUNTAIN PRIDE; California and adjacent Nevada; forming mats 6–12 in (15–30 cm) tall, woody below; leaves ⅝–1½ in (1.5–4 cm), elliptic to ovate, minutely serrate, coriaceous; flowers ¾–1¼ in (2–3 cm), rosy red; *P. pinifolius* New Mexico to Arizona and Mexico; stems to 16 in (40 cm), numerous, woody below; leaves filiform, to ½ in (1 cm); flowers 1–1¼ in (2.5–3 cm), scarlet; 'Mersea Yellow': bright yellow; *P. procerus* SMALL-FLOWERED PENSTEMON; northwestern N America; stem 4–16 in (10–40 cm), slender; leaves ¾–2½ in (2–6 cm) lanceolate to oblanceolate or oblong, deep green, thin; flowers blue-purple; *P. rupicola* ROCK PENSTEMON; Washington to California; mat-forming, woody below, to 4 in (10 cm); leaves ⅜–¾ in (0.8–2 cm), elliptic to orbicular, minutely serrate-dentate, very glaucous, thick, glabrous or canescent; flowers 1¼ in (3 cm), deep rose; 'Albus': white; 'Diamond Lake': large, rich pink; 'Pink Dragon': light salmon-pink; 'Roseus': pink; *P. serrulatus* CASCADE PENSTEMON; S Alaska to Oregon; subshrub, 12–28 in (30–70 cm); leaves ¾–3½ in (2–9 cm), broadly lanceolate to spathulate, subentire to serrate or shallowly laciniate; flowers ⅝–1 in (1.5–2.5 cm), deep blue to dark purple; 'Albus': white. *Cultivars*: 'Alice Hindley': mauve and white; 'Amethyst': amethyst-blue; 'Andenken an Friedrich Hahn': deep wine red; 'Apple Blossom': small white, tipped pink; 'Burgundy': deep wine-purple; 'Edithae': shrubby, prostrate, deep lilac; 'Evelyn': neat, with narrow leaves and slim rose-pink flowers with pale striped throats; 'Firebird': clear red; 'Hidcote Pink': rose pink, throat white with dark pink streaks; 'Hidcote White': white; 'Hopley's Variegated': variegated form of 'Alice Hindley'; 'Maurice Gibb': rich cerise with a white throat; 'Mother of Pearl': white flushed purple; 'Old Candy Pink': vibrant pink; 'Osprey': pink, throat cream; 'Pink Endurance': candy-pink, with honey lines at throat;

'Prairie Fire': orange-red; 'Shoenholz-eri': deep red; 'Six Hills': prostrate with fleshy gray-green leaves, lilac; 'Sour Grapes': tinted purple; 'Weald Beacon': tinted blue.

pentamerous with parts in groups of five, or multiples of five; often written 5-merous.

pentaploid a polyploid with five sets of chromosomes.

Pentas (from Greek *pente*, five, referring to the characteristic number of floral parts). Rubiaceae. Tropical Arabia and Africa, Madagascar. Some 30 or 40 species, perennial or, rarely, biennial herbs or shrubs with ovate to lanceolate leaves. Produced at various times of year in crowded, much-branched cymes or flat-topped corymbs, the flowers are small, tubular to cylindric, with a spreading limb of five, ovate to oblong lobes. Grow in sun or light shade. Minimum temperature 50°F (10°C). Plant in a sandy, fertile mix. Water and feed freely in spring and summer. Keep moist in winter. Increase by soft stem-tip cuttings taken in late spring and inserted in a heated case. *P. lanceolata* (syn. *P. carnea*); STAR-CLUSTER, EGYPTIAN STAR-CLUSTER; Yemen to E Africa; herb or subshrub, to 6½ ft (2 m), erect or prostrate; flowers pink or magenta to lilac or, occasionally, white to 1½ in (4 cm) in dense, domed clusters.

Peperomia (from Greek *peperi*, pepper, and *homoios*, resembling, referring to its resemblance to the closely allied genus *Piper*). Piperaceae. Pantropical. RADIATOR PLANT. About 1000 species, small, generally evergreen, succulent herbs (those listed here are perennial). They are grown for their handsome, fleshy leaves, and, less commonly, for their narrow spikes of very small flowers. Suitable for the home, warm greenhouse or conservatory (minimum temperature 59°F/15°C). Grow in pots or hanging baskets in a porous but moisture-retentive medium rich in fibrous organic matter. Provide a moderately humid but buoyant atmosphere, with shade or bright indirect light. When in growth liquid-feed semi-weekly and water by drenching

thoroughly and allowing the medium to dry partially between waterings; in winter, keep just moist. Propagate by division, leaf or stem cuttings, or by seed.

P. argyreia (syn. *P. sandersii*); WATERMELON PLANT, WATERMELON PEPPER; northern S America to Brazil; stem to 8 in (20 cm), erect, dark red; leaves to 2¾ in (7 cm), broadly ovate, concave, acute at apex, rounded at base, peltate, silver-gray above with dark green stripes along main veins; *P. caperata* EMERALD-RIPPLE PEPPER, GREEN-RIPPLE PEPPER, LITTLE-FANTASY PEPPER; Brazil; stem erect to 8 in (20 cm); leaves 2¼ in (3.2 cm), cordate, broadly acute to rounded at apex, rounded or auriculate at base, often peltate, dark glossy green, veins impressed, in rippling folds; 'Tricolor': leaves with a wide cream edge, marked pink at base; 'Variegata': edged cream; *P. clusiifolia* West Indies, perhaps Venezuela; erect to 10 in (25 cm); leaves 3 in (7.5 cm), obovate to elliptic, broadly acute to rounded at apex, tapered to often clasping base, green or tinged purple, margin flushed maroon; 'Variegata': leaves light green, variegated cream toward edge, with a red margin; *P. fraseri* FLOWERING PEPEROMIA; Colombia and Ecuador; to 16 in (40 cm), erect; leaves 1½ in (3.5 cm), broadly ovate to suborbicular, acute at apex, cordate at base, tinged purple on veins, pale green beneath with bright red to pink veins and pink spots; flowers bright white, fragrant, mignonette-like, in spikes to 1½ in (4 cm); *P. glabella* C and S America, West Indies; to 8 in (20 cm), erect or sprawling; leaves 1½ in (3.8 cm), broadly elliptic to obovate, rounded to obtusely acute at apex, broadly tapered to rounded at base, green, often black-spotted, fleshy; 'Variegata': leaves edged or variegated off-white; *P. griseo-argentea* IVY-LEAF PEPEROMIA, SILVER-LEAF PEPPER, PLATINUM PEPPER; Brazil; to 8 in (20 cm), erect; leaves 1½ in (3.8 cm), cordate, broadly acute to rounded at apex, auriculate or rounded at base, often peltate, gray-green above, paler beneath, coriaceous, veins deeply impressed above; 'Nigra': leaves corrugated, metallic black; *P. magnoliifolia* Panama, northern S America and West Indies; differs from *P. obtusifolia* in its more upright habit and leaves more

contracted to rather acute apex; 'Greengold': leaves spattered green and yellow; 'Variegata': leaves variegated lime green; *P. marmorata* S Brazil; to 12 in (30 cm), stem erect; leaves 4 in (10 cm), ovate, obtuse to acute at apex, deeply cordate to auriculate at base with overlapping lobes, green above with silver-gray or white patterns between veins, coriaceous; 'Silver Heart': leaves dappled silver between veins; *P. metallica* Peru; to 6 in (15 cm), erect; leaves 1 in (2.5 cm), elliptic, acute at apex, broadly tapered to rounded at base, green tinged brown with silvery-green band above, tinged red beneath, succulent; *P. obtusifolia* BABY RUBBER PLANT, AMERICAN RUBBER PLANT, PEPPER-FACE; Mexico to northern S America and West Indies; stoloniferous, stem rooting, ascending, to 6 in (15 cm); leaves 4 in (10 cm), elliptic to obovate, rounded to emarginate at apex, cuneate at base; 'Alba': cream new growth and stem and petioles dotted red; 'Minima': dwarf, dense, with shiny leaves; 'Variegata': leaves more pointed, variegated pale green and marked cream toward margin; *P. rotundifolia* C and S America, West Indies; to 10 in (25 cm), creeping; leaves orbicular to broadly elliptic, rounded or cordate at base, ⅝ in (1.5 cm), green, paler beneath, sparsely hairy, fleshy; var. *pilosior*: more densely hairy, leaves with pale green reticulate pattern above; *P. rubella* West Indies; erect to 6 in (15 cm); leaves in whorls to ½ in (1 cm), elliptic, broadly acute to rounded at apex, broadly tapered to rounded at base, light to dark green above, flushed pink, convex and sparsely hairy beneath; *P. scandens* origin unknown; stem 24 in (60 cm)+, scandent, stout; leaves to 3 in (7.5 cm), ovate to suborbicular, long-acuminate at apex, truncate to subcordate at base.

pepo a multicarpellate fruit with fleshy pulp and a hard exocarp derived from the receptacle.

pepper dust a repellent to cats and dogs, sprinkled on and around plants and beds.

peppers annual or short-lived perennials, natives of tropical America, grown for their edible, often highly decorative fruits; they include the SWEET PEPPER (*Capsicum annuum* Grossum Group), the CHILI PEPPER (*Capsicum annuum* Longum Group) and the HOT PEPPER (*Capsicum frutescens*). Cultivars of sweet pepper may be red, yellow, orange or purple, ripening from green in warm conditions; they come in a range of shapes, round, tapering or irregularly oblong or bell-shaped and measuring 1¼–6 in (3–15 cm) long and 1¼–2¾ in (3–7 cm) in diameter.

Chili peppers have narrow, pointed fruits, ripening to bright red, with a hot flavor which increases in intensity with maturity. Sweet and chili pepper plants grow up to 30 in (75 cm) tall. Hot peppers are branching perennials, grown as annuals, which may reach 5 ft (1.5 m) in height and bear small red, orange or yellow fruits that are highly pungent; they need a long growing season.

For best results, peppers require a minimum temperature of 68°F (20°C) with 70–75% humidity, so greenhouse protection is desirable. Fruit set is adversely affected at 86°F (30°C) and above.

Sow under protection at 68°F (20°C) in mid-March for indoor cropping, one month later for outdoor cropping, either in trays for pricking out or direct into small pots or cell modules. Plant when 4 in (10 cm) high, 15–18 in (38–45 cm) apart, for sweet and chili peppers, 24 in (60 cm) apart for hot peppers. Plants normally branch naturally, but the terminal shoot may be pinched out to ensure a bushy habit. Most cultivars do not require staking, unless thay are over 30 in (75 cm) tall. Mulch the plants, water sparingly but regularly, and apply liquid feed every 14 days; keep damped down where under protection.

Peppers can be picked when still green, and are ready when glossy and smooth. They may be left on the plant to turn color, and generally are sweeter once ripened. Sweet peppers last well on the plant, and also freeze well. chili peppers may be left to shrivel on the plant and can be kept for long periods.

Chili pepper 'Anaheim'

See *Capsicum*. Possible problems: aphids, red spider mite; gray mold; blossom end rot.

perch see *rod*

perennial a plant that persists for more than two seasons. The term is most usually applied to herbaceous ornamentals, but, strictly, is applicable also to trees and woody shrubs.

Pereskia (for Nicholas Claude Fabry de Peiresc [1580–1637], councillor at Aix and patron of science). Cactaceae. S Mexico, C America, north and west S America, Brazil. 16 species, spiny trees, shrubs and woody climbers. They are true cacti, but lack obviously succulent stems; moreover, they bear "leaflike" leaves that are scarcely succulent. The flowers are rotate, showy and borne in panicles and corymbs. They are followed by berry- to pearlike fruit. Provide a minimum temperature of 50°F (10°C). Plant in a mildly acidic to neutral, gritty medium; shade in hot weather and maintain low humidity. Water freely in summer; keep dry from midfall until early spring, except for light misting on warm days in late winter. *P. aculeata* tropical America; woody climber to 33 ft (10 m); leaves lanceolate to elliptic or ovate, to 4½ in (11 cm), spines stipular or at areoles on older growth only; flowers 1–2 in (2.5–5 cm) in diameter, scented, white or nearly so; 'Godseffiana': leaves variegated yellow to peach-colored and purple-tinted beneath.

perfect a bisexual flower or an organ with all its constituent members.

perfoliate of a sessile leaf with basal lobes united and surrounding the stem, which then passes through the blade.

pergola a tall structure upon which climbing and rambling plants are grown. It normally consists of vertical brick or timber pillars supporting horizontal beams. Double pergolas are often constructed one to each side of a pathway and linked by cross pieces to form a covered walk.

perianth the collective term for the floral envelopes, the corolla and calyx; especially when the two are not clearly differentiated.

Pericallis (from Greek *peri*, around, and *kallos*, beauty). Compositae. Canary Islands. About 14 species, perennial herbs, subshrubs or shrubs with daisylike flower heads. The florists' cineraria, *P. × hybrida*, is the most frequently seen in cultivation, flowering within about six months from seed, and valued for the exceptional profusion of bloom which sometimes covers the plant so densely as to obscure the foliage. In warmer climates with frost-free winters and warm dry springs, *P. × hybrida* is sometimes used as bedding but is more usually grown as a winter-flowering house or cool conservatory plant and discarded after blooming. Available in a wide range of cultivars and seed races, from compact Grandiflora and Multiflora types to the more graceful, branching 'Stellata' forms, which carry the blooms clear of the mound of foliage.

Surface sow seed in early to late summer in a sandy, soilless propagating medium and germinate in light shade at 55°F (13°C). Prick out individually into small pots containing a low-fertility loam-based mix, and pot on successively into a medium-fertility potting mix. Ensure excellent drainage and water freely but carefully; plants collapse rapidly if overwatered. Liquid feed semiweekly when roots have filled the pots. Shade in summer, maintaining cool, humid and well-ventilated conditions at temperatures of no more than 59°F (15°C). Overwinter at 45–50°F (7–10°C), increasing temperatures to about 61°F (16°C) if necessary, to hasten flowering once buds have formed. The two species listed here need gritty soil in full sun with low humidity and a minimum temperature of 41°F (5°C). Increase by seed or stem cuttings in summer or fall.

P. cruenta Tenerife; white-woolly perennial herb to 3¼ ft (1 m); leaves ovate to triangular-cordate, 2–6 in (5–15 cm) wide, toothed, pink to purple-tomentose beneath; flower heads

1–1½ in (2.4–4 cm) in diameter, ray florets pink to maroon or purple, disk florets dark purple; *P.* × *hybrida* FLORIST'S CINERARIA; a variable complex of hybrids between *P. lanata* and *P. cruenta* and possibly other species—perennial herbs, often grown as annuals, forming compact cushions or openly branched plants to 3¼ ft (1 m); leaves ovate to suborbicular, often light green; flower heads to 2 in (5 cm) in diameter, florets white to pink, red, maroon, deep purple, violet, lilac and blue, ray florets sometimes bicolored, with white base and colored apex; numerous cultivars and seed races are available with flowers in a wide range of bright colors; *P. lanata* S Tenerife; white-hairy subshrub to 3¼ ft (1 m), ascending to procumbent; leaves to 6 in (15 cm), broadly ovate-cordate to suborbicular, toothed or pinnatifid; flower heads 1¼–2 in (3–5 cm) in diameter, violet-scented, ray florets mauve, disk florets purple.

pericarp the wall of a ripened ovary or fruit, sometimes differentiated into exocarp, mesocarp and endocarp.

periderm an outer layer of protective tissue on stems and roots which may consist of cork, cork cambium and phelloderm.

perigone the perianth, especially when undifferentiated; or anything surrounding a reproductive structure.

perigynous of flowers in which the perianth and stamens are apparently basally united and borne on the margins of a cup-shaped rim, itself borne on the receptacle of a superior ovary.

Perilla (derivation of name obscure). Labiatae. India to Japan. Some 6 species, fast-growing, half hardy annuals, grown for their ornamental and often aromatic foliage. Grow in rich, well-drained but moisture-retentive soil in full sun. Propagate from seed sown under glass in early spring, to plant out in early summer. Pinch out young plants to encourage bushiness. *P. frutescens* Himalaya to E Asia, naturalized Ukraine; to 3¼ ft (1 m), erect, pubescent; leaves 1¾–4¾ in (4.5–12 cm), broadly ovate, acuminate, corrugated, deeply serrate, green sometimes

speckled purple; 'Atropurpurea': leaves deep red-purple; var. *crispa*: leaves laciniate-dentate, dark bronze or purple with crisped, fringed margins; f. *rosea*: leaves crenate, variegated red-pink.

perlite, perlag heat-expanded granules of volcanic aluminosilicate mineral, used as a potting-mix ingredient or separately as a medium for rooting cuttings or for hydroculture. It has a stable structure and high porosity, with negligible nutrient content and cation-exchange capacity, and is a useful additive for improving drainage and aeration. The coarser formulation is known as perlag.

permaculture derived from the words permanent and culture; describing a philosophy and the practice of a holistic approach to cultivation. In the context of horticulture, permaculture involves working with the natural elements, with minimal labor input and high regard to conserving or enhancing the natural qualities of land and landscape. The tenets of permaculture extend beyond horticultural practices.

permanent wilting point the level of soil moisture content at which transpiration ceases and plants remain wilted even in a humid environment.

Perovskia (for the 19th-century Turkestani statesman, B. A. Perovskii). Labiatae. Asia Minor, Iran, C Asia, Himalaya. 7 species, deciduous, perennial, aromatic shrubs or subshrubs with deeply toothed or laciniate, gray-green leaves and, in summer and fall, panicles of many small, tubular flowers. All species are tolerant of dry chalk soil, suited to maritime situations and hardy to 5°F (–15°C), although stems above ground may be killed by frost. The best foliage effects are obtained on new growth and plants should be cut back almost to the base in spring. Grow in perfectly drained soil, in full sun. Propagate by softwood cuttings in

late spring, or from heeled cuttings of lateral shoots in summer.

P. abrotanoides Afghanistan, W Himalaya; to 3¼ ft (1 m); leaves to 2¾ in (7 cm), oval to oblong, bipinnatisect, gray-green; panicle to 16 in (40 cm), flowers 4–6 per whorl, calyx violet, corolla pink; *P. atriplicifolia* Afghanistan, Pakistan; to 60 in (150 cm); leaves to 2½ in (6 cm), lanceolate to cuneate, gray-green crenate or coarsely toothed; panicle narrow, flowers soft blue; 'Blue Mist', earlier flowering with light blue flowers, and 'Blue Spire', deeply cut leaves, lavender-blue flowers in a larger panicle; *P.* 'Hybrida' *P. abrotanoides* × *P. atriplicifolia*; leaves to 2 in (5 cm), ovate, pinnatisect to bipinnatisect, gray-green; inflorescence a long panicle of lavender-blue flowers.

perpetual plants that flower more or less continually over a long period, especially greenhouse carnations.

Persea (name used by Theophrastus for an Egyptian tree). Tropical and subtropical America, Macaronesia, SE Asia. Lauraceae. 150 species, evergreen trees or shrubs with large, entire leaves and small, yellow-green flowers massed in panicles. The fruit is a berry or drupe, ellipsoid to pyriform, with a leathery skin, richly oily flesh and a single, large nut. In cool temperate zones, *P. americana* is occasionally grown for interest, although plants are prone to leaf spotting, take up to seven years to flower, and, if grown from seed, are likely to produce fruit of inferior quality. Grow in a well-drained, medium- fertility, loam-based mix. Syringe daily in summer and water moderately when in growth, less in winter. Maintain a minimum temperature of 50°F (10°C). To germinate, plant the seed with the pointed end about ½ in (1 cm) above the surface of the potting mix. Keep moist and shaded at 59–68°F (15–20°C). Move into full light following germination, which may take up to six months. Propagate also by greenwood cuttings in a closed

seedling splits avocado stone

Persea from seed

case with bottom heat. *P. americana* AVOCADO PEAR, AGUACATE, ALLIGATOR PEAR, PALTA; C America; to 66 ft (20 m); leaves 4–10 in (10–25 cm), ovate to elliptic, subcoriaceous to papery, dull dark-green above, paler beneath; fruit ¾–4¾ in (2–12 cm), oblong-ovoid to pyriform, skin leathery, glossy dark green, pale-punctate, to dark purple-green and tuberculate, flesh lime green to yellow, firm, smooth and oily; seed ovoid, 1½ in (4 cm); numerous cultivars are grown commercially.

Persicaria (from Latin *persica*, peach, a reference to the shape of the leaves). Polygonaceae. Temperate Northern Hemisphere. FLEECE-FLOWER, KNOTWEED. Some 150 species, annual or perennial herbs or rarely shrubs, some aquatic. Stems appear jointed, often arising from rhizomes or stolons. The flowers, produced in spring and summer, are small, mostly with five petaloid segments; borne in usually spikelike terminal or axillary inflorescences. The small achenes have three angles or wings and are enclosed by the persistent perianth.

Persicaria is a diverse genus with species suited to the border, rock or wild garden. Although most have invasive potential, this can often be used to advantage in larger landscape plantings.

In cool, moist semi-shade, *P. campanulata* is a beautiful and robust perennial, bearing small, elegant, bell-shaped blooms over long periods in summer. In the herbaceous border the vigorous clump-forming *P. bistorta* is valued for its large, weed-smothering foliage and dense spikes of soft pink blooms; *P. milletii* is similar, but more compact. These border species flower for longer periods in moist soil. *P. amplexicaulis* is a stout, clump-forming perennial extending its period of interest from the first flush of bloom in midsummer often through until first frosts. *P. microcephala* 'Red Dragon' is a striking plant for an open site while *P. virginiana* (Variegata Group) 'Painter's Palette' is an equally remarkable foliage plant for cool, moist and semi-shaded places. The latter cultivar associates especially with hardy ferns, hostas, the smaller bamboos and grasses such as *Hakonechloa macra* 'Alboaurea'. Lower, mat-forming

species, such as *P. affinis* and *P. vaccinii-folia*, make good groundcover for the front of herbaceous borders and areas of the rock garden where their spread will not threaten less robust alpines. These last two are valuable for their late flowers, which dry to rich chestnut shades and persist into winter, creating a fine contrast with the rusty tints of the fading foliage. The attractively marked foliage of the creeping *P. capitata* also provides good low cover. It may need protection in zones experiencing winter temperatures below about 23°F (–5°C), or can be treated as a half-hardy annual. Most species are hardy to between 5 to –4°F (–15 and –20°C). Propagate perennials by division or increase by seed sown in a cold frame in spring.

P. affinis (syn. *Bistorta affinis*); Himalaya; low, mat-forming perennial to 10 in (25 cm); leaves 1⅛–4 in (3–10 cm), mostly basal, elliptic to oblanceolate, dark green, red-bronze to brown in fall; flowers in dense, erect spikes, 2–2¾ in (5–7 cm), pale pink to crimson or deep salmon red, often becoming darker with age; *P. amplexicaulis* (syn. *Bistorta amplexicaulis*); Himalaya; perennial to 3¼ ft (1 m), rootstock woody; leaves 3⅛–10 in (8–25 cm), ovate to lanceolate, acuminate, cordate at base, downy beneath, long-stalked or stem-clasping; flowers in loose spikes to 3⅛ in (8 cm), rose-red to purple or white; *P. bistorta* BISTORT, SNAKEWEED, EASTER LEDGES; Europe, N and W Asia; perennial to 24 in (60 cm), rootstock stout; leaves 4–8 in (10–20 cm), ovate to oblong, obtuse, truncate at base, wavy, long-stalked or sessile; flowers in dense, cylindrical spikes, rose, pale pink or white; *P. campanulata* LESSER KNOTWEED; Himalaya; creeping perennial to 3¼ ft (1 m); leaves 1⅜–4¾ in (3.5–12 cm), lanceolate to elliptic, white to pink-brown, hairy beneath; flowers in loosely branched, nodding panicles, pink to dark rose-red or white, fragrant; *P. capitata* Himalaya; perennial to 3 in (7.5 cm) with creeping rooting

stems to 12 in (30 cm), glandular-hairy; leaves to 1 in (2.5 cm) ovate to elliptic, green with a purple-bronze V-shaped marking; flowers pink in small, dense, rounded heads; *P. milletii* Himalayas to SW China; stem to 20 in (50 cm); leaves to 12 in (30 cm); linear-lanceolate to oblong, petiole winged, upper leaves clasping; flowers crimson in broad cylindrical to rounded head; *P. vacciniifolia* Himalaya; trailing perennial; stem woody, much-branched, to 12 in (30 cm); leaves ¼–1 in (1–2.5 cm), ovate or elliptic, glaucous beneath, petiole short; flowers in loose, erect spikes, pink; *P. virginiana* (syn. *Tovara virginiana*); Japan, Himalaya, NE US; perennial to 47 in (120 cm), glabrous to roughly hairy; leaves 3⅛–6 in (8–15 cm) ovate to elliptic, acuminate to rounded, glabrous to roughly pubescent; flowers in slender spikes, green-white or tinged pink and dark red bracts; 'Painter's Palette': leaves splashed and mottled with dark green, lime, gray, cream, pale yellow, salmon pink and maroon-black; 'Variegatum': leaves variegated ivory and primrose yellow.

**Persicaria
milletii**

persistent neither falling off nor withering.

perule a bud scale.

pest in its widest sense, any organism that causes harm or damage to humans, their animals, plants or possessions, even if only by annoyance. Invariably, the term is used more narrowly for animal organisms, as opposed to pathogens that cause disease, or weeds. Generally, a pest is considered to be of economic importance when it causes a reduction in yield of 5–10%; for gardeners, the relative importance of a particular pest is determined by circumstances. Methods of pest control can be broadly divided into those that are nonchemical and essentially preventive, and those that are chemical and mostly curative. nonchemical methods include cultural, mechanical, physical, legislative and biological control.

pesticides substances that kill animal organisms such as insects, eelworms, mites, slugs and snails, and rodents; but also used more generally to include chemicals for the control of plant diseases and weeds. They can be naturally occurring materials, a purified concentrate of such materials, or manufactured substances not found in nature. The term covers acaricides, algicides, bactericides, fungicides, herbicides, insecticides, molluscicides and nematicides. Pesticides are prepared in different ways to ensure efficiency, such as sprays, aerosols, dusts, smokes, seed dressing, fogging, injection, and weed wiping, cf. *biological controls*, *cultural controls*.

petal one of the modified leaves of the corolla, generally brightly colored and often providing a place on which pollinators may alight.

petal fall also known as blossom fall. See *bud stages*.

petaloid, petalody flower parts that take the form of petals in color, shape or texture, such as the calyces or stamens of double flowers.

Petasites (from Greek *petasos*, a broad-brimmed hat, referring to the shape of the leaves). Compositae. Northern temperate regions. BUTTERBUR, SWEET COLTSFOOT. Some 15 species, hardy, rhizomatous, perennial herbs with broad, stalked, basal leaves and buttonlike flower heads in a dense panicle, produced usually before the leaves. Although invasive, some *Petasites* are not without value in the garden. *P. fragrans* (not reliably hardy where temperatures fall below 5°F/−15°C) has strongly vanilla-scented flowers carried in midwinter, with or just before the leaves. Good groundcover for wilder areas of the garden, it tolerates drier conditions than other species. In moist and shady areas of the wild or woodland garden the hardy *P. japonicus* makes stately and impressive colonies, especially at the waterside. Both species may be confined by planting in sunken tubs or

barrels, although best effects are obtained *en masse*. Propagate by division or seed.

P. fragrans WINTER HELIOTROPE; C Mediterranean; to 12 in (30 cm); leaves reniform to cordate, lobed, glabrous above, pubescent beneath, toothed; flower heads white-pink, vanilla-scented; *P. japonicus* Korea, China, Japan, naturalized Europe; to 3¼ ft (1 m); leaves to 32 in (80 cm) in diameter, reniform to cordate, more or less lobed, glabrous above, pubescent beneath, toothed; flower heads pale mauve to almost white; var. *giganteus*: syn. *P. giganteus*, leaves 3–5 ft (0.9–1.5 m) across on petioles to 6½ ft (2 m); 'Nishiki-buki': leaves spotted milky yellow to cream.

petiolate, petioled furnished with a petiole.

petiole the leaf stalk.

petiolule the stalk of a leaflet.

Petrea (for Lord Robert James Petrie [1714–1743] of Thorndon, Essex, owner of one of the best private collections of exotics in Europe, supervised by Phillip Miller). Verbenaceae. Tropical America and Mexico; *P. volubilis* naturalized in India. 30 species, evergreen lianes, shrubs, or small trees with elongate racemes in summer. The flowers consist of a showy campanulate calyx with five linear-oblong lobes and a hypocrateriform corolla, darker than the calyx, with five rounded lobes. Under glass, grow in direct sun or bright filtered light with medium to high humidity and a winter minimum temperature of 50°F (10°C). Mist frequently in warm sunny weather. Plant in large tubs, open beds or under and through staging in a freely draining, nonalkaline medium enriched with leaf mold. Propagate by layering (both simple and air) or semi-hardened nodal cuttings inserted in sand with bottom heat and misted regularly. *P. volubilis* BLUEBIRD VINE, PURPLE WREATH, SAND PAPER VINE; C America and Lesser Antilles, introduced elsewhere; woody vine to

undershrub, to 39 ft (12 m); leaves to 8 in (21 cm), oblong to elliptic, subcoriaceous, scurfy to bumpy and bristly, deep green; inflorescence to 14 in (36 cm), calyx lilac, lobes to ¾ in (1.8 cm), corolla to ⅜ in (0.8 cm), indigo to amethyst.

Petrocosmea (from Greek *petros*, rock, and *kosmos*, decoration, referring to the natural habitat). Gesneriaceae. Asia. Some 29 species, perennial, rhizomatous herbs with hairy leaves in basal rosettes. Produced in summer, the flowers are solitary or clustered on scapose inflorescences, and resemble those of *Saintpaulia*. Near hardy to 10°F (−12°C) and elsewhere suitable for an alpine house. Grow in light shade in a fibrous, gritty, acidic mix. Keep moist and cool in summer; protect from damp and drafts from fall til spring. Increase by seed or by leaf cuttings in late spring. *P. kerrii* Thailand; leaves to 4 in (10 cm), ovate to oblong; flowers white, lobes blotched yellow at base.

Petrorhagia (from Greek *petros*, rock, and *rhagas*, fissure referring to the habitat). Caryophyllaceae. Eurasia, especially in the E Mediterranean. 25–30 species, summer-flowering annual or perennial herbs, resembling *Gypsophila*. Suitable for rock gardens, dry walls, raised beds and for border edging. Hardy to 5°F (−15°C). Grow in sun in well-drained, sandy soil. Propagate by seed sown in late winter, or by soft stem cuttings of nonflowering shoots in early summer. *P. saxifraga* S and C Europe; mat-forming perennial to 16 in (40 cm); leaves linear; inflorescence loose delicate, petals ¼–½ in (5–10 mm), pale pink with deeper veins, limb indented; includes cultivars with double and single, pure white, pale rose and deep pink flowers.

Petroselinum (from Greek *petros*, a rock, and *selinon*, parsley or celery). Umbelliferae. Europe. 3 species, biennial herbs with aromatic, ternately compound leaves and small, white or green-yellow flowers in compound umbels. *P. crispum* is PARSLEY (q.v.).

petiolule (leaflet stalk)

petiole (leaf stalk)

Compound leaf

P

Petunia (from the Brazilian *Petum*, a name applied to the closely related tobacco plant, *Nicotiana*). Solanaceae. Tropical S America. Some 35 species, downy annual or perennial herbs, subshrubs or shrubs with salverform to funnelform flowers. Colorful, half-hardy annuals used for bedding in borders, tubs and window boxes or cultivated in pots under glass for winter and early spring flowering. The dwarf types make particularly good edging plants, while the trailing cultivars are suitable for hanging baskets and as summer groundcover in borders; a single plant may cover up to 11 sq. ft (1 m²) of soil. Grandiflora Hybrids generally have fewer and larger flowers than the Multiflora types, but are less weather-resistant, spotting badly after rain: F1 hybrids of both types show increased vigor and uniformity.

All species tolerate poor soil and maritime exposure. They require plenty of sunshine and settled, dry summer weather to make a good display, although recent developments such as the 'Resisto' and 'Plum Crazy' mixtures show greatly improved performance in windy, rainy conditions. Propagate from seed pressed lightly on to the surface of a finely sieved seed mix: sow from late summer to fall for winter- to early spring-flowering pot plants, and from late winter to early spring for summer bedding. Germinate at 59–68°F (15–20°C) and keep evenly moist, watering from below when necessary. Prick out both large and small

Petunia Resisto Series
Some modern strains of petunia combine resistance to weather damage with qualities of continual flowering and brilliant color range.

seedlings in seed mixtures to retain the balance of color. Harden off in a cold frame for planting out after the last frosts. Increase also from softwood cuttings in late summer or early fall, or in spring from stock plants, cut back and top-dressed in late winter and then forced under gentle heat. Cuttings were the most common method of increasing cultivars until reliable seed races became available, and are still useful for the double-flowered and ruffle-edge sorts which do not always come true from seed. Affected by a range of viruses that cause leaf mosaic, mottling and failure to flower, including those viruses common to many of the Solanaceae, such as cucumber mosaic, tobacco mosaic and potato viruses X and Y.

P. × *hybrida* PETUNIA; a complex group of hybrids, thought to be *P. axillaris* × *P. integrifolia*—they are basically bushy plants, grown as annuals and covered with short, clammy hairs; the leaves are ovate to elliptic and the showy flowers funnel-shaped with a broad, spreading limb; among the most popular half-hardy bedding plants, petunias range in habit from the erect and robust to the small, low-growing or cascading; in flower size, from dwarf (to 2 in (5 cm) in diameter) to giant (to 6 in (15 cm) in diameter); in form, from single to semi-double, double and heavily crisped and ruffled; in flower color, from white to cream, blush, pale pink to deep rose, magenta, deep crimson, dark red, plum, deep purple, mauve, lilac and blue, and many cultivars are bicolored, with a contrasting throat or dark veins; two of the most successful new races are the Million Bells Series, miniatures with a low, bushy habit, neat foliage and flowers to 1¼ in (3 cm) across in shades of purple, magenta, and the Surfinia Series, with a cascading habit and masses of flowers to 2½ in (6 cm) diam., in various colors.

pF a logarithmic scale used as a common basis of expressing water content in soil. The range varies from about pF 2 for wet, well-drained soil to pF 7 for excessively dry soil.

pH a scale for the degree of acidity of a substance; the negative index of the logarithm of hydrogen ion concentration. Of special relevance to soil. pH

7.0 represents the neutral condition; pH values below this indicate acidity, and those above it, alkalinity. Soil pH may be measured by simple colorimetric methods or with a pH meter. See *soil*.

Phacelia (from Greek *phakelos*, a cluster, referring to the arrangement of the flowers). Hydrophyllaceae. Western N America, E US, S America. SCORPION WEED. 150 species, annual, biennial and perennial, downy to glandular-pubescent herbs, with pinnatifid, pinnatisect or entire leaves and 5-lobed, shortly tubular flowers in terminal cymes or racemes in summer. The following thrive in poor sandy soil, and, if overwintered in pots in the cool greenhouse at 41–45°F (5–7°C), are also useful for early spring flowers. Sow seed under glass in early spring or *in situ* in late spring in moderately fertile well-drained soil in sun.

P. campanularia CALIFORNIA BLUEBELL; S California; glandular-hispid annual, 6–16 in (15–40 cm); flowers to 1 in (2.5 cm), broadly campanulate-funnelform, dark blue spotted white at the base of each lobe, sometimes wholly white; *P. tanacetifolia* FIDDLE-NECK; California to Mexico; hispidulous annual, 6–48 in (15–120 cm); flowers to ⅝ in (1.5 cm), deeply campanulate, blue to lilac or mauve.

Phaedranassa (from Greek *phaidros*, bright, and *anassa*, lady, referring to the beauty of the flowers). Amaryllidaceae. S America. QUEEN LILY. 6 species, bulbous, herbaceous perennials with stalked, narrow to broadly oblong leaves. Produced in spring and summer in scapose umbels, the flowers are drooping, narrow and funnel-shaped or nearly cylindric, with five lobes spreading from the apex. Plant in fall, with the bulb neck at soil level, in a mix of equal parts loam, leaf mold, and sharp sand; keep cool and just moist until growth begins, then water moderately and grow in full light at a minimum temperature of 45°F (7°C). Dry off as foliage dies down in late summer or fall, and keep cool and dry over winter until growth resumes in early spring. Propagate by offsets and seed. *P. carnioli* S America; to 24 in (60 cm); flowers 6–10, to 2 in (5 cm), glaucous crimson, tipped

P

green with yellow fringe.

Phaius (from Greek *phaios*, gray, referring to the flowers which darken with age or damage). Orchidaceae. Indomalaya, S China, Tropical Australia. Some 50 species, large evergreen perennial herbs, with or without pseudobulbs. The leaves are large, elliptic to lanceolate and plicately ribbed. Carried in spring and summer on an axillary, erect raceme, the flowers consist of spreading, oblong to oblanceolate tepals and a funnelform lip. Grow in shaded, humid conditions with a minimum temperature of 59°F (15°C). Plant in a fast-draining mix of bark, leaf mold, charcoal, garden compost and a little dried FYM. Water throughout the year, allowing a slight drying between waterings and avoiding wetting of foliage. Re-pot every third year and increase by division.

P. flavus (syn. *P. maculatus*); India, Malaysia, Java; leaves spotted pale yellow, 16–19 in (40–48 cm); flowers 2½–3 in (6–8 cm) in diameter, yellow, rarely white, lip streaked red-brown; *P. tankervilleae* (syn. *P. grandifolius*, *P. wallichii*); Himalaya to Australia; leaves 12–39 in (30–100 cm), unspotted; flowers 4–5 in (10–12.5 cm) in diameter, tepals white, green or rose beneath, rusty red, yellow-brown, or white above, lip interior pink to burgundy, base yellow, exterior white, midlobe red-orange or white and pink.

Phalaenopsis (from Greek *phalaina*, moth, and *opsis*, appearance). Orchidaceae. Asia, Australasia. MOTH ORCHID. About 50 species, evergreen, perennial herbs. They are more or less stemless with a few, large and leathery, obovate to elliptic leaves in two loose ranks with, at their bases, numerous aerial roots. The flowers are borne in erect to arching racemes; the sepals are spreading, elliptic to broadly spathulate and usually smaller than petals; the lip is 3-lobed, the lateral lobes erect, the midlobe fleshy with an anchor- or arrow-shaped tip ending in hornlike projections or filaments.

Epiphytes for the intermediate or warm greenhouse, for growing cases (especially *P. cornu-cervi* and *P. violacea*) and for warm, shaded and humid positions in the home. They are valued

Phalaenopsis cornu-cervi
This delicate, star-shaped phalaenopsis requires specialist care and will often only succeed when grown in a closed case.

for their beautiful mothlike flowers matched, in some species, by superbly marked foliage (*P. schilleriana* and *P. stuartiana*). Many grexes are now offered. Grow in pots, baskets or on rafts. The medium should consist of coarse bark, perlag and charcoal. Aerial roots are common and should be encouraged by frequent mistings (periodically, with a dilute feed); never mist at temperatures below 64°F (18°C), since rots will be encouraged by an accumulation of moisture in the growth axis. A humid, buoyant atmosphere is essential, as is shade. Drench pots throughout the year whenever the medium begins to dry out. Propagate by meristem culture or by plantlets sometimes produced on old inflorescences. The genus is also easily raised from seed.

P. amabilis (syn. *P. grandiflora*); East Indies, Australia; leaves glossy green; inflorescence to 3¼ ft (1 m); flowers to 4 in (10 cm) in diameter, fragrant, tepals white, often pink below, lip white, base red, margins yellow, midlobe cruciform, side projections triangular, with 2 yellow-tipped appendages, callus yellow dotted red; *P. cornu-cervi* SE Asia; leaves olive green; inflorescence to 16 in (40 cm), stalk compressed; flowers waxy yellow to yellow-green, sepals marked red-brown, blotches stripes and spots cinnamon, lip fleshy, white, midlobe anchor-shaped, lateral lobes red-brown or striped cinnamon; *P. equestris* Philippines, Taiwan; leaves dark green above, often flushed rose-purple beneath; inflorescence arched, simple or branched, to 12 in (30 cm); flowers to 1½ in (4 cm) in diameter, tepals rose or

white suffused rose, lip deep pink to purple, midlobe ovate, concave, apex fleshy, callus yellow, spotted red, lateral lobes marked yellow; *P. gigantea* Borneo, Sabah; leaves glossy mid-green; inflorescence to 16 in (40 cm), flowers scented, cream to dull yellow, tepals blotched and lined maroon to dark purple, lip fleshy, white, striped, or lined magenta, midlobe ovate; *P. hieroglyphica* Philippines; leaves dark green; inflorescence pendent or arched; tepals white lined red-purple, apex tinted green, lip to ¾ in (2 cm), midlobe truncate, apex jagged; *P. lueddemanniana* Philippines; leaves dull olive green; inflorescence erect or pendent, to 12 in (30 cm), branched or simple, flexuous, becoming horizontal; flowers to 2½ in (6 cm) in diameter, tepals white, laterally or horizontally striped brown-purple, lip to 1 in (2.5 cm), carmine, base yellow, midlobe oblong to ovate, apical callus white, downy; *P. parishii* Himalaya, Vietnam; leaves dark green; inflorescence erect or arching, to 6 in (15 cm); tepals white, lip with midlobe purple, triangular, lateral lobes white or yellow, spotted brown or purple; *P. sanderiana* Philippines; leaves dark green above, marked silver-gray beneath; inflorescence to 32 in (80 cm), axis purple, branched or simple, flowers to 3 in (7.5 cm) in diameter, color and marking variable, tepals pink, dappled white, or wholly white, lip with midlobe triangular, white or yellow, striped purple or brown, apex with 2 filiform projections, callus horseshoe-shaped, yellow or white, spotted red, brown, or purple, lateral lobes white spotted pink; *P. schilleriana* Philippines; leaves dark green, mottled silver-gray above, purple beneath; inflorescence branching, pendent; flowers to 3 in (8 cm) in diameter, fragrant, white to pink, mauve and rose-purple, tepals edged white, lateral sepals spotted carmine-purple at base, lip midlobe white to magenta, anchor-shaped, lateral lobes yellow at base, dotted red-brown; *P. stuartiana* Philippines; leaves green blotched gray above, purple beneath; inflorescence branched, pendent, to 24 in (60 cm); flowers to 2½ in (6 cm) in diameter, fragrant, petals white, sepals white to yellow-green, dotted red-brown at base, lip anchor-shaped, white stained green to yellow spotted brown to orange; *P. violacea* Sumatra, Borneo, Malaysia; leaves glossy light green; inflorescence ascending or arched, thick, jointed, to 5 in (12.5 cm), usually shorter; flowers few, to 1¾ in (4.5 cm) in diameter, often fragrant, tepals amethyst fading to white or lime green at apex, lip midlobe oblong, apiculate, violet tipped with white down, central crest yellow, lateral lobes yellow; column white or amethyst.

Phalaris (Classical Greek name for a kind of grass). Gramineae. Temperate regions. Some 15 species, annual or perennial grasses with slender culms, narrow leaves and silky, spikelike to ovoid panicles in summer. Hardy to between 5 to –4°F (–15 and –20°C). Grow in sun or light shade. Tolerant of most soils and sites from pond margins to dry borders. Sometimes invasive; they can be confined where necessary by planting in a sunken, bottomless half barrel. Propagate by division. *P. arundinacea* REED CANARY GRASS, RIBBON GRASS; Eurasia, N America, S Africa; reedlike, fast-spreading rhizomatous perennial, to 5 ft (1.5 m); leaves to 14 in × ¾ in (35 × 1.8 cm), glabrous; inflorescence narrow, to 6½ in (17 cm); 'Dwarf's Garters': as var. *picta* 'Picta' but dwarf, to 12 in (30 cm); var. *picta* includes 'Picta': GARDENER'S GARTERS, invasive, leaves striped white, usually predominantly on one side of leaf; 'Luteopicta': small, with leaves striped golden-yellow; 'Feesey': small, less invasive, with light green leaves, boldly striped white, and a pink-tinted inflorescence; 'Streamlined': leaves mainly green, edged white; 'Tricolor': leaves white-striped with a strong pink flush.

phanerogam a spermatophyte; a plant reproducing by means of seeds not spores; cf. *cryptogam*.

phanerophyte a plant whose latent buds are located more than 20 in (50 cm) above the soil surface.

Phaseolus (Latin diminutive of Greek *phaselos*, name used by Dioscorides for a kind of bean). Leguminosae. New World. BEAN. Over 20 species, annual or perennial, usually climbing herbs with trifoliolate leaves,

pealike flowers and—usually—edible pods and seeds; see *beans*. *P. coccineus* is the SCARLET RUNNER BEAN; *P. lunatus* the LIMA BEAN; *P. vulgaris* the KIDNEY BEAN, HARICOT, COMMON BEAN, FRENCH BEAN or DWARF STRING, FLAGEOLET, SNAP BEAN.

phellem see *cork*.

Phellodendron (from Greek *phellos*, cork, and *dendron*, tree, referring to the corky bark of some species). Rutaceae. Temperate and subtropical E Asia. 10 species, aromatic, deciduous trees, their bark often thick and corky. They are grown for their handsome, pinnate foliage and fall color. Small, yellow-green flowers are carried in terminal panicles in early summer, and give rise to pea-sized, black fruits. They perform best in zones where summers are long and hot. The pungently aromatic foliage gives fine, clear yellow fall tints, and, on female trees, the black fruits often persist well into winter. Grow in deep, fertile, moisture-retentive but well-drained soil in an open position in full sun. Although hardy to at least –4°F (–20°C), the young growth is sometimes damaged by late spring frosts. Propagate by seed in fall, or by softwood or heeled semi-ripe cuttings in summer rooted in a closed case with bottom heat. Alternatively, take root cuttings in late winter.

P. amurense N China, Manchuria; to 50 ft (15 m); bark pale gray, corky; leaflets 2–4 in (5–10 cm), broadly ovate to lanceolate, dark glossy green above, glaucous beneath, turning yellow in fall; *P. chinense* C China; to 33 ft (10 m), bark thin, dark gray-brown; leaflets 2¾–5½ in (7–14 cm), oblong to lanceolate, yellow-green above, light green and tomentose beneath.

phelloderm a layer of parenchymatous tissue found on the inside of the cork cambium.

phellogen see *cork cambium*.

Phenakospermum (Greek *phenax*, a cheat or impostor, and *sperma*, seed). Strelitziaceae. Brazil, Guyana. 1 species, *P. guianense*, a giant herb to 33 ft (10 m), closely resembling *Ravenala* and *Strelitzia nicolai* except stems less

prominent, leaf blades to 6½ ft (2 m), dark glossy green, midrib often tinted coral-red, more elliptic to ovate than oblong to lanceolate. The inflorescence is terminal with white flowers amid carinate, deflexed bracts. Cultivate as for *Heliconia*.

phenomenal berry see *hybrid berries*.

phenotype the external appearance of an organism, which may vary according to its environment; for example, the foliage type of water crowsfoot (*Ranunculus aquatilis*) where growing in different depths and speeds of water; cf. *genotype*.

pheromone a chemical produced by an insect to induce a specific behavioral response, such as mating, in other insects of the same species. Pheromones are often useful in biological control or integrated pest management systems.

The principal types of pheromones are aggregation, sex, dispersal or spacing, alarm and trail pheromones. Aggregation pheromones stimulate individuals to aggregate for shelter, oviposition, colonization, feeding, or as a prelude to swarming or dispersal; they are widespread among insects such as cockroaches, bees, wasps and many beetles. Sex pheromones can be produced by either sex but they are most commonly produced by "calling" females to attract males; these

Pheromone trap
The sticky inner surface of traps are impregnated with synthetic pheromone, which lures the males of tortricid moths, an apple pest.

P

attractants or lures are often found in butterflies and moths. Dispersal or spacing pheromones are used by insects to prevent overexploitation of a food source; for example, the apple fruit fly applies the pheromone to the surface of apples and other host fruits after depositing eggs to deter other females from ovipositing. Alarm pheromones are characteristic of social insects such as wasps, bees and ants and are used to alert the colony to the presence of intruders; aphids secrete alarm pheromones when they are being attacked by predators. Trail pheromones occur commonly in social insects, particularly ants and termites; on locating a source of food, a worker ant lays down a pheromone trail back to the nest.

Once identified chemically, most pheromones can be prepared synthetically and the resulting compounds have a potential use in insect control for monitoring populations, mass trapping or mating disruption. Simple cardboard traps are available for pests including codling moth and other tortricids on apple, pea moth on peas, gypsy moth, fruit flies in citrus and peach orchards and Japanese beetle. By gathering information on populations, spraying can be more effectively timed and the total amount of insecticide required reduced.

Philadelphus (probably for Ptolemy Philadelphus (ruled 285–246 BC), patron of the arts and sciences). Hydrangeaceae (Philadelphaceae). C and N America, Caucasus, E Asia. MOCK ORANGE. 60 species, deciduous shrubs with peeling bark, ovate to lanceolate leaves and, in spring and summer, rounded, 4-petalled flowers with many stamens, usually fragrant and pale, in racemes, panicles, cymes, or solitary. They are easily grown in moderately fertile soil, including thin, chalky soil. Most will tolerate winter temperatures of at least 5°F (–15°C). They flower best in full sun. Cut back old shoots after flowering. Increase by softwood cuttings.

P. coronarius S Europe, Caucasus; shrub to 10 ft (3 m), bark dark brown, slowly peeling; current growth downy becoming glabrous; leaves 1¾–3½ in (4.5–9 cm), ovate, mostly glabrous, irregularly and shallowly toothed, apex acuminate; flowers 5–9 in short terminal racemes, creamy white, strongly fragrant, 1–1¼ in (2.5–3 cm) across; cultivars include 'Aureus', compact, with golden yellow to lime green leaves; 'Dianthiflorus', dwarf, with double flowers and narrow petals; 'Maculiformis', with 1¼ in (3 cm) flowers, with petals red at base; 'Salicifolius', with narrower leaves and tips of petals bearing a few hairs—may be of hybrid origin; 'Variegatus', with leaves edged white; *P. × cymosus* erect shrub to 8 ft (2.5 m); bark brown, not peeling; leaves ovate, sparsely toothed, hairy beneath; flowers white to cream, sometimes tinted rose, 1½–4 in (4–10 cm) in diameter, cupped to spreading, fragrant in cymes of 1–5; some stamens petal-like; cultivars include 'Nuée Blanche', with single to semi-double, creamy, fragrant, profuse flowers; 'Perle Blanche', of compact habit, with single to semi-double, fragrant flowers; 'Voie Lactée', vigorous, with large leaves and flowers, to 2 in (5 cm), freely produced and with reflexed petals; *P. delavayi* SW China; shrub to 13 ft (4 m); bark gray-brown, gray or chestnut-brown, not peeling; current growth glaucous; leaves ovate-lanceolate or ovate-oblong, acuminate, ¾–3 in (2–8 cm), serrate or entire, sparsely bristly above, shaggy-hairy beneath; flowers in raceme of 5–9, 1–1½ in (2.5–3.5 cm) across, disk-shaped, pure white, fragrant; calyx purple-tinted; includes 'Nymans Variety', with plum-colored calyx; *P. × lemoinei*. (*P. coronarius* × *P. microphyllus*); low compact shrub, bark peeling; leaves ⅝–1 in (1.5–2.5 cm), ovate, glabrous above, sparsely bristly below, apex acuminate, toothed; flowers usually in threes, fragrant, cross-shaped, about 1¼ in (3 cm) across, petals notched; cultivars range from arching to upright in habit, with 1–⅝ in (2.5–1.5 cm) leaves, mottled and variegated to smooth dark green, and 1–2½ in (2.5–6 cm) flowers, white to creamy, fragrant to very fragrant, and with petals sometimes waved, dentate or cut; *P. microphyllus*

SW US; erect shrub to 3¼ ft (1 m); new growth adpressed-pubescent, bark chestnut-brown, shiny, soon flaking; leaves ½–⅝ in (1–1.5 cm), oval-elliptic or lanceolate, entire and ciliate, glabrate above, softly shaggy-hairy beneath; flowering shoots ⅝–1½ in (1.5–4 cm) long, with 1 or rarely 2 pure white, very fragrant, cross-shaped, flowers about 1¼ in (3 cm) wide; *P. × polyanthus* (*P. insignis* × *P. lemoinei*); erect shrub, bark dark brown, peeling; new growth sparsely shaggy; leaves 1½ × 2 in (3.5 × 5 cm), ovate, apex acuminate, entire or with a few sharp teeth, sparsely bristly beneath; flowers 3–5 in cymes or corymbs cross-shaped, about 1¼ in (3 cm) across; cultivars include 'Favorite', to 6½ ft (2 m), with large, cross-shaped, cupped flowers, serrate petals and yellow stamens; and 'Pavillon Blanc', a low bush, with arching branches and creamy-white, fragrant flowers. *P. × purpureomaculatus* (*P. × lemoinei* × *P. coulteri*); shrub to 5 ft (1.5 m), bark black-brown, peeling in second year; new growth hairy; leaves ½–1½ in (1–3.5 cm), broadly ovate, tip acute, more or less entire, with a few scattered hairs beneath; flowers solitary or in threes or fives, fragrant, disk-shaped, 1–1¼ in (2.5–3 cm) across, white, purple at center; cultivars include 'Galathée', with arching branches and solitary flowers, with a pink center and 'Nuage Rose', with wide-opening flowers, with a pink center; *P. × virginalis* stiffly upright to 8 ft (2.5 m); bark gray, peeling when old; new growth hairy; leaves 1½–2¾ in (4–7 cm), ovate, apex shortly acuminate, becoming glabrous above, shaggy beneath; flowers in raceme, usually double, pure white, very fragrant, 1½–2 in (4–5 cm) wide; cultivars include 'Fleur de Neige', to 3¼ ft (1 m), with 1½ in (4 cm), semi-double flowers and yellow stamens; 'Fraicheur', with large, very double, creamy, profuse flowers; 'Glacier', with creamy, very double, late flowers and 'Schneestrum', fast-growing, with pure white double flowers. *Cultivars and*

Philadelphus coronarius "Aurea"

hybrids: 'Beauclerk' to 6½ ft (2 m), with pineapple-scented flowers to 3 in (8 cm), with a purple center and broad petals; 'Bicolore', dwarf, with 1¼ in (3 cm) leaves and creamy flowers with a purple center; 'Boule d'Argent', of compact habit, with 1½ in (4 cm), semi-double flowers in cymes of 5–7, scarcely fragrant; 'Buckley's Quill' (Frosty Morn' × 'Bouquet Blanc'), also known as 'Faxonii', of arching habit, and with cross-shaped flowers; 'Burfordiensis', to 10 ft (3 m), with 2¾ in (7 cm) flowers in raceme of 5–9, and conspicuous, yellow stamens; 'Etoile Rose', with flowers carmine at center fading at apex, scarcely fragrant; 'Frosty Morn', frost-tolerant, and with 1¼ in (3 cm), double flowers; 'Mont Blanc', to 3¼ ft (1 m), with cross-shaped, pure white flowers of a strong fragrance; 'Mrs. E. L. Robinson', with large, fragrant flowers; 'Patricia' (resembles *P. lewisii*), with leathery, dark green leaves and very fragrant flowers in raceme of 3–7; 'Slavinii', rounded bush to 10 ft (3 m), with 2½–3¾ in (6.5–9.5 cm) leaves and 2⅓ in (6 cm), cross-shaped, abundant flowers; 'Splendor' (possibly *P. inodorus* var. *grandiflorus* × *P. lewisii* var. *gordonianus*), of full, rounded habit, with single, wide-opening, slightly fragrant flowers with rounded petals; 'Stenopetalus' (possibly a form of *P. pubescens*), with campanulate flowers; 'Thelma' (origin unknown, possibly *P. purpurascens*), of low, graceful habit, with 1 in (2.5 cm) leaves and ⅝ in (1.5 cm), campanulate flowers; and 'Virginal', with double flowers in loose heads.

× **Philageria** (*Philesia* × *Lapageria*) Liliaceae (Philesiaceae). One garden hybrid, × *P. veitchii* (*P. magellanica* × *L.rosea*), a scrambling shrub, similar in habit to *Lapageria* but more shrubby and less vigorously climbing. The flowers are drooping and consist of three outer tepals to 1½ in (4 cm) long, fleshy, dull red deep or magenta with a glaucous bloom, and three inner tepals to 2½ in (6 cm) long, bright rose and more faintly bloomed. Cultivate as for *Lapageria*. Propagate by simple layering.

Philesia (from Greek *phileo*, to love, from the beauty of the flower). Liliaceae (Philesiaceae). Chile. 1 species, *P. magellanica*, a branching, erect shrubby

evergreen, 12–39 in (30–100 cm), with a dense, rather boxlike habit. The leaves are ⅝–1½ in (1.5–3.5 cm) long, oblong to lanceolate, leathery and deep glossy green. Produced in summer and early fall, the pendent flowers are narrowly campanulate with six tepals—these are 2½ in (6 cm) long and pink to purple-red, sometimes faintly flecked orange-pink. Cultivate as for *Lapageria*. Propagate by removal of suckers or by greenwood or semiripe cuttings in summer in a closed shaded case.

Phillyrea (Greek name for the genus). Oleaceae. Mediterranean to Asia Minor. MOCK PRIVET. 4 species, evergreen shrubs, with glossy green, glabrous leaves and small, fragrant, green-white flowers, resembling those of *Osmanthus*. These are followed by fleshy, ovoid, blue-black fruits. Cultivate as for *Osmanthus*.

P. angustifolia Mediterranean; shrub to 10 ft (3 m); leaves linear to lanceolate, usually entire; 'Rosmarinifolia': leaves narrower, smaller, gray-green, somewhat glaucous; *P. latifolia* Mediterranean; shrub or small tree to 30 ft (9 m); leaves ovate to lanceolate, dentate or entire; 'Buxifolia': leaves small, obovate; 'Spinosa': leaves spiny-dentate, ovate.

Philodendron (from Greek *phileo*, to love, and *dendron*, tree, alluding to the climbing or epiphytic habit). Araceae. Tropical America. 350+ species, epiphytic or terrestrial evergreen perennials, some climbing with long, slender, rooting stems, some with leaves in a dense basal rosette, or along or crowning a stout, unbranched stem. The leaves are often large, entire or lobed to pinnatifid to pedate, oblong or ovate, cordate to sagittate, coriaceous and usually dark, glossy green. They differ in size and shape in the juvenile and adult states. The inflorescence is *Monstera*-like and gives rise to white, orange or red berries.

Grow in an open, fertile, moisture-retentive mix of loam, coir or bark, leaf mold and coarse sand. Maintain a day temperature of 68–81°F (20–27°C), falling to 59–68°F (15–20°C) at night when in growth, with a winter minimum of 59°F (15°C). Site in part-shade or in filtered

Philodendron
Some species of this large genus are self supporting, but this climber specimen typically clasps and entwines tree trunks.

light, ensuring protection from bright summer sun; provide good air circulation, but avoid drafts. Mist frequently when in growth and water moderately, reducing as temperatures fall in winter. When plants are in full growth and roots have filled the pots, feed regularly with a 10:10:5 NPK liquid fertilizer. Train climbers on moss poles, wire cylinders filled with the potting medium, or canes. Smaller species will also trail, making good ground-cover and cascade plants for baskets and planters. The larger species may be pruned, or their stem tips repropagated, to create bushier, more or less freestanding specimens. Propagate by air layering, or by stem tip or leaf bud cuttings rooted in individual small pots in a closed case with a bottom heat of 68–77°F (20–25°C).

P. bipennifolium (syn. *P. panduraeforme*) of gardens; FIDDLELEAF, PANDA PLANT; SE Brazil; stems climbing, tall, internodes long; leaves to 18 × 6 in (45 × 15 cm), reflexed, 5-lobed, glossy dark green, terminal lobe long, to 10 × 4 in (25 × 10 cm), obovate, lateral lobes angular, obtuse, basal lobes broadly oblong-triangular; *P. cordatum* HEART-LEAF PHILODENDRON; SE Brazil; stems tall, climbing, internodes short; leaves 18 × 10 in (45 × 25 cm), reflexed, ovate-triangular, base sagittate, basal lobes round to angular, margins undulate; *P. domesticum* (syn. *P. hastatum*) of gardens; ELEPHANTS EAR; origin unknown; stems climbing; leaves to 24 × 12 in (60 × 30 cm), reflexed, elongate-

P

triangular, sagittate, undulate, glossy bright green, basal lobes rounded-oblong to triangular; 'Variegatum': leaves splashed yellow, cream and green; *P. erubescens* BLUSHING PHILODENDRON, RED-LEAF PHILODENDRON; Colombia; stems tall, climbing, purple or red-purple when young, with deep pink to pink-brown bracts; leaves to 16 in (40 cm), reflexed, ovate-triangular, base shortly sagittate to cordate, somewhat coriaceous, glossy dark green above, coppery-purple beneath; 'Burgundy': leaves to 12 in (30 cm), flushed red with burgundy veins, with a cordate to hastate base and claret stems; 'Golden Erubescens': climber, with thin, round stems and gold leaves, tinted pink beneath and when young; 'Imperial Red': leaves dark purple to red; and 'Red Emerald', vigorous, with claret stems and long-cordate leaves to 16 in (40 cm), dark green with red ribs beneath, shiny, and with long, rich red petioles; *P. imbe* (syn. *P. sellowianum*); SE Brazil; stem climbing, red-purple; leaves 13 × 7 in (33 × 18 cm), reflexed, ovate-oblong, cordate to sagittate, glossy above, basal lobes rounded; 'Goldiana': leaves long-ovate, rich green with gold speckles, red beneath, yellow when young, and with short petioles; 'Variegatum': leaves irregularly blotched green, dark green and cream; 'Weber's Self-heading': climber, with thick, very shiny, oblanceolate leaves, with a light green midrib, ribs red beneath, and petioles red spotted yellow-green; *P. melanochrysum* (syn. *P. andreanum*); BLACK-GOLD PHILODENDRON; Colombia; climbing; leaves 39 × 12 in (100 × 30 cm), reflexed to pendent, oblong-lanceolate or narrow-ovate, sagittate, acuminate, velvety black-green above, veins pale green, copper-colored when young; *P. pedatum* (syn. *P. laciniatum*, *P. laciniosum*); S Venezuela, Surinam to SE Brazil; stems tall, climbing; leaves reflexed, ovate in outline, irregularly pinnatifid, terminal lobe 18 × 12 in (45 × 30 cm), median segments elliptic, obovate or rhombic, lateral segments to 5 per side, oblong, obtuse, basal lobes 11 × 6½ in (27 × 17 cm), widely spreading; 'Purple Green': leaves flushed red-purple; *P. pinnatilobum* (syn. *P.* 'Fernleaf'); Brazil; climbing; leaves to 20 in (50 cm) across, erect, ovate-orbicular, pinnatifid, lateral segments ⅝ in (1.5 cm) across, to 13 per

side, narrow, acuminate, basal lobes bifid; *P. radiatum* (syn. *P. dubium*) of gardens; DUBIA PHILODENDRON; C America; climbing; leaves to 36 × 28 in (90 × 70 cm), reflexed, ovate in outline, cordate-sagittate, deeply pinnatifid, terminal lobe with 8 pairs oblong or further 3-parted segments, basal lobes 5-parted; *P. sagittifolium* (syn. *P. sagittatum*) of gardens; SE Mexico; stems climbing; leaves to 24 × 12 in (60 × 30 cm), long triangular-oblong, sagittate, subcoriaceous, glossy bright green, basal lobes to 5 in (12.5 cm), triangular, obtuse; *P. scandens* (syn. *P. cordatum*) of gardens; HEART-LEAF PHILODENDRON; Mexico and West Indies to SE Brazil; stems slender, climbing, becoming pendent; leaves (3(–12) in 8(–30 cm) × 2½–9 in (6–23 cm), reflexed, ovate-cordate, acuminate, glossy green above, green or red-purple beneath; f. *micans*: leaves bronze above, red to red-brown beneath, and basal lobes larger and slightly overlapping; subsp. *oxycardium*: juvenile leaves glossy brown when immature, green when mature; 'Variegatum': leaves dark green marbled off-white and green-gray.

Phlebodium (diminutive of Greek *phlebion*, vein). Polypodiaceae. Tropical America. Some 10 species, epiphytic ferns with thick and fleshy, creeping rhizomes and pinnately divided fronds bearing circular sori. Provide a minimum temperature of 45°F (7°C) and bright, indirect light. Plant in an open, soilless medium with added coarse bark. Keep moist and humid in warm weather, rather dry in cooler conditions. Propagate by division of rhizomes or by spores—these are freely produced and often sow themselves. *P. aureum* GOLDEN POLYPODY, RABBIT'S FOOT FERN, HARE'S FOOT FERN; tropical America; rhizome thick, hard and creeping; fronds 12–39 in (30–100 cm), deeply pinnatifid, segments linear to oblong or strap-shaped, sea green to glaucous blue-green, sori golden yellow.

Phlomis (from Greek *phlomos*, mullein, alluding to the woolly stems

and leaves of some species). Labiatae. Mediterranean to C Asia and China. About 100 species, downy, felted or woolly herbs or ever-green shrubs with tubular, 2-lipped and hooded flowers in summer; these arise from conspicuous and persistent calyces bunched in axillary whorls. The herbaceous species are hardy to 5°F (–15°C). With a sheltered position and good drainage, The shrubby species will tolerate temperatures almost as low. Grow in full sun in well-drained soil, with shelter from cold winds. The large-leaved *P. russeliana* tolerates light shade. Cut back shrubby species after flowering. Herbaceous perennials may be cut down in fall, although the dead flowering stems are sometimes left for winter interest. Propagate shrubby species by softwood cuttings in summer, or by semiripe cuttings in a sandy propagating mix in a cold frame in fall; increase also by simple layering. Divide herbaceous species in fall or spring. Sow seed in spring at 59–64°F (15–18°C).

P. cashmeriana Kashmir, West Himalaya; to 36 in (90 cm); stem densely woolly; leaves 5–9 in (13–23 cm), ovate-lanceolate, obtuse, broadly rounded at base, downy, white beneath; flowers pale lilac; *P. chrysophylla* Lebanon; low evergreen subshrub; leaves to 2½ in (6 cm), broadly elliptic to oblong-ovate, truncate to cordate at base, yellow-pubescent, golden and downy when young; flowers golden yellow; *P. fruticosa* JERUSALEM SAGE; Mediterranean west to Sardinia; spreading subshrub or shrub to 51 in (130 cm), tawny-hairy to felty; leaves 1¼–3½ in (3–9 cm), ovate to lanceolate, truncate or cuneate at base, dull sage green, rugose above, woolly beneath, entire or crenulate; flowers golden yellow; *P. italica* Balearic Islands, *not* native to Italy; subshrub to 20 in (50 cm); leaves to 4 in (10 cm), oblong to bluntly scutate or lanceolate, obtuse, white- to golden-felted, shallow-crenate; flowers pink or pale lilac; *P. longifolia* Anatolia, Syria, Lebanon, Cyprus; hairy shrub to 51 in (130 cm); leaves 1¼–2¾ in (3–7 cm), lanceolate to

Phlomis
fruticosa

oblong or ovate, cordate or subcordate at base, crenulate or crenate-serrate, green tomentose above, gray to yellow-tomentose beneath; flowers yellow; *P. russeliana* W Syria; to 3¼ ft (1 m); leaves 2½–8 in (6–20 cm), broadly ovate, obtuse, crenate, cordate at base, gray-green, thinly stellate-tomentose above, hoary beneath, long-stalked; flowers golden yellow.

Phlox (from Greek *phlox*, the name used for *Lychnis* by Theophrastus). Polemoniaceae. N America. PHLOX. 67 species, herbaceous to shrubby, evergreen or deciduous annuals or perennials. They vary widely in habit, from tufted and cushion-forming to tall and clumped. The leaves may be needle-like or ovate to lanceolate. The flowers are produced in late spring and summer in terminal corymbs or panicles (sometimes solitary in smaller species); they consist of a slender, short tube and a spreading limb of five, obovate lobes.

Grown for their tall, stately habit and generous masses of flowers, the taller herbaceous types, such as *P. paniculata* and *P. maculata*, have long been mainstays of the herbaceous and mixed border in summer, valued for their often intensely fragrant blooms in a wide range of colors from pure white through shades of pink to crimson and purple. They are also suitable for less formal situations, in the light dappled shade of the woodland edge. Grow in full sun or part shade in deep, moisture-retentive fertile soil that is rich in organic matter. Top-dress with a balanced fertilizer and mulch with well-rotted organic matter in spring. Staking is usually necessary only in exposed situations; deadhead to prevent self-sown seedlings which are usually of inferior quality. Divide in early spring. Alternatively, take stem cuttings in spring from forced rootstocks; increase also by root cuttings in late winter.

Most of the lower-growing types are suited to the rock garden and peat terrace, forming mats of foliage which become dense carpets of often brilliant color when in flower; the more vigorous species such as *P. subulata* and the slightly less rampant *P. douglasii* make good groundcover in the rock garden or at path edges, and are especially useful for softening hard lines at the border front. The smaller cushion-forming species such as *P. caespitosa* are suitable in scale for sink and trough plantings. Grow in fertile, well-drained soil enriched with leaf mold; *P. stolonifera*, *P. adsurgens* and *P.* × *procumbens* are calcifuge. Most species grow in full sun or in light shade in drier soil; *P. divaricata* prefers some shade. Clip over after flowering to remove dead flower heads. In an alpine house, grow in pans in a mix of equal parts loam, leaf mold and sharp sand. Propagate trailing species by removal of rooted sections in spring or early fall, cushion types by cuttings of nonflowering shoots in spring. Increase also by seed. The annual species such as *P. drummondii* and its cultivars are useful as seasonal fillers in the border or for bedding. Sow under glass in spring and harden off before planting out after the last frost.

P. adsurgens Oregon, N California; slender perennial; stem prostrate to ascending, to 12 in (30 cm); leaves ½–¾ in (1–2 cm), rounded to narrowly ovate, glabrous; inflorescence lax, few-flowered, hairy; flowers to 1 in (2.5 cm) in diameter, pink or purple; includes cultivars with lavender to deep pink flowers some with gray-green leaves and a dense, creeping habit; *P. amoena* SE US; perennial, decumbent to erect, to 24 in (60 cm); leaves to 2 in (5 cm), oblong to lanceolate, pilose; flowers magenta, red-purple, pink or white, crowded in a terminal cluster subtended by leafy bracts; *P. bifida* SAND PHLOX, tufted perennial to 8 in (20 cm); leaves to 1¼–2½ in (3–6 cm), distant, linear to narrowly elliptic, ciliate, pilose; flowers sweet-scented, ⅜–⅓ in (0.9–1.4 cm), lavender to white, lobes cleft; includes cultivars with fragrant white to pale lavender flowers and a low, compact, mat-forming habit; *P. divaricata* BLUE PHLOX, WILD SWEET WILLIAM; SE US; perennial to 18 in (45 cm), spreading; leaves to 2 in (5 cm), oblong to ovate or narrowly lanceolate; inflorescence a compound cyme, flowers ½–¾ in (1.2–1.8 cm), to 1½ in (4 cm) in diameter, lavender to pale violet or white, tube sometimes darker inside, lobes cleft to erose; includes cultivars with white and clear blue flowers; *P. douglasii* NW US; perennial to 8 in (20 cm) tall, usually less, loosely tufted, glandular-hairy; leaves ½ in (1–1.2 cm), stiff, subulate to linear, pointed; inflorescence 1–3 in (2.5–7.5 cm), 1–3-flowered; flowers strongly fragrant, white, lavender or pink, ½ in (1–1.3 cm), lobes about ⅓ in (7.5 mm), obovate, includes numerous cultivars

TYPES OF PHLOX

Border (P. paniculata 'Eva Cullum')

Alpine (P. douglasii 'Crackerjack')

Annual (P. drummondii 'Sternenzauber')

with flowers in shades of white, pink, crimson, magenta, mauve and lavender, some with a darker 'eye' or tint; *P. drummondii* ANNUAL PHLOX, DRUMMOND PHLOX; US (E Texas); annual, 4–20 in (10–50 cm) tall, hairy, sometimes glandular; leaves narrowly oblanceolate to ovate; flowers grouped in clusters ¹/₂–⁷/₈ in (1–2.2 cm), purple, violet, pink, lavender, red or white, rarely pale yellow, often paler inside tube with markings around throat; cultivars and seed races include tall to dwarf plants with flowers in shades of white, pink, red and purple and combinations thereof, some with cut and fringed margins; *P. hoodii* northwest N America; dwarf, tufted, mat-forming perennial to 2¹/₂ in (6 cm) high; leaves to ¹/₂ in (1 cm), subulate, tomentose; flowers solitary, white to pink, magenta or palest violet; *P. maculata* MEADOW PHLOX, WILD SWEET WILLIAM; US; rhizomatous perennial, 14–28 in (35–70 cm) tall, glabrous to minutely hairy; stem often red-spotted; leaves 2¹/₂–5 in (6.5–13 cm), linear to ovate; inflorescence a many-flowered panicle, flowers often sweetly scented, ³/₄–1 in (1.8–2.5 cm), pink, purple or white, sometimes with a dark purple ring in throat; includes cultivars with white to pink or lilac flowers, often fragrant and with a dark ring or blotch in the throat; *P. paniculata* GARDEN PHLOX; US; erect perennial 24–39 in (60–100 cm) tall, subglabrous to puberulent; leaves ¹/₂–4³/₄ in (1.2–12 cm) ovate or lanceolate to elliptic, toothed, ciliate; inflorescence a terminal, compound cyme, many-flowered, flowers ³/₄–1¹/₈ in (2–2.8 cm), blue, lavender, pink or white; many cultivars ranging in habit from medium to tall with flowers in large, cylindrical to pyramidal heads and ranging in color from white to pink, purple or red, often with darker throats; some, for example 'Harlequin', have variegated leaves; *P.* × *procumbens* (*P. stolonifera* × *P. subulata*); decumbent clump-forming perennial, 6–10 in (15–25 cm) tall; leaves to 1 in (2.5 cm), oblanceolate to elliptic; inflorescence a lax, flat panicle, flowers bright purple; includes selections with a dense habit, dark green to variegated leaves and pale rose to lilac-pink flowers; *P. stolonifera* CREEPING PHLOX; E US; creeping perennial, forming 6–10 in (15–25 cm) tall mats; leaves to 1³/₄ in

(4.5 cm), obovate and long-stalked to oblong, sessile; inflorescence lax, about 6-flowered, glandular-hairy, flowers to 1 in (2.5 cm), violet to lavender or purple to lilac; includes cultivars with flowers in shades of white, rose, mauve, violet and blue, some with yellow 'eyes'; *P. subulata* CREEPING PHLOX, MOSS PHLOX, MOUNTAIN PHLOX, MOSS PINK; E US; downy perennial, forming dense mats or cushions to 20 in (50 cm) downy; leaves ¹/₄–³/₄ in (0.5–2 cm), rigid, needlelike to subulate; inflorescence a few-flowered, terminal, bracteate cyme; flowers to ⁵/₈ in (1.5 cm), white, pink or lavender; includes cultivars with white, rose, carmine and violet flowers, many with a darker 'eye', some fragrant.

Phoenix (Greek word for the date palm). Palmae. Africa, Asia. DATE PALM. Some 17 species, large, evergreen palms with solitary or clustered trunks clothed with persistent leaf bases or scars. The leaves are pinnate with tough-textured, narrow leaflets, the lowermost reduced to spines. Erect to arching, the inflorescences bear cream-yellow or pale orange flowers. These are followed by oblong-ellipsoid to ovoid, 1-seeded fruits, their skin waxy and shiny, the mesocarp fleshy or pasty and often sweetly edible.

P. dactylifera and *P. canariensis* withstand full sun and dry atmospheres, and are tolerant of a wide range of soil types. In frost-free zones, they are excellent trees for specimen and avenue plantings. In colder areas, younger examples can be used for dot planting in bedding schemes and for containers on terraces; overwinter in cool greenhouse conditions and move outdoors after the last frosts. In mild locations (min. 0°F/ –18°C), young plants may survive outside all year, especially if the base is lagged with thick sacking. *P. roebelinii* requires a minimum temperature of 55°F (13°C), bright light and a well-drained, fibrous, loam-based medium. Water and feed plentifully in warm weather; keep rather dry at other times. This is a graceful palm ideally suited to cultivation in the home when young. Older plants are a popular choice for large containers in public buildings, and for interior landscaping. Propagate from seed, after soaking for

24 hours, with a bottom heat of 68–81° (20–27°C).

P. canariensis CANARY ISLAND DATE, CANARY DATE PALM; Canary Islands; trunk to 50 ft × 36 in (15 × 0.9 m), solitary with oblong scars, these wider than long; leaves to 20 ft (6 m), rachis sometimes twisted, pinnae crowded, regularly spaced; fruit ³/₄ in (2 cm), oblong-ellipsoid, yellow tinged red; *P. dactylifera* DATE, DATE PALM; cultigen, probably originating in W Asia and N Africa; trunk to 100 ft (30 m), slender, suckering, scars as long as wide, or longer; leaves to 10 ft (3 m), rachis rigid, pinnae 12 × ³/₄ in (30 × 2 cm), to 80 on each side, regularly spaced or clustered, rigid; fruit 1¹/₂–2³/₄ in (4–7 cm), oblong-ellipsoid, yellow to brown, edible; *P. roebelinii* MINIATURE DATE PALM, PYGMY DATE PALM, ROEBELIN PALM; Laos; stem to 6¹/₂ ft (2 m), slender at base, expanding toward crown, often leaning, roots forming a basal mass; leaves to 4 ft (1.2 m), pinnae to 10 × ¹/₂ in (25 × 1 cm), gray-green, regularly spaced, drooping, silver-scurfy; fruit to ¹/₂ in (1 cm), ellipsoid, black.

Phormium (from Greek *phormion*, a woven mat—referring to the use made of the fiber). Agavaceae. New Zealand. FLAX LILY. 2 species, large or giant evergreen, perennial herbs with basal clumps of tough-textured, keeled, sword-shaped leaves. Carried in summer, in tall, dark-stalked and tiered panicles, the flowers are tubular and consist of six tepals, their tips curved upward and the stamens protruding. Hardy to 0°F (–18°C), especially if given a deep winter mulch of bracken litter or leaf mold. The typical plants and larger cultivars are unsurpassed in their dramatic evergreen foliage and the scale of their inflorescences. They do particularly well by the sea. Smaller cultivars like 'Bronze Baby' contrast strikingly with silver-gray foliage (*Artemisia* and *Stachys*, for example), provide a rich and exotic foil for the glowing, late summer tones of bronze-leaved *Ligularia* and the smaller *Kniphofia* cultivars, and sit well with such copper and bronze sedges as *Uncinia* and the New Zealand *Carex*. Grow in full sun in moderately fertile, moisture-retentive but well drained soil. Propagate by division or by seed.

Phormium cookianum 'Dazzler'
One of a number of cultivars that, being relatively short and contained, are more suitable for smaller gardens.

P. cookianum MOUNTAIN FLAX; leaves to 60 × 2½ in (150 × 6 cm), flexible, dark olive green, base red-tinted; inflorescence to 6½ ft (2 m), often inclined, flowers 1–1½ in (2.5–4 cm), green tinged orange or yellow; cultivars range in height from dwarf (12 in (30 cm)) to large (5 ft (1.5 m) with narrow to broad leaves, some solid plum-purple or bronze, others striped or flushed white, cream, yellow, lime, orange, copper, rose-pink and maroon. *P. tenax* NEW ZEALAND FLAX, NEW ZEALAND HEMP; leaves to 10 ft (3 m) × 2–4¾ in (5–12 cm), stiff, olive green, margin red or orange, base pale; inflorescence to 16 ft (5 m), usually erect, flowers to 2½ in (6 cm), dull red; many cultivars including dwarf to tall plants from 14 to 48 in (35–120 cm) with narrow to broad leaves tinted, striped or solidly stained purple-bronze, wine red, red, pink, copper, orange, gold, yellow, cream, white and lime.

phosphate a salt of phosphoric acid; a form in which phosphorus is applied as a nutrient. See *phosphorus*.

phosphorus (abbreviation P) a major (macro-) nutrient, important in plant enzyme reactions, and a constituent of cell nuclei; it is essential for cell division and the development of meristem tissue, and is commonly associated with healthy root growth. Plant requirements vary, legumes, for example, having a high demand.

Phosphorus naturally originates from the weathering of rocks, and some is held in organic matter from which it is slowly mineralized. It is stored in most soils and forms insoluble compounds under extreme acidity or alkalinity; availability is related to rooting capacity, young seedlings being more prone to shortage than mature plants. Symbiotic mycorrhiza often aid phosphorus uptake in deficient soil.

Due to its immobility, rarely more than 20–30% of added phosphorus is taken up from fertilizer application so that acute soil deficiency is rare on cultivated ground; long-established grazing land receiving minimal fertilizer dressing is often low in phosphorus.

Symptoms of deficiency are reduced growth rate, especially shortly after crop emergence during a cold spell; in some instances, there is a tendency to dull, blue/green leaves, often purple and with marginal scorch in older ones.

Phosphorus fertilizers include rock phosphate (26% P_2O_5), triple superphosphate (44% P_2O_5), bone-meal (20% P_2O_5), fish, blood and bone (8% P_2O_5) and compound Growmore (7% P_2O_5). Forms of ammonium phosphate are very high in phosphorus and are used in concentrated fertilizer and liquid feed.

Photinia (from Greek *photeinos*, shining, referring to the leaves). Rosaceae. E and SE Asia north to Himalaya, W US. CHRISTMAS BERRY. To 60 species, deciduous and evergreen trees and shrubs with small, white to cream, 5-petalled flowers massed in terminal corymbs or short panicles in late spring and summer. These are followed by small, orange-red pomes. Hardy to 5°F (–15°C). Grow in well-drained, fertile soil in sun or light shade. Protect evergreens from cold winds that may scorch foliage. Deciduous species tend to be calcifuge; evergreens are tolerant of calcareous soil. *P. davidiana* will grow in a range of soils including heavy clay, and will tolerate a degree of drought. Propagate deciduous species from seed sown in fall, cultivars and evergreen species by semiripe basal cuttings rooted with bottom heat in a closed case.

P. davidiana W China; evergreen shrub to 16 ft (5 m); leaves to 4 in (10 cm), lanceolate to oblanceolate, entire, tough, smooth dark green; 'Palette': leaves blotched cream, dark green and lime, flushed or streaked pink at first; var. *undulata* 'Fructo Lutea': fruit bright yellow. *P.* × *fraseri* (*P. glauca* × *P. serratifolia*); vigorous evergreen shrub; leaves 2¾–3½ in (7–9 cm), elliptic to ovate, small-toothed, coppery red at first, becoming shiny dark green; 'Red Robin': leaves deep glowing red at first, becoming dark shiny green; *P. glabra* JAPANESE PHOTINIA; Japan; evergreen shrub, 10–20 ft (3–6 m); leaves 2–3 in (5–8 cm), elliptic to narrowly obovate, red at first, becoming dark shining green; 'Parfait': leaves pink at first, becoming green edged white; 'Rosea-marginata': leaves variegated green, white, gray and pink; *P.* 'Redstart' *P. davidiana* var. *undulata* 'Fructo Lutea' × *P.* × *fraseri* 'Robusta'; large shrub or small tree; leaves to 4½ in (11 cm), bright red at first, becoming dark green, finely toothed above; *P. serratifolia* China, Taiwan; evergreen shrub to tree, 16–39 ft (5–12 m); leaves to 4 in (10 cm), ovate to obovate, saw-toothed, becoming leathery, copper red becoming glossy dark green; *P. villosa* Japan, Korea, China; deciduous shrub or small tree to 16 ft (5 m); leaves 1¼–3 in (3–8 cm), obovate to lanceolate dark ovate, apex long-tapered, leathery, teeth glandular-tipped.

photoperiodic lighting see *supplementary light*.

photoperiodism the influence of day length on plant growth, frequently concerning aspects of reproduction, especially flowering. By reason of this phenomenon, life cycles may be manipulated, and beneficial effects are extended to certain insect pollinators. Photoperiodic responses in plants are often related to the avoidance of seasonal stress factors, such as drought and cold, and are associated with leaf growth, dormancy, storage-organ formation and leaf fall.

Scientific knowledge of the mechanism of photoperiodism is incomplete; most of what is known concerns the effects of day length on flowering. In general, plants growing far from the equator respond to longer day lengths than those growing close to it. Response relative to latitude can occur within a species, sometimes quite precisely, as with soybean varieties grown in the

United States which only achieve optimum performance within an approximately 50-mile range of latitude.

True day-neutral plants where flowering is unaffected by day length are probably rare; cucumber (*Cucumis sativa*) and haricot (*Phaseolus vulgaris*) are two examples. Short-day plants (SDPs) flower in response to days shorter than a certain critical length. Cocklebur (*Xanthium strumarium*) is an example of an SDP, which will flower after just one short day. Spinach (*Spinacia oleracea*) is a long day-plant (LDP), responding to a single inductive long day. More common are species requiring several cycles of the appropriate photoperiod for floral induction.

Among SDPs is *Kalanchoe blossfeldiana*, which has a precise requirement, and the sunflower (*Helianthus annuus*), which will eventually flower in days longer than the critical length. A precise LDP is hibiscus (e.g. *Hibiscus syriacus*), while spring wheat (*Triticum aestivum*) is an LDP not totally dependent on a critical day length. There are subvariations; several species respond to various combinations of day lengths, for instance, long days followed by short days promote flowering in *Kalanchoe laxiflora*, while short days followed by long days are required by white clover (*Trifolium repens*).

The great majority of plants must reach a certain stage of development to respond to day length; henbane (*Hyoscyamus niger*) must be 10–30 days old before it can respond to long days, and many trees will not flower until they are tens of years old.

For all the response types, it is the length of night or darkness, rather than day length, which is the critical factor and it appears that the plant pigment phytochrome inhibits flowering in SDPs, while promoting it in LDPs. This phenomenon makes possible the artificial manipulation of flowering time in practical horticulture, the best-known example of which in Britain is the supply of all-year-round chrysanthemums. Chrysanthemums are SDPs, which are naturally induced to flower by the shortening days of late summer. However, when grown in controlled conditions under glass, they can be prevented from flowering until required by using artificial lights to extend day lengths or, more efficiently, to provide one or several brief night breaks. When flowering is required, the night breaks are suspended and a few long nights allow flowering to be induced. In the long days (short nights) of summer, flowering can be induced by artificially lengthening the nights with blackouts in a greenhouse.

photosynthesis a complex chemical process, promoting the production in green plants of organic substances, such as sugars and starches, from water and atmospheric carbon dioxide. It is the source of energy for plant activity. The process involves the activation by sunlight of the green pigment chlorophyll. Photosynthesis, (carbon assimilation) takes place principally in the leaves, into which carbon dioxide diffuses through stomata, and free oxygen is discharged as a product of the reaction.

phototropism directional growth of a plant in response to light. See *tropism*.

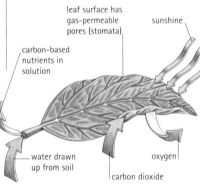

leaf surface has gas-permeable pores (stomata)

sunshine

carbon-based nutrients in solution

water drawn up from soil

oxygen

carbon dioxide

Photosynthesis

Phragmipedium (from Greek *phragma*, partition, and *pedilon*, slipper, referring to the trilocular ovary and the slipper-shaped lip). Orchidaceae. C and S America. LADY-SLIPPER. Some 20 species, evergreen perennial herbs with narrowly strap-shaped leaves in a basal fan. The flowers are borne several to a stem in spring and summer. They resemble those of *Paphiopedilum* but have a more inflated lip, with the petals often narrower and drooping—in some species, greatly attenuated and spiraling. The genus was formerly included variously in *Cypripedium*, *Paphiopedilum*, and *Selenipedium*. Cultivate as for warm-growing *Paphiopedilum*.

P. besseae Colombia, NE Peru; flow- ers to 2½ in (6 cm) in diameter; dorsal sepal ovate-lanceolate, petals oblong-elliptic, larger, all bright scarlet; lip strongly pouched, fiery red to golden yellow or peach; *P. caudatum* Mexico to Peru, Venezuela, Colombia, Ecuador; flowers to 50 in (125 cm) across; dorsal sepal white to yellow-green with dark green veins, to 6 × 1¼ in (15 × 3 cm), lanceolate, acute, arched over lip, strongly undulate to spiraled, petals purple-brown to green-brown, to 24 × ½ in (60 × 1 cm), linear-lanceolate, pendulous, spiraling, lip yellow near base, apex tinted pink or maroon, veined green, to 2¾ × ¾ in (7 × 2 cm), lateral lobes strongly incurved, spotted green; *P. grande* (*P. longifolium* × *P. caudatum*); flowers green-brown with very long petals; *P. lindenii* Colombia, Peru, Ecuador; resembles *P. caudatum* except lip not pouched, similar to petals, wider at base; *P. lindleyanum* Venezuela, Guyana; sepals pale green or yellow-green, veined red-brown, downy below, dorsal sepal to 1½ × ¾ in (3.5 × 2 cm), elliptic, obtuse, concave, petals yellow-green at base, white-green toward apex, margins and veins flushed purple toward apex, to 2⅛ × ½ in (5.5 × 1 cm), linear-oblong, apex rounded, undulate; lip pale yellow-green with yellow-brown venation, to 1¼ × ⅝ in (3 × 1.5 cm), lateral lobes spotted light purple; *P. longifolium* Costa Rica, Panama, Colombia, Ecuador; dorsal sepal pale yellow-green, veined dark green or rose, edged white, to 2½ × ¾ in (6 × 2 cm), lanceolate, acute, erect or curved forward, sometimes undulate, petals pale yellow-green, margins rose-purple, to 4¾ × ½ in (12 × 1 cm), spreading, linear to lanceolate, twisted, lip yellow-green, to 2½ × ⅜ in (6 × 1.5 cm), margins spotted pale rose to magenta; *P. schlimii* Colombia; tepals white flushed rose-pink, dorsal sepal to ¾ × ½ in (2 × 1 cm), ovate-oblong, obtuse, concave, petals slightly longer, spreading, spotted pink at base, elliptic, lip rose-pink, lateral lobes incurved, streaked white and rose-carmine; *P.* × *sedenii* (*P. longifolium* × *P. schlimii*); sepals ivory white, flushed pale rose, exterior rose-pink, petals white, margins tinged rose-pink, twisted, lip rose-pink, lobes white spotted rose.

Phragmites (from Greek *phragma*, fence or screen, referring to the screening effect of many plants growing together along streams). Gramineae. Cosmopolitan. REED. 4 species, rhizomatous perennial grasses; culms clumped, reedy; leaves linear, flat; inflorescence a large, terminal, plumed panicle produced in summer and early fall. Occurring in marsh, fen and riverside habitats in temperate and tropical zones, *P. australis* is an elegant perennial, valued for the soft and showy flowering panicles—these retain their beautiful metallic sheen even on drying—and for the golden russet fall colors. The species is invasive and hardy to −4°F (−20°C) and below. It thrives in deep, moisture-retentive soil, but is generally suitable only for the larger landscape, unless confined in containers, or used as a marginal or submerged aquatic. Propagate by division. *P. australis* (syn. *P. communis*); GIANT REED, CARRIZO; cosmopolitan; culms robust, to 11½ ft (3.5 m); leaves to 24 × 2 in+ (60 × 5 cm+), arching, mid- to gray-green; inflorescence erect to nodding, silky gray tinged pearly pink-brown to purple, then brown, to 18 in (45 cm); 'Rubra': inflorescence crimson-tinted; 'Striatopictus': leaves bright green striped pale yellow; 'Variegatus': leaves striped bright yellow, fading to white.

Phuopsis (from its resemblance to *Valeriana phu*). Rubiaceae. Caucasus. 1 species, *P. stylosa*, a slender mat-forming perennial herb to 12 in (30 cm), with whorls of narrow-lanceolate, slender-pointed and spiny-ciliate leaves. Produced in summer, the clustered flowers are scented, small and pink, with a tubular corolla and five oblong to ovate, obtuse lobes. Suitable for groundcover in the rock garden, and on banks. Hardy to −4°F (−20°C). Grow in moist, gritty but well-drained soil in full sun, or light shade. Propagate by removal of rooted stems, by semiripe cuttings or from seed sown in fall.

Phygelius (from Greek, *phyge*, flight—so-named because it long evaded the researches of botanists). Scrophulariaceae. South Africa. 2 species, evergreen or semi-evergreen shrubs and subshrubs with ovate to lanceolate, serrate leaves and, in summer, narrowly tubular flowers hung in terminal panicles. Hardy to

23°F (−5°C), they are usually treated as herbaceous perennials in areas where temperatures fall much below freezing in winter. In warm-areas or if given the protection of a south-facing wall, *P. capensis* will thrive in its naturally shrubby form and may be trained as a wall shrub and tied into trellis supports. Plant in a sunny site with moderately fertile, light soil. Where the ground freezes, provide a heavy winter mulch. Cut out dead wood in spring. Sow seed in spring at 59–64°F (15–18°C) and overwinter young stock in frost-free conditions. Alternatively, take semiripe cuttings in late summer.

P. aequalis to 3¼ ft (1 m); flowers dusky pink, throat orange, lobes crimson; 'Yellow Trumpet': flowers pale creamy yellow; *P. capensis* CAPE FIGWORT, CAPE FUCHSIA; to 10 ft (3 m), somewhat sprawling; flowers pale orange to deep red; 'Coccineus': flowers rich orange with orange-red lobes; *P. × rectus* (*P. aequalis* × *P. capensis*); varied group of hybrids from 20–60 in (50–150 cm) tall, erect to loosely scrambling with flowers ranging from pale cream, to lime green, pale pink, coral-red, dusky pink, salmon, scarlet and orange.

phyllary one of the bracts that subtends a flower or inflorescence, composing an involucre.

phylloclade a stem or branch, flattened and functioning as a leaf.

Phyllocladus (from Greek *phyllon*, leaf, and *klados*, young branch or shoot, referring to the leaflike shoots). Phyllocladaceae. Malaysia, Indonesia, New Guinea, Tasmania, New Zealand. CELERY PINE. 5 species, evergreen, coniferous trees or shrubs with modified leaflike shoots (phylloclades), which are leathery, incised and often deeply or shallowly toothed. Plant in a free-draining, acidic to neutral medium with additional sand and grit. Grow in full sun in a cool, moist environment. This tree withstands mild frosts. It needs a cool, humid environment in full sun. Propagate by seed or semiripe cuttings. *P. trichomanoides*

TANEKAHA; New Zealand; tree to 66 ft (20 m); phylloclades, ovate to 12 in (30 cm), dark green above, glaucous beneath, tough pinnately lobed with segments roughly rhombic and shallowly crenate.

flattened stem is a phyllode

phyllode an expanded petiole, taking on the function of a leaf blade, as in *Acacia*.

Acacia glaucoptera

Phyllodoce (for a sea nymph of Greek mythology, one of Cyrene's attendants, mentioned by Virgil). Ericaceae. Arctic and alpine regions of Northern Hemisphere. 8 species, dwarf, evergreen shrubs with small, linear, revolute and leathery leaves. Produced in late spring and early summer, the flowers are pitcher- or bell-shaped and nod in racemes or clusters. Suitable for the peat terrace and for cool, damp, peaty niches in the rock garden. Hardy to 5°F (−15°C). Grow in moist but well-drained, peaty, acidic soil, in partial shade or in bright indirect light. Protect in areas that experience prolonged frosts. Trim over after blooming. Propagate by semiripe heel cuttings or softwood tip cuttings in late summer. Increase also by seed in spring, or by layering.

P. aleutica Japan; dwarf, decumbent or scandent; flowers to ⅜ in (8 mm), pale yellow-green, pitcher-shaped, downy, with pink anthers; subsp. *glanduliflora*: Alaska; YELLOW MOUNTAIN HEATHER; flowers fragrant, yellow to olive with purple anthers; *P. caerulea* (syn. *P. taxifolia*); Asia, Europe and US; 4–14 in (10–35 cm), erect or scandent; flowers ¼–½ in (7–12 mm), lilac to purple-pink, pitcher-shaped; *P. empetriformis* PINK MOUNTAIN HEATHER; British Colombia to California; low, diffuse, mat-forming shrub, 4–15 in (10–38 cm); flowers ¼–⅜ in (5–9 mm), bell-shaped, rose-pink; *P. × intermedia*. (*P. empetriformis* × *P. aleutica*) subsp. *glanduliflora*; western N America; dense, bushy subshrub, 6–9 in (15–23 cm); flowers mauve to purple-red or yellow-pink, ovate-campanulate to pitcher-shaped; 'Drummondii': flat habit,

P

dark purple flowers; 'Fred Stoker': flowers light purple; *P. nipponica* North Japan; small, branched, suberect shrub, 2¾–9 in (7–23 cm); flowers rose to white, bell-shaped; var. *amabilis*: calyx lobes red, corolla red- or pink-tipped.

Phyllostachys (from Greek *phyllon*, leaf, and *stachys*, spike, for the 'leafy' inflorescence). Gramineae. China, India, Burma. Some 80 species of medium and large bamboos; see *bamboos*.

phyllotaxy the arrangement of plant organs on an axis. Commonly describes leaves on a stem.

phylloxerids (Hemiptera: Phylloxeridae) a small family of sap-sucking insects, related to aphids, which are important pests of grapes, oak and pecans.

The VINE LOUSE or GRAPE PHYLLOXERID (*Daktulosphaira vitifolii*) is a North American species, introduced into Europe about 1863. Infested vines develop galls on the roots and leaves followed by rapid collapse and death. American vines have both foliar and root-feeding forms but in Europe the life cycle is restricted to subterranean forms. In the 19th-century, serious epidemics were eventually overcome by grafting European grape vines on to resistant rootstocks from North America.

The OAK PHYLLOXERIDS (*Phylloxera glabra* and other species.) infest the underside of oak leaves in summer, causing yellow and brown spots to develop; severe infestations cause extensive browning of foliage followed by premature leaf-fall. Older trees are seldom harmed but young trees may become seriously weakened and can be protected by contact or systemic insecticides recommended for aphid control.

Pecans are cultivated in the southern states of the US for their nuts. They are subject to infestation by the PECAN PHYLLOXERA (*P. devastatrix*), which causes extensive galling of leaves, shoots and nuts; the PECAN LEAF PHYLLOXERA (*P. notabilis*) is less serious on mature trees but can be damaging to young nursery trees.

Physalis (from Greek *physa*, bladder or bellows, referring to the inflated calyx). Solanaceae. Cosmopolitan, especially Americas. GROUND CHERRY, HUSK TOMATO. Some 80 species, annual or perennial herbs. Produced in summer, the flowers are solitary, white tinged violet or yellow, campanulate to rotate and 5-lobed. After pollination, the calyx develops into a colorful, inflated and ribbed bladder or lantern, enclosing the berrylike fruit. The hardy *P. alkekengi* is used for decoration and provides a vivid orange display in the fall garden; it is also used for drying, with the stems cut when the calyces begin to color and air-dried. *P. peruviana* yields the dessert fruit, Cape gooseberry; it is not reliably hardy beyond areas that are frost-free or almost so, but in temperate zones can be grown for fruit in a cool greenhouse. Both species are easily cultivated in well-drained soil, in sun or light shade. Propagate by division or seed.

P. alkekengi JAPANESE LANTERN, WINTER CHERRY, BLADDER CHERRY; C and S Europe, W Asia to Japan; perennial to 24 in (60 cm), thinly glandular-pubescent; calyx to ¾ in (2 cm), becoming inflated, lanternlike to 2 in (5 cm), orange; fruit to ⅔ in (17 mm), red to scarlet, inedible; var. *franchetii* 'Variegata': leaves deeply bordered cream and yellow-green; *P. peruviana* CAPE GOOSEBERRY, PURPLE GROUND CHERRY; tropical S America; perennial to 3¼ ft (1 m); calyx becoming ovoid, pubescent to 1½ in (4 cm), ultimately withered and thinly papery; fruit edible, globose, yellow to purple, to ¾ in (2 cm) in diameter.

physic garden usually, an alternative name for a botanic garden; strictly, a garden primarily concerned with the collection, cultivation and study of medicinal plants, such as were established in Europe as adjuncts to faculties of medicine in the 16th and 17th centuries.

physiological disorder a condition harmful to growth, flowering or fruiting, not caused by pest

Physiological disorder
(drought causing fruit split)

or disease attack, often associated with defects in growing conditions.

physiology the study of the functions of living organisms.

Physocarpus (from Greek *physa*, bladder, and *karpos*, fruit, referring to the inflated follicles). N America, NE Asia. NINEBARK. 10 species, deciduous shrubs with exfoliating bark and palmately lobed leaves. Produced in early summer in terminal corymbs, the flowers are small, white to light pink with five, rounded petals. Hardy to –13°F (–25°C). Grow in moist, moderately fertile, acidic soil in full sun. Prune after flowering, thinning out old and overcrowded shoots by cutting back to ground level. Propagate by removal of suckers, by seed, or from softwood cuttings in a closed case with bottom heat. *P. opulifolius* NINEBARK; central and east N America; to 10 ft (3 m); bark brown, shredded; leaves to 3 in (7.5 cm), oval to rounded, cordate at base glabrous, double-toothed, usually 3-lobed; flowers often pale pink, or white tinged with rose, in many-flowered corymbs; 'Dart's Gold': bright gold leaves, flowers white washed pink; 'Luteus': leaves golden at first, later olive green or tinted bronze.

Physostegia (from Greek *physa*, a bladder, and *stege*, a covering). Labiatae. N America. OBEDIENT PLANT, FALSE DRAGON HEAD. 12 species, erect perennial herbs. They flower in summer and early fall, producing spikes of tubular and hooded, 2-lipped flowers. If pushed to one side on the spike, a flower will remain there, hence the popular name 'obedient plant'. Fully hardy. Plant in rich fertile loamy soil with abundant water. Propagate by division when dormant. Sow seed in fall in a cold frame. *P. virginiana* central and south US and NE Mexico; erect to 70 in (180 cm), often shorter; flowers red-violet, lavender or white, usually spotted and streaked purple; includes short and tall cultivars, some with variegated leaves and flowers ranging in color from white to pale rose, deep pink, lilac, lavender or claret.

Physostegia virginiana 'Variegata'
The obedient plant is so-called because its flowers will remain in a new position if they are moved on the stalk.

Phyteuma (name used by Dioscorides for an aphrodisiac plant, meaning simply 'the plant'). Campanulaceae. Europe, Asia. HORNED RAMPION. Some 40 species, summer-flowering perennial herbs. The flowers are produced in compact terminal spikes or heads, usually subtended by bracts. They consist of five, linear lobes, the whole head appearing spiky. Fully hardy. Plant in sun in fast-draining, gritty neutral or slightly alkaline soil in the rock garden. Propagate by division in spring or after flowering, or by seed in fall. *P. scheuchzeri* Alps; to 16 in (40 cm); inflorescence spherical, bracts linear, leafy, flowers dark blue.

phytochrome a plant pigment involved in the developmental responses of plants to light. It exists in two interchangeable forms depending upon the ratio of red to far-red light. See *photoperiodism*.

Phytolacca (from Greek *phyton*, plant, and French *lac*, lake, a red pigment, from the crimson juice of the berries.) Phytolaccaceae. Temperate and warm regions. POKEWEED. 35 species, perennial herbs, shrubs and trees. In summer, they bear small, apetalous flowers in erect or drooping spikelike racemes. These are followed by wine-red to purple-black, berries. Fully hardy and suitable for the open woodland garden, for massed plantings and as a specimen in the shrub and mixed border. Its tinted, forked stems and garnet spikes of toxic fruits are especially striking in late summer. Grow in moisture-retentive, fertile soil in full sun or light shade. Propagate by seed sown in fall or spring or by division. *P. americana* PIGEON BERRY, POKEWEED, RED INK PLANT; N and C America; herbaceous perennial, to 13 ft (4 m); stem purple-red, dichotomously branching; leaves to 12 in (30 cm), becoming purple-pink to yellow in fall; fruit glossy, green becoming red then purple-black in erect persistent spikes.

phytophthora a genus of parasitic fungi allied to the downy mildews. Of wide importance is POTATO BLIGHT (*Phytophthora infestans*) which spreads rapidly in warm wet seasons. First signs are brown dead patches on the leaf tips or edges which enlarge to cause withering; haulm becomes affected with brownish black patches and all growth may collapse and rot. Tubers become infected by washed-down spores and develop rot before lifting and in store. Weather conditions conducive to infection are two consecutive 24-hour periods during which the minimum temperature is 50°F (10°C) and for no less than 11 hours the relative humidity is at least 89%. Avoid by choosing resistant cultivars including 'Cara', 'Estima', 'Maris Peer' and 'Wilja' or control with fungicide sprays of protectant copper-based products and mancozeb. Other *Phytophthora* diseases include RED CORE DISEASE of strawberry (*P. fragariae*), which is soil inhabiting and persistent, causing loss of root function; CROWN ROT of apple and strawberry (*P. cactorum*); STEM AND FRUIT ROT of red pepper (*P. capsici*); ROOT ROT of many woody plants (*P. cinnamomi*); DOWNY MILDEW of Lima bean (*P. phaseoli*) and LILAC BLIGHT and APPLE FRUIT ROT (*P. syringae*). The majority of phytophthoras are dispersed by water and are therefore important as soilborne diseases, *P. infestans* and *P. phaseoli* are dispersed by airborne spores, thereby causing rapidly spreading epidemics. See *root rot*.

phytoplasmas (formerly known as MYCOPLASMAS, MYCOPLASMA-LIKE ORGANISMS, MLOs) are microorganisms that lack a true cell wall. Allied to bacteria, they attack plants to cause YELLOWS and other diseases transmitted by leafhoppers. They are morphologically similar to the Mycoplasmataceae (animal pathogens and saprophytes) which are related to the Spiroplasmataceae (which cause CITRUS STUBBORN DISEASE, etc.), but phytoplasmas are not thought to be closely related to these families. The true taxonomic position of phytoplasmas is not yet settled.

ASTER YELLOWS is a well-known disease in North America, Europe and Japan, formerly thought to be caused by a virus, but in 1967 shown to be an example of a group of similar plant diseases caused by phytoplasmas. These cannot be grown in artificial culture and their identification depends on symptoms, microscopic examination and transmission and inoculation studies. Infection is transmitted by the feeding of leafhoppers (e.g. *Macrosteles*) migrating from herbaceous perennials; such ornamentals particularly affected include the composites *Calendula*, *Callistephus*, *Chrysanthemum*, *Gaillardia*, *Gerbera* and *Tagetes*. Others are *Anemone*, *Delphinium*, *Gypsophila*, *Phlox* and *Primula*. ASTER YELLOWS is more common in warmer climates such as southern and eastern Europe, where insect vectors are numerous; and it causes yellowing, dwarfing, proliferation of shoots and malformation and greening of flowers, which can be lethal on some hosts while others recover. In North America the disease is considered to be caused by a different strain of phytoplasma to those occurring in Europe. Vegetable diseases caused by ASTER YELLOWS phytoplasma are LETTUCE PHYLLODY, ONION PROLIFERATION YELLOWS of beet, carrot, celery, zucchini and spinach, and VIRESCENCE (GREENING) of brassicas. CORN BUSHY STUNT and STRAWBERRY WITCHES' BROOM occur in north and north west America but are not known in Europe.

HYDRANGEA VIRESCENCE (GREEN FLOWER) is an important disease in Europe, and *Lonicera*, *Jasminum* and *Vaccinium* species are affected by WITCHES' BROOM. 'GREEN PETAL' of strawberries and trifolium clover is a linked condition caused by a phytoplasma.

Other diseases thought to be caused by phytoplasma include APPLE PROLIFERATION, APPLE RUBBERY WOOD, APRICOT CHLOROTIC LEAF ROLL, BLACK CURRANT REVERSION, LITTLE CHERRY,

cherry moliére disease, ELM PHLOEM NECROSIS, GRAPEVINE FLAVESCENCE DORÉE (transmitted by the N American leafhopper, *Scaphoideus litoralis*), PALM LETHAL YELLOWING, PEACH YELLOWS, PEACH ROSETTE, PEAR DECLINE, and RUBUS STUNT.

phytotoxicity the poisonous effects of a substance on plants, as may occur from adverse reaction to a pesticide. Stage and state of growth and environmental conditions, especially bright sunlight, may predispose plants to phytotoxicity.

Picea (from Latin *pix*, pitch, obtained from the resin of *P. abies*). Pinaceae. Northern Hemisphere except Africa. SPRUCE. Some 35 species, resinous evergreen, coniferous trees. The crown is conical in outline, often domed or columnar in older specimens. The branches are borne in more or less horizontal whorls. Needlelike leaves are carried in spirals, usually pressed forward on the branchlets. The cones are ovoid to cylindric with large, usually thin scales obscuring the very short bracts, green to purple, ripening pale to dark brown, becoming pendulous after pollination. Most species are hardy to −22°F (−30°C) or lower. Cultivate as for *Abies*, except that spruces are more tolerant of exposure and less tolerant of shade; they should therefore be planted in the open. They are also more tolerant of poor, peaty soil. As with other conifers, propagation is better from seed than grafts; in *Picea breweriana* this is especially important, grafted plants never making good trees. Seed should be wild-collected or from extensive single-species plantings. Propagate dwarf cultivars by cuttings; if grafted on normal root-stocks, they grow too vigorously.

Several rust fungi, mostly species of *Chrysomyxa*, affect spruce, especially *P. abies*, but none is a serious problem. Those occurring in Britain are *Chrysomyxa abietis* and *C. ledi* var. *rhododendri*, both of which cause yellow bands on the needles. *C.abietis* is only known to infect spruce, on which it produces the teliospore stage, whereas *C. ledi* var. *rhododendri* produces uredio- and teliospores on rhododendron and aeciospores on spruce. The most

important pests of spruce are common to Europe and North America. These include the green spruce aphid, which can cause complete defoliation of several species. This is the most serious pest of spruce in gardens, particularly in warmer areas and following mild winters. Spruce gall adelgids induce ½–1¼ in (1–3 cm) pineapple-shaped galls to develop. The European spruce sawfly and the spruce budworm are destructive pests of opening buds and young shoots in North America.

P. abies NORWAY SPRUCE; N and C America; to 180 ft (55 m); bark red-brown to gray or purple, flaking in thin plates; crown conical, columnar with age, branches level or drooping and upcurved, branchlets pendulous; leaves ½–1 in (1–2.5 cm), dark green, obtuse; cones cylindric, green or purplish, ripening brown, 3–7 in (8–18 cm) × 1¼–1½ in (3–4 cm), to × 2–2½ in (5–6 cm) open; scales rhombic. Upright, conical selections include the slender, to 66 ft (20 m)-tall 'Cupressina' and 'Viminalis', and the broadly conical 'Pyramidata'; sparse forms include the irregularly branched 'Virgata' (SNAKE-BRANCH SPRUCE) and 'Cranstonii'; weeping forms include the very pendulous 'Frohburg' and 'Inversa' and the semi-prostrate 'Lorely'; notable low-growers (to 16 ft (5 m)) include the narrow-conic 'Concinna', the broad-conic 'Conica' and the profusely coning 'Acrocona'; dwarf selections include the very slow-growing 'Clanbrassiliana' (10 ft (3 m) in 180 years), the irregular 'Pachyphylla' and 'Pygmaea', and the more regular 'Elegans' and 'Humilis'; globose dwarfs include the stoutly branched 'Nana Compacta' and 'Pyramidalis Gracilis' and the finer 'Gregoryana' and 'Hystrix'; flat-topped dwarfs include the slow-growing 'Little Gem' (¾ in (2 cm) per annum) and the mat-forming 'Repens'; cultivars noted for needle color include the yellow to gold 'Aurea' and 'Aurescens', the steel-blue 'Coerulea' and the dwarf, gold-variegated 'Callensis' and 'Helen Cordes'; *P. breweriana* BREWER'S SPRUCE; N California and S Oregon; to 115 ft (35 m), slow-growing; bark gray or purple-gray, becoming scaly; crown ovoid-conic; branches horizontal, upward-pointing, branchlets pendulous; leaves flattened, obtuse, 1–1½ in (2.5–3.5 cm), glossy

Picea glauca 'Coerulea'
A densely conical cultivar of white spruce, with dull blue-green leaves tinged silver-blue. A suitable choice for smaller gardens.

deep green above, 2 white stomatal bands beneath, somewhat curved; cones 3–5½ in (8–14 cm) × ¾–1 in (2–2.5 cm), opening to 1¼–1½ in (3–4 cm) across, cylindric, purple then red-brown, resinous; scales large, obovate, apex rounded; *P. engelmannii* ENGELMANN SPRUCE; western N America; to 150 ft (45 m); bark thin, buff, splitting into small plates, resinous; crown conic to narrowly acute; branches in dense whorls, upward-pointing, branchlets pendulous; leaves straight or curved, blue-green or glaucous, soft, flexible ⅝–1¼ in (1.5–3 cm), forward-pointing; cones 1¼–2 in (3–5 cm) × ½ in (1 cm); ovoid to cylindric, tapering, green to light brown; scales very thin, obtuse; 'Argentea', with gray leaves, tinged silver; 'Fendleri', with pendulous branches and leaves to 1¼ in (3 cm); 'Glauca', upright, with vivid blue leaves; 'Microphylla', dwarf, bushy, compact; 'Snake', of highly irregular upright habit, tinged blue; f. *glauca*, with intense glaucous blue leaves; *P. glauca* WHITE SPRUCE; Canada, far NE US; to 80 ft (25 m); bark light gray becoming darker with white cracks; crown conic; branches level or descending, with upward-growing tips; branchlets dense; leaves stiff, dull blue-green, ½–¾ in (10–18 mm), imbricate to spreading; cones 1¼–2 in (3–5 cm) × ½ in (1 cm), ovoid to cylindric, tapering, green to light brown; scales very thin obtuse; 'Aureospicata', with yellow young shoots, later green; 'Coerulea', to 6½ ft (2 m), densely pyramidal, leaves tinged silver-blue; 'Hendersonii', similar to 'Coerulea', with young shoots lateral, later pendulous; 'Pendula', weeping, upright leader, with very pendulous red branches and leaves tinged blue; var. *albertiana*, from Canadian Rocky Mountains, to 150 ft (45 m), with pubescent shoots, leaves to 1 in (2.5 cm), and ovoid cones to 1½ in (4 cm); 'Conica', to 13 ft (4 m), dense, conical, with permanently juvenile, very slender, curved leaves, 4½–⅝ in (11–15 cm) × ¼ in (0.5 mm); 'Gnome', slow-growing mutation of 'Conica' (to 2 in (5 cm) per annum); 'Laurin', small, dense, mutation of 'Conica'; *P. likiangensis* LIJIANG SPRUCE; SW China, SE Tibet, E Assam; to 165 ft (50 m); bark gray, smooth to scaly or shallow-fissured; crown open, broadly conic; branches level to ascending; leaves ⅜–⅝ in (8–15 mm), sharp, dark green to blue-green, flattened, keeled, 2 blue-white stomatal lines beneath, 2 faint bands above, forward-growing, loosely imbricate; cones oval-cylindric, 2¾–5 in (7–13 cm) × 1¼ in (3 cm), red to purple; scales thin, obovate, finely toothed; *P. mariana* BLACK SPRUCE; northern N America; to 66 ft (20 m)+; bark red-brown to gray-brown, exfoliating in thin flakes; crown conic; branches downswept; leaves densely arranged, ¼–⅝ in (0.5–1.5 cm), blue-green above, off-white stomatal stripes beneath, stiff, obtuse; cones ¾–1½ in (2–4 cm) × ⅝ in (1.5 cm), fusiform, mauve, becoming gray-brown, persisting; scales woody, rounded, margins finely toothed; 'Argenteovariegata', with some leaves almost completely white; 'Aurea', with leaves tinged gold; 'Beissneri', dwarf, slow-growing to 16 ft (5 m), similar to 'Doumettii' but with broader leaves tinged blue; 'Doumettii', dwarf to 20 ft (6 m), globose-conic when young, becoming irregular, with a dense crown and bright blue-green leaves; 'Fastigiata', conical dwarf, with slender, ascending branches; 'Nana', very dwarf and globose to 20 in (50 cm), slow-growing to 1¼ in (3 cm) per annum, more than one clone in cultivation; 'Pendula', upright leader with weeping branches; *P. morrisonicola* TAIWAN SPRUCE; Taiwan; to 130 ft (40 m); shoots sparse, pendulous; leaves ½–¾ in (10–20 mm), slender, sharply acuminate, glossy dark green; cones 2–3 in (5–8 cm) × ⅝–¾ in (1.5–2 cm), oblong-cylindric;

scales obovate, obtuse; *P. omorika* SERBIAN SPRUCE; Balkans; to 115 ft (35 m); bark orange-brown to purple-brown, becoming cracked and flaking in fine plates; crown conic to narrowly spire-like; branches downswept to upcurved; branchlets dense, more or less pendulous; leaves ½–¾ in (10–20 mm), flattened, keeled, dark to blue-green, with 2 silver-gray bands beneath; cones 1¼–2¾ in (3–7 cm) × ¾ in (2 cm), fusiform, purple, ripening red-brown, scales closely adpressed, broadly obtuse, finely toothed; 'Expansa', vigorous procumbent dwarf, with branch ends slightly ascending; 'Gnom', broadly conical dwarf, slow-growing to 1¼ in (3 cm) per annum; 'Nana', globose to broadly conic-pyramidal dwarf; 'Pendula', slender and upright, with pendulous branches; *P. orientalis* ORIENTAL SPRUCE, CAUCASIAN SPRUCE, Caucasus, NE Turkey; to 165 ft (50 m); bark smooth, pink-gray, becoming cracked; forming small raised plates; crown conic, dense, to ovoid-columnar; branches slightly ascending; leaves ¼–⅜ in (0.5–0.8 cm), slightly flattened, blunt, bevelled, dark green, adpressed to stamen above; cones 2 in (5 cm) × 3½–⅝ in (9–1.5 cm), purple, ripening, brown, cylindric-conic to fusiform; scales obovate, obtuse, entire, to ⅝ in (15 mm) wide; 'Atrovirens', with very dark green leaves; 'Aurea', with gold young leaves, later dark green, with gold tint; 'Aurea Compacta', broadly pyramidal and compact semi-dwarf, with gold upper leaves and green lower leaves; 'Compacta', broadly conical dwarf; 'Gracilis', very dense dwarf, oval in growth, to 20 ft (6 m), slow-growing (to 2¾ in (7 cm) per annum); 'Nana', globose dwarf to 3¼ ft (1 m), very slow-growing (to 1 in (2.5 cm) per annum); 'Nutans', spreading, weeping and irregular in growth, with very dark green leaves; 'Pendula', compact and slow-growing, with nodding twigs; *P. pungens* BLUE SPRUCE, COLORADO SPRUCE; US (S Rocky Mountains); to 130 ft (40 m) or more; bark purple-gray, deeply grooved, forming thick scales; crown dense, conic to columnar-conic; lower branches downswept; leaves ¾–1 in (2–2.5 cm), radial, assurgent, gray-green to bright pale blue, thickly glaucous, stiff, pungent; cones 2½–4¾ in (6–12 cm) × 1–1¼ in (2.5–3 cm), oblong-

cylindric, bloomed violet, ripening light brown; scales thick-based with thin tips, flexible, emarginate, finely toothed and undulate; blue-leaved upright cultivars include the short-needled 'Microphylla', 'Endtz', 'Oldenburg', the very blue 'Koster' and 'Moerheimii' and the compact 'Fat Albert'; notable blue-tinted dwarfs include the globose 'Globosa' and 'Pumila' and the slow-growing 'Montgomery'. 'Glauca Procumbens' is almost recumbent and 'Glauca Pendula' an irregular, graceful weeping form; yellow and green selections include the sulfur 'Aurea' and the dark green 'Viridis'; forma *glauca* is the group name for all plants with glaucous, blue-gray leaves; *P. sitchensis* SITKA SPRUCE; N America (Pacific coast); to 300 ft (90 m); bark red-gray, exfoliating in coarse scales; crown broad, conic, branches straight, branchlets moderately pendulous; leaves ⅜–1 in (15–25 mm), dark green, with 2 blue-white stomatal bands beneath, sharply pointed, flattened, slightly keeled; cones 1¼–4 in (3–10 cm) × ⅝ in (1.5 cm) when closed, to 1½ in (3.5 cm) broad, cylindric-oblong, pale green, ripening beige; scales very thin oblong to rhombic, undulate, serrate; 'Compacta', broadly conic, dense dwarf to 6½ ft (2 m), with spreading branches and young shoots tinted yellow; 'Microphylla', dwarf, very slow-growing, to 10 in (25 cm) after 10 years, upright and narrowly conic; 'Nana', slow-growing dwarf, of open habit, with leaves tinted blue; *P. smithiana* HIMALAYAN SPRUCE, MORINDA SPRUCE; W Himalaya; to 180 ft (55 m); bark dull gray-purple, grooved, slitting into round scales; crown conic, columnar with age; branches horizontal, shoots pendulous; leaves loosely radial, 1¼–2 in (3–5 cm), dark green, apex acuminate; cones 4–6 in (10–16 cm), cylindric, curved, tapered, shiny pale green, ripening brown, resinous; scales semi-circular, woody, entire, to 1 in (2.5 cm) wide.

pick, pickax a short-handled tool with a thick, centrally fixed head fashioned as a narrow, curving blade with two working points. It is used from a stooping position to break up soil, rock or concrete. A pick has two pointed heads, a pickax, one pointed and one chisel-shaped head.

picotte describing flowers where the

petals have a thin band of contrasting color at their edges. It is used, for example, of carnations and sweet peas.

picturesque a late 18th-century style of British Landscape gardening, fostered by the Reverend William Gilpin and the landscapers Richard Payne Knight and Uvedale Price. It sought to bring subtleties of texture, color, and light and shade into designs, such as might be achieved by a painter.

Pieris (named for the *Pierides*, (Muses)). Ericaceae. E Asia, Himalaya, E US, W Indies. Some 7 species, evergreen trees or shrubs. The new growth is often tinged red, coral or bronze-pink. The leaves are ovate-elliptic to lanceolate and leathery. Produced in spring in erect or drooping, terminal or axillary racemes or panicles, the flowers are small, white, pitcher-shaped, 5-lobed and often scented. Hardy to 5°F (−15°C). Grow in moisture-retentive, well-drained soil that is nonalkaline and humus-rich, in dappled shade or in sun. Give a position with protection to the north and east, sheltered from strong winds and frost; the young foliage is particularly vulnerable to frost, although damaged specimens will usually regenerate giving a second, less spectacular display of colored foliage. Flower buds formed in fall may drop prematurely due to frost or insufficient soil moisture. Propagate by semiripe or softwood basal cuttings in summer; treat with 0.8% IBA and root in a closed case with bottom heat.

P. floribunda FETTERBUSH; SE US; shrub to about 6½ ft (2 m); bark gray to gray-brown; leaves 1¼–3 in (3–8 cm), elliptic to ovate, serrate and ciliate, sharp-tipped, dull green above, sparsely glandular-hirsute; panicles 2–4 in (5–10 cm); includes the later-flowering 'Elongata', with flowers in a long terminal panicle, and the early-flowering, compact 'Spring Snow'; *P. formosa* SW China, Vietnam, Himalaya, Nepal; shrub or small tree, 8–16 ft (2.5–5 m);

bark gray to gray-brown; leaves 1–4 in (2.5–10 cm), elliptic or obovate, finely serrate, sharp-tipped or blunt, coriaceous, lustrous, sparsely glandular-hirsute; panicles or racemes erect to drooping to 6 in (15 cm), flowers sometimes pink-tinged, urceolate to cylindric, hairy; var. *forrestii*: syn. *P. forrestii*, to 10 ft (3 m), with scarlet new growth, leaves elliptic-lanceolate, acuminate, finely serrate, 2½–4 in (6–10 cm)-long, flowers fragrant, in a drooping terminal panicle; 'Wakehurst': to 18 ft (5.4 m), hardy, vigorous, with oblong-elliptic to oblanceolate, bright red leaves, fading to pink before turning deep green, with serrate margins and flowers in large clusters; *P. japonica* LILY OF THE VALLEY BUSH; Japan, Taiwan, E China; shrub or small tree, 9–13 ft (2.7–4 m), bark gray to brown; leaves 1–4 in (2.5–10 cm), obovate to lanceolate, serrate, coriaceous, sharp-tipped to blunt, emerging pink to red or bronze, hardening dark and lustrous green; racemes or panicles to 4¾ in (12 cm), erect to drooping, axillary, flowers sometimes tinged pink; plants formerly known as *P. taiwanensis* usually have bronze-red young growth, tougher, matt green leaves with sparser teeth and a spreading to erect panicle—they include 'Crispa', a small, slow-growing shrub with curled or wavy leaves; 'Bert Chandler', with pale pink young leaves, turning glossy yellow-white then dark green; 'Compacta', compact, dense, to 6 ft (1.8 m), with small leaves; 'Christmas Cheer', early-flowering, with white and deep rose flowers; 'Firecrest', with bright red young growth; 'Flamingo', with bronze-red young growth and deep pink flowers; 'Forest Flame', compact, with oblanceolate finely serrate leaves, and red young growth changing to pink, ivory, then pale green; 'Snowdrift', with bronze-red young growth and abundant flowers on a long, upright panicle; and 'Variegata', with small leaves variegated cream to silver, flushed pink at first, and white flowers.

Pieris 'Forest Flame'

Pilea (from Greek *pilos*, cap, referring to the shape of the larger sepal, which in some species covers the achene). Urticaceae. Tropics (except Australia). Some 600 species, annual or perennial herbs grown for their ornamental foliage. The flowers are very small and inconspicuous. Attractive pot plants for the home or warm conservatory (minimum temperature 50°F/10°C). The trailing species are suitable for small hanging baskets and as groundcover in a greenhouse. Some of the smaller species are especially suited to the close conditions of the terrarium and bottle garden. Grow in bright indirect light or part shade in an open, porous and freely draining soilless medium, rich in organic matter, or in a medium-fertility loam-based mix with additional sharp sand. Keep evenly moist (not wet), and humid when in full growth, and liquid feed every two or three weeks. Reduce water in winter. Do not allow plants to dry out. Site them away from drafts. Re-pot annually in spring; plants often degenerate in their third or fourth year and should then be replaced. Propagate by stem cuttings in spring.

P. cadierei Vietnam; spreading to erect perennial herb or subshrub to 20 in (50 cm); branchlets green tinted pink; leaves to 3⅓ in (8.5 cm), obovate to oblong-oblanceolate, dentate, silver on a dark green ground or wholly metallic; 'Minima': dwarf, with small, elliptic, deep olive green leaves with raised patches of silver; *P. involucrata* FRIENDSHIP PLANT; C and S South America; trailing to erect herb; leaves to 2½ in (6 cm), ovate to obovate, marked bronze, silver or red; 'Coral': stem tinged red; leaves long, ovate, glossy, crenate, copper above, tinged purple beneath; 'Liebmannii': leaves tinged silver; 'Moon Valley': leaves ovate, quilted, crenate, tinged bronze, with a broad silver band along middle and edges dotted silver; 'Norfolk': small, dense; leaves broad, oval, bronze to black-green, with raised silver bands; 'Silver Tree': with white, hairy stalks, ovate, quilted, crenate leaves, tinged bronze, with a broad silver band along middle and sides dotted silver; *P. microphylla* ARTILLERY PLANT, GUNPOWDER PLANT, PISTOL PLANT; Mexico to Brazil; annual or short-lived perennial to 12 in (30 cm); stems slender, translucent, densely branched; leaves very small, crowded, mossy, obovate to orbicular, pale green; 'Variegata': with leaves blotched white and pink; *P. repens* BLACK-LEAF PANAMICA; creeping herb to 12 in (30 cm); leaves to 1½ in (3.5 cm), obovate to suborbicular, obtuse or rounded, glabrous or pilose, crenate, dark; 'Black Magic: mat-forming, with small, round, wavy, green leaves shaded dark bronze.

Pileostegia (from Greek *pilos*, felt, and *stege*, roof, referring to the form of the corolla). Hydrangeaceae. E Asia. 4 species, climbing or prostrate evergreen shrubs, related to *Hydrangea* and *Schizophragma*, but distinguished in having flowers all alike in terminal, corymbose panicles. These are produced in summer and fall and are small and pale with numerous showy stamens. A useful, hardy climber for a north- or east-facing wall, although it flowers more profusely in sun. Propagate by nodal stem and tip cuttings taken from young growth as the foliage expands; treat with rooting hormone and root in a closed case with bottom heat. Increase also by seed and layering. Otherwise, cultivate as for *Decumaria*. *P. viburnoides* India; 20–33 ft (6–10 m); stem self-clinging; leaves 2–7 in (5–18 cm), narrowly oblong to ovate-lanceolate, coriaceous, glossy dark green; panicle to 6 in (15 cm), crowded, flowers, white, stamens conspicuous.

pillar an upright form of trained fruit tree.

pilose covered with diffuse, soft, slender hairs.

Pilosocereus (from Latin *pilosus*, hairy, and *Cereus*). Cactaceae. US (Florida), Mexico, Caribbean region, and tropical S America (especially E Brazil). About 45 species, shrubs and trees with succulent, ribbed stems often covered in long, woolly hairs. Opening at dusk, the flowers are tubular to campanulate with numerous stamens. Provide a minimum temperature of 50°F (10°C). Plant in an acidic medium containing more than 50% grit. Grow in full sun and maintain low humidity. In winter, water only to avoid shrivelling. Increase by stem cuttings. *P. leuco-*

cephalus (syn. *P. palmeri*); E Mexico, C America; eventually a tree to 20 ft (6 m); stem 2–4 in (5–10 cm) in diameter, ribbed, clothed with white hairs, spines pale brown or yellow at first; flowers 2½–3 in (6–8 cm), outer tepals purple-brown, inner tepals pale pink.

pilosulous slightly pilose.

Pimelea (from Greek *pimele*, fat, referring to the oily seeds). Thymelaeaceae. Australasia (New Zealand, Australia, Timor, Lord Howe Island). RICE FLOWER. 80 species, compact evergreen shrubs or herbs, often with decussate leaves. The flowers are tubular with four spreading lobes and silky-hairy; they are borne in terminal heads, to 2 in (5 cm) across and surrounded by colored bracts. Hardy to 41°F (5°C). Grow in neutral to slightly acidic soil with perfect drainage. Water moderately when in growth, and allow to become rather dry when temperatures drop. Good direct light and ventilation are essential in winter. Flowers are borne on the tips of shoots made in the previous season; deadhead and prune after flowering. Propagate by heeled, semi-ripe cuttings in summer, or by softwood cuttings in spring, in a closed case. *P. ferruginea* W Australia; erect shrub to 6½ ft (2 m); leaves to ½ in (12 mm), ovate or oblong, shiny green above, often hairy beneath, revolute; flowers rose-pink, in heads to 1½ in (4 cm) across.

pin-eyed see *heterostyly*.

pinching the removal of the growing tip of a plant with the finger and thumb, to prevent growth extension from that point and to encourage the formation of side shoots. See *break*, *stopping*.

Pinellia (for Giovanni Vincenzo Pinelli [1535–1601], of the Botanic Garden, Naples). Araceae. China, Japan. 6 species of low, cormous, perennial herbs. The leaves are simple to compound. Produced in summer, the flowers are minute and packed on a slender spadix enclosed by a narrow, hooded spathe. Cultivate as for *Arisaema*. *P. ternata* Japan, Korea, China; leaflets 1¼–4¾ in (3–12 cm), ovate-elliptic to oblong; spathe to 2¾ in (7 cm), green, tube ⅝–¾ in (1.5–2 cm),

limb curved at apex, spadix appendix to 4 in (10 cm), erect, purple below.

pine needles leaves of pine trees. These decay slowly and are suitable as a ground mulch where acidic soil conditions are desirable, or for making a leaf mold for use in acidic potting mix.

pinery a low greenhouse, heated by a hot bed and often built as a pit. Pineries were used throughout the 18th and 19th centuries for the growing of pineapples, and sometimes strawberries.

pinetum an arboretum devoted to conifers.

Pinguicula (from Latin *pinguis*, fat, from the greasy appearance of leaves). Lentibulariaceae. BUTTERWORT Europe, Circumboreal, Americas to Antarctic. 46 species, evergreen or deciduous, carnivorous perennial herbs. Borne in a low, flat rosette, the leaves act as living flypaper, secreting sticky mucilage and digestive enzymes. Solitary, 2-lipped and spurred, the slender-stalked flowers are produced in spring and summer. All species require an acidic mix of peat, sand and chopped sphagnum moss, a humid atmosphere and full sun. When in growth, keep them permanently wet by standing the containers in rainwater; when dormant, keep damp and cool (frost-tender species may grow continuously). Apart from the European species, all listed here require a minimum temperature of 50°F (10°C). The European species are essentially hardy to 0°F (−18°C) and prefer cold winter conditions which they survive in the form of tight resting buds. With care, they may be established outdoors in wet, acidic pockets of the rock garden or beside bog-garden pools. Increase by division of resting buds in early spring, division of leaf rosettes in late spring, or by surface-sown seed or leaf cuttings. *P. alpina* Arctic, mountains of Europe; leaves 1–1½ in (2.5–4 cm), elliptic to lanceolate-oblong, yellow-green; flowers white with yellow spots on palate; *P. filifolia* Cuba; leaves 3–6 in (8–15 cm), erect, linear to filiform; flowers white, pink, blue, purple

P

or pale lilac; *P. grandiflora* W Europe; leaves 1¼–1½ in (3–4 cm), oblong to ovate, yellow-green; flowers purple to pink or white, white at throat; *P. longifolia* mountains of S Europe; leaves 2½–5 in (6–13 cm), lowermost elliptic, others linear-lanceolate, somewhat undulate; flowers lilac to pale blue, spotted white at base of lower lip; *P. moranensis* Mexico; leaves 2½–4½ in (6–11 cm), round to broadly and bluntly ovate; flowers crimson to magenta or pink, throat white with darker markings at base of lobes; *P. vulgaris* NW and C Europe; leaves ¾–1¾ in (2–4.5 cm), oblong to ovate, yellow-green; flowers violet, throat white.

pink bud see *bud stages*.

pinks the term garden pink describes a group of *Dianthus* descended from the COTTAGE PINK (*Dianthus plumarius*), which has been cultivated in Europe for more than 500 years. Garden pinks are typically represented by the cultivar 'Mrs. Sinkins', which blooms for about two weeks in early summer and must be allowed to grow naturally without stopping. Modern pinks are mainly of the *D.* × *allwoodii* type, derived from crossing garden pinks with perpetual flowering carnations. These should be pinched to induce a bushy habit and flushes of blooms. They are classified as SELFS, with one color; BICOLORS, with a central eye of contrasting color; LACED or SCOTTISH PINKS, with a ring of contrasting color besides a central eye; and FANCIES, with streaks or stripes

Garden pink (Dianthus 'Mrs. Sinkins')
This old-fashioned pink, with its shaggy petals and powerful scent, is popular in cottage-garden style plantings.

of contrasting color.

Plant in early spring spaced 12 in (30 cm) apart; they should survive for at least three years. Propagate by cuttings, taken at flowering time and comprising four pairs of leaves trimmed just below a joint; insert into a peat/sand or peat/perlite mix and maintain at 59°F (15°C). Annual and biennial pinks (*D.chinensis* and *D.* × *heddeweggii*) are seed-raised for bedding.

pinna (plural pinnae) the primary division of a pinnately compound leaf.

pinnate a featherlike arrangement of leaflets in two rows along the axis. Bipinnate refers to a leaf whose leaflets are themselves pinnately divided.

pinnatifid pinnately cleft nearly to the midrib in broad divisions, but without separating into distinct leaflets or pinnae.

pinnatisect deeply and pinnately cut to, or near to, the midrib; the divisions, narrower than when pinnatifid, and not truly distinct segments.

pinnule the ultimate division of a (generally pinnate) compound leaf.

Pinus (Classical Latin name for this tree). Pinaceae. PINE. Cosmopolitan. About 110 species, evergreen coniferous trees and shrubs. The bark is furrowed or scaly, usually thick and resinous. Needlelike leaves are borne in bundles. The male cones are cylindric, catkinlike and produced in spirally arranged clusters. The female cones are solitary or whorled, ovoid or cylindric to subglobose and composed of spirally arranged, woody scales.

Pines are excellent trees for parks and gardens. The diversity of species and cultivars means that at least one pine can be found for most situations, from extreme cold and drought to coastal sites, temperate woodlands, stony banks and rock gardens. The needs and suitability of each species are described below. Most listed here are fully hardy and show a preference for full sun and well-drained soil, including poor sandy and gravelly substrates. Increase by seed sown in fall or spring, by grafting in late summer,

winter or early spring, and by layering.

Many different rust fungi can affect pines and several are widespread. The white pine blister rust, *Cronartium ribicola*, causes a devastating disease of the American white pines, especially *Pinus strobus*. Other less serious rusts include the pine twisting rust, *Melampsora populnea*, which mainly affects *Pinus sylvestris*; the pine resin-top rust, *Endocronartium pini* also on *P. sylvestris*, may girdle and kill the branches. A needle rust is caused by *Coleosporium tussilaginis*, and needle cast by the fungus *Lophodermium* spp., the latter is worst in cool, damp areas on species adapted to drier conditions. Pines can also be affected by armillaria root rot and phytophthora root rot. In Britain the most serious disease of plantation conifers, including pines, is fomes root and butt rot *Heterobasidion annosum*, although this and many of the other diseases to which the trees are susceptible are unlikely to be a problem on isolated garden trees. Important pests include the pine shoot moth, pine adelgids, several species of sawflies including the fox-colored or European pine sawfly and the conifer spinning mite.

P. aristata BRISTLECONE PINE; W US; to 60 ft (18 m); crown with ascending, whorled, dense branches; bark dark gray, becoming fissured, rust-brown; needles 5, 1–1½ in (2.5–4 cm) × ¹⁄₁₆ in (1 mm), grooved, with flecks of white resin, bright green, blue-white on inner surface in first year of growth, darker later, densely arranged; cones dark purple, maturing cylindric-ovoid, brown, 2–4 in (5–10 cm); *P. armandii* ARMAND PINE; C & W China; to 130 ft (40 m); branches horizontal, spreading widely; bark thin, gray to green-gray, smooth, becoming cracked; needles 5, 4–7 in (10–18 cm), bright glossy green, inner face white-green to glaucous blue, thin, flexible, spreading or pendulous, often kinked near the base, dentate; cones cylindric to oblong-conic, in groups of 1–3, 3–8 in (8–20 cm) × 1½–4½ in (4–11 cm), erect, pendulous in the second year, scales yellow-brown; *P. banksiana* JACK PINE; N America; to 75 ft (23 m); crown regular, ovoid-conic; bark scaly, fissured, orange-gray to red-brown; shoots flexible; needles 2, twisted, spreading, ¾–2 in (2–5 cm) × ¹⁄₁₆ in (1.5 mm), light green to yellow-green, obscurely serrate; cones 1¼–2½ in (3–6.5 cm) × ¾ in (2 cm), ovoid-conic, often in pairs, yellow-buff fading to gray; 'Annae': needles tinted yellow; 'Compacta': dense and fast-growing dwarf; 'Tucker's Dwarf': denser than 'Compacta'; 'Uncle Fogy': prostrate, fast-growing; *P. bungeana* LACEBARK PINE; C & N China; to 80 ft (25 m), often multi-stemmed, slow growing; bark white to gray-green, smooth, exfoliating to reveal cream or pale yellow; needles 3, 2–3½ in (5–9 cm) × ¹⁄₁₆ in (2 mm), hard, shiny, sharply acuminate, dark yellow-green on outer face, pale gray-green on inner face, smelling of turpentine when crushed; cones bluntly ovoid, 1½–2½ in (4–6.5 cm) × 1¼–2 in (3–5 cm); *P. cembra* AROLLA PINE, SWISS PINE; C Europe; to 80 ft (25 m); crown dense, narrowly columnar to ovoid, often branched from ground; bark smooth, gray-green, becoming brown suffused gray, furrowed; branches densely twiggy; needles stiff, 5, 2½–4½ in (6–11 cm), dark green, inner surface blue-white, serrulate; cones resinous, obtuse-ovate, 1½–3 in (4–7.5 cm) × 1½ in (4 cm), purple when young; seeds edible; 'Aurea': needles yellow; 'Compacta Glauca': compact; needles tinted blue; 'Jermyns': compact, conic, very slow-growing; 'Monophylla': slow-growing, irregular dwarf; 'Nana': tightly pyramidal dwarf; needles tinted blue; 'Pendula': pendulous; 'Pygmaea': dwarf; 'Variegata': needles stippled yellow, sometimes entirely yellow; *P. cembroides* MEXICAN STONE PINE, PINYON PINE; Mexico, US; to 50 ft (15 m); crown domed; bark thick, deeply rectangularly fissured, black-brown, branches outspread; needles 2–3, clustered at shoot tips, 1¼–2½ in (3–6 cm), entire, olive green; cones globose, 1¼–1½ in (3–4 cm), bright green when young, turning orange- or buff-brown; seeds edible; 'Blandsfortiana': very slow-growing dwarf; *P. contorta* BEACH PINE; Coastal NW US; to 80 ft (25 m), shrubby on poor sites; crown domed, columnar or ovoid; young trees conical, bushy at base; bark red to yellow-brown, fissured into small squares; needles 2, densely arranged, twisted, yellow to dark green, 1½–2 in (4–5 cm) × ¹⁄₁₆ in (1.5 mm); cones ovoid, 1¼–2¾ in (3–7 cm), yellow-brown; 'Compacta': upright, dense; needles

dark green; 'Frisian Gold': needles tinted gold; 'Pendula': weeping; subspecies *latifolia*: LODGEPOLE PINE; to 100 ft (30 m); bark thick, ridged, needles 3 in (8 cm), more spreading, brighter green; *P. coulteri* BIG-CONE PINE; Mexico, California; to 100 ft (30 m); crown broad conic, becoming ovoid; branches erect to spreading; bark brown to black with scaly ridges; needles 3, 8 in–12½ in (20–32 cm) × ¹⁄₁₆ in (2 mm), gray or blue-green, stiff, finely serrate; cones yellow-brown, ovoid-conic, 8–16 in (20–40 cm) × 6 in (15 cm), woody; *P. densiflora* JAPANESE RED PINE; Japan, Korea; to 115 ft (35 m); crown conic at first, later wide-spreading, irregular, rounded when mature; bark rust-brown, scaly, fissured and gray at base; needles 2, 2¾–4 in (7–10 cm), slender, bright green; cones buff to pale brown, ovoid, 1½–2½ in (4–6 cm); 'Alice Verkade': habit dwarf, tightly globose; 'Aurea': needles with gold tint or spots; 'Globosa': slow-growing, hardy and hemispherical to 3¼ ft (1 m); 'Umbraculifera': very slow-growing umbrella form, needles bright green; *P. halepensis* ALEPPO PINE; Mediterranean; to 66 ft (20 m); crown conic to umbrella-shaped, becoming globose, stem often bowed or twisted; bark silver-gray, becoming red-brown, fissured; needles 2, spreading, 2½–4 in (6–10 cm), stiff, very slender; *P. heldreichii* (syn. *P. leucodermis*); BOSNIAN PINE; Balkans, SE Italy, Greece; tree to 80 ft (25 m); crown ovoid conic; bark ash gray, splitting into furrows, exposing yellow-gray patches; needles 2, 2½–3½ in (6–9 cm) × ¹⁄₁₆ in (2 mm), spiny-tipped, stiff, curved forward, glossy dark green, dentate; cones ovoid, yellow-brown; 'Aureopicta': needles tipped yellow; 'Compact Gem': compact and slow-growing dwarf; *P.* × *holfordiana* (*P. veitchii* × *P. wallichiana*); to 100 ft (30 m); differs from *P. wallichiana* in its downy young shoots and wider cones with scales not reflexed; *P. jeffreyi* JEFFREY PINE; W US; to 180 ft (55 m); crown dome-shaped, conic; bark black-brown, splitting in large plates; branches

stout, spreading; needles 3, 5½–11 in (14–27 cm) × ¹⁄₁₆ in (2 mm), matt gray-green, finely serrate; cones ovoid-conical, 4–10 in (10–24 cm) × 2½–3 in (6–8 cm); buff to brown; *P. longaeva* ANCIENT PINE; NW US; to 66 ft (20 m); crown conic, becoming rough, twisted; bark chocolate brown, in plates, branches erect to pendulous; needles 5, ¾–1½ in (2–4 cm) × ¹⁄₁₆ in (1 mm), green with white lines on inner faces; cones ovoid to cylindric, red-brown, 2–4½ in (5–11 cm); differs from *P. aristata* in lacking resin drops on the foliage; *P. montezumae* ROUGH-BARKED MEXICAN PINE, MONTEZUMA PINE; Mexico, Guatemala; to 115 ft (35 m); crown columnar to conic, becoming rounded; bark rust-brown, rough, fissured; needles 5, rarely 4–6, erect or pendent, 6–12 in (15–30 cm) × ¹⁄₁₆ in (2 mm), green; cones 4¾–10 in (12–25 cm), broadly cylindrical-conical to ovoid-conical, yellow to rust-brown; *P. mugo* MOUNTAIN PINE, MUGO PINE; C Europe, Balkans; shrub to 20 ft (6 m); crown conic; branches erect or decumbent; bark gray-brown, scaly; needles 2, often bowed, twisted, 1¼–2¾ in (3–7 cm) × ¹⁄₁₆–⅛ in (2–3mm), dark green; cones ¾–2½ in (2–6 cm) × 1¼ in (3 cm), ovoid to conic, gray-brown; 'Aurea': semi-dwarf to 3¼ ft (1 m), needles gold in winter; 'Compacta': dense and globose with ascending shoots; 'Hesse': cushion-forming dwarf, needles slightly twisted; 'Humpy': very compact, rounded, slow-growing dwarf; 'Mops': broadly upright dwarf to 5 ft (1.5 m), slow-growing, dense; 'Ophir': flattened-globose to 24 in (60 cm), yellow in winter; 'Prostrata': prostrate; 'Slavinii': mat-forming with ascending branch tips, needles dense, tinted blue; 'Variegata': needles stippled yellow; 'Winter Gold': wide and low, needles twisted, tinted gold in winter; *P. muricata* BISHOP PINE; California; to 130 ft (40 m); crown broadly conic, rounded when mature; bark red-brown, deeply splitting; branches spreading; needles 2–3,

Pinus coulteri

4¾–6 in (12–15 cm) × ¹/₁₆ in (2 mm), twisted, green; cones glossy, 1½–3½ in (4–9 cm) × 1¼–2¾ in (3–7 cm), ovoid, scales with a thick, recurved thorn; *P. nigra* AUSTRIAN PINE, BLACK PINE; SE Europe; to 130 ft (40 m)+; crown ovoid-conic, becoming flat-topped or rounded, very dense; bark gray to dark gray-brown, deeply fissured; needles 2, dark green, stiff, 3–5½ in (8–14 cm) × ¹/₁₆ in (2 mm), straight or bowed, finely toothed; cones 2–3 in (5–8 cm) × ¾–2 in (2–5 cm), yellow-gray to buff, glossy; 'Aurea': needles gold at first; 'Geant de Suisse': columnar-fastigiate; needles very long, to 7 in (18 cm); 'Globosa': semi-dwarf, slow-growing, rounded; 'Hornibrookiana': compact, globose, mound-forming dwarf; 'Variegata': needles stippled gold; subsp. *laricio* 'Wurstle': compactly globose; needles long, vivid green; witches' broom; subsp. *maritima*: CORSICAN PINE; to 180 ft (55 m) in wild, 150 ft (45 m) in cultivation, needles 4¾–7 in (12–18 cm), slender, gray-green; *P. parviflora* JAPANESE WHITE PINE; Japan; to 66 ft (20 m); crown ovoid-conic, compact, usually spreading; bark gray-black, smooth, exfoliating in small plates; needles 5, 1¼–2½ in (3–6 cm), curved, twisted, stiff, finely toothed, glossy dark green with blue-white lines on inner surfaces; cones ovoid to cylindric, to 4 × 1¼ in (10 × 3 cm), leathery-woody, wrinkled, rust-brown; 'Adcock's Dwarf': diminutive and slow-growing, to 30 in (75 cm), forms a congested, gray-green bun; 'Blue Giant': vigorous, to 50 ft (15 m), ascending, needles tinted blue; 'Glauca Nana': semi-dwarf, to 3¼ ft (1 m), needles short, strongly tinted blue; *P. peuce* MACEDONIAN PINE; BALKAN PINE; South Balkans, Greece, Albania; to 115 ft (35 m); crown ovoid-conic; bole often branched from base; bark smooth, gray, thick, deeply ridged; needles 5, 2¾–4 in (7–10 cm) × ¹/₁₆ in (1 mm), pendulous, blue-green, finely serrate; cones resinous, pendulous, 2¾–6 in (7–15 cm) × 1¼–2¾ in (3–7 cm), cylindric, pale brown; *P. pinaster* MARITIME PINE; Atlantic Europe to Greece, Mediterranean; to 115 ft (35 m); crown ovoid-conic, becoming broad rounded or irregular, bark thick, rust-brown, deeply fissured; branches level to pendulous; needles 2, to ⅛ in (2.5 mm) wide, yellow- or gray-green, stiff, shiny,

finely dentate; cones 3–7 in (8–18 cm) × 1½–4½ in (4–11 cm), ovoid-conic, red-brown and shiny; *P. pinea* STONE PINE; Mediterranean; to 80 ft (25 m); crown domed, umbrella-shaped; bark scaly, orange, red- to yellow-brown, with deep furrows; branches horizontal, upswept; needles 2, 4¾–7 in (12–18 cm) × ¹/₁₆ in (2 mm), twisted, blue-gray to glossy green; cones ovoid to subglobose, 3–6 in (8–15 cm) × 2½–4 in (6–10 cm);. 'Fragilis': widely cultivated for edible seed in South Europe; *P. ponderosa* PONDEROSA PINE, WESTERN YELLOW PINE; W US, SW Canada; to 165 ft (50 m); bark thick, yellow-brown, deeply fissured; branches stout, whorled, spreading; needles 3, spreading straight or gently curved, 4½–9 in (11–22 cm) × ¹/₁₆ in (1.5–2 mm), dull green; cones green or purple at first, later brown, 2½–4 in (6–10 cm) × 1½–3 in (4–8 cm); *P. pumila* DWARF SIBERIAN PINE; NE Asia; prostrate shrub, to 10 ft (3 m), or small tree to 20 ft (6 m); needles 5, 1½–3 in (4–8 cm) × ¹/₁₆ in (1 mm), twisted, densely arranged, glossy, green on outer face with blue-white lines on interior face, finely toothed or entire; cones clustered, ovoid, 1¼–2½ in (3–6 cm) × 1¼ in (3 cm), violet-black when young, red to yellow-brown when mature; 'Dwarf Blue': dwarf, irregular, ascending, needles twisted, tinted blue; 'Globe': very dense globose form, needles tinted silver; 'Nana': dense and globose semi-dwarf; *P. radiata* (syn. *P. insignis*); MONTEREY PINE; US (California); to 150 ft (45 m); crown ovoid-conic, becoming rounded, dense; young bark purple-gray, becoming gray to dark brown, deeply fissured; needles 3, 4–6 in (10–16 cm) × ¹/₁₆ in (1 mm), bright green; cones 2½–6 in (6–16 cm) × 1½–4½ in (4–11 cm), glossy yellow-brown, becoming gray; *P. rigida* PITCH PINE, NORTHERN PITCH PINE; NE US, SE Canada tree to 80 ft (25 m); crown irregular, rounded, open, bark dark gray or red-brown, deeply furrowed; branches level; needles 3, yellow-green to pale green, stout, twisted, becoming dark gray-green, 2¾–5½ in (7–14 cm) × ¹/₁₆–⅛ in (2–2.5 mm); cones ovoid-conic, 1½–2¾ in (4–7 cm) × 1¼–2½ in (3–6 cm), pale brown; *P. strobus* WEYMOUTH PINE, EASTERN WHITE PINE; SE Canada, E US; to 165 ft (50 m); crown broadly conic; bark gray-green to

brown, fissured; branches horizontal; needles 5, blue-green, 2¾–5 in (7–13 cm), obtuse, serrate; cones pink-brown, pendulous, narrowly cylindric, 3–6 in (8–16 cm) × ¾ in (2 cm); numerous cultivars—dwarfs include the blue-tinted 'Billaw', 'Blue Shag' and 'Pumila' and the Nana Group ('Nana', 'Pygmaea', 'Radiata', 'Umbraculifera') with light green needles, some dwarfs (e.g. 'Sea Urchin') developed from witches' brooms; upright pyramidal cultivars include the tortuous 'Fastigiata' and the gold-needled 'Hillside Winter Gold'; 'Pendula': weeping; 'Alba': new growth pure white; *P. sylvestris* SCOTS PINE; Siberia to East Asia, Europe; to 100 ft (30 m), rarely 130 ft (40 m); crown ovoid to conic, becoming rounded and often limited to upper trunk as a loosely tiered, flat canopy; bark thin, red-brown, exfoliating to show rust-brown beneath, thick and fissured at base; needles 2, 1½–4 in (4–10 cm) × ¹/₁₆ in (2 mm), twisted, blue to pale gray-green, finely serrate; cones ovoid to conic, 1¼–2¾ in (3–7 cm) × ¾–1½ in (2–4 cm), buff to gray-brown; many cultivars—dwarfs include the blue-tinted conic 'Glauca Nana', and 'Compressa', and the vivid blue 'Doone Valley'; 'Globosa Viridis' and the yellow-needled 'Moseri' are pyramidal dwarf forms; prostrate, creeping dwarfs include the blue-tinted 'Hillside Creeper' and the very dark green 'Repens' and 'Saxatilis'; 'Lodge Hill' and 'Oppdal' are irregular dwarfs derived from witches' brooms, 'Gold Coin' and 'Gold Medal' are richly gold in winter; notable cultivars of normal growth include the pyramidal 'Fastigiata' and the vivid blue of 'Mt. Vernon Blue'; weeping forms include 'Mitsch Weeping' and 'Pendula'. Tinted cultivars include the silver 'Argentea Compacta' and 'Alba', the gold-tinted 'Aurea', 'Beissneriana' and 'Nisbet's Gem', the soft white 'Nivea' and the stippled white 'Variegata'; *P. thunbergii* JAPANESE BLACK PINE; Japan, South Korea to 100 ft (30 m); crown open, with few, long, level or sinuous branches; bark black-gray, furrowed; needles 2, 2¾–5½ in (7–14 cm) × ¹/₁₆ in (2 mm), densely arranged, spreading, twisted, dark green; cones 1¼–2¾ in (3–7 cm) × 1¼ in (3 cm), ovoid-conic, pink to buff; 'Majestic Beauty': dense

P

and compact, resistant to salt and smog damage; 'Pygmaea': compact dwarf to 5 ft (1.5 m), needles long, rich green; *P. virginiana* SCRUB PINE, VIRGINIA PINE; E US; tree to 50 ft (15 m) or shrub, trunk to 20 in (50 cm) diameter; bark thin, furrowed; branches irregular, spreading, often twisted; needles 2, 1½–2¾ in (4–7 cm), yellow-green to dark green, twisted, stiff, sharp, finely serrated; cones oblong to conic, 1¼–2¾ in (3–7 cm), yellow-buff to rust-brown; *P. wallichiana* (syn. *P. excelsa*, *P. griffithii*); HIMALAYAN PINE, BLUE PINE, BHUTAN PINE; Himalaya; to 165 ft (50 m); crown conic, or irregular; bark gray-brown, becoming fissured; upper branches whorled, ascending; needles 5, hanging downward, flexible, gray-green to waxy blue, to 8 in (20 cm) × ¹⁄₁₆ in (1 mm); cones becoming pendulous, cylindric, 5½–11 in (14–28 cm) × 1½–4 in (4–10 cm), green, ripening buff or yellow-brown; 'Umbraculifera': low-growing, mushroom-headed dwarf.

pip (1) a single growth or stem of lily-of-the-valley (*Convallaria majalis*); (2) a florist's term for a single flower in a cluster or truss, especially auriculas and other primulas; (3) a popular name for the seeds of apples, pears, citrus fruits.

single lily-of-the-valley stem

Pip

Piper (classical Latin name.) Piperaceae. Pantropical. PEPPER. More than 1000 species, erect, evergreen shrubs, climbers and small trees, rarely more herblike, often with a pungent odor. They produce very small flowers in cylindric spikes, followed by brightly colored berries harvested in some species for pepper. Those here are grown for their foliage and general habit. Suitable for the warm greenhouse or conservatory. Grow in humid, shady conditions in a fertile, moist medium. Propagate by seed, or by semiripe cuttings in sand in a closed case.

P. magnificum LACQUERED PEPPER; Peru; shrub, erect, to 3¼ ft (1 m); leaves 6 in (15 cm), ovate to broadly elliptic or suborbicular, rounded or broadly acute at apex, cordate to auriculate at base, glossy deep green, bright maroon beneath with white margin and veins, quilted; *P. ornatum* CELEBES PEPPER; Sulawesi; shrub, spreading, creeping or weakly climbing, to 16 ft (5 m); leaves 3¾ in (9.5 cm), broadly cordate to suborbicular, peltate, rounded or acute and attenuate at apex, rounded to cordate at base, finely mottled dark green, pink and silver above, flushed maroon beneath.

piping a method of taking cuttings of pinks, done in early summer by pulling a young vegetative shoot out at a node.

Piptanthus (from Greek *piptein*, to fall, and *anthos*, flower; the calyx, corolla and stamens fall off together, leaving the young pod without a calyx at base). Leguminosae. Himalaya. 2 species, evergreen or semi-deciduous shrubs or small trees, usually with green stems. The leaves are trifoliolate, with narrow leaflets, silky at first, later dark, shining green. Pealike, bright yellow flowers are carried in loose or congested, racemes in spring and summer. Hardy to 5°F (–15°C). Where frosts are prolonged, these shrubs become deciduous and may suffer some damage to their rather tender hollow branches—given adequate protection at the roots, they will resprout from the base. Grow in full sun in moderately fertile, well-drained soil. Prune *Piptanthus* after flowering to remove old and overcrowded growth at ground level. Sow seed under glass when ripe or in early spring.

P. nepalensis Himalaya; leaflets subglabrous to puberulent beneath; flowers bright yellow, standard occasionally with purple-brown or gray markings); *P. tomentosus* (SW China; leaflets thickly silky-tomentose especially beneath; flowers lemon-yellow.

Pistacia (from the Greek name for the nut, *pistake*). Anacardiaceae. Mediterranean, C Asia to Japan, Malaysia, Mexico, S US. PISTACHIO. About 9 species, deciduous or evergreen, dioecious trees and shrubs, usually with pinnate leaves. Produced in spring and summer in axillary clusters, the flowers are inconspicuous but give rise to small, single-seeded drupes. These contain an edible nut in some species. *P. terebinthus* is hardy to 10°F (–12°C). *P. lentiscus* needs wall protection in cool regions. Plant in a sunny position, in well-drained deep but light soil. Both are drought-tolerant. Sow seed in late winter early spring in a loam-based seed propagating medium at 77°F (25°C).

P. lentiscus MASTIC, LENTISCO, CHIOS MASTIC; Mediterranean except NE Africa; tree or shrub to 13 ft (4 m), evergreen; leaves coriaceous, leaflets 4–6, rarely more, ⅝–2 in (1.5–5 cm), ovate, oblong-lanceolate or elliptic; fruit red becoming black; *P. terebinthus* CYPRUS TURPENTINE, TEREBINTE, TEREBINTHO; Iberia to Turkey, Morocco to Egypt; tree or shrub, 6½–20 ft (2–6 m), deciduous; leaves glossy, aromatic, 4–8 in (10–20 cm), leaflets 6–12, 1¼–2 in (3–5 cm), ovate-lanceolate, to oblong; fruit purple, wrinkled.

Pistia (from Greek *pistos*, water, referring to the habitat). Araceae. Pantropical, now a widespread weed of rivers and lakes, first recorded on the Nile, possibly having originated from Lake Victoria. SHELL FLOWER, WATER LETTUCE. 1 species, *P. stratiotes*, an evergreen, floating aquatic, forming dense, freely offsetting rosettes. The roots are fine, feathery and hang in spreading bunches from their undersides. To 8 × 2¾ in (20 × 7 cm), the leaves are broadly wedge-shaped with a rounded, truncate or retuse apex. They are blue-green and fluted above, pearly and prominently ribbed beneath, filled with spongy tissue toward the base and covered with fine, water-repellent hairs. The inflorescence is typical of the Araceae but very small, nestling in the leaf axils. Grow as a free-floating aquatic in heated aquariums or greenhouse pools (minimum temperature 50°F/10°C) in full sun or bright, indirect light in soft water. These plants may be grown outdoors in summer on garden ponds. In fall, bring a few clean and healthy rosettes under cover and overwinter them in bright, frost-free conditions on a pan of wet coir and sand. Propagate by removal of plantlets.

P

613

pistil one of the female reproductive organs of a flower, together making up the gynostemium, and usually composed of ovary, style and stigma. A simple pistil consists of one carpel, a compound pistil of two or more.

Pistil

stamens

simple pistil comprises ovary at base of the style, and stigma at the tip

pistillate a unisexual, female flower bearing a pistil or pistils but no functional stamens.

pistillode a sterile, vestigial pistil remaining in a staminate flower.

pitch resinous exudate.

pitcher a tubular or cuplike vessel, usually a modified leaf. In several carnivorous genera, these are trapping adaptations.

Pisum (the classical Latin name). Leguminosae. Mediterranean, W Asia. PEA. 5 species, annual herbs, often climbing by means of tendrils. The flowers are typically papilionaceous— "pealike"; the fruit a legume containing subglobose seeds. See *peas. P. sativum* is the GARDEN PEA; its variety *macrocarpon*, is the EDIBLE-PODDED PEA, SNOW PEA, MANGE TOUT, or SUGAR PEA .

pit a type of frame or greenhouse constructed with the floor sunk below ground level so that the frame light or roof is at or just above soil level, thus providing wind protection and conserving heat. Pits are a feature of walled gardens in particular, and traditionally were maintained on large estates.

Pitcairnia (for Dr. William Pitcairn [1711–1791], London doctor). Bromeliaceae. C and S America. 260 species, evergreen, terrestrial perennial herbs, occasionally lithophytic or epiphytic. Borne usually in loose basal clumps, the leaves are tough-textured but pliable, oblong-lanceolate to linear and slender-stalked. Showy, tubular flowers are carried in racemes or panicles, often amid colorful bracts. Cultivate as for *Billbergia. P. andreana* Colombia; leaves to 14 in (35 cm), scaly beneath; flowers orange, yellow near apex); *P. heterophylla* (Mexico to Peru; leaves to 28 in (70 cm), flowers pink-red.

pitchfork see *fork.*

Pittosporum (from Greek *pitta*, pitch, and *sporos*, seed, referring to the sticky, resinous coating found on the seeds). Pittosporaceae. Australasia and South Africa to S and E Asia and Hawaii. About 200 species, evergreen trees and shrubs, with thinly leathery to fleshy leaves and small, often sweetly scented flowers produced singly or in corymbs, umbels or clusters from late spring to early fall. *P. tenuifolium* and *P. tobira* are among the hardiest species, tolerating temperatures as low as 14°F (−10°C), and lower with wall shelter: *P. crassifolium* and *P. undulatum* are hardy to about 23°F (−5°C). Grow in well-drained soil in full sun. All species need shelter from cold, drying winds and will benefit from the protection of a deep dry mulch of bracken litter at the root. Under glass, water moderately, maintain good ventilation and provide a winter minimum temperature at about 41°F (5°C). They regenerate freely from old wood and, if necessary, can be cut quite hard back in spring to remove frost-damaged growth. Propagate by seed sown in fall or spring. Increase also by semiripe basal cuttings, rooted in a closed case with bottom heat at 59–64°F (15–18°C) in summer, or by basal ripewood cuttings in late fall in a cold frame.

P. crassifolium KARO, CARO, EVERGREEN PITTOSPORUM; New Zealand; shrub or small tree to 16(–33) ft (5(–10) m), crown columnar, young twigs tomentose; leaves 2–2¾ in (5–7 cm), oblong to elliptic or obovate, leathery, dark green above, white- or buff-tomentose beneath when young, margins thickened; flowers dark crimson to purple, in terminal clusters; 'Variegatum': leaves variegated white; *P. tenuifolium* TAWHIWHI, KOHUHU; New Zealand; tree to 33 ft (10 m), trunk slender; leaves 1–4 in (2.5–10 cm), elliptic, obovate or oblong, glabrous, flat or undulate, pale green; inflorescence axillary, 1- to few-flowered, flowers small, dark maroon to purple-black, fragrant; 'Garnetii', with 1½–2½ in (4–6 cm), ovate-elliptic, gray-green leaves with a white wavy margin sometimes with pink spots; 'Golden King', with 1¼–2 in (3–5 cm), ovate to broadly ovate, pale golden-green leaves; 'Purpureum', with leaves green at first, dark purple-bronze when mature, very wavy; 'Tom Thumb', small, compact, with 1¼–2½ in (3–6 cm), oblong-elliptic, dark purple-bronze leaves with very wavy margins; 'Variegatum', leaves green with a cream margin. *P. tobira* JAPANESE MOCK ORANGE, TOBIRA, JAPANESE PITTOSPORUM; China, Japan; shrub or small tree to 16 ft (5 m); leaves 1¼–4 in (3–10 cm), obovate, apex rounded, base cuneate, leathery, dark green and glossy, revolute; inflorescence terminal, umbellate, 2–3 in (5–7.5 cm) in diameter, flowers orange-blossom-scented, 1 in (2.5 cm) in diameter, cream-white to lemon-yellow; *P. undulatum* VICTORIAN BOX, ORANGE BERRY PITTOSPORUM, CHEESEWOOD; E Australia; tree, 30–46 ft (9–14 m); leaves 3–6 in (8–15 cm), acuminate, laurellike, shiny dark green above, pale beneath, margins wavy; flowers ½–¾ in (1.2–1.8 cm) in diameter, fragrant, cream-white in clustered umbels; 'Variegatum': leaves with white margins.

Pityrogramma (from Greek *pityron*, chaff or bran, and *gramma*, line, referring to the scaly linear sori). Pteridaceae (Adiantaceae). Americas and Africa. About 40 species, evergreen or deciduous ferns. The rhizomes are short-creeping and scaly, giving rise to loose clumps or tufts of fronds. These have wiry, dark and glossy stipes and 2–3 times pinnately compound blades whose undersides are often covered in metallic farina. Grow in light shade in a humid, buoyant atmosphere with a minimum temperature of 50°F (10°C). Pot tightly in a soilless mix rich in coarse bark and grit. Water and syringe freely in summer; keep just moist in winter. Increase by division or spores.

P. calomelanos ILVER FERN; tropical America, now pantropical; stipes 8–22 in (20–55 cm), dark purple, farinaceous when young; frond blade to 24 × 12 in (60 × 30 cm), ovate, bipinnate or tripinnatifid at base, undersurface covered in silver-white farina; *P. chrysophylla*

P

GOLDEN FERN; West Indies and S America, widely naturalized as a subtropical weed; stipes to twice length of blade, dark brown, tinged black; frond blade 8–24 in (20–60 cm), ovate to ovate-triangular, bipinnate or more compound, undersurface covered in golden farina.

Plantago (the Latin name for these plants). Plantaginaceae. Cosmopolitan. PLANTAIN. 200+ species, annual, biennial or perennial herbs and shrublets with basal rosettes of broadly spathulate leaves, or, in caulescent species, stems covered in finer, narrower leaves. Inconspicuous, grainlike flowers are carried in taperlike, stalked spikes. Although better known to most gardeners for the common and persistent lawn weeds it numbers, *Plantago* includes some attractive alpine species whose slender leaves are covered in fine silvery down. These are hardy to 0°F (–18°C) and are suitable for the rock garden, crevices, scree or warm, gritty soil in full sun. The more robust and familiar *P. major* is fully hardy and its cultivars are sometimes grown in the herbaceous border, in moderately fertile soil in sun. Propagate by seed or division.

P. arborescens Canary Islands; dwarf shrub to 24 in (60 cm); stem woody, much-branched; leaves ¾–1½ in (2–4 cm), crowded, linear to filiform, dark green, hairy; *P. major* COMMON PLANTAIN, WHITE-MAN'S FOOT, CART-TRACK-PLANT; Eurasia, naturalized worldwide; perennial herb, sparingly pubescent; leaves 2–8 in (5–20 cm), rosulate, spreading, broadly obovate, stalked, with prominent veins, tough, puckered; 'Atropurpurea': leaves purple tinged bronze to purple; 'Rosularis': ROSE PLANTAIN, monstrous in form, with a stout scape and apical coma of green leaves to 3½ in (9 cm) in diameter, replacing flowers; 'Rubrifolia': large leaves, flushed wine red; 'Variegata': leaves variegated cream and green; *P. nivalis* S Spain; perennial herb; leaves rosulate, linear to narrowly lanceolate, covered in silky white hairs.

plant breeder's rights (abbrev. PBR) the protection afforded plant breeders by the formal official registration and cataloging of new cultigens. It prevents unauthorized propagation of the new plant and enables the breeder to collect royalties. The requirement is covered by plant variety protection laws.

planting and transplanting both terms describe the moving of plants from one growing position to another. Planting usually means the setting out of newly propagated trees, shrubs, herbaceous plants, bulbs and corms, and certain vegetables into a place where they will establish to maturity. Transplanting more often refers to the moving of established plants from one place to another, or the moving of nursery specimens, either in open ground or in containers, during the course of production for sale.

Most nursery stock is established in containers for sale, thus extending the planting season over that of more expensive bare root or root-balled plants. The system is particularly useful for genera that resent root disturbance, for example *Magnolia*, *Cytisus*, *Elaeagnus* and *Cistus*. Plants purchased in containers should be carefully inspected to ensure that their root systems have not become woody and constricted; it is also important to ascertain that they have not been too recently potted and may therefore suffer severe check on transplanting. Rapid establishment after planting will be best achieved with plants that are robust and evidently well-fed and whose roots fully explore the container medium without being pot-bound.

The year-round availability of containerized plants invites planting during unfavorable conditions, such as summer heat and drought, and thought should be given as to the wisdom of attempting to establish purchases during such periods unless the utmost after-care can be provided. Field-grown plants are available for planting during periods of lowest growth activity but, as with those available in containers, this must not be attempted when the ground is frozen or water-logged. Some plants, such as hollies and daphnes, are difficult to handle successfully as bare-root specimens and these, together with species that produce fibrous root systems, such as rhododendrons, are suitably prepared by careful lifting and ball-wrapping as an alternative to containerizing. Where a large number of plants is required, for example, for hedging, field-grown bare-rootstock is usually cheapest.

Mid- and late fall is generally the best time to plant or transplant since the soil is relatively warm and usually sufficiently moist to encourage early rooting. Winter or spring planting may subject young plants to strong winds, frost damage and water-logging, and allows for only minimal growth before a drought period in early summer. In very exposed locations, spring planting may nevertheless be the best course to avoid winter damage, with special precautions taken to aid establishment. Most evergreens are best spring-planted. The majority of herbaceous species can be planted in the fall, but those susceptible to cold or wet should be held over until spring. Bearded irises should be planted mid- to late summer and many woodland plants, such as primulas, set out immediately after flowering.

Where bare root plants are received during periods unsuitable for planting, they should be heeled-in, if possible, or stored in a cool shed with care taken to ensure that the roots do not dry out. Leaving any packing intact is helpful.

Where moderately large trees or shrubs require transplanting in a garden, preparations should be made six to twelve months in advance by

Plantago major 'Rubrifolia'
Cultivars of the common plantain bred for larger leaves in red and purple hues make attractive foliage plants for the border.

P

Planting depth

Most containerized plants should be planted with the top of their rootball level with the surrounding soil. A cane is a useful guide.

taking out a trench around half the root system and refilling it to encourage the production of additional fibrous roots. When the tree or shrub is finally undercut, the ground must be moist and a thick polythene sheet used to cover the root ball during transportation.

Plants being planted out from under protection must be thoroughly hardened off, especially in the case of frost-tender bedding and vegetable subjects.

Planting sites should be well-prepared to ensure good texture and fertility; this can be done by incorporating well-rotted organic matter throughout the cultivation depth well in advance of planting. A light dressing of general compound fertilizer applied just before planting is worthwhile, and removal of perennial weeds at planting stage is most important.

Ensure that stock is well-watered before planting, and that the planting hole is larger than the specimen it is to receive. Always remove plants from containers, gently teasing out compacted roots. Bare root plants should have soil settled around the roots; this can be achieved by continually shaking the specimen up and down as planting proceeds. Small plants are firmed by hand, trees and shrubs with the foot, and in all cases the plant should be planted to the same depth as at its previous site. A thorough watering-in should be provided.

For most garden situations, firm staking of trees is desirable, although there is evidence that unstaked trees develop stronger root systems on exposed sites. For all plants, it is worth

considering the erection of a temporary shelter screen to aid establishment. Where rabbits are a threat, tree guards should be fitted. All planting and transplanting operations should include provision of a ground mulch to eliminate weed competition and conserve soil moisture. This can either be a layer of organic material, kept clear of the immediate base of the plant, or a thick black polythene sheet.

planting board usually, a device for accurately positioning a tree, consisting of a narrow piece of wood, up to 3¼ ft (1 m) long, with one V-notch at the center point and one at each end. The central notch is placed against a cane marking the required plant position, and canes then inserted into the ground within each of the two end notches. The board and central cane are removed while the planting hole is prepared. The planting board is then repositioned within the two end canes to locate the original planting point, and to assist in restoring the soil level.

The term is also sometimes used to refer to a wooden plank put down to reduce soil compaction during planting operations.

planting house, plant house a greenhouse fitted with benches for the cultivation of pot plants.

plantlet a small plant with leaves, and often roots, produced upon certain plants as a means of increase. Some plantlets detach naturally (e.g. bryophyllums), others need to be brought into contact with the soil (e.g. *Tolmiea*).

plant lice a term often applied to aphids and related sap-sucking insects, such as adelgids and phylloxerids.

plant physiology the study of the life processes or functions of plants. It is one of the most important divisions of botanical science.

plantsman formerly, a nurseryman or florist; the term is now used to describe an expert gardener who is primarily a plant connoisseur, often one with a preference for growing individual plants or specific groups of plants over general gardening.

plant window a glazed structure built within a room, usually in front of a window or else with a source of artificial light, as a virtual indoor greenhouse. It is most often of narrow construction and must have facilities for ventilation and access, as provided by sliding panels. Akin to a Wardian case.

plash see *pleach*.

Platanus (classical name from the Greek *platys*, broad, in allusion to the broad, flat leaves). Platanaceae. Mostly N America; one in each of SE Europe to SW Asia, and Indochina. PLANE, SYCAMORE, BUTTONWOOD, PLANE TREE. 7 species, deciduous trees with thin bark, flaking in plates to reveal patches of paler new bark, large, palmately lobed leaves and bristly, brown-green flowers in stalked and pendulous, spherical heads. Planes are large, fast-growing and long-lived trees, with decorative bark and a remarkable tolerance of air pollution and compacted soil. *P.* × *hispanica* is a much-planted street tree. One parent, *P. orientalis*, is a finer tree, with a more rugged crown and deeply cut leaves, but is slower-growing, while the other parent, *P. occidentalis*, is large and fast-growing but susceptible to disease. Hardy to −10°F (−23°C). The natural habitat of all planes is on river gravels and silt with ready access to water, but, given access to ground water, they tolerate drought well, making large trees in dry southern Europe and California. The short, fine, stiff hairs, shed from the leaves in spring, and the fruit in fall have been implicated in bronchial problems; effects are likely to be worse in dry climates. Propagate by seed, cuttings or layers; pre-treat moistened seed of the species at 36°F (2°C) for two months and sow in early spring in a cold frame for frost protection. Seed of *P.* × *hispanica* is often infertile. Heeled hardwood cuttings taken in fall at leaf fall are easily rooted in a cold frame. Plane anthracnose causes sporadic dieback of shoots, occasionally spreading to make large cankers on branches. It is aggravated in cool, damp summers and on those species less adapted to such conditions—*P. occidentalis* is the most likely to be attacked by it in Britain, while *P. orientalis* is virtually immune. *P. × hispanica* varies in susceptibility between clones.

P. × hispanica LONDON PLANE; *P. occidentalis × P. orientalis*; to 165 ft (50 m); bark peeling off in flakes, cream weathering to gray; leaves usually truncate to shallowly cordate at the base, 3- or 5-lobed, 4¾–10 in (12–25 cm) wide, lobes triangular, sinuately toothed to entire; fruit usually in groups of 2; 'Augustine Henry', with pendulous lower branches and 10–14 in (25–35 cm) wide, 5-lobed, slightly blue-green leaves, tomentose beneath at first; 'Cantabrigiensis', with smaller, more deeply lobed leaves, more delicate in all respects; 'Hispanica', with leaves to 12 in (30 cm) wide, normally 5-lobed, with lobes toothed, veins tomentose beneath, and fruit grouped 1–2; 'Kelseyana', with yellow-variegated leaves; 'Mirkovec', with leaves becoming red-tinged in summer, purple-red in fall; 'Pyramidalis', of upright, conical habit, with rougher bark and leaves mostly 3-lobed, with lobes slightly toothed—close to *P. occidentalis*; 'Sutternii', with leaves white-blotched and speckled over the entire surface; and 'Tremonia', of quite narrow, conical habit, very fast-growing; *P. occidentalis* BUTTONWOOD, AMERICAN SYCAMORE, AMERICAN PLANE; SE US; to 165 ft (50 m); bark exfoliating in small plates; leaves generally 3-lobed, 4–7 in (10–18 cm) wide, coarsely sinuate, occasionally entire, base obtuse to cuneate, tomentose beneath at first; fruit usually solitary, occasionally in pairs; *P. × acerifolia* was often grown and sold under this name; includes var. *glabrata*, with smaller, tougher, more deeply lobed leaves, with lobes long acuminate and often entire; *P. orientalis* ORIENTAL PLANE; SE Europe to Asia Minor; to 100 ft (30 m); bark exfoliating in large plates; leaves deeply 5–7-lobed, occasionally 3-lobed on younger shoots, 4–8 in (10–20 cm) wide, lobes longer than wide, base cuneate or truncated; fruit in groups of 3–4 or more, occasionally in pairs; includes var. *insularis*, CYPRIAN PLANE, from Crete, with 5, deep leaf lobes, further lobed with ascending teeth, and long acuminate, and 'Cuneata', with leaves deeply incised

and lobes entire or themselves lobed.

Platycarya (from Greek *platys*, broad, and *karya*, nut, alluding to the winged fruit). Juglandaceae. C and S China. 1 species, *P. strobilacea*, a deciduous tree or shrub to 39 ft (12 m). The leaves are pinnate and 6–12 in (15–30 cm) long; the leaflets are ovate to lanceolate, finely tapered, biserrate and 1½–4 in (4–10 cm) long. The male inflorescence is a slender, erect catkin, 2–3 in (5–8 cm) long; the female inflorescence is a cone-like catkin, ovoid to oblong, and about 1¼ in (3 cm) long. A small to medium-sized tree, which prefers warm dry continental climates where temperatures do not drop below about 10°F (–12°C) in winter. Propagate from ripe or stratified seed, by layering or by splice/veneer grafting on to *Carya* stock.

Platycerium (from Greek *platys*, broad, and *keras*, a horn, referring to the fronds). Polypodiaceae. Tropical Asia and Australasia. STAGHORN FERN, ELKHORN FERN, ANTELOPE EARS. Perhaps 18 species, epiphytic or lithophytic, evergreen ferns. The fronds are of two types: (1) sterile—mantlelike, stalkless, conspicuously veined and variously lobed on the upper margin, these fronds are produced in succession, overlapping each other, clasping the substrate and (the older ones) decaying to create a pocket of moist, fertile humus; (2) fertile—pendulous, stalked, forked and lobed like a elk's or stag's horn, with the spores carried in large, brown velvety patches on the undersides.

These are large, epiphytic ferns suitable for the home, greenhouse or conservatory (minimum temperature 50°F/10°C). All will grow in pots in a soilless medium rich in coarse bark. They will also thrive mounted on wood or bark slabs and stout branches, and tied in place until their spreading sterile fronds have clasped the surface. Encase the roots in an envelope of planting medium and sphagnum moss prior to mounting. *P. bifurcatum* and other clump-forming species can be grown in baskets and will colonize their outer surfaces. Grow in dappled sun or light shade. High humidity is ideal, but these ferns will tolerate the dry atmosphere of the

home if they are frequently syringed, plunged and watered. Keep moist in warm weather, rather dry in winter. Propagate clump-formers by division, larger, nonclumping species (e.g. *P. grande*) by spores. Scraped from the undersides of the drooping fertile fronds and sown thinly on a sterile substrate, spores will soon develop prothalli; these may enter a rest period of up to one year before moving to the next generation.

P. bifurcatum COMMON STAGHORN FERN, ELKHORN FERN; SE Asia, Polynesia, subtropical Australia; clump-forming; sterile fronds to 24 × 18 in (60 × 45 cm), rounded, entire, wavy, or shallowly lobed, papery; fertile fronds to 36 in (90 cm), pendent, base cuneate, 2 or 3 (occasionally to 5) × forked, leathery, segments strap-shaped, obtuse, stellate-pubescent; *P. grande* STAGHORN FERN; Malaysia, Australia, Philippines; solitary; sterile fronds to 42 × 70 in (110 × 180 cm), suborbicular to reniform, upper margin to 5 times deeply and irregularly dichotomously lobed, lower margin entire, papery, bronze to green, strongly veined; fertile fronds to 70 in (180 cm), pendent, cuneate below, 2 × forked, leathery, dividing into strap-shaped segments each to 12 in (30 cm); *P. hillii* ELKHORN FERN; Australia (Queensland), New Guinea; clump-forming sterile fronds to 16 × 10 in (40 × 24 cm), adpressed, rounded and shallowly lobed at upper margin; fertile fronds to 28 in (70 cm)+, erect or suberect, broadly cuneate to spathulate in lower part, irregularly forked or palmately lobed above, dark green, segments narrowly elliptic to obovate; *P. superbum* STAGHORN FERN; Australia; solitary; sterile fronds to 63 × 60 in (160 × 150 cm), spreading, cuneate, apex truncate, to 4 times forked or lobed, gray to green; fertile fronds to 6½ ft (2 m), spreading to pendent, cuneate below, to 5 times forked, segments to 12 in (30 cm) ribbonlike, often twisted.

Platycodon (from Greek *platys*, broad, and *kodon*, bell, alluding to the form of the flower). Campanulaceae. China, Manchuria, Japan. BALLOON FLOWER, CHINESE BELLFLOWER. 1 species, *P. grandiflorus*, a perennial herb with clumped, branching stems erect to

P

28 in (70 cm). The leaves are elliptic-lanceolate, dentate and blue-green. Produced in summer singly or in few-flowered corymbs, the terminal flowers are to 1½ in (4 cm) across and sky blue, azure, white or opal-pink. In bud, the flower is inflated like a gray to slate blue balloon; on opening, it is broadly campanulate, with five spreading, ovate-acuminate lobes. Suitable for the herbaceous border and rock garden and hardy to between 5 and −4°F (−15 and −20°C); mulch with bracken or leaf mold where low temperatures are prolonged. It tolerates a range of soils but fares best in deep, well-drained, loamy soil in sun or light, dappled shade. Propagate by seed sown in spring by basal cuttings with a piece of root attached; also by careful division.

Platystemon (from Greek *platys*, broad, and *stemon*, stamen, referring to the expanded filaments). Papaveraceae. N America (California). CALIFORNIA POPPY, CREAMCUPS. 1 species, *P. californicus*, an annual herb to 12 in (30 cm) tall with erect or decumbent, loose, spreading branches. To 3 in (7.5 cm) long, the leaves are linear to oblong-lanceolate, entire, stem-clasping, gray-green and densely pubescent. Produced in summer, the flowers are terminal, solitary and to 1 in (2.5 cm) in diameter, with six, ovate to rounded, cream to yellow petals and numerous yellow stamens. Suitable for edging borders or for sowing in drifts in the rock garden. Cultivate as for annual *Papaver*.

pleach a term derived from "plash" or "plait" to describe hedge-making by laying, or, sometimes, the training of woody plants against a wall. The term is now used more specifically to describe the formation of a narrow screen or hedge by training new flexible branches along wires and pruning out surplus growth annually. In many cases, the pleaching is restricted to the upper parts of trees, especially lime, hornbeam, or yew, so that a dense green hedge is produced some distance from ground level supported on pillar-like trunks.

pleasance an enclosed park of the Middle Ages, intended for sport, recreation, and aesthetic pleasure, often including water and architectural features as well as trees.

pleasure garden in 18th- and 19th-century England, a public garden used, chiefly at night, for commercial concerts, firework displays, banquets, and other entertainments.

Plectranthus (from Greek *plektron*, spur, and *anthos*, flower: the corolla often has a basal spur). Labiatae. Africa, Asia, Australia. 350 species, annual or perennial herbs, subshrubs or shrubs. They are usually aromatic and minutely clammy-hairy. Small, tubular and 2-lipped, the flowers are whorled or clustered in spikes. Provide a minimum temperature of 50°F (10°C) and bright light. The trailing species and cultivars are easily grown in large hanging baskets, or planted as groundcover under glass. Large plants can be pruned hard after flowering. Propagate by cuttings of new growth taken at any time of the year, by removal of rooted branches of the trailing species, or from seed sown under glass in spring.

P. amboinicus SOUP MINT, MEXICAN MINT, INDIAN MINT, COUNTRY BORAGE, FRENCH THYME, SPANISH THYME; tropics to South Africa; decumbent, many-stemmed, aromatic, perennial herb to 5 ft (1.5 m); leaves 1¾ in (4.5 cm), ovate, pubescent glandular-toothed, rounded, crenulate; flowers lilac, mauve or white; a form with white-edged leaves is in cultivation; *P. argentatus* Australia; spreading, more or less hairy shrub to 3¼ ft (1 m); leaves 2–4½ in (5–11 cm), canescent, ovate, crenate, glandular; flowers pale blue-white; 'Green Silver' is a widely cultivated clone; *P. forsteri* New Caledonia, Fiji, East Australia Island; decumbent, aromatic, perennial herb, stems straggling, to 3¼ ft (1 m); leaves ⅝–1½ in (1.5–3.5 cm), ovate to broad-ovate, pubescent, glandular beneath, crenate or serrate; flowers pale to mid-blue or mauve; includes 'Marginatus', syn. 'Variegatus', with leaves variegated cream and small, white flowers; a gold-variegated form is widely cultivated under the name *P. coleoides*; *P. madagascariensis* South Africa, Mozambique and Madagascar; procumbent or decumbent semi-succulent herb, stem to 3¼ ft (1 m), rooting; leaves ⅝–1¾ in (1.5–4.5 cm), slightly succulent, ovate to subrotund, strigose above, tomentose beneath, glandular-dotted, obtuse to rounded, crenate to dentate; flowers white or mauve, to purple, often dotted with red glands; a fragrant-leaved variegated form is grown as a trailing plant under the name 'Variegated Mintleaf' or, incorrectly, as *P. coleoides* 'Variegata'; *P. oertendahlii* South Africa; freely branching, semi-succulent, perennial herb; stem decumbent, to 3¼ ft (1 m), rooting, glandular-tomentose; leaves 1¼–1½ in (3–4 cm), semi-succulent, ovate to suborbicular, sparingly villous, purple beneath, crenate, ciliate; flowers white or suffused with mauve; 'Variegatus': leaves to 1½ in (4 cm), green-bronze, variegated silver and off-white, particularly at edges.

Pleioblastus (from Greek *pleios*, many, and *blastos*, buds, alluding to the branches which are borne several per node). Gramineae. China, Japan. Some 20 species of dwarf to medium-sized bamboos with short or far-running rhizomes. See *bamboos*.

Pleione (for Pleione, mother of the Pleiades). Orchidaceae. India to Taiwan, Thailand. INDIAN CROCUS. Some 16 species, deciduous, epiphytic or terrestrial perennial herbs. They consist of one or two pseudobulbs only, these near-spherical to box- or flask-shaped and topped with one or two plicately veined and oblong-lanceolate leaves. Solitary and disproportionately large, the flowers appear in spring. The tepals are usually oblong to oblanceolate. The lip is broadly funnel-shaped and often fringed and crested.

These small and beautiful orchids will thrive in an alpine house and cold greenhouse. *P. formosana* has been grown successfully outdoors to 0°F (−18°C) in pockets of perfectly drained peaty soil in the rockery, with minimal winter protection. Re-pot annually at the end of a cool dry rest in a fairly dense bark-based medium rich in leaf mold. Commence watering to promote root and bud development. After flowering, keep moist and well-fed in bright, airy conditions to ensure full leaf and pseudobulb formation. As the leaves wither, reduce water and temperatures. Increase by division and by plantlets. (the latter may develop at the apex of the pseudobulb, especially where plants have been grown in over-warm, moist conditions).

P. bulbocodioides (syn. *P. pogonioides*); China; flowers pink to rose-purple or magenta, lip marked dark purple; *P. formosana* (syn. *P. pricei*); E China, Taiwan; flowers white, lilac or magenta, lip white, typically stained or marked yellow; *P. forrestii* China, N Burma; flowers pale golden yellow or white, lip spotted brown or crimson; *P. hookeriana* C Nepal to S China; sepals and petals lilac-pink to rose, sometimes dotted pale violet, rarely white, lip white, dotted yellow-brown or purple, lamellae and disk yellow; *P. humilis* Burma, NE India; flowers white, lip spotted and streaked bronze or blood red, central zone pale yellow; *P.* × *lagenaria P. maculata* × *P. praecox*; SW China; petals and sepals pink to rose-purple, lip white, central patch yellow, margins blotched purple. *P. limprichtii* SW China, N Burma; flowers rose-pink to magenta, lip paler, spotted ocher or crimson, lamellae white; *P. praecox* Indochina, Burma; flowers white to rose-purple, lamellae yellow; *P. yunnanensis* N Burma, China; flowers pale lavender to rose-pink, rarely white; lip flecked red or purple. In addition to the species and natural hybrid described above, numerous grexes and clones of *Pleione* are grown. Among the finest are: *P.* Shantung (flowers deep yellow or white flushed with pink; the best-known and most vigorous clone is the large-flowered, apricot 'Muriel Harberd'; 'Desert Sands' has creamy-yellow tepals blushing pink and a red-spotted, golden lip; 'Fieldfare' has large pale yellow flowers; *P.* Stromboli (flowers mostly dark red-pink; 'Fireball' is one of the most intensely colored of all *Pleione* clones); *P.* Versailles (flowers very pale mauve-pink to deep rose-pink; the clone 'Bucklebury' is particularly fine and very floriferous).

Pleiospilos (from Greek *pleios*, full, and *spilos*, dot, referring to the leaf surface, which is often covered in dots). Aizoaceae. South Africa. LIVING GRANITE, LIVING ROCK, STONE MIMICRY PLANT. 4 species, highly succulent, stemless, clump-forming perennials.

Solid and similar in texture to lumps of granite, the leaves are usually carried in an opposite or decussate arrangement, one to two pairs per shoot. They are very thick, flat above, the apex obtuse to acute, the bases united and gray-green or dark green with translucent dots. Yellow to orange and often scented of coconut, the daisylike flowers open in bright sun. Cultivate as for *Conophytum*.

P. bolusii MIMICRY PLANT, LIVING ROCK; leaves, 1½–2¾ in (4–7 cm) long, 1¼–1½ in (3–3.5 cm) thick, upper surface broader than long, lower surfaces rounded, apex thickened and drawn over upper surface, red or brown-green with numerous dots; flowers golden yellow; *P. nelii* SPLITROCK, CLEFTSTONE, MIMICRY PLANT; close to *P. bolusii* in size; leaves 2–4, rounded below, drawn over upper surface so that leaf is hemispherical, dark gray-green, densely dotted; flowers salmon pink to yellow to orange; *P. simulans* leaves 2½–3 in (6–8 cm), usually paired, ovate-triangular, tip thickened beneath, not drawn over upper surface, red-, yellow-, or brown-green, spotted, undulating and tuberculate; flowers yellow, sometimes orange, fragrant.

plicate folded lengthwise; pleated, as a closed fan, a term usually applied to leaves for example those of *Veratrum*.

ploidy the number of chromosome sets of a nucleus, cell, or organism.

plug (1) a seedling raised in a single unit of a cellular seed tray. Also often called modules, plugs are a means of planting or potting up with minimal root disturbance; (2) a small piece of turf used for vegetative propagation of lawns; (3) of fruits, such as the raspberry, where the flesh can be detached, leaving the plug around which it is formed.

Plug plant

Plumbago (from Latin *plumbum*, lead; the plant was thought to be a cure for lead poisoning). Plumbaginaceae. Warm and tropical regions. LEADWORT. 15 species, shrubs and perennial or annual herbs. The flowers are

produced at various times of year in branching, spicate racemes; the corolla tube is long and slender with a limb of five, spreading lobes. Grow *P. auriculata* in a well-drained, high-fertility, loam-based mix in direct sunlight, with a winter minimum of 45°F (7°C); ventilate freely when conditions allow at temperatures above 50°F (10°C). Water plentifully and liquid-feed semiweekly when in full growth. Keep just moist in winter. Tie to supports as growth proceeds. Prune hard in late winter, either to the base or by cutting lateral growth hard back to a more permanent framework of branches. Grow *P. indica* in bright filtered light or in sun, with some shade in summer, maintaining moderate to high humidity, with a minimum temperature of 59°F (15°C). For summer flowers, cut back to within 4–6 in (10–15 cm) of the base in spring; given some heat, unpruned specimens will bloom in late winter. Propagate *P. auriculata* by semiripe cuttings of non-flowering lateral growth with a heel. Propagate *P. indica* by basal cuttings and root cuttings, and by seed in spring.

P. auriculata (syn. *P. capensis*); CAPE LEADWORT; South Africa; shrub, stems long-arching, somewhat scandent; spikes short, flowers to 1½ in (4 cm), pale blue; *P. indica* (syn. *P. rosea*); SE Asia; herb or subshrub, semi-scandent or erect; spikes 4–12 in (10–30 cm), flowers to 1 in (2.5 cm), deep rosy pink to pale red or purple.

Plumeria (for Charles Plumier [1646–1706], French traveler and writer on the flora of tropical America). Apocynaceae. Tropical Americas. FRANGIPANI, PAGODA TREE, WEST INDIAN JASMINE, TEMPLE TREE, NOSEGAY. 8 species, deciduous shrubs and small trees with a sparse, candelabra-like crown of cylindrical, swollen, gray-green branches and plentiful milky sap. The leaves are oblong or lanceolate-elliptic. Borne usually on bare branches in terminal thyrses, the flowers are fragrant, salverform or funnelform, with five, spreading, ovate-elliptic lobes. Grow in full sun in a dry atmosphere with a minimum temperature of 50°F (10°C).

P

Plant in a fertile, loam-based medium with additional grit and sand. Water and feed generously in spring and summer. Keep dry in winter when blooms may be produced on bare branches. The soft, thick stems will bleed profusely if broken. Propagate by stem tip cuttings before leaves emerge in spring. Allow the cut surface to dry for several days before inserting in a moist but well-drained medium.

P. alba WEST INDIAN JASMINE; Puerto Rico, Lesser Antilles; to 20 ft (6 m) tall; leaves to 12 in (30 cm), lanceolate; flowers to 2½ in (6 cm) in diameter, yellow with white center; *P. rubra* NOSEGAY, FRANGIPANI, TEMPLE TREE, PAGODA TREE; Mexico to Panama; to 23 ft (7 m); leaves to 16 in (40 cm), obovate; flowers typically rose-pink with a yellow throat, but highly variable in color, to 4 in (10 cm) in diameter; includes forms and cultivars with flowers in shades and mixtures of white, yellow, gold, copper, peach, salmon, rose, cerise and deep red, often with a yellow or white throat.

plumose featherlike; with long, fine hairs, which themselves have fine secondary hairs.

plumule the axis (stem) of an embryo or seedling.

plums the fruits of selected *Prunus* species. The plum grown in Britain and Europe is classified as *P. × domestica*, and is considered to have arisen from hybridization between *P. cerasifera* and *P. spinosa* in southwest Asia/southeast Europe. The Romans introduced different types of plum into Britain, from which seedlings arose in the wild incorporating the indigenous *P. institia* and *P. spinosa*. Until the 16th century, the fruit was eaten dried and preserved.

The main groups of plums belong to *P. domestica*, with wide variations in shape, size and color, within which several types are distinguishable, including greengage types, with green, round fruits of sweet flavor; transparent gage types, where the stone is visible; and prune types, which are purple-skinned, usually have a high sugar content and are suitable for drying; DAMSONS, which are selections from *P. institia*; see *damson*; CHERRY PLUMS, which are very

early flowering, red- and yellow-fruited selections from *P. cerasifera*; of more indifferent cooking quality, some are grown in Britain for foliage effect (e.g. *P. cerasifera* 'Pissardii') and as rootstocks (e.g. 'Myrobalan B'); SALICINE PLUMS, which produce round, large fruits of red, yellow and purple, are selections from *P. salicina*, the Japanese plum, and are widely grown in Japan, southern Europe, South Africa and California.

Other minor groups are identifiable, including the Mirabelle plums of France, which are selections of the species *P. institia* (see *bullace*) and gage-type plums such as 'Imperial Gage' (syn. 'Denniston's Superb').

In North America, the native species *P. americana*, *P. angustifolia*, *P. munsoniana*, *P. nigra* and *P. subcordata* have given rise to a number of disease-resistant cultivars that are suited to both cold and hot conditions.

Plums are widely grown in gardens and the cultivar 'Victoria' is generally successful; a sunny but sheltered site and reasonable freedom from spring frosts will encourage good pollination and improve fruiting potential. In Britain, the southern and particularly the drier southeast counties offer suitable climates for the widest range of cultivars, and wall culture is advisable for consistently good results with the best gages and gage types. For all plums, highly alkaline soil should be avoided, and for longevity of trees, continuously good husbandry is necessary in sandy soil.

Propagation is by budding or grafting predominantly on to moderately vigorous 'St. Julien A' and moderately dwarfing 'Pixy' rootstocks; the older vigorous rootstocks 'Myrobalan B' and 'Brompton' are occasionally used. In the US, seedling 'Myrobalan' is the normal rootstock, or 'Brompton' or 'St. Julien' where incompatibility occurs; the European plums are suited especially to New York State and east coast regions, while the Japanese types are preferred on the west coast.

Fertility in European plums falls into three distinct categories. Class A: cultivars entirely failing to set with their own pollen; class B: cultivars setting a poor crop (2–5%) with their own pollen; class C: cultivars setting a full crop with their own pollen. Cultivars

in classes A and B require at least one other suitable cultivar close by as a pollen source for cross-pollination; these requirements should be considered at the time of purchasing planting stock. The presence of bees and other pollinating insects is paramount and sheltered growing conditions are therefore desirable.

Fruit-thinning to 4–6 in (10–15 cm) apart is essential when a good set has occurred, but should be delayed until stoning has taken place.

The introduction of less vigorous rootstocks, producing smaller trees, has greatly increased the possibility of successful cultivation in gardens. Of free standing forms the pyramid is the best choice on account of space economy, ease of management and lesser likelihood of branch breakage. The bush form is, however, suitable but standards and half standards produce trees unreasonably large for the average-sized garden. Fan training is a very successful form for plums, as it allows for full temperature benefit where grown against a wall or fence. Training in the cordon form is less suitable because of a lack of sufficiently dwarfing rootstock. In the US, large vase-shaped bushes are favored, and sometimes also center-leader trees.

Since growth commences early, planting is best done in late fall or no later than late winter; trees should be staked and tied. Planting distances in gardens should be approximately 11½ ft (3.5 m) for bushes, 10 ft (3 m) for pyramids and 9 ft (2.75 m) for spindles. Fan trees require a wall or fence height of at least 5½ ft (1.75 m) and a span of 10 ft (3 m) minimum, with at least 10 ft (3 m) between trees.

Pruning of established trees should always be done during the summer when there is less risk of infection from silver leaf; early summer is the ideal time, while fruitlets are still small. Wounds over 1 in (2.5 cm) in diameter should be sealed immediately with a suitable paint, the potential benefit outweighing the observation that painted wounds heal more slowly. Steady production of young growth is essential for fruit quality, and on bush trees and spindles, pruning consists of removing any low, crowded, crossing or damaged growths or branches,

Fan-training a plum
Careful spacing and tying-in of the shoots will maximize the amount of ripening sunshine that will fall on the fruits.

keeping the number of cuts to a minimum. On pyramids, summer pruning consists of cutting all laterals and leaders, other than the central one, to 8 in (20 cm), and all sublaterals to 6 in (15 cm), once the shoots are well-ripened. An established fan should be lightly pruned between bud break and flowering in the spring to remove unhealthy, badly-placed or congested growth. Early summer training and pruning entails tying in suitable laterals to the support wires in order to develop and maintain good shape. Surplus side shoots should be pinched or cut to 6 leaves, and these pruned shoots require further shortening to 3 leaves in late summer.

Watering and mulching are advantageous. Gather fruit when firmly ripe preferably picking a tree over two or three times for dessert samples rather than clearing a whole crop. Broken branches should be pruned off as soon as noticed, and wounds painted.

Possible problems: aphids, birds, plum moth (see moth), red spider mite, winter moth; bacterial canker (see *bacterial diseases*), brown rot, silver leaf; gumming.

plunge to sink potted plants, usually up to their rims, into a bed of sand, gravel, or soil, known as a plunge bed, in order to protect them from extremes of temperature, to reduce water loss and to maintain stability in wind.

plur-, pluri- a prefix denoting "many," as plurilocular, meaning many-celled.

pneumatophore a porous apogeotropic root, usually taking the function of a respiratory organ. It is found in plants of wet places, e.g. mangroves.

Poa (Greek name for pasture grass). Gramineae. Cool temperate regions. MEADOWGRASS, SPEAR GRASS. 500 species of mostly perennial, sometimes dioecious hardy grasses; variable habit, stems slender to robust; leaves narrow, folded to flat, or bristled. Inflorescence paniculate. *P. annua* ANNUAL MEADOWGRASS. Europe, US. Annual or biennial; stems to 12 in (30 cm), smooth, creeping or erect; leaves to ⅛ in (3.5 mm) diam., linear, flat, smooth. Inflorescence a panicle to 2¾ in (7 cm), pyramidal, loose; spikelets to ¼ in (5.5 mm) with 3–7 flowers. Common as a weed plant in gardens, especially in turf; *P. alpina* ALPINE MEADOWGRASS; C Asia; tufted perennial, stems to 20 in (50 cm), glabrous, smooth; leaves to 2 × ⅛ in (5 × 0.3 cm), linear, thick, flattened; panicles to 2¾ in (7 cm), ovoid, dense; spikelets to ⅜ in (1 cm) with 3–7 flowers. In var. *vivipera* spikelets are replaced with numerous live plantlets. Grown in rock gardens or at the front of a border.

Grow *Poa* spp. in moderately fertile soil in sun or part-shade. Remove flowered stems to prevent seeding. Propagate from seed in spring or fall.

pod a general term for any dry, dehiscent fruit.

Podalyria (named for Podalyrius, son of Aesculapius, celebrated in Greek mythology as a skilful physician). Leguminosae. South Africa. 25 species, downy shrubs with simple leaves and fragrant, pealike flowers. Grow in a medium-fertility loam-based mix with additional leaf mold. Water moderately, giving a dilute liquid feed semiweekly when in growth. Maintain a winter minimum temperature of 45°F (7°C), with good ventilation. Propagate from seed, or by cuttings of short lateral shoots with a heel, in a sandy propagating mix in a closed case with bottom heat. *P. calyptrata* to 10 ft (3 m); leaves to 2 in (5 cm), elliptic or obovate, gray-green, thinly pubescent; flowers to 1¼ in (3 cm), petals light pink to lavender-purple, purple at base, keel white.

Podocarpus (from Greek *pous*, foot, and *karpos*, fruit, referring to the fleshy receptacle at the base of the seed). Podocarpaceae. Mexico, C and S America, central and South Africa, Asia (Himalaya to Japan), Australasia. PODOCARP, YELLOW-WOOD. About 100 species, evergreen, coniferous shrubs and trees. They vary widely in habit from dwarf and densely bushy to tall and erect to weeping. The foliage ranges in size and shape from small to large, from needlelike to broadly rhombic or lanceolate-falcate, and in color from dull yellow-olive to deep, glaucous sea green. In the female, cones develop fleshy, beadlike arils. The following species are hardy to 0°F (−18°C), but suffer in exposed sites and hard winters. For this reason, they tend to be grown as young, shrubby plants in sheltered rock gardens. *P. alpinus* and *P. nivalis* are especially suited to such positions. However, in mild, humid, maritime climates, some, like *P. salignus*, will attain considerable stature. Plant in moist, acidic to neutral, gritty soil in full sun. Propagation is generally similar to that for *Taxus*, by seed or cuttings; seed may need to be stratified for up to a year. Cuttings should include an erect lead shoot for good shape; side shoots produce prostrate plants.

P. alpinus TASMANIAN PODOCARP; SE Australia (northern southwest Victoria, Tasmania; shrub to 10 ft (3 m), branches level or upswept; leaves linear-oblong, ¼–½ in (6–12 mm), dark buff green above, tinged blue beneath, obtuse to apiculate, midrib keeled; receptacle vivid red; *P. latifolius* YELLOWWOOD; Africa (S Sudan to S Natal); tree to 100 ft (30 m), or shrubby, bark dark gray, smooth, exfoliating in long strips; leaves linear-elliptic, 1½–4 in (4–10 cm) on mature trees, longer on young trees, straight or falcate, rigid, dark glossy green to green tinged blue above, midrib distinct beneath; receptacle red tinged purple; *P. macrophyllus* BUDDHIST PINE, KUSAMAKI, SOUTHERN YEW; S China, Japan; tree to 50 ft (15 m), or shrub to 6½ ft (2 m); leaves broadly linear-lanceolate, 3–4 in (8–10 cm) on mature trees, longer on young trees, green tinged yellow beneath, midrib distinct, bluntly acute; receptacle red; 'Angustifolius': leaves narrower;

P

'Argenteus': leaves bordered white; *P. nivalis* alpine totara; S New Zealand; resembles *P. alpinus*, but leaves elliptic, wider; shrub, erect to prostrate or procumbent, to 6½ × 10 ft (2 × 3 m) wide; leaves ¼–¾ in (6–18 mm), obtuse, rigid, margins thickened; receptacle red; 'Bronze': leaves tinged yellow-bronze, especially when young; 'County Park Fire': foliage creamy yellow to gold flushed bronze-red to pink; *P. salignus* WILLOWLEAF PODOCARP, WILLOW PODOCARP; S Chile; tree, to 66 ft (20 m), or shrub in cold areas, bark fibrous; branches arching, foliage somewhat weeping; adult leaves narrow-lanceolate, more or less falcate, 3–4¾ in (8–12 cm), shiny above, paler beneath, juvenile leaves straighter, 2–4 in (5–10 cm); receptacle dark red to violet; *P. totara* TOTARA; New Zealand; tree, to 100 ft (30 m); bark dark brown, to silver-gray, thick, exfoliating in strips; leaves 6–10 in (15–25 cm), linear-lanceolate, straight to falcate, sharply spined, coriaceous, stiff, green tinged yellow-gray and ridged above, with raised midrib beneath; receptacle fleshy, orange-red to bright red; 'Aureus': leaves yellow-green.

Podophyllum (from Greek *pous*, foot and *phyllon*, leaf—the leaves were thought to resemble a duck's foot in outline). Berberidaceae. Eastern N America to E Asia and Himalaya. Around 5 species, perennial herbs with tuberlike rhizomes. The leaves are large, peltate and palmately lobed, standing over or beneath the terminal flowers like a parasol or ruff. Produced singly or a few together in spring and early summer, the flowers are cup- or bud-like with six to nine petals. They give rise to large, fleshy, ovoid berries. These are hardy plants for the woodland or wild garden, or for moist and shaded borders. Grow in deep, humus-rich, damp soil, in filtered light or shade. Propagate by division, from cuttings of the rhizome, or from fresh, ripe seed.

P. hexandrum (syn. *P. emodi*); W China, Himalaya; leaves to 10 in (25 cm) across, 3–5-lobed, toothed, often flushed red-bronze at first—marbled red-bronze or brown in cultivar Majus; flowers solitary, erect, appearing before leaves mature, white to rose-pink; fruit red; *P. peltatum* MAY APPLE, WILD MANDRAKE; eastern N America south to

Texas; leaves 12 in (30 cm) across, lobes 5–9, cleft, finely hairy beneath; flowers nodding, fragrant, white to rose; fruit green-yellow, rarely red; *P. pleianthum* (syn. *Dysosma pleiantha*); C and SE China; differs from *P. versipelle* in having glossy mid-green leaves to 24 in (60 cm) in diameter, shallowly and bluntly lobed, and appallingly malodorous, dark amber flowers; *P. versipelle* China, Tibet; leaves 16 in (40 cm) across, irregularly deeply divided, 5–8-lobed, finely toothed; flowers nodding, dull orange-bronze to deep crimson, malodorous.

Podranea (an anagram of *Pandorea*, a genus in which these vines were once included). Bignoniaceae. South Africa. 2 species, evergreen climbing shrubs with pinnate leaves and clusters of funnel- to bell-shaped flowers in summer. Cultivate as for *Bignonia*. *P. ricasoliana* PINK TRUMPET VINE, PORT ST. JOHN CLIMBER, RICASOL PODRANEA; flowers to 2½ in (6 cm) long, pale pink striped red, fragrant.

pod-spot any of several fungal diseases that cause spots on the pods of peas and beans, and may also affect leaves, stems and flowers. *Aschochyta* and *Mycosphaerella* are commonly responsible, and damage may be severe in wet seasons. Infection of pods invariably leads to infection of seed, which may be disfigured, and this gives rise to diseased seedlings. Badly infected haulm should be burnt and the growing site rested.

Pogonatherum (Greek, meaning *bearded with bristles*). Gramineae. Tropical Asia. 3 species, low-growing, clump-forming to spreading, bamboo-like grasses with many very slender culms. A delightful miniature 'bamboo', *Pogonatherum* forms a mop of culms, dense with narrow, bright green leaves. It favors moist soil rich in garden compost, leaf mold, or composted bark, shade, a minimum temperature of 50°F (10°C) and frequent misting. Plants will regenerate readily if cut hard back. Propagate by division. *P. paniceum* BAMBOO GRASS; India, China, Malaysia; culms 6–16 in (15–40 cm), simple or branched, tufted, slender, leafy; leaves to ¾ in (2 cm), linear-lanceolate, bright fresh green.

poisonous plants many plants contain chemicals that are poisonous to humans and animals. In some plants, every part is poisonous; in others, poison may be concentrated primarily in one type of organ—for example, rhizome or rootstocks (as in *Convallaria* and *Iris*), fruit (as in *Daphne*), or foliage (as in *Ruta*). In some cases, the poisonous parts of a plant can be rendered innocuous by cooking; with cassava or manioc (*Manihot esculenta*), this is achieved by combining cooking with crushing of the starchy roots to expel the prussic acid within them.

The lethal uses of some plant poisons are well-known, for example, the curare and wourate arrow poisons from *Strychnos toxicaria* in South America, and *S. nux-vomica* as the source of strychnine. Hemlock *Conium maculatum* and angel's trumpet *Brugmansia arborea* are recorded as intentionally administered poisons. However, some poisons, like the morphine of *Papaver somniferum*, and equally curare, have become useful drugs and anaesthetics.

A great many garden plants are poisonous, but incidents of serious effects are rare. It is important that possible risks are understood, but the subject should be seen in perspective to avoid unnecessary alarm and the spoiling of enjoyment of gardens and gardening.

Young children are most at risk from plant poisoning because they frequently put things into their mouths and colorful flowers or berries may be especially attractive to them. A sensible rule is that if a plant is not a recognized food it must not be eaten, and children must be taught this. Mushrooms and 'toadstools' should never be eaten unless definitely identified as harmless.

Adults are most at risk of poisoning from physical contact with plants and sap during weeding and pruning. This type of poisoning usually produces a skin reaction known as contact dermatitis, ranging from mild irritation to chronic blistering. The responsible mechanisms can be divided into five groups: (a) mechanical irritants, such as cactus spines; (b) stings, such as those produced by stinging nettles (*Urtica dioica*), where a toxin is mechanically injected; (c) phototoxins, which are chemicals activated by sunlight, produced, for example, by rue (*Ruta graveolens*), and giant hogweed (*Heracleum mantegazzianum*), the sap of which can give rise to skin blisters and cause permanent scarring; (d) allergens inducing immediate or delayed sensitization, for example, chrysanthemum (*Dendranthema* × *grandiflorum*) *Primula obconica*, ivy (*Hedera helix*) and poison ivy (*Toxicodendron radicans*). Hayfever falls into the allergen-produced group of symptoms and is the result of allergy to wind-borne pollen; (e) direct irritants, as a result of which any person is likely to have a reaction if the concentration of toxin is sufficient, for example, irritation from the sap of *Daphne*, *Euphorbia* and *Ranunculus* species.

Contact with potentially dermatitic plants can be avoided by wearing protective clothing. Where poisoning by swallowing is suspected or evident, medical advice must be obtained, taking samples of the plants where known.

Young pets are notoriously adventurous and should be kept away from potentially hazardous plants. Poisoning of livestock is often more serious due to the large quantities ingested and the longer time spent in digestion. Thoughtless disposal of prunings into fields accessible to livestock is an important cause of sporadic poisoning. Particularly hazardous are hedge trimmings from plants such as box (*Buxus sempervirens*), laburnum (*Laburnum anagyroides*), cherry laurel (*Prunus laurocerasus*), privet (*Ligustrum* species), *Rhododendron* species and yew (*Taxus baccata*). Dried remains of many poisonous plants can have the same or a greater level of toxicity.

In the UK, there exists a voluntary Code of Recommended Retail Practice relating to the labelling of potentially harmful plants, which is intended to help gardeners purchase plants wisely. Individuals must always exercise proper responsibility for their own safety and that of children and animals within the garden environment. At the same time, gardeners have a duty to take reasonable steps to avoid exposure to risk.

The following is a selective list of poisonous species often found in gardens. The letters in parentheses indicate the types of potential risk. For external effects: (S) skin irritant; (E) eye irritant. For internal effects: (P) poisonous when ingested i.e. known to present *any* level of hazard from mild illness to, occasionally, severe poisoning. *Aconitum* (P/S); *Aesculus* (P); *Agrostemma githago* (P); *Alstroemeria* (S); *Aquilegia* (P); *Arum* (P/S/E); *Altropa* (P/S); *Brugmansia* (P); *Caladium* (P); *Calla* (P/S/E); *Catharanthus roseus* (P); *Colchicum* (P); *Convallaria majalis* (P); × *Cupressocyparis leylandii* (S); *Daphne* (P/S); *Datura* (P/S); *Delphinium* (inc. *Consolida*) (P); *Dendranthema* (S); *Dictamnus* (S); *Dieffenbachia* (P/S/E); *Digitalis* (P); *Echium* (S); *Euonymus* (P); *Euphorbia* (P/S/E)—poinsettia does not present a serious hazard; *Ficus carica* (S/E); *Fremontodendron* (S/E); *Gaultheria* (P); *Gloriosa superba* (P); *Hedera* (P/S); *Helleborus* (P/S); *Heracleum mantegazzianum* (severe skin irritant in bright sunlight); *Hippeastrum* (P); *Hyacinthus* (S); *Hyoscyamus* (P); *Ipomoea* (P); *Iris* (P/S); *Juniperus sabina* (P); *Kalmia* (P); + *Laburnocytisus* 'Adamii' (P); *Laburnum* (P); *Lantana* (P/S); *Ligustrum* (P); *Lobelia* (P/S/E); *Lupinus* (P); *Monstera deliciosa* (P/S/E); *Narcissus* (P/S); *Nerium oleander* (P); *Ornithogalum* (P/S); *Phytolacca* (P/S); *Polygonatum* (P); *Primula obconica* (S); *Prunus laurocerasus* (P); *Rhamnus* (inc. *Frangula*) (P/S); *Rhus verniciflua*, *R.radicans*, *R. succedanea* (P/S, severe); *Ricinus communis* (P); *Ruta* (severe skin irritant in bright sunlight); *Schefflera* (S); *Solandra* (P); *Solanum* (most species) (P); *Spartium junceum* (P); *Symphoricarpos* (P); *Taxus* (P); *Thuja* (P/S); *Tulipa* (S); *Veratrum* (P); *Wisteria* (P). All of these plants are safe to grow provided they are treated with respect. They are ornamental plants not food plants.

Leaves are toxic and can irritate skin and eyes

Dieffenbachia seguine

pole see *rod*.

Polemonium (name used by Dioscorides, possibly for the early Athenian philosopher Polemon, or perhaps from *polemos*, war). Polemoniaceae. Temperate to Arctic regions, Northern Hemisphere, southern S America. JACOB'S LADDER, SKY PILOT. 25 species, annuals or perennial herbs, often muskily scented. The leaves are usually pinnate. Borne in spring and summer in axillary or terminal cymes, the flowers are narrowly funnelform to rotate-campanulate and 5-petaled. Hardy to –10°F (–23°C), the following species are suitable for the herbaceous and mixed border and the wild garden. Plant in sun or part shade in moist, well-drained and fertile soil. Deadhead to prevent self-seeding. Propagate species by seed in fall, cultivars by division in spring.

P. brandegei W US; erect perennial 4–12 in (10–30 cm), densely glandular-pubescent and muskily aromatic; flowers bright yellow to pale gold or white, funnelform with a very narrow tube; *P. caeruleum* JACOB'S LADDER, GREEK VALERIAN, CHARITY; N America, N Europe, N Asia; perennial 12–36 in (30–90 cm) tall, glandular-pubescent above; flowers rotate to campanulate, blue, rarely white; *P. carneum* W US; erect perennial, 4–16 in (10–40 cm); flowers pink or yellow, sometimes dark purple to lavender, rarely pink, white or blue; *P. foliosissimum* LEAFY JACOB'S LADDER; erect perennial, 16–48 in (40–120 cm), sparsely villous, glandular above; flowers campanulate, blue-violet, cream, white, or—var. *flavum*—yellow and tawny-red outside; *P. pulcherrimum* NW America; perennial, 20 in–10 ft (0.5–3 m), erect; flowers campanulate, blue to violet or white, tube yellow inside. *Cultivars.* Hybrids and cultivars range in height from 8–39 in (20–100 cm), in flower color from white to pale rose, rich pink, lilac, mauve and pale blue to azure; there are also some striking white and yellow leaf variegations.

polesaw a saw blade attached to a long pole, used to cut branches of tall trees.

Polianthes (from Greek *polios*, bright, and *anthos*, flower). Agavaceae. Mexico. 13 species, evergreen perennial herbs with thick, bulblike bases,

P

short rhizomes and thickened roots. Tough and thinly fleshy, the leaves are lanceolate or linear. Borne in terminal, bracteate, spikelike racemes, the flowers are cylindrical to narrowly funnel-shaped with six segments. Frost-tender, tuberous perennials, *Polianthes* usually flowers in midsummer, but, with successional plantings and given protection and a minimum temperature of 59°F (15°C), may be forced to bloom throughout the year; *P. tuberosa* has long been valued for its spikes of very strongly scented, waxen-white flowers. In cool temperate climates, *Polianthes* is grown in the warm, sheltered flower border, to be lifted and dried off in fall and overwintered in sand in frost free conditions. Otherwise, grow in bright direct sunlight in a greenhouse or conservatory. Plant in a mix of fibrous loam with sand, well-rotted manure and leaf mold or equivalent; give bottom heat of about 59–64°F (15–18°C), keeping the potting mix just moist until the leaves appear. Water plentifully when in full growth, and feed semiweekly with liquid fertilizer. Dry off after the leaves fade in winter. Propagate by seed or offsets in spring. *P. geminiflora* to 28 in (70 cm); flowers to 1 in (2.5 cm), bright orange-red, nodding in a lax raceme; *P. tuberosa* TUBEROSE; only known as a cultigen, having been cultivated in pre-Columbian Mexico; to 4 ft (1.2 m); flowers very fragrant, in a lax spike to 3¼ ft (1 m), pure waxy white, 1¼–2½ in (3–6 cm); 'Excelsior Double Pearl', an improved form of 'The Pearl'; 'Single Mexican', with single flowers with up to 5 spikes, long-lasting; 'The Pearl', with double, highly fragrant flowers; var. *gracilis*, of more slender habit, with narrower leaves, a perianth with a long slender tube and linear segments.

pollard to cut back annually all branches of a tree to the main trunk, usually up to a height of about 6½ ft (2 m). It is practiced to contain tree spread, as with planes (*Platanus*), or to produce a decorative mophead effect, as with willows (*Salix*).

pollen the microspores, spores or grains producing male gametes and borne by an anther in a flowering plant.

pollen beetles (*Meligethes* species) (Coleoptera: Nitidulidae) small, shiny, black or green-bronze beetles, up to ⅛ in (3mm) long, with clubbed antennae; both adults and larvae feed on pollen. The larvae of common species, such as *Meligethes aeneus* and *M.viridescens*, feed in the flower buds of brassicas and related plants, such as mustard and oil seed rape, causing a reduction in the seed crop. From spring onward, adults invade the flowers of a wide variety of garden plants, including roses, sweet peas, marrows, runner beans and daffodils. Although the adult beetles cause no direct damage, problems arise when infested cut flowers are brought indoors, and infested blooms are down-marked on the show bench. Cut flowers for the house should be tapped gently to dislodge as many beetles as possible, and then placed for a few hours during the day in a shed or outhouse where most of the remaining beetles will fly to windows or open doors. Blooms intended for exhibition can be enclosed in fine netting before opening to exclude beetles.

Pollen beetles

pollenizer a plant that provides pollen.

pollinating insects the most important insect pollinators are found in the order Hymenoptera, which includes sawflies, wasps, bees, ants and, particularly, the cosmopolitan honey bee (*Apis mellifera*) and bumble bees (*Bombus* species); some solitary bees, such as leaf-cutting bees (*Megachile* species) and mason bees (*Osmia* species), are also useful. Among the Diptera, blowflies and hoverflies play a significant role. Blowflies are easily reared in captivity and have been used in plant breeding programs under greenhouse protection for crops, such as brassicas, onions and carrots. Some beetles (Coleoptera), for example, pollen beetles, and various species of

thrips (Thysanoptera) pollinate flowers but any benefit may be offset by injury to the blooms. Butterflies and moths (Lepidoptera) are important pollinators of flowers with long tubular corollas.

pollination the transfer of pollen grains from an anther to a stigma, a process that precedes fertilization and the production of seed. It may involve either self-pollination, if pollen is transferred within the same flower, or cross-pollination where the transfer is between different flowers on the same plant or to flowers on another plant of the same species. Many flowers have processes and structures developed to ensure cross-pollination, such as nectar production to attract insects, mechanisms to ensure pollen distribution (as in *Viola* and *Salvia*), and profuse pollen production for wind distribution (as in many grasses). There are adaptations to ensure self-pollination, such as the maturing of anthers and stigmas at the same time. Intervention by gardeners can effect improved pollination, for example, dusting between open flowers of peach with a brush or rabbit's tail. Such action can also be a means of making controlled crosses in plant breeding.

pollinator (1) an agent or means of pollen transfer, for example insects, birds, bats, or wind; (2) used in fruit growing to describe a cultivar planted to ensure fruit set on another cultivar that is self-sterile or partially so.

pollinium a regular mass of more or less coherent pollen grains.

polycarbonate see *greenhouse*.

Polygala (name used by Dioscorides, from Greek *polys*, much, and *gala*, milk; these plants were believed to promote the secretion of milk). Polygalaceae. Widespread. MILKWORT, SENECA, SNAKEROOT. 500 species, annual or perennial herbs and shrubs or, rarely, trees. The pealike flowers consist of two inner, petal-like sepals (wings) and three to five petals, the lowermost petal (keel) often crested. The hardy *P. calcarea* and *P. chamaebuxus* are suitable for the rock garden. Some alpine species, such as *P. vayredae*, do not thrive in mild damp winters and may be more successfully grown in an alpine house. Tender species, such as *P. myrtifolia*, need the protection of the cool greenhouse in cool temperate zones. Grow in part shade or in sun in moisture-retentive but well-drained soil. Under glass, grow in bright filtered light, providing shade from the hottest summer sun and good ventilation. Water plentifully and feed semiweekly with dilute liquid feed when in full growth. Keep just moist in winter with a minimum temperature of 41°F (5°C). Cut leggy specimens hard back in late winter. Propagate by seed in spring or by softwood or semiripe cuttings in a sandy propagating mix in a closed case with gentle bottom heat.

P. calcarea W Europe; perennial herb, erect to 8 in (20 cm), rosette leaves spathulate to obovate, stem leaves smaller, linear-lanceolate; flowers usually blue or white; *P. chamaebuxus* C Europe to Italy; evergreen, low-growing shrub, 2–6 in (5–15 cm); leaves ⅝–1¼ in (1.5–3 cm), elliptic to obovate, leathery, somewhat glossy; flowers with wings cream-white to pink, rosy purple or yellow, keel yellow; *P. myrtifolia* South Africa; erect, much-branched shrub, 3¼–8 ft (1–2.5 m); leaves 1–2 in (2.5–5 cm), elliptic-oblong or obovate; flowers green-white veined purple, or wholly rich purple; *P. vayredae* E Pyrenees; perennial to 2 in (5 cm); leaves ¾–1 in (2–2.5 cm), linear-lanceolate; flowers pink-purple with a yellow-tinged keel.

polygamodioecious (1) a plant that is functionally dioecious but contains some perfect flowers in its inflorescence; (2) a species that has perfect and imperfect flowers on separate individuals.

polygamous describing a plant that has male (staminate), female (pistillate) and hermaphrodite flowers, on the same or separate plants of the same species, for example ash (*Fraxinus excelsior*).

Polygonatum (from Greek *polys*, many, and *gony* joint, referring to the many-jointed rhizome; name used by Dioscorides). Liliaceae (Convallariaceae). SOLOMON'S SEAL. N US,

Europe, Asia. Some 30 species, rhizomatous, perennial herbs with erect to arching stems clothed with alternate, opposite, or whorled, ovate to linear leaves. The flowers are tubular with six, erect to spreading segments, and usually nod or hang from the leaf axils. The berries are blue-black or red. The following species are hardy and tolerant of a range of conditions, excepting heat and drought. However, they are best grown in fertile, humus-rich, moist but well-drained soil in cool, semi-shade or shade. Leave undisturbed once planted and allow large clumps to establish for best effects. *P. hookeri* is suited to damp pockets in the rock garden and to alpine sinks and troughs. Propagate by division or by seed in fall. Larvae of the saw fly will strip foliage in summer.

P. biflorum (syn. *P. canaliculatum*, *P. commutatum*); E US, south central Canada; stem 16 in–6½ ft (40 cm–2 m), erect or arched; leaves 1½–7 in (4–18 cm), alternate, narrow-lanceolate to broadly elliptic, glaucous beneath; flowers drooping, ½–1 in (1–2.3 cm), green-white; *P. hookeri* E Himalaya, China; stem 2–4 in (5–10 cm), more or less erect; leaves crowded, alternate, ⅝–¾ in (1.5–2 cm), linear to narrow-elliptic; flowers solitary, erect, to ¾ in (2 cm), purple or lilac-pink; *P. × hybridum* (*P. multiflorum × P. odoratum*); intermediate between parents; common in cultivation, includes 'Flore Pleno', with double flowers, and 'Striatum' with creamy white striped leaves; *P. multiflorum* Europe, Asia; stem to 36 in (90 cm), arched; leaves 2–6 in (5–15 cm), alternate, elliptic-oblong to ovate; flowers ½–¾ in (1–2 cm), drooping, white tipped green; *P. odoratum* (syn. *P. officinale*); Europe, Asia; stem to 34 in (85 cm), arched; leaves 4–4¾ in (10–12 cm) lanceolate to ovate, alternate, ascending; flowers 2–4 per axil, drooping, fragrant ½–¾ in (1–2 cm), white tipped green; includes 'Gilt Edge', with leaves edged yellow; var. *plurifolium* 'Variegatum', with red stems when young and leaves narrowly edged creamy white; *P. verticillatum* Europe, temperate Asia,

Afghanistan; stem 8–39 in (20–100 cm), erect; leaves 2½–6 in (6.5–15 cm), opposite or whorled, linear-lanceolate to narrowly ovate; flowers to ⅝ in (1.5 cm), drooping, 1–3 per axil, green-white.

Polygonum (from Greek *polys*, many, and *gony*, joint; the stems have conspicuously swollen nodes). Polygonaceae. Northern temperate regions with 1 species also found in southern South America. KNOTWEED, SMARTWEED. Some 20 species, annual or perennial herbs, some becoming shrubby. The stems appear jointed. Produced in summer in axillary, rarely terminal, cymes, the flowers are small, funnel- or bell-shaped and usually consist of five segments. The achenes are small and three-angled, enclosed by persistent perianth or partly protruding.

Many species formerly found in *Polygonum* are now included in *Persicaria* and of the remaining species few are suitable for use as garden plants and most have the potential to become weedy. Among those sometimes grown as ornamentals the most appealing is *P. scoparium*, an attractive curiosity with weak, horsetail-like stems, incorrectly grown for many years as *P. equisetiforme*, under which name it may still be offered. A native of Corsica and Sardinia it requires a sheltered spot in zones experiencing winter temperatures below about 23°F (–5°C) but will often shoot from the base if cut back by frost.

P. forrestii China, Kashmir, Myanmar; creeping perennial to 8 in (20 cm); leaves suborbicular or reniform, cordate at base, blade to 1½ in (4 cm) on long petiole. Flowers small and white to yellowish, borne in summer on terminal, corymbose

Polygonatum
multiflorum

cymes; *P. scoparium* (syn. *P. equisetiforme*) misapplied; Corsica and Sardinia; branching perennial to 3¼ ft (1 m) or so, rootstock becoming woody; leaves falling quickly leaving wiry, green stems, naked but for small, reddish ochreae at the nodes. The flowers are

P

small and white—often pink in wild plants—but highly fragrant, carried in lax spikes in the summer.

polymorphic occurring in more than two distinct forms; possessing variety in some morphological feature.

polyploid a plant with more than the normal two sets of chromosomes as the genetic components of its cells. It arises from a multiplying of the chromosomes complement at the time of fertilization. See *triploid*, *tetraploid*.

Polypodium (from Greek *polys*, much, and *pous*, foot). Polypodiaceae. Mainly temperate Northern Hemisphere. POLYPODY. Some 75 species, epiphytic, lithophytic or terrestrial ferns, evergreen or semi-deciduous with creeping, scaly rhizomes. The fronds are entire to pinnate or pinnatifid. Hardy to 0°F (–18°C) and easily established in the fern border, mixed border, or (*P. vulgare*) on dry stone walls. Although they favor moist, lightly shaded conditions, they will tolerate drought and direct sunlight. Propagate by division or spores.

P. cambricum SOUTHERN POLYPODY; Europe; differs from *P. vulgare* in its broader, softer fronds; 5–20 in (13–50 cm) × 2¾–4 in (7–10 cm), pinnatifid, deltoid or oblong, base truncate, segments to ⅜ in (9 mm) wide; includes numerous cultivars with finely dissected, plumose, forked, lacerate and crested fronds; *P. glycyrrhiza* LICORICE FERN; Alaska to California; fronds to 14 × ⅜ in (35 × 1.5 cm), pinnate to pinnatifid, lanceolate to elliptic or oblong, caudate or attenuate, thin-textured, segments to 2½ × ½ in (6 × 1 cm), alternate, falcate, linear, base dilated, notched; includes crested and lacerated and narrow, elongated cultivars; *P. polypodioides* RESURRECTION FERN; Americas, South Africa; fronds to 6 × 2½ in (15 × 6 cm), deltoid or oblong, apex attenuate to acute, margins rolling inward during dry weather, somewhat leathery, segments to 10 × ¼ in (25 × 5 mm), distant, spreading, linear or oblong, apex obtuse, base dilated, entire or notched, scaly; *P. scouleri* LEATHERY POLYPODY, COAST POLYPODY; N America; fronds to 16 × 6 in (40 × 15 cm), ovate to deltoid, thick-textured

and rigid, segments to 14 pairs, spreading, linear to oblong, margin entire to notched or undulate and cartilaginous; *P. virginianum* ROCK AMERICAN WALL FERN, POLYPODY; N America, E Asia; fronds to 10 × 2¾ in (25 × 7 cm), arching or pendent, lanceolate or deltoid to oblong, leathery to thin-textured, segments to 1½ × ½ in (4 × 1 cm), to 25 pairs, alternate to subopposite, lanceolate to linear or oblong, entire to notched and undulate; includes 'Bipinnatifidum', with regularly and deeply lacerated pinnae, plumose; *P. vulgare* WALL POLYPODY, ADDER'S FERN, WALL FERN, GOLDEN MAIDENHAIR; N America, Europe, Africa, E Asia; fronds to 12 × 6 in (30 × 15 cm), ascending to erect, lanceolate to ovate or oblong or linear, glabrous, thin-textured to subcoriaceous, segments to 2½ in × ¼ in (6 cm × 7 mm), close, spreading, horizontal to ascending, oblong to linear, obtuse, entire to dentate; includes cultivars with plumose, crested, forked, lacerated and pinnately cut fronds.

Polyscias (from Greek *polys*, many, and *skias*, shadow, i.e. sunshade or canopy, referring to the sometimes large and many-branched, spreading inflorescences). Araliaceae. Old World Tropics. About 100 species, evergreen shrubs or trees. Clustered toward the branch ends, the leaves are simple to trifoliolate or pinnate. Small, pale flowers are borne in umbels or heads in compound inflorescences. Cultivation as for *Schefflera*. *P. filicifolia* FERN-LEAF ARALIA, HOTITO; probable cultigen originating in E Malaysia or the West Pacific, now widespread in warmer regions; large erect shrub; leaves 9–17-foliolate, leaflets narrowly elliptic to linear-lanceolate, stalked, deeply cut or pinnatifid, to 4 in (10 cm), bright green, midribs tinted purple, shallowly toothed; white-variegated cultivars are grown; *P. guilfoylei* GERANIUM ARALIA, COFFEE TREE; probable cultigen originating in E Malaysia or the West Pacific, now widespread in warmer regions; erect shrub or treelet to 20 ft (6 m), little-branched; leaves to 24 in (60 cm), leaflets 5–9, stalked, rotund to broadly ovate or oblong-elliptic, to 6 in (15 cm), irregularly spiny-toothed often obscurely lobed, margins white or cream; includes cultivars with crisped,

finely cut and variegated leaves; *P. scutellaria* possible cultigen originating in E Malaysia or the West Pacific, now widespread in warmer regions; shrub or small tree to 20 ft (6 m); leaves to 12 in (30 cm), leaflets 1–3(–5), broadly elliptic or orbicular, often shieldlike, to 11 in (28 cm) wide, apex rounded, the base obtuse to cordate, entire or minutely spiny-toothed, sometimes lobed; includes cultivars with finely toothed or cut and variegated leaves.

Polystichum (from Greek *polys*, many, and *stix*, a row, referring to the regular rows of sori seen on many species). Dryopteridaceae. Cosmopolitan. HOLLY FERN. More than 175 species, small to medium-sized terrestrial ferns, evergreen to semi-deciduous, with shaggy-scaly rhizomes and 1–3-pinnate fronds. Most species are hardy to –22°F (–30°C) or lower, but where harsh winters are common, it may be wise to mulch their bases thickly and to cover the crown with dried leaves or bracken. *Polystichum* will tolerate part sun for up to six hours a day in moist soil. In full shade, it will tolerate quite dry conditions once the fronds are developed. Preferred pH is 6.5 to 7.5; in very acidic soil, some species, such as *P. setiferum*, gradually lose vigor. Propagate by spores or division in spring. Increase also by bulbil-like plantlets, where produced.

P. acrostichoides CHRISTMAS FERN; N America; fronds 8–20 in (20–50 cm) × 2–4¾ in (5–12 cm), linear-lanceolate, pinnae alternate, 20–35 each side, linear-oblong, acutely auriculate at base, minutely spinose-dentate, dark green, with hairlike scales beneath; *P. aculeatum* Europe; fronds 12–36 in (30–90 cm) × 2–9 in (5–22 cm), lanceolate, rigid, pinnae to 50 per side, pinnate or pinnatifid, pinnules small, serrate, decurrent; *P. lonchitis* NORTHERN HOLLY FERN; Europe; fronds 8–24 in (20–60 cm) × 1¼–2¾ in (3–7 cm), linear-lanceolate, rigid, coriaceous, pinnae 25–40 each side, lanceolate, slightly curved, auriculate on upper side at base, serrate, dark green above, scaly beneath, very shortly stalked; *P. proliferum* MOTHER SHIELD FERN; Australia; rhizome trunklike with age; fronds to 39 × 12 in (100 × 30 cm), bipinnate to tripinnate, dark green, with proliferous buds near apex, pinnules spiny-serrate; *P. setiferum* HEDGE FERN; S, W and C Europe; fronds 39–48 in (30–120 cm) × 4–10 in (10–25 cm), lanceolate, soft, pinnae to 4½–1 in (11–2.5 cm), to 40 per side, pinnules serrate, stipitate; rachis bearing bulbils; includes many cultivars with crested, finely dissected, narrowed and pointed, proliferous and densely congested feathery fronds; *P. tsussimense* NE Asia; fronds 10–16 in (25–40 cm) × 4–8 in (10–20 cm), broadly lanceolate to oblong-ovate, acuminate, pinnules ¼–⅝ in (7–15 mm), ovate to oblong-ovate, mucronate, spinose-dentate, glabrous and glaucous above.

polythene a thermoplastic material of versatile use in gardening. It is available in various sheet thicknesses, opaque or colored, and also in molded form. Sheet polythene is used for cladding greenhouses and frames; types incorporating an ultraviolet light inhibitor will last longer. Low continuous polythene tunnels are suitable for advancing crops such as strawberries. Black sheet may be used as a weed-inhibiting soil mulch, and clear sheet as a ground mulch for raising soil temperature or for advancing maturity of crops, such as carrots and potatoes—in such instances, the sheet may be perforated. Polythene sheet is also an excellent means of protecting rooting cuttings and of insulating greenhouses in winter, especially in bubble form. Thick gauge sheet is used as a pool liner. It is also fabricated into flimsy or rigid plant containers. Polythene waste should be disposed of through approved collection agencies and never burnt because the process emits toxic gases.

polytunnel a greenhouse clad with polythene sheet.

pome a multiloculate fruit, formed by the fusion of an inferior ovary and the hypanthium, from which the flesh, which is tough but not woody or bony, is derived.

pome fruit the fruit of apple, pear, quince, medlar, and some other members of the family Rosaceae.

pomology the science and practice of fruit-growing.

pomona a treatise on fruits.

pompon applied especially to types of dahlia and chrysanthemum with small globular flowers composed of tight-packed florets. See *chrysanthemum, dahlia*.

Poncirus (Latinized form of French *poncire*, a type of citrus). Rutaceae. C and N China. 1 species, *P. trifoliata*, TRIFOLIATE ORANGE, HARDY ORANGE, a fast-growing, small, deciduous tree with many, interlacing, green twiggy branches armed with formidable thorns. The leaves are trifoliolate, the terminal leaflet 1¼–2½ in (3–6 cm) × ⅝–1 in (1.5–2.5 cm) and obovate-cuneate. Borne in early spring, the flowers are solitary and scented with waxy, white, oblong petals to 1¼ in (3 cm). Roughly spherical and 1¼–2 in (3–5 cm) in diameter, the fruit is dull lemon-yellow and fragrant when ripe, with a thick, rough peel covered in copious oil glands; the pulp is very acidic. Hardy to 5°F (–15°C), this shrub is valued for its interlacing branch pattern, orange blossom flowers and curious, inedible fruit. It is also used for hedging and as a frost-resistant root-stock for *Citrus*. Grow in well-drained fertile soil in sun. Prune if necessary to remove any dead or damaged wood in spring; clip hedges in early summer. Propagate by seed, removed from flesh when ripe and sown in a cold frame in fall. Increase also by semiripe cuttings in summer.

pond see *water gardening*.

Pontederia (for Giulio Pontedera [1688–1757], professor of botany at Padua). Pontederiaceae. N and S America, mostly eastern. PICKEREL WEED, WAMPEE. 5 species, perennial, aquatic or semi-aquatic, marginal herbs with emergent, lanceolate to sagittate or hastate leaves. Small and zygomorphic, with a 2-lipped tubular perianth, the flowers are borne in dense, scapose spikes in spring and summer. A hardy, marginal aquatic. Grow in full sun. Plant in the pond or lake bed, at its margins or in large, submerged baskets containing a fertile, loam-based medium. Remove dead foliage after the last frosts. Propagate

by division in spring. *P. cordata* (PICKEREL weed, wampee; eastern N America to Caribbean; aquatic perennial, 16–39 in (40–100 cm); leaves to 7 in (18 cm), emergent, erect, ovate to lanceolate with a cordate to sagittate base and long stalks; flowers to ¾ in (2 cm) across, blue, lilac or white, crowded in cylindric spikes to 7 in (18 cm).

Populus (classical Latin vernacular name for the genus). Salicaceae. Europe, Asia, N Africa, N America. ASPEN, POPLAR, COTTONWOOD. Some 35 species, deciduous, dioecious trees with ovate to lanceolate or triangular leaves. The flowers are borne in pendulous catkins before leaves, the male catkins denser than the females. Tufted with white hairs, the minute seeds are released in billowing, cotton-downlike masses in late spring or early summer.

A large genus of Northern Hemisphere natives, from a wide variety of habitats, *Populus* shares many characteristics with the closely related *Salix*, and requires careful selection and siting. Most species produce debris in the form of seed 'cotton', twigs and leaves, and most have greedy and extensive root systems. They are best suited to forestry and to the broader landscape, where they are undeniably useful as windbreaks and visual screens. One commonly used fastigiate poplar for this purpose, *P. nigra* 'Italica', is probably the least suitable, having fragile branches, and being particularly prone to basal rots that may cause sudden collapse; *P. nigra* 'Plantierensis' has stronger and lower branches, and a denser head. While selected cultivars may be suitable for large gardens, they should be sited at least 130 ft (40 m) from buildings, drains, walls and roads, especially in clay soil, since they are known to cause extensive damage to foundations and drainage systems.

Many *Populus* species are useful on difficult sites. *P. alba* and its cultivars and *P. × canescens* are tolerant of salt-laden winds (but not of saline conditions at the roots). *P. tremula* tolerates extremely alkaline soil. *P. × canadensis* 'Regenerata' is tolerant of urban pollution and may be pollarded, where it has outgrown its allotted space. *P. tremula* is sometimes used to improve heavy soil in neglected woodland. The young foliage of some, notably *P. balsamifera*, *P. × jackii* 'Gileadensis' (balm of Gilead), and *P. trichocarpa*, emits a pleasant, light balsam scent, especially after rain. Others color well in fall, among them *P. × canadensis*, *P. maximowiczii* and *P. tremuloides*. Grow in deep, fertile, and well-drained, near neutral soil. Mound planting is advised on wet sites. Propagate by hardwood cuttings, suckers, layers or root cuttings. Sow newly ripened seed in moist silt. All species hybridize readily. The most serious disease is bacterial canker.

P. alba WHITE POPLAR, SILVER-LEAVED POPLAR, ABELE; S, C and E Europe, N Africa to C Asia; to 100 ft (30 m), crown broad, bark smooth, gray suckering; leaves 2½–4¾ in (6–12 cm), ovate, base subcordate, those on long shoots lobed, coarsely toothed, on short shoots serrate ovate to elliptic-oblong, dark green and glabrous above, white-woolly beneath; 'Globosa', a tall shrub with a broadly rounded habit and pink young leaves; 'Intertexta', with dull white young leaves becoming yellow-speckled; 'Nivea', a juvenile form, with chalk white young twigs, leaf undersides and petioles, and deeply lobed leaves; 'Paletzkyana', with leaves deeply lobed; 'Pendula', with pendent branches; 'Pyramidalis', a tall, narrowly conical tree, with large, lobed leaves, often glabrous beneath; 'Raket', slender, columnar, with a gray stem and leaves glossy green above, silvery-gray beneath; 'Richardii', with leaves golden-yellow above; var. *subintegerrima*, with leaves almost entire; *P. balsamifera* BALSAM POPLAR; N US, Canada, Russia; to 100 ft (30 m); suckering from base; young twigs glabrous; buds and new growth covered in a fragrant resin; leaves 2¾–4¾ in (7–12 cm), oval to ovate-lanceolate, base rounded, cordate or broadly cuneate, apex acute, glossy mid-green, white or pale green beneath, subcoriaceous, more or less crenate, glabrous; 'Aurora', with yellow white leaves, spotted dark green; *P. × berolinensis P. laurifolia × P. nigra* 'Italica'; BERLIN POPLAR; to 80 ft (25 m), slenderly columnar; leaves 2¾–4¾ in (7–12 cm), broadly ovate or rhombic-ovate, long-acuminate, base rounded or cuneate, crenate to serrate, bright glossy green above, paler beneath,

more or less glabrous; *P. × canadensis* (*P. deltoides × P. nigra*); CANADIAN POPLAR; tall, fast-growing tree to 100 ft (30 m), crown broad; leaves 2¾–4 in (7–10 cm), triangular to ovate, long-acuminate, base truncate, sparsely toothed, and sometimes with 1 or 2 glands, margins crenate, initially ciliate, petioles tinged red; 'Aurea', with golden yellow leaves, becoming yellow-green, and red petioles; 'Eugenei', to 165 ft (50 m), columnar, with pale bark, 2–3 in (5–8 cm), triangular to rhombic, short-acuminate leaves, coppery-brown when young; 'Marilandica', MAY POPLAR, with a short trunk, broad, rounded crown, spreading, often crooked branches, growing downward, and leaves brown when young, soon pale green, to 4 in (10 cm), rhombic to triangular-ovate, apex slenderly acute, entire; 'Robusta', columnar, with ascending, almost whorled branches, young twigs green, becoming red, finely hairy, and leaves red-brown when young, 4–4¾ in (10–12 cm), glossy, tough, triangular, with to 2 basal glands, rounded teeth, and petioles becoming red; 'Serotina', LATE POPLAR, BLACK ITALIAN POPLAR, to 130 ft (40 m), with a broadly conical, open crown, brown, flexible, glabrous young twigs, with 2¾–4 in (7–10 cm), ovate to triangular leaves, not borne until spring, with a truncate base, red-brown when young, matt dark green when mature, with petioles tinged red; *P. × canescens* (*P. alba × P. tremula*); GRAY POPLAR; natural hybrid; Russia (Georgia), Iran to C Europe; to 150 ft (45 m), crown rounded, bark yellow-gray, scarred, young twigs gray-woolly, soon glabrous; leaves 2½–4¾ in (6–12 cm), triangular-ovate, base cordate, dark green above, gray-woolly beneath, ciliate, teeth glandular, rounded, petioles ½–3 in (1–7.5 cm), woolly to glabrous; 'Aureovariegata', slow-growing, with leaves marbled yellow, and 'Pyramidalis', with a broadly conical crown, gray-green bark, upper branches steeply ascending, and lower branches spreading; *P. deltoides* EASTERN COTTON-WOOD, NECKLACE POPLAR; E and C

US; to 100 ft (30 m), crown broad, bark pale green-yellow, young twigs ribbed, glabrous, buds sticky, balsam-scented; leaves 2¾–7 in (7–18 cm), deltoid-ovate to rhombic, base cordate to truncate, often with 2–5 glands, apex acute, densely ciliate, teeth coarse, glandular, petioles tinged red; subsp. *wislizenii*, with 2–4 in (5–10 cm), triangular to broadly ovate, short-acuminate leaves, with base slightly cuneate or rounded, lacking glands, coarsely crenate, and more or less glabrous; *P. lasiocarpa* CHINESE NECKLACE POPLAR; SW China; to 80 ft (25 m), crown rounded; young twigs angular, densely woolly at first; leaves 6–14 in (15–35 cm), ovate, acute, base cordate, glandular-crenate, glossy gray-green above, paler and downy beneath, veins red, petioles 2–4 in (5–10 cm), red; *P. maximowiczii* JAPANESE POPLAR; north central China, Japan, Korea; to 130 ft (40 m), crown broad, bark gray, deeply fissured; young twigs red, hairy; leaves 2½–4¾ in (6–12 cm), elliptic to oval-elliptic, apex abruptly acuminate to a twisted cusp, base slightly cordate to rounded, matt dark green and wrinkled above, pale green beneath, glandular-serrate and ciliate, veins hairy, somewhat leathery; *P. nigra* BLACK POPLAR; W Europe, N Africa, Siberia; to 100 ft (30 m); crown broad, rounded, trunk often thickly knotted, bark deeply fissured; leaves 2–4 in (5–10 cm), rhombic, triangular or ovate, sometimes wider than long, apex slenderly acuminate, base cuneate or truncate, green, paler beneath, finely crenate; 'Afghanica', columnar, with bark almost white with age, gray young twigs, initially hairy, and triangular-ovate leaves, with a broadly cuneate base; subsp. *betulifolia*, DOWNY BLACK POPLAR, MANCHESTER POPLAR, with brown-orange young twigs, initially hairy, smaller leaves, tapering gently to acute apex, hairy when young, and yellow-green petioles; 'Charkowensis', with oblong, broad, pyramidal crown, ascending branches, and sparsely pubescent young branches; 'Italica', LOMBARDY POPLAR, ITALIAN POPLAR, PYRAMIDAL POPLAR,

white leaf underside

Populus alba

P

columnar, with branches steeply ascending, young twigs brown at apex, later gray, small, rounded-rhombic leaves and petioles tinged red; 'Gigantea', as 'Italica' but broader, with orange winter twigs; 'Lombardy Gold', with golden leaves; 'Plantierensis', of columnar habit, but less so than 'Italica', with hairy young twigs, small leaves, and hairy petioles tinged red; *P. szechuanica* W China; to 130 ft (40 m) in wild; young twigs red-brown, angular; leaves 2¾–8 in (7–20 cm), tinged red at first, oblong to broadly ovate, crenate, teeth with apical glands, apex acuminate, base rounded, or slightly cordate, bright green above, white-silver beneath, veins red; *P. tremula* EUROPEAN ASPEN, ASPEN; NW Europe to N Africa, Siberia; to 66 ft (20 m), crown broad, much-branched, bark fissured and dark gray with age, suckering; leaves 1¼–4¾ in (3–12 cm), oval to suborbicular, acute, base with 2 glands, truncate or cordate, undulate, crenate, gray-green above, very pale beneath, petioles slender; includes the narrow, upright 'Erecta', 'Pendula', a small tree, with pendulous twigs, and 'Purpurea', with leaves tinged red; *P. tremuloides* QUAKING ASPEN; Canada to Mexico; to 66 ft (20 m), trunk slender, bark very pale yellow-gray, suckering, young twigs red-brown; leaves 1¼–2¾ in (3–7 cm), broadly oval to suborbicular, short-acuminate, base truncate to broadly cuneate, finely serrate, ciliate, dark glossy above, blue-green beneath; *P. trichocarpa* BLACK COTTONWOOD, WESTERN BALSAM POPLAR; western N America; to 115 ft (35 m), slenderly pyramidal, crown open, bark smooth, yellow-gray, young twigs olive-brown, glabrous to hairy, slightly angular; leaves 3–10 in (8–25 cm), ovate to rhombic-oblong, slenderly acuminate, base rounded to truncate, leathery, shallowly toothed, dark green and glabrous above, white or pale brown beneath; 'Fritz Pauley', a female clone, 'Pendula', with weeping branches, and 'Scott Pauley', a male clone.

Porana (native name in E Indies). Convolvulaceae. Tropical Asia, Australia. Some 20 species, slender, twining herbs or shrubs with cordate-ovate leaves and small, campanulate or funnelform flowers in terminal panicles or cymes in summer. Cultivate as for tender, perennial *Ipomoea* species. *P. paniculata* BRIDAL-BOUQUET, CHRIST VINE, SNOW CREEPER, SNOW-IN-THE-JUNGLE, WHITE CORALLITA; N India, Upper Burma; liane to 30 ft (9 m); leaves cordate, to 6 in (15 cm), white-pubescent beneath; panicles large, pendulous, flowers to ⅜ in (8 mm), white.

poricidal a form of dehiscence in which the pollen is released through pores at the apex of the anther.

porous tube rubber or polythene tubing with micropores, buried in soil to provide subirrigation; see *irrigation*.

porrect extending or stretching outward and forward.

Portulaca (from *portilaca*, Latin name used by Pliny). Portulacaceae. Widely distributed in warm and tropical regions. PURSLANE, ROSE MOSS. 40 species, fleshy or trailing, mostly annual herbs. Opening in bright sunlight in spring and summer, the flowers consist of four to six, spreading, brightly colored petals and many stamens. *P. grandiflora* is grown for its fleshy, mosslike foliage and for the profusion of individually short-lived, brightly colored flowers carried over long periods in summer. Ideal as a low-growing seasonal filler in flower beds and borders, as edging and in window boxes and other containers, it is easily grown from seed sown *in situ* in spring, in low-nutrient, freely draining, sandy soil in full sun. *P. grandiflora* ROSE MOSS, MOSS ROSE, SUN PLANT, ELEVEN-O'CLOCK;

Portulaca grandiflora 'Cloudbeater Mix'
Plant breeding programs have extended the color range, flowering time and robustness of these undemanding bedding annuals.

Brazil, Argentina, Uruguay; stem prostrate or ascending, to 12 in (30 cm); leaves cylindrical, to 1 in (2.5 cm), thick, fleshy, tinted red when grown in full sun; flowers single to double, rose, red, crimson, scarlet, orange, apricot, gold, yellow, white, sometimes striped or bicolored, 1 in (2.5 cm) in diameter, opening in sunlight; numerous seed races and cultivars are available.

post-emergence used to describe herbicides that are applied after the emergence of a crop from the soil.

posterior at or toward the back or adaxial surface.

post-harvest, post-storage diseases various parasitic diseases and nonparasitic disorders that are liable to affect fresh fruit, vegetables and flower bulbs from the time of harvesting until they are used by the consumer. Diseases such as FRUIT BROWN ROT and POTATO BLIGHT are caused by pathogens which may affect plants during the growing season and also attack their fruit or tubers at maturity. Others, such as BLUE MOLD of citrus and RHIZOPUS ROT of tomato, are diseases specific to harvested produce and their incidence is strongly influenced by damage during growth or handling and the conditions under which produce is stored.

Post-harvest disorders are caused by unfavorable environmental factors before and after harvest, of which extremes of temperature are probably the most important, resulting in chilling or overheating.

post-hole borer a large diameter augerlike tool, usually mechanically operated to facilitate the boring of holes for fence posts.

potager a kitchen garden of vegetables and fruits laid out for ornamental effect, often with the beds edged with low hedges, as in a parterre.

Potamogeton (from Greek *potamos*, river, and *geiton*, neighbor, referring to the natural habitat). Potamogetonaceae. Cosmopolitan. About 90 species, aquatic perennial herbs. The shoots arise from creeping rhizomes rooted in the bottom of the pond,

P

stream or river. The leaves are submerged and/or floating, and variable in shape and size. Small, apetalous, green flowers are produced either above the water or submerged in fleshy spikes. Hardy aquatics suitable for large, cold water aquariums and outdoor pools. Plant the stems in sandy loam and plunge in neutral to alkaline water. Give full sun or strong light. Remove fading foliage and thin colonies when necessary. Propagate by stem cuttings in spring/summer or by scaly resting buds in spring where produced.

P. crispus CURLED PONDWEED; Europe, naturalized E US and California; leaves submerged, to 4 in (10 cm), narrow-oblong, crisped or undulate; *P. lucens* SHINING PONDWEED; Europe, W Africa; leaves submerged, to 8 in (20 cm), narrow-elliptic to obovate-elliptic, tips acuminate or cuspidate, translucent, undulate; *P. natans* BROAD-LEAVED PONDWEED; Europe, N US; floating leaves to 5 in (12.5 cm), broadly oval, with flexible joint at base, petioles often longer than blade; submerged leaves reduced, linear.

potassium (abbreviation K) a major (macro-) nutrient, important in plant metabolism. It is highly mobile in soil, and although effectively held by the cationic exchange capacity of most soils, it is leached on free-draining, acidic and sandy soil. On cropped sites, potassium is commonly in short supply and replenishment through fertilizer application is regularly required; as a base dressing, it should always be applied to balance applications of nitrogen.

Apples, gooseberries and red currants, potatoes, beans, spinach and tomatoes are notably affected by potassium deficiency, which is mostly seen well into the growing season. Symptoms of deficiency are restricted shoot growth, leading to die-back in fruit trees. In most crops, there is marginal scorch of older leaves, often with curling, and this may be preceded by spotting and chlorosis.

Potassium deficiency

Flowers and fruits drop excessively, and fruits are invariably small and of poor quality; in tomatoes, the fruit quality defects known as 'greenback' and 'blotchy ripening' are symptoms of potassium deficiency. Cure is by prevention only.

Potassium fertilizers include: potassium chloride (60% K_2O) which is the least expensive but potentially toxic where excessively applied, and some plants, especially tomatoes, gooseberries and red currants, are susceptible to chloride damage; potassium nitrate (44% K_2O, 13% N), which is expensive and mostly used in liquid feeds; and potassium sulfate (50% K_2O), which is more expensive than potassium chloride but widely used and available as sulfate of potash. Potassium is not stored in high quantity in organic matter.

potato (*Solanum tuberosum*) a short-lived herbaceous perennial cultivated as an annual for its swollen, underground stem tubers. The potato originated in the Andean highlands, being cultivated by the Incas for over 2000 years before the arrival of the Spanish in the 16th century. It was first recorded in Europe in 1587 and rapidly became a staple crop in Ireland and much of northern Europe. It was taken to North America by immigrants from Scotland and Ireland in the early 18th century.

Potatoes are widely cultivated in temperate and tropical regions throughout the world for human consumption and stock feed, and there is large genetic variability within the species. It is a versatile food crop, amenable to processing. However, if developing tubers are exposed to light, they become green and poisonous, as are the green berries produced after flowering.

Tuber formation proceeds better under cooler conditions and potatoes are a difficult crop to grow in hot humid lowlands. Temperatures around 72°F (22°C) favor early growth; during later development, temperatures around 64°F (18°C) are optimal. High soil temperature can retard stolon initiation and tuberization, which is generally best in the range 61–68°F (16–20°C). Potato foliage is very susceptible to damage by frost.

Propagation is through healthy 'seed' tubers, true seed generally producing unacceptable levels of variability in resulting tubers. The use of microtubers produced *in vitro* by tissue culture is a possibility.

In temperate regions, potatoes can be harvested throughout the summer months and tubers stored to extend the season; it is also possible to obtain earlier harvests of immature or "new"' potatoes, which have a superior flavor to the later crop.

Potatoes require a frost-free site, preferably with slightly acidic soil, and they should be grown on at least a three-year rotation to avoid the buildup of eelworm. Good quality "seed" tubers, certified as virus free, should be chosen and growth can be started by the process of "sprouting' or "chitting," which is particularly useful for advancing development of early cultivars. During the latter part of winter, tubers are stood in shallow trays in a well-lit, cool but frost-free environment. The dormant buds or "eyes" are concentrated at what is often referred to as the "rose" end and these should be placed uppermost in the trays to encourage strong shoots about 1 in (2.5 cm) long prior to planting. Chitting will take about six weeks. For early potatoes of good size, the number of sprouts per tuber should be restricted to two or three by rubbing off the excess at planting; for later main crops, all shoots should be retained for higher yield. Seed-tuber size can significantly affect final yield and tuber size, and ideally seed tubers should be approximately the size of a hen's egg.

Planting can commence in early spring, starting with early cultivars, the chitted tubers planted rose end uppermost either in drills 4–4¾ in (10–12 cm) deep or in individual planting holes, before covering with ¾–1¼ in (2–3 cm) of soil. As a general guide, earlies should be planted closer together than later main crops; typically, early potatoes are planted approximately 14 in (35 cm) apart in rows 14–18 in (35–45 cm) apart, whereas row spacing for later cultivars should be increased to 30 in (75 cm).

Planting can be advanced by planting under cloches or by covering with perforated clear plastic film or nonwoven polypropylene 'fleece'. An uncovered early crop can be protected from late frost by covering exposed shoots with straw or by drawing a thin layer of soil over them.

Potatoes should be earthed-up during growth to prevent greening of tubers; the process also serves to kill off weed seedlings. A single operation when plants are about 8 in (20 cm) high is usually sufficient, drawing soil to approximately 4 in (10 cm) depth around the stems.

Early cultivars in particular can be grown in large containers, of 12 in (30 cm) width and depth minimum. These can be placed on a patio or held in a cool greenhouse for early cropping. Chitted tubers are placed in the containers on 4–5 in (10–13 cm) depth of fertile garden soil or potting mix and covered to a similar depth, with further soil or other medium added when the plants are about 6 in (15 cm) high. Crops can be raised in carefully managed, large, black polythene sacks with drainage holes.

Developing tubers should be kept well-supplied with water and, depending on growing conditions, will be ready to harvest 90–120 days from planting. Potatoes may be lifted as required; the entire crop is removed, including the smallest tubers, which may otherwise contribute to a weed and disease problem in following seasons. Potatoes for storage should be left in the ground for a couple of weeks after the haulm has been removed to allow the skins to harden; tubers should be allowed to dry thoroughly before storing in a cool dark environment between 39–50°F (4–10°C) with high humidity.

flowers give rise to green berries

top-growth known as "haulm"

edible tubers

Potato plant

Cultivars vary in time taken to reach maturity, disease resistance, flavor and skin color. In the UK, they are commonly categorized as first earlies (e.g. 'Accent', 'Epicure', 'Foremost'); second earlies (e.g. 'Charlotte', 'Estima', 'Maris Bard'); and maincrop (e.g. 'Desiree', 'Maxine', 'Navan'). Some are often referred to as salad potatoes (e.g. 'Pink Fir Apple', 'Ratte'). Cultivars in the US are categorized as early (e.g. 'Red Norland', 'Irish Cobbler', 'Yukon Gold'); maincrop (e.g. 'All Blue', 'Chieftain', 'Russet Burbank'); and late season (e.g. 'Bintje', 'McNeilly Everbearing', 'Yellow Finn'). Possible problems: cutworms, eelworm, slugs, wireworms; blight (see *phytophthora*), scab, virus, wart disease; hollow heart, internal rust spot.

potato planter a tool for planting potatoes and other tubers or bulbs, which has two triangular scoop-shaped blades that hold the tuber or bulb in a V-shaped cradle while the tool is inserted into the soil. The tuber or bulb is released when the handles are pulled together and the blades open.

pot-bound describes a pot-grown plant whose roots have completely explored the growing medium and are densely packed into the container, often becoming woody and constricted. The condition should be avoided by timely potting-on or planting out, because affected plants are likely to be starved and their potential for producing a vigorous, strong root system after planting out is much reduced.

Potentilla (from Latin *potens*, powerful, referring to the plant's alleged medicinal properties). Rosaceae. Northern Hemisphere. CINQUEFOIL, FIVE-FINGER. About 500 species, mostly perennial but some annual and biennial herbs and shrubs, with palmate, pinnate or trifoliate leaves. Produced in spring and summer, the flowers are usually saucer-shaped, solitary or in terminal or axillary clusters, and 4-, 5-, or 6-parted.

Those listed here are hardy to –13°F (–25°C). The shrubby *P. fruticosa* and its numerous cultivars form loose and floriferous mounds, suitable for the front of the shrub border, for mass planting as groundcover, and also as low informal hedging. The summer and fall blooms of the border perennials, largely derived from *P. nepalensis*, *P. atrosanguinea*, and *P. recta*, are held on slender stems well above the foliage; these are selected for their warm and brilliant shades of yellow, terra cotta, vermilion, mahogany and deep crimson, and are well-suited to strong color schemes and to cottage gardens. The alpine species are suitable for crevices and scree in the rock garden, or for growing on walls; some species, such as *P. alba*, form low mats of gray or silver foliage, carrying their flowers on short stems. *P. nitida* is small and neat and well-suited to sink or trough plantings.

Grow in well-drained soil in full sun to part-shade; too rich a soil will produce soft foliar growth at the expense of flowers. Grow small alpines in poor gritty soil or on scree in full sun, or in an alpine house, using a low fertility loam-based mix, with added grit. Prune shrubby species in early spring, removing weak growth at ground level and cutting back strong growth by half or one third. Old neglected plants may be rejuvenated by cutting hard back, although this may be more safely done in two or more stages. Trim hedges in spring. Propagate herbaceous species by seed sown in fall or early spring, or by division in spring or fall. Remove rooted runners to increase alpine species. Propagate shrubby species by softwood cuttings in summer and, except for cultivars, by seed in fall.

P. alba C, S and E Europe; low-growing, spreading perennial herb to 4 in (10 cm); leaves palmate, leaflets 5, ¾–2½ in (2–6 cm), oblong to obovate-lanceolate, apex toothed, glabrous above, silvery silky beneath at first; flowers to 1 in (2.5 cm) in diameter, white; *P. atrosanguinea* Himalaya; hairy perennial to 36 in (90 cm); leaflets 3, to 3 in (7.5 cm), elliptic-ovate to obovate, toothed, silky above, white-hairy beneath; flowers to 1¼ in (3 cm) in diameter, deep purple-red;

Potentilla atrosanguinea
The Himalayan cinquefoil is representative of the herbaceous potentillas, prized for their bright color range and long flowering.

includes var. *argyrophylla*, with yellow or yellow-orange flowers; hybrids derived from these and (in some cases) *P. nepalensis* include 'Etna', to 18 in (45 cm), with leaves tinted silver and deep crimson flowers; 'Fire-dance', compact, with deep coral flowers; 'Gibson's Scarlet', with bright scarlet flowers; and 'Mons. Rouillard', with double, dark copper flowers; *P. aurea* Alps, Pyrenees; mat-forming perennial to 12 in (30 cm), silvery hairy; leaves digitate, leaflets 5, silver-hairy on margins and veins beneath, oblong, toothed at tip; flowers to ¾ in (2 cm) in diameter, golden yellow, base deeper; 'Aurantiaca', with sunset yellow flowers, 'Florepleno', with double, light gold flowers, and 'Gold-klumpen', with bright gold flowers with an orange ring; *P. crantzii* ALPINE CINQUEFOIL; N US, N, C and S Europe; perennial herb to 8 in (20 cm), rootstock woody; leaves digitate, leaflets 3 or 5, ¾ in (2 cm), obovate to cuneate, toothed at apex, green, hairless above, hairy beneath; flowers to 1 in (2.5 cm) in diameter, yellow, often orange spotted at base; *P. fruticosa* SHRUBBY CINQUEFOIL, GOLDEN HARDHACK, WIDDY; Northern Hemisphere; deciduous, much-branched shrub, to 60 in (150 cm); leaves pinnate or trifoliate, leaflets 3 or 5, to 1 in (2.5 cm), ovate to lanceolate, light to mid-green, silky; flowers to 1½ in (4 cm) in diameter, bright yellow or white; var. *mandschurica*, low-growing, to 18 in (45 cm), with gray silky hairy leaves and white flowers to 1 in (2.5 cm) in diameter; many cultivars and hybrids of *P. fruticosa* are available, ranging in habit from the dwarf and compact to the large and robust, from low and spreading to upright, in foliage from small- to large-leaved, bright green to lime, variegated or silver and silkily hairy, and in flower color from white to cream, palest primrose, buttercup yellow, rich gold, tangerine, vermilion, fiery red, apricot, pink and bicolors; *P. megalantha* Japan; softly hairy tufted perennial to 12 in (30 cm); leaves to 3 in (8 cm) wide, leaflets 3, broad obovate, coarsely crenate, hairy beneath; flowers to 1½ in (4 cm) in diameter, bright yellow; *P. nepalensis* W Himalaya; perennial herb, stem leafy, erect, to 24 in (60 cm); leaflets 5, 1¼–3 in (3–8 cm), obovate or elliptic-obovate, coarsely toothed, hairy; flowers 1 in (2.5 cm) in diameter, purple-red or crimson, base darker; 'Flammenspiel', with red flowers narrowly edged yellow; 'Miss Willmott', with cherry red flowers; 'Roxana', with red buds and salmon pink flowers; *P. neumanniana* N, W and C Europe; mat-forming, perennial to 4 in (10 cm), stem woody, procumbent; leaves digitate, leaflets 5–7, to 1½ in (4 cm), obovate, dentate; flowers to 1 in (2.5 cm) in diameter, yellow; 'Goldrausch', to 4 in (10 cm), with bright gold flowers; 'Nana', to 3 in (7.5 cm), with vivid green leaves and gold flowers; *P. nitida* SW and SE Alps; tufted, silver-gray, downy perennial to 4 in (10 cm); leaflets 3, to ½ in (1 cm), oblanceolate to obovate, apex usually 3-toothed, silvery-silky; flowers 1 in (2.5 cm)+ in diameter, white or pink, base deeper; 'Alannah', with pale pink flowers, 'Alba', with white flowers, 'Compacta', very dwarf, to 2 in (5 cm), with large, gold flowers, 'Lissadel', with vivid pink flowers, and 'Rubra', with deep rose flowers; *P. recta* Europe, Caucasus, Siberia, naturalized eastern N America; perennial; stem to 18 in (45 cm), velvety hairy, with glandular hairs; leaves digitate, leaflets 5–7, to 1½ in (3.5 cm), oblong-lanceolate, green, serrate to pinnatisect; flowers yellow, to 1 in (2.5 cm) in diameter, many in flat corymbs; 'Macrantha', with large, bright yellow flowers in loose clusters; *P. × tonguei* (*P. anglica × P. nepalensis*); stem procumbent, not rooting; leaflets 3–5, obovate, dark green; flowers apricot with carmine-red eye.

pot herb refers to herblike plants that are edible rather than medicinal. See *herbs*.

× **Potinara** (*Brassavola* × *Cattleya* × *Laelia* × *Sophronitis*). Orchidaceae. Quadri-generic hybrids made from species and hybrids of these genera and named after a French orchid grower, Monsieur Potin. The plants are small and compact with flowers in shades of yellow, orange and red.

pot-in-pot a method of displaying creeping or trailing plants, in which two or more pots of different sizes are filled with growing medium and partially embedded inside one another, with plants or cuttings grown in the smallest pot and around the edges of the larger one(s) to produce a cascade effect.

potpourri dried aromatic petals and leaves, often mixed with spices used to scent rooms or clothes.

pots and potting plants were grown in pots by the early Egyptians, Greeks and Chinese and traditionally made from baked clay. Old hand-made pots can be identified by the uneven finish and rather ridged surface inside the pots. terra cotta pots were produced from the late 1940s by mechanized manufacturing methods. Various plastics have replaced clay or terra cotta, except in the case of decorative tubs and containers, and most plants grow equally well in either.

Pot types and uses Conventionally shaped pots are usually classified by internal diameter at the rim, although commercial growers often describe containers by capacity—e.g. 1¾ or 3½ pints (1 or 2 liter), which relates to the volume of growing medium needed to fill them.

References are sometimes made to the practice of grading pots according to the number that could be made from a cast of clay. The largest size, made from one cast, was of 18 in (45 cm) in diameter and known as a "number one"; 32 pots measuring 6 in (16 cm) in diameter could be produced from the same amount of clay and these were known as "32s." Very small sizes were often referred to as "thumbs"—2½ in (6 cm)—and "thimbles"—(2 in (5 cm).

P

Special sizes and shapes are produced for particular uses. The pan (seed pan or mini-pot) is less than half the depth of a normal pot and used for seed-sowing or for small bulbs and shallow-rooting plants such as alpines. Half-pots are half the depth of a normal pot and often used for plants such as azaleas. Long toms are much deeper in proportion to width, and are used for plants with early developing tap roots, those that produce deep roots and resent restriction or disturbance, and those that demand perfect drainage, as can be provided with a deep layer of crocks. All pots must have adequate drainage holes. With terra cotta sorts it is usual to place a layer of broken pots, known as crocks, over the drainage holes, to form a shallow layer at the bottom of the pot. Plastic pots are not normally crocked and are generally more suited to capillary watering.

Plastic pots are light, clean, and easy to handle but although the potting medium dries out less quickly than in clay pots, accurate assessment of water requirements is more difficult. Polypropylene is the plastic widely used, but for large container pots, a proportion of polyethylene (polythene) is used for added strength in cold weather. Polythene is used for inexpensive, collapsible, fold-flat pots.

Clay pots are attractive, and useful where their weight provides stability, for example for tall plants. Plants that need good drainage, such as alpines and many orchids, benefit from the porosity of clay pots.

Peat pots are available for plant raising, and are generally made of a mixture of sphagnum moss peat and wood fiber. They are useful for plants, such as *Salvia*, sweet peas and runner beans. Roots eventually grow through the walls and the pots disintegrate when planted out. Expandable pellets of fertilized compressed peat held in a net are available for rooting cuttings and the direct sowing of seeds, which can be later planted into conventional pots intact. Care must be taken to keep these peat containers moist at all times. Durable containers made solely of compressed paper or wood fiber are available as alternatives to peat-based ones.

Bitumenized cardboard pots, known as 'whale-hides', are used for ring culture; these consist of bottomless tubes, approximately 9 in (23 cm) in diameter at the top and tapered toward the bottom to hold the potting medium. They are stood on an aggregate, especially for the ring culture of tomatoes, cucumbers, and peppers. Versions with bottoms are available for plants requiring a large pot, such as chrysanthemums. Both types are discarded after one season.

Potting The initial placing of seedling plants in pots is known as potting-off or potting-up, while moving potted plants to larger containers is known as potting-on or re-potting. Young and rapidly growing plants need potting-on fairly frequently to avoid growth being checked, slow-growing plants less often. Plants that cannot be potted-on due to limits on the possible size and weight of container can often be maintained by replacing the top and bottom layers of the potting medium each year, and by regular feeding. Established plants should be potted-up or re-potted when they are about to start growth or are growing actively; with young plants, the best time to move them is when the roots have fully explored the growing medium but have not yet started to spiral round the pot. Overpotting (using a pot that is too large) must be avoided because the unexplored potting medium may remain too wet. Normally, choose a pot one or two sizes larger than the existing pot.

A few plants succeed best if the roots are restricted, for example, sansevierias are best re-potted only when the roots fill the pot and start to emerge from the medium; aspidistras are not repotted frequently, and the variegated form is usually better if slightly starved and pot-bound. Cacti can be re-potted less frequently than most plants, and these, together with bromeliads, orchids and other epiphytic or partly epiphytic groups, require relatively small pots for their size. In general, large woody plants should be potted more firmly than those with soft growth, while soil-based potting media can be firmed much more than peat-based types. Newly potted plants will appreciate moister

and shadier conditions than usual for a few days after moving.

pot-thick the arrangement of container-grown plants on a bed or greenhouse bench so that their pots are touching.

potting machine a device used in commercial nurseries to fill pots mechanically with potting medium and thus increase the speed of the potting operation.

potting media (singular: potting medium) used to describe mineral and organic substances suitable for growing containerized plants. In some European countries, the term is synonymous with substrate. The word "compost" is widely used in the UK as a general term for potting, seed, and cutting media, but in the US it usually refers only to the product of a compost pile. The term "compost" traditionally describes all soil-based potting mixes, especially the John Innes "composts." Lightweight media primarily based on peat are often referred to as "mixes." particularly in the US.

Potting media are classified as either soil- or loam-based if they contain mineral soil, and soilless or loam-less if they are based on lightweight ingredients, such as peat or composted bark. In the past, gardeners used their own special recipes, in which a wide range of materials were added to soil, including leaf mold, animal manures, mortar, wood ashes, sand and grit. To overcome variable results, research in the 1930s by W.J.C. Lawrence and J. Newell at the John Innes Horticultural Research Institute, Hertford, England led to development of the standard John Innes products; these are based on loam, sterilized to kill weed seeds and reduce the incidence of soilborne pests and diseases, and generally produce reliable results.

Advances in producing containerized nursery stock in the late 1950s led to the development of soilless mixes, based on peat. These overcame the difficulties of obtaining bulk supplies of good-quality loam and reduced the labor costs of sterilizing and handling.

Soil-based media, such as the John Innes range, confer the possible advan-

P

tage of container wind-stability; they are also often considered more tolerant of over- and under-watering, and have better nutrient-storage capacity. However, batches are likely to be more variable than those of soilless mixes due to the difficulty of standardizing loam texture and organic content.

There are three basic formulations of John Innes "composts" (*see table*): seed compost for germinating seeds; cutting compost for rooting cuttings; and potting composts for growing on plants, designated JIP-1, JIP-2 and JIP-3. The potting composts contain increasing amounts of base fertilizers to accommodate varying degrees of plant vigor and seasonal changes in growth rate.

For the higher fertility JIP-2 and JIP-3, the quantities of fertilizer in JIP-1 are doubled and tripled, respectively. Hoof and horn, superphosphate and potassium sulfate can be obtained ready-mixed as 'John Innes Base' fertilizers.

Loams suitable for John Innes "composts" should be of clay texture, contain fibrous organic matter, and have a pH value of between 5.5 and 6.5. It is essential that the loam is pasteurized, by steaming, at around 180°F (82°C) maintained for 10 minutes. This heat treatment, which is aimed at killing most harmful insects and diseases and weed seeds, must be carefully controlled to avoid risk of producing substances toxic to plants.

Sphagnum peats are the most suitable, since they retain water and provide aeration. Coconut fiber or coir appears to be a generally satisfactory substitute for peat as an ingredient of John Innes "compost," where used at the same volume. The sand will improve drainage and should be a coarse grade and nonalkaline.

Ideally, John Innes products should be used within four weeks of making, since changes in the forms and amounts of available nitrogen and the pH can occur; successful storage will depend on moisture content, temperature and the amounts of organic nitrogen added. Mixing the fertilizers into the medium shortly before use will minimize storage problems.

The low-fertility seed medium is used for seed-sowing and pricking out

and JIP-1, a medium-fertility product, for potting into 3½-in (9-cm) pots. JIP-2 and JIP-3 are used for growing more vigorous plants and for potting into larger pot sizes, and for large tubs and window boxes.

Lime-hating plants can be successfully grown in a medium termed JIS-A, which is the John Innes seed medium with ground limestone replaced by ⅝ oz/ft³ (0.6 kg/m³) of sulfur.

Soilless mixes are usually based on peat blended with materials such as sand, perlite and vermiculite. Some soilless media are mixes of different grades of peat. Peat is deficient in the principal plant nutrients and these are added as fertilizers; lime is also included to neutralize natural acidity. The use of peat is contentious due to actual and potential damage caused to the natural environment during harvest; of special concern is sphagnum peat taken from raised bogs.

The search for alternatives to peat has included developments with waste materials, such as straw, sewage sludge, municipal refuse, and animal wastes. However, the quality of different batches of media derived from these types of organic materials can be variable and they can deteriorate during storage. In addition, there are potential health risks if contaminated residues persist in the medium and it is advisable to handle any organic material with care; always wear gloves or wash hands when handling such mixes, and avoid dusty conditions by working in a

well-ventilated area.

Composted bark and coir are well-tried peat alternatives, as are pine needles and leaf mold. When using growing media based upon these materials, or ones in which they are used as additives, special attention needs to be given to avoid overwatering and early starvation of nutrients.

Coarse sands or grits can be added to peat to change the physical properties of the mix and to increase its weight in order to improve the stability of tall plants growing in pots; very fine sands can reduce aeration and drainage, and suitable types should also be nonalkaline. Perlite and vermiculite can be used as a light-weight substitute for sand in soilless mixes. Mixes containing 50% or more perlite are very useful for rooting cuttings, especially under mist. Unlike perlite, vermiculite contains some potassium and magnesium and can absorb mineral elements such as calcium, magnesium, potassium and ammonium nitrogen from added fertilizers, which will reduce the loss of these nutrients through leaching. Particles of vermiculite are less stable than perlite, but normally last long enough for plants that are regularly re-potted. Also used in peat mixes are polystyrene granules, expanded aggregates made from clays, shales and pulverized fuel ash, and flocks of rock wool.

Lime is added variously to peat mixes as a mixture of ground chalk or limestone and ground magnesium limestone, both to reduce acidity and

Composition of the John Innes range:

	parts/volume	fertilizer	oz/ft³ (kg/m³)
SEED			
loam	2		
peat	1	grnd. limestone	⅝ (0.6)
sand	1	superphosphate	1¼ (1.2)
CUTTING			
loam	1		
peat	2	nil	
sand	1		
POTTING (JIP-1)			
loam	7	grnd. limestone	⅝ (0.6)
peat	3	hoof and horn	1¼ (1.2)
sand	2	superphosphate	1¼ (1.2)
		potass. sulfate	⅝ (0.6)

P

as a source of calcium and magnesium. Nitrogen, phosphorus and potassium are applied either as soluble inorganic fertilizers, such as potassium nitrate and superphosphate, which usually require frequent replenishment, or in a slow-release form. Trace elements are usually added in slow-release form as powdered glass frits or as soluble chemicals.

potting off, potting on, potting up see *pots and potting*.

potting stick a short, thick rounded stick used to firm potting media down the sides of large pots when potting-on or re-potting specimens with a large root-ball.

pot worms see *enchytraeid worms*.

powdery mildew a type of pathogenic fungus characteristically showing as white mycelium on the surface of green tissues of a host plant, with powdery spores. The fungus is mostly external on its host and feeds by penetrating the epidermal cells. The mildews are obligate parasites, and may overwinter in the buds of deciduous and perennial plants or in resting structures on fallen leaves. Symptoms of powdery mildew infection may include chlorosis, stunting and distortion, all of which appear before obvious signs of the pathogen. As infection progresses, there can be loss of vigor and reduction in quality of foliage, flowers and fruit.

Unlike most other fungal pathogens of plants, the powdery mildews are capable of developing on their hosts in the absence of free water; their geographical distribution reflects their adaptation to drier conditions.

Species of powdery mildews are often restricted to certain host families, and within species there may be pathotypes affecting different cultivars.

Plants commonly affected by powdery mildews include apple (parasitized by *Podosphaera leucotricha*), crucifers (*Erysiphe cruciferarum*), cucurbits (*E. cichoracearum* and *Sphaerotheca fuliginea*), *Euonymus japonicus* (*Oidium euonymi-japonici*), gooseberry (*Microsphaera grossulariae* and *Sphaerotheca mors-uvae*), grapevine (*Uncinula necator*), hazelnut (*Phyllactinea guttata*), *Lagerstroemia*

(*Erysiphe lagerstroemiae*), oak (*Microsphaera alphitoides*), pea (*Erysiphe pisi*), peach and rose (*Sphaerotheca pannosa*) and strawberry (*S. macularis*), as well as very many ornamental garden plants.

Despite their importance as pathogens of flowering plants, only one species of powdery mildew (*Erysiphe graminis*) is known to occur on monocotyledons, but this has many specialized pathotypes.

Control measures involve the removal of infected plant debris, pruning affected shoots and growing resistant varieties. Dusting or spraying with sulfur is a traditional remedy but can cause injury to some ornamental plants and certain cultivars of apples, gooseberries and vines. Some systemic fungicides are available to gardeners for use as preventative sprays on ornamentals.

praemorse, premorse raggedly or irregularly truncated, as if gnawed or bitten.

Pratia (for M. C. Prat-Bernon of the French navy, who accompanied Freycinet on his second round-the-world voyage, but died in 1817, a few days after the expedition set sail). Campanulaceae. Australia, New Zealand, tropical Africa, S America. About 20 species, dwarf, perennial herbs with slender, creeping stems, very small leaves and, in summer, delicate, 2-lipped flowers followed by berries. Grow in a sheltered position (minimum temperature 9°F/−13°C), in sun or light, part-day shade, in gritty, moist soil. In an alpine house, grow in pans in a mix of equal parts loam, leaf mold and sharp sand. Water plentifully when in growth and keep just moist in winter. Propagate by seed in fall in a sandy propagating mix, or by division.

P. angulata New Zealand; leaves suborbicular, succulent, serrate; flowers to ½ in (1 cm), subsessile, white with purple veins; 'Ohau': large, white flowers and bright red fruit; *P. pedunculata* Australia; leaves ovate or orbicular, with few teeth; flowers to ¼ in (7 mm), blue, on pedicels longer than leaves; 'County Park': bright blue flowers; *P. perpusilla* New Zealand; leaves minute, oblong or ovate-oblong, acute or obtuse, fleshy, dentate, glabrous or

short-pubescent; flowers to ¼ in (6 mm), white, more or less sessile; 'Fragrant Carpet': white, fragrant flowers; 'Summer Meadows': bronze-tinted leaves, fragrant, white flowers.

precocious appearing or developing early, usually applied to flowers that open before the leaves emerge.

pre-emergence used to describe herbicides that are applied after sowing but before the emergence of a crop from the soil or, in the case of perennial crops, before shoot emergence. The herbicides may be of contact or selective residual action.

prepared describes bulbs that have been treated, usually with heat, while dormant, so as to advance growth and/or flowering, for example hyacinths, shallots.

pre-sowing a method of preparing seeds for sowing, whereby they are fixed to a sheet fabric, such as paper, which rots after being covered with soil, leaving the germinating seeds to develop; it is designed to ensure proper spacing and is used for grass, vegetables and annual flowers.

pricking lightly forking the soil among growing plants to stir and break up the surface for aeration and improved water penetration. It is also done to aerate lawns.

pricking out the operation of transferring very young seedlings from the site where they have germinated to other containers or beds, in order to provide more space for growth. Great care should be taken to handle only the seed leaves and to ensure that the roots are mostly intact and gently settled in with a dibber and by subsequent watering.

prilled granules small solid globules of fertilizer or herbicide. These are designed to aid even distribution, and may allow for slow release of the effective ingredient as the outer casing decomposes.

primary infection the first infection by a pathogen after a period of dormancy.

P

priming the preparation of seeds prior to sowing by promoting the partial imbibition of water to aid germination and establishment. Priming has been successful with crops such as carrot, parsnip and celery. Polyethylene glycol 600 is an example of a substance used to activate processes *leading* to germination, and after which seeds can be stored dry. Primed seeds germinate more quickly and evenly after sowing.

primocane the stem of a biennial cane fruit, such as raspberry, in its first, nonfruiting year. cf. *floricane*.

Primula (the diminutive form of the Latin *primus*, first; from the mediaeval Latin name for the cowslip, *Primula veris*, meaning 'first little thing of spring'). Primulaceae. PRIMROSE. Northern Hemisphere, Ethiopia, tropical mts. to Java and New Guinea, southern S America. 400 species, small or dwarf perennial herbs. The leaves are usually borne in basal clumps or rosettes. Produced at various times of year, the flowers may be solitary or clustered and short-stalked, or carried in scapose heads, spikes and umbels. The corolla is cuplike to tubular, with a limb of 5, spreading or incurved lobes.

Almost without exception, primulas like relatively cool, humid summers with a ready supply of soil moisture when in growth. Most need well-aerated soil that allows excess moisture to drain freely away during the winter months to avoid risk of root rots. A fertile loam with additional organic matter and coarse sand is a good starting point for most primulas and can be adapted to suit individual requirements. The majority of European and American species enjoy or at least tolerate sun, while the Asiatics generally need light shade unless the soil remains constantly cool and moist. Propagation is by seed, division, cuttings, root cuttings, leaf bud cuttings and, increasingly, by micropropagation. With the possible exceptions of *P. vialii* and *P. denticulata*,

Primula japonica 'Postford White'

seed germination in primulas is inhibited at temperatures above 68°F (20°C), and seed of many species needs stratification. Primulas are relatively free from pests and diseases. The most damaging pests are vine weevil, red spider mite and aphid, particularly root aphid, and slugs. The main diseases, generally avoided by good hygiene and cultural conditions, are botrytis, root rots and viruses.

In terms of individual cultural requirements, primulas can be divided into nine groups—1. full sun; permanently moist soil

2. full sun or part-shade; moist but fast-draining soil

3. part-shade; moist but well-drained soil

4. part-shade; well-drained, gritty loam

5. full sun or part-shade; gritty, alkaline soil

6. part-shade; gritty, alkaline soil

7. full or part-shade; moist and humus-rich, neutral to acidic soil

8. sun or part-shade; humus-rich, neutral to acidic soil with grit

9. part-shade; humus-rich neutral to acidic soil with grit

In addition to these groups, there are the Auricula Primulas (see *auriculas*), the Polyanthus Primulas or Pruhonicensis Hybrids derived from *P. vulgaris*, *P. veris*, *P. juliae* and related species, and those species such as *P. malacoides*, *P. obconica* and *P. sinensis*, (which, for all that they conform to cultivation group 4, are commonly grown under glass and in the home).

Polyanthus Primulas are available in a number of named series with an extensive color range. They are raised from seed and treated as biennials, used for bedding. They include the exceptionally large flowered Regal series; the Pacific series, both dwarf and giant, with fragrant, brilliant, velvety flowers, and the low growing Posy series, predominantly pastel with contrasting centers. Surface sow seed in late spring, keep constantly moist and germinate at temperatures no higher than 68°F (20°C); prick out and grow on to plant out in late fall. *P. malacoides*, *P. obconica* and *P. sinensis* are decorative

pot plants for winter and spring flowering. Sow seed between early summer and early fall for a succession of bloom; use a soilless propagating mix and germinate at 59°F (15°C). Grow on in the shaded frame in a medium-fertility loam-based mix with additional leaf mold and grit. Bring under glass in late fall, or before first frost and maintain good light and ventilation with a minimum temperature range of 41–45°F (5–7°C). *P. kewensis* is less commonly grown but requires similar treatment.

The group numbers given in each description refer to the cultivation requirements outlined above.

P. allionii France and Italian Maritime Alps; leaves cushion-forming, oblanceolate to rounded, entire or finely toothed, fleshy, viscid, hairy; scapes very short; flowers 1–5, tubular, $\frac{5}{8}$–1$\frac{1}{4}$ in (1.5–3 cm) diameter, pale pink to red-purple with white eye, or wholly white; group 5; *P. alpicola* Tibet; leaves elliptic to spathulate, finely toothed; scape 6–20 in (15–50 cm), flowers to 1 in (2.5 cm) diameter, bell-shaped, pendent, white, yellow, purple or violet, eye farinose, fragrant; var. *luna*: flowers soft yellow; group 7; *P. aurantiaca* SW China; leaves oblanceolate to obovate, finely toothed; scape to 12 in (30 cm), tinged red; flowers whorled, $\frac{5}{8}$ in (1.5 cm) diameter, tubular, red-orange; group 1 or 7; *P. aureata* Nepal; leaves broadly spathulate to oblong, toothed, farinose; scapes very short; flowers to 10, to 1$\frac{1}{2}$ in (4 cm) diameter, flat, cream to yellow, eye dark yellow; subspecies *fimbriata*: flowers pale cream-yellow, with orange eye, lobes deeply toothed; group 8; *P. auricula* Alps, Carpathians, Apennines; leaves rounded to obovate, sometimes farinose, entire to dentate, fleshy; scapes $\frac{1}{2}$–6 in (1–16 cm); flowers 2–30, $\frac{5}{8}$–1 in (1.5–2.5 cm) diameter, flat deep yellow, fragrant; group 5 or 6, see also *Auriculas*; *P. bulleyana* SW China; leaves ovate to lanceolate, toothed; scapes to 24 in (60 cm); flowers many per whorl, to $\frac{3}{4}$ in (2 cm) diameter, tubular, deep orange; group 1 or 7; *P. chionantha* subsp. *melanops* China; leaves lanceolate, toothed, farinose beneath; scape 8–14 in (20–35 cm); flowers 6–12, to $\frac{3}{4}$ in (2 cm) diameter, purple, eye black, to $\frac{3}{4}$ in (2 cm) diameter, fragrant, narrowly funnel-shaped, pendent; group 1 or 7; *P. chungensis* China, Bhutan,

Assam; leaves elliptic to oblong-obovate, toothed and shallowly lobed; scapes to 24 in (60 cm); flowers whorled, to ³/₄ in (1.8 cm) diameter, tubular, pale orange, tube red, fragrant; group 1 or 7; *P. clarkei* Kashmir; leaves rounded to broadly ovate, toothed; scape usually absent; flowers to ³/₄ in (2 cm) diameter, flat, rose-pink, eye yellow; group 8; *P. clusiana* W Austrian Alps; leaves oblong to obovate, leathery, entire, ciliate, shiny above, gray-green beneath; scapes ¹/₂–2 in (1–5 cm), glandular-hairy; flowers 1–4, ⁵/₈–1¹/₂ in (1.5–4 cm) diameter, tubular, bright rose, fading to lilac, throat glandular, eye white; group 8; *P. denticulata* DRUMSTICK PRIMULA; Afghanistan to Tibet and Burma; leaves obovate to spathulate, finely toothed; scapes 4–12 in (10–30 cm); flowers in a tight, rounded head, each to ²/₃ in (1.7 cm) diameter, flat, pale purple to red-purple, sometimes white, eye yellow; group 1 or 3; *P. elatior* OXLIP; Europe to Near East; leaves ovate to oblong or elliptic, crenate to jaggedly toothed, downy beneath; scapes 4–12 in (10–30 cm); flowers many, ³/₄–1 in (2–2.5 cm), yellow, throat green-yellow to orange, tubular, fragrant; group 1, 7 or 9; *P. farinosa* Scotland and Central Sweden to Central Spain to Bulgaria, North Asia and North Pacific; leaves oblanceolate to elliptic, entire or finely toothed, farinose; scape 1¹/₄–8 in (3–20 cm); flowers 2 to many, ³/₈–²/₃ in (0.8–1.6 cm) diameter, lilac-pink, rarely purple or white, throat yellow, tubular; group 8; *P. flaccida* China; leaves elliptic or obovate, finely toothed, downy; scapes 8–16 in (20–40 cm); flowers 5–15, to 1 in (2.5 cm) diameter, lavender to violet, tubular, farinose, pendent; group 7 or 8); *P. florindae* (Tibet; leaves broadly ovate, toothed; scapes to 36 in (90 cm); flowers many, to ³/₄ in (2 cm) diameter, yellow, creamy-farinose within and on calyx, fragrant, funnel-shaped; group 1 or 7); *P. forrestii* (China; leaves ovate to elliptic, toothed, rugose above, farinose beneath; scapes 6–9 in (15–22 cm); flowers 10–25, to ³/₄ in (2 cm) diameter, flat, yellow, eye orange; group 8; *P. frondosa* Balkans; leaves spathulate or obovate, finely toothed, farinose; scapes 2–4³/₄ in (5–12 cm); flowers 1–30, flat, rose-lilac to red-purple, to ⁵/₈ in (1.5 cm) diameter,

eye and tube yellow; group 8; *P. gracilipes* Nepal, Tibet; leaves oblong-spathulate to elliptic, irregularly toothed; scapes absent; flowers solitary, ¹/₂–1¹/₂ in (1–4 cm) diameter, bright pink-purple, eye small, green- to orange-yellow with narrow white border, tubular, lobes toothed; group 8; *P. hirsuta* (syn. *P. rubra*); Central Alps, Pyrenees; leaves obovate to rounded, toothed, fleshy, glandular-hairy, sticky; scape ¹/₂–2³/₄ in (1–7 cm); flowers 1–15, to 1 in (2.5 cm) diameter, flat, pale lilac to deep purple-red, usually with white center; group 8; *P. ioessa* Tibet; leaves narrowly oblong to spathulate, toothed; scapes 4–12 in (10–30 cm); flowers 2–8, to 1 in (2.5 cm) diameter, funnel-shaped, pink-mauve to violet or white, fragrant, calyx almost black, farinose; group 7; *P. japonica* CANDELABRA PRIMULA; Japan; leaves obovate to broadly spathulate, finely toothed; scapes to 18 in (45 cm); flowers in tiered whorls, to ³/₄ in (2 cm) diameter, tubular, purple-red, crimson, pink to white; Miller's Crimson': crimson; 'Postford White': white with a yellow eye; 'Valley Red': bright red; other candelabra-type primulas include *P. aurantiaca, P. bulleyana, P. chungensis, P. prolifera, P. pulverulenta*; group 1 or 7; *P. kewensis*.(*P. floribunda* × *P. verticillata*); garden origin; leaves obovate to spathulate, finely toothed, thinly farinose; scapes to 12 in (30 cm); flowers whorled, to ³/₄ in (2 cm) diameter, tubular, yellow, fragrant; group 4; *P. malacoides* FAIRY PRIMROSE, BABY PRIMROSE; China; leaves broadly oblong to ovate, shallowly lobed and toothed; scapes 8–12 in (20–30 cm); flowers whorled, to ⁵/₈ in (1.5 cm) diameter, flat, mauve to pink, red, or white; group 4; *P. marginata* Alps; leaves obovate to oblong, toothed, leathery, fleshy, farinose on margins; scape ³/₄–4³/₄ in (2–12 cm); flowers 2–20, ⁵/₈–1¹/₄ in (1.5–3 cm) diameter, lilac to lavender or blue, sometimes violet or pink, shallow funnel-shaped, faintly fragrant, eye white-farinose; 'Prichard's Variety': lilac to purple, eye white-farinose; group 5; *P. modesta* Japan; leaves elliptic to spathulate, wavy-toothed, yellow-farinose; scapes 1–5 in (2.5–12.5 cm); flowers 2–15, to ⁵/₈ in (1.5 cm) diameter, pink-purple, tubular; var. *fauriae*: smaller, white-farinose flowers pink-purple with a yellow eye; group 8; *P. nana* Himalaya; leaves spathulate to

ovate, irregularly toothed or lobed, wavy; scapes absent; flowers solitary, to 1¹/₄ in (3 cm) diameter, blue, lilac, pink or white, eye orange-yellow edged white; group 8; *P. nutans* Mountains of North Asia, North Russia, North Scandinavia, Alaska, South West Yukon; leaves oblong to ovate to orbicular, entire or finely toothed, fleshy; scapes ³/₄–12 in (2–30 cm); flowers 1–10, ¹/₂–³/₄ in (1–2 cm) diameter, lilac to pink-purple, eye yellow, pendent; group 7 or 8; *P. obconica* GERMAN PRIMROSE, POISON PRIMROSE; China; leaves ovate to elliptic to oblong, finely toothed or lobed, hairy; scapes 6–6¹/₂ in (15–17 cm); flowers 10–15, to 1 in (2.5 cm) diameter, flat, pale-lilac or purple, eye yellow; group 4; *P. palinuri* S Italy; leaves broadly spathulate to oblong-ovate toothed, fleshy, viscid, aromatic, glandular-hairy; scapes 3–8 in (8–20 cm); flowers 5–25, to 1¹/₄ in (3 cm) diameter, narrowly funnel-shaped, deep yellow, throat with white, farinose ring; group 5; *P. petiolaris* Himalaya; leaves spathulate, finely toothed; scapes 1¹/₄–2 in (3–5 cm), flowers many, ⁵/₈ in (1.5 cm) diameter, tubular, pink, eye yellow with thin white border, lobes 3-toothed; group 8; *P. polyneura* China; leaves ovate to orbicular, more or less downy; scapes to 9 in (23 cm); flowers 10–50 per umbel, each to 1 in (2.5 cm) diameter, tubular pale rose to rich rose-red to crimson or purple, eye yellow; group 7; *P.* Pruhonicensis Hybrids POLYANTHUS; the name here is taken to cover several groups of hybrids between *P. juliae, P. veris, P. elatior* and *P. vulgaris*, all of which have interbred producing a vast range of plants in many colors and conforming to either the primrose-type habit or the cow-oxlip with stalked umbels. *P.* × *pruhoniciana* (*P. juliae* × *P. vulgaris*) (*P.* × *helenae*) covers the early spring primulas with flowers in red, purple, pink and white, often with white or yellow eyes. *P.* × *margotae* (*P. juliae* × *P.* Elatior Hybrids) have leaves often flushed purple-bronze and pink, red or purple flowers in short-stalked umbels. For example 'Garryarde Guinevere' (leaves bronze; flowers lilac-pink. Elatior Hybrids (*P.* × *polyantha*) are strictly hybrids between members of *Primula* section Vernales. These are the polyanthuses with stalked umbels of flowers in shades of gold, pale yellow, bronze, brown and red.

Included here are the gold and silver-laced forms with small, virtually black flowers edged in golden yellow and silver-white; *P.* × *pubescens* (*P. auricula* × *P. hirsuta*); a group including many popular cultivars in a wide range of colors, among them shades of white, yellow, pink, red, purple and brown, sometimes with a differently colored eye; they differ basically from *P. hirsuta* in having farinose, sometimes entire leaves and a slightly farinose calyx; group 2 or 8; *P. reidii* Himalaya; leaves oblong or lanceolate, crenate or lobed, hairy; scapes 2½–6 in (6–15 cm); flowers 3–10, ¾–1 in (2–2.5 cm) diameter, white, bell- to urn-shaped, fragrant, pendent; var. *williamsii*: more robust, flowers pale blue to white; group 8; *P. rosea* Himalaya; leaves tinted red-bronze at first, emerging with or after flowers, obovate to oblanceolate; scapes 1¼–4 in (3–10 cm); flowers 4–12, ½–¾ in (1–2 cm) diameter, flat, rose-pink to red; group 1 or 7; *P. secundiflora* W China; leaves oblong to obovate or oblanceolate, toothed, farinose beneath; scapes 12–24 in (30–60 cm); flowers 10–20, nodding to one side, ⅝–1 in (1.5–2.5 cm) diameter, funnel-shaped, red-purple or deep rose-red; group 1 or 7; *P. sieboldii* N E Asia; leaves ovate to oblong, with toothed lobes; scapes to 12 in (30 cm); flowers 6–10, 1–1¼ in (2.5–3 cm) diameter, flat, white, pink or purple, eye white; includes numerous cultivars with flowers ranging in color from white to bright cerise and wisteria blue; some of the best have cut or toothed corolla lobes, in the pure white 'Kuisakigarri', for example, they are so delicately fimbriate as to resemble snowflakes; group 7; *P. sikkimensis* Nepal to SW China; leaves elliptic or oblong to oblanceolate, toothed; scapes 6–36 in (15–90 cm); flowers many, to 1 in (2.5 cm) diameter, yellow or cream-white, pendent, funnel-shaped, variably fragrant, calyx yellow-farinose; group 1 or 7; *P. sinensis* China; leaves broadly ovate to rounded, hairy, lobed and toothed, often red beneath; scapes 4–6 in (10–15 cm); flowers whorled, ¾–2 in (2–5 cm) diameter, flat, purple, pink or white with a yellow eye and entire or incised lobes; group 4; *P. sonchifolia* W China; leaves oblong to obovate,

toothed and lobed; scapes to 12 in (30 cm); flowers 3–20, to 1 in (2.5 cm) diameter, tubular, blue to purple with a yellow eye and white-edged, sometimes toothed lobes; group 8; *P. veris* COWSLIP; Europe, W Asia; leaves ovate to oblong-ovate, crenate or entire; scapes 2½–12 in (6–30 cm); flowers 2–16, ½–⅝ in (1–1.5 cm) diameter, tubular, yellow, fragrant with an orange mark at base of each lobe; group 1 or 3; *P. verticillata* SW Arabian Peninsula, NE Africa; leaves lanceolate to ovate-lanceolate, sharply and finely toothed, white-farinose beneath; scapes 4–24 in (10–60 cm); flowers many, whorled, each to ¾ in (2 cm) diameter, bell-shaped, yellow, fragrant; group 4; *P. vialii* (China; leaves broadly lanceolate to oblong, hairy, toothed; scape 12–16 in (30–40 cm); flowers pointing downward in a dense, narrowly conical spike, each to ½ in (1 cm) diameter, tubular, calyx, red in bud, later pink, corolla blue to violet; group 1 or 3; *P. vulgaris* PRIMROSE; W & S Europe; leaves oblanceolate to obovate, toothed, downy; scapes absent; flowers 1–1½ in (2.5–4 cm) diameter, solitary, short-stalked, flat, sometimes fragrant, pale yellow, throat more or less orange; cultivars include forms with single, double or hose-in-hose flowers, in a wide range of colors. 'Jack in the Green': abnormality with a leafy calyx; group 1 or 3; *P. warshenewskiana* C Asia to Himalaya; leaves oblong to oblanceolate, finely toothed, dark green; scapes short; flowers 1–8, to ½ in (1.2 cm) diameter, flat, bright rose or pink with yellow eye surrounded by narrow white zone; group 8; *P. whitei* (syn. *P. bhutanica*); E Himalaya; leaves oblong to spathulate, finely toothed, slightly farinose; scapes short; flowers 5–10, to 1 in (2.5 cm) diameter, tubular to bell-shaped, blue to violet, eye white or yellow-green, lobes toothed; 'Sheriff's Variety' differs in its more conspicuously toothed flowers; group 8.

Proboscidea (from Greek *proboskis*, snout, referring to the beaked fruit).

Pedaliaceae. S America north to central US. UNICORN PLANT, DEVIL'S-CLAW, ELEPHANT-TUSK, PROBOSCIS FLOWER. About 9 species, clammy-hairy, muskily scented, annual or perennial herbs. The flowers are funnelform to campanulate, with a spreading limb of five lobes. The fruit is a woody capsule with large, curving horns at its apex. Cultivate as for *Martynia*. *P. fragrans* SWEET UNICORN PLANT; Mexico; flowers fragrant violet- to red-purple, upper lobes often blotched with darker purple, lower lobe with bright yellow band.

proliferation (1) the presence of an abnormal number of organs in a flower or of an abnormal number of flowers or flower heads on a stem. See *hen and chickens*, *hose-in-hose*; (2) a stage in micropropagation, where new cells develop from tissue, such as an excised meristem; (3) a form of natural vegetative reproduction whereby plantlets or offsets (foliar embryos) are produced on leaves or stems of the mother plant, for example *Tolmiea menziesii*, *Asplenium bulbiferum*. Also known as vivipary; (4) a disease of apples and onions caused by *phytoplasma* (q.v.).

Proliferation on
Tolmeia menziesii

propagating frame a garden frame where used for a similar purpose to a propagating case but constructed at ground level outdoors. It is used for sowing and rooting hardy specimens. A propagating frame allows for progressive hardening off as the covering lights are variably raised or removed. It should be sited in a sheltered position out of full sun, and provided with shading and insulation against cold as necessary.

propagating house a greenhouse devoted to propagation, commonly including mist-propagation equipment and propagating cases.

propagation the increase of plants by seed or vegetative means. See *cuttings*, *division*, *grafting*, *layering*, *micropropagation*, *scooping*, *scoring*, *seed sowing*.

propagation case an enclosed box-like structure used for seed raising and the rooting of cuttings within a green-house, usually with wooden walls about 12–16 in (30–40 cm) high and a glass or sometimes plastic-clad detachable cover, fitted tightly to retain a humid environment. It is usually mounted on a greenhouse benching, and may feature an electrically heated warming cable; this is fitted beneath an overall layer of rooting medium or a covering of sand, upon which containers of seed or cuttings are stood. The term close case (sometimes closed case) is an alternative description.

propagator a purpose-built portable propagating unit, consisting of a stout plastic seed tray to which is fitted a molded translucent plastic dome. There are small ventilators in the top of the dome, and some propagators have warming cables incorporated in their base.

propagule any part of a plant used for propagation.

propping a method of support for leaning trees or long low branches, in which the ground is used as a firm base for a timber or metal crutch.

prickle a small, weak thornlike outgrowth from the bark or outer layers, generally irregularly arranged.

procumbent trailing loosely or lying flat along the surface of the ground, without rooting.

proliferous producing buds or off-shoots; especially from unusual organs, for example plants or plantlets produced from stolons or runners.

prop root a root that arises adventitiously from the stem of a plant, descends to and roots in the ground and supports the stem.

Prostanthera (from Greek *prostheke*, appendage, and Latin *anthera*, anther, from the spurlike projections on the anthers). Labiatae. SE Australia, Tasmania. MINT BUSH. About 50 species, viscid, usually aromatic ever-green shrubs or small trees. Produced in summer in leafy racemes or termi-nal panicles, the flowers are shortly tubular and 2-lipped, the upper lip 2-lobed and hooded, the lower lip 3-lobed. Free-flowering, dependable shrubs for the cool greenhouse and conservatory. Grow in a medium-fer-tility loam-based mix. Give direct light, maintain low humidity and water plentifully when in full growth. Keep just frost-free and almost dry in winter. Container-grown plants can be moved outdoors in late spring, making fine patio specimens. Prune out exhausted growth after flowering. Propagate from seed in spring or by semiripe cuttings in late summer.

P. ovalifolia E Australia; erect shrub, to 13 ft (4 m); leaves to ⅝ in (1.5 cm), oval to ovate, glaucous; flowers numer-ous in short terminal racemes, purple, mauve or white tinted lilac; *P. rotundifo-lia* ROUND-LEAVED MINT BUSH; SE and S Australia; erect shrub to 10 ft (3 m); leaves orbicular to ovate, obscurely dentate or crenate, dark green above; flowers in short, loose, racemes, violet or lilac; 'Chelsea Pink': aromatic, gray-green leaves and pale rose flowers with mauve anthers.

prostrate lying flat on the ground; the Latin equivalent *prostratus, -a,-um* is frequently encountered as a botanical and cultivar name.

protandry the shedding of pollen before the stigma of the same flower is receptive, which discourages self-polli-nation; cf. *protogyny*.

Protea (for Proteus, the ancient Greek sea god, famed for his ability to change shape, a reference to their diversity of form). Proteaceae. South Africa. 115 species, evergreen shrubs or small trees with leathery leaves and slender flowers packed in terminal, conelike heads surrounded by tough, brightly colored bracts. Grow in full light with low humidity and good air circulation. Use a perfectly drained, low-nutrient potting mix, comprising equal parts peat and grit, with addi-tional charcoal; ensure pH is 6.5 or lower. Proteas are extremely sensitive to nitrates and phosphates, which can be toxic even at moderate levels. Con-versely, they may suffer from magne-sium deficiencies: apply dilute liquid feed of magnesium sulfate and urea in spring and fall and water plentifully but judiciously when in flower and full growth. Maintain a winter minimum temperature of 41–45°F (5–7°C) with a summer maximum at about 81°F (27°C). Propagate by seed sown fresh in fall, in a 2:3 mix of peat and grit in individual small pots in the frost-free cold frame or cool greenhouse. Keep seedlings moist but not waterlogged and ensure full ventilation. Avoid root disturbance. Root semiripe cut-tings in summer.

P. cynaroides KING PROTEA; shrub to 6½ ft (2 m); inflorescence 4¾–12 in (12–30 cm), goblet-shaped resembling a globe artichoke, bracts to 4¾ in (12 cm), ovate-lanceolate, deep crimson to pink or cream, silky; *P. magnifica* small shrub; inflorescence turbinate-obovoid, to 6 in (15 cm), bracts creamy pubescent to tomentose, ovate-lanceo-late to linear-lanceolate, white-ciliate; *P. neriifolia* shrub to 10 ft (3 m); inflores-cence goblet-shaped, to 5 in (13 cm), bracts 5½ in (14 cm), oblong to spathu-late, incurved, pink to dark rose, tipped with long black hairs; *P. repens* low shrub or small tree to 13 ft (4 m); inflo-rescence goblet-shaped, to 3½ in (9 cm) in diameter, bracts creamy white, sometimes tinged dark red or pink, glabrous, resinous.

protection (1) any measure taken to make conditions tolerable for tender plants grown in a climate to which they are not adapted, or to guard hardier plants from vagaries of weather. Protected cultivation involves growing plants under some form of cover, such as a cloche, frame, or greenhouse; (2) the protection of plants against pests and diseases, as in "crop protection."

prothallus the gametophyte genera-tion of ferns and other cryptogams, a delicate liverwort-like structure.

protogyny the development of a receptive stigma before pollen shedding by the same flower, which discourages self-pollination; cf. *protandry*.

protoplasm the contents of living cells. Protoplasm is composed of water, proteins, lipids, sugars, a variety

P

of other organic compounds, and mineral salts.

proximal the part nearest to the axis, thus the base of a leaf is proximal; cf. *distal*.

proximate close together.

Prunella (from *Prunella*, pre-Linnaean name for the genus; the origin is obscure but may stem from *Die Breaune*, German for quinsy, a throat infection which these plants allegedly cured). Labiatae. Eurasia, N Africa, N America. SELFHEAL, HEAL ALL. 7 species, decumbent perennial herbs. Produced in spring and summer, whorled in dense spikelets or heads, the flowers are tubular and 2-lipped, the upper lip erect and somewhat hooded, the lower lip shorter, deflexed and 3-lobed. Fully hardy, grow in fully exposed areas or partial shade. It is also useful for groundcover and for meadow and other naturalistic plantings. Propagate from seed or lengths of rooted stem. *P. grandiflora* Europe; sparsely pubescent, to 24 in (60 cm); leaves to 4 in (10 cm), ovate to lanceolate, entire or crenulate; flowers ¾–1¼ in (18–30 mm), lips deep mauve to violet, tube paler to off-white; 'Alba': white; 'Rotkäppchen': carmine; 'Loveliness': pale lilac; 'White Loveliness': white; 'Loveliness Pink': pink.

pruner usually, a pruning tool used for branch lopping, where a movable blade cuts against a fixed one. See *long arm pruner*.

pruning the practice of cutting out parts of plants for specific purposes, carried out almost entirely on woody plants. The main purposes of pruning are to remove dead, diseased or unsightly growth, to maintain a manageable and attractive shape, to prevent overcrowding of other plants, to improve the size or quality of flowers and fruits, and to enhance vigor.

Pruning requirements differ according to species, and special consideration should be given to timing.

Evergreens Cutting evergreens may be necessary or beneficial for rejuvenation, shaping and the removal of dead or diseased parts. Young growth

is often more readily damaged by extremes of temperature and strong sunlight, and pruning of examples such as *Laurus*, *Rosmarinus* and evergreen *Cotoneaster* should therefore be undertaken in late spring.

Rhododendrons and camellias can be suitably pruned by removing flowering branches; special care should be taken to cut back to buds or shoots because there may be no regrowth from old bare wood.

Conifers have a natural tendency for lower branches to die as the trees age and pruning can improve the overall appearance. Occasionally, pruning to improve shape may be desirable, but otherwise this group requires little attention, except when grown as hedging; vigorous young specimens can have crowns removed. Conifers are best pruned when they are in a slow-growing phase.

Deciduous plants Deciduous woody ornamentals such as *Amelanchier*, *Hamamelis*, *Potentilla*, *Viburnum*, *Hibiscus* and *Chaenomeles*, which bear flowers on short shoots and spurs of an established framework, require no more than occasional cutting for shaping, tidying and renovation. This is best carried out in late winter or spring, outside the flowering period. The majority of deciduous shrubs that benefit from regular attention, especially as a means of encouraging a good supply of flowering shoots, may be considered in two main groups. The first group comprises those blooming from mid-summer onward on wood produced in the current season, for example, *Buddleja davidii*, *Caryopteris* × *clandonensis*,

Eccremocarpus scaber. *Hydrangea paniculata* and *Spiraea japonica*; these should have their flowered shoots pruned in early spring, cutting back to within one or two buds of the previous season's growth. Within this group are those which may or may not form a woody framework, depending on locality, such as *Ceratostigma willmottianum*, *Perovskia atriplicifolia*, *Leycesteria formosa*, *Rubus cockburnianus*, *Cotinus coggygria* and hardy fuchsias; these should have all stems cut back to a few inches from ground level, a procedure known as stooling. Bright-stemmed *Salix* and *Cornus* may be stooled, or headed back on an upright stem or 'leg', using the procedure known as pollarding. *Paulownia tomentosa* produces leaves many times normal size if stooled or pollarded. Pruning should be delayed until the danger of frost is past.

The second group comprises the large number of summer-flowering woody plants, such as *Philadelphus*, *Deutzia*, *Buddleja*, *Kerria*, *Hydrangea* × *macrophylla* and *Weigela*, which bear blooms on shoots produced in the previous season. These respond to the thinning out of old branches and crowded shoots, and the removal of faded flower trusses, immediately after blooming. Earlier-flowering subjects in this group, such as *Jasminum nudiflorum*, *Forsythia* and *Prunus triloba*, should have flowered shoots cut out soon after blooming to encourage vigorous replacement growth over the longest possible growing season. Deadheading is a suitable method of pruning heathers and lavender.

Roses Roses are pruned according

Pruning deciduous shrubs
Prune shrubs such as *Deutzia* (left), which flower on the previous season's growth, by removing old wood and thinning shoots after flowering. Shrubs that flower on the current season's growth, such as *Hydrangea paniculata* (right) can be pruned to a framework in early spring.

P

to type, for example, shrub roses should have old, diseased or dead wood removed, with some trimming to maintain shape, while modern bush roses, like hybrid teas and floribundas, need cutting back moderately hard, or sometimes severely, to produce good growth and flowers the next season. Prune when dormant, between leaf fall and budbreak; never in frosty conditions. See *roses*.

Climbers Pruning of woody climbers can be made difficult by tangled growth. With wisterias and ornamental vines, it may be possible to spread out a permanent stout framework of growth and shorten all side growths to it. Climbers with weaker stems, such as *Clematis*, *Jasminum* and *Lonicera*, may require more drastic pruning of the previous season's flowered growth, which is borne on tangles of old bare stems, and severe thinning or pruning of a few selected leads to near ground level may be necessary. Timing is relative to flowering habit.

Fruit For fruit trees and bushes, the objective is to build a strong framework in the formative years, and to ensure a regular supply of replacement shoots or spurs capable of producing sufficient blossom for a full crop of good-quality fruit. The removal of diseased parts and the maintenance of controlled growth with branches open to air and sunlight, are also important reasons for pruning.

Pome and stone fruits flower on wood that is usually one or more years old, and pruning of branches, shoots and spurs of established trees should aim at producing a balance of old and new wood. Currants and gooseberries bear flowers mainly on shoots of the previous year, but also on older wood and spurs. In pruning established black currants, about one third of the total number of branches is removed annually to encourage the production of young wood, which fruits best. Other currants and gooseberries should have leaders reduced to about half their length, and laterals cut back short. Summer-fruiting raspberries bear fruit on laterals arising on canes produced in the previous year, and these are cut to ground level after cropping. Fall-fruiting raspberries bear fruit on canes of the current year, and are pruned to

ground level in late winter. Blackberries and hybrid berries, although their canes are perennial, are pruned on the replacement system in the same way as summer-fruiting raspberries.

The pruning of apples, pears, gooseberries and currants is carried out during dormancy. Stone fruits are pruned in spring and summer in order to avoid exposure to the active stages of silver leaf disease and bacterial canker. Additional summer pruning is an essential means of restricting vigorous growth with intensive tree forms, and of developing and maintaining good structure in gooseberries and red- and white-currants. See *renewal pruning*, *summer pruning*.

Pruning techniques All pruning cuts should be made cleanly, with sharp tools, directly above a growth bud or close to where another branch arises. It is good practice to make pruning cuts to shoots and small branches slope down from a bud at an angle of 45°. The wounds left by the removal of large branches are likely to heal more rapidly if the cut is made a little distance from the trunk, beyond the slight swelling that encircles its base. Care must be taken to ensure that branches which are being removed with a saw do not break and tear bark from the main limb. A branch should first be cut off a short distance from the trunk and two further cuts then made; with each cut, a shallow undercut from the lower surface of the branch should be followed by a second complete cut from above, just a little nearer the trunk or limb. The branch will snap off cleanly and the short remaining stub can be removed without risk of damage.

Wound dressing with special paints may protect from infection, and this is an important requirement for stone fruits, but untreated wounds heal faster, and large wounds are only briefly protected since paint cover soon cracks.

Root pruning The roots of established fruit trees may be cut to reduce growth and encourage fruiting. This practice was more common before the advent of dwarfing rootstocks, but it is still an effective treatment for older trees, including shy flowering ornamentals, albeit less convenient than bark ringing. A trench 18–24 in (45–60 cm)

deep should be dug encircling the tree beneath the branch extremities, and exposed thicker roots severed. The provision of subsequent support may be advisable as anchorage is weakened.

pruning knife a pocket knife used for light pruning, more usually by experts, with one folding blade that is slightly curved.

pruning saw a narrow bladed saw, used for pruning small branches. The blade and handle may be straight or angled, or more usually curved. See *Grecian saw*.

pruning shears see *secateurs*.

pruinose thickly frosted with white or blue-gray bloom, usually on a dark ground color.

Prunus (the Classical Latin name for these plants). Rosaceae. ALMOND, CHERRY, CHERRY LAUREL, NECTARINE, PEACH, PLUM, ARICOT. N Temperate regions, S America. 430 species, deciduous and evergreen trees and shrubs. Produced between fall and early summer (predominantly spring), the flowers consist of five rounded and spreading petals and numerous stamens; they are usually white, pink or red. They give rise to fleshy drupes with hard stones. In some cases these fruits are edible and important crops—see *almond*, *apricot*, *cherry*, *peaches and nectarines*, *plums*.

Grown for their attractive habit and form, their decorative bark, their fine fall colors and for their unrivalled display of blossom which, with judicious selection of species and cultivars, can be extended almost throughout the year, from the late fall and winter blooms of *P. subhirtella* 'Autumnalis', through late spring and early summer with the late-flowering Japanese cherries such as 'Fugenzo' and 'Shirofugen', and into summer with the intermittent flushes of blossom on *P. cerasus* 'Semperflorens'. Most flower in spring. *P. cerasifera* and its cultivars, and *P. davidiana* are among the earliest to flower: the former with spectacular combinations of bridal white blossom and wine red new growth, the latter blooming soon after New Year in a mild season.

P

The shrubby species, *P. incisa*, *P.* × *cistena* and *P. spinosa*, are used for hedging, the last especially useful in cold, exposed and maritime areas. When grown as shrubs, *P. cerasifera* and its dark-leaved cultivars also make excellent hedging plants. The evergreen *P. laurocerasus* and *P. lusitanica* are often used as informal screens and in more manicured hedging. Both make good game cover and are often planted as understory in woodland. *P. laurocerasus* is extremely tolerant of shade and tree drip. Species grown primarily for their beautiful peeling bark include *P. serrula*, a glossy deep mahogany-red, and *P. maackii*, a shining, translucent amber to gold. The Japanese Flowering Cherries (Sato-zakura Group), contribute a range of form and habit, from the upright narrow columns of 'Amanogawa' and stiffly ascending branches of 'Sekiyama', to the small weeping domes of 'Kiku-shidare'. The flowers may be large or small, single, semi-double or double, regular or ragged, sweetly fragrant or almond-scented, snow white, cream, pale rose, pink, pale red, pale lilac or purple-pink. This group includes many small trees for the confined spaces of urban gardens, where their tolerance of pollution is especially useful. Most color well in fall, in shades of yellow and tawny orange, and many also have bronzed new growth, in beautiful contrast to the emergent blossom.

The following are fully hardy. Grow them in well-drained moisture-retentive soil, siting deciduous species in full sun to ensure good flowering and fall color. *P. glandulosa* and *P. triloba* thrive when trained against a sheltered south-facing wall. Plant evergreens in sun to semi-shade. Stake standard specimen trees until established, especially in areas exposed to wind, and protect young stems from rabbits and hares. With the exception of *P. laurocerasus*, which becomes chlorotic on shallow chalk, most grow particularly well in calcareous soil. Prune if necessary in late summer, ensuring a long enough period for wounds to heal before the onset of winter. Cut back the flowered shoots of *P. glandulosa* and *P. triloba* to 2–3 buds from the base, especially if grown as wall or forcing shrubs. If grown as a flowering hedge, trim after

flowering. Cut back *P. laurocerasus* and *P. lusitanica* with secateurs in spring or late summer; neglected specimens can be rejuvenated by cutting hard back into old wood in spring.

Propagate species by seed; they may hybridize and not come true, although seed-raised specimens are generally longer-lived. Collect seed when ripe, remove flesh and stratify in damp coir or sand for 10–14 weeks (3–4 weeks for *P. dulcis* and *P. armeniaca*) prior to sowing. Alternatively sow outdoors in a cold frame in fall and protect from rodents. Propagate shrubby species such as *P. glandulosa*, *P. laurocerasus*, *P. pumila*, *P. tenella* and *P. triloba* by simple layering in early spring. Cultivars are propagated commercially by budding or grafting—the Japanese and large-flowered cherries on to *P. avium*; bird cherry types, such as *P. cornuta*, *P. serotina* and *P. virginiana*, on to *P. padus*. Species such as *P. cerasifera*, *P. incisa*, *P. spinosa* and *P. subhirtella*, can be propagated by semiripe heel cuttings in summer, in a closed case with bottom heat Most species can be propagated by softwood cuttings taken when plants are growing strongly, in spring and early summer, treated with hormone-rooting powder, and rooted with mist and bottom heat.

Ornamental *Prunus* species are affected to various degrees by the same pests and diseases that attack the edible species (q.v.).

P. × *amygdalopersica* (*P. dulcis* × *P. persica*); tree or shrub; leaves similar to *P. dulcis*, coarsely toothed; flowers to 2 in (5 cm) diameter, light pink; fruit peach-like, dry; 'Pollardii': flowers large, rich pink; *P. armeniaca* APRICOT; North China; tree to 33 ft (10 m); leaves to 4¾ in (12 cm), orbicular or ovate, glabrous, toothed; flowers to 1½ in (4 cm) diameter, white or pink; fruit to 2 in (5 cm), white to orange-red or yellow, downy; *P. avium* BIRD CHERRY, GEAN, WILD CHERRY; Europe, Asia; tree to 66 ft (20 m); leaves to 4 in (10 cm), oblong-ovate, acuminate, toothed; flowers 1 in (2.5 cm) diameter, white; fruit ¾ in (2 cm), dark maroon; 'Plena': flowers double, pure white; *P.* × *blireana* *P. cerasifera* 'Atropurpurea' × *P. mume*; garden origin; shrub or small tree to 15 ft (4.5 m); young leaves bronze-red at first; flowers 1¼ in (3 cm) diameter,

bright rose, double; 'Moseri': leaves light red flushed brown; flowers small, pale pink; *P. campanulata* BELL-FLOWERED CHERRY, TAIWAN CHERRY, FORMOSAN, CHERRY; South Japan, Taiwan; small tree; bark purple-brown; leaves to 4½ in (11 cm), elliptic acuminate, toothed; flowers to 1¼ in (3 cm) diameter, dark rose-red, bell-shaped, nodding; fruit ½ in (1 cm) diameter, black-purple; 'Okame' (*P. campanulata* × *P. incisa*): leaves small, dark green, flaming orange in fall; flowers shocking pink; *P. cerasifera* CHERRY PLUM, MYROBALAN; Asia Minor, Caucasus; large shrub or tree to 30 ft (9 m), often spiny; leaves to 2½ in (6.5 cm), ovate to obovate, toothed; flowers to 1 in (2.5 cm), pure white; fruit to 1¼ in (3 cm) diameter, round red to yellow, somewhat pruinose; 'Pissardii': leaves emerging dark red, later deep purple to red-bronze; flowers white, buds pink, profuse, appearing before foliage; fruit maroon; *P. cerasus* SOUR CHERRY; SE Europe to W Asia; shrub or tree to 20 ft (6 m); leaves 2½ in (6 cm), narrowly ovate to elliptic, finely toothed, dark green, glossy; flowers to 1 in (2.5 cm) diameter, white; fruit ¾ in (1.8 cm) diameter, dark red; var. *austera*: MORELLO CHERRY; tree to 30 ft (9 m), somewhat pendulous; flowers to 2½ in (6 cm) diameter; fruit black-red; var. *caproniana*: AMARELLE CHERRY, KENTISH RED CHERRY, tree to 30 ft (9 m); fruit globose, light red; var. *marasca*: MARASCHINO CHERRY; arching tree; fruit black-red, small; *P.* × *cistena* *P. cerasifera* 'Atropurpurea' × *P. pumila*; garden origin; shrub to 8 ft (2.5 m); leaves to 2½ in (6 cm), obovate to lanceolate, red-brown, toothed; flowers white, calyx red-brown; fruit black-purple; 'Crimson Dwarf': dense, upright, to 4 ft (1.2 m) high; leaves red tinted bronze, crimson when young; flowers shell pink, calyx dark red; *P. davidiana* DAVID'S PEACH; China; tree to 30 ft (9 m); leaves to ½ in (1 cm), lanceolate, tapering finely, dark green and shiny, sharp-toothed; flowers 1 in (2.5 cm) diameter, white or pale pink; fruit 1¼ in (3 cm) diameter, yellow to red, downy; *P. domestica* (*P. spinosa* × *P. cerasifera*) subspecies *divaricata*, PLUM, COMMON PLUM; S Europe, Asia; tree to 39 ft (12 m), sometimes spiny; leaves to 4 in (10 cm), elliptic or oblong, downy

Prunus glandulosa 'Alba Plena'
This flowering almond is of modest size and suitable for the mixed border or for wall training. It bears large double white flowers.

at first; flowers to 1 in (2.5 cm) diameter, white; fruit to 3 in (8 cm), yellow or red to blue-black or violet-purple, pruinose, flesh green or yellow; *P. dulcis* ALMOND; Syria to N Africa; tree to 30 ft (9 m); leaves to 5 in (13 cm), lanceolate, tapering narrowly, finely toothed; flowers palest pink to deep rose, to 2 in (5 cm); fruit to 2½ in (6.5 cm), green, with thin, tough flesh and velvety skin; numerous cultivars with single or double flowers in tones of white, pale pink, rose and magenta; *P. glandulosa* DWARF FLOWERING ALMOND; China, Japan; shrub to 6½ ft (2 m); leaves to 2¾ in (7 cm), oblong to lanceolate, finely toothed with glandular stipules; flowers to ¾ in (2 cm) diameter, red becoming pink or white; fruit ½ in (1 cm), dark red; 'Alba Plena': flowers double, large, white; 'Sinensis': flowers large, double, bright pink; *P.* 'Hillieri' (*P. incisa* × *P. sargentii*); garden origin; densely branched tree to 30 ft (9 m); leaves bronze at first, coloring brilliantly in fall, toothed; flowers 1¼ in (3 cm) diameter, pink, calyx bronze-red; *P. incisa* FUJI CHERRY; Japan; tree to 16 ft (5 m); leaves to 2 in (5 cm), obovate or ovate, downy on veins, sharply toothed; flowers produced in late winter and early spring, to ¾ in (2 cm) diameter, white to rose, petals notched; fruit to ⅜ in (0.8 cm), purple-black; 'February Pink': young growth red-tinted, fall color good; flowers pale pink, produced early in the year; *P. insititia* BULLACE; branches often spiny; fruit small, usually dark purple; *P. laurocerasus* CHERRY LAUREL, LAUREL; SE Europe, Asia Minor; evergreen

shrub or tree to 20 ft (6 m); leaves to 10 in (25 cm), oblong to elliptic, glossy and dark green, thick and rather rigid; flowers white, small, in dense racemes to 4 in (10 cm); fruit ⅜ in (0.8 cm), plum red to black; 'Aureovariegata': leaves tipped yellow; 'Castlewellan': leaves slightly contorted, speckled white; 'Otto Luyken': compact and low-growing, spreading shrub to 3¼ ft (1 m); leaves narrow glossy dark green; free-flowering; 'Schipkaensis': broad, goblet shaped, to 6½ ft (2 m); leaves large; very hardy; *P. lusitanica* PORTUGAL LAUREL, LAUREL; Iberian Peninsula; evergreen shrub of wide, bushy habit, or tree to 66 ft (20 m); branchlets red; leaves to 4¾ in (12 cm), oblong to ovate, somewhat toothed, thinly coriaceous dark green, shiny above; flowers to ½ in (1 cm) diameter, white, erect, in racemes to 6 in (15 cm); fruit ⅜ in (8 mm), red to dark purple or black; subsp. *azorica*: AZORES LAUREL CHERRY; Azores; shrub or small tree to 13 ft (4 m); leaves to 4 in (10 cm), ovate to elliptic; racemes shorter, fewer-flowered; 'Variegata': leaves edged white, sometimes flushed pink in winter; *P. maackii* AMUR CHERRY, MANCHURIAN CHERRY; Korea, Manchuria; tree to 52 ft (16 m); bark golden to russet, pellucid, papery, peeling; leaves 4 in (10 cm), elliptic or oblong; flowers small, white, in dense racemes; fruit ⅛ in (4 mm), dry, black; 'Amber Beauty': bark golden; *P. mahaleb* ST. LUCIE CHERRY; Europe, Asia Minor; tree to 30 ft (9 m); leaves 1¾ in (4.5 cm), broadly ovate to rounded, toothed; flowers ½ in (1.4 cm) diameter, white, in racemes; fruit ¼ in (0.6 cm), black; 'Albomarginata': leaves edged white; 'Aurea': leaves splashed yellow; *P. mume* JAPANESE APRICOT, MEI; Japan; tree to 30 ft (9 m); branchlets glossy; leaves to 4 in (10 cm), broad, toothed; flowers to 1¼ in (3 cm), pale rose; fruit to 1¼ in (3 cm) diameter, somewhat downy, yellow; 'Beni-shi-dori': flowers double, intense pink, fading later, fragrant; 'Omoi-no-wac': flowers semi-double, cup-shaped, white, occasional petal or even whole flower pink; *P. padus* BIRD CHERRY, EUROPEAN BIRD CHERRY; Europe, Asia; tree to 5 ft (1.5 m); leaves to 3½ in (9 cm), obovate to elliptic, toothed; flowers to ⅜ in (1.5 cm) diameter, white with toothed petals, in racemes to 4¾

in (12 cm); fruit pea-sized, black; 'Plena': flowers semi-double, large, long-lasting; 'Watereri': flowers white, large, almond-scented in pendulous racemes; var. *commutata*: medium-sized tree; leaves coarser, crenate; racemes to 6 in (15 cm); *P. pensylvanica* PIN CHERRY, BIRD CHERRY, RED CHERRY; N America; tree to 30 ft (9 m); leaves 3½ in (9 cm), narrowly ovate, acuminate, with glandular teeth; flowers ⅝ in (1.5 cm), white; fruit ¼ in (0.6 cm) diameter, red; *P. persica* PEACH; China; small tree to 26 ft (8 m); leaves to 6 in (15 cm), elliptic to lanceolate, tapering narrowly; flowers pink to white, to 1½ in (3.5 cm) diameter; fruit to 2¾ in (7 cm) diameter, downy, yellow blushed red, fragrant, very juicy; numerous cultivars grown for their fruit; the following are ornamental—'Klara Mayer': shrub-like; flowers double, to 1½ in (4 cm), strong red-pink; fruit pale green, tinted red; 'Russel's Red': habit dense; flowers double, striking red; 'Palace Peach': flowers double, small, deepest red; 'Peppermint Stick': flowers double, white, striped red; 'Dianthifolia': flowers very large, semi-double, petal narrow, striped deep red; *P. sargentii* Japan; spreading tree to 60 ft (18 m); leaves to 4 in (10 cm), broadly oblong-elliptic to obovate, tapering, sharply toothed, somewhat, glaucous beneath; flowers to 1½ in (4 cm) diameter, blush-pink with cut petals; fruit to ½ in (1 cm), glossy crimson; 'Columnaris': columnar, to 33 ft (10 m); bark mahogany; leaves flaming red and gold in fall; flowers single, pink; 'Accolade': *P. sargentii* × *P. subhirtella*; habit flat-topped, older plants somewhat pendulous; flowers semi-double, to 1½ in (4 cm) diameter, shocking pink in pendulous clusters; *P.* Sato-zakura Group JAPANESE FLOWERING CHERRIES; most probably derived from *P. serrulata*; 'Amanogawa': narrowly erect, to 20 ft (6 m); flowers single or semi-double, pale pink, fragrant; 'Kanzan': syn. 'Sekiyama'; ascending to spreading, to 39 ft (12 m); leaves lightly tinted red-bronze at first, yellow and copper in fall; flowers large, double, pink in hanging clusters; 'Kiku-shidare-zakura': syn. 'Cheal's Weeping'; small weeping tree; flowers double, clear deep pink; 'Shogetsu': small with a wide-spreading, flattened crown; flowers large, double, fringed, blush pink opening white; 'Shi-

P

rofugen': wide and spreading, flat-crowned; flowers large, double, pink in bud, opening white; 'Shirotae': small, spreading to pendulous; flowers large, single to semi-double, white with a hawthornlike fragrance; 'Ukon': habit erect to spreading; leaves coloring well in fall; flowers large, semi-double, creamy white tinted primrose yellow; 'Uzuza-kura': syn. 'Hokusai'; spreading, vigorous; fall color good; flowers large, semi-double, shell pink developing a dark stain in center with age; 'Yae-marasakizakura': syn. 'Yae-Murasaki'; small, slow-growing; leaves brilliant orange in fall; flowers semi-double, purple-red in bud, opening purple-pink, very freely produced; *P. serrula* BIRCH-BARK CHERRY; SW China; tree to 50 ft (15 m); bark shiny mahogany-brown, peeling and birchlike; leaves to 3 in (7.5 cm), lanceolate, finely toothed; flowers ¾ in (2 cm) diameter, white; fruit ½ in (1 cm), bright red; *P. serrulata* ORIENTAL CHERRY; China; tree to 10 ft (3 m); leaves to 5 in (13 cm), ovate, tapering narrowly, finely toothed; flowers 1½ in (3.5 cm) diameter, pure white, double; fruit small, black; var. *spontanea*: HILL CHERRY, JAPANESE MOUNTAIN CHERRY; Japan; to 60 ft (18 m); bark brown or gray with conspicuous lenticels; leaves bronze when young; flowers to 1 in (2.5 cm), diameter, white or pink, petals incised; *P. spinosa* SLOE, BLACKTHORN; Europe, N Africa, Asia Minor; very spiny shrub or small tree to 26 ft (8 m); leaves to 2 in (5 cm), elliptic to oblong or obovate, finely toothed; flowers to ¾ in (2 cm) diameter, white; fruit to ⅝ in (1.5 cm), black, pruinose; *P. × subhirtella* WINTER FLOWERING CHERRY, SPRING CHERRY, HIGAN CHERRY, ROSE-BUD CHERRY; Japan; tree to 60 ft (18 m) with a flat to somewhat weeping crown; branchlets slender, cascading; leaves to 3 in (8 cm), ovate to lanceolate, tapering, toothed, coloring richly in fall; flowers to ¾ in (1.8 cm) diameter, pale pink to white with cut petals, appearing at leaf fall and and often again before new leaves; fruit to ⅜ in (9 mm), purple-black; 'Autumnalis': habit spreading, to 16 ft (5 m); leaves deeply serrate, red and orange in fall; flowers produced in fall, late winter and early spring, semi-double, petals somewhat frilled, opening white, pink in bud, almond-scented; *P. tenella* DWARF RUSSIAN ALMOND; C Europe to E

Siberia; low, bushy shrub to 5 ft (1.5 m); leaves to 3½ in (9 cm), obovate or oblong, somewhat thick and glossy, coarsely toothed; flowers to ⅝ in (1.5 cm) across, rose-red; fruit 1 in (2.5 cm), gray-yellow, velvety; 'Fire Hill': dwarf, to 30 in (75 cm) high, forms thickets of thin erect stem; flowers intense red-ink, profuse; *P. tomentosa* MANCHU CHERRY; Kasmir, China, Tibet; shrub to 8 ft (2.5 m); young shoots downy; leaves to 2 in (5 cm), obovate to oblong, slightly rugose, downy above, densely so beneath, toothed; flowers to 1 in (2.3 cm) diameter, white or pink; fruit ½ in (1.2 cm), subglobose, hairy, red; *P. triloba* FLOWER-ING ALMOND; China; shrub or small tree to 15 ft (4.5 m); branches brown, often rodlike and erect; leaves to 2½ in (6 cm), ovate or obovate, often trilobed, coarsely toothed; flowers to 1 in (2.5 cm) diameter, pink to white, often double; fruit ½ in (13 mm) diameter, red, downy; 'Multiplex': flowers double, pink; *P. virginiana* CHOKE CHERRY; N America; shrub to 11½ ft (3.5 m), or rarely small tree; leaves to 3 in (8 cm), broadly obovate or elliptic, very finely toothed; flowers ½ in (1 cm) diameter, white, in dense racemes; fruit dark red to black; 'Schubert': habit dense, spreading to 20 ft (6 m) high; leaves becoming purple-brown in summer; *P. × yedoensis P. × subhirtella × P. speciosa*; POTOMAC CHERRY, YOSHINO CHERRY; small tree to 50 ft (15 m), broadly upright; bark smooth; leaves to 4¾ in (12 cm), elliptic, tapering, toothed, stalk yellow with red hairs; flowers to 1½ in (3.5 cm) diameter, pure white in racemes; fruit pea-sized, black; 'Moer-heimii': shrublike, to 10 ft (3 m), weeping; twigs pendulous, gray; flowers pink fading to white; to ¾ in (2 cm) diameter; late-flowering; 'Shidare Yoshino': syn. 'Pendula'; habit weeping; flowers snow white, profuse.

Pseuderanthemum (from Greek *pseudo*, false, and *Eranthemum*, a closely related genus with which this one is much confused). Acanthaceae. Tropics. Some 60 species, evergreen herbs, sub-shrubs and shrubs, differing from *Eran-themum* in their inconspicuous floral bracts and overlapping, not twisted corolla lobes. Cultivate as for *Eranthemum*.

P. atropurpureum Polynesia, naturalized tropical America; slender shrub to 5 ft (1.5 m); leaves 4–6 in

(10–15 cm), linear to ovate-elliptic, dark purple to deep metallic green; flowers to 1 in (2.5 cm), white, spotted rose or purple at base; 'Variegatum': leaves bronze-purple, marked pink and variegated cream-yellow, flowers magenta marked red; *P. reticulatum* Polynesia; subshrub to 3¼ ft (1 m); leaves to 11 in (27 cm), ovate-lanceo-late, undulate, dark green net-veined cream-yellow; flowers to 1¼ in (3 cm), flushed and spotted damson.

pseudobulb the water-storing thickened bulblike stems found in many sympodial orchids. Pseudobulbs vary in shape and size and usually grow actively for only one season, persisting thereafter as backbulbs.

pseudocarp see *accessory fruit*.

pseudogamy development of an embryo following pollination but not fertilization.

Pseudogynoxys (literally a 'false *Gynoxys*'—the name of another genus of South American Compositae). Compositae. Tropical S America. About 13 species, evergreen perennial shrubs or climbers with daisylike flower heads. A vigorous evergreen climber suited to the cool to the inter-mediate greenhouse or conservatory, where it will rapidly cover walls and pillars with deep green foliage and cheer-ful orange-red flower heads. Plant in a moist, but not wet, loam-based fertile mix in semi-shade or full sun. Feed semiweekly in spring and summer. Trim back shoots after flowering. Increase by seed or semiripe nodal cuttings. *P. chenopodioides* (syn. *Senecio chenopodioides*, *S. confusus*); MEXICAN FLAMEVINE, ORANGE-GLOW VINE, TRAILING GROUNDSEL, MEXICAN FIREVINE, MEXICAN DAISY; Colombia; climbing shrub to 20 ft (6 m); leaves narrowly ovate, dentate, light green, glabrous; flower heads to 2 in (5 cm) in diameter, bright orange to flame, usually fragrant.

Pseudolarix (from Greek *pseudo*, false, and *Larix*, which it resembles). Pinaceae. E China. GOLDEN LARCH. 1 species, *P. amabilis*, a deciduous, conifer-ous tree, to 130 ft (40 m). The crown is broadly conic with horizontal

P

branches, the bole covered with rust-brown, narrow-ridged bark, becoming gray and fissured in old trees. The leaves are whorled or spiraled, needle-like, 1¼–2¾ in (3–7 cm) long and pale green becoming rich gold in fall. A difficult tree to grow well in cool-temperate regions: if planted out when small, it is easily scorched and may be killed by 23°F (–5°C). Good trees are found only in southern England yet the 100 ft (30 m) trees in New Jersey and New York show clearly that very cold winters are no problem where summers are long and hot. The golden larch fares best in warm, sheltered sites in fertile, deep soil, around pH 5–6, with about 40 in (1,000 mm) rainfall. Avoid exposure to dry winds, and fast-drying soil. Propagation as for *Larix*.

Pseudopanax (from Greek *pseudo*, false, and *Panax*.) Araliaceae. New Zealand and associated islands, Tasmania, Chile. LANCEWOOD. 12–20 species, evergreen trees or shrubs, some with distinct kinds of foliage in different life-stages. The leaves are simple or palmately compound, the blades entire or variously toothed. Small, pale flowers are borne in umbels on large, compound inflorescences. The following species tolerate temperatures down to at least 23°F (–5°C), provided that they are given a warm, sheltered location. Cultivate in fertile, well-drained soil, giving full sun or part-shade. Large plants respond well to heavy pruning and to careful transplanting. In cold areas, grow in large containers in the conservatory or cool to intermediate greenhouse (winter minimum 45–50°F/ 7–10°C), giving strong, filtered light in summer and low humidity; ventilate whenever possible. Water moderately in summer, sparingly in winter. Propagate from seed in fall, by semiripe cuttings in summer or by air-layering.

P. arboreus FIVE-FINGER, PUAHOU, WHAUWHAUPAKU; New Zealand; round-headed tree to 26 ft (8 m), trunk slender, branches pointed upward; leaflets 3–7, thick, narrowly oblong to oblong-obovate, to 8 in (20 cm), coarsely toothed, dark glossy green above; *P. crassifolius* LANCEWOOD, HOROEKA; New Zealand; tree to 50 ft (15 m) tall, usually erect, slender and

unbranched when young; juvenile leaves to 39 in (100 cm), linear, tough to rigid, sinuately toothed, downward pointing, olive to flesh pink mottled black to maroon or silver-gray, sometimes solid black-brown with an orange-pink midrib; adult-leaves simple or 3–5-foliate, upright, linear to linear-obovate, leathery, to 8 in (20 cm), sinuate or coarsely toothed; *P. ferox* TOOTHED LANCEWOOD; New Zealand; resembling *P. crassifolius* but to 23 ft (7 m); leaves always simple, in adults to 6 in (15 cm) or so; juvenile leaves to 18 in (45 cm), jaggedly toothed; *P. laetus* New Zealand; shrub or small tree, to 20 ft (6 m) or so; leaves 5–7-foliolate, petioles purple-red, to 10 in (25 cm), leaflets obovate, thick, to 12 in (30 cm), stalked, toothed above.

Pseudosasa (from Greek *pseudos*, false, and *Sasa*). Gramineae. China, Japan, Korea. 6 species of tall or short bamboos; the rhizomes are usually spreading and running but in colder climates may become shorter and congested, giving the culms a clumped appearance; see *bamboos*.

pseudostem an erect aerial 'stem' apparently furnished with leaves but in fact composed of the packed or overlapping sheaths and stalks of essentially basal leaves. It is a common feature of the families Musaceae, Zingiberaceae, Heliconiaceae, Strelitziaceae and Cannaceae.

Pseudotsuga (from Greek *pseudo-*, false, and *Tsuga*). Pinaceae. Western N America south to Mexico; E Asia from S Japan to Taiwan and SW China. DOUGLAS FIR. 8 species, evergreen coniferous trees. The crown is conic, becoming irregular with age in exposure, the branches long, spreading or sweeping downward, and the branchlets and shoots somewhat drooping. The bark is smooth, dark purple-gray, with resin blisters when young, becoming very thick, deeply fissured and corky red-brown with paler fissures on mature trees. The needlelike leaves are radially arranged with their short stalks twisted to position the leaves more or less pectinately. Ovoid to cylindric, the cones are pendulous, green, pink or

purple, with a pale or violet bloom, ripening brown, often resinous. The following species is an important timber tree. Fully hardy, it should be planted in moist but well-drained, acidic to neutral soil. Increase by seed, or (cultivars) by grafting on stocks of typical *P. menziesii*. Leaf-cast fungus can partly defoliate trees of *P. menziesii* subsp. *glauca*, and more particularly its var. *caesia*, but severe attacks are rare in gardens. Adelgids attack several species.

P. menziesii (syn. *P. douglasii*, *P. taxifolia*); DOUGLAS FIR, GREEN DOUGLAS FIR; SW British Colombia, to west central California; to 330 ft (100 m), bark green-brown with resin blisters, becoming red-brown, corky, fissured, crown dense, conic, more slender and open in vigorous trees, spirelike, branches level or gently downswept, branchlets drooping, shoots aromatic; leaves ⅝–1½ in (1.5–4 cm), bright green above, two dull white bands beneath, blunt, rounded; cone 2½–4¾ in (6–12 cm), green; subsp. *glauca*: BLUE DOUGLAS FIR, COLORADO DOUGLAS FIR, C and S US, to 130 ft (40 m), leaves strongly upswept, ⅝–1 in (1.5–2.5 cm) gray-green to blue-green, with stomatal bands above as well as beneath, cultivars including dwarf and tall clones with blue to silver-white foliage; var. *caesia*: GRAY-DOUGLAS FIR, FRASER RIVER DOUGLAS FIR, leaves dull gray-green with some stomata above, gray-white beneath.

Psychopsis (from Greek *psyche*, butterfly, and *opsis*, appearance referring to the flower shape). Orchidaceae. C and S America. BUTTERFLY ORCHID. 5 species, evergreen epiphytic perennial herbs, closely allied to and formerly included in *Oncidium*. The pseudobulbs are circular to ovoid and laterally compressed. Each bears a leathery, oblong to lanceolate leaf, often dotted or mottled red-brown. The flowers are produced at various times of year, singly in long succession atop a wiry raceme. They consist of a large, frilled and near-circular lip, broadly scimitar-shaped, with decurved lateral sepals and very slender petals and dorsal sepal, arising like antennae. Provide full sunlight and high summer temperatures (86–104°F/30–40°C). Pot in an open mixture of equal parts coarse bark and charcoal, surrounding the leaf base with fresh sphagnum at first to promote rooting. Alternatively, mount on rafts or cork slabs. Suspend plants in a dry, airy position, water freely during the growing period and give a weak foliar feed every third week. Once pseudobulbs are completed, withhold water, providing only a heavy misting every few days. Provide a minimum winter temperature of 64°F (18°C). Do not remove flower spikes, which may continue to produce flowers even though they appear spent. Propagation is by division, although plants seldom become large enough to warrant this.

P. krameriana (syn. *Oncidium krameri-anum*, *O. nodosum*, *O.papilio* var. *krameri-anum*); Costa Rica, Panama, Ecuador, Peru, Colombia; flowers to 4³⁄₄ in (12 cm) in diameter, showy; sepals deep red-brown with golden yellow margins or bands; lip deep red-brown; *P. lim-minghei* (syn. *Oncidium limminghei*); Brazil, Venezuela; flowers to 2 in (5 cm) in diameter; sepals dull red-brown; petals bright red-brown barred with pale yellow-brown; lip cream-yellow spotted orange-brown; *P. papilio* (syn. *Oncidium papilio*); Trinidad, Venezuela, Colombia, Ecuador, Peru; flowers to 6 in (15 cm) in diameter; dorsal sepal and petals purple-brown mottled yellow-green; lateral sepals bright chestnut-red, barred or blotched deep yellow; lip yellow spotted orange-brown, apex golden yellow bordered or heavily mottled red-brown at margins.

psyllids (Hemiptera: Psyllidae and allied families) small sap-feeding insects up to ¹⁄₈ in (3 mm) long, the adults of which have two pairs of wings and are usually very active. The flat-bodied nymphs are known as suckers, and produce drops of honeydew and conspicuous white waxy threads; some have toxic saliva which induces various forms of galling. Most species are host-specific. Psyllids common to Europe and North America include the APPLE SUCKER (*Psylla mali*), PEAR SUCKER (*P. pyricola*), BOX SUCKER (*P. buxi*) and BAY SUCKER (*Trioza alacris*).

Apple suckers overwinter as straw-colored, elongate-oval eggs on the bark of apple. Hatching occurs in spring and nymphs crawl into the opening buds where they feed between developing leaves and blossoms. There is only one generation each year. In severe attacks, the blossoms turn brown; this can be mistaken for frost damage. Pear suckers differ from apple suckers in that they overwinter as adults and pass through three generations each year. Spring infestations are associated with death of blossoms and black sooty molds growing on the excreted honey-dew; later generations may cause premature defoliation in late summer and death of developing fruit buds in fall.

Box suckers prevent shoot extension and the resultant cupped leaves form tight clusters resembling small cabbages, in which the developing nymphs may be found in the spring. The nymphs of the bay sucker live in curled over leaf edges of bay laurel. In severe attacks, leaves shrivel prematurely and shoots are killed; this type of damage is most serious on young trees under five years old.

Other psyllids include the ALDER SUCKER (*P. alni*); the BLUE-GREEN GUM SUCKER (*Ctenarytaina eucalypti*), introduced into Europe, South Africa and New Zealand from Australia, and sometimes a serious pest of nursery trees; and the CITRUS SUCKER (*Trioza erytreae*), prevalent on citrus in eastern and southern parts of Africa. In North America, the POTATO PSYLLID (*Paratnoza cockerelli*) is an important pest of potato and tomato, causing leaves to become curled and yellow, a condition known as 'psyllid yellows'. Severe attacks cause loss of yield.

Psyllids are best controlled by using systemic insecticides which are effective against aphids. Apple sucker eggs may also be controlled with winter washes applied to apple trees in the dormant season.

Psyllid (pear sucker)

Ptelea (Greek name for the elm tree). Rutaceae. N America. HOP TREE, SHRUBBY TREFOIL. About 11 species, shrubs or small trees, with trifoliolate, muskily aromatic leaves, small, starry green flowers in summer and winged fruit. Hardy to at least 5°F (−15°C). Grow in fertile, well-drained but moisture-retentive soil in full sun or light part-day shade. Sow seed outdoors in fall, or in spring following three months of stratification at 41°F (5°C). Root softwood cuttings in early summer. *P. trifoliata* HOP TREE, STINKING ASH, WATER ASH; E and C US; shrub or tree to 26 ft (8 m); leaflets 1¹⁄₂–4³⁄₄ in (4–12 cm), ovate to oblanceolate; fruit ³⁄₄–1 in (2–2.5 cm), suborbicular, rounded or notched at base; 'Aurea': leaves soft yellow, later lime; 'Glauca': leaves glaucous.

pteridophytes a division of non-flowering vascular plants. They reproduce by spores in the process of alternation of generations. Among these are ferns, club mosses, and horse-tails. There are 365 genera organized in four classes comprising 2,000 species.

Pteris (from the Greek word for fern, *pteron*, wing, referring to the feathery fronds). Pteridaceae. Subtropics and tropics. BRAKE, TABLE FERN, DISH FERN. About 280 species, terrestrial, rhizomatous ferns. The fronds are slender-stalked and loosely clumped, the blades pinnately divided with narrow segments, the lowermost segments often forked or themselves divided. The following species are widely grown as house plants and will tolerate neglect and low temperatures. For best results, grow in dappled light to deep shade, with a minimum temperature of 50°F (10°C) and a humid but buoyant atmosphere. Plant in a porous, soilless, acidic to neutral medium. Keep just moist in cool winters. Water, feed and syringe generously in spring and summer. Propagate by division or spores.

P. argyraea tropics; fronds pinnate to pinnatisect, dark green with a broad silver-white central stripes, terminal pinna 6–12 in (15–30 cm) × 1¹⁄₂ in (3.5 cm), segments linear-oblong; *P. cretica* Old World tropics and subtropics; fronds with 1–5 pairs of simple or forked pinnae, pinnae 4–8 in (10–20 cm), linear to lanceolate; var. *albolineata*: fronds striped and edged white; 'Childsii': fronds bright green, lobed, waved or frilled; 'Cristata': compact, fronds crested; 'Wilsonii': fronds compact, bright green, lobed and heavily crested, giving a fanlike appearance; *P. ensiformis* SWORD BRAKE; Himalaya

P

to Japan, Philippines, Polynesia and tropical Australia; fronds bipinnate, 6–12 in (15–30 cm) × 3–6 in (8–15 cm), terminal pinna 2–4 in (5–10 cm), slightly compound with central portion entire, lateral pinnae to 4–5 pairs, cut into 2–6 obovate-oblong pinnules to ½ in (12 mm) wide, dentate; 'Arguta': fronds dark green with central, silver-white markings; 'Victoriae': fronds with a white zone flanking the midrib on either side; *P. multifida* SPIDER BRAKE, SPIDER FERN; E Asia, introduced America; fronds pedate, 2-pinnate at base, pinnatisect above, 8–20 in (20–50 cm) long, 4–10 in (10–25 cm) broad, pinnae elongate-pinnatisect, decurrent, to ¼ in (5 mm) broad, long-attenuate; *P. tremula* AUSTRALIAN BRAKE, SHAKING BRAKE, TENDER BRAKE, TURAWERA, POOR-MAN'S CIBOTIUM; New Zealand, Australia, Fiji; fronds 3–4 pinnate at base, 12–36 in (30–90 cm) × 8–28 in (20–70 cm); pinnules to ¾ in (2 cm), narrowly oblong to linear, dentate, ultimate segments linear to 1½ × ¼ in (3.5 × 0.5 cm), toothed.

Pterocarya (from Greek *pteron*, wing, and *karyon*, nut, referring to the winged fruit). Juglandaceae. Caucasus to E and SE Asia. WINGNUT. Some 10 species, deciduous trees with handsome pinnate leaves and long, green catkins in summer. Hardy to about 10°F (−12°C) and tolerant of soil compaction. The root system may be too invasive for smaller gardens. *P. fraxinifolia* grows well in damp soil. Most frost-resistant and vigorous is probably the hybrid wingnut, *P. × rehderiana*, which has a tendency to spread by suckering. Propagate from seed, by suckers or by layering; root cuttings are sometimes successful.

P. fraxinifolia CAUCASIAN WALNUT; Caucasus to N Iraq; to 80 ft (25 m), often multi-stemmed, bark gray-black, deeply furrowed; young twigs olive-brown, slightly pubescent; leaves 8–16 in (20–40 cm), leaflets 11–21, oval-oblong to oblong-lanceolate, 3–4¾ in (8–12 cm); 'Albomaculata': young leaves speckled white; *P. × rehderiana* (*P. fraxinifolia × P. stenoptera*); to 100 ft (30 m), suckering; young twigs red-brown; leaves about 8 in (20 cm), rachis partially winged, leaflets 11–21, narrow-oblong, 2½–4¾ in (6–12 cm); *P. stenoptera* China; to 80 ft (25 m); young

twigs tawny pubescent; leaves 8–16 in (20–40 cm), rachis winged, sometimes serrate, leaflets 11–23, oval-oblong to narrow-oblong, serrulate.

Pteroceltis (from Greek *pteron*, wing, and *Celtis*). Ulmaceae. N and C China. 1 species, *P. tartarinowii*, a deciduous tree to 33 ft (10 m), with a broad crown and pale gray bark, peeling in flakes. To 4 in (10 cm) long, the leaves are ovate-oblong to ovate-lanceolate and serrate. The flowers are inconspicuous, the fruits circular, broad-winged, and to ¾ in (2 cm) wide. Cultivate as for *Celtis*.

Pterocephalus (from Greek *pteron*, wing, and *kephale*, head). Dipsacaceae. Mediterranean to C and E Asia. Some 25 species, annual or perennial herbs, subshrubs and shrubs with entire or pinnately lobed leaves. Produced in summer, the flower heads are rounded, flattened, long-stalked and subtended by narrow bracts. The flowers are pink to purple, the outermost conspicuously 2-lipped and larger than those at the center. The following is an undemanding, hardy mat-forming perennial with attractive foliage, flowers and seed heads. It is suitable for sunny well-drained situations in the rock garden, where it may self-seed when conditions suit. Propagate by seed, or by softwood or semiripe cuttings. *P. perennis* Greece; cushion-forming perennial, to 4 in (10 cm), usually shorter, tufted; leaves to 1½ in (4 cm), ovate to oblong, crenate to lyrate; flowers purple-pink in heads to 1½ in (4 cm) in diameter, on 2–2¾ in (5–7 cm) stalks.

Pterostyrax (from Greek *pteron*, wing, and *Styrax*). Styracaceae. Japan, China, Burma. EPAULETTE TREE. 3 species, deciduous shrubs or trees with drooping racemes or panicles of bell-like flowers in summer. Hardy to −4°F (−20°C) and fast-growing. The fragrant-flowered *P. hispida* is a small tree with shedding gray bark, which gives off a foetid odor when bruised. Grow in deep acidic soil, in sun or semi-shade, allowing ample room for the branches to spread; if necessary, prune to shape after flowering. Sow ripe seed, after stratification at 41°F (5°C) for three months. Increase also

by semiripe cuttings in late summer. *P. hispida* EPAULETTE TREE; Japan, China; tree to 50 ft (15 m) or shrub to 15–20 ft (4.5–6 m), bark gray, peeling, aromatic; leaves 2¾–6½ in (7–17 cm), oval to obovate; flowers white, in downy, pendulous panicles 4¾–10 in (12–25 cm) long.

puberulent, puberulous minutely pubescent; covered with minute, soft hairs.

pubescent generally hairy; more specifically, covered with short, fine, soft hairs.

puddling (1) the breakdown of soil surface structure by the impact of raindrops; (2) the practice of dipping the roots of transplants into a slurry of soil and water, traditionally held to aid establishment and discourage root pests; (3) sometimes used to describe the application of a heavy flow of water at the time of inserting a transplant; (4) the compression of a clay layer by treading or pounding, to form a natural waterproof lining to a pool.

Pueraria (for M. N. Puerari [1766–1845], professor at Copenhagen). Leguminosae. SE Asia, Japan. Some 20 species, herbaceous or woody twiners with trifoliolate leaves and pea-like flowers. Particularly useful as a rapidly growing screen, or, if unsupported, as groundcover. In good soil, growth may exceed 50 ft (15 m) during a season, as evinced by its performance in the SE US, where it has now become a notorious weed. In areas where winter temperatures fall much below 5°F (−15°C), *P. montana* var. *lobata* may be grown as an annual; given adequate protection at the roots, however, it will re-sprout from the base in spring if cut down by frost. Grow in full sun in most well-drained soils, training the young stems to cover any support. Prune in spring, if necessary, to control spread. Propagate from seed in spring, sown singly in pots in the warm greenhouse; plant out when the danger of frost has passed. *P. montana* var. *lobata* (syn. *P. lobata*, *P. thunbergiana*); JAPANESE ARROWROOT, KUDZU VINE; China, Japan; deciduous, woody, hairy-stemmed vine to 66 ft (20 m); roots

P

tuberous; leaflets to 7 in (18 cm) bright green turning yellow and copper in fall; raceme erect, to 10 in (25 cm); flowers to ⅝ in (1.5 cm), purple fragrant, in summer and fall.

pulhamite a type of artificial rock, noted for its adherence to geological detail, manufactured by James Pulham (1820–98) in the second half of the 19th century. It was made of clinkers and cement and molded into strata and boulders for use in rock garden construction.

Pulmonaria (from Latin *pulmonarius*, relating to the lung, referring to the spotted leaves of *P. officinalis*, which resemble diseased lungs and were thought to be a cure for lung disease). Boraginaceae. Europe, Asia. LUNG-WORT. Some 14 species, bristly-hairy, rhizomatous perennial herbs. The leaves are ovate to elliptic or lanceolate and often spotted or blotched. Produced from late winter to early spring in forked cymes, the flowers are bell-shaped to shortly tubular with five lobes. *Pulmonaria* provides hardy groundcover for open woodland and border edging, and is also suited to plantings in the sunless shade of buildings; in the wild garden, it is a valuable early nectar source for honey bees, especially in massed plantings. Grow in part- to full shade in moist, humus-rich soil. In zones with cool summers, *P. saccharata* may be grown in full sun, provided that the soil remains adequately moist throughout summer. Increase by division in fall or after flowering.

P. angustifolia Europe; leaves to 16 × 2 in (40 × 5 cm), typically unspotted, setose; flowers bright blue; includes cultivars with spotted or unspotted leaves, low-growing or tall, with flowers in shades of deep azure, clear blue, coral red and pink; *P. longifolia* Europe; leaves to 20 × 2½ in (50 × 6 cm), usually spotted silver-white, setose and sparingly glandular above, setose and glandular beneath; flowers violet to blue-violet; includes cultivars with strongly spotted to solid silver leaves and flowers in tones of pale blue and deep azure, some tinted pink, also dusky mauve; *P. montana* (syn. *P. rubra*); Europe; leaves to 20 × 5 in (50 × 12.5 cm), usually unspotted, setose and sparingly glandu-

lar-pubescent above; flowers violet to blue; includes cultivars with white, coral red and pink flowers; *P. officinalis* JERUSALEM COWSLIP; Europe; leaves to 6 × 4 in (16 × 10 cm), spotted white, setose; flowers red to rose-violet or blue; includes cultivars with white, pale blue, pink and opalescent flowers; *P. saccharata* BETHLEHEM SAGE; Europe; leaves to 11 × 4 in (27 × 10 cm), green, usually spotted silver-white, long-setose, glandular-pubescent; flowers white or red-violet to dark violet; includes cultivars with white, pink- or blue-tinted, pale to deep blue, pink-tinted blue, mauve, rich indigo, pink and red flowers.

Pulsatilla (from the Latin *pulso*, strike—meaning obscure). Ranunculaceae. Eurasia, N America. 30 species, clump-forming, perennial herbs with finely dissected, downy leaves. Borne in spring and summer, the flowers are solitary and bowl- to bell-shaped. They consist (usually) of six oblong to elliptic segments with silky-hairy exteriors, and numerous golden stamens in a central boss surrounded by a ring of nectar-secreting staminodes. The globelike fruiting heads are composed of feathery styles. Fine, spring-flowering perennials for the rock garden, alpine sinks and well-drained borders. The seed heads may be cut and used in dried-flower arrangements. All species here are fully hardy and tolerant of alkaline soil. Large plants have a deep woody rootstock and transplant poorly. Plant out young pot-grown specimens in full sun, in humus-rich, gritty, well-drained soil, and leave undisturbed. Increase by fresh seed or root cuttings.

P. alpina ALPINE PASQUE FLOWER; C Europe; 8–18 in (20–45 cm); flowers more or less erect, 1½–2½ in (4–6 cm) in diameter, white flushed blue-purple or palest creamy yellow, sericeous outside; *P. halleri* C and SE Europe, Crimea; to 6 in (15 cm); flowers erect or nearly so, 1½–3½ in (4–9 cm) in diameter, violet-purple to lavender-blue; forms with lacinate petals are cultivated as well as others with semi-double flowers; *P. occidentalis* N America; 4–24 in (10–60 cm); flowers 1½–2½ in (4–6 cm) in diameter, erect, white or cream-white, sometimes flushed purple or blue, exterior villous); *P. pratensis* Central and Eastern Europe;

flower stalks to 4 in (10 cm), slender, hairy, flowers ¾–1½ in (2–4 cm), nodding, campanulate to urceolate with recurved sepal tips, very hairy, pale to deep purple—black-violet in subsp. *nigricans*; *P. vernalis* Europe to Siberia; to 6 in (15 cm); flowers pendent, becoming erect, 1½–2½ in (4–6 cm) in diameter, with brown silky hairs outside and a white outer segment, usually flushed pink or violet-blue outside; *P. vulgaris* PASQUE FLOWER; Great Britain and W France to Sweden, eastward to Ukraine; 1¼–4¾ in (3–12 cm); flowers 1½–3½ in (4–9 cm) in diameter, pale or dark violet, rarely white; many cultivars exist from dwarf to tall, woolly to almost smooth with coarsely to finely dissected leaves, and with flowers large or small, open or closed, erect or nodding, and in tones of white, lilac, mauve, violet, cobalt, plum, blood red and pink.

pulverulent powdery; covered in a fine bloom, dusty, or minutely freckled.

pulvinus a cushion of enlarged tissue, such as found on a stem at the insertion of a petiole.

pumice a light, porous aluminosilicate volcanic mineral, used in potting mixtures to improve drainage and aeration. It has low cation exchange capacity and contains some potassium and sodium.

pumpkins and squashes (*Cucurbitaceae*) loose collective terms for four species of *Cucurbita*: *C. maxima*, *C. argyrosperma* (*C. mixta*), *C. moschata* and *C. pepo*. They are annual herbs, which can be of bushy or more often trailing habit, and are usually separated into summer and fall/winter harvesting groups. Summer squashes are usually boiled or fried when immature, before the rind hardens. Fall and winter squashes and pumpkins are usually baked when mature, or stored for later use. Winter squashes are usually white-fleshed, whereas pumpkins are usually orange-fleshed, with types derived from each of the four species.

Pumpkins embrace cultivars with coarse, strong-flavored flesh, used for pies in the US, for Hallowe'en 'Jack o'lanterns' and for stock feed, and

P

scallop squash
dumpling squash
pumpkin
Turk's turban squash
summer squash
pattypan squash

Pumpkins and squashes

some grow very large. The acorn, buttercup and butternut groups are the most edible.

All pumpkins and squashes are frost-tender. They may be sown directly into the ground in appropriate conditions, otherwise in small pots or cell modules for planting out usually within two weeks of sowing. In frost-susceptible climates, seed must be sown in warm protected conditions for transplanting after the danger of frost is past. Spacing should suit the plant type and cultivar. Bush forms are typically sown on ridges or mounds, 24–36 in (60–90 cm) each way, with 36–48 in (90–120 cm) between rows, leaving one seedling per station when established; for trailers, leave 48–60 in (120–150 cm) between plants and 6½–13 ft (2–4 m) between rows. Planting into a black plastic ground mulch is a useful technique to suppress weed growth and reduce surface evaporation of soil moisture.

Soil should be prepared with well-rotted manure or garden compost. Supplementary feeding with a balanced fertilizer at semiweekly intervals is valuable; foliar feed plants grown under plastic mulch. Irrigation is essential in dry periods.

Suitable cultivars are best stored over winter at temperatures of 50–61°F (10–16°C); curing fruits at 70–81°F (21–27°C) for 2–3 weeks enhances sweetness in cultivars not subject to deterioration. Possible problems: aphids, red spider mite, whiteflies; virus, downy mildew, gray mold.

punctate dotted with minute, translucent impressions, pits or dark spots.

pungent ending in a rigid and sharp long point.

Punica (from the classical Latin name, *Malum punicum*). Punicaceae. E Mediterranean to Himalaya. 2 species, deciduous or semi-evergreen, densely branched shrubs or small trees. The flowers consist of a fleshy, tubular or more or less campanulate calyx with five to eight sepals, five to seven, silky petals, and numerous stamens. The fruit is a globose, pulpy berry packed with flesh-coated seeds inside a thick, leathery shell. Generally requiring long, hot continental summers for its fruit to ripen, *P. granatum* is nevertheless a handsome ornamental for warm south- or southwest-facing walls in regions where frosts are light and short-lived. In Mediterranean climates, it is sometimes used as hedging. Where size and fruit are not priorities, the dwarf var. *nana* is an altogether better garden plant, ideal in scale for patio tubs overwintered under cool glass. It is also hardier than the typical plant and may survive outdoors in sheltered rock gardens and against sun-drenched walls to 0°F (–18°C). Grow in well-drained, fertile, moderately-retentive, loamy soil in full sun. Although it may be cut to the ground by severe frost, given wall protection and a deep mulch at the roots, var. *nana* will re-sprout vigorously from the base. Prune in late spring or summer to remove old or weak wood. Shorten outward-growing shoots from trained specimens in spring at bud break—flowers are carried on the tips of the current year's growth. Propagate by suckers, by semiripe cuttings, by layering, or by grafting on to seedling understock. Increase also by seed in spring. *P. granatum* POMEGRANATE; E Mediterranean to Himalaya; deciduous or semi-evergreen shrub to 6½ ft (2 m), or small tree to 20 ft (6 m); leaves ¾–3 in (2–8 cm), obovate to oblong, pale green, glossy, subcoriaceous, tinted red in fall; flowers to 1¼ in (3 cm) in diameter, silky, crumpled, scarlet; fruit to 4¾ in (12 cm) in diameter, globose, brown-yellow to purple-red, with a leathery rind and a chimneylike, persistent calyx; seeds with an edible fleshy crimson coat; var. *nana*, a dwarf, intricately branched tree, with small leaves, flowers and fruit.

pupa see *chrysalis*.

Puschkinia (for Count Apollo Apollosovich Mussin-Pushkin [d. 1805], Russian chemist who collected plants in the Caucasus and Ararat). Liliaceae (Hyacinthaceae). Caucasus, Turkey, N Iran, N Iraq, Lebanon. 1 species, *P. scilloides*, a small, spring-flowering, bulbous perennial closely related to *Chionodoxa* and *Scilla*. Hardy to about –4°F (–20°C). Grow in sun or partial shade in gritty, well-drained, humus-rich soil. Flowering is usually better where bulbs can dry out in summer. Propagate by offsets when dormant in late summer, or by seed in fall.

pustule a pimplelike or blisterlike eruption.

Puya (from the Chilean vernacular name for the genus). Bromeliaceae. Andean S America, N Brazil, Guyana, Costa Rica. 168 species, perennial, terrestrial herbs, stemless or with long, stout, simple or branched stems. Packed in dense terminal rosettes, the leaves are tough to rigid, linear to narrowly triangular, the margins normally toothed and spinose. The tubular flowers are produced in great abundance in massive, spirelike panicles. Plant in soil rich in grit, sand and leaf mold. Water liberally in hot weather; keep almost dry in winter. Under glass, grow in full sun with a buoyant, dry atmosphere and a minimum temperature of 41°F (5°C). Outdoors, light frosts may be tolerated where plants are kept dry and sheltered (see *Fascicularia*). Increase by seed or by offsets detached after flowering. *P. alpestris* south central Chile; 4–5 ft (1.2–1.5 m) in flower; leaves to 24 in (60 cm), arching, covered in white scales beneath, hooked-spinose; inflorescence sparsely branched on a stout scape, loosely bipinnate, pyramidal; flowers petrol blue with orange-red anthers.

Pycnostachys (from Greek *pyknos*, dense, *stachys*, ear of corn, referring to the density of the flower spikes). Labiatae. Tropical and South Africa, Madagascar. About 40 species, erect perennial herbs or subshrubs. Borne in dense terminal spikes, the flowers consist of a spiny-toothed calyx and a 2-lipped, tubular corolla. Grow from seed in

P

spring, at 55–59°F (13–15°C). Pot into a high-fertility loam-based potting mix. Give bright indirect light, a minimum temperature of 59°F (15°C) and water plentifully. Propagate also by stem cuttings in early summer, or by softwood cuttings in fall, after flowering.

P. dawei tropical Central Africa; to 70 in (180 cm); leaves to 12 in (30 cm), linear to lanceolate, serrate, red-glandular beneath; flowers to 1 in (25 mm), cobalt blue; *P. urticifolia* tropical and South Africa; to 8 ft (2.5 m); leaves 1¾–4¾ in (4.5–12 cm), ovate, crenate to deeply incised-dentate, smooth to hairy; flowers ½–¾ in (12–20 mm), gentian blue, rarely white tinted blue with a purple-red calyx.

Pyracantha (from Greek *pyr*, fire, referring to the color of the berries, and *akanthos*, thorn). Rosaceae. SE Europe to China. FIRETHORN. 7 species, evergreen, viciously thorny shrubs, with obovate to oblong-lanceolate leaves and small, white to cream flowers in dense corymbs in late spring and summer. These give rise to small and spherical, orange to red fruits. Pollution- and exposure-tolerant evergreens for the border, where they form mounds of glossy green foliage, for training against walls, and for thorny and impenetrable hedging. Some, such as *P. atalantoides*, can be trained with a single stem to form small specimen trees. They are grown for the masses of white flowers in spring and early summer and for the profusion of long-lasting, brightly colored berries. Given protection from cold winds, all species are tolerant of temperatures down to at least 5°F (–15°C).

Pyracanthas grown as hedging
With their dense habit and sharp thorns, pyracanthas make excellent flowering and fruiting hedge plants which deter intruders.

Grow in well-drained, moisture-retentive soil, in sun or part-shade. Avoid very hot, sunny south-facing walls for wall-grown plants. Prune free-standing specimens after flowering to restrict size or to remove damaged wood. Clip back formal, wall-trained plants after flowering to give dense cover; otherwise, remove only outward-facing shoots, tying-in new growth in late summer. Cuttings may be taken from late spring onward, but better growth is obtained from fall cuttings: large, branched semihard cuttings (to 12 in (30 cm)), wounded and treated with hormone rooting compound and placed under mist, will root in 3–4 weeks, and will flower and berry the following season. Raise larger numbers of plants for hedging from fresh ripe seed; remove the flesh and sow in a cold frame in fall. Susceptible to pyracantha scab which causes small scabby lesions on twigs, olive-brown spotting on leaves and flowers, and serious disfigurement of the fruit; it is often accompanied by premature leaf drop. Treat with systemic fungicide in spring and early summer. Leaves may also blister and discolor as a result of the larvae of the firethorn leaf miner moth, *Phyllonorycter leucographella*. As yet, there is no specific treatment for this pest, although control measures for other types of leaf miner may succeed.

P. angustifolia SW China; shoots stiff, densely downy in the first year; leaves ⅝–2 in (1.5–5 cm), linear-oblong to obovate, apex rounded and sometimes toothed; fruit to ½ in (1 cm), felted at first, later yellow-orange; 'Gnome': very hardy, of erect, dense habit, with profuse flowers and orange fruit orange; 'Yukon Belle': of dense habit, with persistent orange fruit; *P. atalantoides* SE to W China; branches olive-brown, downy only at first; leaves 1¼–2¾ in (3–7 cm), lanceolate to elliptic or obovate, mostly entire, sometimes small-toothed; fruit ¼–⅜ in (7–8 mm), scarlet-crimson; 'Aurea': yellow fruit; 'Bakeri': red fruit; 'Nana': dwarf, to 3¼ ft (1 m), with red fruit; *P. coccinea* PYRACANTH, SCARLET FIRETHORN, BUISSON ARDENT; Italy to Asia Minor; shoots downy at first; leaves ¾–1½ in (2–4 cm), elliptic to lanceolate; fruit 2–2½ in (5–6 cm), bright scarlet; 'Baker's Red': hardy, with red fruit; 'Kasan': compact, upright, fast-growing

to 16 ft (5 m), with orange fruit; 'Lalandei': upright to 16 ft (5 m), hardy, with profuse, bright orange fruit; 'Lalandei Monrovia': upright, dense, with orange fruit; 'Sparkler': slow-growing, with leaves variegated white and red fruit; *P. rogersiana* SW China; shoots pale downy at first becoming glabrous, red-brown; leaves ¾–1½ in (2–3.5 cm), oblanceolate to narrow obovate, apex rounded and shallow toothed; fruit ⅜–⅜ in (8–9 mm), yellow to orange-red; 'Flava': bright yellow fruit. *Cultivars*: 'Alexander Pendula', to 6 ft (1.8 m), with weeping branches and coral red fruit; 'Apache', forming a compact spreading mound 5 × 6½ ft (1.5 × 2 m), with bright red fruit, resistant to scab and fireblight; 'Brilliant', with bright red fruit; 'Buttercup', spreading, with small, yellow fruit; 'Fiery Cascade', upright, 8 × 10 ft (2.5 × 3 m), with small, shining leaves and small, red, disease-resistant fruit; 'Golden Charmer', to 8 ft (2.4 m), with large, golden yellow fruit, resistant to scab; 'Harlequin', with variegated leaves and red fruit; 'Mohave', upright, to 13 × 16 ft (4 × 5 m), with bright orange fruit, unaffected by bird feeding and resistant to scab and fireblight; 'Navaho', low, dense, with orange-red fruit, resistant to scab; 'Orange Giant', with bright orange fruit; 'Pueblo', spreading, compact, with orange-red fruit, resistant to scab and fireblight; 'Red Column', upright, with small, red fruit; 'Red Cushion', dense, to 3¼ × 6½ ft (1 × 2 m), with mid-red fruit; 'Red Elf', dwarf, compact, mounding, with bright red fruit; 'Red Pillar', vigorous, upright, with orange-red fruit; 'Renault d'Or', with yellow fruit; 'Ruby Mound', low, dense, with orange-red fruit, resistant to scab; 'Shawnee', dense, spreading to 11½ ft (3.5 m), with abundant, yellow-orange fruit, coloring early, resistant to scab and fireblight; 'Soleil d'Or', spreading, with pale green leaves and yellow fruit; 'Sunshine', open, orange fruit; 'Tiny Tim', with dwarf habit, to 3¼ ft (1 m), densely leafy, profuse fruit; 'Watereri', compact, vigorous to 8 ft (2.5 m), with profuse, orange fruit.

pyramid see *dwarf pyramid*.

pyrene the nutlet of a drupe or drupelet; a seed and the bony endocarp that surrounds it.

pyriform pear-shaped.

Pyrola (diminutive of the Latin *Pyrus*, pear, alluding to the supposed similarity of the leaves). Pyrolaceae. Northern temperate regions. SHINLEAF, WINTERGREEN. 15 species, perennial, dwarf herbs with creeping rhizomes and slender-stalked leaves in basal clusters. Borne in summer in scapose, loose racemes, the flowers consist of five, broad, cupped petals. Fully hardy and generally grown in wild gardens; it is also suitable for cool positions in the rock garden, peat terrace, and at the woodland edge. Plant in shade in damp, sandy acidic soil containing leaf mold and pine needles. Avoid disturbance—any damage to the wide-spreading fibrous-feeding roots may cause either death or prevent any further increase in size. Increase by division, or by seed, which germinates infrequently and should be sown in moist sphagnum moss.

P. asarifolia BOG WINTERGREEN; Canada, E US, Asia; to 26 in (65 cm); leaves broadly elliptic to reniform, to 4 in (10 cm), entire or crenate, often purple beneath; flowers pink to crimson; includes var. *purpurea*, from N America, with leaves sometimes red beneath and large, fragrant, bright violet or rose flowers; *P. rotundifolia* Europe, N America; to 10 in (25 cm); leaves round to oval; flowers white.

Pyrostegia (from Greek *pyr*, fire, and *stege*, covering, referring to the fiery corolla). Bignoniaceae. Americas. 3–4 species, lianes climbing by tendrils. The leaves consist of paired leaflets with a tendril between them. Borne in terminal sprays usually in summer, the flowers are showy, tubular to club-shaped, with the curved corolla tube swollen and expanded toward its apex. Grow in sun in a fertile, well-drained medium. Maintain a humid atmosphere and a minimum temperature of about 50°F (10°C). Water plentifully in summer; sparingly in winter. Prune in late winter early spring, cutting back flowered stems to within 12 in (30 cm) of the base. *P. venusta* works well if trained to a single overhead stem, with flowered shoots cut back to 2–3 buds each spring. Propagate by semiripe cuttings of 2–3 nodes in summer.

P. venusta (syn. *Bignonia ignea*, *B.venusta*, *P. ignea*); FLAME VINE, GOLDEN SHOWER, FLAMING TRUMPET, ORANGE-FLOWERED STEPHANOTIS, TANGO; Brazil, Paraguay, Bolivia, NE Argentina; flowers 1½–2½ in (3.5–6 cm) × ⅛ in (0.3 cm), fiery orange.

Pyrus (classical Latin name for the pear). Rosaceae. Europe to E Asia and N Africa. PEAR. About 30 species, deciduous trees and shrubs, occasionally thorny. They are grown for their habit and foliage, their white to cream, 5-petalled flowers borne in spring, and for their fruit, in some cases ornamental, in others, edible (see *pears*).

Most species are hardy to at least 5°F (−15°C) and are tolerant of atmospheric pollution and a range of soil types. The genus includes a number of attractive foliage trees, notably *P. salicifolia* 'Pendula'. *P. communis*, is especially beautiful in flower, and is worth growing for this alone, even in regions where frosts make fruit set unreliable. *P. calleryana* 'Bradford' flowers profusely in spring and colors well in fall, in shades of russet and red. It is commonly grown as a street tree in the US. The narrowly conical *P. calleryana* 'Chanticleer' is more suitable for the smaller garden. Grow in full sun. Propagate cultivars by budding or grafting on to seedling rootstocks of *P. communis*. Propagate species by seed, although progeny may be variable; stratify for 8–10 weeks, at 34°F (1°C), and sow in spring. Temperatures above 59–68°F (15–20°C) in the sowing medium may induce a secondary dormancy. Most of the pests and diseases are as for *pears* (q.v.).

P. amygdaliformis S Europe, Asia Minor; shrub or small tree to 20 ft (6 m); shoots slender, thorny; leaves 1–2¾ in (2.5–7 cm), ovate-obovate, pointed or blunt, coriaceous, entire or finely scalloped, gray-felted at first becoming shiny green, glabrous; fruit ¾–1¼ in (2–3 cm), rounded, yellow-brown; includes var. *oblongifolia*, with elliptic to oblong leaves, with a blunt apex and rounded base, and larger fruit, yellow flushed red; *P. calleryana* CALLERY PEAR; China; tree to 33 ft (10 m); shoots thorny; leaves 1½–3 in (4–8 cm), ovate, short tapered, undulate-scalloped, shiny, glabrous; fruit ½ in (1

cm), rounded, brown, pitted; 'Aristocrat', fast-growing to 43 ft (13 m), broadly pyramidal, with thornless branches, wavy-edged, glossy leaves, brilliant red in fall, plum when young, and red to yellow fruit; 'Autumn Blaze', fast-growing, to 39 ft (12 m), of asymmetrical and open habit, with glossy leaves and crimson fall color; 'Bradford', to 43 ft (13 m), with a broadly ovate, dense crown and red to maroon leaves in fall; 'Capital', to 39 ft (12 m), loosely pyramidal, dense, with rich glossy green leaves, purple in fall; 'Chanticleer', to 43 ft (13 m), with a narrow-conical crown, evenly branched, with glossy green leaves, becoming carmine-scarlet in fall; 'Redspire', to 39 ft (12 m), with a moderately pyramidal crown, upright, well-branched, with long, thick, glossy leaves, colored crimson to purple in fall, and profuse flowers; 'Stone Hill', to 39 ft (12 m), upright, with an oval crown, deep green, shiny leaves, brilliant orange in fall; 'Trinity', to 33 ft (10 m), with a rounded crown, light green, somewhat serrate leaves, orange to red in fall; and 'White House', to 33 ft (10 m), upright, compact, with crown ovate in outline and red to plum leaves in early fall; *P. communis* COMMON PEAR; Europe, Asia Minor; tree to 50 ft (15 m), crown conical, broad, bark dark, fissured to flaking; branches often thorny; branchlets, crabbed; leaves ¾–3 in (2–8 cm), oval-elliptic, pointed, scalloped, soon glabrous, fall color red-yellow; fruit 1–2 in (2.5–5 cm), pyriform or sub-globose, yellow green, flesh bitter; var. *sativa* is the collective name for all edible pear cultivars; *P. salicifolia* WEEPING PEAR, SILVER PEAR; SE Europe, Asia Minor, Caucasus; tree 16–26 ft (5–8 m), shoots slender, arching to pendulous; leaves 1¼–3½ in (3–9 cm), narrowly oblong-elliptic, apex acuminate, entire or sparsely toothed, silvery gray-downy, becoming more or less glabrous above; flowers cream; fruit ¾–1¼ in (2–3 cm), pyriform, green; 'Pendula', with weeping branches and narrow, silvery leaves; 'Silfrozam', with a broadly weeping crown and willowlike, silvery gray leaves.

pyxis a capsule exhibiting circumscissile dehiscence.

quadrate more or less square.

quadripinnate pinnately divided into four pinnae, or groups of four pinnae.

quassia a bitter extract produced by boiling wood fragments of the tree *Picrasma excelsa*. It is used as a nontoxic deterrent to dogs, cats, rabbits, and birds, applied repeatedly in the form of sprays.

quenouille a type of ornamental wall-trained fruit tree, with a central stem and tiers of successively shorter horizontal branches that form a triangle outline.

quercetum a plantation of oak trees.

Quercus (Latin name for this tree). Fagaceae. N America to western tropical S America, N Africa, Europe, and Asia, in temperate and subtropical zones, and tropics at high altitudes. OAK. 600 species, evergreen or deciduous trees or shrubs. The male flowers are inconspicuous and crowded in slender, pendulous catkins. The female flowers are solitary or two to many in a spike. They give rise to a single-seeded nut (acorn). This is ovoid to globose and partly or almost wholly enclosed by a cup-shaped, scale-covered involucre (cupule), composed of adpressed scales.

Oaks are excellent trees for parks and large gardens, having interesting foliage and often good crown shape; most are long-lived and many are large trees. All oaks like warm summers. The constraints of low summer heat affect the range and health of species which can be grown in Britain; oaks from continental E US, China, and Japan are generally of poor vigor and many suffer fall frost damage to the unripened shoots. Of these, the most tolerant is *Q. rubra*, almost as vigorous as in its native E US. *Q. alba* has very rarely been successful in the UK except in the warmest parts of SE England. Conversely, the Mediterranean oaks, adapted to relatively cooler summers during the ice ages, thrive in Britain's climate, responding to the higher rainfall by growing faster in S England than in their native areas.

In the eastern US, all oaks can be grown in either the northeast, or (the less winter-hardy species) in the southeast. None reacts adversely to the hot, humid summer. European oaks retain considerable winter hardiness from ice age adaptations: *Q. petraea* from N England is hardy in Wisconsin and also enjoys the warmer summers there. *Q. cerris* from S Europe is hardy to −10°F (−23°C). No oak shows extreme cold tolerance, and the genus is absent from most of Canada and Siberia.

Growth is best in fertile, deep soils with medium drainage and 15³/₄–57 in (400–1,500 mm) rainfall, but in such a large genus, different oaks can be found to tolerate almost all conditions, from poor, dry, acidic sands, freely drained mountain screes, through heavy damp clays to poorly drained marshy areas and dry chalk. Only acidic deep peats are consistently avoided. Most are sensitive to salt, but *Q. ilex* is often planted in maritime gardens. Most tolerate exposure only moderately, surviving best in a woodland site, among or near other similarly sized trees or shrubs.

Propagation is by seed, or by grafting where seed is unavailable and for desirable cultivars. For grafting, side-graft sucker shoots (preferably erect) on seedlings of a closely related species and bind with tape. Normal branch shoot scions should be avoided if possible, as they have poor apical dominance and may not develop into good trees.

Since many oaks hybridize freely in cultivation, wild-collected seed should be used whenever possible. Even in the wild, hybrids are frequent. Acorn production is usually cyclical: there is low production in most years to defeat parasites and predators, with, more sporadically, a massive crop in the "mast" years, when a high proportion of seed escapes damage. If possible, seed collection should be made in such years; crop assessment can be made from midsummer. Collect the acorns in mid-fall after they drop.

Acorns must be stored moist and cold; they will be killed if they fall below 60% fresh weight. They cannot normally be stored for more than one winter, except in the case of very hardy species; their acorns can be deep-frozen. For freezing, the acorns, which must not be showing any sign of germination, should be *slightly* dried to about 80% fresh weight (to prevent ice damage to the cells) and acclimatized first for a few days at 32°F (0°C), then 23°F (−5°C) and finally −4°F (−20°C). The seed should be stratified for 3–5 months in damp sand refrigerated at 32–36°F (0–2°C) before sowing, stored in plastic bags.

Acorns commonly start to germinate in early winter (even those stored at 32°F (0°C)), establishing a root system (though not a shoot). These sprouting acorns must be planted immediately, the others in early spring. Lay the acorn horizontally at its own thickness under soil surface. Place in a cold frame in deep, narrow pots to accommodate the long taproot. If the seed supply is plentiful and high losses to rodents are acceptable, it is always preferable to avoid checks to growth by planting the acorns directly where the tree is to grow.

Oaks are best planted as small trees, one to two years old and 4–16 in (10–40 cm) tall. Larger, older plants require special nursery treatment; for these, sever the taproot early and regularly (every few weeks) either by cutting under the seedbed with a spade, or by pruning roots that appear at the bottom of the pot; this will encourage the seedling to develop a more fibrous root system. Plant when 3¼–6½ ft (1–2 m) tall; lengthy slowdowns in growth can occur. Water well, protect from rabbits, and weed until established.

Oaks are affected by numerous pests and diseases, though only a few are serious. In North America, oak wilt has caused heavy losses. The red oaks are most affected; white oaks are more resistant and suffer only scattered shoot death and only rarely whole tree death. *Q. robur* is commonly defoliated by

QUERCUS

Name	Distribution	Habit	Bark	Leaves	Fruit
Q. acutissima SAWTHORN OAK	China, Korea, Japan	deciduous tree, seldom exceeding 80 ft (25 m)	ashen to black, corky, fissured	2½–8 in (6–20 cm), lanceolate to obovate, apex long acuminate, base cuneate to rounded, teeth broadly triangular, bristle-tipped, lustrous green above, paler and glabrous beneath	acorns to 1 in (2.5 cm), solitary, ovoid; cupule to 1½ in (3.5 cm) diameter, concealing two-thirds of acorn, covered with long, hairy scales
Q. agrifolia CALIFORNIA LIVE OAK	California	evergreen tree to 80 ft (25 m), often shrubby in cultivation; crown broad	thick, smooth to grooved, gray, red or black	1–2¾ in (2.5–7 cm), ovate-elliptic or broadly elliptic, apex acute, base rounded, spiny-toothed, deep glossy green and rather concave above, paler beneath, glabrous except for tufted hairs in axils of veins	acorns ¾–1½ in (2–3.5 cm), ovoid, acute, solitary; cupule enclosing one-quarter to one-third of acorn, sericeous
Q. alba WHITE OAK	E US	deciduous tree in 150 ft (45 m); crown rounded	pale gray to brown, exfoliating in plates	4–8 in (10–20 cm), obovate, oblong or elliptic, apex abruptly acute, base cuneate, lobes 3–4 per side, entire or sparsely toothed, initially pubescent, dull mid-green above, orange to burgundy in fall, glaucous beneath	acorn ½–1¼ in (1–3 cm), ovoid-oblong; cupule enclosing quarter to one-third of acorn, gray-white, composed of adpressed, compacted, hairy scales

Comments: f. *elongata*: leaves slender, to 10 in (25 cm), orange to purple red in fall. f. *pinnatifida*: leaves deeply pinnatisect, lobes slender, dentate. f. *repanda:* leaves very shallowly lobed. Hybrids between *Q. alba* and *Q. bicolor* are referred to as *Q* × *jackiana*.

Name	Distribution	Habit	Bark	Leaves	Fruit
Q. aliena	Japan, Korea	deciduous tree to 80 ft (25 m)		4–8 in (10–20 cm), obovate to oblong, apex acute to rounded, base cuneate, sinuately dentate, teeth coarse, blunt, 10–15 per side, yellow-green glabrous above, gray-white to blue-green and lightly hairy beneath	acorns ¾–1 in (2–2.5 cm), ovoid, solitary or grouped 2–3; cupule enclosing one third of acorn, gray-tomentose with scales adpressed

Comments: var. *acutiserrata*: leaves smaller and narrower, teeth acute, rather incurved, gland-tipped.

Name	Distribution	Habit	Bark	Leaves	Fruit
Q. alnifolia GOLDEN OAK	Cyprus	evergreen shrub to 6½ ft (2 m) or tree to 25 ft (8 m)	coarsely textured, gray	1–2½ in (2.5–6 cm), broadly obovate to suborbicular, apex and base rounded to subtruncate, denticulate above, glossy dark or livid green above, with ocher or ash-colored felty hairs beneath	acorns 1–1½ in (2.5–3.5 cm), obovoid, mucronate, solitary or paired; cupule small, enclosing to half acorn, scales spreading, long-pubescent, arranged in a broad band
Q. canariensis ALGERIAN OAK, MIRBECK'S OAK	N Africa, Iberian peninsula (not Canaries)	deciduous tree, to 130 ft (40 m) tall in habitat	thick, rugged, black	2–7 in (5–18 cm), oval or obovate, apex rounded, base tapering, rounded or subcordate, margins obtusely lobed or coarsely toothed, coriaceous, rusty-floccose at first, becoming dark green and glabrous above, paler beneath, glabrous except for rusty residual hairs on veins	acorns to 1 in (2.5 cm), solitary, paired or in small clusters; cupule with adpressed downy scales, enclosing one-third of acorn

Q. acutissima   *Q. agrifolia*   *Q. alba*   *Q. alnifolia*

QUERCUS

Name	Distribution	Habit	Bark	Leaves	Fruit
Q. castaneifolia	Caucasus, Iran, N Africa	deciduous tree to 115 ft (35 m); crown large, rounded	brown, rough-textured and corky	leaves 2½–6 in (6–16 cm), narrowly elliptic to oblong-lanceolate, apex acute, base cuneate or rounded, with coarse triangular aristate saw-teeth, deep glossy green above, dull gray-green beneath, glabrous or minutely downy	acorns ¾–1¼ in (2–3 cm), ovoid, often dorsally compressed, solitary or to 5 on a stout stalk; cupule clothed with slender scales (sometimes reflexed), enclosing one-third to one-half of acorn
Q. cerris TURKEY OAK	C and S Europe, Asia Minor	deciduous tree to 140 ft (43 m); crown conical	gray-white, splitting into thick plates	2–4¾ in (5–12 cm), oblong-lanceolate, tapered to an acute apex and a rounded or truncate base, lobes or teeth triangular to lobulate, mucronulate, dark green and stellate-pubescent initially above, lighter and pubescent to tomentose beneath, yellow-brown in fall	acorns in groups of 1–4, to 1½ in (3.5 cm), ellipsoid, apex subtruncate and mucronate; cupule of subulate often spreading or reflexed scales, enclosing one-third of acorn
Comments: 'Argenteovariegata': leaf margins variegated cream-white. 'Aureovariegata': leaves yellow-variegated. 'Pendula': branchlets pendulous.					
Q. coccifera KERMES OAK, GRAIN OAK	W Mediterranean, S Europe, NW Africa	evergreen bushy shrub, usually ¾–5 ft (0.25–1.5 m), rarely a tree 15 ft (4.5 m)	smooth and gray at first, cracked with age	½–1½ in (1.2–3.5 cm), oval, elliptic or oblong, apex acute or rounded, mucronate, base rounded or cordate, becoming leathery, dark and glabrous above, paler and glabrous or with a few hairs in vein axils beneath, margin undulate, with 4–6 pairs of spreading, spinelike teeth	acorns to ⅝ × 1¼ in (1.5 × 3 cm), ovoid or oblong-ovoid, apex attenuate with an apical spine light brown striped darker; cupule enclosing one-half to two-thirds of acorn, scales spiny, often reflexed, lightly puberulent
Comments: ssp. **calliprinos**: PALESTINE OAK, SIND OAK; tree to 40 ft (12 m); leaves larger and more oblong, to 2 in (5 cm); acorn to three-quarters enclosed by cup. East Mediterranean, South West Asia.					
Q. coccinea SCARLET OAK	E US, S Canada	deciduous tree to 100 ft (30 m)	pale gray-brown, cracked into irregular, scaly plates	3–4¾ in (8–12 cm), oval or obovate, rarely oblong, base truncate, rarely cuneate, silky at first, becoming glabrous and glossy, paler and with tufts of hair in vein axils beneath, scarlet in fall, margin deeply pinnately sinuate-dentate or serrate, lobes usually 7	acorns ⅝–1 in (1.5–2.5 cm), ovoid to subspherical, apex and base rounded, with thin red-brown tomentum; cupule turbinate, scales yellow-brown, oval, subglabrous, enclosing one-third to one-half of acorn
Comments: 'Splendens': leaves brilliant scarlet in fall.					
Q. dentata DAIMIO OAK, JAPANESE EMPEROR OAK	NE Asia, Taiwan	deciduous tree, fast-growing to 65–80 ft (20–25 m); crown large, rounded	brown, fissured and split into gray-scaly plates	6–20 in (15–50 cm), orbicular-obovate to oblong-obovate, base attenuate to cordate, apex attenuate or rounded, sinuately lobed, lobes large, rounded, often mucronulate, pale yellow tomentose at first, becoming dark green and glabrous except on nerves above, paler and densely tomentose beneath	acorns ½–1 in (1.2–2.4 cm), ovoid to subglobose, glabrous, apex rounded, mucronate; cupule scales adpressed, upper scales erect to recurved, enclosing more than half of acorn
Comments: 'Pinnatifida': leaves crispate, deeply and narrowly lobed					

Q. canariensis   *Q. castaneifolia*   *Q. cerris* 'Argenteovariegata'   *Q. coccifera*

QUERCUS

Name	Distribution	Habit	Bark	Leaves	Fruit
Q. ellipsoidalis NORTHERN PIN OAK	NE US	deciduous tree to 65 ft (20 m)	gray-brown, fissured into narrow plates	2½–6 in (6–15 cm), obovate or elliptic, base truncate or cuneate, margin deeply lobed, lobes 5–7, oblong, with 1–3 teeth, silky-tomentose at first, becoming glabrous except in vein axils beneath, dark green and shining above, paler beneath, yellow to light brown with red markings in fall	acorns ½–¾ in (1.2–2 cm), solitary or paired, ellipsoid, mucronate, puberulent, chestnut-brown with darker lines; cupule light red-brown, scales adpressed, finely pubescent, enclosing one-third to one-half of acorn
Q. frainetto HUNGARIAN OAK	S Italy, Turkey, Balkans	deciduous tree to 100 ft (30 m)	smooth with small scale-like plates, dark gray; crown large; branches sometimes pendulous	3–10 in (8–25 cm), obovate or oblong-obovate, apex rounded, base subcordate or truncate, margins pinnatifid, lobes 6–10(–12) pairs, sometimes lobulate or sinuate, initially white-yellow-tomentose, becoming glabrous or stellate-pubescent above, paler glaucescent beneath	acorns ½–1½ in (1.25–3.5 cm), oblong-ellipsoid or ovoid-oblong, apex rounded, mucronate; cupule densely tomentose outside, scales adpressed, enclosing up to one-half of acorn
Q. garryana OREGON WHITE OAK	WN America	deciduous tree 33–100 ft (10–30 m); crown rounded, branches crooked, ascending or pendulous	pale gray, shallowly cracked	leaves 4–6 in (10–15 cm), obovate or oblong-obovate, apex rounded, base cuneate, rounded, or subcordate, margins slightly revolute, lobes 3–5 per side, entire or dentate, dark green and glabrous above, paler and soft pubescent beneath	acorns ¾–1 in (2–2.5 cm), ovoid, base truncate, apex rounded, mucronate, glabrous; cupule shallow, puberulent inside, scales adpressed, pubescent
Q. glauca	Japan, China, Laos	evergreen tree 40–80 ft (12–25 m)		2–6 in (5–15 cm), lanceolate or lanceolate-elliptic, apex long-acuminate, base rounded or shortly acuminate, leathery, dark green above, glaucescent, slightly papillose beneath, margin with fine teeth in upper half	acorns ⅔–1 in (17–25 mm) × ¼–½ in (7–10 mm), narrowly ovoid, puberulent at first, becoming glabrous, crowned with persistent styles; cupule slightly glaucous, ashy-puberulent outside, silky inside, with scales forming 7–9 rings
Q. × heterophylla (*Q. phellos* × *Q. rubra*)	US	deciduous tree 65–80 ft (20–25 m)	smooth, pale gray or brown.	4–7 in (10–18 cm), oblong-lanceolate to obovate, apex mucronate, base cuneate, entire or with few shallow teeth, or with 4–6 shallow or deep, often mucronate lobes each side, ultimately glabrous or slightly hairy on veins beneath	acorns closely resembling those of *Q. rubra*

Q

Q. coccinea

Q. dentata

Q. ellipsoidalis

Q. garryana

QUERCUS

Name	Distribution	Habit	Bark	Leaves	Fruit
Q. × hispanica (*Q. cerris* × *Q. suber*)	S France to Portugal and Italy, Balkans	semievergreen tree or shrub to 100 ft (30 m)	less corky than in *Q. suber*	1½–4 in (4–10 cm), oblong-elliptic, acute, margin sinuate-dentate, teeth small, mucronulate, dark green and sparsely hairy above, densely yellow-white tomentose beneath	acorns 1¼–1½ in (3–4 cm), oblong-ovoid, mucronate, mostly glabrous; cupule hemispherical to ovoid, tomentose scales erect to reflexed, enclosing half or more of acorn

Comments: 'Ambrozyana': leaves 2½–4 in (6–10 cm), usually rather small, oblong-obovate, lobes subulate-mucronate, dark green and shining above, gray-tomentose beneath. 'Diversifolia': small tree; bark very corky; leaves 2 × ¾ in (5 × 2 cm), ovate, each side with conspicuous sinus, thus resembling *Q. cerris* leaves, margin lobed in lower half, entire to denticulate above; acorn cup hemispherical, scales more adpressed. 'Fulhamensis': graceful tree; branch more slender and bark less corky; leaves 3–3½ × 1½ in (7.5–9 × 3.5 cm), ovate, apex acute, base rounded to subcordate, margin dentate, teeth 5–8 each side, apex acute, tomentum white. 'Lucombeana': crown conical; bark only slightly corky; leaves resemble those of *Q. cerris*, 2½–4¾ × 1–1½ in (6–12 × 2.5– 4 cm), oblong, coarsely dentate, teeth 6–7(9) each side, green, glabrous, shining above, paler and tomentose beneath; acorn to 1 in (2.5 cm), cupule with lower scales reflexed, upper scales erect, enclosing more than half of acorn.

Name	Distribution	Habit	Bark	Leaves	Fruit
Q. ilex HOLM OAK, EVERGREEN OAK, HOLLY-LEAVED OAK	Mediterranean	evergreen tree to 65 ft (20 m); crown broad, rounded	smooth, gray, becoming shallowly split	¾–3½ in (2–9 cm), narrowly elliptic, ovate-lanceolate or suborbicular, slightly concave beneath, apex acute or obtuse, base attenuate or slightly cordate, entire or with mucronate, acuminate teeth, leathery, subglabrous above, densely pubescent beneath	acorns in groups of 1–3, ⅝–1¼ in (1.5–3 cm), oblong-ovoid to subglobose, mucronate, gray-brown with darker lines, lightly lanate becoming pulverulent; cupule scales adpressed, triangular, obtuse, tomentose, enclosing about half of acorn

Comments: 'Fordii': crown narrow. Leaves 1–1½ in (2.5–3.75 cm), oblong, apex and base attenuate, margin undulate, entire or dentate.

Name	Distribution	Habit	Bark	Leaves	Fruit
Q. imbricaria SHINGLE OAK	E and C US	deciduous tree 50–65 ft (15–20 m); crown conical to rounded	light brown, smooth, split by narrow cracks into plates	4–6½ in (10–17 cm), oblong-lanceolate to ovate, apex acuminate, apiculate, base attenuate or cuneate, entire, often crispate undulate, revolute, occasionally lobed, initially red-puberulent above and thick white-tomentose beneath, becoming dark green, glabrous above, soft-tomentose beneath	acorns ½–⅝ in (1–1.5 cm), subglobose, mucronate, subglabrous to silky-pubescent; cupule scales adpressed, hairy, enclosing up to half of acorn

Name	Distribution	Habit	Bark	Leaves	Fruit
Q. ithaburensis VALLONEA OAK	Syria, Palestine	semi-evergreen to deciduous tree to 80 ft (25 m)	bark furrowed, dark brown	1½–3½ in (4–9 cm), ovate to lanceolate-elliptic, apex acuminate, base subcordate, teeth 5–9 each side, triangular, aristate, gray-tomentose becoming glabrous above, persistent gray-tomentose beneath	acorns clustered 1–3, 1–1¾ in (2.5–4.5 cm), ovoid, apex obtuse or depressed; cupule to 2 × 2 in (5 × 5 cm), with broad, thick, flattened, woody scales enclosing two thirds to nearly all of the acorn

Comments: Subspecies *macrolepis*: leaves more deeply incised; acorn cupule scales more flexible and less woody

Name	Distribution	Habit	Bark	Leaves	Fruit
Q. laurifolia LAUREL OAK	SE US	deciduous to semievergreen tree to 100 ft (30 m)	smooth, dark brown to black, fissured	2½–5 in (6–13 cm), oblong to obovate, apex acute to rounded, base tapered, acute or rounded, margin entire or with to 3 shallow teeth at apex, glossy above, paler and initially pubescent beneath, midvein and petiole yellow	acorns solitary or paired, ½–⅝ in (1–1.5 cm), ovoid-globose, black-brown; cupule scales adpressed, obtuse, enclosing only the base of acorn, subsessile

Q. glauca

Q. × *hispanica* 'Lucombeana'

Q. ilex

Q. imbricaria

QUERCUS

Name	Distribution	Habit	Bark	Leaves	Fruit
Q. macranthera CAUCASIAN OAK, PERSIAN OAK	Caucasus, N Iran	deciduous tree 80–100 ft (25–30 m)		3–8 in (8–20 cm), obovate, apex rounded or blunt, base rounded, subcordate or subcuneate, serrate, teeth 7–11 each side, rounded or obtuse, rarely mucronate, dark green, glabrous above, yellow or red-brown tomentose beneath	acorns 1⅛–1 in (.6–2.5 cm), ovoid-ellipsoid, almost glabrous; cupule scales erect to spreading, lanceolate, pubescent, enclosing half of acorn
Q. macrocarpa BUR OAK, MOSSY- CUP OAK	C and NE US, SE Canada	deciduous tree to 165 ft (50 m); crown rounded	rugose, split into irregular plates, light gray- brown	4–18 in (10–45 cm), obovate to oblong, base attenuate, cuneate or cordate, lyrate, lobes 5–7 per side, dark green and glabrous above, paler, glaucous or white-tomentose beneath, pale-yellow to brown in fall	acorns 1–1½ in (2.5–4 cm), ovoid to hemispherical, mucronate, softly tomentose; cupule hairy, lower scales adpressed, upper scales with free, spreading apices, enclosing half or more of acorn
Q. marilandica BLACKJACK OAK	C and SE US	small deciduous, slow-growing tree, 20–50 ft (6–15 m)	rough, black- brown, split into square plates	4–6½ in (10–17 cm), broadly obovate, apex obtuse, often divided into 3 mucronate lobes, base rounded to cordate, dark green, shining above, paler and red-brown tomentose beneath, yellow to brown in fall	acorns solitary or paired, ½–¾ in (1–2 cm), ovoid; cupule hairy, made up of broad, adpressed scales, enclosing one- to two-thirds of acorn
Q. mongolica	NE Asia	deciduous tree to 100 ft (30 m)		4–8 in (10–20 cm), obovate, apex obtuse, base attenuate, cordate, teeth rounded, glabrous above, glabrous or pubescent on veins beneath	acorns ¾ in (2 cm), ovoid; cupule made up of tuberculate scales, uppermost scales acuminate, ciliate, enclosing one-third of acorn

Comments: Largely represented in cultivation by ssp. **crispula** var. **grosseserrata**: leaves 4–8 in (10–20 cm), teeth acute, sometimes themselves dentate; acorn cupule made of closely adpressed scales, these are not ciliate; native to Japan, Sakhalin, and the Kuriles

Name	Distribution	Habit	Bark	Leaves	Fruit
Q. muehlenbergii YELLOW CHESTNUT OAK, CHINKAPIN OAK	E US	deciduous tree to 65 ft (20 m), rarely 150 ft (45 m)	gray, split into thin, flaky scales	4–7 in (10–18 cm), oblong, obovate or lanceolate, apex acute or acuminate, base cuneate, serrate, teeth acute, pale green flushed bronze at first, subglabrous above, tomentose beneath, becoming glabrous above, white silky-pubescent beneath, orange or scarlet in fall	acorns solitary, ½–1¼ in (1.3–3 cm), ovoid, mucronate, silky-pubescent; cupule made up of tomentose scales, uppermost scales acute, forming fringe, enclosing half of acorn
Q. nigra WATER OAK	SE US	deciduous tree 65–115 ft (20–35 m)	brown, smooth initially, becoming black-brown deeply channeled	1¼–6 in (3–15 cm), obovate with shallowly lobed apex, lobe tips bristle-like, or oblong and entire, leathery, matt blue-green and glabrous above, glabrous but for tufts of hair in axils of veins beneath	acorns solitary, ½–⅝ in (1–1.5 cm), globose to ovoid, black; cupule made up of short, adpressed scales, enclosing up to half of acorn

Q. macranthera

Q. macrocarpa

Q. muehlenbergii

Q. nigra

QUERCUS

Name	Distribution	Habit	Bark	Leaves	Fruit
Q. palustris PIN OAK	NE US, SE Canada	deciduous tree, 66–80(–115) ft (20–25[–35] m); crown dense, ovoid-conical	smooth, gray-brown becoming fissured and ridged	3–6 in (8–15 cm), obovate, apex acute, base attenuate or truncate, pinnately lobed, lobes oblong to triangular, tips slightly lobed and bristlelike, glabrous and glossy above, paler and glabrous except for tufts of green-white hair in vein axils beneath	acorns ½–⅔ in (1.2–1.7 cm), mucronate; cupule saucer-shaped, puberulent, red-brown, enclosing only base of acorn

Comments: 'Pendula': branches pendent.

Name	Distribution	Habit	Bark	Leaves	Fruit
Q. petraea	Europe to W Russia	deciduous tree to 150 ft (45 m); crown regular, trunk reaching far into crown	bark gray to black-brown, furrowed	2½–6½ in (6–17 cm), broadly or narrowly obovate, base attenuate or truncate to subcordate but not auriculate as is *Q. robur*, apex rounded, margin with 4–6 pairs of even, rounded lobes, glossy, glabrous above, paler, glaucous, glabrous to pubescent beneath	acorns clustered, ¾–1¼ in (2–3 cm), ovoid to oblong-ovoid; cupule made up of closely adpressed, pubescent scales

Comments: 'Insecata': leaves laciniate.

Name	Distribution	Habit	Bark	Leaves	Fruit
Q. phellos WILLOW OAK	SE US	deciduous tree to 130 ft (40 m); crown rounded to columnar	bark gray tinted red-brown, glabrous	2¾–4¾ in (7–12 cm), oblong-lanceolate, apex acute, base attenuate, entire, often undulate, dark green above, paler beneath, almost glabrous	acorns to ½ in (1 cm), subglobose, pale yellow-brown; cupule shallow, scales adpressed, gray-tomentose, enclosing only base of acorn.

Name	Distribution	Habit	Bark	Leaves	Fruit
Q. pontica ARMENIAN OAK	NE Turkey, Caucasus	deciduous shrub or small tree, to 20 ft (6 m), rarely 33 ft (10 m)		6–10 in (15–25 cm), obovate to elliptic, apex acute, base attenuate, margin shallowly and irregularly dentate, teeth mucronate, dark green and shining above, paler with sparse hair on veins beneath, midrib yellow	acorns ¾ in (2 cm), ovoid; cupule of triangular, pubescent, adpressed scales, enclosing up to half of acorn

Name	Distribution	Habit	Bark	Leaves	Fruit
Q. robur ENGLISH OAK, COMMON OAK, PEDUNCULATE OAK	Europe to W Russia	deciduous tree 65–100 ft (20–30 m); crown broad, spreading, irregular	gray-brown, deeply fissured	2–5½ in (5–14 cm), oblong to obovate, apex rounded, base attenuate, auriculate, margin with 3–6 pairs of deep, rounded lobes, glabrous dark green above, paler blue-green beneath	acorns solitary or clustered, ⅝–1 in (1.5–2.5 cm), ovoid to oblong-ovoid, apex mucronate; cupule subhemispherical, made up of tightly adpressed, velvety scales, enclosing one-quarter to one-third of fruit

Comments: Cultivars vary in habit, from dwarf to columnar, in color from variegated to yellow or purple throughout, and in leaf from flat to convex, entire to deeply incised and crispate. 'Contorta': dwarf; leaf lobes twisted. f. *fastigiata*: columnar, branchlets erect. 'Pendula': vigorous; branches pendent. 'Atropurpurea': to 33 ft (10 m); leaves plum purple. 'Concordia': leaves golden. 'Salicifolia': slow-growing; leaves elliptic, entire.

Name	Distribution	Habit	Bark	Leaves	Fruit
Q. rubra RED OAK, NORTHERN RED OAK	E N America	deciduous tree to 150 ft (45 m); crown rounded		4–9 in (10–22 cm), oblong to obovate, base attenuate or rounded, margin with 3–5 pairs of lobes, lobes triangular or ovate, acute, sinuses run to midrib, margins irregularly toothed, dark green, glabrous except for red-brown hairs in vein axils, coloring dull red or yellow-brown in fall	acorns ¾–1¼ in (2–3 cm), ovoid, cupule made up of tightly adpressed, short scales, enclosing one-third of acorn

Comments: 'Aurea': leaves golden yellow, becoming slightly green toward fall.

Q. phellos

Q. robur

Q. rubra 'Aurea'

Q. suber

QUERCUS

Name	Distribution	Habit	Bark	Leaves	Fruit
Q. suber CORK OAK	N Africa, S Europe	evergreen tree to 85 ft (26 m)	to 6 in (15 cm) thick, very corky, deeply fissured	to 1½ in (3.5 cm), ovate to lanceolate, apex acute, base sometimes slightly cordate, margin dentate, teeth 5–7 each side, mucronate, dark green, shining, glabrous above, gray-tomentose beneath	acorns solitary or paired, ¾–1¾ in (2–4.5 cm), ovoid or ellipsoid, apex slightly mucronate; cupule sub-hemispherical, lower scales closely adpressed, upper scales spreading enclosing half or more of acorn
Q. × turneri (Q. ilex × Q. robur) **Comments:** 'Pseudoturneri': leaves narrowly oblong-ovate, lobes narrower, more glabrous beneath, remaining green for longer.		semievergreen tree to 80 ft (25 m)		obovate or elliptic, apex acute or obtuse, base rounded to subcordate, margin sinuately-lobed, lobes 5–6, obtuse, leathery, dark green and glabrous above, paler subglabrous but pubescent on veins beneath	acorns, where produced, in clusters of 3–7, to ¾ in (2 cm), ovoid; cupule sub-hemispherical, pubescent, enclosing half of acorn
Q. velutina BLACK OAK	E US, SE Canada	deciduous tree to 100 ft (30 m)	black-brown, deeply fissured, fissures orange at center	2½–10 in (6–25 cm), narrowly ovate to obovate, often misshapen, apex acute, base truncate, deeply 5- or 7-lobed, lobes ovate to triangular, 1–3 bristle-tipped teeth, dark green, glabrous and glossy above, paler, densely tomentose at first beneath	acorns solitary or paired, ⅝–1 in (1.5–2.5 cm), ovoid to subglobose, pale brown; cupule made up of loosely overlapping, hairy scales, enclosing half of acorn

tortrix moths, but the tree merely grows a second flush of leaves; it is also attacked by numerous gall-wasps, but these also do no real harm. *Q. coccifera* is host to the Kermes insect. Acorns are commonly infested by weevils and gall wasps, including the conspicuous "knopper gall" on *Q. robur* and *Q. petraea*; they may account for most of the crop in years of low seed production, but in mast years most of the very large seed crops will escape their attention.

quicklime see *lime*.

quiescence the inability of a seed to germinate, particularly when due to insufficient hydration. It is also used to describe other plant parts that fail to grow due to suboptimal environmental conditions or natural dormancy.

quilled applied to petals that are inrolled into a narrow tube for much of their length, as in certain dahlias and chrysanthemums.

quinate possessing five leaflets emanating from the same point of attachment.

quince (*Cydonia oblonga*) A small deciduous tree belonging to the family Rosaceae. Grown for its golden-yellow fruits, which are downy, strongly aromatic, and of gritty texture, it is used for preserves, in cooking, and as a herbal medicine. The seeds are poisonous. Quince is of uncertain origin but grows wild in Iran, Anatolia, Turkestan, and Transcaucasia; it was highly regarded by the ancient Greeks.

Quince makes an attractive small specimen tree, with white or pale pink flowers in spring and yellow foliage in fall. It may be grown as a standard, bush, fan, or espalier. Selections have been grown as rootstocks for pears for many centuries, and quince is propagated by chip budding onto quince rootstock or by hardwood cuttings or suckers. Trees should be planted about 13 ft (4 m) apart. The flowers are self-fertile, and fruits are best picked when turned golden yellow. Store in a dark, well-ventilated place, unwrapped and separated from other fruits to avoid aroma taint; they will keep for 2–3 months under suitable conditions. Quince bears its fruits on spurs and on shoot tips of the previous year's growth. Apart from the need to remove congested growth, pruning required for established trees is minimal. Possible problems: brown rot, fireblight.

quincunx an arrangement of five trees with one at each corner of a square and one in the center, favored from ancient times to the 17th century. The term is also often loosely applied to a square planting of trees.

Quisqualis (from Latin *quis*, who, and *qualis*, what kind—there was at first some uncertainty as to the family to which this plant belonged.) Combretaceae. Tropical and South Africa, tropical Indomalaysia. Some 17 species of scandent shrubs often climbing by woody hooks (persistent petioles). Borne in spring and summer in racemes or panicles, the flowers are narrowly tubular, with five spreading, oblong lobes. Grow in sun or part-shade in well-drained and not too fertile soil. Provide a minimum temperature of 50°F (10°C) and bright filtered light or full sun with shade during the hottest summer months. Water plentifully when in growth. Reduce water in winter to allow a period of almost dry rest. In late winter, thin congested growth and shorten flowered stems back to the main framework of growth. Propagate by heeled softwood cuttings or by seed. *Q. indica* DRUNKEN SAILOR, RANGOON CREEPER; Old World Tropics; rampant climber; flowers fragrant to 2½ in (6 cm), white becoming pink to red on upper surfaces and within throat over a period of days.

R

rabbits (*Oryctolagus cuniculus*) small burrowing mammals of the family Leporidae that feed on a wide range of wild and cultivated plants, and may graze them to ground level; they also cause damage in gardens by gnawing the bark of young trees, frequently girdling them, and by digging holes in lawns and borders. Rabbits generally live in colonies underground with interconnecting tunnels, but some spend all of their adult lives above ground. They usually breed all the year round, but especially from January to July. There may be 2–5 litters per year, consisting of 3–6 young, which are at first blind and naked of fur but able to leave the nest after 3–4 weeks.

Foxes, stoats, cats, badgers and some large birds of prey are natural enemies. Deliberate introduction of the virus disease myxomatosis, spread by fleas and mosquitoes, initially reduced numbers but rabbits have become partially immune to it. Control by shooting or gassing is not practicable for most gardeners, and humane trapping requires skill.

Fencing is an alternative, effective means of control. In order to be rabbit-proof, it needs to be constructed out of 1 in (2.5 cm) wire mesh, 4–4½ ft (1.2–1.4 m) high, with the bottom 12 in (30 cm) sunk below ground level; of the underground section, the lower 6 in (15 cm) should be bent outward to discourage burrowing. Trees and shrubs may be protected from bark stripping by netting or spiral tree protectors.

Hares cause similar damage to rabbits but they are much more erratic in their attacks since they usually exist only in small numbers. Fences against hares need to be 5–5¾ ft (1.5–1.75 m) high.

raccoon an omnivorous, largely nocturnal climbing animal which in the US can cause severe damage to fruit and vegetables, and also to water lilies. Shooting and trapping are the only effective controls and local advice on procedures should be sought.

Laburnum anagyroides

raceme of flowers

raceme an indeterminate, unbranched and usually elongate inflorescence composed of pedicelled flowers.

rachilla a secondary axis of a compound leaf or inflorescence.

rachis (plural rachises, rachides) the axis of a compound leaf or a compound inflorescence, as an extension of the petiole or peduncle, respectively.

radicchio see *chicory*.

Radermachera (for J.C.M. Radermacher [1757–83], Dutch resident in Java who published a list of Javanese plants). Bignoniaceae. Indomalaysia, S China, Hainan, Taiwan, Ryukyu Islands. About 15 species, trees or shrubs, mostly evergreen with 2–3-pinnate leaves. Tubular, 5-lobed flowers are carried in terminal thyrses in summer. Young examples of the following species are often treated as pot plants, valued for their evergreen, lustrous foliage. Eventually, they will make handsome flowering trees. Grow in sun or part shade. Water moderately when in growth; maintain a winter minimum temperature of 59°F (15°C). Propagate by seed, cuttings or air layering. *R. sinica* S and E Asia; shrub or tree; leaves to 30 in (75 cm), triangular to deltoid, 2-pinnate; segments ovate to rhomboid, somewhat lobed or toothed, glossy, deep green; flowers scented, to 3 in (7.5 cm), deep yellow.

radial symmetry describes the form of a flower that is circular in outline when viewed from above and with flower parts that radiate from a central point, such as a primrose.

radiate (1) spreading outward from a common center; (2) possessing ray florets, as in the typically daisylike capitula of many Compositae.

radical arising directly from the root, rootstock or rootlike stems; usually applied to leaves that are basal rather than cauline.

radicle the rudimentary root of the embryo.

radish (*Raphanus sativus*) an annual or biennial species, variable in size, color and pungency, grown primarily as an annual for its enlarged taproot, which is usually eaten raw; the immature leaves and seed pods are also edible.

The radish probably originated in the eastern Mediterranean region and was important as a food crop in Egypt by 2000 BC. It is widely distributed and adapted to various climatic conditions.

Roots can be available year round from two main types. Small-rooted cultivars are suitable for summer harvest and are globose or long in shape, with red, pink, bicolored or white skins; selections are available for fall/winter sowing with cold or warm protection, and these usually produce less leaf and are slower to mature. Large-rooted types include the white mooli radishes, which are about 8 in (20 cm) long and suitable for summer use, and the hardy Chinese and Spanish types, which may be white-, red-, black- or violet-skinned, round or long, in some cases up to 24 in (60 cm) long, and capable of producing roots up to 1 lb (500 g) in weight. All of the large-rooted types may be eaten raw or cooked.

Small radishes, such as 'French Breakfast' and 'Crystal Ball', can be sown at 10 day intervals from early spring until fall, and the season extended with cloches or other forms of protection. Sow in rows 6 in (15 cm) apart with seeds 1 in (2.5 cm) apart, or sow broadcast. Too dense a stand will result in lanky unproductive plants. Mooli types should not be sown before June to avoid bolting, and these take 10–12 weeks to mature. Large radishes for winter use should be sown in July or August in rows 10 in (25 cm) apart, aiming at a final spacing between plants of 6 in (15 cm). Sow all types $^1/_2$–$^3/_4$ in (13–20 mm) deep.

An open site is preferable, although summer crops tolerate light shade; crop rotation is necessary because, like other members of the family Cruciferae, radishes are liable to club root infection.

Small-rooted types can be sown thinly along the prepared drills of slower germinating vegetables, such as parsnips and parsley, to mark the rows, and these may be progressively pulled as they mature; alternatively, they may be grown as an intercrop in rows between other vegetables. Rapid germination and establishment is essential and summer radishes must be pulled early since they soon become woody; small-rooted types may be ready within a month from sowing. Winter types can be left in the ground until required, or lifted for indoor storage. Possible problems: cabbage root fly, flea beetle.

raffia a flat, fibrous material used for tying plants, including shoot and bud grafts. It is derived from the leaves of certain palms, especially the RAFFIA PALM (*Raphia farinifera*). The term is often used interchangeably with *bass* or *bast* q.v.

raft (1) piece of bark, osmunda fiber or tree fern fiber onto which epiphytic plants are fixed and hung—this method of growing is particularly suitable for orchids with abundant clinging aerial roots and rambling stems and rhizomes e.g. *Bulbophyllum*; (2) a form of training used in bonsai where the principal trunk of the tree is laid on its side and the lateral branches along the exposed side are trained up as if they were themselves individual trees.

ragwort a weed especially of grassland and uncultivated ground; poisonous particularly to cattle and horses when cut and dry. The most common species is *Senecio jacobaea*, a hardy bien-

nial, sometimes perennial, of the family Asteraceae, native in Europe. Erect stems to 5 ft (1.5 m); leaves to 7$^7/_8$ in (20 cm), pinnatifid. Flowers numerous in a dense corymb, capitula to $^3/_4$ in (2 cm), ray florets yellow. In the UK Ragwort is specified as an injurious weed under the Weeds Act 1959. It is not a problem in well-maintained gardens but gardeners need to be aware of the hazard presented if the plant is allowed to establish in uncultivated areas adjoining farmland where livestock is grazed. Plants should be dug out and carefully disposed of.

Ragwort

rain shadow the area immediately to the leeward of a wall, fence, hedge, screen or shelter belt, which receives much less rainfall than the surrounding areas because of its protection from prevailing wind. It is an important consideration in planting and in the provision of irrigation.

raised bed any growing bed formed above ground level, which may range in height from a very shallow construction up to almost 3.3 ft (1 m). All raised beds offer the advantages of good drainage, a growing medium of relatively high temperature, and free root run. Beds up to 12 in (30 cm) high are used in the vegetable garden and for growing strawberries, in a system referred to as the deep bed method. Taller raised beds are appropriate for sites where there is no soil or where its composition or profile is unsuitable for satisfactory plant growth; they are often used for growing alpines, either direct planted or as plunged container-grown specimens.

Raised beds provide opportunities for gardeners who use a wheelchair or otherwise have restricted mobility, and it is possible to grow a wide range of plants, including ornamentals, vegetables and some forms of fruit in this way.

Beds have walls made of brick or cement blocks, or of timber such as old railroad ties; these may have planting holes left during construction in which to establish ornamental trailing plants and to provide side drainage. For most plant use, a foundation layer of rubble is desirable as an aid to drainage. The growing medium can be mixed according to intended use, a soil-based mix being the best choice.

rake a hand implement consisting of a crossbar with short prongs, or 'teeth', fixed to a long handle. Most commonly used, for leveling and preparing seed-beds, is the steel-headed rake, which consists of a head 12–15 in (30–38 cm) wide, with prongs $^1/_4$ in (6 mm) long, mounted on a wooden handle 60 in (150 cm) long. It is sometimes used for forming seed drills, where with the head turned so that the prongs are facing upward a continuous depression can be made in a fine tilth; this is a suitable method where less precise drilling is required, as may be acceptable in the sowing of annual flower beds. Held at the same angle, the rake may then be used for pulling soil back over the sown drills.

The wooden rake consists of a head about 30 in (76 cm) wide, bearing prongs 3 in (8 cm) long, fixed to a 70 in- (177 cm-) long handle, and is particularly useful for levelling ground and pulling off stones and litter. The spring-tined rake has a special purpose in lawn maintenance; it comprises a fan-shaped head about 12 in (30 cm) long, with a number of thin-gauge tensile wire prongs, spring mounted over a central wire bearer, with the end of each prong bent to a common shallow angle. Plastic and bamboo versions are available. It is used for raking out thatch or gathering mowings and, like every other type of rake, is useful for general tidying, such as leaf gathering; for some purposes, a rubber-headed rake is suitable. A very small, short-handled rake is sometimes used as a cultivator in much the same manner as a hand fork.

R

rambler a climbing plant that trails or scrambles in an informal habit; often refers to a type of rose.

ramentaceous stems or leaves possessing small, loose, brownish scales.

ramet (1) an individual member of a clone; (2) an underground tree system giving rise to large suckering colonies.

ramiflorous bearing flowers directly on large branches and leafless twigs, but not the trunk.

ramiform branched, branchlike.

rammer see *potting stick*.

Ramonda (for L.F. Ramond [d. 1827], French botanist and traveler). Gesneriaceae. S Europe. 3 species, stemless, more or less evergreen perennial herbs. Borne in a low, basal rosette, the leaves are rugose and white-hairy. Produced in spring and summer, the flowers are solitary or few together in scapose umbels; they are shallowly tubular with a broad, spreading limb of four to six lobes. Plant in a rock garden and in wall crevices, especially those with a northern exposure. Kept free of dampness in winter, these plants may be hardy to about 5°F (−15°C). They may also be grown in an alpine house or cold frame in shallow pans, with a well-drained neutral or slightly acidic, loam-based potting mix. Outdoors, establish in pockets of gritty and freely draining soil, and position so that water is unable to settle in the leaf rosette. Plants may shrivel under dry conditions but will readily resurrect given water. In winter, keep barely moist. Propagate by seed or by leaf cuttings as for *Saintpaulia*. *R. myconi* (syn. *R. pyrenaica*); Pyrenees; flowers to 1½ in (4 cm) in diameter, 1–6 on glandular-hairy scapes to 4¾ in (12 cm), violet to lilac, rosy pink or white with a yellow center.

rank (1) a vertical row or column, for example of leaves; (2) in taxonomy, the position of a taxon in the hierarchy.

Ranunculus (name used by Pliny, derived from Latin *rana*, frog: several species are aquatic or grow in marshes). Ranunculaceae. BUTTERCUP, CROWFOOT. Cosmopolitan. Some 400 species, annual, biennial and perennial herbs (those here perennial). They vary greatly in size and habit, but most produce simple to palmately lobed leaves in basal clumps. Solitary or carried in cymose panicles, the flowers are bowl-shaped to starry with five or more petals and numerous stamens.

Some of those commonly grown are selections of garden weeds (for example, cultivars of *R. acris*), fully hardy and suited to damp places in sun or part shade in informal borders, woodland or water gardens. Where they prove invasive, cut back the running rhizomes with a spade. Cultivars of the lesser celandine, *R. ficaria*, are charming additions to the woodland garden and equally suited to underplanting in shrubberies and mixed borders. They prefer some shade and moist, humus-rich soil, at least when in growth. They flower in early to midspring and their foliage (often their finest feature) will disappear by summer, when their pea-sized tubers will withstand drought. This species may also become invasive and is easily propagated by tubers taken in summer and fall. Taller and sadly noninvasive, *R. gouanii* has similar requirements. *R. lingua* is an excellent plant for water margins, pools and bog gardens. *R. asiaticus* should be grown as for the tuberous-rooted De Caen and St. Brigid anemones. Its cultivars make beautiful pot plants and cut flowers. Alpine species such as *R. alpestris* and *R. montanus* are hardy and will thrive in sun in a rock garden given moist, gritty soil. *R. crenatus* and *R. glacialis* are harder to please, needing an acidic medium and careful watering. They are perhaps more easily cultivated in the alpine house. *R. lyallii*. *R. amplexicaulis*, *R. bullatus*, *R. calandrinioides* and *R. gramineus* need fast-draining, sandy soil in full sun. They grow well in the more sheltered reaches of the rock garden, gravel garden and silver border. Some of them may become dormant in summer and dislike wet winter conditions. Increase by seed or division.

Ranzania (for Ono Ranzan, [1729–1810] Japanese naturalist). Berberidaceae. Japan (Honshu). 1 species, *R. japonica*, a perennial, rhizomatous herb, 6–16 in (15–40 cm) tall. The compound leaves consist of three leaflets, each ovate to round, 3-lobed and 3–4¾ in (8–12 cm) across. To 1 in (2.5 cm) across, the nodding flowers appear in early summer. They are pale lavender-violet and composed of six petaloid sepals and six small petals each with two nectaries at its base. For cool, humus-rich, moist soils in light woodland, for the shaded rock garden. Hardy to 14°F (−10°C). Propagate from ripe seed in a cold frame—this can take up to 18 months to germinate and a further 3–5 years to flower.

Raoulia (for Edouard F.L. Raoul [1825–52], French botanist). Compositae. New Zealand. About 20 species, dwarf, evergreen perennial herbs or subshrubs, often forming dense cushions or mats. The leaves are very small and usually densely packed or overlapping. Buttonlike, stalkless flower heads with yellow florets appear in spring and summer. Silvery cushion-formers for the rock garden, fine scree and raised beds. Grow in sun in moist, gritty, humus-rich soils. Protect from excessive wet in winter. Hardy to 5°F (−15°C). In the alpine house, grow in pans with a mix of equal parts loam, leaf mold and sharp sand with a top dressing of grit. Water freely when in growth; keep almost dry in winter. Propagate by division of rooted tufts.

R. australis leaves to ⅟₁₆ in (2 mm), spathulate, closely overlapping, silver-pubescent; flower heads to ¼ in (5 mm) in diameter, phyllaries tipped bright yellow; *R. haastii* leaves to ¼ in (5 mm), ovate to linear-oblong, loosely overlapping, pale sea green; flower heads to ⅜ in (9 mm) in diameter, phyllaries tipped white or yellow; *R. hookeri* leaves to ⅟₁₆ in (2 mm), narrowly obovate to spathulate, closely overlapping, silvery white-tomentose toward apex; phyllaries green or straw-colored.

rape see *green manuring*.

Raphanus (name used by Theophrastus for this plant). Cruciferae. Europe, temperate Asia. 8 species, annual, biennial or perennial herbs with pungently flavored and crisply succulent taproots and lyrate to pinnatifid leaves. *R. sativus* is the RADISH (q.v.)

RANUNCULUS

Name	Distribution	Habit	Leaves	Flowers	
R. aconitifolius	W to C Europe	perennial to 24 in (60 cm)	dark green, palmately, 3–5-lobed	few to many, white, to ¾ in (2 cm), across; sepals red or purple beneath	spring

Comments: 'Flore Pleno': WHITE BACHELOR'S BUTTONS, FAIR MAIDS OF FRANCE, FAIR MAIDS OF KENT; flowers fully double, long-lasting. 'Luteus Plenus': flowers double, yellow.

R. acris MEADOW BUTTERCUP	Europe, Asia, naturalized elsewhere	perennial to 3¼ ft (1 m)	with 3–7 deep lobes simple or further divided, dentate, hairy, sometimes marked black	several, glossy golden yellow, to 1 in (2.5 cm) across	spring

Comments: 'Flore Pleno': YELLOW BACHELOR'S BUTTONS; to 36 in (90 cm); flowers double. 'Hedgehog': leaves marked dark brown; flowers pale.

R. alpestris	Europe	perennial, 1¼–4¾ in (3–12 cm)	glossy dark green, orbicular, lobes 3–5, deeply crenate	1–3, white to ¾ in (2 cm) across; sepals tinged red-brown 3–5	spring-summer
R. amplexicaulis	Pyrenees, N Spain	perennial 3–12 in (8–30 cm)	ovate-lanceolate, glaucous, blue-gray; stem leaves amplexicaul	several, white, occasionally pink, ¾–1 in (2–2.5 cm) diameter; petals sometimes more than 5	spring
R. asiaticus	SE Europe, SW Asia	pubescent perennial to 18 in (45 cm)	3-lobed, lobes stalked, divided and toothed	few to several, red, pink, purple, yellow to white, 1¼–2 in (3–5 cm) across; anthers purple-black	spring-summer

Comments: Bloomingdale Hybrids: dwarf; flowers double in shades of pink, yellow, rose, red and white. 'Color Carnival': tall, robust; flowers large, double, many colors. 'Picotee': compact; flowers double, very large, ruffled, in pink, red, orange, white and yellow, picotee edge. 'Pot Dwarf': flowers semidouble and double, in scarlet, pink, salmon, orange and white. 'Superbissimus': tall; flowers large. Tecolote Hybrids: robust; flowers exceptionally large. Victoria Hybrids: flowers large, fully double in wide range of colors.

R. bullatus	Mediterranean to NW Spain and Portugal	perennial; roots tuberous; stem to 12 in (30 cm)	ovate, crenate, bullate	1–2, yellow, 1 in (2.5 cm) across, violet-scented; petals 5–12	fall-spring
R. alandrinioides	Morocco	perennial to 6 in (15 cm)	to 2½ in (6.5 cm), long-petiolate, lanceolate to ovate, entire, undulate, gray-green, glaucous	1–3, white, sometimes flushed pink, to 2 in (5 cm) across	winter-spring
R. renatus	E Alps, Apennines to Balkans and Carpathians	perennial to 6 in (15 cm)	orbicular, weakly cordate, crenate or 3-lobed at apex	1–2, white, to 1 in (2.5 cm) across	spring

R

R. acris 'Flore Pleno'

R. alpestris

R. asiaticus

R. calandrinioides

RANUNCULUS

Name	Distribution	Habit	Leaves	Flowers	
R. ficaria LESSER CELANDINE, PILEWORT	Europe, NW Africa, W Asia, naturalized N America	perennial 2–12 in (5–30 cm) with small, clustered tubers	cordate, angled or crenate, ½–1½ in (1–4 cm), dark green, long-petiolate	solitary to few, brilliant golden-yellow, fading to white, ¾–1¼ in (2–3 cm) across; petals 8–12	spring

Comments: var. *albus*: leaves with a dark marks; flowers very pale yellow, blue-green below. var. *aurantiacus*: leaves heavily marked coppery-bronze; flowers coppery-orange. 'Bowles Double': flowers double, green center on opening, later paler yellow. 'Brazen Hussy': leaves chocolate brown; flowers golden. ssp. *chrysocephalus*: large in all parts. 'Collarette' syn. 'E.A. Bowles': anthers petaloid, forming a tight anemone center. 'Double Bronze': flowers double, yellow, with bronze backs to petals. 'Double Mud': flowers double, upper surface of petals creamy, lower surface tinged gray. *flore-pleno*: flowers double, yellow, petals tinged green beneath. 'Green Petal': flowers with many narrow, wavy-edged green and yellow staminodes; sepals 0. 'Hoskin's Miniature': small; leaves slightly marked silver. 'Lemon Queen': flowers simple, pale yellow, petals tinged bronze beneath. 'Randall's White': upper surface of petals pale cream, lower surface slate-blue. 'Salmon's White': leaves with dark markings; upper surface of petals very pale cream, lower surface slate-blue.

Name	Distribution	Habit	Leaves	Flowers	
R. glacialis	Alps, Pyrenees, Sierra Nevada, Arctic, Iceland, Greenland	perennial, 1½–10 in (4–25 cm)	dark-green, somewhat fleshy, lobes 3, stalked, deeply segmented	1–3, white or pale pink, becoming red after pollination, ¾–1¼ in (2–3 cm) across	spring-summer
R. gouanii	Pyrenees	pubescent perennial to 12 in (30 cm)	leaves 3–5-lobed, lobes obovate, dentate	1–5 per stem, rich yellow, to 1½ in (4 cm) across	spring

Comments: close to *R. montanus*. *R. gouanii* 'Plenus', also known as *R. speciosus* 'Plenus' is, properly, *R. constantinopolitanus* 'Plenus', with double flowers to 1½ in (4 cm) across in chrome yellow with a green center.

Name	Distribution	Habit	Leaves	Flowers	
R. gramineus	S Europe, N Africa	perennial, 8–20 in (20–50 cm)	linear to lanceolate, flat, glaucous	1–3 per stem, citron yellow, to ¾ in (2 cm) across	spring-summer
R. lingua GREATER SPEARWORT	Europe to Siberia	semiaquatic stoloniferous perennial; stem stout, 20–79 in (50–200 cm)	to 8 in (20 cm), ovate to lanceolate, usually toothed	in lax cyme, bright yellow, to 2 in (5 cm) across	summer

Comments: 'Grandiflorus': flowers large, fleshy

Name	Distribution	Habit	Leaves	Flowers	
R. lyallii GIANT BUTTERCUP, MOUNTCOOK LILY	New Zealand	perennial; rootstock thick, roots fleshy; stem stout, to 5 ft (1.5 m)	peltate, 4¾–16 in (12–40 cm) broad, crenate, leathery, dark green, long-petiolate	5–15 in a panicle, white, 2–3 in (5–8 cm) across	summer
R. montanus	Europe (mountains)	glabrous to pubescent rhizomatous perennial, 6–12 in (16–30 cm)	3–5-lobed, lobes obovate, dentate	1–3, glossy golden-yellow, ¾–1¼ in (2–3 cm) across	spring-summer

Comments: 'Molten Gold': dwarf, robust; leaves dark; flowers large, rounded, gold.

R. ficaria flore-pleno

R. gramineus

R. lingua

raphide an elongated, needlelike crystal of calcium oxalate, sometimes in a bundle and found in the vegetative parts of many plants.

raspberry (*Rubus* species) a deciduous woody perennial, with fruits generally red, but also yellow, black or purple. The temperate climate species is the red-fruited *R. idaeus*, named after Mount Ida in Asia Minor, the possible origin of the raspberry. European and North American raspberries are classified respectively into subspecies *vulgatus* (native to much of Europe and northern Asia to Japan), and *strigosus* (which grows wild in North America, in the mountains of Georgia to Pennsylvania, through Maine and Dakota to Canada). The North American subspecies is hardier and has brighter colored fruits.

The AMERICAN BLACK RASPBERRY, (*R. occidentalis*), has a similar natural range to the AMERICAN RED RASPBERRY (*R. idaeus* subspecies *strigosus*), but is not found so far north and also farther south; and it is less hardy. A selection of the HILL RASPBERRY (*R. niveus* 'Mysore') is grown commercially in Florida and harvested from March to May.

Domestication of the raspberry in Europe was mentioned by Roman writers in the 4th century and the fruits were eaten or used for flavoring drinks while the leaves were used for making tea. By the 16th century, raspberries were cultivated in gardens, and during the next century, different forms were described, including red, yellow and white fruited and thornless cultivars. Selection for larger fruits had made considerable progress by the end of the 18th century, and in 1823 the Horticultural Society of London reported that it had 23 cultivars in its collection. Over the next hundred years, nurserymen introduced more selections and chance seedlings.

Some European cultivars were introduced to North America from the end of the 18th century onward, but due to temperature extremes they did not flourish. They were combined with American forms to produce improved cultivars like 'Cuthbert' and 'Willamette'.

Virus disease developed as a serious problem of raspberries in the first half

Cutting back summer raspberries
Canes in their second year which have borne their crop are cut back to the ground, leaving the new season's canes to crop the next year.

of the 20th century, but the work of breeders in both North America and Europe has greatly reduced the incidence of this virus with the introduction of the virus-tolerant cultivar 'Malling Jewel' and a series of others that show resistance to aphid vectors. 'Glen Clova' and 'Glen Prosen' are widely grown as early and late red-fruited cultivars.

The season is lengthened with fall-fruiting or primocane cultivars, such as 'Autumn Bliss', 'Zeva' and 'Heritage'. These fruit on the current season's canes, from late summer until the first fall frosts, and can be grown in areas where severe winter temperature would normally damage growth.

Yellow-fruited raspberries have been known for centuries—'Yellow Antwerp' was one of the first to be selected; more recent cultivars include 'Amber' and 'Golden Queen'. Black raspberries, such as 'Ohio Everbearer' and 'Black Hawk', are grown in North America, but in the UK are susceptible to *Phylophthora* root rots. Purple raspberries, hybrids of red and black types, grow more vigorously than black raspberries and give higher yields, and cultivars such as 'Brandywine' are grown commercially in a limited area in New York State.

Raspberries are self-fertile, so that single cultivars may be planted.

Raspberries are best grown in cool temperate conditions, sheltered from spring frosts and wind; soil moisture content is crucial, and should be adequate to supply water in summer for growing canes and swelling fruit, but

not so high in winter as to asphyxiate roots. Raspberries show iron deficiency on calcareous soils.

Plant canes of certified stock, with a good fibrous root system, during the dormant period, with plants spaced 16 in (40 cm) apart in rows 6½ ft (2 m) apart. In temperate climates, planting should preferably be undertaken in late fall in order to encourage early root growth; in countries with very cold winters, spring planting is usual to avoid winter losses. Plant the canes with the roots 2–2¾ in (5–7 cm) deep, and cut back each cane to 8 in (20 cm); fall-fruiting canes are cut back to ground level.

In gardens, raspberries are usually grown in upright rows, running north-south for uniform light distribution, with post and wire support. For red raspberries, three wires are fixed, along single rows of 7½ ft- (2.3 m-) long posts driven 18 in (45 cm) into the ground, at 28 in (0.7 m), 3¼ ft (1 m) and 5½ ft (1.6 m) above ground level and the canes are tied to the wires. An alternative system is to erect two parallel rows of support posts, with 24 in (60 cm) between each row, and the line of raspberry canes is planted down the center. Wires are attached along each row of posts at 2½ ft (0.75 m) and 5 ft (1.5 m) above ground level, and twine or wire ties fixed across each tier of parallel wires. The raspberry canes grow up through the structure with no tying. Canes of fall-fruiting raspberries are shorter and do not need permanent support. Black and purple raspberries require more space than red ones, and are planted 30–48 in (75–120 cm) apart in rows about 8 ft (2.5 m) apart; they are usually grown without support or attached to a single wire running 18–24 in (45–60 cm) above soil level along a row of posts.

In cold areas such as the central US and east Canada, canes are not tied in until the spring since the winter snow-fall protects them from very low winter temperatures.

Summer-fruiting red raspberries are pruned by cutting out the fruited canes immediately after harvesting, together with any weak ones, to leave about 8–10 canes for every 3.3 ft (1 m) of row; winter-damaged tips are cut out in late winter. Fall-fruiting raspberries are cut to the ground in winter. New canes

R

of black and purple raspberries are tipped in summer to encourage the growth of laterals, which are then pruned back in spring, according to climate and varietal vigor, to increase fruit size. The old fruited canes are usually cut out each winter.

The main nutrients required by raspberries are potassium for fruiting and nitrogen for cane production; $^1/_{16}$–$^1/_8$ oz/sq. ft (15–30 g/m²) of sulfate of ammonia applied in spring is sufficient to meet these requirements, together with a mid-winter dressing of sulfate of potash at $^1/_8$ oz/sq. ft (30 g/m²). Phosphates are needed every third year, applied as superphosphate at $^1/_4$ oz/sq. ft (60 g/m²). An annual mulch of organic matter will help conserve soil moisture and control weeds.

Watering in dry spells as the fruits start to ripen is beneficial. It is also recommended for fall-fruiting raspberries to maintain fruit size and number. Fruits should be harvested when dry, pulled from the stalk, and kept as cool as possible.

Possible problems: aphids, birds, raspberry cane borer (see *longhorn beetles*), raspberry beetle; cane spot.

raspberry beetle (*Byturus tomentosus*) a small brown beetle, about $^1/_8$ in (4 mm) long, which overwinters in the soil as an adult to emerge in late April to early June. The beetles feed upon the petals and stamens of cane fruit flowers, and also apple and hawthorn. Eggs are laid on the fertilized flowers of blackberry, loganberry, raspberry and related fruits. The brownish white maggots, which are up to $^3/_8$ in (8 mm) long, feed on the outside of developing fruits at the stalk end; as the berries ripen they tunnel into the plug and feed inside the fruit. Fully fed larvae go down into the soil to pupate. There is one generation. Control by spraying a recommended insecticide when the larvae are feeding on the outside of the fruits.

Ratibida (derivation of name obscure). Compositae. N America, Mexico. MEXICAN HAT, PRAIRIE CONEFLOWER. 6 species, erect, roughly hairy biennials or perennial herbs. The leaves are pinnate to pinnatifid. Large

and long-stalked, the daisylike flower heads are produced in summer and early fall. The ray florets are long, colorful and somewhat shaggy, the disk florets are small, dark and packed into a prominent rounded or conelike receptacle. Tolerant of drought, heat and high humidity, the following species are hardy and suitable for use in the herbaceous border, as cut flowers, in native plant collections and in other naturalistic plantings. Propagate by seed. The deep taproots make division difficult. *R. columnifera* is often treated as an annual.

R. columnifera LONG-HEAD CONEFLOWER, PRAIRIE CONEFLOWER; British Colombia to New Mexico; receptacle cone-shaped, ray florets to 1 in (2.5 cm), yellow to red or partly to entirely brown-purple ; *R. pinnata* GRAY-HEAD CONEFLOWER, DROOPING CONEFLOWER; central North America; receptacle globose, ray florets to 2 in (5 cm), yellow.

Ravenala (the native name in Madagascar). Strelitziaceae. Madagascar. TRAVELER'S TREE. 1 species, *R. madagascariensis*, a giant, evergreen treelike herb, to 52 ft (16 m). The columnar stems are unbranched, ring-scarred and olive green or gray. The paddle-shaped leaves are to 13 ft (4 m) long, 2 ranked, dull green and become torn along the veins. The petiole bases overlap to form a distinctive fan at the summit of the stem. The flowers resemble those of the larger *Strelitzia* species, but are duller. Cultivate as for the larger *Strelitzia* species.

ray (1) the primary division of an umbel or umbelliform inflorescence; (2) a ray flower, or a circle of ray flowers, or the corolla of a ray flower.

ray flower, ray floret a small flower that has a tubular corolla and a limb that is expanded and flattened in a straplike blade (ligule). Usually occupying the peripheral rings of a radiate Compositae capitulum; cf. *disk floret*.

Rebutia (for P. Rebut, wine-grower and cactus dealer of Chazay d'Azergues). Cactaceae. Bolivia, NW Argentina. Up to 40 species, low-growing cacti with small, globose to shortly cylindric stems—these are tuberculate or weakly ribbed and covered in rather weak spines. Small, funnelform flowers usually appear near the stem-base. Grow in a cool greenhouse (minimum temperature 45°F/7°C) in a gritty, mildly acidic to neutral medium in full sun; ensure a dry atmosphere. Keep dry from midfall until early spring, except for light misting on warm days in later winter.

R. aureiflora NW Argentina; stems depressed-globose to globose, to 2½ in (6 cm) in diameter, often red-tinged; spines to ½ in (1 cm), bristly; flowers about 1½ in (4 cm) in diameter, yellow with white throat, sometimes orange, red or purple; *R. fiebrigii* (syn. *R. muscula*); Bolivia, NW Argentina; stem globose, depressed at apex, 2 in (5 cm) tall; spines to ¾ in (2 cm), brown-tipped; flower ¾–1¼ in (2–3 cm), bright orange to red; *R. krainziana* probably garden origin; stem depressed-globose, 1½ in (4 cm) in diameter; spines about $^1/_{16}$–$^1/_8$ in (1–2 mm), bristly, white; flowers about 1¼ × 1½ in (3 × 4 cm), bright red with violet sheen and violet throat; *R. minuscula* (syn. *R. violaciflora*); N Argentina; stem globose, to about 2 in (5 cm) in diameter; spines $^1/_{16}$–$^1/_8$ in (2–3mm), bristly; flowers to 1½ in (4 cm), variable in color scarlet to purple-red; *R. pygmaea* NW Argentina; stem ovoid to short-cylindric, ½–1¼ in (1–3 cm) × ½–¾ in (1.2–2 cm); spines $^1/_{16}$–$^1/_8$ in (2–3mm); flowers ¾–1 in (18–25 mm), rose-purple; *R. senilis* N Argentina; stem to 2¾ in (7 cm) in diameter, deep green; spines to 1¼ in (3 cm), chalky white or tinged yellow; flowers 1½ in (3.5 cm), carmine with white throat or citron yellow.

ray florets

disk florets

Chrysanthemum

receptacle the enlarged or elongated, and either flat, concave or convex, end of the stem from which the floral parts derive.

recessive a particular heritable characteristic which is masked by the dominance of another characteristic-transmitting component of a gene. For example, dwarfness is recessive and may be carried as a latent characteristic, while tallness is dominant and is expressed in offspring following fertilization; cf. *dominant*.

recurved curved backward and downward.

red spider mites (Acarina: Tetranychidae) small, spiderlike mites, up to $1/16$ in (1 mm) long, red or greenish yellow with darker markings and with four pairs of legs; they are divided into two subfamilies: red spider mites and bryobia mites. Colonies develop on plant foliage and throughout the summer all stages are usually present; overwintering is as eggs or adults depending upon species. Young and adult mites suck sap from plant tissues, producing a characteristic pale mottling of the upper surface of leaves; in severe attacks, leaves become chlorotic, desiccated, bronzed or silvered and usually covered with spun silk webbing.

The FRUIT TREE RED SPIDER MITE *(Panonychus ulmi)*, known as the EUROPEAN RED MITE in America, is an important pest, especially of apples and plums, and it also attacks other deciduous trees and shrubs. Severe infestations cause leaves to become bronzed; premature defoliation follows and on fruit trees loss of yield. Eggs overwinter in bark crevices of woody plants. The CITRUS RED MITE *(P.citri)*, is a worldwide pest of citrus. The GLASS-HOUSE RED SPIDER MITE *(Tetranychus urticae)*, known as the TWO-SPOTTED MITE in North America, is common and very troublesome, attacking a wide range of greenhouse and outdoor plants, including strawberries, peaches and nectarines, cucumbers, beans, carnations, chrysanthemums, fuchsias, orchids and roses. The closely-related CARMINE MITE *(T. cinnabarinus)* is found in similar situations, but is mostly restricted to greenhouses in temperate countries. Both species overwinter as adults. Other injurious species in North

America include the PACIFIC SPIDER MITE *(T. pacificus)*, SCHOENE SPIDER MITE *(T. schoenei)*, the FOUR-SPOTTED MITE *(T.canadensis)*, the STRAWBERRY SPIDER MITE *(T. turkestani)* and the MCDANIEL SPIDER MITE *(T. mcdanieli)*. All the mites attack a wide range of edible and ornamental plants. The LIME MITE *(Eotetranychus tiliarius)* on *Tilia* spp. in Europe attracts attention because, in severe infestations, mites vacate the leaves in late summer and fall and swarm over the trunk, coating it with glistening silk webbing. Other species occur in North America, including the YELLOW SPIDER MITE *(E. carpani borealis)* and the YUMA SPIDER MITE *(E. yumensis)*. The CONIFER SPINNING MITE *(Oligonychus ununguis)*, known as the SPRUCE SPIDER MITE in North America, is an important pest of conifers; affected foliage turns yellow during the summer and in severe attacks needles are shed. Other North American species include the AVOCADO BROWN MITE *(O. punicae)*, the SOUTHERN RED MITE *(O. ilicis)*, the BANKS GRASS MITE *(O.pratensis)* and the AVOCADO RED MITE *(O. yothersi)*.

Red spider mite

Natural enemies play an important part in the control of red spider mites and the red spider predator *(Phytoseiulus persimilis)* is widely used in Europe and North America to control *Tetranychus urticae* in greenhouses. Spraying greenhouse plants with a fine mist of water at frequent intervals helps check populations. The choice of acaricides is restricted for amateur gardeners and red spider mites readily become resistant to the main groups of chemicals. See *mites*.

red currant *(Ribes rubrum* Red Currant Group) a deciduous shrubby plant grown for its translucent berries borne in pendant trusses. The main difference between the red- and white currant is the absence of cyanidin glycosides in the white currant. Each is cultivated in the same manner. Cultivars of both fruits are developed mainly from *Ribes rubrum* and *R. sativum*, and also *R. petraeum, R. vulgare* and *R. multiflorum*, all of which are native to Europe. They are first

recorded in cultivation in the late 15th century, and were introduced into North America in the early 17th century. The red- and white currant grows easily in cool moist climates, requiring a sheltered site that is not readily prone to frost at flowering time. In gardens, it is commonly grown as a bush on a short leg planted 16 sq. ft (1.5 m²), although commercially it is often trained as a higher yielding stooled bush. Red currants and white currants may also be grown as standards, or as cordons, espaliers or fans which may be trained against a fence or on a wired structure as both space-saving and potentially attractive garden features. Single cordons are conveniently spaced 18 in (45 cm) apart. Two-year-old bushes from a certified source are a good choice for planting in fall.

Red currants depend on potash for healthy growth; this should be applied as $7/8$ oz/sq. ft (25 g/m²) of sulfate of potash in late winter. Nitrogen dressing is advisable only on poor soils. Organic mulching and early summer irrigation are highly beneficial. Fruit is produced from buds borne at the base of one-year-old shoots, and the objective is to form a goblet-shaped bush of 8–10 main branches on which fruiting spurs are carried. In the formative years, prune leading shoots to about half their length. On established bushes, laterals should be cut back to two or three buds each winter, with old less fruitful branches selectively removed. Trained forms should have spur growth encouraged by shortening laterals to one or two buds each winter; all current season growth should be shortened to five leaves during early summer. New plants can be established from hardwood cuttings, 12–15 in- (30–38 cm-) long, taken in fall or early winter, and from which all but the top 3 or 4 buds are removed. 'Jonkheer van Tets', 'Red Lake' and 'Stanza' are among well-liked cultivars of red currant which will provide some harvest succession; 'White Grape' is a notable cultivar of white currant.

Possible problems: birds, capsid bug, sawflies; gray mold, leaf spot.

red thread *(Laetisaria fuciformis)* a common disease of turf, especially where conditions of low fertility are

R

combined with hot weather; it is also known as PINK PATCH. RED FESCUE *(Festuca rubra)* and perennial rye-GRASS *(Lolium perenne)* are most often affected. Patches of diseased grass, up to 14 in (35 cm) in diameter, appear pink or red due to needlelike threads of fungus sticking out from the leaves. Nitrogen fertilizer applications can control the disease. See *lawns*.

Reflexed petals
The narrow, swept-back petals of *Dodecatheon meadia* f. *album* have given it its common name of shooting stars.

reel mower a cylinder mower.

reflexed abruptly deflexed at more than a 90° angle.

regular see *actinomorphic*.

regulated pruning a system of pruning involving thinning out and spacing branches and removing weak growth, mostly with a saw, without attention given to leaders, laterals or spurs. It is applied primarily to large vigorous apple trees, and sometimes referred to as saw pruning.

Rehderodendron (for Alfred Rehder [1863–1949], German botanist, dendrologist and gardener, and Greek *dendron*, tree). Styracaceae. S and W China. 9 species, deciduous shrubs or trees with serrulate leaves and white, 5-petalled flowers in axillary leafless panicles or racemes in spring. The fruit is a woody capsule. *R. macrocarpum* is a beautiful small tree, valued for its lemon-scented flowers in mid- to late spring; these are followed by bright red fruits, which resemble miniature coconuts. The glossy leaves often have attractive fall tints. Hardy to 14°F (−10°C). Plant in a sheltered position. Sow seed when ripe, in mid-summer; take semiripe cuttings, and root in a closed case with bottom heat. Otherwise, cultivate as for *Styrax*. *R. macrocarpum* W China; tree to 30 ft (9 m) flowers to 2 in (5 cm) in diameter, finely downy, fragrant, appearing before leaves.

Rehmannia (for Joseph Rehmann [1799–1831], German physician active in St. Petersburg). Gesneriaceae. China. 9 species, hairy perennial herbs with 2-lipped, tubular flowers in terminal racemes in spring and summer. Suitable for permanent outdoor cultivation, in the lightly shaded herbaceous border only where frosts are short-lived. In cooler zones they are best treated as half-hardy, overwintered in frost-free conditions. Alternatively, grow year-round in the alpine house in an open, humus-rich loam. Propagate from seed, root cuttings or cuttings of basal shoots. *R. elata* to 5 ft (1.5 m), usually smaller; leaves lobed, sometimes toothed; flowers 2¾–4 in (7–10 cm), bright rose-purple, throat yellow, spotted red; *R. glutinosa* to 12 in (30 cm), with sticky purple hairs; leaves obovate, coarsely toothed; flowers to 3 in (7.5 cm), red-brown to yellow, striped purple, lobes pale yellow.

Reinwardtia (for K.G.K. Reinwardt [1773–1822], director of the Botanic Garden, Leiden). Linaceae. N India, China. 2 species. *R. indica*, YELLOW FLAX, a glabrous, evergreen shrub or subshrub, to 36 in (90 cm). Produced in late spring and summer, the flowers are bright yellow, 1–2 in (2.5–5 cm) in diameter, broadly funnel-shaped to bowl-shaped and consist of five, rounded petals. Grow in full sun or bright filtered light; water plentifully and feed fortnightly when in full growth. Provide a minimum winter temperature of 45–50°F (7–10°C). Cut back after flowering. Propagate by seed or by softwood cuttings.

rejuvenation pruning the heading back of nonproductive branches on old fruit trees, which results in a mass of new shoots from which a new fruiting framework can be developed.

relative humidity the amount of water vapor present in the air expressed as a percentage of total saturation.

remontant plants that flower and/or fruit more than once during a growing season.

rendzina a very shallow, humus-rich soil overlying chalk or limestone.

renewal pruning a basic system of pruning apples and pears, carried out in order to ensure a successional supply of one-year-old (growth), two-year-old (bud) and three-year-old (fruiting) shoots, thereby restraining the tendency of most cultivars to produce too much fruit bud. On established trees, about one third of the number of one-year-old laterals is left uncut, and the remainder cut back to stubs or completely removed. Budding and fruiting laterals are either left uncut, cut back to stubs or removed completely, according to the balance of growth desired. Leaders are pruned lightly or heavily, depending on general vigor, and always with a view to providing major replacement shoots. See *pruning*.

reniform kidney-shaped in outline.

repand sinuate, with less pronounced undulations.

repellents materials intended to deter animals from attacking plants, while not killing or injuring them. Mechanical methods, especially those intended to repel birds, include devices such as scarecrows, distress-call recordings, mimic birds of prey, and explosives. Chemical repellents have limited use in the garden, except against birds and mammal pests. Lawn seed may be dressed to deter seed-eating birds and several substances are available to repel deer, rabbits, dogs and cats, although most remain effective only for relatively short periods.

replant disease a reduction in growth or yield, often with associated root lesions, seen when plants of the same species are replanted on the same site. In many cases, replant disease is associated with pathogenic soil fungi, for example *Pythium sylvaticum* in specific apple replant disease (SARD). It is also known as soil sickness. Roses are commonly affected and when required to replant on the same site it is advisable to change the soil wherever practicable; the removed soil may be used safely for nonrosaceous plants.

Reseda (from Latin *resedo*, to heal or calm: the Romans applied the plant to external bruises). Resedaceae. Mediterranean, E Africa, SW Asia to NW India. MIGNONETTE. 55 species, herbs, producing erect racemes crowded with small, often fragrant flowers in summer; the flowers are composed of four to eight, entire to cut petals and many stamens. *R. odorata* is valued for its intense, spicy fragrance. It is grown in the annual and cut-flower border (the flowers are remarkably long lived, persisting for many weeks in water in cool conditions) and as a pot plant for the cool greenhouse or conservatory in winter. Sow seed *in situ* in spring, or in fall where temperatures do not fall much below 14°F (–10°C); alternatively, sow in cellular trays and introduce young plants as plugs. For winter/early spring blooms under glass, make successional sowings at monthly intervals from late summer; sow several seeds in small pots, germinate at about 55°F (13°C) and thin to the strongest, potting on into a medium fertility, loam-based medium. Pinch to encourage bushy plants. Grow in full light and maintain good ventilation with a temperature range between 45–55°F (7–13°C); high temperatures will prevent flowering. *R. odorata* MIGNONETTE, SWEET RESEDA, BASTARD ROCKET; Mediterranean; annual, erect to ascending, to 32 in (80 cm); flowers white, sometimes tinged green or yellow or buff, intensely fragrant.

reserve border see *nursery bed*.

residual used of herbicides that persist in soil for some time after application and continue to kill germinating weeds.

resistance the ability of one organism to ward off the harmful effects of another; for example, some plant

species or cultivars may be resistant to disease infection because of thicker surface leaf cells, which prevent ready penetration of a fungus. Gum barriers and antibodies formed after infection may also help protect against disease. Certain tomato cultivars may be resistant to attack by root eelworm. These are important factors in reducing reliance on pesticides in the garden. Another context occurs when pests and diseases become resistant to a particular chemical control treatment; this points to the importance of using alternative substances from time to time. See *immunity*, *insecticides*.

respiration the breakdown of organic molecules in plant cells, during which process energy is released and carbon dioxide produced. It takes place following the absorption of oxygen by a plant cell. Respiration can proceed independent of light intensity. Diffusion of the gases involved occurs through stomata and lenticels.

resting period a period when a plant makes little or no growth, usually in response to environmental conditions of temperature, light or moisture. See *dormancy*, *quiescence*.

resupinate, resupine a leaf or flower inverted by a twisting of 180° of the petiole or stalk.

retaining wall a supporting wall between different levels of a terraced slope.

retarding the process of artificially delaying growth and/or flowering in plants. The retarding method most commonly used is that of storing at low temperature, as may be practiced with lifted stock of lily-of-the-valley, daffodils and flowering shrubs. It can also be achieved by mechanical means (e.g. deblossoming strawberries in order to encourage a later flush).

reticulate netted, i.e. with a closed or open network of anastomosing veins, ribs or coloring.

retrorse turned, curved or bent downward or backward, away from the apex; cf. *introrse*.

Reverted shoots
Variegated-leaved plants such as *Euonymus fortunei* 'Emerald Gaiety' occasionally produce green shoots, which should be cut out.

reversion (1) alteration in a plant's growth back to a less desirable form, as indicated by changes in color or other characteristics. It is commonly encountered in variegated clones where leaves or part of the plant are found to be wholly green or yellow, representing the nature of the plant from which the variegation is a sport or mutant. Such reverted shoots should be cut out. Suckering, seeding and virus infection sometimes produce forms that are mistaken for reverted forms, while circumstances of breeding occasionally result in the expression of normally recessive characteristics, which may be misinterpreted as true genetic reversion to an ancestral species; (2) a disease of black currants, affecting the size and shape of the leaves and causing a reduction in the number of flowers and therefore crop yield. It is caused by an unknown, graft-transmissible agent, which may be a mycoplasma-like organism, probably transmitted by the BLACK CURRANT GALL MITE (*Cecidophyopsis ribis*).

revolute with margins rolled under, i.e. toward the dorsal surface.

reworking changing the scion cultivar of a fruit tree by grafting onto existing branches. See *frame-working*, *grafting*, *top working*.

Rhamnus from the Greek name for the genus, *Rhamnos*). Rhamnaceae. Widely distributed in northern temperate areas, with a few species in E and South Africa and Brazil. BUCKTHORN. 150 species, deciduous or evergreen trees or shrubs. Produced in summer, the small, yellow-green flowers are followed by small berries, red at first and ripening black. Fully hardy, the following will thrive on most fertile soils in full sun, but benefit from some protection from harsh winds. Prune in late winter/early spring only to remove dead and overcrowded wood. Propagate by seed, stratified for 60–90 days at 41°F (5°C) and sown in spring, by semiripe cuttings or by simple layering.

R. alaternus S Portugal to N Africa and SE Russia; evergreen shrub, 3¼–16 ft (1–5 m); leaves 1¼–2¾ in (3–7 cm), ovate to elliptic, coriaceous, more or less serrate, glabrous; 'Argenteovariegata': leaves elliptic to oblong-lanceolate with broad creamy-white margins on leaden green; *R. imeretina* E Turkey, Georgia, Armenia; deciduous shrub, 6½–13 ft (2–4 m); leaves 3–10 in (8–25 cm), elliptic to broadly lanceolate, finely toothed, glabrous and dull green above, pale, velvety beneath, bronze-purple in fall.

Rhaphidophora (from Greek *raphis*, needle, and *phora*, to bear; the cells contain raphides.) (Sometimes spelt *Raphidophora*). Araceae. SE Asia. 70 species, evergreen climbers or creepers intermediate in appearance between the smaller *Monstera* species and *Philodendron*. Cultivate as for the climbing *Philodendron* species and cultivars. *R. celatocaulis* (syn. *Pothos celatocaulis*); SHINGLE PLANT; Borneo; tall climber; leaves of juvenile plants 3⅓–4 in (8.5–10 cm) in 2 ranks, closely adpressed to substrate, overlapping and obscuring stem, entire, elliptic to ovate, coriaceous, blue-green; adult leaves to 16 in (40 cm), entire, pinnatifid or pinnatisect, occasionally perforate.

Rhaphiolepis (from Greek *rhaphis*, needle and *lepis*, scale, referring to the extremely narrow persistent bracteoles on the inflorescence). Rosaceae. Subtropical E Asia. Some 15 species, evergreen shrubs or small trees with tough, glossy dark green leaves. Produced mostly in spring and summer in terminal racemes or panicles, the flowers resemble apple blossoms and consist of five obovate petals and numerous

stamens. They are followed by small, subglobose pomes, often black or purple-black. Hardy to 5°F (–15°C). Grow in a warm sheltered position in full sun. Prune if necessary, after flowering. Propagate by semiripe cuttings, layering, or seed.

R. × *delacourii* (*R. indica* × *R. umbellata*); garden origin; to 6½ ft (2 m); flowers to ¾ in (1.8 cm) in diameter, rose-pink; includes 'Coates' Crimson', with crimson flowers, 'Enchantress', dwarf, with small, rose flowers in late winter-early summer, and 'Majestic Beauty', with large, dark green leaves and milky pink, scented flowers, in clusters to 10 in (25 cm) across; *R. indica* S China; to 3¼ ft (1 m); flowers to ⅝ in (1.6 cm) in diameter, white tinted pale pink toward center, stamens bright red-pink; cultivars include 'Charisma', small tightly branched, with double, soft pink, abundant flowers in late winter–spring, 'Indian Princess', broadly mounding, compact, with bright pink flowers fading to white, in broad clusters, in spring, 'Rosea', with deep pink flowers, 'Snow White', with white flowers in early spring, and 'Springtime', compact, vigorous, with new growth flushed pink-brown and broad, candy pink flowers; *R. umbellata* Japan, Korea; flowers fragrant to ¾ in (2 cm) in diameter, white, stamens bright pink-red; 'Minor': dwarf, small, white, scented flowers, in early spring.

Rhapis (from Greek *rhaphis*, needle, probably referring to the narrow leaf segments). Palmae. China, Japan. LADY PALM. 12 species, small to medium-sized palms. Ultimately, they make a clump of slender, canelike stems, clothed in their upper portions with the remains of fibrous leaf sheaths. The leaves are palmate, dark green and slender-stalked, the leaflets fingerlike, ribbed and folded. Suitable for pot and tub cultivation in the home, greenhouse or conservatory (minimum temperature 50°F/10°C). Plant in a fast-draining, loamy medium, rich in leaf mold. Water, syringe and feed generously in warm conditions. Shade from direct sunlight. Propagate by seed, suckers or division.

R. excelsa (syn. *R. flabelliformis*); GROUND RATTAN, BAMBOO PALM, LADY PALM, MINIATURE FAN PALM, FERN

RHAPIS; probably originally from China but introduced from Japan; stem to 16 ft (5 m); leaf segments 3–10, 8–12 in (20–30 cm) × ⅗ (1.5 cm), tips truncate; includes 'Variegata', with leaves striped ivory to white; many other variegated forms are cultivated and highly prized, particularly in Japan; *R. humilis* REED RHAPIS, SLENDER LADY PALM; S China; differs from *R. excelsa* in leaf segments numbering at least 9, and 6–7 in (15–18 cm) × to ¾ in (2 cm), with more acuminate tips.

rheophyte a plant that grows in running water.

Rheum (from Greek *rheon*, rhubarb). Polygonaceae. Asia. RHUBARB. 50 species, deciduous perennial herbs with tough or woody rhizomes. Produced in basal clumps, the leaves are large and sinuately toothed to palmately lobed, their stalks often thick and differently colored to the leaf blades. Small flowers are massed amid large bracts on tall panicles in late spring and early summer. Impressive specimens for focal plantings in moist borders, at the woodland edge, bog gardens and the margins of pools and streams. Hardy to about 5°F (–15°C). Grow in sun to part shade in humus-rich, moisture-retentive soils. Propagate by division in spring, cutting through the tough fleshy rootstock with a sharp knife or spade. Alternatively, sow seed in fall in the shaded cold frame. *R.* × *hybridum*, RHUBARB (q.v.) is cultivated for its edible leaf stalks.

R. alexandrae W China, Tibet; to 5 ft (1.5 m); leaves to 9 × 5 in (22 × 13 cm), ovate to oblong, base cordate, entire, dark green in neat rosettes, glabrous, petiole slender; inflorescence bracts, yellow-green, subcordate, flowers green-yellow; *R. nobile* SIKKIM RHUBARB; Nepal to SE Tibet; to 6½ ft (2 m); leaves to 12 in (30 cm) in diameter, rounded, base cuneate to rounded, glossy, leathery, dark green veined red, entire, edged red, petiole stout, red; inflorescence bracts cream; flowers green; *R. palmatum* NW China; to 5 ft (1.5 m); leaves 20–36 in (50–90 cm) × 20–28 in (50–70 cm), more or less rounded, palmately lobed, toothed; inflorescence bracts tinted pink to bronze-red, flowers brick red to deep red; includes various forms with leaves deeply and sharply to broadly cut, many flushed bronze-red at first, later coppery olive; two popular forms are 'Atrosanguineum', the whole of which is suffused blood-red, later bronze-red, and *rubrum*, with leaves flushed dark maroon-red when young.

Rhipsalis (from Greek *rhips*, wicker-work, and *-alis*, alluding to the very slender stems). Cactaceae. Tropical America, with one species extending to tropical Africa, Madagascar and Sri Lanka. Up to 50 species, epiphytic or lithophytic cacti. The stems are cylindric, ribbed, angled, winged or flat. They are usually pendulous and segmented, lacking spines and with the younger segments arising singly or in whorls. The flowers are small, rotate and usually white; they are followed by berrylike fruit. Grow in an intermediate greenhouse (minimum temperature 50°F/10°C). Plant in an acidic medium rich in coarse bark and perlite. Shade in summer. Maintain high humidity. Reduce watering in winter. Increase by stem cuttings.

R. baccifera tropical America, Africa, Madagascar, Ceylon; stems cylindric, pendent, $3\frac{1}{4}$–13 ft (1–4 m), $\frac{1}{8}$–$\frac{1}{4}$ in (4–6 mm) in diameter; fruit white or pink; *R. gracilis* E Brazil; stems 4–12 in (10–30 cm) long, $\frac{1}{16}$–$\frac{1}{8}$ in (1–3 mm) in diameter; fruit white to deep red.

rhizoid a structure resembling a root in appearance and function, as found in *Selaginella*.

Rhizome (Zingiber)

rhizome a specialized stem, slender or swollen, branching or simple, subterranean or lying close to the soil surface (except in epiphytes), and producing roots, stems, leaves and inflorescences along its length and at its apex. Rhizomes are common to many perennial herbs.

rhizomorph a rootlike aggregation of fungal threads, or hyphae, often referred to as a 'bootlace' or 'shoe-string', of *Armillaria* species, by means of which the fungus survives and spreads. See *armillaria root rot*.

rhizosphere the zone of soil immediately surrounding plant roots.

Rhodanthe (from Greek *rhodon*, rose, and *anthos*, flower, in reference to the plumose pappus). Compositae. Australia, South Africa. STRAWFLOWER, EVERLASTING. About 50 species, annual or perennial herbs or shrubs, more or less covered in white hairs. Papery, daisylike flower heads appear in summer and dry well. Cultivate as for *Helichrysum bracteatum*. *R. splendidum* SHOWY SUNRAY, SPLENDID EVERLASTING, SILKY-WHITE EVERLASTING; West Australia; tufted annual to 20 in (50 cm); leaves linear, gray-green; flower heads to $2\frac{1}{2}$ in (6 cm) in diameter, phyllaries cream-white, often with a purple band.

Rhodanthemum (from Greek, *rhodo-*, red and *anthemon*, flower). Compositae. N Africa. 5 species. semi-hardy perennial, evergreen subshrubs or tufted, woody-based herbs, usually with silver, finely divided leaves and long-stalked daisylike flower heads in summer. Hardy to 0°F (−18°C), if planted in a sheltered, warm site and protected from winter wet; grow in full sun in free-draining, gritty soil. Propagate by semiripe cuttings in summer. *R. hosmariense* (syn. *Chrysanthemopsis hosmariensis*, *Chrysanthemum hosmariense*, *Leucanthemopsis hosmariensis*); Morocco; low subshrub to 12 × 20 in (30 × 50 cm); leaves finely-divided, silver-gray, flower heads to $1\frac{1}{2}$ in (4 cm), ray florets white and disk florets yellow; *R. maresii* (syn. *Chrysanthemopsis maresii*); Algeria; woody-based, bushy herb or subshrub to 12 in (30 cm) tall, with silver-gray, finely dissected or simple leaves and yellow flower heads ultimately tinged purple to purple-black.

Rhodiola (from Greek *rhodon*, rose, referring to the rose-scented roots of the type species). Crassulaceae. Himalaya, NW China, C Asia, N America, Europe. Around 50 species, perennial herbs with thick, fleshy and scaly rhizomes. The flowering stems arise annually bearing fleshy leaves. Produced in late spring and summer in terminal heads, the small flowers consist of four or five petals and twice as many rather longer stamens. The following species is very hardy and favors a fast-draining position in full sun. It grows well in a rock garden and in wall crevices. Propagation as for *Sedum*. *R. rosea* (syn. *Sedum rosea*); ROSE-ROOT; Northern Hemisphere; 2–12 in (5–30 cm); leaves $\frac{1}{2}$–$1\frac{1}{2}$ in (1–4 cm), glaucous, gray-green, oblong, apex obtuse to acuminate, entire or toothed, often tinged red, base round or slightly cordate; flowers green-yellow, anthers deep yellow to copper.

Rhodochiton (from Greek *rhodon*, rose, and *chiton*, cloak, referring to the large, rosy calyx). Scrophulariaceae. Mexico. Some 3 species, perennial, climbing herbs with pendulous solitary flowers in summer; these have a decorative umbrella-like calyx and a tubular corolla with five, blunt lobes. In cold areas, it may be grown outdoors as an annual (sometimes surviving as a herbaceous perennial in favored situations) or treated as a perennial in cool greenhouses or conservatories. Grow in a sunny, sheltered spot, in rich, well-drained soil. Provide support while plants are still very young. Under glass, water plentifully during the growing season, sparingly in winter, and give a minimum temperature of 41°F (5°C); ventilate freely and shade from direct summer sun. Cut back and re-pot in spring. Sow seed under glass in early spring or as soon as ripe. *R. atrosanguineum* to 20 ft (6 m), slender-stemmed; calyx to $1\frac{1}{4}$ in (3 cm) in diameter, 5-lobed, shallowly-campanulate, rose-pink or mauve, corolla dark blood-red to maroon-black, to $2\frac{1}{2}$ in (6.5 cm), minutely hairy, anthers ash-white.

Rhododendron (the Ancient Greek name for the unrelated rose-flowered oleander, *Nerium oleander*, from *rhodon*, rose and *dendron*, tree). Ericaceae.

R

Rhododendron 'Inga'
This Indian azalea is one of the evergreen rhododendron hybrids, which can be grown in containers under protection or as houseplants.

Cosmopolitan. Some 800 species, trees and shrubs, evergreen or deciduous with simple leaves. Produced in racemes in spring and summer, the flowers are tubular, funnel-shaped or campanulate with 5, more or less spreading lobes.

Species listed are hardy to 0°F (–18°C), but prefer a mild and sheltered site. Plant in dappled sun or light shade in fertile, humus-rich and acidic to neutral soil. Ensure that the root-run is cool and moist, especially in summer. Prune only to keep within bounds (after flowering), or to remove dead or exhausted growth (in early spring). Increase by layering, grafting, or semiripe cuttings in a case in late summer. Affected by powdery mildew, honey fungus, phytophthora root rot, rusts and chlorosis (caused by poor drainage and unsuitable soil pH). Attacked by rodents, weevils and leatherjackets.

Several of the small, evergreen hybrids and cultivars popularly known as azaleas grow well in containers in the cool greenhouse. They can be brought indoors at flowering time. In addition to the species listed opposite, hundreds of hybrids and cultivars have been named. Varying greatly in size and shape, the flowers range in color from pure white to cream, yellow, gold, apricot, salmon, rose, deep pink, cerise, crimson, magenta, mauve, lilac, scarlet, orange and coral red, often spotted, stained or suffused a different color. (*See table facing page.*)

Rhodohypoxis (from Greek *rhodon*, rose, and *Hypoxis*). Hypoxidaceae. SE Africa. 6 species, small perennial herbs with fibrous and fleshy roots and hairy, grasslike leaves in a basal clump. Produced in spring and summer on slender stalks, the solitary flowers consist of a short tube and six, spreading, oblong to obovate lobes. Plant in peaty pockets in the rock garden, or in sinks and troughs. Although hardy to at least 23°F (–5°C), *Rhodohypoxis* is intolerant of winter wet. When grown outside, protect in winter with a propped pane of glass. Otherwise, keep in the alpine house or bulb frame. Grow in sun in a free-draining, acidic to neutral medium, with additional sharp sand and leaf mold; water plentifully when in growth, avoiding the foliage; keep almost completely dry in winter. Propagate by offsets, by division of established clumps, or by seed. *R. baurii* RED STAR; leaves to 6 in (15 cm), usually shorter, flowers 1–2, white, pink or red, to 1½ in (4 cm) diam., lobes hairy.

Rhodothamnus (from Greek *rhodon*, rose, and *thamnos*, a shrub). Ericaceae. E Alps. 1 species, *R. chamaecistus*, an evergreen, dwarf shrub to 16 in (40 cm). The leaves are ¼–⅜ in (0.5–1.5 cm) long, elliptic to oblanceolate, leathery and dark green. Produced in late spring and summer, the flowers are ¾–1¼ in (2–3 cm) in diameter, rose pink, with five spreading lobes and slender stamens tipped with purple-red anthers. For the rock or peat garden; hardy to 5°F (–15°C). Plant in sun or part shade in moist, humus-rich, acidic soils with a cool root run. Propagate from seed, by careful layering, or by semiripe cuttings in late summer.

Rhodotypos (from Greek *rhodon*, rose, and *typos*, type, referring to its resemblance to a rose). Rosaceae. China, Japan. 1 species, *R. scandens*, a spreading, deciduous shrub to 16 ft (5 m). Up to 2½ in (6 cm) long, the leaves are ovate, acuminate, sharply serrate with corrugated veins. Produced in spring and summer, the flowers are solitary, white, to 1½ in (4 cm) in diameter and composed of four, spreading, rounded petals and numerous stamens. They are followed by shiny black berries. Suitable for a border and woodland gardens or other informal plantings. It will tolerate a wide range of soil conditions, shade, and temperatures as low as –4°F (–20°C). For best results, grow in dappled shade in well-drained, moisture-retentive soil. Thin out old flowered shoots to ground level. Propagate by seed sown in fall, or by softwood or semiripe cuttings in a closed case with bottom heat.

Rhoicissus (from Greek *rhoia*, pomegranate, and *Cissus*). Vitaceae. Tropical and southern Africa. 12 species, more or less woody vines climbing by tendrils. The leaves are simple or 3-foliolate, rarely digitately 5-foliolate. Inconspicuous flowers are produced in axillary cymes and followed by small, grapelike fruit. The following species is a useful house or conservatory plant, grown for its attractive, leathery foliage. Cultivate as for the more resilient *Cissus* species, with a minimum temperature of 45°F (7°C). *R. capensis* (syn. *Cissus capensis*, *Vitis capensis*); South Africa; tuberous-rooted evergreen vine; leaves simple, orbicular to reniform, broadly cordate at base, obtuse at apex, bluntly 5-angled, toothed, 3–8 in (8–20 cm) across, leathery, rusty-tomentose when young; fruit very dark red tinged black, glossy.

rhomboid of leaves and tepals, diamond-shaped, angularly oval, the base and apex forming acute angles, and both sides forming obtuse angles.

Rhombophyllum (from Greek *rhombos*, lozenge, and *phyllon*, leaf, referring to the leaf shape). Aizoaceae. South Africa (Cape Province). 3 species, compact succulent perennials, sometimes small shrubs. The leaves are more or less united at the base and semicylindric, keeled below, with the underside pulled forward and chinlike. Their margins are entire or with 1–2 short teeth. The surface is smooth, more or less glossy and deep green with pale translucent dots. Golden-yellow, daisylike flowers are produced a few per stalk from summer to fall. Cultivate as for *Pleiospilos*.

R. rhomboideum leaves 4–5 pairs resting on soil, 1–2 in (2.5–5 cm) × ½–¾ in (1–2 cm), rhombic above, dark gray-green with white dots and pale margins.

R

RHODODENDRON

Name	Distribution	Habit	Leaves	Flowers
R. aberconwayi	SW China	evergreen, to 6½ ft (2 m)	1¼–2½ in (3–6 cm), thick, elliptic	1–1½ in (2.8–3.5 cm), open-campanulate, white to pale rose with purple spots
Comments: 'His Lordship': flowers white with crimson streaks.				
R. albrechtii	Japan	deciduous, to 6½ ft (2 m)	1½–4¾ in (4–12 cm), obovate, ciliate, finely toothed, densely gray-tomentose beneath	to 2 in (5 cm), open-campanulate, red-purple
Comments: 'Michael McLaren': flowers purple, spotted with yellow-green.				
R. arboreum	Himalaya, China to Thailand, S India and Sri Lanka	evergreen tree to 165 ft (50 m)	2½–7½ in (6.5–19 cm), broadly oblong-lanceolate, glabrous and wrinkled above, densely hairy beneath	1¼–2 in (3–5 cm), tubular-campanulate, fleshy, pink to deep crimson or rarely white, often with dark spots
Comments: ssp. *arboreum*: leaves 3–7½ in (8–19 cm), with silvery or white hairs beneath. 'Goat Fell': flowers cherry red with some spots in throat. 'Rubaiyat': flowers red with darker spots. ssp. *cinnamomeum* var. *cinnamomeum*: leaves with off-white or fawn hairs beneath; flowers pink to red, rarely white. 'Sir Charles Lemon': flowers creamy white; leaves dark green above with bright orange-brown hairs beneath. var. *roseum*: similar to var. *cinnamomeum*, but leaves with a 1-layered, fawn to off-white compacted indumentum, flowers tinged red. 'Tony Schilling': flowers deep pink with darker spots. ssp. *delavayi*: leaves 2¾–6 in (7–15.5 cm), off-white to fawn—hairy beneath; flowers red.				
R. argyrophyllum	SW China	evergreen, spreading, to 39 ft (12 m)	¾–2½ in (1.8–6 cm), elliptic to oblanceolate, glabrous above, with thin, silvery to fawn hairs beneath.	1¼–2⅛ in (3–5.5 cm), funnelform-campanulate or open-campanulate, white to pale pink with purple spots
Comments: subsp. *hypoglaucum* 'Heane Wood': flowers white, flushed and spotted with purple, opening from pink buds				
R. augustinii	China	evergreen, bushy shrub or small tree to 33 ft (10 m)	narrowly elliptic to elliptic, usually evergreen, 1½–4½ in (4–11 cm), glabrous above, golden scaly beneath	1–1½ in (2.8–4 cm), openly funnel-shaped, purple, lavender or almost blue, rarely white, with greenish or brownish spots inside
Comments: Electra Group: flowers large, deep blue. 'Tower Court Form': flowers large, lavender-blue, veined red. ssp. *augustinii*: leaves mostly evergreen; flowers lavender to blue. ssp. *chasmanthum*: leaves mostly evergreen; flowers lavender to blue. Exbury form: flowers blue-purple with some yellow spots.				
R. auriculatum	W China	evergreen shrub or tree to 20 ft (6 m)	6–12 in (15–30 cm), oblong-oblanceolate, base auriculate, margin fringed with small glands, villous and glandular beneath	3–4½ in (8–11 cm), fragrant, funnel-shaped, white or cream to pink, tinged green at the base
R. barbatum	Himalaya	evergreen shrub or tree to 20 ft (6 m)	3½–7½ in (9–19 cm), elliptic to obovate, glabrous above, with scattered hairs and glands beneath	1¼–1½ in (3–3.5 cm), fleshy, tubular-campanulate, crimson to blood-red or, rarely, pure white
R. calendulaceum FLAME AZALEA	SE US	much-branched, deciduous shrub to 10 ft (3 m)	1½–3½ in (3.5–9 cm), elliptic to broadly elliptic or ovate-oblong, finely pubescent above, more densely so beneath	to 2 in (5 cm), funnel-shaped, exterior pubescent, orange, red or yellow, more rarely pink

R

R. arboreum

R. argyrophyllum

R. augustinii

R. calendulaceum

RHODODENDRON

Name	Distribution	Habit	Leaves	Flowers
R. calophytum	SW China	evergreen tree to 39 ft (12 m)	5½–12 in (14–30 cm), oblong-oblanceolate, glabrous when mature	1½–2½ in (4–6 cm), open-campanulate, glabrous, pink-white with purple spots and a basal blotch
R. calostrotum	NE India, N Burma, W China	evergreen, low to prostrate, matted or erect shrub, 2–60 in (5–150 cm)	½–1⅓ in (1–3.3 cm), oblong-ovate to almost circular, upper surface usually matt with persistent, dried-out scales, margins bristly, lower surface with dense overlapping scales	¾–1⅛ in (1.8–2.8 cm), magenta, rarely pink or purple, often with darker spots on the upper lobes, exterior hairy and occasionally scaly

Comments: 'Gigha': compact, very free-flowering flowers, large, rosy-crimson. Rock's form: flowers large, blue-purple; foliage purple-tinged. Calciphilum Group: leaves smaller, flowers pink. Nitens Group: pink-purple flowers in June-July, later than other cultivars.

R. catawbiense	E US	evergreen shrub to 10 ft (3 m)	2½–4½ in (6.5–11.5 cm), broadly elliptic to obovate, glabrous when mature	1¼–1¾ in (3–4.5 cm), funnelform to campanulate, usually lilac-purple with faint spots

Comments: 'Catawbiense Album': flowers large, white, opening from lilac buds. 'English Roseum': flowers bright pink, faintly tinged with lilac. 'Lavender Queen': flowers pale lavender. 'Lee's Dark Purple': flowers deep purple. 'Powell Glass': flowers pure white. 'Roseum Elegans': flowers purple-pink. Some of the above forms, heat-resistant and widely grown in the United States, may be hybrids.

R. cinnabarinum	Himalaya to N Burma	evergreen straggling shrub to 23 ft (7 m)	1¼–3½ in (3–9 cm), broadly to narrowly elliptic, scaly or scaleless above, with fleshy scales beneath often tinged red or purple	1–1½ in (2.5–3.5 cm), tubula to campanulate, yellow, orange, red, red and yellow or purple, usually with a waxy bloom

Comments: 'Aestivale': a late-flowering form (July in Great Brita in) with narrow leaves. 'Nepal': flowers red at base, yellow toward margin. Blandfordiiflorum Group: flowers narrowly tubular, red on outside, yellow, apricot or green inside; late-flowering, hardy. Roylei Group: flowers rose-red to purple-red, relatively open; leaves glaucous blue-green. 'Magnificum': flowers large, red-purple tinged with orange. 'Vin Rosé': flowers red with a waxy bloom. ssp. *xanthocodon*: flowers campanulate, yellow, orange, orange with a purple flush or purple. Concatenans Group: flowers campanulate, apricot to coral; leaves glaucous-white beneath, blue-green above. 'Copper': flowers coral-red flushed with orange and red. Purpurellum Group: flowers pale pink-purple, broadly funnel-shaped. *R. cinnabarinum* has been widely used in hybridization; some of the hybrids, previously thought to be interspecific, are now within the species, e.g. 'Conroy' (*R. cinnabarinum* ssp. *cinnabarinum* 'Roylei' × ssp. *xanthocodon*); others involve other species, e.g. Cinnkeys Group (× *R. keysii*); Royal Flush Group and 'Rose Mangles' (both × *R. maddenii* ssp. *maddenii*) and 'Yunncinn' (× *R. yunnanense*).

R. dauricum	E Siberia, Mongolia, N China, Japan	straggling, semievergreen shrub to 5 ft (1.5 m)	leathery, densely scaly beneath, ½–1½ in (1–3.5 cm), elliptic.	½–¾ in (1.4–2 cm), pink or violet-pink

Comments: 'Arctic Pearl': flowers white. 'Hokkaido': flowers large, white, later-flowering. 'Midwinter': flowers bright rose-purple. Sometimes split into 3 species: *R. dauricum*—leaves dark green above, rusty brown beneath, most overwintering. *R. ledebourii*—leaves pale above and beneath, mostly falling in fall, with a few scales on the upper surface; *R. sichotense*—leaves without scales on the upper surface.

R. davidsonianum	W China	evergreen shrub to 16 ft (5 m)	1¼–2½ in (3–6.5 cm), often V-shaped in section, lower surface covered in small brown scales	1 in (2.3–2.7 cm), pink, pink-lavender or lavender

Comments: 'Caerhays Blotched': flowers pale pink with darker spots.

R. calophytum

R. cinnabarinum subsp. *xanthocodon*

R. decorum

RHODODENDRON

Name	Distribution	Habit	Leaves	Flowers
R. decorum	W China, NE Burma, Laos	evergreen shrub or small tree to 20 ft (6 m).	2½–8 in (6–20 cm), oblanceolate to elliptic, glabrous when mature with punctate hair bases beneath	1¾–4½ in (4.5–11 cm), funnelform-campanulate, sparsely glandular outside, densely so within, white to pale pink, with or without green or crimson spots

Comments: ssp. *decorum*: flowers 1½–2½ in (4–6.5 cm), and leaves to 4¾ in (12 cm). 'Cox's Uranium Green': flowers chartreuse green. ssp. *diaprepes*: leaves and flowers larger. 'Gargantua': flowers very large, white, flushed green below.

Name	Distribution	Habit	Leaves	Flowers
R. degronianum	Japan	evergreen shrub to 8 ft (2.5 m)	3–5½ in (8–14 cm), elliptic to oblanceolate, with dense gray to fawn hairs beneath	1¼–1¾ in (3–4.5 cm), widely funnelform-campanulate, pink with conspicuous darker spots

Comments: 'Gerald Loder': flowers white, spotted and flushed with red-purple. ssp. *yakushimanum* see *R. yakushimanum*.

Name	Distribution	Habit	Leaves	Flowers
R. fortunei	China	evergreen shrub or tree to 33 ft (10 m)	3–7 in (8–18 cm), broadly oblanceolate to obovate, glabrous when mature except for persistent hair-bases beneath	2⅛–2¾ in (5.5–7 cm), open-campanulate or funnelform-campanulate, pale pink to almost pure white, exterior glandular or glabrous

Comments: 'John R. Elcock': flowers purple-pink, yellow in throat. 'Sir Charles Butler': flowers pink. ssp. *discolor*: syn. *R. discolor*; leaves oblanceolate; flowers fragrant, pink, funnelform.

Name	Distribution	Habit	Leaves	Flowers
R. fulvum	W China, NE Burma	evergreen shrub or small tree to 26 ft (8 m)	3–9 in (8–22 cm), oblanceolate to elliptic, glabrous above when mature, velvety brown-hairy beneath, appearing granular	1–1¾ in (2.5–4.5 cm), campanulate, white to pink usually with a dark basal blotch, with or without crimson spots

Name	Distribution	Habit	Leaves	Flowers
R. glaucophyllum	Himalaya, W China	shrub to 5 ft (1.5 m)	1½–2½ in (3.5–6 cm), elliptic, upper surface dark brown-green, lower surface white, with pale and dark scales	¾–1¼ in (1.8–3.2 cm), tubular to campanulate, pink or white flushed with pink, scaly outside

Comments: Plants grown under the name *R. shweliense* are usually this species. 'Branklyn': flowers pale pink, bell-shaped. 'Prostratum': low-growing.

Name	Distribution	Habit	Leaves	Flowers
R. glischrum	W China, NE Burma	shrub or small tree to 26 ft (8 m)	4½–12 in (11–30 cm), obovate to elliptic, ciliate, upper surface smooth to wrinkled, with some glandular bristles, lower surface with a dense covering of bristles sometimes also with a thin brown covering of hairs	1¼–2 in (3–5 cm), campanulate, pink to scarlet or occasionally white flushed pink, with purple spots and usually also a basal blotch

Comments: 'Frank Kingdon Ward': flowers purple-pink, spotted purple.

Name	Distribution	Habit	Leaves	Flowers
R. hippophaeoides	W China	erect, evergreen openly branched shrub to 4 ft (1.2 m)	¼–½ in (5–12 mm), narrowly elliptic, oblong or narrowly obovate, aromatic, gray-green above, yellow-green or gray-green with numerous scales beneath	broadly funnel-shaped, pale lavender to deep purple, rarely white

Comments: 'Haba-shan' syn. 'Bei-ma-shan': tall, flowers lavender blue in large trusses.

R. fulvum

R. kaempferi

R. kiusianum

R. lutescens

RHODODENDRON

Name	Distribution	Habit	Leaves	Flowers
R. impeditum	W China	compact, much-branched, evergreen shrub to 3¼ ft (1 m)	⅛–½ in (4–14 mm), aromatic, lower surface pale gray-green speckled with brown or more uniformly brown	⅜–⅝ in (8–15 mm), broadly funnel-shaped, violet to purple, rarely lavender

Comments: Parent of a number of low, blue-flowered hybrids, e.g. Blue Tit Group (× *R. augustinii*).

Name	Distribution	Habit	Leaves	Flowers
R. kaempferi	Japan	semievergreen shrub to 10 ft (3 m)	½–2 in (1–5 cm), entire, strigose	¾–1¼ in (2–3 cm), funnel-shaped, pink or red

Comments: Very similar to *R. indicum*, but with broader leaves. 'Mikado': flowers red with darker spotting in throat.

Name	Distribution	Habit	Leaves	Flowers
R. kiusianum	Japan	semievergreen to deciduous, dwarf shrub to 3¼ ft (1 m)	¼–¾ in (0.5–2 cm), obovate, red-brown strigose	⅝–¾ in (1.5–2 cm), funnel-shaped, usually rose-pink, occasionally purple

Comments: The Obtusum Group of cultivars and the Kurume Azaleas had their origin in this species and its hybrids with *R. kaempferi*. 'Album': flowers white. 'Benichidori': flowers salmon orange. 'Betty Muir': flowers bright pink. 'Chidori': flowers white. 'Hanejiro': flowers white. 'Harunokikari': flowers lavender-blue. 'Harusame': flowers bright pink. 'Hillier's Pink': flowers pink. "Komokul-shan": flowers pale pink, tipped rose pink. 'Muraski Shikibu': flowers hose-in-hose, red-purple.

Name	Distribution	Habit	Leaves	Flowers
R. lacteum	W China	shrub or small tree to 25 ft (7.5 m)	3–6½ in (8–17 cm), elliptic to obovate, with gray-brown hairs beneath	1½–2 in (4–5 cm), widely campanulate, pure yellow, without spots through sometimes with a purple basal blotch

Comments: 'Blackhills': flowers clear yellow, unmarked.

Name	Distribution	Habit	Leaves	Flowers
R. lutescens	W China	semievergreen, straggling shrub to 20 ft (6 m)	2–3½ in (5–9 cm), lanceolate to oblong, bronze-red at first, variably scaly above, with golden scales beneath	¾–1 in (1.8–2.5 cm), pale yellow with green spots in the inside of the upper lobes, funnel-shaped

Comments: Flowers in late winter and early spring. 'Bagshot Sands': hardy and free-flowering; flowers primrose yellow with darker spots. 'Exbury': flowers clear lemon yellow; new growth red, fairly tender.

Name	Distribution	Habit	Leaves	Flowers
R. luteum	E Europe to Caucasus	deciduous shrub to 13 ft (4 m)	2–4 in (5–10 cm), oblong to lanceolate, sticky with adpressed bristles	to 1½ in (3.5 cm), funnel-shaped, yellow, fragrant, exterior glandular-sticky
R. macabeanum	NE India	evergreen tree to 50 ft (15 m)	5½–10 in (14–25 cm), broadly ovate to broadly elliptic, glabrous above when mature, with dense woolly hairs beneath	to 2 in (5 cm), tubular-campanulate, lemon yellow with a purple blotch at the base
R. mallotum	W China, NE Burma	evergreen shrub or small tree to 21 ft (6.5 m)	4–5 in (10–13 cm), broadly oblanceolate to obovate, glabrous above, with dense, red, woolly hairs beneath	1½–1¾ in (4–4.5 cm), fleshy, tubular-campanulate, crimson

R. luteum

R. occidentale

R. orbiculare

RHODODENDRON

Name	Distribution	Habit	Leaves	Flowers
R. maximum	EN America	shrub or small tree to 11½ ft (3.5 m)	4–6 in (10–16 cm), oblanceolate to elliptic, glabrous above, thinly hairy beneath	1–1¼ in (2.5–3 cm), campanulate, white to pink-purple, with yellow-green spots

Comments: 'Summertime': flowers white, flushed red-purple at tips; yellow-green spots in throat.

R. moupinense	W China	evergreen, compact shrub to 3¼ ft (1 m)	1¼–1½ in (3–4 cm), narrowly ovate, elliptic or obovate, green or tinged brown beneath with dense scales, margins bristly	1¼–1½ in (3–4 cm), white, often flushed pink and with dark red spots on the upper part of the tube inside

Comments: Cilpinense Group, hybrids between *R. moupinense* and *R. ciliatum*, are semievergreen, compact shrubs to 5 ft (1.5 m) tall with pink flowers produced in early spring.

R. occidentale	W US	deciduous shrub to 10 ft (3 m)	1¼–3½ in (3–9 cm), elliptic to oblong-lanceolate, ciliate, thinly pubescent	1½–2 in (3.5–5 cm), funnel-shaped, white or sometimes pink, with a yellow blotch, glandular-hairy outside

Comments: 'Crescent City Double': flowers semidouble, cream flushed with apricot. 'Humboldt Picotee': flowers white, edged with rose carmine. 'Leonard Frisbee': flowers white with broad, frilly petals with pink midline, upper petal with yellow flare. 'Miniskirt': dwarf; flowers white, very small, with long red style. 'Stagecoach Frills': flowers frilly, white flushed with pink, with orange-yellow flare.

R. orbiculare	W China	evergreen shrub or tree to 50 ft (15 m)	2¾–5 in (7–12.5 cm), orbicular to ovate, glabrous	1½ in (3.5–4 cm), campanulate, rose-pink

R. oreotrephes	W China	evergreen shrub to 26 ft (8 m)	¾–3 in (2–8 cm), mostly evergreen, circular to elliptic or oblong, blunt, lower surface with dense purple, red-brown or gray scales	1–1⅓ in (2.5–3.4 cm), rose to rose-lavender

Comments: Exquisetum Group: flowers pale mauve-pink spotted red. 'James's White Form': flowers white.

R. ponticum	W and E Mediterranean, widely naturalized in Britain	evergreen shrub to 26 ft (8 m), young shoots glabrous	2½–7 in (6–18 cm), oblanceolate to broadly elliptic, glabrous when mature	1½–2 in (3.5–5 cm), campanulate, lilac-pink to purple, usually with green-yellow spots

Comments: 'Aucubifolium': leaves spotted yellow. 'Cheiranthifolium': leaves very narrow, undulate; flowers small. 'Foliis Purpureis': leaves coppery-purple in winter. 'Variegatum': leaves bordered with cream-white.

R. racemosum	W China	evergreen shrub to 10 ft (3 m)	⅝–2 in (1.5–5 cm), broadly obovate to oblong-elliptic, glabrous above, shining white-papillose beneath, with dense scales	½–¾ in (1–2 cm), openly funnel-shaped, white to pale or deep pink

Comments: 'Forrest': dwarf; flowers pink. 'Glendoick': taller, with deep pink flowers. 'Rock Rose': flowers bright purple-pink. 'White Lace': flowers white.

R

R. racemosum

R. rex subsp. *fictolacteum*

R. sinogrande

R. souliei

RHODODENDRON

Name	Distribution	Habit	Leaves	Flowers
R. rex	W China, NE Burma	evergreen, large shrub or small tree to 39 ft (12 m)	³⁄₄–14¹⁄₂ in (2–37 cm), obovate to oblanceolate, glabrous above, smooth or finely wrinkled, lower surface with a dense fawn to red hairs	campanulate, white, pale yellow or pink, with a crimson basal blotch and spots

Comments: 'Quartz': flowers pink with crimson blotch and spots. 'Roseum': flowers pale rose pink with small dark blotch, opening from deeper pink buds. ssp. *fictolacteum*: syn. *R. fictolacteum*; leaves brown, flowers white or pink. 'Cherry Tip': flowers white, edged with pink, and with crimson blotch spots.

Name	Distribution	Habit	Leaves	Flowers
R. rubiginosum	W China, NE Burma	evergreen shrubs or small trees to 33 ft (10 m) or more	2–4¹⁄₂ in (5–11.5 cm), narrowly elliptic to elliptic or almost lanceolate, glabrous and scaleless above, scaly beneath	²⁄₃–1¹⁄₂ in (1.7–3.8 cm), openly funnel-shaped, pink, mauve-pink or rarely white, flushed with pink-purple, scaly outside

Comments: 'Wakehurst': flowers mallow purple with crimson spots. Desquamatum Group: flowers usually larger and flatter; plants often more compact with slightly larger leaves.

Name	Distribution	Habit	Leaves	Flowers
R. schlippenbachii	Korea, E Russia	deciduous shrub to 16 ft (5 m)	1–4¹⁄₂ in (2.5–11 cm), obovate or broadly ovate, truncate, rounded or notched at apex, sparsely pubescent at first	1¹⁄₄–2¹⁄₂ in (3–6 cm), very openly funnel-shaped, pale pink, upper lobes spotted with red-brown

Comments: 'Prince Charming': flowers rose, flushed with deeper pink and spotted with crimson.

Name	Distribution	Habit	Leaves	Flowers
R. simsii INDIAN AZALEA	NE Burma, China, Taiwan	evergreen to semievergreen shrub to 10 ft (3 m)	¹⁄₂–2³⁄₄ in (1–7 cm), elliptic, ovate to obovate or oblanceolate, sparsely strigose above, more densely so beneath	1–2 in (2.5–5 cm), broadly funnel-shaped, red, spotted

Name	Distribution	Habit	Leaves	Flowers
R. sinogrande	W China, NE Burma	evergreen tree to 33 ft (10 m).	8–36 in (20–90 cm), oblong-oblanceolate to oblong-elliptic, glabrous and wrinkled above when mature, with silvery or fawn hairs beneath	1¹⁄₂–2¹⁄₂ in (4–6 cm), ventricose-campanulate, pale cream to ivory, blotched crimson at base

Name	Distribution	Habit	Leaves	Flowers
R. souliei	W China	evergreen shrub to 16 ft (5 m)	4¹⁄₂–3 in (5.5–8 cm), broadly ovate, glabrous	1–1¹⁄₂ in (2.5–4 cm), openly saucer-shaped, pale purple-pink

Comments: 'Exbury Pink': flowers deep rose pink. 'Windsor Park': flowers white, edged with pink, upper petal with small red blotch at base.

Name	Distribution	Habit	Leaves	Flowers
R. sutchuenense	W China	evergreen shrub to 16 ft (5 m)	4¹⁄₂–10 in (11–25 cm), oblong-lanceolate, glabrous above, floccose along midrib beneath	2–3 in (5–7.5 cm), widely campanulate, pink with darker spots

Comments: 'Seventh Heaven': flowers red-purple, white in center.

R. sutchuenense   **R. thomsonii**   **R. wardii**   **R. yunnanense**

R

RHODODENDRON

Name	Distribution	Habit	Leaves	Flowers
R. thomsonii	Himalaya, W China	evergreen shrub or small tree to 11½ ft (3.5 m)	1¼–4½ in (3–11 cm), orbicular to obovate or elliptic, glabrous, glaucous beneath, sometimes with some red glands	1½–2 in (3.5–5 cm), campanulate, fleshy, deep crimson, usually without darker spots
R. trichostomum	W China	small, intricately branched shrub, 12–60 in (30–150 cm), often forming rounded bushes	½–1¼ in (1.2–3 cm), linear, oblong or oblanceolate, upper surface green; scaly or not, margins usually revolute, lower surface pale brown with golden scales	¼–¾ in (0.6–2 cm), white or pink, tube glabrous outside, with a few scales on exterior
Comments: Ledoides Group: corolla not scaly. 'Collingwood Ingram': flowers red-purple, paler in throat. 'Lakeside': flowers white, flushed with red-purple. 'Quarry Wood': flowers white, flushed with red-purple. 'Rae Berry': flowers clear, pale pink. 'Sweet Bay': flowers white flushed with rose.				
R. venator	W China	shrub to 10 ft (3 m)	3–5½ in (8–14 cm), elliptic to lanceolate, glabrous except for hairs on midrib beneath	to 1½ in (3.5 cm), fleshy, tubular to campanulate, crimson with darker nectar pouches
R. wardii	W China	evergreen shrub or small tree to 26 ft (8 m)	2½–4½ in (6–11 cm), narrowly obovate to broadly ovate, glabrous, somewhat glaucous beneath	1–1½ in (2.5–4 cm), saucer-shaped, white to pale yellow, sometimes with a purple basal blotch
Comments: 'Ellestee': flowers lemon yellow with crimson blotch. Litiense Group: leaves oblong, wavy, glaucous on underside. 'Meadow Pond': flowers primrose yellow with crimson blotch. var. *puralbum*: flowers white.				
R. williamsianum	W China	dwarf, evergreen shrub to 5 ft (1.5 m)	¾–1¾ in (2–4.5 cm), ovate-orbicular, more or less glabrous	1¼–1½ in (3–4 cm), campanulate, pale pink with darker spots
R. yakushi-manum R. degronianum ssp. yakushimanum	**Comments:** much used in recent hybridization as a parent of a range of striking, very hardy hybrids: leaves silvery then dark green, covered in thick, dense, brown-felty hairs beneath; flowers broad, pink fading to white, speckled green within. 'Ken Janeck': plants and leaves larger than usual; flowers pink. 'Koichiro Wada': flowers white opening from pink buds, in dense trusses, freely produced.			
R. yunnanense	Burma, W China	shrub to 20 ft (6 m)	1¼–2¾ in (3–7 cm), evergreen or deciduous, narrowly elliptic or elliptic, scaly beneath, margins and upper surface bristly	¾–1¼ in (2–3 cm), white, pink or lavender, usually densely spotted above with red or yellow

R

rhubarb (*Rheum × hybridum*) a leafy perennial grown for its thick succulent petioles. It is probably a hybrid of *R. rhaponticum* and *R. palmatum* but its origins are unclear. The two likely parents and other *Rheum* species are common in China and elsewhere in the east; *R. officinale* and *R. palmatum* were described in a Chinese herbal of 2700 BC for their strong laxative properties. The culinary use of rhubarb in Europe dates from the 18th century.

The crop is more frequently cultivated in temperate regions, but cultivars have been selected for high elevations in tropical areas. With shortening day length in fall, rhubarb becomes dormant and leaf production is only resumed following exposure to low temperature; the period of exposure required varies between cultivars. Those requiring the shortest cold treatment to break dormancy produce the earliest crops.

Harvesting takes place from the spring, but plants can be forced to produce an early crop of blanched stalks during late winter. On no account should leaves be eaten since they contain a poisonous glycoside. Blanched and natural stalks may be cooked by boiling or baked in pies and tarts, with sugar usually necessary to reduce acidity.

When grown in a well-prepared site, rhubarb plants may extend to 6½ ft (2 m). Soil must be made moisture-retentive through the incorporation of rotted organic matter; good drainage is essential and plants do not thrive in shade.

All rhubarb plants should be re-propagated about every five years by dividing crowns, with a spade, into wedge-shaped pieces, each bearing at least one strong bud; vigorous healthy mother plants of named cultivars should be chosen when possible since long-standing stocks are prone to degeneration from virus infection. Plant during late fall, 30–36 in (75–90 cm) apart, with the buds just showing at the soil surface. Propagation from seed is possible from spring-sowing but the resulting plants are likely to be variable. Plants should be kept well-watered and free from weeds, and provided with a thick layer of organic mulch each fall or spring.

To enable crowns to build up reserves, harvesting should not be carried out during the first growing season. Always retain three or four leaves per plant to sustain the crown. Flowering stems should be removed since they weaken the plant. Early harvests of outdoor crops can be obtained by forcing plants, either by covering with a thick layer of straw during midwinter or by covering individual crowns with a rhubarb pot or something similar to provide protection and to exclude light, thereby blanching the developing leaves. Crowns can also be lifted during fall and early winter and forced under protection in a greenhouse or shed; they must first be exposed to frost in order to break dormancy. The lifted crowns should be replanted in soil in large pots or boxes and brought under protection, where growth will resume at a temperature between 45–61°F (7–16°C). The containers should be positioned where light can be excluded, for example, under a greenhouse bench with an improvised curtain attached. Plants forced *in situ* take time to recover and are best left uncropped the next season; those forced indoors are best discarded.

Recommended cultivars include: (early) 'Hawkes Champagne', 'Timperley Early'; (midseason) 'Prince Albert', 'Canada Red'; (late) 'The Sutton', 'Victoria'. Notable in the US are 'Linneus' and 'Martha Washington'. Possible problems: crown rot virus.

rhubarb pot a tall, upright earthenware pot with a removable lid, specially made for forcing rhubarb.

Rhus (from Greek name for this plant, *rhous*). Anacardiaceae. Temperate and subtropical N America, southern Africa, subtropical E Asia, NE Australia. SUMAC, SUMACH, TAAIBOS. About 200 species, trees and shrubs, deciduous or evergreen, with simple to pinnate or palmatifid leaves and very small flowers massed in panicles or spikes. The species listed here are deciduous with pinnately compound leaves. The fall foliage color is superb, and the ornamental flower and fruiting spikes persist until winter. Hardy to at least –13°F (–25°C). Plant in well-drained, fertile soil in full sun. Propagate by removal of suckers from fall onward, also by 4 in (10 cm) cuttings of

Rhus typhina
Although prone to suckering, the staghorn sumac is valued for its velvety stems, fine-cut leaves and superb fall color.

semiripe shoots with a heel, taken in late summer and inserted in a sandy medium in a propagating frame with bottom heat. Root cuttings will succeed potted vertically in a sandy medium in winter, under glass. Prune only to keep in bounds or to remove damaged or ungainly wood; the brittle wood of the taller shrubs and tree types is prone to storm damage.

R. aromatica FRAGRANT SUMAC, LEMON SUMAC, POLECAT BUSH; SE Canada to S and E US; shrub to 3¼ ft (1 m), prostrate; leaflets 2½ in (3, to 6.5 cm), ovate, serrate; flower spikes to ¾ in (2 cm), yellow; 'Gro-low': very low and spreading, with golden yellow, fragrant flowers; *R. glabra* SCARLET SUMAC, SMOOTH SUMAC, VINEGAR TREE; NE US to S Canada; deciduous shrub or tree, to 13 ft (4 m); leaflets 11–31, to 4½ in (11 cm), oblong to lanceolate, serrate, glabrous, dark green above, blue-green beneath, fiery red in fall; flower spikes dense, to 10 in (25 cm), green turning deep rusty red; 'Flavescens': leaves yellow in fall; 'Laciniata': leaflets deeply and jaggedly cut; *R. typhina* STAGHORN SUMAC, VELVET SUMAC, VIRGINIAN SUMAC; eastern N America; spreading deciduous tree or shrub to 33 ft (10 m); twigs bristly-velvety; leaflets 11–31, to 4½ in (11 cm), oblong to lanceolate, serrate, coarsely hairy, fiery red to orange and gold in fall; flower spikes to 12 in (30 cm), dense rusty-red; 'Dissecta': leaflets pinnately dissected; 'Laciniata': leaflets deeply and jaggedly cut.

rhytidome the periderm and tissues external to it; bark.

ribbed possessing one or more prominent veins or nerves.

Ribes (from the Arabic *ribas* 'sharp-tasting'). Grossulariaceae. Northern temperate regions. CURRANT, GOOSEBERRY. 150 species of small to medium-sized shrubs, mainly deciduous, often thorny. They bear small, 4–5-petaled flowers singly or in racemes in spring. These are followed by small, juicy berries, which, in some cases, are edible. The ornamental *Ribes* species are grown primarily for their flowers, although some also have attractive foliage as in the golden-leaved *R. sanguineum* 'Brocklebankii'. The low-growing evergreen *R. laurifolium* is particularly valuable in the winter garden, bearing dense panicles of green-yellow flowers in late winter/early spring. The most commonly grown species, the spice-scented *R. odoratum* and the rather feline *R. sanguineum*, are reliably hardy where temperatures fall to –13°F (–25°C). *R. speciosum*, with fuchsialike flowers and fine glossy foliage, will tolerate temperatures to 5°F (–15°C), and is suited to wall or pillar training, especially in areas at the limits of hardiness. *R. laurifolium* shows similar cold tolerance, given shelter from cold drying winds. *R. viburnifolium* does not tolerate temperatures much below 23°F (–5°C).

Grow in moderately fertile, moisture-retentive but well-drained soil in sun. *R. sanguineum*

Ribes odoratum (fall color)

'Brocklebankii' performs better in partial shade. *R. laurifolium* is also shade-tolerant. Trim over immediately after flowering to maintain a compact habit and remove a proportion (a quarter to one third) of flowered wood at the base to maintain a supply of younger wood: flowers are carried on the previous season's growth. Older wood in wall-trained specimens of *R. speciosum* should be removed in late summer and new basal growth tied in. Propagate deciduous species by nodal hardwood cuttings in late fall/early winter. Increase *R. laurifolium* by semiripe cuttings in summer.

R. laurifolium W China; evergreen shrub to 5 ft (1.5 m); leaves 2–4 in (5–10 cm), oval or ovate, coarsely toothed, leathery, smooth; flowers green-yellow; fruit red to black, downy; *R. odoratum* CLOVE CURRANT, BUFFALO CURRANT, MISSOURI CURRANT; C US; shrub to 6½ ft (2 m); deciduous or semievergreen; leaves 1¼–3 in (3–8 cm), oval to rounded, 3–5-lobed, toothed; flowers, sweetly scented, yellow; fruit globose, black; *R. sanguineum* WINTER CURRANT; W US to California; to 13 ft (4 m), deciduous shrub, glandular, mustily aromatic; leaves 1–2¾ in (2.5–7 cm), rounded, base cordate, 3–5-lobed, dark green, downy; flowers red or deep rosy pink; fruit glandular, blue-black with white bloom; 'Albescens': flowers white flushed pink, appearing earlier than other cultivars; 'Brocklebankii': leaves yellow; 'Plenum': double, red flowers; 'Pulborough Scarlet': bright mid-pink flowers; 'Pulborough Scarlet Variegated': leaves variegated yellow; 'Tydemans White': bright white flowers; *R. speciosum* FUCHSIA-FLOWERED GOOSEBERRY; California; evergreen shrub to 13 ft (4 m), bristly-thorny; leaves ½–1½ in (1–4 cm), rounded, 3–5-lobed, bluntly toothed, smooth, glossy; flowers pendulous, red, glandular-bristly, with long, red, downward-pointing stamens; fruit glandular-bristly, red; *R. viburnifolium* California; evergreen shrub to 5 ft (1.5 m), stems low often rooting; leaves ¾–1½ in (2–4 cm), broadly ovate to oval, entire or slightly dentate, glandular, turpentine-scented; flowers pink; fruit red.

rice husks a by-product of the processing of rice, useful for ground mulching and as an ingredient of potting mixtures. They provide good aeration and drainage and are especially beneficial when incorporated into mixes for epiphytes.

Richea (for the French naturalist Colonel A.G. Riche, who died in 1791 during the Australian voyage of Admiral d'Entrecasteaux in search of La Perouse). Epacridaceae. Australia, Tasmania. 11 species, evergreen trees or shrubs. Crowded along the stems or tufted at their tips, the leaves are narrow and usually sword-shaped with sheathing bases. The flowers do not open fully, but are waxy and colorful and crowded in simple terminal clusters, spikes or panicles. Hardy to 5°F (–15°C). Grow in moist, humus-rich, acidic soils in partial or dappled shade, or with part-day sun where soils remain moist throughout the summer. Propagate from semiripe cuttings or by seed in fall. *R. scoparia* (Tasmania; bushy, erect shrub to 5 ft (1.5 m); flowers white, pink or orange in dense cylindric racemes to 12 in (30 cm) long).

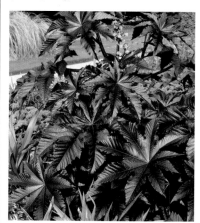

Ricinus communis 'Impala'
This shrub may also be grown as a half-hardy annual, providing exotic foliage for a sub-tropical bedding scheme.

Ricinus (from Latin *ricinus*, a tick, which the seeds resemble). Euphorbiaceae. NE Africa to Middle East, naturalized throughout tropics. 1 species, *R. communis*, CASTOR OIL PLANT, a glabrous shrub to 39 ft (12 m), seldom exceeding 6½ ft (2 m) in cultivation. The leaves are up to 24 in (60 cm) across, rounded in outline and palmately lobed with toothed margins.

In summer, red-green flowers are borne in terminal inflorescences to 6 in (15 cm). These are followed by prickly capsules which split to reveal highly toxic marbled, beadlike seeds. Several cultivars are grown with leaves variously veined, flushed and marbled with yellow, lime green, bronze, purple-red, orange and fiery red. One of the finest is 'Impala' with metallic purple-bronze leaves veined with scarlet, and scarlet flowers. The castor oil plant is often treated as a half-hardy annual, grown each year from seed and planted out after the last frosts. It is valued for its bold foliage, and traditionally used as a dot plant in subtropical bedding. It is also suitable for the cool greenhouse or conservatory. Grow in sun with shelter from wind, in fertile, moisture-retentive but well-drained soil enriched with well-rotted organic matter. Sow seed in spring in individual pots at 68°F (20°C).

riddle a wide-meshed sieve used for sifting soil or coarse materials.

ridger a hand tool shaped like a miniature plow. It is used to produce a furrow into which seeds can be sown.

ridging see *digging*.

rigid paving paving units bedded on mortar, with joints that are sealed with mortar.

ring barking see *bark-ringing*.

ring culture a method of cultivating tomatoes, also used satisfactorily for chrysanthemums and carnations, in which young plants are set into a growing medium contained in bottomless whalehide (q.v.) rings; these measure 9 in (22 cm) in depth and diameter and are stood on a 6 in (15 cm) deep layer of gravel, weathered clinker or similar aggregate. The aggregate is sealed at the base with a polythene sheet in order to prevent root penetration into disease- or pest-infested soil. All water is subsequently applied to the aggregate, and liquid feed to the medium. In this way, nutrition is concentrated within the ring and mainly water-extracting roots develop throughout the aggregate. The method is especially useful on unsuitable soils, and also on solid garden surfaces.

R

681

ringspot an area of visually normal leaf tissue surrounded by one or more rings, which may be darker green, yellow, chlorotic or necrotic. It is usually a virus-disease symptom.

ripeness, ripening used to describe (1) the stage at which fruits reach physiological maturity and are in a condition favorable for eating. In apple fruits, it coincides more or less with maximum respiration rate, at a phase known as the climacteric. Carbon dioxide, water and volatile products, notably ethylene, are evolved at this time; (2) the maturation of young woody shoots on trees and shrubs, or of bulbs, especially onions, which occurs during high summer temperature.

Robinia (for Jean Robin [d. 1629], herbalist to Henry IV of France). Leguminosae. US. Some 20 species, deciduous trees and shrubs with pinnate leaves and pealike, fragrant flowers in pendulous racemes in late spring and early summer. The following will tolerate temperatures to 5°F (–15°C) and atmospheric pollution. Good drainage and shelter from strong winds are necessary. *Robinia* regenerates strongly after pruning, which should be done in late summer to reduce risk of bleeding. Most sucker freely and felled trees will produce coppices. Propagate by seed in spring, scarified or soaked in hot water for 12 hours before sowing, or by removal of rooted suckers. Cultivars can be side-grafted onto seedling rootstock of the species in winter, although suckering may be a problem. Take root cuttings of plants grown on their own roots. Locust borer and locust leaf miner are serious pests in North America.

R. × *ambigua R. pseudoacacia* × *R. viscosa*; differs from *R. pseudoacacia*, in the somewhat glutinous branches with small thorns; flowers pale pink to lavender; *R. hispida* BRISTLY LOCUST, ROSE ACACIA, MOSS LOCUST; SE US; shrub to 7 ft (2.25 m), bristly, suckering; flowers 3–5 in short raceme, pale purple or rose; includes 'Monument', to 13 ft (4 m), compact, conical, sparsely bristled, with racemes to 4 in (10 cm) and large, delicate lilac-pink flowers; *R. kelseyi* ALLEGHANY MOSS; SE US; shrub to 10 ft (3 m), branches bristly at first; racemes to 2½ in (6 cm), crowded, glandular-hairy, flowers lilac to rose; *R. pseudoacacia* BLACK LOCUST, YELLOW LOCUST; E and C US, widely naturalized in temperate regions; tree, to 89 ft (27 m), nearly glabrous; young branches thorny; racemes dense, nodding, to 8 in (20 cm), flowers white to ivory, fragrant, blotched with yellow at base; 'Frisia': a fine small tree with bright golden new foliage, turning a cool lime by midsummer.

robin's pincushion see *bedeguar*.

rocambole (*Allium sativum* var. *ophioscorodon*) a perennial grown for its bulbs, which are used in flavoring in a similar way to garlic. It is propagated vegetatively from both offsets and bulblets produced at the top of its stem. These should be planted 2 in (5 cm) deep and about 8 in (20 cm) apart during early spring, and lifted during the summer months after the foliage dies back. They may be stored in a cool dry place in a similar way to onions.

rock phosphate an inorganic fertilizer made of finely ground phosphate-containing rock (25–40% phosphoric acid). Its usefulness varies according to the source of the rock and processing treatment, and it produces best results in acidic soils.

rock plant an herbaceous, shrubby, or bulbous plant that is suitable for growing in a rock garden. See *alpine*.

rock plant gardening the cultivation of alpine and other rock plants in a garden area specially constructed to simulate natural rock formation. The construction of rock gardens dates from 1772, when the director of what is now the Chelsea Physic Garden in London had placed there about forty tons of stone from the Tower of London, together with lava, brought from Iceland by Sir Joseph Banks, and a topping of flints and chalk. This was the precursor of many such collections of stones, known as 'stoneries' or 'lapideums', which were built largely for their own sake, although an attempt was sometimes made to grow plants on them.

Rock plant gardening (Androsace carnea)
This long established form of gardening provides the fascination and challenges of cultivating plants found naturally at high altitude.

One of the earliest natural-looking rock gardens in England was built in the early 1800s by William Beckford in a quarry at Fonthill, Wiltshire. In the UK and North America interest and achievements in rock gardening evolved throughout the 19th century. Today, rock gardeners in the UK, US, and Canada cultivate rock plants with great seriousness under the aegis of The Alpine Garden Society and the American Rock Garden Society. There are various ways in which rock plants can be grown in the garden, accommodating interest on a large or small scale.

Rock gardens This is the most common form of rock plant growing. The cheapest and most natural-looking features are those made by exposing existing rock, but the incorporation of any existing mound, slope or change of level is a highly-desired opportunity. Artificially created mounds in a flat scene look contrived, especially in a small garden, but this effect can be minimized by making gentle slopes or by creating a surrounding pavement of flat rocks. A south or west outlook is best, but a northwest-facing rock garden still provides good west-facing planting pockets; alternatively, a mound of smaller rocks can be gently stepped on both sides, offering a variety of growing conditions, perhaps with one short, sharp slope and a second long, gentle one. In all cases, the site must be open to good light.

Arrange the stones as they would be found in a natural outcrop, but with some positioned as if they have rolled to the bottom of the slope. Incorporate

R

some flat stones for standing upon while tending plants, and, in the larger rock garden, plan discreet gravel or stone-based paths. Ensure good drainage, and at each level set the largest stones into the bank first, deeply enough to be stable to stand upon and tilted slightly backward so that rain will run off the top surface to the plants' roots. Smaller stones are placed on either side, their tops more or less level, but always with the strata lying in straight lines. The second layer of rocks uses some of the first layer as a base, together with an excavated section of bank. As each stone is positioned, soil must be packed firmly at its back and in any vertical and horizontal crevices. Adjacent rocks should be butted up close but the distance between each cluster of rocks can be varied. It is easiest to plant alpines in the crevices as building progresses.

All true alpines need a well-drained growing medium, which can be packed into the rock crevices; a generally suitable mixture is three parts loam to two parts grit and one part coir or leaf mold. Plants need little feeding and some thrive in very dry and poor soil.

MATERIALS Whenever possible, local stone should be chosen since it will harmonize with the landscape, as well as being relatively cheap to transport. When this is not possible, matching the colors of existing house and garden stone or brick may be a consideration. A mixture of sizes is best, with several bold blocks and some large, flat pieces included.

Limestone is an interesting rock, which varies in consistency and color, producing flowing lines where it has been worn by running water; it is also quite easy to cut. A disadvantage of its weathering is that the surrounding soil becomes alkaline, thus precluding the cultivation of some desirable plants. In Britain, conservation measures justifiably restrict the supply of the choicest rock, which was formerly obtained at the cost of severe damage to surface limestone pavements, but quarried limestone is available. Tufa is a water-retentive form of limestone, deposited by dripping water or mineral springs; it has no strata, is soft to cut and although it hardens on exposure to the air can be easily penetrated by the roots of plants. It is generally used for special situations, including sinks or troughs, where holes 1–2 in (2.5–5 cm) wide and 2 in (5 cm) deep are drilled at a 45° angle and filled with equal parts tufa debris, soil and leaf mold.

Sandstone is a more angular rock, available in a wide range of colors, including soft pinks and yellows; it has obvious strata and can be split easily. Its main advantage is that it absorbs moisture, which it will release into surrounding soil in dry spells and which makes it relatively cool. As sandstone weathers, it produces acidic residues, and mosses and lichens will establish on its surface.

Slate can be used to dramatic effect, echoing natural outcrops, where strata point almost vertically upward; it consists of relatively thin layers of easily split, gray rock.

Granite is least satisfactory because it is heavy, hard to cut or split, and does not weather. It has few strata lines, and if crevices develop, they tend to be vertical and unsuitable for planting.

Scree and moraine beds These are made to simulate particular natural rocky habitats. Scree is a sloping area of stone fragments at the base of a rock face, formed by deposits of weathered rock and notable for its perfect drainage and lack of moisture. Moraine is an accumulation of rock fragments, with sand or silt particles, which arises from the grinding action of a glacier on bedrock; it is well-drained but retains moisture, becoming a damp habitat.

Scree beds may be sited either running between large rocks or as separate features. They can be made with a deep layer of stone fragments and chips laid over 8 in (20 cm) of very gritty soil, which in turn tops a well-drained foundation. Moraine can be constructed by digging out a site to about 24 in (60 cm) deep and placing coarse drainage material to a depth of 12 in (30 cm). Inverted turves are placed on top of this layer as a moisture reservoir, and a very gritty soil mix is added to a depth of 8 in (20 cm). The site is finished with 2 in (5 cm) of coarse gravel into which is laid a 1¼ in (3 cm)-deep subsurface watering system comprising plastic pipes with small widely spaced perforations. Scree depends on rainfall or overhead watering; moraine relies mainly on its subterranean watering system which should be used in hot dry weather. Both scree and moraine benefit from occasional overhead fine spray in very hot weather.

Crevice planting (alpine campanula)
This alpine campanula is being established by wedging a stone in the base of the crevice and packing gritty soil around the plant.

Raised beds These provide a more formal way of growing scree plants, allowing a large number to be grown in a small space. They can be any size or shape, built against a wall or in the form of an island bed, and may be partitioned to provide both acidic and alkaline growing conditions. Dry-stone retaining walls, built to a height up to 3¼ ft (1 m), are best since plants can be grown in narrow cracks between the stones. A gritty soil mix is used to fill the bed, topped with a 2 in (5 cm) layer of coarse gravel. A few pieces of rock protruding from the finished level provide an authentic-looking miniature landscape.

Walls A variety of trailing rock plants can be grown in the gaps between the stones of a dry wall. The top of a brick wall can be used if it has a coping at least 12 in (30 cm) wide and a narrow trough specially built on top of it. The trough is filled with a mixture of two parts fibrous loam to one part leaf mold and one part sharp sand; slow-release fertilizer is added to this.

Paving Alpine plants can be grown where soil rather than cement is used between paving slabs in courtyards, terraces, patios, and in paths laid on sand. Planting should be done during construction, or if the paving is already in place, holes can be made in the cement and gritty soil trickled into the opening.

Sink or trough gardens Old stone sinks and animal drinking troughs provide excellent foundations for growing alpine plants, but original ones are scarce and new ones very expensive. Artificial troughs can be made using discarded glazed white sinks, simulating natural stone with a coating of hypertufa; the mix is plastered over a layer of bonding agent, such as tile cement. The same material can be used to construct a trough using cardboard boxes as molds, with a smaller sized box placed inside another. See *hypertufa*.

Alpine house
A greenhouse bench brings these attractive plants closer to the eye while protecting them from harmful winter wet.

Alpine houses Alpine houses are a means of growing mountain plants with protection from winter rain, severe frost and icy winds. They permit the cultivation of slightly tender species and the propagation, growing and establishment of young plants. They can also be used for the display of spring-flowering alpines and dwarf bulbs, which often flower two or three weeks earlier in containers than in the garden outside. Another use in summer is for drying and ripening many dwarf bulbs, which need summer heat when dormant to ensure regular flowering.

The alpine house should be situated in an open site and, where possible, orientated north/south. Typically, it is unheated, very well-ventilated but draft-free; wooden structures are preferable to aluminum, which gives rise to condensation and drips.

Thermostatically controlled heating will provide plants with the protection against very low temperatures afforded by snow cover in their natural habitat, and prevent freezing of pots. Protection in summer with external blinds or a layer of green plastic netting is desirable, coverings that are easily removed on dull days. Plants are best kept on sturdy benches covered with shingle.

Frames Frames allow perfect water control and protection from winter damage for plants starting growth in fall, and can be used for the propagation, growing and storage of all types of rock plants. They can also be used to hold plants not currently on display; these are trimmed over after flowering, repotted if necessary and stood out until flower buds reappear.

Containers in frames are best plunged in a well-drained bed of ashes, sand or bark fiber, to reduce water loss and protect roots and pots from frost. By watering the bed in which pots are planted, rather than the pots themselves, even plants drying off over the summer can be given the minute amount of moisture they require for optimum growth in the next season. Plants within frames need plenty of air movement, so lights should only be closed in periods of frost or fog; they will also need shading in high summer.

Rock wool a lightweight material manufactured from spun mineral fibers, with high air-filled porosity and low nutrient content or nutrient-holding capacity. There are water-absorbent and water-repellent forms, both available in granules and suitable for use as growing-media additives; the water-absorbent form is widely used for soilless cultivation of greenhouse crops and for propagation. Rock wool is also available as slabs or blocks, and as small modules for rooting cuttings.

rod an outmoded linear measure of land, referred to in old gardening literature, and equivalent to about 16 ft (5 m). It is often loosely used to mean an area about 54 sq. ft (5 m²). It is also known as a pole or perch.

Rodgersia (for US admiral John Rodgers [1812–1882], commander of the expedition on which *R. podophylla*

was discovered). Saxifragaceae. Nepal, China, Japan. 6 species, rhizomatous perennial herbs. The leaves are large and basal, with stout stalks, palmate or pinnate blades and leathery, toothed leaflets. Numerous, small, white, red or purple flowers are carried in dense panicles in summer. Hardy foliage plants for damp borders, bog gardens and pond margins; leaves often emerging bronze or becoming so later in the season. The plumelike flowers are fine and the seed heads become red-tinted in fall. Plant in moist humus-rich soils, in sun or part shade, with shelter from strong winds. Mulch annually to conserve moisture and give a balanced slow-release fertilizer. Water plentifully in drought. Propagate by division in early spring.

R. aesculifolia China; to 6½ ft (2 m); leaves palmate, leaflets acute and coarsely toothed at apex, veins rusty-tomentose; flowers white; *R. pinnata* SW China; to 47 in (120 cm); leaves pinnate, leaflets obovate-lanceolate, flowers red; 'Superba': tall, with leaves tinted bronze to purple and rose flowers; *R. podophylla* Japan, Korea; to 47 in (120 cm); leaves palmate, turning bronze in fall, leaflets cleft and toothed at apex; flowers cream; 'Rotlaub': leaves tinted red; *R. sambucifolia* China; to 35 in (90 cm); leaves pinnate, leaflets acute; flowers white or pink.

rogue any plant with characteristics that deviate from those desired or expected. Rogueing is the culling of such plants, used especially for the removal of atypical or diseased bulbs.

Rohdea (for Michael Rohde [1782–1812], physician and botanist of Bremen). Liliaceae. SW China, Japan. 2 species. *R. japonica*, a rhizomatous perennial herb. The leaves are 12–16 in (30–40 cm) long, dark green, thick and strap-shaped and loosely 2-ranked in a basal rosette. Fleshy, white or yellow-green flowers emerge in a short dense spike in early spring. They are followed by red or yellow berries. Numerous variegated cultivars of this plant are available with leaves variously striped or edged gold, cream and white. They are highly prized in Japan. Grow in cool but frost-free, airy conditions in bright, indirect light. Plant in a loamy mix rich in leaf mold

R

and garden compost. Keep evenly moist. Propagate by seed or division.

roller a large garden hand-tool, comprising a wide, smooth-surfaced wheel mounted on an axle and fixed to a handle; used as an aid in the preparation of level sites, especially prior to laying paving. Modern garden rollers come in various weights, are made of metal or of plastic (sometimes filled with water) and are usually a little longer in width than diameter. Rollers are constructed so as to be pushed or pulled.

Rolling lawns, traditionally done to disperse worm casts and level minor surface undulations, is not recommended because of the deleterious effects of consolidation, particularly on heavy soil; the small roller built into a cylinder mower is adequate for levelling, and certain types of rollers fitted with spikes are effective for aerating the surface layers. Light rollers have a place in aiding seedbed preparation, after initial cultivation, but treading is invariably a more effective technique; such rollers may prove more effective for lawn seedbed preparation.

Romneya (for Rev. T. Romney Robinson [1792–1882], astronomer in Armagh, Ireland). Papaveraceae. California, Mexico. MATILIJA POPPY; CALIFORNIA TREE POPPY. 1 species, *R. coulteri*, a woody-based, suckering perennial herb 8 in–6 1/2 ft (20–200 cm) tall. The leaves are to 6 in (15 cm) long, pinnately lobed and toothed, gray-blue and glaucous. Produced in summer, the flowers are to 6 in (15 cm) in diameter, white and fragrant, with six obovate, silky petals and many golden stamens. The flowers unfurl from tough, podlike calyces. In plants sometimes named var. *trichocalyx*, these are covered in sharp bristles. Such plants also tend to have more finely divided, steely blue foliage. Hardy to 14°F (–10°C) if given sharp drainage and a warm, sunny, sheltered site. Cut back in spring before the appearance of the new growth. This plant may become invasive. Propagate by root cuttings in late winter or by rooted suckers in spring.

Romulea (for Romulus, founder and first King of Rome). Iridaceae.

Mediterranean north to SW England; South Africa, and at high altitudes in C and E Africa north to the Mediterranean. Some 80 species, spring-flowering, crocuslike, perennial cormous herbs. Where they can be kept dry in summer (when dormant), the European and Asiatic species are hardy to 14°F (–10°C); they are best planted at the base of a south-facing wall or niche in the rock garden. *R. bulbocodium* is slightly more cold-tolerant. The South African species, with the possible exception of the alpine *R. macowanii*, are probably more safely grown under glass or in the bulb frame in cool temperate zones. Grow in full sun, in sandy soil. Under glass, use a loam-based mix with additional sharp sand and leaf mold; grow in direct sunlight, with good ventilation, and water moderately when in growth. Dry off gradually as the foliage dies down. Propagate by seed in fall, or in spring for *R. macowanii*. Increase also by offsets.

R. bulbocodium (syn. *R. grandiflora*, *R. clusiana*); Mediterranean, Portugal, NW Spain, Bulgaria; flowers 1–6 per scape; perianth 7/8–2 in (2.25–5 cm), bright violet, rarely white, tube 1/8–3/8 in (0.3–0.8 cm), yellow, orange or white within or at throat: var. *crocea*: flowers yellow; var. *leichtliniana*: flowers white with a yellow throat; var. *subpalustris*: flowers tinted purple-blue, with a white throat; *R. flava* (syn. *R. bulbocodioides*); South Africa; flowers 1–4 per scape; perianth 7/8–1 1/2 in (2.25–4 cm), yellow-green, occasionally white or tinted blue or pink, tube yellow within and at throat; *R. macowanii* (syn. *R. longituba*); South Africa; flowers 1–3 per scape; perianth 1 1/4–4 in (3–10 cm), golden yellow, tube deep orange-yellow within and at throat; *R. nivalis* Lebanon; flowers 1–3 per scape; perianth to 1 in (2.5 cm), lilac to mauve, tube to 1/8 in (0.3 cm), yellow within and at throat; *R. sabulosa* South Africa; flowers 1–4 per scape; perianth to 1 1/4–2 1/8 in (3–5.5 cm), bright scarlet, tube with a dark white- or pink-edge blotch within and at throat.

Rondeletia (for W.G. Rondelet [1507–1566], French scholar, physician, and specialist in fish and algae). Rubiaceae. C to S America, Polynesia.

Some 150 species, shrubs or trees with axillary or terminal panicles, cymes or corymbs of funnel- to salverform, 4–6-lobed flowers in summer. Grow in the intermediate greenhouse (minimum temperature 55°F/13°C), in a loam-based medium, in bright filtered light. Water plentifully when in growth, sparingly in winter. Propagate by semiripe cuttings in a closed case with bottom heat in fall. *R. amoena* Mexico, Panama, Guatemala; shrub to 5 ft (1.5 m), or tree to 46 ft (14 m); flowers white to pink, to 5/8 in (1.5 cm) in many-flowered cymes or panicles.

roof gardens the practice of constructing gardens on the rooftops of buildings dates back to ancient times. The Hanging Gardens of Babylon, built about 600 BC, were terraced gardens arranged in a stepped pyramid over elaborate state rooms. There were rooftop gardens in Roman cities such as Pompeii, balcony gardens in Constantinople, and roof gardens made by the Aztecs in Mexico. On a smaller scale, roof terraces with potted plants have probably always been a common feature of private houses in the Mediterranean and other dry mild regions. In the 20th century, Le Corbusier and Frank Lloyd Wright are among architects to have promoted rooftop gardens.

Ecologically, roof gardens contribute to an increase in air humidity, and help to purify the air and filter dust in towns. However, proper consideration must be given during the planning stage to factors such as access, weight of soil and containers, roof waterproofing and durability, drainage and also local by-laws.

Plants can be grown on roofs in large tubs, boxes and other containers, or, in some instances, in beds. Growing media should be fertile, soil-based and with good moisture-retention properties since rapid drying out is inevitable; an adequate water supply is necessary. Screening from wind is essential for the protection of plants and users—panels of fine wire mesh or similar material will reduce wind force and sheets of strengthened glass are often used.

A very wide range of shrubs and small trees can be grown, provided large containers are available. Species

R

685

with strong branch structure and natural adaptation to hot dry conditions are a good choice; rock-garden plants, heathers and low-growing shrubs can be effective. Even vegetables and soft fruit can be grown with adequate protection and watering facilities, and growing bags are suitable in some instances. Maximum use should be made of climbing plants against walls, chimney stacks, and, if possible, on arbor-type structures.

Similar considerations apply to gardening on balconies, where long narrow window boxes, growing bags and smaller containers are a suitable choice.

rond-point a circular open space in a large formal garden, from which alleys or avenues radiate and several vistas are presented.

root the axis of a plant that serves to anchor it and absorb nutrients from the soil; usually geotropic, subterranean and derived from the radicle. Roots may also be adventitious or aerial.

root aphids the roots of various plants are subject to attack by aphids, invariably attended by ants. In severe infestations, plant growth is checked and wilting occurs. Most root aphids are light-colored and covered with white powdery wax. Some, such as the ARTICHOKE TUBER APHID (*Trama troglodytes*) live on roots continuously, but for most species root-feeding represents one phase in their annual migratory life cycle; for example, the LETTUCE ROOT APHID (*Pemphigus bursarius*) migrates from leaf petiole galls on Lombardy poplars to the roots of lettuce. Other species injurious to garden plants include the AURICULA ROOT APHID (*P. auriculae*), which infests the roots of auriculas and primulas, especially in pots; the ELDER APHID (*Aphis sambuci*), which migrates from elder to *Dianthus* species, *Lychnis* species, London pride (*Saxifraga umbrosa*) and many weeds; and the HAWTHORN-CARROT APHID (*Dysaphis crataegi*), which

attacks the roots of carrots and parsnips.

In North America, the WOOLLY APHID (*Eriosoma lanigerum*) has a bark-infesting form as well as one that attacks the roots of hosts, such as apple, *Cotoneaster* and *Pyracantha*; in Europe only the bark feeding form occurs. Another injurious pest in North America is the STRAWBERRY ROOT APHID (*Aphis forbesi*); several other species of root aphids attack ornamentals, such as asters, calendulas, cosmos, dahlias, primulas and sweet peas.

Root aphids may be controlled by applying soil drenches of a recommended aphicide. Pot plants may be treated by washing the roots and dipping them in similar insecticides. Some lettuce cultivars are resistant to the lettuce root aphid, for example the butterheads 'Avondefiance' and 'Sabine'. See *woolly aphid*.

rootball the mass of roots and growing medium formed by a plant, especially a container-grown one, but also applicable to plants lifted from the open ground.

root-bound see *pot-bound*.

Root aphid

root crop a vegetable crop grown for its edible roots or tubers, such as carrot, parsnip and potato.

root cuttings see *cuttings*.

root dipping the practice of immersing the roots of transplants into a recommended pesticide solution subject to local approvals. It is also applied to the dipping of bare-root trees or shrubs into a water-retentive polymer or alginate in order to prevent their desiccation. See *puddling*.

root flies, maggots Common to Europe and North America, root flies are some of the most serious vegetable pests and include CABBAGE ROOT FLY (*Delia radicum*), ONION FLY (*D. antiqua*), BEAN SEED FLY (*D. platura*) and CARROT FLY (*Psila rosae*). All the *Delia* species have adult forms about ¼ in (6 mm) long, which are of similar appearance

Barrier against root flies
A physical barrier protects these young carrots from the low-flying adult flies, preventing them from laying eggs on the crop.

to the HOUSEFLY (*Musca domestica*). Root fly attacks are best prevented by treating the soil around the plants with granules of recommended insecticides subject to local pesticide approvals. Correct timing is important and varies with different species. On a small scale, physical barriers such as horticultural fleece are effective against cabbage root fly, onion fly and carrot fly, and peas and beans may be protected from bean seed fly by seed dressing subject to local pesticide approvals. See *bean seed fly, cabbage root fly, carrot fly, chrysanthemum stool miner, onion fly*.

root grafting see *grafting*.

root hairs specialized epidermal cells situated a short distance behind the root tip, which increase the root's capacity to absorb water and mineral salts. Root hairs are short-lived and continually being produced as root growth proceeds.

root house an ornamental garden feature of Victorian gardens, formed from the bases of tree trunks, and often thatched.

rooting hormone see *cuttings* (synthetic hormones).

rootlet a small or secondary root.

root nodules small galls of different shapes that occur on the roots of certain plants, in particular members of the Leguminosae, and are produced by the reaction of the host to infection by various nitrogen-fixing microorganisms; they are beneficial. See *nitrogen*.

R

root pruning see *pruning*.

root restriction reducing the root run of a plant by planting it in a confined space in order to contain vegetative growth and induce flowering.

root rot decay of plant roots encouraged primarily by disease organisms, often in unfavorable soil conditions such as waterlogging. Fleshy roots, such as beet, carrot and turnip, may develop soft rots, caused by the bacterium *Erwinia carotovora*, or hard dry rots, such as those caused by the fungi *Leptosphaeria maculans* on rutabaga and *Alternaria radicina* on carrot (BLACK ROT). Many different fungi, including *Colletotrichum*, *Fusarium*, *Phoma*, *Phytophthora*, *Pythium*, *Rhizoctonia* and *Verticillium*, cause root rots of herbaceous plants and some are also responsible for damping-off in seedlings. Root rots caused by *Phytophthora* species commonly affect fruit trees and ornamental trees and shrubs. HONEY FUNGUS (*Armillaria mellea*), WHITE ROOT ROT FUNGUS (*Rosellinia necatrix*) and VIOLET ROOT ROT (*Helicobasidium brebissonii*) are other root rots with a wide host range. See *armillaria root rot*, *black rot*, *violet root rot*.

root run the area of soil explored by a plant's roots.

root spiralization the root configuration developed by plants left too long in a pot or container. See *pot-bound*.

rootstock (1) a woody or fleshy plant upon which a shoot or bud from a chosen specimen is grafted. The rootstock thereby provides the root system of the new plant. Besides facilitating propagation, root-stocks may influence growth and other characteristics in the new individual, such as ultimate size and early bearing in fruit trees and resistance to soilborne pest infestations in tomatoes. Widely used examples of clonal rootstocks are the EMLA selections for apple, Quince for pear and Myrobalan for plum. Many ornamental plants are grafted onto seedlings of the same or closely related species, see *EMLA*; (2) botanically, a rhizome, as in some ferns; (3) loose descriptive term for the crown and root system of a compact plant.

root vegetable see *root crop*.

roridulous covered with small, translucent prominences, giving the appearance of dewdrops.

Rosa (the Classical Latin name for the rose). Rosaceae. ROSE. N Hemisphere. Some 150 species, mostly deciduous shrubs, erect, arching or scrambling, with prickly and/or bristly stems. The leaves are pinnate, trifoliate or simple. Solitary or corymbose, the flowers consist of 4 or 5(–7), usually obovate and spreading petals (8–14 in semidouble, and 15–30+ in double flowers), and numerous stamens. In some species and many cultivars, flowering is remontant (occurs at least twice per season). Known as hips or heps, the fruits are usually waxy, fleshy, brightly colored and crowned with remnants of the sepals.

The following are fully hardy. Plant in sun or light shade in well-drained, fertile soil. Avoid sites that have deteriorated, where other roses have grown. Feed generously in late winter and mulch with garden compost. Continue to feed at regular intervals between midspring and late summer. Remove spent flower heads unless the hips are decorative. Prune in late winter or early spring. Pruning requirements vary, but can be broadly described as follows—remove any dead, damaged, weak or spent growth for all species and hybrids. Old Garden and Groundcover Roses usually need only a light trim. Modern Bush and Miniature Roses can be divested of as much as two thirds of the previous season's growth. Modern Shrub and Climbing Roses, ramblers and species usually need only a light prune. Increase by budding (bud grafting) in summer or by hardwood cuttings in fall. Affected by powdery mildew, black spot and rose rust; also canker and crown gall, rose anthracnose and die-back. Pests include aphids, Japanese beetles and chafers, rose curculio,

fuller beetles, froghoppers and leafhoppers, leaf miners, leaf-rolling sawflies, rose scale, rose slugworms and shoot or pith borers.

Roses are divided into three principal groups, the first includes the species described in detail in the table below; the other two groups comprise hybrids and cultivars so numerous that only brief generalizations can be made here. Each group is further divided.

SPECIES ROSES

Species—all rose species and their varieties and cultivars, including shrub roses and climbers.

Species Hybrids—hybrids between species and clearly showing their influence. Flowers usually single, borne in one phase. Hips often handsome.

OLD GARDEN ROSES

Alba—large shrubs. Foliage gray-green. Flowers semidouble or double, 5–7 per cluster in midsummer. Hardy. Good for border and specimen planting.

Bourbon—shrubs, loosely branched and open. Remontant—flowers usually double, produced in threes in summer and fall. Can be trained to climb: good for borders and for growing on fences, walls and stakes and pillars.

China—sparsely branched shrubs with pointed, glossy leaflets. Remontant—flowers single or double, solitary or in clusters of 2–13 in summer and fall. Good for sheltered borders and walls.

Damask—lax, open shrubs. Flowers very fragrant, semidouble to double, solitary or in 5–7 in loose clusters in summer. Good for borders.

Gallica—dense, freely branching shrubs. Leaves dull green. Flowers single to double, richly colored, usually in threes, in summer. Good for borders and hedging.

Hybrid Perpetual—vigorous, freely branching shrubs. Leaves usually olive green. Remontant—flowers double, solitary or in threes in summer and fall. Good for beds and borders.

Moss—loosely branched shrubs with mosslike, fuzzy growth on stems and calyces. Flowers double in summer.

Noisette—climbing shrubs with smooth stems and glossy leaves. Remontant—flowers usually double, somewhat spicily scented, to 9 per

decorative hips

Rosa canina

MODERN BUSH-TYPE ROSES

Hybrid Tea
Vigorous, remontant, flowers single to fully double, usually borne singly on stout stems. Good for borders and for cutting.

Floribunda ('Westerland')
Vigorous, remontant, flowers single to fully double, free-flowering, flowers clustered at stem tips. Good for borders and as hedging.

Patio ('Sweet Magic')
Dwarf floribundas, compact, cluster-flowered, remontant, flowers often unscented. Good in containers and as low hedges.

Miniature ('Stacey Sue')
Very compact, small-leaved, often sparsely thorned, remontant, flowers rarely scented. Good in raised beds and containers.

Polyantha ('The Fairy')
Compact, remontant, small flowers, single or double, in loose sprays over a long season. Very suitable for mixed plantings.

Groundcover ('Snow Carpet')
Spreading and trailing, many remontant, the best flowering along the entire length of stem; good for groundcover and on banks.

cluster in summer and fall. Good for sheltered, warm walls.

Portland—erect shrubs. Remontant—flowers semidouble to double, solitary or in threes in summer and fall. Good for borders.

Provence (Centifolia)—loose, thorny shrubs. Leaves dark green. Flowers scented, usually double, solitary or in threes in summer. Good for borders.

Sempervirens—semievergreen climbers. Leaves glossy, bright pale to mid-green. Flowers semidouble to double, many, in late summer. Good for pergolas and fences, also for naturalizing.

Tea—shrubs and climbers. Leaves glossy, pale green. Remontant—flowers semidouble to double, pointed, spicily scented, slender-stemmed, solitary or in threes in summer and fall. Good for sheltered borders.

MODERN ROSES

Shrub—varied category of bush roses, mostly remontant and attaining

$3\frac{1}{4}$–$6\frac{1}{2}$ ft (1–2 m) in height. Flowers single or double, solitary or in sprays, in summer and fall. Good for beds and specimen planting.

Hybrid Tea (Large-flowered Bush)—vigorous shrubs. Remontant—flowers usually double, large, and pointed, solitary or in threes, in summer and fall. Good for borders and for cutting.

Floribunda (Cluster-flowered Bush)—vigorous, free-flowering shrub. Remontant—flowers single or double, 3–25 per spray in summer and fall. Good for borders and hedges.

Patio (Dwarf Floribunda)—small, compact shrubs (to 24 × 24 in [60 × 60 cm]). Patio roses are remontant—flowers single to double, 3–11 per spray in summer and fall. Good for beds, hedging and containers.

Miniature Bush—dwarf bush (growing to 18 × 16 in [45 × 40 cm]). Leaves very small. Remontant—flowers small, single to double, 3–11 per

spray. Good for containers and small gardens.

Polyantha—compact, resilient shrubs. Remontant—flowers small, single or double, 7–15 per spray in summer and fall. Good for borders.

Groundcover—stems long, trailing or spreading, more or less prostrate. Groundcover roses often remontant—flowers single to double, in clusters of 3–11 in summer and fall. Good for low to medium groundcover, threading through low shrubs and for beds, banks and walls.

Climbing—vigorous climbers with rather rigid stems. Sometimes remontant—flowers single to double, solitary or clustered, from late spring to fall. Good for walls, fences and pergolas.

Rambler—climbers with robust, lax stems. Flowers single to double, in clusters of 3–21 in summer. Good for walls, pergolas and trees.

(*See table, facing page.*)

R

ROSA

Name	Distribution	Habit	Leaves	Flowers	Fruit
R. × alba (*R. gallica* × *R. arvensis* or *R. corymbifera* or *R. canina* × *R. damascena*) WHITE ROSE, WHITE ROSE OF YORK	garden origin	stout, arching, 6–8 ft (1.8–2.5 m), prickles scattered, hooked, often mixed with bristles	leaflets 5(–7), dull green, ovate to round, shortly acuminate to obtuse, glabrous above, downy beneath, toothed	1–3 per cluster, semidouble or double, 2½–3 in (6–8 cm) across, fragrant; sepals with lobes and leafy tips, glandular-bristly, reflexed; petals white to pale pink	¾–1 in (2–2.5 cm), more or less spherical, red

Comments: 'Alba Maxima': JACOBITE ROSE, CHESHIRE ROSE; flowers double, pink fading to cream. 'Alba Semiplena': semidouble, white.

Name	Distribution	Habit	Leaves	Flowers	Fruit
R. banksiae BANKSIAN ROSE, LADY BANKS'S ROSE	W and C China	strong, climbing to 39 ft (12 m), more or less unarmed	leaflets ¾–2½ in (2–6.5 cm), 3–7, oblong-lanceolate to elliptic-ovate, acute or obtuse, glossy above, sometimes downy beneath, margin wavy, toothed	many per umbel-like cyme, single or double, fragrant, 1–1¼ in (2.5–3 cm) across; sepals entire, reflexed; petals creamy white to lemon or pale primrose yellow	¼ in (0.7 cm), spherical, dull red

Comments: var. *banksiae*: flowers double, white, violet-scented. var. *normalis*: flowers single, white, very fragrant, and stem usually prickly. 'Lutea': stem generally unarmed; leaflets usually 5; flowers double, yellow, slightly fragrant. 'Lutescens': flowers single, yellow, highly scented.

Name	Distribution	Habit	Leaves	Flowers	Fruit
R. californica	W US to Mexico (Baja California)	erect, 5–10 ft (1.5–3 m) tall, red-brown, prickles stout, broad-based, recurved in pairs, with bristles on young shoots.	leaflets ½–1½ in (1–3.5 cm), 5–7, ovate to broadly elliptic, obtuse, hairless or downy above, downy and often glandular beneath, toothed	in clusters, single, fragrant, 1½ in (3.7–4 cm) across; sepals entire, hairy on the back, erect; petals deep pink to bright crimson	to ⅝ in (1.5 cm), spherical with a neck, smooth

Name	Distribution	Habit	Leaves	Flowers	Fruit
R. × centifolia PROVENCE ROSE, CABBAGE ROSE, HOLLAND ROSE	garden origin	to 6½ ft (2 m), prickles many small, almost straight and larger, hooked	leaflets 5–7, dull green, broadly ovate to almost round, glabrous above, downy beneath, glandular-toothed	1 to few, double, globose, very fragrant, 2½–3 in (6–8 cm) across; sepals lobed, glandular; spreading; petals usually pink, more rarely white or dark red	ellipsoidal or spherical, red

Comments: A complex hybrid involving *R. gallica, R. moschata, R. canina* and *R. × damascena*. 'Bullata': leaflets crinkled, tinged brown above when young; flowers pink. 'Cristata': sepals divided, providing each pink flower with a green fringe. 'Muscosa': COMMON MOSS ROSE; calyx and flower-stalks bearing a mass of many-branched, green, scented glands forming the so-called 'moss'.

Name	Distribution	Habit	Leaves	Flowers	Fruit
R. chinensis CHINA ROSE, BENGAL ROSE	garden origin	dwarf to more or less climbing to 20 ft (6 m), prickles absent or scattered, hooked, flattened	leaflets 1–2½ in (2.5–6 cm), 3–5, lanceolate to broadly ovate, acuminate, glossy and hairless above, hairless beneath except for downy midrib, margins with simple teeth	solitary or in clusters, single or semidouble, 2 in (5 cm) across, often fragrant; sepals entire or lobed, smooth or glandular, reflexed; petals pale pink to scarlet or crimson	⅝–¾ in (1.5–2 cm), ovoid to pear-shaped, green-brown to scarlet

Comments: Repeat-flowering, contributing this feature to European roses when it was introduced around 1800. 'Minima' (syn. 'Pompon de Paris'): FAIRY ROSE, PYGMY ROSE; 8–20 in (20–50 cm); flowers *circa* 1¼ in (3 cm) across, rose-red, single or double, petals pointed. Cultivars now included in *R. × odorata:* 'Mutabilis': 3¼–5½ ft (1–1.7 m); leaflets tinged purple or coppery when young; flowers single, fragrant, 1¾–2½ in (4.5–6 cm) across, petals yellow with an orange back, turning coppery salmon-pink and eventually deep pink, and 'Viridiflora': GREEN ROSE; petals green streaked with purple-red, stamens and pistils mutated to leafy, narrow, toothed segments.

R. 'Maiden's Blush' (Alba)

R. × *centifolia* 'Muscosa'

R. × *centifolia*

R. × *damascena* var. *semperflorens*

R

ROSA

Name	Distribution	Habit	Leaves	Flowers	Fruit
R. × damascena (*R. gallica × R. moschata*) SUMMER DAMASK ROSE	Asia Minor	to 7 ft (2.2 m), prickles dense, stout, curved, bristles stiff	leaflets 5(–7), gray-green, ovate to elliptic, acute to obtuse, downy beneath, toothed	in clusters of up to 12, semidouble, fragrant; sepals lobed, with slender tips, glandular and hairy, reflexed; petals pink	1 in (2.5 cm), turbinate, red, bristly

Comments: var. *semperflorens*: FALL DAMASK ROSE, FOUR SEASONS ROSE, QUATRE SAISONS ROSE, MONTHLY ROSE; flowers produced in fall. var. *versicolor*: YORK AND LANCASTER ROSE; flowers loosely double, petals deep pink or very pale pink or partly deep pink and partly pale pink. 'Trigintipetala' (syn. 'Professeur Emile Perrot'): KAZANLIK ROSE; flowers semidouble, *circa* 3 in (8 cm) across, red. 'Portlandica': PORTLAND ROSE; flowers semidouble, bright red, faintly scented, produced from midsummer to fall.

R. 'Dupontii' DUPONT ROSE; SNOW-BUSH ROSE	garden origin	**Comments:** Differs from *R. moschata* in its smaller size (6½–10 ft (2–3 m) tall), leaflets with compound teeth, flowers single, 2½–3 in (6–7.5 cm) across, creamy pink with sepals glandular beneath.			

R. ecae	NE Afghanistan, NW Pakistan and adjacent Russia, N China	much-branched, erect, suckering, to 5 ft (1.5 m), prickles dense, straight, flattened, red-tinged	aromatic, leaflets ⅛–⅜ in (0.4–0.8 cm), 5–9, elliptic to obovate or more or less orbicular, obtuse, glandular beneath, teeth often glandular	solitary, single, 6½–10 ft (2–3 m) across; sepals entire, hairless, spreading or deflexed; petals deep yellow	¼–½ in (0.5–1 cm), spherical, shiny red-brown, smooth and hairless

Comments: 'Golden Chersonese': *R. ecae × R. xanthina* 'Canary Bird'; to 6½ ft (2 m), with the aromatic leaves and deep yellow flowers of *R. ecae*. 'Helen Knight': *R. ecae × R. pimpinellifolia* 'Grandiflora'; stems red-brown to 10 ft (3 m) with support; flowers large, yellow.

R. filipes	W China	arching and climbing to 28 ft (9 m), purple when young, prickles few, small, hooked	coppery when young; leaflets 1½–3 in (3.5–8 cm), 5–7, narrowly ovate to narrowly elliptic, acuminate, hairless or downy on veins beneath, toothed	to 100 or more in large clusters, single, fragrant, ¾–1 in (2–2.5 cm) across; sepals lobed, glandular and slightly downy or hairless, reflexed; petals creamy or white	⅜–⅝ in (0.8–1.5 cm), spherical to ellipsoid, orange to crimson-scarlet

Comments: 'Kiftsgate': fast-growing climber; very free-flowering, inflorescence to 18 in (45 cm) across, flowers white to cream.

R. foetida AUSTRIAN BRIAR, AUSTRIAN YELLOW ROSE	SW and WC Asia	erect or arching, 3¼–10 ft (1–3 m), then gray-brown, prickles few, straight or curved, mixed with bristles	leaflets ⅝–1½ in (1.5–4 cm), 5–9, elliptic to obovate, obtuse to subacute, bright green and subglabrous above, dull green, downy and somewhat glandular beneath, teeth few, compound, glandular	solitary or 2–4, single, 2–3 in (5–7.5 cm) across, malodorous; sepals entire or lobed, apex expanded, hairless or glandular-bristly, erect; petals deep yellow	to ½ in (1 cm), spherical, red, smooth or bristly

Comments: 'Bicolor': AUSTRIAN COPPER BRIAR; petals coppery red inside and yellow-buff on the back; branches occasionally revert to the yellow-flowered form. 'Persiana': PERSIAN DOUBLE YELLOW; flowers very double, yellow, freely produced, smaller than those of *R. foetida*.

R. × *damascena* 'Portlandica'   *R.* 'Dupontii'   *R. ecae*   *R. filipes* 'Kiftsgate'

ROSA

Name	Distribution	Habit	Leaves	Flowers	Fruit
R. gallica FRENCH ROSE, RED ROSE	S and C Europe to Caucasus	erect, shrubby, suckering, 20–79 in (50–200 cm), green to dull red, prickles slender, curved to hooked, bristles glandular	leaflets 3–7, leathery, broadly elliptic to almost orbicular, dark green above, hairy and glandular beneath, teeth compound, usually glandular	solitary, or 2–4, single or semidouble, fragrant, 1½–3 in (4–8 cm) across; sepals lobed, glandular, reflexed; petals rose-pink or crimson	to ½ in (1 cm), spherical to ellipsoid, brick red, glandular-bristly

Comments: var. *officinalis*: syn. *R. officinalis*; APOTHECARIES' ROSE, OFFICINAL ROSE, RED ROSE OF LANCASTER; flowers semidouble, crimson, very fragrant. 'Versicolor' flowers semidouble 2¾–3½ in (7–9 cm) across, striped white, pink and red; often reverts; often confused with *R.* × *damascena* 'Versicolor'.

Name	Distribution	Habit	Leaves	Flowers	Fruit
R. glauca *R. rubrifolia*	C and S Europe	erect to arching 5–10 ft (1.5–3 m) tall, dark red and bloomy when young, prickles sparse, straight or decurved, broad-based, bristles sometimes present	leaflets ¾–1¾ in (2–4.5 cm), 5–9, leaden gray-green to blue-green, often tinged pink to purple-red, glaucous, ovate to narrowly elliptic, acute, hairless, toothed	solitary or 2–12, single, 1–1½ in (2.5–4 cm) across; sepals entire or lobed, smooth or glandular-bristly, spreading; petals pale to deep pink, white at base	½–⅝ in (1.3–1.5 cm), ovoid to subglobose, brown-red, smooth or with sparse glandular bristles
R. laevigata CHEROKEE ROSE	S China, Taiwan, Vietnam, Laos, Cambodia, Burma, naturalized S US	green, climbing to 33 ft (10 m) or more, prickles scattered, stout, red-brown, hooked	leaflets 1¼–3½ in (3–9 cm), 3–5, lanceolate to elliptic or ovate, leathery, acute or acuminate, glossy above, midrib sometimes prickly beneath, toothed	solitary, single, fragrant, 2–4 in (5–10 cm) across; sepals entire, bristly, erect; petals white or creamy white	1½ in (3.5–4 cm), pear-shaped, orange-red to red, bristly
R. longicuspis	NE India, W China, Burma	scrambling and climbing to 20 ft (6 m), tinged red when young, prickles short, curved or hooked or absent	tinged red when young; leaflets 2–4 in (5–10 cm) 3–7, narrowly ovate to elliptic, leathery, acuminate, occasionally downy on midrib beneath, toothed	to 15 in (38 cm) a loose cluster, single, smelling of bananas, to 2 in (5 cm) across; sepals lobed, hairy and glandular; petals white, silky beneath	⅝–¾ in (1.5–2 cm), broadly ellipsoid to spherical, red to orange, often hairy and glandular
R. moschata MUSK ROSE	unknown in the wild; widely cultivated	arching or semiclimbing, purple or red-tinged 10–33 ft (3–10 m), prickles few, scattered, straight or slightly curved	leaflets 1¼–2¾ in (3–7 cm), 5–7, broadly ovate to broadly elliptic, acute or acuminate, shiny and hairless above, downy or not on veins beneath, toothed	in few-flowered loose clusters, single, with a musky scent, 1¼–2⅛ in (3–5.5 cm) across; sepals entire lobed, hairy, reflexed; petals white or cream, reflexing with age	to ⅝ in (1.5 cm), subglobose to ovoid, orange-red, usually downy and sometimes glandular

R. foetida 'Persiana'

R. gallica var. officinalis 'Versicolor'

R. glauca

R. laevigata

R

ROSA

Name	Distribution	Habit	Leaves	Flowers	Fruit
R. moyesii	W China	erect, bristly below, stout, red-brown 6½–11½ ft (2–3.5m), prickles pale, scattered, stout, broad-based	leaflets ½–1½ in (1–4 cm), 7–13, broadly elliptic to ovate, acute, dark green above, somewhat glaucous beneath, hairless except for midrib beneath, toothed	1–2(–4), single, 1½–2½ in (4–6.5 cm) across; sepals entire, expanded at tip, hairy and sparsely glandular; petals pink to blood-red	1½–2⅓ in (3.8–6 cm), bottle-shaped, with a neck, orange-red, glandular-bristly at least toward the base

Comments: Parent of 'Geranium'; compact; leaflets paler green; flowers scarlet, fruit broader, crimson with a shorter neck and 'Sealing Wax': flowers pink; fruit large, bright red. var. *fargesii*: flowers pink to rose-red; leaflets shorter and wider, obtuse.

Name	Distribution	Habit	Leaves	Flowers	Fruit
R. multiflora JAPANESE ROSE, BABY ROSE	Japan, Korea,	arching, trailing or sometimes climbing 10–16 ft (3–5 m), prickles many small, stout, decurved	leaflets ⅝–2 in (1.5–5 cm), 5–11, obovate or elliptic, acute, acuminate or obtuse, sometimes downy beneath, toothed	few to many in branched clusters, single, with a fruity scent, ⅝–1¼ in (1.5–3 cm) across; sepals lobed, glandular-bristly; petals cream, fading to white, occasionally pink	¼ in (0.6–0.7 cm), ovoid to spherical, red

Comments: 'Carnea': flowers double, flesh-pink. 'Grevillei': SEVEN SISTERS ROSE; flowers in clusters of 25 to 50, usually double, deep pink-purple fading to white. 'Wilsonii': flowers single, white, var. *cathayensis*: flowers single, rosy pink, to 1½ in (4 cm) across, in rather flat clusters.

Name	Distribution	Habit	Leaves	Flowers	Fruit
R. pimpinellifolia BURNET ROSE, SCOTCH ROSE	Europe, Asia	suckering, 36–79 in (90–200 cm), purple-brown, prickles dense straight, slender, bristles stiff	leaflets ¼–¾ in (0.6–2 cm), 5–11, broadly elliptic to broadly obovate to orbicular, obtuse, midvein sometimes downy beneath, teeth glandular	solitary, single or double, 1½–2½ in (3.8–6 cm) across; sepals entire, narrow, margin woolly, erect; petals creamy white	¼–⅝ in (0.7–1.5 cm), spherical or almost so, dark brown becoming black, smooth

Comments: 'Andrewsii': flowers double, rose-pink. 'Grandiflora': flowers 2¾–3 in (7–7.5 cm) across. 'Hispida': flowers 2–2¾ in (5–7 cm) across, opening pale yellow, fading to cream.

Name	Distribution	Habit	Leaves	Flowers	Fruit
R. primula	C Asia to N China	erect, slender, to 10 ft (3 m), red-brown when young, prickles stout, straight, somewhat compressed, broad-based	very aromatic; leaflets ¼–¾ in (0.6–2 cm), 7–13, elliptic to obovate or oblanceolate, acute or obtuse, with large glands beneath, teeth compound, glandular	solitary, single, 1–1¾ in (2.5–4.5 cm) across; sepals entire, hairless, erect; petals primrose-yellow	½–⅝ in (1–1.5 cm), spherical to turbinate, brown-red to maroon, smooth

Name	Distribution	Habit	Leaves	Flowers	Fruit
R. roxburghii BURR ROSE, CHESTNUT ROSE, CHINQUAPIN ROSE	China			double, pink, darker in the center	

Comments: The typical plant was originally introduced from Chinese gardens and is rarely grown. More commonly seen is f. *normalis*, with spreading, rather stiff stems to 16 ft (5 m)+ with sparse, straight or hooked prickles. The leaflets are ½–1 in (1–2.5 cm) long, narrowly ovate to obovate, hairless and toothed. Solitary, single and fragrant, the flowers are 2–3 in (5–7.5 cm) across with lobed, downy and prickly sepals and mid- to deep pink petals. The fruit is 1¼–1½ in (3–4 cm) long, flattened spherical, yellow-green and prickly.

R. moschata

R. moyesii

R. pimpinellifolia 'Double White'

R. pimpinellifolia 'Grandiflora'

R

ROSA

Name	Distribution	Habit	Leaves	Flowers	Fruit
R. rubiginosa *R. eglanteria* EGLANTINE, SWEET BRIAR	Europe, N Africa, W Asia	branches arching, 6½–10 ft (2–3 m), dense, bearing many, stout, hooked prickles and stiff bristles	aromatic; leaflets ½–1¼ in (1–3 cm), 5–9, dark green, ovate to rounded, glandular and downy beneath, teeth compound	1–7, single, fragrant, 1–2 in (2.5–5 cm) across; sepals lobed, glandular-bristly, erect; petals pale to deep pink	½–1 in (1–2.5 cm), ovoid to subglobose, red or orange, smooth or glandular-bristly
R. rugosa HEDGEHOG ROSE, JAPANESE ROSE	E Russia, Korea, Japan, N China	stems erect, stout, 4–8 ft (1.2–2.5 m), downy when young, densely prickly and bristly	leaflets 1–2 in (2.5–5 cm), 5–9, dark green, oblong to elliptic, acute, wrinkled above, downy beneath with conspicuous veins, teeth shallow	1 to few, single, fragrant, 2½–3½ in (6–9 cm) across; sepals entire, expanded at tip, downy, erect; petals purple-pink	¾–1 in (2–2.5 cm), subglobose, with a neck at the top, red to orange-red, smooth

Comments: 'Alba': flowers single, white, opening from pale pink buds; very free-fruiting. var. *alboplena*: flowers double, white. var. *rosea*: flowers single, rose-pink.

Name	Distribution	Habit	Leaves	Flowers	Fruit
R. sericea	Himalaya, NE India, N Bhutan, SW and C China	upright or somewhat spreading 6½–13 ft (2–4 m), gray or brown, prickles straight or curved, often upward-pointing, red-tinged with broad bases, mixed with slender bristles	leaflets ¼–1¼ in (0.6–3 cm), 7–11, elliptic, oblong or obovate, obtuse or acute, hairy or not beneath, toothed above	solitary, on short lateral shoots, single, 1–2½ in (2.5–6 cm) across; sepals entire, hairless or silky; petals usually 5, white or cream, notched	⅜–⅝ in (0.8–1.5 cm), spherical to pear-shaped, dark crimson, scarlet, orange or yellow, smooth

Comments: ssp. *omeiensis* f. *pteracantha*: stem with very broad-based prickles forming interrupted wings along stems, bright red at first, hardening gray-brown.

Name	Distribution	Habit	Leaves	Flowers	Fruit
R. wichurana MEMORIAL ROSE	Japan, Korea, E China, Taiwan	procumbent, trailing or climbing 10–20 ft (3–6 m), prickles strong, curved	leaflets 5–9, dark green, elliptic to broadly ovate or rounded, obtuse, hairless except for midrib beneath	6–10 in loose clusters, toothed single, fragrant, 1–2 in (2.5–5 cm) across; sepals entire or lobed, often downy or slightly glandular; petals white	½–⅝ in (1–1.5 cm), ovoid or spherical, orange-red to dark red

Comments: 'Variegata': erect to clambering, leaflets cream with pink tips when young, turning green, marked with cream and tinted red.

Name	Distribution	Habit	Leaves	Flowers	Fruit
R. willmottiae *R. gymnocarpa* var. *willmottiae*	W and NW China	erect or arching to 10 ft (3 m), glaucous-pruinose, becoming red-brown, prickles slender, straight, mostly in pairs	leaflets ¼–⅝ in (0.6–1.5 cm), 7–9, obovate to oblong or almost round, obtuse, hairless, toothed	usually solitary, single, slightly fragrant, 1–1½ in (2.5–3.8 cm) across; sepals entire, hairless; petals purple-pink	½–¾ in (1–1.8 cm), ovoid, pear-shaped or more or less spherical, orange-red

Comments: 'Wisley': flowers deeper pink with narrower petals and the sepals persistent in fruit.

R. primula

R. rugosa var. *rosea*

R. xanthina 'Canary Bird'

R

ROSA

Name	Distribution	Habit	Leaves	Flowers	Fruit
R. × wintoniensis (*R. moyesii* × *R. setipoda*)	garden origin	**Comments:** Differs from *R. moyesii* in clusters of 7–10 flowers with petal crimson, white at base, and aromatic leaves.			
R. xanthina	N China, Korea	5–11½ ft (1.5–3.5 m), erect, brown to gray-brown, prickles straight or slightly curved, broad-based, sometimes much flattened on non-flowering shoots	leaflets ³⁄₈–³⁄₄ in (0.8–2 cm), 7–13, broadly elliptic to obovate to orbicular, obtuse, hairy beneath, toothed	solitary, rarely 2, semidouble, 1½–2 in (3.8–5 cm) across; sepals entire, acuminate, leafy and toothed, more or less hairless; petals bright yellow	½–⁵⁄₈ in (1.2–1.5 cm), spherical or broadly ellipsoid, brown red or maroon, smooth and hairless

Comments: 'Canary Bird': neat foliage and larger, freely produced bright yellow flowers. f. *hugonis*: leaflets elliptic to obovate, flower-stalks hairless bearing single flowers 1½–2½ in (4–6 cm) across. f. *spontanea*: flowers single, 2–2½ in (5–6 cm) across.

Roscoea (for William Roscoe [1753–1831], founder of the Liverpool Botanic Garden). Zingiberaceae. China, Himalaya. Some 17 species, perennial, rhizomatous herbs with lanceolate to strap-shaped leaves, their bases enveloping each other to form a pseudostem. Short terminal spikes of showy flowers are produced in summer and early fall. The corolla is tubular with three petals, the uppermost erect and hooded, the lateral petals hanging either side of a showy, 2-lobed lip. Hardy to −4°F (−20°C) if mulched in winter. Grow in part shade and in rich, moist but well-drained acidic, peaty loam. Propagate by division in spring.

R. alpina Kashmir, Nepal; to 12 in (30 cm); flowers pink or mauve, to 1¼ in (3 cm) in diameter; *R. cautleoides* W China; to 22 in (55 cm); flowers pale yellow, to 2 in (5 cm) diam.; *R. humeana* SW China; to 13 in (34 cm); flowers purple or lilac, to 2 in (5 cm) diam.; *R. purpurea* Himalaya, Sikkim; to 12 in (30 cm); flowers pale purple or white with dark purple markings, to 2½ in (6 cm) diam.

rose a perforated cap attached to the spout of a watering can in order to produce a spray of water. Roses may be round or oval in surface outline and are fitted with the distribution holes uppermost for a fine spray when watering newly sown seed or seedlings, and pointed downward for a more drenching application when watering newly potted or established open-ground plants.

rosemary (*Rosmarinus officinalis*) an evergreen perennial, up to 6½ ft (2 m) in height, with procumbent forms. A native of the Mediterranean region, it has been cultivated for centuries for the aromatic oils distilled from the flowers and leaves; the fresh or dried leaves are used for flavoring meat. Grow in a sheltered sunny site, in pots in areas subject to severe cold. Prune after flowering to contain habit. Propagate from softwood or semiripe cuttings in summer.

rosette leaves radiating from a common crown or center.

Rosmarinus (from Latin *ros*, dew, and *marinus*, of the sea, from the maritime habitat). Labiatae. S Europe, N Africa. 2 species, very aromatic evergreen shrubs with crowded, linear to oblong, leathery leaves with revolute margins. The flowers are 2-lipped, small and borne in short axillary racemes at various times of year, but usually in early spring and late summer. *R. officinalis*, ROSEMARY (q.v.) has been an important constituent of herb gardens for centuries, and is an attractive evergreen shrub for hot, dry, sheltered positions, particularly on stony, calcareous soils. It is hardy to −10°F (−23°C). *R. officinalis* Mediterranean; to 6½ ft (2 m), erect or procumbent; leaves ⅜–1½ in (1.5–4 cm), dark green, leathery, white-tomentose beneath, margins strongly revolute; flowers pale blue to lilac; includes cultivars with white, pink and deep blue flowers, prostrate to tall and narrowly erect, some with white or yellow variegated leaves.

Rossioglossum (for J. Ross, who collected orchids in Mexico in the 1830s). Orchidaceae. Mexico to Panama. 6 species, epiphytic orchids with clumped, ovoid pseudobulbs and broadly elliptic to ovate, leathery leaves. Carried on basal racemes, the flowers are large and waxy, with spreading tepals, usually wavy and with tigerlike coloring. The lip is smaller with a bumpy callus. Provide a minimum temperature of 50°F (10°C). Pot every two years in a dense, bark-based medium containing some leaf mold, coir and sphagnum. Place in a cool, well-ventilated and brightly lit situation, avoiding sunscorch and wetting of the foliage. Water and feed copiously when in growth to encourage the plumpest possible pseudobulbs. On their completion, withhold water, except when it is necessary to prevent excessive shrivelling. Flower spikes will develop in late summer and fall, blooming in winter. Repot and recommence watering on first appearance of new growth. Propagate by division when repotting. *R. grande* (syn. *Odontoglossum grande*); CLOWN ORCHID; Guatemala, Mexico; raceme 5½–12 in (14–30 cm), 2–8-flowered; flowers to 6 in (15 cm) in diameter, long-lived, waxy; sepals linear-lanceolate, yellow, barred and flecked rust to chestnut brown, narrow, wavy; petals oblanceolate, yellow, basal half solidly deep red-brown, broader than sepals; lip cream-white or cream-yellow, banded red-brown, fan-shaped callus yellow, protuberances eyelike, ringed with brick red.

R

rostellum (1) any small beaklike structure; (2) the tissue separating anther from stigma in Orchidaceae.

rosulate (of leaves) arranged in a rosette.

rotate wheel-shaped.

rotation the practice of changing the position of annual crops in a garden each season for a period of several years. Rotation reduces the likelihood of a buildup of soilborne pests and diseases, and helps make the most efficient use of nutrients as different crops absorb surpluses left by others. It also aids weed control where some dense canopy crops smother seedlings and through the continual cultivation required for crops such as potatoes. It is especially advocated for the vegetable garden, where crops from the same family are likely to suffer from the same pests and diseases; legumes, onions and miscellaneous crops are grouped to follow potatoes which in turn follow brassicas over three years.

Strict adherence to such rotation is often impractical in a small garden where there may be limited areas of particular crops and where extended cropping may be practiced using covering methods and a range of cultivars. Moreover, clubroot disease and potato cyst eelworm, for example, can persist in the soil for much longer than three years. The general principle of rotation is advisable, although also worthy of consideration is the view that crops may be grown continually on the same site until pest or disease problems arise and at that point moved elsewhere;

Crop rotation
Planting certain vegetable groups together on a different site each year can lessen the risk of soilborne pests and diseases.

this, however, obviates other sound advantages of rotation.

Rothmannia (for Dr. Georgius Rothmann [1739–1778], explorer, botanist and pupil of Linnaeus). Rubiaceae. Tropical Africa, Madagascar, Asia. 30 species, shrubs or small trees grown for their *Gardenia*-like flowers produced in summer. Cultivate as for *Gardenia*. *R. capensis* (CANDLEWOOD; South Africa; evergreen tree to 46 ft (14 m); leaves to 4 in (10 cm), lustrous dark green; flowers white or cream to yellow, fragrant, to 3 in (8 cm), funnel-shaped).

rototiller a powered cultivator with rotating blades. Rototillers are suitable for cultivating large areas but are capable of producing a semipermeable pan at operating depth when used continually on heavy soils, especially under wet conditions.

rotund rounded, curved like the arc of a circle.

rough leaves the first true leaves produced by a seedling, used particularly when describing a suitable stage of growth at which to prick out or apply pesticide treatment.

rove beetles (Coleoptera: Staphylinidae) a worldwide family of about 20,000 species. Most are black or brown, but some are brightly colored; slender and elongate beetles varying in length from $1/16$–$1\frac{1}{4}$ in (1–30 mm); their most characteristic feature is their very short wing cases, which give a flexibility unusual in beetles. Many fly readily and they are found in a wide variety of habitats, including moss, dung, carrion, decaying vegetable matter, flowers, under bark and in birds' nests.

Many species are predacious as both adults and larvae, exerting natural control of various pests, and several species have been recorded feeding on the eggs and larvae of the cabbage root fly; especially active in this way are *Aleochara* species. *Oligoa flavicornis*, with small, shiny black adults up to $1/16$ in (1 mm) in length, is a predator of the fruit tree red spider mite. Familiar in Europe and North America is the DEVIL'S COACH HORSE (*Staphylinus olens*), which is up to $1\frac{1}{4}$ in (30 mm) long.

Roystonea (for General Roy Stone [1836–1905], US military engineer in Puerto Rico). Palmae. Caribbean Islands and continental coasts. ROYAL PALM. 12 species, palms with columnar trunks and pinnate leaves, their bases forming a distinct crown-shaft. Used in landscaping in the lowland tropics, and for avenue and specimen plantings. Although sometimes grown in sheltered subtropical gardens, they seldom achieve their full stature. *R. regia* is a slender and elegant palm when young, suitable for pot and tub cultivation in the warm greenhouse (minimum temperature 59°F/15°C). Propagate by seed. *R. regia* CUBAN ROYAL; Cuba; trunk to 80 ft (25 m), thickened in middle, often swollen at base, sometimes leaning or crooked; lower leaves curved downward, covering the crown shaft, pinnae to $3\frac{1}{4}$ ft (1 m) × $\frac{3}{4}$–$1\frac{1}{2}$ in (2–4 cm) in 2 rows and differing planes.

Rubus (the Classical Latin name). Rosaceae. BLACKBERRY, BRAMBLE, RASPBERRY. Cosmopolitan. Some 250 species, evergreen or deciduous, erect, scrambling, trailing or prostrate shrubs and shrublets, usually bristly and prickly. The leaves are simple, lobed or pinnately to palmately divided. Produced in spring and summer in clusters, racemes and panicles, the flowers consist of 4 or 5 broad and spreading petals and numerous stamens. They are followed by aggregate fruits composed of many, fleshy drupelets. The following are hardy to –13°F (–25°C), with the exception of *R. squarrosus*, which will not survive below 0°F (–18°C). All prefer fertile, well-drained soil in sun or light shade. Train climbers on walls, fences and trellis or among larger shrubs and over tree stumps. *R. tricolor* is an excellent groundcover. *R. cockburnianus* and *R. thibetanus* are striking silver shrubs for the winter garden. Cut out old and exhausted stems of all species in early spring. Increase by seed. Propagate evergreens by semiripe cuttings in a heated case; deciduous species by softwood or hardwood cuttings; also by layering. See *blackberry*, *dewberry*, *hybrid berries* and *raspberry*. (See table overleaf.)

Rudbeckia (for Olof Rudbeck the elder [1630–1702], and Olof Rudbeck

695

RUBUS

Name	Distribution	Habit	Stems	Leaves	Flowers	Fruit
R. 'Benenden' R. 'Tridel'; (R. deliciosus × R. trilobus)	garden origin	erect, vigorous deciduous shrub to 10 ft (3 m)	branches arching; bark peeling	3–5-lobed, broad, bright green, downy	to 2 in (5 cm) diameter, solitary, axillary; petals broad, bright white	
R. biflorus	Himalaya	deciduous shrub to 10 ft (3 m)	stems erect, white-glaucous, with straight prickles	to 10 in (25 cm); petiole and rachis bristly; leaflets 3–5, ovate to elliptic, to 4 in (10 cm), acute or acuminate, sharply toothed, dark green above, white-tomentose beneath	white, ½–⅔ in (1–1.7 cm) diameter, terminal and axillary	yellow
R. cockburnianus	N and C China	deciduous shrub to 10 ft (3 m).	stems erect, much-branched, strongly white-glaucous, sparsely prickly; branches arching	pinnate, to 8 in (20 cm); petioles white-woolly, with hooked prickles; leaflets 9, to 2½ in (6 cm), ovate, or rhomboid or oval-lanceolate, acuminate, serrate, white-tomentose beneath	purple, small, in terminal panicles to 4¾ in (12 cm)	black
R. henryi **Comments:** var. bambusarum: leaflets 3, narrowly lanceolate, to 5 in (12.5 cm).	C and W China	scrambling evergreen shrub to 20 ft (6 m)	stems slender, with a few prickles, tomentose-floccose when young	trilobed, to 6 in (15 cm), glabrous above, white-tomentose beneath, lobes to 1 in (2.5 cm), narrow, long-acuminate, serrate	pink, to ¾ in (2 cm) diameter, in 6–10-flowered, glandular raceme to 3 in (7.5 cm)	shiny black
R. idaeus RASPBERRY, RED RASPBERRY, WILD RASPBERRY, EUROPEAN RASPBERRY, FRAMBOISE	Europe, N Asia, Japan	to 5 ft (1.5 m), erect	stems erect, bloomed, bristly and softly hairy, usually with weak prickles	usually pinnate; leaflets 3–7 ovate or oblong, occasionally somewhat lobed, all shortly acuminate, cordate at the base, glabrescent above, white-tomentose beneath	white, to ½ in (1 cm) diameter, in few-flowered, leafy, terminal and axillary racemes	red or orange

Comments: 'Aureus': low-growing; leaves clear bright yellow. 'Phyllanthus': flowers replaced by tasselled green shoots, inflorescence divided. var. strigosus: AMERICAN RASPBERRY; densely glandular-bristly. 'Albus': fruit orange-yellow.

R. laciniatus CUT-LEAVED BRAMBLE, CUT-LEAF BLACKBERRY, PARSLEY-LEAVED BRAMBLE	origin unknown	scrambling, deciduous shrub	stems robust, angled, pubescent with stout, recurved prickles	leaflets 3–5, divided into pairs of laciniate segments, glabrous or pubescent beneath	pink-white, in large terminal panicles, petals toothed	black

Comments: 'Elegans': leaves small, upper leaf surface hairy; flowers and fruit rare.

R. 'Benenden'

R. cockburnianus

R. henryi var. bambusarum

R. spectabilis 'Olympic Double'

RUBUS

Name	Distribution	Habit	Stems	Leaves	Flowers	Fruit
R. odoratus FLOWERING RASPBERRY, THIMBLEBERRY, PURPLE-FLOWERING RASPBERRY	E N America	vigorous, deciduous shrub to 10 ft (3 m)	stems woody, erect, with pale brown, peeling bark, glandular, pubescent, without prickles	to 10 in (25 cm), 5-lobed, cordate at base, serrate, pubescent beneath	fragrant, pink-purple, to 2 in (5 cm) diameter, in many-flowered panicles	red or orange
Comments: 'Albus': bark light; leaves pale; flowers white.						
R. pentalobus	Taiwan	spreading or prostrate shrub	stems brown-pubescent, sparsely prickly	wrinkled, ovate to orbicular, to 8 in (20 cm), cordate, lobes 3–5, sharply serrate, pilose to glabrous above, tomentose or subglabrous beneath	white, solitary	red
Comments: 'Emerald Carpet': carpet-forming.						
R. spectabilis SALMONBERRY	W N America	deciduous shrub to 6½ ft (2 m)	stems erect, glabrous, with fine prickles	to 6 in (15 cm); leaflets 3, ovate, to 4 in (10 cm), long-acuminate, serrate, glabrous	pink to maroon, ¾–1½ in (2–3.5 cm) diameter, usually solitary	orange-yellow
Comments: 'Flore Pleno': flowers large, double.						
R. squarrosus	New Zealand	sprawling evergreen shrub	stems slender, glossy, red-brown, fiercely prickly	to 6 in (15 cm), slender-stalked; leaflets 3–5, linear-lanceolate, toothed, often reduced to midrib only or a vestigial blade terminating midrib, tinted red-brown	yellow-white, small in panicles	orange-red
R. thibetanus GHOST BRAMBLE	W China	deciduous shrub to 6½ ft (2 m), resembling a shorter, finer *R. cockburnianus*	stems slender, silver to purple-pruinose, bristly	to 9 in (23 cm); leaflets 7–13, oval or ovate, to 2 in (5 cm), coarsely serrate, mid- to gray-green to silvery above, bright, white-tomentose beneath; terminal leaflet pinnately lobed	purple, to ½ in (1.2 cm) diameter, solitary or in few-flowered terminal racemes	black, pruinose
Comments: often sold under the cultivar name 'Silver Fern'.						
R. tricolor	W China	prostrate, semievergreen shrub	stems with dense, buff bristles	to 4 in (10 cm), acute, cordate at base, serrate, dark green above, tomentose and bristly beneath	white, to 1 in (2.5 cm) diameter, solitary or in small, few-flowered terminal panicles	bright red
Comments: 'Betty Ashburner': *R. tricolor* × *R. fockeanus*; leaves large, rounded, with crinkled edges, shiny. 'Kenneth Ashburner': stems long; leaves pointed, shiny; vigorous.						
R. ulmifolius BRAMBLE	W & C Europe	vigorously scrambling shrub	stems robust, arching, bloomed, with straight or hooked prickles	leaflets 3–5, white-hairy beneath	inflorescence racemelike; petals pink or white, crumpled	red to purple-black
Comments: 'Bellidiflorus': flowers double. 'Variegatus': leaves variegated.						

the younger [1660–1740], the former a Swedish physician/botanist and founder of the Uppsala botanic garden, the latter also a professor at Uppsala—both were friends, patrons and colleagues of Linnaeus). Compositae. N America, now widespread as garden escape. CONEFLOWER. About 15 species, usually perennial, rarely annual or biennial herbs with simple or branched stems and large, daisylike flower heads in summer and fall. Fully hardy. Grow in moderately fertile and moisture-retentive garden soil in sun or part-day shade. Propagate by division or removal of rooted basal portions of stem; also (cultivars) by seed sown under glass in early spring. Plant out seedlings in late spring. The seed races are often treated as annuals, flowering in their first year.

R. fulgida SE US; perennial herb to 3¼ ft (1 m); flower heads to 2¾ in (7 cm) in diameter, receptacle hemispherical to conic, ray florets yellow to orange, disk florets purple-brown; *R. hirta* BLACK-EYED SUSAN, MARGUERITE JAUNE; central US; biennial or short-lived perennial herb to 6½ ft (2 m); flower heads to 3½ in (9 cm) in diameter, receptacle conic, ray florets to 1½ in (4 cm), pale yellow, darker at base, disk florets purple-brown; includes cultivars and seed races with single and double flower heads with large ray florets in shades of gold,

R

some stained or solidly over-laid with brown, bronze or coppery red; the disk florets range in color from bright green to mahogany and black-brown; *R. laciniata* N America; perennial herb to 10 ft (3 m), mostly glabrous and glaucous; flower heads solitary, receptacle hemispheric to conic, ray florets to 2½ in (6 cm), yellow, disk florets yellow-green or gray-green; includes cultivars with short (24 in [60 cm]) to tall (6½ ft [2 m]) habits and large flower heads in shades of yellow and gold.

ruderal a plant that grows in waste materials or on waste land.

rudimentary fragmentary, imperfectly developed.

Ruellia (for Jean de la Ruelle of Soissons [1474–1537], botanist and physician to Francois I, author of *De Natura Plantarum* [1536]). Acanthaceae. Tropical America, Africa, Asia and temperate N America. Some 150 species, perennial herbs, subshrubs or shrubs with 5-lobed, tubular to funnelform flowers in spring and summer. Cultivate as for *Crossandra*. *R. devosiana* Brazil; pubescent subshrub to 18 in (45 cm), leaves with silvery white veins above purple-tinted beneath; flowers white flushed lavender, tube slender, lobes veined purple; *R. graecizans* S America; bushy subshrub to 24 in (60 cm) or more, spreading; flowers to 1 in (2.5 cm), scarlet; *R. macrantha* CHRISTMAS PRIDE; Brazil; bushy subshrub, erect to 6½ ft (2 m); flowers to 3 in (7.5 cm), crimson to lavender-rose, throat paler with red veins; *R. makoyana* MONKEY PLANT, TRAILING VELVET PLANT; Brazil; spreading herb to 24 in (60 cm); leaves tinted violet above and veined silvery gray, purple beneath; flowers to 2 in (5 cm), rosy carmine.

rufescent, rufous reddish-brown.

rugose wrinkled by irregular lines and veins.

rugulose finely rugose.

Rumex (name used by Pliny). Polygonaceae. Northern temperate regions. DOCK, SORREL. 200 species, annual, biennial or perennial herbs, rarely shrubs, with variously shaped leaves and panicles or racemes of very small, rusty-red-green flowers. COMMON SORREL, *R. acetosa*, and the more drought-tolerant FRENCH SORREL, *R. scutatus*, are valued for their sharply flavored leaves, used raw in salads or cooked. Treated as annuals or short-term perennials (replace every third or fourth year), they are easily grown and have a long harvesting season. Grow in sun on any moderately fertile and well-drained soil. Sow seed in spring and thin to 4 in (10 cm), where the whole plant is to be harvested, or to 10 in (25 cm) for perennial crops. Leaves can be harvested about eight weeks from sowing. *R. sanguineus* is the ornamental BLOODY DOCK, a native of Europe, Asia and N Africa. It grows to 3¼ ft (1 m) tall, with bold, oblong and puckered, glossy olive leaves, the veins stained with dark blood red. Fully hardy, it prefers a damp or wet situation and full sun. Increase by seed or division. Allowed to set seed, it may become invasive.

ruminate appearing as if chewed.

runcinate a leaf, petal or petal-like structure, usually oblanceolate in outline and with sharp, prominent teeth or broad, incised lobes pointing backward toward the base, away from a generally acute apex.

runner a common term for a stolon; especially used of strawberries.

creeping, rooting stem (stolon or runner)

parent plant

plantlet potted up

new plantlet

Strawberry runners

run off (1) rain or irrigation water that is not absorbed by soil or evaporated, and therefore a potential cause of erosion; (2) the stage of surface saturation of a plant that results from spraying.

Ruschia (for Ernest Rusch of Lichtenstein Farm, Namaqualand). Aizoaceae. South Africa (Cape Province, Namibia. 360 species, evergreen shrubs, shrublets and perennial herbs with succulent leaves and daisy-like flowers in summer. Cultivate as for *Lampranthus*.

R. acuminata shrublet to 8 in (20 cm); leaves ⅝–1 in (1.5–2.5 cm), tinged blue, spotted, roughly papillose; flowers 1¼ in (3 cm) in diameter, white to pale pink; *R. crassa* shrub ascending or prostrate; leaves blue-green, covered in short hairs, ½–¾ in (1–2 cm) long, apiculate; flowers ⅞ in (2.2 cm) in diameter, white; *R. macowanii* shrublet, 6–8 in (15–20 cm), prostrate; leaves ¾–1½ in (2–3.5 cm), swollen; flowers ⅞ in (2.2 cm) in diameter, pink with darker stripes.

Ruscus (name used by Virgil). Liliaceae (Asparagaceae). Azores, N Africa, Madeira, W Europe to Caspian Sea. BUTCHER'S BROOM. 6 species, evergreen perennial herbs with clumped shrublike stems bearing cladophylls. Fleshy at first, these later become hard and rigid. The true leaves are minute and scalelike. The cladophylls are rhombic to ovate-lanceolate, usually acute to sharply pointed and crowded. Very small, pale flowers are borne on the midrib of the cladophylls. When plants of both sexes are grown together, bright red berries may be produced.

Ruscus tolerates a range of soil conditions, including chalk and heavy clay, and particularly dry shade. Dried stems are used in floral arrangements, taking on red tints when dried in glycerine. They are often dyed dark green. Hardy to –4°F (–20°C). Propagate by division or by seed, which may take up to 18 months to germinate.

R. aculeatus BUTCHER'S BROOM, BOX HOLLY, JEW'S MYRTLE; Mediterranean and Black Sea north to Great Britain, west to Azores; 12–50 in (30–125 cm), erect, densely clumped and branched, branches green, cladophylls to 1 in (2.5 cm), ovate, sharply pointed, crowded, dark glossy green at first, becoming dry and matt, rigid.

Russelia (for Dr. Alexander Russell, physician, traveler and author of *Natural History of Aleppo* [1756]). Scrophulariaceae. Mexico, Cuba to Colombia. 52 species, evergreen shrubs and subshrubs with many erect to pendent, slender green stems, the leaves sometimes reduced to scales. In summer, they bear masses of tubular, 2-lipped flowers. A superb basket plant for the cool to intermediate greenhouse (minimum temperature 50°F/10°C). Grow in full sun in a fast-draining loam-based mix with additional sand. Water very sparingly in cold weather. Propagate from seed and by division or layering (each drooping tip of *R. equisetiformis* that touches damp ground is likely to root); alternatively, increase by greenwood cuttings.

R. equisetiformis (syn. *R. juncea*; CORAL FOUNTAIN, FIRECRACKER PLANT, FOUNTAIN PLANT; Mexico; shrub to 5 ft (1.5 m) with a weeping habit; branches many, green, slender; leaves very small, scalelike, short-lived; flowers bright coral red to scarlet, to 1¼ in (3 cm).

russeting the formation of rough brown patches of cork on the surface of fruits, mainly apples and pears, resulting from genetic characteristic, environmental conditions or disease. Apple varieties which naturally have a rough brown skin are called russets.

rust a fungal plant disease organism typified by orange-red, yellow or white powdery spore masses on affected plants. The term is often confusingly used to describe any red/brown discoloration of foliage.

Morphologically identical rusts are sometimes restricted to one host genus when each is referred to as *formae speciales* (f.sp.). Within a special form of a rust, there may be races which only attack certain cultivars of the host and these are known as pathogenic races or pathotypes.

Rusts are parasites on seed plants and ferns and include many of the most important diseases of cereals, vegetables and trees. Well-known garden rusts include those of *Antirrhinum*, apple (cedar-apple rust), leek, bean, chrysanthemum, carnation, hollyhock, mint, *Pelargonium*, and rose.

Rust fungi are most commonly found on the green, aerial parts of plants, the foliage and stems; infection is often localized to where pustules containing spore masses of the fungus have burst through the epidermis of the plant. Spores may be orange, whitish, yellow, brown or black, and occasionally gelatinous, depending on species. Affected plants are always weakened and heavy infection can cause stunted growth. Some rusts may spread internally in their hosts causing systemic infections that persist from one season to another, for example, mint rust.

A feature of many rusts is the dependence of their reproductive phase on infection of two different types of plants, which may be of a different botanical family; these are called alternate hosts. Such heteroecious rusts include WHEAT/BARBERRY RUST (*Puccinia graminis*) and JUNIPER/PEAR RUST (*Gymnosporangium* spp). It is sometimes possible to prevent infection of a cultivated host plant by eradicating non-crop alternate hosts in the vicinity; for example, the control of PINE BLISTER RUST can be achieved by the eradication of *Ribes*. When the whole life cycle occurs on one kind of host, the rust is termed autoecious, for example, ROSE RUSTS (*Phragmidium* species) and MINT RUST (*Puccinia menthae*).

During the development of their host plants, rusts can produce up to five different types of spore, and life cycles vary according to which ones are present.

CHRYSANTHEMUM WHITE RUST (*Puccinia horiana*), which originated in Japan, has caused serious damage in Europe to its confined host range of Asiatic *Chrysanthemum*, including cultivars of florist's chrysanthemums. It was introduced into England in 1963 on infected cuttings and from around that time also spread to Argentina, Australia, New Zealand, South Africa and the US. The name is descriptive of the rust pustules formed mainly on the undersides of leaves, but any green tissues and flowers are liable to infection. It is spread by airborne spores and is highly contagious in cool, moist conditions. Quarantine measures in the UK were successful until the late 1980s, by which time the disease had become common on the continent of Europe. Strict control of propagation premises prevents outbreaks in new areas of cultivation, but once established on outdoor chrysanthemums, there is little chance of eradicating the disease and nearby greenhouse specimens will be at risk. The hot water treatment of lifted stools will kill infected tissue. There are several different strains of chrysanthemum white rust fungus.

CHRYSANTHEMUM BROWN RUST (*Puccinia chrysanthemi*), sometimes called BLACK RUST because of the very dark-colored spore pustules, is also of Japanese origin and was first found in the UK nearly a century ago. It has no alternate host and occurs worldwide, although it is not usually common or serious enough to warrant control measures.

The fact that some *Berberis* species are alternate hosts for WHEAT RUST (*Puccinia graminis*) has led to barberry being the subject of quarantine measures in several countries, legislation requiring the destruction of certain species of *Berberis* and restrictions on their importation and interstate movement. The rust forms cup-shaped orange bodies on the underside of the leaves and sometimes on the fruits. Some species, such as *B.thunbergii*, are immune from infection by wheat rust and have been widely planted in N America. *Mahonia* species can be infected by wheat rust, but *M.aquifolium* and *M. bealei* are highly resistant and the western North American *M.repens* is immune from infection.

SEMPERVIVUM RUST (*Endophyllum sempervivi*) is systemic and infects the leaves and grows down into the roots, the first symptoms being a stunting or abnormal elongation of the leaves. It is not possible to cure infected plants and they should be destroyed as soon as possible. Neighboring healthy plants of *Sempervivum* and *Echeveria* should be given a protective spray of an approved fungicide.

On junipers, the *Gymnosporangium* rusts cause a range of symptoms, from relatively minor needle infections to witches' brooms and large galls, but their importance as garden diseases mainly depends on their effect on their rosaceous hosts, which is most damaging when fruits are infected. The most economically important is AMERICAN

R

699

CEDAR-APPLE RUST *(G. juniperae-virgini-anae)*, for the damage it causes to apples rather than any harm to its natural hosts, the red cedar *(J.virginiana)*, the southern red cedar *(J. silicicola)*, and the Rocky Mountain juniper *(J.scopulorum)*. This rust is confined to the US and Canada.

Another important NORTH AMERICAN JUNIPER RUST is *G.clavipes*, quince rust, which attacks junipers of the *J. oxycedrus* and *J.sabina* alliances, in particular *J.virginiana* and *J.horizontalis*, and has a wide range of alternate host genera including *Amelanchier*, *Chaenomeles*, *Cotoneaster*, *Crataegus*, *Cydonia*, *Malus*, *Photinia* and *Pyrus*. A similar host range of junipers and Rosaceae is infected in North America by *G.globosum*, known mainly as a serious disease of *Crataegus*, but also found on *Malus*, *Pyrus* and *Sorbus*.

PEAR RUST *(G. fuscum)* and MEDLAR RUST *(G. confusum)* are Eurasian species which have now spread, probably in the form of latent infection of their host, *J.sabina*, to North America. The case of JAPANESE PEAR RUST *(G.asiaticum)* in recent years illustrates the potential for intercontinental movement of plant diseases in commerce. It was found on *Juniperus chinensis* bonsai imported into England from Japan and investigations showed that the fungus was capable of infecting the EUROPEAN PEAR *(Pyrus communis)*. It is not currently established in the UK or mainland Europe.

HOLLYHOCK RUST *(Puccinia malvacearum)* is found worldwide, and although HOLLYHOCK *(Alcea rosea)* is most commonly infected, other members of Malvacae are susceptible, including species growing wild. All green parts are liable to infection, which is characterized by bright yellow or orange spots with reddish centers. On the underside of leaves, infected areas bear circular pin-head-sized pustules; these bear spores in the presence of moisture, which are distributed by air current. Where affected areas coalesce, portions of the leaf may fall out. The disease overwinters in crowns and on plant debris. There are no resistant cultivars, but vigorously growing seedlings are less susceptible than old plants, and regular re-sowing is advisable, as is the removal of the first

leaves. Recommended protectant fungicide spraying from 5–6 in (12.5–15.0 cm) high is worthwhile, and severely diseased plants should be removed and burned.

PELARGONIUM RUST *(Puccinia pelargonii-zonalis)* was first observed in Britain in 1965 and is now established nationally. In the UK, it only affects zonal pelargoniums, first showing as white spots on the underside of leaves and yellow spots on the upper-sides. Brown masses of spores later develop on the undersurfaces in the presence of moisture, and are spread by air current, especially in a humid environment. Control measures include purchasing healthy stock, good greenhouse ventilation and careful watering, and spraying or dusting with an approved fungicide.

ROSE RUST *(Phragmidium* species) infection is most commonly by *P. tuberculatum*, which attacks all sorts of roses. Although distributed throughout Britain, it mostly occurs in southern and eastern England, where it weakens the plant especially in wet seasons. On rose species, the first sign of infection may be bright orange rust patches up to 1 in- (2.5 cm)-long on stems and leaf stalks in early spring; on cultivars, leaf infection in May is more usual as a first sign. Rose rust overwinters as special spores on fallen leaves, plant debris and mulching material, and on soil and other surfaces. Regular pruning, with removal of infected shoots, and the gathering of and burning of fallen leaves are useful means of reducing infection level. Spraying with a recommended fungicide in mid-April before overwintered spores germinate is advisable, and where the disease is prevalent, subsequent summer treatment should be applied.

LEEK RUST *(Puccinia porrii)* is common on leeks and occasionally severe. Diseased plants should be destroyed, and raising and growing carried out on a different site each year. Avoidance of high-nitrogen feeding and very close spacing will reduce the incidence of infection.

MINT RUST *(Puccinia menthae)* occurs widely on cultivated and wild mint, the rhizomes and stems becoming infected in late fall and winter; affected shoots are stunted and bear yellow leaves.

Healthy mother plants should be identified for propagation; when suspect plants must be used, rhizomes should be washed and then immersed in water at 112°F (44°C) for 10 minutes, before plunging in cold water.

Apart from the destruction of alternate hosts, the enforcement of quarantine and hygiene measures, hot water treatment, and cultivar resistance, the control of rusts is possible with systemic chemicals, and those recommended for garden use should be sought.

rustication a style of stonework in which surfaces are left rough and the joints are deeply recessed.

rustic work refers to ornamental garden features made of timber in the form of branches, with bark intact or removed. The term may be used for garden furniture, fencing, pergolas and archways.

Ruta (the Classical Latin name). Rutaceae. Macaronesia, E Europe, SW Asia. RUE. 8 species, pungently aromatic, woody-based perennial herbs and small shrubs with finely 2–3-× pinnately cut leaves. Produced in spring and summer, the small flowers consist of four, outspread, yellow petals with incurved tips. Rue has long been cultivated as a bitter medicinal herb, and is often held to have magical properties, particularly if obtained by theft. It is highly decorative, with glaucous, deeply divided leaves and curious yellow flowers. When handled in sunlight, all parts may cause blistering or dermatitis. Hardy to –10°F (–23°C). Grow in full sun or part-shade in well-drained soil. Cut back damaged or exhausted growth in spring. Propagate from semiripe cuttings taken in late summer, or from seed sown as soon as ripe. *R. graveolens* RUE, HERB OF GRACE; Balkan Peninsula, SE Europe; intensely aromatic, glaucous sea green to blue subshrub or shrub 8–20 in (20–50 cm); leaves finely divided, segments usually obovate, to ½ in (1 cm) long; includes 'Blue Curl', dwarf, bushy, with lacy and curling, ice-blue leaves, 'Blue Mound', mound-forming, with tinted blue leaves, 'Jackman's Blue', with leaves distinctly glaucous blue-green, and 'Variegata', with leaves edged with creamy white.

S

Sabal (from a native American name). Palmae. PALMETTO. N Carolina through Florida and West Indies to E Texas and Colombia. Some 14 species, small to medium-sized palms with palmate leaves. They are usually stemless and clump-forming, but may produce short trunks. Grow in full sun or light shade in a free-draining, sandy medium. In winter keep frost-free and fairly dry, and in summer warm and moist. Propagate by seed or by rooted suckers. *S. minor* DWARF PALMETTO, SCRUB PALMETTO, BUSH PALMETTO; SE US; leaves to 5 ft (1.5 m), blue-green, segments to 60 × 2 in (152 × 5 cm), filaments few or none; *S. palmetto* BLUE PALMETTO, CABBAGE PALMETTO, CABBAGE TREE, COMMON PALMETTO; SE US; to 100 ft (30 m); leaves to 6½ ft (2 m), green, segments to 32 × 1½ in (80 × 4 cm), with many filaments.

sac see *locule*.

sage (*Salvia officinalis*) a perennial subshrub, native of the Mediterranean region; it is widely cultivated for its aromatic leaves, which are used in cooking and in medicines. The plant grows to about 24 in (60 cm) high, and bears gray-green foliage with predominantly purple-blue flowers in summer. Plant 18–24 in (45–60 cm) apart. To avoid legginess, propagate every four or five years by softwood cuttings taken in early summer, or by semiripe cuttings with a heel taken in late summer to early fall; earthing up of established plants produces rooted shoots. Leaves are used fresh but they also dry well. Trim shoots back after

Sage

flowering to retain a compact bush. There are variegated and colored foliage selections, many of which are less hardy, but all sages can be grown as ornamental plants.

Sagina procumbens
This common weed species can be troublesome as an unsightly, persistent invader of paving joints, rock gardens and lawns.

Sagina (Latin meaning "fodder," referring originally to *Spergula arvensis*, a plant cultivated for fodder). Caryophyllaceae. Widespread in northern temperate regions, also occurring on tropical mountains. PEARLWORT. About 20 species, small, low-growing, annual or perennial herbs, carpeting or hummock-forming, with narrow leaves and small, green to white flowers. Suitable for the interstices of paving, pans in an alpine house, open sites in a rock garden, scree and trough plantings. Hardy to 59°F (15°C). Grow in sun in gritty, moist soil. Propagate by seed in fall or by division in spring. *S. boydii* NW Europe; densely cushion-forming, glabrous perennial; leaves crowded, rigid, recurved, glossy dark green. *Sagina procumbens* is a perennial very common in gardens, where it can become a troublesome weed. The needlelike leaves are borne on sideshoots that spread from a central rosette. It thrives in acidic, silty soil low in organic matter, and spreads by means of very fine seed. Control in beds by the application of a deep mulch or, when suitable and recommended, by application of glyphosate. In lawns it may be mistaken for moss. Commercial lawn herbicides provide effective control in such a situation.

Sagittaria (from Latin *sagittarius*, armed with arrows, referring to the leaf shape). ARROWHEAD. Alismataceae. Temperate and tropical regions. 20 species, aquatic, perennial herbs with a swollen rootstock, sagittate leaves and white, 3-petalled flowers in racemes or panicles in spring and summer. Hardy aquatics, these plants have the same cultural requirements as *Alisma*. Propagate by division in spring. *S. latifolia* WAPATO, DUCK POTATO; US; leaves to 12 in (30 cm); scape to 4 ft (1.2 m); flowers 1¼–1½ in (3–4 cm) in diameter; 'Flore Pleno': double-flowered; *S. sagittifolia* OLD WORLD ARROWHEAD; Eurasia; leaves to 10 in (25 cm); scape to 3¼ ft (1 m); flowers to 1 in (2.5 cm) in diameter, spotted purple; 'Flore Pleno': double-flowered.

sagittate arrow- or spear-shaped; where the equal and approximately triangular basal lobes point downward or toward the stalk; cf. *hastate*.

Saintpaulia (for Baron Walter von Saint Paul-Illaire [1860–1910], who discovered *S. ionantha*). Gesneriaceae. Tropical E Africa. AFRICAN VIOLET. 20 species, small perennial herbs with thinly fleshy, hairy leaves in low rosettes, their blades suborbicular to elliptic, the petioles slender and succulent. Produced in cymes at various times of year, the flowers are 2-lipped and consist of five, spreading, oblong to rounded lobes and bright yellow anthers.

Saintpaulias require a temperature range of 63–77°F (17–25°C) all year round, with an overnight drop of no more than 9°F (5°C) for active growth. Prolonged exposure to temperatures below 50°F (10°C) or above 86°F (30°C) may prove fatal. Grow in shade, indirect light or bright filtered light.

When in active growth, water plentifully. If room temperatures fall below 55°F (13°C) during winter, water only moderately. Saintpaulias require medium to high humidity. Stand plants over wet pebbles in trays or surround pots with continuously damp leaf mold or coir. Give soluble or liquid balanced fertilizers while the plant is in active growth. Plant in open, well-drained, soilless potting medium, with a pH range of 6.5–7.0.

S

Saintpaulias prefer to be slightly pot-bound. As a plant matures, a 'neck' develops when spent leaves are removed from the main stem. Repot the plant into a clean pot of the same size by cutting away the bottom third or half of the rootball, thus lowering the plant into the fresh potting medium for new roots to grow from the main stem. When the 'neck' is too long for this treatment, cut through the main stem ¾ in (2 cm) below the leaves, trim the stem below the leaves into a cone shape and pot into a small pot with the leaf-stalks just clear of the potting medium. Place the pot in a covered, heated propagator.

To propagate from leaves, break a mature leaf away cleanly from the main stem using a sharp side-ways tug. Cut the leafstalk to 2 in (5 cm) and insert at a slight angle into potting medium in a 2 in (5 cm) pot; place in bright indirect light in a covered, heated propagator. The leaf will root in 3–4 weeks and plantlets will appear 8–10 weeks after potting. Separate the plantlets from the mother leaf when they are 2 in (5 cm) tall and have at least four leaves, and pot into individual 2 in (5 cm) pots. The trimmed leaf will also root in water, but must be potted into potting medium when the roots are no longer than ⅝ in (1.5 cm).

Sow fresh seed on the surface of moist potting medium, cover with clear plastic film, and place in bright filtered or bright indirect light at a temperature of 77°F (25°C). On germination, reduce the temperature to 68°F (20°C). When seedlings have four leaves, prick out into a small tray for growing on. Cultivars do not come true from seed.

S. ionantha AFRICAN VIOLET, USAMBARA VIOLET; Tanzania; leaves to 2 in (5 cm), ovate or oblong-ovate, crenate, dark green often tinted red-purple above, pale or purple-tinted beneath, hairy; flowers to 1 in (2.5 cm) in diameter, light blue to blue-violet, or white with a violet throat. *S.* cultivars (*Standard*) 'Dupont Blue': violet-blue; 'Glacier': single to semidouble, star-shaped, white with pale cream stamens; 'Hawaii': single, star-shaped, deep royal-blue, fringed silver-white; 'Marguerite': large, pale pink, wavy; 'Porcelain': single, white with blue blotches. (*Dwarf and miniature*) 'Love Bug': semidouble, wine-red; 'Pip Squeak': pale

pink; 'Wee Hope': semidouble, white with a blue center. (*Trailing*) 'Ding Dong Trail': campanulate, pale pink with deeper shading in throat; 'Magic Trail': mid-green, quilted leaves; 'Snowy Trail': semidwarf, semidouble, white flowers; 'Trail's Delight': leaves, edged and blotched white; 'Winding Trail': dwarf, flowers double, blue and white.

salad plant any vegetable or fruit eaten raw in salads; e.g. lettuce, tomato, cucumber, radish, celery and salad onion, but also soft green vegetables, especially where grown as 'cut and come again' crops.

salicetum a collection of willows (*Salix* species); known popularly as a sally garden in the 19th century.

salinity soluble salt concentration of a soil or potting mix, usually measured by electric conductivity. See *conductivity*.

Salix (Classical Latin name for Willow; also Celtic *sal*, near, and *lis*, water). Salicaceae. WILLOW, OSIER, SALLOW. Cosmopolitan except Australia, chiefly temperate regions. Around 300 species, deciduous trees and shrubs. These plants vary greatly in habit, from dwarf, creeping shrubs to medium-sized, weeping trees. Minute flowers are carried in dense, hairy catkins usually appearing before or with the foliage in spring. There are willows suited to a variety of soils and situations, and to a number of uses in the garden. Although generally undemanding in cultivation, they should be

chosen with care—the larger-growing trees may cause problems in drainage systems, and the rapid growth rate of many makes them weak-branched and prone to wind and storm damage. Debris is shed throughout the year, and the genus is predisposed to a range of pests and diseases, many of which reduce the natural life span. That said, willows have strong ornamental and functional values in the garden, which may be categorized as follows:

(a) Weeping willows. Especially beautiful at the waterside; they include *S. babylonica* and *S.* × *sepulcralis*. For smaller spaces, *S. caprea* 'Kilmarnock' and *S. purpurea* 'Pendula' are excellent.

(b) Ornamental catkins. Usually medium to large shrubs, flowering in spring. This group includes *S. aegyptiaca*, *S. caprea*, *S. daphnoides* 'Aglaia', *S. fargesii*, *S. gracilistyla*, *S. hastata*, *S. lanata*, *S. magnifica*, *S. pentandra* and *S. purpurea*.

(c) Colored stems. The young growth has distinctive coloring, and is particularly useful in the winter garden or beside lakes. Members of this group should be grown as stools or low pollards (stubs), cut back hard in late winter/early spring every one to three years. They include cultivars of *S. alba*, *S. daphnoides* and *S. irrorata*.

(d) Ornamental foliage. This group includes gray-leaved plants such as *S. alba* var. *sericea*, *S. elaeagnos*, *S. helvetica*, *S. lanata*, and those with scented leaves such as *S. pentandra*.

(e) Dwarf and alpine species. Suitable for a rock garden, including low-growing or creeping plants that

Salix caprea 'Kilmarnock'
This very compact weeping tree is formed by top-grafting several shoots (see right) onto the top of a rootstock grown as a straight, vertical main stem, usually 5–6 ft (1.5–1.8 m) tall. The resulting growth arches over then cascades to form a narrow crown that widens with age.

SALIX

Name	Distribution	Habit	Shoots	Leaves	Catkins
S. alba WHITE WILLOW	Europe, N Africa, C Asia	tree to 80 ft (25 m)	light gray-pink to olive, gray-hairy at first	to 4 in (10 cm), lanceolate, serrulate, blue-green beneath, silky white-hairy at first	to 2½ in (6 cm)

Comments: var. *caerulea*: CRICKET BAT WILLOW; leaves to 4 in (10 cm), hairless when mature, blue-green above, glaucous beneath; var. *sericea*: SILVER WILLOW: leaves to 4 in (10 cm), silver-white; var. *vitellina*: GOLDEN WILLOW; twigs bright orange-yellow in winter, bright orange-red in

Name	Distribution	Habit	Shoots	Leaves	Catkins
S .babylonica WEEPING WILLOW	Asia	tree to 40 ft (12 m) with long, weeping branches	tinted green	to 6 in (16 cm), narrowly lanceolate, serrulate, deep green above, gray-green beneath	to ¾ in (2 cm)

Comments: 'Crispa': leaves twisted into rings, slow-growing; 'Pendula': gracefully weeping, scab-resistant. The PEKING WILLOW, var. *pekinensis*, (syn. *S. matsudana*) differs in its erect to arching branches and leaves with blue-green undersides. It in turn contains the cultivar 'Tortuosa' (DRAGON'S CLAW WILLOW), an erect shrub or tree to 13 ft (4 m) with corkscrewlike stems and branches and much-twisted leaves—a popular florist's plant.

Name	Distribution	Habit	Shoots	Leaves	Catkins
S. 'Boydii' (*S. lapponum* × *S. reticulata*)	Great Britain	dwarf shrub	hairy	more or less round, gray-hairy with prominent veins	
S. caprea KILMARNOCK WILLOW, GOAT WILLOW, PUSSY WILLOW	Europe to NE Asia	tree or shrub to 33 ft (10 m)	stout smooth, yellow-brown	to 4¾ in (12 cm), broadly oval, toothed, deep green above, gray-green and downy beneath	to 1 in (2.5 cm), ovoid, with soft, silver hairs and golden anthers

Comments: Includes several weeping cultivars; the best-known, 'Kilmarnock', is grown as a small, grafted standard with a dome of weeping branches.

Name	Distribution	Habit	Shoots	Leaves	Catkins
S. daphnoides VIOLET WILLOW	Europe to Asia	tree or tall shrub to 33 ft (10 m)	red- or purple-brown to violet and thickly glaucous	to 4 in (10 cm), oblong to lanceolate, serrate, dark green above, glaucous beneath	to 1¼ in (3 cm), silver and silky, produced before leaves

Comments: Cut hard back each spring to encourage heads of frosted, violet wands for the following winter.

Name	Distribution	Habit	Shoots	Leaves	Catkins
S. elaeagnos ROSEMARY WILLOW, HOARY WILLOW	C Europe to Asia Minor	tall shrub or small tree to 20 ft (6 m)	twigs wandlike, gray-velvety then smooth and red-brown	to 6 in (15 cm), narrowly lanceolate, silver at first becoming dark, glossy green above, white-felted beneath	to 2½ in (6 cm), appearing before or with leaves
S. fargesii	China	shrub to 10 ft (3 m)	glossy purple to red-brown with large, red winter buds	to 6 in (15 cm), elliptic, glossy and dark with sunken veins above, silky beneath	to 4¾ in (12 cm)
S. fragilis CRACK WILLOW, BRITTLE WILLOW	Europe, N Asia, naturalized N America	tree to 80 ft (25 m)	smooth, olive-brown, easily broken at their joints	to 6 in (15 cm), lanceolate, dark green above, more or less glaucous beneath	to 2¾ in (7 cm), drooping, appearing with leaves

S

S. alba

S. alba var. *vitellina* 'Britzensis'

S. babylonica var. *pekinensis* 'Tortuosa'

S. caprea

SALIX

Name	Distribution	Habit	Shoots	Leaves	Catkins
S. gracilistyla ROSEGOLD PUSSY WILLOW	Japan, Korea, Manchuria	erect shrub to 10 ft (3 m)	white-hairy at first	to 4¾ in (12 cm), narrowly oblong, covered in gray silky hairs at first, becoming smooth above, persisting well into fall	to 2 in (5 cm), appearing before leaves, gray-silky with red then bright yellow anthers

Comments: 'Melanostachys' is highly distinctive, with smooth twigs and leaves and black-brown catkins with rust then golden anthers.

S. hastata HALBERD WILLOW	C Europe to NE Asia	erect, dense shrub to 5 ft (1.5 m)	smooth, sometimes red- or purple-tinted	to 3 in (8 cm), oval to broadly oblong, base cordate, dull green above with a yellow-tinted midrib, glaucous beneath	to 2½ in (6 cm)

Comments: 'Wehrhahnii': slow-growing, spreading, small to medium shrub with many silver to golden yellow catkins in early spring. *S. apoda* differs from this species in its bright green, obovate leaves.

S. helvetica SWISS WILLOW	Alps	low, and densely branched shrub	gray-downy becoming more or less smooth, red-brown	1¼–2½ in (3–6 cm), obovate to oblanceolate, thickly gray-downy at first becoming smooth and glossy above	to 1½ in (4 cm), before or with leaves

Comments: A fine silver-leaved shrub for the large rock garden.

S. integra	Korea, Japan	very similar to *S. purpurea*, with slender, slightly weeping branches		oblong, bright pale to mid-green thus differing from *S. purpurea*	

Comments: 'Hakuro-nishiki' to 6½ ft (2 m), somewhat weeping especially if grafted as a standard; leaves pink and white at first becoming bright green boldly splashed with pure white.

S. lanata WOOLLY WILLOW	Arctic and Subarctic Europe and Asia	slow-growing shrub to 3¼ ft (1 m)	ascending, woolly at first becoming gnarled	¾–2¾ in (2–7 cm), broadly oval to obovate, densely gray- to white-hairy, becoming smoother above	to 2 in (5 cm), with golden anthers

Comments: 'Stuartii': dwarf, gnarled shrub with yellow twigs and orange-tinted buds, its leaves smaller but catkins larger than in typical *S. lanata*.

S. magnifica	China	large shrub or tree to 20 ft (6 m)	purple to red	to 10 in (25 cm), oval to obovate with a cordate base, sage green above, glaucous beneath with red veins	to 8 in (20 cm), narrow and ascending, ivory to yellow deepening to brick red and maroon at the tip

Comments: A remarkable species with *Magnolia*-like foliage and catkins that resemble glowing tapers.

S. pentandra BAY WILLOW, LAUREL WILLOW	Europe, naturalized E US	tree or shrub to 33 ft (10 m)	glossy brown-green, buds yellow	2–4¾ in (5–12 cm), elliptic, base cordate or rounded, finely toothed, leathery, glossy dark green above, pale beneath	to 2 in (5 cm)

Comments: The foliage is aromatic when young or crushed.

S. daphnoides   *S. gracilistyla* 'Melanostachys'   *S. hastata* 'Wehrhahnii'   *S. helvetica*

SALIX

Name	Distribution	Habit	Shoots	Leaves	Catkins
S. purpurea PURPLE OSIER, PURPLE WILLOW, BASKET WILLOW	Europe, N Africa to E Asia	shrub or tree to 16 ft (5 m) with a somewhat arching habit	usually purple when young, downy at first then glossy	to 4 in (10 cm), lanceolate to oblong, serrulate, dull blue-green above, paler and glaucous beneath	to 1¼ in (3 cm), narrow, curving, anthers red becoming purple-black

Comments: The inner wood of young shoots is usually yellow. Includes 'Pendula', with long, weeping branches; often trained as a standard.

Name	Distribution	Habit	Shoots	Leaves	Catkins
S. repens CREEPING WILLOW	Europe, Asia Minor, Siberia	shrub to 5 ft (1.5 m) with creeping stems and ascending branches		½–1½ in (1–3.5 cm), narrowly elliptic to ovate or oblong, covered in white silky hairs at first, often becoming glabrous and dull gray-green above	to 1 in (2.5 cm)

Comments: var. *argentea*: syn. *S. arenaria*, dwarf shrub with leaves densely coated in silver hairs; native to coastal regions, it grows well in maritime gardens and in sandy soil.

Name	Distribution	Habit	Shoots	Leaves	Catkins
S. reticulata	N Europe, N America, N Asia	dwarf, creeping and mat-forming shrublet		½–1½ in (1–4 cm), rounded, wrinkled to reticulate and dark green above, white-felted beneath	½–1¼ in (1–3 cm)

Comments: Suitable for damper places in the rock garden.

Name	Distribution	Habit	Shoots	Leaves	Catkins
S. × rubens (*S. alba* × *S. fragilis*)	C Europe	fast-growing shrub or tree to 33 ft (10 m)	olive tinted yellow or red	to 6 in (16 cm), lanceolate, toothed, more or less glaucous beneath	

Comments: Includes 'Basfordiana': branches or stems rodlike, orange-red in winter, especially if stooled in spring; 'Sanguinea': branches or stems sealing wax red in winter, especially if stooled in spring.

Name	Distribution	Habit	Shoots	Leaves	Catkins
S. × sepulcralis WEEPING WILLOW (*S. alba* 'Tristis' × *S. babylonica*)	garden origin	tree to 33 ft (10 m), slightly less weeping than *S. babylonica*	bark more fissured than in *S. babylonica*	with a glandular apex to the petiole, thus differing from *S. babylonica*	

Comments: var. *chrysocoma*: strongly weeping, twigs yellow, leaves bright green—the most commonly cultivated weeping willow.

Name	Distribution	Habit	Shoots	Leaves	Catkins
S. udensis *S. sachalinensis*	Japan, E Russia	tree or shrub to 16 ft (5 m)	hoary at first then smooth shiny and chestnut brown	to 4 in (10 cm), narrowly lanceolate, dark green above, blue-green and slightly hairy beneath	to 1¼ in (3 cm)

Comments: 'Sekka': a fasciated form with sporadic flattened and curling stems, used in flower arranging.

Name	Distribution	Habit	Shoots	Leaves	Catkins
S. viminalis COMMON OSIER	Eurasia	upright tree or shrub to 20 ft (6 m)	glossy, yellow-green	to 6 in (15 cm), slender, linear, tapered, dark green, silver-hairy beneath	to 1½ in (3.5 cm), borne before leaves, green with yellow anthers

Comments: often stooled for screening and for the production of willow wands.

S. pentandra

S. repens

S. reticulata

S. × *sepulcralis* var. *chrysocoma*

make good groundcover; among them, *S. apoda*, *S. arctica*, *S.* 'Boydii' (a suitable trough plant), *S. glaucosericea*, *S.* × *grahamii* (vigorous), *S. helvetica*, *S. herbacea* (one of the smallest), *S. hylematica*, *S. lanata*, *S. reticulata* (will grow in full shade, tolerant of dry conditions).

Willows tolerate a wide range of climates, and many species will thrive where temperatures regularly fall to −13°F (−25°C). *S. magnifica* may suffer below 14°F (−10°C). Most require ample moisture and rarely thrive on shallow chalk. Grow in full sun. Propagate from cuttings: with a few exceptions (e.g. *S. caprea*), 12-in (30-cm) hardwood cuttings of one-year-old wood root easily at any time (usually late fall/early spring) and in any soil. Take semiripe cuttings of dwarf creepers during summer; these species can also be divided or increased by spontaneous layers. Pendulous cultivars are usually grafted. Seed is frequently sterile; fertile seed rapidly loses viability and there is a strong risk that the progeny will in any case be hybrid.

The large willow aphid infests willows in Europe; the giant bark aphid infests trees in North America. Willows across the Northern Hemisphere can become seriously infested by the willow scale and those in North America may also be invaded by several other species of scale insects. The willow bean sawfly and hazel sawfly commonly infest willows in Europe. Various leaf beetles, including flea beetles, also attack willows in both continents.

Anthracnose is particularly serious on weeping willows especially in wet seasons. Small brown spots occur on the leaves which fall prematurely, and black cankers on the shoots result in dieback. The disease is spread by spores produced on the leaves and shoots, and although it may be useful to collect and burn fallen leaves the cankers on the shoots are often too numerous for pruning to be an effective control. Regular sprays of Bordeaux mixture or other copper fungicide commencing when the leaves unfold should have some effect. Watermark disease, a name referring to the characteristic discoloration of the wood, is caused by the bacterium *Erwinia salicis*, and is particularly important on cultivars of *Salix alba*.

The first symptom is the sudden appearance of bright red leaves during hot summer weather. The affected branches die back to produce a 'stag's head' and a sticky liquid containing bacteria oozes from the bark. The only control method is to fell severely affected trees to prevent such spread occurring. The rust fungus *Melampsora* also affects willows, causing stem cankers: control by spraying with Bordeaux mixture. Willow heart rot is caused by a bracket fungus which gains entry through wounded branches, mostly on old trees. Willows can also be affected by armillaria, root rot, crown gall, silver leaf and tar spot.

Salpiglossis (from Greek *salpinx*, tube, and *glossa*, tongue, from the resemblance of the style to a tongue in the corolla throat). Solanaceae. S Andes. 2 species, erect, clammy-pubescent annual, biennial or perennial herbs with 5-lobed, funnel-shaped flowers in summer. Used for bedding schemes, as late winter- and spring-flowering pot plants and for cut flowers. If sown *in situ*, thin to 9–12 in (22–30 cm) apart. Pot plants should be allowed to dry slightly between waterings. *S. sinuata* PAINTED TONGUE; to 24 in (60 cm); flowers to 2½ × 2 in (6 × 5 cm), yellow to ocher, mauve-scarlet or violet-blue with darker purple veins and marking. *Cultivars* Bolero Hybrids, dwarf, vigorous, with flowers in a range of rich colors; Casino Hybrids, dwarf, compact, with flowers veined in shades of red, yellow, orange, rose and purple; 'Kew Blue', dwarf, with abundant, rich blue flowers veined golden-yellow; and Splash Hybrids, compact, tolerant, with abundant flowers in a range of colors.

salsify (*Tragopogon porrifolius*) VEGETABLE OYSTER, OYSTER PLANT a biennial grown primarily for its creamy-white taproots, which are used as a winter vegetable and eaten hot or cold after boiling. Sow fresh seed March–May, ½ in (10 mm) deep,

in rows 6 in (15 cm) apart; thin to 4 in (10 cm) apart. Lift for use from October onward, or store in boxes of sand kept in a cool building.

Also edible are the young shoots, or chards, of overwintered plants and the mauve flower buds and flowering shoots. Chards can be produced by cutting the plants down to ground level in fall, and earthing up to 5 in (13 cm) deep or covering with a similar depth of straw; use in salads or lightly cooked. Pick the flower buds just before opening, with about 4 in (10 cm) length of stem, and cook as for asparagus. Possible problems: white blister.

salt (1) the chemical compound formed as the reaction product of an acid and a base. Most inorganic fertilizers are salts. The name of the salt of a particular acid is derived from the name of the acid: nitric acid forms nitrates; sulfuric acid, sulfates; phosphoric acid, phosphates; carbonic acid, carbonates; silicic acid, silicates. The first part of the full name of a salt indicates the base in the reaction, for example, *potassium* sulfate. (2) Salt commonly refers to sodium chloride, which has a number of horticultural associations: in deflocculating clay soil; as a nutrient supplement (at very low dosage) for crops such as beet, asparagus and sea kale; as a partial weedkiller; and as a phytotoxic compound from sea spray or from winter road dressings.

Salvia (Classical Latin name, from *salvare*, to save or heal, alluding to the supposed medicinal properties of certain species). Labiatae. SAGE. Cosmopolitan. Some 900 or more species, perennial, annual or biennial herbs, shrubs or subshrubs. The flowers are tubular and two-lipped, the upper lip arching and hoodlike, the lower lip spreading and 3-lobed. They emerge from bell-shaped calyces, disposed in whorls arranged in spikes, racemes and panicles.

A number of species are annuals or treated as annuals in cool temperate gardens, including *S. coccinea* and *S. splendens*, used in

trimmed top growth

Salsify roots

SALVIA

Name	Distribution	Habit	Leaves	Flowers
S. argentea	Mediterranean	short-lived perennial or biennial herb, more or less stemless	to 8 in (20 cm), low-lying, ovate to oblong, tip rounded, base tapering, margins scalloped to lobed, thick-textured, rugose and thickly covered in shaggy, silver-white hairs	white to yellow flecked pink to violet in a spreading panicle to 3¼ ft (1 m) tall

Comments: very intolerant of winter wet.

Name	Distribution	Habit	Leaves	Flowers
S. blancoana	Morocco, Spain	evergreen shrub to 3¼ ft (1 m)	to 3½ in (9 cm), oblong-elliptic, silver-hairy	pale blue to violet, sometimes streaked white, on leafless stalks
S. blepharophylla	Mexico	perennial herb or subshrub to 16 in (40 cm)	to 2 in (5 cm), ovate to deltoid, glossy and more or less hairless	red, protruding from purple to maroon calyces in loose racemes to 4¾ in (12 cm)
S. bulleyana	China	more or less stemless perennial herb	to 4¾ in (12 cm), ovate, base cordate to hastate, margins crenate, dark green covered in sparse hairs	yellow with purple to maroon lips in racemes to 24 in (60 cm) tall
S. discolor	Peru	strongly aromatic and clammy perennial herb or subshrub to 5 ft (1.5 m)	to 2½ in (6 cm), oblong-ovate, leathery, shiny dark green above, silver-white beneath	indigo to black, protruding from silver calyces in narrow terminal racemes

Comments: Hardy to 0°F (−18°C) if planted in a sheltered, sunny site, thickly mulched in winter and treated as an herbaceous perennial.

Name	Distribution	Habit	Leaves	Flowers
S. farinacea MEALY SAGE	Texas, Mexico	erect, mealy-downy, perennial herb to 24 in (60 cm) tall	to 3 in (8 cm), ovate to oblong or lanceolate, margins wavy to notched, minutely hairy	blue to lavender or deep purple, emerging from similarly colored, hairy calyces in an interrupted, terminal raceme

Comments: Hardy to 20°F (−7°C), but usually treated as a half-hardy annual in cultivation. Includes cultivars with white, opal, pale blue, dark blue and purple flowers.

Name	Distribution	Habit	Leaves	Flowers
S. fulgens	Mexico	freely branching perennial herb or evergreen subshrub to 3¼ ft (1 m) tall	2½–4¾ in (6–12 cm), ovate to deltoid, toothed or notched, white-hairy beneath	bright red to deep scarlet, in terminal racemes in late summer
S. greggii FALL SAGE	Texas, Mexico	evergreen, glandular-hairy subshrub or perennial herb erect to 3¼ ft (1 m)	to 1¼ in (3 cm), ovate to elliptic or oblong, entire, tough	red to purple or magenta-pink (more rarely, yellow or white) in racemes to 8 in (20 cm)

Comments: Flowers in late summer and fall; has hybridized with *S. microphylla*.

S

S. argentea

S. discolor

S. farinacea

S. fulgens

SALVIA

Name	Distribution	Habit	Leaves	Flowers
S. involucrata	Mexico	glandular-hairy, woody-based perennial herb to 3¼ ft (1 m)	to 5½ in (14 cm), ovate, base usually cordate, glabrous to hairy	pink to red or purple, in racemes to 12 in (30 cm) long in late summer and fall

Comments: Frost-tender and treated as half-hardy. Includes 'Bethellii': flowers deep cerise with paler lips, amid pink to red bracts. 'Deschampsiana': flowers rose-pink, from red calyces and bracts.

S. jurisicii	Macedonia	white-hairy, perennial herb to 24 in (60 cm)	ovate to oblong, pinnately cut into narrow lobes	white to pink or deep violet in loosely branched racemes to 8 in (20 cm)

S. leucantha MEXICAN BUSH SAGE	Mexico to Tropical America	evergreen, erect perennial subshrub or herb, to 3¼ ft (1 m)	to 4 in (10 cm), linear-lanceolate to oblong and finely tapering, rugose above, white-downy beneath	white, woolly, from downy mauve to violet calyces in racemes to 10 in (24 cm)

Comments: Frost-tender.

S. microphylla *S. grahamii*	Mexico	evergreen subshrub or shrub to 48 in (120 cm)	⅝–1½ in (1.5–4 cm), ovate to elliptic, fresh green, glabrous to thinly hairy	deep crimson, pink, magenta or purple, emerging from purple-tinted calyces in racemes to 6 in (15 cm) in late summer

Comments: Half hardy. Includes var. *microphylla*, with cerise flowers; *S.* × *jamensis* 'James Compton' (a cross with *S. greggii*) has large, dark crimson flowers.

S. nemorosa	Europe to C Asia	clump-forming, perennial herb, erect to 3¼ ft (1 m)	to 4 in (10 cm), ovate to lanceolate or oblong, rugose, glandular-hairy	violet to purple or pink to white amid purple bracts in dense, branched spikes to 16 in (40 cm)

S. officinalis SAGE, COMMON SAGE	Mediterranean, N Africa	bushy, intensely aromatic subshrub or shrub to 3¼ ft (1 m)	to 2½ in (6 cm), oblong to elliptic, finely rugose and minutely hairy, typically gray-green	violet-blue to mauve or, rarely, pink to white, amid gray-green to purple-tinted bracts in terminal racemes to 4 in (10 cm)

Comments: Zone 6. The herb sage, widespread in cultivation and with numerous cultivars, varying mostly in leaf coloring—from deep purple-tinted to silver-white, to pure gold, or moss green and gold-variegated, to cream-variegated or gray-green zoned yellow to cream and pink to purple-red.

S. patens	Mexico	glandular-hairy, perennial herb, erect to 3¼ ft (1 m)	to 8 in (20 cm), ovate to deltoid, base hastate to cordate, downy, mid-green	large, deep to pale blue, lilac or white in loose, erect and branching racemes to 16 in (40 cm)

S. pratensis MEADOW CLARY *S. haematodes*	Europe	glandular-hairy perennial herb, often short-lived, to 3¼ ft (1 m)	to 6 in (15 cm), ovate to oblong, apex blunt, base cordate, margins toothed to scalloped, rugose, hairy	violet, lavender, white or pink in panicles to 18 in (45 cm)

Comments: Fully hardy.

S. greggii

S. involucrata 'Bethellii'

S. patens

S. splendens Cleopatra Series

SALVIA

Name	Distribution	Habit	Leaves	Flowers
S. rutilans PINEAPPLE-SCENTED SAGE	known only in cultivation	strongly pineapple-scented, bushy perennial herb or subshrub to 32 in (80 cm)	to 4 in (10 cm), ovate to oblong-lanceolate, more or less toothed, fresh green	pink to scarlet, usually produced in fall or winter in erect racemes
Comments: Frost-tender. Probably a form of the Central American *S. elegans*, and often listed as a cultivar of this species under the name 'Scarlet Pineapple'.				
S. sclarea CLARY	Europe to C Asia	erect, aromatic glandular-hairy, biennial to perennial herb to 3¼ ft (1 m) tall	to 9 in (23 cm), ovate to oblong, base cordate, toothed to erose, rugose	cream to pink, lilac, blue or mauve, amid large, white, mauve or pink bracts in tall branching spikes in summer
Comments: Usually grown as an annual; var. *turkestanica*: stems and bracts purple-pink, flowers white flecked with pink.				
S. splendens SCARLET SAGE	Brazil	erect, sparsely branched annual to perennial herb, 8–39 in (20–100 cm) tall	to 6 in (15 cm), ovate-lanceolate, mid-green, more or less glabrous	large, scarlet, from scarlet calyces amid red to maroon bracts in terminal, unbranched or branched spikes to 7 in (18 cm)
Comments: Frost-tender and widely cultivated as a half-hardy annual. Available in tall, slender or short, bushy forms with flowers in shades of white, pink, crimson, scarlet, blood red and dark violet-purple.				
S. uliginosa BOG SAGE	Brazil, Uruguay, Argentina	branched, perennial herb, erect to 6½ ft (2 m)	to 3½ in (9 cm), lanceolate-oblong, entire to serrate, mid-green	bright blue in long racemes in fall
Comments: Zone 9. Needs moist soil.				
S. viridis *S. horminum*	Mediterranean	erect, bushy annual herb, 8–39 in (20–100 cm), more or less glandular-hairy	to 2 in (5 cm), ovate to oblong	small, white to lilac or purple, from green to purple calyces amid showy, papery bracts in shades of white, pink, lilac or purple, sometimes with contrasting veins, in erect spikes in summer
Comments: A popular annual.				

summer bedding. *S. viridis* provides blooms for cutting to use fresh or air dried, as does *S. sclarea*. Several species usually grown as annuals, (notably *S. farinacea* and *S. patens*), are almost hardy and will behave as perennials given a warm, sheltered and well-drained position. Other Mexican and Central American species (e.g. *S. blepharophylla*, *S. involucrata* and *S. leucantha*) might be tried outdoors in similar conditions. In cooler regions they are amenable to large pot cultivation in the cool glasshouse or conservatory. Some salvias, such as the 'black'-flowered *S. discolor*, may be cut down to the base during winter but will re-sprout in milder climates if given a deep protective mulch. Shrubby species that are able to survive temperatures down to 14°F (−10°C) unharmed include *S. blancoana* and *S. officinalis*. Several other shrubby species will survive to 23°F

(−5°C), e.g. *S. greggii*, *S. microphylla* and *S. guaranitica*. All shrubby salvia species prefer well-drained, loamy soil in a sunny, sheltered position. The more tender species may be kept alive outdoors to 0°F (−18°C) through careful siting against south-facing walls, mulching, wrapping, etc.

Cuttings root readily and soon make flowering-size plants—when winters are harsh, it is an easy matter to keep a few rooted cuttings alive under glass. In winter, the herbaceous species are more likely to suffer from excess moisture than from low temperatures. They prefer well-drained situations in lighter, sandier soil, which benefits from a mulch of organic matter each spring. Several species are nonetheless reliable and easy perennials for any soil; these include *S. nemorosa* and *S. pratensis*. Biennials can be sown *in situ* with a view to their eventual size at

flowering—some, like *S. sclarea* and *S. argentea* form rosettes of very large leaves. The latter needs very fast-draining, gritty soil. Annuals can also be sown outside *in situ* in late spring after the last frosts, although it is more usual to sow *S. splendens* under glass in early spring. All shrubby and most herbaceous salvias are propagated easily from softwood cuttings taken at any stage of the growing season. All can be grown from seed sown under glass in spring.

salverform of a corolla with a long, slim tube and an abruptly expanded, flattened limb.

Salvinia (for Antonio Mario Salvini [1633–1729], professor of Greek at Florence). Salviniaceae. Widespread in tropical and warm-temperate zones. 10 species, free-floating, aquatic ferns with

S

oblong, hairy or papillose leaves arranged along threadlike stems. The individual plants are small, but soon proliferate to form large colonies. The best-known species is *Salvinia natans*. Cultivate as for *Azolla*, but in frost-free conditions.

samara a one-seeded, indehiscent, winged fruit, as found in maple or ash.

Sambucus (the Latin name, perhaps from *sambuca*, a kind of harp, made from elder wood). Caprifoliaceae. Temperate and subtropical Northern Hemisphere, E and NW Africa, S America, E Australia, Tasmania. ELDER, ELDER-BERRY. Some 25 species, deciduous shrubs or small trees with pinnately compound leaves and flat-topped cymose corymbs or panicles of small cream-white flowers in spring and summer. These are followed by glossy, dark berries.

Sambucus species tolerate a wide range of soils (including chalk), atmospheric pollution, coastal situations and shade, the temperate species being able to withstand temperatures down to at least −13°F (−25°C); *S. canadensis* grows where winter temperatures drop to −29°F (−34°C). Plant in sun or part shade. Golden-leaved cultivars color earlier in sun, but retain their color better in cool moist shade. Propagate from hardwood cuttings taken in winter, with a heel so as not to expose the pith. For best foliage effects on plants grown as medium-sized shrubs, prune to the ground in late winter.

S. canadensis AMERICAN ELDER, SWEET ELDER; eastern N America; shrub to 11 ft (3.5 m), often suckering; leaflets (5–)7(–11), serrate, lowermost often lobed, glabrous or lanuginose beneath; inflorescence to 8 in (20 cm) in diameter, flowers ivory; fruit purple-black; cultivars include 'Acutiloba', with finely dissected, deep green leaves; 'Argenteomarginata', with leaves edged silver; 'Aurea', with pale green shoots, golden yellow leaves, and red, sweet fruit; 'Chlorocarpa', with pale yellow-green leaves and light green fruit; 'Maxima', robust, tall-growing, with an inflorescence to 40 cm (16 in) in diameter and

tinted red; and 'Rubra', with pale red fruit; *S. nigra* BLACK ELDER, ELDER-BERRY, EUROPEAN ELDER, BOURTREE, COMMON ELDER; Europe, N Africa, SW Asia; shrub or small tree to 33 ft (10 m); leaflets 3–9, to 4¾ × 2½ in (12 × 6 cm), ovate to elliptic, serrate, sparsely pubescent on veins beneath, dark green above; flowers cream, muskily scented, in flat-topped inflorescences to 8 in (20 cm) in diameter; fruit shiny purple-black; cultivars include 'Alba', with pellucid chalky-white fruit; 'Albopunctata', with leaves splashed white, especially at margins; 'Albovariegata', with leaves coarsely speckled white; 'Argentea', with white leaves, reverse-variegated green; 'Asplenifolia', with fernlike leaves; 'Aurea', with golden to lime green leaves; 'Aureomarginata', with leaves edged gold to yellow-green; f. *laciniata*: leaflets finely laciniate; 'Linearis': leaflets irregularly cut to midrib and blade often reduced to midrib; 'Marginata': leaflets broadly edged gold at first, later margined pale yellow to cream; 'Pulverulentula': leaves striped, spotted and splashed pure white, appearing wholly white at first; f. *porphyrophylla* 'Guincho Purple': leaves leaden purple-black to wine red; flowers bright white with purple stamens; *S. racemosa* EUROPEAN RED ELDER, RED-BERRIED ELDER; Europe, Asia Minor, Siberia, W Asia; shrub to 11 ft (3.5 m); leaves to 9 in (23 cm), leaflets 5, to 4 × 1¾ in (10 × 4.5 cm), oval or ovate, acuminate, scabrous, serrate; flowers pale green to yellow-white in bluntly pyramidal panicles to 3 in (7.5 cm); fruit scarlet; cultivars include 'Aurea', with bright yellow leaves; 'Goldenlocks', with golden-yellow, deeply cut leaves, lasting well in bright sun; 'Laciniata', with green leaves and leaflets deeply slashed, in narrow segments; 'Plumosa', with purple new growth and deeply incised leaflets with fine, slender teeth; 'Plumosa Aurea', resembling 'Plumosa', but with foliage striking gold throughout and new growth often tinted purple-red; 'Sutherland Gold': leaves gold, finely cut; and 'Tenuifolia', dwarf suckering shrub, with finely incised leaves and fil-

iform leaflets, curling in frothy masses.

Sanchezia (for Josef Sanchez, professor of botany at Cadiz [18th century]). Acanthaceae. C and S America. Some 20 species, perennial herbs and soft-stemmed shrubs with handsome foliage and 5-lobed, tubular flowers amid colorful bracts in summer. Provide a minimum temperature of 50°F (10°C), bright, indirect light and medium to high humidity. Water and feed freely in spring and summer, but only sparingly during winter. Prune after flowering. Increase by semiripe cuttings. *S. speciosa* (syn. *S. nobilis*); Ecuador, Peru; evergreen, glabrous shrub to 7½ ft (2.25 m); leaves to 12 in (30 cm), glossy dark green, veins sunken and outlined white or yellow; panicles tinted purple, bracts bright red, flowers yellow.

sand soil with particles ranging in diameter between ¹⁄₁₆ in (2 mm) (very coarse) and ¹⁄₅₀₀ in (0.05 mm) (very fine), mainly derived from solid rocks, such as quartz and sandstone; see *soil*. In gardening parlance, sharp sand is the coarse, angular grade around ⅛ in (3mm) diameter, used in potting media and for cutting mixes; fine sand may be used on capillary benches and as a top dressing for lawns.

sand-bed see *capillary bed*.

Sandersonia (for John Sanderson [1820–1891], honorary secretary of the Horticultural Society of Natal). Liliaceae (Colchicaceae). South Africa. 1 species, *S. aurantiaca* CHINESE LANTERN LILY, CHRISTMAS BELLS, a summer-flowering perennial herb with tuberous roots. To 30 in (75 cm) tall, the stems are erect and clothed with tendril-tipped leaves. Solitary and axillary, the ¾-in- (2-cm-) long flowers are broadly campanulate to urceolate and warm orange. Cultivate as for *Gloriosa*.

sandstone a type of sedimentary rock, of which the harder kinds are valuable for rock garden construction. It contains no lime, and so is useful for calcifuges. See *rock plant gardening*.

Sanguinaria (from Latin *sanguis*, blood, referring to the orange-red latex). Papaveraceae. Eastern N Amer-

Double samara (sycamore)

ica. BLOODROOT, RED PUCCOON.
1 species, *S. canadensis*, a perennial herb
4–24 in (10–60 cm) tall. The leaves are
long-stalked and gray-green, rounded
to reniform with much-scalloped margins. Produced in spring, the flowers
are solitary, to 3 in (7.5 cm) in diameter
and cup- to bowl-shaped with 8–12,
oblong to obovate, white petals (more
in the double 'Florepleno'). This plant
is suitable for a rock garden, woodland
garden, peaty borders and for pot culture in an alpine house. *Sanguinaria* will
tolerate at least 14°F (–20°C) and
a soil pH range of 5–7. Plant in sun
or part shade, in well-drained soil, containing leaf mold, composted bark and
peat. Increase by division of well-established clumps in early spring, alternatively by seed.

Sanguisorba (from Latin *sanguis*,
blood, and *sorbeo*, to soak up, referring
to the plant's alleged styptic qualities
and its former use as an infusion to
prevent bleeding). Rosaceae. Temperate Northern Hemisphere. BURNET.
Some 18 species, rhizomatous perennial herbs or small shrubs with pinnate,
saw-toothed leaves and small, white,
green or pink flowers in dense, bottle-
brush-like spikes in summer. Fully
hardy. Grow in damp, fertile soil in sun
to part shade. Propagate by division in
spring or by seed in spring or fall.

S. canadensis CANADIAN BURNET;
N America; to 6½ ft (2 m); flowers
white, in cylindric spikes to 8 in (20
cm); *S. obtusa* (Japan; to 20 in (50 cm);
flowers pale rose, in nodding spikes to
2¾ in (7 cm); 'Alba': flowers white; *S.
officinalis* GREAT BURNET, BURNET
BLOODWORT; W Europe, Mongolia,
Japan, China, N America; to 3¼ ft (1
m); flowers dark red to black-purple, in
oval or cylindric heads to 1¼ in (3 cm).

Sansevieria (after the Prince of
Sanseviero [1710–1771]). Agavaceae.
Tropical and subtropical Africa, Madagascar, India, East Indies. MOTHER-IN-
LAW'S TONGUE, SNAKE PLANT,
BOWSTRING HEMP. Around 70 species,
evergreen, perennial herbs with tough
and succulent, linear-cylindrical to
ovate or lanceolate leaves in loose tufts
or low rosettes. Carried in narrow
racemes, the flowers are pale, with
narrow

perianth segments, and are infrequently produced in cultivation. They
may be followed by colorful berries.
Maintained at a minimum temperature
of 50°F (10°C), with plenty of light,
Sansevieria is extremely tolerant of dry
atmospheres and neglect. Pot in a
porous, well-drained medium of pH
6.0–7.0. Water sparingly in winter.
Propagate by division or by leaf
cuttings in spring, placing 2 in (5 cm)
deep, transverse sections of leaf in 2:1
sand/coir in a propagating case with
bottom heat of 64°F (18°C). Variegated plants usually revert to green
when produced from leaf cuttings.

S. cylindrica Angola; leaves 3–4 to a
shoot, in 2 ranks, 30 in (75 cm)+, 1 in
(25 mm) thick, semiterete, straight or
slightly arching, banded when young;
S. trifasciata MOTHER-IN-LAW'S TONGUE,
SNAKE PLANT; Nigeria; leaves to 30+ ×
2¾ in (75+ × 7 cm), erect, stiff, linear to
lanceolate, in clusters of 1–2 or more
per shoot, sometimes forming rosettes,
flat, with a yellow-green sharp tip and
margins, banded pale and dark green
or yellow; 'Hahnii': dwarf with shorter,
broader leaves in open rosettes;
'Golden Hahnii': leaves banded gray
and margins banded cream; 'Silver
Hahnii': leaves pale green tinted silver;
var. *laurentii*: leaves as for type but
with bright yellow margins.

**Santolina pinnata subsp. neapolitana
'Sulphurea'**
The dense habit of this santolina lends itself
to use as low hedging. The flower buds may
be shorn for a more formal look.

Santolina (from Latin *sanctum linum*,
holy flax, old name for *S. virens*). Compositae. Mediterranean. 18 species,
small, aromatic evergreen shrubs with
silky to felty, entire to finely dissected

leaves and long-stalked buttonlike
flower heads in late spring and
summer. Hardy to –10°F (–23°C).
Plant in full sun in fast-draining,
medium- to low-fertility soil, with shelter from harsh winds. Trim over after
flowering to give shape and rejuvenate.
Prune out exhausted and frost-damaged wood in spring. These shrubs tolerate shearing and may be used for
edging the herb garden and in parterres and knot gardens. Propagate by
semiripe cuttings in a sandy propagating mix in the cold frame.

S. chamaecyparissus LAVENDER
COTTON; 4–20 in (10–50 cm); leaves
¾–1½ in (2–4 cm), narrow, much
divided and feathery with short, tight
segments, gray- to white-felted; flower
heads bright yellow; includes very
dwarf, compact, silver and pale-flowered
cultivars; *S. pinnata* 16–32 in (40–80
cm); leaves ¾–1½ in (2–4 cm), narrow,
pinnately divided, green; flower heads
white to cream or pale butter yellow;
includes cultivars with silver leaves.

sap the fluid contained in the cells
and vascular system of plants. It is a
variable solution of water, salts, and
complex organic molecules.

sap beetles (Coleoptera: Nitidulidae)
small beetles that feed on the sap of
tree wounds, damaged fruits and vegetables, and fermenting plant fluids.
Sap beetles are closely related to
pollen beetles. In North America, the
DUSTY SAP BEETLE (*Carpophilus lugubris*),
the CORN SAP BEETLE (*C. dimidiatus*)
and certain other species feed on corn,
while *Glischrochilus quadrisignatus* feeds
in large numbers on vegetable and
fruit debris. Some related species
occur in the UK but are of no great
significance.

sap-drawer (1) a shoot left unpruned
on the side or underside of a branch
during formative pruning, in order to
provide nourishment for the branch
without competing with it; (2) a branch
retained during top-working to
maintain a flow of sap.

saprophyte a plant deriving nutrition directly from dead or decayed
organic matter and usually lacking
chlorophyll.

S

711

sapling a young tree at any stage of growth between a strongly developed seedling and the stage at which the heartwood becomes hard.

Saponaria (from medieval Latin *sapo*, soap—the roots of *S. officinalis* produce lather when rubbed under water, and were once used as a soap substitute). Caryophyllaceae. Widespread throughout Europe and SW Asia, with most species in the mountains of S Europe. SOAPWORT. About 20 species, perennial herbs, rarely annuals. Those listed here are tall and erect or low and cushion-forming with flat, 5-parted flowers in summer. *Saponaria* includes robust perennials, such as *S. officinalis* and *S. ocymoides*, together with dwarf, tufted species like *S. caespitosa*. *S. officinalis*, especially in its double forms, is grown in cottage gardens and other informal and naturalistic plantings, in sun or light shade, in moderately fertile, well-drained soil. *S. ocymoides* is well-suited to the border front, path edge and dry walls. Other compact mat- and cushion-forming species are grown in the rock garden, in troughs and in the alpine house. Grow alpine *Saponaria* species in sun in gritty, well-drained but moisture-retentive soil. Trim over after flowering. Propagate by seed during spring or fall, or by softwood cuttings taken after flowering and rooted in a closed case with gentle bottom heat. Increase also by division in spring or fall.

S. caespitosa C Pyrenees; densely tufted, slightly hairy perennial to 6 in (15 cm), with woody stock; flowers pink-purple; *S. ocymoides* S Europe, Spain to Balkans; mat-forming, hairy perennial to 6 in (15 cm); flowers red, pink or white; *S. officinalis* SOAPWORT; widespread in Europe; robust, glabrous, perennial to 24 in (60 cm); flowers pink, red or white; some cultivars with double flowers and variegated leaves; *S. pumilio* E Alps, SE Carpathians; densely tufted, glabrous perennial with woody stock; flowers pink-purple or white; the hybrid *S. × olivana*, with *S. pumilio*, *S. caespitosa* and *S. ocymoides* in its parentage, is easier to grow—it has the attractive cushion habit of *S. pumilio*, and large, pale pink flowers.

sap-rot see *wood rots*.

sapwood the outer, functional xylem layers of a woody stem; cf. *heartwood*. The term is also used, more loosely, to describe young, nonwoody shoots.

Sarcococca (from Greek *sarx*, flesh, and *kokkos*, berry, an allusion to the fleshy fruits). Buxaceae. SE Asia, Himalaya, W China. CHRISTMAS BOX, SWEET BOX. 11 species, small, evergreen shrubs with suckering stems, tough and shiny, neat foliage, small, pale and fragrant winter flowers and glossy berries. They grow best in partial shade, but will tolerate full sun given sufficient moisture. All are hardy to –10°F (–23°C), but prefer a sheltered site and some winter protection where frosts are hard and prolonged. Propagate by division of rooted suckers or by hardwood cuttings taken in fall and inserted into a cold frame.

S. confusa origin unknown; 10 in–6½ ft (0.25–2 m); leaves 1¼–2½ in (3–6.5 cm), elliptic to lanceolate or ovate, thinly leathery, dark green above, pale green beneath; male flowers with cream-colored anthers; fruit ripening from red to black; *S. hookeriana* Himalaya to W China; 10 in–6 ft (0.25–1.8 m); leaves to 2¼ in (5.5 cm), coriaceous, rugose, dull green, ovate to lanceolate; male flowers with deep pink anthers; fruit black; var. *digyna*: spreading and suckering, 12 in–3¼ ft (0.3–1 m), with 1½–3 in (4–8 cm), narrowly elliptic to oblong leaves and purple-black fruit; var. *humilis*: 8–20 in (0.2–0.5 m) tall, with 1½–2¾ in (3.5–7 cm), elliptic leaves; *S. ruscifolia* W China, Tibet; to 3¼ ft (1 m); leaves 1¼–2¼ in (3–5.5 cm), dark green, broadly ovate and tapering; male flowers with cream-colored anthers; fruit red.

sarmentose producing long, slender stolons.

Sarracenia (for Dr. M. Sarrazin de l'Etang [1659–1734], physician at the court of Quebec, who sent plants of *S. purpurea* to Tournefort). Sarraceniaceae. Eastern N America. PITCHER PLANT. 8 species, carnivorous perennial herbs.

Prey is trapped in much the same way as it is for *Cephalotus*, *Darlingtonia* and *Nepenthes*. The leaves are developed as pitcherlike traps and are erect to decumbent, elongate ('trumpet-shaped') or squat, with a broad lateral wing and a terminal lid or hood. The pitcher mouth has a distinct thickened margin. The whole may be green or yellow-green, often variously marked red or brown, especially on veins, sometimes with many translucent white spots toward the apex. The color tends to intensify when plants are grown in full sun. Lanternlike flowers nod on slender scapes, usually in spring.

Grow in full sun in buoyant, humid conditions with a minimum temperature of 45°F (7°C). Plant in an acidic, soilless medium high in sphagnum, leaf mold and sand. Keep moist in winter, when the leaves are often lost. From spring to fall, keep constantly wet, standing the containers in water and misting or watering overhead frequently. Always use rainwater. *S. purpurea* is certainly hardy outdoors to –10°F (–23°C), as may be other species and hybrids. It succeeds in a sunny, sheltered position in wet areas of the bog garden, or stood, containerized, on the marginal shelves of pools (again, it is essential that the water should be soft—plants in small ponds filled by tap water will fail). Increase by division in late winter.

S. flava YELLOW PITCHER PLANT, YELLOW TRUMPET, TRUMPETS; Virginia to Florida, Louisiana; pitchers 12–48 in (30–120 cm), erect, trumpet-shaped, wide at mouth, lid erect, rounded, yellow green, often veined red on lid, especially at base, sometimes wholly red or maroon; flowers yellow; *S. leucophylla* WHITE TRUMPET; SE and C US; pitchers to 48 in (120 cm), erect, trumpet-shaped, slender, green below, white netted with green, maroon or red above, lid erect, undulate, hairy within; flowers red-purple; *S. minor* (HOODED PITCHER PLANT; S Carolina to Florida; pitchers 10–18(–39) in (25–45[–100]

Sarcococca hookeriana

cm), erect, trumpet-shaped, green with purple veins and translucent white patches above, wings broad, lid concave, hooded, bending over mouth; flowers yellow; *S. psittacina* LOBSTER-POT PITCHER PLANT; SE US; pitchers to 6 in (15 cm), prostrate, apex curved inward, green, veined and marked red-purple above with distinct translucent patches, wings broad, lid forming an inflated, round hood; flowers red-purple; *S. purpurea* COMMON PITCHER PLANT, HUNTSMAN'S CUP; New Jersey north to Canadian Arctic, naturalized in Europe, especially Eire; pitchers 4–12 in (10–30 cm), decumbent, squat, curved and erect above, inflated above, narrowed below, green with red, or purple veins and markings, or entirely green, wing broad, lid entire, erect; flowers dark red or yellow; subsp. *venosa*: pitchers squatter, heavily veined and stained red; *S. rubra* SWEET TRUMPET PLANT, SWEET PITCHER PLANT; SE US; pitchers 4–18 in (10–45 cm), erect to sprawling, trumpet-shaped, narrow, green, becoming bronze- to copper-colored with maroon veins above, wing broad, lid bending over pitcher mouth, elliptic, rim and throat glistening with nectar; flowers red to maroon.

Sasa (from *zasa*, Japanese name for the smaller bamboos). Gramineae. Japan, Korea, China. About 40 small or medium-sized bamboos with running rhizomes; see *bamboos*.

Sasaella (diminutive of *Sasa*). Gramineae. Japan. Some 12 species of small, running bamboos; see *bamboos*.

Sasamorpha (from its resemblance to the related *Sasa*). Gramineae. Far East. About 6 species of medium-sized, usually glabrous bamboos; see *bamboos*.

Sassafras (from Spanish *salsafras*). Lauraceae. E N America, E Asia. 3 species of hardy, deciduous, aromatic trees to 100 ft (30 m). Leaves alternate, entire, 1–3-lobed. Bark deeply fissured. Flowers generally dioecious, yellow-green, borne in clustered racemes. Fruit an ovoid drupe on a stout fleshy stalk. This is a good specimen tree for sheltered woodland or in a lawn. Propagate from fresh seed sown in fall, or in spring after stratification; increase

also by root cuttings or suckers. *S. albidum* E N America, to 66 ft (20 m). Dark-green aromatic leaves, 6 in (15 cm) long, turning yellow to orange or purple in fall. Pollinated flowers on female plants bear red-stalked, dark-blue fruits ½ in (1 cm) long. Young growth may be damaged by frost.

Satureja (from *Satureja*, name used by Pliny). Labiatae. Temperate and warm temperate Northern Hemisphere. SAVORY. 30 species, annual herbs or perennial subshrubs with tubular, 2-lipped flowers. Among the most fragrant of herbs, savory is usually grown in an herb garden, but is also suitable for edging in an herbaceous border or for hot, dry and sunny situations on the rock garden or terrace. It is hardy to 14°F (−10°C) and needs full sun and well-drained soil. Propagate by division in spring, or by softwood cuttings in summer. *S. montana* (WINTER SAVORY; S Europe; shrublet to 20 in (50 cm); leaves small, tough, gray-green; flowers white to pale violet; 'Nana': dwarf; 'Procumbens': creeping).

Sauromatum (from the Greek *sauros*, lizard, a reference to the spathe and the petioles, which resemble a mottled lizard skin). Araceae. E and W Africa, E Asia. 2 species, perennial herbs with circular tubers and long-stalked, pedately compound leaves. The malodorous inflorescence usually appears before the foliage—numerous minute cream flowers cover the base of a long, tapering spadix, the whole arrangement more or less enveloped by a narrow spathe, bulbous at the base, reflexed and ribbonlike at its tip. The tubers are sometimes grown as curios in the home, with neither soil nor water, their spathes developing with astonishing speed. They should be planted and fed immediately after they have flowered. Grow in a fertile and well-drained medium, rich in organic matter. Water as the new leaf appears and withhold water as it dies down. Keep dry but not arid when dormant in winter, maintaining a minimum temperature of 41–45°F (5–7°C). They might equally be attempted outdoors in sheltered sites at 0°F (−18°C). Propagate by removal of offsets or by seed. *S. guttatum* (syn.

S. venosum); MONARCH OF THE EAST, VOODOO LILY, RED CALLA; Himalaya, S India; leafstalk to 28 in (70 cm), mottled maroon; spathe tube 2–4 in (5–10 cm), blade 12–28 in (30–70 cm), soon becoming reflexed, twisted and undulate, yellow-green to ocher spotted and mottled blood-red to dark maroon, spadix to 14 in (35 cm), narrowly cylindric, maroon or bronze).

sawdust wood particles resulting from sawing, used as a soil improver or surface mulch. It is a variable product and should be applied only after composting or weathering to prevent nitrogen deficiency in soil into which it is incorporated, and in order to neutralize possible toxins. The carbon:nitrogen ratio is higher than that of bark. The physical properties of sawdust depend on grade, and very fine samples can adversely affect drainage and aeration. Its cation exchange capacity is moderately high but low in nutrients.

Sawfly damage
Larvae of the common gooseberry sawfly may also feed on red currants and white currants. They can defoliate bushes if not noticed early.

S

sawflies (Hymenoptera: Tenthredinidae and some other families) insects up to ¾ in (20 mm) long, mainly black or yellow-brown, sometimes brightly colored with yellow and black predominating; females have a saw-edged ovipositor for inserting eggs into plant tissues. All sawfly larvae feed on plants, many being host specific. Most feed openly on the foliage, others are leaf miners, leaf rollers, stem borers, fruit feeders, or live inside galls. Unlike most other hymenopterous insects, there is no constriction between the thorax and abdomen. The larvae resemble caterpillars of moths and butterflies, but they have more abdominal legs, from six to eight pairs compared to five pairs or fewer in the Lepidoptera.

Roses are host to several open-feeding sawflies. The BANDED SAWFLY (*Allantus cinctus*), known as the CURLED ROSE SAWFLY in the US, has yellow-brown larvae, up to ½ in (12 mm) long, which feed with the hind part of their body raised in the air and, when at rest, remain curled up on the underside of leaves. The EUROPEAN LARGE ROSE SAWFLY (*Arge ochropus*) has blue-green larvae with black spots, as has the more common *Arge pagana*. The ANTLER SAWFLY (*Cladius difformis*), known as the BRISTLY ROSE SLUGWORM in the US, has yellow-green larvae, up to ½ in (12 mm) long, with bodies covered in stiff hairs; the adult males have hornlike projections on the antennae.

The COMMON GOOSEBERRY SAWFLY (*Nematus ribesii*), known as the IMPORTED CURRANT WORM in the US, has green larvae, with black heads and black spots. This species can cause complete defoliation of the host plants. A related European species, the ARUNCUS SAWFLY (*N. spiraea*), has pale green larvae up to ¾ in (20 mm) long, which can completely skeletonize the leaves of its only host *Aruncus dioicus*.

Pines may be attacked by many species of sawfly, including the LARGE PINE SAWFLY (*Diprion pini*) in Europe, with yellow-green larvae, up to 1 in (25 mm) long, which feed in groups on the needles; the PINE SAWFLY (*D.simile*), imported into North America from Europe; and the FOX-COLORED SAWFLY (*Neodiprion sertifer*), known as the EUROPEAN PINE SAWFLY in the US, which has gray-green larvae with a pale line along the back and a black line along each side.

Raspberry foliage is attacked by the RASPBERRY SAWFLY (*Priophorus morio*), which has grayish-green larvae, up to ½ in (12 mm) long. Other defoliating European species include the HAZEL SAWFLY (*Croesus septentrionalis*), with black-spotted green-blue larvae, up to 1 in (25 mm) long, which attack birch, hazel, alders, poplars, and willows; the IRIS SAWFLY (*Rhadinoceraea micans*), with gray-brown larvae, up to ¾ in (20 mm) long, which attack wild and cultivated water-side irises, especially *Iris pseudocorus* and *I. laevigata*; and the SOLOMON'S SEAL SAWFLY (*Phymato-*

cera aterrima), with blue-gray larvae, up to ¾ in (20 mm) long, which feed on polygonatums during early summer.

Examples of sawflies with leaf-mining larvae include the BIRCH LEAFMINER (*Fenusa pusilla*) in Europe and North America, causing blisterlike mines, and the raspberry leaf-mining sawflies (*Metallus* species), in Europe, which live in irregularly-shaped mines on raspberry and blackberry. The ROSE LEAF-ROLLING SAWFLY (*Blennocampa phyllocolpa*) causes tight rolling of rose leaves, but a leaf rolling habit is not common among sawflies. Some European sawflies cause galling, for example, the WILLOW BEAN-GALL SAWFLY (*Pontania proxima*), known as the WILLOW RED GALL SAWFLY in North America, which causes galls up to ¼ in (6 mm) long—these resemble bean seeds and protrude from both sides of the leaves of willows; a related species, the WILLOW PEA-GALL SAWFLY (*P. viminalis*), is responsible for pea-shaped galls on the same host.

Several sawflies are of considerable economic importance as pests of fruit. These include the APPLE SAWFLY (*Hoplocampa testudinea*) in Europe and North America, with cream-white larvae, up to ⅝ in (15 mm) long, which tunnel into apple fruitlets; in Europe, the PLUM SAWFLY (*H.flava*) has similar larvae which bore into plums and damsons in spring and early summer. In North America, the CHERRY FRUIT SAWFLY (*H. cookei*) has yellow-white larvae, up to ¼ in (6 mm) long, which enter the fruits of cherries and plums and occasionally those of peaches and apricots.

Small infestations of sawflies can be removed by hand-picking. Otherwise, caterpillars of open-feeding species should be controlled by applying recommended insecticides. Species with larvae that become hidden must be killed at the adult stage before egg-laying; for example, preventive sprays should be applied against the leaf-rolling sawfly in late spring. See *slugworms*.

Saxegothaea (after Prince Albert of Saxe-Coburg-Gotha [1819–61], Prince Consort). Podocarpaceae. Chilean Andes, Patagonia. 1 species, *S. conspicua*, PRINCE ALBERT'S YEW, a coniferous evergreen tree or shrub to 66 ft (20 m)

or more. The bark is brown, suffused gray and flaking; the branches are whorled with pendulous tips. The leaves are linear to lanceolate, ⅝–1¼ in (1.5–3 cm) long, coriaceous and dark green above with blue-white bands beneath, and a spiny tip. To ½ in (1 cm) long, the mature female cones are blue-gray to glaucous brown. Hardy to 5°F (−15°C). Plant in moist, acidic soil in a sheltered, humid environment.

saxicolous growing on or among rocks.

Saxifraga (from Latin *saxum*, rock, and *fragere*, to break: under the doctrine of the signatures, saxifrages with kidney-shaped leaves were used as a cure for kidney or bladder stones). Saxifragaceae. SAXIFRAGE. Europe, Asia, N America, mainly in arctic and mountainous; extending into S America via the Andes. Some 370 species, dwarf or small annual to perennial herbs (those here perennial or monocarpic). Many are alpines. They range widely in habit from miniature cushion plants to carpeters, rosette-formers and loose clumps. The leaves may be needle- or scalelike, or toothed and lobed, tongue- or strap-shaped, or larger and broader. The flowers are solitary or carried in cymes, racemes or panicles. They consist usually of 5 spreading, rounded petals.

All of the following are hardy to −10°F (−23°C). For many, the greatest threat is not cold, but overly wet conditions. One exception to this is *S. fortunei*, a handsome foliage plant that favors mild climates and damp, acidic soil. It associates well with sedges, hostas and ferns. Plant form and habit reflect natural habitat: the cushion habit generally relates to species occurring in the arctic and high mountain ranges, while those with softer, widespreading foliage mats are typical of the more sheltered montane conditions that prevail in areas of late snow melt. Taller, leafy-stemmed species are generally found in meadows, in open woodlands, and at woodland margins. The presence of lime-encrustation, secreted by ducts or hydathodes on the leaf surface, usually indicates a plant that prefers very rocky or gritty, rather dry and alkaline conditions. In terms of

S

SAXIFRAGA

Name	Distribution	Habit	Leaves	Flowers
S. aizoides YELLOW MOUNTAIN SAXIFRAGE, YELLOW SAXIFRAGE	Iceland, Scandinavia, N Britain, Alps, Apennines	2¾–8 in (7–20 cm), forming loose cushions	⅛–¾ in (4–22 mm), linear to oblong, fleshy, ciliate, covered in a thin, chalky crust	yellow, often spotted orange-red, sometimes orange or brick red, in hairy, stalked racemes

Comments: Group 1. Grow in moist soil; protect from harsh sunlight. var. **atrorubens**: flowers dark red.

S. × apiculata (*S. marginata* × *S. sancta*)	garden origin	densely cushion-forming, to 4 in (10 cm)	to ½ in (12 mm), linear to lanceolate, bright green	yellow in small clusters on short, erect stems

Comments: Group 2. Grow in moist but well-drained soil on the rock garden, in pans or troughs and sinks. Protect from burning sun. 'Alba': flowers white; 'Gregor Mendel': leaves glossy pale green; flowers pale yellow. 'Primrose Bee': flowers large, pale yellow.

S. × arco-valleyi (*S. lilacina* × *S. marginata*)	garden origin	forms small, tight and domed cushions	to ½ in (10 mm), oblong to linear, silver-gray	cuplike, pale pink to bright red, solitary, short-stalked

Comments: Group 3. Grow on the rock garden and in alpine sinks and pans, in moist, gritty soil; protect from scorching sun. 'Arco': pale pink. 'Dainty Dame': bright rose-lilac fading to white flushed pink. 'Ophelia': white. 'Silver Edge': leaves gray-green edged white; flowers pale lilac.

S. × borisii (*S. ferdinandi-coburgi* × *S. marginata*)	garden origin	cushion-forming, to 3 in (8 cm) high	to ½ in (10 mm), linear, gray-green or dark green	usually pale yellow, sometimes white or rich yellow, large, in red-tinted cymes

Comments: Group 3. Grow in gritty soil on the rock garden or in alpine sinks and pans; keep damp and protect from burning sun.

S. × boydii (*S. aretioides* × *S. burseriana*)	garden origin	low-growing, forming tight cushions to 3 in (8 cm)	linear to lanceolate, silver-green	vivid yellow, solitary or a few on short, red-tinted stems

Comments: Group 3. For the rock garden or alpine sink. 'Aretiastrum' (syn. 'Valerie Finnis'): cushions small, dense; flowers deep sulfur-yellow.

S. brunonis *S. brunoniana*	Himalaya	deciduous or semievergreen, mat-forming, with threadlike, red runners	lanceolate, rigid, soft green, in rosettes	yellow, in panicles to 6 in (15 cm)

Comments: Group 1. Grow in moist soil; protect from harsh sun.

S. bryoides MOSSY SAXIFRAGE	Europe (mountains)	forms dense mats of spherical leaf rosettes	⅛–¼ in (3.5–5 mm), oblong to lanceolate, pointed, hairy	white spotted orange, with orange stain at center, solitary on short stems

Comments: Group 4. Rock gardens and alpine sinks; gritty soil, full sun.

S. burseriana BURSER'S SAXIFRAGE	E Alps	stems numerous, woody-based, forming dense cushions	¼–½ in (6–12 mm), packed in low cones, narrowly lanceolate, silver-gray, with a thin, chalky crust	solitary, large, white on short, erect, hairy red stems

Comments: Group 3. Rock gardens, alpine sinks and pans in moist, gritty soil with full sun. 'Crenata': petals crenate. 'Gloria': flowers large, white with yellow centers on bright red stalks. 'His Majesty' (× *irvingii*): rosettes silver-gray; flowers large, rounded, pink, flushed white.

S. × *apiculata* 'Gregor Mendel'

S. × *boydii* 'Hindhead Seedling'

S. burseriana

S

SAXIFRAGA

Name	Distribution	Habit	Leaves	Flowers
S. callosa *S. lingulata* LIMESTONE SAXIFRAGE	NE Spain, SW Alps, Apennines	forms tight leaf rosettes to 6 in (16 cm) diameter, each dying after flowering but replaced by new growths on short stolons	1¹⁄₂–2³⁄₄ in (4–7 cm), linear, covered in a chalky gray-white crust	white, sometimes spotted red, many borne together in erect to arching panicles to 16 in (40 cm) long

Comments: Group 4. Grow in crevices and ledges on the rock garden and in alpine sinks; needs full sun and fast-draining, alkaline soil. 'Albida' (syn. 'Albertii'): rosettes silver, inflorescence large, white. 'Leichtlinii': flowers rose-red. 'Rosea': flowers rosc-red. 'Superba': flowers large, in arching, plumelike inflorescence; cream-white.

Name	Distribution	Habit	Leaves	Flowers
S. cochlearis	Maritime Alps	leaf rosettes numerous, ⁵⁄₈–3 in (1.5–8 cm) diameter, forming a dense cushion	to 1³⁄₄ in (4.5 cm), spathulate to oblanceolate, fleshy, tough, gray-green, chalk-encrusted	white, sometimes spotted red, many together in loose panicles to 12 in (30 cm)

Comments: Group 4. For the rock garden and alpine sinks and troughs; full sun in alkaline, gritty soil. 'Major': flowers larger. 'Minor': tight silvery hummocks.

Name	Distribution	Habit	Leaves	Flowers
S. cotyledon JUNGFRAU SAXIFRAGE, GREAT ALPINE ROCKFOIL	Scandinavia and Iceland, Pyrenees, Alps	leaf rosettes 2³⁄₄–4³⁄₄ in (7–12 cm) diameter, with daughter-rosettes on short runners	³⁄₄–3 in (2–8 cm), oblong to oblanceolate, margins toothed, covered in a chalky crust	white, sometimes spotted or veined red, many in broadly pyramidal panicles

Comments: Group 2. For the rock, scree or gravel garden.

Name	Distribution	Habit	Leaves	Flowers
S. cuneifolia SHIELD-LEAVED SAXIFRAGE	Mountains of S and SC Europe	stems prostrate, loosely carpeting with leaves in rosettes	¹⁄₂–1¹⁄₄ in (1–3 cm), broadly obovate to cuneate, fleshy, glossy bright green above, red-purple beneath, toothed	white, often with yellow basal patch and sometimes red spots, in loose panicles to 10 in (25 cm)

Comments: Group 1. Will thrive in most situations but prefers moist, fertile soil and protection from harsh sun. 'Variegata': leaves variegated creamy white to yellow.

Name	Distribution	Habit	Leaves	Flowers
S. exarata FURROWED SAXIFRAGE	C & S Europe, Caucasus	shoots leafy, to 1¹⁄₂ in (4 cm), forming dense, spreading cushions	to ¹⁄₂ in (10 mm), reniform, deeply divided into 3–5, pointed and furrowed lobes, bright green	white to dull cream, sometimes tinted red, 2–5 together on short, erect stalks

Comments: Group 1. Grow in moist but well-drained soil with protection from harsh sun. In ssp. **moschata** (syn. *S. moschata*), the leaf segments are not furrowed and the flowers are cream, sometimes tinted red. 'Cloth of Gold': leaves solid, bright gold—best in light shade.

Name	Distribution	Habit	Leaves	Flowers
S. ferdinandi-coburgi	E Macedonia	leaves crowded, forming dense cushions	¹⁄₈–³⁄₈ in (4–8 mm), linear, pointed, covered with thick chalk crust	bright yellow, 3–5 together on a hairy, red-tinted stem 1¹⁄₄–4³⁄₄ in (3–12 cm) tall

Comments: Group 3. For the rock garden and alpine sinks and pans in moist, gritty soil with protection from scorching sun.

S. cotyledon

S. cuneifolia

S. exarata subsp. *moschata*
'Cloth of Gold'

SAXIFRAGA

Name	Distribution	Habit	Leaves	Flowers
S. fortunei	Japan	loosely clump-forming	6 in (15 cm), rounded, toothed, glossy and thinly fleshy, apple green tinted bronze or copper and slender stalks to 8 in (20 cm) long	white with one or two lower petals far longer than upper petals, in a loose, airy, red-tinted panicle to 20 in (50 cm) tall

Comments: Group 1. Grow in dappled sun to shade in moist, neutral to acidic soil rich in leaf mold—a fine companion for sedges, ferns, small bamboos and hostas in the damp or woodland garden. 'Rubrifolia': leaves tinted coppery red; 'Wada': leaves beet red.

Name	Distribution	Habit	Leaves	Flowers
S. federici-augusti	Balkan Peninsula	forms dense rosettes of spreading leaves	½–1½ in (12–35 mm), oblanceolate, gray-green covered in chalky crust	bright red to deep maroon, more or less concealed by pink to wine red sepals and leafy bracts in erect then nodding, hairy raceme to 4 in (10 cm) tall

Comments: Group 4. For the rock garden or alpine trough in gritty, alkaline soil. ssp. **grisebachii**. (syn. **S. grisebachii**) inflorescence cherry red to maroon. 'Wisley': more vigorous and brightly colored with the inflorescence bracts deep purple red and tipped bright green.

Name	Distribution	Habit	Leaves	Flowers
S. × geum (*S. hirsuta × S. umbrosa*)	garden origin	forms loose mats of spreading leaf rosettes	¾–2½ in (2–6 cm), broadly oblong to spathulate, crenulate, hairy	small, pink in bud, opening white spotted pink, in loose, frothy, red-tinted panicles to 7 in (18 cm) tall

Comments: Group 1. Grow in dappled sun or part-shade in moist, fertile soil.

Name	Distribution	Habit	Leaves	Flowers
S. granulata FAIR MAIDS OF FRANCE, MEADOW SAXIFRAGE, BULBOUS SAXIFRAGE	Europe	rosette-forming, bulbiferous	¼–¾ in (0.6–2 cm), reniform to cordate, toothed, glandular-hairy, slightly fleshy, short-stalked	white, sometimes red-veined in few-branched panicles 4–12 in (10–30 cm) tall

Comments: Group 1. Grow in moist soil; protect from harsh sun. 'Flore Pleno': flowers sterile with many petals.

Name	Distribution	Habit	Leaves	Flowers
S. hirsuta KIDNEY SAXIFRAGE	SW Europe and Iceland	loosely mat-forming with sprawling and rooting stems	⅝–1½ in (1.5–4 cm), reniform to rounded, crenate to bluntly toothed, soft pale green, stained purple-red beneath, slender-stalked	small, white, faintly spotted pink in loose, narrow, red-tinted panicles 4¾–16 in (12–40 cm)

Comments: Group 1. Grow in sun or shade in moist, fertile soil.

Name	Distribution	Habit	Leaves	Flowers
S. juniperifolia	Bulgaria	stems short, columnar with densely packed leaves, forming dense cushions	⅜–½ in (9–13 mm), linear, pointed, persisting long after death	bright yellow, 3–8 on hairy stems 1¼–2½ in (3–6 cm) long

Comments: Group 3/4. For the rock garden and alpine sink, in gritty soil in sun.

Name	Distribution	Habit	Leaves	Flowers
S. × kellereri	garden origin	leaf rosettes cushion-forming	¾ in (17 mm), cuneate, gray-green, tightly packed	pink, 1–3 together on short stalks

Comments: Group 3. For the rock garden or alpine sink in sun in gritty soil.

S

S. fortunei

S. federici-augusti **subsp. grisebachii** 'Wisley'

S. × geum

SAXIFRAGA

Name	Distribution	Habit	Leaves	Flowers
S. longifolia PYRENEAN SAXIFRAGE	Pyrenees	leaves form a single, broad rosette, dying after flowering and producing no daughter rosettes	2½–4½ in (6–11 cm), linear, fleshy, pale gray-green, with a thick chalk crust	small, white, sometimes spotted red, packed in a cylindrical to conical panicle to 24 in (60 cm)

Comments: Group 4. For the rock garden or alpine sink in full sun in gritty, alkaline soil. Increase by seed. 'Magnifica': rosettes to 6 in (15 cm) diameter; panicle very large and showy. 'Walpole's Variety': smaller, blue-gray rosettes; flowers in short white spikes.

Name	Distribution	Habit	Leaves	Flowers
S. oppositifolia PURPLE MOUNTAIN SAXIFRAGE	Arctic, high mountains of Europe, Asia and N America	stems short, woody, freely branched, forming dense mats and cushions	¼–⅜ in (0.5–0.8 cm), oblong, blunt, bristly, rigid, dark dull green, chalky	solitary, short-stalked, pink to deep purple fading to white

Comments: Group 1. For the rock garden and alpine sinks, in an open, sunny position in gritty, acidic soil. Includes cultivars with white, pale rose, pink, crimson and deep magenta flowers, some with silvery foliage.

Name	Distribution	Habit	Leaves	Flowers
S. paniculata *S. aizoon* LIFELONG SAXIFRAGE	Pyrenees, SW Alps north to Lapland and Iceland	mat-forming	to 1½ in (4 cm), oblong to lanceolate, in hemispherical rosettes, margins inrolled, chalky	creamy-white, sometimes red-spotted in panicles to 12 in (30 cm)

Comments: Group 4. For the rock garden and alpine troughs; grow in full sun in gritty, alkaline soil. Includes cultivars with pure white, pink-spotted, rose and cream to lemon yellow flowers, some with fine, silvery foliage.

Name	Distribution	Habit	Leaves	Flowers
S. rosacea **Comments:** Group 1. Tolerant of most conditions; it includes many forms and popular garden hybrids. Similar to *S. exarata*.	NW and C Europe	variable, low-growing, stems short and forming dense, compact cushions or longer and trailing in mats with dead leaves persistent	½–¾ in (1–2 cm), obovate to cuneate, bright green to red-tinted, usually cut into 5 or more pointed segments	white to pink or dark red, 2–5 on erect, slender scapes to 2½ in (6 cm).

Name	Distribution	Habit	Leaves	Flowers
S. rotundifolia ROUND-LEAVED SAXIFRAGE	Europe (SW France to Black Sea and Aegean), Caucasus	rhizomatous, forming loose, spreading rosettes	⅝–1¾ in (1.5–4.5 cm), rounded, base deeply cordate, smooth to hairy, crenate to sharp-toothed or palmately lobed, slender-stalked	white, usually spotted crimson-purple, shading to orange-yellow at base in loose, spreading panicles 6–28 in (15–70 cm)

Comments: Group 1. Grow in light shade or dappled sun in moist, fertile soil.

Name	Distribution	Habit	Leaves	Flowers
S. sancta	NE Greece	differs from *S. juniperifolia* in its shorter leaves (to ½ in/10 mm), and glabrous inflorescence	**Comments:** Group 3/4.	

S. oppositifolia   *S. sancta*   *S. stolonifera*   *S.* **'Tumbling Waters'**

SAXIFRAGA

Name	Distribution	Habit	Leaves	Flowers
S. stolonifera MOTHER OF THOUSANDS, STRAWBERRY GERANIUM	China, Japan	rosette-forming, spreading by long, thin, red stolons	to 2½ in (6 cm), round, mid-green with silvery veins above, flushed red beneath, bristly, long-stalked	white, lower petals longer than upper, in loose panicles to 16 in (40 cm)
Comments: Group 1. Grow in shade or dappled sun in moist, fertile soil. A good groundcover plant more commonly used as a houseplant and for hanging baskets. *S.* 'Tricolor' ('Magic Carpet'): leaves variegated green, pink, red and silver.				
S. taygetea	SW Greece, Balkans	forms loose, spreading rosettes, similar to *S. rotundifolia*	¼–½ in (5–13 mm), rounded, crenate, smooth to downy, mid-green, slender-stalked	white spotted pink or purple-red, in loose panicles to 8 in (20 cm)
Comments: Group 1.				
S. 'Tumbling Waters'	garden origin	mat-forming with tight low rosettes	to 3 in (8 cm), narrow, with a chalky crust	white, crowded in an arching, conical panicle to 20 in (50 cm) long
Comments: Group 4. For ledges and crevices in the rock garden or alpine sink in sun and in gritty alkaline soil. A spectacular cultivar, each rosette dies after flowering but is replaced by offsets.				
S. umbrosa	Pyrenees	stems short, bearing leaf rosettes forming loose cushions	to 1¼ in (3 cm), oblong to obovate, crenate, tough to thinly fleshy, smooth, ciliate, short-stalked	white spotted crimson in loose, red-tinted panicles to 14 in (35 cm)
Comments: Group 1. Will grow in sun or shade in most soil. *S.* 'Clarence Elliott': dwarf compact; flowers very small, rose-pink. 'Primuloides': to 6 in (15 cm); leaves primroselike; flowers rose-pink.				
S. × urbium (*S. umbrosa × S. hirsuta*) LONDON PRIDE	garden origin	like *S. umbrosa*, but petioles longer and leaves more strongly toothed	white spotted red-pink or flushed pink, in panicles to 10 in (25 cm)	**Comments:** Group 1. Good low groundcover, tolerant of most conditions.

cultural requirements, saxifrages can be broken down into four groups; (1) plants needing protection from fierce sun and moist soil; (2) plants suitable for rock gardens and scree, needing some shade and well-drained soil; (3) plants suitable for well-drained pockets in a rock garden, sink garden, alpine trough and pans in an alpine house, needing shade from fierce sun and moist but never wet soil; (4) plants suitable for a rock garden, sink garden, alpine trough and pans in an alpine house, needing full sun and impeccably drained, alkaline soil.

Increase by division, by cuttings of non-flowering rosettes, by soft tip cuttings of *S. oppositifolia* and by seed (the only practicable means for monocarpic species such as *S. longifolia*). Seed is surface sown when ripe, or in spring after stratification.

scab includes various fungal diseases, the most damaging of which occur on apple, pear and potato. Scab typically shows as a discrete superficial lesion, involving localized severe roughening, pitting or cracking, and abnormal thickening of the surface layers, with or without the development of cork.

APPLE SCAB (*Venturia inaequalis*) and PEAR SCAB (*Venturia pirina*) are restricted to their individual fruit hosts but are very similar in life cycle and the damage caused. The skin of infected young fruits develops blackish brown blotches, and in severe cases fruits may be completely covered, with cracks developing and resultant misshapen young apples; the disease is superficial. Infected leaves show brown or olive green spots and may fall prematurely, reducing growth and also fruiting in the following season; ornamental *Malus* leaves are particularly affected. The fungi overwinter in scabby shoot pustules and in special fruiting bodies on fallen leaves. Disposing of fallen leaves contributes to control, as does regular pruning for improved air circulation and removing infected shoots. Regular sprays of recommended fungicide provide effective control. Among resistant apple cultivars are 'Discovery', 'Lane's Prince Albert' and 'Sunset'; resistant pear cultivars include 'Jargonelle' and 'Catillac'.

COMMON POTATO SCAB (*Streptomyces scabies*) causes unsightly, generally raised, scabby patches on the surface of tubers; different strains probably cause different forms of scabbing. The corky scabs largely prevent infection spreading into the tuber flesh, and because the skin can be peeled for cooking, the disease is tolerable. Common scab occurs predominantly in light soils, especially when these remain dry during tuber initiation, and is encouraged by high lime

infected spotting

Scab

S

content. Fungicide treatment is not appropriate, and attention should be paid to maintaining soil organic-matter content and to irrigation. Resistant cultivars include 'Arran Pilot' 'Maris Peer' and 'King Edward', while those susceptible include 'Desiree', 'Majestic' and 'Maris Piper'. Powdery scab of potatoes is caused by the fungus *Spongospora subterranea*, and symptoms are similar; avoidance of infected seed is the only practical control measure.

scaberulous finely or minutely scabrous.

Scabiosa (from Latin *scabies*, itch, a disease these plants were thought to cure). Dipsacaceae. Europe, Asia, Africa, mainly Mediterranean. PINCUSHION FLOWER, SCABIOUS. 80 species, annual or perennial herbs with flowers in slender-stalked hemispherical, heads subtended by involucral bracts. The following species are hardy to −10°F (−23°C). Grow in sun in moderately fertile, well-drained soil, preferably circumneutral or alkaline. Deadhead to prolong flowering and lift and divide perennials every third or fourth year to maintain vigor. *S. graminifolia* should be given a warm, sunny position in the rock garden with excellent drainage. Propagate by seed. Perennials may also be increased by division or by basal cuttings in spring.

S. atropurpurea MOURNFUL WIDOW, SWEET SCABIOUS, PINCUSHION FLOWER, EGYPTIAN ROSE; South Africa; annual 24–36 in (60–90 cm); flowers dark purple to deep crimson, fragrant, in heads to 2 in (5 cm) in diameter; includes 'Blue Cockade', to 36 in (90 cm), with double, globe-shaped, rich blue, fragrant flowers, 'Chile Black', with darkest purple-black flowers, 'Grandiflora', with large flower heads, and 'Nana', slightly dwarf and much-branched; *S. caucasica* Caucasus; perennial to 24 in (60 cm); flowers pale blue, in heads to 3 in (7.5 cm) in diameter; includes wide range of cultivars and seed races—tall or short, with flowers in shades of white, cream, lavender and blue, good for cutting; *S. columbaria* subsp. *ochroleuca* (syn. *S. ochroleuca*); Europe, W Asia; biennial or perennial to 30 in (75 cm); flowers primrose yellow to creamy white in

heads to 2½ in (6 cm) across; *S. graminifolia* S Europe; perennial to 16 in (40 cm) forming loose mats; leaves grasslike; flowers blue-violet to rose in heads to 1½ in (4 cm) in diameter; *S. lucida* C Europe; perennial to 12 in (30 cm); flowers rose-lilac to pale pink in dense heads to 1½ in (4 cm) in diameter; For *S. rumelica*, see *Knautia macedonica*.

scabrid a little scabrous, or rough.

scabridulous minutely scabrid.

scabrous rough, harsh to the touch because of minute projections, scales, tiny teeth or bristles.

Scadoxus (name derived from Greek *skiadion*, parasol (i.e. umbel), and *doxa*, glory). Amaryllidaceae. Tropical Arabia and Africa to S Namibia and E Cape. BLOOD LILY. 9 species bulbous or rhizomatous herbs differing from *Haemanthus* in their leaves, ovate to lanceolate and not 2-ranked. Cultivate as for *Haemanthus*, maintaining slightly higher temperatures and humidity. *S. multiflorus* (syn. *Haemanthus coccineus*, *H.multiflorus*; tropical and South Africa, Yemen; scape to 30 in (75 cm), spathe valves colorless or tinged red, soon withering, umbel more or less spherical, flowers scarlet, fading pink; subsp. *katherinae*: syn. *Haemanthus katherinae*, flowers larger); *S. puniceus* (syn. *Haemanthus magnificus*, *H.natalensis*, *H.puniceus*; ROYAL PAINT BRUSH; E and South Africa; scape to 16

Scaevola aemula
A frost-tender scrambling perennial often used in hanging baskets. Its oddly shaped flowers are produced continuously over many months.

in (40 cm); spathe valves red, umbel conical, flowers scarlet to green-yellow).

Scaevola (from Latin *scaevus*, left-

handed; alluding to one-sided, fan-shaped corolla. Goodeniaceae. Australia, Polynesia. 90 species of short-lived perennials or herbs or shrubs, some scrambling. Leaves alternate; flowers solitary in leaf axils or few-flowered cymes, fan-shaped, corolla tube split to base on upper side. Frost tender, but in temperate climates suitable for growing under protection, in hanging baskets or as patio plants. Propagate from seed sown at 66–75°F (19–24°C) in spring, or from softwood cuttings taken in late spring or summer. *S. aemula* FAIRY FAN FLOWER, S and E Australia. Perennial to 27½ in (70 cm). Stems ascending or procumbent, glabrous to pubescent. Leaves to 1¾ × 1¼ in (4.5 × 3 cm), variably lanceolate or oblong to ovate. Basal leaves spoon-shaped, toothed. Flowers solitary to 1 in (2.5 cm) across borne in leafy racemes, purple to blue in summer.

scaffold branch a main structural branch of a tree used to support renewable fruiting laterals or spurs.

scald damage caused to plant tissues by unsatisfactory atmospheric temperature or humidity, or toxic pollutants produced by paraffin or gas burners. Sun scald is a variation where leaves, stems and fruits may be damaged as a result of sudden exposure to hot sunshine, especially in cases where the plant surface is wet. Damage takes the form of chlorotic or brown blotches or spots on leaves and shoots, discoloration of bark, shrivelling fruits, as occurs with grapes (cf. *shanking*), and pale areas on tomatoes and sometimes apples and plums. The condition can be particularly troublesome in plants grown in greenhouses, and attention should be paid to shading and watering.

Superficial scald describes a physiological disorder in apples where death of surface cells leads to browning of the skin during storage. It is encountered during hot, dry growing conditions and in the UK is significant on the cultivar 'Bramley's Seedling'.

Sun scorch is separately identified, referring to the withering of shoots as a result of exposure to hot sunshine.

scale see *trichome*.

scaling see *cuttings*.

scale leaves specialized, scalelike leaves, including those covering buds or forming bulbs.

scale insects

(Hemiptera: Coccoidea) sap-sucking insects, some of which excrete copious amounts of honeydew, which is known to encourage the growth of sooty molds. Adult males are winged, with well-developed antennae and legs; the females are wingless, with scalelike bodies lacking well-defined divisions, and legs and antennae absent or reduced. The female lays eggs once in her lifetime; these are protected by a white, cottony, waxy egg sac (as in mealybugs), extruded from the rear end of the female's body, or, more typically, deposited without any white wax under the female's protective scale or shell. The first-stage nymph, known as a crawler, has functional legs and is often the only means of natural dispersal of the species; once its stylets are inserted, the subsequent nymphal stages and the adult female move infrequently (mealybugs, however, retain their mobility).

The GREENHOUSE ORTHEZIA (*Orthezia insignis*) attacks a wide range of greenhouse plants in Europe, North America and Australia, and the mobile nymphs and adults resemble mealybugs; the female insects carry conspicuous white egg sacs attached to their abdomens. The COTTONY CUSHION or FLUTED SCALE (*Icerya purchasi*), so-called because of its conspicuous longitudinally grooved white egg sacs, which can be up to ½ in (10 mm) long, is a serious pest of citrus and also attacks many other plants, including acacia, cytisus, and roses. The BEECH SCALE (*Cryptococcus fagisuga*) in Europe and North America is a widespread pest of beech, where it can be identified by the conspicuous, white, waxy powder on the trunks and branches; it can predispose the bark to infection by fungi (*Nectria* species).

Other scale insects of importance have either soft or armored scales. The soft scales have a waxy covering, which remains part of the body wall and

scale leaves

Lily bulb

cannot be separated from it; some species are large and rounded, others are broad and flattened. The soft scales common to Europe and North America include BROWN SCALE (*Parthenolecanium corni*), known as the EUROPEAN FRUIT SCALE in the US, which is up to ¼ in (5 mm) long, with brown oval convex scales. It infests peach, nectarine, currants, grape vines and many ornamental plants. The SOFT SCALE (*Coccus hesperidum*) is up to ⅛ in (4 mm) long, with flat, elongate-oval scales. It usually lies alongside the main vein on the underside of the leaves of abutilons, bay laurel, camellias, *Citrus*, *Clematis*, escallonias, ferns, *Ficus*, *Hibiscus*, hippeastrums, hollies, ivies, oleanders, poinsettias, *Stephanotis* and many other ornamental plants. The HEMISPHERICAL SCALE (*Saissetia coffeae*), up to ⅛ in (4 mm) long, with a hemispherical shell, infests asparagus ferns, begonias, carnations, clerodendrons, codiaeums, cycads, ferns, *Ficus*, oleanders, orchids, *Stephanotis* and other ornamental plants. Other unarmored scale insects in North America include the TERRAPIN SCALE (*Mesolecanium nigrofasciatum*), a dark red-brown, hemispherical scale, which attacks fruits and shade trees; the BLACK SCALE (*Saissetia oleae*), up to ¼ in (6 mm), with large black or dark brown rounded scales, which is a serious pest of citrus, olive, grapefruit and greenhouse plants; and the CITRICOLA SCALE (*Coccus pseudomagnoliarum*), with flattish scales, at first transparent but later darkening, which also attacks *Citrus*.

Some species of unarmored scales are conspicuous because of their 'woolly' egg sacs; these scale insects are known as WOOLLY SCALES (*Pulvinaria* species). The most widespread in Europe are the HORSE CHESTNUT SCALE (*P. regalis*), on horse chestnuts, limes, elms, sycamores, magnolias, maples, *Cornus* and other ornamental plants; the WOOLLY VINE SCALE (*P. vitis*) on currants and gooseberries; and the CUSHION SCALE (*Chloropulvinaria floccifera*) on camellia and holly. The COTTONY PEACH SCALE (*P. amygdali*), on orchard trees, and the

COTTONY MAPLE SCALE (*P. innumerabilis*), on maples and other trees and shrubs, are widespread in North America.

The armored scales have a hard, waxy scalelike covering, which can be separated from the body, and several species are common to Europe and North America. The MUSSEL SCALE (*Lepidosaphes ulmi*), known as the OYSTERSHELL SCALE in the US, is up to 3mm (⅛ in) long, with mussel-shaped blackish-brown scales. It infests the woody stems and branches of plants such as *Ceanothus*, cotoneasters, ornamental and fruiting apples and pears, box, and various other trees and shrubs. The OYSTERSHELL SCALE (*Quadraspidiotus ostreaeformis*), known as the EUROPEAN FRUIT SCALE in the US, is found on the bark of a wide range of trees and shrubs, especially apple, pear, peach, plum, birch, poplar and horse chestnut. The CAMELLIA SCALE (*Hemiberlesia rapax*), known as the GREEDY SCALE in the US, has circular scales, up to ¹⁄₁₆ in (2 mm) across. This insect infests a wide range of plants, including begonias, camellias, citrus, deciduous fruits, cacti and orchids. The OLEANDER SCALE (*Aspidiotus nerii*) has circular scales, up to ¹⁄₁₆ in (2 mm) across with a yellow center and pale edges. It infests the underside of leaves of many plants, including acacias, ornamental asparagus, aucubas, azaleas, pot *Cyclamen*, dracaenas, ericas, fatsias, *Ficus*, laurels, oleanders and palms. The EUONYMUS SCALE (*Unaspis euonymi*), with female scales similar to those of mussel scales, infests the woody stems of *Euonymus japonica*; the SCURFY SCALE (*Aulacaspis rosae*), known as the ROSE SCALE in the US, has round, flat, opaque white scales, up to ⅛ in (3mm) across, and forms dense colonies on the woody stems of certain species of rose. In North America, there are several other species of armored scales, particularly on citrus and deciduous fruits.

Scale insects are relatively immobile and most garden infestations are introduced on plant material; all newly acquired plants should therefore be inspected carefully. Recommended systemic insecticides control most infestations, while scale insects on deciduous trees and shrubs can also be controlled by applying appropriate winter washes in the dormant season.

S

scandent climbing.

scape an erect, leafless stalk arising at or near the base of the plant and bearing a terminal inflorescence or solitary flower; such inflorescences are described as *scapose*.

scarification (1) the removal of thatch and moss from a lawn using a spring-tined rake or a special tool, known as a scarifier, which has short metal, crescent-shaped teeth or sturdy brushes; see *lawns*; (2) mechanical or chemical treatment of hard-coated seeds, such as those of the family Leguminosae, before sowing to permit imbibition and improve germination. See *seeds and seed sowing*.

scarious thin, dry and shriveled; consisting of more or less translucent tissue.

Schefflera (for J. G. Scheffler [1722–1811], physician in Danzig). Araliaceae. Warmer regions of the world, with the greatest numbers of species in the Americas and S and E Asia to the Pacific. IVY TREE, SCHEF-FLERA, UMBRELLA TREE. Over 700 species, evergreen trees and shrubs, some climbers, some epiphytic. The leaves are usually palmately compound; the flowers are small, green to creamy white or red and borne in umbels on massive panicles. Popular foliage plants cultivated in the intermediate to hot greenhouse or as house plants. Large specimens of *S. actinophylla* are common in offices and public buildings, where they adapt well to hydroponic cultivation. *S. elliptica* and *S. pueckleri* are sold as young rooted leads trained on moss poles. *S. elegantissima* (usually sold in its juvenile form) is the well-known houseplant *Dizygotheca*.

Maintain a minimum winter temperature of 55°F (13°C). Give strong, filtered light all year round. Under glass, maintain medium to high humidity, syringing plants 2–3 times daily in hot weather. When grown as house plants, sponge the foliage occasionally to remove dust and stand in trays of damp pebbles or in groups to create a

scape (unbranched flower stem)

Leucojum vernum

humid microclimate. Water moderately, allowing the medium to become slightly dry between waterings. Feed monthly during the growing season with a dilute liquid fertilizer. Plants tolerate hard cutting back.

Sow ripe seed during fall in a humid atmosphere at a temperature of 68–75°F (20–24°C). Alternatively, propagate by air-layering or by sectional stem cuttings and softwood cuttings rooted with bottom heat in spring and summer.

S. actinophylla AUSTRALIAN IVY-PALM, OCTOPUS-TREE, UMBRELLA-TREE; Australia, New Guinea; erect, glabrous shrub or small tree to 40 ft (12 m); leaflets to 7–16, to 12 × 4 in (30 × 10 cm), oblong, entire, stalked, bright green and glossy above, obtuse; juvenile leaflets fewer, smaller, toothed, acute; includes variegated cultivars; *S. arboricola* Taiwan; glabrous epiphytic shrub or liane; leaflets 7–11, obovate, entire, to 4½ × 1¾ in (11 × 4.5 cm), stalked, bright green and semiglossy above, obtuse; juveniles differ in leaflets with short, widely spaced teeth; includes variegated cultivars; *S. digitata* New Zealand; spreading shrub or tree to 26 ft (8 m), glabrescent; young branches red-purple; leaflets 7–10, thin, to 8 × 2½ in (20 × 6 cm), narrowly obovate, shortly stalked, sharply toothed, leaflets in juvenile plants 5, more or less pinnatifid, lobes toothed, pink beneath; *S. elegantissima* (syn. *Dizygotheca elegantissima*); FALSE ARALIA, PETIT BOUX CALEDONIEN; New Caledonia; glabrous, sparsely branching trees to 50 ft (15 m) with dark bark; juvenile stage to 6½ ft (2 m), unbranched; stem and petioles dark green spotted white; leaflets 7–11, linear, to 9 × 1¼ in (23 × 3 cm), coarsely serrate, dark green to chocolate brown above, dark brown-green beneath, midrib white; adults with leaflets oblong, to 10 × 3 in (25 × 8 cm), stalked, obtuse, broadly toothed, sinuate or entire; *S. pueckleri* S and SE Asia; erect, glabrescent, spreading tree to 60 ft × 24 in (18 × 0.6 m) or scandent; leaflets 5–10, narrowly oblong to 10 × 3 in (25 × 8 cm), resembling *S. actinophylla* but upper surface darker and glossier, yellow-green beneath, always entire; variegated cultivars are grown.

Schima (name said to be derived from the Arabic). Theaceae. S Asia. 2 species. *S. wallichii* (syn. *S. argentea*, *S. superba*), a frost-tender, summer-flowering evergreen tree to 130 ft (40 m) tall. The leaves are 2¾–10 in (7–24 cm) long, elliptic to oblong, entire or wavy. Red-purple at first, they become dark green and thinly coriaceous. Scarlet in bud, the fragrant flowers are to 2½ in (6.5 cm) across and open purple-cream to white, with small, circular petals and many yellow stamens. Grow in freely draining, humus-rich, nonalkaline soil, in full sun or light dappled shade, in a position sheltered from cold drying winds. Under glass, water plentifully when in full growth, at other times moderately; maintain a winter minimum temperature of 37–41°F (3–5°C). Propagate by seed sown ripe, or by semiripe cuttings in summer, rooted in a closed case with bottom heat.

Schinus (from Greek *schinos*, name used for *Pistacia lentiscus*). Anacardiaceae. S America, Uruguay to Mexico, naturalized in S US, Canary Islands, China. Around 30 species, evergreen, resinous shrubs and trees with pinnate or simple leaves and small flowers massed in panicles in summer. When plants of both sexes are grown together, the females sometimes bear colorful, pea-sized berries. The graceful, weeping *S. molle* is widely planted in more or less frost-free climates for shade and ornament. *S. terebinthifolius*, often used as a street tree and lawn specimen in warm climates, is of more rigid aspect, and makes a round-headed tree, its fruit clusters showy in winter. Plant both species in well-drained soil and full sun with wall protection. Increase by seed in spring or by semiripe cuttings.

S. molle PEPPER TREE, PERUVIAN MASTIC TREE, MOLLE; Brazil, Uruguay, Paraguay, N Argentina; tree to 50 ft (15 m); branches slender, pendulous; leaves 4–12 in (10–30 cm), leaflets lanceolate, serrate; flowers pale yellow; fruit rose-pink; *S. terebinthifolius* BRAZILIAN PEPPER TREE, CHRISTMASBERRY TREE, AROEIRA; Venezuela to Argentina; shrub or small tree to 23 ft (7 m); leaves 4–6½ in (10–17 cm), leaflets 1¼–2½ in (3–6 cm), oval-lanceolate to obovate; flowers white; fruit red.

Schisandra (from Greek *schizo*, to split, and *aner*, man, referring to the distinctly separated anther cells). Schisandraceae. E Asia, Eastern N America. 25 species, deciduous or evergreen climbing shrubs with twining stems and oblong to lanceolate leaves. Produced in spring, the flowers are small, cup-shaped and composed of numerous tepals. Where plants of both sexes are cultivated together, the female flowers develop into slender, pendulous spikes bearing bright red, berrylike fruit. The following are hardy to 0°F (−18°C), but may need the protection of a south- or west-facing wall, or of larger trees and shrubs in areas that experience prolonged frosts and harsh winds. Grow in fertile, well-drained but moisture-retentive soil with some protection from intense sunlight; slightly acidic soil is preferred. Topdress annually with organic material, and water plentifully during dry periods, particularly wall-grown specimens. Walls and trellis apart, these shrubs will also scramble through trees and shrubs and over large rocks. Prune in late winter or spring to remove dead wood and to train or limit to the allocated space. Sow seed in cold frames in the fall or root semiripe cuttings in summer. Alternatively, layer long shoots during the fall, severing plants from parent material the following year.

S. chinensis China; flowers to ½ in (1.25 cm) diameter, pale rose to bright pink, fragrant; *S. coccinea* BAY STAR VINE, WILD SARSAPARILLA; SE US; flowers to ½ in (1 cm) in diameter, crimson; *S. grandiflora* N India, Bhutan, Nepal; flowers 1 in (2.5 cm) in diameter, fragrant, white, cream or pale rose; var. *cathayensis*: flowers rose-pink; *S. henryi* C and S China; flowers white; *S. propinqua* C and W China, Himalaya; flowers to ⅝ in (1.5 cm) in diameter, orange-red; var. *sinensis*: flowers smaller, somewhat yellow, cold-resistant; *S. rubriflora* flowers deep scarlet.

schist rock composed of layers of different minerals, which splits into thin plates.

Schizanthus (from Greek *schizo*, to cut, and *anthos*, flower, referring to the deeply cut corolla). Solanaceae. Chile. BUTTERFLY FLOWER, POOR MAN'S

Schizanthus pinnatus 'Hit Parade'
These free-flowering annuals make excellent conservatory plants. They do best in full light but become leggy at high temperatures.

ORCHID. 12 species, glandular-hairy annual herbs with pinnately cut leaves and cymes of showy, 5-lobed and 2-lipped flowers. For outdoor cultivation, sow *in situ* in spring in a sunny, sheltered spot in light, well-drained, fertile soil. Alternatively, sow under glass 7–8 weeks before planting out; harden off before planting out. For pot culture, sow at 55–59°F (13–15°C) between fall and spring. Grow in a medium-fertility, loam-based mix, repotting regularly. Give cool, airy conditions in full sun, and ventilate when temperatures rise above 50°F (10°C). Water sparingly in winter, plentifully in spring and summer. *Schizanthus* is prone to a number of virus diseases, in particular tomato spotted wilt, which causes severe bronzing and wilting of the upper leaves; control aphid infestations and destroy affected plants. *S. pinnatus* annual 8–20 in (20–50 cm); flowers violet to pink, middle upper lip with yellow throat with violet markings; there are many cultivars, hybrids and seed races tall or dwarf plants with large flowers in a range of colors: white, flesh-pink, golden-yellow centered, shades of crimson, amber, pink and mauve to mauve-blue.

schizocarp a dry, usually dehiscent syncarpous ovary which splits into separate, one-seeded halves, at maturity.

Schizopetalon (from Greek *schizo*, to cut, and *petalon*, petal, referring to the lobed petals). Cruciferae. Chile. 5 species, hairy herbs with pinnately lobed leaves and, in summer, racemes

of fragrant flowers each composed of four clawed and deeply cut petals. Grow in well-drained, fertile soil in full sun. Sow under glass at 55–59°F (13–15°C); prick out into individual pots in order to minimize root disturbance on setting out. Plant out after the last frost. For pot plants, sow in early fall in a well-drained, medium-fertility loam-based mix. Maintain a minimum temperature of 50°F (10°C). Water sparingly, increasing quantities when temperatures rise in spring; apply dilute liquid feed when pots are well-filled with roots. *S. walkeri* perennial treated as an annual to 18 in (45 cm); leaves to 5½ in (14 cm), deeply pinnatifid; flowers almond-scented, petals white, fimbriate.

Schizophragma (from Greek *schizo*, to split, and *phragma*, fence, referring to the fruits, which split and fragment between the ribs). Hydrangeaceae. Himalaya to Japan, Taiwan. 4 species, deciduous climbing and creeping shrubs, attaching themselves by means of short, adhesive, aerial roots. The leaves are basically ovate with a tapering tip and a rounded to heart-shaped base. The flowers are carried in flat-topped, branching terminal cymes in summer. Each inflorescence branch bears a long-stalked peripheral enlarged sepal. Ovate to rhombic and white to cream, these sepals appear petal-like and form a showy outer ring encompassing the smaller white fertile flowers. These magnificent climbing shrubs resemble a larger, showier *Hydrangea petiolaris*, whose cultural requirements they share.

S. hydrangeoides Japan, Korea; to 33 ft (10 m); leaves 3–5 in (8–12.5 cm), coarsely toothed; inflorescence to 8 in (20 cm) in diameter, sterile outer sepals 1–1½ in (2.5–3.5 cm), white to ivory; 'Roseum': outer sepals tinted rose; *S. integrifolium* C and W China; 33–50 ft (10–15 m); leaves 4–7 in (10–18 cm), entire or sparsely toothed; inflorescence to 12 in (30 cm) in diameter, sterile outer sepals 2½–2¾ in (6.5–7.25 cm), white. For *S. viburnoides*, see *Pileostegia viburnoides*.

Schizostylis (from Greek *schizo*, to split or cut and *stylis*, style). Iridaceae. South Africa. KAFFIR LILY. 1 species, *S. coccinea*, a perennial, cormous herb,

S

723

8–24 in (20–60 cm) tall, with narrowly sword-shaped leaves and 2-ranked spikes of flowers in late summer and fall. These are scarlet, pink, salmon or white, the perianth tube to 1¼ in (3 cm), slender at the base and abruptly widened at the throat. The lobes are ovate to lanceolate and about 1¼ in (3 cm) long. Plant in a sunny position in moist soil, including sodden, heavy clay. Although hardy to between 23°–14°F (–5 and –10°C), kaffir lilies are also grown in cool greenhouses, for long-lasting cut flowers. Numerous cultivars are available. Increase by division in spring.

Schlumbergera 'Spectabile Coccineum'
This epiphytic cactus makes an undemanding house plant which, with care, is long-lived and regular-flowering. It is easily propagated from stem cuttings.

Schlumbergera (for Frédéric Schlumberger, a well-known collector of cacti at Chateau des Anthieux, near Rouen, and a patron of horticultural botany). Cactaceae. SE Brazil. 6 species, epiphytic or lithophytic cacti. The stems are branched and arching, composed of numerous flattened segments, sometimes with small, bristly spines. Borne usually in winter and spring at the stem tips, the flowers are tubular with several ranks of overlapping and reflexed tepals, an expanded limb and prominent stamens. These cacti, and especially the hybrid *S.* × *buckleyi*, are popular as flowering house plants, with more than 200 cultivars named. Maintain a minimum temperature of 50°F (10°C). Grow in an open acidic to neutral, soilless medium. In spring and summer, shade from direct sun, provide high humidity and water frequently. From late summer until spring, admit full sun, keep cool and

draft-free and water sparingly. Propagate by stem cuttings.

S. × *buckleyi* (*S. truncata* × *S. russelliana*; syn. *S. bridgesii*); HOLIDAY CACTUS; garden origin; stem segments to 2 in (5 cm), crenate; flowers purple, magenta, pink, white, red, orange or yellow, to 2½ in (6.5 cm); *S. truncata* (SE Brazil; stem segments to 3 in (8 cm), serrate; flowers to 2¾ in (7 cm), magenta to rose or red.

Schoenoplectus (from Greek *schoinos*, rush, and *pleko*, braid, alluding to the mat-forming rhizomes of some species). Cyperaceae. Cosmopolitan. BULRUSH. 80 species, annual or perennial, grasslike, rhizomatous herbs with reduced leaves, rushlike stems and small, brown flowers in dense heads. *S. lacustris* (syn. *Scirpus lacustris*) is the widespread and well-known bulrush, a perennial with clumps of terete stems 3¼–10 ft (1–3 m) tall. Fully hardy, it soon establishes itself in damp or wet places in sun or part-shade. The white-banded cultivar 'Zebrinus' is an especially attractive addition to the pond or streamside. Increase by division in spring.

Schwantesia (for Dr. M. H. G. Schwantes [1881–1960], professor at the University of Kiel). Aizoaceae. South Africa. 10 species, many-headed, cushion-forming perennial succulents with fleshy, toothed leaves and daisylike flowers opening on bright days in summer and fall. Cultivate as for *Lithops*. *S. ruedebuschii* leaves erect, to 2 in (5 cm), navicular, margins more or less rounded, suffused blue-green with white mottling, tip expanded and blunt, with broad teeth; flowers light yellow.

Sciadopitys (from Greek *skiadeion*, parasol, and *pitys*, a pine tree: the leaves resemble the spokes of an umbrella). Sciadopityaceae. Japan. JAPANESE UMBRELLA PINE, UMBRELLA PINE. 1 species, *S. verticillata*, an evergreen coniferous tree to 130 ft (40 m) tall. The crown is conical with tiered branches. Distinctly whorled along the branchlets and at their tips, the glossy mid-green needles are 2¾–4¾ in (7–12 cm) long and linear. Hardy to –22°F (–30°C) but best in mild, damp areas with warm, humid summers.

Grow in acidic to neutral soil. Increase by seed or cuttings.

sciarid flies see *fungus gnats*.

Scilla (classical name for *Urginea maritima*). Liliaceae (Hyacinthaceae). South Africa, Asia, Europe. SQUILL. Some 90 species, bulbous herbs—those listed below are perennial and small to medium-sized, with scapose spikes of flowers, generally blue to mauve, star- or bell-like and produced in spring, summer and fall.

Most are hardy to 14°F (–10°C) at least. *S. peruviana* needs protection in regions experiencing temperatures below about 23°F (–5°C). The South African species need cool greenhouse protection in cool temperate zones. Grow in freely draining but humus-rich soil, with adequate moisture when in growth, in sun or dappled shade. Propagate by offsets, by seed when ripe or by division of established clumps as the foliage dies back.

S. fallalis S, W and C Europe, NW Africa to C Asia, Iran, Iraq; fall-flowering; scapes 2–12 in (5–30 cm); flowers with tepals ⅛–¼ in (3–5 mm), spreading, lilac to pink; 'Alba': white; 'Praecox': large, purple-blue; and 'Rosea': pink; *S. bifolia* C and S Europe, Turkey; early spring-flowering; scape 3–6 in (7.5–15 cm); flowers with tepals ¼–½ in (5–10 mm), ovate to elliptic, tips hooded, blue to purple-blue; *S. litardieri* (syn. *S. pratensis*, *S. amethystina*); Balkans; early summer-flowering; scape 2–6 in (5–15 cm); flowers with tepals ⅛–¼ in (4–6 mm), ovate, blue-violet or pink; *S. mischtschenkoana* (syn. *S. tubergeniana*); Iran, Russia; early spring-flowering; scapes 1–3, 2–4 in (5–10 cm); flowers with tepals ½–⅝ in (1–1.5 cm), oblong to elliptic, obtuse, white-blue with a darker stripe; *S. natalensis* South Africa; summer-flowering; scape to 16 in (40 cm); flowers with tepals ¼–½ in (6–10 mm), elliptic to oblong, obtuse, spreading, light violet-blue or occasionally pink or white; *S. peruviana* SW Europe, W Africa; early summer-flowering; scape 6–10 in (15–25 cm); flowers with tepals ⅜–⅝ in (8–15 mm), deep violet-blue to dull purple-brown, or white; *S. scilloides* (syn. *S. chinensis*); China, Korea, Taiwan, Japan, Ryukyu Islands; flowers during late summer or fall;

S

scape 8–16 in (20–40 cm); flowers with tepals ⅛–⅛ in (3–4 mm), narrowly oblong, acute, spreading, pale pink or mauve-pink; *S. siberica* SIBERIAN SQUILL; S Russia, naturalized in C Europe; early spring-flowering; scapes 4–8 in (10–20 cm); flowers rotate or broadly bowl-shaped, pendent, with tepals ½–¾ in (1–2 cm), elliptic to oblong, obtuse, bright-blue with a darker median band; 'Alba': white flowers; 'Spring Beauty': deep blue, long-lasting, scented. See also *Ledebouria* and *Hyacinthoides*.

Scindapsus (name used in ancient Greece for ivylike plant) Araceae. SE Asia, Pacific, Brazil. About 40 species, evergreen trailers and climbers with adhesive adventitious roots. They resemble *Epipremnum* in most respects. Cultivate as for the smaller *Philodendron* species. *S. pictus* Java to Borneo; stems to 40 ft (12 m)+, slender; leaves 2½–7 in (6–18 cm), broadly ovate to lanceolate, coriaceous, dull green; 'Argyraeus': SATIN POTHOS, with 2¾–4 in (7–10 cm), ovate to cordate, silky deep green leaves with silver spots. For *S. aureus*, see *Epipremnum aureum*.

scion a shoot or bud cut from a chosen specimen for the purpose of grafting or budding on to a root-stock, in order to produce a new individual.

scion-rooting the production of roots by a scion, as may occur when a grafted plant is established with the graft union below soil level. Scion-rooting is undesirable where the rootstock is required to transmit a characteristic such as dwarfness, so depth of planting can be critical.

sclerotium (plural: sclerotia) a resistant, usually rounded, fungal resting body, composed of a compact mass of mycelia. Most sclerotium are dark-colored. Diameter varies with type from less than 0.1 mm (¹⁄₁,₀₀₀ in)—e.g., *Verticillium*—to a few inches (several centimeters) in diameter—e.g., *Sclerotinia*.

scooping a method of bulb propagation, especially suitable for hyacinths, involving scooping out the inner portion of the basal plate of the parent bulb with a knife or sharpened spoon to leave a sound outer rim, dusting the

Scooping hyacinth bulbs
Scoop out the inner part of the bulb's basal plate, leaving the outer rim intact. Sit the bulbs in a dish of sand, and keep moist in a dark, warm place. Bulblets should form on the cut surface.

cut surface with fungicide and then placing the bulb base upward in a container of moist sand for storage in a dark, warm place. Bulblets arise around the edge of the scooped area and are removed when of handleable size to grow on. See *scoring*.

scorch, scorching the discoloration and death of plant tissue, especially leaf margins, resulting from disease or any of a wide range of environmental factors, including strong sunlight, contact with chemical substances, salt spray and strong wind.

scoria porous volcanic mineral with properties similar to perlite, used in crushed form in potting media or as a substrate in hydroculture.

scoring a method of propagating bulbs, similar in principle to scooping, but with the base plate scored with two shallow cuts, which are made at right angles to each other across the diameter of the base of the bulb. See *scooping*.

scorzonera (*Scorzonera hispanica*) COMMON VIPER'S GRASS, a hardy perennial grown for its black skinned roots. Scorzonera has broader leaves and yellow flowers, and may be raised and grown in a similar manner to *salsify* (q.v.), to harvest selectively over two seasons. The flower buds are plump and succulent.

scrambler a long stemmed plant, often equipped with prickles, which climbs through shrubs and trees.

scree see *rock garden plants*.

screen a barrier designed to provide privacy, as an ornamental feature, to mask unwanted views, or to protect from sound, or wind. Visual screens may consist of tree belts, hedges, tall individual plant specimens, fences, or walls. Aural screens are effective only when large areas are available to accommodate several rows of tall, dense evergreen trees. Screens used for ornament can be developed from

S

Scoring large fritillary bulbs
Cut two wedges of tissue across the base and basal plate of the bulb, at right-angles. Dust the cut surfaces with fungicide. Rest the bulb on sand, and keep moist in a warm, dark place.

plantings, or made of materials such as wire or wooden lattice work, trellis or pierced wall blocks, any of which may be covered with plants. Screen walls composed of relatively thick blocks of concrete, earthenware, or other materials, incorporating pierced patterns, allow a partial view while reducing wind flow. See *windbreaks*.

scrim a fine cotton mesh used as a shading fabric for greenhouses. It has now largely been superseded by more durable materials.

Scrophularia (from medieval Latin *scrofula*, referring to its supposed ability to cure scrofula—the roots of some species resemble scrofulous tumors). Scrophulariaceae. Northern temperate regions. FIGWORT. Some 200 species, fetid herbs and subshrubs with 4-angled, erect stems and small, squally tubular and 2-lipped flowers in terminal, paniculate cymes in summer. *S. auriculata* 'Variegata' is a bold, perennial foliage plant for waterside plantings or damp borders in sun or part-shade. It is fully hardy. Propagate by division in spring. Attacked by figwort weevil, which may skeletonize foliage. *S. auriculata* (syn. *S. aquatica*); WATER BETONY, WATER FIGWORT; W Europe; perennial to 3¼ ft (1 m); leaves 2–10 in (5–25 cm), ovate to oblong, sometimes lobed at base; flowers red-brown; 'Variegata': leaves dark green marked cream.

scutate shaped like a shield.

Scutellaria (from Latin *scutella*, a small shield or dish, descriptive of the crest or pouch on the upper calyx lip). Labiatae. Cosmopolitan, through temperate regions and tropical montane, with the exception of South Africa. HELMET FLOWER, SKULLCAP. Some 300 species, largely summer-flowering annual or perennial herbs, erect or sprawling with terminal spikes or racemes of tubular and hooded, 2-lipped flowers. The following are hardy to 0°F (–18°C). They need a sunny position. The shorter species are ideal for the front of a border or the rock garden. Propagate by division or seed sown outside in late spring.

S. indica Japan, Korea, China; slender, very white-hairy, procumbent

perennial, 8–16 in (20–40 cm); flowers ¾ in (1.8–2 cm), pale purple-blue; var. *japonica*: larger flowers, lilac to blue; *S. orientalis* SE Europe, mountains of SE Spain; sprawling, subshrubby perennial to 18 in (45 cm), gray-woolly; flowers ⅝–1¼ in (1.5–3 cm), yellow, sometimes spotted red or with lip red, occasionally pink or bright red to purple; *S. scordiifolia* E Europe, Siberia; erect, basally branched perennial, 4–12 in (10–30 cm), hairy; flowers ¾ in (1.8–2 cm), violet-blue.

scythe a large hand-tool for cutting rough grass and newly sown lawns. It consists of a curved, sharpened blade attached to a handle, with two handgrips. The scythe is held with both hands, and cutting is achieved by a swinging movement, with the blade kept parallel to the ground. The grass hook, another hand-tool, is in effect a short-handled scythe. The grass hook's blade is slightly curved, and the tool is used with one hand.

sea kale (*Crambe maritima*) a deep-rooting perennial herbaceous plant, native to northern Europe, especially seaboard areas. Sea kale makes a handsome ornamental plant in gardens, reaching 30 in (75 cm) in height, and is grown especially as a vegetable crop for its edible stems, which have a characteristic flavor when eaten raw or cooked (after blanching). The young flower heads and young leaves may also be eaten raw.

Grass hook

Grow in an organically rich, open site, raised either from seed or from root cuttings or thongs. Plants from spring-sown seed may be variable and germination can be very slow. Thongs, selected from plants at least three-years-old, are lifted in November and pencil-thick side roots cut into portions 3–6 in (7.5–15 cm) long with a sloping cut at the lower end. These should be stored in moist sand in a cool building until March, when buds will appear at the upper cut end. The buds are reduced to the strongest one and the thongs planted with a dibber 1 in (2.5 cm) below soil level, with 15 in (38 cm) between plants.

Sea kale can be forced after its third season. This can be done *in situ* between November and January. Cover the crowns first with dry litter and then with a special earthenware forcing pot (which should be about 15 in (38 cm) high and fitted with a lid) or any upturned container that is large enough and effectively excludes light. Stems are ready after about 12 weeks and should be cut with a knife. Alternatively, roots can be lifted after the first frost, lightly trimmed and packed into boxes or large pots and moved to a dark place, within a building or greenhouse, at a temperature of 61–68°F (16–20°C). The planted containers must be kept moist and stems are useable within a few weeks.

Possible problems: flea beetle; clubroot.

seaweed a useful bulky manure, which can be incorporated fresh or after composting, or dried. There are liquid preparations for use as supplementary feeds. An average analysis of the nutrient content of fresh seaweed is around 0.5% nitrogen, 0.1% phosphate and 1.0% potash, together with a content of trace elements and alginates, which have a beneficial effect on soil structure. The strap-shaped kelps (*Laminaria* species) are richer in plant nutrients than bladderwrack (*Fucus vesiculosus*). Calcified seaweeds concentrate calcium carbonate in their cell walls, and are dried and crushed to produce an organic liming agent and soil conditioner with nutrient content.

Sea kale
All aerial parts can be eaten when young, but the stems are most palatable, especially from crowns forced in the spring.

S

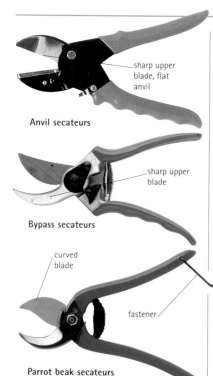

Anvil secateurs

sharp upper blade, flat anvil

Bypass secateurs

sharp upper blade

Parrot beak secateurs

curved blade

fastener

secateurs (pruning shears in the US) small shears used for pruning. They are available in three designs: anvil, bypass and parrot-beak. Anvil secateurs have a straight-edged blade that cuts against a thickened bar or anvil; these must be kept sharp to avoid crush damage to stems. Bypass and parrot-beak types have a scissorlike action which makes a clean cut. All are available in light or heavy duty grade, the latter being suitable for woody pruning.

secondary growth (1) new or extension shoots produced by a tree or shrub after summer pruning. The term is applied especially to fruit trees; (2) new growth from the tip of a shoot that had apparently stopped developing earlier in the same season; (3) used botanically to describe the extension of vascular systems, through the formation of new tissue, that arises from activity of the cambium. It results in stem thickening, also known as secondary thickening.

secondary organism an organism that invades diseased tissues after they have been killed by a primary pathogen. Bacteria, fungi, nematodes and mites are examples of secondary organisms.

sectio, section in plant classification, the rank of taxa between subgenus and series, for example *Rhododendron* subgenus *Rhododendron* section *Pogonanthum*.

secund with all the parts along one side of the axis.

sedge peat peat formed from the remains of sedges, reeds, mosses and heathers. It is usually coarser and darker than sphagnum moss peat and less tractable for use in potting media; it is also generally less acidic and has a lower water-holding capacity, cf. *sphagnum peat*.

Sedum (from Latin *sedere*, to sit, a reference to the way some species attach themselves to rocks and walls). Crassulaceae. Northern temperate and tropical mountain regions. Over 300 species, ranging from annual to perennial herbs and subshrubs. They vary widely in habit and size, but usually have clumped stems with succulent leaves and terminal, branching cymes of small, starry flowers in spring and summer.

The hardy perennials *S. spectabile* and *S. telephium*, together with their hybrids and cultivars, are among the finest plants for late summer and fall borders. Most species can withstand frost to at least 5°F (–15°C); *S. spurium* tolerates temperatures to 23°F (–5°C). A number of species—for example, those native to the hot dry Americas—need protection from frost, and these are best-grown as house or greenhouse plants, with a winter minimum of 41°F (5°C). Among the frost-tender species are several fine foliage plants; for example, *S. morganianum*, which is suitable for hanging baskets. Most species are drought-tolerant. Plant open-ground species in fertile, well-drained soil, in full sun. Grow tender species in a gritty mix in direct light and with good ventilation. Propagate by cuttings, by division in spring and early summer or by seed.

S. acre STONE CROP, WALL PEPPER; widespread Europe, Turkey and N Africa, naturalized E US; loosely tufted or mat-forming perennial 2–4¾ in (5–12 cm); stem slender, erect or trailing; leaves ⅛–¼ in (3–6 mm), overlapping, triangular, blunt, thick; flowers

yellow; 'Aureum': leaves variegated pale yellow; 'Elegans': shoots striped silver at tips; *S. aizoon* N Asia, naturalized in N and C Europe; herbaceous perennial, 12–16 in (30–40 cm); stems few, erect, mostly unbranched; leaves 2–3 in (50–80 mm), oblong to lanceolate, flowers golden yellow; 'Euphorbioides': more compact and robust than type, with flowers of a stronger yellow; *S. caeruleum* W Mediterranean Islands; bushy annual, 2–8 in (5–20 cm); stems erect, hairy above; leaves about ½ in (10 mm), oblong to linear, subterete, suffused red; flowers white at base, blue above; *S. kamtschaticum* Japan; similar to *S. aizoon* except 2–12 in (5–30 cm); rhizome stout, stem branched below; leaves ¾–1½ in (20–40 mm), obovate to lanceolate, apex coarsely toothed; 'Variegatum': leaves edged white and tinged pink, flowers yellow, turning crimson; *S. lydium* W and C Turkey; differs from *S. tenellum* in having rooting stems; leaves linear, to ¼ in (6 mm), tipped red; flowers many; *S. morganianum* BURRO'S TAIL, DONKEY'S TAIL; origin obscure, probably Mexico; evergreen perennial to 2½ in (6 cm); stems numerous, prostrate or pendulous, sparsely branched; leaves to ¾ in (18 mm), very succulent, glaucous, overlapping, oblong to lanceolate, subcylindric, tips pointed incurved; flowers deep pink; *S. obtusatum* California; loose hummock-forming perennial, 1¼–12 in (3–30 cm); leaves ¼–1 in (5–25 mm), in loose rosettes at stem tips, spathulate, glaucous, blunt to rounded, tinged red; flowers pale yellow-orange; *S. palmeri* Mexico; sprawling, evergreen perennial, 6–9 in (15–22 cm); stems arching, branching, naked below, scarred; leaves ⅛–⅝ in (2.5–15 mm), spathulate, glaucous, in loose rosettes; flowers deep orange; *S. rupestre* C and W Europe; mat-forming, evergreen perennial, 6–14 in (15–35 cm); stems horizontal, woody; leaves ½ in (12 mm), linear, terete; flowers bright yellow; 'Cristatum': leaves crested; 'Minus': dwarf; 'Monstrosum Cristatum': a fasciated form, with stem thin at base, widening toward the top edge, along which gray-green leaves are borne; 'Viride': green leaves and yellow flowers; *S. sempervivoides* Armenia, Georgia, Caucasus; erect, hairy biennial, to 8 in (20 cm); leaves ½–1¼ in (10–30 mm), ovate,

S

pointed, tinged purple, in a basal rosette; flowers bright red; *S. spathulifolium* western N America; clump-forming perennial, 3½–6 in (9–15 cm), stems short, often forming long runners; leaves about ¾ in (18 mm), scattered or in compact rosettes at stem tips, spathulate, blunt, gray-glaucous; flowers yellow; 'Aureum': leaves gray, tinged pink and flecked yellow; 'Cape Blanco': compact, with pale silver-gray leaves; 'Carneum': leaves tinged crimson; 'Purpureum': glaucous gray leaves flushed purple; 'Roseum': flowers rose; *S. spectabile* syn. *Hylotelephium spectabile*; ICE PLANT; China, Korea; glaucous, pale sea green perennial to 20 in (50 cm); stems clumped, erect; leaves to 4 in (10 cm), ovate-elliptic, crenate; flowers pale pink to deep rusty red; includes cultivars with white, deep pink and pale rose flowers, some with leaves very pale and glaucous or variegated; *S. spurium* Caucasus, N Iran, naturalized in Europe; evergreen mat-forming, perennial to 6 in (15 cm); stem much-branched, finely hairy, creeping; leaves 1 in (25 mm), obovate, toothed, fringed; flowers white, pink or red purple; 'Atropurpureum': leaves burgundy; flowers rose-red; 'Bronze Carpet': leaves bronze; 'Coccineum': scarlet-red flowers; 'Green Mantle': leaves forming fresh green ground-cover, flowerless; 'Purpurteppich': compact, leaves plum purple; 'Roseum': flowers rose-pink; 'Schorbuser Blut': leaves bronze with age, flowers large, very dark red; 'Variegatum': leaves edged pink and cream; var. *album*: flowers white; *S. telephium* (syn. *Hylotelephium telephium*); ORPINE, LIVE FOREVER; to 24 in (60 cm), erect; leaves to 2¾ in (7 cm), oblong or ovate, slightly toothed; flowers purple-red; includes cultivars with burgundy-red leaves and deep red flowers; *S. tenellum* N Iran, Caucasus; ascending, tufted perennial, 2–3 in (5–8 cm); stem woody, bare below, creeping and ascending; leaves ⅛ in (3mm), overlapping, oblong, terete, smooth; flowers white suffused red. *Cultivars* 'Autumn Joy': flowers bright salmon pink becoming bronze; 'Ruby Glow': leaves purple-gray, flowers rich ruby red; 'Vera Jameson': leaves deep purple; flowers pale pink. See also *Rhodiola*.

seed a ripened, fertilized ovule; an embryonic plant.

seedbed an area of soil prepared for seed sowing. Firming and raking provide a level, fine tilth, ensuring good aeration and water penetration and facilitating the sowing of seeds at an even depth. A stale seedbed is a prepared area left unsown for a period to allow weed seeds to germinate. The seedling weeds are destroyed with a minimum of disturbance to the bed, possibly using a contact herbicide. The crop is then sown with the benefit of a reduced level of competition from weed growth, and less need for early cultivations.

seed box, seed tray a container used for sowing seeds, pricking out seedlings and for the insertion of cuttings; of standard dimension 14–6½ (35 × 17 cm) × 2–3 in (5–7.5 cm) deep depending on purpose; half trays are available. Plastic has largely replaced wood as the preferred manufacturing material. It is easier to clean and stack and more durable; available thicknesses of plastic vary, depending on price and intended use. Some trays are made as cellular units, which may or may not need supporting in sturdier trays; the cells may be of a size suitable for direct sowing or cutting insertion, or large enough for growing on individual plants to planting size. All types must have drainage holes in the base.

seed dressing a pesticide applied as a coating to seeds prior to sowing, to control seed-borne diseases and to protect against certain pests and diseases that attack germinating seeds or young seedlings. Formerly, home treatments by the gardener were advocated, but, in the interests of safety, it is now recommended that seed is purchased ready-dressed, where available, and instructions on safe handling followed.

seed leaf see *cotyledon*.

seedling a young plant that develops from a seed.

seed-raised plants grown from seed, as distinct from those grown by vegetative methods.

seeds and seed sowing seeds are the means of sexual reproduction in plants, as opposed to vegetative or asexual means. By allowing for recombination of genes following fertilization, they facilitate variation and selection of characteristics. A seed contains an embryonic plant, with root and shoot, and food reserves to support it during the periods of germination and initial growth. Viable seeds are living organisms that maintain a species through a period of dormancy, and offer a means of dispersal over time and distance and protection during unfavorable conditions.

The term seed is used loosely to describe all forms of dispersal unit. Strictly speaking, the only true seeds are those in which the ovary wall is dehiscent, for example *Delphinium*, *Lupinus*, *Aquilegia*, *Allium*. In many cases, the dispersal unit is a dry indehiscent fruit, for example *Hibiscus*, *Lavatera*, *Malva*, or a succulent indehiscent fruit, for example *Prunus*, *Malus*, *Ribes*. Sometimes the dispersal unit is a false fruit, when a part other than the ovary wall develops as a result of fertilization, for example *Fragaria*. To germinate naturally, seeds must be mature and provided with suitable environmental conditions.

Environmental control of germination The four main environmental factors influencing germination are water, light, temperature and gases.

WATER For the majority of seeds, the first step in germination is rehydration of the seed tissues. Since water availability can be unpredictable, its shortage is the most common cause of seed or seedling death. Seeds are naturally hygroscopic and the rate of water uptake or imbibition is mainly determined by properties of the seed coat. If the growing medium becomes waterlogged, germination may be suppressed, due to reduced oxygen availability; this risk is increased if the germination period is prolonged—for example, by sub-optimal temperatures.

LIGHT Most seeds germinate equally well in the light or dark. However, some will only germinate if given a light stimulus and a very few will germinate only in the dark. The photo reversible pigment phytochrome allows plants to detect information about their light environment. While the seeds of certain species respond in a particular way to light—for example, small-seeded annual weeds are usually promoted by light—the response is often dependent on other factors, especially temperature. Thus, an individual seed may be insensitive to light at one temperature, but will only germinate at a different temperature if first given a light stimulus. In the garden situation, sown seed is usually covered, with the primary objectives of moisture conservation and protection from predators; the exclusion of light rarely presents difficulties.

TEMPERATURE For all seeds, at any given time, there is a maximum and minimum temperature above and below which germination cannot occur. At a point between these temperatures, there is a specific temperature or narrow band of temperatures which allows for maximum germination in the shortest time, and this is the so-called optimum temperature. Temperate species generally have lower optimum germination temperatures than tropical species, but the range of temperature over which germination may occur can vary considerably, even within a single batch of stored seeds. The seeds of wild plants often fail to germinate under constant temperature conditions.

GASES As a rule, seeds germinate best in air, and germination is suppressed if the carbon dioxide level is raised or the oxygen level lowered; the gaseous atmosphere that surrounds seeds probably plays a significant role in controlling the germination of buried seeds in the natural environment. The seeds of certain aquatic species, such as North American wild rice (*Zizania* species), germinate best if completely submerged in water under more or less anaerobic conditions.

Dormancy Dormancy is a highly variable character controlled by the interaction of genetic and environmental factors:

(a) innate or primary dormancy is expressed when seeds are freshly harvested, and develops during seed development and maturation. It may be enforced, when germination fails because of unsuitable environmental conditions, or physiological when seeds fail to germinate without a prolonged treatment, such as growth-regulator application or chilling. Seed coat impermeability is a true form of innate dormancy.

(b) induced or secondary dormancy describes the condition under which seeds able to germinate are subsequently switched into a dormant state; for example, a combination of high temperature and darkness can often induce a state of dormancy.

Overcoming innate seed dormancy

SCARIFICATION Various methods exist for penetrating hard seed coats:

(1) chipping—using a scalpel and forceps, a small shallow cut is made in the seed coat to allow the entry of water when the seed is sown. To avoid risk of damage, the cut should be located at a site on the seed surface well away from the axis;

(2) filing—used as an alternative to chipping for large-seeded species with particularly thick seed coats;

(3) acid treatment—concentrated sulfuric acid is effective for degrading hard impermeable testas. However, it is only a suitable treatment for commercial operations, when appropriate safety precautions can be taken;

(4) abrasives—rubbing seeds between sheets of sandpaper is effective in some cases, as is tumbling seeds in rotating drums lined with abrasive;

(5) hot water—some species respond positively to simple hot water treatment, in which a volume of seed is plunged into an equal volume of recently boiled water, and left to stand until cool. The proportion of seeds that have swollen is assessed.

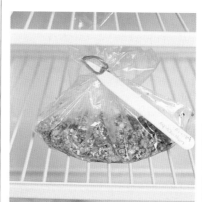

Overcoming seed dormancy
Many seeds need a period of chilling, or cold stratification, before they will germinate. A domestic refrigerator can be used.

STRATIFICATION Very many species of trees and shrubs, as well as many herbaceous species, have seeds with coats that are mechanically resistant to germination. The seed coats will allow water to penetrate but the embryo will not germinate until the hard seed coat splits and the embryo has undergone a period of cold stratification. In a few species, splitting can be achieved by exposure for two weeks at temperatures of 68–77°F (20–25°C). Many other species require exposure for up to twelve weeks at 59–68°F (15–20°C), followed by a period of 12–18 weeks' exposure at between 32–50°F (0–10°C).

The treatment is known as stratification because of the traditional practice of carrying it out in strata of sand and seed in deep pits in the garden, and this remains a suitable method. Alternatively, very small quantities of seed can be mixed with a well-aerated, free-draining medium and placed in a nylon net bag; this is tied loosely but securely and buried just below the soil surface outdoors, carefully marked. Another method is to place the seeds in large pots, in two levels separated by ¾–1¼ in (2–3 cm) layers of sand or a sand/peat mixture, and plunge well below the soil surface. Similar benefit can be achieved by storing container-ized seeds within a refrigerator.

Viability and storage Seeds of the majority of species used in horti-culture are tolerant of desiccation, and it is important to reduce moisture content to a low level as soon as possible after harvest. The optimum moisture content (expressed on a fresh weight basis) for survival of most desiccation-tolerant seeds is in the range of 5–8%.

Desiccation-intolerant seeds will die if dried, for example, SYCAMORE (*Acer pseudoplatanus*), oak (*Quercus* species) and SWEET CHESTNUT (*Castanea sativa*). Such seeds must be maintained at a high-moisture content, equivalent to a relative humidity of not less than 98%. Oxygen must be available when seeds are stored at a high-moisture content.

Lowering the temperature tends to improve storage life. As a rule of thumb, a 5° reduction in the ambient range (say, 50–84°F/10–29°C) results in an approximate doubling of lifespan; lower limits apply to tropical and moist seeds.

S

The realization that desiccation-tolerant seeds may be stored for anything between several decades to several thousand years, providing that moisture content and temperature are properly controlled, has led to the widespread use of seed banks.

Seed quality Many types of seeds are now covered by statutory regulations detailing minimum germination standards. Storage conditions in warehouses or on display racks in shops or warm houses may significantly reduce viability. For seeds stored in such condition, especially when self-gathered or held over from previous years, a quick germination test is often justified. A weighed or counted sample from the measured bulk is set to germinate in containers covered with glass, plastic or cling film; these are placed in a propagator maintained at 68–75°F (20–24°C). For seeds the size of cereal grains or smaller, a bedding of moist absorbent paper should be laid flat in the container; for larger seeds, sand should be used.

After ten days, the number of seeds that have germinated or begun to germinate is counted and the likely total viable number in the batch calculated.

Outdoor bed sowing Sowing directly in the open ground requires preparation of a level seedbed, which is achieved by raking and cross raking ground previously cultivated by digging or forking, and by weathering. Except in wet soil, treading is a helpful means of breaking down clods, but great care must be made not to compact the soil, which impedes drainage and aeration. A wide wooden rake is a valuable aid to levelling and removing large debris. The finished seedbed should be moist and friable to a depth of at least 2 in (5 cm).

There are two methods of sowing seed outdoors—in drills or broadcast. Drills can best be marked out with the aid of a strong garden line pulled taught between two canes. Suitable depth is achieved by pulling the edge of a swan-necked or similar hoe along the line; the same effect can be obtained with a thick cane. For short rows in, for example, narrow beds or frames, a board can be used instead of a garden line. For informal areas, such as an annual flower bed, suitable drills can be made by pushing the reverse side of a metal rake head into the bed and spacing the row intervals by eye. In gardens, seed may be sown from the hand, packet or from a specially designed dispenser; a wheeled drilling device is suitable for larger undertakings. Seed should be sown thinly under most circumstances, and in some cases it can be sown at spaced stations for economy.

Container sowing Sowing in containers requires the tray, pot, pan or cellular-tray modules to be over-filled with potting mix, which is then struck off level and settled by gently tapping it on the bench. The medium is then gently pressed down with a shaped firmer so that the surface is level, and the seed sown broadcast by the methods described. Cell- and thimble-sized plugs may be sown direct to overcome the inevitable damage and growth check caused by pricking out. It is usual to cover sown seeds with sieved soil to the depth of the seed, but this is rarely essential, and some subjects, such as begonias, coleus, *Impatiens* and primulas, should not be covered. The containers should be lightly watered, either with a fine overhead spray, or, when appropriate, by steeping the container in a larger vessel of water so that moisture is absorbed by capillary action. In all cases, very fine seed, such as that of *Begonia*, may be mixed with sand to aid even distribution. A sheet of glass or clear plastic placed over the container will enhance humidity, and covering with a sheet of newspaper reduces water loss by evaporation. Small numbers of seed containers can be accommodated in a commercial seed-tray-sized propagator, which should have a built-in heating element; optimum germination temperature varies according to species.

seep hose, soaker hose small-bore, flexible irrigation tubing from which water leaks or oozes to produce a continuous wet band of soil. It may consist of plastic tubing with durable stitching along one side, or compressed rubber tubing where water oozes from pores in the tube wall. See *irrigation*.

segment a discrete portion of an organ or appendage which is deeply divided, or compound.

Selaginella (diminutive of *Selago*, the old name for another club moss). Selaginellaceae. Tropics and subtropics worldwide, with a few species also in temperate zones, extending rarely to Arctic. LITTLE CLUB MOSS, SPIKE MOSS. Over 700 species, evergreen mosslike plants with bushy and creeping to slender and scrambling stems, clothed with overlapping, scalelike leaves. *Selaginella* species occur in a range of habitats but most—with the exception of specialized desert natives, such as *S. lepidophylla*—are found in moist soil in humid shaded forest, both tropical and temperate. They are grown for their beautiful foliage, usually in a range of rich vibrant greens; several have golden or variegated cultivars and some, such as *S. uncinata* and the climbing *S. willdenovii*, have foliage of luminescent electric blue. Compact cultivars, for example, *S. kraussiana* 'Brownii', may be grown in bottle gardens and terraria. Plant in fast-draining, soilless potting mixes that are open, porous and rich in organic matter. Keep the medium evenly moist but not constantly wet, and maintain high humidity. Shade from direct sun. Provide a minimum temperature of 50°F (10°C). *S. lepidophylla* will grow in similar conditions, although it is usually sold as a dry, dead or half-dead curio, which unfurls quickly when made wet. It is difficult to maintain in cultivation. Propagate by division, alternatively by layers.

S. kraussiana TRAILING SPIKEMOSS, SPREADING CLUB MOSS, MAT SPIKEMOSS; South Africa; stem 6–12 in (15–30 cm), trailing, jointed, copiously pinnate, branches erect to outspread, compound; leaves bright green; includes 'Aurea', with bright golden green foliage, and 'Variegata', with foliage splashed ivory to pale yellow; *S. lepidophylla* RESURRECTION PLANT, ROSE-OF-JERICHO; Texas and Arizona south to Peru; stems 2–4 in (5–10 cm), frondlike, in a rosette; leaves dark green, drying or aging rusty brown; dried, the fronds will roll into a tight, brown ball, unfurling if wet; *S. martensii* Mexico; stem 6–12 in (15–30 cm), trailing, branches decompound, fan-shaped to pinnate; leaves bright green; includes 'Albolineata', with some leaves wholly or partially white, and 'Albovariegata', with white-tipped leaves; *S. uncinata*

S

PEACOCK MOSS, RAINBOW FERN, BLUE SPIKE MOSS; China; stem 12–24 in (30–60 cm), trailing, rooting, slender, branches alternate, pinnate, short, leaves iridescent blue; *S. willldenovii* PEACOCK FERN; Old World tropics; stems to 13 ft (4 m), scandent, branched from base; pinnae 12–24 in (30–60 cm), deltoid, and decompound; leaves bronze to kingfisher blue with an iridescent sheen.

selection see *cultivar*.

selective herbicides and other pesticides that suppress or kill some weeds or pests without seriously affecting others.

Selenicereus (from Greek *selene*, the moon, and *Cereus*, referring to the nocturnal flowers). Cactaceae. Tropical America and the Caribbean region. Some 20 species, lithophytic or epiphytic cacti, with slender and ribbed, spiny and clambering stems. Their flowers, which are very large and funnelform, open at night. During spring and summer, shade these cacti from direct sunlight, and maintain high humidity and good water supplies. In fall and winter, admit full light, reduce water and provide a minimum temperature of 50–59°F (10–15°C). Pot plants in a fast-draining, acidic mix rich in coarse bark and sand. Provide support. Increase *Selenicereus* by stem cuttings.

S. grandiflorus QUEEN OF THE NIGHT; Jamaica, Cuba; stem to 13 ft × 1¼ in (4 m × 3 cm); flowers 6½–12 (17–30 cm) × 4¾–6½ in (12–17 cm), outer tepals pale yellow or brown-tinged, inner white.

self a loose term used by some specialist growers to describe flowers of one color.

self-compatible, self-fertile a flower or plant that is capable of self-fertilization.

self-fertilization fertilization resulting from self-pollination; cf. *cross-fertilization*.

self-incompatible, self-sterile a flower or plant that is incapable of self-fertilization.

selfing the act of artificially pollinating a plant with its own pollen.

self-pollination the transfer of pollen from the anthers to the stigma of the same flower or a different flower of the same plant; a process often used to imply self-fertilization; cf. *cross-pollination*.

Self-seeding
Foxgloves (*Digitalis* spp.) are renowned self-seeders. This can be either useful or a nuisance depending on the situation.

self-seeding the establishment of a succeeding generation from the germination of naturally sown seed shed by the spent flowers of a mother plant.

self-sterile incapable of producing viable seed after self-fertilization.

Semele (named for the daughter of Kadmos and mother of Dionysos). Liliaceae (Asparagaceae). Canary Islands. CLIMBING BUTCHER'S BROOM. 1 species, *S. androgyna*, a robust, climbing, evergreen, perennial herb with clumped stems to 23 ft (7 m) tall. The true leaves are scalelike and soon wither, becoming dry and prickly. The stem branches are clothed with leaflike cladophylls; these are dark green, rigid to semipliable, 1–2¾ in (2.5–7 cm) long and broadly ovate to lanceolate. Small cream to buff flowers are carried along the margins of the cladophylls and give rise to orange-red berries. Grow in a gritty but fertile medium in bright, filtered light in frost-free conditions; provide strong support and water moderately. Flowers are carried on year-old growth and fruit will not ripen for another twelve months, therefore pruning should be restricted, with shoots removed only when necessary to confine to allotted space. Propagate by division.

Semiaquilegia (from Latin *semi-*, half, and *Aquilegia*, to which it is closely related). Ranunculaceae. E Asia. 7 species, low perennial herbs closely related to *Aquilegia*, from which they differ in their petals—these are gibbous or slightly saccate at the base, not spurred. Hardy and suitable for the rock garden. Cultivate as for the smaller *Aquilegia* species. *S. ecalcarata* (W China; to 18 in (45 cm); flowers wine red to purple).

Semiarundinaria (from its similarity to *Arundinaria*.). Gramineae. Far East. 10 or more species of tall bamboos; see *bamboos*.

semiterete a semicylindrical form; terete on one side, but flattened on the other, as some petioles.

semidouble see *double*.

semiripe see *cuttings*.

Sempervivum (from Latin *semper*, forever, and *vivere*, to live). Crassulaceae. Europe, N Africa, W Asia. HOUSE LEEK. 42 species, small, stoloniferous perennial herbs with thickly fleshy, short leaves in low and dense basal rosettes. The flowers are bell- to star-shaped and carried in terminal, long-stemmed cymes. *Sempervivum* species are suitable for a rock garden, scree and alpine house. Drought-tolerant, they thrive in rock crevices, walls, rooftops and paths. All species are hardy to 5°F (–15°C) and will tolerate snow cover. Most will not tolerate warm, high-humidity climates like the North American Gulf Coast. Small and hairy species, such as *S. arachnoideum* may need protection from winter wet. Grow in well-drained gritty soil in sun. Propagate by division, stem cuttings, offsets or seed. Affected by rust.

S. arachnoideum Pyrenees to Carpathians; rosettes around 2 in (5 cm) in diameter, tight, with dense white arachnoid hairs; leaves ¼–½ in (7–12 mm), obovate-oblong or oblanceolate; flowering stem to 4¾ in (12 cm), flowers bright rose-red; *S. ciliosum* Bulgaria; rosettes ¾–2 in (2–5 cm) in diameter, somewhat closed; leaves to 1 in (2.4 cm), gray-green, hairy, incurved, convex on both surfaces; flowering stem to 4 in

S

(10 cm), flowers yellow; *S. erythraeum* SW Bulgaria; rosettes flat, 1¼–2½ in (3–6 cm) in diameter; leaves about ¾ in (2 cm), spathulate-obovate, with a short point, glandular-hairy, gray-purple; flowers red-purple dashed white above, red on back; 'Red Velvet': velvety, pale purple-pink leaves; 'Glasnevin': blue-purple leaves, tinged green, pink, and gray. *S. giuseppii* Spain; rosettes ¾ in (2 cm) in diameter, compact; leaves ⅝ in (1.6 cm), obovate, hairy, green, apex brown; flowers red, edged white; *S. grandifolium* W and C Alps; rosettes 2–8 in (5–20 cm) in diameter, lax, flat; leaves oblong-triangular, abruptly pointed, hairy, dark green, tinged red at tip, smelling of resin; flowering stem 6–12 in (15–30 cm), flowers yellow, stained purple at base; *S. montanum* C Europe; rosettes dense, open, clustered, ⅝–1½ in (1.5–3.5 cm) in diameter; leaves about ½ in (1 cm), dark green, dull, very fleshy, finely hairy, oblanceolate, pointed; flowers red-purple, white, hairy below; *S. tectorum* C Europe; rosettes large, 2–4 in (5–10 cm) in diameter, open, rather flat, offsets numerous; leaves ¾–1½ in (2–4 cm), apex with distinct dark markings, glabrous, oblanceolate, thick, bristle-tipped; flowering stem to 12 in (30 cm), hairy, inflorescence large, many-flowered, flowers dull rose; 'Atropurpureum': dark violet leaves; 'Nigrum': with leaves with conspicuous red-purple tips; 'Red Flush': leaves flushed red; 'Sunset': leaves orange-red; 'Triste': leaves red-brown. See also *Jovibarba*.

Senecio (from Latin *senex*, old man, referring to the usually white or gray, hairy pappus). Compositae. Cosmopolitan. About 1000 species, trees, shrubs, lianes and herbs, varying greatly in size and habit, but generally hairy and with daisylike, usually yellow, flower heads. Some of the more commonly seen species are grown for their white or silver foliage. *S. cineraria*, for example, is frequently used as an annual in summer bedding; although, given a warm sunny situation in well-drained soil, many of its cultivars will tolerate several degrees of frost, becoming perennial subshrubs. Grow them in sunny positions in moderately fertile and well-drained soil. Propagate by seed or by semiripe cuttings in coarse

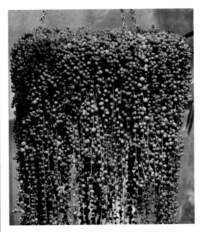

Senecio rowleyanus
This species is very different from most senecios, with trailing stems of beadlike leaves that make it ideal for hanging baskets.

sharp sand in the greenhouse or cold frame. True annuals, such as *S. elegans*, are valued for their magenta or purple daisy flower heads, an uncommon color in the genus, but shared with the slightly frost-tender perennial *S. pulcher*. Their requirements are similar to those of *S. cineraria*, but they do not flower well where summers are very hot and/or humid.

Species that require greenhouse protection in cool temperate zones can be categorized as succulents and nonsucculents. Nonsucculents include the evergreen vining species, *S. macroglossus*, which thrives outdoors in warm, dry, essentially frost-free climates. Under glass, grow in a freely draining medium-fertility potting mix in full sun, with good ventilation and a minimum temperature of 45°F (7°C). Water moderately and feed fortnightly with dilute liquid feed when in full growth. Allow a dry rest, cut back as necessary and re-pot after flowering.

The succulent species show great diversity of form and habit, and are grown primarily for their range of beautiful pastel-colored and often chalky or waxy bloomed foliage. They include trailing species with long strands of curious, globose leaves, such as *S. rowleyanus*, well-suited for hanging baskets in the home or under glass, and taller species with sausage- or candelabra-like stems, such as *S. articulatus*. Grow them in a medium rich in sand and grit. Provide full sun and good ventilation; water moderately when in

full growth, allowing the medium to become almost dry between waterings. When dormant, they need water only to prevent shrivelling. Maintain a minimum temperature of 45°F (7°C). Propagate by seed, division and cuttings.

S. articulatus CANDLE PLANT, HOT-DOG CACTUS, SAUSAGE CRASSULA; South Africa; perennial succulent to 24 in (60 cm); stem with cylindric, swollen joints to ¾ × ½ in (2 × 1.2 cm), glaucous blue with dark lines; leaves to 2 in (5 cm), deeply 3–5-lobed, fleshy, glaucous; flower heads white; *S. cineraria* DUSTY MILLER; W and C Mediterranean; perennial shrub to 20 in (50 cm)+, much-branched, densely white-tomentose; leaves to 6 in (15 cm), ovate or lanceolate, dentate to pinnate; flower heads typically yellow; includes cultivars selected for their habit and intensely silver and finely cut foliage; *S. elegans* South Africa; annual to 24 in (60 cm), clammy-hairy, erect or diffuse, branched; leaves to 3 in (8 cm), oblong, subentire or toothed, lyrate, pinnatifid; flower heads purple, rarely white. *S. grandiflorus* South Africa; perennial herb to 5 ft (1.5 m); leaves to 6 in (15 cm), pinnately divided, lobes linear, entire or dentate; flower heads purple; *S. macroglossus* NATAL IVY, WAX VINE; eastern South Africa to Mozambique and Zimbabwe; slender, twining perennial herb to 6½ ft (2 m); stem somewhat succulent; leaves to 3 in (8 cm), deltoid, hastate, 3-lobed, somewhat succulent; flower heads cream or pale yellow; includes 'Variegatus', with leaves variegated cream; *S. pulcher* South Brazil, Uruguay, Argentina; perennial herb to 24 in (60 cm), lanate at first; leaves to 8 in (20 cm), in a rosette, elliptic to lanceolate, lobed to toothed; flower heads large, violet or purple; *S. scandens* E Asia; climbing perennial to 16 ft (5 m), woody at base; leaves to 4 in (10 cm), deltoid to hastate, incised to toothed, pubescent; flower heads yellow; *S. serpens* BLUE-CHALK-STICKS; South Africa; perennial succulent shrub to 12 in (30 cm), stems glaucous blue, branched below; leaves linear to lanceolate, more or less cylindric, obtuse, grooved above; flower heads white; *S. smithii* Chile, Falkland Islands; perennial to 4 ft (1.2 m); stem erect, stout, usually branched above, woolly; basal leaves to 14 in (35 cm),

S

oblong to cordate, dentate, woolly; flower heads white. See also *Brachyglottis*, *Delairea*, *Pericallis* and *Pseudogynoxis*.

senescence the physiological changes that occur following maturity of a plant or plant organ, ultimately resulting in tissue death.

Senna (from Arabic *sanā*). Leguminosae. Tropics and subtropics, few temperate. Some 260 species, shrubs, trees and herbs. The leaves are pinnate and the flowers racemose, with five, broad, clawed and, usually, yellow petals. Treatment as for *Cassia*. *S. artemisioides* (syn. *Cassia artemisioides*); SILVER CASSIA, WORM-WOOD SENNA, SHOWER CASSIA; Australia; shrub 3¼–10 ft (1–3 m); leaves 1¼–2½ in (3–6 cm), gray-green, leaflets narrow, downy; flowers fragrant, rich yellow; *S. corymbosa* (syn. *Cassia corymbosa*); S US, Uruguay, Argentina; shrub or small tree to 13 ft (4 m), erect or producing procumbent runners; leaves 16–38 in (40–95 cm), dull yellow-green, glabrous, leaflets oblong to obovate; flowers golden-yellow; *S. didymobotrya* (syn. *Cassia didymobotrya*); S India, Sri Lanka, Malaysia, tropical Africa, naturalized neotropics; diffuse shrub 24 in–15 ft (60 cm–5 m); leaves 4–20 in (10–50 cm), leaflets elliptic to oblong, downy; flowers yellow; *S. siamea* (syn. *Cassia siamea*); KASSOD TREE; C and S America; diffusely branched, swift-growing tree; leaves 4–14 in (10–35 cm), leaflets ovate, oblong to elliptic, dark yellow-green and glabrous above, paler and thinly hairy beneath; flowers yellow with dark-hued sepal.

sensible heat see *field heat*.

sensitive (1) refers to plants that respond to the stimulus of touch, such as certain carnivorous plants, and *Mimosa pudica*, in which all the leaflets fold together following contact with an object. This phenomenon is also seen in some flowers where stamens or stigmas may move on contact with visiting insects to the benefit of pollination, for example in the families Berberidaceae and Scrophulariaceae; see *haptonasty*, *haptotropism*. (2) it is a plant that develops severe disease when exposed to a pathogen.

sensu in the sense of; often used before the first author cited in a homonym where two or more authors are contrasted by "non" and "nec"; for example, *Mimulus luteus* sensu Greene non L., where Linnaeus's taxon is the one to which the name should correctly be applied.

sensu lato in the broad sense; a taxon when it is cited in such a way as to signify its broadest interpretation, i.e. embracing variants.

sensu stricto in the narrow sense; a taxon when it is cited in such a way as to signify only its type.

sepal one of the members of the outer floral envelope, enclosing and protecting the inner floral parts; the segments composing the calyx, sometimes leafy, sometimes bract- or scalelike, sometimes petaloid.

septate see *locular*.

sequestrol, sequestrene a complex organic compound used to bind an element tightly, altering its typical properties so that it is not subject to reactions in the soil which normally make it unavailable for plant uptake. Sequestrol treatment is an effective means of making trace elements available, especially manganese and iron, which in highly alkaline soil are insoluble and cause so-called lime-induced chlorosis of leaves. The compounds are also known as chelates, and manufacturers' instructions usually recommend several applications to overcome a nutrient deficiency.

Sequoia (after Sequoyah, son of an English trader and a Cherokee mother, inventor of a syllabary for transcribing the Cherokee language). Cupressaceae. W US (Oregon to California, within 30 km (18 miles) of the Pacific). CALIFORNIA REDWOOD, COAST REDWOOD. 1 species, *S. sempervirens*, an evergreen coniferous tree to 360 ft (110 m) tall in habitat. The crown is conic becoming columnar; the bole is to 27¾ ft (8.5 m) in diameter and the bark red-brown, thick, fibrous and spongy. The leaves are scalelike or ½–¾ in (1–2 cm) long, 2-ranked, linear to oblong and deep

green to blue-gray. Cultivars include the weeping 'Pendula' and the dwarf, sprawling to weeping 'Prostrata'. Treat as for *Abies*, although this tree is more sensitive to exposure to dry winds. *Sequoia* does best in cool humid areas; it may scorch in cold, dry weather but without lasting harm. Most soils are suitable. It is intolerant of pollution.

Sequoiadendron (from *Sequoia* and Greek *dendron*, tree). Cupressaceae. W US (western slopes of Sierra Nevada, California). BIG TREE, GIANT SEQUOIA, SIERRA REDWOOD. 1 species, *S. giganteum*, an evergreen, coniferous tree to 312 ft (95 m) tall; its bole is to 33 ft (10 m) in diameter and covered in thick, spongy, rust brown bark. The crown is conic and irregularly spreading with age; the branches are curved downward with upturned tips. The leaves are up to ¼ in (0.6 cm) long, scalelike to subulate, acute and green suffused gray. It includes pendulous, glaucous, variegated and dwarf cultivars. Hardy to about –22°F (–30°C); soil type, altitude and exposure seem to have little effect on growth, although it does not flourish on shallow chalky soil in exposed areas, or thrive in polluted cities. Light shade is acceptable in early years only. Increase by seed or cuttings.

seriate in a row or whorl. The term is generally prefixed by a number, for example monoseriate, in one row.

sericeous silky; covered with fine, soft, adpressed hairs.

series in plant classification, the category of taxa intermediate in rank between section and species, for example *Saxifraga* section *Porphyrion*, series *Juniperifoliae*.

Seriphidium (diminutive of Greek *seriphon*, a type of wormwood). Compositae. North temperate regions. Some 60 species of aromatic annual to perennial herbs and shrubs resembling *Artemisia*. Cultivate as for *Artemisia*. *S. canum* (syn. *Artemisia cana*); western N America; shrub to 3¼ ft (1 m); leaves silvery gray-pubescent, to 2½ in (6 cm), linear to oblanceolate, acute or acuminate, entire or occasionally irregularly 3-dentate or pinnatifid, sometimes

S

viscid; *S. maritimum* (syn. *Artemisia maritima*); W and N European coasts; perennial herb to 5 ft (1.5 m), strongly aromatic, pale gray- to white-tomentose, occasionally glabrescent; leaves to 1¾ × 1¼ in (4.5 × 3 cm), 2–3-pinnatisect, segments to ⅝ in (15 mm), spathulate to linear; *S. palmeri* California, Baja California; subshrub to 10 ft (3 m); leaves to 4¾ in (12 cm), pinnatifid, lobes 3–9, linear to lanceolate, revolute, densely tomentose beneath; *S. vallesiacum* (syn. *Artemisia vallesiaca*); S Switzerland and S France to N Italy; strongly aromatic perennial to 6½ ft (2 m), densely gray- to white-tomentose; leaves 3–4 pinnatisect, lobes to ¼ in (5 mm), linear, often pinnatisect.

Serissa (from the old Indian name). Rubiaceae. SE Asia. 1 species, *S. foetida* (syn. *S. japonica*), an evergreen, densely branched shrub to 24 in (60 cm) tall. The branches are initially pubescent and the leaves to ¼–¾ in (0.5–2 cm) long, ovate, tough, dark glossy green and fetid. Produced in spring and summer, the flowers are to ½ in (1 cm) long, white and funnel-shaped. It includes cultivars with dwarf habit and minute leaves, double flowers, pink flowers and variegated leaves. Grow in the cool greenhouse (minimum temperature 45°F/7°C), in direct sunlight or with bright filtered light. Use a pH-neutral mix. Water moderately when in growth, less at other times. *Serissa* responds to clipping into formal shapes, after flowering or in winter. Propagate from softwood cuttings in spring or from semiripe cuttings in fall.

serpentine wall a wall built in a regularly curving line, creating sheltered positions for fruit trees and tender shrubs. It usually consists of only one row of bricks with no buttresses. It is sometimes called crinkle-crankle.

serrate essentially dentate, but with forward-pointing teeth resembling those of a saw. Biserrate is when the teeth are themselves serrate.

Serratula (from Latin *serratula*, a little saw, referring to the leaf margins). Compositae. Europe to N Africa and Japan. About 70 species, erect, perennial herbs with pinnately divided leaves

and small thistlelike flower heads in late summer and fall. Fully hardy. Grow in well-drained soil in sun. Propagate by seed or division. *S. seoanei* (syn. *S. shawii*); SW Europe; stem to 3¼ ft (1 m); leaves dark green and scurfy with narrow, serrate segments; flower heads ⅝–¾ in (1.5–2 cm) in diameter, purple-pink.

serrulate minutely or finely serrate.

Sesleria (for Leonardo Sesler [d. 1785], Venetian physician and owner of a botanic garden). Gramineae. Europe. MOOR GRASS. 23 species, tufted perennial grasses with narrow, flat leaves and spikelike, cylindrical to globose inflorescences, often tinted blue, gray or white. These small, hardy grasses are grown for their attractive foliage and short flower spikes. They tolerate a wide range of soils and exposures, but prefer full sunlight and work especially well planted in rockeries, among paving or at the edges of borders. Propagate by division.

S. albicans BLUE MOOR GRASS; W and C Europe; leaves (1/16–)1/8(–1/4) in ((1.5–)2.5–3(–5) mm) wide, gray-green or green, flat or plicate; *S. fallalis* (syn. *S. elongata*); FALL MOOR GRASS; N and E Italy to C Albania; leaves up to 1/8 in (4 mm) wide, usually flat, glabrous, glaucescent; *S. caerulea* (syn. *S. uliginosa*); BLUE MOOR GRASS; C Sweden and NW Russia southward to Bulgaria; leaves lying rather flat in a loose, spreading tussock, bright blue and glaucous above, usually green beneath, ¼–3 (2–8 cm) × 1/16–1/4 in (0.2–0.5 cm), flat, tip blunt; *S. heufleriana* BALKAN MOOR GRASS; eastern C Europe; leaves 1/16–1/8(–1/4) in (2–3(–7) mm) wide, strongly glaucous above when young, the uppermost ⅝–1/8(–1/4) in (1.5–3(–5) cm); *S. nitida* GRAY MOOR GRASS; C and S Italy and Sicily; leaves 1/8–1/4 in (3.5–6 mm) wide, flat, rarely convolute, glabrous, pale blue-green, glaucescent, with rough margins, the uppermost 1½–3 in (3.5–7.5 cm).

sessile stalkless, usually of a leaf lacking a petiole.

set (1) formerly, any cutting, sucker, or graft material, or a young plant intended for bedding out; nowadays,

reserved for potato and other tubers, and small onion or shallot bulbs, grown for planting; (2) \ flowers that have been fertilized and are starting to develop fruit or seed. See *dry set*.

seta a bristle, or bristle-shaped organ.

setaceous either bearing bristles, or bristlelike.

Setaria (from Latin *seta*, a bristle, referring to the bristles of the inflorescence). Gramineae. Tropics, subtropics, warm temperate zones. Some 100 species, annual or perennial grasses. In summer and fall they produce densely cylindrical and bristly, nodding panicles. Among the most ornamental of grasses, grown for their large arching flower spikes. For dried-flower arrangements, these should be cut when green. Sow seed *in situ* in spring in well-drained soil in full sun. *S. italica* (syn. *Panicum italicum*; FOXTAIL MILLET, ITALIAN MILLET, JAPANESE MILLET; warm temperate Asia; annual, to 5 ft (1.5 m); inflorescence erect to pendent, cylindric, to 12 × 1¼ in (30 × 3 cm), spikelets bristled, white, cream, yellow, purple-red, brown to black).

setiform bristle-shaped.

setose covered with sharply pointed bristles.

Simulated granite sets

set(t)s small rectangles of shaped natural or artificial stone, used for making paths.

setulose finely or minutely setose.

sewage sludge processed human excrement and industrial effluent from sewage works; a potential source of organic matter for the improvement of soil structure and the provision of nutrients. Raw sludge is rich in nitrogen and phosphate, but should not be considered for garden use. Treated sludge is sometimes offered as an odorless powder, which contains up to 7.0% nitrogen and 4.0% phosphate. It is variable according to source and processing method and is difficult to re-wet; there is some risk of heavy metal contamination, which can cause long-term soil pollution, and also, when treatment is deficient, risk of transmission of human pathogens.

sexual propagation propagation by means of seed (except, in the case of apomixis) or spores.

shade house any structure used for the cultivation of plants requiring partial shade for acclimatization. Shade houses may be clad with narrow wooden laths, plastic strapping or netting made of extruded plastic or woven nylon. See *lathhouse*.

shade plants refers to plants that will generally grow satisfactorily in situations where sunlight is reduced because of permanent, temporary or partial shadow from taller plants or buildings. Considerations of climate and soil conditions, especially nutrient and water availability, are relevant to shaded sites. The incorporation of bulky organic matter, where practicable, will aid plant establishment in heavily shaded areas especially. The following selection of plants warrant trialing in places of restricted sunlight, under climatic conditions similar to those of the UK.

For deep, dry shade: *Aucuba japonica*, *Hypericum calycinum*, *Hedera helix*, *Daphne laureola*, *Mahonia aquifolium*, *Ruscus aculeatus*, *Vinca minor* and *V. major*. For deep shade, with some moisture: *Prunus laurocerasus*, *Skimmia japonica*, *Buxus sempervirens*, *Taxus baccata*, *Lonicera nitida*, *Gaultheria shallon*, *Ilex aquifolium*, *Sarcococca humilis* and *S. ruscifolia*; also among perennials: the Solomon's seals (*Polygonatum* spp.), bergenias, pulmonarias, bluebells (*Hyacinthoides non-scripta*), and ferns such as *Dryopteris filix-mas* and *Phyllitis scolopendrium*. For north-facing walls or fences: *Jasminum nudiflorum*, *Chaenomeles* spp., *Garrya elliptica*, *Hydrangea petiolaris*, *Clematis* 'Nellie Moser'; and among perennials: hostas, hellebores, epimediums, lamiums and *Ajuga reptans*.

Greenhouse shading
These slatted wooden blinds with vents are a very expensive option. The efficient method of operation is applicable to cheaper systems.

shading the provision of shade in greenhouses and frames; an important factor in preventing excessive temperature rise and water loss, and in protecting against the effects of sunscorch. Movable blinds are the best choice, fixed so that shading can be selectively applied. Roller systems are ideal, made of wooden lath or nylon, but cheaper methods can be devised using translucent fabric, especially for small greenhouses. Wattle hurdles are suitable for covering frames. A useful, alternative method of shading is to apply a special paint to glass for the duration of the brightest summer months. Shading the south side of a greenhouse is most important. See *lathhouse*, *shade house*.

shallot see *onion*.

shanking a disorder of grapes where the short stalk of each fruit withers and the fruits fail to develop. It is caused by water imbalance in the soil or inadequate nutrition.

shards see *crocks*.

sharp (1) soil, sometimes used to describe one that is free-draining, with a high sand or stone content; (2) drainage, denoting fast and free drainage achieved either by crocking or the incorporation of sand, stone chips, or rubble; (3) sand, particles with angular edges, as opposed to those with rounded edges.

shears a two-bladed tool, of scissor action, with short or long handles in varying planes to the blades, used for trimming grass and hedges. Pruning shears in the US are secateurs in Europe.

sheath a tubular structure surrounding a plant part; most often, the basal part of a leaf surrounding the stem in Gramineae and other monocot families, either as a tube, or with overlapping edges and therefore tubelike and distinct from the leaf blade.

sheet composting see *green manuring*.

shell house a garden house with walls lined with shells, occasionally created during the 18th and 19th centuries.

shells crushed sea shells are sometimes used to raise the pH of growing media and to improve aeration. They can also be used mixed with grit to cover greenhouse staging. See *oyster shells*.

shelter belt a row of trees or shrubs, over 15 ft (4.5 m) high, grown principally for wind protection, but also suitable for screening, noise reduction and, incidentally, as a wildlife habitat. Plantings less than 15 ft (4.5 m) high are better described as hedges, which are more likely to be subject to regular pruning or trimming. Due to shadow and competition effects, shelter belts are only suitable around the perimeter of very large gardens, although small gardens can gain much benefit from shelter belts established on adjacent land. For maximum effect, shelter belts should consist of two or three stagger-planted rows. Suitable evergreen species include the Monterey pine (*Pinus radiata*), especially for milder coastal areas, and the Austrian pine (*P. nigra*); suitable deciduous species include the Italian alder (*Alnus cordata*) and the Swedish whitebeam (*Sorbus intermedia*). Mixed plantings of suitable species are visually the most acceptable and extend opportunity for wildlife.

Shepherdia (for John Shepherd [1764–1836], British botanist). Elaeagnaceae. N America. BUFFALO BERRY. 3 species, deciduous or evergreen,

S

dioecious shrubs with scaly twigs and foliage and inconspicuous flowers followed by brightly colored berries. Fully hardy, tolerant of poor dry soil and saline conditions, the following species is grown for its silver foliage and attractive fruits. Cultivate as for *Hippophaë. S. argentea* SILVER BUFFALO BERRY; N America; deciduous shrub to 13 ft (4 m); leaves 1¼–2 in (3–5 cm), oblong, silvery; flowers small, white-yellow; fruit pea-sized, bright red, glossy with silvery scales, edible; 'Xanthocarpa': fruit yellow.

Shibataea (for Keita Shibata [1897–1949], Japanese botanist and biochemist). Gramineae. Far East. 8 species, squat, shrubby bamboos; see *bamboos*.

shingle (1) small sea-worn pebbles, suitable for covering greenhouse staging; (2) a small rectangular piece of thin wood, used for roofing and fencing.

shoddy waste from wool mills, used as an organic manure for its humus content and slowly released nitrogen. It is not widely available to amateur gardeners. Pure wool shoddy contains 12–15% nitrogen, but the inclusion of cotton and dirt in poor grades can lower the nitrogen content to 2.0%.

shoot (1) the first vertical growth of a seedling or, more loosely, a young stem or lateral growth; (2) applied equally to side growths, twigs, or branches.

short-day plant see *photoperiodism*.

Shortia (for Dr. Charles W. Short [1794–1863], botanist, of Kentucky). Diapensiaceae. N America, E Asia. 6 species, evergreen perennial herbs with long-stalked, rounded and toothed leaves and solitary, bell-shaped and fringed flowers in spring. Hardy to at least 5°F (–15°C), suitable for rock gardens, for an acidic border or for a moist, open woodland garden. Each spring provide an acidic mulch such as pine needles. The glossy evergreen foliage assumes bronze tints in winter. Propagate by division in spring. *S. galacifolia* OCONEE BELLS; N America; to 4¾ in (12 cm), flowers solitary,

to 1 in (2.5 cm) in diameter, white and red ultimately flushed rose, pink or blue, funnelform, lobes crenate; *S. soldanelloides* FRINGED GALAX, FRINGE-BELL; Japan; 2½–4 in (6.5–10 cm), flowers to 1 in (2.5 cm) in diameter, broadly campanulate, deep rose at center fading to white on lobes, lobes lacerate.

shot-hole a symptom of several different bacterial or fungal diseases, in which the affected fragments of leaves fall out, leaving small holes.

shot-hole borer see *bark beetles*.

shredder a powered machine with cutting blades that reduces woody and fibrous prunings and similar garden waste to shreds or chips. These may be added to a compost pile or used as a mulch.

shrub a woody-stemmed plant with a number of branches arising at or a little above ground level, but lacking a conspicuous trunk.

shrubbery a garden area devoted to shrubs, traditionally evergreens. Today, shrubberies are less fashionable than shrub borders—mixed plantings of shrubs, bulbs and perennials.

shrublet a small shrub or a dwarf, woody-based and closely branched plant.

Sibiraea (for the Siberian native distribution of *S. altaiensis*, the type species). Rosaceae. SE Europe, Siberia, W China. Deciduous shrubs with small, white to cream flowers in terminal, long-branched racemes in spring and summer. Hardy to at least –4°F (–20°C). Grow in sun in well-drained soil. Cut old or weak shoots back to the base after flowering. Propagate by seed, softwood cuttings or by simple layering. *S. laevigata* (syn. *S. altaiensis*) Siberia, W China, Balkans; erect to 5 ft (1.5 m); leaves to 4 in (10 cm), oblong to lanceolate, soft blue-green; flowers white in slender panicle to 4¾ in (12 cm).

damaged tissue falls away

Shot-hole

sickle a hand tool consisting of a semicircular blade fixed to a short handle, used for cutting rough grass and weeds, especially in awkward places.

Sidalcea (from *Sida*, a genus of the Malvaceae, and *Alcea*). Malvaceae. Western N America. FALSE MALLOW, PRAIRIE MALLOW. 20 species, annual and perennial herbs with rounded, palmately lobed or dissected leaves (both types often on the same plant) and mallowlike flowers in terminal spikes or racemes in summer. Hardy to at least 5°F (–15°C). It will grow in full sun in most soils, heavy clay included. Cut back right after flowering unless seed is needed. Propagate by division or seed in spring. *S. malviflora* CHECKERBLOOM; Oregon, California, Baja California; perennial erect to 32 in (80 cm); petals ½–1 in (1–2.5 cm), pink or lilac, usually white-veined; includes many cultivars, low-growing or to 3¼ ft (1 m) or more, with spikes of flowers in shades of white, pale pink, rose, salmon, red and purple-red.

side dressing see *top dressing*.

Sideritis (name used by Discorides, derived from Greek *sideros*, iron, referring to its supposed medicinal properties in the treatment of iron-inflicted injuries). Labiatae. Mediterranean, Atlantic Islands. Some 100 species, hairy annual or perennial herbs, sub-shrubs, or shrubs bearing terminal spikes of whorled, tubular and 2-lipped flowers. The following frost-tender species is very drought-tolerant and can be used in hot, dry and sunny situations and for landscape plantings in warm, semiarid climates. Elsewhere, grow in a cool, well-ventilated greenhouse with full sun and in a perfectly drained, gritty and humus-rich medium. Root softwood cuttings of new growth in early summer in a sandy propagating mix. *S. candicans* (Canary Islands, Maderia; shrub, to 36 in (90 cm), much-branched, white-tomentose; flowers yellow, tipped red to brown).

side shooting cutting or rubbing out side shoots, especially those between the leaf stalks and stem of tomatoes.

S

sieve a usually circular device that consists of a raised rim across which is fixed a wire-mesh covering with

Sieving
A fine-mesh sieve being used to lightly cover newly sown seeds. The device can be easily made by covering a frame with a suitably perforated rigid material.

$\frac{1}{8}$–$\frac{1}{4}$ in (3–6 mm) perforations (much smaller than in a riddle). It is used to separate coarse particles and stones from growing-media ingredients, and for covering newly sown seed.

sigmoid, sigmoidal S-shaped, curving in one direction and then in the other.

Silene (a classical plant name of obscure origin, used by medieval botanists more or less in our modern sense). Caryophyllaceae. Widespread in Northern Hemisphere, also in South Africa and S America. CAMPION, CATCHFLY. About 500 species, annual, biennial or perennial herbs, often woody at base. Produced in spring and summer the flowers have five, spreading petals each with an entire, notched or cleft limb and a narrow claw. The low-growing species are suited to rock gardens, screes and troughs; most are hardy to at least 5°F (−15°C), although the tightly tufted species are more safely grown in an alpine house. *S. uniflora* is an excellent edging plant for paths, terraces and dry gardens. It thrives in maritime conditions. Shear over after flowering. Others, such as *S. armeria*, *S. coeli-rosa* and the long-blooming *S. pendula*, are hardy annuals. Grow in moisture-retentive but well-drained fertile soil in sun. Propagate annuals by seed sown *in situ*; perennials by division or basal cuttings.

S. acaulis MOSS CAMPION; circumpolar Arctic regions, mountains of W and C Europe and N America; dwarf perennial forming mosslike tufts or mats; flowers solitary, small deep pink or white; *S. alpestris* E Alps, Balkans; loosely tufted, hairy perennial to 8 in (20 cm); flowers small, fringed, white flushed pink; *S. armeria* C and S Europe; annual or biennial to 16 in (40 cm), glaucous; flowers to $\frac{5}{8}$ in (1.5 cm) across, bright pink; *S. coeli-rosa* Mediterranean, naturalized elsewhere in Europe; glabrous annual to 20 in (50 cm); flowers to $1\frac{1}{4}$ in (3 cm) diameter, pink-purple with white "eye" and deeply notched petals; includes 'Blue Angel', with clear blue flowers with dark eye, 'Candida', with white flowers, 'Kermesina', with red flowers, 'Nana', dwarf, 'Oculata', with light pink flowers with purple eye, and 'Rose Angel', with bright rose flowers with dark eye. *S. dioica* RED CAMPION; Europe; perennial with spreading leafy shoots and erect flowering stem to 32 in (80 cm); flowers to $\frac{3}{4}$ in (2 cm) across, red with deeply cleft petals; hybridizes freely with the white-flowered *S. latifolia*; includes 'Compacta', neat, low and dense, 'Florepleno', with double flowers, 'Graham's Delight', tall, to 36 in (90 cm), with leaves striped cream, 'Minikin', compact, with bright dusky pink flowers, 'Richmond', with deep rose-pink flowers, 'Roseaplena', tall, with double, large, dusky pink flowers, 'Tresevern Gold', with leaves variegated gold, and 'Variegata', with leaves striped white and pale pink flowers; *S. elisabethae* Italian Alps; tufted, hairy woody-based perennial to 10 in (25 cm); flowers white with deeply cut petals; *S. hookeri* Oregon, California; tufted, gray-hairy prostrate perennial; flowers pink or purple with white rays and deeply cut petals; *S. pendula* Mediterranean, often naturalized elsewhere; glandular-hairy annual with weak, branching, ascending stem to 8 in (20 cm); flowers to $\frac{3}{4}$ in (1.8 cm) across, petals cut, usually pink; includes 'Compacta', dense, to 4 in (10 cm) high, 'Ruberrima', compact, with deep pink flowers, 'Ruberrima Bonnettii', stem glabrous, flushed purple, with bright pink flowers, and 'Triumph', to 8 in (20 cm), with double, red flowers; *S. schafta* Caucasus; mat-forming, hairy perennial with ascending flowering stem to 10 in (25 cm); flowers to $\frac{3}{4}$ in (2 cm) diameter, red-purple with cleft petals;

includes 'Deep Rose', with rosy magenta flowers, 'Shelly Pink', with palest pink flowers, and 'Splendens', tall, with rose-pink flowers; *S. uniflora* (syn. *S. maritima*); coasts of Atlantic and arctic Europe; mat-forming perennial; leaves to $\frac{3}{4}$ in (2 cm), lanceolate-elliptic, gray-green, glaucous; flowers to $\frac{3}{4}$ in (2 cm) across with a large, inflated calyx, petals deeply cleft, usually white, anthers dark; includes 'Robin Whitebreast', with large white double flowers, resembling a small carnation, 'Rosea', with flowers palest pink, and 'Silver Lining', prostrate, to 8 in (20 cm), with leaves finely edged silver.

silicle, silicula, silicule a short siliqua, no more than twice as long as broad.

siliqua, silique a thin, 2-carpeled fruit, three or more times as long as wide, dehiscing longitudinally and leaving a central frame of tissue (septum). Siliquas are peculiar to the Cruciferae.

Silphium (from Greek *silphion*, name used by Hippocrates for a plant which produced gum-resin, perhaps asafoetida). Compositae. Eastern N America. PRAIRIE DOCK, ROSINWEED. About 23 species, coarse, hairy perennial herbs with pinnately lobed leaves and daisylike flower heads in late summer and fall. Fully hardy. Grow in deep, moisture-retentive, moderately fertile soil, which is not too nitrogen-rich, in sun or dappled shade. Propagate by seed or by division in early spring. *S. laciniatum* COMPASS-PLANT; C South US; $3\frac{1}{4}$–10 ft (1–3 m), glandular, hairy; leaves broadly and deeply pinnately cut, fernlike, standing erect and orienting themselves with the margins pointing north/south and the flat surfaces east/west, thus avoiding full exposure to midday sun; flower heads to $4\frac{3}{4}$ in (12 cm) across, ray florets pale gold, disk florets yellow-orange.

silt fine soil particles $\frac{1}{500}$ to $\frac{1}{12,500}$ in (0.05 to 0.002 mm) in diameter. See *soils*.

silvanberry see *hybrid berries*.

silver leaf (*Chondrostereum purpureum*) a fungal disease of rosaceous trees,

distinctive sheen

Silver leaf on plum

especially plum and its cultivar 'Victoria', characterized by a silvery sheen on leaves and die-back of branches with discoloration of the wood. Silver leaf is a wound parasite, with the spores entering only through pruning cuts and breakages. Silvering is due to air accumulation, with toxins that cause a separation of tissue layers. Flat, overlapping bracket-shaped fruiting bodies develop on dead wood, on which the fungus can live as a saprophyte. The spores are wind-borne and new infections occur most readily between September and May; hence, it is recommended that necessary pruning on susceptible trees is carried out during high summer when natural gums resist infection and spore production is low. Dying branches should be cut back into sound wood with no sign of discoloration. However, if all branches show silvering, the tree should be dug out and burned.

silviculture the practice and science of woodland management for commercial purposes, and also for wildlife conservation.

Silybum (name used by Dioscorides). Compositae. Mediterranean, Europe and mountains of E Africa. 2 species, annual or biennial herbs with pinnately lobed, white-veined or variegated and spiny leaves and thistlelike flower heads in summer. Sow in summer or early fall. It is hardy to 5°F (–15°C). Grow in well-drained fertile soil in an open site in full sun. *S. marianum* BLESSED MARY'S THISTLE, HOLY THISTLE, OUR LADY'S MILK THISTLE; Mediterranean, SW Europe to Afghanistan; biennial to 5 ft (1.5 m); leaves dark green, glossy, marbled white, 10–20 in (25–50 cm), deeply lobed and spiny; flower heads purple.

simple not divided or branched.

Sinarundinaria (from *sino*, Chinese, and *Arundinaria*). Gramineae. China, Himalaya. 12 or more species of clumping bamboos; see *bamboos*.

singling the removal of seedlings from a sown row to leave plants at their final spacing. Particularly used to describe vegetable crops, where it is also referred to as thinning.

single applied to flowers with the normal number of petals for the species; not double or semidouble.

sink garden see *rock plant gardening*.

Sinningia (for Wilhelm Sinning [1792–1874], Prussian horticulturist and botanist). Gesneriaceae. Mexico to Argentina and Brazil. Some 40 species, tuberous or rhizomatous perennial herbs and shrubs (those listed here are squatly tuberous, downy, deciduous herbs). Typically large, thinly fleshy and densely hairy, the leaves are carried in a basal rosette or on annual stems. Produced in summer, the flowers are narrowly tubular to broadly bell-shaped with a spreading, 2-lipped limb, the upper lip 2-lobed, the lower lip 3-lobed.

Pot individual tubers in shallow containers with a fibrous potting medium, covering them to a depth of ³/₄–1¹/₄ in (2–3 cm). Apply water sparingly at first, increasing the amount as growth progresses and watering copiously once plants are in full growth. Maintain a temperature of 68–74°F (20–23°C) until flowering, then move to cooler temperatures for display. Apply a balanced liquid feed monthly throughout the growing season. Frequent damping down during hot weather is beneficial, although the foliage is easily marked by water and syringing must be carried out cautiously; full sunlight will also damage the leaves. Gradually withhold water after flowering until foliage dies back and the root ball is quite dry; store tubers in a cool, dry place (at 45°F/7°C) until the following season. *S. speciosa* and its many hybrids and cultivars are the florist's gloxinias, dependable and free-flowering houseplants. *S. canescens* is grown in collections of caudiciform succulents (i.e. alongside such plants as *Adenium*), and is altogether more tolerant of bright sunlight and arid conditions than the other species. Propagate by seed sown on a finely graded propagating mix, maintaining high humidity and a temperature of 64–68°F (18–20°C); germination will occur within 2–3 weeks. Increase the temperature to 68–74°F (20–23°C) after germination and prick out into seed trays or individual pots. Maintain a constant supply of water to avoid initiation of dormancy—for example, by using capillary matting. Seed and seedlings are very small. Tubers may also be cut up, each segment with a bud. Cuttings of emerging shoots may be rooted in a closed case with bottom heat. Leaf cuttings may be made; tubers are produced at the cut edge, the old leaf decaying in the process.

S. aggregata (syn. *Rechsteineria aggregate*), Brazil; to 24 in (60 cm); flowers to 1¹/₄ in (3 cm), cylindric, red-orange, throat yellow-orange, spotted with red; *S. barbata* (syn. *S. carolinae*); Brazil; to 24 in (60 cm); flowers to 1¹/₄ in (3 cm), white, cylindric, inflated at base; *S. canescens* (syn. *S. leucotricha*, *Rechsteineria canescens*); Brazil; tuber large, exposed, gouty; stems to 10 in (25 cm); leaves to 6 in (15 cm), whorled, oblong-obovate, gray-green, densely white-pubescent; flowers to 1¹/₄ in (3 cm), cylindric, pink to orange to red, hairy, lobes maroon-violet, marked brown-black; *S. cardinalis* (syn. *Rechsteineria cardinalis*); Brazil; to 12 in (30 cm); flowers to 2 in (5 cm), bright red, pubescent; 'Feuerschein': pale tangerine-red to scarlet flowers; 'Innocence': compact, with bright green leaves and snow white flowers; 'Splendens': large, bright scarlet flowers; *S. concinna* Brazil; flowers trumpet-shaped, lilac above, pale mauve to yellow-brown below, purple-spotted inside, upper lobes deep purple, lower lobes paler. *S. speciosa* (syn. *Gloxinia speciosa*, *S. regina*); CINDERELLA'S SLIPPERS; Brazil; to 12 in (30 cm); flowers 1¹/₂–3 in (4–8 cm), stoutly bell-shaped with a broad, spreading limb, purple, lavender, red or white in wild, variously colored in cultivation; hybrids and cultivars include Fyfiana Group, with large, campanulate, erect flowers, white, through pink, yellow and orange, to red and violet, variously blotched and striped; 'Blanche de

S

Meru', white, fringed pink; 'Boonwood Yellow Bird', yellow; 'Chic', flame-red; 'Mont Blanc', pure white; 'Violacea', deep violet-blue; Maxima Group, with large, nodding flowers; 'Buell's Blue Slipper', trumpet-shaped, curved, mauve-blue flowers; 'Buell's Queen Bee', white with a bright pink blotch on either side of throat; 'Pink Slipper', rose-pink, with a dark center and spotted throat.

Sinofranchetia (for Adrien René Franchet [1834–1900], French botanist). C and W China. Lardizabalaceae. 1 species, *S. chinensis*, fast-growing, deciduous, dioecious twining shrub to 33 ft (10 m). The leaves consist of three leaflets, each to 5½ in (14 cm) long, ovate, entire, dark green above, blue-green beneath. Small, dull white flowers are carried in pendulous racemes, 4–12 in (10–30 cm1) long, in late spring. They are followed by globose, lavender-purple berries. Cultivate as for *Holboellia*.

sinuate of the outline of a margin, wavy, alternatively concave and convex, cf. *undulate*.

sinus the indentation or space between two divisions, for example between lobes.

siphunculi a pair of hornlike structures on the rear end of the abdomen of aphids. They differ in shape and size and so are useful characteristics in determining species. Siphunculi function as anti-predatory devices, secreting a fluid that physically interferes with predators and also produces alarm pheromones.

Sisyrinchium (name used by Theophrastus for a plant related to *Iris*). Iridaceae. N, C and S America, with 1 species in Ireland; also Australia, New Zealand and Hawaiian Islands, probably naturalized in these countries. About 90 species, perennial herbs with clumped fans of 2-ranked, linear to sword-shaped leaves. Short-lived, starry to cup-shaped flowers are carried in clusters on slender stalks from spring to summer. Those species described here are hardy to between 14–5°F (–10 and –15°C). Grow in

freely draining, sandy loam soil with additional organic matter. *S. californicum*, *S. bellum* and *S. angustifolium* prefer moist soil, but still need good drainage. Position in full sun or part-day shade. Most species will self-seed if conditions suit. Propagate by seed during spring or fall, alternatively by division in early spring.

S. angustifolium (syn. *S. anceps*, *S. graminoides*, *S. iridoides*); BLUE-EYED GRASS; SE US; 6–18 in (15–45 cm); flowers about ⅝ in (1.5 cm) in diameter, blue, yellow in center; *S. bermudianum* BLUE-EYED GRASS; West Indies; 6–18 in (15–45 cm); flowers ⅝ in (1.5 cm) in diameter, blue, yellow in center; *S. californicum* (syn. *S. boreale*, *S. brachypus*); W US; to 16 in (40 cm); leaves gray-green; flowers to 1½ in (3.5 cm) in diameter, bright yellow, sometimes turning orange on drying; *S. idahoense* var. *bellum* (syn. *S. bellum*, *S. eastwoodiae*); CALIFORNIA BLUE-EYED GRASS; California; 4–20 in (10–50 cm); flowers to ¾ in (2 cm) in diameter, violet-blue with purple veins; *S. striatum* (syn. *S. lutescens*); Argentina, Chile; 16–32 in (40–80 cm); flowers to 1¼ in (3 cm) in diameter, cream or pale yellow, veined with brown; 'Aunt May': leaves green tinged gray, striped cream. For *S. douglasii*, see *Olsynium douglasii*.

Skimmia (from *shikimi*, the Japanese name). Rutaceae. Himalaya through E and SE Asia. 4 species, evergreen dioecious shrubs or small trees with leathery, aromatic leaves, dense panicles of small, white flowers from winter to summer and, where plants of both sexes are present, brightly colored berries. Fully hardy and tolerant of a wide range of conditions, including heavy atmospheric pollution. They thrive in partial shade in free-draining rich soil. Most will grow fairly well in fully exposed sunny places, but the leaves may yellow, fading and scorching at their margins. Propagate from cuttings of new growth taken in early summer and given bottom heat, or from semiripe wood placed in a cold frame in late summer. *Skimmia* will also grow from seed sown outside in spring.

S. anquetilia Afghanistan, Pakistan, India, Nepal; creeping or erect, shrub, 12 in–6½ ft (30 cm–2 m); leaves to 7 in (18 cm), oblanceolate to oblong

or elliptic, pale green or yellow-green; inflorescence globose, 2 in (5 cm) in diameter, flowers green-yellow to yellow, unpleasantly scented; fruit orange or red; *S.* × *confusa*. (*S. anquetilia* × *S. japonica*); garden origin; spreading shrub, 20 in–10 ft (0.5–3 m); leaves 2¾–6 in (7–15 cm), oblanceolate to narrowly elliptic; inflorescence to 6 in (15 cm), pyramidal; flowers sweetly scented, creamy white to white; fruit red; includes 'Kew Green', with all-male, creamy-yellow flowers, and 'Isabella', with female, white flowers and red berries; *S. japonica* Japan, China; erect or low shrub, 20 in–23 ft (0.5–7 m); leaves oblanceolate to elliptic, entire to obscurely crenate, dark to yellow-green; male inflorescence well-developed, female and hermaphrodite inflorescences 1–5-flowered, flowers very sweetly scented white, sometimes flushed pink or red; fruit red; 'Bowles' Dwarf Male': to 12 in (30 cm), with wide leaves, tinted red in winter, and abundant flowers; 'Bronze Knight': male, of open habit, tall, with long leaves, tinted red in winter, and flowers red in bud; 'Fortunei': angular habit, slow-growing, with abundant fruit; 'Nana Femina': female, of stiff, dense, mound-forming habit, with large, broad, thick, twisted, deep green leaves, flowers in large, round heads and abundant fruit; 'Nana Mascula': as 'Nana Femina', but male and more erect, smaller, slow-growing, with small, less twisted leaves and white flowers in dense heads; 'Rubella': male, with bright red leaves in winter, especially upper leaves, and flowers red in bud in a loose panicle; *S. laureola* Nepal, Burma, China; low, creeping shrub or erect tree, 20 in–43 ft (0.5–13 m); leaves oblanceolate to narrowly elliptic, very dark green; inflorescence globose to pyramidal, flowers sweetly scented, creamy or green-white; fruit black; 'Fragrant Cloud': wide-spreading dwarf to 18 in (45 cm), with more pointed, bright green leaves and abundant flowers.

skirret (*Sium sisarum*) a moisture-loving perennial of the Umbelliferae family, grown for its edible tuberous roots, which are slender, gray-skinned and with a flavor characteristic of carrot. Sow in spring for harvesting in

S

fall or winter, or in late summer for use the following spring; alternatively, prepare root cuttings in early spring. Plant in a moisture-retentive site, with plants spaced 8 in (20 cm) apart in rows 18 in (45 cm) apart; irrigate if necessary. Skirret roots should be eaten young before they become woody. They may be lifted and stored in boxes of moist sand, kept within a building.

slasher a long handled billhook.

sleepy disease refers to some kinds of wilt disease, especially those affecting tomatoes.

slime molds lower fungi whose vegetative bodies consist of a plasmodium or a multinucleate mass of protoplasm. They are nonparasitic, but may be unsightly on low-growing plants, such as turf grasses, strawberries, and small ornamentals.

slip a colloquial term for a shoot, especially a cutting. The term is sometimes used more specifically to mean a cutting with a heel, or a shoot separated with roots attached, otherwise known as an Irishman's cutting.

slit drains rectangular plastic pipes capable of absorbing water along their length, laid to a relatively shallow depth in drainage systems.

slitting (1) making short horizontal

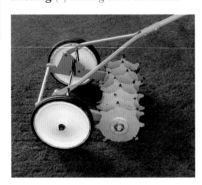

Slitting a lawn
These mechanical slitters make light work of aerating a large area. Aeration is essential in maintaining a fine lawn.

cuts in a lawn with a sharp-bladed slitting machine, in order to improve aeration; (2) making vertical incisions in the bark of a fruit tree where the bark has become so hardened as to prevent an

increase in girth, thereby restricting overall growth; (3) a form of wounding treatment applied to semiripe or hardwood cuttings to encourage growth. See *cuttings*.

slow-release fertilizer formulations that break down slowly in the soil, releasing nutrients over a long period. This may occur naturally as with a number of organic fertilizers, such as hoof and horn, that depend upon bacterial action for their activity, or it may be manufactured by coating individual granules with resin or sulfur. Slow-release substances are particularly useful for plants growing over a long period in containers. Also known as controlled release.

slugs and snails (Mollusca: Gastropoda) soft-bodied, unsegmented animals that secrete a slimy mucus from epidermal glands and a large slime gland opening below the mouth. The body is divided into a head, bearing tentacles and eyes, a muscular foot and a visceral hump. In snails, the hump is spiraled and protected by a shell; most slugs have either lost the shell completely or have a small internal shell, a notable exception being *Testacella* species, which have a small caplike external shell at the rear end of the body (they are unusual in being carnivorous, preying mostly on earthworms). Slugs feed mostly at night and, providing the temperature is above freezing, will continue to do so throughout the winter. The main period of activity is during spring, summer and fall, although they remain inactive during conditions of drought, drying winds, very low temperatures and heavy rain, sheltering under stones, logs, leaf litter or in the soil.

Breeding can occur throughout the year, but most eggs are laid during late summer and fall. The eggs are opaque white or transparent, and are deposited in clusters of 10–50 in small cavities in the soil. Young slugs resemble the adults in shape; at first, the young feed mainly on rotting vegetable material but as they mature they eat an increasing amount of living plant material. Plants particularly susceptible to attack include tulips, *Dianthus*, *Gladiolus*, *Iris*, *Hosta*, hyacinth, lily, *Delphinium*, sweet

pea seedlings, ripening strawberry fruits and many annuals and low-growing plants. Among vegetables especially prone to attack are peas, beans, lettuce, celery and potato tubers.

The GARDEN SLUG (*Arion hortensis*), which is dark gray to black, up to 1½ in (40 mm) long, and with a yellow-orange foot, is a common European pest, attacking plants both above and below ground; it is typical of types that have no keel.

Some slugs have a keel or ridge only on the posterior half of the dorsal surface. Included in this group are the GREAT SLUG (*Limax maximus*), known as the SPOTTED GARDEN SLUG in the US, a black-gray slug up to 8 in (200 mm) long; the CELLAR SLUG (*L. flavus*), known as the TAWNY GARDEN SLUG in the US, which is yellow-gray and up to 4 in (100 mm) long, producing yellow slime; and the FIELD SLUG (*Deroceras reticulatus*), known as the GRAY GARDEN SLUG in the US, which is mottled light gray-brown in color and up to 2 in (50 mm) long, with a chalky white slime.

Slugs with a well-developed keel down the back are known as KEELED SLUGS (*Milax* species); many of these are subterranean and attack the underground parts of plants, such as the tubers of potatoes and the bulbs of tulips. *M. budapestensis*, a dark brown or black slug up to 4 in (100 mm) long with a tripartite colored foot, is a serious pest in northern Europe, whereas *M. gagates*, although present in Europe, appears to be more important in North America, where it is known as the GREENHOUSE SLUG. Specimens of *M. gagates* have a pale foot and can reach a length of 2½ in (60 mm).

Slugs and snails are abundant in most gardens, particularly if the soil is moist with a high organic content. Numbers may be reduced by good garden hygiene, including the removal of weeds and dead vegetation. Measures may be taken to encourage useful predators, such as thrushes, frogs, shrews, hedgehogs and ground and rove beetles. Cultivation of the soil and disturbance of places where slugs are sheltering will help to expose them to these predators. Where slugs are persistent pests, the application of mulches should be reviewed and dressings of manure or

S

organic composts might usefully be replaced by inorganic fertilizers. Susceptible plants or crops should be protected from slugs and snails by using liquid or pelleted forms of recommended molluscicides. Pellets are poisonous to cats, dogs and birds and should be scattered thinly, covered by netting or hidden under raised covers. As an alternative to poisonous baits, slugs may be trapped by placing cabbage leaves, grapefruit skins or hollowed-out potato tubers on the ground. Slugs shelter in such places during the day, and can be collected and killed by dropping them into a strong salt solution. A nonchemical treatment, which employs a microscopic eelworm *Phas-marhabditis hermaphrodita*, is available; it infects slugs to release a destructive bacterium. Treatment should be applied in the evening during March–April or September–October by watering. Earthworms, birds, insects and mammals are not affected.

Small black keeled slugs can damage maincrop potatoes; treat with molluscicide when they surface during warm moist weather. Less susceptible cultivars include 'Wilja', 'Charlotte' and 'Estima'.

slugworms (Hymenoptera: Tenthredinidae) certain sawfly larvae bearing a superficial resemblance to slugs. The PEAR AND CHERRY SLUGWORM (*Caliroa cerasi*) is a cosmopolitan species, occurring in Australasia, North and South America and Europe. The larvae, which taper from front to rear end, are shiny black, up to ⅝ in (15 mm) long and covered with slime. They feed on the upper surface of leaves, removing all the tissue except the main veins and the lower epidermis. Plants attacked include ornamental and fruiting varieties of cherry, pear, plum and, occasionally, apple, almond, hawthorn, quince and rowan. The ROSE SLUG SAWFLY (*Endelomyia aethiops*)—a widespread pest in Europe and North America—has soft, pale green larvae, up to ⅝ in (15 mm) long. They infest mostly the underside of rose leaves, leaving the upper epidermis and main veins intact; when plants are grown in deep shade, the larvae

eaten tunnels

Slug damage on potato

may feed on both leaf surfaces. Also damaged by other species of slugworm are oak, lime, willow, poplar, birch and beech. Slugworms may be controlled with recommended contact insecticides when the larvae are first noticed. See *sawflies*.

Smilacina (diminutive of *Smilax*). Liliaceae (Convallariaceae). N America, C America, Asia. FALSE SOLOMON'S SEAL, SOLOMON'S FEATHERS, SOLOMON'S PLUME. 25 species, perennial herbs, distinguished from the related *Polygonatum* by the racemose or paniculate terminal inflorescence and free, spreading tepals, and from *Maianthemum* by its floral parts in threes, not twos. Suited to the woodland garden and other shaded situations, and hardy to at least –4°F (–20°C). Grow in deep, fertile, humus-rich and moisture-retentive soil that is neutral to slightly acidic and does not dry out when plants are in leaf. Propagate by division.

S. racemosa FALSE SPIKENARD, SOLOMON'S ZIGZAG, TREACLEBERRY; N America, Mexico; stems to 36 in (90 cm), arching; leaves to 6 in (15 cm), lanceolate to elliptic or ovate; panicles to 6 in (15 cm), many-flowered, flowers small, white, sometimes tinged green in frothy terminal panicles; fruit green to red, sometimes mottled red or purple.

Smilax (Greek name). Liliaceae (Smilacaceae). Tropics, temperate Asia, US. GREEN-BRIER, CATBRIER. Some 200 species, dioecious, perennial, evergreen or deciduous, climbing or scrambling vines. The stems are often prickly; the leaves are leathery, smooth and conspicuously veined. The flowers are green to white, small and carried in clusters and racemes during spring and summer. They give rise to spherical berries. Florists' smilax is usually *Asparagus asparagoides*. Grow in semiwooded or woodland locations in damp, fertile soil rich in leaf mold. All are hardy to –4°F (–20°C) and should be allowed to scramble through trees and shrubs and over tree stumps, or be trained on walls, in sun or part to deep shade. Propagate by division or by seed.

S. aspera Canary Islands, S Europe to Ethiopia and India; evergreen to 50 ft (15 m); stems zigzag, angled, spiny; leaves 1½–4½ in (4–11 cm), narrowly to broadly lanceolate, triangular, ovate, oblong or kidney-shaped, abruptly narrowed above the usually cordate base, 5–9-veined, shiny on both surfaces with margins and veins prickly; fruit black or red; 'Maculata': with leaves blotched white; *S. china* Korea, Japan; deciduous climber to 5 m (16 ft), stems sparsely prickly or unarmed; leaves to 3 in (8 cm), broadly ovate to orbicular, sometimes wider than long, apex abruptly acuminate, base somewhat cordate, leathery or papery, 5–7-veined; fruit red; *S. glauca* SAWBRIER, WILD SARSAPARILLA; SE US; climbing deciduous or semievergreen shrub, stems spiny, often glaucous; leaves 1½–5 in (4–13 cm), ovate to lanceolate, broadly tapered or cordate at base, glaucous beneath, 7-veined, often mottled or streaked in a paler or darker silvery tone; fruit black, glaucous; *S. laurifolia* LAUREL-LEAVED GREENBRIER, BLASPHEME VINE, BAMBOO VINE; SE US; evergreen climber, stems prickly below; leaves 2–8 in (5–20 cm), narrowly ovate to oblong-lanceolate, thick-textured, 3-veined; fruit black; *S. rotundifolia* COMMON GREENBRIER, COMMON CATBRIER, BULLBRIER, HORSE BRIER; E US; high-climbing, thinly woody, deciduous or partly evergreen vine to 33 ft (10 m), stems 4-angled, prickly; leaves 2–6 in (5–15 cm), broadly ovate to circular, base round to cordate, thick-textured, 5-veined, dark green; fruit blue to black.

smoke a pesticide applied as fine dry particles which are produced and activated by igniting a mixture of the pesticide, an oxidant and combustible material. Subject to local pesticide approvals; used in greenhouses, which must be kept shut during treatment.

smother crop a crop that makes rapid dense growth and suppresses germinating weed seeds beneath its canopy.

smuts a group of diseases characterized by the formation of conspicuous masses of very dark sootlike spores. Smut fungi are particularly common on grasses, sedges and cereal crops, but only of relatively minor impor-

S

tance in horticulture, occurring on annuals, herbaceous plants, bulbs and vegetables; they do not attack shrubs and trees, apart from unusual forms that occur on palms. The fungi usually spread within the tissues of the infected plant before spore production occurs. They rarely kill their hosts but infected plants can be severely stunted. The most serious smut diseases of garden plants are those affecting bulbs and corms; for example, ONION SMUT, which leads to loss in yield and the formation of poor quality bulbs, and flower smuts, such as CARNATION ANTHER SMUT and SCILLA SMUT, in which the flowers are disfigured by masses of dark spores. Maize smut is a spectacular disease with a worldwide distribution, but it is uncommon in the UK. The best control for the disease is to destroy smutted plants and dispose of any debris, thereby reducing infection in the following season. Also, avoid growing related plants in the same place continually. Spores may be very long-lived in the soil.

Smyrnium (name used by Dioscorides, from Greek *smyrna*, myrrh, referring to the smell of the plants). Umbelliferae. W Europe, Mediterranean. 7 species, glabrous biennial or monocarpic herbs with ternately compound leaves and small, yellow flowers in compound umbels on branching stems, sometimes subtended by colorful leaves and bracts. The following species is ideal for naturalizing in light, open woodland, or among shrubs. A hardy biennial, it prefers a moist, fertile site with filtered sun. Sow seed *in situ* in fall or spring. *S. perfoliatum* S Europe to Czech Republic; 16–60 in (40–150 cm); leaves bright green; upper leaves lime green to golden, stem clasping; umbels golden yellow.

snag (1) a short stump of a shoot or branch left after accidental breakage or faulty pruning; (2) the short piece of rootstock stem retained after beheading of the stock (carried out once a grafted scion bud has established), and to which the developing scion shoot is tied for early support.

snails see *slugs*.

snow mold (*Monographella nivalis*) a common disease of lawns, especially where a high proportion of ANNUAL MEADOW GRASS (*Poa annua*) exists. It can occur at any time of year but is most severe in October and during mild spells in winter, and may appear following a thaw in places where snow has been trodden upon. Small patches of yellowing grass turn brown on death and gradually enlarge and coalesce; in moist weather, the patches become covered with white or pink cottonlike fungal growth. The disease is encouraged by lack of aeration and excessive nitrogen feeding after August. Scarifying, spiking and regular mowing will mitigate against the disease, and it is worthwhile dispersing heavy dew on susceptible sites. Treatment with a recommended fungicide, applied as a preventive each month from August, offers some protection, but none are approved for garden use in the UK.

soakaway a pit filled with rubble or stones and, ideally, lined with brick, placed at the lowest point of a drainage system to collect excess water.

soap sometimes used as an insecticide against aphids and red spider mite, especially in the form of soft soap made from vegetable oil and potash. It is also used as an adjuvant or spreader. For both purposes more effective substances are available.

soboliferous clump-forming; producing suckering lateral shoots from below ground, usually applied to shrubs and small trees, for example *Aesculus parviflora*.

Sobralia (for the Spanish botanist Dr. Francisco Sobral [fl. 1790]). Orchidaceae. C and S America. Some 100 species, evergreen perennial herbs. The stems are tall, clumped and reedlike, and clothed with plicate, lanceolate leaves. Produced in spring and summer in terminal clusters, the flowers are large and showy, basically resembling those of *Cattleya* in shape. Pot in a coarse bark mix, with leaf mold, garden compost, and dried FYM. Maintain a minimum temperature of 59°F (15°C). Provide full sunlight or, when in bloom, light shade. Water and

feed freely when in growth (which is often continuous); at other times, keep just moist. Propagate by division after flowering. *S. macrantha* Mexico to Costa Rica; stems 3¼–6½ ft (1–2 m); flowers to 10 in (25 cm) in diameter, fleshy, short-lived, fragrant, tepals rose-purple, lip rose-purple, white at base, center tinged yellow, apex rounded, broad and frilly; many clones have been recorded, among them white, deep magenta and crimson forms.

sodding US term for turfing lawns.

sod-lifter see *turfing iron*.

soft fruit a group name for bush and cane fruits, such as black currants and raspberries, and also strawberries; cf. *top fruit*.

soft rot a general term for those bacterial and fungal diseases that cause a soft and slimy decay of plant tissues. Storage rots of root crops and other vegetables, fruits, bulbs and corms can be caused by bacteria, mostly *Erwinia* species, or fungi such as *Rhizopus*. Soft rots can occur on growing plants, especially in very humid conditions under glass or on the sappy growth of garden plants caused by excess nitrogen. They often follow infection by the gray mold fungus (*Botrytis cinerea*). See *gray mold*.

soft water water that is relatively free of dissolved mineral salts, especially calcium. It is of relevance to gardening as collected rainwater.

softwood (1) a common name for coniferous trees that produce relatively softwood when compared to broad-leaved deciduous trees; also descriptive of their timber; cf. *hardwood*; (2) soft, green, young plant shoots that contain no woody tissue and which may be induced to root as cuttings.

soil the outermost part of the earth's crust, formed from weathering of rock, the growth of vegetation and the decomposition of plant and animal remains. It comprises a complex mixture of inert minerals, chemicals and organic materials intimately colonized by living organisms.

The deeper a soil is excavated, the

lower the percentage of organic matter present, and the more the material resembles its mineral origins; the horticultural terms 'topsoil' and 'subsoil' relate to this distribution.

Soil classification Soils can vary enormously in make-up and behavior, depending on their location, history and husbandry. Extensive survey work in many countries has led to the recognition and naming of numerous natural soil types based on consistent characteristics, such as the presence and depth of different layers and soil geology. Maps showing the distribution of soil types, or "soil series," can be used to assess the soil in a given area, and to make inferences about qualities, such as the likely ease of working, fertility and drainage.

An alternative approach to soil classification is the "land use capability index" based on direct assessment of general physical qualities only, such as aspect, stoniness, drainage and topography. This system classifies land in seven appraisal grades, covering a range of potential productivity under good management.

Of more relevance to gardening is the classification of soil texture.

Soil texture Soil texture describes

Soil texture
Rubbing moist soil between fingers and thumb gives a guide to soil texture. Sandy soil feels gritty, clay soil smooth and sticky.

the makeup of soil, based on the relative proportions of variously-sized mineral particles in the root zone. Particles larger than $1/16$ in (2.0 mm) in size are classified as stones; those between $1/500$ and $1/16$ in (0.05 mm and 2.0 mm) as sand; those between $1/500$ and $1/12,500$ in (0.002 mm and 0.05 mm) as silt; and those less than $1/12,500$ in (0.002 mm) as clay.

Soils composed of a very high proportion of sand particles are referred

to as light soils. They do not aggregate well and are therefore susceptible to erosion; they are also drought-prone and poor in nutrient retention. They have the advantages of being relatively early-warming, and are usually freely draining and easily cultivated.

Soils in which clay particles predominate are referred to as heavy soils. They are potentially more fertile than sandy soils, showing greater facility in holding certain nutrients in chemical combination, in binding together particles, and in moisture retention. However, they are relatively slow to warm, susceptible to compaction and poor drainage, and are liable to bake hard in summer. Special care is needed in cultivation.

Silt soils are made up of intermediate-sized particles and are of smooth and silky texture. Although potentially fertile and more moisture-retentive than sand, they are unstable and liable to compaction.

Peat soils are formed from incompletely decomposed sedges or mosses. They are naturally wet and usually acidic, but when drained and dressed with fertilizer, can become highly fertile. Limestone or chalk soils are typically shallow and free-draining, alkaline and of moderate fertility. See *loam*.

Soil structure The structure of a soil relates to how well the soil particles are aggregated into crumbs, with a network of pores of different size connecting them, through which water, nutrients and air circulate. Soil structure is influenced by a great variety of factors: the presence of lime, nutrient fertilizers, and organic matter derived from animal and plant residues; the physical effects of frost, wetting and drying; the activity of plant roots, earthworms and microorganisms; and cultivation practices. Structure is at its most vulnerable when a soil is wet and liable to compaction; timely cultivation is important in producing a good tilth.

Soil nutrients Mineral nutrients required for plant growth are normally absorbed in solution from the soil. Those needed in relatively large quantities and known as macronutrients are nitrogen, potassium, phosphorus, magnesium, calcium and sulfur. Micronutrients or trace elements, which are also essential but only required in small amounts, are iron, manganese, copper,

zinc, boron, molybdenum and chlorine. Nitrogen and potassium are the most readily depleted by intensive cropping, phosphorus rather less so. Soil nutrients may be supplemented by the application of organic or inorganic fertilizers. Dressings of bulky organic manure, and the practice of green manuring, are valuable means of maintaining nutrient fertility in well-managed gardens.

Soil pH A term commonly used in horticulture to describe levels of acidity, especially in soil and other growing media. pH values refer to the negative logarithm of the hydrogen ion concentration of an aqueous suspension. Soil acidity is recorded on a scale between pH 0 and pH 14, where the pH value increases as acidity decreases. pH 7 represents a neutral condition and scale points above it are less acidic, or more alkaline. Acidity has several direct and indirect effects on the relationship between soil and plant growth. It affects the solubility and availability of soil minerals; the existence of soil microorganisms, which may be involved in the breakdown of organic matter or be present as plant pathogens; the state of soil structure; and the well-being of plant roots. A pH value of 7 indicates a neutral condition. For many horticultural purposes, a pH of 6.5 is recommended as optimum. Whereas most plants tolerate a wide pH range, some genera, such as *Erica* and *Rhododendron*, consist of species that thrive in acidic soil, and these are known as calcifuges. Plants that do well in soil of high lime content—for example, *Betula* and *Delphinium*—are known as calcicoles.

Soil pH can be raised by the application of lime. The lowering of soil pH is more challenging and best attempted by applying flowers of sulfur, or iron or aluminum sulfate, in line with recommendations resulting from soil testing.

Soil water Water is held in soil as a film around individual soil particles and in the spaces between them. In a well-balanced soil, water is held in fine pores and air in large ones. A soil that is holding the maximum amount of water possible after drainage is said to be at field capacity. Winter rain replenishes the water lost in the growing season and brings soil up to field

S

capacity. Waterlogging occurs when the amount of rain or irrigation exceeds drainage rate. It commonly occurs where a compacted layer exists beneath the topsoil, either due to a naturally-occurring impervious seam or due to compression resulting from surface treading or machinery traffic; a naturally high ground water table can also give rise to waterlogging. Under such conditions, oxygen in the soil is displaced, causing damage to and eventual death of roots if the situation is prolonged. Extreme fluctuation in water level can be detrimental to root growth. To maintain satisfactory plant growth, the gardener must take care to produce a balance between good water-holding capacity and drainage in the soil, as well as taking measures to replenish water that is lost during the growing season through uptake by plants and evaporation.

Salt levels Soil water contains many dissolved mineral salts, some of which are plant nutrients. Where these are present in too high concentrations, they can be damaging to plants and such a soil is termed "saline." Soil salinity can be determined by measuring the electrical conductivity of the soil; the less resistance there is to a current, the higher the salt levels. The term conductivity is therefore often used instead of salinity.

High salt levels make it harder for plant roots to extract water, causing drought stress; symptoms are a blueing of foliage, small stunted leaves and poor growth. Some salts are more harmful than others and sodium is regarded as the most detrimental.

Heavy dressing of soluble fertilizers can increase soil salinity to damaging levels, particularly in the case of plants with shallow, poorly developed roots and germinating seedlings. Soil salt levels quickly fall as a result of leaching, achieved by flooding treatment in greenhouses where crops are continually grown and fed in the border soil, but resulting naturally from rainfall outdoors.

Soil temperature The temperature of the soil is an important consideration for both the hardiness and growth rate of plants. In summer, soil is generally cooler than the air, and in winter, warmer. Soil temperature is affected by depth, texture and the amount of water held; wet soil tends to be comparatively cold and slow to warm up in spring. Thick ground mulches influence soil temperature, making the soil warmer in winter and colder in summer and slowing the rate of temperature change; their use favors the growing of warm-climate plants in areas with cold winters, and cold-climate plants in areas with hot summers. Thin mulches do not behave in the same way, although black polyethylene, which absorbs heat from the sun, can raise soil temperatures in summer and is helpful in speeding the growth of crops that need warmth, such as corn.

Soil life Soil is intimately colonized by many forms of life feeding off organic remains, chemical reactions, and each other. These organisms are involved in many essential functions, such as release of plant nutrients and improvement of soil structure. Soil organisms may be categorized as soil microflora (bacteria and actinomycetes), soil flora (fungi and algae), soil microfauna (protozoa) and soil fauna (worms and arthropods).

Bacteria and actinomycetes are present in vast numbers in most soil. Some of these form symbiotic relationships with plants, for example, with nitrogen-fixers such as alder (*Alnus*) and members of the family Leguminosae. Many types of bacteria play essential roles in both the breakdown and build-up of organic compounds within the soil that are required for plant growth.

Algae need minerals and light, and therefore occur near the soil surface. They play an important role in colonizing bare ground, in initiating the build-up of organic matter and in binding soil particles together.

Fungi colonize the soil with their growth strands, and are important for the breakdown of complex organic matter. They prefer soil to be well aerated, and usually grow better in acidic conditions.

Mycorrhizae are a special group of symbiotic fungi that live in and extend a plant's root system. They extract nutrients that roots cannot extract and, in return, receive carbohydrates. Mycorrhizae are particularly useful in improving phosphorus uptake in deficient soil.

Most of the soil fauna prefer open, aerated soil and many live in litter above soil. Their food supply consists largely of dead and living plants and other soil organisms, and they play a vital part in the breakdown of organic matter, which eventually becomes humus.

Small soil animals indirectly influence the production of organic glues that bind soil particles together; large soil animals are important in improving aeration and helping to distribute organic matter and other organisms, such as fungi.

Worms are important soil organisms. Nematodes, which are usually too small to see with the eye, live in soil water films and, in dry conditions, form cysts in which they can survive for many years. Some feed on bacteria, fungi and insects, while others attack plants. Earthworms have a profound effect on soil formation, fertility, structure and aeration; they are most common in loam soil, and in undisturbed pasture rather than cultivated land. They are intolerant of drought, frost, and dry or sandy soil, and need reasonable aeration. Most require calcium and are unable to survive in very acidic soil; they feed upon dead and decaying plant remains and are encouraged by the addition of organic waste. Earthworm action aids drainage and water infiltration, helps bind soil together and decomposes organic matter into mineral nutrients. Through their casts, they help transfer nutrients and fine soil particles from depth to the topsoil.

soil block a small block of compressed soil-based growing medium, into which seeds may be directly sown or seedlings pricked out. Soil blocks are formed into modules in a mold. They have the disadvantage of drying out rapidly and, for best results, a commercial block-maker should be used and care taken in judging the correct moisture content of the medium used.

soil conditioner, soil ameliorant any material that improves soil structure, including animal manure, garden compost, and leaf mold, and inert materials, such as lime, gypsum,

S

coarse sand or grit. Synthetic soil stabilizers such as polyvinyl alcohol, cellulose acetate, and polyacrylamide may be used to prevent soil capping.

soilless cultivation methods of growing plants without soil, particularly using peat/sand, coir, or bark mixes, but also including hydroponics, rock-wool and straw-bale culture.

soil mark the usually noticeable mark on the stem of a plant that indicates the soil level before it was lifted from the open ground or removed from a container. It is an essential guide to correct replanting depth.

soil moisture deficit the amount of water required to return a soil to field capacity.

soil profile a vertical section of soil at a particular site, running from the surface to the underlying parent rock.

soil sickness see *replant disease*.

soil sterilization the destruction of plant-damaging or competitive soil-borne organisms, such as insects, pathogenic fungi, some viruses and weeds, through the application of heat, usually in the form of steam, or chemicals. The process is, strictly speaking, partial sterilization.

Heat treatment is generally more effective than chemicals for sterilizing loam for seed and potting mixes and commercial electrical soil sterilizers or steaming systems improvised by the gardener may be used. The effectiveness of soil sterilization by these methods depends on the level and duration of temperature; a useful treatment is to heat moist soil to between 160°F (71°C) and 174°F (79°C) for 10 minutes, thus achieving pasteurization.

Soils with extreme pH levels or high organic-matter content should not be treated. Chemical sterilants vary in their range of effectiveness, and the most useful are not suitable for garden use. To overcome pest or disease problems in greenhouse border soil, the best course for the amateur is to resort to container growing or re-soiling.

soil structure see *soil*.

soil warming see *bottom heat*.

Solandra (for Daniel Carlsson Solander [1733–1782], botanist). Solanaceae. Tropical America. CHALICE VINE. 8 species, shrubby climbers with leathery leaves and very large and waxy, funnel-shaped and 5-lobed flowers. These are produced usually in spring and summer and are headily scented, especially at night. Provide a minimum temperature of 50°F (10°C). Plant in well-drained, fertile soil, in full sun or part shade. To induce flowering, stimulate an initial period of shoot growth, then reduce watering until plants almost reach wilting point. Shorten long, vigorous shoots annually in late winter/early spring, removing weak growth altogether (flowering occurs on the current year's wood). Water plentifully during the summer months, sparingly in winter. Propagate by seed in spring and from greenwood cuttings.

S. grandiflora Jamaica, Puerto Rico, Lesser Antilles; evergreen shrub, to 16 ft (5 m)+; flowers white, becoming yellow to pink tinged yellow, to 9 in (23 cm), lobes undulate to crenate; *S. guttata* Mexico; evergreen climbing shrub, to 6½ ft (2 m)+; flowers to 10¼ in (26 cm), throat pale yellow, spotted or striped purple, lobes' crispate; many plants labelled as *S. guttata* are *S. maxima*; *S. maxima* (syn. *S. hartwegii*); Mexico, C America, Colombia, Venezuela; evergreen to deciduous shrub, to 13 ft (4 m); flowers yellow, to 8 in (20 cm), tube with five purple veins, lobes reflexed.

Solanum (Latin name for this plant). Solanaceae. Cosmopolitan, particularly tropical America. NIGHT-SHADE. The 1400 species of herbs, shrubs, trees or vines. vary greatly in habit, but most are toxic, rank and clammy to hairy. The flowers are star- to bell-shaped with five lobes. The fruit is a berry.

The hardiest climbers include the semievergreen, fast growing *S. crispum* (to at least 23°F/−5°C) and its slightly tougher cultivar 'Glasnevin' (to at least 14°F/−10°C), along with the more tender *S. laxum* and its handsome cultivar 'Album' (although this last is known to have survived to 14°F/−10°C). Grow in full sun against walls or fences in fertile soil. Tie in to trellis or wires.

Solanum crispum 'Glasnevin'
This close relative of the potato, tomato, and eggplant is a hardy, vigorous, semievergreen ornamental climber, producing masses of showy flowers for several months in summer.

S. wendlandii and *S. seaforthianum* are handsome climbers, requiring greenhouse conditions in temperate climates. Protect from the fiercest summer sun. Grow in the greenhouse border or in large pots in a medium-fertility, loam-based mix, providing a minimum temperature of 50°F (10°C). Ventilate freely as temperatures rise above 59°F (15°C); water plentifully and feed established plants when in full growth, reducing water in winter. Tie in periodically as growth progresses. Prune all climbers immediately after flowering, or in spring before growth begins, shortening strong stems and removing weak and crowded shoots. Propagate by seed in spring or by softwood or greenwood cuttings in a closed case with bottom heat or under mist.

The poisonous fruits of the frost-tender shrublets *S. capsicastrum* and *S. pseudocapsicum* (WINTER CHERRIES) give a colorful display over the winter period in cool rooms or in window boxes where temperatures do not fall far below freezing. Sow seed in early spring at 64°F (18°C), pot into a medium-fertility loam-based mix, pinching out for bushy plants. Grow in the cool greenhouse or stand out for the summer, feeding fortnightly during the summer months. Bring indoors before the first frost into a minimum temperature of 50°F (10°C). Good light and humidity (a daily syringe) will prevent premature fruit drop. After berry drop, water sparingly and cut back in spring; these plants are, however, generally produced from seed each year.

S. quitoense, a large shrub with magnificent mauve foliage and yellow-

S

orange fruit, is cultivated in the high altitude tropics for fruit and juice production. *S. muricatum*, has larger fruit and can grow at lower altitudes. Grow under glass in cool-temperate regions and give minimum night temperatures of 45–50°F (7–10°C): ventilate freely and water carefully as both overwatering and underwatering will soon cause foliage wilt. Propagate from seed, by cuttings and by grafting. *S.* × *burbankii* (WONDERBERRY) is grown for its edible berries, which resemble black currants. Grow in sun in fertile and well-drained soil. Sow seed in situ in spring, thinning to a final spacing of 24 in (60 cm), in rows 30–36 in (75–90 cm) apart. Irrigate in dry periods. Thrives at temperatures of 64–77°F (18–25°C) with high humidity. In temperate climates grow under greenhouse protection. See also *aubergines* [eggplants](*S. melongena*), *potatoes* (*S. tuberosum*). For *S. rantonnetii*, see *Lycianthes rantonnetii*.

S. capsicastrum FALSE JERUSALEM CHERRY; Brazil; shrublet to 24 in (60 cm), downy; leaves 1½–2¾ in (4–7 cm), oblong to lanceolate, entire to undulate; flowers small, white; fruit ½–1 in (1–2.5 cm), ovoid, pointed, orange to scarlet or creamy yellow); *S. crispum* (Chile; coarse semievergreen vigorous shrub, climbing to 13 ft (4 m), branches stout and glandular; flowers fragrant, to 1¼ in (3 cm) in diameter, lilac-blue, anthers yellow; includes 'Glasnevin', of vigorous habit, with deep blue flowers with golden-yellow stamens in large clusters; *S. laxum* POTATO VINE; Brazil; slender, deciduous vine, flowers star-shaped, ¾–1 in (2–2.5 cm) in diameter, white tinted lilac-blue, stamens lemon-yellow; includes 'Album', with dark green, purple-tinted leaves and pure white, long-lasting flowers; *S. melanocerasum* GARDEN HUCKLEBERRY; origin unknown; widely cultivated in west tropical Africa; annual herb, to 30 in (75 cm); flowers to ½ in (1 cm) in diameter, thick, white, anthers brown; fruit ½–⅝ in (1–1.5 cm) in diameter, black; *S. muricatum* PEPINO, MELON PEAR, MELON SHRUB; Andes; perennial herb or shrub, erect or ascending, to 3¼ ft (1 m)+; flowers to 1½ in (4 cm) in diameter, violet-purple or white with purple markings; fruit pendent, to 4 in (10 cm), ovoid to ellipsoid, white or pale green marked purple, flesh yellow,

aromatic, edible; *S. pseudocapsicum* CHRISTMAS CHERRY, JERSULAM CHERRY, WINTER CHERRY; Madeira, widely naturalized; small, bushy shrub, 3¼–6½ ft (1–2 m), thinly tomentose when young; leaves neat, dark green to mid-green; flowers star-shaped, ½ in (1 cm) in diameter, white; fruit ½–⅝ in (1–1.5 cm) in diameter, globose, bright orange, when ripe, succulent, toxic; includes 'Cherry Jubilee', with white, yellow and orange fruit, 'Giant Red Cherry', with orange-scarlet fruit, to 1 in (2.5 cm), and 'Patersonii', of dwarf, spreading habit, with abundant fruit; *S. quitoense* NARANJILLA, LULO; S America; shrubby scrambler or shrub, to 6½ ft (2 m), densely stellate-pubescent, sometimes armed, all parts flushed purple and purple-hairy; flowers ¼ in (6 mm) in diameter, white; fruit tomato-shaped, 1 in (4 cm)+ in diameter, orange, fleshy juicy, green; *S. seaforthianum* ST. VINCENT LILAC, GLYCINE, ITALIAN JASMINE; S America, widely cultivated and naturalized in subtropics and tropics; vine to 20 ft (6 m), branches slender, glabrous or sparsely pubescent; flowers campanulate to rotate, to ¾ in (2 cm) in diameter, blue, purple, pink or white; *S. wendlandii* POTATO VINE, GIANT POTATO CREEPER, PARADISE FLOWER; Costa Rica; vine to 16 ft (5 m)+, thick branches, sparsely armed with short hooklike spines; flowers rotate, 2 in (5 cm) in diameter, lilac-blue with paler interstices.

Soldanella (from Italian *soldo*, a coin, referring to the shape of the leaf). Primulaceae. Alps, Carpathians, Balkans. 10 species, dwarf, alpine perennial herbs with very small slender-stalked, round and smooth leaves and solitary flowers. These are nodding and bell-shaped with toothed to fringed margins. They appear in spring, often penetrating the snow blanket in their native areas. Grow in sharply drained, humus-rich soil with a neutral to slightly acidic pH. Give an open position with a cool aspect, avoiding strong midday sun. Drier winter conditions may be provided by a propped pane of glass. Otherwise, grow in an alpine house or cold frame, in a gritty medium with added leaf mold, giving bright, filtered light, cool temperatures and good ventilation; water plentifully in the

summer months. Propagate from fresh seed or by division in spring.

S. alpina Pyrenees, Alps to the Tirol; flowers violet or blue-violet, with crimson marks inside, to ⅝ in (15 mm), cut to middle or beyond, lobes each cut into 4–5 lobules; *S. minima* S Alps; flowers to ⅝ in (15 mm), campanulate, divided to quarter of its length, pale violet or lilac to almost white, tinted with lilac streaks; *S. montana* N Alps, Carpathians, Balkans peninsula; flowers to ⅝ in (15 mm), divided to three-quarters of its length, blue to lilac, lobes deeply, divided into 3–4 narrow lobules; *S. villosa* Pyrenees; flowers to ⅝ in (15 mm), violet, divided to three-quarters length, lobes deeply cut into 3–5 lobules.

Soleirolia (for M. Soleirol, a military man, who collected extensively in Corsica [early 19th century]). Urticaceae. W Mediterranean Islands, naturalized W Europe. 1 species, *S. soleirolii* (BABY'S TEARS, IRISH MOSS, MIND-YOUR-OWN-BUSINESS, CORSICAN CURSE), a dwarf evergreen perennial herb, creeping and mat-forming. The stems are delicate, intricately branching, translucent and rooting. The leaves are 1/16–⅛ in (2–4 mm) long and rounded; the flowers minute. It includes cultivars that have white-variegated, silver-gray, lime and golden leaves. Low, compact groundcover for under the greenhouse bench, terraria, and pots. It can become invasive. It is generally considered frost-tender, but may survive temperatures of 9°F (–13°C), especially in damp, equable climates. Grow in a porous, humus-rich medium, with additional grit if necessary; keep evenly moist when in full growth, but reduce water as temperatures and light levels drop in winter. Grow in bright, filtered light or part shade. Container-grown plants should be fed occasionally with dilute liquid fertilizer. Propagate by division.

Solenostemon (from Greek *solen*, tube and *stemon*, stamen—the stamens are united into the corolla tube). Labiatae. Tropical Africa and Asia. 60 species, shrubby perennial herbs with rather succulent stems and softly hairy, ovate and toothed leaves, often beautifully marked and colored. Small, 2-lipped flowers are borne in slender, branched spikes. *S. scutellarioides* and its many colorful cultivars and hybrids have long been familiar to gardeners as 'coleus'—striking foliage plants for year-round indoor display, for permanent outdoor bedding in frost-free climates and for half-hardy bedding use in colder areas. Although easily raised from seed, to perpetuate true leaf color, vegetative propagation is necessary. Root softwood cuttings of young side shoots in early summer under mist or in a closed frame. Pinch back young plants two or three times throughout the season to enhance their shape and foliage. They prefer a winter minimum temperature of 50°F (10°C), a rich, loam-based potting medium, plentiful water and bright, indirect light. They thrive in the home.

S. scutellarioides (syn. *Coleus blumei*, *C.hybridus*, *C.pumilus*, *C.scutellarioides*, *C. verschaffeltii*); COLEUS, PAINTED NETTLE; Malaysia, SE Asia; perennial herb or subshrub, procumbent or erect to 3¼ ft (1 m); stems semisucculent, 4-angled; leaves ovate to deltoid or oblong, crenate, dentate or incised, minutely downy; flowers small, blue-violet, in spikes; the 'coleus' of florists, with many cultivars and seed races ranging in habit from dwarf or trailing to tall; height from 8–24 in (20–60 cm); leaves 1¼–6 in (3–15 cm) long, oak-leafed to heart-shaped or saberlike, edges sometimes deeply serrated or frilled, in a wide range of brilliant colors including bright pink, rose, scarlet, ivory, dark green, purple and black with edges and markings golden, white, lilac, salmon, lemon, cream, burgundy, copper, lime and mixtures thereof.

Solidago (from Latin *solidus*, whole, from its traditional healing properties). Compositae. Northern Hemisphere, particularly N America; a few in S America, Eurasia and Macaronesia. GOLDENROD. About 100 species, hardy perennial herbs with clumped, erect stems, clothed with narrow, toothed leaves and terminating in spreading panicles of numerous, small, buttonlike and golden flower heads in late summer. Suitable for the larger herbaceous border; its hybrids and cultivars are greatly valued for their tolerance of a range of conditions in cultivation and for their late summer color. Grow in

moderately fertile and retentive soil in sun or part shade. Propagate by division. *S. virgaurea* Europe; to 3¼ ft (1 m); flower heads to ½ in (1 cm) in diameter, golden, many in a thyrse or panicle with ascending racemose branches; subsp. *alpestris*: to 8 in (20 cm), with few, large flower heads in compact, spikelike racemes. Cultivars: smaller cultivars include the 12 in (30 cm) yellow 'Golden Dwarf', the 12 in (30 cm) 'Queenie' ('Golden Thumb') with variegated gold and green leaves, the 16 in (40 cm) light gold 'Laurin', the deep gold 20 in (50 cm) semidwarf 'Golden Gate', and the early-flowering 20 in (50 cm) 'Praecox'; taller cultivars include the 28 in (70 cm) buttercup-yellow 'Leraft', the 32 in (80 cm) deep yellow 'Ledsham' and the paler gold 32 in (80 cm) 'Goldschleier'.

× **Solidaster** (*Aster* × *Solidago*). Compositae. Garden origin. An intergeneric hybrid more or less intermediate between its parents, × *S. luteus* is a perennial to 3¼ ft (1 m) tall, with daisy-like flower heads to ½ in (1 cm) in diameter in corymbose panicles, the ray florets canary yellow, becoming creamy yellow with age, and the disk florets golden yellow. Lacking the vigor and coarseness of its *Solidago* parent, and with flowers that mature to a softer, more creamy yellow, × *Solidaster* is suitable for the sunny herbaceous or cut-flower border. Propagate by division or basal cuttings.

solitary refers to either a single (i.e. lone) flower that constitutes a whole inflorescence, or a single flower in an axil.

solitary bees (Hymenoptera: Apoidea) a group of mainly beneficial garden insects differing from social bees in that each female constructs and provisions her own nest without the assistance of her offspring. Nest sites vary according to the type of bee, but include tunnels which they excavate in soil or rotten wood, hollow plant stems, and empty snail shells. In most species, the female dies once the nest is complete and the next generation of bees may not emerge until the following year. Solitary bees are useful pollinating insects of fruit trees and bushes; those

most likely to be seen in gardens are the BURROWING BEES (*Andrena* species), which sometimes nest in lawns and paths. Solitary bees do little damage to lawns and soon disappear once the nesting season is over, so they should be left unmolested. See *leaf-cutter bees*.

Sollya (for R. H. Solly [1778–1858], botanical anatomist and physiologist). Pittosporaceae. Australia. 3 species, evergreen, slender-stemmed climbing shrubs with narrow, dark green leaves and cymes of nodding, bell-shaped flowers with five obovate petals, produced from late spring to fall. *Sollya* will tolerate light frosts, provided the wood is well-ripened. In cold regions, it may be grown in a cool greenhouse or conservatory. Plant in a humus-rich, moisture-retentive but well-drained medium in full sun or part shade. Provide support. Under glass, shade from the hottest sun; water moderately when in full growth, less in winter; maintain a minimum temperature of 41°F (5°C). Propagate by seed sown at 68°F (20°C), or by greenwood cuttings during early summer. *S. heterophylla* BLUEBELL CREEPER, AUSTRALIAN BLUEBELL; W Australia; 20 in–5 ft (0.5–1.5 m); flowers to ¾ in (2 cm) across, bright blue.

soluble fertilizer a type of fertilizer that readily dissolves in water; used in solution for liquid feeding, including foliar application, and also in solid form as a base or top dressing.

Sonerila (from the native Malabar name for one species). Melastomataceae. SE Asia, S China. Some 100 species, tender herbs and subshrubs, often fleshy-stemmed with deeply veined and marked leaves and spikes of rounded, rose-pink flowers. Grow in a coarse, open, soilless medium with leaf mold or other organic matter, sharp sand and charcoal. Admit bright filtered light and maintain high humidity. Keep evenly moist, but never saturated. Provide a minimum temperature of 59°F (15°C). Propagate by cuttings in late winter/early spring. *S. margaritacea* (Java to Burma; procumbent, red-stemmed herb to 12 in (30 cm); leaves to 4¾ in (12 cm), oblong to lanceolate, claret to dark green above with pearly-white spots or zones in lines between veins, pale with red-

S

purple veins beneath; flowers to ⅝ in (1.5 cm) in diameter, rose).

soot residue collected during the sweeping of domestic chimneys; useful as a minor nitrogenous fertilizer (containing 2–4% nitrogen) and for improving soil structure provided it has been weathered for at least three months to remove toxic ingredients, such as sulfur, and then stored dry. It can be prepared as a liquid feed by filling a porous bag, which is then suspended in a tank of water. Traditionally, soot is suggested for sprinkling around susceptible plants as a slug and snail deterrent.

sooty bark (*Cryptostroma corticale*) a fungal disease of SYCAMORE (*Acer pseudoplatanus*) and other *Acer* species, the leaves of affected trees wilting and the bark lifting to reveal masses of black spores. The fate of a tree depends on the extent of bark infection. Although widespread in Europe and N America, the disease is erratic in appearance, occurring in hot summers when trees are under water stress. Infection probably takes place through wounds, such as those inflicted by squirrels, and these animals may be vectors.

sooty blotch a fungal disease (*Gloeodes pomigena*) of top fruits, characterized by black spots on affected fruits.

sooty mold a superficial black fungal growth that develops on leaves and stems. It is formed by various fungi, especially species of *Alternaria*, *Capnodium* and *Cladosporium*, that grow on the sticky honeydew excreted by aphids, mealybugs, whiteflies, some scale insects and some other sap-sucking insects. The sooty molds are not parasitic and prevention is by control of the honeydew-producing insects. On house plants and greenhouse plants, the mold can be wiped off.

Sophora (from Arabic *sophera*, a tree with pea flowers). Leguminosae. Cosmopolitan. Some 52 species, deciduous or evergreen trees, shrubs or robust woody-based herbs with pinnate leaves and clusters of pealike flowers in spring and summer. The late-flowering, fra-grant *S. japonica* tolerates heat and drought, poor soil and city conditions; when mature, it will withstand temperatures as low as –13°F (–25°C). *S. microphylla* and *S. tetraptera* need the shelter of a south-facing wall and excellent drainage. They are hardy to about 14°F (–10°C). Grow all in full sun. Propagate from seed sown fresh or in early spring under glass; pre-soaking in hot water may improve germination. Cultivars of *S. japonica* are grafted on seedling understock of the type. Take softwood or semiripe cuttings of semi-evergreens. Increase also by air-layering.

S. japonica JAPANESE PAGODA TREE, CHINESE SCHOLAR TREE; China, Korea; deciduous tree to 80 ft (25 m); leaflets 1–2 in (2.5–5 cm), in 3–8 pairs, ovate to lanceolate, dark green; panicle terminal, 6–10 in (15–25 cm), flowers to ½ in (1.3 cm), creamy-white fragrant; 'Columnaris'; columnar; 'Pendula': weeping; 'Regent': heat-tolerant, vigorous, oval-crowned, to 60 ft (18 m) tall, with large, glossy dark green leaves and white flowers, produced from an early age; 'Variegata': leaves edged pale cream; 'Violacea': flowers flushed violet; *S. microphylla* New Zealand; evergreen tree to 30 ft (9 m), branches flexuous, tangled; leaflets to ⅜ in (0.8 cm), to 30 pairs, closely opposite, ovate to oblong, dark green; flowers to 1¾ in (4.5 cm), golden-yellow, rather tubular, clustered; *S. tetraptera* KOWHAI; New Zealand; evergreen or semideciduous shrub or tree, 15–40 ft (4.5–12 m); branchlets yellow-hairy, slender; leaflets ⅝–1½ in (1.5–3.5 cm), 10–20 pairs, ovate to oblong, sericeous; flowers 1–2 in (2.5–5 cm), somewhat tubular, golden-yellow, pendulous.

× **Sophrolaeliocattleya** (*Sophronitis* × *Laelia* × *Cattleya*). Orchidaceae. Trigeneric hybrids. The plants are usually smaller than those of other *Cattleya* hybrids and tolerate slightly cooler conditions. The flowers are mostly intense, glowing colors of various shades of red.

Sophronitis (from Greek *sophron*, modest, referring to the small flowers and habit). Orchidaceae. E Brazil, Paraguay. 9 species, dwarf, evergreen, perennial epiphytic herbs. The pseudobulbs are small and clumped, each bearing a leathery, oblong to elliptic leaf. Produced from fall to spring, either singly or in terminal clusters, the flowers are disproportionately large, brightly colored and basically *Cattleya*-like in form. An exquisite dwarf orchid for well-ventilated situations in light shade in a cool house or growing cases (minimum temperature of 50°F/10°C). Pot in small clay pans in a fine-bark mix with added sphagnum moss, charcoal and sterilized leaf mold. Alternatively, attach to rafts or cork slabs. Water throughout the year, allowing a slight drying between each application; mist growing plants in warm weather. Propagate by division. *S. coccinea* (syn. *S. grandiflora*, *S. militaris*); E Brazil; pseudobulbs to 1½ in (4 cm); leaves to 2½ in (6 cm); flowers to 3 in (7.5 cm) in diameter, usually vivid scarlet, the lip marked yellow at the base.

Sorbaria (from Latin, supposedly resembling *Sorbus*). Rosaceae. E Asia. FALSE SPIRAEA. 4 species, deciduous shrubs with freely suckering, slender stems, fine, pinnate leaves and foamy panicles of small, creamy white flowers during summer. Hardy to at least 5°F (–15°C). Grow in sun or dappled shade, in fertile, moisture-retentive soil, with protection from cold winds. Prune in early spring, cutting back the previous year's growth to 2–3 buds, and removing old and weak branches at ground level. This species suckers very freely and may prove invasive. Propagate by removal of suckers in fall or winter. *S. sorbifolia* E Siberia, Manchuria, N China, Korea, Japan; to 10 ft (3 m); leaves to 10 in (25 cm), leaflets to 3½ in (9 cm), lanceolate or oblong, tapering finely.

Sorbus (from Latin *sorbum*, the fruit of *Sorbus domestica*, a name used by Pliny). Rosaceae. MOUNTAIN ASH. N Hemisphere. Some 100 species, deciduous trees or shrubs with simple to pinnately lobed or pinnate leaves and small, white to cream or, rarely, pink flowers borne in spring on terminal corymbs. These are followed by small, usually rounded pomes, often brightly colored and persisting well into fall and winter. The following are fully hardy and valued for foliage, flowers and fruit. They will thrive in most fertile, well-

SORBUS

Name	Distribution	Habit	Leaves	Fruit
S. alnifolia KOREAN MOUNTAIN ASH	Japan, Korea	tree, to 66 ft (20 m); crown erect at first, becoming conical to rounded with age, young stems red-brown, shiny, sometimes hairy at first	2–4 in (5–10 cm), ovate-elliptic, acuminate, saw-toothed, bright green, glabrous beneath, scarlet to orange in fall	pea-sized, red and yellow
S. americana AMERICAN MOUNTAIN ASH	C & E US	tree to 33 ft (10 m) or shrubby, branches red-brown, buds large, glutinous	to 10 in (25 cm), pinnate with 11–17 oblong-lanceolate leaflets, serrate, bright green, slightly downy when young, gray-green beneath, turning golden-yellow in fall	globose, to ¼ in (0.5 cm), scarlet-red
S. aria WHITEBEAM	Europe	tree 20–40 ft (6–12 m), often with multiple stems; crown broadly conical, young shoots and buds gray-felted	simple, elliptic-ovate, 3–4¾ in (8–12 cm), coriaceous, silver-white at first, then dull sea green above and white-felted beneath	to ½ in (1.2 cm), oval to rounded, orange-red, with powdery coating

Comments: 'Aurea': leaves white at first becoming golden yellow. 'Lutescens': young leaves silvery, slightly yellow above becoming silver-green, lower leaf surfaces remaining white. 'Magnifica': leaves large, dark green waxy above, white-felted beneath. 'Majestica': crown spreading, leaves large, dull green above, white beneath becoming green, fruit dark orange-red.

Name	Distribution	Habit	Leaves	Fruit
S. aucuparia EUROPEAN MOUNTAIN ASH, ROWAN	Europe to Asia Minor, Siberia	tree, 16–50 ft (5–15 m), occasionally with multiple stems; young shoots soon glabrous, gray-brown	to 8 in (20 cm), leaflets 9–15 to 2½ in (6 cm), oblong-lanceolate, pointed, roughly senate, dull green, glabrous, gray-green, slightly hairy beneath	¼ in (0.75 cm), bright red

Comments: var. *edulis* 'Rossica Major': vigorous; branches tightly ascending; leaflets 3 × 1 in (8 × 2.5 cm), petiole red, woolly. var. *xanthocarpa*: fruit orange-yellow.

Name	Distribution	Habit	Leaves	Fruit
S. cashmiriana	Himalaya, Kashmir	tree to 33 ft (10 m); shoots glabrous, red.	leaflets 15–19, ¾–1¼ in (2–3 cm), oval-elliptic to oblong, long-tapered, rough, margins serrate, dark green glabrous above, pale green beneath, midrib and rachis brown-hairy at first becoming red	to ¾ in (1.8 cm), white
S. commixta	Korea, Japan	tree to 23 ft (7 m)+, upright at first; buds glabrous, gummy; shoots red brown	leaflets 11–15, 1½–3 in (4–8 cm), elliptic-lanceolate, long-tapered, coarsely serrate, early foliage brown, becoming pale green, blue green beneath becoming yellow-red with age	¼ in (0.75 cm), globose, scarlet

Comments: 'Ethel's Gold': fruit golden-amber, long-lasting.

Name	Distribution	Habit	Leaves	Fruit
S. decora	NE US	shrub or tree to 33 ft (10 m)	leaflets usually 15, to 2¾ in (7 cm), elliptic to oval-lanceolate, blunt or slightly tapered, dark blue-green, glabrous above, paler beneath, soon glabrous, petiole and midrib red	to ½ in (1 cm), subglobose, red

S

S. alnifola

S. americana

S. aucuparia **var.** *xantho-carpa*

S. commixta

SORBUS

Name	Distribution	Habit	Leaves	Fruit
S. esserteauana	W China	tree, 26–50 ft (8–15 m); buds red, white-hairy	7–11 in (18–29 cm); leaflets 11–13, 2½–4 in (6–10 cm), oblong-lanceolate, coriaceous, bright green above, densely downy beneath, turning red in fall	⅜ in (0.8 cm), globose, bright red

Comments: 'Flava': fruit orange-yellow. 'Winter Cheer': fruit yellow later orange-red, long-lasting.

Name	Distribution	Habit	Leaves	Fruit
S. hupehensis	C & W China	tree to 33 ft (10 m); buds glabrous, shoots soon becoming so	leaflets 13–17, ¾–2 in (2–5 cm), elliptic-oblong, tips finely serrate, blue-green above, becoming pink- to red-tinted in fall, gray-green beneath	⅜ in (0.8 cm), globose, white becoming pink

Comments: 'Coral Fire': leaves red in fall, fruit coral red; hardy. 'Pink Pagoda (syn. 'November Pink'): vigorous small tree, fruit white-pink becoming purple-red, persistent. var. *obtusa*, syn. 'Rosea': leaves pale blue-green tinted pink then flame in fall, fruit pink, persistent.

Name	Distribution	Habit	Leaves	Fruit
S. insignis	Himalaya, Sikkim	small tree	to 12 in (30 cm), leaflets 9–13, 2–4 in (5–10 cm), elliptic-oblong, the central leaflets larger, lightly toothed; buds covered in rust-colored silky hairs	pink
S. intermedia	Scandinavia	tree to 40 ft (12 m), occasionally shrubby; young shoots densely tomentose, becoming glabrous	to 33 ft (10 m) broadly ovate, blunt, thin, base rounded to wedge-shaped, lobed or occasionally pinnatisect below, serrate, waxy above, gray-woolly beneath	½ in (1.3 cm), ellipsoid, orange-red
S. 'Joseph Rock'		erect, to 30 ft (9 m)	pinnate, to 2½ × 6 in (6 × 16 cm), vibrant orange to plum in fall, leaflets 15–19, narrowly oblong to serrate	cream to gold
S. latifolia SERVICE TREE OF FONTAINEBLEAU	Europe	vigorous tree to 50 ft (15 m)+; crown broadly conical, branches shiny olive-brown	2¾–4 in (7–10 cm), round-ovate, pinnately lobed, serrate, dull dark green above, yellow-gray-tomentose beneath	⅝ in (1.5 cm), ellipsoid, brown-speckled
S. pohuashanensis	N China	small tree, twigs and buds hairy	leaflets 11–15, 1¼–2½ in (3–6 cm), elliptic to oblong-lanceolate, acute, tips sharply toothed, gray-green downy beneath; stipules very large, ovate	¼–⅜ in (6–8 mm), rounded, orange-red

Comments: Parent of the hybrids *S.* 'Chinese Lace': small tree; leaflets deeply toothed giving lacelike effect, rich fall color; fruit red, glossy, in wide clusters, and *S.* × *kewensis* (*S. pohuashanensis* × *S. esserteauana*): low, leaflets long, deeply cut, rich green, purple in fall, gray beneath; fruit oval, bright red.

S. decora

S. hupehensis var. *obtusa*

S. 'Joseph Rock'

S. prattii

SORBUS

Name	Distribution	Habit	Leaves	Fruit
S. prattii	W China	tree to 26 ft (8 m); twigs glabrous	leaflets 21–27, $^3/_4$–1$^1/_4$ in (2–3 cm), blue-green and downy beneath, tips toothed	$^3/_8$ in (0.8 cm), white
Comments: var. *subarachnoidea* (syn. *S. munda*): leaves covered in rusty weblike down beneath.				
S. reducta	W China, Burma	dwarf, suckering shrub 6–16 in (15–40 cm); shoots slender, thinly bristled	2$^3/_4$–4 in (7–10 cm), leaflets 9–15, $^5/_8$–1 in (1.5–2.5 cm), ovate to elliptic, serrate, slightly downy above, glabrous beneath turning bronze-red in fall	$^1/_4$ in (0.6 cm), globose, carmine
Comments: Suitable for the large rock garden or wild garden.				
S. sargentiana	W China	tree 23–33 ft (7–10 m), buds gummy, slightly downy; shoots stout	large, 8–10 in (20–25 cm), leaflets 7–11, 3–5 in (8–13 cm), oblong-lanceolate, serrate, downy beneath, turning brilliant orange to red in fall	$^1/_4$ in (0.6 cm), red
Comments: 'Warleyensis': leaflets smaller, petiole red; fruit smaller.				
S. scalaris	China	large shrub or small tree to 20 ft (6 m), shoots downy	4–8 in (10–20 cm), leaflets 21–37, $^3/_4$–1$^1/_4$ in (2–3 cm), narrowly-oblong, apex slightly toothed, deep green above, gray-felted beneath, turning red-purple in fall	to $^1/_4$ in (0.6 cm), globose, bright red
S. scopulina	W US	shrub to 13 ft (4 m), erect, rigid; buds black, downy	leaflets 11–15, 1$^1/_4$–2$^1/_2$ in (3–6 cm), oblong-lanceolate, serrate, glabrous, green above, blue-green beneath	$^1/_4$ in (0.5 cm), globose, glossy red
S. thibetica	China	conical tree to 66 ft (20 m)	large, oval, gray-white at first, later deep green above and silvery-white beneath	rounded, red-brown
Comments: 'John Mitchell': leaves to 6 × 6 in (15 × 15 cm), rounded, silvery-white beneath; fruit pear-shaped, orange tinted red.				
S. × thuringiaca (*S. aria* × *S. aucuparia*)	Germany	broadly conical tree to 40 ft (12 m)	dark green, oval, serrate, with 1–4 lobes or leaflets at base	small, red
Comments: 'Fastigiata': crown narrow, upright at first, later spreading.				
S. vestita *S. cuspidata*	Himalaya	broadly conical tree to 40 ft (12 m); branches glabrous purple-brown	to 9 × 6 in (22 × 16 cm) or larger, elliptic-oblong, tapered, serrate, coriaceous, gray-green above, white-felted beneath	to $^3/_4$ in (2 cm), globose, orange-red
S. vilmorinii	China	fine shrub or small tree to 20 ft (6 m), branches spreading, buds and shoots downy, red-brown	3–4$^3/_4$ in (8–12 cm), leaflets 11–31, $^5/_8$–1 in (1.5–2.5 cm), elliptic, upper margins sharply serrate, glabrous above, gray-green beneath	$^3/_8$ in (0.8 cm), globose, red becoming pink

S

S. reducta

S. sargentiana

S. vestita

S. vilmorinii

drained soils—smaller species and those with pinnate leaves tend to suffer in dry positions. All prefer full sun. Propagate cultivars by T-budding or chip-budding in summer, or by whip and tongue grafting in winter. Species are occasionally grafted on to *Crataegus* rootstock—a practice to be discouraged, since such plants almost invariably lean. Increase also by softwood cuttings in spring and early summer, treated with rooting hormone and in a closed case with bottom heat or under mist. Propagation from seed is complicated by dormancy. Collect berries as they begin to color, remove flesh and sow seed immediately, in boxes or pots in a north-facing cold frame. Bring under glass as germination commences, and prick out on development of the second leaf. Return pots containing ungerminated seeds to the frame for a second winter: there may be a second crop of seedlings the following spring. Affected by fireblight.

sorus (pl. *sori*) in ferns, a cluster of sporangia, generally found on the underside of the leaf blade.

sour a colloquial expression for soil in poor condition because of strong acidity, but more usually waterlogging, giving rise to poor structure.

southern stem rot (*Corticium rolfsii*), CROWN ROT, SOUTHERN WILT, SOUTHERN BLIGHT, is a fungal disease which in warm climate gardens may attack vegetables, herbaceous and bulbous plants, and, occasionally, greenhouse crops in cooler climates. The characteristic symptom of the disease is rotting of the stem at soil level, leading to yellowing and wilting of shoots and eventual collapse of the entire plant; it can also cause post-harvest rotting. Infection is encouraged by wet soil that is low in nitrogen and organic matter, with undecomposed plant remains present in the top layers. Infected plants should be removed as soon as they are **Sori on fern pinnule**

seen, together with the surrounding soil over a 6 in (15 cm) stretch beyond the diseased area. Long-term control involves rotation, deep cultivation and maintenance of high fertility. It is not currently established in the mainland UK.

spade the principal hand tool for digging, trenching and planting large specimens, consisting of a rectangular metal blade fixed to a long handle. The standard spade has a slightly dished blade of dimensions 12½ × 8 in (32 × 20 cm); medium versions have blades 10 × 6½ in (25 × 16.5 cm), while the border or ladies' spade has a blade 9 × 5½ in (23 × 14 cm). There may be a thickened tread molded along the blade's top edges. In the UK, the blade is usually fashioned at a slight angle to the handle, which is no more than 3¼ ft (1 m) long with a T-, Y- or D-shaped handgrip; elsewhere in Europe and in the US, the blade is fashioned to lie in line with a longer handle. The best quality blades are made of stainless steel.

There are specialized spades for lifting nursery stock, drainage and post-hole digging, and in some localities, spade work is undertaken with a long-handled pointed shovel. See *graft*.

spadix the fleshy axis of a spike; often surrounded or subtended by a spathe, most familiar as the club- or tail-like inflorescence of Araceae.

Spanish garden a style of design derived from the Islamic garden. The major features are courtyards or patios, often with arcaded sides, narrow canals, rectangular pools, fountains, and formal plantings.

Sparaxis (from Greek *sparasso*, to tear, referring to the bracts). Iridaceae. South Africa. 6 species, cormous perennial herbs; those listed here are 4–12 in (10–30 cm) tall with narrow, ribbed leaves. In spring and summer, they produce spikes of funnel-shaped flowers, each 1½–2½ in (4–6 cm) across with six,

spreading segments. Cultivate as for *Ixia*.

S. elegans (syn. *Streptanthera elegans*); flowers with a yellow throat, and vermilion segments fading to pink, each with a violet band, sometimes marked with yellow at edge inside at base; 'Coccinea': flowers orange-red with near-black center; *S. grandiflora* flowers usually red-purple but sometimes white with purple marks, the tube yellow inside, purple outside; *S. tricolor* flowers with a yellow throat and vermilion or salmon segments; 'Alba': flowers white, yellow segments at throat with dark central stripe; 'Honneur de Haarlem': flowers large, deep crimson, petals blotched black in middle with yellow markings; Magic Border Hybrids: hardy, with large flowers in a rich selection of colors, often four colors in one bloom.

Sparganium (name used by Dioscorides for a waterside plant, probably *Butomus*). Sparganiaceae. Northern and southern temperate regions. 21 species, aquatic or marginal perennial herbs with reedlike stems, ribbonlike leaves and small, green flowers arranged tightly in globose heads on simple or branched racemes. Several species of BUR REEDS are grown, notably *S. natans*. They are hardy to at least 5°F (–15°C). Plant in full sun or part shade at the water's edge or in submerged containers. Remove dead foliage and cut back regularly to confine to bounds. Propagate by seed or division.

Sparrmannia (for Dr. Andreas Sparrmann [1748–1820], Swedish traveler, member of Captain Cook's second expedition). Tiliaceae. Tropics, South Africa. Some 4 species, hairy, evergreen shrubs or trees with large leaves. Borne in umbels on long stalks, the flowers consist of four obovate petals with a boss of long and colorful stamens. If touched, these move rapidly outward. Provide a minimum temperature of 50°F (10°C), bright, filtered light and airy conditions. Pot in a fertile, loam-based mix in large containers or borders. Water and feed liberally in spring and summer; in winter, keep rather dry unless in warm conditions. Prune to restrict size in early spring. Increase by soft cuttings in spring, or by seed. *S. africana* AFRICAN HEMP; South Africa; to 20 ft (6 m); leaves 6–12 in (15–30 cm), cordate to ovate, irregularly toothed, bright green, hairy; flowers to 2 in (5 cm) in diameter, white, stamens yellow with red to purple tips.

Spartina (from Greek *spartion*, a grass used for cordage). Gramineae. W and S Europe, NW and South Africa, America, S Atlantic Islands. CORD GRASS, MARSH GRASS. Some 15 species, rhizomatous, perennial grasses. An adaptable, hardy grass found in freshwater swamps, salt marshes and wet prairies. It prefers damp or wet soil, thrives in full sun and will quickly colonize the banks of ponds and streams, flowering and fruiting over the summer and fall. Propagate by division. *S. pectinata* PRAIRIE CORD GRASS, FRESHWATER CORD GRASS, SLOUGH GRASS; N America; to 6½ ft (2 m), stems tufted, robust; leaves to 48 × ⅜ in (120 × 1.5 cm), narrow and arching, scabrous, turning yellow in fall; inflorescence narrow, compact, erect, to 4 in (10 cm); 'Aureomarginata': leaves edged golden yellow.

Spartium (from Greek *sparton*, the rush, which this plant resembles in its wandlike branches and its use as a fiber source). Leguminosae. Mediterranean regions and SW Europe; naturalized elsewhere. 1 species, *S. junceum* (SPANISH BROOM, WEAVER'S BROOM), a deciduous shrub to 10 ft (3 m) tall with erect, rushlike, green branches and small, slender and short-lived leaves. Fragrant, golden yellow, pealike flowers are borne in terminal racemes from spring to fall. *Spartium* is hardy to 14°F (−10°C). Grow in full sun in well-drained but not too fertile soil. Propagate by seed.

spathe a conspicuous leaf or bract subtending a spadix (q.v.) or other inflorescence; of particular importance in Araceae and Palmae.

Spathiphyllum (from Greek *spatha*, spathe, and *phyllon*, leaf, alluding to the leaflike spathe). Araceae. Tropical America, Philippines, Indonesia. PEACE LILY. 36 species, evergreen, perennial

herbs with glossy green, elliptic to lanceolate leaves and showy, long-lasting inflorescences—these consist of a clublike spadix backed by a sail-like spathe. These are ideal plants for the home and interior landscapes. They need growing conditions similar to those of *Dieffenbachia*, but are stemless and should be propagated by division.

S. floribundum SNOWFLOWER; Colombia; leaves to 8 in (20 cm), velvety dark green; spathe recurved, spreading, lanceolate to oblong-elliptic, to 3 in (8 cm), white or green; includes 'Mauna Loa', compact, with deep green leaves and a white, fragrant inflorescence, and 'Mauna Loa Supreme', upright, tall, with rich green leaves; *S. wallisii* Panama, Costa Rica; leaves 10–14¼ in (24–36 cm), bright green; spathe ovate to oblong or elliptic, concave, to 6½ in (17 cm), white, becoming green, scented; the plant usually grown is the cultivar 'Clevelandii' (syn. *S. clevelandii*) with glossy green leaves to 16 in (40 cm) long and erect to slightly spreading, ovate, acuminate spathes, to 7 in (18 cm) and white.

Spathodea (from Greek *spathe*, a sheath, and *-odes*, resembling, referring to calyx form). Bignoniaceae. Tropical Africa. 1 species, *S. campanulata*, (AFRICAN TULIP TREE), a tree to 66 ft (20 m) with large pinnate leaves and terminal racemes of flowers; these are each to 4¾ in (12 cm) deep, scarlet to blood-red and campanulate with crisped lobes. Widely planted in tropical and sub-tropical regions as a park specimen and street tree. In cool temperate zones, it can be grown in the warm greenhouse or conservatory in a well-drained but moisture-retentive, high-fertility medium with full sun and a buoyant atmosphere. Water plentifully when in full growth and maintain a minimum temperature of about 59°F (15°C). Propagate by seed sown in spring or by semiripe cuttings rooted in a closed case with bottom heat.

spathulate, spatulate spatula-shaped, essentially oblong, but attenuated at the base and rounded at the apex.

spawn (1) the mycelium of cultivated mushrooms; (2) offsets of bulbs and

corms, particularly of gladiolus; (3) refers to raspberry suckers or primocane.

species the category of taxa of the lowest principal taxonomic rank, occurring below genus level and usually containing closely related, morphologically similar individuals often found within a distinct geographical range. The species may further be divided into subspecies, variety and forma. It is the basic unit of naming, forming a binomial in combination with the generic name. The species itself is signified by a specific epithet, or trivial name.

specimen a sample of plant material, living, dried and pressed or pickled, taken for purposes of identification, record-making and demonstration.

specimen plant (1) may refer to any plant, but usually a tree or shrub, which is typical of its species or cultivar and growing in prime condition; (2) a plant placed singly as a conspicuous feature.

spermatophyte a seed-bearing plant.

Sphaeralcea (from Greek *sphaira*, a globe, and *akaia*, mallow, referring to the globose fruits). Malvaceae. N and S America. FALSE MALLOW, GLOBE MALLOW. 60 species, annual or perennial, hairy herbs and subshrubs with racemes and panicles of mallowlike flowers in summer. Grow in a gritty medium in a frost-free greenhouse or overwinter in same and plant outdoors in late spring in a warm dry position in full sun. Propagate by seed, by division, or by softwood cuttings.

S. ambigua DESERT MALLOW; SW US; white-hairy, somewhat shrubby perennial to 3¼ ft (1 m); flowers 1¼–2½ in (3–6 cm) diameter, orange; *S. munroana* western US; gray-hairy, erect perennial to 3¼ ft (1 m); flowers 1¼–2 in (3–5 cm) diameter, apricot-pink to pale red or orange.

sphagnum peat peat formed from the remains of sphagnum moss. It has excellent physical properties and is slow to decompose, with a pH level of

S

753

3.5–4.0, a high cation exchange capacity and a low nutrient content. Also known as moss peat; cf. *sedge peat.*

spicate spikelike, or borne in a spikelike inflorescence.

spiciform spike-shaped.

spiculate furnished with fine, fleshy points.

spike an indeterminate inflorescence bearing sessile flowers on an unbranched axis.

spikelet a small spike.

spiking a method of aerating lawns, carried out either with an ordinary digging fork, a hollow-tined fork, or a wheeled spiking machine. See *lawns, slitting.*

spiling making conical holes in soil by inserting a crowbar and rotating it to make a narrow shaft 18–24 in (45–60 cm) deep, which is filled with specially prepared compost. Taprooted vegetables, such as carrots and parsnips, are sown in each hole with the objective of producing excellent specimens for the show bench. The technique is also suitable for raising such vegetables on very stony sites.

spinach (*Spinacia oleracea*) an annual grown for its edible leaves. Believed to have originated in Central Asia, spinach was cultivated in China as early as the 7th century and in Ethiopia by the 14th century. Young leaves can be eaten raw in salads but older leaves are usually served cooked.

It grows best where average temperatures are around 59–64°F (15–18°C), but will withstand much lower temperatures, with young plants tolerating frost down to 16°F (–9°C). It is liable to run to seed in dry weather, especially in soil low in organic matter. There are two forms of spinach, one with round seeds, used for a summer crop, the other a hardier type with prickly seeds, more suited for an overwintered crop; improved modern cultivars are often dual-purpose. With appropriate cultivars and sowing dates, it is possible in most temperate areas to maintain supply throughout the year.

Sow summer spinach at three-weekly intervals from February to May, the overwintered crop in August or September. Sow ³⁄₄ in (2 cm) deep, in rows about 12 in (30 cm) apart, thinning to 6 in (15 cm) apart in the case of summer spinach and to 9 in (22 cm) apart in the case of the winter crop. Harvesting can commence 10–12 weeks from spring-sowing through to late fall; the overwintered crop can be harvested throughout winter until spring, and cloches will improve its quality. Cut-and-come-again is possible under favorable conditions.

NEW ZEALAND SPINACH (*Tetragonia tetragonioides*) is spikier-leaved and half-hardy. A sprawling perennial, cultivated for its edible young shoots and succulent leaves, it was discovered growing wild in New Zealand by James Cook in 1770. It is indigenous to the coastal region of south and Western Australia and Tasmania. It spreads over the ground, producing smaller leaves and is less dependent on moist conditions than true spinach, or leaf beets. The 'seed' consists of a hard, dry, angular fruit, ³⁄₈–³⁄₄ in (8–19 mm) long, containing several true seeds; these are best soaked in water for 24 hours before sowing. For early summer use, raise singly in pots under protection for planting out, at 9–14in² (60–90 cm²) spacings, after any risk of frost has passed.

For spinach beet (perpetual spinach), see *swiss chard.*

Possible problems: downy mildew; leaf spot; spinach blight (see *blight*).

New Zealand spinach

spindlebush a training system for fruit trees, consisting of a cone-shaped framework around a single vertical stem, grafted on to a dwarfing rootstock, and supported by a permanent stake. The side shoots are tied down to induce fruit-bud formation and early cropping. The system is used especially for apples.

spine a modified stem or reduced branch, stiff and sharp pointed.

spinescent (1) bearing or capable of developing spines; (2) terminating in, or modified to, a spinelike tip.

spin trimmer a brush cutter, also called a string trimmer; a powered cutter with a spinning nylon cord or metal blades, used for cutting down weeds and grass, especially lawn edges or around the base of trees.

spinule a small spine.

spinulose bearing small or sparsely distributed spines.

Spiraea (from Greek *speiraia*, a plant used for garlands). Rosaceae. Asia, Europe, N America, Mexico. SPIREA, SPIRAEA, BRIDAL-WREATH. Some 80 species, deciduous shrubs with small, 4–5-petalled, white, pink or carmine flowers in racemes, panicles or corymbs in spring and summer. The following species are fully hardy. Grow in full sun in well-drained, moisture-retentive and moderately fertile soil. With those that flower during spring and early summer on the previous season's wood, prune immediately after flowering, thinning out old and weak growth by cutting back to within an inch or two (a few centimeters) of old wood. Those that flower on the current season's wood can be pruned in early spring, and cut back to ground level. Propagate *Spiraea* from softwood or semiripe nodal cuttings, alternatively take cuttings of ripe wood in fall and root in the cold frame. Thicket-forming species can be increased by rooted suckers in early spring.

S. × *arguta.* (*S.* × *multiflora* × *S. thunbergii*); GARLAND SPIRAEA; erect, to 6¹⁄₂ ft (2 m), rounded, bushy; leaves to 1¹⁄₂ in (4 cm), oblanceolate, light green, serrate, initially downy beneath; flowers snow-white, in crowded corymbs; *S.* × *billardii* (*S. douglasii* × *S. salicifolia*); closer to *S. douglasii* but with leaves acute at apex and base, downy gray beneath; to 6¹⁄₂ ft (2 m); leaves 2–3 in (5–8 cm), oblong to lanceolate; flowers bright

S

pink in narrow, dense panicle to 8 in (20 cm); 'Alba': flowers white; *S. canescens* Himalaya; to 15 ft (4.5 m), habit domed; branches thin, arching or pendulous; leaves ½–1 in (1–2.5 cm), oval or obovate, apex usually blunt and dentate, dull green and sparsely lanuginose above, gray and densely lanuginose beneath; flowers white or dull cream-white, in hemispherical corymbs to 2 in (5 cm) in diameter. *S. douglasii* western N America; erect, to 8 ft (2.5 m), compact, freely suckering; leaves 1½–4 in (4–10 cm), oblong, apex usually obtuse and serrate, dark green above, felty white beneath; flowers deep pink, crowded in erect, tomentose narrowly conical panicles to 8 in (20 cm); *S. japonica* JAPANESE SPIRAEA; Japan, China; to 5 ft (1.5 m), erect; leaves ¾–3 in (2–8 cm), lanceolate to ovate, acute to acuminate, biserrate, glaucescent with downy veins beneath; flowers rose-pink to carmine, rarely white, crowded in flat corymbs; 'Alpina': mound-forming, with rose flowers, in tiny heads; 'Anthony Waterer': upright, dwarf, with deep green leaves, occasionally cream and pink variegated; 'Bullata': dwarf, with dark olive green, coarsely serrate, crinkled leaves and crimson flowers; 'Bumalda': dwarf, with toothed leaves, often cream and pink variegated, and dark pink flowers; 'Goldflame': leaves bronze to copper turning pale gold to lime; 'Golden Princess': leaves neat, emerging copper turning gold to lime; var. *albiflora*: flowers white; 'Allgold': leaves clear gold; *S. prunifolia* BRIDALWREATH SPIRAEA; China, naturalized Japan; upright to 6½ ft (2 m), dense, bushy; branches slender, arching; leaves 1–1¾ in (2.5–4.5 cm), ovate, obtuse to acute, denticulate, bright green above, downy gray beneath; flowers pure white, double, in clusters along branches; *S. thunbergii* China, Japan; densely branching shrub to 3¼ ft (1 m); branchlets wiry, angled; leaves 1–1½ in (2.5–4 cm), linear to lanceolate, acuminate to acute, sparsely and sharply serrulate, pale green, glabrous; flowers pure white, in clusters closely set on slender, nodding branches; *S. trichocarpa* Korea; 3¼–6½ ft (1–2 m); branches rigid, spreading, young branchlets angled, glabrous; leaves 1¼–2½ in (3–6.5 cm), oblong to lanceolate, few-

toothed or entire, vivid green above, somewhat glaucous beneath; flowers white, in rounded corymbs at ends of short, leafy twigs, forming a graceful spray; 'Snow White': bushy, to 5 ft (1.5 m), twigs drooping, leaves large, light green, flowers large, creamy white, in umbrella-shaped heads; *S. trilobata* N Siberia, Turkestan to N China; intricately branching to 4 ft (1.2 m), broad, compact; stems often flexuous, young branchlets slender; leaves ⅜–1 in (1.5–2.75 cm), more or less circular, sometimes cordate, serrate, occasionally 3–5-lobed, blue-green; flowers white, crowded in umbels to 1½ in (4 cm) in diameter at the ends of short, leafy twigs; *S.* × *vanhouttei* (*S. trilobata* × *S. cantoniensis*); to 6½ ft (2 m); stems slender, rodlike, arching; leaves 1¼–1½ in (3–4 cm), rhomboid or obovate, occasionally 3–5-lobed, apex coarsely serrate, dark green above, somewhat glaucous beneath, glabrous; flowers white, in umbellate clusters to 2 in (5 cm) in diameter, borne profusely along branches; *S. veitchii* W and C China; vigorous, to 11 ft (3.5 m); shoots arching, young branches tinted red, lanuginose, striate; leaves to 2 in (5 cm), oblong or obovate, entire, sometimes slightly lanuginose beneath; flowers white, in crowded, dense corymbs to 2½ in (6.5 cm) in diameter.

spit a spade's depth of soil, usually 10–12 in (25–30 cm). The terms top spit, second spit, and third spit refer to the first three 10–12 in (25–30 cm) layers of soil found when working from the surface downward. See *digging*.

spittlebug see *froghoppers*.

split stone a physiological condition of stone fruits, especially peaches, in which calcium deficiency and irregular water supply are implicated.

spoon-type applied to chrysanthemums, especially those in which the quilled florets expand at their ends into a spoon shape.

Spoon-type

sporangium a sac or body that contains or produces spores; used especially of cryptogams.

spore the propagule of fungi, ferns and mosses, often specialized for a particular method of dispersal, and, in effect, similar to seed in higher plants.

sporophyll a leaf, or modified leaf, or leaflike organ, which bears spores.

sporophyte in cryptogams, the vegetative, spore-bearing generation, as opposed to the gametophyte generation.

sport see *mutation*.

spraing a disordered condition of the flesh of potatoes characterized, in cut tubers, by rust-brown arc-shaped streaks arising in concentric or parallel formation. It is most likely to be caused by virus infection.

spray (1) a group of flowers on a single stem, especially chrysanthemums and carnations; (2) a pesticide applied mixed with water in the form of an emulsion, suspension, or solution using various types of spraying equipment. See *spraying and spraying equipment*.

spraying and spraying equipment insecticides, fungicides, and herbicides should be sprayed only when really necessary: when there is a rapid increase in numbers of a particular pest, danger of spread of disease, or competition from weeds that cannot be dealt with by cultivation methods. Cultural controls, such as pruning, removal of plant residue, rotations and manual weeding are alternative measures, as is encouraging natural enemies to provide biological control. When spraying can be justified, care must be taken to avoid excessive use since this will reduce the survival rate of beneficial insects and also because the target organism may become resistant to a chemical

S

that is regularly used; treatments should also be localized as spot applications in order to avoid contamination of a large area with pesticide. Generally, spraying upward through a plant canopy achieves better distribution of a pesticide than drenching from overhead. Pests hidden deep in plant foliage may be controlled by systemic insecticides, while translocated herbicides, such as glyphosate, will move to underground parts of a target weed. It is very important to identify the cause of a problem correctly and to select the most appropriate chemical substance in each instance.

A pesticide is usually formulated with other chemicals, such as surfactants, emulsifiers and "stickers," so that it mixes with water easily, will spread over the plant surface and will resist removal by rain. Some pesticide products are sold as liquids to be poured and measured out by the user, while others are only available as wettable powders or dispersible grains that break up and form a suspension in water; with the user's safety in view, the latter are preferable since there is less risk of small particles being inhaled during preparation.

With most sprayers, the diluted spray liquid is applied to surfaces by forcing it, under pressure, through a small hole or orifice in a nozzle so that it breaks up into droplets. The droplets can vary in size, the largest tending to fall vertically downward due to gravity while the smaller ones may be wind blown some distance as spray drift. Particular care is needed when applying herbicides to avoid drift which may accidentally damage susceptible valued plants.

Many small garden sprayers are fitted with a variable cone nozzle, which can be screwed clockwise to provide a wide-angled fine spray with mostly small droplets, or anti-clockwise to produce a coarser spray or to form a narrow jet of liquid. Inside the cap with the orifice is the swirl plate, which has one or more tangential slots that direct the liquid flow so that it rotates through the orifice. The distance between the swirl plate and the orifice defines the angle of spray. Ideally, the position of the cap should be fixed while spraying with plain water, so that no later adjustments are necessary

which could cause the operator to come into contact with the pesticide.

Other sprayers have a nozzle body and cap into which a variety of fittings can be inserted, enabling a particular volume of liquid to be applied or different spray patterns to be obtained. Deflector and fan nozzles are used to apply herbicides; cone nozzles are more suitable for pesticides and fungicides. The nozzles should always be held to the side and directed down wind to avoid the operator walking into the spray.

All types of sprayer consist of a container, one or more nozzles and a pump or other alternative method of liquid transfer to the nozzle, e.g. gravity. Filters are necessary on all but the most basic equipment, since spray liquid is readily contaminated with dust or other foreign matter.

Hand-operated trigger sprayer Here, a hand-operated trigger is used to draw liquid via a dip tube from a container, of usually less than one-liter capacity, and force it through a cone nozzle to produce an intermittent spray. Some pesticides can be purchased pre-packed in such sprayers.

Pressure pack This type of applicator, often referred to as an "aerosol," consists of a lightweight metal can, containing a pesticide dissolved in a solvent, together with a gas propellant, such as compressed air or butane. When a plastic valve is opened, the pressure forces the liquid to the orifice, from where it issues as a fine spray, the process of atomization being assisted by volatilization of the liquid.

Syringe-type sprayer This is a cylindrical hand-operated pump, with a hose at one end connected to a container, and a nozzle at the other end. By holding the pump firmly in one hand and sliding the handle in and out, liquid is drawn from the container and forced through the nozzle on the compression stroke. This equipment is mainly suitable for spot treatment in gardens.

Compression sprayer This is the most widely used type of garden sprayer, requiring no pumping while spraying. Models have a robust plastic container of $1^3/4$ pints–$2^1/4$ gallons (1–10 liters) capacity, with a removable

hand-operated pump, which also provides a lid for the container. Air above the liquid is pressurized using the pump; this forces the liquid through a flexible delivery hose to a trigger valve on a hand-held lance, at the end of which is usually a variable cone nozzle. Pressure-indicating devices and safety valves avoid over-pressurization. Large sprayers of this type can be carried as a knapsack. Sprayers where compression is achieved by the need for continuous pumping during spraying are less convenient.

Calibration For correct dosage, it is desirable to know the output from a sprayer over a given time and area. This can be obtained by measuring the quantity of water sprayed into a receptacle for one minute, the distance of travel per minute and the width of the nozzle's spray pattern. The output in gallons per square yard will equal the output per minute (gallons per minute) divided by the speed (yards per minute) times the swath (yards).

Maintenance Spraying equipment should always be washed after use and kept dry while in storage. Nozzles, washers and other parts are subject to wear and must be replaced periodically.

It is essential that appropriate protective clothing is worn during spraying operations. The use and storage of chemical substances is widely subject to legal restrictions and local approval of pesticides must be checked. Always read the label for advice on the product being used.

spreader see *adjuvant*.

Sprekelia (for J. H. von Sprekelsen [d. 1764], German botanist). Amaryllidaceae. Mexico. 1 species, *S. formosissima*, (JACOBEAN LILY, ST. JAMES LILY, AZTEC LILY, ORCHID LILY), a bulbous, perennial herb with narrow leaves and solitary, scapose flowers produced in spring and summer. These are typically scarlet (sometimes deep crimson or white) with six perianth segments, the lower three overlapping and partly inrolled at their bases into a loose, waisted cylinder, their free parts narrowly lanceolate and drooping, the upper three are more or less erect, outspread or reflexed, the central one to 1 in (2.5 cm) across and broader than the lateral segments. Within the cylinder, attached to the bases of the segments, are long stamens—these project down, outward and upward and end in large versatile anthers. Provide a minimum temperature of 45°F (7°C). Cultivation otherwise as for *Hippeastrum*.

springtails (Collembola) small wingless insects, $\frac{1}{16}$–$\frac{1}{4}$ in (1–5 mm) long; many species have a forked tail, which when at rest is held under the body, but when released propels the insect into the air. Springtails abound in leaf litter and commonly occur in soil, especially soils that are moist and rich in fungal growth and the organic matter upon which they feed; infrequently, plant leaves may be damaged, especially at the seedling stage, by the biting of pin-sized holes. Springtails are also often found in the potting mix of house plants, but they will not cause damage to the roots or leaves. Some springtails attack mushrooms, making pits and tunnels in the stalk and caps. In most situations, control measures are unnecessary.

sprinkler see *irrigation*.

sprinkle bar see *dribble bar*.

sprouts (1) the small leafy axillary buds of Brussels sprouts; (2) any new shoot, such as the first growth of a potato tuber or the first aerial growth of a seedling, especially the first shoots of vegetables eaten in the seedling stage, of which there is a considerable variety. The Chinese traditionally used MUNG and SOYBEANS (*Vigna radiata* and *Glycine max*); other suitable legumes include the ADZUKI BEAN (*Vigna angularis*), a small-seeded variety of BROAD BEAN (*Vicia faba*), known as SILK BEAN, ALFALFA (*Medicago sativa*), LENTILS (*Lens culinaris*), many kinds of PEA (*Pisum sativum*), ranging from normal GARDEN PEAS to RED-COATED PEAS and YELLOW FODDER PEAS, and the herb FENUGREEK (*Trigonella foenum-graecum*). Several cruciferous plants can be used, including most brassicas, especially CHINESE CABBAGE, SPINACH MUSTARDS, mild-flavored TURNIP, ASIAN MUSTARDS, RADISH (*Raphanus sativus*), and the familiar

MUSTARD AND CRESS. Other candidates include *Perilla frutescens*, WATER PEPPER (*Persicaria hydropiper*) and its relative BUCKWHEAT (*Polygonum fagopyrum*). ONIONS and LEEKS (*Allium* species) and grains of the grass family, including BARLEY (*Hordeum vulgare*) and RYE (*Secale cereale*) may also be used.

There are two kinds of sprouted seeds: seed sprouts which are grown in the dark and used between germination and the first signs of seed leaves, such as those of most beans; seedling sprouts which are allowed to grow into seedlings in the light and are green, for example, mustard and cress. The easiest domestic method of growing seed sprouts is in a jam jar, with the lid replaced by a fine mesh cover held in place by an elastic band. A dessertspoonful of seed—which will expand to 7 or 10 times its bulk when sprouted—is placed at the bottom; it should be rinsed thoroughly by shaking in water and straining well. The lid is secured, and each morning and evening the jar is filled with tepid water, then shaken and drained. A temperature of 55–75°F (13–24°C) must be maintained; sprouting is slower at the lower temperatures but the quality of sprouts is better.

Seed sprouts are usually boiled, steamed or stir-fried, or added to soup, but they can be eaten raw in salads, as are most seedling sprouts when green. Some leguminous seed sprouts, such as those of broad beans, contain toxins that may be harmful if consumed raw in quantity; cooking greatly lessens the toxicity. Ensure that seeds purchased have not been treated with pesticide for sowing outdoors. See *cress, mustard*.

spud a weeding tool with a narrow chisel-shaped blade, which is either straight, as in a thistle spud, or made with a hooklike projection on one side for extracting severed weeds. It may be long- or short-handled.

spur (1) a tubular or saclike basal extension of the perianth, generally projecting backward and nectariferous; (2) a short branch or branchlet, bearing whorls of leaves and fascicled flowers and fruits from closely spaced nodes; often a short shoot terminating in a fruit bud, which may branch to form a

long, pointed "spur"

Larkspur flower

multiple spur or spur system. Some cultivars of apple produce fruit spurs freely at the expense of lateral growths, and pears similarly.

spurred calcarate, furnished with a spur or spurs.

squamate, squamose, squamous covered with scales.

squamulose covered or furnished with small scales.

squarrose rough or hostile as a result of the outward projection of scales, prickles or bracts with reflexed tips perpendicular to the axis; also describes parts spreading sharply at right angles from a common axis.

squash see *pumpkin*.

squirrels (*Sciurus* species) arboreal rodents, of which only the gray squirrel (*S. carolinensis*) of North America, subsequently introduced into Europe, is likely to be a pest in gardens, especially those adjoining woodland. They may make holes in lawns, attack hanging baskets, dig and eat various bulbs, such as those of crocuses, lilies and tulips, attack nuts and fruits, eat the young shoots of various trees and strip bark, especially on beech and sycamore. Commercial control measures are not appropriate in gardens. Fruit cages help to deter attacks on fruits. Dormant bulbs can be protected by wire netting, laid over the soil surface and then removed once the bulb shoots break through. See *gophers*.

Stachys (Greek word for spike, used by Dioscorides in compound words descriptive of flowering spikes). Labiatae. Widespread, especially in temperate

S

zones and the Eastern Hemisphere; also Australasia and tropical/subtropical mountains. BETONY, HEDGE NETTLE, WOUNDWORT. Some 300 species herbs, subshrubs or shrubs, usually hairy and with 2-lipped flowers whorled in erect spikes in summer. Fully hardy and among the most tolerant of silver-leaved plants, especially suitable for low edging. It is easily grown in well-drained soil in full sun. Propagate by division.

S. byzantina (syn. *S. lanata, S. olympica*); LAMB'S TONGUE, WOOLLY BETONY, LAMB'S TAILS, LAMB'S EARS; Caucasus to Iran; low-growing, perennial, densely white-woolly; leaves thick, 1¼–4 in (3–10 cm), narrowed at base, oblong to elliptic; flowering stem erect, 8–36 in (20–90 cm), flowers ⅝–1 in (15–25 mm), purple or pink; includes 'Big Ears', with large, gray leaves, 'Cotton Ball', with fine foliage and no flowers, 'Primrose Heron', with bright gold leaves in spring, 'Silver Carpet', low, with gray, woolly leaves and flowers absent, and 'Striped Phantom', with leaves broadly striped cream.

Stachyurus (from Greek *stachys*, a spike, and *oura*, tail, referring to the shape of the racemes). Stachyuraceae. E Asia, Himalaya. 10 species, deciduous shrubs or small trees with small, campanulate to rounded flowers in narrow, drooping racemes appearing before the leaves in early spring. Both are hardy to about 5°F (–15°C), lower with shelter. Grow in deep, fertile, well-drained leafy soil, in sun or light, dappled shade, with shelter from cold drying winds. Humus-rich acidic soil is preferred, although *Stachyurus* will tolerate some lime. Propagate by fresh seed, by layering or by heeled semiripe cuttings in a closed case or under mist with gentle bottom heat.

S. chinensis China; to 8 ft (2.5 m); leaves 1¼–6 in (3–15 cm), ovate to oblong, crenate; racemes 2–4 in (5–10 cm), flowers pale yellow, more spreading than in *S. praecox* and opening later; 'Magpie': leaves gray-green above, spotted pale green or pink, and with an irregular ivory edge; *S. praecox* Japan; to 6½ ft (2 m); leaves to 5½ in (14 cm), ovate to broadly lanceolate, serrate; racemes 2–3 in (5–8 cm), flowers to ⅜ in (8 mm), yellow.

stage, staging (1) see *bench, benching*. (2) a table or trestle on which exhibits are arranged at a flower show.

stag-headed describing trees suffering from a condition in which the ends of branches die, leaving leafless, woody projections beyond the leafy crown. The condition may be a symptom of disease, poor root condition or old age.

staking the provision of vertical stakes or poles to which the single stem of a plant is secured for support; used more generally for the provision of diverse plant supports. Except in situations of extreme exposure to wind, or on sites prone to vandalism, most trees

Staking
A short stake (with a buckle-and-spacer tie) suits most young trees best. When planting a container-grown tree, the stake can be driven in at an angle, avoiding the rootball.

require staking, at most, only for the period after planting when a specimen is establishing. When stakes are left for more than about 18 months or, in the case of large specimens or mature transplants, 30 months, trees may become weaker and less supple in roots and stem than when not staked. Single stakes should preferably be inserted before planting, on the windward side of the stem, and with the tree secured with ties that do not chafe and which can be adjusted as girth expansion occurs to avoid constriction. See *tree ties*. For most trees, short single stakes are advisable; in some circumstances, however, support may be desirable up to the head of the tree and this can be achieved with a single tall stake, two parallel stakes with a cross member or by guying branches to three short stakes.

Stakes should be driven into the ground to no less than one quarter of their length. Trained fruit trees, such as cordons, fans and espaliers, require stake provision for longer periods of their life to aid development of tree structure.

Herbaceous plants, such as delphiniums, may require individual spikes to be staked, while other plants can be contained by inserting three stakes at regular intervals around the plant's circumference and holding growths in with a soft string tie (commercial metal hoop supports serve the same purpose). Twiggy sticks are suitable for many clump-forming herbaceous plants. Whatever type of staking is used, it should be installed as early as possible, and with the goal of becoming unobtrusive. Careful choice of herbaceous plants will greatly reduce the need for staking.

Ornamental pot plants, such as *Stephanotis*, *Jasminum*, and *Hedera*, can be attractively staked with a tripod of canes or on hoops. For small pot plants, split canes and raffia ties are best; for large flowering specimens of chrysanthemums, bamboo canes are necessary.

In vegetable gardens, maximum yield from peas and beans is achieved with rows that are supported in some way. Although netting is effective, twiggy pea sticks and coppiced bean rods are visually pleasing. Climbing beans can be trained up sticks or bamboo canes, arranged in parallel rows, with opposing sticks or canes tied together near their tops and a line of horizontal canes placed along the points of contact, linking all pairs. An alternative method of staking involves drawing together the tops of four stakes set out in a square, to form a wigwam. Vegetable crops such as tomatoes and Brussels sprouts benefit from staking.

stale seedbed see *seedbed*.

stamen the male floral organ, bearing an anther, generally on a filament, and producing pollen.

staminate of the male; a unisexual, male flower, bearing stamens and no functional pistils.

staminode a sterile stamen or sta-
menlike structure, either rudimentary
or modified and petal-like.

standard (1) a plant grown with a
bare stem or leg surmounted by a head
of branches. The length of stem varies
according to species grown, from 6½ ft
(2 m) for a standard fruit or ornamental tree to 3¼–4¼ ft (1–1.3 m) for
plants such as a standard rose or fuchsia. A half standard tree has a leg
about 3¼ ft (1 m) high. (2) the large,
uppermost petal in flowers of plants
belonging to the Leguminosae subfamily Papilionoideae. (3) an erect or
ascending unit of the inner whorl of
an *Iris* flower. (4) A plant specimen
which serves as the basis for naming
and describing a new cultivar.

standing ground a site on which
plants in containers are kept to harden
off or grow on before planting out or
moving into a display greenhouse.
Standing grounds usually take the
form of beds covered with gravel,
sand, weathered ashes or special
types of irrigation matting.

stand out, stand down to place
newly containerized plants on to a
standing ground, bed or greenhouse
bench on which they are to grow on.

Stanhopea (for the Earl of Stanhope,
president of the London Medico-
Botanical Society 1829–1837). Orchidaceae. C and S America. 55 species,
epiphytic evergreen perennial herbs.
The pseudobulbs are clumped and
flask-shaped, each bearing one or two,
lanceolate to elliptic leaves. Produced
in spring and summer in strongly pendulous racemes, the flowers are large,
thickly waxy, richly scented and short-
lived. They consist of reflexed, wavy
and curling, ovate to lanceolate tepals
and a downward-pointing, fleshy lip,
complex in structure and heavily
marked. The large column arches forward over the lip. Suitable for the cool
or intermediate house (minimum temperature 50°F/10°C). Plant in wooden
baskets, lined with sphagnum and filled
with a coarse bark mix with added leaf
mold and dried manure. Inflorescences
tend to bury themselves and wither
where pots are used; baskets will permit

the racemes to escape. Water and
syringe freely when in growth and suspend in a humid, airy place in bright,
filtered light. Apply a weak foliar feed
every second week when in growth.
Once the new pseudobulbs are fully
developed, reduce water and temperature and remove all shading. Until the
emergence of new growths and roots,
water only to prevent excessive shrivelling. Propagate *Stanhopea* by division.
   S. eburnea (syn. *S. grandiflora*); Brazil,
Guyana, Venezuela, Trinidad, Colom-
bia; flowers to 6 × 4¾ in (15 × 12 cm),
waxy, ivory-white variously dotted
purple; *S. tigrina* Mexico to Brazil;
flowers large, to 8 in (20 cm) in diameter, deep yellow, heavily barred or
blotched purple-brown, strongly fragrant; *S. wardii* Venezuela to Peru,
Mexico to Panama; flowers are over-
poweringly scented of spice or chocolate, to 5½ in (14 cm) in diameter,
green-white to pale yellow or peach,
variously dotted red-purple, orange-
yellow at base.

Stapelia (named for J.B. von Stapel
(d. 1636), Amsterdam doctor and
author on the botanical works of
Theophrastus). Asclepiadaceae. South,
C and E Africa to E India. CARRION
FLOWER, STARFISH FLOWER. 99 species,
perennial herbs with clump-forming
and sprawling, succulent stems. These
are leafless and angled, the ridges flattened and coarsely toothed. Produced
at various times of year, the starfishlike
flowers are deeply 5-lobed. They are
malodorous, fleshy and rugose or
swollen with a lobed corona. Grow in a
cool greenhouse (minimum temperature 50°F/10°C), with low humidity,
direct sunlight from fall to spring and
bright, filtered light in the summer.
Plant in a loam-based medium high in
sand and grit. Keep more or less dry
from midfall to late winter; water sparingly at other times. Liquid feed with a
low-nitrogen fertilizer from late spring
to late summer. Increase by stem cuttings, layers and division.
   S. flavirostris Cape Province, Lesotho;
stem to 6½ (17 cm) × ¾–1¼ in (2–3
cm); flowers 5–6 in (13–16 cm) in
diameter, deeply cleft, tube short, flat,
lobes lanceolate, exterior pubescent,
interior dull purple-red, lower part
hairy with pale yellow or dull purple

lines, tips dull purple, margins with red
or white hairs; *S. gigantea* (syn. *S. nobilis*);
GIANT STAPELIA; South Africa to Tanzania; stem measures 6–8 (15–20 cm) ×
1¼ in (3 cm); flowers are very malodorous, 10–14 in (25–35 cm) in diameter,
flat to campanulate, tube short, dark
red, rugose, lobes deep, ovate-acuminate, attenuate, pale ocher-yellow with
minute crimson wrinkles, sparsely red-
pubescent, margins white-ciliate,
corona dark purple-brown. For *S. variegata*, see *Orbea variegata*.

Staphylea (from Greek *staphyle*, cluster, alluding to the arrangement of the
flowers). Staphyleaceae. North temperate regions. BLADDERNUT. 11 species,
hardy deciduous shrubs or small trees
with pinnate leaves and 5-petalled,
bell-shaped flowers in terminal panicles
in late spring. These give rise to thin-
walled, lobed and inflated capsules.
Hardy to at least 5°F (–15°C) and
tolerant of a range of soil types in
sun or part shade. Prune to restrict
size and shape, immediately after flowering; overgrown specimens can be
rejuvenated by cutting hard back in
winter. Sow ripe seed in fall in the cold
frame. Root softwood or greenwood
cuttings in summer.
   S. colchica Caucasus; shrub to 13 ft (4
m); flowers fragrant, to ⅝ in (1.5 cm),
in panicle 2–4 in (5–10 cm) long and
wide, white; *S. holocarpa* China; shrub to
16 ft (5 m) or tree to 33 ft (10 m); flowers ⅜ in (0.8 cm), rose in bud becoming pure white, in drooping axillary
panicles to 4 in (10 cm); includes var.
rosea, with rose flowers; *S. pinnata* BLAD-
DER-NUT; Europe, Asia Minor; shrub
to 16 ft (5 m); about ½ in (1 cm), in
panicles to 4¾ in (12 cm), white, sepals
tipped red.

Stauntonia (for Sir George Staunton
[1737–1801], Irish physician, diplomat,
and naturalist; he accompanied Lord
Macartney on his Embassy to China in
1793). Lardizabalaceae. E Asia (Burma
to Taiwan and Japan). 16 species, dioecious, evergreen, twining shrubs with
palmately compound leaves and, in
spring and summer, racemes of small,
cup-shaped flowers. These give rise to
fleshy berries. Hardy to 23°F (–5°C);
plant in a sheltered site and cultivate as
for *Akebia*. *S. hexaphylla* S Korea, Japan,

S

Ryukyu Islands; to 33 ft (10 m); leaflets 3–7, to 5½ in (14 cm), ovate to elliptic, dark green, glossy flowers to ¾ in (2 cm), white to ivory, with a violet tint, fragrant; fruit 1–2 in (2.5–5 cm), globose to ovoid, purple.

steckling a young plant of a root vegetable—for example, a beet or carrot; referring particularly to a transplant, such as those specially raised by late sowing for overwintering and seed production.

steeping (1) the practice of soaking seeds or corms with very hard coats before sowing or planting, to ensure rapid germination or sprouting; (2) the preparation of liquid manure by suspending a porous bag of animal manure in a large container of water.

stellate starlike; commonly refers to hairs with branches that radiate in a starlike manner from a common point.

stem and bulb eelworm (*Ditylenchus dipsaci*) a species of eelworm recorded on more than 450 plants, worldwide. Garden plants most frequently attacked by this eelworm are narcissus, hyacinths, tulips, scillas and snow-drops, and also strawberries, potatoes, onions and phlox. Stem and bulb eelworm exists in various biological races, each of which shows a preference for particular groups of plants, although some hosts are common to more than one race.

The adult eelworms are microscopic, slender, wormlike creatures that measure just over ⅟₁₆ in (1 mm) long. Damage to plants generally involves tissues becoming blistered or bloated, with a growth check leading to stunting, twisting of stems and leaves and distortion of flowers. On narcissus, for example, small pale yellow swellings known as "spickels" appear on the leaves, and if the bulb is cut transversely, concentric brown rings can be seen. On tulips, flowers typically bend over, with part of the bloom remaining green, and the foliage becomes ragged and tears easily. Onions infested with stem and bulb eelworm become soft, flabby and swollen in the neck region, a condition known as "onion bloat." On annual and perennial phlox, the

upper leaves become narrowed and crinkled and the stems brittle and stunted. See *eelworms, hot water treatment*.

stem rot a general term for disease affecting plant stems. There may not always be a clear distinction between a stem rot and other types of rot, such as collar rot, foot rot, leaf rot, and root rot, since the same disease organism may attack several different parts of the plant. Basal stem rot is sometimes used to describe a disease that originates from infection at soil level and spreads upward.

Stem-rooting
Many climbing plants, such as this ivy, produce aerial roots that give rise to new plants when stems are in contact with the soil.

stem-rooting applied to plants with stems that produce aerial roots, such as *Hydrangea petiolaris*, and to those with roots on subterranean stems, for example, some lilies.

Stenotaphrum (from Greek *stenos*, narrow, and *taphros*, trench, referring to the depressions in the raceme axis). Gramineae. New and Old World tropics. Some 7 species, annual or perennial grasses with creeping or ascending stems, rooting at nodes. The leaves are linear to oblong, with the blades held perpendicular to the stem and the broad sheaths compressed and overlapping. Used for lawns in the tropics and subtropics. In cooler regions, it is used as a cascading basket plant or as fast-spreading ground-cover in the warm greenhouse or in subtropical bedding. Grow in rich, moisture-retentive soil in sun. Propagate by plugs rooted in moist sand with bottom heat. *S. secundatum* BUFFALO GRASS, ST. AUGUSTINE GRASS; tropical America, W Africa, Pacific

Islands; stems creeping and rooting; leaves to 6 × ⅝ in (15 × 1.5 cm); 'Variegatum': leaves striped pale green and ivory.

Stephanandra (from Greek *stephanos*, crown, and *aner*, male, referring to the disposition of the persistent, numerous, short stamens in the shape of a crown). Rosaceae. E Asia. 4 species, deciduous shrubs, multi-stemmed and graceful with incised to serrate to shallow-lobed leaves, the veins conspicuous and impressed above. Small, star-shaped flowers are produced in corymbose panicles in late spring and early summer. Hardy to –4°F (–20°C). Grow in full sun or semi-shade, in well-drained but moisture-retentive soil; mulch with well-rotted organic matter annually. Prune after flowering to remove old and overcrowded branches; overgrown plants can be cut hard back almost to ground level in winter. Apply a general fertilizer in early spring. Propagate by division when dormant, or by softwood or semiripe cuttings in summer.

S. incisa (Japan, Korea, Taiwan; much-branched shrub to 8 ft (2.5 m); branchlets slender, flexuous, terete; leaves to 2 in (5 cm), ovate or triangular, apex caudate to acute, base cordate, lobes incised or serrate, pilose to glabrescent, pale green beneath; flowers cream-white or yellow, in short, terminal racemes; 'Crispa': dwarf, mound-forming, with arching branches and small, crinkled, fernlike leaves, tinted maroon in fall);

S. tanakae Japan; shrub to 6½ ft (2 m); shoots slender, arching, smooth, and branchlets terete or angled; leaves to 3½ in (9 cm), ovate, shallowly 3- to several-lobed, apex caudate to acuminate, base subcordate, orange and scarlet or bright yellow in fall, scabrous, biserrate, glabrous above, somewhat pubescent on veins beneath; flowers off-white in terminal panicles to 4 in (10 cm).

Stephanotis (from Greek *stephanotis*, a name given to the myrtle used in Ancient Greece for making crowns or garlands (a use to which these flowers are put); equally, the name here derives from *stephanos*, crown, and *otos*, ear, referring to the auricled staminal

S

corona). Asclepiadaceae. Old World tropics. 5 species, twining, glabrous, evergreen shrubs with leathery leaves and large, white, waxy flowers in umbel-like axillary cymes. They are salverform to funnelform, the tube cylindrical, often slightly inflated at base, the limb with 5 spreading lobes. Train on trellis or wire hoops. Grow in a freely draining medium, fertile, moisture-retentive, well-aerated and rich in organic matter. Maintain a minimum temperature of 59°F (15°C) and high humidity. Admit bright filtered light. Water plentifully and feed fortnightly with dilute liquid feed when in full growth, misting frequently in warm weather. In winter keep just moist. Blooms are carried on young shoots, so prune in winter before growth commences, thinning out congested shoots. Propagate by seed, layering or semiripe cuttings. *S. floribunda* FLORADORA, MADAGASCAR JASMINE, BRIDAL WREATH, CHAPLET FLOWER, WAX FLOWER; Madagascar; stems to 13 ft (4 m); leaves to 6 in (15 cm), oval to oblong, dark green; flowers highly fragrant, to 2½ in (6 cm), pure white to ivory.

sterile of sex organs, not producing viable seed and nonfunctional, barren; of shoots and branches, not bearing flowers; of plants, without functional sex organs, or not producing fruit.

Sternbergia (for Count Kaspar Moritz von Sternberg of Prague [1761–1838], botanist, author of *Revisio Saxifragum*, 1819). Amaryllidaceae. Turkey, west to Spain and east to Kashmir. AUTUMN DAFFODIL. 8 species of perennial, bulbous herbs with narrow leaves borne with or after flowers. The flowers are funnel- to goblet-shaped with six segments; they are solitary and scapose, the scapes sometimes below ground at flowering time. With the exception of the winter and spring-flowering *S. fischeriana* and *S. candida*, these are fall-flowering bulbs. *S. lutea* and *S. sicula* are the most reliable species for cultivation in the open, well-suited for a rock garden or border front, in sunny positions and in well-drained soil. All are hardy but dislike wet winter conditions. Plant deeply in full sun on sharply draining soil. Allow to dry out in summer. Propagate by division of offsets when dormant, or from ripe seed.

S. candida SW Turkey; like *S. fischeriana*, but scape 4¾–8 in (12–20 cm); perianth segments 1¾–2 (4.3–5 cm) × ⅜–¾ in (0.9–1.8 cm), obovate, rounded apex, white; flowering winter to spring; *S. clusiana* (syn. *S. macrantha*); Turkey, Jordan, Israel, Iran; scape short, below ground at flowering; perianth segments 1½–3 (3.7–7.5 cm) × ½–4¾ in (1.1–3.3 cm), obovate to oblanceolate, bright yellow to yellow-green; fall-flowering; *S. colchiciflora* SE Spain, Italy, west to Iran; scape below ground at flowering; perianth segments ¾–1½ (2–3.4 cm) × ⅛–½ in (0.4–1.2 cm), linear, pale yellow; fall-flowering; *S. fischeriana* Caucasus to Kashmir; scape 1¼–6 in (3–15 cm); perianth segments ¾–1½ (2–3.5 cm) × ¼–⅜ in (0.5–0.8 cm), oblanceolate, bright yellow; spring-flowering; *S. lutea* GOLDEN CROCUS; Spain to Iran and C Asia; scape 1–8 in (2.5–20 cm); perianth segments 1¼–2¼ (3–5.5 cm) × ½–¾ in (1–2 cm), oblanceolate to obovate, deep yellow; fall-flowering; *S. sicula* (syn. *S. lutea*) subsp. *sicula*, *S. lutea* var. *gracea*, *S. lutea* var. *angustifolia*; Italy, Greece, Aegean Islands, W Turkey; similar to *S. lutea*; scape to 2¾ in (7 cm); perianth segments ¾–1½ (2–3.4 cm) × ⅛–½ in (0.4–1.2 cm), yellow; fall-flowering.

Stewartia (for John Stuart, Earl of Bute [1713–1792]). Theaceae. Eastern N America, E Asia. 9 species, deciduous trees and shrubs with colorful, exfoliating bark, fine fall color and large flowers in summer. These consist of five to eight, spreading, silken petals with a boss of numerous stamens. The genus is also spelt *Stuartia*. Handsome specimens for the woodland garden, or for lawns and shrubberies in cool shady sites. They offer an exceptionally long season of interest, displaying their beautiful branchwork and peeling bark in winter, creamy flowers over long periods in mid- to late summer, and attractive foliage from spring through to the wine reds and fiery orange before leaf fall in fall. Most species tolerate temperatures to 5°F (–15°C). Grow in deep, humus-rich soil that is nonalkaline and moist but not boggy, ensuring a cool root run and light shade at least from the hottest summer sun. Propagate by seed sown fresh in fall in an outdoor seedbed; seed may not germinate until the second spring, since breaking of dormancy requires some months of warmth followed by three months at temperatures of about 41°F (5°C). Take softwood cuttings in summer or heeled semiripe cuttings in late summer; root these in a sandy propagating mix in the cold frame. Alternatively, increase by simple layering.

S. malacodendron SILKY CAMELLIA; SE US; shrub or small tree to 16 ft (5 m); flowers to 4 in (10 cm) in diameter, petals white, fringed, filaments purple, anthers blue-gray; *S. ovata* MOUNTAIN STEWARTIA; SE US; shrub to 16 ft (5 m); flowers 2½–3 in (6–8 cm) across, cup-shaped, petals creamy white, wavy-edged, one often deformed, filaments yellow-white, anthers white, orange or tinted purple; var. *grandiflora*: flowers to 4¾ in (12 cm) in diameter with purple filaments and orange anthers; *S. pseudocamellia* JAPANESE STEWARTIA; Japan; tree to 66 ft (20 m), usually a shrub to 13 ft (4 m) in cultivation; flowers 2–2½ in (5–6 cm) in diameter, broadly cup-shaped, petals white, suborbicular, concave with jagged edges, filaments white, anthers orange-yellow; *S. sinensis* China; tree to 33 ft (10 m); flowers 1½–2 in (4–5 cm) in diameter, cup-shaped, fragrant, petals broadly ovate, white, anthers yellow.

stigma the apical unit of a pistil that receives the pollen and normally differs in texture from the rest of the style.

stigmatose having especially well-developed or conspicuous stigmas.

stilt roots the oblique adventitious support roots of the mangrove, screw pine and other woody plants of warm coastal and flooded places.

stimulus movements see *geotropism*, *haptonasty*, *phototropism*, *sensitive*.

Stipa (from Latin *stipa*, tow or oakum, from the feathery inflorescences). Gramineae. Temperate regions. FEATHER GRASS, SPEAR GRASS, NEEDLE GRASS. Some 300 species, perennial grasses with clumps of short or tall

S

culms, slender leaves and, in summer, large, finely branched panicles. These are large grasses, making specimen features in herbaceous borders and grass gardens. Four are particularly noteworthy: *S. arundinacea*, an Australasian native, acquires rusty orange and yellow-brown leaf tints at the end of the season, lasting well into winter; *S. calamagrostis* carries windswept plumes high above its foliage, late into the year; *S. gigantea* produces spectacular open heads of long-awned, shimmering spikelets; the awns of *S. pennata* are longer still and feathery. They are hardy to at least 5°F (–15°C). European species sometimes suffer in intensely hot, humid summers. They prefer full sun, a rather dry situation, and gritty soil. *S. arundinacea* needs a moist, slightly acidic and porous soil and will grow in sun or partial shade. Propagate by seed or division.

S. arundinacea PHEASANT'S TAIL GRASS, NEW ZEALAND WIND GRASS; E Australia, New Zealand; to 5 ft (1.5 m), culms slender, clumped, upright or arching; leaves to 12 × ¼ in (30 × 0.6 cm), dark bronze-green, acquiring orange-red to rusty spots and streaks often with black eyelike dots from late summer through winter; panicle pendent; spikelets sparse, tinged purple, awns to ⅜ in (8 mm); *S. calamagrostis* (syn. *Achnatherum calamagrostis*); SILVER SPIKE GRASS; C and S Europe; to 48 in (120 cm), culms clumped, robust; leaves to 12 × ¼ in (30 × 0.5 cm), attenuate; panicle to 32 in (80 cm), loose, appearing one-sided and windswept, feathery; spikelets tinged purple, awns to ½ in (1 cm), straight or curved; *S. gigantea* GIANT FEATHER GRASS; C and S Spain, Portugal, NW Africa; to 100 in (250 cm), culms short or absent; leaves to 28 × ⅛ in (70 × 0.3 cm), involute when dry, smooth to slightly rough; panicle to 20 in (50 cm), very long-stalked, loose, open and arching, held high above foliage, very spectacular; spikelets shimmering straw-yellow, awns to 4¾ in (12 cm), rough; *S. pennata* EUROPEAN FEATHER GRASS; S and C Europe to Himalaya; to 24 in (60 cm), culms short or absent; leaves erect to weeping in a tight bunch, to 24 × ¼ in (60 × 0.6 cm), smooth, glabrous above; panicle very loose, rather sparse, spikelets yellow, awn to 11 in (28 cm), plumose.

stipe the stalk of a pistil or a similar small organ; also, the petiole of a fern or palm frond.

stipel, stipella, stipellae the secondary stipule of a compound leaf, i.e. at the base of a leaflet or petiolule.

stipitate provided with, or borne on, a stipe or small stalk or stalklike base.

stipulate possessing stipules.

stipule a leafy or bractlike appendage at the base of a petiole, usually occurring in pairs and soon shed.

stock (1) a group of mother plants, usually selected and maintained for particular qualities, such as virus freedom (hence *certified stock*), ease of propagation, or flower production; (2) see *rootstock*.

stock plant a plant maintained as a source of propagating material.

Stokesia (for the English botanist Jonathon Stokes, MD [1755–1831]). Compositae. SE US. STOKES' ASTER. 1 species, *S. laevis* (syn. *S. cyanea*), an erect, evergreen perennial herb to 3¼ ft (1 m). To 8 in (20 cm) long and borne in basal rosettes, the leaves are elliptic to lanceolate, dark green and entire or spiny toward the base. Daisylike flower heads to 4 in (10 cm) across appear in summer, consisting of white, yellow to pale lavender to deep indigo florets. Cultivars include forms with flower heads of varying size, with colors ranging from white 'Alba', 'Silver Moon') and yellow to blue (the deep blue of 'Blue Danube' and the deep dark blue of 'Wyoming'), lilac 'Blue Star') and purple; some are early-flowering. Where winter temperatures fall as low as –4 to –13°F (–20 to –25°C), mulch with straw or dry bracken litter. Grow *Stokesia* in a warm, sunny position in light, fertile and freely draining soil. Propagate by seed during fall, by division in spring, or from root cuttings in late winter.

stolon an above-ground stem, either aerial or procumbent, that gives rise to new plants at its tip or at intermediate nodes.

stoloniferous producing stolons.

stoloniform resembling a stolon.

stoma (plural stomata) an aperture or pore in the epidermis of a leaf or stem, allowing gaseous exchange.

stomach poison an insecticide which, in order to be effective, must be ingested by an insect feeding upon treated plant parts.

stone the seed(s) with surrounding hardened endocarp in a drupe.

stone fruits a group name for fruits such as apricot, cherry, peach, and plum that contain a hard stone, or endocarp, enclosing and protecting the seed.

stoning the period of grape development when the seeds start to harden.

stony pit a disease of pears, probably caused by a virus, in which leaves become discolored and fruits are deformed with deep irregular pits and internal stony pockets. Inedibility and premature drop result. The disease is also known as dimpling.

Stool (Cornus sericea 'Flaviramea')
Some species of *Cornus, Salix, Rubus, Eucalyptus,* and *Berberis* are stooled to promote growth of ornamental stems or foliage.

stool a group of shoots emerging from the base of a single plant. The term is applied to plants used for propagation, such as chrysanthemums, and to those cut back to produce attractive young woody shoots, for example, *Cornus alba* cultivars.

stooling see *coppicing, layering.*

stopping see *break, pinching*.

storage organ a swollen stem or root, usually subterranean, in which food and moisture are stored, for example, a parsnip root, crocus corm, or dahlia tuber.

storage rot decay in stored plant produce caused by microorganisms, especially bacteria and fungi. Starchy root crops, fruits, vegetables, bulbs and corms have a high moisture content and are therefore particularly susceptible. SOFT ROT BACTERIA (*Erwinia* species) are common on vegetables, while fungi are the most frequent cause of damage to fruits and root crops. Initial infection may occur while the plant is still growing, either through mechanical damage during harvest and transit, or through wounds at the point of attachment to the parent plant. Exposure to temperature extremes can predispose plants to rotting. Often initial infection by a specific pathogen allows invasion by nonspecific organisms, such as *Botrytis*, *Fusarium* and *Rhizopus*, all of which develop rapidly in storage.

Prevention involves controlling pests and diseases on growing crops, choosing correct harvest times, careful handling at all stages and the provision of correct storage conditions.

stove house, stove a greenhouse where the temperature minimum is maintained at 64°F (18°C), used for the cultivation of tropical plants. It is also known as a hot house or warm house.

straight fertilizer a fertilizer that contains one major plant nutrient, such as sulfate of potash; cf. *compound fertilizer*.

strain in traditional usage, a maintained selection of a plant, especially refers to selections raised from seed. The term is invalid under the International Code of Nomenclature for Cultivated Plants, being considered too imprecise.

straining bolt a device used to maintain tension in wires on fences, and on post and wire structures used for supporting plants, especially fruits. A simple form is the threaded bolt which has a looped head to which the wire is fixed by twisting; the bolt is progressively eased through a narrow hole made in the end post by the tightening of a nut, which tensions the wire against its other, fixed, end.

stramineous strawlike, in color, texture or shape.

strangles a form of heat injury of vegetables caused by contact with hot soil.

stratification see *seeds* and *seed sowing*.

straw the dry stalks of barley, wheat, and oats, which can prove beneficial to the garden in several ways. As a soil improver, straw is best chopped, wetted, and added in small amounts to the compost pile, or composted separately by wetting and adding an activator to loose layers. Provided an ample dressing of nitrogen fertilizer is applied, it may be dug into the soil directly. In either of these forms of application, straw is a useful conditioner improving soil structure and water- and nutrient-holding. Used in a dry, untreated form it is also valuable for protecting plants from frost damage, for vegetable clamping, and as a ground mulch. Where specially treated, it is a useful ingredient of growing media; and it has useful effects in controlling algal growth in large ponds. See *blanketweed, straw bale culture*.

straw bale culture a specialized system for growing tomatoes, cucumbers and peppers in a greenhouse. It is a suitable means of overcoming soil-borne disease infection, but is more demanding of initial effort than ring, pot, or growing-bag culture. Straw bales are placed end to end on a plastic sheet laid over the greenhouse border soil and then drenched with water for a period of three weeks at a minimum temperature of 55°F (13°C). High nitrogen fertilizer, such as ammonium nitrate with lime is applied at a rate of 24 oz (680 g) per bale and watered in. A further nitrogenous dressing is applied four days later at a rate of 16 oz (450 g) per bale, and again, after another four days, at a rate of 12 oz (340 g), together with 24 oz (680 g) of a general fertilizer. The fermenting bales are allowed to cool before the addition of a topping of a general compost, into which the crop is planted.

strawberry (*Fragaria × ananassa*) a herbaceous and comparatively short-term crop, which is the quickest fruit to come into bearing after planting. The large-fruited hybrids grown today are of relatively recent origin. Previously, over many centuries, fruits of a few native European species were collected from the wild for eating, including the WILD STRAWBERRY (*F. vesca*), the ALPINE STRAWBERRY (*F. vesca* var. *semperflorens*), *F.moschata* and *F.viridis*.

Modern cultivars are the progeny of very variable species, so that hybrids can be found to suit a wide range of conditions, from the equator to the Arctic Circle, and from sea level to about 10,000 ft (3,000 m). Selection of cultivars with the right response to local day lengths and temperatures is the key to successful cultivation, whether on a large or small scale.

Plants are susceptible to very low temperatures in winters of cool temperate climates and may need protection. Flowers are susceptible to injury by spring frosts, and windy conditions are known to reduce growth, so a sunny sheltered site is best for strawberries. Infection by virus diseases is a serious problem and it is therefore essential to select and plant healthy stock, which has been certified following expert inspection.

Strawberries may be planted in either fall or spring, but spring is preferable in areas with very cold winters. If runners can be obtained for late summer planting, a crop can be taken in the first year after planting; delays reduce the eventual yield, and with later planting flowers are removed in the first season to allow the plant to build up for the following year. Fall-fruiting cultivars can be picked in their first season after planting, although they are generally deblossomed until just after midsummer. Large-fruited cultivars start to initiate flowers in day lengths of about ten hours, continuing until they become dormant, after which a chilling period is needed before flowering when the temperature

S

rises; an ideal time for planting these cultivars in the UK is the first week in August. With everbearers, flowers are initiated at days longer than 12 hours, but once in a flowering phase, flower development will continue even in short days of less than 8 hours. Remontants initiate flowers in short days and crop in summer after fall or spring planting; they then have the ability to produce a second crop in fall. Almost all strawberry cultivars are self-fertile.

Plant in rows 30–36 in (75–90 cm) apart, with individual plants spaced 12–18 in (30–45 cm) apart. Crowns must be positioned at soil level: if placed above it, the roots will dry out, and if placed below, the plants may rot. Runners on large-fruited cultivars are usually removed as they appear, but if left and laid into the row, then a 'matted row' develops, producing a greater number of fruits per unit area, but ones that are smaller and more susceptible to rotting.

Planting on ridges is a satisfactory system, which encourages good establishment by reason of early-warming and good drainage. Planting through slits in a thin-gauge black-polyethylene ground mulch is of further temperature benefit and serves to conserve moisture and suppress weeds; it is advisable to fit low-level irrigation lines beneath the polyethylene, along each row of plants. A polyethylene mulch will also help to keep fruits clean of soil; in the UK, a straw mulch is traditionally used for this purpose, being placed around the plants as the fruits start to swell. Both types of mulch may encourage slugs and this should be borne in mind.

Strawberries need adequate water at three particular stages: after planting, at the end of flowering, and during fruit swelling. In dry conditions, irrigate every seven days to make up for any shortfall in rain. Low level application is advisable since overhead watering encourages fruit rots.

Fruit is picked with the calyx attached, using the thumbnail to sever the stalk, without touching the fruit, which is easily marked by any pressure. In the garden, keep picked fruits in the shade and use as soon as possible.

Strawberries are less suitable for freezing than other soft fruits since they collapse on thawing.

Strawberry

Unless a matted bed is required, runners should be cut off after cropping: removal of runners promotes a multi-crowned plant. Immediately after harvesting is complete, the old leaves are cut off at about 4 in (10 cm) above ground level. They are then removed and burnt in order to destroy pathogens and allow new growth to develop in healthy conditions. This treatment should not be applied to remontant cultivars, from which only the oldest leaves should be removed by hand.

Strawberries propagate naturally by runners. These are produced in quantity in late summer, and, if healthy, may be used for new plantations. However, because of the susceptibility to virus infection, it is generally preferable to buy in plants certified as virus-tested.

Fruiting can be advanced by covering plants with cloches or low plastic tunnels or by growing them in greenhouses. All of these methods give sufficient protection from low temperature in spring encouraging early ripening. One-year-old plants are most suitable since they tend to crop earlier anyway and are less leafy for the limited space under covers. July planting from cold-stored runners guarantees an even earlier crop.

Strawberry plants should be replaced more frequently than those of other soft fruits, in pursuit of fruit quality and the prevention of pest and disease build up. Cultivars with very large fruits and red flesh include 'Hapil' and 'Pegasus' (both midseason). Older English cultivars include the Cambridge series, of which 'Cambridge Favourite' is a reliable midseason cropper. 'Honeoye' is a US-raised early cultivar of good performance. Among the everbearers, 'Aromel' is notably good in Europe.

Possible problems: aphids, eelworm, red spider mite, slugs; gray mold, powdery mildew, virus.

strawberry barrel, strawberry pot a wooden or plastic barrel or earthenware pot, with many planting holes in its sides, into which strawberry plants are set for cropping in restricted areas or on patios.

streak a condition most usually caused by virus infection, in which plant stems, leaves and occasionally fruits show discolored streaks and sometimes sunken spots. In tomatoes, the condition is often due to a combination of virus disease and growing conditions; in healthy plants, it may be caused by magnesium or potash deficiency.

Strelitzia (for Charlotte of Mecklenburg Strelitz [1744–1818], queen to George III). Strelitziaceae. South Africa. BIRD OF PARADISE. 4 species, large or giant perennial, evergreen herbs, more or less stemless and clump-forming or bearing multiple, stout, unbranched stems. The leaves are large, paddle-shaped and 2-ranked. The inflorescence is axillary and long- or short-stalked, the flowers emerging in succession along the upper edge of waxy, rigid beak or boatlike spathes. Each flower consists of three lanceolate, colorful calyx segments and two corolla lobes; the lobes are arrow-shaped and paired to form a projecting 'tongue' enclosing the stamens and style.

In tropical and subtropical areas, plant out into rich deep, loamy soil in full sun, incorporating organic matter at planting to ensure against drying of the root zone. Under glass, pot in a high-fertility loam-based mix, moisture-retentive but well-drained. If planted directly into greenhouse borders, *Strelitzia* will thrive and flower more freely. Water plentifully during summer, providing shade against the fiercest sun and ventilating whenever temperatures rise above 68°F (20°C). Feed pot-grown plants with a dilute liquid fertilizer fortnightly when in growth. In winter, water sparingly and maintain a minimum temperature of 50°F (10°C). Plants may also be grown

S

in the home, given large containers, good light and moderate humidity. Container-grown plants benefit from being placed outdoors on sheltered terraces in summer. Propagate by seed sown in a moist, sandy medium at 68°F (20°C) in spring. Increase also by removal of rooted offsets.

S. × *kewensis* (*S. alba* × *S. reginae*); garden origin; trunk to 5 ft (1.5 m) or absent; spathe long-stalked, calyx pale yellow, corolla blue, lilac-pink at base; *S. nicolai* Natal, NE Cape; stems to 33 ft (10 m), stout, clumped; leaf blades to 6½ ft × 32 in (2 × 0.8 m), oblong or ovate-oblong, petiole to 6½ ft (2 m); inflorescence short-stalked, spathes chestnut-red, pruinose, 16–18 in (40–45 cm), calyx 8 in (20 cm), white; corolla purple-blue, very gummy; *S. reginae* BIRD OF PARADISE, CRANE FLOWER; South Africa; more or less stemless; leaf blades 10–39 (25–100 cm) × 4–12 in (10–30 cm), glaucescent, oblong-lanceolate, petiole, about 3¼ ft (1 m); inflorescence long-stalked, equalling leaves, spathe about 4¾ in (12 cm), green tinted purple and orange, glaucous, calyx to 4 in (10 cm), orange, corolla dark; cultivars include 'Humilis', dwarf (to 32 in/80 cm), closely clump-forming, with ovate-oblong, short-petioled leaves and disproportionately large, short-stalked flowers; 'Kirstenbosch Gold', with pale orange-gold flowers; 'Rutilans', with leaves with red or purple midrib, and brilliantly colored flowers; var. *juncea*, with leaf blades absent or much reduced—the plant appearing spiky and rushlike.

Streptocarpus (from Greek *streptos*, twisted, and *karpos*, fruit). Gesneriaceae. Tropical, C and E Africa, Madagascar, Thailand, SW China to East Indies. CAPE PRIMROSE. 130 species, annual, perennial or monocarpic herbs, rarely subshrubs, often hairy. They range widely in habit—some are shrubby with small, rather fleshy leaves; others may produce a clump of basal, oblong to oblanceolate leaves, or one massive and wrinkled leaf only. Tubular and 2-lipped, the flowers are produced throughout the year in branched cymes. Provide a minimum temperature of 59°F (15°C), moderate to high humidity, shade from direct sunlight

and protection from drafts. Pot in a porous, soilless medium. Water and feed generously during the growing period, taking care not to wet the foliage. During cooler, resting periods, keep barely moist. Increase by seed, leaf cuttings and stem cuttings.

S. caulescens Tanzania, Kenya; perennial; stem upright, branched, fleshy, to 24 in (60 cm); leaves elliptic or ovate, softly hairy, to 2½ in (6.5 cm); flowers to ¾ in (2 cm) in diameter, violet or pale lilac; includes var. *pallescens*, with flowers violet, or striped violet on white; *S.* × *hybridus* a group of popular garden hybrids, in habit generally like *S. rexii*, with puckered, oblanceolate to oblong leaves and large, mauve-purple to rosy crimson flowers; 'Constant Nymph', with pale blue-mauve flowers with darker lines in throat; 'Merton Blue', with blue-mauve flowers with a white throat with yellow patch; 'Eira', with small, semidouble to double, white flowers, tinged mauve on lower lip; 'Lisa', with shell-pink flowers with a white center; 'Nicola', with small, semi-double, deep pink flowers; 'Falling Stars', with small, numerous, sky-blue flowers; 'Wiesmoor', with trumpet-shaped, bright ruby flowers; *S. rexii* (South Africa; rosette- or clump-forming perennial; leaves obovate to strap-shaped, obtuse, to 12 in (30 cm), short-pubescent, bullate, wavy-crenate; inflorescence 1–2-flowered, rarely more, to 8 in (20 cm), flowers to 3 in (7.5 cm), white or pale mauve, palate and lower lip striped purple); *S. saxorum* (Kenya, Tanzania; perennial; stem low to prostrate, hairy, few-branched, fleshy; leaves opposite, elliptic to ovate, ⅝–1¼ in (1.5–3 cm), fleshy, hairy; flowers to 1½ in (3.5 cm), tube white, lobes pale lilac, carried in sparse axillary cymes; *S. wendlandii* South Africa; monocarpic and stemless; leaf solitary, to 30 × 24 in (75 × 60 cm), massive and somewhat pendulous, dark purple-green above, red-purple beneath, hairy, crenate, deeply puckered; inflorescence to 12 in (30 cm), arising from base of leaf, flowers many, ¾ × 1½ in (1.8 × 3.5 cm), flushed blue-purple, interior white, limb blue-purple with 2 deep purple patches on palate.

Streptosolen (from Greek *streptos* twisted, and *solon*, tube, referring to the

twisted corolla tube). Solanaceae. Colombia, Peru. 1 species, *S. jamesonii* MARMALADE BUSH, ORANGE BROWALLIA, FIREBUSH, an erect to weakly climbing or sprawling evergreen, hairy shrub, to 8 ft (2.5 m). The leaves are up to 2 in (5 cm) long and ovate to elliptic. Borne in spring and summer in terminal corymbs, the flowers are funnel-shaped with a long, yellow to orange and spirally twisted tube, to ¾ in (2 cm) long, and a 5-lobed, orange-red limb. Grow under intermediate greenhouse conditions (minimum temperature 45°F/7°C); conservatory plants may be trained to form standards or attractive specimen shrubs for patios during the summer months. Plant in a well-drained, high-fertility loam-based medium. Provide bright filtered light and medium humidity. Water moderately in summer, sparingly in winter. Feed established plants monthly with a dilute liquid fertilizer and ventilate when temperatures exceed 68°F (20°C). Propagate by heeled greenwood cuttings in a closed case with bottom heat in spring/summer.

stress any environmental factor impairing the normal functioning of plants. Drought, waterlogging, extreme cold or heat, unsuitable light conditions, salinity, and mechanical factors are counted among potential major stresses. Any of these can cause loss of plant performance or even death, and may also make plants more susceptible to pest and disease attack.

striate striped with fine longitudinal lines, grooves or ridges.

strig a single cluster of currants.

strigose covered with sharp, stiff, adpressed hairs.

strigulose minutely or finely strigose.

strike to cause a cutting to root, or to increase a plant by means of cuttings. A struck cutting is one that has formed roots.

stringfellowing severe root-pruning of a bare-root fruit tree prior to planting. A system developed in commercial practice, having been found to speed up planting, stimulate stronger roots and obviate the need for staking. Roots are pruned to ¾–2 in (2–5 cm) from the rootstock.

string trimmer see *spin trimmer*.

strip cropping a system of protected growing in which crops are grown in narrow beds or strips with pathways in between. It enables maximum use to be made of cloches and low polyethylene tunnels, since these can be moved from strip to strip during the year according to the development stage of the crops grown.

strobile, strobilus a cone, or dense conelike cluster of sporophylls.

strobiloid, strobiliform shaped like a cone, as in the closely bracteate inflorescence of some Acanthaceae.

Stromanthe (from Greek *stroma*, bed, and *anthos*, flower, describing the inflorescence). Marantaceae. C America to S Brazil. Some 15 species, evergreen perennial herbs. They resemble *Calathea* but bear their small flowers among brightly colored, waxy bracts. Cultivate as for *Calathea*.

S. *sanguinea* Brazil; leaves to 20 in (50 cm), elliptic-oblong, dark green above, purple-red beneath; inflorescence bracts red, calyx orange-red, corolla white.

Strombocactus (from Greek *strombos*, a spinning top, and *cactus*). Cactaceae. Mexico. 1 species, S. *disciformis*, a low-growing cactus with a disk- to turnip-shaped stem to 3 × 6½ in (8 × 17 cm). The tubercles are spiraled, rhomboid and pale gray-green, the spines weak, to ⅝ in (15 mm) and off-white with darker tips. The flowers are funnelform, 1¼ in (3 cm) long and pale yellow to almost white with a red throat. Provide a minimum temperature of 45°F (7°C) and plant in a gritty, neutral medium. Admit full sun and maintain low humidity. Keep dry in winter except for a light misting on warm days in late winter.

Strongylodon (from Greek *strongylos*, round, and *odous*, tooth, an allusion to the rounded teeth of the calyx). Leguminosae (Papilionoideae). SE Asia to Polynesia. Some 20 species, evergreen, twining shrubs with pendulous racemes of pealike flowers with long, sharp beaklike keels. Grow in light shade. Plant in tubs or greenhouse borders in well-drained, neutral to acidic soil, into which leaf mold and well-rotted farmyard manure have been incorporated. Water and syringe plentifully during the growing season (avoid wetting flowers); at other times, allow a slight drying between waterings to discourage continuous weak growth. It is essential to maintain a winter minimum of 59°F (15°C), and to train carefully (along wires, but not too near the glass) and prune lightly, as for young plants of *Wisteria*. Sow in high temperatures (81–86°F/27–30°C) in a closed case; seed is quick to germinate but slow to reach maturity. Air-layering and stem cuttings taken in early summer will usually produce better results.

S. *macrobotrys* JADE VINE, EMERALD CREEPER; Philippines; vigorous evergreen twining liane to 43 ft (13 m); leaves trifoliolate; raceme cylindrical, to 36 in (90 cm), flowers to 3 in (7.5 cm), waxy aquamarine to luminous jade green.

stub (1) the remnant of wood left after a tree shoot is cut back hard, or any short piece of cut or broken branch projecting from a main stem; (2) sometimes the stump of a tree left in the ground after felling. Stubbing out refers to the complete removal of a plant.

stump the base of a felled or fallen tree, complete with roots, left in the ground; also, sometimes the base of a tree still in growth.

stumpery a collection of tree stumps, often interplanted with ferns or woodland plants. Stumperies were an occasional feature of Victorian gardens.

stunt disordered growth in plants, such as dwarfing, contorted shoots and leaves and abnormal flowers, all of which prevent a plant from developing and functioning normally. Stunted growth may be due to environmental conditions, pest infestation or disease, especially virus infection.

style the elongated and narrow part of the pistil, between ovary and stigma.

Stylophorum (from Greek *stylos*, style, and *phoros*, bearing, referring to the columnar style). Papaveraceae. E Asia, eastern N America. 3 species, perennial herbs with yellow or red sap, pinnatifid, incised leaves and poppylike flowers in spring and summer. Suitable for shady places, open woodland or a peat terrace, *Stylophorum* will require some shade, since it may suffer sun scorch in direct sunlight; otherwise, cultivation and propagation are the same as for *Chelidonium*. S. *diphyllum* CELANDINE POPPY, WOOD POPPY; E US; to 20 in (50 cm), downy; leaves 8–22 in (20–55 cm), deeply incised, scalloped and toothed; flowers ocher in terminal clusters.

Styrax (Greek name for this plant). Styracaceae. Americas, Asia, Europe. SNOWBELL, SILVERBELLS, STORAX. Some 100 species, deciduous or evergreen shrubs and small trees with pendulous, white, bell-shaped flowers. These plants are hardy to 5°F (–15°C), especially with the shelter of a south-facing wall, where the wood will ripen during summer. Grow *Styrax* in moist but well-drained, nonalkaline, loamy soil, in sun or part-shade. Propagate from softwood cuttings during summer; treat with hormone rooting powder and root under mist or in a closed case. Alternatively, sow ripe seed and maintain at a temperature of 59–75°F (15–24°C) for 3–5 months, then cold-stratify at 33–41°F (0.5–5°C) for another three months, and bring into germination.

S. *japonicus* China, Japan; shrub or small tree to 33 ft (10 m); flowers 3–6 on short lateral shoots, pendulous on glabrous stalks to 1½ in (3.5 cm), corolla lobes elliptic-oblong, ⅝ in (1.5 cm), pubescent; 'Benibana': a name applied in Japan to all pink-flowered, seed-raised forms; S. *obassia* Japan; to 33 ft (10 m); flowers in terminal racemes, 4–8 in (10–20 cm), stalks ⅜–½ in (8–10 mm), pubescent, corolla lobes ¾ in (2 cm); S. *wilsonii* W China; shrub or small tree to 10 ft (3 m); flowers 3–5, ⅝–¾ in (1.5–1.8 cm) across, short-stalked; corolla lobes ovate-oblong, ⅜ in (0.8 cm).

S

subalpine describing plants that inhabit the zone between foothills and alpine slopes; usually referring to relatively tall herbaceous subjects that are not clearly adapted as a result of their high altitude habitat, cf. *alpine*.

sub- a prefix meaning (1) (in conjunction with a descriptive term) slightly, somewhat, nearly, as in subacute, meaning somewhat or slightly acute; (2) (in conjunction with an anatomical term) below or under, as in subapical, meaning below the apex.

sub-base the basic foundation on which a path or paved area is laid. It may be composed of hard-core, stones or firm soil, topped with sand or gravel, where appropriate.

suberous, suberose corky.

subgenus the category of supplementary taxa intermediate between genus and order.

sub-irrigation methods of irrigating, in which water is delivered below the soil or substrate surface or on to a standing area; as with buried seephose, and systems used in moraine beds and on capillary and flood benches. See *irrigation, rock plant gardening*.

submerged, submersed beneath the water.

subsessile with a partial or minute stalk.

subshrub (1) a very small but truly woody shrub; (2) a perennial herb with a woody base and partially soft stems.

subsoil the layer of the soil profile directly beneath the topsoil; generally of lower organic matter content, inferior fertility and structure. It should not be mixed with the topsoil during cultivation.

subsoiling trenching or digging deeply in order to loosen the subsoil, especially to break up a pan or generally improve drainage.

substrate a material in which plants can be grown or propagated.

subulate awl-shaped, tapering from a narrow base to a fine, sharp point.

successional applied to sowings made at regular intervals or to the planting of cultivars that fruit at different times, to ensure continuity of supply of a crop.

succulent plant a plant with thick, fleshy leaves or stems developed for water storage, usually as an adaptation to arid conditions, although some succulents grow as epiphytes in humid climates and others by the sea. They are mostly tender plants, such as cacti, but include hardy genera, for example, sedums and sempervivums.

Sucker
Suckers arise from the rootstock on grafted roses. Soil must be scraped away until the sucker can be torn off at its point of origin.

sucker (1) a shoot that arises from plant roots or underground stems and, in the case of grafted plants, may be untypical of the scion. Suckers often occur on plums and roses. (2) see *psyllid*.

sucker cutter, suckering iron a tool used to remove unwanted suckers from the roots of grafted trees and shrubs, consisting of a V-shaped blade fixed to a handle. Older versions of the tool take the form of a very narrow spade with a concave sharp blade.

suffrutex see *subshrub*.

suffruticose, suffrutescent of a subshrub; perennial, with a shrubby, woody, persistent base, and soft stem summits.

sulcate lined with deep longitudinal grooves or channels.

sulfate of ammonia see *ammonium sulfate*.

sulfate of magnesium see *magnesium sulfate*.

sulfate of potash see *potassium sulfate*.

sulfur a major (macro-) nutrient; an essential constituent of the protein contained in living cells, and found in the seed oils of Brassicae. Deficiency occurs only very rarely in soil low in organic matter, in areas distant from industrial sulfur dioxide; it is not known in the UK. Refined sulfur dust, in the form of flowers of sulfur, can be used to acidify noncalcareous soil. Sulphur is also used as a broad spectrum inorganic fungicide, especially against powdery mildews; it has some beneficial effect as a foliar feed.

summer pruning pruning carried out mostly between July and August, particularly on trained apple and pear trees, as a means of restricting growth and encouraging fruit bud. Lateral growth of the current season arising from a main stem is cut back to 3 leaves, while that from spurs or existing side shoots is cut back to 1 leaf. Shoots are suitable for pruning when woody and dark brown at their base. Summer pruning is appropriate for trees that fruit on one-year-old wood, for example, fan-trained peaches or plums.

summerhouse a garden house, usually a simple, utilitarian timber building, used as a retreat from the dwelling house, particularly in summer.

sunberry see *hybrid berries*.

sunflower husks milled sunflower husks can be used in potting mixtures to improve drainage and aeration. Nitrogen depletion and toxins are potential problems.

sun frame a simply constructed, temporary wooden frame covering a prepared cutting bed; traditionally about 12 in (30 cm) high at the back and 9 in (23 cm) high at the front; enclosed by glazed or plastic-clad frame lights, and shaded from bright

S

sunlight. Of particular use in propagating plants from softwood cuttings.

sunken garden a part of a larger, usually formal, garden sunk below ground level. About 24 in (60 cm) deep, with edges and walls of stone, it is accessed by steps, and often occupied by a pool, ferns or a knot garden.

sun scald see *scald*.

sun tunnel low continuous tunnel cloches, clad with white fabric stretched and fixed over wire hoops; used to filter harsh sunlight from low row-crops in hot climates.

superior above, uppermost. A superior ovary is one borne above the insertion of the floral envelope and stamens, or of a hypanthium from which it is distinct.

superphosphate, superphosphate of lime an inorganic phosphate fertilizer containing 18–21% P_2O_5, made by treating insoluble rock phosphate with sulfuric acid; the suffix lime refers to gypsum, which comprises about half its bulk, but which will not raise soil pH. Triple superphosphate is a more concentrated form containing 47% P_2O_5. Both types are water soluble and may be used in compound liquid feed. See *phosphate*.

supplementary light artificial light used, in addition to natural light, in greenhouses. Mercury vapor, sodium vapor, or mercury halide lamps are used to accelerate growth (photosynthetic lighting), while tungsten filament lamps are employed for controlling flowering times (photoperiodic lighting). See *photoperiodism*.

Surrey School a term sometimes applied to English gardeners of the latter part of the 19th century, such as William Robinson and Gertrude Jekyll, who disapproved of elaborate Victorian bedding schemes and advocated more natural-looking plantings, including the herbaceous border and woodland gardens.

suspension finely divided particles of a solid or liquid dispersed in a liquid.

Sutherlandia (for James Sutherland [d. 1719], superintendent of the Edinburgh Botanic Garden and author of *Hortus Medicus Edinburgensis* [1683]). Leguminosae. South Africa. Some 5 species, evergreen or deciduous shrubs with pinnate leaves, racemes of showy, pealike flowers in summer and bladderlike seed pods. Given optimum conditions, *S. frutescens* may tolerate temperatures to 23°F (–5°C). Grow in a sheltered position in perfectly drained soil in full sun. Propagate by seed in spring or by semiripe cuttings in a closed case with bottom heat. *S. frutescens* BALLOON PEA, DUCK PLANT; to 4 ft (1.25 m); branches wandlike; leaves thinly downy; flowers to 1¼ in (3.2 cm), scarlet to deep purple; fruit inflated, to 2 in × 1¼ in (5 × 3.2 cm).

swag a climbing plant, especially a rose, trained along a rope slung high between two posts, as in a catenary (q.v.).

swap hook see *sickle*.

sward stretch of turf or lawn.

swath the width of the area covered by a sprayer or duster, or the width of an area of grass cut with a scythe.

swede (rutabaga) (*Brassica napus*, Napobrassica Group) a biennial grown for its large edible root; it is similar to the turnip but with a milder, sweeter flavor and better storage properties. Swede is one of the hardiest of root crops and can be harvested from fall through the winter months, or lifted and stored either outdoors in clamps or in a cool shed. The flesh is usually yellow, and purple-topped roots are best for the garden. They are peeled and sliced for boiling.

Sow in late spring ¾ in (2 cm) deep, in rows 16–18 in (40–45 cm) apart; thin individual plants to 10 in (25 cm) apart. Swedes are often challenging to grow successfully: the season from sowing to maturity is up to 26 weeks and the crop must be kept growing steadily, which demands an open fertile site, ideally of light texture and with access to irrigation.

Possible problems: flea beetle, cabbage root fly; club root, turnip gall

weevil (see *weevils*).

sweet corn (*Zea mays*) an important cereal crop worldwide, of which primitive forms were cultivated more than 5000 years ago. It is grown for its seed-bearing cobs; the seeds are eaten after boiling, either direct from the cob or separated. It is suitable for freezing.

Corn is a warm-season crop that will not withstand frost, usually requiring 70–110 frost-free days from planting to harvest. The optimum temperature ranges are 68–81°F (20–27°C) for germination, and 68–84°F (20–29°C) air temperature for growth. Flowering is promoted by short days, although adaptable cultivars are available. Corn needs a long, warm growing season to succeed, and later maturing cultivars are generally of better quality; the sugar content decreases with maturity and the supersweet cultivars are notable.

Choose moisture-retentive soil in a sheltered site, on which *in situ* sowings can be made in late May or June. Protect with cloches or upturned jam jars for advantage, or with clear polyethylene or fine net film, which can be either slit or removed on crop establishment—net must be removed by the five-leaf stage. Sow seeds 1–1½ in (2.5–4 cm) deep, with two or three seeds per station, either in block formation with approximately 14 in (35 cm) between stations, or in rows 24 in (60 cm) apart with 12 in (30 cm) between stations; thin germinated groups to one plant. For superior results, multi-sow in 3 in (7.5 cm) pots or similar-sized modules in April, in gentle heat, planting out after the risk of frost has passed. Corn is suitable for intercropping with faster-maturing vegetables or low-growing ones, such as marrows.

The plants are wind-pollinated by transference of pollen from the male flowers or "tassels" to the female flowers or "silks." Earthing up for stability is advisable, and ground mulching helps to suppress weeds and conserve moisture; irrigation during seed swelling is beneficial. Each plant yields one or two cobs, which are ready from July to October, when the tassels and silks die away and the cob assumes a 45° angle to the stem. Mature seeds yield a milky juice when squeezed.

Mini cobs can be obtained by planting early maturing cultivars 6 in (15 cm) apart and harvesting the cobs when about 3 in (7.5 cm) long.

Possible problems: fruit fly.

sweet pea (*Lathyrus odoratus*) a tender, climbing annual with winged stems, originating in Crete, Italy and Sicily. Grown for its highly ornamental and fragrant flowers, it has been subjected to much horticultural breeding and selection on both sides of the Atlantic. There is a range of types: (1) tall forms, which reach 6½–10 ft (2–3 m) and depend on support, producing long stemmed blooms primarily for cutting or exhibition. These include the Grandiflora type or Old-fashioned sweet peas, mostly raised before 1900, with dainty well-scented flowers, and now largely superseded by the Spencer types, originating from the early 1900s, with larger frilled or waved standards in great variety. Other tall forms are the Early Multiflora Giganteas, Cuthbertson Floribundas and Galaxy and Mammoth series, which are variously earlier, more tolerant of hot weather and productive of more blooms per stem; (2) dwarf forms, which grow to a maximum of about 6–12 in (15–30 cm), are of bushy habit and need little or no support, producing short-stemmed flowers ideal for a border display. These include the Little Sweetheart series and the prostrate Cupid and Patio series. The Snoopea series is prostrate and without tendrils, reaching a height of about 12 in (30 cm); similar is the Bijou series, suitable for baskets and tubs; (3) semi-dwarf or hedge forms, such as the Jet Set, Knee-hi and Continental series, can reach 3¼ ft (1 m) in height, with flowers larger than the dwarf forms; in most situations they benefit from support.

Sow seed under protection in late September in mild districts, overwintering in a cold, airy frame, or in late winter or spring in cold districts. Nick darker-colored seeds opposite the original point of attachment to aid germination. Sow in trays, or one to three seeds per small pot or cellular-tray module, or in special 2 in (5 cm)-diameter sweet pea tubes, which are 6 in (15 cm) deep; maintain at 59°F

(15°C), before transferring to a frame. Prick out tray-sown seedlings when 1½ in (3.5 cm) high. Pinch out the tips of all fall-sown plants when 4 in (10 cm) high; stop spring-sown plants at the first pair of leaves. Plant out after progressive hardening off.

Set out fall-sown plants in midspring and those from spring-sowings in late spring, 9 in (23 cm) apart. Bush-grown plants are allowed to develop naturally, supported where appropriate with pea-sticks or nets, or with canes arranged as four-legged tents or in parallel rows. These plants are initially tied loosely with wire rings and the side shoots left to grow. Cordon-grown plants produce the best quality blooms and this system is mainly suited to growing for exhibition. Plants are supported on a structure consisting of stout 8 ft (2.5 m) long posts driven in at each end of the row rising 6½ ft (2 m) out of the ground. To the top of each post is fixed a 18 in (45 cm) long cross piece. Two parallel wires are run between the ends of the cross-pieces and to these are secured 7 ft (2.2 m) stakes, spaced 9 in (23 cm) apart at a slight angle. After two weeks' establishment, pinch out the weakest shoots, leaving one strong shoot to be tied to each stake with raffia, a sweet pea ring or tape. Side shoots and tendrils are removed as the plants grow, as are flower stems with less than four buds, and the plants are progressively tied in. When plants reach the top wire, they can be untied, laid down and trained 12–16 in (30–40 cm) up a stake further along the row, thereby facilitating new stem growth to prolong flower production. A supplementary feed of a high potash fertilizer is recommended, and an organic ground mulch keeps the rows weed-free and retentive of moisture.

Early blooms can be obtained by growing fall-sown plants in a cold greenhouse, in pots or border soil, maintaining a minimum temperature of 41–50°F (5–10°C). Early flowering peach or pink cultivars are particularly suitable for this method. Special watch must be kept for attack by aphids, thrips, slugs and snails.

Possible problems: aphids, slugs and snails; gray mold; foot and root rots.

sweet potato (*Ipomoea batatas*) a vigorous, climbing herbaceous perennial, grown as an annual for its edible fleshy, tuberous rootstock. It is of tropical origin, producing an optimum yield in areas with 29½–49¼ in (750–1,250 mm) rainfall, a temperature range of 72–77°F (22–25°C), and good light levels. Although naturally a short-day plant for flower production, tuber initiation and development are not inhibited by variation in day length.

In temperate climates, sweet potatoes should be grown under cover or in a sheltered place outdoors in very favorable locations. Plant tubers in spring 2–2¾ in (5–7 cm) deep in ridges 30 in (75 cm) apart. Alternatively, raise from stem cuttings, inserted to about half their length below a ridge top, or from seed sown at 75°F (24°C) in trays; potted-up seedlings are planted out when 4–6 in (10–15 cm) high. Under cover, the crop can be grown in pots, growing bags, or border soil, provided it is watered regularly. Harvest sweet potatoes grown from tubers 12–16 weeks after planting, when the foliage turns yellow.

swift moths (Lepidoptera: Hepialidae) In Europe, two species are pests in gardens: the GHOST SWIFT MOTH (*Hepialus humuli*), which has forewings up to 2 in (50 mm), silvery-white in males and yellow-brown in females; and the GARDEN SWIFT MOTH (*H. lupulinus*), which is smaller, with a wingspan of up to 1½ in (40 mm) and yellow-brown forewings with white markings (these are less conspicuous in the females).

The moths fly in early summer and fertilized females drop their eggs during flight over suitable vegetation; resulting larvae enter the soil and feed on the roots and underground organs of a wide range of plants. The larvae of the garden swift moth reach maturity and pupate the following year, those of the ghost swift moth a year later. The root-feeding larvae are white, with shiny brown heads, and up to 2½ in (6.5 mm) long. They are particularly prevalent in herbaceous borders, soft fruit plantations and vegetable gardens. Corms, bulbs, tubers, rhizomes and the roots of many plants are frequently attacked, including anemones, asters, carrots, chrysanthemums,

S

dahlias, delphiniums, gladioli, grasses, lettuces, *Narcissus* and other bulbs, *Phlox*, onions, peonies, parsnips, potatoes, pyrethrums, scabious, solidagos, strawberries, raspberries and rudbeckias.

The caterpillars are often seen when old herbaceous borders, strawberry beds, weedy vegetable plots or grassland are dug during the winter. Such areas should be well-cultivated and, if necessary, treated with an appropriate soil insecticide before being resown or replanted, subject to local pesticide approvals. Rigorous weed elimination and routine cultivation can help prevent damage by these pests, since eggs are rarely dropped onto bare or sparsely planted soil.

swiss chard (*Beta vulgaris* subsp. *cicla* var. *flavescens*) SILVER CHARD, SEA KALE BEET, SILVER BEET; a biennial, related to the beet, occurring in a range of forms collectively known as leaf beets. These are cultivated for their edible leaves, which are larger than those of spinach, with swollen midribs and stems; both leaf blades and stems may be used as separate vegetables. Leaf stalks are white, pink, red or silver-colored, according to form; they are sometimes grown as garden ornamentals, notably 'Ruby Chard'. Swiss chard is hardy and less susceptible to drought than spinach, and year-round harvesting is possible; quality is improved by covering with cloches during winter months.

The main sowings are made *in situ*, ³⁄₄ in (2 cm) deep, in March–April in rows 12–15 in (30–38 cm) apart, thinning to 12 in (30 cm) apart; these will supply a crop from summer until flowering the following spring. A July–August sowing will produce a lower-yielding crop, lasting until well into the following summer, and quality is improved if this is module-raised and grown with unheated protection.

SPINACH BEET, PERPETUAL SPINACH is closely related and botanically identified as *Beta vulgaris* subsp. *cicla* var. *cicla*. Grow as individual plants for leaf harvest or as a cut-and-come-again crop. Raise and space as swiss chard.

Possible problems: downy mildew, leaf spot.

switch a long pliable rod used to disperse worm-casts and dew on turf before mowing.

switch plant a plant with long green photosynthetic shoots and greatly reduced or absent leaves; adapted for arid conditions. For example some *Cytisus* species.

swoe a trade name, now in common use, for a hoe, with an angled blade sharpened on three edges, which can be used with both forward and backward motion.

syconium a fruitlike inflorescence characteristic of *Ficus* where the interior of the globose, fleshy, hollow receptacle is lined with flowers.

Sycopsis (from Greek *syke*, fig-tree and *opsis*, appearance). Hamamelidaceae. Himalaya, China, Malaysia. Some 7 species, evergreen shrubs or small trees. They bear heads of flowers in late winter and early spring—these lack petals but have clusters of showy stamens. *Sycopsis* is tolerant of temperatures down to about 5°F (–15°C). Cultivate as for *Hamamelis* and propagate from semiripe cuttings in summer. *S. sinensis* (C China; to 20 ft (6 m); leaves to 4¾ in (12 cm), leathery, ovate to elliptic-lanceolate, tips occasionally serrulate, dark green above, pale beneath; flowers in thick clusters to 1 in (2.5 cm), bracts red-brown, woolly, filaments yellow, anthers red).

symbiosis a mutually beneficial relationship between two or more organisms, eg, mycorrhizal fungi and heaths, mycorrhiza, fig and the fig wasp.

sympetalous see *gamopetalous*.

Symphoricarpos (from Greek *symphorein*, bear together, and, *karpos*, fruit, referring to the arrangement of the berries, sometimes so tightly clustered as to resemble a compound fruit). Caprifoliaceae. N and C America, China. SNOWBERRY, CORALBERRY. Some 17 species, deciduous, suckering shrubs with small, pink or white, bell-shaped flowers in summer. Persisting through winter, the fruits are globose, white, pink, red or purple-black, and juicy with mealy flesh. *Symphoricarpos* withstands a wide range of soil types, urban pollution and maritime conditions. The following species are hardy to at least –13°F (–25°C). They make useful screens and informal hedges, in cold climates, especially in poor soil, even thriving among the roots and under the drip of trees. The suckering habit of species such as *S. albus* renders them suitable for soil stabilization on banks and slopes; the procumbent rooting branches of *S.* × *chenaultii* make dense groundcover. Propagate by division in fall, or by softwood cuttings in summer. Alternatively, place hardwood cuttings in open ground in winter. Prune out weak, dead or crowded shoots each or every other year, in late winter or early spring.

S. albus SNOWBERRY, COMMON SNOWBERRY, WAXBERRY; N America; to 48 in (120 cm); shoots slender, erect, slightly lanuginose; leaves to 2 in (5 cm), oval to oval-oblong, blunt, rounded at base, sometimes lacerate, dark green above, lighter and finely downy beneath; flowers pink, in spikes or clusters; fruit ½ in (12.5 mm) in diameter, globose or ovoid, snow-white; includes variegated cultivars, and var. *laevigatus*, to 71 in (180 cm), forming dense, erect thickets, with glabrous shoots, leaves to 3 in (7.5 cm) and glabrous, and larger fruit; *S.* × *chenaultii* *S. microphyllus* × *S. orbiculatus*; erect to spreading and low, to 6½ ft (2 m)+; shoots densely downy; leaves to ¾ in (2 cm), ovate, dark green above, blue-green beneath, densely soft-pubescent; flowers pink, in short, terminal spikes; fruit red and white-spotted, or white stippled red on exposed side, or wholly pink; *S.* × *doorenbosii* (*S. albus* var. *laevigatus* × *S.* × *chenaultii*); also known as the Doorenbos Hybrids; very vigorous to 6½ ft (2 m); shoots downy; leaves to 1½ in (4 cm), elliptic to broadly ovate, obtuse, dark green and glabrous above, paler and pubescent beneath; flowers white flushing pink, in short racemes;

Swiss chard

fruit to ½ in (1.3 cm) in diameter, globose, white flushed pink on exposed side; includes numerous cultivars suitable for hedging; *S. orbiculatus* CORALBERRY, INDIAN CURRANT; E US, Mexico; to 6½ ft (2 m), erect, branches thin, pubescent at first; leaves to 1¼ in (3 cm), oval to ovate, rounded at base, full dark green above, pubescent, gray-green beneath, tinted red in fall; flowers ivory flushing dull pink, in short clusters; fruit to ¼ in (0.6 cm) in diameter, ovoid-globose, gray-white becoming opaque wine red; includes variegated cultivars.

symphylids (Symphyla) small, white, delicate-looking arthropods, up to ½ in (10 mm) in length, with long antennae and 12 pairs of legs; they resemble miniature centipedes in their general appearance and high activity. They are found in the soil at various depths down to 6½ ft (2 m). Although unable to make burrows themselves, they are adept at moving up and down cracks and fissures, through spaces between soil particles and along earthworm tunnels. They may be abundant in greenhouses, and although outdoor populations are generally lower, numbers may build up to injurious levels in moist soil with a high organic content and open texture.

The most important species is the glasshouse symphylid (*Scutigerella immaculata*), known as the garden symphylan in North America. It feeds on roots, devouring root hairs and smaller roots, its feeding causing rust-colored lesions. Affected plants make little new growth and readily wilt in dry weather. Damaging attacks in amateur greenhouses and gardens are rare in the UK, but susceptible plants include tomatoes, chrysanthemums and lettuce; outdoor susceptible crops include anemones, asparagus, beans, brassicas, celery, marrows, parsley, garden peas, potatoes, strawberries and sweet peas. To confirm the presence of symphylids, plants should be lifted and their roots immersed in a bucket of water—most of the symphylids will float to the top within a few minutes, and should not be confused with springtails. Symphylids may be controlled by drenching the soil with recommended contact insecticides, subject to local pesticide approvals.

Symphytum (from Greek *symphyo*, to grow together, and *phyton*, plant, from the apparent healing powers of the plants). Boraginaceae. Europe to Caucasus and Iran. COMFREY. 35 species, bristly-hairy perennial herbs, with 5-lobed, tubular flowers in arching cymes in spring. Fully hardy, *Symphytum* species make fast-growing groundcover plants for shaded borders and woodland. *S. officinalis* is also grown as green manure. The leaves also make a valuable high-bulk addition to the compost pile. *S. officinalis* is rich in potassium, phosphorus, calcium and nitrogen, and is used in organic gardens as a high-potash tomato feed or for pot plants. Comfrey water is prepared by packing a water butt or other large container with leaves and steeping in water until decayed. Propagate by seed in fall, by division, or by root cuttings.

S. caucasicum Caucasus, Iran; stem to 24 in (60 cm), branched, pilose; leaves to 8 in (20 cm), ovate-lanceolate to oblong-lanceolate; cymes paired, scorpioid, flowers to ⅝ in (14 mm), red-purple becoming blue; *S. grandiflorum* Europe, Caucasus; stem to 16 in (40 cm), ascending-decumbent, shortly pubescent; leaves elliptic or ovate to ovate-lanceolate, base rounded or subcordate; inflorescence many-flowered, flowers to ⅝ in (16 mm), pale yellow or cream; *S. × uplandicum* (*S. asperum × S. officinale*); Caucasus; stem to 6½ ft (2 m); leaves oblong to elliptic-lanceolate, pubescent; flowers to ¾ in (2 cm), rose becoming blue or purple. *Cultivars* 'Goldsmith', to 12 in (30 cm), with leaves edged and splashed gold and cream, flowers blue, white and pink; 'Hidcote Blue', spreading, vigorous, to 18 in (45 cm) high, with rough leaves and soft blue and white flowers, red in bud, later fading; 'Hidcote Pink', to 18 in (45 cm), with pink and white flowers; 'Langthorn's Pink' ('Roseum'), to 4 ft (1.2 m), vigorous, with pink flowers, in clusters on high stem (possibly a hybrid of *S.* 'Rubrum' and *S. × uplandicum*); and 'Rubrum', to 12 in (30 cm), with deep red flowers in early summer.

sympodial a form of growth in which the terminal bud dies or terminates in an inflorescence, and growth is continued by successive secondary axes growing from lateral buds; cf. *monopodial*.

symptom a visible or measurable expression of a disease or disorder, which may be characteristic and an aid to diagnosis.

Synadenium (from Greek *syn*, with, and *aden*, gland). Euphorbiaceae. Tropical America to Mascarenes. 19 species, shrubs or small trees, with fleshy branches containing milky latex and handsome, thinly succulent leaves. The inflorescences are inconspicuous. Cultivate as for the tender, succulent species of *Euphorbia*. *S. grantii* Uganda to Zimbabwe, Mozambique; succulent shrub, to 3 m (10 ft); leaves to 7 in (18 cm), oblanceolate to obovate, blunt to apiculate; 'Rubrum': leaves red above, purple-red beneath, and finely toothed, and red flowers.

synanthous with leaves appearing alongside the flowers; cf. *hysteranthous*.

syncarp an aggregate or multiple fruit produced from the connate or coherent pistils of one or more flowers, and composed of massed and more or less coalescent fruits.

syndrome the totality of symptoms characteristic of a disease or pest infestation.

synergism (1) the combined effect of two or more organisms, which is greater than their separate effects; (2) the increased activity that may result from mixing pesticides, and which is more than the sum of their individual effects.

synflorescence a compound inflorescence, possessing a terminal inflorescence and lateral inflorescences.

syngamy see *fertilization*.

Syngonium (from Greek *syn*, together or joined, and *gone*, womb, alluding to united ovaries). Araceae. Tropical America. 33 species, evergreen epiphytic or terrestrial perennials with climbing or trailing, rooting stems and sagittate to ovate or pedately lobed leaves. These are attractive foliage plants for pots and hanging baskets, suited to the heated conservatory and intermediate to warm greenhouse, but

S

also tolerant of drier atmospheres in the home and other interiors. Grow in an open and well-drained medium, rich in organic matter, and shade from bright direct sunlight; provide a moist moss pole for support and a minimum temperature of 61–64°F (16–18°C). Water moderately, allowing the medium to dry a little between waterings. Pinch out stem tips to encourage branching. Repot in spring, if necessary. Propagate by leaf bud or stem tip cuttings, taken in summer and rooted in a closed case, or by division.

S. auritum Jamaica, Cuba, Hispaniola; juvenile leaves ovate or sagittate to hastate, acute; adult leaves 3–5-pedatisect, lobes 4–12 in (10–30 cm), broadly elliptic, acuminate, somewhat glossy above; includes 'Fantasy', with thick, deep green, shiny, compound leaves, mottled white, with a midlobe with smaller lobes each side, and petiole streaked cream; *S. erythrophyllum* Panama; juvenile leaves 1¼–3½ in (3–9 cm), ovate, cordate, lobes rounded, black-green above, pale green, soon becoming deep violet-purple beneath; adult leaves trisect, segments 4–9 in (10–22 cm), lanceolate-elliptic to ovate, lateral segments to 4 in (10 cm), glossy dark green above, pale green or violet-purple beneath; *S. hoffmannii* Costa Rica to Panama; juvenile leaves sagittate, 1½–7 in (4–18 cm), green with gray veins; adult leaves trisect, segments 3½–11 in (9–28 cm), oblong-elliptic to ovate-oblong or lanceolate, acuminate, somewhat glossy above; *S. podophyllum* (syn. *S. vellozianum*, *S. gracile*, *S. riedelianum*, *S. xanthophilum*); Mexico to Brazil and Bolivia; juvenile leaves 2¾–5½ in (7–14 cm), simple, cordate, acuminate at apex, becoming sagittate or hastate as plant ages, adult leaves pedatisect, segments 3–11, obovate to broad-elliptic, acuminate, dark green above, pale or sometimes glaucescent beneath. *Cultivars*: 'Albolineatum', with leaves heart-shaped with white center and veins when young, later palmate and green; 'Emerald Gem', with shiny dark green leaves, fleshy and sagittate when young; 'Emerald Gem Variegated', with white to pale gray leaves with irregular variegation; 'Imperial White', with leaves tinted blue and white veins; 'Roxanne', of rosette form, later creeping, with

pink-brown petioles and glossy dull green leaves with muddy green center and shading along -white ribs, hastate when young; 'Silver Knight', silver-green leaves; 'Tricolor', dark green leaves with light green and white variegation, hastate and trilobed when young; and 'Trileaf Wonder', leaves marked ash green along lateral veins and midrib.

synonym (abbrev. syn.) one of two or more names used for the same taxon. Synonyms fall into two types: *nomenclatural* synonyms are different names based on the same type; *taxonomic* synonyms are different names based on different types that are later judged to belong to the same taxon.

synsepalum a calyx cup or tube; a discrete structure formed by the fusion of two or more sepals.

synthecology the study of plant communities.

Synthyris (from Greek *syn*, with, and *thyris*, a window, referring to the valves of the capsule). Scrophulariaceae. US. Some 14 species, low-growing, spring-flowering perennial herbs with 4-parted, campanulate flowers in narrow erect racemes. The following species are hardy woodland denizens, tolerating very poor soil under deciduous trees. The leathery clumps of evergreen foliage will, however, be larger and freer-flowering where the growing medium is a gritty, richer mix. Plant in light shade. Propagate from seed in spring and by division after flowering.

S. reniformis SNOW QUEEN, ROUND-LEAVED SYNTHYRIS; to 4 in (10 cm); leaves with shallow, rounded lobes; flowers campanulate; *S. stellata* COLUMBIA SYNTHYRIS; to 8 in (20 cm); leaves deeply toothed or cut; flowers starry.

Syringa (from Greek *syrinx*, the reed, via *Syrinx*, a nymph transformed into a reed, thus an Arcadian reed pipe: a reference to the hollow stems). Oleaceae. E Asia, SE Europe. LILAC. 20 or more species, deciduous trees and shrubs with simple to pinnately compound leaves and, in spring and summer, terminal panicles of small, scented, tubular and 4-lobed flowers.

Lilacs are hardy, sweetly scented,

spring-flowering shrubs and small trees that make good informal hedging or screens. They may be used as a spring backdrop to a summer-flowering border. *S. josikaea* and its hybrids stand shearing well and make good hedging plants. Smaller types, such as *S. meyeri* 'Palibin', are much neater in habit, slowly forming rounded, small-leafed shrubs that look well as single lawn or patio specimens, or in the rock garden. Plant in a sunny, open site, in fertile, neutral to alkaline loams. Prune initially to one leader. In later years, prune after flowering to thin out old and dead wood. Late-flowering tree lilacs, such as *S. reticulata*, may grow as single stems into small trees. Lax, vigorous plants, like *S.* × *hyacinthiflora* and its cultivars, should have stems shortened by one third, since they do not form a terminal bud and naturally fork each year. Old plants of shrubby lilacs respond well to hard cutting back. Mulch and feed well, particularly on poorer, dry soil. Remove flower heads on small plants directly after flowering to increase vigor. On grafted plants, suckers that overtake the scion material may be a problem, especially where *S. vulgaris* is used as stock. Plants grafted on *Ligustrum* tend to be short-lived unless planted with the graft union 2¾–4 in (7–10 cm) below soil level, encouraging the lilac to root. Layers are a better method, producing own root plants. Propagate also from softwood cuttings in mist in summer, by semiripe cuttings later in a cold frame, or (for species) from seed or suckers in spring.

Lilacs are susceptible to leaf spotting and blotching (*Ascochyta* and *Phyllosticta* species, *Heterosporium syringae*); and blight (*Pseudomonas syringae*), which produces blackened young shoots, often confused with frost damage and chlorosis. Insect pests include the lilac leafminer, whose caterpillars live in blister-shaped mines. Other pests prevalent in Europe include the privet thrip which causes silvering of the foliage but this is only serious in young plants. In North America, the lilac borer (*Podosesia syringae*), a clearwing moth with white caterpillars up to 1½ in (35 mm) long, bores into the branches, causing them to wilt.

S. × *chinensis* (*S.* × *persica* × *S. vulgaris*);

CHINESE LILAC; garden origin; to 10 ft (3 m); branches dense, slender, arching; leaves to 3 in (8 cm), ovate, apex acuminate, base rounded or broad-cuneate; flowers in long, nodding axillary panicles, fragrant, lilac, corolla tube to ⅜ in (8 mm), lobes obtuse or acute; includes 'Alba', with white flowers white, 'Bicolor', with slate-gray flowers with a violet-tinted throat, 'Duplex', with double, lilac-purple flowers, 'Metensis', with opalescent flowers, 'Nana', dwarf, and 'Saugeana', with lilac flowers flushed wine red—paler reversions may appear; *S. emodi* HIMALAYAN LILAC; Afghanistan, Himalaya; robust shrub, upright to 16 ft (5 m); branches very erect, thick, warty; leaves to 6 in (15 cm), oblong-elliptic, dark above, pale gray beneath, glabrous; flowers in columnar panicles to 6 in (15 cm), terminal, pale lilac, malodorous, corolla ¼ in (5 mm); includes 'Aurea', with soft yellow leaves, and 'Variegata', with large leaves, bordered gold-green; *S.* × *hyacinthiflora S. oblata* × *S. vulgaris*; garden origin; leaves broad-ovate, emerging bronze as in *S. oblata*, turning purple in fall; flowers scented as in *S. vulgaris*, single or double with lobes somewhat incurved; *S.* × *hyacinthiflora* embraces the Early-Flowering Hybrids or Praecox Hybrids, where one parent is *S. oblata* var. *giraldii*; these produce looser panicles of bloom two weeks before *S. vulgaris*; there are single and double flowers with colors ranging through white, lilac, and powder blue to garnet, magenta and pink, including bicolors, with forms changing color as the buds open; *S. josikaea* HUNGARIAN LILAC; Hungary, Galicia; erect shrub to 13 ft (4 m); branches rigid, warty; leaves to 4¾ in (12 cm), elliptic, ciliate, glossy above, glaucous beneath; flowers in slender panicles to 6 in (15 cm), pubescent, carried erect, deep violet, corolla to ⅝ in (15 mm), lobes held forward; includes 'Eximia', with large, light red flowers and panicle, later tinted pink. 'H. Zabel', compact, with red flowers

fading to white, 'Pallida', with pale violet flowers, 'Rosea', with pink flowers, and 'Rubra', with violet flowers, tinted red; *S.* × *laciniata* (*S. protolaciniata* × *S. vulgaris*); CUT LEAF LILAC; SW Asia; shrub to 6½ ft (2 m); first leaves pinnately cleft or lobed × 3–9, later leaves entire; flowers deep lilac in bud, opening faded mauve with a violet center, in loose axillary panicle to 2¾ in (7 cm), fragrant; *S. meyeri* N China; compact shrub to 5 ft (1.5 m); shoots 4-sided, downy when young; leaves to 1½ in (4 cm), elliptic, veins pubescent beneath; flowers in broad panicles to 3 in (8 cm), corolla tube to ⅝ in (15 mm), very narrow, purple, faintly scented, sometimes flowering twice in a season; includes 'Palibin', compact, with flowers fading from violet to rose-pink on profuse short panicles; *S.* × *persica* PERSIAN LILAC; W Asia, naturalized Asia Minor; thought to be an ancient back-cross between *S.* × *laciniata* and *S. vulgaris*; to 6½ ft (2 m); branches rigid, glabrous; leaves to 2½ in (6 cm), lanceolate, rarely pinnate or 3-lobed; flowers in panicles to 2 × 2 in (5 × 5 cm), lilac, fragrant; includes 'Alba', with white to rose-pink flowers, and 'Rosea', with light to dark pink flowers; *S.* × *prestoniae* (*S. reflexa* × *S. villosa*); garden origin; flowers rose-white to deep lilac in dense, nodding panicles; cultivars include 'Audrey', with pink, single flowers; 'Desdemona', with magenta to blue, single flowers; 'Donald Wyman', sturdy, dense and upright, with flowers in large pyramidal panicles, lavender tinted purple; 'Elinor', with pale lavender flowers in erect panicle, tinted purple in bud; 'James MacFarlane', very hardy and adaptable, free-flowering, with clear pink flowers; 'Hecla', magenta, single; 'Hiawatha', mauve-red flowers, opening rose-pink; 'Isabella', purple-pink flowers in erect panicle; 'Regan', rose-mauve, single flowers; and 'Red-wine', tinted claret; *S. pubescens* subsp. *patula* Korea, N China; deciduous shrub to 10 ft (3 m);

Syringa meyeri trained as standard

young branches flushed purple, sparsely pubescent or glabrous; leaves to 3 in (8 cm), ovate to rhombic or lanceolate, acuminate, glabrous or minutely downy above, paler, pubescent beneath; flowers fragrant in cylindric, terminal, paired panicles to 6 in (15 cm), corolla to ½ in (10 mm), slender, lilac, white within, lobes narrow, reflexed; 'Miss Kim': hardy and compact, dwarf, with glossy dark green leaves, burgundy in fall, and late, pale lilac flowers; *S. reticulata* JAPANESE TREE LILAC; N Japan; small tree with low, domed crown, to 33 ft (10 m); branches shaggy with exfoliating bark; leaves to 6 in (15 cm), ovate, narrow-acuminate, shiny light green above, initially downy beneath; flowers cream, strongly scented of musk in panicle to 12 in (30 cm); cultivars and varieties include 'Ivory Silk', sturdy and compact, with bark with cherry-pink tint and cream flowers; *S. vulgaris* COMMON LILAC; SE Europe; tree or shrub to 23 ft (7 m); leaves ovate, acuminate, to 4¾ in (12 cm), glabrous; flowers in pyramidal, terminal panicles to 4¾ in (12 cm), lilac, highly fragrant, corolla tube to ½ in (10 mm), lobes concave; includes var. *alba*, with white flowers, and 'Aurea', with leaves opening yellow-green; other cultivars include early- and late-flowering, single- and double-flowered whites, pinks, magentas, lilac-mauves and blues, some with white throats or a different color tone in bud, and flowers and panicle of varying sizes and shapes; *S. yunnanensis* SW China; deciduous shrub to 10 ft (3 m), erect, narrow; branches slender, new growth hairy; leaves to 3 in (8 cm), oval or narrowly obovate, acuminate, tapering to base, olive green above, glaucous beneath, ciliate; flowers in terminal pubescent panicles, to 6 in (15 cm), fragrant, shell-pink, fading; includes 'Alba', with white flowers, and 'Rosea', with pink flowers in long, slender particle. For *S. palibiniana* of gardens, see *S. meyeri* 'Palibin'; for *S. palibiniana*, see *S. pubescens* subsp. *patula*.

systemic (1) a pathogen that is not restricted to the surface of a plant or to a point close to the place of infection; (2) a pesticide that is absorbed by a plant and translocated through its vascular system.

S

Tabebuia (from the vernacular Brazilian name for *Tabebuia uliginosa*). Bignoniaceae. C and S America, West Indies. Some 100 species, shrubs or trees with simple or digitately compound leaves and panicles of 2-lipped, tubular to campanulate flowers. Beautiful lawn and park specimens in subtropical and tropical climates, *Tabebuia* species are valued for their showy and often fragrant flowers (on deciduous species, these are carried when the leaves have fallen). Many flower sporadically throughout the year and some, such as *T. rosea*, require a dry resting period to induce flowering. In cool temperate areas they are grown under glass as for *Tecoma*. Propagate by fresh seed, semiripe cuttings or air-layering.

T. chrysotricha Colombia, Brazil; small tree; flowers to 2½ in (6 cm), yellow, with red down; *T. rosea* Mexico to Colombia and N Venezuela; tree to 90 ft (27 m); flowers to 4 in (10 cm), white, pink or lilac with a yellow to white eye.

Tacca (from the Indonesian name for these plants). Taccaceae. SE Asia, W Africa. 10 species, evergreen perennial herbs with starchy rhizomes or tubers and clumped, lanceolate-ovate to decompound leaves. Fleshy, bell-shaped flowers hang in scapose umbels subtended by heavily veined bracts and long, whiskerlike filaments. Grow in filtered light in a humid greenhouse or conservatory, with a minimum temperature of 55–59°F (13–15°C). Pot in a leaf mold and coarse bark mix with a slow-release fertilizer. Water and syringe continuously, giving a monthly diluted foliar fertilizer. Propagate by division, or by sections of old rhizomes, each with an eye. Alternatively, seed may be surface-sown at a temperature of 72–81°F (22–27°C).

T. chantrieri (syn. *T. macrantha, T. lanci-folia, T. roxburghii*); DEVIL FLOWER, BAT FLOWER, CAT'S WHISKERS; Thailand; like *T. integrifolia*, but to 25 in (63 cm), outer bracts green to black, filaments to 10 in (25 cm), olive green to maroon or violet-black; *T. integrifolia* (syn. *T. aspera*); BAT PLANT, BAT FLOWER; E India to S China, south to Sumatra, Borneo, W Java; to 40 in (100 cm), dark purple or red, sometimes brown, outer bracts to 5½ in (14 cm), green to dark purple, stained and veined black, filaments to 8 in (20 cm), pale green shaded violet, darkening as flowering continues to dark brown or purple-black, flowers nodding, purple-black.

tachinid flies (Diptera: Tachinidae) a diverse family of stout, bristled flies, distributed worldwide, ranging in size from ¹⁄₁₆–³⁄₄ in (2–20 mm). The adults are free-living, often frequenting flowers, but the larvae are internal parasites of various other arthropods, especially insects, including larvae and nymphs of beetles, grasshoppers, plant bugs, sawflies, occasionally other flies and most commonly moths and butterflies. Tachinids are important as natural regulators of insect populations, but have been used only to a limited extent in biological control.

Tagetes patula 'Naughty Marietta'
Both French and African marigolds in fact originally hail from Central America. Both are popular with beneficial insects.

Tagetes (from Tages, an Etruscan deity, grandson of Jupiter, said to have taught the Etruscans sooth-saying). Compositae. Tropical and warm America, one species from Africa. MARIGOLD. About 50 species, annual or perennial herbs with glandular, pin-natifid or pinnate leaves and showy, daisylike flower heads in summer. Grow in sun in moderately fertile and well-drained soil. Deadhead to prolong blooming. Sow seed *in situ* in spring for informal effects or earlier under glass for bedding out and containers. Plants begin to bloom about 12–14 weeks from sowing.

T. erecta AFRICAN MARIGOLD, AZTEC MARIGOLD, BIG MARIGOLD; C America; annual to 3¼ ft (1 m); flower heads are 2–4¾ in (5–12 cm) in diameter, ray florets orange to lemon yellow; includes many seed races, tall to dwarf plants with single to double flower heads in shades of orange and yellow; *T. patula* FRENCH MARIGOLD; Guatemala and Mexico; annual to 20 in (50 cm); flower heads to 2 in (5 cm) in diameter, ray florets red-brown, orange, yellow or particolored; includes numerous seed races, among them dwarf and bushy to tall plants with single or double flower heads in shades and combinations of gold, bronze and rusty red.

Talinum (from the native African name, meaning unknown). Portulacaceae. Tropics and subtropics, western N America. FAMEFLOWER. About 50 species, woody-based, succulent annual or perennial herbs with showy, short-lived flowers consisting of five or more silky petals. Hardy to 5°F (–15°C), given perfect drainage. Well-suited to sunny, perfectly drained niches in the rock garden and in troughs. Cultivate as for *Lewisia*. *T. okanoganense* W N America; cushion-forming perennial; leaves cylindrical, fleshy, gray-green; flowers to ¾ in (2 cm) in diameter, white.

Tamarix (Classical Latin name for tamarisk). Tamaricaceae. W Europe and the Mediterranean to E Asia and India. TAMARISK, SALT CEDAR. 54 species, deciduous shrubs or small trees with many slender branches, their branchlets feathery and clothed with very small, green, needle- or scalelike leaves. In summer, they are clothed in powdery masses of tiny pink or white flowers. Most *Tamarix* species occur in coastal habitats, often in saline soil; they are particularly useful in exposed maritime gardens, as hedging and windbreaks or as border specimens. Grow in well-drained soil in full sun.

Cut back after flowering. Propagate by hardwood cuttings of the current year's growth, taken in winter and rooted in a sandy propagating mix in the open frame, or by semiripe cuttings in summer. Increase also by seed.

T. gallica Mediterranean; shrub or small tree, 6½–33 ft (2–10 m) tall with spreading to erect, slender branches; flowers pink in dense, cylindric racemes 1¼–2 in (3–5 cm) long; *T. ramosissima* E Europe to Asia; shrub or small tree to 20 ft (6 m) tall; flowers pink in slender racemes to 1¼ in (3 cm) long; includes cultivars with pale pink to deep rose flowers, some such as 'Rubra' with very feathery, gray-tinted foliage and bright pink flowers.

Tanacetum (from the Medieval Latin name, *tanazita*, itself derived from the Greek *athanasia*, immortality—the herb tansy was scattered in shrouds to discourage worms and maggots). Compositae. N temperate regions. Some 70 species, mostly scented, annual or perennial herbs, occasionally slightly woody, with entire, toothed or dissected leaves that are often covered in hairs and sometimes silvery. The flower heads are daisy- or buttonlike and white, yellow or both.

A number of low-growing, mound-forming species have very attractive white or silver-downy, finely divided foliage, including *T. densum*, *T. haradjanii* and *T. argenteum*. These are suited to the rock garden, raised bed and warm, south-facing, dry walls and banks, or other situations characterized by open, sunny nature and perfect drainage. *T. parthenium*, feverfew, is more commonly grown in the herb garden; it has been of recent interest for its role in the treatment of migraine. *T. coccineum* is grown in the herbaceous and cut-flower border. It tolerates a range of soils, except those that are very heavy or wet, and will thrive in sun (for better flowering) or light dappled shade; it requires the support of pea sticks in the border and, if cut back after flowering, may give a second flush of bloom later in the season. Propagate by seed, and in the case of perennials, by division or from basal cuttings in spring. *T. parthenium* will self-seed, often to the point of nuisance, although self-sown seedlings will transplant readily if

watered in well. As with the smaller alpine species, it can also be increased by soft cuttings with a heel in summer.

T. argenteum Mediterranean; perennial to 12 in (30 cm), white-tomentose; leaves ¾–2¾ in (2–7 cm), rounded to ovate, 1–2-pinnate to entire; flower heads yellow; *T. coccineum* PAINTED DAISY, PYRETHRUM; W Asia, Caucasus; glabrous perennial to 24 in (60 cm); leaves elliptic to oblong, pinnatisect, dark green; flower heads to 2¾ in (7 cm) in diameter, white to pink or purple-red; cultivars include large to dwarf plants with single to double flower heads in tones of pink, rose, scarlet and dark red; *T. densum* Turkey; perennial subshrub to 12 in (30 cm); leaves ¾–2 in (2–5 cm), ovate, 2-pinnatisect, white-tomentose; flower heads small, yellow; *T. haradjanii* Syria, Turkey; silvery white-tomentose perennial subshrub to 12 in (30 cm); leaves to 2 in (5 cm), oblong to elliptic to ovate, finely 2–3-pinnatisect; flower heads yellow; *T. parthenium* FEVERFEW; SE Europe, Caucasus; aromatic, bushy perennial to 16 in (40 cm); leaves 1¼–3 in (3–8 cm), ovate, pinnatisect, cut and toothed, glandular, mid-green; flower heads to ¾ in (2 cm) in diameter, ray florets white, disk florets yellow; includes cultivars with gold to lime green leaves, dwarf and compact to tall, and with single to pompon flower heads.

Tapeinochilus (from Greek *tapeinos*, low, and *cheilos*, lip, referring to the small labellum). Zingiberaceae. New Guinea, Malaysia, Indonesia, NE Australia. Some 15 species, perennial herbs resembling *Costus*. The flowers are yellow to brown with small lips. They are carried in showy, conelike spikes composed of waxy, overlapping and colorful bracts. Cultivate as for *Costus*. *T. ananassae* PINEAPPLE GINGER; Moluccas; 3¼–6½ ft (1–2 m) tall; inflorescence to 8 in (20 cm), bracts scarlet to crimson, closely overlapping with their tips recurved, the whole resembling a pineapple, flowers yellow.

tapis vert an expanse of turf; but also applied to knots or parterres created from dwarf box (*Buxus* species).

taproot the primary root, which conveys nutrients and anchors the plant.

tar oils tar distillates containing hydrocarbon and phenolic oils; formerly available for use mainly as insecticidal sprays during winter, especially on dormant fruit trees, against hibernating insects or eggs, including those of aphids, scale insects and winter moths. Referred to as winter wash. Also effective as eradicants of moss and lichens on tree trunks.

tar spot (*Rhytisma acerinum*) a fungal disease of *Acer* species, causing pale yellow leaf spots on leaves in spring, which develop into conspicuous, large, shiny black blotches with yellow halos by midsummer. It is not usually the cause of serious damage but premature leaf fall can result from heavy infection. The fungus overwinters on fallen leaves and young foliage is infected in spring.

The fungus is highly susceptible to sulfur dioxide in the air, and clean air legislation has resulted in an increased incidence in urban areas.

fungal infection

Acer tar spot

For small ornamental trees that are regularly disfigured, it is worth collecting and burning infected leaves and spraying expanding leaves with an appropriate fungicide in the spring. A similar disease, *Rhytisma salicinum*, affects willows.

tarsonemid mites (Acari: Tarsonemidae) minute mites, up to $\frac{1}{128}$ in (0.25 mm) long, with four pairs of legs and glistening white or caramel-colored bodies. Males are smaller than females and the last pair of legs is held erect to enable them to carry pre-adult female nymphs prior to mating. The females lay relatively large eggs, from which emerge active larvae with only three pairs of legs; the larval stage is followed by nonfeeding preadult nymphs, which are enclosed in their inflated larval skins. The life cycle may be completed in 10–14 days under warm conditions and breeding may occur throughout the year.

T

The BROAD MITE (*Polyphagotarsonemus latus*) is of worldwide distribution and in warmer regions is an important pest of castor oil, citrus, cotton, pepper, potato, rubber and tea; in temperate countries, it infests greenhouse plants, such as eggplant, begonias, browallias, capsicums, chrysanthemums, *Cissus*, *Cyclamen*, dahlias, fatshederas, fuchsias, gerberas, *Impatiens*, pelargoniums and tomatoes. The foliage of infested plants becomes stunted, brittle and puckered, often accompanied by a downward roll of the leaf margin. The blooms of some plants, including gerberas and chrysanthemums, become malformed and lopsided. Begonias are particularly susceptible to infestation by these mites and typically develop a rust-colored scarring on the underside of leaves.

The STRAWBERRY MITE (*Tarsonemus pallidus*), also known as the CYCLAMEN MITE, occurs in Europe and North America. Outdoors, it attacks strawberries and some perennial asters; susceptible greenhouse plants include azaleas, aphelandras, chrysanthemums, *Cissus*, fatshederas, *Ficus*, fuchsias, gloxinias, heliotropes, ivies, pelargoniums, saintpaulias, verbenas, and *Cyclamen*. Symptoms include leaf puckering, distorted flowers, severe stunting of growth and extensive bronzing of young leaves; the leaf margins of *Cyclamen* and *strawberry* are often turned inward.

The BULB SCALE MITE (*Steneotarsonemus laticeps*) attacks *Narcissus*, especially those forced for early flowering, and hippeastrums. The mites congregate in the neck of the bulb, feeding in the spaces between the bulb scales. Emerging leaves first appear a brighter green than those of healthy plants, with yellow or brown streaks at the leaf margins and edges of the flower stem; these later develop into longitudinal scars, which are brown in *Narcissus* and red in hippeastrums. Leaves become curved and both leaves and flower stems are stunted, with buds either failing to open or producing distorted blooms. Heavily-infested plants have the appearance of being dusted with a fine white powder at the leaf bases.

The FERN MITE (*Hemitarsonemus tepidariorum*), which infests greenhouse ferns causing stunting and distortion, and the MUSHROOM MITE (*Tarsonemus myceliophagus*), are other species of tarsonemid mite.

Infested plants should be destroyed, but move carefully since mites readily fall off, spreading infestation. Only healthy plants should be introduced; mites on strawberry runners, *Narcissus* bulbs and some other plants can be controlled by *hot water treatment* (q.v.).

Taxodium (from *Taxus*, the yew, and Greek *eidos*, resemblance: the genus superficially resembles *Taxus*). Cupressaceae. US, Mexico. SWAMP CYPRESS, BALD CYPRESS. 3 species, deciduous coniferous trees to 150 ft (45 m), commonly found in sodden or submerged habitats. The trunk is often buttressed and, when growing in wet conditions, it may be surrounded by exposed, conical roots or *knees*. The bark is stringy, fissured, brown-gray to rusty red and peels in strips. Broadly conic at first, the crown becomes irregular with age. The leaves are scalelike (on the persistent new growths, or throughout in *T. ascendens*) or oblong to lanceolate to linear and 2-ranked along feathery, deciduous branchlets. *T. distichum* and *T. ascendens* are both trees of flooding river bottoms and coastal swamps. In cultivation, neither needs waterlogged soil. They can, nonetheless, be kept in up to 24 in (60 cm) of permanent water, and so are ideal for planting in the pond or lake bed, at pond or lake margins, or on islands. Both species respond to warm summers, and frost damage can occur below about 14°F (−10°C). *T. distichum* is very tolerant of city air and the high pH of chalk streams; its fall color is superb. The more southerly *T. ascendens* is more tender. Propagate by seed or by cuttings during late summer.

T. ascendens POND CYPRESS; SE US; to 80 ft (25 m), 'knees' rarely produced, crown columnar; leaves to ½ in (1 cm), subulate, bright green turning fox red in fall, closely adpressed to slender, erect branchlets; *T. distichum* SWAMP CYPRESS, BALD CYPRESS; SE US; to 130 ft (40 m), 'knees' often produced in wet sites, crown conic; leaves to ¾ in (2 cm), linear to lanceolate-oblong, pale green turning rust red in fall, 2-ranked and spreading on branchlets; var. *imbricatum* 'Nutans': branchlets pendulous.

taxon (plural taxa) a general term for a taxonomic unit or group of any category or rank. Thus, *Buddleja* is a taxon at genus level, *Buddleja davidii* is a taxon at species level and *Buddleja* 'Black Knight' is a taxon at cultivar level.

taxonomy the identification, nomenclature and classification of living things.

Taxus baccata 'Fastigiata'
All plants of this strongly upright yew are vegetatively propagated clones of a sport that arose at Florence Court in Ireland.

Taxus (Latin name for Yew). Taxaceae. Northern temperate zones to Mexico, C Malesia. YEW. 10 species, normally dioecious, slow-growing, evergreen coniferous trees or shrubs. The bark is thin, red-brown, scaly and exfoliates in plates on older stems. The leaves are narrow, linear to oblong or lanceolate to falcate and glossy dark green with a distinct midrib. The leaves and seeds are highly toxic, the latter enclosed by a colorful, fleshy aril open at the apex.

T. baccata is very tolerant of cold and heat, shade and sun, wet and dry exposure, and any pH; it is, however, sometimes damaged, or even killed when temperatures fall to −13°F (−25°C) or lower. It withstands most types of urban pollution, but is sensitive to soil compaction by roads; damage has also been associated with acid rain. It is ideal for shelter, screens and as a dark background for pale flowers, and is the traditional choice for backing the herbaceous border, garden seats and marble statuary, as well as an ideal material for topiary. Old and overgrown specimens can be pruned back savagely to the pole of the central stem. Where *T. baccata* is not hardy, for example, in the NE US and E Canada, its place in gardens is taken by *T. cuspidata* and *T. × media*; these are hardy to at least −31°F (−35°C), but they are also more demanding of summer heat and humidity. *T. mairei* needs very hot, humid summers to grow well.

Seed may require lengthy stratification. However, good seedlings spring up wherever birds void the seeds; when they are first found at about 4 in (10 cm) tall (they form very little fibrous root and will not move easily when larger), put them in pots or line them out. The cultivars are propagated by cuttings, taken as for *Chamaecyparis*, or by grafting on to seedlings; scions must include an erect leading shoot if the upright growth pattern is to be maintained. Side shoots will not develop a leader and remain prostrate.

T. baccata YEW; Europe to Asia Minor; tree to 50 ft (15 m), crown ovoid-conic, becoming domed, much-branched; leaves ⅝–1¼ (1.5–3 cm) × 1/16 in (0.2–0.25 cm), linear-oblong, glossy dark green; aril red; includes many cultivars, among them dwarf to tall clones with spreading and low to tall and fastigiate habit, small to long leaves, sometimes marked cream or wholly yellow to lime, with red to orange or glowing yellow arils; *T. cuspidata* JAPANESE YEW; Japan; to 66 ft (20 m), often a shrub in cultivation; leaves ⅝–1 (1.5–2.5 cm) × 1/16–⅛ in (0.2–0.3 cm), linear, with a pointed tip, banded yellow-green beneath; aril scarlet; range of cultivars as for *T. baccata*; *T. mairei* S China to SE Asia; to 50 ft (15 m), or bushy in cultivation; leaves to ⅝–1½ (1.5–4 cm) × 1/16–⅛ in (0.2–0.3 cm), linear to lanceolate, falcate, yellow-green above; aril red; *T. × media* (*T. baccata* × *T. cuspidata*); garden origin; pyramidal, spreading bush, leaves as for *T. cuspidata*, aril scarlet; range of cultivars as for *T. baccata*.

tayberry see *hybrid berries*.

Tecoma (from the Mexican name for these plants, *tecomaxochitl*). Bignoni-

aceae. From Arizona and Florida to Argentina. TRUMPET BUSH, YELLOW BELLS. Some 12 species, evergreen or semideciduous trees or shrubs with pinnate leaves and tubular flowers. Grow in full light, but provide protection from direct sunlight in summer. Maintain a minimum temperature of 50–55°F (10–13°C). Water moderately in summer, hardly at all in winter. Prune after flowering. Propagate by seed sown in spring, by semiripe cuttings, or simple layering.

T. capensis CAPE HONEYSUCKLE, erect or scrambling shrub or tree, usually evergreen, to 23 ft (7 m) tall with pinnate leaves and, in spring and summer, clusters or racemes of yellow, orange or scarlet, tubular flowers. Grow in full sun on walls and pergolas in more or less frost-free conditions. Water and fertilize generously when in growth, sparingly in winter. Prune after flowering. Propagate by air-layering or by semiripe cuttings. *T. stans* US, C and S America; to 10 ft (3 m); flowers 1¼–2½ in (3–6 cm) long, yellow lined or stained red.

Tecophilaea (for Tecofila Billiotti, daughter of Professor Colla of Turin, *c.*1830). Liliaceae (Tecophilaeaceae). Andes of Chile. 2 species, small cormous perennial herbs with narrow leaves and solitary, salverform to broadly funnel-shaped flowers in spring. Grow in the alpine or cold greenhouse. Plant in a fertile, sandy potting mix, and position in sun; water only when in growth, gradually reduce water after flowering to allow a warm, dry dormancy in

summer. Propagate by offsets or by seed, which will develop more reliably following hand-pollination. *T. cyanocrocus* Chile; flowers 1¼–1½ in (3–3.5 cm), royal blue, veined and often tinted white in neck, sometimes with a white margin; 'Leichtlinii': flowers paler blue with broad white central zone; 'Violacea': flowers deep purple-blue.

Telekia (for Teleki de Szek [fl. 1816]. who founded a great library in Hungary). Compositae. C Europe to Caucasia. 2 species, tall, coarse perennial herbs with heart-shaped, stalked leaves and loose racemes of large, daisylike flower heads in late summer. Fully hardy and suited to waterside or woodland plantings in large gardens, where it will make huge mounds of foliage, and bear long, branched stems of fine-rayed daisies. Grow in moist soil in sun or part shade, and with some shelter from cold winds. Propagate by seed or division. *T. speciosa* C Europe, Caucasus, Balkans, C and S Russia; to 6½ ft (2 m); leaves to 12 in (30 cm), aromatic, coarsely toothed, hairy beneath; flower heads yellow.

Tellima (an anagram of *Mitella*, a closely related genus). Saxifragaceae. Western N America. FRINGE CUPS. 1 species, *T. grandiflora*, a semievergreen, glandular-hairy, perennial herb. The leaves are low-lying, cordate to reniform, 1¼–4 in (3–10 cm) broad and nearly as long, the margins 5–7-lobed and toothed. Produced in late spring, the flowering stem is 8–32 in (20–80 cm) tall and carries a raceme of

Tellima grandiflora and Mitella breweri
Plants in these two genera are closely related, hence the name of one is an anagram of the other. Another example of this way of naming similar genera is *Allium* and *Muilla*.

small, campanulate flowers, their petals fringed and white tinged green to deep red. Fully hardy and a useful ground-cover for moist borders, woodland and rock gardens, in humus-rich soil in shady spots. The cultivar 'Rubra' (syn. 'Purpurea') is strongly tinted purple-red throughout. Cultivate as for *Heuchera*.

Telopea (from Greek *telopos*, seen at a distance, referring to the conspicuous crimson flowers). Proteaceae. Australia. 4 species, evergreen shrubs with leathery leaves and slender flowers packed in terminal heads and surrounded by showy bracts. Grow *Telopea* in a well-drained, slightly acidic sandy loam in full sun or light shade. Ensure that the plants receive ample summer moisture, and provide protection from strong winds. Once established, *Telopea* will benefit from regular light pruning and will stand being cut hard back to rejuvenate. This plant can tolerate light frosts and may be grown in sheltered temperate gardens where the winter temperature seldom falls much below 23°F (−5°C). *Telopea* can be increased by seed.

T. speciosissima WARATAH; E Australia; straggling shrub to 10 ft (3 m); red flowers amid red bracts in a dense, rounded head to 6 in (15 cm) across; *T. truncata* TASMANIAN WARATAH; low spreading shrub or a tree to 26 ft (8 m); flowers rich crimson or yellow in heads to 3 in (8 cm) across.

temperate house a greenhouse where the temperature is maintained at about 55°F (13°C) minimum.

tender used of plants liable to injury or death when subjected to low temperature; cf. *hardy*.

tendril a slender modified branch, leaf or axis that is capable of attaching itself to a support either by twining or adhesion.

tent caterpillars (Lepidoptera) the caterpillars of some moths and butter-flies that feed gregariously, for all or part of their lives, in extensive silk webs or tents; they are also known as WEB-BERS or WEBWORMS. They include the larvae of the LACKEY MOTH (*Malacosoma neustria*), a common European

species, which are blue-gray and hairy, up to 2 in (50 mm) long, with white and orange-red longitudinal stripes; they feed on the foliage of many trees and shrubs, including apple, cherry, pear, plum, alder, blackthorn, elm, hawthorn, hazel, oak, rose and willow. Several closely related North American species, including the EASTERN TENT CATERPILLAR (*M. americanum*), the WESTERN TENT CATERPILLAR (*M. californicum*), the PACIFIC TENT CATERPILLAR (*M. constrictum*), and the SOUTH WESTERN TENT CATERPILLAR (*M. incurvum*), attack a wide range of fruiting and ornamental trees and shrubs.

SMALL ERMINE MOTHS (*Yponomeuta* species) occur in Europe and North America and all have dusky gray cater-pillars spotted with black, up to ½ in (12 mm) long, that feed on plants such as blackthorn, hawthorn, apple, *Euonymus*, bird cherry and willow.

Other common tent caterpillars include the larvae of the HAWTHORN WEBBER (*Scythropia crataegella*) in Europe, which are brown, up to ⅝ in (15 mm) long, and also attack *Cotoneaster horizontalis*; the larvae of the JUNIPER WEBBER (*Dichomeris marginella*), which are red-brown with two white stripes, up to ½ in (12 mm) long, and feed on junipers in Europe and North America; and the larvae of the BROWN-TAIL MOTH (*Euproctis chrysorrhoea*), found in both continents, which are black and hairy, up to 1½ in (37 mm) long, with brown warts bearing tufts of hair and two conspicuous red spots at the posterior end. Brown-tail moth larvae feed on fruit trees, roses, hawthorn, willow and other trees and shrubs, and bear hairs which may cause a painful skin rash. Two other pests of garden crops in North America are the GARDEN WEB-WORM (*Achyra rantalis*), which has green-yellow caterpillars, up to ¾ in (18 mm) long, with black dots on each segment, and the BEET WEBWORM (*Loxostege sticticalis*), which has green to yellow larvae, up to 1 in (25 mm) long, with a black stripe.

Tent caterpillars can be controlled by removing and burning infested branches. Alternatively, the young caterpillars can be sprayed with a recommended contact insecticide, ensuring that sufficient force is applied to penetrate the silk webbing.

tepal a unit of a perianth, which cannot be clearly distinguished as a sepal or petal; for example, the flower segments of *Tulipa*. In orchids, the term is applied to the sepals and petals minus the labellum and was originally coined for this purpose.

teratology the study of plant abnormalities or monstrosities. See *malformations*, *proliferation*.

terete cylindrical, and smoothly circular in cross-section.

ternate leaves, sepals or petals in threes. A ternate leaf is a compound leaf divided into three leaflets; in a biternate leaf, these divisions are themselves divided into three parts; in a triternate leaf, these parts are further divided into three.

Ternstroemia (for Christopher Ternstroem [d. 1748], Swedish natural-ist and traveler in China). Theaceae. Asia, Americas, Africa. 85 species, evergreen trees or shrubs with leathery leaves and 5-petaled flowers with numerous stamens in summer. These are followed by small, red fruit. *T. japonica* may tolerate temperatures to about 14°F (−10°C). Grow in fertile, humus-rich, nonalkaline soil in part shade. Pinch shoot tips to encourage branching and prune to shape in spring before bud break. Propagate by fresh seed or by semiripe cuttings in late summer. *T. japonica* (syn. *T. gymnanthera*); Japan; shrub or small tree to 11½ ft (3.5 m); leaves 1½–2¾ in (4–7 cm), cuneate to obovate, dark green; flowers white with obovate to cuneate petals; fruit to ½ in (1 cm) in diameter, red; includes 'Variegata', with leaves gray-green edged cream becoming red-tinted.

terrace a flat area raised above main ground level; more generally, any level area treated formally, for example, with paving, and often separated from the rest of the garden by a balustrade or low wall; especially such an area adja-cent to a dwelling, acting as a transi-tion between house and garden and which is frequently referred to as a patio. A terrace is also a level area created artificially on a slope, with retaining walls.

Terrarium

terrarium a small enclosed glass container in which ornamental plants are grown, *see* also Wardian case.

terrestrial growing in the soil; a land plant.

Tetranema (from Greek *tetra*, four, and *nema*, thread, referring to the stamens). Scrophulariaceae. Mexico, Guatemala. 2 species, low perennial herbs with long-stalked clusters of small, tubular and 2-lipped flowers in spring and summer. Provide a minimum temperature of 55°F (13°C). Water moderately (avoiding waterlogging) and fertilize mature specimens regularly with a dilute liquid fertilizer. Provide strong filtered light. Grown as house plants, *Tetranema* species will flower sporadically throughout the year on a well-lit windowsill. Propagate from fresh seed (which may take 1–2 months to germinate), or by division in spring. *T. roseum* (syn. *T. mexicanum*); MEXICAN FOXGLOVE, MEXICAN VIOLET; Mexico; leaves to 4¾ in (12 cm), obovate, dark green, somewhat leathery; flowers to ⅝ in (1.5 cm), lilac to mauve with darker markings, on stalks to 8 in (20 cm) tall.

Tetrapanax (from Greek *tetra*, four, and *Panax*, a related genus, in reference to the presence of four petals in the plant originally described). Araliaceae. Asia (Taiwan). RICE-PAPER PLANT, CHINESE RICE-PAPER PLANT. 1 species, *T. papyrifer*, a suckering shrub or small tree to 23 ft (7 m) tall with slender branches. The leaves, to 20 in (50 cm) or more across, are palmately compound, toothed and covered in scurfy pale felt at first. In the cultivar 'Variegata', the leaves are patterned with

cream, white and various shades of green. Produced at various times of year in massive, umbellate panicles, the flowers are small, cream and invested with large, woolly bracts. Hardy to 23°F (–5°C). In colder areas, the top growth may be cut back to ground level during the winter but the base will sprout in spring. Plant in most soils and situations, but allow plenty of room since *Tetrapanax* often creates running and suckering thickets. Where space is restricted, it may be confined to containers on patios or plunged in the border. Plants grown in the open ground may be regularly chopped back. Increase by suckers.

tetraploid a plant with four sets of chromosomes, instead of two sets, as in most plant species; it is annotated 4 ×. Examples of natural tetraploids are *Cyclamen persicum* and the potato.

Tetrastigma (from Greek *tetra*, four, and stigma, referring to the 4-lobed stigma). Vitaceae. Indo-Malaysia to tropical Australia. 90 species, deciduous or evergreen shrubs climbing vigorously by tendrils. The leaves are palmately or pedately compound; the flowers are inconspicuous and followed by inedible grapelike fruits. Suitable for the intermediate greenhouse or conservatory, or for large spaces in the home or in public buildings (minimum temperature 50°F/10°C). Train on strong wires, posts and rafters. Grow in pots, tubs or beds in a high-fertility loam-based mix with added garden compost and leaf mold. Give bright, filtered light or partial shade. During summer, maintain high humidity by syringing or hosing once the foliage is no longer in bright sunshine. Water plants plentifully when in growth; reduce watering in winter. Cut out overcrowded growth during spring. Increase by stem cuttings in summer, by simple layers, or by detached stem tips. *T. voinierianum* (syn. *Cissus voinieriana*, *Vitis voinieriana*); CHESTNUT VINE, LIZARD PLANT; Laos; very vigorous, covered in dense, tawny down, especially at first; stems stout, becoming woody, tendrils simple; leaflets 3–5, tough, tawny-hairy beneath, 4–10 in (10–25 cm), obovate to broadly rhombic, toothed.

tessellated checkered; marked with a grid of small squares.

testa the outer coating of a seed.

tetradynamous having four long stamens and two short as in Cruciferae.

tetramerous with parts in fours, or groups of four; often written as 4-merous.

Teucrium (from Greek *teukrion*, used in Dioscorides and Theophrastus, perhaps derived from the Trojan king Teucer, supposed to have used the plant medicinally). Labiatae. Cosmopolitan, especially Mediterranean to W Asia. GERMANDER, WOOD SAGE. Some 300 species, evergreen, usually aromatic perennial herbs, shrubs and subshrubs with tough leaves and spikes or heads of tubular, 2-lipped flowers in summer. *T. aroanium* and *T. polium* are suited to the rock garden, raised bed and trough, *T. chamaedrys* to border edging, where it will stand light clipping. All three are hardy to 0°F (–18°C). *T. fruticans* is more sensitive to cold and needs the shelter of a warm, sunny wall in sharply draining soil. This species should be mulched in hard winters and the frost-damaged top growth pruned back hard in mid-spring. It is one of the finest silver-leaved shrubs for dry, sheltered gardens. Grow all in full sun in well-drained soil. Protect from excessive wet in winter. Propagate by softwood or semiripe cuttings in a sandy propagating mix.

T. aroanium (Greece; suckering subshrub to 4 in [10 cm]; leaves to ¾ in [2 cm], tomentose; flowers mauve); *T. chamaedrys* (WALL GERMANDER; Europe to Caucasus; perennial herb or subshrub, 4–20 in (10–50 cm) tall; leaves to 1½ in (4 cm), dark green, toothed; flowers pink, red, purple or white; includes cultivars with cream-variegated leaves and compact habit); *T. fruticans* SHRUBBY GERMANDER; Iberia; evergreen shrub to 6½ ft (2 m); leaves to 1 in (2.5 cm), silver-hairy at least beneath; flowers large, blue to lilac or white; *T. polium* Mediterranean to W Asia; perennial procumbent subshrub to 18 in (45 cm); leaves ½–1¼ in (1–3 cm), rugose white-woolly; flowers white, yellow, purple or pink.

T

texsel greens see *cabbage*.

Thalia (for Johann Thal [1542–1583], German botanist). Marantaceae. Tropical and subtropical Americas, tropical Africa. About 12 species, very large, evergreen perennial herbs of wet places. The leaves arise in two ranks from a basal clump, their petioles long, erect and terminating in a kneelike joint, the blades ovate to lanceolate and held more or less horizontally. Bell-like, silken flowers hang from the flexuous branches of tall, slender panicles in summer. Suitable for subtropical gardens, where the bold, gray-green foliage and graceful inflorescences make a dramatic impact in bog gardens or at pond margins. If its roots do not freeze, *T. dealbata* will withstand winter minimums of 19°F (−7°C). Plant in sun or partial shade in moist, fertile soil with plenty of organic matter. *Thalia* grows well with the soil surface either at water level or covered by up to 18 in (45 cm) of water. In cool temperate areas, grow in the greenhouse or conservatory (minimum temperature 50°F/10°C); stand in shallow water or submerge in indoor pools. In summer, these plants can be moved outdoors to small ponds or to water-filled half barrels. Propagate from seed in spring or by division in spring or summer.

T. dealbata S US, Mexico; 5–10 ft (1.5–3 m); leaves to 20 in (50 cm), covered with mealy lead-white bloom; flowers to 3 in (8 cm), violet; *T. geniculata* tropical America, tropical Africa; differs from last in its height, 10–13 ft (3–4 m), its longer, narrower and less mealy leaves and larger flowers in a more strongly pendulous panicle.

Thalictrum (name used by Dioscorides for a plant with coriander-like leaves, possibly a member of this genus). Ranunculaceae. Northern temperate zones, tropical S America, tropical and South Africa, Indonesia. MEADOW RUE. 130 species, perennial herbs with ferny, ternately compound foliage and delicate panicles of small, brushlike flowers during spring and summer. These lack petals, consisting of petal-like sepals and numerous showy stamens. Fully hardy. Plant in dappled shade or, where a cool, damp

root run can be guaranteed, in full sun. Increase by division in spring or from fresh seed sown in summer and fall.

T. aquilegiifolium Europe to Asia; 12–60 in (30–150 cm); sepals green-white, filaments mauve to white, pink or deep purple; *T. chelidonii* Himalaya; 12–100 in (30–250 cm); sepals lilac to white, filaments mauve to white; *T. delavayi* W China to Tibet; to 48 in (120 cm); sepals lilac to white; *T. diffusiflorum* Tibet; to 40 in (100 cm); sepals mauve; *T. flavum* YELLOW MEADOW RUE; S W Europe to N Africa; to 40 in (100 cm); sepals pale yellow; *T. kiusianum* Japan; to 6 in (15 cm); sepals white to purple, stamens lilac; *T. lucidum* Europe to temperate Asia; to 40 in (100 cm); sepals yellow-green; *T. orientale* Greece to Asia Minor; to 12 in (30 cm); sepals white to lilac.

thallophyte a cryptogam consisting principally of a thallus.

thallus an undifferentiated vegetative growth.

Thamnocalamus (from Greek *thamnos*, bush, and *kalamos*, reed). Gramineae. Himalaya, South Africa. Some 6 species of clumping bamboos. See *bamboos*.

thatch organic debris that accumulates at the soil surface in lawns, as a result of mowing or natural senescence or disease of grass plants. It is more prevalent on compacted or poorly drained lawns. See *lawns*.

theca a case; specifically, the pollen sac in flowering plants or the capsule in bryophytes.

Thelocactus (from Greek *thele*, nipple, and *cactus*). Cactaceae. C and N Mexico, SW US. 11 species, low-growing cacti with globose to short-cylindric, ribbed or tuberculate, spiny stems and funnelform flowers. Provide a minimum temperature of 45°F (7°C). Grow in a neutral, gritty medium, in full sun, with low humidity. Keep dry from midfall until early spring, except for light misting on warm days in late winter. Increase by seed or offsets.

T. bicolor SW US; stem depressed-globose, ovoid to cylindric, 2–15 (5–38

cm) × 2–5½ in (5–14 cm), ribbed, spines tinged red, yellow or white; flowers 1¼–2¾ in (3–7 cm), pink to magenta, throat red; *T. leucacanthus* Mexico; stem globose to cylindric, 1¾–6 (4.5–15 cm) × 1–2 in (2.5–5 cm), ribbed and tuberculate, spines tinged yellow; flowers to 2 in (5 cm) in diameter, magenta; *T. setispinus* (syn. *Ferocactus setispinus*); SW US, N E Mexico; stems globose to cylindric, 2¾–4¾ in (7–12 cm) × 2½–3½ in (6–9 cm), ribbed but not tuberculate, spines pale yellow to red-tinged, hooked; flowers to 2 in (5 cm), yellow with a red throat.

Thelypteris (Theophrastean name, from *thelys*, female, and *pteris*, fern). Thelypteridaceae. Temperate regions. 2 species, rhizomatous ferns, with softly scaly rhizomes and lanceolate to deltoid, bipinnatifid fronds, often scaly and gray-hairy above and glandular beneath. Fully hardy. Plant in moist to wet soil with a pH of 5.0 to 7.0, in sun or shade. Increase by division or spores. *T. palustris* MARSH FERN; cosmopolitan; rhizomes long, creeping; sterile fronds 3–15 in (8–38 cm), thin-textured, lanceolate, up to 25 pairs of linear to lanceolate, pinnately divided pinnae, fertile fronds taller, stouter and stiffer with narrower pinnae and stipe usually longer than blade.

Thermopsis (from Greek *thermos*, lupine, and *opsis*, appearance). Leguminosae. S and W US, Siberia, N India, E Asia. 23 species, perennial herbs with trifoliolate leaves and erect racemes of pealike flowers in summer. Suited to large herbaceous and mixed borders, they are hardy to at least 5°F (−15°C). Grow in moderately fertile well-drained soil in sun. Propagate by seed or division.

T. rhombifolia (syn. *T. montana*); Rocky Mountains to New Mexico; 8–39 in (20–100 cm); leaflets hairy beneath; flowers yellow in downy or glabrous racemes; *T. villosa* (syn. *T. caroliniana*); CAROLINA LUPINE; SE US; 20–39 in (50–100 cm); leaflets somewhat glaucous and downy beneath; flowers yellow in downy racemes.

thermostat a device for regulating temperature in greenhouses and propagators. It incorporates a temperature

Thinning seedlings (beets)

Thinning sideshoots (nectarine)

Thinning fruits (peach)

sensor, by which means heating and ventilating equipment can be operated at chosen settings.

therophyte a plant that completes its growth cycle in one season and survives adverse conditions by means of protective seed.

Thespesia (from Greek *thespesios*, divine). Malvaceae. Tropics. PORTIA TREE. 17 species, evergreen trees and shrubs, usually evergreen with large leaves and showy, 5-petaled and cup-shaped flowers. Cultivation is the same as for *Pavonia*. The following species is well-suited to seaside locations in tropical and subtropical regions. *T. populnea* PORTIA TREE; tropics; tree to 39 ft (12 m); leaves cordate; flowers 2½–4 in (6–10 cm) across, yellow with a maroon center.

Thevetia (for Andre Thevet [1502–1592], French monk and traveler in Brazil and Guyana). Apocynaceae. Tropical America, West Indies. 8 species, evergreen shrubs and trees. The leaves resemble those of *Nerium*, but are darker and more glossy. The flowers are funnel-shaped, with a cylindric tube that dilates sharply to a campanulate throat, and broad, spirally overlapping lobes. All parts are highly poisonous. Cultivate as for *Nerium*, but maintain a minimum temperature of 59°F (15°C). *T. peruviana* YELLOW OLEANDER; shrub or small tree to 26 ft (8 m); flowers fragrant, to 2¾ in (7 cm), yellow to orange or peach, rarely white.

thigmonasty, thigmotropism see *haptonasty, haptotropism*.

thin used of soil that is poorly structured and prone to drying, erosion or capping, or otherwise impoverished. Such soils are sometimes alternatively referred to as lean.

thinning (1) the selective removal of plants from a bed, sown row, container, orchard or other plantation, in order to reduce competition for nutrients, moisture and light. Seedling plants are best thinned when they are very young, to allow for typical and steady development of the remaining plants. Thinning outdoor rows of vegetable plants is often referred to as singling; (2) the removal of over-crowded shoots, especially during the pruning of trees and shrubs; (3) the reduction of flower buds, and more usually young fruits, on fruit trees, in order to improve fruit quality, to prevent branch breakage, or to influence cropping pattern.

thistles a group of handsome plants, including the genera *Carduus*, *Onopordum*, and *Silybum*, suitable for carefully chosen places in the garden. The CREEPING THISTLE (*Circium arvensis*) is, however, unwelcome because of its invasive habit; when young, it produces a taproot from which laterals develop sending up shoots from underground buds. The roots are brittle and the plant is readily propagated during cultivating operations; it also perpetuates itself through seed.

A population of creeping thistle can be reduced by repeated cutting of shoots, over a number of years, just before flowering. Forking out requires concentrated effort so that as many root fragments as possible are removed.

Where space can be afforded, a long term mulch with an opaque, durable fabric will reduce a stand of the weed. Most effective as a means of control is herbicide treatment with glyphosate or glyphosate trimesium, applied according to product recommendations; the weedkillers are nonselective and therefore potentially damaging to valued plants, and more than one application is likely to be necessary.

Thlaspi (from Greek *thlao*, to flatten, and *aspis*, shield, alluding to the fruits). Cruciferae. Northern temperate regions. 60 species, annual to perennial, low-growing herbs, those here cushion- or mat-forming with small leaves and racemes of 4-petaled flowers in spring and summer. Grow in scree and moraine in the rock garden, or in sinks and troughs. They will tolerate winter temperatures to 5°F (−15°C), given a gritty and well-drained growing medium. Small plants may exhaust themselves in flowering. Frequent propagation is recommended. Increase by seed or by division in fall.

T. alpinum SW and C Europe; biennial or perennial; flowers white to purple with violet anthers; *T. bulbosum* Greece, Aegean Islands; biennial or perennial with a swollen rootstock; flowers violet; *T. montanum* MOUNTAIN PENNYCRESS; C Europe; perennial; flowers white.

thong a root cutting taken from fleshy rooted plants, such as horseradish and sea kale.

thrips (Thysanoptera) small brown, yellow or black insects, up to ¹⁄₁₆–¹⁄₈ in pale flecking

Western flower thrips on gloxinia

(2–3mm) long, with slender bodies. Most species have wings when adult, which are very narrow and fringed with long hairs; when the insects are in repose, the wings lie more or less parallel along the back. Wingless thrips live in the surface of soil, while winged types are abundant in flowers and on foliage, many species causing considerable damage. Thrips have rasping and sucking mouthparts, which are used to penetrate plant tissue and imbibe the sap; emptied plant cells become filled with air, resulting in characteristic silvering of foliage. In severe infestations, whole leaves may wither and fall prematurely and the seedlings of many plants are particularly vulnerable.

Some thrips attack fruits, scarring the surface; others invade flowers, discoloring them with blotches or streaks, and causing blooms to become malformed or withered. The number of generations varies with species and locations; for example, the onion thrips (*Thrips tabaci*) passes through two generations in cold northern climates, but under glass and in warmer regions the number of generations may increase to twelve. Thrips often swarm in vast numbers, encouraged by dry, settled weather and a temperature of at least 68°F (20°C).

Of the 5000 or more species distributed world-wide, most are plant feeders but some feed on mites, aphids and other small, soft-bodied insects, or on fungal spores.

The ONION THRIPS (*Thrips tabaci*), of which the adults are yellow to dark brown, attacks plants outdoors and under glass, especially onions, brassicas, begonias, cucumber, cinerarias, chrysanthemums, *Cyclamen*, dahlias, gerberas, gloxinias, tomatoes and sweet peas. The GREENHOUSE THRIPS (*Helio-*

thrips haemorrhoidalis*), infests greenhouse plants in temperate countries, including arum lily, azaleas, chrysanthemums, crotons, ferns, fuchsias, orchids, nicotianas, and tomatoes; the adults are dark brown with an orange-colored apex to the abdomen. The WESTERN FLOWER THRIPS (*Frankliniella occidentalis*) infests a similar range of plants, and also attacks seed heads and scars the surface of fruits, especially nectarine. The GLADIOLUS THRIPS (*Thrips simplex*) has dark brown adults, and also infests freesias. The PEAR THRIPS (*Taeniothrips inconsequens*), with dark brown adults, attacks the leaf and blossom buds of pears, plums, cherries, apricots, apples and almond, and causes russeting on the fruit surfaces. The PRIVET THRIPS (*Dendrothrips ornatus*) infests privet and lilac, causing severe silvering of the foliage; the adults are dark brown with alternate light and dark bands on the forewings, giving the insect's back a banded appearance. The LILY THRIPS (*Liothrips vaneeckei*) congregates between the scales of lily bulbs, which develop brown, sunken areas; the shiny black adults are relatively large at up to $1/8$ in (3mm) long.

Other important species in Europe include the PEA THRIPS (*Kakothrips robustus*) and the ROSE THRIPS (*Thrips fuscipennis*). The dark brown pea thrips infests the young leaves, flowers and pods of peas and, to a lesser extent, broad beans, causing loss of yield and undersized, distorted pods, scarred with silvery brown areas. The rose thrips injures the apex of rose blooms in the bud stage, causing the tips of petals to turn brown and wither, with flecking of blooms and silvering of foliage; the adults are yellow to dark brown.

Other North American species that attack garden flowers and vegetable crops include the FLOWER THRIPS (*Frankliniella tritici*); the TOBACCO THRIPS (*F. fusci*); the BEAN THRIPS (*Caliothrips fasciatus*); and the IRIS THRIPS (*F. iridis*). Another species, the CITRUS THRIPS (*Scirtothrips citri*), is a serious pest of citrus, avocado, nectarines and grapes, causing leaf distortion, blindness of buds and scabby fruits.

Some species of thrips, notably onion thrips (*T. tabaci*), tobacco thrips (*F. fusa*) and the western flower thrips

(*F. occidentalis*), are vectors of tomato spotted wilt virus.

Thrips populations build up quickly in hot dry weather, so under-glass infestations can be discouraged by increasing humidity and growing under cooler conditions. Most species can be controlled by recommended contact insecticides. Infested gladioli corms or lily bulbs should be dusted with recommended contact insecticides before storing.

thrum-eyed see *heterostyly*.

Thuja (from Greek *thyia*, referring to a scented gum). Cupressaceae. N America, E Asia. THUJA, RED CEDAR. 5 species of evergreen coniferous trees, ultimately with open, conical crowns, bark exfoliating in long strips and flattened, fanlike sprays of scalelike, aromatic leaves. All species are from cool woodlands with high rainfall or cold, wet coastal or low plains. *T. plicata* grows to very large sizes in areas with cool wet summers; it is smaller and sparser in drier and warmer regions, and does not survive in the hot summers of the eastern US. *T. koraiensis* and *T. standishii* need more sheltered, humid sites. *T. occidentalis* is considerably more cold-tolerant, and can survive in boggy sites too wet for other species. Although completely hardy, *T. koraiensis* is not seen in the far north, and frost hollows are to be avoided for this species and *T. standishii*. All species tolerate clipping and make good hedges. Propagate as for *Chamaecyparis*. The hybrid *T. plicata* × *T. standishii* has been bred in Denmark to introduce resistance to the fungus *Didymascella thujina* to *T. plicata*. Young seedlings of *T. plicata* can be killed by this fungus, but it is easily controlled by applying appropriate fungicides to the seedbed. Damage to older plants, and the other species, is negligible.

T. koraiensis KOREAN THUJA; Korea; tree to 50 ft (15 m), crown conic with trailing then ascending branchlets; leaves green and glandular above with silvery bands beneath; *T. occidentalis* eastern N America; tree to 66 ft (20 m), crown narrowly conic with horizontal branches and spreading, flattened branchlets; leaves yellow-green above, gray-green beneath, becoming yellowy

T

brown; many cultivars available, including dwarf to tall, domed, compact and weeping habits; *T. plicata* WESTERN RED CEDAR; western N America; to 230 ft (70 m), crown conic to columnar, branches horizontal to drooping with erect tips; leaves in flattened sprays, dark green above, gray-white beneath; includes dwarf to tall cultivars, erect and narrowly conic to low and spreading with fan- to thread-like foliage in shades of olive to bronze or with white to yellow variegation; *T. standishii* JAPANESE THUJA; Japan; to 100 ft (30 m), crown broadly conic and open, branchlets spreading to ascending; leaves glandular, dark green to yellow-green.

Thujopsis (from *Thuja* and Greek *opsis*, appearance, referring to the similarity between these two genera). Cupressaceae. C and S Japan. 1 species, *T. dolobrata*, HIBA ARBORVITAE, an evergreen conifer to 100 ft (30 m) with red-brown bark exfoliating in long stringy strips, a conic crown with numerous, layering stems and horizontal to upswept branches. The leaves are scale-like, thick, waxy and glossy green above and white beneath. Raise from cuttings or by seed and plant in a sheltered site where the soil remains damp, preferably in or beside woodland. Although hardly affected by cold or pH, this tree does demand high humidity.

Thunbergia (for Carl Peter Thunberg [1743–1828], Swedish botanist. A student of Linnaeus, he traveled for the Dutch East India Company as a doctor and sent back plants from Japan, Java and South Africa. Thunberg became professor of botany at Uppsala). Acanthaceae. South and tropical Africa, Madagascar, warm Asia. 100 species, perennial shrubs and herbs, most climbing or scrambling; some are treated as annuals in cultivation. Produced at various times of year, the flowers are large and funnel-shaped with a broad, 2-lipped rim of five lobes. *Thunbergia* includes some of the most beautiful climbers for the arches and pergolas of tropical and subtropical gardens; *T. erecta* may be used as a flowering hedge in such climates. For cooler zones, the genus contains many elegant and vigorous specimens for

borders and large containers in the warm greenhouse or conservatory. Some species, such *T. alata* and *T. gregorii*, flower in their first year from seed and are commonly grown as frost-tender annuals. The latter may overwinter at the base of a warm south-facing wall in mild winter areas, especially if cut back and mulched at the end of the season. Grow in a fertile, loam-based mix with additional sharp sand and screened manure, in direct sun but with shade from the strongest summer sun. Train on wires or trellis. Maintain a minimum temperature of 50°F (10°C) and moderate humidity with good air movement. Water plentifully when in growth. Reduce water as light and temperature levels fall, keeping the plants almost dry in winter. Prune lightly in late winter or early spring before growth resumes; hard pruning will severely reduce the production of flowers. Easily propagated by most types of cuttings and by seed.

T. alata BLACK-EYED SUSAN; tropical Africa; twining herb, often grown as an annual; flowers solitary, to $1\frac{1}{2} \times 1\frac{1}{2}$ in (3.75×4 cm), creamy-white or yellow-orange usually with a dark purple-brown throat; includes 'Alba', with white flowers with a dark center, 'Aurantiaca', with orange flowers with a dark center, 'Bakeri', with snow white flowers, and Suzie Hybrids, with orange, yellow or white flowers with a dark eye; *T. capensis* South Africa; sprawling herb or subshrub, sometimes grown as an annual; flowers 4–10 together, to $1\frac{1}{4}$ in (3 cm), creamy yellow; *T. coccinea* India, Nepal, Burma; woody-stemmed climber, 10–26 ft (3–8 m); flowers in pendent racemes 6–18 in (15–45 cm) long, each to 1 in (2.5 cm), orange-red; *T. erecta* BUSH CLOCK VINE, KING'S MANTLE; tropical W to South Africa; erect or twining shrub to $6\frac{1}{2}$ ft (2 m); flowers solitary, 3 in (7 cm), tube yellow-cream, lobes dark blue-violet; includes 'Alba', with white flowers; *T. fragrans* India, Sri Lanka, Australasia; woody-

stemmed, aromatic climber; leaves 2–3 in (5–7.5 cm), triangular-ovate to oblong, base cordate to hastate, entire to toothed; flowers solitary, to $1\frac{1}{4}$–2 in (3–5 cm), white, lobes spreading; includes 'Angel Wings', with snow white, lightly scented flowers; *T. grandiflora* BLUE TRUMPET VINE, SKY VINE, CLOCK VINE, SKYFLOWER, BLUE SKYFLOWER, BENGAL CLOCK VINE; N India; large twining shrub; flowers usually solitary, to 3×3 in (7.5×7.5 cm), blue-violet, sometimes with a paler, or white to golden, throat; includes 'Alba', with white flowers; *T. gregorii* tropical Africa; twining herb, often cultivated as an annual; flowers solitary, $1\frac{3}{4} \times 1\frac{3}{4}$ in (4.5×4.5 cm), orange; *T. mysorensis* India; twining shrub to 20 ft (6 m); flowers in pendent racemes to 16 in (40 cm) long, each to $1\frac{1}{2} \times 2$ in (3.75×5 cm), rich golden yellow with red-brown lobes.

thunderflies see *thrips*.

thunderworms (*Mermis* species) types of eelworm with thin bodies up to 6 in (160 mm) long. They are most often seen in early summer after heavy rain, when the thin, creamy white or blackish worms can be found writhing on the foliage of various low-growing plants as they deposit their eggs. Thunderworms are harmless to plants and animals other than certain plant-feeding insects, such as caterpillars, grasshoppers or earwigs, in the bodies of which eggs hatch to develop as parasites.

thyme (*Thymus* species) a perennial, aromatic, low-growing herb or subshrub, grown for flavoring and as a source of thymol for antiseptics and deodorants. Also useful for ornamental planting and as a bee plant. There are many types. *T. vulgaris* retains its flavor well in slow cooking, and is a useful ingredient of bouquet garni; *T × citriodorus*, the LEMON-SCENTED THYME, and *T. pulegioides* are commonly grown, and *T. herba-barona* has a distinctive caraway flavor. It becomes straggly after a few

Thymus vulgaris

T

783

years and should be repropagated either from spring-sown seed or from cuttings or division in April or May which will produce established plants sooner. Plant 6–12 in (15–30 cm) apart in a sunny, dry, well-drained site. Leaves can be picked year-round to use fresh, or just before flowering for drying.

Thymus (from Greek *thyo*, to perfume: *thymon* or *thymos* used by Dioscorides, probably for this plant). Labiatae. Eurasia. THYME. 350 species, dwarf or low-growing perennial, aromatic herbs and subshrubs with small leaves and tubular, 2-lipped flowers at various times of year.

Thymes are culinary herbs and important bee plants. All are strongly aromatic in favorable locations. They retain their fragrance well on drying, and are used in potpourri, sweet sachets and herb pillows. Plant in dry sunny borders, open scree, troughs, rock gardens, herb gardens and between paving stones, where low-growing species will tolerate treading. Most species are hardy to at least 5°F (–15°C), but, in very cold climates, they should be protected with a dry mulch of bracken litter or evergreen prunings. Plant in well-drained, preferably calcareous soil, in full sun. Clip over after flowering to maintain vigor and compactness. Propagate by division, by simple layering, and from semiripe heel cuttings in spring or summer.

T. caespititius SW Europe; dwarf, mat-forming shrublet; to 2 in (5 cm) tall; leaves to ¼ in (0.6 cm), narrowly spathulate, ciliate; flowers rose, lilac or white; includes 'Aureus', with pale gold leaves; *T. carnosus* Portugal; woody, erect, to 16 in (40 cm); leaves ovate, light green to gray-green, fleshy, hairy beneath; flowers white, lilac or pink; *T.* × *citriodorus* small shrublet, seldom exceeding 8 in (20 cm) with very small, smooth, dark green leaves strongly scented of lemon; includes cultivars with white to cream or silver-marked leaves and solid lime to gold foliage; *T. herba-barona* CARAWAY THYME; Corsica, Sardinia; dwarf, wiry subshrub to 8 in (20 cm); leaves very small, hairy, caraway-scented; flowers pink to mauve; includes strongly caraway- and lemon-scented forms; *T. leucotrichus* Greece, Turkey; creeping, dwarf shrub to 4 in

(10 cm) with very small, pale, hairy, narrow leaves; flowers pink to purple; *T. praecox* S, W and C Europe; mat-forming subshrub to 2 in (5 cm); leaves lanceolate to obovate, ciliate; flowers white, mauve or purple; *T. pseudolanuginosus* origin unknown; stems prostrate; leaves small, gray-green, hairy; flowers pale pink; *T. pulegioides* Europe; highly aromatic dwarf shrub, ascending to 8 in (20 cm); leaves oval to elliptic, hairy beneath; flowers pink to purple; *T. serpyllum* WILD THYME, N Europe; very aromatic dwarf shrublet with small, ovate, ciliate leaves and heads of pink to purple flowers; includes many cultivars, creeping to erect with white to silver- or gold-variegated leaves; *T. vulgaris* Mediterranean; very aromatic, woody, erect to 12 in (30 cm); leaves small, narrow, revolute; flowers white to purple; includes variegated and camphor-scented cultivars.

thyrse, thyrsus an indeterminate, paniculate or racemose primary axis, with determinate cymose or dichasially compound lateral axes.

Tiarella (from Latin *tiara*, little diadem, referring to the shape of the fruit). Saxifragaceae. FALSE MITERWORT, SUGAR SCOOP. Eastern and northwestern N America, 1 species Asia. 5 species, rhizomatous, evergreen perennial herbs with low clumps of long-stalked, rounded to palmately lobed leaves and, in late spring and early summer, erect racemes of small, starlike flowers. Hardy ground-cover with excellent fall color. Its cultivation requirements are as for *Heuchera*, except that it requires more shade and a moist, humus-rich soil. Remove decayed leaves in winter and protect the rhizomes with a mulch of garden compost. *T. cordifolia* FOAM FLOWER; N America; stoloniferous; leaves to 4 in (10 cm), cordate, 3–5-lobed, toothed, hairy bright green, usually with some maroon staining around veins; racemes to 12 in (30 cm) tall; includes cultivars with pink to wine red flowers and bronze to purple-marbled or maroon leaves; *T. wherryi* differs in lacking stolons and its bronze-pink cast.

Tibouchina (native name in Guyana). Melastomataceae. GLORY BUSH. Tropical S America, mostly

Brazil. Some 350 species, evergreen shrubs or subshrubs, usually hairy with rounded, 5-petaled flowers in spring and summer. Plant in freely draining, neutral or (preferably) acidic, moisture-retentive, fertile soil. Admit bright light, but provide some shade from the hottest midsummer sun; water plentifully when in full growth; Keep almost dry in winter, with a minimum temperature of 45–50°F (7–10°C). Propagate by greenwood or semiripe cuttings. *T. urvilleana* (syn. *T. semidecandra*); BRAZILIAN SPIDER FLOWER; Brazil; shrub 6½–16 ft (2–5 m); leaves 2–4 in (5–10 cm), ovate, deep green and finely bristly above, paler and downy beneath; flowers 2¾–4 in (7–10 cm) across, silky, mauve, indigo or violet, stamens pink to purple.

Tigridia (from Latin *tigris*, tiger, in this case referring to the jaguar, whose spotted pelt these flowers resemble). Iridaceae. Mexico, Guatemala. PEACOCK FLOWER, TIGER FLOWER, FLOWER OF TIGRIS. 23 species, perennial bulbous herbs with sword-shaped, plicate leaves. Borne in summer, the flowers are large, showy and shallowly cupped, the three outer segments broadly obovate and spreading, the inner segments smaller and ovate to pandurate. In frost-free regions, these bulbs will grow outdoors all year round in a sunny position in free-draining soil. Elsewhere, plant them outdoors in spring, lifting in fall to be dried off and stored at 46–54°F (8–12°C) in sand. Otherwise, plant in pots or in the border of the cool greenhouse or conservatory. Grow in a warm, sheltered site in full sun, in fertile, well-drained, sandy or gritty soil. Plant in late spring, 4–5 in (10–12.5 cm) deep in light soil, more shallowly in heavier soil or if bulbs are small. Propagate from seed, alternatively by offsets. *T. pavonia* Mexico; 24–50 in (60–125 cm); outer perianth segments 2½–4 in (6–10 cm), orange, bright pink, red, yellow or white, variously spotted red, brown or maroon at base, inner segments of similar ground color but more distinctly marked.

Tilia (from Latin *tilia*, lime, derived from Greek *ptilon*, feather, referring to the flower bract). Tiliaceae. Eastern and central N America, Europe, W, C

T

and E Asia. LINDEN, LIME, BASSWOOD. About 45 species, deciduous trees, usually with cordate, toothed leaves. Produced in summer, the flowers are small, 5-petaled and fragrant, carried in short, pendulous cymes fused for half their length to an oblong to lanceolate, yellow-green bract.

The following are hardy and grow best in fertile, alkaline to neutral soil with medium to good drainage. They suffer when exposed to harsh winds and are best among or not far from other trees. Propagate by root suckers, layering, grafting or from wild-collected seed. Dig up suckers with as good a root as possible, and replant. Layers respond well to rooting hormone, dusted into the wound; cut from the parent tree when well rooted. Grafts should only be used where suckers are too high up for easy layering; side-graft erect suckers onto seedlings of *T. tomentosa* or *T. platyphyllos*. Stocks of *T.* × *vulgaris* should not be used, since they produce dense basal suckers below the graft, and normal branch-shoot scions must not be used, since they lack apical dominance.

The root and stem suckers are not attractive features on specimen trees, and the best limes for use in gardens are those species, like *T. tomentosa* and *T. platyphyllos*, that rarely produce them. These should be grown from seed. Collect seed in midfall from wild trees or extensive single-species plantings; stratify for 3–5(–16) months in damp sand at 32–37°F (0–3°C) before sowing in early spring in a cold frame. Germination takes up to 18 months (particularly if the stratification period is short). Garden-collected seed will probably produce hybrids of dubious parentage and should not be used, except in the search for new cultivars.

T. americana AMERICAN LINDEN, AMERICAN BASSWOOD; N America; to 130 ft (40 m), crown broad, ovoid to rounded; leaves 2½–6 in (6–16 cm), broadly ovate to orbicular, base truncate, apex acuminate, serrate, dark green and glabrous above, paler beneath with prominent veins and tufts

of hairs in their axils; *T. cordata* LITTLELEAF LINDEN, SMALL-LEAVED LIME; Europe; to 130 ft (40 m), usually smaller, crown outspread, suckering; leaves 1¼–2¾ in (3–7 cm), rounded, apex abruptly acuminate, base cordate, serrate, glossy dark green above, somewhat glaucous beneath with tufts of hairs in the vein axils beneath; *T.* × *euchlora* CRIMEAN LINDEN, CAUCASIAN LIME; to 66 ft (20 m), crown rounded, branches arching to pendulous; leaves 2–4 in (5–10 cm), rounded to ovate, apex abruptly acuminate, base cordate, margins finely serrate, glossy dark green above, paler beneath with tawny tufts in the vein axils; *T.* × *europaea* (syn. *T.* × *vulgaris*); EUROPEAN LINDEN, COMMON LIME; to 130 ft (40 m), crown broadly conical; leaves 2–3½ in (5–9 cm), broadly ovate, apex abruptly acuminate, base cordate, dark green, glabrous above, paler with tufts of hairs in vein axils beneath; *T. henryana* China; to 80 ft (25 m); leaves emerging bronze-red, 2–4¾ in (5–12 cm), broadly ovate, apex acuminate, base cordate to truncate with bristly teeth, veins hairy above, with tufts of hairs in veins beneath; *T. mongolica* MONGOLIAN LINDEN; Russia, Mongolia, China; to 66 ft (20 m), usually shorter, branches arching; leaves 1½–2¾ in (4–7 cm), broadly ovate, apex abruptly acuminate, base truncate to cordate, often 3–5-lobed, finely toothed, flushed red at first, hardening glossy, dark green above, somewhat glaucous beneath; *T. oliveri* China; to 80 ft (25 m); leaves 2¾–4½ in (7–11 cm), broadly ovate, apex abruptly acuminate, base cordate or truncate with sparse, glandular teeth, dark green and glabrous above, white-tomentose beneath; *T.* 'Petiolaris' PENDENT WHITE LIME, WEEPING LIME; Europe to Asia Minor; to 100 ft (30 m), crown domed, branches pendulous; leaves 2–4 in (5–10 cm), oval to rounded, apex acute, base cordate, serrate, dark green and slightly downy above, white-tomentose beneath; *T. platyphyllos* LARGE-LEAVED

LINDEN, BROAD-LEAVED LINDEN; Europe to W Asia; to 130 ft (40 m), crown conical to broadly columnar; leaves 1¾–4½ in (4.5–11 cm), rounded to ovate, apex abruptly acuminate, base cordate, serrate, dull dark green above, light green and somewhat downy beneath; includes 'Rubra', with branches coral- to sealing wax-red in winter; *T. tomentosa* SILVER LIME; S Europe to Asia Minor; to 115 ft (35 m), crown dense, ovoid-conical becoming domed with age, branches erect; leaves 2–4½ in (5–11 cm), rounded, apex abruptly and finely acuminate, base cordate, serrate and sometimes lobed, dark green above, gray-tomentose beneath.

Tillandsia (for Dr Elias Tillands [1640–1693], Swedish botanist and physician). Bromeliaceae. S US, C and S America, W Indies. AIR PLANT. Some 400 species, mostly epiphytic, evergreen perennial herbs. They vary greatly in habit and size, from the miniature and mossy to the large rosette-formers. Many species are sparsely rooting, taking much of their moisture and nourishment from the air through gray, absorbent scales that cover the foliage. The leaves may be threadlike or sword-shaped. Each growth produces a terminal spike of showy, short-lived flowers, often surrounded by vividly colored bracts.

T. cyanea and *T. lindenii* need a minimum temperature of 50°F (10°C), with high humidity and protection from full sun. They grow best planted in small pots containing an open, bark-based medium. Water throughout the year, allowing the medium to dry between waterings. Given dry, airy conditions, the remaining species listed here will survive barely frost-free conditions. They prefer, however, a humid and buoyant atmosphere in full sun and temperatures of 45–73°F (7–23°C). They are grown exclusively as epiphytes—wired, pinned or even glued to branches, cork slabs, bromeliad 'trees' and other objects. Given a daily misting with soft water in warm weather, a weekly misting at cold times, an occasional very dilute foliar fertilizer and adequate light, they may thrive for many years as house plants. Under glass, their culture is considerably easier, but avoid keeping these species

Tilia cordata

785

too wet during cool, dull spells. *T. usneoides*, a signature plant of the deep South of the US, is useful for providing light shade in sections of the greenhouse—merely hang it in swags from the roof. It is also a good, live lining material for orchid baskets. Increase all species by division; *T. usneoides* may also be increased by lengths of stem.

T. aeranthos S Brazil, Argentina, Paraguay, Uruguay; to 12 in (30 cm), with a distinct stem; leaves 2½–5½ in (6–14 cm), narrowly triangular and densely gray-scaly; flowers dark blue in an ovoid to cylindric spike with pink-purple bracts; *T. argentea* C America, West Indies; to 10 in (25 cm) in flower, stem more or less absent; leaves 1¼–3½ in (3–9 cm), filiform, silvery-scaly in a dense rosette; flower spike narrow, flowers bright cerise amid red-green bracts; *T. bulbosa* Mexico to Brazil, Ecuador, W Indies; to 9 in (22 cm) in flower, stem absent but swollen leaf bases form a 'bulb'; leaves terete, narrow, snaking, dark green to olive marked maroon; flowers violet amid red bracts in compound spikes; *T. caput-medusae* C America; to 10 in (25 cm) in flower, stem absent but base bulbous; leaves linear to triangular with inrolled margins, snaking, silver-scaly; inflorescence branched with red to pink bracts and violet flowers; *T. cyanea* (Ecuador, Peru; to 12 in (30 cm) in flower, stem absent; leaves linear to triangular, dark green in a low, spreading rosette; flowers large, dark violet, emerging from closely overlapping, 2-ranked, waxy pink bracts in a flattened, elliptic spike; *T. ionantha* Mexico to Nicaragua; to 4 in (10 cm), stems short, clumped; leaves to 2½ in (6 cm), narrowly triangular, mid-green, gray-scaly, the innermost flushed red at flowering; flowers violet-blue in a short, nestling spike amid rose to scarlet bracts; *T. lindenii* Peru; differs from *T. cyanea* in its pink- to purple-tinted, green bracts and royal blue flowers with a white base; *T. recurvata* BALL MOSS; SE US to S America; dwarf, clump-forming with linear, terete, curving, olive and scaly leaves to ¾ in (2 cm) long and white to violet flowers in a very short inflorescence; *T. streptophylla* Mexico to Honduras; to 10 in (25 cm) in flower; leaves strap-shaped to narrowly triangular, silvery-scaly, twisted and curling in a low

Tillandsia argentea
Air plants have become very widely available in recent years. They are often sold secured to ornamental bark, driftwood or even shells.

bulbous-based rosette; flowers purple amid red bracts in branching spikes; *T. usneoides* SPANISH MOSS, OLD MAN'S BEARD; SE US to S America; individual growths composed of three or four, threadlike, silvery-scaly leaves to 1½ in (4 cm) long and connected by wirelike rhizomes in dense, mossy festoons to 3 m (10 ft) long; flowers very small, stalkless, pale blue and yellow-green.

tiller a shoot issuing from the base or roots of a plant; used particularly to describe basal side shoots of grasses.

tilth a fine crumbly structure to the surface layer of a soil with good moisture status, produced by careful preparation, and especially suitable for seed sowing.

tine an individual prong, spike, or tooth on a cultivation tool, such as a fork, rake, or harrow.

tip bearer apple and pear cultivars that produce fruit buds at the tips of one-year-old shoots. During pruning, only shoots longer than 22 cm (9 in)

are cut back. The apple cultivars 'Worcester Pearmain' and 'Bramley's Seedling' are partial tip bearers, and the pear 'Jargonelle' is a tip bearer.

tipburn a disorder of lettuces in which the leaf margins become brown and the plant disfigured, with arrested growth and associated vulnerability to disease infection. The condition arises particularly in light soil outdoors, where there is shortage of water, and under greenhouse conditions of high humidity during bright sunshine.

tipping removing the tip of a shoot during pruning; often used specifically to describe the light pruning of leader shoots of apples.

Tipuana (referring to the Tipuani Valley in Bolivia, where there are large populations of this tree). Leguminosae. S America. 1 species, *T. tipu* (syn. *T. spedosa*), TIPU TREE, YELLOW JACARANDA, ROSE WOOD, PRIDE OF BOLIVIA, an evergreen tree to 115 ft (35 m) tall with pinnate leaves and yellow to apricot or orange, pealike flowers in pendulous panicles. A fast-growing, spring-flowering tree, used in the tropics and subtropics for park and avenue plantings. Cultivate as for tender *Bauhinia*.

tissue culture see *micropropagation*.

Titanopsis (from Greek *titanos*, chalk, and *opsis*, resemblance, referring to the chalklike surface of the leaves of some species). Aizoaceae. South Africa, Namibia. 6 species, highly succulent, rosette- and clump-forming perennial herbs, with thickly fleshy leaves, their

year-old shoots

tip-bearer

short fruiting "spurs" grow from older wood

spur-bearer

Tip-bearing apples
Tip-bearing cultivars do not crop well if trained and pruned into restricted forms such as espaliers, since their fruit is borne chiefly near the apex of one-year-old growth. Free-standing forms such as the bush and standard allow this growth to develop without being shortened.

tips covered with chalky tubercles resembling stone. Yellow or orange, daisylike flowers open in bright weather. Cultivate as for *Pleiospilos*.

T. calcarea leaves to 1 in (2.5 cm), spathulate, tinged white or green-blue, tip truncate with green-red to gray-white tubercles; flowers golden to orange-yellow; *T. schwantesii* leaves to 1¼ in (3 cm), spathulate, gray to blue-green sometimes tinged red, tip rounded to triangular with yellow-brown tubercles; flowers pale yellow.

Tithonia (for Tithonus, companion of Aurora, goddess of the dawn). Compositae. C America. MEXICAN SUN-FLOWER. 10 species, erect, robust annual or perennial herbs and shrubs. Produced in summer and fall, the daisy-like flower heads are solitary and long-stalked with golden-yellow to orange-scarlet ray florets and yellow disk florets. Grow in well-drained, moderately fertile soil in full sun. Provide the support of stakes, irrigate in dry periods and deadhead regularly. Sow seed *in situ* in spring or earlier under glass. *T. rotundifolia* Mexico to Panama; annual, 3¼–13 ft (1–4 m) tall; flower heads to 2¾ in (7 cm) in diameter, ray florets orange to scarlet; seed races are available with single or double flower heads, in shades of pale yellow, gold, orange, burnt orange and flame, the plants seldom exceeding 3¼ ft (1 m), and sometimes with finely cut leaves.

Todea (for Henry Julius Tode, of Mecklenburg [1733–1797], mycologist). Osmundaceae. Australasia, South Africa. 2 species, large ferns with stout, erect rhizomes crowned with bipinnate fronds. Provide a minimum temperature of 50°F (10°C), a humid atmosphere and filtered light or shade. Plant in an acidic to neutral mix rich in bark, leaf mold, and garden compost. Keep moist at all times. Syringe in summer. *T. barbara* (syn. *T. africana*); CREPE FERN, KING FERN; Australasia, South Africa; rhizome to 3¼ ft (1 m) tall, stout, black and fibrous; fronds to 3¼ ft (1 m), pale to deep, shining green, pinnules to 1½ in (4 cm), lanceolate, serrate.

toggle lopper a lopper, or long-arm pruner, with a double pivot for extra leverage, used for cutting thick branches.

Cordon tomatoes
For a cordon (right) an indeterminate variety must be used. The main stem is trained vertically and all sideshoots removed (left). Once the desired height is reached the shoot tip is removed.

tolerance (1) a plant that shows few or no signs of disease when infected by a pathogen; (2) a plant capable of adapting to an environmental stress by altered metabolism or growth; (3) the amount of pesticide allowed by legal regulations to remain on a crop at or after harvesting time, expressed in parts per million.

Tolmiea (for Dr. William Fraser Tolmie [1812–1886], surgeon for the Hudson's Bay Company at Fort Vancouver). Saxifragaceae. Western N America. PIGGYBACK PLANT. 1 species, *T. menziesii*, a viviparous, hairy perennial herb. The leaves are long-stalked, 2–4 in (5–10 cm) long, reniform to cordate, shallowly palmately lobed and toothed. Plantlets develop at the junction of the petiole and leaf blade. Small, green-brown flowers are carried in erect racemes in spring and summer. The popular cultivar 'Taff's Gold' (syn. 'Maculata', 'Variegata') has fresh lime green leaves finely spotted and mottled cream to gold. Hardy to 1°F (–17°C), although often grown as a house plant. Cultivate as for *Heuchera*, but provide shade. Propagate by potting plantlets in a sandy, low-fertility, loam-based medium. Feed and grow in intermediate greenhouse conditions for planting out the following spring, or peg leaves to surrounding soil and detach young plantlets when rooted.

tomato (*Lycopersicon esculentum*) a short-lived perennial cultivated as an annual for its usually bright red, fleshy fruit. It is a variable species with a growth habit ranging from an indeterminate vine, attaining a potential length of around 33 ft (10 m) in one season, to compact, determinate bush types. Fruits are borne in clusters and may be round, lobed, or pear-shaped, varying in size from ¾–4¾ in (2–12 cm) in diameter; cultivated forms are usually red but also orange, yellow and striped. There is a wide choice of cultivars available suited to local conditions. In section, the fruits contain cavities or locules filled with seed-containing gel. Most of the smaller, round-fruited cultivars are bilocular in contrast to the larger-fruited beefsteak types which are multilocular, producing a more lobed fruit. The cherry tomato, *L.esculentum* var. *cerasiforme*, has smaller and more sweetly flavored fruit.

The tomato originated mainly in Ecuador and Peru and, following domestication in Mexico and Central America, was introduced into Europe during the early 16th century. It is adapted to a wide range of conditions but is frost-tender. Optimum temperature for growth is 68–75°F (20–24°C); temperatures below 55°F (13°C) and greater than 81°F (27°C) adversely affect growth. High light levels are required for maximum fruit set and high yields.

Optimum soil temperature for seed germination is 84°F (29°C). Air temperature greater than 100°F (38°C) can destroy pollen and developing embryos. Setting is poor at high night temperatures of 77–81°F (25–27°C), except with specially selected cultivars, while temperatures below 50°F (10°C) increase the rate of flower abortion. Fruit ripens best at 64–75°F (18–24°C), and poorly between 55°F (13°C) and 50°F (10°C). Fresh fruit, picked at an early stage of ripening, can be stored for several days, optimally at a temperature of 55°F (13°C) in conditions of high humidity.

In temperate regions, fresh outdoor tomatoes are only harvestable during the summer months. Commercially, heated greenhouse production serves most of the year, although poor winter light in northern latitudes makes year-round production difficult.

Plants are seed-raised during early spring, under protection at a temperature of 59–64°F (15–18°C), either sown thinly in seed trays and pricked out into 3 in (7.5 cm) pots, or direct into pots, two or three seeds per pot, and thinned to one. Plants are ready to plant 6–8 weeks after sowing, when 6–8 in (15–20 cm) high with the first flowering truss is visible.

For growing outdoors, plants must be hardened off, and bush (determinate) types are the best choice. These have no prominent leading shoot but a number of side branches, giving rise to a bushy plant; they require a minimum of support. Compact forms are available, suitable for growing in pots, hanging baskets or window boxes. For open-ground sites, a sheltered, sunny position is essential, the soil made fertile and moisture-retentive by the incorporation of organic matter, and ground mulch. Plants are set out 18–24 in (45–60 cm) apart.

Better quality and earlier fruit is obtainable under greenhouse protection, where tall (indeterminate) types are usually grown, with cultivars selected for growing either with or without supplementary heating. Plants may be planted direct into the border soil or grown in pots, by ring culture, or in growing bags, set 16–18 in (40–45 cm) apart. They may be trained up tall canes but, more usually, the plants are progressively twisted clockwise around strong soft twine, which is tied to horizontal wires fixed along the roof of the structure and secured to the base of each plant or to a wire peg.

Indeterminate types require the constant removal of side shoots that arise in axils between leaf stalks and the main stem. Thorough and regular watering and supplementary fertilizer necessary from about the time of first fruit set, with a fertilizer high in potash. Pollination is encouraged by shaking the trusses, and plants are stopped at one leaf above the last required truss. In the greenhouse, wide fluctuation of temperature should be avoided; summer ventilation and shading are essential to keep the temperature as near as possible to a maximum of 68°F (20°C).

Possible problems: aphids, eelworm, red spider mite, whiteflies; gray mold, leaf mold, tomato blight (*see* phytophthora); blossom end rot.

tomentose with densely woolly, short, rigid hairs, perceptible to the touch.

tomentum hair or, more specifically, a tomentose pubescence.

Toona Meliaceae. E Asia to Australasia. 6 species, evergreen or deciduous trees formerly included in *Cedrela* (a genus now confined to the neotropics). Hardy to –13°F (–25°C). Plant in fertile, well-drained soil in full sun. Sow seed during fall, or strike root cuttings in late winter in a cold frame. *T. sinensis* (syn. *Cedrela sinensis*; China; deciduous tree to 66 ft (20 m); leaves 1¼–24 in (3–60 cm) long, pinnate, leaflets 2½–5½ in (6–14 cm), ovate to lanceolate, emerging pink to bronze, hardening deep green, turning gold in fall; flowers small, white to cream, fragrant in pendulous panicles; 'Flamingo': leaves emerging vivid pink, turning creamy yellow then bright green).

top draining see *drainage*.

top dressing the application of quick-acting fertilizers to the soil surface around growing plants to stimulate growth; usually carried out in spring; cf. *base dressing*. Care must be taken to avoid leaf contact, which can cause scorching, and to protect against root damage and pollution of ground water. Top dressing of a lawn involves applying sharp sand and organic matter—such as sieved compost, peat, or spent hops—in order to level the surface and encourage root growth. Sometimes known as side dressing.

top fruit a descriptive term for tree fruits, such as apples, cherries, peaches, pears, and plums; cf. *soft fruit*.

topiary the art of cutting or training trees and shrubs into specified shapes, probably dating from the end of the First century BC. Topiary was widely used in Italian gardens of the 16th and 17th centuries, and spread throughout Europe. A wide range of plants was used, including rosemary, juniper, phillyreas, myrtle and privet.

To create an individual specimen or a structured topiary garden can take from between six to ten years. Good soil preparation and a well-drained site in full sunlight are required for vigorous and even growth. Wind shelter is essential, and plenty of space should be left around topiary specimens to allow for maintenance. Topiaries looks best on level ground and, if possible, should be viewed from above. Shaping should begin when plants are very young.

wigwam of canes of equal length ensures that cone is kept vertical

avoid blunting pruners on wire

use pruners or scissors

Simple topiary form
Guides made from bamboo canes and wire are useful aids to trimming geometric shapes such as this box cone.

It is done by temporarily tying shoots down and clipping with pruners or shears against a simple cane template, or against a shaped wire framework, which may be incorporated into the plant as it grows. Shoots must be tied in while young and supple, pinching them back to encourage branching and training new shoots to fill gaps. Yew, holly, bay, privet and box are some of the best candidates for topiary; when established all need clipping once a year, holly and box around midsummer and yew in early fall. Precise clipping is required, geometric and bird or animal designs always with the aid of guiding templates, and working from the top down. Intricate designs require frequent clipping during the formative years. A dressing of slow-release fertilizer applied in spring is beneficial.

Cones These follow the natural shape of many trees and have the advantage that they can later be developed into a more complex shape, such as a spiral. Plants are first cut to shape by eye before setting up a structure of canes as a template.

Square-based styles Geometric shapes, such as pyramids, obelisks and cubes, are easy to commence, but attention must be paid to maintaining strict verticals and horizontals. They can be used for the formal garden, as part of a structural and proportioned plan. Rounded shapes are easier to maintain.

Crowns For these, it is necessary to select plants with four equally vigorous shoots growing out from the central stem at or near a coincident point. The shoots should be bent downward to utilize the tension of the tree itself and give a more resilient curve. Yew or box are most suitable.

Birds The traditional topiary shapes of birds are most satisfactorily produced from box or yew.

topophysis describes the circumstance in propagation when plants raised from cuttings taken from horizontal branches retain a prostrate growth habit.

topping the removal of the growing point of a plant, other than when done purposely to induce the growth of side shoots (which is referred to as stopping).

Topping may, for example, be carried out to restrict the height of a hedge, or to remove aphid-infested shoots of broad beans.

topsoil soil that, in gardens, is usually fertile and suitable for the cultivation of plants, in contrast to subsoil, which is less weathered and of lower organic-matter content. Topsoil varies in depth, and its natural position in the profile should be preserved during digging and levelling operations.

top working see *grafting*.

Torenia (for Olaf Toren, 18th-century Swedish clergyman). Scrophulariaceae. Africa, Asia, with some species naturalized in US. Some 40 species, perennial or annual herbs with short racemes of broadly tubular, 2-lipped flowers in summer. Plant in moist soil in part shade. Cultivate as for *Alonsoa. T. fournieri* BLUE-WINGS, WISHBONE FLOWER; Asia; to 12 in (30 cm), bushy; flowers ¾–2 in (2–5 cm) across, tube violet, upper lip pale blue, throat lilac to purple marked yellow, lower lobes velvety, dark violet to indigo.

Torreya (for Dr John Torrey [1796–1873], American botanist). Cephalotaxaceae. N America (California, Florida) and Asia (Japan to SW China). NUTMEG-YEW. 7 species, evergreen coniferous shrubs or trees with a broadly oval to conic crown and red-brown, finely shredding bark. Lying flat in two ranks, the leaves are narrowly lanceolate and sharp-tipped. Pollinated cones develop as fleshy, drupelike fruits. Hardy to 0°F (–18°C). Provide shelter and high humidity or moist soil—they tolerate woodland shade very well but not exposure to wind; undemanding as to soil pH. Propagate as for *Taxus. T. californica* CALIFORNIA NUTMEG-YEW; California; tree to 66 ft (20 m), crown broadly conic, branches more or less horizontal with pendulous branchlets; leaves to 2 in (5 cm), dark green to olive, aromatic if crushed; fruit 1¼–1½ in (3–4 cm),

purple-green; 'Spreadeagle': low-growing, branching horizontally; 'Variegata': shoots blotched yellow-green.

tortrix moths (Lepidoptera: Tortricidae) small moths with broad, leaflike wings; their larvae, which are usually green with brown or black heads, wriggle backward actively if removed from their concealed sites. Most tortrix moth caterpillars feed within the turned-over edge of a single leaf, or between adjacent leaves held together by silken threads; others bore into fruits or buds, or tunnel into stems.

Several species are common to Europe and North America. The larvae of the CODLING MOTH (*Cydia pomonella*) burrow into apple and pear fruits; the PEA MOTH (*C. nigricana*) causes similar damage to edible peas. The PINE SHOOT MOTH (*Rhyacionia buoliana*) has red-brown larvae, up to ¾ in (20 mm) long, that tunnel into the buds and young shoots of pines, causing them to turn brown and die. The CARNATION TORTRIX (*Cacoecimorpha pronubana*) has yellow to olive green larvae, up to ¾ in (20 mm) long; they feed between leaves fastened together with webbing, on the buds and blooms of carnations, and many other greenhouse plants, including acacias, *Asparagus*, crassulas, *Cyclamen*, euphorbias, grevilleas, as well as outdoors on *Cytisus*, daphnes, *Euonymus*, ivies, laurel and privet. The BUD MOTH (*Spilonota ocellana*), known in the US as the eye spotted bud moth, has red-brown caterpillars that attack buds in spring and later feed on the foliage, tying together leaves of various woody plants, including cotoneasters and fruit trees and bushes. The STRAWBERRY TORTRIX MOTH (*Acleris comariana*) has pale green larvae with brown heads. They are up to ½ in (12 mm) long, and feed in folded or rolled leaves of strawberries, causing them to turn brown and wither. Common to both continents is the FRUIT TREE TORTRIX MOTH (*Archips podana*), which is one of a complex of species that attack the fruits of apple and to a lesser extent those of

larva grazes on leaf surface

Carnation tortrix moth caterpillar

T

pears, plums and cherries. The caterpillars are green with a darker line along the back; typically, they feed between two leaves fastened together with webbing, but more serious damage is caused when they browse the surface of fruits by feeding beneath a leaf attached to the fruit by webbing. They may also attack blackberries, hawthorns, ivies, oaks, raspberries, rhododendrons and roses.

Other important species in Europe are the FLAX TORTRIX (*Cnephasia interjectana*) and the GREEN OAK TORTRIX (*Tortrix viridana*). The flax tortrix has also been recorded in the Canary Islands and Newfoundland; the green-gray to black caterpillars are commonly found in gardens, attacking in particular heleniums, lettuces, phlox, rudbeckias and solidagos. The green oak tortrix larvae sometimes completely defoliates oaks and later pupates in rolled leaves of underlying plants. The adults are green and the larvae gray-green and up to ¾ in (20 mm) long.

Other important North American species include the ASIAN FRUIT MOTH (*Grapholitha molesta*), the GRAPE BERRY MOTH (*Endopiza viteana*) and the omnivorous LEAF ROLLER (*Platynota stultana*). Larvae of the Asian fruit moth attacks shoots, causing blindness, before tunnelling into fruits of peach, quince and apple, plum and pear; the larvae are white, up to ½ in (12 mm) long. The grape berry moth has two generations of gray-green caterpillars, up to ½ in (12 mm) long; the first generation attacks blossoms and small berries, and the second bores into maturing grapes.

Pheromone traps are available for some species, including codling moth, plum moth, carnation tortrix, and pea moth, allowing contact insecticides to be applied against newly hatched larvae at the correct time. In a small garden, the trapping may reduce pest numbers to an acceptable level without the need to resort to spraying. Recommended contact insecticides may be used to control other species. The bacterial spray containing *Bacillus thuringiensis* has been used successfully against some of these pests. In the US, the Asian fruit moth has been adequately controlled by other biological control methods employing hymenopterous parasites. See *codling moth*, *leaf rollers*.

tortuous irregularly bent and twisted.

torulose of a cylindrical, ellipsoid or terete body, swollen and constricted at intervals but less markedly and regularly so than when moniliform.

torus a receptacle; the region bearing the floral parts.

total weedkiller an herbicide that destroys all vegetation with which it comes into contact, for example, sodium chlorate.

town refuse municipal waste originating from household garbage and street cleaning, is sorted by some municipalities, and segregated organic matter may be composted. It has the disadvantages of variability, low nutrient content, some possibility of heavy metal contamination, and usually glass shard content. It is however in principle an environmentally friendly option, and the processed material is sometimes offered mixed with other organic materials. Some local authorities provide collection points for plant waste, woody forms of which may be shredded before composting; this is referred to as GREENWASTE.

trace elements see *nutrients and plant nutrition*.

Trachelium (from Greek *trachelos*, neck; plants reputedly effective against tracheal diseases). Campanulaceae. Mediterranean. 7 species, perennial herbs with tubular, 5-parted flowers in spring and summer. *T. caeruleum*, suitable for the annual and cut-flower border, is doubtfully hardy, but will bloom in its first year from seed if sown under glass in early spring. Grow in sun in moderately fertile, well-drained soil. The tiny, cushion-forming *T. asperuloides* is suitable for crevice plantings in the rock garden and scree, for trough gardens and for small pans in the alpine house. Although hardy to 5°F (−15°C), it needs some protection from winter wet. Grow in perfectly drained, alkaline soil in sun or with light shade at the hottest part of the day. Propagate by seed or by softwood cuttings in sand in a closed case with gentle bottom heat.

T. asperuloides (syn. *Diosphaera asperuloides*); Greece; tufted, mat-forming, to 1¼ in (3 cm); leaves very small, glossy; flowers disproportionately large, solitary or clustered, white suffused mauve to pink; *T. caeruleum* W and C Mediterranean; erect to 3¼ ft (1 m); flowers small, blue, lilac, mauve or white, in dense, terminal umbels.

Trachelospermum (from Greek *trachelos*, neck, and *sperma*, seed). Apocynaceae. India to Japan. 20 species, evergreen climbing shrubs with milky sap. Produced in summer in terminal and axillary cymes, the flowers are tubular with five spreading lobes twisting and over-lapping to the right. Hardy to 5°F (−15°C) with good drainage and wall shelter. Grow in well-drained, moderately retentive soil in sun or with light part-day shade. Prune to remove deadwood and weak growths, and cut back excessively long stems almost to flowering wood. Propagate by seed, by simple layering or by semiripe cuttings in summer.

T. asiaticum Japan, Korea; 16–23 ft (5–7 m); leaves ¾–2 in (2–5 cm), dark glossy green; flowers fragrant, yellow-white, tube ¼–⅜ in (0.7–0.8 cm), ¾ in (2 cm) across limb, lobes obovate; *T. jasminoides* China; to 23 ft (7 m); leaves 1½–3 in (4–7.5 cm), dark shining green; flowers intensely fragrant, white, tube ¼–½ in (0.75–1 cm), 1 in (2.5 cm) across limb, lobes narrow, wavy; 'Japonicum': leaves veined white, turning bronze in fall; 'Minimum': dwarf, with mottled leaves; 'Variegatum': leaves striped white, often tinged pink to red-bronze; 'Wilsonii': leaves flushed red-bronze to maroon in winter.

Trachycarpus (from Greek *trachys*, rough, and *karpos*, fruit, referring to the fruits of some species). Palmae. Subtropical Asia. 6 species, medium-sized to large palms developing columnar trunks clothed with shaggy, brown fibers and petiole bases. The leaves are large, glossy and palmate with many narrow segments. Golden to cream inflorescences are produced by mature plants. One of the few palms suitable for outdoor cultivation in cool temperate zones, *T. fortunei* will withstand frosts to about 14°F (−10°C), with protection from wind. It is an excellent plant, at least when young, for city gardens and container planting. Plant in well-drained but moist, fertile soil in sun or shade. Propagate by seed. *T. fortunei* CHUSAN PALM, CHINESE WINDMILL PALM; FAN PALM; N Burma, China, naturalized Japan; trunk ultimately to 66 ft (20 m); petioles to 3¼ ft (1 m), sharply toothed, leaf blades to 3¼ × 4 ft (1 × 1.25 m), more or less circular, dark green with many, linear-lanceolate segments, their tips drooping; also hardy, *T. wagnerianus* differs in its smaller, more rigid leaves with narrower, fingerlike segments.

Trachymene (from Greek *trachys*, rough, and *mene*, moon, referring to the appearance of the fruit). Umbelliferae. Australia, W Pacific. 12 or more species, annual, biennial or perennial herbs with ternately divided leaves and small flowers in long-stalked umbels during summer. Grow in fertile, well-drained soil, in a sheltered position in sun. Sow seed under glass in early spring or *in situ* in spring. Alternatively, grow in pots of medium-fertility loam-based mix in the cool greenhouse, and provide light shade from strong sun to preserve flower color. *T. coerulea* BLUE LACE FLOWER; W Australia; annual or biennial to 28 in (70 cm); flowers sky blue to pale lavender, slightly fragrant.

Tradescantia (for John Tradescant [d. 1638], and his son, also named John Tradescant [d. 1662], British naturalists, travelers, collectors and gardeners). Commelinaceae. Americas. SPIDER-LILY, SPIDERWORT. 70 species of perennial or very rarely annual or short-lived herbs. They vary greatly in habit, from erect clump-formers to slender creepers and trailers. Most have succulent stems, thinly fleshy leaves and terminal clusters of 3-petaled flowers in spring and summer.

T. virginiana is hardy and suitable for the herbaceous border. Plant in fertile, well-drained and moisture-retentive soil in sun or light dappled shade. Propagate by division. The remaining, tender species make good dense groundcover for greenhouse borders and subtropical bedding. They are also commonly grown as house plants. The trailing species (all except *T. spathacea*) are especially useful for hanging baskets. Grow in freely draining and moderately

fertile soil, kept moist when the plant is in active growth, in sun or bright filtered light with a minimum temperature of about 59°F (15°C). Propagate by division or cuttings.

T. cerinthoides (syn. *T. blossfeldiana*); FLOWERING INCH PLANT; SE Brazil; stems decumbent, rooting; leaves to 6 in (15 cm), elliptic to oblong, more or less fleshy, glossy dark green and hairy to smooth above, green to purple and hairy beneath; flowers purple-pink to white; 'Variegata': leaves variegated; *T. fluminensis* WANDERING JEW; SE Brazil; stems ascending and decumbent or sprawling to hanging and rooting; leaves ⅝–4¾ in (1.5–12 cm), broadly ovate to lanceolate, smooth, green, sometimes flushed purple beneath; flowers white; includes several cultivars very popular as house plants, with leaves striped or zoned white, silver, yellow-cream and pink, sometimes tinted purple; *T. pallida* (syn. *Setcreasea purpurea*); Mexico; stem to 16 in (40 cm), ascending to decumbent; leaves 2¾–6 in (7–15 cm), oblong-lanceolate to elliptic, trough-shaped, thinly fleshy, glaucous, tinted purple-red, smooth to weakly hairy; flowers pink; 'Purpurea': syn. 'Purple Heart', a very popular cultivar with leaves solidly colored deep purple; *T. sillamontana* (syn. *T. pexata*, *T. velutina*); Mexico; stems ascending or decumbent, to 12 in (30 cm); leaves 1¼–2¾ in (3–7 cm), 2-ranked with clasping bases, elliptic to broadly ovate, somewhat succulent, green flushed purple-red, densely woolly; flowers purple-pink; *T. spathacea* (syn. *T. discolor*, *Rhoeo discolor*); MOSES-IN-A-CRADLE,

THREE-MEN-IN-A-BOAT, OYSTER PLANT, BOAT LILY, MOSES IN THE BULRUSHES; Mexico, Belize, Guatemala; stem short, stout, erect; leaves 8–14 in (20–35 cm), lanceolate, semisucculent, glossy, dark green above, purple-tinted beneath, in a loose rosette; inflorescences axillary, each with a pair of purple-green, fleshy bracts arranged like a boat and containing small white flowers; 'Vittata': leaves striped cream to pale yellow or lime; *T. virginiana* SPIDERWORT; E US; stems slender, clumped, purple-tinted, erect to 16 in (40 cm); leaves to 12 in (30 cm), linear to lanceolate, dark green, arching, thinly hairy; flowers in terminal clusters, dark violet, magenta, pink, mauve, indigo, royal blue, sky blue or white; popular hardy perennials—many cultivars are available, some of them hybrids involving several other US species, these are sometimes included in *T. virginiana* or grouped under the name Andersoniana Group; *T. zebrina* (syn. *Zebrina pendula*; Mexico); stems decumbent to creeping, rooting; leaves 1–4 in (2.5–10 cm), ovate to oblong, slightly succulent, dark green usually striped silver above, purple-tinted beneath; flowers pink, magenta or violet; includes cultivars with leaves stained purple or striped and splashed green, pink, red and white.

trailers plants with stems that grow over the soil surface, often rooting as they do so. They include plants such as trailing *Lobelia*, used at the edges of hanging baskets and other containers. Trailing climbers are scrambling plants that grow upward and horizontally,

Tradescantia Andersoniana Group 'Concord Grape' and T. fluminensis 'Variegata'
Hybrids in the Andersoniana Group are hardy, and make useful border perennials, with a long season of flowering. In frost-prone areas, tender species such as *T. fluminensis* and *T. zebrina* are most frequently seen as houseplants, but are also used as summer bedding.

loosely attached to other plants or to structures; they do not have tendrils or aerial roots, neither do they twine.

translocation (1) the movement of water and solutes within the vascular system of a plant; (2) used of a pesticide which is absorbed into a plant's translocation system and distributed to points distant from where it was applied; thus having widespread effect throughout the plant; (3) the movement of a chromosome segment to another location on the same or another chromosome.

transpiration loss of water by evaporation from plant surfaces, occurring chiefly from open stomata. It is a process accentuated by low atmospheric humidity and temperature rise, and can lead to wilting in dry conditions. Antitranspirant sprays are available to reduce growth check on woody transplants and are especially relevant to evergreens.

transplant (1) (verb) to move a seedling or well-developed plant from one position to another; (2) (noun) a young plant grown from seed or cuttings, intended for direct planting outdoors or for growing in a container or a nursery bed.

transplanter see *bulb planter*.

Trapa (a compressed form of the term *calcitrapa*, the caltrop, a 4-spiked iron ball used to maim horses in battle and which the fruit of this genus is said to resemble). Trapaceae. C Europe to E Asia, Africa. WATER CHESTNUT. 15 species, aquatic, perennial herbs with rosettes of leaves floating by means of inflated petioles, and inconspicuous flowers giving rise to nuts. The raw nuts, rich in carbohydrate and fat, contain toxins which must be destroyed by boiling. They are eaten whole or ground as flour. The following species is sometimes cultivated in aquariums and ponds. They are hardy to −10°F (−23°C). Give full sun, slightly acidic water rich in nutrients. Seeds lose viability if allowed to dry and should be stored in water or wet moss. Propagate also by offsets. *T. natans* (JESUIT'S NUT, WATER CALTROP, WATER CHESTNUT;

widespread; leaf blades to 1¼ in (3 cm), broadly ovate to rhombic, toothed, glossy dark green sometimes turning bronze, petioles to 2 in (5 cm), spindle-shaped, pale, radiating in floating rosettes; fruit a 2–4-horned nut.

trapeziform asymmetrical and four-sided, as a trapezium.

treading the compression of soil in a growing area by using one's feet. Treading is an effective aid for improving soil structure in the preparation of a seedbed, where walking or shuffling over the surface breaks down clods (especially in heavy soils) and serves to firm a soft surface (especially in light soils). Treading is also done to firm the soil around trees and shrubs immediately after planting, and where newly planted specimens are subject to 'lifting' out of the ground due to frost action. Treading; should never be carried out on wet soil because compaction can cause impeded drainage and the exclusion of air.

tree a woody, perennial plant with a single main stem, generally branching at some distance from the ground and possessing a more or less distinct, elevated crown.

tree banding the use of bands of grease, hay, sacking or corrugated paper around tree trunks to trap migrating insects, such as winter moths and certain weevils; in the US, it is known as barrier banding. See *grease banding*.

tree guards devices and constructions used to protect trees from bark-gnawing animals, especially rabbits, hares, cattle and deer. They may take the form of metal or wooden enclosures, to protect specimen trees from larger animals. Wire netting or perforated spiral plastic collars are effective around small trees against rabbit and hare damage. Some tall tree guards, in the form of tubes of translucent plastic material, have the added benefit of providing an ideal growing environment for establishing tree seedlings.

tree house platforms, balconies, seats, and small houses constructed in

trees were once popular in both Eastern and Western gardens, where they were sometimes described as roosts, and used for viewing from or as a place for relaxation. A modern US equivalent is the platform or deck that may surround the base of a tree or lead from house level into the crown of a nearby tree. Tree houses are an excellent way of providing garden interest for children.

tree lopper, tree pruner see *long-arm pruner*.

tree surgery the removal of large tree branches that are damaged, diseased or overcrowded and the treatment of wounds resulting from branch breakage; referring to professional operations.

tree ties any means of securing trees to their supports. Tree ties must allow for increasing trunk girth and also aim to prevent chafing on the stake. They can be made of soft rope, or improvised with strong wire threaded

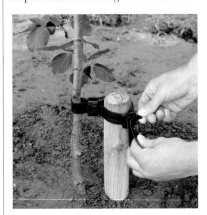

Tree tie
This buckle-and-spacer tie protects the young tree's bark from chafing. It must be checked and loosened regularly to accommodate the increasing girth of the trunk.

through lengths of old water hose. Specially made ties, consisting of plastic straps, are a good choice; the strap passes through a thick buffering band between the tree and stake and is secured with a buckle.

treillage used of trellis and also structures made of trellis, such as arbors, columns, domes and even garden houses and temples.

trellis a construction of diagonally intersecting wooden laths, metal lattice-work or plastic bars, usually forming a 4 in (10 cm) mesh and mounted as variously-sized panels. Trellis has been a feature of garden decoration at least since Roman times, and is useful for creating screens or visually attractive supports for climbing plants, placed either freestanding or against a wall.

trench a vertical-sided furrow or trough made in soil with, depending on the depth required, a spade or draw hoe. Planting in trenches is recommended for certain vegetable crops, such as celery and leeks, and trenches filled with organic matter are also prepared for growing runner beans. Trenches also provide a means of increasing headroom for plants grown under cloches.

trenching see *digging*.

triangulation a method for determining a position using the locations of two fixed points, of known distance from each other, to determine the location of a third point.

tribe a category of taxa intermediate between subfamily and genus.

Trichoderma a genus of soil-dwelling fungi. It contains several species, including *T. viride* and *T. harzianum*, that have antagonistic effects on certain pathogenic fungi.

Trichodiadema (from Greek *thrix*, hair, and *diadema*, crown, referring to the spiny hair-clusters at the tips of the leaves). Aizoaceae. South Africa, Namibia. Some 36 species, succulent shrubs with woody or tuberous roots and terete leaves that terminate in tufts of bristlelike spines. The daisylike flowers open on bright days from spring to late fall. Cultivation is the same as for *Pleiospilos*.

T. densum caudex fleshy, thickened, stems short, mat-forming; leaves to ¾ in (2 cm), papillose, with long, white bristles; flowers crimson); *T. mirabile* (shrublet to 3 in (8 cm), stems white-bristly; leaves to 1 in (2.5 cm), papillose with stiff, dark brown bristles; flowers white.

trichome an epidermal hair or scale, formed of one or more specialized epidermal cells, often glandular-tipped.

Trichopilia (from Greek *thrix*, hair, and *pilion*, a cap, the like of which conceals the anther). Orchidaceae. Tropical C and S America. Some 30 species, epiphytic orchids with laterally compressed, cylindrical to ovoid pseudobulbs and oblong to lanceolate, coriaceous leaves. The flowers are held low or hang down, and consist of linear to lanceolate tepals—often strongly twisted—and a funnel-shaped lip. Grow in the intermediate greenhouse, with a minimum temperature of 54°F (12°C). Pot in pans or baskets in a medium-grade bark mix. Position in good light and high humidity. Impose a short, dry winter rest. Propagate by division.

T. suavis Costa Rica, Panama, Colombia; flowers to 4 in (10 cm) in diameter, delicately fragrant, tepals to 2¼ × ½ in (5.5 × 1 cm), white or cream-white, sometimes spotted pale violet-rose or red, usually undulate but *not* twisted, lip to 2½ × 2 in (6.5 × 5 cm), white or cream-white, often densely spotted pale violet-rose or spotted and lined yellow, throat yellow or yellow-orange, undulate-crisped; *T. tortilis* Guatemala, Honduras, El Salvador, Mexico; flowers to 6 in (15 cm) in diameter, fragrant, waxy, tepals to 3 × ½ in (8 × 1 cm), off-white tinted pale lavender to fleshy purple-brown or yellow-gray with livid blotches, margins much paler, strongly and spirally twisted, lip to 2½ × 1¾ in (6.5 × 4.5 cm), white to pale yellow, throat yellow spotted brown or crimson, margin crisped, undulate.

trichotomous branching regularly by dividing regularly into three.

trickle irrigation, trickle tape see *irrigation*.

Tricyrtis (from Greek *treis*, three, and *kyrtos*, convex; the three outer petals are baglike at the base). Liliaceae (Tricyrtidaceae). E Himalaya to Japan and Taiwan. TOAD LILY. 16 species, deciduous perennial herbs with creeping and tangled rhizomes and clumped, erect to arching stems. The leaves are lanceolate

to elliptic. Borne during late summer and fall in axillary clusters or terminal branching cymes, the flowers are cup- to star-shaped, and composed of six, oblong to lanceolate tepals with swollen bases. Hardy to −10°F (−23°C), especially if thickly mulched in winter. Grow *Tricyrtis* in dappled sun or shade in a sheltered position. Plant in cool, porous soil that is acidic to neutral and rich in leaf mold and garden compost. Keep permanently moist, never wet. Increase *Tricyrtis* by division during spring, alternatively by stem cuttings in late summer (plantlets will develop in the leaf axils).

T. affinis differs from *T. macropoda* in its flowers borne on separate stalks; *T. formosana* (syn. *T. stolonifera*); stems erect; leaves sometimes spotted; inflorescence branched, terminal, flowers to 1¼ in (3 cm) across, widely funnelform to starry, held erect, tepals white to lilac-pink with crimson to mauve spots inside; cultivars include 'Amethystina', with white flowers densely spotted darkest violet, and 'Tojen', a cross with *T. hirta*, with spreading to erect, thinly hairy stems and white to palest rose flowers, yellow and finely purple-spotted at the center and edged with a purple-pink flush; *T. hirta* (syn. *T. japonica*); Japan; stems thickly hairy, erect to 32 in (80 cm); leaves minutely hairy; flowers to 1½ in (4 cm) across, erect, funnelform, solitary or clustered in leaf axils, white with dark purple spots or blotches; includes 'Alba', with white flowers flushed green, 'Lilac Towers', with lilac flowers, 'Miyazaki', with white flowers spotted lilac with sporadic blotches of dark wine red; 'Miyazaki Gold', as 'Miyazaki', but with leaves edged gold, 'Variegata', with leaves edged gold and lavender flowers, and 'White Towers', to 24 in (60 cm), with arching stems and white flowers in most leaf-axils; *T. macrantha* Japan; stems to 36 in (90 cm), arched, drooping, with coarse brown hairs; flowers 1¼–1½ in (3–4 cm), axillary, pendulous, campanulate, yellow with chocolate spots inside; *Subsp. macranthopsis* Japan; stems are 16–32 in (40–80 cm), arching; flowers pendulous, terminal or axillary, to 2 in (5 cm), tubular to campanulate, clear yellow with fine brown spots within; *T. macropoda* China; stem erect, to 28 in (70 cm), occasionally minutely hairy above; flowers to 1¼ in (3 cm), erect, borne in branching cymes, mostly terminal, occasionally axillary, white-purple with small purple spots; *T. ohsumiensis* Japan; stems 8–20 in (20–50 cm), erect, subglabrous; flowers erect, axillary and terminal, ¾–2 in (2–5 cm), broadly funnel-shaped, primrose-yellow, faintly spotted red-brown.

tridentate when the teeth of a margin have teeth which are themselves toothed.

tridynamous when three stamens out of six are longer than the rest.

trifoliate three-leaved, or loosely, with three leaflets.

trifoliolate having three leaflets.

Trifolium (from Latin *tri*, three, and *folium*, leaf). Leguminosae. Temperate and subtropical regions excluding Australasia. CLOVER. Some 230 species, annual, biennial or perennial herbs with creeping to ascending stems, palmately compound leaves and stalked heads of small, pealike flowers in spring and summer. Fully hardy. Grow in moist but well-drained, more or less neutral soil, in full sun. The variegated cultivars listed here are ideal for planting among small to medium-sized perennials, contrasting well with gray, lime green and bronze foliage. However, they have a tendency to become bare and exhausted and should be repropagated frequently. They are also suitable for hanging baskets. Propagate by division or rooted stem sections. *T. pratense* RED CLOVER, PURPLE CLOVER; Europe, naturalized US; erect to decumbent short-lived perennial, 2–8 in (5–20 cm) tall; leaflets ½–1¼ in (1–3 cm), obovate to oblong or rounded, thinly hairy beneath; flowers to ⅝ in (1.5 cm), red-purple to pink or cream; 'Susan Smith': syn. 'Gold Net', pale green leaves, laced and veined with gold; *T. repens* DUTCH CLOVER, SHAMROCK, WHITE CLOVER; Europe, naturalized US; creeping to erect perennial, 2–12 in (5–30 cm) tall; leaflets ¼–¾ in (0.5–2 cm), broadly obovate to rounded, tips notched or truncate, finely toothed; flowers ¼–½ in (0.5–1 cm), white or

pink; 'Atropurpureum': dwarf, with dark purple-red leaflets edged green; 'Aureum': leaflets veined gold; 'Purpurascens': large leaflets, almost solid maroon; forms with a high proportion of leaves with 4 or 5 leaflets are available—'Quinquefolium' has 5 leaflets overlaid with bronze and yellow-veined.

trifurcate with three branches or forked in three.

trigonous a solid body which is triangular but obtusely angled in cross-section.

Trillium (from Greek *tris*, thrice: the leaves and floral parts occur in threes).

Trillium erectum
Trilliums are so-named because many of their plant parts occur in threes: leaves, leafy sepals, and colorful petals. Most are woodland plants that like a moist, shady site.

Liliaceae (Trilliaceae). N America, W Himalaya, NE Asia. TRINITY FLOWER, WAKEROBIN, WOOD LILY, BIRTHROOT. 30 species, deciduous perennial herbs with short, stout rhizomes. The stems arise in spring, unbranched and bearing an apical whorl of three ovate to elliptic leaves. The flowers are solitary, stalked or unstalked and carried above the leaves at the stem's tip. Bell-shaped to narrowly cupped, they consist of three leafy sepals and three broader, colorful petals. Hardy to –20°F (–29°C). They need a sheltered position in dappled sun or shade, and are ideal for the woodland and peat gardens. Plant in open, acidic to neutral soil enriched with leaf mold and garden compost. Keep the roots cool and moist at all times. Mulch in winter. Increase by division or seed.

T. cernuum eastern N America; flowers on pendent pedicels to ¾ in (2 cm), held among or below leaves; petals up to ¾ in (2 cm), undulate, white sometimes flushed rose; *T. chloropetalum* California; leaves mottled maroon; flowers sessile, fragrant, held erect, green to yellow to purple; *T. erectum* eastern N America; flowers borne upright or obliquely on pedicel to 4 in (10 cm), malodorous; sepals light green suffused red-purple, petals up to 3 in (8 cm), spreading or incurved, dark garnet to white; includes 'Ochroleucum', with flowers tinged green, f. *albiflorum*, with white flowers, occasionally flushed rose, and f. *luteum*, with green-yellow flowers stained blood red; *T. grandiflorum* eastern N America; flowers erect on pedicels to 2 in (5 cm), petals up to 3 in (8 cm), undulate, opening pure white, usually flushing pale pink with age; includes double-flowered forms and f. *roseum*, with flowers flushing pink almost immediately and becoming damask when aging; *T. luteum* SE US; leaves mottled; flowers erect, sessile, sweetly scented, petals up to 3½ in (9 cm), erect, cupped, golden or bronzy green; *T. nivale* SE US; ovate; flowers stalked, erect at first, nodding with age, petals up to 1½ in (4 cm), brilliant white; calcicole, flourishing in exposed situations; *T. ovatum* western N America; flowers stalked, borne erect, muskily fragrant; petals spreading rather than erect to spreading as in *T. grandiflorum*, white becoming pink or red; *T. rivale* W US; flowers stalked, erect; petals up to 1 in (2.5 cm), white flushed pink, spotted purple toward base; *T. sessile* NE US; leaves with dark mottling; flowers sessile with pungent odor, petals up to 1¾ in (4.5 cm), erect, maroon; includes 'Rubrum', with crimson-purple flowers, 'Snow Queen', with white flowers, and f. *viridiflorum*, with green-bronze to yellow flowers; *T. undulatum* eastern N America; flowers erect, stalked; sepals dark green bordered maroon, petals up to 1¼ in (3 cm), undulate, white or pale rose-pink, with a dark maroon basal blotch suffusing the veins.

trilocular having three locules.

trimerous with parts in threes; often written as 3-merous.

trimming knife see *pruning knife*.

tripinnate when the ultimate divisions of a bipinnate leaf are themselves pinnate.

triploid a plant that has three sets of chromosomes, instead of two sets as in the majority of plant species. A triploid plant is annotated 3 ×. An example of a triploid is the apple cultivar 'Bramley's Seedling'.

Tripterygium (from Greek *tri-*, three, and *pteryx*, wing, in reference to the 3-winged fruit). Celastraceae. E Asia. 2 species, deciduous climbing shrubs with ovate to elliptic leaves to 6 in (15 cm) long and small flowers in terminal panicles; these are followed by 3-winged fruit in fall. Both *Tripterygium* species are well-adapted to climbing through sturdy trees or over unsightly walls. They flower best in full sun, thrive in moist loamy soil, and will tolerate chalk. *T. regelii* will tolerate cold 5°F (–15°C), but *T. wilfordii* needs the protection of a south-facing wall in places where temperatures fall below 23°F (–5°C). Propagate from seed in fall.

T. regelii Japan, Korea, Manchuria; to 33 ft (10 m); leaves sometimes papillose-pilose on nerves beneath; fruit to ³/₄ in (1.8 cm) in diameter, pale green; *T. wilfordii* Taiwan, E China; to 43 ft (13 m); leaves glabrous, usually glaucous beneath; fruit to ¹/₂ in (1.2 cm) in diameter, purple-red.

triquetrous having a triangular cross-section.

Triteleia (from Greek *tri-*, three and *telos*, end; the parts of the flower are in threes). Liliaceae (Alliaceae). W US. 15 species, perennial, cormous herbs with grasslike leaves and funnel-shaped, 6-lobed flowers borne on slender stalks in scapose umbels. Cultivation is the same as for *Brodiaea*.

T. hyacintha (syn. *Brodiaea hyacintha*, *Brodiaea lactea*); to 28 in (70 cm), flowers usually white, occasionally blue or lilac; *T. ixioides* (syn. *Brodiaea ixioides*, *Brodiaea lutea*); to 24 in (60 cm), flowers golden-yellow; *T. laxa* (syn. *Brodiaea laxa*, *Brodiaea Candida*, *T. candida*); GRASSNUT, TRIPLET LILY; to 30 in (75 cm); flowers deep violet-blue, rarely white; 'Queen

Fabiola': flowers pale violet-blue; *T. peduncularis* (syn. *Brodiaea peduncularis*); stems to 16 in (40 cm), flexuous, flowers white, blue, or tinged lavender.

Tritonia (from Greek *triton*, referring to the variable direction of the stamens of different species). Iridaceae. Tropical and South Africa. 28 species, cormous perennial herbs with fans of sword-shaped, plicate leaves and, in late summer, slender sprays of tubular to cup-shaped flowers. Cultivate as for *Ixia*. *T. crocata* South Africa; 8–20 in (20–50 cm) tall, flowers bright orange, orange-red or pink-orange, the 3 lower lobes with a yellow midline.

Trochodendron (from Greek *trochos*, wheel, and *dendron*, tree, alluding to the stamens which spread like spokes of a wheel). Trochodendraceae. Japan, Korea, Taiwan. 1 species, *T. aralioides*, an evergreen tree or shrub to 66 ft (20 m) tall. To 5¹/₂ in (14 cm) long, the leaves are ovate to oblong, crenate, with a tapering tip, and dark green to olive and glossy. Circular, petal-less, green flowers appear during spring and early summer. *Trochodendron* is hardy to about 14°F (–10°C), provided that it is given shelter from cold drying winds. Grow in a moisture-retentive, moderately fertile, neutral soil in sun or light, part-day shade. Propagate from seed or semiripe cuttings in a closed case with gentle bottom heat or under mist.

Trollius (from German *Trollblume*, globe flower). Ranunculaceae. Northern temperate regions. GLOBE FLOWER. 31 species, perennial herbs that have palmately lobed or divided, toothed leaves. Produced in spring and summer, the buttercup-like flowers are large and rounded with many staminodes and stamens. Fully hardy and suitable for the damp border, bog garden and water margin. Plant in sun in fertile soil that never dries out. Increase by division.

T. × *cultorum* (garden hybrids between *T. europaeus*, *T. asiaticus* and *T. chinensis*); 12–36 in (30–90 cm) tall with large, globe-shaped flowers in shades of yellow, gold, orange and flame; *T. europaeus* GLOBE-FLOWER; Europe, Russia, N America; to 32 in (80 cm) tall; flowers ⁵/₈–2 in (1.5–5 cm) in diam-

eter, globose, lemon-yellow to deep gold; *T. pumilus* Himalaya, Tibet; 2¹/₂–12 in (6–30 cm); flowers ³/₄–1¹/₂ in (2–3.5 cm) in diameter, globose to cup-like, interior yellow-orange, exterior dark wine red or crimson; *T. yunnanensis* W China; to 28 in (70 cm); flowers 1¹/₂–3 in (4–8 cm) in diameter, globose to bowl-shaped, golden yellow to pale orange.

trompe-l'oeil a garden feature intended to deceive the eye, usually by wall paintings, mirrors, ha-has, sunken pools and special plantings.

Tropaeolum tuberosum 'Ken Aslet'
This relative of the common-or-garden nasturtium has an exotic appearance, but can be grown in temperate regions.

Tropaeolum (from Greek *tropaion*, Latin *tropaeum*, trophy, i.e. a sign of victory consisting originally of a wigwam of spears hung with the helmets and shields of the vanquished; gardeners used to grow *T. majus* up pyramids of poles and Linnaeus compared its rounded leaves to shields and the flowers to blood-stained helmets). Tropaeolaceae. S Mexico to Brazil and Patagonia. NASTURTIUM, INDIAN CRESS, CANARY BIRD VINE, CANARY BIRD FLOWER, FLAME FLOWER. Some 86 species, perennial or annual herbs, some tuberous-rooted, most climbing or scrambling. The leaves are rounded and angled to palmately lobed. Produced in summer, the flowers are spurred, with five, clawed petals, the upper two usually smaller than the lower three.

The nasturtium is derived mainly from *T. majus*, although its many

T

cultivars reflect hybridity between this and other species. They range from low-growing dwarf cultivars with a wide color range, for edging and for the flower border, through semitrailing types good for hanging baskets, to taller-climbing types, suited to trellis, fence and other supports. These annuals grow well in sun in well-drained but moisture-retentive soil. Among the perennial species, *T. polyphyllum* is perhaps the hardiest: given full sun and the perfect drainage of a raised bed, it is reliable to about 5°F (−15°C). *T. speciosum* shows similar cold-tolerance. *T. peregrinum* is usually treated as an annual, as for *T. majus*. *T. tricolorum* and *T. tuberosum* will survive short-lived, light frost, given a warm sheltered situation with good drainage. *T. tuberosum* is a short-day plant, and in cool temperate gardens, the late flowers are likely to be spoiled by frost; its large-tubered cultivar 'Ken Aslet' begins to bloom much earlier, in midsummer, and is more desirable for cooler climates. The tubers of these and other slightly tender species, such as *T. pentaphyllum*, may be lifted in fall and stored in cool, dry conditions for replanting in spring. *T. azureum* and *T. tricolorum* work very well in the cool greenhouse or conservatory, trained on pea sticks. Grow in good light, in a neutral or slightly acidic mix of loam, leaf mold and sharp sand. Water plentifully when in growth; withdraw moisture gradually as foliage fades; store the plants more or less dry in their pots over winter. *T. speciosum* differs from other species in that it performs best in areas with cool, moist summers. It favors relatively high rainfall and acidic soil. It is hardy to −10°F (−23°C), but can be difficult to establish: one of the fundamental requirements for success is that the roots and lower stems be cool and shaded. Sow seed of annual species *in situ* or for earlier blooms under glass in late winter/early spring at temperatures of 55–59°F (13–15°C). Propagate perennials with fleshy rhizomes, such as *T. polyphyllum* and *T. speciosum*, by careful division; for tuberous species, separate small tubers when repotting or take basal stem cuttings in spring.

T. azureum Chile; climber to 4 ft (1.2 m), with small tubers; leaves 5-lobed; flowers purple-blue, 1/2–3/4 in (1–2 cm)

in diameter, petals emarginate; *T. majus* INDIAN CRESS, NASTURTIUM; Colombia to Bolivia; vigorous annual climber to 6½ ft (2 m); leaves orbicular, rarely lobed; flowers large, to 2½ in (6 cm), very variable in color, in all shades of red, orange, or yellow (orange in wild plant), petals rounded, claws fimbriate; cultivars include plants ranging in habit from dwarf and bushy to tall and scrambling, some with variegated or deep blue-gray foliage; flowers single to double in shades of cream, yellow, peach, apricot, salmon, pink, orange, scarlet and dark velvety red; *T. pentaphyllum* S America; perennial climber to 20 ft (6 m) with long, beaded tubers, stems and leaf-stalks purple; leaves 5-lobed; flowers 3/4–1¼ in (2–3 cm), in pendent masses, upper sepals spotted, red, petals scarlet; *T. peregrinum* (syn. *T. canariense*); CANARY CREEPER; Peru, Ecuador; perennial climber to 8 ft (2.5 m), treated as a half-hardy annual; leaves usually 5-lobed; flowers to 1 in (2.5 cm) in diameter, petals sulfur or lemon-yellow, upper petals fimbriate-lacerate; *T. polyphyllum* Chile, Argentina; gray-green herbaceous annual or perennial with long rhizome and prostrate or climbing leafy stems to 10 ft (3 m); leaves 5- to 7- or more lobed, glaucous; flowers freely produced, in long masses, petals yellow, orange or ocher; *T. speciosum* FLAME NASTURTIUM, SCOTTISH FLAME FLOWER; Chile; perennial climber to 10 ft (3 m); leaves 5–7-lobed; flowers to 1¼ in (3 cm) across, scarlet, upper petals narrowly wedge-shaped, lower rounded to square, notched; fruit blue; *T. tricolorum* Bolivia, Chile; perennial climber to 6½ ft (2 m), with small tubers; leaves 5–7-lobed; flowers of various colors, calyx urn-shaped, often orange-scarlet, rimmed black, but may be blue, violet, red or yellow with green margin, and yellow within, petals held mostly within calyx, orange, spur red to yellow with a blue or green tip; *T. tuberosum* Peru, Bolivia, Colombia and Ecuador; perennial climber, 6½–10 ft (2–3 m),

with large yellow tubers marbled with purple; leaves 3–5-lobed, gray-green; flowers cup-shaped, calyx red, upper petals rounded, all orange or scarlet; 'Ken Aslet': orange flowers.

tropism growth movement of a plant or organ in the direction of an environmental stimulus, for example, light (phototropism); cf. *nastic movements*.

trough garden see *rock plant gardening*.

trowel a small hand tool with a concave blade about 6 in (15 cm) long with a pointed or rounded end, mounted on a handle 6–12 in (15–30 cm). Used for planting or lifting small plants, and are available in various forms, including some with very narrow blades.

true-breeding used of plants which when self-pollinated give rise to progeny similar to their parent; also known as homozygotic.

true fruit a fruit in which the fruit wall, or pericarp, forms from the wall of the ovary.

true leaves the first leaves to appear after the seed leaves or cotyledons, soon after germination.

trug a shallow oblong basket, usually made with over-lapping strips of wood, with a curved, centrally mounted handle. Also made in plastic, trugs are useful for carrying flowers and produce, plants and small tools. They are sometimes referred to as Sussex trugs.

trullate, trulliform trowel-shaped.

trumpet (1) a description of flowers of tubular shape with a flared opening; (2) a name for the corona of Narcissus flowers, particularly used to define one of its classifying divisions. See *daffodil*.

truncate where the organ is abruptly terminated as if cut cleanly straight across, perpendicular to the midrib.

true leaves

seed leaves

Beech seedling

truncheon an archaic term describing a thick piece of stem used as a cutting or for grafting.

trunk the main stem of a tree; also, the hard, thickened stem of certain primulas and cyclamens, and of tree ferns.

trunk slitting see *bark-bound, slitting.*

truss a compact cluster of flowers or fruits, arising from one position on a stem. The term is applied, for example, to the flower heads of tomatoes, rhododendrons and auriculas.

tryma drupaceous nut with dehiscent exocarp, for example, the walnut.

Tsuga (the Japanese name). Pinaceae. Himalaya, China, Japan and the west and east coasts of N America. HEMLOCK, HEMLOCK SPRUCE. 10 species, evergreen, coniferous trees with horizontal branches, slender branchlets arranged in fine sprays and 2-ranked, linear to needlelike leaves. Cultivation largely as for *Abies.* They will tolerate prolonged dense shade for long periods. Most species require hot, humid summers for full ripening of the shoots (where wood is not fully hardened, trees become shrubby and multistemmed following snow damage to weak stems). All are thin and poor in dry and exposed conditions. Most make excellent informal or formal hedges and screens, especially in semishade.

T. canadensis EASTERN HEMLOCK; N America; to 130 ft (40 m), crown conic; leaves ¼–¾ in (0.6–2 cm), dull green and grooved above, with two gray-white bands beneath; includes dwarf, prostrate, globose, conical and fastigiate cultivars, some with weeping foliage, some variegated; *T. caroliniana* CAROLINA HEMLOCK; SE US; to 130 ft (40 m), crown densely conic; leaves ⅜–⅝ in (0.8–1.5 cm), dark green, grooved above, entire or sometimes notched; includes pyramidal, dwarf, rounded and weeping cultivars; *T. diversifolia* NORTH JAPANESE HEMLOCK; Japan; to 80 ft (25 m) tall, but usually a shrub in cultivation; crown ovoid to conical; leaves ¼–⅝ in (0.5–1.5 cm), linear to oblong, tip often

hooded, dark green, shiny and grooved above, with two white bands beneath; *T. heterophylla* WESTERN HEMLOCK; Alaska to California; to 230 ft (70 m), crown conic; leaves ¼–¾ in (0.5–2 cm), grooved, matt bright green above with two white bands beneath, tip blunt, toothed; includes weeping, narrowly columnar, dwarf, conical and gray-leaved cultivars; *T. mertensiana* MOUNTAIN HEMLOCK; western N America; to 150 ft (45 m), crown narrowly conic; leaves measuring ⅝–1 in (1.5–2.5 cm), thick, keeled or slightly grooved above, often terete, gray-green to blue-green with pale bands on both surfaces; includes dwarf, blue- and silver-leaved cultivars; *T. sieboldii* SOUTHERN JAPANESE HEMLOCK; S Japan; to 100 ft (30 m) or a shrub in cultivation, crown conical to ovoid; leaves ¼–¾ in (0.7–2 cm), yellow-green above, apple green or dull white beneath, notched.

tuber a swollen, generally subterranean stem, branch or root used for storage.

tubercle a small, warty, conical to spherical excrescence.

tuberous bearing tubers, or resembling a tuber.

tufa see *rock plant gardening, hypertufa.*

Tulbaghia (for Ryk Tulbagh [d. 1771], governor of the Cape of Good Hope). Liliaceae (Alliaceae). South Africa. WILD GARLIC, SOCIETY GARLIC. 26 species, perennial herbs, bulbous or fleshy-rooted, with clumps of onion-scented, narrowly strap-shaped leaves. Produced in spring and summer in scapose umbels, the flowers are starlike with an urn-shaped perianth tube, six spreading lobes and a fleshy corona. The species below will tolerate temperatures of 23°F (−5°C) to 14°F (−10°C); they are sometimes given front positions in the herbaceous border, or grown at the base of a warm wall, in well-drained soil in sun, with a dry mulch of bracken litter in winter. In containers, plant in a gritty, loam-based mix in direct sunlight; water plentifully when in active growth, less as plants enter dormancy. Propagate by division or by seed sown when ripe or in spring.

T. capensis leaves mid-green; scapes to 24 in (60 cm), flowers olive green with a maroon corona; *T. natalensis* leaves light green; scape 12 in (30 cm); flowers fragrant, white sometimes tinged lilac with a yellow-orange or green-white corona; *T. violacea* leaves gray-green; scape to 24 in (60 cm), flowers sweetly scented, bright lilac, corona tinged purple, red or white; includes 'Variegata', with gray-green leaves, striped cream to white.

Tulipa (From Turkish *tulbend*, turban, which this flower resembles). Liliaceae (Liliaceae). TULIP. N temperate Old World, especially C Asia. Some 100 species, perennial bulbous herbs with linear to broadly ovate leaves. Produced in spring and early summer, the flowers are solitary and scapose or carried in loose racemes. Bowl-shaped to narrowly bell-like, they are usually held erect and consist of six tepals in two whorls, of which the inner three at least are often blotched or stained in a different color. The introduction of garden tulips into Europe from Turkey dates from the mid-sixteenth century. The plant became the subject of extravagant enthusiasm, and great financial speculation took place in the trade for bulbs throughout the following century, especially in Holland. Commercial production remains important there, and similarly in Lincolnshire in England, in the Western United States and in British Columbia.

The derivation of today's garden cultivars cannot be traced directly to a particular species, although it is probable that many arose from *Tulipa gesneriana* and *T. suaveolens.* There are many early selections of *T. fosteriana, T. kauffmanniana* and *T. greigii.*

Horticulturally, tulips may be grouped into 15 divisions:

(1) *Single early,* cup-shaped, single flowers, often opening wider in sunshine, from early to midspring. (2) *Double early,* long lasting double flowers, opening wide in early to midspring. (3) *Triumph,* conical, single flowers borne on strong stems, and opening to a rounded shape in mid- to late spring. (4) *Darwin hybrids,* large single flowers of variable shape, borne on strong stems in mid- to late spring. (5) *Single late,* single flowers of variable shape, often

T

TULIPA GROUPS

For horticultural purposes, tulips are divided into 15 groups, chiefly defined by their flower characteristics. Group names, such as Single Early, replace the older system of numbered divisions. The Double Late group has also been known as Peony-flowered. The Miscellaneous group contains two loose sections: low-growing, with star-shaped flowers, and slightly taller, with more bowl-shaped flowers.

SINGLE EARLY ('GENERAAL DE WET') **Division one**

DOUBLE EARLY ('ABBA') **Division two**

TRIUMPH ('LUSTIGE WITWE') **Division three**

DARWIN HYBRID ('OLYMPIC FLAME') **Division four**

SINGLE LATE ('UNION JACK') **Division five**

LILY-FLOWERED ('QUEEN OF SHEBA') **Division six**

FRINGED ('HAMILTON') **Division seven**

VIRIDIFLORA ('GOLDEN ARTIST') **Division eight**

REMBRANDT GROUP **Division nine**

PARROT ('FLAMING PARROT') **Division ten**

DOUBLE LATE ('SCARLET BABY') **Division eleven**

KAUFMANNIANA ('GUISEPPE VERDI') **Division twelve**

FOSTERIANA ('SWEETHEART') **Division thirteen**

GREIGII ('PLAISIR') **Division fourteen**

MISCELLANEOUS (T. ORPHANIDEA) **Division fifteen**

TULIPA

Name	Distribution	Stem	Leaves	Flowers
T. acuminata *T. cornuta*	known only in cultivation (Turkey, 18th century)	glabrous, 12–18 in (30–45 cm)	to 8 × 2 in (20 × 5 cm), 3, lanceolate, slightly undulate, glaucous	yellow, sometimes streaked red; tepals 3–5 in (7.5–13 cm), narrowly tapering, apex often convoluted; filaments yellow or white, anthers red-brown

Comments: Closely related to *T. gesneriana* and possibly a variety of that species.

T. armena *T. suaveolens*	Turkey, NW Iran, Iraq, Transcaucasia	to 10 in (25 cm), upper part coarsely hairy	to 6 × 1 in (16 × 2.5 cm), 3–6, lanceolate, glaucous, sometimes downy above, recurved, undulate, margins ciliate	solitary, variable, cup-shaped to bowl-shaped, crimson, vermilion, yellow or multicolored; tepals to 2½ × 1¼ in (6 × 3 cm), rhombic to long-obovate, basal blotch black, navy or yellow-green, sometimes fan-shaped or bordered yellow; stamens yellow or black, filaments narrow-triangular

Comments: Z7

T. aucheriana	Iran	**Comments:** Close to *T. humilis* but flowers opening later, star-shaped, pink, tepals 1¼ × ½ in (3 × 1 cm), basal blotch yellow.		

T. bakeri	Crete	**Comments:** Differs from *T. saxatilis* in the deeper lilac to purple flowers.		

T. biflora *T. polychroma*	Balkans, SE Russia	to 4 in (10 cm), glabrous, brown-green, glaucous	to 6 × ½ in (15 × 1 cm), 2, widely spaced, linear-lanceolate, glaucous, margins and tips tinted claret, sometimes ciliate	fragrant, 1–2, broad-campanulate; tepals to 1¼ × ½ in (3 × 1 cm), narrowly rhombic, cream to ivory, outside gray-green or green-violet, inner tepals with green midrib and yellow basal blotch fringed with yellow cilia; filaments yellow, anthers yellow, tip purple-black

Comments: Late winter–spring.

T. clusiana *T. aitchisonii* LADY TULIP	Iran to Afghanistan, naturalized S Europe	to 12 in (30 cm), glabrous	to 12 × ½ in (30 × 1 cm), 2–5, linear, glaucous	1, rarely 2, opening to form a star; tepals tapering, acute, white to cream, outer tepals to 2½ × ⅝ in (6 × 1.5 cm), exterior carmine, edged white, elliptic, acuminate, basal blotch purple or red; filaments smooth, anthers purple

Comments: 'Cynthia': cream, exterior red with green edge, base purple. var. **chrysantha**: golden-yellow, exterior of tepals stained red or purple-brown, basal blotch absent; stamens yellow; includes 'Tubergen's Gem': yellow, exterior red. var. **stellata**: starry, white with a yellow center.

T. dasystemon	C Asia	to 2 in (5 cm), glabrous	to 4 × ½ in (10 × 1 cm), 2, semisubterranean at flowering, narrowly lanceolate, blue-green, glabrous	solitary; tepals to ¾ × ¼ in (2 × 0.7 cm), narrowly lanceolate, bright yellow, outer tepals with a broad, brown-claret or green band along midrib on the outside, inside pure yellow, inner tepals streaked brown-green along midrib; anthers yellow

Comments: In gardens, the name *T. dasystemon* has been misapplied to *T. tarda*.

T. edulis *Amana edulis*	S Japan, NE China, Korea	to 6 in (15 cm), glabrous, with 2–3 narrow bracts beneath flowers	to 10 × ½ in (25 × 1 cm), to 6	1–2; tepals to 1¼ × ¼ in (3 × 0.6 cm), ivory, exterior veined claret or mauve, basal blotch purple-black edged yellow; filaments glabrous

Comments: Late winter–spring.

T

T. acuminata   *T. biflora*   *T. clusiana* **var. chrysantha**   *T. hageri* 'Splendens'

TULIPA

Name	Distribution	Stem	Leaves	Flowers
T. fosteriana	C Asia	6–20 in (15–50 cm), tinted pink, sometimes hairy	to 12 × 6 in (30 × 16 cm), 3–5, widely spaced, oblong to broadly ovate, glossy green, downy above	solitary, faintly scented; tepals to 7 × 3¼ in (18 × 8.5 cm), lustrous vivid red, long-ovate to narrowly rhombic to broadly lanceolate, tip downy, basal blotch black, fan-shaped or 2–3-pointed, edged yellow; filaments black, triangular, anthers black-violet, pollen purple-brown or yellow

Comments: Fosteriana Hybrids (*T. fosteriana* × *T. greigii* or *T. kaufmanniana*): flowers large, white or yellow. 'Princeps': resembles 'Madame Lefeber' but stem shorter, flowers later. 'Madame Lefeber' ('Red Emperor'): flowers large, tepals to 6 in (15 cm), brilliant red, glossy, basal blotch black with irregular yellow border. Crossed with Darwin tulips to produce Darwin Hybrids, which include Mendel tulips (flowers large, stem stout).

Name	Distribution	Stem	Leaves	Flowers
T. gesneriana	E Europe, Asia Minor	glabrous or finely hairy, to 24 in (60 cm)	to 6 in (15 cm), 2–7, lanceolate to ovate-lanceolate, glaucous, margin ciliate toward apex	solitary, cup-shaped, opening to form a star; tepals 1½–3 in (4–8 cm) (inner tepals wider than outer tepals), purple to dull crimson to yellow, sometimes variegated ('broken'), sometimes with yellow or dark olive basal blotch which may be edged lemon-yellow; filaments glabrous, yellow or purple, anthers yellow or purple

Comments: A complex and variable species, from which most late-flowering cultivars are derived.

Name	Distribution	Stem	Leaves	Flowers
T. greigii	C Asia	to 18 in (45 cm), often tinged pink or brown, hairy	to 12½ × 6 in (32 × 16 cm), 3–5, usually closely set and reflexed, lanceolate, glaucous, stained, veined and streaked maroon above	solitary; tepals to 6 × 4 in (16 × 10 cm), usually vermilion but sometimes claret, orange, yellow, cream or multicolored, rhombic to oblong-obovate, angles rounded, acute, tip downy, basal blotch rhombic, black on red forms, red on yellow forms; filaments black or yellow, anthers black

Comments:

Name	Distribution	Stem	Leaves	Flowers
T. hageri				

Comments: Close to *T. orphanidea*. in range and appearance, except flowers dull red, exterior tinted or marked green. 'Splendens': bronze tinted red, exterior dark red.

Name	Distribution	Stem	Leaves	Flowers
T. humilis	SE Turkey, N & W Iran, N Iraq, Azerbaijan	to 8 in (20 cm)	4–6 × ½ in (10–15 × 1 cm), 2–5, channeled, somewhat glaucous	solitary, or to 3, cup-shaped opening to a star, pale pink, yellow at center; tepals ¾–2 × ½–¾ in (2–5 × 1–2 cm), acute inner tepals longer than outer; filaments yellow or purple, anthers yellow

Comments: 'Eastern Star': rose, flamed bronze green on outer tepals, base yellow. 'Magenta Queen': lilac with yellow center, exterior green and flame. 'Odalisque': light purple, base yellow. 'Persian Pearl': cyclamen-purple, base yellow, exterior light magenta. Violacea Group: deep violet, central blotch may be yellow, black edged yellow, or a very dark navy.

Name	Distribution	Stem	Leaves	Flowers
T. kaufmanniana	C Asia	to 20 in (50 cm), upper part hairy, sometimes glabrous, often tinged red	¾–8 in (2–20 cm) wide, 2–5, closely set, often rosulate, lanceolate to oblanceolate, slightly undulate, pale gray-green, veins darker, glabrous except minutely ciliate margins	1–5, star-shaped to campanulate to cup-shaped, often fragrant; tepals to 4½ × 2 in (11 × 5 cm), white or cream, sometimes shades from yellow to brick-red, outer tepals lanceolate, often recurved, basal blotch yellow, outside red or pink along midrib, inner tepals often erect, long-elliptic or long-rhombic, obtuse, sometimes multicolored, midrib often green or red in lighter-colored forms, basal blotch fan-shaped, bright yellow; filaments yellow, anthers yellow

Comments: Often crossed with *T. fosteriana* and *T. greigii*. 'Lady Killer': white, exterior with a crimson flame, center purple.

T. humilis Violacea Group   *T. linifolia*   *T. marjolletii*   *T. orphanidea* Whittallii Group

TULIPA

Name	Distribution	Stem	Leaves	Flowers
T. linifolia	C Asia, N Iran, Afghanistan	to 12 in (30 cm), glabrous	to 3 × ½ in (8 × 1 cm), 3–8, closely set, linear, falcate, margin often wavy, usually ciliate and pink	solitary, star-shaped; tepals to 2½ × 1½ in (6 × 3.5 cm), rhombic to subovate, scarlet, basal blotch blue-black, truncate, often edged cream to lemon-yellow; filaments yellow or black, anthers gray-yellow

Comments: Batalinii Group (syn. *T. batalinii*) includes 'Apricot Jewel': apricot-orange, interior yellow. 'Bright Gem': sulfur yellow, flushed orange. 'Bronze Charm': sulfur, feathered apricot-bronze. 'Red Gem': bright red, long-lasting. 'Yellow Jewel': pale lemon tinged pink.

Maximowiczii Group differ from the species in their tepals with a black blotch edged white, and black filaments fading to white at apex, anthers mauve or yellow.

Name	Distribution	Stem	Leaves	Flowers
T. marjolletii	SE France	to 20 in (50 cm)	close to *T. gesneriana*.	tepals pale yellow to cream edged pink, exterior flushed rose-mauve, especially along midrib; filaments black, anthers pale yellow

Comments:

Name	Distribution	Stem	Leaves	Flowers
T. orphanidea	E Mediterranean	4–14 in (10–35 cm), glabrous or hairy	to 12 × ⅝ in (30 × 1.5 cm), 2–7, lanceolate, glabrous, margin often claret	1–4, globose; tepals 1¼–2 × ½–¾ in (3–5 × 1–2 cm), elliptic, vermilion to brick-red, outside of outer tepals buff stained green or purple, basal blotch olive to black, sometimes edged yellow; stamens brown or olive

Comments: Closely related to *T. sylvestris*, producing many natural hybrids. *T. orphanidea* is a variable species and may encompass such colorful and valued plants as *T. hageri* and *T. whittallii*. The plant usually offered as *T. orphanidea* has dull orange-brown flowers, the exterior suffused green and mauve. Whittallii Group are a more vivid orange-bronze. 'Flava': yellow, flushed red; very similar to *T. sylvestris*.

Name	Distribution	Stem	Leaves	Flowers
T. praestans	C Asia	4–24 in (10–60 cm), finely downy above	3–6, widely spaced, oblong or lanceolate, pale gray-green, midrib thick, distinctly keeled, margins sometimes undulate, ciliate	1–5, cupped; tepals orange-red, outer tepals 2¾ × 1 in (7 × 2.5 cm), broadly elliptic or subovate, tinged yellow toward base, inner tepals shorter, lanceolate, elliptic or obovate; filaments red, anthers yellow, violet or claret

Comments: 'Fusilier': flowers glowing orange-red, to 4 per stem. 'Unicum': leaves broadly edged white; flowers to 5 per stem, red, base small, yellow, anthers black. 'Van Tubergen's Variety': flowers red, several per stem.

Name	Distribution	Stem	Leaves	Flowers
T. pulchella	Turkey	**Comments:** As for *T. humilis*, but tepals to 1¼ × ⅝ in (3 × 1.5 cm), strongly cupped, mauve, basal blotch navy edged white.		

Name	Distribution	Stem	Leaves	Flowers
T. saxatilis CANDIA TULIP	Crete, W Turkey	6–18 in (15–45 cm), glabrous	4–12 × ¾–2 in (10–30 × 2–5 cm), 2–4, glabrous, lustrous or, rarely, glaucous	1–4, fragrant; tepals 1½–2 × ⅜–1¼ in (4–5 × 1.5–3 cm), elliptic, acute, pink to mauve, basal blotch yellow edged white; stamens yellow

Comments: Bakeri Group: flowers in deeper mauve tones, including 'Lilac Wonder': rosy lilac, base lemon-yellow.

Name	Distribution	Stem	Leaves	Flowers
T. sprengeri	N Turkey	to 12 in (30 cm)	to 10 × 1¼ in (25 × 3 cm), 3–6, linear, glabrous	solitary; tepals brilliant red, acute, tapering toward base, outer tepals 2½ × ⅝ in (6 × 1.5 cm), buff beneath, inner tepals to 1 in (2.5 cm) wide, basal blotch absent; filaments bright red, anthers yellow

Comments: Late-flowering (i.e. late spring–early summer), easily raised from seed and excellent for naturalizing.

T. praestans 'Unicum'

T. saxatilis

T. sprengeri

T. turkestanica

T

TULIPA

Name	Distribution	Stem	Leaves	Flowers
T. sylvestris *T. florentina; T. grisebachiana*	origin unknown; naturalized from Europe and N Africa to C Asia and Siberia	to 18 in (45 cm), glabrous, sometimes tinted red at base	to 10 × 1 in (24 × 2.5 cm), 2–4, widely spaced, declinate, linear, acuminate, channeled, dark green, glabrous, glaucous	1–2, starry; tepals to 2¾ × 1 in (7 × 2.5 cm), lanceolate to subrhombic, acuminate, golden, midrib bordered green, inner tepals convex, sometimes tinged pink; filaments yellow, anthers orange
Comments: 'Major': flowers to 3 per stem, gold, abundant, larger, with 8 petals. 'Tabriz': tall; flowers large, lemon-yellow, sweetly scented.				
T. tarda	C Asia	to 2–4½ in (5–11 cm)	to 4¾ × ⅝ in (12 × 1.5 cm), 3–7, closely set, lanceolate, recurved, bright green, glabrous, margins claret, often ciliate	4–15, broadly star-shaped, fragrant; outer tepals to 1½ × ½ in (3.5 × 1 cm), broadly lanceolate, acute, white, the exterior midrib edged with a broad green stripe shading to purple and yellow, inner tepals 1½ × ¾ in (3.5 × 2 cm), spoon-shaped, acute, interior often yellow toward base; filaments yellow, anthers yellow
Comments:				
T. turkestanica	C Asia	to 12 in (30 cm), very finely white-hairy	to 8 in (20 cm), 2–4, ovate-lanceolate, smooth, gray-green, glaucous	to 12 per stem, to ¾ in (2 cm), sometimes malodorous, ivory to white, base yellow or orange within, exterior of outer tepals stained olive green to gray or slate-mauve; anthers purple, brown or yellow tipped purple
Comments: Very similar to *T. biflora*.				
T. undulatifolia *T. baeotica; T. eichleri*	Balkans, Greece, Turkey, Iran, C Asia	to 20 in (50 cm), hairy	to 7½ × 2¼ in (19 × 5.5 cm), 3–4, widely spaced, linear to lanceolate, reflexed, glaucous, downy, margins crispate or undulate, ciliate	solitary, cup-shaped to broadly campanulate; tepals to 2¾ × 1½ in (7 × 3.5 cm), crimson to dark red, usually paler below, downy, broadly lanceolate to obovate, tapering to downy tip, basal blotch elliptic to rhombic, black to purple, often edged yellow; filaments black, anthers black to yellow
Comments: 'Clare Benedict': bright red, base black, edged yellow, early-flowering. 'Excelsa': large, scarlet, base black, edged yellow.				
T. urumiensis	NW Iran	1–2, to 8 in (20 cm), mostly subterranean, glabrous	4–4¾ × ½ in (10–12 × 1 cm), 2–4 in a flat rosette, plicate, glabrous, glaucous	1–2, cup-shaped, opening to a star in sunlight; tepals to 1½ × ½ in (4 × 1 cm), yellow, outside streaked green or red; stamens and pollen yellow
Comments:				

ovoid or squarish, usually with pointed petals, flowering during late spring and very early summer. (6) *Lily-flowered*, narrow-waisted, single flowers with long, pointed petals often reflexed at the tips, borne on strong stems in late spring. (7) *Fringed*, similar to lily-flowered but with fringed petals. (8) *Viridiflora*, single, variably shaped flowers with partly greenish petals, borne in late spring. (9) *Rembrandt*, mostly old cultivars, similar to Div. 6 with the colors in striped or feathered patterns due to virus infection; flowering in late spring. (10) *Parrot*, large single flowers of variable shape, the petals frilled or fringed and usually twisted; blooming in late spring. (11) *Double late* (Peony flowered), double bowl-shaped flowers in late spring. (12) *Kauffmanniana hybrids*, large single flowers which open wide in sunshine from early to midspring. The leaves are often mottled or striped. (13) *Fosteriana hybrids*, large single flowers

which open wide in sunshine from early to midspring. The leaves are often mottled or striped. (14) *Greigii hybrids*, large single flowers borne in mid- to late spring. The leaves are generally wavy-edged, and always mottled or striped. (15) *Miscellaneous*, other species, their varieties and hybrids, flowering in spring and early summer.

Tulips grow well on sheltered but sunny, well-drained sites that are rich in humus. Some types, including the species and the Kauffmanniana, Fosteriana and Greigii groups, may be left in the ground to flower from year to year, but most hybrid garden tulips are best grown for annual bedding out; after which they may be lifted to discard or replant in the fall for growing to flowering size in about two years. Tulips may be planted much later in the fall than other spring-flowering bulbs, up to mid-November in suitable conditions, setting them out 4–6 in (10–15 cm)

apart and at least 6 in (15 cm) deep. Tulips should not be continually planted on the same ground.

Tulips can be flowered early in 8-in-(20-cm-) wide pots or pans, using top quality bulbs or suitable cultivars, planted early. The containers should be subjected to 10–12 weeks in a cool, dark and damp environment, such as can be provided by burying them outdoors under 2½–3 in (6–8 cm) of soil or sand in a shady site. They should subsequently be removed to a situation out of direct sunlight, and can be introduced gradually to a moderate heating regimen under protection for flower development.

Possible problems: aphids, eelworms, tulip fire (*see* botrytis).

tummelberry see *hybrid berries*.

tunic a bulb or corm covering, usually papery, membranous or fibrous.

tunicate (1) enclosed in a tunic; (2) having concentrically layered coats, the outermost being a tunic, like an onion.

tunnel cloche, tunnel house see *cloche, greenhouse*.

turbinate top-shaped; inversely conical, but contracted near the apex.

turf, sod (1) an area of grass; (2) a piece of lifted grass, primarily used for lawn making (turfing).

turfing iron, sod lifter (US) a spade with a heart-shaped blade, about 10 in (25 cm) long and 8 in (20 cm) wide, set at an angle and fixed to a long handle. Turfing irons are used for cutting and lifting sod.

turf plugger a bulb planter.

turf racer see *edging iron*.

turf seat a raised seat covered with turf, chamomile or thyme, usually built against a wall, or sometimes a grass mound. Turf seats were common in medieval gardens.

turgid filled out or inflated, usually by fluid.

turgor the distension of plant cells by water taken in by osmosis, which results in outward pressure exerted by the protoplasts against the cell walls.

turion a detached winter bud, often thick and fleshy, by which aquatic plants perennate; also, an adventitious shoot or sucker.

turnip (*Brassica rapa* Rapifera Group) a biennial grown as an annual primarily for the swollen edible root, which is flat, round or long in shape, with white or yellow flesh. Native to central and southern Europe, it is widely cultivated in temperate and highland tropical regions; it grows best under cool moist conditions. The root freezes well, either raw or cooked, and turnip tops are a useful substitute for spring greens.

Turnip

The crop should be grown in rotation, like other brassicas, in moisture-retentive soil of high organic-matter content, in a lightly shaded area. Turnip is a fast-maturing crop, harvestable in 6–10 weeks from sowing (although some selections may be ready as small roots even sooner), and it is therefore suitable for catch cropping or inter-cropping.

Sow at 3-week intervals from early spring onward. Very early crops may be obtained from February sowing under cloches. Sow thinly, 1 in (2.5 cm) deep: earlies in rows 8 in (20 cm) apart, thinning individual seedlings to 4 in (10 cm) apart, and later cultivars in rows 12 in (30 cm) apart, thinning to 6 in (15 cm) apart. Sow turnips grown for their tops in fall and early spring. Cut when 6 in (15 cm) high as required.

The crop requires adequate water throughout growth, and summer sowings will bolt if allowed to dry out. Early cultivars are ready when about 2 in (5 cm) in diameter, and quickly deteriorate in quality if left; later ones, sown July–August, are more hardy and can be left in the soil in winter, or lifted and stored in boxes in a cool shed.

Possible problems: aphids, flea beetle, cabbage root fly, turnip gall weevil, (*see* weevils); canker, clubroot, virus.

Tweedia (for J. Tweedie [1775–1862], of Glasgow and Argentina). Asclepiadaceae. S Brazil, Uruguay. 1 species, *T. caerulea* (syn. *Oxypetalum caeruleum*), a twining subshrub to 3¼ ft (1 m) tall. Produced in summer, the flowers are to 1 in (2.5 cm) in diameter, powder-blue becoming lilac, with five outspread and narrow petals. Grow *Tweedia* under glass, maintaining a minimum temperature of 41°F (5°C), in well-drained, moderately fertile soil in sun. Alternatively, treat as an annual and plant out after the last frosts. Propagate *Tweedia* from seed sown under glass during spring.

twiner a climbing plant that twines around a support.

twin-scaling see *cuttings*.

Tylecodon (an anagram of *Cotyledon*). Crassulaceae. South Africa, Namibia. 28 species, succulent perennial subshrubs, usually with swollen stems covered in papery bark and crowned with spreading branches bearing fleshy leaves and panicles of 5-petaled, tubular flowers. These gouty-stemmed plants grow throughout the winter in the Northern Hemisphere, resting in a deciduous state in summer. Cultivate as for *Cotyledon*. *T. paniculatus* (syn. *Cotyledon paniculata*); to 5 ft (1.5 m); flowers orange to red marked yellow and spotted red; *T. reticulatus* (syn. *Cotyledon reticulata*); to 3¼ ft (1 m); flowers yellow-green tipped yellow; *T. wallichii* (syn. *Cotyledon wallichii*); to 4½ ft (1.4 m); flowers yellow-green.

type one of several categories of specimen or, less commonly, an image or description, used by a botanist as the basis of a taxon; the proof of its existence.

Typha (name used by Theophrastus for these or possibly other aquatic plants). Typhaceae. Cosmopolitan. CATTAIL, BULRUSH, REEDMACE. 10 species, aquatic and marginal perennial herbs, with two-ranked, narrowly strap-shaped leaves and scapose inflorescences. Produced during summer and fall, these are composed of many tightly packed and minute flowers, the whole forming a brown, velvety club with a spike at its summit. These plants are suitable for larger water features and lakesides (except for *T. minima*, which is a charming dwarf ideal for small ponds). They are particularly useful as bank stabilizers. For floral decorations, pick the spikes early in the season, while male flowers are still in bloom, and air-dry. Spray with hair lacquer or aerosol fixative.

T. angustifolia LESSER BULRUSH, NARROW-LEAVED REEDMACE; N Hemisphere; to 6½ ft (2 m); leaves ⅛–¼ in (3–6 mm) wide; *T. latifolia* CATTAIL, BULRUSH, GREAT REED-MACE; N Hemisphere; to 6½ ft (2 m), robust; leaves ⅜–¾ in (8–20 mm) wide; *T. minima* DWARF CATTAIL, DWARF REED-MACE; Eurasia; 16–32 in (40–80 cm), slender; leaves to 1/16 in (2 mm) wide.

T

U

U-cordon a cordon formed of two parallel upright or oblique growths branching near the base of a plant, often used as a training method for red currants and gooseberries.

Ulex (name used by Pliny for a type of heather). Leguminosae. W Europe, N Africa. FURZE. 20 species, shrubs, ultimately leafless but with dense branching spines that are green and perform photosynthesis. Fragrant, pealike flowers are produced throughout the year. Hardy to −10°F (−23°C), *U. europaeus* is useful for plantings on land too dry and barren to accommodate other shrubs; more fertile soils will result in lank growth and poor flowering. It is also a valuable soil stabilizer on sandy substrates, an impenetrable barrier, and a useful windbreak in coastal areas and on heathlands. Propagate from seed; also by semiripe cuttings in a sandy propagating mix in the cold frame. *U. europaeus* FURZE, IRISH GORSE, COMMON GORSE, WHIN; W Europe; 24 in–8 ft (0.6–2.5 m), erect or ascending, densely branched, spines to ⅝ in (1.5 cm), dark olive; flowers to ¾ in (2 cm), golden yellow marked red at base of keel, coconut-scented; 'Aureus': foliage golden yellow to lime; 'Flore Pleno': flowers double.

green spines photosynthesize

Ulex europaeus

Ulmus (Classical Latin name). Ulmaceae. Northern temperate regions to Mexico and C Asia. ELM. 45 species, deciduous or semievergreen trees and shrubs (those listed here are hardy deciduous trees), grown for their habit

and foliage. Dutch elm disease (q.v.) has destroyed almost all native elms in both Europe and North America since about 1965. Specimens remain only on the northern fringes of these areas. None of the European or North American indigenous elms show the slightest degree of tolerance to the disease. The disease originated in E Asia and the elms there are resistant; there is less evidence of resistance for Himalayan species, some of which have been diseased in Britain. Asian species grow well in the eastern US, but they do not thrive in the cool summers of northwest Europe or the Pacific northwest. Elms can be hybridized easily in cultivation and some hybrids will resist the disease to a useful extent.

Propagation is by seed for some species, by layers, grafting, or root suckers for others. Seeds can be collected fresh on ripening in early summer and sown immediately without drying; germination then occurs within a few days. Alternatively, the seed can be dried gently and refrigerated for planting the next spring, but germination rates are then lower. The fall-flowering species are treated by the latter method. Layers are pegged from suckers or coppiced plants and, like root suckers, are cut from the parent when a good root system is formed. For grafting, use *U. glabra* or related Asian species for the rootstock; these will not produce suckers from the base.

In addition to Dutch elm disease, this genus is attacked by elm phloem necrosis, a phytoplasma disease with symptoms similar to those of Dutch elm disease, but in which the inner bark is stained yellow, not brown, and smells like oil of wintergreen. It is spread by a leafhopper. Serious epidemics occurred in North America, but it has now declined quite simply due to lack of elms. It has not spread to Europe. The disease is not easily controlled: the use of insecticidal sprays to kill the vectors has been tried, but the volume required to treat large trees is not only impractical but also causes extreme environmental disturbance.

U. americana AMERICAN ELM, WHITE ELM, WATER ELM; eastern N America; to 115 ft (35 m); branches pendulous

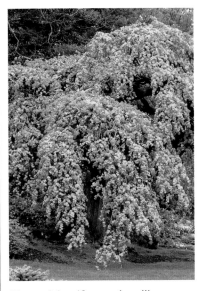

Ulmus glabra 'Camperdownii'
The very compact Camperdown elm, with its weeping habit, is a popular choice for the medium to large garden.

toward tips, bark ash gray, furrowed, twigs downy at first; leaves 2¾–6 in (7–15 cm), oblong to ovate to elliptic, apex acuminate, base unequal, glabrous or scabrous above, downy beneath; includes cultivars with columnar, narrowly upright, vase-shaped and pyramidal crowns, and dark, golden or incised leaves; *U. angustifolia* GOODYER'S ELM; England, France; to 100 ft (30 m), crown rounded with age; leaves 1½–2¾ in (4–7 cm), broadly ovate, glossy above with tufted hairs in vein axils beneath; *U. carpinifolia* EUROPEAN HELD ELM, SMOOTH-LEAVED ELM; S and C Europe; to 100 ft (30 m), pyramidal or narrowly upright; leaves 1½–4 in (4–10 cm), obliquely oval to ovate, biserrate, glabrous above, downy on veins beneath; includes numerous cultivars, tall to dwarf, erect to weeping, narrow to rounded, corky and densely twiggy, with purple, yellow, and white-marked leaves; also includes var. *cornubiensis*, the CORNISH ELM, a narrowly conical tree to 100 ft (30 m), with ovate leaves, glossy dark green and smooth above with conspicuous tufts beneath; *U. glabra* DUTCH ELM, WYCH ELM, SCOTCH ELM; N and C Europe to Asia Minor; to 130 ft (40 m), crown open and spreading, bark fissured with age, young shoots hairy; leaves 2–6 in (5–16 cm), oval to obovate, apex acuminate, occasionally 3-lobed, margins toothed, rough above, downy beneath; includes numerous cultivars, among the most popular are 'Camperdownii', compact and dome-shaped with drooping branches, and 'Exoniensis', erect and conical, to 23 ft (7 m) tall, with irregularly serrate leaves; *U.* × *hollandica* (*U. glabra* × *U. carpinifolia*); HOLLAND ELM; spreading, upright tree to 100 ft (30 m); leaves ovate, serrate, glossy dark green; includes 'Jacqueline Hillier', a densely branched, slow-growing shrub to 6½ ft (2 m), with elliptic to lanceolate, 2-ranked leaves to 1¼ in (3 cm); *U. minor* subsp. *sarniensis* (*U. carpinifolia* × *U.* × *hollandica*); EUROPEAN FIELD ELM, SMOOTH LEATH ELM; differs from *U. carpinifolia* var. *cornubiensis* in its tapering crown with erect branches and broader, biserrate leaves; *U. parvifolia* CHINESE ELM, LACEBARK; China, Korea, Japan; semi-evergreen, to 80 ft (25 m), crown rounded or globose, branchlets slender, bark smooth, flaking in rounded pieces; leaves ¾–2 in (2–5 cm), elliptic to obovate, acute, serrate, coriaceous; includes dwarf, shrubby, slow-growing, pendulous and variegated cultivars; *U. procera* ENGLISH ELM; England; tree to 115 ft (35 m), trunk long and straight, crown tall with rounded heads of foliage on a few large branches, bark with rectangular fissures; leaves 1¼–2¾ in (3–7 cm), rounded to ovate, toothed, scabrous above, bristly beneath, dark green, yellow in fall; includes variegated cultivars; *U. pumila* SIBERIAN ELM; E Siberia, N China, Turkestan; tree or shrub to 33 ft (10 m); leaves ¾–2¾ in (2–7 cm), ovate, serrate, acute to acuminate, deep green and glabrous above, becoming glabrous beneath; includes cultivars with small, rounded, and bushy crowns, some with resistance to Dutch elm disease; *U.* × *vegeta* HUNTINGDON ELM, CHICHESTER ELM; to 130 ft (40 m), trunk thick, short, branching low down, crown open, bark rough; leaves 3–4¾ in (8–12 cm), elliptic, acuminate, biserrate, glabrous above, downy in vein axils beneath.

umbel a flat-topped inflorescence like a corymb, but with all the flowered pedicels (rays) arising from the same point at the apex of the main axis.

umbellate, umbelliform borne in or furnished with an umbel; resembling an umbel.

Umbellularia (from Latin *umbella*, navel, referring to the inflorescence form). Lauraceae. California, Oregon. 1 species, *U. californica*, CALIFORNIA LAUREL, HEADACHE TREE, PEPPERWOOD, an evergreen tree to 80 ft (25 m). The leaves are 2–4¾ in (5–12 cm) long, ovate to oblong or lanceolate, glossy dark green. Produced in stalked umbels in summer, the small flowers give rise to purple berries. The leaves are intensely aromatic when bruised, and on warm days the whole plant exudes a fragrance which may cause dizziness, headaches, and nausea. Given protection from frost when young and some shelter from cold drying winds, it will tolerate temperatures to 5°F/–15°C. Grow in moisture-retentive but well-drained nonalkaline soils with full sun. Propagate from seed sown when ripe in fall, by simple layering, or by semiripe cuttings in a shaded closed case with bottom heat.

umbellule the umbel that terminates a compound umbel.

umbilicate with a more or less central depression, like a navel.

umbo a rough, conical projection, arising from the center of a surface, as in the raised part of the scale in a pine cone.

umbonate bossed; orbicular, with a point projecting from the center.

umbraculiferous shaped like a parasol.

uncinate hooked.

Uncinia (from Latin *uncinatus*, hooked, referring to the seed heads). Cyperaceae. Southern Hemisphere. 35 species, evergreen, tufted grass-like herbs with finely hooked seed-heads. The following species resembles the New Zealand *Carex*, whose cultivation requirements it shares. *U. rubra* New Zealand; leaves linear, finely tapered, arching in dense tussocks to 12 in (30 cm) tall, glossy dark maroon-bronze to blood red.

undercutting severing the roots of lined out trees and shrubs in order to encourage the development of a fibrous root system, most often carried out in advance of lifting for transplanting.

underplanting the establishment of low-growing plants among distinctly taller ones.

undershrub a low shrub.

understory a population of lower-growing trees and shrubs established under a canopy of tall trees in deciduous woodland or tropical rainforest.

undulate wavy, but of a margin's surface rather than outline; cf. *sinuate*.

unguiculate petals and sepals bearing a basal claw.

unijugate see *paired*.

union the point where a scion and rootstock are joined by grafting. It may become swollen when the rate of growth of one component is faster than the other. It is necessary to keep the union above soil level in situations where scion rooting could be a disadvantage.

unisexual either staminate or pistillate; with flowers of one sex only.

united parts usually free or separate held closely or clinging together so as to be scarcely distinguishable.

urceolate an urn-shaped corolla.

urea an organic chemical found in animal urine; it is synthesized as a fertilizer, containing about 45% nitrogen, and used as a liquid fertilizer diluted at

scion

rootstock

calloused bark at point of graft union

Union

flattened flower head

Umbel

1 oz (25 g) per 7 gallons (27 liters) of water. Urea formaldehyde, the product of a chemical reaction between urea and formaldehyde, is an insoluble, slow-release nitrogenous fertilizer.

Urginea (for the African-Arab tribe the Urgin). Liliaceae (Hyacinthaceae). Africa, Mediterranean. 100 species, bulbous perennial herbs with 6-tepaled flowers in scapose racemes in summer and fall. Occasionally successful out of doors in northern Europe, although it is rarely free-flowering in cooler climates. Plant with the bulb neck exposed in very free-draining gritty or sandy soils, in full sunlight; protect from winter wet with a loose mulch of dry bracken or straw. Increase *Urginea* by offsets or seed. *U. maritima* RED SQUILL, SEA ONION; Mediterranean, Portugal; bulb 2–6 in (5–15 cm) in diameter; leaves to 39 in (100 cm), narrow, glaucous; scape to 39 in (100 cm), tinted red, flowers white lined with green or purple-red.

urine liquid waste excreted by animals, which is a quick-acting fertilizer, containing nitrogen and some potassium. It can be diluted with water for use as a liquid plant food or used as an accelerator in compost piles.

Ursinia (for Johann Ursinus of Regensburg [1608–1666], author of *Arboretum Biblicum*). Compositae. South Africa, Ethiopia, Namibia. 40 species, annual and perennial herbs, subshrubs and shrubs with pinnately cut leaves and daisylike flower heads in summer. Cultivate as for *Gazania*. *U. anthemoides* South Africa; thinly hairy annual to 16 in (40 cm); flower heads ⅝–2½ in (1.5–6 cm) in diameter, ray florets yellow or dark purple toward base or coppery yellow beneath, disk florets yellow or purple at apex; *U. chrysanthemoides* South Africa; hairy annual to shrubby perennial to 3¼ ft (1 m); flower heads 1–2½ in (2.5–6 cm) in diameter, ray florets yellow or red throughout or yellow or white above and coppery beneath, disk florets yellow or dark purple at the apex; *U. sericea* S Africa; silvery-hairy procumbent perennial shrub to 28 in (70 cm); flower heads ½–1¼ in (1–3 cm) in diameter, yellow.

Utricularia (from Latin *utriculus*, little bottle or bladder, alluding to the bladderlike traps). Lentibulariaceae. Cosmopolitan. BLADDERWORT. 214 species, perennial carnivorous herbs. They may be aquatic, terrestrial, or epiphytic, with a range of habit and foliage types and 2-lipped, spurred flowers. Prey is caught in very small, bladderlike traps carried on the main growth axis or on rootlike, specialized stems. *U. longifolia* and *U. reniformis* require high humidity, light shade, and a minimum temperature of 50°F/10°C. The planting medium

Uvularia grandiflora
This native of eastern North American forests should thrive in a woodland garden or shady border, or at the water's edge.

should be very open—two parts coarse bark, two parts moss peat, one part perlite, and a little sand. Keep permanently moist, with soft water only. Propagate by division in early summer. They grow well in baskets and shallow pans. *U. vulgaris* is hardy and may be grown outside in still, acidic pools. In aquariums and other containers, it needs to float in soft water out of direct sunlight. It will feed on water fleas.

U. longifolia Brazil; leaves dark green, strap-shaped; flowers to 1¼ in (3 cm), violet blotched orange-yellow; *U. reniformis* Brazil; leaves kidney-shaped; flowers to 1½ in (4 cm), violet with yellow markings; *U. vulgaris* temperate Old World; aquatic perennial with floating stems bearing many small, dark green leaves divided into fine segments; flowers to ¾ in (2 cm), yellow marked red-brown.

utricle a round, inflated sheath or appendage.

Uvularia (from Latin *uvula*, the soft palate, referring to the drooping flowers). Liliaceae (Uvulariaceae). US. MERRY BELLS, BELLWORT. 5 species, rhizomatous, hardy herbaceous perennials with erect to arching stems clothed in oblong-lanceolate to elliptic leaves and hung with narrowly bell-shaped flowers in spring and early summer. These are pendulous and composed of 6 lanceolate and twisted tepals. Suitable for the woodland or rock garden, or at the waterside above water level. Propagate by division of established clumps, or from ripe seed sown in the cold frame.

U. grandiflora to 30 in (75 cm); flowers to ¾ in (2 cm), yellow sometimes tinted green; *U. perfoliata* to 24 in (60 cm); flowers to 1½ in (3.5 cm), yellow, tepals papillose.

Vaccinium (ancient Latin name of disputed origin, used by Virgil and Pliny, perhaps from *bacca*, berry, or a corruption of *Hyacinthus*). Ericaceae. Northern Hemisphere and some tropical highlands. 450 species, shrubs and small trees, evergreen or deciduous, with small, urn- to bell-shaped flowers and spherical berries. Cultivate as for *Arctostaphylos*. See also *blueberry* and *cranberry*.

V. angustifolium LOW-BUSH BLUEBERRY, LATE SWEET BLUEBERRY; northeast N America; deciduous shrublet 3–8 in (8–20 cm) tall; leaves ½–1¼ in (1–3 cm), lanceolate; flowers white tinged green, often streaked red; fruit to ½ in (1.2 cm), blue-black, pruinose, edible; *V. arctostaphylos* CAUCASIAN WHORTLEBERRY; N Asia Minor, W Caucasus; deciduous shrub 3¼–10 ft (1–3 m) tall; leaves 1¼–4 in (3–10 cm), elliptic to oblong, carmine in fall; flowers white tinged green, faintly flushed red; fruit to ½ in (1 cm), purple; *V. corymbosum* BLUEBERRY, HIGH-BUSH BLUEBERRY, SWAMP BLUEBERRY; E US; deciduous shrub to 6½ ft (2 m) tall; leaves 1¼–3 in (3–8 cm), ovate to lanceolate, scarlet in fall; flowers white, sometimes slightly red-tinted; fruit ⅜–⅝ in (0.8–1.5 cm), blue-black, pruinose, edible; *V. glaucoalbum* Sikkim; evergreen shrub to 3¼ ft (1 m) tall; leaves 1¼–3 in (3–8 cm), ovate to oblong; flowers white tinged pink; fruit to ¼ in (0.6 cm), black, pruinose; *V. myrtillus* SOURTOP BLUEBERRY, BILBERRY, WHORTLEBERRY; semideciduous, erect shrub to 20 in (50 cm); leaves ½–1¼ in (1–3 cm), oval to elliptic, finely toothed; flowers tinged green, later red; fruit to ½ in (1 cm), blue-black, pruinose, edible; 'Leucocarpum': fruit off-white; *V. nummularia* Sikkim, Bhutan; evergreen shrub to 16 in (40 cm); leaves ½–1 in (1–2.5 cm), rounded to elliptic; flowers pink; fruit to ¼ in (0.6 cm), black, edible; *V. parvifolium* RED WHORTLEBERRY, RED HUCKLEBERRY; western N America; deciduous shrub, erect to 6½ ft (2 m) or more; leaves ½–¾ in (1–2 cm), ovate to elliptic, red in fall; flowers tinted red-green; fruit to ½ in (1.2 cm), coral red, slightly translucent, edible; *V. vitis-idaea* (COWBERRY, CRANBERRY; northern temperate regions; evergreen, creeping shrub 4–12 in (10–30 cm) tall; leaves ¼–⅝ in (0.6–1.5 cm), obovate to ovate; flowers white to pink; fruit to ¼ in (0.6 cm), bright red, edible.

vaginate possessing or enclosed by a sheath.

Valeriana (Medieval name, perhaps derived from *valere*, to be healthy, referring to its powerful medicinal qualities). Valerianaceae. Widespread. VALERIAN. Some 200 species, perennial herbs and subshrubs with simple to pinnately lobed leaves and small, rotate to campanulate flowers in cymose panicles from spring to fall. The following are hardy and will grow in most soils in sun or part shade. Increase by division or seed.

V. officinalis ALL HEAL, COMMON VALERIAN, GARDEN HELIOTROPE; Europe, W Asia; herb to 5 ft (1.5 m), strongly attractive to cats; leaves pinnate or pinnatisect; flowers pink or white; *V. phu* Caucasus; differs from *V. officinalis* in its undivided or irregularly and sparsely divided lower leaves, the leaf divisions tend to be broader, the flowers are white; includes 'Aurea', with brilliant golden yellow leaves, turning lime green by midsummer. Red valerian is *Centranthus ruber* (syn. *Valeriana rubra*).

Vallea (for Felice Valle [d. 1747], author of *Florula Corsicae* [1761]). Elaeocarpaceae. Andes. 1 species, *V. stipularis*, an evergreen shrub to 16 ft (5 m) tall. The heart-shaped leaves are 1¼–4¾ in (3–12 cm) long. Borne in short cymes in late summer, the flowers are cup-shaped, to ⅝ in (1.5 cm) long and pale rose with darker veins. Hardy to about 23°F (−5°C). Cultivation is the same as for *Crinodendron*.

Vallisneria (for Antonio Vallinieri de Vallisnera [1661–1730], professor at the University of Padua). Hydrocharitaceae. Widespread. EEL GRASS, VALLIS. 2 aquatic perennial herbs, evergreen and bottom-rooting, with a clump of translucent green, ribbonlike leaves and inconspicuous flowers. Suitable for warm or cold aquariums. Plant the base in the substrate; grow in neutral to acidic water; give good light, especially from above. Propagate by division of the runners from parent plants.

V. americana (syn. *V. gigantea*) E US, E Asia to Australia; leaves to 6½ ft × ¾ in (2 m × 2 cm); male flowers with stamens partially or wholly united; *V. spiralis* EEL GRASS, TAPE GRASS; cosmopolitan; leaves to 6½ ft × ½ in (2 m × 1 cm); male flowers with free stamens; 'Torta': leaves spirally twisted.

valvate (1) describing parts with touching but not overlapping margins; (2) opening by or pertaining to valves.

valve one of the parts into which a dehiscent fruit or capsule splits at maturity.

Vancouveria (for Captain George Vancouver, Royal Navy [1758–1798], British navigator and explorer). Berberidaceae. W US. 3 species, perennial herbs resembling a smaller and more delicate *Epimedium*. The foliage is finely divided and often assumes attractive purple-red tints. Cultivate as for *Epimedium*.

V. chrysantha SW Oregon; differs from *V. hexandra* in its yellow flowers; *V. hexandra* Washington to California; deciduous, 4–16 in (10–40 cm) tall; flowers white with red-spotted sepals.

Vanda (Sanskrit name for *Vanda tessellata*.) Orchidaceae. Asia. 35 species, evergreen, epiphytic perennials with long stems clothed by 2-ranked, strapshaped leaves and bearing abundant aerial roots. Produced at various times of year in axillary racemes, the flowers consist of five obovate tepals and a smaller, tonguelike lip. *V. coerulea* is suitable for the cool house or conservatory (minimum temperature 50°F/10°C). The remainder need a minimum temperature of 59°F (15°C). Pot in baskets or orchid pots, containing the coarsest bark-based mix and with perfect drainage. Rooting into the substrate serves largely to anchor the plant: a healthy growth of aerial roots is essential. Older specimens may have bare stem bases, in which case cut away the lower portion of stem altogether, replanting the healthy, leafy, rooting summit. The old base may then produce new shoots. In summer, provide light shade in warm, humid conditions; water and mist frequently, applying diluted foliar fertilizer when in full growth. In winter, reduce temperatures and humidity, admitting maximum light. Increase by stem cuttings and offsets.

V. coerulea India, Burma, Thailand; flowers 2¾–4 in (7–10 cm), pale to deep lilac-blue, obscurely checkered, lip darker; *V. denisoniana* Burma, Thailand; flowers fragrant, to 2 in (5 cm) in diameter, lime green to ivory, often mottled or spotted ginger, lip marked cinnamon to orange at base; *V. rothschildiana* Garden hybrid between *V. coerulea* and *Euanthe sanderiana* with large, broad-tepaled flowers in deep lavender blue with darker, checkered markings; *V. tessellata* (syn. *V. roxburghii*) India, Burma to Malaysia; flowers 1½–2 in (4–5 cm) in diameter, cream, yellow-green or very pale lilac-blue, checkered brown, lip violet to blue edged white; *V. tricolor* (syn. *V. suavis*) Java, Laos; flowers fragrant, 2–3 in (5–7.5 cm) in diameter, usually pale yellow or cream dotted red-brown or purple-red, lip magenta to mauve. For *V. sanderiana*, see *Euanthe sanderiana*; for *V. teres*, see *Papilionanthe teres*.

variability, variation the deviation of plant characteristics from a type as a result of alteration to hereditary material that may arise as adaptations to, for example, environmental change or pest or disease influence. It is the process by which evolution occurs.

variegation the occurrence of patterns in plant leaves and, in some cases, stems and flowers, due especially to differences in distribution of the amount or composition of chlorophyll; in the case of multicolored leaf patterns, other pigments, such as anthocyanin, carotenoids, and xanthophylls, are involved. Variegation is usually an abnormal condition, due to mutation or, less frequently, infection by viruses. It can, however, be a normal character of a species, breeding true from one

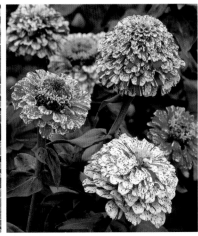

Variegation in foliage and flowers
There are many popular variegated-leaved garden plants with gold, cream, or white leaf centers or margins, such as *Daphne* x *burkwoodii* 'Astrid' (left); variegated flowers, such as these 'Peppermint Stick' zinnias (right), are less common.

generation to the next, as in the case of the white-edged leaves and bracts of the summer annual *Euphorbia marginata*. Species of *Maranta* and *Calathea*, *Pilea cadierei*, and *Silybum marianum* are examples of natural variegation.

Mutations that inhibit chlorophyll production are the most likely cause when areas of white tissue occur sporadically during development of otherwise normal green foliage. Such mutations may be under genetic control and repeated as new leaves develop, or they may arise as a single event directly affecting one chlorophyll-producing cell component. Genetically controlled repeat mutations are evident in *Acer pseudoplatanus* 'Leopoldii', a form of maple which has leaves striped and flecked pink-white, and also in the white and green marbled leaves of the annual *Tropaeolum majus* 'Alaska'. This kind of variegation may be transmitted by seed, providing the parent flowers are self-pollinated.

Chlorophyll mutations not genetically controlled may dominate, through cell divisions, individual seams of a multilayered shoot apex, resulting in layers of white and normal green tissues; these are known as chimeras. Shoots with white layers overlying green will produce leaves with white "skins" and green "cores," and because the skin tissues develop a broad band of cells around the leaf margins, the margins will be white while the central areas of the leaves remain green; the

reverse arrangement of green-over-white shoots produces leaves with green margins and white centers. Variegations of this kind are usually stable, although, occasionally, individual layers will separate and hence entirely green or white shoots and leaves will result. Shoots with entirely green leaves are said to have "reverted" and, since they are more vigorous than the variegated kind, they should be pruned out at the earliest opportunity. All white shoots will not survive on their own if used as cuttings. Variegated plants of the layered or chimera kind include the Norway maple, *Acer platanoides* 'Drummondii', *Philadelphus coronarius* 'Variegatus', *Cornus mas* 'Variegata', and *Aralia elata* 'Variegata'. Perennial herbaceous plants with layered variegation include *Symphytum* x *uplandicum* 'Variegatum', and many cultivars of *Hosta*. Greenhouse plants, such as *Pelargonium*, *Ficus*, and *Codiaeum*, have equally attractive leaf variegations.

Sometimes, apples and chrysanthemums have sectorial chimeras of a different color, in which one kind of tissue lies alongside another and not over or under it. Such chimeras, with more regular patterning, flecking or color alteration, may be perpetuated as ornamentals, as in *Camellia* 'Donckelaeri' and certain rhododendrons. Chimeras that display layered variegation cannot be propagated by seed. Vegetative propagation sometimes gives rise to curious results, as in the sword

V

plant, *Sansevieria trifasciata*, where the popular yellow-edged form *S. trifasciata laurentii* is a chimera and will not reproduce from cuttings, new plants will revert to the plain form.

Some chimeras are produced by grafting—for example, + *Laburnocytisus adamii*, which is created by grafting laburnum *(Laburnum anagyroides)* on to the broom *Chamaecytisus purpureus*. The stock tissue becomes mingled with that of the scion, so that the tree produces, at random, laburnum growths and flowers, broom growth and flowers, and intermediate growth with laburnum-like flowers tinged purple like those of the broom.

Mutations that affect the chemical composition of chlorophyll are generally responsible for plants that produce golden-colored foliage. The golden tissues may occur alone and breed true from seed as in *Tanacetum parthenium* 'Aureum' and Bowles' golden grass, *Milium effusum* 'Aureum', but in many kinds of conifers, such as *Thuja occidentalis* 'Rheingold' and *Cupressus macrocarpa* 'Goldcrest', it must be passed from one generation to the next by vegetative propagation. Golden tissues also occur in combination with layers of green or even white to produce chimeras. *Elaeagnus pungens* 'Maculata' is an example of an evergreen shrub whose leaves have golden centers and green margins. The reverse arrangement—green centers and golden margins—is present in *Elaeagnus pungens* 'Dicksonii'. Similar reciprocal golden variegations are found in cultivars of *Euonymus* and *Hedera*.

Viruses are responsible for relatively few plant variegations; for example, abutilon mosaic virus causes the striking golden-mosaic leaves in *Abutilon striatum* 'Thomsonii' and other abutilons, and the greater periwinkle, *Vinca major*, and common bugle, *Ajuga reptans*, may be infected with vein-clearing virus to produce variegated forms.

Viruses are also responsible for certain kinds of flower variegation where the normal base color of the petals is broken or flecked with different color pigments, as in the Bizarre Group of tulips and forms of the common wallflower and Algerian iris, *Iris unguicularis*. Some flower variegations, however, such as the Damask rose 'York and Lancaster',

Antirrhinum 'Bizarre Hybrids', and *Zinnia* 'Peppermint Stick', are known to be the visible expression of mutant genes. Propagation of virus-transmitted variegation needs to be by vegetative means.

Abnormal leaf variegations may be induced by deficiency of minerals, such as magnesium or iron, or by herbicide action, but such variegations are transient with no ornamental value.

variety, varietas (abbrev. var.) the category of taxa intermediate between subspecies and forma.

vascular plant a plant with strands of cells that form a system for conducting fluids throughout its roots and aerial parts—for example, ferns, horsetails and seed-producing plants—as distinct from algae, fungi, liverworts, and mosses.

vascular wilt a disease in which the pathogen is almost entirely confined to the vascular system. Wilting is a characteristic symptom, but may not always occur. *Verticillium* species often cause typical wilt diseases.

vase see *goblet*.

vector an organism that transmits a pathogen to a plant or animal.

vegetable (1) a general description of plant forms, distinguishing them from animal forms; (2) generally, a plant grown for its edible leaves, stems, roots, bulbs or tubers. However, tomatoes, cucumbers, squashes, eggplants, peppers, and sweet corn cobs are technically fruits; rhubarb is also regarded as a fruit, because of the manner of its culinary use, although it is commonly grown in the vegetable garden.

Vegetative buds on peach

vegetative bud a bud that normally produces only a shoot, as opposed to a fruit bud.

vegetative propagation, vegetative reproduction the increase of a plant by asexual means, from vegetative parts of the plant; a process that normally results in a population of genetically identical individuals. It occurs naturally in the case of bulbils, apomicts, cormlets, offsets, plantlets, and runners, and it may also be brought about by artificial means through cuttings, division, budding, grafting, and layering.

vein an externally visible strand of vascular tissues.

veitchberry see *hybrid berries*.

velamen the corky epidermis of aerial roots in some epiphytes, through which atmospheric moisture is absorbed.

Veltheimia (for August Ferdinand Graf von Veltheim [1741–1801], German patron of botany). Liliaceae (Hyacinthaceae). South Africa. 2 species, bulbous perennial herbs. The bulbs are large, bearing a rosette of thinly fleshy, broadly lanceolate to strap-shaped, undulate leaves. Tubular flowers hang in a dense, torchlike raceme at the top of a stout scape from fall to spring. Plant the bulbs with their necks just above soil level. Grow in sun or bright indirect light, in a freely draining medium, with additional coarse sharp sand, and at a minimum temperature of 41°F (5°C). Water moderately and regularly when in growth, allowing the surface of the medium to dry between waterings. Give an occasional diluted low-nitrogen liquid fertilizer; reduce water gradually as foliage fades to allow near-dry dormancy in summer. Propagate by offsets when dormant, by seed, or by leaf cuttings; mature leaves will form bulbs at their bases if inserted in damp sharp sand.

V. bracteata (syn. *V. viridifolia*) leaves glossy green; scape to 18 in (45 cm), purple spotted yellow-green; flowers to 1½ in (4 cm), pink-purple sometimes tinged yellow; *V. capensis* (syn. *V. glauca*, *V. roodeae*) leaves glaucous; scape to 12 in (30 cm) or more, flecked purple, glaucous, flowers to 1¼ in (3 cm), white spotted red to dull pink, tipped cream or pink with a green or claret apex, to deep and solid coral red.

velutinous coated with fine soft hairs, giving the appearance and texture of velvet.

venation the arrangement or disposition of veins on the surface of an organ.

ventilator a hinged window or louver unit used to admit air to a greenhouse in order to control temperature and humidity. See *greenhouse*.

ventral attached or relating to the inner or adaxial surface or part of an organ; sometimes wrongly applied to the undersurface.

ventricose swollen or inflated on one side.

Veratrum (from Latin *vere*, truly, and *ater*, black, from the color of the root). Liliaceae (Melanthiaceae). Northern temperate regions. 20 species, perennial herbs with erect stems clothed with broad, plicate leaves and terminating in dense panicles of small, 6-parted flowers in summer. Hardy to about −4°F (−20°C), especially if given a protective mulch when dormant in winter. Grow in deep, fertile, moisture-retentive soils, rich in well-rotted organic matter. In moist soils, *Veratrum* will tolerate full sun. However, best foliage effects are obtained in partial shade with shelter from drying winds. Propagate by division. Alternatively, take ¼-in (6-mm) root sections, each with a bud, and root in a sandy propagating mix in the cold frame. Seed germination may be erratic and seedling plants may take up to ten years to reach maturity.

V. album Europe, N Africa, N Asia; 3¼–6½ ft (1–2 m); flowers greenwhite; *V. nigrum* S Europe, Asia, Siberia; 24–48 in (60–120 cm); flowers purple-black.

Verbascum (Latin name used by Pliny). Scrophulariaceae. Europe, N Africa, W and C Asia. MULLEIN. 300 species, annual, biennial, or perennial herbs and subshrubs, usually hairy, often glandular. The flowers are produced from spring to fall in erect spikes or panicles; they consist of five rounded and rather silky petals and hairy anthers.

They are grown for their erect spikes of flowers in summer; a number also have white- or golden-felted foliage, and although these are more commonly used to give height at the back of the herbaceous border, their beautiful rosettes are worthy of positions to the front of borders where they will not be overgrown or overlooked. One of the most attractive of the rosette-formers, *V. olympicum*, may take two years to achieve its full stature, forming a silverwhite rosette up to a yard across, before producing majestic whitestemmed candelabra. Most *Verbascum* species, particularly the alpine *V. dumulosum*, are sun-loving and favor dry soils; they will not tolerate wet soils in winter. Given good drainage, most are hardy to 5°F (−15°C). Many are not reliably perennial, but those that can usually be counted on include *V. nigrum*, *V. chaixii*, and subshrubby species, such as *V. dumulosum*. Grow alpine species in a sharply drained medium and protect from winter moisture with a propped pane or open cloche; alternatively, grow in the alpine house in a sandy, low-fertility alpine mix. Remove spent flowering spikes to encourage a second flush of flowers. Sow seed in late spring/early summer in the cold frame; if seed is sown earlier, biennial species may flower and die in the same season. Increase cultivars by root cuttings in late winter. The subshrubby species may be propagated by semiripe cuttings of lateral shoots in late summer in the cold frame.

V. bombyciferum Asia Minor; white-felty biennial to 70 in (180 cm); leaves to 20 in (50 cm), forming large rosettes; flowers sulfur yellow with white-hairy stamens, in muchbranched, woolly spikes; *V. chaixii* NETTLE-LEAVED MULLEIN; S Europe, E Europe, Russia; graytomentose perennial to 40 in (100 cm); leaves to 12 in (30 cm), sometimes lobed; inflorescence usu-

ally branched, flowers yellow with violet-hairy stamens; *V. densiflorum* (syn. *V. thapsiforme*) Europe, Siberia; biennial to 6½ ft (2 m), gray- or yellow-tomentose; leaves to 18 in (45 cm); inflorescence dense, usually unbranched, flowers yellow with white-yellow-hairy stamens; *V. dumulosum* SW Turkey; perennial, low-growing, muchbranched subshrub to 12 in (30 cm), gray-green and covered with white, yellow, or creamy-brown felt; leaves ½–2 in (1–5 cm); inflorescence 10–30-flowered, flowers lemon yellow with a central ring of coral or brick red. *V. lychnitis* WHITE MULLEIN; Europe, W Asia; sparsely gray-tomentose biennial to 60 in (150 cm); leaves to 12 in (30 cm), green above, white beneath; flowers in a narrow panicle, bright yellow or white, stamens with white or yellow hairs; *V. nigrum* DARK MULLEIN; Europe, Asia; sparingly hairy perennial to 40 in (100 cm) tall; leaves to 16 in (40 cm), hairy beneath; flowers yellow with violet-hairy stamens, in slender, branched or unbranched spikes; *V. olympicum* Turkey; densely whitewoolly perennial or biennial to 70 in (180 cm); tall; leaves to 28 in (70 cm); flowers golden yellow with white-hairy stamens in candelabra-like branching spikes). Numerous hybrids and cultivars are available. Among the finest are: 'Cotswold Beauty', to 4 ft (1.2 m), with pale buff to amber flowers with purple-hairy anthers; 'Gainsborough', to 4½ ft (1.4 m), with silvergray leaves and sulfur to primrose yellow flowers; 'Helen Johnson', to 3¼ ft (1 m), with gray leaves and peach to pale rust flowers; 'Mont Blanc', to 3¼ ft (1 m), with silky white leaves and pure white flowers; and 'Pink Domino', to 3¼ ft (1 m), with rosy pink flowers with a darker eye.

Verbena (Latin *verbena*, classical name for certain sacred herbs, probably of *V. officinalis* of Europe; common name "vervain" said to be derived from the Celtic words *fer*, to remove, and *faen*, stone, referring to its use in treating bladder stones). Verbenaceae. Tropical and subtropical America. VERVAIN.

Verbascum
'Helen
Johnson'

250 species, annual or perennial herbs and subshrubs. The leaves are usually toothed to pinnately lobed. Produced during summer in corymbs or branching spikes, the flowers are small and tubular with a limb of five lobes. *V.* × *hybrida*, *V. rigida* and their cultivars are valued for their tight heads of often brilliantly colored flowers, used in bedding, in the annual border, and in hanging baskets or other containers. *V. bonariensis* will bloom in its first year from seed and is often treated as an annual, although it is well-suited to herbaceous borders where, given good drainage, it will tolerate temperatures to between 23 and 14°F (−5 and −10°C). Grow in full sun in any moderately fertile and moisture-retentive soil. Propagate by seed in fall or spring, and grow at a minimum night temperature of 45–50°F (7–10°C); increase also by stem cuttings in late summer, rooted in a closed case with gentle bottom heat. Increase perennials also by division.

V. bonariensis (syn. *V. patagonica*) PURPLE TOP, SOUTH AMERICAN VERVAIN, TALL VERBENA; S America; slender, erect annual or perennial herb to 6½ ft (2 m) tall; leaves to 5 in (13 cm), oblong to lanceolate, toothed, rugose above, white-hairy beneath; flowers blue, violet, lavender or mauve in short spikes terminating the branches of a long-stalked, forking panicle; *V.* × *hybrida* COMMON GARDEN VERBENA, FLORIST'S VERBENA; garden origin; perennial herb usually grown as an annual, 8–39 in (20–100 cm), erect or low to trailing; leaves to 3 in (8 cm), ovate to lanceolate, toothed to incised, dark green, rugose; flowers fragrant, white to purple, blue, vermilion, scarlet, crimson, red, pink, or yellow, sometimes with a white or yellow mouth, in elongated spikes or large, flat corymbs; numerous cultivars and seed races are available, popular for half-hardy bedding and covering the wide range of habits and colors described above; *V. peruviana* (syn. *V. chamaedrifolia*, *V. chamaedrioides*, *V. coccinea*;; Argentina to S Brazil; creeping, small perennial; leaves to 2 in (5 cm), ovate to oblong, toothed, rough; flowers bright scarlet or crimson, sometimes pink or striped white; *V. rigida* (syn. *V. venosa*) VEINED VERBENA; S Brazil, Argentina; erect or spreading, rigid perennial herb to

24 in (60 cm); leaves to 3 in (7.5 cm), oblong, toothed, rugose, dark green; flowers purple, magenta, or lavender-blue in short spikes, usually terminating the three, candelabra-like branches of a long-stalked panicle; *V. tenera* Brazil to Argentina; low, shrubby perennial with tufted, decumbent stems; leaves to 1 in (2.5 cm), oval to ovate, hairy, finely pinnately divided; flowers rose-violet edged white in elongated spikes.

verge the edge of a lawn; sometimes also a narrow strip of turf alongside a bed, border, or path.

vermicide a pesticide active against earthworms.

vermicompost casts from worms (especially those fed on organic waste material), which can be used as a potting medium ingredient. Vermicompost has good structural stability and useful nutrient content.

vermiculate worm-shaped, with a pattern of impressed, close, wavy lines.

vermiculite an aluminosilicate mineral, heat-treated to form expanded or "exfoliated" granules with very low bulk density and a laminated structure that allows for good aeration and water retention; it is used in potting media or for rooting cuttings. The cation exchange capacity is high and there are useful levels of magnesium and potassium. Industrial grades should be avoided for horticultural use due to possible high alkalinity.

vernal appearing in spring.

vernalization the treatment of seed, bulbs, or plants in order to break dormancy and induce or hasten growth or flowering, most commonly involving low-temperature storage or the application of the growth-influencing plant hormones known as gibberellins.

vernation the arrangement of leaves in the bud.

Veronica (perhaps named for St. Veronica). Scrophulariaceae. Northern temperate regions. SPEEDWELL, BIRD'S-EYE. 250 species, annual or perennial

herbs and subshrubs. Small, bell-shaped to rotate and 4-parted the flowers are produced singly in the leaf axils or in slender racemes from spring to summer. Hardy to −10°F (−23°C) and suited to a range of situations, from the rock garden to the herbaceous border. Increase by division or seed.

V. austriaca Europe; perennial, stems 10–20 in (25–50 cm), erect or decumbent, more or less hairy; leaves linear to rounded, pinnately cut; inflorescence axillary, flowers bright blue; includes subsp. *teucrium*, syn. *V. teucrium*, with royal blue and sky blue flowers; *V. cinerea* E Mediterranean, Asia Minor; tufted to spreading, white-tomentose perennial subshrub; leaves to ⅝ in (1.5 cm), linear, silvery-tomentose; raceme to 1¼ in (3 cm), flowers dark blue sometimes tinged purple, white in center; *V. fruticans* ROCK SPEEDWELL; Europe; woody-based perennial, erect to 6 in (15 cm); leaves ½–¾ in (1–2 cm), obovate to oblong, entire to serrate; flowers deep blue stained red in center in short, capitate racemes; *V. gentianoides* Caucasus, SW Asia; erect perennial to 32 in (80 cm); leaves to 4 in (10 cm), linear to broadly ovate; flowers white or pale blue to lilac with dark blue veins, or wholly dark blue, or white faintly tinted blue, in terminal racemes to 12 in (30 cm); a variegated cultivar is also grown; *V. longifolia* (syn. *V. exaltata*) Europe, naturalized eastern N America; erect perennial to 40 in (100 cm); leaves 1¼–4¾ in (3–12 cm), linear to lanceolate, saw-toothed; flowers pale blue to lilac, bright blue to rich mauve in some cultivars, in long, slender spikes; *V. pectinata* (E Balkans, Asia Minor; evergreen, perennial, mat-forming subshrub to 6 in (15 cm) tall; leaves to ¾ in (2 cm), elliptic to oblong, saw-toothed to incised; flowers deep blue with a white eye, or pink, in axillary racemes to 6 in (15 cm) long; *V. prostrata* Europe; mat-forming perennial; leaves ½–1 in (1–2.5 cm), linear to ovate, entire to toothed; flowers pale to deep blue in dense erect spikes; includes cultivars with flowers in blue, lavender, and pink, some with yellow leaves; *V. spicata* (Europe; erect or ascending perennial to 24 in (60 cm) tall; leaves ¾–3 in (2–8 cm), linear to ovate, crenate to entire, mid-green, hairy; flowers clear blue with purple stamens in dense, terminal racemes to 12 in (30 cm); includes white, dark blue, pink, dark rose, and dwarf cultivars; closely related is *V. incana*, SILVER SPEEDWELL, which differs in being covered in fine, silvery white hairs. For *V. perfoliata*, see *Parahebe perfoliata*; for *V. virginica*, see *Veronicastrum virginicum*.

Veronicastrum (somewhat similar to *Veronica*). Scrophulariaceae. NE Asia, eastern N America. 2 species, erect perennial herbs with whorled leaves and *Veronica*-like flowers produced in summer. Cultivate as for *Veronica*. *V. virginicum* (syn. *Veronica virginica*; eastern N America; CULVER'S ROOT, BLACKROOT, BOWMAN'S ROOT; 24–70 in (60–180 cm) tall; leaves lanceolate to oblanceolate, serrate, glabrous; flowers blue, white or pink with protruding stamens, crowded in slender spikes to 12 in (30 cm) long).

verrucose warty.

verticil a ring or whorl of three or more parts at one node.

verticillate forming or appearing to form a whorl.

verticillium wilt see *wilt*.

Vestia (for L. C. de Vest [1776–1840], professor at Graz, Austria). Solanaceae. Chile. 1 species, *V. foetida* (syn. *V. lycioides*), musky scented evergreen, glabrous shrub 3¼–10 ft (1–3 m) tall with pendent, tubular to funnel-shaped and yellow-green flowers in summer). Where temperatures go below 10°F (–12°C), plant outdoors against a warm, sheltered wall or grow in the cool greenhouse. Site in sun or part-day shade in well-drained, fertile soil. Propagate from seed in spring and by greenwood cuttings rooted with bottom heat in summer.

vestigial of a part or organ that was functional and fully developed in ancestral forms, but is now reduced and obsolete.

viability the ability to live and grow, used especially for the capacity of seeds to germinate. See *seeds and seed sowing*.

Viburnum (Classical Latin name of *V. lantana*). Caprifoliaceae. ARROW-WOOD, WAYFARING TREE. Temperate Northern Hemisphere, extending into Malaysia and S America. At least 150 species, deciduous or evergreen shrubs or small trees. The flowers are small, white or cream, and sometimes flushed pink or wholly pink. They are borne at various times of year in corymbs, sometimes with sterile and showy ray flowers, or in umbels or axillary and terminal panicles. The corolla is rotate, campanulate, or cylindric and 5-lobed. The fruit is a drupe, usually small and glossy, and colored red, blue, or black.

Viburnum includes some of the most choice and valuable shrubs in cultivation. They are grown for their beautiful flowers, usually white, sometimes in showy "lacecap" corymbs and often very fragrant, especially in the winter-flowering species and hybrids. Some bear highly ornamental fruits. Almost all species grown for their fruits are self-incompatible and require pollination by seedlings of a different clone, or by related species flowering at the same time (*V. opulus* is a notable exception). Many of the deciduous species have exceptional fall tints, among them *V. acerifolium*, *V. lantana*, and *V. opulus*. The evergreens, with the possible exception of *V. rhytidophyllum*, generally require a milder climate than the deciduous species (min. temp. –10°F/–23°C), but include a number of species with handsome foliage, such as *V. davidii* and *V. cinnamomifolium*.

They tend to be used in shrubberies and mixed borders, but many are worthy of specimen plantings, especially those *V. plicatum* cultivars with tiered habit and "lacecap" flowers, such as 'Mariesii'. The evergreen *V. tinus* flowers in winter, but it is the deciduous or semideciduous winter-flowerers that are outstanding—both beautiful *and* fragrant. Among these are *V. farreri*, *V. grandiflorum*, and their hybrid offspring, *V. × bodnantense*. In some years, they will bloom from early fall until spring, the flowers withstanding hard frosts without damage. Following on chronologically are the semievergreen *V. × burkwoodii*, which flowers from early winter, its blooms slightly more frost-tender but equally sweetly scented, and *V. × juddii*, *V. carlesii*, and *V. × carlcephalum* which flower in spring and are all hardy to –20°F (–29°C).

Plant in any deep, rich, moisture-retentive soil, in sun or semishade. Shelter winter-flowering species from north and east winds, and position them so that they avoid early morning sun on flowers and young growth after frost. Propagate deciduous species by softwood cuttings in early summer, also by hardwood cuttings in early fall, in the cold frame, or by French layering. Propagate evergreens from semiripe cuttings in summer. Prune evergreens in late spring, deciduous species after flowering, to maintain shape, prevent overcrowding, and remove dead or damaged wood. Viburnum aphids cause tight curling of the leaves. The eggs overwinter on the plant: treat with a tar-oil winter wash before the buds break. Viburnum whitefly infests the underside of the leaves of *V. tinus* and may cause sooty molds.

Victoria (for Queen Victoria [1819–1901]) Nymphaeaceae. Tropical S America. 2 species of giant aquatic herbs, annual or perennial, prickly with stout rhizomes. Leaves large, floating, orbicular, peltate, smooth above; margins up-turned vertically to form a distinct rim. Flowers floating, to 12 in (30 cm) diameter, white turning pink or red on second day, fragrant; sepals 4, petals numerous, *c.* 200 stamens. Fruit large, prickly, berrylike, many seeded.

Victoria is usually grown as an annual, and requires a water temperature of 70–75°F (21–24°C) and full light. Collect seeds when ripe and overwinter in distilled water at 64°F (18°C); sow in midwinter or early spring in a low-fertility loam, and immerse in water at 84–90°F (29–32°C). *V. amazonica* ROYAL WATER LILY, leaves to 6½ ft (2 m) diam., spiny, tinged purple beneath, rim to 6 in (15 cm) deep. Sepals prickly, tinged red-purple. Flowers as described above; night blooming, for two nights only. Amazon region.

Vigna (for Dominico Vigna [d. 1647], professor of botany at Pisa). Leguminosae. Tropics, subtropics. 150 species, erect, twining or creeping herbs with trifoliolate leaves and pealike flowers in summer. *V. caracalla* is suitable for outdoor cultivation in frost-free areas in fertile, well-drained soil in sun; otherwise,

VIBURNUM

Name	Distribution	Habit	Leaves	Flowers	Fruits
V. acerifolium DOCKMACKIE	Eastern N America	erect, deciduous shrub to 6 ft (1.8 m)	to 4 in (10 cm), maplelike, rounded or cordate at base, downy beneath, carmine in fall, 3-lobed, lateral lobes narrowly tapering, toothed	white, in long-stalked terminal cymes to 3 in (7.5 cm) diam. in summer	ovoid, ⅓ in (8.5 mm), red, later purple-black
V. betulifolium	W & C China	deciduous shrub to 11½ ft (3.5 m)	to 4 in (10 cm), ovate to rhomboid or elliptic-oblong, finely tapering, coarsely serrate, glabrous and rich green above, paler beneath	white, in cymes to 4 in (10 cm) diam. in summer	to ¼ in (7 mm), rounded, bright red
V. bitchiuense	Japan, Korea	deciduous shrub to 10 ft (3 m), habit open upright	to 2¾ in (7 cm), ovate or oblong, usually obtuse, subcordate at base, slightly dentate, hairy, densely so beneath	pink, later white, in lax infl. to 2¾ in (7 cm) diam. in spring	black
V. × bodnantense (*V. farreri × V. grandiflorum*)	garden origin	deciduous shrub to 10 ft (3 m), of upright habit	to 4 in (10 cm), lanceolate to ovate or obovate, acute, serrate, soon glabrous	sweetly fragrant, rich rose-red, later fading to white with a strong flush of pink, in dense 2¾-in-(7-cm-) diam. clusters from fall to spring	

Comments: 'Dawn': the type of the cross. 'Pink Dawn': flowers pink, rose in bud, intensely fragrant.

Name	Distribution	Habit	Leaves	Flowers	Fruits
V. × burkwoodii (*V. carlesii × V. utile*)	garden origin	semi-evergreen shrub to 8 ft (2.5 m), of open and divaricate habit	to 4 in (10 cm), ovate to elliptic, acute, rounded or somewhat cordate at base, obscurely toothed, glossy dark green and scabrous above, pale brown-hairy beneath	fragrant, pink-white, later pure white, in rounded, terminal, many-flowered clusters to 3½ in (9 cm) diam. in spring	

Comments: 'Anne Russell': flowers in rounded corymbs, pink in bud, opening white, fragrant. 'Chenaultii': more compact; leaves more persistent, often bronze-brown in fall; flowers pale pink, later white. 'Fulbrook': as 'Anne Russell' but Leaves pale green, infl. Larger, conical, later-flowering. 'Park Farm Hybrid': habit broader; leaves more ovate to lanceolate, to 4 in (10 cm), entire to slightly serrate, hairy beneath; flowers pink at first, later pure white, in cymes to 4¾ in (12 cm) diam.

Name	Distribution	Habit	Leaves	Flowers	Fruits
V. × carlcephalum (*V. carlesii × V. macrocephalum*)	garden origin	vigorous, deciduous shrub to 8 ft (2.5 m)	close to *V. carlesii* but larger, to 4¾ in (12 cm), somewhat glossy, paler beneath, tinged red in fall	pink, later white and pink-flushed, in dense trusses to 6 in (15 cm) diam. in spring	
V. carlesii	Korea, Japan	rounded deciduous shrub to 8 ft (2.5 m)	to 3½ in (9 cm), broad-ovate, acute, somewhat cordate at base, irregular-serrate, dull green above, gray-green, downy beneath	fragrant, pink, later white, in terminal, rounded clusters to 3 in (7.5 cm) diam. in spring	to ¼ in (7 mm), ovoid, compressed, black

Comments: 'Diana': vigorous, compact; leaves tinged chocolate when young; flowers red, then pink, somewhat purple-flushed, later white.

V. acerifolium

V. × bodnantense **'Dawn'**

V. × burkwoodii **'Anne Russell'**

V. × carlcephalum

V

VIBURNUM

Name	Distribution	Habit	Leaves	Flowers	Fruits
V. cinnamomifolium	China	evergreen shrub, sometimes a tree, to 20 ft (6 m)	to 6 in (15 cm), elliptic-oblong, tapering, more or less entire, leathery and dark green with 3 sunken veins above	cream-white, in lax cymes to 6 in (15 cm) diam. in summer	to ⅛ in (4 mm), ovoid, blue-black, shiny

Comments: Differs from the next species in its thinner-textured, entire leaves and the fruit color. It needs more shelter than *V. davidii* and thrives in moist shade.

Name	Distribution	Habit	Leaves	Flowers	Fruits
V. davidii	W China	densely branched evergreen shrub to 5 ft (1.5 m)	to 6 in (15 cm), leathery, narrowly oval to obovate, obscurely toothed toward apex, dark green above, paler beneath, more or less glabrous with 3 distinct veins	dull white, in dense, stiff cymes to 3 in (7.5 cm) diam. in summer	to ¼ in (6.5 mm), narrow-ovoid, metallic blue

Comments: As with many *Viburnum* species, plants of both sexes are needed if the beautiful fruits are to form.

Name	Distribution	Habit	Leaves	Flowers	Fruits
V. dilatatum	Japan, China	erect deciduous shrub to 10 ft (3 m)+	to 4¾ in (12 cm), broadly ovate, rounded or obovate, apex abruptly short-acuminate, base rounded to somewhat cordate, toothed, hairy	pure white, very abundant, in downy cymes to 4¾ in (12 cm) diam. in summer	⅓ in (8.5 mm), rounded-ovoid, bright red

Comments: 'Catskill': to 6 ft (1.8 m), broad, compact; leaves to 5½ in (14 cm), orange-yellow to red in fall; fruit dark red.

Name	Distribution	Habit	Leaves	Flowers	Fruits
V. farreri *V. fragrans*	N China	upright deciduous shrub to 10 ft (3 m)+	to 4 in (10 cm), obovate or ovate, acute, coarsely toothed, tough, glabrous except for downy vein axils beneath	fragrant, white or pink-tinged, in dense terminal and axillary panicles to 2 in (5 cm) diam. in winter	brilliant red, later black

Comments: 'Candidissimum': flowers pure white. 'Nanum': dwarf; leaves small; flowers pink, scented, sparse.

Name	Distribution	Habit	Leaves	Flowers	Fruits
V. grandiflorum	Himalaya, W China	deciduous shrub or small tree, of broad and somewhat stocky habit	to 4 in (10 cm), firm, narrowly oval, acute, tapered at base, finely toothed, woolly beneath	fragrant, bright rose-pink at first, later nearly pure white, in dense corymbs to 3 in (7.5 cm) diam. in winter and spring	to ¾ in (2 cm), ovoid, black-purple

Comments: 'Snow White': flowers white, sometimes becoming pink. f. *foetens*: leaves glabrous beneath, smaller panicles of white flowers in winter, fruits black-purple.

Name	Distribution	Habit	Leaves	Flowers	Fruits
V. × juddii (*V. bitchiuense* × *V. carlesii*)	garden origin	intermediate between parents—broad, deciduous shrub to 5 ft (1.5 m)	more oblong than in *V. carlesii*	more numerous than in *V. carlesii*, in somewhat laxer and broader corymbs in spring	

Name	Distribution	Habit	Leaves	Flowers	Fruits
V. lantana WAYFARING TREE, TWISTWOOD	Europe, N Africa, Asia Minor, Caucasus, NW Iran	upright, deciduous shrub 15 ft (4.5 m), occasionally treelike	to 4¾ in (12 cm), broadly ovate to oblong, apex acute or somewhat blunt, cordate at base, finely toothed, velvety-hairy above, at least at first, densely hairy beneath	white, in cymes to 4 in (10 cm) diam. in spring and summer	oblong, ⅓ in (8.5 mm), red later black, glossy

V. davidii　　　　*V. farreri*　　　　*V. × juddii*　　　　*V. opulus* 'Compactum'

VIBURNUM

Name	Distribution	Habit	Leaves	Flowers	Fruits
V. lentago SHEEPBERRY	Eastern N America	robust deciduous shrub or small tree to 30 ft (9 m)	to 4 in (10 cm), ovate to obovate, apex tapering, base cuneate or rounded, sharply toothed, glossy dark green, lighter beneath, glabrous except for scurfy veins, bright red in fall; petiole winged	creamy white, in terminal cymes to 4½ in (11 cm) diam. in spring and summer	ovoid, to ⅝ in (16 mm), blue-black, pruinose

Comments: 'Pink Beauty': fruit pink, later almost violet.

Name	Distribution	Habit	Leaves	Flowers	Fruits
V. odoratissimum	India, Burma, China, Japan, Philippines	shrub to 33 ft (10 m), evergreen	to 5½ in (14 cm), coriaceous, glabrous, ovate to obovate, glossy green	sweetly fragrant, white, in terminal cymes to 4 in (10 cm) in spring and summer	to ½ in (10 mm), oblong-ovoid, slightly com- pressed, red ripening black

Comments: 'Nanum': habit dwarf, somewhat tender.

Name	Distribution	Habit	Leaves	Flowers	Fruits
V. opulus EUROPEAN CRANBERRY BUSH, GUELDER ROSE, CRAMPBARK	Europe, NW Africa, Asia Minor, Caucasus, C Asia	deciduous shrub to 15 ft (4.5 m), thicket- forming; stems erect, gray; bark thin	to 4 in (10 cm), maplelike, lobes 3–5, acute, coarsely and irregularly toothed, dark green and glabrous above, lanuginose beneath, turning wine-red to carmine in fall	creamy white, in two forms—small and fertile, and sterile and showy, to ¾ in (2 cm) diam., in flat cymes to 3 in (7.5 cm) diam. in summer	to ⅓ in (8.5 mm) diam., globose, bright red

Comments: 'Aureum': leaves emerging bronze, becoming deep yellow yellow, then lime green. 'Compactum': dense and compact, to 5 ft (1.5 m) high; leaves small, glossy, maroon in fall; flowers and fruit abundant. 'Roseum': syn. 'Sterile', 'Snowball'; habit rounded, to 13 ft (4 m); leaves tinted purple in fall; flowers large, double, sterile, in "snowball" heads, white or green tinted, sometimes turning pink. 'Xanthocarpum': leaves pale; fruit bright green at first, later pale ocher.

Name	Distribution	Habit	Leaves	Flowers	Fruits
V. plicatum	Japan, China	deciduous bushy shrub to 10 ft (3 m) branches mostly horizontal	4 in (10 cm), broadly ovate to elliptic-obovate, base round to broadly cuneate, crenate, plicately veined, deep green above, downy beneath, dark red to violet-brown in fall	white, small and fertile or sterile and showy (to 1½ in/4 cm diam.), in flat umbels to 4 in (10 cm) diam. in summer	rounded- ovoid, coral red, later blue-black. Summer.

Comments: f. *tomentosum*: branches horizontally spreading and overlapping; leaves wine red in fall; fruit blue-black. 'Mariesii': low, spreading; branches tiered; inflorescences large, resembling a lacecap *Hydrangea* with outer flowers larger and sterile. 'Nanum Semperflorens': syn. 'Watanabe'; dwarf, to 20 in (0.5 m); leaves richly colored in fall; flowers white, a fine 'lacecap' form.

Name	Distribution	Habit	Leaves	Flowers	Fruits
V. 'Pragense' (*V. rhytidophyllum* × *V. utile*)	garden origin	evergreen shrub to 8 ft (2.5 m); shoots somewhat thin, spreading to slightly nodding	to 4 in (10 cm), elliptic to lanceolate, shiny green and somewhat rugose above, densely tomentose beneath		

Name	Distribution	Habit	Leaves	Flowers	Fruits
V. rhytidophyllum	C & W China	evergreen shrub to 20 ft (6 m)	to 8 in (20 cm), ovate to oblong, tough, shiny and finely rugose above, gray- to tawny-felted beneath	dull yellow-white in tawny-felted, umbel-like trusses to 8 in (20 cm) diam., in spring and summer	ovoid, red ripening black

V. plicatum 'Mariesii'

V. rhytidophyllum

V. sieboldii

V. tinus 'Variegatum'

VIBURNUM

Name	Distribution	Habit	Leaves	Flowers	Fruits
V. sargentii *V. opulus* var. *sargentii*	NE Asia	deciduous shrub to 10 ft (3 m)	to 4¾ in (12 cm), 3-lobed, maplelike, emerging bronze becoming rich yellow-green, turning yellow to red in fall	white to cream, sterile and fertile in lacecap cymes to 4 in (10 cm) diam. in spring and summer	subglobose, light red

Comments: Differs from *V. opulus* in flowers with purple, not yellow, anthers. Includes 'Onondaga', with leaves emerging bronze and turning purple-red in fall, blush pink flower buds and pure white, larger, outer sterile flowers.

Name	Distribution	Habit	Leaves	Flowers	Fruits
V. sieboldii	Japan	deciduous shrub or small tree to 10 ft (3 m)	to 4¾ in (12 cm), obovate to oblong, serrate, glossy and smooth above	creamy white in long-stalked cymes to 4 in (10 cm) diam. in spring and summer	ovoid, pink later blue-black
V. tinus LAURUSTINUS	S Europe, N Africa	evergreen shrub to 11½ ft (3.5 m)	to 4 in (10 cm), ovate to ovate-oblong, entire, shiny dark green above, paler beneath	pink-brown in bud, opening white to palest pink in domed, terminal cymes to 4 in (10 cm) diam., in winter and spring	ovoid, indigo to black

Comments: Includes numerous cultivars, some compact and bushy, some with white- to cream- or yellow-variegated leaves, others with pink-to red-tinted flowers. One of the most popular is 'Eve Price', dense and compact with red-stained flower buds, pink-tinted flowers and blue fruits.

grow in the warm greenhouse. Propagate by seed. *V. caracalla* SNAIL FLOWER, CORKSCREW FLOWER; S America; twining perennial to 20 ft (6 m); flowers to 2 in (5 cm), fragrant, white or yellow with purple-pink wings, the keel coiled like a snail shell.

See also beans.

villous with shaggy pubescence.

Vinca (contraction of ancient Latin name *vinca pervinca*, from *vincio*, bind, wind around, in reference to making wreaths, whence late Middle English *per wynke* and Modern English *periwinkle*). Apocynaceae. Europe, W Asia. PERIWINKLE. 6 species, low, evergreen perennial herbs and subshrubs with long and slender, arching to creeping stems and smooth, dark green leaves. Solitary flowers are produced in the leaf axils from winter to summer; they are funnel-shaped with 5 spreading lobes. Hardy, trailing groundcover. They will grow in almost any soil in sun or shade and, once established, spread rapidly. They may be propagated by division of rooted shoots, or by cuttings. The overwintering shoots of *V. major* can be cut away in late winter before new growth begins. These plants are poisonous.

V. major GREATER PERIWINKLE; fertile shoots arching, to 12 in (30 cm); flowers 1¼–2 in (3–5 cm) across, blue-purple or violet; *V. minor* LESSER PERIWINKLE; fertile shoots more or less erect, to 8 in (20 cm); flowers to 1¼ in (3 cm) across, blue, violet or rich mauve. Both the above species include cultivars with variegated leaves and single and double flowers in shades of pale blue, dark blue, indigo and violet; those derived from *V. minor* may also show strong mauves and purple-reds. For *Vinca rosea*, see *Catharanthus roseus*.

vine a climbing plant.

vine eye (1) a broad, flat, wedge-shaped nail with a hole through which wire can be passed; used to support climbing plants on brick walls. It is driven into the mortar at suitable spacing; (2) a single-node cutting of a grape vine, traditionally taken with the bud in the middle of a short length of internode and inserted horizontally into the rooting medium.

vine weevil (*Otiorhynchus sulcatus*) a widespread pest of many garden plants, especially those grown in pots or other containers. Under greenhouse conditions, tubers of *Cyclamen*, *Begonia*, and *Sinningia* are particularly vulnerable to the feeding grubs, with coleus, crassulas, ferns, fuchsias, *Impatiens*, pelargoniums, primulas, and saintpaulias are also attacked. In gardens, heucheras, primroses, polyanthus, strawberries, saxifrages, and sedums may be severely damaged. Fully grown grubs are about ½ in (10 mm) long but curled; they are plump, legless, and creamy-white with a brown head (see photo, p.826). Larvae are active from late summer to spring, when they feed on roots and burrow into tubers; on woody plants, they remove outer tissue from the stem base and large roots. The first indication of infestation is usually a collapse of the plant.

The adult beetles are flightless, about ⅜ in (9 mm) long and dull black with speckles. They move slowly and eat notches in the leaf margins of a wide range of plants; especially rhododendrons and camellias, where they feed mostly among the lower branches at night. Outdoors, they are active from spring until fall, and egg-laying occurs mainly in June–August. They gain access to greenhouses through open doors or ventilators or on potted plants moved from outside standing areas; they are proficient climbers.

Vine weevil grubs are tolerant of many insecticides, particularly once they are large enough to be most damaging. However, good results can be

Vine weevil

achieved by drenching the growing medium with a recommended insecticide or pathogenic nematode in early August. On a small scale, control vine weevil by picking out and destroying grubs found in the rootballs of container-grown plants (which will then need repotting).

Biological control with the nematodes *Heterorhabditis megidis* and *Steinernema kraussei* is worthwhile in gardens, including greenhouses. These microscopic eelworms are applied in a water suspension, as a drench in late summer when the growing medium temperature is 57–68°F (14–20°C); a moist, open medium gives best results. The nematodes enter the bodies of larvae and transmit a fatal bacteria. They are available commercially.

Adult weevils can be controlled by trapping in corrugated cardboard rolls, placed among greenhouse plants, or by shaking them from the plants on to newspaper at night. Recommended insecticide sprays can be applied to the foliage and growing medium surface, at night, as soon as damage is first noticed.

vinery a traditional greenhouse designed for grape vines, with a wide, airy span and low side-walls of often less than 3¼ ft (1 m) in height. Often constructed as a lean-to, a vinery allows relatively easy access to all parts of the vine, with minimal need for ladders. Vinery-type greenhouses have been used for commercial tomato-growing, in spans 8–30 ft (8.5–9.2 m) wide and 4½–5½ ft (1.4–1.7 m) high to the gutters (12³⁄₄ ft [3.9 m]) to the ridge).

Viola (Classical Latin name, variant of the Greek *ion*, a name applied to a number of plants, including violets). Violaceae. VIOLET. Temperate regions, especially N Temperate & Andes, Sandwich Is. Some 500 species, annual or perennial herbs and small shrubs. Axillary and solitary, the flowers nod on erect stalks. They consist of five petals, the two uppermost often larger and outspread, the two outer, lower petals smaller, the central, lower petal often differently colored and shaped. The flowers are usually spurred.

With the exception of the Parma violets, violets are quite frost-hardy (to at least 14°F/–10°C). Grow them in cool, moist but well-drained soil, in partial or dappled shade, with protection from scorching winds. An acidic to neutral pH is ideal. Propagate from rooted runners, by division immediately after flowering or in fall, or by cuttings. For winter flowers, protect open-ground plants with cloches, or plant in the cold frame in early fall, or in pots in the cold greenhouse, ensuring maximum light and ventilation but with protection from frost and cold winds. Violets will not thrive in high temperatures, and the range should be 41–50°F (5–10°C), never above 59°F (15°C). Parma violets should be given such winter treatment as a matter of course in all but the mildest areas.

The term 'Pansy', from the French *pensées*, referred originally to *V. tricolor*, which has a long history in cultivation. Several modern violettas have been derived from crosses between named violas and *V. cornuta* and *V. c.* 'Alba', by using colchicine. All have the characteristic compact, tufted foliage and delicate fragrant blooms of the true violetta. All pansies have a single-stemmed root system, while violas originating from crosses between *V. lutea*, *V. altaica*, and *V. cornuta* have either a multistemmed root system, or an underground stolon system. Elongated leaves with a sprawling habit, flowers with a short spur or "horn," and little or no scent, are signs of a pansy; rounded leaves, short-jointed stems, long flower spurs, fragrance, and a neat compact habit are sure signs of a true bedding viola.

The garden pansies, *V. × wittrockiana*, usually treated as annuals or biennials, are commonly used for bedding and edging. Some selections, such as the Ice Queen, Floral Dance, and Universal series, are useful for color throughout the winter in mild climates; they also make colorful and attractive plants for window boxes, pots, and tubs. The garden violas, of compact form and perennial habit, make neat edging plants, or can be given foreground positions in herbaceous beds and borders. They can be used to good effect in the underplanting of the shrub border. The species violas and the violettas are well-suited in scale to the rock garden, or in windowboxes and pots, violettas also being useful for bedding in the smaller garden. Those blooming early in the season make a good carpet under taller spring-flowering bulbs. With hybrids, the strongest and most floriferous plants are obtained if treated as biennials, sown in fall for spring planting after overwintering in a well-ventilated cold frame or in summer for fall plantings. For one-year plants, sow at any time from midwinter onward, thinly in pans of sandy propagating medium, covering lightly. Germinate at seeds 68–77°F (20–25°C)—higher temperatures will cause failure; grow at 50°F (10°C), keeping the potting mix moist at all times. Show and exhibition cultivars, or other particularly attractive plants, may be propagated from cuttings as for named violas, or by simple layering, new roots appearing at nodes. Where violas and violettas are treated as perennials, they require a well-drained but moisture-retentive soil, with a pH between 5.5 and 7, and a cool root run. Position them in sun or, in warmer areas, in part shade. Full sun can be tolerated with sufficient moisture at the root; too-deep shade will result in straggling, etiolated plants. When necessary, cut back; flowering will resume in 2–3 weeks. For container culture, grow in a medium fertility loam-based mix. Cultivars can be propagated from cuttings, preferably taken in late summer or early fall. Mature growth is hollow-stemmed and difficult to root: cut back hard to generate good cutting material about one month before propagating. Take nodal cuttings of young growth and insert in a soilless propagating medium in a shaded and well-ventilated cold frame. Violettas and those species of compact habit and a fibrous root system can be divided in late spring or in early fall after cutting back to ensure short, strong shoots.

The rust fungus *Puccinia violae* is more common on species than on hybrids. The fungus mycelium is perennial in the rootstocks, so infected plants are best destroyed. The smut *Urocystis violae* produces black spore masses in large swellings on the leaves and stalks; affected plants should be destroyed and the site kept free of violas for several years. The violet leaf midge causes abnormal thickening and rolling of the leaves and can be severely debilitating. Pick off and destroy affected leaves and treat with insecticide.

(See table overleaf.)

VIOLA

Name	Distribution	Habit	Leaves	Flowers
V. aetolica	Balkans	perennial herb 2–16 in (5–40 cm)	to ¾ in (2 cm), ovate to lanceolate, crenate	to ¾ in (2 cm), yellow, the upper petals sometimes tipped violet
V. biflora TWIN-FLOWERED VIOLET	Europe to N Asia, N America	creeping to weakly erect perennial herb to 8 in (20 cm)	reniform to cordate, toothed	to ⅝ in (1.5 cm), yellow, lower petals veined or streaked brown to purple-black
V. calcarata	C Europe	perennial herb to 2½ in (6 cm)	to 1½ in (4 cm), elliptic to lanceolate, base cuneate, crenate	large and slender-spurred, blue to mauve, lilac or yellow, with a yellow center
V. canadensis CANADA VIOLET, TALL WHITE VIOLET	N America	erect perennial herb, 2–12 in (5–30 cm)	ovate, sparsely hairy, toothed	white with a yellow center and purple back, the lower petals sometimes flushed purple throughout

Comments: Pure white and dwarf forms are also grown.

V. cornuta HORNED VIOLET, VIOLA, BEDDING PANSY		perennial, 4–12 in (10–30 cm), prostrate to ascending	ovate with a truncate to cordate base and crenate margins	¾–1½ in (2–4 cm) diam., the petals broadly wedge-shaped and violet to pale lilac-blue

Comments: Many cultivars are available, including dwarf and compact to larger and rather sprawling plants, some with variegated leaves, and flowers ranging from white to opal, silvery lilac, pale blue, lilac, mauve and dark violet.

V. cucullata MARSH BLUE VIOLET *V. obliqua*		spreading perennial herb to 6 in (15 cm)	to 3½ in (9 cm) wide, ovate-cordate to reniform, crenate	to 1½ in (4 cm), blue-violet with a white eye, or wholly white, or pale blue

Comments: Includes cultivars with flowers red-eyed and white, white with violet or sky blue eyes, and rose to red.

V. elatior	C Europe, W Asia	erect perennial herb, 8–20 in (20–50 cm)	to 3½ in (9 cm), broadly lanceolate, toothed	to 1 in (2.5 cm), pale blue with a white center
V. gracilis *V. olympica*	Balkans, Greece to Asia Minor	low-perennial to 4 in (10 cm)	oblong to broadly ovate, more or less toothed, with large, pinnately divided stipules	to 1½ in (4 cm) across, deep violet with a yellow center

Comments: Cultivars with larger and white flowers are available.

V. hederacea AUSTRALIAN VIOLET, TRAILING VIOLET *Erpetion reniforme; V. reniforme*	Australia	stemless or creeping and mat-forming perennial herb seldom more than 2¾ in (7 cm) high	to 1¼ in (3 cm) across, ovate-cordate to reniform, entire to toothed	to ¾ in (2 cm), blue-violet or white **Comments:** Needs protection in winter and is well-suited to a shady, cool and moist situation in the cold or alpine house.
V. labradorica LABRADOR VIOLET	N N America, Greenland	clump-forming, spreading perennial to 2 in (5 cm)	ovate-cordate to reniform, dark green	small, typically mauve with a paler throat overlaid with darker veins, rarely blue, lilac or white

V. biflora   *V. cornuta*   *V. odorata*   *V. pedata*

VIOLA

Name	Distribution	Habit	Leaves	Flowers
V. lutea MOUNTAIN PANSY	W & C Europe	creeping to mat-forming perennial herb to 4 in (10 cm) tall	to 1¼ in (3 cm), ovate-cordate to lanceolate	to 1¼ in (3 cm), similar to *V. tricolor* but wholly yellow, or with upper petals sometimes purple, or the whole flower violet

Comments: For the rock garden or alpine house, in free-draining soil in sun.

Name	Distribution	Habit	Leaves	Flowers
V. odorata ENGLISH VIOLET, GARDEN VIOLET, SWEET VIOLET	Europe	spreading perennial herb to 6 in (15 cm)	broadly ovate-cordate to reniform, crenate	fragrant, to ¾ in (2 cm), dark violet, lilac, white or yellow

Comments: Includes numerous cultivars ranging in flower size, form and color.

Name	Distribution	Habit	Leaves	Flowers
V. palmata EARLY BLUE VIOLET, WILD OKRA	US	spreading perennial herb to 4 in (10 cm)	palmately lobed with 5–11, toothed segments	pale violet with a white eye overlaid with darker veins

Comments: Plant in a dry, fast-draining situation.

Name	Distribution	Habit	Leaves	Flowers
V. pedata BIRD'S FOOT VIOLET, CROWFOOT VIOLET, PANSY VIOLET	E N America	thick-rooted, clump-forming perennial to 6 in (15 cm)	palmately divided into 3–5, cleft, narrow segments	deep, velvety purple, the lower petals paler than the upper with dark veins

Comments: White-flowered forms are grown, likewise 'Bicolor', with flowers half dark violet, half pale lilac. Although hardy, this species fares better in the alpine house grown in an acidic, sandy medium.

Name	Distribution	Habit	Leaves	Flowers
V. sororia WOOLLY BLUE VIOLET	E N America	perennial herb, erect or spreading, to 3 in (8 cm)	2–4 in (5–10 cm) across, ovate to rounded, crenate, hairy beneath, pale to mid-green	to 1 in (2.5 cm), deep violet-blue with a white eye overlaid with darker veins

Comments: 'Albiflora': flowers pure white. 'Freckles': flowers white flecked and spotted pale blue.

Name	Distribution	Habit	Leaves	Flowers
V. tricolor HEARTSEASE, JOHNNY JUMP-UP, LOVE-IN-IDLENESS, WILD PANSY	Europe, Asia	annual, biennial or perennial herb, erect and bushy or sprawling to spreading, 2–12 in (5–30 cm)	ovate-cordate to lanceolate, crenate	¾–1½ in (2–4 cm), upper 2 petals typically violet to mauve, lateral petals white striped violet-black, lowest petals white with yellow bases overlaid with violet-black; forms with violet, pale mauve, yellow and bicolored flowers are common

Comments: Many cultivars are known, one of the finest is 'Bowles' Black', with velvety black flowers.

Name	Distribution	Habit	Leaves	Flowers
V. × wittrockiana PANSY, LADIES'-DELIGHT, HEARTSEASE, STEPMOTHER'S FLOWER	garden origin	erect and bushy to sprawling annual, biennial or short-lived perennial herb 2½–8 in (6–20 cm)	2–4¾ in (5–12 cm), ovate-cordate to spathulate-lanceolate, crenate	to 3 in (8 cm) across, the petals rounded and overlapping, in a wide range of colors

Comments: One of the most popular hardy bedding plants with many cultivars and seed races, ranging in flowering time (winter to summer), longevity, size and color, including pure tones and mixtures of white, pale blue, azure, indigo, violet, mauve, lilac, opal, pale rose, red, orange and yellow.

V. tricolor

*V. × **wittrockiana*** 'Padparadja'

*V. × **wittrockiana*** Princess Series

*V. × **wittrockiana*** Crystal Bowl Series

violet root rot (*Helicobasidium brebissonii*, syn. *H. purpureum*) a fungal disease, in which strands of violet- or purple-colored mycelium cover the roots, crown, and stem bases of plants, in which small dark resting bodies occur, as well as in the surrounding soil. Plants become yellow, stunted, and may wilt and die. A wide range of plants is affected, including asparagus, beet, carrot, celery, clover, parsnip, potato, rutabaga, strawberry, sugar beet, and turnip, as well as ornamentals, weeds, and young trees. The disease may perpetuate in the soil for many years, especially in acidic waterlogged conditions. Control by rotation, removing crop debris and burning affected roots.

virescence greening of tissue that is normally devoid of chlorophyll; often a symptom of *phytoplasma* (q.v.) infection.

virgate long, slim, and straight, like a rod or wand.

viridarium a medieval garden or park planted with trees.

viroid one of the smallest pathogens known, akin to viruses and transmitted mainly by grafting and other vegetative propagation methods. Viroids are the cause of a number of diseases with symptoms similar to those of viruses, including CITRUS EXOCORTIS, CHRYSANTHEMUM STUNT, COCONUT CADANG-CADANG, CUCUMBER PALE FRUIT, HOP STUNT, and POTATO SPINDLE TUBER.

viruses noncellular obligately parasitic pathogens, visible only under the electron microscope, responsible for a wide range of plant diseases. Viruses multiply only in living cells, since they are dependent on their host's body processes; they disrupt cells, alter metabolic activity, and usually cause a variety of symptoms. Almost any plant may be attacked. Some viruses can infect a wide host range, causing very different symptoms, of varying severity, in different plants.

Reduction in growth is the most common symptom, and may be associated with stunting, loss of vigor, decreased yield, loss of flower potential, or crop failure. Where fruit trees and ornamentals such as pelargoniums are hosts, infection may not be obvious, and it is then termed "latent." Most conspicuous is color change; this is particularly noticeable in leaves, which develop chlorotic and yellow patterns, such as mosaics, mottles, blotches, spots, ringspots, vein-banding, and vein-yellowing. Flower-breaking—for example, the light streaks on dark petals apparent in "broken" tulips—may also occur. Leaf variegation of some garden cultivars is viral in origin—for example, *Lonicera japonica* 'Aureoreticulata' and *Jasminum officinale* 'Aureum'. Flower malformations, leaf-rolling, leaf-curling, leaf-narrowing, abortion of reproductive organs, abnormal branching, rosetting, and enations are malformations caused by viruses. Tissue death may occur as local lesions, or it may affect phloem, stem tips, or buds, or the internal tissue of organs such as tubers. Wilting or withering may result. Many of these symptoms are similar to those caused by fungal or bacterial diseases; environmental effects and mineral deficiencies can also produce comparable symptoms.

For example, three plant viruses—TOBACCO MOSAIC VIRUS, CUCUMBER MOSAIC VIRUS, and CYMBIDIUM MOSAIC VIRUS—are considered here in more detail:

TOBACCO MOSAIC VIRUS (TMV) and the closely related tomato mosaic virus occur worldwide and are capable of infecting species from more than 150 genera in 30 families, which are economically important chiefly in Solanaceae. Leaf mottling and malformation, stunting, and reduced yield are the usual symptoms of infection.

TMV is a highly infectious virus, which can survive in plant debris in soil for many years and infect roots directly; it is spread by contact between plants, particularly during cultural operations, and in seed. Use of fresh or steam-sterilized soil for susceptible crops is advisable, as is thorough hand-washing and sterilization of tools before and after working on plants. Resistant tomato cultivars are available.

CUCUMBER MOSAIC VIRUS (CMV) also occurs worldwide and can infect more than 775 species in 86 families, especially cucurbits, tomato, pepper, spinach, many other vegetables, and ornamentals, including gladioli, lilies, delphiniums and petunias. Leaf mosaic, leaf malformation, stunting, color-breaking and sterility of flowers and severe reduction in yield are the major symptoms, and are most severe in outdoor plants in summer. Aphid vectors are the most important means of transmission, but spread by seed and mechanical means also occurs during cultural operations, and the virus can overwinter in many weeds and crop plants. Isolation of susceptible crops, aphid control, and weed elimination are standard control measures, together with the use of resistant or tolerant cultivars.

CYMBIDIUM MOSAIC VIRUS, which has spread worldwide as a result of interest in orchid-growing, has no known natural vector and is typically transmitted on cutting implements, and probably also on hands during cultural operations. Typical symptoms are long, well-defined yellow and black streaks on leaves and a marked reduction in size and number of flowers. It affects many other orchids and is sometimes associated with other orchid viruses.

Aphids, leafhoppers, mites, nematodes, fungi, and parasitic plants can all serve as virus vectors. Because of their intimate relationship with plant cells, viruses are virtually impossible to eliminate by chemical means; they are not affected by antibiotics and no viricides are commercially available. Insecticides, nematicides, and fungicides can reduce spread by vectors; disinfection of tools, hands, and greenhouse wires is an additional useful cultural measure. Avoiding sources of infection, by using certified seed or planting material, is the most important measure of control. Also vital is the prompt removal and destruction of infected plants, and the elimination of weeds that may act as a reservoir of infection.

Virus-free plants can be produced by heat treatment or meristem culture.

viscid covered in a sticky or gelatinous exudation.

Vitaliana (for Donati Vitaliano [1717–1762], prof. of botany at Turin). Primulaceae. Mountains of S and WC Europe. 1 species, *V. primuliflora* (syn. *Douglasia vitaliana*), a mat-forming, tufted, evergreen perennial herb. The leaves are small, narrow, and silvery. Produced in spring, the flowers are solitary, stalkless, and bright yellow to rich gold; they consist of a short tube and a limb to 1 in (2.5 cm) across, of 5 segments. Cultivate as for *Androsace*.

Vitex (the Latin name used by Pliny for *V. agnus-castus*). Verbenaceae. Mostly tropics, some temperate. 250 species, trees and shrubs (those here deciduous small aromatic trees and shrubs) with digitate leaves and small, tubular, and 2-lipped flowers in racemes and panicles in late summer and fall. Given the shelter of a warm wall with good drainage and protection from cold drying winds, they will tolerate temperatures to between 23 and 14°F (−5 and −10°C). Increase by semiripe cuttings.

V. agnus-castus CHASTE TREE; S Europe; to 16 ft (5 m); leaflets 5–9, with gray-white hairs beneath; flowers fragrant, lavender, lilac or white; *V. negundo* E Africa, E Asia; to 28 ft (8.5 m) leaflets 3–5, white-hairy beneath; flowers lilac to lavender.

viticulture the practice and science of cultivating grape vines.

Vitis (name used by the Romans for the grapevine). Vitaceae. Northern Hemisphere, especially N America. GRAPE, VINE. 65 species, deciduous shrubs mostly climbing by tendrils. The leaves are simple to palmately lobed and toothed. Small, green-white flowers in spring and summer give rise to succulent berries, usually pruinose and sometimes edible. The ornamental species are usually found in rich, damp woodland soils. They are hardy vigorous vines, ideally suited to clothing pergolas, trellis, and fences and for creating covered walkways. They will also climb and cascade through sturdy trees and, with support, make good wall plants. They are grown primarily for their luxuriant and often very attractive foliage, although some, such as *V. davidii*, with distinctive prickly stems, also bear edible fruits. The edible grape, *V. vinifera*, has given rise to clones with beautiful foliage. Many other species are valued for their brilliance in fall, including the spectacular, large-leaved *V. coignetiae*, and *V. davidii*, *V. amurensis*, and *V. thunbergii*.

Grow in deep, moist, well-drained, moderately fertile soil in full sun or partial shade (sun and warmth are needed for fruit ripening and good fall colors). Prune in midwinter, before the sap begins to rise. In a restricted space, most species can be trained to a permanent framework and cut back to between one or two buds to form a spur system that becomes increasingly picturesque with age. Excessive new growth is removed (i.e., new shoots stopped at 5–6 leaves in midsummer as the basal growth begins to ripen), frequently giving rise to attractive contrasts between new and mature foliage. Propagate by hardwood cuttings in late winter, rooted in a closed case with bottom heat at 64–70°F (18–21°C); also by simple layers, or by seed, following a six-week stratification period at or below 23°F (−5°C).

V. amurensis AMUR GRAPE; NE Asia, vigorous vine to 50 ft (15 m); leaves 4–10 in (10–25 cm), 5-lobed, midlobe broadly ovate, acuminate, slightly hairy beneath, turning rich crimson and purple in fall; fruit black, glaucous, bitter; *V. coignetiae* CRIMSON GLORY VINE; Japan, Korea; vigorous vine to 80 ft (25 m); leaves to 12 in (30 cm), rounded, obscurely 3–5-lobed, toothed, thick-textured, rather puckered with impressed veins but more or less smooth above, brown-scurfy beneath, turning metallic bronze and then fiery red to glowing scarlet in fall; fruit purple-black, glaucous, scarcely edible; *V. davidii* China; vigorous vine to 50 ft (15 m), young shoots with spinelike bristles; leaves to 10 in (25 cm), ovate to cordate, toothed, tip tapered, glossy dark green above, glaucous beneath, brilliant red in fall; fruit black, edible; includes 'Veitchii', with leaves tinged bronze in summer, and var. *cyanocarpa*, with fruit thickly blue-pruinose; *V. thunbergii* temperate E Asia; moderately vigorous vine; leaves 2¾–6 in (7–15 cm), cordate at base with 3–5, ovate, toothed lobes, dull dark green turning rich crimson in fall, woolly beneath; fruit purple-black, glaucous; *V. vinifera* COMMON GRAPE VINE; S and C Europe, W Asia; vigorous vine to 65 ft (20 m); leaves 2–6 in (5–15 cm), rounded in outline, palmately 3–7-lobed, toothed, base cordate, becoming glabrous above, hairy beneath; fruit

large, sweet and edible green, yellow, purple-red or purple-black; a widespread and much-developed fruit crop (see *grapes*), with many hybrids and cultivars; ornamental cultivars include 'Brant', a fruiting hybrid with large, deeply lobed leaves that turn deep purple-red during fall, except for yellow-green veins and margins, 'Ciotat' (syn. 'Apiifolia'), with finely cut and deeply lobed leaves, and 'Purpurea', with plum leaves turning a rich dark purple to garnet in fall.

viviparous developing plantlets.

vivipary (1) the development of plantlets on nonfloral organs—for example, plantlets on the leaves of *Kalanchoe daigremontiana* (see *foliar embryo*, *proliferation)*; (2) the germination of seeds within a fruit still attached to the parent plant, that occurs in some *Poa* species; (3) the production of living offspring, as occurs in *aphids* (q.v.).

Vriesea (for W. de Vriese [1807–1862], Dutch botanist). Bromeliaceae. C and S America. 249 species, evergreen perennial herbs with strap-shaped, glossy leaves, their bases overlapping and forming a funnel or vase. From its center, a raceme or spike arises clothed with brightly colored bracts and bearing small flowers. Cultivate as for *Aechmea*.

V. fenestralis SE Brazil; leaves to 20 in (50 cm), pale green netted with dark green lines, sometimes spotted red-brown and scaly beneath; floral bracts green, spotted, flowers white-green; *V. fosteriana* Brazil; leaves to 28 in (70 cm), green, banded maroon beneath; floral bracts yellow, flowers pale green tipped purple; *V. hieroglyphica* (Brazil; leaves to 32 in (80 cm), broadly banded dark green or purple; floral bracts yellow-green, flowers yellow); *V. psittacina* leaves to 20 in (50 cm), green covered in pale scales; floral bracts yellow tipped green or red tipped yellow to wholly red or yellow-green, flowers yellow sometimes tipped green; *V. splendens* (E Venezuela to Surinam; FLAMING SWORD; leaves to 32 in (80 cm), dark green with broad, dark purple-brown bands; floral bracts flaming scarlet to orange, flowers yellow.

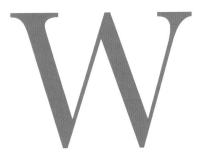

Wahlenbergia (for Georg Wahlenberg [1780–1851] of Uppsala, author of *Flora Lapponica*). Campanulaceae. ROCK BELL. Cosmopolitan. 150 species, annual or perennial herbs with bell-shaped, 5-lobed flowers in summer. Hardy to 0°F (−18°C). Plant in full sun in moist, sandy, and acidic soil. *W. albomarginata* is more safely grown in the alpine house in damp, cool temperate gardens. Propagate by seed, or alternatively by division.

W. albomarginata New Zealand; tufted perennial to 12 in (30 cm); leaves to ³⁄₄ in (2 cm), hairy; flowers white to pale blue or pale slate blue; *W. congesta* New Zealand; mat-forming perennial; leaves to 1 in (2.5 cm), glabrous; flowers pale blue to white.

Waldsteinia (for Count Franz Adam Waldstein von Wartenburg [1759–1823], Austrian botanist, who published in cooperation with the Hungarian botanist Kitaibel an outstanding work on Hungarian flora in 1799–1812). Rosaceae. Northern temperate regions. 6 species resembling yellow-flowered *Fragaria*. Suitable for the rock garden, the front of the flower border, and the woodland edge; *W. ternata* will cover banks. Hardy to at least 5°F (−15°C). Grow in part shade, or sun where soils stay moist in summer. Propagate by division of rooted runners in early spring, or by seed.

W. fragarioides BARREN STRAWBERRY; E US; leaves bronze; flowers to ³⁄₄ in (2 cm) in diameter; *W. ternata* (leaves hairy; flowers to ⅝ in (1.5 cm) diam.

walk a path created primarily as a feature, possibly between trees, under a pergola or arbor, or linking dominant features in a garden. In Renaissance gardens, walks were aggrandized into alleys and avenues, and usually terminated in some focal point.

wall case a very narrow lean-to greenhouse used to protect wall-trained fruit trees, such as peaches and apricots.

wall nail a nail with a strip of soft lead attached to its head. The lead strip can be bent around wires to support climbing plants on brick walls, with the nail being driven into the mortar. It is also known as a lead-headed wall nail.

walnut (*Juglans regia*; ENGLISH WALNUT, PERSIAN WALNUT) a large tree reaching 60 ft (18 m) or more, grown as a broad-crowned, attractive ornamental tree and for its nuts; its native area stretches from the Balkan peninsula to Kashmir. It is self-fertile and wind-pollinated, but male and female flowers may mature at different times and pollination is therefore more likely when two cultivars are established; flowers and shoots are susceptible to damage at temperatures between 27 and 28°F (−2 and −3°C). Fruit ripening is variable, but immature nuts are suitable for pickling.

Plant young trees 40–60 ft (12–18 m) apart, taking care to keep the taproot intact and to reject potbound specimens. Establishment is slow, and trees may be trained as center leader standards for best ornamental effect, or contained, for example, as a goblet form, in smaller gardens. Pruning must only be carried out in the completely dormant season, and minimal attention is required for established trees. Walnuts for pickling are picked in summer before the shells harden; mature nuts are harvested in early fall on release from their casings, and should be stored dry in a cool, airy, slightly humid environment.

Propagation is possible from seed but is best done by chip budding or grafting cultivar scions on to BLACK WALNUT (*J. nigra*) seedlings.

Possible problems: aphids, caterpillars.

Wardian case originally a wooden-sided, glazed container with a pitched roof, developed by Nathaniel Bagshaw Ward in the early 19th century for transporting actively growing plants over long distances. Widely used by Victorian plant-hunters for transporting collections from overseas, it was subsequently adopted in various forms for the indoor cultivation of plants, especially those requiring high humidity; modern versions are bottle gardens and terrariums. It is also called a fern case.

warm house see *stove house*.

wart disease (*Synchytrium endobioticum*) a destructive fungal disease of potatoes, highly localized worldwide. It was first formally recorded in 1869 in Czechoslovakia and England, and has since been recognized in most of north and central Europe, the Indian subcontinent, New Zealand and South Africa. Wart disease probably originated in South America, where it occurs. It has been successfully eradicated in the eastern US, following outbreaks from 1918 onward, and in North America it is only established in Newfoundland.

The fungus is soilborne and can survive there for up to 30 years; resting bodies germinate in wet conditions, giving rise to infection of the "eyes" and young sprouts of potato tubers early in the growing season. Cells near the site of infection enlarge, and irregular cauliflower-like galls develop on the seed tuber, stems, young tubers, and sometimes aerial stems and foliage. Underground, the galls are whitish and turn green if exposed to light. The disease flourishes in wet seasons, when it can result in total loss of crop; it is also spread in soil on machinery, tools, and footwear, and the manure of animals fed with diseased tubers can also be infectious.

In Britain, the control of wart disease has been effected by the growing of resistant cultivars, made available through government-certified seed programs; as a result, the majority of cultivars now grown are of the immune type, selected during breeding by official laboratory testing. The disease is rare in commercial crops and only of limited occurrence in private gardens and allotments. Of nonimmune cultivars, only 'King Edward' and 'Red King Edward' are grown to any extent in Britain, but these are of limited susceptibility. Although permitted, it is not advisable to grow nonimmune cultivars. Extreme vigilance is necessary, especially as regards the appearance of new races of the pathogen; these exist on the continent of Europe, in the ex-Soviet republics, and in Newfoundland, and can infect immune cultivars.

Most countries impose strict import regulations on soil and, especially, on seed potatoes.

Washingtonia (for George Washington [1732–1799], first president of the US). Palmae. SW US, N Mexico. 2 species, tall palms with columnar stems, scarred below and clothed above with coarse, rusty fibers. The leaves are large and palmate, composed of numerous, dark green, linear segments. They are frequently seen as avenue trees in the dry tropics and subtropics. They show great tolerance of transplanting, despite their deep root system, and grow rapidly even when young. Grow in frost-free conditions with full sun and free-draining soil. Water container-grown plants frequently in spring and summer. Propagate *Washingtonia* by fresh seed.

W. filifera COTTON PALM, DESERT FAN PALM, CALIFORNIA FAN PALM; S California, Arizona, N Mexico; to 50 ft (15 m); petioles to 6½ ft (2 m), toothed at base, leaf blades to 6½ ft (2 m), segments tipped with white filaments; *W. robusta* SOUTHERN WASHINGTONIA, MEXICAN WASHINGTONIA; NW Mexico; to 80 ft (25 m); petioles toothed throughout, leaf blades to 3¼ ft (1 m), segments drooping, with white filaments when young.

wasps winged insects of the order Hymenoptera, frequently troublesome in home gardens. The common wasp (*Vespula vulgaris*) is the best known species of social wasp, which also includes the hornet (*Vespa crabro*). Adult common wasps in the worker caste are approximately ⅝ in (15 mm) long and brightly banded in yellow and black. Wasps perform a beneficial function in spring and early summer, feeding their grubs mainly on insects, some of which are pests of garden plants. However, they cause serious damage to tree fruits and grapes in late summer, usually following primary damage by birds; dahlias are sometimes attacked by gnawing on the stems. In some seasons, wasps are a serious pest of honey bee hives.

Wasp damage

The overwintered queen leaves hibernation in spring and builds a nest of a paperlike material, made by chewing small pieces of wood; the nest is constructed as an outer covering protecting combs of downward-facing cells, into each of which an egg is laid. During mid- to late summer, males and young queens are produced and the fertilized queens fly off to hibernate. A reduced number of female workers and males are active until killed by frosts in late fall. Nests are not recolonized the following year.

Control of wasps in and around gardens is by destroying nests with recommended chemicals, applied strictly according to instructions; when possible, trained operators should be engaged.

watercress (*Nasturtium officinale*) a hardy aquatic and wet-soil perennial, native throughout Europe, especially in limestone areas that give rise to pure springs running at a constant temperature of around 50°F (10°C). It is grown as a salad vegetable for its pungent-tasting leaves, which are rich in vitamins and minerals, particularly iron.

The availability of suitable free-flowing uncontaminated water in back yards or residential gardens is rare. If special care is taken to keep the crop constantly moist, watercress can be successfully grown in a trench, 12 in (30 cm) deep and 24 in (60 cm) wide; prepare with a 4-in (10-cm) layer of rotted organic matter topped off with a similar depth of fertile soil. Cuttings from purchased bunches root easily in a container of water, and these are set out 6 in (15 cm) apart; pinching out the growing tips will encourage bushy growth.

Watercress can also be grown in well-crocked 8-in (20-cm) pots, filled with loam-based growing mix; plant a number of well-rooted cuttings per pot. Keep thoroughly watered by standing container in a shallow tray of water and replenishing daily. Protect all crops from wind and frost to maintain good quality.

Possible problems: aphids, flea beetle; virus.

water gardening there are existing records of decorative pools and water features dating from 3000 BC in ancient Egypt. The Chinese grew water lilies in pools, lakes, urns, and vases by the 10th century AD, and water was a vital element in the design of Persian and Indian gardens. In succeeding centuries, water was used primarily for the effect of stillness and its mirroring qualities; fountains and waterfalls were used to add movement to gardens. Plants seldom featured until the early 18th century, and the cultivation of tropical and temperate water lilies followed. The type of water gardening in which cultivation of plants and care of fish predominate did not develop in Europe and North America until the end of the 19th century.

Siting A pool should be sited in a sheltered position, where cold air does not accumulate, and away from trees so that aquatic plants and fish can benefit from full sunshine. Even a shallow pool can present danger to small children, and should be sited within visible range to enable supervision. For the best effect, construct the pool at a naturally low point in the yard, carefully distributing excavated soil to emphasize a low spot.

Types of pool An informal pool may take any irregular nonangular shape; a few sweeping curves are much more attractive than a number of smaller ones. The pool should be edged with natural materials, such as stones or turf, with marginal moisture-loving plants established to soften the outline. Blending with a rock garden creates an impressive ornamental feature.

Watercress cuttings

A formal pool may be raised or sunken, incorporating coping or paving stones and made to a geometric shape. Such features usually look best with fewer plants, in particular species of more rigid form; fountains are valuable complements. Formal pools make good focal points, and can be attractively situated near a wall where water spouts and sculptures can be added.

In small areas, such as a patio, it is possible to construct a water feature by utilizing a large ornamental container and planting it with a miniature water lily and other dwarf species, such as *Typha minima*, the DWARF REED MACE, and *Mimulus ringens*, together with floating plants that will need reducing from time to time.

On spacious sites, a bog garden can be created adjacent to a pool by laying impermeable sheeting shallowly beneath an absorbent, highly organic growing medium. This should be kept constantly moist, either using the pool or by means of buried irrigation lines.

Choice of plants Plants for water gardens may be considered under group headings. **Oxygenators** are submerged fast-growing species, usually established from a bunch of cuttings planted in an individual pot container. They help keep a pool clear of algae and are essential if fish are stocked, for which purpose *Myriophyllum* and *Lagarosiphon* species are particularly effective. **Deep water plants** succeed in water depths from 12 to 36 in (30–90 cm), and are most commonly represented by the water lilies (*Nymphaea* species). *Aponogeton*, *Nymphoides*, and *Orontium* species are also suitable. **Surface floaters**, such as *Lemna trisulca* and *Trapa natans*, add character and balance but must be prevented from completely covering the water surface. Marginals include the aquatic irises and dwarf rushes. Bog plants, such as *Caltha* and *Myosotis* species, thrive in waterlogged soil.

Construction Pools can be made with flexible liners of synthetic rubber or plastic; butyl rubber is more durable than polythene or PVC and its long life justifies its expense. To obtain the correct liner dimensions, take the maximum width of the intended pool plus twice the maximum depth, and the maximum length plus twice the maxi-

mum depth. To provide a turned-over flap at the finished edges, an extra 6 in (15 cm) should be allowed around the edge of the liner sheet.

The pool site may be marked out with a rope or hose. The hole should then be excavated with sloping sides and with shelves constructed at various depths to accommodate a range of plants; ensure that the finished edges are perfectly level all around to prevent seepage. The completed hole must be lined with fiberglass wadding or plastered with fine sand to protect the sheet from puncturing. The liner is then draped over the hole, anchored all around with large stones and slowly filled with water. Surplus sheet should be trimmed and the pool edged with stones protruding above the water by 2 in (5 cm) or so. Preformed rigid fiberglass or plastic liners are available, and care must be taken to ensure that these are set level all around.

By incorporating moving water and fish and carefully maintaining a balanced plant population of various, contrasting forms, a special garden feature can be created that is both ornamental and peaceful to observe, while functioning as an attraction for wildlife.

water-holding polymers polyacrylamides, polyvinyl alcohols and starches are specifically manufactured to increase water retention in soil or substrates. They are of particular value in hanging baskets and patio containers.

watering can a spouted can for watering plants, made of either galvanized iron or plastic. See *irrigation, rose*.

waterlogged the state of a growing substance when saturated with water. It may result from compaction, natural defects in the soil profile, the lie of the land, or other factors that prevent drainage. It is a common cause of root death. See *drainage*.

watermelons (*Citrullus lanatus*) a vining annual of subtropical natural habitat, grown for its large, rounded-oblong, edible fruits, mottled or striped, light and dark green. Cultivars may be red-fleshed or yellow/orange fleshed. For best results, watermelons require a temperature of 77–86°F (25–30°C). In

temperate climates, they may be grown under cover as sweet melons (q.v.), although plants are extremely vigorous. Sown seed requires a temperature of at least 72°F (22°C) for germination.

water shoot a vigorous upright shoot growing from an adventitious

Water shoots
Vigorous regrowth following hard pruning is typical of *Syringa vulgaris*, enabling lilacs to be renovated. These shoots need thinning.

bud on the upper surface of a tree or shrub branch, especially near a large pruning wound. In fruit trees, they are unproductive and often congesting, but are sometimes used for bending to encourage fruit bud formation, or as replacement shoots in some pruning systems.

water soaked describing plant lesions that are soft and watery, such as those caused by *Sclerotinia* or bacterial soft rots.

waterworks various systems for displaying water motion in lakes, pools, canals, and formal basins. Most commonly employed are fountains and cascades, but there is also a wide range of other contrivances, including the modern bubbler.

Watsonia (for Sir William Watson [1715–1758], British scientist). Iridaceae. South Africa. 52 species, cormous perennial herbs with sword-shaped leaves. Produced in summer in 2-ranked spikes, the flowers are tubular and curving with six tepals. Slightly frost-tender and more safely grown in the cool greenhouse in cool temperate areas; however, in areas where temperatures only rarely fall to 23°F (–5°C), most species can be grown outside with a protective mulch of bracken litter. They are generally best left undisturbed, but spring- and early summer-flowering species that rest during late summer are sometimes lifted and stored in a cool, frost-free place in winter. The late summer and fall-flowering species are more or less evergreen, and should not be dried out. Grow in a sunny position in a light, well-drained, sandy loam. Provide plentiful water when in growth. Apply a slow-release fertilizer in summer. Propagate by seed or offsets.

W. borbonica (syn. *W. pyramidata*) 3¼–6½ ft (1–2 m); flowers to 2½ in (6 cm) across, slightly scented, pale to deep pink or purple with white lines at the base of each tepal, rarely wholly white; *W. fourcadei* 3¼–6½ ft (1–2 m); flowers to 2½ in (6 cm) across, pink, orange, or vermilion, rarely purple, sometimes with a paler tube; *W. meriana* 20 in–6½ ft (0.5–2 m); flowers to 1½ in (4 cm) across, orange, red, pink, purple, rarely yellow; *W. pillansii* (syn. *W. beatricis*) 20 in–4 ft (0.5–1.2 m); flowers to 2½ in (6 cm) across, orange or orange-red.

wattle a construction of pliable, woody plant stems (for example, young willow or hazel branches), mostly used in the form of hurdles for fencing.

weaning the gradual acclimatization of vegetatively propagated plants from a rooting environment, especially cuttings rooted in a mist unit and micropropagated plants raised by tissue culture. It is sometimes referred to as acclimatization.

webbers, webworms see *tent caterpillars*.

weed a plant growing where it is not wanted. Weeds are found in habitats disturbed by human activity, and are usually native species, although some garden plants and lawn grasses have the potential to become weeds because of their free-seeding habit or invasive growth. Annual weeds complete their life cycle in one year, and many can produce several generations during that time. Perennial weeds perpetuate themselves from year to year by means of rhizomes, bulbs, tubers, and taproots.

weed wiper a device for smearing individual weeds with herbicide, often in the form of a specially-made glove. It is particularly suitable for applying translocated herbicides on a small scale.

weep holes small, round drainage holes set into the base of a brick or block retaining wall to provide drainage.

weeping (1) describing the growth habit of trees and shrubs with pendulous branches or twigs; (2) the phenomena of bleeding and gumming.

weevils (Coleoptera: mostly Curculionidae) the largest family in the animal kingdom, with over 40,000 described species. The head of a weevil is elongated at the front to form a snout, with the mouthparts at the tip and with the antennae, which are often elbowed and with a terminal club, in varying positions along its length. Some weevils have long snouts that facilitate feeding; females also use their snouts to make deep incisions in plant tissue in which they deposit eggs. The larvae are all plant feeders; they are remarkably uniform, the fleshy grubs are off-white in color, with a well-developed yellow-brown head capsule, and devoid of legs. Some weevil larvae feed openly on foliage, or in rolled leaf portions or as leafminers; many are root-feeders; still others are wood- or shoot-borers, seed- or fruit-eaters, or live in galls on roots or stems. When fully fed, the larvae pupate, usually in the soil, but sometimes within the tissues of the host plant.

The BOLL WEEVIL (*Anthonomus grandis grandis*) is the most serious pest of cotton in the US, while other *Anthonomus* species attack garden plants. The larvae of the STRAWBERRY BLOSSOM WEEVIL (*A. rubi*), a European species, feed on wilted buds; the adults are black and up to ⅛ in (3 mm) long. The STRAWBERRY BUD WEEVIL (*A. signatus*) of North America attacks strawberries in a similar way. The larvae of another European species, the APPLE BLOSSOM WEEVIL (*A. pomorum*), feed on apple blossom buds; the adults are up to ⅛ in (4 mm) long, with a white

Apple blossom weevil

V-shaped mark on their backs. In the US, the larvae of the PEPPER WEEVIL (*A. eugenii*) destroy pepper buds; the adults are black and up to ⅛ in (3 mm) long. Also important in North America is the PLUM CURCULIO (*Conotrachelus nenuphar*), whose brown weevils, up to ¼ in (6 mm) long, feed on foliage and puncture the fruit of stone fruits, apples, and pears, while the larvae bore into fruit. Larvae of the BLACK WALNUT CURCULIO (*C. retentus*) tunnel into walnuts; the BUTTERNUT CURCULIO (*C. juglandis*) causes similar damage to walnuts and butternuts; and the larvae of the QUINCE CURCULIO (*C. crataegi*) invade the fruits of quince. Other North American weevil pests include the CARROT WEEVIL (*Listronotus oregonensis*), whose larvae bore into the roots and stems of carrots, celery, parsley, and parsnips, and the VEGETABLE WEEVIL (*Listorderes costirostris obliquus*), whose adults and larvae feed on the foliage and roots of various vegetable crops, including carrots, turnips, potatoes, and tomatoes.

Species prevalent in Europe include the APPLE SHOOT CUTTER (*Rhynchites caeruleus*) whose bright blue weevils, up to ⅛ in (4 mm) long, attack apple and other fruit trees, depositing eggs in soft shoots that are then partially or completely severed. The APPLE FRUIT RHYNCHITES (*R. aequatus*) are small, red-brown weevils that deposit eggs in apple fruitlets into which the larvae then tunnel. The STRAWBERRY RHYNCHITES (*R. germanicus*) are metallic blue-green weevils, up to ⅛ in (3 mm) long, which sever the leaves and blossoms of strawberries and other plants, such as raspberry, blackberry, geum, potentillas, and helianthemum. The larvae of the NUT WEEVIL (*Curculio nucum*) feed on the kernels of hazel nuts. The TURNIP GALL WEEVIL (*Ceuthorrhynchus pleurostigma*), a dull black weevil up to ⅛ in (3 mm) long, has larvae that live in marble-shaped galls just below soil level on the taproots of brassicas, especially cabbages, savoys, turnips, and rutabaga.

PEA AND BEAN WEEVILS (*Sitona species*) are common in both Europe and North America. The adults are black with yellow-brown scales that give a

W

825

Vine weevil larvae
Damage to the roots by these C-shaped grubs can prove fatal to plants. The larvae are often imported into the garden via purchases of container-grown specimens.

striped appearance. They feed on the leaf margins, removing symmetrical U-shaped notches from broad beans and, to a lesser extent, from garden peas and sweet peas; the larvae feed in the root nodules. Other species of weevil are *leaf miners* (q.v.), *leaf weevils* (q.v.), leaf rovers, and wingless weevils.

Wingless weevils Several medium to large weevils are flightless, with absent or vestigial wings, and with a comparatively short snout. The most important are *Otiorhynchus* species, whose largely nocturnal adults feed on leaves, buds, and shoots, while their larvae attack underground parts of plants. The larvae have slightly curved, creamy white, legless bodies, with red-brown heads, and may be up to $^1/_2$ in (12 mm) long, according to species; when fully fed, they pupate in the soil. The principal pest species common to Europe and North America are the VINE, or YEW, WEEVIL (*O. sulcatus*), with black adults up to $^3/_8$ in (9 mm) long; the CLAY-COLORED WEEVIL (*O. singularis*), with brown adults up to $^1/_4$ in (7 mm) long; and the STRAWBERRY ROOT WEEVILS (*O. nugostriatus* and *O. ovatus*), with adults similar to the vine weevil but smaller. Other major European species include another STRAWBERRY ROOT WEEVIL (*O. rugifrons*), and the RED-LEGGED WEEVIL (*O. clavipes*), which has black adults up to $^1/_2$ in (13 mm) long, with red legs.

Clay-colored weevil adults attack a wide range of plants, including apples, currants, raspberries, rhododendrons, roses, spruces, and other conifers, causing ring barking and damage to buds and new growths. The larvae are less injurious than those of the vine weevil, but they are difficult to distinguish from one another. The strawberry root weevils are common in woodlands and hedgerows but seldom damage garden plants except strawberries, whose roots the larvae may sever. Red-legged weevil adults attack soft and tree fruits and roses, and their larvae damage the roots of strawberries and potted plants.

The STRAWBERRY CROWN BORER (*Tyloderma fragariae*), with dark brown adults up to $^1/_8$ in (4 mm) long, is an important pest of strawberries in the eastern US; its larvae bore into and may destroy the crowns of the plants.

Methods of weevil control include clearing plant debris, in which adults shelter, trapping with corrugated paper or burlap, grease banding the trunks of young trees, and, for strawberries, long rotation and burning off foliage after cropping. Recommended persistent contact insecticides can be used in potting mixes, or as a spray when leaf damage is first noticed. The parasitic eelworms *Heterorhabditis megidis* and *Steinernema kraussei* are useful biological control agents, and the fungus *Metarhizium anisopliae*, applied as a spore drench, may prove to be effective. See *vine weevil*.

Weigela (for Christian Ehrenfried van Weigel [1748–1831], German botanist, professor at Greifswald). Caprifoliaceae. E Asia. 10 species, deciduous shrubs with corymbs of bell- to funnel-shaped, 5-lobed flowers in spring and summer. Hardy to –9°F (–23°C). Plant in fertile, moist but well-drained soil, preferably in sun, or in partial shade. Prune after flowering to maintain vigor, thinning out exhausted shoots to ground level, and shorten the strongest shoots to within an inch or two of old wood. Propagate in early summer from softwood basal cuttings rooted in a sandy propagating mix in the cold frame, or in summer by semiripe cuttings with a heel, at 59°F (15°C). Alternatively, take 8-in (20-cm) hardwood cuttings in fall after leaf fall, and place in a sheltered nursery bed.

W. florida Korea, N China, Japan; to 10 ft (3 m) flowers to 1$^1/_2$ in (4 cm), dark rose-red, paler within; includes numerous hybrids and cultivars, small or large with variegated, dark green or purple-red-tinted leaves and white, pink, or dark carmine flowers; *W. middendorfiana* Japan, N China; to 5 ft (1.5 m); flowers to 1$^1/_2$ in (4 cm), yellow; *W. praecox* Japan, Korea; to 6$^1/_2$ ft (2 m); flowers to 1$^1/_2$ in (4 cm), purple-pink to carmine; includes tall and short cultivars, some with variegated leaves, early-flowering with white, pink, carmine, and red flowers, the exteriors often darker.

Weldenia (for L. von Welden [1780–1853], Austrian soldier and student of the Alpine flora). Commelinaceae. Mexico, Guatemala. 1 species, *W. candida*, a tuberous-rooted, perennial herb, stemless with a basal rosette of linear to lanceolate leaves 2–8 in (5–20 cm) long. Produced in clusters in spring and summer, the flowers are 2–2$^1/_2$ in (5–6 cm) long and white or blue with ovate segments. A choice perennial for the alpine house, plant in a deep pot of freely draining loam-based medium. Keep dry but not arid during winter rest. Resume watering in spring, and water freely in summer, reducing supplies as the leaves wither after flowering. Propagate by seed or by division.

wellhead the structure built at the top of a water well, often finely carved and used as a garden ornament.

wettable powder a pesticide formulation in which the active chemical constituent is adsorbed onto an inert carrier, ground to a fine powder, and a surfactant added; the resultant product is insoluble and forms a suspension when vigorously stirred in water to form a substance for spraying.

wetter, wetting agent see *adjuvant*.

whalehide a trade name, now in common use for the bitumenized cardboard used to make plant containers, especially bottomless pots for

Whalehide pot

W

the ring culture of tomatoes. Some forms of whalehide pots degrade more quickly than others and are suitable for leaving intact at planting time.

wheelbarrow a large open-topped container, with sloping sides, mounted on a frame, at one end of which is an axle usually bearing one wheel. At the opposite end, the frame is fashioned to form two handles, below which are two legs for supporting the container when stationary. It is used for transporting soil, bulky manure, or garden waste. See *ballbarrow*.

whetstone a shaped stone for sharpening cutting tools, especially scythes and sickles.

whip a young seedling or grafted tree, without lateral growths.

white blister (*Albugo* species) a fungal disease confusingly sometimes called white rust, which is the accepted common name of the true rust, *Puccinia horiana*, on chrysanthemum. *Albugo* is closely related to the downy mildews, and similarly encouraged by humid weather. It can overwinter in the remains of infected plants by means of resting bodies.

Albugo candida infects members of the Cruciferae family and has strains restricted to certain hosts. Incidence of the disease varies from year to year on cultivated plants, but the following vegetables are prone to infection: brassicas in general, horseradish, radish, and watercress. Ornamental hosts include alyssums, aubretias, honesty, and wallflower, and the disease is also commonly seen on the weed shepherd's purse (*Capsella bursa-pastoris*). The first signs of infection are small raised white pustules on the foliage, which spread in concentric rings and become powdery; the edge of the infected area may turn blackish as the infection progresses and, in severe infections, distortion of the host occurs. It may be necessary to destroy affected plants to check spread; frequent protective treatment with a recommended fungicide may be warranted, subject to local pesticide approvals.

A. tragopogonis infects members of the Compositae, on which it causes yellow spotting followed by white pustules and stunting of plants. It is the most important disease of salsify and scorzonera, and there are no effective control measures. Gerberas, feverfew, ragwort, and sunflower are also hosts.

white bud see *bud stages*.

white currant see *red currant*.

whiteflies (Hemiptera: Aleyrodidae) small, sap-sucking, mothlike insects, up to $\frac{1}{16}$ in (2 mm) long, with two pairs of rounded wings covered with a white, powdery wax. All stages are found on the underside of leaves, the elongated, slightly curved eggs suspended by a short pedicel and, in several species, deposited in complete or partial circles. In all species, both adults and larvae excrete large quantities of honeydew that fall on underlying leaves; a heavy infestation weakens affected plants, which become coated with unsightly black, sooty mold. Some species of whitefly cause leaf spotting.

The GLASSHOUSE WHITEFLY (*Trialeurodes vaporariorum*) is a cosmopolitan species living under glass and, in warmer climates, also outdoors. It attacks a wide range of plants. Adults live for about a month, and the length of life cycle varies according to temperature, usually about three weeks at 68°F (20°C). Other species common to Europe and North America include the RHODODENDRON WHITEFLY (*Dialeurodes chittendeni*), which attacks smooth-leaved rhododendrons, and the AZALEA WHITEFLY (*Pealius azaleae*), which infests hairy-leaved evergreen azaleas. In Europe, brassicas may become infested with the CABBAGE WHITEFLY (*Aleyrodes proletella*), and *Viburnum tinus* with the VIBURNUM WHITEFLY (*Aleurotuba jelinekii*), which overwinters as conspicuous black pupae fringed with a frill of white wax. Several other species are present in North America, including TOBACCO WHITEFLY (*Bemisia tabaci*); and CITRUS WHITEFLY (*Dialeurodes citri*), which is one of several species that attack citrus.

Infestations should be controlled with recommended contact or systemic insecticides, applied as soon as symptoms

Viburnum whitefly

are first noticed. To guard against resistance, from time to time use sprays from different insecticide groups. The GLASSHOUSE WHITEFLY (*T. vaporariorum*) may be controlled biologically by introducing the parasite *Encarsia formosa*, a minute, winged, chalcid wasp now widely available to gardeners. The parasite is self-perpetuating at temperatures above 75°F (24°C), and it is likely to die out over the winter period.

whorl three or more organs arranged in a circle at one node or around the same axis.

wide-span house a greenhouse with a span of 60 ft (18 m) or more.

white rot (*Sclerotium cepivorum*) affects onions, garlic, and to a lesser extent shallots and leeks. First symptoms are yellowing of the foliage and wilting, due to root destruction. White, fluffy mycelium develops around the neck of the bulb, and the bulb eventually shrivels. Small black resting bodies of the fungus form to perpetuate the disease in the soil. Contaminated land must be avoided, and care taken to destroy infected tissue and prevent movement of the soil from an infected site.

widger a small tool shaped like a tapering spatula, for use in pricking out seedlings.

wild and woodland gardening a form of gardening based on the concept of using indigenous or appropriate exotic plants in an informal way, the aim frequently being to create, under a controlled regimen of good husbandry, an image of the surrounding natural environment. It was popularized from the late 19th century by William Robinson, Gertrude Jekyll, and others, but its progenitors can be traced back to medieval times, when informally managed areas were allowed to flourish within the ramparts of castles and fortified dwellings. In the US, many woodland gardens were started in the late 20th century.

Site selection is of fundamental importance in creating a successful woodland garden, and consideration

827

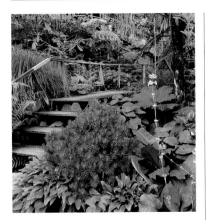

Woodland garden
A moist, shady, sheltered spot offers the opportunity to design with bold foliage forms and textures.

must be given to the composition and maturity of the existing area. The native woodlands of eastern North America offer a suitable selection of canopy species, with a wide range of oaks as well as black walnut, butternut, and forest species of hickory. In the west, the available native woodland is largely dominated by coniferous species, which can provide excellent growing conditions.

In Britain and mainland Europe, oaks (*Quercus robur* and *Q. petraea*) provide a good environment due to their longevity, deep-rootedness, and relatively open canopy, which creates an ideal balance of shelter and shade. Occasional trees of beech or ash will not be detrimental, but large numbers are likely to result in too dense a canopy, while the shallow root systems of beech and the spreading roots of ash can suppress understory plantings. Excellent woodland gardens can be created in pine woods, but these may prove too dark in late winter and early spring when many plants are growing vigorously; judicious thinning is advisable.

Mature woodland is always to be preferred for the creation of a woodland garden, and in its design, informality is paramount. The aim should be to develop three tiers of vegetation: a canopy of large trees; a woody understory of shade-demanding shrubs and small trees, such as rhododendrons; and hardy herbaceous and bulbous plants. Existing trees must be healthy and structurally sound, and any necessary removal or thinning

undertaken as a first step. When appropriate, crown-thinning can be used to increase the levels of light without substantially altering the appearance of the woodland. There must be a balance between wooded and open areas, since not all plants require the same degree of shade; glades provide a vital change of environment, which adds to the woodland garden experience. Bold groups of herbaceous plants, added in drifts among the woody plantings, extend interest, as well as providing weed-suppressing groundcover. Suitable species include primroses (*Primula vulgaris*), snowdrops (*Galanthus nivalis*), wood anemones (*Anemone nemorosa*), Solomon's seal (*Polygonatum*), lungwort (*Pulmonaria*), comfrey (*Symphytum*), and hellebores (*Helleborus*).

Before undertaking bed preparation, efforts must be made to eradicate perennial weeds. If the soil is poorly structured and impoverished, as is frequently the case where coniferous species predominate, ground preparation must be thorough. On a small scale, single digging is adequate, but where larger beds are required, it is advisable to use machinery, such as a pedestrian-operated rotary cultivator. In all cases, generous quantities of organic matter must be incorporated into the soil. After planting, the beds should be mulched to a minimum depth of 2 in (50 mm). Leaf mold is particularly suitable as a mulch if available in sufficient quantity; alternatively, very well-rotted manure, garden compost, bark, or wood chips may be used. During establishment, new plantings will need regular watering, with repeated applications to beds of herbaceous plants and bulbs during spring and summer.

wilderness an area of a garden allowed to develop with minimum control, often contrived by dense planting of shrubs and trees crossed by a maze of intersecting paths. Wildernesses were popular from the mid-17th to the 18th century.

wilding a self-sown plant.

× **Wilsonara** Orchidaceae. Garden hybrids between *Cochlioda*, *Odontoglossum*

and *Oncidium*. They have laterally compressed pseudobulbs, more or less strap-shaped leaves, and tall, branching sprays of small flowers with crisped tepals in shades of yellow, cream, and white marked brown to deep mauve. Cultivate as for *Odontoglossum*.

wilt used to describe a collapsed condition in a plant evidently due to disease. Various species of plant pathogens are described as wilt, and the following are commonly of concern to gardeners:

ASTER WILT (*Fusarium oxysporum* f.sp. *callistephi*) China asters are susceptible to this rapid wilting disease, where the stems are found to be blackened, frequently covered with white or pinkish fungal growth. The disease is most prevalent in poorly-drained soils and is persistent. Control is by prevention through the avoidance of planting infected stock or planting on contaminated sites, rotation, and destruction of infected plants. Resistant cultivars are available.

BLOSSOM WILT a symptom of fungal infection of leaves and flowers on tree fruits, notably by the brown rot fungi (*Monilinia* species).

CLEMATIS WILT (*Phoma clematidina*). Clematis, especially Jackmanii types and some other large-flowered cultivars, are susceptible and may be affected by wilting or die back of shoots. Some species, including *C. montana*, are resistant. Although cultural effects are possible, fungal infection is the major cause. The fungus enters lower parts of the plant and symptoms range from a flagging of upper shoots, blackening of leaf stalks, to general collapse, although the plant is rarely killed outright in one season. Wilted shoots should be cut back to remove apparently infected tissue, and new shoots should be sprayed with a recommended fungicide.

FUSARIUM WILT (*Fusarium oxysporum* f.sp. *lycopersici*) is a term used to describe a troublesome disease of tomatoes, the fungus entering roots from the soil and giving rise to brown discoloration of the root vascular system. Yellowing and wilting of the aerial parts follow. Soil sterilization or container growing are control methods.

PEONY WILT (*Botrytis paeoniae*) a common cause of dieback and often death if the plants are sufficiently weakened: Shoots turn brown from spring or early summer, in wet seasons especially, and under some conditions fluffy fungal growth grows profusely at the stem bases. Resting fungal bodies may be formed to perpetuate infection in the soil. Infected tissue should be cut out as soon as noticed, and destroyed. In herbaceous peonies, this requires cutting below soil level. Sprays of a recommended fungicide may be worthwhile.

withering

VERTICILLIUM WILT a soilborne fungal disease most frequently caused by *Verticillium albo-atrum* and *V. dahliae*, which has a very wide host range and is most troublesome on young plants. *V. dahliae*, usually included in *V. albo-atrum* in the US, is mostly responsible for damage to woody plants, and resting bodies may remain viable in the soil for several years even in the absence of host plants. Symptoms appear first on older leaves as yellowed or dull foliage, later becoming necrotic and desiccated, and the leaves may curl and bend downward. The wilting symptom is initially reversible, but as the disease takes hold, permanent wilting occurs and the vascular strands of plants become stained, and some plants, such as tomatoes, produce adventitious roots on the stem. Damage to trees and shrubs falls into two categories: in acute wilt, there is a sudden wilting and dieback of the foliage, with leaves remaining on the plant; chronic wilt is slower or progressive, with often one-sided wilting of the leaves, crown dieback over several years, and early leaf fall. *Acer* is particularly susceptible, and other commonly affected woody plants include ash, beech, *Cercis*, *Cotinus*, *Cornus*, elm, laburnum, *Rhus*, *Robinia*, rose, and *Rubus*; also herbaceous plants such as *Antirrhinum*, eggplant, *Aster*, chrysanthemums, *Dahlia*, *Fuchsia*, mint, and tomato.

Complete removal of affected debris and root material is vital, together with good weed control, as several broadleafed weed hosts allow it to persist. There is no reliable chemical control

Peony wilt

and affected plants are best removed and burned. The soil should be changed or sterilized and susceptible plants avoided.

Dutch elm disease (q.v.) is a serious vascular wilt disease caused by the fungus *Ophiostoma novo-ulmi*.

wilting the loss of turgor in plant cells that results in drooping and possibly eventual death of plant parts. It occurs when transpiration exceeds water uptake, and can result from lack of water, or from the withdrawal of water by parasites. Wilting may be a symptom of disease or disorder caused by root damage and/or blocking of vascular tissue.

wind-rocking root disturbance caused by the movement of plants in wind; a potential cause of long term instability and root damage.

wind-throw the uprooting of plants, particularly trees, by wind.

windbreak, windscreen a barrier established to reduce the force of strong winds, thereby preventing physical damage to plants and structures; it also reduces water loss through transpiration and evaporation. A windbreak may consist of living plants or take the form of a fabricated screen. The most effective barriers are those that are 60% permeable, since damaging eddies occur to leeward and windward of a solid barrier. A windbreak is

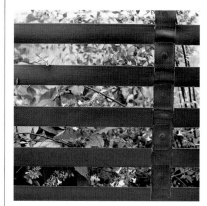

Windbreak fabric
Permeable screening provides effective protection from wind; unlike a solid barrier, eddies do not form in its lee.

most beneficial for a distance to leeward of up to 10 times its height, and it affects wind speeds up to 1½ times its height.

windfall fruit that drops to the ground because of wind or ripeness; occasionally, also trees or branches brought down by wind.

window box a plant display container, primarily designed for use on external window ledges or narrow balconies and therefore narrowly oblong. Window boxes are also suitable for the sides of patios, deck railings, or for placing within or on top of porches. For an attractive display, they can be planted in a similar way to hanging baskets. Regular attention should be paid to deadheading, watering, and supplementary fertilizers.

wing (1) a thin, flat, often membranous extension or appendage or an organ; (2) a lateral petal of a papilionaceous flower.

winged pyramid a decorative form of fruit tree, trained on a metal framework to form a conical shape.

winter annual an annual plant that germinates in the fall and overwinters and dies during the following summer.

winter garden (1) an outdoor garden planned for attractiveness in winter, utilizing flowering plants, including many fragrant types, as well as plants with colored stems or conspicuous bark or fruit and evergreen foliage; (2) an entire garden under shelter, taking the form of a large-scale conservatory, with paths between extensive beds and trees sited among other plants. Winter gardens were popular in the 19th century.

winter moths (Lepidoptera: Geometridae) a group of moths, most active between September and March, in which females are wingless and males winged. Female moths emerge from pupae in the soil, crawl up the trunks of host plants, and deposit eggs either singly or in groups, depending upon species. The caterpillars are of the looper type, known in North America as cankerworms or inchworms. They feed openly within loose silk webbing, on the buds, flower trusses, and foliage of various trees and shrubs. As well as causing extensive defoliation and damage to flower buds, they also bite holes in the fruitlets of fruit trees; these callous over and, on mature fruits, appear as corky areas, often developing into deep, scarred clefts. Apples, pears, plums, cherries, and their ornamental cultivars are often attacked, as well as many ornamental trees and shrubs, especially beech, *Cotoneaster*, dogwood, elm, hawthorn, hazel, hornbeam, linden, rhododendron, rose, sycamore, and willow. Fully-fed caterpillars drop to the ground in early summer on silken threads and pupate in the soil.

One of the most prevalent species in North America and Europe is the WINTER MOTH, *Operophtera brumata*, whose green looper caterpillars are up to 1 in (25 mm) long, with a light green or yellow stripe along each side and one along the back. The MARCH MOTH, *Alsophila aescularia*, is a European species with more slender caterpillars; the closely-related FALL CANKERWORM (*A. pometaria*) occurs in North America. Both species lay eggs as a bracelet of about 100 eggs encircling a twig. March moths appear in late winter to early spring and the fall cankerworm in winter. The MOTTLED UMBER MOTH (*Erannis defoliaria*) is a common European species with conspicuous red-brown and yellow caterpillars, up to 1¼ in (30 mm) long, which feed more openly than the other species. A close relative, the LINDEN LOOPER (*E. tiliaria*), occurs in North America. The SPRING CANKERWORM (*Paleacrita vernala*) is also prevalent, with moths that appear in spring followed by slender larvae colored light green, brown or black with white lines down the back.

Winter moths can be controlled, where feasible, by grease banding tree trunks in fall to prevent wingless females from ascending to deposit eggs. Alternatively, apply recommended contact insecticides just as the buds open.

winter wash see tar oils.

wirestem used to describe the damping-off of brassicas caused by the fungus *Rhizoctonia solani*, which is visible as a constricted red-brown stem lesion at soil level. See *damping-off*.

wireworms (Coleoptera: Elateridae) the larvae of click beetles, or skipjacks, which, when turned on their backs, right themselves using a mechanism under the thorax that throws them into the air with an audible click. The beetles are often dark brown or black, elongate and oval in shape, tapering toward the hind end, and seldom exceed ½ in (13 mm) in length. *Agriotes* species are the most important wireworm pests in Europe. The COMMON CLICK BEETLE (*A. lineatus*) and the GARDEN CLICK BEETLE (*Athous haemorrhoidalis*) are often the most prevalent species in gardens. In North America, the WHEAT WIREWORM (*Agriotes mancus*) and *Limonius*, *Ctenicera*, and *Conoderus* species are the principal pests.

Their natural habitat is permanent grassland, but females also lay eggs in cereal crops and weedy soil. The larvae are shiny golden-brown, cylindrical, hard-bodied grubs, up to 1 in (25 mm) long, with strong mandibles, three small pairs of thoracic legs, and a characteristic projection on the underside of the terminal segment. Larvae of *Agriotes* species are distinguished by a dark spot on each side of the terminal segment. The larvae feed in the soil for up to five years, depending on species, and attack a wide range of plants, including anemones, carnations, chrysanthemums, dahlias, gladioli, primulas, brassicas, beans, beets, carrots, lettuce, onions, potatoes, strawberries, corn, tomatoes, and turnips. Feeding occurs in bouts, peaking in spring and fall. Seedlings and young plants are particularly vulnerable, the wireworms attacking roots and stems at or just below soil level, causing wilting and death. Potato tubers are tunneled deeply and the base of tomato stems bored into and the pith invaded; the fibrous roots of fruit trees and nursery stock can also be damaged.

Infestation is most troublesome in the first few years after the cultivation of grassland, and also in weedy arable

Wireworms

land. Such areas should be plowed or dug early in the season and cultivated several times. Repeated clean cultivation of vegetable and fruit areas and rigorous weed control will deter egg-laying. Subject to local pesticide approvals, drenches, sprays, or granules of recommended insecticide applied to the soil before replanting or sowing can be effective, and suitable seed dressing will protect some vegetable crops during early growth. Potatoes and carrots must be lifted early from affected sites.

Wisteria (for Caspar Wistar [1761–1818], Professor of Anatomy at the University of Pennsylvania). Leguminosae. E Asia, E US. 10 species, deciduous, twining shrubs with pinnate leaves composed of ovate to oblong leaflets, and pendulous racemes of pealike flowers in spring and summer. Hardy climbers suited to walls, arches, arbors, and pergolas. With careful pruning and a little support, *W. floribunda* and *W. sinensis* can also be grown as "freestanding" lawn specimens. Equally, they may be left unhindered to scramble through tall trees. Plant in a sunny position, but with protection from early morning sun in frosty periods and with shelter from cold winds. All species are hardy to at least 5°F (–15°C), but are more reliably hardy given the additional warmth of a wall. Grow in a deep, fertile, well-drained but moisture-retentive soil.

Prune to encourage the formation of flowering spurs close to the main framework of the plant. Once the desired framework is achieved, cut back all shoots to 5–6 buds in midsummer, about two months after flowering; any subsequent twining growth and late-flowering shoots are again cut back to 2–3 buds in late fall or winter to form flowering spurs for the following season. The flower buds are quite apparent in winter, being rounder and plumper than the vegetative buds. Any basal shoots not required for propagation by layering should be removed.

Propagate by simple layering, or by basal cuttings of side shoots in early to midsummer, in a closed case with

Pruning wisteria to improve flowering
Wisteria should be pruned in both summer and winter, gradually shortening long, whippy growths (unless needed to extend the framework) to encourage the formation of flower buds and hence a fine display, as in this *Wisteria* x *formosa* (right).

bottom heat. Increase also by bench grafting, making an apical wedge graft onto seedling stock of *W. sinensis* in late winter. Plunge the pot in a closed case with bottom heat at 64–68°F (18–20°C). When established, repot, ensuring that the graft union is below the soil surface to encourage the scion to root. Seed-raised plants are variable and may, in some cases, take up to 20 years to bear flowers of poor quality that are then obscured by foliage. If this method is attempted, sow seed in spring at 50–55°F (10–13°C), after presoaking in hot water for about 18 hours. Seeds are poisonous. The aphid-borne wisteria vein mosaic virus causes yellow mottling or spotting of leaves. Late frosts will kill the developing racemes, but these are often replaced by a second flush.

W. brachybotrys 'Shiro-kapitan' (syn. *W. venusta*) SILKY WISTERIA; Japan; stems twining counterclockwise, to 30 ft (9 m); racemes 4–6 in (10–15 cm), flowers to 1 in (2.5 cm) across, white or purple, highly fragrant, on silky, hairy stalks; *W. floribunda* JAPANESE WISTERIA; Japan; stem twining clockwise, to 26 ft (8 m); racemes 16–48 in (40–120 cm), flowering gradually from base, flowers to ¾ in (2 cm) across, fragrant, typically lilac-blue, also darkest violet, blue, lilac, pink, red, or white; includes numerous cultivars with large or small flowers, some double, in a wide range of colors, some with very long racemes; *W.* x *formosa* (*W. floribunda* × *W. sinensis*) stem twining clockwise; raceme to 10 in (25 cm), flowers strongly fragrant, blooming all at once, to ¾ in (2 cm) across, standard pale violet, wings and keel darker); *W. japonica* Japan, Korea; racemes 6–12 in (15–30 cm), often branching, flowers to ½ in (1.3 cm) across, white or cream to rose; *W. sinensis* CHINESE WISTERIA; China; stems to 33 ft (10 m), twining counterclockwise; racemes 6–12 in (15–30 cm), flowers to 1 in (2.5 cm) across, faintly scented, blue-violet, includes white, pale blue, dark blue, lilac, mauve and purple-black cultivars with single and double flowers.

witches' broom the development of an abnormally large number of shoots, mainly on woody plants, often growing in the form of a broom or, on trees in particular, as a tangled mass of branching stems, usually with reduced or abnormally shaped leaves. They are mainly produced following infection by fungi, including rusts, but mycoplasma-like organisms may also be responsible. Mite infestation of the growing points of plants can cause witches' brooms, as can damage by other factors, such as low temperature. Dwarf mistletoes (*Arceuthobium* species) attack many conifers in western North America, causing damaging witches' brooms.

wonderberry see *Solanum*.

wood, woody lignified plant tissue that forms rigid stems and branches, giving the plant a robust structure.

wood ash the product of burning wood or other vegetable material which, although variable, is useful in containing 4–15% potash, as well as phosphate, iron, magnesium, and manganese in small amounts. Ash from herbaceous material or young woody growths is richest in potassium. Wood ash should be applied immediately or stored dry. It slightly increases the alkalinity of soil and should be well-incorporated, especially on heavy soils, to avoid damage to the surface soil structure.

wood bud see *vegetative bud*.

wood chips, wood shavings waste wood fragments produced during milling or from the shredding of prunings. It may be used satisfactorily as a degradable path covering or a mulch around plants. If incorporated into the topsoil, it can cause nitrogen depletion as it decomposes. It is unlikely to transmit, or encourage the development of, honey fungus.

woodchuck (*Marmota monax*) a North American mammal of the marmot tribe that devours salads, other vegetables, and flowers in the garden; it is also known as a groundhog. It is usually deterred by construction of low wire fencing, buried 6 in (15 cm) below ground level and extending 3¼ ft (1 m) above it. Shooting, trapping, or gassing can be carried out in badly infested areas, but advice on appropriate local laws and procedures must be taken.

woodland garden see *wild and woodland gardening*.

woodlice (Crustacea: Isopoda) crustaceans possessing a hard, segmented, convex body up to ½ in (12 mm) long, one pair of antennae, and seven pairs of walking legs. Woodlice are also known as sowbugs, pillbugs, or slaters. They are restricted to damp places and mainly nocturnal activity. Immature woodlice resemble adults, except in size; during the breeding season, females have four pairs of plates that project inward between the rear legs to form a brood chamber in which up to 50 eggs are laid, and then newly hatched young are carried.

Woodlice feed mostly on decaying vegetable matter and are generally beneficial in accelerating the breakdown of plant remains. They sometimes attack living plants, especially seedlings under glass, which may be severed at soil level, and they may bite irregularly shaped holes in the leaves, stems, flowers, and fruit of older plants.

Some species roll into a ball for protection, including the COMMON PILLBUG (*Armadillidium vulgare*) in North America and Europe, which has light gray to black adults up to $^1/_2$ in (12 mm) long.

Woodlice are numerous where daytime shelter is available, and where plant damage occurs, these sites should be reduced. On a small scale, woodlice may be successfully trapped in inverted flower pots or scooped-out potato tubers, provided the traps are examined daily and all the woodlice destroyed. Recommended contact insecticides applied to the soil surface are effective, as are certain slug baits, but both methods of control should only be employed when essential.

Woodwardia (for Thomas Jenkinson Woodward [1745–1820], English botanist). Blechnaceae. Eurasia, N America. CHAIN FERN. 10 species of mostly large hardy ferns. Rhizomes short, creeping to erect, stout, densely paleate, woody. Fronds deciduous, several or many, in a crown; monomorphic or dimorphic; blades uniform, once pinnate, sparsely scaly; pinnae lobed or coarsely pinnatifid, linear. Bulbils may be produced near the tips of fronds or on the upper surface. Sori on underside of pinnae are in chainlike arrangement. Suitable for moist, shady banks. Grow in damp soil in partial shade with some shelter from cold winds. Propagate from spores sown in late summer at 16°C/61°F, or from bulbils or by division in spring. *W. radicans* EUROPEAN CHAIN FERN Evergreen with arching, broadly lance-shaped, dark green fronds to 6½ ft (2 m); pinnatifid pinnae to 12 in (30 cm), ovate to lance-shaped. Atlantic islands.

woolly aphid (*Eriosoma lanigerum*). The woolly aphid is a cosmopolitan

Woodlouse

species, occurring in most of the apple-growing countries of the world. Besides apples, it also attacks cotoneasters, crab apples, pyracanthas, and occasionally hawthorn and *Sorbus*. The purple-brown aphids, covered with a fluffy, white waxy material, live in cracks and crevices in the bark of their host plants and are also found on young shoots and around old pruning scars. As well as reducing the vigor of the trees, the aphids cause localized swelling of the bark, which leads to deformed and gnarled twigs and branches. These damaged areas are often split open by frosts, allowing the entry of diseases such as *Gloeosporium* spp. and apple canker. In North America and some other regions, woolly aphids also attack the roots, causing gall-like swellings. Where this occurs, such damage is considered more serious, particularly on young trees, than injury to the aerial parts. Unlike most other aphid species, woolly aphids overwinter on the tree as immature nymphs rather than eggs. Winter wash treatments are not very effective against this species, and it is better to apply a systemic insecticide when signs of renewed woolly aphid activity become visible during spring.

worcesterberry a hybrid fruit in the genus *Ribes*, thus related to the gooseberry and black currant. Its parentage is not definitely known but it is considered most likely to be *R. grossularia*

Woolly aphids
These creatures, pests mainly of woody plants, secrete a fluffy white waxy substance that surrounds and protects them, making them difficult to spray or wash off.

(gooseberry) crossed with R. × *succirubrum*. The latter is *R. divaricatum* × *R. niveum*, and was first described in 1907. Worcesterberry is similar to the gooseberry in habit and is cultivated in the same way. The fruits are dull red and are used for cooking. 'Jochelbeere', raised in Germany by crossing gooseberry and *R. succirubrum*, is considered to be identical.

wounding the removal of a sliver of bark at the base of a cutting, or slitting vertically, to encourage rooting. A similar process of wounding stems is often beneficial in propagation by layering.

Wound held open by matchstick to encourage rooting

wrenching the practice of loosening a young established plant in its growing position, by use of hand tools or plow or similar. The objective is to break or disturb roots, in order to encourage by regrowth a compact, fibrous rootball for easier transplanting. The procedure may be carried out over more than one season and has particular relevance to field production of woody nursery stock.

Wounded stem

Wulfenia (for Franz Xavier Freiherr von Wulfen [1728–1805], Austrian botanist). Scrophulariaceae. SE Europe, W Asia, Himalaya. 5 species of hardy perennial herbs, tufted, nearly glabrous. Leaves mostly basal and radical or alternate, undivided, petiolate, crenate, or dentate. Inflorescence a raceme, terminal, spicate, bracteate on an unbranched stem. Flowers small, blue or purple, axillary; calyx 5-lobed, corolla with short tube, upper lip entire or emarginated, lower lip 3-lobed, short; stamens 2, attached at throat of corolla. Fruit a 4-valved capsule.

This is an attractive plant for rock gardens on a moist site. Propagate *Wulfenia* from spring- or fall-sown seed, or by division. *W. amherstiana* Afghanistan, W Himalayas. Evergreen perennial with rosettes of obovate-oblong, scalloped, conspicuously veined, dark green leaves, 2–6 in (5–15 cm) long. Erect stems bear lax, one-sided racemes of purple flowers, 1½–8 in (4–20 cm), during summer.

W

X

Xanthoceras (from Greek *xanthos*, yellow, and *keras*, horn, referring to the hornlike growths between the petals). Sapindaceae. N China. 2 species, deciduous shrubs and small trees with fissured bark, yellow wood, and pinnate leaves. Borne in spring and summer in erect panicles, the flowers consist of five broad and spreading petals. Hardy to −10°F (−23°C). Plant in any fertile, well-drained soil in sun and with shelter from harsh winds. To flower well, this tree needs a long, hot summer; it is often grown against south-facing walls in cooler, cloudier areas. Increase by seed in fall, or by rooted suckers in early spring. *X. sorbifolium* erect shrub to 23 ft (7 m); flowers to ¾ in (2 cm) wide, white with the center stained green to yellow then red.

Xanthorhiza (from Greek *xanthos*, yellow, and *rhiza*, root). Ranunculaceae. E N America. 1 species, *X. simplicissima*, a deciduous, running, and suckering woody-based perennial herb or shrub to 32 in (80 cm). The stems are thin and sparsely branched with yellow wood. The leaves are to 7 in (18 cm) long, 1–2-pinnate with narrowly elliptic to lanceolate, toothed leaflets. They emerge purple, become midgreen, and turn bronze in fall. Small, star-shaped, and purple-brown, the flowers are produced in slender, drooping panicles in spring. Excellent, medium-height groundcover hardy to −20°F (−29°C). Plant in sun or shade on a moist, fertile soil. Older plants can be rejuvenated by shearing to ground level in spring. Increase by division.

Xanthorrhoea (from Greek *xanthos*, yellow, and *rheo*, to flow, referring to the resin produced by the plants). Liliaceae (Xanthorrhoeaceae). Australia. BLACK BOY, GRASS TREE. 15 species, large evergreen perennial herbs and shrubs with thick, dark, and fibrous cylindrical trunks composed of countless hard, compacted leaf bases. Carried in a dense, terminal crown, the leaves are long and needlelike. Small, white flowers are carried in tapering, clublike spikes. Several species are grown, all superficially very similar, including *X. australis*, *X. arborea* and *X. preisii*. They may reach a height of 13 ft (4 m) with leaves to 5 ft (1.5 m) long, but are painfully slow-growing. Grow these rare and remarkable plants in a fast-draining, acidic to neutral medium. Provide a minimum temperature of 50°F (10°C), full sun, and a dry atmosphere. Water freely in hot weather, sparingly at other times. Increase either by offsets or by seed.

— flower panicles

Xanthoceras sorbifolium

Xanthosoma (Greek *xanthos*, yellow, and *soma*, body, referring to yellow tissues of some species). Araceae. Tropical America. YAUTIA, TANNIA. 50 species, large, tuberous perennial herbs with stout-stalked, cordate to sagittate leaves dull, *Arum*-like inflorescences. Cultivate as for *Alocasia*.

X. sagittifolium YAUTIA; native range unknown, widespread in cultivation in tropics; leaf blades to 36 in (90 cm), broadly arrow-shaped, glaucous above, petiole to 3¼ ft (1 m); includes cultivars with leaves veined, edged, and splashed with white and gold; *X. violaceum* BLUE TARO, BLUE TANNIA; native range unknown, widespread through cultivation in tropics; leaf blades to 28 in (70 cm), broadly arrow-shaped, glaucous, margins and veins flushed dark purple, petiole to 6½ ft (2 m).

Xeranthemum (from Greek *xeros*, dry, and *anthos*, flower). Compositae. Mediterranean to W Asia. 6 species, erect, annual summer-flowering herbs with daisylike flower heads, papery and pearly in texture and lasting well when dried. Sow seed *in situ* in spring on a fertile, well-drained soil in sun. *X. annuum* IMMORTELLE; SE Europe to W Asia, naturalized elsewhere; stem 10–30 in (25–75 cm); leaves to 2½ in (6 cm), linear to oblong, white-tomentose; flower heads 1¼–2 in (3–5 cm) in diameter, bright pink or white; seed races include plants with white, pink, rose, red, and purple flower heads.

Xerophyllum (from Greek *xeros*, dry, and *phyllon*, leaf; the leaves are dry and grasslike). Liliaceae (Melanthiaceae). N America. 3 species, rhizomatous perennial herbs with tufts of linear, rough-edged leaves and pyramidal racemes of long-stalked, star-shaped flowers in summer. Hardy to −20°F (−29°C). Grow in an acidic soil, permanently moist and enriched with leaf mold, in full sun. Increase by seed or division. *X. tenax* ELK GRASS, BEAR GRASS, INDIAN BASKET GRASS, SQUAW GRASS; western N America; to 71 in (180 cm); flowers to ⅝ in (1.5 cm) across, white to cream with violet stamens.

xerophyte a plant adapted to survival in an arid habitat.

Xerophyte
Plants adapted to extreme desert conditions, such as this agave, are low-maintenance plants for containers on a sunny patio.

yard, yard gardening in the US, "yard" is the usual name for what in the UK is known as a "garden"; the term "yard gardening" is occasionally used to denote cultivation in courtyard situations.

yellows disease characterized by a general yellowing of foliage or other yellow-colored symptoms, caused by various fungi, bacteria and phytoplasma-like organisms. *Fusarium oxysporum* f.sp. *conglutinans* causes CABBAGE YELLOWS, a form of the disease that is particularly destructive to cabbage and other brassicas in the US. Plant roots are infected from the soil, and at high temperatures the fungus progresses rapidly through the vascular system, causing the leaves to turn yellow-green, with the lower ones curling and dying. The pathogen can survive many years in the soil and it spreads in crop debris, soil, and drainage water or on implements. The best control is by the choice of resistant cultivars.

F. oxysporum f.sp. *gladioli* causes a VASCULAR WILT DISEASE, gladiolus yellow, in which the plants turn yellow and die during the growing season, and there is rotting of corms. Freesias are also susceptible, and the symptoms on corms of these and gladiolus are seen when the tunic is removed to reveal circular, black sunken areas around the base, with irregularly concentric ridges. The disease is encouraged by heavy manuring and insufficient ripening before storage. Yellowed plants should be disposed of, together with a shovelful of the surrounding soil, as soon as noticed.

Xanthomonas campestris pv. *hyacinthi* is a bacterium causing yellows of hyacinths. It is an occasional problem; affected plants fail to sprout, the growth is stunted or the bulbs rotten; further signs are brown striping and rotting of the leaves and flower stalks. The disease spreads from plant to plant and diseased ones should be carefully removed.

Aster yellows, palm lethal yellowing, and peach yellows are phytoplasma diseases. See *phytoplasma*.

yostaberry see *jostaberry*.

youngberry see *hybrid berries*.

Yucca (from *yucca*, the native name for *Manihot esculenta*, named by Gerard, who mistook the genus for *Manihot*). Agavaceae. N and C America, West Indies. 40 species, large evergreen perennial herbs, shrubs, or trees. Where present, the stems are stout, cylindrical, sparsely branched, and scarred by the traces of dead leaves (these may also persist in a dense collar). In age, they may become massive and freely branched above. The leaves are sword-shaped to needlelike, thick, and tough but pliable, or slender and rigid; they are commonly glaucous and gray-green, clothing the stems or arranged in dense, terminal rosettes. The waxy, bell-shaped flowers are usually fragrant at night and hang in stately spirelike panicles arising from the crown in summer.

All described below prefer full sun, a sheltered position, and a fast-draining, sandy soil with minimal winter wetness. *Y. filamentosa*, *Y. filifera*, *Y. glauca*, *Y. gloriosa*, and *Y. recurvifolia*, hardy to −20°F (−29°C), are superb plants for border and outdoor container plantings. *Y. gloriosa* soon forms a large and free-flowering stand and is perhaps better used for specimen plantings in lawns. In cool temperate cultivation, *Y. rostrata* and *Y. whipplei* are smaller, finer plants, ideal for sheltered, dry rockeries, for the base of a south-facing wall, or for a silver border. Although hardy to 0°F (−18°C), they will both suffer unless planted on a very lean, sandy soil and protected from prolonged cold and wet. Of the remaining species, most will only thrive above 20°F (−7°C), or in a cool greenhouse or conservatory (minimum temperature 45°F/7°C), where they associate well with cacti and succulents. *Y. elephantipes* is a popular and durable houseplant, sold in the form of rooted and sprouting stem sections. It tolerates more shade and moisture than the other tender species. Increase by seed sown in heat, by division, by removal of rooted suckers, and, where possible, by stem cuttings.

Y. aloifolia DAGGER PLANT, SPANISH BAYONET; SE US, West Indies; stems to 26 ft (8 m), slender, sometimes branching; leaves to 16 × 2½ in (40 × 6 cm), rigid, flat, sharply pointed, and minutely toothed; flowers to 2 × 4 in (5 × 10 cm), cream tinged purple or lined green at base; includes 'Marginata', with leaves edged yellow, 'Quadricolor', with leaves striped yellow and white, and 'Tricolor', with leaves striped yellow, sometimes with white central stripe; *Y. brevifolia* JOSHUA TREE; California to SW Utah; stem to 30 ft (9 m) or more, often branching, bark deeply fissured; leaves to 16 × 1½ in (40 × 4 cm), stiletto-like, rigid, minutely toothed; flowers to 2¾ in (7 cm), green tinged yellow to cream, malodorous; *Y. elephantipes* Mexico, Guatemala; differs from *Y. aloifolia* in its taller, freely branching and stouter stems; leaves to 39 × 2¾ in (100 × 7 cm), semirigid, base swollen, minutely

Yucca gloriosa
The Spanish dagger is a superb plant for mild coastal gardens, sending up an impressive flower spike once mature.

toothed; flowers to 1½ in (4 cm), white or cream; *Y. filamentosa* ADAM'S NEEDLE, SPOONLEAF YUCCA, NEEDLE PALM; US; stems short or absent, clump-forming and suckering; leaves to 30 × 4 in (75 × 10 cm), sword-shaped, stiff, margins bearing wavy to curling threads and fibers; inflorescence 3¼–13 ft (1–4 m), flowers to 2 in (5 cm), white tinged yellow; includes 'Bright Edge', to 24 in (60 cm). with leaves broadly edged yellow, 'Elegantissima', erect to 4 ft (1.2 m), with white flowers, 'Garland's Gold', with leaves with a central gold stripe, similar to 'Mediostriata', 'Nobilis', with large and very glaucous leaves, a tall and massive inflorescence, and flowers tinted red, 'Rosenglocken', with flowers tinted rose, 'Starburst', forming low rosettes with cream-edged leaves, and 'Variegata', with white leaf margins becoming pink-tinged, and center of leaves glaucous green; *Y. filifera* (syn. *Y. flaccida)*; much-branched shrub to 33 ft (10 m); leaves to 22 × 1½ in (55 × 4 cm), linear-lanceolate, glaucous, somewhat flexible and reflexed above middle, margins with straight, not curling, threads; flowers to 2 in (5 cm), creamy white; includes 'Golden Sword', with leaves edged yellow; *Y. glauca* western C US; stems absent or very short; leaves to 24 × 2 in (60 × 5 cm), linear, rigid, smooth, and glaucous, margins white to gray, bearing sparse straight threads; flowers to

2½ in (6 cm), creamy white tinged green or brown; includes 'Rosea', with flowers tinged rose); *Y. gloriosa* SPANISH DAGGER, ROMAN CANDLE, PALM LILY; SE US; stem to 8 ft (2.5 m), thick, rarely branching but suckering freely; leaves to 24 × 2¾ in (60 × 7 cm), narrowly lanceolate, smooth, stiff, glaucous, entire; flowers to 2¾ in (7 cm), creamy white sometimes tinged red or green; cultivars include: 'Variegata', with leaves striped creamy yellow; and 'Vittorio Emmanuel II', low and compact, with flowers strongly tinted red in bud; *Y. recurvifolia* SE US; similar to *Y. gloriosa* but with stems often branching, leaves to 36 in (90 cm) long and recurved, and a more open inflorescence; includes 'Marginata', with leaves edged yellow, and 'Variegata', with leaves with a central yellow stripe; *Y. rostrata* N Mexico, S US; stem absent or to 10 ft (3 m), solitary or several in a clump, leaf rosettes dense; leaves 8–24 in (20–60 cm) × ¼–½ in (0.5–1.3 cm), linear, sharply pointed, rigid, somewhat glaucous with a thin pale yellow margin, entire or minutely toothed; flowers to 2½ in (6 cm), white; *Y. smalliana* ADAM'S NEEDLE, BEAR GRASS; S California to Florida; resembles *Y. filamentosa* but with narrower and flatter leaves, the marginal threads distinctly curled, a finely hairy inflorescence axis and white flowers; includes 'Maxima', tall, with an inflorescence with large,

Propagating yucca from offsets
In spring, the small suckers or offsets that form around the crown can be detached with a portion of root and potted.

leafy bracts, and 'Variegata', with leaves striped yellow; *Y. whipplei* OUR LORD'S CANDLE; W California, Baja California, Mexico, Arizona; stem usually absent, leaf rosettes dense; leaves 12–36 in (30–90 cm) × ½–2¾ in (1–7 cm), linear, glaucous, rigid, pungent, margins minutely toothed; flowers to 2½ in (6.5 cm), creamy white often tipped green; young plants resemble *Y. rostrata*.

Yushania (after the Yushan mountains in Taiwan). Gramineae. E Asia. 2 species, clump-forming bamboos. See *bamboos.*

Zaluzianskya (Scrophulariaceae). S Africa. 35 species, sticky, hairy annual or perennial herbs or subshrubs with short-stalked flowers in late spring and summer; these are tubular with a spreading limb of 5 broad lobes. Hardy to 0°F (−18°C) in a sheltered, sunny position. Grow in sandy, fast-draining soil. Avoid wet conditions. In places where winters are harsh, over-winter young plants in an unheated greenhouse. Increase by stem tip cuttings in spring. *Z. ovata* bushy, low-growing evergreen perennial to 4 × 12 in (10 × 30 cm); leaves to 1¼ in (3 cm), ovate to oblong, toothed, mid-green with short, gray hairs; flowers to ¾ in (2 cm) diam., pure white with deep wine red reverses to lobes.

Zamia (from Greek *zamia*, loss, echoing Pliny's description of the withered appearance of fir cones). Zamiaceae. Americas. 30 species, evergreen cycads, with swollen subterranean stems or small, cylindrical trunks. The leaves are pinnately compound with tough leaflets. Male cones tend to be narrow and scurfy, the females squatter, resembling a hand grenade. Where plants of both sexes cone together, the females may produce small, hard nuts with a brightly colored, fleshy coating. Grow in frost-free conditions with bright indirect light to full sun. Plant in a free-draining, loam-based mix with additional sand, leaf mold, and composted bark; water, feed, and syringe freely in warm weather, at other times keep rather dry. Both are excellent foliage plants for the home and cool greenhouse. Where temperatures stay above 20°F (−7°C), they are resilient candidates for landscaping. Propagate by seed sown in warmth with the fleshy coat removed, or by rooted offsets. *Z. furfuracea* CARDBOARD PALM; Mexico; stem subterranean or stout, short; leaves to 3¼ ft (1 m), leaflets to 4¾ in (12 cm), obovate to oblong, tip broad, bluntly toothed, rigid, olive green, scurfy); *Z. pumila* (syn. *Z. angustifolia*, *Z. integrifolia)*; COONTIE, FLORIDA ARROWROOT, SEMINOLE BREAD; stem subterranean or short, swollen and sometimes multiheaded; leaves to 3¼ ft (1 m), leaflets 2–4¾ in (5–12 cm), linear to oblanceolate or oblong, tip broad and blunt to slender and pointed, minutely toothed, somewhat pliable, dark green, glossy.

Zamioculcas (a combination of *Zamia*, which this aroid very broadly resembles, and *culcas*, the Arabic name for *Colocasia*). Araceae. Tropical Africa. 1 species, *Z. zamiifolia*, an evergreen or partially deciduous perennial herb. The pinnate leaves are 12–39 in (30–100 cm) long and stand erect in tight clumps. The petioles are succulent and swollen at their bases. The leaflets are 2–6 in (5–15 cm) long, broadly ovate to elliptic or lanceolate, closely set, glossy dark green, and somewhat fleshy. A handsome foliage plant, tolerant of temperatures to 50°F (10°C) and dry conditions. Where cool drought continues, however, the leaves may drop, leaving only their swollen bases as storage vessels. For luxuriant, year-round growth, plant in a fertile soilless medium; position in bright, indirect light, keep evenly moist, and maintain a minimum temperature of 59°F (15°C). Increase by inserting mature leaflets in a moist, soilless mix with bottom heat, or by division.

Zantedeschia (for Giovanni Zantedeschi [1773–1846], Italian botanist and physician). Araceae. South Africa, some widely naturalized elsewhere. CALLA LILY, ARUM LILY. 6 species, perennial herbs usually evergreen and with short, thick rhizomes. The leaves arise in a basal clump and are usually heart- or arrow-shaped or, less commonly, lanceolate. Produced during summer, the inflorescence consists of numerous minute flowers packed at the base of a club-shaped spadix, the whole surrounded by a showy, broadly funnel-shaped spathe. *Z. aethiopica* is hardy to 0°F (−18°C), especially the cultivar 'Crowborough'. It will grow in sun or part shade with year-round moisture in most fertile soils, and will also thrive with its roots fully or partially submerged in water in ponds, lakes, or half-barrels. The remaining species and cultivars require bright, frost-free conditions. Plant them in a porous, fertile, and preferably soilless medium. As new growth emerges, increase water; fertilize and water liberally when in full leaf. After flowering, decrease water supplies. Dry off as the foliage withers and keep virtually dry over winter. Increase by offsets.

Z. aethiopica ARUM LILY; leaf blades to 16 in (40 cm); spathe to 10 in (25 cm), white, spadix yellow; includes the large and hardy, pure white 'Crowborough', and 'Green Goddess' with large spathes stained and streaked with green; *Z. albomaculata* leaf blades to 18 in (45 cm), with white spots or blotches or plain; spathe to 4¾ in (12 cm), white to ivory, pale yellow, or pink; *Z. elliottiana* leaves densely spotted; spathe golden yellow; *Z. rehmannii* leaves to 16 in (40 cm), lanceolate; spathe to 4¾ in (12 cm), white, pink, or plum, sometimes with a darker throat. Numerous hybrids and cultivars have been developed within this genus, including plants tall and dwarf, with leaves spotted and unspotted and spathes in tones of white, cream, yellow, peach, pink, red, and plum. In some, the throat is far darker (e.g., purple-black) or paler.

Zantedeschia elliottiana
Numerous colorful hybrids have been developed from the golden arum, with both plain and spotted leaves.

Zanthoxylum (from Greek *xanthos*, yellow, and *xylon*, wood). Rutaceae. Widespread in warmer areas. PRICKLY ASH. Some 250 species, deciduous or evergreen prickly trees and shrubs with aromatic, usually pinnate foliage, small, cymose flowers and fleshy or leathery fruit. Hardy to at least 5°F (−15°C). Plant in full sun or semishade on a deep, moist, and fertile soil. Increase by seed in fall, by semiripe cuttings in fall, or by root cuttings in late winter. *Z. piperitum* JAPAN PEPPER; N China, Korea, Japan; shrub or tree to 20 ft (6 m); leaflets 11–23, to 1½ in (3.5 cm), ovate, tip toothed; *Z. simulans* China, Taiwan; spreading shrub or small tree to 10 ft (3 m); leaflets 7–11, to 2 in (5 cm), ovate to oblong, serrate.

peppercorn-like berries

Zanthoxylum simulans

Zauschneria (for Johann Baptist Zauschner [1737–1799], professor in Prague). Onagraceae. SW US, Mexico. 4 species, low-growing, evergreen perennial subshrubs with small leaves covered in gray down. Produced in summer, the flowers are tubular to trumpet-shaped with a limb of 4 flared lobes. Hardy to 0°F (−18°C). Plant in sandy, free-draining soil in full sun. Protect from hard frosts and wet weather with fleece or a dry mulch. Increase by stem cuttings in spring. *Z. californica* (syn. *Z. cana*, *Epilobium canum*); HUMMINGBIRD'S TRUMPET, CALIFORNIA FUCHSIA; SW US to Mexico; 8–24 in (20–60 cm), covered in gray to silver down; flowers vermilion to scarlet; 'Album': flowers white; 'Dublin', syn. 'Glasnevin': flowers long, flame-colored.

Zea (from Greek *zea*, a type of cereal). Gramineae. C America, native origin unclear, now widespread through cultivation. 4 species, large annual or, rarely, perennial grasses. The stem is usually tall, thick and unbranched, sheathed by the overlapping bases of arching strap-shaped leaves. The male inflorescence has several tassel-like racemes in a terminal panicle. The female inflorescence is axillary and enveloped by tough spathes (husks). It develops as a stoutly cylindrical "cone" of tightly packed, juicy grains, tipped with a plume of long, silky styles. The ornamental cultivars are treated as half-hardy annuals. Sow seed under glass in late winter or early spring and plant out after the last frost. In regions with long, hot summers, seed may be sown *in situ* in late spring. Grow in sunny, warm, and sheltered conditions in a moist, fertile soil. As the cobs near maturity, plants prefer hotter, drier weather. See *sweet corn*. *Z. mays* CORN, MAIZE, SWEET CORN; 3¼–12 ft (1–4 m); leaves to 36 in (90 cm); female inflorescence to 8 in (20 cm), grains to ½ in (1 cm), yellow; ornamental cultivars include plants with pink and white-striped leaves, others with small cobs, some with blue-black or wine-red grains, or grains in a mixture of colors (the highly decorative INDIAN CORN) and is used in dried-flower arrangements.

Zelkova (from the local name for *Z. carpinifolia*). Ulmaceae. Crete, Caucasus, E Asia. 5 species, deciduous trees with smooth to scaly, gray bark and many branches usually drawn gently upward in a rounded or gobletlike crown atop a short, clean trunk. Ovate to elliptic, saw-toothed and distinctly veined, the leaves turn gold, amber, or red in fall. Inconspicuous green flowers give rise to dry, nutlike drupes. The following species are hardy to 0°F (−18°C), but prefer a sheltered situation. Plant in sun in a deep, fertile soil with plentiful moisture. *Z. serrata* makes a beautiful bonsai. Increase by seed sown in fall.

Z. abelicea Crete; to 50 ft (15 m); branchlets white-hairy; leaves ⅜–2 in (1.5–5 cm), ovate to oblong, obtuse, cordate to rounded at base, triangular-toothed, somewhat hairy at first; *Z. carpinifolia* CAUCASIAN ELM; Caucasus; to 115 ft (35 m), branchlets densely downy; leaves ¾–2¾ in (2–7 cm), elliptic to oblong, acute, rounded or subcordate at base, teeth obtuse, ciliate, with scattered hairs above, paler and downy beneath; *Z. serrata* JAPANESE ZELKOVA, SAW LEAF ZELKOVA; Japan, Taiwan, E China; to 115 ft (35 m), branchlets tinged purple-gray, slightly hairy; leaves 1¼–2¾ in (3–7 cm), oblong-elliptic, acuminate, rounded or somewhat cordate at base, teeth acute, ciliate, sometimes thinly hairy above, pale green and glossy beneath with hairy veins; includes dwarf, compact, shapely and variegated cultivars.

Zenobia (for Zenobia, Queen of Palmyra, *c.* AD 266). Ericaceae. SE US. 1 species, *Z. pulverulenta*, a deciduous or semievergreen shrub, 20–71 in (50–180 cm) tall. The leaves are ¾–2¾ in (2–7 cm) long, ovate to broadly elliptic, entire or toothed, blue-green and somewhat glaucous. Bell-shaped, sparkling white, and sweetly fragrant, the flowers hang on slender stalks in summer. Cultivate as for *Leucothoë*.

white-throated flowers

Zephyranthes (from Greek *zephyros*, the west wind, and *anthos*, flower—the genus originates in the Western Hemisphere). Amaryllidaceae. Americas. RAIN FLOWER, RAIN LILY, ZEPHYR LILY. 71 species, bulbous perennial herbs with narrowly strap-shaped to grassy leaves and solitary, funnel-shaped flowers usually appearing before or with the leaves in late spring or fall. In favored locations where temperatures stay above 0°F (−18°C), the following species may grow outdoors in fast-draining soils at the base of a south-facing wall. Otherwise, grow under glass with a minimum temperature of 45°F (7°C). Pot in a sandy, loam-based mix and position in full sun. Keep dry and warm once the leaves have faded. After a period of dry

Zephyranthes grandiflora

Z

837

rest, resume watering and lower temperatures to induce flowering and new growth. Increase by seed or division.

Z. atamasca ATAMASCO LILY; SE US; to 12 in (30 cm), flowers to 3 in (8 cm), pure white or tinged purple; *Z. candida* Argentina, Uruguay; to 10 in (25 cm), flowers to 2 in (5 cm), pure white or slightly rose-tinged on the exterior; *Z. citrina* tropical America; to 5 in (13 cm), flowers to 2 in (5 cm), bright yellow; *Z. grandiflora* Mexico; to 12 in (30 cm), flowers 3 in (8 cm), bright pink with a white throat; *Z. rosea* Cuba; to 6 in (15 cm), flowers to 2½ in (6 cm), bright rose.

Zigadenus (from Greek *zygon*, yoke, and *aden*, gland—a pair of glands is typically present at the base of the tepals). Liliaceae (Melanthiaceae). N America, N Asia. DEATH CAMAS, ZYGADENE. 18 species, bulbous or thickly rhizomatous perennial herbs with narrowly strap-shaped leaves and erect spikes of star-shaped flowers in summer. Cultivate as for *Camassia*.

Z. elegans WHITE CAMAS, ALAKALI GRASS; N America; to 36 in (90 cm), flowers ⅝–¾ in (1.6–2 cm) diam. green-white; *Z. fremontii* STAR ZYGADENE, STAR LILY; SW US; to 36 in (90 cm), flowers ¾–1¼ in (2–3 cm) diam., off-white to ivory.

zinc an essential plant micronutrient, its lack can cause shoot dwarfing and dieback in fruit with small, narrow leaves. It is most common in high sunlight climates, and in alkaline soils or those rich in phosphorus; citrus fruits are susceptible.

Zinc toxicity is possible if organic manure is contaminated with "heavy metals"; severe chlorosis and interveinal necrosis are likely symptoms. Acidifying contaminated soil and planting *Thlaspi caerulescens* (ALPINE PENNYCRESS) can help remove zinc and cadmium.

Zingiber (from Greek *Zingiberi*, probably derived from an Indian word). Zingiberaceae. Tropical Asia. GINGER. About 100 species of perennial herbs with branching, thick, aromatic rhizomes and leafy, reedlike stems. Leaves in 2 ranks, usually lanceolate, aromatic. Flowers borne on erect scape, single, in axils of colorful waxy bracts; petals 3,

with posterior broader than lateral petals, lip 3-lobed. Fruit a 3-valved fleshy capsule.

Useful in tropical greenhouse collections, with low light but high temperature and humidity. Requires space on account of lax growth. Propagate from fresh seed, sown at 64°F (18°C) or by division in the spring. *Z. officinale* COMMON GINGER. To 5 ft (1.5 m); leaves 6 × ⅝ in (15 × 1.5 cm), sessile, lanceolate, acuminate; flowers in dense ellipsoid spike, scape 6–8 in (15–20 cm). Corolla a yellow-green tube 1 in (2.5 cm), petals to ¾ in (1.8 cm) deep, purple with yellow spots and stripes. Grown for culinary root and stem ginger. Tropical Asia.

Zinnia (for Johann Gottfried Zinn [1727–1759], professor of botany at Gottingen). Compositae. S US to Argentina, particularly Mexico. Some 20 species, annual or perennial herbs or low shrubs with brightly colored daisylike flower heads in summer. Annuals, they thrive on most soils in full sun. Avoid damp conditions. Deadhead frequently. Sow seed under glass in early spring, and plant out after the last frosts. *Z. elegans* Mexico; erect annual to 3¼ ft (1 m); flower heads

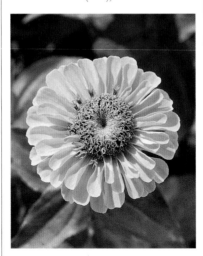

Zinnia elegans 'Envy'
Most cultivars of this native Mexican species prefer sun, but the strikingly colored 'Envy' tolerates some shade.

1½–3 in (4–8 cm) across, ray florets red, white, yellow, orange, pink, scarlet, lilac, or purple, disk florets yellow and black; a highly developed and popular garden annual with many seed races ranging from tall (32 in/ 80 cm) to dwarf (8 in/20 cm) with large or small flower heads, single or double, ruffled or dahlia-like, in a wide spectrum of colors.

zones see *hardiness*.

zygomorphic bilaterally symmetrical, having only one plane of symmetry by which it can be divided into two equal halves.

Zygopetalum (from Greek, *zygon*, yoke, and *petalon*, petal, referring to the fusion of the tepals at the base of the column). Orchidaceae. C and S America. 20 species, evergreen epiphytic or terrestrial orchids. Those listed here have clumped, ovoid to conical pseudobulbs and lanceolate to strap-shaped leaves. Produced in spring and summer on tall, erect racemes, the flowers are waxy, often fragrant with spreading oblong to lanceolate tepals and an obovate to fan-shaped lip with a fleshy, ridged callus. Cultivate as for *Odontoglossum*, except at slightly higher temperatures.

Z. crinitum E Brazil; inflorescence to 20 in (50 cm), flowers strongly fragrant, tepals to 1 in (2.7 cm), gray-green or yellow-green streaked and spotted chestnut brown, lip to 2 in (5 cm), white veined red or purple, veins branching, hairy, callus white; *Z. intermedium* Peru, Bolivia, Brazil; inflorescence to 20 in (50 cm), flowers hyacinth-scented, tepals to 1½ in (3.7 cm) equal, green or yellow-green blotched red-brown or purple to maroon, lip to 1½ in (3.5 cm), white with radiating, broken lilac to deep purple-violet lines, callus mauve; *Z. mackayi* Brazil; differs from *Z. intermedium* in its taller inflorescence and unequal petals and sepals.

zygote the cell resulting from the union of gametes at fertilization, from which an embryo develops.

Zingiber officinale

Z

Some Common Pests and Diseases of Garden Plants

Diagnostic Charts

Plants growing strongly are less likely to succumb to pests, diseases, and disorders than those that struggle. Good performance can be encouraged by careful choice of plants for the location and climate, by the establishment of a well planned and prepared site, and by continuous maintenance with watchfulness and good technique. Pests and diseases thrive on neglected plants. See *cultural controls*.

Problems are bound to arise even under good management, but in the amateur garden, some loss of quantity and quality in edible crops can be tolerated. Where pest and disease control is essential because of competition, threat, or unsightliness, the first consideration should be the use of so-called mechanical methods like protection within physical barriers, trapping, and hand-picking—all of which are perfectly feasible and effective on a small scale. The next most suitable means of control is with the use of predators and

parasites, a good selection of which are now available to the gardener for reducing the numbers of some specific pests. See *biological controls*.

The last resort should be to chemical substances, most usually applied as sprays, dusts, or fogs. The range is wide, but the authorized use of specific substances is under constant review in the interests of safety and protection of the natural environment. For these and other reasons, the retail availability of generic substances, and of commercial products and formulations, is continually changing; the sensible and practical course for the gardener is to refer to what is currently offered and recommended by retailers. See *pesticides*.

In all of these considerations, the correct identification of pests and diseases is vital. The following selective groups of descriptions provide a means of deciding the most likely cause of some more commonly observed symptoms.

FRUITS (TREE)

Symptoms	Possible causes	Symptoms	Possible causes
APPLE		**CHERRIES**	
Ripening fruit with maggot holes and tunneling.	codling moth larvae	Leaves and shoots severely distorted.	aphids
Leaves and shoots distorted.	aphids	Leaves eaten; blossom and young fruits damaged.	winter moth larvae
Swellings on woody stems with white woolly masses.	woolly aphids	Leaves with a silver sheen. Tree parts die progressively.	silver leaf
Leaves eaten; blossom and young fruits damaged.	winter moth larvae	Bark oozes resin-colored gum. Small brown spots on leaves with holes developing.	bacterial canker
Leaves with white powdery fungal growth, mostly on the upper sides and especially at shoot tips; leaves may curl inward.	powdery mildew	**PEACHES**	
Leaves, stems, and fruits with brownish felty patches; early defoliation. Black scabby patches on fruits, which may be cracked and distorted.	scab	Leaves thicken and blister and turn red. White fungal bloom on the leaves. Early defoliation.	peach leaf curl
		Leaves and shoots severely distorted.	aphids
Bark areas sunken and discolored, often near a bud, joint, or wound. Rings of loose flaky tissue bearing white pustules in summer, red pustules in winter. Infected shoots die.	canker	Leaf surfaces show progressive pale mottling. Premature leaf fall. Sometimes a fine silk webbing apparent.	red spider mite
Fruitlets tunneled and fall early in midsummer. Some damaged fruits remain to maturity, but are misshapen, with a long ribbon scar.	sawfly larvae	**PEAR**	
		Leaves and shoots distorted.	aphids
		Fruitlets turn black and fall.	gall midge larvae
Fruits developing soft brown areas penetrating the flesh. Concentric rings of cream pustules. Fruits fall or shrivel on the tree.	brown rot	Leaves, stems and fruits with brownish felty patches; early defoliation. Black scabby patches on fruits which may be cracked and distorted.	scab

FRUITS (TREE)

Symptoms	Possible causes	Symptoms	Possible causes
PEAR (CONT.)		**PLUM**	
Fruits developing soft brown areas penetrating the flesh. Concentric rings of cream pustules. Fruits fall or shrivel on the tree.	brown rot	Leaves with a silver sheen. Tree parts die progressively.	silver leaf
Leaves turn brown to black, wither, and die, but remain attached. Individual limbs affected; oozing cankers appear. Progressive decline of the tree.	fireblight	Bark oozes resin-colored gum. Small brown spots on leaves with holes developing.	bacterial canker
		Leaves and shoots severely distorted; sticky foliage. Black sooty mold.	aphids
		Fruits ripen prematurely and fall. Pink maggot within the fruit.	plum moth larvae
		Buds destroyed between fall and spring.	bullfinches

FRUIT (SOFT)

Symptoms	Possible causes	Symptoms	Possible causes
CURRANTS		**RASPBERRIES**	
Leaves, especially at shoot tips, coated with white powdery fungus. Shoots and leaves wither and die.	American gooseberry mildew (see powdery mildew)	Leaves distorted.	aphids
		Ripened fruits dried at the stalk end. Small maggot within the flesh.	raspberry beetle larvae
Leaf upper surfaces with dark brown spots; premature defoliation. Loss of vigor.	leaf spot	Foliage yellowed, mottled, and streaked. Stunted/dwarfed growth. Poor cropping.	virus
Bark lifted. Small fuzzy gray fungal patches. Stems die back.	*Botrytis* gray mold	Purple spots with silvery central areas on stems, leaves, and flower stalks. Dieback of canes may occur.	cane spot
Leaves distorted, with reddening in some cases.	aphids		
Buds much enlarged, and fail to open.	big bud mite	**STRAWBERRIES**	
GOOSEBERRIES		Leaves distorted; growth checked.	aphids
Leaves and shoots distorted.	aphids	Leaf surfaces show progressive pale mottling. Foliage withered and fine silk webbing may be apparent.	red spider mite
Leaves eaten; bushes defoliated, especially from their centers.	sawfly larvae	Foliage yellowed and puckered. Stunted growth, and poor cropping.	virus
Buds destroyed between fall and spring.	bullfinches	Fruits rotted, with fuzzy gray fungal growth.	*Botrytis* gray mold
Leaves, especially at shoot tips, and developing fruits coated with white powdery fungus. Shoots and leaves wither and die.	American gooseberry mildew (see powdery mildew)		
Bark lifted. Small fuzzy gray fungal patches. Stems die back.	*Botrytis* gray mold		

Vegetables

Symptoms	Possible causes	Symptoms	Possible causes
BRASSICAS		**PEAS AND BEANS**	
Foliage eaten; hearts bored into.	cabbage caterpillars	Leaf margins conspicuously scalloped with U-shaped notches.	pea and been weevil adults
Foliage yellow and puckered, with dense colonies of gray/white insects.	mealy cabbage aphids, treat as aphids	Leaves and pods of peas silver-flecked and finely mottled.	thrips
Leaves with yellow spots becoming brown or gray; concentric rings from which holes develop.	leaf spot	Leaf undersides and shoot tips with dense colonies of black insects.	aphids
Plants discolored, wilted, and stunted; grossly swollen roots.	clubroot	Leaves of broad beans with brown spots and streaks.	*Botrytis* chocolate spot
Plants wilted and collapsed; taproots tunneled, fine roots destroyed.	cabbage rootfly	Leaves and stems of runner and kidney beans with water-soaked patches and angular spots each with a pale halo.	bacterial halo blight
Seedling leaves with neat round holes.	flea beetle	Pea pods with dark sunken blotches.	pod spot
		Pea seeds damaged as they develop in the pod.	pea moth larvae
		Roots of runner and kidney beans infested with colonies of white-wax-covered insects.	root aphids
		Seeds of runner and kidney beans fail to germinate.	bean seed fly

Vegetables (Bulbs, Roots, and Tubers)

Symptoms	Possible causes	Symptoms	Possible causes
CARROTS		Leaves with pale, rounded areas; tips discolored and withered.	downy mildew
Leaves distorted; growth checked.	aphids	Leaves yellow; white fluffy fungus at stem base and roots.	white rot
Seedlings wilt and die; plants stunted, foliage reddened. Tap roots tunneled.	carrot fly	Young plants collapse, usually in groups, with yellow drooping leaves.	onion fly larvae
LEEKS		**PARSNIPS**	
Young plants abnormally swollen, stunted, and thick-necked; rot in later stages.	stem and bulb eelworm	Roots cracked and blackened, especially at the shoulders; rot developing.	canker
Leaves yellow in places with bright orange spots and blotches.	rust		
ONIONS		**POTATOES**	
Bulbs developing gray rot on the necks in storage.	neck rot	Lower leaves discolor and die; growth stunted and weak; plants die down prematurely; tubers small.	potato cyst eelworm
Plants abnormally swollen, stunted, and thick-necked.	stem and bulb eelworm	Leaves with yellow, brown patches; haulm dies progressively; tubers rot.	potato blight

ORNAMENTALS

Symptoms	Possible causes	Symptoms	Possible causes
SEEDS		**FOLIAGE**	
developing seeds damaged	moth larvae	eaten (clean holes, perforations, skeletonizing, notching)	birds; beetle adults; butterfly/moth larvae; deer; earwigs; leaf-cutter bees; millepedes; rabbits/hares; sawfly larvae; slugs/snails; slugworms; weevil adults; woodlice
tunneled	beetle larvae		
germinating seed damaged	millepedes; wireworms		
BULBS, CORMS AND TUBERS		finely mottled surface	thrips
eaten/tunneled	bulb fly larvae; cutworms; millepedes; slugs; vine weevil larvae; wireworms	finely mottled surface with defoliation and fine webbing	red spider mite
		tunneled	leaf miner
internal discoloration	bulb scale mite; stem and bulb eelworm	fuzzy gray fungal growth	*Botrytis* gray mold
rotted	daffodil basal rot; *Phytophthora* root rots; violet root rot	marginal yellowing/scorch	drought; high temperature; nutrient deficiency; pesticide damage; waterlogging
ROOTS		overall or interveinal yellowing	drought; nutrient deficiency; waterlogging
constricted/rotted	*Pythium*/*Phytophthora* damping off; foot and root rots; *Fusarium* wilt; *Verticillium* wilt; waterlogging	puckered/blistered/distorted	aphids; hormone weedkiller; peach leaf curl; psyllids; stem and bulb eelworm
eaten/tunneled	cockchafers (*see* chafers); cutworms; leatherjackets; millepedes; slugs; symphylids; vine weevil larvae; wireworms; woodlice	rolled	aphids; sawfly larvae; tortrix moth larvae
		silvered	silver leaf
		spots/discolored patches	leaf spot; leaf and bud eelworm; rust; scab
fungal fruiting bodies/compacted black strands	honey fungus	sticky/black mold	aphids; scale insects; whitefly
galled	clubroot; crown gall; *Phylloxerid* vine louse; rootknot eelworm; woolly aphids	white fungal growth	powdery mildew; downy mildew
		woolly masses	adelgids; mealy bugs; woolly aphids
woolly masses	root aphids	yellow variegation/mottle/mosaic/streaking/ring-spotting	virus
STEMS AND SHOOTS		**FLOWERS**	
distorted	aphids; capsids; froghoppers; hormone weedkiller; mechanical wounding; rust; stem and bulb eelworm	failure to open	drought; gall midge larvae; high temperature
		buds blackened	frost
galled	clubroot; crown gall; gall mites; leafy gall	petals and flower buds lacerated/eaten	birds; beetle adults; earwigs; weevil adults
gnawed	beetle adults; cockchafers (*see* chafers); cutworms; deer; millepedes; rabbits/hares; slugs/snails; springtails; voles; weevil adults and larvae; woodlice	small/distorted/streaked	virus
		spotted/withered	*Botrytis* gray mold
		uneven opening/distortion	moth larvae; capsid bugs; leaf and bud eelworm; gall midge larvae
sticky/black mold	aphids; whitefly; scale insects		
wilted/tunneled/withered/dead	bark beetle; canker; drought; Dutch elm disease; fireblight; fly larvae; *Botrytis* gray mold; moth larvae; waterlogging	white flecks on petals	*Botrytis* gray mold; red spider mite; thrips

LEAF ARRANGEMENTS 1

TERMINOLOGY

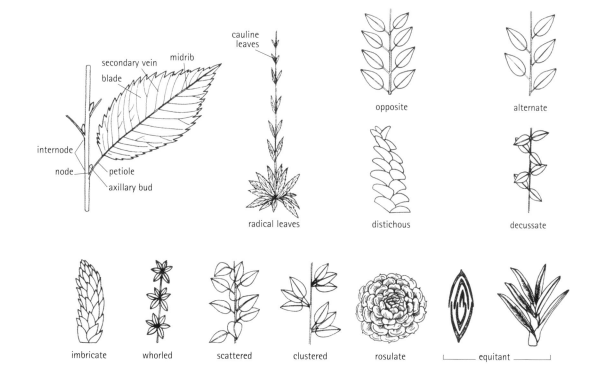

secondary vein

blade

midrib

cauline leaves

internode

node

petiole

axillary bud

radical leaves

opposite

alternate

distichous

decussate

imbricate · whorled · scattered · clustered · rosulate · equitant

COMPOUND LEAVES

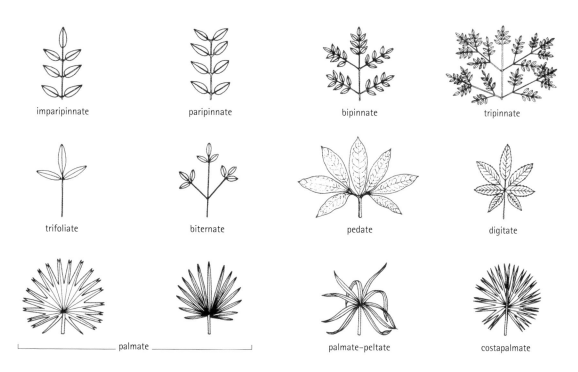

imparipinnate

paripinnate

bipinnate

tripinnate

trifoliate

biternate

pedate

digitate

palmate

palmate-peltate

costapalmate

LEAF ARRANGEMENTS 2

INSERTION

petiolate

sessile

amplexicaul

peltate

perfoliate

connate–perfoliate

sheathing

decurrent

LIGULES

auricled

hairy

STIPULES

leafy

scalelike

glandular

spinose or filiform

sheathing

protective

LEAF ATTITUDES

curved

recurved

reflexed

deflexed

revolute

carinate

involute

plicate

conduplicate

LEAF-LIKE ORGANS

phyllode

leafy petiole

phylloclades

Leaf shapes 1

Whole leaves

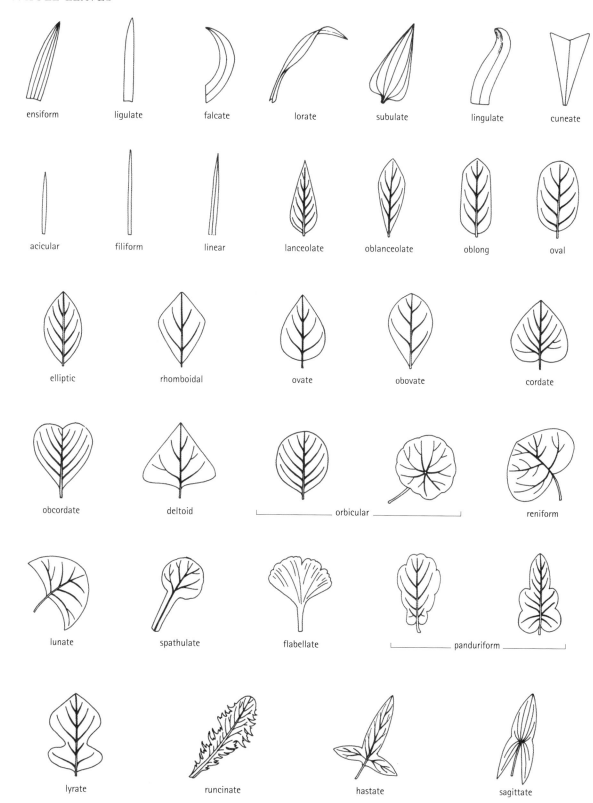

ensiform	ligulate	falcate	lorate	subulate	lingulate	cuneate
acicular	filiform	linear	lanceolate	oblanceolate	oblong	oval
elliptic	rhomboidal		ovate	obovate		cordate
obcordate	deltoid		orbicular			reniform
lunate	spathulate		flabellate	panduriform		
lyrate		runcinate		hastate		sagittate

LEAF SHAPES 2

LEAF TIPS

acuminate

acute

abruptly acute

apiculate

aristate

caudate

cirrhose

cuspidate

pungent

mucronate

mucronulate

obtuse

rounded

truncate

premorse

retuse

emarginate

cleft

LEAF BASES

acute

acuminate

attenuate

cuneate

cordate

reniform

hastate

sagittate

auriculate

rounded

obtuse

truncate

unequal

oblique

LEAF MARGINS

MARGINS

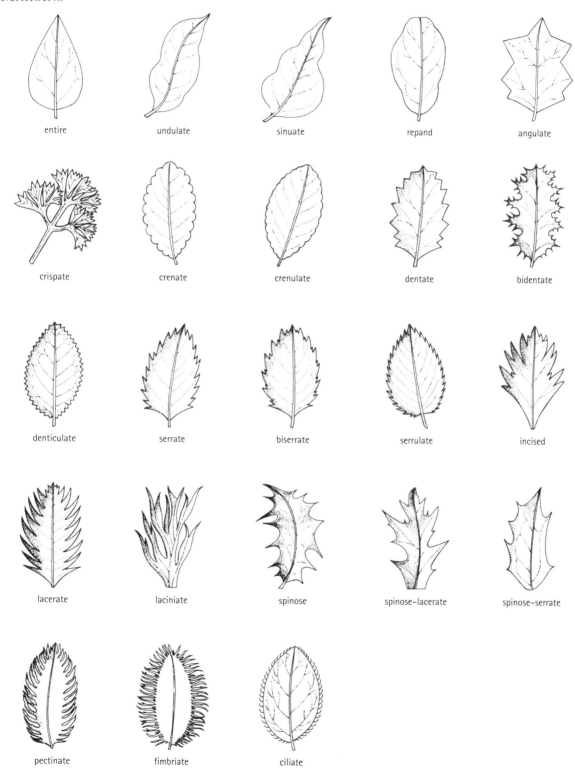

entire

undulate

sinuate

repand

angulate

crispate

crenate

crenulate

dentate

bidentate

denticulate

serrate

biserrate

serrulate

incised

lacerate

laciniate

spinose

spinose–lacerate

spinose–serrate

pectinate

fimbriate

ciliate

Leaf lobing and veining

Lobing

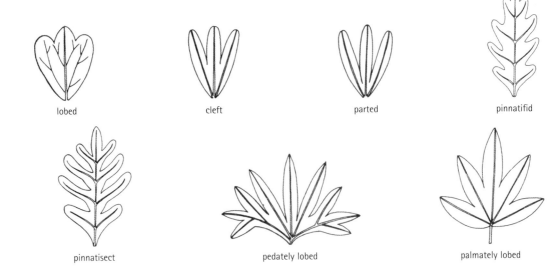

lobed

cleft

parted

pinnatifid

pinnatisect

pedately lobed

palmately lobed

Venation

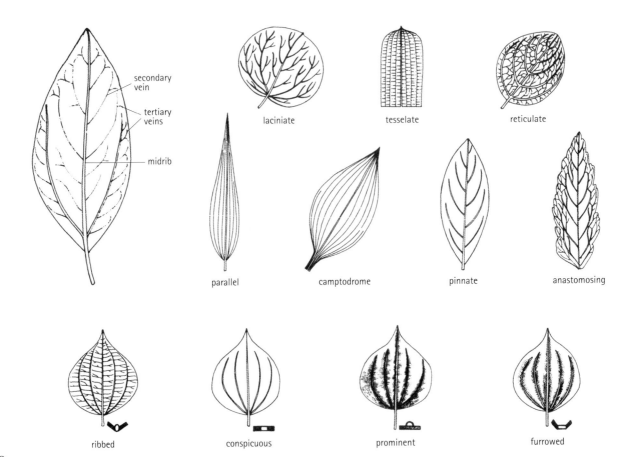

secondary vein

tertiary veins

midrib

laciniate

tesselate

reticulate

parallel

camptodrome

pinnate

anastomosing

ribbed

conspicuous

prominent

furrowed

FLOWER FORMS AND ARRANGEMENTS 1

PARTS OF THE FLOWER

stigma — anther ⎤
pistil style — filament ⎦ stamen
ovary — petal
sepal

└ corolla (inner floral envelope) ┘
└──── calyx (outer floral envelope) ────┘

polypetalous flower

(a) (b) (c) (d)

position of ovary
(a) ovary superior, perianth and stamens hypogynous
(b) ovary superior, petals and stamens perigynous
(c) ovary partly inferior, petals and stamens epigynous
(d) ovary inferior, petals and stamens epigynous

gamopetalous flower

unisexual flowers (*Salix*) ♂ ♀

anther

basifixed stamen

connective

filament

dorsifixed stamen

sessile stigma

composite capitulum
└──── (face, left: section, right) ────┘

ray floret

disk floret

849

Flower forms and arrangements 2

Perianth forms

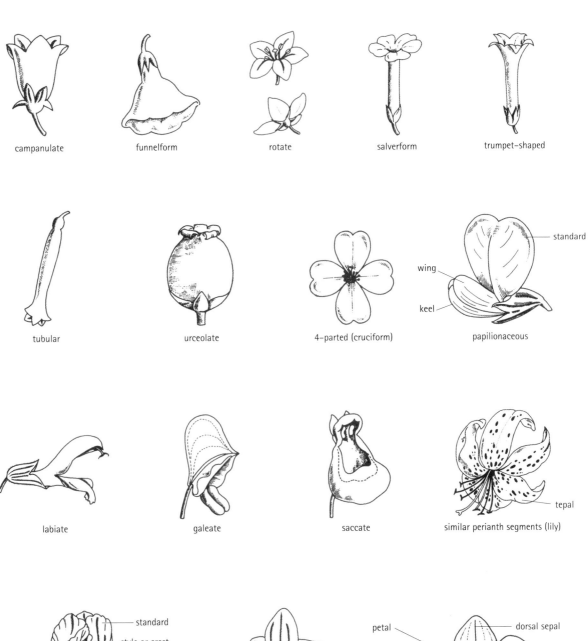

campanulate

funnelform

rotate

salverform

trumpet-shaped

tubular

urceolate

4-parted (cruciform)

papilionaceous

standard

wing

keel

labiate

galeate

saccate

similar perianth segments (lily)

tepal

standard

style or crest

stigma

beard

fall

dissimilar perianth segments (iris)

corona

amaryllidaceous

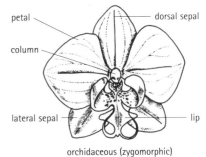

petal

column

dorsal sepal

lateral sepal

lip

orchidaceous (zygomorphic)

Fruits 1

cupular fruit

nuts

nutlets

hep (hip)

balausta

pepo

berry

pome

hesperidium

drupe

accessory fruit (with seed enlarged)

aggregate fruit

syconium, e.g., *Ficus* (complete syconium)
and *Dorstenia* (partial syconium)

sororsis (multiple fruit, e.g., *Morus, Ananas*)

Fruits 2

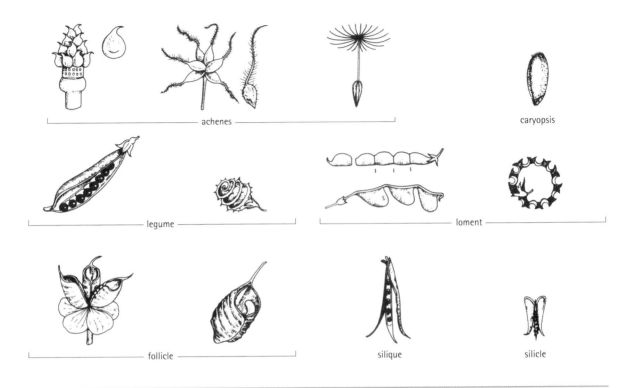

achenes

caryopsis

legume

loment

follicle

silique

silicle

Capsules (showing different modes of dehiscence)

loculicidal

septicidal

septifragal

porocidal

valvate

circumscissile (pyxis)

utricle

schizocarp

samara

strobilus (conifer)

strobilus (angiosperm, e.g., *Humulus*)

INFLORESCENCES

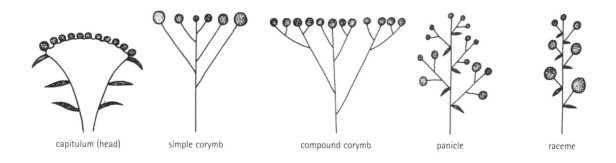

capitulum (head) simple corymb compound corymb panicle raceme

CYMES

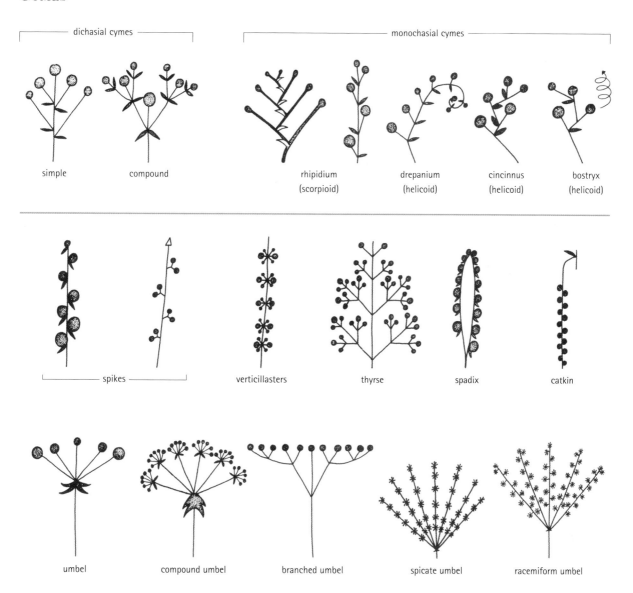

dichasial cymes monochasial cymes

simple compound rhipidium (scorpioid) drepanium (helicoid) cincinnus (helicoid) bostryx (helicoid)

spikes verticillasters thyrse spadix catkin

umbel compound umbel branched umbel spicate umbel racemiform umbel

Bud stages

Apple, pear, plum and cherry

(a) *dormant* (b) *swelling* (c) *breaking* (d) *burst*

(e) *mouse ear* (f) *green cluster* (g) *pink bud*

(h) *petal fall* (i) *fruitlet* (j) *cot split (plum)*

Black currant

(k) *grape*

Gooseberry

(l) *early flower* (m) *fruit set* (n) *fruit swelling*

Raspberry

(o) *green bud* (p) *fruitlet*

Apple, pear, plum and cherry: (a) no sign of growth (b) bud scales just beginning to part (c) bud scales opening (d) leaf tips apparent at top of the bud (e) leaves fully defined (f) small green flower buds visible among expanding leaf clusters (g) unopened flowers within pink-colored buds (=*white bud* in pear, plum, and cherry) (h) most flowering over (i) small swelling fruits visible (= (j) in plums, accompanied by a splitting off of the yellow calyx). **Black currant**—*dormant, breaking, burst* similar to apple, etc. (k) leaves about 1 in (25 mm) across, flower clusters in unopened green bud, reminiscent of bunches of grapes. **Gooseberry**—*dormant, breaking* similar to apple, etc. (l) flower buds just showing (m) flowers fully open (n) three weeks after fruit set. **Raspberry**—*dormant, burst* similar to apple, etc. (o) leaves opened and green flower buds showing (p) green fruits swelling.

INDEX
OF COMMON NAMES

This index excludes common names of edible plants that appear as main text entries (e.g., apple) unless that name also happens to cover some ornamentals (e.g., onion *Allium*). When a common name applies to an entire genus, its specific variants are not usually listed. Thus "pine" is given below as *Pinus*. Readers seeking the Bhutan pine (*Pinus wallichiana*) should look under *Pinus* in the main text, where the name stands after its Latin equivalent. Exceptions to this rule appear below (e.g., screw pine *Pandanus*). When a name applies to more than one plant, the more common application of the name is given first (e.g., mother-in-law's tongue *Sansevieria*, *Dieffenbachia*).